# BBC FOOTBALL YEARBOOK

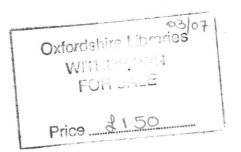

## 2003/2004



BBC BOOKS

First published 2003


ISBN 0 563 48760 7

Published by BBC Books, BBC Worldwide Ltd,
Woodlands, 80 Wood Lane, London W12 0TT

Commissioning editor: Ben Dunn
Project editor: Christopher Tinker
Data interpretation and design: Tony Warner
Data collation: Peter Watts, John Haines
Design: John-Paul Warner
Picture and data research: Stephen Hall

Printed and bound in Great Britain by Butler & Tanner Ltd, Frome

# Most football fact books try to settle the argument...

**... this one aims to give you 50 ways to continue it.**
To be a fan is to join that greatest debate, contradicting the TV pundit and arguing around the finality of the league table, armed only with the evidence of your own eyes and the moral certainty which comes from living every second of that last tortuous season.

Sometimes the more of an expert you are, the more certain you are that the league tables lie. So it is that in the season ended in 2003, **Arsene Wenger** can argue that you should combine FA Cup *and* the League to measure the top English club. In Scotland **Celtic** fans can point to odds-defying performances in the UEFA Cup to set against **Rangers'** treble, while **Milan** will wave their Champions League trophy in the face of **Juvé's** Serie A triumph.

And that's just the clubs... individual players provoke even deeper debate!

### Just who is the best forward?

**A** A player who scores the most goals in a season?
**B** A player who plays less often but scores more goals per game?
**C** Or a player who scores a higher percentage of his team's goals?

*Or shouldn't a case be made for the forward with a better all-round contribution to his team's 'Attacking Power'...*
**D** For example, a player whose team scores more goals when he is on the pitch?
**E** Or a player who can point to the highest total of both assists and goals?

There is no definitive answer but if we gave you the names of **Henry, Larsson, van Nistlerooy, Beattie** and **Scholes** you'd have an idea of which one best fitted each of the descriptions **A–E** above.

You can check the answers in this book. And that wouldn't be a bad way to start to explore it, for this is a new kind of football book, with three main differences:
**1.** It turns football facts into charts that compare players and clubs;
**2.** It extends coverage to the top leagues in Europe;
**3.** And it's full of colour pictures reliving the drama of the season.

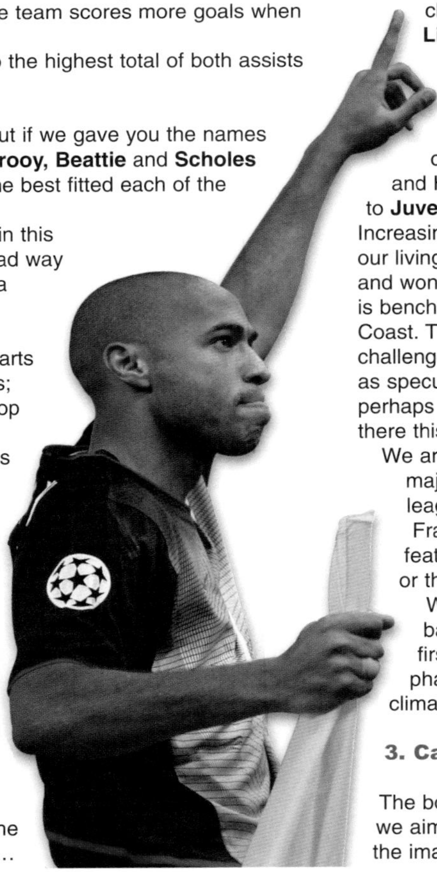

### 1. There's a new breed of football fact...

You'll hear it quoted in the TV studio and embellishing radio commentary; you'll see it increasingly in our papers as the peg behind a story or preview. It may highlight a particular player's importance or compare strengths of teams playing in different divisions. The following should seem familiar...

- How important is **Patrick Vieira** to **Arsenal** – look at their average points total when he does and doesn't play?
- What's the gap between **United's** crowd-pulling power and **Madrid's** – check out their stadium capacity and season's crowds?
- Where is the next **van Nistlerooy** playing now – study the leading European Strike Rates?
- Who are the **top shot-stoppers** in the Premiership?

Fly
Emirates

They all pluck the headline from a ream of stats to give an insight into the value of a player or unearth an unlikely explanation for a club's run of success.

We have turned these nuggets into charts that reveal more about the strengths and failings of every club. They are ever more relevant now that football is a squad game and the fan has a different view of the best XI from his team's manager.

Mostly, we want to find ways to take that chart of top defensive performances at one club and compare them to the rest of the division; to test the **West Brom** chants of '**Hoult** for England' and find out whether **Liverpool** are hitting more shots on goal than **Chelsea**?

### 2. Into Europe...

The next step is to take **Rangers'** strengths and chart them against Premiership clubs or sides in Spain and Holland. To find ways of comparing **Davids'** importance to **Juventus** against **Ronaldinho's** for **Paris St Germain.** Increasingly we're more likely to find **Inter Milan** performing in our living rooms than say **Nottingham Forest.** We are watching and wondering why a South American star of the World Cup is benched in favour of an unknown talent from Africa's West Coast. There's an added excitement in following **Deportivo's** challenge for La Liga in the back pages of a Monday newspaper, as speculation links their midfield star with your team...or perhaps there's a big name from here you want to follow over there this season!

We are taking a greater interest in international stars, and the major clubs and leagues of Europe where they play. Our league coverage extends to the top divisions in Spain, Italy, France, Holland and Germany and other top clubs will be featured in the pages devoted to the **Champions League** or the **UEFA Cup.**

We hope the material adds vital background to that ball-winner signed from the middle reaches of the French first division. It should also mark your card for the first phase of the **Champions League** and this season's climax – **Euro 2004.**

### 3. Capturing the moment...

The book tells each club's story of success and woe and we aim to recall the thrill of those important moments with the images that filled the back pages that week.

Over 900 colour pictures lift the book, illustrating the passion, the elation and the despair that football brings to our lives. We have charted the story of 22 clubs in pictures, match headlines and brief snippets of news, using images from the games to capture the drama, or the expression on the face behind the headline.

The league position accents these stories and their compilation became a fascinating insight into the 'biorhythms' that lie behind each club's season.

It will also help you to put faces to the chart-toppers and players to watch out for. You may admire the form of **Laurent Robert** but struggle to picture him if you're not a **Newcastle** fan. Our 'teams of the season' have player portraits to jog your memory.

## What you'll find inside

The three points above explain how and why this book does a different job from the other fine fact-filled books you will find on the shelves. *They* provide a worthy record of football in Britain over the last 150 years, often going down into non-league football and make a very good job of it too. *We* turn a brighter light on the season ended in 2003 and reflect the media spotlight on football. Like the media, our coverage is more extensive for the top leagues and strongest clubs – hardly surprising, as leading sides play nearly half as many games again as their rivals do.

Two guiding principles lie behind our coverage:
- **Is it going to excite and inform us?**
- **Is the depth of information comparable across Europe?**

We could get reliable data from 11 European leagues but the first principle argues that Spain's La Liga gets in and the Swiss League is left out.

Portugal has thrown up one of the clubs of 2003 in Porto but the data from Portugal isn't reliable to the same depth for us to make our key comparisons. They fell foul of our second principle.

We decided to pack in more coverage of 11 divisions, the top four in **England**, the top two in **Scotland** and the top divisions from the more successful European football nations – **Spain**, **Italy**, **Germany**, **France** and **Holland**.

For international coverage we have taken the top 27 countries from the FIFA Rankings plus the 3 home countries, Scotland, Wales and Northern Ireland, not currently in the top 30. We have followed these through the season after the World Cup. Not surprisingly the international teams we cover include all those supplying most players to the top leagues.

Many sides in the Premiership boast current Internationals from sides fancied for the **Euro 2004** or the next **World Cup.** We put a nationality against all featured players and note those that have won caps for any top 30 International sides in the last season.

## How to use the book

Following the example of our papers and broadcasters, this book hunts out a headline from the hard information. We believe in providing editorial hooks into what is still comprehensive data to highlight the impressive, noteworthy and downright astonishing performances. After all, life is short and the season is long.

We take the objective facts of the football season but sort them editorially, choosing key criteria to chart the best and worst performances by and within a club. For example Goalscorers are sorted by **Strike Rate** – the number of minutes played in league games divided by the number of goals scored. The charts opposite explain how the book works in more detail.

## Start with your favourite team

We suggest you start with your team and see the story of their season and how key players contributed to success or failure. Then you can expand your view to other clubs and review your star defender against a rival team's.

**Divisional Round-ups** chart your club in their division comparing qualities such as attacking and defending ability or the size of their crowds. Individual players are also exposed to division-wide scrutiny, so see how many of your team chart in the divisional player tables.

**Arsenal** fans can find out how **Henry** fares when his Strike Rate is compared to the best in Spain or just how consistent **Campbell's** record is when judged against Italy's defensive masters. You can follow the club through the FA Cup or see how **Vieira** measures up to opponents in the Champions League. From that starting point of your team we hope to whisk you into a voyage of discovery that intrigues, surprises and leads you deeper into a different take on European football and your club's place within it.

- **We won't** try to change your mind about which defender your manager should have definitely let go this summer…
- **We will** sharpen your thinking about who to buy to replace him.
- **We won't** challenge your view that it should all have been so different in 2002/03…
- **We will** give you an insight into where it actually went wrong!

## And finally…

…a huge 'thank you' to **Tony Warner**, **Peter Watts**, **Steve Hall** and **John-Paul Warner** of Warner Leach and to **John Haines** of Sportsgrid, for their help in expanding on my ideas, interpreting scarily demanding plans and reworking crude designs into a professional book.

Also to **Action Images** and several other unsung stars who worked all season and then all night to get us through a break-neck production cycle in the fortnight after the Spanish kicked the final ball of the season.

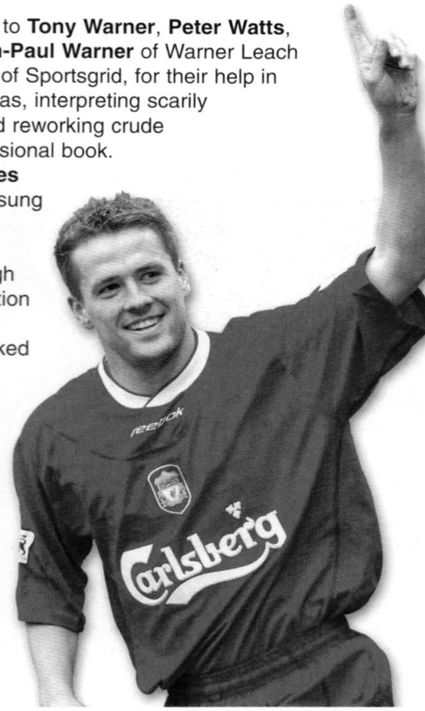
Carlsberg

The greatest compliment I can pay their efforts is to have this book live up to what was one of the most thrilling football seasons in living memory.

Terry Pratt, 2003

# How to use the book – table explanations

## KEY PLAYERS - GOALSCORERS

FRIENDS PROVIDENT
9

| 1 James Beattie | |
|---|---|
| **Goals in the League** | 23 |
| **Goals in all competitions** | 24 |
| **Assists** League goals scored by team-mates where he delivered the final pass | 2 |
| **Contribution to Attacking Power** Average number of minutes between League team goals while on pitch | 76 |
| **Player Strike Rate** Average number of minutes between League goals scored by player | 139 |
| **Club Strike Rate** Average minutes between League goals scored by club | 80 |

| | PLAYER | GOALS LGE | GOALS ALL | ASSISTS | POWER | S RATE |
|---|---|---|---|---|---|---|
| 2 | Brett Ormerod | 5 | 9 | 4 | 62 | 351 mins |
| 3 | Fabrice Fernandes | 3 | 4 | 4 | 82 | 985 mins |
| 4 | Anders Svensson | 2 | 4 | 4 | 79 | 1106 mins |
| 5 | Michael Svensson | 2 | 4 | 1 | 71 | 1509 mins |

**The Club Goalscorers** table looks at the records of each club's most deadly scorers. The table is topped by the player with the best **Strike Rate,** which measures the average number of minutes between his League goals. We divide his minutes on the pitch in League games by the goals he scores.

Here, **Beattie** has the best Strike Rate in Southampton, with a goal on average every 139 minutes over the season. The table also features other notable players with the next best Strike Rates and all players – not just forwards – are eligible. A player must have played in a minimum number of League games to qualify for the chart – in the Premiership, it is 12 'counting' League games.

You can work out any players' Strike Rate by dividing their minutes played in League games (recorded in the Player Appearance table) by the League goals they scored.
This table also notes goals scored and **Assists** where a player made the final pass to a colleague to score in a Premier League game.

Finally, it gives a feel for the team's overall potency when that player is on the pitch in his **Attacking Power** rating. This measures how often his team scores in numbers of minutes between League goals. So when **Ormerod** is on the pitch, Saints score, on average, every 62 minutes. You can compare this with the **Club Strike Rate**, which gives Southampton's average for the season. Here, the club rate is only 80 minutes, showing that Southampton score more often when Ormerod is contributing to the team's attack.

## KEY PLAYERS - MIDFIELDERS

| 1 Lee Cartwright | |
|---|---|
| **Goals in the League** | 2 |
| **Goals in all competitions** | 2 |
| **Defensive Rating** Average number of mins between League goals conceded while on the pitch | 62 |
| **Contribution to Attacking Power** Average number of minutes between League team goals while on pitch | 54 |
| **Scoring Difference** Defensive Rating minus Contribution to Attacking Power | 8 |

| | PLAYER | GOALS LGE | GOALS ALL | DEF RATE | ATT POWER | SCORE DIFF |
|---|---|---|---|---|---|---|
| 2 | Paul McKenna | 3 | 3 | 61 | 56 | 5 mins |
| 3 | Dickson Etuhu | 6 | 6 | 59 | 54 | 5 mins |
| 4 | Eddie Lewis | 5 | 6 | 61 | 59 | 2 mins |
| 5 | Eric Skora | 0 | 1 | 57 | 73 | -16 mins |

**The Club Midfielders** table is the record of each club's key midfield players. We allocate a position of Forward, Midfield, Defender or Goalkeeper to each player and where important players can play in more than one role we get our data team to make a call. So in the Premiership Paul Scholes is a forward and John-Arne Riise is shown as a midfield player.

The player who has the best record in both, helping the team score goals and preventing goals against, tops the table. In this example **Cartwright** from Preston is top. When he is playing, the team scores a League goal on average every **54 minutes** as shown in his Attacking Power. The team concedes a League goal when he is on the pitch every **62 minutes** and this is shown as his **Defensive Rating**. By subtracting Cartwright's Attacking Power from his Defensive Rating, we are left with a difference of **8 minutes**. It is like a 'personal goal difference' and we have called this his **Scoring Difference**. It can be a positive or a negative figure. **Skora's** Scoring Difference is a minus figure, –16 minutes, which means Preston has been more likely to lose goals than score them when he is on the pitch. The higher the positive figure, the better the team's goals record while he is on the pitch.

### Team of the Season

The Team of the Season is usually a visual guide to a club's Chart-Topping players in a 4-4-2 formation. The Goalkeeper and four Defenders are chosen by the best Defensive Ratings; the four best Scoring Differences make up the Midfielders and usually the two best Forwards are selected by Strike Rate.

Beckham

CG 27 SD +83

In the Premiership we have decided to run the 4-4-1-1 formation adopted by many teams. We then rate the withdrawn Forward by Attacking Power and the spearhead striker by Strike Rate. In cases where the same player tops both these criteria, we use the second-rated player for the other role. It's a guide to the players gaining the best results in each club based only on the games they played. Ideally, it will throw up some major differences from the manager's first XI!

In each League's Divisional Round-up we do something different and highlight those out-performing their team-mates. We compare a player's stats against the team average (or in a striker's case, the next highest) and weight it to take account that differences can fluctuate wildly at struggling clubs. It means a stunning performance by one player in a poor team will still be recognised. Across the top seven Divisions we cover, we run a European Inter-League Team of the Season. You can find this on page 498.

### Chart-Topping Defenders

The Chart-Topping Defenders table shows the top 30 defending records across the division. Every division we cover charts both the club records and the top individuals in each position.

## CHART-TOPPING DEFENDERS

Westcoast

| 1 Matthew Upson - Reading | |
|---|---|
| **Goals Conceded in the League** The number of League goals conceded while he was on the pitch | 5 |
| **Goals Conceded in all competitions** The number of goals conceded while he was on the pitch in all competitions | 8 |
| **Clean Sheets** In games when he played at least 70 mins | 8 |
| **Defensive Rating** Average number of minutes between League goals conceded while on pitch | 90 |
| **Club Defensive Rating** Average mins between League goals conceded by the club this season | 230 |

| | PLAYER | CLUB | CON: LGE | ALL | CS | CDR | DEF RATE |
|---|---|---|---|---|---|---|---|
| 2 | Taggart | Leicester | 24 | 24 | 12 | 104 | 115 mins |
| 3 | Irwin | Wolves | 34 | 43 | 20 | 94 | 111 mins |
| 4 | Davidson | Leicester | 22 | 30 | 10 | 104 | 110 mins |

The Division I defenders table is topped by **Matthew Upson** who was then playing for Reading. He only played the minimum number of 12 **Counting Games** to qualify for this chart but conceded less League goals in proportion to his time on the pitch than any other defender in the division. Reading conceded just one goal on average for every 230 minutes Upson was playing for them. This is Upson's **Defensive Rating**. He was in the sort of form that persuaded Steve Bruce to sign him and Sven to pick him for England.

This chart obviously features more players from teams with good Goals Against records but still throws up players who have significantly outperformed their **Club Defensive Rating**. All clubs have both top individuals and a note of their Club Defensive Rating record on their club pages.

We also tally Goals Conceded and **Clean Sheets** (games where the team didn't concede any goals) by each player. To have a Clean Sheet recorded against his name a defender or keeper must have played for at least 70 minutes of the game. Playing at least 70 minutes qualifies as a Counting Game.

# CONTENTS...

**493** **Mark your Champions League card for the season. Shearer shone, Zidane sparkled; but which banker keeps delivering Euro success?**

**150** **When the championship changed hands three times in just 90 nerve-shredding minutes and took all Britain's 5-Live listeners to the wire...**

**95** **Who split Henry and van Nistlerooy in the Premiership Forwards Strike Rate charts?**

**135** **Big squads are bad for your league health – it's true! Which club fielded 26 different midfield players over the season? Clue – it wasn't Madrid (just 10) or Juventus (only 9) Oh and they play in blue!**

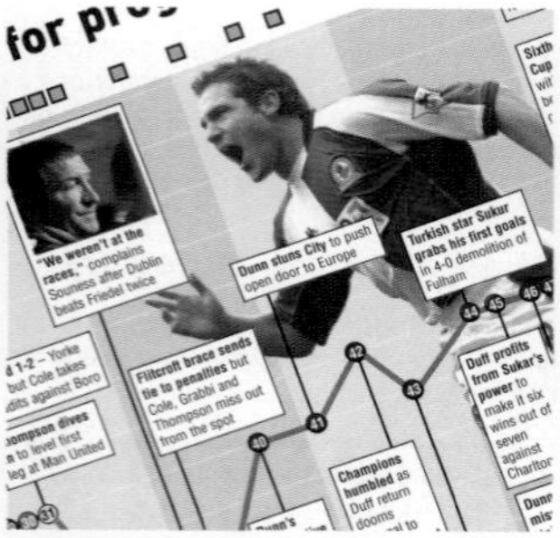

## CLUBS

**497** **Is Buffon safer than Cudicini? The great club keepers of Europe display their records before the Euro 2004 selection battle...**

**10** **Moments which decided the Premiership – even the greatest clubs have patches that are far from purple. We track the football 'biorhythms' of your club over 80 glorious pages!**

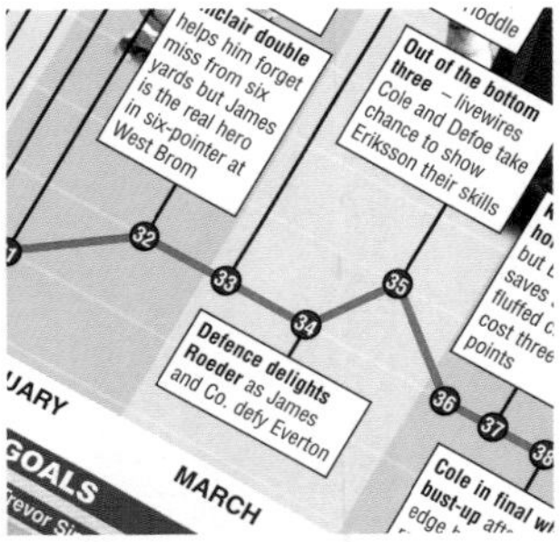

Out of the bottom three – livewires Cole and Defoe take chance to show Eriksson their skills
Defence delights Roeder as James and Co. defy Everton
MARCH

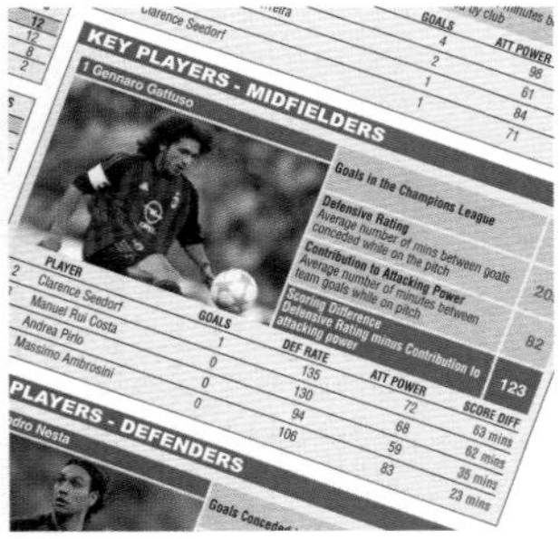

KEY PLAYERS - MIDFIELDERS
PLAYERS - DEFENDERS

# MANCHESTER UNITED

**NICKNAME:** RED DEVILS

**KEY:** Won, Drawn, Lost

| No | Comp | Opponent | Venue | Result | Score | Scorers |
|---|---|---|---|---|---|---|
| 1 | ecql1 | Zalaegerszeg | A | L | 0-1 | |
| 2 | lge | West Brom | H | W | 1-0 | Solskjaer 78 |
| 3 | lge | Chelsea | A | D | 2-2 | Beckham 26; Giggs 66 |
| 4 | ecql2 | Zalaegerszeg | H | W | 5-0 | van Nistelrooy 6,77 pen; Beckham 15; Scholes 21; Solskjaer 83 |
| 5 | lge | Sunderland | A | D | 1-1 | Giggs 7 |
| 6 | lge | Middlesbrough | H | W | 1-0 | van Nistelrooy 28 pen |
| 7 | lge | Bolton | H | L | 0-1 | |
| 8 | lge | Leeds | A | L | 0-1 | |
| 9 | ecgf | Maccabi Haifa | H | W | 5-2 | Giggs 11; Solskjaer 35; Veron 46; van Nistelrooy 54; Forlan 89 pen |
| 10 | lge | Tottenham | H | W | 1-0 | van Nistelrooy 63 pen |
| 11 | ecgf | B Leverkusen | A | W | 2-1 | van Nistelrooy 31,42 |
| 12 | lge | Charlton | A | W | 3-1 | Scholes 54; Giggs 82; van Nistelrooy 90 |
| 13 | ecgf | Olympiakos | H | W | 4-0 | Giggs 19,66; Veron 26; Solskjaer 77 |
| 14 | lge | Everton | H | W | 3-0 | Scholes 86,90; van Nistelrooy 90 pen |
| 15 | lge | Fulham | A | D | 1-1 | Solskjaer 61 |
| 16 | ecgf | Olympiakos | A | W | 3-2 | Blanc 21; Veron 59; Scholes 84 |
| 17 | lge | Aston Villa | H | D | 1-1 | Forlan 77 |
| 18 | ecgf | Maccabi Haifa | A | L | 0-3 | |
| 19 | lge | Southampton | H | W | 2-1 | Neville, P 15; Forlan 85 |
| 20 | wr3 | Leicester | H | W | 2-0 | Beckham 80 pen; Richardson 90 |
| 21 | lge | Man City | A | L | 1-3 | Solskjaer 8 |
| 22 | ecgf | B Leverkusen | H | W | 2-0 | Veron 42; van Nistelrooy 69 |
| 23 | lge | West Ham | A | D | 1-1 | van Nistelrooy 38 |
| 24 | lge | Newcastle | H | W | 5-3 | Scholes 25; van Nistelrooy 38,45,53; Solskjaer 55 |
| 25 | ecgd | Basel | A | W | 3-1 | van Nistelrooy 62,63; Solskjaer 68 |
| 26 | lge | Liverpool | A | W | 2-1 | Forlan 64,67 |
| 27 | wr4 | Burnley | A | W | 2-0 | Forlan 35; Solskjaer 66 |
| 28 | lge | Arsenal | H | W | 2-0 | Veron 22; Scholes 73 |
| 29 | ecgd | Deportivo | H | W | 2-0 | van Nistelrooy 8,55 |
| 30 | lge | West Ham | H | W | 3-0 | Solskjaer 15; Veron 17; Schemmel 61 og |
| 31 | wqf | Chelsea | H | W | 1-0 | Forlan 80 |
| 32 | lge | Blackburn | A | L | 0-1 | |
| 33 | lge | Middlesbrough | A | L | 1-3 | Giggs 60 |
| 34 | lge | Birmingham | H | W | 2-0 | Forlan 37; Beckham 74 |
| 35 | lge | Sunderland | H | W | 2-1 | Beckham 81; Scholes 90 |
| 36 | facr3 | Portsmouth | H | W | 4-1 | van Nistelrooy 5 pen,81 pen; Beckham 17; Scholes 90 |
| 37 | wsfl1 | Blackburn | H | D | 1-1 | Scholes 58 |
| 38 | lge | West Brom | A | W | 3-1 | van Nistelrooy 8; Scholes 23; Solskjaer 55 |
| 39 | lge | Chelsea | H | W | 2-1 | Scholes 39; Forlan 90 |
| 40 | wsfl2 | Blackburn | A | W | 3-1 | Scholes 30,42; van Nistelrooy 77 pen |
| 41 | facr4 | West Ham | H | W | 6-0 | Giggs 8,30; van Nistelrooy 49,58; Neville, P 50; Solskjaer 69 |
| 42 | lge | Southampton | A | W | 2-0 | van Nistelrooy 15; Giggs 22 |
| 43 | lge | Birmingham | A | W | 1-0 | van Nistelrooy 56 |
| 44 | lge | Man City | H | D | 1-1 | van Nistelrooy 18 |
| 45 | facr5 | Arsenal | H | L | 0-2 | |
| 46 | ecgd | Juventus | H | W | 2-1 | Brown 4; van Nistelrooy 85 |
| 47 | lge | Bolton | A | D | 1-1 | Solskjaer 90 |
| 48 | ecgd | Juventus | A | W | 3-0 | Giggs 15,41; van Nistelrooy 63 |
| 49 | wf | Liverpool | N | L | 0-2 | |
| 50 | lge | Leeds | H | W | 2-1 | Radebe 20 og; Silvestre 79 |
| 51 | ecgd | Basel | H | D | 1-1 | Neville, G 53 |
| 52 | lge | Aston Villa | A | W | 1-0 | Beckham 12 |
| 53 | ecgd | Deportivo | A | L | 0-2 | |
| 54 | lge | Fulham | H | W | 3-0 | van Nistelrooy 45 pen,68,90 |
| 55 | lge | Liverpool | H | W | 4-0 | van Nistelrooy 5 pen,65 pen; Giggs 78; Solskjaer 90 |
| 56 | ecqfl1 | Real Madrid | A | L | 1-3 | van Nistelrooy 52 |
| 57 | lge | Newcastle | A | W | 6-2 | Solskjaer 32; Scholes 34,38,52; Giggs 44; van Nistelrooy 58 pen |
| 58 | lge | Arsenal | A | D | 2-2 | van Nistelrooy 24; Giggs 63 |
| 59 | lge | Blackburn | H | W | 3-1 | van Nistelrooy 20; Scholes 42,60 |
| 60 | ecqfl2 | Real Madrid | H | W | 4-3 | van Nistelrooy 43; Helguera 53 og; Beckham 71,84 |
| 61 | lge | Tottenham | A | W | 2-0 | Scholes 69; van Nistelrooy 90 |
| 62 | lge | Charlton | H | W | 4-1 | Beckham 11; van Nistelrooy 32,37,53 |
| 63 | lge | Everton | A | W | 2-1 | Beckham 43; van Nistelrooy 78 pen |

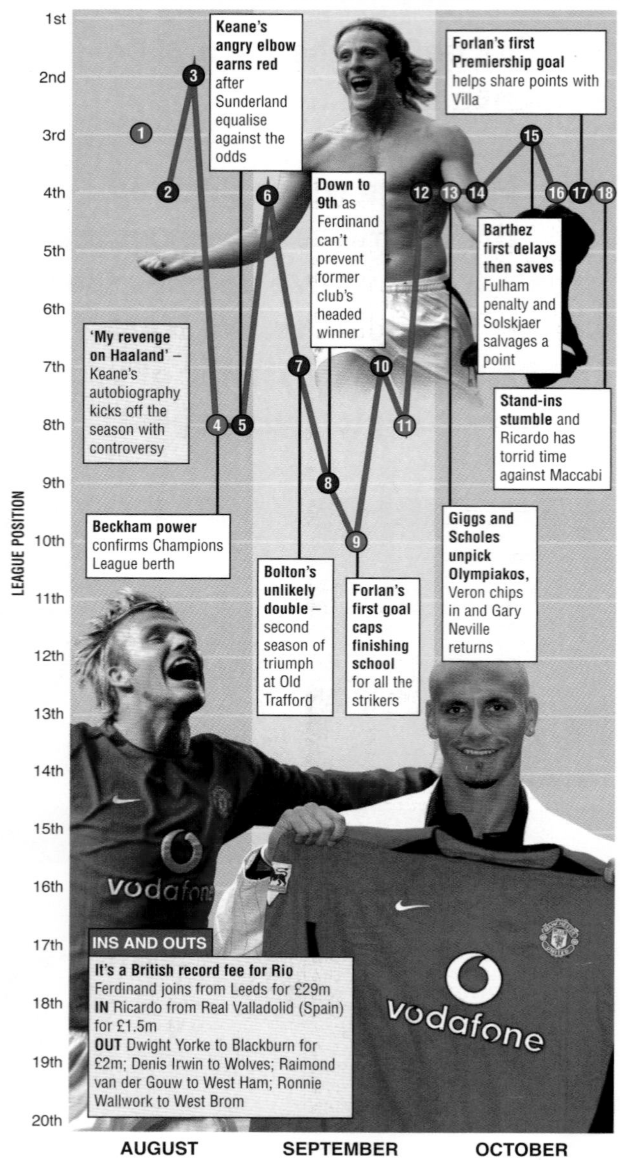

1st
2nd
3rd
4th
5th
6th
7th
8th
9th
10th
11th
12th
13th
14th
15th
16th
17th
18th
19th
20th
LEAGUE POSITION
Keane's angry elbow earns red after Sunderland equalise against the odds
Forlan's first Premiership goal helps share points with Villa
Down to 9th as Ferdinand can't prevent former club's headed winner
Barthez first delays then saves Fulham penalty and Solskjaer salvages a point
'My revenge on Haaland' – Keane's autobiography kicks off the season with controversy
Stand-ins stumble and Ricardo has torrid time against Maccabi
Beckham power confirms Champions League berth
Bolton's unlikely double – second season of triumph at Old Trafford
Forlan's first goal caps finishing school for all the strikers
Giggs and Scholes unpick Olympiakos, Veron chips in and Gary Neville returns
vodafone
vodafone
AUGUST
SEPTEMBER
OCTOBER


**INS AND OUTS**

**It's a British record fee for Rio** Ferdinand joins from Leeds for £29m
**IN** Ricardo from Real Valladolid (Spain) for £1.5m
**OUT** Dwight Yorke to Blackburn for £2m; Denis Irwin to Wolves; Raimond van der Gouw to West Ham; Ronnie Wallwork to West Brom

Home, Away, Neutral

## ATTENDANCES

**HOME GROUND:** OLD TRAFFORD **CAPACITY:** 67750 **AVERAGE LEAGUE AT HOME:** 67604

| | | | | | | | | | | | |
|---|---|---|---|---|---|---|---|---|---|---|---|
| 49 | Liverpool | 75000 | 39 | Chelsea | 67606 | 37 | Blackburn | 62740 | 21 | Man City | 34649 |
| 62 | Charlton | 67721 | 30 | West Ham | 67555 | 48 | Juventus | 59111 | 42 | Southampton | 32085 |
| 54 | Fulham | 67706 | 6 | Middlesbro | 67508 | 31 | Chelsea | 57985 | 32 | Blackburn | 30475 |
| 19 | Southampton | 67691 | 36 | Portsmouth | 67222 | 57 | Newcastle | 52164 | 25 | Basel | 29500 |
| 28 | Arsenal | 67650 | 45 | Arsenal | 67209 | 20 | Leicester | 47848 | 43 | Birmingham | 29479 |
| 44 | Man City | 67646 | 41 | West Ham | 67181 | 5 | Sunderland | 47586 | 40 | Blackburn | 29048 |
| 2 | West Brom | 67645 | 50 | Leeds | 67135 | 26 | Liverpool | 44250 | 47 | Bolton | 27409 |
| 34 | Birmingham | 67640 | 29 | Deportivo | 67014 | 52 | Aston Villa | 42602 | 38 | West Brom | 27129 |
| 55 | Liverpool | 67639 | 13 | Olympiakos | 66902 | 3 | Chelsea | 41541 | 18 | Charlton | 26630 |
| 14 | Everton | 67629 | 51 | Basel | 66870 | 63 | Everton | 40168 | 12 | Maccabi Haifa | 22500 |
| 59 | Blackburn | 67626 | 4 | Zalaegerszeg | 66814 | 1 | Zalaegerszeg | 40000 | 11 | B Leverkusen | 22500 |
| 7 | Bolton | 67623 | 60 | Real Madrid | 66708 | 8 | Leeds | 39622 | 27 | Burnley | 22034 |
| 24 | Newcastle | 67619 | 56 | Real Madrid | 66708 | 58 | Arsenal | 38164 | 15 | Fulham | 18103 |
| 17 | Aston Villa | 67619 | 22 | B Leverkusen | 66185 | 61 | Tottenham | 36073 | 16 | Olympiakos | 15000 |
| 10 | Tottenham | 67611 | 46 | Juventus | 66073 | 23 | West Ham | 35049 | 53 | Deportivo | 7120 |
| 35 | Sunderland | 67609 | 9 | Maccabi Haifa | 63439 | 33 | Middlesboro | 34673 | | | |

## GOAL ATTEMPTS

**FOR**
Goal attempts recorded in League games

| | HOME | AWAY | TOTAL | AVE |
|---|---|---|---|---|
| shots on target | 173 | 122 | 295 | 7.8 |
| shots off target | 133 | 95 | 228 | 6.0 |
| TOTAL | 306 | 217 | 523 | 13.8 |

**Ratio of goals to shots** Average number of shots on target per League goal scored: **4.0**

**Accuracy rating** Average percentage of total goal attempts which were on target: **56.4**

**AGAINST**
Goal attempts recorded in League games

| | HOME | AWAY | TOTAL | AVE |
|---|---|---|---|---|
| shots on target | 73 | 85 | 158 | 4.2 |
| shots off target | 78 | 122 | 200 | 5.3 |
| TOTAL | 151 | 207 | 358 | 9.4 |

**Ratio of goals to shots** Average number of shots on target per League goal scored: **4.6**

**Accuracy rating** Average percentage of total goal attempts which were on target: **44.1**

# Best-ever Championship says Fergie

**Final Position: 1st**

KEY: ● League ● Champions Lge ● UEFA Cup ● FA Cup ○ League Cup ● Other

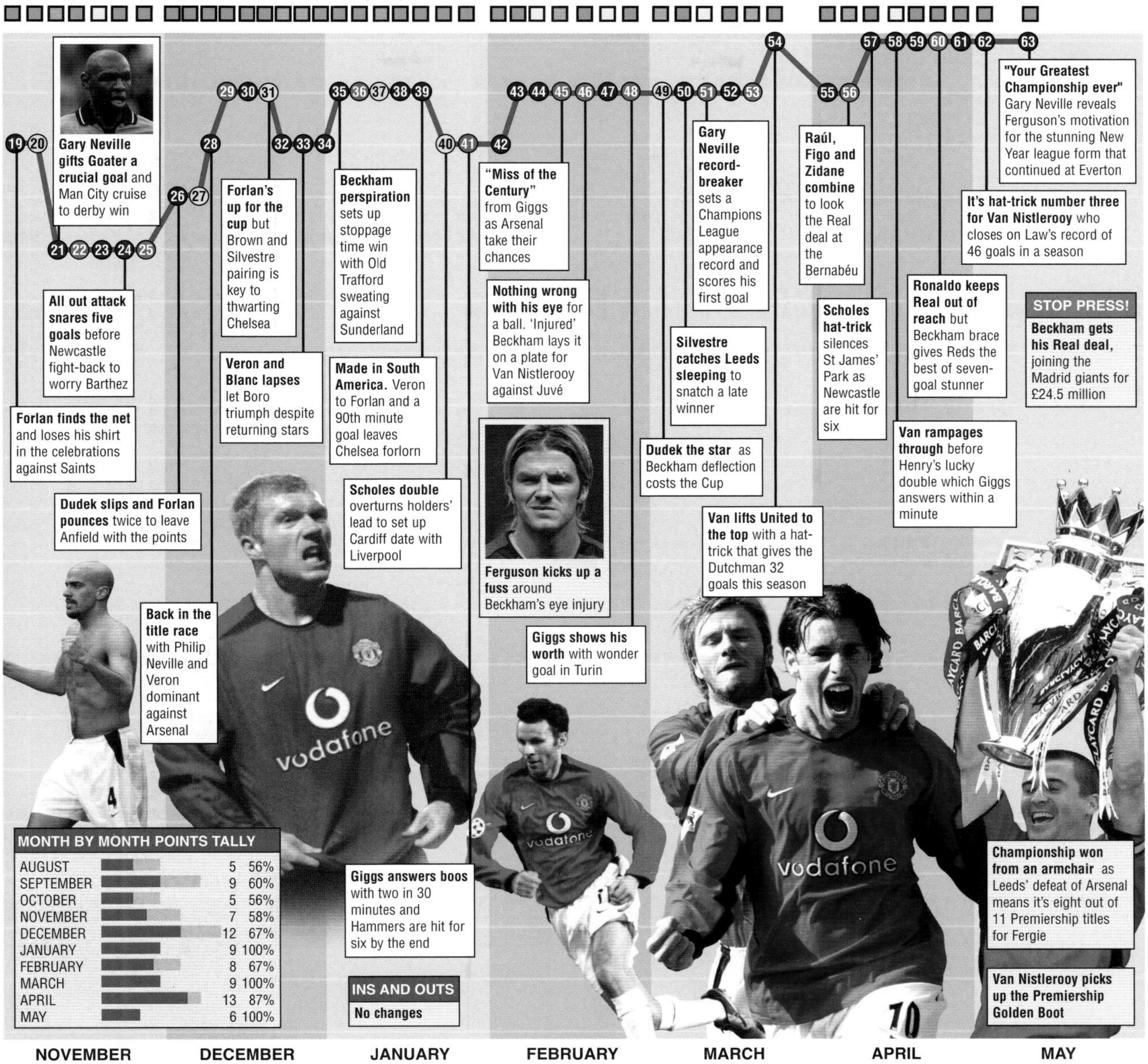
19 20 21 22 23 24 25 26 27 28 29 30 31 32 33 34 35 36 37 38 39 40 41 42 43 44 45 46 47 48 49 50 51 52 53 54 55 56 57 58 59 60 61 62 63
NOVEMBER
DECEMBER
JANUARY
FEBRUARY
MARCH
APRIL
MAY
vodafone

**Forlan finds the net** and loses his shirt in the celebrations against Saints

**Gary Neville gifts Goater a crucial goal** and Man City cruise to derby win

**All out attack snares five goals** before Newcastle fight-back to worry Barthez

**Dudek slips and Forlan pounces** twice to leave Anfield with the points

**Back in the title race** with Philip Neville and Veron dominant against Arsenal

**Forlan's up for the cup** but Brown and Silvestre pairing is key to thwarting Chelsea

**Veron and Blanc lapses** let Boro triumph despite returning stars

**Beckham perspiration** sets up stoppage time win with Old Trafford sweating against Sunderland

**Made in South America.** Veron to Forlan and a 90th minute goal leaves Chelsea forlorn

**Scholes double** overturns holders' lead to set up Cardiff date with Liverpool

**Giggs answers boos** with two in 30 minutes and Hammers are hit for six by the end

**"Miss of the Century"** from Giggs as Arsenal take their chances

**Nothing wrong with his eye** for a ball. 'Injured' Beckham lays it on a plate for Van Nistlerooy against Juvé

**Ferguson kicks up a fuss** around Beckham's eye injury

**Giggs shows his worth** with wonder goal in Turin

**Gary Neville record-breaker** sets a Champions League appearance record and scores his first goal

**Silvestre catches Leeds sleeping** to snatch a late winner

**Dudek the star** as Beckham deflection costs the Cup

**Van lifts United to the top** with a hat-trick that gives the Dutchman 32 goals this season

**Raúl, Figo and Zidane combine** to look the Real deal at the Bernabéu

**Scholes hat-trick** silences St James' Park as Newcastle are hit for six

**Ronaldo keeps Real out of reach** but Beckham brace gives Reds the best of seven-goal stunner

**Van rampages through** before Henry's lucky double which Giggs answers within a minute

**It's hat-trick number three for Van Nistlerooy** who closes on Law's record of 46 goals in a season

**"Your Greatest Championship ever"** Gary Neville reveals Ferguson's motivation for the stunning New Year league form that continued at Everton

**STOP PRESS!**
**Beckham gets his Real deal,** joining the Madrid giants for £24.5 million

**Championship won from an armchair** as Leeds' defeat of Arsenal means it's eight out of 11 Premiership titles for Fergie

**Van Nistlerooy picks up the Premiership Golden Boot**

**MONTH BY MONTH POINTS TALLY**

| | | |
|---|---|---|
| AUGUST | 5 | 56% |
| SEPTEMBER | 9 | 60% |
| OCTOBER | 5 | 56% |
| NOVEMBER | 7 | 58% |
| DECEMBER | 12 | 67% |
| JANUARY | 9 | 100% |
| FEBRUARY | 8 | 67% |
| MARCH | 9 | 100% |
| APRIL | 13 | 87% |
| MAY | 6 | 100% |

**INS AND OUTS**
No changes

## DISCIPLINARY RECORDS

**1 Phil Neville**

| | |
|---|---|
| League Yellow | 7 |
| League Red | 0 |
| League Total | 7 |
| All Comps Yellow | 13 |
| All Comps Red | 0 |
| TOTAL | 13 |

League Average **238** mins between cards

vodafone

| | PLAYER | LEAGUE Y | LEAGUE R | TOTAL Y | TOTAL R | AVE |
|---|---|---|---|---|---|---|
| 2 | Keane | 4 | 1 | 7 | 1 | 352 |
| 3 | Forlan | 2 | 0 | 2 | 0 | 423 |
| 4 | Beckham | 5 | 0 | 7 | 0 | 503 |
| 5 | Fortune | 1 | 0 | 3 | 0 | 509 |
| 6 | Neville, G | 3 | 0 | 6 | 0 | 608 |
| 7 | Brown | 3 | 0 | 4 | 0 | 617 |
| 8 | Solskjaer | 4 | 0 | 5 | 0 | 651 |
| 9 | Scholes | 4 | 0 | 8 | 0 | 684 |
| 10 | Blanc | 2 | 0 | 2 | 0 | 712 |
| 11 | Ferdinand | 3 | 0 | 5 | 0 | 812 |
| 12 | van Nistelrooy | 3 | 0 | 5 | 0 | 965 |
| 13 | Butt | 1 | 0 | 2 | 0 | 1217 |
| 14 | Silvestre | 2 | 0 | 3 | 0 | 1458 |
| 15 | Veron | 1 | 0 | 6 | 0 | 1757 |
| | Other | 1 | 0 | 4 | 0 | |
| | TOTAL | 46 | 1 | 82 | 1 | |

## GOALS

**1 Ruud van Nistelrooy**

| | |
|---|---|
| League | 25 |
| FA Cup | 4 |
| League Cup | 1 |
| Europe | 14 |
| Other | 0 |
| TOTAL | 44 |

League Average **116** mins between goals

vodafone

| | PLAYER | LGE | FAC | LC | Euro | TOT | AVE |
|---|---|---|---|---|---|---|---|
| 2 | Scholes | 14 | 1 | 3 | 2 | 20 | 195 |
| 3 | Solskjaer | 9 | 1 | 1 | 4 | 15 | 289 |
| 4 | Giggs | 8 | 2 | 0 | 5 | 15 | 356 |
| 5 | Forlan | 6 | 0 | 2 | 1 | 9 | 140 |
| 6 | Beckham | 6 | 1 | 1 | 3 | 11 | 420 |
| 7 | Veron | 2 | 0 | 0 | 4 | 6 | 879 |
| 8 | Neville, P | 1 | 1 | 0 | 0 | 2 | 1666 |
| 9 | Silvestre | 1 | 0 | 0 | 0 | 1 | 2916 |
| 10 | Richardson | 0 | 0 | 1 | 0 | 1 | |
| 11 | Neville, G | 0 | 0 | 0 | 1 | 1 | |
| 12 | Blanc | 0 | 0 | 0 | 1 | 1 | |
| 13 | Brown | 0 | 0 | 0 | 1 | 1 | |
| | Other | 2 | 0 | 0 | 1 | 3 | |
| | TOTAL | 74 | 10 | 9 | 37 | 130 | |

## SQUAD APPEARANCES

| Match | 1 2 3 4 5 | 6 7 8 9 10 | 11 12 13 14 15 | 16 17 18 19 20 | 21 22 23 24 25 | 26 27 28 29 30 | 31 32 33 34 35 | 36 37 38 39 40 | 41 42 43 44 45 | 46 47 48 49 50 | 51 52 53 54 55 | 56 57 58 59 60 | 61 62 63 |
|---|---|---|---|---|---|---|---|---|---|---|---|---|---|
| Venue | A H A H A | H H A H H | A A H H A | A H A H H | A H A H A | A A H H H | H A A H H | H H A H A | H A A H H | H A A N H | H A A H H | A A A H H | A H A |
| Competition | C L L C L | L L L C L | C L C L L | C L C L W | L C L L C | L W L C L | W L L L L | F W L L W | F L L L F | C L C W L | C L C L L | C L L L C | L L L |
| Result | L W D W D | W L L W W | W W W W D | W D L W W | L W D W W | W W W W W | W L L W W | W D W W W | W W W D L | W D W L W | D W L W W | L W D W W | W W W |

**Goalkeepers**
Fabien Barthez
Roy Carroll
Ricardo Lopez Felipe
Ben Williams

**Defenders**
Laurent Blanc
Wes Brown
Rio Ferdinand
Mark Lynch
David May
Gary Neville
John O'Shea
Lee Roche
Mikael Silvestre

**Midfielders**
David Beckham
Nicky Butt
Luke Chadwick
Darren Fletcher
Quinton Fortune
Ryan Giggs
Roy Keane
Phil Neville
Danny Pugh
Keiron Richardson
Michael Stewart
Paul Tierney
Mads Timms
Juan Sebastian Veron

**Forwards**
Jimmy Davis
Diego Forlan
Daniel Nardiello
Paul Scholes
Ole Gunnar Solskjaer
Ruud van Nistelrooy
Danny Webber

KEY: On all match | On bench | Subbed or sent off (Counting game) | Subbed or sent off (playing less than 70 minutes) | Subbed on from bench (Counting Game) | Subbed on (playing less than 70 minutes) | Subbed on and then subbed or sent off (Counting Game) | Subbed on and then subbed or sent off (playing less than 70 minutes) | Not in 16

## KEY PLAYERS - GOALSCORERS

**1 Ruud van Nistelrooy**

| | |
|---|---|
| **Goals in the League** | 25 |
| **Goals in all competitions** | 44 |
| **Assists** League goals scored by team-mates where he delivered the final pass | 4 |
| **Contribution to Attacking Power** Average number of minutes between League team goals while on pitch | 45 |
| **Player Strike Rate** Average number of minutes between League goals scored by player | 116 |
| **Club Strike Rate** Average minutes between League goals scored by club | 46 |

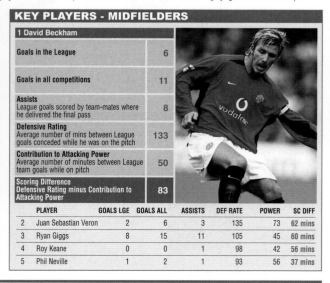

| | PLAYER | GOALS LGE | GOALS ALL | ASSISTS | POWER | S RATE |
|---|---|---|---|---|---|---|
| 2 | Paul Scholes | 14 | 20 | 4 | 40 | 195 mins |
| 3 | Ole Gunnar Solskjaer | 9 | 15 | 9 | 43 | 289 mins |
| 4 | Ryan Giggs | 8 | 15 | 11 | 45 | 356 mins |
| 5 | David Beckham | 6 | 11 | 8 | 50 | 420 mins |

## KEY PLAYERS - MIDFIELDERS

**1 David Beckham**

| | |
|---|---|
| **Goals in the League** | 6 |
| **Goals in all competitions** | 11 |
| **Assists** League goals scored by team-mates where he delivered the final pass | 8 |
| **Defensive Rating** Average number of mins between League goals conceded while he was on the pitch | 133 |
| **Contribution to Attacking Power** Average number of minutes between League team goals while on pitch | 50 |
| **Scoring Difference** Defensive Rating minus Contribution to Attacking Power | 83 |

| | PLAYER | GOALS LGE | GOALS ALL | ASSISTS | DEF RATE | POWER | SC DIFF |
|---|---|---|---|---|---|---|---|
| 2 | Juan Sebastian Veron | 2 | 6 | 3 | 135 | 73 | 62 mins |
| 3 | Ryan Giggs | 8 | 15 | 11 | 105 | 45 | 60 mins |
| 4 | Roy Keane | 0 | 0 | 1 | 98 | 42 | 56 mins |
| 5 | Phil Neville | 1 | 2 | 1 | 93 | 56 | 37 mins |

## PLAYER APPEARANCES

| | AGE (on 01/07/03) | IN THE SQUAD | COUNTING GAMES | MINUTES ON PITCH | IN THE SQUAD | MINUTES ON PITCH | THIS SEASON | NATIONAL SIDE |
|---|---|---|---|---|---|---|---|---|
| **Goalkeepers** | | | | | | | | |
| Fabien Barthez | 32 | 31 | 27 | 2539 | 48 | 3955 | 6 | France (2) |
| Roy Carroll | 25 | 12 | 8 | 836 | 24 | 1376 | - | N Ireland |
| Ricardo L Felipe | 31 | 29 | 0 | 45 | 48 | 339 | 1 | Spain (2) |
| Ben Williams | 20 | 3 | 0 | 0 | 5 | 0 | - | England |
| **Defenders** | | | | | | | | |
| Laurent Blanc | 37 | 23 | 14 | 1424 | 37 | 2270 | - | France |
| Wes Brown | 23 | 23 | 19 | 1851 | 37 | 2835 | 1 | England (7) |
| Rio Ferdinand | 24 | 28 | 27 | 2438 | 46 | 4035 | 5 | England (7) |
| Mark Lynch | 21 | 0 | 0 | 0 | 2 | 90 | - | England |
| David May | 33 | 5 | 0 | 1 | 14 | 182 | - | England |
| Gary Neville | 28 | 28 | 18 | 1825 | 47 | 3319 | 5 | England (7) |
| John O'Shea | 22 | 36 | 22 | 2288 | 60 | 3760 | 7 | Rep of Ireland (15) |
| Lee Roche | 22 | 2 | 0 | 22 | 7 | 67 | - | England |
| Mikael Silvestre | 25 | 34 | 31 | 2916 | 54 | 4621 | 8 | France (2) |
| **Midfielders** | | | | | | | | |
| David Beckham | 28 | 32 | 27 | 2518 | 53 | 4097 | 6 | England (7) |
| Nicky Butt | 28 | 20 | 11 | 1217 | 33 | 1997 | 5 | England (7) |
| Luke Chadwick | 22 | 6 | 0 | 28 | 13 | 158 | - | England |
| Darren Fletcher | 19 | 4 | 0 | 0 | 10 | 163 | - | Scotland |
| Quinton Fortune | 26 | 14 | 4 | 509 | 22 | 902 | - | South Africa |
| Ryan Giggs | 29 | 37 | 30 | 2848 | 60 | 4597 | - | Wales |
| Roy Keane | 31 | 21 | 19 | 1763 | 32 | 2699 | - | Rep of Ireland |
| Phil Neville | 26 | 35 | 15 | 1666 | 59 | 3152 | 3 | England (7) |
| Danny Pugh | 20 | 3 | 0 | 6 | 14 | 233 | - | England |
| Keiron Richardson | 18 | 9 | 0 | 43 | 19 | 248 | - | England |
| Michael Stewart | 22 | 6 | 0 | 1 | 17 | 148 | - | England |
| Paul Tierney | 20 | 2 | 0 | 0 | 4 | 0 | - | England |
| Mads Timms | 18 | 0 | 0 | 0 | 1 | 12 | - | Denmark |
| Juan S Veron | 28 | 26 | 17 | 1757 | 43 | 3148 | 2 | Argentina (5) |
| **Forwards** | | | | | | | | |
| Jimmy Davis | 20 | 1 | 0 | 0 | 2 | 0 | - | England |
| Diego Forlan | 24 | 34 | 5 | 842 | 58 | 1667 | 2 | Uruguay (28) |
| Daniel Nardiello | 20 | 0 | 0 | 0 | 5 | 103 | - | England |
| Paul Scholes | 28 | 33 | 30 | 2736 | 53 | 4077 | 8 | England (7) |
| O Gunnar Solskjaer | 30 | 37 | 27 | 2604 | 58 | 3763 | 10 | Norway (24) |
| R van Nistelrooy | 27 | 34 | 32 | 2897 | 53 | 4338 | 8 | Holland (6) |
| Danny Webber | 21 | 0 | 0 | 0 | 2 | 19 | - | England |

KEY: LEAGUE ALL COMPS CAPS (FIFA RANKING)

## TEAM OF THE SEASON

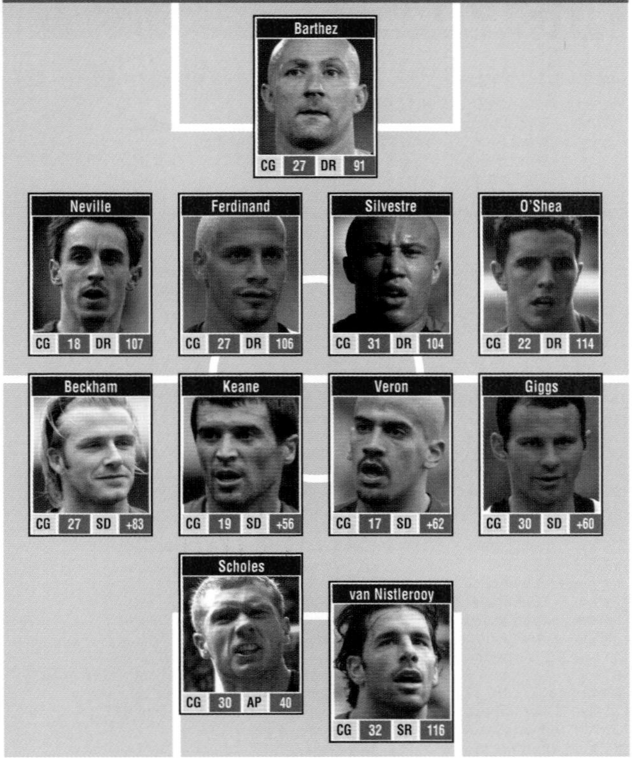

Barthez
CG 27 DR 91
Neville
CG 18 DR 107
Ferdinand
CG 27 DR 106
Silvestre
CG 31 DR 104
O'Shea
CG 22 DR 114
Beckham
CG 27 SD +83
Keane
CG 19 SD +56
Veron
CG 17 SD +62
Giggs
CG 30 SD +60
Scholes
CG 30 AP 40
van Nistlerooy
CG 32 SR 116


**KEY:** DR = Defensive Rate, SD = Scoring Difference AP = Attacking Power SR = Strike Rate, CG=Counting Games – League games playing at least 70 minutes

## TOP POINT EARNERS

| 1 David Beckham | |
|---|---|
| **Counting Games** League games when he played at least 70 minutes | 27 |
| **Average points** Average League points taken in Counting games | 2.33 |
| **Club Average points** Average points taken in League games | 2.18 |

| | PLAYER | GAMES | PTS |
|---|---|---|---|
| 2 | Roy Keane | 19 | 2.32 |
| 3 | Paul Scholes | 30 | 2.30 |
| 4 | Rio Ferdinand | 27 | 2.30 |
| 5 | Wes Brown | 19 | 2.26 |
| 6 | Mikael Silvestre | 31 | 2.23 |
| 7 | John O'Shea | 22 | 2.23 |
| 8 | Gary Neville | 18 | 2.22 |
| 9 | Ruud van Nistelrooy | 32 | 2.16 |
| 10 | Ryan Giggs | 30 | 2.10 |

## KEY PLAYERS - DEFENDERS

| 1 John O'Shea | |
|---|---|
| **Goals Conceded** The number of League goals conceded while he was on the pitch | 20 |
| **Goals Conceded in all competitions** The number goals conceded while he was on the pitch in all competitions | 36 |
| **League minutes played** Number of minutes played in league matches | 2288 |
| **Clean Sheets** In games when he played at least70 mins | 10 |
| **Defensive Rating** Average number of mins between League goals conceded while he was on the pitch | 114 |
| **Club Defensive Rating** Average number of mins between League goals conceded by the club this season | 101 |

| | PLAYER | CON LGE | CON ALL | MINS | C SHEETS | DEF RATE |
|---|---|---|---|---|---|---|
| 2 | Gary Neville | 17 | 35 | 1825 | 8 | 107 mins |
| 3 | Rio Ferdinand | 23 | 44 | 2438 | 9 | 106 mins |
| 4 | Mikael Silvestre | 28 | 51 | 2916 | 11 | 104 mins |
| 5 | Wes Brown | 20 | 33 | 1851 | 6 | 93 mins |

## KEY PLAYERS - GOALKEEPERS

| 1 Roy Carroll | |
|---|---|
| **Goals Conceded in the League** The number of League goals conceded while he was on the pitch | 6 |
| **Goals Conceded in all competitions** The number of goals conceded while he was on the pitch in all competitions | 9 |
| **League minutes played** Number of minutes played in league matches | 836 |
| **Clean Sheets** In games when he played at least 70 mins | 3 |
| **Goals to Shots Ratio** The average number of shots on target per each League goal conceded | 5.5 |
| **Defensive Rating** Ave number of mins between League goals conceded while on the pitch | 139 |

| 2 Fabien Barthez | |
|---|---|
| **Goals Conceded in the League** The number of League goals conceded while he was on the pitch | 28 |
| **Goals Conceded in all competitions** The number of goals conceded while he was on the pitch in all competitions | 46 |
| **League minutes played** Number of minutes played in league matches | 2539 |
| **Clean Sheets** In games when he played at least 70 mins | 9 |
| **Goals to Shots Ratio** The average number of shots on target per each League goal conceded | 4.3 |
| **Defensive Rating** Ave number of mins between League goals conceded while on the pitch | 91 |

# ARSENAL

**NICKNAME:** THE GUNNERS

KEY: Won / Drawn / Lost

| No | Comp | Opponent | Venue | Res | Score | Scorers |
|---|---|---|---|---|---|---|
| 1 | facs | Liverpool | N | W | 1-0 | Silva 69 |
| 2 | lge | Birmingham | H | W | 2-0 | Henry 9; Wiltord 23 |
| 3 | lge | West Ham | A | D | 2-2 | Henry 64; Wiltord 88 |
| 4 | lge | West Brom | H | W | 5-2 | Cole 2; Lauren 21; Wiltord 24,77; Aliadiere 89 |
| 5 | lge | Chelsea | A | D | 1-1 | Toure 59 |
| 6 | lge | Man City | H | W | 2-1 | Wiltord 25; Henry 42 |
| 7 | lge | Charlton | A | W | 3-0 | Henry 44; Wiltord 66; Edu 88 |
| 8 | ecga | B Dortmund | H | W | 2-0 | Bergkamp 61; Ljungberg 77 |
| 9 | lge | Bolton | H | W | 2-1 | Henry 26; Kanu 90 |
| 10 | ecga | PSV Eindhoven | A | W | 4-0 | Silva 1; Ljungberg 66; Henry 81,90 |
| 11 | lge | Leeds | A | W | 4-1 | Kanu 9,87; Toure 20; Henry 47 |
| 12 | ecga | Auxerre | A | W | 1-0 | Silva 48 |
| 13 | lge | Sunderland | H | W | 3-1 | Kanu 3,9; Vieira 45 |
| 14 | lge | Everton | A | L | 1-2 | Ljungberg 8 |
| 15 | ecga | Auxerre | H | L | 1-2 | Kanu 53 |
| 16 | lge | Blackburn | H | L | 1-2 | Edu 45 |
| 17 | ecga | B Dortmund | A | L | 1-2 | Henry 18 |
| 18 | lge | Fulham | A | W | 1-0 | Marlet 31 og |
| 19 | wr3 | Sunderland | H | L | 2-3 | Pires 12; Jeffers 32 |
| 20 | lge | Newcastle | H | W | 1-0 | Wiltord 25 |
| 21 | ecga | PSV Eindhoven | H | D | 0-0 | |
| 22 | lge | Tottenham | H | W | 3-0 | Henry 13; Ljungberg 55; Wiltord 71 |
| 23 | lge | Southampton | A | L | 2-3 | Bergkamp 36; Pires 80 |
| 24 | ecgb | Roma | A | W | 3-1 | Henry 6,70,75 |
| 25 | lge | Aston Villa | H | W | 3-1 | Pires 17; Henry 49,81 pen |
| 26 | lge | Man Utd | A | L | 0-2 | |
| 27 | ecgb | Valencia | H | D | 0-0 | |
| 28 | lge | Tottenham | A | D | 1-1 | Pires 45 pen |
| 29 | lge | Middlesbrough | H | W | 2-0 | Campbell 45; Pires 90 |
| 30 | lge | West Brom | A | W | 2-1 | Jeffers 48; Henry 85 |
| 31 | lge | Liverpool | H | D | 1-1 | Henry 79 pen |
| 32 | lge | Chelsea | H | W | 3-2 | Bergkamp 9; Van Bronckhorst 81; Henry 82 |
| 33 | facr3 | Oxford | H | W | 2-0 | Bergkamp 15; McNiven 67 og |
| 34 | lge | Birmingham | A | W | 4-0 | Henry 6,70; Pires 29; Lauren 67 |
| 35 | lge | West Ham | H | W | 3-1 | Henry 14 pen,71,87 |
| 36 | facr4 | Farnborough | A | W | 5-1 | Campbell 19; Jeffers 23,68; Bergkamp 74; Lauren 79 |
| 37 | lge | Liverpool | A | D | 2-2 | Pires 8; Bergkamp 63 |
| 38 | lge | Fulham | H | W | 2-1 | Pires 17,90 |
| 39 | lge | Newcastle | A | D | 1-1 | Henry 36 |
| 40 | facr5 | Man Utd | A | W | 2-0 | Edu 35; Wiltord 52 |
| 41 | ecgb | Ajax | H | D | 1-1 | Wiltord 5 |
| 42 | lge | Man City | A | W | 5-1 | Bergkamp 5; Pires 12; Henry 15; Campbell 19; Vieira 53 |
| 43 | ecgb | Ajax | A | D | 0-0 | |
| 44 | lge | Charlton | H | W | 2-0 | Jeffers 26; Pires 45 |
| 45 | facqf | Chelsea | H | D | 2-2 | Jeffers 36; Henry 45 |
| 46 | ecgb | Roma | H | D | 1-1 | Vieira 12 |
| 47 | lge | Blackburn | A | L | 0-2 | |
| 48 | ecgb | Valencia | A | L | 1-2 | Henry 49 |
| 49 | lge | Everton | H | W | 2-1 | Cygan 8; Vieira 64 |
| 50 | facqfr | Chelsea | A | W | 3-1 | Terry 25 og; Wiltord 34; Lauren 82 |
| 51 | lge | Aston Villa | A | D | 1-1 | Ljungberg 56 |
| 52 | facsf | Sheff Utd | H | W | 1-0 | Ljungberg 34 |
| 53 | lge | Man Utd | H | D | 2-2 | Henry 51,62 |
| 54 | lge | Middlesbrough | A | W | 2-0 | Wiltord 48; Henry 82 |
| 55 | lge | Bolton | A | D | 2-2 | Wiltord 47; Pires 56 |
| 56 | lge | Leeds | H | L | 2-3 | Henry 31; Bergkamp 63 |
| 57 | lge | Southampton | H | W | 6-1 | Pires 9,23,47; Pennant 16,19,26 |
| 58 | lge | Sunderland | A | W | 4-0 | Henry 7; Ljungberg 39,78,88 |
| 59 | facf | Southampton | N | W | 1-0 | Pires 37 |

LEAGUE POSITION
1st
2nd
3rd
4th
5th
6th
7th
8th
9th
10th
11th
12th
13th
14th
15th
16th
17th
18th
19th
20th
AUGUST
SEPTEMBER
OCTOBER
**Ljundberg's scoring return** helps edge past Dortmund 2-0 in Champions League opener
**Thirty games unbeaten** is a new Premiership record. Kanu's brace helps beat Sunderland
**Edu strikes at both ends** but Blackburn's Yorke has the final say
**Toure's debut goal** earns ten-men a point at Chelsea
**14 in a row** is a top division record for wins on the bounce
**Gilberto's fastest ever goal** against PSV beats Del Piero's Champions League record
**Wonderboy** Rooney's 25 yarder ends record run. The unbeaten run of 30 Premiership games and 23 games unbeaten away, both fall to 90th minute strike
**Silva-ware strike** as debut goal from Gilberto clinches the Cup in Cardiff
**Kanu double beats Leeds and Chesterfield,** whose Football League all time record for scoring in 46 consecutive matches is surpassed in this 4-1 win
CYGAN
18


**INS AND OUTS**

**Star Silva signs**
Brazil's World cup star Gilberto Silva 25 joins from Athletico Mineiro for £4.5m
**IN** Pascal Cygan £2.1m from Lille
**OUT** Richard Wright £3.5m to Everton

Home / Away / Neutral

## ATTENDANCES

**HOME GROUND:** HIGHBURY **CAPACITY:** 38500 **AVERAGE LEAGUE AT HOME:** 38041

| | | | | | | | | | | | |
|---|---|---|---|---|---|---|---|---|---|---|---|
| 59 | Southampton | 73726 | 5 | Chelsea | 40037 | 2 | Birmingham | 38018 | 42 | Man City | 34960 |
| 24 | Roma | 70000 | 14 | Everton | 39038 | 44 | Charlton | 38015 | 8 | B Dortmund | 34907 |
| 26 | Man Utd | 67650 | 53 | Man Utd | 38164 | 29 | Middlesboro | 38003 | 27 | Valencia | 34793 |
| 1 | Liverpool | 67337 | 22 | Tottenham | 38152 | 9 | Bolton | 37974 | 54 | Middlesboro | 34724 |
| 40 | Man Utd | 67209 | 56 | Leeds | 38127 | 4 | West Brom | 37920 | 23 | Southampton | 31797 |
| 52 | Sheff Utd | 59170 | 20 | Newcastle | 38120 | 13 | Sunderland | 37902 | 47 | Blackburn | 29840 |
| 39 | Newcastle | 52157 | 45 | Chelsea | 38104 | 6 | Man City | 37878 | 34 | Birmingham | 29505 |
| 17 | B Dortmund | 52000 | 32 | Chelsea | 38096 | 28 | Tottenham | 36076 | 55 | Bolton | 27253 |
| 43 | Ajax | 51025 | 25 | Aston Villa | 38090 | 46 | Roma | 35472 | 30 | West Brom | 27025 |
| 48 | Valencia | 50000 | 31 | Liverpool | 38074 | 33 | Oxford | 35432 | 7 | Charlton | 26080 |
| 37 | Liverpool | 43660 | 16 | Blackburn | 38064 | 41 | Ajax | 35427 | 10 | PSV | 24000 |
| 51 | Aston Villa | 42602 | 35 | West Ham | 38053 | 21 | PSV | 35274 | 12 | Auxerre | 23000 |
| 50 | Chelsea | 41456 | 57 | Southampton | 38052 | 15 | Auxerre | 35206 | 19 | Sunderland | 19059 |
| 11 | Leeds | 40199 | 38 | Fulham | 38050 | 36 | Farnborough | 35108 | 18 | Fulham | 18800 |
| 58 | Sunderland | 40188 | 49 | Everton | 38042 | 3 | West Ham | 35048 | | | |

## GOAL ATTEMPTS

**FOR**
Goal attempts recorded in League games

| | HOME | AWAY | TOTAL | AVE |
|---|---|---|---|---|
| shots on target | 190 | 125 | 315 | 8.3 |
| shots off target | 129 | 82 | 211 | 5.6 |
| TOTAL | 319 | 207 | 526 | 13.8 |

**Ratio of goals to shots** Average number of shots on target per League goal scored: **3.7**

**Accuracy rating** Average percentage of total goal attempts which were on target: **59.9**

**AGAINST**
Goal attempts recorded in League games

| | HOME | AWAY | TOTAL | AVE |
|---|---|---|---|---|
| shots on target | 65 | 103 | 168 | 4.4 |
| shots off target | 65 | 125 | 190 | 5.0 |
| TOTAL | 130 | 228 | 358 | 9.4 |

**Ratio of goals to shots** Average number of shots on target per League goal scored: **4.0**

**Accuracy rating** Average percentage of total goal attempts which were on target: **46.9**

# Cup glory and plaudits for Henry

**Final Position: 2nd**

KEY: ● League ● Champions Lge ● UEFA Cup ● FA Cup ○ League Cup ● Other

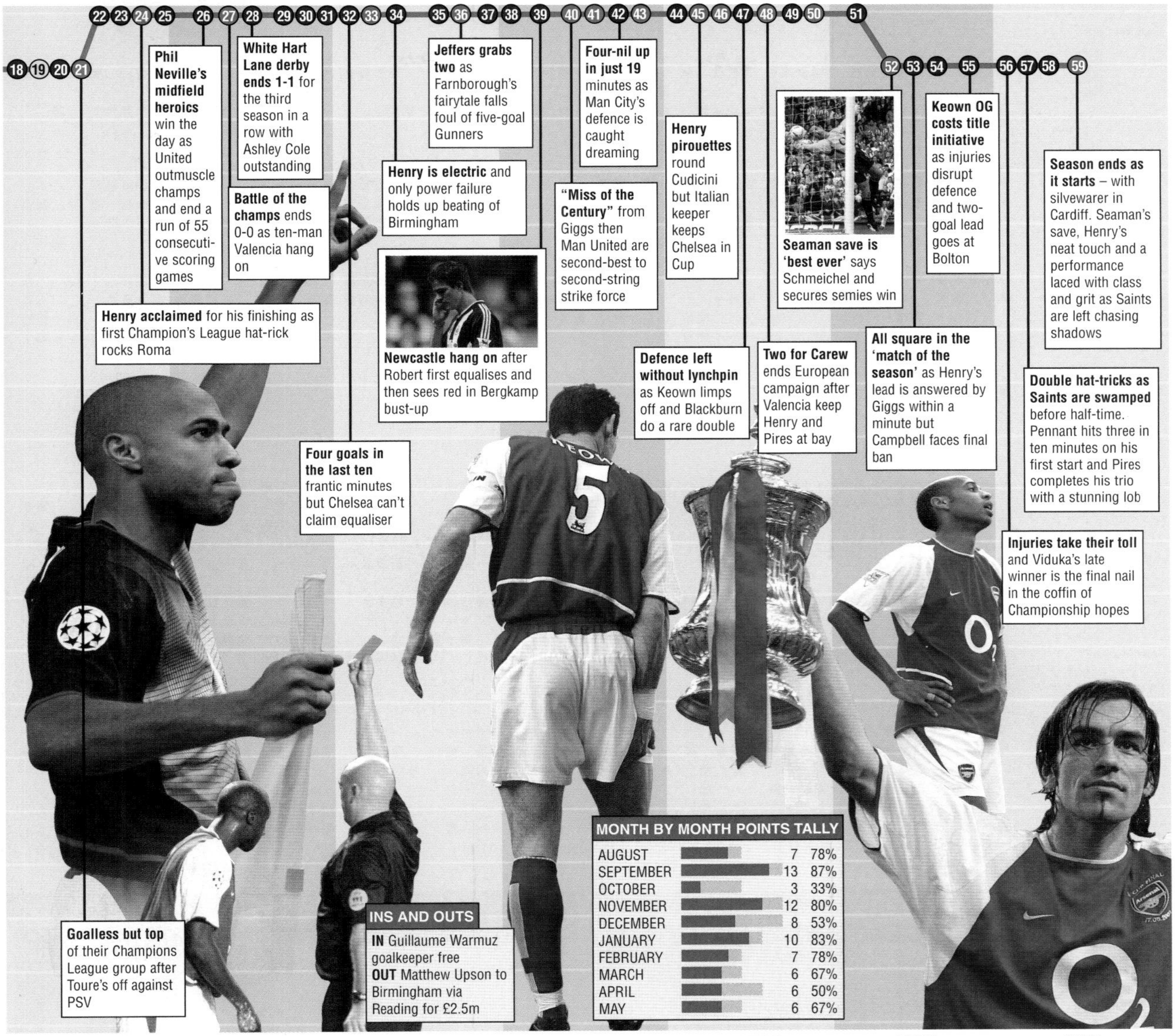

**Goalless but top** of their Champions League group after Toure's off against PSV

**Henry acclaimed** for his finishing as first Champion's League hat-rick rocks Roma

**Phil Neville's midfield heroics** win the day as United outmuscle champs and end a run of 55 consecuti-ve scoring games

**Battle of the champs** ends 0-0 as ten-man Valencia hang on

**White Hart Lane derby ends 1-1** for the third season in a row with Ashley Cole outstanding

**Four goals in the last ten** frantic minutes but Chelsea can't claim equaliser

**Henry is electric** and only power failure holds up beating of Birmingham

**Jeffers grabs two** as Farnborough's fairytale falls foul of five-goal Gunners

**Newcastle hang on** after Robert first equalises and then sees red in Bergkamp bust-up

**"Miss of the Century"** from Giggs then Man United are second-best to second-string strike force

**Four-nil up in just 19** minutes as Man City's defence is caught dreaming

**Henry pirouettes** round Cudicini but Italian keeper keeps Chelsea in Cup

**Defence left without lynchpin** as Keown limps off and Blackburn do a rare double

**Two for Carew** ends European campaign after Valencia keep Henry and Pires at bay

**Seaman save is 'best ever'** says Schmeichel and secures semies win

**All square in the 'match of the season'** as Henry's lead is answered by Giggs within a minute but Campbell faces final ban

**Keown OG costs title initiative** as injuries disrupt defence and two-goal lead goes at Bolton

**Injuries take their toll** and Viduka's late winner is the final nail in the coffin of Championship hopes

**Double hat-tricks as Saints are swamped** before half-time. Pennant hits three in ten minutes on his first start and Pires completes his trio with a stunning lob

**Season ends as it starts** – with silvewarer in Cardiff. Seaman's save, Henry's neat touch and a performance laced with class and grit as Saints are left chasing shadows

**INS AND OUTS**

**IN** Guillaume Warmuz goalkeeper free
**OUT** Matthew Upson to Birmingham via Reading for £2.5m

**MONTH BY MONTH POINTS TALLY**

| Month | Points | % |
|---|---|---|
| AUGUST | 7 | 78% |
| SEPTEMBER | 13 | 87% |
| OCTOBER | 3 | 33% |
| NOVEMBER | 12 | 80% |
| DECEMBER | 8 | 53% |
| JANUARY | 10 | 83% |
| FEBRUARY | 7 | 78% |
| MARCH | 6 | 67% |
| APRIL | 6 | 50% |
| MAY | 6 | 67% |

NOVEMBER DECEMBER JANUARY FEBRUARY MARCH APRIL MAY

## DISCIPLINARY RECORDS

**1 Patrick Vieira**

| | |
|---|---|
| League Yellow | 7 |
| League Red | 1 |
| League Total | 8 |
| All Comps Yellow | 12 |
| All Comps Red | 1 |
| TOTAL | 13 |

League Average
254
mins between cards

| | PLAYER | LEAGUE | | TOTAL | | AVE |
|---|---|---|---|---|---|---|
| 2 | Parlour | 4Y | 0R | 4Y | 0R | 319 |
| 3 | Keown | 6 | 0 | 7 | 0 | 325 |
| 4 | Edu | 3 | 0 | 4 | 0 | 333 |
| 5 | Luzhny | 3 | 0 | 3 | 0 | 356 |
| 6 | Henry | 9 | 0 | 11 | 0 | 366 |
| 7 | Lauren | 6 | 0 | 8 | 0 | 382 |
| 8 | Cygan | 3 | 0 | 5 | 1 | 476 |
| 9 | Cole | 5 | 0 | 7 | 0 | 540 |
| 10 | Campbell | 3 | 2 | 4 | 2 | 586 |
| 11 | Bergkamp | 3 | 0 | 3 | 0 | 598 |
| 12 | Toure | 1 | 0 | 3 | 1 | 909 |
| 13 | Van Bronckhorst | 1 | 0 | 2 | 0 | 962 |
| 14 | Wiltord | 1 | 0 | 2 | 0 | 2352 |
| | Other | 1 | 0 | 4 | 0 | |
| | TOTAL | 56 | 3 | 79 | 5 | |

## GOALS

**1 Thierry Henry**

| | |
|---|---|
| League | 24 |
| FA Cup | 1 |
| League Cup | 0 |
| Europe | 7 |
| Other | 0 |
| TOTAL | 32 |

League Average
137
mins between goals

| | PLAYER | LGE | FAC | LC | Euro | TOT | AVE |
|---|---|---|---|---|---|---|---|
| 2 | Pires | 14 | 1 | 1 | 0 | 16 | 128 |
| 3 | Wiltord | 10 | 2 | 0 | 1 | 13 | 235 |
| 4 | Ljungberg | 6 | 1 | 0 | 2 | 9 | 266 |
| 5 | Kanu | 5 | 0 | 0 | 1 | 6 | 171 |
| 6 | Bergkamp | 5 | 2 | 0 | 1 | 8 | 359 |
| 7 | Vieira | 3 | 0 | 0 | 1 | 4 | 679 |
| 8 | Pennant | 3 | 0 | 0 | 0 | 3 | 49 |
| 9 | Edu | 2 | 1 | 0 | 0 | 3 | 500 |
| 10 | Toure | 2 | 0 | 0 | 0 | 2 | 455 |
| 11 | Jeffers | 2 | 3 | 1 | 0 | 6 | 181 |
| 12 | Lauren | 2 | 2 | 0 | 0 | 4 | 1148 |
| 13 | Campbell | 2 | 1 | 0 | 0 | 3 | 1465 |
| 14 | Van Bronckhorst | 1 | 0 | 0 | 0 | 1 | 962 |
| 15 | Cole | 1 | 0 | 0 | 0 | 1 | 2702 |
| | Other | 3 | 2 | 0 | 2 | 8 | |
| | TOTAL | 85 | 16 | 2 | 15 | 119 | |

## SQUAD APPEARANCES

| Match | Venue | Competition | Result |
|---|---|---|---|
| 1 | N | O | W |
| 2 | H | L | W |
| 3 | A | L | D |
| 4 | H | L | W |
| 5 | A | L | D |
| 6 | H | L | W |
| 7 | A | L | W |
| 8 | H | C | W |
| 9 | H | L | W |
| 10 | A | C | W |
| 11 | A | L | W |
| 12 | A | C | W |
| 13 | H | L | W |
| 14 | A | L | L |
| 15 | H | C | L |
| 16 | H | L | L |
| 17 | A | C | L |
| 18 | A | L | W |
| 19 | H | W | L |
| 20 | H | L | W |
| 21 | H | C | D |
| 22 | H | L | W |
| 23 | A | L | L |
| 24 | A | C | W |
| 25 | H | L | W |
| 26 | A | L | L |
| 27 | H | C | D |
| 28 | A | L | D |
| 29 | H | L | W |
| 30 | A | L | W |
| 31 | H | L | D |
| 32 | H | L | W |
| 33 | H | F | W |
| 34 | A | L | W |
| 35 | H | L | W |
| 36 | A | F | W |
| 37 | A | L | D |
| 38 | H | L | W |
| 39 | A | L | D |
| 40 | A | F | W |
| 41 | H | C | D |
| 42 | A | L | W |
| 43 | A | C | D |
| 44 | H | L | W |
| 45 | H | F | D |
| 46 | H | C | D |
| 47 | A | L | L |
| 48 | A | C | L |
| 49 | H | L | W |
| 50 | A | F | W |
| 51 | A | L | D |
| 52 | H | F | W |
| 53 | H | L | D |
| 54 | A | L | W |
| 55 | A | L | D |
| 56 | H | L | L |
| 57 | H | L | W |
| 58 | A | L | W |
| 59 | N | F | W |

**Goalkeepers**
Craig Holloway
David Seaman
Rami Shaaban
Stuart Taylor
Guillaume Warmuz

**Defenders**
Sol Campbell
Ashley Cole
Pascal Cygan
Ryan Garry
Justin Hoyte
Martin Keown
Bisan Lauren
Oleg Luzhny
Igors Stepanovs
Sebastian Svard
Efstathios Tavlaridis
Matthew Upson
Moritz Volz

**Midfielders**
David Bentley
Edu
Fredrik Ljungberg
Ray Parlour
Jermaine Pennant
Robert Pires
Steven Sidwell
Gilberto Silva
Kolo Toure
G Van Bronckhorst
Patrick Vieira

**Forwards**
Jeremie Aliadiere
Dennis Bergkamp
Thierry Henry
Francis Jeffers
Nwankwo Kanu
Jerome Thomas
Sylvain Wiltord

KEY: ■ On all match · ■ On bench · ⏮ Subbed or sent off (Counting game) · « Subbed or sent off (playing less than 70 minutes) · ⏭ Subbed on from bench (Counting Game) · » Subbed on (playing less than 70 minutes) · ⏭⏮ Subbed on and then subbed or sent off (Counting Game) · »« Subbed on and then subbed or sent off (playing less than 70 minutes) · □ Not in 16

## KEY PLAYERS - GOALSCORERS

**1 Robert Pires**

| | |
|---|---|
| **Goals in the League** | 14 |
| **Goals in all competitions** | 16 |
| **Assists** League goals scored by team-mates where he delivered the final pass | 3 |
| **Contribution to Attacking Power** Average number of minutes between League team goals while on pitch | 37 |
| **Player Strike Rate** Average number of minutes between League goals scored by player | 128 |
| **Club Strike Rate** Average minutes between League goals scored by club | 40 |

| | PLAYER | GOALS LGE | GOALS ALL | ASSISTS | POWER | S RATE |
|---|---|---|---|---|---|---|
| 2 | Thierry Henry | 24 | 32 | 21 | 39 | 137 mins |
| 3 | Sylvain Wiltord | 10 | 13 | 4 | 45 | 235 mins |
| 4 | Fredrik Ljungberg | 6 | 9 | 2 | 51 | 266 mins |
| 5 | Dennis Bergkamp | 5 | 8 | 9 | 43 | 359 mins |

## KEY PLAYERS - MIDFIELDERS

**1 Robert Pires**

| | |
|---|---|
| **Goals in the League** | 14 |
| **Goals in all competitions** | 16 |
| **Assists** League goals scored by team-mates where he delivered the final pass | 3 |
| **Defensive Rating** Average number of mins between League goals conceded while he was on the pitch | 89 |
| **Contribution to Attacking Power** Average number of minutes between League team goals while on pitch | 37 |
| **Scoring Difference** Defensive Rating minus Contribution to Attacking Power | 52 |

| | PLAYER | GOALS LGE | GOALS ALL | ASSISTS | DEF RATE | POWER | SC DIFF |
|---|---|---|---|---|---|---|---|
| 2 | Fredrik Ljungberg | 6 | 9 | 2 | 100 | 52 | 48 mins |
| 3 | Gilberto Silva | 0 | 3 | 2 | 84 | 43 | 41 mins |
| 4 | Patrick Vieira | 3 | 4 | 3 | 75 | 42 | 33 mins |
| 5 | Ray Parlour | 0 | 0 | 0 | 71 | 44 | 27 mins |

## PLAYER APPEARANCES

| | AGE (on 01/07/03) | IN THE SQUAD | COUNTING GAMES | MINUTES ON PITCH | IN THE SQUAD | MINUTES ON PITCH | THIS SEASON | NATIONAL SIDE |
|---|---|---|---|---|---|---|---|---|
| **Goalkeepers** | | | | | | | | |
| Craig Holloway | 18 | 1 | 0 | 0 | 2 | 0 | - | England |
| David Seaman | 39 | 28 | 28 | 2520 | 44 | 3825 | 2 | England (7) |
| Rami Shaaban | 28 | 9 | 2 | 223 | 14 | 403 | - | Sweden |
| Stuart Taylor | 22 | 29 | 7 | 677 | 46 | 1082 | - | England |
| Guillaume Warmuz | 32 | 9 | 0 | 27 | 12 | 27 | - | France |
| **Defenders** | | | | | | | | |
| Sol Campbell | 28 | 33 | 32 | 2930 | 49 | 4370 | 3 | England (7) |
| Ashley Cole | 22 | 31 | 30 | 2702 | 45 | 3872 | 6 | England (7) |
| Pascal Cygan | 29 | 23 | 15 | 1430 | 40 | 2484 | - | France |
| Ryan Garry | 19 | 2 | 1 | 90 | 3 | 100 | - | England |
| Justin Hoyte | 18 | 1 | 0 | 1 | 1 | 1 | - | England |
| Martin Keown | 36 | 25 | 21 | 1954 | 37 | 2779 | - | England |
| Bisan Lauren | 26 | 28 | 25 | 2296 | 45 | 3737 | - | Cameroon |
| Oleg Luzhny | 34 | 28 | 11 | 1069 | 42 | 1598 | - | Ukraine |
| Igors Stepanovs | 27 | 4 | 2 | 180 | 14 | 360 | - | Latvia |
| Sebastian Svard | 20 | 0 | 0 | 0 | 2 | 156 | - | Denmark |
| Efstathios Tavlaridis | 23 | 1 | 0 | 15 | 3 | 105 | - | Greece |
| Matthew Upson | 24 | 2 | 0 | 0 | 4 | 90 | 4 | England (7) |
| Moritz Volz | 20 | 0 | 0 | 0 | 2 | 10 | - | Germany |
| **Midfielders** | | | | | | | | |
| David Bentley | 18 | 0 | 0 | 0 | 1 | 14 | - | England |
| Edu | 25 | 19 | 7 | 1000 | 35 | 1643 | - | Brazil |
| Fredrik Ljungberg | 26 | 21 | 16 | 1598 | 35 | 2481 | 4 | Sweden (20) |
| Ray Parlour | 30 | 19 | 12 | 1276 | 31 | 1971 | - | England |
| Jermaine Pennant | 20 | 6 | 1 | 146 | 11 | 258 | - | England |
| Robert Pires | 29 | 27 | 15 | 1788 | 43 | 2998 | 2 | France (2) |
| Steven Sidwell | 20 | 0 | 0 | 0 | 1 | 0 | - | England |
| Gilberto Silva | 26 | 36 | 33 | 3018 | 52 | 4156 | 6 | Brazil (1) |
| Habib Kolo Toure | 22 | 30 | 6 | 909 | 47 | 1473 | - | Ivory Coast |
| G Van Bronckhorst | 28 | 22 | 8 | 962 | 35 | 1549 | 3 | Holland (6) |
| Patrick Vieira | 27 | 24 | 22 | 2038 | 42 | 3556 | 6 | France (2) |
| **Forwards** | | | | | | | | |
| Jeremie Aliadiere | 20 | 3 | 0 | 26 | 4 | 26 | - | France |
| Dennis Bergkamp | 34 | 30 | 19 | 1794 | 43 | 2590 | - | Holland |
| Thierry Henry | 25 | 37 | 37 | 3299 | 55 | 4636 | 8 | France (2) |
| Francis Jeffers | 22 | 24 | 1 | 362 | 41 | 1029 | 1 | England (7) |
| Nwankwo Kanu | 26 | 18 | 6 | 857 | 30 | 1247 | - | Nigeria |
| Jerome Thomas | 20 | 0 | 0 | 0 | 1 | 0 | - | England |
| Sylvain Wiltord | 29 | 37 | 24 | 2352 | 57 | 3624 | 8 | France (2) |

**KEY:** LEAGUE ALL COMPS CAPS (FIFA RANKING)

## TEAM OF THE SEASON

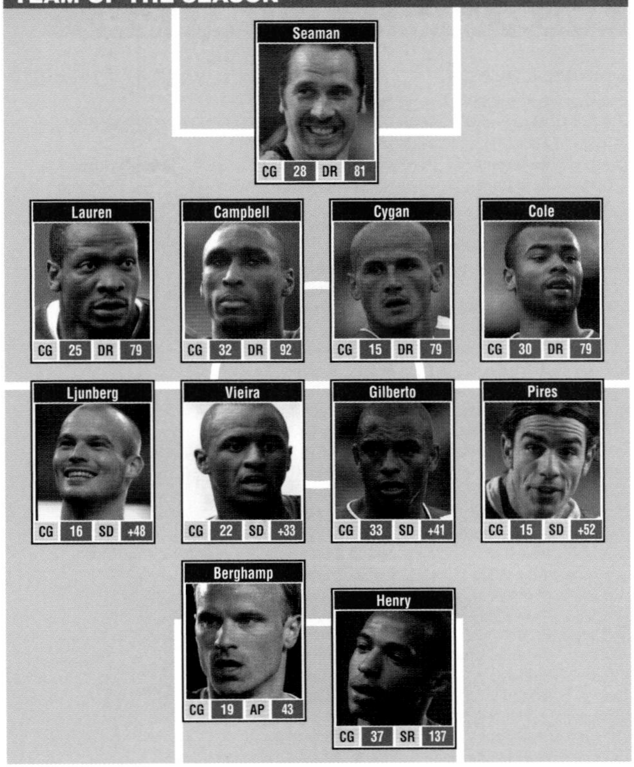
Seaman
CG 28 DR 81
Lauren
CG 25 DR 79
Campbell
CG 32 DR 92
Cygan
CG 15 DR 79
Cole
CG 30 DR 79
Ljunberg
CG 16 SD +48
Vieira
CG 22 SD +33
Gilberto
CG 33 SD +41
Pires
CG 15 SD +52
Berghamp
CG 19 AP 43
Henry
CG 37 SR 137

**KEY:** DR = Defensive Rate, SD = Scoring Difference AP = Attacking Power SR = Strike Rate, CG=Counting Games – League games playing at least 70 minutes

## TOP POINT EARNERS

**1 Sol Campbell**

| | |
|---|---|
| **Counting Games** League games when he played at least 70 minutes | 32 |
| **Average points** Average League points taken in Counting games | 2.25 |
| **Club Average points** Average points taken in League games | 2.05 |

| | PLAYER | GAMES | PTS |
|---|---|---|---|
| 2 | Sylvain Wiltord | 24 | 2.21 |
| 3 | Patrick Vieira | 22 | 2.14 |
| 4 | Martin Keown | 21 | 2.14 |
| 5 | Thierry Henry | 37 | 2.08 |
| 6 | David Seaman | 28 | 2.07 |
| 7 | Gilberto Silva | 33 | 2.06 |
| 8 | Dennis Bergkamp | 19 | 2.00 |
| 9 | Ashley Cole | 30 | 1.97 |
| 10 | Bisan Lauren | 25 | 1.92 |

## KEY PLAYERS - DEFENDERS

**1 Sol Campbell**

| | |
|---|---|
| **Goals Conceded** The number of League goals conceded while he was on the pitch | 32 |
| **Goals Conceded in all competitions** The number goals conceded while he was on the pitch in all competitions | 44 |
| **League minutes played** Number of minutes played in league matches | 2930 |
| **Clean Sheets** In games when he played at least70 mins | 9 |
| **Defensive Rating** Average number of mins between League goals conceded while he was on the pitch | 92 |
| **Club Defensive Rating** Average number of mins between League goals conceded by the club this season | 81 |

| | PLAYER | CON LGE | CON ALL | MINS | C SHEETS | DEF RATE |
|---|---|---|---|---|---|---|
| 2 | Pascal Cygan | 18 | 28 | 1430 | 4 | 79 mins |
| 3 | Ashley Cole | 34 | 40 | 2702 | 9 | 79 mins |
| 4 | Bisan Lauren | 29 | 41 | 2296 | 4 | 79 mins |
| 5 | Martin Keown | 25 | 28 | 1954 | 5 | 78 mins |

## KEY PLAYERS - GOALKEEPERS

**1 David Seaman**

| | |
|---|---|
| **Goals Conceded in the League** The number of League goals conceded while he was on the pitch | 31 |
| **Goals Conceded in all competitions** The number of goals conceded while he was on the pitch in all competitions | 39 |
| **League minutes played** Number of minutes played in league matches | 2520 |
| **Clean Sheets** In games when he played at least 70 mins | 8 |
| **Goals to Shots Ratio** The average number of shots on target per each League goal conceded | 3.9 |
| **Defensive Rating** Ave number of mins between League goals conceded while on the pitch | 81 |

**2 Stuart Taylor**

| | |
|---|---|
| **Goals Conceded in the League** The number of League goals conceded while he was on the pitch | 9 |
| **Goals Conceded in all competitions** The number of goals conceded while he was on the pitch in all competitions | 16 |
| **League minutes played** Number of minutes played in league matches | 677 |
| **Clean Sheets** In games when he played at least 70 mins | 1 |
| **Goals to Shots Ratio** The average number of shots on target per each League goal conceded | 3.6 |
| **Defensive Rating** Ave number of mins between League goals conceded while on the pitch | 75 |

# NEWCASTLE UNITED

NICKNAME: THE MAGPIES

KEY: Won / Drawn / Lost

| | | | | | | |
|---|---|---|---|---|---|---|
| 1 | ecql1 | Zeljeznicar | A | W | 1-0 | Dyer 56 |
| 2 | lge | West Ham | H | W | 4-0 | Lua Lua 61,72; Shearer 76; Solano 86 |
| 3 | lge | Man City | A | L | 0-1 | |
| 4 | ecql2 | Zeljeznicar | H | W | 4-0 | Dyer 24; Lua Lua 37; Viana 74; Shearer 80 |
| 5 | lge | Liverpool | A | D | 2-2 | Speed 81; Shearer 89 |
| 6 | lge | Leeds | H | L | 0-2 | |
| 7 | lge | Chelsea | A | L | 0-3 | |
| 8 | ecge | Dinamo Kiev | A | L | 0-2 | |
| 9 | lge | Sunderland | H | W | 2-0 | Bellamy 2; Shearer 39 |
| 10 | ecge | Feyenoord | H | L | 0-1 | |
| 11 | lge | Birmingham | A | W | 2-0 | Solano 34; Ameobi 90 |
| 12 | ecge | Juventus | A | L | 0-2 | |
| 13 | lge | West Brom | H | W | 2-1 | Shearer 45,69 |
| 14 | lge | Blackburn | A | L | 2-5 | Shearer 35 pen,48 |
| 15 | ecge | Juventus | H | W | 1-0 | Griffin 62 |
| 16 | lge | Charlton | H | W | 2-1 | Griffin 37; Robert 59 |
| 17 | ecge | Dinamo Kiev | H | W | 2-1 | Speed 58; Shearer 69 pen |
| 18 | lge | Middlesbrough | H | W | 2-0 | Ameobi 19; Caldwell, S 87 |
| 19 | wr3 | Everton | H | L | 2-3* | Dyer 77,78; Pistone 100 og (*on penalties) |
| 20 | lge | Arsenal | A | L | 0-1 | |
| 21 | ecge | Feyenoord | A | W | 3-2 | Bellamy 45,90; Viana 49 |
| 22 | lge | Southampton | H | W | 2-1 | Ameobi 41; Hughes 54 |
| 23 | lge | Man Utd | A | L | 3-5 | Bernard 35; Shearer 52; Bellamy 74 |
| 24 | ecga | Inter Milan | H | L | 1-4 | Solano 72 |
| 25 | lge | Everton | H | W | 2-1 | Shearer 86; Tie 89 og |
| 26 | lge | Aston Villa | A | W | 1-0 | Shearer 82 |
| 27 | ecga | Barcelona | A | L | 1-3 | Ameobi 24 |
| 28 | lge | Southampton | A | D | 1-1 | Bellamy 50 |
| 29 | lge | Fulham | H | W | 2-0 | Solano 8; Bellamy 70 |
| 30 | lge | Bolton | A | L | 3-4 | Shearer 8,79; Ameobi 71 |
| 31 | lge | Tottenham | H | W | 2-1 | Speed 17; Shearer 58 |
| 32 | lge | Liverpool | H | W | 1-0 | Robert 13 |
| 33 | facr3 | Wolverhampton | A | L | 2-3 | Jenas 40; Shearer 43 pen |
| 34 | lge | West Ham | A | D | 2-2 | Bellamy 9; Jenas 81 |
| 35 | lge | Man City | H | W | 2-0 | Shearer 1; Bellamy 65 |
| 36 | lge | Bolton | H | W | 1-0 | Jenas 18 |
| 37 | lge | Tottenham | A | W | 1-0 | Jenas 90 |
| 38 | lge | Arsenal | H | D | 1-1 | Robert 53 |
| 39 | ecga | B Leverkusen | A | W | 3-1 | Ameobi 5,15; LuaLua 32 |
| 40 | lge | Leeds | A | W | 3-0 | Dyer 17,48; Shearer 54 |
| 41 | ecga | B Leverkusen | H | W | 3-1 | Shearer 5,11,36 pen |
| 42 | lge | Chelsea | H | W | 2-1 | Hasselbaink 31 og; Bernard 53 |
| 43 | lge | Middlesbrough | A | L | 0-1 | |
| 44 | ecga | Inter Milan | A | D | 2-2 | Shearer 42,49 |
| 45 | lge | Charlton | A | W | 2-0 | Shearer 33 pen; Solano 49 |
| 46 | ecga | Barcelona | H | L | 0-2 | |
| 47 | lge | Blackburn | H | W | 5-1 | Solano 24; Robert 61; Jenas 85; Gresko 89 og; Bellamy 90 |
| 48 | lge | Everton | A | L | 1-2 | Robert 40 |
| 49 | lge | Man Utd | H | L | 2-6 | Jenas 21; Ameobi 86 |
| 50 | lge | Fulham | A | L | 1-2 | Shearer 39 |
| 51 | lge | Aston Villa | H | D | 1-1 | Solano 37 |
| 52 | lge | Sunderland | A | W | 1-0 | Solano 43 pen |
| 53 | lge | Birmingham | H | W | 1-0 | Viana 42 |
| 54 | lge | West Brom | A | D | 2-2 | Jenas 43; Viana 80 |

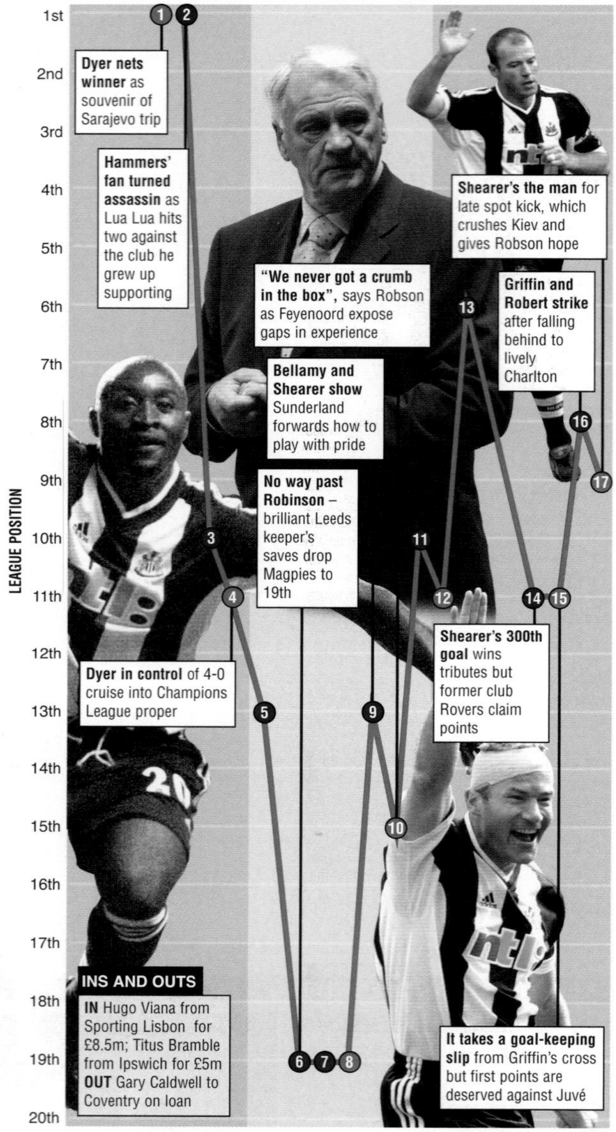

LEAGUE POSITION
1st
2nd
3rd
4th
5th
6th
7th
8th
9th
10th
11th
12th
13th
14th
15th
16th
17th
18th
19th
20th
AUGUST
SEPTEMBER
OCTOBER
**Dyer nets winner** as souvenir of Sarajevo trip
**Hammers' fan turned assassin** as Lua Lua hits two against the club he grew up supporting
**"We never got a crumb in the box"**, says Robson as Feyenoord expose gaps in experience
**Shearer's the man** for late spot kick, which crushes Kiev and gives Robson hope
**Griffin and Robert strike** after falling behind to lively Charlton
**Bellamy and Shearer show** Sunderland forwards how to play with pride
**No way past Robinson** – brilliant Leeds keeper's saves drop Magpies to 19th
**Dyer in control** of 4-0 cruise into Champions League proper
**Shearer's 300th goal** wins tributes but former club Rovers claim points
INS AND OUTS
**IN** Hugo Viana from Sporting Lisbon for £8.5m; Titus Bramble from Ipswich for £5m **OUT** Gary Caldwell to Coventry on loan
**It takes a goal-keeping slip** from Griffin's cross but first points are deserved against Juvé


Home / Away / Neutral

## ATTENDANCES

HOME GROUND: ST JAMES' PARK CAPACITY: 52200 AVERAGE LEAGUE AT HOME: 51923

| | | | | | | | | | | | |
|---|---|---|---|---|---|---|---|---|---|---|---|
| 23 | Man Utd | 67619 | 46 | Barcelona | 51883 | 5 | Liverpool | 43241 | 19 | Everton | 34584 |
| 44 | Inter Milan | 53459 | 22 | Southampton | 51812 | 8 | Dinamo Kiev | 42500 | 4 | Zeljeznicar | 34067 |
| 9 | Sunderland | 52181 | 6 | Leeds | 51730 | 10 | Feyenoord | 40540 | 26 | Aston Villa | 33446 |
| 49 | Man Utd | 52164 | 16 | Charlton | 51670 | 41 | B Leverkusen | 40508 | 28 | Southampton | 32061 |
| 38 | Arsenal | 52157 | 25 | Everton | 51607 | 17 | Dinamo Kiev | 40185 | 11 | Birmingham | 29072 |
| 42 | Chelsea | 52157 | 29 | Fulham | 51576 | 48 | Everton | 40031 | 33 | Wolves | 27316 |
| 35 | Man City | 52152 | 18 | Middlesboro | 51558 | 40 | Leeds | 40025 | 30 | Bolton | 27314 |
| 32 | Liverpool | 52147 | 2 | West Ham | 51072 | 7 | Chelsea | 39746 | 14 | Blackburn | 27307 |
| 53 | Birmingham | 52146 | 24 | Inter Milan | 50108 | 20 | Arsenal | 38120 | 54 | West Brom | 27036 |
| 31 | Tottenham | 52145 | 12 | Juventus | 49700 | 37 | Tottenham | 36084 | 45 | Charlton | 26728 |
| 13 | West Brom | 52142 | 15 | Juventus | 48370 | 34 | West Ham | 35048 | 39 | B Leverkusen | 22500 |
| 47 | Blackburn | 52106 | 27 | Barcelona | 45100 | 1 | Zeljeznicar | 35000 | 50 | Fulham | 17900 |
| 51 | Aston Villa | 52015 | 52 | Sunderland | 45067 | 43 | Middlesboro | 34814 | | | |
| 36 | Bolton | 52005 | 21 | Feyenoord | 45000 | 3 | Man City | 34776 | | | |

## GOAL ATTEMPTS

**FOR** – Goal attempts recorded in League games

| | HOME | AWAY | TOTAL | AVE |
|---|---|---|---|---|
| shots on target | 167 | 112 | 279 | 7.3 |
| shots off target | 108 | 100 | 208 | 5.5 |
| TOTAL | 275 | 212 | 487 | 12.8 |

| | |
|---|---|
| **Ratio of goals to shots** Average number of shots on target per League goal scored | 4.4 |
| **Accuracy rating** Average percentage of total goal attempts which were on target | 57.3 |

**AGAINST** – Goal attempts recorded in League games

| | HOME | AWAY | TOTAL | AVE |
|---|---|---|---|---|
| shots on target | 96 | 131 | 227 | 6.0 |
| shots off target | 73 | 112 | 185 | 4.9 |
| TOTAL | 169 | 243 | 412 | 10.8 |

| | |
|---|---|
| **Ratio of goals to shots** Average number of shots on target per League goal scored | 4.7 |
| **Accuracy rating** Average percentage of total goal attempts which were on target | 55.1 |

# Robson's young stars come of age

**Final Position: 3rd**

**KEY:** ● League ● Champions Lge ● UEFA Cup ● FA Cup ○ League Cup ● Other

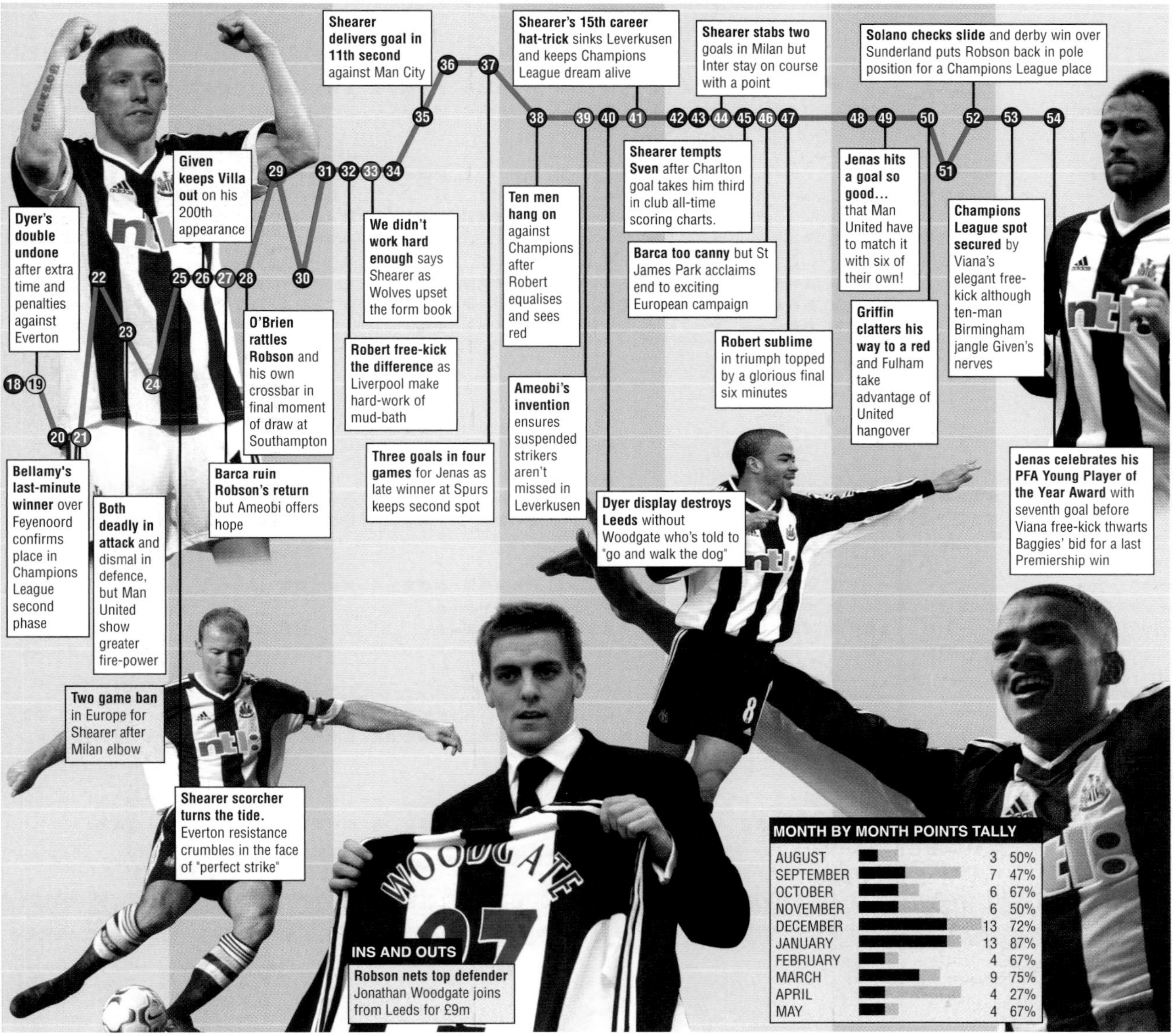

18 19 20 21 22 23 24 25 26 27 28 29 30 31 32 33 34 35 36 37 38 39 40 41 42 43 44 45 46 47 48 49 50 51 52 53 54
**Dyer's double undone** after extra time and penalties against Everton
**Bellamy's last-minute winner** over Feyenoord confirms place in Champions League second phase
**Both deadly in attack** and dismal in defence, but Man United show greater fire-power
**Given keeps Villa out** on his 200th appearance
**Barca ruin Robson's return** but Ameobi offers hope
**O'Brien rattles Robson** and his own crossbar in final moment of draw at Southampton
**Two game ban** in Europe for Shearer after Milan elbow
**Shearer scorcher turns the tide.** Everton resistance crumbles in the face of "perfect strike"
**Shearer delivers goal in 11th second** against Man City
**We didn't work hard enough** says Shearer as Wolves upset the form book
**Robert free-kick the difference** as Liverpool make hard-work of mud-bath
**Three goals in four games** for Jenas as late winner at Spurs keeps second spot
**Shearer's 15th career hat-trick** sinks Leverkusen and keeps Champions League dream alive
**Ten men hang on** against Champions after Robert equalises and sees red
**Ameobi's invention** ensures suspended strikers aren't missed in Leverkusen
**Dyer display destroys Leeds** without Woodgate who's told to "go and walk the dog"
**Shearer stabs two** goals in Milan but Inter stay on course with a point
**Shearer tempts Sven** after Charlton goal takes him third in club all-time scoring charts.
**Barca too canny** but St James Park acclaims end to exciting European campaign
**Robert sublime** in triumph topped by a glorious final six minutes
**Solano checks slide** and derby win over Sunderland puts Robson back in pole position for a Champions League place
**Jenas hits a goal so good...** that Man United have to match it with six of their own!
**Griffin clatters his way to a red** and Fulham take advantage of United hangover
**Champions League spot secured** by Viana's elegant free-kick although ten-man Birmingham jangle Given's nerves
**Jenas celebrates his PFA Young Player of the Year Award** with seventh goal before Viana free-kick thwarts Baggies' bid for a last Premiership win
WOODGATE
27
INS AND OUTS
**Robson nets top defender** Jonathan Woodgate joins from Leeds for £9m
NOVEMBER
DECEMBER
JANUARY
FEBRUARY
MARCH
APRIL
MAY


**MONTH BY MONTH POINTS TALLY**

| | | |
|---|---|---|
| AUGUST | 3 | 50% |
| SEPTEMBER | 7 | 47% |
| OCTOBER | 6 | 67% |
| NOVEMBER | 6 | 50% |
| DECEMBER | 13 | 72% |
| JANUARY | 13 | 87% |
| FEBRUARY | 4 | 67% |
| MARCH | 9 | 75% |
| APRIL | 4 | 27% |
| MAY | 4 | 67% |

## DISCIPLINARY RECORDS

**1 Andrew Griffin**

| | |
|---|---|
| League Yellow | 8 |
| League Red | 1 |
| League Total | 9 |
| All Comps Yellow | 9 |
| All Comps Red | 1 |
| TOTAL | 10 |

**League Average**
**223**
**mins between cards**

| | PLAYER | LEAGUE | | TOTAL | | AVE |
|---|---|---|---|---|---|---|
| 2 | Viana | 4Y | 0R | 5Y | 0R | 268 |
| 3 | Dabizas | 3 | 1 | 6 | 1 | 286 |
| 4 | Speed | 5 | 0 | 5 | 0 | 390 |
| 5 | Robert | 4 | 1 | 4 | 1 | 414 |
| 6 | Bramble | 3 | 0 | 4 | 0 | 415 |
| 7 | Bernard | 5 | 0 | 7 | 0 | 430 |
| 8 | Shearer | 7 | 0 | 8 | 0 | 437 |
| 9 | Ameobi | 2 | 0 | 4 | 0 | 478 |
| 10 | LuaLua | 1 | 0 | 3 | 0 | 515 |
| 11 | Woodgate | 1 | 0 | 1 | 0 | 861 |
| 12 | Caldwell, S | 1 | 0 | 2 | 0 | 1168 |
| 13 | O'Brien | 1 | 0 | 1 | 0 | 2233 |
| 14 | Solano | 1 | 0 | 1 | 0 | 2277 |
| 15 | Jenas | 1 | 0 | 1 | 0 | 2280 |
| | Other | 3 | 0 | 6 | 1 | |
| | **TOTAL** | **50** | **3** | **67** | **4** | |

## GOALS

**1 Alan Shearer**

| | |
|---|---|
| League | 17 |
| FA Cup | 1 |
| League Cup | 0 |
| Europe | 7 |
| Other | 0 |
| TOTAL | 25 |

**League Average**
**180**
**mins between goals**

| | PLAYER | LGE | FAC | LC | Euro | TOT | AVE |
|---|---|---|---|---|---|---|---|
| 2 | Bellamy | 7 | 0 | 0 | 2 | 9 | 350 |
| 3 | Solano | 7 | 0 | 0 | 1 | 8 | 325 |
| 4 | Jenas | 6 | 1 | 0 | 0 | 7 | 380 |
| 5 | Robert | 5 | 0 | 0 | 0 | 5 | 414 |
| 6 | Ameobi | 5 | 0 | 0 | 3 | 8 | 191 |
| 7 | LuaLua | 2 | 0 | 0 | 2 | 4 | 258 |
| 8 | Speed | 2 | 0 | 0 | 1 | 3 | 975 |
| 9 | Viana | 2 | 0 | 0 | 2 | 4 | 537 |
| 10 | Dyer | 2 | 0 | 2 | 2 | 6 | 1474 |
| 11 | Bernard | 2 | 0 | 0 | 0 | 2 | 1077 |
| 12 | Hughes | 1 | 0 | 0 | 0 | 1 | 3139 |
| 13 | Griffin | 1 | 0 | 0 | 1 | 2 | 2014 |
| 14 | Caldwell, S | 1 | 0 | 0 | 0 | 1 | 1168 |
| | Other | 3 | 0 | 1 | 0 | 4 | |
| | **TOTAL** | **63** | **2** | **3** | **21** | **89** | |

## SQUAD APPEARANCES

| Match | 1 | 2 | 3 | 4 | 5 | 6 | 7 | 8 | 9 | 10 | 11 | 12 | 13 | 14 | 15 | 16 | 17 | 18 |
|---|---|---|---|---|---|---|---|---|---|---|---|---|---|---|---|---|---|---|
| Venue | A | H | A | H | A | H | A | A | H | H | A | A | H | A | H | H | H | H |
| Competition | C | L | L | C | L | L | L | C | L | C | L | C | L | L | C | L | C | L |
| Result | W | W | L | W | D | L | L | L | W | L | W | L | W | L | W | W | W | W |

| Match | 19 | 20 | 21 | 22 | 23 | 24 | 25 | 26 | 27 | 28 | 29 | 30 | 31 | 32 | 33 | 34 | 35 | 36 |
|---|---|---|---|---|---|---|---|---|---|---|---|---|---|---|---|---|---|---|
| Venue | H | A | A | H | A | H | H | A | A | A | H | A | H | H | A | A | H | H |
| Competition | W | L | C | L | L | C | L | L | C | L | L | L | L | L | F | L | L | L |
| Result | L | L | W | W | L | L | W | W | L | D | W | L | W | W | L | D | W | W |

| Match | 37 | 38 | 39 | 40 | 41 | 42 | 43 | 44 | 45 | 46 | 47 | 48 | 49 | 50 | 51 | 52 | 53 | 54 |
|---|---|---|---|---|---|---|---|---|---|---|---|---|---|---|---|---|---|---|
| Venue | A | H | A | A | H | H | A | A | A | H | H | A | H | A | H | A | H | A |
| Competition | L | L | C | L | C | L | L | C | L | C | L | L | L | L | L | L | L | L |
| Result | W | D | W | W | W | W | L | D | W | L | W | L | L | L | D | W | W | D |

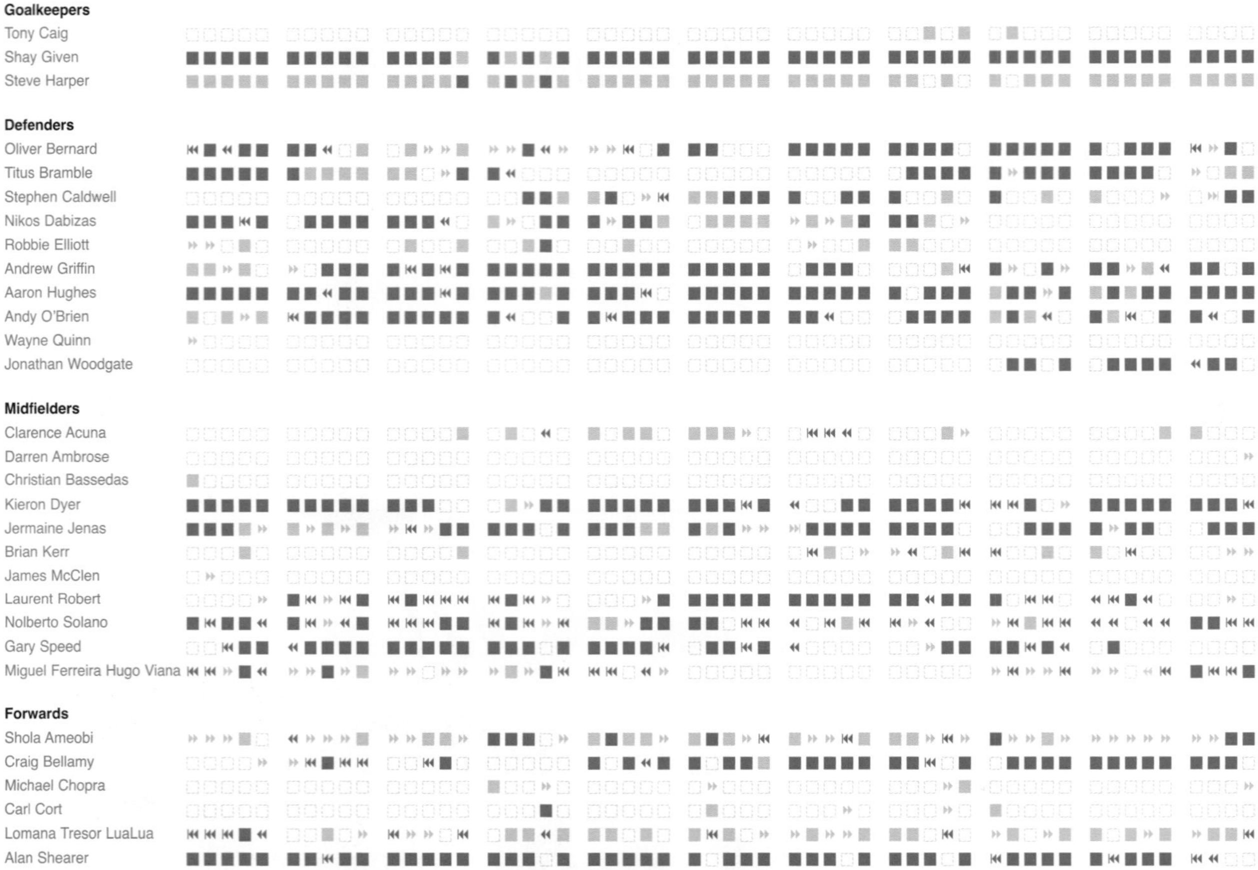
Goalkeepers
Tony Caig
Shay Given
Steve Harper
Defenders
Oliver Bernard
Titus Bramble
Stephen Caldwell
Nikos Dabizas
Robbie Elliott
Andrew Griffin
Aaron Hughes
Andy O'Brien
Wayne Quinn
Jonathan Woodgate
Midfielders
Clarence Acuna
Darren Ambrose
Christian Bassedas
Kieron Dyer
Jermaine Jenas
Brian Kerr
James McClen
Laurent Robert
Nolberto Solano
Gary Speed
Miguel Ferreira Hugo Viana
Forwards
Shola Ameobi
Craig Bellamy
Michael Chopra
Carl Cort
Lomana Tresor LuaLua
Alan Shearer

KEY: On all match · On bench · Subbed or sent off (Counting game) · Subbed or sent off (playing less than 70 minutes) · Subbed on from bench (Counting Game) · Subbed on (playing less than 70 minutes) · Subbed on and then subbed or sent off (Counting Game) · Subbed on and then subbed or sent off (playing less than 70 minutes) · Not in 16

## KEY PLAYERS - GOALSCORERS

| 1 Alan Shearer | |
|---|---|
| **Goals in the League** | 17 |
| **Goals in all competitions** | 25 |
| **Assists** League goals scored by team-mates where he delivered the final pass | 4 |
| **Contribution to Attacking Power** Average number of minutes between League team goals while on pitch | 55 |
| **Player Strike Rate** Average number of minutes between League goals scored by player | 180 |
| **Club Strike Rate** Average minutes between League goals scored by club | 54 |

9

| | PLAYER | GOALS LGE | GOALS ALL | ASSISTS | POWER | S RATE |
|---|---|---|---|---|---|---|
| 2 | Nolberto Solano | 7 | 8 | 5 | 58 | 325 mins |
| 3 | Craig Bellamy | 7 | 9 | 7 | 53 | 350 mins |
| 4 | Jermaine Jenas | 6 | 7 | 3 | 54 | 380 mins |
| 5 | Laurent Robert | 5 | 5 | 7 | 55 | 414 mins |

## KEY PLAYERS - MIDFIELDERS

| 1 Laurent Robert | |
|---|---|
| **Goals in the League** | 5 |
| **Goals in all competitions** | 5 |
| **Assists** League goals scored by team-mates where he delivered the final pass | 7 |
| **Defensive Rating** Average number of mins between League goals conceded while he was on the pitch | 80 |
| **Contribution to Attacking Power** Average number of minutes between League team goals while on pitch | 56 |
| **Scoring Difference** Defensive Rating minus Contribution to Attacking Power | 24 |

32

| | PLAYER | GOALS LGE | GOALS ALL | ASSISTS | DEF RATE | POWER | SC DIFF |
|---|---|---|---|---|---|---|---|
| 2 | Jermaine Jenas | 6 | 7 | 3 | 74 | 54 | 20 mins |
| 3 | Kieron Dyer | 2 | 6 | 4 | 72 | 55 | 17 mins |
| 4 | Gary Speed | 2 | 3 | 2 | 65 | 50 | 15 mins |
| 5 | Nolberto Solano | 7 | 8 | 5 | 71 | 58 | 13 mins |

## PLAYER APPEARANCES

| | AGE (on 01/07/03) | IN THE SQUAD | COUNTING GAMES | MINUTES ON PITCH | IN THE SQUAD | MINUTES ON PITCH | THIS SEASON | NATIONAL SIDE |
|---|---|---|---|---|---|---|---|---|
| **Goalkeepers** | | | | | | | | |
| Tony Caig | 29 | 3 | 0 | 0 | 3 | 0 | - | England |
| Shay Given | 27 | 38 | 38 | 3420 | 54 | 4590 | 9 | Rep of Ireland (15) |
| Steve Harper | 29 | 35 | 0 | 0 | 51 | 300 | - | England |
| **Defenders** | | | | | | | | |
| Oliver Bernard | 23 | 30 | 23 | 2153 | 45 | 3056 | - | France |
| Titus Bramble | 21 | 21 | 13 | 1246 | 32 | 1902 | - | England |
| Stephen Caldwell | 22 | 16 | 13 | 1168 | 24 | 1383 | 1 | Scotland (64) |
| Nikos Dabizas | 29 | 24 | 12 | 1146 | 35 | 1985 | - | Greece |
| Robbie Elliott | 29 | 7 | 0 | 19 | 12 | 141 | - | England |
| Andrew Griffin | 24 | 29 | 21 | 2014 | 45 | 3202 | - | England |
| Aaron Hughes | 23 | 36 | 35 | 3139 | 52 | 4222 | 7 | N Ireland (111) |
| Andy O'Brien | 24 | 30 | 25 | 2233 | 45 | 3211 | 3 | Rep of Ireland (15) |
| Wayne Quinn | 26 | 0 | 0 | 0 | 1 | 3 | - | England |
| Jonathan Woodgate | 23 | 10 | 9 | 861 | 10 | 861 | 5 | England (7) |
| **Midfielders** | | | | | | | | |
| Clarence Acuna | 27 | 9 | 1 | 150 | 17 | 298 | - | Chile |
| Darren Ambrose | 19 | 1 | 0 | 15 | 1 | 15 | - | England |
| Christian Bassedas | 30 | 0 | 0 | 0 | 1 | 0 | - | Argentina |
| Kieron Dyer | 24 | 35 | 32 | 2947 | 48 | 4036 | 4 | England (7) |
| Jermaine Jenas | 20 | 34 | 23 | 2280 | 48 | 3079 | 3 | England (7) |
| Brian Kerr | 21 | 8 | 3 | 307 | 15 | 388 | 1 | Scotland (64) |
| James McClen | 24 | 1 | 0 | 4 | 1 | 4 | - | England |
| Laurent Robert | 28 | 27 | 23 | 2071 | 40 | 3056 | - | France |
| Nolberto Solano | 28 | 34 | 22 | 2277 | 49 | 3299 | - | Peru |
| Gary Speed | 33 | 24 | 20 | 1950 | 36 | 3030 | 5 | Wales (50) |
| Hugo Viana | 20 | 23 | 10 | 1074 | 36 | 1656 | 3 | Portugal (14) |
| **Forwards** | | | | | | | | |
| Shola Ameobi | 21 | 37 | 7 | 956 | 52 | 1379 | - | England |
| Craig Bellamy | 23 | 30 | 27 | 2452 | 37 | 2982 | 4 | Wales (50) |
| Michael Chopra | 19 | 3 | 0 | 9 | 6 | 77 | - | England |
| Carl Cort | 25 | 1 | 0 | 5 | 5 | 132 | - | England |
| LuaLua | 22 | 26 | 4 | 515 | 42 | 1061 | - | England |
| Alan Shearer | 33 | 35 | 34 | 3063 | 48 | 4211 | - | England |

KEY: LEAGUE ALL COMPS CAPS (FIFA RANKING)

## TEAM OF THE SEASON

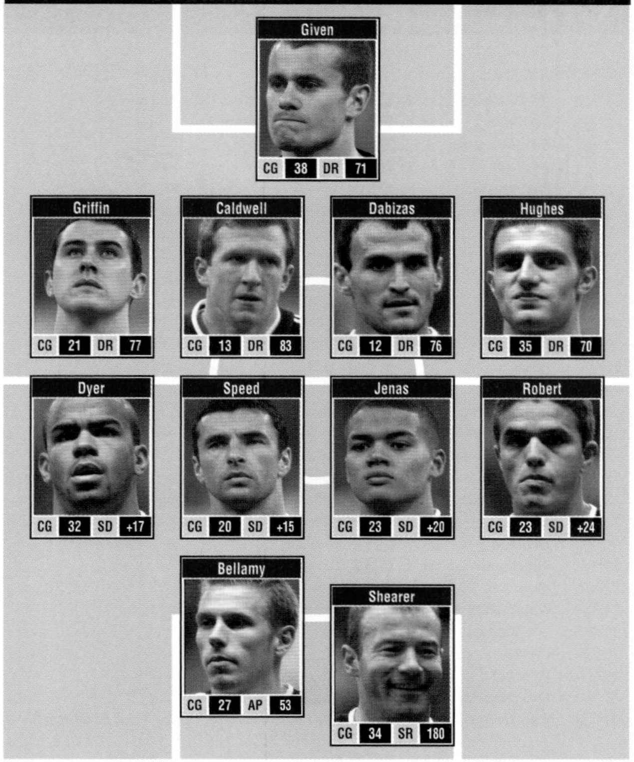

Given
CG 38 DR 71
Griffin
CG 21 DR 77
Caldwell
CG 13 DR 83
Dabizas
CG 12 DR 76
Hughes
CG 35 DR 70
Dyer
CG 32 SD +17
Speed
CG 20 SD +15
Jenas
CG 23 SD +20
Robert
CG 23 SD +24
Bellamy
CG 27 AP 53
Shearer
CG 34 SR 180


KEY: DR = Defensive Rate, SD = Scoring Difference AP = Attacking Power SR = Strike Rate, CG=Counting Games – League games playing at least 70 minutes

## TOP POINT EARNERS

**1 Stephen Caldwell**

| | |
|---|---|
| **Counting Games** League games when he played at least 70 minutes | 13 |
| **Average points** Average League points taken in Counting games | 2.31 |
| **Club Average points** Average points taken in League games | 1.82 |

| | PLAYER | GAMES | PTS |
|---|---|---|---|
| 2 | Andrew Griffin | 21 | **2.05** |
| 3 | Laurent Robert | 23 | **2.04** |
| 4 | Nolberto Solano | 22 | **2.00** |
| 5 | Craig Bellamy | 27 | **1.93** |
| 6 | Nikos Dabizas | 12 | **1.83** |
| 7 | Shay Given | 38 | **1.82** |
| 8 | Aaron Hughes | 35 | **1.80** |
| 9 | Alan Shearer | 34 | **1.79** |
| 10 | Gary Speed | 20 | **1.75** |

## KEY PLAYERS - DEFENDERS

**1 Stephen Caldwell**

| | |
|---|---|
| **Goals Conceded** The number of League goals conceded while he was on the pitch | 14 |
| **Goals Conceded in all competitions** The number goals conceded while he was on the pitch in all competitions | 18 |
| **League minutes played** Number of minutes played in league matches | 1168 |
| **Clean Sheets** In games when he played at least70 mins | 6 |
| **Defensive Rating** Average number of mins between League goals conceded while he was on the pitch | 83 |
| **Club Defensive Rating** Average number of mins between League goals conceded by the club this season | 71 |

| | PLAYER | CON LGE | CON ALL | MINS | C SHEETS | DEF RATE |
|---|---|---|---|---|---|---|
| 2 | Andrew Griffin | 26 | 51 | 2014 | 8 | **77 mins** |
| 3 | Nikos Dabizas | 15 | 31 | 1146 | 6 | **76 mins** |
| 4 | Aaron Hughes | 45 | 65 | 3139 | 13 | **70 mins** |
| 5 | Oliver Bernard | 31 | 47 | 2153 | 9 | **69 mins** |

## KEY PLAYERS - GOALKEEPERS

**1 Shay Given**

| | |
|---|---|
| **Goals Conceded in the League** The number of League goals conceded while he was on the pitch | 48 |
| **Goals Conceded in all competitions** The number of goals conceded while he was on the pitch in all competitions | 71 |
| **League minutes played** Number of minutes played in league matches | 3420 |
| **Clean Sheets** In games when he played at least 70 mins | 14 |
| **Goals to Shots Ratio** The average number of shots on target per each League goal conceded | 4.7 |
| **Defensive Rating** Ave number of mins between League goals conceded while on the pitch | 71 |

**2 Steve Harper**

| | |
|---|---|
| **Goals Conceded in the League** The number of League goals conceded while he was on the pitch | – |
| **Goals Conceded in all competitions** The number of goals conceded while he was on the pitch in all competitions | 4 |
| **League minutes played** Number of minutes played in league matches | 0 |
| **Clean Sheets** In games when he played at least 70 mins | – |
| **Goals to Shots Ratio** The average number of shots on target per each League goal conceded | – |
| **Defensive Rating** Ave number of mins between League goals conceded while on the pitch | – |

# CHELSEA

**NICKNAME:** THE BLUES

KEY: Won / Drawn / Lost

| | | | | | | |
|---|---|---|---|---|---|---|
| 1 | lge | **Charlton** | A | W | 3-2 | Zola 43; Cole 85; Lampard 89 |
| 2 | lge | **Man Utd** | H | D | 2-2 | Gallas 3; Zenden 45 |
| 3 | lge | **Southampton** | A | D | 1-1 | Lampard 79 |
| 4 | lge | **Arsenal** | H | D | 1-1 | Zola 33 |
| 5 | lge | **Blackburn** | A | W | 3-2 | Gronkjaer 37; Zola 51,80 |
| 6 | lge | **Newcastle** | H | W | 3-0 | Gudjohnsen 14,58; Zola 25 |
| 7 | uc1rl1 | **Viking** | H | W | 2-1 | Hasselbaink 43; De Lucas 69 |
| 8 | lge | **Fulham** | A | D | 0-0 | |
| 9 | lge | **West Ham** | H | L | 2-3 | Hasselbaink 20 pen; Zola 74 |
| 10 | uc1rl2 | **Viking** | A | L | 2-4 | Lampard 45; Terry 62 |
| 11 | lge | **Liverpool** | A | L | 0-1 | |
| 12 | lge | **Man City** | A | W | 3-0 | Zola 69,84; Hasselbaink 86 |
| 13 | lge | **West Brom** | H | W | 2-0 | Hasselbaink 30; Le Saux 54 |
| 14 | lge | **Tottenham** | A | D | 0-0 | |
| 15 | wr3 | **Gillingham** | H | W | 2-1 | Cole 20,52 |
| 16 | lge | **Birmingham** | H | W | 3-0 | Gudjohnsen 3,31; Zola 42 |
| 17 | lge | **Middlesbrough** | H | W | 1-0 | Babayaro 47 |
| 18 | lge | **Bolton** | A | D | 1-1 | Hasselbaink 90 |
| 19 | lge | **Sunderland** | H | W | 3-0 | Gallas 58; Desailly 84; Hasselbaink 89 |
| 20 | wr4 | **Everton** | H | W | 4-1 | Hasselbaink 26,71; Petit 44; Stanic 69 |
| 21 | lge | **Everton** | A | W | 3-1 | Stanic 5; Hasselbaink 28; Gronkjaer 90 |
| 22 | lge | **Middlesbrough** | A | D | 1-1 | Terry 42 |
| 23 | wqf | **Man Utd** | A | L | 0-1 | |
| 24 | lge | **Aston Villa** | H | W | 2-0 | Gudjohnsen 42; Lampard 57 |
| 25 | lge | **Southampton** | H | D | 0-0 | |
| 26 | lge | **Leeds** | A | L | 0-2 | |
| 27 | lge | **Arsenal** | A | L | 2-3 | Stanic 85; Petit 86 |
| 28 | facr3 | **Middlesbrough** | H | W | 1-0 | Stanic 40 |
| 29 | lge | **Charlton** | H | W | 4-1 | Hasselbaink 3 pen; Gallas 11; Gudjohnsen 34; Le Saux 54 |
| 30 | lge | **Man Utd** | A | L | 1-2 | Gudjohnsen 30 |
| 31 | facr4 | **Shrewsbury** | A | W | 4-0 | Zola 40,75; Cole 53; Morris 80 |
| 32 | lge | **Leeds** | H | W | 3-2 | Gudjohnsen 57; Lampard 80; Matteo 83 og |
| 33 | lge | **Tottenham** | H | D | 1-1 | Zola 40 |
| 34 | lge | **Birmingham** | A | W | 3-1 | Zola 44; Gudjohnsen 49; Hasselbaink 69 pen |
| 35 | facr5 | **Stoke** | A | W | 2-0 | Hasselbaink 52; Gronkjaer 76 |
| 36 | lge | **Blackburn** | H | L | 1-2 | Hasselbaink 90 |
| 37 | lge | **Newcastle** | A | L | 1-2 | Lampard 37 |
| 38 | facqf | **Arsenal** | A | D | 2-2 | Terry 3; Lampard 84 |
| 39 | lge | **West Brom** | A | W | 2-0 | Stanic 38; Zola 56 |
| 40 | lge | **Man City** | H | W | 5-0 | Hasselbaink 37; Terry 43; Stanic 58; Lampard 69; Gallas 79 |
| 41 | facqfr | **Arsenal** | H | L | 1-3 | Terry 79 |
| 42 | lge | **Sunderland** | A | W | 2-1 | Zola 52; Cole 85 |
| 43 | lge | **Bolton** | H | W | 1-0 | Cole 58 |
| 44 | lge | **Aston Villa** | A | L | 1-2 | Terry 89 |
| 45 | lge | **Everton** | H | W | 4-1 | Gudjohnsen 25; Hasselbaink 48; Gronkjaer 62; Zola 90 |
| 46 | lge | **Fulham** | H | D | 1-1 | Goma 39 og |
| 47 | lge | **West Ham** | A | L | 0-1 | |
| 48 | lge | **Liverpool** | H | W | 2-1 | Desailly 14; Gronkjaer 27 |

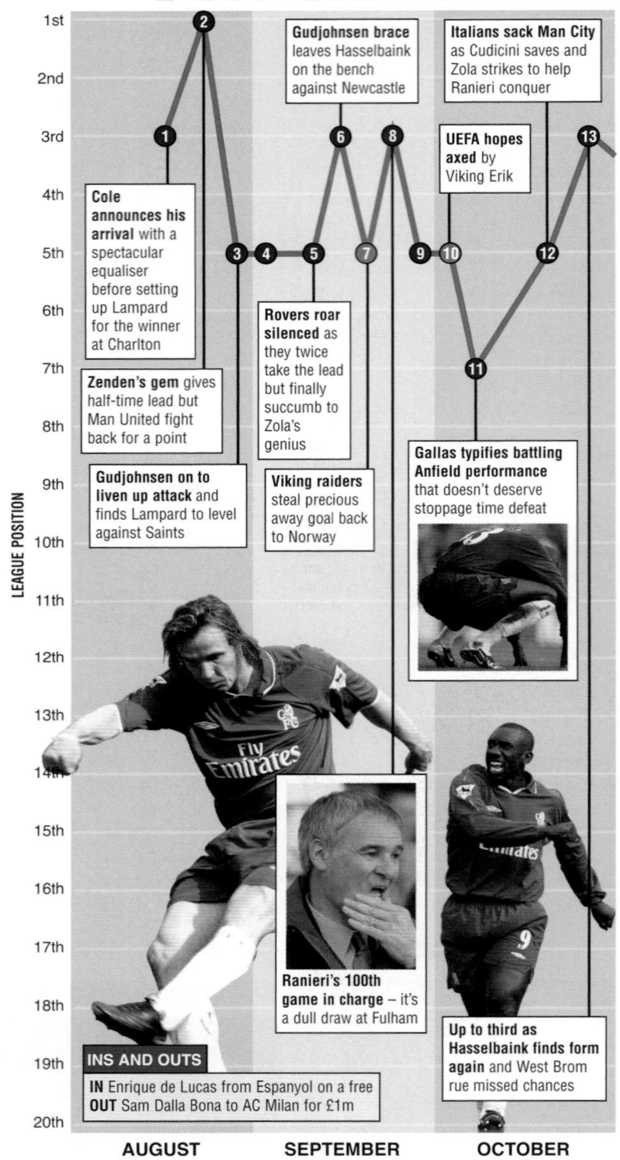
1st
2nd
3rd
4th
5th
6th
7th
8th
9th
10th
11th
12th
13th
14th
15th
16th
17th
18th
19th
20th
LEAGUE POSITION
**Cole announces his arrival** with a spectacular equaliser before setting up Lampard for the winner at Charlton
**Zenden's gem** gives half-time lead but Man United fight back for a point
**Gudjohnsen on to liven up attack** and finds Lampard to level against Saints
**Gudjohnsen brace** leaves Hasselbaink on the bench against Newcastle
**Rovers roar silenced** as they twice take the lead but finally succumb to Zola's genius
**Viking raiders** steal precious away goal back to Norway
**Ranieri's 100th game in charge** – it's a dull draw at Fulham
**Italians sack Man City** as Cudicini saves and Zola strikes to help Ranieri conquer
**UEFA hopes axed** by Viking Erik
**Gallas typifies battling Anfield performance** that doesn't deserve stoppage time defeat
**Up to third as Hasselbaink finds form again** and West Brom rue missed chances
**INS AND OUTS**
**IN** Enrique de Lucas from Espanyol on a free
**OUT** Sam Dalla Bona to AC Milan for £1m
AUGUST
SEPTEMBER
OCTOBER

Home / Away / Neutral

## ATTENDANCES

**HOME GROUND:** STAMFORD BRIDGE **CAPACITY:** 42449 **AVERAGE LEAGUE AT HOME:** 39784

| | | | | | | | | | | | |
|---|---|---|---|---|---|---|---|---|---|---|---|
| 30 | Man Utd | 67606 | 46 | Fulham | 40792 | 9 | West Ham | 38929 | 34 | Birmingham | 29475 |
| 23 | Man Utd | 57985 | 26 | Leeds | 40122 | 24 | Aston Villa | 38284 | 22 | Middlesbro | 29160 |
| 37 | Newcastle | 52157 | 4 | Arsenal | 40037 | 38 | Arsenal | 38104 | 15 | Gillingham | 28033 |
| 11 | Liverpool | 43856 | 42 | Sunderland | 40011 | 27 | Arsenal | 38096 | 39 | West Brom | 27024 |
| 48 | Liverpool | 41911 | 43 | Bolton | 39852 | 29 | Charlton | 37284 | 35 | Stoke | 26615 |
| 2 | Man Utd | 41541 | 6 | Newcastle | 39746 | 14 | Tottenham | 36049 | 1 | Charlton | 25640 |
| 41 | Arsenal | 41456 | 32 | Leeds | 39738 | 16 | Birmingham | 35237 | 18 | Bolton | 25476 |
| 33 | Tottenham | 41384 | 25 | Southampton | 39428 | 47 | West Ham | 35042 | 5 | Blackburn | 22999 |
| 40 | Man City | 41105 | 21 | Everton | 39396 | 12 | Man City | 34953 | 8 | Fulham | 16504 |
| 13 | West Brom | 40893 | 44 | Aston Villa | 39358 | 20 | Everton | 32322 | 7 | Viking | 15772 |
| 45 | Everton | 40875 | 17 | Middlesboro | 39064 | 3 | Southampton | 31208 | 31 | Shrewsbury | 7950 |
| 36 | Blackburn | 40850 | 19 | Sunderland | 38946 | 28 | Middlesboro | 29796 | 10 | Viking | 5000 |

## GOAL ATTEMPTS

**FOR**
Goal attempts recorded in League games

| | HOME | AWAY | TOTAL | AVE |
|---|---|---|---|---|
| shots on target | 136 | 116 | 252 | 6.6 |
| shots off target | 118 | 100 | 218 | 5.7 |
| TOTAL | 254 | 216 | 470 | 12.4 |

**Ratio of goals to shots**
Average number of shots on target per League goal scored: **3.7**

**Accuracy rating**
Average percentage of total goal attempts which were on target: **53.6**

**AGAINST**
Goal attempts recorded in League games

| | HOME | AWAY | TOTAL | AVE |
|---|---|---|---|---|
| shots on target | 78 | 105 | 183 | 4.8 |
| shots off target | 60 | 116 | 176 | 4.6 |
| TOTAL | 138 | 221 | 359 | 9.4 |

**Ratio of goals to shots**
Average number of shots on target per League goal scored: **4.8**

**Accuracy rating**
Average percentage of total goal attempts which were on target: **51.0**

# Zola earns Champions League finale

**Final Position: 4th**

KEY: ● League ● Champions Lge ● UEFA Cup ● FA Cup ○ League Cup ● Other

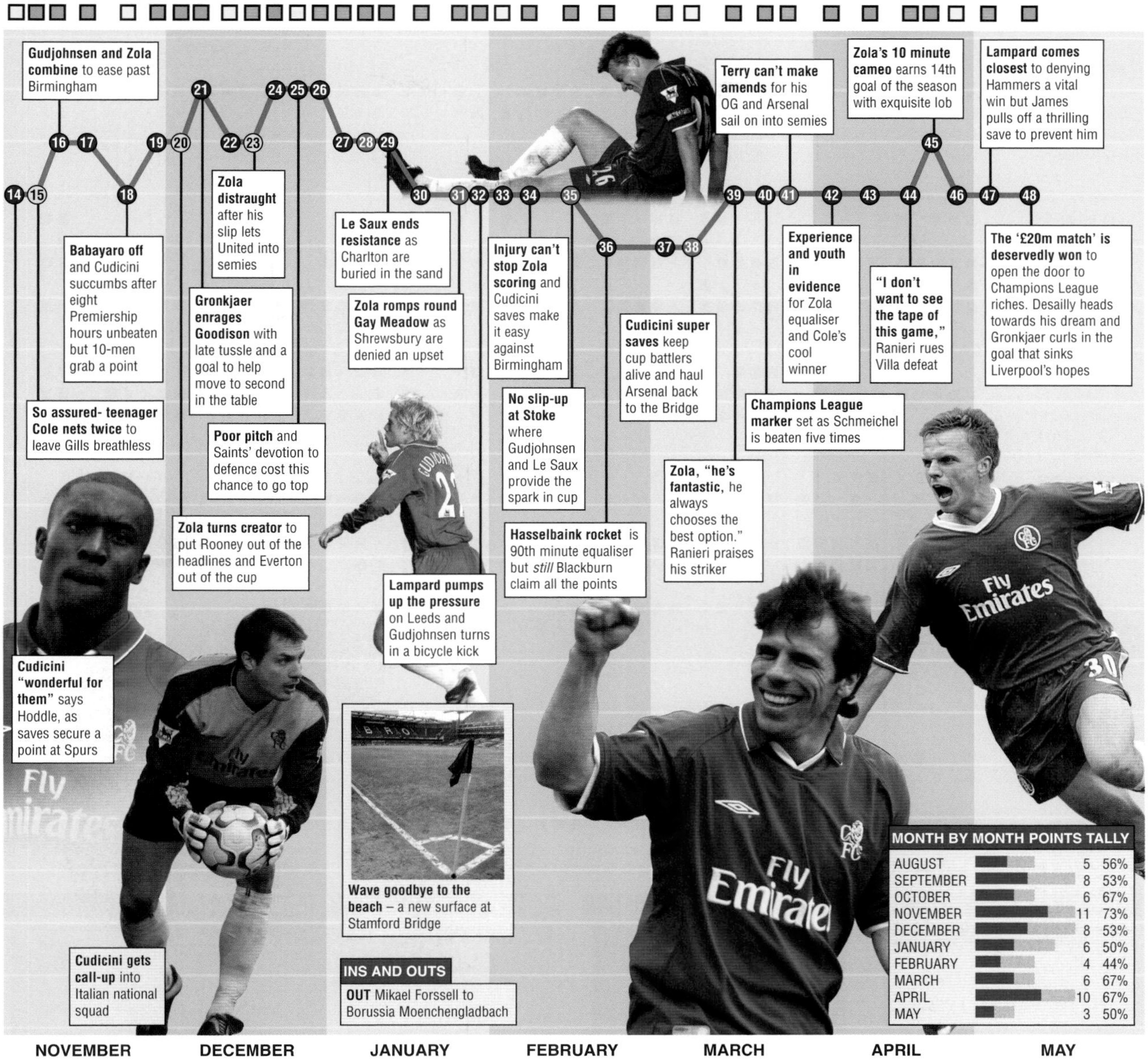

14 15 16 17 18 19 20 21 22 23 24 25 26 27 28 29 30 31 32 33 34 35 36 37 38 39 40 41 42 43 44 45 46 47 48
**Gudjohnsen and Zola combine** to ease past Birmingham
**Zola distraught** after his slip lets United into semis
**Le Saux ends resistance** as Charlton are buried in the sand
**Terry can't make amends** for his OG and Arsenal sail on into semies
**Zola's 10 minute cameo** earns 14th goal of the season with exquisite lob
**Lampard comes closest** to denying Hammers a vital win but James pulls off a thrilling save to prevent him
**Babayaro off** and Cudicini succumbs after eight Premiership hours unbeaten but 10-men grab a point
**Gronkjaer enrages Goodison** with late tussle and a goal to help move to second in the table
**Zola romps round Gay Meadow** as Shrewsbury are denied an upset
**Injury can't stop Zola scoring** and Cudicini saves make it easy against Birmingham
**Cudicini super saves** keep cup battlers alive and haul Arsenal back to the Bridge
**Experience and youth in evidence** for Zola equaliser and Cole's cool winner
**"I don't want to see the tape of this game,"** Ranieri rues Villa defeat
**The '£20m match' is deservedly won** to open the door to Champions League riches. Desailly heads towards his dream and Gronkjaer curls in the goal that sinks Liverpool's hopes
**No slip-up at Stoke** where Gudjohnsen and Le Saux provide the spark in cup
**Champions League marker** set as Schmeichel is beaten five times
**So assured- teenager Cole nets twice** to leave Gills breathless
**Poor pitch** and Saints' devotion to defence cost this chance to go top
**Zola, "he's fantastic,** he always chooses the best option." Ranieri praises his striker
**Zola turns creator** to put Rooney out of the headlines and Everton out of the cup
**Hasselbaink rocket** is 90th minute equaliser but *still* Blackburn claim all the points
**Lampard pumps up the pressure** on Leeds and Gudjohnsen turns in a bicycle kick
**Cudicini "wonderful for them"** says Hoddle, as saves secure a point at Spurs
**Wave goodbye to the beach** – a new surface at Stamford Bridge
**Cudicini gets call-up** into Italian national squad
NOVEMBER
DECEMBER
JANUARY
FEBRUARY
MARCH
APRIL
MAY


**INS AND OUTS**

**OUT** Mikael Forssell to Borussia Moenchengladbach

**MONTH BY MONTH POINTS TALLY**

| | | |
|---|---|---|
| AUGUST | 5 | 56% |
| SEPTEMBER | 8 | 53% |
| OCTOBER | 6 | 67% |
| NOVEMBER | 11 | 73% |
| DECEMBER | 8 | 53% |
| JANUARY | 6 | 50% |
| FEBRUARY | 4 | 44% |
| MARCH | 6 | 67% |
| APRIL | 10 | 67% |
| MAY | 3 | 50% |

## DISCIPLINARY RECORDS

**1 Mario Stanic**

| | |
|---|---|
| League Yellow | 4 |
| League Red | 0 |
| League Total | 4 |
| All Comps Yellow | 6 |
| All Comps Red | 0 |
| TOTAL | 6 |

**League Average**
**254**
mins between cards

| | PLAYER | LEAGUE 6Y | LEAGUE OR | TOTAL 6Y | TOTAL OR | AVE |
|---|---|---|---|---|---|---|
| 2 | De Lucas | 6 | 0 | 6 | 0 | 266 |
| 3 | Petit | 6 | 0 | 6 | 0 | 342 |
| 4 | Gronkjaer | 5 | 0 | 5 | 0 | 346 |
| 5 | Babayaro | 3 | 1 | 4 | 1 | 369 |
| 6 | Desailly | 6 | 0 | 6 | 0 | 449 |
| 7 | Terry | 3 | 0 | 5 | 0 | 472 |
| 8 | Zenden | 2 | 0 | 2 | 0 | 493 |
| 9 | Le Saux | 4 | 0 | 4 | 0 | 542 |
| 10 | Hasselbaink | 4 | 0 | 4 | 0 | 595 |
| 11 | Morris | 3 | 0 | 4 | 0 | 600 |
| 12 | Gallas | 5 | 0 | 5 | 0 | 648 |
| 13 | Melchiot | 4 | 0 | 4 | 0 | 707 |
| 14 | Lampard | 3 | 0 | 3 | 0 | 1102 |
| 15 | Gudjohnsen | 1 | 0 | 2 | 0 | 2026 |
| | Other | 4 | 0 | 6 | 1 | |
| | TOTAL | 63 | 1 | 72 | 2 | |

## GOALS

**1 Gianfranco Zola**

| | |
|---|---|
| League | 14 |
| FA Cup | 2 |
| League Cup | 0 |
| Europe | 0 |
| Other | 0 |
| TOTAL | 16 |

**League Average**
**188**
mins between goals

| | PLAYER | LGE | FAC | LC | Euro | TOT | AVE |
|---|---|---|---|---|---|---|---|
| 2 | Hasselbaink | 11 | 1 | 2 | 1 | 15 | 216 |
| 3 | Gudjohnsen | 10 | 0 | 0 | 0 | 10 | 203 |
| 4 | Lampard | 6 | 1 | 0 | 1 | 8 | 551 |
| 5 | Stanic | 4 | 1 | 1 | 0 | 6 | 255 |
| 6 | Gronkjaer | 4 | 1 | 0 | 0 | 5 | 433 |
| 7 | Gallas | 4 | 0 | 0 | 0 | 4 | 810 |
| 8 | Terry | 3 | 2 | 0 | 1 | 6 | 473 |
| 9 | Cole | 3 | 1 | 2 | 0 | 6 | 131 |
| 10 | Le Saux | 2 | 0 | 0 | 0 | 2 | 1085 |
| 11 | Desailly | 2 | 0 | 0 | 0 | 2 | 1347 |
| 12 | Zenden | 1 | 0 | 0 | 0 | 1 | 986 |
| 13 | Babayaro | 1 | 0 | 0 | 0 | 1 | 1479 |
| 14 | Petit | 1 | 0 | 1 | 0 | 2 | 2052 |
| 15 | Morris | 0 | 1 | 0 | 0 | 1 | |
| | Other | 2 | 0 | 0 | 1 | 3 | |
| | TOTAL | 68 | 10 | 6 | 4 | 88 | |

## SQUAD APPEARANCES

| Match | 1 | 2 | 3 | 4 | 5 | 6 | 7 | 8 | 9 | 10 | 11 | 12 | 13 | 14 | 15 | 16 | 17 | 18 | 19 | 20 | 21 | 22 | 23 | 24 |
|---|---|---|---|---|---|---|---|---|---|---|---|---|---|---|---|---|---|---|---|---|---|---|---|---|
| Venue | A | H | A | H | A | H | H | A | H | A | A | A | H | A | H | H | H | A | H | H | A | A | A | H |
| Competition | L | L | L | L | L | L | E | L | L | E | L | L | L | L | W | L | L | L | L | W | L | L | W | L |
| Result | W | D | D | D | W | W | W | D | L | L | L | W | W | D | W | W | W | D | W | W | W | D | L | W |

| Match | 25 | 26 | 27 | 28 | 29 | 30 | 31 | 32 | 33 | 34 | 35 | 36 | 37 | 38 | 39 | 40 | 41 | 42 | 43 | 44 | 45 | 46 | 47 | 48 |
|---|---|---|---|---|---|---|---|---|---|---|---|---|---|---|---|---|---|---|---|---|---|---|---|---|
| Venue | H | A | A | H | H | A | A | H | H | A | A | H | A | A | A | H | H | A | H | A | H | H | A | H |
| Competition | L | L | L | F | L | L | F | L | L | L | F | L | L | F | L | L | F | L | L | L | L | L | L | L |
| Result | D | L | L | W | W | L | W | W | D | W | W | L | L | D | W | W | L | W | W | L | W | D | L | W |

**Goalkeepers**
Carlo Cudicini
Ed de Goey
Rhys Evans
Lenny Pidgely

**Defenders**
Celestine Babayaro
Winston Bogarde
Marcel Desailly
Albert Ferrer
William Gallas
Robert Huth
Joel Kitamirike
Graeme Le Saux
Mario Melchiot
John Terry

**Midfielders**
Enrique De Lucas
Jesper Gronkjaer
Jo Keenan
Frank Lampard
Jody Morris
Alexis Nicolas
Emmanuel Petit
Mario Stanic
Boudewijn Zenden

**Forwards**
Gabriele Ambrosetti
Carlton Cole
Eidur Gudjohnsen
Jimmy-Floyd Hasselbaink
Filipe Oliveira
Gianfranco Zola

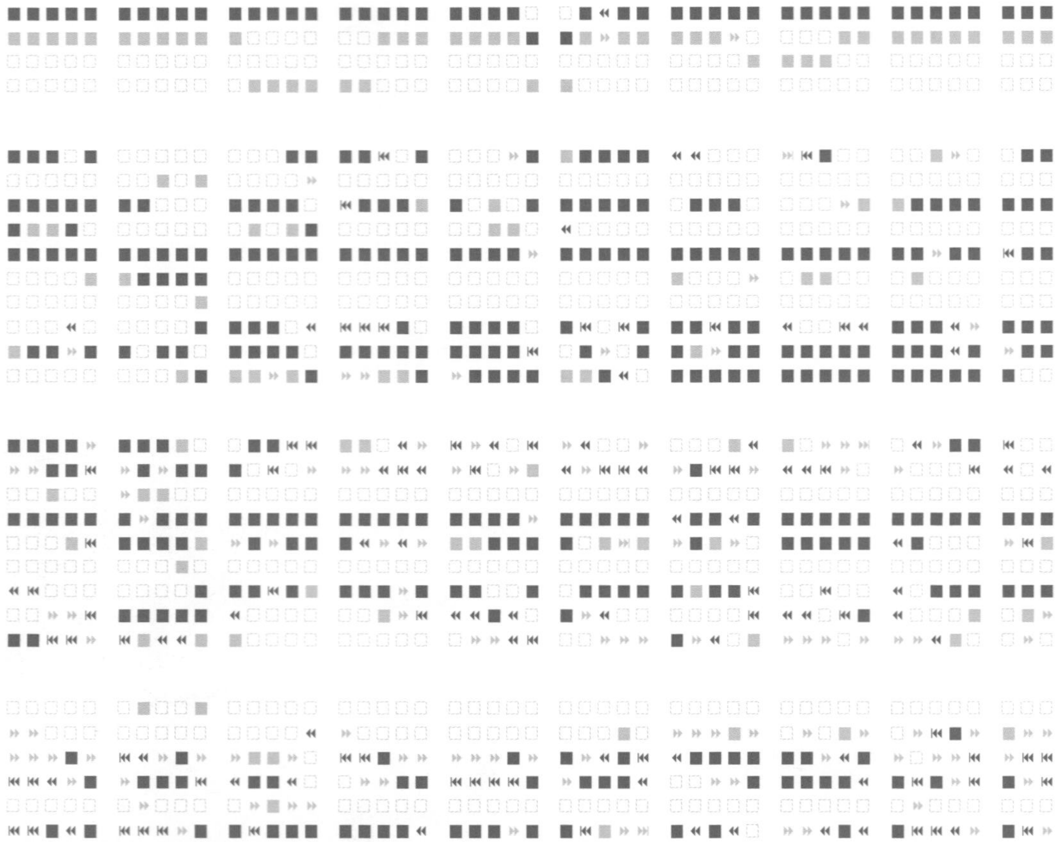

KEY: On all match · On bench · Subbed or sent off (Counting game) · Subbed or sent off (playing less than 70 minutes) · Subbed on from bench (Counting Game) · Subbed on (playing less than 70 minutes) · Subbed on and then subbed or sent off (Counting Game) · Subbed on and then subbed or sent off (playing less than 70 minutes) · Not in 16

## KEY PLAYERS - GOALSCORERS

**1 Gianfranco Zola**

| | |
|---|---|
| **Goals in the League** | 14 |
| **Goals in all competitions** | 16 |
| **Assists** League goals scored by team-mates where he delivered the final pass | 7 |
| **Contribution to Attacking Power** Average number of minutes between League team goals while on pitch | 64 |
| **Player Strike Rate** Average number of minutes between League goals scored by player | 188 |
| **Club Strike Rate** Average minutes between League goals scored by club | 50 |

ZOLA
25

| | PLAYER | GOALS LGE | GOALS ALL | ASSISTS | POWER | S RATE |
|---|---|---|---|---|---|---|
| 2 | Eidur Gudjohnsen | 10 | 10 | 2 | 41 | 203 mins |
| 3 | Jimmy-Floyd Hasselbaink | 11 | 15 | 7 | 50 | 216 mins |
| 4 | Jesper Gronkjaer | 4 | 5 | 4 | 46 | 433 mins |
| 5 | John Terry | 3 | 6 | 2 | 45 | 473 mins |

## KEY PLAYERS - MIDFIELDERS

**1 Enrique Martinez De Lucas**

| | |
|---|---|
| **Goals in the League** | 0 |
| **Goals in all competitions** | 1 |
| **Assists** League goals scored by team-mates where he delivered the final pass | 0 |
| **Defensive Rating** Average number of mins between League goals conceded while he was on the pitch | 114 |
| **Contribution to Attacking Power** Average number of minutes between League team goals while on pitch | 57 |
| **Scoring Difference** Defensive Rating minus Contribution to Attacking Power | 57 |

Fly
Emirates

| | PLAYER | GOALS LGE | GOALS ALL | ASSISTS | DEF RATE | POWER | SC DIFF |
|---|---|---|---|---|---|---|---|
| 2 | Jody Morris | 0 | 1 | 1 | 100 | 53 | 47 mins |
| 3 | Emmanuel Petit | 1 | 2 | 5 | 93 | 51 | 42 mins |
| 4 | Frank Lampard | 6 | 8 | 3 | 89 | 49 | 40 mins |
| 5 | Jesper Gronkjaer | 4 | 5 | 4 | 79 | 47 | 32 mins |

## PLAYER APPEARANCES

| | AGE (on 01/07/03) | IN THE SQUAD | COUNTING GAMES | MINUTES ON PITCH | IN THE SQUAD | MINUTES ON PITCH | THIS SEASON | NATIONAL SIDE |
|---|---|---|---|---|---|---|---|---|
| **Goalkeepers** | | | | | | | | |
| Carlo Cudicini | 29 | 36 | 36 | 3240 | 46 | 4114 | - | Italy |
| Ed de Goey | 36 | 31 | 2 | 197 | 38 | 222 | - | Holland |
| Rhys Evans | 21 | 2 | 0 | 0 | 4 | 0 | - | Wales |
| Lenny Pidgely | 18 | 7 | 0 | 0 | 8 | 0 | - | England |
| **Defenders** | | | | | | | | |
| Celestine Babayaro | 24 | 21 | 16 | 1479 | 26 | 1884 | - | Nigeria |
| Winston Bogarde | 32 | 1 | 0 | 0 | 3 | 22 | - | Holland |
| Marcel Desailly | 34 | 32 | 30 | 2694 | 37 | 2874 | 7 | France (2) |
| Albert Ferrer | 33 | 8 | 2 | 225 | 10 | 315 | - | Spain |
| William Gallas | 25 | 38 | 36 | 3241 | 48 | 4141 | 7 | France (2) |
| Robert Huth | 18 | 6 | 2 | 180 | 11 | 367 | - | Germany |
| Joel Kitamirike | 19 | 0 | 0 | 0 | 1 | 0 | - | Uganda |
| Graeme Le Saux | 34 | 28 | 23 | 2170 | 34 | 2681 | - | England |
| Mario Melchiot | 26 | 36 | 30 | 2831 | 43 | 3372 | 1 | Holland (6) |
| John Terry | 22 | 28 | 15 | 1418 | 37 | 2228 | 2 | England (7) |
| **Midfielders** | | | | | | | | |
| Enrique De Lucas | 24 | 29 | 15 | 1597 | 35 | 1926 | - | Spain |
| Jesper Gronkjaer | 25 | 31 | 13 | 1733 | 40 | 2279 | - | Holland |
| Jo Keenan | 20 | 3 | 0 | 2 | 4 | 2 | - | England |
| Frank Lampard | 25 | 38 | 36 | 3307 | 48 | 4127 | 6 | England (7) |
| Jody Morris | 24 | 31 | 18 | 1800 | 40 | 2259 | - | England |
| Alexis Nicolas | 20 | 1 | 0 | 0 | 1 | 0 | - | England |
| Emmanuel Petit | 32 | 25 | 22 | 2052 | 33 | 2623 | 4 | France (2) |
| Mario Stanic | 31 | 21 | 7 | 1019 | 28 | 1540 | 4 | Croatia (26) |
| Boudewijn Zenden | 26 | 23 | 6 | 986 | 31 | 1221 | 9 | Holland (6) |
| **Forwards** | | | | | | | | |
| Gabriele Ambrosetti | 29 | 0 | 0 | 0 | 2 | 0 | - | Italy |
| Carlton Cole | 19 | 17 | 2 | 394 | 20 | 505 | - | England |
| Eidur Gudjohnsen | 24 | 37 | 19 | 2026 | 46 | 2396 | - | Iceland |
| J-Floyd Hasselbaink | 31 | 36 | 22 | 2381 | 44 | 3077 | 4 | Holland (6) |
| Filipe Oliveira | 19 | 4 | 0 | 6 | 6 | 41 | - | Portugal |
| Gianfranco Zola | 37 | 38 | 26 | 2629 | 47 | 3265 | - | Italy |

KEY: LEAGUE ALL COMPS CAPS (FIFA RANKING)

## TEAM OF THE SEASON

Cudicini
CG 36 DR 90
Melchiot
CG 30 DR 105
Desailly
CG 30 DR 90
Terry
CG 15 DR 101
Le Saux
CG 23 DR 109
Morris
CG 18 SD +47
Lampard
CG 36 SD +40
Petit
CG 22 SD +42
De Lucas
CG 15 SD +57
Gudjohnsen
CG 19 AP 41
Zola
CG 26 SR 188


KEY: DR = Defensive Rate, SD = Scoring Difference AP = Attacking Power SR = Strike Rate, CG=Counting Games – League games playing at least 70 minutes

## TOP POINT EARNERS

**1 Jimmy-Floyd Hasselbaink**

| | |
|---|---|
| **Counting Games** League games when he played at least 70 minutes | 22 |
| **Average points** Average League points taken in Counting games | 2.00 |
| **Club Average points** Average points taken in League games | 1.76 |

| | PLAYER | GAMES | PTS |
|---|---|---|---|
| 2 | Graeme Le Saux | 23 | 2.00 |
| 3 | Jesper Gronkjaer | 13 | 1.92 |
| 4 | Marcel Desailly | 30 | 1.87 |
| 5 | John Terry | 15 | 1.87 |
| 6 | Enrique Martinez De Lucas | 15 | 1.87 |
| 7 | Jody Morris | 18 | 1.83 |
| 8 | Mario Melchiot | 30 | 1.83 |
| 9 | Carlo Cudicini | 36 | 1.83 |
| 10 | William Gallas | 36 | 1.75 |

## KEY PLAYERS - DEFENDERS

**1 Graeme Le Saux**

| | |
|---|---|
| **Goals Conceded** The number of League goals conceded while he was on the pitch | 20 |
| **Goals Conceded in all competitions** The number goals conceded while he was on the pitch in all competitions | 28 |
| **League minutes played** Number of minutes played in league matches | 2170 |
| **Clean Sheets** In games when he played at least70 mins | 8 |
| **Defensive Rating** Average number of mins between League goals conceded while he was on the pitch | 109 |
| **Club Defensive Rating** Average number of mins between League goals conceded by the club this season | 90 |

Fly Emirates


| | PLAYER | CON LGE | CON ALL | MINS | C SHEETS | DEF RATE |
|---|---|---|---|---|---|---|
| 2 | Mario Melchiot | 27 | 34 | 2831 | 13 | 105 mins |
| 3 | John Terry | 14 | 26 | 1418 | 5 | 101 mins |
| 4 | Marcel Desailly | 30 | 31 | 2694 | 9 | 90 mins |
| 5 | William Gallas | 38 | 51 | 3241 | 11 | 85 mins |

## KEY PLAYERS - GOALKEEPERS

Fly Emirates


**1 Carlo Cudicini**

| | |
|---|---|
| **Goals Conceded in the League** The number of League goals conceded while he was on the pitch | 36 |
| **Goals Conceded in all competitions** The number of goals conceded while he was on the pitch in all competitions | 49 |
| **League minutes played** Number of minutes played in league matches | 3240 |
| **Clean Sheets** In games when he played at least 70 mins | 12 |
| **Goals to Shots Ratio** The average number of shots on target per each League goal conceded | 4.8 |
| **Defensive Rating** Ave number of mins between League goals conceded while on the pitch | 90 |

**2 Ed de Goey**

| | |
|---|---|
| **Goals Conceded in the League** The number of League goals conceded while he was on the pitch | 3 |
| **Goals Conceded in all competitions** The number of goals conceded while he was on the pitch in all competitions | 3 |
| **League minutes played** Number of minutes played in league matches | 197 |
| **Clean Sheets** In games when he played at least 70 mins | 1 |
| **Goals to Shots Ratio** The average number of shots on target per each League goal conceded | 3.3 |
| **Defensive Rating** Ave number of mins between League goals conceded while on the pitch | 66 |

# LIVERPOOL

**NICKNAME:** THE REDS

KEY: Won / Drawn / Lost

| | | | | | | |
|---|---|---|---|---|---|---|
| 1 | facs | Arsenal | N | L | 0-1 | |
| 2 | lge | Aston Villa | A | W | 1-0 | Riise 47 |
| 3 | lge | Southampton | H | W | 3-0 | Diouf 4,50; Murphy 90 pen |
| 4 | lge | Blackburn | A | D | 2-2 | Murphy 30; Riise 76 |
| 5 | lge | Newcastle | H | D | 2-2 | Hamann 54; Owen 73 pen |
| 6 | lge | Birmingham | H | D | 2-2 | Murphy 25; Gerrard 49 |
| 7 | lge | Bolton | A | W | 3-2 | Baros 45,72; Heskey 88 |
| 8 | ecgb | Valencia | A | L | 0-2 | |
| 9 | lge | West Brom | H | W | 2-0 | Baros 56; Riise 90 |
| 10 | ecgb | Basel | H | D | 1-1 | Baros 34 |
| 11 | lge | Man City | A | W | 3-0 | Owen 4,64,89 |
| 12 | ecgb | S Moscow | H | W | 5-0 | Heskey 7,89; Cheyrou 13; Hyypia 27; Diao 80 |
| 13 | lge | Chelsea | H | W | 1-0 | Owen 90 |
| 14 | lge | Leeds | A | W | 1-0 | Diao 66 |
| 15 | ecgb | S Moscow | A | W | 3-1 | Owen 29,70,90 |
| 16 | lge | Tottenham | H | W | 2-1 | Murphy 71; Owen 86 pen |
| 17 | ecgb | Valencia | H | L | 0-1 | |
| 18 | lge | West Ham | H | W | 2-0 | Owen 28,55 |
| 19 | wr3 | Southampton | H | W | 3-1 | Berger 45; Diouf 57; Baros 60 |
| 20 | lge | Middlesbrough | A | L | 0-1 | |
| 21 | ecgb | Basel | A | D | 3-3 | Murphy 61; Smicer 64; Owen 85 |
| 22 | lge | Sunderland | H | D | 0-0 | |
| 23 | lge | Fulham | A | L | 2-3 | Hamann 62; Baros 86 |
| 24 | uc3rl1 | Vitesse Arnhem | A | W | 1-0 | Owen 26 |
| 25 | lge | Man Utd | H | L | 1-2 | Hyypia 82 |
| 26 | wr4 | Ipswich | H | W | 5-4* | Diouf 54 pen (*on penalties) |
| 27 | lge | Charlton | A | L | 0-2 | |
| 28 | uc3rl2 | Vitesse Arnhem | H | W | 1-0 | Owen 20 |
| 29 | lge | Sunderland | A | L | 1-2 | Baros 69 |
| 30 | wqf | Aston Villa | A | W | 4-3 | Murphy 27,90; Baros 54; Gerrard 67 |
| 31 | lge | Everton | H | D | 0-0 | |
| 32 | lge | Blackburn | H | D | 1-1 | Riise 17 |
| 33 | lge | Arsenal | A | D | 1-1 | Murphy 70 pen |
| 34 | lge | Newcastle | A | L | 0-1 | |
| 35 | facr3 | Man City | A | W | 1-0 | Murphy 47 pen |
| 36 | wsfl1 | Sheff Utd | A | L | 1-2 | Mellor 35 |
| 37 | lge | Aston Villa | H | D | 1-1 | Owen 38 |
| 38 | lge | Southampton | A | W | 1-0 | Heskey 14 |
| 39 | wsfl2 | Sheff Utd | H | W | 2-0 | Diouf 8; Owen 107 |
| 40 | facr4 | Crystal Palace | A | D | 0-0 | |
| 41 | lge | Arsenal | H | D | 2-2 | Riise 52; Henchoz 90 |
| 42 | lge | West Ham | A | W | 3-0 | Baros 6; Gerrard 9; Heskey 67 |
| 43 | facr4r | Crystal Palace | H | L | 0-2 | |
| 44 | lge | Middlesbrough | H | D | 1-1 | Riise 74 |
| 45 | uc4rl1 | Auxerre | A | W | 1-0 | Hyypia 73 |
| 46 | lge | Birmingham | A | L | 1-2 | Owen 77 |
| 47 | uc4rl2 | Auxerre | H | W | 2-0 | Owen 67; Murphy 72 |
| 48 | wf | Man Utd | N | W | 2-0 | Gerrard 38; Owen 85 |
| 49 | lge | Bolton | H | W | 2-0 | Diouf 44; Owen 67 |
| 50 | ucqfl1 | Celtic | A | D | 1-1 | Heskey 17 |
| 51 | lge | Tottenham | A | W | 3-2 | Owen 51; Heskey 72; Gerrard 82 |
| 52 | ucqfl2 | Celtic | H | L | 0-2 | |
| 53 | lge | Leeds | H | W | 3-1 | Owen 12; Murphy 20; Gerrard 72 |
| 54 | lge | Man Utd | A | L | 0-4 | |
| 55 | lge | Fulham | H | W | 2-0 | Heskey 36; Owen 59 |
| 56 | lge | Everton | A | W | 2-1 | Owen 31; Murphy 64 |
| 57 | lge | Charlton | H | W | 2-1 | Hyypia 86; Gerrard 90 |
| 58 | lge | West Brom | A | W | 6-0 | Owen 15,49,61,67; Baros 47,84 |
| 59 | lge | Man City | H | L | 1-2 | Baros 59 |
| 60 | lge | Chelsea | A | L | 1-2 | Hyypia 11 |

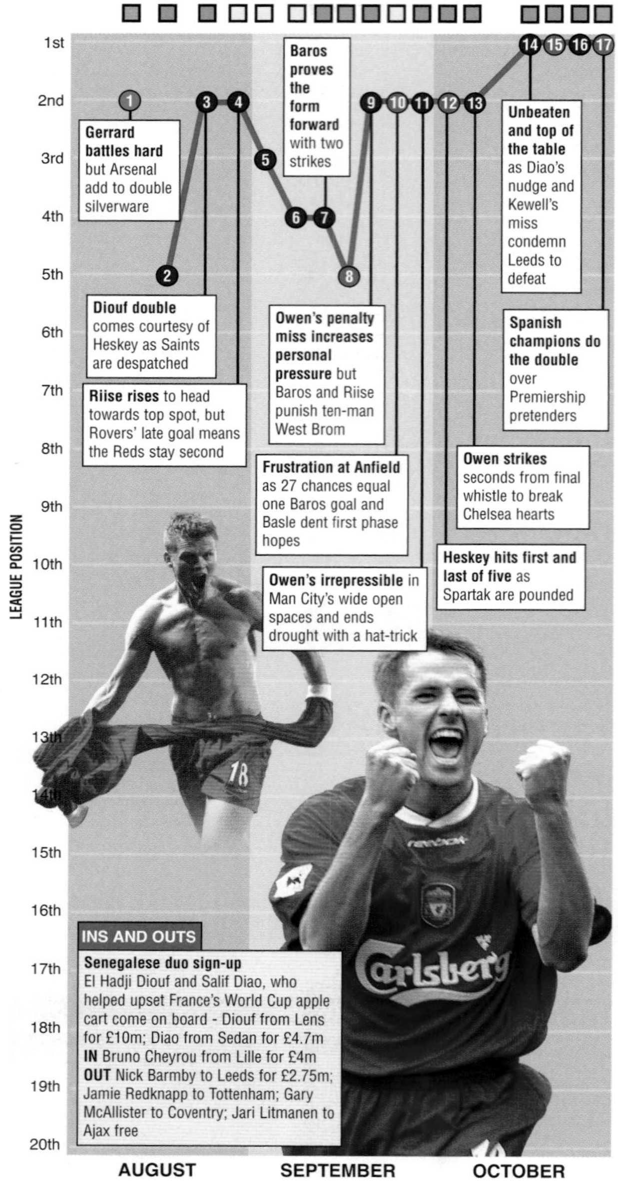

1st
2nd
3rd
4th
5th
6th
7th
8th
9th
10th
11th
12th
13th
14th
15th
16th
17th
18th
19th
20th
LEAGUE POSITION
**Gerrard battles hard** but Arsenal add to double silverware
**Diouf double** comes courtesy of Heskey as Saints are despatched
**Riise rises** to head towards top spot, but Rovers' late goal means the Reds stay second
**Baros proves the form forward** with two strikes
**Owen's penalty miss increases personal pressure** but Baros and Riise punish ten-man West Brom
**Frustration at Anfield** as 27 chances equal one Baros goal and Basle dent first phase hopes
**Owen's irrepressible** in Man City's wide open spaces and ends drought with a hat-trick
**Heskey hits first and last of five** as Spartak are pounded
**Owen strikes** seconds from final whistle to break Chelsea hearts
**Unbeaten and top of the table** as Diao's nudge and Kewell's miss condemn Leeds to defeat
**Spanish champions do the double** over Premiership pretenders
AUGUST
SEPTEMBER
OCTOBER


**INS AND OUTS**

**Senegalese duo sign-up**
El Hadji Diouf and Salif Diao, who helped upset France's World Cup apple cart come on board - Diouf from Lens for £10m; Diao from Sedan for £4.7m
**IN** Bruno Cheyrou from Lille for £4m
**OUT** Nick Barmby to Leeds for £2.75m; Jamie Redknapp to Tottenham; Gary McAllister to Coventry; Jari Litmanen to Ajax free

## ATTENDANCES

Home / Away / Neutral

**HOME GROUND:** ANFIELD **CAPACITY:** 45000 **AVERAGE LEAGUE AT HOME:** 43242

| | | | | | | | | | | | |
|---|---|---|---|---|---|---|---|---|---|---|---|
| 48 | Man Utd | 75000 | 5 | Newcastle | 43241 | 12 | S Moscow | 40812 | 36 | Sheff Utd | 30095 |
| 54 | Man Utd | 67639 | 37 | Aston Villa | 43210 | 14 | Leeds | 40197 | 21 | Basel | 30000 |
| 1 | Arsenal | 67337 | 6 | Birmingham | 43113 | 56 | Everton | 40162 | 46 | Birmingham | 29449 |
| 50 | Celtic | 59759 | 32 | Blackburn | 43075 | 30 | Aston Villa | 38530 | 4 | Blackburn | 29207 |
| 34 | Newcastle | 52147 | 22 | Sunderland | 43074 | 33 | Arsenal | 38074 | 35 | Man City | 28586 |
| 25 | Man Utd | 44250 | 3 | Southampton | 43058 | 10 | Basel | 37634 | 7 | Bolton | 27328 |
| 52 | Celtic | 44238 | 53 | Leeds | 43021 | 29 | Sunderland | 37118 | 58 | West Brom | 27128 |
| 59 | Man City | 44220 | 8 | Valencia | 43000 | 51 | Tottenham | 36077 | 24 | Vitesse | 27000 |
| 16 | Tottenham | 44084 | 44 | Middlesboro | 42247 | 19 | Southampton | 35870 | 27 | Charlton | 26694 |
| 18 | West Ham | 44048 | 55 | Fulham | 42120 | 11 | Man City | 35141 | 26 | Ipswich | 26305 |
| 31 | Everton | 44025 | 57 | Charlton | 42010 | 43 | Crystal Palace | 35109 | 40 | Crystal Palace | 26054 |
| 13 | Chelsea | 43856 | 60 | Chelsea | 41911 | 42 | West Ham | 35033 | 28 | Vitesse | 23576 |
| 39 | Sheff Utd | 43837 | 17 | Valencia | 41831 | 20 | Middlesboro | 34747 | 45 | Auxerre | 20452 |
| 9 | West Brom | 43830 | 49 | Bolton | 41462 | 47 | Auxerre | 34252 | 23 | Fulham | 18144 |
| 41 | Arsenal | 43660 | 2 | Aston Villa | 41183 | 38 | Southampton | 32104 | 15 | S Moscow | 15000 |

## GOAL ATTEMPTS

**FOR**
Goal attempts recorded in League games

| | HOME | AWAY | TOTAL | AVE |
|---|---|---|---|---|
| shots on target | 162 | 103 | 265 | 7.0 |
| shots off target | 128 | 99 | 227 | 6.0 |
| TOTAL | 290 | 202 | 492 | 12.9 |

**Ratio of goals to shots** Average number of shots on target per League goal scored: **4.3**

**Accuracy rating** Average percentage of total goal attempts which were on target: **53.9**

**AGAINST**
Goal attempts recorded in League games

| | HOME | AWAY | TOTAL | AVE |
|---|---|---|---|---|
| shots on target | 76 | 97 | 173 | 4.6 |
| shots off target | 68 | 103 | 171 | 4.5 |
| TOTAL | 144 | 200 | 344 | 9.1 |

**Ratio of goals to shots** Average number of shots on target per League goal scored: **4.2**

**Accuracy rating** Average percentage of total goal attempts which were on target: **50.3**

# League Cup joy but too much pain

**Final Position: 5th**

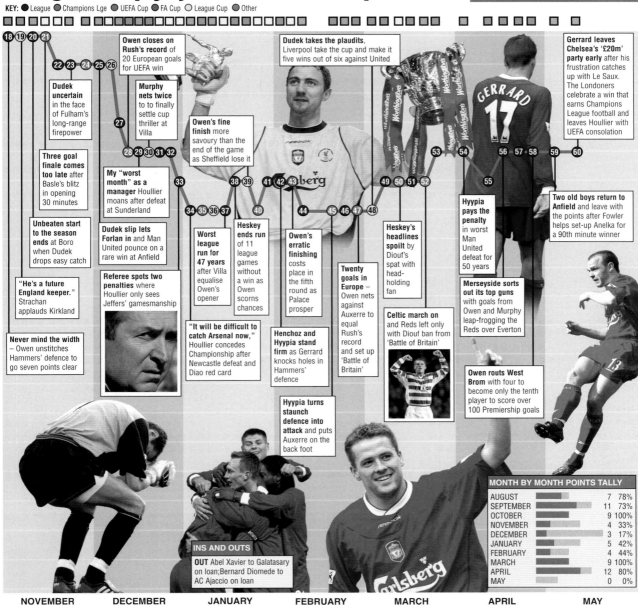

**KEY:** ● League ● Champions Lge ● UEFA Cup ● FA Cup ○ League Cup ● Other

**Never mind the width** – Owen unstitches Hammers' defence to go seven points clear

**"He's a future England keeper."** Strachan applauds Kirkland

**Unbeaten start to the season ends** at Boro when Dudek drops easy catch

**Three goal finale comes too late** after Basle's blitz in opening 30 minutes

**Dudek uncertain** in the face of Fulham's long-range firepower

**Owen closes on Rush's record** of 20 European goals for UEFA win

**Murphy nets twice** to to finally settle cup thriller at Villa

**My "worst month" as a manager** Houllier moans after defeat at Sunderland

**Dudek slip lets Forlan in** and Man United pounce on a rare win at Anfield

**Referee spots two penalties** where Houllier only sees Jeffers' gamesmanship

**"It will be difficult to catch Arsenal now,"** Houllier concedes Championship after Newcastle defeat and Diao red card

**Worst league run for 47 years** after Villa equalise Owen's opener

**Owen's fine finish** more savoury than the end of the game as Sheffield lose it

**Heskey ends run** of 11 league games without a win as Owen scorns chances

**Henchoz and Hyypia stand firm** as Gerrard knocks holes in Hammers' defence

**Owen's erratic finishing** costs place in the fifth round as Palace prosper

**Dudek takes the plaudits**, Liverpool take the cup and make it five wins out of six against United

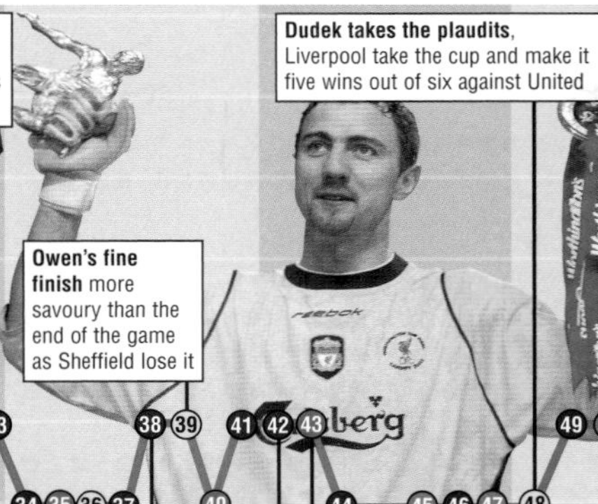

**Hyypia turns staunch defence into attack** and puts Auxerre on the back foot

**Twenty goals in Europe** – Owen nets against Auxerre to equal Rush's record and set up 'Battle of Britain'

**Heskey's headlines spoilt** by Diouf's spat with head-holding fan

**Celtic march on** and Reds left only with Diouf ban from 'Battle of Britain'

**Hyypia pays the penalty** in worst Man United defeat for 50 years

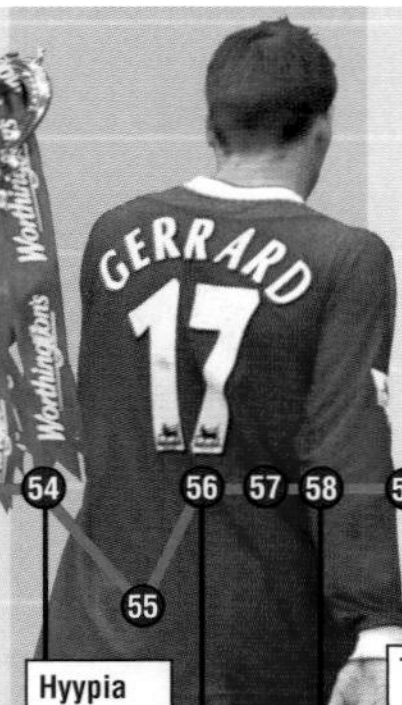

**Merseyside sorts out its top guns** with goals from Owen and Murphy leap-frogging the Reds over Everton

**Owen routs West Brom** with four to become only the tenth player to score over 100 Premiership goals

**Gerrard leaves Chelsea's '£20m' party early** after his frustration catches up with Le Saux. The Londoners celebrate a win that earns Champions League football and leaves Houllier with UEFA consolation

**Two old boys return to Anfield** and leave with the points after Fowler helps set-up Anelka for a 90th minute winner

**INS AND OUTS**

**OUT** Abel Xavier to Galatasary on loan;Bernard Diomede to AC Ajaccio on loan

**MONTH BY MONTH POINTS TALLY**

| | | |
|---|---|---|
| AUGUST | 7 | 78% |
| SEPTEMBER | 11 | 73% |
| OCTOBER | 9 | 100% |
| NOVEMBER | 4 | 33% |
| DECEMBER | 3 | 17% |
| JANUARY | 5 | 42% |
| FEBRUARY | 4 | 44% |
| MARCH | 9 | 100% |
| APRIL | 12 | 80% |
| MAY | 0 | 0% |

NOVEMBER DECEMBER JANUARY FEBRUARY MARCH APRIL MAY

## DISCIPLINARY RECORDS

**1 Salif Diao**

| | |
|---|---|
| League Yellow | 4 |
| League Red | 1 |
| League Total | 5 |
| All Comps Yellow | 6 |
| All Comps Red | 1 |
| TOTAL | 7 |

League Average 246 mins between cards

| | PLAYER | LEAGUE Y | LEAGUE R | TOTAL Y | TOTAL R | AVE |
|---|---|---|---|---|---|---|
| 2 | Diouf | 6Y | 0R | 9Y | 0R | 312 |
| 3 | Hamann | 7 | 0 | 9 | 1 | 363 |
| 4 | Murphy | 7 | 0 | 10 | 0 | 451 |
| 5 | Smicer | 2 | 0 | 6 | 0 | 471 |
| 6 | Gerrard | 5 | 1 | 6 | 1 | 477 |
| 7 | Henchoz | 3 | 0 | 8 | 0 | 537 |
| 8 | Traore | 4 | 0 | 8 | 0 | 668 |
| 9 | Heskey | 3 | 0 | 3 | 0 | 685 |
| 10 | Carragher | 4 | 0 | 4 | 0 | 752 |
| 11 | Cheyrou | 1 | 0 | 1 | 0 | 763 |
| 12 | Baros | 2 | 0 | 2 | 0 | 768 |
| 13 | Riise | 1 | 0 | 1 | 0 | 2902 |
| 14 | Hyypia | 0 | 1 | 1 | 1 | 3154 |
| | Other | 0 | 0 | 1 | 0 | |
| | TOTAL | 49 | 3 | 75 | 4 | |

## GOALS

**1 Michael Owen**

| | |
|---|---|
| League | 19 |
| FA Cup | 0 |
| League Cup | 2 |
| Europe | 7 |
| Other | 0 |
| TOTAL | 28 |

League Average 149 mins between goals

| | PLAYER | LGE | FAC | LC | Euro | TOT | AVE |
|---|---|---|---|---|---|---|---|
| 2 | Baros | 9 | 0 | 2 | 1 | 12 | 171 |
| 3 | Murphy | 7 | 1 | 2 | 2 | 12 | 452 |
| 4 | Riise | 6 | 0 | 0 | 0 | 6 | 484 |
| 5 | Heskey | 5 | 0 | 0 | 3 | 8 | 411 |
| 6 | Gerrard | 5 | 0 | 2 | 0 | 7 | 573 |
| 7 | Hyypia | 3 | 0 | 0 | 2 | 5 | 1051 |
| 8 | Diouf | 3 | 0 | 3 | 0 | 6 | 626 |
| 9 | Hamann | 2 | 0 | 0 | 0 | 2 | 1273 |
| 10 | Henchoz | 1 | 0 | 0 | 0 | 1 | 1613 |
| 11 | Diao | 1 | 0 | 0 | 1 | 2 | 1231 |
| 12 | Mellor | 0 | 0 | 1 | 0 | 1 | |
| 13 | Cheyrou | 0 | 0 | 0 | 1 | 1 | |
| 14 | Berger | 0 | 0 | 1 | 0 | 1 | |
| 15 | Smicer | 0 | 0 | 0 | 1 | 1 | |
| | Other | 0 | 0 | 0 | 0 | 0 | |
| | TOTAL | 61 | 1 | 13 | 18 | 93 | |

## SQUAD APPEARANCES

| Match | 1 | 2 | 3 | 4 | 5 | 6 | 7 | 8 | 9 | 10 | 11 | 12 | 13 | 14 | 15 | 16 | 17 | 18 | 19 | 20 | 21 | 22 | 23 | 24 | 25 | 26 | 27 | 28 | 29 | 30 |
|---|---|---|---|---|---|---|---|---|---|---|---|---|---|---|---|---|---|---|---|---|---|---|---|---|---|---|---|---|---|---|
| Venue | N | A | H | A | H | H | A | A | H | H | A | H | H | A | A | H | H | H | H | A | A | H | A | A | H | H | A | H | A | A |
| Competition | O | L | L | L | L | L | L | C | L | C | L | C | L | L | C | L | C | L | W | L | C | L | L | E | L | W | L | E | L | W |
| Result | L | W | W | D | D | D | W | L | W | D | W | W | W | W | W | W | L | W | W | L | D | D | L | W | L | W | L | W | L | W |

| Match | 31 | 32 | 33 | 34 | 35 | 36 | 37 | 38 | 39 | 40 | 41 | 42 | 43 | 44 | 45 | 46 | 47 | 48 | 49 | 50 | 51 | 52 | 53 | 54 | 55 | 56 | 57 | 58 | 59 | 60 |
|---|---|---|---|---|---|---|---|---|---|---|---|---|---|---|---|---|---|---|---|---|---|---|---|---|---|---|---|---|---|---|
| Venue | H | H | A | A | A | A | H | A | H | A | H | A | H | H | A | A | H | N | H | A | A | H | H | A | H | A | H | A | H | A |
| Competition | L | L | L | L | F | W | L | L | W | F | L | L | F | L | E | L | E | W | L | E | L | E | L | L | L | L | L | L | L | L |
| Result | D | D | D | L | W | L | D | W | W | D | D | W | L | D | W | L | W | W | W | D | W | L | W | L | W | W | W | W | L | L |

**Goalkeepers**
Pegguy Arphexad
Jurzy Dudek
Chris Kirkland

**Defenders**
Markus Babbel
Jamie Carragher
Stephane Henchoz
Sami Hyypia
Jon Otsemobor
Djimi Traore
Gregory Vignal
Abel Xavier

**Midfielders**
Patrik Berger
Igor Biscan
Bruno Cheyrou
Salif Diao
Bernard Diomede
Steven Gerrard
Dietmar Hamann
Danny Murphy
John Arne Riise
Vladimir Smicer
John Welsh

**Forwards**
Milan Baros
El Hadji Diouf
Emile Heskey
Neil Mellor
Michael Owen

KEY: On all match · On bench · Subbed or sent off (Counting game) · Subbed or sent off (playing less than 70 minutes) · Subbed on from bench (Counting Game) · Subbed on (playing less than 70 minutes) · Subbed on and then subbed or sent off (Counting Game) · Subbed on and then subbed or sent off (playing less than 70 minutes) · Not in 16

## KEY PLAYERS - GOALSCORERS

**1 Michael Owen**

| | |
|---|---|
| **Goals in the League** | 19 |
| **Goals in all competitions** | 28 |
| **Assists** League goals scored by team-mates where he delivered the final pass | 4 |
| **Contribution to Attacking Power** Average number of minutes between League team goals while on pitch | 55 |
| **Player Strike Rate** Average number of minutes between League goals scored by player | 149 |
| **Club Strike Rate** Average minutes between League goals scored by club | 56 |

| | PLAYER | GOALS LGE | GOALS ALL | ASSISTS | POWER | S RATE |
|---|---|---|---|---|---|---|
| 2 | Milan Baros | 9 | 12 | 4 | 46 | 171 mins |
| 3 | Emile Heskey | 5 | 8 | 3 | 54 | 411 mins |
| 4 | Danny Murphy | 7 | 12 | 6 | 58 | 452 mins |
| 5 | John Arne Riise | 6 | 6 | 4 | 53 | 484 mins |

## KEY PLAYERS - MIDFIELDERS

**1 John Arne Riise**

| | |
|---|---|
| **Goals in the League** | 6 |
| **Goals in all competitions** | 6 |
| **Assists** League goals scored by team-mates where he delivered the final pass | 4 |
| **Defensive Rating** Average number of mins between League goals conceded while he was on the pitch | 88 |
| **Contribution to Attacking Power** Average number of minutes between League team goals while on pitch | 54 |
| **Scoring Difference** Defensive Rating minus Contribution to Attacking Power | 34 |

| | PLAYER | GOALS LGE | GOALS ALL | ASSISTS | DEF RATE | POWER | SC DIFF |
|---|---|---|---|---|---|---|---|
| 2 | Steven Gerrard | 5 | 7 | 8 | 87 | 54 | 33 mins |
| 3 | Dietmar Hamann | 2 | 2 | 1 | 82 | 51 | 31 mins |
| 4 | Danny Murphy | 7 | 12 | 6 | 81 | 59 | 22 mins |
| 5 | Salif Diao | 1 | 2 | 1 | 77 | 65 | 12 mins |

## PLAYER APPEARANCES

| | AGE (on 01/07/03) | IN THE SQUAD | COUNTING GAMES | MINUTES ON PITCH | IN THE SQUAD | MINUTES ON PITCH | THIS SEASON | NATIONAL SIDE |
|---|---|---|---|---|---|---|---|---|
| **Goalkeepers** | | | | | | | | |
| Pegguy Arphexad | 30 | 17 | 0 | 0 | 26 | 0 | - | France |
| Jerzy Dudek | 30 | 36 | 30 | 2700 | 57 | 4146 | 6 | Poland (29) |
| Chris Kirkland | 22 | 23 | 8 | 720 | 37 | 1314 | - | England |
| **Defenders** | | | | | | | | |
| Abel Xavier | 30 | 4 | 4 | 360 | 6 | 557 | - | Portugal |
| Markus Babbel | 30 | 7 | 1 | 135 | 19 | 411 | - | Germany |
| Jamie Carragher | 25 | 38 | 32 | 3009 | 59 | 4675 | 1 | England (7) |
| Stephane Henchoz | 28 | 19 | 17 | 1613 | 32 | 2753 | - | Switzerland |
| Sami Hyypia | 29 | 36 | 35 | 3154 | 56 | 4984 | - | Finland |
| Jon Otsemobor | 20 | 0 | 0 | 0 | 2 | 69 | - | England |
| Djimi Traore | 23 | 38 | 28 | 2673 | 58 | 4020 | - | France |
| Gregory Vignal | 21 | 1 | 0 | 12 | 4 | 243 | - | France |
| **Midfielders** | | | | | | | | |
| Patrik Berger | 29 | 4 | 0 | 39 | 9 | 141 | - | Czech Republic |
| Igor Biscan | 25 | 17 | 2 | 275 | 34 | 521 | - | Croatia |
| Bruno Cheyrou | 25 | 27 | 7 | 763 | 44 | 1294 | 3 | France (2) |
| Salif Diao | 26 | 32 | 10 | 1231 | 52 | 2101 | 2 | Senegal (29) |
| Bernard Diomede | 29 | 0 | 0 | 0 | 1 | 0 | - | France |
| Steven Gerrard | 23 | 35 | 30 | 2867 | 54 | 4577 | 8 | England (7) |
| Dietmar Hamann | 29 | 30 | 28 | 2545 | 44 | 3551 | 3 | Germany (4) |
| Danny Murphy | 26 | 36 | 36 | 3162 | 56 | 4856 | 3 | England (7) |
| John Arne Riise | 22 | 38 | 31 | 2902 | 58 | 4510 | 10 | Norway (24) |
| Vladimir Smicer | 30 | 29 | 4 | 943 | 45 | 1733 | 8 | Czech Republic (13) |
| John Welsh | 19 | 0 | 0 | 0 | 2 | 38 | - | England |
| **Forwards** | | | | | | | | |
| Milan Baros | 21 | 33 | 12 | 1537 | 54 | 2149 | 9 | Czech Republic (13) |
| El Hadji Diouf | 22 | 34 | 16 | 1877 | 55 | 3163 | 2 | Senegal (29) |
| Emile Heskey | 25 | 32 | 18 | 2056 | 52 | 3385 | 7 | England (7) |
| Neil Mellor | 20 | 6 | 0 | 102 | 15 | 319 | - | England |
| Michael Owen | 23 | 36 | 30 | 2835 | 55 | 4427 | 9 | England (7) |

**KEY:** LEAGUE ALL COMPS CAPS (FIFA RANKING)

## TEAM OF THE SEASON

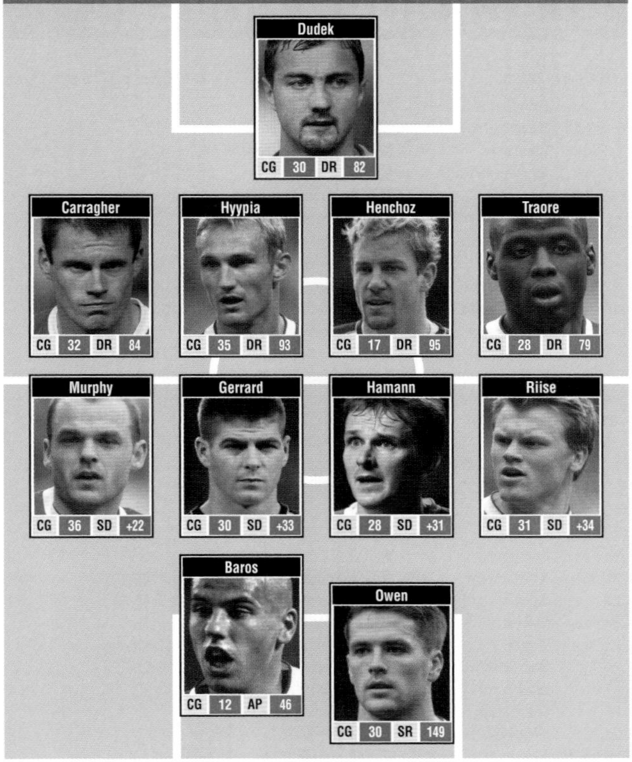

Dudek
CG 30 DR 82
Carragher
CG 32 DR 84
Hyypia
CG 35 DR 93
Henchoz
CG 17 DR 95
Traore
CG 28 DR 79
Murphy
CG 36 SD +22
Gerrard
CG 30 SD +33
Hamann
CG 28 SD +31
Riise
CG 31 SD +34
Baros
CG 12 AP 46
Owen
CG 30 SR 149


**KEY:** DR = Defensive Rate, SD = Scoring Difference AP = Attacking Power SR = Strike Rate, CG=Counting Games – League games playing at least 70 minutes

## TOP POINT EARNERS

**1 Emile Heskey**

| | |
|---|---|
| **Counting Games** League games when he played at least 70 minutes | 18 |
| **Average points** Average League points taken in Counting games | 2.00 |
| **Club Average points** Average points taken in League games | 1.68 |

| | PLAYER | GAMES | PTS |
|---|---|---|---|
| 2 | Jurzy Dudek | 30 | 1.90 |
| 3 | Dietmar Hamann | 28 | 1.89 |
| 4 | El Hadji Diouf | 16 | 1.88 |
| 5 | John Arne Riise | 31 | 1.81 |
| 6 | Djimi Traore | 28 | 1.79 |
| 7 | Michael Owen | 30 | 1.77 |
| 8 | Steven Gerrard | 30 | 1.77 |
| 9 | Sami Hyypia | 35 | 1.74 |
| 10 | Jamie Carragher | 32 | 1.72 |

## KEY PLAYERS - DEFENDERS

**1 Stephane Henchoz**

| | |
|---|---|
| **Goals Conceded** The number of League goals conceded while he was on the pitch | 17 |
| **Goals Conceded in all competitions** The number goals conceded while he was on the pitch in all competitions | 26 |
| **League minutes played** Number of minutes played in league matches | 1613 |
| **Clean Sheets** In games when he played at least70 mins | 6 |
| **Defensive Rating** Average number of mins between League goals conceded while he was on the pitch | 95 |
| **Club Defensive Rating** Average number of mins between League goals conceded by the club this season | 83 |

Carlsberg


| | PLAYER | CON LGE | CON ALL | MINS | C SHEETS | DEF RATE |
|---|---|---|---|---|---|---|
| 2 | Sami Hyypia | 34 | 53 | 3154 | 14 | 93 mins |
| 3 | Jamie Carragher | 36 | 53 | 3009 | 11 | 84 mins |
| 4 | Djimi Traore | 34 | 50 | 2673 | 10 | 79 mins |

## KEY PLAYERS - GOALKEEPERS

**1 Chris Kirkland**

| | |
|---|---|
| **Goals Conceded in the League** The number of League goals conceded while he was on the pitch | 8 |
| **Goals Conceded in all competitions** The number of goals conceded while he was on the pitch in all competitions | 14 |
| **League minutes played** Number of minutes played in league matches | 720 |
| **Clean Sheets** In games when he played at least 70 mins | 2 |
| **Goals to Shots Ratio** The average number of shots on target per each League goal conceded | 4.9 |
| **Defensive Rating** Ave number of mins between League goals conceded while on the pitch | 90 |

**2 Jurzy Dudek**

| | |
|---|---|
| **Goals Conceded in the League** The number of League goals conceded while he was on the pitch | 33 |
| **Goals Conceded in all competitions** The number of goals conceded while he was on the pitch in all competitions | 48 |
| **League minutes played** Number of minutes played in league matches | 2700 |
| **Clean Sheets** In games when he played at least 70 mins | 12 |
| **Goals to Shots Ratio** The average number of shots on target per each League goal conceded | 4.1 |
| **Defensive Rating** Ave number of mins between League goals conceded while on the pitch | 82 |

# BLACKBURN ROVERS

NICKNAME: ROVERS

KEY: Won / Drawn / Lost

| | | | | | | |
|---|---|---|---|---|---|---|
| 1 | lge | **Sunderland** | H | D | 0-0 | |
| 2 | lge | **Birmingham** | A | W | 1-0 | Yorke 13 |
| 3 | lge | **Liverpool** | H | D | 2-2 | Dunn 16; Grabbi 84 |
| 4 | lge | **Middlesbrough** | A | L | 0-1 | |
| 5 | lge | **Chelsea** | H | L | 2-3 | Dunn 17 pen; Thompson 44 |
| 6 | lge | **Man City** | A | D | 2-2 | Thompson 25; Cole 54 |
| 7 | uc1rl1 | **CSKA Sofia** | H | D | 1-1 | Grabbi 25 |
| 8 | lge | **Leeds** | H | W | 1-0 | Flitcroft 23 |
| 9 | lge | **West Brom** | A | W | 2-0 | Yorke 72 pen; Duff 76 |
| 10 | uc1rl2 | **CSKA Sofia** | A | D | 3-3 | Thompson 30; Ostenstad 56; Duff 57 |
| 11 | lge | **Tottenham** | H | L | 1-2 | Ostenstad 57 |
| 12 | lge | **Newcastle** | H | W | 5-2 | Dunn 3 pen,8; Taylor 54,73; Yorke 62 |
| 13 | lge | **Arsenal** | A | W | 2-1 | Edu 6 og; Yorke 53 |
| 14 | uc2rl1 | **Celtic** | A | L | 0-1 | |
| 15 | lge | **Aston Villa** | H | D | 0-0 | |
| 16 | wr3 | **Walsall** | H | W | 5-4* | Grabbi 45 pen; Roper 105 og (*on penalties) |
| 17 | lge | **Southampton** | A | D | 1-1 | Cole 90 |
| 18 | uc2rl2 | **Celtic** | H | L | 0-2 | |
| 19 | lge | **Everton** | H | L | 0-1 | |
| 20 | lge | **Charlton** | A | L | 1-3 | Thompson 60 |
| 21 | lge | **Fulham** | H | W | 2-1 | Yorke 35; Brevett 77 og |
| 22 | wr4 | **Rotherham** | H | W | 4-0 | Yorke 12,39; Cole 16; Duff 43 |
| 23 | lge | **Bolton** | A | D | 1-1 | Short 90 |
| 24 | lge | **Everton** | A | L | 1-2 | Cole 6 |
| 25 | wqf | **Wigan** | A | W | 2-0 | Cole 16,80 |
| 26 | lge | **Man Utd** | H | W | 1-0 | Flitcroft 40 |
| 27 | lge | **Liverpool** | A | D | 1-1 | Cole 77 |
| 28 | lge | **West Ham** | H | D | 2-2 | Duff 4; Cole 78 |
| 29 | lge | **Middlesbrough** | H | W | 1-0 | Yorke 57 |
| 30 | facr3 | **Aston Villa** | A | W | 4-1 | Jansen 17,60; Yorke 52,71 |
| 31 | wsfl1 | **Man Utd** | A | D | 1-1 | Thompson 61 |
| 32 | lge | **Sunderland** | A | D | 0-0 | |
| 33 | lge | **Birmingham** | H | D | 1-1 | Duff 19 |
| 34 | wsfl2 | **Man Utd** | H | L | 1-3 | Cole 12 |
| 35 | facr4 | **Sunderland** | H | D | 3-3 | Cole 14,73; Yorke 90 |
| 36 | lge | **West Ham** | A | L | 1-2 | Yorke 38 |
| 37 | lge | **Aston Villa** | A | L | 0-3 | |
| 38 | facr4r | **Sunderland** | A | L | 0-3* | Flitcroft 50,90 (*on penalties) |
| 39 | lge | **Southampton** | H | W | 1-0 | Thompson 26 |
| 40 | lge | **Chelsea** | A | W | 2-1 | Yorke 86; Dunn 90 |
| 41 | lge | **Man City** | H | W | 1-0 | Dunn 13 |
| 42 | lge | **Arsenal** | H | W | 2-0 | Duff 21; Tugay 52 |
| 43 | lge | **Newcastle** | A | L | 1-5 | Duff 54 |
| 44 | lge | **Fulham** | A | W | 4-0 | Dunn 37 pen; Duff 53; Sukur 42,54 |
| 45 | lge | **Charlton** | H | W | 1-0 | Duff 34 |
| 46 | lge | **Man Utd** | A | L | 1-3 | Berg 25 |
| 47 | lge | **Bolton** | H | D | 0-0 | |
| 48 | lge | **Leeds** | A | W | 3-2 | Dunn 38 pen; Cole 69; Todd 78 |
| 49 | lge | **West Brom** | H | D | 1-1 | Duff 11 |
| 50 | lge | **Tottenham** | A | W | 4-0 | Yorke 5; Hignett 45; Duff 48; Cole 60 |

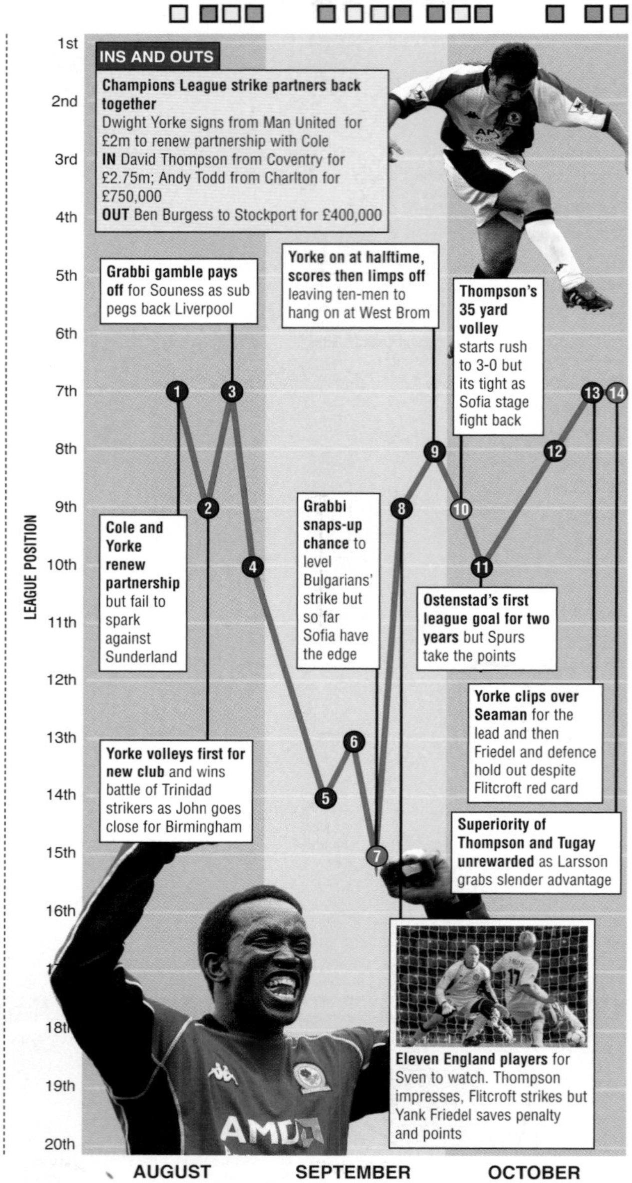

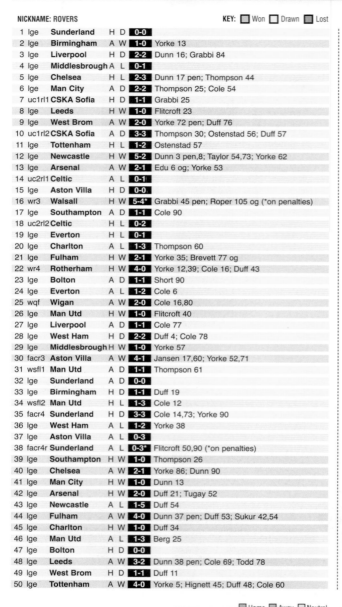

1st
2nd
3rd
4th
5th
6th
7th
8th
9th
10th
11th
12th
13th
14th
15th
16th
19th
20th
LEAGUE POSITION
INS AND OUTS
Champions League strike partners back together
Dwight Yorke signs from Man United for £2m to renew partnership with Cole
IN David Thompson from Coventry for £2.75m; Andy Todd from Charlton for £750,000
OUT Ben Burgess to Stockport for £400,000
Grabbi gamble pays off for Souness as sub pegs back Liverpool
Yorke on at halftime, scores then limps off leaving ten-men to hang on at West Brom
Thompson's 35 yard volley starts rush to 3-0 but its tight as Sofia stage fight back
Cole and Yorke renew partnership but fail to spark against Sunderland
Grabbi snaps-up chance to level Bulgarians' strike but so far Sofia have the edge
Ostenstad's first league goal for two years but Spurs take the points
Yorke clips over Seaman for the lead and then Friedel and defence hold out despite Flitcroft red card
Yorke volleys first for new club and wins battle of Trinidad strikers as John goes close for Birmingham
Superiority of Thompson and Tugay unrewarded as Larsson grabs slender advantage
Eleven England players for Sven to watch. Thompson impresses, Flitcroft strikes but Yank Friedel saves penalty and points
AUGUST
SEPTEMBER
OCTOBER


Home / Away / Neutral

## ATTENDANCES

HOME GROUND: EWOOD PARK CAPACITY: 30475 AVERAGE LEAGUE AT HOME: 26224

| | | | | | | | | | | | |
|---|---|---|---|---|---|---|---|---|---|---|---|
| 46 | Man Utd | 67626 | 26 | Man Utd | 30475 | 12 | Newcastle | 27307 | 15 | Aston Villa | 23004 |
| 31 | Man Utd | 62740 | 17 | Southampton | 30059 | 1 | Sunderland | 27122 | 5 | Chelsea | 22999 |
| 14 | Celtic | 59553 | 42 | Arsenal | 29840 | 19 | Everton | 26469 | 21 | Fulham | 21096 |
| 43 | Newcastle | 52106 | 18 | Celtic | 29689 | 11 | Tottenham | 26203 | 10 | CSKA Sofia | 20000 |
| 27 | Liverpool | 43075 | 3 | Liverpool | 29207 | 20 | Charlton | 26152 | 7 | CSKA Sofia | 18300 |
| 40 | Chelsea | 40850 | 37 | Aston Villa | 29171 | 8 | Leeds | 25415 | 25 | Wigan | 16922 |
| 13 | Arsenal | 38064 | 34 | Man Utd | 29048 | 9 | West Brom | 25170 | 38 | Sunderland | 15745 |
| 48 | Leeds | 38062 | 47 | Bolton | 28862 | 28 | West Ham | 24998 | 35 | Sunderland | 14315 |
| 24 | Everton | 36578 | 41 | Man City | 28647 | 39 | Southampton | 24896 | 44 | Fulham | 14017 |
| 32 | Sunderland | 36529 | 4 | Middlesboro | 28270 | 23 | Bolton | 24556 | 22 | Rotherham | 11220 |
| 50 | Tottenham | 36036 | 2 | Birmingham | 27563 | 30 | Aston Villa | 23884 | 16 | Walsall | 9486 |
| 36 | West Ham | 34743 | 45 | Charlton | 27506 | 29 | Middlesbro | 23413 | | | |
| 6 | Man City | 34130 | 49 | West Brom | 27470 | 33 | Birmingham | 23331 | | | |

## GOAL ATTEMPTS

**FOR**
Goal attempts recorded in League games

| | HOME | AWAY | TOTAL | AVE |
|---|---|---|---|---|
| shots on target | 119 | 87 | 206 | 5.4 |
| shots off target | 126 | 99 | 225 | 5.9 |
| TOTAL | 245 | 186 | 431 | 11.3 |

| | |
|---|---|
| **Ratio of goals to shots** Average number of shots on target per League goal scored | 4.0 |
| **Accuracy rating** Average percentage of total goal attempts which were on target | 47.8 |

**AGAINST**
Goal attempts recorded in League games

| | HOME | AWAY | TOTAL | AVE |
|---|---|---|---|---|
| shots on target | 90 | 135 | 225 | 5.9 |
| shots off target | 82 | 87 | 169 | 4.4 |
| TOTAL | 172 | 222 | 394 | 10.4 |

| | |
|---|---|
| **Ratio of goals to shots** Average number of shots on target per League goal scored | 5.2 |
| **Accuracy rating** Average percentage of total goal attempts which were on target | 57.1 |

# European spot reward for progress

**Final Position: 6th**

KEY: ● League ● Champions Lge ● UEFA Cup ● FA Cup ○ League Cup ● Other

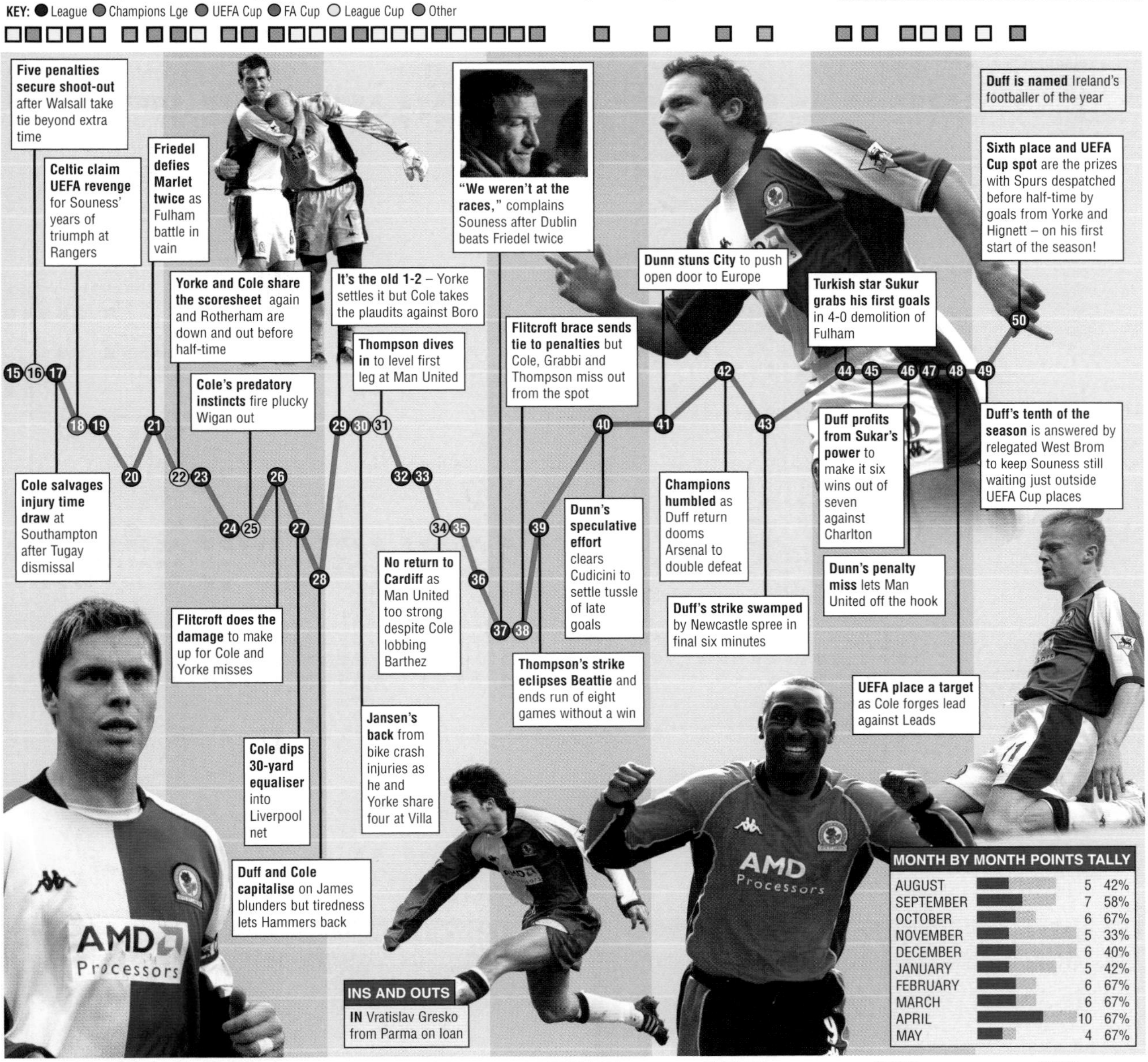

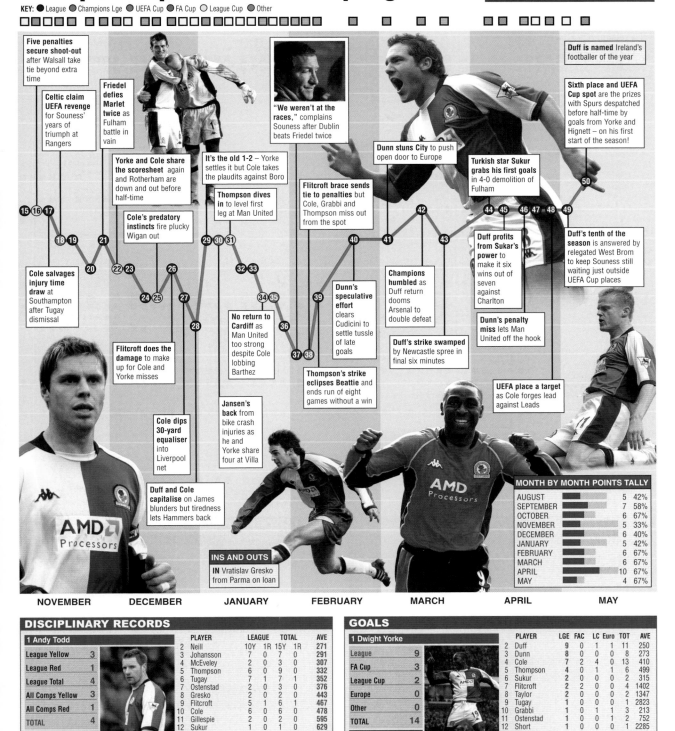

**Five penalties secure shoot-out** after Walsall take tie beyond extra time
**Celtic claim UEFA revenge** for Souness' years of triumph at Rangers
**Friedel defies Marlet twice** as Fulham battle in vain
**Cole salvages injury time draw** at Southampton after Tugay dismissal
**Yorke and Cole share the scoresheet** again and Rotherham are down and out before half-time
**Cole's predatory instincts** fire plucky Wigan out
**Flitcroft does the damage** to make up for Cole and Yorke misses
**Cole dips 30-yard equaliser** into Liverpool net
**Duff and Cole capitalise** on James blunders but tiredness lets Hammers back
**It's the old 1-2** – Yorke settles it but Cole takes the plaudits against Boro
**Thompson dives in** to level first leg at Man United
**Jansen's back** from bike crash injuries as he and Yorke share four at Villa
**No return to Cardiff** as Man United too strong despite Cole lobbing Barthez
**"We weren't at the races,"** complains Souness after Dublin beats Friedel twice
**Flitcroft brace sends tie to penalties** but Cole, Grabbi and Thompson miss out from the spot
**Thompson's strike eclipses Beattie** and ends run of eight games without a win
**Dunn's speculative effort** clears Cudicini to settle tussle of late goals
**Dunn stuns City** to push open door to Europe
**Champions humbled** as Duff return dooms Arsenal to double defeat
**Duff's strike swamped** by Newcastle spree in final six minutes
**Turkish star Sukur grabs his first goals** in 4-0 demolition of Fulham
**Duff profits from Sukar's power** to make it six wins out of seven against Charlton
**Dunn's penalty miss** lets Man United off the hook
**UEFA place a target** as Cole forges lead against Leads
**Duff is named** Ireland's footballer of the year
**Sixth place and UEFA Cup spot** are the prizes with Spurs despatched before half-time by goals from Yorke and Hignett – on his first start of the season!
**Duff's tenth of the season** is answered by relegated West Brom to keep Souness still waiting just outside UEFA Cup places
15 16 17 18 19 20 21 22 23 24 25 26 27 28 29 30 31 32 33 34 35 36 37 38 39 40 41 42 43 44 45 46 47 48 49 50
INS AND OUTS
**IN** Vratislav Gresko from Parma on loan
NOVEMBER
DECEMBER
JANUARY
FEBRUARY
MARCH
APRIL
MAY


**MONTH BY MONTH POINTS TALLY**

| | | |
|---|---|---|
| AUGUST | 5 | 42% |
| SEPTEMBER | 7 | 58% |
| OCTOBER | 6 | 67% |
| NOVEMBER | 5 | 33% |
| DECEMBER | 6 | 40% |
| JANUARY | 5 | 42% |
| FEBRUARY | 6 | 67% |
| MARCH | 6 | 67% |
| APRIL | 10 | 67% |
| MAY | 4 | 67% |

## DISCIPLINARY RECORDS

**1 Andy Todd**

| | |
|---|---|
| League Yellow | 3 |
| League Red | 1 |
| League Total | 4 |
| All Comps Yellow | 3 |
| All Comps Red | 1 |
| TOTAL | 4 |

League Average
173
mins between cards

| | PLAYER | LEAGUE | | TOTAL | | AVE |
|---|---|---|---|---|---|---|
| 2 | Neill | 10Y | 1R | 15Y | 1R | 271 |
| 3 | Johansson | 7 | 0 | 7 | 0 | 291 |
| 4 | McEveley | 2 | 0 | 3 | 0 | 307 |
| 5 | Thompson | 6 | 0 | 9 | 0 | 332 |
| 6 | Tugay | 7 | 1 | 7 | 1 | 352 |
| 7 | Ostenstad | 2 | 0 | 3 | 0 | 376 |
| 8 | Gresko | 2 | 0 | 2 | 0 | 443 |
| 9 | Flitcroft | 5 | 1 | 6 | 1 | 467 |
| 10 | Cole | 6 | 0 | 6 | 0 | 478 |
| 11 | Gillespie | 2 | 0 | 2 | 0 | 595 |
| 12 | Sukur | 1 | 0 | 1 | 0 | 629 |
| 13 | Berg | 2 | 0 | 2 | 0 | 637 |
| 14 | Duff | 3 | 0 | 3 | 0 | 749 |
| 15 | Short | 2 | 0 | 2 | 0 | 1142 |
| | Other | 5 | 0 | 9 | 0 | |
| | **TOTAL** | **65** | **4** | **80** | **4** | |

## GOALS

**1 Dwight Yorke**

| | |
|---|---|
| League | 9 |
| FA Cup | 3 |
| League Cup | 2 |
| Europe | 0 |
| Other | 0 |
| TOTAL | 14 |

League Average
258
mins between goals

| | PLAYER | LGE | FAC | LC | Euro | TOT | AVE |
|---|---|---|---|---|---|---|---|
| 2 | Duff | 9 | 0 | 1 | 1 | 11 | 250 |
| 3 | Dunn | 8 | 0 | 0 | 0 | 8 | 273 |
| 4 | Cole | 7 | 2 | 4 | 0 | 13 | 410 |
| 5 | Thompson | 4 | 0 | 1 | 1 | 6 | 499 |
| 6 | Sukur | 2 | 0 | 0 | 0 | 2 | 315 |
| 7 | Flitcroft | 2 | 2 | 0 | 0 | 4 | 1402 |
| 8 | Taylor | 2 | 0 | 0 | 0 | 2 | 1347 |
| 9 | Tugay | 1 | 0 | 0 | 0 | 1 | 2823 |
| 10 | Grabbi | 1 | 0 | 1 | 1 | 3 | 213 |
| 11 | Ostenstad | 1 | 0 | 0 | 1 | 2 | 752 |
| 12 | Short | 1 | 0 | 0 | 0 | 1 | 2285 |
| 13 | Hignett | 1 | 0 | 0 | 0 | 1 | 113 |
| 14 | Berg | 1 | 0 | 0 | 0 | 1 | 1275 |
| 15 | Todd | 1 | 0 | 0 | 0 | 1 | 693 |
| | Other | 2 | 2 | 1 | 0 | 5 | |
| | **TOTAL** | **52** | **9** | **10** | **4** | **75** | |

## SQUAD APPEARANCES

| Match | 1 | 2 | 3 | 4 | 5 | 6 | 7 | 8 | 9 | 10 | 11 | 12 | 13 | 14 | 15 | 16 | 17 | 18 | 19 | 20 | 21 | 22 | 23 | 24 | 25 |
|---|---|---|---|---|---|---|---|---|---|---|---|---|---|---|---|---|---|---|---|---|---|---|---|---|---|
| Venue | H | A | H | A | H | A | H | H | A | A | H | H | A | A | H | H | A | H | H | A | H | H | A | A | A |
| Competition | L | L | L | L | L | L | E | L | L | E | L | L | L | E | L | W | L | E | L | L | L | W | L | L | W |
| Result | D | W | D | L | L | D | D | W | W | D | L | W | W | L | D | W | D | L | L | L | W | W | D | L | W |

| Match | 26 | 27 | 28 | 29 | 30 | 31 | 32 | 33 | 34 | 35 | 36 | 37 | 38 | 39 | 40 | 41 | 42 | 43 | 44 | 45 | 46 | 47 | 48 | 49 | 50 |
|---|---|---|---|---|---|---|---|---|---|---|---|---|---|---|---|---|---|---|---|---|---|---|---|---|---|
| Venue | H | A | H | H | A | A | A | H | H | H | A | A | A | H | A | H | H | A | A | H | A | H | A | H | A |
| Competition | L | L | L | L | F | W | L | L | W | F | L | L | F | L | L | L | L | L | L | L | L | L | L | L | L |
| Result | W | D | D | W | W | D | D | D | L | D | L | L | L | W | W | W | W | L | W | W | L | D | W | D | W |

**Goalkeepers**
Brad Friedel
Alan Kelly
Alan Miller
Ryan Robinson

**Defenders**
Henning Berg
Stig Inge Bjornebye
John Curtis
Nils-Eric Johansson
James McEveley
Lucas Neill
Marc Sebastien Pelzer
Craig Short
Martin Taylor
Andy Todd
Hakan Unsal

**Midfielders**
Neil Danns
John Douglas
Damien Duff
David Dunn
Garry Flitcroft
Keith Gillespie
Vratislav Gresko
Craig Hignett
Alan Mahon
Marc Richards
David Thompson
Kerimoglu Tugay

**Forwards**
Andy Cole
Paul Gallagher
Corrado Grabbi
Matthew Jansen
Egil Ostenstad
Hakan Sukur
Dwight Yorke

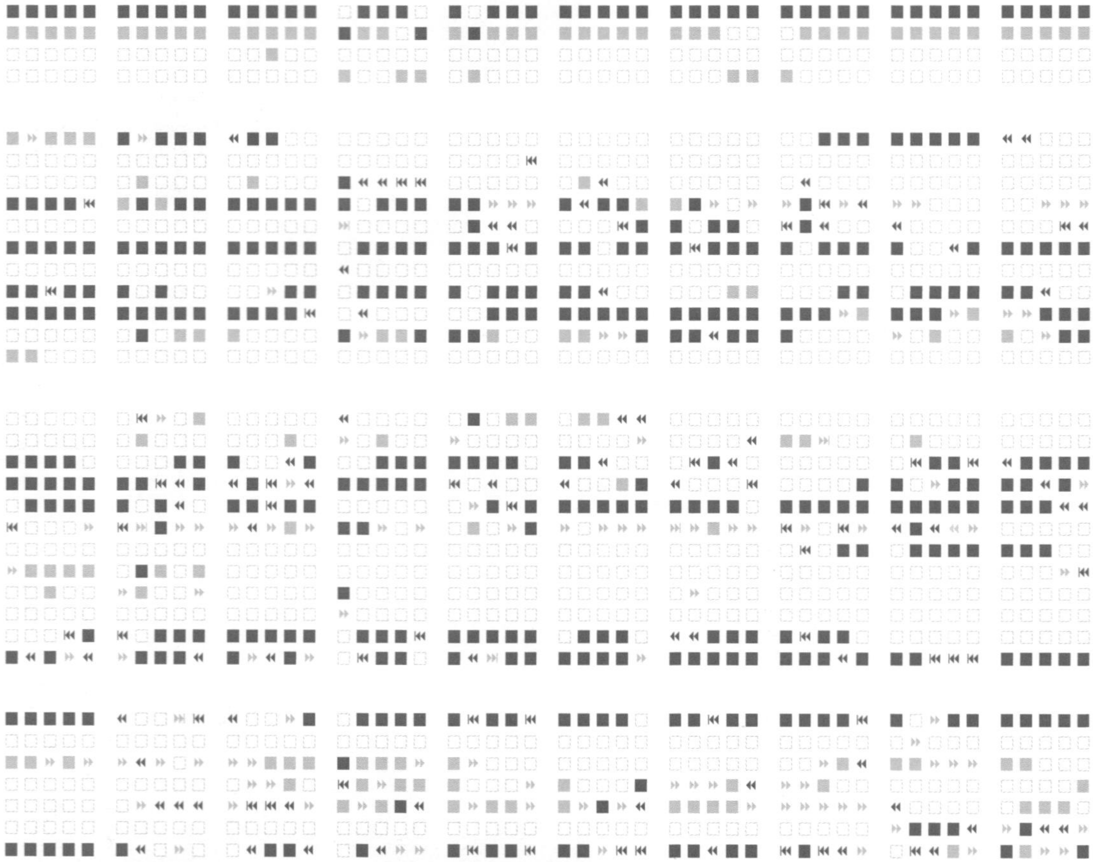

KEY: On all match | On bench | Subbed or sent off (Counting game) | Subbed or sent off (playing less than 70 minutes) | Subbed on from bench (Counting Game) | Subbed on (playing less than 70 minutes) | Subbed on and then subbed or sent off (Counting Game) | Subbed on and then subbed or sent off (playing less than 70 minutes) | Not in 16

## KEY PLAYERS - GOALSCORERS

**1 Damien Duff**

| | |
|---|---|
| Goals in the League | 9 |
| Goals in all competitions | 11 |
| Assists<br>League goals scored by team-mates where he delivered the final pass | 5 |
| Contribution to Attacking Power<br>Average number of minutes between League team goals while on pitch | 70 |
| Player Strike Rate<br>Average number of minutes between League goals scored by player | 250 |
| Club Strike Rate<br>Average minutes between League goals scored by club | 66 |

| | PLAYER | GOALS LGE | GOALS ALL | ASSISTS | POWER | S RATE |
|---|---|---|---|---|---|---|
| 2 | Dwight Yorke | 9 | 14 | 3 | 61 | 258 mins |
| 3 | David Dunn | 8 | 8 | 4 | 62 | 273 mins |
| 4 | Andy Cole | 7 | 13 | 6 | 75 | 410 mins |
| 5 | David Thompson | 4 | 6 | 4 | 71 | 499 mins |

## KEY PLAYERS - MIDFIELDERS

**1 Kerimoglu Tugay**

| | |
|---|---|
| Goals in the League | 1 |
| Goals in all competitions | 1 |
| Assists<br>League goals scored by team-mates where he delivered the final pass | 2 |
| Defensive Rating<br>Average number of mins between League goals conceded while he was on the pitch | 88 |
| Contribution to Attacking Power<br>Average number of minutes between League team goals while on pitch | 63 |
| Scoring Difference<br>Defensive Rating minus Contribution to Attacking Power | 25 |

| | PLAYER | GOALS LGE | GOALS ALL | ASSISTS | DEF RATE | POWER | SC DIFF |
|---|---|---|---|---|---|---|---|
| 2 | Damien Duff | 8 | 10 | 5 | 83 | 70 | 13 mins |
| 3 | David Dunn | 9 | 9 | 4 | 75 | 62 | 13 mins |
| 4 | Garry Flitcroft | 2 | 4 | 0 | 76 | 64 | 12 mins |
| 5 | David Thompson | 4 | 6 | 4 | 80 | 71 | 9 mins |

## PLAYER APPEARANCES

| | AGE (on 01/07/03) | IN THE SQUAD | COUNTING GAMES | MINUTES ON PITCH | IN THE SQUAD | MINUTES ON PITCH | THIS SEASON | NATIONAL SIDE |
|---|---|---|---|---|---|---|---|---|
| **Goalkeepers** | | | | | | | | |
| Brad Friedel | 32 | 37 | 37 | 3330 | 47 | 4260 | - | United States |
| Alan Kelly | 34 | 36 | 1 | 90 | 46 | 300 | - | Rep of Ireland |
| Alan Miller | 33 | 1 | 0 | 0 | 1 | 0 | - | England |
| Ryan Robinson | 20 | 3 | 0 | 0 | 7 | 0 | - | England |
| **Defenders** | | | | | | | | |
| Henning Berg | 33 | 20 | 12 | 1275 | 23 | 1506 | 7 | Norway (24) |
| Stig Inge Bjornebye | 33 | 0 | 0 | 0 | 1 | 81 | - | Norway |
| John Curtis | 24 | 7 | 2 | 303 | 10 | 468 | - | England |
| Nils-Eric Johansson | 23 | 32 | 18 | 2043 | 43 | 2711 | 5 | Sweden (20) |
| James McEveley | 17 | 9 | 5 | 614 | 15 | 1110 | - | England |
| Lucas Neill | 25 | 34 | 33 | 2991 | 45 | 4011 | - | Australia |
| Marc Seb Pelzer | 22 | 0 | 0 | 0 | 1 | 29 | - | Germany |
| Craig Short | 35 | 27 | 24 | 2285 | 32 | 2555 | - | England |
| Martin Taylor | 23 | 35 | 28 | 2693 | 44 | 3533 | - | England |
| Andy Todd | 28 | 20 | 6 | 693 | 29 | 1353 | - | England |
| Hakan Unsal | 30 | 2 | 0 | 0 | 2 | 0 | 4 | Turkey (8) |
| **Midfielders** | | | | | | | | |
| Neil Danns | 20 | 5 | 0 | 47 | 11 | 313 | - | England |
| John Douglas | 21 | 4 | 0 | 2 | 11 | 210 | - | Rep of Ireland |
| Damien Duff | 24 | 26 | 23 | 2247 | 31 | 2616 | 7 | Rep of Ireland (15) |
| David Dunn | 23 | 29 | 20 | 2184 | 37 | 2788 | 1 | England (7) |
| Garry Flitcroft | 30 | 33 | 30 | 2803 | 40 | 3402 | - | England |
| Keith Gillespie | 28 | 26 | 7 | 1190 | 37 | 1774 | 6 | N Ireland (111) |
| Vratislav Gresko | 25 | 10 | 10 | 887 | 10 | 887 | - | Slovakia |
| Craig Hignett | 33 | 8 | 1 | 113 | 10 | 203 | - | England |
| Alan Mahon | 25 | 3 | 0 | 30 | 6 | 153 | - | Rep of Ireland |
| Marc Richards | 20 | 0 | 0 | 0 | 1 | 41 | - | England |
| David Thompson | 25 | 23 | 22 | 1997 | 32 | 2812 | - | England |
| Kerimoglu Tugay | 32 | 37 | 28 | 2823 | 48 | 3740 | 10 | Turkey (8) |
| **Forwards** | | | | | | | | |
| Andy Cole | 31 | 34 | 31 | 2873 | 43 | 3640 | - | England |
| Paul Gallagher | 18 | 1 | 0 | 13 | 1 | 13 | - | England |
| Corrado Grabbi | 27 | 24 | 0 | 213 | 31 | 482 | - | Italy |
| Matthew Jansen | 25 | 12 | 0 | 78 | 21 | 350 | - | England |
| Egil Ostenstad | 31 | 26 | 4 | 752 | 38 | 1038 | - | Norway |
| Hakan Sukur | 31 | 10 | 4 | 629 | 10 | 629 | 4 | Turkey (8) |
| Dwight Yorke | 31 | 35 | 20 | 2319 | 45 | 3049 | - | Trinidad & Tobago |

KEY: LEAGUE ALL COMPS CAPS (FIFA RANKING)

## TEAM OF THE SEASON

Friedel
CG 37 DR 83
Neill
CG 33 DR 91
Short
CG 24 DR 79
Berg
CG 12 DR 85
Johansson
CG 18 DR 82
Flitcroft
CG 30 SD +12
Tugay
CG 28 SD +25
Dunn
CG 20 SD +13
Duff
CG 23 SD +13
Cole
CG 31 AP 75
Yorke
CG 20 SR 258


KEY: DR = Defensive Rate, SD = Scoring Difference AP = Attacking Power SR = Strike Rate, CG=Counting Games – League games playing at least 70 minutes

## TOP POINT EARNERS

**1 Henning Berg**

| | |
|---|---|
| **Counting Games** League games when he played at least 70 minutes | 12 |
| **Average points** Average League points taken in Counting games | 2.58 |
| **Club Average points** Average points taken in League games | 1.58 |

| | PLAYER | GAMES | PTS |
|---|---|---|---|
| 2 | David Dunn | 20 | 1.65 |
| 3 | Brad Friedel | 37 | 1.62 |
| 4 | Lucas Neill | 33 | 1.61 |
| 5 | Garry Flitcroft | 30 | 1.60 |
| 6 | Kerimoglu Tugay | 28 | 1.54 |
| 7 | Martin Taylor | 28 | 1.54 |
| 8 | Andy Cole | 31 | 1.52 |
| 9 | Craig Short | 24 | 1.46 |
| 10 | Nils-Eric Johansson | 18 | 1.44 |

## KEY PLAYERS - DEFENDERS

**1 Lucas Neill**

| | |
|---|---|
| **Goals Conceded** The number of League goals conceded while he was on the pitch | 33 |
| **Goals Conceded in all competitions** The number goals conceded while he was on the pitch in all competitions | 50 |
| **League minutes played** Number of minutes played in league matches | 2991 |
| **Clean Sheets** In games when he played at least70 mins | 13 |
| **Defensive Rating** Average number of mins between League goals conceded while he was on the pitch | 91 |
| **Club Defensive Rating** Average number of mins between League goals conceded by the club this season | 80 |

| | PLAYER | CON LGE | CON ALL | MINS | C SHEETS | DEF RATE |
|---|---|---|---|---|---|---|
| 2 | Henning Berg | 15 | 20 | 1275 | 7 | 85 mins |
| 3 | Nils-Eric Johansson | 25 | 36 | 2043 | 7 | 82 mins |
| 4 | Craig Short | 29 | 32 | 2285 | 10 | 79 mins |
| 5 | Martin Taylor | 34 | 49 | 2693 | 11 | 79 mins |

## KEY PLAYERS - GOALKEEPERS

**1 Brad Friedel**

| | |
|---|---|
| **Goals Conceded in the League** The number of League goals conceded while he was on the pitch | 40 |
| **Goals Conceded in all competitions** The number of goals conceded while he was on the pitch in all competitions | 57 |
| **League minutes played** Number of minutes played in league matches | 3330 |
| **Clean Sheets** In games when he played at least 70 mins | 15 |
| **Goals to Shots Ratio** The average number of shots on target per each League goal conceded | 5.4 |
| **Defensive Rating** Ave number of mins between League goals conceded while on the pitch | 83 |

**2 Alan Kelly**

| | |
|---|---|
| **Goals Conceded in the League** The number of League goals conceded while he was on the pitch | 3 |
| **Goals Conceded in all competitions** The number of goals conceded while he was on the pitch in all competitions | 5 |
| **League minutes played** Number of minutes played in league matches | 90 |
| **Clean Sheets** In games when he played at least 70 mins | 0 |
| **Goals to Shots Ratio** The average number of shots on target per each League goal conceded | 3 |
| **Defensive Rating** Ave number of mins between League goals conceded while on the pitch | 30 |

# EVERTON

**NICKNAME: THE TOFFEES**

KEY: Won / Drawn / Lost

| | | | | | | |
|---|---|---|---|---|---|---|
| 1 | lge | **Tottenham** | H | D | 2-2 | Pembridge 37; Radzinski 81 |
| 2 | lge | **Sunderland** | A | W | 1-0 | Campbell 28 |
| 3 | lge | **Birmingham** | H | D | 1-1 | Cunningham 90 og |
| 4 | lge | **Man City** | A | L | 1-3 | Unsworth 28 pen |
| 5 | lge | **Southampton** | A | L | 0-1 | |
| 6 | lge | **Middlesbrough** | H | W | 2-1 | Campbell 33,77 |
| 7 | lge | **Aston Villa** | A | L | 2-3 | Radzinski 51; Campbell 66 |
| 8 | lge | **Fulham** | H | W | 2-0 | Campbell 44; Gravesen 45 |
| 9 | wr2 | **Wrexham** | A | W | 3-0 | Campbell 25; Rooney 82,88 |
| 10 | lge | **Man Utd** | A | L | 0-3 | |
| 11 | lge | **Arsenal** | H | W | 2-1 | Radzinski 21; Rooney 89 |
| 12 | lge | **West Ham** | A | W | 1-0 | Carsley 70 |
| 13 | lge | **Leeds** | A | W | 1-0 | Rooney 80 |
| 14 | wr3 | **Newcastle** | A | W | 3-2* | Campbell 11; Watson 85; Unsworth 112 pen (*on penalties) |
| 15 | lge | **Charlton** | H | W | 1-0 | Radzinski 31 |
| 16 | lge | **Blackburn** | A | W | 1-0 | Campbell 19 |
| 17 | lge | **West Brom** | H | W | 1-0 | Radzinski 35 |
| 18 | lge | **Newcastle** | A | L | 1-2 | Campbell 17 |
| 19 | wr4 | **Chelsea** | A | L | 1-4 | Naysmith 80 |
| 20 | lge | **Chelsea** | H | L | 1-3 | Naysmith 43 |
| 21 | lge | **Blackburn** | H | W | 2-1 | Carsley 12; Rooney 25 |
| 22 | lge | **Liverpool** | A | D | 0-0 | |
| 23 | lge | **Birmingham** | A | D | 1-1 | Radzinski 45 |
| 24 | lge | **Bolton** | H | D | 0-0 | |
| 25 | lge | **Man City** | H | D | 2-2 | Watson 6; Radzinski 90 |
| 26 | facr3 | **Shrewsbury** | A | L | 1-2 | Alexandersson 60 |
| 27 | lge | **Tottenham** | A | L | 3-4 | McBride 10; Watson 58; Radzinski 74 |
| 28 | lge | **Sunderland** | H | W | 2-1 | McBride 51,57 |
| 29 | lge | **Bolton** | A | W | 2-1 | Watson 33,39 |
| 30 | lge | **Leeds** | H | W | 2-0 | Unsworth 56 pen; Radzinski 68 |
| 31 | lge | **Charlton** | A | L | 1-2 | McBride 69 |
| 32 | lge | **Southampton** | H | W | 2-1 | Radzinski 83,90 |
| 33 | lge | **Middlesbrough** | A | D | 1-1 | Watson 23 |
| 34 | lge | **West Ham** | H | D | 0-0 | |
| 35 | lge | **Arsenal** | A | L | 1-2 | Rooney 56 |
| 36 | lge | **Newcastle** | H | W | 2-1 | Rooney 18; Unsworth 65 pen |
| 37 | lge | **West Brom** | A | W | 2-1 | Weir 23; Campbell 45 |
| 38 | lge | **Liverpool** | H | L | 1-2 | Unsworth 58 pen |
| 39 | lge | **Chelsea** | A | L | 1-4 | Carsley 77 |
| 40 | lge | **Aston Villa** | H | W | 2-1 | Campbell 59; Rooney 90 |
| 41 | lge | **Fulham** | A | L | 0-2 | |
| 42 | lge | **Man Utd** | H | L | 1-2 | Campbell 8 |

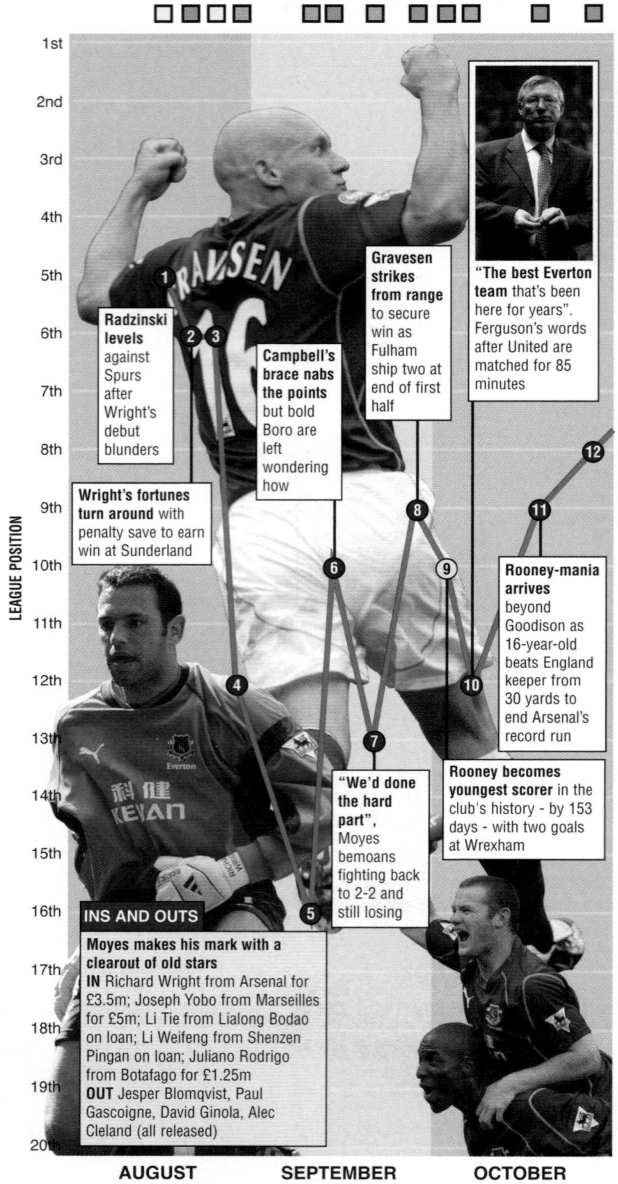

LEAGUE POSITION
1st
2nd
3rd
4th
5th
6th
7th
8th
9th
10th
11th
12th
13th
14th
15th
16th
17th
18th
19th
20th
Radzinski levels against Spurs after Wright's debut blunders
Wright's fortunes turn around with penalty save to earn win at Sunderland
Campbell's brace nabs the points but bold Boro are left wondering how
Gravesen strikes from range to secure win as Fulham ship two at end of first half
"The best Everton team that's been here for years". Ferguson's words after United are matched for 85 minutes
Rooney-mania arrives beyond Goodison as 16-year-old beats England keeper from 30 yards to end Arsenal's record run
Rooney becomes youngest scorer in the club's history - by 153 days - with two goals at Wrexham
"We'd done the hard part", Moyes bemoans fighting back to 2-2 and still losing
INS AND OUTS
Moyes makes his mark with a clearout of old stars
IN Richard Wright from Arsenal for £3.5m; Joseph Yobo from Marseilles for £5m; Li Tie from Lialong Bodao on loan; Li Weifeng from Shenzen Pingan on loan; Juliano Rodrigo from Botafago for £1.25m
OUT Jesper Blomqvist, Paul Gascoigne, David Ginola, Alec Cleland (all released)
AUGUST
SEPTEMBER
OCTOBER


Home / Away / Neutral

## ATTENDANCES

**HOME GROUND: GOODISON PARK  CAPACITY: 40200  AVERAGE LEAGUE AT HOME: 38491**

| | | | | | | | | | | | |
|---|---|---|---|---|---|---|---|---|---|---|---|
| 10 | Man Utd | 67629 | 1 | Tottenham | 40120 | 21 | Blackburn | 36578 | 23 | Birmingham | 29505 |
| 18 | Newcastle | 51607 | 17 | West Brom | 40113 | 32 | Southampton | 36569 | 5 | Southampton | 29190 |
| 22 | Liverpool | 44025 | 36 | Newcastle | 40031 | 27 | Tottenham | 36070 | 37 | West Brom | 27039 |
| 39 | Chelsea | 40875 | 24 | Bolton | 39480 | 4 | Man City | 34835 | 31 | Charlton | 26623 |
| 42 | Man Utd | 40168 | 20 | Chelsea | 39396 | 14 | Newcastle | 34584 | 16 | Blackburn | 26469 |
| 40 | Aston Villa | 40167 | 11 | Arsenal | 39038 | 8 | Fulham | 34371 | 29 | Bolton | 25119 |
| 25 | Man City | 40163 | 35 | Arsenal | 38042 | 12 | West Ham | 34117 | 41 | Fulham | 18385 |
| 38 | Liverpool | 40162 | 2 | Sunderland | 37698 | 33 | Middlesboro | 32473 | 9 | Wrexham | 13420 |
| 13 | Leeds | 40161 | 15 | Charlton | 37621 | 6 | Middlesboro | 32440 | 26 | Shrewsbury | 7800 |
| 34 | West Ham | 40158 | 28 | Sunderland | 37409 | 19 | Chelsea | 32322 | | | |
| 30 | Leeds | 40153 | 3 | Birmingham | 37197 | 7 | Aston Villa | 30023 | | | |

## GOAL ATTEMPTS

**FOR** Goal attempts recorded in League games

| | HOME | AWAY | TOTAL | AVE |
|---|---|---|---|---|
| shots on target | 130 | 95 | 225 | 5.9 |
| shots off target | 118 | 89 | 207 | 5.4 |
| **TOTAL** | **248** | **184** | **432** | **11.4** |

**Ratio of goals to shots** Average number of shots on target per League goal scored: **4.7**

**Accuracy rating** Average percentage of total goal attempts which were on target: **52.1**

**AGAINST** Goal attempts recorded in League games

| | HOME | AWAY | TOTAL | AVE |
|---|---|---|---|---|
| shots on target | 96 | 136 | 232 | 6.1 |
| shots off target | 90 | 95 | 185 | 4.9 |
| **TOTAL** | **186** | **231** | **417** | **11.0** |

**Ratio of goals to shots** Average number of shots on target per League goal scored: **4.7**

**Accuracy rating** Average percentage of total goal attempts which were on target: **55.6**

# Rooney headlines Moyes' hard work

**Final Position: 7th**

KEY: ● League ● Champions Lge ● UEFA Cup ● FA Cup ○ League Cup ● Other

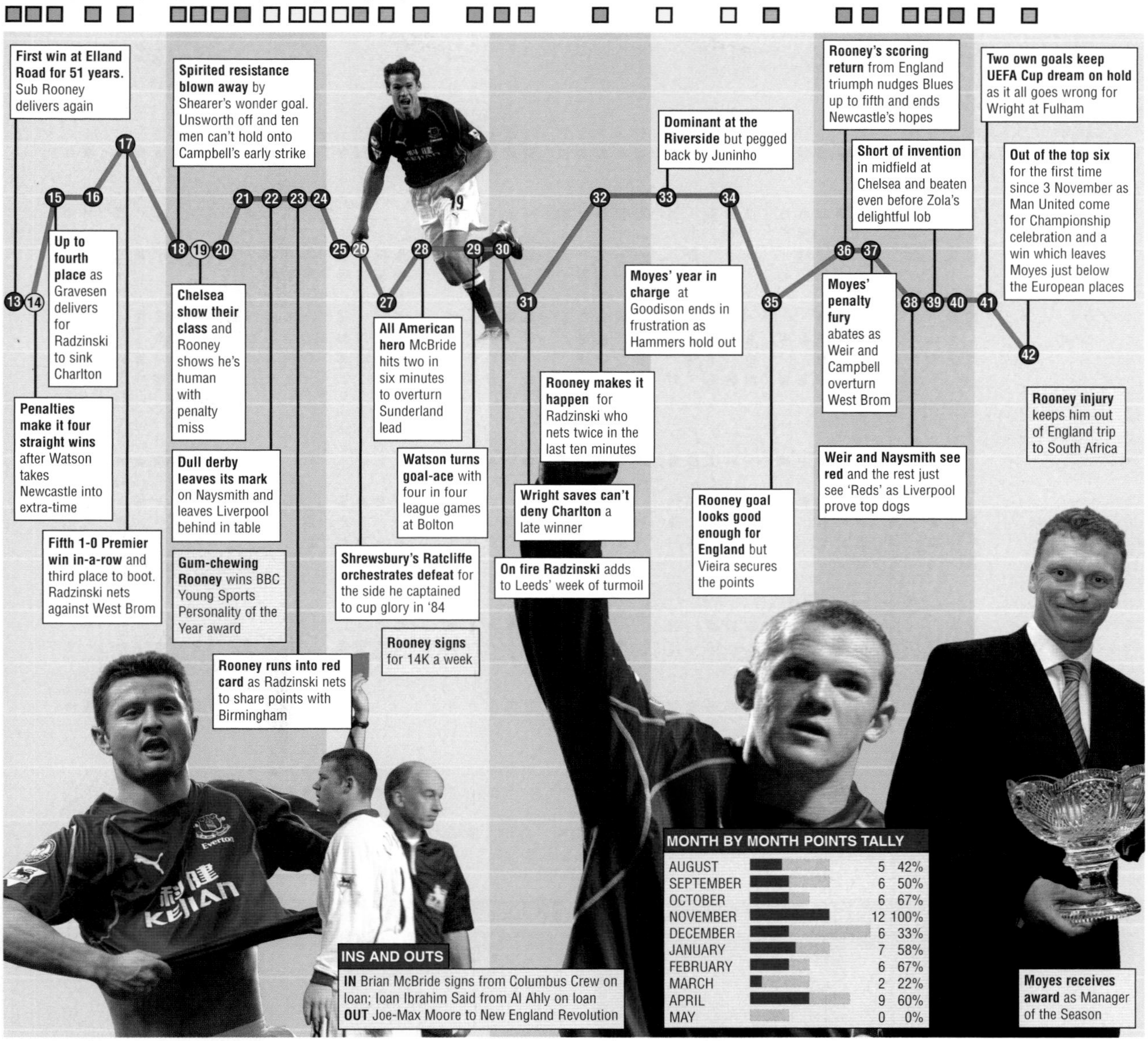

**First win at Elland Road for 51 years.** Sub Rooney delivers again
**Penalties make it four straight wins** after Watson takes Newcastle into extra-time
**Up to fourth place** as Gravesen delivers for Radzinski to sink Charlton
**Fifth 1-0 Premier win in-a-row** and third place to boot. Radzinski nets against West Brom
**Spirited resistance blown away** by Shearer's wonder goal. Unsworth off and ten men can't hold onto Campbell's early strike
**Chelsea show their class** and Rooney shows he's human with penalty miss
**Dull derby leaves its mark** on Naysmith and leaves Liverpool behind in table
**Gum-chewing Rooney** wins BBC Young Sports Personality of the Year award
**Rooney runs into red card** as Radzinski nets to share points with Birmingham
**Shrewsbury's Ratcliffe orchestrates defeat** for the side he captained to cup glory in '84
**Rooney signs** for 14K a week
**All American hero** McBride hits two in six minutes to overturn Sunderland lead
**Watson turns goal-ace** with four in four league games at Bolton
**On fire Radzinski** adds to Leeds' week of turmoil
**Wright saves can't deny Charlton** a late winner
**Rooney makes it happen** for Radzinski who nets twice in the last ten minutes
**Moyes' year in charge** at Goodison ends in frustration as Hammers hold out
**Dominant at the Riverside** but pegged back by Juninho
**Rooney goal looks good enough for England** but Vieira secures the points
**Rooney's scoring return** from England triumph nudges Blues up to fifth and ends Newcastle's hopes
**Moyes' penalty fury** abates as Weir and Campbell overturn West Brom
**Short of invention** in midfield at Chelsea and beaten even before Zola's delightful lob
**Weir and Naysmith see red** and the rest just see 'Reds' as Liverpool prove top dogs
**Two own goals keep UEFA Cup dream on hold** as it all goes wrong for Wright at Fulham
**Out of the top six** for the first time since 3 November as Man United come for Championship celebration and a win which leaves Moyes just below the European places
**Rooney injury** keeps him out of England trip to South Africa
**Moyes receives award** as Manager of the Season
13 14 15 16 17 18 19 20 21 22 23 24 25 26 27 28 29 30 31 32 33 34 35 36 37 38 39 40 41 42
NOVEMBER
DECEMBER
JANUARY
FEBRUARY
MARCH
APRIL
MAY


### INS AND OUTS

**IN** Brian McBride signs from Columbus Crew on loan; loan Ibrahim Said from Al Ahly on loan
**OUT** Joe-Max Moore to New England Revolution

### MONTH BY MONTH POINTS TALLY

| | | |
|---|---|---|
| AUGUST | 5 | 42% |
| SEPTEMBER | 6 | 50% |
| OCTOBER | 6 | 67% |
| NOVEMBER | 12 | 100% |
| DECEMBER | 6 | 33% |
| JANUARY | 7 | 58% |
| FEBRUARY | 6 | 67% |
| MARCH | 2 | 22% |
| APRIL | 9 | 60% |
| MAY | 0 | 0% |

## DISCIPLINARY RECORDS

**1 Wayne Rooney**

| | |
|---|---|
| League Yellow | 6 |
| League Red | 1 |
| League Total | 7 |
| All Comps Yellow | 8 |
| All Comps Red | 1 |
| TOTAL | 9 |

League Average
210
mins between cards

| | PLAYER | LEAGUE | | TOTAL | | AVE |
|---|---|---|---|---|---|---|
| 2 | Gravesen | 11Y | 0R | 12Y | 0R | **246** |
| 3 | Weir | 7 | 2 | 8 | 2 | **282** |
| 4 | Naysmith | 4 | 1 | 4 | 1 | **419** |
| 5 | Unsworth | 5 | 1 | 5 | 1 | **462** |
| 6 | Hibbert | 4 | 0 | 5 | 0 | **512** |
| 7 | Gemmill | 2 | 0 | 2 | 0 | **532** |
| 8 | Li Tie | 4 | 0 | 4 | 0 | **549** |
| 9 | Stubbs | 4 | 1 | 5 | 1 | **588** |
| 10 | Pembridge | 2 | 0 | 2 | 0 | **826** |
| 11 | Campbell | 3 | 0 | 3 | 0 | **911** |
| 12 | Watson | 1 | 0 | 2 | 0 | **1332** |
| 13 | Carsley | 1 | 0 | 2 | 0 | **1865** |
| 14 | Yobo | 0 | 1 | 0 | 1 | **1881** |
| 15 | Wright | 1 | 0 | 1 | 0 | **2970** |
| | Other | 3 | 0 | 4 | 0 | |
| | **TOTAL** | **58** | **7** | **67** | **7** | |

## GOALS

**1 Tomasz Radzinski**

| | |
|---|---|
| League | 11 |
| FA Cup | 0 |
| League Cup | 0 |
| Europe | 0 |
| Other | 0 |
| TOTAL | 11 |

League Average
209
mins between goals

| | PLAYER | LGE | FAC | LC | Euro | TOT | AVE |
|---|---|---|---|---|---|---|---|
| 2 | Campbell | **10** | 0 | 2 | 0 | 12 | 274 |
| 3 | Rooney | **6** | 0 | 2 | 0 | 8 | 261 |
| 4 | Watson | **5** | 0 | 1 | 0 | 6 | 266 |
| 5 | Unsworth | **4** | 0 | 1 | 0 | 5 | 693 |
| 6 | McBride | **4** | 0 | 0 | 0 | 4 | 139 |
| 7 | Carsley | **3** | 0 | 0 | 0 | 3 | 622 |
| 8 | Pembridge | **1** | 0 | 0 | 0 | 1 | 1653 |
| 9 | Gravesen | **1** | 0 | 0 | 0 | 1 | 2711 |
| 10 | Naysmith | **1** | 0 | 1 | 0 | 2 | 2098 |
| 11 | Weir | **1** | 0 | 0 | 0 | 1 | 2539 |
| 12 | Alexandersson | **0** | 1 | 0 | 0 | 1 | |
| | Other | 1 | 0 | 0 | 0 | 1 | |
| | **TOTAL** | **48** | **1** | **7** | **0** | **56** | |

## SQUAD APPEARANCES

| Match | 1 | 2 | 3 | 4 | 5 | 6 | 7 | 8 | 9 | 10 | 11 | 12 | 13 | 14 | 15 | 16 | 17 | 18 | 19 | 20 | 21 | 22 | 23 | 24 | 25 | 26 | 27 | 28 | 29 | 30 | 31 | 32 | 33 | 34 | 35 | 36 | 37 | 38 | 39 | 40 | 41 | 42 |
|---|---|---|---|---|---|---|---|---|---|---|---|---|---|---|---|---|---|---|---|---|---|---|---|---|---|---|---|---|---|---|---|---|---|---|---|---|---|---|---|---|---|---|
| Venue | H | A | H | A | A | H | A | H | A | A | H | A | A | A | H | A | H | A | A | H | H | A | A | H | H | A | A | H | A | H | A | H | A | H | A | H | A | H | A | H | A | H |
| Competition | L | L | L | L | L | L | L | L | W | L | L | L | L | W | L | L | L | L | W | L | L | L | L | L | L | F | L | L | L | L | L | L | L | L | L | L | L | L | L | L | L | L |
| Result | D | W | D | L | L | W | L | W | W | L | W | W | W | W | W | W | W | L | L | L | W | D | D | D | D | L | L | W | W | W | L | W | D | D | L | W | W | L | L | W | L | L |

**Goalkeepers**

Espen Baardsen
Paul Gerrard
Steve Simonsen
Richard Wright

**Defenders**

Tony Hibbert
Li Li Weifeng
Gary Naysmith
Alessandro Pistone
Ibrahim Said
Alan Stubbs
David Unsworth
David Weir
Joseph Yobo

**Midfielders**

Niclas Alexandersson
Lee Carsley
Peter Clarke
Scot Gemmill
Thomas Gravesen
Li Tie
Tobias Linderoth
Kevin McLeod
Leon Osman
Mark Pembridge
Steve Watson

**Forwards**

Kevin Campbell
Nick Chadwick
Duncan Ferguson
Brian McBride
Tomasz Radzinski
Juliano Rodrigo
Wayne Rooney

KEY: On all match | On bench | Subbed or sent off (Counting game) | Subbed or sent off (playing less than 70 minutes) | Subbed on from bench (Counting Game) | Subbed on (playing less than 70 minutes) | Subbed on and then subbed or sent off (Counting Game) | Subbed on and then subbed or sent off (playing less than 70 minutes) | Not in 16

## KEY PLAYERS - GOALSCORERS

**1 Tomasz Radzinski**

| | |
|---|---|
| Goals in the League | 11 |
| Goals in all competitions | 11 |
| Assists<br>League goals scored by team-mates where he delivered the final pass | 4 |
| Contribution to Attacking Power<br>Average number of minutes between League team goals while on pitch | 71 |
| **Player Strike Rate**<br>**Average number of minutes between League goals scored by player** | **209** |
| Club Strike Rate<br>Average minutes between League goals scored by club | 71 |

| | PLAYER | GOALS LGE | GOALS ALL | ASSISTS | POWER | S RATE |
|---|---|---|---|---|---|---|
| 2 | Wayne Rooney | 6 | 8 | 4 | 65 | 261 mins |
| 3 | Steve Watson | 5 | 6 | 0 | 57 | 266 mins |
| 4 | Kevin Campbell | 10 | 12 | 4 | 73 | 274 mins |
| 5 | Lee Carsley | 3 | 3 | 1 | 77 | 622 mins |

## KEY PLAYERS - MIDFIELDERS

**1 Steve Watson**

| | |
|---|---|
| Goals in the League | 5 |
| Goals in all competitions | 6 |
| Assists<br>League goals scored by team-mates where he delivered the final pass | 0 |
| Defensive Rating<br>Average number of mins between League goals conceded while he was on the pitch | 70 |
| Contribution to Attacking Power<br>Average number of minutes between League team goals while on pitch | 57 |
| **Scoring Difference**<br>**Defensive Rating minus Contribution to Attacking Power** | **13** |

| | PLAYER | GOALS LGE | GOALS ALL | ASSISTS | DEF RATE | POWER | SC DIFF |
|---|---|---|---|---|---|---|---|
| 2 | Lee Carsley | 3 | 3 | 1 | 81 | 78 | 3 mins |
| 3 | Thomas Gravesen | 1 | 1 | 8 | 71 | 71 | 0 mins |
| 4 | Mark Pembridge | 1 | 1 | 1 | 72 | 72 | 0 mins |
| 5 | Li Tie | 0 | 0 | 4 | 63 | 71 | -8 mins |

## PLAYER APPEARANCES

| | AGE (on 01/07/03) | IN THE SQUAD | COUNTING GAMES | MINUTES ON PITCH | IN THE SQUAD | MINUTES ON PITCH | THIS SEASON | NATIONAL SIDE |
|---|---|---|---|---|---|---|---|---|
| **Goalkeepers** | | | | | | | | |
| Espen Baardsen | 25 | 4 | 1 | 90 | 5 | 90 | - | Norway |
| Paul Gerrard | 30 | 22 | 2 | 180 | 22 | 180 | - | England |
| Steve Simonsen | 24 | 15 | 2 | 180 | 18 | 180 | - | England |
| Richard Wright | 25 | 33 | 33 | 2970 | 37 | 3360 | 1 | England (7) |
| **Defenders** | | | | | | | | |
| Tony Hibbert | 22 | 24 | 21 | 2050 | 26 | 2140 | - | England |
| Li Li Weifeng | 25 | 6 | 1 | 90 | 8 | 180 | - | China PR |
| Gary Naysmith | 24 | 33 | 22 | 2098 | 37 | 2453 | 9 | Scotland (64) |
| Alessandro Pistone | 27 | 17 | 10 | 945 | 19 | 1155 | - | Italy |
| Ibrahim Said | 22 | 1 | 0 | 0 | 1 | 0 | - | Egypt |
| Alan Stubbs | 31 | 36 | 31 | 2940 | 40 | 3158 | - | England |
| David Unsworth | 29 | 34 | 29 | 2772 | 38 | 3161 | - | England |
| David Weir | 33 | 34 | 27 | 2539 | 37 | 2839 | 2 | Scotland (64) |
| Joseph Yobo | 22 | 30 | 19 | 1881 | 32 | 2061 | - | Nigeria |
| **Midfielders** | | | | | | | | |
| Niclas Alexandersson | 31 | 13 | 2 | 309 | 14 | 354 | 5 | Sweden (20) |
| Lee Carsley | 29 | 27 | 20 | 1865 | 30 | 2165 | 9 | Rep of Ireland (15) |
| Peter Clarke | 21 | 0 | 0 | 0 | 1 | 90 | - | England |
| Scot Gemmill | 32 | 23 | 8 | 975 | 26 | 1161 | 6 | Scotland (64) |
| Thomas Gravesen | 27 | 35 | 28 | 2711 | 37 | 2846 | 10 | Denmark (10) |
| Li Tie | 25 | 34 | 21 | 2197 | 38 | 2418 | - | China PR |
| Tobias Linderoth | 24 | 10 | 2 | 299 | 11 | 337 | 4 | Sweden (20) |
| Kevin McLeod | 22 | 1 | 0 | 0 | 4 | 1 | - | England |
| Leon Osman | 22 | 3 | 0 | 2 | 3 | 2 | - | England |
| Mark Pembridge | 32 | 24 | 17 | 1653 | 26 | 1688 | 6 | Wales (50) |
| Steve Watson | 29 | 23 | 13 | 1332 | 24 | 1414 | - | England |
| **Forwards** | | | | | | | | |
| Kevin Campbell | 33 | 37 | 27 | 2735 | 40 | 3017 | - | England |
| Nick Chadwick | 20 | 1 | 0 | 16 | 1 | 16 | - | England |
| Duncan Ferguson | 31 | 10 | 0 | 188 | 11 | 206 | - | Scotland |
| Brian McBride | 31 | 8 | 5 | 555 | 8 | 555 | 2 | United States (10) |
| Tomasz Radzinski | 29 | 30 | 23 | 2300 | 34 | 2607 | - | Canada |
| Juliano Rodrigo | 26 | 5 | 0 | 55 | 5 | 55 | - | Brazil |
| Wayne Rooney | 17 | 34 | 13 | 1566 | 38 | 1894 | 5 | England (7) |

**KEY:** LEAGUE ALL COMPS CAPS (FIFA RANKING)

## TEAM OF THE SEASON

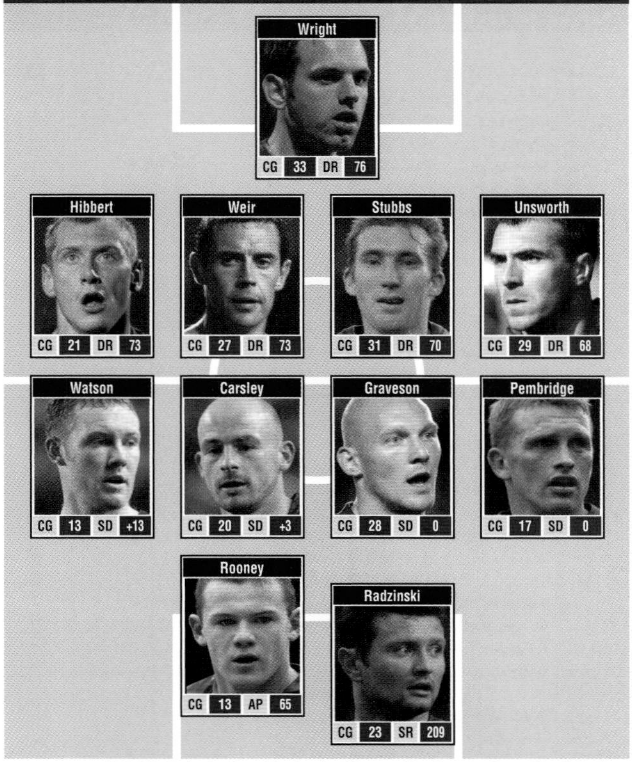
Wright
CG 33 DR 76
Hibbert
CG 21 DR 73
Weir
CG 27 DR 73
Stubbs
CG 31 DR 70
Unsworth
CG 29 DR 68
Watson
CG 13 SD +13
Carsley
CG 20 SD +3
Graveson
CG 28 SD 0
Pembridge
CG 17 SD 0
Rooney
CG 13 AP 65
Radzinski
CG 23 SR 209

**KEY:** DR = Defensive Rate, SD = Scoring Difference AP = Attacking Power SR = Strike Rate, CG=Counting Games – League games playing at least 70 minutes

## TOP POINT EARNERS

**1 Steve Watson**

| | |
|---|---|
| **Counting Games** League games when he played at least 70 minutes | 13 |
| **Average points** Average League points taken in Counting games | 1.85 |
| **Club Average points** Average points taken in League games | 1.55 |

| | PLAYER | GAMES | PTS |
|---|---|---|---|
| 2 | Lee Carsley | 20 | 1.80 |
| 3 | Mark Pembridge | 17 | 1.76 |
| 4 | Tomasz Radzinski | 23 | 1.74 |
| 5 | Tony Hibbert | 21 | 1.71 |
| 6 | Joseph Yobo | 19 | 1.68 |
| 7 | Richard Wright | 33 | 1.67 |
| 8 | David Unsworth | 29 | 1.66 |
| 9 | Kevin Campbell | 27 | 1.59 |
| 10 | Alan Stubbs | 31 | 1.58 |

## KEY PLAYERS - DEFENDERS

**1 Tony Hibbert**

| | |
|---|---|
| **Goals Conceded** The number of League goals conceded while he was on the pitch | 28 |
| **Goals Conceded in all competitions** The number goals conceded while he was on the pitch in all competitions | 28 |
| **League minutes played** Number of minutes played in league matches | 2050 |
| **Clean Sheets** In games when he played at least70 mins | 8 |
| **Defensive Rating** Average number of mins between League goals conceded while he was on the pitch | 73 |
| **Club Defensive Rating** Average number of mins between League goals conceded by the club this season | 70 |

| | PLAYER | CON LGE | CON ALL | MINS | C SHEETS | DEF RATE |
|---|---|---|---|---|---|---|
| 2 | David Weir | 35 | 44 | 2539 | 6 | 73 mins |
| 3 | Alan Stubbs | 42 | 47 | 2940 | 9 | 70 mins |
| 4 | David Unsworth | 41 | 50 | 2772 | 8 | 68 mins |

## KEY PLAYERS - GOALKEEPERS

**1 Richard Wright**

| | |
|---|---|
| **Goals Conceded in the League** The number of League goals conceded while he was on the pitch | 39 |
| **Goals Conceded in all competitions** The number of goals conceded while he was on the pitch in all competitions | 48 |
| **League minutes played** Number of minutes played in league matches | 2970 |
| **Clean Sheets** In games when he played at least 70 mins | 11 |
| **Goals to Shots Ratio** The average number of shots on target per each League goal conceded | 5.2 |
| **Defensive Rating** Ave number of mins between League goals conceded while on the pitch | 76 |

**2 Paul Gerrard**

| | |
|---|---|
| **Goals Conceded in the League** The number of League goals conceded while he was on the pitch | 2 |
| **Goals Conceded in all competitions** The number of goals conceded while he was on the pitch in all competitions | 2 |
| **League minutes played** Number of minutes played in league matches | 180 |
| **Clean Sheets** In games when he played at least 70 mins | 0 |
| **Goals to Shots Ratio** The average number of shots on target per each League goal conceded | 4.5 |
| **Defensive Rating** Ave number of mins between League goals conceded while on the pitch | 90 |

# SOUTHAMPTON

**NICKNAME:** THE SAINTS

KEY: Won / Drawn / Lost

| | | | | | | |
|---|---|---|---|---|---|---|
| 1 | lge | **Middlesbrough** | H | D | 0-0 | |
| 2 | lge | **Liverpool** | A | L | 0-3 | |
| 3 | lge | **Chelsea** | H | D | 1-1 | Fernandes 51 |
| 4 | lge | **Tottenham** | A | L | 1-2 | Taricco 29 og |
| 5 | lge | **Everton** | H | W | 1-0 | Pahars 71 pen |
| 6 | lge | **West Brom** | A | L | 0-1 | |
| 7 | lge | **Charlton** | H | D | 0-0 | |
| 8 | lge | **Bolton** | A | D | 1-1 | Bridge 82 |
| 9 | wr2 | **Tranmere** | H | W | 6-1 | Marsden 1; Ormerod 25,42,67; Fernandes 52; Svensson, M 65 |
| 10 | lge | **Man City** | H | W | 2-0 | Ormerod 1,41 |
| 11 | lge | **Aston Villa** | A | W | 1-0 | Beattie 48 pen |
| 12 | lge | **Fulham** | H | W | 4-2 | Beattie 26 pen,42,53; Ormerod 72 |
| 13 | lge | **Man Utd** | A | L | 1-2 | Fernandes 18 |
| 14 | wr3 | **Liverpool** | A | L | 1-3 | Delgado 55 |
| 15 | lge | **Blackburn** | H | D | 1-1 | Beattie 38 pen |
| 16 | lge | **Newcastle** | A | L | 1-2 | Beattie 2 |
| 17 | lge | **Arsenal** | H | W | 3-2 | Beattie 45,59 pen; Delgado 67 |
| 18 | lge | **West Ham** | A | W | 1-0 | Beattie 90 |
| 19 | lge | **Birmingham** | H | W | 2-0 | Beattie 60 pen,83 |
| 20 | lge | **Newcastle** | H | D | 1-1 | Marsden 52 |
| 21 | lge | **Leeds** | A | D | 1-1 | Fernandes 89 |
| 22 | lge | **Chelsea** | A | D | 0-0 | |
| 23 | lge | **Sunderland** | H | W | 2-1 | Beattie 73; Tessem 90 |
| 24 | lge | **Tottenham** | H | W | 1-0 | Beattie 82 |
| 25 | facr3 | **Tottenham** | H | W | 4-0 | Svensson, M 13; Tessem 50; Svensson, A 56; Beattie 80 |
| 26 | lge | **Middlesbrough** | A | D | 2-2 | Beattie 40,60 |
| 27 | lge | **Liverpool** | H | L | 0-1 | |
| 28 | facr4 | **Millwall** | H | D | 1-1 | Davies 90 |
| 29 | lge | **Sunderland** | A | W | 1-0 | Beattie 50 |
| 30 | lge | **Man Utd** | H | L | 0-2 | |
| 31 | facr4r | **Millwall** | A | D | 0-2 | Oakley 21,102 |
| 32 | lge | **Blackburn** | A | L | 0-1 | |
| 33 | facr5 | **Norwich** | H | W | 2-0 | Svensson, A 71; Tessem 74 |
| 34 | lge | **Everton** | A | L | 1-2 | Beattie 33 |
| 35 | lge | **West Brom** | H | W | 1-0 | Beattie 8 |
| 36 | facqf | **Wolverhampton** | H | W | 2-0 | Marsden 56; Butler 81 og |
| 37 | lge | **Fulham** | A | D | 2-2 | Beattie 81; Svensson, M 90 |
| 38 | lge | **Aston Villa** | H | D | 2-2 | Beattie 40; Davies 90 |
| 39 | lge | **West Ham** | H | D | 1-1 | Beattie 44 |
| 40 | facsf | **Watford** | A | W | 2-1 | Ormerod 43; Robinson 80 og |
| 41 | lge | **Leeds** | H | W | 3-2 | Ormerod 31; Beattie 45; Svensson, A 53 |
| 42 | lge | **Birmingham** | A | L | 2-3 | Svensson, A 26; Ormerod 77 |
| 43 | lge | **Charlton** | A | L | 1-2 | Beattie 90 |
| 44 | lge | **Bolton** | H | D | 0-0 | |
| 45 | lge | **Arsenal** | A | L | 1-6 | Tessem 35 |
| 46 | lge | **Man City** | A | W | 1-0 | Svensson, M 34 |
| 47 | facf | **Arsenal** | N | L | 0-1 | |

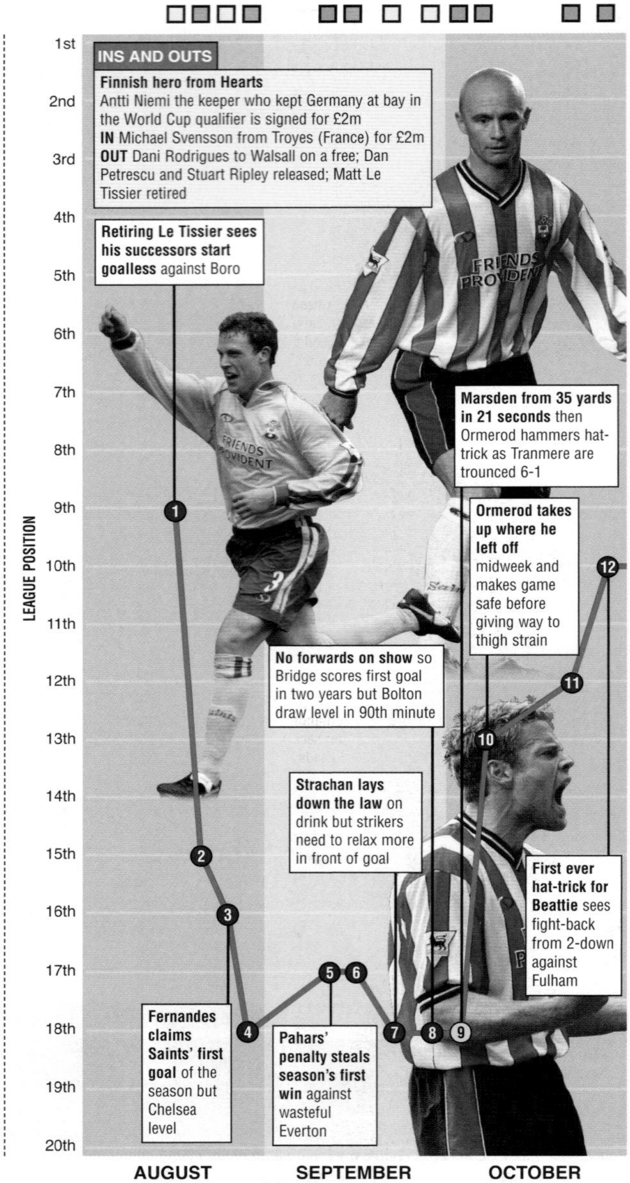

1st
2nd
3rd
4th
5th
6th
7th
8th
9th
10th
11th
12th
13th
14th
15th
16th
17th
18th
19th
20th
LEAGUE POSITION
INS AND OUTS
Finnish hero from Hearts Antti Niemi the keeper who kept Germany at bay in the World Cup qualifier is signed for £2m
IN Michael Svensson from Troyes (France) for £2m
OUT Dani Rodrigues to Walsall on a free; Dan Petrescu and Stuart Ripley released; Matt Le Tissier retired
Retiring Le Tissier sees his successors start goalless against Boro
Marsden from 35 yards in 21 seconds then Ormerod hammers hat-trick as Tranmere are trounced 6-1
Ormerod takes up where he left off midweek and makes game safe before giving way to thigh strain
No forwards on show so Bridge scores first goal in two years but Bolton draw level in 90th minute
Strachan lays down the law on drink but strikers need to relax more in front of goal
First ever hat-trick for Beattie sees fight-back from 2-down against Fulham
Fernandes claims Saints' first goal of the season but Chelsea level
Pahars' penalty steals season's first win against wasteful Everton
AUGUST
SEPTEMBER
OCTOBER


Home / Away / Neutral

## ATTENDANCES

**HOME GROUND:** ST MARY'S STADIUM **CAPACITY:** 32085 **AVERAGE LEAGUE AT HOME:** 30680

| | | | | | | | | | | | |
|---|---|---|---|---|---|---|---|---|---|---|---|
| 47 | Arsenal | 73726 | 29 | Sunderland | 34102 | 3 | Chelsea | 31208 | 12 | Fulham | 26188 |
| 13 | Man Utd | 67691 | 27 | Liverpool | 32104 | 19 | Birmingham | 31132 | 43 | Charlton | 25894 |
| 16 | Newcastle | 51812 | 30 | Man Utd | 32085 | 33 | Norwich | 31103 | 11 | Aston Villa | 25817 |
| 2 | Liverpool | 43058 | 20 | Newcastle | 32061 | 10 | Man City | 31009 | 7 | Charlton | 25714 |
| 40 | Watford | 42602 | 41 | Leeds | 32032 | 44 | Bolton | 30950 | 25 | Tottenham | 25589 |
| 22 | Chelsea | 39428 | 39 | West Ham | 31941 | 15 | Blackburn | 30059 | 32 | Blackburn | 24896 |
| 45 | Arsenal | 38052 | 35 | West Brom | 31915 | 5 | Everton | 29190 | 28 | Millwall | 23809 |
| 21 | Leeds | 36687 | 24 | Tottenham | 31890 | 42 | Birmingham | 29115 | 8 | Bolton | 22692 |
| 34 | Everton | 36569 | 38 | Aston Villa | 31888 | 18 | West Ham | 28844 | 37 | Fulham | 18031 |
| 14 | Liverpool | 35870 | 17 | Arsenal | 31797 | 1 | Middlesboro | 28341 | 9 | Tranmere | 16603 |
| 4 | Tottenham | 35573 | 36 | Wolves | 31715 | 26 | Middlesboro | 27443 | 31 | Millwall | 10197 |
| 46 | Man City | 34957 | 23 | Sunderland | 31423 | 6 | West Brom | 26383 | | | |

## GOAL ATTEMPTS

**FOR** — Goal attempts recorded in League games

| | HOME | AWAY | TOTAL | AVE |
|---|---|---|---|---|
| shots on target | 123 | 94 | 217 | 5.7 |
| shots off target | 115 | 114 | 229 | 6.0 |
| TOTAL | 238 | 208 | 446 | 11.7 |

| | |
|---|---|
| **Ratio of goals to shots** Average number of shots on target per League goal scored | 5.0 |
| **Accuracy rating** Average percentage of total goal attempts which were on target | 48.7 |

**AGAINST** — Goal attempts recorded in League games

| | HOME | AWAY | TOTAL | AVE |
|---|---|---|---|---|
| shots on target | 90 | 157 | 247 | 6.5 |
| shots off target | 103 | 94 | 197 | 5.2 |
| TOTAL | 193 | 251 | 444 | 11.7 |

| | |
|---|---|
| **Ratio of goals to shots** Average number of shots on target per League goal scored | 5.4 |
| **Accuracy rating** Average percentage of total goal attempts which were on target | 55.6 |

# Final adds gloss to league finish

Final Position: **8th**

KEY: ● League ● Champions Lge ● UEFA Cup ● FA Cup ○ League Cup ● Other

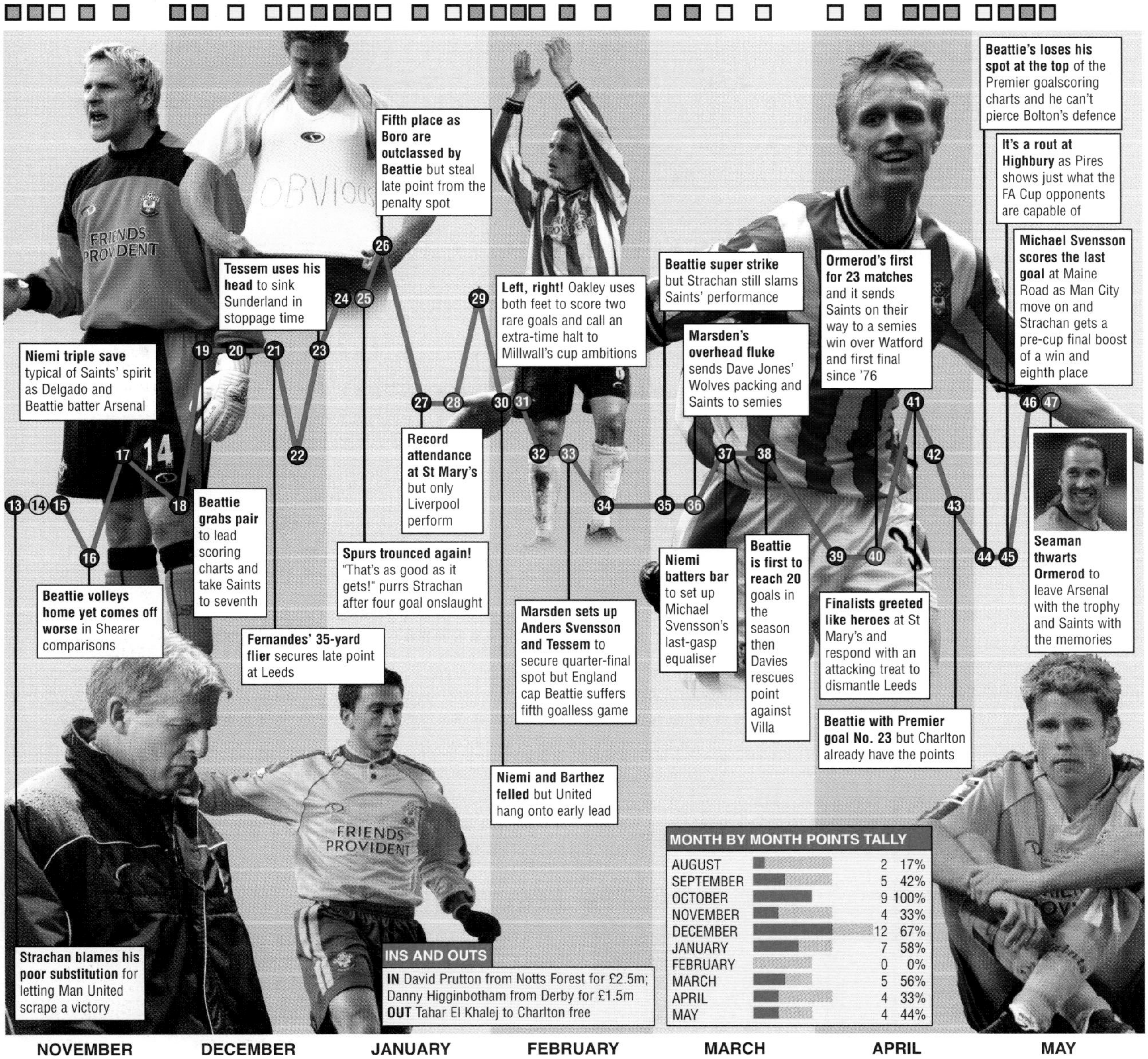
Niemi triple save typical of Saints' spirit as Delgado and Beattie batter Arsenal
Beattie volleys home yet comes off worse in Shearer comparisons
Strachan blames his poor substitution for letting Man United scrape a victory
Beattie grabs pair to lead scoring charts and take Saints to seventh
Tessem uses his head to sink Sunderland in stoppage time
Fernandes' 35-yard flier secures late point at Leeds
Fifth place as Boro are outclassed by Beattie but steal late point from the penalty spot
Spurs trounced again! "That's as good as it gets!" purrs Strachan after four goal onslaught
Record attendance at St Mary's but only Liverpool perform
Left, right! Oakley uses both feet to score two rare goals and call an extra-time halt to Millwall's cup ambitions
Niemi and Barthez felled but United hang onto early lead
Marsden sets up Anders Svensson and Tessem to secure quarter-final spot but England cap Beattie suffers fifth goalless game
Beattie super strike but Strachan still slams Saints' performance
Marsden's overhead fluke sends Dave Jones' Wolves packing and Saints to semies
Niemi batters bar to set up Michael Svensson's last-gasp equaliser
Beattie is first to reach 20 goals in the season then Davies rescues point against Villa
Ormerod's first for 23 matches and it sends Saints on their way to a semies win over Watford and first final since '76
Finalists greeted like heroes at St Mary's and respond with an attacking treat to dismantle Leeds
Beattie with Premier goal No. 23 but Charlton already have the points
Beattie's loses his spot at the top of the Premier goalscoring charts and he can't pierce Bolton's defence
It's a rout at Highbury as Pires shows just what the FA Cup opponents are capable of
Michael Svensson scores the last goal at Maine Road as Man City move on and Strachan gets a pre-cup final boost of a win and eighth place
Seaman thwarts Ormerod to leave Arsenal with the trophy and Saints with the memories
NOVEMBER
DECEMBER
JANUARY
FEBRUARY
MARCH
APRIL
MAY

**INS AND OUTS**

**IN** David Prutton from Notts Forest for £2.5m; Danny Higginbotham from Derby for £1.5m
**OUT** Tahar El Khalej to Charlton free

**MONTH BY MONTH POINTS TALLY**

| | | |
|---|---|---|
| AUGUST | 2 | 17% |
| SEPTEMBER | 5 | 42% |
| OCTOBER | 9 | 100% |
| NOVEMBER | 4 | 33% |
| DECEMBER | 12 | 67% |
| JANUARY | 7 | 58% |
| FEBRUARY | 0 | 0% |
| MARCH | 5 | 56% |
| APRIL | 4 | 33% |
| MAY | 4 | 44% |

## DISCIPLINARY RECORDS

**1 Marian Pahars**

| | |
|---|---|
| League Yellow | 3 |
| League Red | 1 |
| League Total | 4 |
| All Comps Yellow | 3 |
| All Comps Red | 1 |
| TOTAL | 4 |

League Average
115
mins between cards

| | PLAYER | LEAGUE | | TOTAL | | AVE |
|---|---|---|---|---|---|---|
| 2 | Williams | 4Y | 1R | 4Y | 1R | 179 |
| 3 | Marsden | 8 | 0 | 11 | 0 | 329 |
| 4 | Prutton | 2 | 0 | 2 | 0 | 443 |
| 5 | Bridge | 6 | 0 | 6 | 0 | 508 |
| 6 | Ormerod | 3 | 0 | 4 | 0 | 585 |
| 7 | Svensson, M | 4 | 1 | 5 | 1 | 603 |
| 8 | Svensson, A | 3 | 0 | 3 | 0 | 737 |
| 9 | Telfer | 3 | 0 | 4 | 0 | 797 |
| 10 | Delap | 2 | 0 | 2 | 0 | 950 |
| 11 | Fernandes | 3 | 0 | 4 | 0 | 985 |
| 12 | Beattie | 3 | 0 | 6 | 0 | 1067 |
| 13 | Dodd | 1 | 0 | 1 | 0 | 1134 |
| 14 | Oakley | 2 | 0 | 2 | 0 | 1253 |
| | Other | 2 | 0 | 2 | 0 | |
| | TOTAL | 49 | 3 | 59 | 3 | |

## GOALS

**1 James Beattie**

| | |
|---|---|
| League | 23 |
| FA Cup | 1 |
| League Cup | 0 |
| Europe | 0 |
| Other | 0 |
| TOTAL | 24 |

League Average
139
mins between goals

| | PLAYER | LGE | FAC | LC | Euro | TOT | AVE |
|---|---|---|---|---|---|---|---|
| 2 | Ormerod | 5 | 1 | 3 | 0 | 9 | 351 |
| 3 | Fernandes | 3 | 0 | 1 | 0 | 4 | 985 |
| 4 | Svensson, A | 2 | 2 | 0 | 0 | 4 | 1106 |
| 5 | Tessem | 2 | 2 | 0 | 0 | 4 | 560 |
| 6 | Svensson, M | 2 | 1 | 1 | 0 | 4 | 1509 |
| 7 | Delgado | 1 | 0 | 1 | 0 | 2 | 187 |
| 8 | Bridge | 1 | 0 | 0 | 0 | 1 | 3049 |
| 9 | Pahars | 1 | 0 | 0 | 0 | 1 | 460 |
| 10 | Davies, K | 1 | 1 | 0 | 0 | 2 | 155 |
| 11 | Marsden | 1 | 1 | 1 | 0 | 3 | 2632 |
| 12 | Oakley | 0 | 2 | 0 | 0 | 2 | |
| | Other | 1 | 2 | 0 | 0 | 3 | |
| | TOTAL | 43 | 13 | 7 | 0 | 63 | |

## SQUAD APPEARANCES

| Match | 1 | 2 | 3 | 4 | 5 | 6 | 7 | 8 | 9 | 10 | 11 | 12 | 13 | 14 | 15 | 16 | 17 | 18 | 19 | 20 | 21 | 22 | 23 | 24 | 25 | 26 | 27 | 28 | 29 | 30 | 31 | 32 | 33 | 34 | 35 | 36 | 37 | 38 | 39 | 40 | 41 | 42 | 43 | 44 | 45 | 46 | 47 |
|---|---|---|---|---|---|---|---|---|---|---|---|---|---|---|---|---|---|---|---|---|---|---|---|---|---|---|---|---|---|---|---|---|---|---|---|---|---|---|---|---|---|---|---|---|---|---|---|
| Venue | H | A | H | A | H | A | H | A | H | H | A | H | A | A | H | A | H | A | H | H | A | A | H | H | H | A | H | H | A | H | A | A | H | A | H | H | A | H | H | A | H | A | A | H | A | A | N |
| Competition | L | L | L | L | L | L | L | L | W | L | L | L | L | W | L | L | L | L | L | L | L | L | L | L | F | L | L | F | L | L | F | L | F | L | L | F | L | L | L | F | L | L | L | L | L | L | F |
| Result | D | L | D | L | W | L | D | D | W | W | W | W | L | L | D | L | W | W | W | D | D | D | W | W | W | D | L | D | W | L | D | L | W | L | W | W | D | D | D | W | W | L | L | D | L | W | L |

**Goalkeepers**
Alan Blayney
Paul Jones
Neil Moss
Antti Niemi

**Defenders**
Chris Baird
Francis Benali
Wayne Bridge
Jason Dodd
Tahar El Khalej
Marcus Hall
Danny Higginbotham
Claus Lundekvam
Gary Monk
Michael Svensson
Paul Williams

**Midfielders**
Federico Arias
Aaron Davies
Rory Delap
Fabrice Fernandes
Chris Marsden
Matthew Oakley
David Prutton
Anders Svensson
Paul Telfer
Jo Tessem

**Forwards**
James Beattie
Kevin Davies
Augustin Delgado
Andrei Kanchelskis
Brett Ormerod
Marian Pahars

KEY: On all match | On bench | Subbed or sent off (Counting game) | Subbed or sent off (playing less than 70 minutes) | Subbed on from bench (Counting Game) | Subbed on (playing less than 70 minutes) | Subbed on and then subbed or sent off (Counting Game) | Subbed on and then subbed or sent off (playing less than 70 minutes) | Not in 16

## KEY PLAYERS - GOALSCORERS

**1 James Beattie**

| | |
|---|---|
| **Goals in the League** | 23 |
| **Goals in all competitions** | 24 |
| **Assists** League goals scored by team-mates where he delivered the final pass | 2 |
| **Contribution to Attacking Power** Average number of minutes between League team goals while on pitch | 76 |
| **Player Strike Rate** Average number of minutes between League goals scored by player | 139 |
| **Club Strike Rate** Average minutes between League goals scored by club | 80 |

FRIENDS PROVIDENT

| | PLAYER | GOALS LGE | GOALS ALL | ASSISTS | POWER | S RATE |
|---|---|---|---|---|---|---|
| 2 | Brett Ormerod | 5 | 9 | 4 | 62 | 351 mins |
| 3 | Fabrice Fernandes | 3 | 4 | 4 | 82 | 985 mins |
| 4 | Anders Svensson | 2 | 4 | 4 | 79 | 1106 mins |
| 5 | Michael Svensson | 2 | 4 | 1 | 71 | 1509 mins |

## KEY PLAYERS - MIDFIELDERS

**1 Rory Delap**

| | |
|---|---|
| **Goals in the League** | 0 |
| **Goals in all competitions** | 0 |
| **Assists** League goals scored by team-mates where he delivered the final pass | 1 |
| **Defensive Rating** Average number of mins between League goals conceded while he was on the pitch | 106 |
| **Contribution to Attacking Power** Average number of minutes between League team goals while on pitch | 90 |
| **Scoring Difference** Defensive Rating minus Contribution to Attacking Power | 16 |

FRIENDS PROVIDENT

| | PLAYER | GOALS LGE | GOALS ALL | ASSISTS | DEF RATE | POWER | SC DIFF |
|---|---|---|---|---|---|---|---|
| 2 | Matthew Oakley | 0 | 2 | 3 | 81 | 76 | 5 mins |
| 3 | Fabrice Fernandes | 3 | 4 | 4 | 80 | 82 | -2 mins |
| 4 | Chris Marsden | 1 | 3 | 3 | 91 | 94 | -3 mins |
| 5 | Anders Svensson | 2 | 4 | 4 | 67 | 79 | -12 mins |

## PLAYER APPEARANCES

| | AGE (on 01/07/03) | IN THE SQUAD | COUNTING GAMES | MINUTES ON PITCH | IN THE SQUAD | MINUTES ON PITCH | THIS SEASON | NATIONAL SIDE |
|---|---|---|---|---|---|---|---|---|
| **Goalkeepers** | | | | | | | | |
| Alan Blayney | 21 | 6 | 0 | 0 | 8 | 0 | - | N Ireland |
| Paul Jones | 36 | 38 | 13 | 1175 | 46 | 1291 | 6 | Wales (50) |
| Neil Moss | 28 | 2 | 0 | 0 | 2 | 0 | - | England |
| Antti Niemi | 31 | 29 | 25 | 2245 | 37 | 2969 | - | Finland |
| **Defenders** | | | | | | | | |
| Chris Baird | 21 | 3 | 1 | 159 | 4 | 245 | 5 | N Ireland (111) |
| Francis Benali | 34 | 2 | 2 | 180 | 4 | 390 | - | England |
| Wayne Bridge | 22 | 34 | 34 | 3049 | 40 | 3589 | 6 | England (7) |
| Jason Dodd | 32 | 19 | 10 | 1134 | 24 | 1427 | - | England |
| Tahar El Khalej | 35 | 2 | 0 | 4 | 2 | 4 | - | Morocco |
| Marcus Hall | 27 | 3 | 0 | 0 | 3 | 0 | - | England |
| D Higginbotham | 24 | 11 | 3 | 379 | 15 | 469 | - | England |
| Claus Lundekvam | 30 | 33 | 32 | 2905 | 41 | 3655 | 10 | Norway (24) |
| Gary Monk | 24 | 2 | 0 | 65 | 2 | 65 | - | England |
| Michael Svensson | 27 | 37 | 33 | 3017 | 46 | 3857 | 9 | Sweden (20) |
| Paul Williams | 32 | 31 | 10 | 898 | 39 | 988 | - | England |
| **Midfielders** | | | | | | | | |
| Federico Arias | 24 | 1 | 0 | 0 | 2 | 0 | - | Argentina |
| Aaron Davies | 19 | 1 | 0 | 0 | 1 | 0 | - | Wales |
| Rory Delap | 27 | 25 | 20 | 1900 | 31 | 2227 | 2 | Rep of Ireland (15) |
| Fabrice Fernandes | 23 | 38 | 33 | 2955 | 46 | 3559 | - | France |
| Chris Marsden | 34 | 30 | 28 | 2632 | 39 | 3311 | - | England |
| Matthew Oakley | 25 | 35 | 26 | 2506 | 44 | 3300 | - | England |
| David Prutton | 21 | 12 | 9 | 887 | 12 | 887 | - | England |
| Anders Svensson | 26 | 36 | 21 | 2212 | 44 | 2894 | 9 | Sweden (20) |
| Paul Telfer | 31 | 37 | 26 | 2393 | 44 | 3053 | - | Scotland |
| Jo Tessem | 31 | 30 | 6 | 1119 | 39 | 1373 | 3 | Norway (24) |
| **Forwards** | | | | | | | | |
| James Beattie | 25 | 38 | 35 | 3201 | 47 | 3974 | 2 | England (7) |
| Kevin Davies | 26 | 14 | 1 | 155 | 19 | 237 | - | England |
| Augustin Delgado | 28 | 8 | 1 | 187 | 9 | 277 | - | Ecuador |
| Andrei Kanchelskis | 34 | 2 | 0 | 36 | 4 | 56 | - | |
| Brett Ormerod | 26 | 37 | 14 | 1756 | 45 | 2269 | - | England |
| Marian Pahars | 26 | 10 | 3 | 460 | 11 | 483 | - | Latvia |

KEY: LEAGUE ALL COMPS CAPS (FIFA RANKING)

## TEAM OF THE SEASON

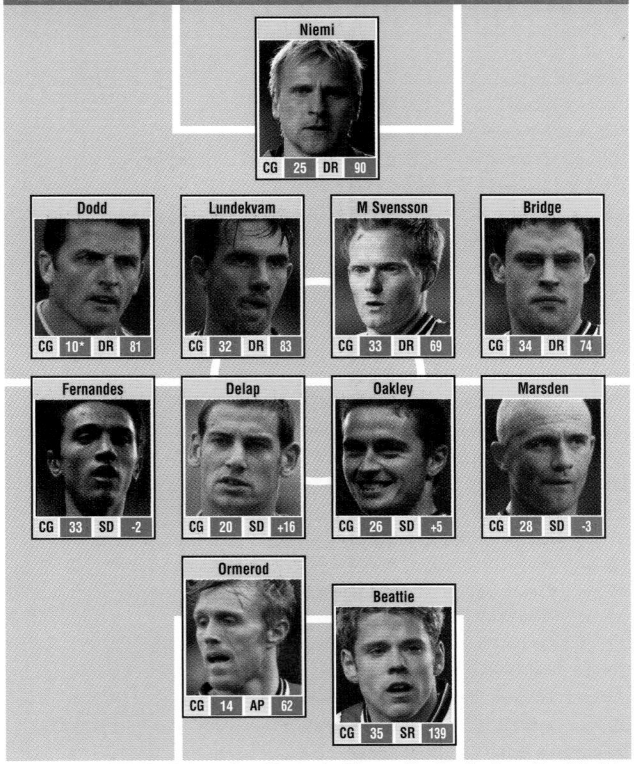

Niemi
CG 25 DR 90
Dodd
CG 10* DR 81
Lundekvam
CG 32 DR 83
M Svensson
CG 33 DR 69
Bridge
CG 34 DR 74
Fernandes
CG 33 SD -2
Delap
CG 20 SD +16
Oakley
CG 26 SD +5
Marsden
CG 28 SD -3
Ormerod
CG 14 AP 62
Beattie
CG 35 SR 139


KEY: DR = Defensive Rate, SD = Scoring Difference AP = Attacking Power SR = Strike Rate, CG=Counting Games – League games playing at least 70 minutes

## TOP POINT EARNERS

**1 Brett Ormerod**

| | |
|---|---|
| **Counting Games** League games when he played at least 70 minutes | 14 |
| **Average points** Average League points taken in Counting games | 1.79 |
| **Club Average points** Average points taken in League games | 1.37 |

| | PLAYER | GAMES | PTS |
|---|---|---|---|
| 2 | Rory Delap | 20 | 1.60 |
| 3 | Antti Niemi | 25 | 1.48 |
| 4 | Claus Lundekvam | 32 | 1.47 |
| 5 | Fabrice Fernandes | 33 | 1.45 |
| 6 | Wayne Bridge | 34 | 1.44 |
| 7 | Chris Marsden | 28 | 1.43 |
| 8 | James Beattie | 35 | 1.43 |
| 9 | Michael Svensson | 33 | 1.42 |
| 10 | Anders Svensson | 21 | 1.29 |

## KEY PLAYERS - DEFENDERS

**1 Claus Lundekvam**

| | |
|---|---|
| **Goals Conceded** The number of League goals conceded while he was on the pitch | 35 |
| **Goals Conceded in all competitions** The number goals conceded while he was on the pitch in all competitions | 42 |
| **League minutes played** Number of minutes played in league matches | 2905 |
| **Clean Sheets** In games when he played at least70 mins | 11 |
| **Defensive Rating** Average number of mins between League goals conceded while he was on the pitch | 83 |
| **Club Defensive Rating** Average number of mins between League goals conceded by the club this season | 74 |

FRIENDS PROVIDENT


| | PLAYER | CON LGE | CON ALL | MINS | C SHEETS | DEF RATE |
|---|---|---|---|---|---|---|
| 2 | Wayne Bridge | 41 | 47 | 3049 | 12 | 74 mins |
| 3 | Michael Svensson | 44 | 52 | 3017 | 10 | 69 mins |
| | Did not play sufficient counting games: | | | | | |
| | Jason Dodd | 14 | 18 | 1134 | 5 | 81 mins |

## KEY PLAYERS - GOALKEEPERS

**1 Antti Niemi**

| | |
|---|---|
| **Goals Conceded in the League** The number of League goals conceded while he was on the pitch | 25 |
| **Goals Conceded in all competitions** The number of goals conceded while he was on the pitch in all competitions | 32 |
| **League minutes played** Number of minutes played in league matches | 2245 |
| **Clean Sheets** In games when he played at least 70 mins | 9 |
| **Goals to Shots Ratio** The average number of shots on target per each League goal conceded | 6.2 |
| **Defensive Rating** Ave number of mins between League goals conceded while on the pitch | 90 |

**2 Paul Jones**

| | |
|---|---|
| **Goals Conceded in the League** The number of League goals conceded while he was on the pitch | 21 |
| **Goals Conceded in all competitions** The number of goals conceded while he was on the pitch in all competitions | 22 |
| **League minutes played** Number of minutes played in league matches | 1175 |
| **Clean Sheets** In games when he played at least 70 mins | 4 |
| **Goals to Shots Ratio** The average number of shots on target per each League goal conceded | 4.4 |
| **Defensive Rating** Ave number of mins between League goals conceded while on the pitch | 56 |

# MANCHESTER CITY

**NICKNAME:** BLUES/CITIZENS

**KEY:** Won / Drawn / Lost

| | | | | | | |
|---|---|---|---|---|---|---|
| 1 | lge | Leeds | A | L | 0-3 | |
| 2 | lge | Newcastle | H | W | 1-0 | Huckerby 36 |
| 3 | lge | Aston Villa | A | L | 0-1 | |
| 4 | lge | Everton | H | W | 3-1 | Anelka 14,16,85 |
| 5 | lge | Arsenal | A | L | 1-2 | Anelka 28 |
| 6 | lge | Blackburn | H | D | 2-2 | Anelka 80; Goater 90 |
| 7 | lge | West Ham | A | D | 0-0 | |
| 8 | lge | Liverpool | H | L | 0-3 | |
| 9 | wr2 | Crewe | H | W | 3-2 | Berkovic 69; Walker 84 og; Huckerby 86 |
| 10 | lge | Southampton | A | L | 0-2 | |
| 11 | lge | Chelsea | H | L | 0-3 | |
| 12 | lge | Birmingham | A | W | 2-0 | Sun Jihai 24; Anelka 89 |
| 13 | lge | West Brom | A | W | 2-1 | Anelka 51; Goater 71 |
| 14 | wr3 | Wigan | A | L | 0-1 | |
| 15 | lge | Man Utd | H | W | 3-1 | Anelka 5; Goater 26,51 |
| 16 | lge | Charlton | H | L | 0-1 | |
| 17 | lge | Middlesbrough | A | L | 1-3 | Anelka 68 |
| 18 | lge | Bolton | H | W | 2-0 | Howey 24; Berkovic 56 |
| 19 | lge | Sunderland | A | W | 3-0 | Foe 44; Sun Jihai 63; Goater 87 |
| 20 | lge | Charlton | A | D | 2-2 | Foe 73,87 |
| 21 | lge | Tottenham | H | L | 2-3 | Howey 29; Benarbia 90 |
| 22 | lge | Aston Villa | H | W | 3-1 | Foe 15,80; Benarbia 78 |
| 23 | lge | Fulham | A | W | 1-0 | Anelka 84 |
| 24 | lge | Everton | A | D | 2-2 | Anelka 33; Foe 83 |
| 25 | facr3 | Liverpool | H | L | 0-1 | |
| 26 | lge | Leeds | H | W | 2-1 | Goater 29; Jensen 50 |
| 27 | lge | Newcastle | A | L | 0-2 | |
| 28 | lge | Fulham | H | W | 4-1 | Anelka 21; Benarbia 47; Foe 61; Wright-Phillips 70 |
| 29 | lge | West Brom | H | L | 1-2 | Gilchrist 22 og |
| 30 | lge | Man Utd | A | D | 1-1 | Goater 87 |
| 31 | lge | Arsenal | H | L | 1-5 | Anelka 87 |
| 32 | lge | Blackburn | A | L | 0-1 | |
| 33 | lge | Birmingham | H | W | 1-0 | Fowler 72 |
| 34 | lge | Chelsea | A | L | 0-5 | |
| 35 | lge | Bolton | A | L | 0-2 | |
| 36 | lge | Middlesbrough | H | D | 0-0 | |
| 37 | lge | Tottenham | A | W | 2-0 | Sommeil 3; Barton 21 |
| 38 | lge | Sunderland | H | W | 3-0 | Foe 36,80; Fowler 38 |
| 39 | lge | West Ham | H | L | 0-1 | |
| 40 | lge | Liverpool | A | W | 2-1 | Anelka 74 pen,90 |
| 41 | lge | Southampton | H | L | 0-1 | |

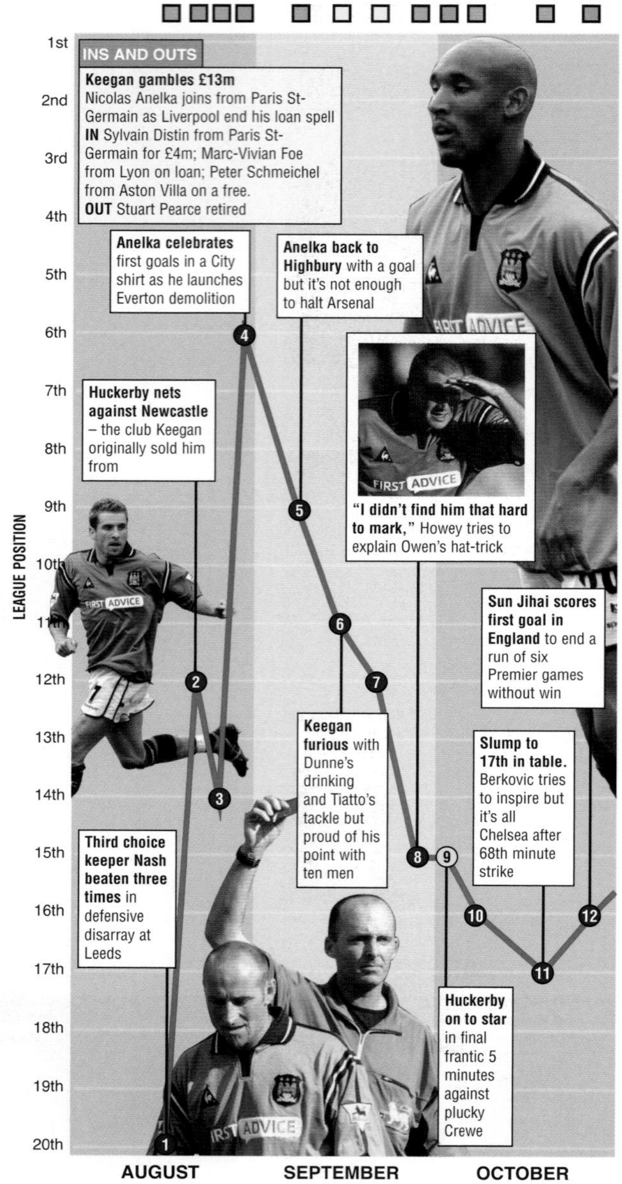

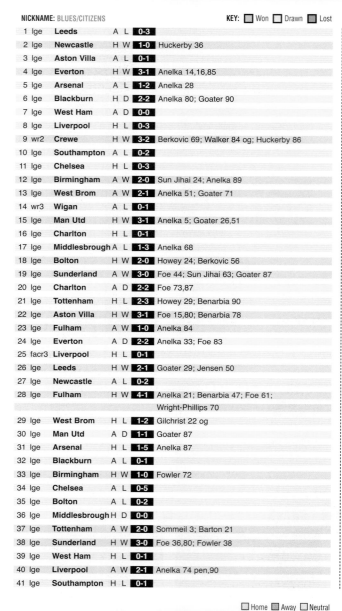

1st
2nd
3rd
4th
5th
6th
7th
8th
9th
10th
11th
12th
13th
14th
15th
16th
17th
18th
19th
20th
LEAGUE POSITION
INS AND OUTS
**Keegan gambles £13m** Nicolas Anelka joins from Paris St-Germain as Liverpool end his loan spell **IN** Sylvain Distin from Paris St-Germain for £4m; Marc-Vivian Foe from Lyon on loan; Peter Schmeichel from Aston Villa on a free. **OUT** Stuart Pearce retired
**Anelka celebrates** first goals in a City shirt as he launches Everton demolition
**Anelka back to Highbury** with a goal but it's not enough to halt Arsenal
**Huckerby nets against Newcastle** – the club Keegan originally sold him from
**"I didn't find him that hard to mark,"** Howey tries to explain Owen's hat-trick
**Sun Jihai scores first goal in England** to end a run of six Premier games without win
**Keegan furious** with Dunne's drinking and Tiatto's tackle but proud of his point with ten men
**Slump to 17th in table.** Berkovic tries to inspire but it's all Chelsea after 68th minute strike
**Third choice keeper Nash beaten three times** in defensive disarray at Leeds
**Huckerby on to star** in final frantic 5 minutes against plucky Crewe
1
2
3
4
5
6
7
8
9
10
11
12
AUGUST
SEPTEMBER
OCTOBER


Home / Away / Neutral

## ATTENDANCES

**HOME GROUND:** MAINE ROAD **CAPACITY:** 35150 **AVERAGE LEAGUE AT HOME:** 34560

| | | | | | | | | | | | |
|---|---|---|---|---|---|---|---|---|---|---|---|
| 30 | Man Utd | 67646 | 31 | Arsenal | 34960 | 33 | Birmingham | 34596 | 32 | Blackburn | 28647 |
| 27 | Newcastle | 52152 | 41 | Southampton | 34957 | 21 | Tottenham | 34563 | 25 | Liverpool | 28586 |
| 40 | Liverpool | 44220 | 11 | Chelsea | 34953 | 38 | Sunderland | 34357 | 13 | West Brom | 27044 |
| 34 | Chelsea | 41105 | 26 | Leeds | 34884 | 6 | Blackburn | 34130 | 35 | Bolton | 26949 |
| 1 | Leeds | 40195 | 18 | Bolton | 34860 | 22 | Aston Villa | 33991 | 20 | Charlton | 26434 |
| 24 | Everton | 40163 | 4 | Everton | 34835 | 3 | Aston Villa | 33494 | 9 | Crewe | 21820 |
| 5 | Arsenal | 37878 | 39 | West Ham | 34815 | 16 | Charlton | 33455 | 23 | Fulham | 17937 |
| 19 | Sunderland | 36511 | 36 | Middlesboro | 34793 | 28 | Fulham | 33260 | 14 | Wigan | 15007 |
| 37 | Tottenham | 36075 | 2 | Newcastle | 34776 | 17 | Middlesboro | 31510 | | | |
| 8 | Liverpool | 35141 | 29 | West Brom | 34675 | 10 | Southampton | 31009 | | | |
| 7 | West Ham | 35050 | 15 | Man Utd | 34649 | 12 | Birmingham | 29316 | | | |

## GOAL ATTEMPTS

**FOR** – Goal attempts recorded in League games

| | HOME | AWAY | TOTAL | AVE |
|---|---|---|---|---|
| shots on target | 141 | 88 | 229 | 6.0 |
| shots off target | 112 | 89 | 201 | 5.3 |
| TOTAL | 253 | 177 | 430 | 11.3 |

| | |
|---|---|
| **Ratio of goals to shots** Average number of shots on target per League goal scored | 4.9 |
| **Accuracy rating** Average percentage of total goal attempts which were on target | 53.3 |

**AGAINST** – Goal attempts recorded in League games

| | HOME | AWAY | TOTAL | AVE |
|---|---|---|---|---|
| shots on target | 90 | 124 | 214 | 5.6 |
| shots off target | 62 | 88 | 150 | 3.9 |
| TOTAL | 152 | 212 | 364 | 9.6 |

| | |
|---|---|
| **Ratio of goals to shots** Average number of shots on target per League goal scored | 4.0 |
| **Accuracy rating** Average percentage of total goal attempts which were on target | 58.8 |

# Top-half farewell for Maine Road

**Final Position: 9th**

KEY: ● League ● Champions Lge ● UEFA Cup ● FA Cup ○ League Cup ● Other

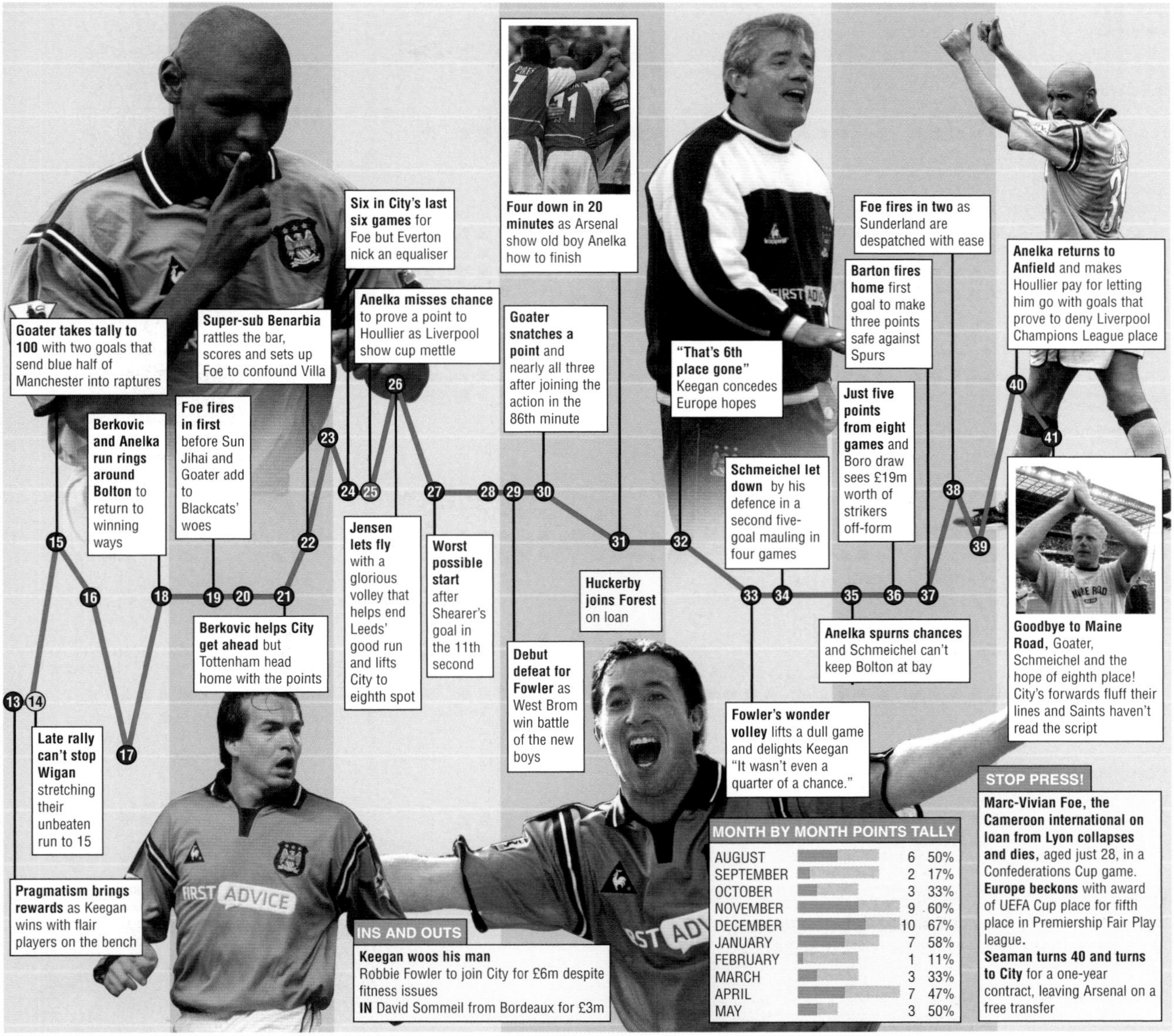

**Pragmatism brings rewards** as Keegan wins with flair players on the bench

**Late rally can't stop Wigan** stretching their unbeaten run to 15

**Goater takes tally to 100** with two goals that send blue half of Manchester into raptures

**Berkovic and Anelka run rings around Bolton** to return to winning ways

**Foe fires in first** before Sun Jihai and Goater add to Blackcats' woes

**Berkovic helps City get ahead** but Tottenham head home with the points

**Super-sub Benarbia** rattles the bar, scores and sets up Foe to confound Villa

**Six in City's last six games** for Foe but Everton nick an equaliser

**Jensen lets fly** with a glorious volley that helps end Leeds' good run and lifts City to eighth spot

**Anelka misses chance** to prove a point to Houllier as Liverpool show cup mettle

**Worst possible start** after Shearer's goal in the 11th second

**Debut defeat for Fowler** as West Brom win battle of the new boys

**Goater snatches a point** and nearly all three after joining the action in the 86th minute

**Four down in 20 minutes** as Arsenal show old boy Anelka how to finish

**Huckerby joins Forest** on loan

**"That's 6th place gone"** Keegan concedes Europe hopes

**Fowler's wonder volley** lifts a dull game and delights Keegan "It wasn't even a quarter of a chance."

**Schmeichel let down** by his defence in a second five-goal mauling in four games

**Anelka spurns chances** and Schmeichel can't keep Bolton at bay

**Just five points from eight games** and Boro draw sees £19m worth of strikers off-form

**Barton fires home** first goal to make three points safe against Spurs

**Foe fires in two** as Sunderland are despatched with ease

**Anelka returns to Anfield** and makes Houllier pay for letting him go with goals that prove to deny Liverpool Champions League place

**Goodbye to Maine Road,** Goater, Schmeichel and the hope of eighth place! City's forwards fluff their lines and Saints haven't read the script

### INS AND OUTS

**Keegan woos his man**
Robbie Fowler to join City for £6m despite fitness issues
**IN** David Sommeil from Bordeaux for £3m

### MONTH BY MONTH POINTS TALLY

| | | |
|---|---|---|
| AUGUST | 6 | 50% |
| SEPTEMBER | 2 | 17% |
| OCTOBER | 3 | 33% |
| NOVEMBER | 9 | 60% |
| DECEMBER | 10 | 67% |
| JANUARY | 7 | 58% |
| FEBRUARY | 1 | 11% |
| MARCH | 3 | 33% |
| APRIL | 7 | 47% |
| MAY | 3 | 50% |

### STOP PRESS!

**Marc-Vivian Foe, the Cameroon international on loan from Lyon collapses and dies,** aged just 28, in a Confederations Cup game.
**Europe beckons** with award of UEFA Cup place for fifth place in Premiership Fair Play league.
**Seaman turns 40 and turns to City** for a one-year contract, leaving Arsenal on a free transfer

NOVEMBER DECEMBER JANUARY FEBRUARY MARCH APRIL MAY

## DISCIPLINARY RECORDS

**1 Danny Tiatto**

| | |
|---|---|
| League Yellow | 3 |
| League Red | 1 |
| League Total | 4 |
| All Comps Yellow | 3 |
| All Comps Red | 1 |
| TOTAL | 4 |

League Average
222
mins between cards

| | PLAYER | LEAGUE | | TOTAL | | AVE |
|---|---|---|---|---|---|---|
| 2 | Barton | 2Y | 0R | 2Y | 0R | 304 |
| 3 | Sun Jihai | 6 | 1 | 6 | 1 | 317 |
| 4 | Benarbia | 5 | 1 | 5 | 1 | 343 |
| 5 | Wright-Phillips | 4 | 2 | 4 | 2 | 355 |
| 6 | Jensen | 7 | 1 | 7 | 1 | 356 |
| 7 | Dunne | 5 | 0 | 5 | 0 | 411 |
| 8 | Foe | 7 | 0 | 8 | 0 | 443 |
| 9 | Horlock | 4 | 0 | 5 | 0 | 513 |
| 10 | Distin | 5 | 0 | 5 | 0 | 612 |
| 11 | Sommeil | 2 | 0 | 2 | 0 | 630 |
| 12 | Berkovic | 2 | 0 | 3 | 0 | 1077 |
| 13 | Howey | 1 | 0 | 1 | 0 | 2007 |
| 14 | Schmeichel | 1 | 0 | 1 | 0 | 2610 |
| | Other | 4 | 0 | 4 | 0 | |
| | TOTAL | 58 | 6 | 61 | 6 | |

## GOALS

**1 Nicolas Anelka**

| | |
|---|---|
| League | 15 |
| FA Cup | 0 |
| League Cup | 0 |
| Europe | 0 |
| Other | 0 |
| TOTAL | 15 |

League Average
225
mins between goals

| | PLAYER | LGE | FAC | LC | Euro | TOT | AVE |
|---|---|---|---|---|---|---|---|
| 2 | Foe | 9 | 0 | 0 | 0 | 9 | 345 |
| 3 | Goater | 7 | 0 | 0 | 0 | 7 | 188 |
| 4 | Benarbia | 3 | 0 | 0 | 0 | 3 | 687 |
| 5 | Sun Jihai | 2 | 0 | 0 | 0 | 2 | 1112 |
| 6 | Howey | 2 | 0 | 0 | 0 | 2 | 1004 |
| 7 | Fowler | 2 | 0 | 0 | 0 | 2 | 484 |
| 8 | Berkovic | 1 | 0 | 1 | 0 | 2 | 2154 |
| 9 | Sommeil | 1 | 0 | 0 | 0 | 1 | 1260 |
| 10 | Huckerby | 1 | 0 | 1 | 0 | 2 | 582 |
| 11 | Jensen | 1 | 0 | 0 | 0 | 1 | 2854 |
| 12 | Barton | 1 | 0 | 0 | 0 | 1 | 609 |
| 13 | Wright-Phillips | 1 | 0 | 0 | 0 | 1 | 2131 |
| | Other | 1 | 0 | 1 | 0 | 2 | |
| | TOTAL | 47 | 0 | 3 | 0 | 50 | |

## SQUAD APPEARANCES

| Match | 1 | 2 | 3 | 4 | 5 | 6 | 7 | 8 | 9 | 10 | 11 | 12 | 13 | 14 | 15 | 16 | 17 | 18 | 19 | 20 | 21 | 22 | 23 | 24 | 25 | 26 | 27 | 28 | 29 | 30 | 31 | 32 | 33 | 34 | 35 | 36 | 37 | 38 | 39 | 40 | 41 |
|---|---|---|---|---|---|---|---|---|---|---|---|---|---|---|---|---|---|---|---|---|---|---|---|---|---|---|---|---|---|---|---|---|---|---|---|---|---|---|---|---|---|
| Venue | A | H | A | H | A | H | A | H | H | A | H | A | A | A | H | H | A | H | A | A | H | H | A | A | H | H | A | H | H | A | H | A | H | A | A | H | A | H | H | A | H |
| Competition | L | L | L | L | L | L | L | L | W | L | L | L | L | W | L | L | L | L | L | L | L | L | L | L | F | L | L | L | L | L | L | L | L | L | L | L | L | L | L | L | L |
| Result | L | W | L | W | L | D | D | L | W | L | L | W | W | L | W | L | L | W | W | D | L | W | W | D | L | W | L | W | L | D | L | L | W | L | L | D | W | W | L | W | L |

**Goalkeepers**
Kevin Ellegaard
Tim Flowers
Brian Murphy
Carlo Nash
Peter Schmeichel
Nicholas Weaver

**Defenders**
Mikkel Bischoff
Sylvain Distin
Richard Dunne
Steve Howey
Niclas Jensen
Lucien Mettomo
Paul Ritchie
David Sommeil
Sun Jihai
Gerard Wiekens

**Midfielders**
Joey Barton
Djamel Belmadi
Ali Benarbia
Eyal Berkovic
Marc-Vivien Foe
Kevin Horlock
Stephen Jordan
Karim Kerkar
Chris Shuker
Danny Tiatto

**Forwards**
Nicolas Anelka
Robbie Fowler
Shaun Goater
Darren Huckerby
Jonathan Macken
Vicente Matias Vuoso
Sean Wright-Phillips

KEY: On all match · On bench · Subbed or sent off (Counting game) · Subbed or sent off (playing less than 70 minutes) · Subbed on from bench (Counting Game) · Subbed on (playing less than 70 minutes) · Subbed on and then subbed or sent off (Counting Game) · Subbed on and then subbed or sent off (playing less than 70 minutes) · Not in 16

## KEY PLAYERS - GOALSCORERS

**1 Shaun Goater**

| | |
|---|---|
| **Goals in the League** | 7 |
| **Goals in all competitions** | 7 |
| **Assists** League goals scored by team-mates where he delivered the final pass | 2 |
| **Contribution to Attacking Power** Average number of minutes between League team goals while on pitch | 59 |
| **Player Strike Rate** Average number of minutes between League goals scored by player | 188 |
| **Club Strike Rate** Average minutes between League goals scored by club | 73 |

FIRST ADVICE

| | PLAYER | GOALS LGE | GOALS ALL | ASSISTS | POWER | S RATE |
|---|---|---|---|---|---|---|
| 2 | Nicolas Anelka | 15 | 15 | 5 | 73 | 225 mins |
| 3 | Marc-Vivien Foe | 9 | 9 | 0 | 70 | 345 mins |
| 4 | Ali Benarbia | 3 | 3 | 6 | 71 | 687 mins |
| 5 | Steve Howey | 2 | 2 | 0 | 64 | 1004 mins |

## KEY PLAYERS - MIDFIELDERS

**1 Ali Benarbia**

| | |
|---|---|
| **Goals in the League** | 3 |
| **Goals in all competitions** | 3 |
| **Assists** League goals scored by team-mates where he delivered the final pass | 6 |
| **Defensive Rating** Average number of mins between League goals conceded while he was on the pitch | 69 |
| **Contribution to Attacking Power** Average number of minutes between League team goals while on pitch | 71 |
| **Scoring Difference** Defensive Rating minus Contribution to Attacking Power | -2 |

| | PLAYER | GOALS LGE | GOALS ALL | ASSISTS | DEF RATE | POWER | SC DIFF |
|---|---|---|---|---|---|---|---|
| 2 | Marc-Vivien Foe | 9 | 9 | 0 | 66 | 71 | -5 mins |
| 3 | Kevin Horlock | 0 | 0 | 3 | 62 | 73 | -11 mins |
| 4 | Eyal Berkovic | 1 | 2 | 9 | 60 | 74 | -14 mins |

## PLAYER APPEARANCES

| | AGE (on 01/07/03) | IN THE SQUAD | COUNTING GAMES | MINUTES ON PITCH | IN THE SQUAD | MINUTES ON PITCH | THIS SEASON | NATIONAL SIDE |
|---|---|---|---|---|---|---|---|---|
| **Goalkeepers** | | | | | | | | |
| Kevin Ellegaard | 23 | 1 | 0 | 0 | 1 | 0 | - | Denmark |
| Tim Flowers | 36 | 3 | 0 | 0 | 4 | 0 | - | England |
| Brian Murphy | 20 | 1 | 0 | 0 | 1 | 0 | - | Rep of Ireland |
| Carlo Nash | 29 | 38 | 9 | 810 | 41 | 900 | - | England |
| Peter Schmeichel | 39 | 29 | 29 | 2610 | 31 | 2790 | - | Denmark |
| Nicholas Weaver | 24 | 4 | 0 | 0 | 4 | 0 | - | England |
| **Defenders** | | | | | | | | |
| Mikkel Bischoff | 21 | 6 | 0 | 60 | 7 | 60 | - | Denmark |
| Sylvain Distin | 25 | 34 | 34 | 3060 | 36 | 3183 | - | France |
| Richard Dunne | 23 | 33 | 21 | 2056 | 34 | 2146 | 4 | Rep of Ireland (15) |
| Steve Howey | 31 | 24 | 22 | 2007 | 26 | 2115 | - | England |
| Niclas Jensen | 28 | 36 | 31 | 2854 | 39 | 3124 | 10 | Denmark (10) |
| Lucien Mettomo | 31 | 6 | 3 | 321 | 8 | 420 | 2 | Cameroon (18) |
| Paul Ritchie | 27 | 2 | 0 | 0 | 3 | 0 | - | Scotland |
| David Sommeil | 28 | 14 | 14 | 1260 | 14 | 1260 | - | France |
| Sun Jihai | 25 | 34 | 21 | 2224 | 37 | 2473 | - | China PR |
| Gerard Wiekens | 30 | 14 | 4 | 423 | 16 | 585 | - | Holland |
| **Midfielders** | | | | | | | | |
| Joey Barton | 20 | 8 | 7 | 609 | 8 | 609 | - | England |
| Djamel Belmadi | 27 | 10 | 1 | 335 | 10 | 335 | - | France |
| Ali Benarbia | 34 | 37 | 20 | 2060 | 40 | 2324 | - | Algeria |
| Eyal Berkovic | 31 | 27 | 21 | 2154 | 29 | 2294 | - | Israel |
| Marc-Vivien Foe | 28 | 35 | 34 | 3106 | 38 | 3376 | 1 | Cameroon (18) |
| Kevin Horlock | 30 | 35 | 19 | 2053 | 38 | 2290 | 3 | N Ireland (111) |
| Stephen Jordan | 21 | 1 | 0 | 22 | 1 | 22 | - | England |
| Karim Kerkar | 26 | 2 | 0 | 0 | 2 | 0 | - | France |
| Chris Shuker | 21 | 5 | 0 | 109 | 5 | 109 | - | England |
| Danny Tiatto | 23 | 16 | 9 | 891 | 16 | 891 | - | Australia |
| **Forwards** | | | | | | | | |
| Nicolas Anelka | 24 | 38 | 37 | 3378 | 41 | 3648 | - | France |
| Robbie Fowler | 28 | 13 | 9 | 968 | 13 | 968 | - | England |
| Shaun Goater | 33 | 35 | 12 | 1316 | 38 | 1463 | - | Bermuda |
| Darren Huckerby | 27 | 23 | 3 | 582 | 26 | 642 | - | England |
| Jonathan Macken | 25 | 7 | 0 | 101 | 7 | 101 | - | England |
| V Matias Vuoso | 21 | 3 | 0 | 0 | 5 | 0 | - | Argentina |
| S Wright-Phillips | 21 | 34 | 20 | 2131 | 37 | 2342 | - | England |

KEY: LEAGUE ALL COMPS CAPS (IN THE SQUAD)

## TEAM OF THE SEASON

Schmeichel
CG 29 DR 69
Jensen
CG 31 DR 62
Distin
CG 34 DR 70
Dunne
CG 21 DR 71
Sommeil
CG 14 DR 63
Berkovic
CG 21 SD -14
Foe
CG 34 SD -5
Bernabia
CG 20 SD -2
Horlock
CG 19 SD -11
Anelka
CG 37 AP 73
Goater
CG 12 SR 188


KEY: DR = Defensive Rate, SD = Scoring Difference AP = Attacking Power SR = Strike Rate, CG=Counting Games – League games playing at least 70 minutes

## TOP POINT EARNERS

**1 Shaun Goater**

| | |
|---|---|
| **Counting Games** League games when he played at least 70 minutes | 12 |
| **Average points** Average League points taken in Counting games | 1.83 |
| **Club Average points** Average points taken in League games | 1.34 |

| | PLAYER | GAMES | PTS |
|---|---|---|---|
| 2 | Richard Dunne | 21 | 1.71 |
| 3 | Steve Howey | 22 | 1.55 |
| 4 | Kevin Horlock | 19 | 1.42 |
| 5 | Sylvain Distin | 34 | 1.41 |
| 6 | Marc-Vivien Foe | 34 | 1.41 |
| 7 | Peter Schmeichel | 29 | 1.41 |
| 8 | Sun Jihai | 21 | 1.38 |
| 9 | Ali Benarbia | 20 | 1.35 |
| 10 | Nicolas Anelka | 37 | 1.35 |

## KEY PLAYERS - DEFENDERS

**1 Richard Dunne**

| | |
|---|---|
| **Goals Conceded** The number of League goals conceded while he was on the pitch | 29 |
| **Goals Conceded in all competitions** The number goals conceded while he was on the pitch in all competitions | 30 |
| **League minutes played** Number of minutes played in league matches | 2056 |
| **Clean Sheets** In games when he played at least70 mins | 6 |
| **Defensive Rating** Average number of mins between League goals conceded while he was on the pitch | 71 |
| **Club Defensive Rating** Average number of mins between League goals conceded by the club this season | 63 |

FIRST ADVICE


| | PLAYER | CON LGE | CON ALL | MINS | C SHEETS | DEF RATE |
|---|---|---|---|---|---|---|
| 2 | Sylvain Distin | 44 | 45 | 3060 | 10 | 70 mins |
| 3 | David Sommeil | 20 | 20 | 1260 | 4 | 63 mins |
| 4 | Niclas Jensen | 46 | 50 | 2854 | 7 | 62 mins |
| 5 | Steve Howey | 33 | 35 | 2007 | 6 | 61 mins |

## KEY PLAYERS - GOALKEEPERS

**1 Peter Schmeichel**

| | |
|---|---|
| **Goals Conceded in the League** The number of League goals conceded while he was on the pitch | 38 |
| **Goals Conceded in all competitions** The number of goals conceded while he was on the pitch in all competitions | 41 |
| **League minutes played** Number of minutes played in league matches | 2610 |
| **Clean Sheets** In games when he played at least 70 mins | 9 |
| **Goals to Shots Ratio** The average number of shots on target per each League goal conceded | 4.1 |
| **Defensive Rating** Ave number of mins between League goals conceded while on the pitch | 69 |

**2 Carlo Nash**

| | |
|---|---|
| **Goals Conceded in the League** The number of League goals conceded while he was on the pitch | 16 |
| **Goals Conceded in all competitions** The number of goals conceded while he was on the pitch in all competitions | 17 |
| **League minutes played** Number of minutes played in league matches | 810 |
| **Clean Sheets** In games when he played at least 70 mins | 1 |
| **Goals to Shots Ratio** The average number of shots on target per each League goal conceded | 3.6 |
| **Defensive Rating** Ave number of mins between League goals conceded while on the pitch | 51 |

# TOTTENHAM HOTSPUR

NICKNAME: SPURS

KEY: Won / Drawn / Lost

| | | | | | | |
|---|---|---|---|---|---|---|
| 1 | lge | Everton | A | D | 2-2 | Etherington 63; Ferdinand 75 |
| 2 | lge | Aston Villa | H | W | 1-0 | Redknapp 26 |
| 3 | lge | Charlton | A | W | 1-0 | Davies 7 |
| 4 | lge | Southampton | H | W | 2-1 | Ferdinand 10; Sheringham 90 pen |
| 5 | lge | Fulham | A | L | 2-3 | Richards 35; Sheringham 43 |
| 6 | lge | West Ham | H | W | 3-2 | Davies 62; Sheringham 71 pen; Gardner 89 |
| 7 | lge | Man Utd | A | L | 0-1 | |
| 8 | lge | Middlesbrough | H | L | 0-3 | |
| 9 | wr2 | Cardiff | H | W | 1-0 | Sheringham 30 |
| 10 | lge | Blackburn | A | W | 2-1 | Keane 5; Redknapp 88 |
| 11 | lge | Bolton | H | W | 3-1 | Keane 58,73; Davies 90 |
| 12 | lge | Liverpool | A | L | 1-2 | Richards 82 |
| 13 | lge | Chelsea | H | D | 0-0 | |
| 14 | wr3 | Burnley | A | L | 1-2 | Poyet 17 |
| 15 | lge | Sunderland | A | L | 0-2 | |
| 16 | lge | Arsenal | A | L | 0-3 | |
| 17 | lge | Leeds | H | W | 2-0 | Sheringham 12; Keane 41 |
| 18 | lge | Birmingham | A | D | 1-1 | Sheringham 55 |
| 19 | lge | West Brom | H | W | 3-1 | Ziege 3; Keane 30; Poyet 80 |
| 20 | lge | Arsenal | H | D | 1-1 | Ziege 11 |
| 21 | lge | Man City | A | W | 3-2 | Perry 38; Davies 48; Poyet 84 |
| 22 | lge | Charlton | H | D | 2-2 | Keane 68; Iversen 87 |
| 23 | lge | Newcastle | A | L | 1-2 | Dabizas 73 og |
| 24 | lge | Southampton | A | L | 0-1 | |
| 25 | facr3 | Southampton | A | L | 0-4 | |
| 26 | lge | Everton | H | W | 4-3 | Poyet 15; Keane 50,68,83 |
| 27 | lge | Aston Villa | A | W | 1-0 | Sheringham 69 |
| 28 | lge | Newcastle | H | L | 0-1 | |
| 29 | lge | Chelsea | A | D | 1-1 | Sheringham 18 |
| 30 | lge | Sunderland | H | W | 4-1 | Poyet 14; Doherty 45; Davies 67; Sheringham 84 |
| 31 | lge | Fulham | H | D | 1-1 | Sheringham 40 pen |
| 32 | lge | West Ham | A | L | 0-2 | |
| 33 | lge | Liverpool | H | L | 2-3 | Taricco 47; Sheringham 87 |
| 34 | lge | Bolton | A | L | 0-1 | |
| 35 | lge | Birmingham | H | W | 2-1 | Keane 7; Poyet 88 |
| 36 | lge | Leeds | A | D | 2-2 | Sheringham 37; Keane 39 |
| 37 | lge | Man City | H | L | 0-2 | |
| 38 | lge | West Brom | A | W | 3-2 | Keane 45,85; Sheringham 63 |
| 39 | lge | Man Utd | H | L | 0-2 | |
| 40 | lge | Middlesbrough | A | L | 1-5 | Redknapp 60 |
| 41 | lge | Blackburn | H | L | 0-4 | |

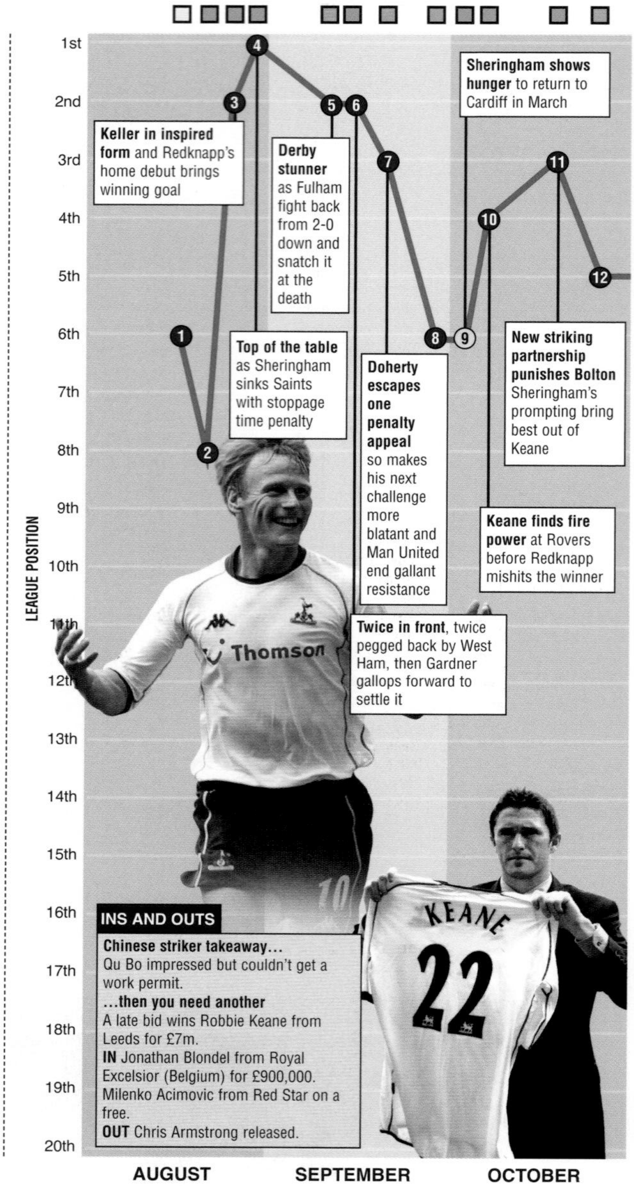

1st
2nd
3rd
4th
5th
6th
7th
8th
9th
10th
11th
12th
13th
14th
15th
16th
17th
18th
19th
20th
LEAGUE POSITION
Keller in inspired form and Redknapp's home debut brings winning goal
Top of the table as Sheringham sinks Saints with stoppage time penalty
Derby stunner as Fulham fight back from 2-0 down and snatch it at the death
Doherty escapes one penalty appeal so makes his next challenge more blatant and Man United end gallant resistance
Twice in front, twice pegged back by West Ham, then Gardner gallops forward to settle it
Sheringham shows hunger to return to Cardiff in March
New striking partnership punishes Bolton Sheringham's prompting bring best out of Keane
Keane finds fire power at Rovers before Redknapp mishits the winner
Thomson
KEANE
22
AUGUST
SEPTEMBER
OCTOBER


**INS AND OUTS**

**Chinese striker takeaway...**
Qu Bo impressed but couldn't get a work permit.
**...then you need another**
A late bid wins Robbie Keane from Leeds for £7m.
**IN** Jonathan Blondel from Royal Excelsior (Belgium) for £900,000. Milenko Acimovic from Red Star on a free.
**OUT** Chris Armstrong released.

Home / Away / Neutral

## ATTENDANCES

HOME GROUND: WHITE HART LANE  CAPACITY: 36214  AVERAGE LEAGUE AT HOME: 35897

| | | | | | | | | | | | |
|---|---|---|---|---|---|---|---|---|---|---|---|
| 7 | Man Utd | 67611 | 33 | Liverpool | 36077 | 19 | West Brom | 35958 | 38 | West Brom | 26899 |
| 23 | Newcastle | 52145 | 20 | Arsenal | 36076 | 11 | Bolton | 35909 | 3 | Charlton | 26461 |
| 12 | Liverpool | 44084 | 37 | Man City | 36075 | 17 | Leeds | 35718 | 10 | Blackburn | 26203 |
| 29 | Chelsea | 41384 | 30 | Sunderland | 36075 | 4 | Southampton | 35573 | 25 | Southampton | 25589 |
| 1 | Everton | 40120 | 39 | Man Utd | 36073 | 2 | Aston Villa | 35384 | 34 | Bolton | 23084 |
| 15 | Sunderland | 40024 | 26 | Everton | 36070 | 32 | West Ham | 35049 | 9 | Cardiff | 22723 |
| 36 | Leeds | 39560 | 35 | Birmingham | 36058 | 31 | Fulham | 34704 | 5 | Fulham | 16757 |
| 27 | Aston Villa | 38576 | 13 | Chelsea | 36049 | 21 | Man City | 34563 | 14 | Burnley | 13512 |
| 16 | Arsenal | 38152 | 22 | Charlton | 36043 | 24 | Southampton | 31890 | | | |
| 28 | Newcastle | 36084 | 41 | Blackburn | 36036 | 40 | Middlesboro | 30230 | | | |
| 8 | Middlesboro | 36082 | 6 | West Ham | 36005 | 18 | Birmingham | 29505 | | | |

## GOAL ATTEMPTS

**FOR** – Goal attempts recorded in League games

| | HOME | AWAY | TOTAL | AVE |
|---|---|---|---|---|
| shots on target | 127 | 84 | 211 | 5.6 |
| shots off target | 119 | 70 | 189 | 5.0 |
| TOTAL | 246 | 154 | 400 | 10.5 |

**Ratio of goals to shots** Average number of shots on target per League goal scored: **4.1**

**Accuracy rating** Average percentage of total goal attempts which were on target: **52.8**

**AGAINST** – Goal attempts recorded in League games

| | HOME | AWAY | TOTAL | AVE |
|---|---|---|---|---|
| shots on target | 126 | 154 | 280 | 7.4 |
| shots off target | 98 | 84 | 182 | 4.8 |
| TOTAL | 224 | 238 | 462 | 12.2 |

**Ratio of goals to shots** Average number of shots on target per League goal scored: **4.5**

**Accuracy rating** Average percentage of total goal attempts which were on target: **60.6**

# Hoddle sees need for 'fresh blood'

Final Position: **10th**

KEY: ● League ● Champions Lge ● UEFA Cup ● FA Cup ○ League Cup ● Other

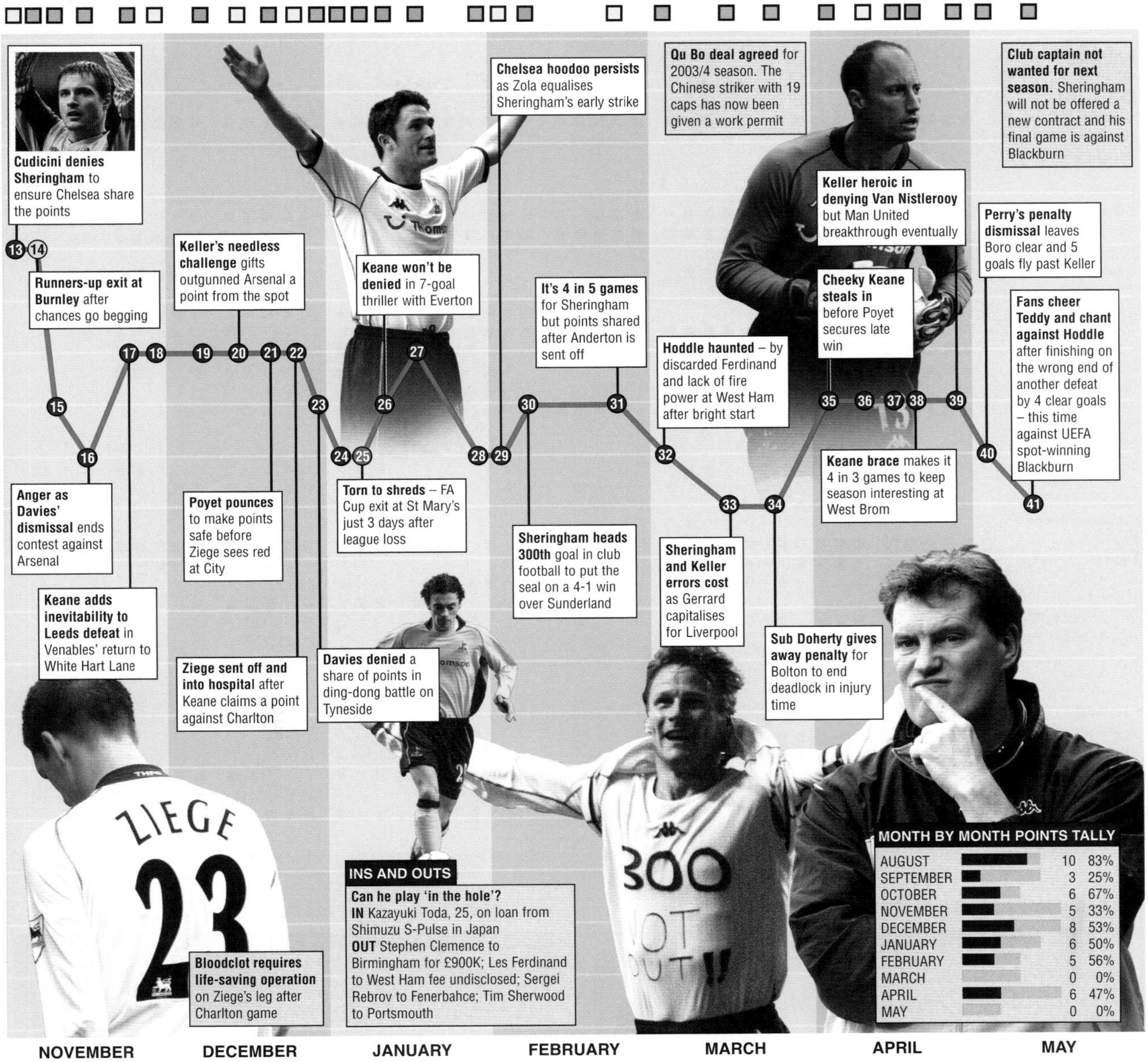
**Cudicini denies Sheringham** to ensure Chelsea share the points
**Runners-up exit at Burnley** after chances go begging
**Anger as Davies' dismissal** ends contest against Arsenal
**Keane adds inevitability to Leeds defeat** in Venables' return to White Hart Lane
**Keller's needless challenge** gifts outgunned Arsenal a point from the spot
**Poyet pounces** to make points safe before Ziege sees red at City
**Ziege sent off and into hospital** after Keane claims a point against Charlton
**Bloodclot requires life-saving operation** on Ziege's leg after Charlton game
**Keane won't be denied** in 7-goal thriller with Everton
**Davies denied** a share of points in ding-dong battle on Tyneside
**Torn to shreds** – FA Cup exit at St Mary's just 3 days after league loss
**Chelsea hoodoo persists** as Zola equalises Sheringham's early strike
**It's 4 in 5 games** for Sheringham but points shared after Anderton is sent off
**Sheringham heads 300th** goal in club football to put the seal on a 4-1 win over Sunderland
**Qu Bo deal agreed** for 2003/4 season. The Chinese striker with 19 caps has now been given a work permit
**Hoddle haunted** – by discarded Ferdinand and lack of fire power at West Ham after bright start
**Sheringham and Keller errors cost** as Gerrard capitalises for Liverpool
**Sub Doherty gives away penalty** for Bolton to end deadlock in injury time
**Keller heroic in denying Van Nistlerooy** but Man United breakthrough eventually
**Cheeky Keane steals in** before Poyet secures late win
**Keane brace** makes it 4 in 3 games to keep season interesting at West Brom
**Club captain not wanted for next season.** Sheringham will not be offered a new contract and his final game is against Blackburn
**Perry's penalty dismissal** leaves Boro clear and 5 goals fly past Keller
**Fans cheer Teddy and chant against Hoddle** after finishing on the wrong end of another defeat by 4 clear goals – this time against UEFA spot-winning Blackburn
ZIEGE
23
300
NOT
OUT!!
NOVEMBER
DECEMBER
JANUARY
FEBRUARY
MARCH
APRIL
MAY

**INS AND OUTS**

**Can he play 'in the hole'?**
**IN** Kazayuki Toda, 25, on loan from Shimuzu S-Pulse in Japan
**OUT** Stephen Clemence to Birmingham for £900K; Les Ferdinand to West Ham fee undisclosed; Sergei Rebrov to Fenerbahce; Tim Sherwood to Portsmouth

**MONTH BY MONTH POINTS TALLY**

| | | |
|---|---|---|
| AUGUST | 10 | 83% |
| SEPTEMBER | 3 | 25% |
| OCTOBER | 6 | 67% |
| NOVEMBER | 5 | 33% |
| DECEMBER | 8 | 53% |
| JANUARY | 6 | 50% |
| FEBRUARY | 5 | 56% |
| MARCH | 0 | 0% |
| APRIL | 6 | 47% |
| MAY | 0 | 0% |

## DISCIPLINARY RECORDS

**1 Christian Ziege**

| | |
|---|---|
| League Yellow | 7 |
| League Red | 2 |
| League Total | 9 |
| All Comps Yellow | 7 |
| All Comps Red | 2 |
| TOTAL | 9 |

League Average
90
mins between cards

| | PLAYER | LEAGUE | | TOTAL | | AVE |
|---|---|---|---|---|---|---|
| | | 5Y | 0R | 5Y | 0R | |
| 2 | Freund | | | | | **239** |
| 3 | Perry | 3 | 1 | 3 | 1 | **322** |
| 4 | Poyet | 4 | 1 | 4 | 1 | **370** |
| 5 | Davies | 7 | 1 | 7 | 1 | **374** |
| 6 | Anderton | 3 | 1 | 3 | 1 | **389** |
| 7 | Bunjevcevic | 7 | 0 | 8 | 0 | **393** |
| 8 | Redknapp | 3 | 0 | 3 | 0 | **427** |
| 9 | Richards | 5 | 0 | 6 | 0 | **454** |
| 10 | Doherty | 2 | 0 | 2 | 0 | **493** |
| 11 | Acimovic | 1 | 0 | 1 | 0 | **498** |
| 12 | Gardner | 2 | 0 | 2 | 0 | **498** |
| 13 | Taricco | 3 | 0 | 3 | 0 | **558** |
| 14 | Thatcher | 1 | 0 | 2 | 0 | **807** |
| 15 | Keller | 4 | 0 | 4 | 0 | **832** |
| | Other | 7 | 0 | 8 | 0 | |
| | **TOTAL** | **64** | **6** | **68** | **6** | |

## GOALS

**1 Robbie Keane**

| | |
|---|---|
| League | 13 |
| FA Cup | 0 |
| League Cup | 0 |
| Europe | 0 |
| Other | 0 |
| TOTAL | 13 |

League Average
189
mins between goals

| | PLAYER | LGE | FAC | LC | Euro | TOT | AVE |
|---|---|---|---|---|---|---|---|
| 2 | Sheringham | **12** | 0 | 1 | 0 | 13 | 247 |
| 3 | Davies | **5** | 0 | 0 | 0 | 5 | 599 |
| 4 | Poyet | **5** | 0 | 1 | 0 | 6 | 371 |
| 5 | Redknapp | **3** | 0 | 0 | 0 | 3 | 427 |
| 6 | Richards | **2** | 0 | 0 | 0 | 2 | 1137 |
| 7 | Ziege | **2** | 0 | 0 | 0 | 2 | 409 |
| 8 | Ferdinand | **2** | 0 | 0 | 0 | 2 | 200 |
| 9 | Iversen | **1** | 0 | 0 | 0 | 1 | 778 |
| 10 | Etherington | **1** | 0 | 0 | 0 | 1 | 1313 |
| 11 | Doherty | **1** | 0 | 0 | 0 | 1 | 987 |
| 12 | Taricco | **1** | 0 | 0 | 0 | 1 | 1675 |
| 13 | Gardner | **1** | 0 | 0 | 0 | 1 | 996 |
| 14 | Perry | **1** | 0 | 0 | 0 | 1 | 1290 |
| | Other | 1 | 0 | 0 | 0 | 1 | |
| | **TOTAL** | **51** | **0** | **2** | **0** | **53** | |

## SQUAD APPEARANCES

| Match | 1 | 2 | 3 | 4 | 5 | 6 | 7 | 8 | 9 | 10 | 11 | 12 | 13 | 14 | 15 | 16 | 17 | 18 | 19 | 20 | 21 | 22 | 23 | 24 | 25 | 26 | 27 | 28 | 29 | 30 | 31 | 32 | 33 | 34 | 35 | 36 | 37 | 38 | 39 | 40 | 41 |
|---|---|---|---|---|---|---|---|---|---|---|---|---|---|---|---|---|---|---|---|---|---|---|---|---|---|---|---|---|---|---|---|---|---|---|---|---|---|---|---|---|---|
| Venue | A | H | A | H | A | H | A | H | H | A | H | A | H | A | A | A | H | A | H | H | A | H | A | A | A | H | A | H | A | H | H | A | H | A | H | A | H | A | H | A | H |
| Competition | L | L | L | L | L | L | L | L | W | L | L | L | L | W | L | L | L | L | L | L | L | L | L | L | F | L | L | L | L | L | L | L | L | L | L | L | L | L | L | L | L |
| Result | D | W | W | W | L | W | L | L | W | W | W | L | D | L | L | L | W | D | W | D | W | D | L | L | L | W | W | L | D | W | D | L | L | L | W | D | L | W | L | L | L |

**Goalkeepers**
Robert Burch
Lars Hirschfeld
Kasey Keller
Gavin Kelly
Neil Sullivan

**Defenders**
Goran Bunjevcevic
Stephen Carr
Gary Doherty
Anthony Gardner
Ron Henry
Ledley King
Chris Perry
Dean Richards
Mauricio Taricco
Ben Thatcher
Christian Ziege

**Midfielders**
Milenko Acimovic
Darren Anderton
Jonathan Blondel
Stephen Clemence
Simon Davies
Matthew Etherington
Steffen Freund
Gustavo Poyet
Jamie Redknapp
Rohan Ricketts
Kazuyuki Toda
Mark Yeates

**Forwards**
Les Ferdinand
Steffen Iversen
Robbie Keane
Serguei Rebrov
Teddy Sheringham
Jamie Slabber

KEY: On all match · On bench · Subbed or sent off (Counting game) · Subbed or sent off (playing less than 70 minutes) · Subbed on from bench (Counting Game) · Subbed on (playing less than 70 minutes) · Subbed on and then subbed or sent off (Counting Game) · Subbed on and then subbed or sent off (playing less than 70 minutes) · Not in 16

## KEY PLAYERS - GOALSCORERS

**1 Robbie Keane**

| | |
|---|---|
| Goals in the League | 13 |
| Goals in all competitions | 13 |
| Assists<br>League goals scored by team-mates where he delivered the final pass | 2 |
| Contribution to Attacking Power<br>Average number of minutes between League team goals while on pitch | 68 |
| Player Strike Rate<br>Average number of minutes between League goals scored by player | 189 |
| Club Strike Rate<br>Average minutes between League goals scored by club | 67 |

| | PLAYER | GOALS LGE | GOALS ALL | ASSISTS | POWER | S RATE |
|---|---|---|---|---|---|---|
| 2 | Teddy Sheringham | 12 | 13 | 4 | 78 | 247 mins |
| 3 | Gustavo Poyet | 5 | 6 | 3 | 68 | 371 mins |
| 4 | Jamie Redknapp | 3 | 3 | 1 | 67 | 427 mins |
| 5 | Simon Davies | 5 | 5 | 4 | 63 | 599 mins |

## KEY PLAYERS - MIDFIELDERS

**1 Darren Anderton**

| | |
|---|---|
| Goals in the League | 0 |
| Goals in all competitions | 0 |
| Assists<br>League goals scored by team-mates where he delivered the final pass | 6 |
| Defensive Rating<br>Average number of mins between League goals conceded while he was on the pitch | 65 |
| Contribution to Attacking Power<br>Average number of minutes between League team goals while on pitch | 62 |
| Scoring Difference<br>Defensive Rating minus Contribution to Attacking Power | 3 |

Thomson

| | PLAYER | GOALS LGE | GOALS ALL | ASSISTS | DEF RATE | POWER | SC DIFF |
|---|---|---|---|---|---|---|---|
| 2 | Jamie Redknapp | 3 | 3 | 1 | 58 | 67 | -9 mins |
| 3 | Simon Davies | 5 | 5 | 4 | 53 | 64 | -11 mins |
| 4 | Steffen Freund | 0 | 0 | 0 | 60 | 75 | -15 mins |
| 5 | Gustavo Poyet | 5 | 6 | 3 | 52 | 69 | -17 mins |

## PLAYER APPEARANCES

| | AGE (on 01/07/03) | IN THE SQUAD | COUNTING GAMES | MINUTES ON PITCH | IN THE SQUAD | MINUTES ON PITCH | THIS SEASON | NATIONAL SIDE |
|---|---|---|---|---|---|---|---|---|
| **Goalkeepers** | | | | | | | | |
| Robert Burch | - | 1 | 0 | 0 | 1 | 0 | - | England |
| Lars Hirschfeld | 24 | 16 | 0 | 0 | 18 | 0 | - | Canada |
| Kasey Keller | 33 | 37 | 37 | 3330 | 40 | 3600 | 1 | United States (10) |
| Gavin Kelly | 22 | 1 | 1 | 90 | 1 | 90 | - | England |
| Neil Sullivan | 33 | 21 | 0 | 0 | 22 | 0 | 2 | Scotland (64) |
| **Defenders** | | | | | | | | |
| Goran Bunjevcevic | 30 | 37 | 28 | 2752 | 40 | 2932 | - | Serbia & Montenegro |
| Stephen Carr | 26 | 30 | 29 | 2655 | 32 | 2835 | 6 | Rep of Ireland (15) |
| Gary Doherty | 23 | 20 | 9 | 987 | 23 | 1041 | 9 | Rep of Ireland (15) |
| Anthony Gardner | 22 | 15 | 10 | 996 | 16 | 1086 | - | England |
| Ron Henry | 19 | 1 | 0 | 0 | 1 | 0 | - | England |
| Ledley King | 22 | 25 | 24 | 2224 | 26 | 2314 | 1 | England (7) |
| Chris Perry | 30 | 26 | 13 | 1290 | 28 | 1425 | - | England |
| Dean Richards | 29 | 26 | 25 | 2273 | 27 | 2363 | - | England |
| Mauricio Taricco | 30 | 24 | 16 | 1675 | 26 | 1830 | - | Argentina |
| Ben Thatcher | 27 | 17 | 7 | 807 | 19 | 987 | - | England |
| Christian Ziege | 31 | 12 | 7 | 817 | 12 | 817 | - | Germany |
| **Midfielders** | | | | | | | | |
| Milenko Acimovic | 26 | 31 | 3 | 498 | 33 | 588 | - | Slovenia |
| Darren Anderton | 31 | 20 | 17 | 1556 | 22 | 1632 | - | England |
| Jonathan Blondel | 19 | 2 | 0 | 12 | 3 | 12 | 1 | Belgium (16) |
| Stephen Clemence | 25 | 2 | 0 | 0 | 3 | 90 | - | England |
| Simon Davies | 23 | 36 | 32 | 2995 | 39 | 3246 | 7 | Wales (50) |
| Matt Etherington | 21 | 24 | 13 | 1313 | 26 | 1462 | - | England |
| Steffen Freund | 33 | 19 | 12 | 1199 | 21 | 1348 | - | Germany |
| Gustavo Poyet | 35 | 28 | 17 | 1854 | 30 | 2034 | - | Uruguay |
| Jamie Redknapp | 30 | 17 | 12 | 1281 | 17 | 1281 | - | England |
| Rohan Ricketts | 20 | 2 | 0 | 0 | 2 | 0 | - | England |
| Kazuyuki Toda | 25 | 10 | 1 | 190 | 10 | 190 | - | Japan |
| Mark Yeates | - | 1 | 0 | 0 | 1 | 0 | - | England |
| **Forwards** | | | | | | | | |
| Les Ferdinand | 36 | 13 | 2 | 400 | 15 | 446 | - | England |
| Steffen Iversen | 27 | 24 | 6 | 778 | 27 | 889 | 8 | Norway (24) |
| Robbie Keane | 22 | 30 | 27 | 2457 | 33 | 2681 | 7 | Rep of Ireland (15) |
| Sergei Rebrov | 29 | 2 | 0 | 0 | 2 | 0 | - | Ukraine |
| Teddy Sheringham | 37 | 36 | 31 | 2969 | 38 | 3149 | - | England |
| Jamie Slabber | 18 | 2 | 0 | 12 | 2 | 12 | - | England |

KEY: LEAGUE ALL COMPS CAPS (IN THE SQUAD)

## TEAM OF THE SEASON

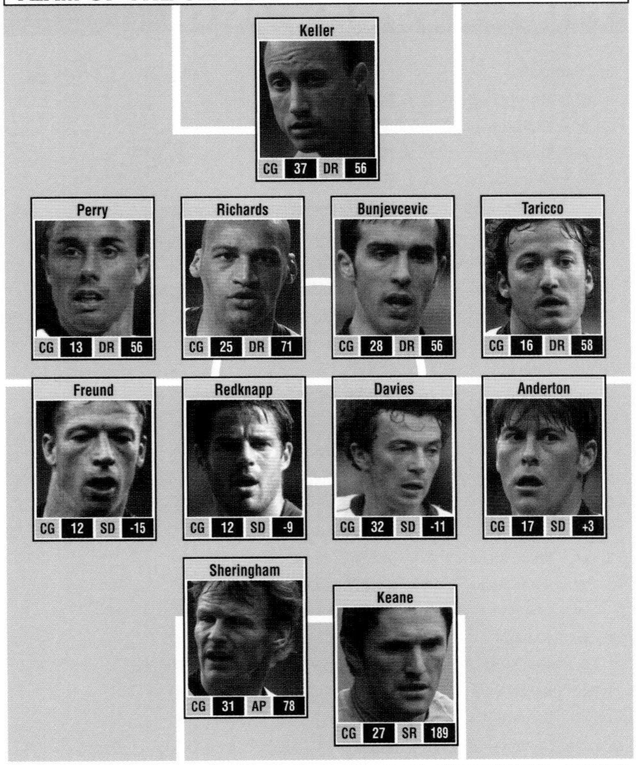

Keller
CG 37 DR 56
Perry
CG 13 DR 56
Richards
CG 25 DR 71
Bunjevcevic
CG 28 DR 56
Taricco
CG 16 DR 58
Freund
CG 12 SD -15
Redknapp
CG 12 SD -9
Davies
CG 32 SD -11
Anderton
CG 17 SD +3
Sheringham
CG 31 AP 78
Keane
CG 27 SR 189


KEY: DR = Defensive Rate, SD = Scoring Difference AP = Attacking Power SR = Strike Rate, CG=Counting Games – League games playing at least 70 minutes

## TOP POINT EARNERS

**1 Jamie Redknapp**

| | |
|---|---|
| **Counting Games** League games when he played at least 70 minutes | 12 |
| **Average points** Average League points taken in Counting games | 1.92 |
| **Club Average points** Average points taken in League games | 1.32 |

| | PLAYER | GAMES | PTS |
|---|---|---|---|
| 2 | Darren Anderton | 17 | 1.53 |
| 3 | Dean Richards | 25 | 1.52 |
| 4 | Teddy Sheringham | 31 | 1.39 |
| 5 | Simon Davies | 32 | 1.38 |
| 6 | Mauricio Taricco | 16 | 1.38 |
| 7 | Goran Bunjevcevic | 28 | 1.36 |
| 8 | Kasey Keller | 37 | 1.35 |
| 9 | Chris Perry | 13 | 1.31 |
| 10 | Robbie Keane | 27 | 1.30 |

## KEY PLAYERS - DEFENDERS

**1 Dean Richards**

| | |
|---|---|
| **Goals Conceded** The number of League goals conceded while he was on the pitch | 32 |
| **Goals Conceded in all competitions** The number goals conceded while he was on the pitch in all competitions | 32 |
| **League minutes played** Number of minutes played in league matches | 2273 |
| **Clean Sheets** In games when he played at least70 mins | 5 |
| **Defensive Rating** Average number of mins between League goals conceded while he was on the pitch | 71 |
| **Club Defensive Rating** Average number of mins between League goals conceded by the club this season | 55 |

Thomson


| | PLAYER | CON LGE | CON ALL | MINS | C SHEETS | DEF RATE |
|---|---|---|---|---|---|---|
| 2 | Mauricio Taricco | 29 | 33 | 1675 | 3 | 58 mins |
| 3 | Goran Bunjevcevic | 49 | 51 | 2752 | 4 | 56 mins |
| 4 | Chris Perry | 23 | 26 | 1290 | 1 | 56 mins |
| 5 | Stephen Carr | 50 | 56 | 2655 | 3 | 53 mins |

## KEY PLAYERS - GOALKEEPERS

**1 Kasey Keller**

| | |
|---|---|
| **Goals Conceded in the League** The number of League goals conceded while he was on the pitch | 60 |
| **Goals Conceded in all competitions** The number of goals conceded while he was on the pitch in all competitions | 66 |
| **League minutes played** Number of minutes played in league matches | 3330 |
| **Clean Sheets** In games when he played at least 70 mins | 5 |
| **Goals to Shots Ratio** The average number of shots on target per each League goal conceded | 4.6 |
| **Defensive Rating** Ave number of mins between League goals conceded while on the pitch | 56 |

**2 Gavin Kelly**

| | |
|---|---|
| **Goals Conceded in the League** The number of League goals conceded while he was on the pitch | 2 |
| **Goals Conceded in all competitions** The number of goals conceded while he was on the pitch in all competitions | 2 |
| **League minutes played** Number of minutes played in league matches | 90 |
| **Clean Sheets** In games when he played at least 70 mins | 0 |
| **Goals to Shots Ratio** The average number of shots on target per each League goal conceded | 2.5 |
| **Defensive Rating** Ave number of mins between League goals conceded while on the pitch | 45 |

# MIDDLESBROUGH

**NICKNAME:** BORO

KEY: Won / Drawn / Lost

| | | | | | | |
|---|---|---|---|---|---|---|
| 1 | lge | Southampton | A | D | 0-0 | |
| 2 | lge | Fulham | H | D | 2-2 | Maccarone 31,50 |
| 3 | lge | Blackburn | H | W | 1-0 | Job 90 |
| 4 | lge | Man Utd | A | L | 0-1 | |
| 5 | lge | Sunderland | H | W | 3-0 | Nemeth 15,66; Maccarone 37 |
| 6 | lge | Everton | A | L | 1-2 | Nemeth 10 |
| 7 | lge | Birmingham | H | W | 1-0 | Queudrue 28 |
| 8 | lge | Tottenham | A | W | 3-0 | Maccarone 32; Geremi 55; Job 58 |
| 9 | wr2 | Brentford | A | W | 4-1 | Marinelli 18; Whelan 20; Wilson 75; Downing 76 |
| 10 | lge | Bolton | H | W | 2-0 | Ehiogu 23; Geremi 69 |
| 11 | lge | Charlton | A | L | 0-1 | |
| 12 | lge | Leeds | H | D | 2-2 | Job 25; Southgate 83 |
| 13 | lge | Newcastle | A | L | 0-2 | |
| 14 | wr3 | Ipswich | A | L | 1-3 | Queudrue 88 |
| 15 | lge | Liverpool | H | W | 1-0 | Southgate 82 |
| 16 | lge | Chelsea | A | L | 0-1 | |
| 17 | lge | Man City | H | W | 3-1 | Ehiogu 53; Boksic 62; Geremi 84 |
| 18 | lge | West Brom | A | L | 0-1 | |
| 19 | lge | West Ham | H | D | 2-2 | Nemeth 58; Ehiogu 88 |
| 20 | lge | Chelsea | H | D | 1-1 | Geremi 32 |
| 21 | lge | Arsenal | A | L | 0-2 | |
| 22 | lge | Man Utd | H | W | 3-1 | Boksic 45; Nemeth 48; Job 85 |
| 23 | lge | Aston Villa | A | L | 0-1 | |
| 24 | lge | Blackburn | A | L | 0-1 | |
| 25 | facr3 | Chelsea | A | L | 0-1 | |
| 26 | lge | Southampton | H | D | 2-2 | Whelan 73; Maccarone 82 pen |
| 27 | lge | Fulham | A | L | 0-1 | |
| 28 | lge | Aston Villa | H | L | 2-5 | Maccarone 33; Greening 35 |
| 29 | lge | Liverpool | A | D | 1-1 | Geremi 38 |
| 30 | lge | Sunderland | A | W | 3-1 | Riggott 21,29; Christie 59 |
| 31 | lge | Everton | H | D | 1-1 | Juninho 74 |
| 32 | lge | Newcastle | H | W | 1-0 | Geremi 62 |
| 33 | lge | Leeds | A | W | 3-2 | Maccarone 36 pen; Juninho 45; Geremi 64 |
| 34 | lge | Charlton | H | D | 1-1 | Christie 57 |
| 35 | lge | West Brom | H | W | 3-0 | Christie 36; Greening 76; Nemeth 76 |
| 36 | lge | Man City | A | D | 0-0 | |
| 37 | lge | Arsenal | H | L | 0-2 | |
| 38 | lge | West Ham | A | L | 0-1 | |
| 39 | lge | Birmingham | A | L | 0-3 | |
| 40 | lge | Tottenham | H | W | 5-1 | Christie 23; Juninho 26; Nemeth 28; Maccarone 51,75 |
| 41 | lge | Bolton | A | L | 1-2 | Ricketts 61 |

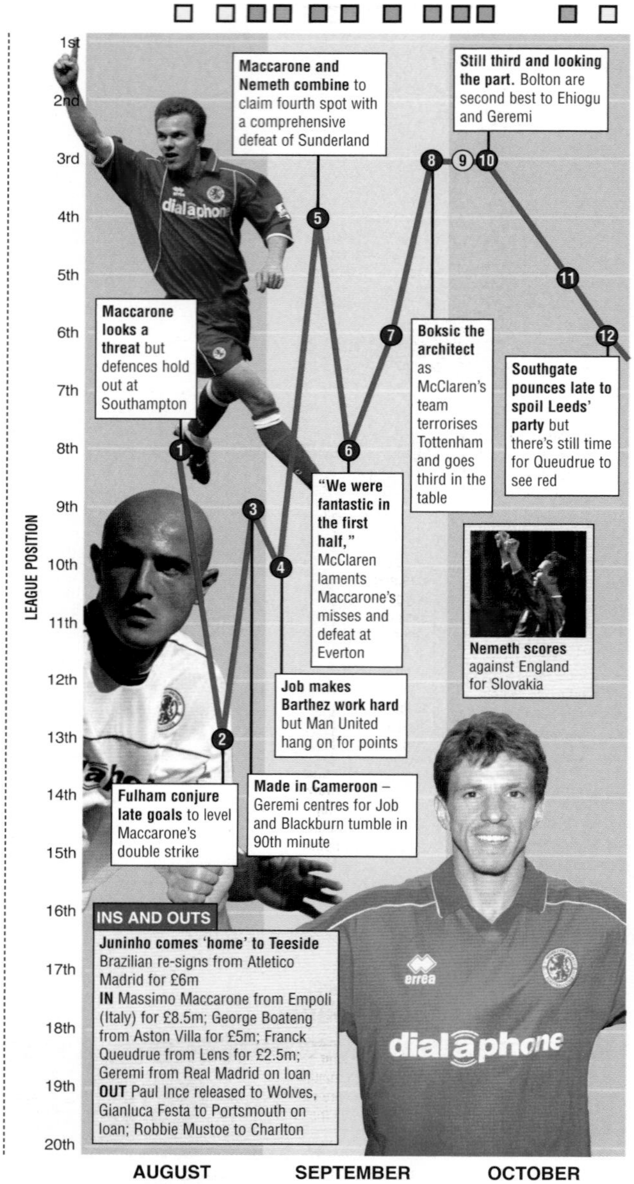

1st
2nd
3rd
4th
5th
6th
7th
8th
9th
10th
11th
12th
13th
14th
15th
16th
17th
18th
19th
20th
LEAGUE POSITION
AUGUST
SEPTEMBER
OCTOBER
**Maccarone and Nemeth combine** to claim fourth spot with a comprehensive defeat of Sunderland
**Still third and looking the part.** Bolton are second best to Ehiogu and Geremi
**Maccarone looks a threat** but defences hold out at Southampton
**Boksic the architect** as McClaren's team terrorises Tottenham and goes third in the table
**Southgate pounces late to spoil Leeds' party** but there's still time for Queudrue to see red
**"We were fantastic in the first half,"** McClaren laments Maccarone's misses and defeat at Everton
**Nemeth scores** against England for Slovakia
**Job makes Barthez work hard** but Man United hang on for points
**Fulham conjure late goals** to level Maccarone's double strike
**Made in Cameroon** – Geremi centres for Job and Blackburn tumble in 90th minute
dialaphone
errea


**INS AND OUTS**

**Juninho comes 'home' to Teeside** Brazilian re-signs from Atletico Madrid for £6m

**IN** Massimo Maccarone from Empoli (Italy) for £8.5m; George Boateng from Aston Villa for £5m; Franck Queudrue from Lens for £2.5m; Geremi from Real Madrid on loan

**OUT** Paul Ince released to Wolves, Gianluca Festa to Portsmouth on loan; Robbie Mustoe to Charlton

Home / Away / Neutral

## ATTENDANCES

**HOME GROUND:** RIVERSIDE STADIUM **CAPACITY:** 34820 **AVERAGE LEAGUE AT HOME:** 31025

| | | | | | | | | | | | |
|---|---|---|---|---|---|---|---|---|---|---|---|
| 4 | Man Utd | 67508 | 15 | Liverpool | 34747 | 35 | West Brom | 30187 | 26 | Southampton | 27443 |
| 13 | Newcastle | 51558 | 37 | Arsenal | 34724 | 7 | Birmingham | 29869 | 41 | Bolton | 27241 |
| 29 | Liverpool | 42247 | 12 | Leeds | 34723 | 25 | Chelsea | 29796 | 18 | West Brom | 27029 |
| 30 | Sunderland | 42134 | 22 | Man Utd | 34673 | 20 | Chelsea | 29160 | 11 | Charlton | 26271 |
| 33 | Leeds | 39073 | 23 | Aston Villa | 33637 | 34 | Charlton | 29080 | 24 | Blackburn | 23413 |
| 16 | Chelsea | 39064 | 31 | Everton | 32473 | 39 | Birmingham | 28821 | 14 | Ipswich | 14417 |
| 21 | Arsenal | 38003 | 6 | Everton | 32440 | 2 | Fulham | 28588 | 27 | Fulham | 14253 |
| 8 | Tottenham | 36082 | 5 | Sunderland | 32155 | 1 | Southampton | 28341 | 9 | Brentford | 7558 |
| 38 | West Ham | 35019 | 17 | Man City | 31510 | 19 | West Ham | 28283 | | | |
| 32 | Newcastle | 34814 | 10 | Bolton | 31005 | 3 | Blackburn | 28270 | | | |
| 36 | Man City | 34793 | 40 | Tottenham | 30230 | 28 | Aston Villa | 27546 | | | |

## GOAL ATTEMPTS

**FOR**
Goal attempts recorded in League games

| | HOME | AWAY | TOTAL | AVE |
|---|---|---|---|---|
| shots on target | 105 | 71 | 176 | 4.6 |
| shots off target | 133 | 73 | 206 | 5.4 |
| TOTAL | 238 | 144 | 382 | 10.1 |

**Ratio of goals to shots** Average number of shots on target per League goal scored: **3.7**

**Accuracy rating** Average percentage of total goal attempts which were on target: **46.1**

**AGAINST**
Goal attempts recorded in League games

| | HOME | AWAY | TOTAL | AVE |
|---|---|---|---|---|
| shots on target | 100 | 137 | 237 | 6.2 |
| shots off target | 106 | 71 | 177 | 4.7 |
| TOTAL | 206 | 208 | 414 | 10.9 |

**Ratio of goals to shots** Average number of shots on target per League goal scored: **5.4**

**Accuracy rating** Average percentage of total goal attempts which were on target: **57.2**

# Juninho return lights up Riverside

Final Position: **11th**

KEY: ● League ● Champions Lge ● UEFA Cup ● FA Cup ○ League Cup ● Other

**Newcastle ride their luck** to win and Queudrue is sent off for second time
**All change for cup** and all over in first half at Ipswich
**Job knocks himself out** in the search for an equaliser but Baggies hang onto points
**Unbeaten leaders tumble** at the Riverside as Southgate stab wounds Liverpool's ambitions
**Trio of strikers all score** against Man United as McClaren's tactics undo Ferguson
**Hammers pegged back by Ehiogu.** Unbeaten home record saved by his late leap
**Schwarzer on stop form** until Campbell starts Arsenal's challenge
**Wilson sent off after 25 minutes** but Villa are made to fight all the way
**Windass' challenge on Cudicini** provides talking point but keeper is the only thing to hit Chelsea net
**Now it's 11 hours** without an away goal. Blackburn is another unhappy away day
**Villa take advantage** of absent old boys Southgate and Ehiogu to end unbeaten home record
**First penalty in 63 matches** and Maccarone denies Saints from the spot
**Juninho helps reserves to 9-0** win in front of 20,000 fans
**Ex-Derby duo share the derby spoils** with first goals in triumph over Sunderland
**Geremi curls in** half-time lead at Anfield before Riise ensures a share of the points
**Juninho slides in** the equaliser to rule at the Riverside
**Alen Boksic announces his retirement**
INS AND OUTS
**Derby duo join**
**IN** Malcolm Christie and Chris Riggott from Derby for £3m
INS AND OUTS
**Ricketts signs late**
**IN** Michael Ricketts chooses Boro over Spurs for £4m
**Christie poaches** the goal that keeps it just one Riverside defeat in 16
**Juninho's drive and Geremi's chip** club Leeds into submission
**Geremi nods winner** but Juninho sparks derby win that dents Newcastle's hopes
**Albion tormented** by Juninho and fellow Brazilian Doriva on his debut
**Doriva mugged by Henry,** who proves the difference in Arsenal's vital victory
**Now no goal in four games** as Birmingham leap-frog over Boro
**Goal drought ends in style** as Spurs are put to the sword and McClaren celebrates a birthday rise to tenth place
**Ricketts applies the law** of the ex-player scoring against his old club but Bolton's comfort level is increased by Queudrue's dismissal
13 14 15 16 17 18 19 20 21 22 23 24 25 26 27 28 29 30 31 32 33 34 35 36 37 38 39 40 41
NOVEMBER
DECEMBER
JANUARY
FEBRUARY
MARCH
APRIL
MAY

**MONTH BY MONTH POINTS TALLY**

| | | |
|---|---|---|
| AUGUST | 5 | 56% |
| SEPTEMBER | 9 | 60% |
| OCTOBER | 4 | 44% |
| NOVEMBER | 6 | 40% |
| DECEMBER | 5 | 33% |
| JANUARY | 1 | 8% |
| FEBRUARY | 4 | 67% |
| MARCH | 8 | 67% |
| APRIL | 4 | 27% |
| MAY | 3 | 50% |

## DISCIPLINARY RECORDS

**1 Luke Wilkshire**

| | |
|---|---|
| League Yellow | 2 |
| League Red | 1 |
| League Total | 3 |
| All Comps Yellow | 2 |
| All Comps Red | 1 |
| TOTAL | 3 |

League Average
198
mins between cards

| | PLAYER | LEAGUE | | TOTAL | | AVE |
|---|---|---|---|---|---|---|
| 2 | Queudrue | 10Y | 3R | 10Y | 3R | 199 |
| 3 | Stockdale | 3 | 0 | 3 | 0 | 361 |
| 4 | Ehiogu | 6 | 0 | 6 | 0 | 445 |
| 5 | Boateng | 5 | 0 | 5 | 0 | 490 |
| 6 | Ricketts | 1 | 0 | 1 | 0 | 546 |
| 7 | Boksic | 2 | 0 | 2 | 0 | 555 |
| 8 | Greening | 6 | 0 | 6 | 0 | 562 |
| 9 | Maccarone | 3 | 0 | 3 | 0 | 727 |
| 10 | Juninho | 1 | 0 | 1 | 0 | 801 |
| 11 | Southgate | 3 | 0 | 3 | 0 | 1074 |
| 12 | Geremi | 2 | 0 | 2 | 0 | 1483 |
| 13 | Parnaby | 1 | 0 | 1 | 0 | 1783 |
| 14 | Job | 1 | 0 | 1 | 0 | 1944 |
| 15 | Schwarzer | 1 | 0 | 1 | 0 | 3420 |
| | Other | 8 | 1 | 14 | 1 | |
| | TOTAL | 55 | 5 | 61 | 5 | |

## GOALS

**1 Massimo Maccarone**

| | |
|---|---|
| League | 9 |
| FA Cup | 0 |
| League Cup | 0 |
| Europe | 0 |
| Other | 0 |
| TOTAL | 9 |

League Average
242
mins between goals

| | PLAYER | LGE | FAC | LC | Euro | TOT | AVE |
|---|---|---|---|---|---|---|---|
| 2 | Nemeth | 7 | 0 | 0 | 0 | 7 | 211 |
| 3 | Geremi | 7 | 0 | 0 | 0 | 7 | 424 |
| 4 | Job | 4 | 0 | 0 | 0 | 4 | 486 |
| 5 | Christie | 4 | 0 | 0 | 0 | 4 | 205 |
| 6 | Ehiogu | 3 | 0 | 0 | 0 | 3 | 891 |
| 7 | Juninho | 3 | 0 | 0 | 0 | 3 | 267 |
| 8 | Southgate | 2 | 0 | 0 | 0 | 2 | 1612 |
| 9 | Riggott | 2 | 0 | 0 | 0 | 2 | 198 |
| 10 | Boksic | 2 | 0 | 0 | 0 | 2 | 555 |
| 11 | Greening | 2 | 0 | 0 | 0 | 2 | 1688 |
| 12 | Whelan | 1 | 0 | 1 | 0 | 2 | 350 |
| 13 | Ricketts | 1 | 0 | 0 | 0 | 1 | 546 |
| 14 | Queudrue | 1 | 0 | 1 | 0 | 2 | 2596 |
| 15 | Downing | 0 | 0 | 1 | 0 | 1 | |
| | Other | 0 | 0 | 2 | 0 | 2 | |
| | TOTAL | 48 | 0 | 5 | 0 | 53 | |

## SQUAD APPEARANCES

| Match | 1 | 2 | 3 | 4 | 5 | 6 | 7 | 8 | 9 | 10 | 11 | 12 | 13 | 14 | 15 | 16 | 17 | 18 | 19 | 20 | 21 | 22 | 23 | 24 | 25 | 26 | 27 | 28 | 29 | 30 | 31 | 32 | 33 | 34 | 35 | 36 | 37 | 38 | 39 | 40 | 41 |
|---|---|---|---|---|---|---|---|---|---|---|---|---|---|---|---|---|---|---|---|---|---|---|---|---|---|---|---|---|---|---|---|---|---|---|---|---|---|---|---|---|---|
| Venue | A | H | H | A | H | A | H | A | A | H | A | H | A | A | H | A | H | A | H | H | A | H | A | A | A | H | A | H | A | A | H | H | A | H | H | A | H | A | A | H | A |
| Competition | L | L | L | L | L | L | L | L | W | L | L | L | L | W | L | L | L | L | L | L | L | L | L | L | F | L | L | L | L | L | L | L | L | L | L | L | L | L | L | L | L |
| Result | D | D | W | L | W | L | W | W | W | W | L | D | L | L | W | L | W | L | D | D | L | W | L | L | L | D | L | L | D | W | D | W | W | D | W | D | L | L | L | W | L |

**Goalkeepers**
Mark Crossley
Brad Jones
Sam Russell
Mark Schwarzer

**Defenders**
Colin Cooper
Andrew Davies
Ugo Ehiogu
Jason Gavin
Phil Gulliver
David Murphy
Franck Queudrue
Chris Riggott
Gareth Southgate
Robbie Stockdale
Tony Vidmar

**Midfielders**
George Boateng
Brian Close
Guidoni Junior Doriva
John Eustace
Geremi
Jonathan Greening
Juninho
Carlos Marinelli
Stuart Parnaby
Luke Wilkshire
Mark Wilson

**Forwards**
Alen Boksic
Jamie Cade
Malcolm Christie
Craig Dove
Stuart Downing
Joseph-Desire Job
Allan Johnston
Massimo Maccarone
Szilard Nemeth
Michael Ricketts
Noel Whelan
Dean Windass

KEY: ■ On all match ■ On bench ⏮ Subbed or sent off (Counting game) « Subbed or sent off (playing less than 70 minutes) ⏭ Subbed on from bench (Counting Game) » Subbed on (playing less than 70 minutes) Subbed on and then subbed or sent off (Counting Game) Subbed on and then subbed or sent off (playing less than 70 minutes) Not in 16

## KEY PLAYERS - GOALSCORERS

| 1 Szilard Nemeth | |
|---|---|
| **Goals in the League** | 7 |
| **Goals in all competitions** | 7 |
| **Assists** League goals scored by team-mates where he delivered the final pass | 1 |
| **Contribution to Attacking Power** Average number of minutes between League team goals while on pitch | 70 |
| **Player Strike Rate** Average number of minutes between League goals scored by player | 211 |
| **Club Strike Rate** Average minutes between League goals scored by club | 71 |

dialaphone

| | PLAYER | GOALS LGE | GOALS ALL | ASSISTS | POWER | S RATE |
|---|---|---|---|---|---|---|
| 2 | Massimo Maccarone | 9 | 9 | 6 | 64 | 242 mins |
| 3 | Geremi Sorele Nitjap Fotso | 7 | 7 | 8 | 70 | 424 mins |
| 4 | Joseph-Desire Job | 4 | 4 | 4 | 81 | 486 mins |
| 5 | Ugo Ehiogu | 3 | 3 | 0 | 78 | 891 mins |

## KEY PLAYERS - MIDFIELDERS

| 1 Geremi Sorele Nitjap Fotso | |
|---|---|
| **Goals in the League** | 7 |
| **Goals in all competitions** | 7 |
| **Assists** League goals scored by team-mates where he delivered the final pass | 8 |
| **Defensive Rating** Average number of mins between League goals conceded while he was on the pitch | 85 |
| **Contribution to Attacking Power** Average number of minutes between League team goals while on pitch | 71 |
| **Scoring Difference** Defensive Rating minus Contribution to Attacking Power | 14 |

| | PLAYER | GOALS LGE | GOALS ALL | ASSISTS | DEF RATE | POWER | SC DIFF |
|---|---|---|---|---|---|---|---|
| 2 | Jonathan Greening | 2 | 2 | 3 | 77 | 72 | 5 mins |
| 3 | George Boateng | 0 | 0 | 0 | 72 | 70 | 2 mins |
| 4 | Stuart Parnaby | 0 | 0 | 2 | 59 | 78 | -19 mins |

## PLAYER APPEARANCES

| | AGE (on 01/07/03) | IN THE SQUAD | COUNTING GAMES | MINUTES ON PITCH | IN THE SQUAD | MINUTES ON PITCH | THIS SEASON | NATIONAL SIDE |
|---|---|---|---|---|---|---|---|---|
| **Goalkeepers** | | | | | | | | |
| Mark Crossley | 34 | 29 | 0 | 0 | 32 | 180 | 5 | Wales (50) |
| Brad Jones | 21 | 9 | 0 | 0 | 9 | 0 | - | United States |
| Sam Russell | 20 | 0 | 0 | 0 | 2 | 0 | - | England |
| Mark Schwarzer | 30 | 38 | 38 | 3420 | 39 | 3510 | - | Australia |
| **Defenders** | | | | | | | | |
| Colin Cooper | 36 | 27 | 13 | 1405 | 30 | 1655 | - | England |
| Andrew Davies | 18 | 2 | 1 | 90 | 4 | 180 | - | England |
| Ugo Ehiogu | 30 | 32 | 29 | 2672 | 32 | 2672 | 1 | England (7) |
| Jason Gavin | 23 | 2 | 0 | 0 | 3 | 90 | - | Rep of Ireland |
| Phil Gulliver | 20 | 0 | 0 | 0 | 1 | 0 | - | |
| David Murphy | 19 | 8 | 2 | 307 | 8 | 307 | - | England |
| Franck Queudrue | 24 | 31 | 28 | 2596 | 33 | 2776 | - | France |
| Chris Riggott | 22 | 5 | 4 | 395 | 5 | 395 | - | England |
| Gareth Southgate | 32 | 36 | 36 | 3224 | 37 | 3314 | 7 | England (7) |
| Robbie Stockdale | 23 | 18 | 11 | 1085 | 19 | 1162 | 1 | Scotland (64) |
| Tony Vidmar | 33 | 15 | 9 | 896 | 18 | 1166 | - | Australia |
| **Midfielders** | | | | | | | | |
| George Boateng | 27 | 28 | 27 | 2450 | 28 | 2450 | 1 | Holland (6) |
| Brian Close | 21 | 0 | 0 | 0 | 2 | 25 | - | N Ireland |
| Guidoni Doriva | 31 | 8 | 3 | 339 | 8 | 339 | - | Brazil |
| John Eustace | 23 | 1 | 0 | 4 | 1 | 4 | - | England |
| Geremi | 24 | 33 | 33 | 2967 | 34 | 3057 | 2 | Cameroon (18) |
| Jonathan Greening | 24 | 38 | 37 | 3375 | 39 | 3465 | - | England |
| Juninho | 30 | 10 | 8 | 801 | 10 | 801 | - | Brazil |
| Carlos Marinelli | 21 | 12 | 2 | 292 | 14 | 447 | - | Argentina |
| Stuart Parnaby | 20 | 21 | 18 | 1783 | 23 | 1963 | - | England |
| Luke Wilkshire | 21 | 22 | 5 | 596 | 24 | 776 | - | Australia |
| Mark Wilson | 24 | 12 | 3 | 311 | 15 | 511 | - | England |
| **Forwards** | | | | | | | | |
| Alen Boksic | 33 | 20 | 11 | 1110 | 21 | 1120 | 1 | Croatia (26) |
| Jamie Cade | 19 | 0 | 0 | 0 | 1 | 25 | - | England |
| Malcolm Christie | 24 | 12 | 7 | 818 | 12 | 818 | - | England |
| Craig Dove | 19 | 0 | 0 | 0 | 2 | 20 | - | England |
| Stuart Downing | 18 | 3 | 0 | 58 | 4 | 103 | - | England |
| Joseph-Desire Job | 25 | 30 | 17 | 1944 | 31 | 1989 | 2 | Cameroon (18) |
| Allan Johnston | 29 | 0 | 0 | 0 | 2 | 180 | 2 | Scotland (64) |
| M Maccarone | 23 | 37 | 22 | 2181 | 38 | 2181 | 1 | Italy (12) |
| Szilard Nemeth | 24 | 32 | 12 | 1477 | 34 | 1632 | - | Hungary |
| Michael Ricketts | 24 | 9 | 4 | 546 | 9 | 546 | - | England |
| Noel Whelan | 28 | 20 | 0 | 350 | 22 | 478 | - | England |
| Dean Windass | 34 | 4 | 0 | 35 | 6 | 160 | - | England |

**KEY:** LEAGUE ALL COMPS CAPS (FIFA RANKING)

## TEAM OF THE SEASON

Schwarzer
CG 38 DR 78
Cooper
CG 13 DR 88
Ehiogu
CG 29 DR 92
Southgate
CG 36 DR 85
Queudrue
CG 28 DR 76
Parnaby
CG 18 SD -19
Geremi
CG 33 SD +14
Boateng
CG 27 SD +2
Greening
CG 37 SD +5
Maccarone
CG 22 AP 64
Nemeth
CG 12 SR 211


**KEY:** DR = Defensive Rate, SD = Scoring Difference AP = Attacking Power SR = Strike Rate, CG=Counting Games – League games playing at least 70 minutes

## TOP POINT EARNERS

**1 Massimo Maccarone**

| | |
|---|---|
| **Counting Games** League games when he played at least 70 minutes | 22 |
| **Average points** Average League points taken in Counting games | 1.41 |
| **Club Average points** Average points taken in League games | 1.29 |

| | PLAYER | GAMES | PTS |
|---|---|---|---|
| 2 | Geremi Sorele Nitjap Fotso | 33 | 1.39 |
| 3 | Ugo Ehiogu | 29 | 1.38 |
| 4 | Jonathan Greening | 37 | 1.32 |
| 5 | Colin Cooper | 13 | 1.31 |
| 6 | George Boateng | 27 | 1.30 |
| 7 | Mark Schwarzer | 38 | 1.29 |
| 8 | Joseph-Desire Job | 17 | 1.29 |
| 9 | Franck Queudrue | 28 | 1.29 |
| 10 | Gareth Southgate | 36 | 1.28 |

## KEY PLAYERS - DEFENDERS

**1 Ugo Ehiogu**

| | |
|---|---|
| **Goals Conceded** The number of League goals conceded while he was on the pitch | 29 |
| **Goals Conceded in all competitions** The number goals conceded while he was on the pitch in all competitions | 29 |
| **League minutes played** Number of minutes played in league matches | 2672 |
| **Clean Sheets** In games when he played at least70 mins | 10 |
| **Defensive Rating** Average number of mins between League goals conceded while he was on the pitch | 92 |
| **Club Defensive Rating** Average number of mins between League goals conceded by the club this season | 78 |

| | PLAYER | CON LGE | CON ALL | MINS | C SHEETS | DEF RATE |
|---|---|---|---|---|---|---|
| 2 | Colin Cooper | 16 | 21 | 1405 | 5 | 88 mins |
| 3 | Gareth Southgate | 38 | 39 | 3224 | 9 | 85 mins |
| 4 | Franck Queudrue | 34 | 38 | 2596 | 8 | 76 mins |

## KEY PLAYERS - GOALKEEPERS

dialaphone


**1 Mark Schwarzer**

| | |
|---|---|
| **Goals Conceded in the League** The number of League goals conceded while he was on the pitch | 44 |
| **Goals Conceded in all competitions** The number of goals conceded while he was on the pitch in all competitions | 45 |
| **League minutes played** Number of minutes played in league matches | 3420 |
| **Clean Sheets** In games when he played at least 70 mins | 10 |
| **Goals to Shots Ratio** The average number of shots on target per each League goal conceded | 5.4 |
| **Defensive Rating** Ave number of mins between League goals conceded while on the pitch | 78 |

**1 Mark Crossley**

| | |
|---|---|
| **Goals Conceded in the League** The number of League goals conceded while he was on the pitch | – |
| **Goals Conceded in all competitions** The number of goals conceded while he was on the pitch in all competitions | 4 |
| **League minutes played** Number of minutes played in league matches | 0 |
| **Clean Sheets** In games when he played at least 70 mins | – |
| **Goals to Shots Ratio** The average number of shots on target per each League goal conceded | – |
| **Defensive Rating** Ave number of mins between League goals conceded while on the pitch | – |

# CHARLTON ATHLETIC

**NICKNAME:** THE ADDICKS

KEY: Won / Drawn / Lost

| | | | | | | |
|---|---|---|---|---|---|---|
| 1 | lge | Chelsea | H | L | 2-3 | Konchesky 7; Rufus 34 |
| 2 | lge | Bolton | A | W | 2-1 | Bart-Williams 26 pen; Euell 67 |
| 3 | lge | Tottenham | H | L | 0-1 | |
| 4 | lge | West Ham | A | W | 2-0 | Jensen 3; Fortune 43 |
| 5 | lge | Aston Villa | A | L | 0-2 | |
| 6 | lge | Arsenal | H | L | 0-3 | |
| 7 | lge | Southampton | A | D | 0-0 | |
| 8 | lge | Man Utd | H | L | 1-3 | Jensen 45 |
| 9 | wr2 | Oxford | H | L | 5-6* | (*on penalties) |
| 10 | lge | Fulham | A | L | 0-1 | |
| 11 | lge | Middlesbrough | H | W | 1-0 | Euell 4 |
| 12 | lge | Newcastle | A | L | 1-2 | Bartlett 30 |
| 13 | lge | Sunderland | H | D | 1-1 | Rowett 77 |
| 14 | lge | Everton | A | L | 0-1 | |
| 15 | lge | Man City | A | W | 1-0 | Bartlett 79 |
| 16 | lge | Blackburn | H | W | 3-1 | Konchesky 59; Rufus 74; Euell 90 |
| 17 | lge | Leeds | A | W | 2-1 | Lisbie 80; Parker 90 |
| 18 | lge | Liverpool | H | W | 2-0 | Euell 36; Konchesky 78 |
| 19 | lge | Man City | H | D | 2-2 | Euell 51 pen; Jensen 63 |
| 20 | lge | Birmingham | A | D | 1-1 | Jensen 37 |
| 21 | lge | Tottenham | A | D | 2-2 | Euell 14,49 |
| 22 | lge | West Brom | H | W | 1-0 | Lisbie 6 |
| 23 | facr3 | Exeter | H | W | 3-1 | Johansson 25,61; Euell 72 pen |
| 24 | lge | Chelsea | A | L | 1-4 | Euell 42 pen |
| 25 | lge | Bolton | H | D | 1-1 | Fish 47 |
| 26 | lge | West Ham | H | W | 4-2 | Jensen 42; Parker 45,52; Kishishev 90 |
| 27 | facr4 | Fulham | A | L | 0-3 | |
| 28 | lge | West Brom | A | W | 1-0 | Bartlett 60 |
| 29 | lge | Sunderland | A | W | 3-1 | Fish 24; Proctor 29 og,32 og |
| 30 | lge | Everton | H | W | 2-1 | Kishishev 19; Lisbie 83 |
| 31 | lge | Aston Villa | H | W | 3-0 | Euell 52; Johansson 87,90 |
| 32 | lge | Arsenal | A | L | 0-2 | |
| 33 | lge | Newcastle | H | L | 0-2 | |
| 34 | lge | Middlesbrough | A | D | 1-1 | Johansson 26 |
| 35 | lge | Leeds | H | L | 1-6 | Euell 45 pen |
| 36 | lge | Blackburn | A | L | 0-1 | |
| 37 | lge | Birmingham | H | L | 0-2 | |
| 38 | lge | Liverpool | A | L | 1-2 | Bartlett 47 |
| 39 | lge | Southampton | H | W | 2-1 | Parker 32; Lisbie 50 |
| 40 | lge | Man Utd | A | L | 1-4 | Jensen 13 |
| 41 | lge | Fulham | H | L | 0-1 | |

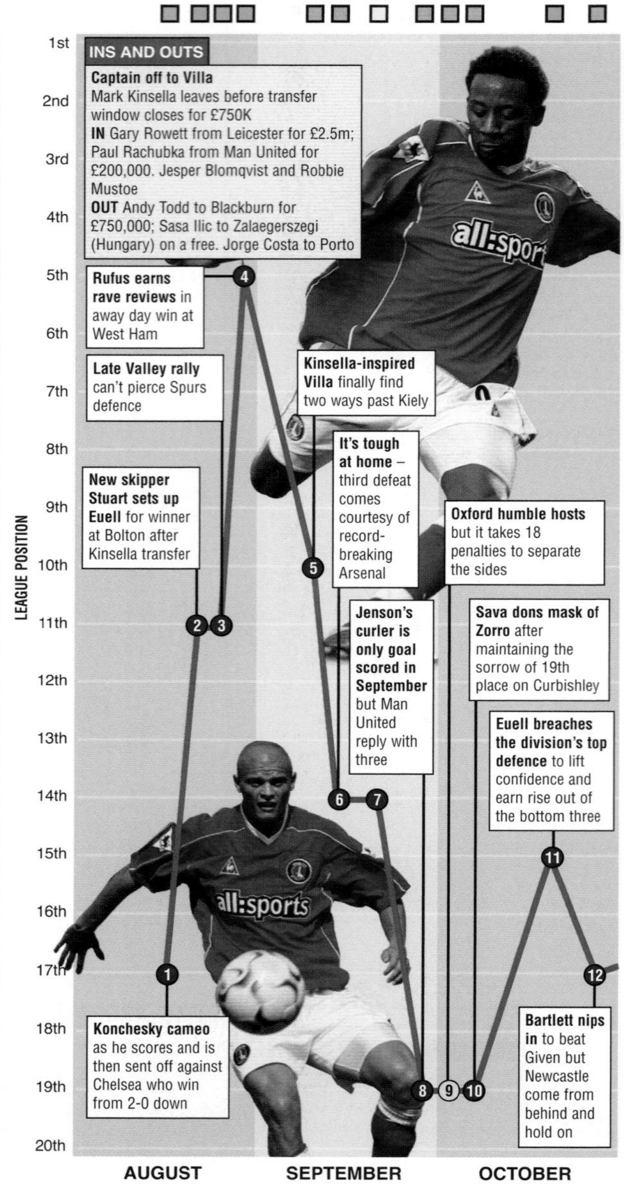
1st
2nd
3rd
4th
5th
6th
7th
8th
9th
10th
11th
12th
13th
14th
15th
16th
17th
18th
19th
20th
LEAGUE POSITION
INS AND OUTS
**Captain off to Villa** Mark Kinsella leaves before transfer window closes for £750K
**IN** Gary Rowett from Leicester for £2.5m; Paul Rachubka from Man United for £200,000. Jesper Blomqvist and Robbie Mustoe
**OUT** Andy Todd to Blackburn for £750,000; Sasa Ilic to Zalaegerszegi (Hungary) on a free. Jorge Costa to Porto
**Rufus earns rave reviews** in away day win at West Ham
**Late Valley rally** can't pierce Spurs defence
**New skipper Stuart sets up Euell** for winner at Bolton after Kinsella transfer
**Konchesky cameo** as he scores and is then sent off against Chelsea who win from 2-0 down
**Kinsella-inspired Villa** finally find two ways past Kiely
**It's tough at home** – third defeat comes courtesy of record-breaking Arsenal
**Jenson's curler is only goal scored in September** but Man United reply with three
**Oxford humble hosts** but it takes 18 penalties to separate the sides
**Sava dons mask of Zorro** after maintaining the sorrow of 19th place on Curbishley
**Euell breaches the division's top defence** to lift confidence and earn rise out of the bottom three
**Bartlett nips in** to beat Given but Newcastle come from behind and hold on
1
2
3
4
5
6
7
8
9
10
11
12
AUGUST
SEPTEMBER
OCTOBER

Home / Away / Neutral

## ATTENDANCES

**HOME GROUND:** THE VALLEY **CAPACITY:** 26700 **AVERAGE LEAGUE AT HOME:** 26255

| | | | | | | | | | | | |
|---|---|---|---|---|---|---|---|---|---|---|---|
| 40 | Man Utd | 67721 | 34 | Middlesboro | 29080 | 13 | Sunderland | 26284 | 37 | Birmingham | 25732 |
| 12 | Newcastle | 51670 | 20 | Birmingham | 28837 | 35 | Leeds | 26274 | 7 | Southampton | 25714 |
| 38 | Liverpool | 42010 | 36 | Blackburn | 27506 | 11 | Middlesboro | 26271 | 1 | Chelsea | 25640 |
| 32 | Arsenal | 38015 | 33 | Newcastle | 26728 | 31 | Aston Villa | 26257 | 2 | Bolton | 21753 |
| 14 | Everton | 37621 | 18 | Liverpool | 26694 | 22 | West Brom | 26196 | 23 | Exeter | 18107 |
| 24 | Chelsea | 37284 | 8 | Man Utd | 26630 | 16 | Blackburn | 26152 | 10 | Fulham | 14720 |
| 21 | Tottenham | 36043 | 30 | Everton | 26623 | 28 | West Brom | 26113 | 27 | Fulham | 12203 |
| 29 | Sunderland | 36024 | 5 | Aston Villa | 26483 | 41 | Fulham | 26108 | 9 | Oxford | 9494 |
| 17 | Leeds | 35537 | 3 | Tottenham | 26461 | 6 | Arsenal | 26080 | | | |
| 15 | Man City | 33455 | 19 | Man City | 26434 | 25 | Bolton | 26057 | | | |
| 4 | West Ham | 32424 | 26 | West Ham | 26340 | 39 | Southampton | 25894 | | | |

## GOAL ATTEMPTS

**FOR** – Goal attempts recorded in League games

| | HOME | AWAY | TOTAL | AVE |
|---|---|---|---|---|
| shots on target | 121 | 84 | 205 | 5.4 |
| shots off target | 87 | 62 | 149 | 3.9 |
| TOTAL | 208 | 146 | 354 | 9.3 |

| | |
|---|---|
| **Ratio of goals to shots** Average number of shots on target per League goal scored | 4.6 |
| **Accuracy rating** Average percentage of total goal attempts which were on target | 57.9 |

**AGAINST** – Goal attempts recorded in League games

| | HOME | AWAY | TOTAL | AVE |
|---|---|---|---|---|
| shots on target | 128 | 132 | 260 | 6.8 |
| shots off target | 120 | 84 | 204 | 5.4 |
| TOTAL | 248 | 216 | 464 | 12.2 |

| | |
|---|---|
| **Ratio of goals to shots** Average number of shots on target per League goal scored | 4.6 |
| **Accuracy rating** Average percentage of total goal attempts which were on target | 56.0 |

# Mid-season surge ends in a slide

**Final Position: 12th**

KEY: League, Champions Lge, UEFA Cup, FA Cup, League Cup, Other

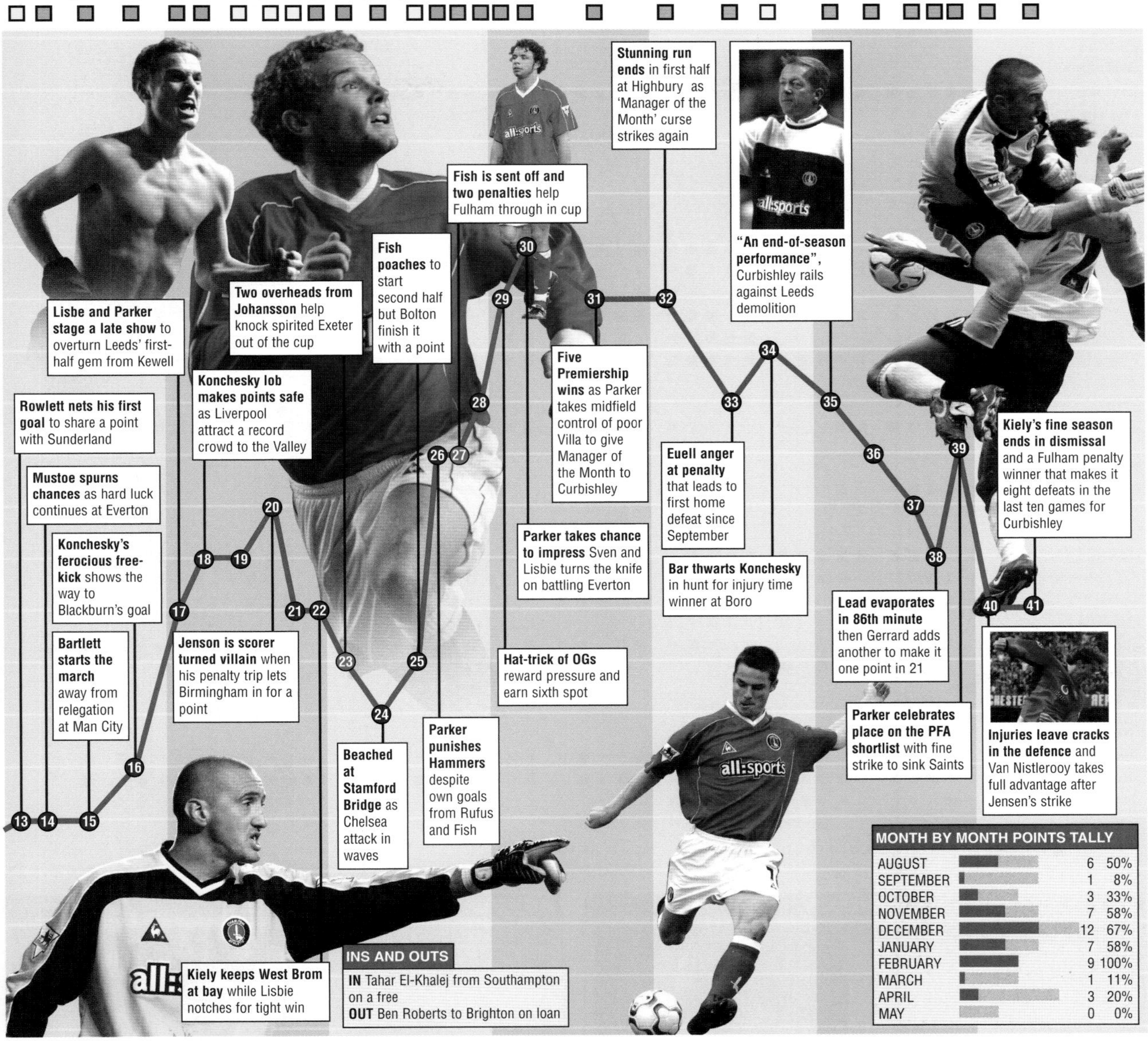

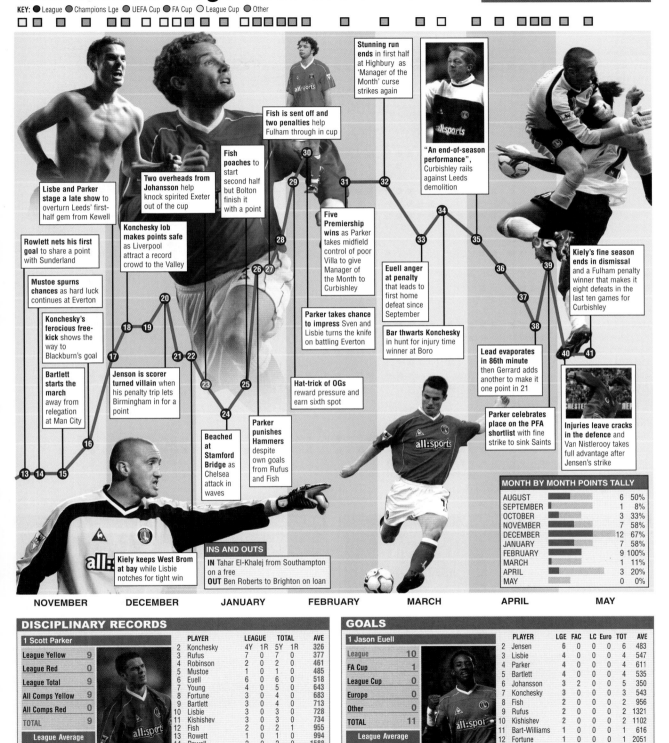

**Rowlett nets his first goal** to share a point with Sunderland
**Mustoe spurns chances** as hard luck continues at Everton
**Bartlett starts the march** away from relegation at Man City
**Konchesky's ferocious free-kick** shows the way to Blackburn's goal
**Lisbe and Parker stage a late show** to overturn Leeds' first-half gem from Kewell
**Konchesky lob makes points safe** as Liverpool attract a record crowd to the Valley
**Two overheads from Johansson** help knock spirited Exeter out of the cup
**Jenson is scorer turned villain** when his penalty trip lets Birmingham in for a point
**Kiely keeps West Brom at bay** while Lisbie notches for tight win
**Beached at Stamford Bridge** as Chelsea attack in waves
**Fish poaches** to start second half but Bolton finish it with a point
**Parker punishes Hammers** despite own goals from Rufus and Fish
**Fish is sent off and two penalties** help Fulham through in cup
**Hat-trick of OGs** reward pressure and earn sixth spot
**Parker takes chance to impress** Sven and Lisbie turns the knife on battling Everton
**Five Premiership wins** as Parker takes midfield control of poor Villa to give Manager of the Month to Curbishley
**Stunning run ends** in first half at Highbury as 'Manager of the Month' curse strikes again
**Euell anger at penalty** that leads to first home defeat since September
**Bar thwarts Konchesky** in hunt for injury time winner at Boro
**"An end-of-season performance"**, Curbishley rails against Leeds demolition
**Lead evaporates in 86th minute** then Gerrard adds another to make it one point in 21
**Parker celebrates place on the PFA shortlist** with fine strike to sink Saints
**Kiely's fine season ends in dismissal** and a Fulham penalty winner that makes it eight defeats in the last ten games for Curbishley
**Injuries leave cracks in the defence** and Van Nistlerooy takes full advantage after Jensen's strike
NOVEMBER
DECEMBER
JANUARY
FEBRUARY
MARCH
APRIL
MAY


### INS AND OUTS

**IN** Tahar El-Khalej from Southampton on a free
**OUT** Ben Roberts to Brighton on loan

### MONTH BY MONTH POINTS TALLY

| | | |
|---|---|---|
| AUGUST | 6 | 50% |
| SEPTEMBER | 1 | 8% |
| OCTOBER | 3 | 33% |
| NOVEMBER | 7 | 58% |
| DECEMBER | 12 | 67% |
| JANUARY | 7 | 58% |
| FEBRUARY | 9 | 100% |
| MARCH | 1 | 11% |
| APRIL | 3 | 20% |
| MAY | 0 | 0% |

## DISCIPLINARY RECORDS

**1 Scott Parker**

| | |
|---|---|
| League Yellow | 9 |
| League Red | 0 |
| League Total | 9 |
| All Comps Yellow | 9 |
| All Comps Red | 0 |
| TOTAL | 9 |

League Average 271 mins between cards

| | PLAYER | LEAGUE | | TOTAL | | AVE |
|---|---|---|---|---|---|---|
| 2 | Konchesky | 4Y | 1R | 5Y | 1R | 326 |
| 3 | Rufus | 7 | 0 | 7 | 0 | 377 |
| 4 | Robinson | 2 | 0 | 2 | 0 | 461 |
| 5 | Mustoe | 1 | 0 | 1 | 0 | 485 |
| 6 | Euell | 6 | 0 | 6 | 0 | 518 |
| 7 | Young | 4 | 0 | 5 | 0 | 643 |
| 8 | Fortune | 3 | 0 | 4 | 0 | 683 |
| 9 | Bartlett | 3 | 0 | 4 | 0 | 713 |
| 10 | Lisbie | 3 | 0 | 3 | 0 | 728 |
| 11 | Kishishev | 3 | 0 | 3 | 0 | 734 |
| 12 | Fish | 2 | 0 | 2 | 1 | 955 |
| 13 | Rowett | 1 | 0 | 1 | 0 | 994 |
| 14 | Powell | 2 | 0 | 2 | 0 | 1588 |
| 15 | Kiely | 1 | 1 | 1 | 1 | 1680 |
| | Other | 3 | 0 | 4 | 0 | |
| | TOTAL | 54 | 2 | 59 | 3 | |

## GOALS

**1 Jason Euell**

| | |
|---|---|
| League | 10 |
| FA Cup | 1 |
| League Cup | 0 |
| Europe | 0 |
| Other | 0 |
| TOTAL | 11 |

League Average 311 mins between goals

| | PLAYER | LGE | FAC | LC | Euro | TOT | AVE |
|---|---|---|---|---|---|---|---|
| 2 | Jensen | 6 | 0 | 0 | 0 | 6 | 483 |
| 3 | Lisbie | 4 | 0 | 0 | 0 | 4 | 547 |
| 4 | Parker | 4 | 0 | 0 | 0 | 4 | 611 |
| 5 | Bartlett | 4 | 0 | 0 | 0 | 4 | 535 |
| 6 | Johansson | 3 | 2 | 0 | 0 | 5 | 350 |
| 7 | Konchesky | 3 | 0 | 0 | 0 | 3 | 543 |
| 8 | Fish | 2 | 0 | 0 | 0 | 2 | 956 |
| 9 | Rufus | 2 | 0 | 0 | 0 | 2 | 1321 |
| 10 | Kishishev | 2 | 0 | 0 | 0 | 2 | 1102 |
| 11 | Bart-Williams | 1 | 0 | 0 | 0 | 1 | 616 |
| 12 | Fortune | 1 | 0 | 0 | 0 | 1 | 2051 |
| 13 | Rowett | 1 | 0 | 0 | 0 | 1 | 994 |
| | Other | 2 | 0 | 0 | 0 | 2 | |
| | TOTAL | 45 | 3 | 0 | 0 | 48 | |

## SQUAD APPEARANCES

| Match | 1 | 2 | 3 | 4 | 5 | 6 | 7 | 8 | 9 | 10 | 11 | 12 | 13 | 14 | 15 | 16 | 17 | 18 | 19 | 20 | 21 | 22 | 23 | 24 | 25 | 26 | 27 | 28 | 29 | 30 | 31 | 32 | 33 | 34 | 35 | 36 | 37 | 38 | 39 | 40 | 41 |
|---|---|---|---|---|---|---|---|---|---|---|---|---|---|---|---|---|---|---|---|---|---|---|---|---|---|---|---|---|---|---|---|---|---|---|---|---|---|---|---|---|---|
| Venue | H | A | H | A | A | H | A | H | H | A | H | A | H | A | A | H | A | H | H | A | A | H | H | A | H | H | A | A | A | H | H | A | H | A | H | A | H | A | H | A | H |
| Competition | L | L | L | L | L | L | L | L | W | L | L | L | L | L | L | L | L | L | L | L | L | L | F | L | L | L | F | L | L | L | L | L | L | L | L | L | L | L | L | L | L |
| Result | L | W | L | W | L | L | D | L | L | L | W | L | D | L | W | W | W | W | D | D | D | W | W | L | D | W | L | W | W | W | W | L | L | D | L | L | L | L | W | L | L |

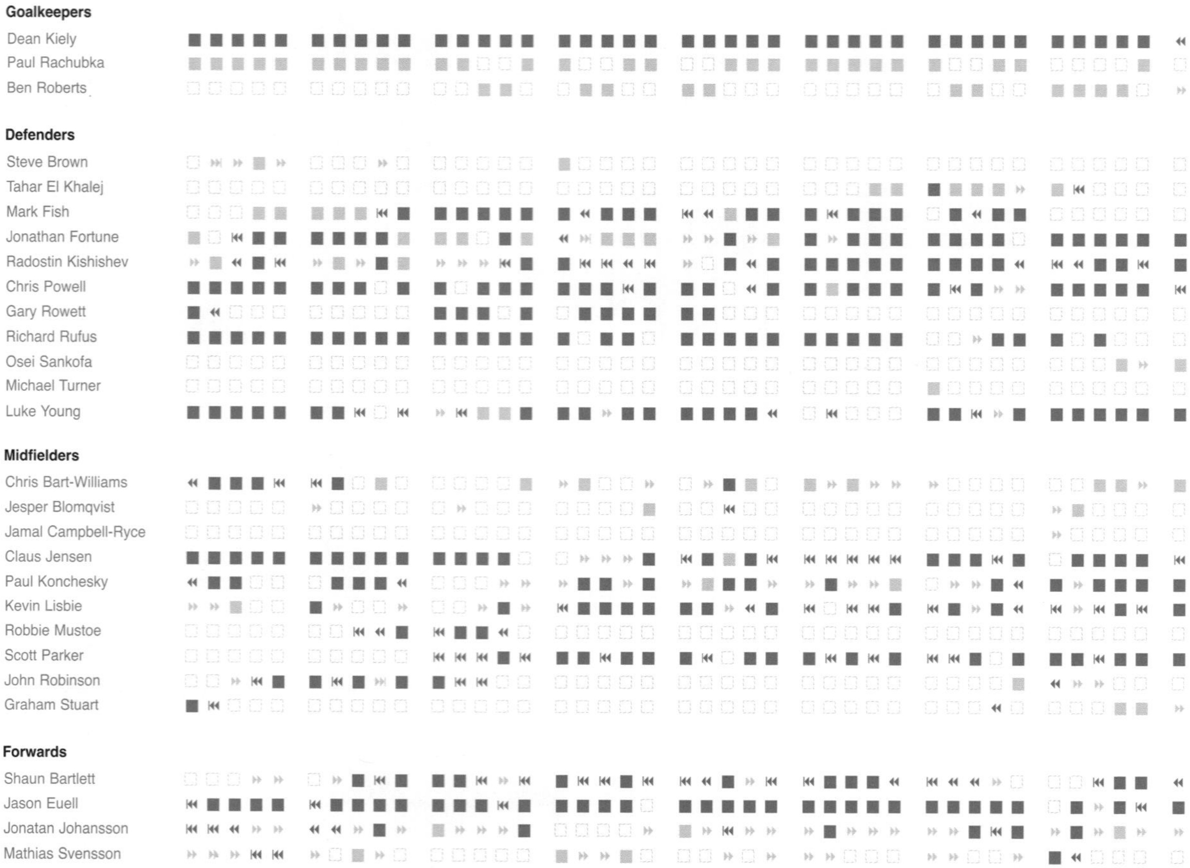

Goalkeepers
Dean Kiely
Paul Rachubka
Ben Roberts
Defenders
Steve Brown
Tahar El Khalej
Mark Fish
Jonathan Fortune
Radostin Kishishev
Chris Powell
Gary Rowett
Richard Rufus
Osei Sankofa
Michael Turner
Luke Young
Midfielders
Chris Bart-Williams
Jesper Blomqvist
Jamal Campbell-Ryce
Claus Jensen
Paul Konchesky
Kevin Lisbie
Robbie Mustoe
Scott Parker
John Robinson
Graham Stuart
Forwards
Shaun Bartlett
Jason Euell
Jonatan Johansson
Mathias Svensson


KEY: On all match / On bench / Subbed or sent off (Counting game) / Subbed or sent off (playing less than 70 minutes) / Subbed on from bench (Counting Game) / Subbed on (playing less than 70 minutes) / Subbed on and then subbed or sent off (Counting Game) / Subbed on and then subbed or sent off (playing less than 70 minutes) / Not in 16

## KEY PLAYERS - GOALSCORERS

**1 Jason Euell**

| | |
|---|---|
| **Goals in the League** | 10 |
| **Goals in all competitions** | 11 |
| **Assists** League goals scored by team-mates where he delivered the final pass | 3 |
| **Contribution to Attacking Power** Average number of minutes between League team goals while on pitch | 72 |
| **Player Strike Rate** Average number of minutes between League goals scored by player | 311 |
| **Club Strike Rate** Average minutes between League goals scored by club | 76 |

| | PLAYER | GOALS LGE | GOALS ALL | ASSISTS | POWER | S RATE |
|---|---|---|---|---|---|---|
| 2 | Claus Jensen | 6 | 6 | 7 | 74 | 483 mins |
| 3 | Shaun Bartlett | 4 | 4 | 2 | 69 | 535 mins |
| 4 | Paul Konchesky | 3 | 3 | 1 | 81 | 543 mins |
| 5 | Kevin Lisbie | 4 | 4 | 5 | 70 | 547 mins |

## KEY PLAYERS - MIDFIELDERS

**1 Scott Parker**

| | |
|---|---|
| **Goals in the League** | 4 |
| **Goals in all competitions** | 4 |
| **Assists** League goals scored by team-mates where he delivered the final pass | 4 |
| **Defensive Rating** Average number of mins between League goals conceded while he was on the pitch | 63 |
| **Contribution to Attacking Power** Average number of minutes between League team goals while on pitch | 70 |
| **Scoring Difference** Defensive Rating minus Contribution to Attacking Power | -7 |

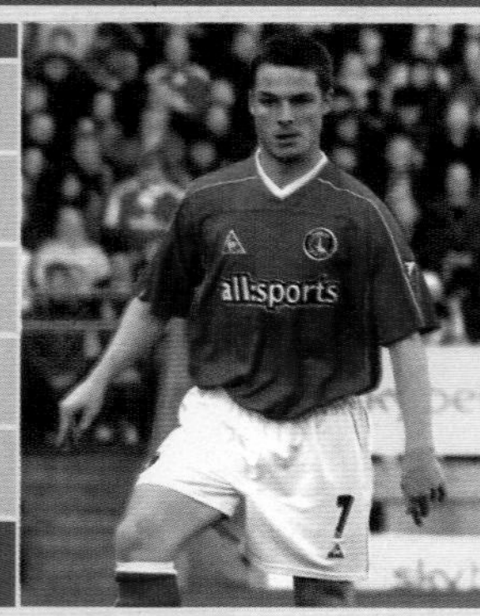

all:sports


| | PLAYER | GOALS LGE | GOALS ALL | ASSISTS | DEF RATE | POWER | SC DIFF |
|---|---|---|---|---|---|---|---|
| 2 | Kevin Lisbie | 4 | 4 | 5 | 61 | 71 | -10 mins |
| 3 | Claus Jensen | 6 | 6 | 7 | 57 | 74 | -17 mins |
| 4 | Paul Konchesky | 3 | 3 | 1 | 53 | 82 | -29 mins |

## PLAYER APPEARANCES

| | AGE (on 01/07/03) | IN THE SQUAD | COUNTING GAMES | MINUTES ON PITCH | IN THE SQUAD | MINUTES ON PITCH | THIS SEASON | NATIONAL SIDE |
|---|---|---|---|---|---|---|---|---|
| **Goalkeepers** | | | | | | | | |
| Dean Kiely | 32 | 38 | 37 | 3361 | 41 | 3661 | 6 | Rep of Ireland (15) |
| Paul Rachubka | 22 | 25 | 0 | 0 | 28 | 0 | - | England |
| Ben Roberts | 28 | 13 | 0 | 60 | 13 | 60 | - | England |
| **Defenders** | | | | | | | | |
| Steve Brown | 31 | 5 | 1 | 129 | 6 | 155 | - | England |
| Tahar El Khalej | 35 | 9 | 2 | 195 | 9 | 195 | - | Morocco |
| Mark Fish | 29 | 28 | 20 | 1911 | 31 | 2092 | - | South Africa |
| Jonathan Fortune | 22 | 35 | 22 | 2051 | 38 | 2280 | - | England |
| Radostin Kishishev | 28 | 37 | 21 | 2204 | 40 | 2504 | - | Bulgaria |
| Chris Powell | 33 | 37 | 34 | 3177 | 38 | 3177 | - | England |
| Gary Rowett | 29 | 12 | 11 | 994 | 12 | 994 | - | England |
| Richard Rufus | 28 | 30 | 29 | 2642 | 33 | 2942 | - | England |
| Osei Sankofa | 18 | 3 | 0 | 18 | 3 | 18 | - | England |
| Michael Turner | 19 | 1 | 0 | 0 | 1 | 0 | - | England |
| Luke Young | 23 | 34 | 28 | 2574 | 36 | 2735 | - | England |
| **Midfielders** | | | | | | | | |
| Chris Bart-Williams | 29 | 22 | 6 | 616 | 25 | 725 | - | England |
| Jesper Blomqvist | 29 | 5 | 0 | 56 | 6 | 131 | - | Sweden |
| J Campbell-Ryce | 20 | 1 | 0 | 5 | 1 | 5 | - | England |
| Claus Jensen | 26 | 35 | 32 | 2897 | 38 | 3088 | 9 | Denmark (10) |
| Paul Konchesky | 22 | 31 | 14 | 1630 | 34 | 1930 | 1 | England (7) |
| Kevin Lisbie | 24 | 33 | 22 | 2186 | 34 | 2201 | - | England |
| Robbie Mustoe | 35 | 6 | 5 | 485 | 7 | 530 | - | England |
| Scott Parker | 22 | 28 | 27 | 2445 | 29 | 2521 | 1 | England (7) |
| John Robinson | 31 | 14 | 9 | 922 | 15 | 997 | - | Wales |
| Graham Stuart | 32 | 6 | 2 | 213 | 6 | 213 | - | England |
| **Forwards** | | | | | | | | |
| Shaun Bartlett | 30 | 31 | 19 | 2140 | 34 | 2388 | - | South Africa |
| Jason Euell | 26 | 36 | 35 | 3112 | 39 | 3412 | - | England |
| Jonatan Johansson | 27 | 34 | 7 | 1050 | 37 | 1336 | - | Finland |
| Mathias Svensson | 28 | 18 | 3 | 425 | 21 | 505 | - | Sweden |

KEY: LEAGUE ALL COMPS CAPS (FIFA RANKING)

## TEAM OF THE SEASON

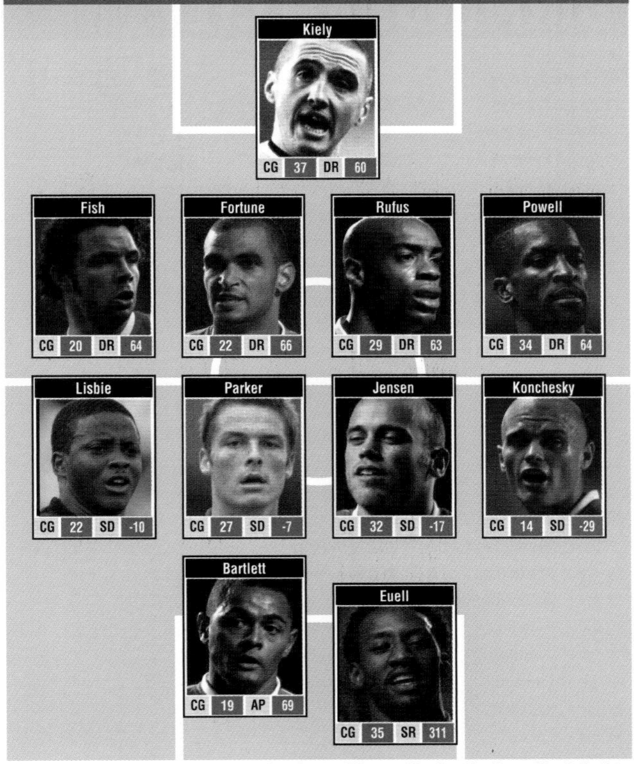

Kiely
CG 37 DR 60
Fish
CG 20 DR 64
Fortune
CG 22 DR 66
Rufus
CG 29 DR 63
Powell
CG 34 DR 64
Lisbie
CG 22 SD -10
Parker
CG 27 SD -7
Jensen
CG 32 SD -17
Konchesky
CG 14 SD -29
Bartlett
CG 19 AP 69
Euell
CG 35 SR 311


KEY: DR = Defensive Rate, SD = Scoring Difference AP = Attacking Power SR = Strike Rate, CG=Counting Games – League games playing at least 70 minutes

## TOP POINT EARNERS

**1 Shaun Bartlett**

| | |
|---|---|
| **Counting Games** League games when he played at least 70 minutes | 19 |
| **Average points** Average League points taken in Counting games | 1.79 |
| **Club Average points** Average points taken in League games | 1.29 |

| | PLAYER | GAMES | PTS |
|---|---|---|---|
| 2 | Radostin Kishishev | 21 | 1.71 |
| 3 | Kevin Lisbie | 22 | 1.59 |
| 4 | Mark Fish | 20 | 1.50 |
| 5 | Scott Parker | 27 | 1.41 |
| 6 | Chris Powell | 34 | 1.41 |
| 7 | Jason Euell | 35 | 1.37 |
| 8 | Richard Rufus | 29 | 1.34 |
| 9 | Dean Kiely | 37 | 1.32 |
| 10 | Jonathan Fortune | 22 | 1.18 |

## KEY PLAYERS - DEFENDERS

**1 Jonathan Fortune**

| | |
|---|---|
| **Goals Conceded** The number of League goals conceded while he was on the pitch | 31 |
| **Goals Conceded in all competitions** The number goals conceded while he was on the pitch in all competitions | 33 |
| **League minutes played** Number of minutes played in league matches | 2051 |
| **Clean Sheets** In games when he played at least70 mins | 4 |
| **Defensive Rating** Average number of mins between League goals conceded while he was on the pitch | 66 |
| **Club Defensive Rating** Average number of mins between League goals conceded by the club this season | 61 |

| | PLAYER | CON LGE | CON ALL | MINS | C SHEETS | DEF RATE |
|---|---|---|---|---|---|---|
| 2 | Mark Fish | 30 | 33 | 1911 | 4 | 64 mins |
| 3 | Chris Powell | 50 | 50 | 3177 | 8 | 64 mins |
| 4 | Richard Rufus | 42 | 46 | 2642 | 7 | 63 mins |
| 5 | Radostin Kishishev | 36 | 40 | 2204 | 5 | 61 mins |

## KEY PLAYERS - GOALKEEPERS

**1 Dean Kiely**

| | |
|---|---|
| **Goals Conceded in the League** The number of League goals conceded while he was on the pitch | 56 |
| **Goals Conceded in all competitions** The number of goals conceded while he was on the pitch in all competitions | 60 |
| **League minutes played** Number of minutes played in league matches | 3361 |
| **Clean Sheets** In games when he played at least 70 mins | 8 |
| **Goals to Shots Ratio** The average number of shots on target per each League goal conceded | 4.6 |
| **Defensive Rating** Ave number of mins between League goals conceded while on the pitch | 60 |

**2 Ben Roberts**

| | |
|---|---|
| **Goals Conceded in the League** The number of League goals conceded while he was on the pitch | 1 |
| **Goals Conceded in all competitions** The number of goals conceded while he was on the pitch in all competitions | 1 |
| **League minutes played** Number of minutes played in league matches | 60 |
| **Clean Sheets** In games when he played at least 70 mins | 0 |
| **Goals to Shots Ratio** The average number of shots on target per each League goal conceded | 7 |
| **Defensive Rating** Ave number of mins between League goals conceded while on the pitch | 60 |

# BIRMINGHAM CITY

**NICKNAME: THE BLUES**

KEY: Won / Drawn / Lost

| | | | | | | |
|---|---|---|---|---|---|---|
| 1 | lge | Arsenal | A | L | 0-2 | |
| 2 | lge | Blackburn | H | L | 0-1 | |
| 3 | lge | Everton | A | D | 1-1 | John 49 pen |
| 4 | lge | Leeds | H | W | 2-1 | Devlin 32; Johnson, D 58 |
| 5 | lge | Liverpool | A | D | 2-2 | Morrison 60,90 |
| 6 | lge | Aston Villa | H | W | 3-0 | Morrison 32; Enckelman 77 og; Horsfield 83 |
| 7 | lge | Middlesbrough | A | L | 0-1 | |
| 8 | lge | Newcastle | H | L | 0-2 | |
| 9 | wr2 | Leyton Orient | A | W | 3-2 | John 16,26,77 |
| 10 | lge | West Ham | A | W | 2-1 | John 3,43 |
| 11 | lge | West Brom | A | D | 1-1 | Moore 84 og |
| 12 | lge | Man City | H | L | 0-2 | |
| 13 | lge | Bolton | H | W | 3-1 | Purse 61; Savage 72; Horsfield 81 |
| 14 | wr3 | Preston | H | L | 0-2 | |
| 15 | lge | Chelsea | A | L | 0-3 | |
| 16 | lge | Fulham | H | D | 0-0 | |
| 17 | lge | Sunderland | A | W | 1-0 | Morrison 89 |
| 18 | lge | Tottenham | H | D | 1-1 | Kenna 68 |
| 19 | lge | Southampton | A | L | 0-2 | |
| 20 | lge | Fulham | A | W | 1-0 | Kirovski 7 |
| 21 | lge | Charlton | H | D | 1-1 | Devlin 67 pen |
| 22 | lge | Everton | H | D | 1-1 | Kirovski 45 |
| 23 | lge | Man Utd | A | L | 0-2 | |
| 24 | lge | Leeds | A | L | 0-2 | |
| 25 | facr3 | Fulham | A | L | 1-3 | John 90 |
| 26 | lge | Arsenal | H | L | 0-4 | |
| 27 | lge | Blackburn | A | D | 1-1 | John 83 |
| 28 | lge | Bolton | A | L | 2-4 | Savage 44; Morrison 60 |
| 29 | lge | Man Utd | H | L | 0-1 | |
| 30 | lge | Chelsea | H | L | 1-3 | Savage 87 pen |
| 31 | lge | Liverpool | H | W | 2-1 | Clemence 34; Morrison 68 |
| 32 | lge | Aston Villa | A | W | 2-0 | Lazaridis 74; Horsfield 76 |
| 33 | lge | Man City | A | L | 0-1 | |
| 34 | lge | West Brom | H | W | 1-0 | Horsfield 90 |
| 35 | lge | Tottenham | A | L | 1-2 | Devlin 77 pen |
| 36 | lge | Sunderland | H | W | 2-0 | Hughes 43; Dugarry 60 |
| 37 | lge | Charlton | A | W | 2-0 | Dugarry 20; Savage 55 pen |
| 38 | lge | Southampton | H | W | 3-2 | Dugarry 75,82; Hughes 79 |
| 39 | lge | Middlesbrough | H | W | 3-0 | Dugarry 18; Clemence 40; Lazaridis 80 |
| 40 | lge | Newcastle | A | L | 0-1 | |
| 41 | lge | West Ham | H | D | 2-2 | Horsfield 80; John 8 |

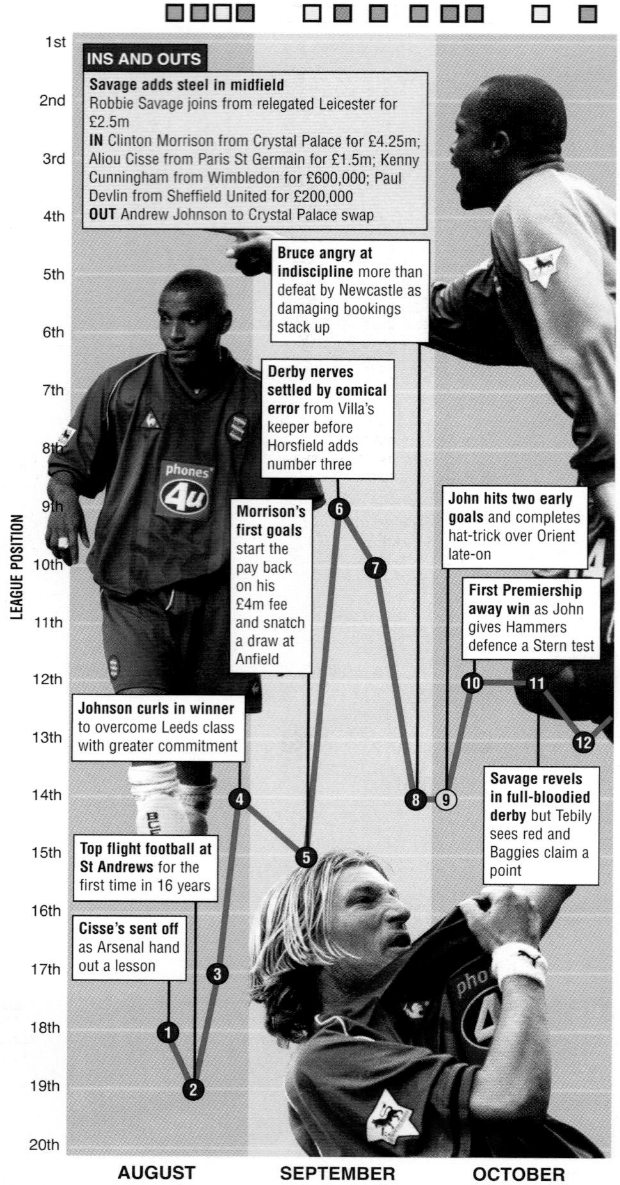

1st
2nd
3rd
4th
5th
6th
7th
8th
9th
10th
11th
12th
13th
14th
15th
16th
17th
18th
19th
20th
LEAGUE POSITION
INS AND OUTS
Savage adds steel in midfield
Robbie Savage joins from relegated Leicester for £2.5m
IN Clinton Morrison from Crystal Palace for £4.25m; Aliou Cisse from Paris St Germain for £1.5m; Kenny Cunningham from Wimbledon for £600,000; Paul Devlin from Sheffield United for £200,000
OUT Andrew Johnson to Crystal Palace swap
Bruce angry at indiscipline more than defeat by Newcastle as damaging bookings stack up
Derby nerves settled by comical error from Villa's keeper before Horsfield adds number three
Morrison's first goals start the pay back on his £4m fee and snatch a draw at Anfield
John hits two early goals and completes hat-trick over Orient late-on
First Premiership away win as John gives Hammers defence a Stern test
Johnson curls in winner to overcome Leeds class with greater commitment
Savage revels in full-blooded derby but Tebily sees red and Baggies claim a point
Top flight football at St Andrews for the first time in 16 years
Cisse's sent off as Arsenal hand out a lesson
AUGUST
SEPTEMBER
OCTOBER

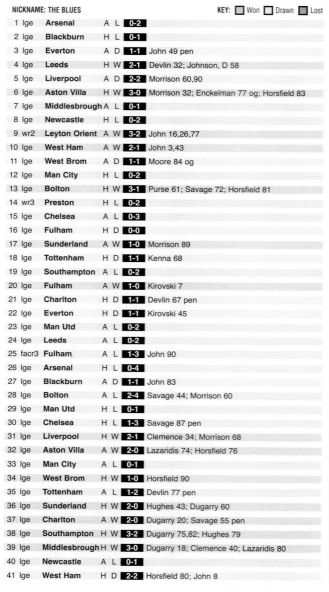

Home / Away / Neutral

## ATTENDANCES

HOME GROUND: ST ANDREWS CAPACITY: 29505 AVERAGE LEAGUE AT HOME: 28855

| | | | | | | | | | | | |
|---|---|---|---|---|---|---|---|---|---|---|---|
| 23 | Man Utd | 67640 | 33 | Man City | 34596 | 31 | Liverpool | 29449 | 16 | Fulham | 26164 |
| 40 | Newcastle | 52146 | 19 | Southampton | 31132 | 12 | Man City | 29316 | 37 | Charlton | 25732 |
| 5 | Liverpool | 43113 | 7 | Middlesboro | 29869 | 36 | Sunderland | 29132 | 28 | Bolton | 24288 |
| 32 | Aston Villa | 42602 | 18 | Tottenham | 29505 | 38 | Southampton | 29115 | 27 | Blackburn | 23331 |
| 24 | Leeds | 40034 | 22 | Everton | 29505 | 8 | Newcastle | 29072 | 20 | Fulham | 14962 |
| 17 | Sunderland | 38803 | 41 | West Ham | 29505 | 21 | Charlton | 28837 | 14 | Preston | 12241 |
| 1 | Arsenal | 38018 | 26 | Arsenal | 29505 | 39 | Middlesboro | 28821 | 25 | Fulham | 9203 |
| 3 | Everton | 37197 | 6 | Aston Villa | 29505 | 4 | Leeds | 27634 | 9 | Leyton Orient | 3615 |
| 35 | Tottenham | 36058 | 29 | Man Utd | 29479 | 2 | Blackburn | 27563 | | | |
| 15 | Chelsea | 35237 | 30 | Chelsea | 29475 | 13 | Bolton | 27224 | | | |
| 10 | West Ham | 35010 | 34 | West Brom | 29449 | 11 | West Brom | 27021 | | | |

## GOAL ATTEMPTS

**FOR** — Goal attempts recorded in League games

| | HOME | AWAY | TOTAL | AVE |
|---|---|---|---|---|
| shots on target | 94 | 70 | 164 | 4.3 |
| shots off target | 73 | 88 | 161 | 4.2 |
| TOTAL | 167 | 158 | 325 | 8.6 |

| | |
|---|---|
| **Ratio of goals to shots** Average number of shots on target per League goal scored | 4.0 |
| **Accuracy rating** Average percentage of total goal attempts which were on target | 50.5 |

**AGAINST** — Goal attempts recorded in League games

| | HOME | AWAY | TOTAL | AVE |
|---|---|---|---|---|
| shots on target | 85 | 129 | 214 | 5.6 |
| shots off target | 76 | 70 | 146 | 3.8 |
| TOTAL | 161 | 199 | 360 | 9.5 |

| | |
|---|---|
| **Ratio of goals to shots** Average number of shots on target per League goal scored | 4.4 |
| **Accuracy rating** Average percentage of total goal attempts which were on target | 59.4 |

# Dugarry lifts Midlands' top dogs

**Final Position: 13th**

KEY: ● League ● Champions Lge ● UEFA Cup ● FA Cup ○ League Cup ● Other

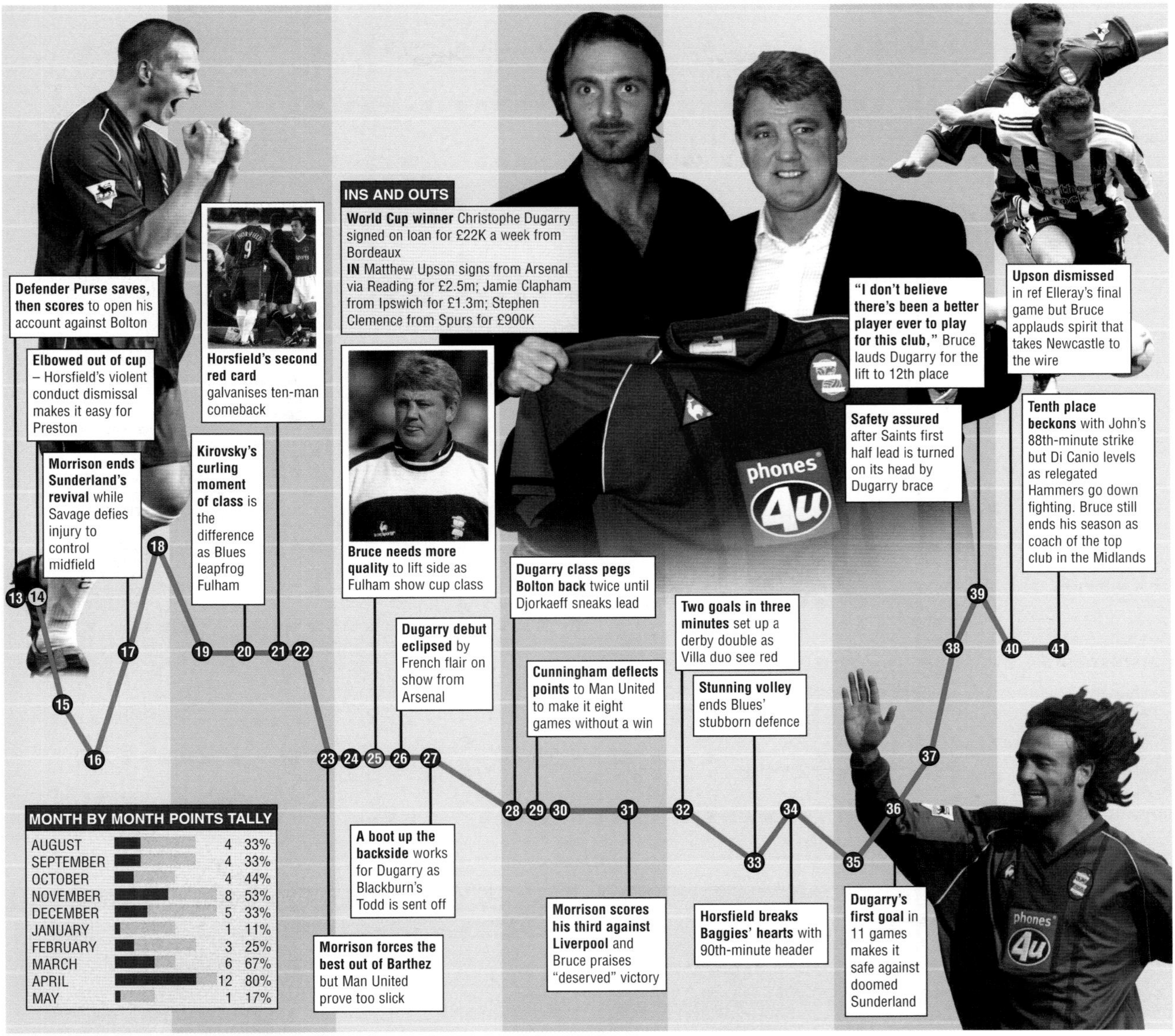

**Defender Purse saves, then scores** to open his account against Bolton
**Elbowed out of cup** – Horsfield's violent conduct dismissal makes it easy for Preston
**Morrison ends Sunderland's revival** while Savage defies injury to control midfield
**Kirovsky's curling moment of class** is the difference as Blues leapfrog Fulham
**Horsfield's second red card** galvanises ten-man comeback
INS AND OUTS
**World Cup winner** Christophe Dugarry signed on loan for £22K a week from Bordeaux
**IN** Matthew Upson signs from Arsenal via Reading for £2.5m; Jamie Clapham from Ipswich for £1.3m; Stephen Clemence from Spurs for £900K
**Bruce needs more quality** to lift side as Fulham show cup class
**Dugarry debut eclipsed** by French flair on show from Arsenal
**A boot up the backside** works for Dugarry as Blackburn's Todd is sent off
**Morrison forces the best out of Barthez** but Man United prove too slick
**Dugarry class pegs Bolton back** twice until Djorkaeff sneaks lead
**Cunningham deflects points** to Man United to make it eight games without a win
**Morrison scores his third against Liverpool** and Bruce praises "deserved" victory
**Two goals in three minutes** set up a derby double as Villa duo see red
**Stunning volley** ends Blues' stubborn defence
**Horsfield breaks Baggies' hearts** with 90th-minute header
**"I don't believe there's been a better player ever to play for this club,"** Bruce lauds Dugarry for the lift to 12th place
**Safety assured** after Saints first half lead is turned on its head by Dugarry brace
**Dugarry's first goal** in 11 games makes it safe against doomed Sunderland
**Upson dismissed** in ref Elleray's final game but Bruce applauds spirit that takes Newcastle to the wire
**Tenth place beckons** with John's 88th-minute strike but Di Canio levels as relegated Hammers go down fighting. Bruce still ends his season as coach of the top club in the Midlands


**MONTH BY MONTH POINTS TALLY**

| | | |
|---|---|---|
| AUGUST | 4 | 33% |
| SEPTEMBER | 4 | 33% |
| OCTOBER | 4 | 44% |
| NOVEMBER | 8 | 53% |
| DECEMBER | 5 | 33% |
| JANUARY | 1 | 11% |
| FEBRUARY | 3 | 25% |
| MARCH | 6 | 67% |
| APRIL | 12 | 80% |
| MAY | 1 | 17% |

NOVEMBER DECEMBER JANUARY FEBRUARY MARCH APRIL MAY

## DISCIPLINARY RECORDS

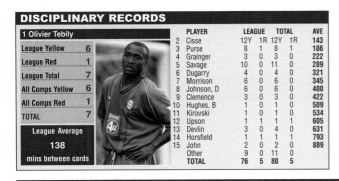

**1 Olivier Tebily**

| | |
|---|---|
| League Yellow | 6 |
| League Red | 1 |
| League Total | 7 |
| All Comps Yellow | 6 |
| All Comps Red | 1 |
| TOTAL | 7 |

League Average **138** mins between cards

| | PLAYER | LEAGUE | | TOTAL | | AVE |
|---|---|---|---|---|---|---|
| | | Y | R | Y | R | |
| 2 | Cisse | 12 | 1 | 12 | 1 | 143 |
| 3 | Purse | 8 | 1 | 8 | 1 | 186 |
| 4 | Grainger | 3 | 0 | 3 | 0 | 222 |
| 5 | Savage | 10 | 0 | 11 | 0 | 289 |
| 6 | Dugarry | 4 | 0 | 4 | 0 | 321 |
| 7 | Morrison | 6 | 0 | 6 | 0 | 345 |
| 8 | Johnson, D | 6 | 0 | 6 | 0 | 400 |
| 9 | Clemence | 3 | 0 | 3 | 0 | 422 |
| 10 | Hughes, B | 1 | 0 | 1 | 0 | 509 |
| 11 | Kirovski | 1 | 0 | 1 | 0 | 534 |
| 12 | Upson | 1 | 1 | 1 | 1 | 605 |
| 13 | Devlin | 3 | 0 | 4 | 0 | 631 |
| 14 | Horsfield | 1 | 1 | 1 | 1 | 793 |
| 15 | John | 2 | 0 | 2 | 0 | 889 |
| | Other | 9 | 0 | 11 | 0 | |
| | **TOTAL** | **76** | **5** | **80** | **5** | |

## GOALS

**1 Clinton Morrison**

| | |
|---|---|
| League | 6 |
| FA Cup | 0 |
| League Cup | 0 |
| Europe | 0 |
| Other | 0 |
| TOTAL | 6 |

League Average **346** mins between goals

| | PLAYER | LGE | FAC | LC | Euro | TOT | AVE |
|---|---|---|---|---|---|---|---|
| 2 | Dugarry | 5 | 0 | 0 | 0 | 5 | 257 |
| 3 | Horsfield | 5 | 0 | 0 | 0 | 5 | 317 |
| 4 | John | 5 | 1 | 3 | 0 | 9 | 356 |
| 5 | Savage | 4 | 0 | 0 | 0 | 4 | 725 |
| 6 | Devlin | 3 | 0 | 0 | 0 | 3 | 631 |
| 7 | Hughes | 2 | 0 | 0 | 0 | 2 | 220 |
| 8 | Lazaridis | 2 | 0 | 0 | 0 | 2 | 885 |
| 9 | Clemence | 2 | 0 | 0 | 0 | 2 | 633 |
| 10 | Kirovski | 2 | 0 | 0 | 0 | 2 | 267 |
| 11 | Purse | 1 | 0 | 0 | 0 | 1 | 1678 |
| 12 | Kenna | 1 | 0 | 0 | 0 | 1 | 3048 |
| 13 | Johnson, D | 1 | 0 | 0 | 0 | 1 | 2403 |
| | Other | 2 | 0 | 0 | 0 | 2 | |
| | **TOTAL** | **41** | **1** | **3** | **0** | **45** | |

## SQUAD APPEARANCES

| Match | 1 | 2 | 3 | 4 | 5 | 6 | 7 | 8 | 9 | 10 | 11 | 12 | 13 | 14 | 15 | 16 | 17 | 18 | 19 | 20 |
|---|---|---|---|---|---|---|---|---|---|---|---|---|---|---|---|---|---|---|---|---|
| Venue | A | H | A | H | A | H | A | H | A | A | A | H | H | H | A | H | A | H | A | A |
| Competition | L | L | L | L | L | L | L | L | W | L | L | L | L | W | L | L | L | L | L | L |
| Result | L | L | D | W | D | W | L | L | W | W | D | L | W | L | L | D | W | D | L | W |

| Match | 21 | 22 | 23 | 24 | 25 | 26 | 27 | 28 | 29 | 30 | 31 | 32 | 33 | 34 | 35 | 36 | 37 | 38 | 39 | 40 | 41 |
|---|---|---|---|---|---|---|---|---|---|---|---|---|---|---|---|---|---|---|---|---|---|
| Venue | H | H | A | A | A | H | A | A | H | H | H | A | A | H | A | H | A | H | H | A | H |
| Competition | L | L | L | L | F | L | L | L | L | L | L | L | L | L | L | L | L | L | L | L | L |
| Result | D | D | L | L | L | L | D | L | L | L | W | W | L | W | L | W | W | W | W | L | D |

**Goalkeepers**

Ian Bennett
Clint Davies
Andy Marriott
Nico Vaesen

**Defenders**

Aliou Cisse
Jamie Clapham
Ferdinand Coly
Kenny Cunningham
Nicky Eaden
Martin Grainger
Michael Johnson
Jeff Kenna
Darren Purse
Matthew Sadler
Olivier Tebily
Matthew Upson
Steve Vickers

**Midfielders**

Darren Carter
Stephen Clemence
Paul Devlin
Bryan Hughes
Jonathan Hutchinson
Damien Johnson
Jovan Kirovski
Stan Lazaridis
Darryl Powell
Robbie Savage
Piotr Swierczewski
Curtis Woodhouse

**Forwards**

Christophe Dugarry
Craig Fagan
Geoff Horsfield
Stern John
Tommy Mooney
Clinton Morrison

KEY: On all match · On bench · Subbed or sent off (Counting game) · Subbed or sent off (playing less than 70 minutes) · Subbed on from bench (Counting Game) · Subbed on (playing less than 70 minutes) · Subbed on and then subbed or sent off (Counting Game) · Subbed on and then subbed or sent off (playing less than 70 minutes) · Not in 16

## KEY PLAYERS - GOALSCORERS

**1 Christophe Dugarry**

| | |
|---|---|
| **Goals in the League** | 5 |
| **Goals in all competitions** | 5 |
| **Assists** League goals scored by team-mates where he delivered the final pass | 1 |
| **Contribution to Attacking Power** Average number of minutes between League team goals while on pitch | 67 |
| **Player Strike Rate** Average number of minutes between League goals scored by player | 257 |
| **Club Strike Rate** Average minutes between League goals scored by club | 83 |

| | PLAYER | GOALS LGE | GOALS ALL | ASSISTS | POWER | S RATE |
|---|---|---|---|---|---|---|
| 2 | Geoff Horsfield | 5 | 5 | 2 | 63 | 317 mins |
| 3 | Clinton Morrison | 6 | 6 | 2 | 98 | 346 mins |
| 4 | Stern John | 5 | 9 | 5 | 93 | 356 mins |
| 5 | Paul Devlin | 3 | 3 | 1 | 67 | 631 mins |

## KEY PLAYERS - MIDFIELDERS

**1 Paul Devlin**

| | |
|---|---|
| **Goals in the League** | 3 |
| **Goals in all competitions** | 3 |
| **Assists** League goals scored by team-mates where he delivered the final pass | 1 |
| **Defensive Rating** Average number of mins between League goals conceded while he was on the pitch | 76 |
| **Contribution to Attacking Power** Average number of minutes between League team goals while on pitch | 68 |
| **Scoring Difference** Defensive Rating minus Contribution to Attacking Power | 8 |

| | PLAYER | GOALS LGE | GOALS ALL | ASSISTS | DEF RATE | POWER | SC DIFF |
|---|---|---|---|---|---|---|---|
| 2 | Stan Lazaridis | 2 | 2 | 6 | 80 | 80 | 0 mins |
| 3 | Stephen Clemence | 2 | 2 | 2 | 67 | 74 | -7 mins |
| 4 | Robbie Savage | 4 | 4 | 5 | 69 | 78 | -9 mins |
| 5 | Damien Johnson | 1 | 1 | 0 | 73 | 86 | -13 mins |

## PLAYER APPEARANCES

| | AGE (on 01/07/03) | IN THE SQUAD | COUNTING GAMES | MINUTES ON PITCH | IN THE SQUAD | MINUTES ON PITCH | THIS SEASON | NATIONAL SIDE |
|---|---|---|---|---|---|---|---|---|
| **Goalkeepers** | | | | | | | | |
| Ian Bennett | 31 | 37 | 10 | 900 | 40 | 1080 | - | England |
| Clint Davies | 20 | 1 | 0 | 0 | 1 | 0 | - | England |
| Andy Marriott | 32 | 9 | 1 | 90 | 9 | 90 | - | Wales |
| Nico Vaesen | 33 | 29 | 27 | 2430 | 32 | 2520 | - | Belgium |
| **Defenders** | | | | | | | | |
| Aliou Cisse | 27 | 21 | 21 | 1864 | 21 | 1864 | 2 | Senegal (29) |
| Jamie Clapham | 27 | 16 | 16 | 1440 | 16 | 1440 | - | England |
| Ferdinand Coly | 29 | 2 | 0 | 67 | 3 | 157 | 2 | Senegal (29) |
| Kenny Cunningham | 32 | 31 | 30 | 2763 | 32 | 2853 | 8 | Rep of Ireland (15) |
| Nicky Eaden | 31 | 2 | 0 | 0 | 2 | 0 | - | England |
| Martin Grainger | 30 | 9 | 7 | 668 | 10 | 758 | - | England |
| Michael Johnson | 30 | 13 | 3 | 441 | 13 | 441 | - | Jamaica |
| Jeff Kenna | 32 | 37 | 31 | 3048 | 39 | 3228 | 2 | Rep of Ireland (15) |
| Darren Purse | 26 | 23 | 19 | 1678 | 24 | 1768 | - | England |
| Matthew Sadler | 18 | 2 | 1 | 157 | 4 | 292 | - | England |
| Olivier Tebily | 27 | 12 | 10 | 969 | 13 | 1059 | - | Ivory Coast |
| Matthew Upson | 24 | 14 | 13 | 1211 | 14 | 1211 | 4 | England (7) |
| Steve Vickers | 35 | 6 | 4 | 392 | 7 | 482 | - | England |
| **Midfielders** | | | | | | | | |
| Darren Carter | 19 | 14 | 2 | 389 | 16 | 452 | - | England |
| Stephen Clemence | 25 | 15 | 13 | 1266 | 15 | 1266 | - | England |
| Paul Devlin | 31 | 33 | 17 | 1893 | 35 | 1960 | 9 | Scotland (64) |
| Bryan Hughes | 27 | 25 | 10 | 949 | 27 | 1062 | - | England |
| Jon Hutchinson | 21 | 4 | 1 | 90 | 6 | 270 | - | England |
| Damien Johnson | 24 | 30 | 26 | 2403 | 32 | 2514 | 8 | N Ireland (111) |
| Jovan Kirovski | 27 | 22 | 4 | 534 | 25 | 675 | 3 | United States (10) |
| Stan Lazaridis | 30 | 33 | 15 | 1770 | 35 | 1950 | - | Australia |
| Darryl Powell | 26 | 14 | 2 | 355 | 17 | 625 | - | Jamaica |
| Robbie Savage | 28 | 33 | 32 | 2899 | 34 | 2989 | 4 | Wales (50) |
| Piotr Swierczewski | 31 | 3 | 0 | 39 | 3 | 39 | 3 | Poland (29) |
| Curtis Woodhouse | 23 | 5 | 0 | 47 | 7 | 137 | - | England |
| **Forwards** | | | | | | | | |
| Christophe Dugarry | 31 | 16 | 12 | 1284 | 16 | 1284 | - | France |
| Craig Fagan | 20 | 2 | 0 | 10 | 5 | 114 | - | England |
| Geoff Horsfield | 29 | 31 | 13 | 1587 | 33 | 1767 | - | England |
| Stern John | 26 | 33 | 17 | 1778 | 36 | 1899 | - | Trinidad & Tobago |
| Tommy Mooney | 31 | 3 | 0 | 6 | 3 | 6 | - | England |
| Clinton Morrison | 24 | 28 | 20 | 2073 | 31 | 2208 | 3 | Rep of Ireland (15) |

KEY: LEAGUE | ALL COMPS | CAPS (FIFA RANKING)

## TEAM OF THE SEASON

Vaesen
CG 27 DR 68
Cisse
CG 21 DR 78
Cunningham
CG 30 DR 79
Upson
CG 13 DR 76
Purse
CG 19 DR 76
Devlin
CG 17 SD +8
Savage
CG 32 SD -9
Clemence
CG 13 SD -7
Lazaridis
CG 15 SD 0
Horsfield
CG 13 AP 63
Dugarry
CG 12 SR 257

KEY: DR = Defensive Rate, SD = Scoring Difference AP = Attacking Power SR = Strike Rate, CG=Counting Games – League games playing at least 70 minutes

## TOP POINT EARNERS

**1 Matthew Upson**

| | |
|---|---|
| **Counting Games** League games when he played at least 70 minutes | 13 |
| **Average points** Average League points taken in Counting games | 1.69 |
| **Club Average points** Average points taken in League games | 1.26 |

| | PLAYER | GAMES | PTS |
|---|---|---|---|
| 2 | Kenny Cunningham | 30 | 1.50 |
| 3 | Geoff Horsfield | 13 | 1.46 |
| 4 | Stephen Clemence | 13 | 1.46 |
| 5 | Jamie Clapham | 16 | 1.44 |
| 6 | Paul Devlin | 17 | 1.41 |
| 7 | Christophe Dugarry | 12 | 1.33 |
| 8 | Stan Lazaridis | 15 | 1.33 |
| 9 | Robbie Savage | 32 | 1.31 |
| 10 | Damien Johnson | 26 | 1.31 |

## KEY PLAYERS - DEFENDERS

**1 Kenny Cunningham**

| | |
|---|---|
| **Goals Conceded** The number of League goals conceded while he was on the pitch | 35 |
| **Goals Conceded in all competitions** The number goals conceded while he was on the pitch in all competitions | 37 |
| **League minutes played** Number of minutes played in league matches | 2763 |
| **Clean Sheets** In games when he played at least70 mins | 9 |
| **Defensive Rating** Average number of mins between League goals conceded while he was on the pitch | 79 |
| **Club Defensive Rating** Average number of mins between League goals conceded by the club this season | 70 |

phones 4u

| | PLAYER | CON LGE | CON ALL | MINS | C SHEETS | DEF RATE |
|---|---|---|---|---|---|---|
| 2 | Aliou Cisse | 24 | 24 | 1864 | 4 | 78 mins |
| 3 | Darren Purse | 22 | 24 | 1678 | 4 | 76 mins |
| 4 | Matthew Upson | 16 | 16 | 1211 | 5 | 76 mins |
| 5 | Jeff Kenna | 44 | 49 | 3048 | 8 | 69 mins |

## KEY PLAYERS - GOALKEEPERS

**1 Nico Vaesen**

| | |
|---|---|
| **Goals Conceded in the League** The number of League goals conceded while he was on the pitch | 36 |
| **Goals Conceded in all competitions** The number of goals conceded while he was on the pitch in all competitions | 39 |
| **League minutes played** Number of minutes played in league matches | 2430 |
| **Clean Sheets** In games when he played at least 70 mins | 5 |
| **Goals to Shots Ratio** The average number of shots on target per each League goal conceded | 4 |
| **Defensive Rating** Ave number of mins between League goals conceded while on the pitch | 68 |

**2 Ian Bennett**

| | |
|---|---|
| **Goals Conceded in the League** The number of League goals conceded while he was on the pitch | 11 |
| **Goals Conceded in all competitions** The number of goals conceded while he was on the pitch in all competitions | 15 |
| **League minutes played** Number of minutes played in league matches | 900 |
| **Clean Sheets** In games when he played at least 70 mins | 4 |
| **Goals to Shots Ratio** The average number of shots on target per each League goal conceded | 5.8 |
| **Defensive Rating** Ave number of mins between League goals conceded while on the pitch | 82 |

# FULHAM

NICKNAME: THE COTTAGERS

KEY: Won / Drawn / Lost

| | | | | | | |
|---|---|---|---|---|---|---|
| 1 | lge | Bolton | H | W | 4-1 | Saha 11 pen; Legwinski 32,79; Marlet 37 pen |
| 2 | lge | Middlesbrough | A | D | 2-2 | Davis 89; Sava 90 |
| 3 | lge | West Brom | A | L | 0-1 | |
| 4 | lge | Tottenham | H | W | 3-2 | Inamoto 68; Malbranque 83 pen; Legwinski 90 |
| 5 | lge | Sunderland | A | W | 3-0 | Inamoto 33; Hayles 54; Marlet 78 |
| 6 | uc1rl1 | Hajduk Split | A | W | 1-0 | Malbranque 50 |
| 7 | lge | Chelsea | H | D | 0-0 | |
| 8 | lge | Everton | A | L | 0-2 | |
| 9 | uc1rl2 | Hajduk Split | H | D | 2-2 | Marlet 19; Malbranque 43 pen |
| 10 | lge | Charlton | H | W | 1-0 | Sava 36 |
| 11 | lge | Man Utd | H | D | 1-1 | Marlet 35 |
| 12 | lge | West Ham | H | L | 0-1 | |
| 13 | lge | Southampton | A | L | 2-4 | Clark 16; Malbranque 24 |
| 14 | uc2rl1 | Dinamo Zagreb | A | W | 3-0 | Boa Morte 36; Marlet 60; Hayles 78 |
| 15 | lge | Arsenal | H | L | 0-1 | |
| 16 | wr3 | Bury | H | W | 3-1 | Stolcers 40,53; Clark 73 |
| 17 | lge | Aston Villa | A | L | 1-3 | Boa Morte 51 |
| 18 | uc2rl2 | Dinamo Zagreb | H | W | 2-1 | Malbranque 80; Boa Morte 90 |
| 19 | lge | Birmingham | A | D | 0-0 | |
| 20 | lge | Liverpool | H | W | 3-2 | Sava 5,68; Davis 38 |
| 21 | uc3rl1 | Hertha Berlin | A | L | 1-2 | Marlet 53 |
| 22 | lge | Blackburn | A | L | 1-2 | Marlet 60 |
| 23 | wr4 | Wigan | A | L | 1-2 | Boa Morte 86 |
| 24 | lge | Leeds | H | W | 1-0 | Djetou 10 |
| 25 | uc3rl2 | Hertha Berlin | H | D | 0-0 | |
| 26 | lge | Birmingham | H | L | 0-1 | |
| 27 | lge | Newcastle | A | L | 0-2 | |
| 28 | lge | West Ham | A | D | 1-1 | Sava 49 |
| 29 | lge | Man City | H | L | 0-1 | |
| 30 | facr3 | Birmingham | H | W | 3-1 | Sava 11; Goldbaek 22; Saha 46 |
| 31 | lge | Bolton | A | D | 0-0 | |
| 32 | lge | Middlesbrough | H | W | 1-0 | Davis 39 |
| 33 | facr4 | Charlton | H | W | 3-0 | Malbranque 59,66 pen,87 pen |
| 34 | lge | Man City | A | L | 1-4 | Malbranque 2 |
| 35 | lge | Arsenal | A | L | 1-2 | Malbranque 29 |
| 36 | lge | Aston Villa | H | W | 2-1 | Malbranque 14 pen; Harley 36 |
| 37 | facr5 | Burnley | H | D | 1-1 | Malbranque 45 |
| 38 | lge | West Brom | H | W | 3-0 | Saha 72; Wome 74; Malbranque 77 pen |
| 39 | lge | Tottenham | A | D | 1-1 | King 15 og |
| 40 | facr5r | Burnley | A | L | 0-3 | |
| 41 | lge | Sunderland | H | W | 1-0 | Saha 85 |
| 42 | lge | Southampton | H | D | 2-2 | Saha 44; Svensson, M 52 og |
| 43 | lge | Man Utd | A | L | 0-3 | |
| 44 | lge | Blackburn | H | L | 0-4 | |
| 45 | lge | Liverpool | A | L | 0-2 | |
| 46 | lge | Newcastle | H | W | 2-1 | Legwinski 69; Clark 86 |
| 47 | lge | Leeds | A | L | 0-2 | |
| 48 | lge | Chelsea | A | D | 1-1 | Boa Morte 66 |
| 49 | lge | Everton | H | W | 2-0 | Stubbs 34 og; Wright 43 og |
| 50 | lge | Charlton | A | W | 1-0 | Saha 31 pen |

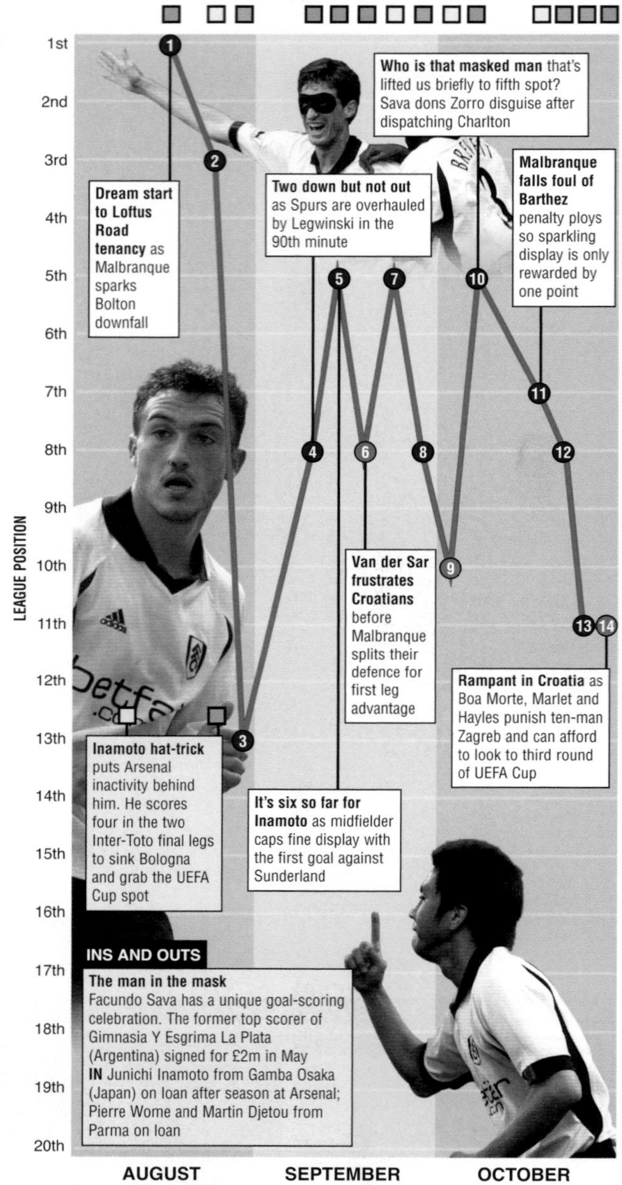
LEAGUE POSITION
1st
2nd
3rd
4th
5th
6th
7th
8th
9th
10th
11th
12th
13th
14th
15th
16th
17th
18th
19th
20th
AUGUST
SEPTEMBER
OCTOBER
Dream start to Loftus Road tenancy as Malbranque sparks Bolton downfall
Who is that masked man that's lifted us briefly to fifth spot? Sava dons Zorro disguise after dispatching Charlton
Two down but not out as Spurs are overhauled by Legwinski in the 90th minute
Malbranque falls foul of Barthez penalty ploys so sparkling display is only rewarded by one point
Van der Sar frustrates Croatians before Malbranque splits their defence for first leg advantage
Rampant in Croatia as Boa Morte, Marlet and Hayles punish ten-man Zagreb and can afford to look to third round of UEFA Cup
Inamoto hat-trick puts Arsenal inactivity behind him. He scores four in the two Inter-Toto final legs to sink Bologna and grab the UEFA Cup spot
It's six so far for Inamoto as midfielder caps fine display with the first goal against Sunderland

**INS AND OUTS**

**The man in the mask**
Facundo Sava has a unique goal-scoring celebration. The former top scorer of Gimnasia Y Esgrima La Plata (Argentina) signed for £2m in May
**IN** Junichi Inamoto from Gamba Osaka (Japan) on loan after season at Arsenal; Pierre Wome and Martin Djetou from Parma on loan

Home / Away / Neutral

## ATTENDANCES

HOME GROUND: LOFTUS ROAD CAPACITY: 18800 AVERAGE LEAGUE AT HOME: 16706

| | | | | | | | | | | | |
|---|---|---|---|---|---|---|---|---|---|---|---|
| 43 | Man Utd | 67706 | 2 | Middlesboro | 28588 | 42 | Southampton | 18031 | 10 | Charlton | 14720 |
| 27 | Newcastle | 51576 | 13 | Southampton | 26188 | 29 | Man City | 17937 | 21 | Hertha Berlin | 14477 |
| 45 | Liverpool | 42120 | 19 | Birmingham | 26164 | 46 | Newcastle | 17900 | 32 | Middlesboro | 14253 |
| 48 | Chelsea | 40792 | 50 | Charlton | 26108 | 24 | Leeds | 17494 | 44 | Blackburn | 14017 |
| 35 | Arsenal | 38050 | 3 | West Brom | 25462 | 36 | Aston Villa | 17092 | 37 | Burnley | 13062 |
| 47 | Leeds | 37220 | 31 | Bolton | 25156 | 4 | Tottenham | 16757 | 33 | Charlton | 12203 |
| 5 | Sunderland | 35432 | 6 | Hajduk Split | 25000 | 7 | Chelsea | 16504 | 40 | Burnley | 11635 |
| 28 | West Ham | 35025 | 22 | Blackburn | 21096 | 1 | Bolton | 16388 | 30 | Birmingham | 9203 |
| 39 | Tottenham | 34704 | 15 | Arsenal | 18800 | 41 | Sunderland | 16286 | 18 | Dinamo Zagreb | 7700 |
| 8 | Everton | 34371 | 9 | Hajduk Split | 18500 | 12 | West Ham | 15858 | 23 | Wigan | 7615 |
| 34 | Man City | 33260 | 49 | Everton | 18385 | 38 | West Brom | 15799 | 16 | Bury | 6700 |
| 14 | D Zagreb | 30000 | 20 | Liverpool | 18144 | 25 | Hertha Berlin | 15161 | | | |
| 17 | Aston Villa | 29563 | 11 | Man Utd | 18103 | 26 | Birmingham | 14962 | | | |

## GOAL ATTEMPTS

**FOR**
Goal attempts recorded in League games

| | HOME | AWAY | TOTAL | AVE |
|---|---|---|---|---|
| shots on target | 99 | 81 | 180 | 4.7 |
| shots off target | 101 | 85 | 186 | 4.9 |
| TOTAL | 200 | 166 | 366 | 9.6 |

| | |
|---|---|
| **Ratio of goals to shots** Average number of shots on target per League goal scored | 4.4 |
| **Accuracy rating** Average percentage of total goal attempts which were on target | 49.2 |

**AGAINST**
Goal attempts recorded in League games

| | HOME | AWAY | TOTAL | AVE |
|---|---|---|---|---|
| shots on target | 87 | 129 | 216 | 5.7 |
| shots off target | 77 | 81 | 158 | 4.2 |
| TOTAL | 164 | 210 | 374 | 9.8 |

| | |
|---|---|
| **Ratio of goals to shots** Average number of shots on target per League goal scored | 4.3 |
| **Accuracy rating** Average percentage of total goal attempts which were on target | 57.8 |

# Home loan takes its toll on Tigana

Final Position: **14th**

KEY: ● League ● Champions Lge ● UEFA Cup ● FA Cup ○ League Cup ● Other

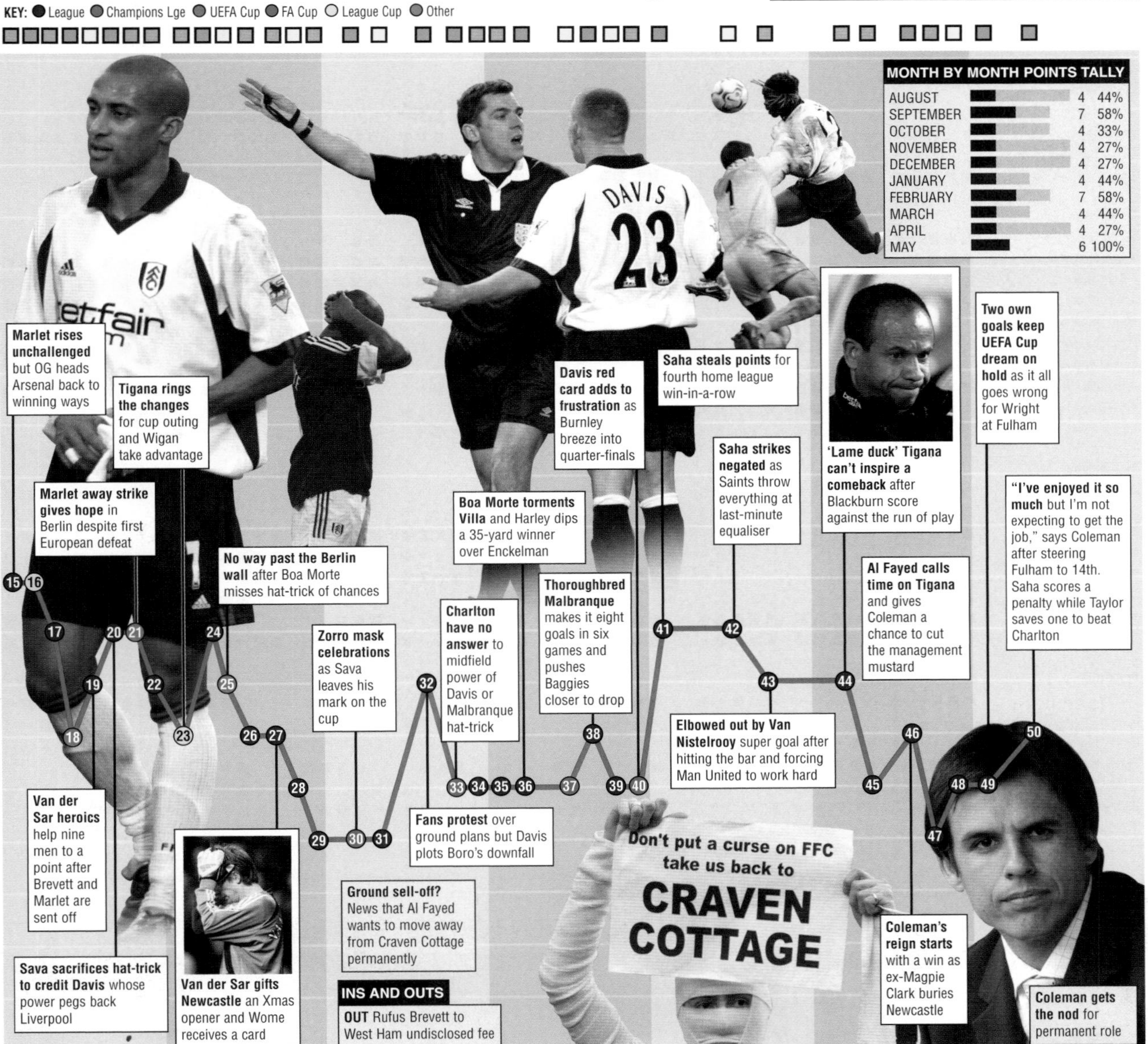
Marlet rises unchallenged but OG heads Arsenal back to winning ways
Tigana rings the changes for cup outing and Wigan take advantage
Marlet away strike gives hope in Berlin despite first European defeat
No way past the Berlin wall after Boa Morte misses hat-trick of chances
Van der Sar heroics help nine men to a point after Brevett and Marlet are sent off
Sava sacrifices hat-trick to credit Davis whose power pegs back Liverpool
Van der Sar gifts Newcastle an Xmas opener and Wome receives a card
Zorro mask celebrations as Sava leaves his mark on the cup
Ground sell-off? News that Al Fayed wants to move away from Craven Cottage permanently
INS AND OUTS
OUT Rufus Brevett to West Ham undisclosed fee
Charlton have no answer to midfield power of Davis or Malbranque hat-trick
Fans protest over ground plans but Davis plots Boro's downfall
Boa Morte torments Villa and Harley dips a 35-yard winner over Enckelman
Davis red card adds to frustration as Burnley breeze into quarter-finals
Thoroughbred Malbranque makes it eight goals in six games and pushes Baggies closer to drop
Saha steals points for fourth home league win-in-a-row
DAVIS
23
Saha strikes negated as Saints throw everything at last-minute equaliser
Elbowed out by Van Nistelrooy super goal after hitting the bar and forcing Man United to work hard
Don't put a curse on FFC take us back to
CRAVEN COTTAGE
'Lame duck' Tigana can't inspire a comeback after Blackburn score against the run of play
Al Fayed calls time on Tigana and gives Coleman a chance to cut the management mustard
Coleman's reign starts with a win as ex-Magpie Clark buries Newcastle
Two own goals keep UEFA Cup dream on hold as it all goes wrong for Wright at Fulham
"I've enjoyed it so much but I'm not expecting to get the job," says Coleman after steering Fulham to 14th. Saha scores a penalty while Taylor saves one to beat Charlton
Coleman gets the nod for permanent role
NOVEMBER
DECEMBER
JANUARY
FEBRUARY
MARCH
APRIL
MAY

**MONTH BY MONTH POINTS TALLY**

| | | |
|---|---|---|
| AUGUST | 4 | 44% |
| SEPTEMBER | 7 | 58% |
| OCTOBER | 4 | 33% |
| NOVEMBER | 4 | 27% |
| DECEMBER | 4 | 27% |
| JANUARY | 4 | 44% |
| FEBRUARY | 7 | 58% |
| MARCH | 4 | 44% |
| APRIL | 4 | 27% |
| MAY | 6 | 100% |

## DISCIPLINARY RECORDS

**1 Pierre Nled Wome**

| | |
|---|---|
| League Yellow | 5 |
| League Red | 1 |
| League Total | 6 |
| All Comps Yellow | 5 |
| All Comps Red | 1 |
| TOTAL | 6 |

League Average
172
mins between cards

| | PLAYER | LEAGUE | | TOTAL | | AVE |
|---|---|---|---|---|---|---|
| | | 3Y | 0R | 3Y | 0R | |
| 2 | Hayles | | | | | 186 |
| 3 | Boa Morte | 9 | 0 | 9 | 0 | 242 |
| 4 | Clark | 3 | 0 | 3 | 0 | 258 |
| 5 | Brevett | 5 | 1 | 6 | 1 | 291 |
| 6 | Melville | 6 | 0 | 8 | 0 | 374 |
| 7 | Finnan | 6 | 0 | 7 | 0 | 480 |
| 8 | Harley | 2 | 0 | 2 | 0 | 495 |
| 9 | Goma | 3 | 1 | 3 | 1 | 620 |
| 10 | Legwinski | 4 | 0 | 5 | 0 | 722 |
| 11 | Marlet | 2 | 1 | 2 | 1 | 781 |
| 12 | Davis | 3 | 0 | 3 | 1 | 828 |
| 13 | Djetou | 2 | 0 | 3 | 0 | 892 |
| 14 | Ouaddou | 1 | 0 | 2 | 0 | 932 |
| 15 | Malbranque | 3 | 0 | 3 | 0 | 1015 |
| | Other | 2 | 2 | 4 | 2 | |
| | **TOTAL** | **59** | **6** | **68** | **7** | |

## GOALS

**1 Steed Malbranque**

| | |
|---|---|
| League | 6 |
| FA Cup | 4 |
| League Cup | 0 |
| Europe | 3 |
| Other | 0 |
| TOTAL | 13 |

League Average
508
mins between goals

| | PLAYER | LGE | FAC | LC | Euro | TOT | AVE |
|---|---|---|---|---|---|---|---|
| 2 | Saha | **5** | 1 | 0 | 0 | 6 | 231 |
| 3 | Sava | **5** | 1 | 0 | 0 | 6 | 218 |
| 4 | Marlet | **4** | 0 | 0 | 3 | 7 | 586 |
| 5 | Legwinski | **4** | 0 | 0 | 0 | 4 | 722 |
| 6 | Davis | **3** | 0 | 0 | 0 | 3 | 829 |
| 7 | Inamoto | **2** | 0 | 0 | 0 | 2 | 426 |
| 8 | Clark | **2** | 0 | 1 | 0 | 3 | 388 |
| 9 | Boa Morte | **2** | 0 | 1 | 2 | 5 | 1091 |
| 10 | Wome | **1** | 0 | 0 | 0 | 1 | 1035 |
| 11 | Harley | **1** | 0 | 0 | 0 | 1 | 990 |
| 12 | Hayles | **1** | 0 | 0 | 1 | 2 | 558 |
| 13 | Djetou | **1** | 0 | 0 | 0 | 1 | 1785 |
| 14 | Stolcers | **0** | 0 | 2 | 0 | 2 | |
| 15 | Goldbaek | **0** | 1 | 0 | 0 | 1 | |
| | Other | 4 | 0 | 0 | 0 | 4 | |
| | **TOTAL** | **41** | **7** | **4** | **9** | **61** | |

## SQUAD APPEARANCES

| Match | Venue | Competition | Result |
|---|---|---|---|
| 1 | H | L | W |
| 2 | A | L | D |
| 3 | A | L | L |
| 4 | H | L | W |
| 5 | A | L | W |
| 6 | A | E | W |
| 7 | H | L | D |
| 8 | A | L | L |
| 9 | H | E | D |
| 10 | H | L | W |
| 11 | H | L | D |
| 12 | H | L | L |
| 13 | A | L | L |
| 14 | A | E | W |
| 15 | H | L | L |
| 16 | H | W | W |
| 17 | A | L | L |
| 18 | H | E | W |
| 19 | A | L | D |
| 20 | H | L | W |
| 21 | A | E | L |
| 22 | A | L | L |
| 23 | A | W | L |
| 24 | H | L | W |
| 25 | H | E | D |
| 26 | H | L | L |
| 27 | A | L | L |
| 28 | A | L | D |
| 29 | H | L | L |
| 30 | H | F | W |
| 31 | A | L | D |
| 32 | H | L | W |
| 33 | H | F | W |
| 34 | A | L | L |
| 35 | A | L | L |
| 36 | H | L | W |
| 37 | H | F | D |
| 38 | H | L | W |
| 39 | A | L | D |
| 40 | A | F | L |
| 41 | H | L | W |
| 42 | H | L | D |
| 43 | A | L | L |
| 44 | H | L | L |
| 45 | A | L | L |
| 46 | H | L | W |
| 47 | A | L | L |
| 48 | A | L | D |
| 49 | H | L | W |
| 50 | A | L | W |

**Goalkeepers**
Martin Herrera
Maik Taylor
Glyn Thompson
Edwin Van der Sar

**Defenders**
Rufus Brevett
Steve Finnan
Alain Goma
Jon Harley
Mark Hudson
Zatyiah Knight
Dean Leacock
Andy Melville
Abdeslam Ouaddou
Pierre Nlend Wome

**Midfielders**
Lee Clark
John Collins
Sean Davis
Martin Djetou
Bjarne Goldbaek
Junichi Inamoto
Sylvain Legwinski
Steed Malbranque

**Forwards**
Luis Boa Morte
Elvis Hammond
Barry Hayles
Steve Marlet
Louis Saha
Facundo Sava
Andrejs Stolcers
Callum Willock

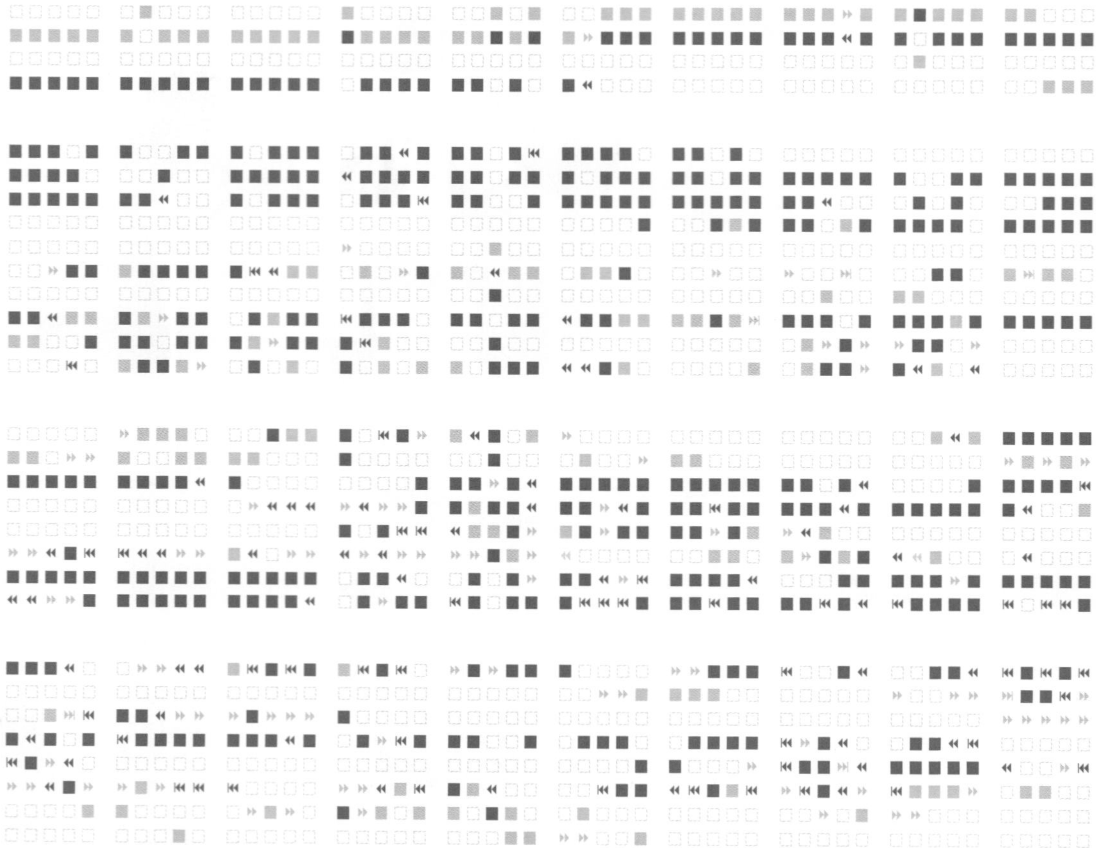

KEY: On all match · On bench · Subbed or sent off (Counting game) · Subbed or sent off (playing less than 70 minutes) · Subbed on from bench (Counting Game) · Subbed on (playing less than 70 minutes) · Subbed on and then subbed or sent off (Counting Game) · Subbed on and then subbed or sent off (playing less than 70 minutes) · Not in 16

## KEY PLAYERS - GOALSCORERS

**1 Louis Saha**

| | |
|---|---|
| Goals in the League | 5 |
| Goals in all competitions | 6 |
| Assists<br>League goals scored by team-mates where he delivered the final pass | 2 |
| Contribution to Attacking Power<br>Average number of minutes between League team goals while on pitch | 82 |
| **Player Strike Rate**<br>**Average number of minutes between League goals scored by player** | **231** |
| Club Strike Rate<br>Average minutes between League goals scored by club | 83 |

| | PLAYER | GOALS LGE | GOALS ALL | ASSISTS | POWER | S RATE |
|---|---|---|---|---|---|---|
| 2 | Steed Malbranque | 6 | 13 | 5 | 84 | **508 mins** |
| 3 | Steve Marlet | 4 | 7 | 1 | 83 | **586 mins** |
| 4 | Sylvain Legwinski | 4 | 4 | 2 | 90 | **722 mins** |
| 5 | Sean Davis | 3 | 3 | 1 | 77 | **829 mins** |

## KEY PLAYERS - MIDFIELDERS

**1 Sean Davis**

| | |
|---|---|
| Goals in the League | 3 |
| Goals in all competitions | 3 |
| Assists<br>League goals scored by team-mates where he delivered the final pass | 1 |
| Defensive Rating<br>Average number of mins between League goals conceded while he was on the pitch | 78 |
| Contribution to Attacking Power<br>Average number of minutes between League team goals while on pitch | 78 |
| **Scoring Difference**<br>**Defensive Rating minus Contribution to Attacking Power** | **0** |

| | PLAYER | GOALS LGE | GOALS ALL | ASSISTS | DEF RATE | POWER | SC DIFF |
|---|---|---|---|---|---|---|---|
| 2 | Steed Malbranque | 6 | 13 | 5 | 69 | 85 | **-16 mins** |
| 3 | Sylvain Legwinski | 4 | 4 | 2 | 70 | 90 | **-20 mins** |
| 4 | Martin Djetou | 1 | 1 | 1 | 58 | 94 | **-36 mins** |

## PLAYER APPEARANCES

| | AGE (on 01/07/03) | IN THE SQUAD | COUNTING GAMES | MINUTES ON PITCH | IN THE SQUAD | MINUTES ON PITCH | THIS SEASON | NATIONAL SIDE |
|---|---|---|---|---|---|---|---|---|
| **Goalkeepers** | | | | | | | | |
| Martin Herrera | 32 | 17 | 1 | 142 | 24 | 142 | - | Argentina |
| Maik Taylor | 31 | 36 | 17 | 1597 | 48 | 2227 | 8 | N Ireland (111) |
| Glyn Thompson | 22 | 1 | 0 | 0 | 1 | 0 | - | England |
| Edwin Van der Sar | 32 | 22 | 18 | 1681 | 27 | 2131 | 6 | Holland (6) |
| **Defenders** | | | | | | | | |
| Rufus Brevett | 33 | 20 | 19 | 1746 | 26 | 2266 | - | England |
| Steve Finnan | 27 | 32 | 32 | 2880 | 40 | 3573 | - | England |
| Alain Goma | 30 | 29 | 27 | 2481 | 37 | 3201 | - | France |
| Jon Harley | 23 | 13 | 11 | 990 | 17 | 1350 | - | England |
| Mark Hudson | 21 | 0 | 0 | 0 | 2 | 12 | - | England |
| Zatyiah Knight | 23 | 25 | 13 | 1279 | 32 | 1421 | - | England |
| Dean Leacock | 19 | 3 | 0 | 0 | 4 | 90 | - | England |
| Andy Melville | 34 | 35 | 23 | 2249 | 46 | 3137 | 7 | Wales (50) |
| Abdeslam Ouaddou | 24 | 16 | 9 | 932 | 24 | 1416 | - | Morocco |
| Pierre Nlend Wome | 24 | 18 | 9 | 1035 | 28 | 1339 | 2 | Cameroon (18) |
| **Midfielders** | | | | | | | | |
| Lee Clark | 30 | 16 | 7 | 775 | 24 | 1038 | - | England |
| John Collins | 35 | 15 | 0 | 27 | 20 | 223 | - | Scotland |
| Sean Davis | 23 | 28 | 27 | 2486 | 37 | 3180 | 1 | England (7) |
| Martin Djetou | 28 | 27 | 16 | 1785 | 37 | 2467 | - | France |
| Bjarne Goldbaek | 34 | 14 | 8 | 733 | 22 | 1117 | - | Denmark |
| Junichi Inamoto | 23 | 25 | 3 | 852 | 36 | 1334 | 4 | Japan (23) |
| Sylvain Legwinski | 29 | 35 | 30 | 2889 | 43 | 3548 | - | France |
| Steed Malbranque | 23 | 37 | 32 | 3047 | 47 | 3834 | - | Belgium |
| **Forwards** | | | | | | | | |
| Luis Boa Morte | 25 | 30 | 22 | 2181 | 39 | 2713 | 3 | Portugal (14) |
| Elvis Hammond | 22 | 12 | 3 | 409 | 14 | 409 | - | Ghana |
| Barry Hayles | 31 | 15 | 4 | 558 | 19 | 780 | - | Jamaica |
| Steve Marlet | 29 | 28 | 25 | 2343 | 36 | 2927 | 8 | France (2) |
| Louis Saha | 24 | 17 | 12 | 1155 | 20 | 1391 | - | France |
| Facundo Sava | 28 | 29 | 9 | 1091 | 39 | 1716 | - | Argentina |
| Andrejs Stolcers | 28 | 10 | 0 | 61 | 17 | 260 | - | Latvia |
| Callum Willock | 21 | 3 | 0 | 54 | 6 | 54 | - | England |

KEY: LEAGUE ALL COMPS CAPS (FIFA RANKING)

## TEAM OF THE SEASON

Van der Sar
CG 18 DR 70
Finnan
CG 32 DR 67
Goma
CG 27 DR 67
Melville
CG 23 DR 73
Brevett
CG 19 DR 67
Djetou
CG 16 SD -36
Davis
CG 27 SD 0
Malbranque
CG 32 SD -16
Legwinski
CG 30 SD -20
Marlet
CG 25 AP 83
Saha
CG 12 SR 231


**KEY:** DR = Defensive Rate, SD = Scoring Difference AP = Attacking Power SR = Strike Rate, CG=Counting Games – League games playing at least 70 minutes

## TOP POINT EARNERS

**1 Louis Saha**

| | |
|---|---|
| **Counting Games** League games when he played at least 70 minutes | 12 |
| **Average points** Average League points taken in Counting games | 1.58 |
| **Club Average points** Average points taken in League games | 1.26 |

| | PLAYER | GAMES | PTS |
|---|---|---|---|
| 2 | Martin Djetou | 16 | 1.44 |
| 3 | Maik Taylor, M | 17 | 1.41 |
| 4 | Andy Melville | 23 | 1.39 |
| 5 | Sean Davis | 27 | 1.37 |
| 6 | Steed Malbranque | 32 | 1.28 |
| 7 | Steve Finnan | 32 | 1.25 |
| 8 | Sylvain Legwinski | 30 | 1.23 |
| 9 | Edwin Van der Sar | 18 | 1.22 |
| 10 | Alain Goma | 27 | 1.19 |

## KEY PLAYERS - DEFENDERS

**1 Andy Melville**

| | |
|---|---|
| **Goals Conceded** The number of League goals conceded while he was on the pitch | 31 |
| **Goals Conceded in all competitions** The number goals conceded while he was on the pitch in all competitions | 40 |
| **League minutes played** Number of minutes played in league matches | 2249 |
| **Clean Sheets** In games when he played at least70 mins | 7 |
| **Defensive Rating** Average number of mins between League goals conceded while he was on the pitch | 73 |
| **Club Defensive Rating** Average number of mins between League goals conceded by the club this season | 68 |

betfair.com


| | PLAYER | CON LGE | CON ALL | MINS | C SHEETS | DEF RATE |
|---|---|---|---|---|---|---|
| 2 | Alain Goma | 37 | 42 | 2481 | 7 | 67 mins |
| 3 | Steve Finnan | 43 | 51 | 2880 | 8 | 67 mins |
| 4 | Rufus Brevett | 26 | 31 | 1746 | 5 | 67 mins |
| 5 | Zatyiah Knight | 21 | 25 | 1279 | 3 | 61 mins |

## KEY PLAYERS - GOALKEEPERS

**1 Edwin Van der Sar**

| | |
|---|---|
| **Goals Conceded in the League** The number of League goals conceded while he was on the pitch | 24 |
| **Goals Conceded in all competitions** The number of goals conceded while he was on the pitch in all competitions | 29 |
| **League minutes played** Number of minutes played in league matches | 1681 |
| **Clean Sheets** In games when he played at least 70 mins | 5 |
| **Goals to Shots Ratio** The average number of shots on target per each League goal conceded | 3.5 |
| **Defensive Rating** Ave number of mins between League goals conceded while on the pitch | 70 |

**2 Maik Taylor**

| | |
|---|---|
| **Goals Conceded in the League** The number of League goals conceded while he was on the pitch | 23 |
| **Goals Conceded in all competitions** The number of goals conceded while he was on the pitch in all competitions | 31 |
| **League minutes played** Number of minutes played in league matches | 1597 |
| **Clean Sheets** In games when he played at least 70 mins | 6 |
| **Goals to Shots Ratio** The average number of shots on target per each League goal conceded | 4.4 |
| **Defensive Rating** Ave number of mins between League goals conceded while on the pitch | 69 |

# LEEDS UNITED

**NICKNAME:** UNITED

KEY: Won / Drawn / Lost

| | | | | | | |
|---|---|---|---|---|---|---|
| 1 | lge | **Man City** | H | W | 3-0 | Barmby 15; Viduka 45; Keane 80 |
| 2 | lge | **West Brom** | A | W | 3-1 | Kewell 39; Bowyer 53; Viduka 70 |
| 3 | lge | **Sunderland** | H | L | 0-1 | |
| 4 | lge | **Birmingham** | A | L | 1-2 | Bowyer 50 |
| 5 | lge | **Newcastle** | A | W | 2-0 | Viduka 5; Smith 86 |
| 6 | lge | **Man Utd** | H | W | 1-0 | Kewell 66 |
| 7 | uc1rl1 | **Zaporizhya** | H | W | 1-0 | Smith 79 |
| 8 | lge | **Blackburn** | A | L | 0-1 | |
| 9 | lge | **Arsenal** | H | L | 1-4 | Kewell 85 |
| 10 | uc1rl2 | **Zaporizhya** | A | D | 1-1 | Barmby 77 |
| 11 | lge | **Aston Villa** | A | D | 0-0 | |
| 12 | lge | **Liverpool** | H | L | 0-1 | |
| 13 | lge | **Middlesbrough** | A | D | 2-2 | Viduka 9 pen; Bowyer 56 |
| 14 | uc2rl1 | **Hapoel Tel-Aviv** | H | W | 1-0 | Kewell 81 |
| 15 | lge | **Everton** | H | L | 0-1 | |
| 16 | wr3 | **Sheff Utd** | A | L | 1-2 | Yates 24 og |
| 17 | lge | **West Ham** | A | W | 4-3 | Barmby 11; Kewell 28,41; Viduka 45 |
| 18 | uc2rl2 | **Hapoel Tel-Aviv** | A | W | 4-1 | Smith 30,54,62,83 |
| 19 | lge | **Bolton** | H | L | 2-4 | Smith 4; Kewell 84 |
| 20 | lge | **Tottenham** | A | L | 0-2 | |
| 21 | uc3rl1 | **Malaga** | A | D | 0-0 | |
| 22 | lge | **Charlton** | H | L | 1-2 | Kewell 42 |
| 23 | lge | **Fulham** | A | L | 0-1 | |
| 24 | uc3rl2 | **Malaga** | H | L | 1-2 | Bakke 22 |
| 25 | lge | **Bolton** | A | W | 3-0 | Mills 12; Fowler 16; Wilcox 75 |
| 26 | lge | **Southampton** | H | D | 1-1 | Kewell 74 |
| 27 | lge | **Sunderland** | A | W | 2-1 | Milner 51; Fowler 80 pen |
| 28 | lge | **Chelsea** | H | W | 2-0 | Woodgate 30; Milner 45 |
| 29 | lge | **Birmingham** | H | W | 2-0 | Bakke 6; Viduka 67 |
| 30 | facr3 | **Scunthorpe** | A | W | 2-0 | Viduka 32 pen; Bakke 68 |
| 31 | lge | **Man City** | A | L | 1-2 | Kewell 90 |
| 32 | lge | **West Brom** | H | D | 0-0 | |
| 33 | facr4 | **Gillingham** | A | D | 1-1 | Smith 49 |
| 34 | lge | **Chelsea** | A | L | 2-3 | Kewell 18; Lucic 66 |
| 35 | lge | **Everton** | A | L | 0-2 | |
| 36 | facr4r | **Gillingham** | H | W | 2-1 | Viduka 11; Bakke 58 |
| 37 | lge | **West Ham** | H | W | 1-0 | Johnson, Seth 20 |
| 38 | facr5 | **Crystal Palace** | A | W | 2-1 | Kelly 32; Kewell 73 |
| 39 | lge | **Newcastle** | H | L | 0-3 | |
| 40 | lge | **Man Utd** | A | L | 1-2 | Viduka 64 |
| 41 | facqf | **Sheff Utd** | A | L | 0-1 | |
| 42 | lge | **Middlesbrough** | H | L | 2-3 | Viduka 24,76 |
| 43 | lge | **Liverpool** | A | L | 1-3 | Viduka 44 |
| 44 | lge | **Charlton** | A | W | 6-1 | Kewell 12,76; Harte 34 pen; Viduka 42,53,56 pen |
| 45 | lge | **Tottenham** | H | D | 2-2 | Viduka 31,76 pen |
| 46 | lge | **Southampton** | A | L | 2-3 | Kewell 80; Barmby 90 |
| 47 | lge | **Fulham** | H | W | 2-0 | Viduka 4,49 |
| 48 | lge | **Blackburn** | H | L | 2-3 | Viduka 21; Smith 90 |
| 49 | lge | **Arsenal** | A | W | 3-2 | Kewell 5; Harte 49; Viduka 88 |
| 50 | lge | **Aston Villa** | H | W | 3-1 | Harte 8; Barmby 81; Viduka 90 |

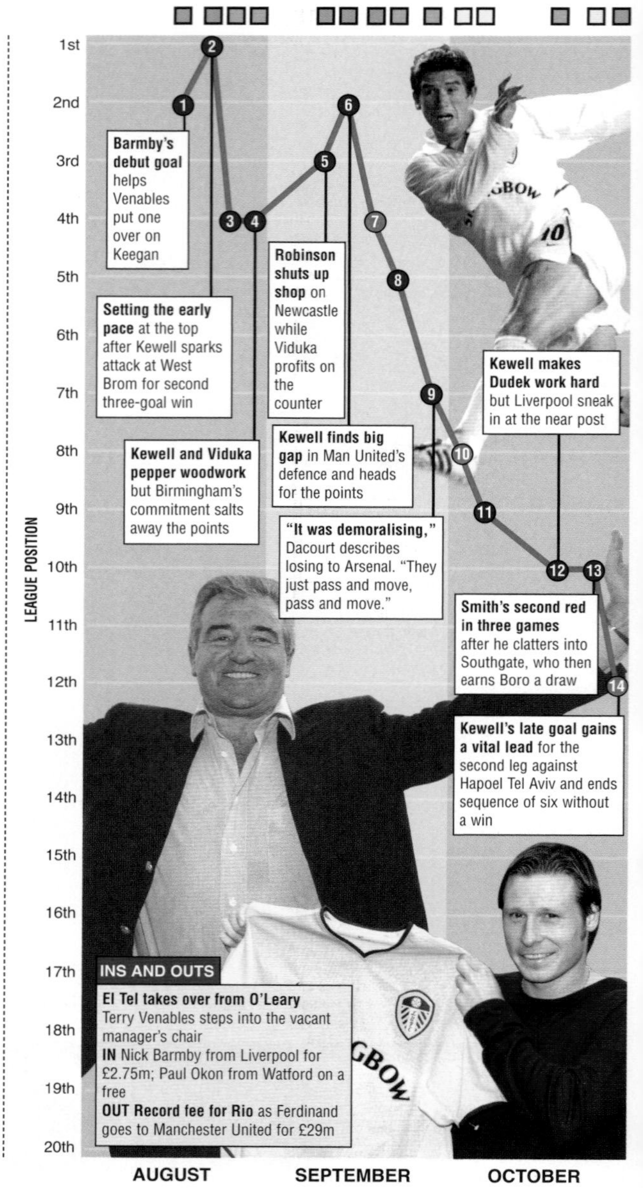

1st
2nd
3rd
4th
5th
6th
7th
8th
9th
10th
11th
12th
13th
14th
15th
16th
17th
18th
19th
20th
LEAGUE POSITION
**Barmby's debut goal** helps Venables put one over on Keegan
**Setting the early pace** at the top after Kewell sparks attack at West Brom for second three-goal win
**Kewell and Viduka pepper woodwork** but Birmingham's commitment salts away the points
**Robinson shuts up shop** on Newcastle while Viduka profits on the counter
**Kewell finds big gap** in Man United's defence and heads for the points
**"It was demoralising,"** Dacourt describes losing to Arsenal. "They just pass and move, pass and move."
**Kewell makes Dudek work hard** but Liverpool sneak in at the near post
**Smith's second red in three games** after he clatters into Southgate, who then earns Boro a draw
**Kewell's late goal gains a vital lead** for the second leg against Hapoel Tel Aviv and ends sequence of six without a win
INS AND OUTS
**El Tel takes over from O'Leary** Terry Venables steps into the vacant manager's chair
**IN** Nick Barmby from Liverpool for £2.75m; Paul Okon from Watford on a free
**OUT Record fee for Rio** as Ferdinand goes to Manchester United for £29m
AUGUST
SEPTEMBER
OCTOBER


Home / Away / Neutral

## ATTENDANCES

**HOME GROUND:** ELLAND ROAD **CAPACITY:** 40205 **AVERAGE LEAGUE AT HOME:** 39120

| | | | | | | | | | | | |
|---|---|---|---|---|---|---|---|---|---|---|---|
| 40 | Man Utd | 67135 | 39 | Newcastle | 40025 | 22 | Charlton | 35537 | 2 | West Brom | 26618 |
| 5 | Newcastle | 51730 | 3 | Sunderland | 39929 | 21 | Malaga | 35000 | 44 | Charlton | 26274 |
| 27 | Sunderland | 44029 | 34 | Chelsea | 39738 | 31 | Man City | 34884 | 8 | Blackburn | 25415 |
| 43 | Liverpool | 43021 | 32 | West Brom | 39708 | 13 | Middlesboro | 34723 | 41 | Sheff Utd | 24633 |
| 50 | Aston Villa | 40205 | 6 | Man Utd | 39622 | 24 | Malaga | 34123 | 38 | Crystal Palace | 24512 |
| 9 | Arsenal | 40199 | 45 | Tottenham | 39560 | 11 | Aston Villa | 33505 | 25 | Bolton | 23378 |
| 12 | Liverpool | 40197 | 42 | Middlesboro | 39073 | 17 | West Ham | 33297 | 23 | Fulham | 17494 |
| 1 | Man City | 40195 | 49 | Arsenal | 38127 | 46 | Southampton | 32032 | 10 | Zaporizhya | 12000 |
| 15 | Everton | 40161 | 48 | Blackburn | 38062 | 14 | Tel-Aviv | 31867 | 33 | Gillingham | 11093 |
| 35 | Everton | 40153 | 47 | Fulham | 37220 | 7 | Zaporizhya | 30000 | 30 | Scunthorpe | 8329 |
| 37 | West Ham | 40126 | 26 | Southampton | 36687 | 36 | Gillingham | 29359 | 18 | Tel-Aviv | 3000 |
| 28 | Chelsea | 40122 | 19 | Bolton | 36627 | 4 | Birmingham | 27634 | | | |
| 29 | Birmingham | 40034 | 20 | Tottenham | 35718 | 16 | Sheff Utd | 26663 | | | |

## GOAL ATTEMPTS

**FOR**
Goal attempts recorded in League games

| | HOME | AWAY | TOTAL | AVE |
|---|---|---|---|---|
| shots on target | 110 | 96 | 206 | 5.4 |
| shots off target | 143 | 66 | 209 | 5.5 |
| TOTAL | 253 | 162 | 415 | 10.9 |

| | |
|---|---|
| **Ratio of goals to shots** Average number of shots on target per League goal scored | 3.6 |
| **Accuracy rating** Average percentage of total goal attempts which were on target | 49.6 |

**AGAINST**
Goal attempts recorded in League games

| | HOME | AWAY | TOTAL | AVE |
|---|---|---|---|---|
| shots on target | 91 | 133 | 224 | 5.9 |
| shots off target | 119 | 96 | 215 | 5.7 |
| TOTAL | 210 | 229 | 439 | 11.6 |

| | |
|---|---|
| **Ratio of goals to shots** Average number of shots on target per League goal scored | 3.9 |
| **Accuracy rating** Average percentage of total goal attempts which were on target | 51.0 |

# El Tel pays price of past ambition

**Final Position: 15th**

KEY: ● League ● Champions Lge ● UEFA Cup ● FA Cup ○ League Cup ● Other

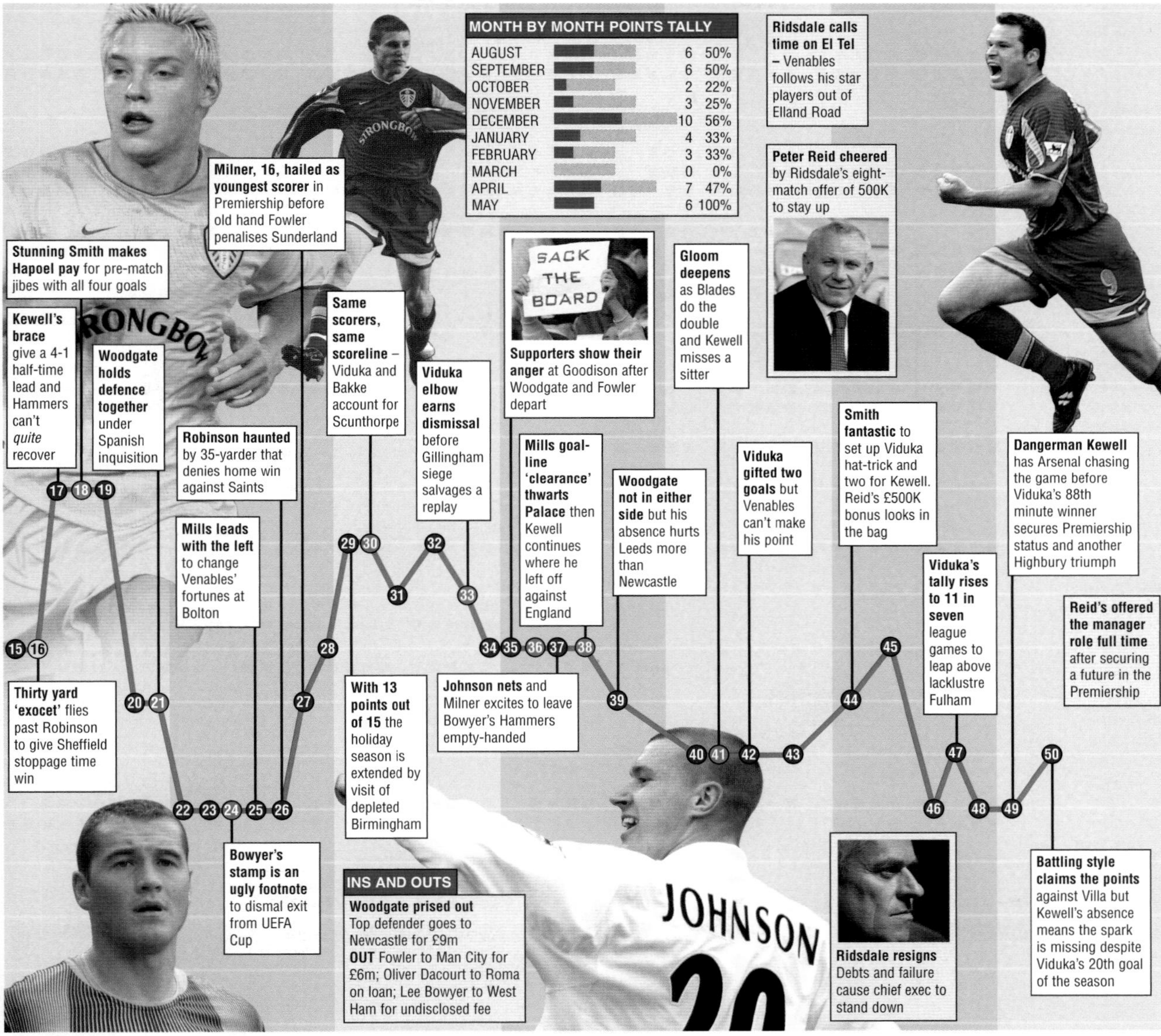
Stunning Smith makes Hapoel pay for pre-match jibes with all four goals
Kewell's brace give a 4-1 half-time lead and Hammers can't *quite* recover
Woodgate holds defence together under Spanish inquisition
Milner, 16, hailed as youngest scorer in Premiership before old hand Fowler penalises Sunderland
Robinson haunted by 35-yarder that denies home win against Saints
Mills leads with the left to change Venables' fortunes at Bolton
Thirty yard 'exocet' flies past Robinson to give Sheffield stoppage time win
Bowyer's stamp is an ugly footnote to dismal exit from UEFA Cup
Same scorers, same scoreline – Viduka and Bakke account for Scunthorpe
With 13 points out of 15 the holiday season is extended by visit of depleted Birmingham
Viduka elbow earns dismissal before Gillingham siege salvages a replay
SACK THE BOARD
Supporters show their anger at Goodison after Woodgate and Fowler depart
Mills goal-line 'clearance' thwarts Palace then Kewell continues where he left off against England
Johnson nets and Milner excites to leave Bowyer's Hammers empty-handed
Woodgate not in either side but his absence hurts Leeds more than Newcastle
Gloom deepens as Blades do the double and Kewell misses a sitter
Ridsdale calls time on El Tel – Venables follows his star players out of Elland Road
Peter Reid cheered by Ridsdale's eight-match offer of 500K to stay up
Viduka gifted two goals but Venables can't make his point
Smith fantastic to set up Viduka hat-trick and two for Kewell. Reid's £500K bonus looks in the bag
Viduka's tally rises to 11 in seven league games to leap above lacklustre Fulham
Dangerman Kewell has Arsenal chasing the game before Viduka's 88th minute winner secures Premiership status and another Highbury triumph
Reid's offered the manager role full time after securing a future in the Premiership
Battling style claims the points against Villa but Kewell's absence means the spark is missing despite Viduka's 20th goal of the season
Ridsdale resigns Debts and failure cause chief exec to stand down
JOHNSON 20
15 16 17 18 19 20 21 22 23 24 25 26 27 28 29 30 31 32 33 34 35 36 37 38 39 40 41 42 43 44 45 46 47 48 49 50

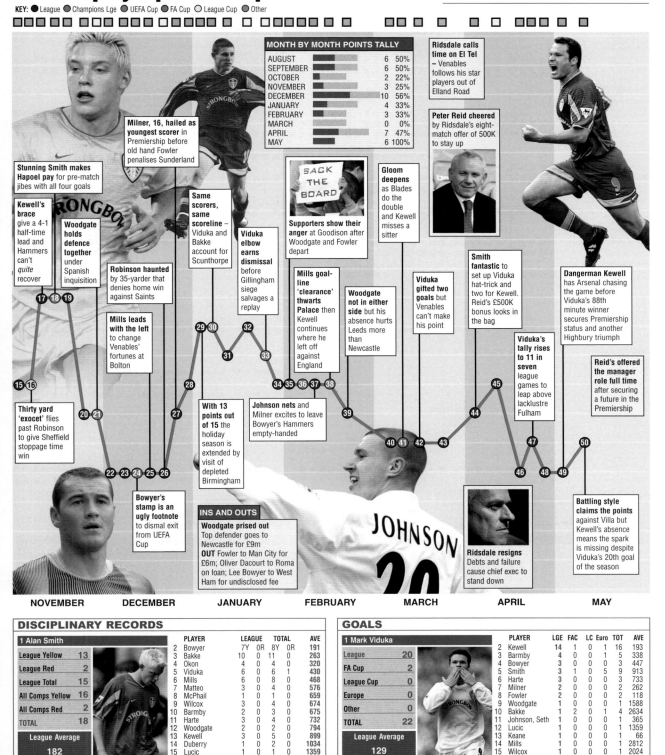

**MONTH BY MONTH POINTS TALLY**

| | | |
|---|---|---|
| AUGUST | 6 | 50% |
| SEPTEMBER | 6 | 50% |
| OCTOBER | 2 | 22% |
| NOVEMBER | 3 | 25% |
| DECEMBER | 10 | 56% |
| JANUARY | 4 | 33% |
| FEBRUARY | 3 | 33% |
| MARCH | 0 | 0% |
| APRIL | 7 | 47% |
| MAY | 6 | 100% |

**INS AND OUTS**

**Woodgate prised out**
Top defender goes to Newcastle for £9m
**OUT** Fowler to Man City for £6m; Oliver Dacourt to Roma on loan; Lee Bowyer to West Ham for undisclosed fee

NOVEMBER DECEMBER JANUARY FEBRUARY MARCH APRIL MAY

## DISCIPLINARY RECORDS

**1 Alan Smith**

| | |
|---|---|
| League Yellow | 13 |
| League Red | 2 |
| League Total | 15 |
| All Comps Yellow | 16 |
| All Comps Red | 2 |
| TOTAL | 18 |

League Average
182
mins between cards

| | PLAYER | LEAGUE | | TOTAL | | AVE |
|---|---|---|---|---|---|---|
| 2 | Bowyer | 7Y | 0R | 8Y | 0R | 191 |
| 3 | Bakke | 10 | 0 | 11 | 0 | 263 |
| 4 | Okon | 4 | 0 | 4 | 0 | 320 |
| 5 | Viduka | 6 | 0 | 6 | 1 | 430 |
| 6 | Mills | 6 | 0 | 8 | 0 | 468 |
| 7 | Matteo | 3 | 0 | 4 | 0 | 576 |
| 8 | McPhail | 1 | 0 | 1 | 0 | 659 |
| 9 | Wilcox | 3 | 0 | 4 | 0 | 674 |
| 10 | Barmby | 2 | 0 | 3 | 0 | 675 |
| 11 | Harte | 3 | 0 | 4 | 0 | 732 |
| 12 | Woodgate | 2 | 0 | 2 | 0 | 794 |
| 13 | Kewell | 3 | 0 | 5 | 0 | 899 |
| 14 | Duberry | 1 | 0 | 2 | 0 | 1034 |
| 15 | Lucic | 1 | 0 | 1 | 0 | 1359 |
| | Other | 8 | 0 | 13 | 0 | |
| | TOTAL | 73 | 2 | 92 | 3 | |

## GOALS

**1 Mark Viduka**

| | |
|---|---|
| League | 20 |
| FA Cup | 2 |
| League Cup | 0 |
| Europe | 0 |
| Other | 0 |
| TOTAL | 22 |

League Average
129
mins between goals

| | PLAYER | LGE | FAC | LC | Euro | TOT | AVE |
|---|---|---|---|---|---|---|---|
| 2 | Kewell | 14 | 1 | 0 | 1 | 16 | 193 |
| 3 | Barmby | 4 | 0 | 0 | 1 | 5 | 338 |
| 4 | Bowyer | 3 | 0 | 0 | 0 | 3 | 447 |
| 5 | Smith | 3 | 1 | 0 | 5 | 9 | 913 |
| 6 | Harte | 3 | 0 | 0 | 0 | 3 | 733 |
| 7 | Milner | 2 | 0 | 0 | 0 | 2 | 262 |
| 8 | Fowler | 2 | 0 | 0 | 0 | 2 | 118 |
| 9 | Woodgate | 1 | 0 | 0 | 0 | 1 | 1588 |
| 10 | Bakke | 1 | 2 | 0 | 1 | 4 | 2634 |
| 11 | Johnson, Seth | 1 | 0 | 0 | 0 | 1 | 365 |
| 12 | Lucic | 1 | 0 | 0 | 0 | 1 | 1359 |
| 13 | Keane | 1 | 0 | 0 | 0 | 1 | 66 |
| 14 | Mills | 1 | 0 | 0 | 0 | 1 | 2812 |
| 15 | Wilcox | 1 | 0 | 0 | 0 | 1 | 2024 |
| | Other | 0 | 1 | 1 | 0 | 2 | |
| | TOTAL | 58 | 7 | 1 | 8 | 74 | |

## SQUAD APPEARANCES

| Match | 1 | 2 | 3 | 4 | 5 | 6 | 7 | 8 | 9 | 10 | 11 | 12 | 13 | 14 | 15 | 16 | 17 | 18 | 19 | 20 | 21 | 22 | 23 | 24 | 25 |
|---|---|---|---|---|---|---|---|---|---|---|---|---|---|---|---|---|---|---|---|---|---|---|---|---|---|
| Venue | H | A | H | A | A | H | H | A | H | A | A | H | A | H | H | A | A | A | H | A | A | H | A | H | A |
| Competition | L | L | L | L | L | L | E | L | L | E | L | L | L | E | L | W | L | E | L | L | E | L | L | E | L |
| Result | W | W | L | L | W | W | W | L | L | D | D | L | D | W | L | L | W | W | L | L | D | L | L | L | W |

| Match | 26 | 27 | 28 | 29 | 30 | 31 | 32 | 33 | 34 | 35 | 36 | 37 | 38 | 39 | 40 | 41 | 42 | 43 | 44 | 45 | 46 | 47 | 48 | 49 | 50 |
|---|---|---|---|---|---|---|---|---|---|---|---|---|---|---|---|---|---|---|---|---|---|---|---|---|---|
| Venue | H | A | H | H | A | A | H | A | A | A | H | H | A | H | A | A | H | A | A | H | A | H | H | A | H |
| Competition | L | L | L | L | F | L | L | F | L | L | F | L | F | L | L | F | L | L | L | L | L | L | L | L | L |
| Result | D | W | W | W | W | L | D | D | L | L | W | W | W | L | L | L | L | L | W | D | L | W | L | W | W |

**Goalkeepers**
Nigel Martyn
Paul Robinson

**Defenders**
Shane Cansdell-Sherriff
Michael Duberry
Ian Harte
Gary Kelly
Matthew Kilgallon
Teddy Lucic
Dominic Matteo
Danny Mills
Lucas Radebe
Frazier Richardson
Jonathan Woodgate

**Midfielders**
Eirik Bakke
Nick Barmby
David Batty
Lee Bowyer
Jacob Burns
Olivier Dacourt
Seth Johnson
Simon Johnson
Harry Kewell
Jamie McMaster
Stephen McPhail
James Milner
Paul Okon
Sanfelix Raul Bravo
Jason Wilcox

**Forwards**
Michael Bridges
Robbie Fowler
Robbie Keane
Harpal Singh
Alan Smith
Mark Viduka

KEY: On all match · On bench · Subbed or sent off (Counting game) · Subbed or sent off (playing less than 70 minutes) · Subbed on from bench (Counting Game) · Subbed on (playing less than 70 minutes) · Subbed on and then subbed or sent off (Counting Game) · Subbed on and then subbed or sent off (playing less than 70 minutes) · Not in 16

## KEY PLAYERS - GOALSCORERS

**1 Mark Viduka**

| | |
|---|---|
| Goals in the League | 20 |
| Goals in all competitions | 22 |
| Assists<br>League goals scored by team-mates where he delivered the final pass | 3 |
| Contribution to Attacking Power<br>Average number of minutes between League team goals while on pitch | 52 |
| Player Strike Rate<br>Average number of minutes between League goals scored by player | 129 |
| Club Strike Rate<br>Average minutes between League goals scored by club | 59 |

STRONGBOW

| | PLAYER | GOALS LGE | GOALS ALL | ASSISTS | POWER | S RATE |
|---|---|---|---|---|---|---|
| 2 | Harry Kewell | 14 | 16 | 9 | 56 | 193 mins |
| 3 | Nick Barmby | 4 | 5 | 2 | 58 | 338 mins |
| 4 | Lee Bowyer | 3 | 3 | 1 | 74 | 447 mins |
| 5 | Ian Harte | 3 | 3 | 4 | 52 | 733 mins |

## KEY PLAYERS - MIDFIELDERS

**1 Harry Kewell**

| | |
|---|---|
| Goals in the League | 14 |
| Goals in all competitions | 16 |
| Assists<br>League goals scored by team-mates where he delivered the final pass | 9 |
| Defensive Rating<br>Average number of mins between League goals conceded while he was on the pitch | 60 |
| Contribution to Attacking Power<br>Average number of minutes between League team goals while on pitch | 56 |
| Scoring Difference<br>Defensive Rating minus Contribution to Attacking Power | 4 |

| | PLAYER | GOALS LGE | GOALS ALL | ASSISTS | DEF RATE | POWER | SC DIFF |
|---|---|---|---|---|---|---|---|
| 2 | Eirik Bakke | 1 | 4 | 4 | 59 | 56 | 3 mins |
| 3 | Nick Barmby | 4 | 5 | 2 | 59 | 59 | 0 mins |
| 4 | Jason Wilcox | 1 | 1 | 2 | 55 | 55 | 0 mins |
| 5 | Paul Okon | 0 | 0 | 0 | 67 | 71 | -4 mins |

## PLAYER APPEARANCES

| | AGE (on 01/07/03) | IN THE SQUAD | COUNTING GAMES | MINUTES ON PITCH | IN THE SQUAD | MINUTES ON PITCH | THIS SEASON | NATIONAL SIDE |
|---|---|---|---|---|---|---|---|---|
| **Goalkeepers** | | | | | | | | |
| Nigel Martyn | 36 | 38 | 0 | 0 | 50 | 0 | - | England |
| Paul Robinson | 23 | 38 | 38 | 3420 | 50 | 4500 | 7 | England (7) |
| **Defenders** | | | | | | | | |
| S Cansdell-Sherriff | 20 | 1 | 0 | 0 | 1 | 0 | - | Australia |
| Michael Duberry | 27 | 22 | 11 | 1034 | 31 | 1482 | - | England |
| Ian Harte | 25 | 32 | 22 | 2198 | 44 | 2998 | 7 | Rep of Ireland (15) |
| Gary Kelly | 28 | 35 | 24 | 2189 | 46 | 3064 | 3 | Rep of Ireland (15) |
| Matthew Kilgallon | 19 | 5 | 0 | 6 | 10 | 36 | - | England |
| Teddy Lucic | 30 | 21 | 14 | 1359 | 25 | 1635 | 6 | Sweden (20) |
| Dominic Matteo | 29 | 20 | 19 | 1729 | 24 | 2073 | - | Scotland |
| Danny Mills | 26 | 35 | 30 | 2812 | 44 | 3443 | 9 | England (7) |
| Lucas Radebe | 34 | 22 | 16 | 1517 | 30 | 2058 | - | South Africa |
| Frazier Richardson | 20 | 2 | 0 | 0 | 4 | 25 | - | England |
| Jonathan Woodgate | 23 | 19 | 17 | 1588 | 25 | 2100 | 5 | England (7) |
| **Midfielders** | | | | | | | | |
| Eirik Bakke | 25 | 34 | 28 | 2634 | 45 | 3510 | 8 | Norway (24) |
| Nick Barmby | 29 | 26 | 12 | 1351 | 32 | 1715 | - | England |
| David Batty | 34 | 1 | 0 | 0 | 1 | 0 | - | England |
| Lee Bowyer | 26 | 16 | 15 | 1341 | 22 | 1881 | 1 | England (7) |
| Jacob Burns | 25 | 3 | 1 | 126 | 8 | 126 | - | Australia |
| Olivier Dacourt | 28 | 10 | 2 | 369 | 13 | 496 | 3 | France (2) |
| Seth Johnson | 24 | 13 | 3 | 365 | 18 | 640 | - | England |
| Simon Johnson | 20 | 7 | 1 | 134 | 8 | 134 | - | England |
| Harry Kewell | 24 | 31 | 30 | 2698 | 41 | 3530 | - | Australia |
| Jamie McMaster | 20 | 6 | 0 | 53 | 10 | 53 | - | Australia |
| Stephen McPhail | 23 | 13 | 4 | 659 | 20 | 948 | 6 | Rep of Ireland (15) |
| James Milner | 17 | 22 | 1 | 523 | 27 | 592 | - | England |
| Paul Okon | 31 | 17 | 14 | 1281 | 26 | 1780 | - | Australia |
| Sanfelix Raul Bravo | 22 | 9 | 4 | 399 | 10 | 489 | - | Spain |
| Jason Wilcox | 31 | 26 | 21 | 2024 | 34 | 2725 | - | England |
| **Forwards** | | | | | | | | |
| Michael Bridges | 24 | 6 | 1 | 145 | 12 | 214 | - | England |
| Robbie Fowler | 28 | 8 | 1 | 236 | 11 | 326 | - | England |
| Robbie Keane | 22 | 3 | 0 | 66 | 3 | 66 | 7 | Rep of Ireland (15) |
| Harpal Singh | 21 | 0 | 0 | 0 | 1 | 0 | - | England |
| Alan Smith | 22 | 33 | 28 | 2738 | 43 | 3632 | 3 | England (7) |
| Mark Viduka | 27 | 33 | 27 | 2583 | 41 | 3177 | - | Australia |

KEY: LEAGUE ALL COMPS CAPS (FIFA RATING)

## TEAM OF THE SEASON

Robinson
CG 38 DR 60
Mills
CG 30 DR 62
Woodgate
CG 17 DR 84
Matteo
CG 19 DR 64
Harte
CG 22 DR 69
Wilcox
CG 21 SD 0
Barmby
CG 12 SD 0
Bakke
CG 28 SD +3
Kewell
CG 30 SD +4
Smith
CG 28 AP 70
Viduka
CG 27 SR 129


**KEY:** DR = Defensive Rate, SD = Scoring Difference AP = Attacking Power SR = Strike Rate, CG=Counting Games – League games playing at least 70 minutes

## TOP POINT EARNERS

**1 Ian Harte**

| | |
|---|---|
| **Counting Games** League games when he played at least 70 minutes | 22 |
| **Average points** Average League points taken in Counting games | 1.64 |
| **Club Average points** Average points taken in League games | 1.24 |

| | PLAYER | GAMES | PTS |
|---|---|---|---|
| 2 | Mark Viduka | 27 | 1.44 |
| 3 | Dominic Matteo | 19 | 1.42 |
| 4 | Danny Mills | 30 | 1.40 |
| 5 | Gary Kelly | 24 | 1.38 |
| 6 | Jason Wilcox | 21 | 1.33 |
| 7 | Eirik Bakke | 28 | 1.29 |
| 8 | Harry Kewell | 30 | 1.27 |
| 9 | Paul Robinson | 38 | 1.24 |
| 10 | Paul Okon | 14 | 1.21 |

## KEY PLAYERS - DEFENDERS

**1 Jonathan Woodgate**

| | |
|---|---|
| **Goals Conceded** The number of League goals conceded while he was on the pitch | 19 |
| **Goals Conceded in all competitions** The number goals conceded while he was on the pitch in all competitions | 21 |
| **League minutes played** Number of minutes played in league matches | 1588 |
| **Clean Sheets** In games when he played at least70 mins | 6 |
| **Defensive Rating** Average number of mins between League goals conceded while he was on the pitch | 84 |
| **Club Defensive Rating** Average number of mins between League goals conceded by the club this season | 60 |

RONGBOW


| | PLAYER | CON LGE | CON ALL | MINS | C SHEETS | DEF RATE |
|---|---|---|---|---|---|---|
| 2 | Ian Harte | 32 | 39 | 2198 | 7 | 69 mins |
| 3 | Dominic Matteo | 27 | 29 | 1729 | 6 | 64 mins |
| 4 | Danny Mills | 45 | 53 | 2812 | 9 | 62 mins |
| 5 | Teddy Lucic | 23 | 27 | 1359 | 3 | 59 mins |

## KEY PLAYERS - GOALKEEPERS

**1 Paul Robinson**

| | |
|---|---|
| **Goals Conceded in the League** The number of League goals conceded while he was on the pitch | 57 |
| **Goals Conceded in all competitions** The number of goals conceded while he was on the pitch in all competitions | 67 |
| **League minutes played** Number of minutes played in league matches | 3420 |
| **Clean Sheets** In games when he played at least 70 mins | 10 |
| **Goals to Shots Ratio** The average number of shots on target per each League goal conceded | 3.9 |
| **Defensive Rating** Ave number of mins between League goals conceded while on the pitch | 60 |

MARTYN


**2 Nigel Martyn**

| | |
|---|---|
| **Goals Conceded in the League** The number of League goals conceded while he was on the pitch | – |
| **Goals Conceded in all competitions** The number of goals conceded while he was on the pitch in all competitions | – |
| **League minutes played** Number of minutes played in league matches | 0 |
| **Clean Sheets** In games when he played at least 70 mins | – |
| **Goals to Shots Ratio** The average number of shots on target per each League goal conceded | – |
| **Defensive Rating** Ave number of mins between League goals conceded while on the pitch | – |

# ASTON VILLA

**NICKNAME:** THE VILLANS

KEY: Won / Drawn / Lost

| | | | | | | |
|---|---|---|---|---|---|---|
| 1 | lge | Liverpool | H | L | 0-1 | |
| 2 | lge | Tottenham | A | L | 0-1 | |
| 3 | lge | Man City | H | W | 1-0 | Vassell 64 |
| 4 | lge | Bolton | A | L | 0-1 | |
| 5 | lge | Charlton | H | W | 2-0 | De La Cruz 70; Moore 83 |
| 6 | lge | Birmingham | A | L | 0-3 | |
| 7 | lge | Everton | H | W | 3-2 | Hendrie 7,48; Dublin 85 |
| 8 | lge | Sunderland | A | L | 0-1 | |
| 9 | wr2 | Luton | H | W | 3-0 | De La Cruz 8; Dublin 25,48 |
| 10 | lge | Leeds | H | D | 0-0 | |
| 11 | lge | Southampton | H | L | 0-1 | |
| 12 | lge | Man Utd | A | D | 1-1 | Mellberg 35 |
| 13 | lge | Blackburn | A | D | 0-0 | |
| 14 | wr3 | Oxford | A | W | 3-0 | Taylor 74; Barry 77; Dublin 86 |
| 15 | lge | Fulham | H | W | 3-1 | Angel 20; Allback 66; Leonhardsen 83 |
| 16 | lge | West Brom | A | D | 0-0 | |
| 17 | lge | West Ham | H | W | 4-1 | Hendrie 29; Leonhardsen 59; Dublin 72; Vassell 80 |
| 18 | lge | Arsenal | A | L | 1-3 | Hitzlsperger 64 |
| 19 | wr4 | Preston | H | W | 5-0 | Vassell 44,55; Dublin 80; Angel 84; Hitzlsperger 87 |
| 20 | lge | Newcastle | H | L | 0-1 | |
| 21 | lge | West Brom | H | W | 2-1 | Vassell 16; Hitzlsperger 90 |
| 22 | wqf | Liverpool | H | L | 3-4 | Vassell 23 pen; Hitzlsperger 72; Dublin 84 |
| 23 | lge | Chelsea | A | L | 0-2 | |
| 24 | lge | Man City | A | L | 1-3 | Dublin 41 |
| 25 | lge | Middlesbrough | H | W | 1-0 | Dublin 11 |
| 26 | lge | Bolton | H | W | 2-0 | Dublin 8; Vassell 80 |
| 27 | facr3 | Blackburn | H | L | 1-4 | Angel 41 |
| 28 | lge | Liverpool | A | D | 1-1 | Dublin 49 pen |
| 29 | lge | Tottenham | H | L | 0-1 | |
| 30 | lge | Middlesbrough | A | W | 5-2 | Vassell 24,81; Gudjonsson 31; Barry 48; Dublin 90 |
| 31 | lge | Blackburn | H | W | 3-0 | Dublin 2,40; Barry 81 |
| 32 | lge | Fulham | A | L | 1-2 | Barry 3 |
| 33 | lge | Charlton | A | L | 0-3 | |
| 34 | lge | Birmingham | H | L | 0-2 | |
| 35 | lge | Man Utd | H | L | 0-1 | |
| 36 | lge | Southampton | A | D | 2-2 | Hendrie 30; Vassell 36 |
| 37 | lge | Arsenal | H | D | 1-1 | Toure 70 og |
| 38 | lge | West Ham | A | D | 2-2 | Vassell 35 pen; Leonhardsen 53 |
| 39 | lge | Chelsea | H | W | 2-1 | Allback 11,78 |
| 40 | lge | Newcastle | A | D | 1-1 | Dublin 69 |
| 41 | lge | Everton | A | L | 1-2 | Allback 49 |
| 42 | lge | Sunderland | H | W | 1-0 | Allback 80 |
| 43 | lge | Leeds | A | L | 1-3 | Gudjonsson 40 |

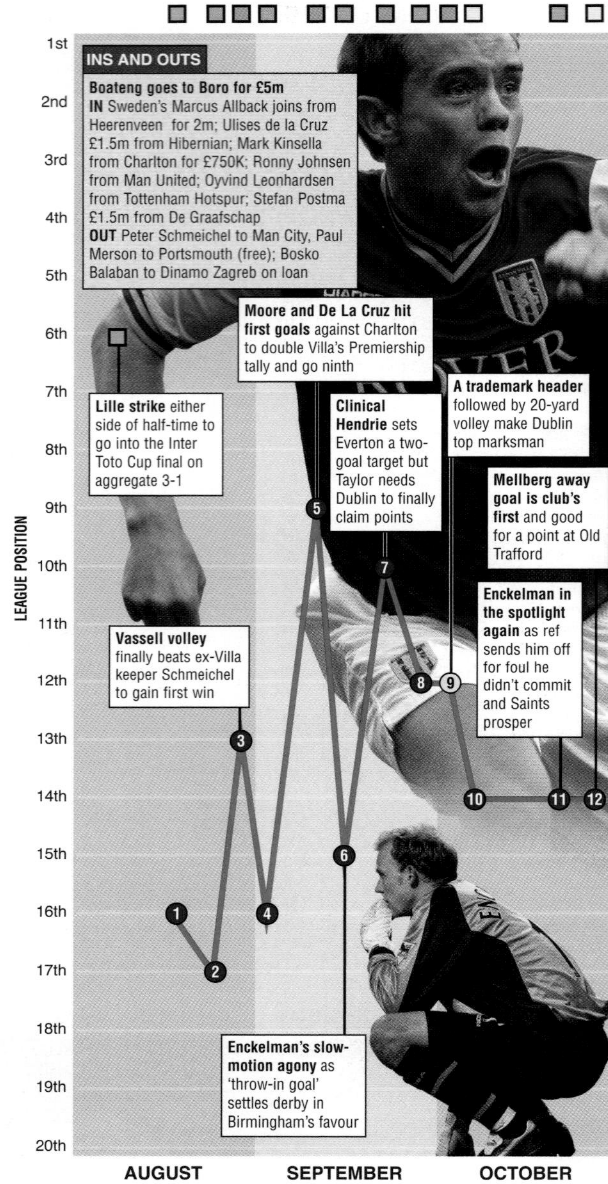
1st
2nd
3rd
4th
5th
6th
7th
8th
9th
10th
11th
12th
13th
14th
15th
16th
17th
18th
19th
20th
LEAGUE POSITION
INS AND OUTS
Boateng goes to Boro for £5m
IN Sweden's Marcus Allback joins from Heerenveen for 2m; Ulises de la Cruz £1.5m from Hibernian; Mark Kinsella from Charlton for £750K; Ronny Johnsen from Man United; Oyvind Leonhardsen from Tottenham Hotspur; Stefan Postma £1.5m from De Graafschap
OUT Peter Schmeichel to Man City, Paul Merson to Portsmouth (free); Bosko Balaban to Dinamo Zagreb on loan
Moore and De La Cruz hit first goals against Charlton to double Villa's Premiership tally and go ninth
A trademark header followed by 20-yard volley make Dublin top marksman
Lille strike either side of half-time to go into the Inter Toto Cup final on aggregate 3-1
Clinical Hendrie sets Everton a two-goal target but Taylor needs Dublin to finally claim points
Mellberg away goal is club's first and good for a point at Old Trafford
Enckelman in the spotlight again as ref sends him off for foul he didn't commit and Saints prosper
Vassell volley finally beats ex-Villa keeper Schmeichel to gain first win
Enckelman's slow-motion agony as 'throw-in goal' settles derby in Birmingham's favour
1
2
3
4
5
6
7
8
9
10
11
12
AUGUST
SEPTEMBER
OCTOBER

Home / Away / Neutral

## ATTENDANCES

**HOME GROUND:** VILLA PARK **CAPACITY:** 43275 **AVERAGE LEAGUE AT HOME:** 34975

| | | | | | | | | | | | |
|---|---|---|---|---|---|---|---|---|---|---|---|
| 12 | Man Utd | 67619 | 39 | Chelsea | 39358 | 3 | Man City | 33494 | 5 | Charlton | 26483 |
| 40 | Newcastle | 52015 | 29 | Tottenham | 38576 | 20 | Newcastle | 33446 | 33 | Charlton | 26257 |
| 28 | Liverpool | 43210 | 22 | Liverpool | 38530 | 17 | West Ham | 33279 | 11 | Southampton | 25817 |
| 35 | Man Utd | 42602 | 23 | Chelsea | 38284 | 36 | Southampton | 31888 | 27 | Blackburn | 23884 |
| 34 | Birmingham | 42602 | 18 | Arsenal | 38090 | 26 | Bolton | 31838 | 19 | Preston | 23042 |
| 37 | Arsenal | 42602 | 42 | Sunderland | 36963 | 7 | Everton | 30023 | 13 | Blackburn | 23004 |
| 1 | Liverpool | 41183 | 2 | Tottenham | 35384 | 15 | Fulham | 29563 | 4 | Bolton | 22501 |
| 8 | Sunderland | 40492 | 38 | West Ham | 35029 | 6 | Birmingham | 29505 | 9 | Luton | 20833 |
| 21 | West Brom | 40391 | 24 | Man City | 33991 | 31 | Blackburn | 29171 | 32 | Fulham | 17092 |
| 43 | Leeds | 40205 | 25 | Middlesboro | 33637 | 30 | Middlesboro | 27546 | 14 | Oxford | 12177 |
| 41 | Everton | 40167 | 10 | Leeds | 33505 | 16 | West Brom | 27091 | | | |

## GOAL ATTEMPTS

**FOR**
Goal attempts recorded in League games

| | HOME | AWAY | TOTAL | AVE |
|---|---|---|---|---|
| shots on target | 125 | 104 | 229 | 6.0 |
| shots off target | 132 | 113 | 245 | 6.4 |
| TOTAL | 257 | 217 | 474 | 12.5 |

**Ratio of goals to shots**
Average number of shots on target per League goal scored: **5.5**

**Accuracy rating**
Average percentage of total goal attempts which were on target: **48.3**

**AGAINST**
Goal attempts recorded in League games

| | HOME | AWAY | TOTAL | AVE |
|---|---|---|---|---|
| shots on target | 85 | 130 | 215 | 5.7 |
| shots off target | 111 | 104 | 215 | 5.7 |
| TOTAL | 196 | 234 | 430 | 11.3 |

**Ratio of goals to shots**
Average number of shots on target per League goal scored: **4.6**

**Accuracy rating**
Average percentage of total goal attempts which were on target: **50.0**

# Taylor resigns after late escape

Final Position: **16th**

KEY: ● League ● Champions Lge ● UEFA Cup ● FA Cup ○ League Cup ● Other

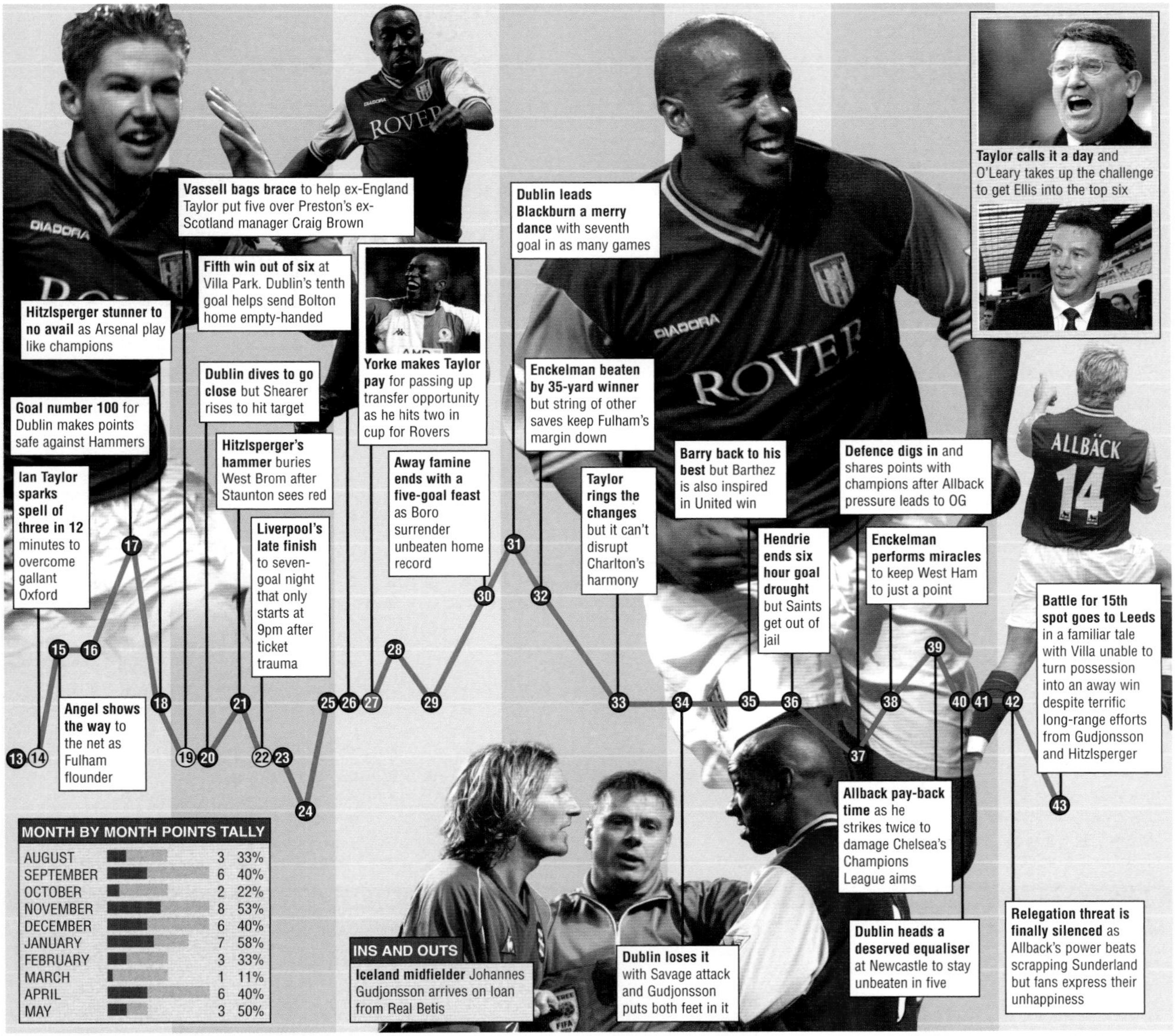

13 14 15 16 17 18 19 20 21 22 23 24 25 26 27 28 29 30 31 32 33 34 35 36 37 38 39 40 41 42 43


**Ian Taylor sparks spell of three in 12 minutes** to overcome gallant Oxford

**Angel shows the way** to the net as Fulham flounder

**Goal number 100** for Dublin makes points safe against Hammers

**Hitzlsperger stunner to no avail** as Arsenal play like champions

**Vassell bags brace** to help ex-England Taylor put five over Preston's ex-Scotland manager Craig Brown

**Fifth win out of six** at Villa Park. Dublin's tenth goal helps send Bolton home empty-handed

**Dublin dives to go close** but Shearer rises to hit target

**Hitzlsperger's hammer** buries West Brom after Staunton sees red

**Liverpool's late finish** to seven-goal night that only starts at 9pm after ticket trauma

**Yorke makes Taylor pay** for passing up transfer opportunity as he hits two in cup for Rovers

**Away famine ends with a five-goal feast** as Boro surrender unbeaten home record

**Dublin leads Blackburn a merry dance** with seventh goal in as many games

**Enckelman beaten by 35-yard winner** but string of other saves keep Fulham's margin down

**Taylor rings the changes** but it can't disrupt Charlton's harmony

**Dublin loses it** with Savage attack and Gudjonsson puts both feet in it

**Barry back to his best** but Barthez is also inspired in United win

**Hendrie ends six hour goal drought** but Saints get out of jail

**Defence digs in** and shares points with champions after Allback pressure leads to OG

**Enckelman performs miracles** to keep West Ham to just a point

**Allback pay-back time** as he strikes twice to damage Chelsea's Champions League aims

**Dublin heads a deserved equaliser** at Newcastle to stay unbeaten in five

**Battle for 15th spot goes to Leeds** in a familiar tale with Villa unable to turn possession into an away win despite terrific long-range efforts from Gudjonsson and Hitzlsperger

**Relegation threat is finally silenced** as Allback's power beats scrapping Sunderland but fans express their unhappiness

**Taylor calls it a day** and O'Leary takes up the challenge to get Ellis into the top six

**INS AND OUTS**

**Iceland midfielder** Johannes Gudjonsson arrives on loan from Real Betis

**MONTH BY MONTH POINTS TALLY**

| | | |
|---|---|---|
| AUGUST | 3 | 33% |
| SEPTEMBER | 6 | 40% |
| OCTOBER | 2 | 22% |
| NOVEMBER | 8 | 53% |
| DECEMBER | 6 | 40% |
| JANUARY | 7 | 58% |
| FEBRUARY | 3 | 33% |
| MARCH | 1 | 11% |
| APRIL | 6 | 40% |
| MAY | 3 | 50% |

NOVEMBER DECEMBER JANUARY FEBRUARY MARCH APRIL MAY

## DISCIPLINARY RECORDS

**1 Johannnes Gudjonsson**

| | |
|---|---|
| League Yellow | 4 |
| League Red | 1 |
| League Total | 5 |
| All Comps Yellow | 4 |
| All Comps Red | 1 |
| TOTAL | 5 |

League Average
156
mins between cards

| | PLAYER | LEAGUE | | TOTAL | | AVE |
|---|---|---|---|---|---|---|
| 2 | Taylor | 4Y | 0R | 5Y | 0R | 230 |
| 3 | Staunton | 8 | 1 | 8 | 1 | 231 |
| 4 | Hendrie | 7 | 0 | 7 | 0 | 261 |
| 5 | Barry | 10 | 0 | 10 | 0 | 301 |
| 6 | Dublin | 5 | 1 | 5 | 1 | 333 |
| 7 | Wright | 2 | 0 | 2 | 0 | 376 |
| 8 | Allback | 2 | 0 | 2 | 0 | 496 |
| 9 | Edwards | 1 | 0 | 1 | 0 | 507 |
| 10 | Moore | 1 | 0 | 1 | 0 | 531 |
| 11 | Crouch | 1 | 0 | 1 | 0 | 591 |
| 12 | Leonhardsen | 2 | 0 | 2 | 0 | 610 |
| 13 | Hadji | 1 | 0 | 1 | 0 | 616 |
| 14 | De La Cruz | 2 | 0 | 2 | 0 | 625 |
| 15 | Hitzlsperger | 3 | 0 | 3 | 0 | 683 |
| | Other | 13 | 1 | 13 | 1 | |
| | TOTAL | 66 | 4 | 67 | 4 | |

## GOALS

**1 Dion Dublin**

| | |
|---|---|
| League | 10 |
| FA Cup | 0 |
| League Cup | 5 |
| Europe | 0 |
| Other | 0 |
| TOTAL | 15 |

League Average
200
mins between goals

| | PLAYER | LGE | FAC | LC | Euro | TOT | AVE |
|---|---|---|---|---|---|---|---|
| 2 | Vassell | 8 | 0 | 3 | 0 | 11 | 313 |
| 3 | Allback | 5 | 0 | 0 | 0 | 5 | 198 |
| 4 | Hendrie | 4 | 0 | 0 | 0 | 4 | 458 |
| 5 | Barry | 3 | 0 | 1 | 0 | 4 | 1006 |
| 6 | Leonhardsen | 3 | 0 | 0 | 0 | 3 | 407 |
| 7 | Gudjonsson, J | 2 | 0 | 0 | 0 | 2 | 391 |
| 8 | Hitzlsperger | 2 | 0 | 2 | 0 | 4 | 1025 |
| 9 | Mellberg | 1 | 0 | 0 | 0 | 1 | 3420 |
| 10 | Angel | 1 | 1 | 1 | 0 | 3 | 782 |
| 11 | De La Cruz | 1 | 0 | 1 | 0 | 2 | 1251 |
| 12 | Moore | 1 | 0 | 0 | 0 | 1 | 531 |
| 13 | Taylor | 0 | 0 | 1 | 0 | 1 | |
| | Other | 1 | 0 | 0 | 0 | 1 | |
| | TOTAL | 42 | 1 | 14 | 0 | 57 | |

## SQUAD APPEARANCES

| Match | 1 | 2 | 3 | 4 | 5 | 6 | 7 | 8 | 9 | 10 | 11 | 12 | 13 | 14 | 15 | 16 | 17 | 18 | 19 | 20 | 21 | 22 |
|---|---|---|---|---|---|---|---|---|---|---|---|---|---|---|---|---|---|---|---|---|---|---|
| Venue | H | A | H | A | H | A | H | A | H | H | H | A | A | A | H | A | H | A | H | H | H | H |
| Competition | L | L | L | L | L | L | L | L | W | L | L | L | L | W | L | L | L | L | W | L | L | W |
| Result | L | L | W | L | W | L | W | L | W | D | L | D | D | W | W | D | W | L | W | L | W | L |

| Match | 23 | 24 | 25 | 26 | 27 | 28 | 29 | 30 | 31 | 32 | 33 | 34 | 35 | 36 | 37 | 38 | 39 | 40 | 41 | 42 | 43 |
|---|---|---|---|---|---|---|---|---|---|---|---|---|---|---|---|---|---|---|---|---|---|
| Venue | A | A | H | H | H | A | H | A | H | A | A | H | H | A | H | A | H | A | A | H | A |
| Competition | L | L | L | L | F | L | L | L | L | L | L | L | L | L | L | L | L | L | L | L | L |
| Result | L | L | W | W | L | D | L | W | W | L | L | L | L | D | D | D | W | D | L | W | L |

**Goalkeepers**
Peter Enckelman
Wayne Henderson
Stefan Postma

**Defenders**
Alpay Ozalan
Gareth Barry
Ulises De La Cruz
Mark Delaney
Rob Edwards
Ronny Johnsen
Olof Mellberg
Liam Ridgewell
Steve Staunton
Alan Wright

**Midfielders**
Stephen Cooke
J Gudjonsson
Moustapha Hadji
Lee Hendrie
Tomas Hitzlsperger
Mark Kinsella
Oyvind Leonhardsen
Jlloyd Samuel
Ian Taylor
Peter Whittingham

**Forwards**
Marcus Allback
Juan Pablo Angel
Michael Boulding
Peter Crouch
Dion Dublin
Stefan Moore
Darius Vassell

KEY: On all match · On bench · Subbed or sent off (Counting game) · Subbed or sent off (playing less than 70 minutes) · Subbed on from bench (Counting Game) · Subbed on (playing less than 70 minutes) · Subbed on and then subbed or sent off (Counting Game) · Subbed on and then subbed or sent off (playing less than 70 minutes) · Not in 16

## KEY PLAYERS - GOALSCORERS

**1 Dion Dublin**

| | |
|---|---|
| Goals in the League | 10 |
| Goals in all competitions | 15 |
| Assists<br>League goals scored by team-mates where he delivered the final pass | 2 |
| Contribution to Attacking Power<br>Average number of minutes between League team goals while on pitch | 68 |
| Player Strike Rate<br>Average number of minutes between League goals scored by player | 200 |
| Club Strike Rate<br>Average minutes between League goals scored by club | 81 |

ROVER

| | PLAYER | GOALS LGE | GOALS ALL | ASSISTS | POWER | S RATE |
|---|---|---|---|---|---|---|
| 2 | Darius Vassell | 8 | 11 | 3 | 80 | 313 mins |
| 3 | Lee Hendrie | 4 | 4 | 2 | 107 | 458 mins |
| 4 | Gareth Barry | 3 | 4 | 6 | 81 | 1006 mins |
| 5 | Tomas Hitzlsperger | 2 | 4 | 2 | 66 | 1025 mins |

## KEY PLAYERS - MIDFIELDERS

**1 Tomas Hitzlsperger**

| | |
|---|---|
| Goals in the League | 2 |
| Goals in all competitions | 4 |
| Assists<br>League goals scored by team-mates where he delivered the final pass | 2 |
| Defensive Rating<br>Average number of mins between League goals conceded while he was on the pitch | 71 |
| Contribution to Attacking Power<br>Average number of minutes between League team goals while on pitch | 66 |
| Scoring Difference<br>Defensive Rating minus Contribution to Attacking Power | 5 |

ROVER
12

| | PLAYER | GOALS LGE | GOALS ALL | ASSISTS | DEF RATE | POWER | SC DIFF |
|---|---|---|---|---|---|---|---|
| 2 | Jlloyd Samuel | 0 | 0 | 2 | 73 | 73 | 0 mins |
| 3 | Lee Hendrie | 4 | 4 | 2 | 92 | 108 | -16 mins |
| 4 | Mark Kinsella | 0 | 0 | 1 | 81 | 126 | -45 mins |

## PLAYER APPEARANCES

| | AGE (on 01/07/03) | IN THE SQUAD | COUNTING GAMES | MINUTES ON PITCH | IN THE SQUAD | MINUTES ON PITCH | THIS SEASON | NATIONAL SIDE |
|---|---|---|---|---|---|---|---|---|
| **Goalkeepers** | | | | | | | | |
| Peter Enckelman | 26 | 37 | 32 | 2926 | 40 | 3196 | - | Finland |
| Wayne Henderson | 19 | 1 | 0 | 0 | 3 | 0 | - | Rep of Ireland |
| Stefan Postma | 26 | 38 | 5 | 493 | 43 | 673 | - | Holland |
| **Defenders** | | | | | | | | |
| Alpay Ozalan | 30 | 5 | 5 | 450 | 5 | 450 | 10 | Turkey (8) |
| Gareth Barry | 22 | 35 | 33 | 3018 | 40 | 3468 | 2 | England (7) |
| Ulises De La Cruz | 28 | 25 | 9 | 1251 | 29 | 1518 | - | Ecuador |
| Mark Delaney | 27 | 12 | 12 | 1059 | 13 | 1149 | 4 | Wales (50) |
| Rob Edwards | 20 | 12 | 4 | 507 | 14 | 575 | - | England |
| Ronny Johnsen | 34 | 27 | 21 | 2043 | 30 | 2313 | 8 | Norway (24) |
| Olof Mellberg | 25 | 38 | 38 | 3420 | 41 | 3690 | 8 | Sweden (20) |
| Liam Ridgewell | 18 | 3 | 0 | 0 | 4 | 22 | - | England |
| Steve Staunton | 34 | 27 | 22 | 2087 | 30 | 2333 | - | Rep of Ireland |
| Alan Wright | 31 | 11 | 6 | 752 | 12 | 842 | - | England |
| **Midfielders** | | | | | | | | |
| Stephen Cooke | 20 | 4 | 0 | 32 | 4 | 32 | - | England |
| J Gudjonsson | 23 | 11 | 7 | 781 | 11 | 781 | - | Iceland |
| Moustapha Hadji | 31 | 12 | 5 | 616 | 13 | 706 | - | Morocco |
| Lee Hendrie | 26 | 31 | 18 | 1832 | 35 | 2184 | - | England |
| Tomas Hitzlsperger | 21 | 31 | 19 | 2049 | 35 | 2245 | - | Germany |
| Mark Kinsella | 30 | 22 | 13 | 1382 | 27 | 1677 | 9 | Rep of Ireland (15) |
| Oyvind Leonhardsen | 32 | 20 | 11 | 1220 | 24 | 1469 | 8 | Norway (24) |
| Jlloyd Samuel | 22 | 38 | 32 | 3056 | 43 | 3497 | - | England |
| Ian Taylor | 35 | 13 | 9 | 921 | 16 | 1068 | - | England |
| Peter Whittingham | 18 | 4 | 1 | 214 | 4 | 214 | - | England |
| **Forwards** | | | | | | | | |
| Marcus Allback | 30 | 27 | 7 | 992 | 31 | 1005 | 9 | Sweden (20) |
| Juan Pablo Angel | 27 | 22 | 5 | 782 | 26 | 910 | - | Colombia |
| Michael Boulding | 27 | 1 | 0 | 0 | 1 | 0 | - | England |
| Peter Crouch | 22 | 20 | 4 | 591 | 22 | 591 | - | England |
| Dion Dublin | 34 | 29 | 19 | 1998 | 34 | 2439 | - | England |
| Stefan Moore | 19 | 19 | 3 | 531 | 21 | 662 | - | England |
| Darius Vassell | 23 | 33 | 23 | 2502 | 37 | 2746 | 8 | England (7) |

KEY: LEAGUE ALL COMPS CAPS (FIFA RANKING)

## TEAM OF THE SEASON

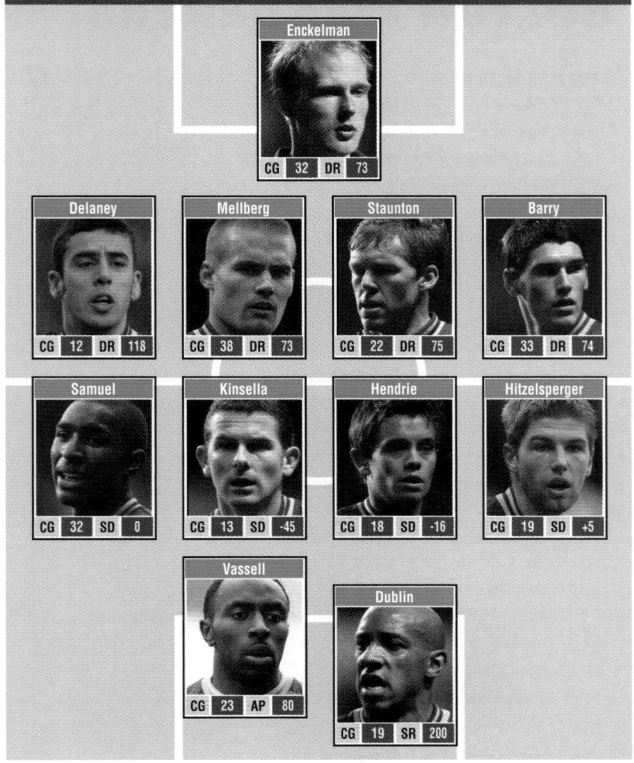
Enckelman
CG 32 DR 73
Delaney
CG 12 DR 118
Mellberg
CG 38 DR 73
Staunton
CG 22 DR 75
Barry
CG 33 DR 74
Samuel
CG 32 SD 0
Kinsella
CG 13 SD -45
Hendrie
CG 18 SD -16
Hitzelsperger
CG 19 SD +5
Vassell
CG 23 AP 80
Dublin
CG 19 SR 200

KEY: DR = Defensive Rate, SD = Scoring Difference AP = Attacking Power SR = Strike Rate, CG=Counting Games – League games playing at least 70 minutes

## TOP POINT EARNERS

**1 Dion Dublin**

| | |
|---|---|
| **Counting Games** League games when he played at least 70 minutes | 19 |
| **Average points** Average League points taken in Counting games | 1.32 |
| **Club Average points** Average points taken in League games | 1.18 |

| | PLAYER | GAMES | PTS |
|---|---|---|---|
| 2 | Jlloyd Samuel | 32 | 1.28 |
| 3 | Darius Vassell | 23 | 1.26 |
| 4 | Mark Delaney | 12 | 1.25 |
| 5 | Gareth Barry | 33 | 1.24 |
| 6 | Tomas Hitzlsperger | 19 | 1.21 |
| 7 | Peter Enckelman | 32 | 1.19 |
| 8 | Ronny Johnsen | 21 | 1.19 |
| 9 | Olof Mellberg | 38 | 1.18 |
| 10 | Steve Staunton | 22 | 1.18 |

## KEY PLAYERS - DEFENDERS

**1 Mark Delaney**

| | |
|---|---|
| **Goals Conceded** The number of League goals conceded while he was on the pitch | 9 |
| **Goals Conceded in all competitions** The number goals conceded while he was on the pitch in all competitions | 9 |
| **League minutes played** Number of minutes played in league matches | 1059 |
| **Clean Sheets** In games when he played at least70 mins | 4 |
| **Defensive Rating** Average number of mins between League goals conceded while he was on the pitch | 118 |
| **Club Defensive Rating** Average number of mins between League goals conceded by the club this season | 73 |

ROVER

| | PLAYER | CON LGE | CON ALL | MINS | C SHEETS | DEF RATE |
|---|---|---|---|---|---|---|
| 2 | Steve Staunton | 28 | 28 | 2087 | 5 | 75 mins |
| 3 | Gareth Barry | 41 | 49 | 3018 | 8 | 74 mins |
| 4 | Olof Mellberg | 47 | 55 | 3420 | 9 | 73 mins |
| 5 | Ronny Johnsen | 30 | 30 | 2043 | 3 | 68 mins |

## KEY PLAYERS - GOALKEEPERS

**1 Peter Enckelman**

| | |
|---|---|
| **Goals Conceded in the League** The number of League goals conceded while he was on the pitch | 40 |
| **Goals Conceded in all competitions** The number of goals conceded while he was on the pitch in all competitions | 44 |
| **League minutes played** Number of minutes played in league matches | 2926 |
| **Clean Sheets** In games when he played at least 70 mins | 7 |
| **Goals to Shots Ratio** The average number of shots on target per each League goal conceded | 4.6 |
| **Defensive Rating** Ave number of mins between League goals conceded while on the pitch | 73 |

**2 Stefan Postma**

| | |
|---|---|
| **Goals Conceded in the League** The number of League goals conceded while he was on the pitch | 7 |
| **Goals Conceded in all competitions** The number of goals conceded while he was on the pitch in all competitions | 11 |
| **League minutes played** Number of minutes played in league matches | 493 |
| **Clean Sheets** In games when he played at least 70 mins | 2 |
| **Goals to Shots Ratio** The average number of shots on target per each League goal conceded | 3.6 |
| **Defensive Rating** Ave number of mins between League goals conceded while on the pitch | 70 |

# BOLTON WANDERERS

**NICKNAME: THE TROTTERS**

KEY: Won / Drawn / Lost

| | | | | | | |
|---|---|---|---|---|---|---|
| 1 | lge | Fulham | A | L | 1-4 | Ricketts 4 pen |
| 2 | lge | Charlton | H | L | 1-2 | Djorkaeff 2 |
| 3 | lge | Aston Villa | H | W | 1-0 | Ricketts 55 pen |
| 4 | lge | Man Utd | A | W | 1-0 | Nolan 77 |
| 5 | lge | Liverpool | H | L | 2-3 | Gardner 54; Ivan Campo 87 |
| 6 | lge | Arsenal | A | L | 1-2 | Farrelly 47 |
| 7 | lge | Southampton | H | D | 1-1 | Djorkaeff 90 |
| 8 | wr2 | Bury | H | L | 0-1 | |
| 9 | lge | Middlesbrough | A | L | 0-2 | |
| 10 | lge | Tottenham | A | L | 1-3 | Djorkaeff 63 |
| 11 | lge | Sunderland | H | D | 1-1 | Babb 80 og |
| 12 | lge | Birmingham | A | L | 1-3 | Okocha 72 |
| 13 | lge | West Brom | H | D | 1-1 | Frandsen 89 |
| 14 | lge | Leeds | A | W | 4-2 | Pedersen 3,90; Djorkaeff 80; Ricketts 89 pen |
| 15 | lge | Chelsea | H | D | 1-1 | Pedersen 63 |
| 16 | lge | Man City | A | L | 0-2 | |
| 17 | lge | Blackburn | H | D | 1-1 | Okocha 8 |
| 18 | lge | Leeds | H | L | 0-3 | |
| 19 | lge | West Ham | A | D | 1-1 | Ricketts 65 |
| 20 | lge | Newcastle | H | W | 4-3 | Okocha 5; Gardner 9; Ricketts 45,63 |
| 21 | lge | Everton | A | D | 0-0 | |
| 22 | lge | Aston Villa | A | L | 0-2 | |
| 23 | facr3 | Sunderland | H | D | 1-1 | Ricketts 18 |
| 24 | lge | Fulham | H | D | 0-0 | |
| 25 | facr3r | Sunderland | A | L | 0-0 | |
| 26 | lge | Charlton | A | D | 1-1 | Djorkaeff 85 |
| 27 | lge | Newcastle | A | L | 0-1 | |
| 28 | lge | Everton | H | L | 1-2 | Facey 90 |
| 29 | lge | Birmingham | H | W | 4-2 | Cunningham 12 og; Pedersen 46; Djorkaeff 84; Facey 87 |
| 30 | lge | West Brom | A | D | 1-1 | Pedersen 18 |
| 31 | lge | Man Utd | H | D | 1-1 | N'Gotty 62 |
| 32 | lge | Liverpool | A | L | 0-2 | |
| 33 | lge | Sunderland | A | W | 2-0 | Okocha 50; Pedersen 55 |
| 34 | lge | Tottenham | H | W | 1-0 | Okocha 90 pen |
| 35 | lge | Man City | H | W | 2-0 | Pedersen 32; Campo 51 |
| 36 | lge | Chelsea | A | L | 0-1 | |
| 37 | lge | West Ham | H | W | 1-0 | Okocha 38 |
| 38 | lge | Blackburn | A | D | 0-0 | |
| 39 | lge | Arsenal | H | D | 2-2 | Djorkaeff 74; Keown 84 og |
| 40 | lge | Southampton | A | D | 0-0 | |
| 41 | lge | Middlesbrough | H | W | 2-1 | Frandsen 10; Okocha 21 |

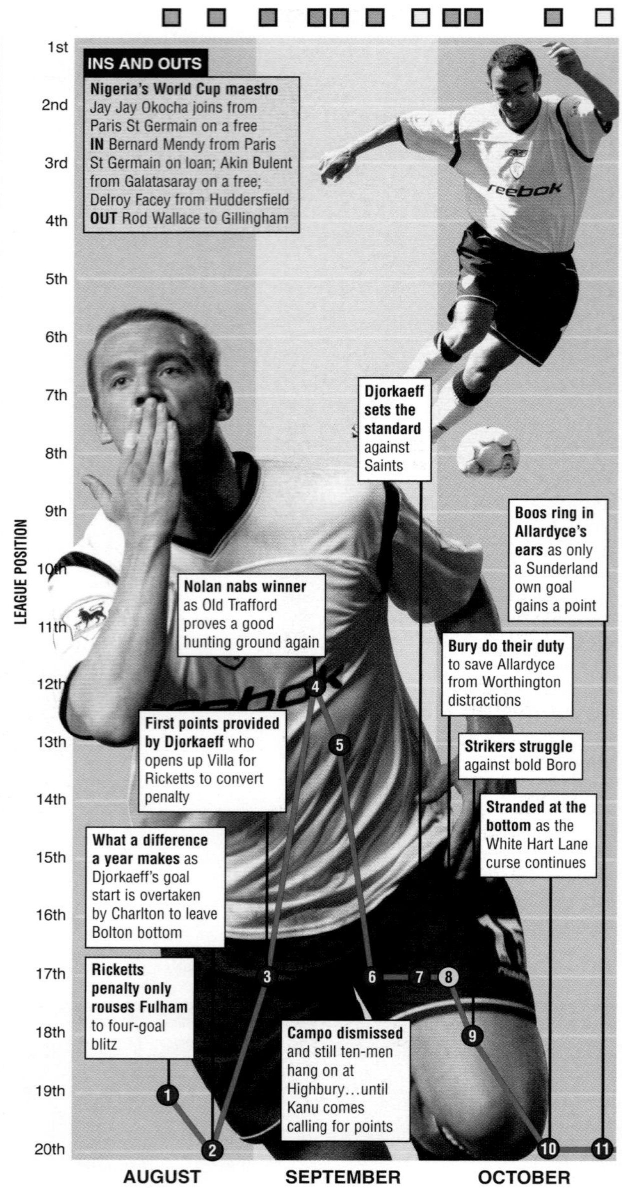

1st
2nd
3rd
4th
5th
6th
7th
8th
9th
10th
11th
12th
13th
14th
15th
16th
17th
18th
19th
20th
LEAGUE POSITION
INS AND OUTS
Nigeria's World Cup maestro Jay Jay Okocha joins from Paris St Germain on a free
IN Bernard Mendy from Paris St Germain on loan; Akin Bulent from Galatasaray on a free; Delroy Facey from Huddersfield
OUT Rod Wallace to Gillingham
Djorkaeff sets the standard against Saints
Boos ring in Allardyce's ears as only a Sunderland own goal gains a point
Nolan nabs winner as Old Trafford proves a good hunting ground again
Bury do their duty to save Allardyce from Worthington distractions
First points provided by Djorkaeff who opens up Villa for Ricketts to convert penalty
Strikers struggle against bold Boro
Stranded at the bottom as the White Hart Lane curse continues
What a difference a year makes as Djorkaeff's goal start is overtaken by Charlton to leave Bolton bottom
Ricketts penalty only rouses Fulham to four-goal blitz
Campo dismissed and still ten-men hang on at Highbury...until Kanu comes calling for points
1
2
3
4
5
6
7
8
9
10
11
AUGUST
SEPTEMBER
OCTOBER


Home / Away / Neutral

## ATTENDANCES

**HOME GROUND: REEBOK STADIUM CAPACITY: 27410 AVERAGE LEAGUE AT HOME: 25017**

| | | | | | | | | | | | |
|---|---|---|---|---|---|---|---|---|---|---|---|
| 4 | Man Utd | 67623 | 22 | Aston Villa | 31838 | 35 | Man City | 26949 | 11 | Sunderland | 23036 |
| 27 | Newcastle | 52005 | 9 | Middlesboro | 31005 | 30 | West Brom | 26933 | 7 | Southampton | 22692 |
| 33 | Sunderland | 42124 | 40 | Southampton | 30950 | 26 | Charlton | 26057 | 3 | Aston Villa | 22501 |
| 32 | Liverpool | 41462 | 38 | Blackburn | 28862 | 15 | Chelsea | 25476 | 2 | Charlton | 21753 |
| 36 | Chelsea | 39852 | 31 | Man Utd | 27409 | 24 | Fulham | 25156 | 1 | Fulham | 16388 |
| 21 | Everton | 39480 | 5 | Liverpool | 27328 | 28 | Everton | 25119 | 25 | Sunderland | 14550 |
| 6 | Arsenal | 37974 | 20 | Newcastle | 27314 | 17 | Blackburn | 24556 | 8 | Bury | 12621 |
| 14 | Leeds | 36627 | 39 | Arsenal | 27253 | 29 | Birmingham | 24288 | 23 | Sunderland | 10123 |
| 10 | Tottenham | 35909 | 41 | Middlesboro | 27241 | 13 | West Brom | 23630 | | | |
| 19 | West Ham | 34892 | 12 | Birmingham | 27224 | 18 | Leeds | 23378 | | | |
| 16 | Man City | 34860 | 37 | West Ham | 27160 | 34 | Tottenham | 23084 | | | |

## GOAL ATTEMPTS

**FOR** – Goal attempts recorded in League games

| | HOME | AWAY | TOTAL | AVE |
|---|---|---|---|---|
| shots on target | 127 | 77 | 204 | 5.4 |
| shots off target | 133 | 91 | 224 | 5.9 |
| **TOTAL** | **260** | **168** | **428** | **11.3** |

**Ratio of goals to shots** – Average number of shots on target per League goal scored: **5.0**

**Accuracy rating** – Average percentage of total goal attempts which were on target: **47.7**

**AGAINST** – Goal attempts recorded in League games

| | HOME | AWAY | TOTAL | AVE |
|---|---|---|---|---|
| shots on target | 96 | 122 | 218 | 5.7 |
| shots off target | 79 | 77 | 156 | 4.1 |
| **TOTAL** | **175** | **199** | **374** | **9.8** |

**Ratio of goals to shots** – Average number of shots on target per League goal scored: **4.3**

**Accuracy rating** – Average percentage of total goal attempts which were on target: **58.3**

# Foreign legion's thrilling finale

Final Position: **17th**

KEY: ● League ● Champions Lge ● UEFA Cup ● FA Cup ○ League Cup ● Other

**Allardyce loses to 'old pal' Bruce** despite Okocha equaliser

### INS AND OUTS

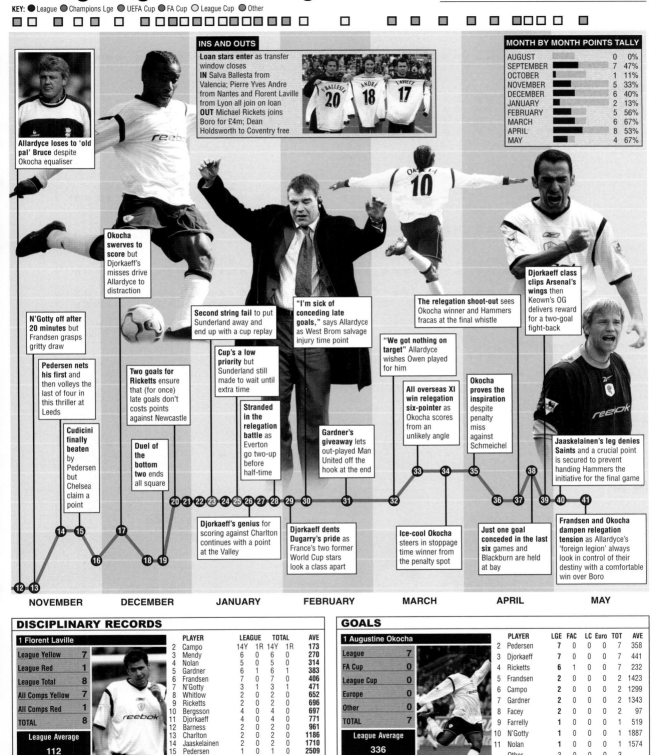

**Loan stars enter** as transfer window closes
**IN** Salva Ballesta from Valencia; Pierre Yves Andre from Nantes and Florent Laville from Lyon all join on loan
**OUT** Michael Rickets joins Boro for £4m; Dean Holdsworth to Coventry free

S BALLESTA
20
ANDRÉ
18
LAVILLE
17

### MONTH BY MONTH POINTS TALLY

| Month | Points | % |
|---|---|---|
| AUGUST | 0 | 0% |
| SEPTEMBER | 7 | 47% |
| OCTOBER | 1 | 11% |
| NOVEMBER | 5 | 33% |
| DECEMBER | 6 | 40% |
| JANUARY | 2 | 13% |
| FEBRUARY | 5 | 56% |
| MARCH | 6 | 67% |
| APRIL | 8 | 53% |
| MAY | 4 | 67% |

10

**N'Gotty off after 20 minutes** but Frandsen grasps gritty draw

**Pedersen nets his first** and then volleys the last of four in this thriller at Leeds

**Cudicini finally beaten** by Pedersen but Chelsea claim a point

**Okocha swerves to score** but Djorkaeff's misses drive Allardyce to distraction

**Two goals for Ricketts** ensure that (for once) late goals don't costs points against Newcastle

**Duel of the bottom two** ends all square

**Second string fail** to put Sunderland away and end up with a cup replay

**Cup's a low priority** but Sunderland still made to wait until extra time

**Stranded in the relegation battle** as Everton go two-up before half-time

**Djorkaeff's genius** for scoring against Charlton continues with a point at the Valley

**Djorkaeff dents Dugarry's pride** as France's two former World Cup stars look a class apart

**"I'm sick of conceding late goals,"** says Allardyce as West Brom salvage injury time point

**Gardner's giveaway** lets out-played Man United off the hook at the end

**"We got nothing on target"** Allardyce wishes Owen played for him

**All overseas XI win relegation six-pointer** as Okocha scores from an unlikely angle

**Ice-cool Okocha** steers in stoppage time winner from the penalty spot

**Okocha proves the inspiration** despite penalty miss against Schmeichel

**The relegation shoot-out** sees Okocha winner and Hammers fracas at the final whistle

**Just one goal conceded in the last six** games and Blackburn are held at bay

**Djorkaeff class clips Arsenal's wings** then Keown's OG delivers reward for a two-goal fight-back

**Jaaskelainen's leg denies Saints** and a crucial point is secured to prevent handing Hammers the initiative for the final game

**Frandsen and Okocha dampen relegation tension** as Allardyce's 'foreign legion' always look in control of their destiny with a comfortable win over Boro

NOVEMBER DECEMBER JANUARY FEBRUARY MARCH APRIL MAY

## DISCIPLINARY RECORDS

**1 Florent Laville**

| | |
|---|---|
| League Yellow | 7 |
| League Red | 1 |
| League Total | 8 |
| All Comps Yellow | 7 |
| All Comps Red | 1 |
| TOTAL | 8 |

League Average
112
mins between cards

| | PLAYER | LEAGUE | | TOTAL | | AVE |
|---|---|---|---|---|---|---|
| 2 | Campo | 14Y | 1R | 14Y | 1R | 173 |
| 3 | Mendy | 6 | 0 | 6 | 0 | 270 |
| 4 | Nolan | 5 | 0 | 5 | 0 | 314 |
| 5 | Gardner | 6 | 1 | 6 | 1 | 383 |
| 6 | Frandsen | 7 | 0 | 7 | 0 | 406 |
| 7 | N'Gotty | 3 | 1 | 3 | 1 | 471 |
| 8 | Whitlow | 2 | 0 | 2 | 0 | 652 |
| 9 | Ricketts | 2 | 0 | 2 | 0 | 696 |
| 10 | Bergsson | 4 | 0 | 4 | 0 | 697 |
| 11 | Djorkaeff | 4 | 0 | 4 | 0 | 771 |
| 12 | Barness | 2 | 0 | 2 | 0 | 961 |
| 13 | Charlton | 2 | 0 | 2 | 0 | 1186 |
| 14 | Jaaskelainen | 2 | 0 | 2 | 0 | 1710 |
| 15 | Pedersen | 1 | 0 | 1 | 0 | 2509 |
| | Other | 5 | 0 | 9 | 1 | |
| | **TOTAL** | **72** | **4** | **76** | **5** | |

## GOALS

**1 Augustine Okocha**

| | |
|---|---|
| League | 7 |
| FA Cup | 0 |
| League Cup | 0 |
| Europe | 0 |
| Other | 0 |
| TOTAL | 7 |

League Average
336
mins between goals

| | PLAYER | LGE | FAC | LC | Euro | TOT | AVE |
|---|---|---|---|---|---|---|---|
| 2 | Pedersen | 7 | 0 | 0 | 0 | 7 | 358 |
| 3 | Djorkaeff | 7 | 0 | 0 | 0 | 7 | 441 |
| 4 | Ricketts | 6 | 1 | 0 | 0 | 7 | 232 |
| 5 | Frandsen | 2 | 0 | 0 | 0 | 2 | 1423 |
| 6 | Campo | 2 | 0 | 0 | 0 | 2 | 1299 |
| 7 | Gardner | 2 | 0 | 0 | 0 | 2 | 1343 |
| 8 | Facey | 2 | 0 | 0 | 0 | 2 | 97 |
| 9 | Farrelly | 1 | 0 | 0 | 0 | 1 | 519 |
| 10 | N'Gotty | 1 | 0 | 0 | 0 | 1 | 1887 |
| 11 | Nolan | 1 | 0 | 0 | 0 | 1 | 1574 |
| | Other | 3 | 0 | 0 | 0 | 3 | |
| | **TOTAL** | **41** | **1** | **0** | **0** | **42** | |

## SQUAD APPEARANCES

| Match | 1 | 2 | 3 | 4 | 5 | 6 | 7 | 8 | 9 | 10 | 11 | 12 | 13 | 14 | 15 | 16 | 17 | 18 | 19 | 20 | 21 | 22 | 23 | 24 | 25 | 26 | 27 | 28 | 29 | 30 | 31 | 32 | 33 | 34 | 35 | 36 | 37 | 38 | 39 | 40 | 41 |
|---|---|---|---|---|---|---|---|---|---|---|---|---|---|---|---|---|---|---|---|---|---|---|---|---|---|---|---|---|---|---|---|---|---|---|---|---|---|---|---|---|---|
| Venue | A | H | H | A | H | A | H | H | A | A | H | A | H | A | H | A | H | H | A | H | A | A | H | H | A | A | A | H | H | A | H | A | A | H | H | A | H | A | H | A | H |
| Competition | L | L | L | L | L | L | L | W | L | L | L | L | L | L | L | L | L | L | L | L | L | L | F | L | F | L | L | L | L | L | L | L | L | L | L | L | L | L | L | L | L |
| Result | L | L | W | W | L | L | D | L | L | L | D | L | D | W | D | L | D | L | D | W | D | L | D | D | L | D | L | L | W | D | D | L | W | W | W | L | W | D | D | D | W |

**Goalkeepers**
Jussi Jaaskelainen
Kevin Poole

**Defenders**
Anthony Barness
Gudni Bergsson
Ramos Ivan Campo
Simon Charlton
David Holdsworth
Nicky Hunt
Florent Laville
Danny Livesey
Bernard Mendy
Bruno N'Gotty
Leam Richardson
Paul Warhurst
Michael Whitlow

**Midfielders**
Akin Bulent
Youri Djorkaeff
Gareth Farrelly
Per Frandsen
Ricardo Gardner
Kevin Nolan
Augustine Okocha
Jeff Smith
Nicky Southall
Stig Tofting

**Forwards**
Pierre-Yves Andre
Chris Armstrong
Delroy Facey
Dean Holdsworth
Jermaine Johnson
Henrik Pedersen
Michael Ricketts
Ioan Ballesta Salva
Jonathan Walters

KEY: ■ On all match ■ On bench ⏮ Subbed or sent off (Counting game) « Subbed or sent off (playing less than 70 minutes) ⏭ Subbed on from bench (Counting Game) » Subbed on (playing less than 70 minutes) Subbed on and then subbed or sent off (Counting Game) Subbed on and then subbed or sent off (playing less than 70 minutes) □ Not in 16

## KEY PLAYERS - GOALSCORERS

| 1 Michael Ricketts | |
|---|---|
| Goals in the League | 6 |
| Goals in all competitions | 7 |
| Assists<br>League goals scored by team-mates where he delivered the final pass | 0 |
| Contribution to Attacking Power<br>Average number of minutes between League team goals while on pitch | 73 |
| Player Strike Rate<br>Average number of minutes between League goals scored by player | 232 |
| Club Strike Rate<br>Average minutes between League goals scored by club | 83 |

| | PLAYER | GOALS LGE | GOALS ALL | ASSISTS | POWER | S RATE |
|---|---|---|---|---|---|---|
| 2 | Augustine Okocha | 7 | 7 | 1 | 73 | **336 mins** |
| 3 | Henrik Pedersen | 7 | 7 | 3 | 86 | **358 mins** |
| 4 | Youri Djorkaeff | 7 | 7 | 6 | 79 | **441 mins** |
| 5 | Ramos Ivan Campo | 2 | 2 | 0 | 89 | **299 mins** |

## KEY PLAYERS - MIDFIELDERS

| 1 Per Frandsen | |
|---|---|
| Goals in the League | 2 |
| Goals in all competitions | 2 |
| Assists<br>League goals scored by team-mates where he delivered the final pass | 2 |
| Defensive Rating<br>Average number of mins between League goals conceded while he was on the pitch | 73 |
| Contribution to Attacking Power<br>Average number of minutes between League team goals while on pitch | 75 |
| Scoring Difference<br>Defensive Rating minus Contribution to Attacking Power | -2 |

| | PLAYER | GOALS LGE | GOALS ALL | ASSISTS | DEF RATE | POWER | SC DIFF |
|---|---|---|---|---|---|---|---|
| 2 | Augustine Okocha | 7 | 7 | 1 | 71 | 74 | **-3 mins** |
| 3 | Youri Djorkaeff | 7 | 7 | 6 | 73 | 79 | **-6 mins** |
| 4 | Ricardo Gardner | 2 | 2 | 2 | 71 | 90 | **-19 mins** |
| 5 | Kevin Nolan | 1 | 1 | 2 | 61 | 112 | **-51 mins** |

## PLAYER APPEARANCES

| | AGE (on 01/07/03) | IN THE SQUAD | COUNTING GAMES | MINUTES ON PITCH | IN THE SQUAD | MINUTES ON PITCH | THIS SEASON | NATIONAL SIDE |
|---|---|---|---|---|---|---|---|---|
| **Goalkeepers** | | | | | | | | |
| Jussi Jaaskelainen | 28 | 38 | 38 | 3420 | 41 | 3420 | - | Iceland |
| Kevin Poole | 39 | 38 | 0 | 0 | 41 | 300 | - | England |
| **Defenders** | | | | | | | | |
| Anthony Barness | 31 | 33 | 20 | 1923 | 34 | 2013 | - | England |
| Gudni Bergsson | 37 | 31 | 31 | 2790 | 31 | 2790 | - | Iceland |
| Ramos Ivan Campo | 29 | 33 | 29 | 2598 | 36 | 2898 | - | Spain |
| Simon Charlton | 31 | 33 | 25 | 2372 | 33 | 2372 | - | England |
| David Holdsworth | 34 | 0 | 0 | 0 | 1 | 90 | - | England |
| Nicky Hunt | 19 | 0 | 0 | 0 | 2 | 131 | - | England |
| Florent Laville | 29 | 10 | 10 | 900 | 10 | 900 | - | France |
| Danny Livesey | 18 | 7 | 0 | 77 | 9 | 240 | - | England |
| Bernard Mendy | 21 | 23 | 17 | 1624 | 25 | 1793 | - | France |
| Bruno N'Gotty | 32 | 24 | 19 | 1887 | 25 | 2007 | - | France |
| Leam Richardson | 23 | 0 | 0 | 0 | 1 | 0 | - | England |
| Paul Warhurst | 33 | 7 | 3 | 397 | 8 | 472 | - | England |
| Michael Whitlow | 35 | 20 | 13 | 1305 | 22 | 1442 | - | England |
| **Midfielders** | | | | | | | | |
| Akin Bulent | 23 | 2 | 0 | 6 | 5 | 143 | - | Turkey |
| Youri Djorkaeff | 35 | 36 | 34 | 3084 | 37 | 3204 | - | France |
| Gareth Farrelly | 27 | 8 | 5 | 519 | 10 | 670 | - | Rep of Ireland |
| Per Frandsen | 33 | 36 | 31 | 2846 | 36 | 2846 | 1 | Denmark (10) |
| Ricardo Gardner | 24 | 32 | 27 | 2685 | 32 | 2685 | - | Jamaica |
| Kevin Nolan | 21 | 35 | 14 | 1574 | 38 | 1742 | - | England |
| Augustine Okocha | 29 | 32 | 25 | 2355 | 33 | 2372 | - | Nigeria |
| Jeff Smith | 23 | 2 | 0 | 0 | 5 | 300 | - | England |
| Nicky Southall | 31 | 2 | 0 | 0 | 2 | 0 | - | England |
| Stig Tofting | 33 | 15 | 1 | 288 | 18 | 571 | - | Denmark |
| **Forwards** | | | | | | | | |
| Pierre-Yves Andre | 29 | 11 | 0 | 188 | 11 | 188 | - | France |
| Chris Armstrong | 32 | 1 | 0 | 0 | 2 | 52 | - | England |
| Delroy Facey | 23 | 12 | 0 | 193 | 14 | 328 | - | England |
| Dean Holdsworth | 34 | 14 | 2 | 373 | 15 | 406 | - | England |
| Jermaine Johnson | 23 | 2 | 0 | 24 | 3 | 83 | - | Jamaica |
| Henrik Pedersen | 28 | 35 | 23 | 2509 | 36 | 2547 | - | Denmark |
| Michael Ricketts | 24 | 22 | 12 | 1393 | 23 | 1483 | - | England |
| Ioan Ballesta Salva | 28 | 8 | 1 | 144 | 8 | 144 | - | Spain |
| Jonathan Walters | 19 | 5 | 0 | 41 | 8 | 157 | - | England |

KEY: LEAGUE ALL COMPS CAPS (FIFA RANKING)

## TEAM OF THE SEASON

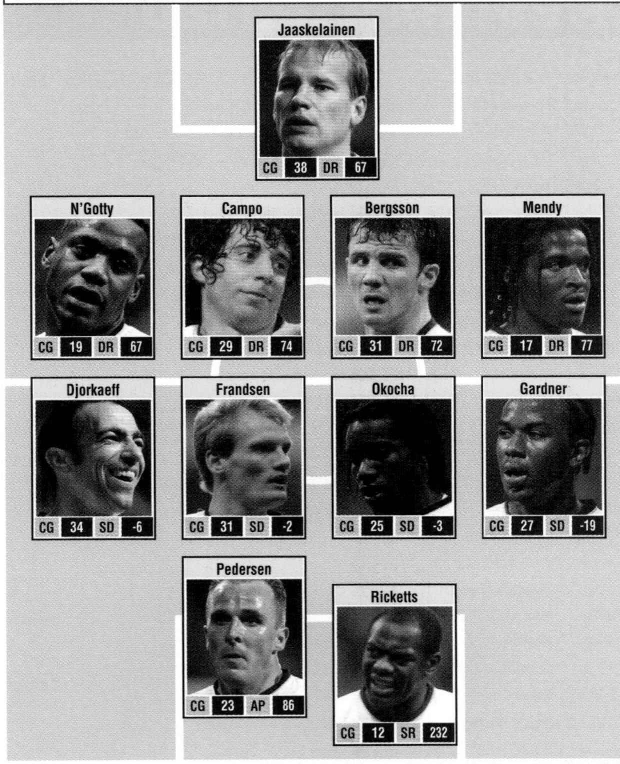

Jaaskelainen
CG 38 DR 67
N'Gotty
CG 19 DR 67
Campo
CG 29 DR 74
Bergsson
CG 31 DR 72
Mendy
CG 17 DR 77
Djorkaeff
CG 34 SD -6
Frandsen
CG 31 SD -2
Okocha
CG 25 SD -3
Gardner
CG 27 SD -19
Pedersen
CG 23 AP 86
Ricketts
CG 12 SR 232


**KEY:** DR = Defensive Rate, SD = Scoring Difference AP = Attacking Power SR = Strike Rate, CG=Counting Games – League games playing at least 70 minutes

## TOP POINT EARNERS

**1 Bernard Mendy**

| | |
|---|---|
| **Counting Games** League games when he played at least 70 minutes | 17 |
| **Average points** Average League points taken in Counting games | 1.59 |
| **Club Average points** Average points taken in League games | 1.16 |

| | PLAYER | GAMES | PTS |
|---|---|---|---|
| 2 | Henrik Pedersen | 23 | 1.57 |
| 3 | Bruno N'Gotty | 19 | 1.42 |
| 4 | Augustine Okocha | 25 | 1.40 |
| 5 | Per Frandsen | 31 | 1.35 |
| 6 | Gudni Bergsson | 31 | 1.23 |
| 7 | Jussi Jaaskelainen | 38 | 1.16 |
| 8 | Michael Whitlow | 13 | 1.15 |
| 9 | Youri Djorkaeff | 34 | 1.15 |
| 10 | Ramos Ivan Campo | 29 | 1.14 |

## KEY PLAYERS - DEFENDERS

**1 Bernard Mendy**

| | |
|---|---|
| **Goals Conceded** The number of League goals conceded while he was on the pitch | 21 |
| **Goals Conceded in all competitions** The number goals conceded while he was on the pitch in all competitions | 22 |
| **League minutes played** Number of minutes played in league matches | 1624 |
| **Clean Sheets** In games when he played at least70 mins | 5 |
| **Defensive Rating** Average number of mins between League goals conceded while he was on the pitch | 77 |
| **Club Defensive Rating** Average number of mins between League goals conceded by the club this season | 67 |

| | PLAYER | CON LGE | CON ALL | MINS | C SHEETS | DEF RATE |
|---|---|---|---|---|---|---|
| 2 | Ramos Ivan Campo | 35 | 39 | 2598 | 8 | 74 mins |
| 3 | Gudni Bergsson | 39 | 39 | 2790 | 10 | 72 mins |
| 4 | Bruno N'Gotty | 28 | 30 | 1887 | 7 | 67 mins |
| 5 | Anthony Barness | 30 | 31 | 1923 | 3 | 64 mins |

## KEY PLAYERS - GOALKEEPERS

**1 Jussi Jaaskelainen**

| | |
|---|---|
| **Goals Conceded in the League** The number of League goals conceded while he was on the pitch | 51 |
| **Goals Conceded in all competitions** The number of goals conceded while he was on the pitch in all competitions | 51 |
| **League minutes played** Number of minutes played in league matches | 3420 |
| **Clean Sheets** In games when he played at least 70 mins | 10 |
| **Goals to Shots Ratio** The average number of shots on target per each League goal conceded | 4.3 |
| **Defensive Rating** Ave number of mins between League goals conceded while on the pitch | 67 |

**2 Kevin Poole**

| | |
|---|---|
| **Goals Conceded in the League** The number of League goals conceded while he was on the pitch | – |
| **Goals Conceded in all competitions** The number of goals conceded while he was on the pitch in all competitions | 4 |
| **League minutes played** Number of minutes played in league matches | 0 |
| **Clean Sheets** In games when he played at least 70 mins | – |
| **Goals to Shots Ratio** The average number of shots on target per each League goal conceded | – |
| **Defensive Rating** Ave number of mins between League goals conceded while on the pitch | – |

# WEST HAM UNITED

NICKNAME: THE HAMMERS

KEY: Won Drawn Lost

| | | | | | | |
|---|---|---|---|---|---|---|
| 1 | lge | Newcastle | A | L | 0-4 | |
| 2 | lge | Arsenal | H | D | 2-2 | Cole 43; Kanoute 53 |
| 3 | lge | Charlton | H | L | 0-2 | |
| 4 | lge | West Brom | H | L | 0-1 | |
| 5 | lge | Tottenham | A | L | 2-3 | Kanoute 66; Sinclair 77 |
| 6 | lge | Man City | H | D | 0-0 | |
| 7 | lge | Chelsea | A | W | 3-2 | Defoe 39; di Canio 47,83 |
| 8 | wr2 | Chesterfield | A | W | 5-4* | Defoe 13 (*on penalties) |
| 9 | lge | Birmingham | H | L | 1-2 | Cole 16 |
| 10 | lge | Sunderland | A | W | 1-0 | Sinclair 22 |
| 11 | lge | Fulham | A | W | 1-0 | di Canio 90 pen |
| 12 | lge | Everton | H | L | 0-1 | |
| 13 | lge | Liverpool | A | L | 0-2 | |
| 14 | wr3 | Oldham | H | L | 0-1 | |
| 15 | lge | Leeds | H | L | 3-4 | di Canio 21,50 pen; Sinclair 74 |
| 16 | lge | Man Utd | H | D | 1-1 | Defoe 86 |
| 17 | lge | Aston Villa | A | L | 1-4 | di Canio 70 |
| 18 | lge | Southampton | H | L | 0-1 | |
| 19 | lge | Middlesbrough | A | D | 2-2 | Cole 46; Pearce 76 |
| 20 | lge | Man Utd | A | L | 0-3 | |
| 21 | lge | Bolton | H | D | 1-1 | Pearce 17 |
| 22 | lge | Fulham | H | D | 1-1 | Sinclair 63 pen |
| 23 | lge | Blackburn | A | D | 2-2 | Taylor 24 og; Defoe 86 |
| 24 | facr3 | Nottm Forest | H | W | 3-2 | Defoe 26,83; Cole 61 |
| 25 | lge | Newcastle | H | D | 2-2 | Cole 14; Defoe 45 |
| 26 | lge | Arsenal | A | L | 1-3 | Defoe 40 |
| 27 | lge | Charlton | A | L | 2-4 | Rufus 19 og; Sinclair 62 |
| 28 | facr4 | Man Utd | A | L | 0-6 | |
| 29 | lge | Blackburn | H | W | 2-1 | di Canio 58 pen; Defoe 89 |
| 30 | lge | Liverpool | H | L | 0-3 | |
| 31 | lge | Leeds | A | L | 0-1 | |
| 32 | lge | West Brom | A | W | 2-1 | Sinclair 45,67 |
| 33 | lge | Tottenham | H | W | 2-0 | Ferdinand 32; Carrick 47 |
| 34 | lge | Everton | A | D | 0-0 | |
| 35 | lge | Sunderland | H | W | 2-0 | Defoe 24; Kanoute 65 |
| 36 | lge | Southampton | A | D | 1-1 | Defoe 83 |
| 37 | lge | Aston Villa | H | D | 2-2 | Sinclair 15; Kanoute 65 |
| 38 | lge | Bolton | A | L | 0-1 | |
| 39 | lge | Middlesbrough | H | W | 1-0 | Sinclair 77 |
| 40 | lge | Man City | A | W | 1-0 | Kanoute 81 |
| 41 | lge | Chelsea | H | W | 1-0 | di Canio 71 |
| 42 | lge | Birmingham | A | D | 2-2 | Ferdinand 66; di Canio 89 |

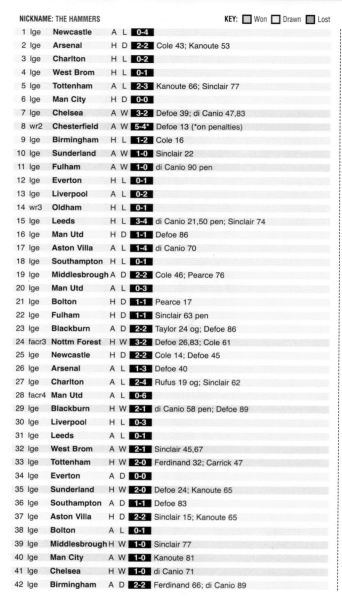

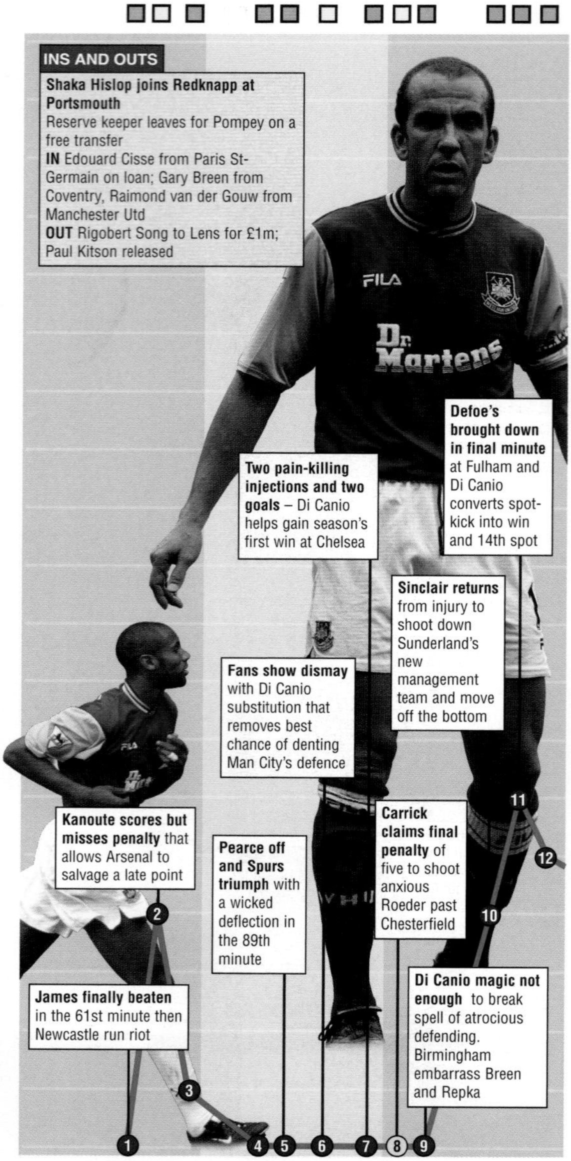
INS AND OUTS
Shaka Hislop joins Redknapp at Portsmouth
Reserve keeper leaves for Pompey on a free transfer
IN Edouard Cisse from Paris St-Germain on loan; Gary Breen from Coventry, Raimond van der Gouw from Manchester Utd
OUT Rigobert Song to Lens for £1m; Paul Kitson released
LEAGUE POSITION
Defoe's brought down in final minute at Fulham and Di Canio converts spot-kick into win and 14th spot
Two pain-killing injections and two goals – Di Canio helps gain season's first win at Chelsea
Sinclair returns from injury to shoot down Sunderland's new management team and move off the bottom
Fans show dismay with Di Canio substitution that removes best chance of denting Man City's defence
Kanoute scores but misses penalty that allows Arsenal to salvage a late point
Pearce off and Spurs triumph with a wicked deflection in the 89th minute
Carrick claims final penalty of five to shoot anxious Roeder past Chesterfield
James finally beaten in the 61st minute then Newcastle run riot
Di Canio magic not enough to break spell of atrocious defending. Birmingham embarrass Breen and Repka
1 2 3 4 5 6 7 8 9 10 11 12
AUGUST
SEPTEMBER
OCTOBER

Home Away Neutral

## ATTENDANCES

HOME GROUND: UPTON PARK CAPACITY: 35050 AVERAGE LEAGUE AT HOME: 34405

| | | | | | | | | | | | |
|---|---|---|---|---|---|---|---|---|---|---|---|
| 20 | Man Utd | 67555 | 16 | Man Utd | 35049 | 4 | West Brom | 34957 | 18 | Southampton | 28844 |
| 28 | Man Utd | 67181 | 33 | Tottenham | 35049 | 21 | Bolton | 34892 | 19 | Middlesboro | 28283 |
| 1 | Newcastle | 51072 | 25 | Newcastle | 35048 | 40 | Man City | 34815 | 38 | Bolton | 27160 |
| 10 | Sunderland | 44352 | 2 | Arsenal | 35048 | 29 | Blackburn | 34743 | 32 | West Brom | 27042 |
| 13 | Liverpool | 44048 | 41 | Chelsea | 35042 | 12 | Everton | 34117 | 27 | Charlton | 26340 |
| 34 | Everton | 40158 | 30 | Liverpool | 35033 | 15 | Leeds | 33297 | 23 | Blackburn | 24998 |
| 31 | Leeds | 40126 | 35 | Sunderland | 35033 | 17 | Aston Villa | 33279 | 14 | Oldham | 21919 |
| 7 | Chelsea | 38929 | 37 | Aston Villa | 35029 | 3 | Charlton | 32424 | 11 | Fulham | 15858 |
| 26 | Arsenal | 38053 | 22 | Fulham | 35025 | 36 | Southampton | 31941 | 8 | Chesterfield | 7102 |
| 5 | Tottenham | 36005 | 39 | Middlesboro | 35019 | 24 | Nottm Forest | 29612 | | | |
| 6 | Man City | 35050 | 9 | Birmingham | 35010 | 42 | Birmingham | 29505 | | | |

## GOAL ATTEMPTS

**FOR** – Goal attempts recorded in League games

| | HOME | AWAY | TOTAL | AVE |
|---|---|---|---|---|
| shots on target | 113 | 82 | 195 | 5.1 |
| shots off target | 118 | 102 | 220 | 5.8 |
| TOTAL | 231 | 184 | 415 | 10.9 |

**Ratio of goals to shots** – Average number of shots on target per League goal scored: **4.6**

**Accuracy rating** – Average percentage of total goal attempts which were on target: **47.0**

**AGAINST** – Goal attempts recorded in League games

| | HOME | AWAY | TOTAL | AVE |
|---|---|---|---|---|
| shots on target | 80 | 129 | 209 | 5.5 |
| shots off target | 94 | 82 | 176 | 4.6 |
| TOTAL | 174 | 211 | 385 | 10.1 |

**Ratio of goals to shots** – Average number of shots on target per League goal scored: **3.5**

**Accuracy rating** – Average percentage of total goal attempts which were on target: **54.3**

# Bubble bursts for 'too good' team

**Final Position: 18th**

KEY: ● League ● Champions Lge ● UEFA Cup ● FA Cup ○ League Cup ● Other

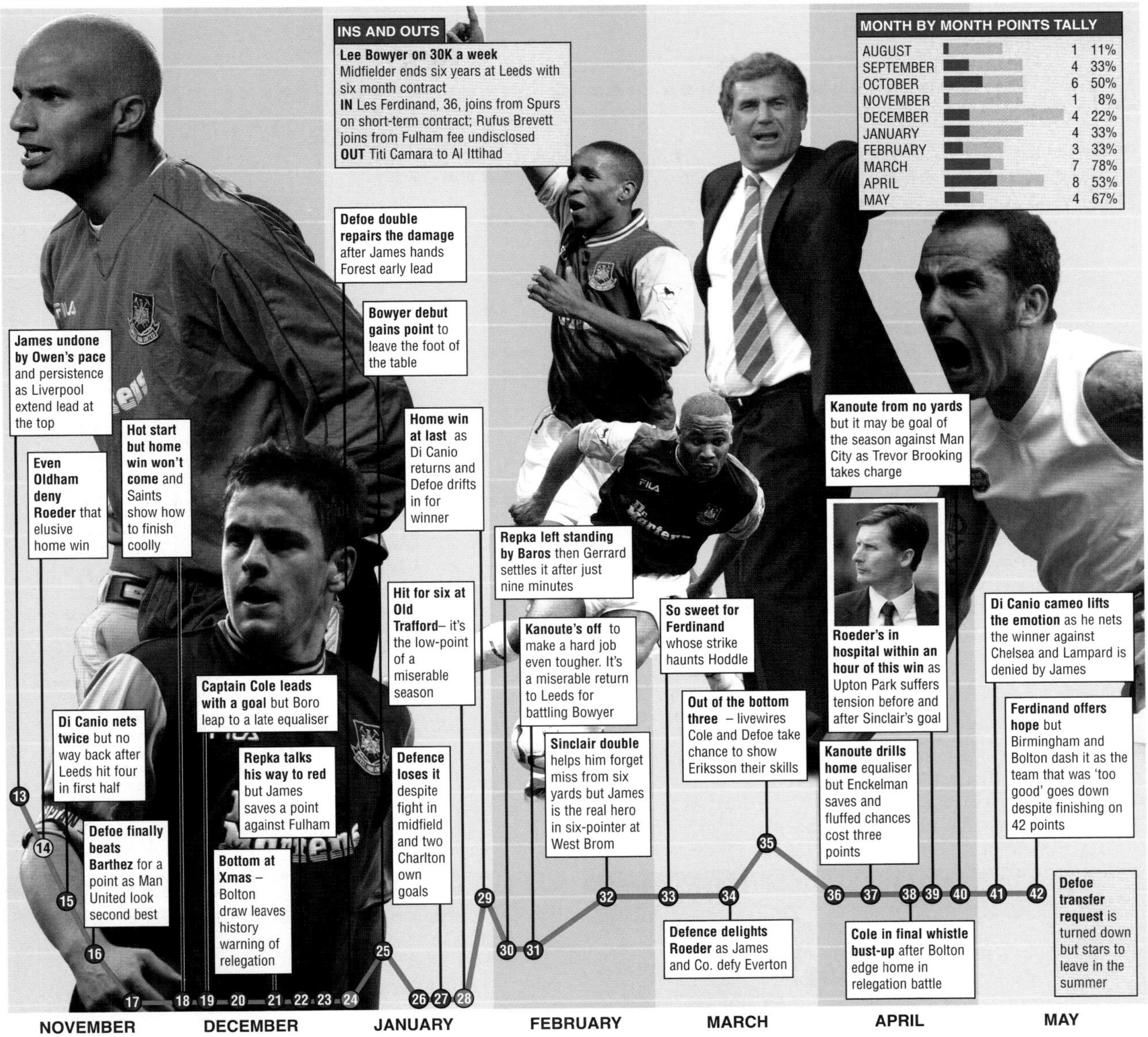
INS AND OUTS
**Lee Bowyer on 30K a week** Midfielder ends six years at Leeds with six month contract
**IN** Les Ferdinand, 36, joins from Spurs on short-term contract; Rufus Brevett joins from Fulham fee undisclosed
**OUT** Titi Camara to Al Ittihad
MONTH BY MONTH POINTS TALLY
AUGUST 1 11%
SEPTEMBER 4 33%
OCTOBER 6 50%
NOVEMBER 1 8%
DECEMBER 4 22%
JANUARY 4 33%
FEBRUARY 3 33%
MARCH 7 78%
APRIL 8 53%
MAY 4 67%
**James undone by Owen's pace** and persistence as Liverpool extend lead at the top
**Even Oldham deny Roeder** that elusive home win
**Hot start but home win won't come** and Saints show how to finish coolly
**Di Canio nets twice** but no way back after Leeds hit four in first half
**Defoe finally beats Barthez** for a point as Man United look second best
**Captain Cole leads with a goal** but Boro leap to a late equaliser
**Repka talks his way to red** but James saves a point against Fulham
**Bottom at Xmas** – Bolton draw leaves history warning of relegation
**Defoe double repairs the damage** after James hands Forest early lead
**Bowyer debut gains point** to leave the foot of the table
**Home win at last** as Di Canio returns and Defoe drifts in for winner
**Hit for six at Old Trafford**– it's the low-point of a miserable season
**Defence loses it** despite fight in midfield and two Charlton own goals
**Repka left standing by Baros** then Gerrard settles it after just nine minutes
**Kanoute's off** to make a hard job even tougher. It's a miserable return to Leeds for battling Bowyer
**Sinclair double** helps him forget miss from six yards but James is the real hero in six-pointer at West Brom
**So sweet for Ferdinand** whose strike haunts Hoddle
**Out of the bottom three** – livewires Cole and Defoe take chance to show Eriksson their skills
**Defence delights Roeder** as James and Co. defy Everton
**Kanoute from no yards** but it may be goal of the season against Man City as Trevor Brooking takes charge
**Roeder's in hospital within an hour of this win** as Upton Park suffers tension before and after Sinclair's goal
**Kanoute drills home** equaliser but Enckelman saves and fluffed chances cost three points
**Cole in final whistle bust-up** after Bolton edge home in relegation battle
**Di Canio cameo lifts the emotion** as he nets the winner against Chelsea and Lampard is denied by James
**Ferdinand offers hope** but Birmingham and Bolton dash it as the team that was 'too good' goes down despite finishing on 42 points
**Defoe transfer request** is turned down but stars to leave in the summer
13 14 15 16 17 18 19 20 21 22 23 24 25 26 27 28 29 30 31 32 33 34 35 36 37 38 39 40 41 42
NOVEMBER
DECEMBER
JANUARY
FEBRUARY
MARCH
APRIL
MAY

## DISCIPLINARY RECORDS

**1 Tomas Repka**

| | |
|---|---|
| League Yellow | 12 |
| League Red | 1 |
| League Total | 13 |
| All Comps Yellow | 13 |
| All Comps Red | 1 |
| TOTAL | 14 |

League Average 211 mins between cards

| | PLAYER | LEAGUE | | TOTAL | | AVE |
|---|---|---|---|---|---|---|
| | | 4Y | 0R | 4Y | 0R | |
| 2 | Bowyer | | | | | 216 |
| 3 | Cisse | 6 | 0 | 6 | 0 | 257 |
| 4 | Minto | 3 | 0 | 4 | 0 | 278 |
| 5 | Cole | 10 | 0 | 10 | 0 | 319 |
| 6 | Brevett | 3 | 0 | 3 | 0 | 365 |
| 7 | Johnson | 3 | 0 | 3 | 0 | 429 |
| 8 | Lomas | 3 | 1 | 3 | 1 | 563 |
| 9 | Kanoute | 1 | 1 | 1 | 1 | 564 |
| 10 | Carrick | 4 | 0 | 4 | 0 | 633 |
| 11 | Schemmel | 2 | 0 | 4 | 0 | 677 |
| 12 | di Canio | 2 | 0 | 3 | 0 | 679 |
| 13 | Winterburn | 2 | 0 | 2 | 0 | 701 |
| 14 | Pearce | 1 | 2 | 2 | 2 | 777 |
| 15 | Breen | 1 | 0 | 1 | 0 | 866 |
| | Other | 9 | 0 | 13 | 0 | |
| | TOTAL | 66 | 5 | 76 | 5 | |

## GOALS

**1 Trevor Sinclair**

| | |
|---|---|
| League | 9 |
| FA Cup | 0 |
| League Cup | 0 |
| Europe | 0 |
| Other | 0 |
| TOTAL | 9 |

League Average 356 mins between goals

| | PLAYER | LGE | FAC | LC | Euro | TOT | AVE |
|---|---|---|---|---|---|---|---|
| 2 | di Canio | 9 | 0 | 0 | 0 | 9 | 151 |
| 3 | Defoe | 8 | 2 | 1 | 0 | 11 | 353 |
| 4 | Kanoute | 5 | 0 | 0 | 0 | 5 | 226 |
| 5 | Cole | 4 | 1 | 0 | 0 | 5 | 799 |
| 6 | Ferdinand | 2 | 0 | 0 | 0 | 2 | 438 |
| 7 | Pearce | 2 | 0 | 0 | 0 | 2 | 1166 |
| 8 | Carrick | 1 | 0 | 0 | 0 | 1 | 2533 |
| | Other | 2 | 0 | 0 | 0 | 4 | |
| | TOTAL | 42 | 3 | 1 | 0 | 48 | |

## SQUAD APPEARANCES

| Match | Venue | Competition | Result |
|---|---|---|---|
| 1 | A | L | L |
| 2 | H | L | D |
| 3 | H | L | L |
| 4 | H | L | L |
| 5 | A | L | L |
| 6 | H | L | D |
| 7 | A | L | W |
| 8 | A | W | W |
| 9 | H | L | L |
| 10 | A | L | W |
| 11 | A | L | W |
| 12 | H | L | L |
| 13 | A | L | L |
| 14 | H | W | L |
| 15 | H | L | L |
| 16 | H | L | D |
| 17 | A | L | L |
| 18 | H | L | L |
| 19 | A | L | D |
| 20 | A | L | L |
| 21 | H | L | D |
| 22 | H | L | D |
| 23 | A | L | D |
| 24 | H | F | W |
| 25 | H | L | D |
| 26 | A | L | L |
| 27 | A | L | L |
| 28 | A | F | L |
| 29 | H | L | W |
| 30 | H | L | L |
| 31 | A | L | L |
| 32 | A | L | W |
| 33 | H | L | W |
| 34 | A | L | D |
| 35 | H | L | W |
| 36 | A | L | D |
| 37 | H | L | D |
| 38 | A | L | L |
| 39 | H | L | W |
| 40 | A | L | W |
| 41 | H | L | W |
| 42 | A | L | D |

**Goalkeepers**
Stephen Bywater
David James
Raimond van der Gouw

**Defenders**
Gary Breen
Rufus Brevett
Christian Dailly
Glen Johnson
Vladimir Labant
Scott Minto
Ian Pearce
Tomas Repka
Sebastien Schemmel
Nigel Winterburn

**Midfielders**
Lee Bowyer
Michael Carrick
Edouard Cisse
Joe Cole
Anton Ferdinand
Don Hutchison
Steve Lomas
John Moncur
Trevor Sinclair

**Forwards**
Titi Camara
Jermain Defoe
Paolo di Canio
Les Ferdinand
Richard Garcia
Frederic Kanoute
Youssef Sofiane

KEY: On all match · On bench · Subbed or sent off (Counting game) · Subbed or sent off (playing less than 70 minutes) · Subbed on from bench (Counting Game) · Subbed on (playing less than 70 minutes) · Subbed on and then subbed or sent off (Counting Game) · Subbed on and then subbed or sent off (playing less than 70 minutes) · Not in 16

## KEY PLAYERS - GOALSCORERS

**1 Paolo di Canio**

| | |
|---|---|
| Goals in the League | 9 |
| Goals in all competitions | 9 |
| Assists<br>League goals scored by team-mates where he delivered the final pass | 3 |
| Contribution to Attacking Power<br>Average number of minutes between League team goals while on pitch | 79 |
| Player Strike Rate<br>Average number of minutes between League goals scored by player | 151 |
| Club Strike Rate<br>Average minutes between League goals scored by club | 81 |

| | PLAYER | GOALS LGE | GOALS ALL | ASSISTS | POWER | S RATE |
|---|---|---|---|---|---|---|
| 2 | Jermain Defoe | 8 | 11 | 6 | 76 | 353 mins |
| 3 | Trevor Sinclair | 9 | 9 | 1 | 78 | 356 mins |
| 4 | Joe Cole | 4 | 5 | 4 | 86 | 799 mins |
| 5 | Ian Pearce | 2 | 2 | 1 | 86 | 1166 mins |

## KEY PLAYERS - MIDFIELDERS

**1 Steve Lomas**

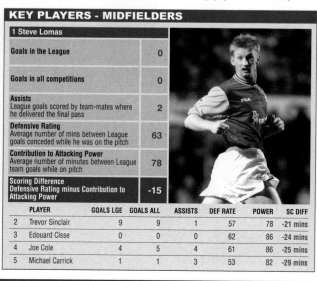

| | |
|---|---|
| Goals in the League | 0 |
| Goals in all competitions | 0 |
| Assists<br>League goals scored by team-mates where he delivered the final pass | 2 |
| Defensive Rating<br>Average number of mins between League goals conceded while he was on the pitch | 63 |
| Contribution to Attacking Power<br>Average number of minutes between League team goals while on pitch | 78 |
| Scoring Difference<br>Defensive Rating minus Contribution to Attacking Power | -15 |

| | PLAYER | GOALS LGE | GOALS ALL | ASSISTS | DEF RATE | POWER | SC DIFF |
|---|---|---|---|---|---|---|---|
| 2 | Trevor Sinclair | 9 | 9 | 1 | 57 | 78 | -21 mins |
| 3 | Edouard Cisse | 0 | 0 | 0 | 62 | 86 | -24 mins |
| 4 | Joe Cole | 4 | 5 | 4 | 61 | 86 | -25 mins |
| 5 | Michael Carrick | 1 | 1 | 3 | 53 | 82 | -29 mins |

## PLAYER APPEARANCES

| | AGE (on 01/07/03) | IN THE SQUAD | COUNTING GAMES | MINUTES ON PITCH | IN THE SQUAD | MINUTES ON PITCH | THIS SEASON | NATIONAL SIDE |
|---|---|---|---|---|---|---|---|---|
| **Goalkeepers** | | | | | | | | |
| Stephen Bywater | 22 | 4 | 0 | 0 | 4 | 0 | - | England |
| David James | 32 | 38 | 38 | 3420 | 43 | 3900 | 9 | England (7) |
| van der Gouw | 40 | 34 | 0 | 0 | 39 | 0 | - | Holland |
| **Defenders** | | | | | | | | |
| Gary Breen | 29 | 28 | 9 | 866 | 33 | 1299 | 10 | Rep of Ireland (15) |
| Rufus Brevett | 33 | 13 | 12 | 1095 | 13 | 1095 | - | England |
| Christian Dailly | 29 | 32 | 23 | 2091 | 37 | 2372 | 11 | Scotland (64) |
| Glen Johnson | 18 | 17 | 14 | 1288 | 18 | 1299 | - | England |
| Vladimir Labant | 29 | 1 | 0 | 20 | 1 | 20 | - | Slovakia |
| Scott Minto | 31 | 15 | 9 | 835 | 18 | 1099 | - | England |
| Ian Pearce | 29 | 35 | 25 | 2332 | 39 | 2658 | - | England |
| Tomas Repka | 29 | 35 | 30 | 2754 | 38 | 2886 | - | Czech Republic |
| Seb Schemmel | 28 | 18 | 15 | 1355 | 22 | 1691 | - | France |
| Nigel Winterburn | 39 | 25 | 14 | 1403 | 28 | 1607 | - | England |
| **Midfielders** | | | | | | | | |
| Lee Bowyer | 26 | 10 | 9 | 865 | 11 | 955 | 1 | England (7) |
| Michael Carrick | 21 | 30 | 28 | 2533 | 35 | 3013 | - | England |
| Edouard Cisse | 25 | 30 | 14 | 1545 | 35 | 1883 | - | France |
| Joe Cole | 21 | 36 | 36 | 3194 | 41 | 3674 | 5 | England (7) |
| Anton Ferdinand | 18 | 1 | 0 | 0 | 1 | 0 | - | England |
| Don Hutchison | 32 | 16 | 0 | 127 | 17 | 127 | 4 | Scotland (64) |
| Steve Lomas | 29 | 29 | 24 | 2253 | 32 | 2553 | 5 | N Ireland (111) |
| John Moncur | 36 | 14 | 0 | 73 | 16 | 73 | - | England |
| Trevor Sinclair | 30 | 38 | 35 | 3203 | 42 | 3582 | 2 | England (7) |
| **Forwards** | | | | | | | | |
| Titi Camara | 30 | 15 | 0 | 68 | 19 | 192 | - | Guinea |
| Jermain Defoe | 20 | 38 | 29 | 2821 | 43 | 3301 | - | England |
| Paolo di Canio | 35 | 18 | 15 | 1358 | 19 | 1478 | - | Italy |
| Les Ferdinand | 36 | 14 | 5 | 876 | 14 | 876 | - | England |
| Richard Garcia | 21 | 7 | 0 | 0 | 10 | 22 | - | Australia |
| Frederic Kanoute | 25 | 17 | 10 | 1129 | 17 | 1129 | - | France |
| Youssef Sofiane | 18 | 0 | 0 | 0 | 3 | 0 | - | France |

KEY: LEAGUE ALL COMPS CAPS (FIFA RANKING)

## TEAM OF THE SEASON

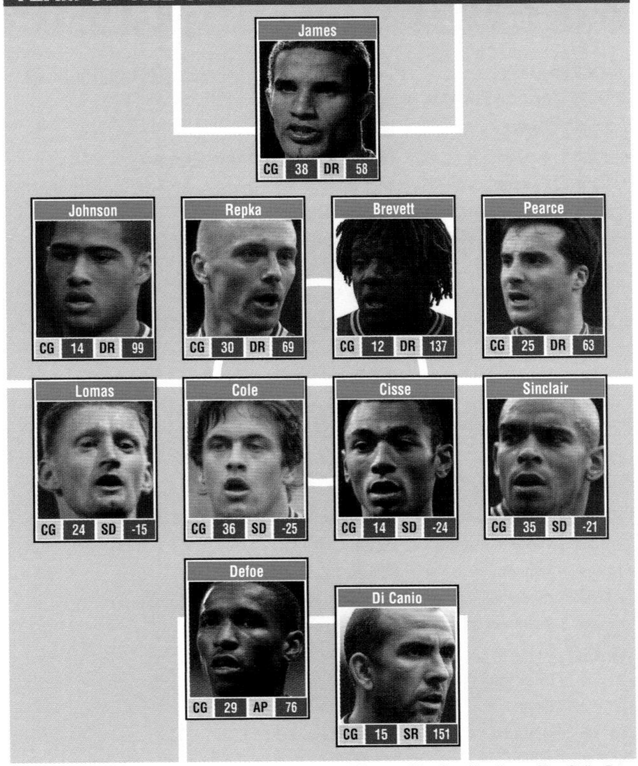
James
CG 38 DR 58
Johnson
CG 14 DR 99
Repka
CG 30 DR 69
Brevett
CG 12 DR 137
Pearce
CG 25 DR 63
Lomas
CG 24 SD -15
Cole
CG 36 SD -25
Cisse
CG 14 SD -24
Sinclair
CG 35 SD -21
Defoe
CG 29 AP 76
Di Canio
CG 15 SR 151

KEY: DR = Defensive Rate, SD = Scoring Difference AP = Attacking Power SR = Strike Rate, CG=Counting Games – League games playing at least 70 minutes

## TOP POINT EARNERS

**1 Rufus Brevett**

| | |
|---|---|
| **Counting Games** League games when he played at least 70 minutes | 12 |
| **Average points** Average League points taken in Counting games | 1.83 |
| **Club Average points** Average points taken in League games | 1.11 |

| | PLAYER | GAMES | PTS |
|---|---|---|---|
| 2 | Glen Johnson | 14 | 1.79 |
| 3 | Steve Lomas | 24 | 1.33 |
| 4 | Tomas Repka | 30 | 1.30 |
| 5 | Jermain Defoe | 29 | 1.17 |
| 6 | Ian Pearce | 25 | 1.12 |
| 7 | David James | 38 | 1.11 |
| 8 | Trevor Sinclair | 35 | 1.11 |
| 9 | Joe Cole | 36 | 1.08 |
| 10 | Michael Carrick | 28 | 1.04 |

## KEY PLAYERS - DEFENDERS

**1 Rufus Brevett**

| | |
|---|---|
| **Goals Conceded** The number of League goals conceded while he was on the pitch | 8 |
| **Goals Conceded in all competitions** The number goals conceded while he was on the pitch in all competitions | 8 |
| **League minutes played** Number of minutes played in league matches | 1095 |
| **Clean Sheets** In games when he played at least70 mins | 6 |
| **Defensive Rating** Average number of mins between League goals conceded while he was on the pitch | 137 |
| **Club Defensive Rating** Average number of mins between League goals conceded by the club this season | 58 |

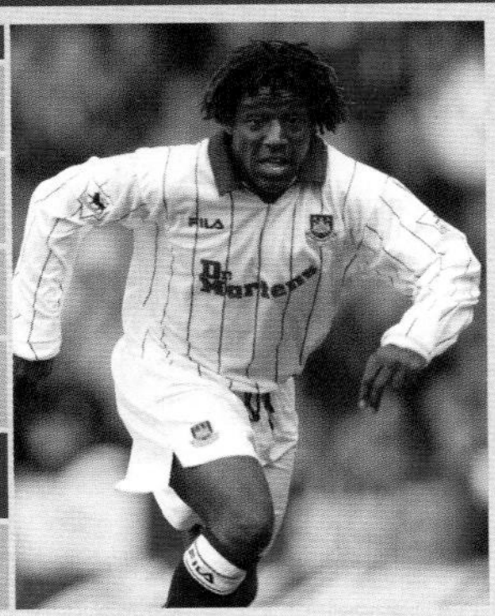

| | PLAYER | CON LGE | CON ALL | MINS | C SHEETS | DEF RATE |
|---|---|---|---|---|---|---|
| 2 | Glen Johnson | 13 | 13 | 1288 | 6 | 99 mins |
| 3 | Tomas Repka | 40 | 41 | 2754 | 9 | 69 mins |
| 4 | Ian Pearce | 37 | 46 | 2332 | 6 | 63 mins |
| 5 | Sebastien Schemmel | 25 | 28 | 1355 | 1 | 54 mins |

## KEY PLAYERS - GOALKEEPERS

**1 David James**

| | |
|---|---|
| **Goals Conceded in the League** The number of League goals conceded while he was on the pitch | 59 |
| **Goals Conceded in all competitions** The number of goals conceded while he was on the pitch in all competitions | 69 |
| **League minutes played** Number of minutes played in league matches | 3420 |
| **Clean Sheets** In games when he played at least 70 mins | 9 |
| **Goals to Shots Ratio** The average number of shots on target per each League goal conceded | 3.5 |
| **Defensive Rating** Ave number of mins between League goals conceded while on the pitch | 58 |

**2 Raimond van der Gouw**

| | |
|---|---|
| **Goals Conceded in the League** The number of League goals conceded while he was on the pitch | – |
| **Goals Conceded in all competitions** The number of goals conceded while he was on the pitch in all competitions | – |
| **League minutes played** Number of minutes played in league matches | 0 |
| **Clean Sheets** In games when he played at least 70 mins | – |
| **Goals to Shots Ratio** The average number of shots on target per each League goal conceded | – |
| **Defensive Rating** Ave number of mins between League goals conceded while on the pitch | – |

# WEST BROMWICH ALBION

**NICKNAME:** BAGGIES

KEY: Won / Drawn / Lost

| | | | | | | |
|---|---|---|---|---|---|---|
| 1 | lge | Man Utd | A | L | 0-1 | |
| 2 | lge | Leeds | H | L | 1-3 | Marshall 89 |
| 3 | lge | Arsenal | A | L | 2-5 | Dobie 51; Roberts 87 |
| 4 | lge | Fulham | H | W | 1-0 | Moore 48 |
| 5 | lge | West Ham | A | W | 1-0 | Roberts 28 |
| 6 | lge | Southampton | H | W | 1-0 | Gregan 79 |
| 7 | lge | Liverpool | A | L | 0-2 | |
| 8 | lge | Blackburn | H | L | 0-2 | |
| 9 | wr2 | Wigan | A | L | 1-3 | Hughes 88 |
| 10 | lge | Newcastle | A | L | 1-2 | Balis 26 |
| 11 | lge | Birmingham | H | D | 1-1 | Roberts 87 |
| 12 | lge | Chelsea | A | L | 0-2 | |
| 13 | lge | Man City | H | L | 1-2 | Clement 62 |
| 14 | lge | Bolton | A | D | 1-1 | Dobie 17 |
| 15 | lge | Aston Villa | H | D | 0-0 | |
| 16 | lge | Everton | A | L | 0-1 | |
| 17 | lge | Middlesbrough | H | W | 1-0 | Dichio 72 |
| 18 | lge | Tottenham | A | L | 1-3 | Dobie 73 |
| 19 | lge | Aston Villa | A | L | 1-2 | Koumas 29 |
| 20 | lge | Sunderland | H | D | 2-2 | Dichio 27; Koumas 33 |
| 21 | lge | Arsenal | H | L | 1-2 | Dichio 3 |
| 22 | lge | Charlton | A | L | 0-1 | |
| 23 | facr3 | Bradford | H | W | 3-1 | Dichio 4,11,19 |
| 24 | lge | Man Utd | H | L | 1-3 | Koumas 6 |
| 25 | lge | Leeds | A | D | 0-0 | |
| 26 | facr4 | Watford | A | L | 0-1 | |
| 27 | lge | Charlton | H | L | 0-1 | |
| 28 | lge | Man City | A | W | 2-1 | Clement 18; Moore 71 |
| 29 | lge | Bolton | H | D | 1-1 | Johnson 90 |
| 30 | lge | Fulham | A | L | 0-3 | |
| 31 | lge | West Ham | H | L | 1-2 | Dichio 50 |
| 32 | lge | Southampton | A | L | 0-1 | |
| 33 | lge | Chelsea | H | L | 0-2 | |
| 34 | lge | Birmingham | A | L | 0-1 | |
| 35 | lge | Middlesbrough | A | L | 0-3 | |
| 36 | lge | Everton | H | L | 1-2 | Balis 18 pen |
| 37 | lge | Sunderland | A | W | 2-1 | McInnes 39,42 |
| 38 | lge | Tottenham | H | L | 2-3 | Dichio 24; Clement 61 |
| 39 | lge | Liverpool | H | L | 0-6 | |
| 40 | lge | Blackburn | A | D | 1-1 | Koumas 54 |
| 41 | lge | Newcastle | H | D | 2-2 | Dobie 57,72 |

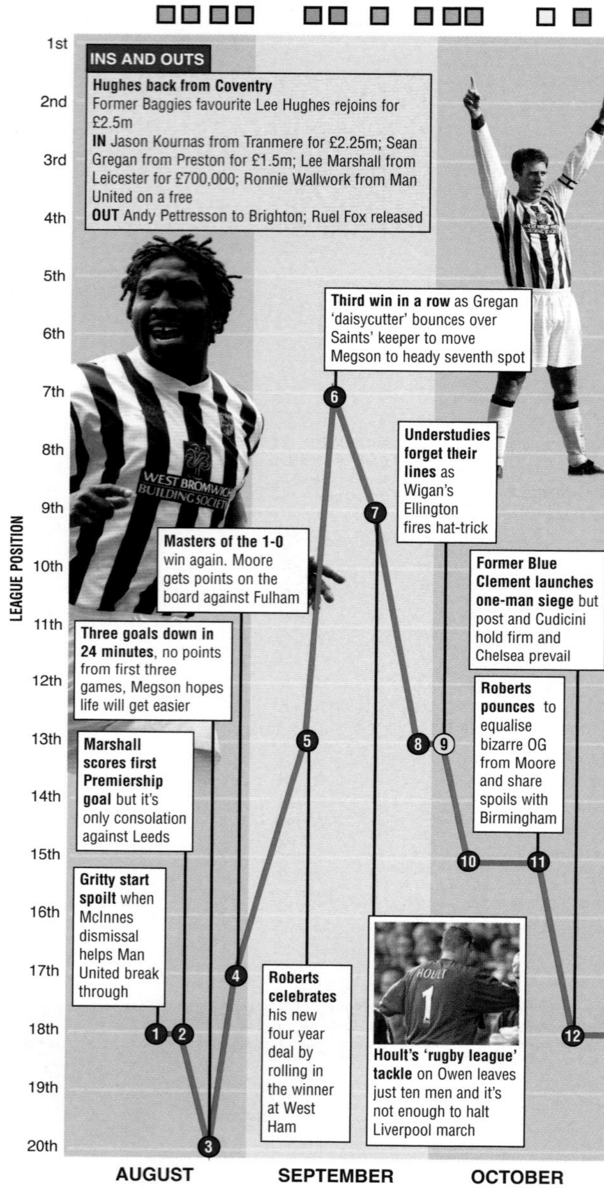

LEAGUE POSITION
1st
2nd
3rd
4th
5th
6th
7th
8th
9th
10th
11th
12th
13th
14th
15th
16th
17th
18th
19th
20th
INS AND OUTS
Hughes back from Coventry
Former Baggies favourite Lee Hughes rejoins for £2.5m
IN Jason Kournas from Tranmere for £2.25m; Sean Gregan from Preston for £1.5m; Lee Marshall from Leicester for £700,000; Ronnie Wallwork from Man United on a free
OUT Andy Pettresson to Brighton; Ruel Fox released
Third win in a row as Gregan 'daisycutter' bounces over Saints' keeper to move Megson to heady seventh spot
Understudies forget their lines as Wigan's Ellington fires hat-trick
Masters of the 1-0 win again. Moore gets points on the board against Fulham
Former Blue Clement launches one-man siege but post and Cudicini hold firm and Chelsea prevail
Three goals down in 24 minutes, no points from first three games, Megson hopes life will get easier
Roberts pounces to equalise bizarre OG from Moore and share spoils with Birmingham
Marshall scores first Premiership goal but it's only consolation against Leeds
Gritty start spoilt when McInnes dismissal helps Man United break through
Roberts celebrates his new four year deal by rolling in the winner at West Ham
Hoult's 'rugby league' tackle on Owen leaves just ten men and it's not enough to halt Liverpool march
AUGUST
SEPTEMBER
OCTOBER


Home / Away / Neutral

## ATTENDANCES

**HOME GROUND:** THE HAWTHORNS **CAPACITY:** 27130 **AVERAGE LEAGUE AT HOME:** 26731

| | | | | | | | | | | | |
|---|---|---|---|---|---|---|---|---|---|---|---|
| 1 | Man Utd | 67645 | 28 | Man City | 34675 | 41 | Newcastle | 27036 | 27 | Charlton | 26113 |
| 10 | Newcastle | 52142 | 32 | Southampton | 31915 | 17 | Middlesboro | 27029 | 4 | Fulham | 25462 |
| 7 | Liverpool | 43830 | 35 | Middlesboro | 30187 | 21 | Arsenal | 27025 | 8 | Blackburn | 25170 |
| 12 | Chelsea | 40893 | 34 | Birmingham | 29449 | 33 | Chelsea | 27024 | 14 | Bolton | 23630 |
| 19 | Aston Villa | 40391 | 40 | Blackburn | 27470 | 11 | Birmingham | 27021 | 23 | Bradford | 19909 |
| 16 | Everton | 40113 | 24 | Man Utd | 27129 | 29 | Bolton | 26933 | 26 | Watford | 16975 |
| 25 | Leeds | 39708 | 39 | Liverpool | 27128 | 38 | Tottenham | 26899 | 30 | Fulham | 15799 |
| 3 | Arsenal | 37920 | 15 | Aston Villa | 27091 | 20 | Sunderland | 26703 | 9 | Wigan | 6558 |
| 37 | Sunderland | 36025 | 13 | Man City | 27044 | 2 | Leeds | 26618 | | | |
| 18 | Tottenham | 35958 | 31 | West Ham | 27042 | 6 | Southampton | 26383 | | | |
| 5 | West Ham | 34957 | 36 | Everton | 27039 | 22 | Charlton | 26196 | | | |

## GOAL ATTEMPTS

**FOR**
Goal attempts recorded in League games

| | HOME | AWAY | TOTAL | AVE |
|---|---|---|---|---|
| shots on target | 108 | 92 | 200 | 5.3 |
| shots off target | 108 | 92 | 200 | 5.3 |
| TOTAL | 216 | 184 | 400 | 10.5 |

**Ratio of goals to shots** Average number of shots on target per League goal scored: **6.9**

**Accuracy rating** Average percentage of total goal attempts which were on target: **50.0**

**AGAINST**
Goal attempts recorded in League games

| | HOME | AWAY | TOTAL | AVE |
|---|---|---|---|---|
| shots on target | 92 | 156 | 248 | 6.5 |
| shots off target | 100 | 92 | 192 | 5.1 |
| TOTAL | 192 | 248 | 440 | 11.6 |

**Ratio of goals to shots** Average number of shots on target per League goal scored: **3.8**

**Accuracy rating** Average percentage of total goal attempts which were on target: **56.4**

# Adventure ends with pride and fall

Final Position: **19th**

KEY: ● League ● Champions Lge ● UEFA Cup ● FA Cup ○ League Cup ● Other

**INS AND OUTS**

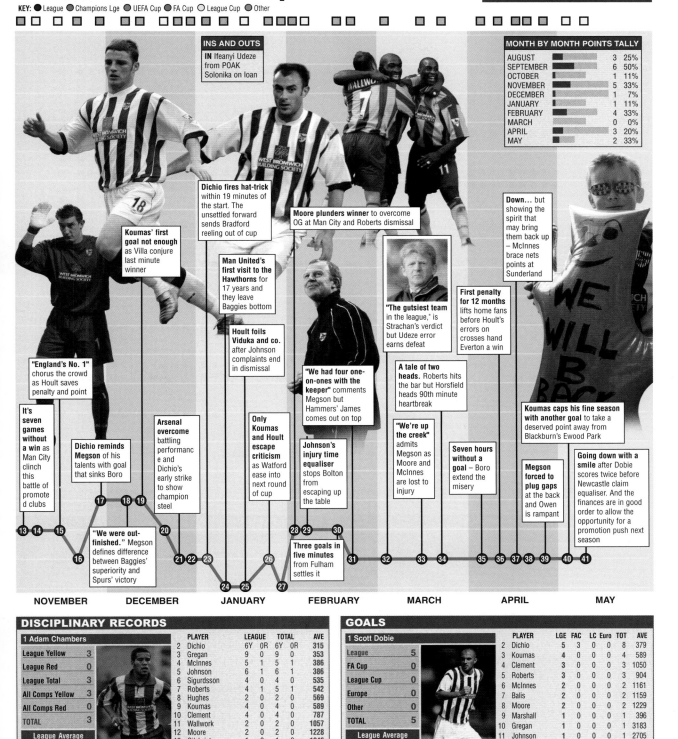

**IN** Ifeanyi Udeze from POAK Solonika on loan

**MONTH BY MONTH POINTS TALLY**

| | | |
|---|---|---|
| AUGUST | 3 | 25% |
| SEPTEMBER | 6 | 50% |
| OCTOBER | 1 | 11% |
| NOVEMBER | 5 | 33% |
| DECEMBER | 1 | 7% |
| JANUARY | 1 | 11% |
| FEBRUARY | 4 | 33% |
| MARCH | 0 | 0% |
| APRIL | 3 | 20% |
| MAY | 2 | 33% |

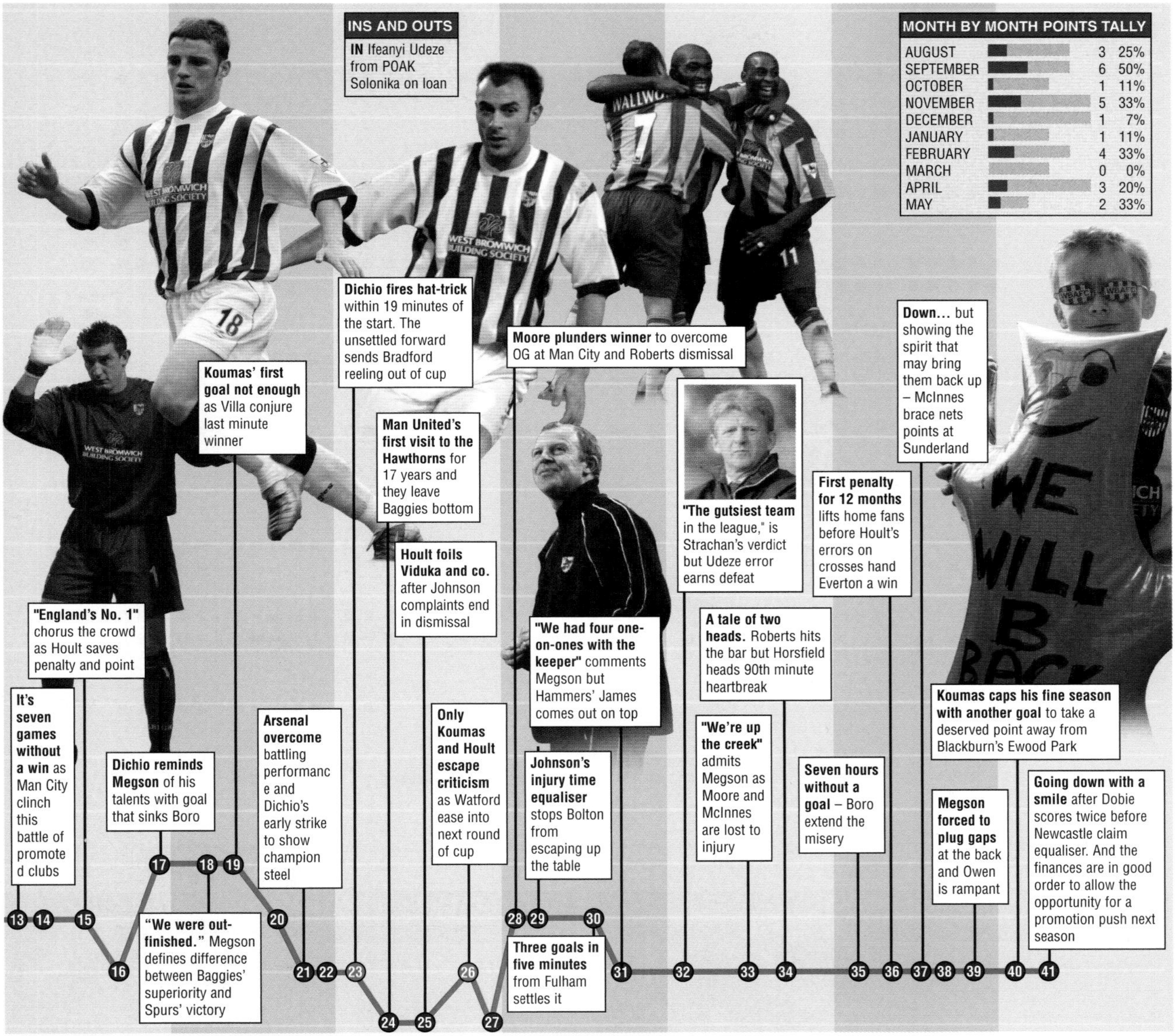
WALLWO
7
11
WEST BROMWICH BUILDING SOCIETY
WE WILL B BACK
It's seven games without a win as Man City clinch this battle of promote d clubs
"England's No. 1" chorus the crowd as Hoult saves penalty and point
"We were out-finished." Megson defines difference between Baggies' superiority and Spurs' victory
Dichio reminds Megson of his talents with goal that sinks Boro
Koumas' first goal not enough as Villa conjure last minute winner
Arsenal overcome battling performanc e and Dichio's early strike to show champion steel
Dichio fires hat-trick within 19 minutes of the start. The unsettled forward sends Bradford reeling out of cup
Man United's first visit to the Hawthorns for 17 years and they leave Baggies bottom
Hoult foils Viduka and co. after Johnson complaints end in dismissal
Only Koumas and Hoult escape criticism as Watford ease into next round of cup
Moore plunders winner to overcome OG at Man City and Roberts dismissal
Johnson's injury time equaliser stops Bolton from escaping up the table
Three goals in five minutes from Fulham settles it
"We had four one-on-ones with the keeper" comments Megson but Hammers' James comes out on top
"The gutsiest team in the league," is Strachan's verdict but Udeze error earns defeat
"We're up the creek" admits Megson as Moore and McInnes are lost to injury
A tale of two heads. Roberts hits the bar but Horsfield heads 90th minute heartbreak
Seven hours without a goal – Boro extend the misery
First penalty for 12 months lifts home fans before Hoult's errors on crosses hand Everton a win
Down... but showing the spirit that may bring them back up – McInnes brace nets points at Sunderland
Megson forced to plug gaps at the back and Owen is rampant
Koumas caps his fine season with another goal to take a deserved point away from Blackburn's Ewood Park
Going down with a smile after Dobie scores twice before Newcastle claim equaliser. And the finances are in good order to allow the opportunity for a promotion push next season
13 14 15 16 17 18 19 20 21 22 23 24 25 26 27 28 29 30 31 32 33 34 35 36 37 38 39 40 41
NOVEMBER
DECEMBER
JANUARY
FEBRUARY
MARCH
APRIL
MAY

## DISCIPLINARY RECORDS

**1 Adam Chambers**

| | |
|---|---|
| League Yellow | 3 |
| League Red | 0 |
| League Total | 3 |
| All Comps Yellow | 3 |
| All Comps Red | 0 |
| TOTAL | 3 |

League Average 298 mins between cards

| | PLAYER | LEAGUE | | TOTAL | | AVE |
|---|---|---|---|---|---|---|
| 2 | Dichio | 6Y | 0R | 6Y | 0R | 315 |
| 3 | Gregan | 9 | 0 | 9 | 0 | 353 |
| 4 | McInnes | 5 | 1 | 5 | 1 | 386 |
| 5 | Johnson | 6 | 1 | 6 | 1 | 386 |
| 6 | Sigurdsson | 4 | 0 | 4 | 0 | 535 |
| 7 | Roberts | 4 | 1 | 5 | 1 | 542 |
| 8 | Hughes | 2 | 0 | 2 | 0 | 569 |
| 9 | Koumas | 4 | 0 | 4 | 0 | 589 |
| 10 | Clement | 4 | 0 | 4 | 0 | 787 |
| 11 | Wallwork | 2 | 0 | 2 | 0 | 1057 |
| 12 | Moore | 2 | 0 | 2 | 0 | 1228 |
| 13 | Gilchrist | 1 | 0 | 1 | 0 | 1946 |
| 14 | Hoult | 0 | 1 | 0 | 1 | 3275 |
| | Other | 0 | 0 | 0 | 0 | |
| | TOTAL | 52 | 4 | 53 | 4 | |

## GOALS

**1 Scott Dobie**

| | |
|---|---|
| League | 5 |
| FA Cup | 0 |
| League Cup | 0 |
| Europe | 0 |
| Other | 0 |
| TOTAL | 5 |

League Average 241 mins between goals

| | PLAYER | LGE | FAC | LC | Euro | TOT | AVE |
|---|---|---|---|---|---|---|---|
| 2 | Dichio | 5 | 3 | 0 | 0 | 8 | 379 |
| 3 | Koumas | 4 | 0 | 0 | 0 | 4 | 589 |
| 4 | Clement | 3 | 0 | 0 | 0 | 3 | 1050 |
| 5 | Roberts | 3 | 0 | 0 | 0 | 3 | 904 |
| 6 | McInnes | 2 | 0 | 0 | 0 | 2 | 1161 |
| 7 | Balis | 2 | 0 | 0 | 0 | 2 | 1159 |
| 8 | Moore | 2 | 0 | 0 | 0 | 2 | 1229 |
| 9 | Marshall | 1 | 0 | 0 | 0 | 1 | 396 |
| 10 | Gregan | 1 | 0 | 0 | 0 | 1 | 3183 |
| 11 | Johnson | 1 | 0 | 0 | 0 | 1 | 2705 |
| 12 | Hughes | 0 | 0 | 1 | 0 | 1 | |
| | Other | 0 | 0 | 0 | 0 | 0 | |
| | TOTAL | 29 | 3 | 1 | 0 | 33 | |

## SQUAD APPEARANCES

| Match | 1 | 2 | 3 | 4 | 5 | 6 | 7 | 8 | 9 | 10 | 11 | 12 | 13 | 14 | 15 | 16 | 17 | 18 | 19 | 20 | 21 | 22 | 23 | 24 | 25 | 26 | 27 | 28 | 29 | 30 | 31 | 32 | 33 | 34 | 35 | 36 | 37 | 38 | 39 | 40 | 41 |
|---|---|---|---|---|---|---|---|---|---|---|---|---|---|---|---|---|---|---|---|---|---|---|---|---|---|---|---|---|---|---|---|---|---|---|---|---|---|---|---|---|---|
| Venue | A | H | A | H | A | H | A | H | A | A | H | A | H | A | H | A | H | A | A | H | H | A | H | H | A | A | H | A | H | A | H | A | H | A | A | H | A | H | H | A | H |
| Competition | L | L | L | L | L | L | L | L | W | L | L | L | L | L | L | L | L | L | L | L | L | L | F | L | L | F | L | L | L | L | L | L | L | L | L | L | L | L | L | L | L |
| Result | L | L | L | W | W | W | L | L | L | L | D | L | L | D | D | L | W | L | L | D | L | L | W | L | D | L | L | W | D | L | L | L | L | L | L | L | W | L | L | D | D |

**Goalkeepers**
Russell Hoult
Brian Jensen
Joe Murphy

**Defenders**
Igor Balis
Adam Chambers
James Chambers
Neil Clement
Phil Gilchrist
Des Lyttle
Lee Marshall
Darren Moore
Larus Sigurdsson
Ifeanyi Udeze
Ronnie Wallwork

**Midfielders**
Matt Collins
Lloyd Dyer
Sean Gregan
Andy Johnson
Batista
Jason Koumas
Derek McInnes

**Forwards**
Danny Dichio
Scott Dobie
Lee Hughes
Jason Roberts
Bob Taylor
Matt Turner

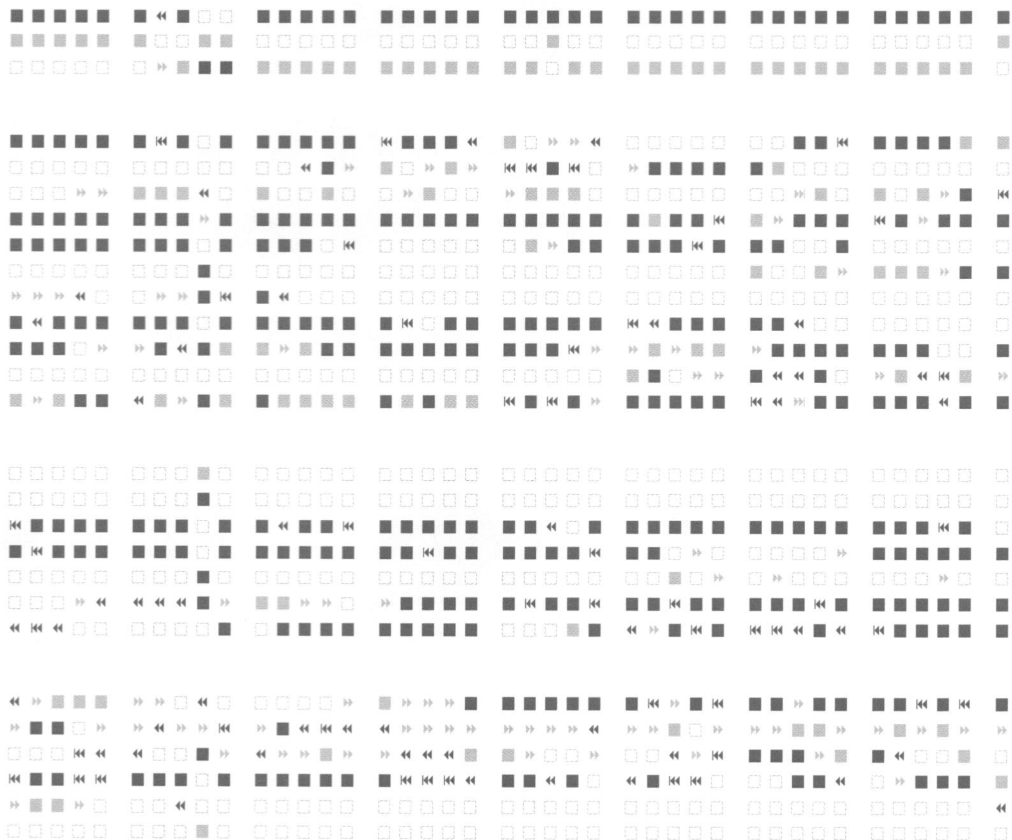

KEY: On all match · On bench · Subbed or sent off (Counting game) · Subbed or sent off (playing less than 70 minutes) · Subbed on from bench (Counting Game) · Subbed on (playing less than 70 minutes) · Subbed on and then subbed or sent off (Counting Game) · Subbed on and then subbed or sent off (playing less than 70 minutes) · Not in 16

## KEY PLAYERS - GOALSCORERS

**1 Danny Dichio**

| | |
|---|---|
| **Goals in the League** | 5 |
| **Goals in all competitions** | 8 |
| **Assists** League goals scored by team-mates where he delivered the final pass | 0 |
| **Contribution to Attacking Power** Average number of minutes between League team goals while on pitch | 105 |
| **Player Strike Rate** Average number of minutes between League goals scored by player | 379 |
| **Club Strike Rate** Average minutes between League goals scored by club | 118 |

| | PLAYER | GOALS LGE | GOALS ALL | ASSISTS | POWER | S RATE |
|---|---|---|---|---|---|---|
| 2 | Jason Koumas | 4 | 4 | 5 | 117 | 589 mins |
| 3 | Jason Roberts | 3 | 3 | 1 | 113 | 904 mins |
| 4 | Neil Clement | 3 | 3 | 1 | 116 | 1050 mins |
| 5 | Igor Balis | 2 | 2 | 0 | 115 | 1159 mins |

## KEY PLAYERS - MIDFIELDERS

**1 Andy Johnson**

| | |
|---|---|
| **Goals in the League** | 1 |
| **Goals in all competitions** | 1 |
| **Assists** League goals scored by team-mates where he delivered the final pass | 1 |
| **Defensive Rating** Average number of mins between League goals conceded while he was on the pitch | 51 |
| **Contribution to Attacking Power** Average number of minutes between League team goals while on pitch | 108 |
| **Scoring Difference** Defensive Rating minus Contribution to Attacking Power | -57 |

| | PLAYER | GOALS LGE | GOALS ALL | ASSISTS | DEF RATE | POWER | SC DIFF |
|---|---|---|---|---|---|---|---|
| 2 | Jason Koumas | 4 | 4 | 5 | 54 | 118 | -64 mins |
| 3 | Derek McInnes | 2 | 2 | 2 | 49 | 116 | -67 mins |
| 4 | Sean Gregan | 1 | 1 | 0 | 53 | 122 | -69 mins |

## PLAYER APPEARANCES

| | AGE (on 01/07/03) | IN THE SQUAD | COUNTING GAMES | MINUTES ON PITCH | IN THE SQUAD | MINUTES ON PITCH | THIS SEASON | NATIONAL SIDE |
|---|---|---|---|---|---|---|---|---|
| **Goalkeepers** | | | | | | | | |
| Russell Hoult | 30 | 37 | 36 | 3275 | 39 | 3455 | - | England |
| Brian Jensen | 28 | 8 | 0 | 0 | 10 | 0 | - | Denmark |
| Joe Murphy | 22 | 31 | 1 | 146 | 33 | 236 | 1 | Rep of Ireland (15) |
| **Defenders** | | | | | | | | |
| Igor Balis | 33 | 31 | 25 | 2318 | 32 | 2324 | - | Slovakia |
| Adam Chambers | 22 | 16 | 9 | 894 | 18 | 991 | - | England |
| James Chambers | 22 | 19 | 3 | 305 | 21 | 350 | - | England |
| Neil Clement | 24 | 38 | 34 | 3149 | 41 | 3374 | - | England |
| Phil Gilchrist | 29 | 23 | 22 | 1946 | 25 | 2081 | - | England |
| Des Lyttle | 31 | 9 | 2 | 204 | 10 | 294 | - | England |
| Lee Marshall | 24 | 9 | 2 | 396 | 10 | 486 | - | England |
| Darren Moore | 29 | 29 | 26 | 2457 | 31 | 2630 | - | England |
| Larus Sigurdsson | 30 | 35 | 22 | 2141 | 38 | 2354 | - | Iceland |
| Ifeanyi Udeze | 22 | 13 | 4 | 508 | 14 | 508 | - | Nigeria |
| Ronnie Wallwork | 25 | 38 | 21 | 2115 | 41 | 2379 | - | England |
| **Midfielders** | | | | | | | | |
| Matt Collins | 21 | 0 | 0 | 0 | 1 | 0 | - | England |
| Lloyd Dyer | 20 | 0 | 0 | 0 | 1 | 90 | - | England |
| Sean Gregan | 29 | 36 | 35 | 3183 | 38 | 3318 | - | England |
| Andy Johnson | 29 | 32 | 30 | 2705 | 34 | 2885 | 4 | Wales (50) |
| Batista | 31 | 4 | 0 | 30 | 5 | 120 | - | Portugal |
| Jason Koumas | 23 | 34 | 23 | 2357 | 37 | 2627 | 3 | Wales (50) |
| Derek McInnes | 32 | 30 | 24 | 2321 | 31 | 2378 | 2 | Scotland (64) |
| **Forwards** | | | | | | | | |
| Danny Dichio | 28 | 32 | 17 | 1895 | 35 | 2135 | - | England |
| Scott Dobie | 24 | 36 | 4 | 1203 | 39 | 1302 | - | England |
| Lee Hughes | 27 | 28 | 6 | 1139 | 29 | 1229 | - | England |
| Jason Roberts | 25 | 33 | 29 | 2712 | 35 | 2823 | - | Grenada |
| Bob Taylor | 36 | 6 | 0 | 115 | 6 | 115 | - | England |
| Matt Turner | 21 | 0 | 0 | 0 | 1 | 0 | - | England |

**KEY:** LEAGUE ALL COMPS CAPS (FIFA RANKING)

## TEAM OF THE SEASON

Hoult
CG 36 DR 54
Wallwork
CG 21 DR 54
Moore
CG 26 DR 63
Gilchrist
CG 22 DR 56
Clement
CG 34 DR 52
Koumas
CG 23 SD -64
Johnson
CG 30 SD -57
McInnes
CG 24 SD -67
Gregan
CG 35 SD -69
Roberts
CG 29 AP 113
Dichio
CG 17 SR 379

**KEY:** DR = Defensive Rate, SD = Scoring Difference AP = Attacking Power SR = Strike Rate, CG=Counting Games – League games playing at least 70 minutes

## TOP POINT EARNERS

| 1 Darren Moore | |
|---|---|
| **Counting Games** League games when he played at least 70 minutes | 26 |
| **Average points** Average League points taken in Counting games | 0.81 |
| **Club Average points** Average points taken in League games | 0.68 |

| | PLAYER | GAMES | PTS |
|---|---|---|---|
| 2 | Ronnie Wallwork | 21 | 0.76 |
| 3 | Neil Clement | 34 | 0.76 |
| 4 | Phil Gilchrist | 22 | 0.73 |
| 5 | Andy Johnson | 30 | 0.73 |
| 6 | Igor Balis | 25 | 0.72 |
| 7 | Russell Hoult | 36 | 0.72 |
| 8 | Sean Gregan | 35 | 0.71 |
| 9 | Jason Roberts | 29 | 0.69 |
| 10 | Derek McInnes | 24 | 0.67 |

## KEY PLAYERS - DEFENDERS

| 1 Darren Moore | |
|---|---|
| **Goals Conceded** The number of League goals conceded while he was on the pitch | 39 |
| **Goals Conceded in all competitions** The number goals conceded while he was on the pitch in all competitions | 41 |
| **League minutes played** Number of minutes played in league matches | 2457 |
| **Clean Sheets** In games when he played at least70 mins | 6 |
| **Defensive Rating** Average number of mins between League goals conceded while he was on the pitch | 63 |
| **Club Defensive Rating** Average number of mins between League goals conceded by the club this season | 53 |

| | PLAYER | CON LGE | CON ALL | MINS | C SHEETS | DEF RATE |
|---|---|---|---|---|---|---|
| 2 | Phil Gilchrist | 35 | 37 | 1946 | 5 | 56 mins |
| 3 | Ronnie Wallwork | 39 | 44 | 2115 | 2 | 54 mins |
| 4 | Neil Clement | 60 | 64 | 3149 | 6 | 52 mins |
| 5 | Larus Sigurdsson | 41 | 46 | 2141 | 2 | 52 mins |

## KEY PLAYERS - GOALKEEPERS

| 1 Russell Hoult | |
|---|---|
| **Goals Conceded in the League** The number of League goals conceded while he was on the pitch | 61 |
| **Goals Conceded in all competitions** The number of goals conceded while he was on the pitch in all competitions | 63 |
| **League minutes played** Number of minutes played in league matches | 3275 |
| **Clean Sheets** In games when he played at least 70 mins | 6 |
| **Goals to Shots Ratio** The average number of shots on target per each League goal conceded | 3.8 |
| **Defensive Rating** Ave number of mins between League goals conceded while on the pitch | 54 |

| 2 Joe Murphy | |
|---|---|
| **Goals Conceded in the League** The number of League goals conceded while he was on the pitch | 4 |
| **Goals Conceded in all competitions** The number of goals conceded while he was on the pitch in all competitions | 7 |
| **League minutes played** Number of minutes played in league matches | 146 |
| **Clean Sheets** In games when he played at least 70 mins | 0 |
| **Goals to Shots Ratio** The average number of shots on target per each League goal conceded | 1.8 |
| **Defensive Rating** Ave number of mins between League goals conceded while on the pitch | 37 |

# SUNDERLAND

**NICKNAME:** MACKEMS/BLACKCATS

**KEY:** Won / Drawn / Lost

| | | | | | | |
|---|---|---|---|---|---|---|
| 1 | lge | Blackburn | A | D | 0-0 | |
| 2 | lge | Everton | H | L | 0-1 | |
| 3 | lge | Leeds | A | W | 1-0 | McAteer 46 |
| 4 | lge | Man Utd | H | D | 1-1 | Flo 70 |
| 5 | lge | Middlesbrough | A | L | 0-3 | |
| 6 | lge | Fulham | H | L | 0-3 | |
| 7 | lge | Newcastle | A | L | 0-2 | |
| 8 | lge | Aston Villa | H | W | 1-0 | Bellion 69 |
| 9 | wr2 | Cambridge | A | W | 7-0 | Reyna 21; McCann 26; Arca 54; Stewart 63,65; Flo 75,82 |
| 10 | lge | Arsenal | A | L | 1-3 | Craddock 83 |
| 11 | lge | West Ham | H | L | 0-1 | |
| 12 | lge | Bolton | A | D | 1-1 | Gray 45 |
| 13 | lge | Charlton | A | D | 1-1 | Flo 15 |
| 14 | wr3 | Arsenal | A | W | 3-2 | Kyle 56; Stewart 70; Williams 72 |
| 15 | lge | Tottenham | H | W | 2-0 | Phillips 60; Flo 62 |
| 16 | lge | Liverpool | A | D | 0-0 | |
| 17 | lge | Birmingham | H | L | 0-1 | |
| 18 | lge | Chelsea | A | L | 0-3 | |
| 19 | wr4 | Sheff Utd | A | L | 0-2 | |
| 20 | lge | Man City | H | L | 0-3 | |
| 21 | lge | Liverpool | H | W | 2-1 | McCann 36; Proctor 85 |
| 22 | lge | West Brom | A | D | 2-2 | Phillips 56,64 |
| 23 | lge | Leeds | H | L | 1-2 | Proctor 34 |
| 24 | lge | Southampton | A | L | 1-2 | Flo 77 |
| 25 | lge | Man Utd | A | L | 1-2 | Veron 4 og |
| 26 | facr3 | Bolton | A | D | 1-1 | Phillips 63 |
| 27 | lge | Blackburn | H | D | 0-0 | |
| 28 | facr3r | Bolton | H | W | 0-0 | Arca 99; Proctor 100 |
| 29 | lge | Everton | A | L | 1-2 | Kilbane 34 |
| 30 | facr4 | Blackburn | A | D | 3-3 | Stewart 2; Proctor 52; Phillips 70 |
| 31 | lge | Southampton | H | L | 0-1 | |
| 32 | lge | Charlton | H | L | 1-3 | Phillips 81 pen |
| 33 | facr4r | Blackburn | H | W | 3-0* | Phillips 10; McCann 79 (*on penalties) |
| 34 | lge | Tottenham | A | L | 1-4 | Phillips 26 |
| 35 | facr5 | Watford | H | L | 0-1 | |
| 36 | lge | Middlesbrough | H | L | 1-3 | Phillips 56 |
| 37 | lge | Fulham | A | L | 0-1 | |
| 38 | lge | Bolton | H | L | 0-2 | |
| 39 | lge | West Ham | A | L | 0-2 | |
| 40 | lge | Chelsea | H | L | 1-2 | Thornton 12 |
| 41 | lge | Birmingham | A | L | 0-2 | |
| 42 | lge | West Brom | H | L | 1-2 | Stewart 70 |
| 43 | lge | Man City | A | L | 0-3 | |
| 44 | lge | Newcastle | H | L | 0-1 | |
| 45 | lge | Aston Villa | A | L | 0-1 | |
| 46 | lge | Arsenal | H | L | 0-4 | |

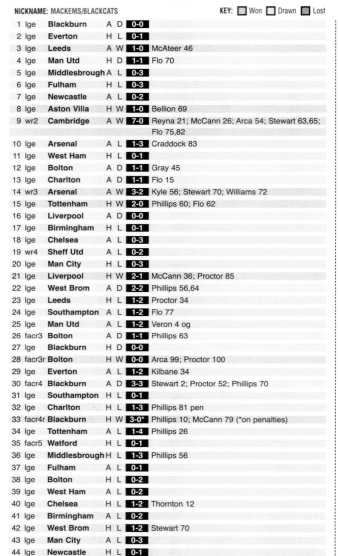

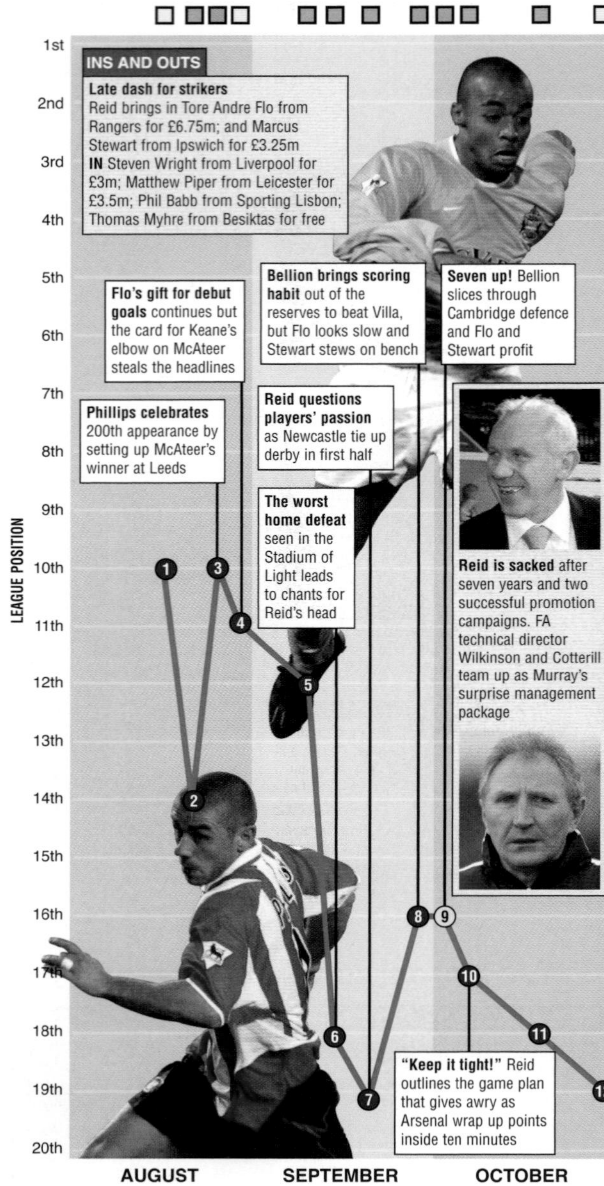
1st
2nd
3rd
4th
5th
6th
7th
8th
9th
10th
11th
12th
13th
14th
15th
16th
17th
18th
19th
20th
LEAGUE POSITION
AUGUST
SEPTEMBER
OCTOBER
INS AND OUTS
**Late dash for strikers** Reid brings in Tore Andre Flo from Rangers for £6.75m; and Marcus Stewart from Ipswich for £3.25m
**IN** Steven Wright from Liverpool for £3m; Matthew Piper from Leicester for £3.5m; Phil Babb from Sporting Lisbon; Thomas Myhre from Besiktas for free
**Flo's gift for debut goals** continues but the card for Keane's elbow on McAteer steals the headlines
**Bellion brings scoring habit** out of the reserves to beat Villa, but Flo looks slow and Stewart stews on bench
**Seven up!** Bellion slices through Cambridge defence and Flo and Stewart profit
**Phillips celebrates** 200th appearance by setting up McAteer's winner at Leeds
**Reid questions players' passion** as Newcastle tie up derby in first half
**The worst home defeat** seen in the Stadium of Light leads to chants for Reid's head
**Reid is sacked** after seven years and two successful promotion campaigns. FA technical director Wilkinson and Cotterill team up as Murray's surprise management package
**"Keep it tight!"** Reid outlines the game plan that gives awry as Arsenal wrap up points inside ten minutes

Home / Away / Neutral

## ATTENDANCES

**HOME GROUND:** STADIUM OF LIGHT **CAPACITY:** 48300 **AVERAGE LEAGUE AT HOME:** 39697

| | | | | | | | | | | | |
|---|---|---|---|---|---|---|---|---|---|---|---|
| 25 | Man Utd | 67609 | 40 | Chelsea | 40011 | 42 | West Brom | 36025 | 22 | West Brom | 26703 |
| 7 | Newcastle | 52181 | 3 | Leeds | 39929 | 32 | Charlton | 36024 | 13 | Charlton | 26284 |
| 4 | Man Utd | 47586 | 18 | Chelsea | 38946 | 6 | Fulham | 35432 | 12 | Bolton | 23036 |
| 44 | Newcastle | 45067 | 17 | Birmingham | 38803 | 39 | West Ham | 35033 | 14 | Arsenal | 19059 |
| 11 | West Ham | 44352 | 10 | Arsenal | 37902 | 43 | Man City | 34357 | 37 | Fulham | 16286 |
| 23 | Leeds | 44029 | 2 | Everton | 37698 | 31 | Southampton | 34102 | 33 | Blackburn | 15745 |
| 16 | Liverpool | 43074 | 29 | Everton | 37409 | 5 | Middlesboro | 32155 | 28 | Bolton | 14550 |
| 36 | Middlesboro | 42134 | 21 | Liverpool | 37118 | 24 | Southampton | 31423 | 30 | Blackburn | 14315 |
| 38 | Bolton | 42124 | 45 | Aston Villa | 36963 | 41 | Birmingham | 29132 | 26 | Bolton | 10123 |
| 8 | Aston Villa | 40492 | 27 | Blackburn | 36529 | 1 | Blackburn | 27122 | 9 | Cambridge | 8175 |
| 46 | Arsenal | 40188 | 20 | Man City | 36511 | 19 | Sheff Utd | 27068 | | | |
| 15 | Tottenham | 40024 | 34 | Tottenham | 36075 | 35 | Watford | 26916 | | | |

## GOAL ATTEMPTS

**FOR** — Goal attempts recorded in League games

| | HOME | AWAY | TOTAL | AVE |
|---|---|---|---|---|
| shots on target | 97 | 63 | 160 | 4.2 |
| shots off target | 101 | 60 | 161 | 4.2 |
| TOTAL | 198 | 123 | 321 | 8.4 |

**Ratio of goals to shots** Average number of shots on target per League goal scored: **7.6**

**Accuracy rating** Average percentage of total goal attempts which were on target: **49.8**

**AGAINST** — Goal attempts recorded in League games

| | HOME | AWAY | TOTAL | AVE |
|---|---|---|---|---|
| shots on target | 122 | 143 | 265 | 7 |
| shots off target | 108 | 63 | 171 | 4.5 |
| TOTAL | 230 | 206 | 436 | 11.5 |

**Ratio of goals to shots** Average number of shots on target per League goal scored: **4.1**

**Accuracy rating** Average percentage of total goal attempts which were on target: **60.8**

# Managers 4, wins 4 – a record low

Final Position: **20th**

KEY: ● League ● Champions Lge ● UEFA Cup ● FA Cup ○ League Cup ● Other

INS AND OUTS
IN Mart Poom from Derby, fee undisclosed; Talel el Karkouri from Paris St Germain on loan
Phillips first of the season then Flo makes it safe and Quinn says his goodbyes
Macho wins praise for point at Anfield but forwards can't muster a shot
Stewart engineers fight-back to oust Arsenal's second-string
Wilkinson sees his fringe players go down to his former club Sheffield United
Fifth game without a goal. Phillips and Flo flop again and Man City find it easy
Proctor rewards manager's faith as his winner against Liverpool helps rise out of relegation places
Proctor rises at one end but fells Kewell at the other to let in Leeds
Macho keeps Man United at bay until the 81st minute when Beckham and Scholes steal points
Character shows as Phillips goal ensures Bolton are forced to a replay
Kilbane hits first of season but Everton take charge in second half
Arca leaves it 'til extra time to snatch win that proves cup's a low priority
Own goal farce puts Charlton clear as a pair from Proctor plus one from Wright leave Sorensen no chance and Wilkinson bottom
Sorensen saves twice from the spot as dogged Blackburn are finally knocked out on penalties
Just two points out of 27 after Spurs ease beyond Phillips' and Sorensen's resistance
Phillips' goal run peters out against his old side and twice taken penalty sees Watford through
All change again! Former Eire boss Mick McCarthy takes over as Wilkinson and Cotterill are sacked by Bob Murray
Sunderland suffer despite management changes. Hammers show benefits of keeping faith
McCarthy can't halt losing streak as relegation tussle turns on Sorensen blunder
Relegated at Birmingham and the reason is clear – more defeats than goals scored!
Twelfth defeat in a row as Man City ease to three goal win
The lowest points total in Premiership history although McCarthy's battlers are unlucky to lose at Villa
"We were hopeless," admits McCarthy after nine games in charge and nine defeats. Arsenal hit four to show the gulf in class
13 14 15 16 17 18 19 20 21 22 23 24 25 26 27 28 29 30 31 32 33 34 35 36 37 38 39 40 41 42 43 44 45 46
NOVEMBER
DECEMBER
JANUARY
FEBRUARY
MARCH
APRIL
MAY


**MONTH BY MONTH POINTS TALLY**

| | | |
|---|---|---|
| AUGUST | 5 | 42% |
| SEPTEMBER | 3 | 25% |
| OCTOBER | 1 | 11% |
| NOVEMBER | 5 | 33% |
| DECEMBER | 4 | 27% |
| JANUARY | 1 | 8% |
| FEBRUARY | 0 | 0% |
| MARCH | 0 | 0% |
| APRIL | 0 | 0% |
| MAY | 0 | 0% |

## DISCIPLINARY RECORDS

**1 Jason McAteer**

| | |
|---|---|
| League Yellow | 3 |
| League Red | 0 |
| League Total | 3 |
| All Comps Yellow | 3 |
| All Comps Red | 0 |
| TOTAL | 3 |

League Average
235
mins between cards

| | PLAYER | LEAGUE | | TOTAL | | AVE |
|---|---|---|---|---|---|---|
| 2 | Williams | 5Y | 0R | 6Y | 0R | 243 |
| 3 | McCann | 10 | 0 | 10 | 0 | 246 |
| 4 | Wright | 8 | 0 | 8 | 0 | 272 |
| 5 | Stewart | 2 | 1 | 2 | 1 | 282 |
| 6 | El Karkouri | 2 | 0 | 2 | 0 | 325 |
| 7 | McCartney | 4 | 0 | 6 | 0 | 376 |
| 8 | Bjorklund | 4 | 0 | 4 | 0 | 398 |
| 9 | Kyle | 2 | 0 | 2 | 0 | 429 |
| 10 | Kilbane | 6 | 0 | 7 | 0 | 442 |
| 11 | Proctor | 2 | 0 | 3 | 0 | 507 |
| 12 | Piper | 1 | 0 | 2 | 0 | 785 |
| 13 | Phillips | 3 | 0 | 3 | 0 | 914 |
| 14 | Reyna | 1 | 0 | 1 | 0 | 925 |
| 15 | Craddock | 2 | 0 | 3 | 0 | 1125 |
| | Other | 4 | 0 | 6 | 0 | |
| | TOTAL | 59 | 1 | 68 | 1 | |

## GOALS

**1 Kevin Phillips**

| | |
|---|---|
| League | 6 |
| FA Cup | 3 |
| League Cup | 0 |
| Europe | 0 |
| Other | 0 |
| TOTAL | 9 |

League Average
457
mins between goals

| | PLAYER | LGE | FAC | LC | Euro | TOT | AVE |
|---|---|---|---|---|---|---|---|
| 2 | Flo | 4 | 0 | 2 | 0 | 6 | 508 |
| 3 | Proctor | 2 | 2 | 0 | 0 | 4 | 508 |
| 4 | Thornton | 1 | 0 | 0 | 0 | 1 | 945 |
| 5 | Kilbane | 1 | 0 | 0 | 0 | 1 | 2657 |
| 6 | McCann | 1 | 1 | 1 | 0 | 3 | 2465 |
| 7 | Bellion | 1 | 0 | 0 | 0 | 1 | 587 |
| 8 | Craddock | 1 | 0 | 0 | 0 | 1 | 2250 |
| 9 | Stewart | 1 | 1 | 3 | 0 | 5 | 847 |
| 10 | Gray | 1 | 0 | 0 | 0 | 1 | 2786 |
| 11 | McAteer | 1 | 0 | 0 | 0 | 1 | 706 |
| 12 | Arca | 0 | 1 | 1 | 0 | 2 | |
| 13 | Reyna | 0 | 0 | 1 | 0 | 1 | |
| 14 | Williams | 0 | 0 | 1 | 0 | 1 | |
| 15 | Kyle | 0 | 0 | 1 | 0 | 1 | |
| | Other | 1 | 0 | 0 | 0 | 1 | |
| | TOTAL | 21 | 8 | 10 | 0 | 39 | |

## SQUAD APPEARANCES

| Match | 1 | 2 | 3 | 4 | 5 | 6 | 7 | 8 | 9 | 10 | 11 | 12 | 13 | 14 | 15 | 16 | 17 | 18 | 19 | 20 | 21 | 22 | 23 | 24 | 25 | 26 | 27 | 28 | 29 | 30 | 31 | 32 | 33 | 34 | 35 | 36 | 37 | 38 | 39 | 40 | 41 | 42 | 43 | 44 | 45 | 46 |
|---|---|---|---|---|---|---|---|---|---|---|---|---|---|---|---|---|---|---|---|---|---|---|---|---|---|---|---|---|---|---|---|---|---|---|---|---|---|---|---|---|---|---|---|---|---|---|
| Venue | A | H | A | H | A | H | A | H | A | A | H | A | A | A | H | A | H | A | A | H | H | A | H | A | A | A | H | H | A | A | H | H | H | A | H | H | A | H | A | H | A | H | A | H | A | H |
| Competition | L | L | L | L | L | L | L | L | W | L | L | L | L | W | L | L | L | L | W | L | L | L | L | L | L | F | L | F | L | F | L | L | F | L | F | L | L | L | L | L | L | L | L | L | L | L |
| Result | D | L | W | D | L | L | L | W | W | L | L | D | D | W | W | D | L | L | L | L | W | D | L | L | L | D | D | W | L | D | L | L | W | L | L | L | L | L | L | L | L | L | L | L | L | L |

**Goalkeepers**
Michael Ingham
Jurgen Macho
Thomas Myhre
Mart Poom
Thomas Sorensen
Craig Turns

**Defenders**
Phil Babb
Joachim Bjorklund
Clifford Byrne
Ben Clark
Jody Craddock
Elliot Dickman
Talal El Karkouri
Michael Gray
George McCartney
Richard Ryan
Emerson Thome
Stanislav Varga
Stephen Wright

**Midfielders**
Julio Arca
Chris Black
Thomas Butler
Kevin Kilbane
Jason McAteer
Gavin McCann
Nicolas Medina
John Oster
Claudio Reyna
Mark Rossiter
Stefan Schwarz
Paul Thirlwell
Sean Thornton
Darren Williams

**Forwards**
David Bellion
Tore Andre Flo
Kevin Kyle
Kevin Phillips
Matthew Piper
Mike Proctor
Niall Quinn
Marcus Stewart

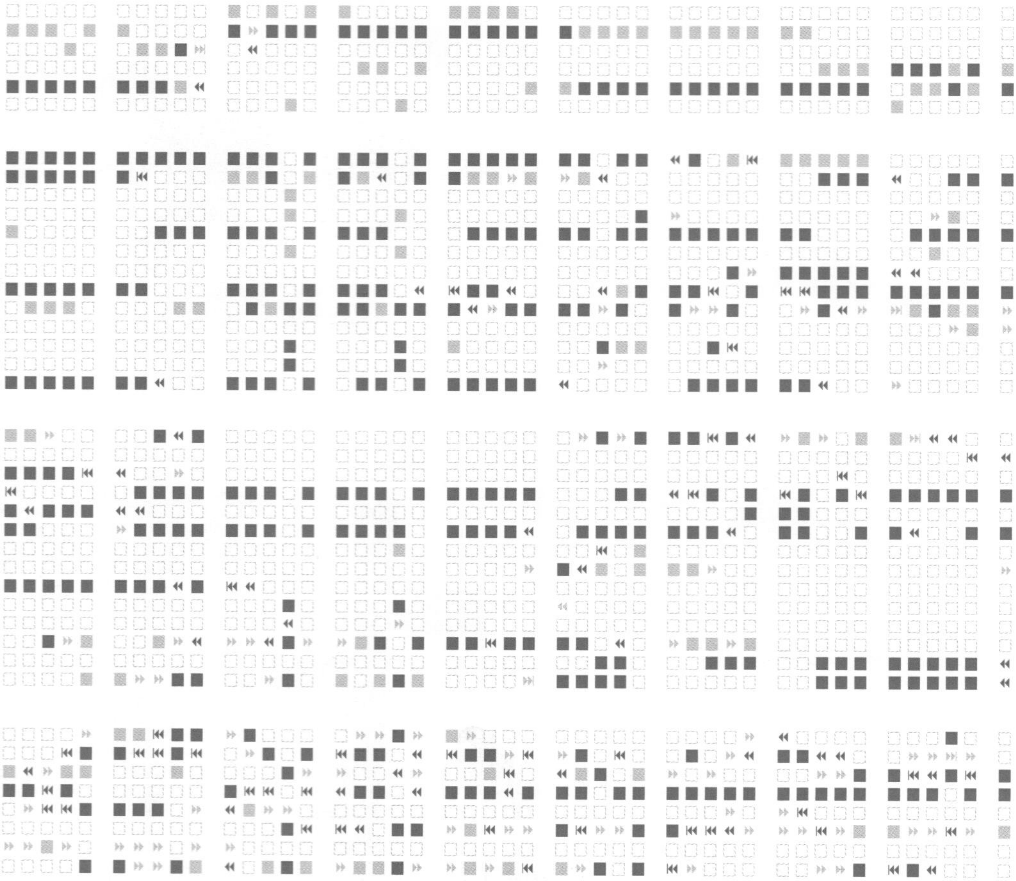

KEY: On all match / On bench / ⏮ Subbed or sent off (Counting game) / « Subbed or sent off (playing less than 70 minutes) / ⏭ Subbed on from bench (Counting Game) / » Subbed on (playing less than 70 minutes) / Subbed on and then subbed or sent off (Counting Game) / Subbed on and then subbed or sent off (playing less than 70 minutes) / Not in 16

## KEY PLAYERS - GOALSCORERS

**1 Kevin Phillips**

| | |
|---|---|
| Goals in the League | 6 |
| Goals in all competitions | 9 |
| Assists<br>League goals scored by team-mates where he delivered the final pass | 5 |
| Contribution to Attacking Power<br>Average number of minutes between League team goals while on pitch | 152 |
| Player Strike Rate<br>Average number of minutes between League goals scored by player | 457 |
| Club Strike Rate<br>Average minutes between League goals scored by club | 163 |

| | PLAYER | GOALS LGE | GOALS ALL | ASSISTS | POWER | S RATE |
|---|---|---|---|---|---|---|
| 2 | Tore Andre Flo | 4 | 6 | 2 | 135 | 508 mins |
| 3 | Jody Craddock | 1 | 1 | 0 | 140 | 2250 mins |
| 4 | Gavin McCann | 1 | 3 | 2 | 136 | 2465 mins |
| 5 | Kevin Kilbane | 1 | 1 | 3 | 147 | 2657 mins |

## KEY PLAYERS - MIDFIELDERS

**1 Gavin McCann**

| | |
|---|---|
| Goals in the League | 1 |
| Goals in all competitions | 3 |
| Assists<br>League goals scored by team-mates where he delivered the final pass | 2 |
| Defensive Rating<br>Average number of mins between League goals conceded while he was on the pitch | 59 |
| Contribution to Attacking Power<br>Average number of minutes between League team goals while on pitch | 137 |
| Scoring Difference<br>Defensive Rating minus Contribution to Attacking Power | -78 |

| | PLAYER | GOALS LGE | GOALS ALL | ASSISTS | DEF RATE | POWER | SC DIFF |
|---|---|---|---|---|---|---|---|
| 2 | Kevin Kilbane | 1 | 1 | 3 | 52 | 148 | -96 mins |
| 3 | Darren Williams | 0 | 1 | 0 | 49 | 243 | -194 mins |
| | Did not play sufficient counting games: | | | | | | |
| | Claudio Reyna | 0 | 1 | 0 | 66 | 231 | -165 mins |

## PLAYER APPEARANCES

| | AGE (on 01/07/03) | IN THE SQUAD | COUNTING GAMES | MINUTES ON PITCH | IN THE SQUAD | MINUTES ON PITCH | THIS SEASON | NATIONAL SIDE |
|---|---|---|---|---|---|---|---|---|
| **Goalkeepers** | | | | | | | | |
| Michael Ingham | 22 | 8 | 0 | 0 | 8 | 0 | 7 | (0) |
| Jurgen Macho | 25 | 25 | 12 | 1144 | 32 | 1414 | - | Austria |
| Thomas Myhre | 29 | 5 | 1 | 102 | 6 | 192 | 1 | Norway (24) |
| Mart Poom | 31 | 12 | 4 | 360 | 12 | 360 | - | Estonia |
| Thomas Sorensen | 27 | 25 | 20 | 1814 | 31 | 2234 | 8 | Denmark (10) |
| Craig Turns | 20 | 1 | 0 | 0 | 3 | 0 | - | England |
| **Defenders** | | | | | | | | |
| Phil Babb | 32 | 32 | 25 | 2313 | 36 | 2654 | 2 | Rep of Ireland (15) |
| Joachim Bjorklund | 32 | 28 | 17 | 1593 | 30 | 1716 | - | Sweden |
| Clifford Byrne | 21 | 0 | 0 | 0 | 1 | 0 | - | Rep of Ireland |
| Ben Clark | 20 | 3 | 0 | 72 | 6 | 162 | - | England |
| Jody Craddock | 27 | 26 | 25 | 2250 | 31 | 2730 | - | England |
| Elliot Dickman | 24 | 1 | 0 | 0 | 3 | 0 | - | England |
| Talal El Karkouri | 26 | 8 | 6 | 651 | 9 | 683 | - | Morocco |
| Michael Gray | 28 | 33 | 30 | 2786 | 37 | 3144 | - | England |
| George McCartney | 22 | 31 | 15 | 1505 | 37 | 1840 | 7 | N Ireland (111) |
| Richard Ryan | 18 | 3 | 0 | 60 | 3 | 60 | - | Rep of Ireland |
| Emerson Thome | 31 | 3 | 0 | 68 | 8 | 488 | - | Brazil |
| Stanislav Varga | 30 | 0 | 0 | 0 | 3 | 241 | - | Slovakia |
| Stephen Wright | 23 | 26 | 23 | 2182 | 29 | 2407 | - | England |
| **Midfielders** | | | | | | | | |
| Julio Arca | 22 | 18 | 7 | 784 | 23 | 1197 | - | Argentina |
| Chris Black | 20 | 2 | 1 | 129 | 2 | 129 | - | England |
| Thomas Butler | 22 | 7 | 6 | 567 | 8 | 598 | - | England |
| Kevin Kilbane | 26 | 30 | 29 | 2657 | 34 | 3047 | 9 | Rep of Ireland (15) |
| Jason McAteer | 32 | 9 | 6 | 706 | 10 | 796 | 2 | Rep of Ireland (15) |
| Gavin McCann | 25 | 30 | 26 | 2465 | 35 | 2975 | - | England |
| Nicolas Medina | | 0 | 0 | 0 | 3 | 89 | - | Argentina |
| John Oster | 24 | 5 | 0 | 111 | 9 | 208 | 3 | Wales (50) |
| Claudio Reyna | 29 | 11 | 10 | 925 | 12 | 990 | - | United States |
| Mark Rossiter | 20 | 0 | 0 | 0 | 3 | 191 | - | Rep of Ireland |
| Stefan Schwarz | 34 | 0 | 0 | 0 | 2 | 71 | - | Sweden |
| Paul Thirlwell | 24 | 23 | 9 | 1155 | 28 | 1360 | - | England |
| Sean Thornton | 20 | 11 | 10 | 945 | 14 | 1275 | - | Rep of Ireland |
| Darren Williams | 26 | 21 | 12 | 1217 | 26 | 1697 | - | England |
| **Forwards** | | | | | | | | |
| David Bellion | 20 | 14 | 4 | 587 | 17 | 799 | - | France |
| Tore Andre Flo | 30 | 30 | 19 | 2032 | 33 | 2225 | 6 | Norway (24) |
| Kevin Kyle | 22 | 21 | 7 | 858 | 28 | 1182 | 5 | Scotland (64) |
| Kevin Phillips | 29 | 32 | 29 | 2743 | 36 | 3133 | - | England |
| Matthew Piper | 21 | 14 | 7 | 785 | 15 | 830 | - | England |
| Mike Proctor | 22 | 25 | 9 | 1015 | 32 | 1564 | - | England |
| Niall Quinn | 36 | 9 | 0 | 188 | 9 | 188 | - | Retired |
| Marcus Stewart | 30 | 26 | 7 | 847 | 32 | 1327 | - | England |

KEY: LEAGUE ALL COMPS CAPS (FIFA RANKING)

## TEAM OF THE SEASON

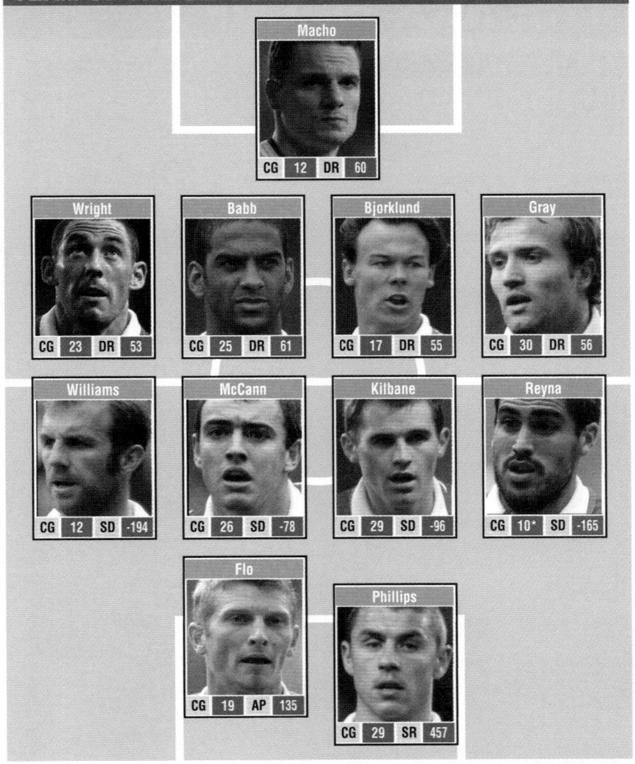
Macho
CG 12 DR 60
Wright
CG 23 DR 53
Babb
CG 25 DR 61
Bjorklund
CG 17 DR 55
Gray
CG 30 DR 56
Williams
CG 12 SD -194
McCann
CG 26 SD -78
Kilbane
CG 29 SD -96
Reyna
CG 10* SD -165
Flo
CG 19 AP 135
Phillips
CG 29 SR 457

KEY: DR = Defensive Rate, SD = Scoring Difference AP = Attacking Power SR = Strike Rate, CG=Counting Games – League games playing at least 70 minutes

## TOP POINT EARNERS

**1 Phil Babb**

| | |
|---|---|
| **Counting Games** League games when he played at least 70 minutes | 25 |
| **Average points** Average League points taken in Counting games | 0.76 |
| **Club Average points** Average points taken in League games | 0.50 |

| | PLAYER | GAMES | PTS |
|---|---|---|---|
| 2 | Jurgen Macho | 12 | 0.75 |
| 3 | Stephen Wright | 23 | 0.61 |
| 4 | George McCartney | 15 | 0.60 |
| 5 | Joachim Bjorklund | 17 | 0.59 |
| 6 | Gavin McCann | 26 | 0.58 |
| 7 | Tore Andre Flo | 19 | 0.58 |
| 8 | Kevin Phillips | 29 | 0.52 |
| 9 | Michael Gray | 30 | 0.50 |
| 10 | Kevin Kilbane | 29 | 0.48 |

## KEY PLAYERS - DEFENDERS

**1 Phil Babb**

| | |
|---|---|
| **Goals Conceded** The number of League goals conceded while he was on the pitch | 38 |
| **Goals Conceded in all competitions** The number goals conceded while he was on the pitch in all competitions | 43 |
| **League minutes played** Number of minutes played in league matches | 2313 |
| **Clean Sheets** In games when he played at least70 mins | 6 |
| **Defensive Rating** Average number of mins between League goals conceded while he was on the pitch | 61 |
| **Club Defensive Rating** Average number of mins between League goals conceded by the club this season | 53 |

| | PLAYER | CON LGE | CON ALL | MINS | C SHEETS | DEF RATE |
|---|---|---|---|---|---|---|
| 2 | Michael Gray | 50 | 56 | 2786 | 4 | 56 mins |
| 3 | Joachim Bjorklund | 29 | 29 | 1593 | 3 | 55 mins |
| 4 | Stephen Wright | 41 | 44 | 2182 | 3 | 53 mins |
| 5 | Jody Craddock | 43 | 50 | 2250 | 4 | 52 mins |

## KEY PLAYERS - GOALKEEPERS

**1 Jurgen Macho**

| | |
|---|---|
| **Goals Conceded in the League** The number of League goals conceded while he was on the pitch | 19 |
| **Goals Conceded in all competitions** The number of goals conceded while he was on the pitch in all competitions | 24 |
| **League minutes played** Number of minutes played in league matches | 1144 |
| **Clean Sheets** In games when he played at least 70 mins | 2 |
| **Goals to Shots Ratio** The average number of shots on target per each League goal conceded | 5.1 |
| **Defensive Rating** Ave number of mins between League goals conceded while on the pitch | 60 |

**2 Thomas Sorensen**

| | |
|---|---|
| **Goals Conceded in the League** The number of League goals conceded while he was on the pitch | 37 |
| **Goals Conceded in all competitions** The number of goals conceded while he was on the pitch in all competitions | 43 |
| **League minutes played** Number of minutes played in league matches | 1814 |
| **Clean Sheets** In games when he played at least 70 mins | 4 |
| **Goals to Shots Ratio** The average number of shots on target per each League goal conceded | 3.5 |
| **Defensive Rating** Ave number of mins between League goals conceded while on the pitch | 49 |

# THE AXA FA CUP

## 1ST ROUND

| | |
|---|---|
| **Barnsley 1**<br>Dyer 17<br>6,857 | **Blackpool 4**<br>Hills 37<br>Murphy 49<br>Dalglish 50<br>Taylor 70 |
| **Barrow 2**<br>Holt 16<br>Salmon 49 | **Moor Green 0**<br>2,650 |
| **Bournemouth 2**<br>Thomas 38<br>Elliott 73 | **Doncaster 1**<br>Gill, R 71<br>5,371 |
| **Bristol Rovers 0**<br>4,135 | **Runcorn 0** |
| **Bury 0**<br>2,987 | **Plymouth 3**<br>Evans 19<br>Nelson 32 og<br>Wotton 86 |
| **Carlisle 2**<br>Foran 56<br>Farrell 67 | **Lincoln 1**<br>Futcher 87<br>4,388 |
| **Chesterfield 1**<br>Davies 74<br>3,703 | **Morecambe 2**<br>Elam 43<br>Thompson 90 |
| **Colchester 0**<br>2,901 | **Chester 1**<br>Tate 83 |
| **Dag & Red 3**<br>McDougald 14<br>Shipp 18,24 | **Havant & W 2**<br>Haughton 21,27<br>1,546 |
| **Dover 0**<br>4,186 | **Oxford 1**<br>Oldfield 22 |
| **Farnborough 5**<br>Baptiste 2,35<br>Taggart 6<br>Charlery 13<br>Piper, L 21 | **Harrogate 1**<br>Hunter 11<br>1,090 |
| **Forest Green 0**<br>2,147 | **Exeter 0** |
| **Hereford 0**<br>4,005 | **Wigan 1**<br>Green 90 |
| **Heybridge 0**<br>2,046 | **Bristol City 7**<br>Roberts 16,40<br>Tinnion 40<br>Murray 45,61<br>Lita 66,82 |
| **Hull City 0**<br>7,803 | **Macclesfield 3**<br>Tipton 12<br>Lightbourne 27<br>Whitaker 76 |
| **Kidderminster 2**<br>Setchell 58 og<br>Broughton 77 | **Rushden & D 2**<br>Duffy 45,71<br>3,079 |
| **Leyton Orient 1**<br>Martin 25<br>3,605 | **Margate 1**<br>Keister 42 |
| **Luton 4**<br>Spring 3<br>Brkovic 45,65<br>Thorpe 45 | **Guiseley 0**<br>5,248 |
| **Northampton 3**<br>Harsley 10<br>Gabbiadini 35<br>Asamoah 68 | **Boston 2**<br>Battersby 56<br>Higgins 82<br>4,373 |
| **Northwich 0**<br>1,724 | **Scunthorpe 3**<br>Torpey 38,48,72 pen |
| **Oldham 2**<br>Low 18<br>Hall, F 90<br>5,802 | **Burton 2**<br>Webster 42 pen<br>Dudley 59 |
| **Port Vale 0**<br>5,507 | **Crewe 1**<br>Ashton 85 |
| **Rochdale 3**<br>Connor 3<br>Platt 12<br>Beech 61 | **Peterborough 2**<br>Fenn 83<br>Clarke, A 88<br>2,566 |
| **Scarborough 0**<br>2,084 | **Cambridge 0** |
| **Shrewsbury 4**<br>Jemson 32<br>Wilding 39,74<br>Tolley, J 89 | **Stafford 0**<br>5,114 |
| **Slough 1**<br>Bubb 30<br>1,687 | **Harrogate Railway 2**<br>Smith 53<br>Davey 68 |
| **Southend 1**<br>Lee 3 og<br>4,984 | **Hartlepool 1**<br>Barron 23 |
| **Southport 4**<br>Pickford 43,60<br>Thomson, P 75<br>Lane 90 | **Notts County 2**<br>Allsopp 8,41<br>3,519 |
| **Stevenage 1**<br>Howell 6 | **Hastings 0**<br>1,821 |
| **Stockport 4**<br>Beckett 24<br>Fradin 42<br>Burgess 57 pen,80 | **St Albans City 1**<br>Browne 68<br>3,303 |
| **Swindon 1**<br>Gurney 85 | **Huddersfield 0**<br>4,210 |
| **Team Bath 2**<br>Heiniger 71<br>Kamara-Taylor 83<br>5,469 | **Mansfield 4**<br>Lawrence 19,36<br>Tisdale 43<br>Christie 56 |
| **Tiverton 1**<br>Pears 18<br>1,840 | **Crawley 1**<br>McDonnell 36 |
| **Torquay 5**<br>Russell, A 6 pen<br>Gritton 43,62<br>Osei-Kuffour 76<br>Fowler 89 | **Boreham W 0**<br>2,739 |
| **Tranmere 2**<br>Barlow 7<br>Howarth 62<br>5,592 | **Cardiff 2**<br>Collins 34<br>Kavanagh 44 |
| **Vauxhall Motors 0**<br>3,507 | **QPR 0** |
| **Wrexham 0**<br>3,442 | **Darlington 2**<br>Conlon 59<br>Liddle, C 70 |
| **Wycombe 2**<br>Rammell 12<br>Brown 26<br>5,673 | **Brentford 4**<br>O'Connor 3<br>Somner 9<br>Vine 42,52 |
| **Yeovil 0**<br>6,455 | **Cheltenham 2**<br>Alsop 8<br>Devaney 64 |
| **York 2**<br>Duffield 21,88<br>2,948 | **Swansea 1**<br>Murphy 80 |

### 1st Round replays

| | |
|---|---|
| **Burton 2**<br>Moore 84,110<br>3,416 | **Oldham 2**<br>Wijnhard 50<br>Eyres, D 116 |
| Oldham win 5-4 on penalties | |
| **Cambridge 2**<br>Wanless 31<br>Hotte 97 og | **Scarborough 1**<br>Jordan 90<br>3,373 |
| **Cardiff 2**<br>Campbell 60<br>Collins 68 | **Tranmere 1**<br>Mellon 45<br>6,853 |
| **Crawley 3**<br>McDonnell 66,80<br>Bagnall 87 | **Tiverton 2**<br>Pears 8,64<br>3,907 |
| **Exeter 2**<br>Sheldon 25<br>Lock 85 | **Forest Green 1**<br>Richardson 20<br>2,951 |
| **Hartlepool 1**<br>Richardson 63<br>4,080 | **Southend 2**<br>Bramble 88<br>Cort 89 |
| **Margate 1**<br>Keister 51 pen | **Leyton Orient 0**<br>2,048 |
| **QPR 1**<br>Thomson 18<br>5,336 | **Vauxhall Motors 1**<br>Brazier 22 |
| Vauxhall Motors win 4-3 on penalties | |
| **Runcorn 1**<br>Barrett 19 og<br>2,444 | **Bristol Rovers 3**<br>Grazioli 17<br>Carlisle 108<br>Gilroy 118 |
| **Rushden & D 2**<br>Duffy 36<br>Wardley 67 | **Kidderminster 1**<br>Broughton 73<br>3,391 |

## 2ND ROUND

| | |
|---|---|
| **Blackpool 3**<br>Hazell 21 og<br>Taylor 56<br>Murphy 90 | **Torquay 1**<br>Gritton 8<br>5,014 |
| **Bristol Rovers 1**<br>Allen 73<br>4,369 | **Rochdale 1**<br>Platt 6 |
| **Cambridge 2**<br>Tann 5,45<br>5,076 | **Northampton 2**<br>Stamp 55<br>Hargreaves 83 |
| **Crawley 1**<br>McDonnell 3<br>4,516 | **Dag & Red 2**<br>McDougald 26<br>Janney 88 |
| **Crewe 3**<br>Rix 6<br>Brammer 63 pen<br>Ashton 78 | **Mansfield 0**<br>4,563 |
| **Darlington 4**<br>Hodgson 2<br>Offiong 38,63<br>Conlon 46 | **Stevenage 1**<br>Howell 4<br>3,351 |
| **Exeter 3**<br>McConnell 20<br>Walker 62 pen<br>Moor 85 | **Rushden & D 1**<br>Lowe 71<br>2,277 |
| **Harrogate Railway 1**<br>Davey 78<br>3,500 | **Bristol City 3**<br>Walker 20 og<br>Murray 53<br>Roberts 90 |
| **Macclesfield 2**<br>Lightbourne 82<br>Tipton 90 | **Vauxhall Motors 0**<br>2,972 |
| **Margate 0**<br>1,362 | **Cardiff 3**<br>Thorne 28<br>Boland 34<br>Fortune-West 88 |
| **Morecambe 3**<br>Bentley 28,45<br>Rigoglioso 57<br>4,293 | **Chester 2**<br>Bolland 25<br>Clare 42 |
| **Oldham 1**<br>Haining 83<br>4,416 | **Cheltenham 2**<br>Yates 17<br>Brayson 20 |
| **Oxford 1**<br>Louis 65 | **Swindon 0**<br>11,645 |
| **Scunthorpe 0**<br>3,590 | **Carlisle 0** |
| **Shrewsbury 3**<br>van Blerk 7<br>Jemson 19,76 | **Barrow 1**<br>Housham 60<br>4,210 |
| **Southend 1**<br>Rawle 53<br>5,721 | **Bournemouth 1**<br>Broadhurst 41 |
| **Southport 0**<br>2,534 | **Farnborough 3**<br>Piper, L 26<br>Carroll 39<br>Green 76 |
| **Stockport 0**<br>3,571 | **Plymouth 3**<br>Stonebridge 9<br>Friio 14<br>Wotton 72 pen |
| **Wigan 3**<br>Ellington 37,64<br>Flynn 86 | **Luton 0**<br>4,544 |
| **York 1**<br>Bullock 63<br>3,517 | **Brentford 2**<br>McCammon 35<br>Hunt 87 |

### 2nd Round replays

| | |
|---|---|
| **Bournemouth 3**<br>Fletcher, S 39<br>Holmes 80<br>Browning 89 | **Southend 2**<br>Bramble 42<br>Rawle 45<br>5,456 |
| **Northampton 0**<br>4,591 | **Cambridge 1**<br>Riza 79 |
| **Rochdale 3**<br>Platt 34<br>Connor 48<br>McCourt 80 | **Bristol Rovers 2**<br>Barrett 19<br>Tait 51<br>2,206 |
| **Carlisle 0**<br>6,809 | **Scunthorpe 1**<br>Carruthers 25 |

## 3RD ROUND

| | |
|---|---|
| **Arsenal 2**<br>Bergkamp 15<br>McNiven 67 og | **Oxford 0**<br>35,432 |
| **Aston Villa 1**<br>Angel 41<br>23,884 | **Blackburn 4**<br>Jansen 17,60<br>Yorke 52,71 |
| **Blackpool 1**<br>Popovic 10 og<br>9,062 | **Crystal P 2**<br>Black 56,64 |
| **Bolton 1**<br>Ricketts 18<br>10,123 | **Sunderland 1**<br>Phillips 63 |
| **Bournemouth 0**<br>7,252 | **Crewe 0** |
| **Brentford 1**<br>Hunt 36 | **Derby 0**<br>8,709 |
| **Cambridge 1**<br>Youngs 49<br>6,864 | **Millwall 1**<br>Claridge 60 |
| **Cardiff 2**<br>Earnshaw 76<br>Campbell 90<br>16,013 | **Coventry 2**<br>Mills 27<br>McAllister 55 pen |
| **Charlton 3**<br>Johansson 25,61<br>Euell 72 pen | **Exeter 1**<br>Gaia 49<br>18,107 |
| **Chelsea 1**<br>Stanic 40 | **Middlesbro 0**<br>29,796 |
| **Darlington 2**<br>Nicolls 13<br>Clark 37<br>4,260 | **Farnborough 3**<br>Baptiste 10<br>Carroll 19,60 |
| **Fulham 3**<br>Sava 11<br>Goldbaek 22<br>Saha 46 | **Birmingham 1**<br>John 90<br>9,203 |
| **Gillingham 4**<br>King 12,18 pen<br>Ipoua 41<br>Hope 75 | **Sheff Wed 1**<br>Sibon 4<br>6,434 |
| **Grimsby 2**<br>Cooke 57 pen<br>Mansaram 87<br>5,350 | **Burnley 2**<br>Moore, A 14<br>Weller 18 |
| **Ipswich 4**<br>Clapham 2<br>Bent, D 65,77<br>Ambrose 75 | **Morecambe 0**<br>18,529 |
| **Leicester 2**<br>Elliott 45<br>Dickov 75 | **Bristol City 0**<br>25,868 |
| **Macclesfield 0**<br>4,244 | **Watford 2**<br>Helguson 24<br>Pennant 61 |
| **Man City 0**<br>28,586 | **Liverpool 1**<br>Murphy 47 pen |
| **Man Utd 4**<br>van Nistelrooy 5 pen,<br>81 pen<br>Scholes 90<br>Beckham 17 | **Portsmouth 1**<br>Stone 39<br>67,222 |

**Norwich 3 Brighton 1**
Mulryne 57,81 — Pethick 49
McVeigh 71 — 17,205

**Plymouth 2 Dag & Red 2**
Stonebridge 44 — Terry 13
Wotton 61 — McDougald 67
11,885

**Preston 1 Rochdale 2**
Anderson 48 — McEvilly 35
8,762 — Simpson 54

**Rotherham 0 Wimbledon 3**
4,527 — Shipperley 36
McAnuff 85
Morgan 90

**Scunthorpe 0 Leeds 2**
8,329 — Viduka 32 pen
Bakke 68

**Sheff Utd 4 Cheltenham 0**
Murphy 9 — 9,166
McGovern 20
Kabba 62,84

**Shrewsbury 2 Everton 1**
Jemson 39,89 — Alexandersson 60
7,800

**Southampton 4 Tottenham 0**
Svensson, M 13 — 25,589
Tessem 50
Svensson, A 56
Beattie 80

**Stoke 3 Wigan 0**
Greenacre 20,67 — 9,618
Iwelumo 31

**Walsall 0 Reading 0**
5,987

**West Brom 3 Bradford 1**
Dichio 4,11,19 — Danks 80
19,909

**West Ham 3 Nottm Forest 2**
Defoe 26,83 — Harewood 17
Cole 61 — Reid 50
29,612

**Wolves 3 Newcastle 2**
Ince 6 — Jenas 40
Kennedy 28 — Shearer 43 pen
Ndah 49 — 27,316

### 3rd Round replays

**Burnley 4 Grimsby 0**
Moore, I 25,90 — 5,436
Little 79
Blake 86 pen

**Coventry 3 Cardiff 0**
Fowler 21 — 11,997
Holdsworth, Dean 57
Bothroyd 89

**Crewe 2 Bournemouth 2**
Jones 29 — Hayter 38
Sodje 120 — Fletcher, S 98
4,540

**Dag & Red 2 Plymouth 0**
Shipp 20 — 4,530
McDougald 85

**Millwall 3 Cambridge 2**
Claridge 60 pen — Kitson 58
Robinson 70 — Youngs 61
Ifill 77 — 7,031

**Reading 1 Walsall 1**
Aranalde 32 og — Wrack 7
8,767
Walsall win 4-1 on penalties

**Sunderland 2 Bolton 0**
Arca 99 — 14,550
Proctor 100

**A double by patched-up veteran striker** Jemson caused the shock of the round as Shrewsbury beat Everton. The Shrews struggling in the Third Division are managed by Kevin Ratcliffe who captained Everton to FA Cup final glory in 1984.

**The holders show no mercy** to Conference League minnows Farnborough despite them switching the tie to Highbury. After Lee is sent off in the 28th minute it proves all too easy for Arsenal, who run in five.

**Goals by both Svenssons** (Michael and Anders) plus 2 more from striking duo Tessem and Beattie swamped a Spurs side that were a poor reflection of their proud cup history. Saints were irrepressible and turned in the performance of the round.

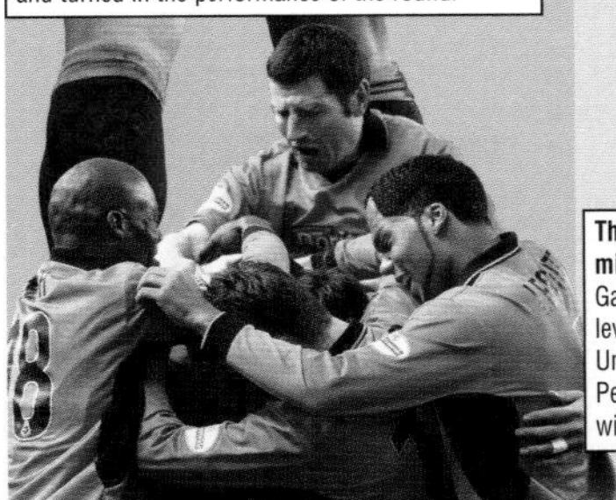

**Three goals down after 65 minutes,** Ipswich hit back through Gaardsoe, Miller and Bent to draw level 5 minutes later. Then Sheffield United's Warnock sent on sub Peschisolido and he slid home the winner in the 89th minute.

**Ndah scored the winning goal of 5** in a thriller at Molineux that saw Wolves surrender a 2-goal lead but battle back to secure a win against Premiership high-flyers Newcastle.

**Ndah's 2 first-half goals** put the scent of cup glory in Wolves' nostrils and 2 more by Miller helped them pull away from Division 1 rivals Leicester.

**FA Cup 3rd Round regulars** Dagenham have gone one stage better. They took Plymouth to a replay and then took them apart with a deflected goal by Shipp and a McDonald header improving on the 2-2 draw in Devon.

**Ten-man Palace first frustrated and then subdued Liverpool** who couldn't score against the Eagles in 180 minutes of cup football. The first tie finished 0-0 before Gray scored in the Anfield replay on his 100th appearance for Palace. Then a Henchoz OG settled it.

## 4TH ROUND

**Blackburn 3 Sunderland 3**
Cole 14,73 — Stewart 2
Yorke 90 — Proctor 52
14,315 — Phillips 70

**Brentford 0 Burnley 3**
9,563 — Blake 52
Cook 86
Little 89

**Crystal P 0 Liverpool 0**
26,054

**Farnborough 1 Arsenal 5**
Baptiste 71 — Campbell 19
35,108 — Jeffers 23,68
Bergkamp 74
Lauren 79

**Fulham 3 Charlton 0**
Malbranque 59, — 12,203
66 pen,87 pen

**Gillingham 1 Leeds 1**
Sidibe 82 — Smith 49
11,093

**Man Utd 6 West Ham 0**
Giggs 8,30 — 67,181
van Nistelrooy 49,58
Neville, P 50
Solskjaer 69

**Norwich 1 Dag & Red 0**
Abbey 90 — 21,164

**Rochdale 2 Coventry 0**
Connor 33 — 9,156
Griffiths 47

**Sheff Utd 4 Ipswich 3**
Brown 19,64 — Gaardsoe 66
Jagielka 32 — Miller, T 68 pen
Peschisolido 89 — Bent, M 70
12,757

**Shrewsbury 0 Chelsea 4**
7,950 — Zola 40,75
Cole 53
Morris 80

**Southampton 1 Millwall 1**
Davies 90 — Claridge 17
23,809

**Stoke 3 Bournemouth 0**
Iwelumo 45 pen,51 — 12,004
Hoekstra 84

**Walsall 1 Wimbledon 0**
Zdrillic 75 — 6,693

**Watford 1 West Brom 0**
Helguson 80 — 16,975

**Wolves 4 Leicester 1**
Ndah 5,45 — Dickov 29 pen
Miller 51,71 — 28,164

### 4th Round replays

**Leeds 2 Gillingham 1**
Viduka 11 — Ipoua 86
Bakke 58 — 29,359

**Liverpool 0 Crystal P 2**
35,109 — Gray 55
Henchoz 79 og

**Millwall 1 Southampton 2**
Reid 37 — Oakley 21,102
10,197

**Sunderland 2 Blackburn 2**
Phillips 10 — Flitcroft 50,90
McCann 79 — 15,745
Sunderland win 3-0 on penalties

## 5TH ROUND

**Man Utd** 0
67,209
**Arsenal** 2
Edu 35
Wiltord 52

**Goal gapes for Giggs but** in 1999's semi-final Giggs scored a 'goal of the century' against Arsenal; here he added a miss of similar proportions before Edu's deflection and Wiltord's sharpness made United pay for his profligacy.

**Stoke** 0
26,615
**Chelsea** 2
Hasselbaink 52
Gronkjaer 76

**Sheff Utd** 2
Mooney 37
Ndlovu 56
**Walsall** 0
17,510

**Warnock's luck** extends to getting his Sheffield United side pulled out of the hat first. After that his players have proved good enough to beat Leeds, Liverpool and the rest at Bramall Lane. The 9th home tie of the year ended Walsall's hopes.

**Crystal P** 1
Gray 34
24,512
**Leeds** 2
Kelly 32
Kewell 73

**Palace manager Francis admits he was wrong** about Johnson's disallowed shot being 6 inches over the line, "…if you see it, it's about 2 foot over," he said. Instead Kewell's glorious run and finish in the 73rd minute sends Leeds through.

**Sunderland** 0
26,916
**Watford** 1
Smith, T 65 pen

**Fulham** 1
Malbranque 45
**Burnley** 1
Moore, A 4
13,062

**Burnley** 3
Taylor 27
Moore, I 35
Diallo 52
**Fulham** 0
11,635

**Southampton** 2
Svensson, A 71
Tessem 74
**Norwich** 0
31,103

**Wolves** 3
Ndah 32
Miller 79
Proudlock 90
**Rochdale** 1
Melaugh 52
23,921

BRISCOE

## QUARTER FINALS

**Arsenal** 2 **Chelsea** 2
Jeffers 36 Terry 3
Henry 45 Lampard 84
38,104

**Chelsea** 1 **Arsenal** 3
Terry 79 Terry 25 og
41,456 Wiltord 34
Lauren 82

**Vieira dominates replay battle** with former colleague Petit.
Chelsea had fought back against Henry's predatory instincts to earn a 2-2 draw at Highbury but were well beaten in the Stamford Bridge replay. Even Cygan's sending off in the 66th minute didn't influence the margin of victory.

**Sheff Utd** 1 **Leeds** 0
Kabba 78 24,633

**A second cup victory over Leeds** and another semi-final in an astonishing season for Sheffield United and their outspoken manager Warnock. Kabba, whose pace unsettled Leeds throughout a poor game, scored the goal that leaves the Blades still hoping for league and cup glory.

KABBA
SMITH

**Watford** 2 **Burnley** 0
Smith, T 74 20,336
Glass 80

TOSHIBA

**With the promise of semi-final riches at stake**, nerves played the major role in the first hour of this match between cash-strapped Division I clubs. Finally Watford struck gold through goals from Smith and Glass.

**Southampton** 2 **Wolves** 0
Marsden 56 31,715
Butler 81 og

**Old boy Marsden** can't have hit many weaker shots than the overhead kick that put former club Wolves behind at St Mary's. They conceded an even softer second when Butler steered a cross into his own net and Saints are in an FA Cup semi-final for the first time in 17 years.

## SEMI FINALS

**Arsenal** 1 **Sheff Utd** 0
Ljungberg 34 59,170

**The 'double Double'** remains a very real possibility after Seaman's astonishing stretch keeps Peschisolido's header out and saves Arsenal from extra time before a tough midweek league game against Man United.
The header from point-blank range seemed destined to be the Sheffield's equaliser but Seaman reached out almost in slow motion to palm it away.
Earlier Arsenal had taken advantage of referee Poll's decision not to stop play after a clumsy challenge on striker Allison and Wiltord followed up a shot which clipped the post, to cut-back for Ljungberg to finish.

**Watford** 1 **Southampton** 2
Gayle 88 Ormerod 43
42,602 Robinson 80 og

**Next Cardiff and then Europe beckon** for Saints now that they have overcome Watford to reach a first FA Cup final since 1976.
The Hertfordshire side caused Jones to make an important save at 1-0 but Ormerod had already put Southampton on their way with a first goal for 23 games and nearly six months. He also set up the second when his cross was slid home by Beattie.

## THE FINAL

**Arsenal** 1 **Southampton** 0
Pires 37 73,726

**Arsenal managed a rare defence of the FA Cup** thanks to a first-half strike from the alert Pires and a fine second-half save from Seaman.

After the disappointment of letting the Championship slip away over the final weeks of the season, Arsenal rallied without injured skipper Vieira and made it very hard for Saints in attack. The one time they really succeeded in getting behind the Arsenal defence, Seaman pawed away Ormerod's fierce shot at the near post in the 83rd minute.

The game had started with a bang after Henry strode past Lundekvam despite being pulled back and forced Niemi into a one-handed save. Had he gone down it would have been a penalty and a dismissal for the defender.

Saints kept Arsenal at bay after that with young fullback Baird helping to subdue Arsenal's left flank in only his second start for Strachan. However the Londoners took the lead their domination deserved when Henry's touch released Bergkamp who slipped the ball back to Ljungberg. The Swede was striving for a third consecutive FA Cup final goal but his shot was blocked only to run to Pires, who shot low past Niemi.

# THE PREMIERSHIP ROUND-UP

## STADIUM CAPACITY AND HOME CROWDS

| | TEAM | CAPACITY | AVE | HIGH | LOW |
|---|---|---|---|---|---|
| 1 | Man Utd | 67750 | 99.78 | 67721 | 67135 |
| 2 | Newcastle | 52200 | 99.47 | 52181 | 51072 |
| 3 | Tottenham | 36214 | 99.12 | 36084 | 34704 |
| 4 | Arsenal | 38500 | 98.81 | 38164 | 37878 |
| 5 | West Brom | 27130 | 98.53 | 27129 | 25170 |
| 6 | Charlton | 26700 | 98.34 | 26728 | 25640 |
| 7 | Man City | 35150 | 98.32 | 35141 | 33260 |
| 8 | West Ham | 35050 | 98.16 | 35050 | 28844 |
| 9 | Birmingham | 29505 | 97.80 | 29505 | 26164 |
| 10 | Leeds | 40205 | 97.30 | 40205 | 35537 |
| 11 | Liverpool | 45000 | 96.09 | 44250 | 41462 |
| 12 | Everton | 40200 | 95.75 | 40168 | 32440 |
| 13 | Southampton | 32085 | 95.62 | 32104 | 25714 |
| 14 | Chelsea | 42449 | 93.72 | 41911 | 35237 |
| 15 | Bolton | 27410 | 91.27 | 27409 | 21753 |
| 16 | Middlesbrough | 34820 | 89.10 | 34814 | 27443 |
| 17 | Fulham | 18800 | 88.87 | 18800 | 14017 |
| 18 | Blackburn | 30475 | 86.05 | 30475 | 21096 |
| 19 | Sunderland | 48300 | 82.19 | 47586 | 34102 |
| 20 | Aston Villa | 43275 | 80.82 | 42602 | 25817 |

**Key:** Average. The percentage of each stadium filled in League games over the season (AVE), the stadium capacity and the highest and lowest crowds recorded.

## AWAY ATTENDANCE

| | TEAM | AVE | HIGH | LOW |
|---|---|---|---|---|
| 1 | Man Utd | 99.18 | 52164 | 18103 |
| 2 | Arsenal | 98.02 | 67650 | 18800 |
| 3 | Liverpool | 97.92 | 67639 | 18144 |
| 4 | Newcastle | 96.82 | 67619 | 17900 |
| 5 | Man City | 95.72 | 67646 | 17937 |
| 6 | Tottenham | 95.08 | 67611 | 16757 |
| 7 | Sunderland | 95.07 | 67609 | 16286 |
| 8 | West Brom | 94.77 | 67645 | 15799 |
| 9 | Chelsea | 94.71 | 67606 | 16504 |
| 10 | Leeds | 94.70 | 67135 | 17494 |
| 11 | West Ham | 94.60 | 67555 | 15858 |
| 12 | Everton | 94.47 | 67629 | 18385 |
| 13 | Bolton | 94.14 | 67623 | 16388 |
| 14 | Aston Villa | 94.10 | 67619 | 17092 |
| 15 | Birmingham | 93.14 | 67640 | 14962 |
| 16 | Middlesbrough | 92.66 | 67508 | 14253 |
| 17 | Blackburn | 91.48 | 67626 | 14017 |
| 18 | Southampton | 90.06 | 67691 | 18031 |
| 19 | Fulham | 89.60 | 67706 | 21096 |
| 20 | Charlton | 88.92 | 67721 | 14720 |

**Key:** Average. How close each club has come to filling grounds in its away league matches (AVE) and the highest and lowest crowds recorded.

## CLUB STRIKE FORCE

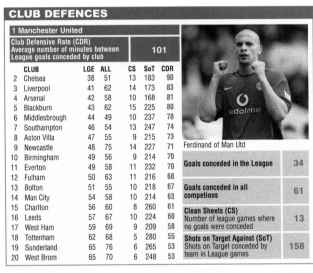

Henry, Pires and Bergkamp of Arsenal

| | |
|---|---|
| Goals scored in the League | 85 |
| Goals scored in all competions | 119 |
| Shots on target (SoT) Shots on target hit by the team recorded in League games | 315 |

**1 Arsenal**

| | |
|---|---|
| Club Strike Rate (CSR) Average number of minutes between League goals scored by club | 40 |

| | CLUB | LGE | ALL | SoT | CSR |
|---|---|---|---|---|---|
| 2 | Man Utd | 74 | 130 | 295 | 46 |
| 3 | Chelsea | 68 | 88 | 252 | 50 |
| 4 | Newcastle | 63 | 89 | 279 | 54 |
| 5 | Liverpool | 61 | 93 | 265 | 56 |
| 6 | Leeds | 58 | 74 | 206 | 59 |
| 7 | Blackburn | 52 | 75 | 206 | 66 |
| 8 | Tottenham | 51 | 53 | 211 | 67 |
| 9 | Everton | 48 | 56 | 225 | 71 |
| 10 | Middlesbrough | 48 | 53 | 176 | 71 |
| 11 | Man City | 47 | 50 | 229 | 73 |
| 12 | Charlton | 45 | 48 | 205 | 76 |
| 13 | Southampton | 43 | 63 | 217 | 80 |
| 14 | Aston Villa | 42 | 57 | 229 | 81 |
| 15 | West Ham | 42 | 46 | 195 | 81 |
| 16 | Birmingham | 41 | 45 | 164 | 83 |
| 17 | Bolton | 41 | 42 | 204 | 83 |
| 18 | Fulham | 41 | 61 | 180 | 83 |
| 19 | West Brom | 29 | 33 | 200 | 118 |
| 20 | Sunderland | 21 | 39 | 160 | 163 |
| | TOTAL: LEAGUE: 1000 | | AL COMPS: 1314 | | |

## CLUB DEFENCES

**1 Manchester United**

| | |
|---|---|
| Club Defensive Rate (CDR) Average number of minutes between League goals conceded by club | 101 |

| | CLUB | LGE | ALL | CS | SoT | CDR |
|---|---|---|---|---|---|---|
| 2 | Chelsea | 38 | 51 | 13 | 183 | 90 |
| 3 | Liverpool | 41 | 62 | 14 | 173 | 83 |
| 4 | Arsenal | 42 | 58 | 10 | 168 | 81 |
| 5 | Blackburn | 43 | 62 | 15 | 225 | 80 |
| 6 | Middlesbrough | 44 | 49 | 10 | 237 | 78 |
| 7 | Southampton | 46 | 54 | 13 | 247 | 74 |
| 8 | Aston Villa | 47 | 55 | 9 | 215 | 73 |
| 9 | Newcastle | 48 | 75 | 14 | 227 | 71 |
| 10 | Birmingham | 49 | 56 | 9 | 214 | 70 |
| 11 | Everton | 49 | 58 | 11 | 232 | 70 |
| 12 | Fulham | 50 | 63 | 11 | 216 | 68 |
| 13 | Bolton | 51 | 55 | 10 | 218 | 67 |
| 14 | Man City | 54 | 58 | 10 | 214 | 63 |
| 15 | Charlton | 56 | 60 | 8 | 260 | 61 |
| 16 | Leeds | 57 | 67 | 10 | 224 | 60 |
| 17 | West Ham | 59 | 69 | 9 | 209 | 58 |
| 18 | Tottenham | 62 | 68 | 5 | 280 | 55 |
| 19 | Sunderland | 65 | 76 | 6 | 265 | 53 |
| 20 | West Brom | 65 | 70 | 6 | 248 | 53 |

Ferdinand of Man Utd

| | |
|---|---|
| Goals conceded in the League | 34 |
| Goals conceded in all competions | 61 |
| Clean Sheets (CS) Number of league games where no goals were conceded | 13 |
| Shots on Target Against (SoT) Shots on Target conceded by team in League games | 158 |

## CLUB GOAL ATTEMPTS

### GOAL ATTEMPTS – FOR

**KEY:** Shots on Target (SoT), Shots Off Target (SO) Total shots (Tot) Ratio of shots on target to goals (SG) Accuracy Rating (AR)

| | CLUB | SoT | SO | Tot | SG | AR |
|---|---|---|---|---|---|---|
| 1 | Arsenal | 315 | 211 | 526 | 3.7 | 59.9 |
| 2 | Man Utd | 295 | 228 | 523 | 4 | 56.4 |
| 3 | Liverpool | 265 | 227 | 492 | 4.3 | 53.9 |
| 4 | Newcastle | 279 | 208 | 487 | 4.4 | 57.3 |
| 5 | Aston Villa | 229 | 245 | 474 | 5.5 | 48.3 |
| 6 | Chelsea | 252 | 218 | 470 | 3.7 | 53.6 |
| 7 | Southampton | 217 | 229 | 446 | 5 | 48.7 |
| 8 | Everton | 225 | 207 | 432 | 4.7 | 52.1 |
| 9 | Blackburn | 206 | 225 | 431 | 4 | 47.8 |
| 10 | Man City | 229 | 201 | 430 | 4.9 | 53.3 |
| 11 | Bolton | 204 | 224 | 428 | 5 | 47.7 |
| 12 | Leeds | 206 | 209 | 415 | 3.6 | 49.6 |
| 13 | West Ham | 195 | 220 | 415 | 4.6 | 47.0 |
| 14 | Tottenham | 211 | 189 | 400 | 4.1 | 52.8 |
| 15 | West Brom | 200 | 200 | 400 | 6.9 | 50.0 |
| 16 | Middlesbrough | 176 | 206 | 382 | 3.7 | 46.1 |
| 17 | Fulham | 180 | 186 | 366 | 4.4 | 49.2 |
| 18 | Charlton | 205 | 149 | 354 | 4.6 | 57.9 |
| 19 | Birmingham | 164 | 161 | 325 | 4 | 50.5 |
| 20 | Sunderland | 160 | 161 | 321 | 7.6 | 49.8 |

### GOAL ATTEMPTS – AGAINST

**KEY:** Shots on Target (SoT), Shots Off Target (SO) Total shots (Tot) Ratio of shots on target to goals (SG) Accuracy Rating (AR)

| | CLUB | SoT | SO | Tot | SG | AR |
|---|---|---|---|---|---|---|
| 1 | Liverpool | 173 | 171 | 344 | 4.2 | 50.3 |
| 2 | Arsenal | 168 | 190 | 358 | 4 | 46.9 |
| 3 | Man Utd | 158 | 200 | 358 | 4.6 | 44.1 |
| 4 | Chelsea | 183 | 176 | 359 | 4.8 | 51.0 |
| 5 | Birmingham | 214 | 146 | 360 | 4.4 | 59.4 |
| 6 | Man City | 214 | 150 | 364 | 4 | 58.8 |
| 7 | Bolton | 218 | 156 | 374 | 4.3 | 58.3 |
| 8 | Fulham | 216 | 158 | 374 | 4.3 | 57.8 |
| 9 | West Ham | 209 | 176 | 385 | 3.5 | 54.3 |
| 10 | Blackburn | 225 | 169 | 394 | 5.2 | 57.1 |
| 11 | Newcastle | 227 | 185 | 412 | 4.7 | 55.1 |
| 12 | Middlesbrough | 237 | 177 | 414 | 5.4 | 57.2 |
| 13 | Everton | 232 | 185 | 417 | 4.7 | 55.6 |
| 14 | Aston Villa | 215 | 215 | 430 | 4.6 | 50.0 |
| 15 | Sunderland | 265 | 171 | 436 | 4.1 | 60.8 |
| 16 | Leeds | 224 | 215 | 439 | 3.9 | 51.0 |
| 17 | West Brom | 248 | 192 | 440 | 3.8 | 56.4 |
| 18 | Southampton | 247 | 197 | 444 | 5.4 | 55.6 |
| 19 | Tottenham | 280 | 182 | 462 | 4.5 | 60.6 |
| 20 | Charlton | 260 | 204 | 464 | 4.6 | 56.0 |

## CLUB DISCIPLINARY RECORDS

Purse kicks his way to two yellows

| | |
|---|---|
| League Yellow | 76 |
| League Red | 5 |
| League Total | 81 |
| All Competitions Yellow | 80 |
| All Competitions Red | 5 |
| TOTAL | 85 |

**1 Birmingham**

| | |
|---|---|
| Cards Average in League Average number of minutes between a card being shown of either colour | 42 |

| | CLUB | LEAGUE | | TOTAL | | AVE |
|---|---|---|---|---|---|---|
| 2 | Bolton | 72 Y | 4 R | 76 Y | 5 R | 45 |
| 3 | Leeds | 73 | 2 | 92 | 3 | 46 |
| 4 | West Ham | 66 | 5 | 76 | 5 | 48 |
| 5 | Aston Villa | 66 | 4 | 67 | 4 | 49 |
| 6 | Tottenham | 64 | 6 | 68 | 6 | 49 |
| 7 | Blackburn | 65 | 4 | 80 | 4 | 50 |
| 8 | Chelsea | 63 | 1 | 72 | 2 | 53 |
| 9 | Everton | 58 | 7 | 67 | 7 | 53 |
| 10 | Fulham | 59 | 6 | 68 | 7 | 53 |
| 11 | Man City | 58 | 6 | 61 | 6 | 53 |
| 12 | Middlesbrough | 55 | 5 | 61 | 5 | 57 |
| 13 | Sunderland | 59 | 1 | 68 | 1 | 57 |
| 14 | Arsenal | 56 | 3 | 79 | 5 | 58 |
| 15 | Charlton | 54 | 2 | 59 | 3 | 61 |
| 16 | West Brom | 52 | 4 | 53 | 4 | 61 |
| 17 | Newcastle | 50 | 3 | 67 | 4 | 65 |
| 18 | Liverpool | 49 | 3 | 75 | 4 | 66 |
| 19 | Southampton | 49 | 3 | 59 | 3 | 66 |
| 20 | Man Utd | 46 | 1 | 82 | 1 | 73 |
| | TOTAL | 1190 | 75 | 1410 | 84 | |

## CHART-TOPPING MIDFIELDERS

vodafone

| 1 David Beckham - Manchester United | |
|---|---|
| **Goals scored in the League** | 6 |
| **Assists** in league games | 8 |
| **Defensive Rating** Av number of mins between League goals conceded while on the pitch | 133 |
| **Contribution to Attacking Power** Average number of minutes between League team goals while on pitch | 50 |
| **Scoring Difference** Defensive Rating minus Contribution to Attacking Power | 83 |

| | PLAYER | CLUB | GOALS | ASS | DEF R | POWER | SCORE DIFF |
|---|---|---|---|---|---|---|---|
| 2 | Veron | Man Utd | 2 | 3 | 135 | 73 | 62 mins |
| 3 | Giggs | Man Utd | 8 | 11 | 105 | 45 | 60 mins |
| 4 | De Lucas | Chelsea | 0 | 0 | 114 | 57 | 57 mins |
| 5 | Keane | Man Utd | 0 | 1 | 98 | 42 | 56 mins |
| 6 | Pires | Arsenal | 14 | 3 | 89 | 37 | 52 mins |
| 7 | Ljungberg | Arsenal | 6 | 2 | 100 | 52 | 48 mins |
| 8 | Morris | Chelsea | 0 | 1 | 100 | 53 | 47 mins |
| 9 | Petit | Chelsea | 1 | 5 | 93 | 51 | 42 mins |
| 10 | Silva | Arsenal | 0 | 2 | 84 | 43 | 41 mins |
| 11 | Lampard | Chelsea | 6 | 3 | 89 | 49 | 40 mins |
| 12 | Neville, P | Man Utd | 1 | 1 | 93 | 56 | 37 mins |
| 13 | Riise | Liverpool | 6 | 4 | 88 | 54 | 34 mins |
| 14 | Vieira | Arsenal | 3 | 3 | 75 | 42 | 33 mins |
| 15 | Gerrard | Liverpool | 5 | 8 | 87 | 54 | 33 mins |
| 16 | Gronkjaer | Chelsea | 4 | 4 | 79 | 47 | 32 mins |
| 17 | Hamann | Liverpool | 2 | 1 | 82 | 51 | 31 mins |
| 18 | Parlour | Arsenal | 0 | 0 | 71 | 44 | 27 mins |
| 19 | Tugay | Blackburn | 1 | 2 | 88 | 63 | 25 mins |
| 20 | Robert | Newcastle | 5 | 7 | 80 | 56 | 24 mins |

The Divisional Round-up charts combine the records of chart-topping keepers, defenders, midfield players and forwards, from every club in the division.. The one above is for **the Chart-topping Midfielders**. The players are ranked by their Scoring Difference although other attributes are shown for you to compare.

## CHART-TOPPING GOALSCORERS

vodafone

| 1 Ruud van Nistelrooy - Manchester United | |
|---|---|
| **Goals scored in the League (GL)** | 25 |
| **Goals scored in all competitions (GA)** | 44 |
| **Contribution to Attacking Power (AP)** Average number of minutes between League team goals while on pitch | 45 |
| **Player Strike Rate** Average number of minutes between League goals scored by player | 116 |
| **Club Strike Rate (CSR)** Average minutes between League goals scored by club | 46 |

| | PLAYER | CLUB | GOALS: LGE | ALL | POWER | CSR | S RATE |
|---|---|---|---|---|---|---|---|
| 2 | Pires | Arsenal | 14 | 16 | 37 | 40 | 128 mins |
| 3 | Viduka | Leeds | 20 | 22 | 52 | 59 | 129 mins |
| 4 | Henry | Arsenal | 24 | 32 | 39 | 40 | 137 mins |
| 5 | Beattie | Southampton | 23 | 24 | 76 | 80 | 139 mins |
| 6 | Owen | Liverpool | 19 | 28 | 55 | 56 | 149 mins |
| 7 | di Canio | West Ham | 9 | 9 | 79 | 81 | 151 mins |
| 8 | Baros | Liverpool | 9 | 12 | 46 | 56 | 171 mins |
| 9 | Shearer | Newcastle | 17 | 25 | 55 | 54 | 180 mins |
| 10 | Zola | Chelsea | 14 | 16 | 64 | 50 | 188 mins |
| 11 | Goater | Man City | 7 | 7 | 59 | 73 | 188 mins |
| 12 | Keane | Tottenham | 13 | 13 | 68 | 67 | 189 mins |
| 13 | Kewell | Leeds | 14 | 16 | 56 | 59 | 193 mins |
| 14 | Scholes | Man Utd | 14 | 20 | 40 | 46 | 195 mins |
| 15 | Dublin | Aston Villa | 10 | 15 | 68 | 81 | 200 mins |
| 16 | Gudjohnsen | Chelsea | 10 | 10 | 41 | 50 | 203 mins |
| 17 | Radzinsk | Everton | 11 | 11 | 71 | 71 | 209 mins |
| 18 | Nemeth | Middlesbrough | 7 | 7 | 70 | 71 | 211 mins |
| 19 | Hasselbaink | Chelsea | 11 | 15 | 50 | 50 | 216 mins |
| 20 | Anelka | Man City | 15 | 15 | 73 | 73 | 225 mins |

**The Chart-topping Goalscorers** measures the players by Strike Rate. They are most likely to be Forwards but Midfield players and even Defenders do come through the club tables. It is not a measure of the number of League goals scored - although that is also noted - but how often on average they have scored.

## CHART-TOPPING DEFENDERS

FILA

| 1 Rufus Brevett - West Ham | |
|---|---|
| **Goals Conceded in the League** The number of League goals conceded while he was on the pitch | 8 |
| **Goals Conceded in all competitions** The number of goals conceded while he was on the pitch in all competitions | 8 |
| **Clean Sheets** In games when he played at least 70 mins | 6 |
| **Defensive Rating** Average number of minutes between League goals conceded while on pitch | 58 |
| **Club Defensive Rating** Average mins between League goals conceded by the club this season | 137 |

| | PLAYER | CLUB | CON: LGE | ALL | CS | CDR | DEF RATE |
|---|---|---|---|---|---|---|---|
| 2 | Delaney | Aston Villa | 9 | 9 | 4 | 73 | 118 mins |
| 3 | O'Shea | Man Utd | 20 | 36 | 10 | 101 | 114 mins |
| 4 | Le Saux | Chelsea | 20 | 28 | 8 | 90 | 109 mins |
| 5 | Neville, G | Man Utd | 17 | 35 | 8 | 101 | 107 mins |
| 6 | Ferdinand | Man Utd | 23 | 44 | 9 | 101 | 106 mins |
| 7 | Melchiot | Chelsea | 27 | 34 | 13 | 90 | 105 mins |
| 8 | Silvestre | Man Utd | 28 | 51 | 11 | 101 | 104 mins |
| 9 | Terry | Chelsea | 14 | 26 | 5 | 90 | 101 mins |
| 10 | Johnson | West Ham | 13 | 13 | 6 | 58 | 99 mins |
| 11 | Henchoz | Liverpool | 17 | 26 | 6 | 83 | 95 mins |
| 12 | Hyypia | Liverpool | 34 | 53 | 14 | 83 | 93 mins |
| 13 | Brown | Man Utd | 20 | 33 | 6 | 101 | 93 mins |
| 14 | Campbell | Arsenal | 32 | 44 | 9 | 81 | 92 mins |
| 15 | Ehiogu | M'boro | 29 | 29 | 10 | 78 | 92 mins |
| 16 | Neill | Blackburn | 33 | 50 | 13 | 80 | 91 mins |
| 17 | Desailly | Chelsea | 30 | 31 | 9 | 90 | 90 mins |
| 18 | Cooper | M'boro | 16 | 21 | 5 | 78 | 88 mins |
| 19 | Berg | Blackburn | 15 | 20 | 7 | 80 | 85 mins |
| 20 | Gallas | Chelsea | 38 | 51 | 11 | 90 | 85 mins |

**The Chart-topping Defenders** are resolved by their Defensive Rating, how often their team concedes a goal while they are playing. All these rightly favour players at the best performing clubs because good players win matches. However, good players in lower-table clubs will chart where they have lifted the team's performance.

## CHART-TOPPING GOALKEEPERS

| 1 Fabien Barthez - Manchester United | |
|---|---|
| **Goals conceded in the League (CL)** | 28 |
| **Goals conceded in all comps (CA)** | 46 |
| **Counting Games** League games when he played at least 70 minutes | 27 |
| **Clean Sheets** In games when he played at least 70 mins | 9 |
| **Goals to Shots Ratio (GSR)** The average number of shots on target per each League goal conceded | 4.3 |
| **Defensive Rating** Average number of minutes between League goals conceded while on pitch | 91 |

| | PLAYER | CLUB | CG | CON: LGE | ALL | CS | GSR | DEF RATE |
|---|---|---|---|---|---|---|---|---|
| 2 | Niemi | Ston | 25 | 25 | 32 | 9 | 6.2 | 90 mins |
| 3 | Cudicini | Chelsea | 36 | 36 | 49 | 12 | 4.8 | 90 mins |
| 4 | Friedel | Blackburn | 37 | 40 | 57 | 15 | 5.4 | 83 mins |
| 5 | Dudek | Liverpool | 30 | 33 | 48 | 12 | 4.1 | 82 mins |
| 6 | Seaman | Arsenal | 28 | 31 | 39 | 8 | 3.9 | 81 mins |
| 7 | Schwarzer | Middlesbrough | 38 | 44 | 45 | 10 | 5.4 | 78 mins |
| 8 | Wright | Everton | 33 | 39 | 48 | 11 | 5.2 | 76 mins |
| 9 | Enckelman | Aston Villa | 32 | 40 | 44 | 7 | 4.6 | 73 mins |
| 10 | Given | Newcastle | 38 | 48 | 71 | 14 | 4.7 | 71 mins |
| 11 | Van der Sar | Fulham | 18 | 24 | 29 | 5 | 3.5 | 70 mins |
| 12 | Taylor, M | Fulham | 17 | 23 | 31 | 6 | 4.4 | 69 mins |
| 13 | Schmeichel | Man City | 29 | 38 | 41 | 9 | 4.1 | 69 mins |
| 14 | Vaesen | Birmingham | 27 | 36 | 39 | 5 | 4 | 68 mins |
| 15 | Jaaskelainen | Bolton | 38 | 51 | 51 | 10 | 4.3 | 67 mins |
| 16 | Macho | Sunderland | 12 | 19 | 24 | 2 | 5.1 | 60 mins |
| 17 | Kiely | Charlton | 37 | 56 | 60 | 8 | 4.5 | 60 mins |
| 18 | Robinson | Leeds | 38 | 57 | 67 | 10 | 3.9 | 60 mins |
| 19 | James | West Ham | 38 | 59 | 69 | 9 | 3.5 | 58 mins |
| 20 | Jones | Southampton | 13 | 21 | 22 | 4 | 4.4 | 56 mins |

**The Chart-topping Goalkeepers** are positioned by their Defensive Rating. We also show Clean Sheets where the team has not conceded and the Keeper has played all or most (at least 70 minutes) of the game. Now teams use several keepers in a season, not every team will necessarily chart on this page.

## FINAL LEAGUE TABLE

| | HOME | | | | | | AWAY | | | | | TOTAL | | | |
|---|---|---|---|---|---|---|---|---|---|---|---|---|---|---|---|
| | P | W | D | L | F | A | W | D | L | F | A | F | A | DIF | PTS |
| Man Utd | 38 | 16 | 2 | 1 | 42 | 12 | 9 | 6 | 4 | 32 | 22 | 74 | 34 | 40 | 83 |
| Arsenal | 38 | 15 | 2 | 2 | 47 | 20 | 8 | 7 | 4 | 38 | 22 | 85 | 42 | 43 | 78 |
| Newcastle | 38 | 15 | 2 | 2 | 36 | 17 | 6 | 4 | 9 | 27 | 31 | 63 | 48 | 15 | 69 |
| Chelsea | 38 | 12 | 5 | 2 | 41 | 15 | 7 | 5 | 7 | 27 | 23 | 68 | 38 | 30 | 67 |
| Liverpool | 38 | 9 | 8 | 2 | 30 | 16 | 9 | 2 | 8 | 31 | 25 | 61 | 41 | 20 | 64 |
| Blackburn | 38 | 9 | 7 | 3 | 24 | 15 | 7 | 5 | 7 | 28 | 28 | 52 | 43 | 9 | 60 |
| Everton | 38 | 11 | 5 | 3 | 28 | 19 | 6 | 3 | 10 | 20 | 30 | 48 | 49 | -1 | 59 |
| Southampton | 38 | 9 | 8 | 2 | 25 | 16 | 4 | 5 | 10 | 18 | 30 | 43 | 46 | -3 | 52 |
| Man City | 38 | 9 | 2 | 8 | 28 | 26 | 6 | 4 | 9 | 19 | 28 | 47 | 54 | -7 | 51 |
| Tottenham | 38 | 9 | 4 | 6 | 30 | 29 | 5 | 4 | 10 | 21 | 33 | 51 | 62 | -11 | 50 |
| Middlesbrough | 38 | 10 | 7 | 2 | 36 | 21 | 3 | 3 | 13 | 12 | 23 | 48 | 44 | 4 | 49 |
| Charlton | 38 | 8 | 3 | 8 | 26 | 30 | 6 | 4 | 9 | 19 | 26 | 45 | 56 | -11 | 49 |
| Birmingham | 38 | 8 | 5 | 6 | 25 | 23 | 5 | 4 | 10 | 16 | 26 | 41 | 49 | -8 | 48 |
| Fulham | 38 | 11 | 3 | 5 | 26 | 18 | 2 | 6 | 11 | 15 | 32 | 41 | 50 | -9 | 48 |
| Leeds | 38 | 7 | 3 | 9 | 25 | 26 | 7 | 2 | 10 | 33 | 31 | 58 | 57 | 1 | 47 |
| Aston Villa | 38 | 11 | 2 | 6 | 25 | 14 | 1 | 7 | 11 | 17 | 33 | 42 | 47 | -5 | 45 |
| Bolton | 38 | 7 | 8 | 4 | 27 | 24 | 3 | 6 | 10 | 14 | 27 | 41 | 51 | -10 | 44 |
| West Ham | 38 | 5 | 7 | 7 | 21 | 24 | 5 | 5 | 9 | 21 | 35 | 42 | 59 | -17 | 42 |
| West Brom | 38 | 3 | 5 | 11 | 17 | 34 | 3 | 3 | 13 | 12 | 31 | 29 | 65 | -36 | 26 |
| Sunderland | 38 | 3 | 2 | 14 | 11 | 31 | 1 | 5 | 13 | 10 | 34 | 21 | 65 | -44 | 19 |

## PLAYER DISCIPLINARY RECORD

| League Yellow | 12 |
|---|---|
| League Red | 1 |
| League Total | 13 |
| All Competitions Yellow | 12 |
| All Competitions Red | 1 |
| TOTAL ALL COMPETITIONS | 13 |

**1 Olivier Tebily - Birmingham**

Cards Average
Average number of minutes between a card being shown of either colour: **143**

| | PLAYER | | LEAGUE | | TOTAL | | AVE |
|---|---|---|---|---|---|---|---|
| | | | 12Y | 1R | 12Y | 1R | |
| 2 | Cisse | Birmingham | 12Y | 1R | 12Y | 1R | 143 |
| 3 | Wome | Fulham | 5 | 1 | 5 | 1 | 172 |
| 4 | Campo | Bolton | 14 | 1 | 14 | 1 | 173 |
| 5 | Smith | Leeds | 13 | 2 | 16 | 2 | 182 |
| 6 | Purse | Birmingham | 8 | 1 | 8 | 1 | 186 |
| 7 | Bowyer | Leeds | 7 | 0 | 8 | 0 | 191 |
| 8 | Queudrue | M'boro | 10 | 3 | 10 | 3 | 199 |
| 9 | Repka | West Ham | 12 | 1 | 13 | 1 | 211 |
| 10 | Rooney | Everton | 6 | 1 | 8 | 1 | 223 |
| 11 | Griffin | Newcastle | 8 | 1 | 9 | 1 | 223 |
| 12 | Staunton | Aston Villa | 8 | 1 | 8 | 1 | 231 |
| 13 | Neville, P | Man Utd | 7 | 0 | 13 | 0 | 238 |
| 14 | Freund | Tottenham | 5 | 0 | 5 | 0 | 239 |
| 15 | Boa Morte | Fulham | 9 | 0 | 9 | 0 | 242 |
| 16 | Williams | Sunderland | 5 | 0 | 6 | 0 | 243 |
| 17 | Gravesen | Everton | 11 | 0 | 12 | 0 | 246 |
| 18 | Diao | Liverpool | 4 | 1 | 6 | 1 | 246 |
| 19 | McCann | Sunderland | 10 | 0 | 10 | 0 | 246 |
| 20 | Vieira | Arsenal | 7 | 1 | 12 | 1 | 254 |

## PREMIERSHIP CHART-TOPPING POINT EARNERS

| | PLAYER | TEAM | GAMES | POINTS | AVE |
|---|---|---|---|---|---|
| 2 | Beckham | Man Utd | 27 | 63 | 2.33 |
| 3 | Keane | Man Utd | 19 | 44 | 2.32 |
| 4 | Caldwell, S | Newcastle | 13 | 30 | 2.31 |
| 5 | Scholes | Man Utd | 30 | 69 | 2.30 |
| 6 | Ferdinand | Man Utd | 27 | 62 | 2.30 |
| 7 | Brown | Man Utd | 19 | 43 | 2.26 |
| 8 | Campbell | Arsenal | 32 | 72 | 2.25 |
| 9 | Silvestre | Man Utd | 31 | 69 | 2.23 |
| 10 | O'Shea | Man Utd | 22 | 49 | 2.23 |
| 11 | Neville, G | Man Utd | 18 | 40 | 2.22 |
| 12 | Wiltord | Arsenal | 24 | 53 | 2.21 |
| 13 | van Nistelrooy | Man Utd | 32 | 69 | 2.16 |
| 14 | Vieira | Arsenal | 22 | 47 | 2.14 |
| 15 | Keown | Arsenal | 21 | 45 | 2.14 |
| 16 | Giggs | Man Utd | 30 | 63 | 2.10 |
| 17 | Henry | Arsenal | 37 | 77 | 2.08 |
| 18 | Seaman | Arsenal | 28 | 58 | 2.07 |
| 19 | Barthez | Man Utd | 27 | 56 | 2.07 |
| 20 | Silva | Arsenal | 33 | 68 | 2.06 |

**1 Henning Berg - Blackburn**

| | |
|---|---|
| Counting Games<br>League games where he played at least 70 minutes | 12 |
| Total League Points<br>Taken in Counting Games | 31 |
| Average League Points<br>Taken in Counting Games | 2.58 |

## TEAM OF THE SEASON

Barthez
Man Utd
CG 27 DR 91
Delaney
Aston Villa
CG 12 DR 118
Campbell
Arsenal
CG 32 DR 92
Woodgate
Leeds
CG 17 DR 84
Brevett
West Ham
CG 12 DR 137
Beckham
Man Utd
CG 27 SD 83
Tugay
Blackburn
CG 28 SD 25
Davis
Fulham
CG 27 SD 0
McCann
Sunderland
CG 26 SD -78
Viduka
Leeds
CG 27 AP 129
van Nistelrooy
Man Utd
CG 32 SR 116


**The Team of the Season** in each League's Divisional Round-up is different to those at club level. It doesn't just mirror the Chart-topping performances but highlights Keepers, Defenders, Midfield players and Forwards who are dramatically out-performing their team-mates. We compare their key rating to the club average see below: -

- **The Division Team's goalkeeper** has to be the player with the highest Defensive Rating as he often plays most or all the games in a league season.
- **The Division Team's defenders** are also tested by Defensive Rating but against their co-defender's Ratings. We weight it to take into account the fact that differences can fluctuate wildly at the bottom of a division.
- **The Division Team's midfield** all have good Scoring Differences compared to the average Ratings of their colleagues. In all cases these players must have played at least a minimum of Counting Games.
- **The Divisional Team strikeforce** is made up of the two players who have the biggest gap in Strike Rate between themselves and their next forward. These are weighted again, as lower sides may not even have a second charting forward.

NATIONWIDE FOOTBALL DIVISION ONE CHAMPIONS

# PORTSMOUTH

Final Position: **1st**

**NICKNAME:** POMPEY

KEY: ☐ Won ☐ Drawn ☐ Lost

| | | | | | | |
|---|---|---|---|---|---|---|
| 1 | div1 | Nottm Forest | H | W | 2-0 | Burton 7; Pericard 44 |
| 2 | div1 | Sheff Utd | A | D | 1-1 | Burton 25 |
| 3 | div1 | Crystal Palace | A | W | 3-2 | Foxe 68; Crowe 69,70 |
| 4 | div1 | Watford | H | W | 3-0 | Merson 42 pen; Todorov 45; Burton 47 |
| 5 | div1 | Grimsby | A | W | 1-0 | Burchill 83 |
| 6 | div1 | Brighton | H | W | 4-2 | Taylor 3; Merson 25 pen; Todorov 45; Crowe 52 |
| 7 | div1 | Gillingham | A | W | 3-1 | Merson 30; Burchill 45; O'Neil 79 |
| 8 | wcr1 | Peterborough | H | W | 2-0 | Quashie 25; Primus 76 |
| 9 | div1 | Millwall | H | W | 1-0 | Todorov 50 |
| 10 | div1 | Wimbledon | H | W | 4-1 | Pericard 2; Todorov 30; Williams 38 og; Taylor 71 |
| 11 | div1 | Norwich | A | L | 0-1 | |
| 12 | div1 | Bradford | H | W | 3-0 | Quashie 17,58; Pericard 21 |
| 13 | wcr2 | Wimbledon | H | L | 1-3 | Pericard 5 |
| 14 | div1 | Rotherham | A | W | 3-2 | Pericard 14; Todorov 23; Merson 45 pen |
| 15 | div1 | Coventry | H | D | 1-1 | Pericard 50 |
| 16 | div1 | Burnley | A | W | 3-0 | Quashie 21; Todorov 58; Harper 86 |
| 17 | div1 | Preston | H | W | 3-2 | Stone 23; Merson 26 pen; Taylor 34 |
| 18 | div1 | Leicester | H | L | 0-2 | |
| 19 | div1 | Wolves | A | D | 1-1 | Merson 56 |
| 20 | div1 | Derby | A | W | 2-1 | Todorov 27; Burchill 51 |
| 21 | div1 | Stoke | H | W | 3-0 | Burchill 49; Pericard 87; Todorov 90 |
| 22 | div1 | Sheff Wed | A | W | 3-1 | Todorov 11,50; O'Neil 64 |
| 23 | div1 | Walsall | H | W | 3-2 | Quashie 45; Todorov 58; Taylor 76 |
| 24 | div1 | Reading | A | D | 0-0 | |
| 25 | div1 | Stoke | A | D | 1-1 | Crowe 74 |
| 26 | div1 | Ipswich | H | D | 1-1 | Todorov 19 |
| 27 | div1 | Crystal Palace | H | D | 1-1 | Merson 27 |
| 28 | div1 | Nottm Forest | A | W | 2-1 | Taylor 56; Pericard 87 |
| 29 | div1 | Watford | A | D | 2-2 | Burton 54; Harper 58 |
| 30 | facr3 | Man Utd | A | L | 1-4 | Stone 39 |
| 31 | div1 | Sheff Utd | H | L | 1-2 | O'Neil 78 |
| 32 | div1 | Brighton | A | D | 1-1 | Todorov 64 |
| 33 | div1 | Grimsby | H | W | 3-0 | Ayegbeni 4; Ford 75 og; Quashie 90 |
| 34 | div1 | Derby | H | W | 6-2 | Merson 3; Ayegbeni 17,80; Taylor 22; Todorov 73,86 |
| 35 | div1 | Leicester | A | D | 1-1 | Taylor 65 |
| 36 | div1 | Gillingham | H | W | 1-0 | De Zeeuw 58 |
| 37 | div1 | Millwall | A | W | 5-0 | Ayegbeni 15,25; Sherwood 31; Todorov 45; Merson 72 pen |
| 38 | div1 | Wimbledon | A | L | 1-2 | Merson 26 |
| 39 | div1 | Norwich | H | W | 3-2 | Ayegbeni 57; Todorov 59,72 |
| 40 | div1 | Wolves | H | W | 1-0 | Stone 4 |
| 41 | div1 | Coventry | A | W | 4-0 | Caldwell, G 14 og; Stone 17; Harper 23; Merson 68 |
| 42 | div1 | Preston | A | D | 1-1 | Ayegbeni 5 |
| 43 | div1 | Walsall | A | W | 2-1 | Harper 15; Todorov 33 |
| 44 | div1 | Sheff Wed | H | L | 1-2 | Bradbury 20 |
| 45 | div1 | Burnley | H | W | 1-0 | Todorov 73 |
| 46 | div1 | Ipswich | A | L | 0-3 | |
| 47 | div1 | Reading | H | W | 3-0 | Pericard 19,45; Todorov 71 |
| 48 | div1 | Rotherham | H | W | 3-2 | Merson 11 pen; Todorov 22,45 |
| 49 | div1 | Bradford | A | W | 5-0 | Festa 20; Todorov 48,50,58 pen; Stone 67 |

☐ Home ☐ Away ☐ Neutral

## ATTENDANCES

**HOME GROUND:** FRATTON PARK **CAPACITY:** 19600 **AVERAGE LEAGUE AT HOME:** 18916

| | | | | | | | | | | | |
|---|---|---|---|---|---|---|---|---|---|---|---|
| 30 | Man Utd | 67222 | 33 | Grimsby | 19428 | 17 | Preston | 18637 | 25 | Stoke | 13330 |
| 35 | Leicester | 31775 | 48 | Rotherham | 19420 | 1 | Nottm Forest | 18510 | 13 | Wimbledon | 11754 |
| 46 | Ipswich | 29396 | 39 | Norwich | 19221 | 12 | Bradford | 18459 | 38 | Wimbledon | 10356 |
| 28 | Nottm Forest | 28165 | 45 | Burnley | 19221 | 3 | Crystal Palace | 18315 | 37 | Millwall | 9697 |
| 19 | Wolves | 27022 | 27 | Crystal Palace | 19217 | 4 | Watford | 17901 | 7 | Gillingham | 8797 |
| 20 | Derby | 26587 | 26 | Ipswich | 19130 | 23 | Walsall | 17701 | 14 | Rotherham | 8604 |
| 24 | Reading | 23462 | 18 | Leicester | 19107 | 9 | Millwall | 17201 | 8 | Peterborough | 8581 |
| 11 | Norwich | 21335 | 49 | Bradford | 19088 | 42 | Preston | 16665 | 43 | Walsall | 7899 |
| 40 | Wolves | 19558 | 6 | Brighton | 19031 | 22 | Sheff Wed | 16602 | 32 | Brighton | 6848 |
| 47 | Reading | 19535 | 31 | Sheff Utd | 18872 | 2 | Sheff Utd | 16093 | 5 | Grimsby | 5770 |
| 44 | Sheff Wed | 19524 | 15 | Coventry | 18837 | 16 | Burnley | 15788 | | | |
| 36 | Gillingham | 19521 | 10 | Wimbledon | 18837 | 29 | Watford | 15048 | | | |
| 34 | Derby | 19503 | 21 | Stoke | 18701 | 41 | Coventry | 13922 | | | |

## KEY PLAYERS - GOALSCORERS

1 Svetoslav Todorov

| | |
|---|---|
| **Goals in the League** | 26 |
| **Goals in all competitions** | 26 |
| **Contribution to Attacking Power** Average number of minutes between League team goals while on pitch | 40 |
| **Player Strike Rate** The total number of minutes he was on the pitch for every League goal scored | 143 |
| **Club Strike Rate** Average number of minutes between League goals scored by club | 43 |

| | PLAYER | GOALS LGE | GOALS ALL | POWER | S RATE |
|---|---|---|---|---|---|
| 2 | Vincent Pericard | 9 | 10 | 41 | 188 mins |
| 3 | Paul Merson | 12 | 12 | 41 | 318 mins |
| 4 | Steve Stone | 4 | 5 | 49 | 382 mins |
| 5 | Matthew Taylor | 7 | 7 | 42 | 450 mins |

## KEY PLAYERS - MIDFIELDERS

1 Kevin Harper

| | |
|---|---|
| **Goals in the League** | 4 |
| **Goals in all competitions** | 4 |
| **Defensive Rating** Average number of mins between League goals conceded while on the pitch | 117 |
| **Contribution to Attacking Power** Average number of minutes between League team goals while on pitch | 39 |
| **Scoring Difference** Defensive Rating minus Contribution to Attacking Power | 78 |

| | PLAYER | GOALS LGE | GOALS ALL | DEF RATE | ATT POWER | SCORE DIFF |
|---|---|---|---|---|---|---|
| 2 | Carl Robinson | 0 | 0 | 127 | 56 | 71 mins |
| 3 | Tim Sherwood | 1 | 1 | 96 | 37 | 59 mins |
| 4 | Hayden Foxe | 1 | 1 | 94 | 43 | 51 mins |
| 5 | Paul Merson | 12 | 12 | 91 | 42 | 49 mins |

## KEY PLAYERS - DEFENDERS

1 Arjan De Zeeuw

| | |
|---|---|
| **Goals Conceded in League** | 31 |
| **Goals Conceded in all competitions** | 31 |
| **Clean Sheets** In League games when he played at least 70 mins | 13 |
| **Defensive Rating** Ave number of mins between League goals conceded while on the pitch | 99 |
| **Club Defensive Rating** Average number of mins between League goals conceded by the club this season | 92 |

| | PLAYER | CON LGE | CON ALL | CLN SHEETS | DEF RATE |
|---|---|---|---|---|---|
| 2 | Gianluca Festa | 25 | 28 | 10 | 92 mins |
| 3 | Matthew Taylor | 35 | 42 | 11 | 90 mins |
| 4 | Linvoy Primus | 39 | 46 | 12 | 90 mins |
| 5 | Lassina Diabate | 19 | 21 | 1 | 75 mins |

## KEY GOALKEEPER

1 Shaka Hislop

| | |
|---|---|
| **Goals Conceded in the League** | 45 |
| **Goals Conceded in all competitions** | 52 |
| **Clean Sheets** In games when he played at least 70 mins | 15 |
| **Goals to Shots Ratio** The average number of shots on target per each League goal conceded | 4.7 |
| **Defensive Rating** Ave number of mins between League goals conceded while on the pitch | 91 |

## MONTHY POINTS TALLY

| Month | Points | % |
|---|---|---|
| AUGUST | 16 | 89% |
| SEPTEMBER | 15 | 83% |
| OCTOBER | 10 | 67% |
| NOVEMBER | 13 | 72% |
| DECEMBER | 7 | 47% |
| JANUARY | 2 | 17% |
| FEBRUARY | 10 | 83% |
| MARCH | 13 | 72% |
| APRIL | 12 | 67% |
| MAY | 3 | 100% |

## TOP POINT EARNERS

| | PLAYER | GAMES | AV PTS |
|---|---|---|---|
| 1 | Kevin Harper | 17 | 2.47 |
| 2 | Vincent Pericard | 14 | 2.29 |
| 3 | Arjan De Zeeuw | 32 | 2.28 |
| 4 | Tim Sherwood | 17 | 2.24 |
| 5 | Gianluca Festa | 25 | 2.24 |
| 6 | Paul Merson | 42 | 2.17 |
| 7 | Svetoslav Todorov | 42 | 2.17 |
| 8 | Matthew Taylor | 35 | 2.14 |
| 9 | Shaka Hislop | 45 | 2.11 |
| 10 | Lassina Diabate | 13 | 2.08 |
| | CLUB AVERAGE: | | 2.13 |

## LEAGUE APPEARANCES, BOOKINGS AND CAPS

| | AGE (on 01/07/03) | IN THE SQUAD | COUNTING GAMES | MINUTES ON PITCH | YELLOW CARDS | RED CARDS | THIS SEASON | HOME COUNTRY |
|---|---|---|---|---|---|---|---|---|
| **Goalkeepers** | | | | | | | | |
| Shaka Hislop | 34 | 46 | 45 | 4095 | 1 | 0 | - | Trinidad & Tobago |
| Yoshikatsu Kawaguchi | 27 | 46 | 0 | 45 | 0 | 0 | 1 | Japan (23) |
| **Defenders** | | | | | | | | |
| Lewis Buxton | 19 | 1 | 0 | 1 | 0 | 0 | - | Wales |
| Jason Crowe | 24 | 19 | 4 | 723 | 2 | 0 | - | England |
| Arjan De Zeeuw | 33 | 38 | 32 | 3072 | 5 | 0 | - | Holland |
| Lassina Diabate | 28 | 34 | 13 | 1423 | 7 | 0 | - | Ivory Coast |
| Gianluca Festa | 34 | 28 | 25 | 2297 | 3 | 0 | - | Italy |
| Eddie Howe | 25 | 1 | 0 | 8 | 0 | 0 | - | England |
| Linvoy Primus | 29 | 44 | 38 | 3516 | 3 | 0 | - | England |
| Paul Ritchie | 27 | 13 | 6 | 727 | 3 | 0 | - | Scotland |
| Efstathios Tavlaridis | 23 | 6 | 2 | 262 | 2 | 0 | - | Greece |
| Matthew Taylor | 21 | 35 | 35 | 3150 | 7 | 0 | - | England |
| Carl Tiler | 33 | 2 | 0 | 10 | 0 | 0 | - | England |
| Jamie Vincent | 28 | 2 | 0 | 0 | 0 | 0 | - | England |
| **Midfielders** | | | | | | | | |
| Neil Barrett | 21 | 1 | 0 | 0 | 0 | 0 | - | England |
| Chris Clarke | - | 1 | 0 | 0 | 0 | 0 | - | England |
| Shaun Cooper | 19 | 5 | 0 | 0 | 0 | 0 | - | England |
| Hayden Foxe | 26 | 32 | 29 | 2738 | 5 | 0 | - | Australia |
| Kevin Harper | 27 | 40 | 17 | 2101 | 4 | 0 | - | England |
| Markus Heikkinen | 24 | 4 | 0 | 67 | 0 | 0 | - | Finland |
| Ceri Hughes | 32 | 6 | 4 | 411 | 1 | 0 | - | |
| Paul Merson | 35 | 45 | 42 | 3816 | 4 | 0 | - | England |
| Gary O'Neil | 20 | 40 | 9 | 1337 | 0 | 0 | - | England |
| Courtney Pitt | 21 | 2 | 0 | 0 | 0 | 0 | - | England |
| Nigel Quashie | 24 | 42 | 41 | 3745 | 12 | 0 | - | England |
| Carl Robinson | 26 | 21 | 9 | 888 | 1 | 0 | 1 | Wales (50) |
| Tim Sherwood | 34 | 17 | 17 | 1530 | 4 | 0 | - | England |
| Steve Stone | 31 | 19 | 17 | 1529 | 4 | 0 | - | England |
| **Forwards** | | | | | | | | |
| Yakubu Ayegbeni | 20 | 14 | 11 | 1049 | 0 | 0 | - | Nigeria |
| Lee Bradbury | 28 | 3 | 2 | 218 | 0 | 0 | - | England |
| Mark Burchill | 22 | 26 | 2 | 448 | 0 | 0 | - | Scotland |
| Deon Burton | 26 | 22 | 7 | 926 | 1 | 0 | - | Jamaica |
| Vincent Pericard | 20 | 36 | 14 | 1693 | 1 | 0 | - | France |
| Svetoslav Todorov | 24 | 45 | 42 | 3715 | 4 | 0 | - | Bulgaria |

KEY: LEAGUE BOOKINGS CAPS (FIFA RANKING)

## GOALS

| 1 S Todorov | |
|---|---|
| League | 26 |
| FA Cup | 0 |
| League Cup | 0 |
| Other | 0 |
| TOTAL | 26 |

| | PLAYER | LGE | FAC | LC | Oth | TOT |
|---|---|---|---|---|---|---|
| 2 | Merson | 12 | 0 | 0 | 0 | 12 |
| 3 | Pericard | 9 | 0 | 1 | 0 | 10 |
| 4 | Ayegbeni | 7 | 0 | 0 | 0 | 7 |
| 5 | Taylor | 7 | 0 | 0 | 0 | 7 |
| 6 | Quashie | 5 | 0 | 1 | 0 | 6 |
| 7 | Burchill | 4 | 0 | 0 | 0 | 4 |
| 8 | Crowe | 4 | 0 | 0 | 0 | 4 |
| 9 | Stone | 4 | 1 | 0 | 0 | 5 |
| 10 | Burton | 4 | 0 | 0 | 0 | 4 |
| 11 | Harper | 4 | 0 | 0 | 0 | 4 |
| | Other | 11 | 0 | 1 | 0 | 12 |
| | TOTAL | 97 | 1 | 3 | 0 | 101 |

## TEAM OF THE SEASON

| GOALKEEPER | GAMES | DEF RATE |
|---|---|---|
| Shaka Hislop | 45 | 91 |
| **DEFENDERS** | **GAMES** | **DEF RATE** |
| Arjan De Zeeuw | 32 | 99 |
| Gianluca Festa | 25 | 92 |
| Matthew Taylor | 35 | 90 |
| Linvoy Primus | 38 | 90 |
| **MIDFIELDERS** | **GAMES** | **SCORE DIFF** |
| Kevin Harper | 17 | 78 |
| Carl Robinson | 9 | 71 |
| Tim Sherwood | 17 | 59 |
| Hayden Foxe | 29 | 51 |
| **GOALSCORERS** | **GAMES** | **STRIKE RATE** |
| Svetoslav Todorov | 42 | 143 |
| Vincent Pericard | 14 | 188 |

Games = games playing at least 70 minutes

## SQUAD APPEARANCES

| Match | 1 | 2 | 3 | 4 | 5 | 6 | 7 | 8 | 9 | 10 | 11 | 12 | 13 | 14 | 15 | 16 | 17 | 18 | 19 | 20 | 21 | 22 | 23 | 24 | 25 |
|---|---|---|---|---|---|---|---|---|---|---|---|---|---|---|---|---|---|---|---|---|---|---|---|---|---|
| Venue | H | A | A | H | A | H | A | H | H | H | A | H | H | A | H | A | H | H | A | A | H | A | H | A | A |
| Competition | L | L | L | L | L | L | L | W | L | L | L | L | W | L | L | L | L | L | L | L | L | L | L | L | L |
| Result | W | D | W | W | W | W | W | W | W | W | L | W | L | W | D | W | W | L | D | W | W | W | W | D | D |

| Match | 26 | 27 | 28 | 29 | 30 | 31 | 32 | 33 | 34 | 35 | 36 | 37 | 38 | 39 | 40 | 41 | 42 | 43 | 44 | 45 | 46 | 47 | 48 | 49 |
|---|---|---|---|---|---|---|---|---|---|---|---|---|---|---|---|---|---|---|---|---|---|---|---|---|
| Venue | H | H | A | A | A | H | A | H | H | A | H | A | A | H | H | A | A | A | H | H | A | H | H | A |
| Competition | L | L | L | L | F | L | L | L | L | L | L | L | L | L | L | L | L | L | L | L | L | L | L | L |
| Result | D | D | W | D | L | L | D | W | W | D | W | W | L | W | W | W | D | W | L | W | L | W | W | W |

**Goalkeepers**
Shaka Hislop
Yoshikatsu Kawaguchi

**Defenders**
Lewis Buxton
Jason Crowe
Arjan De Zeeuw
Lassina Diabate
Gianluca Festa
Eddie Howe
Linvoy Primus
Paul Ritchie
Efstathios Tavlaridis
Matthew Taylor
Carl Tiler
Jamie Vincent

**Midfielders**
Neil Barrett
Chris Clarke
Shaun Cooper
Hayden Foxe
Kevin Harper
Markus Heikkinen
Ceri Hughes
Paul Merson
Gary O'Neil
Courtney Pitt
Nigel Quashie
Carl Robinson
Tim Sherwood
Steve Stone

**Forwards**
Yakubu Ayegbeni
Lee Bradbury
Mark Burchill
Deon Burton
Vincent Pericard
Svetoslav Todorov

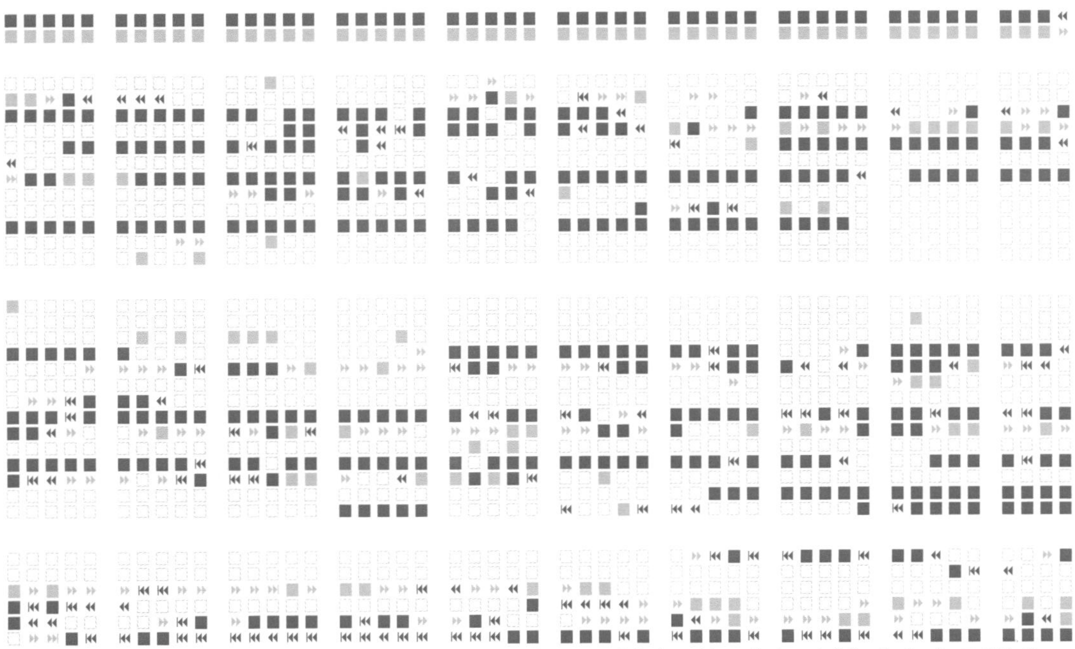

KEY: ■ On all match ■ On bench
⏮ Subbed or sent off (Counting game)
« Subbed or sent off (playing less than 70 minutes)
» Subbed on from bench (Counting Game)
» Subbed on (playing less than 70 minutes)
» Subbed on and then subbed or sent off (Counting Game)
» Subbed on and then subbed or sent off (playing less than 70 minutes)
Not in 16

# LEICESTER CITY

Final Position: **2nd**

**NICKNAME:** THE FOXES

KEY: ☐Won ☐Drawn ☐Lost

| | | | | | | |
|---|---|---|---|---|---|---|
| 1 | div1 | Watford | H | W | 2-0 | Deane 47,54 |
| 2 | div1 | Stoke | A | W | 1-0 | Scowcroft 7 |
| 3 | div1 | Ipswich | A | L | 1-6 | Stevenson 45 |
| 4 | div1 | Reading | H | W | 2-1 | Deane 3; Dickov 4 pen |
| 5 | div1 | Crystal Palace | A | D | 0-0 | |
| 6 | div1 | Gillingham | H | W | 2-0 | Lewis 10; Dickov 42 |
| 7 | div1 | Wimbledon | A | W | 3-2 | Benjamin 43; Izzet 45 pen; Stewart 80 |
| 8 | wcr1 | Hull City | A | W | 4-2 | Rogers 18,97; Dickov 91; Scowcroft 99 |
| 9 | div1 | Derby | H | W | 3-1 | Izzet 27; Deane 79; Dickov 87 |
| 10 | div1 | Bradford | H | W | 4-0 | Deane 27; Elliott 28; Dickov 68 pen; Scowcroft 90 |
| 11 | div1 | Sheff Wed | A | D | 0-0 | |
| 12 | div1 | Wolves | H | W | 1-0 | Dickov 5 pen |
| 13 | wcr2 | Sheff Wed | A | W | 2-1 | Izzet 90; Benjamin 97 |
| 14 | div1 | Norwich | A | D | 0-0 | |
| 15 | div1 | Burnley | H | L | 0-1 | |
| 16 | div1 | Nottm Forest | A | D | 2-2 | Deane 23; Dickov 41 |
| 17 | div1 | Coventry | H | W | 2-1 | Taggart 76; Deane 89 |
| 18 | div1 | Portsmouth | A | W | 2-0 | Scowcroft 13; Elliott 39 |
| 19 | wcr3 | Man Utd | A | L | 0-2 | |
| 20 | div1 | Walsall | H | W | 2-0 | Heath 57; Scowcroft 67 |
| 21 | div1 | Millwall | A | D | 2-2 | Heath 1; Stewart 3 |
| 22 | div1 | Rotherham | H | W | 2-1 | Dickov 50; Stewart 64 |
| 23 | div1 | Preston | A | L | 0-2 | |
| 24 | div1 | Grimsby | A | W | 2-1 | Scowcroft 2; Izzet 74 |
| 25 | div1 | Sheff Utd | H | D | 0-0 | |
| 26 | div1 | Millwall | H | W | 4-1 | Scowcroft 10,52; Elliott 25; Dickov 78 |
| 27 | div1 | Brighton | A | W | 1-0 | Deane 72 |
| 28 | div1 | Ipswich | H | L | 1-2 | Dickov 55 pen |
| 29 | div1 | Watford | A | W | 2-1 | Elliott 34; Deane 66 |
| 30 | facr3 | Bristol City | H | W | 2-0 | Elliott 45; Dickov 75 |
| 31 | div1 | Stoke | H | D | 0-0 | |
| 32 | div1 | Gillingham | A | L | 2-3 | Sinclair 50; Wright 61 |
| 33 | facr4 | Wolves | A | L | 1-4 | Dickov 29 pen |
| 34 | div1 | Reading | A | W | 3-1 | Dickov 17,26 pen; Heath 34 |
| 35 | div1 | Crystal Palace | H | W | 1-0 | Dickov 77 |
| 36 | div1 | Walsall | A | W | 4-1 | Dickov 41; Scowcroft 45,85; Elliott 72 |
| 37 | div1 | Portsmouth | H | D | 1-1 | Benjamin 9 |
| 38 | div1 | Wimbledon | H | W | 4-0 | Dickov 34 pen,90; Benjamin 48,48 |
| 39 | div1 | Derby | A | D | 1-1 | Deane 26 |
| 40 | div1 | Bradford | A | D | 0-0 | |
| 41 | div1 | Sheff Wed | H | D | 1-1 | McLaren 50 og |
| 42 | div1 | Preston | H | W | 2-1 | Deane 43,56 |
| 43 | div1 | Burnley | A | W | 2-1 | Dickov 79; Benjamin 83 |
| 44 | div1 | Coventry | A | W | 2-1 | McKinlay 48; Scowcroft 68 |
| 45 | div1 | Grimsby | H | W | 2-0 | Benjamin 61; Davidson 71 |
| 46 | div1 | Nottm Forest | H | W | 1-0 | Wright 37 |
| 47 | div1 | Rotherham | A | D | 1-1 | Benjamin 75 |
| 48 | div1 | Brighton | H | W | 2-0 | Izzet 10; Stewart 45 |
| 49 | div1 | Sheff Utd | A | L | 1-2 | Deane 4 |
| 50 | div1 | Norwich | H | D | 1-1 | Benjamin 20 |
| 51 | div1 | Wolves | A | D | 1-1 | Benjamin 86 pen |

☐Home ☐Away ☐Neutral

## ATTENDANCES

**HOME GROUND:** THE WALKERS STADIUM **CAPACITY:** 32100 **AVERAGE LEAGUE AT HOME:** 29230

| | | | | | | | | | | | |
|---|---|---|---|---|---|---|---|---|---|---|---|
| 19 | Man Utd | 47848 | 42 | Preston | 30713 | 31 | Stoke | 25038 | 2 | Stoke | 14028 |
| 12 | Wolves | 32082 | 6 | Gillingham | 30067 | 10 | Bradford | 24651 | 23 | Preston | 13048 |
| 46 | Nottm Forest | 32065 | 16 | Nottm Forest | 29497 | 39 | Derby | 24307 | 40 | Bradford | 11531 |
| 48 | Brighton | 31909 | 51 | Wolves | 28190 | 4 | Reading | 22978 | 21 | Millwall | 10772 |
| 26 | Millwall | 31904 | 33 | Wolves | 28164 | 11 | Sheff Wed | 22219 | 13 | Sheff Wed | 10472 |
| 37 | Portsmouth | 31775 | 41 | Sheff Wed | 27463 | 49 | Sheff Utd | 21277 | 47 | Rotherham | 9888 |
| 22 | Rotherham | 31714 | 3 | Ipswich | 27374 | 14 | Norwich | 20952 | 36 | Walsall | 8741 |
| 50 | Norwich | 31639 | 17 | Coventry | 27139 | 18 | Portsmouth | 19107 | 32 | Gillingham | 8609 |
| 38 | Wimbledon | 31438 | 35 | Crystal Palace | 27005 | 34 | Reading | 17156 | 24 | Grimsby | 7310 |
| 28 | Ipswich | 31426 | 25 | Sheff Utd | 26718 | 44 | Coventry | 16610 | 8 | Hull City | 7061 |
| 9 | Derby | 31049 | 15 | Burnley | 26254 | 29 | Watford | 16017 | 27 | Brighton | 6592 |
| 1 | Watford | 31022 | 30 | Bristol City | 25868 | 5 | Crystal Palace | 15440 | 7 | Wimbledon | 2165 |
| 45 | Grimsby | 31014 | 20 | Walsall | 25243 | 43 | Burnley | 14554 | | | |

## KEY PLAYERS - GOALSCORERS

1 Brian Deane

| | |
|---|---|
| Goals in the League | 13 |
| Goals in all competitions | 13 |
| Contribution to Attacking Power<br>Average number of minutes between League team goals while on pitch | 59 |
| Player Strike Rate<br>The total number of minutes he was on the pitch for every League goal scored | 180 |
| Club Strike Rate<br>Average number of minutes between League goals scored by club | 55 |

| | PLAYER | GOALS LGE | GOALS ALL | POWER | S RATE |
|---|---|---|---|---|---|
| 2 | Trevor Benjamin | 9 | 10 | 56 | 188 mins |
| 3 | Paul Dickov | 18 | 21 | 54 | 198 mins |
| 4 | James Scowcroft | 10 | 11 | 55 | 381 mins |
| 5 | Jordan Stewart | 4 | 4 | 52 | 625 mins |

## KEY PLAYERS - MIDFIELDERS

1 Mustafa Izzet

| | |
|---|---|
| Goals in the League | 4 |
| Goals in all competitions | 5 |
| Defensive Rating<br>Average number of mins between League goals conceded while on the pitch | 126 |
| Contribution to Attacking Power<br>Average number of minutes between League team goals while on pitch | 50 |
| Scoring Difference<br>Defensive Rating minus Contribution to Attacking Power | 76 |

| | PLAYER | GOALS LGE | GOALS ALL | DEF RATE | ATT POWER | SCORE DIFF |
|---|---|---|---|---|---|---|
| 2 | Billy McKinlay | 1 | 1 | 123 | 59 | 64 mins |
| 3 | Andrew Impey | 0 | 0 | 104 | 56 | 48 mins |
| 4 | Jordan Stewart | 4 | 4 | 93 | 54 | 39 mins |

## KEY PLAYERS - DEFENDERS

1 Gerry Taggart

| | |
|---|---|
| Goals Conceded in League | 24 |
| Goals Conceded in all competitions | 24 |
| Clean Sheets<br>In League games when he played at least 70 mins | 12 |
| Defensive Rating<br>Ave number of mins between League goals conceded while on the pitch | 115 |
| Club Defensive Rating<br>Average number of mins between League goals conceded by the club this season | 104 |

| | PLAYER | CON LGE | CON ALL | CLN SHEETS | DEF RATE |
|---|---|---|---|---|---|
| 2 | Callum Davidson | 22 | 30 | 10 | 110 mins |
| 3 | Alan Rogers | 33 | 41 | 18 | 104 mins |
| 4 | Matt Elliott | 37 | 43 | 17 | 103 mins |
| 5 | Frank Sinclair | 28 | 36 | 14 | 98 mins |

## KEY GOALKEEPER

1 Ian Walker

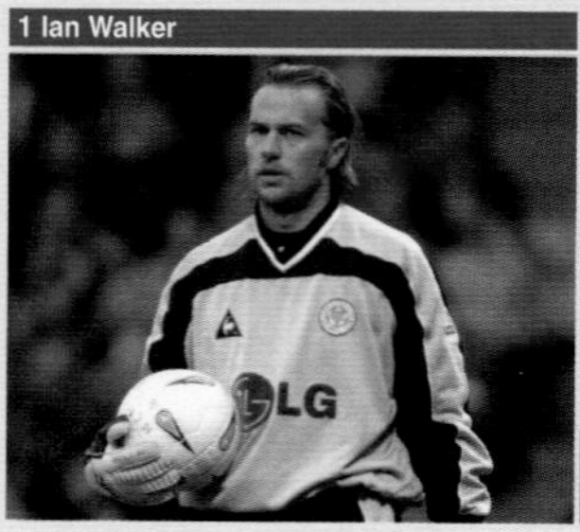

| | |
|---|---|
| Goals Conceded in the League | 40 |
| Goals Conceded in all competitions | 49 |
| Clean Sheets<br>In games when he played at least 70 mins | 19 |
| Goals to Shots Ratio<br>The average number of shots on target per each League goal conceded | 5.9 |
| Defensive Rating<br>Ave number of mins between League goals conceded while on the pitch | 103 |

## MONTHY POINTS TALLY

| | | |
|---|---|---|
| AUGUST | 13 | 72% |
| SEPTEMBER | 16 | 89% |
| OCTOBER | 8 | 53% |
| NOVEMBER | 13 | 62% |
| DECEMBER | 10 | 67% |
| JANUARY | 7 | 47% |
| FEBRUARY | 10 | 83% |
| MARCH | 12 | 67% |
| APRIL | 11 | 61% |
| MAY | 1 | 33% |

## TOP POINT EARNERS

| | PLAYER | GAMES | AV PTS |
|---|---|---|---|
| 1 | Callum Davidson | 25 | 2.24 |
| 2 | Mustafa Izzet | 35 | 2.23 |
| 3 | Gerry Taggart | 28 | 2.07 |
| 4 | James Scowcroft | 42 | 2.02 |
| 5 | Ian Walker | 46 | 2.00 |
| 6 | Jordan Stewart | 22 | 2.00 |
| 7 | Frank Sinclair | 29 | 1.97 |
| 8 | Andrew Impey | 26 | 1.96 |
| 9 | Matt Elliott | 42 | 1.95 |
| 10 | Paul Dickov | 40 | 1.95 |
| | CLUB AVERAGE: | | 2.00 |

## GOALS

| 1 Paul Dickov | |
|---|---|
| League | 16 |
| FA Cup | 2 |
| League Cup | 1 |
| Other | 0 |
| TOTAL | 19 |

LG

| | PLAYER | LGE | FAC | LC | Oth | TOT |
|---|---|---|---|---|---|---|
| 2 | Deane | 13 | 0 | 0 | 0 | 13 |
| 3 | Scowcroft | 10 | 0 | 1 | 0 | 11 |
| 4 | Benjamin | 9 | 0 | 1 | 0 | 10 |
| 5 | Elliott | 5 | 1 | 0 | 0 | 6 |
| 6 | Stewart | 4 | 0 | 0 | 0 | 4 |
| 7 | Izzet | 4 | 0 | 1 | 0 | 5 |
| 8 | Heath | 3 | 0 | 0 | 0 | 3 |
| 9 | Wright | 2 | 0 | 0 | 0 | 2 |
| 10 | Lewis | 1 | 0 | 0 | 0 | 1 |
| 11 | Davidson | 1 | 0 | 0 | 0 | 1 |
| | Other | 5 | 0 | 2 | 0 | 7 |
| | TOTAL | 73 | 3 | 6 | 0 | 82 |

## TEAM OF THE SEASON

| GOALKEEPER | GAMES | DEF RATE |
|---|---|---|
| Ian Walker | 46 | 103 |
| **DEFENDERS** | **GAMES** | **DEF RATE** |
| Gerry Taggart | 28 | 115 |
| Callum Davidson | 25 | 110 |
| Alan Rogers | 36 | 104 |
| Matt Elliott | 42 | 103 |
| **MIDFIELDERS** | **GAMES** | **SCORE DIFF** |
| Mustafa Izzet | 35 | 76 |
| Billy McKinlay | 27 | 64 |
| Andrew Impey | 26 | 48 |
| Jordan Stewart | 22 | 39 |
| **GOALSCORERS** | **GAMES** | **STRIKE RATE** |
| Brian Deane | 24 | 180 |
| Trevor Benjamin | 14 | 188 |

Games = games playing at least 70 minutes

## LEAGUE APPEARANCES, BOOKINGS AND CAPS

| | AGE (on 01/07/03) | IN THE SQUAD | COUNTING GAMES | MINUTES ON PITCH | YELLOW CARDS | RED CARDS | THIS SEASON | HOME COUNTRY |
|---|---|---|---|---|---|---|---|---|
| **Goalkeepers** | | | | | | | | |
| Tim Flowers | 36 | 22 | 0 | 13 | 0 | 0 | - | England |
| Paul Murphy | 20 | 4 | 0 | 0 | 0 | 0 | - | Rep of Ireland |
| Michael Price | 20 | 1 | 0 | 0 | 0 | 0 | - | England |
| Simon Royce | 31 | 2 | 0 | 0 | 0 | 0 | - | England |
| Ian Walker | 31 | 46 | 46 | 4127 | 1 | 0 | 2 | England (7) |
| **Defenders** | | | | | | | | |
| Jon Ashton | 20 | 6 | 1 | 73 | 0 | 0 | - | England |
| Callum Davidson | 27 | 30 | 25 | 2422 | 7 | 1 | 3 | Scotland (64) |
| Matt Elliott | 34 | 44 | 42 | 3816 | 2 | 0 | - | Scotland |
| Matt Heath | 22 | 30 | 8 | 783 | 2 | 0 | - | England |
| Lee Marshall | 24 | 1 | 1 | 90 | 0 | 0 | - | England |
| Alan Rogers | 26 | 41 | 36 | 3416 | 4 | 0 | - | England |
| Frank Sinclair | 31 | 36 | 29 | 2743 | 12 | 1 | - | Jamaica |
| Gerry Taggart | 32 | 37 | 28 | 2770 | 11 | 2 | 1 | N Ireland (111) |
| **Midfielders** | | | | | | | | |
| Andrew Impey | 31 | 37 | 26 | 2500 | 6 | 0 | - | England |
| Mustafa Izzet | 28 | 38 | 35 | 3278 | 13 | 1 | - | Turkey |
| Matthew Jones | 22 | 11 | 2 | 289 | 1 | 0 | 2 | Wales (50) |
| Junior Lewis | 29 | 13 | 5 | 533 | 0 | 0 | - | England |
| Billy McKinlay | 34 | 37 | 27 | 2701 | 9 | 0 | - | Scotland |
| Chris O'Grady | 17 | 3 | 0 | 1 | 0 | 0 | - | England |
| Stefan Oakes | 24 | 9 | 1 | 195 | 1 | 0 | - | England |
| Martin Reeves | 21 | 7 | 0 | 50 | 0 | 0 | - | England |
| John Stevenson | 20 | 24 | 0 | 119 | 0 | 0 | - | England |
| Jordan Stewart | 21 | 41 | 22 | 2500 | 3 | 0 | - | England |
| Nicky Summerbee | 31 | 39 | 5 | 1077 | 0 | 1 | - | England |
| Tom Williamson | 18 | 2 | 0 | 0 | 0 | 0 | - | England |
| **Forwards** | | | | | | | | |
| Trevor Benjamin | 24 | 40 | 14 | 1688 | 5 | 0 | - | England |
| Brian Deane | 35 | 32 | 24 | 2335 | 5 | 1 | - | England |
| Paul Dickov | 30 | 42 | 40 | 3556 | 13 | 0 | - | England |
| Tom Petrescu | 16 | 1 | 0 | 19 | 0 | 0 | - | Finland |
| James Scowcroft | 29 | 43 | 42 | 3807 | 5 | 0 | - | England |
| Tommy Wright | 18 | 16 | 3 | 440 | 2 | 0 | - | England |

KEY: LEAGUE BOOKINGS CAPS (FIFA RANKING)

## SQUAD APPEARANCES

| Match | 1 | 2 | 3 | 4 | 5 | 6 | 7 | 8 | 9 | 10 | 11 | 12 | 13 | 14 | 15 | 16 | 17 | 18 | 19 | 20 | 21 | 22 | 23 | 24 | 25 | 26 | 27 | 28 | 29 | 30 | 31 | 32 | 33 | 34 | 35 | 36 | 37 | 38 | 39 | 40 | 41 | 42 | 43 | 44 | 45 | 46 | 47 | 48 | 49 | 50 | 51 |
|---|---|---|---|---|---|---|---|---|---|---|---|---|---|---|---|---|---|---|---|---|---|---|---|---|---|---|---|---|---|---|---|---|---|---|---|---|---|---|---|---|---|---|---|---|---|---|---|---|---|---|---|
| Venue | H | A | A | H | A | H | A | A | H | H | A | H | A | A | H | A | H | A | A | H | A | H | A | A | H | H | A | H | A | H | H | A | A | A | H | A | H | H | A | A | H | H | A | A | H | H | A | H | A | H | A |
| Competition | L | L | L | L | L | L | L | W | L | L | L | L | W | L | L | L | L | L | W | L | L | L | L | L | L | L | L | L | L | F | L | L | F | L | L | L | L | L | L | L | L | L | L | L | L | L | L | L | L | L | L |
| Result | W | W | L | W | D | W | W | D | W | W | D | W | D | D | L | D | W | W | L | W | D | W | L | W | D | W | W | L | W | W | D | L | L | W | W | W | D | W | D | D | D | W | W | W | W | W | D | W | L | D | D |

**Goalkeepers**
Tim Flowers
Paul Murphy
Michael Price
Simon Royce
Ian Walker

**Defenders**
Jon Ashton
Callum Davidson
Matt Elliott
Matt Heath
Lee Marshall
Alan Rogers
Frank Sinclair
Gerry Taggart

**Midfielders**
Andrew Impey
Muzzy Izzet
Matthew Jones
Junior Lewis
Billy McKinlay
Chris O'Grady
Stefan Oakes
Martin Reeves
John Stevenson
Jordan Stewart
Nicky Summerbee
Tom Williamson

**Forwards**
Trevor Benjamin
Brian Deane
Paul Dickov
Tom Petrescu
James Scowcroft
Tommy Wright

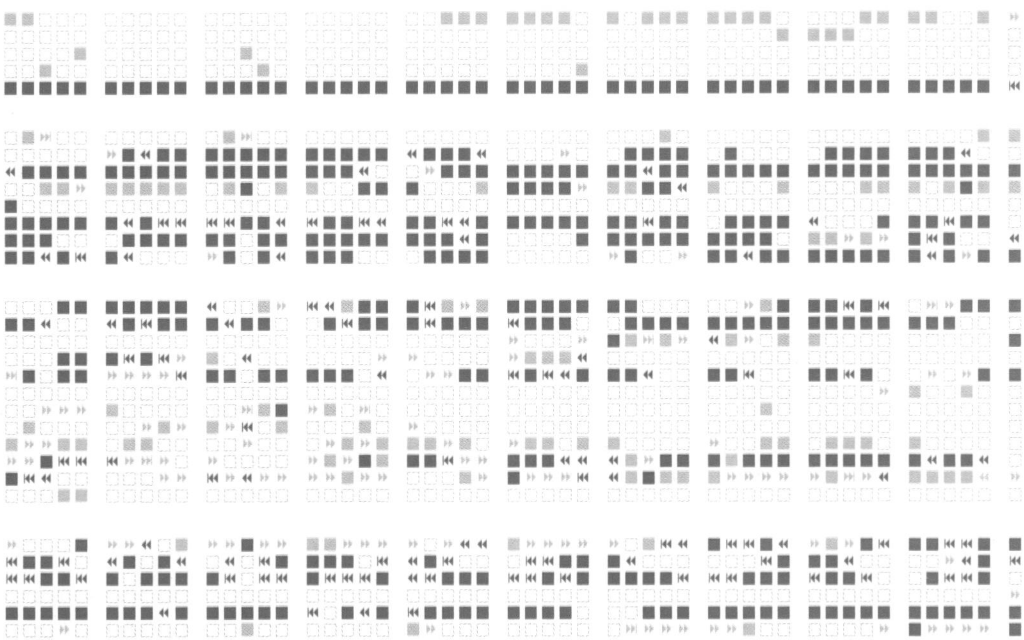

KEY: On all match / On bench
Subbed or sent off (Counting game) / Subbed or sent off (playing less than 70 minutes)
Subbed on from bench (Counting Game) / Subbed on (playing less than 70 minutes)
Subbed on and then subbed or sent off (Counting Game) / Subbed on and then subbed or sent off (playing less than 70 minutes)
Not in 16

# SHEFFIELD UNITED

Final Position: **3rd**

**NICKNAME:** THE BLADES

**KEY:** ☐ Won ☐ Drawn ☐ Lost

| | | | | | | |
|---|---|---|---|---|---|---|
| 1 | div1 | **Coventry** | A | L | 1-2 | Asaba 12 |
| 2 | div1 | **Portsmouth** | H | D | 1-1 | Ndlovu 13 |
| 3 | div1 | **Walsall** | H | D | 1-1 | McGovern 40 |
| 4 | div1 | **Burnley** | A | W | 1-0 | Onuora 35 |
| 5 | div1 | **Millwall** | H | W | 3-1 | Asaba 76; Tonge 82; Ndlovu 90 |
| 6 | div1 | **Sheff Wed** | A | L | 0-2 | |
| 7 | div1 | **Norwich** | A | W | 3-2 | Brown 2; Tonge 7; Asaba 31 pen |
| 8 | wcr1 | **York** | H | W | 1-0 | McGovern 13 |
| 9 | div1 | **Rotherham** | H | W | 1-0 | Ndlovu 74 |
| 10 | div1 | **Grimsby** | H | W | 2-1 | Allison 81; Tonge 88 |
| 11 | div1 | **Gillingham** | A | D | 1-1 | Allison 60 |
| 12 | div1 | **Watford** | H | L | 1-2 | Allison 10 |
| 13 | wcr2 | **Wycombe** | H | W | 4-1 | Boulding 15; Brown 48,87; Montgomery 86 |
| 14 | div1 | **Wolves** | A | W | 3-1 | Tonge 45,50; Allison 48 |
| 15 | div1 | **Brighton** | A | W | 4-2 | Brown 70; Asaba 78,86 pen,88 pen |
| 16 | div1 | **Stoke** | H | W | 2-1 | Handyside 62 og; Brown 70 pen |
| 17 | div1 | **Wimbledon** | H | D | 1-1 | Asaba 90 |
| 18 | div1 | **Derby** | A | L | 1-2 | Murphy 23 |
| 19 | div1 | **Nottm Forest** | A | L | 0-3 | |
| 20 | wcr3 | **Leeds** | H | W | 2-1 | Jagielka 90; Ndlovu 90 |
| 21 | div1 | **Ipswich** | H | D | 0-0 | |
| 22 | div1 | **Bradford** | A | W | 5-0 | Kabba 14; Windass 40; Murphy 59; Brown 80 pen; Asaba 88 |
| 23 | div1 | **Crystal Palace** | H | W | 2-1 | Windass 45; Allison 89 |
| 24 | wcr4 | **Sunderland** | H | W | 2-0 | Murphy 54; Allison 56 |
| 25 | div1 | **Leicester** | A | D | 0-0 | |
| 26 | div1 | **Reading** | A | W | 2-0 | Harley 59; Windass 76 |
| 27 | wcqf | **Crystal Palace** | H | W | 3-1 | Asaba 35; Peschisolido 86,88 |
| 28 | div1 | **Preston** | H | W | 1-0 | Alexander 58 og |
| 29 | div1 | **Walsall** | A | W | 1-0 | Brown 72 |
| 30 | div1 | **Coventry** | H | D | 0-0 | |
| 31 | facr3 | **Cheltenham** | H | W | 4-0 | Murphy 9; McGovern 20; Kabba 62,84 |
| 32 | wcsfl1 | **Liverpool** | H | W | 2-1 | Tonge 76,81 |
| 33 | div1 | **Portsmouth** | A | W | 2-1 | Ndlovu 24; Brown 87 |
| 34 | div1 | **Sheff Wed** | H | W | 3-1 | Kabba 62; Brown 65; Allison 78 |
| 35 | wcsfl2 | **Liverpool** | A | L | 0-2 | (aet) |
| 36 | facr4 | **Ipswich** | H | W | 4-3 | Brown 19,64; Jagielka 32; Peschisolido 89 |
| 37 | div1 | **Millwall** | A | L | 0-1 | |
| 38 | div1 | **Ipswich** | A | L | 2-3 | Ndlovu 45; Windass 50 |
| 39 | facr5 | **Walsall** | H | W | 2-0 | Mooney 37; Ndlovu 56 |
| 40 | div1 | **Reading** | H | L | 1-3 | Brown 3 |
| 41 | div1 | **Norwich** | H | L | 0-1 | |
| 42 | div1 | **Rotherham** | A | W | 2-1 | Brown 17 pen; Kabba 62 |
| 43 | div1 | **Grimsby** | A | W | 4-1 | Windass 12; Kabba 25; Kozluk 32; Brown 86 |
| 44 | facqf | **Leeds** | H | W | 1-0 | Kabba 78 |
| 45 | div1 | **Burnley** | H | W | 4-2 | Brown 17,36; Ndlovu 66,72 |
| 46 | div1 | **Stoke** | A | D | 0-0 | |
| 47 | div1 | **Brighton** | H | W | 2-1 | Windass 5; Brown 34 |
| 48 | div1 | **Derby** | H | W | 2-0 | Tonge 18; Kabba 55 |
| 49 | div1 | **Gillingham** | H | D | 2-2 | Kabba 44; Peschisolido 81 |
| 50 | div1 | **Crystal Palace** | A | D | 2-2 | Popovic 21 og; Kabba 87 |
| 51 | div1 | **Wimbledon** | A | L | 0-1 | |
| 52 | facsf | **Arsenal** | A | L | 0-1 | |
| 53 | div1 | **Nottm Forest** | H | W | 1-0 | Asaba 62 |
| 54 | div1 | **Preston** | A | L | 0-2 | |
| 55 | div1 | **Leicester** | H | W | 2-1 | Asaba 15,90 |
| 56 | div1 | **Wolves** | H | D | 3-3 | Peschisolido 2,90; Brown 56 pen |
| 57 | div1 | **Bradford** | H | W | 3-0 | Brown 60,79 pen; Ndlovu 64 |
| 58 | div1 | **Watford** | A | L | 0-2 | |
| 59 | d1po1 | **Nottm Forest** | A | D | 1-1 | Brown 58 pen |
| 60 | d1po2 | **Nottm Forest** | H | W | 4-3 | Brown 60; Kabba 68; Peschisolido 112; Walker 117 og |
| 61 | d1pof | **Wolves** | N | L | 0-3 | |

☐ Home ☐ Away ☐ Neutral

## ATTENDANCES

**HOME GROUND:** BRAMALL LANE **CAPACITY:** 30370 **AVERAGE LEAGUE AT HOME:** 18069

| | | | | | | | | | | | |
|---|---|---|---|---|---|---|---|---|---|---|---|
| 61 | Wolves | 69473 | 19 | Nottm Forest | 22579 | 45 | Burnley | 17359 | 5 | Millwall | 13024 |
| 52 | Arsenal | 59170 | 56 | Wolvers | 22211 | 40 | Reading | 16884 | 4 | Burnley | 12868 |
| 35 | Liverpool | 43837 | 27 | Crystal Palace | 22211 | 23 | Crystal Palace | 16686 | 36 | Ipswich | 12757 |
| 60 | Nottm Forest | 30212 | 55 | Leicester | 21277 | 28 | Preston | 16342 | 42 | Rotherham | 10797 |
| 32 | Liverpool | 30095 | 30 | Coventry | 20465 | 12 | Watford | 16301 | 29 | Walsall | 10459 |
| 59 | Nottm Forest | 29064 | 7 | Norwich | 20074 | 2 | Portsmouth | 16093 | 31 | Cheltenham | 9166 |
| 34 | Sheff Wed | 28179 | 9 | Rotherham | 19948 | 21 | Ipswich | 15884 | 37 | Millwall | 9102 |
| 6 | Sheff Wed | 27075 | 47 | Brighton | 19357 | 49 | Gillingham | 15799 | 11 | Gillingham | 7497 |
| 24 | Sunderland | 27068 | 41 | Norwich | 19020 | 50 | Crystal Palace | 15377 | 43 | Grimsby | 6897 |
| 25 | Leicester | 26718 | 33 | Portsmouth | 18872 | 16 | Stoke | 15163 | 15 | Brighton | 6810 |
| 20 | Leeds | 26663 | 1 | Coventry | 18839 | 54 | Preston | 14793 | 8 | York | 4675 |
| 38 | Ipswich | 26151 | 26 | Reading | 18534 | 46 | Stoke | 14449 | 13 | Wycombe | 4389 |
| 44 | Leeds | 24633 | 48 | Derby | 18401 | 58 | Watford | 14230 | 51 | Wimbledon | 1325 |
| 14 | Wolves | 24625 | 57 | Bradford | 18297 | 10 | Grimsby | 14208 | | | |
| 18 | Derby | 23525 | 39 | Walsall | 17510 | 3 | Walsall | 14011 | | | |
| 53 | Nottm Forest | 23317 | 17 | Wimbledon | 17372 | 22 | Bradford | 13364 | | | |

## KEY PLAYERS - GOALSCORERS

1 Carl Asaba

| | |
|---|---|
| **Goals in the League** | 11 |
| **Goals in all competitions** | 12 |
| **Contribution to Attacking Power** Average number of minutes between League team goals while on pitch | 63 |
| **Player Strike Rate** The total number of minutes he was on the pitch for every League goal scored | 150 |
| **Club Strike Rate** Average number of minutes between League goals scored by club | 58 |

| | PLAYER | GOALS LGE | GOALS ALL | POWER | S RATE |
|---|---|---|---|---|---|
| 2 | Michael Brown | 16 | 22 | 54 | 214 mins |
| 3 | Steve Kabba | 7 | 11 | 45 | 225 mins |
| 4 | Dean Windass | 6 | 6 | 47 | 251 mins |
| 5 | Wayne Allison | 6 | 7 | 61 | 255 mins |

## KEY PLAYERS - MIDFIELDERS

1 Philip Jagielka

| | |
|---|---|
| **Goals in the League** | 0 |
| **Goals in all competitions** | 2 |
| **Defensive Rating** Average number of mins between League goals conceded while on the pitch | 86 |
| **Contribution to Attacking Power** Average number of minutes between League team goals while on pitch | 55 |
| **Scoring Difference** Defensive Rating minus Contribution to Attacking Power | 31 |

| | PLAYER | GOALS LGE | GOALS ALL | DEF RATE | ATT POWER | SCORE DIFF |
|---|---|---|---|---|---|---|
| 2 | Stuart McCall | 0 | 0 | 83 | 54 | 29 mins |
| 3 | Michael Brown | 16 | 22 | 80 | 54 | 26 mins |
| 4 | Michael Tonge | 6 | 8 | 82 | 58 | 24 mins |
| 5 | Robert Ullathorne | 0 | 0 | 66 | 58 | 8 mins |

## KEY PLAYERS - DEFENDERS

1 Steve Yates

| | |
|---|---|
| **Goals Conceded in League** | 12 |
| **Goals Conceded in all competitions** | 13 |
| **Clean Sheets** In League games when he played at least 70 mins | 1 |
| **Defensive Rating** Ave number of mins between League goals conceded while on the pitch | 81 |
| **Club Defensive Rating** Average number of mins between League goals conceded by the club this season | 80 |

| | PLAYER | CON LGE | CON ALL | CLN SHEETS | DEF RATE |
|---|---|---|---|---|---|
| 2 | Robert Kozluk | 33 | 44 | 6 | 80 mins |
| 3 | Robert Page | 37 | 54 | 11 | 79 mins |
| 4 | John Curtis | 11 | 19 | 4 | 79 mins |
| 5 | Shaun Murphy | 48 | 54 | 11 | 78 mins |

## KEY GOALKEEPER

1 Patrick Kenny

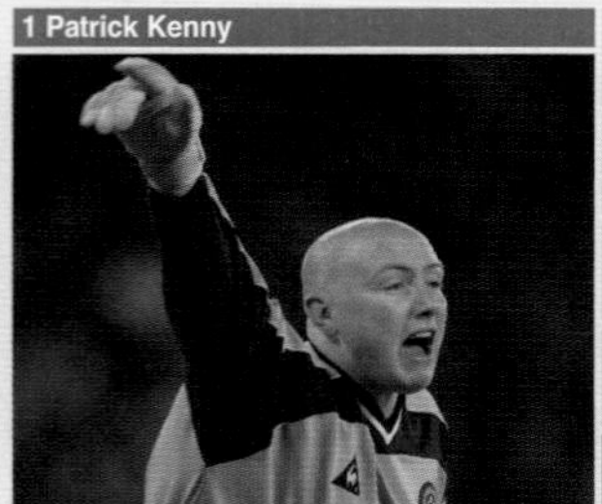

| | |
|---|---|
| **Goals Conceded in the League** | 50 |
| **Goals Conceded in all competitions** | 64 |
| **Clean Sheets** In games when he played at least 70 mins | 13 |
| **Goals to Shots Ratio** The average number of shots on target per each League goal conceded | 4.6 |
| **Defensive Rating** Ave number of mins between League goals conceded while on the pitch | 81 |

## MONTHY POINTS TALLY

| | | |
|---|---|---|
| AUGUST | 8 | 53% |
| SEPTEMBER | 13 | 62% |
| OCTOBER | 13 | 72% |
| NOVEMBER | 10 | 67% |
| DECEMBER | 17 | 81% |
| JANUARY | 15 | 83% |
| FEBRUARY | 6 | 33% |
| MARCH | 17 | 81% |
| APRIL | 11 | 46% |
| MAY | 4 | 33% |

## TOP POINT EARNERS

| | PLAYER | GAMES | AV PTS |
|---|---|---|---|
| 1 | Dean Windass | 14 | 2.43 |
| 2 | Steve Kabba | 12 | 2.17 |
| 3 | Stuart McCall | 26 | 1.92 |
| 4 | Philip Jagielka | 39 | 1.92 |
| 5 | Robert Page | 32 | 1.84 |
| 6 | Michael Tonge | 39 | 1.79 |
| 7 | Michael Brown | 37 | 1.78 |
| 8 | Shaun Murphy | 41 | 1.78 |
| 9 | Patrick Kenny | 45 | 1.78 |
| 10 | Nick Montgomery | 12 | 1.75 |
| | CLUB AVERAGE: | | 1.74 |

## GOALS

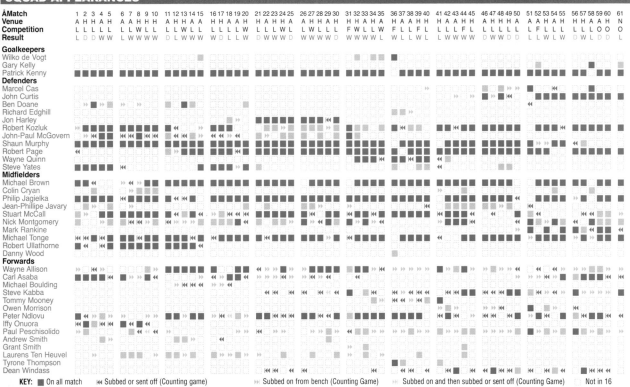

| 1 Michael Brown | |
|---|---|
| League | 16 |
| FA Cup | 2 |
| League Cup | 2 |
| Other | 2 |
| TOTAL | 22 |

| | PLAYER | LGE | FAC | LC | Oth | TOT |
|---|---|---|---|---|---|---|
| 2 | Asaba | 11 | 0 | 1 | 0 | 12 |
| 3 | Ndlovu | 8 | 1 | 1 | 0 | 10 |
| 4 | Kabba | 7 | 3 | 0 | 1 | 11 |
| 5 | Windass | 6 | 0 | 0 | 0 | 6 |
| 6 | Tonge | 6 | 0 | 2 | 0 | 8 |
| 7 | Allison | 6 | 0 | 1 | 0 | 7 |
| 8 | Peschisolido | 3 | 1 | 2 | 1 | 7 |
| 9 | Murphy | 2 | 1 | 1 | 0 | 4 |
| 10 | Harley | 1 | 0 | 0 | 0 | 1 |
| 11 | Onuora | 1 | 0 | 0 | 0 | 1 |
| | Other | 5 | 3 | 4 | 1 | 13 |
| | TOTAL | 72 | 11 | 14 | 5 | 102 |

## TEAM OF THE SEASON

| GOALKEEPER | GAMES | DEF RATE |
|---|---|---|
| Patrick Kenny | 45 | 81 |
| **DEFENDERS** | **GAMES** | **DEF RATE** |
| Steve Yates | 10 | 81 |
| Robert Kozluk | 29 | 80 |
| Robert Page | 32 | 79 |
| John Curtis | 9 | 79 |
| **MIDFIELDERS** | **GAMES** | **SCORE DIFF** |
| Philip Jagielka | 39 | 31 |
| Stuart McCall | 26 | 29 |
| Michael Brown | 37 | 26 |
| Michael Tonge | 39 | 24 |
| **GOALSCORERS** | **GAMES** | **STRIKE RATE** |
| Carl Asaba | 13 | 150 |
| Steve Kabba | 12 | 225 |

Games = games playing at least70 minutes

## LEAGUE APPEARANCES, BOOKINGS AND CAPS

| | AGE (on 01/07/03) | IN THE SQUAD | COUNTING GAMES | MINUTES ON PITCH | YELLOW CARDS | RED CARDS | THIS SEASON | HOME COUNTRY |
|---|---|---|---|---|---|---|---|---|
| **Goalkeepers** | | | | | | | | |
| Wilko de Vogt | 27 | 2 | 0 | 0 | 0 | 0 | - | Holland |
| Gary Kelly | 36 | 1 | 1 | 90 | 0 | 0 | - | England |
| Patrick Kenny | 24 | 45 | 45 | 4050 | 1 | 0 | - | England |
| **Defenders** | | | | | | | | |
| Marcel Cas | 31 | 8 | 3 | 329 | 0 | 0 | - | Holland |
| John Curtis | 24 | 12 | 9 | 865 | 0 | 0 | - | England |
| Ben Doane | 23 | 8 | 1 | 227 | 0 | 0 | - | England |
| Richard Edghill | 28 | 2 | 0 | 20 | 0 | 0 | - | England |
| Jon Harley | 23 | 10 | 7 | 728 | 3 | 1 | - | England |
| Robert Kozluk | 25 | 40 | 29 | 2641 | 1 | 0 | - | England |
| John-Paul McGovern | - | 22 | 6 | 818 | 0 | 0 | - | Scotland |
| Shaun Murphy | 32 | 44 | 41 | 3736 | 5 | 0 | - | Australia |
| Robert Page | 28 | 35 | 32 | 2940 | 6 | 0 | 4 | Wales (50) |
| Wayne Quinn | 26 | 7 | 5 | 491 | 3 | 1 | - | England |
| Steve Yates | 33 | 16 | 10 | 966 | 0 | 0 | - | England |
| **Midfielders** | | | | | | | | |
| Michael Brown | 26 | 40 | 37 | 3423 | 8 | 0 | - | England |
| Colin Cryan | 22 | 7 | 0 | 27 | 0 | 0 | - | Rep of Ireland |
| Philip Jagielka | 20 | 42 | 39 | 3625 | 3 | 1 | - | England |
| Jean-Phillipe Javary | 25 | 16 | 2 | 219 | 0 | 0 | - | France |
| Stuart McCall | 39 | 37 | 26 | 2650 | 5 | 0 | - | Scotland |
| Nick Montgomery | 22 | 35 | 12 | 1370 | 1 | 0 | - | England |
| Mark Rankine | 33 | 7 | 4 | 443 | 0 | 0 | - | England |
| Michael Tonge | 20 | 44 | 39 | 3606 | 6 | 0 | - | England |
| Robert Ullathorne | 31 | 12 | 10 | 987 | 3 | 0 | - | England |
| Danny Wood | 19 | 0 | 0 | 0 | 0 | 0 | - | England |
| **Forwards** | | | | | | | | |
| Wayne Allison | 34 | 38 | 12 | 1532 | 0 | 0 | - | England |
| Carl Asaba | 30 | 29 | 13 | 1654 | 0 | 0 | - | England |
| Michael Boulding | 27 | 6 | 1 | 243 | 0 | 0 | - | England |
| Steve Kabba | 22 | 27 | 12 | 1577 | 2 | 0 | - | England |
| Tommy Mooney | 31 | 5 | 1 | 182 | 0 | 0 | - | England |
| Owen Morrison | 21 | 10 | 3 | 310 | 0 | 0 | - | N Ireland |
| Peter Ndlovu | 30 | 42 | 26 | 2778 | 4 | 1 | - | Zimbabwe |
| Iffy Onuora | 35 | 8 | 5 | 466 | 0 | 1 | - | Scotland |
| Paul Peschisolido | 32 | 33 | 2 | 676 | 2 | 0 | - | Canada |
| Grant Smith | 23 | 1 | 0 | 0 | 0 | 0 | - | Scotland |
| Andrew Smith | 22 | 6 | 0 | 47 | 0 | 0 | - | |
| Laurens Ten Heuvel | 27 | 14 | 0 | 163 | 1 | 0 | - | Holland |
| Tyrone Thompson | 22 | 2 | 0 | 0 | 0 | 0 | - | England |
| Dean Windass | 34 | 22 | 14 | 1506 | 3 | 0 | - | England |

KEY: LEAGUE BOOKINGS CAPS (FIFA RANKING)

## SQUAD APPEARANCES

| ÅMatch | 1 | 2 | 3 | 4 | 5 | 6 | 7 | 8 | 9 | 10 | 11 | 12 | 13 | 14 | 15 | 16 | 17 | 18 | 19 | 20 | 21 | 22 | 23 | 24 | 25 | 26 | 27 | 28 | 29 | 30 |
|---|---|---|---|---|---|---|---|---|---|---|---|---|---|---|---|---|---|---|---|---|---|---|---|---|---|---|---|---|---|---|
| Venue | A | H | H | A | H | A | A | H | H | H | A | H | H | A | A | H | H | A | A | H | H | A | H | H | A | A | H | H | A | H |
| Competition | L | L | L | L | L | L | L | W | L | L | L | L | W | L | L | L | L | L | L | W | L | L | L | W | L | L | W | L | L | L |
| Result | L | D | D | W | W | L | W | W | W | W | D | L | W | W | W | W | D | L | L | W | D | W | W | W | D | W | W | W | W | D |

| ÅMatch | 31 | 32 | 33 | 34 | 35 | 36 | 37 | 38 | 39 | 40 | 41 | 42 | 43 | 44 | 45 | 46 | 47 | 48 | 49 | 50 | 51 | 52 | 53 | 54 | 55 | 56 | 57 | 58 | 59 | 60 | 61 |
|---|---|---|---|---|---|---|---|---|---|---|---|---|---|---|---|---|---|---|---|---|---|---|---|---|---|---|---|---|---|---|---|
| Venue | H | H | A | H | A | H | A | A | H | H | H | A | A | H | H | A | H | H | H | A | A | A | H | A | H | H | H | A | A | H | N |
| Competition | F | W | L | L | W | F | L | L | F | L | L | L | L | F | L | L | L | L | L | L | L | F | L | L | L | L | L | L | O | O | O |
| Result | W | W | W | W | L | W | L | L | W | L | L | W | W | W | W | D | W | W | D | D | L | L | W | L | W | D | W | L | D | D | L |

**Goalkeepers**
Wilko de Vogt
Gary Kelly
Patrick Kenny
**Defenders**
Marcel Cas
John Curtis
Ben Doane
Richard Edghill
Jon Harley
Robert Kozluk
John-Paul McGovern
Shaun Murphy
Robert Page
Wayne Quinn
Steve Yates
**Midfielders**
Michael Brown
Colin Cryan
Philip Jagielka
Jean-Phillipe Javary
Stuart McCall
Nick Montgomery
Mark Rankine
Michael Tonge
Robert Ullathorne
Danny Wood
**Forwards**
Wayne Allison
Carl Asaba
Michael Boulding
Steve Kabba
Tommy Mooney
Owen Morrison
Peter Ndlovu
Iffy Onuora
Paul Peschisolido
Andrew Smith
Grant Smith
Laurens Ten Heuvel
Tyrone Thompson
Dean Windass

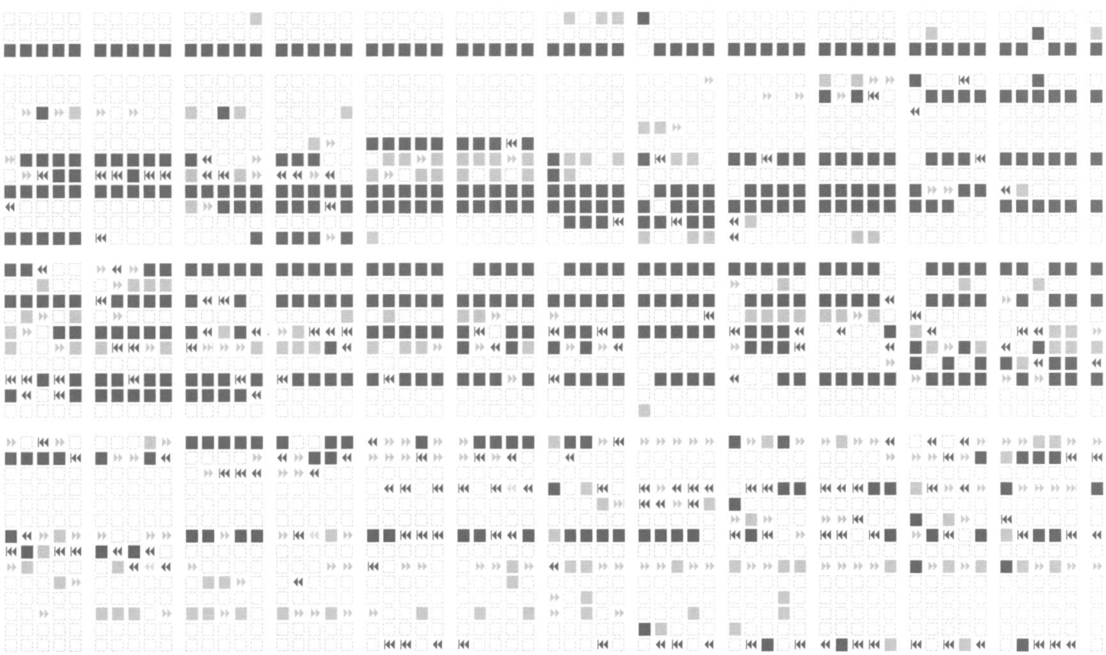

KEY: On all match; On bench; Subbed or sent off (Counting game); Subbed or sent off (playing less than 70 minutes); Subbed on from bench (Counting Game); Subbed on (playing less than 70 minutes); Subbed on and then subbed or sent off (Counting Game); Subbed on and then subbed or sent off (playing less than 70 minutes); Not in 16

# READING

Final Position: **4th**

**NICKNAME:** THE ROYALS

KEY: ☐ Won ☐ Drawn ☐ Lost

| | | | | | | |
|---|---|---|---|---|---|---|
| 1 | div1 | **Derby** | A | L | 0-3 | |
| 2 | div1 | **Sheff Wed** | H | W | 2-1 | Cureton 47,77 |
| 3 | div1 | **Coventry** | H | L | 1-2 | Cureton 13 pen |
| 4 | div1 | **Leicester** | A | L | 1-2 | Cureton 20 pen |
| 5 | div1 | **Burnley** | H | W | 3-0 | Cureton 55,90; Butler 87 |
| 6 | div1 | **Walsall** | A | W | 2-0 | Hughes 79,90 |
| 7 | div1 | **Rotherham** | A | D | 0-0 | |
| 8 | wcr1 | **Cambridge** | A | L | 1-3 | Upson 89 |
| 9 | div1 | **Wimbledon** | H | L | 0-1 | |
| 10 | div1 | **Norwich** | H | L | 0-2 | |
| 11 | div1 | **Wolves** | A | W | 1-0 | Hughes 58 |
| 12 | div1 | **Stoke** | H | D | 1-1 | Rougier 12 |
| 13 | div1 | **Grimsby** | A | W | 3-0 | Hughes 13; Forster 32; Pouton 90 og |
| 14 | div1 | **Ipswich** | H | W | 3-1 | Forster 28,40,69 |
| 15 | div1 | **Preston** | A | L | 0-1 | |
| 16 | div1 | **Bradford** | H | W | 1-0 | Shorey 71 |
| 17 | div1 | **Millwall** | H | W | 2-0 | Forster 6; Hughes 90 |
| 18 | div1 | **Gillingham** | A | W | 1-0 | Rougier 82 |
| 19 | div1 | **Watford** | H | W | 1-0 | Watson 61 |
| 20 | div1 | **Crystal Palace** | A | W | 1-0 | Forster 39 |
| 21 | div1 | **Brighton** | A | W | 1-0 | Salako 22 |
| 22 | div1 | **Portsmouth** | H | D | 0-0 | |
| 23 | div1 | **Sheff Utd** | H | L | 0-2 | |
| 24 | div1 | **Nottm Forest** | A | L | 0-2 | |
| 25 | div1 | **Coventry** | A | L | 0-2 | |
| 26 | div1 | **Derby** | H | W | 2-1 | Tyson 5; Cureton 90 |
| 27 | facr3 | **Walsall** | A | D | 0-0 | |
| 28 | div1 | **Sheff Wed** | A | L | 2-3 | Forster 9; Butler 19 |
| 29 | facr3r | **Walsall** | H | L | 1-4* | Aranalde 32 og (*on penalties) |
| 30 | div1 | **Walsall** | H | D | 0-0 | |
| 31 | div1 | **Leicester** | H | L | 1-3 | Hughes 54 |
| 32 | div1 | **Burnley** | A | W | 5-2 | Sidwell 37,79; Salako 45,52; Henderson 90 |
| 33 | div1 | **Gillingham** | H | W | 2-1 | Chadwick 13; Salako 88 |
| 34 | div1 | **Millwall** | A | W | 2-0 | Forster 45; Henderson 83 |
| 35 | div1 | **Sheff Utd** | A | W | 3-1 | Forster 35,81; Williams 74 |
| 36 | div1 | **Rotherham** | H | W | 3-0 | Harper 15; Hughes 32; Forster 40 |
| 37 | div1 | **Wimbledon** | A | L | 0-2 | |
| 38 | div1 | **Norwich** | A | W | 1-0 | Kenton 74 og |
| 39 | div1 | **Wolves** | H | L | 0-1 | |
| 40 | div1 | **Crystal Palace** | H | W | 2-1 | Brown 66; Harper 90 |
| 41 | div1 | **Ipswich** | A | L | 1-3 | Forster 16 |
| 42 | div1 | **Bradford** | A | W | 1-0 | Forster 66 |
| 43 | div1 | **Brighton** | H | L | 1-2 | Cureton 84 |
| 44 | div1 | **Preston** | H | W | 5-1 | Forster 30,42,58; Shorey 57 pen; Henderson 90 |
| 45 | div1 | **Nottm Forest** | H | W | 1-0 | Hughes 74 |
| 46 | div1 | **Portsmouth** | A | L | 0-3 | |
| 47 | div1 | **Grimsby** | H | W | 2-1 | Little 2; Hughes 22 |
| 48 | div1 | **Watford** | A | W | 3-0 | Rougier 27; Henderson 70; Cureton 90 |
| 49 | div1 | **Stoke** | A | L | 0-1 | |
| 50 | d1po1 | **Wolves** | A | L | 1-2 | Forster 25 |
| 51 | d1po2 | **Wolves** | H | L | 0-1 | |

☐ Home ☐ Away ☐ Neutral

## ATTENDANCES

**HOME GROUND:** MADJESKI STADIUM **CAPACITY:** 24200 **AVERAGE LEAGUE AT HOME:** 16011

| | | | | | | | | | | | |
|---|---|---|---|---|---|---|---|---|---|---|---|
| 1 | Derby | 33016 | 25 | Coventry | 19526 | 36 | Rotherham | 14816 | 42 | Bradford | 11385 |
| 50 | Wolves | 27678 | 14 | Ipswich | 19524 | 3 | Coventry | 14712 | 33 | Gillingham | 11030 |
| 24 | Nottm Forest | 25831 | 38 | Norwich | 18970 | 32 | Burnley | 14420 | 29 | Walsall | 8767 |
| 11 | Wolves | 25560 | 23 | Sheff Utd | 18534 | 10 | Norwich | 14335 | 18 | Gillingham | 8511 |
| 41 | Ipswich | 24108 | 40 | Crystal Palace | 18063 | 44 | Preston | 14012 | 34 | Millwall | 7038 |
| 51 | Wolves | 24060 | 28 | Sheff Wed | 17715 | 12 | Stoke | 13646 | 21 | Brighton | 6817 |
| 22 | Portsmouth | 23462 | 19 | Watford | 17465 | 2 | Sheff Wed | 13638 | 7 | Rotherham | 6154 |
| 4 | Leicester | 22978 | 31 | Leicester | 17156 | 17 | Millwall | 13081 | 27 | Walsall | 5987 |
| 45 | Nottm Forest | 21612 | 35 | Sheff Utd | 16884 | 15 | Preston | 13021 | 13 | Grimsby | 5582 |
| 49 | Stoke | 20477 | 26 | Derby | 16299 | 16 | Bradford | 12110 | 6 | Walsall | 5327 |
| 47 | Grimsby | 20273 | 43 | Brighton | 16133 | 5 | Burnley | 12009 | 37 | Wimbledon | 3869 |
| 39 | Wolves | 19731 | 20 | Crystal Palace | 15712 | 48 | Watford | 11814 | 8 | Cambridge | 2696 |
| 46 | Portsmouth | 19535 | 9 | Wimbledon | 14832 | 30 | Walsall | 11786 | | | |

## KEY PLAYERS - GOALSCORERS

1 Jamie Cureton

| | |
|---|---|
| Goals in the League | 9 |
| Goals in all competitions | 9 |
| Contribution to Attacking Power<br>Average number of minutes between League team goals while on pitch | 80 |
| Player Strike Rate<br>The total number of minutes he was on the pitch for every League goal scored | 152 |
| Club Strike Rate<br>Average number of minutes between League goals scored by club | 68 |

| | PLAYER | GOALS LGE | GOALS ALL | POWER | S RATE |
|---|---|---|---|---|---|
| 2 | Nick Forster | 16 | 17 | 65 | 189 mins |
| 3 | Andrew Hughes | 9 | 9 | 70 | 391 mins |
| 4 | John Salako | 4 | 4 | 66 | 727 mins |
| 5 | Luke Chadwick | 1 | 1 | 60 | 1158 mins |

## KEY PLAYERS - MIDFIELDERS

1 Ricky Newman

| | |
|---|---|
| Goals in the League | 0 |
| Goals in all competitions | 0 |
| Defensive Rating<br>Average number of mins between League goals conceded while on the pitch | 108 |
| Contribution to Attacking Power<br>Average number of minutes between League team goals while on pitch | 71 |
| Scoring Difference<br>Defensive Rating minus Contribution to Attacking Power | 37 |

| | PLAYER | GOALS LGE | GOALS ALL | DEF RATE | ATT POWER | SCORE DIFF |
|---|---|---|---|---|---|---|
| 2 | Andrew Hughes | 9 | 9 | 98 | 70 | 28 mins |
| 3 | John Salako | 4 | 4 | 94 | 66 | 28 mins |
| 4 | Luke Chadwick | 1 | 1 | 83 | 61 | 22 mins |
| 5 | Kevin Watson | 1 | 1 | 104 | 84 | 20 mins |

## KEY PLAYERS - DEFENDERS

1 Matthew Upson

| | |
|---|---|
| Goals Conceded in League | 5 |
| Goals Conceded in all competitions | 8 |
| Clean Sheets<br>In League games when he played at least 70 mins | 8 |
| Defensive Rating<br>Ave number of mins between League goals conceded while on the pitch | 230 |
| Club Defensive Rating<br>Average number of mins between League goals conceded by the club this season | 90 |

| | PLAYER | CON LGE | CON ALL | CLN SHEETS | DEF RATE |
|---|---|---|---|---|---|
| 2 | Nicky Shorey | 43 | 49 | 18 | 89 mins |
| 3 | Adrian Williams | 36 | 40 | 14 | 89 mins |
| 4 | Steve Brown | 22 | 26 | 6 | 77 mins |
| 5 | John Mackie | 28 | 32 | 6 | 68 mins |

## KEY GOALKEEPER

1 Marcus Hahnemann

| | |
|---|---|
| Goals Conceded in the League | 38 |
| Goals Conceded in all competitions | 45 |
| Clean Sheets<br>In games when he played at least 70 mins | 18 |
| Goals to Shots Ratio<br>The average number of shots on target per each League goal conceded | 5.5 |
| Defensive Rating<br>Ave number of mins between League goals conceded while on the pitch | 97 |

## MONTHY POINTS TALLY

| | | |
|---|---|---|
| AUGUST | 9 | 50% |
| SEPTEMBER | 5 | 28% |
| OCTOBER | 9 | 75% |
| NOVEMBER | 15 | 100% |
| DECEMBER | 4 | 27% |
| JANUARY | 3 | 20% |
| FEBRUARY | 15 | 100% |
| MARCH | 9 | 50% |
| APRIL | 12 | 67% |
| MAY | 0 | 0% |

## TOP POINT EARNERS

| | PLAYER | GAMES | AV PTS |
|---|---|---|---|
| 1 | Matthew Upson | 12 | 2.17 |
| 2 | Steve Brown | 18 | 2.06 |
| 3 | Ricky Newman | 19 | 2.00 |
| 4 | Luke Chadwick | 12 | 2.00 |
| 5 | John Salako | 29 | 1.86 |
| 6 | Kevin Watson | 21 | 1.81 |
| 7 | Marcus Hahnemann | 41 | 1.78 |
| 8 | James Harper | 30 | 1.77 |
| 9 | Andrew Hughes | 39 | 1.77 |
| 10 | Nick Forster | 30 | 1.77 |
| | CLUB AVERAGE: | | 1.72 |

## LEAGUE APPEARANCES, BOOKINGS AND CAPS

| | AGE (on 01/07/03) | IN THE SQUAD | COUNTING GAMES | MINUTES ON PITCH | YELLOW CARDS | RED CARDS | THIS SEASON | HOME COUNTRY |
|---|---|---|---|---|---|---|---|---|
| **Goalkeepers** | | | | | | | | |
| Jamie Ashdown | 22 | 35 | 1 | 90 | 0 | 0 | - | England |
| Marcus Hahnemann | 31 | 43 | 41 | 3690 | 4 | 0 | 1 | United States (10) |
| Phil Whitehead | 33 | 9 | 4 | 360 | 0 | 0 | - | England |
| Jamie Young | - | 2 | 0 | 0 | 0 | 0 | - | England |
| **Defenders** | | | | | | | | |
| Steve Brown | 31 | 21 | 18 | 1697 | 4 | 0 | - | England |
| Peter Castle | 16 | 1 | 0 | 12 | 0 | 0 | - | England |
| John Mackie | 27 | 38 | 20 | 1896 | 8 | 1 | - | England |
| Nicky Shorey | 22 | 45 | 43 | 3843 | 4 | 0 | - | England |
| Alex Smith | 27 | 1 | 0 | 11 | 0 | 0 | - | England |
| Matthew Upson | 24 | 15 | 12 | 1149 | 4 | 0 | 4 | England (7) |
| Adrian Viveash | 33 | 10 | 3 | 382 | 0 | 1 | - | England |
| Adrian Whitbread | 31 | 1 | 1 | 90 | 0 | 0 | - | England |
| Adrian Williams | 31 | 37 | 35 | 3193 | 5 | 0 | 2 | Wales (50) |
| **Midfielders** | | | | | | | | |
| Darren Campbell | 17 | 1 | 0 | 12 | 0 | 0 | - | England |
| Luke Chadwick | 22 | 15 | 12 | 1158 | 0 | 0 | - | England |
| Joe Gamble | 21 | 1 | 0 | 0 | 0 | 0 | - | Rep of Ireland |
| James Harper | 22 | 37 | 30 | 2886 | 0 | 0 | - | England |
| Andrew Hughes | 25 | 43 | 39 | 3522 | 3 | 0 | - | England |
| Sam Igoe | 27 | 19 | 6 | 783 | 4 | 0 | - | England |
| Glen Little | 27 | 6 | 4 | 455 | 0 | 0 | - | England |
| Graeme Murty | 28 | 44 | 43 | 3915 | 2 | 0 | - | England |
| Ricky Newman | 32 | 32 | 19 | 2048 | 9 | 0 | - | England |
| Phil Parkinson | 35 | 8 | 0 | 82 | 0 | 0 | - | England |
| Anthony Rougier | 31 | 25 | 10 | 1120 | 5 | 0 | - | Trinidad & Tobago |
| John Salako | 34 | 43 | 29 | 2908 | 2 | 0 | - | England |
| Steven Sidwell | 20 | 15 | 10 | 1032 | 1 | 0 | - | England |
| Kevin Watson | 29 | 36 | 21 | 2191 | 4 | 0 | - | England |
| **Forwards** | | | | | | | | |
| Martin Butler | 28 | 23 | 11 | 1091 | 4 | 0 | - | England |
| Jamie Cureton | 27 | 37 | 11 | 1369 | 0 | 0 | - | England |
| Nick Forster | 29 | 40 | 30 | 3029 | 3 | 0 | - | England |
| Darius Henderson | 21 | 25 | 1 | 524 | 1 | 0 | - | England |
| Nathan Tyson | 21 | 27 | 4 | 875 | 2 | 1 | - | England |

KEY: LEAGUE BOOKINGS CAPS (FIFA RANKING)

## GOALS

**1 Nick Forster**

| | |
|---|---|
| League | 16 |
| FA Cup | 0 |
| League Cup | 0 |
| Other | 1 |
| TOTAL | 17 |

| | PLAYER | LGE | FAC | LC | Oth | TOT |
|---|---|---|---|---|---|---|
| 2 | Cureton | 9 | 0 | 0 | 0 | 9 |
| 3 | Hughes | 9 | 0 | 0 | 0 | 9 |
| 4 | Henderson | 4 | 0 | 0 | 0 | 4 |
| 5 | Salako | 4 | 0 | 0 | 0 | 4 |
| 6 | Rougier | 3 | 0 | 0 | 0 | 3 |
| 7 | Butler | 2 | 0 | 0 | 0 | 2 |
| 8 | Harper | 2 | 0 | 0 | 0 | 2 |
| 9 | Sidwell | 2 | 0 | 0 | 0 | 2 |
| 10 | Shorey | 2 | 0 | 0 | 0 | 2 |
| 11 | Watson | 1 | 0 | 0 | 0 | 1 |
| | Other | 7 | 1 | 1 | 0 | 9 |
| | TOTAL | 61 | 1 | 1 | 1 | 64 |

## TEAM OF THE SEASON

| GOALKEEPER | GAMES | DEF RATE |
|---|---|---|
| Marcus Hahnemann | 41 | 97 |
| **DEFENDERS** | **GAMES** | **DEF RATE** |
| Matthew Upson | 12 | 230 |
| Nicky Shorey | 43 | 89 |
| Adrian Williams | 35 | 89 |
| Steve Brown | 18 | 77 |
| **MIDFIELDERS** | **GAMES** | **SCORE DIFF** |
| Ricky Newman | 19 | 37 |
| Andrew Hughes | 39 | 28 |
| John Salako | 29 | 28 |
| Luke Chadwick | 12 | 22 |
| **GOALSCORERS** | **GAMES** | **STRIKE RATE** |
| Jamie Cureton | 11 | 152 |
| Nick Forster | 30 | 189 |

Games = games playing at least 70 minutes

## SQUAD APPEARANCES

| Match | 1 | 2 | 3 | 4 | 5 | 6 | 7 | 8 | 9 | 10 | 11 | 12 | 13 | 14 | 15 | 16 | 17 | 18 | 19 | 20 | 21 | 22 | 23 | 24 | 25 | 26 | 27 | 28 | 29 | 30 | 31 | 32 | 33 | 34 | 35 | 36 | 37 | 38 | 39 | 40 | 41 | 42 | 43 | 44 | 45 | 46 | 47 | 48 | 49 | 50 | 51 |
|---|---|---|---|---|---|---|---|---|---|---|---|---|---|---|---|---|---|---|---|---|---|---|---|---|---|---|---|---|---|---|---|---|---|---|---|---|---|---|---|---|---|---|---|---|---|---|---|---|---|---|---|
| Venue | A | H | H | A | H | A | A | A | H | H | A | H | A | H | A | H | H | A | H | A | A | H | H | A | A | H | A | A | H | H | H | A | H | A | A | H | A | A | H | H | A | A | H | H | H | A | H | A | A | A | H |
| Competition | L | L | L | L | L | L | L | W | L | L | L | L | L | L | L | L | L | L | L | L | L | L | L | L | L | L | F | L | F | L | L | L | L | L | L | L | L | L | L | L | L | L | L | L | L | L | L | L | L | O | O |
| Result | L | W | L | L | W | W | D | L | L | L | W | D | W | W | L | W | W | W | W | W | W | D | L | L | L | W | D | L | L | D | L | W | W | W | W | W | L | W | L | W | L | W | L | W | W | L | W | W | L | L | L |

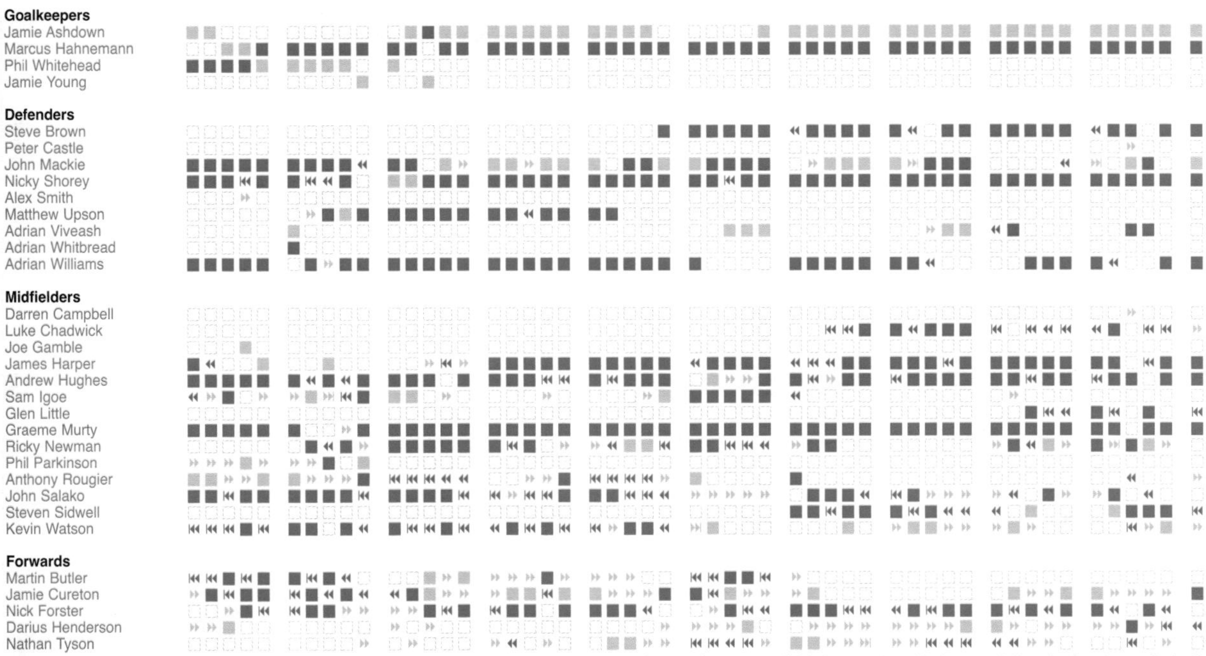
Goalkeepers
Jamie Ashdown
Marcus Hahnemann
Phil Whitehead
Jamie Young
Defenders
Steve Brown
Peter Castle
John Mackie
Nicky Shorey
Alex Smith
Matthew Upson
Adrian Viveash
Adrian Whitbread
Adrian Williams
Midfielders
Darren Campbell
Luke Chadwick
Joe Gamble
James Harper
Andrew Hughes
Sam Igoe
Glen Little
Graeme Murty
Ricky Newman
Phil Parkinson
Anthony Rougier
John Salako
Steven Sidwell
Kevin Watson
Forwards
Martin Butler
Jamie Cureton
Nick Forster
Darius Henderson
Nathan Tyson

KEY: ■ On all match ■ On bench
⏮ Subbed or sent off (Counting game) ⏪ Subbed or sent off (playing less than 70 minutes)
⏭ Subbed on from bench (Counting Game) ⏩ Subbed on (playing less than 70 minutes)
Subbed on and then subbed or sent off (Counting Game) Subbed on and then subbed or sent off (playing less than 70 minutes)
Not in 16

# WOLVERHAMPTON WANDERERS

Final Position: **5th**

**NICKNAME:** WOLVES

**KEY:** ☐Won ☐Drawn ☐Lost

| | | | | | | |
|---|---|---|---|---|---|---|
| 1 | div1 | Bradford | A | D | 0-0 | |
| 2 | div1 | Walsall | H | W | 3-1 | Cameron 10,55; Newton 85 |
| 3 | div1 | Burnley | H | W | 3-0 | Blake 1; Irwin 49; Cooper 87 |
| 4 | div1 | Derby | A | W | 4-1 | Rae 19,88; Cooper 78; Miller 90 |
| 5 | div1 | Sheff Wed | H | D | 2-2 | Blake 61; Sturridge 69 |
| 6 | div1 | Wimbledon | A | L | 2-3 | Ingimarsson 14; Sturridge 70 |
| 7 | wcr1 | Swansea | A | W | 3-2 | Blake 16; Pollet 34; Rae 78 |
| 8 | div1 | Crystal Palace | A | L | 2-4 | Ingimarsson 30; Blake 70 |
| 9 | div1 | Reading | H | L | 0-1 | |
| 10 | div1 | Preston | H | W | 4-0 | Blake 22,84; Sturridge 44; Miller 86 |
| 11 | div1 | Leicester | A | L | 0-1 | |
| 12 | wcr2 | Rotherham | A | L | 2-4* | Newton 44 Pen; Miller 56; Rae 68; Scott 119 og (*on penalties) |
| 13 | div1 | Sheff Utd | H | L | 1-3 | Ullathorne 35 og |
| 14 | div1 | Stoke | A | W | 2-0 | Cameron 78; Blake 90 |
| 15 | div1 | Grimsby | H | W | 4-1 | Irwin 30; Miller 66; Ndah 71; Sturridge 90 |
| 16 | div1 | Gillingham | A | W | 4-0 | Cameron 28 pen; Blake 45,52,59 |
| 17 | div1 | Watford | A | D | 1-1 | Cooper 90 |
| 18 | div1 | Portsmouth | H | D | 1-1 | Sturridge 62 |
| 19 | div1 | Brighton | H | D | 1-1 | Miller 76 |
| 20 | div1 | Coventry | A | W | 2-0 | Lescott 38; Rae 77 |
| 21 | div1 | Nottm Forest | H | W | 2-1 | Miller 76; Sturridge 80 |
| 22 | div1 | Rotherham | A | D | 0-0 | |
| 23 | div1 | Norwich | H | W | 1-0 | Cole 37 |
| 24 | div1 | Coventry | H | L | 0-2 | |
| 25 | div1 | Millwall | A | D | 1-1 | Kennedy 5 |
| 26 | div1 | Burnley | A | L | 1-2 | Butler 85 |
| 27 | div1 | Bradford | H | L | 1-2 | Ndah 54 |
| 28 | div1 | Derby | H | D | 1-1 | Ince 66 |
| 29 | facr3 | Newcastle | H | W | 3-2 | Ince 6; Kennedy 28; Ndah 49 |
| 30 | div1 | Walsall | A | W | 1-0 | Ndah 64 |
| 31 | div1 | Wimbledon | H | D | 1-1 | Miller 43 |
| 32 | facr4 | Leicester | H | W | 4-1 | Ndah 5,45; Miller 51,71 |
| 33 | div1 | Sheff Wed | A | W | 4-0 | Proudlock 24,42; Miller 67; Sturridge 89 |
| 34 | div1 | Brighton | A | L | 1-4 | Miller 65 |
| 35 | facr5 | Rochdale | H | W | 3-1 | Ndah 32; Miller 79; Proudlock 90 |
| 36 | div1 | Ipswich | A | W | 4-2 | Miller 12,64; Naylor 74; Ndah 81 |
| 37 | div1 | Preston | A | W | 2-0 | Ndah 53; Miller 83 |
| 38 | div1 | Watford | H | D | 0-0 | |
| 39 | div1 | Crystal Palace | H | W | 4-0 | Miller 40,83,90 pen; Sturridge 77 |
| 40 | div1 | Ipswich | H | D | 1-1 | Ince 48 |
| 41 | facqf | Southampton | A | L | 0-2 | |
| 42 | div1 | Reading | A | W | 1-0 | Miller 44 |
| 43 | div1 | Portsmouth | A | L | 0-1 | |
| 44 | div1 | Stoke | H | D | 0-0 | |
| 45 | div1 | Gillingham | H | W | 6-0 | Blake 16; Cameron 22; Kennedy 37,45; Miller 45,48 |
| 46 | div1 | Rotherham | H | D | 0-0 | |
| 47 | div1 | Grimsby | A | W | 1-0 | Blake 13 |
| 48 | div1 | Nottm Forest | A | D | 2-2 | Blake 9; Cameron 26 |
| 49 | div1 | Millwall | H | W | 3-0 | Newton 5,80; Cameron 78 |
| 50 | div1 | Norwich | A | W | 3-0 | Ndah 52; Sturridge 74; Miller 90 |
| 51 | div1 | Sheff Utd | A | D | 3-3 | Ndah 10; Sturridge 45,62 pen |
| 52 | div1 | Leicester | H | D | 1-1 | Miller 57 |
| 53 | d1po1 | Reading | H | W | 2-1 | Newton 75; Naylor 83 |
| 54 | d1po2 | Reading | A | W | 1-0 | Rae 81 |
| 55 | d1pof | Sheff Utd | N | W | 3-0 | Kennedy 6; Blake 22; Miller 45 |

☐Home ☐Away ☐Neutral

## ATTENDANCES

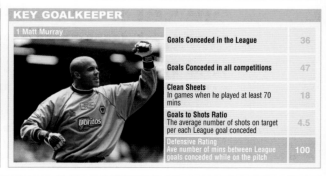

**HOME GROUND:** MOLINEUX **CAPACITY:** 28500 **AVERAGE LEAGUE AT HOME:** 25745

| | | | | | | | | | | | |
|---|---|---|---|---|---|---|---|---|---|---|---|
| 55 | Sheff Utd | 69473 | 40 | Ipswich | 26901 | 15 | Grimsby | 23875 | 1 | Bradford | 13223 |
| 11 | Leicester | 32082 | 28 | Derby | 26442 | 31 | Wimbledon | 23716 | 30 | Walsall | 11037 |
| 41 | Southampton | 31715 | 39 | Crystal Palace | 26010 | 10 | Preston | 23696 | 16 | Gillingham | 10036 |
| 4 | Derby | 29954 | 46 | Rotherham | 25944 | 19 | Brighton | 23016 | 25 | Millwall | 9091 |
| 52 | Leicester | 28190 | 27 | Bradford | 25812 | 51 | Sheff Utd | 22211 | 34 | Brighton | 6754 |
| 32 | Leicester | 28164 | 23 | Norwich | 25753 | 33 | Sheff Wed | 21381 | 22 | Rotherham | 6736 |
| 21 | Nottm Forest | 27953 | 24 | Coventry | 25577 | 50 | Norwich | 20843 | 12 | Rotherham | 5064 |
| 2 | Walsall | 27904 | 9 | Reading | 25560 | 42 | Reading | 19731 | 47 | Grimsby | 4983 |
| 36 | Ipswich | 27700 | 44 | Stoke | 25235 | 43 | Portsmouth | 19558 | 7 | Swansea | 4799 |
| 53 | Reading | 27678 | 45 | Gillingham | 25171 | 20 | Coventry | 18998 | 6 | Wimbledon | 3223 |
| 29 | Newcastle | 27316 | 3 | Burnley | 25031 | 26 | Burnley | 18641 | | | |
| 48 | Nottm Forest | 27209 | 13 | Sheff Utd | 24625 | 8 | Crystal Palace | 16961 | | | |
| 5 | Sheff Wed | 27096 | 38 | Watford | 24591 | 14 | Stoke | 16885 | | | |
| 18 | Portsmouth | 27022 | 54 | Reading | 24060 | 17 | Watford | 16524 | | | |
| 49 | Millwall | 27015 | 35 | Rochdale | 23921 | 37 | Preston | 16070 | | | |

## KEY PLAYERS - GOALSCORERS

1 Nathan Blake

| | |
|---|---|
| **Goals in the League** | 12 |
| **Goals in all competitions** | 14 |
| **Contribution to Attacking Power** Average number of minutes between League team goals while on pitch | 41 |
| **Player Strike Rate** The total number of minutes he was on the pitch for every League goal scored | 150 |
| **Club Strike Rate** Average number of minutes between League goals scored by club | 51 |

| | PLAYER | GOALS LGE | GOALS ALL | POWER | S RATE |
|---|---|---|---|---|---|
| 2 | Kenny Miller | 19 | 24 | 51 | 159 mins |
| 3 | Dean Sturridge | 11 | 11 | 51 | 161 mins |
| 4 | George Ndah | 7 | 11 | 51 | 205 mins |
| 5 | Colin Cameron | 7 | 7 | 46 | 360 mins |

## KEY PLAYERS - MIDFIELDERS

1 Paul Ince

| | |
|---|---|
| **Goals in the League** | 2 |
| **Goals in all competitions** | 3 |
| **Defensive Rating** Average number of mins between League goals conceded while on the pitch | 115 |
| **Contribution to Attacking Power** Average number of minutes between League team goals while on pitch | 52 |
| **Scoring Difference** Defensive Rating minus Contribution to Attacking Power | 63 |

| | PLAYER | GOALS LGE | GOALS ALL | DEF RATE | ATT POWER | SCORE DIFF |
|---|---|---|---|---|---|---|
| 2 | Mark Kennedy | 3 | 5 | 106 | 56 | 50 mins |
| 3 | Shaun Newton | 3 | 5 | 101 | 56 | 45 mins |
| 4 | Alex Rae | 3 | 6 | 81 | 58 | 23 mins |
| 5 | Kevin Cooper | 3 | 3 | 73 | 51 | 22 mins |

## KEY PLAYERS - DEFENDERS

1 Denis Irwin

| | |
|---|---|
| **Goals Conceded in League** | 34 |
| **Goals Conceded in all competitions** | 43 |
| **Clean Sheets** In League games when he played at least 70 mins | 20 |
| **Defensive Rating** Ave number of mins between League goals conceded while on the pitch | 111 |
| **Club Defensive Rating** Average number of mins between League goals conceded by the club this season | 94 |

| | PLAYER | CON LGE | CON ALL | CLN SHEETS | DEF RATE |
|---|---|---|---|---|---|
| 2 | Mark Clyde | 13 | 13 | 4 | 99 mins |
| 3 | Joleon Lescott | 42 | 53 | 20 | 94 mins |
| 4 | Lee Naylor | 29 | 42 | 15 | 94 mins |
| 5 | Paul Butler | 31 | 44 | 15 | 89 mins |

## KEY GOALKEEPER

1 Matt Murray

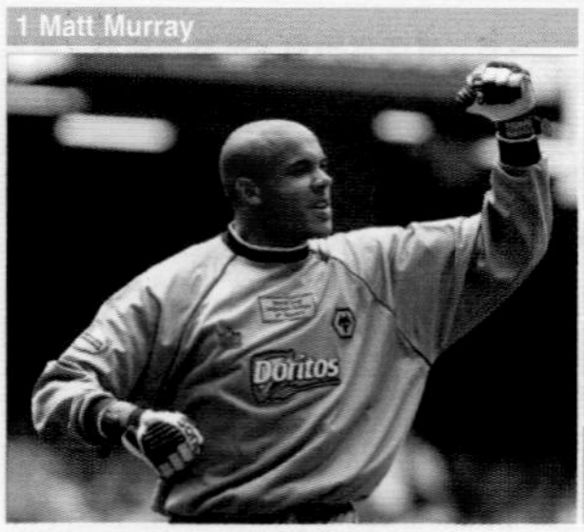

| | |
|---|---|
| **Goals Conceded in the League** | 36 |
| **Goals Conceded in all competitions** | 47 |
| **Clean Sheets** In games when he played at least 70 mins | 18 |
| **Goals to Shots Ratio** The average number of shots on target per each League goal conceded | 4.5 |
| **Defensive Rating** Ave number of mins between League goals conceded while on the pitch | 100 |

## MONTHY POINTS TALLY

| | | |
|---|---|---|
| AUGUST | 11 | 61% |
| SEPTEMBER | 6 | 40% |
| OCTOBER | 10 | 67% |
| NOVEMBER | 10 | 56% |
| DECEMBER | 4 | 27% |
| JANUARY | 11 | 73% |
| FEBRUARY | 13 | 72% |
| MARCH | 11 | 52% |
| APRIL | 12 | 67% |
| MAY | 10 | 83% |

## TOP POINT EARNERS

| | PLAYER | GAMES | AV PTS |
|---|---|---|---|
| 1 | Kenny Miller | 31 | 2.00 |
| 2 | Colin Cameron | 25 | 1.92 |
| 3 | Nathan Blake | 19 | 1.84 |
| 4 | Denis Irwin | 41 | 1.80 |
| 5 | Paul Ince | 33 | 1.76 |
| 6 | Shaun Newton | 22 | 1.73 |
| 7 | Lee Naylor | 30 | 1.73 |
| 8 | Paul Butler | 29 | 1.72 |
| 9 | Joleon Lescott | 44 | 1.70 |
| 10 | Mark Kennedy | 30 | 1.70 |
| | CLUB AVERAGE: | | 1.65 |

## GOALS

| 1 Kenny Miller | |
|---|---|
| League | 19 |
| FA Cup | 3 |
| League Cup | 1 |
| Other | 1 |
| TOTAL | 24 |

| | PLAYER | LGE | FAC | LC | Oth | TOT |
|---|---|---|---|---|---|---|
| 2 | Blake | 12 | 0 | 1 | 1 | 14 |
| 3 | Sturridge | 11 | 0 | 0 | 0 | 11 |
| 4 | Ndah | 7 | 4 | 0 | 0 | 11 |
| 5 | Cameron | 7 | 0 | 0 | 0 | 7 |
| 6 | Newton | 3 | 0 | 1 | 1 | 5 |
| 7 | Cooper | 3 | 0 | 0 | 0 | 3 |
| 8 | Rae | 3 | 0 | 2 | 1 | 6 |
| 9 | Kennedy | 3 | 1 | 0 | 1 | 5 |
| 10 | Ince | 2 | 1 | 0 | 0 | 3 |
| 11 | Irwin | 2 | 0 | 0 | 0 | 2 |
| | Other | 9 | 1 | 2 | 1 | 13 |
| | TOTAL | 81 | 10 | 7 | 6 | 104 |

## TEAM OF THE SEASON

| GOALSCORER | GAMES | DEF RATE |
|---|---|---|
| Matt Murray | 40 | 100 |
| **DEFENDERS** | **GAMES** | **DEF RATE** |
| Denis Irwin | 41 | 111 |
| Mark Clyde | 14 | 99 |
| Joleon Lescott | 44 | 94 |
| Lee Naylor | 30 | 94 |
| **MIDFIELDERS** | **GAMES** | **SCORE DIFF** |
| Paul Ince | 33 | 63 |
| Mark Kennedy | 30 | 50 |
| Shaun Newton | 22 | 45 |
| Alex Rae | 27 | 23 |
| **GOALSCORERS** | **GAMES** | **STRIKE RATE** |
| Nathan Blake | 19 | 150 |
| Kenny Miller | 31 | 159 |

Games = games playing at least 70 minutes

## LEAGUE APPEARANCES, BOOKINGS AND CAPS

| | AGE (on 01/07/03) | IN THE SQUAD | COUNTING GAMES | MINUTES ON PITCH | YELLOW CARDS | RED CARDS | THIS SEASON | HOME COUNTRY |
|---|---|---|---|---|---|---|---|---|
| **Goalkeepers** | | | | | | | | |
| Ian Feuer | 32 | 2 | 0 | 0 | 0 | 0 | - | United States |
| Matt Murray | 22 | 46 | 40 | 3600 | 0 | 0 | - | England |
| Michael Oakes | 29 | 41 | 6 | 540 | 0 | 0 | - | England |
| Lewis Solly | 19 | 3 | 0 | 0 | 0 | 0 | - | England |
| **Defenders** | | | | | | | | |
| Paul Butler | 30 | 43 | 29 | 2763 | 6 | 0 | - | Rep of Ireland |
| Mohamed Camara | 28 | 1 | 0 | 0 | 0 | 0 | - | Guinea |
| Mark Clyde | 20 | 25 | 14 | 1281 | 1 | 0 | - | N Ireland |
| Sean Connelly | 33 | 1 | 0 | 0 | 0 | 0 | - | England |
| Marc Edworthy | 30 | 30 | 17 | 1721 | 3 | 0 | - | England |
| Denis Irwin | 37 | 43 | 41 | 3780 | 3 | 0 | - | Rep of Ireland |
| Joleon Lescott | 20 | 44 | 44 | 3960 | 1 | 0 | - | England |
| Lee Naylor | 23 | 36 | 30 | 2727 | 0 | 0 | - | England |
| Ludovic Pollet | 33 | 10 | 2 | 180 | 1 | 0 | - | France |
| **Midfielders** | | | | | | | | |
| Keith Andrews | 22 | 13 | 1 | 276 | 1 | 0 | - | Rep of Ireland |
| Sammy Clingan | 19 | 1 | 0 | 0 | 0 | 0 | - | N Ireland |
| Kevin Cooper | 28 | 33 | 12 | 1385 | 5 | 0 | - | England |
| Paul Ince | 35 | 37 | 33 | 3102 | 11 | 0 | - | England |
| Ivar Ingimarsson | 25 | 18 | 10 | 886 | 2 | 0 | - | Iceland |
| Mark Kennedy | 27 | 31 | 30 | 2753 | 4 | 0 | - | Rep of Ireland |
| John Melligan | 22 | 2 | 0 | 4 | 0 | 0 | - | Rep of Ireland |
| Shaun Newton | 27 | 35 | 22 | 2422 | 3 | 0 | - | England |
| Alex Rae | 33 | 43 | 27 | 2660 | 10 | 0 | - | Scotland |
| **Forwards** | | | | | | | | |
| Nathan Blake | 31 | 23 | 19 | 1797 | 3 | 1 | 3 | Wales (50) |
| Colin Cameron | 30 | 35 | 25 | 2521 | 3 | 0 | 5 | Scotland (64) |
| Carlton Cole | 19 | 7 | 3 | 418 | 0 | 0 | - | England |
| Kenny Miller | 23 | 46 | 31 | 3028 | 5 | 0 | 4 | Scotland (64) |
| George Ndah | 28 | 26 | 12 | 1435 | 6 | 0 | - | England |
| Adam Proudlock | 22 | 19 | 3 | 459 | 0 | 0 | - | England |
| Dean Sturridge | 29 | 42 | 16 | 1767 | 4 | 0 | - | England |

KEY: LEAGUE BOOKINGS CAPS (FIFA RANKING)

## SQUAD APPEARANCES

| Match | 1 2 3 4 5 | 6 7 8 9 10 | 11 12 13 14 15 | 16 17 18 19 20 | 21 22 23 24 25 | 26 27 28 29 30 | 31 32 33 34 35 | 36 37 38 39 40 | 41 42 43 44 45 | 46 47 48 49 50 | 51 52 53 54 55 |
|---|---|---|---|---|---|---|---|---|---|---|---|
| Venue | A H H A H | A A A H H | A A H A H | A A H H A | H A H H A | A H H H A | H H A A H | A A H H H | A A A H H | H A A H A | A H H A N |
| Competition | L L L L L | L W L L L | L W L L L | L L L L L | L L L L L | L L L F L | L F L L F | L L L L L | F L L L L | L L L L L | L L O O O |
| Result | D W W W D | L W L L W | L L L W W | W D D D W | W D W L D | L L D W W | D W W L W | W W D W D | L W L D W | D W D W W | D D W W W |

**Goalkeepers**: Ian Feuer, Matt Murray, Michael Oakes, Lewis Solly

**Defenders**: Paul Butler, Mohamed Camara, Mark Clyde, Sean Connelly, Marc Edworthy, Denis Irwin, Joleon Lescott, Lee Naylor, Ludovic Pollet

**Midfielders**: Keith Andrews, Sammy Clingan, Kevin Cooper, Paul Ince, Ivar Ingimarsson, Mark Kennedy, John Melligan, Shaun Newton, Alex Rae

**Forwards**: Nathan Blake, Colin Cameron, Carlton Cole, Kenny Miller, George Ndah, Adam Proudlock, Dean Sturridge

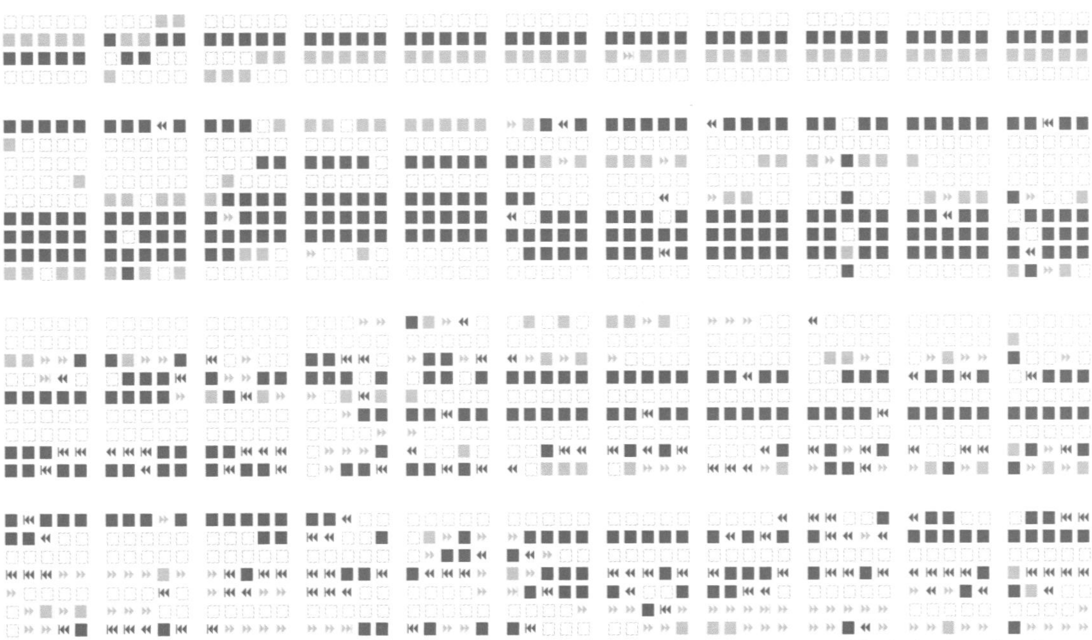

KEY: On all match; On bench; Subbed or sent off (Counting game); Subbed or sent off (playing less than 70 minutes); Subbed on from bench (Counting Game); Subbed on (playing less than 70 minutes); Subbed on and then subbed or sent off (Counting Game); Subbed on and then subbed or sent off (playing less than 70 minutes); Not in 16

# NOTTINGHAM FOREST

Final Position: **6th**

NICKNAME: THE REDS

KEY: ☐Won ☐Drawn ☐Lost

| | | | | | | |
|---|---|---|---|---|---|---|
| 1 | div1 | Portsmouth | A | L | 0-2 | |
| 2 | div1 | Preston | H | D | 2-2 | Johnson, D 68; Jess 82 |
| 3 | div1 | Sheff Wed | H | W | 4-0 | Johnson, D 2; Lester 47; Scimeca 68,71 |
| 4 | div1 | Walsall | A | L | 1-2 | Prutton 83 |
| 5 | div1 | Wimbledon | H | W | 2-0 | Johnson, D 15,45 |
| 6 | div1 | Coventry | A | W | 1-0 | Scimeca 15 |
| 7 | wcr1 | Kidderminster | H | W | 4-0 | Lester 23,69 pen; Scimeca 45; Johnson, D 50 |
| 8 | div1 | Watford | H | L | 0-1 | |
| 9 | div1 | Gillingham | H | W | 4-1 | Harewood 4,15 pen,66; Johnson, D 38 |
| 10 | div1 | Grimsby | A | W | 3-0 | Johnson, D 17,85 pen,90 |
| 11 | div1 | Stoke | A | D | 2-2 | Dawson, M 35; Johnson, D 45 |
| 12 | div1 | Rotherham | H | W | 3-2 | Johnson, D 2,39; Bopp 18 |
| 13 | wcr2 | Walsall | H | L | 1-2 | Johnson, D 79 |
| 14 | div1 | Millwall | A | W | 2-1 | Johnson, D 64,85 |
| 15 | div1 | Derby | A | D | 0-0 | |
| 16 | div1 | Leicester | H | D | 2-2 | Johnson, D 76 pen; Lester 90 |
| 17 | div1 | Norwich | A | D | 0-0 | |
| 18 | div1 | Sheff Utd | H | W | 3-0 | Lester 54,61; Harewood 63 |
| 19 | div1 | Crystal Palace | A | D | 0-0 | |
| 20 | div1 | Bradford | H | W | 3-0 | Lester 18; Johnson, D 25; Louis-Jean 36 |
| 21 | div1 | Wolves | A | L | 1-2 | Harewood 45 |
| 22 | div1 | Brighton | H | W | 3-2 | Harewood 8; Johnson, D 45; Lester 76 |
| 23 | div1 | Ipswich | H | W | 2-1 | Johnson, D 5,63 |
| 24 | div1 | Burnley | A | L | 0-1 | |
| 25 | div1 | Bradford | A | L | 0-1 | |
| 26 | div1 | Reading | H | W | 2-0 | Johnson, D 4; Harewood 67 |
| 27 | div1 | Sheff Wed | A | L | 0-2 | |
| 28 | div1 | Portsmouth | H | L | 1-2 | Dawson, M 90 |
| 29 | div1 | Walsall | H | D | 1-1 | Thompson 15 |
| 30 | facr3 | West Ham | A | L | 2-3 | Harewood 17; Reid 50 |
| 31 | div1 | Coventry | H | D | 1-1 | Williams 33 |
| 32 | div1 | Preston | A | D | 1-1 | Johnson, D 16 |
| 33 | div1 | Wimbledon | A | W | 3-2 | Harewood 29,32; Johnson, D 90 |
| 34 | div1 | Crystal Palace | H | W | 2-1 | Dawson, M 4; Harewood 59 |
| 35 | div1 | Stoke | H | W | 6-0 | Harewood 13,24,28,45 pen; Johnson, D 53; Jess 85 |
| 36 | div1 | Watford | A | D | 1-1 | Huckerby 66 |
| 37 | div1 | Gillingham | A | W | 4-1 | Huckerby 7,17; Harewood 46; Thompson 55 |
| 38 | div1 | Grimsby | H | D | 2-2 | Reid 23; Williams 90 |
| 39 | div1 | Brighton | A | L | 0-1 | |
| 40 | div1 | Derby | H | W | 3-0 | Harewood 13,49 pen; Huckerby 15 |
| 41 | div1 | Norwich | H | W | 4-0 | Huckerby 11; Harewood 22; Williams 56; Brennan 82 |
| 42 | div1 | Ipswich | A | W | 4-3 | Thompson 27; Harewood 29,75; Naylor 33 og |
| 43 | div1 | Leicester | A | L | 0-1 | |
| 44 | div1 | Wolves | H | D | 2-2 | Johnson, D 40; Dawson, M 74 |
| 45 | div1 | Sheff Utd | A | L | 0-1 | |
| 46 | div1 | Reading | A | L | 0-1 | |
| 47 | div1 | Burnley | H | W | 2-0 | Dawson, M 75; Johnson, D 90 |
| 48 | div1 | Millwall | H | D | 3-3 | Jess 19; Bopp 22; Johnson, D 72 |
| 49 | div1 | Rotherham | A | D | 2-2 | Lester 63; Westcarr 66 |
| 50 | d1po1 | Sheff Utd | H | D | 1-1 | Johnson, D 55 |
| 51 | d1po2 | Sheff Utd | A | L | 3-4 | Johnson 30; Reid 58; Page 119 og |

☐Home ☐Away ☐Neutral

## ATTENDANCES

HOME GROUND: CITY GROUND CAPACITY: 30602 AVERAGE LEAGUE AT HOME: 24436

| | | | | | | | | | | | |
|---|---|---|---|---|---|---|---|---|---|---|---|
| 43 | Leicester | 32065 | 41 | Norwich | 27296 | 46 | Reading | 21612 | 6 | Coventry | 13732 |
| 15 | Derby | 30547 | 44 | Wolvers | 27209 | 3 | Sheff Wed | 21129 | 32 | Preston | 13508 |
| 51 | Sheff Utd | 30212 | 27 | Sheff Wed | 26362 | 17 | Norwich | 20986 | 25 | Bradford | 12245 |
| 40 | Derby | 29725 | 34 | Crystal Palace | 26012 | 20 | Bradford | 19653 | 14 | Millwall | 10501 |
| 30 | West Ham | 29612 | 26 | Reading | 25831 | 19 | Crystal Palace | 18971 | 49 | Rotherham | 9942 |
| 42 | Ipswich | 29503 | 38 | Grimsby | 25507 | 1 | Portsmouth | 18510 | 37 | Gillingham | 7277 |
| 16 | Leicester | 29497 | 47 | Burnley | 25403 | 2 | Preston | 18065 | 10 | Grimsby | 7072 |
| 48 | Millwall | 29463 | 12 | Rotherham | 25089 | 36 | Watford | 17934 | 39 | Brighton | 6830 |
| 22 | Brighton | 29137 | 23 | Ipswich | 24898 | 8 | Watford | 17865 | 13 | Walsall | 6343 |
| 50 | Sheff Utd | 29064 | 31 | Coventry | 24487 | 5 | Wimbledon | 16431 | 4 | Walsall | 5096 |
| 29 | Walsall | 28441 | 35 | Stoke | 24085 | 9 | Gillingham | 16073 | 7 | Kidderminster | 4498 |
| 28 | Portsmouth | 28165 | 45 | Sheff Utd | 23317 | 11 | Stoke | 14554 | 33 | Wimbledon | 3382 |
| 21 | Wolvers | 27953 | 18 | Sheff Utd | 22579 | 24 | Burnley | 13869 | | | |

## KEY PLAYERS - GOALSCORERS

1 David Johnson

| | |
|---|---|
| Goals in the League | 25 |
| Goals in all competitions | 29 |
| Contribution to Attacking Power<br>Average number of minutes between League team goals while on pitch | 47 |
| Player Strike Rate<br>The total number of minutes he was on the pitch for every League goal scored | 136 |
| Club Strike Rate<br>Average number of minutes between League goals scored by club | 50 |

| | PLAYER | GOALS LGE | GOALS ALL | POWER | S RATE |
|---|---|---|---|---|---|
| 2 | Marlon Harewood | 20 | 21 | 49 | 189 mins |
| 3 | Jack Lester | 7 | 9 | 61 | 265 mins |
| 4 | Eoin Jess | 3 | 3 | 54 | 543 mins |
| 5 | John Thompson | 3 | 3 | 48 | 547 mins |

## KEY PLAYERS - MIDFIELDERS

1 Gareth Williams

| | |
|---|---|
| Goals in the League | 3 |
| Goals in all competitions | 3 |
| Defensive Rating<br>Average number of mins between League goals conceded while on the pitch | 89 |
| Contribution to Attacking Power<br>Average number of minutes between League team goals while on pitch | 47 |
| Scoring Difference<br>Defensive Rating minus Contribution to Attacking Power | 42 |

| | PLAYER | GOALS LGE | GOALS ALL | DEF RATE | ATT POWER | SCORE DIFF |
|---|---|---|---|---|---|---|
| 2 | Andrew Reid | 1 | 3 | 79 | 46 | 33 mins |
| 3 | David Prutton | 1 | 1 | 89 | 58 | 31 mins |
| 4 | Eugen Bopp | 2 | 2 | 68 | 45 | 23 mins |
| 5 | John Thompson | 3 | 3 | 61 | 48 | 13 mins |

## KEY PLAYERS - DEFENDERS

1 Jon Olav Hjelde

| | |
|---|---|
| Goals Conceded in League | 19 |
| Goals Conceded in all competitions | 22 |
| Clean Sheets<br>In League games when he played at least 70 mins | 7 |
| Defensive Rating<br>Ave number of mins between League goals conceded while on the pitch | 90 |
| Club Defensive Rating<br>Average number of mins between League goals conceded by the club this season | 83 |

| | PLAYER | CON LGE | CON ALL | CLN SHEETS | DEF RATE |
|---|---|---|---|---|---|
| 2 | Matthieu Louis-Jean | 41 | 49 | 13 | 87 mins |
| 3 | Riccardo Scimeca | 41 | 51 | 13 | 85 mins |
| 4 | Jim Brennan | 48 | 56 | 14 | 83 mins |
| 5 | Michael Dawson | 41 | 47 | 11 | 83 mins |

## KEY GOALKEEPER

1 Darren Ward

| | |
|---|---|
| Goals Conceded in the League | 48 |
| Goals Conceded in all competitions | 58 |
| Clean Sheets<br>In games when he played at least 70 mins | 14 |
| Goals to Shots Ratio<br>The average number of shots on target per each League goal conceded | 5.1 |
| Defensive Rating<br>Ave number of mins between League goals conceded while on the pitch | 84 |

## MONTHY POINTS TALLY

| | | |
|---|---|---|
| AUGUST | 10 | 56% |
| SEPTEMBER | 13 | 72% |
| OCTOBER | 6 | 40% |
| NOVEMBER | 13 | 72% |
| DECEMBER | 3 | 20% |
| JANUARY | 3 | 25% |
| FEBRUARY | 9 | 100% |
| MARCH | 11 | 61% |
| APRIL | 8 | 38% |
| MAY | 2 | 22% |

## TOP POINT EARNERS

| | PLAYER | GAMES | AV PTS |
|---|---|---|---|
| 1 | Jon Olav Hjelde | 17 | 1.94 |
| 2 | Gareth Williams | 38 | 1.76 |
| 3 | Marlon Harewood | 41 | 1.71 |
| 4 | Michael Dawson | 37 | 1.70 |
| 5 | Riccardo Scimeca | 38 | 1.66 |
| 6 | Jim Brennan | 44 | 1.66 |
| 7 | David Johnson | 38 | 1.66 |
| 8 | Matthieu Louis-Jean | 39 | 1.64 |
| 9 | Darren Ward | 45 | 1.62 |
| 10 | Andrew Reid | 22 | 1.55 |
| | CLUB AVERAGE: | | 1.61 |

## GOALS

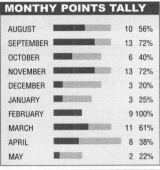

| 1 David Johnson | |
|---|---|
| League | 25 |
| FA Cup | 0 |
| League Cup | 2 |
| Other | 2 |
| TOTAL | 29 |

| | PLAYER | LGE | FAC | LC | Oth | TOT |
|---|---|---|---|---|---|---|
| 2 | Harewood | 20 | 1 | 0 | 0 | 21 |
| 3 | Lester | 7 | 0 | 2 | 0 | 9 |
| 4 | Huckerby | 5 | 0 | 0 | 0 | 5 |
| 5 | Dawson | 5 | 0 | 0 | 0 | 5 |
| 6 | Williams | 3 | 0 | 0 | 0 | 3 |
| 7 | Thompson | 3 | 0 | 0 | 0 | 3 |
| 8 | Scimeca | 3 | 0 | 1 | 0 | 4 |
| 9 | Jess | 3 | 0 | 0 | 0 | 3 |
| 10 | Bopp | 2 | 0 | 0 | 0 | 2 |
| 11 | Prutton | 1 | 0 | 0 | 0 | 1 |
| | Other | 5 | 1 | 0 | 4 | 10 |
| | TOTAL | 82 | 2 | 5 | 6 | 95 |

## TEAM OF THE SEASON

| GOALKEEPER | GAMES | DEF RATE |
|---|---|---|
| Darren Ward | 45 | 84 |
| **DEFENDERS** | **GAMES** | **DEF RATE** |
| Jon Olav Hjelde | 17 | 90 |
| Matthieu Louis-Jean | 39 | 87 |
| Riccardo Scimeca | 38 | 85 |
| Jim Brennan | 44 | 83 |
| **MIDFIELDERS** | **GAMES** | **SCORE DIFF** |
| Gareth Williams | 38 | 42 |
| Andrew Reid | 22 | 33 |
| David Prutton | 24 | 31 |
| Eugen Bopp | 10 | 23 |
| **GOALSCORERS** | **GAMES** | **STRIKE RATE** |
| David Johnson | 38 | 136 |
| Marlon Harewood | 41 | 189 |

Games = games playing more than 70 minutes

## LEAGUE APPEARANCES, BOOKINGS AND CAPS

| | AGE (on 01/07/03) | IN THE SQUAD | COUNTING GAMES | MINUTES ON PITCH | YELLOW CARDS | RED CARDS | THIS SEASON | HOME COUNTRY |
|---|---|---|---|---|---|---|---|---|
| **Goalkeepers** | | | | | | | | |
| Barry Roche | 21 | 46 | 1 | 90 | 0 | 0 | - | Rep of Ireland |
| Darren Ward | 29 | 46 | 45 | 4050 | 0 | 0 | - | England |
| **Defenders** | | | | | | | | |
| Jim Brennan | 26 | 45 | 44 | 3980 | 1 | 0 | - | Canada |
| Michael Dawson | 19 | 38 | 37 | 3394 | 7 | 0 | - | England |
| Chris Doig | 22 | 39 | 6 | 581 | 0 | 0 | - | Scotland |
| Marcus Hall | 27 | 1 | 1 | 90 | 0 | 0 | - | England |
| Jon Olav Hjelde | 30 | 39 | 17 | 1705 | 4 | 1 | - | Norway |
| Matthieu Louis-Jean | 27 | 42 | 39 | 3580 | 7 | 0 | - | France |
| Wes Morgan | 19 | 1 | 0 | 0 | 0 | 0 | - | England |
| Davy Oyen | 27 | 6 | 0 | 52 | 0 | 0 | - | Belgium |
| Gregor Robertson | 19 | 0 | 0 | 0 | 0 | 0 | - | Scotland |
| Riccardo Scimeca | 28 | 40 | 38 | 3472 | 4 | 0 | - | England |
| Des Walker | 37 | 33 | 26 | 2470 | 4 | 0 | - | England |
| **Midfielders** | | | | | | | | |
| Eugen Bopp | 19 | 28 | 10 | 952 | 2 | 0 | - | Germany |
| Brian Cash | 20 | 1 | 0 | 1 | 0 | 0 | - | Rep of Ireland |
| David Prutton | 21 | 24 | 24 | 2142 | 9 | 2 | - | England |
| Andrew Reid | 20 | 42 | 22 | 2042 | 5 | 0 | - | Rep of Ireland |
| John Thompson | 22 | 28 | 16 | 1640 | 3 | 0 | - | Rep of Ireland |
| Gareth Williams | 21 | 40 | 38 | 3467 | 3 | 0 | 4 | Scotland (64) |
| **Forwards** | | | | | | | | |
| Mickael Curier | 20 | 0 | 0 | 0 | 0 | 0 | - | France |
| Matt Bodkin | 19 | 1 | 0 | 0 | 0 | 0 | - | England |
| Marlon Harewood | 23 | 44 | 41 | 3785 | 7 | 0 | - | England |
| Darren Huckerby | 27 | 9 | 9 | 790 | 3 | 0 | - | England |
| Eoin Jess | 32 | 45 | 15 | 1630 | 2 | 0 | - | Scotland |
| David Johnson | 26 | 43 | 38 | 3405 | 4 | 0 | - | England |
| Jack Lester | 27 | 34 | 19 | 1852 | 7 | 2 | - | England |
| Craig Westcarr | 18 | 21 | 2 | 264 | 1 | 0 | - | England |

KEY: LEAGUE BOOKINGS CAPS (FIFA RANKING)

## SQUAD APPEARANCES

| Match | 1 | 2 | 3 | 4 | 5 | 6 | 7 | 8 | 9 | 10 | 11 | 12 | 13 | 14 | 15 | 16 | 17 | 18 | 19 | 20 | 21 | 22 | 23 | 24 | 25 | 26 | 27 | 28 | 29 | 30 | 31 | 32 | 33 | 34 | 35 | 36 | 37 | 38 | 39 | 40 | 41 | 42 | 43 | 44 | 45 | 46 | 47 | 48 | 49 | 50 | 51 |
|---|---|---|---|---|---|---|---|---|---|---|---|---|---|---|---|---|---|---|---|---|---|---|---|---|---|---|---|---|---|---|---|---|---|---|---|---|---|---|---|---|---|---|---|---|---|---|---|---|---|---|---|
| Venue | A | H | H | A | H | A | H | H | H | A | A | H | H | A | A | H | A | H | A | H | A | H | H | A | A | H | A | H | H | A | H | A | A | H | H | A | A | H | A | H | H | A | A | H | A | A | H | H | A | H | A |
| Competition | L | L | L | L | L | L | W | L | L | L | L | L | W | L | L | L | L | L | L | L | L | L | L | L | L | L | L | L | L | F | L | L | L | L | L | L | L | L | L | L | L | L | L | L | L | L | L | L | L | O | O |
| Result | L | D | W | L | W | W | W | L | W | W | D | W | L | W | D | D | D | W | D | W | L | W | W | L | L | W | L | L | D | L | D | D | W | W | W | D | W | D | L | W | W | W | L | D | L | L | W | D | D | D | D |

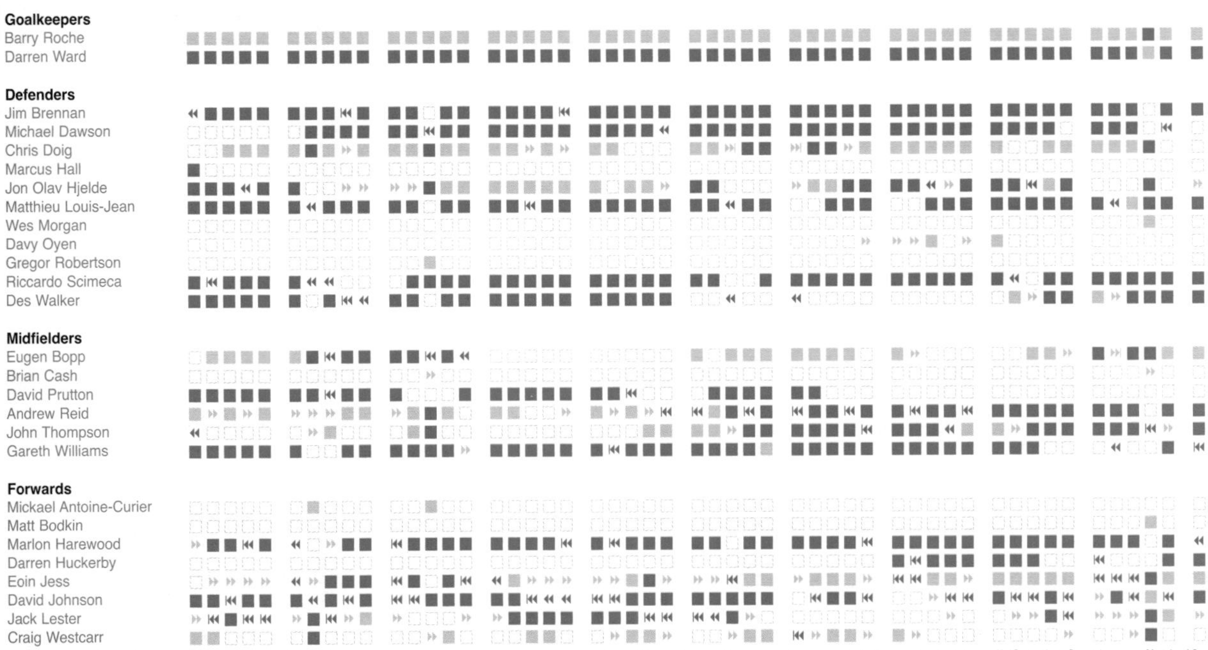

Goalkeepers
Barry Roche
Darren Ward
Defenders
Jim Brennan
Michael Dawson
Chris Doig
Marcus Hall
Jon Olav Hjelde
Matthieu Louis-Jean
Wes Morgan
Davy Oyen
Gregor Robertson
Riccardo Scimeca
Des Walker
Midfielders
Eugen Bopp
Brian Cash
David Prutton
Andrew Reid
John Thompson
Gareth Williams
Forwards
Mickael Antoine-Curier
Matt Bodkin
Marlon Harewood
Darren Huckerby
Eoin Jess
David Johnson
Jack Lester
Craig Westcarr


KEY: ■ On all match ■ On bench
⏮ Subbed or sent off (Counting game)
« Subbed or sent off (playing less than 70 minutes)
⏭ Subbed on from bench (Counting Game)
» Subbed on (playing less than 70 minutes)
Subbed on and then subbed or sent off (Counting Game)
Subbed on and then subbed or sent off (playing less than 70 minutes)
Not in 16

# IPSWICH TOWN

Final Position: **7th**

**NICKNAME:** TRACTOR BOYS

KEY: ☐Won ☐Drawn ☐Lost

| | | | | | | |
|---|---|---|---|---|---|---|
| 1 | div1 | **Walsall** | A | W | 2-0 | Ambrose 37; Bent, M 62 |
| 2 | ucql1 | **Beggen** | A | W | 1-0 | Stewart 90 |
| 3 | div1 | **Leicester** | H | W | 6-1 | Holland 45,56; Ambrose 69; George 75; Counago 85,90 |
| 4 | div1 | **Millwall** | A | D | 1-1 | Bent, D 55 |
| 5 | div1 | **Bradford** | H | L | 1-2 | Bent, D 14 |
| 6 | ucql2 | **Beggen** | H | W | 8-1 | Miller, T 3,19; Counago 18,24,74; Brown 41; McGreal 60; Ambrose 79 |
| 7 | div1 | **Preston** | A | D | 0-0 | |
| 8 | div1 | **Norwich** | H | D | 1-1 | Counago 90 |
| 9 | uc1rl1 | **FK Sartid** | H | D | 1-1 | Armstrong 56 |
| 10 | div1 | **Stoke** | A | L | 1-2 | Gunnarsson 68 og |
| 11 | wcr2 | **Brighton** | H | W | 3-1 | Bent, D 13; Counago 22; Ambrose 45 |
| 12 | div1 | **Derby** | H | L | 0-1 | |
| 13 | uc1rl2 | **FK Sartid** | A | W | 1-0 | Bent, M 9 pen |
| 14 | div1 | **Wimbledon** | A | W | 1-0 | Ambrose 90 |
| 15 | div1 | **Grimsby** | A | L | 0-3 | |
| 16 | div1 | **Sheff Wed** | H | W | 2-1 | Counago 30,35 |
| 17 | div1 | **Reading** | A | L | 1-3 | Ambrose 62 |
| 18 | div1 | **Burnley** | H | D | 2-2 | McGreal 2; Ambrose 15 |
| 19 | div1 | **Gillingham** | H | L | 0-1 | |
| 20 | uc2rl1 | **Slovan Liberec** | H | W | 1-0 | Bent, D 67 |
| 21 | div1 | **Crystal Palace** | H | L | 1-2 | Ambrose 39 |
| 22 | wcr3 | **Middlesbrough** | H | W | 3-1 | Gaardsoe 2; Clapham 40; Bent, D 44 |
| 23 | div1 | **Sheff Utd** | A | D | 0-0 | |
| 24 | uc2rl2 | **Slovan Liberec** | A | L | 2-4* | (*on penalties) |
| 25 | div1 | **Watford** | A | W | 2-0 | Armstrong 51; Clapham 57 |
| 26 | div1 | **Coventry** | H | W | 2-1 | Bent, D 10; Counago 83 |
| 27 | div1 | **Nottm Forest** | A | L | 1-2 | Williams 89 og |
| 28 | wcr4 | **Liverpool** | A | L | 4-5* | Miller, T 14 (*on penalties) |
| 29 | div1 | **Rotherham** | H | L | 1-2 | Wilnis 11 |
| 30 | div1 | **Brighton** | A | D | 1-1 | Magilton 78 |
| 31 | div1 | **Watford** | H | W | 4-2 | Miller, T 23; Naylor 40; Counago 67; Bent, M 87 |
| 32 | div1 | **Portsmouth** | A | D | 1-1 | Gaardsoe 54 |
| 33 | div1 | **Leicester** | A | W | 2-1 | Gaardsoe 84; Ambrose 88 |
| 34 | div1 | **Walsall** | H | W | 3-2 | Counago 45,85; Gaardsoe 60 |
| 35 | div1 | **Millwall** | H | W | 4-1 | Miller, T 57,87 pen; Wright 75; Bent, M 79 |
| 36 | facr3 | **Morecambe** | H | W | 4-0 | Clapham 2; Bent, D 65,77; Ambrose 75 |
| 37 | div1 | **Burnley** | A | D | 1-1 | Counago 22 |
| 38 | div1 | **Preston** | H | W | 3-0 | Bent, M 30; Bent, D 74,86 |
| 39 | facr4 | **Sheff Utd** | A | L | 3-4 | Gaardsoe 66; Miller, T 68 pen; Bent, M 70 |
| 40 | div1 | **Bradford** | A | L | 0-2 | |
| 41 | div1 | **Sheff Utd** | H | W | 3-2 | Bent, D 57,88; Ambrose 78 |
| 42 | div1 | **Wolves** | H | L | 2-4 | Bent, M 2; Holland 45 |
| 43 | div1 | **Grimsby** | H | D | 2-2 | Bent, D 12,89 |
| 44 | div1 | **Norwich** | A | W | 2-0 | Wilnis 72; Bent, D 90 |
| 45 | div1 | **Wolves** | A | D | 1-1 | Naylor 84 |
| 46 | div1 | **Stoke** | H | D | 0-0 | |
| 47 | div1 | **Crystal Palace** | A | D | 1-1 | Bent, M 67 |
| 48 | div1 | **Sheff Wed** | A | W | 1-0 | Holland 17 |
| 49 | div1 | **Reading** | H | W | 3-1 | Gaardsoe 1; Holland 31; Magilton 70 |
| 50 | div1 | **Brighton** | H | D | 2-2 | Bent, M 20; Reuser 85 |
| 51 | div1 | **Gillingham** | A | W | 3-1 | Counago 32,73; Bent, M 78 |
| 52 | div1 | **Nottm Forest** | H | L | 3-4 | Miller, T 14,26 pen; Bent, M 60 |
| 53 | div1 | **Coventry** | A | W | 4-2 | Bent, M 51,69; Counago 55,65 |
| 54 | div1 | **Portsmouth** | H | W | 3-0 | Reuser 11; Miller, T 27; Counago 30 |
| 55 | div1 | **Rotherham** | A | L | 1-2 | Counago 31 |
| 56 | div1 | **Wimbledon** | H | L | 1-5 | Bent, D 79 |
| 57 | div1 | **Derby** | A | W | 4-1 | Counago 32; Bent, D 37; Magilton 41; Holland 90 |

☐Home ☐Away ☐Neutral

## ATTENDANCES

**HOME GROUND:** PORTMAN ROAD **CAPACITY:** 30000 **AVERAGE LEAGUE AT HOME:** 25454

| | | | | | | | | | | | |
|---|---|---|---|---|---|---|---|---|---|---|---|
| 33 | Leicester | 31426 | 21 | Crystal Palace | 24941 | 17 | Reading | 19524 | 11 | Brighton | 13266 |
| 52 | Nottm Forest | 29503 | 27 | Nottm Forest | 24898 | 32 | Portsmouth | 19130 | 39 | Sheff Utd | 12757 |
| 54 | Portsmouth | 29396 | 48 | Sheff Wed | 24726 | 36 | Morecambe | 18529 | 40 | Bradford | 12080 |
| 8 | Norwich | 29112 | 38 | Preston | 24666 | 6 | Beggen | 17462 | 51 | Gillingham | 8508 |
| 57 | Derby | 28785 | 46 | Stoke | 24547 | 9 | FK Sartid | 16933 | 4 | Millwall | 8097 |
| 42 | Wolves | 27700 | 12 | Derby | 24439 | 25 | Watford | 16184 | 55 | Rotherham | 7519 |
| 3 | Leicester | 27374 | 19 | Gillingham | 24176 | 20 | Slovan Lib | 16138 | 24 | Slovan Liberec | 6509 |
| 45 | Wolves | 26901 | 43 | Grimsby | 24118 | 13 | FK Sartid | 16000 | 30 | Brighton | 6377 |
| 34 | Walsall | 26550 | 49 | Reading | 24108 | 47 | Crystal Palace | 15990 | 1 | Walsall | 5353 |
| 28 | Liverpool | 26305 | 26 | Coventry | 23633 | 23 | Sheff Utd | 15884 | 15 | Grimsby | 4688 |
| 41 | Sheff Utd | 26151 | 16 | Sheff Wed | 23410 | 37 | Burnley | 15501 | 14 | Wimbledon | 3238 |
| 50 | Brighton | 26078 | 31 | Watford | 22985 | 7 | Preston | 15357 | 2 | Beggen | 2971 |
| 35 | Millwall | 26040 | 29 | Rotherham | 22770 | 10 | Stoke | 14587 | | | |
| 56 | Wimbledon | 25564 | 18 | Burnley | 22736 | 22 | Middlesboro | 14417 | | | |
| 5 | Bradford | 25457 | 44 | Norwich | 21243 | 53 | Coventry | 13968 | | | |

## KEY PLAYERS - GOALSCORERS

1 Pablo Gonzalez Counago

| | |
|---|---|
| **Goals in the League** | 17 |
| **Goals in all competitions** | 21 |
| **Contribution to Attacking Power** Average number of minutes between League team goals while on pitch | 45 |
| **Player Strike Rate** The total number of minutes he was on the pitch for every League goal scored | 140 |
| **Club Strike Rate** Average number of minutes between League goals scored by club | 53 |

| | PLAYER | GOALS LGE | GOALS ALL | POWER | S RATE |
|---|---|---|---|---|---|
| 2 | Darren Bent | 12 | 17 | 59 | 194 mins |
| 3 | Marcus Bent | 11 | 13 | 46 | 204 mins |
| 4 | Darren Ambrose | 8 | 11 | 55 | 249 mins |
| 5 | Tommy Miller | 6 | 10 | 41 | 349 mins |

## KEY PLAYERS - MIDFIELDERS

1 Jermaine Wright

| | |
|---|---|
| **Goals in the League** | 1 |
| **Goals in all competitions** | 1 |
| **Defensive Rating** Average number of mins between League goals conceded while on the pitch | 68 |
| **Contribution to Attacking Power** Average number of minutes between League team goals while on pitch | 48 |
| **Scoring Difference** Defensive Rating minus Contribution to Attacking Power | 20 |

| | PLAYER | GOALS LGE | GOALS ALL | DEF RATE | ATT POWER | SCORE DIFF |
|---|---|---|---|---|---|---|
| 2 | Matt Holland | 6 | 6 | 64 | 53 | 11 mins |
| 3 | Darren Ambrose | 8 | 11 | 64 | 55 | 9 mins |
| 4 | Jim Magilton | 3 | 3 | 61 | 57 | 4 mins |

## KEY PLAYERS - DEFENDERS

1 Hermann Hreidarsson

| | |
|---|---|
| **Goals Conceded in League** | 31 |
| **Goals Conceded in all competitions** | 40 |
| **Clean Sheets** In League games when he played at least 70 mins | 5 |
| **Defensive Rating** Ave number of mins between League goals conceded while on the pitch | 75 |
| **Club Defensive Rating** Average number of mins between League goals conceded by the club this season | 66 |

| | PLAYER | CON LGE | CON ALL | CLN SHEETS | DEF RATE |
|---|---|---|---|---|---|
| 2 | Jamie Clapham | 33 | 38 | 5 | 70 mins |
| 3 | Thomas Gaardsoe | 46 | 52 | 9 | 70 mins |
| 4 | Tommy Miller | 30 | 38 | 4 | 70 mins |
| 5 | Fabian Wilnis | 40 | 47 | 6 | 68 mins |

## KEY GOALKEEPER

1 Andy Marshall

| | |
|---|---|
| **Goals Conceded in the League** | 56 |
| **Goals Conceded in all competitions** | 65 |
| **Clean Sheets** In games when he played at least 70 mins | 9 |
| **Goals to Shots Ratio** The average number of shots on target per each League goal conceded | 4.3 |
| **Defensive Rating** Ave number of mins between League goals conceded while on the pitch | 64 |

## MONTHY POINTS TALLY

| Month | Points | % |
|---|---|---|
| AUGUST | 13 | 72% |
| SEPTEMBER | 6 | 33% |
| OCTOBER | 13 | 54% |
| NOVEMBER | 10 | 48% |
| DECEMBER | 12 | 57% |
| JANUARY | 10 | 67% |
| FEBRUARY | 4 | 33% |
| MARCH | 16 | 67% |
| APRIL | 6 | 40% |
| MAY | 3 | 100% |

## TOP POINT EARNERS

| | PLAYER | GAMES | AV PTS |
|---|---|---|---|
| 1 | Tommy Miller | 20 | 1.90 |
| 2 | Fabian Wilnis | 27 | 1.74 |
| 3 | Thomas Gaardsoe | 35 | 1.69 |
| 4 | Christopher Makin | 29 | 1.66 |
| 5 | Pablo Counago | 20 | 1.60 |
| 6 | Hermann Hreidarsson | 24 | 1.58 |
| 7 | Andy Marshall | 40 | 1.55 |
| 8 | Marcus Bent | 20 | 1.50 |
| 9 | Matt Holland | 45 | 1.49 |
| 10 | Jamie Clapham | 25 | 1.48 |
| | CLUB AVERAGE: | | 1.52 |

## GOALS

| 1 Pablo Counago | |
|---|---|
| League | 17 |
| FA Cup | 0 |
| League Cup | 1 |
| Other | 3 |
| TOTAL | 21 |

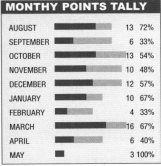

| | PLAYER | LGE | FAC | LC | Oth | TOT |
|---|---|---|---|---|---|---|
| 2 | Bent, D | 12 | 2 | 2 | 1 | 17 |
| 3 | Bent, M | 11 | 1 | 0 | 1 | 13 |
| 4 | Ambrose | 8 | 1 | 1 | 1 | 11 |
| 5 | Miller, T | 6 | 1 | 1 | 2 | 10 |
| 6 | Holland | 6 | 0 | 0 | 0 | 6 |
| 7 | Gaardsoe | 4 | 1 | 1 | 0 | 6 |
| 8 | Magilton | 3 | 0 | 0 | 0 | 3 |
| 9 | Reuser | 2 | 0 | 0 | 0 | 2 |
| 10 | Wilnis | 2 | 0 | 0 | 0 | 2 |
| 11 | Naylor | 2 | 0 | 0 | 0 | 2 |
| | Other | 7 | 1 | 1 | 4 | 13 |
| | TOTAL | 80 | 7 | 7 | 12 | 106 |

## TEAM OF THE SEASON

| GOALKEEPER | GAMES | DEF RATE |
|---|---|---|
| Andy Marshall | 40 | 64 |
| **DEFENDERS** | **GAMES** | **DEF RATE** |
| Hermann Hreidarsson | 24 | 75 |
| Jamie Clapham | 25 | 70 |
| Thomas Gaardsoe | 35 | 70 |
| Tommy Miller | 20 | 70 |
| **MIDFIELDERS** | **GAMES** | **SCORE DIFF** |
| Jermaine Wright | 25 | 20 |
| Matt Holland | 45 | 11 |
| Darren Ambrose | 19 | 9 |
| Jim Magilton | 33 | 4 |
| **GOALSCORERS** | **GAMES** | **STRIKE RATE** |
| Pablo Gonzalez Counago | 20 | 140 |
| Darren Bent | 19 | 194 |

Games = games playing at least 70 minutes

## LEAGUE APPEARANCES, BOOKINGS AND CAPS

| | AGE (on 01/07/03) | IN THE SQUAD | COUNTING GAMES | MINUTES ON PITCH | YELLOW CARDS | RED CARDS | THIS SEASON | HOME COUNTRY |
|---|---|---|---|---|---|---|---|---|
| **Goalkeepers** | | | | | | | | |
| Paul Gerrard | 30 | 5 | 5 | 450 | 0 | 0 | - | England |
| Andy Marshall | 28 | 45 | 40 | 3600 | 1 | 0 | - | England |
| Lewis Price | 18 | 1 | 0 | 0 | 0 | 0 | - | England |
| James Pullen | 21 | 41 | 1 | 90 | 0 | 0 | - | England |
| **Defenders** | | | | | | | | |
| Wayne Brown | 25 | 10 | 7 | 653 | 0 | 0 | - | England |
| Jamie Clapham | 27 | 26 | 25 | 2295 | 1 | 0 | - | England |
| Aidan Collins | - | 2 | 0 | 17 | 0 | 0 | - | England |
| Thomas Gaardsoe | 23 | 40 | 35 | 3231 | 5 | 0 | - | Denmark |
| Hermann Hreidarsson | 28 | 28 | 24 | 2336 | 5 | 1 | - | Iceland |
| Christopher Makin | 36 | 33 | 29 | 2782 | 9 | 1 | - | England |
| John McGreal | 31 | 16 | 14 | 1314 | 3 | 0 | - | England |
| Tommy Miller | 24 | 32 | 20 | 2093 | 3 | 0 | - | England |
| Matthew Richards | 18 | 19 | 9 | 1006 | 0 | 0 | - | England |
| Mark Venus | 36 | 12 | 5 | 602 | 3 | 0 | - | England |
| Fabian Wilnis | 32 | 41 | 27 | 2709 | 3 | 0 | - | Holland |
| **Midfielders** | | | | | | | | |
| Nabil Abidallah | 20 | 7 | 0 | 0 | 0 | 0 | - | Holland |
| Darren Ambrose | 19 | 35 | 19 | 1990 | 2 | 0 | - | England |
| Matt Bloomfield | 19 | 1 | 0 | 0 | 0 | 0 | - | England |
| Dean Bowditch | 17 | 11 | 0 | 82 | 0 | 0 | - | England |
| Matt Holland | 29 | 45 | 45 | 4050 | 3 | 0 | - | England |
| Ulrich Le Pen | 29 | 0 | 0 | 0 | 0 | 0 | - | France |
| Jim Magilton | 34 | 41 | 33 | 3242 | 2 | 0 | - | N Ireland |
| Justin Miller | 22 | 1 | 0 | 27 | 0 | 0 | - | South Africa |
| Antonio Murray | 18 | 1 | 0 | 10 | 0 | 0 | - | England |
| Martijn Reuser | 28 | 19 | 7 | 815 | 1 | 0 | - | Holland |
| Ian Westlake | 19 | 8 | 0 | 52 | 0 | 0 | - | England |
| Jermaine Wright | 27 | 45 | 25 | 2663 | 1 | 0 | - | England |
| **Forwards** | | | | | | | | |
| Alun Armstrong | 28 | 22 | 4 | 776 | 0 | 0 | - | England |
| Darren Bent | 19 | 38 | 19 | 2328 | 1 | 0 | - | England |
| Marcus Bent | 25 | 34 | 20 | 2247 | 2 | 0 | - | England |
| Pablo Counago | 23 | 40 | 20 | 2386 | 5 | 2 | - | Spain |
| Finidi George | 32 | 12 | 1 | 365 | 0 | 0 | - | Nigeria |
| Richard Logan | 21 | 0 | 0 | 0 | 0 | 0 | - | England |
| Richard Naylor | 26 | 21 | 6 | 969 | 0 | 0 | - | England |
| Marcus Stewart | 30 | 4 | 2 | 227 | 0 | 0 | - | England |

KEY: LEAGUE BOOKINGS CAPS(FIFA RANKING)

## SQUAD APPEARANCES

| Match | 1 | 2 | 3 | 4 | 5 | 6 | 7 | 8 | 9 | 10 | 11 | 12 | 13 | 14 | 15 | 16 | 17 | 18 | 19 | 20 | 21 | 22 | 23 | 24 | 25 | 26 | 27 | 28 | 29 | 30 | 31 | 32 | 33 | 34 | 35 | 36 | 37 | 38 | 39 | 40 | 41 | 42 | 43 | 44 | 45 | 46 | 47 | 48 | 49 | 50 | 51 | 52 | 53 | 54 | 55 | 56 | 57 |
|---|---|---|---|---|---|---|---|---|---|---|---|---|---|---|---|---|---|---|---|---|---|---|---|---|---|---|---|---|---|---|---|---|---|---|---|---|---|---|---|---|---|---|---|---|---|---|---|---|---|---|---|---|---|---|---|---|---|
| Venue | A | A | H | A | H | H | A | H | H | A | H | H | A | A | A | H | A | H | H | H | H | H | A | A | A | H | A | A | H | A | H | A | A | H | H | H | A | H | A | A | H | H | H | A | A | H | A | A | H | H | A | H | A | H | A | H | A |
| Competition | L | E | L | L | L | C | L | L | E | L | W | L | E | L | L | L | L | L | L | E | L | W | L | E | L | L | L | W | L | L | L | L | L | L | L | F | L | L | F | L | L | L | L | L | L | L | L | L | L | L | L | L | L | L | L | L | L |
| Result | W | W | W | D | L | W | D | D | D | L | W | L | W | W | L | W | L | D | L | W | L | W | D | L | W | W | L | L | L | D | W | D | W | W | W | W | D | W | L | L | W | L | D | W | D | D | D | W | W | D | W | L | W | W | L | L | W |

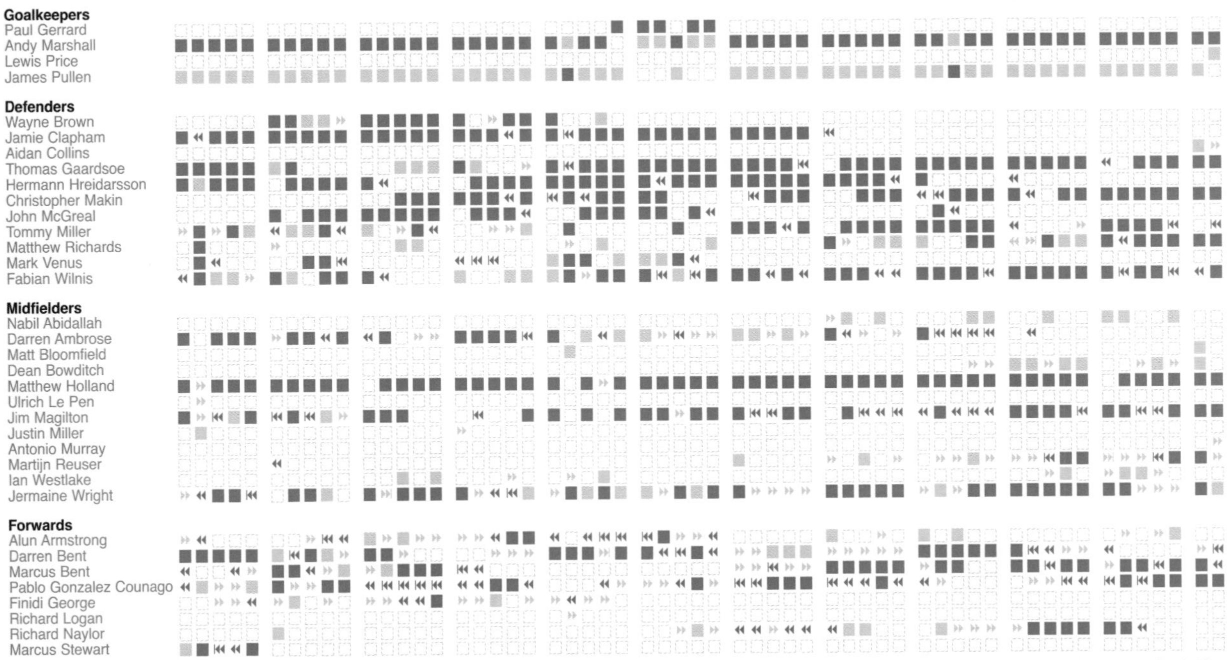
Goalkeepers
Paul Gerrard
Andy Marshall
Lewis Price
James Pullen
Defenders
Wayne Brown
Jamie Clapham
Aidan Collins
Thomas Gaardsoe
Hermann Hreidarsson
Christopher Makin
John McGreal
Tommy Miller
Matthew Richards
Mark Venus
Fabian Wilnis
Midfielders
Nabil Abidallah
Darren Ambrose
Matt Bloomfield
Dean Bowditch
Matthew Holland
Ulrich Le Pen
Jim Magilton
Justin Miller
Antonio Murray
Martijn Reuser
Ian Westlake
Jermaine Wright
Forwards
Alun Armstrong
Darren Bent
Marcus Bent
Pablo Gonzalez Counago
Finidi George
Richard Logan
Richard Naylor
Marcus Stewart

KEY: On all match; On bench; Subbed or sent off (Counting game); Subbed or sent off (playing less than 70 minutes); Subbed on from bench (Counting Game); Subbed on (playing less than 70 minutes); Subbed on and then subbed or sent off (Counting Game); Subbed on and then subbed or sent off (playing less than 70 minutes); Not in 16

# NORWICH CITY

Final Position: **8th**

**NICKNAME:** THE CANARIES

KEY: Won Drawn Lost

| | | | | | | |
|---|---|---|---|---|---|---|
| 1 | div1 | Grimsby | H | W | 4-0 | Mulryne 30,59; McVeigh 41,70 |
| 2 | div1 | Rotherham | A | D | 1-1 | Nielsen 87 |
| 3 | div1 | Brighton | A | W | 2-0 | McVeigh 58; Easton 68 |
| 4 | div1 | Gillingham | H | W | 1-0 | McVeigh 40 |
| 5 | div1 | Stoke | A | D | 1-1 | Drury 47 |
| 6 | div1 | Watford | H | W | 4-0 | McVeigh 29; Roberts 49; Mulryne 66; Nielsen 87 |
| 7 | div1 | Sheff Utd | H | L | 2-3 | McVeigh 85; Mackay 90 |
| 8 | wcr1 | Cheltenham | H | L | 0-3 | |
| 9 | div1 | Ipswich | A | D | 1-1 | Mackay 79 |
| 10 | div1 | Reading | A | W | 2-0 | McVeigh 2; Mulryne 5 |
| 11 | div1 | Portsmouth | H | W | 1-0 | Roberts 81 |
| 12 | div1 | Preston | A | W | 2-1 | Nielsen 34; McVeigh 53 |
| 13 | div1 | Leicester | H | D | 0-0 | |
| 14 | div1 | Millwall | H | W | 3-1 | Nielsen 42,59; Kenton 72 |
| 15 | div1 | Coventry | A | D | 1-1 | McVeigh 90 |
| 16 | div1 | Bradford | A | L | 1-2 | Abbey 70 |
| 17 | div1 | Nottm Forest | H | D | 0-0 | |
| 18 | div1 | Wimbledon | A | L | 2-4 | Henderson 71; Nielsen 79 |
| 19 | div1 | Sheff Wed | H | W | 3-0 | Roberts 31 pen,82; McVeigh 44 |
| 20 | div1 | Crystal Palace | H | W | 2-0 | McVeigh 9; Roberts 87 |
| 21 | div1 | Burnley | A | L | 0-2 | |
| 22 | div1 | Derby | H | W | 1-0 | Mackay 82 |
| 23 | div1 | Wolves | A | L | 0-1 | |
| 24 | div1 | Crystal Palace | A | L | 0-2 | |
| 25 | div1 | Walsall | H | W | 2-1 | Mackay 55; Mulryne 60 |
| 26 | div1 | Brighton | H | L | 0-1 | |
| 27 | div1 | Grimsby | A | D | 1-1 | Abbey 51 |
| 28 | div1 | Rotherham | H | D | 1-1 | McVeigh 59 |
| 29 | facr3 | Brighton | H | W | 3-1 | Mulryne 57,81; McVeigh 71 |
| 30 | div1 | Watford | A | L | 1-2 | Cox 53 og |
| 31 | facr4 | Dag & Red | H | W | 1-0 | Abbey 90 |
| 32 | div1 | Stoke | H | D | 2-2 | Roberts 2; Mackay 23 |
| 33 | div1 | Sheff Wed | A | D | 2-2 | Healy 18; Roberts 43 |
| 34 | facr5 | Southampton | A | L | 0-2 | |
| 35 | div1 | Sheff Utd | A | W | 1-0 | McVeigh 69 |
| 36 | div1 | Gillingham | A | L | 0-1 | |
| 37 | div1 | Ipswich | H | L | 0-2 | |
| 38 | div1 | Reading | H | L | 0-1 | |
| 39 | div1 | Portsmouth | A | L | 2-3 | Easton 58; Rivers 62 |
| 40 | div1 | Coventry | H | W | 2-0 | Nedergaard 33; Drury 90 |
| 41 | div1 | Millwall | A | W | 2-0 | Mackay 8; Abbey 38 |
| 42 | div1 | Nottm Forest | A | L | 0-4 | |
| 43 | div1 | Wimbledon | H | W | 1-0 | Healy 40 |
| 44 | div1 | Bradford | H | W | 3-2 | Rivers 49 pen,86; Abbey 54 |
| 45 | div1 | Derby | A | L | 1-2 | McVeigh 10 |
| 46 | div1 | Burnley | H | W | 2-0 | Nedergaard 3; Abbey 67 |
| 47 | div1 | Walsall | A | D | 0-0 | |
| 48 | div1 | Wolves | H | L | 0-3 | |
| 49 | div1 | Leicester | A | D | 1-1 | Rivers 74 |
| 50 | div1 | Preston | H | W | 2-0 | Mears 46 og; Mulryne 63 |

Home Away Neutral

## ATTENDANCES

**HOME GROUND:** CARROW ROAD **CAPACITY:** 21468 **AVERAGE LEAGUE AT HOME:** 20348

| | | | | | | | | | | | |
|---|---|---|---|---|---|---|---|---|---|---|---|
| 49 | Leicester | 31639 | 48 | Wolves | 20843 | 1 | Grimsby | 19869 | 12 | Preston | 13550 |
| 34 | Southampton | 31103 | 26 | Brighton | 20687 | 28 | Rotherham | 19452 | 30 | Watford | 13338 |
| 9 | Ipswich | 29112 | 19 | Sheff Wed | 20667 | 39 | Portsmouth | 19221 | 8 | Cheltenham | 13285 |
| 42 | Nottm Forest | 27296 | 4 | Gillingham | 20588 | 33 | Sheff Wed | 19114 | 16 | Bradford | 12888 |
| 23 | Wolves | 25753 | 6 | Watford | 20563 | 35 | Sheff Utd | 19020 | 27 | Grimsby | 8306 |
| 45 | Derby | 23643 | 22 | Derby | 20522 | 38 | Reading | 18970 | 36 | Gillingham | 7935 |
| 11 | Portsmouth | 21335 | 14 | Millwall | 20448 | 44 | Bradford | 18536 | 2 | Rotherham | 7687 |
| 37 | Ipswich | 21243 | 50 | Preston | 20232 | 29 | Brighton | 17205 | 47 | Walsall | 7018 |
| 31 | Dag & Red | 21164 | 32 | Stoke | 20186 | 24 | Crystal Palace | 16791 | 41 | Millwall | 6854 |
| 43 | Wimbledon | 21059 | 7 | Sheff Utd | 20074 | 15 | Coventry | 16409 | 3 | Brighton | 6730 |
| 17 | Nottm Forest | 20986 | 46 | Burnley | 20026 | 21 | Burnley | 16282 | 18 | Wimbledon | 3908 |
| 13 | Leicester | 20952 | 40 | Coventry | 20009 | 5 | Stoke | 14931 | | | |
| 20 | Crystal Palace | 20907 | 25 | Walsall | 19872 | 10 | Reading | 14335 | | | |

## KEY PLAYERS - GOALSCORERS

1 Paul McVeigh

| | |
|---|---|
| **Goals in the League** | 14 |
| **Goals in all competitions** | 15 |
| **Contribution to Attacking Power** Average number of minutes between League team goals while on pitch | 74 |
| **Player Strike Rate** The total number of minutes he was on the pitch for every League goal scored | 229 |
| **Club Strike Rate** Average number of minutes between League goals scored by club | 69 |

| | PLAYER | GOALS LGE | GOALS ALL | POWER | S RATE |
|---|---|---|---|---|---|
| 2 | Iwan Roberts | 7 | 7 | 69 | 415 mins |
| 3 | Phillip Mulryne | 6 | 8 | 68 | 465 mins |
| 4 | Malcolm Mackay | 6 | 6 | 75 | 544 mins |
| 5 | Mark Rivers | 4 | 4 | 73 | 570 mins |

## KEY PLAYERS - MIDFIELDERS

1 Phillip Mulryne

| | |
|---|---|
| **Goals in the League** | 6 |
| **Goals in all competitions** | 8 |
| **Defensive Rating** Average number of mins between League goals conceded while on the pitch | 100 |
| **Contribution to Attacking Power** Average number of minutes between League team goals while on pitch | 68 |
| **Scoring Difference** Defensive Rating minus Contribution to Attacking Power | 32 |

| | PLAYER | GOALS LGE | GOALS ALL | DEF RATE | ATT POWER | SCORE DIFF |
|---|---|---|---|---|---|---|
| 2 | Gary Holt | 0 | 0 | 84 | 68 | 16 mins |
| 3 | Mark Rivers | 4 | 4 | 88 | 74 | 14 mins |
| 4 | Darel Russell | 0 | 0 | 72 | 60 | 12 mins |
| 5 | Clint Easton | 2 | 2 | 70 | 67 | 3 mins |

## KEY PLAYERS - DEFENDERS

1 Steen Nedergaard

| | |
|---|---|
| **Goals Conceded in League** | 30 |
| **Goals Conceded in all competitions** | 35 |
| **Clean Sheets** In League games when he played at least 70 mins | 17 |
| **Defensive Rating** Ave number of mins between League goals conceded while on the pitch | 99 |
| **Club Defensive Rating** Average number of mins between League goals conceded by the club this season | 84 |

| | PLAYER | CON LGE | CON ALL | CLN SHEETS | DEF RATE |
|---|---|---|---|---|---|
| 2 | Adam Drury | 43 | 49 | 18 | 91 mins |
| 3 | Darren Kenton | 37 | 40 | 13 | 86 mins |
| 4 | Craig Fleming | 30 | 33 | 9 | 82 mins |
| 5 | Malcolm Mackay | 40 | 46 | 12 | 82 mins |

## KEY GOALKEEPER

1 Robert Green

| | |
|---|---|
| **Goals Conceded in the League** | 49 |
| **Goals Conceded in all competitions** | 55 |
| **Clean Sheets** In games when he played at least 70 mins | 18 |
| **Goals to Shots Ratio** The average number of shots on target per each League goal conceded | 5.5 |
| **Defensive Rating** Ave number of mins between League goals conceded while on the pitch | 84 |

## MONTHY POINTS TALLY

| Month | Points | % |
|---|---|---|
| AUGUST | 14 | 78% |
| SEPTEMBER | 10 | 56% |
| OCTOBER | 6 | 40% |
| NOVEMBER | 9 | 60% |
| DECEMBER | 4 | 27% |
| JANUARY | 7 | 58% |
| FEBRUARY | 5 | 33% |
| MARCH | 12 | 50% |
| APRIL | 5 | 33% |
| MAY | 3 | 100% |

## TOP POINT EARNERS

| | PLAYER | GAMES | AV PTS |
|---|---|---|---|
| 1 | Steen Nedergaard | 32 | 1.81 |
| 2 | Clint Easton | 19 | 1.68 |
| 3 | Paul McVeigh | 32 | 1.66 |
| 4 | Phillip Mulryne | 29 | 1.66 |
| 5 | Adam Drury | 43 | 1.58 |
| 6 | Darren Kenton | 35 | 1.57 |
| 7 | Mark Rivers | 23 | 1.57 |
| 8 | Iwan Roberts | 31 | 1.55 |
| 9 | Gary Holt | 45 | 1.53 |
| 10 | Robert Green | 46 | 1.50 |
| | CLUB AVERAGE: | | 1.50 |

## LEAGUE APPEARANCES, BOOKINGS AND CAPS

| | AGE (on 01/07/03) | IN THE SQUAD | COUNTING GAMES | MINUTES ON PITCH | YELLOW CARDS | RED CARDS | THIS SEASON | HOME COUNTRY |
|---|---|---|---|---|---|---|---|---|
| **Goalkeepers** | | | | | | | | |
| Paul Crichton | 34 | 41 | 0 | 0 | 0 | 0 | - | Wales |
| Robert Green | 23 | 46 | 46 | 4140 | 0 | 0 | - | England |
| Arran Lee-Barrett | 23 | 5 | 0 | 0 | 0 | 0 | - | England |
| **Defenders** | | | | | | | | |
| Keith Briggs | 21 | 5 | 1 | 113 | 0 | 0 | - | England |
| Leigh Bromby | 23 | 8 | 4 | 405 | 1 | 0 | - | England |
| Adam Drury | 24 | 45 | 43 | 3906 | 2 | 0 | - | England |
| Neil Emblen | 32 | 15 | 3 | 436 | 1 | 0 | - | England |
| Craig Fleming | 31 | 35 | 26 | 2452 | 4 | 0 | - | England |
| Darren Kenton | 24 | 40 | 35 | 3193 | 8 | 0 | - | England |
| Malcolm Mackay | 31 | 42 | 35 | 3266 | 2 | 0 | - | Scotland |
| Steen Nedergaard | 33 | 35 | 32 | 2958 | 5 | 0 | - | Denmark |
| **Midfielders** | | | | | | | | |
| Clint Easton | 25 | 30 | 19 | 1820 | 2 | 0 | - | England |
| Paul Heckingbottom | 25 | 16 | 6 | 711 | 1 | 0 | - | England |
| Gary Holt | 30 | 45 | 45 | 4050 | 3 | 0 | - | Scotland |
| Phillip Mulryne | 25 | 33 | 29 | 2790 | 7 | 0 | 2 | N Ireland (111) |
| Mark Rivers | 27 | 34 | 23 | 2280 | 0 | 0 | - | England |
| Darel Russell | 22 | 31 | 16 | 1511 | 5 | 0 | - | England |
| Jason Shackell | 19 | 5 | 2 | 180 | 0 | 0 | - | England |
| Dean Sinclair | 18 | 4 | 1 | 84 | 0 | 0 | - | England |
| Nicky Southall | 31 | 9 | 4 | 430 | 1 | 0 | - | England |
| Daryl Sutch | 31 | 1 | 0 | 0 | 0 | 0 | - | England |
| **Forwards** | | | | | | | | |
| Zema Abbey | 26 | 34 | 10 | 1216 | 3 | 0 | - | England |
| David Healy | 23 | 13 | 9 | 854 | 2 | 0 | 8 | N Ireland (111) |
| Ian Henderson | 18 | 21 | 3 | 573 | 3 | 0 | - | England |
| Ryan Jarvis | 16 | 3 | 1 | 164 | 0 | 0 | - | England |
| Chris Llewellyn | 23 | 8 | 2 | 238 | 0 | 0 | - | Wales |
| Paul McVeigh | 25 | 44 | 32 | 3207 | 4 | 0 | 7 | N Ireland (111) |
| David Nielsen | 26 | 36 | 11 | 1405 | 1 | 0 | - | Denmark |
| Alex Notman | 23 | 8 | 1 | 250 | 1 | 0 | - | Scotland |
| Iwan Roberts | 35 | 44 | 31 | 2908 | 3 | 0 | - | Wales |

KEY: LEAGUE BOOKINGS CAPS (FIFA RANKING)

## GOALS

**1 Paul McVeigh**

| | |
|---|---|
| League | 14 |
| FA Cup | 1 |
| League Cup | 0 |
| Other | 0 |
| TOTAL | 15 |

| | PLAYER | LGE | FAC | LC | Oth | TOT |
|---|---|---|---|---|---|---|
| 2 | Roberts | 7 | 0 | 0 | 0 | 7 |
| 3 | Mackay | 6 | 0 | 0 | 0 | 6 |
| 4 | Mulryne | 6 | 2 | 0 | 0 | 8 |
| 5 | Nielsen | 6 | 0 | 0 | 0 | 6 |
| 6 | Abbey | 5 | 1 | 0 | 0 | 6 |
| 7 | Rivers | 4 | 0 | 0 | 0 | 4 |
| 8 | Easton | 2 | 0 | 0 | 0 | 2 |
| 9 | Nedergaard | 2 | 0 | 0 | 0 | 2 |
| 10 | Drury | 2 | 0 | 0 | 0 | 2 |
| 11 | Healy | 2 | 0 | 0 | 0 | 2 |
| | Other | 4 | 0 | 0 | 0 | 4 |
| | TOTAL | 60 | 4 | 0 | 0 | 64 |

## TEAM OF THE SEASON

| GOALKEEPER | GAMES | DEF RATE |
|---|---|---|
| Robert Green | 46 | 84 |
| **DEFENDERS** | **GAMES** | **DEF RATE** |
| Steen Nedergaard | 32 | 99 |
| Adam Drury | 43 | 91 |
| Darren Kenton | 35 | 86 |
| Craig Fleming | 26 | 82 |
| **MIDFIELDERS** | **GAMES** | **SCORE DIFF** |
| Phillip Mulryne | 29 | 32 |
| Gary Holt | 45 | 16 |
| Mark Rivers | 23 | 14 |
| Darel Russell | 16 | 12 |
| **GOALSCORERS** | **GAMES** | **STRIKE RATE** |
| Paul McVeigh | 32 | 229 |
| Iwan Roberts | 31 | 415 |

Games = games playing at least 70 minutes

## SQUAD APPEARANCES

| Match | 1 | 2 | 3 | 4 | 5 | 6 | 7 | 8 | 9 | 10 | 11 | 12 | 13 | 14 | 15 | 16 | 17 | 18 | 19 | 20 | 21 | 22 | 23 | 24 | 25 |
|---|---|---|---|---|---|---|---|---|---|---|---|---|---|---|---|---|---|---|---|---|---|---|---|---|---|
| Venue | H | A | A | H | A | H | H | H | A | A | H | A | H | H | A | A | H | A | H | H | A | H | A | A | H |
| Competition | L | L | L | L | L | L | L | W | L | L | L | L | L | L | L | L | L | L | L | L | L | L | L | L | L |
| Result | W | D | W | W | D | W | L | L | D | W | W | W | D | W | D | L | D | L | W | W | L | W | L | L | W |

| Match | 26 | 27 | 28 | 29 | 30 | 31 | 32 | 33 | 34 | 35 | 36 | 37 | 38 | 39 | 40 | 41 | 42 | 43 | 44 | 45 | 46 | 47 | 48 | 49 | 50 |
|---|---|---|---|---|---|---|---|---|---|---|---|---|---|---|---|---|---|---|---|---|---|---|---|---|---|
| Venue | H | A | H | H | A | H | H | A | A | A | A | H | H | A | H | A | A | H | H | A | H | A | H | A | H |
| Competition | L | L | L | F | L | F | L | L | F | L | L | L | L | L | L | L | L | L | L | L | L | L | L | L | L |
| Result | L | D | D | W | L | W | D | D | L | W | L | L | L | L | W | W | L | W | W | L | W | D | L | D | W |

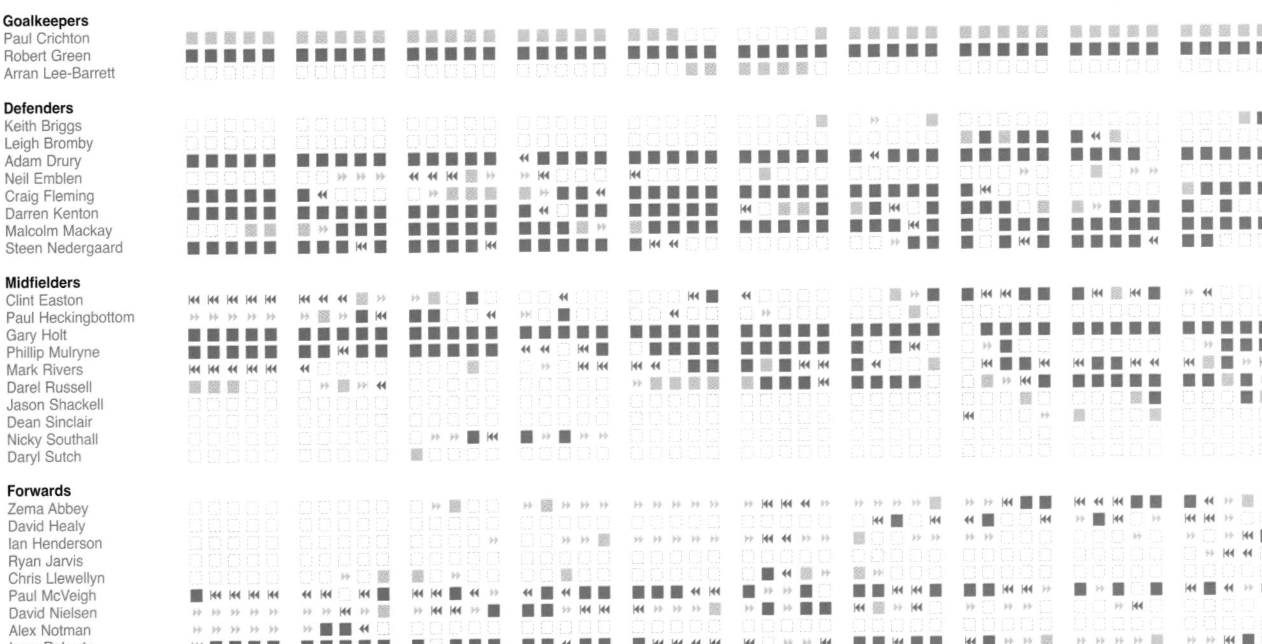
Goalkeepers
Paul Crichton
Robert Green
Arran Lee-Barrett
Defenders
Keith Briggs
Leigh Bromby
Adam Drury
Neil Emblen
Craig Fleming
Darren Kenton
Malcolm Mackay
Steen Nedergaard
Midfielders
Clint Easton
Paul Heckingbottom
Gary Holt
Phillip Mulryne
Mark Rivers
Darel Russell
Jason Shackell
Dean Sinclair
Nicky Southall
Daryl Sutch
Forwards
Zema Abbey
David Healy
Ian Henderson
Ryan Jarvis
Chris Llewellyn
Paul McVeigh
David Nielsen
Alex Notman
Iwan Roberts

KEY: On all match · On bench · Subbed or sent off (Counting game) · Subbed or sent off (playing less than 70 minutes) · Subbed on from bench (Counting Game) · Subbed on (playing less than 70 minutes) · Subbed on and then subbed or sent off (Counting Game) · Subbed on and then subbed or sent off (playing less than 70 minutes) · Not in 16

# MILLWALL

Final Position: **9th**

**NICKNAME:** THE LIONS

KEY: Won / Drawn / Lost

| | | | | | | |
|---|---|---|---|---|---|---|
| 1 | div1 | Rotherham | H | L | 0-6 | |
| 2 | div1 | Watford | A | D | 0-0 | |
| 3 | div1 | Gillingham | A | L | 0-1 | |
| 4 | div1 | Ipswich | H | D | 1-1 | May 4 |
| 5 | div1 | Sheff Utd | A | L | 1-3 | Ifill 89 |
| 6 | div1 | Grimsby | H | W | 2-0 | Claridge 7,60 |
| 7 | div1 | Brighton | H | W | 1-0 | Ward 73 |
| 8 | wcr1 | Rushden & D | A | L | 4-5* | (*on penalties) |
| 9 | div1 | Portsmouth | A | L | 0-1 | |
| 10 | div1 | Burnley | A | D | 2-2 | Livermore 31; Davies 64 |
| 11 | div1 | Walsall | H | L | 0-3 | |
| 12 | div1 | Coventry | A | W | 3-2 | Davies 38; Kinet 50; Harris 85 |
| 13 | div1 | Nottm Forest | H | L | 1-2 | Davies 44 |
| 14 | div1 | Wimbledon | H | D | 1-1 | Nethercott 82 |
| 15 | div1 | Norwich | A | L | 1-3 | Claridge 50 |
| 16 | div1 | Derby | H | W | 3-0 | Wise 43; Harris 81 pen,90 |
| 17 | div1 | Sheff Wed | A | W | 1-0 | Claridge 19 |
| 18 | div1 | Reading | A | L | 0-2 | |
| 19 | div1 | Preston | H | W | 2-1 | Ifill 10; Wise 16 |
| 20 | div1 | Leicester | H | D | 2-2 | Reid 28; Wise 81 |
| 21 | div1 | Stoke | A | W | 1-0 | Reid 2 |
| 22 | div1 | Bradford | H | W | 1-0 | Harris 82 |
| 23 | div1 | Crystal Palace | A | L | 0-1 | |
| 24 | div1 | Leicester | A | L | 1-4 | Claridge 1 |
| 25 | div1 | Wolves | H | D | 1-1 | Roberts 43 |
| 26 | div1 | Gillingham | H | D | 2-2 | Ryan 41; Harris 58 |
| 27 | div1 | Rotherham | A | W | 3-1 | Harris 40; Reid 48; Claridge 58 |
| 28 | div1 | Ipswich | A | L | 1-4 | Reid 64 |
| 29 | facr3 | Cambridge | A | D | 1-1 | Claridge 60 |
| 30 | div1 | Watford | H | W | 4-0 | Claridge 10; Ryan 41; Ifill 78; Sweeney 89 |
| 31 | facr3r | Cambridge | H | W | 3-2 | Claridge 60 pen; Robinson 70; Ifill 77 |
| 32 | div1 | Grimsby | A | W | 2-0 | Claridge 43,84 pen |
| 33 | facr4 | Southampton | A | D | 1-1 | Claridge 17 |
| 34 | div1 | Sheff Utd | H | W | 1-0 | Ifill 63 |
| 35 | facr4r | Southampton | H | L | 1-2 | Reid 37 |
| 36 | div1 | Preston | A | L | 1-2 | Kinet 88 |
| 37 | div1 | Reading | H | L | 0-2 | |
| 38 | div1 | Brighton | A | L | 0-1 | |
| 39 | div1 | Portsmouth | H | L | 0-5 | |
| 40 | div1 | Burnley | H | D | 1-1 | Sadlier 84 |
| 41 | div1 | Walsall | A | W | 2-1 | Harris 59; Ifill 62 |
| 42 | div1 | Wimbledon | A | L | 0-2 | |
| 43 | div1 | Norwich | H | L | 0-2 | |
| 44 | div1 | Sheff Wed | H | W | 3-0 | Reid 42,45; Ifill 54 |
| 45 | div1 | Bradford | A | W | 1-0 | Harris 90 |
| 46 | div1 | Stoke | H | W | 3-1 | Harris 19; Roberts 49; Livermore 55 |
| 47 | div1 | Derby | A | W | 2-1 | Harris 6; McCammon 63 |
| 48 | div1 | Wolves | A | L | 0-3 | |
| 49 | div1 | Crystal Palace | H | W | 3-2 | Harris 39 pen; McCammon 43; Cahill 74 |
| 50 | div1 | Nottm Forest | A | D | 3-3 | Nethercott 25; Cahill 67; Harris 87 |
| 51 | div1 | Coventry | H | W | 2-0 | Craig 51; Cahill 54 |

Home / Away / Neutral

## ATTENDANCES

**HOME GROUND:** THE NEW DEN **CAPACITY:** 20146 **AVERAGE LEAGUE AT HOME:** 8511

| | | | | | | | | | | | |
|---|---|---|---|---|---|---|---|---|---|---|---|
| 24 | Leicester | 31904 | 18 | Reading | 13081 | 25 | Wolves | 9091 | 37 | Reading | 7038 |
| 50 | Nottm Forest | 29463 | 5 | Sheff Utd | 13024 | 30 | Watford | 9030 | 31 | Cambridge | 7031 |
| 48 | Wolves | 27015 | 10 | Burnley | 11878 | 7 | Brighton | 8822 | 29 | Cambridge | 6864 |
| 28 | Ipswich | 26040 | 2 | Watford | 11187 | 46 | Stoke | 8725 | 43 | Norwich | 6854 |
| 33 | Southampton | 23809 | 26 | Gillingham | 10947 | 22 | Bradford | 8510 | 38 | Brighton | 6751 |
| 47 | Derby | 21014 | 20 | Leicester | 10772 | 14 | Wimbledon | 8248 | 6 | Grimsby | 6677 |
| 15 | Norwich | 20448 | 45 | Bradford | 10676 | 16 | Derby | 8116 | 41 | Walsall | 6647 |
| 23 | Crystal Palace | 19301 | 49 | Crystal Palace | 10670 | 4 | Ipswich | 8097 | 27 | Rotherham | 6448 |
| 9 | Portsmouth | 17201 | 13 | Nottm Forest | 10501 | 19 | Preston | 7554 | 40 | Burnley | 6045 |
| 17 | Sheff Wed | 16791 | 35 | Southampton | 10197 | 3 | Gillingham | 7543 | 32 | Grimsby | 4993 |
| 21 | Stoke | 13776 | 39 | Portsmouth | 9697 | 11 | Walsall | 7525 | 42 | Wimbledon | 2952 |
| 12 | Coventry | 13562 | 51 | Coventry | 9220 | 44 | Sheff Wed | 7338 | 8 | Rushden & D | 2731 |
| 36 | Preston | 13117 | 34 | Sheff Utd | 9102 | 1 | Rotherham | 7177 | | | |

## KEY PLAYERS - GOALSCORERS

**1 Neil Harris**

| | |
|---|---|
| **Goals in the League** | 12 |
| **Goals in all competitions** | 12 |
| **Contribution to Attacking Power** Average number of minutes between League team goals while on pitch | 67 |
| **Player Strike Rate** The total number of minutes he was on the pitch for every League goal scored | 252 |
| **Club Strike Rate** Average number of minutes between League goals scored by club | 69 |

| | PLAYER | GOALS LGE | GOALS ALL | POWER | S RATE |
|---|---|---|---|---|---|
| 2 | Steven Reid | 6 | 7 | 69 | 289 mins |
| 3 | Steve Claridge | 9 | 12 | 74 | 316 mins |
| 4 | Paul Ifill | 6 | 7 | 70 | 669 mins |
| 5 | Dennis Wise | 3 | 3 | 62 | 828 mins |

## KEY PLAYERS - MIDFIELDERS

**1 Dennis Wise**

| | |
|---|---|
| **Goals in the League** | 3 |
| **Goals in all competitions** | 3 |
| **Defensive Rating** Average number of mins between League goals conceded while on the pitch | 67 |
| **Contribution to Attacking Power** Average number of minutes between League team goals while on pitch | 62 |
| **Scoring Difference** Defensive Rating minus Contribution to Attacking Power | 5 |

| | PLAYER | GOALS LGE | GOALS ALL | DEF RATE | ATT POWER | SCORE DIFF |
|---|---|---|---|---|---|---|
| 2 | Andy Roberts | 2 | 2 | 61 | 62 | -1 mins |
| 3 | Matt Lawrence | 0 | 0 | 57 | 62 | -5 mins |
| 4 | Steven Reid | 6 | 7 | 64 | 72 | -8 mins |
| 5 | Christophe Kinet | 2 | 2 | 50 | 84 | -34 mins |

## KEY PLAYERS - DEFENDERS

**1 Paul Robinson**

| | |
|---|---|
| **Goals Conceded in League** | 19 |
| **Goals Conceded in all competitions** | 25 |
| **Clean Sheets** In League games when he played at least 70 mins | 4 |
| **Defensive Rating** Ave number of mins between League goals conceded while on the pitch | 61 |
| **Club Defensive Rating** Average number of mins between League goals conceded by the club this season | 60 |

| | PLAYER | CON LGE | CON ALL | CLN SHEETS | DEF RATE |
|---|---|---|---|---|---|
| 2 | Stuart Nethercott | 52 | 52 | 9 | 58 mins |
| 3 | Robert Ryan | 57 | 63 | 9 | 57 mins |
| 4 | Darren Ward | 60 | 66 | 9 | 56 mins |

## KEY GOALKEEPER

**1 Tony Warner**

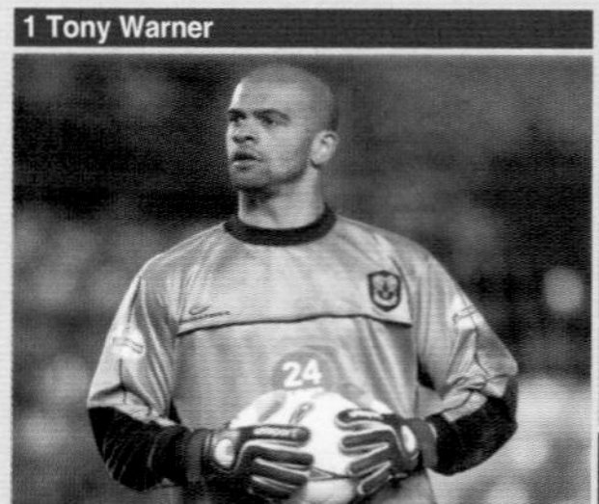

| | |
|---|---|
| **Goals Conceded in the League** | 69 |
| **Goals Conceded in all competitions** | 75 |
| **Clean Sheets** In games when he played at least 70 mins | 13 |
| **Goals to Shots Ratio** The average number of shots on target per each League goal conceded | 4.1 |
| **Defensive Rating** Ave number of mins between League goals conceded while on the pitch | 60 |

## MONTHY POINTS TALLY

| | | |
|---|---|---|
| AUGUST | 5 | 28% |
| SEPTEMBER | 8 | 44% |
| OCTOBER | 7 | 47% |
| NOVEMBER | 10 | 67% |
| DECEMBER | 5 | 33% |
| JANUARY | 11 | 61% |
| FEBRUARY | 3 | 20% |
| MARCH | 7 | 39% |
| APRIL | 13 | 72% |
| MAY | 3 | 100% |

## TOP POINT EARNERS

| | PLAYER | GAMES | AV PTS |
|---|---|---|---|
| 1 | Dennis Wise | 26 | 1.77 |
| 2 | Andy Roberts | 29 | 1.59 |
| 3 | Neil Harris | 30 | 1.57 |
| 4 | Robert Ryan | 32 | 1.56 |
| 5 | Stuart Nethercott | 33 | 1.52 |
| 6 | David Livermore | 40 | 1.50 |
| 7 | Paul Ifill | 44 | 1.48 |
| 8 | Steve Claridge | 27 | 1.48 |
| 9 | Tony Warner | 46 | 1.43 |
| 10 | Steven Reid | 19 | 1.42 |
| | CLUB AVERAGE: | | 1.43 |

## LEAGUE APPEARANCES, BOOKINGS AND CAPS

| | AGE (on 01/07/03) | IN THE SQUAD | COUNTING GAMES | MINUTES ON PITCH | YELLOW CARDS | RED CARDS | THIS SEASON | HOME COUNTRY |
|---|---|---|---|---|---|---|---|---|
| **Goalkeepers** | | | | | | | | |
| Willy Gueret | 29 | 46 | 0 | 0 | 0 | 0 | - | France |
| Tony Warner | 29 | 46 | 46 | 4140 | 1 | 0 | - | England |
| **Defenders** | | | | | | | | |
| Sergei Baltacha | 23 | 3 | 1 | 107 | 1 | 0 | - | Ukraine |
| Ronnie Bull | 22 | 26 | 5 | 677 | 2 | 0 | - | England |
| Tony Craig | - | 6 | 1 | 146 | 2 | 0 | - | England |
| Joe Dolan | 23 | 2 | 2 | 169 | 0 | 0 | - | England |
| Alan Dunne | 20 | 7 | 3 | 287 | 0 | 0 | - | Rep of Ireland |
| Glen Johnson | 18 | 8 | 7 | 643 | 0 | 0 | - | England |
| Stuart Nethercott | 30 | 37 | 33 | 3024 | 4 | 0 | - | England |
| Marcus Phillips | 20 | 15 | 4 | 415 | 0 | 0 | - | England |
| Matthew Rees | 20 | 3 | 0 | 0 | 0 | 0 | - | Wales |
| Paul Robinson | 21 | 18 | 12 | 1151 | 2 | 0 | 7 | England (7) |
| Robert Ryan | 26 | 45 | 32 | 3258 | 3 | 0 | - | Rep of Ireland |
| David Tuttle | 31 | 6 | 1 | 90 | 1 | 0 | - | England |
| Darren Ward | 24 | 41 | 36 | 3334 | 2 | 0 | - | England |
| **Midfielders** | | | | | | | | |
| Tim Cahill | 23 | 11 | 8 | 816 | 3 | 0 | - | Australia |
| Marvin Elliot | 18 | 3 | 0 | 24 | 0 | 0 | - | England |
| Charlie Hearn | 19 | 15 | 4 | 515 | 1 | 0 | - | England |
| Christophe Kinet | 24 | 33 | 9 | 1091 | 2 | 0 | - | Belgium |
| Matt Lawrence | 29 | 34 | 30 | 2731 | 7 | 1 | - | England |
| Ben May | 19 | 15 | 2 | 429 | 3 | 0 | - | England |
| Steven Reid | 22 | 20 | 19 | 1735 | 3 | 0 | - | England |
| Andy Roberts | 29 | 38 | 29 | 2737 | 4 | 0 | - | England |
| Peter Sweeney | 18 | 9 | 0 | 102 | 0 | 0 | - | Scotland |
| Dennis Wise | 36 | 30 | 26 | 2483 | 7 | 0 | - | England |
| **Forwards** | | | | | | | | |
| Moses Ashikodi | 16 | 6 | 1 | 118 | 1 | 0 | - | England |
| Kevin Braniff | 20 | 19 | 3 | 446 | 0 | 0 | - | N Ireland |
| Steve Claridge | 37 | 45 | 27 | 2847 | 3 | 0 | - | England |
| Kevin Davies | 26 | 10 | 5 | 585 | 3 | 0 | - | England |
| Neil Harris | 25 | 40 | 30 | 3022 | 7 | 0 | - | England |
| Paul Ifill | 23 | 45 | 44 | 4016 | 9 | 0 | - | England |
| David Livermore | 23 | 42 | 40 | 3642 | 15 | 1 | - | England |
| Mark McCammon | 24 | 7 | 5 | 505 | 1 | 0 | - | England |
| Richard Sadlier | 24 | 5 | 0 | 226 | 0 | 0 | - | Rep of Ireland |

KEY: LEAGUE BOOKINGS CAPS (FIFA RANKING)

## GOALS

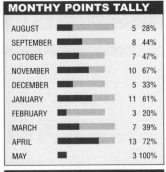

| 1 Neil Harris | |
|---|---|
| League | 12 |
| FA Cup | 0 |
| League Cup | 0 |
| Other | 0 |
| TOTAL | 12 |

| | PLAYER | LGE | FAC | LC | Oth | TOT |
|---|---|---|---|---|---|---|
| 2 | Claridge | 9 | 3 | 0 | 0 | 12 |
| 3 | Reid | 6 | 1 | 0 | 0 | 7 |
| 4 | Ifill | 6 | 1 | 0 | 0 | 7 |
| 5 | Cahill | 3 | 0 | 0 | 0 | 3 |
| 6 | Davies, K | 3 | 0 | 0 | 0 | 3 |
| 7 | Wise | 3 | 0 | 0 | 0 | 3 |
| 8 | Kinet | 2 | 0 | 0 | 0 | 2 |
| 9 | McCammon | 2 | 0 | 0 | 0 | 2 |
| 10 | Livermore | 2 | 0 | 0 | 0 | 2 |
| 11 | Nethercott | 2 | 0 | 0 | 0 | 2 |
| | Other | 9 | 1 | 0 | 0 | 10 |
| | TOTAL | 59 | 6 | 0 | 0 | 65 |

## TEAM OF THE SEASON

| GOALKEEPER | GAMES | DEF RATE |
|---|---|---|
| Tony Warner | 46 | 60 |
| **DEFENDERS** | **GAMES** | **DEF RATE** |
| Paul Robinson | 12 | 61 |
| Stuart Nethercott | 33 | 58 |
| Robert Ryan | 32 | 57 |
| Darren Ward | 36 | 56 |
| **MIDFIELDERS** | **GAMES** | **SCORE DIFF** |
| Dennis Wise | 26 | 5 |
| Andy Roberts | 29 | -1 |
| Matt Lawrence | 30 | -5 |
| Steven Reid | 19 | -8 |
| **GOALSCORERS** | **GAMES** | **STRIKE RATE** |
| Neil Harris | 30 | 252 |
| Steve Claridge | 27 | 316 |

Games = games playing at least 70 minutes

## SQUAD APPEARANCES

| Match | 1 | 2 | 3 | 4 | 5 | 6 | 7 | 8 | 9 | 10 | 11 | 12 | 13 | 14 | 15 | 16 | 17 | 18 | 19 | 20 | 21 | 22 | 23 | 24 | 25 | 26 | 27 | 28 | 29 | 30 | 31 | 32 | 33 | 34 | 35 | 36 | 37 | 38 | 39 | 40 | 41 | 42 | 43 | 44 | 45 | 46 | 47 | 48 | 49 | 50 | 51 |
|---|---|---|---|---|---|---|---|---|---|---|---|---|---|---|---|---|---|---|---|---|---|---|---|---|---|---|---|---|---|---|---|---|---|---|---|---|---|---|---|---|---|---|---|---|---|---|---|---|---|---|---|
| Venue | H | A | A | H | A | H | H | A | A | A | H | A | H | H | A | H | A | A | H | H | A | H | A | A | H | H | A | A | A | H | H | A | A | H | H | A | H | A | H | H | A | A | H | H | A | H | A | A | H | A | H |
| Competition | L | L | L | L | L | L | L | W | L | L | L | L | L | L | L | L | L | L | L | L | L | L | L | L | L | L | L | L | F | L | F | L | F | L | F | L | L | L | L | L | L | L | L | L | L | L | L | L | L | L | L |
| Result | L | D | L | D | L | W | W | L | L | D | L | W | L | D | L | W | W | L | W | D | W | W | L | L | D | D | W | L | D | W | W | W | D | W | D | L | L | L | L | D | W | L | L | W | W | W | W | L | W | D | W |

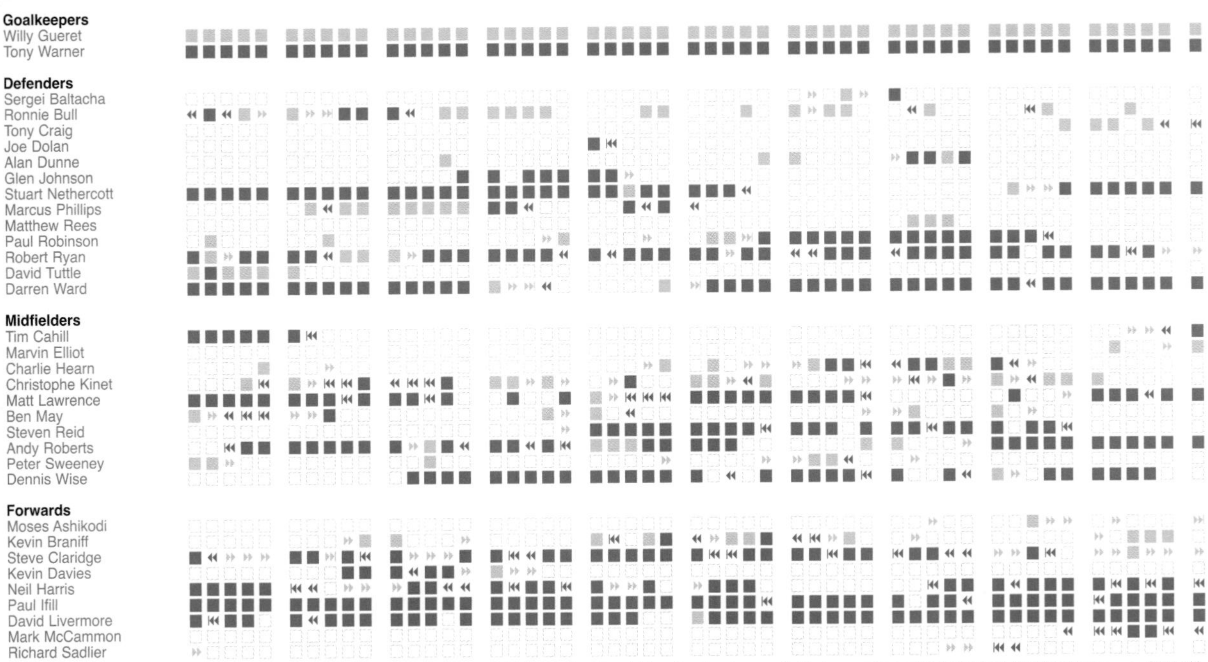
Goalkeepers
Willy Gueret
Tony Warner
Defenders
Sergei Baltacha
Ronnie Bull
Tony Craig
Joe Dolan
Alan Dunne
Glen Johnson
Stuart Nethercott
Marcus Phillips
Matthew Rees
Paul Robinson
Robert Ryan
David Tuttle
Darren Ward
Midfielders
Tim Cahill
Marvin Elliot
Charlie Hearn
Christophe Kinet
Matt Lawrence
Ben May
Steven Reid
Andy Roberts
Peter Sweeney
Dennis Wise
Forwards
Moses Ashikodi
Kevin Braniff
Steve Claridge
Kevin Davies
Neil Harris
Paul Ifill
David Livermore
Mark McCammon
Richard Sadlier

KEY: On all match | On bench | Subbed or sent off (Counting game) | Subbed or sent off (playing less than 70 minutes) | Subbed on from bench (Counting Game) | Subbed on (playing less than 70 minutes) | Subbed on and then subbed or sent off (Counting Game) | Subbed on and then subbed or sent off (playing less than 70 minutes) | Not in 16

# WIMBLEDON

Final Position: **10th**

NICKNAME: THE DONS/WOMBLES

KEY: ☐ Won ☐ Drawn ☐ Lost

| | | | | | | |
|---|---|---|---|---|---|---|
| 1 | div1 | Gillingham | H | L | 0-1 | |
| 2 | div1 | Grimsby | A | D | 0-0 | |
| 3 | div1 | Watford | A | L | 2-3 | Nowland 17; Francis 84 |
| 4 | div1 | Brighton | H | W | 1-0 | Shipperley 73 pen |
| 5 | div1 | Nottm Forest | A | L | 0-2 | |
| 6 | div1 | Wolves | H | W | 3-2 | Shipperley 3,76; Gray 55 |
| 7 | div1 | Leicester | H | L | 2-3 | Williams 10; Shipperley 15 |
| 8 | wcr1 | Southend | A | W | 4-1 | Andersen 45; Tapp 65; Shipperley 68,90 |
| 9 | div1 | Reading | A | W | 1-0 | McAnuff 90 |
| 10 | div1 | Portsmouth | A | L | 1-4 | Shipperley 10 |
| 11 | div1 | Coventry | H | L | 0-1 | |
| 12 | div1 | Burnley | A | L | 0-1 | |
| 13 | wcr2 | Portsmouth | A | W | 3-1 | McAnuff 6; Leigertwood 16; Shipperley 58 |
| 14 | div1 | Ipswich | H | L | 0-1 | |
| 15 | div1 | Millwall | A | D | 1-1 | Nethercott 71 og |
| 16 | div1 | Crystal Palace | H | D | 2-2 | Shipperley 76; Agyemang 79 |
| 17 | div1 | Sheff Utd | A | D | 1-1 | Connolly 12 |
| 18 | div1 | Rotherham | H | W | 2-1 | Shipperley 19; Connolly 60 |
| 19 | div1 | Norwich | H | W | 4-2 | Shipperley 24; Connolly 42,45,83 pen |
| 20 | wcr3 | Rotherham | H | L | 1-3 | Agyemang 35 |
| 21 | div1 | Bradford | A | W | 5-3 | Connolly 30,45,49,61; Darlington 89 |
| 22 | div1 | Walsall | H | W | 3-2 | McAnuff 25; Shipperley 69 pen; Francis 90 |
| 23 | div1 | Derby | A | L | 2-3 | Shipperley 7; Connolly 88 |
| 24 | div1 | Sheff Wed | H | W | 3-0 | Morgan 42; Connolly 63; Shipperley 89 |
| 25 | div1 | Preston | A | W | 5-3 | Connolly 40,65 pen; McAnuff 72,82; Reo-Coker 90 |
| 26 | div1 | Walsall | A | L | 0-2 | |
| 27 | div1 | Stoke | H | D | 1-1 | Connolly 82 |
| 28 | div1 | Watford | H | D | 0-0 | |
| 29 | facr3 | Rotherham | A | W | 3-0 | Shipperley 36; McAnuff 85; Morgan 90 |
| 30 | div1 | Grimsby | H | D | 3-3 | Agyemang 67; Darlington 69; Francis 73 |
| 31 | div1 | Wolves | A | D | 1-1 | Francis 46 |
| 32 | facr4 | Walsall | A | L | 0-1 | |
| 33 | div1 | Nottm Forest | H | L | 2-3 | Gray 59; Francis 63 |
| 34 | div1 | Brighton | A | W | 3-2 | Connolly 39,79; Volz 48 |
| 35 | div1 | Bradford | H | D | 2-2 | Ainsworth 47; Shipperley 71 |
| 36 | div1 | Leicester | A | L | 0-4 | |
| 37 | div1 | Reading | H | W | 2-0 | Francis 31; Tapp 85 |
| 38 | div1 | Portsmouth | H | W | 2-1 | Agyemang 66; Ainsworth 87 |
| 39 | div1 | Coventry | A | D | 2-2 | Connolly 12; Shipperley 76 |
| 40 | div1 | Gillingham | A | D | 3-3 | Connolly 4; Reo-Coker 79; Shipperley 87 pen |
| 41 | div1 | Millwall | H | W | 2-0 | Shipperley 19; Agyemang 90 |
| 42 | div1 | Crystal Palace | A | W | 1-0 | Andersen 45 |
| 43 | div1 | Rotherham | A | L | 1-2 | Connolly 59 |
| 44 | div1 | Norwich | A | L | 0-1 | |
| 45 | div1 | Sheff Wed | A | L | 2-4 | Connolly 54; Agyemang 55 |
| 46 | div1 | Sheff Utd | H | W | 1-0 | Shipperley 38 |
| 47 | div1 | Derby | H | L | 0-2 | |
| 48 | div1 | Stoke | A | L | 1-2 | Shipperley 51 |
| 49 | div1 | Preston | H | W | 2-0 | Shipperley 60,65 |
| 50 | div1 | Ipswich | A | W | 5-1 | Shipperley 28; Nowland 60; Connolly 83,85; Tapp 88 |
| 51 | div1 | Burnley | H | W | 2-1 | Connolly 55,81 |

☐ Home ☐ Away ☐ Neutral

## ATTENDANCES

HOME GROUND: SELHURST PARK CAPACITY: 26309 AVERAGE LEAGUE AT HOME: 2786

| | | | | | | | | | | | |
|---|---|---|---|---|---|---|---|---|---|---|---|
| 36 | Leicester | 31438 | 12 | Burnley | 12259 | 2 | Grimsby | 4625 | 24 | Sheff Wed | 2131 |
| 23 | Derby | 25597 | 39 | Coventry | 11796 | 29 | Rotherham | 4527 | 11 | Coventry | 2077 |
| 50 | Ipswich | 25564 | 13 | Portsmouth | 11754 | 19 | Norwich | 3908 | 51 | Burnley | 1972 |
| 31 | Wolves | 23716 | 21 | Bradford | 10615 | 37 | Reading | 3869 | 47 | Derby | 1934 |
| 44 | Norwich | 21059 | 38 | Portsmouth | 10356 | 33 | Nottm Forest | 3382 | 27 | Stoke | 1697 |
| 10 | Portsmouth | 18837 | 3 | Watford | 10292 | 14 | Ipswich | 3238 | 30 | Grimsby | 1336 |
| 45 | Sheff Wed | 17649 | 15 | Millwall | 8248 | 6 | Wolves | 3223 | 46 | Sheff Utd | 1325 |
| 17 | Sheff Utd | 17372 | 40 | Gillingham | 7884 | 41 | Millwall | 2952 | 22 | Walsall | 1255 |
| 5 | Nottm Forest | 16431 | 32 | Walsall | 6693 | 28 | Watford | 2643 | 35 | Bradford | 1178 |
| 9 | Reading | 14832 | 26 | Walsall | 6596 | 8 | Southend | 2634 | 49 | Preston | 1053 |
| 42 | Crystal Palace | 13713 | 16 | Crystal Palace | 6538 | 4 | Brighton | 2522 | 18 | Rotherham | 849 |
| 48 | Stoke | 12587 | 34 | Brighton | 6111 | 1 | Gillingham | 2476 | 20 | Rotherham | 664 |
| 25 | Preston | 12415 | 43 | Rotherham | 5896 | 7 | Leicester | 2165 | | | |

## KEY PLAYERS - GOALSCORERS

1 David Connolly

| | |
|---|---|
| Goals in the League | 24 |
| Goals in all competitions | 24 |
| Contribution to Attacking Power<br>Average number of minutes between League team goals while on pitch | 46 |
| Player Strike Rate<br>The total number of minutes he was on the pitch for every League goal scored | 102 |
| Club Strike Rate<br>Average number of minutes between League goals scored by club | 54 |

| | PLAYER | GOALS LGE | GOALS ALL | POWER | S RATE |
|---|---|---|---|---|---|
| 2 | Neil Shipperley | 20 | 24 | 54 | 198 mins |
| 3 | Damian Francis | 6 | 6 | 56 | 442 mins |
| 4 | Jobi McAnuff | 4 | 6 | 53 | 663 mins |
| 5 | Alex Tapp | 2 | 3 | 67 | 985 mins |

## KEY PLAYERS - MIDFIELDERS

1 Nigel Reo-Coker

| | |
|---|---|
| Goals in the League | 2 |
| Goals in all competitions | 2 |
| Defensive Rating<br>Average number of mins between League goals conceded while on the pitch | 55 |
| Contribution to Attacking Power<br>Average number of minutes between League team goals while on pitch | 49 |
| Scoring Difference<br>Defensive Rating minus Contribution to Attacking Power | 6 |

| | PLAYER | GOALS LGE | GOALS ALL | DEF RATE | ATT POWER | SCORE DIFF |
|---|---|---|---|---|---|---|
| 2 | Jobi McAnuff | 4 | 6 | 59 | 53 | 6 mins |
| 3 | Damian Francis | 6 | 6 | 60 | 56 | 4 mins |
| 4 | Robert Gier | 0 | 0 | 47 | 49 | -2 mins |
| 5 | Alex Tapp | 2 | 3 | 64 | 68 | -4 mins |

## KEY PLAYERS - DEFENDERS

1 Ben Chorley

| | |
|---|---|
| Goals Conceded in League | 11 |
| Goals Conceded in all competitions | 11 |
| Clean Sheets<br>In League games when he played at least 70 mins | 3 |
| Defensive Rating<br>Ave number of mins between League goals conceded while on the pitch | 76 |
| Club Defensive Rating<br>Average number of mins between League goals conceded by the club this season | 55 |

| | PLAYER | CON LGE | CON ALL | CLN SHEETS | DEF RATE |
|---|---|---|---|---|---|
| 2 | Peter Hawkins | 63 | 66 | 10 | 59 mins |
| 3 | Trond Andersen | 54 | 57 | 7 | 57 mins |
| 4 | Darren Holloway | 23 | 28 | 1 | 54 mins |
| 5 | Mark Williams | 38 | 39 | 6 | 53 mins |

## KEY GOALKEEPER

1 Kelvin Davis

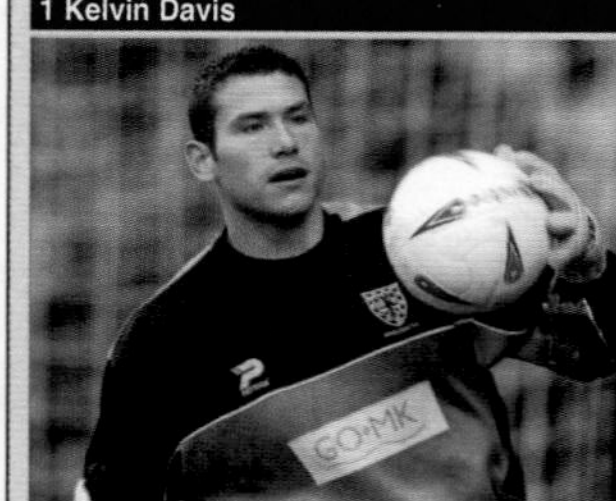

| | |
|---|---|
| Goals Conceded in the League | 75 |
| Goals Conceded in all competitions | 81 |
| Clean Sheets<br>In games when he played at least 70 mins | 10 |
| Goals to Shots Ratio<br>The average number of shots on target per each League goal conceded | 3.2 |
| Defensive Rating<br>Ave number of mins between League goals conceded while on the pitch | 55 |

## MONTHY POINTS TALLY

| Month | Points | % |
|---|---|---|
| AUGUST | 7 | 39% |
| SEPTEMBER | 6 | 33% |
| OCTOBER | 9 | 50% |
| NOVEMBER | 12 | 67% |
| DECEMBER | 5 | 42% |
| JANUARY | 5 | 42% |
| FEBRUARY | 4 | 33% |
| MARCH | 14 | 58% |
| APRIL | 9 | 50% |
| MAY | 3 | 100% |

## TOP POINT EARNERS

| | PLAYER | GAMES | AV PTS |
|---|---|---|---|
| 1 | David Connolly | 27 | **1.70** |
| 2 | Nigel Reo-Coker | 30 | **1.57** |
| 3 | Mikele Leigertwood | 27 | **1.52** |
| 4 | Peter Hawkins | 41 | **1.49** |
| 5 | Neil Shipperley | 43 | **1.44** |
| 6 | Alex Tapp | 21 | **1.43** |
| 7 | Trond Andersen | 33 | **1.42** |
| 8 | Jobi McAnuff | 29 | **1.41** |
| 9 | Kelvin Davis | 46 | **1.41** |
| 10 | Jermaine Darlington | 28 | **1.39** |
| | **CLUB AVERAGE:** | | **1.41** |

## LEAGUE APPEARANCES, BOOKINGS AND CAPS

| | AGE (on 01/07/03) | IN THE SQUAD | COUNTING GAMES | MINUTES ON PITCH | YELLOW CARDS | RED CARDS | THIS SEASON | HOME COUNTRY |
|---|---|---|---|---|---|---|---|---|
| **Goalkeepers** | | | | | | | | |
| Kelvin Davis | 26 | 46 | 46 | 4140 | 1 | 0 | - | England |
| Shane Gore | 21 | 20 | 0 | 0 | 0 | 0 | - | England |
| Paul Heald | 34 | 26 | 0 | 0 | 0 | 0 | - | England |
| **Defenders** | | | | | | | | |
| Trond Andersen | 28 | 38 | 33 | 3061 | 4 | 0 | 11 | Norway (24) |
| Ben Chorley | 20 | 13 | 9 | 833 | 3 | 0 | - | England |
| Jermaine Darlington | 29 | 37 | 28 | 2746 | 2 | 0 | - | England |
| Heikki Haara | 20 | 2 | 1 | 90 | 0 | 0 | - | Finland |
| Peter Hawkins | 24 | 45 | 41 | 3735 | 5 | 0 | - | England |
| Darren Holloway | 25 | 18 | 13 | 1233 | 2 | 0 | - | England |
| Mikele Leigertwood | 20 | 34 | 27 | 2433 | 1 | 0 | - | England |
| Dean Lewington | 19 | 4 | 0 | 2 | 0 | 0 | - | England |
| Moritz Volz | 20 | 10 | 10 | 900 | 2 | 0 | - | Germany |
| Mark Williams | 32 | 23 | 22 | 2032 | 5 | 1 | 6 | N Ireland (111) |
| Christopher Willmott | 25 | 18 | 5 | 450 | 1 | 0 | - | England |
| **Midfielders** | | | | | | | | |
| Gareth Ainsworth | 30 | 15 | 7 | 740 | 1 | 0 | - | England |
| Damian Francis | 24 | 35 | 28 | 2650 | 4 | 0 | - | England |
| Robert Gier | 22 | 38 | 28 | 2494 | 2 | 1 | - | England |
| Michael Gordon | 18 | 3 | 0 | 27 | 0 | 0 | - | England |
| Nico Herzig | 19 | 2 | 0 | 0 | 0 | 0 | - | Germany |
| Malvin Kamara | 19 | 5 | 0 | 39 | 1 | 0 | - | England |
| Par Karlsson | 25 | 5 | 1 | 190 | 0 | 0 | - | Sweden |
| Jobi McAnuff | 21 | 31 | 29 | 2650 | 2 | 0 | - | Jamaica |
| Hakan Mild | 32 | 1 | 0 | 0 | 0 | 0 | - | Sweden |
| Nigel Reo-Coker | 19 | 36 | 30 | 2750 | 2 | 0 | - | England |
| Alex Tapp | 21 | 33 | 21 | 1970 | 4 | 0 | - | England |
| **Forwards** | | | | | | | | |
| Patrick Agyemang | 22 | 37 | 9 | 1271 | 3 | 0 | - | England |
| David Connolly | 26 | 28 | 27 | 2443 | 1 | 0 | 5 | Rep of Ireland (15) |
| Wayne Gray | 22 | 44 | 10 | 1238 | 1 | 0 | - | England |
| Lionel Morgan | 20 | 15 | 2 | 465 | 0 | 0 | - | England |
| Adam Nowland | 22 | 27 | 6 | 947 | 3 | 1 | - | England |
| Neil Shipperley | 28 | 46 | 43 | 3966 | 4 | 0 | - | England |

**KEY:** LEAGUE BOOKINGS CAPS (FIFA RANKING)

## GOALS

**1 David Connolly**

| | |
|---|---|
| League | 24 |
| FA Cup | 0 |
| League Cup | 0 |
| Other | 0 |
| TOTAL | 24 |

| | PLAYER | LGE | FAC | LC | Oth | TOT |
|---|---|---|---|---|---|---|
| 2 | Shipperley | 20 | 1 | 3 | 0 | 24 |
| 3 | Francis | 6 | 0 | 0 | 0 | 6 |
| 4 | Agyemang | 5 | 0 | 1 | 0 | 6 |
| 5 | McAnuff | 4 | 1 | 1 | 0 | 6 |
| 6 | Gray | 2 | 0 | 0 | 0 | 2 |
| 7 | Nowland | 2 | 0 | 0 | 0 | 2 |
| 8 | Tapp | 2 | 0 | 1 | 0 | 3 |
| 9 | Darlington | 2 | 0 | 0 | 0 | 2 |
| 10 | Reo-Coker | 2 | 0 | 0 | 0 | 2 |
| 11 | Ainsworth | 2 | 0 | 0 | 0 | 2 |
| | Other | 5 | 1 | 2 | 0 | 8 |
| | **TOTAL** | **76** | **3** | **8** | **0** | **87** |

## TEAM OF THE SEASON

| GOALKEEPER | GAMES | DEF RATE |
|---|---|---|
| Kelvin Davis | 46 | 55 |
| **DEFENDERS** | **GAMES** | **DEF RATE** |
| Beb Chorley | 9 | 76 |
| Peter Hawkins | 41 | 59 |
| Trond Andersen | 33 | 57 |
| Darren Holloway | 13 | 54 |
| **MIDFIELDERS** | **GAMES** | **SCORE DIFF** |
| Nigel Reo-Coker | 30 | 6 |
| Jobi McAnuff | 29 | 6 |
| Damian Francis | 28 | 4 |
| Robert Gier | 28 | -2 |
| **GOALSCORERS** | **GAMES** | **STRIKE RATE** |
| David Connolly | 27 | 102 |
| Neil Shipperley | 43 | 198 |

Games = games playing at least 70 minutes

## SQUAD APPEARANCES

| Match | 1 | 2 | 3 | 4 | 5 | 6 | 7 | 8 | 9 | 10 | 11 | 12 | 13 | 14 | 15 | 16 | 17 | 18 | 19 | 20 | 21 | 22 | 23 | 24 | 25 |
|---|---|---|---|---|---|---|---|---|---|---|---|---|---|---|---|---|---|---|---|---|---|---|---|---|---|
| Venue | H | A | A | H | A | H | H | A | A | A | H | A | A | H | A | H | A | H | H | H | A | H | A | H | A |
| Competition | L | L | L | L | L | L | L | W | L | L | L | L | W | L | L | L | L | L | L | W | L | L | L | L | L |
| Result | L | D | L | W | L | W | L | W | W | L | L | L | W | L | D | D | D | W | W | L | W | W | L | W | W |

| Match | 26 | 27 | 28 | 29 | 30 | 31 | 32 | 33 | 34 | 35 | 36 | 37 | 38 | 39 | 40 | 41 | 42 | 43 | 44 | 45 | 46 | 47 | 48 | 49 | 50 | 51 |
|---|---|---|---|---|---|---|---|---|---|---|---|---|---|---|---|---|---|---|---|---|---|---|---|---|---|---|
| Venue | A | H | H | A | H | A | A | H | A | H | A | H | H | A | A | H | A | A | A | A | H | H | A | H | A | H |
| Competition | L | L | L | F | L | L | F | L | L | L | L | L | L | L | L | L | L | L | L | L | L | L | L | L | L | L |
| Result | L | D | D | W | D | D | L | L | W | D | L | W | W | D | D | W | W | L | L | L | W | L | L | W | W | W |

**Goalkeepers**
Kelvin Davis
Shane Gore
Paul Heald

**Defenders**
Trond Andersen
Ben Chorley
Jermaine Darlington
Heikki Haara
Peter Hawkins
Darren Holloway
Mikele Leigertwood
Dean Lewington
Moritz Volz
Mark Williams
Christopher Willmott

**Midfielders**
Gareth Ainsworth
Damian Francis
Robert Gier
Michael Gordon
Nico Herzig
Malvin Kamara
Par Karlsson
Jobi McAnuff
Hakan Mild
Nigel Reo-Coker
Alex Tapp

**Forwards**
Patrick Agyemang
David Connolly
Wayne Gray
Lionel Morgan
Adam Nowland
Neil Shipperley

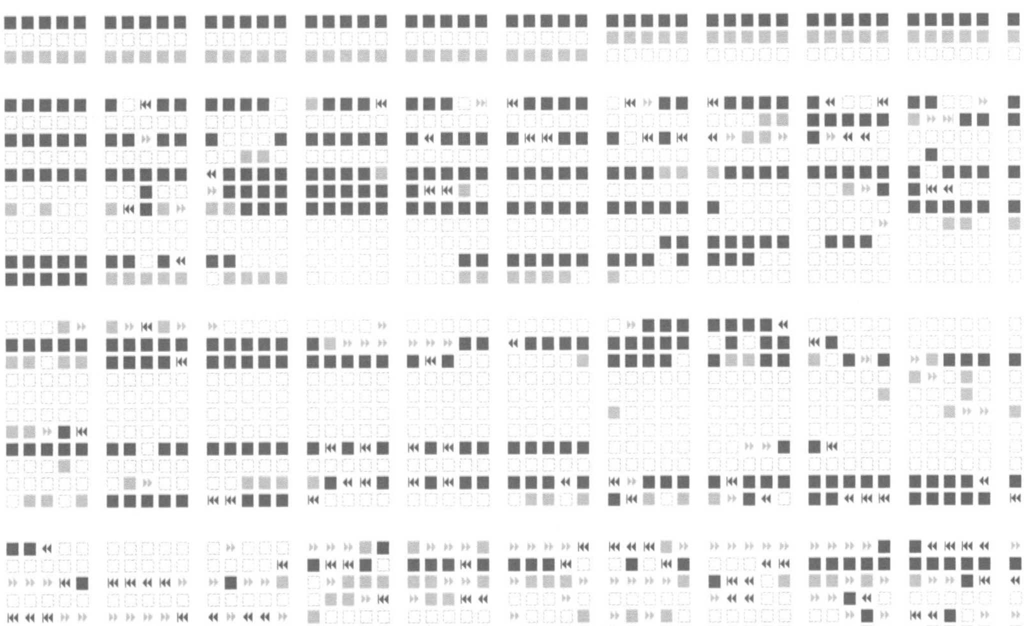

**KEY:** On all match | On bench | Subbed or sent off (Counting game) | Subbed or sent off (playing less than 70 minutes) | Subbed on from bench (Counting Game) | Subbed on (playing less than 70 minutes) | Subbed on and then subbed or sent off (Counting Game) | Subbed on and then subbed or sent off (playing less than 70 minutes) | Not in 16

# GILLINGHAM

Final Position: **11th**

NICKNAME: THE GILLS

KEY: Won / Drawn / Lost

| | | | | | | |
|---|---|---|---|---|---|---|
| 1 | div1 | **Wimbledon** | A | W | 1-0 | Ipoua 48 |
| 2 | div1 | **Derby** | H | W | 1-0 | Shaw 16 |
| 3 | div1 | **Millwall** | H | W | 1-0 | Ipoua 61 |
| 4 | div1 | **Norwich** | A | L | 0-1 | |
| 5 | div1 | **Preston** | H | D | 1-1 | Saunders 62 |
| 6 | div1 | **Leicester** | A | L | 0-2 | |
| 7 | div1 | **Portsmouth** | H | L | 1-3 | James 67 |
| 8 | wcr1 | **Torquay** | A | W | 1-0 | Hessenthaler 69 |
| 9 | div1 | **Brighton** | A | W | 4-2 | Shaw 11,36; Perpetuini 12; James 90 |
| 10 | div1 | **Nottm Forest** | A | L | 1-4 | Hessenthaler 5 |
| 11 | div1 | **Sheff Utd** | H | D | 1-1 | Shaw 16 |
| 12 | div1 | **Crystal Palace** | A | D | 2-2 | Perpetuini 23; Mullins 66 og |
| 13 | wcr2 | **Stockport** | A | W | 2-1 | Ipoua 25; Johnson, T 113 |
| 14 | div1 | **Coventry** | H | L | 0-2 | |
| 15 | div1 | **Rotherham** | A | D | 1-1 | Wallace 17 |
| 16 | div1 | **Watford** | H | W | 3-0 | Sidibe 2; Ipoua 33; James 90 |
| 17 | div1 | **Ipswich** | A | W | 1-0 | Sidibe 34 |
| 18 | div1 | **Wolves** | H | L | 0-4 | |
| 19 | div1 | **Grimsby** | A | D | 1-1 | Saunders 89 |
| 20 | wcr3 | **Chelsea** | A | L | 1-2 | King 90 |
| 21 | div1 | **Reading** | H | L | 0-1 | |
| 22 | div1 | **Sheff Wed** | H | D | 1-1 | Johnson, T 24 |
| 23 | div1 | **Walsall** | A | L | 0-1 | |
| 24 | div1 | **Stoke** | H | D | 1-1 | Shaw 52 |
| 25 | div1 | **Bradford** | A | W | 3-1 | King 59 pen,74; Wallace 90 |
| 26 | div1 | **Sheff Wed** | A | W | 2-0 | Wallace 5; Smith 74 |
| 27 | div1 | **Burnley** | H | W | 4-2 | Wallace 17; Smith 41,45; King 64 |
| 28 | div1 | **Millwall** | A | D | 2-2 | Saunders 8; King 60 pen |
| 29 | facr3 | **Sheff Wed** | H | W | 4-1 | King 12,18 pen; Ipoua 41; Hope 75 |
| 30 | div1 | **Derby** | A | D | 1-1 | Ipoua 57 |
| 31 | div1 | **Leicester** | H | W | 3-2 | Shaw 32; Elliott 45 og; Sidibe 86 |
| 32 | facr4 | **Leeds** | H | D | 1-1 | Sidibe 82 |
| 33 | div1 | **Preston** | A | L | 0-3 | |
| 34 | facr4r | **Leeds** | A | L | 1-2 | Ipoua 86 |
| 35 | div1 | **Reading** | A | L | 1-2 | Wallace 10 |
| 36 | div1 | **Grimsby** | H | W | 3-0 | Wallace 6,14; Hope 45 |
| 37 | div1 | **Portsmouth** | A | L | 0-1 | |
| 38 | div1 | **Norwich** | H | W | 1-0 | Wallace 75 |
| 39 | div1 | **Brighton** | H | W | 3-0 | Shaw 47; Johnson, T 60 pen; Southall 76 |
| 40 | div1 | **Nottm Forest** | H | L | 1-4 | Wallace 79 |
| 41 | div1 | **Wimbledon** | H | D | 3-3 | Shaw 59,80; Wallace 75 |
| 42 | div1 | **Rotherham** | H | D | 1-1 | Wallace 22 |
| 43 | div1 | **Watford** | A | W | 1-0 | Shaw 65 |
| 44 | div1 | **Wolves** | A | L | 0-6 | |
| 45 | div1 | **Sheff Utd** | A | D | 2-2 | Osborn 53; Shaw 69 |
| 46 | div1 | **Ipswich** | H | L | 1-3 | Smith 28 |
| 47 | div1 | **Stoke** | A | D | 0-0 | |
| 48 | div1 | **Walsall** | H | L | 0-1 | |
| 49 | div1 | **Burnley** | A | L | 0-2 | |
| 50 | div1 | **Bradford** | H | W | 1-0 | Shaw 29 |
| 51 | div1 | **Coventry** | A | D | 0-0 | |
| 52 | div1 | **Crystal Palace** | H | W | 2-1 | King 3; Nosworthy 5 |

Home / Away / Neutral

## ATTENDANCES

HOME GROUND: PRIESTFIELD STADIUM CAPACITY: 12500 AVERAGE LEAGUE AT HOME: 8081

| | | | | | | | | | | | |
|---|---|---|---|---|---|---|---|---|---|---|---|
| 6 | Leicester | 30067 | 47 | Stoke | 12746 | 21 | Reading | 8511 | 48 | Walsall | 6972 |
| 34 | Leeds | 29359 | 33 | Preston | 12121 | 46 | Ipswich | 8508 | 9 | Brighton | 6733 |
| 20 | Chelsea | 28033 | 32 | Leeds | 11093 | 24 | Stoke | 8150 | 23 | Walsall | 6630 |
| 44 | Wolves | 25171 | 35 | Reading | 11030 | 22 | Sheff Wed | 8028 | 29 | Sheff Wed | 6434 |
| 17 | Ipswich | 24176 | 28 | Millwall | 10947 | 38 | Norwich | 7935 | 50 | Bradford | 6281 |
| 30 | Derby | 22769 | 25 | Bradford | 10711 | 27 | Burnley | 7905 | 15 | Rotherham | 6094 |
| 4 | Norwich | 20588 | 43 | Watford | 10492 | 41 | Wimbledon | 7884 | 19 | Grimsby | 5715 |
| 37 | Portsmouth | 19521 | 18 | Wolves | 10036 | 5 | Preston | 7785 | 1 | Wimbledon | 2476 |
| 26 | Sheff Wed | 17715 | 52 | Crystal Palace | 9315 | 14 | Coventry | 7722 | 13 | Stockport | 2396 |
| 10 | Nottm Forest | 16073 | 39 | Brighton | 9178 | 3 | Millwall | 7543 | 8 | Torquay | 1981 |
| 45 | Sheff Utd | 15799 | 7 | Portsmouth | 8797 | 11 | Sheff Utd | 7497 | | | |
| 12 | Crystal Palace | 15699 | 2 | Derby | 8775 | 42 | Rotherham | 7284 | | | |
| 51 | Coventry | 14795 | 16 | Watford | 8728 | 40 | Nottm Forest | 7277 | | | |
| 49 | Burnley | 14031 | 31 | Leicester | 8609 | 36 | Grimsby | 7158 | | | |

## KEY PLAYERS - GOALSCORERS

1 Rod Wallace

| | |
|---|---|
| Goals in the League | 11 |
| Goals in all competitions | 11 |
| Contribution to Attacking Power<br>Average number of minutes between League team goals while on pitch | 54 |
| Player Strike Rate<br>The total number of minutes he was on the pitch for every League goal scored | 133 |
| Club Strike Rate<br>Average number of minutes between League goals scored by club | 74 |

| | PLAYER | GOALS LGE | GOALS ALL | POWER | S RATE |
|---|---|---|---|---|---|
| 2 | Paul Shaw | 12 | 12 | 68 | 304 mins |
| 3 | Guy Ipoua | 4 | 7 | 74 | 484 mins |
| 4 | Mamady Sidibe | 3 | 4 | 104 | 695 mins |
| 5 | David Perpetuini | 2 | 2 | 84 | 717 mins |

## KEY PLAYERS - MIDFIELDERS

1 Nayron Nosworthy

SEAFRANCE

| | |
|---|---|
| Goals in the League | 1 |
| Goals in all competitions | 1 |
| Defensive Rating<br>Average number of mins between League goals conceded while on the pitch | 82 |
| Contribution to Attacking Power<br>Average number of minutes between League team goals while on pitch | 80 |
| Scoring Difference<br>Defensive Rating minus Contribution to Attacking Power | 2 |

| | PLAYER | GOALS LGE | GOALS ALL | DEF RATE | ATT POWER | SCORE DIFF |
|---|---|---|---|---|---|---|
| 2 | Andy Hessenthaler | 1 | 2 | 72 | 72 | 0 mins |
| 3 | Nicky Southall | 1 | 1 | 59 | 63 | -4 mins |
| 4 | Paul Smith | 4 | 4 | 63 | 72 | -9 mins |
| 5 | Mark Saunders | 3 | 3 | 52 | 63 | -11 mins |

## KEY PLAYERS - DEFENDERS

1 Barry Ashby

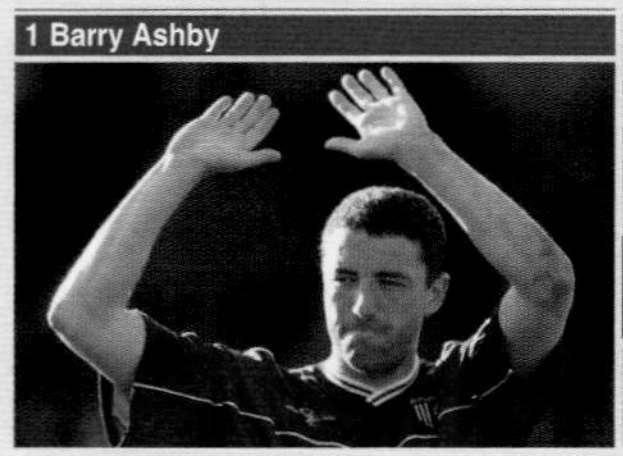

| | |
|---|---|
| Goals Conceded in League | 47 |
| Goals Conceded in all competitions | 52 |
| Clean Sheets<br>In League games when he played at least 70 mins | 11 |
| Defensive Rating<br>Ave number of mins between League goals conceded while on the pitch | 70 |
| Club Defensive Rating<br>Average number of mins between League goals conceded by the club this season | 64 |

| | PLAYER | CON LGE | CON ALL | CLN SHEETS | DEF RATE |
|---|---|---|---|---|---|
| 2 | Chris Hope | 65 | 72 | 13 | 64 mins |
| 3 | Roland Edge | 48 | 51 | 10 | 62 mins |
| 4 | David Perpetuini | 28 | 33 | 2 | 51 mins |

## KEY GOALKEEPER

1 Jason Brown

| | |
|---|---|
| Goals Conceded in the League | 46 |
| Goals Conceded in all competitions | 52 |
| Clean Sheets<br>In games when he played at least 70 mins | 12 |
| Goals to Shots Ratio<br>The average number of shots on target per each League goal conceded | 4.7 |
| Defensive Rating<br>Ave number of mins between League goals conceded while on the pitch | 75 |

## MONTHY POINTS TALLY

| | | |
|---|---|---|
| AUGUST | 10 | 56% |
| SEPTEMBER | 8 | 44% |
| OCTOBER | 10 | 56% |
| NOVEMBER | 3 | 17% |
| DECEMBER | 10 | 83% |
| JANUARY | 8 | 67% |
| FEBRUARY | 6 | 33% |
| MARCH | 9 | 38% |
| APRIL | 5 | 33% |
| MAY | 3 | 100% |

## TOP POINT EARNERS

| | PLAYER | GAMES | AV PTS |
|---|---|---|---|
| 1 | Jason Brown | 38 | 1.55 |
| 2 | Guy Ipoua | 18 | 1.50 |
| 3 | Nicky Southall | 21 | 1.48 |
| 4 | Mamady Sidibe | 21 | 1.48 |
| 5 | Andy Hessenthaler | 28 | 1.46 |
| 6 | Nayron Nosworthy | 37 | 1.46 |
| 7 | Paul Shaw | 39 | 1.46 |
| 8 | Roland Edge | 31 | 1.45 |
| 9 | Paul Smith | 45 | 1.38 |
| 10 | Barry Ashby | 36 | 1.36 |
| | CLUB AVERAGE: | | 1.35 |

## GOALS

**1 Paul Shaw**

| | |
|---|---|
| League | 12 |
| FA Cup | 0 |
| League Cup | 0 |
| Other | 0 |
| TOTAL | 12 |

| | PLAYER | LGE | FAC | LC | Oth | TOT |
|---|---|---|---|---|---|---|
| 2 | Wallace | 11 | 0 | 0 | 0 | 11 |
| 3 | King | 4 | 2 | 1 | 0 | 7 |
| 4 | Smith | 4 | 0 | 0 | 0 | 4 |
| 5 | Ipoua | 4 | 2 | 1 | 0 | 7 |
| 6 | Saunders | 3 | 0 | 0 | 0 | 3 |
| 7 | James | 3 | 0 | 0 | 0 | 3 |
| 8 | Sidibe | 3 | 1 | 0 | 0 | 4 |
| 9 | Perpetuini | 2 | 0 | 0 | 0 | 2 |
| 10 | Johnson, T | 2 | 0 | 1 | 0 | 3 |
| 11 | Hessenthaler | 1 | 0 | 1 | 0 | 2 |
| | Other | 7 | 1 | 0 | 0 | 8 |
| | TOTAL | 56 | 6 | 4 | 0 | 66 |

## TEAM OF THE SEASON

| GOALKEEPER | GAMES | DEF RATE |
|---|---|---|
| Jason Brown | 38 | 75 |
| **DEFENDERS** | **GAMES** | **DEF RATE** |
| Barry Ashby | 36 | 70 |
| Chris Hope | 46 | 64 |
| Roland Edge | 31 | 62 |
| David Perpetuini | 12 | 51 |
| **MIDFIELDERS** | **GAMES** | **SCORE DIFF** |
| Nayron Nosworthy | 37 | 2 |
| Andy Hessenthaler | 28 | 0 |
| Nicky Southall | 21 | -4 |
| Paul Smith | 45 | -9 |
| **GOALSCORERS** | **GAMES** | **STRIKE RATE** |
| Rod Wallace | 13 | 133 |
| Paul Shaw | 39 | 304 |

Games = games playing at least 70 minutes

## LEAGUE APPEARANCES, BOOKINGS AND CAPS

| | AGE (on 01/07/03) | IN THE SQUAD | COUNTING GAMES | MINUTES ON PITCH | YELLOW CARDS | RED CARDS | THIS SEASON | HOME COUNTRY |
|---|---|---|---|---|---|---|---|---|
| **Goalkeepers** | | | | | | | | |
| Vince Bartram | 34 | 44 | 8 | 707 | 0 | 0 | - | England |
| Jason Brown | 21 | 40 | 38 | 3433 | 2 | 0 | - | England |
| Danny Knowles | - | 1 | 0 | 0 | 0 | 0 | - | England |
| **Defenders** | | | | | | | | |
| Barry Ashby | 32 | 38 | 36 | 3284 | 3 | 0 | - | England |
| Guy Butters | 33 | 5 | 0 | 0 | 0 | 0 | - | England |
| Andrew Crofts | 19 | 1 | 0 | 0 | 0 | 0 | - | England |
| Roland Edge | 24 | 34 | 31 | 2954 | 1 | 0 | - | England |
| Chris Hope | 30 | 46 | 46 | 4140 | 3 | 0 | - | England |
| Mark Patterson | 34 | 3 | 1 | 135 | 0 | 0 | - | England |
| Adrian Pennock | 32 | 5 | 2 | 199 | 0 | 0 | - | England |
| David Perpetuini | 24 | 40 | 12 | 1434 | 4 | 0 | - | England |
| Richard Rose | 20 | 16 | 0 | 20 | 0 | 0 | - | England |
| **Midfielders** | | | | | | | | |
| Andy Hessenthaler | 37 | 33 | 28 | 2599 | 12 | 1 | - | England |
| Leon Johnson | 22 | 37 | 7 | 811 | 1 | 0 | - | England |
| Nayron Nosworthy | 22 | 40 | 37 | 3448 | 5 | 1 | - | England |
| Simon Osborn | 31 | 18 | 11 | 1201 | 0 | 0 | - | England |
| Mark Saunders | 32 | 34 | 25 | 2533 | 1 | 1 | - | England |
| Paul Smith | 31 | 45 | 45 | 4011 | 4 | 0 | - | England |
| Nicky Southall | 31 | 24 | 21 | 2020 | 2 | 0 | - | England |
| Daniel Spiller | 22 | 31 | 5 | 544 | 1 | 0 | - | England |
| John Wallis | 17 | 2 | 0 | 0 | 0 | 0 | - | England |
| Ben White | 21 | 1 | 0 | 0 | 0 | 0 | - | England |
| **Forwards** | | | | | | | | |
| Jones Awuah | - | 6 | 0 | 108 | 0 | 0 | - | England |
| Akwasi Edusei | - | 4 | 0 | 23 | 0 | 0 | - | England |
| Guy Ipoua | 27 | 37 | 18 | 1936 | 7 | 0 | - | Cameroon |
| Kevin James | 23 | 20 | 6 | 675 | 2 | 1 | - | England |
| Tommy Johnson | 32 | 26 | 9 | 1204 | 3 | 0 | - | England |
| Marlon King | 23 | 10 | 9 | 802 | 2 | 0 | - | England |
| Paul Shaw | 29 | 43 | 39 | 3642 | 3 | 0 | - | England |
| Mamady Sidibe | 23 | 30 | 21 | 2084 | 3 | 0 | - | France |
| Rod Wallace | 33 | 22 | 13 | 1464 | 1 | 0 | - | England |

KEY: LEAGUE BOOKINGS CAPS (FIFA RANKING)

## SQUAD APPEARANCES

| Match | 1 | 2 | 3 | 4 | 5 | 6 | 7 | 8 | 9 | 10 | 11 | 12 | 13 | 14 | 15 | 16 | 17 | 18 | 19 | 20 | 21 | 22 | 23 | 24 | 25 | 26 | 27 | 28 | 29 | 30 | 31 | 32 | 33 | 34 | 35 | 36 | 37 | 38 | 39 | 40 | 41 | 42 | 43 | 44 | 45 | 46 | 47 | 48 | 49 | 50 | 51 | 52 |
|---|---|---|---|---|---|---|---|---|---|---|---|---|---|---|---|---|---|---|---|---|---|---|---|---|---|---|---|---|---|---|---|---|---|---|---|---|---|---|---|---|---|---|---|---|---|---|---|---|---|---|---|---|
| Venue | A | H | H | A | H | A | H | A | A | A | H | A | A | H | A | H | A | H | A | A | H | H | A | H | A | A | H | A | H | A | H | H | A | A | A | H | A | H | H | H | H | H | A | A | A | H | A | H | A | H | A | H |
| Competition | L | L | L | L | L | L | L | W | L | L | L | L | W | L | L | L | L | L | L | W | L | L | L | L | L | L | L | L | F | L | L | F | L | F | L | L | L | L | L | L | L | L | L | L | L | L | L | L | L | L | L | L |
| Result | W | W | W | L | D | L | L | W | W | L | D | D | D | L | D | W | W | L | D | L | L | D | L | D | W | W | W | D | W | D | W | D | L | L | L | W | L | W | W | L | D | D | W | L | D | L | D | L | L | W | D | W |

**Goalkeepers**
Vince Bartram
Jason Brown
Danny Knowles

**Defenders**
Barry Ashby
Guy Butters
Andrew Crofts
Roland Edge
Chris Hope
Mark Patterson
Adrian Pennock
David Perpetuini
Richard Rose

**Midfielders**
Andy Hessenthaler
Leon Johnson
Nayron Nosworthy
Simon Osborn
Mark Saunders
Paul Smith
Nicky Southall
Daniel Spiller
John Wallis
Ben White

**Forwards**
Jones Awuah
Akwasi Edusei
Guy Ipoua
Kevin James
Tommy Johnson
Marlon King
Paul Shaw
Mamady Sidibe
Rod Wallace

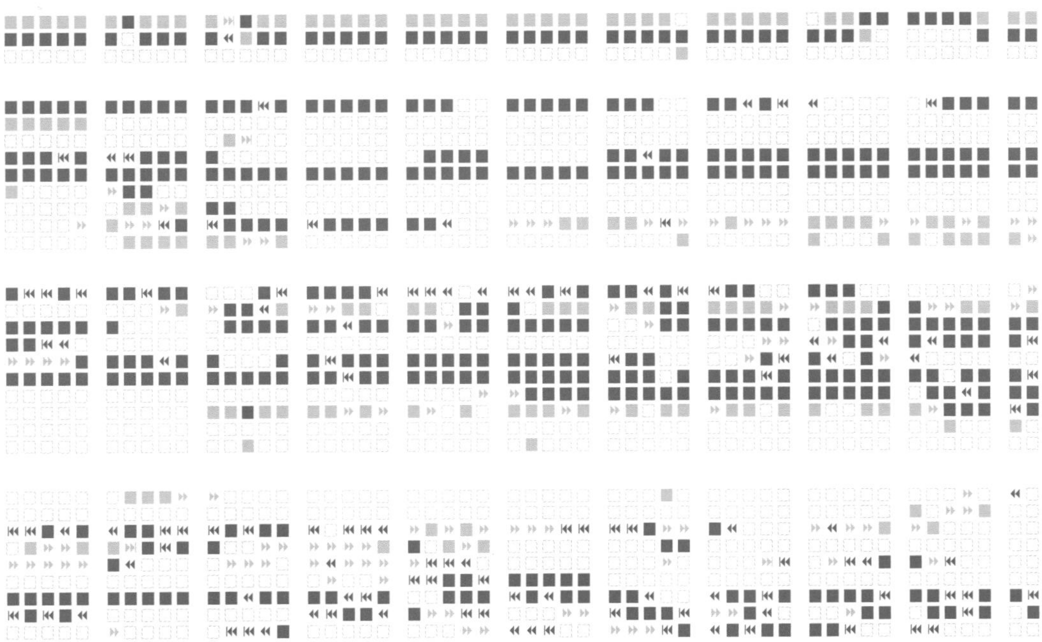

KEY: On all match; On bench; Subbed or sent off (Counting game); Subbed or sent off (playing less than 70 minutes); Subbed on from bench (Counting Game); Subbed on (playing less than 70 minutes); Subbed on and then subbed or sent off (Counting Game); Subbed on and then subbed or sent off (playing less than 70 minutes); Not in 16

# PRESTON NORTH END 12th

NICKNAME: THE LILYWHITES

KEY: ☐Won ☐Drawn ☐Lost

| | | | | | | |
|---|---|---|---|---|---|---|
| 1 | div1 | Crystal Palace | H | L | 1-2 | Fuller 67 |
| 2 | div1 | Nottm Forest | A | D | 2-2 | Fuller 30; Etuhu 48 |
| 3 | div1 | Rotherham | A | D | 0-0 | |
| 4 | div1 | Stoke | H | W | 4-3 | Healy 11,24; Fuller 60; Cresswell 90 |
| 5 | div1 | Gillingham | A | D | 1-1 | Cresswell 90 |
| 6 | div1 | Ipswich | H | D | 0-0 | |
| 7 | wcr1 | Scunthorpe | H | W | 2-1 | Alexander 22 pen; Fuller 115 |
| 8 | div1 | Sheff Wed | H | D | 2-2 | Fuller 13; Cresswell 84 |
| 9 | div1 | Watford | H | D | 1-1 | Cresswell 72 |
| 10 | div1 | Derby | A | W | 2-0 | Etuhu 41; Healy 77 |
| 11 | div1 | Wolves | A | L | 0-4 | |
| 12 | div1 | Norwich | H | L | 1-2 | Cresswell 51 |
| 13 | wcr2 | Macclesfield | A | W | 2-1 | Skora 34; Jackson 90 |
| 14 | div1 | Bradford | A | D | 1-1 | Alexander 39 pen |
| 15 | div1 | Walsall | A | D | 3-3 | Healy 38; Lucketti 75; Alexander 88 |
| 16 | div1 | Reading | H | W | 1-0 | Cresswell 22 |
| 17 | div1 | Portsmouth | A | L | 2-3 | Cresswell 12; Alexander 47 pen |
| 18 | div1 | Burnley | H | W | 3-1 | Fuller 3,66; McKenna 62 |
| 19 | wcr3 | Birmingham | A | W | 2-0 | Fuller 59; Lewis 80 |
| 20 | div1 | Millwall | A | L | 1-2 | Fuller 89 |
| 21 | div1 | Grimsby | A | D | 3-3 | Cresswell 27; Alexander 84 pen; Etuhu 88 |
| 22 | div1 | Brighton | H | D | 2-2 | Lucketti 16; Cresswell 36 |
| 23 | div1 | Leicester | H | W | 2-0 | Fuller 48,90 |
| 24 | div1 | Coventry | A | W | 2-1 | Cresswell 7; Lewis 88 |
| 25 | wcr4 | Aston Villa | A | L | 0-5 | |
| 26 | div1 | Wimbledon | H | L | 3-5 | Leigertwood 11 og; McKenna 41; Alexander 56 pen |
| 27 | div1 | Grimsby | H | W | 3-0 | Alexander 12 pen; Cresswell 26; Healy 59 |
| 28 | div1 | Sheff Utd | A | L | 0-1 | |
| 29 | div1 | Rotherham | H | L | 0-2 | |
| 30 | div1 | Crystal Palace | A | L | 0-2 | |
| 31 | div1 | Stoke | A | L | 1-2 | Abbott 90 |
| 32 | facr3 | Rochdale | H | L | 1-2 | Anderson 48 |
| 33 | div1 | Ipswich | A | L | 0-3 | |
| 34 | div1 | Nottm Forest | H | D | 1-1 | Cartwright 30 |
| 35 | div1 | Gillingham | H | W | 3-0 | Lewis 29; Alexander 38 pen; Ashby 55 og |
| 36 | div1 | Millwall | H | W | 2-1 | Lewis 15; Cartwright 25 |
| 37 | div1 | Wolves | H | L | 0-2 | |
| 38 | div1 | Sheff Wed | A | W | 1-0 | Cresswell 79 |
| 39 | div1 | Watford | A | W | 1-0 | Alexander 19 pen |
| 40 | div1 | Derby | H | W | 4-2 | Alexander 14; Etuhu 22; Koumantarakis 39; Cresswell 51 |
| 41 | div1 | Leicester | A | L | 1-2 | Lewis 20 |
| 42 | div1 | Walsall | H | W | 5-0 | Alexander 14 pen; Etuhu 28; Cresswell 63; Koumantarakis 73,85 |
| 43 | div1 | Portsmouth | H | D | 1-1 | McKenna 89 |
| 44 | div1 | Coventry | H | D | 2-2 | Cresswell 27; Abbott 90 |
| 45 | div1 | Burnley | A | L | 0-2 | |
| 46 | div1 | Brighton | A | W | 2-0 | Jackson 71; Cresswell 86 |
| 47 | div1 | Reading | A | L | 1-5 | Mears 83 |
| 48 | div1 | Sheff Utd | H | W | 2-0 | Etuhu 61; Lewis 87 |
| 49 | div1 | Wimbledon | A | L | 0-2 | |
| 50 | div1 | Bradford | H | W | 1-0 | Abbott 13 |
| 51 | div1 | Norwich | A | L | 0-2 | |

☐Home ☐Away ☐Neutral

## ATTENDANCES

HOME GROUND: DEEPDALE CAPACITY: 23500 AVERAGE LEAGUE AT HOME: 13853

| | | | | | | | | | | | |
|---|---|---|---|---|---|---|---|---|---|---|---|
| 41 | Leicester | 30713 | 18 | Burnley | 16046 | 24 | Coventry | 13313 | 42 | Walsall | 11170 |
| 10 | Derby | 29257 | 29 | Rotherham | 15452 | 14 | Bradford | 13215 | 39 | Watford | 11101 |
| 33 | Ipswich | 24666 | 4 | Stoke | 15422 | 36 | Millwall | 13117 | 32 | Rochdale | 8762 |
| 11 | Wolves | 23696 | 6 | Ipswich | 15357 | 22 | Brighton | 13068 | 5 | Gillingham | 7785 |
| 25 | Aston Villa | 23042 | 31 | Stoke | 14862 | 23 | Leicester | 13048 | 20 | Millwall | 7554 |
| 51 | Norwich | 20232 | 48 | Sheff Utd | 14793 | 44 | Coventry | 13026 | 3 | Rotherham | 6885 |
| 38 | Sheff Wed | 18912 | 1 | Crystal Palace | 14663 | 16 | Reading | 13021 | 15 | Walsall | 6832 |
| 17 | Portsmouth | 18637 | 47 | Reading | 14012 | 27 | Grimsby | 12420 | 46 | Brighton | 6669 |
| 30 | Crystal Palace | 18484 | 40 | Derby | 14003 | 26 | Wimbledon | 12415 | 21 | Grimsby | 5774 |
| 2 | Nottm Forest | 18065 | 50 | Bradford | 13652 | 9 | Watford | 12408 | 7 | Scunthorpe | 5594 |
| 43 | Portsmouth | 16665 | 8 | Sheff Wed | 13632 | 45 | Burnley | 12245 | 13 | Macclesfield | 2036 |
| 28 | Sheff Utd | 16342 | 12 | Norwich | 13550 | 19 | Birmingham | 12241 | 49 | Wimbledon | 1053 |
| 37 | Wolves | 16070 | 34 | Nottm Forest | 13508 | 35 | Gillingham | 12121 | | | |

## KEY PLAYERS - GOALSCORERS

1 Ricardo Fuller

| | |
|---|---|
| Goals in the League | 9 |
| Goals in all competitions | 11 |
| Contribution to Attacking Power<br>Average number of minutes between League team goals while on pitch | 63 |
| Player Strike Rate<br>The total number of minutes he was on the pitch for every League goal scored | 176 |
| Club Strike Rate<br>Average number of minutes between League goals scored by club | 61 |

| | PLAYER | GOALS LGE | GOALS ALL | POWER | S RATE |
|---|---|---|---|---|---|
| 2 | Richard Cresswell | 16 | 16 | 59 | 226 mins |
| 3 | David Healy | 5 | 5 | 54 | 240 mins |
| 4 | Graham Alexander | 10 | 11 | 59 | 405 mins |
| 5 | Dickson Etuhu | 6 | 6 | 54 | 479 mins |

## KEY PLAYERS - MIDFIELDERS

1 Lee Cartwright

| | |
|---|---|
| Goals in the League | 2 |
| Goals in all competitions | 2 |
| Defensive Rating<br>Average number of mins between League goals conceded while on the pitch | 62 |
| Contribution to Attacking Power<br>Average number of minutes between League team goals while on pitch | 54 |
| Scoring Difference<br>Defensive Rating minus Contribution to Attacking Power | 8 |

| | PLAYER | GOALS LGE | GOALS ALL | DEF RATE | ATT POWER | SCORE DIFF |
|---|---|---|---|---|---|---|
| 2 | Paul McKenna | 3 | 3 | 61 | 56 | 5 mins |
| 3 | Dickson Etuhu | 6 | 6 | 59 | 54 | 5 mins |
| 4 | Eddie Lewis | 5 | 6 | 61 | 59 | 2 mins |
| 5 | Eric Skora | 0 | 1 | 57 | 73 | -16 mins |

## KEY PLAYERS - DEFENDERS

1 Michael Jackson

| | |
|---|---|
| Goals Conceded in League | 23 |
| Goals Conceded in all competitions | 24 |
| Clean Sheets<br>In League games when he played at least 70 mins | 7 |
| Defensive Rating<br>Ave number of mins between League goals conceded while on the pitch | 75 |
| Club Defensive Rating<br>Average number of mins between League goals conceded by the club this season | 59 |

| | PLAYER | CON LGE | CON ALL | CLN SHEETS | DEF RATE |
|---|---|---|---|---|---|
| 2 | Rob Edwards | 33 | 34 | 7 | 65 mins |
| 3 | Chris Lucketti | 62 | 71 | 13 | 62 mins |
| 4 | Tyrone Mears | 21 | 21 | 4 | 62 mins |
| 5 | Graham Alexander | 67 | 76 | 13 | 60 mins |

## KEY GOALKEEPER

1 Jonathan Gould

| | |
|---|---|
| Goals Conceded in the League | 14 |
| Goals Conceded in all competitions | 14 |
| Clean Sheets<br>In games when he played at least 70 mins | 5 |
| Goals to Shots Ratio<br>The average number of shots on target per each League goal conceded | 4.6 |
| Defensive Rating<br>Ave number of mins between League goals conceded while on the pitch | 77 |

## MONTHY POINTS TALLY

| Month | Points | % |
|---|---|---|
| AUGUST | 6 | 40% |
| SEPTEMBER | 9 | 43% |
| OCTOBER | 8 | 53% |
| NOVEMBER | 14 | 67% |
| DECEMBER | 3 | 17% |
| JANUARY | 1 | 8% |
| FEBRUARY | 6 | 67% |
| MARCH | 13 | 72% |
| APRIL | 10 | 48% |
| MAY | 0 | 0% |

## TOP POINT EARNERS

| | PLAYER | GAMES | AV PTS |
|---|---|---|---|
| 1 | Michael Jackson | 18 | **1.61** |
| 2 | Rob Edwards | 22 | **1.59** |
| 3 | Richard Cresswell | 39 | **1.44** |
| 4 | Dickson Etuhu | 28 | **1.43** |
| 5 | Eddie Lewis | 30 | **1.43** |
| 6 | Chris Lucketti | 43 | **1.40** |
| 7 | Graham Alexander | 45 | **1.36** |
| 8 | David Lucas | 18 | **1.33** |
| 9 | Ricardo Fuller | 18 | **1.33** |
| 10 | Paul McKenna | 34 | **1.29** |
| | **CLUB AVERAGE:** | | **1.33** |

## LEAGUE APPEARANCES, BOOKINGS AND CAPS

| | AGE (on 01/07/03) | IN THE SQUAD | COUNTING GAMES | MINUTES ON PITCH | YELLOW CARDS | RED CARDS | THIS SEASON | HOME COUNTRY |
|---|---|---|---|---|---|---|---|---|
| **Goalkeepers** | | | | | | | | |
| Jonathan Gould | 34 | 15 | 11 | 1078 | 0 | 0 | - | England |
| Andrew Lonergan | 19 | 12 | 0 | 0 | 0 | 0 | - | England |
| David Lucas | 25 | 38 | 18 | 1757 | 0 | 1 | - | England |
| Teuvo Moilanen | 29 | 27 | 14 | 1305 | 0 | 0 | - | Finland |
| Kelham O'Hanlon | 41 | 0 | 0 | 0 | 0 | 0 | - | Rep of Ireland |
| **Defenders** | | | | | | | | |
| Graham Alexander | 31 | 45 | 45 | 4050 | 6 | 0 | 10 | Scotland (64) |
| Brian Barry-Murphy | 24 | 2 | 2 | 180 | 0 | 0 | - | Rep of Ireland |
| Marlon Broomes | 25 | 36 | 21 | 1946 | 1 | 0 | - | Scotland |
| Adam Eaton | 23 | 2 | 0 | 3 | 0 | 0 | - | England |
| Rob Edwards | 30 | 29 | 22 | 2138 | 2 | 0 | - | Wales |
| Michael Jackson | 29 | 31 | 18 | 1730 | 6 | 1 | - | England |
| Chris Lucketti | 31 | 43 | 43 | 3869 | 6 | 0 | - | England |
| Tyrone Mears | 20 | 27 | 12 | 1305 | 2 | 0 | - | England |
| Colin Murdock | 28 | 27 | 24 | 2131 | 10 | 0 | 3 | N Ireland (111) |
| Brian O'Neil | 30 | 8 | 5 | 466 | 1 | 0 | - | Scotland |
| **Midfielders** | | | | | | | | |
| Iain Anderson | 25 | 10 | 0 | 116 | 0 | 0 | - | Scotland |
| John Bailey | 19 | 5 | 0 | 13 | 0 | 0 | - | England |
| Lee Cartwright | 30 | 29 | 11 | 1182 | 0 | 0 | - | England |
| Dickson Etuhu | 21 | 40 | 28 | 2871 | 6 | 0 | - | Algeria |
| Michael Keane | 20 | 8 | 0 | 121 | 0 | 0 | - | Rep of Ireland |
| Eddie Lewis | 29 | 39 | 30 | 2974 | 6 | 0 | 2 | United States (10) |
| Alan McCormack | 19 | 2 | 0 | 0 | 0 | 0 | - | Rep of Ireland |
| Paul McKenna | 25 | 43 | 34 | 3361 | 7 | 0 | - | England |
| Mark Rankine | 33 | 31 | 10 | 1059 | 0 | 1 | - | England |
| Eric Skora | 21 | 42 | 23 | 2494 | 7 | 1 | - | France |
| **Forwards** | | | | | | | | |
| Pawel Abbott | 21 | 20 | 5 | 679 | 0 | 0 | - | Poland |
| Richard Cresswell | 25 | 42 | 39 | 3617 | 7 | 0 | - | England |
| Ricardo Fuller | 23 | 18 | 18 | 1587 | 1 | 1 | - | Jamaica |
| David Healy | 23 | 28 | 12 | 1202 | 4 | 0 | 8 | N Ireland (111) |
| G Koumantarakis | 29 | 10 | 7 | 747 | 0 | 0 | - | South Africa |
| Simon Lynch | 21 | 19 | 5 | 770 | 2 | 0 | - | Canada |
| Joe O'Neill | 20 | 8 | 7 | 619 | 2 | 0 | - | Scotland |

**KEY:** LEAGUE BOOKINGS CAPS (FIFA RANKING)

## GOALS

| 1 R Cresswell | |
|---|---|
| League | 16 |
| FA Cup | 0 |
| League Cup | 0 |
| Other | 0 |
| TOTAL | 16 |

| | PLAYER | LGE | FAC | LC | Oth | TOT |
|---|---|---|---|---|---|---|
| 2 | Alexander | **10** | 0 | 1 | 0 | 11 |
| 3 | Fuller | **9** | 0 | 2 | 0 | 11 |
| 4 | Etuhu | **6** | 0 | 0 | 0 | 6 |
| 5 | Lewis | **5** | 0 | 1 | 0 | 6 |
| 6 | Healy | **5** | 0 | 0 | 0 | 5 |
| 7 | Koumantarakis | **3** | 0 | 0 | 0 | 3 |
| 8 | McKenna | **3** | 0 | 0 | 0 | 3 |
| 9 | Abbott | **3** | 0 | 0 | 0 | 3 |
| 10 | Cartwright | **2** | 0 | 0 | 0 | 2 |
| 11 | Lucketti | **2** | 0 | 0 | 0 | 2 |
| | Other | 4 | 1 | 2 | 0 | 7 |
| | **TOTAL** | **68** | **1** | **6** | **0** | **75** |

## TEAM OF THE SEASON

| GOALKEEPER | GAMES | DEF RATE |
|---|---|---|
| Jonathan Gould | 11 | 77 |
| **DEFENDERS** | **GAMES** | **DEF RATE** |
| Michael Jackson | 18 | 75 |
| Rob Edwards | 22 | 65 |
| Chris Lucketti | 43 | 62 |
| Tyrone Mears | 12 | 62 |
| **MIDFIELDERS** | **GAMES** | **SCORE DIFF** |
| Lee Cartwright | 11 | 8 |
| Paul McKenna | 34 | 5 |
| Dickson Etuhu | 28 | 5 |
| Eddie Lewis | 30 | 2 |
| **GOALSCORERS** | **GAMES** | **STRIKE RATE** |
| Ricardo Fuller | 18 | 176 |
| Richard Cresswell | 39 | 226 |

Games = games playing more than 70 minutes

## SQUAD APPEARANCES

| Match | 1 | 2 | 3 | 4 | 5 | 6 | 7 | 8 | 9 | 10 | 11 | 12 | 13 | 14 | 15 | 16 | 17 | 18 | 19 | 20 | 21 | 22 | 23 | 24 | 25 | 26 | 27 | 28 | 29 | 30 | 31 | 32 | 33 | 34 | 35 | 36 | 37 | 38 | 39 | 40 | 41 | 42 | 43 | 44 | 45 | 46 | 47 | 48 | 49 | 50 | 51 |
|---|---|---|---|---|---|---|---|---|---|---|---|---|---|---|---|---|---|---|---|---|---|---|---|---|---|---|---|---|---|---|---|---|---|---|---|---|---|---|---|---|---|---|---|---|---|---|---|---|---|---|---|
| Venue | H | A | A | H | A | H | H | H | H | A | A | H | A | A | A | H | A | H | A | A | A | H | H | A | A | H | H | A | H | A | A | H | A | H | H | H | H | A | A | H | A | H | H | H | A | A | A | H | A | H | A |
| Competition | L | L | L | L | L | L | W | L | L | L | L | L | W | L | L | L | L | L | W | L | L | L | L | L | W | L | L | L | L | L | L | F | L | L | L | L | L | L | L | L | L | L | L | L | L | L | L | L | L | L | L |
| Result | L | D | D | W | D | D | D | D | D | W | L | L | W | D | D | W | L | W | W | L | D | D | W | W | L | L | W | L | L | L | L | L | L | D | W | W | L | W | W | W | L | W | D | D | L | W | L | W | L | W | L |

**Goalkeepers**
Jonathan Gould
Andrew Lonergan
David Lucas
Teuvo Moilanen
Kelham O'Hanlon

**Defenders**
Graham Alexander
Brian Barry-Murphy
Marlon Broomes
Adam Eaton
Rob Edwards
Michael Jackson
Chris Lucketti
Tyrone Mears
Colin Murdock
Brian O'Neil

**Midfielders**
Iain Anderson
John Bailey
Lee Cartwright
Dickson Etuhu
Michael Keane
Eddie Lewis
Alan McCormack
Paul McKenna
Mark Rankine
Eric Skora

**Forwards**
Pawel Abbott
Richard Cresswell
Ricardo Fuller
David Healy
George Koumantarakis
Simon Lynch
Joe O'Neill

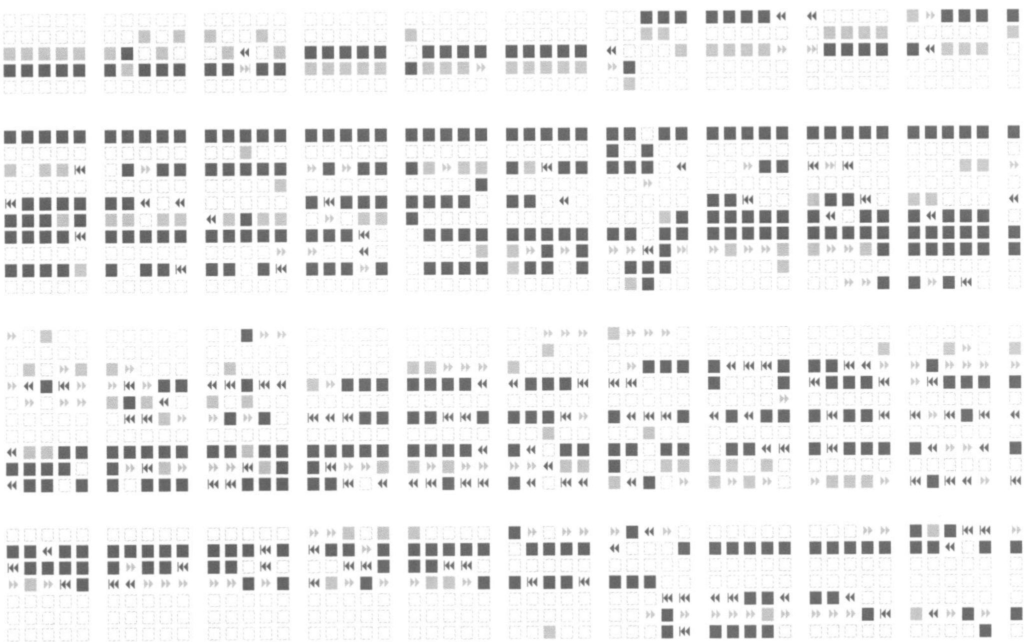

**KEY:** On all match · On bench · Subbed or sent off (Counting game) · Subbed or sent off (playing less than 70 minutes) · Subbed on from bench (Counting Game) · Subbed on (playing less than 70 minutes) · Subbed on and then subbed or sent off (Counting Game) · Subbed on and then subbed or sent off (playing less than 70 minutes) · Not in 16

# WATFORD

Final Position: **13th**

**NICKNAME:** THE HORNETS

KEY: ☐ Won ☐ Drawn ☐ Lost

| | | | | | | |
|---|---|---|---|---|---|---|
| 1 | div1 | **Leicester** | A | L | 0-2 | |
| 2 | div1 | **Millwall** | H | D | 0-0 | |
| 3 | div1 | **Wimbledon** | H | W | 3-2 | Webber 30; Robinson 41; Nielsen 85 |
| 4 | div1 | **Portsmouth** | A | L | 0-3 | |
| 5 | div1 | **Coventry** | H | W | 5-2 | Glass 5; Smith 34; Webber 40; Nielsen 63; Robinson 71 |
| 6 | div1 | **Norwich** | A | L | 0-4 | |
| 7 | div1 | **Walsall** | H | W | 2-0 | Smith 71; Foley 89 |
| 8 | wcr1 | **Luton** | H | L | 1-2 | Foley 84 |
| 9 | div1 | **Nottm Forest** | A | W | 1-0 | Cox 45 |
| 10 | div1 | **Preston** | A | D | 1-1 | Robinson 30 |
| 11 | div1 | **Crystal Palace** | H | D | 3-3 | Ardley 27; Hyde 38; Helguson 46 |
| 12 | div1 | **Sheff Utd** | A | W | 2-1 | Cox 35 pen; Helguson 37 |
| 13 | div1 | **Brighton** | H | W | 1-0 | Helguson 39 |
| 14 | div1 | **Grimsby** | H | W | 2-0 | Foley 12; Smith, T 90 |
| 15 | div1 | **Gillingham** | A | L | 0-3 | |
| 16 | div1 | **Sheff Wed** | H | W | 1-0 | Helguson 42 |
| 17 | div1 | **Stoke** | A | W | 2-1 | Helguson 18; Cox 37 |
| 18 | div1 | **Wolves** | H | D | 1-1 | Cox 67 |
| 19 | div1 | **Rotherham** | A | L | 1-2 | Foley 60 |
| 20 | div1 | **Ipswich** | H | L | 0-2 | |
| 21 | div1 | **Reading** | A | L | 0-1 | |
| 22 | div1 | **Burnley** | H | W | 2-1 | Helguson 40; Smith, T 72 pen |
| 23 | div1 | **Derby** | A | L | 0-3 | |
| 24 | div1 | **Ipswich** | A | L | 2-4 | Smith, T 50; Cox 75 |
| 25 | div1 | **Bradford** | H | W | 1-0 | Cox 90 pen |
| 26 | div1 | **Wimbledon** | A | D | 0-0 | |
| 27 | div1 | **Leicester** | H | L | 1-2 | Helguson 29 |
| 28 | div1 | **Portsmouth** | H | D | 2-2 | Hyde 51; Cox 81 |
| 29 | facr3 | **Macclesfield** | A | W | 2-0 | Helguson 24; Pennant 61 |
| 30 | div1 | **Millwall** | A | L | 0-4 | |
| 31 | div1 | **Norwich** | H | W | 2-1 | Nielsen 45; Helguson 90 |
| 32 | facr4 | **West Brom** | H | W | 1-0 | Helguson 80 |
| 33 | div1 | **Coventry** | A | W | 1-0 | Hyde 60 |
| 34 | div1 | **Rotherham** | H | L | 1-2 | Smith, T 62 |
| 35 | facr5 | **Sunderland** | A | W | 1-0 | Smith, T 65 pen |
| 36 | div1 | **Walsall** | A | L | 0-2 | |
| 37 | div1 | **Wolves** | A | D | 0-0 | |
| 38 | div1 | **Nottm Forest** | H | D | 1-1 | Helguson 13 |
| 39 | div1 | **Preston** | H | L | 0-1 | |
| 40 | facqf | **Burnley** | H | W | 2-0 | Smith, T 74; Glass 80 |
| 41 | div1 | **Grimsby** | A | L | 0-1 | |
| 42 | div1 | **Gillingham** | H | L | 0-1 | |
| 43 | div1 | **Stoke** | H | L | 1-2 | Helguson 67 |
| 44 | div1 | **Sheff Wed** | A | D | 2-2 | Smith, T 33; Norville 82 |
| 45 | div1 | **Burnley** | A | W | 7-4 | Brown 13; Hyde 16; Cox 26; Chopra 29,40,61,90 |
| 46 | div1 | **Crystal Palace** | A | W | 1-0 | Hunt 45 og |
| 47 | facsf | **Southampton** | H | L | 1-2 | Gayle 88 |
| 48 | div1 | **Bradford** | A | L | 1-2 | Helguson 41 |
| 49 | div1 | **Derby** | H | W | 2-0 | Chopra 18; Ardley 85 |
| 50 | div1 | **Brighton** | A | L | 0-4 | |
| 51 | div1 | **Reading** | H | L | 0-3 | |
| 52 | div1 | **Sheff Utd** | H | W | 2-0 | Cox 64; Fitzgerald 79 |

☐ Home ☐ Away ☐ Neutral

## ATTENDANCES

**HOME GROUND:** VICARAGE ROAD **CAPACITY:** 22011 **AVERAGE LEAGUE AT HOME:** 13400

| | | | | | | | | | | | |
|---|---|---|---|---|---|---|---|---|---|---|---|
| 47 | Southampton | 42602 | 32 | West Brom | 16975 | 31 | Norwich | 13338 | 3 | Wimbledon | 10292 |
| 1 | Leicester | 31022 | 18 | Wolves | 16524 | 25 | Bradford | 12579 | 45 | Burnley | 10208 |
| 35 | Sunderland | 26916 | 12 | Sheff Utd | 16301 | 43 | Stoke | 12570 | 30 | Millwall | 9030 |
| 37 | Wolves | 24591 | 20 | Ipswich | 16184 | 10 | Preston | 12408 | 15 | Gillingham | 8728 |
| 24 | Ipswich | 22985 | 27 | Leicester | 16017 | 11 | Crystal Palace | 12153 | 36 | Walsall | 7705 |
| 23 | Derby | 21653 | 13 | Brighton | 15305 | 49 | Derby | 11909 | 50 | Brighton | 6841 |
| 6 | Norwich | 20563 | 16 | Sheff Wed | 15058 | 51 | Reading | 11814 | 19 | Rotherham | 6790 |
| 40 | Burnley | 20336 | 28 | Portsmouth | 15048 | 17 | Stoke | 11215 | 41 | Grimsby | 4847 |
| 38 | Nottm Forest | 17934 | 34 | Rotherham | 15025 | 2 | Millwall | 11187 | 29 | Macclesfield | 4244 |
| 4 | Portsmouth | 17901 | 52 | Sheff Utd | 14230 | 48 | Bradford | 11145 | 26 | Wimbledon | 2643 |
| 9 | Nottm Forest | 17865 | 8 | Luton | 14171 | 5 | Coventry | 11136 | | | |
| 21 | Reading | 17465 | 46 | Crystal Palace | 14051 | 39 | Preston | 11101 | | | |
| 33 | Coventry | 17393 | 22 | Burnley | 13977 | 7 | Walsall | 10528 | | | |
| 44 | Sheff Wed | 17086 | 14 | Grimsby | 13821 | 42 | Gillingham | 10492 | | | |

## KEY PLAYERS - GOALSCORERS

1 Heidar Helguson

| | |
|---|---|
| **Goals in the League** | 11 |
| **Goals in all competitions** | 13 |
| **Contribution to Attacking Power** Average number of minutes between League team goals while on pitch | 95 |
| Player Strike Rate The total number of minutes he was on the pitch for every League goal scored | 218 |
| **Club Strike Rate** Average number of minutes between League goals scored by club | 77 |

| | PLAYER | GOALS LGE | GOALS ALL | POWER | S RATE |
|---|---|---|---|---|---|
| 2 | Tommy Smith | 7 | 9 | 67 | 336 mins |
| 3 | Neil Cox | 9 | 9 | 71 | 399 mins |
| 4 | Micah Hyde | 4 | 4 | 77 | 818 mins |
| 5 | Allan Nielsen | 3 | 3 | 65 | 877 mins |

## KEY PLAYERS - MIDFIELDERS

1 Jamie Hand

| | |
|---|---|
| **Goals in the League** | 0 |
| **Goals in all competitions** | 0 |
| **Defensive Rating** Average number of mins between League goals conceded while on the pitch | 84 |
| **Contribution to Attacking Power** Average number of minutes between League team goals while on pitch | 73 |
| Scoring Difference Defensive Rating minus Contribution to Attacking Power | 11 |

| | PLAYER | GOALS LGE | GOALS ALL | DEF RATE | ATT POWER | SCORE DIFF |
|---|---|---|---|---|---|---|
| 2 | Paolo Vernazza | 0 | 0 | 58 | 67 | -9 mins |
| 3 | Allan Nielsen | 3 | 3 | 57 | 66 | -9 mins |
| 4 | Paul Robinson | 3 | 3 | 65 | 81 | -16 mins |
| 5 | Neal Ardley | 2 | 2 | 57 | 75 | -18 mins |

## KEY PLAYERS - DEFENDERS

1 Lloyd Doyley

| | |
|---|---|
| **Goals Conceded in League** | 22 |
| **Goals Conceded in all competitions** | 24 |
| **Clean Sheets** In League games when he played at least 70 mins | 8 |
| Defensive Rating Ave number of mins between League goals conceded while on the pitch | 85 |
| **Club Defensive Rating** Average number of mins between League goals conceded by the club this season | 59 |

| | PLAYER | CON LGE | CON ALL | CLN SHEETS | DEF RATE |
|---|---|---|---|---|---|
| 2 | Sean Dyche | 34 | 36 | 7 | 60 mins |
| 3 | Neil Cox | 61 | 65 | 11 | 59 mins |
| 4 | Wayne Brown | 24 | 24 | 3 | 47 mins |

## KEY GOALKEEPER

1 Alec Chamberlain

| | |
|---|---|
| **Goals Conceded in the League** | 68 |
| **Goals Conceded in all competitions** | 72 |
| **Clean Sheets** In games when he played at least 70 mins | 10 |
| **Goals to Shots Ratio** The average number of shots on target per each League goal conceded | 4 |
| Defensive Rating Ave number of mins between League goals conceded while on the pitch | 56 |

## MONTHY POINTS TALLY

| | | |
|---|---|---|
| AUGUST | 7 | 39% |
| SEPTEMBER | 11 | 61% |
| OCTOBER | 12 | 80% |
| NOVEMBER | 4 | 27% |
| DECEMBER | 4 | 27% |
| JANUARY | 10 | 67% |
| FEBRUARY | 7 | 47% |
| MARCH | 5 | 24% |
| APRIL | 9 | 43% |
| MAY | 3 | 100% |

## TOP POINT EARNERS

| | PLAYER | GAMES | AV PTS |
|---|---|---|---|
| 1 | Jamie Hand | 15 | 2.00 |
| 2 | Lloyd Doyley | 20 | 1.80 |
| 3 | Allan Nielsen | 28 | 1.61 |
| 4 | Paolo Vernazza | 12 | 1.50 |
| 5 | Sean Dyche | 22 | 1.45 |
| 6 | Paul Robinson | 32 | 1.41 |
| 7 | Neil Cox | 40 | 1.35 |
| 8 | Tommy Smith | 21 | 1.33 |
| 9 | Neal Ardley | 42 | 1.29 |
| 10 | Stephen Glass | 24 | 1.21 |
| | CLUB AVERAGE: | | 1.30 |

## GOALS

| 1 Heidar Helguson | |
|---|---|
| League | 11 |
| FA Cup | 2 |
| League Cup | 0 |
| Other | 0 |
| TOTAL | 13 |

| | PLAYER | LGE | FAC | LC | Oth | TOT |
|---|---|---|---|---|---|---|
| 2 | Cox | 9 | 0 | 0 | 0 | 9 |
| 3 | Smith, T | 7 | 2 | 0 | 0 | 9 |
| 4 | Chopra | 5 | 0 | 0 | 0 | 5 |
| 5 | Hyde | 4 | 0 | 0 | 0 | 4 |
| 6 | Nielsen | 3 | 0 | 0 | 0 | 3 |
| 7 | Foley | 3 | 0 | 1 | 0 | 4 |
| 8 | Robinson | 3 | 0 | 0 | 0 | 3 |
| 9 | Ardley | 2 | 0 | 0 | 0 | 2 |
| 10 | Webber | 2 | 0 | 0 | 0 | 2 |
| 11 | Fitzgerald | 1 | 0 | 0 | 0 | 1 |
| | Other | 4 | 3 | 0 | 0 | 7 |
| | TOTAL | 54 | 7 | 1 | 0 | 62 |

## TEAM OF THE SEASON

| GOALKEEPER | GAMES | DEF RATE |
|---|---|---|
| Alec Chamberlain | 42 | 56 |
| **DEFENDERS** | **GAMES** | **DEF RATE** |
| Lloyd Doyley | 20 | 85 |
| Sean Dyche | 22 | 60 |
| Neil Cox | 40 | 59 |
| Wayne Brown | 12 | 47 |
| **MIDFIELDERS** | **GAMES** | **SCORE DIFF** |
| Jamie Hand | 15 | 11 |
| Paolo Vernazza | 12 | -9 |
| Allan Nielsen | 28 | -9 |
| Paul Robinson | 32 | -16 |
| **GOALSCORERS** | **GAMES** | **STRIKE RATE** |
| Heidar Helguson | 26 | 218 |
| Tommy Smith | 21 | 336 |

Games = games playing at least 70 minutes

## LEAGUE APPEARANCES, BOOKINGS AND CAPS

| | AGE (on 01/07/03) | IN THE SQUAD | COUNTING GAMES | MINUTES ON PITCH | YELLOW CARDS | RED CARDS | THIS SEASON | HOME COUNTRY |
|---|---|---|---|---|---|---|---|---|
| **Goalkeepers** | | | | | | | | |
| Alec Chamberlain | 39 | 46 | 42 | 3780 | 2 | 0 | - | England |
| Richard Lee | 20 | 46 | 4 | 360 | 0 | 0 | - | England |
| **Defenders** | | | | | | | | |
| Wayne Brown | 25 | 21 | 12 | 1125 | 0 | 0 | - | England |
| Neil Cox | 31 | 40 | 40 | 3590 | 5 | 0 | - | England |
| Lloyd Doyley | 20 | 29 | 20 | 1874 | 0 | 0 | - | Rep of Ireland |
| Sean Dyche | 32 | 25 | 22 | 2023 | 5 | 1 | - | England |
| Jack Smith | 19 | 5 | 0 | 38 | 0 | 0 | - | England |
| **Midfielders** | | | | | | | | |
| Neal Ardley | 30 | 43 | 42 | 3764 | 2 | 0 | - | England |
| Gary Fisken | 21 | 4 | 1 | 210 | 1 | 0 | - | England |
| Stephen Glass | 27 | 35 | 24 | 2358 | 2 | 0 | - | Scotland |
| Elliot Godfrey | 20 | 2 | 0 | 5 | 0 | 0 | - | Canada |
| Jamie Hand | 19 | 26 | 15 | 1671 | 9 | 0 | - | England |
| Micah Hyde | 28 | 37 | 37 | 3271 | 6 | 1 | - | Jamaica |
| Jerel Ifil | 21 | 5 | 1 | 90 | 0 | 0 | - | England |
| Richard Johnson | 29 | 14 | 4 | 500 | 2 | 0 | - | Australia |
| Gavin Mahon | 26 | 28 | 13 | 1197 | 0 | 0 | - | England |
| Anthony McNamee | 19 | 33 | 1 | 435 | 0 | 0 | - | England |
| Allan Nielsen | 32 | 35 | 28 | 2630 | 3 | 1 | - | Denmark |
| Jermaine Pennant | 20 | 13 | 12 | 1022 | 0 | 0 | - | England |
| Paul Robinson | 24 | 39 | 32 | 3174 | 12 | 1 | 7 | England (7) |
| Sam Swonell | 20 | 3 | 1 | 79 | 0 | 0 | - | England |
| Paolo Vernazza | 23 | 33 | 12 | 1211 | 3 | 0 | - | England |
| **Forwards** | | | | | | | | |
| Michael Chopra | 19 | 5 | 3 | 295 | 0 | 0 | - | England |
| Lee Cook | 20 | 5 | 3 | 262 | 0 | 0 | - | England |
| Scott Fitzgerald | 23 | 4 | 1 | 147 | 0 | 0 | - | England |
| Dominic Foley | 27 | 20 | 5 | 678 | 4 | 1 | - | Rep of Ireland |
| Marcus Gayle | 32 | 32 | 27 | 2578 | 2 | 0 | - | England |
| Heidar Helguson | 25 | 31 | 26 | 2393 | 6 | 0 | - | Iceland |
| Gifton Noel-Williams | 23 | 17 | 7 | 808 | 1 | 0 | - | England |
| Jason Norville | 19 | 13 | 5 | 599 | 0 | 0 | - | Trinidad & Tobago |
| Tommy Smith | 23 | 35 | 21 | 2349 | 1 | 0 | - | England |
| Danny Webber | 21 | 12 | 9 | 917 | 0 | 0 | - | England |

KEY: LEAGUE BOOKINGS CAPS (FIFA RANKING)

## SQUAD APPEARANCES

| Match | 1 | 2 | 3 | 4 | 5 | 6 | 7 | 8 | 9 | 10 | 11 | 12 | 13 | 14 | 15 | 16 | 17 | 18 | 19 | 20 | 21 | 22 | 23 | 24 | 25 | 26 | 27 | 28 | 29 | 30 | 31 | 32 | 33 | 34 | 35 | 36 | 37 | 38 | 39 | 40 | 41 | 42 | 43 | 44 | 45 | 46 | 47 | 48 | 49 | 50 | 51 | 52 |
|---|---|---|---|---|---|---|---|---|---|---|---|---|---|---|---|---|---|---|---|---|---|---|---|---|---|---|---|---|---|---|---|---|---|---|---|---|---|---|---|---|---|---|---|---|---|---|---|---|---|---|---|---|
| Venue | A | H | H | A | H | A | H | H | A | A | H | A | H | H | A | H | A | H | A | H | A | H | A | A | H | A | H | H | A | A | H | H | A | H | A | A | A | H | H | H | A | H | H | A | A | A | H | A | H | A | H | H |
| Competition | L | L | L | L | L | L | L | W | L | L | L | L | L | L | L | L | L | L | L | L | L | L | L | L | L | L | L | L | F | L | L | F | L | L | F | L | L | L | L | F | L | L | L | L | L | L | F | L | L | L | L | L |
| Result | L | D | W | L | W | L | W | L | W | D | D | W | W | W | L | W | W | D | L | L | L | W | L | L | W | D | L | D | W | L | W | W | W | L | W | L | D | D | L | W | L | L | L | D | W | W | L | L | W | L | L | W |

**Goalkeepers**
Alec Chamberlain
Richard Lee

**Defenders**
Wayne Brown
Neil Cox
Lloyd Doyley
Sean Dyche
Jack Smith

**Midfielders**
Neal Ardley
Gary Fisken
Stephen Glass
Elliot Godfrey
Jamie Hand
Micah Hyde
Jerel Ifil
Richard Johnson
Gavin Mahon
Anthony McNamee
Allan Nielsen
Jermaine Pennant
Paul Robinson
Sam Swonell
Paolo Vernazza

**Forwards**
Michael Chopra
Lee Cook
Scott Fitzgerald
Dominic Foley
Marcus Gayle
Heidar Helguson
Gifton Noel-Williams
Jason Norville
Tommy Smith
Danny Webber

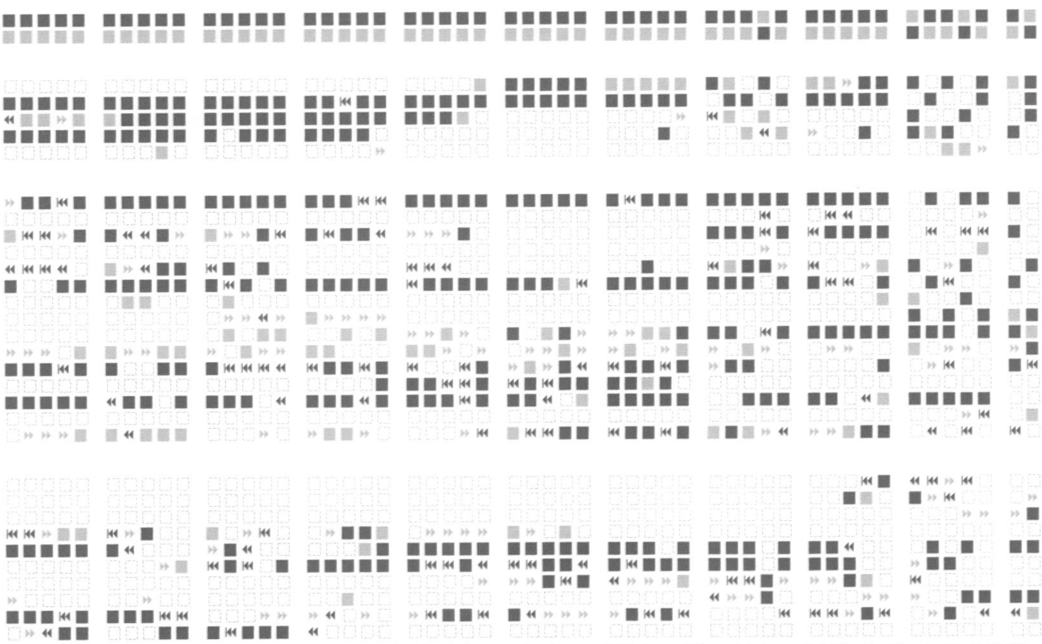

KEY: ■ On all match ■ On bench
⏮ Subbed or sent off (Counting game) « Subbed or sent off (playing less than 70 minutes)
» Subbed on from bench (Counting Game) » Subbed on (playing less than 70 minutes)
» Subbed on and then subbed or sent off (Counting Game) » Subbed on and then subbed or sent off (playing less than 70 minutes)
□ Not in 16

# CRYSTAL PALACE

Final Position: **14th**

**NICKNAME:** THE EAGLES

KEY: Won Drawn Lost

| | | | | | | |
|---|---|---|---|---|---|---|
| 1 | div1 | **Preston** | A | W | 2-1 | Powell 68; Kabba 85 |
| 2 | div1 | **Bradford** | H | D | 1-1 | Popovic 80 |
| 3 | div1 | **Portsmouth** | H | L | 2-3 | Freedman 39; Popovic 42 |
| 4 | div1 | **Coventry** | A | L | 0-1 | |
| 5 | div1 | **Leicester** | H | D | 0-0 | |
| 6 | div1 | **Burnley** | A | D | 0-0 | |
| 7 | wcr1 | **Plymouth** | H | W | 2-1 | Powell 21; Johnson 113 |
| 8 | div1 | **Wolves** | H | W | 4-2 | Routledge 1; Freedman 35,60 pen; Thomson 71 |
| 9 | div1 | **Derby** | H | L | 0-1 | |
| 10 | div1 | **Watford** | A | D | 3-3 | Mullins 23,44; Robinson 40 og |
| 11 | div1 | **Sheff Wed** | A | D | 0-0 | |
| 12 | div1 | **Gillingham** | H | D | 2-2 | Granville 47; Routledge 70 |
| 13 | wcr2 | **Cheltenham** | H | W | 7-0 | Adebola 19,73; Mullins 46; Popovic 52; Freedman 55,90; Walker 74 og |
| 14 | div1 | **Stoke** | A | D | 1-1 | Adebola 77 |
| 15 | div1 | **Wimbledon** | A | D | 2-2 | Gray 15; Johnson 69 |
| 16 | div1 | **Brighton** | H | W | 5-0 | Johnson 4,35,55 pen; Freedman 51 pen; Gray 57 |
| 17 | div1 | **Walsall** | A | W | 4-3 | Johnson 29,64,90; Freedman 58 |
| 18 | div1 | **Ipswich** | A | W | 2-1 | Johnson 19; Butterfield 78 |
| 19 | wcr3 | **Coventry** | H | W | 3-0 | Johnson 20,75; Gray 89 |
| 20 | div1 | **Nottm Forest** | H | D | 0-0 | |
| 21 | div1 | **Norwich** | A | L | 0-2 | |
| 22 | div1 | **Grimsby** | H | W | 2-0 | Derry 39; Adebola 61 |
| 23 | div1 | **Reading** | H | L | 0-1 | |
| 24 | div1 | **Sheff Utd** | A | L | 1-2 | Riihilahti 69 |
| 25 | wcr4 | **Oldham** | H | W | 2-0 | Black 11,74 |
| 26 | div1 | **Millwall** | H | W | 1-0 | Granville 73 |
| 27 | div1 | **Norwich** | H | W | 2-0 | Adebola 6; Black 27 |
| 28 | wcqf | **Sheff Utd** | A | L | 1-3 | Page 82 og |
| 29 | div1 | **Rotherham** | A | W | 3-1 | Black 12,51; Gray 45 |
| 30 | div1 | **Portsmouth** | A | D | 1-1 | Gray 30 |
| 31 | div1 | **Preston** | H | W | 2-0 | Black 38,55 |
| 32 | div1 | **Coventry** | H | D | 1-1 | Akinbiyi 72 |
| 33 | facr3 | **Blackpool** | A | W | 2-1 | Black 56,64 |
| 34 | div1 | **Burnley** | H | D | 1-1 | Popovic 62 pen |
| 35 | facr4 | **Liverpool** | H | D | 0-0 | |
| 36 | div1 | **Leicester** | A | L | 0-1 | |
| 37 | facr4r | **Liverpool** | A | W | 2-0 | Gray 55; Henchoz 79 og |
| 38 | div1 | **Nottm Forest** | A | L | 1-2 | Johnson 75 pen |
| 39 | facr5 | **Leeds** | H | L | 1-2 | Gray 34 |
| 40 | div1 | **Sheff Wed** | H | D | 0-0 | |
| 41 | div1 | **Wolverhampton** | A | L | 0-4 | |
| 42 | div1 | **Derby** | A | W | 1-0 | Black 61 |
| 43 | div1 | **Bradford** | A | L | 1-2 | Whelan 24 |
| 44 | div1 | **Ipswich** | H | D | 1-1 | Johnson 20 |
| 45 | div1 | **Reading** | A | L | 1-2 | Johnson 76 |
| 46 | div1 | **Wimbledon** | H | L | 0-1 | |
| 47 | div1 | **Walsall** | H | W | 2-0 | Freedman 54 pen; Routledge 89 |
| 48 | div1 | **Brighton** | A | D | 0-0 | |
| 49 | div1 | **Sheff Utd** | H | D | 2-2 | Adebola 15; Whelan 22 |
| 50 | div1 | **Watford** | H | L | 0-1 | |
| 51 | div1 | **Grimsby** | A | W | 4-1 | Routledge 18; Whelan 34; Gray 35; Freedman 89 |
| 52 | div1 | **Rotherham** | H | D | 0-0 | |
| 53 | div1 | **Millwall** | A | L | 2-3 | Freedman 22; Roberts 49 og |
| 54 | div1 | **Stoke** | H | W | 1-0 | Adebola 82 |
| 55 | div1 | **Gillingham** | A | L | 1-2 | Freedman 30 pen |

Home Away Neutral

## ATTENDANCES

**HOME GROUND:** SELHURST PARK **CAPACITY:** 26309 **AVERAGE LEAGUE AT HOME:** 16866

| | | | | | | | | | | | |
|---|---|---|---|---|---|---|---|---|---|---|---|
| 37 | Liverpool | 35109 | 20 | Nottm Forest | 18971 | 4 | Coventry | 15526 | 33 | Blackpool | 9062 |
| 36 | Leicester | 27005 | 31 | Preston | 18484 | 52 | Rotherham | 15508 | 19 | Coventry | 8102 |
| 35 | Liverpool | 26054 | 3 | Portsmouth | 18315 | 5 | Leicester | 15440 | 25 | Oldham | 7431 |
| 38 | Nottm Forest | 26012 | 45 | Reading | 18063 | 49 | Sheff Utd | 15377 | 29 | Rotherham | 6829 |
| 41 | Wolves | 26010 | 32 | Coventry | 17362 | 2 | Bradford | 15205 | 48 | Brighton | 6786 |
| 18 | Ipswich | 24941 | 8 | Wolves | 16961 | 9 | Derby | 14948 | 15 | Wimbledon | 6538 |
| 39 | Leeds | 24512 | 27 | Norwich | 16791 | 1 | Preston | 14663 | 7 | Plymouth | 6385 |
| 42 | Derby | 22682 | 40 | Sheff Wed | 16707 | 14 | Stoke | 14214 | 17 | Walsall | 6368 |
| 28 | Sheff Utd | 22211 | 24 | Sheff Utd | 16686 | 50 | Watford | 14051 | 13 | Cheltenham | 4901 |
| 16 | Brighton | 21796 | 34 | Burnley | 16344 | 46 | Wimbledon | 13713 | 51 | Grimsby | 4707 |
| 21 | Norwich | 20907 | 11 | Sheff Wed | 16112 | 6 | Burnley | 12407 | | | |
| 22 | Grimsby | 20093 | 54 | Stoke | 16064 | 10 | Watford | 12153 | | | |
| 26 | Millwall | 19301 | 44 | Ipswich | 15990 | 43 | Bradford | 11016 | | | |
| 30 | Portsmouth | 19217 | 23 | Reading | 15712 | 53 | Millwall | 10670 | | | |
| 47 | Walsall | 19102 | 12 | Gillingham | 15699 | 55 | Gillingham | 9315 | | | |

## KEY PLAYERS - GOALSCORERS

**1 Andrew Johnson**

| | |
|---|---|
| **Goals in the League** | 11 |
| **Goals in all competitions** | 14 |
| **Contribution to Attacking Power** Average number of minutes between League team goals while on pitch | 70 |
| **Player Strike Rate** The total number of minutes he was on the pitch for every League goal scored | 193 |
| **Club Strike Rate** Average number of minutes between League goals scored by club | 70 |

| | PLAYER | GOALS LGE | GOALS ALL | POWER | S RATE |
|---|---|---|---|---|---|
| 2 | Dougie Freedman | 9 | 11 | 66 | 228 mins |
| 3 | Thomas Black | 6 | 10 | 69 | 335 mins |
| 4 | Julian Gray | 5 | 8 | 71 | 499 mins |
| 5 | Dele Adebola | 5 | 7 | 73 | 560 mins |

## KEY PLAYERS - MIDFIELDERS

**1 Aki Riihilahti**

| | |
|---|---|
| **Goals in the League** | 1 |
| **Goals in all competitions** | 1 |
| **Defensive Rating** Average number of mins between League goals conceded while on the pitch | 91 |
| **Contribution to Attacking Power** Average number of minutes between League team goals while on pitch | 69 |
| **Scoring Difference** Defensive Rating minus Contribution to Attacking Power | 22 |

| | PLAYER | GOALS LGE | GOALS ALL | DEF RATE | ATT POWER | SCORE DIFF |
|---|---|---|---|---|---|---|
| 2 | Julian Gray | 5 | 8 | 89 | 71 | 18 mins |
| 3 | Thomas Black | 6 | 10 | 84 | 69 | 15 mins |
| 4 | Stephen Thomson | 1 | 1 | 79 | 66 | 13 mins |
| 5 | Shaun Derry | 1 | 1 | 80 | 76 | 4 mins |

## KEY PLAYERS - DEFENDERS

**1 Kit Symons**

| | |
|---|---|
| **Goals Conceded in League** | 23 |
| **Goals Conceded in all competitions** | 28 |
| **Clean Sheets** In League games when he played at least 70 mins | 6 |
| **Defensive Rating** Ave number of mins between League goals conceded while on the pitch | 84 |
| **Club Defensive Rating** Average number of mins between League goals conceded by the club this season | 80 |

| | PLAYER | CON LGE | CON ALL | CLN SHEETS | DEF RATE |
|---|---|---|---|---|---|
| 2 | Danny Granville | 33 | 36 | 9 | 82 mins |
| 3 | Danny Butterfield | 51 | 57 | 13 | 80 mins |
| 4 | Darren Powell | 40 | 46 | 11 | 79 mins |
| 5 | Hayden Mullins | 49 | 56 | 13 | 78 mins |

## KEY GOALKEEPER

**1 Alex Kolinko**

| | |
|---|---|
| **Goals Conceded in the League** | 28 |
| **Goals Conceded in all competitions** | 33 |
| **Clean Sheets** In games when he played at least 70 mins | 10 |
| **Goals to Shots Ratio** The average number of shots on target per each League goal conceded | 3.8 |
| **Defensive Rating** Ave number of mins between League goals conceded while on the pitch | 87 |

## MONTHY POINTS TALLY

| Month | Points | % |
|---|---|---|
| AUGUST | 6 | 33% |
| SEPTEMBER | 9 | 50% |
| OCTOBER | 11 | 73% |
| NOVEMBER | 10 | 48% |
| DECEMBER | 16 | 76% |
| JANUARY | 6 | 50% |
| FEBRUARY | 4 | 27% |
| MARCH | 8 | 33% |
| APRIL | 8 | 44% |
| MAY | 0 | 0% |

## TOP POINT EARNERS

| | PLAYER | GAMES | AV PTS |
|---|---|---|---|
| 1 | Thomas Black | 16 | 1.63 |
| 2 | Alex Kolinko | 27 | 1.59 |
| 3 | Julian Gray | 22 | 1.50 |
| 4 | Aki Riihilahti | 13 | 1.46 |
| 5 | Shaun Derry | 33 | 1.33 |
| 6 | Hayden Mullins | 42 | 1.31 |
| 7 | Danny Butterfield | 44 | 1.30 |
| 8 | Dele Adebola | 25 | 1.28 |
| 9 | Andrew Johnson | 22 | 1.27 |
| 10 | Darren Powell | 33 | 1.27 |
| | CLUB AVERAGE: | | 1.28 |

## GOALS

| 1 Andrew Johnson | |
|---|---|
| League | 11 |
| FA Cup | 0 |
| League Cup | 3 |
| Other | 0 |
| TOTAL | 14 |

| | PLAYER | LGE | FAC | LC | Oth | TOT |
|---|---|---|---|---|---|---|
| 2 | Freedman | 9 | 0 | 2 | 0 | 11 |
| 3 | Black | 6 | 2 | 2 | 0 | 10 |
| 4 | Gray | 5 | 2 | 1 | 0 | 8 |
| 5 | Adebola | 5 | 0 | 2 | 0 | 7 |
| 6 | Routledge | 4 | 0 | 0 | 0 | 4 |
| 7 | Popovic | 3 | 0 | 1 | 0 | 4 |
| 8 | Whelan | 3 | 0 | 0 | 0 | 3 |
| 9 | Mullins | 2 | 0 | 1 | 0 | 3 |
| 10 | Granville | 2 | 0 | 0 | 0 | 2 |
| 11 | Thomson | 1 | 0 | 0 | 0 | 1 |
| | Other | 8 | 1 | 3 | 0 | 12 |
| | TOTAL | 59 | 5 | 15 | 0 | 79 |

## TEAM OF THE SEASON

| GOALKEEPER | GAMES | DEF RATE |
|---|---|---|
| Alex Kolinko | 27 | 87 |
| **DEFENDERS** | **GAMES** | **DEF RATE** |
| Kit Symons | 20 | 84 |
| Danny Granville | 26 | 82 |
| Danny Butterfield | 44 | 80 |
| Darren Powell | 33 | 79 |
| **MIDFIELDERS** | **GAMES** | **SCORE DIFF** |
| Aki Riihilahti | 13 | 22 |
| Julian Gray | 22 | 18 |
| Thomas Black | 16 | 15 |
| Stephen Thomson | 13 | 13 |
| **GOALSCORERS** | **GAMES** | **STRIKE RATE** |
| Andrew Johnson | 22 | 193 |
| Dougie Freedman | 20 | 228 |

Games = games playing at least 70 minutes

## LEAGUE APPEARANCES, BOOKINGS AND CAPS

| | AGE (on 01/07/03) | IN THE SQUAD | COUNTING GAMES | MINUTES ON PITCH | YELLOW CARDS | RED CARDS | THIS SEASON | HOME COUNTRY |
|---|---|---|---|---|---|---|---|---|
| **Goalkeepers** | | | | | | | | |
| Cedric Berthelin | 26 | 19 | 8 | 740 | 0 | 0 | - | France |
| Matt Clarke | 29 | 6 | 6 | 520 | 0 | 0 | - | England |
| Lance Cronin | 17 | 8 | 0 | 0 | 0 | 0 | - | England |
| Alex Kolinko | 28 | 42 | 27 | 2430 | 1 | 0 | - | Latvia |
| Nikolaos Michopoulos | 33 | 15 | 5 | 450 | 0 | 0 | - | Greece |
| Sven Scheuer | 32 | 1 | 0 | 0 | 0 | 0 | - | Germany |
| **Defenders** | | | | | | | | |
| Will Antwi | 20 | 10 | 0 | 37 | 0 | 0 | - | England |
| Dean Austin | 33 | 9 | 1 | 144 | 0 | 0 | - | England |
| Gary Borrowdale | 17 | 23 | 7 | 754 | 1 | 0 | - | England |
| Danny Butterfield | 23 | 46 | 44 | 4055 | 3 | 0 | - | England |
| Curtis Fleming | 34 | 11 | 7 | 762 | 1 | 0 | - | Rep of Ireland |
| Andrew Frampton | 23 | 3 | 0 | 12 | 0 | 0 | - | England |
| Danny Granville | 28 | 38 | 26 | 2694 | 9 | 1 | - | England |
| David Hunt | 20 | 5 | 0 | 121 | 0 | 0 | - | England |
| Hayden Mullins | 24 | 43 | 42 | 3845 | 12 | 0 | - | England |
| Tony Popovic | 30 | 37 | 33 | 3070 | 4 | 0 | - | Australia |
| Darren Powell | 27 | 38 | 33 | 3152 | 11 | 0 | - | England |
| Jamie Smith | 28 | 2 | 1 | 96 | 0 | 0 | - | England |
| Kit Symons | 32 | 26 | 20 | 1926 | 0 | 0 | - | Wales |
| Sam Togwell | 18 | 1 | 0 | 1 | 0 | 0 | - | England |
| **Midfielders** | | | | | | | | |
| Thomas Black | 26 | 45 | 16 | 2012 | 4 | 0 | - | England |
| Shaun Derry | 25 | 39 | 33 | 3182 | 4 | 0 | - | England |
| Julian Gray | 23 | 36 | 22 | 2495 | 1 | 0 | - | England |
| Gavin Heeroo | 18 | 1 | 0 | 0 | 0 | 0 | - | Mauritius |
| Richard Howell | 20 | 1 | 1 | 90 | 0 | 0 | - | |
| Aki Riihilahti | 26 | 27 | 13 | 1457 | 3 | 0 | - | Finland |
| Wayne Routledge | 18 | 30 | 10 | 1422 | 3 | 1 | - | England |
| Andrejs Rubins | 24 | 6 | 0 | 50 | 0 | 0 | - | |
| Robert Smith | 20 | 0 | 0 | 0 | 0 | 0 | - | England |
| Stephen Thomson | 25 | 29 | 13 | 1582 | 3 | 0 | - | Scotland |
| Ben Watson | 18 | 7 | 3 | 341 | 0 | 0 | - | England |
| **Forwards** | | | | | | | | |
| Dele Adebola | 28 | 39 | 25 | 2802 | 1 | 0 | - | Nigeria |
| Adeola Akinbiyi | 28 | 11 | 3 | 433 | 0 | 0 | - | England |
| Dougie Freedman | 28 | 30 | 20 | 2052 | 1 | 0 | - | Scotland |
| Andrew Johnson | 22 | 29 | 22 | 2125 | 1 | 0 | - | England |
| Steve Kabba | 22 | 4 | 0 | 80 | 0 | 0 | - | England |
| Noel Whelan | 28 | 8 | 3 | 508 | 2 | 0 | - | England |
| Gareth Williams | 20 | 10 | 0 | 63 | 0 | 0 | - | Wales |

## SQUAD APPEARANCES

| Match | 1 | 2 | 3 | 4 | 5 | 6 | 7 | 8 | 9 | 10 | 11 | 12 | 13 | 14 | 15 | 16 | 17 | 18 | 19 | 20 | 21 | 22 | 23 | 24 | 25 | 26 | 27 | 28 | 29 | 30 | 31 | 32 | 33 | 34 | 35 | 36 | 37 | 38 | 39 | 40 | 41 | 42 | 43 | 44 | 45 | 46 | 47 | 48 | 49 | 50 | 51 | 52 | 53 | 54 | 55 |
|---|---|---|---|---|---|---|---|---|---|---|---|---|---|---|---|---|---|---|---|---|---|---|---|---|---|---|---|---|---|---|---|---|---|---|---|---|---|---|---|---|---|---|---|---|---|---|---|---|---|---|---|---|---|---|---|
| Venue | A | H | H | A | H | A | H | H | H | A | A | H | H | A | A | H | A | A | H | H | A | H | H | A | H | H | H | A | A | A | H | H | A | H | H | A | A | A | H | H | A | A | A | H | A | H | H | A | H | H | A | H | A | H | A |
| Competition | L | L | L | L | L | L | W | L | L | L | L | L | W | L | L | L | L | L | W | L | L | L | L | L | W | L | L | W | L | L | L | L | F | L | F | L | F | L | F | L | L | L | L | L | L | L | L | L | L | L | L | L | L | L | L |
| Result | W | D | L | L | D | D | D | W | L | D | D | D | W | D | D | W | W | W | W | D | L | W | L | L | W | W | W | L | W | D | W | D | W | D | D | L | W | L | L | D | L | W | L | D | L | L | W | D | D | L | W | D | L | W | L |

**Goalkeepers**
Cedric Berthelin
Matt Clarke
Lance Cronin
Alex Kolinko
Nikolaos Michopoulos
Sven Scheuer
**Defenders**
Will Antwi
Dean Austin
Gary Borrowdale
Danny Butterfield
Curtis Fleming
Andrew Frampton
Danny Granville
David Hunt
Hayden Mullins
Tony Popovic
Darren Powell
Jamie Smith
Kit Symons
Sam Togwell
**Midfielders**
Thomas Black
Shaun Derry
Julian Gray
Gavin Heeroo
Richard Howell
Aki Riihilahti
Wayne Routledge
Andrejs Rubins
Robert Smith
Stephen Thomson
Ben Watson
**Forwards**
Dele Adebola
Adeola Akinbiyi
Dougie Freedman
Andrew Johnson
Steve Kabba
Noel Whelan
Gareth Williams

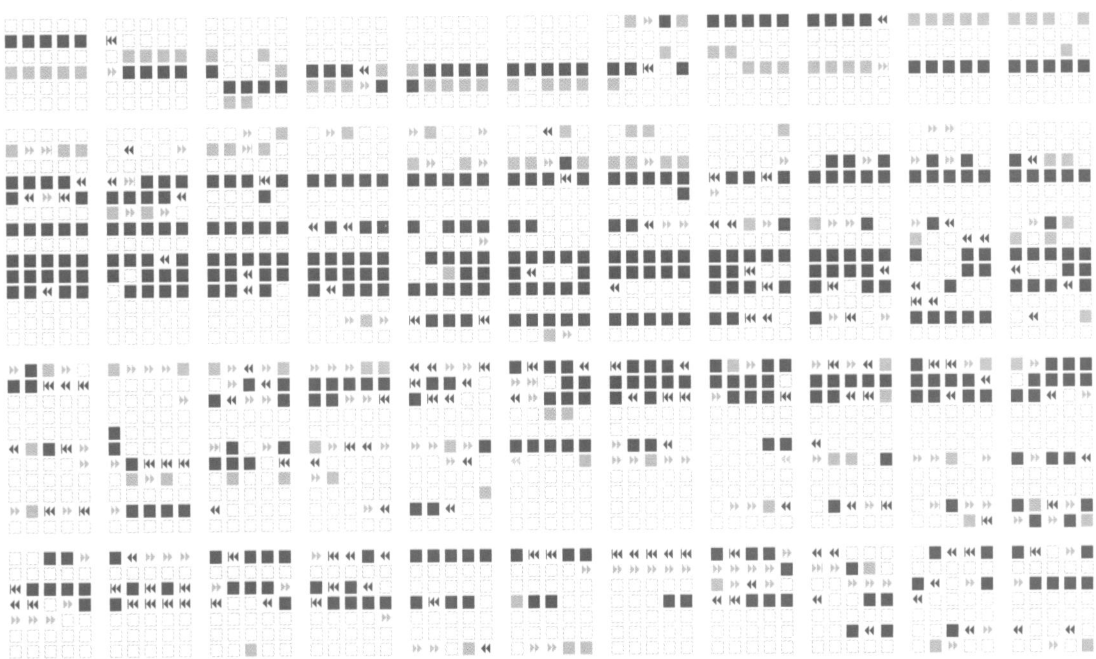

KEY: On all match; On bench; Subbed or sent off (Counting game); Subbed or sent off (playing less than 70 minutes); Subbed on from bench (Counting Game); Subbed on (playing less than 70 minutes); Subbed on and then subbed or sent off (Counting Game); Subbed on and then subbed or sent off (playing less than 70 minutes); Not in 16

# ROTHERHAM UNITED

Final Position: **15th**

**NICKNAME:** THE MERRY MILLERS

KEY: Won / Drawn / Lost

| No | Comp | Opponent | Venue | Result | Score | Scorers |
|---|---|---|---|---|---|---|
| 1 | div1 | Millwall | A | W | 6-0 | Byfield 23,52,80,81; McIntosh 43; Sedgwick 71 |
| 2 | div1 | Norwich | H | D | 1-1 | Lee 68 |
| 3 | div1 | Preston | H | D | 0-0 | |
| 4 | div1 | Sheff Wed | A | W | 2-1 | Lee 30 pen; Garner 89 |
| 5 | div1 | Derby | H | W | 2-1 | Lee 65,82 |
| 6 | div1 | Bradford | A | L | 2-4 | Barker, R 71; Robins 80 |
| 7 | div1 | Reading | H | D | 0-0 | |
| 8 | wcr1 | Carlisle | H | W | 3-1 | Monkhouse 50; Robins 68; Warne 89 |
| 9 | div1 | Sheff Utd | A | L | 0-1 | |
| 10 | div1 | Walsall | A | W | 4-3 | Byfield 14,22; Lee 29,77 pen |
| 11 | div1 | Brighton | H | W | 1-0 | Lee 20 |
| 12 | div1 | Nottm Forest | A | L | 2-3 | Barker, R 43; Byfield 58 |
| 13 | wcr2 | Wolves | H | W | 4-2* | Barker, R 4,93; Robins 78 pen; Swailes 85 (*on penalties) |
| 14 | div1 | Portsmouth | H | L | 2-3 | Byfield 33; Lee 72 pen |
| 15 | div1 | Gillingham | H | D | 1-1 | Ashby 13 og |
| 16 | div1 | Grimsby | A | D | 0-0 | |
| 17 | div1 | Stoke | H | W | 4-0 | Barker, R 15,53; Lee 39; Swailes 87 |
| 18 | div1 | Wimbledon | A | L | 1-2 | Lee 89 |
| 19 | div1 | Coventry | A | L | 1-2 | Daws 38 |
| 20 | wcr3 | Wimbledon | A | W | 3-1 | Monkhouse 51; Barker, R 75; Lee 85 |
| 21 | div1 | Watford | H | W | 2-1 | McIntosh 41; Barker, R 67 |
| 22 | div1 | Burnley | H | D | 0-0 | |
| 23 | div1 | Leicester | A | L | 1-2 | McIntosh 66 |
| 24 | div1 | Wolves | H | D | 0-0 | |
| 25 | wcr4 | Blackburn | A | L | 0-4 | |
| 26 | div1 | Ipswich | A | W | 2-1 | Talbot 25; Barker, R 45 |
| 27 | div1 | Burnley | A | W | 6-2 | Lee 12,59; Mullin 27,30; Byfield 84,89 |
| 28 | div1 | Crystal Palace | H | L | 1-3 | Byfield 69 |
| 29 | div1 | Preston | A | W | 2-0 | Robins 56; Barker, R 85 |
| 30 | div1 | Millwall | H | L | 1-3 | Hurst 81 |
| 31 | div1 | Sheff Wed | H | L | 0-2 | |
| 32 | facr3 | Wimbledon | H | L | 0-3 | |
| 33 | div1 | Norwich | A | D | 1-1 | Garner 33 |
| 34 | div1 | Bradford | H | W | 3-2 | McIntosh 21; Garner 50; Byfield 60 pen |
| 35 | div1 | Derby | A | L | 0-3 | |
| 36 | div1 | Watford | A | W | 2-1 | McIntosh 69; Swailes 75 |
| 37 | div1 | Coventry | H | W | 1-0 | Byfield 33 |
| 38 | div1 | Reading | A | L | 0-3 | |
| 39 | div1 | Sheff Utd | H | L | 1-2 | Lee 81 pen |
| 40 | div1 | Walsall | H | D | 0-0 | |
| 41 | div1 | Brighton | A | L | 0-2 | |
| 42 | div1 | Gillingham | A | D | 1-1 | Warne 12 |
| 43 | div1 | Grimsby | H | L | 0-1 | |
| 44 | div1 | Wimbledon | H | W | 2-1 | Robins 19; Branston 48 |
| 45 | div1 | Wolves | A | D | 0-0 | |
| 46 | div1 | Stoke | A | L | 0-2 | |
| 47 | div1 | Leicester | H | D | 1-1 | Lee 54 |
| 48 | div1 | Crystal Palace | A | D | 0-0 | |
| 49 | div1 | Ipswich | H | W | 2-1 | Mullin 85; Robins 87 |
| 50 | div1 | Portsmouth | A | L | 2-3 | Branston 16; Swailes 29 |
| 51 | div1 | Nottm Forest | H | D | 2-2 | Lee 55; Robins 69 |

Home / Away / Neutral

## ATTENDANCES

**HOME GROUND:** MILLMOOR **CAPACITY:** 11500 **AVERAGE LEAGUE AT HOME:** 7521

| | | | | | | | | | | | |
|---|---|---|---|---|---|---|---|---|---|---|---|
| 23 | Leicester | 31714 | 38 | Reading | 14816 | 49 | Ipswich | 7519 | 16 | Grimsby | 6418 |
| 35 | Derby | 26257 | 27 | Burnley | 14121 | 42 | Gillingham | 7284 | 43 | Grimsby | 6239 |
| 45 | Wolves | 25944 | 19 | Coventry | 13179 | 1 | Millwall | 7177 | 7 | Reading | 6154 |
| 12 | Nottm Forest | 25089 | 6 | Bradford | 12385 | 17 | Stoke | 7078 | 15 | Gillingham | 6094 |
| 4 | Sheff Wed | 22873 | 31 | Sheff Wed | 11480 | 34 | Bradford | 6939 | 44 | Wimbledon | 5896 |
| 26 | Ipswich | 22770 | 25 | Blackburn | 11220 | 3 | Preston | 6885 | 40 | Walsall | 5792 |
| 9 | Sheff Utd | 19948 | 39 | Sheff Utd | 10797 | 28 | Crystal Palace | 6829 | 13 | Wolves | 5064 |
| 46 | Stoke | 19553 | 51 | Nottm Forest | 9942 | 21 | Watford | 6790 | 10 | Walsall | 4648 |
| 33 | Norwich | 19452 | 47 | Leicester | 9888 | 24 | Wolves | 6736 | 32 | Wimbledon | 4527 |
| 50 | Portsmouth | 19420 | 14 | Portsmouth | 8604 | 11 | Brighton | 6696 | 8 | Carlisle | 2902 |
| 48 | Crystal Palace | 15508 | 5 | Derby | 8408 | 37 | Coventry | 6524 | 18 | Wimbledon | 849 |
| 29 | Preston | 15452 | 2 | Norwich | 7687 | 41 | Brighton | 6468 | 20 | Wimbledon | 664 |
| 36 | Watford | 15025 | 22 | Burnley | 7575 | 30 | Millwall | 6448 | | | |

## KEY PLAYERS - GOALSCORERS

1 Darren Byfield

BODYLINE

| | |
|---|---|
| Goals in the League | 13 |
| Goals in all competitions | 13 |
| Contribution to Attacking Power<br>Average number of minutes between League team goals while on pitch | 66 |
| Player Strike Rate<br>The total number of minutes he was on the pitch for every League goal scored | 164 |
| Club Strike Rate<br>Average number of minutes between League goals scored by club | 67 |

| | PLAYER | GOALS LGE | GOALS ALL | POWER | S RATE |
|---|---|---|---|---|---|
| 2 | Alan Lee | 15 | 16 | 69 | 219 mins |
| 3 | Richard Barker | 7 | 10 | 60 | 300 mins |
| 4 | Guy Branston | 2 | 2 | 92 | 603 mins |
| 5 | Darren Garner | 3 | 3 | 61 | 614 mins |

## KEY PLAYERS - MIDFIELDERS

1 Martin McIntosh

BODYLINE
T··Mobile·

| | |
|---|---|
| Goals in the League | 5 |
| Goals in all competitions | 5 |
| Defensive Rating<br>Average number of mins between League goals conceded while on the pitch | 64 |
| Contribution to Attacking Power<br>Average number of minutes between League team goals while on pitch | 64 |
| Scoring Difference<br>Defensive Rating minus Contribution to Attacking Power | 0 |

| | PLAYER | GOALS LGE | GOALS ALL | DEF RATE | ATT POWER | SCORE DIFF |
|---|---|---|---|---|---|---|
| 2 | Nick Daws | 1 | 1 | 65 | 67 | -2 mins |
| 3 | Darren Garner | 3 | 3 | 58 | 61 | -3 mins |
| 4 | Chris Sedgwick | 1 | 1 | 63 | 68 | -5 mins |
| 5 | Curtis Woodhouse | 0 | 0 | 69 | 160 | -91 mins |

## KEY PLAYERS - DEFENDERS

1 Shaun Barker

| | |
|---|---|
| Goals Conceded in League | 14 |
| Goals Conceded in all competitions | 14 |
| Clean Sheets<br>In League games when he played at least 70 mins | 2 |
| Defensive Rating<br>Ave number of mins between League goals conceded while on the pitch | 71 |
| Club Defensive Rating<br>Average number of mins between League goals conceded by the club this season | 67 |

| | PLAYER | CON LGE | CON ALL | CLN SHEETS | DEF RATE |
|---|---|---|---|---|---|
| 2 | Guy Branston | 17 | 22 | 3 | 71 mins |
| 3 | Paul Hurst | 59 | 71 | 13 | 67 mins |
| 4 | Chris Swailes | 60 | 73 | 12 | 64 mins |
| 5 | Marvin Bryan | 18 | 22 | 4 | 64 mins |

## KEY GOALKEEPER

1 Mike Pollitt

T··Mobile

| | |
|---|---|
| Goals Conceded in the League | 52 |
| Goals Conceded in all competitions | 65 |
| Clean Sheets<br>In games when he played at least 70 mins | 12 |
| Goals to Shots Ratio<br>The average number of shots on target per each League goal conceded | 3.7 |
| Defensive Rating<br>Ave number of mins between League goals conceded while on the pitch | 69 |

## MONTHY POINTS TALLY

| Month | Points | % |
|---|---|---|
| AUGUST | 11 | 61% |
| SEPTEMBER | 10 | 56% |
| OCTOBER | 6 | 33% |
| NOVEMBER | 8 | 44% |
| DECEMBER | 9 | 50% |
| JANUARY | 4 | 33% |
| FEBRUARY | 6 | 40% |
| MARCH | 5 | 33% |
| APRIL | 6 | 33% |
| MAY | 1 | 33% |

## TOP POINT EARNERS

| | PLAYER | GAMES | AV PTS |
|---|---|---|---|
| 1 | John Mullin | 25 | 1.60 |
| 2 | Darren Byfield | 17 | 1.53 |
| 3 | Rob Scott | 21 | 1.48 |
| 4 | Darren Garner | 17 | 1.47 |
| 5 | Chris Sedgwick | 37 | 1.46 |
| 6 | Chris Swailes | 42 | 1.36 |
| 7 | Mike Pollitt | 40 | 1.33 |
| 8 | Paul Hurst | 44 | 1.32 |
| 9 | Martin McIntosh | 42 | 1.29 |
| 10 | Alan Lee | 35 | 1.29 |
| | CLUB AVERAGE: | | 1.28 |

## GOALS

**1 Alan Lee**

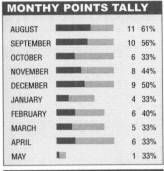

| | |
|---|---|
| League | 15 |
| FA Cup | 0 |
| League Cup | 1 |
| Other | 0 |
| TOTAL | 16 |

| | PLAYER | LGE | FAC | LC | Oth | TOT |
|---|---|---|---|---|---|---|
| 2 | Byfield | 13 | 0 | 0 | 0 | 13 |
| 3 | Barker, R | 7 | 0 | 3 | 0 | 10 |
| 4 | McIntosh | 5 | 0 | 0 | 0 | 5 |
| 5 | Robins | 5 | 0 | 2 | 0 | 7 |
| 6 | Garner | 3 | 0 | 0 | 0 | 3 |
| 7 | Swailes | 3 | 0 | 1 | 0 | 4 |
| 8 | Mullin | 3 | 0 | 0 | 0 | 3 |
| 9 | Branston | 2 | 0 | 0 | 0 | 2 |
| 10 | Talbot | 1 | 0 | 0 | 0 | 1 |
| 11 | Sedgwick | 1 | 0 | 0 | 0 | 1 |
| | Other | 4 | 0 | 3 | 0 | 7 |
| | TOTAL | 62 | 0 | 10 | 0 | 72 |

## TEAM OF THE SEASON

| GOALKEEPER | GAMES | DEF RATE |
|---|---|---|
| Mike Pollitt | 40 | 69 |
| **DEFENDERS** | **GAMES** | **DEF RATE** |
| Shaun Barker | 11 | 71 |
| Guy Branston | 13 | 71 |
| Paul Hurst | 44 | 67 |
| Chris Swailes | 42 | 64 |
| **MIDFIELDERS** | **GAMES** | **SCORE DIFF** |
| Martin McIntosh | 42 | 0 |
| Nick Daws | 29 | -2 |
| Darren Garner | 17 | -3 |
| Chris Sedgwick | 37 | -5 |
| **GOALSCORERS** | **GAMES** | **STRIKE RATE** |
| Darren Byfield | 17 | 164 |
| Alan Lee | 35 | 219 |

Games = games playing at least 70 minutes

## LEAGUE APPEARANCES, BOOKINGS AND CAPS

| | AGE (on 01/07/03) | IN THE SQUAD | COUNTING GAMES | MINUTES ON PITCH | YELLOW CARDS | RED CARDS | THIS SEASON | HOME COUNTRY |
|---|---|---|---|---|---|---|---|---|
| **Goalkeepers** | | | | | | | | |
| Ian Gray | 28 | 44 | 6 | 527 | 1 | 0 | - | England |
| Mike Pollitt | 31 | 42 | 40 | 3613 | 3 | 1 | - | England |
| **Defenders** | | | | | | | | |
| Shaun Barker | - | 11 | 11 | 990 | 1 | 0 | - | England |
| Chris Beech | 27 | 12 | 1 | 99 | 0 | 0 | - | |
| Guy Branston | 24 | 22 | 13 | 1206 | 7 | 1 | - | England |
| Marvin Bryan | 27 | 21 | 11 | 1147 | 2 | 0 | - | England |
| Danny Hudson | 24 | 4 | 0 | 0 | 0 | 0 | - | England |
| Paul Hurst | 28 | 46 | 44 | 3940 | 1 | 0 | - | England |
| Rob Scott | 29 | 23 | 21 | 1956 | 6 | 0 | - | England |
| Chris Swailes | 32 | 44 | 42 | 3825 | 7 | 1 | - | England |
| **Midfielders** | | | | | | | | |
| Nick Daws | 33 | 41 | 29 | 2729 | 0 | 0 | - | England |
| Gareth Farrelly | 27 | 6 | 6 | 520 | 0 | 0 | - | Rep of Ireland |
| Darren Garner | 31 | 30 | 17 | 1841 | 6 | 0 | - | England |
| Martin McIntosh | 32 | 42 | 42 | 3774 | 11 | 0 | - | Scotland |
| Andy Monkhouse | 22 | 28 | 8 | 1007 | 1 | 0 | - | England |
| Chris Sedgwick | 23 | 44 | 37 | 3469 | 7 | 0 | - | England |
| Curtis Woodhouse | 23 | 12 | 10 | 959 | 3 | 0 | - | England |
| **Forwards** | | | | | | | | |
| Richard Barker | 28 | 46 | 21 | 2101 | 4 | 0 | - | England |
| Darren Byfield | 26 | 42 | 17 | 2129 | 6 | 0 | - | England |
| William Hoskins | - | 1 | 0 | 0 | 0 | 0 | - | England |
| Alan Lee | 24 | 41 | 35 | 3284 | 12 | 0 | 3 | Rep of Ireland (15) |
| John Mullin | 27 | 36 | 25 | 2683 | 7 | 1 | - | England |
| Mark Robins | 33 | 28 | 6 | 696 | 0 | 0 | - | England |
| Stewart Talbot | 30 | 25 | 6 | 781 | 4 | 0 | - | England |
| Paul Warne | 30 | 46 | 17 | 2108 | 5 | 0 | - | England |

**KEY:** LEAGUE BOOKINGS CAPS (FIFA RANKING)

## SQUAD APPEARANCES

| Match | 1 | 2 | 3 | 4 | 5 | 6 | 7 | 8 | 9 | 10 | 11 | 12 | 13 | 14 | 15 | 16 | 17 | 18 | 19 | 20 | 21 | 22 | 23 | 24 | 25 |
|---|---|---|---|---|---|---|---|---|---|---|---|---|---|---|---|---|---|---|---|---|---|---|---|---|---|
| Venue | A | H | H | A | H | A | H | H | A | A | H | A | H | H | H | A | H | A | A | A | H | H | A | H | A |
| Competition | L | L | L | L | L | L | L | W | L | L | L | L | W | L | L | L | L | L | L | W | L | L | L | L | W |
| Result | W | D | D | W | W | L | D | W | L | W | W | L | W | L | D | D | W | L | L | W | W | D | L | D | L |

| Match | 26 | 27 | 28 | 29 | 30 | 31 | 32 | 33 | 34 | 35 | 36 | 37 | 38 | 39 | 40 | 41 | 42 | 43 | 44 | 45 | 46 | 47 | 48 | 49 | 50 | 51 |
|---|---|---|---|---|---|---|---|---|---|---|---|---|---|---|---|---|---|---|---|---|---|---|---|---|---|---|
| Venue | A | A | H | A | H | H | H | A | H | A | A | H | A | H | H | A | A | H | H | A | A | H | A | H | A | H |
| Competition | L | L | L | L | L | L | F | L | L | L | L | L | L | L | L | L | L | L | L | L | L | L | L | L | L | L |
| Result | W | W | L | W | L | L | L | D | W | L | W | W | L | L | D | L | D | L | W | D | L | D | D | W | L | D |

**Goalkeepers**
Ian Gray
Mike Pollitt

**Defenders**
Shaun Barker
Chris Beech
Guy Branston
Marvin Bryan
Danny Hudson
Paul Hurst
Rob Scott
Chris Swailes

**Midfielders**
Nick Daws
Gareth Farrelly
Darren Garner
Martin McIntosh
Andy Monkhouse
Chris Sedgwick
Curtis Woodhouse

**Forwards**
Richard Barker
Darren Byfield
William Hoskins
Alan Lee
John Mullin
Mark Robins
Stewart Talbot
Paul Warne

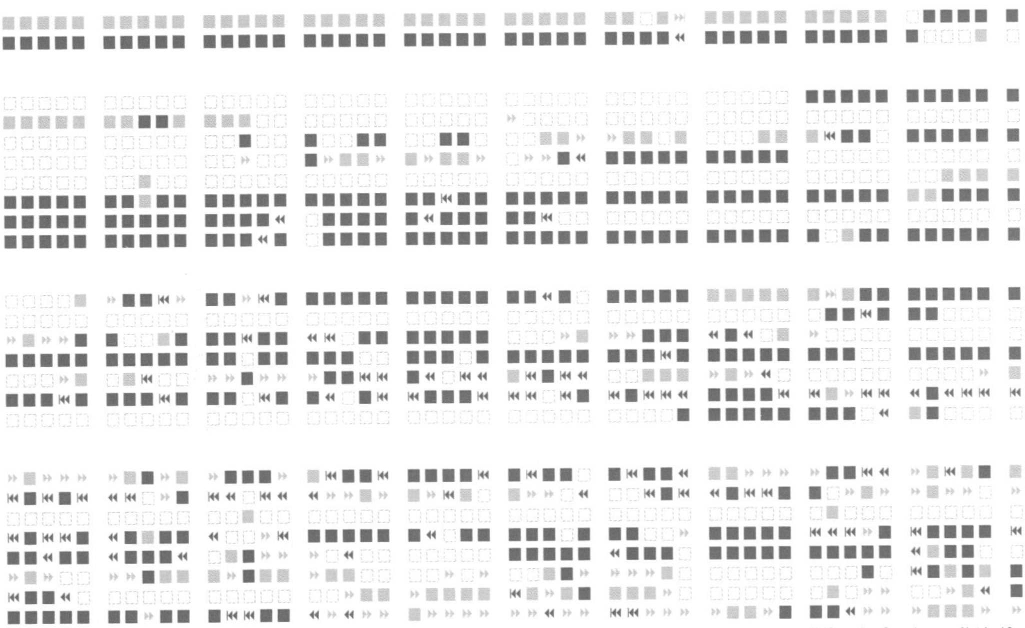

**KEY:** On all match | On bench | Subbed or sent off (Counting game) | Subbed or sent off (playing less than 70 minutes) | Subbed on from bench (Counting Game) | Subbed on (playing less than 70 minutes) | Subbed on and then subbed or sent off (Counting Game) | Subbed on and then subbed or sent off (playing less than 70 minutes) | Not in 16

# BURNLEY

Final Position: **16th**

NICKNAME: THE CLARETS

KEY: Won / Drawn / Lost

| | | | | | | |
|---|---|---|---|---|---|---|
| 1 | div1 | Brighton | H | L | 1-3 | Briscoe 89 |
| 2 | div1 | Wolves | A | L | 0-3 | |
| 3 | div1 | Sheff Utd | H | L | 0-1 | |
| 4 | div1 | Reading | A | L | 0-3 | |
| 5 | div1 | Crystal Palace | H | D | 0-0 | |
| 6 | div1 | Derby | A | W | 2-1 | Blake 50 pen; Barton 55 og |
| 7 | wcr1 | Blackpool | H | W | 3-0 | West 13; Papadopoulos 63,74 |
| 8 | div1 | Stoke | H | W | 2-1 | Gnohere 76; Papadopoulos 82 |
| 9 | div1 | Millwall | H | D | 2-2 | West 17 pen; Moore, I 85 |
| 10 | div1 | Bradford | A | D | 2-2 | Blake 58; Taylor 76 |
| 11 | div1 | Wimbledon | H | W | 1-0 | Little 50 |
| 12 | wcr2 | Huddersfield | A | W | 1-0 | Papadopoulos 103 |
| 13 | div1 | Sheff Wed | A | W | 3-1 | Taylor 8; Little 56; Moore, I 60 |
| 14 | div1 | Walsall | H | W | 2-1 | Blake 42; Davis, S 69 |
| 15 | div1 | Leicester | A | W | 1-0 | Moore, I 54 |
| 16 | div1 | Ipswich | A | D | 2-2 | Gnohere 6; Papadopoulos 90 |
| 17 | div1 | Portsmouth | H | L | 0-3 | |
| 18 | div1 | Grimsby | A | L | 5-6 | Taylor 22,49; Moore, I 31; Blake 45,83 pen |
| 19 | div1 | Preston | A | L | 1-3 | Taylor 51 |
| 20 | wcr3 | Tottenham | H | W | 2-1 | Blake 57; Davis, S 61 |
| 21 | div1 | Coventry | H | W | 3-1 | Blake 15 pen; Grant 35; Davenport 86 og |
| 22 | div1 | Rotherham | A | D | 0-0 | |
| 23 | div1 | Norwich | H | W | 2-0 | McGregor 59; Little 85 |
| 24 | div1 | Watford | A | L | 1-2 | Taylor 76 |
| 25 | wcr4 | Man Utd | H | L | 0-2 | |
| 26 | div1 | Nottm Forest | H | W | 1-0 | Briscoe 28 |
| 27 | div1 | Rotherham | H | L | 2-6 | Davis, S 67,78 |
| 28 | div1 | Gillingham | A | L | 2-4 | Taylor 28; Blake 76 pen |
| 29 | div1 | Wolves | H | W | 2-1 | Taylor 24; West 32 |
| 30 | div1 | Brighton | A | D | 2-2 | Little 44; Moore, I 71 |
| 31 | facr3 | Grimsby | A | D | 2-2 | Moore, A 14; Weller 18 |
| 32 | div1 | Ipswich | H | D | 1-1 | Blake 66 pen |
| 33 | facr3r | Grimsby | H | W | 4-0 | Moore, I 25,90; Little 79; Blake 86 pen |
| 34 | div1 | Crystal Palace | A | D | 1-1 | Taylor 44 |
| 35 | facr4 | Brentford | A | W | 3-0 | Blake 52; Cook 86; Little 89 |
| 36 | div1 | Reading | H | L | 2-5 | Moore, I 55; West 90 |
| 37 | div1 | Coventry | A | W | 1-0 | Cox 35 |
| 38 | facr5 | Fulham | A | D | 1-1 | Moore, A 4 |
| 39 | div1 | Derby | H | W | 2-0 | Moore, I 8; Taylor 23 |
| 40 | facr5r | Fulham | H | W | 3-0 | Taylor 27; Moore, I 35; Diallo 52 |
| 41 | div1 | Stoke | A | W | 1-0 | West 56 |
| 42 | div1 | Millwall | A | D | 1-1 | Moore, I 18 |
| 43 | facqf | Watford | A | L | 0-2 | |
| 44 | div1 | Sheff Utd | A | L | 2-4 | Taylor 64; Blake 90 |
| 45 | div1 | Walsall | A | L | 2-3 | Blake 74 pen; Little 90 |
| 46 | div1 | Leicester | H | L | 1-2 | Sinclair 90 og |
| 47 | div1 | Grimsby | H | D | 1-1 | Moore, A 52 |
| 48 | div1 | Bradford | H | L | 0-2 | |
| 49 | div1 | Watford | H | L | 4-7 | Taylor 15,39,45; Davis, S 35 |
| 50 | div1 | Preston | H | W | 2-0 | Papadopoulos 42; Blake 61 |
| 51 | div1 | Norwich | A | L | 0-2 | |
| 52 | div1 | Portsmouth | A | L | 0-1 | |
| 53 | div1 | Gillingham | H | W | 2-0 | Taylor 28; Diallo 50 |
| 54 | div1 | Nottm Forest | A | L | 0-2 | |
| 55 | div1 | Sheff Wed | H | L | 2-7 | Blake 42 pen,53 |
| 56 | div1 | Wimbledon | A | L | 1-2 | Taylor 27 |

Home / Away / Neutral

## ATTENDANCES

HOME GROUND: TURF MOOR CAPACITY: 22619 AVERAGE LEAGUE AT HOME: 13976

| | | | | | | | | | | | |
|---|---|---|---|---|---|---|---|---|---|---|---|
| 15 | Leicester | 26254 | 19 | Preston | 16046 | 21 | Coventry | 13470 | 28 | Gillingham | 7905 |
| 54 | Nottm Forest | 25403 | 17 | Portsmouth | 15788 | 47 | Grimsby | 13445 | 22 | Rotherham | 7575 |
| 2 | Wolves | 25031 | 32 | Ipswich | 15501 | 38 | Fulham | 13062 | 7 | Blackpool | 7448 |
| 16 | Ipswich | 22736 | 39 | Derby | 15063 | 14 | Walsall | 12907 | 30 | Brighton | 6502 |
| 6 | Derby | 22342 | 1 | Brighton | 14738 | 41 | Stoke | 12874 | 45 | Walsall | 6327 |
| 25 | Man Utd | 22034 | 10 | Bradford | 14561 | 3 | Sheff Utd | 12868 | 42 | Millwall | 6045 |
| 43 | Watford | 20336 | 46 | Leicester | 14554 | 5 | Crystal Palace | 12407 | 12 | Huddersfield | 5887 |
| 51 | Norwich | 20026 | 36 | Reading | 14420 | 11 | Wimbledon | 12259 | 18 | Grimsby | 5620 |
| 52 | Portsmouth | 19221 | 8 | Stoke | 14244 | 50 | Preston | 12245 | 33 | Grimsby | 5436 |
| 29 | Wolves | 18641 | 27 | Rotherham | 14121 | 4 | Reading | 12009 | 31 | Grimsby | 5350 |
| 55 | Sheff Wed | 17435 | 53 | Gillingham | 14031 | 9 | Millwall | 11878 | 56 | Wimbledon | 1972 |
| 44 | Sheff Utd | 17359 | 24 | Watford | 13977 | 40 | Fulham | 11635 | | | |
| 13 | Sheff Wed | 17004 | 26 | Nottm Forest | 13869 | 48 | Bradford | 11095 | | | |
| 34 | Crystal Palace | 16344 | 37 | Coventry | 13659 | 49 | Watford | 10208 | | | |
| 23 | Norwich | 16282 | 20 | Tottenham | 13512 | 35 | Brentford | 9563 | | | |

## KEY PLAYERS - GOALSCORERS

1 Gareth Taylor

| | |
|---|---|
| Goals in the League | 16 |
| Goals in all competitions | 17 |
| Contribution to Attacking Power<br>Average number of minutes between League team goals while on pitch | 60 |
| Player Strike Rate<br>The total number of minutes he was on the pitch for every League goal scored | 213 |
| Club Strike Rate<br>Average number of minutes between League goals scored by club | 64 |

| | PLAYER | GOALS LGE | GOALS ALL | POWER | S RATE |
|---|---|---|---|---|---|
| 2 | Robbie Blake | 13 | 16 | 56 | 227 mins |
| 3 | Ian Moore | 9 | 12 | 66 | 327 mins |
| 4 | Glen Little | 5 | 7 | 63 | 522 mins |
| 5 | Steve Davis | 4 | 5 | 53 | 531 mins |

## KEY PLAYERS - MIDFIELDERS

1 Alan Moore

| | |
|---|---|
| Goals in the League | 1 |
| Goals in all competitions | 3 |
| Defensive Rating<br>Average number of mins between League goals conceded while on the pitch | 61 |
| Contribution to Attacking Power<br>Average number of minutes between League team goals while on pitch | 56 |
| Scoring Difference<br>Defensive Rating minus Contribution to Attacking Power | 5 |

| | PLAYER | GOALS LGE | GOALS ALL | DEF RATE | ATT POWER | SCORE DIFF |
|---|---|---|---|---|---|---|
| 2 | Paul Cook | 0 | 1 | 69 | 69 | 0 mins |
| 3 | Tony Grant | 1 | 1 | 45 | 56 | -11 mins |
| 4 | Glen Little | 5 | 7 | 46 | 64 | -18 mins |
| 5 | Paul Weller | 0 | 1 | 42 | 62 | -20 mins |

## KEY PLAYERS - DEFENDERS

1 Ian Cox

| | |
|---|---|
| Goals Conceded in League | 34 |
| Goals Conceded in all competitions | 39 |
| Clean Sheets<br>In League games when he played at least 70 mins | 6 |
| Defensive Rating<br>Ave number of mins between League goals conceded while on the pitch | 58 |
| Club Defensive Rating<br>Average number of mins between League goals conceded by the club this season | 46 |

| | PLAYER | CON LGE | CON ALL | CLN SHEETS | DEF RATE |
|---|---|---|---|---|---|
| 2 | Drissa Diallo | 20 | 23 | 4 | 56 mins |
| 3 | David Gnohere | 54 | 59 | 6 | 51 mins |
| 4 | Lee Briscoe | 52 | 57 | 8 | 48 mins |
| 5 | Mark McGregor | 42 | 45 | 5 | 48 mins |

## KEY GOALKEEPER

1 Nikolaos Michopoulos

| | |
|---|---|
| Goals Conceded in the League | 19 |
| Goals Conceded in all competitions | 19 |
| Clean Sheets<br>In games when he played at least 70 mins | 4 |
| Goals to Shots Ratio<br>The average number of shots on target per each League goal conceded | 4.1 |
| Defensive Rating<br>Ave number of mins between League goals conceded while on the pitch | 59 |

## MONTHY POINTS TALLY

| Month | Points | % |
|---|---|---|
| AUGUST | 1 | 7% |
| SEPTEMBER | 14 | 78% |
| OCTOBER | 13 | 62% |
| NOVEMBER | 10 | 56% |
| DECEMBER | 7 | 39% |
| JANUARY | 9 | 60% |
| FEBRUARY | 10 | 67% |
| MARCH | 5 | 21% |
| APRIL | 6 | 29% |
| MAY | 0 | 0% |

## TOP POINT EARNERS

| | PLAYER | GAMES | AV PTS |
|---|---|---|---|
| 1 | Ian Cox | 20 | 1.80 |
| 2 | Paul Cook | 13 | 1.54 |
| 3 | Tony Grant | 23 | 1.48 |
| 4 | Lee Briscoe | 24 | 1.46 |
| 5 | David Gnohere | 28 | 1.43 |
| 6 | Robbie Blake | 26 | 1.38 |
| 7 | Drissa Diallo | 12 | 1.33 |
| 8 | Marlon Beresford | 33 | 1.33 |
| 9 | Graham Branch | 27 | 1.30 |
| 10 | Ian Moore | 27 | 1.30 |
| | CLUB AVERAGE: | | 1.20 |

## GOALS

| 1 Gareth Taylor | |
|---|---|
| League | 16 |
| FA Cup | 1 |
| League Cup | 0 |
| Other | 0 |
| TOTAL | 17 |

| | PLAYER | LGE | FAC | LC | Oth | TOT |
|---|---|---|---|---|---|---|
| 2 | Blake | 13 | 2 | 1 | 0 | 16 |
| 3 | Moore, I | 9 | 3 | 0 | 0 | 12 |
| 4 | Little | 5 | 2 | 0 | 0 | 7 |
| 5 | West | 4 | 0 | 1 | 0 | 5 |
| 6 | Davis, S | 4 | 0 | 1 | 0 | 5 |
| 7 | Papadopoulos | 3 | 0 | 3 | 0 | 6 |
| 8 | Gnohere | 2 | 0 | 0 | 0 | 2 |
| 9 | Grant | 1 | 0 | 0 | 0 | 1 |
| 10 | Diallo | 1 | 1 | 0 | 0 | 2 |
| 11 | McGregor | 1 | 0 | 0 | 0 | 1 |
| | Other | 6 | 4 | 0 | 0 | 10 |
| | TOTAL | 65 | 13 | 6 | 0 | 84 |

## TEAM OF THE SEASON

| GOALKEEPER | GAMES | DEF RATE |
|---|---|---|
| Nikolaos Michopoulos | 12 | 59 |
| **DEFENDERS** | **GAMES** | **DEF RATE** |
| Ian Cox | 20 | 58 |
| Drissa Diallo | 12 | 56 |
| David Gnohere | 28 | 51 |
| Lee Briscoe | 24 | 48 |
| **MIDFIELDERS** | **GAMES** | **SCORE DIFF** |
| Alan Moore | 10 | 5 |
| Paul Cook | 13 | 0 |
| Tony Grant | 23 | -11 |
| Glen Little | 25 | -18 |
| **GOALSCORERS** | **GAMES** | **STRIKE RATE** |
| Gareth Taylor | 37 | 213 |
| Robbie Blake | 26 | 227 |

Games = games playing at least 70 minutes

## LEAGUE APPEARANCES, BOOKINGS AND CAPS

| | AGE (on 01/07/03) | IN THE SQUAD | COUNTING GAMES | MINUTES ON PITCH | YELLOW CARDS | RED CARDS | THIS SEASON | HOME COUNTRY |
|---|---|---|---|---|---|---|---|---|
| **Goalkeepers** | | | | | | | | |
| Marlon Beresford | 33 | 36 | 33 | 3024 | 2 | 0 | - | England |
| Nikolaos Michopoulos | 33 | 29 | 12 | 1116 | 0 | 0 | - | Greece |
| **Defenders** | | | | | | | | |
| Lee Briscoe | 27 | 32 | 24 | 2519 | 4 | 0 | - | England |
| Ian Cox | 32 | 29 | 20 | 1968 | 5 | 0 | - | England |
| Earl Davis | 20 | 3 | 2 | 180 | 0 | 0 | - | England |
| Steve Davis | 34 | 26 | 22 | 2123 | 5 | 0 | - | England |
| Drissa Diallo | 30 | 14 | 12 | 1127 | 2 | 0 | - | Mauritania |
| David Gnohere | 24 | 33 | 28 | 2743 | 9 | 2 | - | France |
| Andrew Leeson | 19 | 3 | 0 | 0 | 0 | 0 | - | England |
| Mark McGregor | 26 | 38 | 21 | 2028 | 4 | 1 | - | Wales |
| Dean West | 30 | 41 | 39 | 3619 | 4 | 1 | - | England |
| **Midfielders** | | | | | | | | |
| Gordon Armstrong | 35 | 12 | 1 | 242 | 2 | 0 | - | England |
| Richard Chaplow | 18 | 6 | 2 | 273 | 0 | 0 | - | England |
| Paul Cook | 36 | 31 | 13 | 1457 | 4 | 1 | - | England |
| Tony Grant | 28 | 38 | 23 | 2480 | 7 | 0 | - | England |
| Lenny Johnrose | 33 | 6 | 3 | 393 | 1 | 0 | - | England |
| Glen Little | 27 | 34 | 25 | 2611 | 8 | 0 | - | England |
| Brad Maylett | 22 | 14 | 1 | 245 | 1 | 0 | - | England |
| Alan Moore | 28 | 29 | 10 | 1342 | 0 | 0 | - | Rep of Ireland |
| Matthew O'Neill | 19 | 12 | 3 | 393 | 0 | 0 | - | England |
| Joel Pilkington | 18 | 4 | 0 | 0 | 0 | 0 | - | England |
| Andrew Waine | 20 | 6 | 0 | 43 | 0 | 0 | - | England |
| Paul Weller | 28 | 34 | 22 | 2436 | 4 | 0 | - | England |
| **Forwards** | | | | | | | | |
| Robbie Blake | 27 | 46 | 26 | 2946 | 2 | 0 | - | England |
| Graham Branch | 31 | 35 | 27 | 2659 | 7 | 0 | - | England |
| Ian Moore | 26 | 47 | 27 | 2946 | 3 | 1 | - | England |
| D Papadopoulos | 21 | 38 | 3 | 968 | 2 | 0 | - | Greece |
| Andy Payton | 35 | 14 | 0 | 15 | 0 | 0 | - | England |
| Mark Rasmussen | 19 | 6 | 0 | 12 | 0 | 0 | - | England |
| Gareth Taylor | 30 | 40 | 37 | 3409 | 11 | 1 | 4 | Wales (50) |

KEY: LEAGUE BOOKINGS CAPS (FIFA RANKING)

## SQUAD APPEARANCES

| Match | 1 | 2 | 3 | 4 | 5 | 6 | 7 | 8 | 9 | 10 | 11 | 12 | 13 | 14 | 15 | 16 | 17 | 18 | 19 | 20 | 21 | 22 | 23 | 24 | 25 | 26 | 27 | 28 |
|---|---|---|---|---|---|---|---|---|---|---|---|---|---|---|---|---|---|---|---|---|---|---|---|---|---|---|---|---|
| Venue | H | A | H | A | H | A | H | H | H | A | H | A | A | H | A | A | H | A | A | H | H | A | H | A | H | H | H | A |
| Competition | L | L | L | L | L | L | W | L | L | L | L | W | L | L | L | L | L | L | L | W | L | L | L | L | W | L | L | L |
| Result | L | L | L | L | D | W | W | W | D | D | W | D | W | W | W | D | L | L | L | W | W | D | W | L | L | W | L | L |

| Match | 29 | 30 | 31 | 32 | 33 | 34 | 35 | 36 | 37 | 38 | 39 | 40 | 41 | 42 | 43 | 44 | 45 | 46 | 47 | 48 | 49 | 50 | 51 | 52 | 53 | 54 | 55 | 56 |
|---|---|---|---|---|---|---|---|---|---|---|---|---|---|---|---|---|---|---|---|---|---|---|---|---|---|---|---|---|
| Venue | H | A | A | H | H | A | A | H | A | A | H | H | A | A | A | A | A | H | H | H | H | H | A | A | H | A | H | A |
| Competition | L | L | F | L | F | L | F | L | L | F | L | F | L | L | F | L | L | L | L | L | L | L | L | L | L | L | L | L |
| Result | W | D | D | D | W | D | W | L | W | D | W | W | W | D | L | L | L | L | D | L | L | W | L | L | W | L | L | L |

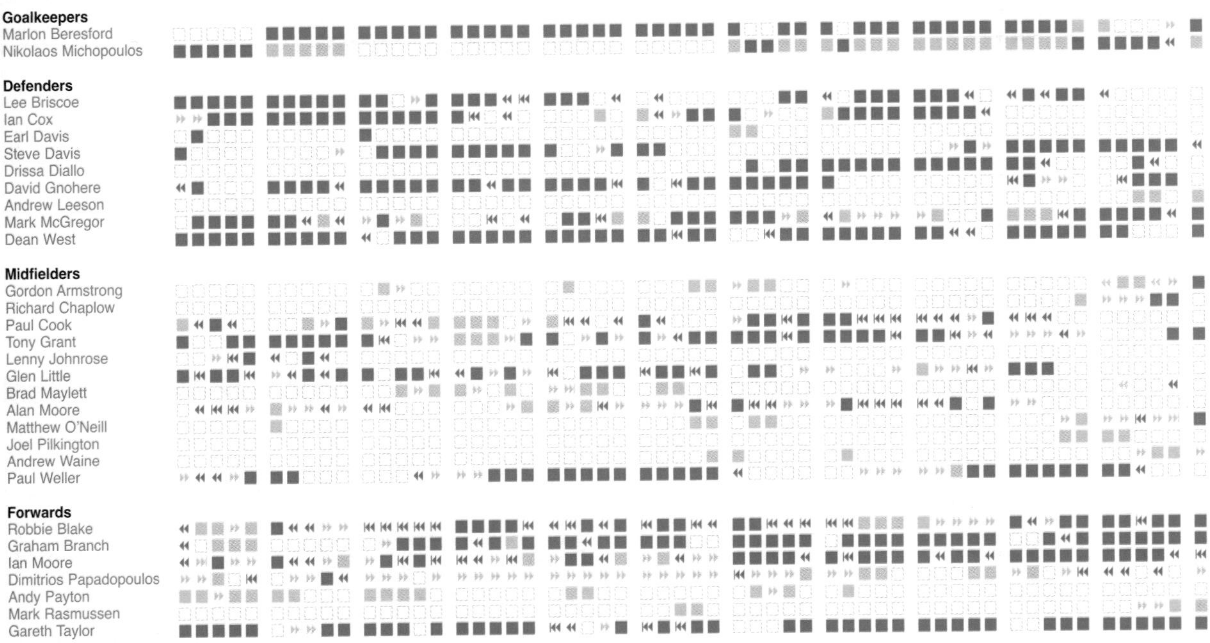

KEY: On all match · On bench · Subbed or sent off (Counting game) · Subbed or sent off (playing less than 70 minutes) · Subbed on from bench (Counting Game) · Subbed on (playing less than 70 minutes) · Subbed on and then subbed or sent off (Counting Game) · Subbed on and then subbed or sent off (playing less than 70 minutes) · Not in 16

# WALSALL

Final Position: **17th**

**NICKNAME:** THE SADDLERS

**KEY:** Won / Drawn / Lost

| | | | | | | |
|---|---|---|---|---|---|---|
| 1 | div1 | Ipswich | H | L | 0-2 | |
| 2 | div1 | Wolves | A | L | 1-3 | Herivelto 67 |
| 3 | div1 | Sheff Utd | A | D | 1-1 | Corica 23 |
| 4 | div1 | Nottm Forest | H | W | 2-1 | Sonner 25 pen; Wrack 90 |
| 5 | div1 | Brighton | A | W | 2-0 | Corica 6; Leitao 7 |
| 6 | div1 | Reading | H | L | 0-2 | |
| 7 | div1 | Watford | A | L | 0-2 | |
| 8 | wcr1 | Shrewsbury | H | W | 1-0 | Leitao 23 |
| 9 | div1 | Bradford | H | L | 0-1 | |
| 10 | div1 | Rotherham | H | L | 3-4 | Zdrilic 15,44; Leitao 62 |
| 11 | div1 | Millwall | A | W | 3-0 | Zdrilic 22; Wrack 35; Leitao 76 |
| 12 | div1 | Sheff Wed | H | W | 1-0 | Simpson 44 |
| 13 | wcr2 | Nottm Forest | A | W | 2-1 | Leitao 21; Junior 24 |
| 14 | div1 | Derby | A | D | 2-2 | Corica 63; Aranalde 90 pen |
| 15 | div1 | Burnley | A | L | 1-2 | Birch 79 |
| 16 | div1 | Preston | H | D | 3-3 | Leitao 20; Junior 26; Aranalde 44 pen |
| 17 | div1 | Coventry | A | D | 0-0 | |
| 18 | div1 | Crystal Palace | H | L | 3-4 | Corica 2; Junior 5,53 |
| 19 | div1 | Stoke | H | W | 4-2 | Leitao 51,57; Junior 66; Aranalde 84 pen |
| 20 | wcr3 | Blackburn | A | L | 4-5* | Aranalde 67 pen; Zdrilic 98 (*on penalties) |
| 21 | div1 | Leicester | A | L | 0-2 | |
| 22 | div1 | Wimbledon | A | L | 2-3 | Junior 42; Sonner 80 pen |
| 23 | div1 | Gillingham | H | W | 1-0 | Junior 7 |
| 24 | div1 | Portsmouth | A | L | 2-3 | Sonner 31 pen,68 pen |
| 25 | div1 | Grimsby | H | W | 3-1 | Junior 27; Leitao 66; Wrack 87 |
| 26 | div1 | Wimbledon | H | W | 2-0 | Wrack 11; Junior 62 |
| 27 | div1 | Norwich | A | L | 1-2 | Easton 50 og |
| 28 | div1 | Sheff Utd | H | L | 0-1 | |
| 29 | div1 | Ipswich | A | L | 2-3 | Wrack 68,89 |
| 30 | div1 | Nottm Forest | A | D | 1-1 | Ainsworth 64 |
| 31 | facr3 | Reading | H | D | 0-0 | |
| 32 | div1 | Wolves | H | L | 0-1 | |
| 33 | facr3r | Reading | A | W | 4-1* | Wrack 7 (*on penalties) |
| 34 | div1 | Reading | A | D | 0-0 | |
| 35 | facr4 | Wimbledon | H | W | 1-0 | Zdrilic 75 |
| 36 | div1 | Brighton | H | W | 1-0 | Leitao 7 |
| 37 | div1 | Leicester | H | L | 1-4 | Matias 87 |
| 38 | facr5 | Sheff Utd | A | L | 0-2 | |
| 39 | div1 | Watford | H | W | 2-0 | Junior 25; Leitao 86 |
| 40 | div1 | Stoke | A | L | 0-1 | |
| 41 | div1 | Bradford | A | W | 2-1 | Robinson 49; Matias 73 |
| 42 | div1 | Rotherham | A | D | 0-0 | |
| 43 | div1 | Millwall | H | L | 1-2 | Junior 85 |
| 44 | div1 | Burnley | H | W | 3-2 | Leitao 24; Birch 33; Matias 66 |
| 45 | div1 | Preston | A | L | 0-5 | |
| 46 | div1 | Crystal Palace | A | L | 0-2 | |
| 47 | div1 | Portsmouth | H | L | 1-2 | Junior 45 |
| 48 | div1 | Gillingham | A | W | 1-0 | Leitao 49 |
| 49 | div1 | Coventry | H | D | 0-0 | |
| 50 | div1 | Norwich | H | D | 0-0 | |
| 51 | div1 | Grimsby | A | W | 1-0 | Junior 47 |
| 52 | div1 | Derby | H | W | 3-2 | Junior 3,51,70 |
| 53 | div1 | Sheff Wed | A | L | 1-2 | Matias 56 |

Home / Away / Neutral

## ATTENDANCES

**HOME GROUND:** BESCOT STADIUM **CAPACITY:** 11050 **AVERAGE LEAGUE AT HOME:** 6982

| | | | | | | | | | | | |
|---|---|---|---|---|---|---|---|---|---|---|---|
| 30 | Nottm Forest | 28441 | 45 | Preston | 11170 | 49 | Coventry | 7337 | 31 | Reading | 5987 |
| 2 | Wolves | 27904 | 32 | Wolves | 11037 | 50 | Norwich | 7018 | 25 | Grimsby | 5888 |
| 29 | Ipswich | 26550 | 41 | Bradford | 10893 | 48 | Gillingham | 6972 | 42 | Rotherham | 5792 |
| 14 | Derby | 25247 | 7 | Watford | 10528 | 16 | Preston | 6832 | 1 | Ipswich | 5353 |
| 21 | Leicester | 25243 | 28 | Sheff Utd | 10459 | 12 | Sheff Wed | 6792 | 6 | Reading | 5327 |
| 53 | Sheff Wed | 20864 | 40 | Stoke | 10409 | 35 | Wimbledon | 6693 | 4 | Nottm Forest | 5096 |
| 27 | Norwich | 19872 | 20 | Blackburn | 9486 | 43 | Millwall | 6647 | 9 | Bradford | 4678 |
| 46 | Crystal Palace | 19102 | 33 | Reading | 8767 | 23 | Gillingham | 6630 | 10 | Rotherham | 4648 |
| 24 | Portsmouth | 17701 | 37 | Leicester | 8741 | 26 | Wimbledon | 6596 | 51 | Grimsby | 4618 |
| 38 | Sheff Utd | 17510 | 52 | Derby | 8416 | 5 | Brighton | 6519 | 8 | Shrewsbury | 3847 |
| 17 | Coventry | 14544 | 36 | Brighton | 8413 | 19 | Stoke | 6391 | 22 | Wimbledon | 1255 |
| 3 | Sheff Utd | 14011 | 47 | Portsmouth | 7899 | 18 | Crystal Palace | 6368 | | | |
| 15 | Burnley | 12907 | 39 | Watford | 7705 | 13 | Nottm Forest | 6343 | | | |
| 34 | Reading | 11786 | 11 | Millwall | 7525 | 44 | Burnley | 6327 | | | |

## KEY PLAYERS - GOALSCORERS

1 Jose Luis Junior

| | |
|---|---|
| Goals in the League | 15 |
| Goals in all competitions | 16 |
| Contribution to Attacking Power<br>Average number of minutes between League team goals while on pitch | 71 |
| Player Strike Rate<br>The total number of minutes he was on the pitch for every League goal scored | 157 |
| Club Strike Rate<br>Average number of minutes between League goals scored by club | 73 |

| | PLAYER | GOALS LGE | GOALS ALL | POWER | S RATE |
|---|---|---|---|---|---|
| 2 | Jorge Leitao | 11 | 13 | 68 | 324 mins |
| 3 | Danny Sonner | 4 | 4 | 68 | 447 mins |
| 4 | Darren Wrack | 6 | 7 | 74 | 629 mins |
| 5 | Steve Corica | 4 | 4 | 62 | 693 mins |

## KEY PLAYERS - MIDFIELDERS

1 Fitzroy Simpson

| | |
|---|---|
| Goals in the League | 1 |
| Goals in all competitions | 1 |
| Defensive Rating<br>Average number of mins between League goals conceded while on the pitch | 54 |
| Contribution to Attacking Power<br>Average number of minutes between League team goals while on pitch | 54 |
| Scoring Difference<br>Defensive Rating minus Contribution to Attacking Power | 0 |

| | PLAYER | GOALS LGE | GOALS ALL | DEF RATE | ATT POWER | SCORE DIFF |
|---|---|---|---|---|---|---|
| 2 | Steve Corica | 4 | 4 | 59 | 63 | -4 mins |
| 3 | Vinny Samways | 0 | 0 | 80 | 86 | -6 mins |
| 4 | Martyn O'Connor | 0 | 0 | 59 | 68 | -9 mins |
| 5 | Danny Sonner | 4 | 4 | 60 | 69 | -9 mins |

## KEY PLAYERS - DEFENDERS

1 Anthony Barras

| | |
|---|---|
| Goals Conceded in League | 20 |
| Goals Conceded in all competitions | 21 |
| Clean Sheets<br>In League games when he played at least 70 mins | 6 |
| Defensive Rating<br>Ave number of mins between League goals conceded while on the pitch | 68 |
| Club Defensive Rating<br>Average number of mins between League goals conceded by the club this season | 60 |

| | PLAYER | CON LGE | CON ALL | CLN SHEETS | DEF RATE |
|---|---|---|---|---|---|
| 2 | Ian Roper | 51 | 55 | 11 | 68 mins |
| 3 | Danny Hay | 37 | 43 | 6 | 61 mins |
| 4 | Zigor Aranalde | 56 | 62 | 12 | 61 mins |
| 5 | Darren Bazeley | 66 | 72 | 11 | 57 mins |

## KEY GOALKEEPER

1 James Walker

| | |
|---|---|
| Goals Conceded in the League | 56 |
| Goals Conceded in all competitions | 62 |
| Clean Sheets<br>In games when he played at least 70 mins | 13 |
| Goals to Shots Ratio<br>The average number of shots on target per each League goal conceded | 3.8 |
| Defensive Rating<br>Ave number of mins between League goals conceded while on the pitch | 65 |

## MONTHY POINTS TALLY

| Month | Points | % |
|---|---|---|
| AUGUST | 7 | 39% |
| SEPTEMBER | 9 | 50% |
| OCTOBER | 6 | 33% |
| NOVEMBER | 7 | 39% |
| DECEMBER | 6 | 40% |
| JANUARY | 7 | 39% |
| FEBRUARY | 6 | 40% |
| MARCH | 7 | 39% |
| APRIL | 11 | 61% |
| MAY | 0 | 0% |

## TOP POINT EARNERS

| | PLAYER | GAMES | AV PTS |
|---|---|---|---|
| 1 | Anthony Barras | 14 | 1.50 |
| 2 | Vinny Samways | 12 | 1.50 |
| 3 | Fitzroy Simpson | 15 | 1.33 |
| 4 | Jose Luis Junior | 21 | 1.33 |
| 5 | Jorge Leitao | 38 | 1.29 |
| 6 | Steve Corica | 24 | 1.21 |
| 7 | Ian Roper | 37 | 1.19 |
| 8 | James Walker | 40 | 1.18 |
| 9 | Zigor Aranalde | 38 | 1.16 |
| 10 | Danny Sonner | 19 | 1.16 |
| | CLUB AVERAGE: | | 1.17 |

## GOALS

| 1 Jose Luis Junior | |
|---|---|
| League | 15 |
| FA Cup | 0 |
| League Cup | 1 |
| Other | 0 |
| TOTAL | 16 |

| | PLAYER | LGE | FAC | LC | Oth | TOT |
|---|---|---|---|---|---|---|
| 2 | Leitao | 11 | 0 | 2 | 0 | 13 |
| 3 | Wrack | 6 | 1 | 0 | 0 | 7 |
| 4 | Sonner | 4 | 0 | 0 | 0 | 4 |
| 5 | Corica | 4 | 0 | 0 | 0 | 4 |
| 6 | Zdrilic | 3 | 1 | 1 | 0 | 5 |
| 7 | Aranalde | 3 | 0 | 1 | 0 | 4 |
| 8 | Matias | 3 | 0 | 0 | 0 | 3 |
| 9 | Birch | 2 | 0 | 0 | 0 | 2 |
| 10 | Herivelto | 1 | 0 | 0 | 0 | 1 |
| 11 | Ainsworth | 1 | 0 | 0 | 0 | 1 |
| | Other | 4 | 0 | 0 | 0 | 4 |
| | TOTAL | 57 | 2 | 5 | 0 | 64 |

## TEAM OF THE SEASON

| GOALKEEPER | GAMES | DEF RATE |
|---|---|---|
| James Walker | 40 | 65 |
| **DEFENDERS** | **GAMES** | **DEF RATE** |
| Anthony Barras | 14 | 68 |
| Ian Roper | 37 | 68 |
| Zigor Aranalde | 38 | 61 |
| Danny Hay | 23 | 61 |
| **MIDFIELDERS** | **GAMES** | **SCORE DIFF** |
| Fitzroy Simpson | 15 | 0 |
| Steve Corica | 24 | -4 |
| Vinny Samways | 12 | -6 |
| Martyn O'Connor | 28 | -9 |
| **GOALSCORERS** | **GAMES** | **STRIKE RATE** |
| Jose Luis Junior | 21 | 157 |
| Jorge Leitao | 38 | 324 |

Games = games playing at least 70 minutes

## LEAGUE APPEARANCES, BOOKINGS AND CAPS

| | AGE (on 01/07/03) | IN THE SQUAD | COUNTING GAMES | MINUTES ON PITCH | YELLOW CARDS | RED CARDS | THIS SEASON | HOME COUNTRY |
|---|---|---|---|---|---|---|---|---|
| **Goalkeepers** | | | | | | | | |
| Matthew Harris | 19 | 4 | 0 | 0 | 0 | 0 | - | England |
| James Walker | 29 | 41 | 40 | 3612 | 1 | 2 | - | England |
| Gavin Ward | 33 | 45 | 5 | 529 | 1 | 0 | - | England |
| **Defenders** | | | | | | | | |
| Zigor Aranalde | 30 | 40 | 38 | 3423 | 5 | 0 | - | Spain |
| Anthony Barras | 32 | 31 | 14 | 1356 | 1 | 0 | - | England |
| Darren Bazeley | 30 | 46 | 41 | 3736 | 4 | 0 | - | England |
| Matthew Carbon | 28 | 30 | 17 | 1724 | 2 | 0 | - | England |
| Neil Emblen | 32 | 5 | 2 | 276 | 1 | 0 | - | England |
| Matthew Gadsby | 23 | 1 | 0 | 0 | 0 | 0 | - | England |
| Danny Hay | 28 | 30 | 23 | 2257 | 5 | 1 | - | Australia |
| Ludovic Pollet | 33 | 5 | 4 | 377 | 1 | 0 | - | France |
| Ian Roper | 26 | 41 | 37 | 3490 | 11 | 0 | - | England |
| **Midfielders** | | | | | | | | |
| Gareth Ainsworth | 30 | 5 | 2 | 243 | 0 | 1 | - | England |
| Steve Corica | 30 | 45 | 24 | 2770 | 4 | 0 | - | Australia |
| Jean-Phillipe Javary | 25 | 1 | 0 | 0 | 0 | 0 | - | France |
| Jamie Lawrence | 33 | 5 | 3 | 340 | 0 | 0 | - | England |
| Roberto Martinez | 29 | 9 | 2 | 223 | 2 | 1 | - | Spain |
| Martyn O'Connor | 35 | 35 | 28 | 2788 | 7 | 1 | - | England |
| Carl Robinson | 26 | 12 | 9 | 869 | 1 | 1 | 1 | Wales (50) |
| Vinny Samways | 34 | 13 | 12 | 1114 | 2 | 0 | - | England |
| Chris Shuker | 21 | 6 | 2 | 260 | 0 | 0 | - | England |
| Fitzroy Simpson | 33 | 30 | 15 | 1517 | 3 | 0 | - | Jamaica |
| Danny Sonner | 31 | 28 | 19 | 1788 | 5 | 1 | - | England |
| Craig Stanley | 20 | 0 | 0 | 0 | 0 | 0 | - | England |
| Mark Wright | 21 | 10 | 2 | 198 | 1 | 0 | - | England |
| **Forwards** | | | | | | | | |
| Gary Birch | 21 | 22 | 6 | 704 | 1 | 0 | - | England |
| Andrew Bishop | 20 | 1 | 0 | 0 | 0 | 0 | - | England |
| Moreira Herivelto | 27 | 7 | 0 | 73 | 0 | 0 | - | Brazil |
| Jose Luis Junior | 26 | 38 | 21 | 2351 | 6 | 0 | - | Brazil |
| Jorge Leitao | 29 | 44 | 38 | 3562 | 4 | 0 | - | Portugal |
| Pedro Miguel Matias | 29 | 30 | 6 | 972 | 2 | 0 | - | Spain |
| Danni Rodrigues | 23 | 1 | 0 | 14 | 0 | 0 | - | Portuguese |
| Darren Wrack | 27 | 43 | 41 | 3775 | 4 | 0 | - | England |
| David Zdrilic | 29 | 32 | 9 | 1042 | 1 | 0 | - | Australia |

**KEY:** LEAGUE BOOKINGS CAPS (FIFA RANKING)

## SQUAD APPEARANCES

| | | | | | | | | | | | |
|---|---|---|---|---|---|---|---|---|---|---|---|
| **Match** | 1 2 3 4 5 | 6 7 8 9 10 | 11 12 13 14 15 | 16 17 18 19 20 | 21 22 23 24 25 | 26 27 28 29 30 | 31 32 33 34 35 | 36 37 38 39 40 | 41 42 43 44 45 | 46 47 48 49 50 | 51 52 53 |
| **Venue** | H A A H A | H A H H H | A H A A A | H A H H A | A A H A H | H A H A A | H H A A H | H H A H A | A A H H A | A H A H H | A H A |
| **Competition** | L L L L L | L L W L L | L L W L L | L L L L W | L L L L L | L L L L L | F L F L F | L L F L L | L L L L L | L L L L L | L L L |
| **Result** | L L D W W | L L W L L | W W W D L | D D L W L | L L W L W | W L L L D | D L W D W | W L L W L | W D L W L | L L W D D | W W L |

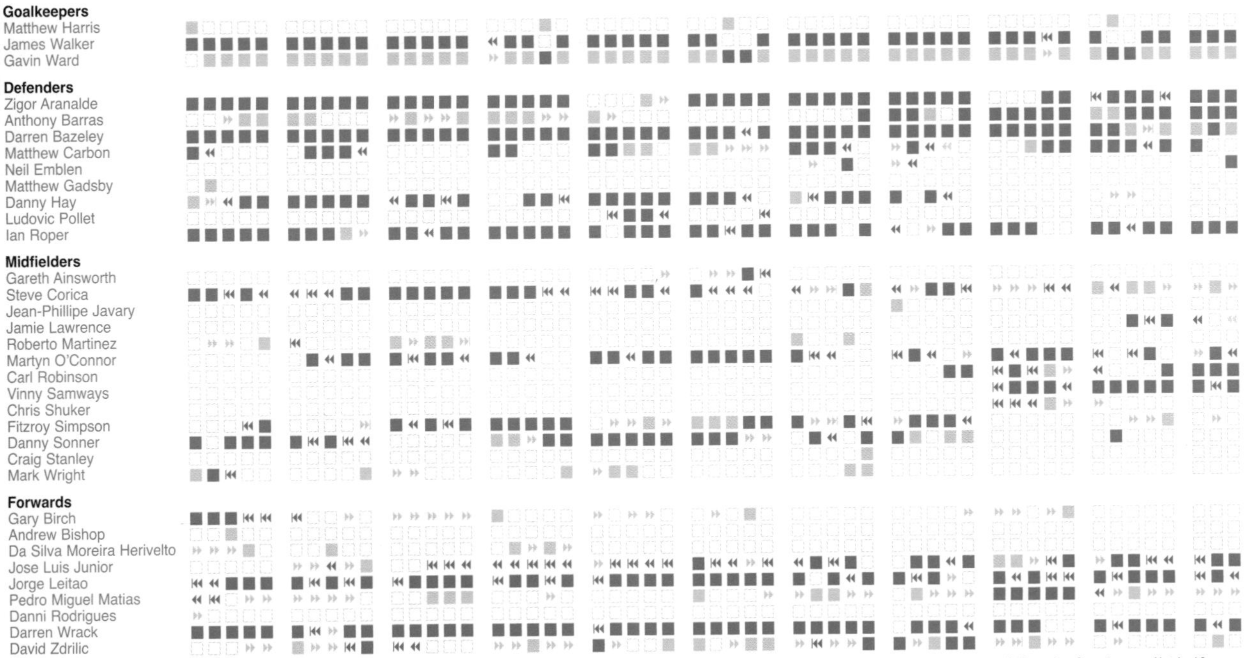
Goalkeepers
Matthew Harris
James Walker
Gavin Ward
Defenders
Zigor Aranalde
Anthony Barras
Darren Bazeley
Matthew Carbon
Neil Emblen
Matthew Gadsby
Danny Hay
Ludovic Pollet
Ian Roper
Midfielders
Gareth Ainsworth
Steve Corica
Jean-Phillipe Javary
Jamie Lawrence
Roberto Martinez
Martyn O'Connor
Carl Robinson
Vinny Samways
Chris Shuker
Fitzroy Simpson
Danny Sonner
Craig Stanley
Mark Wright
Forwards
Gary Birch
Andrew Bishop
Da Silva Moreira Herivelto
Jose Luis Junior
Jorge Leitao
Pedro Miguel Matias
Danni Rodrigues
Darren Wrack
David Zdrilic

**KEY:** On all match; On bench; Subbed or sent off (Counting game); Subbed or sent off (playing less than 70 minutes); Subbed on from bench (Counting Game); Subbed on (playing less than 70 minutes); Subbed on and then subbed or sent off (Counting Game); Subbed on and then subbed or sent off (playing less than 70 minutes); Not in 16

# DERBY COUNTY

# 18th

NICKNAME: THE RAMS

KEY: Won / Drawn / Lost

| | | | | | | |
|---|---|---|---|---|---|---|
| 1 | div1 | Reading | H | W | 3-0 | Lee 61; Ravanelli 63; Christie 72 |
| 2 | div1 | Gillingham | A | L | 0-1 | |
| 3 | div1 | Grimsby | A | W | 2-1 | Bolder 43,74 |
| 4 | div1 | Wolves | H | L | 1-4 | Christie 45 |
| 5 | div1 | Rotherham | A | L | 1-2 | Strupar 47 |
| 6 | div1 | Stoke | H | W | 2-0 | Christie 82,84 |
| 7 | div1 | Burnley | H | L | 1-2 | Bolder 8 |
| 8 | wcr1 | Mansfield | A | W | 3-1 | Morris 10; Christie 70; Evatt 78 |
| 9 | div1 | Leicester | A | L | 1-3 | Riggott 22 |
| 10 | div1 | Crystal Palace | A | W | 1-0 | Kinkladze 82 |
| 11 | div1 | Preston | H | L | 0-2 | |
| 12 | div1 | Ipswich | A | W | 1-0 | Carbonari 45 |
| 13 | wcr2 | Oldham | H | L | 1-2 | Higginbotham 17 pen |
| 14 | div1 | Walsall | H | D | 2-2 | Christie 19,53 |
| 15 | div1 | Bradford | A | D | 0-0 | |
| 16 | div1 | Nottm Forest | H | D | 0-0 | |
| 17 | div1 | Millwall | A | L | 0-3 | |
| 18 | div1 | Sheff Utd | H | W | 2-1 | McLeod 36; Burton 86 |
| 19 | div1 | Sheff Wed | A | W | 3-1 | Morris 7,29; McLeod 48 |
| 20 | div1 | Portsmouth | H | L | 1-2 | Higginbotham 16 pen |
| 21 | div1 | Brighton | A | L | 0-1 | |
| 22 | div1 | Wimbledon | H | W | 3-2 | Elliott 17; Burton 47; Morris 80 |
| 23 | div1 | Norwich | A | L | 0-1 | |
| 24 | div1 | Watford | H | W | 3-0 | Morris 4; Riggott 62; Burton 71 |
| 25 | div1 | Brighton | H | W | 1-0 | Higginbotham 30 pen |
| 26 | div1 | Coventry | A | L | 0-3 | |
| 27 | div1 | Grimsby | H | L | 1-3 | Morris 32 |
| 28 | div1 | Reading | A | L | 1-2 | Burley 8 pen |
| 29 | div1 | Wolves | A | D | 1-1 | Christie 15 |
| 30 | facr3 | Brentford | A | L | 0-1 | |
| 31 | div1 | Gillingham | H | D | 1-1 | Zavagno 64 pen |
| 32 | div1 | Stoke | A | W | 3-1 | Christie 50; Zavagno 74; Morris 90 |
| 33 | div1 | Rotherham | H | W | 3-0 | Kinkladze 16; Bolder 45; McLeod 49 |
| 34 | div1 | Portsmouth | A | L | 2-6 | Morris 58; Kinkladze 71 pen |
| 35 | div1 | Sheff Wed | H | D | 2-2 | Bolder 53,70 |
| 36 | div1 | Burnley | A | L | 0-2 | |
| 37 | div1 | Leicester | H | D | 1-1 | Burley 90 |
| 38 | div1 | Crystal Palace | H | L | 0-1 | |
| 39 | div1 | Preston | A | L | 2-4 | Ravanelli 75,90 |
| 40 | div1 | Bradford | H | L | 1-2 | Morris 28 |
| 41 | div1 | Nottm Forest | A | L | 0-3 | |
| 42 | div1 | Sheff Utd | A | L | 0-2 | |
| 43 | div1 | Norwich | H | W | 2-1 | Burley 24; Kenton 57 og |
| 44 | div1 | Wimbledon | A | W | 2-0 | Valakari 29; Boertien 58 |
| 45 | div1 | Millwall | H | L | 1-2 | Kinkladze 8 |
| 46 | div1 | Coventry | H | W | 1-0 | Ravanelli 62 |
| 47 | div1 | Watford | A | L | 0-2 | |
| 48 | div1 | Walsall | A | L | 2-3 | Valakari 59; Ravanelli 83 |
| 49 | div1 | Ipswich | H | L | 1-4 | Lee 22 |

Home / Away / Neutral

## ATTENDANCES

HOME GROUND: PRIDE PARK CAPACITY: 34000 AVERAGE LEAGUE AT HOME: 25469

| | | | | | | | | | | | |
|---|---|---|---|---|---|---|---|---|---|---|---|
| 1 | Reading | 33016 | 14 | Walsall | 25247 | 19 | Sheff Wed | 19747 | 48 | Walsall | 8416 |
| 9 | Leicester | 31049 | 12 | Ipswich | 24439 | 34 | Portsmouth | 19503 | 5 | Rotherham | 8408 |
| 16 | Nottm Forest | 30547 | 37 | Leicester | 24307 | 42 | Sheff Utd | 18401 | 17 | Millwall | 8116 |
| 4 | WolveS | 29954 | 46 | Coventry | 23921 | 32 | Stoke | 17308 | 21 | Brighton | 6845 |
| 41 | Nottm Forest | 29725 | 40 | Bradford | 23735 | 28 | Reading | 16299 | 3 | Grimsby | 5810 |
| 11 | Preston | 29257 | 43 | Norwich | 23643 | 36 | Burnley | 15063 | 8 | Mansfield | 5788 |
| 49 | Ipswich | 28785 | 18 | Sheff Utd | 23525 | 10 | Crystal Palace | 14948 | 44 | Wimbledon | 1934 |
| 27 | Grimsby | 27141 | 31 | Gillingham | 22769 | 39 | Preston | 14003 | | | |
| 20 | Portsmouth | 26587 | 38 | Crystal Palace | 22682 | 15 | Bradford | 13385 | | | |
| 29 | WolveS | 26442 | 7 | Burnley | 22342 | 26 | Coventry | 13185 | | | |
| 35 | Sheff Wed | 26311 | 6 | Stoke | 21723 | 47 | Watford | 11909 | | | |
| 33 | Rotherham | 26257 | 24 | Watford | 21653 | 13 | Oldham | 9029 | | | |
| 25 | Brighton | 25786 | 45 | Millwall | 21014 | 2 | Gillingham | 8775 | | | |
| 22 | Wimbledon | 25597 | 23 | Norwich | 20522 | 30 | Brentford | 8709 | | | |

## KEY PLAYERS - GOALSCORERS

1 Malcolm Christie

| | |
|---|---|
| Goals in the League | 8 |
| Goals in all competitions | 9 |
| Contribution to Attacking Power<br>Average number of minutes between League team goals while on pitch | 78 |
| Player Strike Rate<br>The total number of minutes he was on the pitch for every League goal scored | 254 |
| Club Strike Rate<br>Average number of minutes between League goals scored by club | 75 |

| | PLAYER | GOALS LGE | GOALS ALL | POWER | S RATE |
|---|---|---|---|---|---|
| 2 | Fabrizio Ravanelli | 5 | 5 | 71 | 288 mins |
| 3 | Lee Morris | 8 | 9 | 73 | 294 mins |
| 4 | Georgiou Kinkladze | 4 | 4 | 71 | 518 mins |
| 5 | Adam Bolder | 6 | 6 | 74 | 573 mins |

## KEY PLAYERS - MIDFIELDERS

1 Paul Boertien

| | |
|---|---|
| Goals in the League | 1 |
| Goals in all competitions | 1 |
| Defensive Rating<br>Average number of mins between League goals conceded while on the pitch | 58 |
| Contribution to Attacking Power<br>Average number of minutes between League team goals while on pitch | 71 |
| Scoring Difference<br>Defensive Rating minus Contribution to Attacking Power | -13 |

| | PLAYER | GOALS LGE | GOALS ALL | DEF RATE | ATT POWER | SCORE DIFF |
|---|---|---|---|---|---|---|
| 2 | Robert Lee | 2 | 2 | 55 | 71 | -16 mins |
| 3 | Adam Bolder | 6 | 6 | 57 | 75 | -18 mins |
| 4 | Georgiou Kinkladze | 4 | 4 | 51 | 71 | -20 mins |
| 5 | Craig Burley | 3 | 3 | 53 | 75 | -22 mins |

## KEY PLAYERS - DEFENDERS

1 Chris Riggott

Pedigree


| | |
|---|---|
| Goals Conceded in League | 26 |
| Goals Conceded in all competitions | 29 |
| Clean Sheets<br>In League games when he played at least 70 mins | 8 |
| Defensive Rating<br>Ave number of mins between League goals conceded while on the pitch | 73 |
| Club Defensive Rating<br>Average number of mins between League goals conceded by the club this season | 56 |

| | PLAYER | CON LGE | CON ALL | CLN SHEETS | DEF RATE |
|---|---|---|---|---|---|
| 2 | Danny Higginbotham | 27 | 30 | 7 | 73 mins |
| 3 | Richard Jackson | 25 | 25 | 3 | 63 mins |
| 4 | Warren Barton | 57 | 60 | 7 | 54 mins |
| 5 | Steve Elliott | 38 | 39 | 3 | 50 mins |

## KEY GOALKEEPER

1 Mart Poom

Pedigree


| | |
|---|---|
| Goals Conceded in the League | 12 |
| Goals Conceded in all competitions | 15 |
| Clean Sheets<br>In games when he played at least 70 mins | 5 |
| Goals to Shots Ratio<br>The average number of shots on target per each League goal conceded | 5.7 |
| Defensive Rating<br>Ave number of mins between League goals conceded while on the pitch | 97 |

## MONTHY POINTS TALLY

| | | |
|---|---|---|
| AUGUST | 9 | 50% |
| SEPTEMBER | 9 | 50% |
| OCTOBER | 6 | 33% |
| NOVEMBER | 6 | 40% |
| DECEMBER | 6 | 40% |
| JANUARY | 5 | 42% |
| FEBRUARY | 4 | 33% |
| MARCH | 1 | 6% |
| APRIL | 9 | 50% |
| MAY | 0 | 0% |

## TOP POINT EARNERS

| | PLAYER | GAMES | AV PTS |
|---|---|---|---|
| 1 | Mart Poom | 13 | **1.77** |
| 2 | Malcolm Christie | 21 | **1.43** |
| 3 | Danny Higginbotham | 21 | **1.43** |
| 4 | Chris Riggott | 20 | **1.25** |
| 5 | Georgiou Kinkladze | 21 | **1.24** |
| 6 | Warren Barton | 31 | **1.23** |
| 7 | Paul Boertien | 39 | **1.23** |
| 8 | Ian Evatt | 15 | **1.20** |
| 9 | Adam Murray | 13 | **1.15** |
| 10 | Robert Lee | 31 | **1.13** |
| | **CLUB AVERAGE:** | | **1.13** |

## GOALS

| 1 Malcolm Christie | |
|---|---|
| League | 8 |
| FA Cup | 0 |
| League Cup | 1 |
| Other | 0 |
| TOTAL | 9 |

| | PLAYER | LGE | FAC | LC | Oth | TOT |
|---|---|---|---|---|---|---|
| 2 | Morris | **8** | 0 | 1 | 0 | 9 |
| 3 | Bolder | **6** | 0 | 0 | 0 | 6 |
| 4 | Ravanelli | **5** | 0 | 0 | 0 | 5 |
| 5 | Kinkladze | **4** | 0 | 0 | 0 | 4 |
| 6 | McLeod | **3** | 0 | 0 | 0 | 3 |
| 7 | Burley | **3** | 0 | 0 | 0 | 3 |
| 8 | Burton | **3** | 0 | 0 | 0 | 3 |
| 9 | Riggott | **2** | 0 | 0 | 0 | 2 |
| 10 | Valakari | **2** | 0 | 0 | 0 | 2 |
| 11 | Higginbotham | **2** | 0 | 1 | 0 | 3 |
| | Other | 9 | 0 | 1 | 0 | 10 |
| | **TOTAL** | **55** | **0** | **4** | **0** | **59** |

## TEAM OF THE SEASON

| GOALKEEPER | GAMES | DEF RATE |
|---|---|---|
| Mart Poom | 13 | 97 |
| **DEFENDERS** | **GAMES** | **DEF RATE** |
| Chris Riggott | 20 | 73 |
| Danny Higginbotham | 21 | 73 |
| Richard Jackson | 15 | 63 |
| Warren Barton | 31 | 54 |
| **MIDFIELDERS** | **GAMES** | **SCORE DIFF** |
| Paul Boertien | 39 | -13 |
| Robert Lee | 31 | -16 |
| Adam Bolder | 35 | -18 |
| Georgiou Kinkladze | 21 | -20 |
| **GOALSCORERS** | **GAMES** | **STRIKE RATE** |
| Malcolm Christie | 21 | 254 |
| Fabrizio Ravanelli | 15 | 288 |

Games = games playing at least 70 minutes

## LEAGUE APPEARANCES, BOOKINGS AND CAPS

| | AGE (on 01/07/03) | IN THE SQUAD | COUNTING GAMES | MINUTES ON PITCH | YELLOW CARDS | RED CARDS | THIS SEASON | HOME COUNTRY |
|---|---|---|---|---|---|---|---|---|
| **Goalkeepers** | | | | | | | | |
| Lee Camp | 18 | 5 | 0 | 45 | 0 | 0 | - | England |
| Lee Grant | 20 | 44 | 25 | 2376 | 1 | 0 | - | England |
| Andy Oakes | 26 | 29 | 5 | 561 | 0 | 0 | - | England |
| Mart Poom | 31 | 13 | 13 | 1159 | 0 | 1 | - | Estonia |
| **Defenders** | | | | | | | | |
| Warren Barton | 34 | 39 | 31 | 3094 | 5 | 2 | - | England |
| Horacio Carbonari | 26 | 2 | 1 | 135 | 0 | 0 | - | Argentina |
| Steve Elliott | 24 | 27 | 21 | 1892 | 9 | 0 | - | England |
| Ian Evatt | 21 | 33 | 15 | 1582 | 2 | 0 | - | England |
| Danny Higginbotham | 24 | 23 | 21 | 1980 | 1 | 0 | - | England |
| Tom Huddlestone | 16 | 3 | 0 | 0 | 0 | 0 | - | England |
| Richard Jackson | 23 | 27 | 15 | 1582 | 1 | 0 | - | England |
| Pablo Mills | 19 | 20 | 11 | 1206 | 2 | 0 | - | England |
| Brian O'Neil | 30 | 6 | 2 | 223 | 1 | 0 | - | Scotland |
| Chris Riggott | 22 | 22 | 20 | 1887 | 2 | 0 | - | England |
| Paul Ritchie | 27 | 7 | 7 | 630 | 1 | 0 | - | Scotland |
| Luciano Zavagno | 25 | 11 | 5 | 559 | 1 | 0 | - | Argentina |
| **Midfielders** | | | | | | | | |
| Paul Boertien | 24 | 44 | 39 | 3612 | 8 | 0 | - | England |
| Adam Bolder | 22 | 45 | 35 | 3439 | 9 | 0 | - | England |
| Craig Burley | 31 | 22 | 20 | 1867 | 3 | 0 | 1 | Scotland (64) |
| Francois Grenet | 28 | 3 | 2 | 220 | 1 | 0 | - | France |
| Lee Holmes | 16 | 4 | 0 | 30 | 0 | 0 | - | England |
| Lewis Hunt | 20 | 12 | 6 | 683 | 3 | 0 | - | England |
| Georgiou Kinkladze | 40 | 37 | 21 | 2071 | 3 | 0 | - | Georgia |
| Robert Lee | 37 | 36 | 31 | 2910 | 11 | 1 | - | England |
| Adam Murray | 21 | 32 | 13 | 1523 | 4 | 1 | - | England |
| Chris Palmer | 19 | 3 | 0 | 0 | 0 | 0 | - | England |
| Gary Twigg | 19 | 17 | 0 | 126 | 1 | 0 | - | Scotland |
| Simo Valakari | 30 | 7 | 5 | 438 | 0 | 0 | - | Finland |
| **Forwards** | | | | | | | | |
| Deon Burton | 26 | 7 | 4 | 426 | 2 | 0 | - | Jamaica |
| Nick Chadwick | 20 | 6 | 2 | 360 | 0 | 0 | - | England |
| Malcolm Christie | 24 | 24 | 21 | 2028 | 3 | 1 | - | England |
| Izale McLeod | 18 | 35 | 17 | 1783 | 7 | 0 | - | England |
| Tommy Mooney | 31 | 8 | 6 | 639 | 0 | 0 | - | England |
| Lee Morris | 23 | 34 | 25 | 2352 | 4 | 0 | - | England |
| Fabrizio Ravanelli | 34 | 21 | 15 | 1439 | 1 | 0 | - | Italy |
| Marvin Robinson | 23 | 3 | 0 | 33 | 0 | 0 | - | England |
| Branko Strupar | 33 | 9 | 4 | 380 | 0 | 0 | - | Belgium |
| Marcus Tudgay | 20 | 15 | 0 | 94 | 1 | 0 | - | England |

KEY: LEAGUE BOOKINGS CAPS (FIFA RANKING)

## SQUAD APPEARANCES

| Match | 1 | 2 | 3 | 4 | 5 | 6 | 7 | 8 | 9 | 10 | 11 | 12 | 13 | 14 | 15 | 16 | 17 | 18 | 19 | 20 | 21 | 22 | 23 | 24 | 25 | 26 | 27 | 28 | 29 | 30 | 31 | 32 | 33 | 34 | 35 | 36 | 37 | 38 | 39 | 40 | 41 | 42 | 43 | 44 | 45 | 46 | 47 | 48 | 49 |
|---|---|---|---|---|---|---|---|---|---|---|---|---|---|---|---|---|---|---|---|---|---|---|---|---|---|---|---|---|---|---|---|---|---|---|---|---|---|---|---|---|---|---|---|---|---|---|---|---|---|
| Venue | H | A | A | H | A | H | H | A | A | A | H | A | H | H | A | H | A | H | A | H | A | H | A | H | H | A | H | A | A | A | H | A | H | A | H | A | H | H | A | H | A | A | H | A | H | H | A | A | H |
| Competition | L | L | L | L | L | L | L | W | L | L | L | L | W | L | L | L | L | L | L | L | L | L | L | L | L | L | L | L | L | F | L | L | L | L | L | L | L | L | L | L | L | L | L | L | L | L | L | L | L |
| Result | W | L | W | L | L | W | L | W | L | W | L | W | D | D | D | D | L | W | W | L | L | W | L | W | W | L | L | L | D | L | D | W | W | L | D | L | D | L | L | L | L | L | W | W | L | W | L | L | L |

**Goalkeepers**
Lee Camp
Lee Grant
Andy Oakes
Mart Poom
**Defenders**
Warren Barton
Horacio Carbonari
Steve Elliott
Ian Evatt
Danny Higginbotham
Tom Huddlestone
Richard Jackson
Pablo Mills
Brian O'Neil
Chris Riggott
Paul Ritchie
Luciano Zavagno
**Midfielders**
Paul Boertien
Adam Bolder
Craig Burley
Francois Grenet
Lee Holmes
Lewis Hunt
Georgiou Kinkladze
Robert Lee
Adam Murray
Chris Palmer
Gary Twigg
Simo Valakari
**Forwards**
Deon Burton
Nick Chadwick
Malcolm Christie
Izale McLeod
Tommy Mooney
Lee Morris
Fabrizio Ravanelli
Marvin Robinson
Branko Strupar
Marcus Tudgay

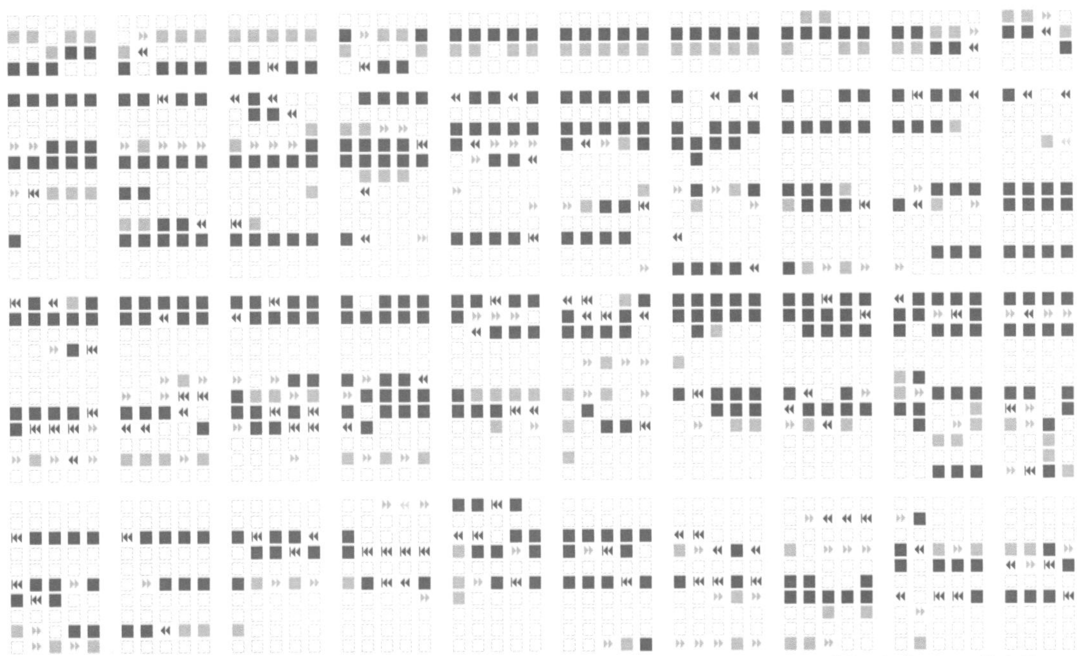

KEY: On all match; On bench; Subbed or sent off (Counting game); Subbed or sent off (playing less than 70 minutes); Subbed on from bench (Counting Game); Subbed on (playing less than 70 minutes); Subbed on and then subbed or sent off (Counting Game); Subbed on and then subbed or sent off (playing less than 70 minutes); Not in 16

# BRADFORD CITY

Final Position: **19th**

**NICKNAME:** THE BANTAMS

KEY: ☐ Won ☐ Drawn ☐ Lost

| | | | | | | |
|---|---|---|---|---|---|---|
| 1 | div1 | Wolves | H | D | 0-0 | |
| 2 | div1 | Crystal Palace | A | D | 1-1 | Evans 75 |
| 3 | div1 | Stoke | A | L | 1-2 | Gray 90 |
| 4 | div1 | Grimsby | H | D | 0-0 | |
| 5 | div1 | Ipswich | A | W | 2-1 | Evans 24; Proctor 83 |
| 6 | div1 | Rotherham | H | W | 4-2 | Ward 23,85; Uhlenbeek 47; Proctor 55 |
| 7 | wcr1 | Wrexham | A | L | 1-2 | Cadamarteri 82 |
| 8 | div1 | Walsall | A | W | 1-0 | Gray 53 |
| 9 | div1 | Leicester | A | L | 0-4 | |
| 10 | div1 | Burnley | H | D | 2-2 | Gray 17; Proctor 89 |
| 11 | div1 | Coventry | H | D | 1-1 | Evans 25 |
| 12 | div1 | Portsmouth | A | L | 0-3 | |
| 13 | div1 | Preston | H | D | 1-1 | Proctor 20 |
| 14 | div1 | Derby | H | D | 0-0 | |
| 15 | div1 | Sheff Wed | A | L | 1-2 | Warnock 44 |
| 16 | div1 | Norwich | H | W | 2-1 | Reid 41,55 |
| 17 | div1 | Reading | A | L | 0-1 | |
| 18 | div1 | Brighton | A | L | 2-3 | Gray 49,90 pen |
| 19 | div1 | Wimbledon | H | L | 3-5 | Facey 8; Standing 31,45 |
| 20 | div1 | Nottm Forest | A | L | 0-3 | |
| 21 | div1 | Sheff Utd | H | L | 0-5 | |
| 22 | div1 | Millwall | A | L | 0-1 | |
| 23 | div1 | Gillingham | H | L | 1-3 | Gray 42 |
| 24 | div1 | Nottm Forest | H | W | 1-0 | Molenaar 42 |
| 25 | div1 | Watford | A | L | 0-1 | |
| 26 | div1 | Stoke | H | W | 4-2 | Gray 20 pen,89; Handyside 67 og; Jorgensen 70 |
| 27 | div1 | Wolves | A | W | 2-1 | Jorgensen 51; Gray 59 |
| 28 | facr3 | West Brom | A | L | 1-3 | Danks 80 |
| 29 | div1 | Rotherham | A | L | 2-3 | Jorgensen 2; Gray 62 pen |
| 30 | div1 | Grimsby | A | W | 2-1 | Gray 57; Jorgensen 90 |
| 31 | div1 | Ipswich | H | W | 2-0 | Jorgensen 62; Forrest 68 |
| 32 | div1 | Wimbledon | A | D | 2-2 | Jorgensen 30; Ward 60 |
| 33 | div1 | Brighton | H | L | 0-1 | |
| 34 | div1 | Coventry | A | W | 2-0 | Gray 22; Jorgensen 83 |
| 35 | div1 | Walsall | H | L | 1-2 | Forrest 62 |
| 36 | div1 | Leicester | H | D | 0-0 | |
| 37 | div1 | Crystal Palace | H | W | 2-1 | Atherton 70; Francis 73 |
| 38 | div1 | Derby | A | W | 2-1 | Jorgensen 14; Lawrence 90 |
| 39 | div1 | Sheff Wed | H | D | 1-1 | Gray 32 pen |
| 40 | div1 | Reading | H | L | 0-1 | |
| 41 | div1 | Burnley | A | W | 2-0 | Jorgensen 18; Gray 89 |
| 42 | div1 | Norwich | A | L | 2-3 | Forrest 42; Jorgensen 68 pen |
| 43 | div1 | Millwall | H | L | 0-1 | |
| 44 | div1 | Watford | H | W | 2-1 | Jorgensen 13; Gray 43 pen |
| 45 | div1 | Gillingham | A | L | 0-1 | |
| 46 | div1 | Preston | A | L | 0-1 | |
| 47 | div1 | Sheff Utd | A | L | 0-3 | |
| 48 | div1 | Portsmouth | H | L | 0-5 | |

☐ Home ☐ Away ☐ Neutral

## ATTENDANCES

**HOME GROUND:** BRADFORD & BINGLEY STADIUM **CAPACITY:** 25136 **AVERAGE LEAGUE AT HOME:** 12500

| | | | | | | | | | | | |
|---|---|---|---|---|---|---|---|---|---|---|---|
| 27 | Wolves | 25812 | 26 | Stoke | 14575 | 6 | Rotherham | 12385 | 35 | Walsall | 10893 |
| 5 | Ipswich | 25457 | 10 | Burnley | 14561 | 24 | Nottm Forest | 12245 | 23 | Gillingham | 10711 |
| 9 | Leicester | 24651 | 39 | Sheff Wed | 14452 | 17 | Reading | 12110 | 43 | Millwall | 10676 |
| 38 | Derby | 23735 | 46 | Preston | 13652 | 31 | Ipswich | 12080 | 19 | Wimbledon | 10615 |
| 28 | West Brom | 19909 | 14 | Derby | 13385 | 11 | Coventry | 11655 | 22 | Millwall | 8510 |
| 20 | Nottm Forest | 19653 | 21 | Sheff Utd | 13364 | 36 | Leicester | 11531 | 29 | Rotherham | 6939 |
| 48 | Portsmouth | 19088 | 1 | Wolves | 13223 | 33 | Brighton | 11520 | 18 | Brighton | 6319 |
| 42 | Norwich | 18536 | 13 | Preston | 13215 | 40 | Reading | 11385 | 45 | Gillingham | 6281 |
| 12 | Portsmouth | 18459 | 16 | Norwich | 12888 | 44 | Watford | 11145 | 30 | Grimsby | 5582 |
| 47 | Sheff Utd | 18297 | 25 | Watford | 12579 | 41 | Burnley | 11095 | 8 | Walsall | 4678 |
| 15 | Sheff Wed | 17191 | 34 | Coventry | 12525 | 37 | Crystal Palace | 11016 | 7 | Wrexham | 2232 |
| 2 | Crystal Palace | 15205 | 3 | Stoke | 12424 | 4 | Grimsby | 10914 | 32 | Wimbledon | 1178 |

## KEY PLAYERS - GOALSCORERS

1 Claus Jorgensen

| | |
|---|---|
| **Goals in the League** | 11 |
| **Goals in all competitions** | 11 |
| **Contribution to Attacking Power** Average number of minutes between League team goals while on pitch | 74 |
| **Player Strike Rate** The total number of minutes he was on the pitch for every League goal scored | 236 |
| **Club Strike Rate** Average number of minutes between League goals scored by club | 81 |

| | PLAYER | GOALS LGE | GOALS ALL | POWER | S RATE |
|---|---|---|---|---|---|
| 2 | Andy Gray | 15 | 15 | 83 | 262 mins |
| 3 | Paul Evans | 3 | 3 | 79 | 474 mins |
| 4 | Michael Standing | 2 | 2 | 66 | 694 mins |
| 5 | Ashley Ward | 3 | 3 | 70 | 708 mins |

## KEY PLAYERS - MIDFIELDERS

1 Jamie Lawrence

| | |
|---|---|
| **Goals in the League** | 1 |
| **Goals in all competitions** | 1 |
| **Defensive Rating** Average number of mins between League goals conceded while on the pitch | 76 |
| **Contribution to Attacking Power** Average number of minutes between League team goals while on pitch | 81 |
| **Scoring Difference** Defensive Rating minus Contribution to Attacking Power | -5 |

| | PLAYER | GOALS LGE | GOALS ALL | DEF RATE | ATT POWER | SCORE DIFF |
|---|---|---|---|---|---|---|
| 2 | Michael Standing | 2 | 2 | 50 | 66 | -16 mins |
| 3 | Gus Uhlenbeek | 1 | 1 | 59 | 76 | -17 mins |
| 4 | Andy Gray | 15 | 15 | 58 | 84 | -26 mins |
| 5 | Paul Evans | 3 | 3 | 47 | 79 | -32 mins |

## KEY PLAYERS - DEFENDERS

1 Peter Atherton

| | |
|---|---|
| **Goals Conceded in League** | 31 |
| **Goals Conceded in all competitions** | 31 |
| **Clean Sheets** In League games when he played at least 70 mins | 5 |
| **Defensive Rating** Ave number of mins between League goals conceded while on the pitch | 71 |
| **Club Defensive Rating** Average number of mins between League goals conceded by the club this season | 57 |

| | PLAYER | CON LGE | CON ALL | CLN SHEETS | DEF RATE |
|---|---|---|---|---|---|
| 2 | David Wetherall | 23 | 23 | 4 | 64 mins |
| 3 | Simon Francis | 33 | 36 | 5 | 61 mins |
| 4 | Lewis Emanuel | 36 | 39 | 5 | 61 mins |
| 5 | Wayne Jacobs | 29 | 32 | 2 | 57 mins |

## KEY GOALKEEPER

1 Aidan Davison

| | |
|---|---|
| **Goals Conceded in the League** | 52 |
| **Goals Conceded in all competitions** | 57 |
| **Clean Sheets** In games when he played at least 70 mins | 7 |
| **Goals to Shots Ratio** The average number of shots on target per League goal conceded | 3.8 |
| **Defensive Rating** Ave number of mins between League goals conceded while on the pitch | 58 |

## MONTHY POINTS TALLY

| Month | Points | % |
|---|---|---|
| AUGUST | 9 | 50% |
| SEPTEMBER | 5 | 28% |
| OCTOBER | 5 | 33% |
| NOVEMBER | 0 | 0% |
| DECEMBER | 9 | 60% |
| JANUARY | 3 | 33% |
| FEBRUARY | 7 | 58% |
| MARCH | 11 | 46% |
| APRIL | 3 | 20% |
| MAY | 0 | 0% |

## TOP POINT EARNERS

| | PLAYER | GAMES | AV PTS |
|---|---|---|---|
| 1 | Michael Standing | 13 | 1.54 |
| 2 | Ashley Ward | 23 | 1.43 |
| 3 | Aidan Davison | 32 | 1.38 |
| 4 | Peter Atherton | 24 | 1.33 |
| 5 | Jamie Lawrence | 15 | 1.27 |
| 6 | Claus Jorgensen | 28 | 1.25 |
| 7 | Danny Cadamarteri | 13 | 1.23 |
| 8 | Lewis Emanuel | 22 | 1.23 |
| 9 | Gus Uhlenbeek | 41 | 1.20 |
| 10 | Andy Myers | 20 | 1.20 |
| | CLUB AVERAGE: | | 1.13 |

## GOALS

| 1 Andy Gray | |
|---|---|
| League | 15 |
| FA Cup | 0 |
| League Cup | 0 |
| Other | 0 |
| TOTAL | 15 |

| | PLAYER | LGE | FAC | LC | Oth | TOT |
|---|---|---|---|---|---|---|
| 2 | Jorgensen | 11 | 0 | 0 | 0 | 11 |
| 3 | Proctor | 4 | 0 | 0 | 0 | 4 |
| 4 | Forrest | 3 | 0 | 0 | 0 | 3 |
| 5 | Evans | 3 | 0 | 0 | 0 | 3 |
| 6 | Ward | 3 | 0 | 0 | 0 | 3 |
| 7 | Reid | 2 | 0 | 0 | 0 | 2 |
| 8 | Standing | 2 | 0 | 0 | 0 | 2 |
| 9 | Facey | 1 | 0 | 0 | 0 | 1 |
| 10 | Francis | 1 | 0 | 0 | 0 | 1 |
| 11 | Molenaar | 1 | 0 | 0 | 0 | 1 |
| | Other | 5 | 1 | 1 | 0 | 7 |
| | TOTAL | 51 | 1 | 1 | 0 | 53 |

## TEAM OF THE SEASON

| GOALKEEPER | GAMES | DEF RATE |
|---|---|---|
| Aidan Davison | 32 | 58 |
| **DEFENDERS** | **GAMES** | **DEF RATE** |
| Peter Atherton | 24 | 71 |
| David Wetherall | 16 | 64 |
| Simon Francis | 22 | 61 |
| Lewis Emanuel | 22 | 61 |
| **MIDFIELDERS** | **GAMES** | **SC DIFF** |
| Jamie Lawrence | 15 | -5 |
| Michael Standing | 13 | -16 |
| Gus Uhlenbeek | 41 | -17 |
| Andy Gray | 43 | -26 |
| **GOALSCORERS** | **GAMES** | **STRIKE RATE** |
| Claus Jorgensen | 28 | 236 |
| Ashley Ward | 23 | 708 |

Games = games playing at least 70 minutes

## LEAGUE APPEARANCES, BOOKINGS AND CAPS

| | AGE (on 01/07/03) | IN THE SQUAD | COUNTING GAMES | MINUTES ON PITCH | YELLOW CARDS | RED CARDS | THIS SEASON | HOME COUNTRY |
|---|---|---|---|---|---|---|---|---|
| **Goalkeepers** | | | | | | | | |
| Steve Banks | 31 | 13 | 7 | 676 | 0 | 0 | - | England |
| Nicky Beach | 18 | 2 | 0 | 0 | 0 | 0 | - | England |
| Dave Beasant | 44 | 4 | 0 | 0 | 0 | 0 | - | England |
| Neil Bennett | 22 | 1 | 0 | 0 | 0 | 0 | - | England |
| Aidan Davison | 35 | 42 | 32 | 3014 | 0 | 0 | - | N Ireland |
| Stefan Magnusson | 22 | 8 | 0 | 0 | 0 | 0 | - | Denmark |
| Boaz Myhill | 20 | 7 | 2 | 180 | 0 | 0 | - | England |
| Gary Walsh | 35 | 13 | 3 | 270 | 0 | 0 | - | England |
| **Defenders** | | | | | | | | |
| Peter Atherton | 33 | 26 | 24 | 2195 | 9 | 1 | - | England |
| Mark Bower | 23 | 45 | 33 | 3089 | 10 | 1 | - | England |
| Lewis Emanuel | 19 | 31 | 22 | 2179 | 2 | 0 | - | England |
| Simon Francis | 18 | 29 | 22 | 2002 | 4 | 1 | - | England |
| Wayne Jacobs | 34 | 26 | 17 | 1661 | 6 | 1 | - | England |
| Robert Molenaar | 34 | 30 | 26 | 2542 | 6 | 0 | - | Holland |
| Andy Myers | 29 | 26 | 20 | 1936 | 1 | 0 | - | England |
| Andy Tod | 31 | 8 | 3 | 348 | 0 | 0 | - | Scotland |
| David Wetherall | 32 | 17 | 16 | 1470 | 3 | 0 | - | Scotland |
| Jake Wright | 17 | 1 | 0 | 0 | 0 | 0 | - | England |
| **Midfielders** | | | | | | | | |
| Paul Evans | 28 | 23 | 14 | 1422 | 7 | 0 | 2 | Wales (50) |
| Craig Fishlock | 20 | 10 | 0 | 0 | 0 | 0 | - | England |
| Andy Gray | 25 | 44 | 43 | 3930 | 7 | 0 | 4 | Scotland (64) |
| Thomas Kearney | 21 | 4 | 3 | 329 | 3 | 0 | - | England |
| Jamie Lawrence | 33 | 16 | 15 | 1373 | 6 | 1 | - | England |
| Andy Lee | 20 | 5 | 0 | 8 | 0 | 0 | - | England |
| Fraser McHugh | 21 | 4 | 1 | 135 | 0 | 0 | - | England |
| Thomas Penford | 18 | 5 | 0 | 57 | 0 | 0 | - | England |
| Paul Reid | 24 | 21 | 6 | 598 | 0 | 0 | - | Australia |
| Michael Standing | 22 | 40 | 13 | 1388 | 3 | 0 | - | England |
| Gus Uhlenbeek | 32 | 42 | 41 | 3731 | 7 | 1 | - | Holland |
| Stephen Warnock | 21 | 12 | 12 | 1080 | 5 | 0 | - | England |
| **Forwards** | | | | | | | | |
| Danny Cadamarteri | 23 | 21 | 13 | 1291 | 1 | 1 | - | England |
| Marc Danks | 19 | 8 | 0 | 18 | 0 | 0 | - | England |
| Danny Ekoku | 17 | 10 | 0 | 0 | 0 | 0 | - | England |
| Delroy Facey | 23 | 6 | 5 | 501 | 1 | 0 | - | England |
| Danny Forrest | 18 | 21 | 9 | 1022 | 2 | 0 | - | England |
| Claus Jorgensen | 27 | 35 | 28 | 2597 | 5 | 0 | - | Denmark |
| Carricondo Juanjo | 24 | 18 | 2 | 304 | 0 | 0 | - | Spain |
| Ben Muirhead | 20 | 11 | 4 | 468 | 0 | 0 | - | England |
| Mike Proctor | 22 | 12 | 9 | 900 | 1 | 0 | - | England |
| Kevin Sanasy | 18 | 6 | 0 | 8 | 0 | 0 | - | England |
| Harpal Singh | 21 | 3 | 2 | 225 | 0 | 0 | - | England |
| Laurens Ten Heuvel | 27 | 6 | 2 | 304 | 1 | 0 | - | Holland |
| Graeme Tomlinson | 27 | 1 | 0 | 0 | 0 | 0 | - | England |
| Ashley Ward | 32 | 24 | 23 | 2123 | 7 | 0 | - | England |

## SQUAD APPEARANCES

| Match | 1 | 2 | 3 | 4 | 5 | 6 | 7 | 8 | 9 | 10 | 11 | 12 | 13 | 14 | 15 | 16 | 17 | 18 | 19 | 20 | 21 | 22 | 23 | 24 | 25 | 26 | 27 | 28 | 29 | 30 | 31 | 32 | 33 | 34 | 35 | 36 | 37 | 38 | 39 | 40 | 41 | 42 | 43 | 44 | 45 | 46 | 47 | 48 |
|---|---|---|---|---|---|---|---|---|---|---|---|---|---|---|---|---|---|---|---|---|---|---|---|---|---|---|---|---|---|---|---|---|---|---|---|---|---|---|---|---|---|---|---|---|---|---|---|---|
| Venue | H | A | A | H | A | H | A | A | A | H | H | A | H | H | A | H | A | A | H | A | H | A | H | H | A | H | A | A | A | A | H | A | H | A | H | H | H | A | H | H | A | A | H | H | A | A | A | H |
| Competition | L | L | L | L | L | L | W | L | L | L | L | L | L | L | L | L | L | L | L | L | L | L | L | L | L | L | L | F | L | L | L | L | L | L | L | L | L | L | L | L | L | L | L | L | L | L | L | L |
| Result | D | D | L | D | W | W | L | W | L | D | D | L | D | D | L | W | L | L | L | L | L | L | L | W | L | W | W | L | L | W | W | D | L | W | L | D | W | W | D | L | W | L | L | W | L | L | L | L |

**Goalkeepers**
Steve Banks
Nicky Beach
Dave Beasant
Neil Bennett
Aidan Davison
Stefan Magnusson
Boaz Myhill
Gary Walsh
**Defenders**
Peter Atherton
Mark Bower
Simon Francis
Wayne Jacobs
Robert Molenaar
Andy Myers
Andy Tod
David Wetherall
Jake Wright
**Midfielders**
Paul Evans
Craig Fishlock
Andy Gray
Thomas Kearney
Jamie Lawrence
Andy Lee
Fraser McHugh
Thomas Penford
Paul Reid
Michael Standing
Gus Uhlenbeek
Stephen Warnock
**Forwards**
Danny Cadamarteri
Marc Danks
Danny Ekoku
Lewis Emanuel
Delroy Facey
Danny Forrest
Claus Jorgensen
Carricondo Juanjo
Ben Muirhead
Mike Proctor
Kevin Sanasy
Harpal Singh
Laurens Ten Heuvel
Graeme Tomlinson
Ashley Ward

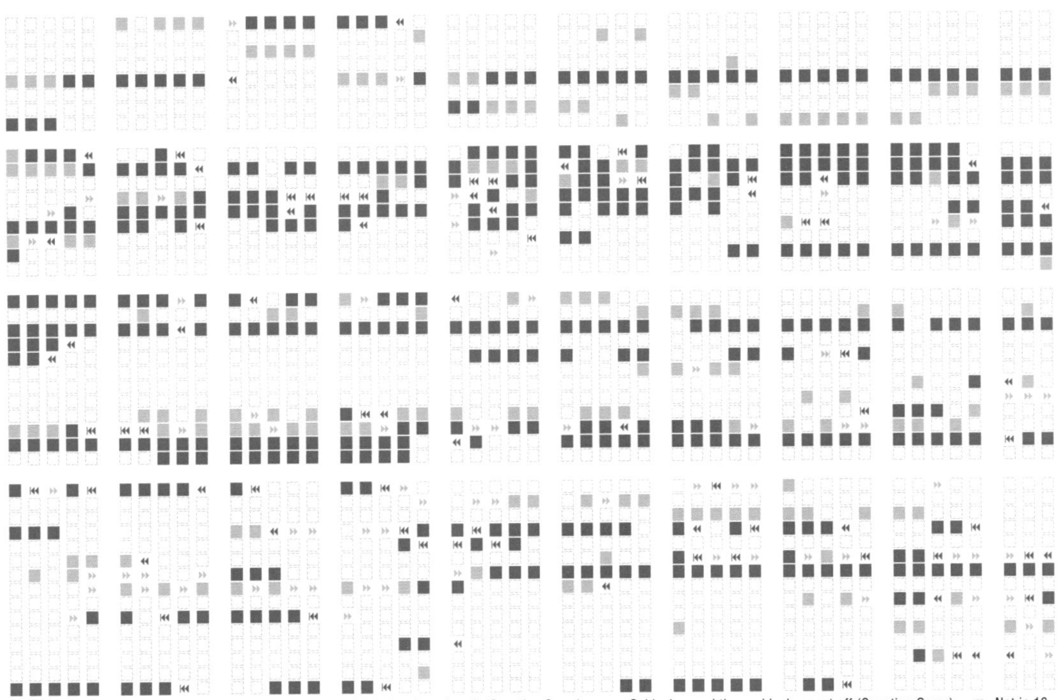

KEY: On all match
On bench
⏮ Subbed or sent off (Counting game)
« Subbed or sent off (playing less than 70 minutes)
⏭ Subbed on from bench (Counting Game)
» Subbed on (playing less than 70 minutes)
Subbed on and then subbed or sent off (Counting Game)
Subbed on and then subbed or sent off (playing less than 70 minutes)
Not in 16

# COVENTRY CITY

Final Position: **20th**

**NICKNAME:** THE SKY BLUES

KEY: Won / Drawn / Lost

| | | | | | | |
|---|---|---|---|---|---|---|
| 1 | div1 | **Sheff Utd** | H | W | 2-1 | Bothroyd 15; McSheffrey 40 |
| 2 | div1 | **Brighton** | A | D | 0-0 | |
| 3 | div1 | **Reading** | A | W | 2-1 | Davenport 74; Bothroyd 82 |
| 4 | div1 | **Crystal Palace** | H | W | 1-0 | Hughes 4 pen |
| 5 | div1 | **Watford** | A | L | 2-5 | McSheffrey 86; Eustace 90 |
| 6 | div1 | **Nottm Forest** | H | L | 0-1 | |
| 7 | wcr1 | **Colchester** | H | W | 3-0 | McSheffrey 1; McAllister 14; Mills 83 |
| 8 | div1 | **Grimsby** | H | W | 3-2 | Mills 48; McAllister 68 pen; Bothroyd 86 |
| 9 | div1 | **Sheff Wed** | H | D | 1-1 | Normann 76 |
| 10 | div1 | **Wimbledon** | A | W | 1-0 | McAllister 8 pen |
| 11 | div1 | **Bradford** | A | D | 1-1 | Bothroyd 83 |
| 12 | div1 | **Millwall** | H | L | 2-3 | McSheffrey 30; Mills 45 |
| 13 | wcr2 | **Rushden & D** | H | W | 8-0 | McSheffrey 9,35,50; Mills 24,45; Bothroyd 61,85; Betts 80 pen |
| 14 | div1 | **Gillingham** | A | W | 2-0 | Bothroyd 46; Pipe 53 |
| 15 | div1 | **Portsmouth** | A | D | 1-1 | Davenport 61 |
| 16 | div1 | **Norwich** | H | D | 1-1 | Partridge 22 |
| 17 | div1 | **Walsall** | H | D | 0-0 | |
| 18 | div1 | **Leicester** | A | L | 1-2 | Partridge 53 |
| 19 | div1 | **Rotherham** | H | W | 2-1 | McAllister 38,82 |
| 20 | wcr3 | **Crystal Palace** | A | L | 0-3 | |
| 21 | div1 | **Burnley** | A | L | 1-3 | McAllister 66 pen |
| 22 | div1 | **Wolves** | H | L | 0-2 | |
| 23 | div1 | **Ipswich** | A | L | 1-2 | Eustace 74 |
| 24 | div1 | **Preston** | H | L | 1-2 | Davenport 80 |
| 25 | div1 | **Stoke** | A | W | 2-1 | Bothroyd 16,21 |
| 26 | div1 | **Wolves** | A | W | 2-0 | McAllister 8; Partridge 65 |
| 27 | div1 | **Derby** | H | W | 3-0 | McAllister 30; Hignett 35; Bothroyd 54 |
| 28 | div1 | **Reading** | H | W | 2-0 | Hignett 39; Partridge 52 |
| 29 | div1 | **Sheff Utd** | A | D | 0-0 | |
| 30 | div1 | **Crystal Palace** | A | D | 1-1 | McSheffrey 69 |
| 31 | facr3 | **Cardiff** | A | D | 2-2 | Mills 27; McAllister 55 pen |
| 32 | div1 | **Brighton** | H | D | 0-0 | |
| 33 | facr3r | **Cardiff** | H | W | 3-0 | Fowler 21; Holdsworth, Dean 57; Bothroyd 89 |
| 34 | div1 | **Nottm Forest** | A | D | 1-1 | Sara 87 |
| 35 | facr4 | **Rochdale** | A | L | 0-2 | |
| 36 | div1 | **Watford** | H | L | 0-1 | |
| 37 | div1 | **Burnley** | H | L | 0-1 | |
| 38 | div1 | **Rotherham** | A | L | 0-1 | |
| 39 | div1 | **Bradford** | H | L | 0-2 | |
| 40 | div1 | **Grimsby** | A | W | 2-0 | Ford 17 og; Eustace 63 |
| 41 | div1 | **Sheff Wed** | A | L | 1-5 | Joachim 54 |
| 42 | div1 | **Wimbledon** | H | D | 2-2 | Eustace 21; Joachim 74 |
| 43 | div1 | **Norwich** | A | L | 0-2 | |
| 44 | div1 | **Portsmouth** | H | L | 0-4 | |
| 45 | div1 | **Leicester** | H | L | 1-2 | Jansen 71 |
| 46 | div1 | **Preston** | A | D | 2-2 | Pead 52; Pipe 62 |
| 47 | div1 | **Ipswich** | H | L | 2-4 | Jansen 23; Gordon 44 |
| 48 | div1 | **Walsall** | A | D | 0-0 | |
| 49 | div1 | **Derby** | A | L | 0-1 | |
| 50 | div1 | **Stoke** | H | L | 0-1 | |
| 51 | div1 | **Gillingham** | H | D | 0-0 | |
| 52 | div1 | **Millwall** | A | L | 0-2 | |

Home / Away / Neutral

## ATTENDANCES

**HOME GROUND:** HIGHFIELD ROAD **CAPACITY:** 23500 **AVERAGE LEAGUE AT HOME:** 14812

| | | | | | | | | | | | |
|---|---|---|---|---|---|---|---|---|---|---|---|
| 18 | Leicester | 27139 | 30 | Crystal Palace | 17362 | 37 | Burnley | 13659 | 11 | Bradford | 11655 |
| 26 | Wolves | 25577 | 45 | Leicester | 16610 | 12 | Millwall | 13562 | 5 | Watford | 11136 |
| 34 | Nottm Forest | 24487 | 16 | Norwich | 16409 | 21 | Burnley | 13470 | 52 | Millwall | 9220 |
| 49 | Derby | 23921 | 31 | Cardiff | 16013 | 24 | Preston | 13313 | 35 | Rochdale | 9156 |
| 23 | Ipswich | 23633 | 32 | Brighton | 15951 | 27 | Derby | 13185 | 13 | Rushden & D | 8570 |
| 29 | Sheff Utd | 20465 | 4 | Crystal Palace | 15526 | 19 | Rotherham | 13179 | 20 | Crystal Palace | 8102 |
| 43 | Norwich | 20009 | 51 | Gillingham | 14795 | 46 | Preston | 13026 | 14 | Gillingham | 7722 |
| 41 | Sheff Wed | 19536 | 3 | Reading | 14712 | 25 | Stoke | 12760 | 48 | Walsall | 7337 |
| 28 | Reading | 19526 | 17 | Walsall | 14544 | 50 | Stoke | 12675 | 2 | Brighton | 6816 |
| 22 | Wolves | 18998 | 9 | Sheff Wed | 14178 | 39 | Bradford | 12525 | 38 | Rotherham | 6524 |
| 1 | Sheff Utd | 18839 | 47 | Ipswich | 13968 | 8 | Grimsby | 12403 | 7 | Colchester | 6075 |
| 15 | Portsmouth | 18837 | 44 | Portsmouth | 13922 | 33 | Cardiff | 11997 | 40 | Grimsby | 5736 |
| 36 | Watford | 17393 | 6 | Nottm Forest | 13732 | 42 | Wimbledon | 11796 | 10 | Wimbledon | 2077 |

## KEY PLAYERS - GOALSCORERS

1 Jay Bothroyd

| | |
|---|---|
| **Goals in the League** | 8 |
| **Goals in all competitions** | 11 |
| **Contribution to Attacking Power** Average number of minutes between League team goals while on pitch | 71 |
| **Player Strike Rate** The total number of minutes he was on the pitch for every League goal scored | 258 |
| **Club Strike Rate** Average number of minutes between League goals scored by club | 90 |

| | PLAYER | GOALS LGE | GOALS ALL | POWER | S RATE |
|---|---|---|---|---|---|
| 2 | Gary McSheffrey | 4 | 8 | 93 | 373 mins |
| 3 | Gary McAllister | 7 | 9 | 91 | 498 mins |
| 4 | Ritchie Partridge | 4 | 4 | 83 | 523 mins |
| 5 | John Eustace | 4 | 4 | 99 | 549 mins |

## KEY PLAYERS - MIDFIELDERS

1 Barry Quinn

| | |
|---|---|
| **Goals in the League** | 0 |
| **Goals in all competitions** | 0 |
| **Defensive Rating** Average number of mins between League goals conceded while on the pitch | 135 |
| **Contribution to Attacking Power** Average number of minutes between League team goals while on pitch | 81 |
| **Scoring Difference** Defensive Rating minus Contribution to Attacking Power | 54 |

| | PLAYER | GOALS LGE | GOALS ALL | DEF RATE | ATT POWER | SCORE DIFF |
|---|---|---|---|---|---|---|
| 2 | Ritchie Partridge | 4 | 4 | 75 | 84 | -9 mins |
| 3 | Youssef Safri | 0 | 0 | 71 | 82 | -11 mins |
| 4 | Youssef Chippo | 0 | 0 | 60 | 79 | -19 mins |
| 5 | Gary McAllister | 7 | 9 | 68 | 92 | -24 mins |

## KEY PLAYERS - DEFENDERS

1 Mohammed Konjic

SUBARU

| | |
|---|---|
| **Goals Conceded in League** | 50 |
| **Goals Conceded in all competitions** | 57 |
| **Clean Sheets** In League games when he played at least 70 mins | 13 |
| **Defensive Rating** Ave number of mins between League goals conceded while on the pitch | 75 |
| **Club Defensive Rating** Average number of mins between League goals conceded by the club this season | 67 |

| | PLAYER | CON LGE | CON ALL | CLN SHEETS | DEF RATE |
|---|---|---|---|---|---|
| 2 | Gary Caldwell | 45 | 51 | 10 | 71 mins |
| 3 | Richard Shaw | 35 | 37 | 8 | 70 mins |
| 4 | Dean Gordon | 41 | 48 | 7 | 64 mins |
| 5 | Calum Davenport | 42 | 47 | 6 | 57 mins |

## KEY GOALKEEPER

1 Morten Hyldgaard

| | |
|---|---|
| **Goals Conceded in the League** | 32 |
| **Goals Conceded in all competitions** | 39 |
| **Clean Sheets** In games when he played at least 70 mins | 8 |
| **Goals to Shots Ratio** The average number of shots on target per each League goal conceded | 4.7 |
| **Defensive Rating** Ave number of mins between League goals conceded while on the pitch | 76 |

## MONTHY POINTS TALLY

| Month | Points | % |
|---|---|---|
| AUGUST | 10 | 56% |
| SEPTEMBER | 11 | 61% |
| OCTOBER | 9 | 50% |
| NOVEMBER | 3 | 17% |
| DECEMBER | 13 | 87% |
| JANUARY | 7 | 39% |
| FEBRUARY | 0 | 0% |
| MARCH | 4 | 22% |
| APRIL | 3 | 17% |
| MAY | 0 | 0% |

## TOP POINT EARNERS

| | PLAYER | GAMES | AV PTS |
|---|---|---|---|
| 1 | Barry Quinn | 12 | 1.50 |
| 2 | Youssef Safri | 19 | 1.47 |
| 3 | Jay Bothroyd | 16 | 1.38 |
| 4 | Ritchie Partridge | 20 | 1.35 |
| 5 | Morten Hyldgaard | 27 | 1.30 |
| 6 | Richard Shaw | 27 | 1.19 |
| 7 | Mohammed Konjic | 42 | 1.19 |
| 8 | Gary Caldwell | 35 | 1.09 |
| 9 | Calum Davenport | 25 | 1.08 |
| 10 | Youssef Chippo | 16 | 1.06 |
| | CLUB AVERAGE: | | 1.09 |

## LEAGUE APPEARANCES, BOOKINGS AND CAPS

| | AGE (on 01/07/03) | IN THE SQUAD | COUNTING GAMES | MINUTES ON PITCH | YELLOW CARDS | RED CARDS | THIS SEASON | HOME COUNTRY |
|---|---|---|---|---|---|---|---|---|
| **Goalkeepers** | | | | | | | | |
| Richard Brush | 18 | 1 | 0 | 0 | 0 | 0 | - | England |
| Fabien Debec | 27 | 28 | 11 | 990 | 0 | 0 | - | France |
| Morten Hyldgaard | 25 | 34 | 27 | 2430 | 1 | 0 | - | Denmark |
| Gary Montgomery | 20 | 28 | 8 | 720 | 0 | 0 | - | England |
| Ben Williams | 20 | 1 | 0 | 0 | 0 | 0 | - | England |
| **Defenders** | | | | | | | | |
| Gary Caldwell | 22 | 36 | 35 | 3195 | 4 | 1 | 2 | Scotland (64) |
| Sean Cooney | 19 | 2 | 0 | 12 | 0 | 0 | - | Australia |
| Calum Davenport | 20 | 41 | 25 | 2381 | 4 | 1 | - | England |
| Vicente Mate Engonga | 37 | 13 | 5 | 474 | 0 | 0 | - | Spain |
| Dean Gordon | 30 | 33 | 28 | 2605 | 3 | 1 | - | England |
| Mohammed Konjic | 33 | 42 | 42 | 3758 | 5 | 0 | - | Bosnia |
| Richard Shaw | 34 | 42 | 27 | 2465 | 6 | 0 | - | England |
| Steve Walsh | 38 | 2 | 1 | 94 | 0 | 0 | - | England |
| **Midfielders** | | | | | | | | |
| Tom Bates | 17 | 2 | 0 | 14 | 0 | 0 | - | England |
| Robert Betts | 21 | 3 | 1 | 90 | 0 | 0 | - | England |
| Youssef Chippo | 30 | 29 | 16 | 1727 | 7 | 1 | - | Morocco |
| John Eustace | 23 | 37 | 21 | 2197 | 5 | 0 | - | England |
| Brian Ford | 20 | 0 | 0 | 0 | 0 | 0 | - | Scotland |
| Lee Fowler | 20 | 1 | 1 | 90 | 0 | 0 | - | Wales |
| Craig Hignett | 33 | 8 | 4 | 531 | 2 | 1 | - | England |
| Avun Jephcott | - | 1 | 0 | 4 | 0 | 0 | - | England |
| Brian Kerr | 21 | 3 | 1 | 178 | 0 | 0 | 1 | Scotland (64) |
| Ben Mackey | 20 | 4 | 0 | 48 | 0 | 0 | - | England |
| Gary McAllister | 38 | 41 | 37 | 3486 | 3 | 0 | - | Scotland |
| Jamie McMaster | 20 | 3 | 1 | 135 | 0 | 0 | - | Australia |
| Mark Noon | - | 2 | 0 | 9 | 0 | 0 | - | England |
| Runar Normann | 25 | 5 | 1 | 157 | 0 | 0 | 2 | |
| Isaac Osbourne | 17 | 5 | 1 | 155 | 0 | 0 | - | England |
| Ritchie Partridge | 22 | 27 | 20 | 2091 | 2 | 0 | 1 | Rep of Ireland (15) |
| Craig Pead | 21 | 26 | 14 | 1607 | 3 | 0 | - | England |
| David Pipe | 19 | 24 | 9 | 1088 | 0 | 0 | 1 | Wales (50) |
| Barry Quinn | 24 | 21 | 12 | 1213 | 0 | 0 | - | Rep of Ireland |
| Youssef Safri | 26 | 27 | 19 | 2047 | 7 | 1 | - | Morocco |
| Juan Sara | 24 | 4 | 0 | 131 | 0 | 0 | - | Argentina |
| Eddie Stanford | 18 | 1 | 0 | 18 | 1 | 0 | - | England |
| Gavin Strachan | 24 | 3 | 0 | 25 | 0 | 0 | - | Scotland |
| David Thompson | 25 | 4 | 4 | 359 | 1 | 0 | - | England |
| Andrew Whing | 18 | 14 | 12 | 1126 | 1 | 0 | - | England |
| Christian Yulu | 18 | 3 | 0 | 90 | 0 | 0 | - | France |
| **Forwards** | | | | | | | | |
| Jay Bothroyd | 21 | 34 | 16 | 2065 | 4 | 0 | - | England |
| Laurent Delorge | 23 | 3 | 0 | 59 | 0 | 0 | - | Belgium |
| Dean Holdsworth | 34 | 18 | 11 | 1205 | 1 | 0 | - | England |
| Lee Hughes | 27 | 4 | 2 | 251 | 1 | 0 | - | England |
| Matthew Jansen | 25 | 11 | 7 | 669 | 2 | 0 | - | England |
| Julian Joachim | 28 | 11 | 8 | 869 | 0 | 0 | - | England |
| Gary McSheffrey | 21 | 33 | 11 | 1493 | 4 | 1 | - | England |
| Lee Mills | 32 | 20 | 9 | 1008 | 0 | 0 | - | England |

## GOALS

| 1 Jay Bothroyd | |
|---|---|
| League | 8 |
| FA Cup | 1 |
| League Cup | 2 |
| Other | 0 |
| TOTAL | 11 |

| | PLAYER | LGE | FAC | LC | Oth | TOT |
|---|---|---|---|---|---|---|
| 2 | McAllister | 7 | 1 | 1 | 0 | 9 |
| 3 | Partridge | 4 | 0 | 0 | 0 | 4 |
| 4 | Eustace | 4 | 0 | 0 | 0 | 4 |
| 5 | McSheffrey | 4 | 0 | 4 | 0 | 8 |
| 6 | Davenport | 3 | 0 | 0 | 0 | 3 |
| 7 | Jansen | 2 | 0 | 0 | 0 | 2 |
| 8 | Pipe | 2 | 0 | 0 | 0 | 2 |
| 9 | Joachim | 2 | 0 | 0 | 0 | 2 |
| 10 | Hignett | 2 | 0 | 0 | 0 | 2 |
| 11 | Mills | 2 | 1 | 3 | 0 | 6 |
| | Other | 6 | 2 | 1 | 0 | 9 |
| | TOTAL | 46 | 5 | 11 | 0 | 62 |

## TEAM OF THE SEASON

| GOALKEEPER | GAMES | DEF RATE |
|---|---|---|
| Morten Hyldgaard | 27 | 76 |
| **DEFENDERS** | **GAMES** | **DEF RATE** |
| Mohammed Konjic | 42 | 75 |
| Gary Caldwell | 35 | 71 |
| Richard Shaw | 27 | 70 |
| Dean Gordon | 28 | 64 |
| **MIDFIELDERS** | **GAMES** | **SCORE DIFF** |
| Barry Quinn | 12 | 54 |
| Ritchie Partridge | 20 | -9 |
| Youssef Safri | 19 | -11 |
| Youssef Chippo | 16 | -19 |
| **GOALSCORERS** | **GAMES** | **STRIKE RATE** |
| Jay Bothroyd | 16 | 258 |
| Gary McSheffrey | 11 | 373 |

Games = games playing at least 70 minutes

## SQUAD APPEARANCES

| Match | 1 | 2 | 3 | 4 | 5 | 6 | 7 | 8 | 9 | 10 | 11 | 12 | 13 | 14 | 15 | 16 | 17 | 18 | 19 | 20 | 21 | 22 | 23 | 24 | 25 | 26 |
|---|---|---|---|---|---|---|---|---|---|---|---|---|---|---|---|---|---|---|---|---|---|---|---|---|---|---|
| Venue | H | A | A | H | A | H | H | H | H | A | A | H | H | A | A | H | H | A | H | A | A | H | A | H | A | A |
| Competition | L | L | L | L | L | L | W | L | L | L | L | L | W | L | L | L | L | L | L | W | L | L | L | L | L | L |
| Result | W | D | W | W | L | L | W | W | D | W | D | L | W | W | D | D | D | L | W | L | L | L | L | L | W | W |

| Match | 27 | 28 | 29 | 30 | 31 | 32 | 33 | 34 | 35 | 36 | 37 | 38 | 39 | 40 | 41 | 42 | 43 | 44 | 45 | 46 | 47 | 48 | 49 | 50 | 51 | 52 |
|---|---|---|---|---|---|---|---|---|---|---|---|---|---|---|---|---|---|---|---|---|---|---|---|---|---|---|
| Venue | H | H | A | A | A | H | H | A | A | H | H | A | H | A | A | H | A | H | H | A | H | A | A | H | H | A |
| Competition | L | L | L | L | F | L | F | L | F | L | L | L | L | L | L | L | L | L | L | L | L | L | L | L | L | L |
| Result | W | W | D | D | D | D | W | D | L | L | L | L | L | W | L | D | L | L | L | D | L | D | L | L | D | L |

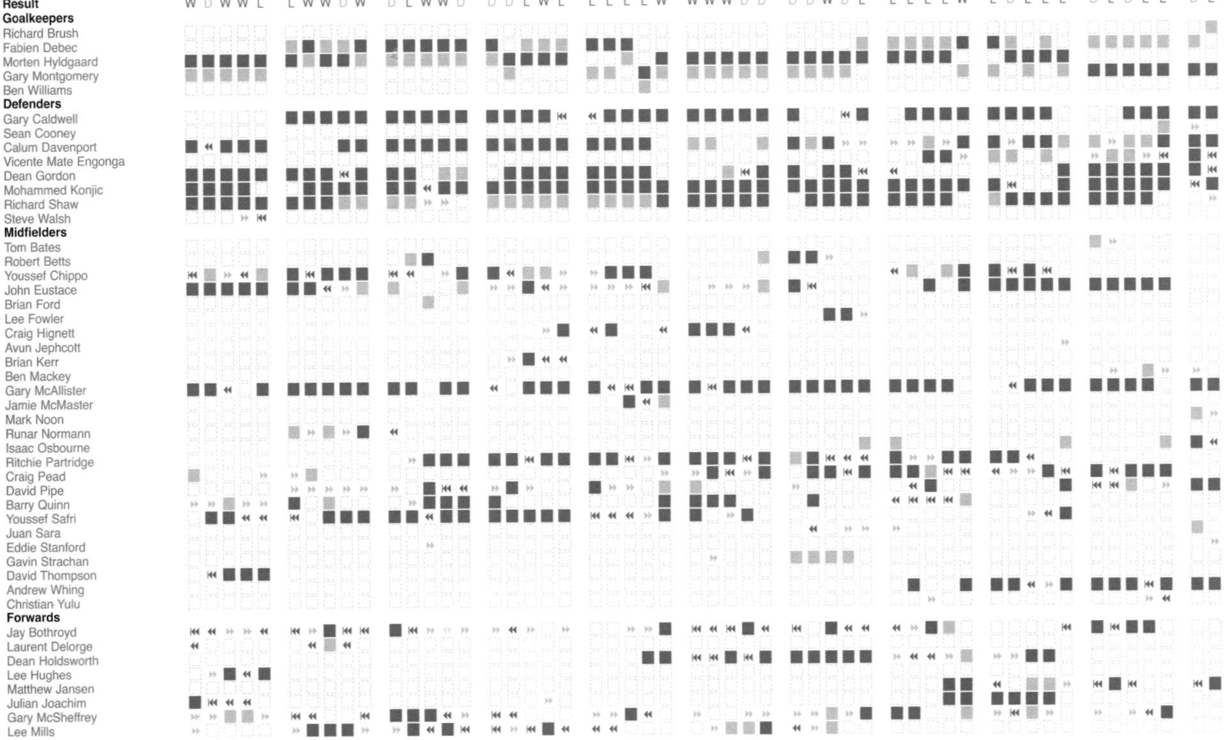
Goalkeepers
Richard Brush
Fabien Debec
Morten Hyldgaard
Gary Montgomery
Ben Williams
Defenders
Gary Caldwell
Sean Cooney
Calum Davenport
Vicente Mate Engonga
Dean Gordon
Mohammed Konjic
Richard Shaw
Steve Walsh
Midfielders
Tom Bates
Robert Betts
Youssef Chippo
John Eustace
Brian Ford
Lee Fowler
Craig Hignett
Avun Jephcott
Brian Kerr
Ben Mackey
Gary McAllister
Jamie McMaster
Mark Noon
Runar Normann
Isaac Osbourne
Ritchie Partridge
Craig Pead
David Pipe
Barry Quinn
Youssef Safri
Juan Sara
Eddie Stanford
Gavin Strachan
David Thompson
Andrew Whing
Christian Yulu
Forwards
Jay Bothroyd
Laurent Delorge
Dean Holdsworth
Lee Hughes
Matthew Jansen
Julian Joachim
Gary McSheffrey
Lee Mills

# STOKE CITY

Final Position: **21st**

**NICKNAME:** THE POTTERS

**KEY:** Won / Drawn / Lost

| | | | | | | |
|---|---|---|---|---|---|---|
| 1 | div1 | Sheff Wed | A | D | 0-0 | |
| 2 | div1 | Leicester | H | L | 0-1 | |
| 3 | div1 | Bradford | H | W | 2-1 | Cooke 4; Marteinsson 43 |
| 4 | div1 | Preston | A | L | 3-4 | Clarke 6 pen,64 pen; Cooke 90 |
| 5 | div1 | Norwich | H | D | 1-1 | Commons 74 |
| 6 | div1 | Derby | A | L | 0-2 | |
| 7 | wcr1 | Bury | A | L | 0-1 | |
| 8 | div1 | Burnley | A | L | 1-2 | Gudjonsson 74 |
| 9 | div1 | Brighton | A | W | 2-1 | Mooney 17 pen; Cooke 76 |
| 10 | div1 | Ipswich | H | W | 2-1 | Shtaniuk 17; Cooke 79 |
| 11 | div1 | Nottm Forest | H | D | 2-2 | Shtaniuk 14; Goodfellow 72 |
| 12 | div1 | Reading | A | D | 1-1 | Vandeurzen 39 |
| 13 | div1 | Crystal Palace | H | D | 1-1 | Iwelumo 85 |
| 14 | div1 | Wolves | H | L | 0-2 | |
| 15 | div1 | Sheff Utd | A | L | 1-2 | Greenacre 84 |
| 16 | div1 | Rotherham | A | L | 0-4 | |
| 17 | div1 | Watford | H | L | 1-2 | Mooney 72 |
| 18 | div1 | Walsall | A | L | 2-4 | Cooke 77,81 |
| 19 | div1 | Grimsby | H | L | 1-2 | Mooney 50 pen |
| 20 | div1 | Portsmouth | A | L | 0-3 | |
| 21 | div1 | Millwall | H | L | 0-1 | |
| 22 | div1 | Gillingham | A | D | 1-1 | Clarke 54 |
| 23 | div1 | Coventry | H | L | 1-2 | Hoekstra 35 |
| 24 | div1 | Portsmouth | H | D | 1-1 | Gunnarsson 34 |
| 25 | div1 | Wimbledon | A | D | 1-1 | Iwelumo 88 |
| 26 | div1 | Bradford | A | L | 2-4 | Marteinsson 9; Henry 23 |
| 27 | div1 | Sheff Wed | H | W | 3-2 | Iwelumo 16,66; Gunnarsson 90 |
| 28 | div1 | Preston | H | W | 2-1 | Gunnarsson 43; Hoekstra 45 |
| 29 | facr3 | Wigan | H | W | 3-0 | Greenacre 20,67; Iwelumo 31 |
| 30 | div1 | Leicester | A | D | 0-0 | |
| 31 | div1 | Derby | H | L | 1-3 | Greenacre 63 |
| 32 | facr4 | Bournemouth | H | W | 3-0 | Iwelumo 45 pen,51; Hoekstra 84 |
| 33 | div1 | Norwich | A | D | 2-2 | Gunnarsson 63; Mills 88 |
| 34 | div1 | Grimsby | A | L | 0-2 | |
| 35 | facr5 | Chelsea | H | L | 0-2 | |
| 36 | div1 | Nottm Forest | A | L | 0-6 | |
| 37 | div1 | Walsall | H | W | 1-0 | Mills 19 |
| 38 | div1 | Burnley | H | L | 0-1 | |
| 39 | div1 | Brighton | H | W | 1-0 | Greenacre 83 |
| 40 | div1 | Ipswich | A | D | 0-0 | |
| 41 | div1 | Sheff Utd | H | D | 0-0 | |
| 42 | div1 | Wolves | A | D | 0-0 | |
| 43 | div1 | Watford | A | W | 2-1 | Hoekstra 34 pen,49 |
| 44 | div1 | Gillingham | H | D | 0-0 | |
| 45 | div1 | Rotherham | H | W | 2-0 | Warhurst 21; Cooke 40 |
| 46 | div1 | Millwall | A | L | 1-3 | Shtaniuk 73 |
| 47 | div1 | Wimbledon | H | W | 2-1 | Gunnarsson 29; Akinbiyi 45 |
| 48 | div1 | Coventry | A | W | 1-0 | Montgomery 57 og |
| 49 | div1 | Crystal Palace | A | L | 0-1 | |
| 50 | div1 | Reading | H | W | 1-0 | Akinbiyi 55 |

Home / Away / Neutral

## ATTENDANCES

**HOME GROUND:** BRITANNIA STADIUM **CAPACITY:** 28000 **AVERAGE LEAGUE AT HOME:** 14631

| | | | | | | | | | | | |
|---|---|---|---|---|---|---|---|---|---|---|---|
| 1 | Sheff Wed | 26746 | 14 | Wolves | 16885 | 2 | Leicester | 14028 | 17 | Watford | 11215 |
| 35 | Chelsea | 26615 | 49 | Crystal Palace | 16064 | 21 | Millwall | 13776 | 37 | Walsall | 10409 |
| 42 | Wolves | 25235 | 27 | Sheff Wed | 16042 | 12 | Reading | 13646 | 29 | Wigan | 9618 |
| 30 | Leicester | 25038 | 4 | Preston | 15422 | 24 | Portsmouth | 13330 | 46 | Millwall | 8725 |
| 40 | Ipswich | 24547 | 15 | Sheff Utd | 15163 | 38 | Burnley | 12874 | 22 | Gillingham | 8150 |
| 36 | Nottm Forest | 24085 | 5 | Norwich | 14931 | 23 | Coventry | 12760 | 16 | Rotherham | 7078 |
| 6 | Derby | 21723 | 28 | Preston | 14862 | 44 | Gillingham | 12746 | 18 | Walsall | 6391 |
| 39 | Brighton | 21023 | 10 | Ipswich | 14587 | 48 | Coventry | 12675 | 9 | Brighton | 6369 |
| 50 | Reading | 20477 | 26 | Bradford | 14575 | 47 | Wimbledon | 12587 | 34 | Grimsby | 5657 |
| 33 | Norwich | 20186 | 11 | Nottm Forest | 14554 | 43 | Watford | 12570 | 7 | Bury | 2581 |
| 45 | Rotherham | 19553 | 41 | Sheff Utd | 14449 | 3 | Bradford | 12424 | 25 | Wimbledon | 1697 |
| 20 | Portsmouth | 18701 | 8 | Burnley | 14244 | 32 | Bournemouth | 12004 | | | |
| 31 | Derby | 17308 | 13 | Crystal Palace | 14214 | 19 | Grimsby | 11488 | | | |

## KEY PLAYERS - GOALSCORERS

**1 Andrew Cooke**

| | |
|---|---|
| Goals in the League | 7 |
| Goals in all competitions | 7 |
| Contribution to Attacking Power<br>Average number of minutes between League team goals while on pitch | 96 |
| Player Strike Rate<br>The total number of minutes he was on the pitch for every League goal scored | 316 |
| Club Strike Rate<br>Average number of minutes between League goals scored by club | 92 |

| | PLAYER | GOALS LGE | GOALS ALL | POWER | S RATE |
|---|---|---|---|---|---|
| 2 | Peter Hoekstra | 4 | 5 | 97 | 510 mins |
| 3 | Chris Greenacre | 3 | 5 | 69 | 554 mins |
| 4 | Clive Clarke | 3 | 3 | 98 | 824 mins |
| 5 | Brynjar Gunnarsson | 4 | 4 | 100 | 852 mins |

## KEY PLAYERS - MIDFIELDERS

**1 Bjarni Gudjonsson**

| | |
|---|---|
| Goals in the League | 1 |
| Goals in all competitions | 1 |
| Defensive Rating<br>Average number of mins between League goals conceded while on the pitch | 67 |
| Contribution to Attacking Power<br>Average number of minutes between League team goals while on pitch | 94 |
| Scoring Difference<br>Defensive Rating minus Contribution to Attacking Power | -27 |

| | PLAYER | GOALS LGE | GOALS ALL | DEF RATE | ATT POWER | SCORE DIFF |
|---|---|---|---|---|---|---|
| 2 | Wayne Thomas | 0 | 0 | 55 | 88 | -33 mins |
| 3 | James O'Connor | 0 | 0 | 57 | 92 | -35 mins |
| 4 | Karl Henry | 1 | 1 | 45 | 101 | -56 mins |

## KEY PLAYERS - DEFENDERS

**1 Marcus Hall**

| | |
|---|---|
| Goals Conceded in League | 30 |
| Goals Conceded in all competitions | 32 |
| Clean Sheets<br>In League games when he played at least 70 mins | 9 |
| Defensive Rating<br>Ave number of mins between League goals conceded while on the pitch | 70 |
| Club Defensive Rating<br>Average number of mins between League goals conceded by the club this season | 60 |

| | PLAYER | CON LGE | CON ALL | CLN SHEETS | DEF RATE |
|---|---|---|---|---|---|
| 2 | Brynjar Gunnarsson | 51 | 54 | 10 | 67 mins |
| 3 | Sergei Shtaniuk | 60 | 63 | 11 | 66 mins |
| 4 | Clive Clarke | 40 | 41 | 5 | 62 mins |
| 5 | Peter Handyside | 66 | 69 | 10 | 60 mins |

## KEY GOALKEEPER

**1 Mark Crossley**

| | |
|---|---|
| Goals Conceded in the League | 7 |
| Goals Conceded in all competitions | 7 |
| Clean Sheets<br>In games when he played at least 70 mins | 7 |
| Goals to Shots Ratio<br>The average number of shots on target per each League goal conceded | 8 |
| Defensive Rating<br>Ave number of mins between League goals conceded while on the pitch | 154 |

## MONTHY POINTS TALLY

| Month | Points | % |
|---|---|---|
| AUGUST | 5 | 28% |
| SEPTEMBER | 8 | 44% |
| OCTOBER | 1 | 7% |
| NOVEMBER | 1 | 7% |
| DECEMBER | 5 | 33% |
| JANUARY | 10 | 67% |
| FEBRUARY | 4 | 27% |
| MARCH | 9 | 50% |
| APRIL | 10 | 56% |
| MAY | 3 | 100% |

## TOP POINT EARNERS

| | PLAYER | GAMES | AV PTS |
|---|---|---|---|
| 1 | Mark Crossley | 12 | 1.67 |
| 2 | Marcus Hall | 23 | 1.35 |
| 3 | Chris Greenacre | 17 | 1.29 |
| 4 | Peter Hoekstra | 19 | 1.26 |
| 5 | Andrew Cooke | 23 | 1.17 |
| 6 | Bjarni Gudjonsson | 25 | 1.16 |
| 7 | Sergei Shtaniuk | 44 | 1.14 |
| 8 | Steve Banks | 14 | 1.14 |
| 9 | Brynjar Gunnarsson | 38 | 1.11 |
| 10 | Peter Handyside | 43 | 1.07 |
| | CLUB AVERAGE: | | 1.09 |

## LEAGUE APPEARANCES, BOOKINGS AND CAPS

| | AGE (on 01/07/03) | IN THE SQUAD | COUNTING GAMES | MINUTES ON PITCH | YELLOW CARDS | RED CARDS | THIS SEASON | HOME COUNTRY |
|---|---|---|---|---|---|---|---|---|
| **Goalkeepers** | | | | | | | | |
| Steve Banks | 31 | 25 | 14 | 1260 | 0 | 0 | - | England |
| Mark Crossley | 34 | 12 | 12 | 1080 | 2 | 0 | 5 | Wales (50) |
| Neil Cutler | 26 | 33 | 20 | 1800 | 0 | 0 | - | England |
| Jani Viander | 27 | 22 | 0 | 0 | 0 | 0 | - | Finland |
| **Defenders** | | | | | | | | |
| Clive Clarke | 23 | 32 | 26 | 2473 | 4 | 0 | - | Rep of Ireland |
| Brynjar Gunnarsson | 27 | 39 | 38 | 3408 | 10 | 1 | - | Iceland |
| Marcus Hall | 27 | 24 | 23 | 2096 | 2 | 0 | - | England |
| Peter Handyside | 28 | 44 | 43 | 3938 | 3 | 1 | - | Scotland |
| Richard Keogh | 16 | 0 | 0 | 0 | 0 | 0 | - | England |
| Frazier Richardson | 20 | 9 | 5 | 559 | 0 | 0 | - | England |
| Sergei Shtaniuk | 31 | 44 | 44 | 3960 | 9 | 1 | - | Belarus |
| Paul Warhurst | 33 | 6 | 2 | 306 | 1 | 0 | - | England |
| Mark Williams | 32 | 9 | 4 | 410 | 1 | 0 | 6 | N Ireland (111) |
| **Midfielders** | | | | | | | | |
| Kristian Commons | 19 | 9 | 6 | 557 | 0 | 0 | - | England |
| Marc Goodfellow | 21 | 25 | 4 | 832 | 0 | 0 | - | England |
| Bjarni Gudjonsson | 24 | 42 | 25 | 2544 | 2 | 0 | - | Iceland |
| Karl Henry | 20 | 29 | 13 | 1314 | 1 | 0 | - | England |
| Petur Marteinsson | 29 | 24 | 6 | 614 | 3 | 1 | - | Iceland |
| Lewis Neal | 21 | 25 | 6 | 713 | 2 | 0 | - | England |
| James O'Connor | 23 | 43 | 43 | 3870 | 11 | 0 | - | Rep of Ireland |
| Wayne Thomas | 24 | 41 | 40 | 3619 | 6 | 1 | - | England |
| Jurgen Vandeurzen | 29 | 22 | 5 | 547 | 0 | 0 | - | Belgium |
| Brian Wilson | 20 | 9 | 4 | 410 | 0 | 0 | - | England |
| **Forwards** | | | | | | | | |
| Adeola Akinbiyi | 28 | 4 | 0 | 229 | 0 | 0 | - | England |
| Andrew Cooke | 29 | 36 | 23 | 2215 | 5 | 0 | - | England |
| Chris Greenacre | 25 | 31 | 17 | 1663 | 1 | 0 | - | England |
| Peter Hoekstra | 30 | 34 | 19 | 2041 | 5 | 0 | - | Holland |
| Chris Iwelumo | 24 | 39 | 11 | 1434 | 3 | 0 | - | Scotland |
| Lee Mills | 32 | 12 | 4 | 578 | 0 | 0 | - | England |
| Tommy Mooney | 31 | 12 | 11 | 977 | 0 | 1 | - | England |

KEY: LEAGUE BOOKINGS CAPS

## GOALS

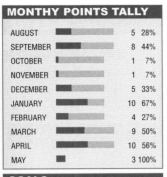

| 1 Andrew Cooke | |
|---|---|
| League | 7 |
| FA Cup | 0 |
| League Cup | 0 |
| Other | 0 |
| TOTAL | 7 |

| | PLAYER | LGE | FAC | LC | Oth | TOT |
|---|---|---|---|---|---|---|
| 2 | Gunnarsson | 4 | 0 | 0 | 0 | 4 |
| 3 | Hoekstra | 4 | 1 | 0 | 0 | 5 |
| 4 | Iwelumo | 4 | 3 | 0 | 0 | 7 |
| 5 | Mooney | 3 | 0 | 0 | 0 | 3 |
| 6 | Shtaniuk | 3 | 0 | 0 | 0 | 3 |
| 7 | Greenacre | 3 | 2 | 0 | 0 | 5 |
| 8 | Clarke | 3 | 0 | 0 | 0 | 3 |
| 9 | Akinbiyi | 2 | 0 | 0 | 0 | 2 |
| 10 | Mills | 2 | 0 | 0 | 0 | 2 |
| 11 | Marteinsson | 2 | 0 | 0 | 0 | 2 |
| | Other | 8 | 0 | 0 | 0 | 8 |
| | TOTAL | 45 | 6 | 0 | 0 | 51 |

## TEAM OF THE SEASON

| GOALKEEPER | GAMES | DEF RATE |
|---|---|---|
| Mark Crossley | 12 | 154 |
| **DEFENDERS** | **GAMES** | **DEF RATE** |
| Marcus Hall | 23 | 70 |
| Brynjar Gunnarsson | 38 | 67 |
| Sergei Shtaniuk | 44 | 66 |
| Clive Clarke | 26 | 62 |
| **MIDFIELDERS** | **GAMES** | **SCORE DIFF** |
| Bjarni Gudjonsson | 25 | -27 |
| Wayne Thomas | 40 | -33 |
| James O'Connor | 43 | -35 |
| Karl Henry | 13 | -56 |
| **GOALSCORERS** | **GAMES** | **STRIKE RATE** |
| Andrew Cooke | 23 | 316 |
| Peter Hoekstra | 19 | 510 |

Games = games playing at least 70 minutes

## SQUAD APPEARANCES

| Match | 1 | 2 | 3 | 4 | 5 | 6 | 7 | 8 | 9 | 10 | 11 | 12 | 13 | 14 | 15 | 16 | 17 | 18 | 19 | 20 | 21 | 22 | 23 | 24 | 25 |
|---|---|---|---|---|---|---|---|---|---|---|---|---|---|---|---|---|---|---|---|---|---|---|---|---|---|
| Venue | A | H | H | A | H | A | A | A | A | H | H | A | H | H | A | A | H | A | H | A | H | A | H | H | A |
| Competition | L | L | L | L | L | L | W | L | L | L | L | L | L | L | L | L | L | L | L | L | L | L | L | L | L |
| Result | D | L | W | L | D | L | L | L | W | W | D | D | D | L | L | L | L | L | L | L | L | D | L | D | D |

| Match | 26 | 27 | 28 | 29 | 30 | 31 | 32 | 33 | 34 | 35 | 36 | 37 | 38 | 39 | 40 | 41 | 42 | 43 | 44 | 45 | 46 | 47 | 48 | 49 | 50 |
|---|---|---|---|---|---|---|---|---|---|---|---|---|---|---|---|---|---|---|---|---|---|---|---|---|---|
| Venue | A | H | H | H | A | H | H | A | A | H | A | H | H | H | A | H | A | A | H | H | A | H | A | A | H |
| Competition | L | L | L | F | L | L | F | L | L | F | L | L | L | L | L | L | L | L | L | L | L | L | L | L | L |
| Result | L | W | W | W | D | L | W | D | L | L | L | W | L | W | D | D | D | W | D | W | L | W | W | L | W |

**Goalkeepers**
Steve Banks
Mark Crossley
Neil Cutler
Jani Viander

**Defenders**
Clive Clarke
Brynjar Gunnarsson
Marcus Hall
Peter Handyside
Richard Keogh
Frazier Richardson
Sergei Shtaniuk
Paul Warhurst
Mark Williams

**Midfielders**
Kristian Commons
Marc Goodfellow
Bjarni Gudjonsson
Karl Henry
Petur Marteinsson
Lewis Neal
James O'Connor
Wayne Thomas
Jurgen Vandeurzen
Brian Wilson

**Forwards**
Adeola Akinbiyi
Andrew Cooke
Chris Greenacre
Peter Hoekstra
Chris Iwelumo
Lee Mills
Tommy Mooney

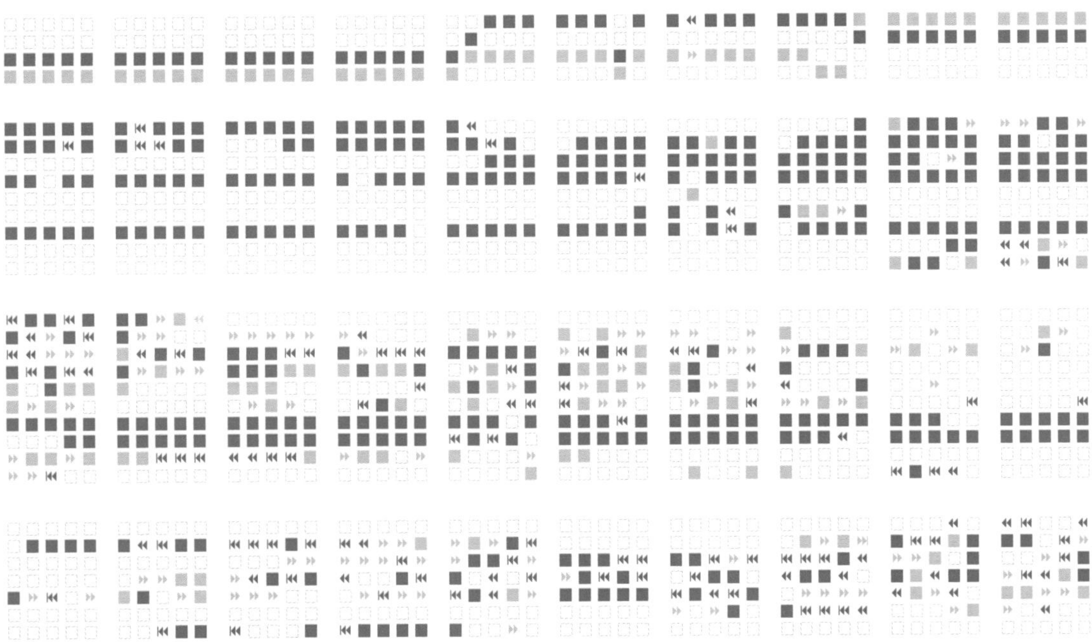

KEY: On all match; On bench; Subbed or sent off (Counting game); Subbed or sent off (playing less than 70 minutes); Subbed on from bench (Counting Game); Subbed on (playing less than 70 minutes); Subbed on and then subbed or sent off (Counting Game); Subbed on and then subbed or sent off (playing less than 70 minutes); Not in 16

# SHEFFIELD WEDNESDAY

Final Position: **22nd**

**NICKNAME: THE OWLS**

KEY: Won / Drawn / Lost

| | | | | | | |
|---|---|---|---|---|---|---|
| 1 | div1 | Stoke | H | D | 0-0 | |
| 2 | div1 | Reading | A | L | 1-2 | Sibon 18 |
| 3 | div1 | Nottm Forest | A | L | 0-4 | |
| 4 | div1 | Rotherham | H | L | 1-2 | Armstrong 8 |
| 5 | div1 | Wolves | A | D | 2-2 | Kuqi 9,63 |
| 6 | div1 | Sheff Utd | H | W | 2-0 | Owusu 73; Kuqi 82 |
| 7 | wcr1 | Rochdale | H | W | 1-0 | Sibon 2 |
| 8 | div1 | Preston | A | D | 2-2 | Kuqi 34; McLaren 75 |
| 9 | div1 | Coventry | A | D | 1-1 | Knight 58 |
| 10 | div1 | Leicester | H | D | 0-0 | |
| 11 | div1 | Crystal Palace | H | D | 0-0 | |
| 12 | div1 | Walsall | A | L | 0-1 | |
| 13 | wcr2 | Leicester | H | L | 1-2 | Sibon 32 |
| 14 | div1 | Burnley | H | L | 1-3 | Donnelly 67 |
| 15 | div1 | Ipswich | A | L | 1-2 | Donnelly 58 |
| 16 | div1 | Bradford | H | W | 2-1 | Sibon 34,86 pen |
| 17 | div1 | Watford | A | L | 0-1 | |
| 18 | div1 | Millwall | H | L | 0-1 | |
| 19 | div1 | Derby | H | L | 1-3 | Hamshaw 61 |
| 20 | div1 | Norwich | A | L | 0-3 | |
| 21 | div1 | Gillingham | A | D | 1-1 | Knight 90 |
| 22 | div1 | Portsmouth | H | L | 1-3 | Knight 27 |
| 23 | div1 | Wimbledon | A | L | 0-3 | |
| 24 | div1 | Brighton | H | D | 1-1 | Kuqi 90 |
| 25 | div1 | Gillingham | H | L | 0-2 | |
| 26 | div1 | Grimsby | A | L | 0-2 | |
| 27 | div1 | Nottm Forest | H | W | 2-0 | Sibon 45; Johnston 55 |
| 28 | div1 | Stoke | A | L | 2-3 | Sibon 23; Proudlock 72 |
| 29 | div1 | Rotherham | A | W | 2-0 | Kuqi 68; Proudlock 90 |
| 30 | facr3 | Gillingham | A | L | 1-4 | Sibon 4 |
| 31 | div1 | Reading | H | W | 3-2 | Quinn 52; Sibon 69; Johnston 71 |
| 32 | div1 | Sheff Utd | A | L | 1-3 | Quinn 47 |
| 33 | div1 | Wolves | H | L | 0-4 | |
| 34 | div1 | Norwich | H | D | 2-2 | Robinson 66; Quinn 76 |
| 35 | div1 | Derby | A | D | 2-2 | Barton 16 og; Crane 83 |
| 36 | div1 | Crystal Palace | A | D | 0-0 | |
| 37 | div1 | Preston | H | L | 0-1 | |
| 38 | div1 | Coventry | H | W | 5-1 | Reddy 8; Kuqi 52,69; McLaren 60; Bradbury 64 |
| 39 | div1 | Leicester | A | D | 1-1 | McLaren 25 |
| 40 | div1 | Ipswich | H | L | 0-1 | |
| 41 | div1 | Bradford | A | D | 1-1 | Crane 82 |
| 42 | div1 | Millwall | A | L | 0-3 | |
| 43 | div1 | Watford | H | D | 2-2 | Bradbury 66 pen; Maddix 90 |
| 44 | div1 | Wimbledon | H | W | 4-2 | Reddy 40; Owusu 48,72; Bradbury 76 |
| 45 | div1 | Portsmouth | A | W | 2-1 | Westwood 76; Reddy 90 |
| 46 | div1 | Grimsby | H | D | 0-0 | |
| 47 | div1 | Brighton | A | D | 1-1 | Holt 16 |
| 48 | div1 | Burnley | A | W | 7-2 | McLaren 3; Westwood 5; Wood 32; Evans, R 47; Haslam 66; Gnohere 73 og; Quinn 80 |
| 49 | div1 | Walsall | H | W | 2-1 | Owusu 66; Quinn 76 |

Home / Away / Neutral

## ATTENDANCES

**HOME GROUND:** HILLSBOROUGH **CAPACITY:** 39814 **AVERAGE LEAGUE AT HOME:** 20326

| | | | | | | | | | | | |
|---|---|---|---|---|---|---|---|---|---|---|---|
| 32 | Sheff Utd | 28179 | 3 | Nottm Forest | 21129 | 16 | Bradford | 17191 | 29 | Rotherham | 11480 |
| 39 | Leicester | 27463 | 49 | Walsall | 20864 | 43 | Watford | 17086 | 13 | Leicester | 10472 |
| 5 | Wolves | 27096 | 20 | Norwich | 20667 | 14 | Burnley | 17004 | 7 | Rochdale | 8815 |
| 6 | Sheff Utd | 27075 | 19 | Derby | 19747 | 18 | Millwall | 16791 | 26 | Grimsby | 8224 |
| 1 | Stoke | 26746 | 38 | Coventry | 19536 | 36 | Crystal Palace | 16707 | 21 | Gillingham | 8028 |
| 27 | Nottm Forest | 26362 | 45 | Portsmouth | 19524 | 22 | Portsmouth | 16602 | 42 | Millwall | 7338 |
| 35 | Derby | 26311 | 34 | Norwich | 19114 | 11 | Crystal Palace | 16112 | 47 | Brighton | 6928 |
| 46 | Grimsby | 26082 | 37 | Preston | 18912 | 28 | Stoke | 16042 | 12 | Walsall | 6792 |
| 40 | Ipswich | 24726 | 24 | Brighton | 18008 | 17 | Watford | 15058 | 30 | Gillingham | 6434 |
| 15 | Ipswich | 23410 | 25 | Gillingham | 17715 | 41 | Bradford | 14452 | 23 | Wimbledon | 2131 |
| 4 | Rotherham | 22873 | 31 | Reading | 17715 | 9 | Coventry | 14178 | | | |
| 10 | Leicester | 22219 | 44 | Wimbledon | 17649 | 2 | Reading | 13638 | | | |
| 33 | Wolves | 21381 | 48 | Burnley | 17435 | 8 | Preston | 13632 | | | |

## KEY PLAYERS - GOALSCORERS

**1 Gerald Sibon**

| | |
|---|---|
| Goals in the League | 6 |
| Goals in all competitions | 9 |
| Contribution to Attacking Power<br>Average number of minutes between League team goals while on pitch | 94 |
| Player Strike Rate<br>The total number of minutes he was on the pitch for every League goal scored | 316 |
| Club Strike Rate<br>Average number of minutes between League goals scored by club | 75 |

| | PLAYER | GOALS LGE | GOALS ALL | POWER | S RATE |
|---|---|---|---|---|---|
| 2 | Shefki Kuqi | 8 | 8 | 81 | 366 mins |
| 3 | Michael Reddy | 3 | 3 | 62 | 375 mins |
| 4 | Allan Johnston | 2 | 2 | 77 | 540 mins |
| 5 | Alan Quinn | 5 | 5 | 70 | 607 mins |

## KEY PLAYERS - MIDFIELDERS

**1 Paul McLaren**

| | |
|---|---|
| Goals in the League | 4 |
| Goals in all competitions | 4 |
| Defensive Rating<br>Average number of mins between League goals conceded while on the pitch | 64 |
| Contribution to Attacking Power<br>Average number of minutes between League team goals while on pitch | 70 |
| Scoring Difference<br>Defensive Rating minus Contribution to Attacking Power | -6 |

| | PLAYER | GOALS LGE | GOALS ALL | DEF RATE | ATT POWER | SCORE DIFF |
|---|---|---|---|---|---|---|
| 2 | Alan Quinn | 5 | 5 | 57 | 71 | -14mins- |
| 3 | Trond Egil Soltvedt | 0 | 0 | 52 | 94 | -42 mins |
| 4 | Tony Crane | 2 | 2 | 51 | 101 | -50 mins |

## KEY PLAYERS - DEFENDERS

**1 Dean Smith**

| | |
|---|---|
| Goals Conceded in League | 16 |
| Goals Conceded in all competitions | 16 |
| Clean Sheets<br>In League games when he played at least 70 mins | 2 |
| Defensive Rating<br>Ave number of mins between League goals conceded while on the pitch | 76 |
| Club Defensive Rating<br>Average number of mins between League goals conceded by the club this season | 57 |

| | PLAYER | CON LGE | CON ALL | CLN SHEETS | DEF RATE |
|---|---|---|---|---|---|
| 2 | David Burrows | 16 | 16 | 4 | 69 mins |
| 3 | Danny Maddix | 32 | 34 | 4 | 62 mins |
| 4 | Leigh Bromby | 38 | 44 | 5 | 61 mins |
| 5 | Brian Barry-Murphy | 25 | 25 | 2 | 61 mins |

## KEY GOALKEEPER

**1 Kevin Pressman**

| | |
|---|---|
| Goals Conceded in the League | 61 |
| Goals Conceded in all competitions | 63 |
| Clean Sheets<br>In games when he played at least 70 mins | 6 |
| Goals to Shots Ratio<br>The average number of shots on target per each League goal conceded | 3.3 |
| Defensive Rating<br>Ave number of mins between League goals conceded while on the pitch | 54 |

## MONTHY POINTS TALLY

| | | |
|---|---|---|
| AUGUST | 2 | 13% |
| SEPTEMBER | 10 | 48% |
| OCTOBER | 3 | 17% |
| NOVEMBER | 1 | 7% |
| DECEMBER | 4 | 27% |
| JANUARY | 6 | 50% |
| FEBRUARY | 3 | 25% |
| MARCH | 6 | 29% |
| APRIL | 11 | 73% |
| MAY | 3 | 100% |

## TOP POINT EARNERS

| | PLAYER | GAMES | AV PTS |
|---|---|---|---|
| 1 | Ashley Westwood | 22 | 1.45 |
| 2 | Dean Smith | 13 | 1.38 |
| 3 | Brian Barry-Murphy | 17 | 1.35 |
| 4 | Paul McLaren | 28 | 1.18 |
| 5 | Michael Reddy | 12 | 1.08 |
| 6 | Gary Monk | 15 | 1.07 |
| 7 | Steven Haslam | 19 | 1.05 |
| 8 | Shefki Kuqi | 30 | 1.03 |
| 9 | Alan Quinn | 32 | 1.00 |
| 10 | Allan Johnston | 12 | 1.00 |
| | CLUB AVERAGE: | | 1.00 |

## LEAGUE APPEARANCES, BOOKINGS AND CAPS

| | AGE (on 01/07/03) | IN THE SQUAD | COUNTING GAMES | MINUTES ON PITCH | YELLOW CARDS | RED CARDS | THIS SEASON | HOME COUNTRY |
|---|---|---|---|---|---|---|---|---|
| **Goalkeepers** | | | | | | | | |
| Paul Evans | 29 | 18 | 7 | 630 | 1 | 0 | - | South Africa |
| Kevin Pressman | 35 | 43 | 36 | 3321 | 0 | 0 | - | England |
| Christopher Stringer | 19 | 31 | 1 | 199 | 0 | 0 | - | England |
| **Defenders** | | | | | | | | |
| Craig Armstrong | 28 | 23 | 15 | 1461 | 3 | 0 | - | England |
| Brian Barry-Murphy | 24 | 17 | 17 | 1530 | 0 | 0 | - | Rep of Ireland |
| Jon Beswetherick | 25 | 6 | 4 | 408 | 1 | 0 | - | England |
| Leigh Bromby | 23 | 30 | 25 | 2311 | 3 | 1 | - | England |
| David Burrows | 34 | 14 | 12 | 1110 | 2 | 0 | - | England |
| Derek Geary | 23 | 27 | 24 | 2166 | 10 | 0 | - | Rep of Ireland |
| Ryan Green | 22 | 8 | 4 | 352 | 0 | 0 | - | Rep of Ireland |
| Steven Haslam | 23 | 35 | 19 | 1845 | 3 | 0 | - | England |
| Ian Hendon | 31 | 11 | 8 | 714 | 2 | 0 | - | England |
| Danny Maddix | 35 | 32 | 21 | 1977 | 8 | 1 | - | England |
| Gary Monk | 24 | 15 | 15 | 1350 | 0 | 0 | - | England |
| Dean Smith | 32 | 14 | 13 | 1215 | 3 | 0 | - | England |
| Ashley Westwood | 26 | 28 | 22 | 1936 | 4 | 0 | - | England |
| Richard Wood | 18 | 4 | 2 | 187 | 0 | 0 | - | England |
| **Midfielders** | | | | | | | | |
| Tony Crane | 20 | 24 | 10 | 1112 | 3 | 0 | - | England |
| Simon Donnelly | 28 | 20 | 5 | 795 | 2 | 0 | - | Scotland |
| Richard Evans | 20 | 7 | 3 | 295 | 0 | 0 | - | Wales |
| Matthew Hamshaw | 21 | 21 | 2 | 535 | 0 | 0 | - | England |
| Paul McLaren | 26 | 37 | 28 | 2798 | 5 | 0 | - | England |
| Philip O'Donnell | 31 | 3 | 0 | 0 | 0 | 0 | - | Scotland |
| Darryl Powell | 26 | 8 | 7 | 643 | 4 | 0 | - | Jamaica |
| Alan Quinn | 24 | 41 | 32 | 3036 | 6 | 1 | - | Rep of Ireland |
| Carl Robinson | 26 | 4 | 4 | 360 | 0 | 0 | 1 | Wales (50) |
| Matthew Shaw | 19 | 0 | 0 | 0 | 0 | 0 | - | England |
| Trond Egil Soltvedt | 36 | 29 | 19 | 1777 | 3 | 0 | - | Norway |
| **Forwards** | | | | | | | | |
| Lee Bradbury | 28 | 11 | 9 | 826 | 0 | 0 | - | England |
| Michele di Piedi | 22 | 2 | 1 | 78 | 0 | 0 | - | Italy |
| Grant Holt | 22 | 7 | 3 | 312 | 2 | 0 | - | England |
| Allan Johnston | 29 | 12 | 12 | 1080 | 1 | 0 | 2 | Scotland (64) |
| Leon Knight | 20 | 26 | 10 | 1319 | 1 | 0 | - | England |
| Shefki Kuqi | 26 | 43 | 30 | 2926 | 1 | 1 | - | Serbia & Montenegro |
| Owen Morrison | 21 | 3 | 0 | 21 | 0 | 0 | - | N Ireland |
| Lloyd Owusu | 26 | 34 | 10 | 1396 | 2 | 0 | - | England |
| Adam Proudlock | 22 | 5 | 3 | 319 | 0 | 0 | - | England |
| Michael Reddy | 23 | 15 | 12 | 1125 | 2 | 0 | - | Rep of Ireland |
| Jon Shaw | 19 | 2 | 0 | 1 | 0 | 0 | - | England |
| Gerald Sibon | 29 | 25 | 19 | 1896 | 6 | 1 | - | Holland |

## GOALS

| 1 Shefki Kuqi | |
|---|---|
| League | 8 |
| FA Cup | 0 |
| League Cup | 0 |
| Other | 0 |
| TOTAL | 8 |

| | PLAYER | LGE | FAC | LC | Oth | TOT |
|---|---|---|---|---|---|---|
| 2 | Sibon | 6 | 1 | 2 | 0 | 9 |
| 3 | Quinn | 5 | 0 | 0 | 0 | 5 |
| 4 | McLaren | 4 | 0 | 0 | 0 | 4 |
| 5 | Owusu | 4 | 0 | 0 | 0 | 4 |
| 6 | Knight | 3 | 0 | 0 | 0 | 3 |
| 7 | Bradbury | 3 | 0 | 0 | 0 | 3 |
| 8 | Reddy | 3 | 0 | 0 | 0 | 3 |
| 9 | Proudlock | 2 | 0 | 0 | 0 | 2 |
| 10 | Crane | 2 | 0 | 0 | 0 | 2 |
| 11 | Johnston | 2 | 0 | 0 | 0 | 2 |
| | Other | 14 | 0 | 0 | 0 | 14 |
| | **TOTAL** | **56** | **1** | **2** | **0** | **59** |

## TEAM OF THE SEASON

| GOALKEEPER | GAMES | DEF RATE |
|---|---|---|
| Kevin Pressman | 36 | 54 |
| **DEFENDERS** | **GAMES** | **DEF RATE** |
| Dean Smith | 13 | 76 |
| David Burrows | 12 | 69 |
| Danny Maddix | 21 | 62 |
| Leigh Bromby | 25 | 61 |
| **MIDFIELDERS** | **GAMES** | **SCORE DIFF** |
| Paul McLaren | 28 | -6 |
| Alan Quinn | 32 | -14 |
| Trond Egil Soltvedt | 19 | -42 |
| Tony Crane | 10 | -50 |
| **GOALSCORERS** | **GAMES** | **STRIKE RATE** |
| Gerald Sibon | 19 | 316 |
| Shefki Kuqi | 30 | 366 |

Games = games playing at least 70 minutes

## SQUAD APPEARANCES

| Match | 1 | 2 | 3 | 4 | 5 | 6 | 7 | 8 | 9 | 10 | 11 | 12 | 13 | 14 | 15 | 16 | 17 | 18 | 19 | 20 | 21 | 22 | 23 | 24 | 25 |
|---|---|---|---|---|---|---|---|---|---|---|---|---|---|---|---|---|---|---|---|---|---|---|---|---|---|
| Venue | H | A | A | H | A | H | H | A | A | H | H | A | H | H | A | H | A | H | H | A | A | H | A | H | H |
| Competition | L | L | L | L | L | L | W | L | L | L | L | L | W | L | L | L | L | L | L | L | L | L | L | L | L |
| Result | D | L | L | L | D | W | W | D | D | D | D | L | D | L | L | W | L | L | L | L | D | L | L | D | L |

| Match | 26 | 27 | 28 | 29 | 30 | 31 | 32 | 33 | 34 | 35 | 36 | 37 | 38 | 39 | 40 | 41 | 42 | 43 | 44 | 45 | 46 | 47 | 48 | 49 |
|---|---|---|---|---|---|---|---|---|---|---|---|---|---|---|---|---|---|---|---|---|---|---|---|---|
| Venue | A | H | A | A | A | H | A | H | H | A | A | H | H | A | H | A | A | H | H | A | H | A | A | H |
| Competition | L | L | L | L | F | L | L | L | L | L | L | L | L | L | L | L | L | L | L | L | L | L | L | L |
| Result | L | W | L | W | L | W | L | L | D | D | D | L | W | D | L | D | L | D | W | W | D | D | W | W |

**Goalkeepers**
Paul Evans
Kevin Pressman
Christopher Stringer
**Defenders**
Craig Armstrong
Brian Barry-Murphy
Jon Beswetherick
Leigh Bromby
David Burrows
Derek Geary
Ryan Green
Steven Haslam
Ian Hendon
Danny Maddix
Gary Monk
Dean Smith
Ashley Westwood
Richard Wood
**Midfielders**
Tony Crane
Simon Donnelly
Richard Evans
Matthew Hamshaw
Paul McLaren
Philip O'Donnell
Darryl Powell
Alan Quinn
Carl Robinson
Matthew Shaw
Trond Egil Soltvedt
**Forwards**
Lee Bradbury
Michele di Piedi
Grant Holt
Allan Johnston
Leon Knight
Shefki Kuqi
Owen Morrison
Lloyd Owusu
Adam Proudlock
Michael Reddy
Jon Shaw
Gerald Sibon

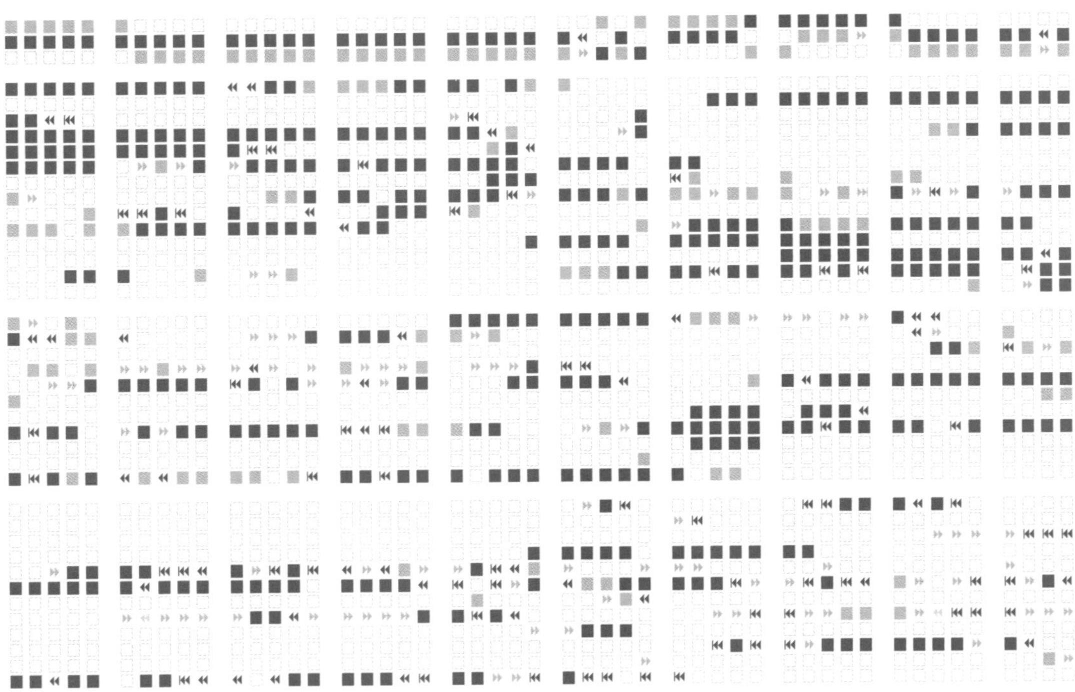

# BRIGHTON & HOVE ALBION

Final Position: **23rd**

**NICKNAME:** THE SEAGULLS

KEY: ☐ Won ☐ Drawn ☐ Lost

| | | | | | | |
|---|---|---|---|---|---|---|
| 1 | div1 | Burnley | A | W | 3-1 | Melton 29; Brooker 65; Zamora 68 |
| 2 | div1 | Coventry | H | D | 0-0 | |
| 3 | div1 | Norwich | H | L | 0-2 | |
| 4 | div1 | Wimbledon | A | L | 0-1 | |
| 5 | div1 | Walsall | H | L | 0-2 | |
| 6 | div1 | Portsmouth | A | L | 2-4 | Cullip 8; Brooker 19 |
| 7 | div1 | Millwall | A | L | 0-1 | |
| 8 | wcr1 | Exeter | H | W | 2-1 | Wilkinson 34; Cullip 103 |
| 9 | div1 | Gillingham | H | L | 2-4 | Carpenter 27; Hart 80 |
| 10 | div1 | Stoke | H | L | 1-2 | Carpenter 79 |
| 11 | div1 | Rotherham | A | L | 0-1 | |
| 12 | wcr2 | Ipswich | A | L | 1-3 | Hammond 8 |
| 13 | div1 | Grimsby | H | L | 1-2 | Zamora 71 |
| 14 | div1 | Watford | A | L | 0-1 | |
| 15 | div1 | Sheff Utd | H | L | 2-4 | Hart 23; Barrett 34 |
| 16 | div1 | Crystal Palace | A | L | 0-5 | |
| 17 | div1 | Bradford | H | W | 3-2 | Zamora 10 pen,55 pen; Rodger 42 |
| 18 | div1 | Wolves | A | D | 1-1 | Zamora 15 |
| 19 | div1 | Derby | H | W | 1-0 | Mayo 89 |
| 20 | div1 | Preston | A | D | 2-2 | Rodger 53; Sidwell 72 |
| 21 | div1 | Nottm Forest | A | L | 2-3 | Sidwell 81; Jones, N 90 |
| 22 | div1 | Reading | H | L | 0-1 | |
| 23 | div1 | Sheff Wed | A | D | 1-1 | Hart 20 |
| 24 | div1 | Ipswich | H | D | 1-1 | Zamora 45 |
| 25 | div1 | Derby | A | L | 0-1 | |
| 26 | div1 | Leicester | H | L | 0-1 | |
| 27 | div1 | Norwich | A | W | 1-0 | Sidwell 38 |
| 28 | div1 | Burnley | H | D | 2-2 | Sidwell 88,89 |
| 29 | div1 | Coventry | A | D | 0-0 | |
| 30 | facr3 | Norwich | A | L | 1-3 | Pethick 49 |
| 31 | div1 | Portsmouth | H | D | 1-1 | Zamora 54 |
| 32 | div1 | Walsall | A | L | 0-1 | |
| 33 | div1 | Wimbledon | H | L | 2-3 | Brooker 3; Zamora 86 |
| 34 | div1 | Wolves | H | W | 4-1 | Zamora 31; Blackwell 45; Brooker 47; Hart 67 |
| 35 | div1 | Bradford | A | W | 1-0 | Zamora 28 |
| 36 | div1 | Millwall | H | W | 1-0 | Rougier 65 |
| 37 | div1 | Gillingham | A | L | 0-3 | |
| 38 | div1 | Stoke | A | L | 0-1 | |
| 39 | div1 | Rotherham | H | W | 2-0 | Hurst 56 og; Zamora 68 |
| 40 | div1 | Nottm Forest | H | W | 1-0 | Brooker 16 |
| 41 | div1 | Sheff Utd | A | L | 1-2 | Carpenter 14 |
| 42 | div1 | Ipswich | A | D | 2-2 | Marshall 66 og; Rougier 81 |
| 43 | div1 | Crystal Palace | H | D | 0-0 | |
| 44 | div1 | Reading | A | W | 2-1 | Brooker 17; Kitson 77 |
| 45 | div1 | Preston | H | L | 0-2 | |
| 46 | div1 | Leicester | A | L | 0-2 | |
| 47 | div1 | Sheff Wed | H | D | 1-1 | Zamora 57 pen |
| 48 | div1 | Watford | H | W | 4-0 | Blackwell 13; Kitson 27; Zamora 72; Oatway 90 |
| 49 | div1 | Grimsby | A | D | 2-2 | Zamora 45 pen; Cullip 47 |

☐ Home ☐ Away ☐ Neutral

## ATTENDANCES

**HOME GROUND:** WITHDEAN STADIUM **CAPACITY:** 7000 **AVERAGE LEAGUE AT HOME:** 6650

| | | | | | | | | | | | |
|---|---|---|---|---|---|---|---|---|---|---|---|
| 46 | Leicester | 31909 | 29 | Coventry | 15951 | 40 | Nottm Forest | 6830 | 5 | Walsall | 6519 |
| 21 | Nottm Forest | 29137 | 14 | Watford | 15305 | 22 | Reading | 6817 | 28 | Burnley | 6502 |
| 42 | Ipswich | 26078 | 1 | Burnley | 14738 | 2 | Coventry | 6816 | 39 | Rotherham | 6468 |
| 25 | Derby | 25786 | 12 | Ipswich | 13266 | 15 | Sheff Utd | 6810 | 49 | Grimsby | 6396 |
| 18 | Wolves | 23016 | 20 | Preston | 13068 | 43 | Crystal Palace | 6786 | 24 | Ipswich | 6377 |
| 16 | Crystal Palace | 21796 | 35 | Bradford | 11520 | 34 | Wolves | 6754 | 10 | Stoke | 6369 |
| 38 | Stoke | 21023 | 37 | Gillingham | 9178 | 36 | Millwall | 6751 | 17 | Bradford | 6319 |
| 27 | Norwich | 20687 | 7 | Millwall | 8822 | 9 | Gillingham | 6733 | 33 | Wimbledon | 6111 |
| 41 | Sheff Utd | 19357 | 32 | Walsall | 8413 | 3 | Norwich | 6730 | 8 | Exeter | 5200 |
| 6 | Portsmouth | 19031 | 47 | Sheff Wed | 6928 | 11 | Rotherham | 6696 | 4 | Wimbledon | 2522 |
| 23 | Sheff Wed | 18008 | 31 | Portsmouth | 6848 | 45 | Preston | 6669 | | | |
| 30 | Norwich | 17205 | 19 | Derby | 6845 | 26 | Leicester | 6592 | | | |
| 44 | Reading | 16133 | 48 | Watford | 6841 | 13 | Grimsby | 6547 | | | |

## KEY PLAYERS - GOALSCORERS

1 Bobby Zamora

| | |
|---|---|
| **Goals in the League** | 14 |
| **Goals in all competitions** | 14 |
| **Contribution to Attacking Power** Average number of minutes between League team goals while on pitch | 78 |
| **Player Strike Rate** The total number of minutes he was on the pitch for every League goal scored | 213 |
| **Club Strike Rate** Average number of minutes between League goals scored by club | 84 |

| | PLAYER | GOALS LGE | GOALS ALL | POWER | S RATE |
|---|---|---|---|---|---|
| 2 | Paul Brooker | 6 | 6 | 86 | 461 mins |
| 3 | Gary Hart | 4 | 4 | 71 | 610 mins |
| 4 | Dean Blackwell | 2 | 2 | 66 | 796 mins |
| 5 | Simon Rodger | 2 | 2 | 71 | 1106 mins |

## KEY PLAYERS - MIDFIELDERS

1 Simon Rodger

| | |
|---|---|
| **Goals in the League** | 2 |
| **Goals in all competitions** | 2 |
| **Defensive Rating** Average number of mins between League goals conceded while on the pitch | 76 |
| **Contribution to Attacking Power** Average number of minutes between League team goals while on pitch | 71 |
| **Scoring Difference** Defensive Rating minus Contribution to Attacking Power | 5 |

| | PLAYER | GOALS LGE | GOALS ALL | DEF RATE | ATT POWER | SCORE DIFF |
|---|---|---|---|---|---|---|
| 2 | Ivar Ingimarsson | 0 | 0 | 84 | 79 | 5 mins |
| 3 | Kerry Mayo | 1 | 1 | 69 | 83 | -14 mins |
| 4 | Steven Sidwell | 5 | 5 | 82 | 99 | -17 mins |
| 5 | Paul Brooker | 6 | 6 | 66 | 87 | -21 mins |

## KEY PLAYERS - DEFENDERS

1 Dean Blackwell

| | |
|---|---|
| **Goals Conceded in League** | 24 |
| **Goals Conceded in all competitions** | 25 |
| **Clean Sheets** In League games when he played at least 70 mins | 6 |
| **Defensive Rating** Ave number of mins between League goals conceded while on the pitch | 66 |
| **Club Defensive Rating** Average number of mins between League goals conceded by the club this season | 62 |

| | PLAYER | CON LGE | CON ALL | CLN SHEETS | DEF RATE |
|---|---|---|---|---|---|
| 2 | Robbie Pethick | 35 | 39 | 4 | 64 mins |
| 3 | Danny Cullip | 62 | 69 | 9 | 63 mins |
| 4 | Nathan Jones | 26 | 28 | 3 | 63 mins |
| 5 | Paul Watson | 62 | 68 | 9 | 62 mins |

## KEY GOALKEEPER

1 Dave Beasant

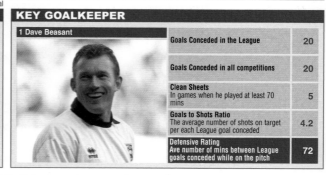

| | |
|---|---|
| **Goals Conceded in the League** | 20 |
| **Goals Conceded in all competitions** | 20 |
| **Clean Sheets** In games when he played at least 70 mins | 5 |
| **Goals to Shots Ratio** The average number of shots on target per each League goal conceded | 4.2 |
| **Defensive Rating** Ave number of mins between League goals conceded while on the pitch | 72 |

## MONTHY POINTS TALLY

| Month | Points | % |
|---|---|---|
| AUGUST | 4 | 22% |
| SEPTEMBER | 3 | 14% |
| OCTOBER | 0 | 0% |
| NOVEMBER | 8 | 44% |
| DECEMBER | 6 | 33% |
| JANUARY | 2 | 22% |
| FEBRUARY | 9 | 60% |
| MARCH | 8 | 38% |
| APRIL | 7 | 47% |
| MAY | 1 | 33% |

## TOP POINT EARNERS

| | PLAYER | GAMES | AV PTS |
|---|---|---|---|
| 1 | Dean Blackwell | 16 | 1.63 |
| 2 | Ivar Ingimarsson | 15 | 1.47 |
| 3 | Simon Rodger | 22 | 1.23 |
| 4 | Bobby Zamora | 33 | 1.21 |
| 5 | Dave Beasant | 16 | 1.19 |
| 6 | Kerry Mayo | 40 | 1.13 |
| 7 | Richard Carpenter | 39 | 1.05 |
| 8 | Paul Watson | 43 | 0.98 |
| 9 | Paul Brooker | 28 | 0.96 |
| 10 | Gary Hart | 23 | 0.96 |
| | CLUB AVERAGE: | | 0.98 |

## GOALS

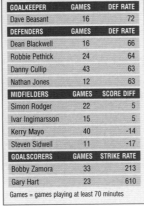

| 1 Bobby Zamora | |
|---|---|
| League | 14 |
| FA Cup | 0 |
| League Cup | 0 |
| Other | 0 |
| TOTAL | 14 |

| | PLAYER | LGE | FAC | LC | Oth | TOT |
|---|---|---|---|---|---|---|
| 2 | Brooker | 6 | 0 | 0 | 0 | 6 |
| 3 | Sidwell | 5 | 0 | 0 | 0 | 5 |
| 4 | Hart | 4 | 0 | 0 | 0 | 4 |
| 5 | Carpenter | 3 | 0 | 0 | 0 | 3 |
| 6 | Rougier | 2 | 0 | 0 | 0 | 2 |
| 7 | Blackwell | 2 | 0 | 0 | 0 | 2 |
| 8 | Rodger | 2 | 0 | 0 | 0 | 2 |
| 9 | Kitson | 2 | 0 | 0 | 0 | 2 |
| 10 | Cullip | 2 | 0 | 1 | 0 | 3 |
| 11 | Mayo | 1 | 0 | 0 | 0 | 1 |
| | Other | 6 | 1 | 2 | 0 | 9 |
| | TOTAL | 49 | 1 | 3 | 0 | 53 |

## TEAM OF THE SEASON

| GOALKEEPER | GAMES | DEF RATE |
|---|---|---|
| Dave Beasant | 16 | 72 |
| **DEFENDERS** | **GAMES** | **DEF RATE** |
| Dean Blackwell | 16 | 66 |
| Robbie Pethick | 24 | 64 |
| Danny Cullip | 43 | 63 |
| Nathan Jones | 12 | 63 |
| **MIDFIELDERS** | **GAMES** | **SCORE DIFF** |
| Simon Rodger | 22 | 5 |
| Ivar Ingimarsson | 15 | 5 |
| Kerry Mayo | 40 | -14 |
| Steven Sidwell | 11 | -17 |
| **GOALSCORERS** | **GAMES** | **STRIKE RATE** |
| Bobby Zamora | 33 | 213 |
| Gary Hart | 23 | 610 |

Games = games playing at least 70 minutes

## LEAGUE APPEARANCES, BOOKINGS AND CAPS

| | AGE (on 01/07/03) | IN THE SQUAD | COUNTING GAMES | MINUTES ON PITCH | YELLOW CARDS | RED CARDS | THIS SEASON | HOME COUNTRY |
|---|---|---|---|---|---|---|---|---|
| **Goalkeepers** | | | | | | | | |
| Dave Beasant | 44 | 17 | 16 | 1440 | 1 | 0 | - | England |
| John Keeley | 41 | 1 | 0 | 0 | 0 | 0 | - | England |
| Michel Kuipers | 29 | 21 | 21 | 1889 | 3 | 1 | - | Holland |
| Will Packham | 22 | 35 | 0 | 0 | 0 | 0 | - | England |
| Andy Petterson | 33 | 15 | 6 | 541 | 0 | 0 | - | Australia |
| Ben Roberts | 28 | 3 | 3 | 270 | 0 | 0 | - | England |
| **Defenders** | | | | | | | | |
| Dean Blackwell | 33 | 22 | 16 | 1591 | 2 | 0 | - | England |
| Guy Butters | 33 | 11 | 6 | 540 | 3 | 0 | - | England |
| Danny Cullip | 26 | 44 | 43 | 3912 | 8 | 0 | - | England |
| Dean Hammond | 20 | 8 | 1 | 91 | 0 | 0 | - | England |
| Adam Hinshelwood | 19 | 19 | 4 | 414 | 0 | 0 | - | England |
| Nathan Jones | 30 | 34 | 12 | 1631 | 3 | 0 | - | Wales |
| Robbie Pethick | 32 | 29 | 24 | 2253 | 3 | 0 | - | England |
| Adam Virgo | 20 | 5 | 4 | 360 | 0 | 0 | - | England |
| Paul Watson | 28 | 44 | 43 | 3852 | 7 | 0 | - | England |
| **Midfielders** | | | | | | | | |
| Paul Brooker | 27 | 41 | 28 | 2768 | 0 | 1 | - | England |
| Richard Carpenter | 30 | 44 | 39 | 3685 | 6 | 0 | - | England |
| Dan Harding | - | 1 | 0 | 0 | 0 | 0 | - | |
| Ivar Ingimarsson | 25 | 15 | 15 | 1350 | 1 | 0 | - | Iceland |
| Kerry Mayo | 25 | 41 | 40 | 3662 | 3 | 0 | - | England |
| Chris McPhee | 20 | 2 | 0 | 30 | 1 | 0 | - | England |
| Stephen Melton | 24 | 10 | 2 | 378 | 0 | 0 | - | England |
| Charlie Oatway | 29 | 45 | 16 | 1708 | 6 | 0 | - | England |
| John Piercy | 23 | 9 | 1 | 111 | 0 | 0 | - | England |
| Simon Rodger | 31 | 28 | 22 | 2211 | 2 | 0 | - | England |
| Paul Rogers | 38 | 18 | 1 | 181 | 0 | 0 | - | England |
| Anthony Rougier | 31 | 6 | 4 | 452 | 0 | 0 | - | Trinidad & Tobago |
| Steven Sidwell | 20 | 12 | 11 | 988 | 2 | 0 | - | England |
| Shaun Wilkinson | 21 | 19 | 4 | 543 | 2 | 0 | - | England |
| **Forwards** | | | | | | | | |
| Graham Barrett | 21 | 33 | 20 | 1882 | 3 | 1 | 1 | Rep of Ireland (15) |
| Gary Hart | 26 | 37 | 23 | 2439 | 7 | 1 | - | England |
| Paul Kitson | 32 | 13 | 5 | 600 | 2 | 0 | - | England |
| Daniel Marney | 21 | 15 | 6 | 653 | 0 | 0 | - | England |
| Daniel Webb | 20 | 5 | 0 | 33 | 0 | 0 | - | England |
| Bobby Zamora | 22 | 34 | 33 | 2986 | 6 | 0 | - | England |

KEY: LEAGUE BOOKINGS CAPS (FIFA RANKING)

## SQUAD APPEARANCES

| Match | 1 | 2 | 3 | 4 | 5 | 6 | 7 | 8 | 9 | 10 | 11 | 12 | 13 | 14 | 15 | 16 | 17 | 18 | 19 | 20 | 21 | 22 | 23 | 24 | 25 | 26 | 27 | 28 | 29 | 30 | 31 | 32 | 33 | 34 | 35 | 36 | 37 | 38 | 39 | 40 | 41 | 42 | 43 | 44 | 45 | 46 | 47 | 48 | 49 |
|---|---|---|---|---|---|---|---|---|---|---|---|---|---|---|---|---|---|---|---|---|---|---|---|---|---|---|---|---|---|---|---|---|---|---|---|---|---|---|---|---|---|---|---|---|---|---|---|---|---|
| Venue | A | H | H | A | H | A | A | H | H | H | A | A | H | A | H | A | H | A | H | A | A | H | A | H | A | H | A | H | A | A | H | A | H | H | A | H | A | A | H | H | A | A | H | A | H | A | H | H | A |
| Competition | L | L | L | L | L | L | L | W | L | L | L | W | L | L | L | L | L | L | L | L | L | L | L | L | L | L | L | L | L | F | L | L | L | L | L | L | L | L | L | L | L | L | L | L | L | L | L | L | L |
| Result | W | D | L | L | L | L | L | D | L | L | L | L | L | L | L | L | W | D | W | D | L | L | D | D | L | L | W | D | D | L | D | L | L | W | W | W | L | L | W | W | L | D | D | W | L | L | D | W | D |

**Goalkeepers**
Dave Beasant
John Keeley
Michel Kuipers
Will Packham
Andy Petterson
Ben Roberts

**Defenders**
Dean Blackwell
Guy Butters
Danny Cullip
Dean Hammond
Adam Hinshelwood
Nathan Jones
Robbie Pethick
Adam Virgo
Paul Watson

**Midfielders**
Paul Brooker
Richard Carpenter
Dan Harding
Ivar Ingimarsson
Kerry Mayo
Chris McPhee
Stephen Melton
Charlie Oatway
John Piercy
Simon Rodger
Paul Rogers
Anthony Rougier
Steven Sidwell
Shaun Wilkinson

**Forwards**
Graham Barrett
Gary Hart
Paul Kitson
Daniel Marney
Daniel Webb
Bobby Zamora

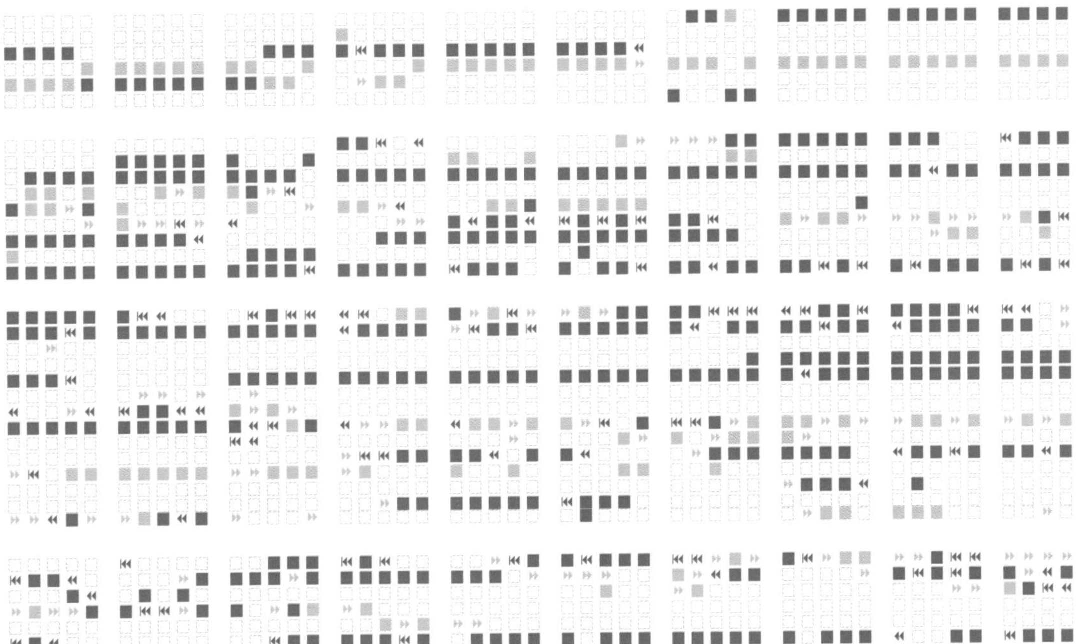

KEY: On all match; On bench; Subbed or sent off (Counting game); Subbed or sent off (playing less than 70 minutes); Subbed on from bench (Counting Game); Subbed on (playing less than 70 minutes); Subbed on and then subbed or sent off (Counting Game); Subbed on and then subbed or sent off (playing less than 70 minutes); Not in 16

# GRIMSBY TOWN

Final Position: **24th**

NICKNAME: THE MARINERS

KEY: Won Drawn Lost

| | | | | | | |
|---|---|---|---|---|---|---|
| 1 | div1 | Norwich | A | L | 0-4 | |
| 2 | div1 | Wimbledon | H | D | 0-0 | |
| 3 | div1 | Derby | H | L | 1-2 | Barnard 36 |
| 4 | div1 | Bradford | A | D | 0-0 | |
| 5 | div1 | Portsmouth | H | L | 0-1 | |
| 6 | div1 | Millwall | A | L | 0-2 | |
| 7 | wcr1 | Chesterfield | H | L | 0-1 | |
| 8 | div1 | Coventry | A | L | 2-3 | Kabba 46; Pouton 69 |
| 9 | div1 | Sheff Utd | A | L | 1-2 | Robinson 9 |
| 10 | div1 | Nottm Forest | H | L | 0-3 | |
| 11 | div1 | Brighton | A | W | 2-1 | Barnard 2; Pouton 80 |
| 12 | div1 | Reading | H | L | 0-3 | |
| 13 | div1 | Ipswich | H | W | 3-0 | Kabba 8,60; Pouton 17 pen |
| 14 | div1 | Watford | A | L | 0-2 | |
| 15 | div1 | Rotherham | H | D | 0-0 | |
| 16 | div1 | Wolves | A | L | 1-4 | Kabba 2 |
| 17 | div1 | Burnley | H | W | 6-5 | Kabba 3,31; Livingstone 28; Campbell 36; Pouton 56 pen; Ford 72 |
| 18 | div1 | Gillingham | H | D | 1-1 | Oster 77 |
| 19 | div1 | Stoke | A | W | 2-1 | Livingstone 14; Campbell 22 |
| 20 | div1 | Preston | H | D | 3-3 | Campbell 3; Ford 59; Mansaram 80 |
| 21 | div1 | Crystal Palace | A | L | 0-2 | |
| 22 | div1 | Leicester | H | L | 1-2 | Oster 54 |
| 23 | div1 | Walsall | A | L | 1-3 | Livingstone 38 |
| 24 | div1 | Preston | A | L | 0-3 | |
| 25 | div1 | Sheff Wed | H | W | 2-0 | Santos 49; Mansaram 52 |
| 26 | div1 | Derby | A | W | 3-1 | Oster 3,64; Soames 89 |
| 27 | div1 | Norwich | H | D | 1-1 | Oster 77 |
| 28 | facr3 | Burnley | H | D | 2-2 | Cooke 57 pen; Mansaram 87 |
| 29 | div1 | Wimbledon | A | D | 3-3 | Boulding 35; Andersen 52 og; Campbell 72 |
| 30 | facr3r | Burnley | A | L | 0-4 | |
| 31 | div1 | Millwall | H | L | 0-2 | |
| 32 | div1 | Bradford | H | L | 1-2 | Boulding 15 |
| 33 | div1 | Portsmouth | A | L | 0-3 | |
| 34 | div1 | Stoke | H | W | 2-0 | Boulding 4; Thompson 40 |
| 35 | div1 | Gillingham | A | L | 0-3 | |
| 36 | div1 | Ipswich | A | D | 2-2 | Groves 8; Boulding 24 |
| 37 | div1 | Coventry | H | L | 0-2 | |
| 38 | div1 | Sheff Utd | H | L | 1-4 | Campbell 34 |
| 39 | div1 | Nottm Forest | A | D | 2-2 | Groves 44; Pouton 48 |
| 40 | div1 | Watford | H | W | 1-0 | Groves 63 |
| 41 | div1 | Rotherham | A | W | 1-0 | Oster 90 |
| 42 | div1 | Burnley | A | D | 1-1 | Campbell 43 |
| 43 | div1 | Leicester | A | L | 0-2 | |
| 44 | div1 | Wolves | H | L | 0-1 | |
| 45 | div1 | Crystal Palace | H | L | 1-4 | Chettle 48 |
| 46 | div1 | Sheff Wed | A | D | 0-0 | |
| 47 | div1 | Walsall | H | L | 0-1 | |
| 48 | div1 | Reading | A | L | 1-2 | Keane 90 |
| 49 | div1 | Brighton | H | D | 2-2 | Keane 23 pen; Hughes 60 |

Home Away Neutral

## ATTENDANCES

HOME GROUND: BLUNDELL PARK CAPACITY: 10033 AVERAGE LEAGUE AT HOME: 5883

| | | | | | | | | | | | |
|---|---|---|---|---|---|---|---|---|---|---|---|
| 43 | Leicester | 31014 | 24 | Preston | 12420 | 49 | Brighton | 6396 | 28 | Burnley | 5350 |
| 26 | Derby | 27141 | 8 | Coventry | 12403 | 41 | Rotherham | 6239 | 31 | Millwall | 4993 |
| 46 | Sheff Wed | 26082 | 19 | Stoke | 11488 | 23 | Walsall | 5888 | 44 | Wolves | 4983 |
| 39 | Nottm Forest | 25507 | 4 | Bradford | 10914 | 3 | Derby | 5810 | 40 | Watford | 4847 |
| 36 | Ipswich | 24118 | 27 | Norwich | 8306 | 20 | Preston | 5774 | 45 | Crystal Palace | 4707 |
| 16 | Wolves | 23875 | 25 | Sheff Wed | 8224 | 5 | Portsmouth | 5770 | 13 | Ipswich | 4688 |
| 48 | Reading | 20273 | 22 | Leicester | 7310 | 37 | Coventry | 5736 | 2 | Wimbledon | 4625 |
| 21 | Crystal Palace | 20093 | 35 | Gillingham | 7158 | 18 | Gillingham | 5715 | 47 | Walsall | 4618 |
| 1 | Norwich | 19869 | 10 | Nottm Forest | 7072 | 34 | Stoke | 5657 | 7 | Chesterfield | 3248 |
| 33 | Portsmouth | 19428 | 38 | Sheff Utd | 6897 | 17 | Burnley | 5620 | 29 | Wimbledon | 1336 |
| 9 | Sheff Utd | 14208 | 6 | Millwall | 6677 | 12 | Reading | 5582 | | | |
| 14 | Watford | 13821 | 11 | Brighton | 6547 | 32 | Bradford | 5582 | | | |
| 42 | Burnley | 13445 | 15 | Rotherham | 6418 | 30 | Burnley | 5436 | | | |

## KEY PLAYERS - GOALSCORERS

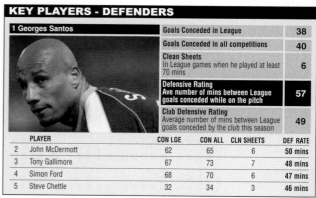

1 Steve Kabba

| | |
|---|---|
| Goals in the League | 6 |
| Goals in all competitions | 6 |
| Contribution to Attacking Power<br>Average number of minutes between League team goals while on pitch | 81 |
| Player Strike Rate<br>The total number of minutes he was on the pitch for every League goal scored | 190 |
| Club Strike Rate<br>Average number of minutes between League goals scored by club | 88 |

| | PLAYER | GOALS LGE | GOALS ALL | POWER | S RATE |
|---|---|---|---|---|---|
| 2 | John Oster | 6 | 6 | 69 | 255 mins |
| 3 | Alan Pouton | 5 | 5 | 74 | 417 mins |
| 4 | Steve Livingstone | 3 | 3 | 71 | 617 mins |
| 5 | Stuart Campbell | 6 | 6 | 83 | 666 mins |

## KEY PLAYERS - MIDFIELDERS

1 Iain Ward

| | |
|---|---|
| Goals in the League | 0 |
| Goals in all competitions | 0 |
| Defensive Rating<br>Average number of mins between League goals conceded while on the pitch | 57 |
| Contribution to Attacking Power<br>Average number of minutes between League team goals while on pitch | 50 |
| Scoring Difference<br>Defensive Rating minus Contribution to Attacking Power | 7 |

| | PLAYER | GOALS LGE | GOALS ALL | DEF RATE | ATT POWER | SCORE DIFF |
|---|---|---|---|---|---|---|
| 2 | John Oster | 6 | 6 | 55 | 70 | -15 mins |
| 3 | Darren Barnard | 2 | 2 | 50 | 75 | -25 mins |
| 4 | Alan Pouton | 5 | 5 | 43 | 74 | -31 mins |
| 5 | Stuart Campbell | 6 | 6 | 51 | 83 | -32 mins |

## KEY PLAYERS - DEFENDERS

1 Georges Santos

| | |
|---|---|
| Goals Conceded in League | 38 |
| Goals Conceded in all competitions | 40 |
| Clean Sheets<br>In League games when he played at least 70 mins | 6 |
| Defensive Rating<br>Ave number of mins between League goals conceded while on the pitch | 57 |
| Club Defensive Rating<br>Average number of mins between League goals conceded by the club this season | 49 |

| | PLAYER | CON LGE | CON ALL | CLN SHEETS | DEF RATE |
|---|---|---|---|---|---|
| 2 | John McDermott | 62 | 65 | 6 | 50 mins |
| 3 | Tony Gallimore | 67 | 73 | 7 | 48 mins |
| 4 | Simon Ford | 68 | 70 | 6 | 47 mins |
| 5 | Steve Chettle | 32 | 34 | 3 | 46 mins |

## KEY GOALKEEPER

1 Danny Coyne

| | |
|---|---|
| Goals Conceded in the League | 85 |
| Goals Conceded in all competitions | 92 |
| Clean Sheets<br>In games when he played at least 70 mins | 9 |
| Goals to Shots Ratio<br>The average number of shots on target per each League goal conceded | 3.5 |
| Defensive Rating<br>Ave number of mins between League goals conceded while on the pitch | 49 |

## MONTHY POINTS TALLY

| | | |
|---|---|---|
| AUGUST | 2 | 11% |
| SEPTEMBER | 3 | 20% |
| OCTOBER | 7 | 39% |
| NOVEMBER | 5 | 33% |
| DECEMBER | 7 | 47% |
| JANUARY | 2 | 13% |
| FEBRUARY | 4 | 33% |
| MARCH | 8 | 44% |
| APRIL | 1 | 6% |
| MAY | 1 | 33% |

## TOP POINT EARNERS

| | PLAYER | GAMES | AV PTS |
|---|---|---|---|
| 1 | John Oster | 17 | **1.24** |
| 2 | Darren Mansaram | 20 | **1.15** |
| 3 | Georges Santos | 23 | **1.04** |
| 4 | Simon Ford | 34 | **1.03** |
| 5 | Steve Livingstone | 17 | **0.94** |
| 6 | Terry Cooke | 13 | **0.92** |
| 7 | Alan Pouton | 22 | **0.91** |
| 8 | Stuart Campbell | 44 | **0.89** |
| 9 | Danny Coyne | 46 | **0.85** |
| 10 | Tony Gallimore | 34 | **0.82** |
| | **CLUB AVERAGE:** | | **0.85** |

## GOALS

**1 Stuart Campbell**

| | |
|---|---|
| League | 6 |
| FA Cup | 0 |
| League Cup | 0 |
| Other | 0 |
| TOTAL | 6 |

| | PLAYER | LGE | FAC | LC | Oth | TOT |
|---|---|---|---|---|---|---|
| 2 | Oster | **6** | 0 | 0 | 0 | 6 |
| 3 | Kabba | **6** | 0 | 0 | 0 | 6 |
| 4 | Pouton | **5** | 0 | 0 | 0 | 5 |
| 5 | Boulding | **4** | 0 | 0 | 0 | 4 |
| 6 | Groves | **3** | 0 | 0 | 0 | 3 |
| 7 | Livingstone | **3** | 0 | 0 | 0 | 3 |
| 8 | Barnard | **2** | 0 | 0 | 0 | 2 |
| 9 | Ford | **2** | 0 | 0 | 0 | 2 |
| 10 | Keane | **2** | 0 | 0 | 0 | 2 |
| 11 | Mansaram | **2** | 1 | 0 | 0 | 3 |
| | Other | 7 | 1 | 0 | 0 | 8 |
| | **TOTAL** | **48** | **2** | **0** | **0** | **50** |

## TEAM OF THE SEASON

| GOALKEEPER | GAMES | DEF RATE |
|---|---|---|
| Danny Coyne | 46 | 49 |
| **DEFENDERS** | **GAMES** | **DEF RATE** |
| Georges Santos | 23 | 57 |
| John McDermott | 33 | 50 |
| Tony Gallimore | 34 | 48 |
| Simon Ford | 34 | 47 |
| **MIDFIELDERS** | **GAMES** | **SCORE DIFF** |
| Iain Ward | 9 | 7 |
| John Oster | 17 | -15 |
| Darren Banard | 18 | -25 |
| Alan Pouton | 22 | -31 |
| **GOALSCORERS** | **GAMES** | **STRIKE RATE** |
| Steve Kabba | 13 | 190 |
| Steve Livingstone | 17 | 617 |

Games = games playing at least 70 minutes

## LEAGUE APPEARANCES, BOOKINGS AND CAPS

| | AGE (on 01/07/03) | IN THE SQUAD | COUNTING GAMES | MINUTES ON PITCH | YELLOW CARDS | RED CARDS | THIS SEASON | HOME COUNTRY |
|---|---|---|---|---|---|---|---|---|
| **Goalkeepers** | | | | | | | | |
| Shaun Allaway | 20 | 38 | 0 | 0 | 0 | 0 | - | England |
| Danny Coyne | 24 | 46 | 46 | 4140 | 0 | 0 | - | Wales |
| Bradley Hughes | 19 | 5 | 0 | 0 | 0 | 0 | - | England |
| Andrew Pettinger | 19 | 1 | 0 | 0 | 0 | 0 | - | England |
| **Defenders** | | | | | | | | |
| Steve Chettle | 34 | 29 | 14 | 1469 | 0 | 0 | - | England |
| Simon Ford | 21 | 40 | 34 | 3195 | 2 | 1 | - | England |
| Tony Gallimore | 31 | 38 | 34 | 3248 | 7 | 1 | - | England |
| Jason Gavin | 23 | 10 | 8 | 769 | 4 | 0 | - | Rep of Ireland |
| John McDermott | 34 | 35 | 33 | 3076 | 3 | 0 | - | England |
| Wes Parker | 19 | 14 | 1 | 199 | 0 | 0 | - | England |
| Paul Raven | 32 | 9 | 3 | 355 | 2 | 1 | - | England |
| Georges Santos | 32 | 27 | 23 | 2162 | 3 | 1 | - | Cape Verde Islands |
| Greg Young | 20 | 1 | 0 | 62 | 0 | 0 | - | England |
| **Midfielders** | | | | | | | | |
| Darren Barnard | 31 | 34 | 18 | 1937 | 4 | 0 | 2 | Wales (50) |
| Stuart Campbell | 25 | 45 | 44 | 3993 | 5 | 0 | - | England |
| Stacy Coldicott | 29 | 31 | 25 | 2387 | 3 | 0 | - | England |
| Paul Groves | 37 | 37 | 30 | 2730 | 3 | 0 | - | England |
| Graham Hockless | 20 | 1 | 0 | 55 | 0 | 0 | - | England |
| Richard Hughes | 24 | 12 | 11 | 1052 | 0 | 0 | - | Scotland |
| Phil Jevons | 23 | 3 | 1 | 90 | 1 | 0 | - | England |
| Michael Keane | 20 | 7 | 6 | 595 | 3 | 0 | - | Rep of Ireland |
| John Oster | 24 | 17 | 17 | 1530 | 1 | 0 | 3 | Wales (50) |
| Alan Pouton | 26 | 25 | 22 | 2084 | 10 | 2 | - | England |
| Jake Sagere | 23 | 1 | 0 | 55 | 0 | 0 | - | United States |
| Iain Ward | 20 | 20 | 9 | 858 | 0 | 0 | - | England |
| **Forwards** | | | | | | | | |
| Chris Bolder | 20 | 17 | 6 | 690 | 0 | 0 | - | England |
| Michael Boulding | 27 | 12 | 9 | 839 | 1 | 0 | - | England |
| Terry Cooke | 26 | 34 | 13 | 1472 | 1 | 0 | - | England |
| Steve Kabba | 22 | 13 | 13 | 1140 | 4 | 0 | - | England |
| Steve Livingstone | 33 | 33 | 17 | 1851 | 6 | 1 | - | England |
| Darren Mansaram | 19 | 36 | 20 | 2032 | 4 | 0 | - | England |
| Paul Robinson | 24 | 14 | 3 | 473 | 1 | 0 | 7 | England (7) |
| Jonathan Rowan | 21 | 19 | 3 | 316 | 1 | 0 | - | England |
| David Soames | 18 | 20 | 0 | 129 | 0 | 0 | - | England |
| Robert Taylor | 32 | 1 | 0 | 18 | 0 | 0 | - | England |
| Chris Thompson | 21 | 11 | 2 | 307 | 0 | 0 | - | England |

**KEY:** LEAGUE BOOKINGS CAPS (FIFA RANKING)

## SQUAD APPEARANCES

| Match | 1 | 2 | 3 | 4 | 5 | 6 | 7 | 8 | 9 | 10 | 11 | 12 | 13 | 14 | 15 | 16 | 17 | 18 | 19 | 20 | 21 | 22 | 23 | 24 | 25 |
|---|---|---|---|---|---|---|---|---|---|---|---|---|---|---|---|---|---|---|---|---|---|---|---|---|---|
| Venue | A | H | H | A | H | A | H | A | A | H | A | H | H | A | H | A | H | H | A | H | A | H | A | A | H |
| Competition | L | L | L | L | L | L | W | L | L | L | L | L | L | L | L | L | L | L | L | L | L | L | L | L | L |
| Result | L | D | L | D | L | L | D | L | L | L | W | L | W | L | D | L | W | D | W | D | L | L | L | L | W |

| Match | 26 | 27 | 28 | 29 | 30 | 31 | 32 | 33 | 34 | 35 | 36 | 37 | 38 | 39 | 40 | 41 | 42 | 43 | 44 | 45 | 46 | 47 | 48 | 49 |
|---|---|---|---|---|---|---|---|---|---|---|---|---|---|---|---|---|---|---|---|---|---|---|---|---|
| Venue | A | H | H | A | A | H | H | A | H | A | A | H | H | A | H | A | A | A | H | H | A | H | A | H |
| Competition | L | L | F | L | F | L | L | L | L | L | L | L | L | L | L | L | L | L | L | L | L | L | L | L |
| Result | W | D | D | D | L | L | L | L | W | L | D | L | L | D | W | W | D | L | L | L | D | L | L | D |

**Goalkeepers**
Shaun Allaway
Danny Coyne
Bradley Hughes
Andrew Pettinger

**Defenders**
Steve Chettle
Simon Ford
Tony Gallimore
Jason Gavin
John McDermott
Wes Parker
Paul Raven
Georges Santos
Greg Young

**Midfielders**
Darren Barnard
Stuart Campbell
Stacy Coldicott
Paul Groves
Graham Hockless
Richard Hughes
Phil Jevons
Michael Keane
John Oster
Alan Pouton
Jake Sagere
Iain Ward

**Forwards**
Chris Bolder
Michael Boulding
Terry Cooke
Steve Kabba
Steve Livingstone
Darren Mansaram
Paul Robinson
Jonathan Rowan
David Soames
Robert Taylor
Chris Thompson

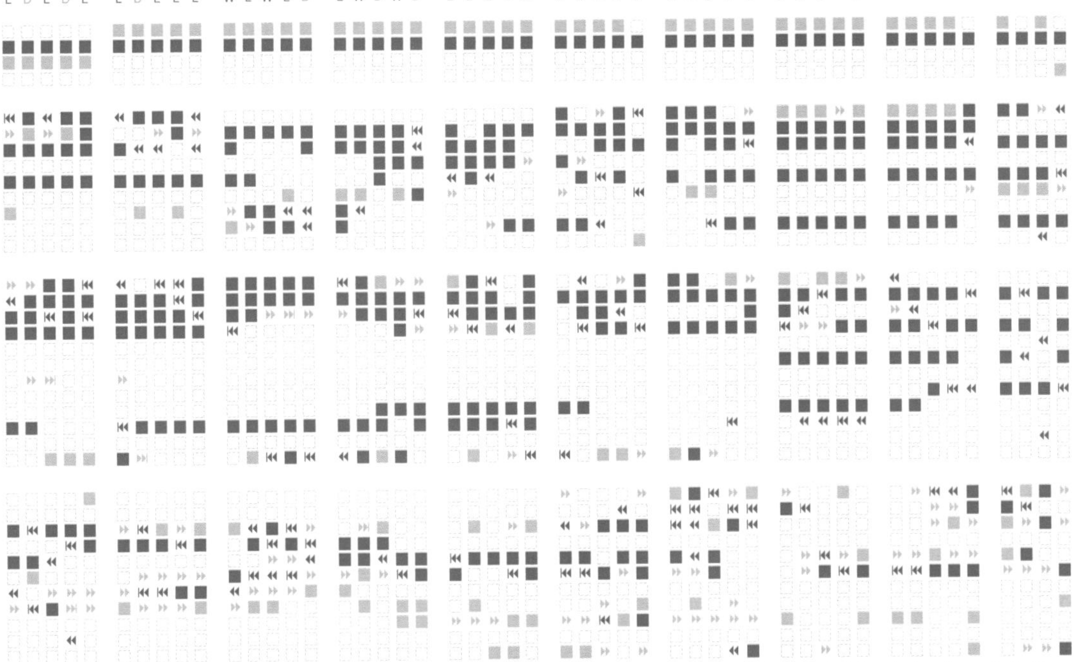

KEY: On all match | On bench | Subbed or sent off (Counting game) | Subbed or sent off (playing less than 70 minutes) | Subbed on from bench (Counting Game) | Subbed on (playing less than 70 minutes) | Subbed on and then subbed or sent off (Counting Game) | Subbed on and then subbed or sent off (playing less than 70 minutes) | Not in 16

# DIVISION ONE ROUND-UP

## STADIUM CAPACITY AND HOME CROWDS

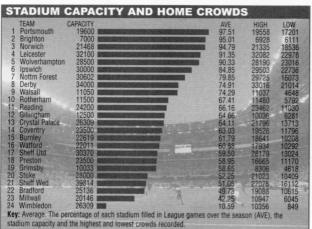

| | TEAM | CAPACITY | AVE | HIGH | LOW |
|---|---|---|---|---|---|
| 1 | Portsmouth | 19600 | 97.51 | 19558 | 17201 |
| 2 | Brighton | 7000 | 95.01 | 6928 | 6111 |
| 3 | Norwich | 21468 | 94.79 | 21335 | 18536 |
| 4 | Leicester | 32100 | 91.35 | 32082 | 22978 |
| 5 | Wolverhampton | 28500 | 90.33 | 28190 | 23016 |
| 6 | Ipswich | 30000 | 84.85 | 29503 | 22736 |
| 7 | Nottm Forest | 30602 | 79.85 | 29725 | 16073 |
| 8 | Derby | 34000 | 74.91 | 33016 | 21014 |
| 9 | Walsall | 11050 | 74.29 | 11037 | 4648 |
| 10 | Rotherham | 11500 | 67.41 | 11480 | 5792 |
| 11 | Reading | 24200 | 66.16 | 23462 | 11030 |
| 12 | Gillingham | 12500 | 64.66 | 10036 | 6281 |
| 13 | Crystal Palace | 26309 | 64.11 | 21796 | 13713 |
| 14 | Coventry | 23500 | 63.03 | 19526 | 11796 |
| 15 | Burnley | 22619 | 61.79 | 18641 | 10208 |
| 16 | Watford | 22011 | 60.88 | 17934 | 10292 |
| 17 | Sheff Utd | 30370 | 59.50 | 28179 | 13024 |
| 18 | Preston | 23500 | 58.95 | 16665 | 11170 |
| 19 | Grimsby | 10033 | 58.65 | 8306 | 4618 |
| 20 | Stoke | 28000 | 52.25 | 21023 | 10409 |
| 21 | Sheff Wed | 39814 | 51.05 | 27075 | 16112 |
| 22 | Bradford | 25136 | 49.73 | 19088 | 10615 |
| 23 | Millwall | 20146 | 42.25 | 10947 | 6045 |
| 24 | Wimbledon | 26309 | 10.59 | 10356 | 849 |

**Key:** Average. The percentage of each stadium filled in League games over the season (AVE), the stadium capacity and the highest and lowest crowds recorded.

## AWAY ATTENDANCE

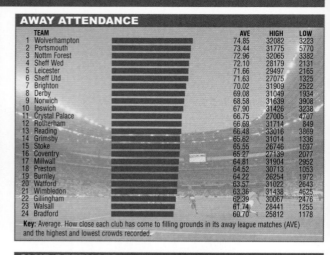

| | TEAM | AVE | HIGH | LOW |
|---|---|---|---|---|
| 1 | Wolverhampton | 74.85 | 32082 | 3223 |
| 2 | Portsmouth | 73.44 | 31775 | 5770 |
| 3 | Nottm Forest | 72.96 | 32065 | 3382 |
| 4 | Sheff Wed | 72.10 | 28179 | 2131 |
| 5 | Leicester | 71.66 | 29497 | 2165 |
| 6 | Sheff Utd | 71.63 | 27075 | 1325 |
| 7 | Brighton | 70.02 | 31909 | 2522 |
| 8 | Derby | 69.08 | 31049 | 1934 |
| 9 | Norwich | 68.58 | 31639 | 3908 |
| 10 | Ipswich | 67.90 | 31426 | 3238 |
| 11 | Crystal Palace | 66.75 | 27005 | 4707 |
| 12 | Rotherham | 66.69 | 31714 | 849 |
| 13 | Reading | 66.48 | 33016 | 3869 |
| 14 | Grimsby | 65.62 | 31014 | 1336 |
| 15 | Stoke | 65.55 | 26746 | 1697 |
| 16 | Coventry | 65.27 | 27139 | 2077 |
| 17 | Millwall | 64.81 | 31904 | 2952 |
| 18 | Preston | 64.52 | 30713 | 1053 |
| 19 | Burnley | 64.22 | 26254 | 1972 |
| 20 | Watford | 63.57 | 31022 | 2643 |
| 21 | Wimbledon | 63.36 | 31438 | 4625 |
| 22 | Gillingham | 62.39 | 30067 | 2476 |
| 23 | Walsall | 61.74 | 28441 | 1255 |
| 24 | Bradford | 60.70 | 25812 | 1178 |

**Key:** Average. How close each club has come to filling grounds in its away league matches (AVE) and the highest and lowest crowds recorded.

## CLUB STRIKE FORCE

Todorov of Portsmouth

**1 Portsmouth**

**Club Strike Rate (CSR)** Average number of minutes between League goals scored by club: **43**

| | CLUB | LGE | ALL | SoT | CSR |
|---|---|---|---|---|---|
| 2 | Nottm Forest | 82 | 93 | 260 | 50 |
| 3 | Wolverhampton | 81 | 104 | 245 | 51 |
| 4 | Ipswich | 80 | 106 | 331 | 52 |
| 5 | Wimbledon | 76 | 87 | 264 | 54 |
| 6 | Leicester | 73 | 82 | 278 | 57 |
| 7 | Sheff Utd | 72 | 102 | 293 | 58 |
| 8 | Preston | 68 | 75 | 284 | 61 |
| 9 | Burnley | 65 | 84 | 232 | 64 |
| 10 | Rotherham | 62 | 72 | 231 | 67 |
| 11 | Reading | 61 | 64 | 217 | 68 |
| 12 | Norwich | 60 | 64 | 255 | 69 |
| 13 | Crystal Palace | 59 | 79 | 231 | 70 |
| 14 | Millwall | 59 | 65 | 270 | 70 |
| 15 | Walsall | 57 | 64 | 231 | 73 |
| 16 | Gillingham | 56 | 66 | 245 | 74 |
| 17 | Sheff Wed | 56 | 59 | 262 | 74 |
| 18 | Derby | 55 | 59 | 229 | 75 |
| 19 | Watford | 54 | 62 | 271 | 77 |
| 20 | Bradford | 51 | 53 | 262 | 81 |
| 21 | Brighton | 49 | 53 | 235 | 84 |
| 22 | Grimsby | 48 | 50 | 205 | 86 |
| 23 | Coventry | 46 | 62 | 261 | 90 |
| 24 | Stoke | 45 | 51 | 206 | 92 |

| | |
|---|---|
| Goals scored in the League | 97 |
| Goals scored in all competions | 101 |
| **Shots on target (SoT)** Shots on target hit by the team recorded in League games | 291 |

## CLUB DEFENCES

**1 Leicester**

**Club Defensive Rate (CDR)** Average number of minutes between League goals conceded by club: **104**

| | CLUB | LGE | ALL | CS | SoT | CDR |
|---|---|---|---|---|---|---|
| 2 | Wolverhampton | 44 | 57 | 20 | 184 | 94 |
| 3 | Portsmouth | 45 | 52 | 16 | 220 | 92 |
| 4 | Reading | 46 | 53 | 19 | 238 | 90 |
| 5 | Norwich | 49 | 55 | 18 | 271 | 84 |
| 6 | Nottm Forest | 50 | 60 | 14 | 258 | 83 |
| 7 | Crystal Palace | 52 | 59 | 15 | 199 | 80 |
| 8 | Sheff Utd | 52 | 69 | 13 | 238 | 80 |
| 9 | Coventry | 62 | 69 | 13 | 252 | 67 |
| 10 | Rotherham | 62 | 75 | 13 | 233 | 67 |
| 11 | Ipswich | 64 | 74 | 10 | 269 | 65 |
| 12 | Gillingham | 65 | 72 | 13 | 269 | 64 |
| 13 | Brighton | 67 | 74 | 10 | 268 | 62 |
| 14 | Millwall | 69 | 75 | 13 | 283 | 60 |
| 15 | Stoke | 69 | 72 | 11 | 226 | 60 |
| 16 | Walsall | 69 | 75 | 14 | 251 | 60 |
| 17 | Preston | 70 | 79 | 13 | 273 | 59 |
| 18 | Watford | 70 | 74 | 13 | 282 | 59 |
| 19 | Bradford | 73 | 78 | 9 | 276 | 57 |
| 20 | Sheff Wed | 73 | 79 | 8 | 265 | 57 |
| 21 | Wimbledon | 73 | 79 | 10 | 243 | 57 |
| 22 | Derby | 74 | 78 | 11 | 270 | 56 |
| 23 | Grimsby | 85 | 92 | 9 | 299 | 49 |
| 24 | Burnley | 89 | 97 | 11 | 285 | 47 |

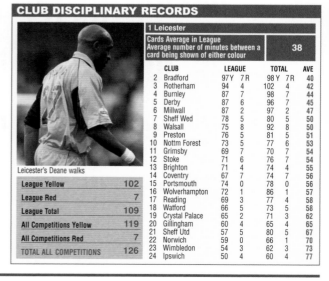

Davidson defending for Leicester

| | |
|---|---|
| Goals conceded in the League | 40 |
| Goals conceded in all competions | 49 |
| **Clean Sheets (CS)** Number of league games where no goals were conceded | 19 |
| **Shots on Target Against (SoT)** Shots on Target conceded by team in League games | 237 |

## CLUB GOAL ATTEMPTS

### GOAL ATTEMPTS – FOR

**KEY:** Shots on Target (SoT), Shots Off Target (SO) Total shots (Tot) Ratio of shots on target to goals (SG) Accuracy Rating (AR)

| | CLUB | SoT | SO | Tot | SG | AR |
|---|---|---|---|---|---|---|
| 1 | Ipswich | 331 | 289 | 620 | 4.1 | 53.4 |
| 2 | Sheff Utd | 293 | 247 | 540 | 4.1 | 54.3 |
| 3 | Preston | 284 | 251 | 535 | 4.2 | 53.1 |
| 4 | Coventry | 261 | 267 | 528 | 5.7 | 49.4 |
| 5 | Leicester | 278 | 250 | 528 | 3.8 | 52.7 |
| 6 | Sheff Wed | 262 | 263 | 525 | 4.7 | 49.9 |
| 7 | Millwall | 270 | 253 | 523 | 4.6 | 51.6 |
| 8 | Portsmouth | 291 | 230 | 521 | 3.0 | 55.9 |
| 9 | Wolverhampton | 245 | 263 | 508 | 3.0 | 48.2 |
| 10 | Nottm Forest | 260 | 244 | 504 | 3.2 | 51.6 |
| 11 | Bradford | 262 | 241 | 503 | 5.1 | 52.1 |
| 12 | Watford | 271 | 216 | 487 | 5.0 | 55.6 |
| 13 | Gillingham | 245 | 241 | 486 | 4.4 | 50.4 |
| 14 | Wimbledon | 264 | 222 | 486 | 3.5 | 54.3 |
| 15 | Norwich | 255 | 223 | 478 | 4.3 | 53.3 |
| 16 | Burnley | 232 | 236 | 468 | 3.6 | 49.6 |
| 17 | Derby | 229 | 237 | 466 | 4.2 | 49.1 |
| 18 | Crystal Palace | 231 | 233 | 464 | 3.9 | 49.8 |
| 19 | Rotherham | 231 | 231 | 462 | 3.7 | 50.0 |
| 20 | Brighton | 235 | 211 | 446 | 4.8 | 52.7 |
| 21 | Reading | 217 | 218 | 435 | 3.6 | 49.9 |
| 22 | Stoke | 206 | 224 | 430 | 4.6 | 47.9 |
| 23 | Grimsby | 205 | 213 | 418 | 4.3 | 49.0 |
| 24 | Walsall | 231 | 181 | 412 | 4.1 | 56.1 |

### GOAL ATTEMPTS – AGAINST

**KEY:** Shots on Target (SoT), Shots Off Target (SO) Total shots (Tot) Ratio of shots on target to goals (SG) Accuracy Rating (AR)

| | CLUB | SoT | SO | Tot | SG | AR |
|---|---|---|---|---|---|---|
| 1 | Wolverhampton | 184 | 175 | 359 | 4.2 | 51.3 |
| 2 | Crystal Palace | 199 | 170 | 369 | 3.8 | 53.9 |
| 3 | Stoke | 226 | 177 | 403 | 3.3 | 56.1 |
| 4 | Rotherham | 233 | 206 | 439 | 3.8 | 53.1 |
| 5 | Walsall | 251 | 203 | 454 | 3.6 | 55.3 |
| 6 | Derby | 270 | 185 | 455 | 3.6 | 59.3 |
| 7 | Reading | 238 | 217 | 455 | 5.2 | 52.3 |
| 8 | Leicester | 237 | 219 | 456 | 5.9 | 52.0 |
| 9 | Portsmouth | 220 | 241 | 461 | 4.9 | 47.7 |
| 10 | Coventry | 252 | 216 | 468 | 4.1 | 53.8 |
| 11 | Wimbledon | 243 | 226 | 469 | 3.3 | 51.8 |
| 12 | Sheff Utd | 238 | 233 | 471 | 4.6 | 50.5 |
| 13 | Brighton | 268 | 216 | 484 | 4.0 | 55.4 |
| 14 | Sheff Wed | 265 | 221 | 486 | 3.6 | 54.5 |
| 15 | Burnley | 285 | 207 | 492 | 3.2 | 57.9 |
| 16 | Preston | 273 | 222 | 495 | 3.9 | 55.2 |
| 17 | Gillingham | 269 | 232 | 501 | 4.1 | 53.7 |
| 18 | Norwich | 271 | 230 | 501 | 5.5 | 54.1 |
| 19 | Nottm Forest | 258 | 247 | 505 | 5.2 | 51.1 |
| 20 | Watford | 282 | 225 | 507 | 4.0 | 55.6 |
| 21 | Bradford | 276 | 235 | 511 | 3.8 | 54.0 |
| 22 | Millwall | 283 | 230 | 513 | 4.1 | 55.2 |
| 23 | Grimsby | 299 | 224 | 523 | 3.5 | 57.2 |
| 24 | Ipswich | 269 | 258 | 527 | 4.2 | 51.0 |

## CLUB DISCIPLINARY RECORDS

Leicester's Deane walks

| | |
|---|---|
| League Yellow | 102 |
| League Red | 7 |
| League Total | 109 |
| All Competitions Yellow | 119 |
| All Competitions Red | 7 |
| TOTAL ALL COMPETITIONS | 126 |

**1 Leicester**

**Cards Average in League** Average number of minutes between a card being shown of either colour: **38**

| | CLUB | LEAGUE | | TOTAL | | AVE |
|---|---|---|---|---|---|---|
| 2 | Bradford | 97Y | 7R | 98 Y | 7R | 40 |
| 3 | Rotherham | 94 | 4 | 102 | 4 | 42 |
| 4 | Burnley | 87 | 7 | 98 | 7 | 44 |
| 5 | Derby | 87 | 6 | 96 | 7 | 45 |
| 6 | Millwall | 87 | 2 | 97 | 2 | 47 |
| 7 | Sheff Wed | 78 | 5 | 80 | 5 | 50 |
| 8 | Walsall | 75 | 8 | 92 | 8 | 50 |
| 9 | Preston | 76 | 5 | 81 | 5 | 51 |
| 10 | Nottm Forest | 73 | 5 | 77 | 6 | 53 |
| 11 | Grimsby | 69 | 7 | 70 | 7 | 54 |
| 12 | Stoke | 71 | 6 | 76 | 7 | 54 |
| 13 | Brighton | 71 | 4 | 74 | 4 | 55 |
| 14 | Coventry | 67 | 7 | 74 | 7 | 56 |
| 15 | Portsmouth | 74 | 0 | 78 | 0 | 56 |
| 16 | Wolverhampton | 72 | 1 | 86 | 1 | 57 |
| 17 | Reading | 69 | 3 | 77 | 4 | 58 |
| 18 | Watford | 66 | 5 | 73 | 5 | 58 |
| 19 | Crystal Palace | 65 | 2 | 71 | 3 | 62 |
| 20 | Gillingham | 60 | 4 | 65 | 4 | 65 |
| 21 | Sheff Utd | 57 | 5 | 80 | 5 | 67 |
| 22 | Norwich | 59 | 0 | 66 | 1 | 70 |
| 23 | Wimbledon | 54 | 3 | 62 | 3 | 73 |
| 24 | Ipswich | 50 | 4 | 60 | 4 | 77 |

## CHART-TOPPING MIDFIELDERS

| 1 Kevin Harper - Portsmouth | |
|---|---|
| **Goals scored in the League** | 4 |
| **Defensive Rating** Av number of mins between League goals conceded while on the pitch | 117 |
| **Contribution to Attacking Power** Average number of minutes between League team goals while on pitch | 39 |
| **Scoring Difference** Defensive Rating minus Contribution to Attacking Power | 78 |

| | PLAYER | CLUB | GOALS | DEF RATE | POWER | S DIFF |
|---|---|---|---|---|---|---|
| 2 | Izzet | Leicester | 4 | 126 | 50 | 76 |
| 3 | Robinson | Portsmouth | 0 | 127 | 56 | 71 |
| 4 | McKinlay | Leicester | 1 | 123 | 59 | 64 |
| 5 | Ince | Wolverhampton | 2 | 115 | 52 | 63 |
| 6 | Sherwood | Portsmouth | 1 | 96 | 37 | 59 |
| 7 | Quinn | Coventry | 0 | 135 | 81 | 54 |
| 8 | Foxe | Portsmouth | 1 | 94 | 43 | 51 |
| 9 | Kennedy | Wolverhampton | 3 | 106 | 56 | 50 |
| 10 | Merson | Portsmouth | 12 | 91 | 42 | 49 |
| 11 | Impey | Leicester | 0 | 104 | 56 | 48 |
| 12 | Newton | Wolverhampton | 3 | 101 | 56 | 45 |
| 13 | Quashie | Portsmouth | 5 | 87 | 43 | 44 |
| 14 | Williams | Nottm Forest | 3 | 89 | 47 | 42 |
| 15 | Stone | Portsmouth | 4 | 90 | 49 | 41 |
| 16 | Stewart | Leicester | 4 | 93 | 54 | 39 |
| 17 | Newman | Reading | 0 | 108 | 71 | 37 |
| 18 | Sidwell | Reading | 2 | 86 | 52 | 34 |
| 19 | Reid | Nottm Forest | 1 | 79 | 46 | 33 |
| 20 | Mulryne | Norwich | 6 | 100 | 68 | 32 |

The Divisional Round-up charts combine the records of chart-topping keepers, defenders, midfield players and forwards, from every club in the division.. The one above is for **the Chart-topping Midfielders**. The players are ranked by their Scoring Difference although other attributes are shown for you to compare.

## CHART-TOPPING GOALSCORERS

GO•MK

| 1 David Connolly - Wimbledon | |
|---|---|
| **Goals scored in the League (GL)** | 24 |
| **Goals scored in all competitions (GA)** | 24 |
| **Contribution to Attacking Power (AP)** Average number of minutes between League team goals while on pitch | 46 |
| **Player Strike Rate** Average number of minutes between League goals scored by player | 102 |
| **Club Strike Rate (CSR)** Average minutes between League goals scored by club | 54 |

| | PLAYER | CLUB | GOALS: LGE | ALL | POWER | CSR | S RATE |
|---|---|---|---|---|---|---|---|
| 2 | Wallace | Gillingham | 11 | 11 | 54 | 74 | 133 mins |
| 3 | Johnson | Nottm Forest | 25 | 29 | 47 | 50 | 136 mins |
| 4 | Counago | Ipswich | 17 | 21 | 45 | 52 | 140 mins |
| 5 | Todorov | Portsmouth | 26 | 26 | 40 | 43 | 143 mins |
| 6 | Asaba | Sheff Utd | 11 | 12 | 63 | 58 | 150 mins |
| 7 | Blake | Wolverhampton | 12 | 14 | 41 | 51 | 150 mins |
| 8 | Junior | Walsall | 15 | 16 | 71 | 73 | 157 mins |
| 9 | Miller | Wolverhampton | 19 | 24 | 51 | 51 | 159 mins |
| 10 | Sturridge | Wolverhampton | 11 | 11 | 51 | 51 | 161 mins |
| 11 | Byfield | Rotherham | 13 | 13 | 66 | 67 | 164 mins |
| 12 | Fuller | Preston | 9 | 11 | 63 | 61 | 176 mins |
| 13 | Deane | Leicester | 13 | 13 | 59 | 57 | 180 mins |
| 14 | Benjamin | Leicester | 9 | 10 | 58 | 57 | 188 mins |
| 15 | Pericard | Portsmouth | 9 | 10 | 41 | 43 | 188 mins |
| 16 | Harewood | Nottm Forest | 20 | 21 | 49 | 50 | 189 mins |
| 17 | Forster | Reading | 16 | 17 | 65 | 68 | 189 mins |
| 18 | Kabba | Grimsby | 6 | 6 | 81 | 86 | 190 mins |
| 19 | Johnson | Crystal Palace | 11 | 14 | 70 | 70 | 193 mins |
| 20 | Bent, D | Ipswich | 12 | 17 | 59 | 52 | 194 mins |

**The Chart-topping Goalscorers** measures the players by Strike Rate. They are most likely to be Forwards but Midfield players and even Defenders do come through the club tables. It is not a measure of the number of League goals scored - although that is also noted - but how often on average they have scored.

## CHART-TOPPING DEFENDERS

Westcoast

| 1 Matthew Upson - Reading | |
|---|---|
| **Goals Conceded in the League** The number of League goals conceded while he was on the pitch | 5 |
| **Goals Conceded in all competitions** The number of goals conceded while he was on the pitch in all competitions | 8 |
| **Clean Sheets** In games when he played at least 70 mins | 8 |
| **Defensive Rating** Average number of minutes between League goals conceded while on pitch | 90 |
| **Club Defensive Rating** Average mins between League goals conceded by the club this season | 230 |

| | PLAYER | CLUB | CON: LGE | ALL | CS | CDR | DEF RATE |
|---|---|---|---|---|---|---|---|
| 2 | Taggart | Leicester | 24 | 24 | 12 | 104 | 115 mins |
| 3 | Irwin | Wolves | 34 | 43 | 20 | 94 | 111 mins |
| 4 | Davidson | Leicester | 22 | 30 | 10 | 104 | 110 mins |
| 5 | Rogers | Leicester | 33 | 41 | 18 | 104 | 104 mins |
| 6 | Elliott | Leicester | 37 | 43 | 17 | 104 | 103 mins |
| 7 | Nedergaard | Norwich | 30 | 35 | 17 | 84 | 99 mins |
| 8 | De Zeeuw | Portsmouth | 31 | 31 | 13 | 92 | 99 mins |
| 9 | Clyde | Wolves | 13 | 13 | 4 | 94 | 99 mins |
| 10 | Sinclair | Leicester | 28 | 36 | 14 | 104 | 98 mins |
| 11 | Lescott | Wolves | 42 | 53 | 20 | 94 | 94 mins |
| 12 | Naylor | Wolves | 29 | 42 | 15 | 94 | 94 mins |
| 13 | Festa | Portsmouth | 25 | 28 | 10 | 92 | 92 mins |
| 14 | Drury | Norwich | 43 | 49 | 18 | 84 | 91 mins |
| 15 | Hjelde | Nottm Forest | 19 | 22 | 7 | 83 | 90 mins |
| 16 | Taylor | Portsmouth | 35 | 42 | 11 | 92 | 90 mins |
| 17 | Primus | Portsmouth | 39 | 46 | 12 | 92 | 90 mins |
| 18 | Shorey | Reading | 43 | 49 | 18 | 90 | 89 mins |
| 19 | Williams | Reading | 36 | 40 | 14 | 90 | 89 mins |
| 20 | Butler | Wolves | 31 | 44 | 15 | 94 | 89 mins |

**The Chart-topping Defenders** are resolved by their Defensive Rating, how often their team concedes a goal while they are playing. All these rightly favour players at the best performing clubs because good players win matches. However, good players in lower-table clubs will chart where they have lifted the team's performance.

## CHART-TOPPING GOALKEEPERS

Britannia

| 1 Mark Crossley - Stoke | |
|---|---|
| **Goals conceded in the League (CL)** | 7 |
| **Goals conceded in all comps (CA)** | 7 |
| **Counting Games** League games when he played at least 70 minutes | 12 |
| **Clean Sheets** In games when he played at least 70 mins | 7 |
| **Goals to Shots Ratio (GSR)** The average number of shots on target per each League goal conceded | 8 |
| **Defensive Rating** Average number of minutes between League goals conceded while on pitch | 154 |

| | PLAYER | CLUB | CG | CON: LGE | ALL | CS | GSR | DEF RATE |
|---|---|---|---|---|---|---|---|---|
| 1 | Crossley | Stoke | 12 | 7 | 7 | 7 | 8 | 154 mins |
| 2 | Walker | Leicester | 46 | 40 | 49 | 19 | 5.9 | 103 mins |
| 3 | Murray | Wolverhampton | 40 | 36 | 47 | 18 | 4.5 | 100 mins |
| 4 | Poom | Derby | 13 | 12 | 15 | 5 | 5.7 | 97 mins |
| 5 | Hahnemann | Reading | 41 | 38 | 45 | 18 | 5.5 | 97 mins |
| 6 | Hislop | Portsmouth | 45 | 45 | 52 | 15 | 4.7 | 91 mins |
| 7 | Kolinko | Crystal Palace | 27 | 28 | 33 | 10 | 3.8 | 87 mins |
| 8 | Ward | Nottm Forest | 45 | 48 | 58 | 14 | 5.1 | 84 mins |
| 9 | Green | Norwich | 46 | 49 | 55 | 18 | 5.5 | 84 mins |
| 10 | Kenny | Sheff Utd | 45 | 50 | 64 | 13 | 4.6 | 81 mins |
| 11 | Gould | Preston | 11 | 14 | 14 | 5 | 4.6 | 77 mins |
| 12 | Hyldgaard | Coventry | 27 | 32 | 39 | 8 | 4.7 | 76 mins |
| 13 | Brown | Gillingham | 38 | 46 | 52 | 12 | 4.7 | 75 mins |
| 14 | Beasant | Brighton | 16 | 20 | 20 | 5 | 4.2 | 72 mins |
| 15 | Pollitt | Rotherham | 40 | 52 | 65 | 12 | 3.7 | 69 mins |
| 16 | Berthelin | Crystal Palace | 8 | 11 | 13 | 2 | 3.5 | 67 mins |
| 17 | Walker | Walsall | 40 | 56 | 62 | 13 | 3.8 | 65 mins |
| 18 | Marshall | Ipswich | 40 | 56 | 65 | 9 | 4.3 | 64 mins |
| 19 | Kuipers | Brighton | 21 | 30 | 30 | 4 | 4.6 | 63 mins |
| 20 | Warner | Millwall | 46 | 69 | 75 | 13 | 4.1 | 60 mins |

**The Chart-topping Goalkeepers** are positioned by their Defensive Rating. We also show Clean Sheets where the team has not conceded and the Keeper has played all or most (at least 70 minutes) of the game. Now teams use several keepers in a season, not every team will necessarily chart on this page.

## FINAL LEAGUE TABLE

| | HOME | | | | | | AWAY | | | | | TOTAL | | | |
|---|---|---|---|---|---|---|---|---|---|---|---|---|---|---|---|
| | P | W | D | L | F | A | W | D | L | F | A | F | A | DIF | PTS |
| Portsmouth | 46 | 17 | 3 | 3 | 52 | 22 | 12 | 8 | 3 | 45 | 23 | 97 | 45 | 52 | **98** |
| Leicester | 46 | 16 | 5 | 2 | 40 | 12 | 10 | 9 | 4 | 33 | 28 | 73 | 40 | 33 | **92** |
| Sheff Utd | 46 | 13 | 7 | 3 | 38 | 23 | 10 | 4 | 9 | 34 | 29 | 72 | 52 | 20 | **80** |
| Reading | 46 | 13 | 3 | 7 | 33 | 21 | 12 | 1 | 10 | 28 | 25 | 61 | 46 | 15 | **79** |
| Wolverhampton | 46 | 9 | 10 | 4 | 40 | 19 | 11 | 6 | 6 | 41 | 25 | 81 | 44 | 37 | **76** |
| Nottm Forest | 46 | 14 | 7 | 2 | 57 | 23 | 6 | 7 | 10 | 25 | 27 | 82 | 50 | 32 | **74** |
| Ipswich | 46 | 10 | 5 | 8 | 49 | 39 | 9 | 8 | 6 | 31 | 25 | 80 | 64 | 16 | **70** |
| Norwich | 46 | 14 | 4 | 5 | 36 | 17 | 5 | 8 | 10 | 24 | 32 | 60 | 49 | 11 | **69** |
| Millwall | 46 | 11 | 6 | 6 | 34 | 32 | 8 | 3 | 12 | 25 | 37 | 59 | 69 | -10 | **66** |
| Wimbledon | 46 | 12 | 5 | 6 | 39 | 28 | 6 | 6 | 11 | 37 | 45 | 76 | 73 | 3 | **65** |
| Gillingham | 46 | 10 | 6 | 7 | 33 | 31 | 6 | 8 | 9 | 23 | 34 | 56 | 65 | -9 | **62** |
| Preston | 46 | 11 | 7 | 5 | 44 | 29 | 5 | 6 | 12 | 24 | 41 | 68 | 70 | -2 | **61** |
| Watford | 46 | 11 | 5 | 7 | 33 | 26 | 6 | 4 | 13 | 21 | 44 | 54 | 70 | -16 | **60** |
| Crystal Palace | 46 | 8 | 10 | 5 | 29 | 17 | 6 | 7 | 10 | 30 | 35 | 59 | 52 | 7 | **59** |
| Rotherham | 46 | 8 | 9 | 6 | 27 | 25 | 7 | 5 | 11 | 35 | 37 | 62 | 62 | 0 | **59** |
| Burnley | 46 | 10 | 4 | 9 | 35 | 44 | 5 | 6 | 12 | 30 | 45 | 65 | 89 | -24 | **55** |
| Walsall | 46 | 10 | 3 | 10 | 34 | 34 | 5 | 6 | 12 | 23 | 35 | 57 | 69 | -12 | **54** |
| Derby | 46 | 9 | 5 | 9 | 33 | 32 | 6 | 2 | 15 | 22 | 42 | 55 | 74 | -19 | **52** |
| Bradford | 46 | 7 | 8 | 8 | 27 | 35 | 7 | 2 | 14 | 24 | 38 | 51 | 73 | -22 | **52** |
| Coventry | 46 | 6 | 6 | 11 | 23 | 31 | 6 | 8 | 9 | 23 | 31 | 46 | 62 | -16 | **50** |
| Stoke | 46 | 9 | 6 | 8 | 25 | 25 | 3 | 8 | 12 | 20 | 44 | 45 | 69 | -24 | **50** |
| Sheff Wed | 46 | 7 | 7 | 9 | 29 | 32 | 3 | 9 | 11 | 27 | 41 | 56 | 73 | -17 | **46** |
| Brighton | 46 | 7 | 6 | 10 | 29 | 31 | 4 | 6 | 13 | 20 | 36 | 49 | 67 | -18 | **45** |
| Grimsby | 46 | 5 | 6 | 12 | 26 | 39 | 4 | 6 | 13 | 22 | 46 | 48 | 85 | -37 | **39** |

## PLAYER DISCIPLINARY RECORD

| | |
|---|---|
| League Yellow | 7 |
| League Red | 1 |
| TOTAL | 8 |

**1 Guy Branston - Rotherham**

| Cards Average<br>Average number of minutes between a card being shown of either colour | 150 |
|---|---|

| | PLAYER | | LY | LR | TOT | AVE |
|---|---|---|---|---|---|---|
| 2 | Pouton | Grimsby | 10 | 2 | 12 | 173 |
| 3 | Harley | Sheff Utd | 3 | 1 | 4 | 182 |
| 4 | Hand | Watford | 9 | 0 | 9 | 185 |
| 5 | Henderson | Norwich | 3 | 0 | 3 | 191 |
| 6 | Gavin | Grimsby | 4 | 0 | 4 | 192 |
| 7 | Prutton | Nottm Forest | 9 | 2 | 11 | 194 |
| 8 | Igoe | Reading | 4 | 0 | 4 | 195 |
| 9 | Talbot | Rotherham | 4 | 0 | 4 | 195 |
| 10 | Lawrence | Bradford | 6 | 1 | 7 | 196 |
| 11 | Hessenthaler | Gillingham | 12 | 1 | 13 | 199 |
| 12 | Evans | Bradford | 7 | 0 | 7 | 203 |
| 13 | Diabate | Portsmouth | 7 | 0 | 7 | 203 |
| 14 | Lester | Nottm Forest | 7 | 2 | 9 | 205 |
| 15 | Elliott | Derby | 9 | 0 | 9 | 210 |
| 16 | Mackie | Reading | 8 | 1 | 9 | 210 |
| 17 | Sinclair | Leicester | 12 | 1 | 13 | 211 |
| 18 | Taggart | Leicester | 11 | 2 | 13 | 213 |
| 19 | Murdock | Preston | 10 | 0 | 10 | 213 |
| 20 | Chippo | Coventry | 7 | 1 | 8 | 215 |

## PREMIERSHIP CHART-TOPPING POINT EARNERS

| | PLAYER | TEAM | GAMES | POINTS | AVE |
|---|---|---|---|---|---|
| 2 | Windass | Sheff Utd | 14 | 34 | 2.43 |
| 3 | Pericard | Portsmouth | 14 | 32 | 2.29 |
| 4 | De Zeeuw | Portsmouth | 32 | 73 | 2.28 |
| 5 | Davidson | Leicester | 25 | 56 | 2.24 |
| 6 | Festa | Portsmouth | 25 | 56 | 2.24 |
| 7 | Sherwood | Portsmouth | 17 | 38 | 2.24 |
| 8 | Izzet | Leicester | 35 | 78 | 2.23 |
| 9 | Merson | Portsmouth | 42 | 91 | 2.17 |
| 10 | Todorov | Portsmouth | 42 | 91 | 2.17 |
| 11 | Upson | Reading | 12 | 26 | 2.17 |
| 12 | Kabba | Sheff Utd | 12 | 26 | 2.17 |
| 13 | Taylor | Portsmouth | 35 | 75 | 2.14 |
| 14 | Hislop | Portsmouth | 45 | 95 | 2.11 |
| 15 | Diabate | Portsmouth | 13 | 27 | 2.08 |
| 16 | Quashie | Portsmouth | 41 | 85 | 2.07 |
| 17 | Foxe | Portsmouth | 29 | 60 | 2.07 |
| 18 | Taggart | Leicester | 28 | 58 | 2.07 |
| 19 | Brown | Reading | 18 | 37 | 2.06 |
| 20 | Scowcroft | Leicester | 42 | 85 | 2.02 |

**1 Kevin Harper - Portsmouth**

| | |
|---|---|
| Counting Games<br>League games where he played at least 70 minutes | 17 |
| Total League Points<br>Taken in Counting Games | 42 |
| Average League Points<br>Taken in Counting Games | 2.47 |

Nationwide


## TEAM OF THE SEASON

Crossley
Stoke
CG 12 DR 154
Doyley
Watford
CG 20 DR 85
Jackson
Preston
CG 18 DR 75
Upson
Reading
CG 12 DR 230
Irwin
Wolves
CG 41 DR 111
Quinn
Coventry
CG 12 SD +54
Harper
Portsmouth
CG 17 SD +78
Hand
Watford
CG 15 SD +11
Mulryn
Norwich
CG 24 SD +32
Wallace
Gillingham
CG 13 SR 133
Connolly
Wimbledon
CG 27 SR 102


**The Team of the Season** in each League's Divisional Round-up is different to those at club level. It doesn't just mirror the Chart-topping performances but highlights Keepers, Defenders, Midfield players and Forwards who are dramatically out-performing their team-mates. We compare their key rating to the club average see below: -

- **The Division Team's goalkeeper** has to be the player with the highest Defensive Rating as he often plays most or all the games in a league season.
- **The Division Team's defenders** are also tested by Defensive Rating but against their co-defender's Ratings. We weight it to take into account the fact that differences can fluctuate wildly at the bottom of a division.
- **The Division Team's midfield** all have good Scoring Differences compared to the average Ratings of their colleagues. In all cases these players must have played at least a minimum of Counting Games.
- **The Divisional Team strikeforce** is made up of the two players who have the biggest gap in Strike Rate between themselves and their next forward. These are weighted again, as lower sides may not even have a second charting forward.

# THE SCOTTISH PREMIERSHIP ROUND-UP

## STADIUM CAPACITY AND HOME CROWDS

| | TEAM | CAPACITY | AVE | HIGH | LOW |
|---|---|---|---|---|---|
| 1 | Rangers | 50420 | 96.81 | 49874 | 45992 |
| 2 | Celtic | 60506 | 94.99 | 59027 | 55204 |
| 3 | Livingston | 10016 | 68.18 | 10004 | 4144 |
| 4 | Hearts | 18300 | 65.89 | 17732 | 8074 |
| 5 | Hibernian | 18700 | 54.3 | 15560 | 7518 |
| 6 | Dundee Utd | 14200 | 53.99 | 12402 | 5572 |
| 7 | Aberdeen | 22200 | 52.91 | 17284 | 8861 |
| 8 | Dundee | 14000 | 52.85 | 11539 | 5363 |
| 9 | Dunfermline | 12510 | 48.98 | 9139 | 4086 |
| 10 | Motherwell | 13742 | 44.28 | 12037 | 3741 |
| 11 | Kilmarnock | 18220 | 40.64 | 16722 | 4021 |
| 12 | Partick | 14538 | 38.91 | 10022 | 3541 |

**Key:** Average. The percentage of each stadium filled in League games over the season (AVE), the stadium capacity and the highest and lowest crowds recorded.

## AWAY ATTENDANCE

| | TEAM | AVE | HIGH | LOW |
|---|---|---|---|---|
| 1 | Rangers | 77.49 | 59027 | 8754 |
| 2 | Celtic | 74.91 | 49874 | 7119 |
| 3 | Hearts | 60.42 | 58450 | 4114 |
| 4 | Aberdeen | 58.72 | 58526 | 4731 |
| 5 | Dundee | 58.62 | 57542 | 4025 |
| 6 | Hibernian | 58.3 | 57512 | 4551 |
| 7 | Kilmarnock | 57.87 | 57469 | 4144 |
| 8 | Dundee Utd | 55.95 | 56907 | 4342 |
| 9 | Dunfermline | 54.89 | 58387 | 3741 |
| 10 | Partick | 54.63 | 57839 | 4746 |
| 11 | Motherwell | 52.86 | 56733 | 4086 |
| 12 | Livingston | 48.07 | 57169 | 3541 |

**Key:** Average. How close each club has come to filling grounds in its away league matches (AVE) and the highest and lowest crowds recorded.

## CLUB STRIKE FORCE

de Boer scores for Rangers

| | |
|---|---|
| Goals scored in the League | 101 |
| Goals scored in all competions | 124 |
| Shots on target (SoT) Shots on target hit by the team recorded in League games | 287 |

**1 Rangers**

| | |
|---|---|
| Club Strike Rate (CSR) Average number of minutes between League goals scored by club | 34 |

| | CLUB | LGE | ALL | SoT | CSR |
|---|---|---|---|---|---|
| 2 | Celtic | 98 | 143 | 272 | 35 |
| 3 | Hearts | 57 | 64 | 223 | 60 |
| 4 | Hibernian | 56 | 64 | 166 | 61 |
| 5 | Dunfermline | 54 | 65 | 182 | 63 |
| 6 | Dundee | 50 | 63 | 189 | 68 |
| 7 | Livingston | 48 | 57 | 195 | 71 |
| 8 | Kilmarnock | 47 | 47 | 149 | 73 |
| 9 | Motherwell | 45 | 58 | 168 | 76 |
| 10 | Aberdeen | 41 | 49 | 142 | 83 |
| 11 | Partick | 37 | 42 | 150 | 92 |
| 12 | Dundee Utd | 35 | 45 | 166 | 98 |

## CLUB DEFENCES

**1 Celtic**

| | |
|---|---|
| Club Defensive Rate (CDR) Average number of minutes between League goals conceded by club | 132 |

| | CLUB | LGE | ALL | CS | SoT | CDR |
|---|---|---|---|---|---|---|
| 2 | Rangers | 28 | 38 | 19 | 134 | 122 |
| 3 | Hearts | 51 | 58 | 11 | 170 | 67 |
| 4 | Aberdeen | 54 | 60 | 8 | 202 | 63 |
| 5 | Kilmarnock | 56 | 57 | 13 | 217 | 61 |
| 6 | Partick | 58 | 61 | 9 | 223 | 59 |
| 7 | Dundee | 60 | 65 | 5 | 215 | 57 |
| 8 | Livingston | 62 | 76 | 6 | 193 | 55 |
| 9 | Hibernian | 64 | 72 | 8 | 176 | 53 |
| 10 | Dundee Utd | 68 | 76 | 5 | 215 | 50 |
| 11 | Dunfermline | 71 | 79 | 5 | 216 | 48 |
| 12 | Motherwell | 71 | 78 | 2 | 221 | 48 |

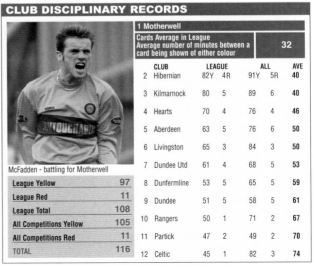

Valgaeren - the heart of the Celtic defence

| | |
|---|---|
| Goals conceded in the League | 34 |
| Goals conceded in all competions | 61 |
| Clean Sheets (CS) Number of league games where no goals were conceded | 13 |
| Shots on Target Against (SoT) Shots on Target conceded by team in League games | 158 |

## CLUB GOAL ATTEMPTS

### GOAL ATTEMPTS – FOR

**KEY:** Shots on Target (SoT), Shots Off Target (SO) Total shots (Tot) Ratio of shots on target to goals (SG) Accuracy Rating (AR)

| | CLUB | SoT | SO | Tot | SG | AR |
|---|---|---|---|---|---|---|
| 1 | Celtic | 272 | 223 | **495** | 2.8 | 54.9 |
| 2 | Dundee | 189 | 160 | **349** | 3.8 | 54.2 |
| 3 | Rangers | 287 | 243 | **530** | 2.8 | 54.2 |
| 4 | Kilmarnock | 149 | 131 | **280** | 3.2 | 53.2 |
| 5 | Hearts | 223 | 201 | **424** | 3.9 | 52.6 |
| 6 | Hibernian | 166 | 152 | **318** | 3 | 52.2 |
| 7 | Dunfermline | 182 | 174 | **356** | 3.4 | 51.1 |
| 8 | Motherwell | 168 | 161 | **329** | 3.7 | 51.1 |
| 9 | Livingston | 195 | 194 | **389** | 4.1 | 50.1 |
| 10 | Dundee Utd | 166 | 168 | **334** | 4.7 | 49.7 |
| 11 | Partick | 150 | 153 | **303** | 4.1 | 49.5 |
| 12 | Aberdeen | 142 | 163 | **305** | 3.5 | 46.6 |

### GOAL ATTEMPTS – AGAINST

**KEY:** Shots on Target (SoT), Shots Off Target (SO) Total shots (Tot) Ratio of shots on target to goals (SG) Accuracy Rating (AR)

| | CLUB | SoT | SO | Tot | SG | AR |
|---|---|---|---|---|---|---|
| 1 | Celtic | 107 | 171 | **278** | 4.1 | 38.5 |
| 5 | Hibernian | 176 | 142 | **318** | 2.8 | 55.3 |
| 2 | Rangers | 134 | 196 | **330** | 4.8 | 40.6 |
| 10 | Aberdeen | 202 | 132 | **334** | 3.7 | 60.5 |
| 3 | Hearts | 170 | 166 | **336** | 3.3 | 50.6 |
| 12 | Partick | 223 | 134 | **357** | 3.8 | 62.5 |
| 11 | Kilmarnock | 217 | 141 | **358** | 3.9 | 60.6 |
| 4 | Livingston | 193 | 166 | **359** | 3.1 | 53.8 |
| 9 | Dundee | 215 | 149 | **364** | 3.6 | 59.1 |
| 8 | Dundee Utd | 215 | 150 | **365** | 3.2 | 58.9 |
| 7 | Dunfermline | 216 | 155 | **371** | 3 | 58.2 |
| 6 | Motherwell | 221 | 174 | **395** | 3.1 | 55.9 |

## CLUB DISCIPLINARY RECORDS

McFadden - battling for Motherwell

| | |
|---|---|
| League Yellow | 97 |
| League Red | 11 |
| League Total | 108 |
| All Competitions Yellow | 105 |
| All Competitions Red | 11 |
| TOTAL | 116 |

**1 Motherwell**

| | |
|---|---|
| Cards Average in League Average number of minutes between a card being shown of either colour | 32 |

| | CLUB | LEAGUE | | ALL | | AVE |
|---|---|---|---|---|---|---|
| 2 | Hibernian | 82Y | 4R | 91Y | 5R | **40** |
| 3 | Kilmarnock | 80 | 5 | 89 | 6 | **40** |
| 4 | Hearts | 70 | 4 | 76 | 4 | **46** |
| 5 | Aberdeen | 63 | 5 | 76 | 6 | **50** |
| 6 | Livingston | 65 | 3 | 84 | 3 | **50** |
| 7 | Dundee Utd | 61 | 4 | 68 | 5 | **53** |
| 8 | Dunfermline | 53 | 5 | 65 | 5 | **59** |
| 9 | Dundee | 51 | 5 | 58 | 5 | **61** |
| 10 | Rangers | 50 | 1 | 71 | 2 | **67** |
| 11 | Partick | 47 | 2 | 49 | 2 | **70** |
| 12 | Celtic | 45 | 1 | 82 | 3 | **74** |

## CHART-TOPPING MIDFIELDERS

| 1 James McNamara - Celtic | |
|---|---|
| **Goals scored in the League** | 1 |
| **Defensive Rating** Av number of mins between League goals conceded while on the pitch | 243 |
| **Contribution to Attacking Power** Average number of minutes between League team goals while on pitch | 39 |
| **Scoring Difference** Defensive Rating minus Contribution to Attacking Power | 204 |

| | PLAYER | CLUB | GOALS | DEF R | POWER | SCORE DIFF |
|---|---|---|---|---|---|---|
| 2 | Guppy | Celtic | 0 | 191 | 31 | 160 mins |
| 3 | Arteta | Rangers | 4 | 189 | 34 | 155 mins |
| 4 | Lennon | Celtic | 0 | 136 | 35 | 101 mins |
| 5 | Lambert | Celtic | 3 | 133 | 36 | 97 mins |
| 6 | Petrov | Celtic | 12 | 129 | 33 | 96 mins |
| 7 | de Boer | Rangers | 16 | 127 | 32 | 95 mins |
| 8 | Mjallby | Celtic | 3 | 129 | 37 | 92 mins |
| 9 | Ferguson, B | Rangers | 16 | 126 | 34 | 92 mins |
| 10 | Thompson | Celtic | 8 | 121 | 37 | 84 mins |
| 11 | Sheerin | Aberdeen | 8 | 79 | 63 | 16 mins |
| 12 | MacFarlane | Hearts | 0 | 80 | 64 | 16 mins |
| 13 | Tosh | Aberdeen | 2 | 75 | 60 | 15 mins |
| 14 | McMullan | Hearts | 1 | 67 | 58 | 9 mins |
| 15 | Zambernardi | Hibernian | 0 | 69 | 60 | 9 mins |
| 16 | Stamp | Hearts | 4 | 65 | 59 | 6 mins |
| 17 | Wiss | Hibernian | 0 | 72 | 67 | 5 mins |
| 18 | Nemsadze | Dundee | 0 | 72 | 68 | 4 mins |
| 19 | Brady | Dundee | 1 | 59 | 61 | -2 mins |
| 20 | Dempsey | Dunfermline | 2 | 54 | 59 | -5 mins |

The Divisional Round-up charts combine the records of chart-topping keepers, defenders, midfield players and forwards, from every club in the division.. The one above is for **the Chart-topping Midfielders**. The players are ranked by their Scoring Difference although other attributes are shown for you to compare.

## CHART-TOPPING GOALSCORERS

| 1 John Hartson - Celtic | |
|---|---|
| **Goals scored in the League** | 18 |
| **Goals scored in all competitions** | 25 |
| **Contribution to Attacking Power** Average number of minutes between League team goals while on pitch | 40 |
| **Player Strike Rate** Average number of minutes between League goals scored by player | 96 |
| **Club Strike Rate (CSR)** Average minutes between League goals scored by club | 20 |

| | PLAYER | CLUB | GOALS: LGE | ALL | POWER | CSR | S RATE |
|---|---|---|---|---|---|---|---|
| 2 | Larsson | Celtic | 28 | 44 | 32 | 20 | 106 mins |
| 3 | Mols | Rangers | 13 | 14 | 36 | 20 | 144 mins |
| 4 | Boyd | Kilmarnock | 12 | 12 | 58 | 42 | 151 mins |
| 5 | Arveladze | Rangers | 15 | 16 | 31 | 20 | 154 mins |
| 6 | Kirk | Hearts | 10 | 11 | 57 | 35 | 155 mins |
| 7 | Sheerin | Aberdeen | 8 | 8 | 63 | 48 | 158 mins |
| 8 | McManus | Hibernian | 11 | 11 | 60 | 35 | 159 mins |
| 9 | Sutton | Celtic | 15 | 19 | 35 | 20 | 163 mins |
| 10 | de Boer | Rangers | 16 | 20 | 31 | 20 | 166 mins |
| 11 | de Vries | Hearts | 15 | 15 | 56 | 35 | 170 mins |
| 12 | Lovell | Dundee | 11 | 14 | 59 | 40 | 173 mins |
| 13 | Crawford | Dunfermline | 18 | 22 | 64 | 37 | 185 mins |
| 14 | McSwegan | Kilmarnock | 11 | 11 | 68 | 42 | 187 mins |
| 15 | McFadden | Motherwell | 13 | 19 | 69 | 44 | 193 mins |
| 16 | Ferguson, B | Rangers | 16 | 18 | 33 | 20 | 197 mins |
| 17 | Lovenkrands | Rangers | 9 | 12 | 37 | 20 | 206 mins |
| 18 | Burns | Partick | 16 | 17 | 96 | 54 | 211 mins |
| 19 | O'Connor | Hibernian | 7 | 9 | 71 | 35 | 214 mins |
| 20 | Petrov | Celtic | 12 | 14 | 32 | 20 | 225 mins |

**The Chart-topping Goalscorers** measures the players by Strike Rate. They are most likely to be Forwards but Midfield players and even Defenders do come through the club tables. It is not a measure of the number of League goals scored - although that is also noted - but how often on average they have scored.

## CHART-TOPPING DEFENDERS

| 1 Sylla - Celtic | |
|---|---|
| **Goals Conceded in the League** The number of League goals conceded while he was on the pitch | 5 |
| **Goals Conceded in all competitions** The number of goals conceded while he was on the pitch in all competitions | 9 |
| **Clean Sheets** In games when he played at least 70 mins | 7 |
| **Defensive Rating** Average number of minutes between League goals conceded while on pitch | 223 |
| **Club Defensive Rating** Average mins between League goals conceded by the club this season | 76 |

| | PLAYER | CLUB | CON: LGE | ALL | CS | CDR | DEF RATE |
|---|---|---|---|---|---|---|---|
| 2 | Muscat | Rangers | 12 | 19 | 14 | 71 | 162 mins |
| 3 | Malcolm | Rangers | 12 | 18 | 11 | 71 | 160 mins |
| 4 | Balde | Celtic | 24 | 41 | 20 | 76 | 134 mins |
| 5 | Moore | Rangers | 23 | 30 | 18 | 71 | 134 mins |
| 6 | Valgaeren | Celtic | 23 | 40 | 19 | 76 | 133 mins |
| 7 | Laursen | Celtic | 15 | 25 | 13 | 76 | 128 mins |
| 8 | Ricksen | Rangers | 26 | 35 | 17 | 71 | 120 mins |
| 9 | Numan | Rangers | 21 | 27 | 10 | 71 | 108 mins |
| 10 | Ross | Rangers | 13 | 17 | 7 | 71 | 108 mins |
| 11 | Amoruso | Rangers | 21 | 26 | 10 | 71 | 101 mins |
| 12 | Hay | Kilmarnock | 12 | 12 | 5 | 35 | 97 mins |
| 13 | Dillon | Kilmarnock | 15 | 16 | 5 | 35 | 80 mins |
| 14 | Maybury | Hearts | 40 | 47 | 11 | 39 | 78 mins |
| 15 | Webster | Hearts | 23 | 24 | 6 | 39 | 75 mins |
| 16 | Pressley | Hearts | 39 | 46 | 9 | 39 | 75 mins |
| 17 | Mahood | Kilmarnock | 42 | 43 | 13 | 35 | 74 mins |
| 18 | Matyus | Hibernian | 17 | 17 | 5 | 31 | 72 mins |
| 19 | Hutchinson | Dundee | 13 | 15 | 2 | 33 | 70 mins |
| 20 | Severin | Hearts | 47 | 50 | 10 | 39 | 68 mins |

**The Chart-topping Defenders** are resolved by their Defensive Rating, how often their team concedes a goal while they are playing. All these rightly favour players at the best performing clubs because good players win matches. However, good players in lower-table clubs will chart where they have lifted the team's performance.

## CHART-TOPPING GOALKEEPERS

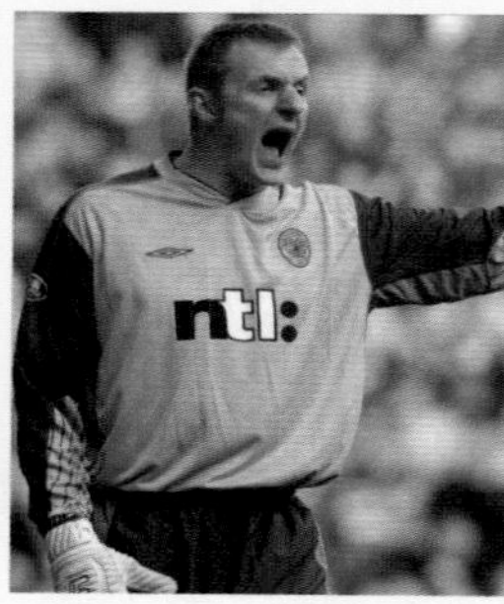
ntl:

| 1 Rab Douglas - Celtic | |
|---|---|
| **Goals conceded in the League (CL)** | 14 |
| **Goals conceded in all comps (CA)** | 34 |
| **Counting Games** League games when he played at least 70 minutes | 20 |
| **Clean Sheets** In games when he played at least 70 mins | 12 |
| **Goals to Shots Ratio (GSR)** The average number of shots on target per each League goal conceded | 4.4 |
| **Defensive Rating** Average number of minutes between League goals conceded while on pitch | 129 |

| | PLAYER | CLUB | CG | CON: LGE | ALL | CS | GSR | DEF RATE |
|---|---|---|---|---|---|---|---|---|
| 2 | Moilanen | Hearts | 14 | 10 | 11 | 5 | 3.6 | 126 mins |
| 3 | Klos | Rangers | 38 | 28 | 38 | 19 | 4.8 | 122 mins |
| 4 | Kjaer | Aberdeen | 22 | 28 | 31 | 6 | 4.1 | 73 mins |
| 5 | Broto | Livingston | 23 | 35 | 46 | 4 | 3.5 | 61 mins |
| 6 | Speroni | Dundee | 38 | 60 | 65 | 5 | 3.6 | 57 mins |
| 7 | Colgan | Hibernian | 30 | 48 | 56 | 6 | 2.7 | 56 mins |
| 8 | Marshall | Kilmarnock | 30 | 48 | 49 | 9 | 3.6 | 56 mins |
| 9 | Arthur | Partick | 35 | 56 | 59 | 8 | 3.8 | 56 mins |
| 10 | Dubourdeau | Motherwell | 22 | 36 | 40 | 1 | 3.2 | 55 mins |
| 11 | Preece | Aberdeen | 15 | 26 | 29 | 2 | 2.9 | 54 mins |
| 12 | Stillie | Dunfermline | 21 | 36 | 43 | 4 | 2.8 | 53 mins |
| 13 | Main | Livingston | 12 | 21 | 21 | 2 | 2.5 | 51 mins |
| 14 | McKenzie | Hearts | 20 | 37 | 39 | 6 | 3.1 | 49 mins |
| 15 | Gallacher, P | Dundee Utd | 34 | 63 | 68 | 4 | 3.1 | 48 mins |
| 16 | Ruitenbeek | Dunfermline | 17 | 35 | 36 | 1 | 3.3 | 44 mins |
| 17 | Woods | Motherwell | 16 | 35 | 38 | 1 | 3.1 | 41 mins |

**The Chart-topping Goalkeepers** are positioned by their Defensive Rating. We also show Clean Sheets where the team has not conceded and the Keeper has played all or most (at least 70 minutes) of the game. Now teams use several keepers in a season, not every team will necessarily chart on this page.

## FINAL LEAGUE TABLE

| | HOME | | | | | | AWAY | | | | | TOTAL | | | |
|---|---|---|---|---|---|---|---|---|---|---|---|---|---|---|---|
| | P | W | D | L | F | A | W | D | L | F | A | F | A | DIF | PTS |
| Rangers | 38 | 18 | 0 | 1 | 55 | 12 | 13 | 4 | 2 | 46 | 16 | 101 | 28 | 73 | 97 |
| Celtic | 38 | 18 | 1 | 0 | 56 | 12 | 13 | 3 | 3 | 42 | 14 | 98 | 26 | 72 | 97 |
| Hearts | 38 | 12 | 3 | 4 | 36 | 24 | 6 | 6 | 7 | 21 | 27 | 57 | 51 | 6 | 63 |
| Kilmarnock | 38 | 9 | 5 | 5 | 26 | 21 | 7 | 4 | 8 | 21 | 35 | 47 | 56 | -9 | 57 |
| Dunfermline | 38 | 9 | 3 | 7 | 32 | 30 | 4 | 4 | 11 | 22 | 41 | 54 | 71 | -17 | 46 |
| Dundee | 38 | 6 | 7 | 6 | 29 | 27 | 4 | 7 | 8 | 21 | 33 | 50 | 60 | -10 | 44 |
| Hibernian | 38 | 8 | 3 | 8 | 28 | 29 | 7 | 3 | 9 | 28 | 35 | 56 | 64 | -8 | 51 |
| Aberdeen | 38 | 5 | 7 | 7 | 19 | 21 | 8 | 3 | 8 | 22 | 33 | 41 | 54 | -13 | 49 |
| Livingston | 38 | 5 | 4 | 10 | 23 | 28 | 4 | 4 | 11 | 25 | 34 | 48 | 62 | -14 | 35 |
| Partick | 38 | 5 | 6 | 8 | 23 | 23 | 3 | 5 | 11 | 14 | 35 | 37 | 58 | -21 | 35 |
| Dundee Utd | 38 | 2 | 7 | 10 | 18 | 32 | 5 | 4 | 10 | 17 | 36 | 35 | 68 | -33 | 32 |
| Motherwell | 38 | 6 | 4 | 9 | 31 | 34 | 1 | 3 | 15 | 14 | 37 | 45 | 71 | -26 | 28 |

## PLAYER DISCIPLINARY RECORD

| | |
|---|---|
| League Yellow | 7 |
| League Red | 1 |
| TOTAL | 8 |

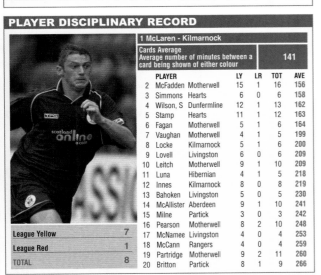

**1 McLaren - Kilmarnock**

**Cards Average**
Average number of minutes between a card being shown of either colour: **141**

| | PLAYER | | LY | LR | TOT | AVE |
|---|---|---|---|---|---|---|
| 2 | McFadden | Motherwell | 15 | 1 | 16 | 156 |
| 3 | Simmons | Hearts | 6 | 0 | 6 | 158 |
| 4 | Wilson, S | Dunfermline | 12 | 1 | 13 | 162 |
| 5 | Stamp | Hearts | 11 | 1 | 12 | 163 |
| 6 | Fagan | Motherwell | 5 | 1 | 6 | 164 |
| 7 | Vaughan | Motherwell | 4 | 1 | 5 | 199 |
| 8 | Locke | Kilmarnock | 5 | 1 | 6 | 200 |
| 9 | Lovell | Livingston | 6 | 0 | 6 | 209 |
| 10 | Leitch | Motherwell | 9 | 1 | 10 | 209 |
| 11 | Luna | Hibernian | 4 | 1 | 5 | 218 |
| 12 | Innes | Kilmarnock | 8 | 0 | 8 | 219 |
| 13 | Bahoken | Livingston | 5 | 0 | 5 | 230 |
| 14 | McAllister | Aberdeen | 9 | 1 | 10 | 241 |
| 15 | Milne | Partick | 3 | 0 | 3 | 242 |
| 16 | Pearson | Motherwell | 8 | 2 | 10 | 248 |
| 17 | McNamee | Livingston | 4 | 0 | 4 | 253 |
| 18 | McCann | Rangers | 4 | 0 | 4 | 259 |
| 19 | Partridge | Motherwell | 9 | 2 | 11 | 260 |
| 20 | Britton | Partick | 8 | 1 | 9 | 266 |

## PREMIERSHIP CHART-TOPPING POINT EARNERS

| | PLAYER | TEAM | GAMES | POINTS | AVE |
|---|---|---|---|---|---|
| 2 | McNamara | Celtic | 13 | 35 | 2.69 |
| 3 | Malcolm | Rangers | 20 | 53 | 2.65 |
| 4 | Laursen | Celtic | 21 | 55 | 2.62 |
| 5 | Agathe | Celtic | 21 | 55 | 2.62 |
| 6 | Lennon | Celtic | 26 | 68 | 2.62 |
| 7 | Moore | Rangers | 34 | 89 | 2.62 |
| 8 | Arveladze | Rangers | 23 | 60 | 2.61 |
| 9 | de Boer | Rangers | 25 | 65 | 2.60 |
| 10 | Valgaeren | Celtic | 34 | 87 | 2.56 |
| 11 | Arteta | Rangers | 20 | 51 | 2.55 |
| 12 | Klos | Rangers | 38 | 97 | 2.55 |
| 13 | Thompson | Celtic | 24 | 61 | 2.54 |
| 14 | Numan | Rangers | 24 | 61 | 2.54 |
| 15 | Sutton | Celtic | 26 | 66 | 2.54 |
| 16 | Larsson | Celtic | 32 | 81 | 2.53 |
| 17 | Balde | Celtic | 36 | 91 | 2.53 |
| 18 | Ferguson, B | Rangers | 35 | 88 | 2.51 |
| 19 | McCann | Rangers | 10 | 25 | 2.50 |
| 20 | Ross | Rangers | 14 | 35 | 2.50 |

DIADORA
ntl:home
Digital TV


**1 Kevin Muscat - Rangers**

| | |
|---|---|
| **Counting Games** League games where he played at least 70 minutes | 22 |
| **Total League Points** Taken in Counting Games | 61 |
| **Average League Points** Taken in Counting Games | 2.77 |

## TEAM OF THE SEASON

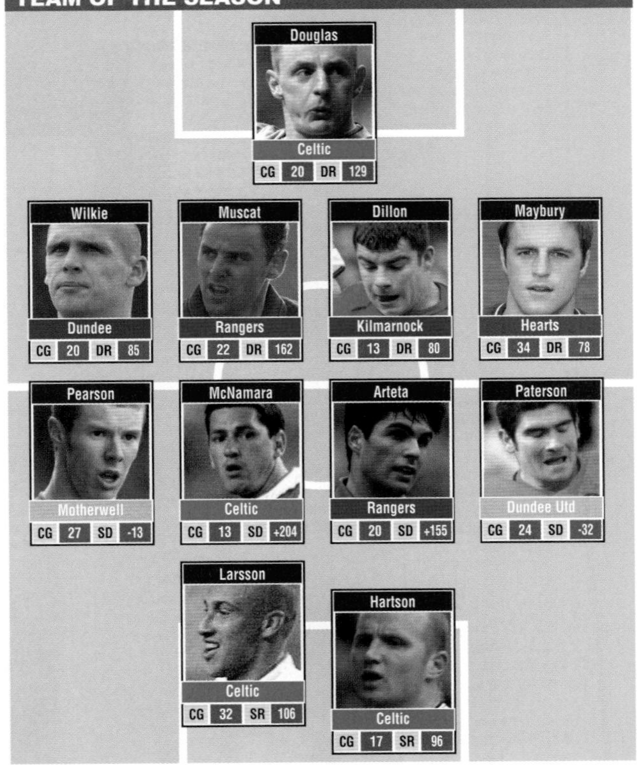

Douglas
Celtic
CG 20 DR 129
Wilkie
Dundee
CG 20 DR 85
Muscat
Rangers
CG 22 DR 162
Dillon
Kilmarnock
CG 13 DR 80
Maybury
Hearts
CG 34 DR 78
Pearson
Motherwell
CG 27 SD -13
McNamara
Celtic
CG 13 SD +204
Arteta
Rangers
CG 20 SD +155
Paterson
Dundee Utd
CG 24 SD -32
Larsson
Celtic
CG 32 SR 106
Hartson
Celtic
CG 17 SR 96


**The Team of the Season** in each League's Divisional Round-up is different to those at club level. It doesn't just mirror the Chart-topping performances but highlights Keepers, Defenders, Midfield players and Forwards who are dramatically out-performing their team-mates. We compare their key rating to the club average see below: -

- **The Division Team's goalkeeper** has to be the player with the highest Defensive Rating as he often plays most or all the games in a league season.
- **The Division Team's defenders** are also tested by Defensive Rating but against their co-defender's Ratings. We weight it to take into account the fact that differences can fluctuate wildly at the bottom of a division.
- **The Division Team's midfield** all have good Scoring Differences compared to the average Ratings of their colleagues. In all cases these players must have played at least a minimum of Counting Games.
- **The Divisional Team strikeforce** is made up of the two players who have the biggest gap in Strike Rate between themselves and their next forward. These are weighted again, as lower sides may not even have a second charting forward.

# HOW RANGERS WON THE LEAGUE

AUGUST
SEPTEMBER
OCTOBER
NOVEMBER
DECEMBER
1st
2nd
ntl:home Digital TV
DIADORA

**INS AND OUTS**

**Arteta in and Flo departs**
**IN** Mikel Arteta from Barcelona for £6m, Kevin Muscat from Wolves
**OUT** Tore Andre Flo joins Sunderland for £6.75m

**Late start to game but season is off and running** with goals from de Boer, Arveladze and sub Lovenkrands sinking Dundee

**Lovenkrands brace makes it safe** at Hibernian in bad-tempered tussle of one red and seven yellows

**De Boer hard work thrown away** in extra-time as UEFA campaign ends in first round. McCann's goal is answered by Zizkov's sub

**Eighth consecutive league win** as Ferguson's sweet strike makes the points safe against struggling Dundee United

**Caniggia hat-trick inspires** the demolition of Dunfermline despite Ruitenbeek's fine performance in goal

**First goals for Mols** mark Kilmarnock for a hammering and Ferguson adds a brace in 6-1 win

**Ferguson penalty prevents defeat** as Aberdeen net their first goals against the Gers for two years

**Under the cosh at Dundee** before Moore makes a telling contribution at both ends

**Ricksen starts rush of goals** in the second half after Hearts are reduced to ten

**Arveladze's first hat-trick** earns a 4-0 lead but it nearly evaporates against ten-man Livingston in second half

**MONTH BY MONTH POINTS TALLY**

| Month | Points | % |
|---|---|---|
| AUGUST | 10 | 83% |
| SEPTEMBER | 15 | 100% |
| OCTOBER | 7 | 78% |
| NOVEMBER | 10 | 83% |
| DECEMBER | 18 | 86% |
| JANUARY | 6 | 100% |
| FEBRUARY | 9 | 100% |
| MARCH | 6 | 67% |
| APRIL | 6 | 67% |
| MAY | 10 | 83% |

**Rangers still top after a six-goal stunner** in which the lead changes hands three times before a Celtic equaliser sees the points shared

**Sutton scores after just 20 seconds** but Rangers hit three before half-time

**New signings enjoy debut** and it's business as usual. Hedman and Laursen come in to help rout Dundee United by five goals

**Motherwell's youngsters spring a surprise** and hang on after Hartson's late consolation

**So easy as Larsson hits hat-trick** and Sutton two as Kilmarnock surrender

**Striking pair clinical** in Hearts demolition. Larsson scores two and Sutton also weighs in

**Sutton's scoring return** to former club makes certain of UEFA progression. Blackburn, seventh in the Premiership, are deservedly beaten

**Hartson hat-trick** answers two from de Vries in a six-goal Boxing Day cracker against Hearts

**Blackburn's performance wins plaudits** but Larsson's goal wins a lead to take to the away leg of this 'Battle of Britain' tie

**UEFA Cup flyer** for Larsson as his hat-trick sends Lithuanian side Suduva tumbling to an eight-goal annihilation

**Celta outgunned** by away goal from Hartson to keep UEFA scalps tumbling. The side third in the La Liga tumble to Scots

**Basle blast two to make sure** their first leg away goal counts double but Sutton's late chance nearly sees O'Neill through to the Champions League proper

**MONTH BY MONTH POINTS TALLY**

| Month | Points | % |
|---|---|---|
| AUGUST | 12 | 100% |
| SEPTEMBER | 12 | 80% |
| OCTOBER | 7 | 78% |
| NOVEMBER | 12 | 100% |
| DECEMBER | 16 | 76% |
| JANUARY | 4 | 67% |
| FEBRUARY | 6 | 100% |
| MARCH | 6 | 100% |
| APRIL | 7 | 58% |
| MAY | 15 | 100% |

**INS AND OUTS**

**Laursen joins from Hibs**
The Danish defender joins for an undisclosed fee
**IN** Magnus Hedman joins from Coventry for £1.5m
**OUT** Morten Wieghorst joins Brondby under the Bosman Rules

**Hartson makes a powerful case** for a starting place with four in this 7-0 demolition of Aberdeen

# HOW CELTIC CAME OH-SO CLOSE

# Gers revel in Scotland's limelight

**Final Position: 1st**

KEY: League, Champions Lge, UEFA Cup, Scottish FA Cup, Scottish League Cup, Other; Won, Drawn, Lost

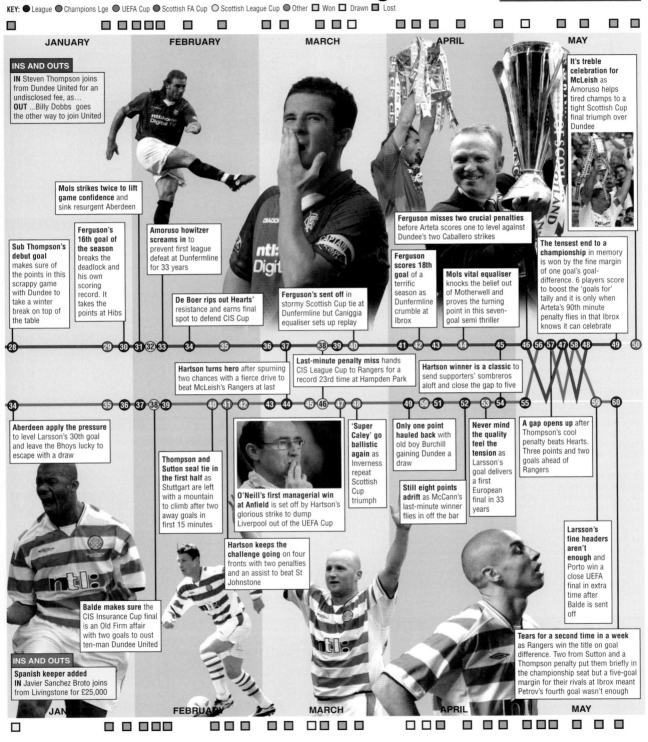

JANUARY FEBRUARY MARCH APRIL MAY

**INS AND OUTS**

**IN** Steven Thompson joins from Dundee United for an undisclosed fee, as...
**OUT** ...Billy Dobbs goes the other way to join United

**It's treble celebration for McLeish** as Amoruso helps tired champs to a tight Scottish Cup final triumph over Dundee

**Mols strikes twice to lift game confidence** and sink resurgent Aberdeen

**Sub Thompson's debut goal** makes sure of the points in this scrappy game with Dundee to take a winter break on top of the table

**Ferguson's 16th goal of the season** breaks the deadlock and his own scoring record. It takes the points at Hibs

**Amoruso howitzer screams in** to prevent first league defeat at Dunfermline for 33 years

**De Boer rips out Hearts'** resistance and earns final spot to defend CIS Cup

**Ferguson's sent off** in stormy Scottish Cup tie at Dunfermline but Caniggia equaliser sets up replay

**Ferguson misses two crucial penalties** before Arteta scores one to level against Dundee's two Caballero strikes

**Ferguson scores 18th goal** of a terrific season as Dunfermline crumble at Ibrox

**Mols vital equaliser** knocks the belief out of Motherwell and proves the turning point in this seven-goal semi thriller

**The tensest end to a championship** in memory is won by the fine margin of one goal's goal-difference. 6 players score to boost the 'goals for' tally and it is only when Arteta's 90th minute penalty flies in that Ibrox knows it can celebrate

**Hartson turns hero** after spurning two chances with a fierce drive to beat McLeish's Rangers at last

**Last-minute penalty miss** hands CIS League Cup to Rangers for a record 23rd time at Hampden Park

**Hartson winner is a classic** to send supporters' sombreros aloft and close the gap to five

**Aberdeen apply the pressure** to level Larsson's 30th goal and leave the Bhoys lucky to escape with a draw

**Thompson and Sutton seal tie in the first half** as Stuttgart are left with a mountain to climb after two away goals in first 15 minutes

**O'Neill's first managerial win at Anfield** is set off by Hartson's glorious strike to dump Liverpool out of the UEFA Cup

**'Super Caley' go ballistic again** as Inverness repeat Scottish Cup triumph

**Only one point hauled back** with old boy Burchill gaining Dundee a draw

**Still eight points adrift** as McCann's last-minute winner flies in off the bar

**Never mind the quality feel the tension** as Larsson's goal delivers a first European final in 33 years

**A gap opens up** after Thompson's cool penalty beats Hearts. Three points and two goals ahead of Rangers

**Hartson keeps the challenge going** on four fronts with two penalties and an assist to beat St Johnstone

**Larsson's fine headers aren't enough** and Porto win a close UEFA final in extra time after Balde is sent off

**Balde makes sure** the CIS Insurance Cup final is an Old Firm affair with two goals to oust ten-man Dundee United

**Tears for a second time in a week** as Rangers win the title on goal difference. Two from Sutton and a Thompson penalty put them briefly in the championship seat but a five-goal margin for their rivals at Ibrox meant Petrov's fourth goal wasn't enough

**INS AND OUTS**

**Spanish keeper added**
**IN** Javier Sanchez Broto joins from Livingstone for £25,000

JANUARY FEBRUARY MARCH APRIL MAY

# Trophies 0... Guts and pride... awesome

**Final Position: 2nd**

# RANGERS

Final Position: **1st**

**NICKNAME:** THE GERS

KEY: Won / Drawn / Lost

| | | | | | | |
|---|---|---|---|---|---|---|
| 1 | prem | **Kilmarnock** | A | D | 1-1 | Arveladze 29 |
| 2 | prem | **Dundee** | H | W | 3-0 | de Boer 11; Arveladze 66; Lovenkrands 87 |
| 3 | prem | **Hibernian** | A | W | 4-2 | de Boer 6; Ferguson 45 pen; Lovenkrands 64,86 |
| 4 | prem | **Aberdeen** | H | W | 2-0 | de Boer 29; Ferguson 77 pen |
| 5 | prem | **Dunfermline** | A | W | 6-0 | Caniggia 11,59,68; Arteta 28; Ricksen 42; Ferguson 56 pen |
| 6 | prem | **Hearts** | H | W | 2-0 | Caniggia 41; Arveladze 78 |
| 7 | prem | **Livingston** | A | W | 2-0 | Ross 61; Ferguson 86 pen |
| 8 | uc1rl1 | **Zizkov** | A | L | 0-2 | |
| 9 | prem | **Partick** | H | W | 3-0 | Lovenkrands 2; de Boer 27,69 |
| 10 | prem | **Dundee Utd** | A | W | 3-0 | Amoruso 22; Ferguson 45; Arveladze 73 |
| 11 | uc1rl2 | **Zizkov** | H | W | 3-1 | de Boer 42,58; McCann 97 |
| 12 | prem | **Celtic** | A | D | 3-3 | Arteta 6; de Boer 56; Arveladze 76 |
| 13 | prem | **Motherwell** | H | W | 3-0 | Amoruso 1; Lovenkrands 72; de Boer 90 |
| 14 | cis3 | **Hibernian** | A | W | 3-2 | Townsley 21 og; Caniggia 24; Lovenkrands 78 |
| 15 | prem | **Kilmarnock** | H | W | 6-1 | Mols 5,15; de Boer 26; Ferguson 34,71 pen; Moore 67 |
| 16 | prem | **Dundee** | A | W | 3-0 | Malcolm 30; Lovenkrands 50; Moore 79 |
| 17 | sccqf | **Dunfermline** | A | W | 1-0 | Caniggia 79 |
| 18 | prem | **Hibernian** | H | W | 2-1 | Mols 11; Arveladze 35 |
| 19 | prem | **Aberdeen** | A | D | 2-2 | Numan 24; Ferguson 78 pen |
| 20 | prem | **Dunfermline** | H | W | 3-0 | McCann 60; Mols 81; Arveladze 83 |
| 21 | prem | **Hearts** | A | W | 4-0 | Ricksen 52,81; Ferguson 79 pen; Hughes 90 |
| 22 | prem | **Livingston** | H | W | 4-3 | Ferguson 8; Arveladze 10,18,46 |
| 23 | prem | **Celtic** | H | W | 3-2 | Moore 10; de Boer 35; Mols 40 |
| 24 | prem | **Dundee Utd** | H | W | 3-0 | Ferguson 13,56,86 pen |
| 25 | prem | **Partick** | A | W | 2-1 | Mols 70; de Boer 79 |
| 26 | prem | **Motherwell** | A | L | 0-1 | |
| 27 | prem | **Kilmarnock** | A | W | 1-0 | Lovenkrands 24 |
| 28 | prem | **Dundee** | H | W | 3-1 | Ferguson 21; de Boer 44; Thompson 82 |
| 29 | scr3 | **Arbroath** | A | W | 3-0 | Ferguson 27; Moore 32; Arveladze 57 |
| 30 | prem | **Hibernian** | A | W | 2-0 | Ferguson 58; Caniggia 85 |
| 31 | prem | **Aberdeen** | H | W | 2-1 | Mols 37,77 |
| 32 | cissf | **Hearts** | A | W | 1-0 | de Boer 27 |
| 33 | prem | **Dunfermline** | A | W | 3-1 | McCann 38; Amoruso 71; Caniggia 90 |
| 34 | prem | **Hearts** | H | W | 1-0 | Severin 41 og |
| 35 | scr4 | **Ayr** | A | W | 1-0 | de Boer 79 |
| 36 | prem | **Livingston** | A | W | 2-1 | Amoruso 8; Arveladze 16 |
| 37 | prem | **Celtic** | A | L | 0-1 | |
| 38 | cisf | **Celtic** | A | W | 2-1 | Caniggia 23; Lovenkrands 35 |
| 39 | prem | **Motherwell** | H | W | 2-0 | Ferguson 18; Lovenkrands 46 |
| 40 | scqf | **Dunfermline** | A | D | 1-1 | Caniggia 31 |
| 41 | prem | **Partick** | H | W | 2-0 | Mols 70,75 |
| 42 | Scqfr | **Dunfermline** | H | W | 3-0 | Lovenkrands 4; Ferguson 19; Arteta 54 |
| 43 | prem | **Dundee Utd** | A | W | 4-1 | de Boer 11,45; Arveladze 18,69 |
| 44 | scsf | **Motherwell** | H | W | 4-3 | Konterman 2; Mols 56; Amoruso 60; Partridge 73 og |
| 45 | prem | **Celtic** | H | L | 1-2 | de Boer 57 |
| 46 | prem | **Dundee** | A | D | 2-2 | Wilkie 1 og; Arteta 85 pen |
| 47 | prem | **Kilmarnock** | H | W | 4-0 | Mols 6,7; Arveladze 59; Caniggia 80 |
| 48 | prem | **Hearts** | A | W | 2-0 | de Boer 65; Lovenkrands 73 |
| 49 | prem | **Dunfermline** | H | W | 6-1 | Mols 4; Caniggia 16; Arveladze 30; de Boer 64; Thompson 67; Arteta 90 pen |
| 50 | scf | **Dundee** | N | W | 1-0 | Amoruso 66 |

Home / Away / Neutral

## ATTENDANCES

**HOME GROUND:** IBROX **CAPACITY:** 50420 **AVERAGE LEAGUE AT HOME:** 48814

| | | | | | | | | | | | |
|---|---|---|---|---|---|---|---|---|---|---|---|
| 12 | Celtic | 59027 | 28 | Dundee | 49112 | 42 | Dunfermline | 24752 | 36 | Livingston | 10004 |
| 37 | Celtic | 58787 | 47 | Kilmarnock | 49036 | 48 | Hearts | 15632 | 7 | Livingston | 10003 |
| 38 | Celtic | 52000 | 18 | Hibernian | 48798 | 19 | Aberdeen | 14915 | 14 | Hibernian | 10000 |
| 50 | Dundee | 50000 | 9 | Partick | 48696 | 1 | Kilmarnock | 13972 | 40 | Dunfermline | 9875 |
| 23 | Celtic | 49874 | 6 | Hearts | 48581 | 30 | Hibernian | 13686 | 35 | Ayr | 9608 |
| 45 | Celtic | 49740 | 20 | Dunfermline | 48431 | 27 | Kilmarnock | 13396 | 46 | Dundee | 9195 |
| 49 | Dunfermline | 49731 | 15 | Kilmarnock | 48368 | 21 | Hearts | 12156 | 5 | Dunfermline | 8948 |
| 31 | Aberdeen | 49667 | 11 | Zizkov | 47646 | 3 | Hibernian | 11663 | 33 | Dunfermline | 8754 |
| 41 | Partick | 49472 | 24 | Dundee Utd | 47639 | 26 | Motherwell | 11234 | 17 | Dunfermline | 8415 |
| 34 | Hearts | 49459 | 2 | Dundee | 47044 | 43 | Dundee Utd | 10271 | 8 | Zizkov | 5500 |
| 13 | Motherwell | 49376 | 22 | Livingston | 45992 | 16 | Dundee | 10124 | 29 | Arbroath | 4125 |
| 39 | Motherwell | 49240 | 32 | Hearts | 31609 | 25 | Partick | 10022 | | | |
| 4 | Aberdeen | 49219 | 44 | Motherwell | 29352 | 10 | Dundee Utd | 10013 | | | |

## KEY PLAYERS - GOALSCORERS

**1 Michael Mols**

ntl:home
Digital TV

| | |
|---|---|
| **Goals in the League** | 13 |
| **Goals in all competitions** | 14 |
| **Contribution to Attacking Power** Average number of minutes between League team goals while on pitch | 36 |
| **Player Strike Rate** The total number of minutes he was on the pitch for every League goal scored | 144 |
| **Club Strike Rate** Average number of minutes between League goals scored by club | 20 |

| | PLAYER | GOALS LGE | GOALS ALL | POWER | S RATE |
|---|---|---|---|---|---|
| 2 | Shota Arveladze | 15 | 16 | 31 | 154 mins |
| 3 | Ronald de Boer | 16 | 20 | 31 | 166 mins |
| 4 | Barry Ferguson | 16 | 18 | 33 | 197 mins |
| 5 | Peter Lovenkrands | 9 | 12 | 37 | 206 mins |

## KEY PLAYERS - MIDFIELDERS

**1 Mikel Arteta**

ntl:home
Digital TV

| | |
|---|---|
| **Goals in the League** | 4 |
| **Goals in all competitions** | 5 |
| **Defensive Rating** Average number of mins between League goals conceded while on the pitch | 189 |
| **Contribution to Attacking Power** Average number of minutes between League team goals while on pitch | 34 |
| **Scoring Difference** Defensive Rating minus Contribution to Attacking Power | 155 |

| | PLAYER | GOALS LGE | GOALS ALL | DEF RATE | ATT POWER | SCORE DIFF |
|---|---|---|---|---|---|---|
| 2 | Ronald de Boer | 16 | 20 | 127 | 32 | 95 mins |
| 3 | Barry Ferguson | 16 | 18 | 126 | 34 | 92 mins |
| 4 | Peter Lovenkrands | 9 | 12 | 125 | 37 | 88 mins |

## KEY PLAYERS - DEFENDERS

**1 Kevin Muscat**

ntl:home

| | |
|---|---|
| **Goals Conceded in League** | 12 |
| **Goals Conceded in all competitions** | 19 |
| **Clean Sheets** In League games when he played at least 70 mins | 14 |
| **Defensive Rating** Ave number of mins between League goals conceded while on the pitch | 162 |
| **Club Defensive Rating** Average number of mins between League goals conceded by the club this season | 71 |

| | PLAYER | CON LGE | CON ALL | CLN SHEETS | DEF RATE |
|---|---|---|---|---|---|
| 2 | Robert Malcolm | 12 | 18 | 11 | 160 mins |
| 3 | Craig Moore | 23 | 30 | 18 | 134 mins |
| 4 | Fernando Ricksen | 26 | 35 | 17 | 120 mins |
| 5 | Arthur Numan | 21 | 27 | 10 | 108 mins |

## KEY GOALKEEPER

**1 Stefan Klos**

ntl:home

| | |
|---|---|
| **Goals Conceded in the League** | 28 |
| **Goals Conceded in all competitions** | 38 |
| **Clean Sheets** In games when he played at least 70 mins | 19 |
| **Goals to Shots Ratio** The average number of shots on target per each League goal conceded | 4.8 |
| **Defensive Rating** Ave number of mins between League goals conceded while on the pitch | 122 |

## DISCIPLINARY RECORDS

| | PLAYER | YELLOW | RED | AVE |
|---|---|---|---|---|
| 1 | McCann | 4 | 0 | 259 |
| 2 | Muscat | 6 | 0 | 324 |
| 3 | Ricksen | 6 | 1 | 445 |
| 4 | Lovenkrands | 4 | 0 | 462 |
| 5 | Moore | 6 | 0 | 513 |
| 6 | Amoruso | 4 | 0 | 528 |
| 7 | Caniggia | 2 | 0 | 544 |
| 8 | Arteta | 3 | 0 | 694 |
| 9 | Ferguson, B | 4 | 0 | 787 |
| 10 | Mols | 2 | 0 | 938 |
| 11 | Malcolm | 2 | 0 | 957 |
| 12 | de Boer | 2 | 0 | 1329 |
| 13 | Ross | 1 | 0 | 1407 |
| | Other | 4 | 0 | |
| | TOTAL | 50 | 1 | |

## TOP POINT EARNERS

| | PLAYER | GAMES | AV PTS |
|---|---|---|---|
| 1 | Stephen Hughes | 5 | 3.00 |
| 2 | Kevin Muscat | 22 | 2.77 |
| 3 | Robert Malcolm | 20 | 2.65 |
| 4 | Craig Moore | 34 | 2.62 |
| 5 | Shota Arveladze | 23 | 2.61 |
| 6 | Ronald de Boer | 25 | 2.60 |
| 7 | Mikel Arteta | 20 | 2.55 |
| 8 | Stefan Klos | 38 | 2.55 |
| 9 | Arthur Numan | 24 | 2.54 |
| 10 | Barry Ferguson | 35 | 2.51 |
| | CLUB AVERAGE: | | 2.55 |

## LEAGUE APPEARANCES, BOOKINGS AND CAPS

| | AGE (on 01/07/03) | IN SQUAD | COUNTING GAMES | MINUTES ON PITCH | YELLOW CARDS | RED CARDS | THIS SEASON | NATIONAL SIDE |
|---|---|---|---|---|---|---|---|---|
| **Goalkeepers** | | | | | | | | |
| Stefan Klos | 31 | 38 | 38 | 3420 | 2 | 0 | - | Germany |
| Allan McGregor | 21 | 38 | 0 | 0 | 0 | 0 | - | Scotland |
| **Defenders** | | | | | | | | |
| Lorenzo Amoruso | 32 | 24 | 23 | 2113 | 4 | 0 | - | Italy |
| Jerome Bonnissel | 30 | 4 | 1 | 170 | 0 | 0 | - | France |
| Andrew Dowie | 20 | 0 | 0 | 0 | 0 | 0 | - | Scotland |
| Dan Eggen | 33 | 2 | 0 | 0 | 0 | 0 | - | Norway |
| Robert Malcolm | 22 | 29 | 20 | 1914 | 2 | 0 | 3 | Scotland (64) |
| Craig Moore | 27 | 35 | 34 | 3078 | 6 | 0 | - | Australia |
| Kevin Muscat | 29 | 23 | 22 | 1947 | 6 | 0 | - | Australia |
| Arthur Numan | 33 | 26 | 24 | 2274 | 1 | 0 | - | Holland |
| Paul Reid | 21 | 1 | 0 | 0 | 0 | 0 | - | England |
| Fernando Ricksen | 26 | 35 | 34 | 3120 | 6 | 1 | 8 | Holland (6) |
| Maurice Ross | 22 | 25 | 14 | 1407 | 1 | 0 | 9 | Scotland (64) |
| **Midfielders** | | | | | | | | |
| Mikel Arteta | 21 | 27 | 20 | 2082 | 3 | 0 | - | Spain |
| Ronald de Boer | 33 | 33 | 25 | 2658 | 2 | 0 | 4 | Holland (6) |
| Barry Ferguson | 25 | 36 | 35 | 3150 | 4 | 0 | 5 | Scotland (64) |
| James Gibson | 23 | 1 | 0 | 0 | 0 | 0 | - | Scotland |
| Stephen Hughes | 20 | 20 | 5 | 659 | 0 | 0 | - | Scotland |
| Alan Hutton | 18 | 2 | 0 | 45 | 0 | 0 | - | England |
| Bert Konterman | 32 | 23 | 3 | 548 | 0 | 0 | - | Holland |
| Russell Latapy | 34 | 17 | 1 | 207 | 0 | 0 | - | Trinidad & Tobago |
| Peter Lovenkrands | 23 | 27 | 16 | 1851 | 4 | 0 | 4 | Denmark (10) |
| Neil McCann | 28 | 18 | 10 | 1039 | 4 | 0 | 1 | Scotland (64) |
| Steve McLean | 20 | 6 | 0 | 38 | 0 | 0 | - | Scotland |
| Christian Nerlinger | 30 | 8 | 0 | 45 | 0 | 0 | - | Germany |
| **Forwards** | | | | | | | | |
| Shota Arveladze | 30 | 30 | 23 | 2303 | 0 | 0 | - | Georgia |
| Claudio Caniggia | 36 | 29 | 6 | 1089 | 2 | 0 | - | Argentina |
| Billy Dodds | 34 | 10 | 0 | 168 | 0 | 0 | - | Scotland |
| Tore Andre Flo | 30 | 4 | 1 | 144 | 0 | 0 | 6 | Norway (24) |
| Michael Mols | 32 | 28 | 16 | 1876 | 2 | 0 | - | Holland |
| Steven Thompson | 24 | 8 | 1 | 245 | 1 | 0 | 7 | Scotland (64) |

KEY: LEAGUE BOOKINGS CAPS (FIFA RANKING)

## GOALS

| | PLAYER | MINS | GOALS | AVE |
|---|---|---|---|---|
| 1 | de Boer | 2658 | 16 | 166 |
| 2 | Ferguson, B | 3150 | 16 | 197 |
| 3 | Arveladze | 2303 | 15 | 154 |
| 4 | Mols | 1876 | 13 | 144 |
| 5 | Lovenkrands | 1851 | 9 | 206 |
| 6 | Caniggia | 1089 | 8 | 136 |
| 7 | Amoruso | 2113 | 4 | 528 |
| 8 | Arteta | 2082 | 4 | 521 |
| 9 | Moore | 3078 | 3 | 1026 |
| 10 | Ricksen | 3120 | 3 | 1040 |
| 11 | Thompson | 245 | 2 | 123 |
| 12 | McCann | 1039 | 2 | 520 |
| 13 | Malcolm | 1914 | 1 | 1914 |
| | Other | | 5 | |
| | TOTAL | | 101 | |

## TEAM OF THE SEASON

| GOALKEEPER | GAMES | DEF RATE |
|---|---|---|
| Stefan Klos | 38 | 122 |
| **DEFENDERS** | **GAMES** | **DEF RATE** |
| Kevin Muscat | 22 | 162 |
| Robert Malcolm | 20 | 160 |
| Craig Moore | 34 | 134 |
| Fernando Ricksen | 34 | 120 |
| **MIDFIELDERS** | **GAMES** | **SCORE DIFF** |
| Mikel Arteta | 20 | 155 |
| Ronald de Boer | 25 | 95 |
| Barry Ferguson | 35 | 92 |
| Peter Lovenkrands | 16 | 88 |
| **GOALSCORERS** | **GAMES** | **STRIKE RATE** |
| Michael Mols | 16 | 144 |
| Shota Arveladze | 23 | 154 |

Games = games playing more than 70 minutes

## SQUAD APPEARANCES

| | 1 | 2 | 3 | 4 | 5 | 6 | 7 | 8 | 9 | 10 | 11 | 12 | 13 | 14 | 15 | 16 | 17 | 18 | 19 | 20 | 21 | 22 | 23 | 24 | 25 |
|---|---|---|---|---|---|---|---|---|---|---|---|---|---|---|---|---|---|---|---|---|---|---|---|---|---|
| Venue | A | H | A | H | A | H | A | A | H | A | H | A | H | A | H | A | A | H | A | H | A | H | H | H | A |
| Competition | L | L | L | L | L | L | L | E | L | L | E | L | L | I | L | L | I | L | L | L | L | L | L | L | L |
| Result | D | W | W | W | W | W | W | L | W | W | W | D | W | W | W | W | W | W | D | W | W | W | W | W | W |

| | 26 | 27 | 28 | 29 | 30 | 31 | 32 | 33 | 34 | 35 | 36 | 37 | 38 | 39 | 40 | 41 | 42 | 43 | 44 | 45 | 46 | 47 | 48 | 49 | 50 |
|---|---|---|---|---|---|---|---|---|---|---|---|---|---|---|---|---|---|---|---|---|---|---|---|---|---|
| Venue | A | A | H | A | A | H | A | A | H | A | A | A | A | H | A | H | H | A | H | H | A | H | A | H | A |
| Competition | L | L | L | S | L | L | I | L | L | S | L | L | I | L | S | L | S | L | S | L | L | L | L | L | S |
| Result | L | W | W | W | W | W | W | W | W | W | W | L | W | W | D | W | W | W | W | L | D | W | W | W | W |

**Goalkeepers**
Stefan Klos
Allan McGregor

**Defenders**
Lorenzo Amoruso
Jerome Bonnissel
Andrew Dowie
Dan Eggen
Robert Malcolm
Craig Moore
Kevin Muscat
Arthur Numan
Paul Reid
Fernando Ricksen
Maurice Ross

**Midfielders**
Mikel Arteta
Ronald de Boer
Barry Ferguson
James Gibson
Stephen Hughes
Alan Hutton
Bert Konterman
Russell Latapy
Peter Lovenkrands
Steve McLean
Christian Nerlinger

**Forwards**
Shota Arveladze
Claudio Caniggia
Billy Dodds
Tore Andre Flo
Neil McCann
Michael Mols
Steven Thompson

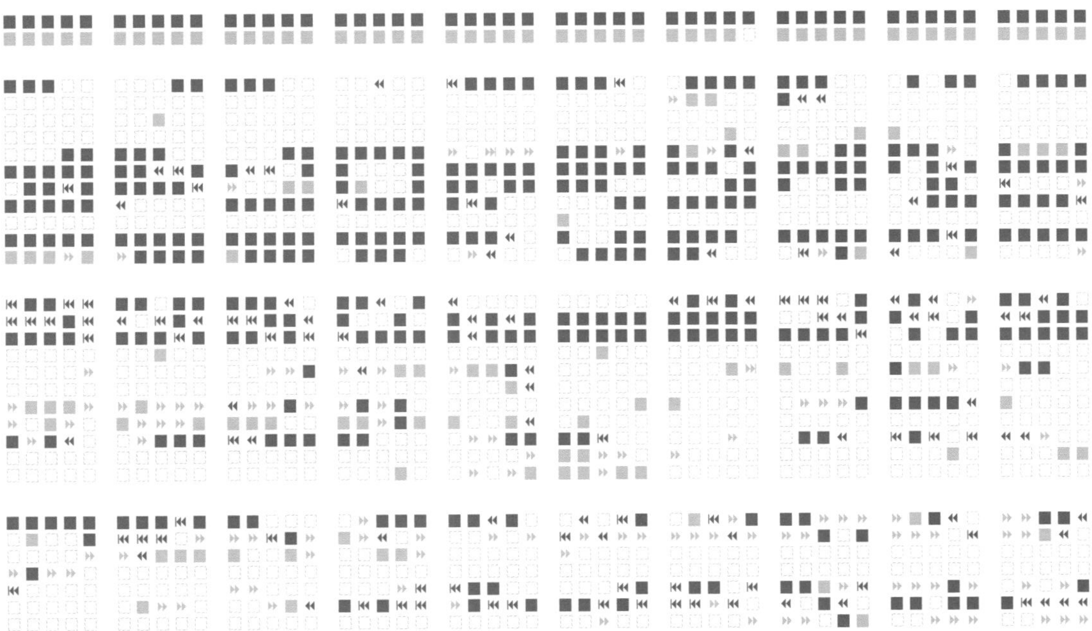

KEY: On all match; Subbed or sent off (Counting game); Subbed on from bench (Counting Game); Subbed on and then subbed or sent off (Counting Game); Not in 16
On bench; Subbed or sent off (playing less than 70 minutes); Subbed on (playing less than 70 minutes); Subbed on and then subbed or sent off (playing less than 70 minutes)

# CELTIC

Final Position: **2nd**

KEY: Won Drawn Lost

**NICKNAME:** THE BHOYS

| | | | | | | |
|---|---|---|---|---|---|---|
| 1 | prem | Dunfermline | H | W | 2-1 | Larsson 41,65 |
| 2 | prem | Aberdeen | A | W | 4-0 | Mjallby 5; Sutton 34; Sylla 53; Lambert 66 |
| 3 | ecql1 | Basel | H | W | 3-1 | Larsson 4 pen; Sutton 51; Sylla 87 |
| 4 | prem | Dundee Utd | H | W | 5-0 | McNamara 24; Sutton 25; Petrov 33; Hartson 79; Larsson 81 |
| 5 | prem | Partick | A | W | 1-0 | Larsson 71 |
| 6 | ecql2 | Basel | A | L | 0-2 | |
| 7 | prem | Livingston | H | W | 2-0 | Larsson 26; Balde 38 |
| 8 | prem | Motherwell | A | L | 1-2 | Hartson 87 |
| 9 | prem | Hibernian | H | W | 1-0 | Hartson 31 |
| 10 | uc1rl1 | FK Suduva | H | W | 8-1 | Larsson 15,23,29; Petrov 27; Sutton 35; Lambert 50; Hartson 71; Valgaeren 82 |
| 11 | prem | Dundee | A | W | 1-0 | Larsson 17 |
| 12 | prem | Kilmarnock | H | W | 5-0 | Larsson 11,20,90 pen; Sutton 14,66 |
| 13 | uc1rl2 | FK Suduva | A | W | 2-0 | Fernandez 12; Thompson 25 |
| 14 | prem | Rangers | H | D | 3-3 | Larsson 39,55; Sutton 77 |
| 15 | prem | Hearts | A | W | 4-1 | Sutton 3; Petrov 9; Larsson 36,41 |
| 16 | cisr3 | Inverness CT | H | W | 4-2 | Maloney 4; Hartson 20,60; Thompson 43 |
| 17 | prem | Dunfermline | A | W | 4-1 | Larsson 25; Thompson 32; Petrov 74; Sutton 84 |
| 18 | uc2rl1 | Blackburn | H | W | 1-0 | Larsson 85 |
| 19 | prem | Aberdeen | H | W | 7-0 | Hartson 26,35,51,81; Larsson 43; Balde 71; Maloney 88 |
| 20 | cisqf | Partick | H | W | 5-4* | Lambert 42 (*on penalties) |
| 21 | prem | Dundee Utd | A | W | 2-0 | Hartson 14; Sutton 88 |
| 22 | uc2rl2 | Blackburn | A | W | 2-0 | Larsson 15; Sutton 68 |
| 23 | prem | Partick | H | W | 4-0 | Sutton 10; Petrov 33,68; Larsson 90 |
| 24 | prem | Livingston | A | W | 2-0 | Larsson 6 pen,83 |
| 25 | uc3rl1 | Celta Vigo | H | W | 1-0 | Larsson 52 |
| 26 | prem | Motherwell | H | W | 3-1 | Larsson 53; Leitch 67 og; Valgaeren 72 |
| 27 | prem | Hibernian | A | W | 1-0 | Petrov 76 |
| 28 | prem | Rangers | A | L | 2-3 | Sutton 1; Hartson 61 |
| 29 | uc3rl2 | Celta Vigo | A | L | 1-2 | Hartson 37 |
| 30 | prem | Kilmarnock | A | D | 1-1 | Valgaeren 66 |
| 31 | prem | Dundee | H | W | 2-0 | Hartson 38; Larsson 54 |
| 32 | prem | Hearts | H | W | 4-2 | Hartson 22,44,68; Larsson 73 |
| 33 | prem | Dunfermline | H | W | 1-0 | Larsson 19 |
| 34 | prem | Aberdeen | A | D | 1-1 | Larsson 30 |
| 35 | scr3 | St Mirren | H | W | 3-0 | Larsson 47,57; Sylla 70 |
| 36 | prem | Dundee Utd | H | W | 2-0 | Hartson 25; Larsson 29 |
| 37 | prem | Partick | A | W | 2-0 | Sutton 7,33 |
| 38 | cissf | Dundee Utd | H | W | 3-0 | Balde 52,90; Larsson 80 |
| 39 | prem | Livingston | H | W | 2-1 | Sylla 77; Sutton 85 |
| 40 | uc4rl1 | Stuttgart | H | W | 3-1 | Lambert 36; Maloney 45; Petrov 68 |
| 41 | scr4 | St Johnstone | H | W | 3-0 | Hartson 32 pen,86 pen; Smith, J 76 |
| 42 | uc4rl2 | Stuttgart | A | L | 2-3 | Thompson 12; Sutton 14 |
| 43 | prem | Hibernian | H | W | 3-2 | Hartson 1,23; Mjallby 90 |
| 44 | prem | Rangers | H | W | 1-0 | Hartson 57 |
| 45 | ucqfl1 | Liverpool | H | D | 1-1 | Larsson 2 |
| 46 | cisf | Rangers | N | L | 1-2 | Larsson 57 |
| 47 | ucqfl2 | Liverpool | A | W | 2-0 | Thompson 45; Hartson 81 |
| 48 | scqf | Inverness CT | A | L | 0-1 | |
| 49 | prem | Dundee | A | D | 1-1 | Thompson 11 |
| 50 | ucsfl1 | Boavista | H | D | 1-1 | Larsson 51 |
| 51 | prem | Kilmarnock | H | W | 2-0 | Larsson 20; Petrov 73 |
| 52 | prem | Hearts | A | L | 1-2 | Larsson 59 |
| 53 | ucsfl2 | Boavista | A | W | 1-0 | Larsson 78 |
| 54 | prem | Rangers | A | W | 2-1 | Thompson 29 pen; Hartson 43 |
| 55 | prem | Dunfermline | A | W | 4-1 | Larsson 21; Petrov 29,32; Thompson 59 pen |
| 56 | prem | Motherwell | A | W | 4-0 | Petrov 36,56; Lambert 61,65 |
| 57 | prem | Hearts | H | W | 1-0 | Thompson 29 |
| 58 | prem | Dundee | H | W | 6-2 | Larsson 14; Thompson 27,30; Maloney 52,63; Mjallby 77 |
| 59 | ucfin | Porto | N | L | 2-3 | Larsson 47,56 |
| 60 | prem | Kilmarnock | A | W | 4-0 | Sutton 16,43; Thompson 54 pen; Petrov 83 |

Home Away Neutral

## ATTENDANCES

**HOME GROUND:** CELTIC PARK **CAPACITY:** 60506 **AVERAGE LEAGUE AT HOME:** 57443

| | | | | | | | | | | | |
|---|---|---|---|---|---|---|---|---|---|---|---|
| 50 | Boavista | 60000 | 58 | Dundee | 57000 | 47 | Liverpool | 44238 | 27 | Hibernian | 12042 |
| 45 | Liverpool | 59759 | 7 | Livingston | 56988 | 10 | FK Suduva | 36824 | 56 | Motherwell | 12037 |
| 18 | Blackburn | 59553 | 51 | Kilmarnock | 56966 | 6 | Basel | 35000 | 53 | Boavista | 11000 |
| 14 | Rangers | 59027 | 4 | Dundee Utd | 56907 | 16 | Inverness CT | 34592 | 21 | Dundee Utd | 10664 |
| 40 | Stuttgart | 59000 | 26 | Motherwell | 56733 | 35 | St Mirren | 29976 | 24 | Livingston | 10002 |
| 44 | Rangers | 58787 | 9 | Hibernian | 56703 | 22 | Blackburn | 29689 | 11 | Dundee | 9483 |
| 19 | Aberdeen | 58526 | 31 | Dundee | 56162 | 20 | Partick | 26333 | 30 | Kilmarnock | 9225 |
| 32 | Hearts | 58450 | 36 | Dundee Utd | 55204 | 41 | St Johnstone | 26205 | 17 | Dunfermline | 9139 |
| 33 | Dunfermline | 58387 | 25 | Celta Vigo | 53726 | 29 | Celta Vigo | 19080 | 49 | Dundee | 9013 |
| 57 | Hearts | 58175 | 59 | Porto | 52972 | 38 | Dundee Utd | 18856 | 55 | Dunfermline | 8923 |
| 23 | Partick | 57839 | 46 | Rangers | 52000 | 2 | Aberdeen | 17284 | 8 | Motherwell | 8448 |
| 43 | Hibernian | 57512 | 28 | Rangers | 49874 | 60 | Kilmarnock | 16722 | 5 | Partick | 8033 |
| 12 | Kilmarnock | 57469 | 54 | Rangers | 49740 | 34 | Aberdeen | 16331 | 37 | Partick | 7119 |
| 1 | Dunfermline | 57415 | 3 | Basel | 49500 | 52 | Hearts | 15855 | 48 | Inverness CT | 6050 |
| 39 | Livingston | 57169 | 42 | Stuttgart | 45000 | 15 | Hearts | 13911 | 13 | FK Suduva | 1200 |

## KEY PLAYERS - GOALSCORERS

1 John Hartson

| | |
|---|---|
| Goals in the League | 18 |
| Goals in all competitions | 25 |
| Contribution to Attacking Power<br>Average number of minutes between League team goals while on pitch | 40 |
| Player Strike Rate<br>The total number of minutes he was on the pitch for every League goal scored | 96 |
| Club Strike Rate<br>Average number of minutes between League goals scored by club | 20 |

| | PLAYER | GOALS LGE | GOALS ALL | POWER | S RATE |
|---|---|---|---|---|---|
| 2 | Henrik Larsson | 28 | 44 | 32 | 106 mins |
| 3 | Chris Sutton | 15 | 19 | 35 | 163 mins |
| 4 | Stilian Petrov | 12 | 14 | 32 | 225 mins |
| 5 | Alan Thompson | 8 | 12 | 36 | 288 mins |

## KEY PLAYERS - MIDFIELDERS

1 Jackie McNamara

| | |
|---|---|
| Goals in the League | 1 |
| Goals in all competitions | 1 |
| Defensive Rating<br>Average number of mins between League goals conceded while on the pitch | 243 |
| Contribution to Attacking Power<br>Average number of minutes between League team goals while on pitch | 39 |
| Scoring Difference<br>Defensive Rating minus Contribution to Attacking Power | 204 |

| | PLAYER | GOALS LGE | GOALS ALL | DEF RATE | ATT POWER | SCORE DIFF |
|---|---|---|---|---|---|---|
| 2 | Steve Guppy | 0 | 0 | 191 | 31 | 160 mins |
| 3 | Neil Lennon | 0 | 0 | 136 | 35 | 101 mins |
| 4 | Paul Lambert | 3 | 6 | 133 | 36 | 97 mins |
| 5 | Stilian Petrov | 12 | 14 | 129 | 33 | 96 mins |

## KEY PLAYERS - DEFENDERS

1 Mohammed Sylla

| | |
|---|---|
| Goals Conceded in League | 5 |
| Goals Conceded in all competitions | 9 |
| Clean Sheets<br>In League games when he played at least 70 mins | 7 |
| Defensive Rating<br>Ave number of mins between League goals conceded while on the pitch | 223 |
| Club Defensive Rating<br>Average number of mins between League goals conceded by the club this season | 76 |

| | PLAYER | CON LGE | CON ALL | CLN SHEETS | DEF RATE |
|---|---|---|---|---|---|
| 2 | Dianbobo Balde | 24 | 41 | 20 | 134 mins |
| 3 | Joos Valgaeren | 23 | 40 | 19 | 133 mins |
| 4 | Ulrik Laursen | 15 | 25 | 13 | 128 mins |

## KEY GOALKEEPER

1 Robert Douglas

| | |
|---|---|
| Goals Conceded in the League | 14 |
| Goals Conceded in all competitions | 34 |
| Clean Sheets<br>In games when he played at least 70 mins | 12 |
| Goals to Shots Ratio<br>The average number of shots on target per each League goal conceded | 4.4 |
| Defensive Rating<br>Ave number of mins between League goals conceded while on the pitch | 129 |

## DISCIPLINARY RECORDS

| | PLAYER | YELLOW | RED | AVE |
|---|---|---|---|---|
| 1 | Sutton | 8 | 1 | 272 |
| 2 | Thompson | 8 | 0 | 288 |
| 3 | Broto | 2 | 0 | 390 |
| 4 | Lennon | 5 | 0 | 488 |
| 5 | Petrov | 5 | 0 | 540 |
| 6 | Sylla | 2 | 0 | 557 |
| 7 | Laursen | 3 | 0 | 642 |
| 8 | Hartson | 2 | 0 | 867 |
| 9 | Agathe | 2 | 0 | 1043 |
| 10 | Balde | 3 | 0 | 1068 |
| 11 | Mjallby | 1 | 0 | 1158 |
| 12 | McNamara | 1 | 0 | 1215 |
| 13 | Lambert | 1 | 0 | 2531 |
| | Other | 2 | 0 | |
| | TOTAL | 45 | 1 | |

## TOP POINT EARNERS

| | PLAYER | GAMES | AV PTS |
|---|---|---|---|
| 1 | Mohammed Sylla | 9 | 3.00 |
| 2 | Jonathan Gould | 2 | 3.00 |
| 3 | Bobby Petta | 2 | 3.00 |
| 4 | Shaun Maloney | 5 | 3.00 |
| 5 | David Fernandez | 3 | 3.00 |
| 6 | Jamie Smith | 3 | 3.00 |
| 7 | Magnus Hedman | 8 | 2.75 |
| 8 | Javier Sanchez Broto | 8 | 2.75 |
| 9 | Steve Guppy | 11 | 2.73 |
| 10 | Jackie McNamara | 13 | 2.69 |
| | CLUB AVERAGE: | | 2.55 |

## GOALS

| | PLAYER | MINS | GOALS | AVE |
|---|---|---|---|---|
| 1 | Larsson | 2967 | 28 | 106 |
| 2 | Hartson | 1735 | 18 | 96 |
| 3 | Sutton | 2451 | 15 | 163 |
| 4 | Petrov | 2701 | 12 | 225 |
| 5 | Thompson | 2304 | 8 | 288 |
| 6 | Lambert | 2531 | 3 | 844 |
| 7 | Mjallby | 1158 | 3 | 386 |
| 8 | Maloney | 620 | 3 | 207 |
| 9 | Sylla | 1114 | 2 | 557 |
| 10 | Balde | 3204 | 2 | 1602 |
| 11 | Valgaeren | 3053 | 2 | 1527 |
| 12 | McNamara | 1215 | 1 | 1215 |
| | Other | | 1 | |
| | TOTAL | | 98 | |

## TEAM OF THE SEASON

| GOALKEEPER | GAMES | DEF RATE |
|---|---|---|
| Robert Douglas | 20 | 129 |
| **DEFENDERS** | **GAMES** | **DEF RATE** |
| Mohammed Sylla | 9 | 223 |
| Dianbobo Balde | 36 | 134 |
| Joos Valgaeren | 34 | 133 |
| Ulrik Laursen | 21 | 128 |
| **MIDFIELDERS** | **GAMES** | **SCORE DIFF** |
| Jackie McNamara | 13 | 204 |
| Steve Guppy | 11 | 160 |
| Neil Lennon | 26 | 101 |
| Paul Lambert | 28 | 97 |
| **GOALSCORERS** | **GAMES** | **STRIKE RATE** |
| John Hartson | 17 | 96 |
| Henrik Larsson | 32 | 106 |

Games = games playing more than 70 minutes

## LEAGUE APPEARANCES, BOOKINGS AND CAPS

| | AGE (on 01/07/03) | IN THE SQUAD | COUNTING GAMES | MINUTES ON PITCH | YELLOW CARDS | RED CARDS | THIS SEASON | NATIONAL SIDE |
|---|---|---|---|---|---|---|---|---|
| **Goalkeepers** | | | | | | | | |
| Javier Sanchez Broto | 31 | 14 | 8 | 781 | 2 | 0 | - | Spain |
| Robert Douglas | 31 | 26 | 20 | 1808 | 0 | 0 | 7 | Scotland (64) |
| Jonathan Gould | 34 | 16 | 2 | 180 | 0 | 0 | - | England |
| Magnus Hedman | 30 | 13 | 8 | 720 | 0 | 0 | 5 | Sweden (20) |
| David Marshall | - | 6 | 0 | 0 | 0 | 0 | - | Scotland |
| **Defenders** | | | | | | | | |
| Dianbobo Balde | 27 | 36 | 36 | 3204 | 3 | 0 | - | France |
| Tommy Boyd | 37 | 0 | 0 | 0 | 0 | 0 | - | Scotland |
| Stephen Crainey | 22 | 37 | 3 | 387 | 0 | 0 | 2 | Scotland (64) |
| John Kennedy | 19 | 1 | 0 | 0 | 0 | 0 | - | Scotland |
| Ulrik Laursen | 27 | 23 | 21 | 1927 | 3 | 0 | - | Denmark |
| Johan Mjallby | 32 | 15 | 12 | 1158 | 1 | 0 | 4 | Sweden (20) |
| Mohammed Sylla | 26 | 19 | 9 | 1114 | 2 | 0 | - | Ivory coast |
| Joos Valgaeren | 27 | 35 | 34 | 3053 | 1 | 0 | 5 | Belgium (16) |
| Stanislav Varga | 30 | 3 | 1 | 90 | 0 | 0 | - | Slovakia |
| **Midfielders** | | | | | | | | |
| Didier Agathe | 27 | 27 | 21 | 2086 | 2 | 0 | - | France |
| Steve Guppy | 34 | 19 | 11 | 1145 | 0 | 0 | - | England |
| Colin Healy | 23 | 1 | 0 | 4 | 0 | 0 | 10 | Rep of Ireland (15) |
| Paul Lambert | 33 | 32 | 28 | 2531 | 1 | 0 | 8 | Scotland (64) |
| Neil Lennon | 32 | 28 | 26 | 2443 | 5 | 0 | - | N Ireland |
| Jackie McNamara | 29 | 27 | 13 | 1215 | 1 | 0 | 5 | Scotland (64) |
| Liam Miller | 22 | 1 | 0 | 0 | 0 | 0 | - | Rep of Ireland |
| Stilian Petrov | 24 | 34 | 29 | 2701 | 5 | 0 | - | Bulgaria |
| Bobby Petta | 28 | 2 | 2 | 161 | 0 | 0 | - | Holland |
| Jamie Smith | 22 | 16 | 3 | 427 | 0 | 0 | 2 | Scotland (64) |
| Alan Thompson | 29 | 29 | 24 | 2304 | 8 | 0 | - | England |
| Ross Wallace | - | 0 | 0 | 0 | 0 | 0 | - | Scotland |
| **Forwards** | | | | | | | | |
| David Fernandez | 27 | 16 | 3 | 408 | 0 | 0 | - | Spain |
| John Hartson | 28 | 29 | 17 | 1735 | 2 | 0 | 6 | Wales (50) |
| Henrik Larsson | 31 | 35 | 32 | 2967 | 1 | 0 | 1 | Sweden (20) |
| Simon Lynch | 21 | 1 | 0 | 0 | 0 | 0 | - | Canada |
| Shaun Maloney | 20 | 36 | 5 | 620 | 0 | 0 | - | Scotland |
| Chris Sutton | 30 | 30 | 26 | 2451 | 8 | 1 | - | England |

KEY: LEAGUE BOOKINGS CAPS (FIFA RANKING)

## SQUAD APPEARANCES

| Match | 1 | 2 | 3 | 4 | 5 | 6 | 7 | 8 | 9 | 10 | 11 | 12 | 13 | 14 | 15 | 16 | 17 | 18 | 19 | 20 | 21 | 22 | 23 | 24 | 25 | 26 | 27 | 28 | 29 | 30 |
|---|---|---|---|---|---|---|---|---|---|---|---|---|---|---|---|---|---|---|---|---|---|---|---|---|---|---|---|---|---|---|
| Venue | H | A | H | H | A | A | H | A | H | H | A | H | A | H | A | H | A | H | H | H | A | A | H | A | H | H | A | A | A | A |
| Competition | L | L | C | L | L | C | L | L | L | E | L | L | E | L | L | I | L | E | L | I | L | E | L | L | E | L | L | L | E | L |
| Result | W | W | W | W | W | L | W | L | W | W | W | W | W | D | W | W | W | W | W | W | W | W | W | W | W | W | W | L | L | D |

| Match | 31 | 32 | 33 | 34 | 35 | 36 | 37 | 38 | 39 | 40 | 41 | 42 | 43 | 44 | 45 | 46 | 47 | 48 | 49 | 50 | 51 | 52 | 53 | 54 | 55 | 56 | 57 | 58 | 59 | 60 |
|---|---|---|---|---|---|---|---|---|---|---|---|---|---|---|---|---|---|---|---|---|---|---|---|---|---|---|---|---|---|---|
| Venue | H | H | H | A | H | H | A | H | H | H | H | A | H | H | H | H | A | A | A | H | H | A | A | A | A | A | H | H | N | A |
| Competition | L | L | L | L | S | L | L | I | L | E | S | E | L | L | E | I | E | S | L | E | L | L | E | L | L | L | L | L | E | L |
| Result | W | W | W | D | W | W | W | W | W | W | W | L | W | W | D | L | W | L | D | D | W | L | W | W | W | W | W | W | L | W |

**Goalkeepers**
Javier Sanchez Broto
Robert Douglas
Jonathan Gould
Magnus Hedman
David Marshall

**Defenders**
Dianbobo Balde
Tommy Boyd
Stephen Crainey
John Kennedy
Ulrik Laursen
Johan Mjallby
Mohammed Sylla
Joos Valgaeren
Stanislav Varga

**Midfielders**
Didier Agathe
Steve Guppy
Colin Healy
Paul Lambert
Neil Lennon
Jackie McNamara
Liam Miller
Stilian Petrov
Bobby Petta
Jamie Smith
Alan Thompson
Ross Wallace

**Forwards**
David Fernandez
John Hartson
Henrik Larsson
Simon Lynch
Shaun Maloney
Chris Sutton

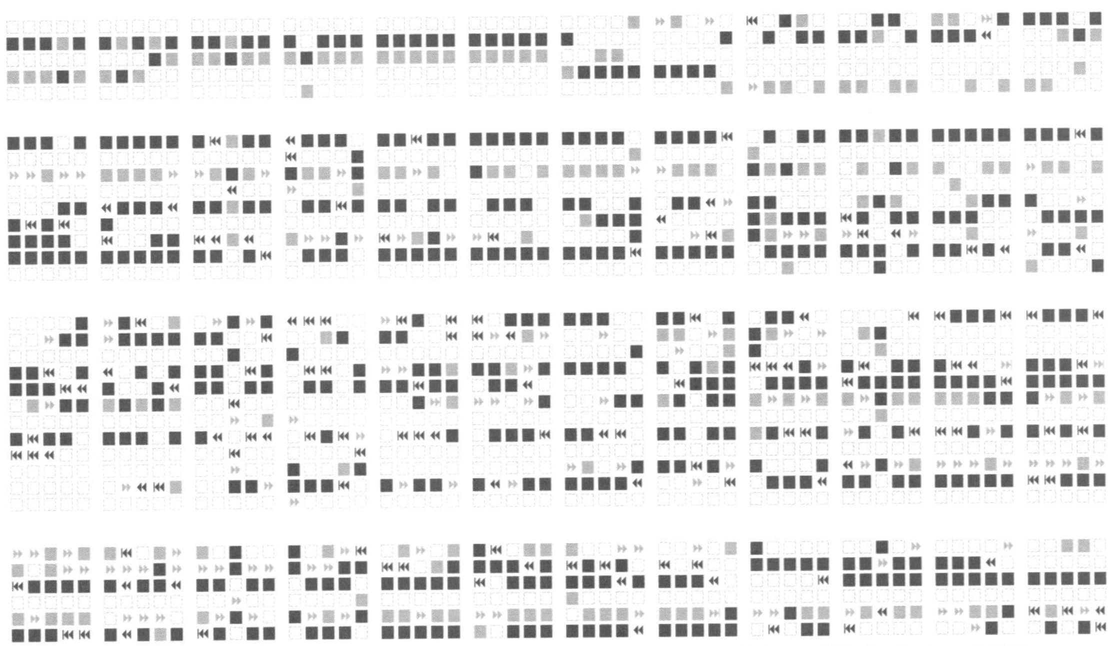

KEY: ■ On all match ■ On bench ⏮ Subbed or sent off (Counting game) « Subbed or sent off (playing less than 70 minutes) ⏭ Subbed on from bench (Counting Game) » Subbed on (playing less than 70 minutes) Subbed on and then subbed or sent off (Counting Game) Subbed on and then subbed or sent off (playing less than 70 minutes) Not in 16

# HEART OF MIDLOTHIAN

Final Position: **3rd**

NICKNAME: THE JAM TARTS

| | | | | | | |
|---|---|---|---|---|---|---|
| 1 | lge | Dundee | A | D | 1-1 | Wales 33 |
| 2 | lge | Hibernian | H | W | 5-1 | Kirk 18; de Vries 40,65,90,90 |
| 3 | lge | Aberdeen | A | D | 1-1 | de Vries 78 |
| 4 | lge | Dunfermline | H | W | 2-0 | Weir 53; de Vries 57 |
| 5 | lge | Kilmarnock | H | D | 1-1 | McMullan 30 |
| 6 | lge | Rangers | A | L | 0-2 | |
| 7 | lge | Motherwell | H | W | 4-2 | de Vries 34; Kirk 63,76; Boyack 74 |
| 8 | lge | Dundee Utd | H | W | 2-0 | Valois 25; de Vries 56 |
| 9 | cis2 | Stirling | A | W | 3-2 | Kirk 11; Valois 38; Pressley 65 pen |
| 10 | lge | Partick | A | D | 2-2 | Valois 37; Severin 79 |
| 11 | lge | Livingston | A | D | 1-1 | Stamp 46 |
| 12 | lge | Celtic | H | L | 1-4 | Wales 89 |
| 13 | cis3 | Ross County | H | W | 3-0 | Pressley 55 pen; Valois 58; Simmons 80 |
| 14 | lge | Dundee | H | L | 1-2 | McKenna 60 |
| 15 | lge | Hibernian | A | W | 2-1 | McKenna 86; Stamp 90 |
| 16 | lge | Aberdeen | H | D | 0-0 | |
| 17 | cisqf | Aberdeen | A | W | 1-0 | McKenna 66 |
| 18 | lge | Dunfermline | A | L | 1-3 | Severin 53 |
| 19 | lge | Kilmarnock | A | W | 1-0 | de Vries 48 |
| 20 | lge | Rangers | H | L | 0-4 | |
| 21 | lge | Motherwell | A | L | 1-6 | Kirk 51 |
| 22 | lge | Livingston | H | W | 2-1 | Kirk 5,70 pen |
| 23 | lge | Partick | H | W | 1-0 | Maybury 90 |
| 24 | lge | Dundee Utd | A | W | 3-0 | de Vries 26; Kirk 41,51 |
| 25 | lge | Celtic | A | L | 2-4 | de Vries 4,66 |
| 26 | lge | Dundee | A | W | 2-1 | Kirk 42; Weir 80 |
| 27 | lge | Hibernian | H | D | 4-4 | Pressley 30 pen; de Vries 62; Weir 90,90 |
| 28 | scr3 | Falkirk | A | L | 0-4 | |
| 29 | lge | Aberdeen | A | W | 1-0 | Wales 90 |
| 30 | lge | Dunfermline | H | W | 3-0 | Severin 45; Wales 49; McKenna 90 |
| 31 | cissf | Rangers | N | L | 0-1 | |
| 32 | lge | Kilmarnock | H | W | 3-0 | Maybury 50; de Vries 55; McKenna 79 |
| 33 | lge | Rangers | A | L | 0-1 | |
| 34 | lge | Motherwell | H | W | 2-1 | McKenna 30; Simmons 72 |
| 35 | lge | Livingston | A | D | 1-1 | Stamp 8 |
| 36 | lge | Dundee Utd | H | W | 2-1 | Webster 69; Kirk 78 |
| 37 | lge | Partick | A | D | 1-1 | Pressley 79 |
| 38 | lge | Celtic | H | W | 2-1 | Stamp 73; McCann 90 |
| 39 | lge | Dunfermline | A | W | 1-0 | Pressley 57 pen |
| 40 | lge | Kilmarnock | A | L | 0-1 | |
| 41 | lge | Celtic | A | L | 0-1 | |
| 42 | lge | Rangers | H | L | 0-2 | |
| 43 | lge | Dundee | H | W | 1-0 | de Vries 78 |

## ATTENDANCES

HOME GROUND: TYNECASTLE PARK CAPACITY: 18300 AVERAGE LEAGUE AT HOME: 12057

| | | | | | | | |
|---|---|---|---|---|---|---|---|
| 25 Celtic | 58450 | 34 Motherwell | 11704 | 26 Dundee | 7340 | | |
| 41 Celtic | 58175 | 8 Dundee Utd | 11532 | 39 Dunfermline | 6968 | | |
| 33 Rangers | 49459 | 4 Dunfermline | 11367 | 11 Livingston | 6512 | | |
| 6 Rangers | 48581 | 30 Dunfermline | 11281 | 19 Kilmarnock | 6511 | | |
| 31 Rangers | 31609 | 32 Kilmarnock | 10426 | 13 Ross County | 6454 | | |
| 27 Hibernian | 17732 | 14 Dundee | 10169 | 10 Partick | 6111 | | |
| 38 Celtic | 15855 | 23 Partick | 9734 | 24 Dundee Utd | 6025 | | |
| 42 Rangers | 15632 | 36 Dundee Utd | 9663 | 37 Partick | 5288 | | |
| 15 Hibernian | 15560 | 29 Aberdeen | 9322 | 18 Dunfermline | 4800 | | |
| 2 Hibernian | 15245 | 40 Kilmarnock | 9019 | 21 Motherwell | 4114 | | |
| 12 Celtic | 13911 | 7 Motherwell | 8578 | 9 Stirling | 2791 | | |
| 3 Aberdeen | 12825 | 22 Livingston | 8074 | | | | |
| 43 Dundee | 12205 | 1 Dundee | 7705 | | | | |
| 20 Rangers | 12156 | 17 Aberdeen | 7576 | | | | |
| 16 Aberdeen | 11920 | 35 Livingston | 7531 | | | | |
| 5 Kilmarnock | 11912 | 28 Falkirk | 7500 | | | | |

■ Home □ Away ▨ Neutral

## KEY PLAYERS - GOALSCORERS

**1 Andy Kirk**

| | | | |
|---|---|---|---|
| Goals in the League | 10 | Player Strike Rate<br>Average number of minutes between League goals scored by player | 155 |
| Contribution to Attacking Power<br>Average number of minutes between League team goals while on pitch | 57 | Club Strike Rate<br>Average number of minutes between League goals scored by club | 35 |

| | PLAYER | LGE GOALS | POWER | STRIKE RATE |
|---|---|---|---|---|
| 2 | Mark de Vries | 15 | 56 | 170 mins |
| 3 | Phil Stamp | 4 | 59 | 490 mins |
| 4 | Kevin McKenna | 5 | 54 | 562 mins |
| 5 | Steven Pressley | 3 | 57 | 973 mins |

## KEY PLAYERS - MIDFIELDERS

**1 Neil MacFarlane**

| | | | |
|---|---|---|---|
| Goals in the League | 0 | Contribution to Attacking Power<br>Average number of minutes between League team goals while on pitch | 64 |
| Defensive Rating<br>Average number of mins between League goals conceded while he was on the pitch | 80 | Scoring Difference<br>Defensive Rating minus Contribution to Attacking Power | 16 |

| | PLAYER | LGE GOALS | DEF RATE | POWER | SCORE DIFF |
|---|---|---|---|---|---|
| 2 | Paul McMullan | 1 | 67 | 58 | 9 mins |
| 3 | Phil Stamp | 4 | 65 | 59 | 6 mins |

## KEY PLAYERS - DEFENDERS

**1 Alan Maybury**

| | | | |
|---|---|---|---|
| Goals Conceded (GC)<br>The number of League goals conceded while he was on the pitch | 40 | Clean Sheets<br>In games when he played at least 70 minutes | 11 |
| Defensive Rating<br>Ave number of mins between League goals conceded while on the pitch | 78 | Club Defensive Rating<br>Average number of mins between League goals conceded by the club this season | 39 |

| | PLAYER | CON LGE | CLEAN SHEETS | DEF RATE |
|---|---|---|---|---|
| 2 | Andy Webster | 23 | 6 | 75 mins |
| 3 | Steven Pressley | 39 | 9 | 75 mins |
| 4 | Austin McCann | 19 | 4 | 66 mins |

## KEY GOALKEEPER

**1 Teuvo Moilanen**

| | |
|---|---|
| Goals Conceded in the League | 10 |
| Defensive Rating<br>Ave number of mins between League goals conceded while on the pitch | 126 |
| Counting Games<br>Games when he played at least 70 mins | 14 |
| Clean Sheets<br>In games when he played at least 70 mins | 5 |

## TOP POINT EARNERS

| | PLAYER | GAMES | AVE |
|---|---|---|---|
| 1 | Mahe | 6 | 2.17 |
| 2 | Kirk | 14 | 1.93 |
| 3 | MacFarlane | 16 | 1.88 |
| 4 | Moilanen | 14 | 1.86 |
| 5 | McCann | 13 | 1.85 |
| 6 | Stamp | 20 | 1.75 |
| 7 | Maybury | 34 | 1.74 |
| 8 | Valois | 35 | 1.69 |
| 9 | Webster | 18 | 1.67 |
| 10 | Niemi | 3 | 1.67 |
| | CLUB AVERAGE: | | 1.66 |

Ave = Average points per match in Counting Games

## DISCIPLINARY RECORDS

| | PLAYER | YELLOW | RED | AVE |
|---|---|---|---|---|
| 1 | Simmons | 6 | 0 | 158 |
| 2 | Stamp | 11 | 1 | 163 |
| 3 | Mahe | 3 | 0 | 230 |
| 4 | Webster | 5 | 1 | 286 |
| 5 | McCann | 3 | 1 | 314 |
| 6 | Maybury | 8 | 1 | 345 |
| 7 | MacFarlane | 4 | 0 | 418 |
| 8 | de Vries | 5 | 0 | 511 |
| 9 | McKenna | 5 | 0 | 562 |
| 10 | Boyack | 3 | 0 | 573 |
| 11 | Pressley | 5 | 0 | 583 |
| 12 | Severin | 5 | 0 | 643 |
| 13 | Valois | 4 | 0 | 811 |
| | Other | 3 | 0 | |
| | TOTAL | 70 | 4 | |

## LEAGUE GOALS

| | PLAYER | MINS | GOALS | AVE |
|---|---|---|---|---|
| 1 | de Vries | 2555 | 15 | 170 |
| 2 | Kirk | 1548 | 10 | 155 |
| 3 | McKenna | 2810 | 5 | 562 |
| 4 | Wales | 1146 | 4 | 287 |
| 5 | Stamp | 1960 | 4 | 490 |
| 6 | Weir | 950 | 4 | 238 |
| 7 | Pressley | 2919 | 3 | 973 |
| 8 | Severin | 3216 | 3 | 1072 |
| 9 | Maybury | 3111 | 2 | 1556 |
| 10 | Valois | 3246 | 2 | 1623 |
| 11 | Simmons | 953 | 1 | 953 |
| 12 | McMullan | 1208 | 1 | 1208 |
| 13 | McCann | 1259 | 1 | 1259 |
| | Other | | 2 | |
| | TOTAL | | 57 | |

## MONTH BY MONTH GUIDE TO THE POINTS

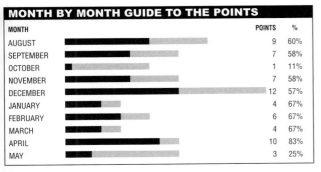

| MONTH | POINTS | % |
|---|---|---|
| AUGUST | 9 | 60% |
| SEPTEMBER | 7 | 58% |
| OCTOBER | 1 | 11% |
| NOVEMBER | 7 | 58% |
| DECEMBER | 12 | 57% |
| JANUARY | 4 | 67% |
| FEBRUARY | 6 | 67% |
| MARCH | 4 | 67% |
| APRIL | 10 | 83% |
| MAY | 3 | 25% |

## TEAM OF THE SEASON

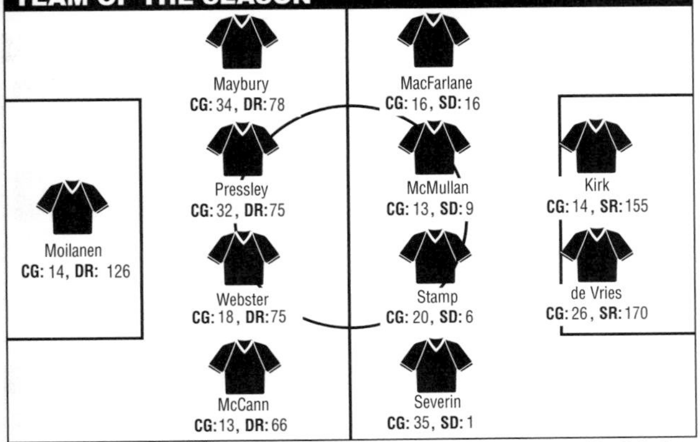
Maybury
CG: 34, DR: 78
MacFarlane
CG: 16, SD: 16
Moilanen
CG: 14, DR: 126
Pressley
CG: 32, DR: 75
McMullan
CG: 13, SD: 9
Kirk
CG: 14, SR: 155
Webster
CG: 18, DR: 75
Stamp
CG: 20, SD: 6
de Vries
CG: 26, SR: 170
McCann
CG: 13, DR: 66
Severin
CG: 35, SD: 1

KEY: DR = Defensive Rate, SD = Scoring Difference, SR = Strike Rate, CG = Counting Games – League games playing at least 70 minutes

## LEAGUE APPEARANCES, BOOKINGS AND CAPS

| | AGE (on 01/07/03) | IN THE SQUAD | COUNTING GAMES | MINUTES ON PITCH | YELLOW CARDS | RED CARDS | THIS SEASON | HOME COUNTRY |
|---|---|---|---|---|---|---|---|---|
| **Goalkeepers** | | | | | | | | |
| Craig Gordon | 20 | 27 | 1 | 90 | 0 | 0 | - | Scotland |
| Roddy McKenzie | 27 | 31 | 20 | 1800 | 0 | 0 | - | Scotland |
| Teuvo Moilanen | 29 | 14 | 14 | 1260 | 0 | 0 | - | Finland |
| Antti Niemi | 31 | 3 | 3 | 270 | 0 | 0 | - | Finland |
| Lee Windrum | 17 | 1 | 0 | 0 | 0 | 0 | - | N Ireland |
| **Defenders** | | | | | | | | |
| David Dunn | 19 | 1 | 1 | 73 | 0 | 0 | - | Scotland |
| John Knox | 19 | 1 | 0 | 52 | 0 | 0 | - | Scotland |
| Stephane Mahe | 34 | 13 | 6 | 690 | 3 | 0 | - | France |
| Alan Maybury | 24 | 35 | 34 | 3111 | 8 | 1 | - | Rep of Ireland |
| Austin McCann | 23 | 24 | 13 | 1259 | 3 | 1 | - | Scotland |
| Kevin McKenna | 22 | 37 | 29 | 2810 | 5 | 0 | - | Canada |
| Steven Pressley | 29 | 33 | 32 | 2919 | 5 | 0 | 8 | Scotland (64) |
| Andy Webster | 21 | 33 | 18 | 1716 | 5 | 1 | 3 | Scotland (64) |
| **Midfielders** | | | | | | | | |
| Steven Boyack | 26 | 29 | 19 | 1719 | 3 | 0 | - | Scotland |
| Liam Fox | 19 | 1 | 0 | 0 | 0 | 0 | - | Scotland |
| Neil Janczyk | 20 | 15 | 1 | 293 | 0 | 0 | - | Scotland |
| Neil MacFarlane | 25 | 23 | 16 | 1673 | 4 | 0 | - | Scotland |
| David McGeown | 19 | 3 | 0 | 45 | 0 | 0 | - | Scotland |
| Paul McMullan | 19 | 18 | 13 | 1208 | 0 | 0 | - | Scotland |
| Robbie Neilson | 23 | 7 | 5 | 450 | 0 | 0 | - | Scotland |
| Wilfred Queifio | - | 3 | 2 | 198 | 0 | 0 | - | Scotland |
| Scott Severin | 24 | 38 | 35 | 3216 | 5 | 0 | 4 | Scotland (64) |
| Stephen Simmons | 21 | 24 | 5 | 953 | 6 | 0 | - | Scotland |
| Phil Stamp | 27 | 25 | 20 | 1960 | 11 | 1 | - | England |
| **Forwards** | | | | | | | | |
| Mark de Vries | 27 | 33 | 26 | 2555 | 5 | 0 | - | Holland |
| Joe Hamill | 19 | 4 | 0 | 111 | 0 | 0 | - | Scotland |
| Andy Kirk | 24 | 31 | 14 | 1548 | 1 | 0 | 4 | N Ireland (111) |
| Robert Sloan | 19 | 1 | 0 | 39 | 0 | 0 | - | Scotland |
| Kevin Twaddle | 31 | 9 | 0 | 216 | 2 | 0 | - | Scotland |
| Jean Louis Valois | 29 | 38 | 35 | 3246 | 4 | 0 | - | France |
| Gary Wales | 24 | 28 | 8 | 1146 | 0 | 0 | - | Scotland |
| Graham Weir | 18 | 25 | 6 | 950 | 0 | 0 | - | Scotland |

KEY: LEAGUE BOOKINGS CAPS

## SQUAD APPEARANCES

| Match | 1 | 2 | 3 | 4 | 5 | 6 | 7 | 8 | 9 | 10 | 11 | 12 | 13 | 14 | 15 | 16 | 17 | 18 | 19 | 20 | 21 | 22 | 23 | 24 | 25 | 26 | 27 | 28 | 29 | 30 | 31 | 32 | 33 | 34 | 35 | 36 | 37 | 38 | 39 | 40 | 41 | 42 | 43 |
|---|---|---|---|---|---|---|---|---|---|---|---|---|---|---|---|---|---|---|---|---|---|---|---|---|---|---|---|---|---|---|---|---|---|---|---|---|---|---|---|---|---|---|---|
| Venue | A | H | A | H | H | A | H | H | A | A | A | H | H | H | A | H | A | A | A | H | A | H | H | A | A | A | H | A | A | H | H | H | A | H | A | H | A | H | A | A | A | H | H |
| Competition | L | L | L | L | L | L | L | L | I | L | L | L | I | L | L | L | I | L | L | L | L | L | L | L | L | L | L | S | L | L | I | L | L | L | L | L | L | L | L | L | L | L | L |
| Result | D | W | D | W | D | L | W | W | W | D | D | L | W | L | W | D | W | L | W | L | L | W | W | W | L | W | D | L | W | W | L | W | L | W | D | W | D | W | W | L | L | L | W |

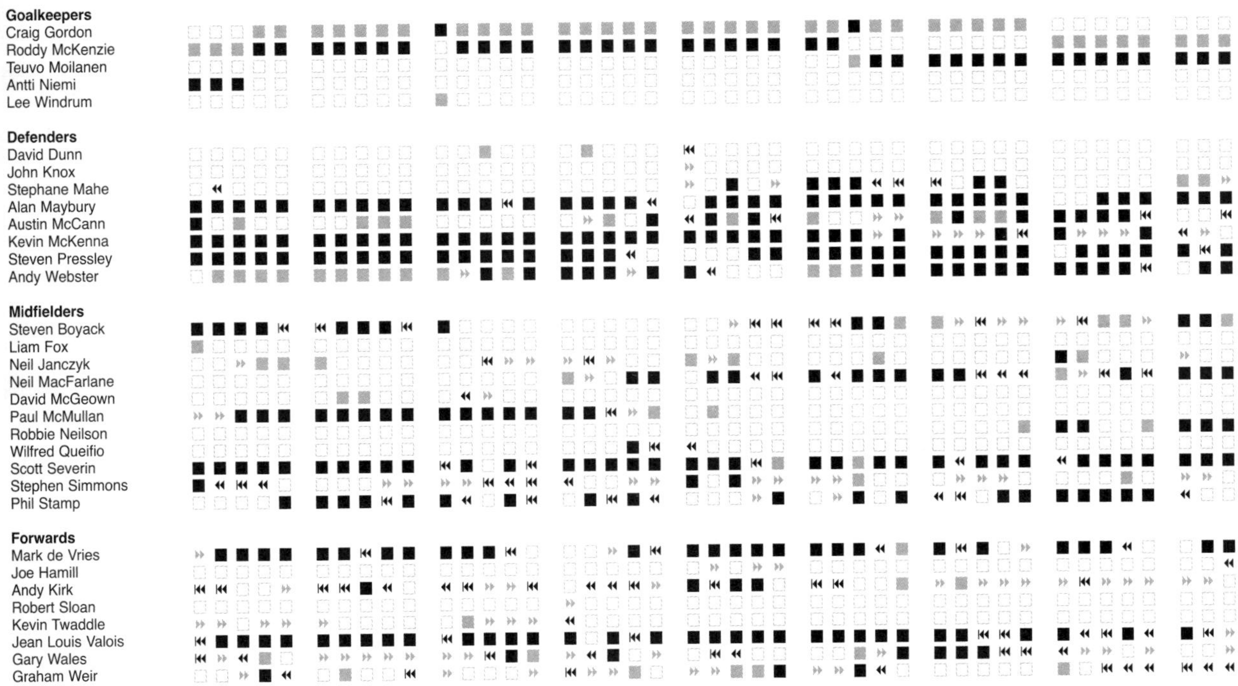
Goalkeepers
Craig Gordon
Roddy McKenzie
Teuvo Moilanen
Antti Niemi
Lee Windrum
Defenders
David Dunn
John Knox
Stephane Mahe
Alan Maybury
Austin McCann
Kevin McKenna
Steven Pressley
Andy Webster
Midfielders
Steven Boyack
Liam Fox
Neil Janczyk
Neil MacFarlane
David McGeown
Paul McMullan
Robbie Neilson
Wilfred Queifio
Scott Severin
Stephen Simmons
Phil Stamp
Forwards
Mark de Vries
Joe Hamill
Andy Kirk
Robert Sloan
Kevin Twaddle
Jean Louis Valois
Gary Wales
Graham Weir

# KILMARNOCK

Final Position: **4th**

NICKNAME: KILLIE

| | | | | | | |
|---|---|---|---|---|---|---|
| 1 | lge | Rangers | H | D | 1-1 | McLaren 79 |
| 2 | lge | Dundee Utd | A | W | 2-1 | Dargo 78; Boyd 81 |
| 3 | lge | Motherwell | H | L | 0-3 | |
| 4 | lge | Livingston | A | W | 1-0 | Boyd 42 |
| 5 | lge | Hearts | A | D | 1-1 | Boyd 44 |
| 6 | lge | Partick | H | W | 1-0 | Canero 41 |
| 7 | lge | Aberdeen | H | D | 2-2 | Mahood 55; McLaughlin 90 |
| 8 | lge | Hibernian | A | L | 0-2 | |
| 9 | cis2 | Airdrie Utd | H | L | 3-4* | (*on penalties) |
| 10 | lge | Celtic | A | L | 0-5 | |
| 11 | lge | Dundee | A | L | 1-2 | Boutal 65 |
| 12 | lge | Dunfermline | H | D | 2-2 | Shields 48; Boyd 75 |
| 13 | lge | Rangers | A | L | 1-6 | Fulton 44 |
| 14 | lge | Dundee Utd | H | L | 1-2 | Fulton 24 |
| 15 | lge | Motherwell | A | W | 1-0 | Boyd 90 |
| 16 | lge | Livingston | H | W | 2-0 | Di Giacomo 64; McSwegan 90 |
| 17 | lge | Hearts | H | L | 0-1 | |
| 18 | lge | Partick | A | L | 0-3 | |
| 19 | lge | Aberdeen | A | W | 1-0 | McSwegan 66 |
| 20 | lge | Dundee | H | W | 2-0 | Fulton 57; Boyd 90 |
| 21 | lge | Celtic | H | D | 1-1 | McLaren 19 |
| 22 | lge | Hibernian | H | W | 2-1 | McSwegan 63; Fulton 88 |
| 23 | lge | Dunfermline | A | W | 2-0 | McSwegan 70; Boyd 88 |
| 24 | lge | Rangers | H | L | 0-1 | |
| 25 | lge | Dundee Utd | A | D | 2-2 | Canero 21; McLaren 67 |
| 26 | scr3 | Motherwell | H | L | 0-1 | |
| 27 | lge | Motherwell | H | W | 1-0 | Boyd 81 pen |
| 28 | lge | Livingston | A | W | 4-0 | McLaren 21,70; Canero 34; Boyd 49 |
| 29 | lge | Hearts | A | L | 0-3 | |
| 30 | lge | Partick | H | W | 1-0 | Canero 45 |
| 31 | lge | Aberdeen | H | W | 2-0 | McSwegan 58; Canero 63 |
| 32 | lge | Dundee | A | D | 2-2 | Canero 51; McSwegan 85 |
| 33 | lge | Dunfermline | H | D | 1-1 | Boyd 81 |
| 34 | lge | Hibernian | H | W | 6-2 | McDonald 11; McSwegan 24,42,47,62; Boyd 90 pen |
| 35 | lge | Celtic | A | L | 0-2 | |
| 36 | lge | Dundee | A | W | 1-0 | Innes 76 |
| 37 | lge | Hearts | H | W | 1-0 | McSwegan 29 |
| 38 | lge | Rangers | A | L | 0-4 | |
| 39 | lge | Dunfermline | A | D | 2-2 | McDonald 26; Boyd 90 |
| 40 | lge | Celtic | H | L | 0-4 | |

## ATTENDANCES

HOME GROUND: RUGBY PARK CAPACITY: 18220 AVERAGE LEAGUE AT HOME: 7404

| | | | | | | | | |
|---|---|---|---|---|---|---|---|---|
| 10 | Celtic | 57469 | 25 | Dundee Utd | 7183 | 11 | Dundee | 5567 |
| 35 | Celtic | 56966 | 39 | Dunfermline | 6896 | **34** | **Hibernian** | **5558** |
| 38 | Rangers | 49036 | **26** | **Motherwell** | **6882** | **12** | **Dunfermline** | **5515** |
| 13 | Rangers | 48368 | **6** | **Partick** | **6848** | **14** | **Dundee Utd** | **5417** |
| **40** | **Celtic** | **16722** | **7** | **Aberdeen** | **6538** | **16** | **Livingston** | **5270** |
| **1** | **Rangers** | **13972** | 32 | Dundee | 6531 | 18 | Partick | 5055 |
| **24** | **Rangers** | **13396** | **17** | **Hearts** | **6511** | **20** | **Dundee** | **4810** |
| 5 | Hearts | 11912 | 2 | Dundee Utd | 6366 | **27** | **Motherwell** | **4457** |
| 29 | Hearts | 10426 | **3** | **Motherwell** | **6164** | 15 | Motherwell | 4439 |
| **21** | **Celtic** | **9225** | 36 | Dundee | 5964 | **9** | **Airdrie Utd** | **4150** |
| **37** | **Hearts** | **9019** | 23 | Dunfermline | 5847 | 28 | Livingston | 4144 |
| 19 | Aberdeen | 8861 | **22** | **Hibernian** | **5814** | **33** | **Dunfermline** | **4021** |
| 8 | Hibernian | 8680 | **31** | **Aberdeen** | **5769** | | | |
| 4 | Livingston | 7416 | **30** | **Partick** | **5651** | | | |

■ Home □ Away ▒ Neutral

## KEY PLAYERS - GOALSCORERS

**1 Kris Boyd**

| | | | |
|---|---|---|---|
| Goals in the League | 12 | Player Strike Rate<br>Average number of minutes between League goals scored by player | 151 |
| Contribution to Attacking Power<br>Average number of minutes between League team goals while on pitch | 58 | Club Strike Rate<br>Average number of minutes between League goals scored by club | 42 |

| | PLAYER | LGE GOALS | POWER | STRIKE RATE |
|---|---|---|---|---|
| 2 | Gary McSwegan | 11 | 68 | 187 mins |
| 3 | Andrew McLaren | 5 | 65 | 369 mins |
| 4 | Peter Canero | 6 | 71 | 465 mins |
| 5 | Steve Fulton | 4 | 75 | 797 mins |

## KEY PLAYERS - MIDFIELDERS

**1 Steve Fulton**

| | | | |
|---|---|---|---|
| Goals in the League | 4 | Contribution to Attacking Power<br>Average number of minutes between League team goals while on pitch | 76 |
| Defensive Rating<br>Average number of mins between League goals conceded while he was on the pitch | 59 | Scoring Difference<br>Defensive Rating minus Contribution to Attacking Power | -17 |

| | PLAYER | LGE GOALS | DEF RATE | POWER | SCORE DIFF |
|---|---|---|---|---|---|
| 2 | Gary Locke | 0 | 55 | 134 | -79 mins |

## KEY PLAYERS - DEFENDERS

**1 Garry Hay**

| | | | |
|---|---|---|---|
| Goals Conceded (GC)<br>The number of League goals conceded while he was on the pitch | 12 | Clean Sheets<br>In games when he played at least 70 minutes | 5 |
| Defensive Rating<br>Ave number of mins between League goals conceded while on the pitch | 97 | Club Defensive Rating<br>Average number of mins between League goals conceded by the club this season | 35 |

| | PLAYER | CON LGE | CLEAN SHEETS | DEF RATE |
|---|---|---|---|---|
| 2 | Shaun Dillon | 15 | 5 | 80 mins |
| 3 | Alan Mahood | 42 | 13 | 74 mins |
| 4 | Chris Innes | 26 | 7 | 68 mins |
| 5 | James Fowler | 38 | 9 | 63 mins |

## KEY GOALKEEPER

**1 Gordon Marshall**

| | |
|---|---|
| Goals Conceded in the League | 48 |
| Defensive Rating<br>Ave number of mins between League goals conceded while on the pitch | 56 |
| Counting Games<br>Games when he played at least 70 mins | 30 |
| Clean Sheets<br>In games when he played at least 70 mins | 9 |

## TOP POINT EARNERS

| | PLAYER | GAMES | AVE |
|---|---|---|---|
| 1 | McDonald | 7 | 2.57 |
| 2 | Dargo | 8 | 2.13 |
| 3 | Murray | 3 | 2.00 |
| 4 | Mitchell | 2 | 2.00 |
| 5 | Meldrum | 7 | 2.00 |
| 6 | Hay | 11 | 2.00 |
| 7 | McLaren | 16 | 1.88 |
| 8 | McSwegan | 20 | 1.85 |
| 9 | Hessey | 4 | 1.75 |
| 10 | Innes | 19 | 1.68 |
| | CLUB AVERAGE: | | 1.50 |

Ave = Average points per match in Counting Games

## DISCIPLINARY RECORDS

| | PLAYER | YELLOW | RED | AVE |
|---|---|---|---|---|
| 1 | McLaren | 12 | 1 | 141 |
| 2 | Locke | 5 | 1 | 200 |
| 3 | Innes | 8 | 0 | 219 |
| 4 | Sanjuan | 1 | 1 | 243 |
| 5 | Di Giacomo | 2 | 0 | 303 |
| 6 | McLaughlin | 5 | 0 | 305 |
| 7 | Boyd | 5 | 0 | 362 |
| 8 | Dillon | 3 | 0 | 398 |
| 9 | McSwegan | 5 | 0 | 412 |
| 10 | Dargo | 2 | 0 | 466 |
| 11 | Fowler | 5 | 0 | 480 |
| 12 | Shields | 5 | 1 | 494 |
| 13 | Marshall | 4 | 0 | 675 |
| | Other | 18 | 1 | |
| | TOTAL | 80 | 5 | |

## LEAGUE GOALS

| | PLAYER | MINS | GOALS | AVE |
|---|---|---|---|---|
| 1 | Boyd | 1811 | 12 | 151 |
| 2 | McSwegan | 2062 | 11 | 187 |
| 3 | Canero | 2790 | 6 | 465 |
| 4 | McLaren | 1845 | 5 | 369 |
| 5 | Fulton | 3187 | 4 | 797 |
| 6 | McDonald | 846 | 2 | 423 |
| 7 | Shields | 2965 | 1 | 2965 |
| 8 | Boutal | 225 | 1 | 225 |
| 9 | Di Giacomo | 606 | 1 | 606 |
| 10 | Dargo | 932 | 1 | 932 |
| 11 | McLaughlin | 1527 | 1 | 1527 |
| 12 | Mahood | 3104 | 1 | 3104 |
| 13 | Innes | 1758 | 1 | 1758 |
| | Other | | 0 | |
| | TOTAL | | 47 | |

## MONTH BY MONTH GUIDE TO THE POINTS

| MONTH | POINTS | % |
|---|---|---|
| AUGUST | 8 | 53% |
| SEPTEMBER | 4 | 33% |
| OCTOBER | 1 | 11% |
| NOVEMBER | 6 | 40% |
| DECEMBER | 13 | 72% |
| JANUARY | 4 | 67% |
| FEBRUARY | 6 | 67% |
| MARCH | 5 | 56% |
| APRIL | 6 | 67% |
| MAY | 4 | 33% |

## TEAM OF THE SEASON

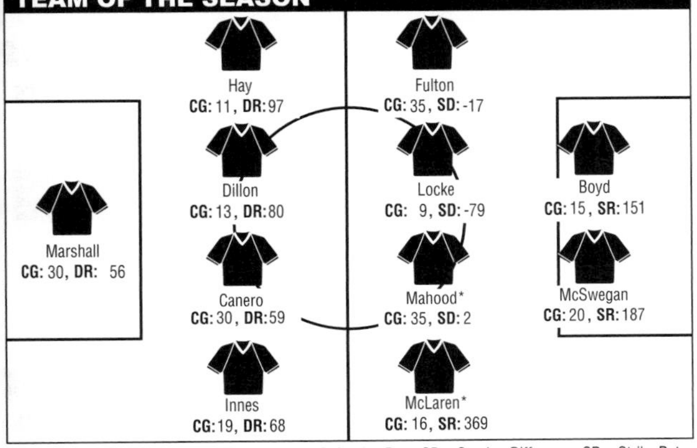
Marshall
CG: 30, DR: 56
Hay
CG: 11, DR: 97
Dillon
CG: 13, DR: 80
Canero
CG: 30, DR: 59
Innes
CG: 19, DR: 68
Fulton
CG: 35, SD: -17
Locke
CG: 9, SD: -79
Mahood*
CG: 35, SD: 2
McLaren*
CG: 16, SR: 369
Boyd
CG: 15, SR: 151
McSwegan
CG: 20, SR: 187

KEY: DR = Defensive Rate, SD = Scoring Difference, SR = Strike Rate,
CG = Counting Games – League games playing at least 70 minutes

## LEAGUE APPEARANCES, BOOKINGS AND CAPS

| | AGE (on 01/07/03) | IN THE SQUAD | COUNTING GAMES | MINUTES ON PITCH | YELLOW CARDS | RED CARDS | THIS SEASON | HOME COUNTRY |
|---|---|---|---|---|---|---|---|---|
| **Goalkeepers** | | | | | | | | |
| Gordon Marshall | 39 | 31 | 30 | 2700 | 4 | 0 | - | Scotland |
| Colin Meldrum | 27 | 29 | 7 | 630 | 0 | 0 | - | Scotland |
| Craig Samson | - | 1 | 0 | 0 | 0 | 0 | - | Scotland |
| Colin Stewart | 23 | 14 | 1 | 90 | 0 | 0 | - | Scotland |
| **Defenders** | | | | | | | | |
| Peter Canero | 22 | 33 | 30 | 2790 | 4 | 0 | - | Scotland |
| Shaun Dillon | 18 | 16 | 13 | 1194 | 3 | 0 | - | Scotland |
| Frederic Dindeleux | 29 | 30 | 24 | 2318 | 1 | 0 | - | France |
| James Fowler | 22 | 32 | 24 | 2404 | 5 | 0 | - | Scotland |
| Garry Hay | 25 | 34 | 11 | 1162 | 1 | 0 | - | Scotland |
| Sean Hessey | 24 | 5 | 4 | 397 | 2 | 1 | - | England |
| Chris Innes | 26 | 23 | 19 | 1758 | 8 | 0 | - | Scotland |
| Alan Mahood | 30 | 35 | 35 | 3104 | 4 | 0 | - | Scotland |
| Barry McLaughlin | 30 | 23 | 16 | 1527 | 5 | 0 | - | Scotland |
| Greg Shields | 26 | 34 | 32 | 2965 | 5 | 1 | - | Scotland |
| **Midfielders** | | | | | | | | |
| Mark Canning | 19 | 3 | 0 | 25 | 0 | 0 | - | Scotland |
| Steve Fulton | 32 | 36 | 35 | 3187 | 4 | 0 | - | Scotland |
| Gary Locke | 28 | 25 | 9 | 1204 | 5 | 1 | - | Scotland |
| Gary McDonald | 21 | 16 | 7 | 846 | 1 | 0 | - | Scotland |
| Ally Mitchell | 34 | 11 | 2 | 373 | 1 | 0 | - | Scotland |
| Stephen Murray | 20 | 18 | 3 | 428 | 0 | 0 | - | Scotland |
| Garcia Sanjuan | 31 | 12 | 5 | 487 | 1 | 1 | - | Spain |
| **Forwards** | | | | | | | | |
| Samuel Boutal | 34 | 3 | 2 | 225 | 0 | 0 | - | France |
| Kris Boyd | 19 | 38 | 15 | 1811 | 5 | 0 | - | Scotland |
| Craig Dargo | 25 | 15 | 8 | 932 | 2 | 0 | - | Scotland |
| Paul Di Giacomo | 21 | 21 | 4 | 606 | 2 | 0 | - | Scotland |
| Andrew McLaren | 30 | 25 | 16 | 1845 | 12 | 1 | - | Scotland |
| Gary McSwegan | 32 | 32 | 20 | 2062 | 5 | 0 | - | Scotland |
| Jose Quitongo | 28 | 12 | 2 | 377 | 0 | 0 | - | Angola |

KEY: LEAGUE BOOKINGS CAPS

## SQUAD APPEARANCES

| Match | 1 | 2 | 3 | 4 | 5 | 6 | 7 | 8 | 9 | 10 | 11 | 12 | 13 | 14 | 15 | 16 | 17 | 18 | 19 | 20 | 21 | 22 | 23 | 24 | 25 | 26 | 27 | 28 | 29 | 30 | 31 | 32 | 33 | 34 | 35 | 36 | 37 | 38 | 39 | 40 |
|---|---|---|---|---|---|---|---|---|---|---|---|---|---|---|---|---|---|---|---|---|---|---|---|---|---|---|---|---|---|---|---|---|---|---|---|---|---|---|---|---|
| Venue | H | A | H | A | A | H | H | A | H | A | A | H | A | H | A | H | H | A | A | H | H | H | A | H | A | H | H | A | A | H | H | A | H | H | A | A | H | A | A | H |
| Competition | L | L | L | L | L | L | L | L | I | L | L | L | L | L | L | L | L | L | L | L | L | L | L | L | L | S | L | L | L | L | L | L | L | L | L | L | L | L | L | L |
| Result | D | W | L | W | D | W | D | L | L | L | L | D | L | L | W | W | L | L | W | W | D | W | W | L | D | L | W | W | L | W | W | D | D | W | L | W | W | L | D | L |

**Goalkeepers**
Gordon Marshall
Colin Meldrum
Craig Samson
Colin Stewart

**Defenders**
Peter Canero
Shaun Dillon
Frederic Dindeleux
James Fowler
Garry Hay
Sean Hessey
Chris Innes
Alan Mahood
Barry McLaughlin
Greg Shields

**Midfielders**
Mark Canning
Steve Fulton
Gary Locke
Gary McDonald
Ally Mitchell
Stephen Murray
Jesus Garcia Sanjuan

**Forwards**
Samuel Boutal
Kris Boyd
Craig Dargo
Paul Di Giacomo
Andrew McLaren
Gary McSwegan
Jose Quitongo

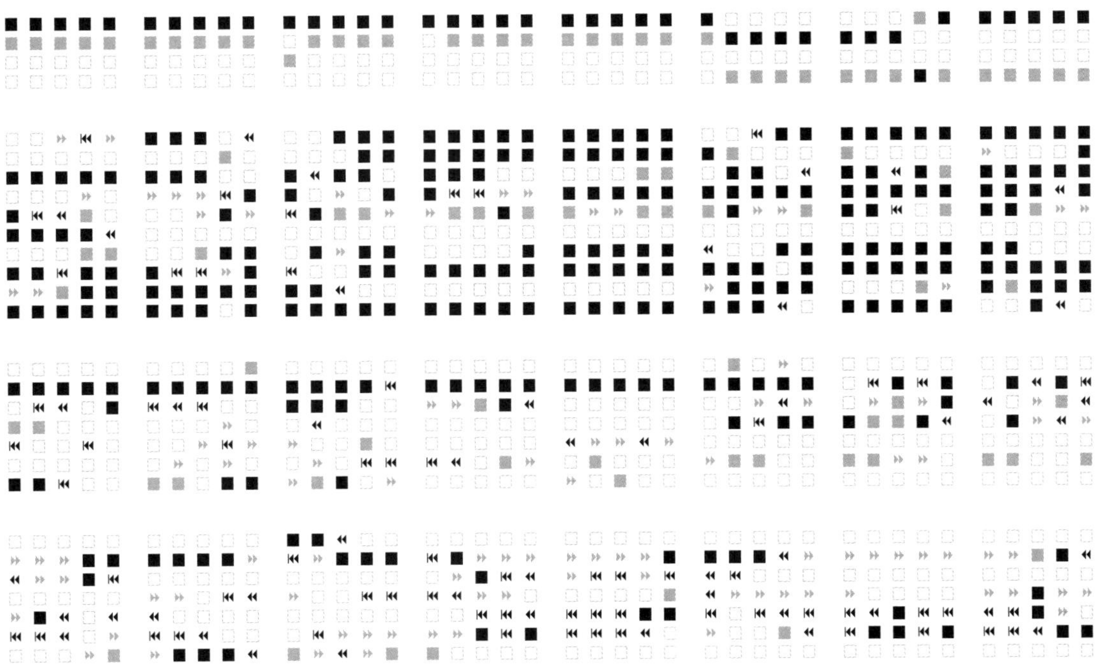

# DUNFERMLINE

Final Position: **5th**

NICKNAME: THE PARS

| | | | | | | |
|---|---|---|---|---|---|---|
| 1 | lge | Celtic | A | L | 1-2 | Dempsey 75 |
| 2 | lge | Livingston | H | W | 2-1 | Crawford 28; Brewster 49 |
| 3 | lge | Dundee | H | W | 4-2 | Crawford 33,79,84; Brewster 68 |
| 4 | lge | Hearts | A | L | 0-2 | |
| 5 | lge | Rangers | H | L | 0-6 | |
| 6 | lge | Hibernian | A | W | 4-1 | Walker 10; Brewster 23,57; Crawford 31 |
| 7 | lge | Dundee Utd | A | W | 2-1 | Dempsey 9; Crawford 16 |
| 8 | lge | Motherwell | H | W | 1-0 | Bullen 73 |
| 9 | cis2 | Cowdenbeath | A | W | 2-1 | Thomson, S M 80; Bullen 101 |
| 10 | lge | Aberdeen | A | L | 1-3 | Bullen 40 |
| 11 | lge | Partick | H | W | 4-1 | Thomson, S M 27; Nicholson 67; Crawford 78,90 |
| 12 | lge | Kilmarnock | A | D | 2-2 | Brewster 43; Bullen 57 |
| 13 | cis3 | Falkirk | H | W | 2-0 | Crawford 1,78 |
| 14 | lge | Celtic | H | L | 1-4 | Brewster 56 |
| 15 | lge | Livingston | A | D | 1-1 | Brewster 47 |
| 16 | cisqf | Rangers | H | L | 0-1 | |
| 17 | lge | Dundee | A | W | 3-2 | Brewster 25; Crawford 74; Dair 84 |
| 18 | lge | Hearts | H | W | 3-1 | Nicholson 65; Bullen 76; Crawford 90 |
| 19 | lge | Rangers | A | L | 0-3 | |
| 20 | lge | Hibernian | H | D | 1-1 | Crawford 66 |
| 21 | lge | Dundee Utd | H | W | 4-1 | Brewster 4,38 pen; Walker 41; Nicholson 55 |
| 22 | lge | Partick | A | L | 0-4 | |
| 23 | lge | Aberdeen | H | W | 3-0 | Crawford 39; Wilson 46; Brewster 63 pen |
| 24 | lge | Kilmarnock | H | L | 0-2 | |
| 25 | lge | Celtic | A | L | 0-1 | |
| 26 | lge | Livingston | H | W | 2-0 | Crawford 45,57 |
| 27 | scr3 | Livingston | A | D | 1-1 | Crawford 62 |
| 28 | lge | Dundee | H | L | 0-1 | |
| 29 | lge | Hearts | A | L | 0-3 | |
| 30 | scr3r | Livingston | H | W | 2-0 | Brewster 67,90 |
| 31 | lge | Rangers | H | L | 1-3 | Brewster 49 |
| 32 | lge | Hibernian | A | W | 3-1 | Mason 20; Crawford 39,55 |
| 33 | lge | Motherwell | A | L | 1-2 | Crawford 53 |
| 34 | scr4 | Hibernian | H | D | 1-1 | Nicholson 58 |
| 35 | lge | Dundee Utd | A | L | 0-3 | |
| 36 | scr4r | Hibernian | A | W | 2-0 | Crawford 57; Wilson, S 79 |
| 37 | lge | Partick | H | D | 0-0 | |
| 38 | lge | Kilmarnock | A | D | 1-1 | Shields 59 og |
| 39 | scqf | Rangers | H | D | 1-1 | Grondin 23 |
| 40 | lge | Motherwell | H | W | 3-0 | Hampshire 18; Nicholson 50; Hunt 77 |
| 41 | Scqfr | Rangers | A | L | 0-3 | |
| 42 | lge | Aberdeen | A | L | 0-1 | |
| 43 | lge | Hearts | H | L | 0-1 | |
| 44 | lge | Celtic | H | L | 1-4 | McNicol 81 |
| 45 | lge | Dundee | A | D | 2-2 | Crawford 54; Bullen 90 |
| 46 | lge | Kilmarnock | H | D | 2-2 | Nicholson 5; Mason 11 |
| 47 | lge | Rangers | A | L | 1-6 | Dair 11 |

## ATTENDANCES

HOME GROUND: EAST END PARK CAPACITY: 12510 AVERAGE LEAGUE AT HOME: 6127

| | | | | | | | | |
|---|---|---|---|---|---|---|---|---|
| 25 | Celtic | 58387 | 16 | Rangers | 8415 | 26 | Livingston | 5218 |
| 1 | Celtic | 57415 | 20 | Hibernian | 7515 | 8 | Motherwell | 4987 |
| 47 | Rangers | 49731 | 43 | Hearts | 6968 | 23 | Aberdeen | 4835 |
| 19 | Rangers | 48431 | 13 | Falkirk | 6933 | 18 | Hearts | 4800 |
| 41 | Rangers | 24752 | 46 | Kilmarnock | 6896 | 2 | Livingston | 4751 |
| 10 | Aberdeen | 11678 | 34 | Hibernian | 6619 | 37 | Partick | 4746 |
| 4 | Hearts | 11367 | 15 | Livingston | 6324 | 21 | Dundee Utd | 4342 |
| 29 | Hearts | 11281 | 7 | Dundee Utd | 6041 | 28 | Dundee | 4237 |
| 42 | Aberdeen | 10033 | 35 | Dundee Utd | 6004 | 22 | Partick | 4110 |
| 39 | Rangers | 9875 | 3 | Dundee | 5901 | 27 | Livingston | 4106 |
| 6 | Hibernian | 9837 | 36 | Hibernian | 5851 | 40 | Motherwell | 4086 |
| 32 | Hibernian | 9175 | 24 | Kilmarnock | 5847 | 38 | Kilmarnock | 4021 |
| 14 | Celtic | 9139 | 11 | Partick | 5522 | 33 | Motherwell | 3741 |
| 5 | Rangers | 8948 | 12 | Kilmarnock | 5515 | 30 | Livingston | 3158 |
| 44 | Celtic | 8923 | 17 | Dundee | 5475 | 9 | Cowdenbeath | 2988 |
| 31 | Rangers | 8754 | 45 | Dundee | 5411 | | | |

Home / Away / Neutral

## KEY PLAYERS - GOALSCORERS

**1 Stevie Crawford**

| | | | |
|---|---|---|---|
| Goals in the League | 18 | Player Strike Rate<br>Average number of minutes between League goals scored by player | 185 |
| Contribution to Attacking Power<br>Average number of minutes between League team goals while on pitch | 64 | Club Strike Rate<br>Average number of minutes between League goals scored by club | 37 |

| | PLAYER | LGE GOALS | POWER | STRIKE RATE |
|---|---|---|---|---|
| 2 | Craig Brewster | 12 | 66 | 259 mins |
| 3 | Lee Bullen | 5 | 58 | 597 mins |
| 4 | Barry Nicholson | 5 | 62 | 674 mins |
| 5 | Jason Dair | 2 | 62 | 972 mins |

## KEY PLAYERS - MIDFIELDERS

**1 Gary Dempsey**

| | | | |
|---|---|---|---|
| Goals in the League | 2 | Contribution to Attacking Power<br>Average number of minutes between League team goals while on pitch | 59 |
| Defensive Rating<br>Average number of mins between League goals conceded while he was on the pitch | 54 | Scoring Difference<br>Defensive Rating minus Contribution to Attacking Power | -5 |

| | PLAYER | LGE GOALS | DEF RATE | POWER | SCORE DIFF |
|---|---|---|---|---|---|
| 2 | Scott Thomson | 1 | 50 | 57 | -7 mins |
| 3 | Lee Bullen | 5 | 49 | 59 | -10 mins |
| 4 | Barry Nicholson | 5 | 49 | 62 | -13 mins |
| 5 | Gary Mason | 2 | 45 | 58 | -13 mins |

## KEY PLAYERS - DEFENDERS

**1 Angus MacPherson**

| | | | |
|---|---|---|---|
| Goals Conceded (GC)<br>The number of League goals conceded while he was on the pitch | 25 | Clean Sheets<br>In games when he played at least 70 minutes | 2 |
| Defensive Rating<br>Ave number of mins between League goals conceded while on the pitch | 53 | Club Defensive Rating<br>Average number of mins between League goals conceded by the club this season | 28 |

| | PLAYER | CON LGE | CLEAN SHEETS | DEF RATE |
|---|---|---|---|---|
| 2 | Andrius Skerla | 55 | 4 | 52 mins |
| 3 | Scott Wilson | 43 | 3 | 49 mins |

## KEY GOALKEEPER

**1 Derek Stillie**

| | |
|---|---|
| Goals Conceded in the League | 36 |
| Defensive Rating<br>Ave number of mins between League goals conceded while on the pitch | 53 |
| Counting Games<br>Games when he played at least 70 mins | 21 |
| Clean Sheets<br>In games when he played at least 70 mins | 4 |

## TOP POINT EARNERS

| | PLAYER | GAMES | AVE |
|---|---|---|---|
| 1 | Dempsey | 9 | 1.89 |
| 2 | Kilgannon | 13 | 1.54 |
| 3 | Thomson, S M | 21 | 1.52 |
| 4 | Wilson, D | 4 | 1.50 |
| 5 | Ruitenbeek | 17 | 1.41 |
| 6 | Wilson, S | 23 | 1.35 |
| 7 | Hampshire | 9 | 1.33 |
| 8 | Bullen | 31 | 1.32 |
| 9 | Skerla | 31 | 1.26 |
| 10 | Nicholson | 37 | 1.24 |
| | **CLUB AVERAGE:** | | **1.21** |

Ave = Average points per match in Counting Games

## DISCIPLINARY RECORDS

| | PLAYER | YELLOW | RED | AVE |
|---|---|---|---|---|
| 1 | Brannan | 2 | 2 | 161 |
| 2 | Wilson, S | 12 | 1 | 162 |
| 3 | Bullen | 7 | 0 | 426 |
| 4 | MacPherson | 3 | 0 | 441 |
| 5 | Hunt | 1 | 0 | 451 |
| 6 | McGroarty | 2 | 0 | 479 |
| 7 | Brewster | 5 | 1 | 518 |
| 8 | Hampshire | 2 | 0 | 534 |
| 9 | Mason | 4 | 0 | 552 |
| 10 | Kilgannon | 1 | 1 | 721 |
| 11 | Grondin | 1 | 0 | 837 |
| 12 | Skerla | 3 | 0 | 951 |
| 13 | Dair | 2 | 0 | 972 |
| | Other | 8 | 0 | |
| | **TOTAL** | **53** | **5** | |

## LEAGUE GOALS

| | PLAYER | MINS | GOALS | AVE |
|---|---|---|---|---|
| 1 | Crawford | 3334 | 18 | 185 |
| 2 | Brewster | 3109 | 12 | 259 |
| 3 | Nicholson | 3368 | 5 | 674 |
| 4 | Bullen | 2986 | 5 | 597 |
| 5 | Dair | 1944 | 2 | 972 |
| 6 | Mason | 2209 | 2 | 1105 |
| 7 | Walker | 1042 | 2 | 521 |
| 8 | Dempsey | 1525 | 2 | 763 |
| 9 | Hampshire | 1069 | 1 | 1069 |
| 10 | Thomson, S M | 1944 | 1 | 1944 |
| 11 | Wilson, S | 2114 | 1 | 2114 |
| 12 | McNicol | 45 | 1 | 45 |
| 13 | Hunt | 451 | 1 | 451 |
| | Other | | 1 | |
| | **TOTAL** | | **54** | |

## MONTH BY MONTH GUIDE TO THE POINTS

| MONTH | POINTS | % |
|---|---|---|
| AUGUST | 6 | 50% |
| SEPTEMBER | 12 | 67% |
| OCTOBER | 7 | 58% |
| NOVEMBER | 8 | 44% |
| DECEMBER | 6 | 40% |
| JANUARY | 4 | 44% |
| FEBRUARY | 7 | 39% |
| MARCH | 6 | 40% |
| APRIL | 3 | 25% |
| MAY | 2 | 17% |

## LEAGUE APPEARANCES, BOOKINGS AND CAPS

| | AGE (on 01/07/03) | IN THE SQUAD | COUNTING GAMES | MINUTES ON PITCH | YELLOW CARDS | RED CARDS | THIS SEASON | HOME COUNTRY |
|---|---|---|---|---|---|---|---|---|
| **Goalkeepers** | | | | | | | | |
| Sean Murdoch | - | 2 | 0 | 0 | 0 | 0 | - | Scotland |
| Marco Ruitenbeek | 35 | 37 | 17 | 1530 | 0 | 0 | - | Holland |
| Derek Stillie | 29 | 35 | 21 | 1890 | 0 | 0 | - | Scotland |
| Scott Thomson | 36 | 2 | 0 | 0 | 0 | 0 | - | Scotland |
| **Defenders** | | | | | | | | |
| Ged Brannan | 31 | 8 | 6 | 647 | 2 | 2 | - | England |
| Ian Campbell | 22 | 2 | 0 | 0 | 0 | 0 | - | Scotland |
| Jason Dair | 29 | 33 | 17 | 1944 | 2 | 0 | - | Scotland |
| Andre Karnebeek | 32 | 6 | 0 | 83 | 1 | 0 | - | Holland |
| Angus MacPherson | 34 | 22 | 12 | 1323 | 3 | 0 | - | Scotland |
| Scott McNicol | 20 | 4 | 0 | 45 | 0 | 0 | - | Australia |
| Andrius Skerla | 26 | 32 | 31 | 2855 | 3 | 0 | - | Lithuania |
| Scott Walker | 28 | 29 | 8 | 1042 | 1 | 0 | - | Scotland |
| Scott Wilson | 26 | 25 | 23 | 2114 | 12 | 1 | - | Scotland |
| **Midfielders** | | | | | | | | |
| Lee Bullen | 32 | 35 | 31 | 2986 | 7 | 0 | - | Scotland |
| Gary Dempsey | 22 | 33 | 9 | 1525 | 1 | 0 | - | Rep of Ireland |
| G Fotheringham | 22 | 1 | 0 | 0 | 0 | 0 | - | Scotland |
| David Grondin | 23 | 13 | 6 | 837 | 1 | 0 | - | France |
| Jim Hamilton | - | 1 | 0 | 22 | 0 | 0 | - | Scotland |
| Noel Hunt | 20 | 12 | 2 | 451 | 1 | 0 | - | Rep of Ireland |
| Sean Kilgannon | 22 | 31 | 13 | 1442 | 1 | 1 | - | Scotland |
| Gary Mason | 23 | 28 | 23 | 2209 | 4 | 0 | - | Scotland |
| Mark McGarty | 20 | 8 | 1 | 218 | 0 | 0 | - | Scotland |
| Chris McGroarty | 22 | 29 | 7 | 959 | 2 | 0 | - | Scotland |
| Kevin McLeish | 22 | 2 | 0 | 7 | 0 | 0 | - | Scotland |
| David Nicholls | 31 | 7 | 1 | 178 | 0 | 0 | - | Scotland |
| Barry Nicholson | 24 | 38 | 37 | 3368 | 3 | 0 | - | Scotland |
| Scott Thomson | 31 | 22 | 21 | 1944 | 1 | 0 | - | Scotland |
| Darren Wilson | - | 4 | 4 | 360 | 1 | 0 | - | Scotland |
| **Forwards** | | | | | | | | |
| Craig Brewster | 36 | 37 | 33 | 3109 | 5 | 1 | - | Scotland |
| Patrick Clark | 22 | 1 | 0 | 0 | 0 | 0 | - | Scotland |
| Stevie Crawford | 29 | 38 | 37 | 3334 | 0 | 0 | 10 | Scotland (64) |
| Steven Hampshire | 23 | 28 | 9 | 1069 | 2 | 0 | - | Scotland |
| Stewart Petrie | 33 | 3 | 0 | 16 | 0 | 0 | - | Scotland |

**KEY:** LEAGUE BOOKINGS CAPS

## TEAM OF THE SEASON

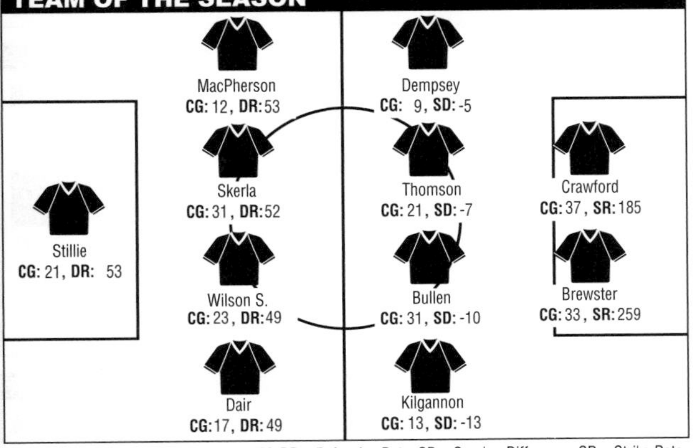

MacPherson
CG: 12, DR: 53
Dempsey
CG: 9, SD: -5
Skerla
CG: 31, DR: 52
Thomson
CG: 21, SD: -7
Crawford
CG: 37, SR: 185
Stillie
CG: 21, DR: 53
Wilson S.
CG: 23, DR: 49
Bullen
CG: 31, SD: -10
Brewster
CG: 33, SR: 259
Dair
CG: 17, DR: 49
Kilgannon
CG: 13, SD: -13


**KEY:** DR = Defensive Rate, SD = Scoring Difference, SR = Strike Rate, CG = Counting Games – League games playing at least 70 minutes

## SQUAD APPEARANCES

| Match | 1 | 2 | 3 | 4 | 5 | 6 | 7 | 8 | 9 | 10 | 11 | 12 | 13 | 14 | 15 | 16 | 17 | 18 | 19 | 20 | 21 | 22 | 23 | 24 | 25 | 26 | 27 | 28 | 29 | 30 | 31 | 32 | 33 | 34 | 35 | 36 | 37 | 38 | 39 | 40 | 41 | 42 | 43 | 44 | 45 | 46 | 47 |
|---|---|---|---|---|---|---|---|---|---|---|---|---|---|---|---|---|---|---|---|---|---|---|---|---|---|---|---|---|---|---|---|---|---|---|---|---|---|---|---|---|---|---|---|---|---|---|---|
| Venue | A | H | H | A | H | A | A | H | A | A | H | A | H | H | A | H | A | H | A | H | H | A | H | H | A | H | A | H | A | H | H | A | A | H | A | A | H | A | H | H | A | A | H | H | A | H | A |
| Competition | L | L | L | L | L | L | L | L | I | L | L | L | I | L | L | I | L | L | L | L | L | L | L | L | L | L | S | L | L | S | L | L | L | S | L | S | L | L | S | L | S | L | L | L | L | L | L |
| Result | L | W | W | L | L | W | W | W | W | L | W | D | W | L | D | L | W | W | L | D | W | L | W | L | L | W | D | L | L | W | L | W | L | D | L | W | D | D | D | W | L | L | L | L | D | D | L |

**Goalkeepers**
Sean Murdoch
Marco Ruitenbeek
Derek Stillie
Scott Thomson

**Defenders**
Ged Brannan
Ian Campbell
Jason Dair
Andre Karnebeek
Angus MacPherson
Scott McNicol
Andrius Skerla
Scott Walker
Scott Wilson

**Midfielders**
Lee Bullen
Gary Dempsey
George Fotheringham
David Grondin
Jim Hamilton
Noel Hunt
Sean Kilgannon
Gary Mason
Mark McGarty
Chris McGroarty
Kevin McLeish
David Nicholls
Barry Nicholson
Scott Thomson
Darren Wilson

**Forwards**
Craig Brewster
Patrick Clark
Stevie Crawford
Steven Hampshire
Stewart Petrie

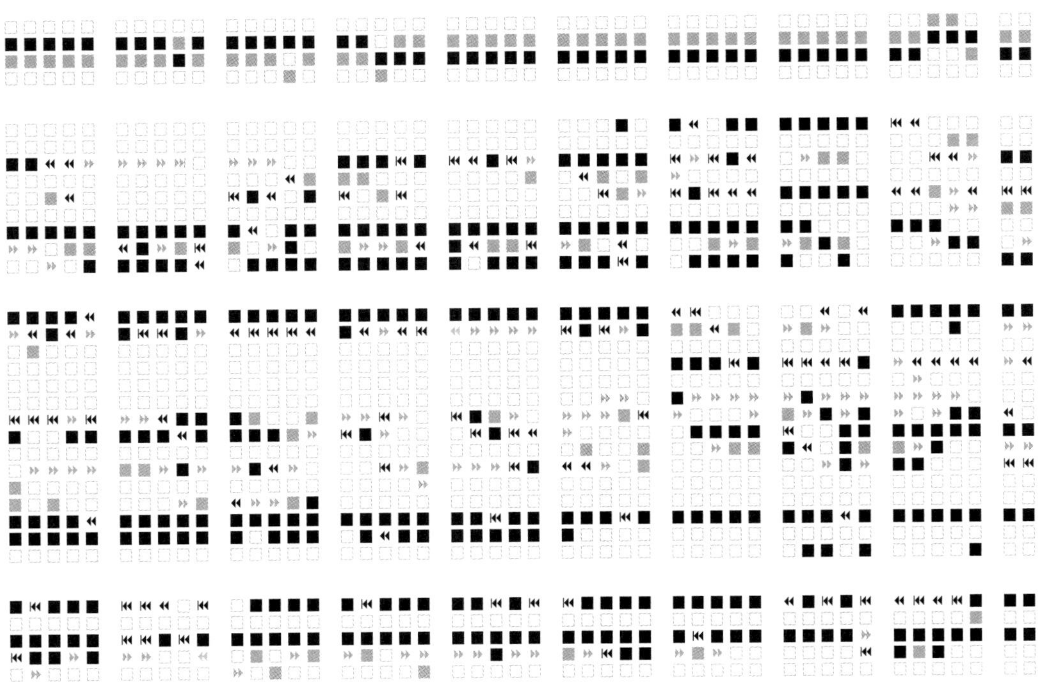

# DUNDEE

Final Position: **6th**

NICKNAME: THE DARK BLUES

| | | | | | | |
|---|---|---|---|---|---|---|
| 1 | lge | Hearts | H | D | 1-1 | Caballero 65 |
| 2 | lge | Rangers | A | L | 0-3 | |
| 3 | lge | Dunfermline | A | L | 2-4 | Novo 21,58 |
| 4 | lge | Hibernian | H | W | 2-1 | Caballero 78; Lovell 90 |
| 5 | lge | Dundee Utd | A | D | 0-0 | |
| 6 | lge | Livingston | H | W | 2-1 | Novo 52; Rae 76 |
| 7 | lge | Partick | A | D | 1-1 | Rae 49 |
| 8 | lge | Celtic | H | L | 0-1 | |
| 9 | cis2 | Queen of South | H | W | 3-1 | Sara 16,39; Caballero 21 |
| 10 | lge | Motherwell | A | D | 1-1 | Lovell 13 |
| 11 | lge | Kilmarnock | H | W | 2-1 | Rae 75; Caballero 90 |
| 12 | lge | Aberdeen | A | D | 0-0 | |
| 13 | cis3 | Partick | A | L | 0-1 | |
| 14 | lge | Hearts | A | W | 2-1 | Lovell 26,67 |
| 15 | lge | Rangers | H | L | 0-3 | |
| 16 | lge | Dunfermline | H | L | 2-3 | Nicholson 8 og; Lovell 19 |
| 17 | lge | Hibernian | A | L | 1-2 | Novo 90 |
| 18 | lge | Dundee Utd | H | W | 3-2 | Caballero 11,30; Hernandez 55 |
| 19 | lge | Livingston | A | D | 1-1 | Novo 72 pen |
| 20 | lge | Partick | H | W | 4-1 | Brady 38; Sara 51; Lovell 67,75 |
| 21 | lge | Kilmarnock | A | L | 0-2 | |
| 22 | lge | Motherwell | H | D | 1-1 | Sara 35 |
| 23 | lge | Celtic | A | L | 0-2 | |
| 24 | lge | Aberdeen | H | L | 1-2 | Milne 87 |
| 25 | lge | Hearts | H | L | 1-2 | Milne 57 |
| 26 | lge | Rangers | A | L | 1-3 | Lovell 23 |
| 27 | scr3 | Partick | A | W | 2-0 | Nemsadze 14; Rae 82 |
| 28 | lge | Dunfermline | A | W | 1-0 | Nicholson 13 og |
| 29 | lge | Dundee Utd | A | D | 1-1 | Novo 30 |
| 30 | scr4 | Aberdeen | H | W | 2-0 | Lovell 22; Novo 41 |
| 31 | lge | Hibernian | H | W | 3-0 | Rae 9; Milne 85; Murray 90 og |
| 32 | lge | Partick | A | W | 3-1 | Milne 15; Mackay 26; Novo 78 |
| 33 | lge | Livingston | H | D | 0-0 | |
| 34 | lge | Kilmarnock | H | D | 2-2 | Wilkie 39; Milne 41 |
| 35 | lge | Aberdeen | A | D | 3-3 | Lovell 16 pen; Caballero 24; Wilkie 81 |
| 36 | scqf | Falkirk | A | D | 1-1 | Novo 66 |
| 37 | lge | Celtic | H | D | 1-1 | Burchill 20 |
| 38 | Scqfr | Falkirk | H | D | 1-1 | Caballero 44; Burchill 94; Lovell 99,107 |
| 39 | lge | Motherwell | A | W | 2-1 | Burchill 2; Milne 24 |
| 40 | scsf | Inverness CT | A | W | 1-0 | Nemsadze 78 |
| 41 | lge | Kilmarnock | H | L | 0-1 | |
| 42 | lge | Rangers | H | D | 2-2 | Caballero 17,28 |
| 43 | lge | Dunfermline | H | D | 2-2 | Lovell 17 pen,58 |
| 44 | lge | Celtic | A | L | 2-6 | Smith 26; Mair 90 |
| 45 | lge | Hearts | A | L | 0-1 | |
| 46 | scf | Rangers | N | L | 0-1 | |

## ATTENDANCES

HOME GROUND: DENS PARK CAPACITY: 14000 AVERAGE LEAGUE AT HOME: 7399

| | | | | | | | | |
|---|---|---|---|---|---|---|---|---|
| 44 | Celtic | 57000 | 42 | Rangers | 9195 | 16 | Dunfermline | 5475 |
| 23 | Celtic | 56162 | 37 | Celtic | 9013 | 43 | Dunfermline | 5411 |
| 46 | Rangers | 50000 | 17 | Hibernian | 8870 | 6 | Livingston | 5391 |
| 26 | Rangers | 49112 | 24 | Aberdeen | 8574 | 20 | Partick | 5363 |
| 2 | Rangers | 47044 | 31 | Hibernian | 8414 | 19 | Livingston | 5307 |
| 40 | Inverness CT | 14429 | 1 | Hearts | 7705 | 27 | Partick | 4825 |
| 12 | Aberdeen | 14003 | 33 | Livingston | 7554 | 21 | Kilmarnock | 4810 |
| 5 | Dundee Utd | 12402 | 30 | Aberdeen | 7549 | 39 | Motherwell | 4693 |
| 45 | Hearts | 12205 | 36 | Falkirk | 7403 | 32 | Partick | 4599 |
| 35 | Aberdeen | 12119 | 25 | Hearts | 7340 | 7 | Partick | 4551 |
| 18 | Dundee Utd | 11539 | 34 | Kilmarnock | 6531 | 28 | Dunfermline | 4237 |
| 29 | Dundee Utd | 10457 | 4 | Hibernian | 6411 | 10 | Motherwell | 4025 |
| 14 | Hearts | 10169 | 41 | Kilmarnock | 5964 | 13 | Partick | 2652 |
| 15 | Rangers | 10124 | 3 | Dunfermline | 5901 | 9 | Queen of South | 2190 |
| 38 | Falkirk | 9562 | 11 | Kilmarnock | 5567 | | | |
| 8 | Celtic | 9483 | 22 | Motherwell | 5527 | | | |

■ Home □ Away ▒ Neutral

## KEY PLAYERS - GOALSCORERS

**1 Steve Lovell**

| | | | |
|---|---|---|---|
| Goals in the League | 11 | Player Strike Rate<br>Average number of minutes between League goals scored by player | 173 |
| Contribution to Attacking Power<br>Average number of minutes between League team goals while on pitch | 59 | Club Strike Rate<br>Average number of minutes between League goals scored by club | 40 |

| | PLAYER | LGE GOALS | POWER | STRIKE RATE |
|---|---|---|---|---|
| 2 | Nacho Novo | 7 | 80 | 344 mins |
| 3 | Fabian Caballero | 8 | 72 | 373 mins |
| 4 | Gavin Rae | 4 | 73 | 795 mins |
| 5 | Lee Wilkie | 2 | 67 | 1520 mins |

## KEY PLAYERS - MIDFIELDERS

**1 Georghi Nemsadze**

| | | | |
|---|---|---|---|
| Goals in the League | 0 | Contribution to Attacking Power<br>Average number of minutes between League team goals while on pitch | 68 |
| Defensive Rating<br>Average number of mins between League goals conceded while he was on the pitch | 72 | Scoring Difference<br>Defensive Rating minus Contribution to Attacking Power | 4 |

| | PLAYER | LGE GOALS | DEF RATE | POWER | SCORE DIFF |
|---|---|---|---|---|---|
| 2 | Garry Brady | 1 | 59 | 61 | -2 mins |
| 3 | Dave Mackay | 1 | 56 | 67 | -11 mins |
| 4 | Juan Sara | 2 | 53 | 84 | -31 mins |

## KEY PLAYERS - DEFENDERS

**1 Tom Hutchinson**

| | | | |
|---|---|---|---|
| Goals Conceded (GC)<br>The number of League goals conceded while he was on the pitch | 13 | Clean Sheets<br>In games when he played at least 70 minutes | 2 |
| Defensive Rating<br>Ave number of mins between League goals conceded while on the pitch | 70 | Club Defensive Rating<br>Average number of mins between League goals conceded by the club this season | 33 |

| | PLAYER | CON LGE | CLEAN SHEETS | DEF RATE |
|---|---|---|---|---|
| 2 | Lee Wilkie | 48 | 5 | 63 mins |
| 3 | Barry Smith | 58 | 5 | 57 mins |
| 4 | Gavin Rae | 56 | 5 | 57 mins |
| 5 | Jonay Hernandez Santos | 51 | 2 | 53 mins |

## KEY GOALKEEPER

**1 Julian Speroni**

| | |
|---|---|
| Goals Conceded in the League | 60 |
| Defensive Rating<br>Ave number of mins between League goals conceded while on the pitch | 57 |
| Counting Games<br>Games when he played at least 70 mins | 38 |
| Clean Sheets<br>In games when he played at least 70 mins | 5 |

## TOP POINT EARNERS

| | PLAYER | GAMES | AVE |
|---|---|---|---|
| 1 | Nemsadze | 20 | 1.60 |
| 2 | Hutchinson | 10 | 1.40 |
| 3 | Burchill | 5 | 1.40 |
| 4 | Wilkie | 32 | 1.34 |
| 5 | Brady | 17 | 1.24 |
| 6 | Mackay | 33 | 1.21 |
| 7 | Speroni | 38 | 1.16 |
| 8 | Smith | 37 | 1.16 |
| 9 | Rae | 34 | 1.12 |
| 10 | Lovell | 19 | 1.11 |
| | **CLUB AVERAGE:** | | **1.16** |

Ave = Average points per match in Counting Games

## DISCIPLINARY RECORDS

| | PLAYER | YELLOW | RED | AVE |
|---|---|---|---|---|
| 1 | Wilkie | 9 | 2 | 276 |
| 2 | Lovell | 6 | 0 | 317 |
| 3 | Khizanishvili | 3 | 1 | 343 |
| 4 | Novo | 5 | 1 | 400 |
| 5 | Burchill | 1 | 0 | 571 |
| 6 | Smith | 5 | 0 | 664 |
| 7 | Hernandez Santos | 3 | 1 | 669 |
| 8 | Rae | 4 | 0 | 794 |
| 9 | Caballero | 3 | 0 | 995 |
| 10 | Sara | 1 | 0 | 1006 |
| 11 | Nemsadze | 2 | 0 | 1012 |
| 12 | Mackay | 3 | 0 | 1032 |
| 13 | Mair | 2 | 0 | 1068 |
| | Other | 4 | 0 | |
| | **TOTAL** | **51** | **5** | |

## LEAGUE GOALS

| | PLAYER | MINS | GOALS | AVE |
|---|---|---|---|---|
| 1 | Lovell | 1905 | 11 | 173 |
| 2 | Caballero | 2985 | 8 | 373 |
| 3 | Novo | 2405 | 7 | 344 |
| 4 | Milne | 1112 | 6 | 185 |
| 5 | Rae | 3178 | 4 | 795 |
| 6 | Sara | 1006 | 2 | 503 |
| 7 | Wilkie | 3039 | 2 | 1520 |
| 8 | Burchill | 571 | 2 | 286 |
| 9 | Hernandez | 2679 | 1 | 2679 |
| 10 | Mackay | 3096 | 1 | 3096 |
| 11 | Smith | 3323 | 1 | 3323 |
| 12 | Mair | 2137 | 1 | 2137 |
| 13 | Brady | 1700 | 1 | 1700 |
| | Other | | 3 | |
| | **TOTAL** | | **50** | |

## MONTH BY MONTH GUIDE TO THE POINTS

| MONTH | POINTS | % |
|---|---|---|
| AUGUST | 5 | 33% |
| SEPTEMBER | 5 | 42% |
| OCTOBER | 7 | 78% |
| NOVEMBER | 4 | 27% |
| DECEMBER | 4 | 22% |
| JANUARY | 3 | 50% |
| FEBRUARY | 4 | 67% |
| MARCH | 6 | 50% |
| APRIL | 4 | 44% |
| MAY | 2 | 17% |

## TEAM OF THE SEASON

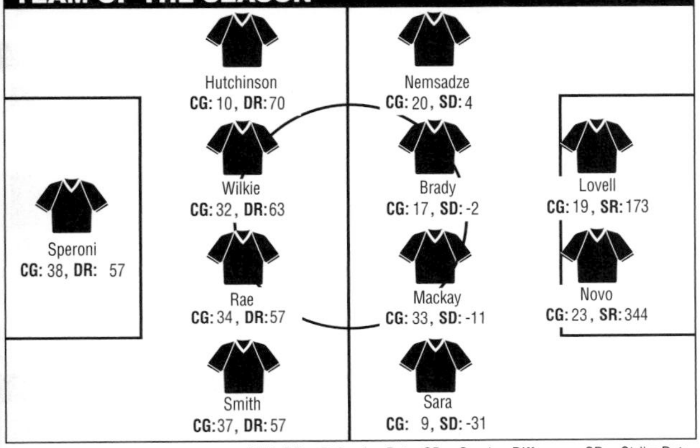
Hutchinson
CG: 10, DR: 70
Nemsadze
CG: 20, SD: 4
Wilkie
CG: 32, DR: 63
Brady
CG: 17, SD: -2
Lovell
CG: 19, SR: 173
Speroni
CG: 38, DR: 57
Rae
CG: 34, DR: 57
Mackay
CG: 33, SD: -11
Novo
CG: 23, SR: 344
Smith
CG: 37, DR: 57
Sara
CG: 9, SD: -31

KEY: DR = Defensive Rate, SD = Scoring Difference, SR = Strike Rate, CG = Counting Games – League games playing at least 70 minutes

## LEAGUE APPEARANCES, BOOKINGS AND CAPS

| | AGE (on 01/07/03) | IN THE SQUAD | COUNTING GAMES | MINUTES ON PITCH | YELLOW CARDS | RED CARDS | THIS SEASON | HOME COUNTRY |
|---|---|---|---|---|---|---|---|---|
| **Goalkeepers** | | | | | | | | |
| James Langfield | 23 | 35 | 0 | 0 | 0 | 0 | - | Scotland |
| Derek Soutar | 22 | 3 | 0 | 0 | 0 | 0 | - | Scotland |
| Julian Speroni | 24 | 38 | 38 | 3420 | 0 | 0 | - | Argentina |
| **Defenders** | | | | | | | | |
| Gavin Beith | 21 | 10 | 0 | 5 | 0 | 0 | - | Scotland |
| Hernandez Santos | 24 | 34 | 30 | 2679 | 3 | 1 | - | Spain |
| Tom Hutchinson | 21 | 15 | 10 | 916 | 0 | 0 | - | England |
| Zurab Khizanishvili | 21 | 26 | 14 | 1372 | 3 | 1 | - | Georgia |
| Lee Mair | 22 | 36 | 23 | 2137 | 2 | 0 | - | Scotland |
| Marcello Marrocco | 34 | 3 | 0 | 0 | 0 | 0 | - | Italy |
| Barry Smith | 29 | 37 | 37 | 3323 | 5 | 0 | - | Scotland |
| Lee Wilkie | 23 | 35 | 32 | 3039 | 9 | 2 | 9 | Scotland (64) |
| **Midfielders** | | | | | | | | |
| Garry Brady | 26 | 32 | 17 | 1700 | 1 | 0 | - | Scotland |
| Kris Brash | 20 | 1 | 0 | 0 | 0 | 0 | - | Scotland |
| Beto Caranza | 31 | 6 | 1 | 141 | 0 | 0 | - | Argentina |
| Dave Mackay | 22 | 35 | 33 | 3096 | 3 | 0 | - | Scotland |
| Georghi Nemsadze | 31 | 27 | 20 | 2025 | 2 | 0 | - | Georgia |
| Gavin Rae | 25 | 38 | 34 | 3178 | 4 | 0 | 1 | Scotland (64) |
| Stephen Robb | 21 | 14 | 0 | 164 | 0 | 0 | - | Scotland |
| Mark Robertson, M | 26 | 7 | 0 | 117 | 1 | 0 | - | Scotland |
| Juan Sara | 24 | 20 | 9 | 1006 | 1 | 0 | - | Argentina |
| **Forwards** | | | | | | | | |
| Mark Burchill | 22 | 11 | 5 | 571 | 1 | 0 | - | Scotland |
| Fabian Caballero | 25 | 36 | 31 | 2985 | 3 | 0 | - | Argentina |
| Barry Forbes | 21 | 6 | 0 | 108 | 1 | 0 | - | Scotland |
| Neil Jablonski | - | 7 | 1 | 107 | 0 | 0 | - | Scotland |
| Steve Lovell | 22 | 28 | 19 | 1905 | 6 | 0 | - | England |
| Steven Milne | 23 | 31 | 9 | 1112 | 1 | 0 | - | Scotland |
| Nacho Novo | 24 | 37 | 23 | 2405 | 5 | 1 | - | Spain |

KEY: LEAGUE BOOKINGS CAPS

## SQUAD APPEARANCES

| Match | 1 | 2 | 3 | 4 | 5 | 6 | 7 | 8 | 9 | 10 | 11 | 12 | 13 | 14 | 15 | 16 | 17 | 18 | 19 | 20 | 21 | 22 | 23 | 24 | 25 | 26 | 27 | 28 | 29 | 30 | 31 | 32 | 33 | 34 | 35 | 36 | 37 | 38 | 39 | 40 | 41 | 42 | 43 | 44 | 45 | 46 |
|---|---|---|---|---|---|---|---|---|---|---|---|---|---|---|---|---|---|---|---|---|---|---|---|---|---|---|---|---|---|---|---|---|---|---|---|---|---|---|---|---|---|---|---|---|---|---|
| Venue | H | A | A | H | A | H | A | H | H | A | H | A | A | A | H | H | A | H | A | H | A | H | A | H | H | A | A | A | A | H | H | A | H | H | A | A | H | H | A | A | H | H | H | A | A | H |
| Competition | L | L | L | L | L | L | L | L | I | L | L | L | I | L | L | L | L | L | L | L | L | L | L | L | L | L | S | L | L | S | L | L | L | L | L | S | L | S | L | S | L | L | L | L | L | S |
| Result | D | L | L | W | D | W | D | L | W | D | W | D | L | W | L | L | L | W | D | W | L | D | L | L | L | L | W | W | D | W | W | W | D | D | D | D | D | D | W | W | L | D | D | L | L | L |

**Goalkeepers**
James Langfield
Derek Soutar
Julian Speroni

**Defenders**
Gavin Beith
Jonay Hernandez Santos
Tom Hutchinson
Zurab Khizanishvili
Lee Mair
Marcello Marrocco
Gavin Rae
Barry Smith
Lee Wilkie

**Midfielders**
Garry Brady
Kris Brash
Beto Caranza
Dave Mackay
Georghi Nemsadze
Stephen Robb
Mark Robertson
Juan Sara

**Forwards**
Mark Burchill
Fabian Caballero
Barry Forbes
Neil Jablonski
Steve Lovell
Steven Milne
Nacho Novo

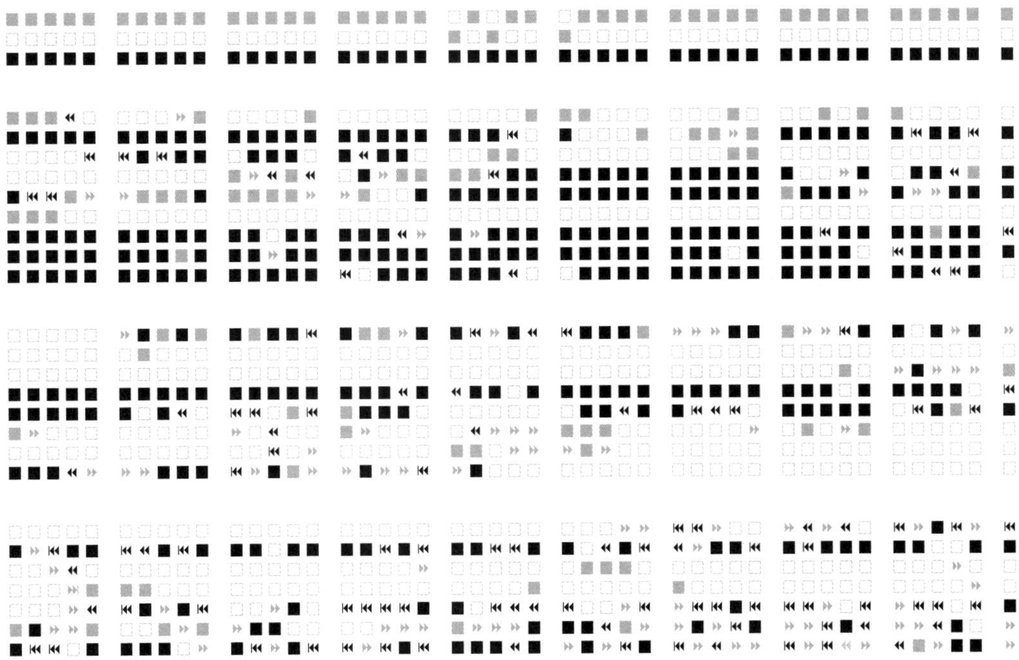

# HIBERNIAN

Final Position: **7th**

NICKNAME: THE HIBEES

| | | | | | | | |
|---|---|---|---|---|---|---|---|
| 1 | lge | Aberdeen | H | L | 1-2 | Luna 31 |
| 2 | lge | Hearts | A | L | 1-5 | Murray 51 |
| 3 | lge | Rangers | H | L | 2-4 | Townsley 35; O'Connor 88 |
| 4 | lge | Dundee | A | L | 1-2 | O'Connor 9 |
| 5 | lge | Motherwell | A | W | 2-0 | Townsley 14,71 |
| 6 | lge | Dunfermline | H | L | 1-4 | Paatelainen 41 |
| 7 | lge | Celtic | A | L | 0-1 | |
| 8 | lge | Kilmarnock | H | W | 2-0 | Murray 8; McManus 11 |
| 9 | cis2 | Alloa | A | W | 2-0 | Brebner 59; O'Connor 72 |
| 10 | lge | Livingston | H | W | 1-0 | Murray 45 |
| 11 | lge | Dundee Utd | H | W | 2-1 | O'Connor 28; Murray 51 |
| 12 | lge | Partick | A | W | 3-0 | O'Connor 43,89; Paatelainen 81 |
| 13 | cis3 | Rangers | H | L | 2-3 | Murray 5; O'Connor 72 |
| 14 | lge | Aberdeen | A | W | 1-0 | Brebner 70 |
| 15 | lge | Hearts | H | L | 1-2 | Paatelainen 36 |
| 16 | lge | Rangers | A | L | 1-2 | McManus 45 |
| 17 | lge | Dundee | H | W | 2-1 | Paatelainen 12,49 pen |
| 18 | lge | Motherwell | H | W | 3-1 | Paatelainen 59; McManus 64; O'Neil 90 pen |
| 19 | lge | Dunfermline | A | D | 1-1 | McManus 57 |
| 20 | lge | Celtic | H | L | 0-1 | |
| 21 | lge | Dundee Utd | A | D | 1-1 | Murray 7 |
| 22 | lge | Livingston | A | W | 2-1 | Murray 55; James 66 |
| 23 | lge | Kilmarnock | A | L | 1-2 | Luna 83 |
| 24 | lge | Partick | H | D | 1-1 | O'Neil 89 pen |
| 25 | lge | Aberdeen | H | W | 2-0 | Paatelainen 70; McManus 85 |
| 26 | lge | Hearts | A | D | 4-4 | Townsley 11; McManus 17; James 89; Brebner 90 |
| 27 | scr3 | Dundee Utd | A | W | 3-2 | Brebner 10,28,87 |
| 28 | lge | Rangers | H | L | 0-2 | |
| 29 | lge | Motherwell | A | L | 1-2 | O'Connor 71 |
| 30 | lge | Dunfermline | H | L | 1-3 | O'Connor 67 |
| 31 | scr4 | Dunfermline | A | D | 1-1 | Murray 42 |
| 32 | lge | Dundee | A | L | 0-3 | |
| 33 | lge | Celtic | A | L | 2-3 | McManus 37,60 |
| 34 | scr4r | Dunfermline | H | L | 0-2 | |
| 35 | lge | Dundee Utd | H | D | 1-1 | McManus 3 |
| 36 | lge | Partick | A | W | 1-0 | McManus 15 |
| 37 | lge | Kilmarnock | A | L | 2-6 | Murray 18; Jack 83 |
| 38 | lge | Livingston | H | D | 2-2 | Orman 44; Riordan 53 |
| 39 | lge | Dundee Utd | A | W | 2-1 | McManus 58 pen; Murray 90 |
| 40 | lge | Aberdeen | H | W | 3-1 | Jack 42; Riordan 61,72 |
| 41 | lge | Motherwell | H | W | 1-0 | Brebner 66 pen |
| 42 | lge | Livingston | A | W | 2-1 | Brown 38,69 |
| 43 | lge | Partick | H | L | 2-3 | Jack 8; Brown 34 |

## ATTENDANCES

HOME GROUND: EASTER ROAD CAPACITY: 18700 AVERAGE LEAGUE AT HOME: 10154

| | | | | | | | | |
|---|---|---|---|---|---|---|---|---|
| 33 | Celtic | 57512 | 10 | Livingston | 9451 | 31 | Dunfermline | 6619 |
| 7 | Celtic | 56703 | 43 | Partick | 9286 | 22 | Livingston | 6501 |
| 16 | Rangers | 48798 | 30 | Dunfermline | 9175 | 4 | Dundee | 6411 |
| 26 | Hearts | 17732 | 11 | Dundee Utd | 9175 | 12 | Partick | 5946 |
| 15 | Hearts | 15560 | 27 | Dundee Utd | 8985 | 5 | Motherwell | 5888 |
| 2 | Hearts | 15245 | 17 | Dundee | 8870 | 34 | Dunfermline | 5851 |
| 28 | Rangers | 13686 | 18 | Motherwell | 8859 | 23 | Kilmarnock | 5814 |
| 1 | Aberdeen | 13340 | 8 | Kilmarnock | 8680 | 21 | Dundee Utd | 5673 |
| 14 | Aberdeen | 12321 | 32 | Dundee | 8414 | 37 | Kilmarnock | 5558 |
| 20 | Celtic | 12042 | 38 | Livingston | 8150 | 42 | Livingston | 5432 |
| 3 | Rangers | 11663 | 40 | Aberdeen | 7904 | 29 | Motherwell | 4999 |
| 25 | Aberdeen | 11604 | 41 | Motherwell | 7809 | 36 | Partick | 4551 |
| 24 | Partick | 10317 | 35 | Dundee Utd | 7518 | 9 | Alloa | 1842 |
| 13 | Rangers | 10000 | 19 | Dunfermline | 7515 | | | |
| 6 | Dunfermline | 9837 | 39 | Dundee Utd | 6758 | | | |

■ Home □ Away ▒ Neutral

## KEY PLAYERS - GOALSCORERS

**1 Tom McManus**

| | | | |
|---|---|---|---|
| Goals in the League | 11 | Player Strike Rate<br>Average number of minutes between League goals scored by player | 159 |
| Contribution to Attacking Power<br>Average number of minutes between League team goals while on pitch | 60 | Club Strike Rate<br>Average number of minutes between League goals scored by club | 35 |

| | PLAYER | LGE GOALS | POWER | STRIKE RATE |
|---|---|---|---|---|
| 2 | Garry O'Connor | 7 | 71 | 214 mins |
| 3 | Mixu Paatelainen | 7 | 58 | 266 mins |
| 4 | Derek Townsley | 4 | 56 | 384 mins |
| 5 | Ian Murray | 8 | 59 | 389 mins |

## KEY PLAYERS - MIDFIELDERS

**1 Yannick Zambernardi**

| | | | |
|---|---|---|---|
| Goals in the League | 0 | Contribution to Attacking Power<br>Average number of minutes between League team goals while on pitch | 60 |
| Defensive Rating<br>Average number of mins between League goals conceded while he was on the pitch | 69 | Scoring Difference<br>Defensive Rating minus Contribution to Attacking Power | 9 |

| | PLAYER | LGE GOALS | DEF RATE | POWER | SCORE DIFF |
|---|---|---|---|---|---|
| 2 | Jarkko Wiss | 0 | 72 | 67 | 5 mins |
| 3 | Ian Murray | 8 | 53 | 60 | -7 mins |
| 4 | Derek Townsley | 4 | 45 | 57 | -12 mins |
| 5 | John O'Neil | 2 | 56 | 75 | -19 mins |

## KEY PLAYERS - DEFENDERS

**1 Jumas Matyus**

| | | | |
|---|---|---|---|
| Goals Conceded (GC)<br>The number of League goals conceded while he was on the pitch | 17 | Clean Sheets<br>In games when he played at least 70 minutes | 5 |
| Defensive Rating<br>Ave number of mins between League goals conceded while on the pitch | 72 | Club Defensive Rating<br>Average number of mins between League goals conceded by the club this season | 31 |

| | PLAYER | CON LGE | CLEAN SHEETS | DEF RATE |
|---|---|---|---|---|
| 2 | Paul Fenwick | 42 | 6 | 63 mins |
| 3 | Alen Orman | 33 | 5 | 62 mins |
| 4 | Craig James | 33 | 4 | 56 mins |
| 5 | Gary Smith | 52 | 5 | 53 mins |

## KEY GOALKEEPER

**1 Nick Colgan**

| | |
|---|---|
| Goals Conceded in the League | 48 |
| Defensive Rating<br>Ave number of mins between League goals conceded while on the pitch | 56 |
| Counting Games<br>Games when he played at least 70 mins | 30 |
| Clean Sheets<br>In games when he played at least 70 mins | 6 |

## TOP POINT EARNERS

| | PLAYER | GAMES | AVE |
|---|---|---|---|
| 1 | Whittaker | 2 | 3.00 |
| 2 | Brown, B | 4 | 2.25 |
| 3 | Matyus | 13 | 2.15 |
| 4 | Andersson | 3 | 2.00 |
| 5 | Luna | 10 | 1.60 |
| 6 | Doumbe | 11 | 1.55 |
| 7 | Wiss | 20 | 1.55 |
| 8 | Fenwick | 28 | 1.54 |
| 9 | Zambernardi | 26 | 1.50 |
| 10 | Thomson | 2 | 1.50 |
| | CLUB AVERAGE: | | 1.34 |

Ave = Average points per match in Counting Games

## DISCIPLINARY RECORDS

| | PLAYER | YELLOW | RED | AVE |
|---|---|---|---|---|
| 1 | Luna | 4 | 1 | 218 |
| 2 | Jack | 5 | 0 | 293 |
| 3 | Brebner | 7 | 1 | 294 |
| 4 | Zambernardi | 7 | 0 | 344 |
| 5 | Paatelainen | 5 | 0 | 372 |
| 6 | O'Neil | 4 | 0 | 375 |
| 7 | Fenwick | 7 | 0 | 376 |
| 8 | Townsley | 4 | 0 | 383 |
| 9 | Smith, G | 6 | 1 | 390 |
| 10 | Orman | 5 | 0 | 411 |
| 11 | McManus | 4 | 0 | 437 |
| 12 | Murray | 7 | 0 | 445 |
| 13 | Wiss | 4 | 0 | 470 |
| | Other | 13 | 1 | |
| | TOTAL | 82 | 4 | |

## LEAGUE GOALS

| | PLAYER | MINS | GOALS | AVE |
|---|---|---|---|---|
| 1 | McManus | 1749 | 11 | 159 |
| 2 | Murray | 3115 | 8 | 389 |
| 3 | O'Connor | 1500 | 7 | 214 |
| 4 | Paatelainen | 1862 | 7 | 266 |
| 5 | Townsley | 1535 | 4 | 384 |
| 6 | Brebner | 2354 | 3 | 785 |
| 7 | Brown, B | 339 | 3 | 113 |
| 8 | Jack | 1469 | 3 | 490 |
| 9 | Riordan | 504 | 3 | 168 |
| 10 | O'Neil | 1502 | 2 | 751 |
| 11 | James | 1843 | 2 | 922 |
| 12 | Luna | 1094 | 2 | 547 |
| 13 | Orman | 2056 | 1 | 2056 |
| | Other | | 0 | |
| | TOTAL | | 56 | |

## MONTH BY MONTH GUIDE TO THE POINTS

| MONTH | POINTS | % |
|---|---|---|
| AUGUST | 3 | 20% |
| SEPTEMBER | 6 | 50% |
| OCTOBER | 9 | 100% |
| NOVEMBER | 7 | 47% |
| DECEMBER | 8 | 44% |
| JANUARY | 1 | 17% |
| FEBRUARY | 0 | 0% |
| MARCH | 4 | 44% |
| APRIL | 4 | 44% |
| MAY | 9 | 75% |

## TEAM OF THE SEASON

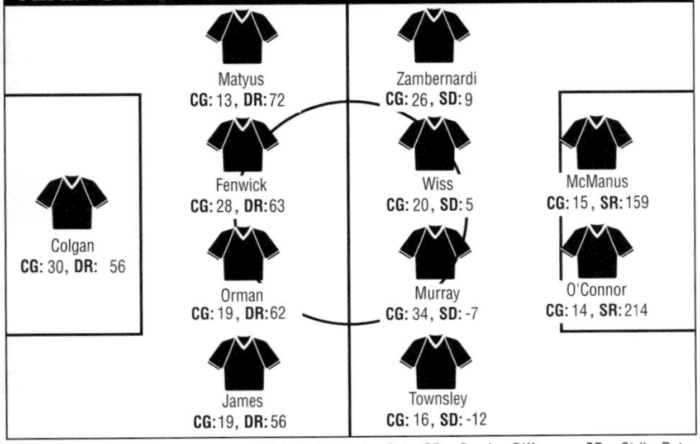
Matyus
CG: 13, DR: 72
Zambernardi
CG: 26, SD: 9
Colgan
CG: 30, DR: 56
Fenwick
CG: 28, DR: 63
Wiss
CG: 20, SD: 5
McManus
CG: 15, SR: 159
Orman
CG: 19, DR: 62
Murray
CG: 34, SD: -7
O'Connor
CG: 14, SR: 214
James
CG: 19, DR: 56
Townsley
CG: 16, SD: -12

**KEY:** DR = Defensive Rate, SD = Scoring Difference, SR = Strike Rate, CG = Counting Games – League games playing at least 70 minutes

## LEAGUE APPEARANCES, BOOKINGS AND CAPS

| | AGE (on 01/07/03) | IN THE SQUAD | COUNTING GAMES | MINUTES ON PITCH | YELLOW CARDS | RED CARDS | THIS SEASON | HOME COUNTRY |
|---|---|---|---|---|---|---|---|---|
| **Goalkeepers** | | | | | | | | |
| Daniel Andersson | 30 | 12 | 3 | 270 | 0 | 0 | - | Sweden |
| Tony Caig | 29 | 24 | 5 | 463 | 0 | 0 | - | England |
| Nick Colgan | 29 | 34 | 30 | 2688 | 4 | 1 | 5 | Rep of Ireland (15) |
| Ian Westwater | 39 | 5 | 0 | 0 | 0 | 0 | - | England |
| **Defenders** | | | | | | | | |
| Grant Brebner | 25 | 35 | 24 | 2354 | 7 | 1 | - | Scotland |
| Mathias Doumbe | 23 | 23 | 11 | 1020 | 1 | 0 | - | France |
| Paul Fenwick | 33 | 33 | 28 | 2637 | 7 | 0 | - | Canada |
| Paul Hilland | - | 1 | 0 | 0 | 0 | 0 | - | |
| Matthias Jack | 34 | 30 | 16 | 1469 | 5 | 0 | - | Germany |
| Craig James | 20 | 25 | 19 | 1843 | 1 | 0 | - | England |
| Jumas Matyus | 28 | 14 | 13 | 1224 | 1 | 0 | - | Hungary |
| Alen Orman | 25 | 25 | 19 | 2056 | 5 | 0 | - | Austria |
| Gary Smith | 32 | 32 | 30 | 2734 | 6 | 1 | - | Scotland |
| Darren Thomson | - | 2 | 2 | 180 | 0 | 0 | - | Scotland |
| **Midfielders** | | | | | | | | |
| Frederic Arpinon | 34 | 11 | 2 | 257 | 1 | 0 | - | France |
| Alistair Brown | - | 1 | 0 | 0 | 0 | 0 | - | Scotland |
| Mark Dempsie | 22 | 6 | 4 | 393 | 1 | 0 | - | Scotland |
| Ian Murray | 22 | 36 | 34 | 3115 | 7 | 0 | 2 | Scotland (64) |
| Kevin Nicol | 21 | 7 | 1 | 104 | 0 | 0 | - | Scotland |
| John O'Neil | 32 | 23 | 16 | 1502 | 4 | 0 | - | Scotland |
| Derek Townsley | 30 | 33 | 16 | 1535 | 4 | 0 | - | England |
| Steven Whittaker | 19 | 5 | 2 | 291 | 0 | 0 | - | Scotland |
| Jarkko Wiss | 31 | 27 | 20 | 1880 | 4 | 0 | - | Finland |
| Yannick Zambernardi | 25 | 28 | 26 | 2411 | 7 | 0 | - | France |
| **Forwards** | | | | | | | | |
| Scott Brown | - | 4 | 4 | 339 | 1 | 0 | - | Scotland |
| Frederic Dacquin | 24 | 3 | 0 | 67 | 0 | 0 | - | France |
| Francisco Luna | - | 18 | 10 | 1094 | 4 | 1 | - | |
| Tom McManus | 22 | 35 | 15 | 1749 | 4 | 0 | - | Scotland |
| Garry O'Connor | 20 | 23 | 14 | 1500 | 3 | 0 | - | Scotland |
| Mixu Paatelainen | 36 | 28 | 20 | 1862 | 5 | 0 | - | Finland |
| Alan Reid | 22 | 12 | 0 | 40 | 0 | 0 | - | Scotland |
| Derek Riordan | 20 | 12 | 4 | 504 | 0 | 0 | - | Scotland |

**KEY:** LEAGUE BOOKINGS CAPS

## SQUAD APPEARANCES

| Match | 1 | 2 | 3 | 4 | 5 | 6 | 7 | 8 | 9 | 10 | 11 | 12 | 13 | 14 | 15 | 16 | 17 | 18 | 19 | 20 | 21 | 22 | 23 | 24 | 25 | 26 | 27 | 28 | 29 | 30 | 31 | 32 | 33 | 34 | 35 | 36 | 37 | 38 | 39 | 40 | 41 | 42 | 43 |
|---|---|---|---|---|---|---|---|---|---|---|---|---|---|---|---|---|---|---|---|---|---|---|---|---|---|---|---|---|---|---|---|---|---|---|---|---|---|---|---|---|---|---|---|
| Venue | H | A | H | A | A | H | A | H | A | H | H | A | H | A | H | A | H | H | A | H | A | A | A | H | H | A | A | H | A | H | A | A | A | H | H | A | A | H | A | H | H | A | H |
| Competition | L | L | L | L | L | L | L | L | I | L | L | L | I | L | L | L | L | L | L | L | L | L | L | L | L | L | S | L | L | L | S | L | L | S | L | L | L | L | L | L | L | L | L |
| Result | L | L | L | L | W | L | L | W | W | W | W | W | L | W | L | L | W | W | D | L | D | W | L | D | W | D | W | L | L | L | D | L | L | L | D | W | L | D | W | W | W | W | L |

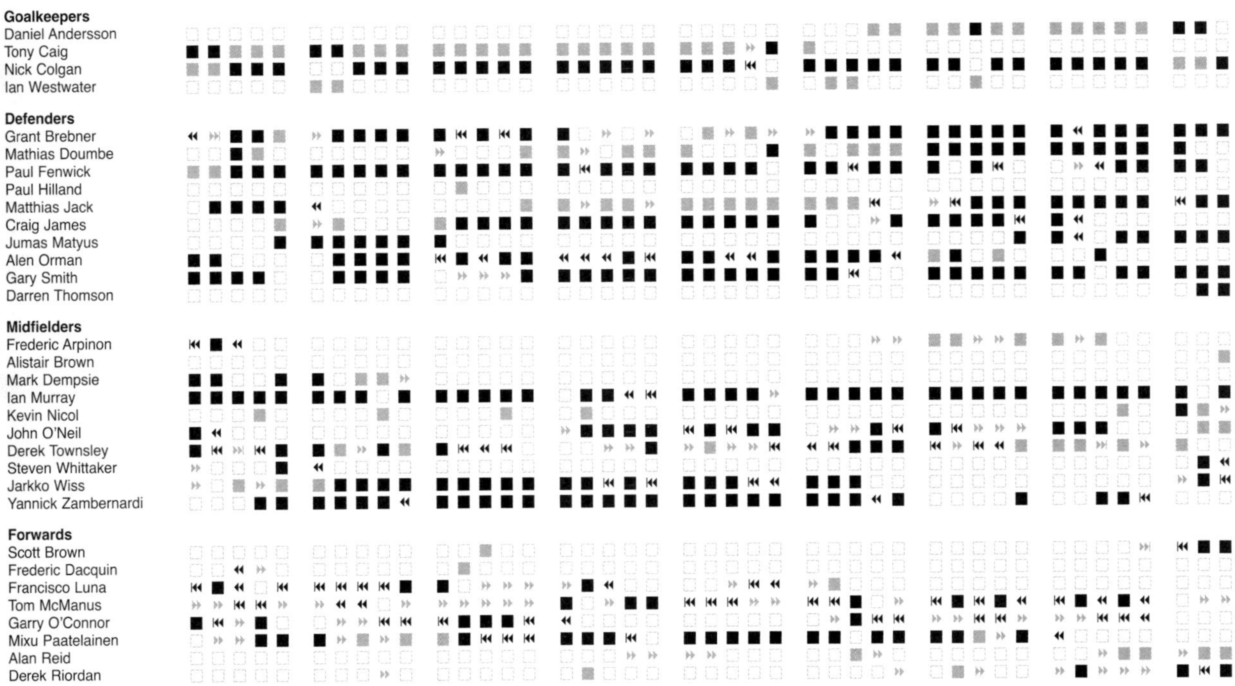
Goalkeepers
Daniel Andersson
Tony Caig
Nick Colgan
Ian Westwater
Defenders
Grant Brebner
Mathias Doumbe
Paul Fenwick
Paul Hilland
Matthias Jack
Craig James
Jumas Matyus
Alen Orman
Gary Smith
Darren Thomson
Midfielders
Frederic Arpinon
Alistair Brown
Mark Dempsie
Ian Murray
Kevin Nicol
John O'Neil
Derek Townsley
Steven Whittaker
Jarkko Wiss
Yannick Zambernardi
Forwards
Scott Brown
Frederic Dacquin
Francisco Luna
Tom McManus
Garry O'Connor
Mixu Paatelainen
Alan Reid
Derek Riordan

# ABERDEEN

Final Position: **8th**

NICKNAME: THE DONS

| | | | | | | |
|---|---|---|---|---|---|---|
| 1 | lge | Hibernian | A | W | 2-1 | Mackie 63; Clark 90 |
| 2 | lge | Celtic | H | L | 0-4 | |
| 3 | ucql1 | Nistru-Unisport | H | W | 1-0 | Mackie 59 |
| 4 | lge | Hearts | H | D | 1-1 | D'Jaffo 72 |
| 5 | lge | Rangers | A | L | 0-2 | |
| 6 | ucql2 | Nistru-Unisport | A | D | 0-0 | |
| 7 | lge | Partick | H | L | 0-1 | |
| 8 | lge | Dundee Utd | H | L | 1-2 | Mackie 2 |
| 9 | lge | Kilmarnock | A | D | 2-2 | D'Jaffo 64; Young, Darren 81 |
| 10 | uc1rl1 | Hertha Berlin | H | D | 0-0 | |
| 11 | lge | Livingston | A | W | 2-1 | Anderson 1; McNaughton 73 |
| 12 | lge | Dunfermline | H | W | 3-1 | Billio 44; D'Jaffo 54; Young, Derek 64 |
| 13 | uc1rl2 | Hertha Berlin | A | L | 0-1 | |
| 14 | lge | Motherwell | A | W | 2-1 | Young, Derek 46; Deloumeaux 83 |
| 15 | lge | Dundee | H | D | 0-0 | |
| 16 | lge | Hibernian | H | L | 0-1 | |
| 17 | lge | Celtic | A | L | 0-7 | |
| 18 | cis3 | Motherwell | H | W | 3-1 | Mike 23; Deloumeaux 24; Michie 42 |
| 19 | lge | Hearts | A | D | 0-0 | |
| 20 | cisqf | Hearts | H | L | 0-1 | |
| 21 | lge | Rangers | H | D | 2-2 | Mike 56; Mackie 74 |
| 22 | lge | Partick | A | L | 1-2 | Mike 84 |
| 23 | lge | Dundee Utd | A | D | 1-1 | McGuire 27 pen |
| 24 | lge | Kilmarnock | H | L | 0-1 | |
| 25 | lge | Motherwell | H | D | 1-1 | Young, Derek 30 |
| 26 | lge | Dunfermline | A | L | 0-3 | |
| 27 | lge | Livingston | H | D | 0-0 | |
| 28 | lge | Dundee | A | W | 2-1 | McGuire 50; Smith 64 og |
| 29 | lge | Hibernian | A | L | 0-2 | |
| 30 | lge | Celtic | H | D | 1-1 | Anderson 51 |
| 31 | scr3 | Queen of South | A | D | 0-0 | |
| 32 | lge | Hearts | H | L | 0-1 | |
| 33 | lge | Rangers | A | L | 1-2 | Tosh 75 |
| 34 | lge | Partick | H | L | 0-1 | |
| 35 | lge | Dundee Utd | H | W | 3-0 | Sheerin 39 pen,71; McGuire 74 |
| 36 | scr3r | Queen of South | H | W | 4-1 | Young, Derek 16; D'Jaffo 22,90; Anderson 25 |
| 37 | scr4 | Dundee | A | L | 0-2 | |
| 38 | lge | Kilmarnock | A | L | 0-2 | |
| 39 | lge | Motherwell | A | W | 1-0 | Sheerin 7 pen |
| 40 | lge | Dundee | H | D | 3-3 | Sheerin 57,64; McGuire 80 |
| 41 | lge | Livingston | A | W | 2-1 | Young, Derek 29; Sheerin 31 |
| 42 | lge | Dunfermline | H | W | 1-0 | Sheerin 10 |
| 43 | lge | Livingston | H | W | 1-0 | Hinds 25 |
| 44 | lge | Hibernian | A | L | 1-3 | Tiernan 88 |
| 45 | lge | Partick | H | W | 2-1 | Hinds 47; McGuire 60 |
| 46 | lge | Motherwell | A | W | 3-2 | Hinds 19; Deloumeaux 26; Sheerin 34 |
| 47 | lge | Dundee Utd | A | W | 2-0 | Mackie 51; Tosh 55 |

## ATTENDANCES

HOME GROUND: PITTODRIE STADIUM CAPACITY: 22200 AVERAGE LEAGUE AT HOME: 11746

| | | | | | | | | |
|---|---|---|---|---|---|---|---|---|
| 17 | Celtic | 58526 | 34 | Partick | 11334 | 20 | Hearts | 7576 |
| 33 | Rangers | 49667 | 27 | Livingston | 11253 | 37 | Dundee | 7549 |
| 5 | Rangers | 49219 | 8 | Dundee Utd | 10724 | 11 | Livingston | 7513 |
| 13 | Hertha Berlin | 30770 | 10 | Hertha Berlin | 10180 | 6 | Nistru-Unisport | 7000 |
| 2 | Celtic | 17284 | 42 | Dunfermline | 10033 | 18 | Motherwell | 6557 |
| 30 | Celtic | 16331 | 45 | Partick | 9960 | 9 | Kilmarnock | 6538 |
| 21 | Rangers | 14915 | 3 | Nistru-Unisport | 9894 | 22 | Partick | 6182 |
| 15 | Dundee | 14003 | 25 | Motherwell | 9569 | 36 | Queen of South | 6150 |
| 1 | Hibernian | 13340 | 32 | Hearts | 9322 | 14 | Motherwell | 6014 |
| 4 | Hearts | 12825 | 35 | Dundee Utd | 9146 | 38 | Kilmarnock | 5769 |
| 7 | Partick | 12591 | 43 | Livingston | 8921 | 41 | Livingston | 5731 |
| 16 | Hibernian | 12321 | 24 | Kilmarnock | 8861 | 31 | Queen of South | 5716 |
| 40 | Dundee | 12119 | 23 | Dundee Utd | 8621 | 39 | Motherwell | 5636 |
| 19 | Hearts | 11920 | 28 | Dundee | 8574 | 26 | Dunfermline | 4835 |
| 12 | Dunfermline | 11678 | 47 | Dundee Utd | 8516 | 46 | Motherwell | 4731 |
| 29 | Hibernian | 11604 | 44 | Hibernian | 7904 | | | |

■ Home □ Away ▒ Neutral

## KEY PLAYERS - GOALSCORERS

**1 Paul Sheerin**

| | | | |
|---|---|---|---|
| Goals in the League | 8 | Player Strike Rate<br>Average number of minutes between League goals scored by player | 158 |
| Contribution to Attacking Power<br>Average number of minutes between League team goals while on pitch | 63 | Club Strike Rate<br>Average number of minutes between League goals scored by club | 48 |

| | PLAYER | LGE GOALS | POWER | STRIKE RATE |
|---|---|---|---|---|
| 2 | Derek Young | 4 | 87 | 502 mins |
| 3 | Darren Mackie | 4 | 81 | 510 mins |
| 4 | Steven Tosh | 2 | 60 | 603 mins |
| 5 | Philip McGuire | 5 | 90 | 633 mins |

## KEY PLAYERS - MIDFIELDERS

**1 Paul Sheerin**

| | | | |
|---|---|---|---|
| Goals in the League | 8 | Contribution to Attacking Power<br>Average number of minutes between League team goals while on pitch | 63 |
| Defensive Rating<br>Average number of mins between League goals conceded while he was on the pitch | 79 | Scoring Difference<br>Defensive Rating minus Contribution to Attacking Power | 16 |

| | PLAYER | LGE GOALS | DEF RATE | POWER | SCORE DIFF |
|---|---|---|---|---|---|
| 2 | Steven Tosh | 2 | 75 | 60 | 15 mins |
| 3 | Darren Young | 1 | 57 | 95 | -38 mins |

## KEY PLAYERS - DEFENDERS

**1 Philip McGuire**

| | | | |
|---|---|---|---|
| Goals Conceded (GC)<br>The number of League goals conceded while he was on the pitch | 49 | Clean Sheets<br>In games when he played at least 70 minutes | 7 |
| Defensive Rating<br>Ave number of mins between League goals conceded while on the pitch | 65 | Club Defensive Rating<br>Average number of mins between League goals conceded by the club this season | 37 |

| | PLAYER | CON LGE | CLEAN SHEETS | DEF RATE |
|---|---|---|---|---|
| 2 | Russell Anderson | 46 | 6 | 63 mins |
| 3 | Eric Deloumeaux | 44 | 6 | 63 mins |
| 4 | Kevin Rutkiewicz | 27 | 3 | 60 mins |
| 5 | Kevin McNaughton | 28 | 2 | 59 mins |

## KEY GOALKEEPER

**1 Peter Kjaer**

| | |
|---|---|
| Goals Conceded in the League | 28 |
| Defensive Rating<br>Ave number of mins between League goals conceded while on the pitch | 73 |
| Counting Games<br>Games when he played at least 70 mins | 22 |
| Clean Sheets<br>In games when he played at least 70 mins | 6 |

## TOP POINT EARNERS

| | PLAYER | GAMES | AVE |
|---|---|---|---|
| 1 | Morrison | 2 | 3.00 |
| 2 | Hinds | 9 | 2.44 |
| 3 | Hart | 8 | 2.38 |
| 4 | Payne | 4 | 2.25 |
| 5 | Sheerin | 14 | 1.79 |
| 6 | Kjaer | 22 | 1.68 |
| 7 | Tiernan | 13 | 1.62 |
| 8 | Tosh | 12 | 1.58 |
| 9 | Bisconti | 8 | 1.50 |
| 10 | Young, Derek | 21 | 1.48 |
| | **CLUB AVERAGE:** | | **1.29** |

Ave = Average points per match in Counting Games

## DISCIPLINARY RECORDS

| | PLAYER | YELLOW | RED | AVE |
|---|---|---|---|---|
| 1 | Fabiano | 4 | 1 | 124 |
| 2 | McAllister | 9 | 1 | 241 |
| 3 | Michie | 3 | 0 | 273 |
| 4 | Bisconti | 3 | 0 | 284 |
| 5 | McGuire | 8 | 0 | 395 |
| 6 | Tosh | 3 | 0 | 402 |
| 7 | Rutkiewicz | 3 | 1 | 404 |
| 8 | McNaughton | 3 | 1 | 411 |
| 9 | Deloumeaux | 5 | 1 | 459 |
| 10 | Anderson | 6 | 0 | 482 |
| 11 | Billio | 1 | 0 | 492 |
| 12 | Young, Darren | 4 | 0 | 497 |
| 13 | Young, Derek | 4 | 0 | 502 |
| | Other | 7 | 0 | |
| | **TOTAL** | **63** | **5** | |

## LEAGUE GOALS

| | PLAYER | MINS | GOALS | AVE |
|---|---|---|---|---|
| 1 | Sheerin | 1260 | 8 | 158 |
| 2 | McGuire | 3165 | 5 | 633 |
| 3 | Young, Derek | 2008 | 4 | 502 |
| 4 | Mackie | 2039 | 4 | 510 |
| 5 | D'Jaffo | 1194 | 3 | 398 |
| 6 | Hinds | 869 | 3 | 290 |
| 7 | Deloumeaux | 2754 | 2 | 1377 |
| 8 | Tosh | 1206 | 2 | 603 |
| 9 | Mike | 1178 | 2 | 589 |
| 10 | Anderson | 2894 | 2 | 1447 |
| 11 | Tiernan | 1440 | 1 | 1440 |
| 12 | Clark | 1798 | 1 | 1798 |
| 13 | McNaughton | 1646 | 1 | 1646 |
| | Other | | 3 | |
| | **TOTAL** | | **41** | |

## MONTH BY MONTH GUIDE TO THE POINTS

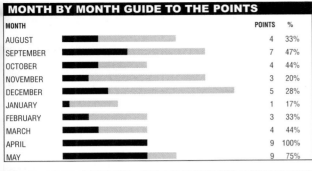

| MONTH | POINTS | % |
|---|---|---|
| AUGUST | 4 | 33% |
| SEPTEMBER | 7 | 47% |
| OCTOBER | 4 | 44% |
| NOVEMBER | 3 | 20% |
| DECEMBER | 5 | 28% |
| JANUARY | 1 | 17% |
| FEBRUARY | 3 | 33% |
| MARCH | 4 | 44% |
| APRIL | 9 | 100% |
| MAY | 9 | 75% |

## TEAM OF THE SEASON

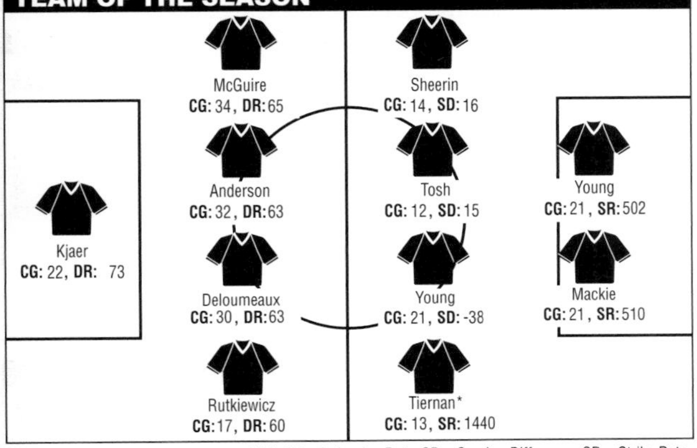
McGuire
CG: 34, DR: 65
Sheerin
CG: 14, SD: 16
Anderson
CG: 32, DR: 63
Tosh
CG: 12, SD: 15
Young
CG: 21, SR: 502
Kjaer
CG: 22, DR: 73
Deloumeaux
CG: 30, DR: 63
Young
CG: 21, SD: -38
Mackie
CG: 21, SR: 510
Rutkiewicz
CG: 17, DR: 60
Tiernan*
CG: 13, SR: 1440

KEY: DR = Defensive Rate, SD = Scoring Difference, SR = Strike Rate, CG = Counting Games – League games playing at least 70 minutes

## LEAGUE APPEARANCES, BOOKINGS AND CAPS

| | AGE (on 01/07/03) | IN THE SQUAD | COUNTING GAMES | MINUTES ON PITCH | YELLOW CARDS | RED CARDS | THIS SEASON | HOME COUNTRY |
|---|---|---|---|---|---|---|---|---|
| **Goalkeepers** | | | | | | | | |
| Ryan Esson | 23 | 9 | 0 | 0 | 0 | 0 | - | Scotland |
| Peter Kjaer | 37 | 27 | 22 | 2032 | 1 | 0 | - | Denmark |
| Mark Peat | 21 | 3 | 0 | 0 | 0 | 0 | - | Scotland |
| David Preece | 26 | 37 | 15 | 1403 | 1 | 0 | - | England |
| **Defenders** | | | | | | | | |
| Russell Anderson | 24 | 33 | 32 | 2894 | 6 | 0 | 4 | Scotland (64) |
| Eric Deloumeaux | 30 | 32 | 30 | 2754 | 5 | 1 | - | France |
| Robbie Hedderman | 21 | 2 | 0 | 0 | 0 | 0 | - | Rep of Ireland |
| James McAllister | 25 | 29 | 26 | 2414 | 9 | 1 | - | Scotland |
| Philip McGuire | 23 | 36 | 34 | 3165 | 8 | 0 | - | Scotland |
| Kevin McNaughton | 20 | 22 | 18 | 1646 | 3 | 1 | 2 | Scotland (64) |
| Scott Morrison | 18 | 2 | 2 | 180 | 0 | 0 | - | Scotland |
| Ross O'Donoghue | 20 | 14 | 1 | 129 | 0 | 0 | - | Scotland |
| Stephen Payne | 19 | 23 | 4 | 401 | 0 | 0 | - | Scotland |
| Kevin Rutkiewicz | 23 | 22 | 17 | 1618 | 3 | 1 | - | Scotland |
| **Midfielders** | | | | | | | | |
| Pat Billio | 29 | 14 | 3 | 492 | 1 | 0 | - | Italy |
| Roberto Bisconti | 29 | 11 | 8 | 854 | 3 | 0 | - | Belgian |
| Christopher Clark | 22 | 27 | 19 | 1798 | 1 | 0 | - | Scotland |
| Alexander Diamond | 18 | 1 | 0 | 45 | 0 | 0 | - | Scotland |
| Robert Duncan | 20 | 1 | 0 | 0 | 0 | 0 | - | Scotland |
| Nicolas Fabiano | 22 | 12 | 4 | 624 | 4 | 1 | - | France |
| Richard Foster | 17 | 2 | 0 | 34 | 0 | 0 | - | Scotland |
| Scott Muirhead | 19 | 2 | 0 | 71 | 0 | 0 | - | Scotland |
| Paul Sheerin | 28 | 14 | 14 | 1260 | 0 | 0 | - | Scotland |
| Kevin Souter | 19 | 2 | 0 | 0 | 0 | 0 | - | Scotland |
| Steven Tosh | 30 | 14 | 12 | 1206 | 3 | 0 | - | Scotland |
| Darren Young | 24 | 26 | 21 | 1988 | 4 | 0 | - | Scotland |
| **Forwards** | | | | | | | | |
| Laurent D'Jaffo | 32 | 24 | 9 | 1194 | 1 | 0 | - | France |
| Michael Hart | 23 | 8 | 8 | 706 | 0 | 0 | - | Scotland |
| Leigh Hinds | 24 | 13 | 9 | 869 | 0 | 0 | - | England |
| Darren Mackie | 21 | 30 | 21 | 2039 | 1 | 0 | - | Scotland |
| Scott Michie | 19 | 26 | 3 | 821 | 3 | 0 | - | Scotland |
| Leon Mike | 21 | 26 | 9 | 1178 | 2 | 0 | - | England |
| Ben Thornley | 28 | 7 | 1 | 264 | 0 | 0 | - | England |
| Fergus Tiernan | 21 | 26 | 13 | 1440 | 0 | 0 | - | Scotland |
| Derek Young | 23 | 29 | 21 | 2008 | 4 | 0 | - | Scotland |

KEY: LEAGUE BOOKINGS CAPS

## SQUAD APPEARANCES

| Match | 1 | 2 | 3 | 4 | 5 | 6 | 7 | 8 | 9 | 10 | 11 | 12 | 13 | 14 | 15 | 16 | 17 | 18 | 19 | 20 | 21 | 22 | 23 | 24 | 25 | 26 | 27 | 28 | 29 | 30 | 31 | 32 | 33 | 34 | 35 | 36 | 37 | 38 | 39 | 40 | 41 | 42 | 43 | 44 | 45 | 46 | 47 |
|---|---|---|---|---|---|---|---|---|---|---|---|---|---|---|---|---|---|---|---|---|---|---|---|---|---|---|---|---|---|---|---|---|---|---|---|---|---|---|---|---|---|---|---|---|---|---|---|
| Venue | A | H | H | H | A | A | H | H | A | H | A | H | A | A | H | H | A | H | A | H | H | A | A | H | H | A | H | A | A | H | A | H | A | H | H | H | A | A | A | H | A | H | H | A | H | A | A |
| Competition | L | L | E | L | L | E | L | L | L | E | L | L | E | L | L | L | L | I | L | I | L | L | L | L | L | L | L | L | L | L | S | L | L | L | L | S | S | L | L | L | L | L | L | L | L | L | L |
| Result | W | L | W | D | L | D | L | L | D | D | W | W | L | W | D | L | L | W | D | L | D | L | D | L | D | L | D | W | L | D | D | L | L | L | W | W | L | L | W | D | W | W | W | L | W | W | W |

**Goalkeepers**
Ryan Esson
Peter Kjaer
Mark Peat
David Preece

**Defenders**
Russell Anderson
Eric Deloumeaux
Robbie Hedderman
James McAllister
Philip McGuire
Kevin McNaughton
Scott Morrison
Ross O'Donoghue
Stephen Payne
Kevin Rutkiewicz

**Midfielders**
Pat Billio
Roberto Bisconti
Alexander Diamond
Robert Duncan
Nicolas Fabiano
Richard Foster
Scott Muirhead
Paul Sheerin
Kevin Souter
Steven Tosh
Darren Young

**Forwards**
Christopher Clark
Laurent D'Jaffo
Michael Hart
Leigh Hinds
Darren Mackie
Scott Michie
Leon Mike
Ben Thornley
Fergus Tiernan
Derek Young

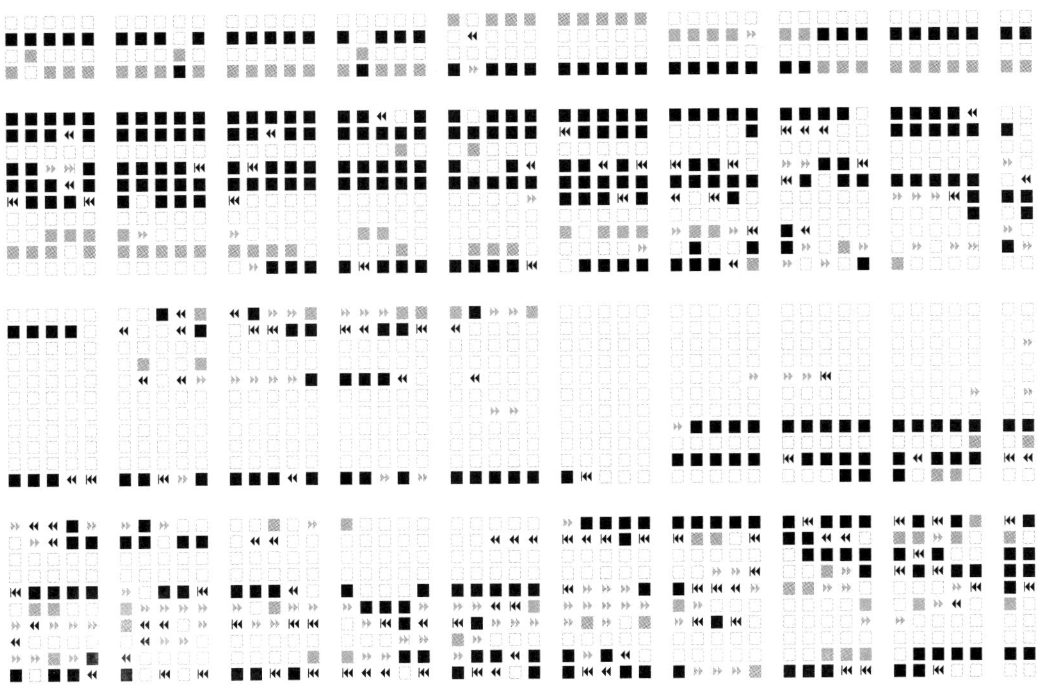

# LIVINGSTONE

Final Position: **9th**

NICKNAME: THE LIVI' LIONS

| | | | | | | |
|---|---|---|---|---|---|---|
| 1 | lge | Motherwell | H | W | 3-2 | Rubio 8; Zarate 34,46 |
| 2 | lge | Dunfermline | A | L | 1-2 | Xausa 90 |
| 3 | ucql1 | Vaduz | A | D | 1-1 | Rubio 51 |
| 4 | lge | Partick | A | D | 2-2 | Rubio 31,76 |
| 5 | lge | Kilmarnock | H | L | 0-1 | |
| 6 | ucql2 | Vaduz | H | D | 0-0 | |
| 7 | lge | Celtic | A | L | 0-2 | |
| 8 | lge | Dundee | A | L | 1-2 | Nemsadze 30 og |
| 9 | lge | Rangers | H | L | 0-2 | |
| 10 | uc1rl1 | Sturm Graz | A | L | 2-5 | Camacho 90; Lovell 90 |
| 11 | lge | Aberdeen | H | L | 1-2 | Xausa 55 |
| 12 | lge | Hibernian | A | L | 0-1 | |
| 13 | uc1rl2 | Sturm Graz | H | W | 4-3 | Wilson 30 pen,90; Xausa 54; Andrews 77 |
| 14 | lge | Hearts | H | D | 1-1 | Wilson 41 |
| 15 | lge | Dundee Utd | A | W | 3-2 | Bollan 68; Wilson 75; Dadi 78 |
| 16 | lge | Motherwell | A | W | 5-1 | Makel 9; Toure-Maman 48,58; Bingham 81; Xausa 90 |
| 17 | lge | Dunfermline | H | D | 1-1 | Toure-Maman 79 |
| 18 | cis3 | St Johnstone | A | W | 1-0 | Dadi 60 |
| 19 | lge | Partick | H | W | 3-0 | Dadi 47; Andrews 51; Bingham 59 |
| 20 | cisqf | Dundee Utd | H | L | 0-2 | |
| 21 | lge | Kilmarnock | A | L | 0-2 | |
| 22 | lge | Celtic | H | L | 0-2 | |
| 23 | lge | Dundee | H | D | 1-1 | Camacho 2 |
| 24 | lge | Rangers | A | L | 3-4 | Zarate 50,87; Wilson 72 |
| 25 | lge | Hearts | A | L | 1-2 | Zarate 63 |
| 26 | lge | Hibernian | H | L | 1-2 | Brinquin 90 |
| 27 | lge | Aberdeen | A | D | 0-0 | |
| 28 | lge | Dundee Utd | H | W | 3-0 | Camacho 8; Andrews 51; Bingham 86 |
| 29 | lge | Motherwell | H | W | 1-0 | Zarate 87 |
| 30 | lge | Dunfermline | A | L | 0-2 | |
| 31 | scr3 | Dunfermline | H | D | 1-1 | Bollan 26 |
| 32 | lge | Partick | A | W | 3-1 | Andrews 35; Zarate 70; McMenamin 80 |
| 33 | lge | Kilmarnock | H | L | 0-4 | |
| 34 | scr3r | Dunfermline | A | L | 0-2 | |
| 35 | lge | Celtic | A | L | 1-2 | Zarate 52 |
| 36 | lge | Rangers | H | L | 1-2 | Dadi 90 |
| 37 | lge | Dundee | A | D | 0-0 | |
| 38 | lge | Hearts | H | D | 1-1 | Rubio 61 |
| 39 | lge | Dundee Utd | A | W | 1-0 | Andrews 87 |
| 40 | lge | Aberdeen | H | L | 1-2 | Lovell 2 |
| 41 | lge | Hibernian | A | D | 2-2 | Wilson 87; O'Brien 89 |
| 42 | lge | Aberdeen | A | L | 0-1 | |
| 43 | lge | Partick | H | W | 3-1 | Xausa 25; Zarate 44; Camacho 50 |
| 44 | lge | Dundee Utd | H | L | 1-2 | Bingham 78 |
| 45 | lge | Hibernian | H | L | 1-2 | Pasquinelli 87 |
| 46 | lge | Motherwell | A | L | 2-6 | Makel 16; McMenamin 54 |

## ATTENDANCES

HOME GROUND: ALMONDVALE STADIUM CAPACITY: 10016 AVERAGE LEAGUE AT HOME: 6828

| | | | | | | | | |
|---|---|---|---|---|---|---|---|---|
| 35 | Celtic | 57169 | **29** | **Motherwell** | **7216** | **13** | **Sturm Graz** | **5208** |
| 7 | Celtic | 56988 | **1** | **Motherwell** | **7124** | **28** | **Dundee Utd** | **5103** |
| 24 | Rangers | 45992 | **14** | **Hearts** | **6512** | 46 | Motherwell | 4790 |
| 27 | Aberdeen | 11253 | **26** | **Hibernian** | **6501** | 2 | Dunfermline | 4751 |
| **36** | **Rangers** | **10004** | **17** | **Dunfermline** | **6324** | 16 | Motherwell | 4342 |
| **9** | **Rangers** | **10003** | **44** | **Dundee Utd** | **6314** | 4 | Partick | 4255 |
| **22** | **Celtic** | **10002** | 39 | Dundee Utd | 6247 | **33** | **Kilmarnock** | **4144** |
| 12 | Hibernian | 9451 | **19** | **Partick** | **6218** | **31** | **Dunfermline** | **4106** |
| 42 | Aberdeen | 8921 | **40** | **Aberdeen** | **5731** | **20** | **Dundee Utd** | **3592** |
| 41 | Hibernian | 8150 | 15 | Dundee Utd | 5572 | 32 | Partick | 3541 |
| 25 | Hearts | 8074 | **45** | **Hibernian** | **5432** | 34 | Dunfermline | 3158 |
| 37 | Dundee | 7554 | 8 | Dundee | 5391 | 10 | Sturm Graz | 2785 |
| **38** | **Hearts** | **7531** | **43** | **Partick** | **5349** | 18 | St Johnstone | 2688 |
| **11** | **Aberdeen** | **7513** | **23** | **Dundee** | **5307** | 3 | Vaduz | 1322 |
| **5** | **Kilmarnock** | **7416** | 21 | Kilmarnock | 5270 | | | |
| **6** | **Vaduz** | **7219** | 30 | Dunfermline | 5218 | | | |

■ Home □ Away ▨ Neutral

## KEY PLAYERS - GOALSCORERS

**1 Rolando Zarate**

| | | | |
|---|---|---|---|
| Goals in the League | 9 | Player Strike Rate<br>Average number of minutes between League goals scored by player | 233 |
| Contribution to Attacking Power<br>Average number of minutes between League team goals while on pitch | 65 | Club Strike Rate<br>Average number of minutes between League goals scored by club | 41 |

| | PLAYER | LGE GOALS | POWER | STRIKE RATE |
|---|---|---|---|---|
| 2 | Barry Wilson | 4 | 73 | 406 mins |
| 3 | Juan Jose Camacho | 3 | 68 | 482 mins |
| 4 | Oscar Rubio | 4 | 65 | 540 mins |
| 5 | David Bingham | 4 | 74 | 559 mins |

## KEY PLAYERS - MIDFIELDERS

**1 Cherif Toure-Maman**

| | | | |
|---|---|---|---|
| Goals in the League | 3 | Contribution to Attacking Power<br>Average number of minutes between League team goals while on pitch | 70 |
| Defensive Rating<br>Average number of mins between League goals conceded while he was on the pitch | 60 | Scoring Difference<br>Defensive Rating minus Contribution to Attacking Power | -10 |

| | PLAYER | LGE GOALS | DEF RATE | POWER | SCORE DIFF |
|---|---|---|---|---|---|
| 2 | Francisco Guinovart | 0 | 61 | 80 | -19 mins |
| 3 | Lee Makel | 2 | 56 | 76 | -20 mins |
| 4 | Julian Maidana | 0 | 53 | 76 | -23 mins |
| 5 | Burton O'Brien | 1 | 48 | 72 | -24 mins |

## KEY PLAYERS - DEFENDERS

**1 Gary Bollan**

| | | | |
|---|---|---|---|
| Goals Conceded (GC)<br>The number of League goals conceded while he was on the pitch | 29 | Clean Sheets<br>In games when he played at least 70 minutes | 4 |
| Defensive Rating<br>Ave number of mins between League goals conceded while on the pitch | 64 | Club Defensive Rating<br>Average number of mins between League goals conceded by the club this season | 32 |

| | PLAYER | CON LGE | CLEAN SHEETS | DEF RATE |
|---|---|---|---|---|
| 2 | Marvin Andrews | 48 | 6 | 62 mins |
| 3 | Oscar Rubio | 39 | 2 | 55 mins |
| 4 | Phillipe Brinquin | 49 | 3 | 50 mins |
| 5 | David McNamee | 22 | 1 | 46 mins |

## KEY GOALKEEPER

**1 Javier Sanchez Broto**

| | |
|---|---|
| Goals Conceded in the League | 35 |
| Defensive Rating<br>Ave number of mins between League goals conceded while on the pitch | 61 |
| Counting Games<br>Games when he played at least 70 mins | 23 |
| Clean Sheets<br>In games when he played at least 70 mins | 4 |

## TOP POINT EARNERS

| | PLAYER | GAMES | AVE |
|---|---|---|---|
| 1 | McMenamin | 2 | 1.50 |
| 2 | McEwan | 2 | 1.50 |
| 3 | Xausa | 11 | 1.36 |
| 4 | Dadi | 9 | 1.33 |
| 5 | Hart | 9 | 1.22 |
| 6 | Bollan | 20 | 1.15 |
| 7 | Makel | 24 | 1.13 |
| 8 | Lovell | 12 | 1.08 |
| 9 | Zarate | 18 | 1.06 |
| 10 | O'Brien | 19 | 1.05 |
| | CLUB AVERAGE: | | 0.92 |

Ave = Average points per match in Counting Games

## DISCIPLINARY RECORDS

| | PLAYER | YELLOW | RED | AVE |
|---|---|---|---|---|
| 1 | Pasquinelli | 3 | 0 | 171 |
| 2 | Lovell | 6 | 0 | 209 |
| 3 | Bahoken | 5 | 0 | 230 |
| 4 | McNamee | 4 | 0 | 253 |
| 5 | Hart | 3 | 0 | 296 |
| 6 | Camacho | 4 | 0 | 361 |
| 7 | Xausa | 4 | 0 | 366 |
| 8 | Wilson | 3 | 1 | 406 |
| 9 | Toure-Maman | 2 | 1 | 418 |
| 10 | Dadi | 3 | 0 | 424 |
| 11 | Bingham | 5 | 0 | 447 |
| 12 | Bollan | 3 | 1 | 460 |
| 13 | Zarate | 3 | 0 | 700 |
| | Other | 17 | 0 | |
| | TOTAL | 65 | 3 | |

## LEAGUE GOALS

| | PLAYER | MINS | GOALS | AVE |
|---|---|---|---|---|
| 1 | Zarate | 2101 | 9 | 233 |
| 2 | Xausa | 1466 | 4 | 367 |
| 3 | Wilson | 1624 | 4 | 406 |
| 4 | Rubio | 2161 | 4 | 540 |
| 5 | Andrews | 2970 | 4 | 743 |
| 6 | Bingham | 2236 | 4 | 559 |
| 7 | Toure-Maman | 1256 | 3 | 419 |
| 8 | Camacho | 1446 | 3 | 482 |
| 9 | Dadi | 1273 | 3 | 424 |
| 10 | McMenamin | 359 | 2 | 180 |
| 11 | Makel | 2360 | 2 | 1180 |
| 12 | Pasquinelli | 514 | 1 | 514 |
| 13 | Brinquin | 2454 | 1 | 2454 |
| | Other | | 4 | |
| | TOTAL | | 48 | |

## MONTH BY MONTH GUIDE TO THE POINTS

| MONTH | POINTS | % |
|---|---|---|
| AUGUST | 4 | 33% |
| SEPTEMBER | 0 | 0% |
| OCTOBER | 7 | 78% |
| NOVEMBER | 5 | 33% |
| DECEMBER | 7 | 39% |
| JANUARY | 3 | 50% |
| FEBRUARY | 0 | 0% |
| MARCH | 5 | 42% |
| APRIL | 1 | 11% |
| MAY | 3 | 25% |

## TEAM OF THE SEASON

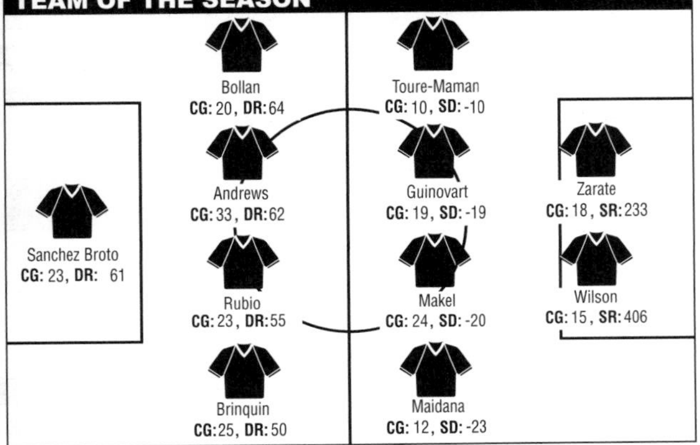

Sanchez Broto
CG: 23, DR: 61
Bollan
CG: 20, DR: 64
Andrews
CG: 33, DR: 62
Rubio
CG: 23, DR: 55
Brinquin
CG: 25, DR: 50
Toure-Maman
CG: 10, SD: -10
Guinovart
CG: 19, SD: -19
Makel
CG: 24, SD: -20
Maidana
CG: 12, SD: -23
Zarate
CG: 18, SR: 233
Wilson
CG: 15, SR: 406


KEY: DR = Defensive Rate, SD = Scoring Difference, SR = Strike Rate, CG = Counting Games – League games playing at least 70 minutes

## LEAGUE APPEARANCES, BOOKINGS AND CAPS

| | AGE (on 01/07/03) | IN THE SQUAD | COUNTING GAMES | MINUTES ON PITCH | YELLOW CARDS | RED CARDS | THIS SEASON | HOME COUNTRY |
|---|---|---|---|---|---|---|---|---|
| **Goalkeepers** | | | | | | | | |
| Javier Broto | 31 | 24 | 23 | 2118 | 1 | 0 | - | Spain |
| Allan Creer | 17 | 0 | 0 | 0 | 0 | 0 | - | Scotland |
| Eamon Fullerton | - | 1 | 0 | 0 | 0 | 0 | - | Scotland |
| Fernando Lopez | - | 5 | 0 | 0 | 0 | 0 | - | Spain |
| Alan Main | 35 | 14 | 12 | 1080 | 0 | 0 | - | Scotland |
| David McEwan | 21 | 33 | 2 | 222 | 0 | 0 | - | Scotland |
| **Defenders** | | | | | | | | |
| Marvin Andrews | 27 | 33 | 33 | 2970 | 2 | 0 | - | Trinidad & Tobago |
| Gary Bollan | 30 | 22 | 20 | 1842 | 3 | 1 | - | Scotland |
| Phillipe Brinquin | 32 | 29 | 25 | 2454 | 3 | 0 | - | France |
| Emmanuel Dorado | 30 | 3 | 1 | 150 | 1 | 0 | - | Argentina |
| Stewart Greacen | 21 | 3 | 0 | 0 | 0 | 0 | - | |
| David McNamee | 22 | 13 | 10 | 1013 | 4 | 0 | - | Scotland |
| Oscar Rubio | 27 | 29 | 23 | 2161 | 2 | 0 | - | Portugal |
| William Snowdon | 20 | 2 | 0 | 0 | 0 | 0 | - | England |
| **Midfielders** | | | | | | | | |
| Guillermo Amor | 35 | 4 | 0 | 136 | 0 | 0 | - | Spain |
| Gustave Bahoken | 24 | 21 | 11 | 1151 | 5 | 0 | - | Cameroon |
| Richard Brittain | 19 | 4 | 0 | 120 | 0 | 0 | - | Scotland |
| Juan Jose Camacho | 22 | 29 | 14 | 1446 | 4 | 0 | - | Spain |
| Stuart Lovell | 31 | 15 | 12 | 1257 | 6 | 0 | - | Australia |
| Julian Maidana | 31 | 12 | 12 | 1067 | 1 | 0 | - | Argentina |
| Lee Makel | 30 | 31 | 24 | 2360 | 2 | 0 | - | England |
| Scott McLaughlin | - | 1 | 1 | 90 | 0 | 0 | - | Scotland |
| Francisco Guinovart | 32 | 36 | 19 | 2252 | 3 | 0 | - | Spain |
| Cherif Toure-Maman | 22 | 30 | 10 | 1256 | 2 | 1 | - | Togo |
| **Forwards** | | | | | | | | |
| David Bingham | 32 | 34 | 22 | 2236 | 5 | 0 | - | Scotland |
| Eugene Dadi | 29 | 23 | 9 | 1273 | 3 | 0 | - | France |
| Michael Hart | 23 | 12 | 9 | 888 | 3 | 0 | - | Scotland |
| Paul McLaughlin | - | 1 | 0 | 0 | 0 | 0 | - | Scotland |
| Colin McMenamin | 22 | 15 | 2 | 359 | 2 | 0 | - | Scotland |
| Burton O'Brien | 22 | 31 | 19 | 1949 | 0 | 0 | - | Scotland |
| Fernando Pasquinelli | - | 6 | 6 | 514 | 3 | 0 | - | Argentina |
| Stephen Whalen | 21 | 1 | 0 | 0 | 0 | 0 | - | Scotland |
| Barry Wilson | 31 | 25 | 15 | 1624 | 3 | 1 | - | Scotland |
| David Xausa | 27 | 32 | 11 | 1466 | 4 | 0 | - | Canada |
| Rolando Zarate | 24 | 34 | 18 | 2101 | 3 | 0 | - | Argentina |

KEY: LEAGUE BOOKINGS CAPS

## SQUAD APPEARANCES

| Match | 1 | 2 | 3 | 4 | 5 | 6 | 7 | 8 | 9 | 10 | 11 | 12 | 13 | 14 | 15 | 16 | 17 | 18 | 19 | 20 | 21 | 22 | 23 | 24 | 25 | 26 | 27 | 28 | 29 | 30 | 31 | 32 | 33 | 34 | 35 | 36 | 37 | 38 | 39 | 40 | 41 | 42 | 43 | 44 | 45 | 46 |
|---|---|---|---|---|---|---|---|---|---|---|---|---|---|---|---|---|---|---|---|---|---|---|---|---|---|---|---|---|---|---|---|---|---|---|---|---|---|---|---|---|---|---|---|---|---|---|
| Venue | H | A | A | A | H | H | A | A | H | A | H | A | H | H | A | A | H | A | H | H | A | H | H | A | A | H | A | H | H | A | H | A | H | A | A | H | A | H | A | H | A | A | H | H | H | A |
| Competition | L | L | E | L | L | E | L | L | L | E | L | L | E | L | L | L | L | I | L | I | L | L | L | L | L | L | L | L | L | L | S | L | L | S | L | L | L | L | L | L | L | L | L | L | L | L |
| Result | W | L | D | D | L | D | L | L | L | L | L | L | W | D | W | W | D | W | W | L | L | L | D | L | L | L | D | W | W | L | D | W | L | L | L | L | D | D | W | L | D | L | W | L | L | L |

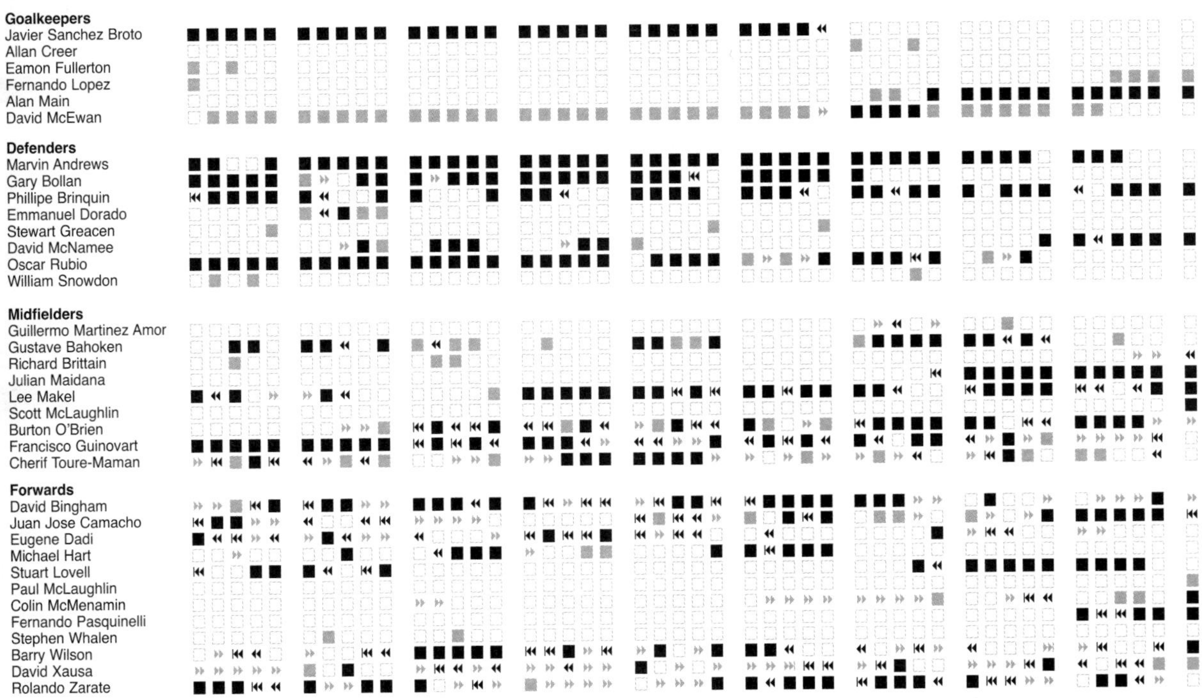

Goalkeepers
Javier Sanchez Broto
Allan Creer
Eamon Fullerton
Fernando Lopez
Alan Main
David McEwan
Defenders
Marvin Andrews
Gary Bollan
Phillipe Brinquin
Emmanuel Dorado
Stewart Greacen
David McNamee
Oscar Rubio
William Snowdon
Midfielders
Guillermo Martinez Amor
Gustave Bahoken
Richard Brittain
Julian Maidana
Lee Makel
Scott McLaughlin
Burton O'Brien
Francisco Guinovart
Cherif Toure-Maman
Forwards
David Bingham
Juan Jose Camacho
Eugene Dadi
Michael Hart
Stuart Lovell
Paul McLaughlin
Colin McMenamin
Fernando Pasquinelli
Stephen Whalen
Barry Wilson
David Xausa
Rolando Zarate

# PARTICK THISTLE

Final Position: **10th**

NICKNAME: THE JAGS

| | | | | | | | |
|---|---|---|---|---|---|---|---|
| 1 | lge | Dundee Utd | H | D | 0-0 | |
| 2 | lge | Motherwell | A | D | 1-1 | Burns 80 |
| 3 | lge | Livingston | H | D | 2-2 | Mitchell 32,63 pen |
| 4 | lge | Celtic | H | L | 0-1 | |
| 5 | lge | Aberdeen | A | W | 1-0 | Lilley 30 |
| 6 | lge | Kilmarnock | A | L | 0-1 | |
| 7 | lge | Dundee | H | D | 1-1 | Mitchell 42 |
| 8 | lge | Rangers | A | L | 0-3 | |
| 9 | cis2 | Berwick | A | W | 3-0 | Hardie 19,32; Buchan 35 |
| 10 | lge | Hearts | H | D | 2-2 | Archibald 27,78 |
| 11 | lge | Dunfermline | A | L | 1-4 | Mitchell 60 pen |
| 12 | lge | Hibernian | H | L | 0-3 | |
| 13 | cis3 | Dundee | H | W | 1-0 | Hardie 83 |
| 14 | lge | Dundee Utd | A | D | 1-1 | Waddell 86 |
| 15 | lge | Motherwell | H | W | 2-0 | Hardie 30; Burns 52 |
| 16 | cisqf | Celtic | A | L | 4-5* | Burns 50 (*on penalties) |
| 17 | lge | Livingston | A | L | 0-3 | |
| 18 | lge | Celtic | A | L | 0-4 | |
| 19 | lge | Aberdeen | H | W | 2-1 | Lilley 32; Hardie 79 |
| 20 | lge | Kilmarnock | H | W | 3-0 | Burns 64,79,87 |
| 21 | lge | Dundee | A | L | 1-4 | Britton 70 |
| 22 | lge | Dunfermline | H | W | 4-0 | Britton 5; Burns 45,52; McLean 70 |
| 23 | lge | Hearts | A | L | 0-1 | |
| 24 | lge | Rangers | H | L | 1-2 | Burns 7 |
| 25 | lge | Hibernian | A | D | 1-1 | Burns 78 |
| 26 | lge | Dundee Utd | H | D | 0-0 | |
| 27 | lge | Motherwell | A | D | 2-2 | Burns 19,49 pen |
| 28 | scr3 | Dundee | H | L | 0-2 | |
| 29 | lge | Livingston | H | L | 1-3 | Burns 39 |
| 30 | lge | Celtic | H | L | 0-2 | |
| 31 | lge | Aberdeen | A | W | 1-0 | Burns 13 |
| 32 | lge | Kilmarnock | A | L | 0-1 | |
| 33 | lge | Dundee | H | L | 1-3 | Buchan 31 |
| 34 | lge | Dunfermline | A | D | 0-0 | |
| 35 | lge | Hibernian | H | L | 0-1 | |
| 36 | lge | Rangers | A | L | 0-2 | |
| 37 | lge | Hearts | H | D | 1-1 | Mitchell 73 |
| 38 | lge | Motherwell | H | W | 3-0 | Burns 29; Britton 68,90 |
| 39 | lge | Livingston | A | L | 1-3 | Lilley 45 |
| 40 | lge | Aberdeen | A | L | 1-2 | Burns 17 pen |
| 41 | lge | Dundee Utd | H | L | 0-1 | |
| 42 | lge | Hibernian | A | W | 3-2 | Britton 29; Rowson 52; Burns 86 |

## ATTENDANCES

HOME GROUND: FIRHILL STADIUM CAPACITY: 14538 AVERAGE LEAGUE AT HOME: 5656

| | | | | | | | | |
|---|---|---|---|---|---|---|---|---|
| 18 | Celtic | 57839 | 14 | Dundee Utd | 6369 | **20** | **Kilmarnock** | **5055** |
| 36 | Rangers | 49472 | **41** | **Dundee Utd** | **6357** | **38** | **Motherwell** | **4870** |
| 8 | Rangers | 48696 | 27 | Motherwell | 6262 | **28** | **Dundee** | **4825** |
| 16 | Celtic | 26333 | 17 | Livingston | 6218 | 34 | Dunfermline | 4746 |
| 5 | Aberdeen | 12591 | **19** | **Aberdeen** | **6182** | **33** | **Dundee** | **4599** |
| 31 | Aberdeen | 11334 | **10** | **Hearts** | **6111** | **7** | **Dundee** | **4551** |
| 25 | Hibernian | 10317 | **12** | **Hibernian** | **5946** | **35** | **Hibernian** | **4551** |
| **24** | **Rangers** | **10022** | 2 | Motherwell | 5788 | **3** | **Livingston** | **4255** |
| 40 | Aberdeen | 9960 | 32 | Kilmarnock | 5651 | **22** | **Dunfermline** | **4110** |
| 23 | Hearts | 9734 | 11 | Dunfermline | 5522 | **29** | **Livingston** | **3541** |
| 42 | Hibernian | 9286 | **15** | **Motherwell** | **5405** | **13** | **Dundee** | **2652** |
| **4** | **Celtic** | **8033** | 21 | Dundee | 5363 | 9 | Berwick | 563 |
| **30** | **Celtic** | **7119** | 39 | Livingston | 5349 | | | |
| 6 | Kilmarnock | 6848 | **37** | **Hearts** | **5288** | | | |
| **1** | **Dundee Utd** | **6375** | **26** | **Dundee Utd** | **5109** | | | |

■ Home □ Away ▨ Neutral

## KEY PLAYERS - GOALSCORERS

**1 Alex Burns**

| | | | |
|---|---|---|---|
| Goals in the League | 16 | Player Strike Rate<br>Average number of minutes between League goals scored by player | 211 |
| Contribution to Attacking Power<br>Average number of minutes between League team goals while on pitch | 96 | Club Strike Rate<br>Average number of minutes between League goals scored by club | 54 |

| | PLAYER | LGE GOALS | POWER | STRIKE RATE |
|---|---|---|---|---|
| 2 | Jamie Mitchell | 5 | 79 | 448 mins |
| 3 | Gerry Britton | 5 | 79 | 480 mins |
| 4 | David Lilley | 3 | 88 | 1003 mins |
| 5 | David Rowson | 1 | 104 | 1145 mins |

## KEY PLAYERS - MIDFIELDERS

**1 Jamie Mitchell**

| | | | |
|---|---|---|---|
| Goals in the League | 5 | Contribution to Attacking Power<br>Average number of minutes between League team goals while on pitch | 80 |
| Defensive Rating<br>Average number of mins between League goals conceded while he was on the pitch | 55 | Scoring Difference<br>Defensive Rating minus Contribution to Attacking Power | -25 |

| | PLAYER | LGE GOALS | DEF RATE | POWER | SCORE DIFF |
|---|---|---|---|---|---|
| 2 | Martin Hardie | 2 | 59 | 87 | -28 mins |
| 3 | Scott Paterson | 0 | 60 | 97 | -37 mins |
| 4 | David Rowson | 1 | 57 | 104 | -47 mins |

## KEY PLAYERS - DEFENDERS

**1 Daniele Chiarini**

| | | | |
|---|---|---|---|
| Goals Conceded (GC)<br>The number of League goals conceded while he was on the pitch | 17 | Clean Sheets<br>In games when he played at least 70 minutes | 4 |
| Defensive Rating<br>Ave number of mins between League goals conceded while on the pitch | 64 | Club Defensive Rating<br>Average number of mins between League goals conceded by the club this season | 34 |

| | PLAYER | CON LGE | CLEAN SHEETS | DEF RATE |
|---|---|---|---|---|
| 2 | Alan Archibald | 53 | 9 | 61 mins |
| 3 | David Lilley | 50 | 8 | 60 mins |
| 4 | Stephen Craigan | 53 | 8 | 60 mins |
| 5 | Jamie Buchan | 35 | 5 | 59 mins |

## KEY GOALKEEPER

**1 Kenny Arthur**

| | |
|---|---|
| Goals Conceded in the League | 56 |
| Defensive Rating<br>Ave number of mins between League goals conceded while on the pitch | 56 |
| Counting Games<br>Games when he played at least 70 mins | 35 |
| Clean Sheets<br>In games when he played at least 70 mins | 8 |

## TOP POINT EARNERS

| | PLAYER | GAMES | AVE |
|---|---|---|---|
| 1 | Ross | 5 | 1.40 |
| 2 | Waddell | 3 | 1.33 |
| 3 | Chiarini | 12 | 1.25 |
| 4 | Britton | 23 | 1.13 |
| 5 | Whyte | 22 | 1.00 |
| 6 | Hardie | 35 | 0.97 |
| 7 | Lilley | 33 | 0.97 |
| 8 | Arthur | 35 | 0.94 |
| 9 | Paterson | 30 | 0.93 |
| 10 | Archibald | 36 | 0.89 |
| | **CLUB AVERAGE:** | | **0.92** |

Ave = Average points per match in Counting Games

## DISCIPLINARY RECORDS

| | PLAYER | YELLOW | RED | AVE |
|---|---|---|---|---|
| 1 | Milne | 3 | 0 | 242 |
| 2 | Britton | 8 | 1 | 266 |
| 3 | Lilley | 6 | 1 | 429 |
| 4 | Hardie | 6 | 0 | 520 |
| 5 | Whyte | 3 | 0 | 682 |
| 6 | Mitchell | 3 | 0 | 746 |
| 7 | Craigan | 4 | 0 | 798 |
| 8 | Archibald | 4 | 0 | 810 |
| 9 | Burns | 4 | 0 | 844 |
| 10 | Buchan | 2 | 0 | 1037 |
| 11 | Chiarini | 1 | 0 | 1080 |
| 12 | Paterson | 2 | 0 | 1358 |
| | Other | 1 | 0 | |
| | **TOTAL** | **47** | **2** | |

## LEAGUE GOALS

| | PLAYER | MINS | GOALS | AVE |
|---|---|---|---|---|
| 1 | Burns | 3379 | 16 | 211 |
| 2 | Mitchell | 2239 | 5 | 448 |
| 3 | Britton | 2398 | 5 | 480 |
| 4 | Lilley | 3008 | 3 | 1003 |
| 5 | Hardie | 3125 | 2 | 1563 |
| 6 | Archibald | 3240 | 2 | 1620 |
| 7 | Rowson | 1145 | 1 | 1145 |
| 8 | McLean | 482 | 1 | 482 |
| 9 | Buchan | 2075 | 1 | 2075 |
| 10 | Waddell | 453 | 1 | 453 |
| | Other | | 0 | |
| | **TOTAL** | | **37** | |

## MONTH BY MONTH GUIDE TO THE POINTS

| MONTH | POINTS | % |
|---|---|---|
| AUGUST | 3 | 25% |
| SEPTEMBER | 5 | 33% |
| OCTOBER | 1 | 11% |
| NOVEMBER | 9 | 60% |
| DECEMBER | 5 | 28% |
| JANUARY | 1 | 17% |
| FEBRUARY | 3 | 33% |
| MARCH | 1 | 11% |
| APRIL | 4 | 44% |
| MAY | 3 | 25% |

## TEAM OF THE SEASON

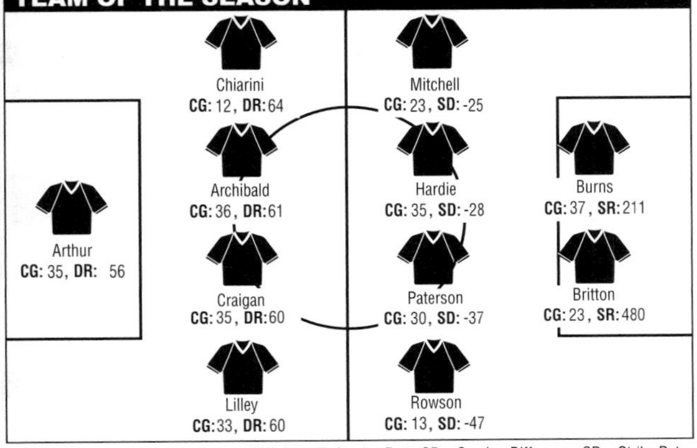
Arthur
CG: 35, DR: 56
Chiarini
CG: 12, DR: 64
Archibald
CG: 36, DR: 61
Craigan
CG: 35, DR: 60
Lilley
CG: 33, DR: 60
Mitchell
CG: 23, SD: -25
Hardie
CG: 35, SD: -28
Paterson
CG: 30, SD: -37
Rowson
CG: 13, SD: -47
Burns
CG: 37, SR: 211
Britton
CG: 23, SR: 480

KEY: DR = Defensive Rate, SD = Scoring Difference, SR = Strike Rate, CG = Counting Games – League games playing at least 70 minutes

## LEAGUE APPEARANCES, BOOKINGS AND CAPS

| | AGE (on 01/07/03) | IN THE SQUAD | COUNTING GAMES | MINUTES ON PITCH | YELLOW CARDS | RED CARDS | THIS SEASON | HOME COUNTRY |
|---|---|---|---|---|---|---|---|---|
| **Goalkeepers** | | | | | | | | |
| Kenny Arthur | 24 | 38 | 35 | 3150 | 0 | 0 | 3 | Scotland (64) |
| Kevin Budinauckas | 28 | 35 | 3 | 273 | 0 | 0 | - | Scotland |
| Steven Pinkowski | 20 | 3 | 0 | 0 | 0 | 0 | - | Scotland |
| **Defenders** | | | | | | | | |
| Alan Archibald | 25 | 36 | 36 | 3240 | 4 | 0 | - | Scotland |
| Jamie Buchan | 26 | 31 | 23 | 2075 | 2 | 0 | - | Scotland |
| Daniele Chiarini | 24 | 13 | 12 | 1080 | 1 | 0 | - | Italy |
| Stephen Craigan | 26 | 36 | 35 | 3195 | 4 | 0 | 4 | N Ireland (111) |
| David Lilley | 25 | 34 | 33 | 3008 | 6 | 1 | - | Scotland |
| Alan McDermott | - | 1 | 0 | 0 | 0 | 0 | - | |
| Kevin McGowne | 33 | 8 | 7 | 630 | 0 | 0 | - | Scotland |
| James McKinstry | 24 | 10 | 3 | 300 | 1 | 0 | - | Scotland |
| Gavin Rushford | - | 2 | 0 | 1 | 0 | 0 | - | Scotland |
| Derek Whyte | 34 | 25 | 22 | 2047 | 3 | 0 | - | Scotland |
| **Midfielders** | | | | | | | | |
| Chic Charnley | 40 | 2 | 0 | 5 | 0 | 0 | - | Scotland |
| Derek Fleming | 29 | 10 | 3 | 436 | 0 | 0 | - | Scotland |
| Andy Gibson | 21 | 32 | 1 | 215 | 0 | 0 | - | Scotland |
| Martin Hardie | 27 | 37 | 35 | 3125 | 6 | 0 | - | Scotland |
| Willie Howie | 20 | 1 | 0 | 0 | 0 | 0 | - | Scotland |
| Danny Lennon | 34 | 13 | 2 | 288 | 0 | 0 | - | Scotland |
| Jamie Mitchell | 27 | 31 | 23 | 2239 | 3 | 0 | - | Scotland |
| Scott Paterson | 25 | 32 | 30 | 2717 | 2 | 0 | - | Scotland |
| Ian Ross | 28 | 7 | 5 | 503 | 0 | 0 | - | Scotland |
| David Rowson | 26 | 13 | 13 | 1145 | 0 | 0 | - | Scotland |
| Paul Walker | 25 | 16 | 2 | 369 | 0 | 0 | - | Scotland |
| **Forwards** | | | | | | | | |
| Gerry Britton | 32 | 33 | 23 | 2398 | 8 | 1 | - | Scotland |
| Alex Burns | 29 | 38 | 37 | 3379 | 4 | 0 | - | Scotland |
| Barry Elliot | 24 | 3 | 0 | 74 | 0 | 0 | - | Scotland |
| Scott McLean | 27 | 12 | 1 | 482 | 0 | 0 | - | Scotland |
| Ken Milne | 23 | 16 | 7 | 726 | 3 | 0 | - | Scotland |
| Ian Morris | 21 | 4 | 0 | 2 | 0 | 0 | - | Scotland |
| Matthew Shields | - | 1 | 0 | 12 | 0 | 0 | - | Scotland |
| Richard Waddell | 22 | 35 | 3 | 453 | 0 | 0 | - | Scotland |

KEY: LEAGUE BOOKINGS CAPS

## SQUAD APPEARANCES

| Match | 1 | 2 | 3 | 4 | 5 | 6 | 7 | 8 | 9 | 10 | 11 | 12 | 13 | 14 | 15 | 16 | 17 | 18 | 19 | 20 | 21 | 22 | 23 | 24 | 25 | 26 | 27 | 28 | 29 | 30 | 31 | 32 | 33 | 34 | 35 | 36 | 37 | 38 | 39 | 40 | 41 | 42 |
|---|---|---|---|---|---|---|---|---|---|---|---|---|---|---|---|---|---|---|---|---|---|---|---|---|---|---|---|---|---|---|---|---|---|---|---|---|---|---|---|---|---|---|
| Venue | H | A | H | H | A | A | H | A | A | H | A | H | H | A | H | A | A | A | H | H | A | H | A | H | A | H | A | H | H | H | A | A | H | A | H | A | H | H | A | A | H | A |
| Competition | L | L | L | L | L | L | L | L | I | L | L | L | I | L | L | I | L | L | L | L | L | L | L | L | L | L | L | S | L | L | L | L | L | L | L | L | L | L | L | L | L | L |
| Result | D | D | D | L | W | L | D | L | W | D | L | L | W | D | W | L | L | L | W | W | L | W | L | L | D | D | D | L | L | L | W | L | L | D | L | L | D | W | L | L | L | W |

**Goalkeepers**
Kenny Arthur
Kevin Budinauckas
Steven Pinkowski

**Defenders**
Alan Archibald
Jamie Buchan
Daniele Chiarini
Stephen Craigan
David Lilley
Alan McDermott
Kevin McGowne
James McKinstry
Gavin Rushford
Derek Whyte

**Midfielders**
Chic Charnley
Derek Fleming
Andy Gibson
Martin Hardie
Willie Howie
Danny Lennon
Jamie Mitchell
Scott Paterson
Ian Ross
David Rowson
Paul Walker

**Forwards**
Gerry Britton
Alex Burns
Barry Elliot
Scott McLean
Ken Milne
Ian Morris
Matthew Shields
Richard Waddell

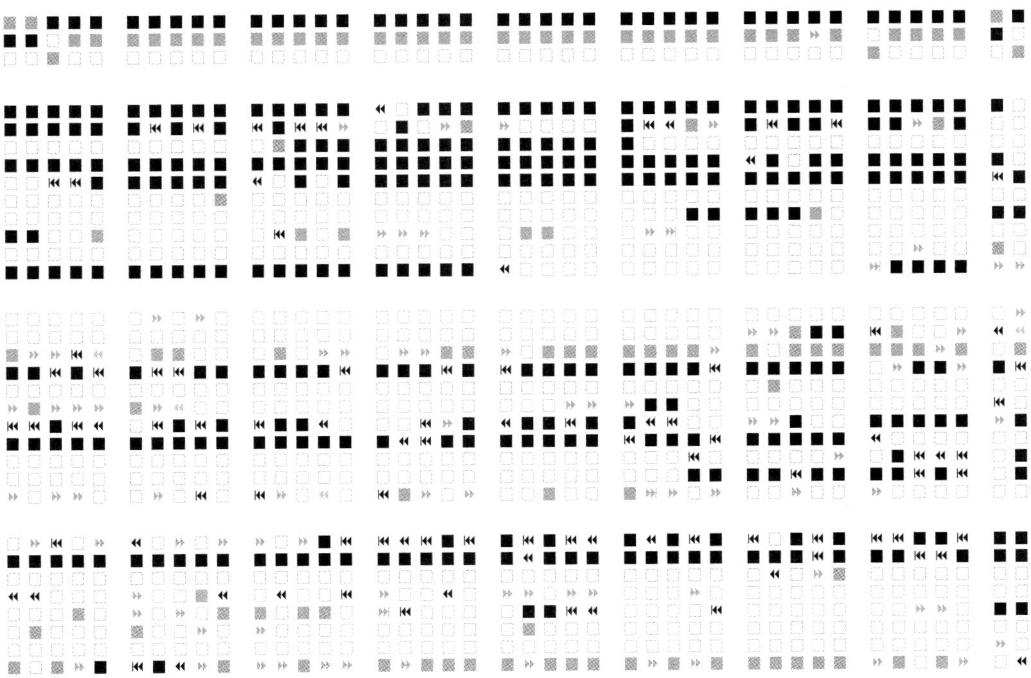

# DUNDEE UNITED

Final Position: **11th**

NICKNAME: THE TERRORS/ ARABS

| | | | | | | |
|---|---|---|---|---|---|---|
| 1 | lge | Partick | A | D | 0-0 | |
| 2 | lge | Kilmarnock | H | L | 1-2 | Thompson 71 |
| 3 | lge | Celtic | A | L | 0-5 | |
| 4 | lge | Motherwell | H | D | 1-1 | McIntyre 47 |
| 5 | lge | Dundee | H | D | 0-0 | |
| 6 | lge | Aberdeen | A | W | 2-1 | Thompson 17,40 |
| 7 | lge | Dunfermline | H | L | 1-2 | Lilley 50 |
| 8 | lge | Hearts | A | L | 0-2 | |
| 9 | cis2 | Queens Park | H | W | 4-1 | O'Donnell 8,37,69; Thompson 72 |
| 10 | lge | Rangers | H | L | 0-3 | |
| 11 | lge | Hibernian | A | L | 1-2 | Thompson 75 |
| 12 | lge | Livingston | H | L | 2-3 | Lilley 45; McIntyre 58 |
| 13 | lge | Partick | H | D | 1-1 | Thompson 13 |
| 14 | cis3 | Airdrie Utd | A | W | 2-1 | Thompson 61,68 |
| 15 | lge | Kilmarnock | A | W | 2-1 | Thompson 7; McIntyre 90 |
| 16 | lge | Celtic | H | L | 0-2 | |
| 17 | cisqf | Livingston | A | W | 2-0 | Lilley 38,73 pen |
| 18 | lge | Motherwell | A | W | 2-1 | Hamilton 1,24 |
| 19 | lge | Dundee | A | L | 2-3 | Hamilton 67; McIntyre 83 |
| 20 | lge | Aberdeen | H | D | 1-1 | Hamilton 37 pen |
| 21 | lge | Dunfermline | A | L | 1-4 | McIntyre 61 |
| 22 | lge | Hibernian | H | D | 1-1 | Wilson 3 |
| 23 | lge | Rangers | A | L | 0-3 | |
| 24 | lge | Hearts | H | L | 0-3 | |
| 25 | lge | Livingston | A | L | 0-3 | |
| 26 | lge | Partick | A | D | 0-0 | |
| 27 | lge | Kilmarnock | H | D | 2-2 | Dodds 31; McIntyre 90 |
| 28 | scr3 | Hibernian | H | L | 2-3 | O'Donnell 70; Hamilton 79 pen |
| 29 | lge | Celtic | A | L | 0-2 | |
| 30 | lge | Motherwell | H | W | 2-1 | Tod 5; Miller 68 |
| 31 | cissf | Celtic | N | L | 0-3 | |
| 32 | lge | Dundee | H | D | 1-1 | Mackay 19 og |
| 33 | lge | Aberdeen | A | L | 0-3 | |
| 34 | lge | Dunfermline | H | W | 3-0 | Easton 38; Tod 47; Ogunmade 89 |
| 35 | lge | Hibernian | A | D | 1-1 | McIntyre 69 |
| 36 | lge | Livingston | H | L | 0-1 | |
| 37 | lge | Hearts | A | L | 1-2 | Griffin 40 |
| 38 | lge | Rangers | H | L | 1-4 | Dodds 71 |
| 39 | lge | Hibernian | H | L | 1-2 | McCracken 32 |
| 40 | lge | Motherwell | A | D | 2-2 | Miller 49; McIntyre 81 |
| 41 | lge | Livingston | A | W | 2-1 | McIntyre 2; Miller 90 |
| 42 | lge | Partick | A | W | 1-0 | Paterson 59 |
| 43 | lge | Aberdeen | H | L | 0-2 | |

## ATTENDANCES

HOME GROUND: TANNADICE PARK CAPACITY: 14200 AVERAGE LEAGUE AT HOME: 7665

| | | | |
|---|---|---|---|
| 3 | Celtic | 56907 | Away |
| 29 | Celtic | 55204 | Away |
| 23 | Rangers | 47639 | Away |
| 31 | Celtic | 18856 | Neutral |
| 5 | Dundee | 12402 | Home |
| 19 | Dundee | 11539 | Away |
| 8 | Hearts | 11532 | Away |
| 6 | Aberdeen | 10724 | Away |
| 16 | Celtic | 10664 | Home |
| 32 | Dundee | 10457 | Home |
| 38 | Rangers | 10271 | Home |
| 10 | Rangers | 10013 | Home |
| 37 | Hearts | 9663 | Away |
| 11 | Hibernian | 9175 | Away |
| 33 | Aberdeen | 9146 | Away |
| 40 | Motherwell | 9056 | Away |
| 28 | Hibernian | 8985 | Home |
| 20 | Aberdeen | 8621 | Home |
| 43 | Aberdeen | 8516 | Home |
| 35 | Hibernian | 7518 | Away |
| 27 | Kilmarnock | 7183 | Home |
| 39 | Hibernian | 6758 | Home |
| 30 | Motherwell | 6672 | Home |
| 1 | Partick | 6375 | Away |
| 13 | Partick | 6369 | Home |
| 2 | Kilmarnock | 6366 | Home |
| 42 | Partick | 6357 | Away |
| 41 | Livingston | 6314 | Away |
| 36 | Livingston | 6247 | Home |
| 7 | Dunfermline | 6041 | Home |
| 24 | Hearts | 6025 | Home |
| 34 | Dunfermline | 6004 | Home |
| 4 | Motherwell | 5795 | Home |
| 22 | Hibernian | 5673 | Home |
| 12 | Livingston | 5572 | Home |
| 15 | Kilmarnock | 5417 | Away |
| 18 | Motherwell | 5381 | Away |
| 26 | Partick | 5109 | Away |
| 25 | Livingston | 5103 | Away |
| 21 | Dunfermline | 4342 | Away |
| 9 | Queens Park | 3600 | Home |
| 17 | Livingston | 3592 | Away |
| 14 | Airdrie Utd | 1768 | Away |

■ Home □ Away ▒ Neutral

## KEY PLAYERS - GOALSCORERS

**1 Steven Thompson**

| | | | |
|---|---|---|---|
| **Goals in the League** | 6 | **Player Strike Rate** Average number of minutes between League goals scored by player | 277 |
| **Contribution to Attacking Power** Average number of minutes between League team goals while on pitch | 110 | **Club Strike Rate** Average number of minutes between League goals scored by club | 57 |

| | PLAYER | LGE GOALS | POWER | STRIKE RATE |
|---|---|---|---|---|
| 2 | James McIntyre | 9 | 91 | 303 mins |
| 3 | Charlie Miller | 3 | 96 | 898 mins |
| 4 | Derek Lilley | 2 | 103 | 1194 mins |
| 5 | Daniel Griffin | 1 | 108 | 1407 mins |

## KEY PLAYERS - MIDFIELDERS

**1 Jamie Paterson**

| | | | |
|---|---|---|---|
| **Goals in the League** | 1 | **Contribution to Attacking Power** Average number of minutes between League team goals while on pitch | 86 |
| **Defensive Rating** Average number of mins between League goals conceded while he was on the pitch | 54 | **Scoring Difference** Defensive Rating minus Contribution to Attacking Power | -32 |

| | PLAYER | LGE GOALS | DEF RATE | POWER | SCORE DIFF |
|---|---|---|---|---|---|
| 2 | Stuart Duff | 0 | 52 | 99 | -47 mins |
| 3 | Craig Easton | 1 | 50 | 99 | -49 mins |

## KEY PLAYERS - DEFENDERS

**1 Gary Bollan**

| | | | |
|---|---|---|---|
| **Goals Conceded (GC)** The number of League goals conceded while he was on the pitch | 20 | **Clean Sheets** In games when he played at least 70 minutes | 2 |
| **Defensive Rating** Ave number of mins between League goals conceded while on the pitch | 59 | **Club Defensive Rating** Average number of mins between League goals conceded by the club this season | 29 |

| | PLAYER | CON LGE | CLEAN SHEETS | DEF RATE |
|---|---|---|---|---|
| 2 | Andy Tod | 17 | 2 | 58 mins |
| 3 | David McCracken | 43 | 2 | 50 mins |
| 4 | Daniel Griffin | 28 | 3 | 50 mins |
| 5 | Jim Lauchlan | 39 | 4 | 49 mins |

## KEY GOALKEEPER

**1 Paul Gallacher**

| | |
|---|---|
| **Goals Conceded in the League** | 63 |
| **Defensive Rating** Ave number of mins between League goals conceded while on the pitch | 48 |
| **Counting Games** Games when he played at least 70 mins | 34 |
| **Clean Sheets** In games when he played at least 70 mins | 4 |

## TOP POINT EARNERS

| | PLAYER | GAMES | AVE |
|---|---|---|---|
| 1 | Combe | 4 | 1.75 |
| 2 | Chiarini | 2 | 1.50 |
| 3 | Hamilton | 4 | 1.25 |
| 4 | Bollan | 13 | 1.15 |
| 5 | McCunnie | 11 | 1.09 |
| 6 | Lilley | 22 | 1.00 |
| 7 | Tod | 10 | 1.00 |
| 8 | Dodds | 5 | 1.00 |
| 9 | Lauchlan | 19 | 0.95 |
| 10 | McIntyre | 30 | 0.90 |
| | **CLUB AVERAGE:** | | **0.84** |

Ave = Average points per match in Counting Games

## DISCIPLINARY RECORDS

| | PLAYER | YELLOW | RED | AVE |
|---|---|---|---|---|
| 1 | Miller | 9 | 1 | 269 |
| 2 | McCunnie | 4 | 0 | 314 |
| 3 | Lauchlan | 6 | 0 | 317 |
| 4 | Tod | 3 | 0 | 327 |
| 5 | Easton | 9 | 0 | 341 |
| 6 | Bollan | 3 | 0 | 390 |
| 7 | Lilley | 6 | 0 | 397 |
| 8 | Smart | 0 | 1 | 506 |
| 9 | McGowne | 2 | 0 | 540 |
| 10 | O'Donnell | 1 | 0 | 609 |
| 11 | Dodds | 1 | 0 | 665 |
| 12 | McIntyre | 3 | 1 | 682 |
| 13 | Griffin | 2 | 0 | 703 |
| | Other | 12 | 1 | |
| | **TOTAL** | **61** | **4** | |

## LEAGUE GOALS

| | PLAYER | MINS | GOALS | AVE |
|---|---|---|---|---|
| 1 | McIntyre | 2730 | 9 | 303 |
| 2 | Thompson | 1660 | 6 | 277 |
| 3 | Hamilton | 739 | 4 | 185 |
| 4 | Miller | 2694 | 3 | 898 |
| 5 | Tod | 981 | 2 | 491 |
| 6 | Lilley | 2387 | 2 | 1194 |
| 7 | Dodds | 665 | 2 | 333 |
| 8 | Paterson | 1883 | 1 | 1883 |
| 9 | Easton | 3070 | 1 | 3070 |
| 10 | Ogunmade | 168 | 1 | 168 |
| 11 | Wilson | 1915 | 1 | 1915 |
| 12 | McCracken | 2160 | 1 | 2160 |
| 13 | Griffin | 1407 | 1 | 1407 |
| | Other | | 1 | |
| | **TOTAL** | | **35** | |

## MONTH BY MONTH GUIDE TO THE POINTS

| MONTH | POINTS | % |
|---|---|---|
| AUGUST | 3 | 20% |
| SEPTEMBER | 3 | 25% |
| OCTOBER | 1 | 11% |
| NOVEMBER | 7 | 47% |
| DECEMBER | 2 | 11% |
| JANUARY | 1 | 17% |
| FEBRUARY | 4 | 44% |
| MARCH | 4 | 44% |
| APRIL | 0 | 0% |
| MAY | 7 | 58% |

## TEAM OF THE SEASON

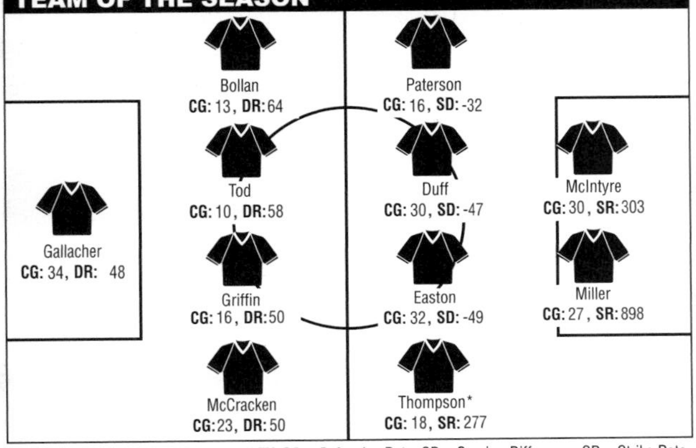
Bollan
CG: 13, DR: 64
Paterson
CG: 16, SD: -32
Tod
CG: 10, DR: 58
Duff
CG: 30, SD: -47
McIntyre
CG: 30, SR: 303
Gallacher
CG: 34, DR: 48
Griffin
CG: 16, DR: 50
Easton
CG: 32, SD: -49
Miller
CG: 27, SR: 898
McCracken
CG: 23, DR: 50
Thompson*
CG: 18, SR: 277

**KEY:** DR = Defensive Rate, SD = Scoring Difference, SR = Strike Rate, CG = Counting Games – League games playing at least 70 minutes

## LEAGUE APPEARANCES, BOOKINGS AND CAPS

| | AGE (on 01/07/03) | IN THE SQUAD | COUNTING GAMES | MINUTES ON PITCH | YELLOW CARDS | RED CARDS | THIS SEASON | HOME COUNTRY |
|---|---|---|---|---|---|---|---|---|
| **Goalkeepers** | | | | | | | | |
| Alan Combe | 29 | 27 | 4 | 418 | 0 | 1 | - | Scotland |
| Paul Gallacher | 23 | 37 | 34 | 3042 | 1 | 0 | 9 | Scotland (64) |
| Paul Jarvie | 21 | 12 | 0 | 0 | 0 | 0 | - | Scotland |
| **Defenders** | | | | | | | | |
| Hasney Aljofree | 24 | 1 | 1 | 90 | 0 | 0 | - | England |
| Gary Bollan | 30 | 14 | 13 | 1170 | 3 | 0 | - | Scotland |
| Daniele Chiarini | 24 | 6 | 2 | 241 | 0 | 0 | - | Italy |
| Warren Cummings | 22 | 15 | 8 | 785 | 1 | 0 | - | Scotland |
| Daniel Griffin | 25 | 17 | 16 | 1407 | 2 | 0 | 3 | N Ireland (111) |
| Jim Lauchlan | 26 | 26 | 19 | 1906 | 6 | 0 | - | Scotland |
| David McCracken | 21 | 31 | 23 | 2160 | 3 | 0 | - | Scotland |
| Jamie McCunnie | 20 | 23 | 11 | 1257 | 4 | 0 | - | Scotland |
| Kevin McGowne | 33 | 13 | 12 | 1080 | 2 | 0 | - | Scotland |
| Andy Tod | 31 | 13 | 10 | 981 | 3 | 0 | - | Scotland |
| Mark Wilson | 19 | 27 | 18 | 1915 | 0 | 0 | - | Scotland |
| **Midfielders** | | | | | | | | |
| Steven Carson | 22 | 10 | 2 | 301 | 0 | 0 | - | N Ireland |
| Aaron Conway | - | 1 | 0 | 11 | 0 | 0 | - | Scotland |
| Stuart Duff | 21 | 38 | 30 | 2863 | 3 | 0 | - | Scotland |
| Craig Easton | 24 | 36 | 32 | 3070 | 9 | 0 | - | Scotland |
| Russell Latapy | 34 | 8 | 1 | 402 | 0 | 0 | - | Trinidad & Tobago |
| Stephen McGowan | - | 1 | 0 | 45 | 0 | 0 | - | Scotland |
| Stephen O'Donnell | 19 | 18 | 5 | 609 | 1 | 0 | - | Scotland |
| Jamie Paterson | 23 | 35 | 16 | 1883 | 1 | 0 | - | Scotland |
| Anastasios Venetis | 32 | 3 | 0 | 84 | 0 | 0 | - | Greece |
| **Forwards** | | | | | | | | |
| Billy Dodds | 34 | 14 | 5 | 665 | 1 | 0 | - | Scotland |
| Arnar Gunnlaugsson | 30 | 8 | 0 | 224 | 0 | 0 | - | Iceland |
| Jim Hamilton | 27 | 17 | 4 | 739 | 1 | 0 | - | Scotland |
| Derek Lilley | 29 | 34 | 22 | 2387 | 6 | 0 | - | Scotland |
| James McIntyre | 31 | 34 | 30 | 2730 | 3 | 1 | - | Scotland |
| Charlie Miller | 27 | 34 | 27 | 2694 | 9 | 1 | - | Scotland |
| Daniel Ogunmade | 19 | 7 | 1 | 168 | 0 | 0 | - | Scotland |
| Allan Smart | 29 | 25 | 1 | 506 | 0 | 1 | - | Scotland |
| Steven Thompson | 24 | 20 | 18 | 1660 | 2 | 0 | 7 | Scotland (64) |
| David Winters | 20 | 1 | 0 | 8 | 0 | 0 | - | Scotland |

**KEY:** LEAGUE BOOKINGS CAPS

## SQUAD APPEARANCES

| Match | 1 | 2 | 3 | 4 | 5 | 6 | 7 | 8 | 9 | 10 | 11 | 12 | 13 | 14 | 15 | 16 | 17 | 18 | 19 | 20 | 21 | 22 |
|---|---|---|---|---|---|---|---|---|---|---|---|---|---|---|---|---|---|---|---|---|---|---|
| Venue | A | H | A | H | H | A | H | A | H | H | A | H | H | A | A | H | A | A | A | H | A | H |
| Competition | L | L | L | L | L | L | L | L | I | L | L | L | L | I | L | L | I | L | L | L | L | L |
| Result | D | L | L | D | D | W | L | L | W | L | L | L | D | W | W | L | W | W | L | D | L | D |

| Match | 23 | 24 | 25 | 26 | 27 | 28 | 29 | 30 | 31 | 32 | 33 | 34 | 35 | 36 | 37 | 38 | 39 | 40 | 41 | 42 | 43 |
|---|---|---|---|---|---|---|---|---|---|---|---|---|---|---|---|---|---|---|---|---|---|
| Venue | A | H | A | A | H | H | A | H | A | H | A | H | A | H | A | H | H | A | A | A | H |
| Competition | L | L | L | L | L | S | L | L | I | L | L | L | L | L | L | L | L | L | L | L | L |
| Result | L | L | L | D | D | L | L | W | L | D | L | W | D | L | L | L | L | D | W | W | L |

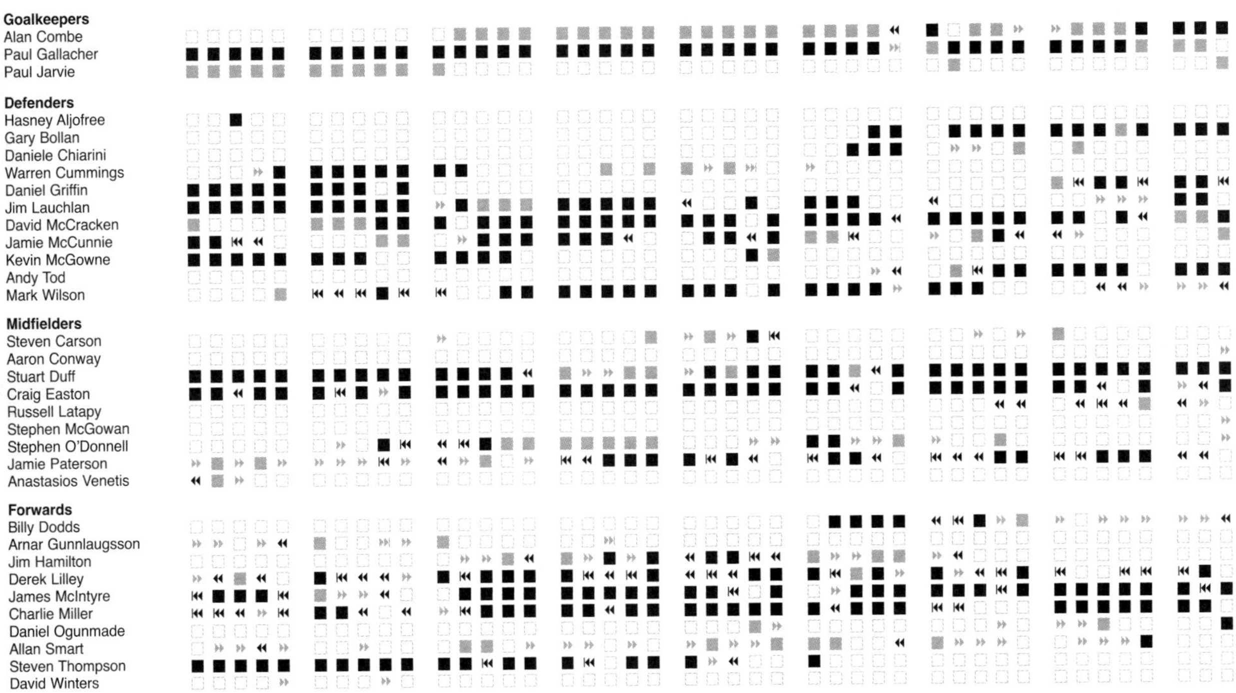
Goalkeepers
Alan Combe
Paul Gallacher
Paul Jarvie
Defenders
Hasney Aljofree
Gary Bollan
Daniele Chiarini
Warren Cummings
Daniel Griffin
Jim Lauchlan
David McCracken
Jamie McCunnie
Kevin McGowne
Andy Tod
Mark Wilson
Midfielders
Steven Carson
Aaron Conway
Stuart Duff
Craig Easton
Russell Latapy
Stephen McGowan
Stephen O'Donnell
Jamie Paterson
Anastasios Venetis
Forwards
Billy Dodds
Arnar Gunnlaugsson
Jim Hamilton
Derek Lilley
James McIntyre
Charlie Miller
Daniel Ogunmade
Allan Smart
Steven Thompson
David Winters

# MOTHERWELL

Final Position: **12th**

NICKNAME: THE WELL

| | | | | | | |
|---|---|---|---|---|---|---|
| 1 | lge | Livingston | A | L | 2-3 | Leitch 50; Lehmann 64 |
| 2 | lge | Partick | H | D | 1-1 | Pearson 82 |
| 3 | lge | Kilmarnock | A | W | 3-0 | Ramsay 66; Pearson 83; McFadden 85 |
| 4 | lge | Dundee Utd | A | D | 1-1 | Pearson 3 |
| 5 | lge | Hibernian | H | L | 0-2 | |
| 6 | lge | Celtic | H | W | 2-1 | Fagen 77; McFadden 79 pen |
| 7 | lge | Hearts | A | L | 2-4 | Lehmann 12; McFadden 27 |
| 8 | lge | Dunfermline | A | L | 0-1 | |
| 9 | cis2 | East Fife | A | W | 2-0 | Lehmann 29; McFadden 66 |
| 10 | lge | Dundee | H | D | 1-1 | McFadden 55 |
| 11 | lge | Aberdeen | H | L | 1-2 | McFadden 39 pen |
| 12 | lge | Rangers | A | L | 0-3 | |
| 13 | lge | Livingston | H | L | 1-5 | Kemas 79 |
| 14 | lge | Partick | A | L | 0-2 | |
| 15 | cis3 | Aberdeen | A | L | 1-3 | Adams 41 |
| 16 | lge | Kilmarnock | H | L | 0-1 | |
| 17 | lge | Dundee Utd | H | L | 1-2 | Lehmann 82 |
| 18 | lge | Hibernian | A | L | 1-3 | Ferguson 47 |
| 19 | lge | Celtic | A | L | 1-3 | Lehmann 74 |
| 20 | lge | Hearts | H | W | 6-1 | Pearson 15; McFadden 19 pen,26; Adams 36; Corrigan 66; Ferguson 90 |
| 21 | lge | Aberdeen | A | D | 1-1 | Kinniburgh 59 |
| 22 | lge | Dundee | A | D | 1-1 | Lehmann 25 |
| 23 | lge | Rangers | H | W | 1-0 | McFadden 65 |
| 24 | lge | Livingston | A | L | 0-1 | |
| 25 | lge | Partick | H | D | 2-2 | Clarkson 9; Partridge 77 |
| 26 | scr3 | Kilmarnock | A | W | 1-0 | McFadden 35 pen |
| 27 | lge | Kilmarnock | A | L | 0-1 | |
| 28 | lge | Dundee Utd | A | L | 1-2 | Adams 20 pen |
| 29 | lge | Hibernian | H | W | 2-1 | Clarkson 31; Fagan 41 |
| 30 | lge | Dunfermline | H | W | 2-1 | Pearson 20; Craig 50 |
| 31 | scr4 | Clyde | A | W | 2-0 | McFadden 41,77 |
| 32 | lge | Hearts | A | L | 1-2 | Lasley 53 |
| 33 | lge | Aberdeen | H | L | 0-1 | |
| 34 | lge | Rangers | A | L | 0-2 | |
| 35 | scqf | Stranraer | A | W | 4-0 | Wright 31 og; McFadden 54; Adams 59; Lehmann 87 |
| 36 | lge | Dunfermline | A | L | 0-3 | |
| 37 | lge | Dundee | H | L | 1-2 | McFadden 77 |
| 38 | scsf | Rangers | N | L | 3-4 | Craig 15; McFadden 27; Adams 90 |
| 39 | lge | Partick | A | L | 0-3 | |
| 40 | lge | Dundee Utd | H | D | 2-2 | Pearson 11; Vaughan 85 |
| 41 | lge | Celtic | H | L | 0-4 | |
| 42 | lge | Hibernian | A | L | 0-1 | |
| 43 | lge | Aberdeen | H | L | 2-3 | Clarkson 16; McFadden 84 pen |
| 44 | lge | Livingston | H | W | 6-2 | Lasley 30,90; Craig 57; McFadden 64,74 pen,75 |

## ATTENDANCES

HOME GROUND: FIR PARK CAPACITY: 13742 AVERAGE LEAGUE AT HOME: 6085

| | | | | | | | | |
|---|---|---|---|---|---|---|---|---|
| 19 | Celtic | 56733 | 26 | Kilmarnock | 6882 | 8 | Dunfermline | 4987 |
| 12 | Rangers | 49376 | 28 | Dundee Utd | 6672 | 39 | Partick | 4870 |
| 34 | Rangers | 49240 | 15 | Aberdeen | 6557 | 44 | Livingston | 4790 |
| 38 | Rangers | 29352 | 25 | Partick | 6262 | 43 | Aberdeen | 4731 |
| 41 | Celtic | 12037 | 3 | Kilmarnock | 6164 | 37 | Dundee | 4693 |
| 32 | Hearts | 11704 | 11 | Aberdeen | 6014 | 35 | Stranraer | 4500 |
| 23 | Rangers | 11234 | 5 | Hibernian | 5888 | 27 | Kilmarnock | 4457 |
| 21 | Aberdeen | 9569 | 4 | Dundee Utd | 5795 | 16 | Kilmarnock | 4439 |
| 40 | Dundee Utd | 9056 | 2 | Partick | 5788 | 13 | Livingston | 4342 |
| 18 | Hibernian | 8859 | 33 | Aberdeen | 5636 | 20 | Hearts | 4114 |
| 7 | Hearts | 8578 | 22 | Dundee | 5527 | 36 | Dunfermline | 4086 |
| 6 | Celtic | 8448 | 14 | Partick | 5405 | 10 | Dundee | 4025 |
| 42 | Hibernian | 7809 | 17 | Dundee Utd | 5381 | 30 | Dunfermline | 3741 |
| 24 | Livingston | 7216 | 31 | Clyde | 5032 | 9 | East Fife | 978 |
| 1 | Livingston | 7124 | 29 | Hibernian | 4999 | | | |

■ Home □ Away ▒ Neutral

## KEY PLAYERS - GOALSCORERS

**1 James McFadden**

| | | | |
|---|---|---|---|
| Goals in the League | 13 | Player Strike Rate<br>Average number of minutes between League goals scored by player | 193 |
| Contribution to Attacking Power<br>Average number of minutes between League team goals while on pitch | 69 | Club Strike Rate<br>Average number of minutes between League goals scored by club | 44 |

| | PLAYER | LGE GOALS | POWER | STRIKE RATE |
|---|---|---|---|---|
| 2 | David Clarkson | 3 | 66 | 400 mins |
| 3 | Stephen Pearson | 6 | 71 | 415 mins |
| 4 | Dirk Lehmann | 5 | 87 | 488 mins |
| 5 | Keith Lasley | 3 | 80 | 589 mins |

## KEY PLAYERS - MIDFIELDERS

**1 Stephen Pearson**

| | | | |
|---|---|---|---|
| Goals in the League | 6 | Contribution to Attacking Power<br>Average number of minutes between League team goals while on pitch | 71 |
| Defensive Rating<br>Average number of mins between League goals conceded while he was on the pitch | 58 | Scoring Difference<br>Defensive Rating minus Contribution to Attacking Power | -13 |

| | PLAYER | LGE GOALS | DEF RATE | POWER | SCORE DIFF |
|---|---|---|---|---|---|
| 2 | James McFadden | 13 | 49 | 70 | -21 mins |
| 3 | David Partridge | 1 | 52 | 82 | -30 mins |
| 4 | Steven Hammell | 0 | 47 | 78 | -31 mins |
| 5 | Keith Lasley | 3 | 45 | 80 | -35 mins |

## KEY PLAYERS - DEFENDERS

**1 William Kinniburgh**

| | | | |
|---|---|---|---|
| Goals Conceded (GC)<br>The number of League goals conceded while he was on the pitch | 21 | Clean Sheets<br>In games when he played at least 70 minutes | 1 |
| Defensive Rating<br>Ave number of mins between League goals conceded while on the pitch | 54 | Club Defensive Rating<br>Average number of mins between League goals conceded by the club this season | 28 |

| | PLAYER | CON LGE | CLEAN SHEETS | DEF RATE |
|---|---|---|---|---|
| 2 | Martyn Corrigan | 71 | 2 | 48 mins |
| 3 | Tony Vaughan | 23 | 0 | 43 mins |

## KEY GOALKEEPER

**1 Francais Dubourdeau**

| | |
|---|---|
| Goals Conceded in the League | 36 |
| Defensive Rating<br>Ave number of mins between League goals conceded while on the pitch | 55 |
| Counting Games<br>Games when he played at least 70 mins | 22 |
| Clean Sheets<br>In games when he played at least 70 mins | 1 |

## TOP POINT EARNERS

| | PLAYER | GAMES | AVE |
|---|---|---|---|
| 1 | Sengewald | 3 | 2.00 |
| 2 | Craig | 5 | 1.80 |
| 3 | Quinn | 3 | 1.67 |
| 4 | Fagan | 7 | 1.14 |
| 5 | McDonald | 3 | 1.00 |
| 6 | Kinniburgh | 12 | 1.00 |
| 7 | Adams | 28 | 0.86 |
| 8 | Pearson | 27 | 0.85 |
| 9 | Clarkson | 13 | 0.85 |
| 10 | Dubourdeau | 22 | 0.82 |
| | CLUB AVERAGE: | | 0.74 |

Ave = Average points per match in Counting Games

## DISCIPLINARY RECORDS

| | PLAYER | YELLOW | RED | AVE |
|---|---|---|---|---|
| 1 | McFadden | 15 | 1 | 156 |
| 2 | Fagan | 5 | 1 | 164 |
| 3 | Vaughan | 4 | 1 | 199 |
| 4 | Leitch | 9 | 1 | 209 |
| 5 | Craig | 3 | 0 | 221 |
| 6 | Pearson | 8 | 2 | 248 |
| 7 | Partridge | 9 | 2 | 260 |
| 8 | Kinniburgh | 4 | 0 | 285 |
| 9 | Lasley | 6 | 0 | 294 |
| 10 | Adams | 8 | 1 | 300 |
| 11 | Ferguson | 2 | 0 | 420 |
| 12 | Lehmann | 5 | 0 | 488 |
| 13 | Ramsey | 3 | 0 | 492 |
| | Other | 16 | 2 | |
| | TOTAL | 97 | 11 | |

## LEAGUE GOALS

| | PLAYER | MINS | GOALS | AVE |
|---|---|---|---|---|
| 1 | McFadden | 2511 | 13 | 193 |
| 2 | Pearson | 2487 | 6 | 415 |
| 3 | Lehmann | 2440 | 5 | 488 |
| 4 | Clarkson | 1201 | 3 | 400 |
| 5 | Lasley | 1767 | 3 | 589 |
| 6 | Craig | 665 | 2 | 333 |
| 7 | Fagan | 989 | 2 | 495 |
| 8 | Adams | 2700 | 2 | 1350 |
| 9 | Ferguson | 840 | 2 | 420 |
| 10 | Kinniburgh | 1141 | 1 | 1141 |
| 11 | Khemas | 314 | 1 | 314 |
| 12 | Corrigan | 3403 | 1 | 3403 |
| 13 | Ramsey | 1476 | 1 | 1476 |
| | Other | | 3 | |
| | TOTAL | | 45 | |

## MONTH BY MONTH GUIDE TO THE POINTS

| MONTH | POINTS | % |
|---|---|---|
| AUGUST | 5 | 33% |
| SEPTEMBER | 4 | 33% |
| OCTOBER | 0 | 0% |
| NOVEMBER | 0 | 0% |
| DECEMBER | 8 | 44% |
| JANUARY | 1 | 17% |
| FEBRUARY | 6 | 67% |
| MARCH | 0 | 0% |
| APRIL | 0 | 0% |
| MAY | 4 | 27% |

## TEAM OF THE SEASON

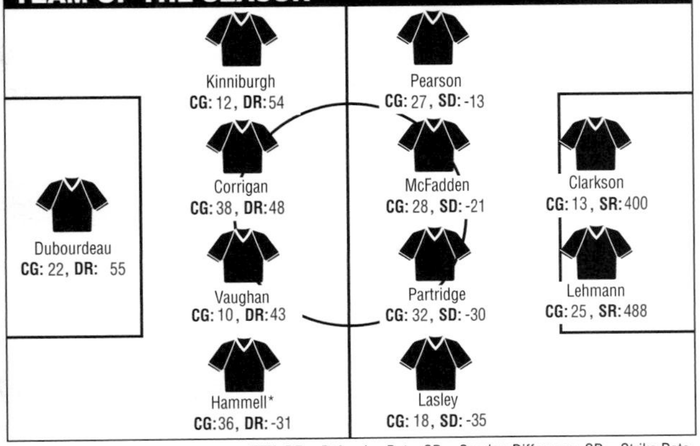

Dubourdeau
CG: 22, DR: 55
Kinniburgh
CG: 12, DR: 54
Corrigan
CG: 38, DR: 48
Vaughan
CG: 10, DR: 43
Hammell*
CG: 36, DR: -31
Pearson
CG: 27, SD: -13
McFadden
CG: 28, SD: -21
Partridge
CG: 32, SD: -30
Lasley
CG: 18, SD: -35
Clarkson
CG: 13, SR: 400
Lehmann
CG: 25, SR: 488


KEY: DR = Defensive Rate, SD = Scoring Difference, SR = Strike Rate, CG = Counting Games – League games playing at least 70 minutes

## LEAGUE APPEARANCES, BOOKINGS AND CAPS

| | AGE (on 01/07/03) | IN THE SQUAD | COUNTING GAMES | MINUTES ON PITCH | YELLOW CARDS | RED CARDS | THIS SEASON | HOME COUNTRY |
|---|---|---|---|---|---|---|---|---|
| **Goalkeepers** | | | | | | | | |
| Francais Dubourdeau | - | 35 | 22 | 1970 | 0 | 1 | - | France |
| Jamie Ewings | 18 | 4 | 0 | 0 | 0 | 0 | - | Scotland |
| Stephen Woods | 33 | 37 | 16 | 1451 | 0 | 0 | - | Scotland |
| **Defenders** | | | | | | | | |
| Martyn Corrigan | 25 | 38 | 38 | 3403 | 2 | 0 | - | Scotland |
| David Cowan | 21 | 22 | 12 | 1285 | 2 | 0 | - | England |
| Brian Dempsie | 20 | 1 | 0 | 66 | 1 | 0 | - | Scotland |
| Chris Higgins | 18 | 1 | 0 | 0 | 0 | 0 | - | Scotland |
| William Kinniburgh | 18 | 27 | 12 | 1141 | 4 | 0 | - | Scotland |
| Kevin McDonald | 20 | 23 | 3 | 356 | 1 | 0 | - | Scotland |
| Paul Quinn | 18 | 7 | 3 | 294 | 0 | 0 | - | Scotland |
| Daniel Sengewald | 27 | 11 | 3 | 420 | 4 | 1 | - | Germany |
| Tony Vaughan | 27 | 12 | 10 | 996 | 4 | 1 | - | England |
| **Midfielders** | | | | | | | | |
| Ross Ballantyne | - | 1 | 0 | 17 | 0 | 0 | - | Scotland |
| David Black | 19 | 1 | 0 | 0 | 0 | 0 | - | Scotland |
| David Clarke | 20 | 2 | 0 | 11 | 0 | 0 | - | Scotland |
| Shaun Fagan | 19 | 24 | 7 | 989 | 5 | 1 | - | Scotland |
| Steven Hammell | 21 | 37 | 36 | 3278 | 6 | 0 | - | Scotland |
| Keith Lasley | 23 | 26 | 18 | 1767 | 6 | 0 | - | Scotland |
| Scott Leitch | 33 | 26 | 22 | 2096 | 9 | 1 | - | Scotland |
| Graeme Mathie | 20 | 1 | 0 | 0 | 0 | 0 | - | Scotland |
| James McFadden | 20 | 30 | 28 | 2511 | 15 | 1 | 4 | Scotland (64) |
| David Partridge | 24 | 32 | 32 | 2864 | 9 | 2 | - | Wales |
| Stephen Pearson | 20 | 29 | 27 | 2487 | 8 | 2 | - | Scotland |
| Douglas Ramsey | 24 | 27 | 14 | 1476 | 3 | 0 | - | Scotland |
| **Forwards** | | | | | | | | |
| Derek Adams | 28 | 32 | 28 | 2700 | 8 | 1 | - | Scotland |
| David Clarkson | 17 | 24 | 13 | 1201 | 0 | 0 | - | Scotland |
| Steven Craig | 22 | 14 | 5 | 665 | 3 | 0 | - | Scotland |
| Steven Ferguson | 26 | 20 | 7 | 840 | 2 | 0 | - | Scotland |
| Darren Jack | 19 | 4 | 0 | 36 | 0 | 0 | - | Scotland |
| Khaled Kemas | 23 | 1 | 0 | 0 | 0 | 0 | - | Algeria |
| Khaled Khemas | 23 | 7 | 2 | 314 | 0 | 0 | - | Algeria |
| Dirk Lehmann | 32 | 32 | 25 | 2440 | 5 | 0 | - | Germany |
| Richard Offiong | 19 | 9 | 0 | 168 | 0 | 0 | - | England |
| Ian Russell | - | 9 | 0 | 100 | 0 | 0 | - | |
| Andrew Scott | 18 | 1 | 0 | 7 | 0 | 0 | - | Scotland |
| Kenneth Wright | 17 | 1 | 0 | 14 | 0 | 0 | - | Scotland |

KEY: LEAGUE BOOKINGS CAPS

## SQUAD APPEARANCES

| Match | 1 | 2 | 3 | 4 | 5 | 6 | 7 | 8 | 9 | 10 | 11 | 12 | 13 | 14 | 15 | 16 | 17 | 18 | 19 | 20 | 21 | 22 | 23 | 24 | 25 | 26 | 27 | 28 | 29 | 30 | 31 | 32 | 33 | 34 | 35 | 36 | 37 | 38 | 39 | 40 | 41 | 42 | 43 | 44 |
|---|---|---|---|---|---|---|---|---|---|---|---|---|---|---|---|---|---|---|---|---|---|---|---|---|---|---|---|---|---|---|---|---|---|---|---|---|---|---|---|---|---|---|---|---|
| Venue | A | H | A | A | H | H | A | A | A | H | H | A | H | A | A | H | H | A | A | H | A | A | H | A | H | A | A | A | H | H | A | A | H | A | A | A | H | A | A | H | H | A | H | H |
| Competition | L | L | L | L | L | L | L | L | I | L | L | L | L | L | I | L | L | L | L | L | L | L | L | L | L | S | L | L | L | L | S | L | L | L | S | L | L | S | L | L | L | L | L | L |
| Result | L | D | W | D | L | W | L | L | W | D | L | L | L | L | L | L | L | L | L | W | D | D | W | L | D | W | L | L | W | W | W | L | L | L | W | L | L | L | L | D | L | L | L | W |

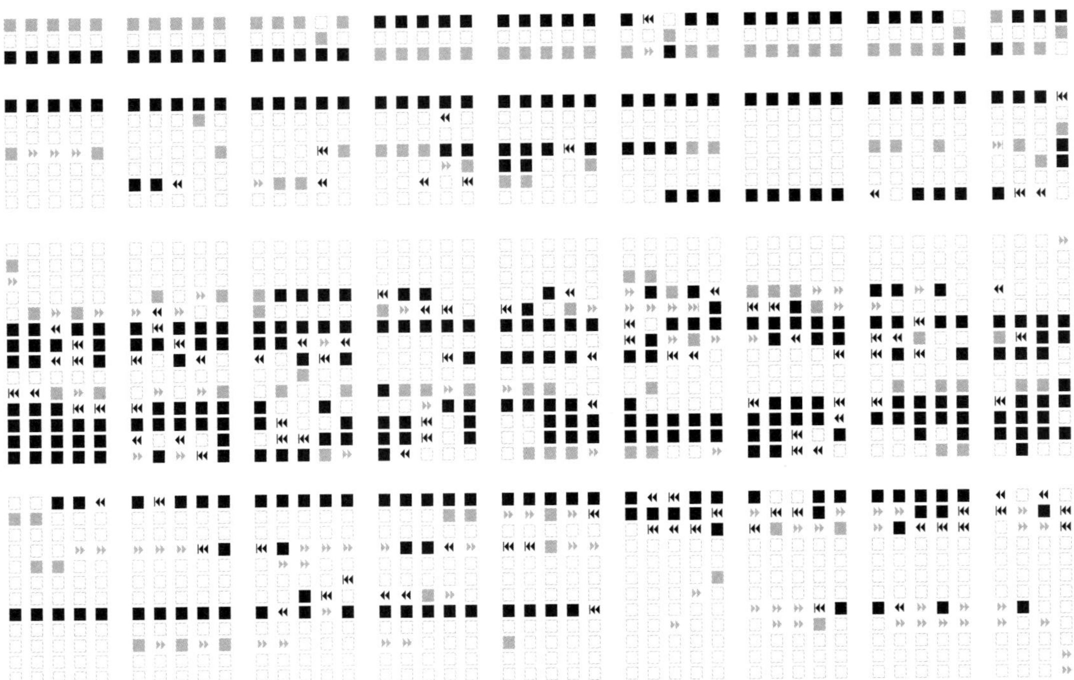

**Goalkeepers**
Francais Dubourdeau
Jamie Ewings
Stephen Woods

**Defenders**
Martyn Corrigan
Brian Dempsie
Chris Higgins
William Kinniburgh
Paul Quinn
Daniel Sengewald
Tony Vaughan

**Midfielders**
Ross Ballantyne
David Black
David Clarke
David Cowan
Shaun Fagan
Steven Hammell
Keith Lasley
Scott Leitch
Graeme Mathie
Kevin McDonald
James McFadden
David Partridge
Stephen Pearson
Douglas Ramsey

**Forwards**
Derek Adams
David Clarkson
Steven Craig
Steven Ferguson
Darren Jack
Khaled Kemas
Khaled Khemas
Dirk Lehmann
Richard Offiong
Ian Russell
Andrew Scott
Kenneth Wright

BELL'S SCOTTISH FOOTBALL LEAGUE FIRST DIVISION CHAMPIONS

# FALKIRK

Final Position: **1st**

NICKNAME: THE BAIRNS

| | | | | | | |
|---|---|---|---|---|---|---|
| 1 | lge | Ayr | A | W | 3-1 | McQuilken 1; Coyle 23; James 80 |
| 2 | lge | St Mirren | H | W | 2-0 | Coyle 9; Lawrie 15 |
| 3 | lge | Inverness CT | A | W | 2-1 | Miller 81; Tosh 90 |
| 4 | lge | Alloa | A | W | 6-1 | McPherson 11; Lawrie 27,53; Samuel 70,75; Coyle 77 |
| 5 | lge | Queen of South | H | W | 3-0 | Lawrie 28; Allan 76 og; Samuel 83 |
| 6 | cis1 | Peterhead | H | W | 2-0 | Lawrie 45; Coyle 51 |
| 7 | lge | Ross County | A | D | 1-1 | Coyle 58 |
| 8 | lge | Clyde | H | W | 2-1 | Coyle 57; McQuilken 68 |
| 9 | cis2 | Ayr | A | W | 2-0 | Samuel 23; Miller 53 |
| 10 | lge | St Johnstone | H | W | 1-0 | James 87 |
| 11 | lge | Arbroath | A | L | 0-2 | |
| 12 | lge | Ayr | H | W | 3-0 | McManus 60 og; Coyle 77,86 |
| 13 | cis3 | Dunfermline | A | L | 0-2 | |
| 14 | lge | St Mirren | A | D | 4-4 | Kerr 12; Miller 18,34,74 |
| 15 | lge | Queen of South | A | D | 1-1 | Henry 57 |
| 16 | lge | Alloa | H | W | 3-0 | Henry 8; Coyle 49; James 77 |
| 17 | lge | Ross County | H | W | 2-0 | Miller 24,89 |
| 18 | lge | Clyde | A | L | 0-2 | |
| 19 | lge | St Johnstone | A | W | 1-0 | James 60 |
| 20 | lge | Arbroath | H | W | 2-1 | Samuel 44; Coyle 60 |
| 21 | lge | Inverness CT | H | D | 1-1 | Hughes 17 |
| 22 | lge | Queen of South | H | W | 5-0 | Miller 19; Henry 25; Coyle 36; Samuel 47,56 |
| 23 | lge | Arbroath | A | W | 4-1 | Samuel 8,16,35; Coyle 48 |
| 24 | scr3 | Hearts | H | W | 4-0 | Samuel 3,17,31; Coyle 13 |
| 25 | lge | St Johnstone | H | D | 1-1 | Henry 62 |
| 26 | lge | Inverness CT | A | W | 4-3 | Coyle 31,73,86; Samuel 33 |
| 27 | lge | St Mirren | H | W | 3-1 | Coyle 16; Henry 58; Samuel 78 |
| 28 | scr4 | Alloa | A | W | 2-0 | Coyle 52; Samuel 62 |
| 29 | lge | Ayr | A | L | 0-1 | |
| 30 | lge | Queen of South | A | L | 1-2 | Miller 57 |
| 31 | lge | Clyde | H | W | 3-0 | McLaughlin 6 og; Halliwell 23 og; Miller 40 |
| 32 | lge | Alloa | H | W | 3-1 | Miller 45 pen; Rodgers 77; Taylor 88 |
| 33 | lge | Ross County | A | W | 1-0 | Miller 18 pen |
| 34 | lge | Clyde | A | D | 0-0 | |
| 35 | Scpqf | Dundee | H | D | 1-1 | Coyle 57 |
| 36 | lge | Alloa | A | W | 3-1 | Coyle 38; Miller 44; Taylor 55 |
| 37 | lge | Ross County | H | W | 3-0 | Miller 15,68; Coyle 85 |
| 38 | Scqfr | Dundee | A | L | 1-4 | Taylor 32 |
| 39 | lge | St Johnstone | A | W | 1-0 | Taylor 55 |
| 40 | lge | Arbroath | H | W | 4-1 | Coyle 25,60,89; Kerr 65 |
| 41 | lge | Ayr | H | W | 3-0 | Miller 10; Taylor 39; McKenzie 87 pen |
| 42 | lge | St Mirren | A | W | 2-1 | Taylor 14; Miller 49 |
| 43 | lge | Inverness CT | H | L | 2-3 | Samuel 6; Taylor 50 |

## ATTENDANCES

HOME GROUND: BROCKVILLE PARK CAPACITY: 7550 AVERAGE LEAGUE AT HOME: 4164

| | | | | | | | | |
|---|---|---|---|---|---|---|---|---|
| 38 | Dundee | 9562 | 31 | Clyde | 3706 | 15 | Queen of South | 3017 |
| 24 | Hearts | 7500 | 19 | St Johnstone | 3696 | 34 | Clyde | 3012 |
| 35 | Dundee | 7403 | 14 | St Mirren | 3661 | 20 | Arbroath | 2675 |
| 43 | Inverness CT | 7300 | 8 | Clyde | 3595 | 30 | Queen of South | 2655 |
| 13 | Dunfermline | 6933 | 37 | Ross County | 3523 | 4 | Alloa | 2613 |
| 39 | St Johnstone | 6542 | 12 | Ayr | 3441 | 3 | Inverness CT | 2267 |
| 10 | St Johnstone | 5872 | 18 | Clyde | 3415 | 33 | Ross County | 2161 |
| 40 | Arbroath | 4950 | 16 | Alloa | 3390 | 6 | Peterhead | 2157 |
| 25 | St Johnstone | 4694 | 26 | Inverness CT | 3322 | 9 | Ayr | 2080 |
| 21 | Inverness CT | 4691 | 32 | Alloa | 3320 | 23 | Arbroath | 1807 |
| 2 | St Mirren | 4360 | 17 | Ross County | 3255 | 29 | Ayr | 1783 |
| 27 | St Mirren | 4206 | 7 | Ross County | 3129 | 36 | Alloa | 1686 |
| 5 | Queen of South | 4091 | 42 | St Mirren | 3062 | 11 | Arbroath | 1115 |
| 41 | Ayr | 4042 | 28 | Alloa | 3059 | | | |
| 22 | Queen of South | 3858 | 1 | Ayr | 3030 | | | |

■ Home □ Away ▒ Neutral

## KEY PLAYERS - GOALSCORERS

**1 Owen Coyle**

| | | | |
|---|---|---|---|
| Goals in the League | 20 | Player Strike Rate<br>Average number of minutes between League goals scored by player | 151 |
| Contribution to Attacking Power<br>Average number of minutes between League team goals while on pitch | 40 | Club Strike Rate<br>Average number of minutes between League goals scored by club | 20 |

| | PLAYER | LGE GOALS | POWER | STRIKE RATE |
|---|---|---|---|---|
| 2 | Collin Samuel | 12 | 40 | 162 mins |
| 3 | Lee Miller | 16 | 40 | 181 mins |
| 4 | Kevin James | 4 | 42 | 263 mins |
| 5 | John Henry | 5 | 43 | 442 mins |

## KEY PLAYERS - MIDFIELDERS

**1 Scott MacKenzie**

| | | | |
|---|---|---|---|
| Goals in the League | 1 | Contribution to Attacking Power<br>Average number of minutes between League team goals while on pitch | 40 |
| Defensive Rating<br>Average number of mins between League goals conceded while he was on the pitch | 106 | Scoring Difference<br>Defensive Rating minus Contribution to Attacking Power | 66 |

| | PLAYER | LGE GOALS | DEF RATE | POWER | SCORE DIFF |
|---|---|---|---|---|---|
| 2 | Mark Kerr | 2 | 100 | 40 | 60 mins |
| 3 | Steven Tosh | 1 | 100 | 42 | 58 mins |
| 4 | David Nicholls | 0 | 95 | 40 | 55 mins |

## KEY PLAYERS - DEFENDERS

**1 Kevin James**

| | | | |
|---|---|---|---|
| Goals Conceded (GC)<br>The number of League goals conceded while he was on the pitch | 8 | Clean Sheets<br>In games when he played at least 70 minutes | 5 |
| Defensive Rating<br>Ave number of mins between League goals conceded while on the pitch | 132 | Club Defensive Rating<br>Average number of mins between League goals conceded by the club this season | 51 |

| | PLAYER | CON LGE | CLEAN SHEETS | DEF RATE |
|---|---|---|---|---|
| 2 | John Hughes | 25 | 11 | 109 mins |
| 3 | James McQuilken | 27 | 11 | 108 mins |
| 4 | Craig McPherson | 28 | 12 | 102 mins |
| 5 | John Henry | 22 | 9 | 100 mins |

## KEY GOALKEEPER

**1 Allan Ferguson**

| | |
|---|---|
| Goals Conceded in the League | 30 |
| Defensive Rating<br>Ave number of mins between League goals conceded while on the pitch | 95 |
| Counting Games<br>Games when he played at least 70 mins | 32 |
| Clean Sheets<br>In games when he played at least 70 mins | 12 |

## TOP POINT EARNERS

| | PLAYER | GAMES | AVE |
|---|---|---|---|
| 1 | Lawrie | 6 | 2.67 |
| 2 | Reid | 4 | 2.50 |
| 3 | Taylor | 6 | 2.50 |
| 4 | Hill | 4 | 2.50 |
| 5 | Henry | 17 | 2.47 |
| 6 | McPherson | 29 | 2.34 |
| 7 | Coyle | 30 | 2.33 |
| 8 | Hughes | 30 | 2.30 |
| 9 | McQuilken | 31 | 2.29 |
| 10 | MacKenzie | 32 | 2.25 |
| | **CLUB AVERAGE:** | | **2.25** |

Ave = Average points per match in Counting Games

## DISCIPLINARY RECORDS

| | PLAYER | YELLOW | RED | AVE |
|---|---|---|---|---|
| 1 | Tosh | 5 | 1 | 233 |
| 2 | James | 2 | 1 | 351 |
| 3 | Rennie | 3 | 0 | 431 |
| 4 | Reid | 1 | 0 | 462 |
| 5 | Nicholls | 3 | 0 | 508 |
| 6 | Hughes | 5 | 0 | 544 |
| 7 | Lawrie | 1 | 0 | 551 |
| 8 | Miller | 4 | 1 | 578 |
| 9 | Kerr | 4 | 0 | 749 |
| 10 | McQuilken | 3 | 0 | 972 |
| 11 | MacKenzie | 2 | 0 | 1437 |
| 12 | Henry | 1 | 0 | 2209 |
| 13 | McPherson | 1 | 0 | 2868 |
| | Other | 3 | 0 | |
| | TOTAL | 38 | 3 | |

## LEAGUE GOALS

| | PLAYER | MINS | GOALS | AVE |
|---|---|---|---|---|
| 1 | Coyle | 3017 | 20 | 151 |
| 2 | Miller | 2892 | 16 | 181 |
| 3 | Samuel | 1948 | 12 | 162 |
| 4 | Taylor | 766 | 6 | 128 |
| 5 | Henry | 2209 | 5 | 442 |
| 6 | Lawrie | 551 | 4 | 138 |
| 7 | James | 1053 | 4 | 263 |
| 8 | McQuilken | 2917 | 2 | 1459 |
| 9 | Kerr | 2999 | 2 | 1500 |
| 10 | Rodgers | 187 | 1 | 187 |
| 11 | McPherson | 2868 | 1 | 2868 |
| 12 | MacKenzie | 2874 | 1 | 2874 |
| 13 | Hughes | 2724 | 1 | 2724 |
| | Other | | 5 | |
| | TOTAL | | 80 | |

## MONTH BY MONTH GUIDE TO THE POINTS

| MONTH | POINTS | % |
|---|---|---|
| AUGUST | 15 | 100% |
| SEPTEMBER | 7 | 78% |
| OCTOBER | 4 | 44% |
| NOVEMBER | 10 | 67% |
| DECEMBER | 7 | 78% |
| JANUARY | 3 | 100% |
| FEBRUARY | 7 | 58% |
| MARCH | 13 | 72% |
| APRIL | 12 | 100% |
| MAY | 3 | 50% |

## TEAM OF THE SEASON

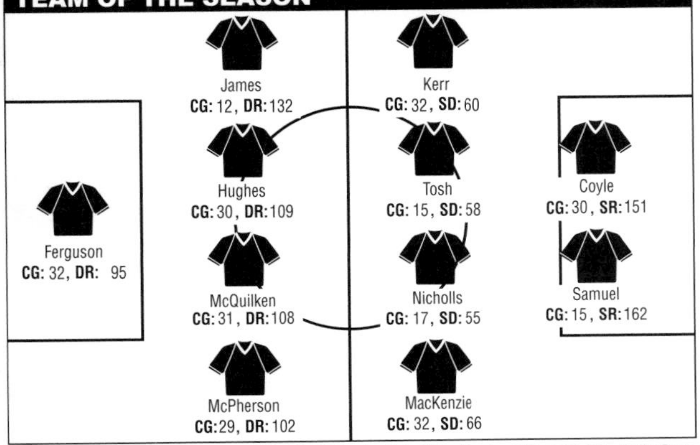

Ferguson
CG: 32, DR: 95
James
CG: 12, DR: 132
Hughes
CG: 30, DR: 109
McQuilken
CG: 31, DR: 108
McPherson
CG: 29, DR: 102
Kerr
CG: 32, SD: 60
Tosh
CG: 15, SD: 58
Nicholls
CG: 17, SD: 55
MacKenzie
CG: 32, SD: 66
Coyle
CG: 30, SR: 151
Samuel
CG: 15, SR: 162


**KEY:** DR = Defensive Rate, SD = Scoring Difference, SR = Strike Rate, CG = Counting Games – League games playing at least 70 minutes

## LEAGUE APPEARANCES, BOOKINGS AND CAPS

| | AGE (on 01/07/03) | IN THE SQUAD | COUNTING GAMES | MINUTES ON PITCH | YELLOW CARDS | RED CARDS | THIS SEASON | HOME COUNTRY |
|---|---|---|---|---|---|---|---|---|
| **Goalkeepers** | | | | | | | | |
| Michael Atai | - | 4 | 0 | 0 | 0 | 0 | - | Scotland |
| Allan Ferguson | 34 | 34 | 32 | 2860 | 0 | 0 | - | Scotland |
| Darren Hill | 21 | 34 | 4 | 360 | 0 | 0 | - | Scotland |
| **Defenders** | | | | | | | | |
| Kevin Christie | 27 | 6 | 1 | 113 | 1 | 0 | - | Scotland |
| Stuart Cringean | - | 17 | 1 | 260 | 1 | 0 | - | Scotland |
| John Henry | 31 | 36 | 17 | 2209 | 1 | 0 | - | Scotland |
| John Hughes | 38 | 31 | 30 | 2724 | 5 | 0 | - | Scotland |
| Kevin James | 27 | 13 | 12 | 1053 | 2 | 1 | - | Scotland |
| Andy Lawrie | 24 | 7 | 6 | 551 | 1 | 0 | - | Scotland |
| Craig McPherson | 31 | 35 | 29 | 2868 | 1 | 0 | - | Scotland |
| James McQuilken | 28 | 35 | 31 | 2917 | 3 | 0 | - | Scotland |
| Brian Reid | 33 | 11 | 4 | 462 | 1 | 0 | - | Scotland |
| Steven Rennie | 21 | 29 | 14 | 1294 | 3 | 0 | - | Scotland |
| **Midfielders** | | | | | | | | |
| Phil Creaney | 20 | 5 | 0 | 37 | 0 | 0 | - | Scotland |
| Mark Kerr | 21 | 36 | 32 | 2999 | 4 | 0 | - | Scotland |
| Scott MacKenzie | 33 | 32 | 32 | 2874 | 2 | 0 | - | Scotland |
| Iain McSween | - | 21 | 0 | 161 | 0 | 0 | - | Scotland |
| David Nicholls | 31 | 17 | 17 | 1525 | 3 | 0 | - | Scotland |
| Stuart Taylor | 28 | 16 | 6 | 766 | 0 | 0 | - | Scotland |
| Steven Tosh | 30 | 16 | 15 | 1399 | 5 | 1 | - | Scotland |
| **Forwards** | | | | | | | | |
| Owen Coyle | 36 | 36 | 30 | 3017 | 1 | 0 | - | Scotland |
| Steven Craig | 22 | 5 | 0 | 60 | 0 | 0 | - | Scotland |
| Lee Miller | 20 | 34 | 31 | 2892 | 4 | 1 | - | Scotland |
| Andy Rodgers | 19 | 31 | 0 | 187 | 0 | 0 | - | Scotland |
| Collin Samuel | 21 | 34 | 15 | 1948 | 0 | 0 | - | Trinidad & Tobago |

**KEY:** LEAGUE BOOKINGS CAPS

## SQUAD APPEARANCES

| Match | 1 | 2 | 3 | 4 | 5 | 6 | 7 | 8 | 9 | 10 | 11 | 12 | 13 | 14 | 15 | 16 | 17 | 18 | 19 | 20 | 21 | 22 | 23 | 24 | 25 | 26 | 27 | 28 | 29 | 30 | 31 | 32 | 33 | 34 | 35 | 36 | 37 | 38 | 39 | 40 | 41 | 42 | 43 |
|---|---|---|---|---|---|---|---|---|---|---|---|---|---|---|---|---|---|---|---|---|---|---|---|---|---|---|---|---|---|---|---|---|---|---|---|---|---|---|---|---|---|---|---|
| Venue | A | H | A | A | H | H | A | H | A | H | A | H | A | A | A | H | H | A | A | H | H | H | A | H | H | A | H | A | A | A | H | H | A | A | H | A | H | A | A | H | H | A | H |
| Competition | L | L | L | L | L | I | L | L | I | L | L | L | I | L | L | L | L | L | L | L | L | L | L | S | L | L | L | S | L | L | L | L | L | L | S | L | L | S | L | L | L | L | L |
| Result | W | W | W | W | W | W | D | W | W | W | L | W | L | D | D | W | W | L | W | W | D | W | W | W | D | W | W | W | L | L | W | W | W | D | D | W | W | L | W | W | W | W | L |

**Goalkeepers**
Michael Atai
Allan Ferguson
Darren Hill

**Defenders**
Kevin Christie
Stuart Cringean
John Henry
John Hughes
Kevin James
Andy Lawrie
Craig McPherson
James McQuilken
Brian Reid
Steven Rennie

**Midfielders**
Phil Creaney
Mark Kerr
Scott MacKenzie
Iain McSween
David Nicholls
Stuart Taylor
Steven Tosh

**Forwards**
Owen Coyle
Steven Craig
Lee Miller
Andy Rodgers
Collin Samuel

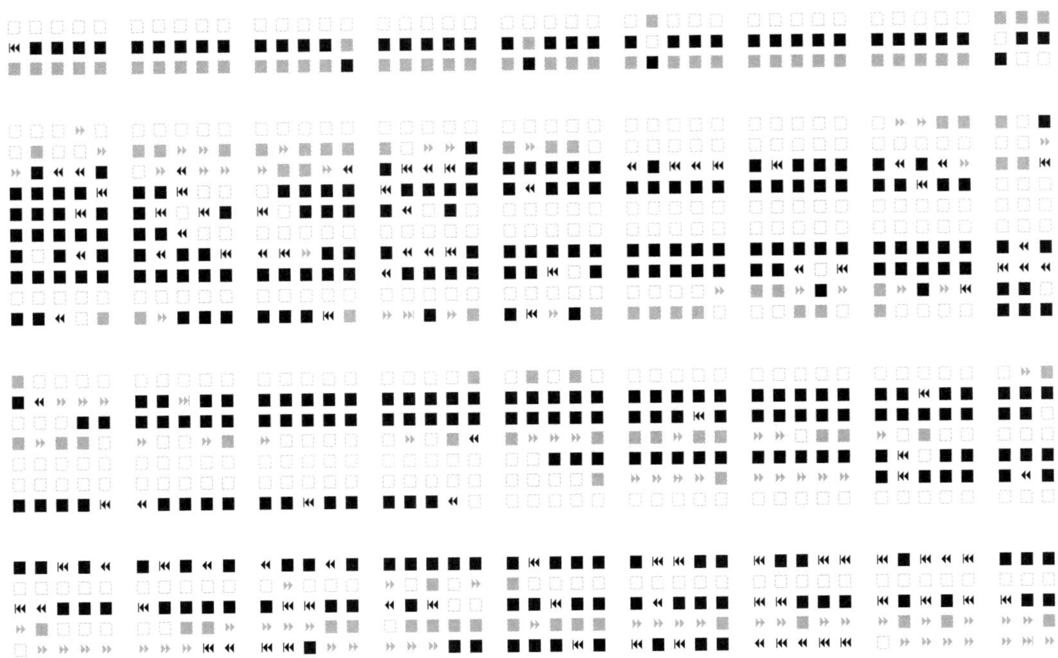

# CLYDE

Final Position: **2nd**

NICKNAME: THE BULLY WEE

| | | | | | | |
|---|---|---|---|---|---|---|
| 1 | lge | Queen of South | A | L | 1-2 | Millen 83 |
| 2 | lge | Ayr | H | W | 1-0 | Hinds 53 |
| 3 | lge | Arbroath | A | D | 1-1 | Fraser 23 |
| 4 | lge | St Mirren | H | L | 2-3 | Keogh 52,78 |
| 5 | lge | Ross County | A | D | 1-1 | Ross 84 |
| 6 | cis1 | Ross County | H | L | 0-1 | |
| 7 | lge | Alloa | H | D | 0-0 | |
| 8 | lge | Falkirk | A | L | 1-2 | Kane, P 90 |
| 9 | lge | Inverness CT | H | W | 3-0 | Nish 30,45; Convery 81 |
| 10 | lge | St Johnstone | A | W | 1-0 | Hinds 19 pen |
| 11 | lge | Queen of South | H | W | 2-1 | Kernaghan 51; Keogh 53 |
| 12 | lge | Ayr | A | D | 1-1 | Keogh 19 |
| 13 | lge | Ross County | H | W | 2-1 | Keogh 6; Ross 37 |
| 14 | lge | St Mirren | A | W | 4-1 | Millen 62; Nish 74,90; Ross 80 |
| 15 | lge | Alloa | A | W | 4-1 | Mensing 15; Nish 17; Fraser 47; Potter 64 |
| 16 | lge | Falkirk | H | W | 2-0 | Hinds 21,27 |
| 17 | lge | Inverness CT | A | L | 0-1 | |
| 18 | lge | St Johnstone | H | L | 1-2 | Hinds 66 |
| 19 | lge | Arbroath | H | W | 3-0 | Hinds 3; Mensing 39; Keogh 43 |
| 20 | lge | Ross County | A | D | 1-1 | Convery 66 |
| 21 | lge | St Mirren | H | W | 3-2 | Falconer 19,24; Keogh 69 |
| 22 | lge | St Johnstone | A | W | 2-1 | Fraser 29; Mensing 55 |
| 23 | scr3 | Gretna | A | W | 2-1 | Millen 30; Hinds 61 |
| 24 | lge | Arbroath | A | W | 2-1 | Falconer 12; Hagen 64 |
| 25 | scr4 | Motherwell | H | L | 0-2 | |
| 26 | lge | Queen of South | A | D | 1-1 | Hagen 70 |
| 27 | lge | Ross County | H | W | 1-0 | Convery 35 |
| 28 | lge | Falkirk | A | L | 0-3 | |
| 29 | lge | St Mirren | A | W | 2-1 | Kernaghan 82; Gilhaney 85 |
| 30 | lge | Alloa | H | D | 2-2 | Keogh 74; Gilhaney 77 |
| 31 | lge | Falkirk | H | D | 0-0 | |
| 32 | lge | Inverness CT | H | W | 4-1 | McConalogue 1; Millen 7; Gilhaney 16; Ross 86 |
| 33 | lge | Ayr | H | W | 3-0 | Millen 25 pen,67 pen; Falconer 88 |
| 34 | lge | Alloa | A | W | 2-1 | McConalogue 28; Keogh 63 |
| 35 | lge | Inverness CT | A | W | 2-1 | Mensing 28; McConalogue 61 |
| 36 | lge | St Johnstone | H | W | 2-1 | Potter 24; Millen 43 |
| 37 | lge | Queen of South | H | D | 2-2 | Keogh 2; Gilhaney 24 |
| 38 | lge | Ayr | A | W | 3-0 | McConalogue 18,50; Hagen 33 |
| 39 | lge | Arbroath | H | W | 4-2 | Keogh 4,42; Hagen 30; Millen 66 |

## ATTENDANCES

HOME GROUND: BROADWOOD STADIUM CAPACITY: 8030 AVERAGE LEAGUE AT HOME: 1320

| | | | | | | | | |
|---|---|---|---|---|---|---|---|---|
| **25** | **Motherwell** | **5032** | **4** | **St Mirren** | **1874** | 23 | Gretna | 973 |
| 28 | Falkirk | 3706 | 38 | Ayr | 1795 | **7** | **Alloa** | **973** |
| 8 | Falkirk | 3595 | 35 | Inverness CT | 1682 | **9** | **Inverness CT** | **936** |
| **16** | **Falkirk** | **3415** | **21** | **St Mirren** | **1500** | **19** | **Arbroath** | **861** |
| 1 | Queen of South | 3206 | 26 | Queen of South | 1375 | 3 | Arbroath | 744 |
| **31** | **Falkirk** | **3012** | **18** | **St Johnstone** | **1367** | 15 | Alloa | 736 |
| 17 | Inverness CT | 2829 | **36** | **St Johnstone** | **1185** | **32** | **Inverness CT** | **703** |
| 14 | St Mirren | 2703 | **2** | **Ayr** | **1077** | 34 | Alloa | 687 |
| 29 | St Mirren | 2683 | **37** | **Queen of South** | **1060** | 24 | Arbroath | 686 |
| 20 | Ross County | 2534 | **13** | **Ross County** | **1047** | **30** | **Alloa** | **665** |
| 22 | St Johnstone | 2455 | **39** | **Arbroath** | **1042** | **6** | **Ross County** | **604** |
| 5 | Ross County | 2059 | **11** | **Queen of South** | **1026** | | | |
| 10 | St Johnstone | 2037 | **33** | **Ayr** | **1015** | | | |
| 12 | Ayr | 1989 | **27** | **Ross County** | **1012** | | | |

■ Home □ Away ▒ Neutral

## KEY PLAYERS - GOALSCORERS

**1 Pat Keogh**

| | | | |
|---|---|---|---|
| Goals in the League | 12 | Player Strike Rate<br>Average number of minutes between League goals scored by player | 182 |
| Contribution to Attacking Power<br>Average number of minutes between League team goals while on pitch | 45 | Club Strike Rate<br>Average number of minutes between League goals scored by club | 25 |

| | PLAYER | LGE GOALS | POWER | STRIKE RATE |
|---|---|---|---|---|
| 2 | Leigh Hinds | 6 | 53 | 261 mins |
| 3 | Andy Millen | 7 | 45 | 380 mins |
| 4 | David Hagen | 4 | 48 | 634 mins |
| 5 | Jack Ross | 4 | 47 | 720 mins |

## KEY PLAYERS - MIDFIELDERS

**1 Jack Ross**

| | | | |
|---|---|---|---|
| Goals in the League | 4 | Contribution to Attacking Power<br>Average number of minutes between League team goals while on pitch | 47 |
| Defensive Rating<br>Average number of mins between League goals conceded while he was on the pitch | 93 | Scoring Difference<br>Defensive Rating minus Contribution to Attacking Power | 46 |

| | PLAYER | LGE GOALS | DEF RATE | POWER | SCORE DIFF |
|---|---|---|---|---|---|
| 2 | John Fraser | 3 | 86 | 48 | 38 mins |
| 3 | Simon Mensing | 4 | 86 | 48 | 38 mins |
| 4 | Paul Kane | 1 | 71 | 63 | 8 mins |

## KEY PLAYERS - DEFENDERS

**1 Alan Kernaghan**

| | | | |
|---|---|---|---|
| Goals Conceded (GC)<br>The number of League goals conceded while he was on the pitch | 25 | Clean Sheets<br>In games when he played at least 70 minutes | 7 |
| Defensive Rating<br>Ave number of mins between League goals conceded while on the pitch | 93 | Club Defensive Rating<br>Average number of mins between League goals conceded by the club this season | 44 |

| | PLAYER | CON LGE | CLEAN SHEETS | DEF RATE |
|---|---|---|---|---|
| 2 | John-Paul Potter | 31 | 9 | 92 mins |
| 3 | Pat Keogh | 24 | 7 | 91 mins |
| 4 | Andy Millen | 31 | 10 | 86 mins |
| 5 | Fabian Bossy | 14 | 2 | 71 mins |

## KEY GOALKEEPER

**1 Bryn Halliwell**

| | |
|---|---|
| Goals Conceded in the League | 34 |
| Defensive Rating<br>Ave number of mins between League goals conceded while on the pitch | 90 |
| Counting Games<br>Games when he played at least 70 mins | 34 |
| Clean Sheets<br>In games when he played at least 70 mins | 10 |

## TOP POINT EARNERS

| | PLAYER | GAMES | AVE |
|---|---|---|---|
| 1 | Convery | 2 | 3.00 |
| 2 | Gilhaney | 5 | 3.00 |
| 3 | McConalogue | 9 | 2.67 |
| 4 | Falconer | 5 | 2.60 |
| 5 | Cosgrove | 8 | 2.25 |
| 6 | Hagen | 26 | 2.19 |
| 7 | Kernaghan | 26 | 2.19 |
| 8 | McLaughlin | 6 | 2.17 |
| 9 | Nish | 9 | 2.11 |
| 10 | Potter | 31 | 2.10 |
| | **CLUB AVERAGE:** | | **2.00** |

Ave = Average points per match in Counting Games

## DISCIPLINARY RECORDS

| | PLAYER | YELLOW | RED | AVE |
|---|---|---|---|---|
| 1 | Falconer | 4 | 0 | 215 |
| 2 | Fraser | 8 | 0 | 322 |
| 3 | Potter | 7 | 1 | 356 |
| 4 | Millen | 5 | 2 | 380 |
| 5 | Bossy | 2 | 0 | 494 |
| 6 | Nish | 2 | 0 | 516 |
| 7 | Kane | 2 | 0 | 534 |
| 8 | Keogh | 4 | 0 | 545 |
| 9 | Mensing | 4 | 0 | 776 |
| 10 | McConalogue | 1 | 0 | 958 |
| 11 | Cosgrove | 1 | 0 | 1053 |
| 12 | Kernaghan | 2 | 0 | 1161 |
| 13 | Hinds | 1 | 0 | 1563 |
| | Other | 2 | 0 | |
| | **TOTAL** | **45** | **3** | |

## LEAGUE GOALS

| | PLAYER | MINS | GOALS | AVE |
|---|---|---|---|---|
| 1 | Keogh | 2181 | 12 | 182 |
| 2 | Millen | 2663 | 7 | 380 |
| 3 | Hinds | 1563 | 6 | 261 |
| 4 | Nish | 1033 | 5 | 207 |
| 5 | McConalogue | 958 | 5 | 192 |
| 6 | Hagen | 2535 | 4 | 634 |
| 7 | Gilhaney | 619 | 4 | 155 |
| 8 | Falconer | 860 | 4 | 215 |
| 9 | Ross | 2878 | 4 | 720 |
| 10 | Mensing | 3105 | 4 | 776 |
| 11 | Fraser | 2582 | 3 | 861 |
| 12 | Convery | 733 | 3 | 244 |
| 13 | Potter | 2854 | 2 | 1427 |
| | Other | | 3 | |
| | **TOTAL** | | **66** | |

## MONTH BY MONTH GUIDE TO THE POINTS

| MONTH | POINTS | % |
|---|---|---|
| AUGUST | 5 | 33% |
| SEPTEMBER | 4 | 44% |
| OCTOBER | 7 | 78% |
| NOVEMBER | 12 | 80% |
| DECEMBER | 4 | 44% |
| JANUARY | 6 | 100% |
| FEBRUARY | 4 | 67% |
| MARCH | 14 | 67% |
| APRIL | 10 | 83% |
| MAY | 6 | 100% |

## TEAM OF THE SEASON

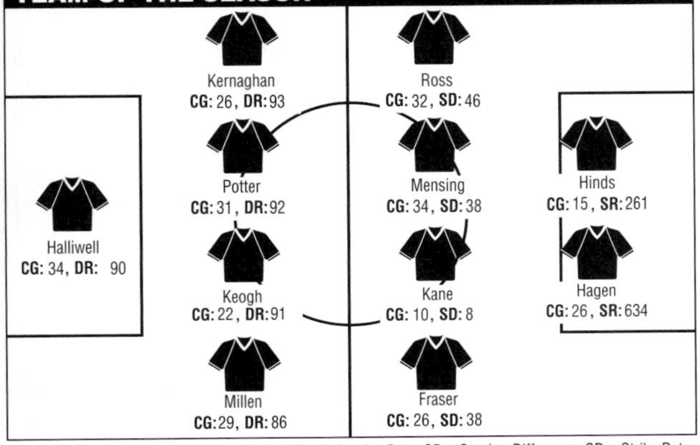
Halliwell
CG: 34, DR: 90
Kernaghan
CG: 26, DR: 93
Potter
CG: 31, DR: 92
Keogh
CG: 22, DR: 91
Millen
CG: 29, DR: 86
Ross
CG: 32, SD: 46
Mensing
CG: 34, SD: 38
Kane
CG: 10, SD: 8
Fraser
CG: 26, SD: 38
Hinds
CG: 15, SR: 261
Hagen
CG: 26, SR: 634

KEY: DR = Defensive Rate, SD = Scoring Difference, SR = Strike Rate,
CG = Counting Games – League games playing at least 70 minutes

## LEAGUE APPEARANCES, BOOKINGS AND CAPS

| | AGE (on 01/07/03) | IN THE SQUAD | COUNTING GAMES | MINUTES ON PITCH | YELLOW CARDS | RED CARDS | THIS SEASON | HOME COUNTRY |
|---|---|---|---|---|---|---|---|---|
| **Goalkeepers** | | | | | | | | |
| Bryn Halliwell | 22 | 35 | 34 | 3060 | 0 | 0 | - | England |
| David McEwan | 21 | 1 | 1 | 90 | 0 | 0 | - | Scotland |
| Allan Morrison | - | 33 | 1 | 90 | 0 | 0 | - | Scotland |
| **Defenders** | | | | | | | | |
| Fabian Bossy | 25 | 29 | 10 | 989 | 2 | 0 | - | France |
| Paul Doyle | - | 4 | 0 | 14 | 0 | 0 | - | Scotland |
| Pat Keogh | 27 | 29 | 22 | 2181 | 4 | 0 | - | Scotland |
| Alan Kernaghan | 36 | 27 | 26 | 2323 | 2 | 0 | - | Rep of Ireland |
| Mark McLaughlin | 27 | 11 | 6 | 576 | 0 | 0 | - | Scotland |
| Andy Millen | 38 | 30 | 29 | 2663 | 5 | 2 | - | Scotland |
| John-Paul Potter | 23 | 33 | 31 | 2854 | 7 | 1 | - | Scotland |
| Brian Smith | 26 | 10 | 4 | 421 | 0 | 0 | - | Scotland |
| **Midfielders** | | | | | | | | |
| John Baird | - | 3 | 0 | 11 | 0 | 0 | - | Scotland |
| Charlie Clark | - | 2 | 0 | 0 | 0 | 0 | - | Scotland |
| Stephen Cosgrove | 22 | 29 | 8 | 1053 | 1 | 0 | - | Scotland |
| David Dunn | 21 | 6 | 2 | 247 | 0 | 0 | - | Scotland |
| John Fraser | 25 | 34 | 26 | 2582 | 8 | 0 | - | Scotland |
| Paul Kane | 38 | 15 | 10 | 1069 | 2 | 0 | - | Scotland |
| Andy McClay | - | 10 | 2 | 221 | 0 | 0 | - | Scotland |
| Simon Mensing | 21 | 36 | 34 | 3105 | 4 | 0 | - | England |
| William Reid | - | 4 | 0 | 18 | 0 | 0 | - | Scotland |
| Jack Ross | 27 | 33 | 32 | 2878 | 1 | 0 | - | Scotland |
| **Forwards** | | | | | | | | |
| Steve Convery | 30 | 26 | 2 | 733 | 0 | 0 | - | Scotland |
| Willie Falconer | 37 | 21 | 5 | 860 | 4 | 0 | - | Scotland |
| Mark Gilhaney | - | 12 | 5 | 619 | 0 | 0 | - | Scotland |
| David Hagen | 30 | 31 | 26 | 2535 | 1 | 0 | - | Scotland |
| Leigh Hinds | 24 | 20 | 15 | 1563 | 1 | 0 | - | England |
| Andy Kane | - | 3 | 0 | 76 | 0 | 0 | - | Scotland |
| S McConalogue | 22 | 19 | 9 | 958 | 1 | 0 | - | Scotland |
| Colin Nish | 22 | 15 | 9 | 1033 | 2 | 0 | - | Scotland |
| Paul Shields | 21 | 14 | 5 | 754 | 0 | 0 | - | Scotland |

KEY: LEAGUE BOOKINGS CAPS

## SQUAD APPEARANCES

| Match | 1 | 2 | 3 | 4 | 5 | 6 | 7 | 8 | 9 | 10 | 11 | 12 | 13 | 14 | 15 | 16 | 17 | 18 | 19 | 20 |
|---|---|---|---|---|---|---|---|---|---|---|---|---|---|---|---|---|---|---|---|---|
| Venue | A | H | A | H | A | H | H | A | H | A | H | A | H | A | A | H | A | H | H | A |
| Competition | L | L | L | L | L | I | L | L | L | L | L | L | L | L | L | L | L | L | L | L |
| Result | L | W | D | L | D | L | D | L | W | W | W | D | W | W | W | W | L | L | W | D |

| Match | 21 | 22 | 23 | 24 | 25 | 26 | 27 | 28 | 29 | 30 | 31 | 32 | 33 | 34 | 35 | 36 | 37 | 38 | 39 |
|---|---|---|---|---|---|---|---|---|---|---|---|---|---|---|---|---|---|---|---|
| Venue | H | A | A | A | H | A | H | A | A | H | H | H | H | A | A | H | H | A | H |
| Competition | L | L | S | L | S | L | L | L | L | L | L | L | L | L | L | L | L | L | L |
| Result | W | W | W | W | L | D | W | L | W | D | D | W | W | W | W | W | D | W | W |

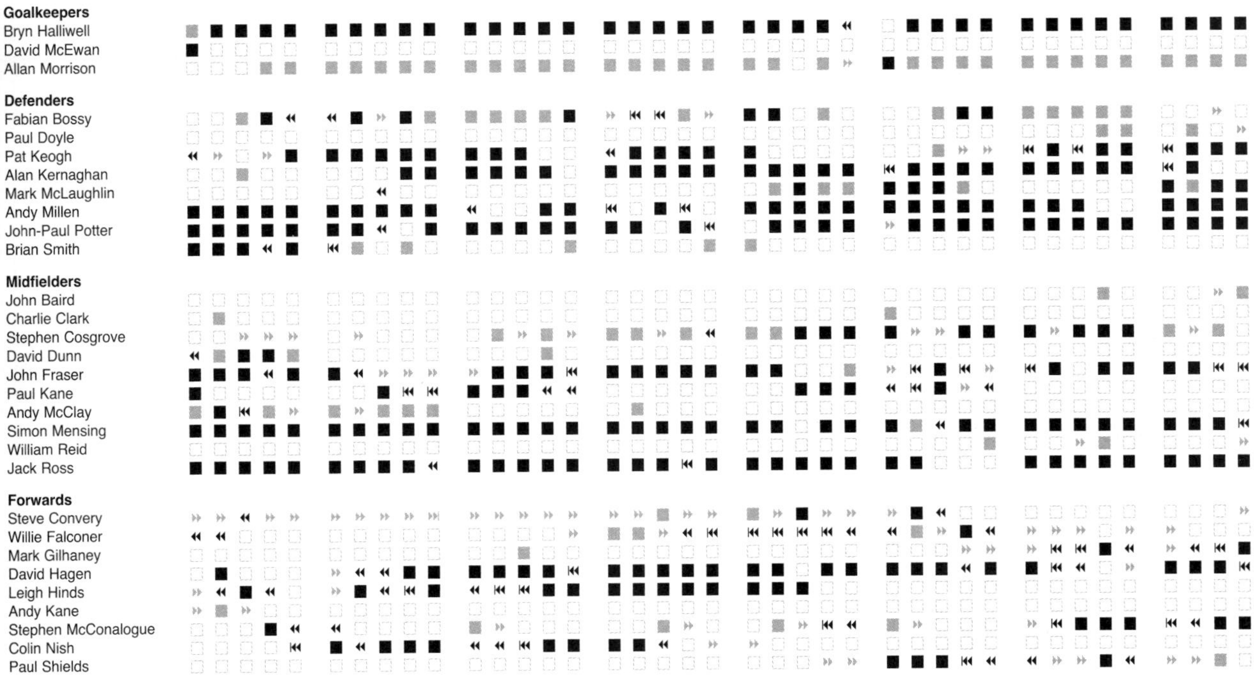
Goalkeepers
Bryn Halliwell
David McEwan
Allan Morrison
Defenders
Fabian Bossy
Paul Doyle
Pat Keogh
Alan Kernaghan
Mark McLaughlin
Andy Millen
John-Paul Potter
Brian Smith
Midfielders
John Baird
Charlie Clark
Stephen Cosgrove
David Dunn
John Fraser
Paul Kane
Andy McClay
Simon Mensing
William Reid
Jack Ross
Forwards
Steve Convery
Willie Falconer
Mark Gilhaney
David Hagen
Leigh Hinds
Andy Kane
Stephen McConalogue
Colin Nish
Paul Shields

# ST JOHNSTONE

Final Position: **3rd**

NICKNAME: THE SAINTS

| | | | | | | |
|---|---|---|---|---|---|---|
| 1 | lge | St Mirren | A | W | 2-0 | Parker 17; Hartley 53 |
| 2 | lge | Inverness CT | H | W | 1-0 | McCaffrey 81 og |
| 3 | lge | Queen of South | A | D | 0-0 | |
| 4 | lge | Arbroath | A | W | 1-0 | Hartley 29 |
| 5 | lge | Alloa | H | W | 2-0 | McCann 10; Connolly 42 |
| 6 | lge | Ayr | A | D | 0-0 | |
| 7 | lge | Ross County | H | D | 1-1 | McCann 30 |
| 8 | cis2 | Stranraer | A | W | 3-1 | McCulloch 17; Hay 99,119 |
| 9 | lge | Falkirk | A | L | 0-1 | |
| 10 | lge | Clyde | H | L | 0-1 | |
| 11 | lge | St Mirren | H | W | 2-0 | Hartley 40; Hay 42 |
| 12 | lge | Inverness CT | A | L | 1-2 | Hay 87 pen |
| 13 | lge | Alloa | A | W | 3-1 | Hay 25,70; Connolly 47 |
| 14 | cis3 | Livingston | H | L | 0-1 | |
| 15 | lge | Arbroath | H | W | 2-0 | Hay 2; Hartley 90 |
| 16 | lge | Ayr | H | L | 0-2 | |
| 17 | lge | Ross County | A | D | 0-0 | |
| 18 | lge | Falkirk | H | L | 0-1 | |
| 19 | lge | Clyde | A | W | 2-1 | Hay 13; Lovenkrands 75 |
| 20 | lge | Queen of South | H | D | 2-2 | Parker 89; Reilly 90 |
| 21 | lge | Alloa | H | W | 3-0 | Seaton 76 og; Forsyth 82; Lovenkrands 84 |
| 22 | lge | Arbroath | A | W | 3-2 | Maxwell 61; Lovenkrands 71; Connolly 79 |
| 23 | lge | Ross County | H | W | 2-0 | Hay 30; Forsyth 53 |
| 24 | lge | Clyde | H | L | 1-2 | Connolly 4 |
| 25 | scr3 | Airdrie Utd | A | D | 1-1 | Baxter 89 |
| 26 | lge | Falkirk | A | D | 1-1 | Hartley 25 |
| 27 | scr3r | Airdrie Utd | H | W | 4-2* | Connolly 34 (*on penalties) |
| 28 | lge | Queen of South | A | W | 2-1 | Robertson, M 77; Noble 87 |
| 29 | lge | Inverness CT | H | W | 2-0 | Hay 84,90 |
| 30 | scr4 | Celtic | A | L | 0-3 | |
| 31 | lge | Alloa | A | W | 2-1 | Dods 25; Connolly 66 |
| 32 | lge | Ayr | A | W | 1-0 | Dods 53 |
| 33 | lge | Arbroath | H | W | 2-1 | MacDonald 22; Murray 90 |
| 34 | lge | Ross County | A | W | 3-2 | Noble 16,37; Hartley 68 |
| 35 | lge | St Mirren | A | W | 3-1 | Maxwell 12; MacDonald 19; Dods 74 |
| 36 | lge | Ayr | H | W | 1-0 | MacDonald 5 |
| 37 | lge | Falkirk | H | L | 0-1 | |
| 38 | lge | Clyde | A | L | 1-2 | Noble 30 |
| 39 | lge | St Mirren | H | D | 1-1 | Noble 73 |
| 40 | lge | Inverness CT | A | W | 2-1 | Maxwell 15; Reilly 57 |
| 41 | lge | Queen of South | H | L | 0-1 | |

## ATTENDANCES

HOME GROUND: MCDIARMID PARK CAPACITY: 10620 AVERAGE LEAGUE AT HOME: 2618

| | | | | | | | | |
|---|---|---|---|---|---|---|---|---|
| 30 | Celtic | 26205 | 24 | Clyde | 2455 | 41 | Queen of South | 2016 |
| 37 | Falkirk | 6542 | 7 | Ross County | 2434 | 15 | Arbroath | 2014 |
| 9 | Falkirk | 5872 | 23 | Ross County | 2400 | 16 | Ayr | 2003 |
| 26 | Falkirk | 4694 | 35 | St Mirren | 2369 | 28 | Queen of South | 1862 |
| 2 | Inverness CT | 3772 | 6 | Ayr | 2320 | 40 | Inverness CT | 1814 |
| 18 | Falkirk | 3696 | 5 | Alloa | 2274 | 32 | Ayr | 1690 |
| 1 | St Mirren | 3694 | 36 | Ayr | 2132 | 19 | Clyde | 1367 |
| 3 | Queen of South | 3137 | 27 | Airdrie Utd | 2105 | 4 | Arbroath | 1350 |
| 34 | Ross County | 2689 | 39 | St Mirren | 2103 | 22 | Arbroath | 1250 |
| 14 | Livingston | 2688 | 21 | Alloa | 2090 | 38 | Clyde | 1185 |
| 17 | Ross County | 2614 | 25 | Airdrie Utd | 2073 | 13 | Alloa | 952 |
| 29 | Inverness CT | 2613 | 20 | Queen of South | 2048 | 31 | Alloa | 884 |
| 12 | Inverness CT | 2541 | 33 | Arbroath | 2038 | 8 | Stranraer | 510 |
| 11 | St Mirren | 2458 | 10 | Clyde | 2037 | | | |

■ Home □ Away ■ Neutral

## KEY PLAYERS - GOALSCORERS

**1 Tommy Lovenkrands**

| | | | |
|---|---|---|---|
| Goals in the League | 3 | Player Strike Rate<br>Average number of minutes between League goals scored by player | 462 |
| Contribution to Attacking Power<br>Average number of minutes between League team goals while on pitch | 69 | Club Strike Rate<br>Average number of minutes between League goals scored by club | 33 |

| | PLAYER | LGE GOALS | POWER | STRIKE RATE |
|---|---|---|---|---|
| 2 | Patrick Connolly | 5 | 56 | 478 mins |
| 3 | Paul Hartley | 6 | 60 | 480 mins |
| 4 | Darren Dods | 3 | 66 | 602 mins |
| 5 | Keigan Parker | 2 | 59 | 839 mins |

## KEY PLAYERS - MIDFIELDERS

**1 Mark Robertson, M**

| | | | |
|---|---|---|---|
| Goals in the League | 1 | Contribution to Attacking Power<br>Average number of minutes between League team goals while on pitch | 55 |
| Defensive Rating<br>Average number of mins between League goals conceded while he was on the pitch | 110 | Scoring Difference<br>Defensive Rating minus Contribution to Attacking Power | 55 |

| | PLAYER | LGE GOALS | DEF RATE | POWER | SCORE DIFF |
|---|---|---|---|---|---|
| 2 | Mark Reilly | 2 | 109 | 72 | 37 mins |

## KEY PLAYERS - DEFENDERS

**1 Stuart McCluskey**

| | | | |
|---|---|---|---|
| Goals Conceded (GC)<br>The number of League goals conceded while he was on the pitch | 10 | Clean Sheets<br>In games when he played at least 70 minutes | 7 |
| Defensive Rating<br>Ave number of mins between League goals conceded while on the pitch | 135 | Club Defensive Rating<br>Average number of mins between League goals conceded by the club this season | 56 |

| | PLAYER | CON LGE | CLEAN SHEETS | DEF RATE |
|---|---|---|---|---|
| 2 | Grant Murray | 26 | 14 | 114 mins |
| 3 | John Robertson, J | 20 | 10 | 112 mins |
| 4 | Ian Maxwell | 27 | 13 | 112 mins |
| 5 | Marc McCulloch | 12 | 5 | 105 mins |

## KEY GOALKEEPER

**1 Kevin Cuthbert**

| | |
|---|---|
| Goals Conceded in the League | 15 |
| Defensive Rating<br>Ave number of mins between League goals conceded while on the pitch | 132 |
| Counting Games<br>Games when he played at least 70 mins | 22 |
| Clean Sheets<br>In games when he played at least 70 mins | 9 |

## TOP POINT EARNERS

| | PLAYER | GAMES | AVE |
|---|---|---|---|
| 1 | McCann | 5 | 2.60 |
| 2 | Robertson, M | 10 | 2.50 |
| 3 | Noble | 6 | 2.50 |
| 4 | MacDonald | 8 | 2.25 |
| 5 | Hartley | 32 | 2.03 |
| 6 | Ferry | 2 | 2.00 |
| 7 | Forsyth | 7 | 2.00 |
| 8 | Cuthbert | 22 | 2.00 |
| 9 | Connolly | 25 | 2.00 |
| 10 | Maxwell | 33 | 1.94 |
| | CLUB AVERAGE: | | 1.86 |

Ave = Average points per match in Counting Games

## DISCIPLINARY RECORDS

| | PLAYER | YELLOW | RED | AVE |
|---|---|---|---|---|
| 1 | Parker | 6 | 0 | 279 |
| 2 | Robertson, M | 3 | 0 | 293 |
| 3 | Hartley | 7 | 1 | 360 |
| 4 | Noble | 2 | 0 | 387 |
| 5 | Maxwell | 6 | 0 | 505 |
| 6 | Reilly | 5 | 0 | 546 |
| 7 | McCluskey | 2 | 0 | 672 |
| 8 | MacDonald | 1 | 0 | 796 |
| 9 | McCann | 1 | 0 | 904 |
| 10 | Murray | 3 | 0 | 990 |
| 11 | Connolly | 2 | 0 | 1194 |
| 12 | McCulloch | 1 | 0 | 1265 |
| 13 | Baxter | 1 | 0 | 1365 |
| | Other | 4 | 1 | |
| | TOTAL | 44 | 2 | |

## LEAGUE GOALS

| | PLAYER | MINS | GOALS | AVE |
|---|---|---|---|---|
| 1 | Hay | 1286 | 9 | 143 |
| 2 | Hartley | 2880 | 6 | 480 |
| 3 | Noble | 775 | 5 | 155 |
| 4 | Connolly | 2389 | 5 | 478 |
| 5 | Maxwell | 3032 | 3 | 1011 |
| 6 | MacDonald | 796 | 3 | 265 |
| 7 | Dods | 1806 | 3 | 602 |
| 8 | Lovenkrands | 1387 | 3 | 462 |
| 9 | McCann | 904 | 2 | 452 |
| 10 | Reilly | 2731 | 2 | 1366 |
| 11 | Forsyth | 716 | 2 | 358 |
| 12 | Parker | 1678 | 2 | 839 |
| 13 | Robertson, M | 881 | 1 | 881 |
| | Other | | 3 | |
| | TOTAL | | 49 | |

## MONTH BY MONTH GUIDE TO THE POINTS

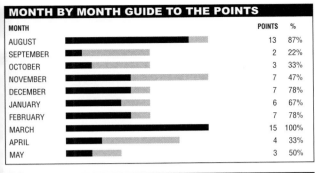

| MONTH | POINTS | % |
|---|---|---|
| AUGUST | 13 | 87% |
| SEPTEMBER | 2 | 22% |
| OCTOBER | 3 | 33% |
| NOVEMBER | 7 | 47% |
| DECEMBER | 7 | 78% |
| JANUARY | 6 | 67% |
| FEBRUARY | 7 | 78% |
| MARCH | 15 | 100% |
| APRIL | 4 | 33% |
| MAY | 3 | 50% |

## TEAM OF THE SEASON

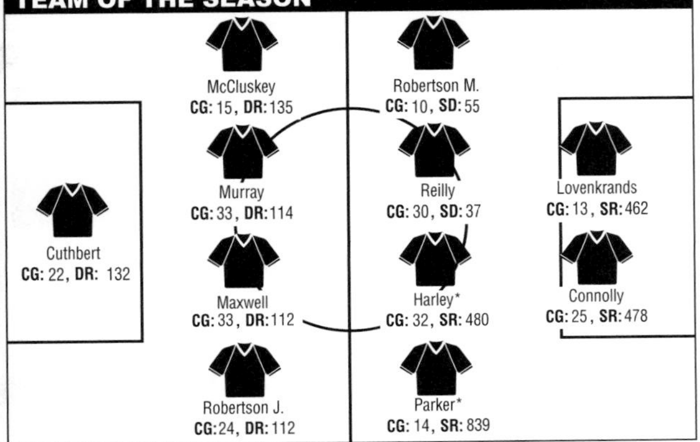
McCluskey
CG: 15, DR:135
Robertson M.
CG: 10, SD: 55
Murray
CG: 33, DR:114
Reilly
CG: 30, SD: 37
Lovenkrands
CG: 13, SR: 462
Cuthbert
CG: 22, DR: 132
Maxwell
CG: 33, DR:112
Harley*
CG: 32, SR: 480
Connolly
CG: 25, SR: 478
Robertson J.
CG:24, DR:112
Parker*
CG: 14, SR: 839

KEY: DR = Defensive Rate, SD = Scoring Difference, SR = Strike Rate, CG = Counting Games – League games playing at least 70 minutes

## LEAGUE APPEARANCES, BOOKINGS AND CAPS

| | AGE (on 01/07/03) | IN THE SQUAD | COUNTING GAMES | MINUTES ON PITCH | YELLOW CARDS | RED CARDS | THIS SEASON | HOME COUNTRY |
|---|---|---|---|---|---|---|---|---|
| **Goalkeepers** | | | | | | | | |
| Kevin Cuthbert | 2004 | 36 | 22 | 1980 | 0 | 0 | - | Scotland |
| Ross Gilpin | 2004 | 0 | 0 | 0 | 0 | 0 | - | Scotland |
| Alan Main | 35 | 22 | 14 | 1260 | 0 | 0 | - | Scotland |
| Simon Miotto | 33 | 14 | 0 | 0 | 0 | 0 | - | Australia |
| **Defenders** | | | | | | | | |
| Mark Baxter | 18 | 19 | 15 | 1365 | 1 | 0 | - | Scotland |
| Darren Dods | 38 | 35 | 19 | 1806 | 1 | 0 | - | Scotland |
| Mark Ferry | 19 | 12 | 2 | 379 | 0 | 0 | - | Scotland |
| Ross Forsyth | - | 19 | 7 | 716 | 0 | 0 | - | Scotland |
| Edward Malone | - | 3 | 1 | 152 | 0 | 0 | - | Scotland |
| Ian Maxwell | - | 34 | 33 | 3032 | 6 | 0 | - | Scotland |
| David McClune | 20 | 10 | 3 | 309 | 0 | 0 | - | |
| Stuart McCluskey | 25 | 17 | 15 | 1345 | 2 | 0 | - | Scotland |
| Marc McCulloch | 23 | 26 | 12 | 1265 | 1 | 0 | - | Scotland |
| Grant Murray | 27 | 33 | 33 | 2970 | 3 | 0 | - | Scotland |
| John Robertson | 27 | 27 | 24 | 2240 | 1 | 0 | - | Scotland |
| James Weir | 34 | 3 | 2 | 175 | 1 | 1 | - | Scotland |
| **Midfielders** | | | | | | | | |
| Martin Maher | - | 3 | 0 | 11 | 0 | 0 | - | Scotland |
| Ryan McCann | 21 | 20 | 5 | 904 | 1 | 0 | - | Scotland |
| Emmanuel Panther | 18 | 6 | 2 | 239 | 0 | 0 | - | Scotland |
| Mark Reilly | 34 | 32 | 30 | 2731 | 5 | 0 | - | Scotland |
| Mark Robertson | 26 | 10 | 10 | 881 | 3 | 0 | - | Scotland |
| Ryan Stevenson | 18 | 14 | 1 | 385 | 0 | 0 | - | England |
| **Forwards** | | | | | | | | |
| Patrick Connolly | 33 | 35 | 25 | 2389 | 2 | 0 | - | Scotland |
| Paul Hartley | 26 | 33 | 32 | 2880 | 7 | 1 | - | Scotland |
| Chris Hay | 28 | 27 | 10 | 1286 | 0 | 0 | - | Scotland |
| Tommy Lovenkrands | 29 | 19 | 13 | 1387 | 1 | 0 | - | Denmark |
| Peter MacDonald | 22 | 14 | 8 | 796 | 1 | 0 | - | Scotland |
| Stuart Noble | 19 | 13 | 6 | 775 | 2 | 0 | - | Scotland |
| Keigan Parker | 21 | 32 | 14 | 1678 | 6 | 0 | - | Scotland |
| Craig Russell | 29 | 8 | 1 | 245 | 0 | 0 | - | England |

KEY: LEAGUE BOOKINGS CAPS

## SQUAD APPEARANCES

| Match | 1 | 2 | 3 | 4 | 5 | 6 | 7 | 8 | 9 | 10 | 11 | 12 | 13 | 14 | 15 | 16 | 17 | 18 | 19 | 20 | 21 | 22 | 23 | 24 | 25 | 26 | 27 | 28 | 29 | 30 | 31 | 32 | 33 | 34 | 35 | 36 | 37 | 38 | 39 | 40 | 41 |
|---|---|---|---|---|---|---|---|---|---|---|---|---|---|---|---|---|---|---|---|---|---|---|---|---|---|---|---|---|---|---|---|---|---|---|---|---|---|---|---|---|---|
| Venue | A | H | A | A | H | A | H | A | A | H | H | A | A | H | H | H | A | H | A | H | H | A | H | H | A | A | H | A | H | A | A | A | H | A | A | H | H | A | H | A | H |
| Competition | L | L | L | L | L | L | L | I | L | L | L | L | L | I | L | L | L | L | L | L | L | L | L | L | S | L | S | L | L | S | L | L | L | L | L | L | L | L | L | L | L |
| Result | W | W | D | W | W | D | D | W | L | L | W | L | W | L | W | L | D | L | W | D | W | W | W | L | D | D | W | W | W | L | W | W | W | W | W | W | L | L | D | W | L |

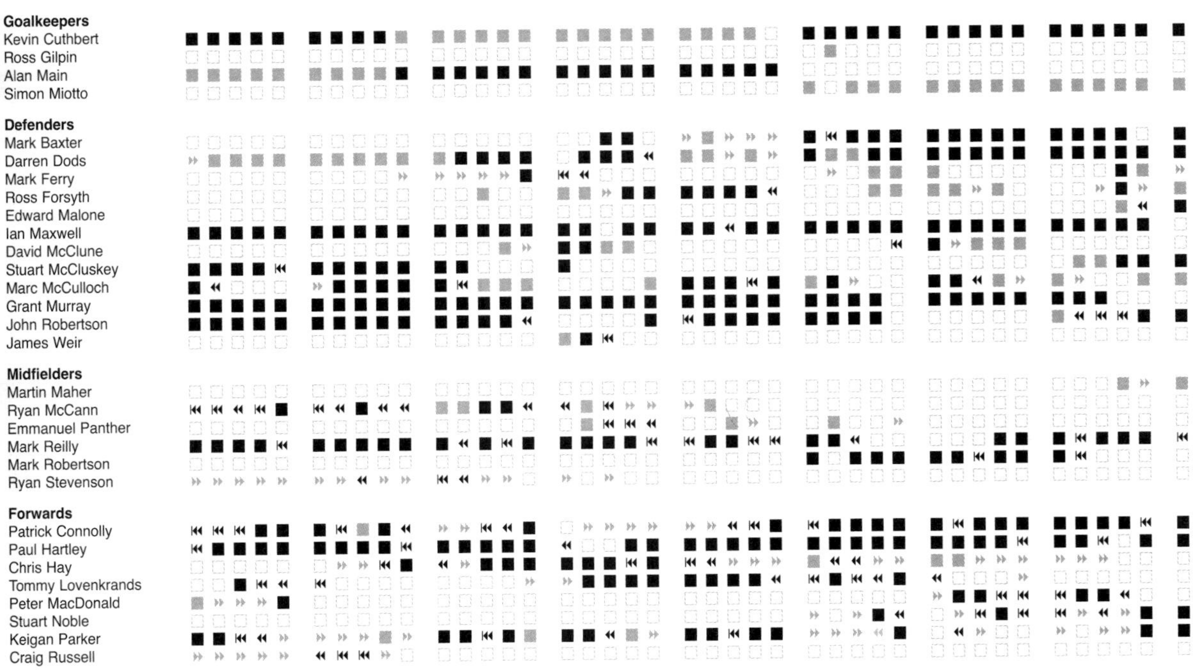
Goalkeepers
Kevin Cuthbert
Ross Gilpin
Alan Main
Simon Miotto
Defenders
Mark Baxter
Darren Dods
Mark Ferry
Ross Forsyth
Edward Malone
Ian Maxwell
David McClune
Stuart McCluskey
Marc McCulloch
Grant Murray
John Robertson
James Weir
Midfielders
Martin Maher
Ryan McCann
Emmanuel Panther
Mark Reilly
Mark Robertson
Ryan Stevenson
Forwards
Patrick Connolly
Paul Hartley
Chris Hay
Tommy Lovenkrands
Peter MacDonald
Stuart Noble
Keigan Parker
Craig Russell

KEY: On all match On bench Not in 16 Subbed off Subbed on from bench

# INVERNESS CT

Final Position: **4th**

NICKNAME: CALEY THISTLE

| | | | | | | |
|---|---|---|---|---|---|---|
| 1 | lge | Alloa | H | D | 0-0 | |
| 2 | lge | St Johnstone | A | L | 0-1 | |
| 3 | lge | Falkirk | H | L | 1-2 | Tokely 23 |
| 4 | lge | Ross County | H | W | 2-0 | Wyness 7,33 |
| 5 | lge | St Mirren | A | W | 4-0 | Robson 9,21; Hart 24; Christie 72 |
| 6 | cis1 | Dumbarton | H | W | 2-0 | Wyness 24; Ritchie 71 |
| 7 | lge | Queen of South | A | W | 3-1 | Mann 7; Wyness 24,48 |
| 8 | lge | Arbroath | H | W | 5-0 | Tokely 6,68; Hart 47; Wyness 50; Ritchie 85 |
| 9 | cis2 | St Mirren | H | W | 3-1 | Hart 13; Wyness 73,86 |
| 10 | lge | Clyde | A | L | 0-3 | |
| 11 | lge | Ayr | H | W | 2-0 | Ritchie 19; Wyness 76 |
| 12 | lge | Alloa | A | W | 6-0 | Wyness 6,19,27; Ritchie 35,71,79 |
| 13 | cis3 | Celtic | A | L | 2-4 | Ritchie 10; Wyness 72 |
| 14 | lge | St Johnstone | H | W | 2-1 | Wyness 45; Hart 61 |
| 15 | lge | St Mirren | H | W | 4-1 | Wyness 7,25; Hart 58; Robson 84 pen |
| 16 | lge | Ross County | A | W | 2-0 | Robson 1; McCulloch 8 og |
| 17 | lge | Queen of South | H | W | 5-3 | Ritchie 6,59,89; Robson 43 pen,49 |
| 18 | lge | Arbroath | A | W | 2-1 | Wyness 23; Hart 71 |
| 19 | lge | Clyde | H | W | 1-0 | Robson 80 |
| 20 | lge | Ayr | A | D | 3-3 | Mann 54; Ritchie 70; Wyness 72 |
| 21 | lge | Falkirk | A | D | 1-1 | MacKenzie 1 og |
| 22 | lge | Alloa | H | D | 1-1 | Mann 5 |
| 23 | lge | St Mirren | A | W | 4-1 | Wyness 14; Tokely 22; Stewart 29; Ritchie 51 |
| 24 | lge | Ayr | H | L | 0-1 | |
| 25 | scr3 | Raith | H | W | 2-0 | Robson 65 pen; Wyness 70 |
| 26 | lge | Falkirk | H | L | 3-4 | Robson 8; Wyness 28; Ritchie 56 |
| 27 | lge | St Johnstone | A | L | 0-2 | |
| 28 | scr4 | Hamilton | H | W | 6-1 | Wyness 8,68; Robson 31,50; Ritchie 49; McCaffrey 72 |
| 29 | lge | Ross County | H | L | 1-5 | Wyness 87 |
| 30 | lge | St Mirren | H | W | 3-1 | Ritchie 25,49,55 |
| 31 | lge | Arbroath | H | W | 2-0 | Ritchie 42; Low 90 |
| 32 | lge | Ross County | A | W | 2-0 | Hart 60; Robson 87 |
| 33 | lge | Queen of South | A | D | 0-0 | |
| 34 | lge | Arbroath | A | W | 3-1 | Hislop 67; Wyness 68,84 |
| 35 | lge | Clyde | A | L | 1-4 | Robson 26 |
| 36 | Scpqf | Celtic | H | W | 1-0 | Wyness 45 |
| 37 | lge | Queen of South | H | W | 1-0 | Tokely 42 |
| 38 | lge | Clyde | H | L | 1-2 | Hislop 63 |
| 39 | SCsf | Dundee | N | L | 0-1 | |
| 40 | lge | Alloa | A | W | 5-1 | Mann 19; Ritchie 28,50,71; Golabek 84 |
| 41 | lge | Ayr | A | L | 0-1 | |
| 42 | lge | St Johnstone | H | L | 1-2 | Hart 7 |
| 43 | lge | Falkirk | A | W | 3-2 | Nicholls 47 og; Mann 79; Christie 82 |

## ATTENDANCES

HOME GROUND: CALEDONIAN PARK CAPACITY: 6500 AVERAGE LEAGUE AT HOME: 2142

| | | | | | | | | |
|---|---|---|---|---|---|---|---|---|
| 13 | Celtic | 34592 | 14 | St Johnstone | 2541 | 1 | Alloa | 1623 |
| 39 | Dundee | 14429 | 3 | Falkirk | 2267 | 7 | Queen of South | 1611 |
| 43 | Falkirk | 7300 | 25 | Raith | 2146 | 33 | Queen of South | 1405 |
| 36 | Celtic | 6050 | 15 | St Mirren | 2023 | 31 | Arbroath | 1396 |
| 16 | Ross County | 5449 | 24 | Ayr | 2021 | 9 | St Mirren | 1194 |
| 21 | Falkirk | 4691 | 30 | St Mirren | 1973 | 41 | Ayr | 1114 |
| 32 | Ross County | 4621 | 28 | Hamilton | 1917 | 10 | Clyde | 936 |
| 2 | St Johnstone | 3772 | 17 | Queen of South | 1855 | 35 | Clyde | 703 |
| 29 | Ross County | 3443 | 42 | St Johnstone | 1814 | 6 | Dumbarton | 667 |
| 26 | Falkirk | 3322 | 11 | Ayr | 1803 | 18 | Arbroath | 653 |
| 23 | St Mirren | 3054 | 8 | Arbroath | 1685 | 34 | Arbroath | 539 |
| 4 | Ross County | 3000 | 38 | Clyde | 1682 | 12 | Alloa | 531 |
| 19 | Clyde | 2829 | 20 | Ayr | 1663 | 40 | Alloa | 485 |
| 27 | St Johnstone | 2613 | 37 | Queen of South | 1656 | | | |
| 5 | St Mirren | 2605 | 22 | Alloa | 1639 | | | |

■ Home □ Away ▒ Neutral

## KEY PLAYERS - GOALSCORERS

**1 Paul Ritchie**

| | | | |
|---|---|---|---|
| Goals in the League | 18 | Player Strike Rate<br>Average number of minutes between League goals scored by player | 133 |
| Contribution to Attacking Power<br>Average number of minutes between League team goals while on pitch | 40 | Club Strike Rate<br>Average number of minutes between League goals scored by club | 22 |

| | PLAYER | LGE GOALS | POWER | STRIKE RATE |
|---|---|---|---|---|
| 2 | Dennis Wyness | 19 | 44 | 158 mins |
| 3 | Barry Robson | 10 | 42 | 296 mins |
| 4 | Richard Hart | 7 | 38 | 333 mins |
| 5 | Robert Mann | 5 | 41 | 567 mins |

## KEY PLAYERS - MIDFIELDERS

**1 Ross Tokely**

| | | | |
|---|---|---|---|
| Goals in the League | 5 | Contribution to Attacking Power<br>Average number of minutes between League team goals while on pitch | 41 |
| Defensive Rating<br>Average number of mins between League goals conceded while he was on the pitch | 75 | Scoring Difference<br>Defensive Rating minus Contribution to Attacking Power | 34 |

| | PLAYER | LGE GOALS | DEF RATE | POWER | SCORE DIFF |
|---|---|---|---|---|---|
| 2 | Barry Robson | 10 | 71 | 43 | 28 mins |
| 4 | Charles Christie | 2 | 81 | 58 | 23 mins |

## KEY PLAYERS - DEFENDERS

**1 Grant Munro**

| | | | |
|---|---|---|---|
| Goals Conceded (GC)<br>The number of League goals conceded while he was on the pitch | 33 | Clean Sheets<br>In games when he played at least 70 minutes | 10 |
| Defensive Rating<br>Ave number of mins between League goals conceded while on the pitch | 80 | Club Defensive Rating<br>Average number of mins between League goals conceded by the club this season | 36 |

| | PLAYER | CON LGE | CLEAN SHEETS | DEF RATE |
|---|---|---|---|---|
| 2 | Robert Mann | 42 | 9 | 68 mins |
| 3 | Stuart McCaffrey | 29 | 6 | 63 mins |

## KEY GOALKEEPER

**1 Mark Brown**

| | |
|---|---|
| Goals Conceded in the League | 45 |
| Defensive Rating<br>Ave number of mins between League goals conceded while on the pitch | 72 |
| Counting Games<br>Games when he played at least 70 mins | 36 |
| Clean Sheets<br>In games when he played at least 70 mins | 12 |

## TOP POINT EARNERS

| | PLAYER | GAMES | AVE |
|---|---|---|---|
| 1 | Bagan | 3 | 2.33 |
| 2 | Ritchie | 24 | 2.17 |
| 3 | Hart | 24 | 2.04 |
| 4 | McBain | 31 | 1.97 |
| 5 | Duncan | 23 | 1.91 |
| 6 | Tokely | 31 | 1.90 |
| 7 | Munro | 28 | 1.89 |
| 8 | Mann | 31 | 1.87 |
| 9 | Wyness | 33 | 1.85 |
| 10 | Robson | 34 | 1.82 |
| | CLUB AVERAGE: | | 1.81 |

Ave = Average points per match in Counting Games

## DISCIPLINARY RECORDS

| | PLAYER | YELLOW | RED | AVE |
|---|---|---|---|---|
| 1 | Robson | 10 | 0 | 296 |
| 2 | Munro | 4 | 1 | 526 |
| 3 | Duncan | 3 | 1 | 554 |
| 4 | McCaffrey | 3 | 0 | 613 |
| 5 | Golabek | 4 | 0 | 757 |
| 6 | Hart | 3 | 0 | 777 |
| 7 | Tokely | 3 | 0 | 956 |
| 8 | Christie | 1 | 0 | 1209 |
| 9 | McBain | 2 | 0 | 1441 |
| 10 | Wyness | 2 | 0 | 1505 |
| 11 | Mann | 1 | 0 | 2837 |
| | Other | 2 | 0 | |
| | TOTAL | 38 | 2 | |

## LEAGUE GOALS

| | PLAYER | MINS | GOALS | AVE |
|---|---|---|---|---|
| 1 | Wyness | 3010 | 19 | 158 |
| 2 | Ritchie | 2387 | 18 | 133 |
| 3 | Robson | 2964 | 10 | 296 |
| 4 | Hart | 2332 | 7 | 333 |
| 5 | Tokely | 2868 | 5 | 574 |
| 6 | Mann | 2837 | 5 | 567 |
| 7 | Hislop | 575 | 2 | 288 |
| 8 | Christie | 1209 | 2 | 605 |
| 9 | Low | 340 | 1 | 340 |
| 10 | Golabek | 3031 | 1 | 3031 |
| 11 | Stewart | 270 | 1 | 270 |
| | Other | | 3 | |
| | TOTAL | | 74 | |

## MONTH BY MONTH GUIDE TO THE POINTS

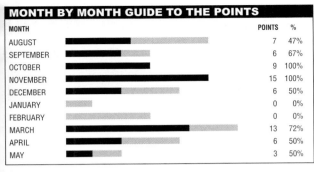

| MONTH | POINTS | % |
|---|---|---|
| AUGUST | 7 | 47% |
| SEPTEMBER | 6 | 67% |
| OCTOBER | 9 | 100% |
| NOVEMBER | 15 | 100% |
| DECEMBER | 6 | 50% |
| JANUARY | 0 | 0% |
| FEBRUARY | 0 | 0% |
| MARCH | 13 | 72% |
| APRIL | 6 | 50% |
| MAY | 3 | 50% |

## TEAM OF THE SEASON

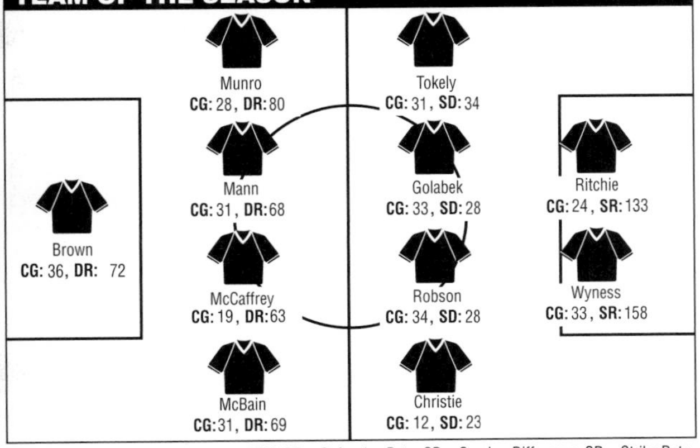
Munro
CG: 28, DR: 80
Tokely
CG: 31, SD: 34
Mann
CG: 31, DR: 68
Golabek
CG: 33, SD: 28
Ritchie
CG: 24, SR: 133
Brown
CG: 36, DR: 72
McCaffrey
CG: 19, DR: 63
Robson
CG: 34, SD: 28
Wyness
CG: 33, SR: 158
McBain
CG: 31, DR: 69
Christie
CG: 12, SD: 23

KEY: DR = Defensive Rate, SD = Scoring Difference, SR = Strike Rate,
CG = Counting Games – League games playing at least 70 minutes

## LEAGUE APPEARANCES, BOOKINGS AND CAPS

| | AGE (on 01/07/03) | IN THE SQUAD | COUNTING GAMES | MINUTES ON PITCH | YELLOW CARDS | RED CARDS | THIS SEASON | HOME COUNTRY |
|---|---|---|---|---|---|---|---|---|
| **Goalkeepers** | | | | | | | | |
| Mark Brown | 22 | 36 | 36 | 3240 | 0 | 0 | - | Scotland |
| Mike Fraser | - | 17 | 0 | 0 | 0 | 0 | - | Scotland |
| Ali Ridgers | 23 | 15 | 0 | 0 | 0 | 0 | - | Scotland |
| Alexander Rodgers | - | 3 | 0 | 0 | 0 | 0 | - | Scotland |
| **Defenders** | | | | | | | | |
| Brian Gilfillan | 18 | 6 | 0 | 24 | 0 | 0 | - | Scotland |
| Robert Mann | 29 | 32 | 31 | 2837 | 1 | 0 | - | Scotland |
| Roy McBain | 28 | 35 | 31 | 2883 | 2 | 0 | - | Scotland |
| Stuart McCaffrey | 24 | 32 | 19 | 1841 | 3 | 0 | - | Scotland |
| Chris Miller | - | 5 | 0 | 0 | 0 | 0 | - | Scotland |
| Grant Munro | 22 | 34 | 28 | 2631 | 4 | 1 | - | Scotland |
| **Midfielders** | | | | | | | | |
| Charles Christie | 37 | 24 | 12 | 1209 | 1 | 0 | - | Scotland |
| Stuart Golabek | 28 | 34 | 33 | 3031 | 4 | 0 | - | Scotland |
| Anthony Low | 19 | 24 | 2 | 340 | 1 | 0 | - | Scotland |
| Barry Robson | 24 | 34 | 34 | 2964 | 10 | 0 | - | Scotland |
| Graham Stewart | 21 | 15 | 1 | 270 | 1 | 0 | - | Scotland |
| Ross Tokely | 24 | 34 | 31 | 2868 | 3 | 0 | - | Scotland |
| **Forwards** | | | | | | | | |
| David Bagan | 26 | 18 | 3 | 462 | 0 | 0 | - | Scotland |
| Russell Duncan | 22 | 27 | 23 | 2218 | 3 | 1 | - | Scotland |
| Richard Hart | 25 | 32 | 24 | 2332 | 3 | 0 | - | Scotland |
| Stephen Hislop | - | 15 | 3 | 575 | 0 | 0 | - | Scotland |
| Liam Keogh | 21 | 31 | 2 | 484 | 0 | 0 | - | Scotland |
| Paul Ritchie | 34 | 36 | 24 | 2387 | 0 | 0 | - | Scotland |
| Dennis Wyness | 26 | 36 | 33 | 3010 | 2 | 0 | - | Scotland |

KEY: LEAGUE BOOKINGS CAPS

## SQUAD APPEARANCES

| Match | 1 | 2 | 3 | 4 | 5 | 6 | 7 | 8 | 9 | 10 | 11 | 12 | 13 | 14 | 15 | 16 | 17 | 18 | 19 | 20 | 21 | 22 | 23 | 24 | 25 | 26 | 27 | 28 | 29 | 30 | 31 | 32 | 33 | 34 | 35 | 36 | 37 | 38 | 39 | 40 | 41 | 42 | 43 |
|---|---|---|---|---|---|---|---|---|---|---|---|---|---|---|---|---|---|---|---|---|---|---|---|---|---|---|---|---|---|---|---|---|---|---|---|---|---|---|---|---|---|---|---|
| Venue | H | A | H | H | A | H | A | H | H | A | H | A | A | H | H | A | H | A | H | A | A | H | A | H | H | H | A | H | H | H | H | A | A | A | A | H | H | H | H | A | A | H | A |
| Competition | L | L | L | L | L | I | L | L | I | L | L | L | I | L | L | L | L | L | L | L | L | L | L | L | S | L | L | S | L | L | L | L | L | L | L | S | L | L | S | L | L | L | L |
| Result | D | L | L | W | W | W | W | W | W | L | W | W | L | W | W | W | W | W | W | D | D | D | W | L | W | L | L | W | L | W | W | W | D | W | L | W | W | L | L | W | L | L | W |

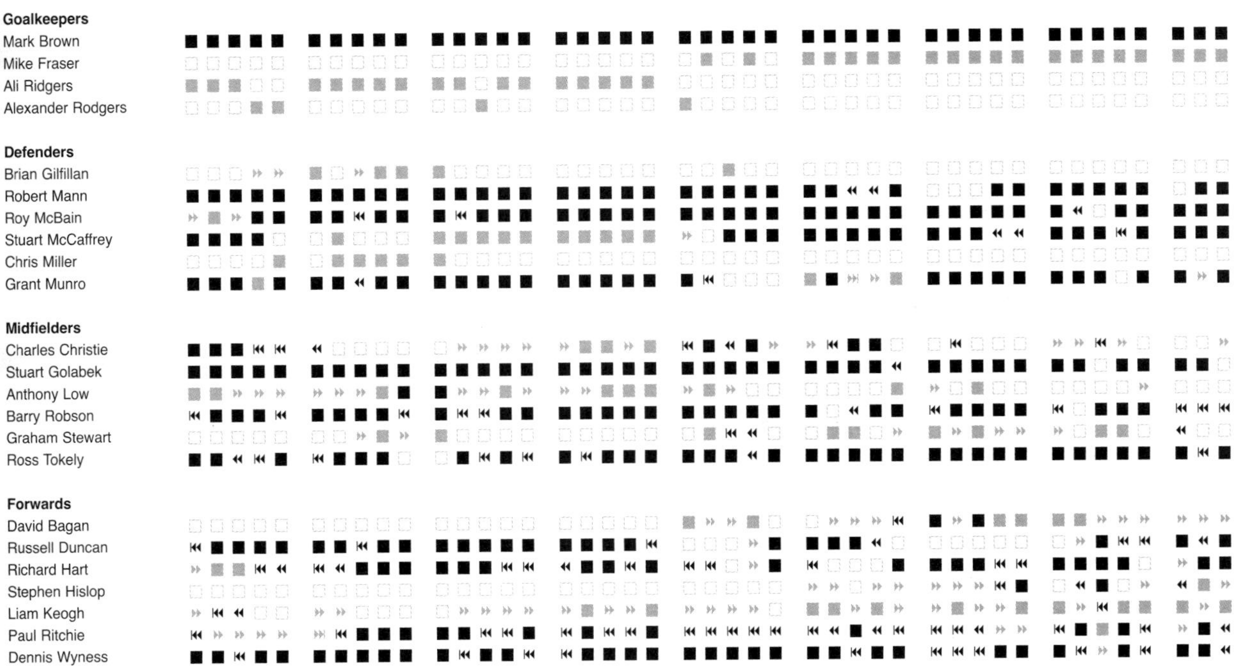
Goalkeepers
Mark Brown
Mike Fraser
Ali Ridgers
Alexander Rodgers
Defenders
Brian Gilfillan
Robert Mann
Roy McBain
Stuart McCaffrey
Chris Miller
Grant Munro
Midfielders
Charles Christie
Stuart Golabek
Anthony Low
Barry Robson
Graham Stewart
Ross Tokely
Forwards
David Bagan
Russell Duncan
Richard Hart
Stephen Hislop
Liam Keogh
Paul Ritchie
Dennis Wyness

# QUEEN OF THE SOUTH

Final Position: **5th**

NICKNAME: THE DOONHAMMER'S

| | | | | | | |
|---|---|---|---|---|---|---|
| 1 | lge | Clyde | H | W | 2-1 | Potter 12 og; Paton 72 |
| 2 | lge | Ross County | A | L | 0-2 | |
| 3 | lge | St Johnstone | H | D | 0-0 | |
| 4 | lge | Ayr | H | L | 1-2 | Bowey 84 |
| 5 | lge | Falkirk | A | L | 0-3 | |
| 6 | cis1 | Forfar | H | W | 2-0 | O'Neill 25 pen; Neilson 60 |
| 7 | lge | Inverness CT | H | L | 1-3 | Weatherson 68 |
| 8 | lge | St Mirren | A | L | 1-2 | Shields 8 |
| 9 | cis2 | Dundee | A | L | 1-3 | Weatherson 29 |
| 10 | lge | Arbroath | H | D | 2-2 | Lyle 5,56 |
| 11 | lge | Alloa | A | W | 1-0 | O'Neill 43 |
| 12 | lge | Clyde | A | L | 1-2 | Thomson 21 |
| 13 | lge | Ross County | H | W | 2-0 | Lyle 11,49 |
| 14 | lge | Falkirk | H | D | 1-1 | McColligan 12 |
| 15 | lge | Ayr | A | W | 1-0 | McLaughlin 58 |
| 16 | lge | Inverness CT | A | L | 3-5 | O'Connor 37,53; O'Neill 73 pen |
| 17 | lge | St Mirren | H | W | 3-0 | O'Connor 35; Paton 41; O'Neill 61 |
| 18 | lge | Arbroath | A | W | 2-1 | Bowey 15; Lyle 46 |
| 19 | lge | Alloa | H | D | 1-1 | McColligan 80 |
| 20 | lge | St Johnstone | A | D | 2-2 | Paton 12; Bowey 73 |
| 21 | lge | Falkirk | A | L | 0-5 | |
| 22 | lge | Ayr | H | D | 1-1 | Weatherson 62 |
| 23 | lge | Alloa | A | D | 3-3 | O'Neill 8; Weatherson 21,62 |
| 24 | scr3 | Aberdeen | H | D | 0-0 | |
| 25 | lge | St Johnstone | H | L | 1-2 | McLaughlin 41 |
| 26 | scr3r | Aberdeen | A | L | 1-4 | Weatherson 90 pen |
| 27 | lge | St Mirren | A | D | 2-2 | O'Neill 50; Bowey 59 |
| 28 | lge | Clyde | H | D | 1-1 | McAlpine 16 |
| 29 | lge | Falkirk | H | W | 2-1 | O'Neill 63 pen; Weatherson 88 |
| 30 | lge | Ayr | A | W | 1-0 | Thomson 26 |
| 31 | lge | Inverness CT | H | D | 0-0 | |
| 32 | lge | St Mirren | H | L | 0-2 | |
| 33 | lge | Arbroath | H | W | 3-0 | O'Neill 13,79; O'Connor 41 |
| 34 | lge | Ross County | A | W | 3-0 | O'Neill 40; O'Connor 73; MacKay 80 og |
| 35 | lge | Inverness CT | A | L | 0-1 | |
| 36 | lge | Arbroath | A | D | 0-0 | |
| 37 | lge | Alloa | H | L | 0-1 | |
| 38 | lge | Clyde | A | D | 2-2 | Thomson 15; Weatherson 74 |
| 39 | lge | Ross County | H | W | 1-0 | O'Connor 31 |
| 40 | lge | St Johnstone | A | W | 1-0 | Lyle 66 |

## ATTENDANCES

HOME GROUND: PALMERSTON PARK CAPACITY: 6412 AVERAGE LEAGUE AT HOME: 2152

| | | | | | | | | |
|---|---|---|---|---|---|---|---|---|
| 26 | Aberdeen | 6150 | 9 | Dundee | 2190 | 7 | Inverness CT | 1611 |
| 24 | Aberdeen | 5716 | 19 | Alloa | 2111 | 13 | Ross County | 1538 |
| 5 | Falkirk | 4091 | 20 | St Johnstone | 2048 | 31 | Inverness CT | 1405 |
| 21 | Falkirk | 3858 | 40 | St Johnstone | 2016 | 28 | Clyde | 1375 |
| 1 | Clyde | 3206 | 34 | Ross County | 1976 | 6 | Forfar | 1158 |
| 3 | St Johnstone | 3137 | 32 | St Mirren | 1911 | 33 | Arbroath | 1108 |
| 14 | Falkirk | 3017 | 27 | St Mirren | 1888 | 38 | Clyde | 1060 |
| 22 | Ayr | 2921 | 37 | Alloa | 1873 | 12 | Clyde | 1026 |
| 2 | Ross County | 2894 | 25 | St Johnstone | 1862 | 11 | Alloa | 658 |
| 4 | Ayr | 2803 | 16 | Inverness CT | 1855 | 18 | Arbroath | 579 |
| 17 | St Mirren | 2663 | 39 | Ross County | 1810 | 23 | Alloa | 561 |
| 29 | Falkirk | 2655 | 10 | Arbroath | 1733 | 36 | Arbroath | 502 |
| 8 | St Mirren | 2492 | 30 | Ayr | 1730 | | | |
| 15 | Ayr | 2234 | 35 | Inverness CT | 1656 | | | |

■ Home □ Away ▒ Neutral

## KEY PLAYERS - GOALSCORERS

**1 Jon O'Neill**

| | | | |
|---|---|---|---|
| Goals in the League | 9 | Player Strike Rate<br>Average number of minutes between League goals scored by player | 199 |
| Contribution to Attacking Power<br>Average number of minutes between League team goals while on pitch | 63 | Club Strike Rate<br>Average number of minutes between League goals scored by club | 36 |

| | PLAYER | LGE GOALS | POWER | STRIKE RATE |
|---|---|---|---|---|
| 2 | Derek Lyle | 6 | 84 | 395 mins |
| 3 | Peter Weatherson | 6 | 73 | 419 mins |
| 4 | Eric Paton | 3 | 69 | 507 mins |
| 5 | Steve Bowey | 4 | 70 | 762 mins |

## KEY PLAYERS - MIDFIELDERS

**1 Robbie Neilson**

| | | | |
|---|---|---|---|
| Goals in the League | 0 | Contribution to Attacking Power<br>Average number of minutes between League team goals while on pitch | 60 |
| Defensive Rating<br>Average number of mins between League goals conceded while he was on the pitch | 64 | Scoring Difference<br>Defensive Rating minus Contribution to Attacking Power | 4 |

| | PLAYER | LGE GOALS | DEF RATE | POWER | SCORE DIFF |
|---|---|---|---|---|---|
| 2 | Joe McAlpine | 1 | 81 | 81 | 0 mins |
| 3 | Steve Bowey | 4 | 71 | 71 | 0 mins |
| 4 | Brian McLaughlin | 2 | 70 | 76 | -6 mins |
| 5 | Jon O'Neill | 9 | 58 | 64 | -6 mins |

## KEY PLAYERS - DEFENDERS

**1 Andrew Aitken**

| | | | |
|---|---|---|---|
| Goals Conceded (GC)<br>The number of League goals conceded while he was on the pitch | 43 | Clean Sheets<br>In games when he played at least 70 minutes | 12 |
| Defensive Rating<br>Ave number of mins between League goals conceded while on the pitch | 73 | Club Defensive Rating<br>Average number of mins between League goals conceded by the club this season | 34 |

| | PLAYER | CON LGE | CLEAN SHEETS | DEF RATE |
|---|---|---|---|---|
| 2 | James Thomson | 36 | 11 | 73 mins |
| 3 | Derek Allan | 23 | 5 | 67 mins |
| 4 | Derek Anderson | 31 | 7 | 65 mins |

## KEY GOALKEEPER

**1 Colin Scott**

| | |
|---|---|
| Goals Conceded in the League | 18 |
| Defensive Rating<br>Ave number of mins between League goals conceded while on the pitch | 78 |
| Counting Games<br>Games when he played at least 70 mins | 16 |
| Clean Sheets<br>In games when he played at least 70 mins | 5 |

## TOP POINT EARNERS

| | PLAYER | GAMES | AVE |
|---|---|---|---|
| 1 | Dawson | 2 | 2.00 |
| 2 | Paton | 13 | 1.69 |
| 3 | Weatherson | 26 | 1.54 |
| 4 | Thomson | 29 | 1.52 |
| 5 | McColligan | 18 | 1.50 |
| 6 | Neilson | 13 | 1.46 |
| 7 | O'Neill | 17 | 1.41 |
| 8 | O'Connor | 10 | 1.40 |
| 9 | Lyle | 24 | 1.38 |
| 10 | McAlpine | 21 | 1.38 |
| | CLUB AVERAGE: | | 1.33 |

Ave = Average points per match in Counting Games

## DISCIPLINARY RECORDS

| | PLAYER | YELLOW | RED | AVE |
|---|---|---|---|---|
| 1 | Neilson | 6 | 1 | 163 |
| 2 | McColligan | 6 | 1 | 272 |
| 3 | O'Neill | 6 | 0 | 298 |
| 4 | Gray | 1 | 0 | 496 |
| 5 | Anderson | 4 | 0 | 506 |
| 6 | Bowey | 6 | 0 | 507 |
| 7 | Lyle | 4 | 0 | 593 |
| 8 | Atkinson | 1 | 0 | 616 |
| 9 | Thomson | 4 | 0 | 657 |
| 10 | McAlpine | 3 | 0 | 671 |
| 11 | Paton | 2 | 0 | 760 |
| 12 | Shields | 1 | 0 | 782 |
| 13 | Aitken | 4 | 0 | 782 |
| | Other | 5 | 1 | |
| | TOTAL | 53 | 3 | |

## LEAGUE GOALS

| | PLAYER | MINS | GOALS | AVE |
|---|---|---|---|---|
| 1 | O'Neill | 1789 | 9 | 199 |
| 2 | Lyle | 2372 | 6 | 395 |
| 3 | O'Connor | 1358 | 6 | 226 |
| 4 | Weatherson | 2511 | 6 | 419 |
| 5 | Bowey | 3047 | 4 | 762 |
| 6 | Paton | 1521 | 3 | 507 |
| 7 | Thomson | 2629 | 3 | 876 |
| 8 | McColligan | 1905 | 2 | 953 |
| 9 | McLaughlin | 1891 | 2 | 946 |
| 10 | Shields | 782 | 1 | 782 |
| 11 | McAlpine | 2014 | 1 | 2014 |
| | Other | | 2 | |
| | TOTAL | | 45 | |

## MONTH BY MONTH GUIDE TO THE POINTS

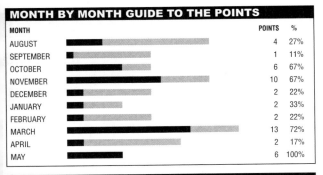

| MONTH | POINTS | % |
|---|---|---|
| AUGUST | 4 | 27% |
| SEPTEMBER | 1 | 11% |
| OCTOBER | 6 | 67% |
| NOVEMBER | 10 | 67% |
| DECEMBER | 2 | 22% |
| JANUARY | 2 | 33% |
| FEBRUARY | 2 | 22% |
| MARCH | 13 | 72% |
| APRIL | 2 | 17% |
| MAY | 6 | 100% |

## TEAM OF THE SEASON

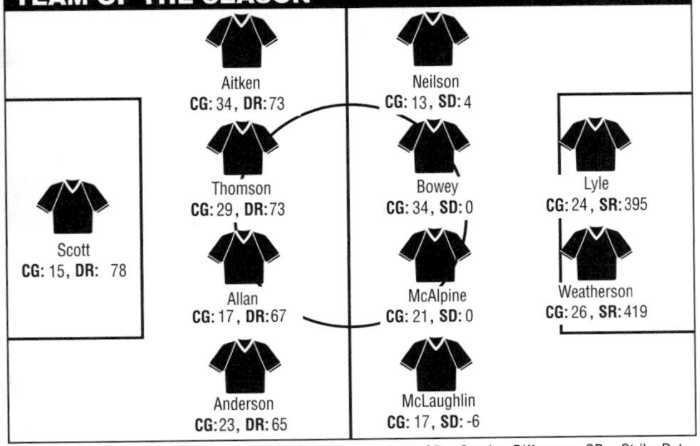
Aitken
CG: 34, DR: 73
Neilson
CG: 13, SD: 4
Thomson
CG: 29, DR: 73
Bowey
CG: 34, SD: 0
Lyle
CG: 24, SR: 395
Scott
CG: 15, DR: 78
Allan
CG: 17, DR: 67
McAlpine
CG: 21, SD: 0
Weatherson
CG: 26, SR: 419
Anderson
CG: 23, DR: 65
McLaughlin
CG: 17, SD: -6

KEY: DR = Defensive Rate, SD = Scoring Difference, SR = Strike Rate, CG = Counting Games – League games playing at least 70 minutes

## LEAGUE APPEARANCES, BOOKINGS AND CAPS

| | AGE (on 01/07/03) | IN THE SQUAD | COUNTING GAMES | MINUTES ON PITCH | YELLOW CARDS | RED CARDS | THIS SEASON | HOME COUNTRY |
|---|---|---|---|---|---|---|---|---|
| **Goalkeepers** | | | | | | | | |
| Jamie Campbell | 22 | 12 | 1 | 90 | 0 | 0 | - | Scotland |
| Andy Goram | 39 | 19 | 18 | 1665 | 0 | 0 | - | Scotland |
| Stuart Robertson | - | 10 | 1 | 90 | 0 | 0 | - | Scotland |
| Colin Scott | 33 | 30 | 15 | 1395 | 1 | 0 | - | Scotland |
| **Defenders** | | | | | | | | |
| Andrew Aitken | 25 | 35 | 34 | 3128 | 4 | 0 | - | Scotland |
| Derek Allan | 28 | 21 | 17 | 1543 | 0 | 0 | - | Scotland |
| Derek Anderson | 31 | 25 | 23 | 2026 | 4 | 0 | - | Scotland |
| Patrick Atkinson | 33 | 19 | 7 | 616 | 1 | 0 | - | England |
| Jonathan Crawford | 33 | 9 | 4 | 426 | 1 | 0 | - | Scotland |
| Alan Gray | 29 | 15 | 5 | 496 | 1 | 0 | - | Scotland |
| Robbie Henderson | - | 5 | 2 | 161 | 1 | 0 | - | |
| Steven Renicks | 27 | 8 | 4 | 360 | 0 | 0 | - | Scotland |
| James Thomson | 32 | 30 | 29 | 2629 | 4 | 0 | - | Scotland |
| **Midfielders** | | | | | | | | |
| Steve Bowey | 28 | 34 | 34 | 3047 | 6 | 0 | - | England |
| Paul Burns | - | 6 | 1 | 133 | 0 | 0 | - | Scotland |
| Ben Dawson | - | 9 | 2 | 243 | 0 | 0 | - | England |
| Sean Ferry | - | 1 | 0 | 0 | 0 | 0 | - | Scotland |
| William Gibson | 18 | 5 | 1 | 115 | 0 | 0 | - | Scotland |
| Peter Heatherson | 38 | 1 | 1 | 90 | 0 | 0 | - | Scotland |
| Thomas Lennox | - | 1 | 0 | 0 | 0 | 0 | - | Scotland |
| Joe McAlpine | 21 | 34 | 21 | 2014 | 3 | 0 | - | Scotland |
| Brian McLaughlin | 29 | 35 | 17 | 1891 | 0 | 0 | - | Scotland |
| Robbie Neilson | 23 | 13 | 13 | 1145 | 6 | 1 | - | Scotland |
| Jon O'Neill | 29 | 32 | 17 | 1789 | 6 | 0 | - | Scotland |
| Eric Paton | 24 | 30 | 13 | 1521 | 2 | 0 | - | Scotland |
| **Forwards** | | | | | | | | |
| Derek Lyle | 22 | 35 | 24 | 2372 | 4 | 0 | - | Scotland |
| Brian McColligan | 22 | 32 | 18 | 1905 | 6 | 1 | - | Scotland |
| Sean O'Connor | 21 | 23 | 10 | 1358 | 0 | 0 | - | England |
| Paul Shields | 21 | 14 | 7 | 782 | 1 | 0 | - | Scotland |
| Peter Weatherson | 23 | 32 | 26 | 2511 | 2 | 1 | - | Scotland |

KEY: LEAGUE BOOKINGS CAPS

## SQUAD APPEARANCES

| Match | 1 | 2 | 3 | 4 | 5 | 6 | 7 | 8 | 9 | 10 | 11 | 12 | 13 | 14 | 15 | 16 | 17 | 18 | 19 | 20 | 21 | 22 | 23 | 24 | 25 | 26 | 27 | 28 | 29 | 30 | 31 | 32 | 33 | 34 | 35 | 36 | 37 | 38 | 39 | 40 |
|---|---|---|---|---|---|---|---|---|---|---|---|---|---|---|---|---|---|---|---|---|---|---|---|---|---|---|---|---|---|---|---|---|---|---|---|---|---|---|---|---|
| Venue | H | A | H | H | A | H | H | A | A | H | A | A | H | H | A | A | H | A | H | A | A | H | A | H | H | A | A | H | H | A | H | H | H | A | A | A | H | A | H | A |
| Competition | L | L | L | L | L | I | L | L | I | L | L | L | L | L | L | L | L | L | L | L | L | L | L | S | L | S | L | L | L | L | L | L | L | L | L | L | L | L | L | L |
| Result | W | L | D | L | L | W | L | L | L | D | W | L | W | D | W | L | W | W | D | D | L | D | D | D | L | L | D | D | W | W | D | L | W | W | L | D | L | D | W | W |

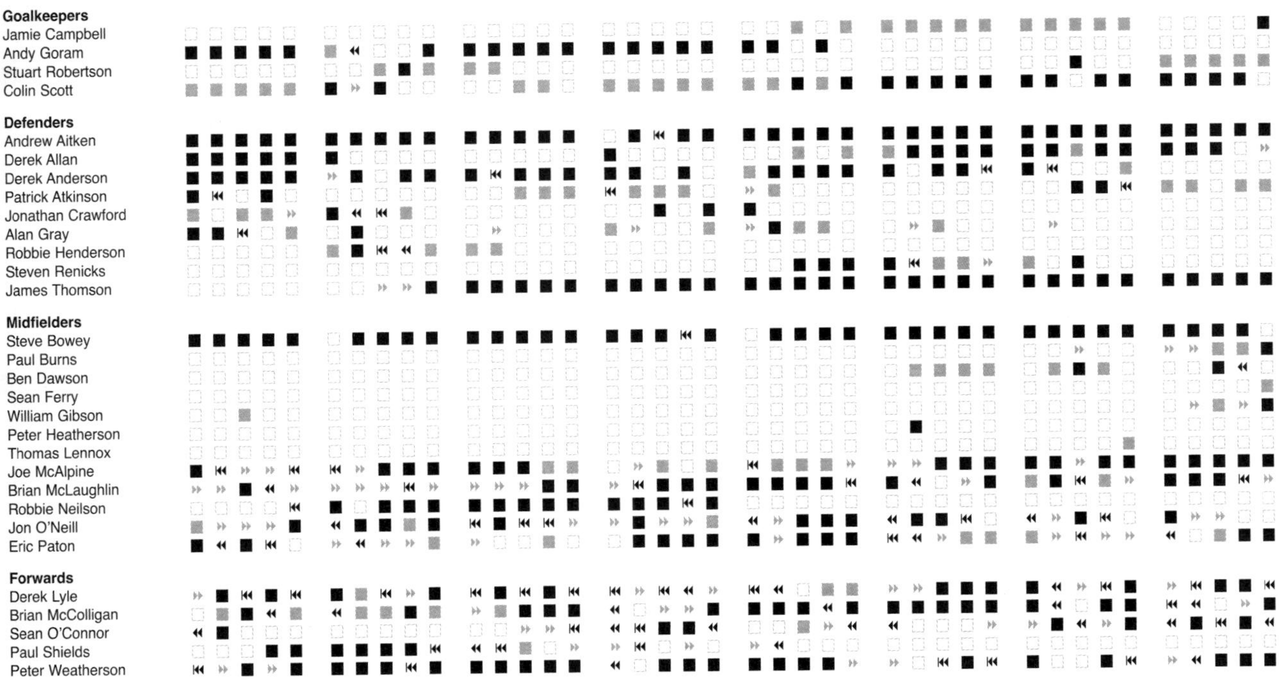
Goalkeepers
Jamie Campbell
Andy Goram
Stuart Robertson
Colin Scott
Defenders
Andrew Aitken
Derek Allan
Derek Anderson
Patrick Atkinson
Jonathan Crawford
Alan Gray
Robbie Henderson
Steven Renicks
James Thomson
Midfielders
Steve Bowey
Paul Burns
Ben Dawson
Sean Ferry
William Gibson
Peter Heatherson
Thomas Lennox
Joe McAlpine
Brian McLaughlin
Robbie Neilson
Jon O'Neill
Eric Paton
Forwards
Derek Lyle
Brian McColligan
Sean O'Connor
Paul Shields
Peter Weatherson

# AYR UNITED

Final Position: **6th**

NICKNAME: THE HONEST MEN

| | | | | | | | |
|---|---|---|---|---|---|---|---|
| 1 | lge | Falkirk | H | L | 1-3 | Kean 66 |
| 2 | lge | Clyde | A | L | 0-1 | |
| 3 | lge | Ross County | H | W | 2-1 | Perry 11 og; Grady 17 |
| 4 | lge | Queen of South | A | W | 2-1 | Campbell 44; Grady 53 |
| 5 | lge | Arbroath | H | W | 1-0 | Sheerin 45 |
| 6 | lge | St Johnstone | H | D | 0-0 | |
| 7 | lge | Alloa | A | W | 1-0 | Chaplain 52 |
| 8 | cis2 | Falkirk | H | L | 0-2 | |
| 9 | lge | St Mirren | H | D | 1-1 | Grady 26 |
| 10 | lge | Inverness CT | A | L | 0-2 | |
| 11 | lge | Falkirk | A | L | 0-3 | |
| 12 | lge | Clyde | H | D | 1-1 | Annand 22 |
| 13 | lge | Arbroath | A | D | 1-1 | Annand 16 |
| 14 | lge | Queen of South | H | L | 0-1 | |
| 15 | lge | St Johnstone | A | W | 2-0 | Craig 34,67 |
| 16 | lge | Alloa | H | W | 3-1 | Sheerin 26; Chaplain 46; Little 87 og |
| 17 | lge | St Mirren | A | L | 0-1 | |
| 18 | lge | Inverness CT | H | D | 3-3 | Chaplain 21; Annand 48; Lovering 52 |
| 19 | lge | Ross County | A | L | 0-1 | |
| 20 | lge | Arbroath | H | W | 4-0 | Campbell 3; Kean 59; McColl 70; Ferguson 89 |
| 21 | lge | Queen of South | A | D | 1-1 | Kean 69 |
| 22 | lge | Inverness CT | A | W | 1-0 | Kean 3 |
| 23 | scr3 | Peterhead | H | W | 2-0 | Black 9; Grady 76 pen |
| 24 | lge | St Mirren | H | D | 0-0 | |
| 25 | lge | Ross County | H | D | 1-1 | Whalen 37 |
| 26 | scr4 | Rangers | H | L | 0-1 | |
| 27 | lge | Falkirk | H | W | 1-0 | Chaplain 30 |
| 28 | lge | Arbroath | A | W | 2-1 | Kean 89,90 |
| 29 | lge | St Johnstone | H | L | 0-1 | |
| 30 | lge | Queen of South | H | L | 0-1 | |
| 31 | lge | Alloa | H | L | 0-1 | |
| 32 | lge | Clyde | A | L | 0-3 | |
| 33 | lge | Alloa | A | W | 3-2 | Whalen 9,69,82 |
| 34 | lge | St Johnstone | A | L | 0-1 | |
| 35 | lge | St Mirren | A | D | 1-1 | Chaplain 37 |
| 36 | lge | Falkirk | A | L | 0-3 | |
| 37 | lge | Inverness CT | H | W | 1-0 | Kean 19 |
| 38 | lge | Clyde | H | L | 0-3 | |
| 39 | lge | Ross County | A | L | 1-4 | Whalen 50 |

## ATTENDANCES

HOME GROUND: SOMERSET PARK CAPACITY: 10250 AVERAGE LEAGUE AT HOME: 1896

| | | | | | | | | |
|---|---|---|---|---|---|---|---|---|
| 26 | Rangers | 9608 | 8 | Falkirk | 2080 | 17 | St Mirren | 1638 |
| 36 | Falkirk | 4042 | 23 | Peterhead | 2040 | 16 | Alloa | 1632 |
| 39 | Ross County | 3449 | 22 | Inverness CT | 2021 | 25 | Ross County | 1486 |
| 11 | Falkirk | 3441 | 15 | St Johnstone | 2003 | 31 | Alloa | 1363 |
| 1 | Falkirk | 3030 | 12 | Clyde | 1989 | 37 | Inverness CT | 1114 |
| 21 | Queen of South | 2921 | 10 | Inverness CT | 1803 | 2 | Clyde | 1077 |
| 4 | Queen of South | 2803 | 38 | Clyde | 1795 | 32 | Clyde | 1015 |
| 24 | St Mirren | 2738 | 27 | Falkirk | 1783 | 7 | Alloa | 619 |
| 9 | St Mirren | 2489 | 5 | Arbroath | 1732 | 28 | Arbroath | 505 |
| 19 | Ross County | 2352 | 30 | Queen of South | 1730 | 33 | Alloa | 454 |
| 6 | St Johnstone | 2320 | 3 | Ross County | 1692 | 13 | Arbroath | 381 |
| 35 | St Mirren | 2248 | 29 | St Johnstone | 1690 | | | |
| 14 | Queen of South | 2234 | 20 | Arbroath | 1664 | | | |
| 34 | St Johnstone | 2132 | 18 | Inverness CT | 1663 | | | |

■ Home □ Away ■ Neutral

## KEY PLAYERS - GOALSCORERS

**1 Edward Annand**

| | | | |
|---|---|---|---|
| Goals in the League | 3 | Player Strike Rate<br>Average number of minutes between League goals scored by player | 489 |
| Contribution to Attacking Power<br>Average number of minutes between League team goals while on pitch | 86 | Club Strike Rate<br>Average number of minutes between League goals scored by club | 48 |

| | PLAYER | LGE GOALS | POWER | STRIKE RATE |
|---|---|---|---|---|
| 2 | Scott Chaplain | 5 | 96 | 600 mins |
| 3 | James Grady | 3 | 96 | 838 mins |
| 4 | Paul Sheerin | 2 | 73 | 849 mins |
| 5 | Mark Campbell | 2 | 97 | 1217 mins |

## KEY PLAYERS - MIDFIELDERS

**1 Paul Sheerin**

| | | | |
|---|---|---|---|
| Goals in the League | 2 | Contribution to Attacking Power<br>Average number of minutes between League team goals while on pitch | 74 |
| Defensive Rating<br>Average number of mins between League goals conceded while he was on the pitch | 81 | Scoring Difference<br>Defensive Rating minus Contribution to Attacking Power | 7 |

| | PLAYER | LGE GOALS | DEF RATE | POWER | SCORE DIFF |
|---|---|---|---|---|---|
| 2 | Iain Nicolson | 0 | 79 | 72 | 7 mins |
| 3 | Scott Chaplain | 5 | 81 | 97 | -16 mins |
| 4 | Neil Murray | 0 | 68 | 92 | -24 mins |

## KEY PLAYERS - DEFENDERS

**1 Willie Lyle**

| | | | |
|---|---|---|---|
| Goals Conceded (GC)<br>The number of League goals conceded while he was on the pitch | 30 | Clean Sheets<br>In games when he played at least 70 minutes | 8 |
| Defensive Rating<br>Ave number of mins between League goals conceded while on the pitch | 87 | Club Defensive Rating<br>Average number of mins between League goals conceded by the club this season | 37 |

| | PLAYER | CON LGE | CLEAN SHEETS | DEF RATE |
|---|---|---|---|---|
| 2 | Mark Campbell | 30 | 6 | 81 mins |
| 3 | David Craig | 32 | 8 | 79 mins |
| 4 | Marc Smyth | 36 | 9 | 77 mins |
| 5 | Allan McManus | 29 | 6 | 77 mins |

## KEY GOALKEEPER

**1 Craig Nelson**

| | |
|---|---|
| Goals Conceded in the League | 38 |
| Defensive Rating<br>Ave number of mins between League goals conceded while on the pitch | 73 |
| Counting Games<br>Games when he played at least 70 mins | 31 |
| Clean Sheets<br>In games when he played at least 70 mins | 8 |

## TOP POINT EARNERS

| | PLAYER | GAMES | AVE |
|---|---|---|---|
| 1 | Nicolson | 13 | 1.54 |
| 2 | Latta | 2 | 1.50 |
| 3 | Kean | 8 | 1.50 |
| 4 | Sheerin | 19 | 1.42 |
| 5 | Smyth | 31 | 1.42 |
| 6 | Lyle | 26 | 1.42 |
| 7 | Dodds | 5 | 1.40 |
| 8 | Murray | 18 | 1.39 |
| 9 | Grady | 26 | 1.38 |
| 10 | Chaplain | 33 | 1.27 |
| | CLUB AVERAGE: | | 1.25 |

Ave = Average points per match in Counting Games

## DISCIPLINARY RECORDS

| | PLAYER | YELLOW | RED | AVE |
|---|---|---|---|---|
| 1 | Lovering | 11 | 2 | 128 |
| 2 | McManus | 8 | 2 | 224 |
| 3 | Annand | 6 | 0 | 244 |
| 4 | Campbell | 8 | 0 | 304 |
| 5 | Grady | 6 | 1 | 359 |
| 6 | Smyth | 6 | 1 | 397 |
| 7 | Sheerin | 2 | 1 | 565 |
| 8 | Lyle | 3 | 1 | 650 |
| 9 | Dunlop | 2 | 0 | 702 |
| 10 | Nicolson | 1 | 0 | 1657 |
| 11 | Murray | 0 | 1 | 1831 |
| 12 | Chaplain | 1 | 0 | 3002 |
| | Other | 0 | 0 | |
| | TOTAL | 54 | 9 | |

## LEAGUE GOALS

| | PLAYER | MINS | GOALS | AVE |
|---|---|---|---|---|
| 1 | Kean | 1265 | 7 | 181 |
| 2 | Chaplain | 3002 | 5 | 600 |
| 3 | Whalen | 984 | 5 | 197 |
| 4 | Annand | 1466 | 3 | 489 |
| 5 | Grady | 2515 | 3 | 838 |
| 6 | Campbell | 2433 | 2 | 1217 |
| 7 | Craig | 2538 | 2 | 1269 |
| 8 | Sheerin | 1697 | 2 | 849 |
| 9 | McColl | 525 | 1 | 525 |
| 10 | Lovering | 1668 | 1 | 1668 |
| 11 | Ferguson | 75 | 1 | 75 |
| | Other | | 2 | |
| | TOTAL | | 34 | |

## MONTH BY MONTH GUIDE TO THE POINTS

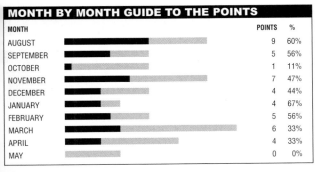

| MONTH | POINTS | % |
|---|---|---|
| AUGUST | 9 | 60% |
| SEPTEMBER | 5 | 56% |
| OCTOBER | 1 | 11% |
| NOVEMBER | 7 | 47% |
| DECEMBER | 4 | 44% |
| JANUARY | 4 | 67% |
| FEBRUARY | 5 | 56% |
| MARCH | 6 | 33% |
| APRIL | 4 | 33% |
| MAY | 0 | 0% |

## TEAM OF THE SEASON

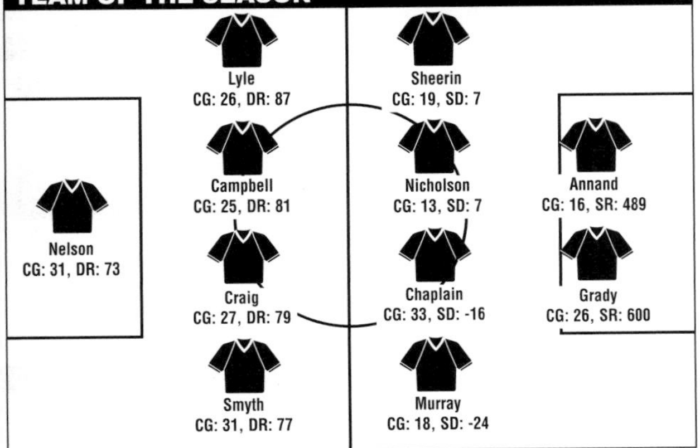
Lyle
CG: 26, DR: 87
Sheerin
CG: 19, SD: 7
Campbell
CG: 25, DR: 81
Nicholson
CG: 13, SD: 7
Annand
CG: 16, SR: 489
Nelson
CG: 31, DR: 73
Craig
CG: 27, DR: 79
Chaplain
CG: 33, SD: -16
Grady
CG: 26, SR: 600
Smyth
CG: 31, DR: 77
Murray
CG: 18, SD: -24

KEY: DR = Diffensive Rate, SD = Scoring Difference, SR = Strike Rate

## LEAGUE APPEARANCES, BOOKINGS AND CAPS

| | AGE (on 01/07/03) | IN THE SQUAD | COUNTING GAMES | MINUTES ON PITCH | YELLOW CARDS | RED CARDS | THIS SEASON | HOME COUNTRY |
|---|---|---|---|---|---|---|---|---|
| **Goalkeepers** | | | | | | | | |
| John Dodds | 21 | 36 | 5 | 450 | 0 | 0 | - | Scotland |
| Craig Nelson | 32 | 32 | 31 | 2790 | 0 | 0 | - | Scotland |
| **Defenders** | | | | | | | | |
| Fabian Bossy | 25 | 1 | 1 | 90 | 0 | 0 | - | France |
| Robert Burgess | 18 | 6 | 0 | 0 | 0 | 0 | - | Scotland |
| Mark Campbell | 25 | 29 | 25 | 2433 | 8 | 0 | - | Scotland |
| David Craig | 34 | 31 | 27 | 2538 | 0 | 0 | - | Scotland |
| Michael Dunlop | 20 | 29 | 13 | 1404 | 2 | 0 | - | Scotland |
| Martin Ferry | 20 | 9 | 1 | 90 | 0 | 0 | - | Rep of Ireland |
| Iain Fulton | 18 | 1 | 0 | 0 | 0 | 0 | - | Scotland |
| Paul Lovering | 27 | 22 | 16 | 1668 | 11 | 2 | - | Scotland |
| Willie Lyle | 19 | 35 | 26 | 2602 | 3 | 1 | - | Scotland |
| Alan McDermott | - | 2 | 1 | 98 | 0 | 0 | - | |
| Stewart McGrady | 17 | 2 | 0 | 58 | 0 | 0 | - | Scotland |
| Allan McManus | 28 | 26 | 24 | 2247 | 8 | 2 | - | Scotland |
| Marc Smyth | 20 | 32 | 31 | 2781 | 6 | 1 | - | N Ireland |
| **Midfielders** | | | | | | | | |
| Aaron Black | 19 | 27 | 3 | 588 | 0 | 0 | - | Scotland |
| Scott Chaplain | 19 | 36 | 33 | 3002 | 1 | 0 | - | Scotland |
| Brian Hamilton | 35 | 4 | 0 | 0 | 0 | 0 | - | Scotland |
| James Latta | 18 | 12 | 2 | 352 | 0 | 0 | - | Scotland |
| Boyd Mullen | 17 | 4 | 0 | 110 | 0 | 0 | - | Scotland |
| Neil Murray | 30 | 30 | 18 | 1831 | 0 | 1 | - | Scotland |
| Iain Nicolson | 26 | 26 | 13 | 1657 | 1 | 0 | - | Scotland |
| Paul Sheerin | 28 | 19 | 19 | 1697 | 2 | 1 | - | Scotland |
| **Forwards** | | | | | | | | |
| Edward Annand | 30 | 20 | 16 | 1466 | 6 | 0 | - | Scotland |
| Craig Conway | 18 | 1 | 0 | 3 | 0 | 0 | - | Scotland |
| Andrew Ferguson | 18 | 5 | 0 | 75 | 0 | 0 | - | Scotland |
| James Grady | 32 | 31 | 26 | 2515 | 6 | 1 | - | Scotland |
| Stuart Kean | 20 | 35 | 8 | 1265 | 0 | 0 | - | Scotland |
| Mark McColl | 18 | 16 | 4 | 525 | 0 | 0 | - | Scotland |
| Aidan McVeigh | 20 | 3 | 0 | 44 | 0 | 0 | - | N Ireland |
| Stephen Whalen | 21 | 13 | 10 | 984 | 0 | 0 | - | Scotland |

KEY: LEAGUE BOOKINGS CAPS

## SQUAD APPEARANCES

| Match | 1 | 2 | 3 | 4 | 5 | 6 | 7 | 8 | 9 | 10 | 11 | 12 | 13 | 14 | 15 | 16 | 17 | 18 | 19 | 20 | 21 | 22 | 23 | 24 | 25 | 26 | 27 | 28 | 29 | 30 | 31 | 32 | 33 | 34 | 35 | 36 | 37 | 38 | 39 |
|---|---|---|---|---|---|---|---|---|---|---|---|---|---|---|---|---|---|---|---|---|---|---|---|---|---|---|---|---|---|---|---|---|---|---|---|---|---|---|---|
| Venue | H | A | H | A | H | H | A | H | H | A | A | H | A | H | A | H | A | H | A | H | A | A | H | H | H | H | H | A | H | H | H | A | A | A | A | A | H | H | A |
| Competition | L | L | L | L | L | L | L | I | L | L | L | L | L | L | L | L | L | L | L | L | L | L | S | L | L | S | L | L | L | L | L | L | L | L | L | L | L | L | L |
| Result | L | L | W | W | W | D | W | L | D | L | L | D | D | L | W | W | L | D | L | W | D | W | W | D | D | L | W | W | L | L | L | L | W | L | D | L | W | L | L |

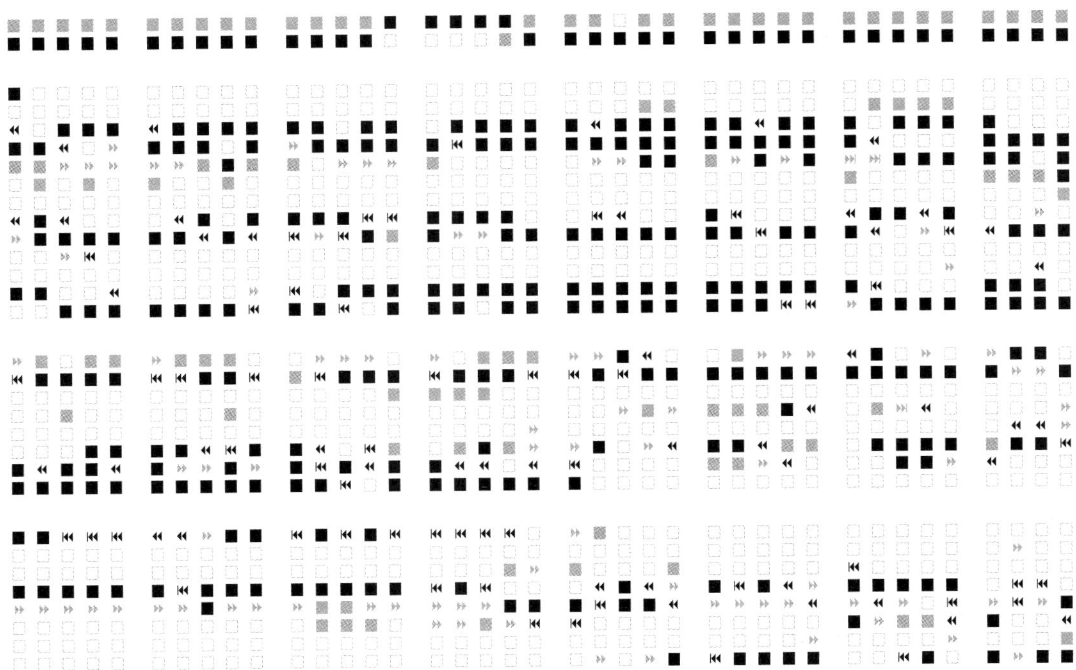

**Goalkeepers**
John Dodds
Craig Nelson

**Defenders**
Fabian Bossy
Robert Burgess
Mark Campbell
David Craig
Michael Dunlop
Martin Ferry
Iain Fulton
Paul Lovering
Willie Lyle
Alan McDermott
Stewart McGrady
Allan McManus
Marc Smyth

**Midfielders**
Aaron Black
Scott Chaplain
Brian Hamilton
James Latta
Boyd Mullen
Neil Murray
Iain Nicolson
Paul Sheerin

**Forwards**
Edward Annand
Craig Conway
Andrew Ferguson
James Grady
Stuart Kean
Mark McColl
Aidan McVeigh
Stephen Whalen

# ST MIRREN

Final Position: **7th**

NICKNAME: BUDDIES/SAINTS

| | | | | | | | |
|---|---|---|---|---|---|---|---|
| 1 | lge | St Johnstone | H | L | 0-2 | |
| 2 | lge | Falkirk | A | L | 0-2 | |
| 3 | lge | Alloa | H | W | 3-1 | Gillies 8; Cameron 81; McKenzie 90 |
| 4 | lge | Clyde | A | W | 3-2 | Junior Mendes 25,29,90 |
| 5 | lge | Inverness CT | H | L | 0-4 | |
| 6 | cis1 | G Morton | A | W | 3-2 | Cameron 55; Lappin 78; Yardley 116 |
| 7 | lge | Arbroath | A | D | 2-2 | Cameron 45; Gillies 66 |
| 8 | lge | Queen of South | H | W | 2-1 | Cameron 19; Weatherson 86 og |
| 9 | cis2 | Inverness CT | A | L | 1-3 | Cameron 24 |
| 10 | lge | Ayr | A | D | 1-1 | Cameron 60 |
| 11 | lge | Ross County | H | D | 1-1 | Junior Mendes 39 |
| 12 | lge | St Johnstone | A | L | 0-2 | |
| 13 | lge | Falkirk | H | D | 4-4 | Robb 53; Cameron 58,66,86 pen |
| 14 | lge | Inverness CT | A | L | 1-4 | Gillies 82 |
| 15 | lge | Clyde | H | L | 1-4 | Robb 24 |
| 16 | lge | Arbroath | H | W | 2-0 | Robb 17; Junior Mendes 20 |
| 17 | lge | Queen of South | A | L | 0-3 | |
| 18 | lge | Ayr | H | W | 1-0 | Junior Mendes 38 |
| 19 | lge | Ross County | A | L | 0-4 | |
| 20 | lge | Alloa | A | W | 3-2 | Gillies 71 pen; Cameron 73,84 |
| 21 | lge | Inverness CT | H | L | 1-4 | Cameron 86 |
| 22 | lge | Clyde | A | L | 2-3 | Gillies 13; Cameron 47 |
| 23 | lge | Ross County | H | W | 1-0 | Cameron 60 |
| 24 | scr3 | Celtic | A | L | 0-3 | |
| 25 | lge | Ayr | A | D | 0-0 | |
| 26 | lge | Alloa | H | D | 1-1 | Roberts 80 |
| 27 | lge | Falkirk | A | L | 1-3 | Denham 56 |
| 28 | lge | Queen of South | H | D | 2-2 | McLean 15; Gillies 51 pen |
| 29 | lge | Inverness CT | A | L | 1-3 | McHale 13 |
| 30 | lge | Clyde | H | L | 1-2 | Roberts 90 |
| 31 | lge | Queen of South | A | W | 2-0 | Gillies 4; Denham 87 |
| 32 | lge | St Johnstone | H | L | 1-3 | Gillies 60 |
| 33 | lge | Arbroath | A | D | 1-1 | Roberts 4 |
| 34 | lge | Arbroath | H | W | 1-0 | Cameron 14 |
| 35 | lge | Ayr | H | D | 1-1 | McKenna 82 |
| 36 | lge | Ross County | A | L | 0-2 | |
| 37 | lge | St Johnstone | A | D | 1-1 | Gillies 26 |
| 38 | lge | Falkirk | H | L | 1-2 | McGinty 62 |
| 39 | lge | Alloa | A | L | 0-4 | |

## ATTENDANCES

HOME GROUND: ST MIRREN PARK CAPACITY: 10800 AVERAGE LEAGUE AT HOME: 2697

| | | | | | | | | |
|---|---|---|---|---|---|---|---|---|
| 24 | Celtic | 29976 | 17 | Queen of South | 2663 | 36 | Ross County | 1967 |
| 6 | G Morton | 4477 | 5 | Inverness CT | 2605 | 31 | Queen of South | 1911 |
| 2 | Falkirk | 4360 | 8 | Queen of South | 2492 | 28 | Queen of South | 1888 |
| 27 | Falkirk | 4206 | 10 | Ayr | 2489 | 4 | Clyde | 1874 |
| 11 | Ross County | 3737 | 12 | St Johnstone | 2458 | 18 | Ayr | 1638 |
| 1 | St Johnstone | 3694 | 19 | Ross County | 2429 | 22 | Clyde | 1500 |
| 13 | Falkirk | 3661 | 32 | St Johnstone | 2369 | 9 | Inverness CT | 1194 |
| 3 | Alloa | 3104 | 23 | Ross County | 2366 | 39 | Alloa | 1084 |
| 38 | Falkirk | 3062 | 35 | Ayr | 2248 | 7 | Arbroath | 1008 |
| 21 | Inverness CT | 3054 | 34 | Arbroath | 2122 | 20 | Alloa | 783 |
| 16 | Arbroath | 3021 | 26 | Alloa | 2105 | 33 | Arbroath | 508 |
| 25 | Ayr | 2738 | 37 | St Johnstone | 2103 | | | |
| 15 | Clyde | 2703 | 14 | Inverness CT | 2023 | | | |
| 30 | Clyde | 2683 | 29 | Inverness CT | 1973 | | | |

■ Home □ Away ▒ Neutral

## KEY PLAYERS - GOALSCORERS

**1 Martin Cameron**

| | | | |
|---|---|---|---|
| Goals in the League | 13 | Player Strike Rate<br>Average number of minutes between League goals scored by player | 178 |
| Contribution to Attacking Power<br>Average number of minutes between League team goals while on pitch | 74 | Club Strike Rate<br>Average number of minutes between League goals scored by club | 39 |

| | PLAYER | LGE GOALS | POWER | STRIKE RATE |
|---|---|---|---|---|
| 2 | Junior Mendes | 6 | 62 | 218 mins |
| 3 | Ricky Gillies | 9 | 82 | 319 mins |
| 4 | Ricky Robb | 3 | 81 | 489 mins |
| 5 | Greig Denham | 2 | 82 | 659 mins |

## KEY PLAYERS - MIDFIELDERS

**1 Hugh Murray**

| | | | |
|---|---|---|---|
| Goals in the League | 0 | Contribution to Attacking Power<br>Average number of minutes between League team goals while on pitch | 72 |
| Defensive Rating<br>Average number of mins between League goals conceded while he was on the pitch | 68 | Scoring Difference<br>Defensive Rating minus Contribution to Attacking Power | -4 |

| | PLAYER | LGE GOALS | DEF RATE | POWER | SCORE DIFF |
|---|---|---|---|---|---|
| 2 | Paul McHale | 1 | 61 | 85 | -24 mins |
| 3 | Ian Ross | 0 | 39 | 67 | -28 mins |
| 4 | Simon Lappin | 0 | 46 | 76 | -30 mins |

## KEY PLAYERS - DEFENDERS

**1 Martin Baker**

| | | | |
|---|---|---|---|
| Goals Conceded (GC)<br>The number of League goals conceded while he was on the pitch | 14 | Clean Sheets<br>In games when he played at least 70 minutes | 3 |
| Defensive Rating<br>Ave number of mins between League goals conceded while on the pitch | 59 | Club Defensive Rating<br>Average number of mins between League goals conceded by the club this season | 23 |

| | PLAYER | CON LGE | CLEAN SHEETS | DEF RATE |
|---|---|---|---|---|
| 2 | Greig Denham | 24 | 4 | 55 mins |
| 3 | Jamie McGowan | 21 | 2 | 53 mins |
| 4 | Kirk Broadfoot | 41 | 4 | 48 mins |
| 5 | Chris Kerr | 21 | 1 | 48 mins |

## KEY GOALKEEPER

**1 Ludovic Roy**

| | |
|---|---|
| Goals Conceded in the League | 34 |
| Defensive Rating<br>Ave number of mins between League goals conceded while on the pitch | 56 |
| Counting Games<br>Games when he played at least 70 mins | 21 |
| Clean Sheets<br>In games when he played at least 70 mins | 5 |

## TOP POINT EARNERS

| | PLAYER | GAMES | AVE |
|---|---|---|---|
| 1 | Murray | 12 | 1.67 |
| 2 | Kerr | 9 | 1.56 |
| 3 | Yardley | 2 | 1.50 |
| 4 | Baltacha | 5 | 1.40 |
| 5 | Roy | 21 | 1.33 |
| 6 | Junior Mendes | 13 | 1.31 |
| 7 | Cameron | 24 | 1.21 |
| 8 | Guy | 14 | 1.21 |
| 9 | McGowan | 12 | 1.17 |
| 10 | Ross | 20 | 1.10 |
| | **CLUB AVERAGE:** | | **1.03** |

Ave = Average points per match in Counting Games

## DISCIPLINARY RECORDS

| | PLAYER | YELLOW | RED | AVE |
|---|---|---|---|---|
| 1 | Dempsie | 5 | 0 | 144 |
| 2 | Murray | 4 | 1 | 230 |
| 3 | Ross | 5 | 0 | 360 |
| 4 | McGowan | 3 | 0 | 373 |
| 5 | Baker | 2 | 0 | 415 |
| 6 | Denham | 3 | 0 | 439 |
| 7 | Lowing | 3 | 0 | 459 |
| 8 | Robb | 3 | 0 | 488 |
| 9 | Broadfoot | 3 | 0 | 654 |
| 10 | Cameron | 3 | 0 | 771 |
| 11 | Mitchell | 1 | 0 | 827 |
| 12 | McGinty | 2 | 0 | 914 |
| 13 | Gillies | 2 | 1 | 957 |
| | Other | 9 | 0 | |
| | **TOTAL** | **48** | **2** | |

## LEAGUE GOALS

| | PLAYER | MINS | GOALS | AVE |
|---|---|---|---|---|
| 1 | Cameron | 2314 | 13 | 178 |
| 2 | Gillies | 2873 | 9 | 319 |
| 3 | Jnr Mendes | 1308 | 6 | 218 |
| 4 | Roberts | 1002 | 3 | 334 |
| 5 | Robb | 1466 | 3 | 489 |
| 6 | Denham | 1318 | 2 | 659 |
| 7 | MacKenzie | 95 | 1 | 95 |
| 8 | McHale | 1099 | 1 | 1099 |
| 9 | McGinty | 1829 | 1 | 1829 |
| 10 | McLean | 500 | 1 | 500 |
| 11 | McKenna | 95 | 1 | 95 |
| | Other | | 1 | |
| | **TOTAL** | | **42** | |

## MONTH BY MONTH GUIDE TO THE POINTS

| MONTH | POINTS | % |
|---|---|---|
| AUGUST | 6 | 40% |
| SEPTEMBER | 5 | 56% |
| OCTOBER | 2 | 22% |
| NOVEMBER | 6 | 40% |
| DECEMBER | 3 | 33% |
| JANUARY | 3 | 50% |
| FEBRUARY | 3 | 25% |
| MARCH | 4 | 27% |
| APRIL | 5 | 42% |
| MAY | 0 | 0% |

## TEAM OF THE SEASON

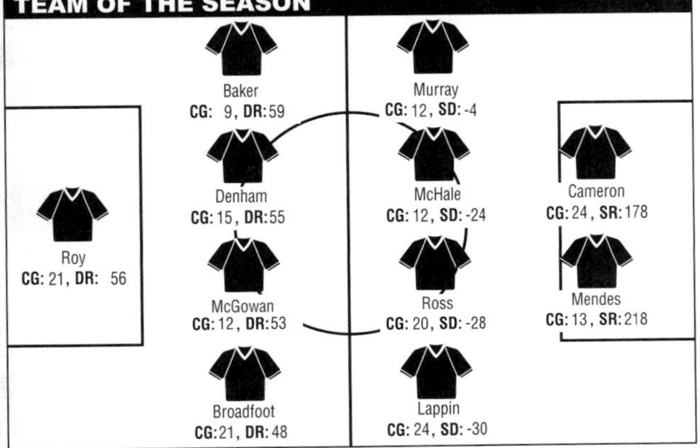
Roy
CG: 21, DR: 56
Baker
CG: 9, DR:59
Denham
CG: 15, DR:55
McGowan
CG: 12, DR:53
Broadfoot
CG:21, DR: 48
Murray
CG: 12, SD: -4
McHale
CG: 12, SD: -24
Ross
CG: 20, SD: -28
Lappin
CG: 24, SD: -30
Cameron
CG: 24, SR: 178
Mendes
CG: 13, SR: 218

KEY: DR = Defensive Rate, SD = Scoring Difference, SR = Strike Rate, CG = Counting Games – League games playing at least 70 minutes

## LEAGUE APPEARANCES, BOOKINGS AND CAPS

| | AGE (on 01/07/03) | IN THE SQUAD | COUNTING GAMES | MINUTES ON PITCH | YELLOW CARDS | RED CARDS | THIS SEASON | HOME COUNTRY |
|---|---|---|---|---|---|---|---|---|
| **Goalkeepers** | | | | | | | | |
| Billy Bald | - | 13 | 1 | 90 | 0 | 0 | - | Scotland |
| Kris Robertson | - | 36 | 14 | 1260 | 0 | 0 | - | Scotland |
| Ludovic Roy | 25 | 23 | 21 | 1890 | 1 | 0 | - | France |
| **Defenders** | | | | | | | | |
| Martin Baker | 29 | 10 | 9 | 831 | 2 | 0 | - | Scotland |
| Sergei Baltacha | 23 | 5 | 5 | 450 | 1 | 0 | - | Ukraine |
| Kirk Broadfoot | 18 | 29 | 21 | 1962 | 3 | 0 | - | Scotland |
| Greig Denham | 26 | 16 | 15 | 1318 | 3 | 0 | - | Scotland |
| Andy Dow | 30 | 16 | 4 | 428 | 0 | 0 | - | Scotland |
| Gerhard Fellner | 33 | 1 | 1 | 90 | 1 | 0 | - | Austria |
| Brian Gordon | 17 | 1 | 0 | 0 | 0 | 0 | - | Scotland |
| Graham Guy | - | 23 | 14 | 1427 | 1 | 0 | - | Scotland |
| Chris Kerr | 24 | 28 | 9 | 1007 | 1 | 0 | - | Scotland |
| David Lowing | - | 28 | 13 | 1379 | 3 | 0 | - | Scotland |
| Jamie McGowan | 32 | 16 | 12 | 1121 | 3 | 0 | - | Scotland |
| Ricky Robb | 20 | 22 | 13 | 1466 | 3 | 0 | - | Scotland |
| Paul Rudden | 22 | 20 | 10 | 1006 | 1 | 0 | - | Scotland |
| **Midfielders** | | | | | | | | |
| Mark Dempsie | 22 | 9 | 8 | 720 | 5 | 0 | - | Scotland |
| Jamie Dunbar | 19 | 24 | 6 | 1011 | 0 | 0 | - | Scotland |
| Jeff Ferguson | 17 | 3 | 0 | 10 | 0 | 0 | - | Scotland |
| David Jack | 19 | 2 | 0 | 10 | 0 | 0 | - | Scotland |
| Simon Lappin | 20 | 34 | 24 | 2498 | 2 | 0 | - | Scotland |
| Scott MacKenzie | 33 | 3 | 1 | 95 | 0 | 0 | - | Scotland |
| Paul McHale | 21 | 13 | 12 | 1099 | 1 | 0 | - | Scotland |
| Graham McWilliam | 17 | 2 | 0 | 13 | 0 | 0 | - | Scotland |
| Ally Mitchell | 34 | 12 | 7 | 827 | 1 | 0 | - | Scotland |
| Alan Muir | 16 | 3 | 1 | 128 | 0 | 0 | - | Scotland |
| Hugh Murray | 24 | 15 | 12 | 1153 | 4 | 1 | - | Scotland |
| Ryan Robinson | 22 | 1 | 0 | 0 | 0 | 0 | - | Scotland |
| Ian Ross | 28 | 20 | 20 | 1800 | 5 | 0 | - | Scotland |
| **Forwards** | | | | | | | | |
| Martin Cameron | 25 | 29 | 24 | 2314 | 3 | 0 | - | Scotland |
| Ricky Gillies | 26 | 33 | 31 | 2873 | 2 | 1 | - | Scotland |
| Junior Mendes | 26 | 17 | 13 | 1308 | 0 | 0 | - | England |
| Brian McGinty | - | 25 | 18 | 1829 | 2 | 0 | - | Scotland |
| David McKenna | 16 | 4 | 0 | 95 | 0 | 0 | - | Scotland |
| Scott McLean | 27 | 7 | 4 | 500 | 0 | 0 | - | Scotland |
| Mark Roberts | 27 | 14 | 9 | 1002 | 0 | 0 | - | Scotland |
| Mark Yardley | 33 | 15 | 2 | 432 | 0 | 0 | - | |

KEY: LEAGUE BOOKINGS CAPS

## SQUAD APPEARANCES

| Match | 1 | 2 | 3 | 4 | 5 | 6 | 7 | 8 | 9 | 10 | 11 | 12 | 13 | 14 | 15 | 16 | 17 | 18 | 19 | 20 | 21 | 22 | 23 | 24 | 25 | 26 | 27 | 28 | 29 | 30 | 31 | 32 | 33 | 34 | 35 | 36 | 37 | 38 | 39 |
|---|---|---|---|---|---|---|---|---|---|---|---|---|---|---|---|---|---|---|---|---|---|---|---|---|---|---|---|---|---|---|---|---|---|---|---|---|---|---|---|
| Venue | H | A | H | A | H | A | A | H | A | A | H | A | H | A | H | H | A | H | A | A | H | A | H | A | A | H | A | H | A | H | A | H | A | H | H | A | A | H | A |
| Competition | L | L | L | L | L | I | L | L | I | L | L | L | L | L | L | L | L | L | L | L | L | L | L | S | L | L | L | L | L | L | L | L | L | L | L | L | L | L | L |
| Result | L | L | W | W | L | W | D | W | L | D | D | L | D | L | L | W | L | W | L | W | L | L | W | L | D | D | L | D | L | L | W | L | D | W | D | L | D | L | L |

**Goalkeepers**
Billy Bald
Kris Robertson
Ludovic Roy
**Defenders**
Martin Baker
Sergei Baltacha
Kirk Broadfoot
Greig Denham
Andy Dow
Gerhard Fellner
Brian Gordon
Graham Guy
Chris Kerr
David Lowing
Jamie McGowan
Ricky Robb
Paul Rudden
**Midfielders**
Mark Dempsie
Jamie Dunbar
Jeff Ferguson
David Jack
Simon Lappin
Scott MacKenzie
Paul McHale
Graham McWilliam
Ally Mitchell
Alan Muir
Hugh Murray
Ryan Robinson
Ian Ross
Trialist
**Forwards**
Martin Cameron
Ricky Gillies
Junior Mendes
Brian McGinty
David McKenna
Scott McLean
Mark Roberts
Mark Yardley

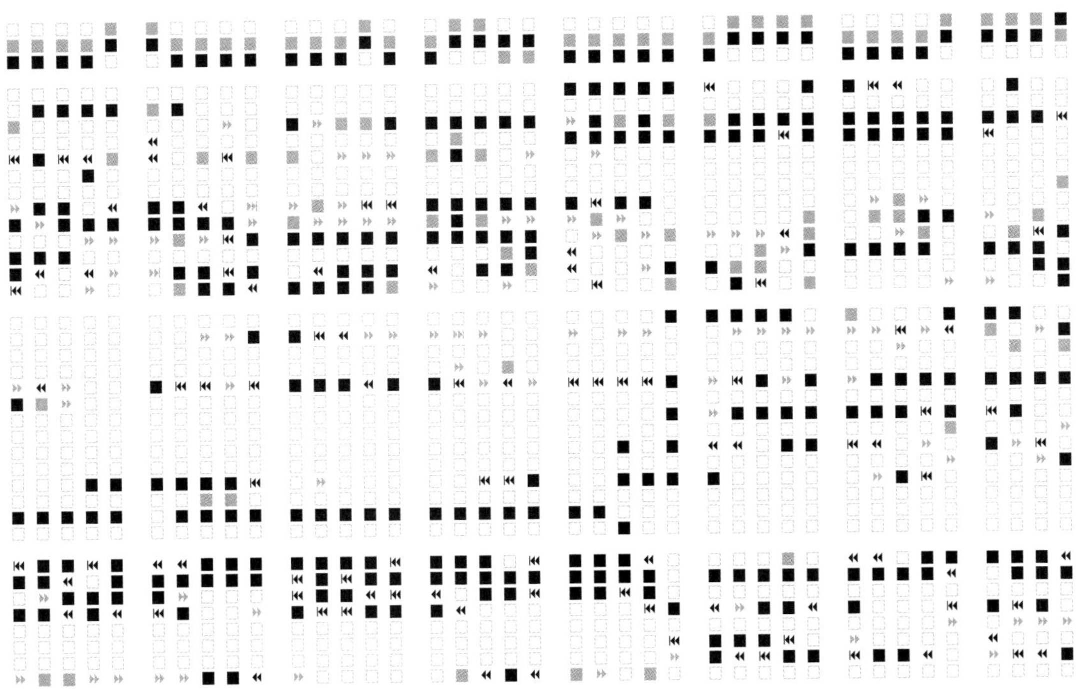

# ROSS COUNTY

Final Position: **8th**

NICKNAME: THE HIGHLANDERS

| | | | | | | |
|---|---|---|---|---|---|---|
| 1 | lge | Arbroath | A | W | 3-0 | Bone 43; Cowie 63; Ferguson 69 |
| 2 | lge | Queen of South | H | W | 2-0 | Ferguson 39; Wood 90 |
| 3 | lge | Ayr | A | L | 1-2 | Gethins 85 |
| 4 | lge | Inverness CT | A | L | 0-2 | |
| 5 | lge | Clyde | H | D | 1-1 | Canning 87 |
| 6 | cis1 | Clyde | A | W | 1-0 | Bone 27 |
| 7 | lge | Falkirk | H | D | 1-1 | Gilbert 88 |
| 8 | lge | St Johnstone | A | D | 1-1 | Bayne 61 |
| 9 | cis2 | Hamilton | H | W | 3-0 | McCulloch 26; Cowie 75; Graham, Alasdair 86 og |
| 10 | lge | Alloa | H | L | 0-1 | |
| 11 | lge | St Mirren | A | D | 1-1 | Irvine 42 |
| 12 | lge | Arbroath | H | W | 4-0 | MacKay 1; Hislop 2,40; Robertson 74 |
| 13 | cis3 | Hearts | A | L | 0-3 | |
| 14 | lge | Queen of South | A | L | 0-2 | |
| 15 | lge | Clyde | A | L | 1-2 | Canning 39 |
| 16 | lge | Inverness CT | H | L | 0-2 | |
| 17 | lge | Falkirk | A | L | 0-2 | |
| 18 | lge | St Johnstone | H | D | 0-0 | |
| 19 | lge | Alloa | A | D | 1-1 | Irvine 38 |
| 20 | lge | St Mirren | H | W | 4-0 | Bayne 44,51,81; Mackay 90 |
| 21 | lge | Ayr | H | W | 1-0 | Bone 59 |
| 22 | lge | Arbroath | A | L | 1-2 | Hislop 86 |
| 23 | lge | Clyde | H | D | 1-1 | Mackay 36 |
| 24 | lge | St Johnstone | A | L | 0-2 | |
| 25 | lge | St Mirren | A | L | 0-1 | |
| 26 | scr3 | G Morton | H | L | 1-2 | Winters 43 |
| 27 | lge | Alloa | H | L | 1-2 | Irvine 88 |
| 28 | lge | Ayr | A | D | 1-1 | Robertson 53 |
| 29 | lge | Inverness CT | A | W | 5-1 | McLeish 13; Ferguson 19 pen; Venetis 39; Robertson 48; Gethins 88 |
| 30 | lge | Clyde | A | L | 0-1 | |
| 31 | lge | Inverness CT | H | L | 0-2 | |
| 32 | lge | Falkirk | H | L | 0-1 | |
| 33 | lge | St Johnstone | H | L | 2-3 | Dods 78 og; Ferguson 81 |
| 34 | lge | Queen of South | H | L | 0-3 | |
| 35 | lge | Falkirk | A | L | 0-3 | |
| 36 | lge | Alloa | A | L | 1-2 | Ferguson 27 |
| 37 | lge | St Mirren | H | W | 2-0 | Ferguson 57; McGarry 80 |
| 38 | lge | Arbroath | H | W | 3-1 | Robertson 16; Winters 20; Bayne 74 |
| 39 | lge | Queen of South | A | L | 0-1 | |
| 40 | lge | Ayr | H | W | 4-1 | McGarry 46,49; Higgins 58; MacKay 78 |

## ATTENDANCES

HOME GROUND: VICTORIA PARK CAPACITY: 5800 AVERAGE LEAGUE AT HOME: 2706

| | | | | | | | | |
|---|---|---|---|---|---|---|---|---|
| 13 | Hearts | 6454 | 8 | St Johnstone | 2434 | 39 | Queen of South | 1810 |
| 16 | Inverness CT | 5449 | 20 | St Mirren | 2429 | 3 | Ayr | 1692 |
| 31 | Inverness CT | 4621 | 24 | St Johnstone | 2400 | 14 | Queen of South | 1538 |
| 11 | St Mirren | 3737 | 25 | St Mirren | 2366 | 28 | Ayr | 1486 |
| 35 | Falkirk | 3523 | 21 | Ayr | 2352 | 15 | Clyde | 1047 |
| 40 | Ayr | 3449 | 26 | G Morton | 2250 | 30 | Clyde | 1012 |
| 29 | Inverness CT | 3443 | 38 | Arbroath | 2204 | 9 | Hamilton | 902 |
| 17 | Falkirk | 3255 | 32 | Falkirk | 2161 | 36 | Alloa | 876 |
| 7 | Falkirk | 3129 | 27 | Alloa | 2096 | 1 | Arbroath | 760 |
| 4 | Inverness CT | 3000 | 12 | Arbroath | 2065 | 6 | Clyde | 604 |
| 2 | Queen of South | 2894 | 5 | Clyde | 2059 | 22 | Arbroath | 580 |
| 33 | St Johnstone | 2689 | 10 | Alloa | 2021 | 19 | Alloa | 445 |
| 18 | St Johnstone | 2614 | 34 | Queen of South | 1976 | | | |
| 23 | Clyde | 2534 | 37 | St Mirren | 1967 | | | |

■ Home □ Away ▒ Neutral

## KEY PLAYERS - GOALSCORERS

**1 Steve Ferguson**

| | | | |
|---|---|---|---|
| Goals in the League | 6 | Player Strike Rate<br>Average number of minutes between League goals scored by player | 255 |
| Contribution to Attacking Power<br>Average number of minutes between League team goals while on pitch | 61 | Club Strike Rate<br>Average number of minutes between League goals scored by club | 39 |

| | PLAYER | LGE GOALS | POWER | STRIKE RATE |
|---|---|---|---|---|
| 2 | Graeme Bayne | 5 | 75 | 380 mins |
| 3 | Steven MacKay | 4 | 64 | 420 mins |
| 4 | Steven McGarry | 3 | 65 | 611 mins |
| 5 | Hugh Robertson | 4 | 78 | 650 mins |

## KEY PLAYERS - MIDFIELDERS

**1 Steven MacKay**

| | | | |
|---|---|---|---|
| Goals in the League | 4 | Contribution to Attacking Power<br>Average number of minutes between League team goals while on pitch | 65 |
| Defensive Rating<br>Average number of mins between League goals conceded while he was on the pitch | 88 | Scoring Difference<br>Defensive Rating minus Contribution to Attacking Power | 23 |

| | PLAYER | LGE GOALS | DEF RATE | POWER | SCORE DIFF |
|---|---|---|---|---|---|
| 2 | Steve Ferguson | 6 | 64 | 61 | 3 mins |
| 3 | Don Cowie | 1 | 70 | 84 | -14 mins |
| 4 | Kenny Gilbert | 1 | 75 | 97 | -22 mins |

## KEY PLAYERS - DEFENDERS

**1 Mark Perry**

| | | | |
|---|---|---|---|
| Goals Conceded (GC)<br>The number of League goals conceded while he was on the pitch | 21 | Clean Sheets<br>In games when he played at least 70 minutes | 5 |
| Defensive Rating<br>Ave number of mins between League goals conceded while on the pitch | 80 | Club Defensive Rating<br>Average number of mins between League goals conceded by the club this season | 35 |

| | PLAYER | CON LGE | CLEAN SHEETS | DEF RATE |
|---|---|---|---|---|
| 2 | Paul Deas | 14 | 3 | 72 mins |
| 3 | Brian Irvine | 38 | 7 | 72 mins |
| 4 | Mark McCulloch | 43 | 7 | 69 mins |
| 5 | Sean Webb | 19 | 1 | 68 mins |

## KEY GOALKEEPER

**1 Tony Bullock**

| | |
|---|---|
| Goals Conceded in the League | 46 |
| Defensive Rating<br>Ave number of mins between League goals conceded while on the pitch | 70 |
| Counting Games<br>Games when he played at least 70 mins | 36 |
| Clean Sheets<br>In games when he played at least 70 mins | 7 |

## TOP POINT EARNERS

| | PLAYER | GAMES | AVE |
|---|---|---|---|
| 1 | Bone | 8 | 1.63 |
| 2 | Winters | 4 | 1.50 |
| 3 | Venetis | 2 | 1.50 |
| 4 | Campbell | 4 | 1.50 |
| 5 | Hannah | 6 | 1.50 |
| 6 | Higgins | 2 | 1.50 |
| 7 | Gethins | 4 | 1.50 |
| 8 | McGarry | 16 | 1.50 |
| 9 | Ferguson | 15 | 1.27 |
| 10 | MacKay | 16 | 1.19 |
| | CLUB AVERAGE: | | 0.97 |

Ave = Average points per match in Counting Games

## DISCIPLINARY RECORDS

| | PLAYER | YELLOW | RED | AVE |
|---|---|---|---|---|
| 1 | Gilbert | 8 | 1 | 215 |
| 2 | Tait | 2 | 1 | 237 |
| 3 | Bone | 3 | 0 | 278 |
| 4 | Perry | 6 | 0 | 281 |
| 5 | Deas | 3 | 0 | 335 |
| 6 | Gethins | 2 | 0 | 344 |
| 7 | Ferguson | 4 | 0 | 383 |
| 8 | Hislop | 2 | 0 | 408 |
| 9 | Irvine | 6 | 0 | 455 |
| 10 | Winters | 1 | 0 | 525 |
| 11 | Canning | 4 | 0 | 533 |
| 12 | Bayne | 3 | 0 | 633 |
| 13 | MacKay | 2 | 0 | 839 |
| | Other | 7 | 1 | |
| | TOTAL | 53 | 3 | |

## LEAGUE GOALS

| | PLAYER | MINS | GOALS | AVE |
|---|---|---|---|---|
| 1 | Ferguson | 1532 | 6 | 255 |
| 2 | Bayne | 1899 | 5 | 380 |
| 3 | MacKay | 1678 | 4 | 420 |
| 4 | Robertson | 2599 | 4 | 650 |
| 5 | McGarry | 1833 | 3 | 611 |
| 6 | Irvine | 2732 | 3 | 911 |
| 7 | Hislop | 817 | 3 | 272 |
| 8 | Canning | 2132 | 2 | 1066 |
| 9 | Gethins | 689 | 2 | 345 |
| 10 | Bone | 834 | 2 | 417 |
| 11 | Cowie | 2017 | 1 | 2017 |
| 12 | Higgins | 387 | 1 | 387 |
| 13 | Winters | 525 | 1 | 525 |
| | Other | | 5 | |
| | TOTAL | | 42 | |

## MONTH BY MONTH GUIDE TO THE POINTS

| MONTH | POINTS | % |
|---|---|---|
| AUGUST | 7 | 47% |
| SEPTEMBER | 2 | 22% |
| OCTOBER | 4 | 44% |
| NOVEMBER | 2 | 13% |
| DECEMBER | 7 | 58% |
| JANUARY | 0 | 0% |
| FEBRUARY | 4 | 44% |
| MARCH | 0 | 0% |
| APRIL | 6 | 50% |
| MAY | 3 | 50% |

## TEAM OF THE SEASON

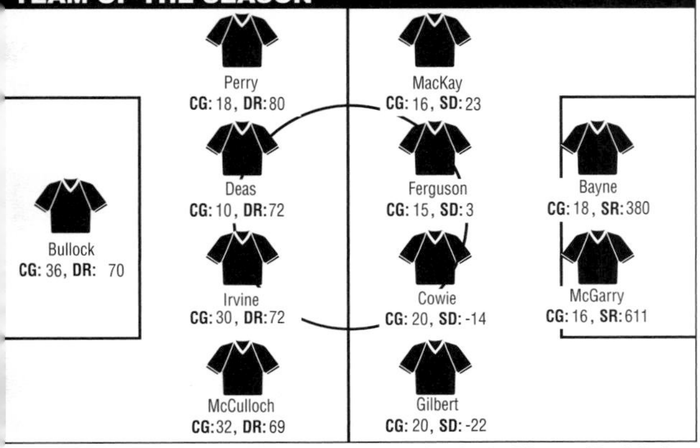
Perry
CG: 18, DR: 80
MacKay
CG: 16, SD: 23
Deas
CG: 10, DR: 72
Ferguson
CG: 15, SD: 3
Bayne
CG: 18, SR: 380
Bullock
CG: 36, DR: 70
Irvine
CG: 30, DR: 72
Cowie
CG: 20, SD: -14
McGarry
CG: 16, SR: 611
McCulloch
CG: 32, DR: 69
Gilbert
CG: 20, SD: -22

**KEY:** DR = Defensive Rate, SD = Scoring Difference, SR = Strike Rate, CG = Counting Games – League games playing at least 70 minutes

## LEAGUE APPEARANCES, BOOKINGS AND CAPS

| | AGE (on 01/07/03) | IN THE SQUAD | COUNTING GAMES | MINUTES ON PITCH | YELLOW CARDS | RED CARDS | THIS SEASON | HOME COUNTRY |
|---|---|---|---|---|---|---|---|---|
| **Goalkeepers** | | | | | | | | |
| Tony Bullock | 31 | 36 | 36 | 3240 | 0 | 0 | - | England |
| Leslie Fridge | 34 | 36 | 0 | 0 | 0 | 0 | - | Scotland |
| **Defenders** | | | | | | | | |
| Martin Canning | 21 | 27 | 22 | 2132 | 4 | 0 | - | Scotland |
| Paul Deas | 31 | 16 | 10 | 1006 | 3 | 0 | - | |
| Brian Irvine | 38 | 33 | 30 | 2732 | 6 | 0 | - | Scotland |
| Mark McCulloch | 28 | 34 | 32 | 2965 | 3 | 0 | - | Scotland |
| Mark Perry | 32 | 21 | 18 | 1687 | 6 | 0 | - | Scotland |
| Hugh Robertson | 28 | 33 | 29 | 2599 | 1 | 0 | - | Scotland |
| Jordan Tait | 23 | 10 | 7 | 712 | 2 | 1 | - | Scotland |
| Sean Webb | - | 27 | 13 | 1289 | 0 | 1 | - | Scotland |
| **Midfielders** | | | | | | | | |
| M Bolochoweckyj | - | 4 | 0 | 11 | 0 | 0 | - | Scotland |
| Craig Campbell | 20 | 9 | 4 | 440 | 0 | 0 | - | Scotland |
| Don Cowie | 20 | 32 | 20 | 2017 | 0 | 0 | - | Scotland |
| Steve Ferguson | 26 | 23 | 15 | 1532 | 4 | 0 | - | Scotland |
| Kenny Gilbert | 28 | 23 | 20 | 1938 | 8 | 1 | - | Scotland |
| David Hannah | 29 | 6 | 6 | 540 | 0 | 0 | - | Scotland |
| Peter Lynch | - | 1 | 0 | 22 | 0 | 0 | - | Scotland |
| Steven MacKay | 22 | 32 | 16 | 1678 | 2 | 0 | - | Scotland |
| Kevin McLeish | 22 | 12 | 8 | 811 | 0 | 0 | - | Scotland |
| Anastasios Venetis | 32 | 9 | 2 | 459 | 0 | 0 | - | Greece |
| **Forwards** | | | | | | | | |
| Graeme Bayne | 23 | 31 | 18 | 1899 | 3 | 0 | - | Scotland |
| Alex Bone | 32 | 16 | 8 | 834 | 3 | 0 | - | Scotland |
| Grant Davidson | - | 3 | 0 | 45 | 1 | 0 | - | Scotland |
| Connor Gethins | - | 19 | 4 | 689 | 2 | 0 | - | Rep of Ireland |
| Sean Higgins | - | 9 | 2 | 387 | 1 | 0 | - | Scotland |
| Steven Hislop | - | 14 | 6 | 817 | 2 | 0 | - | Scotland |
| Steven McGarry | 23 | 35 | 16 | 1833 | 1 | 0 | - | Scotland |
| David Winters | 20 | 12 | 4 | 525 | 1 | 0 | - | Scotland |
| Martin Wood | 20 | 14 | 4 | 582 | 0 | 0 | - | Scotland |

**KEY:** LEAGUE BOOKINGS CAPS

## SQUAD APPEARANCES

| Match | 1 | 2 | 3 | 4 | 5 | 6 | 7 | 8 | 9 | 10 | 11 | 12 | 13 | 14 | 15 | 16 | 17 | 18 | 19 | 20 | 21 | 22 | 23 | 24 | 25 | 26 | 27 | 28 | 29 | 30 | 31 | 32 | 33 | 34 | 35 | 36 | 37 | 38 | 39 | 40 |
|---|---|---|---|---|---|---|---|---|---|---|---|---|---|---|---|---|---|---|---|---|---|---|---|---|---|---|---|---|---|---|---|---|---|---|---|---|---|---|---|---|
| Venue | A | H | A | A | H | A | H | A | H | H | A | H | A | A | A | H | A | H | A | H | H | A | H | A | A | H | H | A | A | A | H | H | H | H | A | A | H | H | A | H |
| Competition | L | L | L | L | L | I | L | L | I | L | L | L | I | L | L | L | L | L | L | L | L | L | L | L | L | S | L | L | L | L | L | L | L | L | L | L | L | L | L | L |
| Result | W | W | L | L | D | W | D | D | W | L | D | W | L | L | L | L | L | D | D | W | W | L | D | L | L | L | L | D | W | L | L | L | L | L | L | L | W | W | L | W |

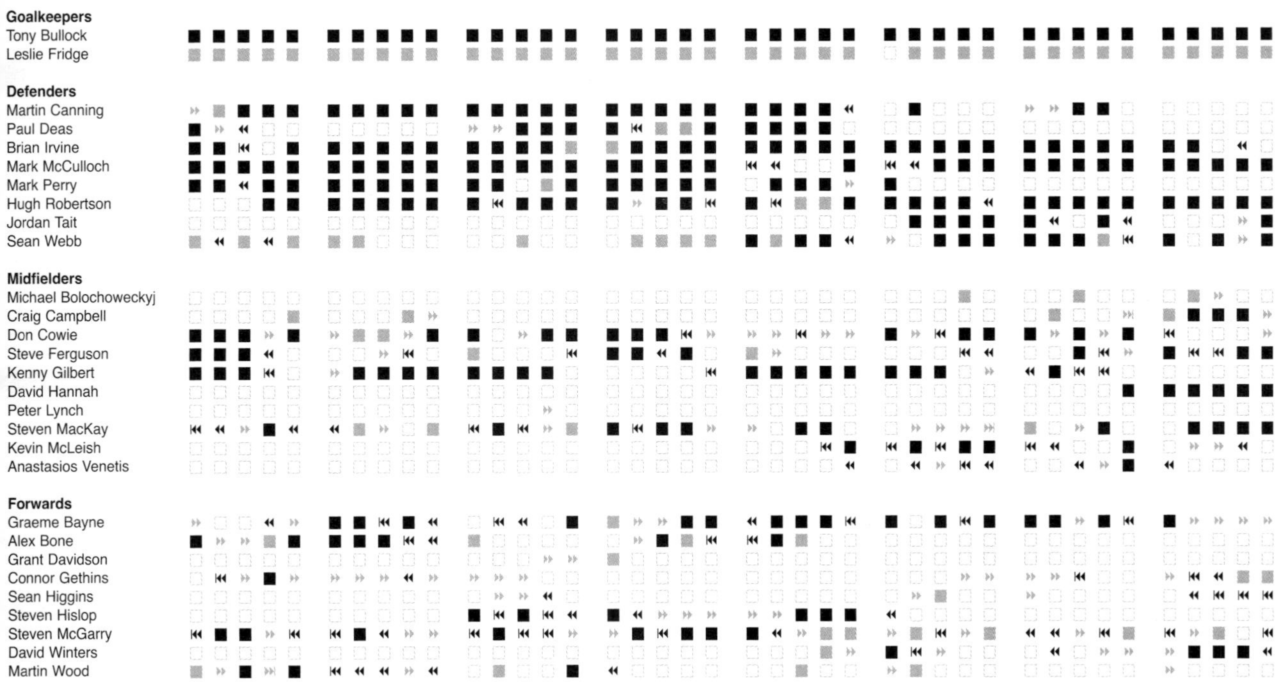
Goalkeepers
Tony Bullock
Leslie Fridge
Defenders
Martin Canning
Paul Deas
Brian Irvine
Mark McCulloch
Mark Perry
Hugh Robertson
Jordan Tait
Sean Webb
Midfielders
Michael Bolochoweckyj
Craig Campbell
Don Cowie
Steve Ferguson
Kenny Gilbert
David Hannah
Peter Lynch
Steven MacKay
Kevin McLeish
Anastasios Venetis
Forwards
Graeme Bayne
Alex Bone
Grant Davidson
Connor Gethins
Sean Higgins
Steven Hislop
Steven McGarry
David Winters
Martin Wood

# ALLOA

**Final Position: 9th**

NICKNAME: THE WASPS

| | | | | | | |
|---|---|---|---|---|---|---|
| 1 | lge | Inverness CT | A | D | 0-0 | |
| 2 | lge | Arbroath | H | L | 0-3 | |
| 3 | lge | St Mirren | A | L | 1-3 | Crabbe 38 pen |
| 4 | lge | Falkirk | H | L | 1-6 | Ferguson, B 5 |
| 5 | lge | St Johnstone | A | L | 0-2 | |
| 6 | cis1 | Raith | A | W | 3-2 | Hutchison 40; Little 65; Hamilton 108 |
| 7 | lge | Clyde | A | D | 0-0 | |
| 8 | lge | Ayr | H | L | 0-1 | |
| 9 | cis2 | Hibernian | H | L | 0-2 | |
| 10 | lge | Ross County | A | W | 1-0 | Evans G 72 |
| 11 | lge | Queen of South | H | L | 0-1 | |
| 12 | lge | Inverness CT | H | L | 0-6 | |
| 13 | lge | Arbroath | A | W | 1-0 | Hamilton 54 |
| 14 | lge | St Johnstone | H | L | 1-3 | Seaton 27 pen |
| 15 | lge | Falkirk | A | L | 0-3 | |
| 16 | lge | Clyde | H | L | 1-4 | Cowan 44 |
| 17 | lge | Ayr | A | L | 1-3 | Cowan 88 |
| 18 | lge | Ross County | H | D | 1-1 | Little 63 |
| 19 | lge | Queen of South | A | D | 1-1 | Hutchison 27 |
| 20 | lge | St Mirren | H | L | 2-3 | Crabbe 9; Thomson 61 |
| 21 | lge | Inverness CT | A | D | 1-1 | Hutchison 45 |
| 22 | lge | St Johnstone | A | L | 0-3 | |
| 23 | lge | Queen of South | H | D | 3-3 | Seaton 10 pen,42 pen; Thomson 75 |
| 24 | scr3 | Cowdenbeath | A | W | 3-2 | Crabbe 53. 74; Thomson 72, |
| 25 | lge | Ross County | A | W | 2-1 | Sloan 4,9 |
| 26 | lge | St Mirren | A | D | 1-1 | Hamilton 43 |
| 27 | scr4 | Falkirk | H | L | 0-2 | |
| 28 | lge | Arbroath | H | W | 3-2 | Little 13; Watson 51; Hutchison 89 |
| 29 | lge | St Johnstone | H | L | 1-2 | Sloan 28 |
| 30 | lge | Falkirk | A | L | 1-3 | Hughes 79 og |
| 31 | lge | Clyde | A | D | 2-2 | Sloan 11; Mensing 86 og |
| 32 | lge | Ayr | A | W | 1-0 | Crabbe 66 |
| 33 | lge | Ayr | H | L | 2-3 | Little 2; Davidson 85 |
| 34 | lge | Falkirk | H | L | 1-3 | Hamilton 10 |
| 35 | lge | Clyde | H | L | 1-2 | Hamilton 23 |
| 36 | lge | Ross County | H | W | 2-1 | Hamilton 12; Sloan 71 |
| 37 | lge | Queen of South | A | W | 1-0 | Thomson 67 |
| 38 | lge | Inverness CT | H | L | 1-5 | Sloan 60 pen |
| 39 | lge | Arbroath | A | W | 1-0 | Ferguson, B 44 |
| 40 | lge | St Mirren | H | W | 4-0 | Sloan 10,31; Seaton 48; Hutchison 88 |

## ATTENDANCES

HOME GROUND: RECREATION PARK CAPACITY: 3100 AVERAGE LEAGUE AT HOME: 828

| | | | | | | | | |
|---|---|---|---|---|---|---|---|---|
| 15 | Falkirk | 3390 | 21 | Inverness CT | 1639 | 31 | Clyde | 665 |
| 30 | Falkirk | 3320 | 17 | Ayr | 1632 | 11 | Queen of South | 658 |
| 3 | St Mirren | 3104 | 1 | Inverness CT | 1623 | 8 | Ayr | 619 |
| 27 | Falkirk | 3059 | 32 | Ayr | 1363 | 23 | Queen of South | 561 |
| 4 | Falkirk | 2613 | 6 | Raith | 1342 | 12 | Inverness CT | 531 |
| 5 | St Johnstone | 2274 | 40 | St Mirren | 1084 | 24 | Cowdenbeath | 529 |
| 19 | Queen of South | 2111 | 7 | Clyde | 973 | 2 | Arbroath | 518 |
| 26 | St Mirren | 2105 | 14 | St Johnstone | 952 | 38 | Inverness CT | 485 |
| 25 | Ross County | 2096 | 29 | St Johnstone | 884 | 33 | Ayr | 454 |
| 22 | St Johnstone | 2090 | 36 | Ross County | 876 | 18 | Ross County | 445 |
| 10 | Ross County | 2021 | 20 | St Mirren | 783 | 39 | Arbroath | 405 |
| 37 | Queen of South | 1873 | 13 | Arbroath | 768 | 28 | Arbroath | 340 |
| 9 | Hibernian | 1842 | 16 | Clyde | 736 | | | |
| 34 | Falkirk | 1686 | 35 | Clyde | 687 | | | |

■ Home □ Away ▨ Neutral

## KEY PLAYERS - GOALSCORERS

**1 Robert Sloan**

| | | | |
|---|---|---|---|
| Goals in the League | 8 | Player Strike Rate<br>Average number of minutes between League goals scored by player | 169 |
| Contribution to Attacking Power<br>Average number of minutes between League team goals while on pitch | 56 | Club Strike Rate<br>Average number of minutes between League goals scored by club | 42 |

| | PLAYER | LGE GOALS | POWER | STRIKE RATE |
|---|---|---|---|---|
| 2 | Scott Crabbe | 3 | 78 | 548 mins |
| 3 | Gareth Hutchison | 4 | 90 | 589 mins |
| 4 | Ross Hamilton | 5 | 84 | 609 mins |
| 5 | Andy Seaton | 4 | 76 | 707 mins |

## KEY PLAYERS - MIDFIELDERS

**1 Derek Ferguson**

| | | | |
|---|---|---|---|
| Goals in the League | 0 | Contribution to Attacking Power<br>Average number of minutes between League team goals while on pitch | 81 |
| Defensive Rating<br>Average number of mins between League goals conceded while he was on the pitch | 55 | Scoring Difference<br>Defensive Rating minus Contribution to Attacking Power | -26 |

| | PLAYER | LGE GOALS | DEF RATE | POWER | SCORE DIFF |
|---|---|---|---|---|---|
| 2 | Ian Little | 3 | 49 | 80 | -31 mins |
| 3 | Martin Christie | 0 | 44 | 86 | -42 mins |
| 4 | Jimmy Fisher | 0 | 37 | 165 | -128 mins |

## KEY PLAYERS - DEFENDERS

**1 Gregg Watson**

| | | | |
|---|---|---|---|
| Goals Conceded (GC)<br>The number of League goals conceded while he was on the pitch | 35 | Clean Sheets<br>In games when he played at least 70 minutes | 7 |
| Defensive Rating<br>Ave number of mins between League goals conceded while on the pitch | 57 | Club Defensive Rating<br>Average number of mins between League goals conceded by the club this season | 23 |

| | PLAYER | CON LGE | CLEAN SHEETS | DEF RATE |
|---|---|---|---|---|
| 2 | Craig Valentine | 66 | 8 | 46 mins |
| 3 | Steven Thomson | 70 | 8 | 45 mins |
| 4 | Andy Seaton | 67 | 5 | 42 mins |

## KEY GOALKEEPER

**1 Derek Soutar**

| | |
|---|---|
| Goals Conceded in the League | 19 |
| Defensive Rating<br>Ave number of mins between League goals conceded while on the pitch | 57 |
| Counting Games<br>Games when he played at least 70 mins | 12 |
| Clean Sheets<br>In games when he played at least 70 mins | 3 |

## TOP POINT EARNERS

| | PLAYER | GAMES | AVE |
|---|---|---|---|
| 1 | Soutar | 12 | 1.67 |
| 2 | Sloan | 14 | 1.64 |
| 3 | Watson | 20 | 1.35 |
| 4 | Ferguson, D | 17 | 1.24 |
| 5 | Ferguson | 5 | 1.20 |
| 6 | Walker | 23 | 1.17 |
| 7 | Valentine | 34 | 1.03 |
| 8 | Seaton | 30 | 1.00 |
| 9 | Davidson | 4 | 1.00 |
| 10 | Hamilton | 33 | 0.97 |
| | CLUB AVERAGE: | | 0.97 |

Ave = Average points per match in Counting Games

## DISCIPLINARY RECORDS

| | PLAYER | YELLOW | RED | AVE |
|---|---|---|---|---|
| 1 | MacDonald | 2 | 1 | 154 |
| 2 | Christie | 7 | 2 | 230 |
| 3 | Davidson | 2 | 0 | 230 |
| 4 | Crabbe | 4 | 0 | 411 |
| 5 | Little | 5 | 0 | 431 |
| 6 | Fisher | 2 | 0 | 493 |
| 7 | Watson | 4 | 0 | 495 |
| 8 | Valentine | 6 | 0 | 508 |
| 9 | Cowan | 1 | 0 | 641 |
| 10 | Ferguson, D | 3 | 0 | 676 |
| 11 | Thomson | 4 | 0 | 787 |
| 12 | Seaton | 3 | 0 | 942 |
| 13 | Hamilton | 3 | 0 | 1014 |
| | Other | 4 | 0 | |
| | TOTAL | 50 | 3 | |

## LEAGUE GOALS

| | PLAYER | MINS | GOALS | AVE |
|---|---|---|---|---|
| 1 | Sloan | 1354 | 8 | 169 |
| 2 | Hamilton | 3044 | 5 | 609 |
| 3 | Hutchison | 2355 | 4 | 589 |
| 4 | Seaton | 2827 | 4 | 707 |
| 5 | Crabbe | 1644 | 3 | 548 |
| 6 | Little | 2157 | 3 | 719 |
| 7 | Thomson | 3150 | 3 | 1050 |
| 8 | Cowan | 641 | 2 | 321 |
| 9 | Ferguson | 491 | 2 | 246 |
| 10 | Watson | 1980 | 1 | 1980 |
| 11 | Evans, G | 416 | 1 | 416 |
| 12 | Davidson | 461 | 1 | 461 |
| | Other | | 2 | |
| | TOTAL | | 39 | |

## MONTH BY MONTH GUIDE TO THE POINTS

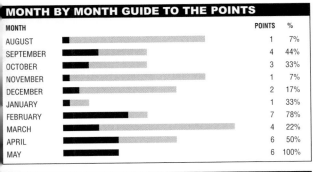

| MONTH | POINTS | % |
|---|---|---|
| AUGUST | 1 | 7% |
| SEPTEMBER | 4 | 44% |
| OCTOBER | 3 | 33% |
| NOVEMBER | 1 | 7% |
| DECEMBER | 2 | 17% |
| JANUARY | 1 | 33% |
| FEBRUARY | 7 | 78% |
| MARCH | 4 | 22% |
| APRIL | 6 | 50% |
| MAY | 6 | 100% |

## TEAM OF THE SEASON

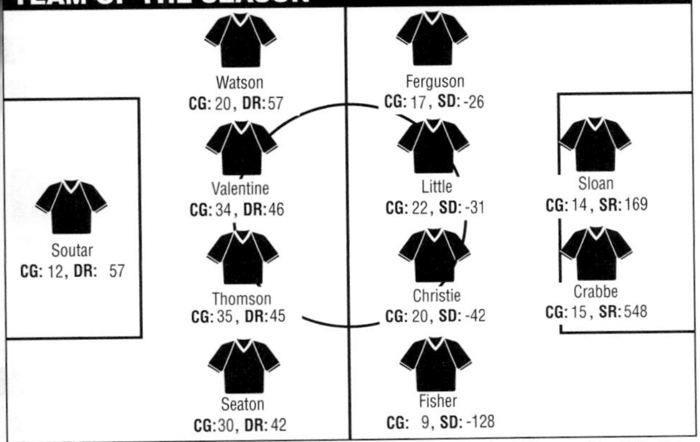

Soutar
CG: 12, DR: 57
Watson
CG: 20, DR: 57
Valentine
CG: 34, DR: 46
Thomson
CG: 35, DR: 45
Seaton
CG: 30, DR: 42
Ferguson
CG: 17, SD: -26
Little
CG: 22, SD: -31
Christie
CG: 20, SD: -42
Fisher
CG: 9, SD: -128
Sloan
CG: 14, SR: 169
Crabbe
CG: 15, SR: 548


KEY: DR = Defensive Rate, SD = Scoring Difference, SR = Strike Rate, CG = Counting Games – League games playing at least 70 minutes

## LEAGUE APPEARANCES, BOOKINGS AND CAPS

| | AGE (on 01/07/03) | IN THE SQUAD | COUNTING GAMES | MINUTES ON PITCH | YELLOW CARDS | RED CARDS | THIS SEASON | HOME COUNTRY |
|---|---|---|---|---|---|---|---|---|
| **Goalkeepers** | | | | | | | | |
| James Evans | 21 | 31 | 16 | 1440 | 0 | 0 | - | Scotland |
| Myles Hogarth | 28 | 26 | 8 | 720 | 0 | 0 | - | Scotland |
| Jim McQueen | 42 | 3 | 0 | 0 | 0 | 0 | - | Scotland |
| Derek Soutar | 22 | 12 | 12 | 1080 | 1 | 0 | - | Scotland |
| **Defenders** | | | | | | | | |
| Mark Cowan | 32 | 31 | 6 | 641 | 1 | 0 | - | Scotland |
| Keith Knox | 38 | 13 | 4 | 424 | 1 | 0 | - | Scotland |
| Andy Seaton | 25 | 33 | 30 | 2827 | 3 | 0 | - | Scotland |
| Steven Thomson | 30 | 35 | 35 | 3150 | 4 | 0 | - | Scotland |
| Craig Valentine | 32 | 34 | 34 | 3049 | 6 | 0 | - | Scotland |
| Gregg Watson | 32 | 27 | 20 | 1980 | 4 | 0 | - | Scotland |
| **Midfielders** | | | | | | | | |
| Martin Christie | 31 | 27 | 20 | 2072 | 7 | 2 | - | Scotland |
| Harry Curran | 36 | 2 | 0 | 0 | 0 | 0 | - | Scotland |
| Ross Elliott | - | 7 | 1 | 184 | 0 | 0 | - | Scotland |
| Browne Ferguson | 22 | 7 | 5 | 491 | 0 | 0 | - | Scotland |
| Derek Ferguson | 35 | 27 | 17 | 2030 | 3 | 0 | - | Scotland |
| Jimmy Fisher | 35 | 18 | 9 | 987 | 2 | 0 | - | Scotland |
| Graeme Gillan | - | 15 | 1 | 194 | 0 | 0 | - | Scotland |
| Kevin Kelbie | - | 1 | 0 | 0 | 0 | 0 | - | Scotland |
| Ian Little | 29 | 28 | 22 | 2157 | 5 | 0 | - | Scotland |
| William MacDonald | - | 11 | 5 | 462 | 2 | 1 | - | Scotland |
| **Forwards** | | | | | | | | |
| Scott Crabbe | 34 | 30 | 15 | 1644 | 4 | 0 | - | Scotland |
| Ryan Davidson | 21 | 16 | 4 | 461 | 2 | 0 | - | Scotland |
| Gareth Evans | 36 | 24 | 0 | 416 | 1 | 0 | - | England |
| Ross Hamilton | 23 | 35 | 33 | 3044 | 3 | 0 | - | Scotland |
| Gareth Hutchison | 31 | 36 | 22 | 2355 | 0 | 0 | - | Scotland |
| Robert Sloan | 19 | 16 | 14 | 1354 | 0 | 0 | - | Scotland |
| James Stevenson | - | 4 | 0 | 121 | 0 | 0 | - | Scotland |
| Richard Walker | - | 29 | 23 | 2273 | 1 | 0 | - | Scotland |

KEY: LEAGUE BOOKINGS CAPS

## SQUAD APPEARANCES

| Match | 1 | 2 | 3 | 4 | 5 | 6 | 7 | 8 | 9 | 10 | 11 | 12 | 13 | 14 | 15 | 16 | 17 | 18 | 19 | 20 |
|---|---|---|---|---|---|---|---|---|---|---|---|---|---|---|---|---|---|---|---|---|
| Venue | A | H | A | H | A | A | A | H | H | A | H | H | A | H | A | H | A | H | A | H |
| Competition | L | L | L | L | L | I | L | L | I | L | L | L | L | L | L | L | L | L | L | L |
| Result | D | L | L | L | L | W | D | L | L | W | L | L | W | L | L | L | L | D | D | L |

| Match | 21 | 22 | 23 | 24 | 25 | 26 | 27 | 28 | 29 | 30 | 31 | 32 | 33 | 34 | 35 | 36 | 37 | 38 | 39 | 40 |
|---|---|---|---|---|---|---|---|---|---|---|---|---|---|---|---|---|---|---|---|---|
| Venue | A | A | H | A | A | A | H | H | H | A | A | A | H | H | H | H | A | H | A | H |
| Competition | L | L | L | S | L | L | S | L | L | L | L | L | L | L | L | L | L | L | L | L |
| Result | D | L | D | W | W | D | L | W | L | L | D | W | L | L | L | W | W | L | W | W |

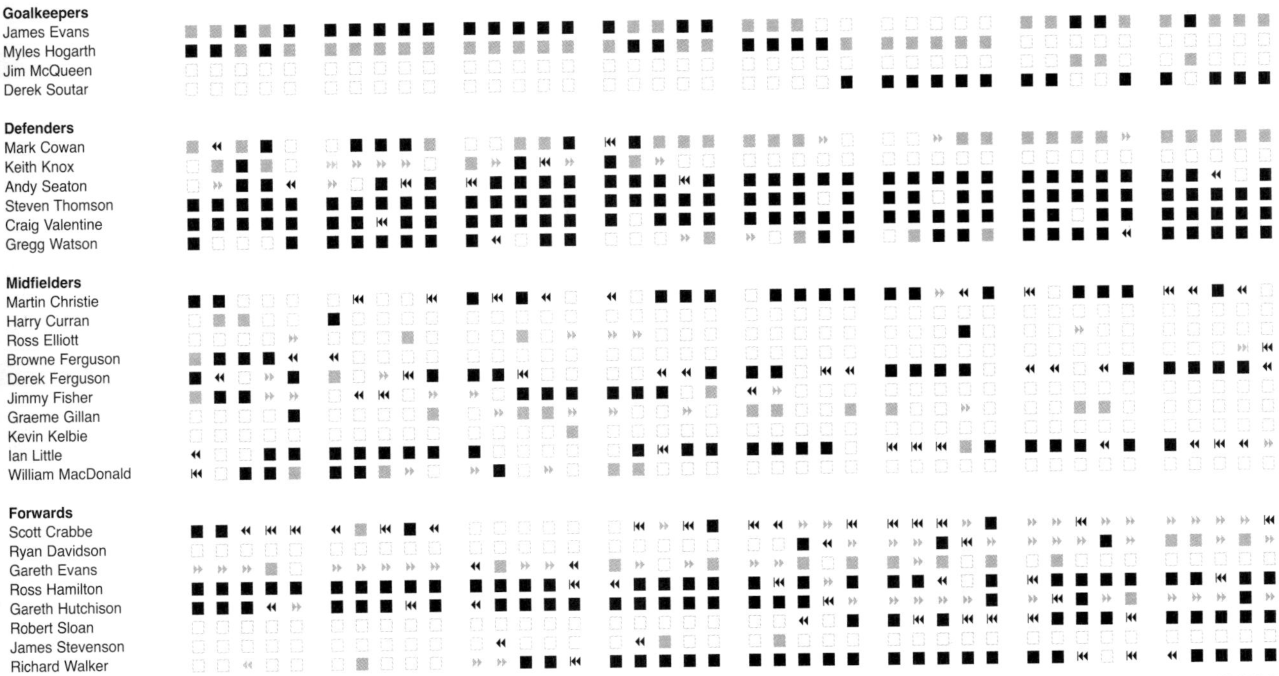

Goalkeepers
James Evans
Myles Hogarth
Jim McQueen
Derek Soutar
Defenders
Mark Cowan
Keith Knox
Andy Seaton
Steven Thomson
Craig Valentine
Gregg Watson
Midfielders
Martin Christie
Harry Curran
Ross Elliott
Browne Ferguson
Derek Ferguson
Jimmy Fisher
Graeme Gillan
Kevin Kelbie
Ian Little
William MacDonald
Forwards
Scott Crabbe
Ryan Davidson
Gareth Evans
Ross Hamilton
Gareth Hutchison
Robert Sloan
James Stevenson
Richard Walker

# ARBROATH

Final Position: **10th**

NICKNAME: THE RED LICHTIES

| | | | | | | | |
|---|---|---|---|---|---|---|---|
| 1 | lge | Ross County | H | L | 0-3 | |
| 2 | lge | Alloa | A | W | 3-0 | McDowell 23; Ritchie 65; Spink 89 |
| 3 | lge | Clyde | H | D | 1-1 | McDowell 75 pen |
| 4 | lge | St Johnstone | H | L | 0-1 | |
| 5 | lge | Ayr | A | L | 0-1 | |
| 6 | cis1 | Berwick | A | L | 2-4 | Feroz 51,87 pen |
| 7 | lge | St Mirren | H | D | 2-2 | Feroz 7; Cusick 88 pen |
| 8 | lge | Inverness CT | A | L | 0-5 | |
| 9 | lge | Queen of South | A | D | 2-2 | Currie 8; Cargill 53 |
| 10 | lge | Falkirk | H | W | 2-0 | Cusick 83; Feroz 85 pen |
| 11 | lge | Ross County | A | L | 0-4 | |
| 12 | lge | Alloa | H | L | 0-1 | |
| 13 | lge | Ayr | H | D | 1-1 | McDowell 72 pen |
| 14 | lge | St Johnstone | A | L | 0-2 | |
| 15 | lge | St Mirren | A | L | 0-2 | |
| 16 | lge | Inverness CT | H | L | 1-2 | Tait 73 |
| 17 | lge | Queen of South | H | L | 1-2 | McDowell 62 |
| 18 | lge | Falkirk | A | L | 1-2 | Spink 53 |
| 19 | lge | Clyde | A | L | 0-3 | |
| 20 | lge | Ross County | H | W | 2-1 | Perry 16 og; Swankie 42 |
| 21 | lge | Ayr | A | L | 0-4 | |
| 22 | lge | St Johnstone | H | L | 2-3 | Brownlie 23; McGlashan 88 |
| 23 | lge | Falkirk | H | L | 1-4 | McGlashan 77 |
| 24 | scr3 | Rangers | H | L | 0-3 | |
| 25 | lge | Clyde | H | L | 1-2 | Dow 76 |
| 26 | lge | Alloa | A | L | 2-3 | Cusick 48; Henslee 76 |
| 27 | lge | Ayr | H | L | 1-2 | Forrest, E 43 |
| 28 | lge | Inverness CT | A | L | 0-2 | |
| 29 | lge | St Johnstone | A | L | 1-2 | Swankie 20 |
| 30 | lge | Inverness CT | H | L | 1-3 | Heenan 45 |
| 31 | lge | Queen of South | A | L | 0-3 | |
| 32 | lge | St Mirren | H | D | 1-1 | Dow 52 |
| 33 | lge | St Mirren | A | L | 0-1 | |
| 34 | lge | Queen of South | H | D | 0-0 | |
| 35 | lge | Falkirk | A | L | 1-4 | Cusick 74 |
| 36 | lge | Ross County | A | L | 1-3 | Brownlie 17 |
| 37 | lge | Alloa | H | L | 0-1 | |
| 38 | lge | Clyde | A | L | 2-4 | McInally 14; Henslee 81 |

## ATTENDANCES

HOME GROUND: GAYFIELD PARK CAPACITY: 6500 AVERAGE LEAGUE AT HOME: 685

| | | | | | | | | |
|---|---|---|---|---|---|---|---|---|
| 35 | Falkirk | 4950 | 28 | Inverness CT | 1396 | 17 | Queen of South | 579 |
| 24 | Rangers | 4125 | 4 | St Johnstone | 1350 | 30 | Inverness CT | 539 |
| 15 | St Mirren | 3021 | 22 | St Johnstone | 1250 | 2 | Alloa | 518 |
| 18 | Falkirk | 2675 | 10 | Falkirk | 1115 | 32 | St Mirren | 508 |
| 36 | Ross County | 2204 | 31 | Queen of South | 1108 | 27 | Ayr | 505 |
| 33 | St Mirren | 2122 | 38 | Clyde | 1042 | 34 | Queen of South | 502 |
| 11 | Ross County | 2065 | 7 | St Mirren | 1008 | 37 | Alloa | 405 |
| 29 | St Johnstone | 2038 | 19 | Clyde | 861 | 13 | Ayr | 381 |
| 14 | St Johnstone | 2014 | 12 | Alloa | 768 | 26 | Alloa | 340 |
| 23 | Falkirk | 1807 | 1 | Ross County | 760 | 6 | Berwick | 263 |
| 9 | Queen of South | 1733 | 3 | Clyde | 744 | | | |
| 5 | Ayr | 1732 | 25 | Clyde | 686 | | | |
| 8 | Inverness CT | 1685 | 16 | Inverness CT | 653 | | | |
| 21 | Ayr | 1664 | 20 | Ross County | 580 | | | |

■ Home □ Away ▒ Neutral

## KEY PLAYERS - GOALSCORERS

**1 John Cusick**

| | | | |
|---|---|---|---|
| Goals in the League | 4 | Player Strike Rate<br>Average number of minutes between League goals scored by player | 357 |
| Contribution to Attacking Power<br>Average number of minutes between League team goals while on pitch | 95 | Club Strike Rate<br>Average number of minutes between League goals scored by club | 54 |

| | PLAYER | LGE GOALS | POWER | STRIKE RATE |
|---|---|---|---|---|
| 2 | Andy Dow | 2 | 130 | 585 mins |
| 3 | John McGlashan | 2 | 157 | 630 mins |
| 4 | Craig Feroz | 2 | 103 | 881 mins |
| 5 | Paul Brownlie | 2 | 96 | 921 mins |

## KEY PLAYERS - MIDFIELDERS

**1 Greg Henslee**

| | | | |
|---|---|---|---|
| Goals in the League | 2 | Contribution to Attacking Power<br>Average number of minutes between League team goals while on pitch | 88 |
| Defensive Rating<br>Average number of mins between League goals conceded while he was on the pitch | 45 | Scoring Difference<br>Defensive Rating minus Contribution to Attacking Power | -43 |

| | PLAYER | LGE GOALS | DEF RATE | POWER | SCORE DIFF |
|---|---|---|---|---|---|
| 2 | John Cusick | 4 | 48 | 95 | -47 mins |
| 3 | Gavin Swankie | 2 | 56 | 108 | -52 mins |
| 4 | Andrew Cargill | 1 | 42 | 116 | -74 mins |
| 5 | John McGlashan | 2 | 41 | 158 | -117 mins |

## KEY PLAYERS - DEFENDERS

**1 Steven Florence**

| | | | |
|---|---|---|---|
| Goals Conceded (GC)<br>The number of League goals conceded while he was on the pitch | 46 | Clean Sheets<br>In games when he played at least 70 minutes | 1 |
| Defensive Rating<br>Ave number of mins between League goals conceded while on the pitch | 44 | Club Defensive Rating<br>Average number of mins between League goals conceded by the club this season | 21 |

| | PLAYER | CON LGE | CLEAN SHEETS | DEF RATE |
|---|---|---|---|---|
| 2 | Andy Dow | 27 | 1 | 43 mins |
| 3 | Jordan Tait | 34 | 2 | 43 mins |
| 4 | John McAulay | 30 | 1 | 43 mins |
| 5 | Innes Ritchie | 71 | 3 | 42 mins |

## KEY GOALKEEPER

**1 Craig Hinchcliffe**

| | |
|---|---|
| Goals Conceded in the League | 77 |
| Defensive Rating<br>Ave number of mins between League goals conceded while on the pitch | 42 |
| Counting Games<br>Games when he played at least 70 mins | 36 |
| Clean Sheets<br>In games when he played at least 70 mins | 3 |

## TOP POINT EARNERS

| | PLAYER | GAMES | AVE |
|---|---|---|---|
| 1 | Spink | 7 | 0.71 |
| 2 | Tait | 16 | 0.69 |
| 3 | Cusick | 13 | 0.69 |
| 4 | Feroz | 18 | 0.67 |
| 5 | McAulay | 9 | 0.67 |
| 6 | Trialist | 6 | 0.67 |
| 7 | McDowell | 8 | 0.63 |
| 8 | Swankie | 11 | 0.55 |
| 9 | Browne | 15 | 0.53 |
| 10 | Brownlie | 16 | 0.50 |
| | CLUB AVERAGE: | | 0.42 |

Ave = Average points per match in Counting Games

## DISCIPLINARY RECORDS

| | PLAYER | YELLOW | RED | AVE |
|---|---|---|---|---|
| 1 | McDowell | 6 | 1 | 153 |
| 2 | Cargill | 9 | 0 | 193 |
| 3 | Cusick | 5 | 1 | 237 |
| 4 | McGlashan | 4 | 0 | 315 |
| 5 | McAulay | 3 | 0 | 428 |
| 6 | Florence | 4 | 0 | 500 |
| 7 | Brownlie | 3 | 0 | 613 |
| 8 | Browne | 2 | 0 | 675 |
| 9 | Currie | 3 | 0 | 775 |
| 10 | Forrest | 1 | 0 | 808 |
| 11 | Ritchie | 3 | 0 | 990 |
| 12 | Henslee | 2 | 0 | 1098 |
| 13 | Feroz | 1 | 0 | 1761 |
| | Other | 4 | 0 | |
| | TOTAL | 50 | 2 | |

## LEAGUE GOALS

| | PLAYER | MINS | GOALS | AVE |
|---|---|---|---|---|
| 1 | McDowell | 1071 | 4 | 268 |
| 2 | Cusick | 1426 | 4 | 357 |
| 3 | Feroz | 1761 | 2 | 881 |
| 4 | Brownlie | 1841 | 2 | 921 |
| 5 | McGlashan | 1260 | 2 | 630 |
| 6 | Henslee | 2197 | 2 | 1099 |
| 7 | Dow | 1170 | 2 | 585 |
| 8 | Spink | 950 | 2 | 475 |
| 9 | Swankie | 1505 | 2 | 753 |
| 10 | McInally | 398 | 1 | 398 |
| 11 | Currie | 2327 | 1 | 2327 |
| 12 | Heenan | 1649 | 1 | 1649 |
| 13 | Tait | 1478 | 1 | 1478 |
| | Other | | 4 | |
| | TOTAL | | 30 | |

## MONTH BY MONTH GUIDE TO THE POINTS

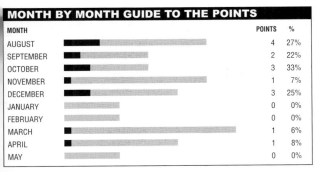

| MONTH | POINTS | % |
|---|---|---|
| AUGUST | 4 | 27% |
| SEPTEMBER | 2 | 22% |
| OCTOBER | 3 | 33% |
| NOVEMBER | 1 | 7% |
| DECEMBER | 3 | 25% |
| JANUARY | 0 | 0% |
| FEBRUARY | 0 | 0% |
| MARCH | 1 | 6% |
| APRIL | 1 | 8% |
| MAY | 0 | 0% |

## TEAM OF THE SEASON

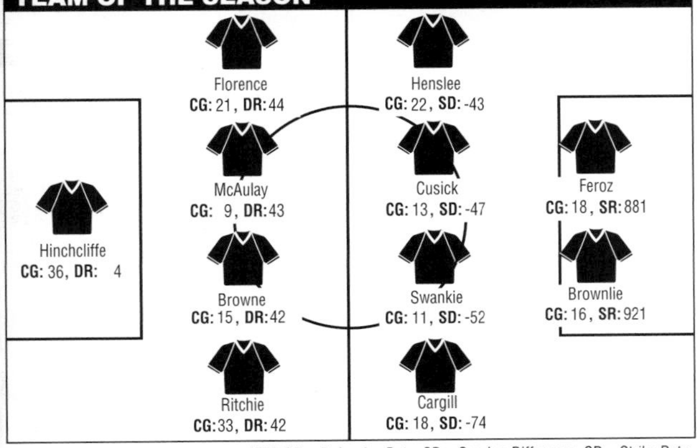
Hinchcliffe
CG: 36, DR: 4
Florence
CG: 21, DR: 44
McAulay
CG: 9, DR: 43
Browne
CG: 15, DR: 42
Ritchie
CG: 33, DR: 42
Henslee
CG: 22, SD: -43
Cusick
CG: 13, SD: -47
Swankie
CG: 11, SD: -52
Cargill
CG: 18, SD: -74
Feroz
CG: 18, SR: 881
Brownlie
CG: 16, SR: 921

KEY: DR = Defensive Rate, SD = Scoring Difference, SR = Strike Rate, CG = Counting Games – League games playing at least 70 minutes

## LEAGUE APPEARANCES, BOOKINGS AND CAPS

| | AGE (on 01/07/03) | IN THE SQUAD | COUNTING GAMES | MINUTES ON PITCH | YELLOW CARDS | RED CARDS | THIS SEASON | HOME COUNTRY |
|---|---|---|---|---|---|---|---|---|
| **Goalkeepers** | | | | | | | | |
| Gary Gow | 26 | 17 | 0 | 0 | 0 | 0 | - | Scotland |
| Craig Hinchcliffe | 31 | 36 | 36 | 3240 | 1 | 0 | - | Scotland |
| Timmy Woodcock | 19 | 17 | 0 | 0 | 0 | 0 | - | Scotland |
| **Defenders** | | | | | | | | |
| Gary Bowman | 28 | 17 | 7 | 940 | 0 | 0 | - | Scotland |
| Paul Browne | 28 | 15 | 15 | 1350 | 2 | 0 | - | Scotland |
| Denis Connaghan | 27 | 4 | 0 | 0 | 0 | 0 | - | Scotland |
| Ross Currie | 21 | 31 | 23 | 2327 | 3 | 0 | - | Scotland |
| Andy Dow | 30 | 13 | 13 | 1170 | 0 | 0 | - | Scotland |
| Steven Florence | 31 | 24 | 21 | 2002 | 4 | 0 | - | Scotland |
| Edward Forrest | 24 | 10 | 9 | 808 | 1 | 0 | - | Scotland |
| Euan Graham | 20 | 14 | 2 | 377 | 0 | 0 | - | Scotland |
| John McAulay | 31 | 32 | 9 | 1286 | 3 | 0 | - | Scotland |
| David McInally | 22 | 12 | 2 | 398 | 2 | 0 | - | Scotland |
| Kenny McMillan | - | 3 | 2 | 183 | 1 | 0 | - | Scotland |
| Innes Ritchie | 29 | 33 | 33 | 2970 | 3 | 0 | - | Scotland |
| Darren Spink | - | 25 | 7 | 950 | 0 | 0 | - | Scotland |
| Jordan Tait | 23 | 17 | 16 | 1478 | 0 | 0 | - | Scotland |
| **Midfielders** | | | | | | | | |
| Andrew Cargill | 27 | 22 | 18 | 1739 | 9 | 0 | - | Scotland |
| John Cusick | 29 | 19 | 13 | 1426 | 5 | 1 | - | Scotland |
| Paul Durno | - | 12 | 2 | 269 | 0 | 0 | - | Scotland |
| Paul Farquharson | - | 2 | 0 | 58 | 0 | 0 | - | Scotland |
| Greg Henslee | 20 | 33 | 22 | 2197 | 2 | 0 | - | Scotland |
| John McGlashan | 36 | 16 | 13 | 1260 | 4 | 0 | - | Scotland |
| Kevin McMullen | - | 10 | 5 | 618 | 0 | 0 | - | Scotland |
| Gavin Swankie | 19 | 31 | 11 | 1505 | 0 | 0 | - | Scotland |
| Trialist2004 | 6 | 6 | 529 | 0 | 0 | - | | |
| **Forwards** | | | | | | | | |
| Paul Brownlie | 25 | 28 | 16 | 1841 | 3 | 0 | - | Scotland |
| Craig Feroz | 25 | 24 | 18 | 1761 | 1 | 0 | - | Scotland |
| Kevin Heenan | 21 | 31 | 13 | 1649 | 0 | 0 | - | Scotland |
| Alan Lawrence | 40 | 2 | 2 | 180 | 0 | 0 | - | Scotland |
| Murray McDowell | 25 | 19 | 8 | 1071 | 6 | 1 | - | |

KEY: LEAGUE BOOKINGS CAPS

## SQUAD APPEARANCES

| Match | 1 | 2 | 3 | 4 | 5 | 6 | 7 | 8 | 9 | 10 | 11 | 12 | 13 | 14 | 15 | 16 | 17 | 18 | 19 | 20 | 21 | 22 | 23 | 24 | 25 | 26 | 27 | 28 | 29 | 30 | 31 | 32 | 33 | 34 | 35 | 36 | 37 | 38 |
|---|---|---|---|---|---|---|---|---|---|---|---|---|---|---|---|---|---|---|---|---|---|---|---|---|---|---|---|---|---|---|---|---|---|---|---|---|---|---|
| Venue | H | A | H | H | A | A | H | A | A | H | A | H | H | A | A | H | H | A | A | H | A | H | H | H | H | A | H | A | A | H | A | H | A | H | A | A | H | A |
| Competition | L | L | L | L | L | I | L | L | L | L | L | L | L | L | L | L | L | L | L | L | L | L | L | S | L | L | L | L | L | L | L | L | L | L | L | L | L | L |
| Result | L | W | D | L | L | L | D | L | D | W | L | L | D | L | L | L | L | L | L | W | L | L | L | L | L | L | L | L | L | L | L | D | L | D | L | L | L | L |

**Goalkeepers**
Gary Gow
Craig Hinchcliffe
Timmy Woodcock

**Defenders**
Gary Bowman
Paul Browne
Denis Connaghan
Ross Currie
Andy Dow
Steven Florence
Edward Forrest
Euan Graham
John McAulay
David McInally
Kenny McMillan
Innes Ritchie
Darren Spink
Jordan Tait

**Midfielders**
Andrew Cargill
John Cusick
Paul Durno
Paul Farquharson
Greg Henslee
John McGlashan
Kevin McMullen
Gavin Swankie

**Forwards**
Paul Brownlie
Craig Feroz
Kevin Heenan
Alan Lawrence
Murray McDowell

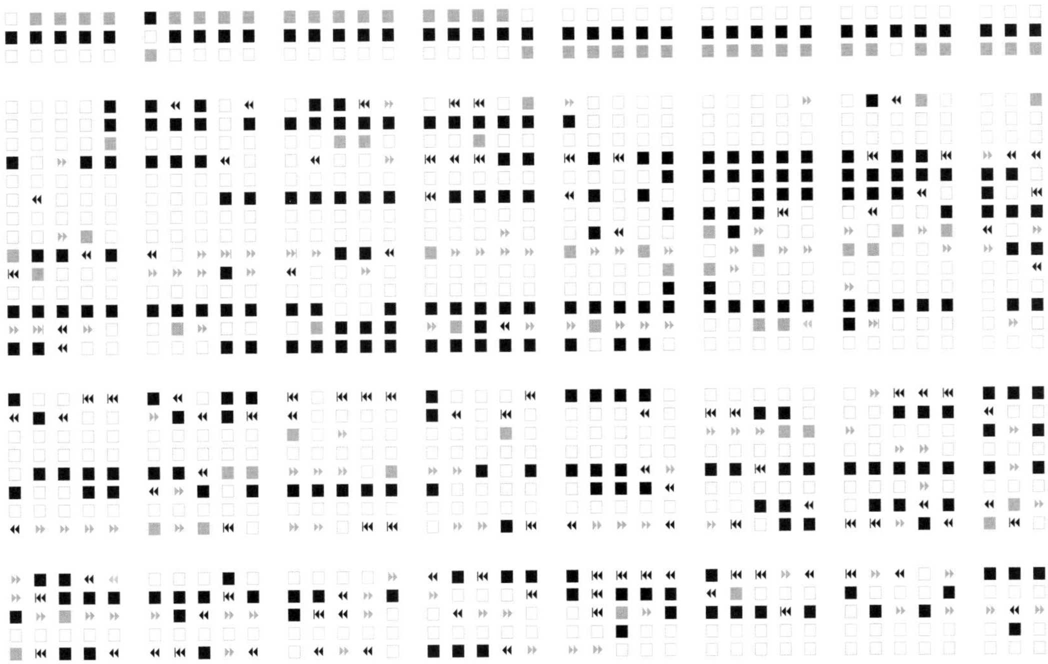

# SCOTTISH LEAGUE DIVISION ONE ROUND-UP

## FINAL LEAGUE TABLE

Division One champions Falkirk were unable to take Motherwell's place in the Bank of Scotland Premiership Division this season as the Scottish FA ruled that their ground would not meet the requirements.

| | | HOME | | | | | AWAY | | | | | TOTAL | | | |
|---|---|---|---|---|---|---|---|---|---|---|---|---|---|---|---|
| | P | W | D | L | F | A | W | D | L | F | A | F | A | DIF | PTS |
| Falkirk | 36 | 15 | 2 | 1 | 46 | 10 | 10 | 4 | 4 | 34 | 22 | 80 | 32 | 48 | 81 |
| Clyde | 36 | 12 | 4 | 2 | 37 | 17 | 9 | 5 | 4 | 29 | 20 | 66 | 37 | 29 | 72 |
| St Johnstone | 36 | 9 | 3 | 6 | 22 | 13 | 11 | 4 | 3 | 27 | 16 | 49 | 29 | 20 | 67 |
| Inverness CT | 36 | 10 | 2 | 6 | 35 | 23 | 10 | 3 | 5 | 39 | 22 | 74 | 45 | 29 | 65 |
| Queen of South | 36 | 6 | 7 | 5 | 22 | 18 | 6 | 5 | 7 | 23 | 30 | 45 | 48 | -3 | 48 |
| Ayr | 36 | 6 | 6 | 6 | 19 | 18 | 6 | 3 | 9 | 15 | 26 | 34 | 44 | -10 | 45 |
| St Mirren | 36 | 6 | 5 | 7 | 24 | 32 | 3 | 5 | 10 | 18 | 39 | 42 | 71 | -29 | 37 |
| Ross County | 36 | 7 | 4 | 7 | 26 | 19 | 2 | 4 | 12 | 16 | 27 | 42 | 46 | -4 | 35 |
| Alloa | 36 | 3 | 2 | 13 | 24 | 49 | 6 | 6 | 6 | 15 | 23 | 39 | 72 | -33 | 35 |
| Arbroath | 36 | 2 | 5 | 11 | 17 | 30 | 1 | 1 | 16 | 13 | 47 | 30 | 77 | -47 | 15 |

## TEAM OF THE SEASON

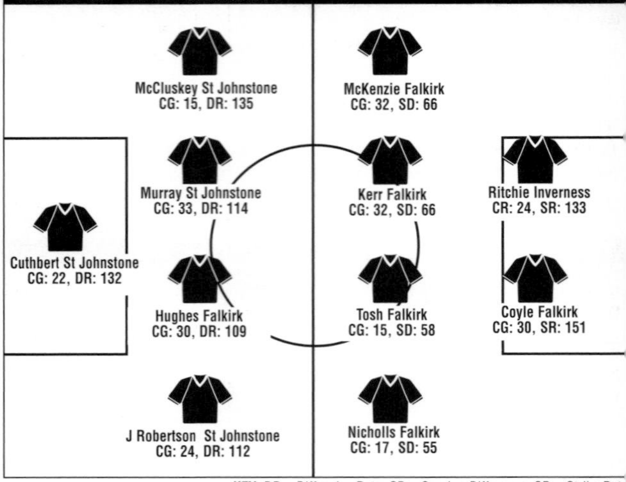

McCluskey St Johnstone
CG: 15, DR: 135
McKenzie Falkirk
CG: 32, SD: 66
Murray St Johnstone
CG: 33, DR: 114
Kerr Falkirk
CG: 32, SD: 66
Ritchie Inverness
CR: 24, SR: 133
Cuthbert St Johnstone
CG: 22, DR: 132
Hughes Falkirk
CG: 30, DR: 109
Tosh Falkirk
CG: 15, SD: 58
Coyle Falkirk
CG: 30, SR: 151
J Robertson St Johnstone
CG: 24, DR: 112
Nicholls Falkirk
CG: 17, SD: 55


**KEY:** DR = Diffensive Rate, SD = Scoring Difference, SR = Strike Rate
Games = CG=Counting Games – League games playing at least 70 minutes

## CLUB STRIKE FORCE

**KEY:** Goals: Total number of goals scored in League.
Club Strike Rate (CSR): Average number of mins between goals scored

| | CLUB | GOALS | CSR |
|---|---|---|---|
| 1 | Falkirk | 80 | 41 mins |
| 2 | Inverness CT | 74 | 44 mins |
| 3 | Clyde | 66 | 49 mins |
| 4 | St Johnstone | 49 | 66 mins |
| 5 | Queen of South | 45 | 72 mins |
| 6 | Ross County | 42 | 77 mins |
| 7 | St Mirren | 42 | 77 mins |
| 8 | Alloa | 39 | 83 mins |
| 9 | Ayr | 34 | 95 mins |
| 10 | Arbroath | 30 | 108 mins |
| | TOTAL | 501 | |

## CLUB DEFENCES

**KEY:** Defensive Rating: Average number of mins between goals conceded. CS: Clean Sheets - Games where no goals were conceded.

| | CLUB | CONCEDED | CLEAN SH | DEF RATE |
|---|---|---|---|---|
| 1 | St Johnstone | 29 | 14 | 112 mins |
| 2 | Falkirk | 32 | 14 | 101 mins |
| 3 | Clyde | 37 | 10 | 88 mins |
| 4 | Ayr | 44 | 9 | 74 mins |
| 5 | Inverness CT | 45 | 12 | 72 mins |
| 6 | Ross County | 46 | 7 | 70 mins |
| 7 | Queen of South | 48 | 12 | 68 mins |
| 8 | St Mirren | 71 | 6 | 46 mins |
| 9 | Alloa | 72 | 8 | 45 mins |
| 10 | Arbroath | 77 | 3 | 42 mins |
| | TOTAL | 501 | 95 | |

## CLUB DISCIPLINARY RECORDS

**KEY:** AVE: Average number of mins between cards

| | CLUB | YELL | RED | TOT | AVE |
|---|---|---|---|---|---|
| 1 | Ayr | 54 | 9 | 63 | 51 mins |
| 2 | Queen of South | 53 | 3 | 56 | 58 mins |
| 3 | Ross County | 53 | 3 | 56 | 58 mins |
| 4 | Alloa | 50 | 3 | 53 | 61 mins |
| 5 | Arbroath | 50 | 2 | 52 | 62 mins |
| 6 | St Mirren | 48 | 2 | 50 | 65 mins |
| 7 | Clyde | 45 | 3 | 48 | 68 mins |
| 8 | St Johnstone | 44 | 2 | 46 | 70 mins |
| 9 | Falkirk | 38 | 3 | 41 | 79 mins |
| 10 | Inverness CT | 38 | 2 | 40 | 81 mins |
| | TOTAL | 473 | 32 | 505 | |

## STADIUM CAPACITY AND HOME CROWDS

| | TEAM | CAPACITY | AVE | HIGH | LOW |
|---|---|---|---|---|---|
| 1 | Falkirk | 7550 | 55.17 | 7300 | 2675 |
| 2 | Ross County | 5800 | 46.66 | 5449 | 1967 |
| 3 | Queen of South | 6412 | 33.56 | 3206 | 1108 |
| 4 | Inverness CT | 6500 | 32.97 | 3443 | 1396 |
| 5 | Alloa | 3100 | 26.71 | 2613 | 340 |
| 6 | St Mirren | 10800 | 24.97 | 3737 | 1638 |
| 7 | St Johnstone | 10620 | 24.65 | 6542 | 2003 |
| 8 | Ayr | 10250 | 18.51 | 3030 | 1114 |
| 9 | Clyde | 8030 | 16.45 | 3415 | 665 |
| 10 | Arbroath | 6500 | 12.22 | 1950 | 381 |

## AWAY ATTENDANCE

| | TEAM | AVE | HIGH | LOW |
|---|---|---|---|---|
| 1 | Falkirk | 40.95 | 6542 | 1115 |
| 2 | St Johnstone | 33.48 | 5872 | 884 |
| 3 | Inverness CT | 32.81 | 7300 | 485 |
| 4 | St Mirren | 30.09 | 4360 | 508 |
| 5 | Clyde | 28.54 | 3706 | 686 |
| 6 | Ayr | 27.58 | 4042 | 381 |
| 7 | Ross County | 25.72 | 3737 | 445 |
| 8 | Queen of South | 24.6 | 4091 | 502 |
| 9 | Arbroath | 24.25 | 4950 | 340 |
| 10 | Alloa | 23.84 | 3390 | 405 |

## TOP GOALSCORERS

**KEY: Strike Rate:** Average number of minutes between League goals scored by player. **Club Strike Rate (CSR):** Average minutes between League goals scored by club. **Contribution to Attacking Power (PWR):** Average mins between League goals scored by club while on pitch.

| | PLAYER | CLUB | GOALS | PWR | CSR | S RATE |
|---|---|---|---|---|---|---|
| 1 | Ritchie | Inverness CT | 18 | 40 | 22 | 133 |
| 2 | Coyle | Falkirk | 20 | 40 | 20 | 151 |
| 3 | Wyness | Inverness CT | 19 | 44 | 22 | 158 |
| 4 | Samuel | Falkirk | 12 | 40 | 20 | 162 |
| 5 | Sloan | Alloa | 8 | 56 | 42 | 169 |
| 6 | Cameron | St Mirren | 13 | 74 | 39 | 178 |
| 7 | Miller | Falkirk | 16 | 40 | 20 | 181 |
| 8 | Keogh | Clyde | 12 | 45 | 25 | 182 |
| 9 | O'Neill | Queen of South | 9 | 63 | 36 | 199 |
| 10 | Junior Mendes | St Mirren | 6 | 62 | 39 | 218 |
| 11 | Ferguson | Ross County | 6 | 61 | 39 | 255 |
| 12 | Hinds | Clyde | 6 | 53 | 25 | 261 |
| 13 | James | Falkirk | 4 | 42 | 20 | 263 |
| 14 | Robson | Inverness CT | 10 | 42 | 22 | 296 |
| 15 | Gillies | St Mirren | 9 | 82 | 39 | 319 |
| 16 | Hart | Inverness CT | 7 | 38 | 22 | 333 |
| 17 | Cusick | Arbroath | 4 | 95 | 54 | 357 |
| 18 | Millen | Clyde | 7 | 45 | 25 | 380 |
| 19 | Bayne | Ross County | 5 | 75 | 39 | 380 |
| 20 | Lyle | Queen of South | 6 | 84 | 36 | 395 |
| 21 | Weatherson | Queen of South | 6 | 73 | 36 | 419 |
| 22 | MacKay | Ross County | 4 | 64 | 39 | 420 |
| 23 | Henry | Falkirk | 5 | 43 | 20 | 442 |
| 24 | Lovenkrands | St Johnstone | 3 | 69 | 33 | 462 |
| 25 | Connolly | St Johnstone | 5 | 56 | 33 | 478 |
| 26 | Hartley | St Johnstone | 6 | 60 | 33 | 480 |
| 27 | Annand | Ayr | 3 | 86 | 48 | 489 |
| 28 | Robb | St Mirren | 3 | 81 | 39 | 489 |
| 29 | Paton | Queen of South | 3 | 69 | 36 | 507 |
| 30 | Crabbe | Alloa | 3 | 78 | 42 | 548 |

## TOP DEFENDERS

**KEY: Defensive Rating (DR)** Average mins between League goals conceded while on pitch. **Club Defensive Rating (CDR):** Average minutes between League goals conceded by club. **Clean Sheets (CS)** - Games where no goals were conceded.

| | PLAYER | CLUB | CONC | CS | CDR | DR |
|---|---|---|---|---|---|---|
| 1 | McCluskey | St Johnstone | 10 | 7 | 56 | 135 |
| 2 | James | Falkirk | 8 | 5 | 51 | 132 |
| 3 | Murray | St Johnstone | 26 | 14 | 56 | 114 |
| 4 | Robertson, J | St Johnstone | 20 | 10 | 56 | 112 |
| 5 | Maxwell | St Johnstone | 27 | 13 | 56 | 112 |
| 6 | Hughes | Falkirk | 25 | 11 | 51 | 109 |
| 7 | McQuilken | Falkirk | 27 | 11 | 51 | 108 |
| 8 | McCulloch | St Johnstone | 12 | 5 | 56 | 105 |
| 9 | McPherson | Falkirk | 28 | 12 | 51 | 102 |
| 10 | Henry | Falkirk | 22 | 9 | 51 | 100 |
| 11 | Dods | St Johnstone | 18 | 5 | 56 | 100 |
| 12 | Baxter | St Johnstone | 14 | 3 | 56 | 98 |
| 13 | Kernaghan | Clyde | 25 | 7 | 44 | 93 |
| 14 | Potter | Clyde | 31 | 9 | 44 | 92 |
| 15 | Keogh | Clyde | 24 | 7 | 44 | 91 |
| 16 | Lyle | Ayr | 30 | 8 | 37 | 87 |
| 17 | Millen | Clyde | 31 | 10 | 44 | 86 |
| 18 | Campbell | Ayr | 30 | 6 | 37 | 81 |
| 19 | Munro | Inverness CT | 33 | 10 | 36 | 80 |
| 20 | Perry | Ross County | 21 | 5 | 35 | 80 |
| 21 | Craig | Ayr | 32 | 8 | 37 | 79 |
| 22 | Smyth | Ayr | 36 | 9 | 37 | 77 |
| 23 | McManus | Ayr | 29 | 6 | 37 | 77 |
| 24 | Rennie | Falkirk | 17 | 6 | 51 | 76 |
| 25 | Aitken | Queen of South | 43 | 12 | 34 | 73 |
| 26 | Thomson | Queen of South | 36 | 11 | 34 | 73 |
| 27 | Deas | Ross County | 14 | 3 | 35 | 72 |
| 28 | Irvine | Ross County | 38 | 7 | 35 | 72 |
| 29 | Bossy | Clyde | 14 | 2 | 44 | 71 |
| 30 | McCulloch | Ross County | 43 | 7 | 35 | 69 |

## TOP MIDFIELDERS

**KEY: Scoring Difference (SD)** Team goals scored while on the pitch minus team goals conceded. **Contribution to Attacking Power:** Average mins between League goals scored by club while on pitch. **Defensive Rating (DR)** Average mins between League goals conceded while on pitch.

| | PLAYER | TEAM | GOALS | DR | PWR | SD |
|---|---|---|---|---|---|---|
| 1 | MacKenzie | Falkirk | 1 | 106 | 40 | 66 |
| 2 | Kerr | Falkirk | 2 | 100 | 40 | 60 |
| 3 | Tosh | Falkirk | 1 | 100 | 42 | 58 |
| 4 | Nicholls | Falkirk | 0 | 95 | 40 | 55 |
| 5 | Robertson, M | St Johnstone | 1 | 110 | 55 | 55 |
| 6 | Ross | Clyde | 4 | 93 | 47 | 46 |
| 7 | Fraser | Clyde | 3 | 86 | 48 | 38 |
| 8 | Mensing | Clyde | 4 | 86 | 48 | 38 |
| 9 | Reilly | St Johnstone | 2 | 109 | 72 | 37 |
| 10 | Tokely | Inverness CT | 5 | 75 | 41 | 34 |
| 11 | Robson | Inverness CT | 10 | 71 | 43 | 28 |
| 12 | McBain | Inverness CT | 0 | 69 | 41 | 28 |
| 13 | Christie | Inverness CT | 2 | 81 | 58 | 23 |
| 14 | MacKay | Ross County | 4 | 88 | 65 | 23 |
| 15 | Kane | Clyde | 1 | 71 | 63 | 8 |
| 16 | Sheerin | Ayr | 2 | 81 | 74 | 7 |
| 17 | Nicolson | Ayr | 0 | 79 | 72 | 7 |
| 18 | Neilson | Queen of South | 0 | 64 | 60 | 4 |
| 19 | Ferguson | Ross County | 6 | 64 | 61 | 3 |
| 20 | McAlpine | Queen of South | 1 | 81 | 81 | 0 |
| 21 | Bowey | Queen of South | 4 | 71 | 71 | 0 |
| 22 | Murray | St Mirren | 0 | 68 | 72 | -4 |
| 23 | McLaughlin | Queen of South | 2 | 70 | 76 | -6 |
| 24 | O'Neill | Queen of South | 9 | 58 | 64 | -6 |
| 25 | Paton | Queen of South | 3 | 61 | 69 | -8 |
| 26 | Cowie | Ross County | 1 | 70 | 84 | -14 |
| 27 | Chaplain | Ayr | 5 | 81 | 97 | -16 |
| 28 | Gilbert | Ross County | 1 | 75 | 97 | -22 |
| 29 | Murray | Ayr | 0 | 68 | 92 | -24 |
| 30 | McHale | St Mirren | 1 | 61 | 85 | -24 |

## PLAYER DISCIPLINARY RECORDS

**KEY: AVE:** Average number of mins between cards

| | PLAYER | TEAM | YELL | RED | TOTAL | AVE |
|---|---|---|---|---|---|---|
| 1 | Lovering | Ayr | 11 | 2 | 13 | 128 |
| 2 | McDowell | Arbroath | 6 | 1 | 7 | 153 |
| 3 | Neilson | Queen of South | 6 | 1 | 7 | 163 |
| 4 | Cargill | Arbroath | 9 | 0 | 9 | 193 |
| 5 | Falconer | Clyde | 4 | 0 | 4 | 215 |
| 6 | Gilbert | Ross County | 8 | 1 | 9 | 215 |
| 7 | McManus | Ayr | 8 | 2 | 10 | 224 |
| 8 | Christie | Alloa | 7 | 2 | 9 | 230 |
| 9 | Murray | St Mirren | 4 | 1 | 5 | 230 |
| 10 | Tosh | Falkirk | 5 | 1 | 6 | 233 |
| 11 | Cusick | Arbroath | 5 | 1 | 6 | 237 |
| 12 | Annand | Ayr | 6 | 0 | 6 | 244 |
| 13 | McColligan | Queen of South | 6 | 1 | 7 | 272 |
| 14 | Parker | St Johnstone | 6 | 0 | 6 | 279 |
| 15 | Perry | Ross County | 6 | 0 | 6 | 281 |
| 16 | Robertson, M | St Johnstone | 3 | 0 | 3 | 293 |
| 17 | Robson | Inverness CT | 10 | 0 | 10 | 296 |
| 18 | O'Neill | Queen of South | 6 | 0 | 6 | 298 |
| 19 | Campbell | Ayr | 8 | 0 | 8 | 304 |
| 20 | McGlashan | Arbroath | 4 | 0 | 4 | 315 |
| 21 | Fraser | Clyde | 8 | 0 | 8 | 322 |
| 22 | Deas | Ross County | 3 | 0 | 3 | 335 |
| 23 | James | Falkirk | 2 | 1 | 3 | 351 |
| 24 | Potter | Clyde | 7 | 1 | 8 | 356 |
| 25 | Grady | Ayr | 6 | 1 | 7 | 359 |
| 26 | Hartley | St Johnstone | 7 | 1 | 8 | 360 |
| 27 | Ross | St Mirren | 5 | 0 | 5 | 360 |
| 28 | McGowan | St Mirren | 3 | 0 | 3 | 373 |
| 29 | Millen | Clyde | 5 | 2 | 7 | 380 |
| 30 | Ferguson | Ross County | 4 | 0 | 4 | 383 |

## CHART TOPPING GOALKEEPERS

**KEY: Defensive Rating (DR)** Average mins between League goals conceded while on pitch. **Clean Sheets (CS)** - Games where no goals were conceded.

| | PLAYER | TEAM | CON | CS | DR |
|---|---|---|---|---|---|
| 1 | Cuthbert | St Johnstone | 15 | 9 | 132 |
| 2 | Ferguson | Falkirk | 30 | 12 | 95 |
| 3 | Main | St Johnstone | 14 | 5 | 90 |
| 4 | Halliwell | Clyde | 34 | 10 | 90 |
| 5 | Scott | Queen of South | 18 | 5 | 78 |
| 6 | Nelson | Ayr | 38 | 8 | 73 |
| 7 | Brown | Inverness CT | 45 | 12 | 72 |
| 8 | Bullock | Ross County | 46 | 7 | 70 |
| 9 | Soutar | Alloa | 19 | 3 | 57 |
| 10 | Goram | Queen of South | 30 | 5 | 56 |
| 11 | Roy | St Mirren | 34 | 5 | 56 |
| 12 | Evans, J | Alloa | 33 | 4 | 44 |
| 13 | Hinchcliffe | Arbroath | 77 | 3 | 42 |
| 14 | Robertson | St Mirren | 33 | 1 | 38 |
| 15 | Hogarth | Alloa | 20 | 1 | 36 |

## TOP POINT EARNERS

**KEY: Counting Games** League games where he played more than 70 minutes. **Total League Points** Taken in Counting Games. **Average League Points** Taken in Counting Games.

| | PLAYER | TEAM | GAMES | POINTS | AVE |
|---|---|---|---|---|---|
| 1 | Henry | Falkirk | 17 | 42 | 2.47 |
| 2 | McPherson | Falkirk | 29 | 68 | 2.34 |
| 3 | Coyle | Falkirk | 30 | 70 | 2.33 |
| 5 | Hughes | Falkirk | 30 | 69 | 2.30 |
| 6 | McQuilken | Falkirk | 31 | 71 | 2.29 |
| 7 | MacKenzie | Falkirk | 32 | 72 | 2.25 |
| 8 | James | Falkirk | 12 | 27 | 2.25 |
| 9 | Nicholls | Falkirk | 17 | 38 | 2.24 |
| 10 | Ferguson | Falkirk | 32 | 71 | 2.22 |
| 11 | Tosh | Falkirk | 15 | 33 | 2.20 |
| 12 | Hagen | Clyde | 26 | 57 | 2.19 |
| 13 | Kernaghan | Clyde | 26 | 57 | 2.19 |
| 14 | Ritchie | Inverness CT | 24 | 52 | 2.17 |
| 15 | Kerr | Falkirk | 32 | 69 | 2.16 |
| 16 | Miller | Falkirk | 31 | 66 | 2.13 |
| 17 | Potter | Clyde | 31 | 65 | 2.10 |
| 18 | Halliwell | Clyde | 34 | 71 | 2.09 |
| 19 | Fraser | Clyde | 26 | 54 | 2.08 |
| 20 | Hinds | Clyde | 15 | 31 | 2.07 |
| 21 | Rennie | Falkirk | 14 | 29 | 2.07 |
| 22 | Keogh | Clyde | 22 | 45 | 2.05 |
| 23 | Hart | Inverness CT | 24 | 49 | 2.04 |
| 24 | Mensing | Clyde | 34 | 69 | 2.03 |
| 25 | Ross | Clyde | 32 | 65 | 2.03 |
| 26 | Hartley | St Johnstone | 32 | 65 | 2.03 |
| 27 | Millen | Clyde | 29 | 58 | 2.00 |
| 28 | Connolly | St Johnstone | 25 | 50 | 2.00 |
| 29 | Cuthbert | St Johnstone | 22 | 44 | 2.00 |
| 30 | Samuel | Falkirk | 15 | 30 | 2.00 |

## NATIONWIDE FOOTBALL DIVISION TWO CHAMPIONS

# WIGAN ATHLETIC

Final Position: **1st**

NICKNAME: THE LATICS

| | | | | | | |
|---|---|---|---|---|---|---|
| 1 | div2 | Cheltenham | A | W | 2-0 | Liddell 6; McCulloch 24 |
| 2 | div2 | Mansfield | H | W | 3-2 | Ellington 26,31; De Vos 64 |
| 3 | div2 | Bristol City | H | W | 2-0 | Green 75; McCulloch 89 |
| 4 | div2 | Notts County | A | W | 2-0 | Liddell 63,75 |
| 5 | div2 | Port Vale | H | L | 0-1 | |
| 6 | div2 | Colchester | A | L | 0-1 | |
| 7 | div2 | Wycombe | H | W | 3-0 | McCulloch 3; Liddell 36,90 |
| 8 | wcr1 | Northampton | A | W | 1-0 | Jarrett 31 |
| 9 | div2 | Chesterfield | A | D | 0-0 | |
| 10 | div2 | Tranmere | A | W | 2-0 | Ellington 53 pen,66 |
| 11 | div2 | Peterborough | H | D | 2-2 | Liddell 38 pen; Ellington 47 |
| 12 | div2 | Barnsley | A | W | 3-1 | Liddell 2; Jackson 12; Green 65 |
| 13 | wcr2 | West Brom | H | W | 3-1 | Ellington 31,60,80 |
| 14 | div2 | Cardiff | H | D | 2-2 | Dinning 25; Ellington 28 |
| 15 | div2 | Plymouth | A | W | 3-1 | Dinning 25,58; Ellington 90 |
| 16 | div2 | Stockport | H | W | 2-1 | Ellington 49; Roberts 61 |
| 17 | div2 | Luton | A | D | 1-1 | De Vos 88 |
| 18 | div2 | QPR | H | D | 1-1 | Liddell 29 |
| 19 | div2 | Crewe | H | W | 2-0 | Liddell 10 pen; Foster 45 og |
| 20 | wcr3 | Man City | H | W | 1-0 | Roberts 35 |
| 21 | div2 | Blackpool | A | W | 2-0 | Dinning 12; Flynn 86 |
| 22 | facr1 | Hereford | A | W | 1-0 | Green 90 |
| 23 | div2 | Brentford | A | W | 1-0 | Roberts 45 |
| 24 | div2 | Northampton | H | W | 1-0 | Roberts 37 |
| 25 | wcr4 | Fulham | H | W | 2-1 | Ellington 20,28 |
| 26 | facr2 | Luton | H | W | 3-0 | Ellington 37,64; Flynn 86 |
| 27 | div2 | Oldham | A | W | 2-0 | Ellington 36; De Vos 60 |
| 28 | wcqf | Blackburn | H | L | 0-2 | |
| 29 | div2 | Huddersfield | H | W | 1-0 | De Vos 45 |
| 30 | div2 | Port Vale | A | W | 1-0 | De Vos 69 |
| 31 | div2 | Swindon | H | W | 2-0 | Teale 42; Ellington 90 |
| 32 | div2 | Notts County | H | W | 3-1 | Dinning 45; De Vos 57; Liddell 73 |
| 33 | facr3 | Stoke | A | L | 0-3 | |
| 34 | div2 | Bristol City | A | W | 1-0 | Kennedy 49 |
| 35 | div2 | Colchester | H | W | 2-1 | De Vos 44; Liddell 74 pen |
| 36 | div2 | Swindon | A | L | 1-2 | McCulloch 55 |
| 37 | div2 | Mansfield | A | W | 2-1 | Ellington 39; Liddell 43 |
| 38 | div2 | Cheltenham | H | D | 0-0 | |
| 39 | div2 | Blackpool | H | D | 1-1 | Liddell 1 |
| 40 | div2 | Wycombe | A | W | 2-0 | McCulloch 9; Liddell 89 pen,89 pen |
| 41 | div2 | Crewe | A | W | 1-0 | Ellington 38 |
| 42 | div2 | Chesterfield | H | W | 3-1 | Teale 25; Dinning 40; Liddell 74 pen |
| 43 | div2 | Tranmere | H | D | 0-0 | |
| 44 | div2 | Peterborough | A | D | 1-1 | Arber 82 og |
| 45 | div2 | Luton | H | D | 1-1 | Roberts 75 |
| 46 | div2 | Stockport | A | D | 1-1 | De Vos 63 |
| 47 | div2 | QPR | A | W | 1-0 | Ellington 47 |
| 48 | div2 | Plymouth | H | L | 0-1 | |
| 49 | div2 | Northampton | A | W | 2-0 | Ellington 9; Liddell 43 pen |
| 50 | div2 | Brentford | H | W | 2-0 | Ellington 57; McCulloch 90 |
| 51 | div2 | Huddersfield | A | D | 0-0 | |
| 52 | div2 | Oldham | H | W | 3-1 | Roberts 9,80; Bullard 71 |
| 53 | div2 | Cardiff | A | D | 0-0 | |
| 54 | div2 | Barnsley | H | W | 1-0 | Dinning 13 |

## ATTENDANCES

HOME GROUND: JJB STADIUM CAPACITY: 25000 AVERAGE LEAGUE AT HOME: 7287

| | | |
|---|---|---|
| 28 | Blackburn | 16922 |
| 20 | Man City | 15007 |
| 47 | QPR | 14703 |
| 53 | Cardiff | 14702 |
| 51 | Huddersfield | 13769 |
| 34 | Bristol City | 13151 |
| 52 | Oldham | 12783 |
| 54 | Barnsley | 12537 |
| 39 | Blackpool | 10546 |
| 12 | Barnsley | 9977 |
| 33 | Stoke | 9618 |
| 43 | Tranmere | 9021 |
| 41 | Crewe | 8917 |
| 15 | Plymouth | 8746 |
| 27 | Oldham | 8269 |
| 10 | Tranmere | 8153 |
| 14 | Cardiff | 8047 |
| 21 | Blackpool | 7676 |
| 25 | Fulham | 7615 |
| 17 | Luton | 7364 |
| 16 | Stockport | 7276 |
| 50 | Brentford | 7204 |
| 48 | Plymouth | 7203 |
| 45 | Luton | 7087 |
| 19 | Crewe | 7086 |
| 46 | Stockport | 6719 |
| 13 | West Brom | 6558 |
| 3 | Bristol City | 6548 |
| 5 | Port Vale | 6532 |
| 30 | Port Vale | 6395 |
| 42 | Chesterfield | 6384 |
| 4 | Notts County | 6302 |
| 18 | QPR | 6241 |
| 38 | Cheltenham | 6171 |
| 31 | Swindon | 6114 |
| 40 | Wycombe | 6052 |
| 24 | Northampton | 6032 |
| 29 | Huddersfield | 6013 |
| 32 | Notts County | 6009 |
| 2 | Mansfield | 5837 |
| 49 | Northampton | 5822 |
| 11 | Peterborough | 5797 |
| 35 | Colchester | 5792 |
| 37 | Mansfield | 5524 |
| 23 | Brentford | 5454 |
| 7 | Wycombe | 5358 |
| 36 | Swindon | 5238 |
| 1 | Cheltenham | 5138 |
| 44 | Peterborough | 4970 |
| 26 | Luton | 4544 |
| 9 | Chesterfield | 4124 |
| 22 | Hereford | 4005 |
| 6 | Colchester | 2721 |
| 8 | Northampton | 2336 |

■ Home □ Away ▨ Neutral

## KEY PLAYERS - GOALSCORERS

**1 Andy Liddell**

| | | | |
|---|---|---|---|
| Goals in the League | 16 | Player Strike Rate<br>Average number of minutes between League goals scored by player | 178 |
| Contribution to Attacking Power<br>Average number of minutes between League team goals while on pitch | 60 | Club Strike Rate<br>Average number of minutes between League goals scored by club | 61 |

| | PLAYER | LGE GOALS | POWER | STRIKE RATE |
|---|---|---|---|---|
| 2 | Nathan Ellington | 15 | 57 | 238 mins |
| 3 | Neil Roberts | 6 | 66 | 387 mins |
| 4 | Tony Dinning | 7 | 58 | 443 mins |
| 5 | Jason De Vos | 8 | 60 | 484 mins |

## KEY PLAYERS - MIDFIELDERS

**1 Jimmy Bullard**

| | | | |
|---|---|---|---|
| Goals in the League | 1 | Contribution to Attacking Power<br>Average number of minutes between League team goals while on pitch | 84 |
| Defensive Rating<br>Average number of mins between League goals conceded while he was on the pitch | 217 | Scoring Difference<br>Defensive Rating minus Contribution to Attacking Power | 133 |

| | PLAYER | LGE GOALS | DEF RATE | POWER | SCORE DIFF |
|---|---|---|---|---|---|
| 2 | Scott Green | 2 | 138 | 52 | 86 mins |
| 3 | Jason De Vos | 8 | 161 | 60 | 101 mins |
| 4 | Tony Dinning | 7 | 163 | 58 | 105 mins |

## KEY PLAYERS - DEFENDERS

**1 Peter Kennedy**

| | | | |
|---|---|---|---|
| Goals Conceded (GC)<br>The number of League goals conceded while he was on the pitch | 9 | Clean Sheets<br>In games when he played at least 70 minutes | 13 |
| Defensive Rating<br>Ave number of mins between League goals conceded while on the pitch | 211 | Club Defensive Rating<br>Average number of mins between League goals conceded by the club this season | 166 |

| | PLAYER | CON LGE | CLEAN SHEETS | DEF RATE |
|---|---|---|---|---|
| 2 | Paul Mitchell | 7 | 6 | 201 mins |
| 3 | Steven McMillan | 15 | 14 | 169 mins |
| 4 | Nicky Eaden | 22 | 20 | 159 mins |
| 5 | Jason Jarrett | 10 | 11 | 151 mins |

## KEY GOALKEEPER

**1 John Filan**

| | |
|---|---|
| Goals Conceded in the League | 25 |
| Defensive Rating<br>Ave number of mins between League goals conceded while on the pitch | 166 |
| Counting Games<br>Games when he played at least 70 mins | 46 |
| Clean Sheets<br>In games when he played at least 70 mins | 25 |

## TOP POINT EARNERS

| | PLAYER | MINS | AVE |
|---|---|---|---|
| 1 | Kennedy | 20 | 2.55 |
| 2 | Roberts | 22 | 2.36 |
| 3 | Mitchell | 11 | 2.36 |
| 4 | Brannan | 3 | 2.33 |
| 5 | Teale | 22 | 2.32 |
| 6 | Jarrett | 22 | 2.32 |
| 7 | Ellington | 40 | 2.25 |
| 8 | Jackson | 42 | 2.24 |
| 9 | Dinning | 33 | 2.24 |
| 10 | Green | 13 | 2.23 |
| | **CLUB AVERAGE:** | | **2.17** |

Ave = Average points per match in Counting Games

## DISCIPLINARY RECORDS

| | PLAYER | YELLOW | RED | AVE |
|---|---|---|---|---|
| 1 | Breckin | 3 | 0 | 231 |
| 2 | Mitchell | 5 | 0 | 281 |
| 3 | Roberts | 7 | 0 | 331 |
| 4 | McCulloch | 8 | 0 | 369 |
| 5 | Baines | 1 | 0 | 495 |
| 6 | McMillan | 5 | 0 | 506 |
| 7 | Jarrett | 4 | 0 | 567 |
| 8 | Dinning | 4 | 1 | 620 |
| 9 | Teale | 4 | 0 | 623 |
| 10 | Jackson | 5 | 1 | 654 |
| 11 | Bullard | 2 | 0 | 758 |
| 12 | De Vos | 5 | 0 | 774 |
| 13 | Kennedy | 2 | 0 | 949 |
| | Other | 9 | 1 | |
| | **TOTAL** | **64** | **3** | |

## LEAGUE GOALS

| | PLAYER | MINS | GOALS | AVE |
|---|---|---|---|---|
| 1 | Liddell | 2854 | 16 | 178 |
| 2 | Ellington | 3572 | 15 | 238 |
| 3 | De Vos | 3870 | 8 | 484 |
| 4 | Dinning | 3102 | 7 | 443 |
| 5 | McCulloch | 2955 | 6 | 493 |
| 6 | Roberts | 2322 | 6 | 387 |
| 7 | Green | 1245 | 2 | 623 |
| 8 | Teale | 2493 | 2 | 1247 |
| 9 | Kennedy | 1898 | 1 | 1898 |
| 10 | Bullard | 1517 | 1 | 1517 |
| 11 | Flynn | 442 | 1 | 442 |
| 12 | Jackson | 3925 | 1 | 3925 |
| | Other | | 2 | |
| | **TOTAL** | | **68** | |

## MONTH BY MONTH GUIDE TO THE POINTS

| MONTH | POINTS | % |
|---|---|---|
| AUGUST | 12 | 67% |
| SEPTEMBER | 11 | 73% |
| OCTOBER | 9 | 60% |
| NOVEMBER | 12 | 100% |
| DECEMBER | 12 | 100% |
| JANUARY | 12 | 80% |
| FEBRUARY | 8 | 67% |
| MARCH | 10 | 48% |
| APRIL | 11 | 73% |
| MAY | 3 | 100% |

## TEAM OF THE SEASON

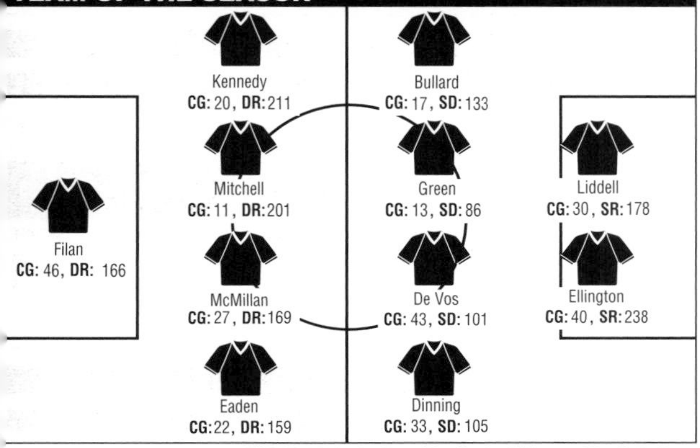
Kennedy
CG: 20, DR: 211
Bullard
CG: 17, SD: 133
Mitchell
CG: 11, DR: 201
Green
CG: 13, SD: 86
Liddell
CG: 30, SR: 178
Filan
CG: 46, DR: 166
McMillan
CG: 27, DR: 169
De Vos
CG: 43, SD: 101
Ellington
CG: 40, SR: 238
Eaden
CG: 22, DR: 159
Dinning
CG: 33, SD: 105

KEY: DR = Defensive Rate, SD = Scoring Difference, SR = Strike Rate, CG = Counting Games – League games playing at least 70 minutes

## LEAGUE APPEARANCES, BOOKINGS AND CAPS

| | AGE | IN THE SQUAD | COUNTING GAMES | MINUTES ON PITCH | YELLOW CARDS | RED CARDS | THIS SEASON | HOME COUNTRY |
|---|---|---|---|---|---|---|---|---|
| **Goalkeepers** | | | | | | | | |
| Dave Beasant | 44 | 15 | 0 | 0 | 0 | 0 | - | England |
| John Filan | 33 | 46 | 46 | 4140 | 3 | 0 | - | Australia |
| Ryan Yeomans | - | 26 | 0 | 0 | 0 | 0 | - | England |
| **Defenders** | | | | | | | | |
| Leighton Baines | 18 | 13 | 5 | 495 | 1 | 0 | - | England |
| Ged Brannan | 31 | 10 | 3 | 429 | 0 | 0 | - | England |
| Ian Breckin | 27 | 33 | 7 | 695 | 3 | 0 | - | England |
| Jason De Vos | 29 | 43 | 43 | 3870 | 5 | 0 | - | Canada |
| Tony Dinning | 28 | 39 | 33 | 3102 | 4 | 1 | - | England |
| Nicky Eaden | 31 | 37 | 37 | 3330 | 3 | 0 | - | England |
| Matt Jackson | 31 | 45 | 42 | 3925 | 5 | 1 | - | England |
| Jason Jarrett | 23 | 41 | 22 | 2271 | 4 | 0 | - | England |
| Peter Kennedy | 29 | 28 | 20 | 1898 | 2 | 0 | 4 | N Ireland (111) |
| Steven McMillan | 27 | 38 | 27 | 2530 | 5 | 0 | - | Scotland |
| Paul Mitchell | 21 | 40 | 11 | 1407 | 5 | 0 | - | England |
| **Midfielders** | | | | | | | | |
| Jimmy Bullard | 24 | 17 | 17 | 1517 | 2 | 0 | - | England |
| Scott Green | 33 | 22 | 13 | 1245 | 0 | 0 | - | England |
| David Moore | - | 2 | 0 | 0 | 0 | 0 | - | England |
| **Forwards** | | | | | | | | |
| Lee Ashcroft | 30 | 4 | 0 | 0 | 0 | 0 | - | England |
| Nathan Ellington | 22 | 42 | 40 | 3572 | 1 | 0 | - | England |
| Michael Flynn | 22 | 27 | 2 | 442 | 1 | 0 | - | Wales |
| Andy Liddell | 30 | 37 | 30 | 2854 | 1 | 1 | - | England |
| Chris Lynch | - | 3 | 0 | 0 | 0 | 0 | - | England |
| Lee McCulloch | 25 | 38 | 32 | 2955 | 8 | 0 | - | England |
| Neil Roberts | 25 | 45 | 22 | 2322 | 7 | 0 | 2 | Wales (50) |
| Gary Teale | 24 | 45 | 22 | 2493 | 4 | 0 | - | Scotland |

KEY: LEAGUE BOOKINGS CAPS

## SQUAD APPEARANCES

| Match | 1 | 2 | 3 | 4 | 5 | 6 | 7 | 8 | 9 | 10 | 11 | 12 | 13 | 14 | 15 | 16 | 17 | 18 | 19 | 20 | 21 | 22 | 23 | 24 | 25 | 26 | 27 | 28 | 29 | 30 | 31 | 32 | 33 | 34 | 35 | 36 | 37 | 38 | 39 | 40 | 41 | 42 | 43 | 44 | 45 | 46 | 47 | 48 | 49 | 50 | 51 | 52 | 53 | 54 |
|---|---|---|---|---|---|---|---|---|---|---|---|---|---|---|---|---|---|---|---|---|---|---|---|---|---|---|---|---|---|---|---|---|---|---|---|---|---|---|---|---|---|---|---|---|---|---|---|---|---|---|---|---|---|---|
| Venue | A | H | H | A | H | A | H | A | A | A | H | A | H | H | A | H | A | H | H | H | A | A | A | H | H | H | A | H | H | A | H | H | A | A | H | A | A | H | H | A | A | H | H | A | H | A | A | H | A | H | A | H | A | H |
| Competition | L | L | L | L | L | L | L | W | L | L | L | L | W | L | L | L | L | L | L | W | L | F | L | L | W | F | L | W | L | L | L | L | F | L | L | L | L | L | L | L | L | L | L | L | L | L | L | L | L | L | L | L | L | L |
| Result | W | W | W | W | L | L | W | W | D | W | D | W | W | D | W | W | D | D | W | W | W | W | W | W | W | W | W | L | W | W | W | W | L | W | W | L | W | D | D | W | W | W | D | D | D | D | W | L | W | W | D | W | D | W |

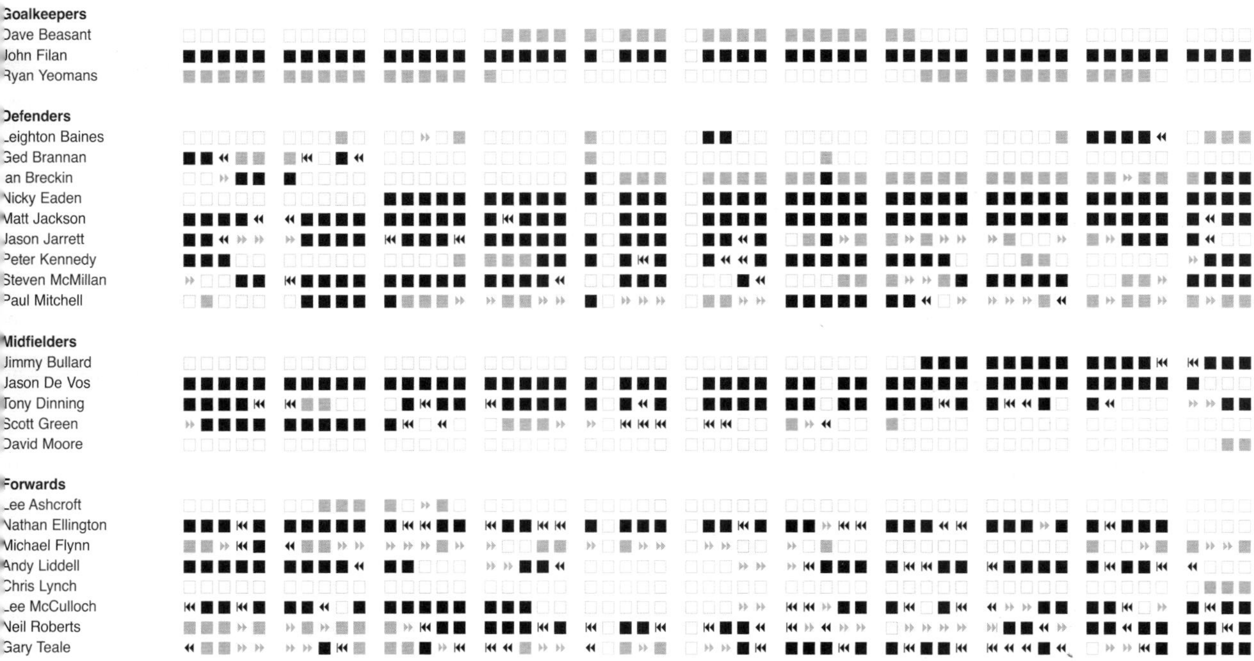
Goalkeepers
Dave Beasant
John Filan
Ryan Yeomans
Defenders
Leighton Baines
Ged Brannan
Ian Breckin
Nicky Eaden
Matt Jackson
Jason Jarrett
Peter Kennedy
Steven McMillan
Paul Mitchell
Midfielders
Jimmy Bullard
Jason De Vos
Tony Dinning
Scott Green
David Moore
Forwards
Lee Ashcroft
Nathan Ellington
Michael Flynn
Andy Liddell
Chris Lynch
Lee McCulloch
Neil Roberts
Gary Teale

# CREWE ALEXANDRA

Final Position: **2nd**

NICKNAME: THE RAILWAYMEN

| | | | | | | |
|---|---|---|---|---|---|---|
| 1 | div2 | Northampton | A | D | 1-1 | Sorvel 30 |
| 2 | div2 | Notts County | H | L | 0-3 | |
| 3 | div2 | Colchester | H | W | 2-0 | Hulse 9; Bell 81 |
| 4 | div2 | Huddersfield | A | D | 1-1 | Hulse 17 |
| 5 | div2 | Cheltenham | H | W | 1-0 | Jack 44 |
| 6 | div2 | Mansfield | A | W | 5-0 | Walker 30; Jack 36; Hulse 38; Foster 47; Lunt 65 |
| 7 | div2 | Chesterfield | H | D | 0-0 | |
| 8 | wcr1 | Port Vale | A | W | 2-0 | Jack 17,20 |
| 9 | div2 | Peterborough | A | D | 0-0 | |
| 10 | div2 | Wycombe | A | W | 2-1 | Hulse 26,32 |
| 11 | div2 | Tranmere | H | W | 2-0 | Curtis 57 og; Hulse 73 |
| 12 | div2 | Cardiff | A | L | 1-2 | Hulse 48 |
| 13 | wcr2 | Man City | A | L | 2-3 | Jack 1; Hulse 85 |
| 14 | div2 | QPR | H | W | 2-0 | Jones 29,69 |
| 15 | div2 | Stockport | A | W | 4-1 | Lunt 6; Hulse 32,84; Jones 53 |
| 16 | div2 | Plymouth | H | L | 0-1 | |
| 17 | div2 | Port Vale | A | W | 2-1 | Hulse 32,81 |
| 18 | div2 | Luton | H | L | 0-1 | |
| 19 | div2 | Wigan | A | L | 0-2 | |
| 20 | div2 | Brentford | H | W | 2-1 | Hulse 21,82 |
| 21 | facr1 | Port Vale | A | W | 1-0 | Ashton 85 |
| 22 | div2 | Blackpool | H | W | 3-0 | Hulse 8; Sodje 59; Tierney 63 |
| 23 | div2 | Bristol City | A | D | 2-2 | Foster 32; Hulse 35 |
| 24 | facr2 | Mansfield | H | W | 3-0 | Rix 6; Brammer 63 pen; Ashton 78 |
| 25 | div2 | Barnsley | H | W | 2-0 | Foster 17; Jack 82 |
| 26 | div2 | Swindon | A | W | 3-1 | Ashton 18; Foster 40; Jack 59 |
| 27 | div2 | Cheltenham | A | W | 4-0 | Ashton 6; Vaughan 38; Jack 40; Brammer 67 pen |
| 28 | div2 | Oldham | H | L | 1-2 | Hulse 56 |
| 29 | div2 | Mansfield | H | W | 2-0 | Walton 60; Miles 90 |
| 30 | facr3 | Bournemouth | A | D | 0-0 | |
| 31 | div2 | Colchester | A | W | 2-1 | Jones 56,62 |
| 32 | facr3r | Bournemouth | H | L | 1-3* | Jones 29; Sodje 120 (*on penalties) |
| 33 | div2 | Huddersfield | H | W | 1-0 | Jones 90 |
| 34 | div2 | Oldham | A | W | 3-1 | Hulse 60,86; Ashton 88 |
| 35 | div2 | Northampton | H | D | 3-3 | Jones 39,70; Vaughan 41 |
| 36 | div2 | Notts County | A | D | 2-2 | Jones 2; Hulse 13 |
| 37 | div2 | Brentford | A | W | 2-1 | Lunt 52,64 pen |
| 38 | div2 | Chesterfield | A | W | 2-0 | Wright 33; Jack 85 |
| 39 | div2 | Wigan | H | L | 0-1 | |
| 40 | div2 | Peterborough | H | L | 0-1 | |
| 41 | div2 | Wycombe | H | W | 4-2 | Ashton 8,62; Lunt 24 pen; Hulse 59 |
| 42 | div2 | Tranmere | A | L | 1-2 | Hulse 47 |
| 43 | div2 | Port Vale | H | D | 1-1 | Sorvel 54 |
| 44 | div2 | Plymouth | A | W | 3-1 | Jack 4; Ashton 13,68 |
| 45 | div2 | Luton | A | W | 4-0 | Ashton 7,21; Vaughan 50; Jack 78 |
| 46 | div2 | Stockport | H | W | 1-0 | Jack 77 |
| 47 | div2 | Blackpool | A | W | 1-0 | Lunt 69 |
| 48 | div2 | Bristol City | H | D | 1-1 | Lunt 15 pen |
| 49 | div2 | Swindon | H | L | 0-1 | |
| 50 | div2 | Barnsley | A | W | 2-1 | Sorvel 34; Hulse 62 |
| 51 | div2 | QPR | A | D | 0-0 | |
| 52 | div2 | Cardiff | H | D | 1-1 | Walker 45 |

## ATTENDANCES

HOME GROUND: THE ALEXANDRA STADIUM CAPACITY: 10118 AVERAGE LEAGUE AT HOME: 6761

| | | | | | | | | |
|---|---|---|---|---|---|---|---|---|
| 13 | Man City | 21820 | 19 | Wigan | 7086 | 27 | Cheltenham | 5548 |
| 51 | QPR | 16921 | **22** | **Blackpool** | **7019** | 21 | Port Vale | 5507 |
| 12 | Cardiff | 13208 | **29** | **Mansfield** | **6931** | **5** | **Cheltenham** | **5488** |
| 23 | Bristol City | 12585 | **11** | **Tranmere** | **6875** | 37 | Brentford | 5424 |
| **52** | **Cardiff** | **9562** | **16** | **Plymouth** | **6733** | **41** | **Wycombe** | **5398** |
| 50 | Barnsley | 9396 | 45 | Luton | 6607 | **3** | **Colchester** | **5138** |
| **28** | **Oldham** | **9006** | 15 | Stockport | 6468 | 26 | Swindon | 4957 |
| **39** | **Wigan** | **8917** | **49** | **Swindon** | **6384** | 10 | Wycombe | 4909 |
| 42 | Tranmere | 8670 | 17 | Port Vale | 6374 | **24** | **Mansfield** | **4563** |
| 4 | Huddersfield | 8467 | **35** | **Northampton** | **6164** | **32** | **Bournemouth** | **4540** |
| **43** | **Port Vale** | **8146** | **2** | **Notts County** | **6141** | 9 | Peterborough | 4345 |
| **48** | **Bristol City** | **7901** | **18** | **Luton** | **6030** | 6 | Mansfield | 4183 |
| 44 | Plymouth | 7777 | **7** | **Chesterfield** | **5837** | 38 | Chesterfield | 3956 |
| **14** | **QPR** | **7683** | **33** | **Huddersfield** | **5819** | 36 | Notts County | 3875 |
| 47 | Blackpool | 7623 | **40** | **Peterborough** | **5704** | 8 | Port Vale | 3765 |
| 34 | Oldham | 7597 | 1 | Northampton | 5694 | 31 | Colchester | 2949 |
| **46** | **Stockport** | **7336** | **20** | **Brentford** | **5663** | | | |
| 30 | Bournemouth | 7252 | **25** | **Barnsley** | **5633** | | | |

■ Home □ Away ▨ Neutral

## KEY PLAYERS - GOALSCORERS

**1 Robert Hulse**

| | | | |
|---|---|---|---|
| Goals in the League | 22 | Player Strike Rate<br>Average number of minutes between League goals scored by player | 142 |
| Contribution to Attacking Power<br>Average number of minutes between League team goals while on pitch | 56 | Club Strike Rate<br>Average number of minutes between League goals scored by club | 54 |

| | PLAYER | LGE GOALS | POWER | STRIKE RATE |
|---|---|---|---|---|
| 2 | Steve Jones | 9 | 64 | 194 mins |
| 3 | Dean Ashton | 9 | 50 | 251 mins |
| 4 | Rodney Jack | 9 | 52 | 346 mins |
| 5 | Kenny Lunt | 7 | 53 | 585 mins |

## KEY PLAYERS - MIDFIELDERS

**1 Paul Tierney**

| | | | |
|---|---|---|---|
| Goals in the League | 1 | Contribution to Attacking Power<br>Average number of minutes between League team goals while on pitch | 36 |
| Defensive Rating<br>Average number of mins between League goals conceded while he was on the pitch | 105 | Scoring Difference<br>Defensive Rating minus Contribution to Attacking Power | 69 |

| | PLAYER | LGE GOALS | DEF RATE | POWER | SCORE DIFF |
|---|---|---|---|---|---|
| 2 | David Vaughan | 3 | 109 | 53 | 56 mins |
| 3 | David Brammer | 1 | 108 | 52 | 56 mins |
| 4 | Richard Walker | 2 | 105 | 56 | 49 mins |
| 5 | Kenny Lunt | 7 | 102 | 54 | 48 mins |

## KEY PLAYERS - DEFENDERS

**1 Steve Foster**

| | | | |
|---|---|---|---|
| Goals Conceded (GC)<br>The number of League goals conceded while he was on the pitch | 26 | Clean Sheets<br>In games when he played at least 70 minutes | 15 |
| Defensive Rating<br>Ave number of mins between League goals conceded while on the pitch | 120 | Club Defensive Rating<br>Average number of mins between League goals conceded by the club this season | 104 |

| | PLAYER | CON LGE | CLEAN SHEETS | DEF RATE |
|---|---|---|---|---|
| 2 | David Walton | 22 | 10 | 113 mins |
| 3 | Efetobore Sodje | 21 | 8 | 95 mins |
| 4 | David Wright | 29 | 11 | 94 mins |

## KEY GOALKEEPER

**1 Clayton Ince**

| | |
|---|---|
| Goals Conceded in the League | 35 |
| Defensive Rating<br>Ave number of mins between League goals conceded while on the pitch | 110 |
| Counting Games<br>Games when he played at least 70 mins | 43 |
| Clean Sheets<br>In games when he played at least 70 mins | 16 |

## TOP POINT EARNERS

| | PLAYER | GAMES | AVE |
|---|---|---|---|
| 1 | Tierney | 14 | 2.36 |
| 2 | Rix | 10 | 2.00 |
| 3 | Little | 2 | 2.00 |
| 4 | Foster | 34 | 2.00 |
| 5 | Bankole | 2 | 2.00 |
| 6 | Walton | 28 | 1.96 |
| 7 | Wright | 30 | 1.93 |
| 8 | Brammer | 38 | 1.92 |
| 9 | Ashton | 23 | 1.91 |
| 10 | Jack | 34 | 1.88 |
| | CLUB AVERAGE: | | 1.87 |

Ave = Average points per match in Counting Games

## DISCIPLINARY RECORDS

| | PLAYER | YELLOW | RED | AVE |
|---|---|---|---|---|
| 1 | Sodje | 3 | 1 | 500 |
| 2 | Hulse | 6 | 0 | 521 |
| 3 | Jones | 2 | 0 | 871 |
| 4 | Brammer | 4 | 0 | 892 |
| 5 | Wright | 3 | 0 | 913 |
| 6 | Foster | 2 | 1 | 1042 |
| 7 | Sorvel | 3 | 0 | 1169 |
| 8 | Rix | 1 | 0 | 1221 |
| 9 | Tierney | 1 | 0 | 1255 |
| 10 | Walker | 1 | 1 | 1367 |
| 11 | Jack | 2 | 0 | 1557 |
| 12 | Lunt | 2 | 0 | 2047 |
| 13 | Walton | 1 | 0 | 2486 |
| | Other | 3 | 0 | |
| | TOTAL | 34 | 3 | |

## LEAGUE GOALS

| | PLAYER | MINS | GOALS | AVE |
|---|---|---|---|---|
| 1 | Hulse | 3129 | 22 | 142 |
| 2 | Jack | 3115 | 9 | 346 |
| 3 | Jones | 1743 | 9 | 194 |
| 4 | Ashton | 2259 | 9 | 251 |
| 5 | Lunt | 4095 | 7 | 585 |
| 6 | Foster | 3128 | 4 | 782 |
| 7 | Sorvel | 3507 | 3 | 1169 |
| 8 | Vaughan | 2615 | 3 | 872 |
| 9 | Walker | 2735 | 2 | 1368 |
| 10 | Miles | 59 | 1 | 59 |
| 11 | Sodje | 2001 | 1 | 2001 |
| 12 | Tierney | 1255 | 1 | 1255 |
| 13 | Brammer | 3568 | 1 | 3568 |
| | Other | | 4 | |
| | TOTAL | | 76 | |

## MONTH BY MONTH GUIDE TO THE POINTS

| MONTH | POINTS | % |
|---|---|---|
| AUGUST | 11 | 61% |
| SEPTEMBER | 8 | 53% |
| OCTOBER | 9 | 60% |
| NOVEMBER | 7 | 58% |
| DECEMBER | 9 | 75% |
| JANUARY | 12 | 100% |
| FEBRUARY | 8 | 53% |
| MARCH | 13 | 62% |
| APRIL | 8 | 53% |
| MAY | 1 | 33% |

## TEAM OF THE SEASON

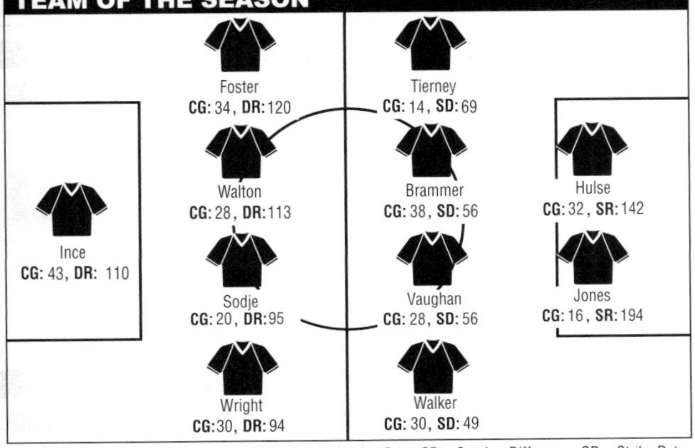
Foster
CG: 34, DR: 120
Tierney
CG: 14, SD: 69
Walton
CG: 28, DR: 113
Brammer
CG: 38, SD: 56
Hulse
CG: 32, SR: 142
Ince
CG: 43, DR: 110
Sodje
CG: 20, DR: 95
Vaughan
CG: 28, SD: 56
Jones
CG: 16, SR: 194
Wright
CG: 30, DR: 94
Walker
CG: 30, SD: 49

KEY: DR = Defensive Rate, SD = Scoring Difference, SR = Strike Rate, CG = Counting Games – League games playing at least 70 minutes

## LEAGUE APPEARANCES, BOOKINGS AND CAPS

| | AGE | IN THE SQUAD | COUNTING GAMES | MINUTES ON PITCH | YELLOW CARDS | RED CARDS | THIS SEASON | HOME COUNTRY |
|---|---|---|---|---|---|---|---|---|
| **Goalkeepers** | | | | | | | | |
| Ademola Bankole | 33 | 42 | 2 | 191 | 0 | 0 | - | Nigeria |
| Clayton Ince | 30 | 43 | 43 | 3859 | 1 | 0 | - | Trinidad & Tobago |
| Danny Milosevic | 25 | 1 | 0 | 50 | 0 | 0 | - | Australia |
| Stuart Tomlinson | 19 | 6 | 0 | 40 | 0 | 0 | - | England |
| **Defenders** | | | | | | | | |
| Sagi Burton | 25 | 4 | 0 | 58 | 0 | 0 | - | England |
| Steve Foster | 22 | 35 | 34 | 3128 | 2 | 1 | - | England |
| Chris McCready | 22 | 12 | 6 | 593 | 0 | 0 | - | England |
| Alex Morris | 20 | 1 | 0 | 0 | 0 | 0 | - | England |
| Efetobore Sodje | 30 | 43 | 20 | 2001 | 3 | 1 | - | Nigeria |
| David Walton | 30 | 34 | 28 | 2486 | 1 | 0 | - | England |
| David Wright | 23 | 31 | 30 | 2740 | 3 | 0 | - | England |
| **Midfielders** | | | | | | | | |
| Lee Bell | 19 | 25 | 2 | 426 | 0 | 0 | - | England |
| David Brammer | 28 | 41 | 38 | 3568 | 4 | 0 | - | England |
| Kenny Lunt | 23 | 46 | 46 | 4095 | 2 | 0 | - | England |
| Stefan Oakes | 24 | 9 | 1 | 215 | 0 | 0 | - | England |
| Ben Rix | 19 | 32 | 10 | 1221 | 1 | 0 | - | England |
| James Robinson | 20 | 3 | 0 | 7 | 0 | 0 | - | England |
| Neil Sorvel | 30 | 44 | 38 | 3507 | 3 | 0 | - | England |
| Paul Tierney | 20 | 20 | 14 | 1255 | 1 | 0 | - | England |
| David Vaughan | 20 | 33 | 28 | 2615 | 1 | 0 | 2 | Wales (50) |
| Richard Walker | 22 | 43 | 30 | 2735 | 1 | 1 | - | England |
| **Forwards** | | | | | | | | |
| Dean Ashton | 19 | 41 | 23 | 2259 | 0 | 0 | - | England |
| Paul Edwards | 20 | 4 | 0 | 16 | 1 | 0 | - | England |
| Robert Hulse | 23 | 39 | 32 | 3129 | 6 | 0 | - | England |
| Rodney Jack | 30 | 38 | 34 | 3115 | 2 | 0 | - | Jamaica |
| Steve Jones | 26 | 38 | 16 | 1743 | 2 | 0 | 3 | N Ireland (111) |
| Colin Little | 30 | 13 | 2 | 225 | 0 | 0 | - | England |
| John Miles | 21 | 10 | 0 | 59 | 0 | 0 | - | England |
| Andy White | 21 | 5 | 0 | 30 | 0 | 0 | - | England |

KEY: LEAGUE BOOKINGS CAPS

## SQUAD APPEARANCES

| Match | 1 | 2 | 3 | 4 | 5 | 6 | 7 | 8 | 9 | 10 | 11 | 12 | 13 |
|---|---|---|---|---|---|---|---|---|---|---|---|---|---|
| Venue | A | H | H | A | H | A | H | A | A | A | H | A | A |
| Competition | L | L | L | L | L | L | L | W | L | L | L | L | W |
| Result | D | L | W | D | W | W | D | W | D | W | W | L | L |

| Match | 14 | 15 | 16 | 17 | 18 | 19 | 20 | 21 | 22 | 23 | 24 | 25 | 26 |
|---|---|---|---|---|---|---|---|---|---|---|---|---|---|
| Venue | H | A | H | A | H | A | H | A | H | A | H | H | A |
| Competition | L | L | L | L | L | L | L | F | L | L | F | L | L |
| Result | W | W | L | W | L | L | W | W | W | D | W | W | W |

| Match | 27 | 28 | 29 | 30 | 31 | 32 | 33 | 34 | 35 | 36 | 37 | 38 | 39 |
|---|---|---|---|---|---|---|---|---|---|---|---|---|---|
| Venue | A | H | H | A | A | H | H | A | H | A | A | A | H |
| Competition | L | L | L | F | L | F | L | L | L | L | L | L | L |
| Result | W | L | W | D | W | L | W | W | D | D | W | W | L |

| Match | 40 | 41 | 42 | 43 | 44 | 45 | 46 | 47 | 48 | 49 | 50 | 51 | 52 |
|---|---|---|---|---|---|---|---|---|---|---|---|---|---|
| Venue | H | H | A | H | A | A | H | A | H | H | A | A | H |
| Competition | L | L | L | L | L | L | L | L | L | L | L | L | L |
| Result | L | W | L | D | W | W | W | W | D | L | W | D | D |

**Goalkeepers**
Ademola Bankole
Clayton Ince
Danny Milosevic
Stuart Tomlinson

**Defenders**
Sagi Burton
Steve Foster
Chris McCready
Alex Morris
Efetobore Sodje
David Walton
David Wright

**Midfielders**
Lee Bell
David Brammer
Kenny Lunt
Stefan Oakes
Ben Rix
James Robinson
Neil Sorvel
Paul Tierney
David Vaughan
Richard Walker

**Forwards**
Dean Ashton
Paul Edwards
Robert Hulse
Rodney Jack
Steve Jones
Colin Little
John Miles
Andy White

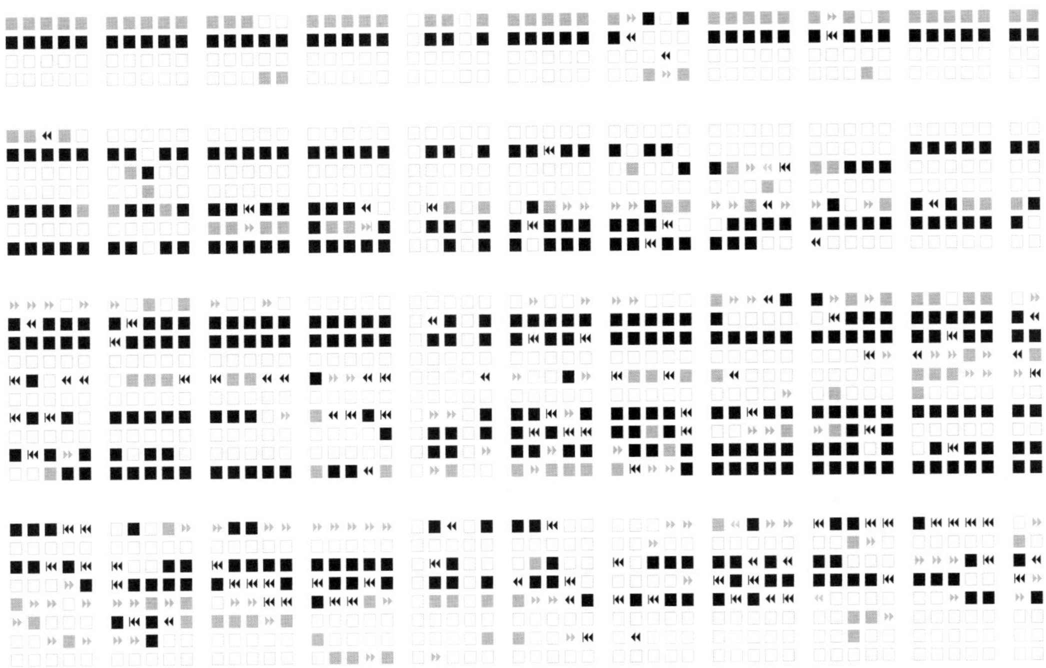

# BRISTOL CITY

Final Position: **3rd**

NICKNAME: THE ROBINS

| | | | | | | |
|---|---|---|---|---|---|---|
| 1 | div2 | Blackpool | H | W | 2-0 | Peacock 77; Murray 90 |
| 2 | div2 | Brentford | A | L | 0-1 | |
| 3 | div2 | Wigan | A | L | 0-2 | |
| 4 | div2 | Wycombe | H | W | 3-0 | Bell 39; Murray 52; Roberts 73 |
| 5 | div2 | Plymouth | A | L | 0-2 | |
| 6 | div2 | Tranmere | H | W | 2-0 | Tinnion 70 pen; Murray 74 |
| 7 | div2 | Northampton | H | W | 3-0 | Peacock 7,76; Clist 87 |
| 8 | wcr1 | Oxford | H | L | 0-1 | |
| 9 | div2 | Cheltenham | A | W | 3-2 | Murray 3; Coles 42; Matthews 53 |
| 10 | div2 | Oldham | A | L | 0-1 | |
| 11 | div2 | QPR | H | L | 1-3 | Murray 10 |
| 12 | div2 | Port Vale | A | W | 3-2 | Beadle 18; Murray 40; Lita 90 |
| 13 | div2 | Chesterfield | H | W | 4-0 | Roberts 26; Hill 63; Murray 90,90 |
| 14 | div2 | Barnsley | A | W | 4-1 | Butler 19; Roberts 29,58,73 |
| 15 | div2 | Swindon | H | W | 2-0 | Murray 11; Tinnion 38 |
| 16 | div2 | Peterborough | A | W | 3-1 | Tinnion 3; Brown, A 17; Murray 90 |
| 17 | div2 | Huddersfield | H | W | 1-0 | Hill 38 |
| 18 | div2 | Colchester | A | D | 2-2 | Peacock 42,58 |
| 19 | facr1 | Heybridge | A | W | 7-0 | Roberts 16,40; Tinnion 40 pen; Murray 45,61; Lita 66,82 |
| 20 | div2 | Mansfield | A | W | 5-4 | Murray 39; Roberts 50,90; Tinnion 87 pen; Lita 90 |
| 21 | div2 | Crewe | H | D | 2-2 | Murray 48; Peacock 84 |
| 22 | div2 | Notts County | H | W | 3-2 | Beadle 33; Murray 57; Peacock 83 |
| 23 | facr2 | Harrogate Rway | A | W | 3-1 | Walker 20 og; Murray 53; Roberts 90 |
| 24 | div2 | Cardiff | A | W | 2-0 | Tinnion 49 pen; Roberts 76 |
| 25 | div2 | Luton | H | D | 1-1 | Beadle 90 |
| 26 | div2 | Plymouth | H | D | 0-0 | |
| 27 | div2 | Stockport | A | W | 4-1 | Peacock 19; Coles 40; Rosenior 45; Beadle 89 |
| 28 | div2 | Wycombe | A | L | 1-2 | Tinnion 87 pen |
| 29 | facr3 | Leicester | A | L | 0-2 | |
| 30 | div2 | Wigan | H | L | 0-1 | |
| 31 | div2 | Tranmere | A | D | 1-1 | Bell 10 |
| 32 | div2 | Stockport | H | D | 1-1 | Roberts 50 |
| 33 | div2 | Blackpool | A | D | 0-0 | |
| 34 | div2 | Colchester | H | L | 1-2 | Fagan 51 |
| 35 | div2 | Brentford | H | D | 0-0 | |
| 36 | div2 | Notts County | A | L | 0-2 | |
| 37 | div2 | Northampton | A | W | 2-1 | Robins 12; Tinnion 35 |
| 38 | div2 | Cheltenham | H | W | 3-1 | Robins 2; Brown, A 20; Rosenior 90 |
| 39 | div2 | Oldham | H | W | 2-0 | Murray 54; Roberts 90 |
| 40 | div2 | QPR | A | L | 0-1 | |
| 41 | div2 | Peterborough | H | W | 1-0 | Robins 73 |
| 42 | div2 | Swindon | A | D | 1-1 | Robins 48 |
| 43 | div2 | Huddersfield | A | W | 2-1 | Hill 17; Peacock 36 |
| 44 | div2 | Barnsley | H | W | 2-0 | Murray 6; Roberts 63 |
| 45 | div2 | Mansfield | H | W | 5-2 | Peacock 13; Murray 32,51,80; Carey 70 |
| 46 | div2 | Crewe | A | D | 1-1 | Roberts 62 |
| 47 | div2 | Luton | A | D | 2-2 | Tinnion 66; Peacock 75 |
| 48 | div2 | Cardiff | H | W | 2-0 | Tinnion 55 pen; Roberts 73 |
| 49 | div2 | Chesterfield | A | L | 0-2 | |
| 50 | div2 | Port Vale | H | W | 2-0 | Murray 31; Peacock 43 |
| 51 | d2po1 | Cardiff | A | L | 0-1 | |
| 52 | d2po2 | Cardiff | H | D | 0-0 | |

## ATTENDANCES

HOME GROUND: ASHTON GATE CAPACITY: 21500 AVERAGE LEAGUE AT HOME: 11889

| | | | | | | | | |
|---|---|---|---|---|---|---|---|---|
| 29 | Leicester | 25868 | 41 | Peterborough | 11231 | 28 | Wycombe | 6785 |
| 51 | Cardiff | 19146 | 39 | Oldham | 11194 | 3 | Wigan | 6548 |
| 26 | Plymouth | 18085 | 34 | Colchester | 11107 | 47 | Luton | 6381 |
| 52 | Cardiff | 16307 | 7 | Northampton | 11104 | 9 | Cheltenham | 5895 |
| 48 | Cardiff | 15615 | 32 | Stockport | 10831 | 36 | Notts County | 5754 |
| 24 | Cardiff | 15239 | 22 | Notts County | 10690 | 10 | Oldham | 5583 |
| 40 | QPR | 14681 | 14 | Barnsley | 10495 | 16 | Peterborough | 5332 |
| 25 | Luton | 14057 | 44 | Barnsley | 10232 | 27 | Stockport | 5100 |
| 15 | Swindon | 13205 | 13 | Chesterfield | 10107 | 20 | Mansfield | 4801 |
| 30 | Wigan | 13151 | 6 | Tranmere | 9849 | 49 | Chesterfield | 4770 |
| 21 | Crewe | 12585 | 4 | Wycombe | 9597 | 37 | Northampton | 4688 |
| 50 | Port Vale | 12410 | 43 | Huddersfield | 9477 | 12 | Port Vale | 4286 |
| 11 | QPR | 12221 | 35 | Brentford | 9084 | 8 | Oxford | 4065 |
| 45 | Mansfield | 12013 | 42 | Swindon | 8629 | 23 | Harrogate Railway | 3500 |
| 5 | Plymouth | 11922 | 46 | Crewe | 7901 | 18 | Colchester | 3338 |
| 1 | Blackpool | 11891 | 31 | Tranmere | 7459 | 19 | Heybridge | 2046 |
| 38 | Cheltenham | 11711 | 33 | Blackpool | 7290 | | | |
| 17 | Huddersfield | 11494 | 2 | Brentford | 7130 | | | |

■ Home □ Away ▒ Neutral

## KEY PLAYERS - GOALSCORERS

**1 Scott Murray**

| | | | |
|---|---|---|---|
| Goals in the League | 19 | Player Strike Rate<br>Average number of minutes between League goals scored by player | 210 |
| Contribution to Attacking Power<br>Average number of minutes between League team goals while on pitch | 53 | Club Strike Rate<br>Average number of minutes between League goals scored by club | 52 |

| | PLAYER | LGE GOALS | POWER | STRIKE RATE |
|---|---|---|---|---|
| 2 | Christian Roberts | 13 | 51 | 212 mins |
| 3 | Lee Peacock | 12 | 56 | 242 mins |
| 4 | Brian Tinnion | 9 | 50 | 319 mins |
| 5 | Aaron Brown | 2 | 56 | 929 mins |

## KEY PLAYERS - MIDFIELDERS

**1 Brian Tinnion**

| | | | |
|---|---|---|---|
| Goals in the League | 9 | Contribution to Attacking Power<br>Average number of minutes between League team goals while on pitch | 50 |
| Defensive Rating<br>Average number of mins between League goals conceded while he was on the pitch | 90 | Scoring Difference<br>Defensive Rating minus Contribution to Attacking Power | 40 |

| | PLAYER | LGE GOALS | DEF RATE | POWER | SCORE DIFF |
|---|---|---|---|---|---|
| 2 | Tommy Doherty | 0 | 92 | 57 | 35 mins |
| 3 | Danny Coles | 2 | 81 | 54 | 27 mins |

## KEY PLAYERS - DEFENDERS

**1 Louis Carey**

| | | | |
|---|---|---|---|
| Goals Conceded (GC)<br>The number of League goals conceded while he was on the pitch | 19 | Clean Sheets<br>In games when he played at least 70 minutes | 7 |
| Defensive Rating<br>Ave number of mins between League goals conceded while on the pitch | 102 | Club Defensive Rating<br>Average number of mins between League goals conceded by the club this season | 86 |

| | PLAYER | CON LGE | CLEAN SHEETS | DEF RATE |
|---|---|---|---|---|
| 2 | Matthew Hill | 40 | 14 | 90 mins |
| 3 | Anthony Butler | 38 | 13 | 89 mins |
| 4 | Joe Burnell | 44 | 15 | 85 mins |
| 5 | Mick Bell | 38 | 12 | 82 mins |

## KEY GOALKEEPER

**1 Steve Phillips**

| | |
|---|---|
| Goals Conceded in the League | 48 |
| Defensive Rating<br>Ave number of mins between League goals conceded while on the pitch | 86 |
| Counting Games<br>Games when he played at least 70 mins | 46 |
| Clean Sheets<br>In games when he played at least 70 mins | 16 |

## TOP POINT EARNERS

| | PLAYER | GAMES | AVE |
|---|---|---|---|
| 1 | Hulbert | 2 | 3.00 |
| 2 | Beadle | 8 | 2.25 |
| 3 | Woodman | 7 | 2.14 |
| 4 | Roberts | 26 | 2.12 |
| 5 | Robins | 5 | 2.00 |
| 6 | Butler | 38 | 1.97 |
| 7 | Tinnion | 28 | 1.93 |
| 8 | Doherty | 32 | 1.91 |
| 9 | Burnell | 40 | 1.88 |
| 10 | Hill | 39 | 1.85 |
| | **CLUB AVERAGE:** | | **1.80** |

Ave = Average points per match in Counting Games

## DISCIPLINARY RECORDS

| | PLAYER | YELLOW | RED | AVE |
|---|---|---|---|---|
| 1 | Rosenior | 3 | 0 | 166 |
| 2 | Brown, A | 5 | 3 | 232 |
| 3 | Doherty | 10 | 1 | 274 |
| 4 | Butler | 9 | 1 | 339 |
| 5 | Beadle | 2 | 0 | 532 |
| 6 | Roberts | 5 | 0 | 552 |
| 7 | Coles | 5 | 1 | 554 |
| 8 | Peacock | 4 | 0 | 725 |
| 9 | Hill | 4 | 0 | 899 |
| 10 | Burnell | 4 | 0 | 931 |
| 11 | Murray | 3 | 0 | 1330 |
| 12 | Tinnion | 1 | 0 | 2873 |
| | Other | 4 | 0 | |
| | TOTAL | 59 | 6 | |

## LEAGUE GOALS

| | PLAYER | MINS | GOALS | AVE |
|---|---|---|---|---|
| 1 | Murray | 3990 | 19 | 210 |
| 2 | Roberts | 2762 | 13 | 212 |
| 3 | Peacock | 2901 | 12 | 242 |
| 4 | Tinnion | 2873 | 9 | 319 |
| 5 | Beadle | 1065 | 4 | 266 |
| 6 | Robins | 442 | 4 | 111 |
| 7 | Hill | 3598 | 3 | 1199 |
| 8 | Coles | 3328 | 2 | 1664 |
| 9 | Brown, A | 1858 | 2 | 929 |
| 10 | Bell | 3118 | 2 | 1559 |
| 11 | Rosenior | 500 | 2 | 250 |
| 12 | Lita | 220 | 2 | 110 |
| 13 | Matthews | 225 | 1 | 225 |
| | Other | | 4 | |
| | TOTAL | | 79 | |

## MONTH BY MONTH GUIDE TO THE POINTS

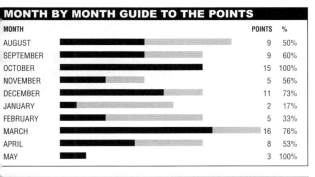

| MONTH | POINTS | % |
|---|---|---|
| AUGUST | 9 | 50% |
| SEPTEMBER | 9 | 60% |
| OCTOBER | 15 | 100% |
| NOVEMBER | 5 | 56% |
| DECEMBER | 11 | 73% |
| JANUARY | 2 | 17% |
| FEBRUARY | 5 | 33% |
| MARCH | 16 | 76% |
| APRIL | 8 | 53% |
| MAY | 3 | 100% |

## TEAM OF THE SEASON

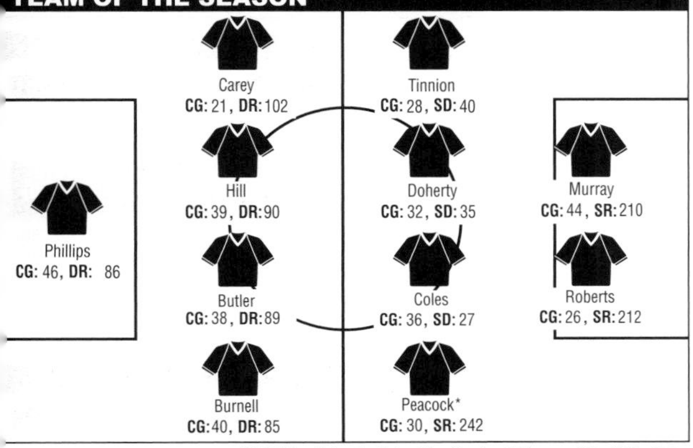
Carey
CG: 21, DR: 102
Tinnion
CG: 28, SD: 40
Hill
CG: 39, DR: 90
Doherty
CG: 32, SD: 35
Murray
CG: 44, SR: 210
Phillips
CG: 46, DR: 86
Butler
CG: 38, DR: 89
Coles
CG: 36, SD: 27
Roberts
CG: 26, SR: 212
Burnell
CG: 40, DR: 85
Peacock*
CG: 30, SR: 242

KEY: DR = Defensive Rate, SD = Scoring Difference, SR = Strike Rate, CG = Counting Games – League games playing at least 70 minutes

## LEAGUE APPEARANCES, BOOKINGS AND CAPS

| | AGE | IN THE SQUAD | COUNTING GAMES | MINUTES ON PITCH | YELLOW CARDS | RED CARDS | THIS SEASON | HOME COUNTRY |
|---|---|---|---|---|---|---|---|---|
| **Goalkeepers** | | | | | | | | |
| Ben Foster | 20 | 4 | 0 | 0 | 0 | 0 | - | England |
| Boaz Myhill | 20 | 17 | 0 | 0 | 0 | 0 | - | England |
| Steve Phillips | 25 | 46 | 46 | 4140 | 0 | 0 | - | England |
| Mike Stowell | 38 | 24 | 0 | 0 | 0 | 0 | - | England |
| **Defenders** | | | | | | | | |
| Kevin Amankwaah | 21 | 3 | 0 | 18 | 0 | 0 | - | England |
| Mick Bell | 31 | 41 | 34 | 3118 | 0 | 0 | - | England |
| Joe Burnell | 22 | 44 | 40 | 3726 | 4 | 0 | - | England |
| Anthony Butler | 30 | 38 | 38 | 3399 | 9 | 1 | - | England |
| Louis Carey | 26 | 26 | 21 | 1929 | 0 | 0 | - | England |
| Clayton Fortune | 20 | 16 | 6 | 597 | 0 | 0 | - | England |
| Matthew Hill | 22 | 43 | 39 | 3598 | 4 | 0 | - | England |
| Darren Jones | 19 | 2 | 0 | 0 | 0 | 0 | - | Wales |
| Mark Lever | 33 | 2 | 0 | 0 | 0 | 0 | - | England |
| Keith Millen | 36 | 3 | 3 | 264 | 0 | 0 | - | England |
| Craig Woodman | 20 | 15 | 7 | 691 | 0 | 0 | - | England |
| **Midfielders** | | | | | | | | |
| Simon Clist | 22 | 6 | 0 | 106 | 0 | 0 | - | England |
| Danny Coles | 21 | 43 | 36 | 3328 | 5 | 1 | - | England |
| Tommy Doherty | 24 | 38 | 32 | 3020 | 10 | 1 | 2 | N Ireland (111) |
| Robin Hulbert | 23 | 13 | 2 | 247 | 0 | 0 | - | England |
| Aaron Shanahan | 20 | 1 | 0 | 0 | 0 | 0 | - | England |
| Brian Tinnion | 35 | 40 | 28 | 2873 | 1 | 0 | - | England |
| **Forwards** | | | | | | | | |
| Peter Beadle | 31 | 31 | 8 | 1065 | 2 | 0 | - | England |
| Aaron Brown | 23 | 41 | 15 | 1858 | 5 | 3 | - | England |
| Albano Correia | 21 | 1 | 0 | 0 | 0 | 0 | - | Portugal |
| Craig Fagan | 20 | 6 | 3 | 396 | 2 | 0 | - | England |
| Leroy Lita | - | 23 | 0 | 220 | 1 | 0 | - | Congo |
| Lee Matthews | 24 | 8 | 1 | 225 | 1 | 0 | - | England |
| Scott Murray | 29 | 45 | 44 | 3990 | 3 | 0 | - | Scotland |
| Lee Peacock | 26 | 37 | 30 | 2901 | 4 | 0 | - | Scotland |
| Christian Roberts | 23 | 44 | 26 | 2762 | 5 | 0 | - | Wales |
| Mark Robins | 33 | 6 | 5 | 442 | 0 | 0 | - | England |
| Liam Rosenior | 18 | 29 | 1 | 500 | 3 | 0 | - | England |

KEY: LEAGUE BOOKINGS CAPS

## SQUAD APPEARANCES

| Match | 1 | 2 | 3 | 4 | 5 | 6 | 7 | 8 | 9 | 10 | 11 | 12 | 13 | 14 | 15 | 16 | 17 | 18 | 19 | 20 | 21 | 22 | 23 | 24 | 25 | 26 |
|---|---|---|---|---|---|---|---|---|---|---|---|---|---|---|---|---|---|---|---|---|---|---|---|---|---|---|
| Venue | H | A | A | H | A | H | H | H | A | A | H | A | H | A | H | A | H | A | A | A | H | H | A | A | H | H |
| Competition | L | L | L | L | L | L | L | W | L | L | L | L | L | L | L | L | L | L | F | L | L | L | F | L | L | L |
| Result | W | L | L | W | L | W | W | L | W | L | L | W | W | W | W | W | W | D | W | W | D | W | W | W | D | D |

| Match | 27 | 28 | 29 | 30 | 31 | 32 | 33 | 34 | 35 | 36 | 37 | 38 | 39 | 40 | 41 | 42 | 43 | 44 | 45 | 46 | 47 | 48 | 49 | 50 | 51 | 52 |
|---|---|---|---|---|---|---|---|---|---|---|---|---|---|---|---|---|---|---|---|---|---|---|---|---|---|---|
| Venue | A | A | A | H | A | H | A | H | H | A | A | H | H | A | H | A | A | H | H | A | A | H | A | H | A | H |
| Competition | L | L | F | L | L | L | L | L | L | L | L | L | L | L | L | L | L | L | L | L | L | L | L | L | O | O |
| Result | W | L | L | L | D | D | D | L | D | L | W | W | W | L | W | D | W | W | W | D | D | W | L | W | L | D |

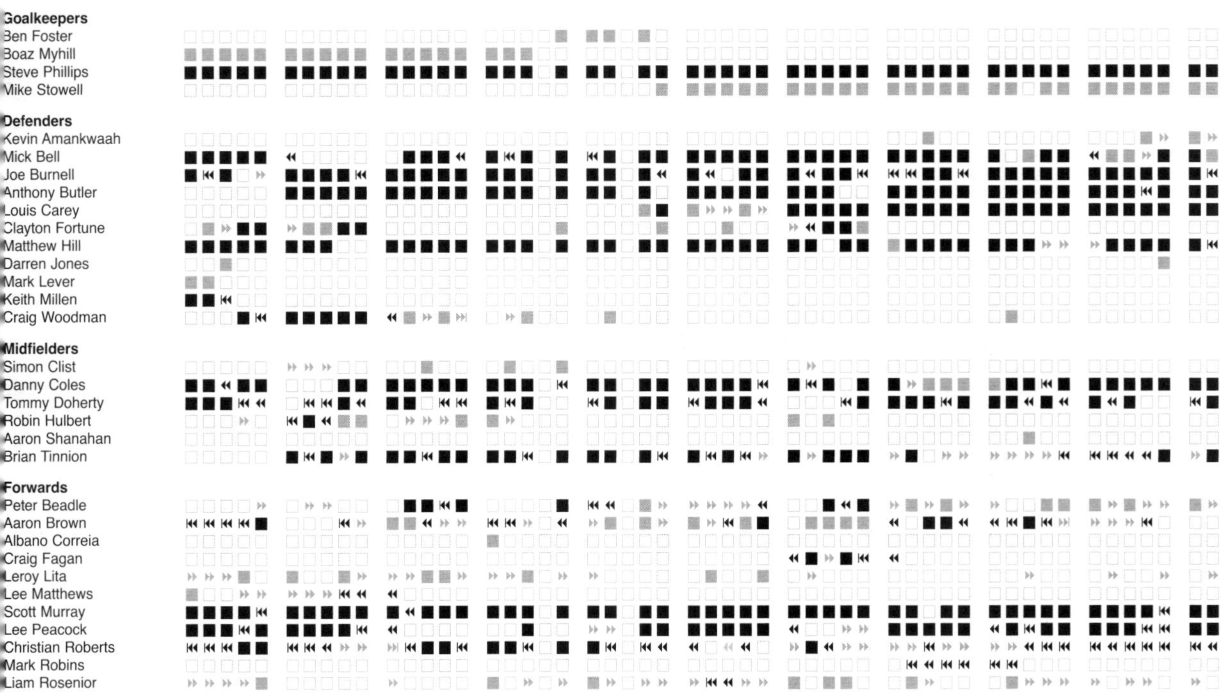
Goalkeepers
Ben Foster
Boaz Myhill
Steve Phillips
Mike Stowell
Defenders
Kevin Amankwaah
Mick Bell
Joe Burnell
Anthony Butler
Louis Carey
Clayton Fortune
Matthew Hill
Darren Jones
Mark Lever
Keith Millen
Craig Woodman
Midfielders
Simon Clist
Danny Coles
Tommy Doherty
Robin Hulbert
Aaron Shanahan
Brian Tinnion
Forwards
Peter Beadle
Aaron Brown
Albano Correia
Craig Fagan
Leroy Lita
Lee Matthews
Scott Murray
Lee Peacock
Christian Roberts
Mark Robins
Liam Rosenior

# QUEENS PARK RANGERS

Final Position: **4th**

NICKNAME: RANGERS

| | | | | | | |
|---|---|---|---|---|---|---|
| 1 | div2 | Chesterfield | H | W | 3-1 | Furlong 72; Langley 88; Gallen 90 |
| 2 | div2 | Stockport | A | D | 1-1 | Connolly 70 pen |
| 3 | div2 | Barnsley | A | L | 0-1 | |
| 4 | div2 | Peterborough | H | W | 2-0 | Gallen 59,70 |
| 5 | div2 | Wycombe | A | L | 1-4 | Furlong 44 |
| 6 | div2 | Plymouth | H | D | 2-2 | Thomas 69; Paquette 90 |
| 7 | div2 | Mansfield | A | W | 4-0 | Furlong 6; Shittu 48; Gallen 85; Thomson 89 |
| 8 | wcr1 | Leyton Orient | A | L | 2-3 | Thomson 70 pen; Gallen 89 |
| 9 | div2 | Swindon | H | W | 2-0 | Gallen 49; Langley 55 |
| 10 | div2 | Huddersfield | H | W | 3-0 | Shittu 4; Williams 31; Carlisle 72 |
| 11 | div2 | Bristol City | A | W | 3-1 | Connolly 23,47; Gallen 52 |
| 12 | div2 | Colchester | H | W | 2-0 | Connolly 39; Gallen 72 |
| 13 | div2 | Crewe | A | L | 0-2 | |
| 14 | div2 | Blackpool | H | W | 2-1 | Langley 17; Clarke, C 65 og |
| 15 | div2 | Cheltenham | A | D | 1-1 | Thomas 11 |
| 16 | div2 | Oldham | H | L | 1-2 | Rose 2 |
| 17 | div2 | Wigan | A | D | 1-1 | Thomson 45 |
| 18 | div2 | Port Vale | A | D | 0-0 | |
| 19 | div2 | Northampton | H | L | 0-1 | |
| 20 | facr1 | Vaux Motors | A | D | 0-0 | |
| 21 | div2 | Luton | A | D | 0-0 | |
| 22 | facr1r | Vaux Motors | H | L | 3-4* | Thomson 18 (*on penalties) |
| 23 | div2 | Cardiff | H | L | 0-4 | |
| 24 | div2 | Notts County | A | L | 0-3 | |
| 25 | div2 | Brentford | H | D | 1-1 | Bircham 18 |
| 26 | div2 | Wycombe | H | W | 2-1 | Rose 12; Gallen 30 |
| 27 | div2 | Tranmere | A | L | 0-3 | |
| 28 | div2 | Peterborough | A | W | 2-0 | Carlisle 44; Langley 79 |
| 29 | div2 | Stockport | H | W | 1-0 | Gallen 89 pen |
| 30 | div2 | Barnsley | H | W | 1-0 | Paquette 11 |
| 31 | div2 | Plymouth | A | W | 1-0 | Paquette 51 |
| 32 | div2 | Tranmere | H | L | 1-2 | Palmer 60 |
| 33 | div2 | Chesterfield | A | W | 4-2 | Paquette 13; Shittu 22; Furlong 83; Thomson 89 |
| 34 | div2 | Northampton | A | D | 1-1 | Furlong 60 |
| 35 | div2 | Port Vale | H | W | 4-0 | Shittu 52; Furlong 61; Padula 79; Gallen 89 |
| 36 | div2 | Mansfield | H | D | 2-2 | Furlong 20; Gallen 90 |
| 37 | div2 | Swindon | A | L | 1-3 | Shittu 15 |
| 38 | div2 | Huddersfield | A | W | 3-0 | Furlong 5,90; Shittu 38 |
| 39 | div2 | Bristol City | H | W | 1-0 | Gallen 19 pen |
| 40 | div2 | Oldham | A | D | 0-0 | |
| 41 | div2 | Cheltenham | H | W | 4-1 | Gallen 40; Duff, M 45 og; Cook 55; Furlong 63 |
| 42 | div2 | Wigan | H | L | 0-1 | |
| 43 | div2 | Blackpool | A | W | 3-1 | Langley 35,65,85 |
| 44 | div2 | Cardiff | A | W | 2-1 | Furlong 64; Langley 89 |
| 45 | div2 | Luton | H | W | 2-0 | McLeod 39,83 |
| 46 | div2 | Brentford | A | W | 2-1 | Shittu 8; Bircham 90 |
| 47 | div2 | Notts County | H | W | 2-0 | Furlong 16; Langley 90 |
| 48 | div2 | Crewe | H | D | 0-0 | |
| 49 | div2 | Colchester | A | W | 1-0 | Furlong 52 |
| 50 | d2po1 | Oldham | A | D | 1-1 | Langley 47 |
| 51 | d2po2 | Oldham | H | W | 1-0 | Furlong 82 |
| 52 | d2pof | Cardiff | N | D | 1-0 | |

## ATTENDANCES

HOME GROUND: LOFTUS ROAD CAPACITY: 19148 AVERAGE LEAGUE AT HOME: 13206

| | | | | | | | | |
|---|---|---|---|---|---|---|---|---|
| 52 | Cardiff | 66096 | 50 | Oldham | 12152 | 37 | Swindon | 7716 |
| 51 | Oldham | 17201 | 19 | Northampton | 11947 | 13 | Crewe | 7683 |
| 48 | Crewe | 16921 | 36 | Mansfield | 11942 | 40 | Oldham | 7242 |
| 45 | Luton | 15786 | 9 | Swindon | 11619 | 15 | Cheltenham | 6382 |
| 25 | Brentford | 15559 | 4 | Peterborough | 11510 | 17 | Wigan | 6241 |
| 16 | Oldham | 15491 | 41 | Cheltenham | 11370 | 28 | Peterborough | 6210 |
| 44 | Cardiff | 15245 | 14 | Blackpool | 11335 | 2 | Stockport | 5881 |
| 26 | Wycombe | 14874 | 30 | Barnsley | 11217 | 34 | Northampton | 5859 |
| 42 | Wigan | 14703 | 10 | Huddersfield | 11010 | 24 | Notts County | 5343 |
| 39 | Bristol City | 14681 | 29 | Stockport | 10387 | 22 | Vauxhall Motors | 5336 |
| 23 | Cardiff | 14345 | 31 | Plymouth | 10249 | 49 | Colchester | 5047 |
| 6 | Plymouth | 14001 | 3 | Barnsley | 9626 | 8 | Leyton Orient | 4981 |
| 35 | Port Vale | 13703 | 21 | Luton | 9477 | 7 | Mansfield | 4581 |
| 47 | Notts County | 13585 | 46 | Brentford | 9168 | 33 | Chesterfield | 4395 |
| 12 | Colchester | 12906 | 38 | Huddersfield | 8695 | 18 | Port Vale | 4394 |
| 1 | Chesterfield | 12603 | 27 | Tranmere | 8434 | 20 | Vauxhall Motors | 3507 |
| 32 | Tranmere | 12249 | 5 | Wycombe | 8383 | | | |
| 11 | Bristol City | 12221 | 43 | Blackpool | 8162 | | | |

■ Home □ Away ▒ Neutral

## KEY PLAYERS - GOALSCORERS

**1 Paul Furlong**

| | | | |
|---|---|---|---|
| Goals in the League | 13 | Player Strike Rate<br>Average number of minutes between League goals scored by player | 189 |
| Contribution to Attacking Power<br>Average number of minutes between League team goals while on pitch | 51 | Club Strike Rate<br>Average number of minutes between League goals scored by club | 60 |

| | PLAYER | LGE GOALS | POWER | STRIKE RATE |
|---|---|---|---|---|
| 2 | Kevin Gallen | 13 | 55 | 281 mins |
| 3 | Richard Langley | 9 | 56 | 373 mins |
| 4 | Danny Shittu | 7 | 57 | 545 mins |
| 5 | Lee Cook | 1 | 63 | 1075 mins |

## KEY PLAYERS - MIDFIELDERS

**1 Richard Langley**

| | | | |
|---|---|---|---|
| Goals in the League | 9 | Contribution to Attacking Power<br>Average number of minutes between League team goals while on pitch | 56 |
| Defensive Rating<br>Average number of mins between League goals conceded while he was on the pitch | 93 | Scoring Difference<br>Defensive Rating minus Contribution to Attacking Power | 37 |

| | PLAYER | LGE GOALS | DEF RATE | POWER | SCORE DIFF |
|---|---|---|---|---|---|
| 2 | Tommy Williams | 1 | 89 | 65 | 24 mins |
| 3 | Danny Shittu | | 7 | 57 | 36 mins |

## KEY PLAYERS - DEFENDERS

**1 Gino Padula**

| | | | |
|---|---|---|---|
| Goals Conceded (GC)<br>The number of League goals conceded while he was on the pitch | 13 | Clean Sheets<br>In games when he played at least 70 minutes | 7 |
| Defensive Rating<br>Ave number of mins between League goals conceded while on the pitch | 116 | Club Defensive Rating<br>Average number of mins between League goals conceded by the club this season | 92 |

| | PLAYER | CON LGE | CLEAN SHEETS | DEF RATE |
|---|---|---|---|---|
| 2 | Clarke Carlisle | 29 | 14 | 102 mins |
| 3 | Marc Bircham | 32 | 14 | 96 mins |
| 4 | Steve Palmer | 45 | 19 | 92 mins |
| 5 | Terell Forbes | 36 | 16 | 87 mins |

## KEY GOALKEEPER

**1 Chris Day**

| | |
|---|---|
| Goals Conceded in the League | 5 |
| Defensive Rating<br>Ave number of mins between League goals conceded while on the pitch | 216 |
| Counting Games<br>Games when he played at least 70 mins | 12 |
| Clean Sheets<br>In games when he played at least 70 mins | 7 |

## TOP POINT EARNERS

| | PLAYER | GAMES | AVE |
|---|---|---|---|
| 1 | Kelly | 6 | 3.00 |
| 2 | McLeod | 7 | 2.57 |
| 3 | Day | 12 | 2.42 |
| 4 | Padula | 15 | 2.33 |
| 5 | Angell | 4 | 2.25 |
| 6 | Paquette | 4 | 2.25 |
| 7 | Oli | 4 | 2.00 |
| 8 | Cook | 13 | 2.00 |
| 9 | Gallen | 40 | 1.98 |
| 10 | Furlong | 25 | 1.96 |
| | CLUB AVERAGE: | | 1.8 |

Ave = Average points per match in Counting Games

## DISCIPLINARY RECORDS

| | PLAYER | YELLOW | RED | AVE |
|---|---|---|---|---|
| 1 | Kelly | 3 | 1 | 149 |
| 2 | Murphy | 2 | 0 | 229 |
| 3 | Bircham | 10 | 1 | 280 |
| 4 | Padula | 5 | 0 | 301 |
| 5 | McLeod | 2 | 0 | 348 |
| 6 | Furlong | 6 | 1 | 351 |
| 7 | Cook | 2 | 1 | 358 |
| 8 | Carlisle | 5 | 2 | 421 |
| 9 | Shittu | 9 | 0 | 424 |
| 10 | Connolly | 2 | 0 | 543 |
| 11 | Langley | 6 | 0 | 560 |
| 12 | Angell | 1 | 0 | 634 |
| 13 | Williams | 3 | 0 | 649 |
| | Other | 15 | 2 | |
| | TOTAL | 71 | 8 | |

## LEAGUE GOALS

| | PLAYER | MINS | GOALS | AVE |
|---|---|---|---|---|
| 1 | Gallen | 3650 | 13 | 281 |
| 2 | Furlong | 2460 | 13 | 189 |
| 3 | Langley | 3361 | 9 | 373 |
| 4 | Shittu | 3817 | 7 | 545 |
| 5 | Paquette | 462 | 4 | 116 |
| 6 | Connolly | 1086 | 4 | 272 |
| 7 | Thomson | 697 | 3 | 232 |
| 8 | Bircham | 3086 | 2 | 1543 |
| 9 | Carlisle | 2951 | 2 | 1476 |
| 10 | McLeod | 697 | 2 | 349 |
| 11 | Thomas | 415 | 2 | 208 |
| 12 | Rose | 2217 | 2 | 1109 |
| 13 | Cook | 1075 | 1 | 1075 |
| | Other | | 5 | |
| | TOTAL | | 69 | |

## MONTH BY MONTH GUIDE TO THE POINTS

| MONTH | POINTS | % |
|---|---|---|
| AUGUST | 8 | 44% |
| SEPTEMBER | 15 | 100% |
| OCTOBER | 5 | 33% |
| NOVEMBER | 2 | 17% |
| DECEMBER | 4 | 33% |
| JANUARY | 12 | 80% |
| FEBRUARY | 8 | 67% |
| MARCH | 13 | 62% |
| APRIL | 13 | 87% |
| MAY | 3 | 100% |

## TEAM OF THE SEASON

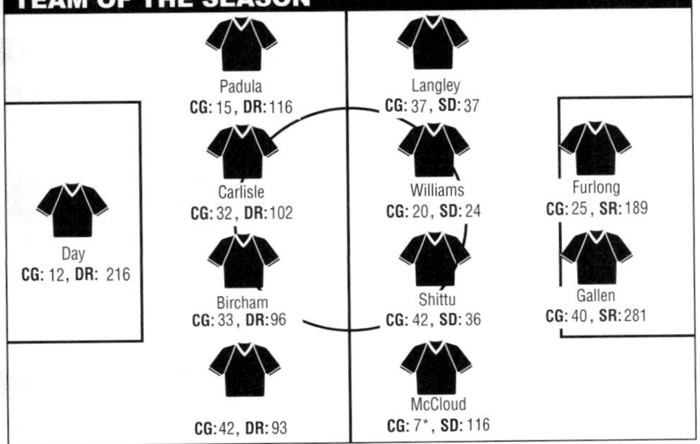
Padula
CG: 15, DR: 116
Langley
CG: 37, SD: 37
Day
CG: 12, DR: 216
Carlisle
CG: 32, DR: 102
Williams
CG: 20, SD: 24
Furlong
CG: 25, SR: 189
Bircham
CG: 33, DR: 96
Shittu
CG: 42, SD: 36
Gallen
CG: 40, SR: 281
CG: 42, DR: 93
McCloud
CG: 7*, SD: 116

KEY: DR = Defensive Rate, SD = Scoring Difference, SR = Strike Rate, CG = Counting Games – League games playing at least 70 minutes

## LEAGUE APPEARANCES, BOOKINGS AND CAPS

| | AGE | IN THE SQUAD | COUNTING GAMES | MINUTES ON PITCH | YELLOW CARDS | RED CARDS | THIS SEASON | HOME COUNTRY |
|---|---|---|---|---|---|---|---|---|
| **Goalkeepers** | | | | | | | | |
| Nicky Culkin | 25 | 27 | 17 | 1530 | 0 | 0 | - | England |
| Chris Day | 27 | 25 | 12 | 1080 | 0 | 0 | - | England |
| Fraser Digby | 36 | 16 | 1 | 160 | 0 | 0 | - | England |
| Simon Royce | 31 | 16 | 15 | 1371 | 0 | 1 | - | England |
| **Defenders** | | | | | | | | |
| Marc Bircham | 25 | 39 | 33 | 3086 | 10 | 1 | - | England |
| Clarke Carlisle | 23 | 36 | 32 | 2951 | 5 | 2 | - | England |
| Terell Forbes | 21 | 40 | 38 | 3411 | 2 | 0 | - | England |
| Stephen Kelly | 19 | 7 | 6 | 597 | 3 | 1 | - | Rep of Ireland |
| Danny Murphy | 20 | 23 | 4 | 458 | 2 | 0 | - | England |
| Gino Padula | 26 | 27 | 15 | 1509 | 5 | 0 | - | Argentina |
| Steve Palmer | 35 | 46 | 46 | 4128 | 3 | 0 | - | England |
| Chris Plummer | 26 | 3 | 0 | 70 | 0 | 0 | - | England |
| Matthew Rose | 27 | 32 | 24 | 2217 | 3 | 0 | - | England |
| Danny Shittu | 22 | 43 | 42 | 3817 | 9 | 0 | - | Nigeria |
| **Midfielders** | | | | | | | | |
| Marcus Bean | 18 | 16 | 4 | 437 | 0 | 1 | - | England |
| Oliver Burgess | 21 | 10 | 1 | 194 | 0 | 0 | - | England |
| Wesley Daly | 19 | 7 | 0 | 241 | 0 | 0 | - | England |
| Brian Fitzgerald | 19 | 1 | 0 | 0 | 0 | 0 | - | England |
| Richard Langley | 23 | 39 | 37 | 3361 | 6 | 0 | - | England |
| Kevin McLeod | 22 | 8 | 7 | 697 | 2 | 0 | - | England |
| Benjamin Walshe | 20 | 1 | 0 | 45 | 0 | 0 | - | England |
| Tommy Williams | 22 | 30 | 20 | 1949 | 3 | 0 | - | England |
| **Forwards** | | | | | | | | |
| Brett Angell | 34 | 23 | 4 | 634 | 1 | 0 | - | England |
| Karl Connolly | 33 | 17 | 9 | 1086 | 2 | 0 | - | England |
| Lee Cook | 20 | 13 | 13 | 1075 | 2 | 1 | - | England |
| Mbombo Doudou | 22 | 18 | 1 | 266 | 1 | 0 | - | Congo DR |
| Paul Furlong | 34 | 35 | 25 | 2460 | 6 | 1 | - | England |
| Kevin Gallen | 27 | 42 | 40 | 3650 | 3 | 0 | - | England |
| Leroy Griffiths | 26 | 11 | 3 | 292 | 1 | 0 | - | England |
| Steve Lovell | 22 | 2 | 0 | 0 | 0 | 0 | - | England |
| Dennis Oli | 19 | 21 | 4 | 692 | 0 | 0 | - | England |
| Richard Paquette | 20 | 22 | 4 | 462 | 0 | 0 | - | England |
| Jerome Thomas | 20 | 6 | 4 | 415 | 1 | 0 | - | England |
| Andy Thomson | 32 | 32 | 4 | 697 | 1 | 0 | - | Scotland |
| Callum Willock | 21 | 3 | 2 | 248 | 0 | 0 | - | England |

KEY: LEAGUE BOOKINGS CAPS

## SQUAD APPEARANCES

| Match | 1 | 2 | 3 | 4 | 5 | 6 | 7 | 8 | 9 | 10 | 11 | 12 | 13 | 14 | 15 | 16 | 17 | 18 | 19 | 20 | 21 | 22 | 23 | 24 | 25 | 26 |
|---|---|---|---|---|---|---|---|---|---|---|---|---|---|---|---|---|---|---|---|---|---|---|---|---|---|---|
| Venue | H | A | A | H | A | H | A | A | H | H | A | H | A | H | A | H | A | A | H | A | A | H | H | A | H | H |
| Competition | L | L | L | L | L | L | L | W | L | L | L | L | L | L | L | L | L | L | L | F | L | F | L | L | L | L |
| Result | W | D | L | W | L | D | W | L | W | W | W | W | L | W | D | L | D | D | L | D | D | L | L | L | D | W |

| Match | 27 | 28 | 29 | 30 | 31 | 32 | 33 | 34 | 35 | 36 | 37 | 38 | 39 | 40 | 41 | 42 | 43 | 44 | 45 | 46 | 47 | 48 | 49 | 50 | 51 | 52 |
|---|---|---|---|---|---|---|---|---|---|---|---|---|---|---|---|---|---|---|---|---|---|---|---|---|---|---|
| Venue | A | A | H | H | A | H | A | A | H | H | A | A | H | A | H | H | A | A | H | A | H | H | A | A | H | N |
| Competition | L | L | L | L | L | L | L | L | L | L | L | L | L | L | L | L | L | L | L | L | L | L | L | O | O | O |
| Result | L | W | W | W | W | L | W | D | W | D | L | W | W | D | W | L | W | W | W | W | W | D | W | D | W | D |

**Goalkeepers**
Nicky Culkin
Chris Day
Fraser Digby
Simon Royce

**Defenders**
Marc Bircham
Clarke Carlisle
Terell Forbes
Stephen Kelly
Danny Murphy
Gino Padula
Steve Palmer
Chris Plummer
Matthew Rose
Danny Shittu

**Midfielders**
Marcus Bean
Oliver Burgess
Wesley Daly
Brian Fitzgerald
Richard Langley
Kevin McLeod
Benjamin Walshe
Tommy Williams

**Forwards**
Brett Angell
Karl Connolly
Lee Cook
Mbombo Doudou
Paul Furlong
Kevin Gallen
Leroy Griffiths
Steve Lovell
Dennis Oli
Richard Paquette
Jerome Thomas
Andy Thomson
Callum Willock

# OLDHAM ATHLETIC

Final Position: **5th**

NICKNAME: THE LATICS

| | | | | | | |
|---|---|---|---|---|---|---|
| 1 | div2 | Cardiff | H | L | 1-2 | Duxbury 90 |
| 2 | div2 | Peterborough | A | W | 1-0 | Killen 62 |
| 3 | div2 | Brentford | A | D | 0-0 | |
| 4 | div2 | Tranmere | H | W | 2-0 | Hill 68; Wijnhard 77 |
| 5 | div2 | Blackpool | A | D | 0-0 | |
| 6 | div2 | Wycombe | H | L | 0-2 | |
| 7 | div2 | Notts County | A | W | 3-1 | Eyres, D 34; Sheridan, D 36; Killen 65 |
| 8 | wcr1 | Notts County | H | W | 3-2 | Killen 10; Carss 45; Wijnhard 80 |
| 9 | div2 | Mansfield | H | W | 6-1 | Wijnhard 10,25 pen,36,70; Corazzin 80; Andrews 84 pen |
| 10 | div2 | Bristol City | H | W | 1-0 | Wijnhard 70 |
| 11 | div2 | Colchester | A | W | 1-0 | Andrews 64 |
| 12 | div2 | Huddersfield | H | W | 4-0 | Wijnhard 1,56; Eyres, D 18; Da Silva 80 |
| 13 | wcr2 | Derby | A | W | 2-1 | Eyres, D 19; Wijnhard 94 pen |
| 14 | div2 | Swindon | A | W | 1-0 | Duxbury 5 |
| 15 | div2 | Port Vale | A | D | 1-1 | Holden 49 |
| 16 | div2 | Luton | H | L | 1-2 | Holden 4 |
| 17 | div2 | QPR | A | W | 2-1 | Low 29; Duxbury 38 |
| 18 | div2 | Northampton | H | W | 4-0 | Andrews 28; Corazzin 61; Eyres, D 71 pen; Eyre, J 84 |
| 19 | div2 | Stockport | H | W | 2-0 | Hall, F 40; Vernon 90 |
| 20 | wcr3 | West Ham | A | W | 1-0 | Corazzin 42 |
| 21 | div2 | Plymouth | A | D | 2-2 | Eyres, D 74 pen; Andrews 76 |
| 22 | facr1 | Burton | H | D | 2-2 | Low 18; Hall, F 90 |
| 23 | div2 | Cheltenham | H | D | 0-0 | |
| 24 | facr1r | Burton | A | W | 5-4* | Wijnhard 50; Eyres, D 116 (*on penalties) |
| 25 | div2 | Barnsley | A | D | 2-2 | Baudet 27; Killen 81 |
| 26 | wcr4 | Crystal Palace | A | L | 0-2 | |
| 27 | facr2 | Cheltenham | H | L | 1-2 | Haining 83 |
| 28 | div2 | Wigan | H | L | 0-2 | |
| 29 | div2 | Chesterfield | A | W | 1-0 | Hall, F 22 |
| 30 | div2 | Blackpool | H | D | 1-1 | Haining 45 |
| 31 | div2 | Crewe | A | W | 2-1 | Corazzin 26; Eyres, D 61 pen |
| 32 | div2 | Tranmere | A | W | 2-1 | Eyres, D 37 pen; Baudet 76 |
| 33 | div2 | Peterborough | H | D | 0-0 | |
| 34 | div2 | Brentford | H | W | 2-1 | Hall, F 22; Duxbury 46 |
| 35 | div2 | Wycombe | A | D | 2-2 | Andrews 26; Carss 84 |
| 36 | div2 | Crewe | H | L | 1-3 | Armstrong 64 |
| 37 | div2 | Cardiff | A | D | 1-1 | Eyres, D 87 |
| 38 | div2 | Plymouth | H | L | 0-1 | |
| 39 | div2 | Stockport | A | W | 2-1 | Murray 9; Eyres, D 89 |
| 40 | div2 | Notts County | H | D | 1-1 | Andrews 44 |
| 41 | div2 | Mansfield | A | W | 1-0 | Hall, F 88 pen |
| 42 | div2 | Bristol City | A | L | 0-2 | |
| 43 | div2 | Colchester | H | W | 2-0 | Eyre, J 13; Eyres, D 19 |
| 44 | div2 | QPR | H | D | 0-0 | |
| 45 | div2 | Luton | A | D | 0-0 | |
| 46 | div2 | Northampton | A | W | 2-0 | Andrews 67,89 |
| 47 | div2 | Port Vale | H | D | 1-1 | Eyres, D 28 |
| 48 | div2 | Barnsley | H | W | 2-1 | Andrews 4; Low 56 |
| 49 | div2 | Cheltenham | A | D | 1-1 | Eyres, D 31 |
| 50 | div2 | Chesterfield | H | W | 4-0 | Andrews 20; Wijnhard 26,75; Eyres, D 79 |
| 51 | div2 | Wigan | A | L | 1-3 | Andrews 1 |
| 52 | div2 | Swindon | H | W | 4-0 | Low 27; Eyres, D 31; Haining 79; Corazzin 83 |
| 53 | div2 | Huddersfield | A | D | 1-1 | Carss 68 |
| 54 | d2po1 | QPR | H | D | 1-1 | Eyres, D 28 |
| 55 | d2po2 | QPR | A | L | 0-1 | |

## ATTENDANCES

HOME GROUND: BOUNDARY PARK  CAPACITY: 13700  AVERAGE LEAGUE AT HOME: 6699

| | | | | | | | | |
|---|---|---|---|---|---|---|---|---|
| 20 | West Ham | 21919 | 12 | Huddersfield | 7643 | 46 | Northampton | 5646 |
| 55 | QPR | 17201 | 36 | Crewe | 7597 | 10 | Bristol City | 5583 |
| 17 | QPR | 15491 | 26 | Crystal Palace | 7431 | 15 | Port Vale | 5563 |
| 51 | Wigan | 12783 | 44 | QPR | 7242 | 18 | Northampton | 5512 |
| 37 | Cardiff | 12579 | 47 | Port Vale | 7209 | 9 | Mansfield | 5490 |
| 54 | QPR | 12152 | 16 | Luton | 6916 | 7 | Notts County | 5435 |
| 53 | Huddersfield | 11271 | 50 | Chesterfield | 6885 | 3 | Brentford | 5356 |
| 25 | Barnsley | 11222 | 52 | Swindon | 6873 | 43 | Colchester | 5223 |
| 42 | Bristol City | 11194 | 38 | Plymouth | 6657 | 2 | Peterborough | 5204 |
| 32 | Tranmere | 9795 | 23 | Cheltenham | 6575 | 34 | Brentford | 5039 |
| 30 | Blackpool | 9415 | 35 | Wycombe | 6226 | 49 | Cheltenham | 4439 |
| 13 | Derby | 9029 | 48 | Barnsley | 6191 | 27 | Cheltenham | 4416 |
| 31 | Crewe | 9006 | 45 | Luton | 6142 | 14 | Swindon | 4326 |
| 28 | Wigan | 8269 | 6 | Wycombe | 5963 | 8 | Notts County | 4205 |
| 19 | Stockport | 8251 | 4 | Tranmere | 5933 | 29 | Chesterfield | 4052 |
| 21 | Plymouth | 8216 | 33 | Peterborough | 5922 | 24 | Burton | 3416 |
| 5 | Blackpool | 8201 | 22 | Burton | 5802 | 11 | Colchester | 3021 |
| 39 | Stockport | 8168 | 41 | Mansfield | 5712 | | | |
| 1 | Cardiff | 8033 | 40 | Notts County | 5657 | | | |

■ Home □ Away ▒ Neutral

## KEY PLAYERS - GOALSCORERS

**1 Clyde Wijnhard**

| | | | |
|---|---|---|---|
| Goals in the League | 10 | Player Strike Rate<br>Average number of minutes between League goals scored by player | 211 |
| Contribution to Attacking Power<br>Average number of minutes between League team goals while on pitch | 62 | Club Strike Rate<br>Average number of minutes between League goals scored by club | 61 |

| | PLAYER | LGE GOALS | POWER | STRIKE RATE |
|---|---|---|---|---|
| 2 | Wayne Andrews | 11 | 59 | 228 mins |
| 3 | David Eyres | 13 | 59 | 264 mins |
| 4 | Lee Duxbury | 4 | 83 | 395 mins |
| 5 | Carlo Corazzin | 4 | 50 | 529 mins |

## KEY PLAYERS - MIDFIELDERS

**1 Joshua Low**

| | | | |
|---|---|---|---|
| Goals in the League | 3 | Contribution to Attacking Power<br>Average number of minutes between League team goals while on pitch | 45 |
| Defensive Rating<br>Average number of mins between League goals conceded while he was on the pitch | 136 | Scoring Difference<br>Defensive Rating minus Contribution to Attacking Power | 91 |

| | PLAYER | LGE GOALS | DEF RATE | POWER | SCORE DIFF |
|---|---|---|---|---|---|
| 2 | Darren Sheridan | 1 | 139 | 52 | 87 mins |
| 3 | Matthew Appleby | 0 | 142 | 62 | 80 mins |
| 4 | Anthony Carss | 2 | 113 | 69 | 44 mins |
| 5 | Paul Murray | 1 | 101 | 67 | 34 mins |

## KEY PLAYERS - DEFENDERS

**1 Clinton Hill**

| | | | |
|---|---|---|---|
| Goals Conceded (GC)<br>The number of League goals conceded while he was on the pitch | 10 | Clean Sheets<br>In games when he played at least 70 minutes | 9 |
| Defensive Rating<br>Ave number of mins between League goals conceded while on the pitch | 149 | Club Defensive Rating<br>Average number of mins between League goals conceded by the club this season | 109 |

| | PLAYER | CON LGE | CLEAN SHEETS | DEF RATE |
|---|---|---|---|---|
| 2 | Fitz Hall | 31 | 16 | 113 mins |
| 3 | Will Haining | 22 | 9 | 101 mins |
| 4 | David Beharall | 25 | 10 | 101 mins |
| 5 | Chris Armstrong | 31 | 12 | 96 mins |

## KEY GOALKEEPER

**1 Leslie Pogliacomi**

| | |
|---|---|
| Goals Conceded in the League | 28 |
| Defensive Rating<br>Ave number of mins between League goals conceded while on the pitch | 117 |
| Counting Games<br>Games when he played at least 70 mins | 36 |
| Clean Sheets<br>In games when he played at least 70 mins | 18 |

## TOP POINT EARNERS

| | PLAYER | GAMES | AVE |
|---|---|---|---|
| 1 | Low | 17 | 2.18 |
| 2 | Killen | 6 | 2.17 |
| 3 | Corazzin | 19 | 2.16 |
| 4 | Eyre, J | 22 | 2.09 |
| 5 | Appleby | 11 | 2.09 |
| 6 | Sheridan, D | 26 | 2.08 |
| 7 | Hill | 16 | 2.06 |
| 8 | Hall, F | 38 | 1.97 |
| 9 | Wijnhard | 24 | 1.96 |
| 10 | Duxbury | 12 | 1.92 |
| | CLUB AVERAGE: | | 1.78 |

Ave = Average points per match in Counting Games

## DISCIPLINARY RECORDS

| | PLAYER | YELLOW | RED | AVE |
|---|---|---|---|---|
| 1 | Appleby | 4 | 1 | 198 |
| 2 | Baudet | 6 | 2 | 214 |
| 3 | Sheridan, D | 8 | 1 | 277 |
| 4 | Hall, F | 9 | 2 | 317 |
| 5 | Killen | 3 | 0 | 364 |
| 6 | Low | 4 | 0 | 409 |
| 7 | Andrews | 6 | 0 | 418 |
| 8 | Eyre, J | 5 | 0 | 463 |
| 9 | Burgess | 1 | 0 | 487 |
| 10 | Eyres, D | 6 | 1 | 490 |
| 11 | Hill | 2 | 1 | 497 |
| 12 | Duxbury | 3 | 0 | 526 |
| 13 | Clegg | 1 | 0 | 608 |
| | Other | 16 | 1 | |
| | TOTAL | 74 | 9 | |

## LEAGUE GOALS

| | PLAYER | MINS | GOALS | AVE |
|---|---|---|---|---|
| 1 | Eyres, D | 3436 | 13 | 264 |
| 2 | Andrews | 2510 | 11 | 228 |
| 3 | Wijnhard | 2111 | 10 | 211 |
| 4 | Duxbury | 1579 | 4 | 395 |
| 5 | Corazzin | 2114 | 4 | 529 |
| 6 | Hall, F | 3488 | 4 | 872 |
| 7 | Low | 1637 | 3 | 546 |
| 8 | Killen | 1093 | 3 | 364 |
| 9 | Haining | 2214 | 2 | 1107 |
| 10 | Carss | 1588 | 2 | 794 |
| 11 | Holden | 275 | 2 | 138 |
| 12 | Baudet | 1713 | 2 | 857 |
| 13 | Eyre, J | 2318 | 2 | 1159 |
| | Other | | 6 | |
| | TOTAL | | 68 | |

## MONTH BY MONTH GUIDE TO THE POINTS

| MONTH | POINTS | % |
|---|---|---|
| AUGUST | 8 | 44% |
| SEPTEMBER | 15 | 100% |
| OCTOBER | 10 | 67% |
| NOVEMBER | 6 | 50% |
| DECEMBER | 7 | 58% |
| JANUARY | 9 | 50% |
| FEBRUARY | 4 | 44% |
| MARCH | 12 | 57% |
| APRIL | 10 | 67% |
| MAY | 1 | 33% |

## TEAM OF THE SEASON

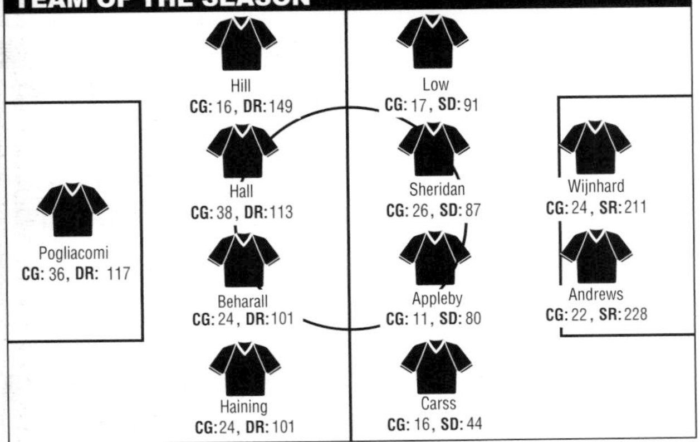
Pogliacomi
CG: 36, DR: 117
Hill
CG: 16, DR: 149
Hall
CG: 38, DR: 113
Beharall
CG: 24, DR: 101
Haining
CG: 24, DR: 101
Low
CG: 17, SD: 91
Sheridan
CG: 26, SD: 87
Appleby
CG: 11, SD: 80
Carss
CG: 16, SD: 44
Wijnhard
CG: 24, SR: 211
Andrews
CG: 22, SR: 228

KEY: DR = Defensive Rate, SD = Scoring Difference , SR = Strike Rate, CG=Counting Games – League games playing at least 70 minutes

## LEAGUE APPEARANCES, BOOKINGS AND CAPS

| | AGE | IN THE SQUAD | COUNTING GAMES | MINUTES ON PITCH | YELLOW CARDS | RED CARDS | THIS SEASON | HOME COUNTRY |
|---|---|---|---|---|---|---|---|---|
| **Goalkeepers** | | | | | | | | |
| David Miskelly | 23 | 44 | 9 | 877 | 0 | 0 | - | Rep of Ireland |
| Brian Murphy | 20 | 3 | 0 | 0 | 0 | 0 | - | Rep of Ireland |
| Leslie Pogliacomi | 27 | 37 | 36 | 3264 | 0 | 1 | - | Australia |
| Duncan Roberts | 24 | 6 | 0 | 0 | 0 | 0 | - | England |
| **Defenders** | | | | | | | | |
| Chris Armstrong | 20 | 33 | 33 | 2970 | 3 | 0 | - | Holland |
| Stuart Balmer | 33 | 1 | 0 | 0 | 0 | 0 | - | Scotland |
| Julien Baudet | 24 | 28 | 17 | 1713 | 6 | 2 | - | France |
| David Beharall | 24 | 39 | 24 | 2514 | 1 | 0 | - | England |
| Lee Duxbury | 33 | 39 | 12 | 1579 | 3 | 0 | - | England |
| Will Haining | 20 | 28 | 24 | 2214 | 2 | 0 | - | Scotland |
| Daniel Hall | 19 | 3 | 0 | 3 | 0 | 0 | - | England |
| Fitz Hall | 22 | 40 | 38 | 3488 | 9 | 2 | - | England |
| Clinton Hill | 24 | 17 | 16 | 1492 | 2 | 1 | - | England |
| **Midfielders** | | | | | | | | |
| Matthew Appleby | 27 | 13 | 11 | 994 | 4 | 1 | - | England |
| Danny Boshell | 22 | 7 | 1 | 102 | 0 | 0 | - | England |
| Anthony Carss | 27 | 29 | 16 | 1588 | 2 | 0 | - | England |
| Michael Clegg | 26 | 16 | 5 | 608 | 1 | 0 | - | England |
| Dean Holden | 23 | 11 | 3 | 275 | 1 | 0 | - | England |
| Joshua Low | 24 | 23 | 17 | 1637 | 4 | 0 | - | England |
| Paul Murray | 26 | 31 | 28 | 2617 | 3 | 0 | - | England |
| Darren Sheridan | 35 | 34 | 26 | 2494 | 8 | 1 | - | England |
| John Sheridan | 38 | 7 | 2 | 294 | 0 | 0 | - | England |
| **Forwards** | | | | | | | | |
| Wayne Andrews | 25 | 39 | 22 | 2510 | 6 | 0 | - | England |
| Ben Burgess | 21 | 10 | 5 | 487 | 1 | 0 | - | Rep of Ireland |
| Carlo Corazzin | 31 | 41 | 19 | 2114 | 3 | 0 | - | Canada |
| Lourenco Da Silva | 20 | 10 | 1 | 233 | 0 | 0 | - | |
| John Eyre | 28 | 35 | 22 | 2318 | 5 | 0 | - | England |
| David Eyres | 39 | 40 | 38 | 3436 | 6 | 1 | - | England |
| Christopher Killen | 21 | 32 | 6 | 1093 | 3 | 0 | - | New Zealand |
| Scott Vernon | 19 | 16 | 1 | 214 | 0 | 0 | - | England |
| Clyde Wijnhard | 29 | 25 | 24 | 2111 | 1 | 0 | - | Holland |

KEY: LEAGUE BOOKINGS CAPS

## SQUAD APPEARANCES

| Match | 1 | 2 | 3 | 4 | 5 | 6 | 7 | 8 | 9 | 10 | 11 | 12 | 13 | 14 | 15 | 16 | 17 | 18 | 19 | 20 | 21 | 22 | 23 | 24 | 25 |
|---|---|---|---|---|---|---|---|---|---|---|---|---|---|---|---|---|---|---|---|---|---|---|---|---|---|
| Venue | H | A | A | H | A | H | A | H | H | H | A | H | A | A | A | H | A | H | H | A | A | H | H | A | A |
| Competition | L | L | L | L | L | L | L | W | L | L | L | L | W | L | L | L | L | L | L | W | L | F | L | F | L |
| Result | L | W | D | W | D | L | W | W | W | W | W | W | D | W | D | L | W | W | W | W | D | D | D | W | D |

| Match | 26 | 27 | 28 | 29 | 30 | 31 | 32 | 33 | 34 | 35 | 36 | 37 | 38 | 39 | 40 | 41 | 42 | 43 | 44 | 45 | 46 | 47 | 48 | 49 | 50 | 51 | 52 | 53 | 54 | 55 |
|---|---|---|---|---|---|---|---|---|---|---|---|---|---|---|---|---|---|---|---|---|---|---|---|---|---|---|---|---|---|---|
| Venue | A | H | H | A | H | A | A | H | H | A | H | A | H | A | H | A | A | H | H | A | A | H | H | A | H | A | H | A | H | A |
| Competition | W | F | L | L | L | L | L | L | L | L | L | L | L | L | L | L | L | L | L | L | L | L | L | L | L | L | L | L | O | O |
| Result | L | L | L | W | D | W | W | D | W | D | L | D | L | W | D | W | L | W | D | D | W | D | W | D | W | L | W | D | D | L |

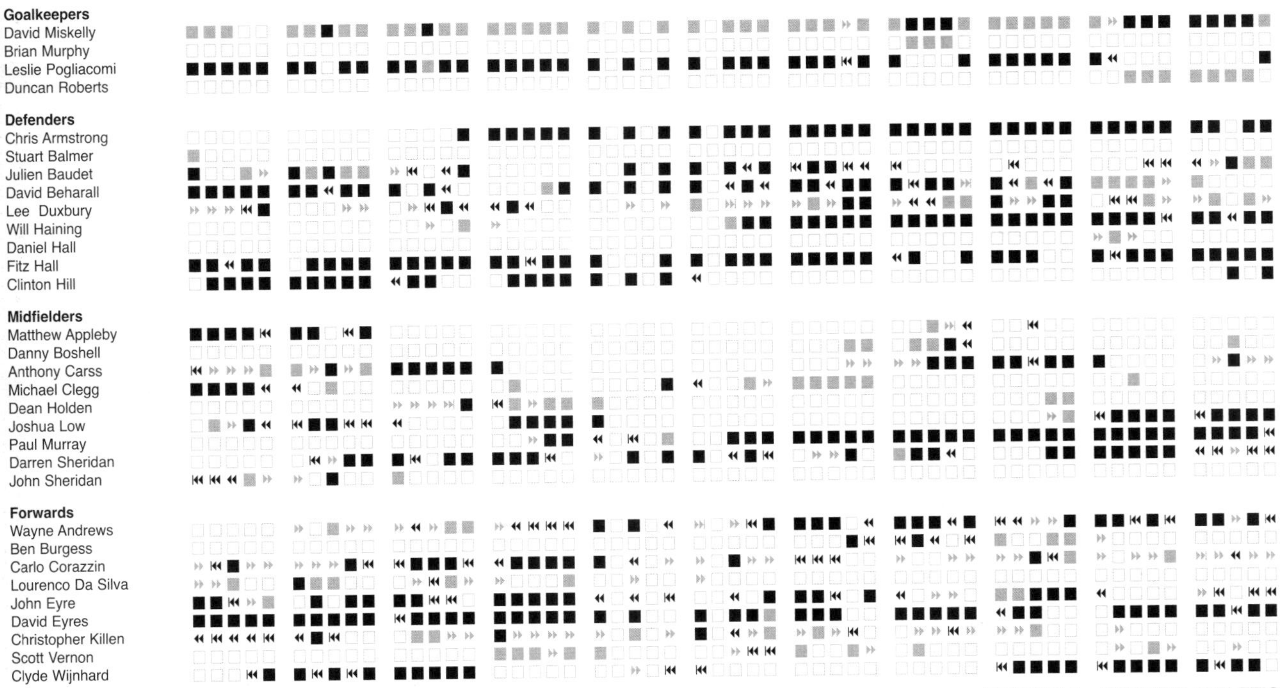
Goalkeepers
David Miskelly
Brian Murphy
Leslie Pogliacomi
Duncan Roberts
Defenders
Chris Armstrong
Stuart Balmer
Julien Baudet
David Beharall
Lee Duxbury
Will Haining
Daniel Hall
Fitz Hall
Clinton Hill
Midfielders
Matthew Appleby
Danny Boshell
Anthony Carss
Michael Clegg
Dean Holden
Joshua Low
Paul Murray
Darren Sheridan
John Sheridan
Forwards
Wayne Andrews
Ben Burgess
Carlo Corazzin
Lourenco Da Silva
John Eyre
David Eyres
Christopher Killen
Scott Vernon
Clyde Wijnhard

# CARDIFF CITY

Final Position: **6th**

NICKNAME: THE BLUEBIRDS

| | | | | | | |
|---|---|---|---|---|---|---|
| 1 | div2 | Oldham | A | W | 2-1 | Campbell 21; Earnshaw 84 |
| 2 | div2 | Port Vale | H | W | 3-1 | Thorne 4; Fortune-West 9; Legg 67 |
| 3 | div2 | Northampton | H | L | 1-2 | Kavanagh 15 |
| 4 | div2 | Swindon | A | W | 1-0 | Fortune-West 27 |
| 5 | div2 | Luton | H | D | 0-0 | |
| 6 | div2 | Cheltenham | A | D | 1-1 | Campbell 11 |
| 7 | wcr1 | Boston | A | W | 5-1 | Earnshaw 25,36,42; Bennett 45 og; Thorne 68 |
| 8 | div2 | Stockport | H | W | 2-1 | Earnshaw 2; Kavanagh 38 |
| 9 | div2 | Brentford | H | W | 2-0 | Legg 28; Earnshaw 73 |
| 10 | div2 | Notts County | A | W | 1-0 | Croft 21 |
| 11 | div2 | Plymouth | A | D | 2-2 | Earnshaw 2,67 |
| 12 | div2 | Crewe | H | W | 2-1 | Earnshaw 84,86 |
| 13 | wcr2 | Tottenham | A | L | 0-1 | |
| 14 | div2 | Wigan | A | D | 2-2 | Earnshaw 19,85 |
| 15 | div2 | Wycombe | H | W | 1-0 | Kavanagh 79 |
| 16 | div2 | Blackpool | A | L | 0-1 | |
| 17 | div2 | Tranmere | H | W | 4-0 | Thorne 29,82; Earnshaw 40 pen; Weston 90 |
| 18 | div2 | Mansfield | A | W | 1-0 | Thorne 70 |
| 19 | div2 | Peterborough | H | W | 3-0 | Kavanagh 19; Earnshaw 54 pen; Weston 58 |
| 20 | div2 | Barnsley | A | L | 2-3 | Earnshaw 23,42 |
| 21 | facr1 | Tranmere | A | D | 2-2 | Collins 34; Kavanagh 44 |
| 22 | div2 | Chesterfield | H | W | 1-0 | Thorne 12 |
| 23 | facr1r | Tranmere | H | W | 2-1 | Campbell 60; Collins 68 |
| 24 | div2 | QPR | A | W | 4-0 | Earnshaw 59,65,87; Campbell 90 |
| 25 | facr2 | Margate | A | W | 3-0 | Thorne 28; Boland 34; Fortune-West 88 |
| 26 | div2 | Bristol City | H | L | 0-2 | |
| 27 | div2 | Colchester | A | W | 2-1 | Earnshaw 45,77 |
| 28 | div2 | Luton | A | L | 0-2 | |
| 29 | div2 | Huddersfield | H | W | 4-0 | Bowen 19,64; Earnshaw 44,73 |
| 30 | div2 | Swindon | H | D | 1-1 | Earnshaw 89 |
| 31 | facr3 | Coventry | H | D | 2-2 | Earnshaw 76; Campbell 90 |
| 32 | facr3r | Coventry | A | L | 0-3 | |
| 33 | div2 | Cheltenham | H | W | 2-1 | Thorne 8; Earnshaw 36 |
| 34 | div2 | Huddersfield | A | L | 0-1 | |
| 35 | div2 | Oldham | H | D | 1-1 | Bowen 35 |
| 36 | div2 | Northampton | A | W | 1-0 | Earnshaw 58 |
| 37 | div2 | Barnsley | H | D | 1-1 | Gordon 90 |
| 38 | div2 | Plymouth | H | D | 1-1 | Earnshaw 42 |
| 39 | div2 | Port Vale | A | W | 2-0 | Gordon 35; Thorne 64 |
| 40 | div2 | Stockport | A | D | 1-1 | Thorne 81 |
| 41 | div2 | Brentford | A | W | 2-0 | Young 52; Earnshaw 78 |
| 42 | div2 | Notts County | H | L | 0-2 | |
| 43 | div2 | Tranmere | A | D | 3-3 | Earnshaw 35,68,90 |
| 44 | div2 | Blackpool | H | W | 2-1 | Earnshaw 44; Mahon 51 |
| 45 | div2 | Mansfield | H | W | 1-0 | Earnshaw 62 |
| 46 | div2 | QPR | H | L | 1-2 | Thorne 78 |
| 47 | div2 | Wycombe | A | W | 4-0 | Thorne 5,81; Mahon 68; Legg 84 |
| 48 | div2 | Chesterfield | A | W | 3-0 | Kavanagh 24; Thorne 35,82 |
| 49 | div2 | Peterborough | A | L | 0-2 | |
| 50 | div2 | Colchester | H | L | 0-3 | |
| 51 | div2 | Bristol City | A | L | 0-2 | |
| 52 | div2 | Wigan | H | D | 0-0 | |
| 53 | div2 | Crewe | A | D | 1-1 | Earnshaw 64 |
| 54 | d2po1 | Bristol City | H | W | 1-0 | Thorne 74 |
| 55 | d2po2 | Bristol City | A | D | 0-0 | |
| 56 | d2pof | QPR | N | D | 0-0 | Campbell 114 |

## ATTENDANCES

HOME GROUND: NINIAN PARK CAPACITY: 22000 AVERAGE LEAGUE AT HOME: 12484

| | | | | | | | | |
|---|---|---|---|---|---|---|---|---|
| 56 | QPR | 66096 | 45 | Mansfield | 13009 | 28 | Luton | 7805 |
| 13 | Tottenham | 22723 | 19 | Peterborough | 12918 | 16 | Blackpool | 7744 |
| 54 | Bristol City | 19146 | 37 | Barnsley | 12759 | 4 | Swindon | 7564 |
| 55 | Bristol City | 16307 | 50 | Colchester | 12633 | 23 | Tranmere | 6853 |
| 31 | Coventry | 16013 | 35 | Oldham | 12579 | 10 | Notts County | 6118 |
| 51 | Bristol City | 15615 | 17 | Tranmere | 12096 | 47 | Wycombe | 5889 |
| 46 | QPR | 15245 | 9 | Brentford | 12032 | 41 | Brentford | 5727 |
| 26 | Bristol City | 15239 | 32 | Coventry | 11997 | 21 | Tranmere | 5592 |
| 52 | Wigan | 14702 | 44 | Blackpool | 11788 | 40 | Stockport | 5385 |
| 24 | QPR | 14345 | 11 | Plymouth | 11606 | 49 | Peterborough | 4984 |
| 38 | Plymouth | 14006 | 33 | Cheltenham | 11605 | 36 | Northampton | 4553 |
| 29 | Huddersfield | 13703 | 8 | Stockport | 11546 | 48 | Chesterfield | 4398 |
| 5 | Luton | 13564 | 42 | Notts County | 11389 | 6 | Cheltenham | 4395 |
| 22 | Chesterfield | 13331 | 20 | Barnsley | 10894 | 39 | Port Vale | 3831 |
| 3 | Northampton | 13321 | 43 | Tranmere | 9637 | 18 | Mansfield | 3441 |
| 2 | Port Vale | 13296 | 53 | Crewe | 9562 | 27 | Colchester | 3096 |
| 12 | Crewe | 13208 | 34 | Huddersfield | 9462 | 7 | Boston | 2280 |
| 15 | Wycombe | 13130 | 14 | Wigan | 8047 | 25 | Margate | 1362 |
| 30 | Swindon | 13062 | 1 | Oldham | 8033 | | | |

## KEY PLAYERS - GOALSCORERS

**1 Robert Earnshaw**

| | | | |
|---|---|---|---|
| Goals in the League | 31 | Player Strike Rate: Average number of minutes between League goals scored by player | 116 |
| Contribution to Attacking Power: Average number of minutes between League team goals while on pitch | 61 | Club Strike Rate: Average number of minutes between League goals scored by club | 61 |

| | PLAYER | LGE GOALS | POWER | STRIKE RATE |
|---|---|---|---|---|
| 2 | Peter Thorne | 13 | 63 | 311 mins |
| 3 | Alan Mahon | 2 | 63 | 571 mins |
| 4 | Andy Legg | 3 | 67 | 770 mins |
| 5 | Graham Kavanagh | 5 | 61 | 770 mins |

## KEY PLAYERS - MIDFIELDERS

**1 Graham Kavanagh**

| | | | |
|---|---|---|---|
| Goals in the League | 5 | Contribution to Attacking Power: Average number of minutes between League team goals while on pitch | 61 |
| Defensive Rating: Average number of mins between League goals conceded while he was on the pitch | 94 | Scoring Difference: Defensive Rating minus Contribution to Attacking Power | 33 |

| | PLAYER | LGE GOALS | DEF RATE | POWER | SCORE DIFF |
|---|---|---|---|---|---|
| 2 | Gareth Whalley | 0 | 89 | 57 | 32 mins |
| 3 | Willie Boland | 0 | 93 | 62 | 31 mins |
| 4 | Andy Legg | 3 | 96 | 68 | 28 mins |
| 5 | Alan Mahon | 2 | 88 | 63 | 25 mins |

## KEY PLAYERS - DEFENDERS

**1 Rhys Weston**

| | | | |
|---|---|---|---|
| Goals Conceded (GC): The number of League goals conceded while he was on the pitch | 31 | Clean Sheets: In games when he played at least 70 minutes | 16 |
| Defensive Rating: Ave number of mins between League goals conceded while on the pitch | 109 | Club Defensive Rating: Average number of mins between League goals conceded by the club this season | 96 |

| | PLAYER | CON LGE | CLEAN SHEETS | DEF RATE |
|---|---|---|---|---|
| 2 | Gary Croft | 33 | 17 | 107 mins |
| 3 | Spencer Prior | 31 | 15 | 101 mins |
| 4 | Daniel Gabbidon | 21 | 8 | 91 mins |
| 5 | Scott Young | 11 | 3 | 91 mins |

## KEY GOALKEEPER

**1 Neil Alexander**

| | |
|---|---|
| Goals Conceded in the League | 36 |
| Defensive Rating: Ave number of mins between League goals conceded while on the pitch | 100 |
| Counting Games: Games when he played at least70 mins | 40 |
| Clean Sheets: In games when he played at least 70 mins | 15 |

## TOP POINT EARNERS

| | PLAYER | GAMES | AVE |
|---|---|---|---|
| 1 | Fortune-West | 4 | 2.25 |
| 2 | Maxwell | 4 | 2.25 |
| 3 | Bowen | 5 | 2.20 |
| 4 | Campbell | 8 | 2.00 |
| 5 | Jenkins | 3 | 2.00 |
| 6 | Weston | 36 | 1.94 |
| 7 | Croft | 39 | 1.90 |
| 8 | Whalley | 14 | 1.86 |
| 9 | Ainsworth | 7 | 1.86 |
| 10 | Gabbidon | 20 | 1.85 |
| | CLUB AVERAGE: | | 1.76 |

Ave = Average points per match in Counting Games

## DISCIPLINARY RECORDS

| | PLAYER | YELLOW | RED | AVE |
|---|---|---|---|---|
| 1 | Bowen | 2 | 0 | 305 |
| 2 | Boland | 11 | 0 | 320 |
| 3 | Kavanagh | 8 | 0 | 481 |
| 4 | Weston | 7 | 0 | 484 |
| 5 | Campbell | 2 | 0 | 500 |
| 6 | Mahon | 2 | 0 | 571 |
| 7 | Fortune-West | 1 | 0 | 638 |
| 8 | Ainsworth | 0 | 1 | 717 |
| 9 | Barker | 4 | 0 | 761 |
| 10 | Prior | 4 | 0 | 783 |
| 11 | Croft | 4 | 0 | 886 |
| 12 | Young | 1 | 0 | 1006 |
| 13 | Legg | 2 | 0 | 1155 |
| | Other | 12 | 1 | |
| | TOTAL | 60 | 2 | |

## LEAGUE GOALS

| | PLAYER | MINS | GOALS | AVE |
|---|---|---|---|---|
| 1 | Earnshaw | 3584 | 31 | 116 |
| 2 | Thorne | 4037 | 13 | 311 |
| 3 | Kavanagh | 3848 | 5 | 770 |
| 4 | Bowen | 610 | 3 | 203 |
| 5 | Campbell | 1001 | 3 | 334 |
| 6 | Legg | 2310 | 3 | 770 |
| 7 | Mahon | 1142 | 2 | 571 |
| 8 | Fortune-West | 638 | 2 | 319 |
| 9 | Gordon | 313 | 2 | 157 |
| 10 | Weston | 3394 | 2 | 1697 |
| 11 | Croft | 3544 | 1 | 3544 |
| 12 | Young | 1006 | 1 | 1006 |
| | Other | | 0 | |
| | TOTAL | | 68 | |

## MONTH BY MONTH GUIDE TO THE POINTS

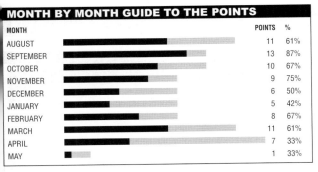

| MONTH | POINTS | % |
|---|---|---|
| AUGUST | 11 | 61% |
| SEPTEMBER | 13 | 87% |
| OCTOBER | 10 | 67% |
| NOVEMBER | 9 | 75% |
| DECEMBER | 6 | 50% |
| JANUARY | 5 | 42% |
| FEBRUARY | 8 | 67% |
| MARCH | 11 | 61% |
| APRIL | 7 | 33% |
| MAY | 1 | 33% |

## TEAM OF THE SEASON

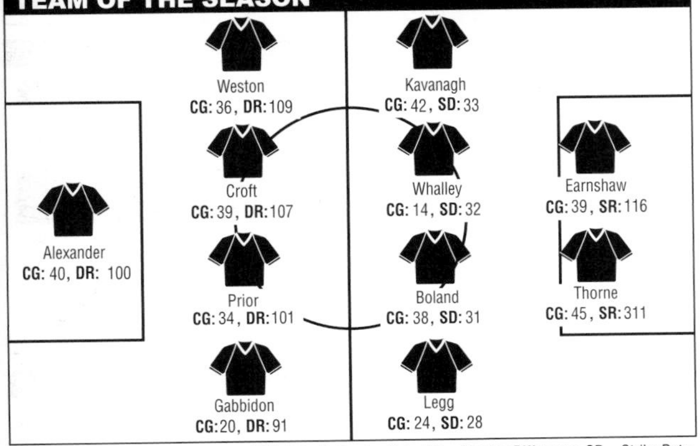
Alexander
CG: 40, DR: 100
Weston
CG: 36, DR: 109
Croft
CG: 39, DR: 107
Prior
CG: 34, DR: 101
Gabbidon
CG: 20, DR: 91
Kavanagh
CG: 42, SD: 33
Whalley
CG: 14, SD: 32
Boland
CG: 38, SD: 31
Legg
CG: 24, SD: 28
Earnshaw
CG: 39, SR: 116
Thorne
CG: 45, SR: 311

**KEY:** DR = Defensive Rate, SD = Scoring Difference, SR = Strike Rate, CG = Counting Games – League games playing at least 70 minutes

## LEAGUE APPEARANCES, BOOKINGS AND CAPS

| | AGE | IN THE SQUAD | COUNTING GAMES | MINUTES ON PITCH | YELLOW CARDS | RED CARDS | THIS SEASON | HOME COUNTRY |
|---|---|---|---|---|---|---|---|---|
| **Goalkeepers** | | | | | | | | |
| Neil Alexander | 25 | 43 | 40 | 3600 | 0 | 0 | 5 | Scotland (64) |
| Martyn Margetson | 31 | 44 | 6 | 540 | 0 | 0 | - | Wales |
| Mark Walton | 34 | 5 | 0 | 0 | 0 | 0 | - | Wales |
| **Defenders** | | | | | | | | |
| Christopher Barker | 23 | 45 | 31 | 3046 | 4 | 0 | - | England |
| Gary Croft | 29 | 45 | 39 | 3544 | 4 | 0 | - | England |
| Daniel Gabbidon | 23 | 24 | 20 | 1920 | 1 | 0 | 3 | Wales (50) |
| Des Hamilton | 26 | 11 | 1 | 201 | 1 | 0 | - | England |
| Stephen Jenkins | 30 | 7 | 3 | 258 | 1 | 0 | - | Wales |
| Spencer Prior | 32 | 39 | 34 | 3134 | 4 | 0 | - | England |
| Rhys Weston | 22 | 39 | 36 | 3394 | 7 | 0 | - | England |
| Scott Young | 27 | 14 | 11 | 1006 | 1 | 0 | - | Wales |
| **Midfielders** | | | | | | | | |
| Gareth Ainsworth | 30 | 9 | 7 | 717 | 0 | 1 | - | England |
| Willie Boland | 27 | 41 | 38 | 3525 | 11 | 0 | - | Rep of Ireland |
| Mark Bonner | 29 | 21 | 6 | 651 | 0 | 0 | - | Wales |
| Jason Bowen | 30 | 20 | 5 | 610 | 2 | 0 | - | Wales |
| Graham Kavanagh | 29 | 44 | 42 | 3848 | 8 | 0 | - | Rep of Ireland |
| Andy Legg | 36 | 43 | 24 | 2310 | 2 | 0 | - | Wales |
| Alan Mahon | 25 | 16 | 12 | 1142 | 2 | 0 | - | Rep of Ireland |
| Leyton Maxwell | 23 | 25 | 4 | 605 | 0 | 0 | - | Wales |
| Gareth Whalley | 29 | 21 | 14 | 1426 | 1 | 0 | - | Rep of Ireland |
| Fan Zhiyi | 33 | 6 | 4 | 448 | 0 | 1 | - | China |
| **Forwards** | | | | | | | | |
| Andy Campbell | 24 | 30 | 8 | 1001 | 2 | 0 | - | England |
| James Collins | 19 | 10 | 0 | 11 | 0 | 0 | - | Wales |
| Robert Earnshaw | 22 | 46 | 39 | 3584 | 3 | 0 | 6 | Wales (50) |
| Leo Fortune-West | 32 | 26 | 4 | 638 | 1 | 0 | - | England |
| Gavin Gordon | 24 | 16 | 1 | 313 | 4 | 0 | - | England |
| Peter Thorne | 30 | 46 | 45 | 4037 | 1 | 0 | - | England |

**KEY:** LEAGUE BOOKINGS CAPS

## SQUAD APPEARANCES

| Match | 1 | 2 | 3 | 4 | 5 | 6 | 7 | 8 | 9 | 10 | 11 | 12 | 13 | 14 | 15 | 16 | 17 | 18 | 19 | 20 | 21 | 22 | 23 | 24 | 25 | 26 | 27 | 28 |
|---|---|---|---|---|---|---|---|---|---|---|---|---|---|---|---|---|---|---|---|---|---|---|---|---|---|---|---|---|
| Venue | A | H | H | A | H | A | A | H | H | A | A | H | A | A | H | A | H | A | H | A | A | H | H | A | A | H | A | A |
| Competition | L | L | L | L | L | L | W | L | L | L | L | L | W | L | L | L | L | L | L | L | F | L | F | L | F | L | L | L |
| Result | W | W | L | W | D | D | W | W | W | W | D | W | L | D | W | L | W | W | W | L | D | W | W | W | W | L | W | L |

| Match | 29 | 30 | 31 | 32 | 33 | 34 | 35 | 36 | 37 | 38 | 39 | 40 | 41 | 42 | 43 | 44 | 45 | 46 | 47 | 48 | 49 | 50 | 51 | 52 | 53 | 54 | 55 | 56 |
|---|---|---|---|---|---|---|---|---|---|---|---|---|---|---|---|---|---|---|---|---|---|---|---|---|---|---|---|---|
| Venue | H | H | H | A | H | A | H | A | H | H | A | A | A | H | A | H | H | H | A | A | A | H | A | H | A | H | A | N |
| Competition | L | L | F | F | L | L | L | L | L | L | L | L | L | L | L | L | L | L | L | L | L | L | L | L | L | O | O | O |
| Result | W | D | D | L | W | L | D | W | D | D | W | D | W | L | D | W | W | L | W | W | L | L | L | D | D | W | D | D |

**Goalkeepers**
Neil Alexander
Martyn Margetson
Mark Walton

**Defenders**
Christopher Barker
Gary Croft
Daniel Gabbidon
Des Hamilton
Stephen Jenkins
Spencer Prior
Rhys Weston
Scott Young

**Midfielders**
Gareth Ainsworth
Willie Boland
Mark Bonner
Jason Bowen
Graham Kavanagh
Andy Legg
Alan Mahon
Leyton Maxwell
Gareth Whalley
Fan Zhiyi

**Forwards**
Andy Campbell
James Collins
Robert Earnshaw
Leo Fortune-West
Gavin Gordon
Peter Thorne

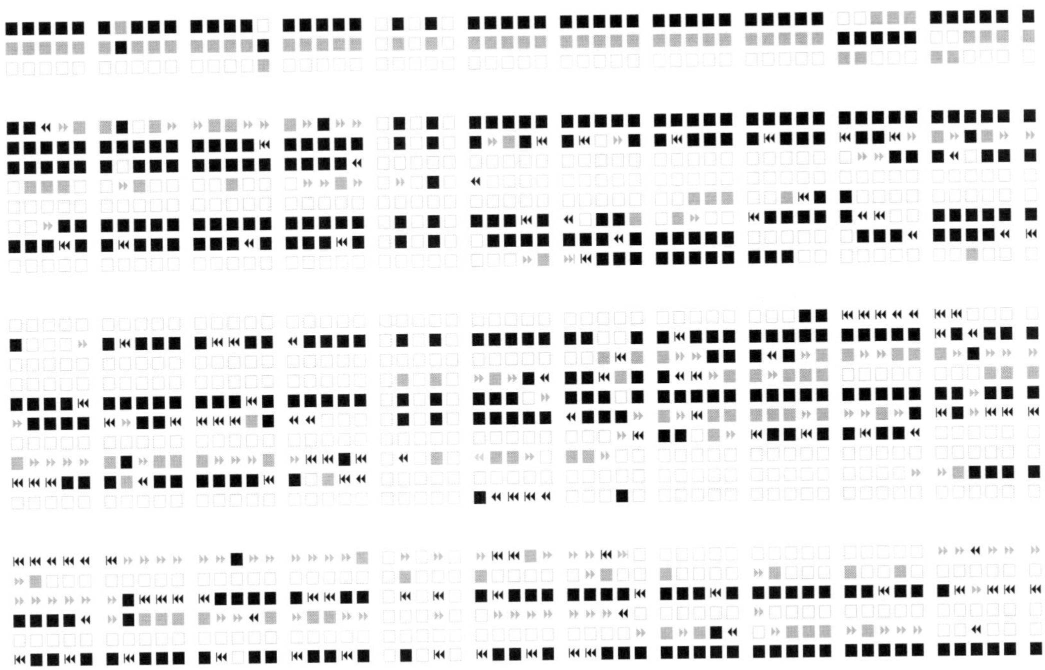

# TRANMERE ROVERS

Final Position: **7th**

NICKNAME: ROVERS

| | | | | | | |
|---|---|---|---|---|---|---|
| 1 | div2 | Port Vale | A | W | 4-1 | Koumas 40; Haworth 45,81; Allen 47 |
| 2 | div2 | Colchester | H | D | 1-1 | Koumas 15 |
| 3 | div2 | Cheltenham | H | W | 1-0 | Barlow 60 |
| 4 | div2 | Oldham | A | L | 0-2 | |
| 5 | div2 | Huddersfield | H | W | 2-1 | Price 71; Gray 77 |
| 6 | div2 | Bristol City | A | L | 0-2 | |
| 7 | div2 | Blackpool | A | L | 0-3 | |
| 8 | wcr1 | Hartlepool | A | W | 2-1 | Haworth 36; Taylor 82 |
| 9 | div2 | Brentford | H | W | 3-1 | Haworth 44,66; Price 85 |
| 10 | div2 | Wigan | H | L | 0-2 | |
| 11 | div2 | Crewe | A | L | 0-2 | |
| 12 | div2 | Stockport | H | W | 1-0 | Haworth 16 |
| 13 | wcr2 | Southampton | A | L | 1-6 | Allen 21 |
| 14 | div2 | Mansfield | A | L | 1-6 | Hay 13 |
| 15 | div2 | Chesterfield | A | L | 0-1 | |
| 16 | div2 | Barnsley | H | W | 1-0 | Allen 2 |
| 17 | div2 | Cardiff | A | L | 0-4 | |
| 18 | div2 | Peterborough | H | D | 1-1 | Hume 53 |
| 19 | div2 | Plymouth | H | W | 2-1 | Roberts 87; Wotton 90 og |
| 20 | div2 | Swindon | A | D | 1-1 | Jones 80 |
| 21 | facr1 | Cardiff | H | D | 2-2 | Barlow 7; Howarth 62 |
| 22 | div2 | Wycombe | A | W | 3-1 | Barlow 63,90; Haworth 67 |
| 23 | facr1r | Cardiff | A | L | 1-2 | Mellon 45 |
| 24 | div2 | Luton | H | L | 1-3 | Roberts 24 |
| 25 | div2 | Northampton | A | W | 4-0 | Haworth 10,66; Taylor 71; Hay 76 |
| 26 | div2 | Notts County | H | D | 2-2 | Allen 1; Haworth 11 |
| 27 | div2 | Huddersfield | A | W | 2-1 | Nicholson 58 pen; Roberts 77 |
| 28 | div2 | QPR | H | W | 3-0 | Haworth 54; Jones 60,71 |
| 29 | div2 | Oldham | H | L | 1-2 | Howarth 59 |
| 30 | div2 | Colchester | A | D | 2-2 | Haworth 38; Mellon 60 |
| 31 | div2 | Bristol City | H | D | 1-1 | Haworth 61 |
| 32 | div2 | QPR | A | W | 2-1 | Robinson 80; Haworth 90 |
| 33 | div2 | Port Vale | H | W | 1-0 | McClare 31 og |
| 34 | div2 | Cheltenham | A | L | 1-3 | Sharps 50 |
| 35 | div2 | Swindon | H | L | 0-1 | |
| 36 | div2 | Plymouth | A | W | 1-0 | Haworth 57 |
| 37 | div2 | Blackpool | H | W | 2-1 | Hume 14,70 |
| 38 | div2 | Brentford | A | W | 2-1 | Hume 20; Sharps 48 |
| 39 | div2 | Wigan | A | D | 0-0 | |
| 40 | div2 | Crewe | H | W | 2-1 | Price 43; Sharps 88 |
| 41 | div2 | Cardiff | H | D | 3-3 | Haworth 47; Hume 78; Jones 89 |
| 42 | div2 | Barnsley | A | D | 1-1 | Nicholson 49 pen |
| 43 | div2 | Peterborough | A | D | 0-0 | |
| 44 | div2 | Chesterfield | H | W | 2-1 | Anderson 30; Hume 51 |
| 45 | div2 | Luton | A | D | 0-0 | |
| 46 | div2 | Wycombe | H | W | 1-0 | Jones 90 |
| 47 | div2 | Notts County | A | W | 1-0 | Haworth 65 |
| 48 | div2 | Northampton | H | W | 4-0 | Nicholson 59 pen; Haworth 60; Anderson 90; Hay 90 |
| 49 | div2 | Mansfield | H | W | 3-1 | Jones 15; Haworth 81; Price 90 |
| 50 | div2 | Stockport | A | W | 3-2 | Nicholson 48 pen; Haworth 70; Jones 81 |

## ATTENDANCES

HOME GROUND: PRENTON PARK CAPACITY: 16789 AVERAGE LEAGUE AT HOME: 7876

| | | | | | | | | |
|---|---|---|---|---|---|---|---|---|
| 13 | Southampton | 16603 | 10 | Wigan | 8153 | 45 | Luton | 6326 |
| 32 | QPR | 12249 | 5 | Huddersfield | 7534 | 18 | Peterborough | 5980 |
| 17 | Cardiff | 12096 | 12 | Stockport | 7513 | 4 | Oldham | 5933 |
| 27 | Huddersfield | 11002 | 2 | Colchester | 7499 | 47 | Notts County | 5715 |
| 49 | Mansfield | 10418 | 33 | Port Vale | 7461 | 1 | Port Vale | 5629 |
| 6 | Bristol City | 9849 | 31 | Bristol City | 7459 | 21 | Cardiff | 5592 |
| 29 | Oldham | 9795 | 48 | Northampton | 7348 | 38 | Brentford | 5396 |
| 41 | Cardiff | 9637 | 50 | Stockport | 7236 | 22 | Wycombe | 5386 |
| 37 | Blackpool | 9111 | 35 | Swindon | 7181 | 20 | Swindon | 5077 |
| 39 | Wigan | 9021 | 19 | Plymouth | 7083 | 25 | Northampton | 4268 |
| 42 | Barnsley | 8786 | 11 | Crewe | 6875 | 43 | Peterborough | 4158 |
| 40 | Crewe | 8670 | 16 | Barnsley | 6855 | 15 | Chesterfield | 4111 |
| 36 | Plymouth | 8590 | 23 | Cardiff | 6853 | 34 | Cheltenham | 3936 |
| 28 | QPR | 8434 | 7 | Blackpool | 6834 | 14 | Mansfield | 3668 |
| 26 | Notts County | 8275 | 46 | Wycombe | 6814 | 30 | Colchester | 2846 |
| 24 | Luton | 8273 | 3 | Cheltenham | 6807 | 8 | Hartlepool | 2778 |
| 44 | Chesterfield | 8238 | 9 | Brentford | 6626 | | | |

■ Home □ Away ▒ Neutral

## KEY PLAYERS - GOALSCORERS

**1 Simon Haworth**

| | | | |
|---|---|---|---|
| Goals in the League | 19 | Player Strike Rate<br>Average number of minutes between League goals scored by player | 196 |
| Contribution to Attacking Power<br>Average number of minutes between League team goals while on pitch | 60 | Club Strike Rate<br>Average number of minutes between League goals scored by club | 63 |

| | PLAYER | LGE GOALS | POWER | STRIKE RATE |
|---|---|---|---|---|
| 2 | Iain Hulme | 6 | 62 | 346 mins |
| 3 | Gary Jones | 7 | 61 | 507 mins |
| 4 | Stuart Barlow | 3 | 57 | 595 mins |
| 5 | Shane Nicholson | 4 | 66 | 762 mins |

## KEY PLAYERS - MIDFIELDERS

**1 Ian Sharps**

| | | | |
|---|---|---|---|
| Goals in the League | 3 | Contribution to Attacking Power<br>Average number of minutes between League team goals while on pitch | 62 |
| Defensive Rating<br>Average number of mins between League goals conceded while he was on the pitch | 93 | Scoring Difference<br>Defensive Rating minus Contribution to Attacking Power | 31 |

| | PLAYER | LGE GOALS | DEF RATE | POWER | SCORE DIFF |
|---|---|---|---|---|---|
| 2 | Micky Mellon | 1 | 67 | 57 | 10 mins |
| 3 | Ryan Taylor | 1 | 61 | 73 | -12 mins |

## KEY PLAYERS - DEFENDERS

**1 Tyrone Loran**

| | | | |
|---|---|---|---|
| Goals Conceded (GC)<br>The number of League goals conceded while he was on the pitch | 13 | Clean Sheets<br>In games when he played at least 70 minutes | 6 |
| Defensive Rating<br>Ave number of mins between League goals conceded while on the pitch | 102 | Club Defensive Rating<br>Average number of mins between League goals conceded by the club this season | 73 |

| | PLAYER | CON LGE | CLEAN SHEETS | DEF RATE |
|---|---|---|---|---|
| 2 | Sean Connelly | 32 | 11 | 91 mins |
| 3 | Gareth Roberts | 39 | 10 | 80 mins |
| 4 | Shane Nicholson | 41 | 10 | 74 mins |
| 5 | Graham Allen | 50 | 11 | 73 mins |

## KEY GOALKEEPER

**1 John Achterberg**

| | |
|---|---|
| Goals Conceded in the League | 45 |
| Defensive Rating<br>Ave number of mins between League goals conceded while on the pitch | 75 |
| Counting Games<br>Games when he played at least 70 mins | 37 |
| Clean Sheets<br>In games when he played at least 70 mins | 9 |

## TOP POINT EARNERS

| | PLAYER | GAMES | AVE |
|---|---|---|---|
| 1 | Anderson | 7 | 2.71 |
| 2 | Loran | 14 | 2.14 |
| 3 | Howarth | 2 | 2.00 |
| 4 | Price | 7 | 2.00 |
| 5 | Feuer | 2 | 2.00 |
| 6 | Sharps | 28 | 1.96 |
| 7 | Nicholson | 32 | 1.94 |
| 8 | Hulme | 17 | 1.94 |
| 9 | Connelly | 32 | 1.91 |
| 10 | Haworth | 40 | 1.83 |
| | CLUB AVERAGE: | | 1.74 |

Ave = Average points per match in Counting Games

## DISCIPLINARY RECORDS

| | PLAYER | YELLOW | RED | AVE |
|---|---|---|---|---|
| 1 | Hinds | 2 | 0 | 249 |
| 2 | Edwards | 4 | 0 | 270 |
| 3 | Gray | 2 | 0 | 374 |
| 4 | Jones | 9 | 0 | 394 |
| 5 | Taylor | 3 | 1 | 399 |
| 6 | Roberts | 7 | 0 | 447 |
| 7 | Mellon | 6 | 0 | 448 |
| 8 | Allen | 6 | 2 | 455 |
| 9 | Haworth | 5 | 2 | 531 |
| 10 | Jackson | 1 | 0 | 540 |
| 11 | Nicholson | 5 | 0 | 609 |
| 12 | Loran | 2 | 0 | 666 |
| 13 | Harrison | 1 | 0 | 707 |
| | Other | 11 | 0 | |
| | TOTAL | 64 | 5 | |

## LEAGUE GOALS

| | PLAYER | MINS | GOALS | AVE |
|---|---|---|---|---|
| 1 | Haworth | 3719 | 19 | 196 |
| 2 | Jones | 3547 | 7 | 507 |
| 3 | Hulme | 2073 | 6 | 346 |
| 4 | Price | 1251 | 4 | 313 |
| 5 | Nicholson | 3047 | 4 | 762 |
| 6 | Barlow | 1785 | 3 | 595 |
| 7 | Hay | 1013 | 3 | 338 |
| 8 | Allen | 3645 | 3 | 1215 |
| 9 | Roberts | 3131 | 3 | 1044 |
| 10 | Sharps | 2591 | 3 | 864 |
| 11 | Koumas | 360 | 2 | 180 |
| 12 | Anderson | 615 | 2 | 308 |
| 13 | Gray | 749 | 1 | 749 |
| | Other | | 6 | |
| | TOTAL | | 66 | |

## MONTH BY MONTH GUIDE TO THE POINTS

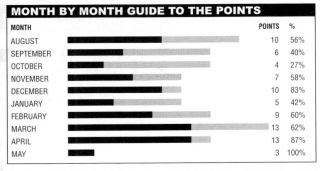

| MONTH | POINTS | % |
|---|---|---|
| AUGUST | 10 | 56% |
| SEPTEMBER | 6 | 40% |
| OCTOBER | 4 | 27% |
| NOVEMBER | 7 | 58% |
| DECEMBER | 10 | 83% |
| JANUARY | 5 | 42% |
| FEBRUARY | 9 | 60% |
| MARCH | 13 | 62% |
| APRIL | 13 | 87% |
| MAY | 3 | 100% |

## TEAM OF THE SEASON

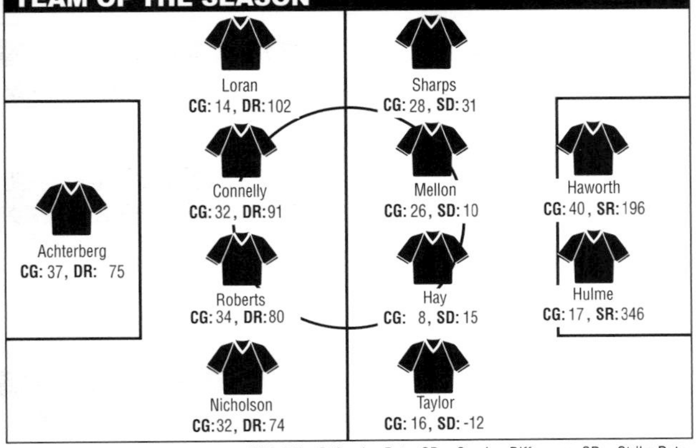
Achterberg
CG: 37, DR: 75
Loran
CG: 14, DR: 102
Connelly
CG: 32, DR: 91
Roberts
CG: 34, DR: 80
Nicholson
CG: 32, DR: 74
Sharps
CG: 28, SD: 31
Mellon
CG: 26, SD: 10
Hay
CG: 8, SD: 15
Taylor
CG: 16, SD: -12
Haworth
CG: 40, SR: 196
Hulme
CG: 17, SR: 346

**KEY:** DR = Defensive Rate, SD = Scoring Difference, SR = Strike Rate, CG = Counting Games – League games playing at least 70 minutes

## LEAGUE APPEARANCES, BOOKINGS AND CAPS

| | AGE | IN THE SQUAD | COUNTING GAMES | MINUTES ON PITCH | YELLOW CARDS | RED CARDS | THIS SEASON | HOME COUNTRY |
|---|---|---|---|---|---|---|---|---|
| **Goalkeepers** | | | | | | | | |
| John Achterberg | 32 | 41 | 37 | 3386 | 0 | 0 | - | Holland |
| Ian Feuer | 32 | 2 | 2 | 180 | 0 | 0 | - | United States |
| Russell Howarth | 21 | 28 | 2 | 214 | 0 | 0 | - | England |
| Eric Nixon | 40 | 7 | 0 | 61 | 0 | 0 | - | England |
| Philip Palethorpe | - | 1 | 0 | 0 | 0 | 0 | - | England |
| Keith Welch | 34 | 7 | 1 | 119 | 0 | 0 | - | England |
| Phil Whitehead | 33 | 6 | 2 | 180 | 0 | 0 | - | England |
| **Defenders** | | | | | | | | |
| Graham Allen | 26 | 42 | 40 | 3645 | 6 | 2 | - | England |
| Sean Connelly | 33 | 33 | 32 | 2917 | 2 | 0 | - | England |
| Christian Edwards | 27 | 13 | 12 | 1080 | 4 | 0 | 1 | Wales (50) |
| Kevin Gray | 31 | 15 | 7 | 749 | 2 | 0 | - | England |
| Richard Hinds | 22 | 25 | 5 | 498 | 2 | 0 | - | England |
| Michael Jackson | 29 | 6 | 6 | 540 | 1 | 0 | - | England |
| Tyrone Loran | 22 | 18 | 14 | 1332 | 2 | 0 | - | Holland |
| Pat McGibbon | 29 | 4 | 4 | 360 | 0 | 0 | - | |
| Alan Navarro | 22 | 5 | 4 | 373 | 1 | 0 | - | England |
| Shane Nicholson | 33 | 38 | 32 | 3047 | 5 | 0 | - | England |
| James Olsen | 21 | 11 | 1 | 123 | 0 | 0 | - | England |
| Gareth Roberts | 25 | 37 | 34 | 3131 | 7 | 0 | - | Wales |
| **Midfielders** | | | | | | | | |
| Iain Anderson | 25 | 7 | 7 | 615 | 0 | 0 | - | Scotland |
| Tom Curtis | 30 | 8 | 7 | 659 | 0 | 0 | - | England |
| Danny Harrison | 20 | 18 | 6 | 707 | 1 | 0 | - | England |
| Alex Hay | 21 | 32 | 8 | 1013 | 1 | 0 | - | England |
| Jason Koumas | 23 | 4 | 4 | 360 | 0 | 0 | 3 | Wales (50) |
| Micky Mellon | 31 | 43 | 26 | 2690 | 6 | 0 | - | England |
| Jason Price | 26 | 27 | 7 | 1251 | 1 | 0 | - | Cardiff |
| Ian Sharps | 22 | 39 | 28 | 2591 | 2 | 0 | - | England |
| Ryan Taylor | 18 | 30 | 16 | 1596 | 3 | 1 | - | England |
| **Forwards** | | | | | | | | |
| Stuart Barlow | 34 | 33 | 17 | 1785 | 1 | 0 | - | England |
| Simon Haworth | 26 | 42 | 40 | 3719 | 5 | 2 | - | Wales |
| Iain Hulme | 19 | 40 | 17 | 2073 | 2 | 0 | - | England |
| Gary Jones | 28 | 40 | 39 | 3547 | 9 | 0 | - | England |
| James McGuire | 19 | 4 | 0 | 0 | 0 | 0 | - | England |
| Andy Parkinson | 24 | 16 | 2 | 314 | 0 | 0 | - | England |
| Adam Proudlock | 22 | 5 | 5 | 450 | 1 | 0 | - | England |
| Andy Robinson | - | 10 | 1 | 143 | 0 | 0 | - | England |

**KEY:** LEAGUE BOOKINGS CAPS

## SQUAD APPEARANCES

| Match | 1 | 2 | 3 | 4 | 5 | 6 | 7 | 8 | 9 | 10 | 11 | 12 | 13 | 14 | 15 | 16 | 17 | 18 | 19 | 20 | 21 | 22 | 23 | 24 | 25 |
|---|---|---|---|---|---|---|---|---|---|---|---|---|---|---|---|---|---|---|---|---|---|---|---|---|---|
| Venue | A | H | H | A | H | A | A | A | H | H | A | H | A | A | A | H | A | H | H | A | H | A | A | H | A |
| Competition | L | L | L | L | L | L | L | W | L | L | L | L | W | L | L | L | L | L | L | L | F | L | F | L | L |
| Result | W | D | W | L | W | L | L | W | W | L | L | W | L | L | L | W | L | D | W | D | D | W | L | L | W |

| Match | 26 | 27 | 28 | 29 | 30 | 31 | 32 | 33 | 34 | 35 | 36 | 37 | 38 | 39 | 40 | 41 | 42 | 43 | 44 | 45 | 46 | 47 | 48 | 49 | 50 |
|---|---|---|---|---|---|---|---|---|---|---|---|---|---|---|---|---|---|---|---|---|---|---|---|---|---|
| Venue | H | A | H | H | A | H | A | H | A | H | A | H | A | A | H | H | A | A | H | A | H | A | H | H | A |
| Competition | L | L | L | L | L | L | L | L | L | L | L | L | L | L | L | L | L | L | L | L | L | L | L | L | L |
| Result | D | W | W | L | D | D | W | W | L | L | W | W | W | D | W | D | D | D | W | D | W | W | W | W | W |

**Goalkeepers**
John Achterberg
Ian Feuer
Russell Howarth
Eric Nixon
Philip Palethorpe
Keith Welch
Phil Whitehead

**Defenders**
Graham Allen
Sean Connelly
Christian Edwards
Kevin Gray
Richard Hinds
Michael Jackson
Tyrone Loran
Pat McGibbon
Alan Navarro
Shane Nicholson
James Olsen
Gareth Roberts

**Midfielders**
Iain Anderson
Tom Curtis
Danny Harrison
Alex Hay
Jason Koumas
Micky Mellon
Jason Price
Ian Sharps
Ryan Taylor

**Forwards**
Stuart Barlow
Simon Haworth
Iain Hulme
Gary Jones
James McGuire
Andy Parkinson
Adam Proudlock
Andy Robinson

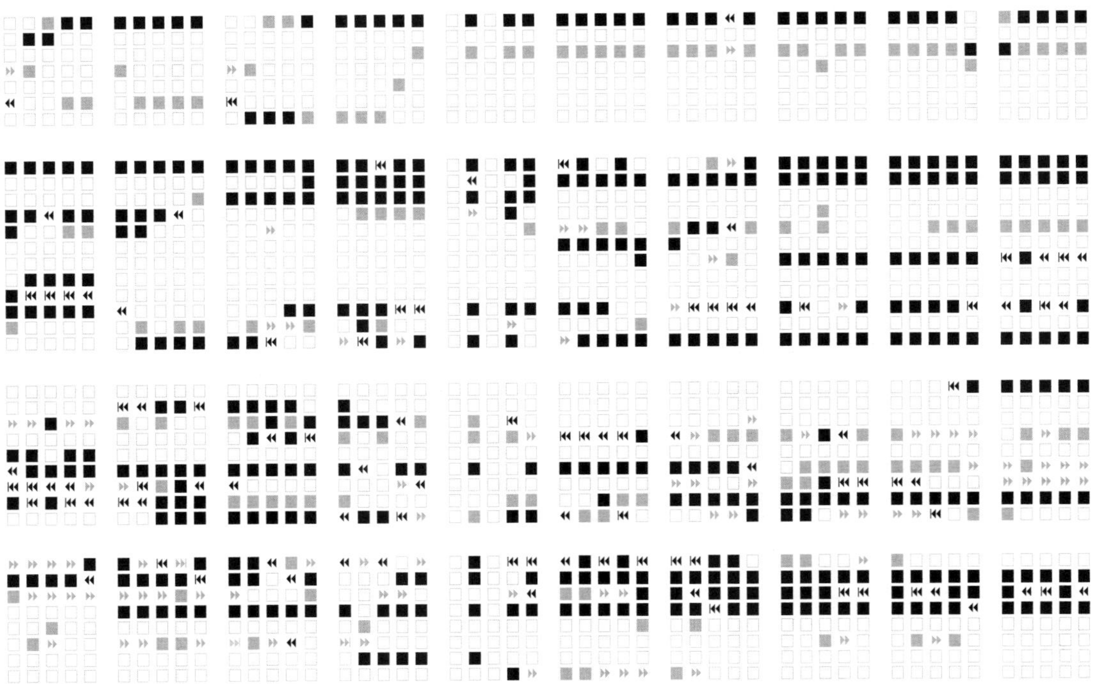

# PLYMOUTH ARGYLE

Final Position: **8th**

NICKNAME: THE PILGRIMS

| | | | | | | |
|---|---|---|---|---|---|---|
| 1 | div2 | Mansfield | A | L | 3-4 | Evans 24; Friio 85; Lowndes 90 |
| 2 | div2 | Huddersfield | H | W | 2-1 | Friio 57; Wotton 90 |
| 3 | div2 | Luton | H | W | 2-1 | McGlinchey 56; Wotton 82 |
| 4 | div2 | Cheltenham | A | W | 2-1 | Coughlan 60; Wotton 75 |
| 5 | div2 | Bristol City | H | W | 2-0 | Wotton 65 pen; Coughlan 81 |
| 6 | div2 | QPR | A | D | 2-2 | Friio 33; Hodges, L 58 |
| 7 | wcr1 | Crystal Palace | A | L | 1-2 | Sturrock 38 |
| 8 | div2 | Barnsley | A | D | 1-1 | Sturrock 38 |
| 9 | div2 | Peterborough | A | L | 0-2 | |
| 10 | div2 | Chesterfield | H | L | 0-1 | |
| 11 | div2 | Cardiff | H | D | 2-2 | Wotton 8; Coughlan 90 |
| 12 | div2 | Wycombe | A | L | 1-2 | Friio 60 |
| 13 | div2 | Northampton | H | D | 0-0 | |
| 14 | div2 | Wigan | H | L | 1-3 | Stonebridge 17 |
| 15 | div2 | Crewe | A | W | 1-0 | Norris 45 |
| 16 | div2 | Blackpool | H | L | 1-3 | Keith 60 |
| 17 | div2 | Brentford | A | D | 0-0 | |
| 18 | div2 | Tranmere | A | L | 1-2 | Adams 6 |
| 19 | div2 | Oldham | H | D | 2-2 | Stonebridge 4; Friio 7 |
| 20 | facr1 | Bury | A | W | 3-0 | Evans 19; Nelson 32 og; Wotton 86 |
| 21 | div2 | Stockport | H | W | 4-1 | Goodwin 6 og,60 og; Keith 13; Adams 42 |
| 22 | div2 | Colchester | A | D | 0-0 | |
| 23 | facr2 | Stockport | A | W | 3-0 | Stonebridge 9; Friio 14; Wotton 72 pen |
| 24 | div2 | Swindon | H | D | 1-1 | Hodges, L 90 pen |
| 25 | div2 | Port Vale | A | W | 2-1 | Evans 2; Keith 40 |
| 26 | div2 | Bristol City | A | D | 0-0 | |
| 27 | div2 | Notts County | H | W | 1-0 | Aljofree 61 |
| 28 | div2 | Cheltenham | H | W | 3-1 | Phillips 22; Stonebridge 34; Norris 53 |
| 29 | facr3 | Dag & Red | H | D | 2-2 | Stonebridge 44; Wotton 61 |
| 30 | facr3r | Dag & Red | A | L | 0-2 | |
| 31 | div2 | QPR | H | L | 0-1 | |
| 32 | div2 | Notts County | A | W | 2-0 | Norris 38,50 |
| 33 | div2 | Mansfield | H | W | 3-1 | Lawrence 2 og; Phillips 68; Evans 84 |
| 34 | div2 | Huddersfield | A | L | 0-1 | |
| 35 | div2 | Oldham | A | W | 1-0 | Evans 39 |
| 36 | div2 | Tranmere | H | L | 0-1 | |
| 37 | div2 | Cardiff | A | D | 1-1 | Wotton 86 |
| 38 | div2 | Luton | A | L | 0-1 | |
| 39 | div2 | Barnsley | H | D | 1-1 | Coughlan 14 |
| 40 | div2 | Peterborough | H | W | 6-1 | Keith 9; Burton 25 og; Gill 42 og; Wotton 45; Friio 62; Bent 72 |
| 41 | div2 | Chesterfield | A | L | 2-3 | Keith 15,74 |
| 42 | div2 | Blackpool | A | D | 1-1 | Keith 29 |
| 43 | div2 | Crewe | H | L | 1-3 | Stonebridge 47 |
| 44 | div2 | Brentford | H | W | 3-0 | Keith 12,47; Smith, G 28 |
| 45 | div2 | Wigan | A | W | 1-0 | Keith 35 |
| 46 | div2 | Colchester | H | D | 0-0 | |
| 47 | div2 | Stockport | A | L | 1-2 | Keith 72 |
| 48 | div2 | Port Vale | H | W | 3-0 | Coughlan 56; Norris 67; Wotton 77 |
| 49 | div2 | Swindon | A | L | 0-2 | |
| 50 | div2 | Northampton | A | D | 2-2 | Norris 19; Stonebridge 55 |
| 51 | div2 | Wycombe | H | W | 1-0 | Lowndes 75 |

## ATTENDANCES

HOME GROUND: HOME PARK CAPACITY: 18600 AVERAGE LEAGUE AT HOME: 8980

| | | | | | | | | |
|---|---|---|---|---|---|---|---|---|
| 26 | Bristol City | 18085 | 13 | Northampton | 8530 | 17 | Brentford | 6431 |
| 37 | Cardiff | 14006 | 39 | Barnsley | 8228 | 7 | Crystal Palace | 6385 |
| 6 | QPR | 14001 | 19 | Oldham | 8216 | 32 | Notts County | 6329 |
| 5 | Bristol City | 11922 | 24 | Swindon | 8111 | 47 | Stockport | 5484 |
| 27 | Notts County | 11901 | 33 | Mansfield | 8030 | 1 | Mansfield | 5309 |
| 29 | Dag & Red | 11885 | 43 | Crewe | 7777 | 50 | Northampton | 5063 |
| 11 | Cardiff | 11606 | 48 | Port Vale | 7775 | 49 | Swindon | 5057 |
| 3 | Luton | 10973 | 21 | Stockport | 7746 | 25 | Port Vale | 4892 |
| 28 | Cheltenham | 10927 | 38 | Luton | 7589 | 4 | Cheltenham | 4713 |
| 31 | QPR | 10249 | 34 | Huddersfield | 7294 | 30 | Dag & Red | 4530 |
| 51 | Wycombe | 10129 | 45 | Wigan | 7203 | 9 | Peterborough | 4208 |
| 8 | Barnsley | 9134 | 46 | Colchester | 7122 | 22 | Colchester | 3714 |
| 2 | Huddersfield | 8953 | 18 | Tranmere | 7083 | 41 | Chesterfield | 3668 |
| 42 | Blackpool | 8772 | 40 | Peterborough | 6931 | 23 | Stockport | 3571 |
| 14 | Wigan | 8746 | 44 | Brentford | 6835 | 20 | Bury | 2987 |
| 16 | Blackpool | 8717 | 15 | Crewe | 6733 | | | |
| 36 | Tranmere | 8590 | 12 | Wycombe | 6708 | | | |
| 10 | Chesterfield | 8547 | 35 | Oldham | 6657 | | | |

■ Home □ Away ▒ Neutral

## KEY PLAYERS - GOALSCORERS

**1 Marino Keith**

| | | | |
|---|---|---|---|
| Goals in the League | 11 | **Player Strike Rate** Average number of minutes between League goals scored by player | 179 |
| **Contribution to Attacking Power** Average number of minutes between League team goals while on pitch | 63 | **Club Strike Rate** Average number of minutes between League goals scored by club | 66 |

| | PLAYER | LGE GOALS | POWER | STRIKE RATE |
|---|---|---|---|---|
| 2 | David Norris | 6 | 73 | 440 mins |
| 3 | Paul Wotton | 8 | 68 | 454 mins |
| 4 | David Friio | 6 | 64 | 483 mins |
| 5 | Ian Stonebridge | 5 | 75 | 500 mins |

## KEY PLAYERS - MIDFIELDERS

**1 Jason Bent**

| | | | |
|---|---|---|---|
| Goals in the League | 1 | **Contribution to Attacking Power** Average number of minutes between League team goals while on pitch | 55 |
| **Defensive Rating** Average number of mins between League goals conceded while he was on the pitch | 91 | **Scoring Difference** Defensive Rating minus Contribution to Attacking Power | 36 |

| | PLAYER | LGE GOALS | DEF RATE | POWER | SCORE DIFF |
|---|---|---|---|---|---|
| 2 | Martin Phillips | 2 | 63 | 53 | 10 mins |
| 3 | David Friio | 6 | 74 | 64 | 10 mins |
| 4 | Brian McGlinchey | 1 | 71 | 95 | -24 mins |

## KEY PLAYERS - DEFENDERS

**1 Hasney Aljofree**

| | | | |
|---|---|---|---|
| **Goals Conceded (GC)** The number of League goals conceded while he was on the pitch | 18 | **Clean Sheets** In games when he played at least 70 minutes | 7 |
| **Defensive Rating** Ave number of mins between League goals conceded while on the pitch | 92 | **Club Defensive Rating** Average number of mins between League goals conceded by the club this season | 80 |

| | PLAYER | CON LGE | CLEAN SHEETS | DEF RATE |
|---|---|---|---|---|
| 2 | Paul Wotton | 46 | 12 | 79 mins |
| 3 | Graham Coughlan | 48 | 12 | 78 mins |
| 4 | David Worrell | 50 | 12 | 78 mins |
| 5 | Steve Adams | 43 | 10 | 75 mins |

## KEY GOALKEEPER

**1 Romain Larrieu**

| | |
|---|---|
| Goals Conceded in the League | 48 |
| **Defensive Rating** Ave number of mins between League goals conceded while on the pitch | 81 |
| **Counting Games** Games when he played at least 70 mins | 43 |
| **Clean Sheets** In games when he played at least 70 mins | 13 |

## TOP POINT EARNERS

| | PLAYER | GAMES | AVE |
|---|---|---|---|
| 1 | Smith | 4 | 2.00 |
| 2 | Connolly | 2 | 2.00 |
| 3 | Malcolm | 3 | 2.00 |
| 4 | Beresford | 3 | 2.00 |
| 5 | Bent | 20 | 1.85 |
| 6 | Lowndes | 5 | 1.80 |
| 7 | Barras | 3 | 1.67 |
| 8 | Sturrock | 5 | 1.60 |
| 9 | Norris | 28 | 1.57 |
| 10 | Aljofree | 17 | 1.53 |
| | CLUB AVERAGE: | | 1.41 |

Ave = Average points per match in Counting Games

## DISCIPLINARY RECORDS

| | PLAYER | YELLOW | RED | AVE |
|---|---|---|---|---|
| 1 | Lowndes | 4 | 0 | 169 |
| 2 | McGlinchey | 4 | 1 | 227 |
| 3 | Friio | 8 | 0 | 362 |
| 4 | Phillips | 3 | 0 | 440 |
| 5 | Aljofree | 3 | 0 | 549 |
| 6 | Wotton | 6 | 0 | 605 |
| 7 | Bernard | 1 | 0 | 636 |
| 8 | Bent | 2 | 1 | 640 |
| 9 | Norris | 4 | 0 | 659 |
| 10 | Worrell | 4 | 0 | 971 |
| 11 | Keith | 2 | 0 | 983 |
| 12 | Evans | 2 | 0 | 1467 |
| 13 | Adams | 2 | 0 | 1613 |
| | Other | 6 | 0 | |
| | TOTAL | 51 | 2 | |

## LEAGUE GOALS

| | PLAYER | MINS | GOALS | AVE |
|---|---|---|---|---|
| 1 | Keith | 1966 | 11 | 179 |
| 2 | Wotton | 3633 | 8 | 454 |
| 3 | Friio | 2898 | 6 | 483 |
| 4 | Norris | 2639 | 6 | 440 |
| 5 | Coughlan | 3727 | 5 | 745 |
| 6 | Stonebridge | 2502 | 5 | 500 |
| 7 | Evans | 2935 | 4 | 734 |
| 8 | Adams | 3227 | 2 | 1614 |
| 9 | Lowndes | 678 | 2 | 339 |
| 10 | Hodges | 3271 | 2 | 1636 |
| 11 | Phillips | 1321 | 2 | 661 |
| 12 | Smith | 345 | 1 | 345 |
| 13 | Sturrock | 743 | 1 | 743 |
| | Other | | 8 | |
| | TOTAL | | 63 | |

## MONTH BY MONTH GUIDE TO THE POINTS

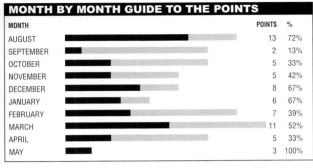

| MONTH | POINTS | % |
|---|---|---|
| AUGUST | 13 | 72% |
| SEPTEMBER | 2 | 13% |
| OCTOBER | 5 | 33% |
| NOVEMBER | 5 | 42% |
| DECEMBER | 8 | 67% |
| JANUARY | 6 | 67% |
| FEBRUARY | 7 | 39% |
| MARCH | 11 | 52% |
| APRIL | 5 | 33% |
| MAY | 3 | 100% |

## TEAM OF THE SEASON

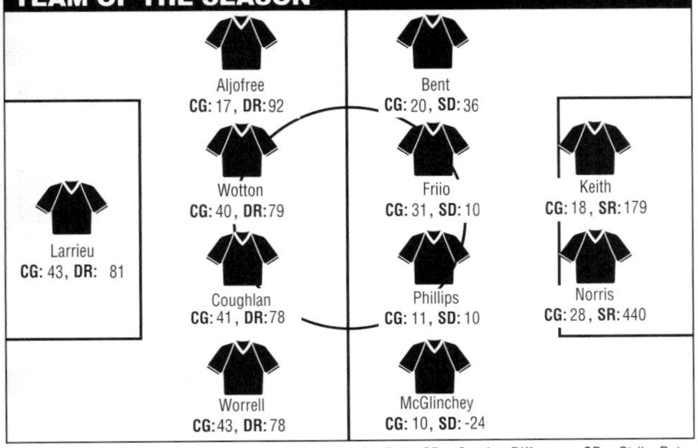

Larrieu
CG: 43, DR: 81
Aljofree
CG: 17, DR: 92
Wotton
CG: 40, DR: 79
Coughlan
CG: 41, DR: 78
Worrell
CG: 43, DR: 78
Bent
CG: 20, SD: 36
Friio
CG: 31, SD: 10
Phillips
CG: 11, SD: 10
McGlinchey
CG: 10, SD: -24
Keith
CG: 18, SR: 179
Norris
CG: 28, SR: 440


KEY: DR = Defensive Rate, SD = Scoring Difference, SR = Strike Rate, CG = Counting Games – League games playing at least 70 minutes

## LEAGUE APPEARANCES, BOOKINGS AND CAPS

| | AGE | IN THE SQUAD | COUNTING GAMES | MINUTES ON PITCH | YELLOW CARDS | RED CARDS | THIS SEASON | HOME COUNTRY |
|---|---|---|---|---|---|---|---|---|
| **Goalkeepers** | | | | | | | | |
| Romain Larrieu | 26 | 43 | 43 | 3870 | 0 | 0 | - | France |
| Luke McCormick | 19 | 43 | 2 | 206 | 0 | 0 | - | England |
| Danny Milosevic | 25 | 1 | 1 | 81 | 0 | 0 | - | Australia |
| Kenny Schofield | - | 2 | 0 | 0 | 0 | 0 | - | England |
| **Defenders** | | | | | | | | |
| Steve Adams | 22 | 38 | 36 | 3227 | 2 | 0 | - | England |
| Hasney Aljofree | 24 | 26 | 17 | 1648 | 3 | 0 | - | England |
| Anthony Barras | 32 | 5 | 3 | 306 | 0 | 0 | - | England |
| Anthony Capaldi | 21 | 1 | 1 | 72 | 0 | 0 | - | N Ireland |
| Paul Connolly | 19 | 2 | 2 | 180 | 1 | 0 | - | England |
| Graham Coughlan | 28 | 43 | 41 | 3727 | 2 | 0 | - | Rep of Ireland |
| Stuart Malcolm | 23 | 3 | 3 | 270 | 0 | 0 | - | Scotland |
| Kieran McAnespie | 23 | 5 | 2 | 197 | 1 | 0 | - | Scotland |
| Craig Taylor | 29 | 1 | 1 | 90 | 1 | 0 | - | England |
| David Worrell | 25 | 44 | 43 | 3887 | 4 | 0 | - | Rep of Ireland |
| Paul Wotton | 25 | 43 | 40 | 3633 | 6 | 0 | - | England |
| **Midfielders** | | | | | | | | |
| Jason Bent | 26 | 27 | 20 | 1920 | 2 | 1 | - | Canada |
| David Beresford | 26 | 24 | 3 | 599 | 0 | 0 | - | England |
| Paul Bernard | 30 | 13 | 6 | 636 | 1 | 0 | - | Scotland |
| Joe Broad | 20 | 9 | 1 | 134 | 0 | 0 | - | England |
| David Friio | 30 | 36 | 31 | 2898 | 8 | 0 | - | France |
| Osvaldo Lopes | 23 | 21 | 3 | 397 | 0 | 0 | - | France |
| Brian McGlinchey | 25 | 26 | 10 | 1138 | 4 | 1 | - | N Ireland |
| Martin Phillips | 27 | 32 | 11 | 1321 | 3 | 0 | - | England |
| Stuart Yetton | - | 1 | 0 | 7 | 0 | 0 | - | England |
| **Forwards** | | | | | | | | |
| Micky Evans | 30 | 43 | 32 | 2935 | 2 | 0 | - | England |
| Lee Hodges | 29 | 39 | 33 | 3271 | 0 | 0 | - | England |
| Marino Keith | 28 | 42 | 18 | 1966 | 2 | 0 | - | Scotland |
| Nathan Lowndes | 26 | 22 | 5 | 678 | 4 | 0 | - | England |
| Marcus Martain | - | 1 | 0 | 0 | 0 | 0 | - | England |
| David Norris | 22 | 33 | 28 | 2639 | 4 | 0 | - | England |
| Grant Smith | 23 | 5 | 4 | 345 | 1 | 0 | - | Scotland |
| Ian Stonebridge | 21 | 38 | 25 | 2502 | 0 | 0 | - | England |
| Blair Sturrock | 21 | 24 | 5 | 743 | 0 | 0 | - | Scotland |

KEY: LEAGUE BOOKINGS CAPS

## SQUAD APPEARANCES

| Match | 1 | 2 | 3 | 4 | 5 | 6 | 7 | 8 | 9 | 10 | 11 | 12 | 13 | 14 | 15 | 16 | 17 | 18 | 19 | 20 | 21 | 22 | 23 | 24 | 25 | 26 | 27 | 28 | 29 | 30 | 31 | 32 | 33 | 34 | 35 | 36 | 37 | 38 | 39 | 40 | 41 | 42 | 43 | 44 | 45 | 46 | 47 | 48 | 49 | 50 | 51 |
|---|---|---|---|---|---|---|---|---|---|---|---|---|---|---|---|---|---|---|---|---|---|---|---|---|---|---|---|---|---|---|---|---|---|---|---|---|---|---|---|---|---|---|---|---|---|---|---|---|---|---|---|
| Venue | A | H | H | A | H | A | A | A | A | H | H | A | H | H | A | H | A | A | H | A | H | A | A | H | A | A | H | H | H | A | H | A | H | A | A | H | A | A | H | H | A | A | H | H | A | H | A | H | A | A | H |
| Competition | L | L | L | L | L | L | W | L | L | L | L | L | L | L | L | L | L | L | L | F | L | L | F | L | L | L | L | L | F | F | L | L | L | L | L | L | L | L | L | L | L | L | L | L | L | L | L | L | L | L | L |
| Result | L | W | W | W | W | D | D | D | L | L | D | L | D | L | W | L | D | L | D | W | W | D | W | D | W | D | W | W | D | L | L | W | W | L | W | L | D | L | D | W | L | D | L | W | W | D | L | W | L | D | W |

**Goalkeepers**
Romain Larrieu
Luke McCormick
Danny Milosevic
Kenny Schofield

**Defenders**
Steve Adams
Hasney Aljofree
Anthony Barras
Anthony Capaldi
Paul Connolly
Graham Coughlan
Stuart Malcolm
Kieran McAnespie
Craig Taylor
David Worrell
Paul Wotton

**Midfielders**
Jason Bent
David Beresford
Paul Bernard
Joe Broad
David Friio
Osvaldo Lopes
Brian McGlinchey
Martin Phillips
Stuart Yetton

**Forwards**
Micky Evans
Lee Hodges
Marino Keith
Nathan Lowndes
Marcus Martain
David Norris
Grant Smith
Ian Stonebridge
Blair Sturrock

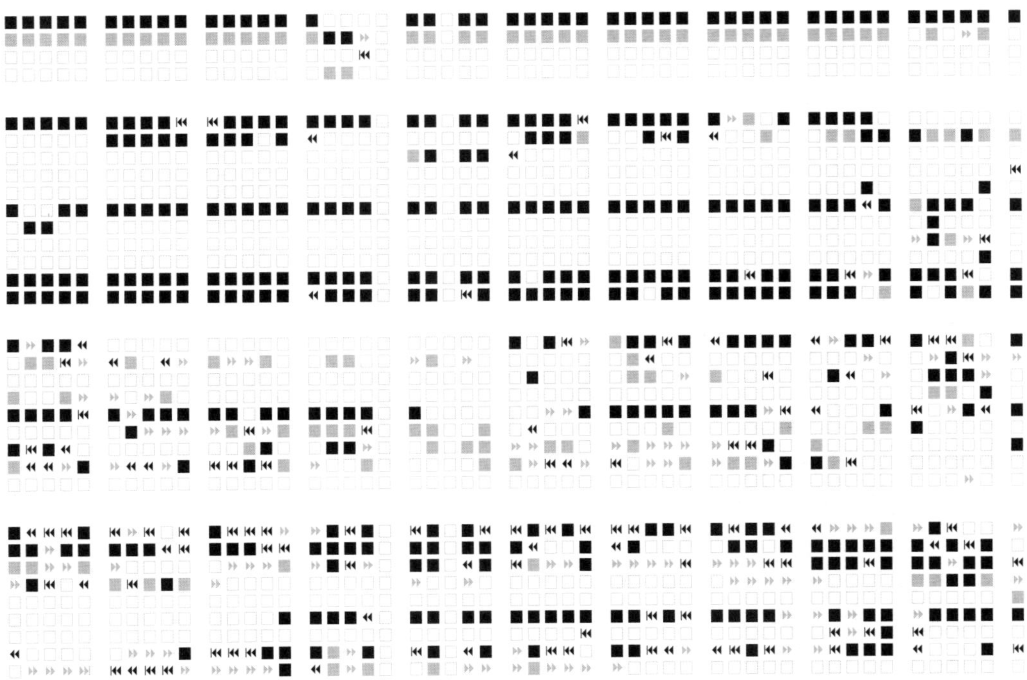

# LUTON TOWN

Final Position: **9th**

NICKNAME: THE HATTERS

| | | | | | | |
|---|---|---|---|---|---|---|
| 1 | div2 | Peterborough | H | L | 2-3 | Crowe 48; Brkovic 82 |
| 2 | div2 | Blackpool | A | L | 2-5 | Howard 6; Thorpe 71 |
| 3 | div2 | Plymouth | A | L | 1-2 | Howard 67 |
| 4 | div2 | Barnsley | H | L | 2-3 | Nicholls 42 pen; Spring 51 |
| 5 | div2 | Cardiff | A | D | 0-0 | |
| 6 | div2 | Chesterfield | H | W | 3-0 | Perrett 36; Howard 69; Crowe 82 |
| 7 | div2 | Brentford | A | D | 0-0 | |
| 8 | wcr1 | Watford | A | W | 2-1 | Spring 30; Howard 40 |
| 9 | div2 | Notts County | H | D | 2-2 | Perrett 78; Howard 86 |
| 10 | div2 | Mansfield | H | L | 2-3 | Howard 85; Nicholls 86 |
| 11 | div2 | Huddersfield | A | W | 1-0 | Howard 90 |
| 12 | div2 | Swindon | H | W | 3-0 | Howard 13; Fotiadis 46; Robinson 86 pen |
| 13 | wcr2 | Aston Villa | A | L | 0-3 | |
| 14 | div2 | Stockport | A | W | 3-2 | Spring 14,74; Fotiadis 71 |
| 15 | div2 | Cheltenham | H | W | 2-1 | Coyne 55; Fotiadis 59 |
| 16 | div2 | Oldham | A | W | 2-1 | Fotiadis 33; Thorpe 58 |
| 17 | div2 | Wigan | H | D | 1-1 | Skelton 24 |
| 18 | div2 | Crewe | A | W | 1-0 | Howard 85 |
| 19 | div2 | Northampton | A | L | 0-3 | |
| 20 | div2 | Port Vale | H | D | 0-0 | |
| 21 | facr1 | Guiseley | H | W | 4-0 | Spring 3; Brkovic 45,65; Thorpe 45 |
| 22 | div2 | QPR | H | D | 0-0 | |
| 23 | div2 | Tranmere | A | W | 3-1 | Spring 70; Brkovic 79; Howard 89 |
| 24 | facr2 | Wigan | A | L | 0-3 | |
| 25 | div2 | Colchester | H | L | 1-2 | Fotiadis 35 |
| 26 | div2 | Bristol City | A | D | 1-1 | Howard 53 |
| 27 | div2 | Cardiff | H | W | 2-0 | Thorpe 80; Howard 90 |
| 28 | div2 | Wycombe | A | W | 2-1 | Howard 21,34 |
| 29 | div2 | Chesterfield | A | L | 1-2 | Brkovic 8 |
| 30 | div2 | Barnsley | A | W | 3-2 | Spring 45; Thorpe 50,64 |
| 31 | div2 | Wycombe | H | W | 1-0 | Spring 57 |
| 32 | div2 | Peterborough | A | D | 1-1 | Howard 12 |
| 33 | div2 | Port Vale | A | W | 2-1 | Thorpe 49; Nicholls 76 pen |
| 34 | div2 | Blackpool | H | L | 1-3 | Thorpe 48 |
| 35 | div2 | Northampton | H | W | 3-2 | Hughes 26,84; Nicholls 58 |
| 36 | div2 | Brentford | H | L | 0-1 | |
| 37 | div2 | Plymouth | H | W | 1-0 | Thorpe 50 |
| 38 | div2 | Notts County | A | L | 1-2 | Thorpe 88 |
| 39 | div2 | Mansfield | A | L | 2-3 | Thorpe 13,82 |
| 40 | div2 | Huddersfield | H | W | 3-0 | Thorpe 50; Holmes 71; Howard 89 |
| 41 | div2 | Wigan | A | D | 1-1 | Howard 57 |
| 42 | div2 | Oldham | H | D | 0-0 | |
| 43 | div2 | Crewe | H | L | 0-4 | |
| 44 | div2 | Tranmere | H | D | 0-0 | |
| 45 | div2 | Cheltenham | A | D | 2-2 | Hughes 12; Forbes 38 |
| 46 | div2 | QPR | A | L | 0-2 | |
| 47 | div2 | Bristol City | H | D | 2-2 | Howard 2,82 |
| 48 | div2 | Colchester | A | W | 5-0 | Howard 14,45,90; Griffiths 21; Nicholls 43 pen |
| 49 | div2 | Stockport | H | D | 1-1 | Howard 61 |
| 50 | div2 | Swindon | A | L | 1-2 | Thorpe 31 |

## ATTENDANCES

HOME GROUND: KENILWORTH ROAD CAPACITY: 9970 AVERAGE LEAGUE AT HOME: 6746

| | | | | | | | | |
|---|---|---|---|---|---|---|---|---|
| 13 | Aston Villa | 20833 | 35 | Northampton | 7048 | 6 | Chesterfield | 6060 |
| 46 | QPR | 15786 | 36 | Brentford | 6940 | 18 | Crewe | 6030 |
| 8 | Watford | 14171 | 16 | Oldham | 6916 | 49 | Stockport | 6010 |
| 26 | Bristol City | 14057 | 38 | Notts County | 6778 | 10 | Mansfield | 6004 |
| 5 | Cardiff | 13564 | 32 | Peterborough | 6760 | 14 | Stockport | 5932 |
| 3 | Plymouth | 10973 | 43 | Crewe | 6607 | 25 | Colchester | 5890 |
| 22 | QPR | 9477 | 34 | Blackpool | 6563 | 19 | Northampton | 5750 |
| 11 | Huddersfield | 9249 | 9 | Notts County | 6456 | 21 | Guiseley | 5248 |
| 30 | Barnsley | 9079 | 50 | Swindon | 6455 | 39 | Mansfield | 4829 |
| 23 | Tranmere | 8273 | 15 | Cheltenham | 6447 | 33 | Port Vale | 4714 |
| 1 | Peterborough | 7860 | 12 | Swindon | 6393 | 29 | Chesterfield | 4638 |
| 27 | Cardiff | 7805 | 47 | Bristol City | 6381 | 24 | Wigan | 4544 |
| 28 | Wycombe | 7740 | 2 | Blackpool | 6377 | 48 | Colchester | 3967 |
| 37 | Plymouth | 7589 | 44 | Tranmere | 6326 | 45 | Cheltenham | 3762 |
| 17 | Wigan | 7364 | 4 | Barnsley | 6230 | | | |
| 31 | Wycombe | 7351 | 42 | Oldham | 6142 | | | |
| 7 | Brentford | 7145 | 40 | Huddersfield | 6122 | | | |
| 41 | Wigan | 7087 | 20 | Port Vale | 6112 | | | |

■ Home □ Away ▒ Neutral

## KEY PLAYERS - GOALSCORERS

**1 Steven Howard**

| | | | |
|---|---|---|---|
| Goals in the League | 22 | Player Strike Rate<br>Average number of minutes between League goals scored by player | 164 |
| Contribution to Attacking Power<br>Average number of minutes between League team goals while on pitch | 61 | Club Strike Rate<br>Average number of minutes between League goals scored by club | 62 |

| | PLAYER | LGE GOALS | POWER | STRIKE RATE |
|---|---|---|---|---|
| 2 | Tony Thorpe | 13 | 66 | 189 mins |
| 3 | Matthew Spring | 6 | 61 | 590 mins |
| 4 | Kevin Nicholls | 5 | 62 | 612 mins |
| 5 | Dean Crowe | 2 | 54 | 792 mins |

## KEY PLAYERS - MIDFIELDERS

**1 Paul Hughes**

| | | | |
|---|---|---|---|
| Goals in the League | 3 | Contribution to Attacking Power<br>Average number of minutes between League team goals while on pitch | 63 |
| Defensive Rating<br>Average number of mins between League goals conceded while he was on the pitch | 86 | Scoring Difference<br>Defensive Rating minus Contribution to Attacking Power | 23 |

| | PLAYER | LGE GOALS | DEF RATE | POWER | SCORE DIFF |
|---|---|---|---|---|---|
| 2 | Steve Robinson | 1 | 77 | 67 | 10 mins |
| 3 | Steven Howard | 22 | 68 | 61 | 7 mins |
| 4 | Matthew Spring | 6 | 64 | 61 | 3 mins |
| 5 | Kevin Nicholls | 5 | 62 | 62 | 0 mins |

## KEY PLAYERS - DEFENDERS

**1 Russell Perrett**

| | | | |
|---|---|---|---|
| Goals Conceded (GC)<br>The number of League goals conceded while he was on the pitch | 21 | Clean Sheets<br>In games when he played at least 70 minutes | 9 |
| Defensive Rating<br>Ave number of mins between League goals conceded while on the pitch | 79 | Club Defensive Rating<br>Average number of mins between League goals conceded by the club this season | 67 |

| | PLAYER | CON LGE | CLEAN SHEETS | DEF RATE |
|---|---|---|---|---|
| 2 | Sol Davis | 39 | 13 | 77 mins |
| 3 | Emmerson Boyce | 39 | 11 | 75 mins |
| 4 | Chris Coyne | 52 | 12 | 66 mins |
| 5 | Allan Neilson | 30 | 4 | 62 mins |

## KEY GOALKEEPER

**1 Cedric Berthelin**

| | |
|---|---|
| Goals Conceded in the League | 9 |
| Defensive Rating<br>Ave number of mins between League goals conceded while on the pitch | 90 |
| Counting Games<br>Games when he played at least 70 mins | 9 |
| Clean Sheets<br>In games when he played at least 70 mins | 3 |

## TOP POINT EARNERS

| | PLAYER | GAMES | AVE |
|---|---|---|---|
| 1 | Skelton | 3 | 2.33 |
| 2 | Fotiadis | 6 | 2.17 |
| 3 | Berthelin | 9 | 2.00 |
| 4 | Hillier | 11 | 1.73 |
| 5 | Hughes | 24 | 1.67 |
| 6 | Griffiths | 3 | 1.67 |
| 7 | Robinson | 20 | 1.65 |
| 8 | Neilson | 18 | 1.50 |
| 9 | Coyne | 36 | 1.50 |
| 10 | Holmes | 6 | 1.50 |
| | CLUB AVERAGE: | | 1.41 |

Ave = Average points per match in Counting Games

## DISCIPLINARY RECORDS

| | PLAYER | YELLOW | RED | AVE |
|---|---|---|---|---|
| 1 | Bayliss | 4 | 0 | 197 |
| 2 | Nicholls | 13 | 1 | 218 |
| 3 | Howard | 12 | 1 | 278 |
| 4 | Brkovic | 9 | 0 | 282 |
| 5 | Perrett | 5 | 0 | 330 |
| 6 | Fotiadis | 2 | 0 | 381 |
| 7 | Hughes | 6 | 0 | 401 |
| 8 | Hillier | 3 | 0 | 412 |
| 9 | Davis, S | 6 | 1 | 427 |
| 10 | Spring | 8 | 0 | 442 |
| 11 | Thorpe | 5 | 0 | 490 |
| 12 | Robinson | 4 | 0 | 517 |
| 13 | Coyne | 5 | 1 | 568 |
| | Other | 5 | 2 | |
| | TOTAL | 87 | 6 | |

## LEAGUE GOALS

| | PLAYER | MINS | GOALS | AVE |
|---|---|---|---|---|
| 1 | Howard | 3614 | 22 | 164 |
| 2 | Thorpe | 2453 | 13 | 189 |
| 3 | Spring | 3539 | 6 | 590 |
| 4 | Nicholls | 3060 | 5 | 612 |
| 5 | Fotiadis | 763 | 5 | 153 |
| 6 | Brkovic | 2541 | 3 | 847 |
| 7 | Hughes | 2407 | 3 | 802 |
| 8 | Crowe | 1583 | 2 | 792 |
| 9 | Perrett | 1652 | 2 | 826 |
| 10 | Griffiths | 257 | 1 | 257 |
| 11 | Forbes | 322 | 1 | 322 |
| 12 | Holmes | 869 | 1 | 869 |
| 13 | Coyne | 3412 | 1 | 3412 |
| | Other | | 2 | |
| | TOTAL | | 67 | |

## MONTH BY MONTH GUIDE TO THE POINTS

| MONTH | POINTS | % |
|---|---|---|
| AUGUST | 4 | 22% |
| SEPTEMBER | 8 | 53% |
| OCTOBER | 13 | 87% |
| NOVEMBER | 5 | 42% |
| DECEMBER | 7 | 58% |
| JANUARY | 6 | 67% |
| FEBRUARY | 10 | 56% |
| MARCH | 5 | 28% |
| APRIL | 7 | 39% |
| MAY | 0 | 0% |

## TEAM OF THE SEASON

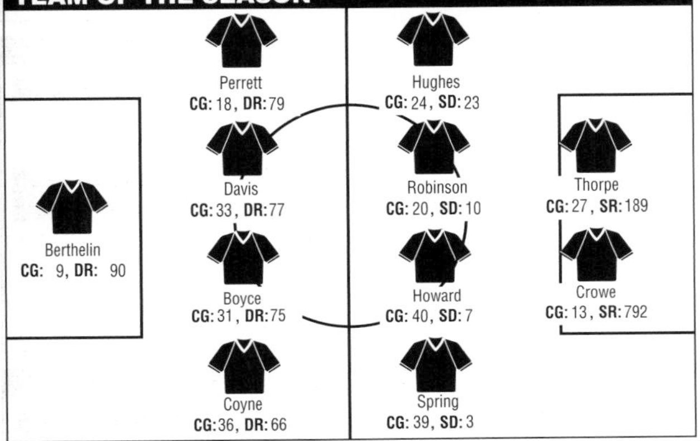
Perrett
CG: 18, DR: 79
Hughes
CG: 24, SD: 23
Davis
CG: 33, DR: 77
Robinson
CG: 20, SD: 10
Thorpe
CG: 27, SR: 189
Berthelin
CG: 9, DR: 90
Boyce
CG: 31, DR: 75
Howard
CG: 40, SD: 7
Crowe
CG: 13, SR: 792
Coyne
CG: 36, DR: 66
Spring
CG: 39, SD: 3

**KEY:** DR = Defensive Rate, SD = Scoring Difference, SR = Strike Rate, CG = Counting Games – League games playing at least 70 minutes

## LEAGUE APPEARANCES, BOOKINGS AND CAPS

| | AGE | IN THE SQUAD | COUNTING GAMES | MINUTES ON PITCH | YELLOW CARDS | RED CARDS | THIS SEASON | HOME COUNTRY |
|---|---|---|---|---|---|---|---|---|
| **Goalkeepers** | | | | | | | | |
| Rob Beckwith | - | 6 | 4 | 360 | 0 | 0 | - | England |
| Cedric Berthelin | 26 | 9 | 9 | 810 | 0 | 0 | - | France |
| Dean Brill | - | 5 | 0 | 0 | 0 | 0 | - | England |
| Carl Emberson | 30 | 39 | 17 | 1678 | 1 | 1 | - | England |
| Lars Hirschfeld | 24 | 6 | 4 | 383 | 0 | 0 | - | Canada |
| Mark Ovendale | 29 | 15 | 5 | 504 | 0 | 0 | - | England |
| Ben Roberts | 28 | 5 | 4 | 405 | 0 | 0 | - | England |
| **Defenders** | | | | | | | | |
| David Bayliss | 27 | 20 | 7 | 789 | 4 | 0 | - | England |
| Emmerson Boyce | 23 | 35 | 31 | 2908 | 0 | 0 | - | England |
| Chris Coyne | 24 | 41 | 36 | 3412 | 5 | 1 | - | Australia |
| Sol Davis | 23 | 34 | 33 | 2995 | 6 | 1 | - | England |
| Joe Deeney | - | 3 | 0 | 0 | 0 | 0 | - | England |
| Kevin Foley | 18 | 2 | 0 | 31 | 0 | 0 | - | England |
| Ian Hillier | 23 | 31 | 11 | 1236 | 3 | 0 | - | England |
| Duncan Jupp | 28 | 8 | 1 | 187 | 0 | 0 | - | Scotland |
| Alan Kimble | 36 | 28 | 8 | 799 | 0 | 0 | - | England |
| Allan Neilson | 30 | 30 | 18 | 1861 | 1 | 0 | - | Wales |
| Russell Perrett | 30 | 24 | 18 | 1652 | 5 | 0 | - | England |
| Christopher Willmott | 25 | 14 | 11 | 1074 | 1 | 0 | - | England |
| **Midfielders** | | | | | | | | |
| Ahmet Brkovic | 28 | 39 | 23 | 2541 | 9 | 0 | - | Croatia |
| Peter Holmes | 22 | 26 | 6 | 869 | 0 | 0 | - | England |
| Steven Howard | 27 | 41 | 40 | 3614 | 12 | 1 | - | England |
| Paul Hughes | 27 | 38 | 24 | 2407 | 6 | 0 | - | England |
| Sam Igoe | 27 | 2 | 2 | 180 | 0 | 0 | - | England |
| Matthew Judge | - | 2 | 0 | 3 | 0 | 0 | - | England |
| Michael Leary | 20 | 5 | 0 | 0 | 0 | 0 | - | England |
| Lee Mansell | 20 | 7 | 0 | 48 | 0 | 0 | - | England |
| Kevin Nicholls | 24 | 36 | 33 | 3060 | 13 | 1 | - | England |
| Pary Okai | - | 1 | 0 | 0 | 0 | 0 | - | England |
| Steve Robinson | 28 | 31 | 20 | 2068 | 4 | 0 | - | England |
| Aaron Skelton | 28 | 10 | 3 | 394 | 0 | 0 | - | England |
| Matthew Spring | 23 | 41 | 39 | 3539 | 8 | 0 | - | England |
| **Forwards** | | | | | | | | |
| Dean Crowe | 24 | 28 | 13 | 1583 | 1 | 0 | - | England |
| Adrian Forbes | 24 | 6 | 3 | 322 | 0 | 1 | - | England |
| Andrew Fotiadis | 25 | 22 | 6 | 763 | 2 | 0 | - | England |
| Carl Griffiths | 31 | 7 | 3 | 257 | 1 | 0 | - | England |
| James Osborn | 19 | 1 | 0 | 0 | 0 | 0 | - | England |
| Tony Thorpe | 29 | 37 | 27 | 2453 | 5 | 0 | - | England |
| Robbie Winters | 28 | 1 | 0 | 45 | 0 | 0 | - | |

## SQUAD APPEARANCES

| Match | 1 | 2 | 3 | 4 | 5 | 6 | 7 | 8 | 9 | 10 | 11 | 12 | 13 | 14 | 15 | 16 | 17 | 18 | 19 | 20 | 21 | 22 | 23 | 24 | 25 | 26 | 27 | 28 | 29 | 30 | 31 | 32 | 33 | 34 | 35 | 36 | 37 | 38 | 39 | 40 | 41 | 42 | 43 | 44 | 45 | 46 | 47 | 48 | 49 | 50 |
|---|---|---|---|---|---|---|---|---|---|---|---|---|---|---|---|---|---|---|---|---|---|---|---|---|---|---|---|---|---|---|---|---|---|---|---|---|---|---|---|---|---|---|---|---|---|---|---|---|---|---|
| Venue | H | A | A | H | A | H | A | A | H | H | A | H | A | A | H | A | H | A | A | H | H | H | A | A | H | A | H | A | A | A | H | A | A | H | H | H | H | A | A | H | A | H | H | H | A | A | H | A | H | A |
| Competition | L | L | L | L | L | L | L | W | L | L | L | L | W | L | L | L | L | L | L | L | F | L | L | F | L | L | L | L | L | L | L | L | L | L | L | L | L | L | L | L | L | L | L | L | L | L | L | L | L | L |
| Result | L | L | L | L | D | W | D | W | D | L | W | W | L | W | W | W | D | W | L | D | W | D | W | L | L | D | W | W | L | W | W | D | W | L | W | L | W | L | L | W | D | D | L | D | D | L | D | W | D | L |

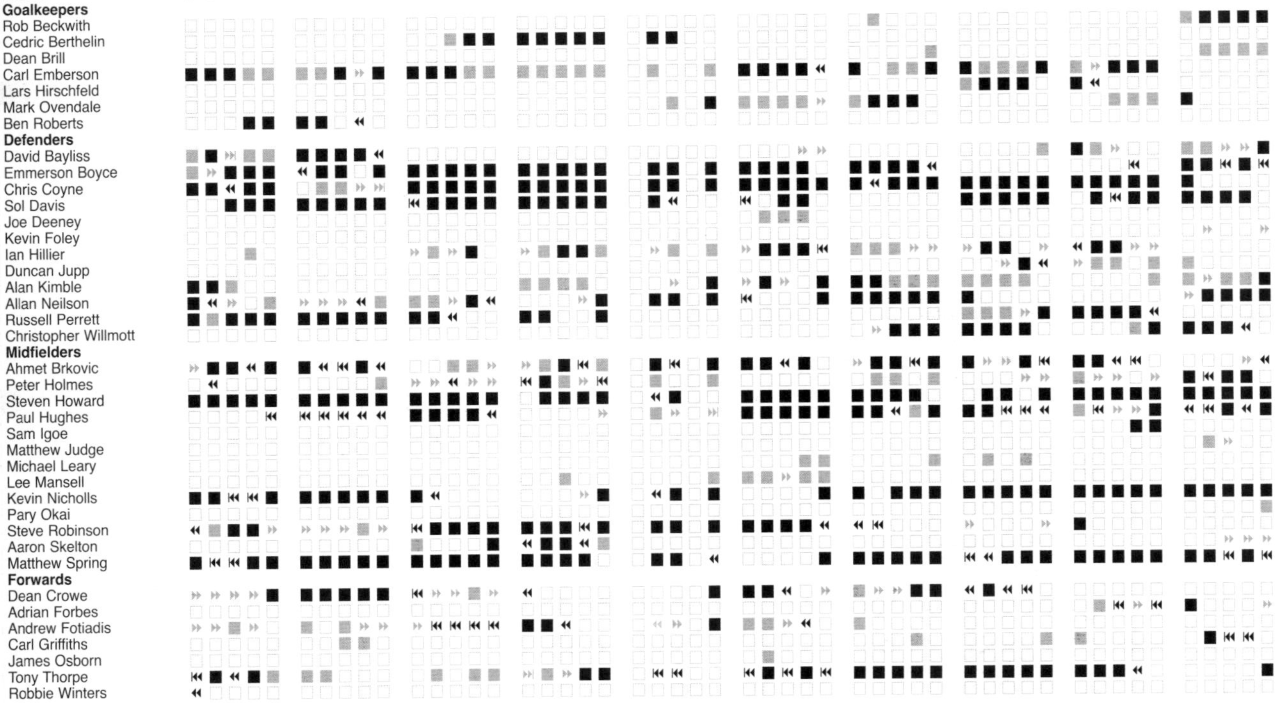
Goalkeepers
Rob Beckwith
Cedric Berthelin
Dean Brill
Carl Emberson
Lars Hirschfeld
Mark Ovendale
Ben Roberts
Defenders
David Bayliss
Emmerson Boyce
Chris Coyne
Sol Davis
Joe Deeney
Kevin Foley
Ian Hillier
Duncan Jupp
Alan Kimble
Allan Neilson
Russell Perrett
Christopher Willmott
Midfielders
Ahmet Brkovic
Peter Holmes
Steven Howard
Paul Hughes
Sam Igoe
Matthew Judge
Michael Leary
Lee Mansell
Kevin Nicholls
Pary Okai
Steve Robinson
Aaron Skelton
Matthew Spring
Forwards
Dean Crowe
Adrian Forbes
Andrew Fotiadis
Carl Griffiths
James Osborn
Tony Thorpe
Robbie Winters

# SWINDON TOWN

Final Position: **10th**

NICKNAME: THE ROBINS

| | | | | | | |
|---|---|---|---|---|---|---|
| 1 | div2 | Barnsley | H | W | 3-1 | Parkin 32,50,87 pen |
| 2 | div2 | Chesterfield | A | W | 4-2 | Invincible 12,39; Sabin 42; Parkin 57 |
| 3 | div2 | Blackpool | A | D | 0-0 | |
| 4 | div2 | Cardiff | H | L | 0-1 | |
| 5 | div2 | Brentford | A | L | 1-3 | Davis 17 |
| 6 | div2 | Stockport | H | L | 0-1 | |
| 7 | div2 | Port Vale | H | L | 1-2 | Gurney 7 |
| 8 | wcr1 | Wycombe | H | L | 1-2 | Willis 100 |
| 9 | div2 | QPR | A | L | 0-2 | |
| 10 | div2 | Cheltenham | A | L | 0-2 | |
| 11 | div2 | Northampton | H | W | 2-0 | Jackson 31; Parkin 79 pen |
| 12 | div2 | Luton | A | L | 0-3 | |
| 13 | div2 | Oldham | H | L | 0-1 | |
| 14 | div2 | Colchester | H | D | 2-2 | Gurney 66; Sabin 68 |
| 15 | div2 | Bristol City | A | L | 0-2 | |
| 16 | div2 | Mansfield | H | W | 2-1 | Parkin 21; Sabin 46 |
| 17 | div2 | Notts County | A | D | 1-1 | Parkin 32 |
| 18 | div2 | Wycombe | A | W | 3-2 | Davis 12; Parkin 79,90 |
| 19 | div2 | Tranmere | H | D | 1-1 | Parkin 2 |
| 20 | facr1 | Huddersfield | H | W | 1-0 | Gurney 85 |
| 21 | div2 | Huddersfield | A | W | 3-2 | Duke 1; Gurney 24 pen; Parkin 89 |
| 22 | div2 | Peterborough | H | D | 1-1 | Parkin 79 pen |
| 23 | facr2 | Oxford | A | L | 0-1 | |
| 24 | div2 | Plymouth | A | D | 1-1 | Gurney 77 |
| 25 | div2 | Crewe | H | L | 1-3 | Parkin 75 pen |
| 26 | div2 | Brentford | H | W | 2-1 | Gurney 2; Parkin 66 |
| 27 | div2 | Wigan | A | L | 0-2 | |
| 28 | div2 | Cardiff | A | D | 1-1 | Parkin 70 |
| 29 | div2 | Chesterfield | H | W | 3-0 | Parkin 33; Invincible 52; Reeves 87 |
| 30 | div2 | Stockport | A | W | 5-2 | Parkin 7; Robinson 12; Reeves 74; Hewlett 85; Sabin 90 |
| 31 | div2 | Blackpool | H | D | 1-1 | Miglioranzi 20 |
| 32 | div2 | Wigan | H | W | 2-1 | Invincible 24; Gurney 35 |
| 33 | div2 | Barnsley | A | D | 1-1 | Invincible 34 |
| 34 | div2 | Tranmere | A | W | 1-0 | Gurney 50 |
| 35 | div2 | Wycombe | H | L | 0-3 | |
| 36 | div2 | Port Vale | A | D | 1-1 | Parkin 54 |
| 37 | div2 | QPR | H | W | 3-1 | Robinson 18; Parkin 64; Heywood 68 |
| 38 | div2 | Northampton | A | L | 0-1 | |
| 39 | div2 | Cheltenham | H | L | 0-3 | |
| 40 | div2 | Mansfield | A | L | 1-2 | Reeves 45 |
| 41 | div2 | Bristol City | H | D | 1-1 | Parkin 66 |
| 42 | div2 | Notts County | H | W | 5-0 | Parkin 43,61,89; Gurney 59; Duke 69 |
| 43 | div2 | Colchester | A | L | 0-1 | |
| 44 | div2 | Peterborough | A | D | 1-1 | Invincible 71 |
| 45 | div2 | Huddersfield | H | L | 0-1 | |
| 46 | div2 | Crewe | A | W | 1-0 | Miglioranzi 75 |
| 47 | div2 | Plymouth | H | W | 2-0 | Invincible 38; Parkin 68 |
| 48 | div2 | Oldham | A | L | 0-4 | |
| 49 | div2 | Luton | H | W | 2-1 | Miglioranzi 41; Parkin 43 |

## ATTENDANCES

HOME GROUND: COUNTY GROUND CAPACITY: 16000 AVERAGE LEAGUE AT HOME: 5440

| | | | | | | | | |
|---|---|---|---|---|---|---|---|---|
| 15 | Bristol City | 13205 | 35 | Wycombe | 6239 | 11 | Northampton | 4719 |
| 28 | Cardiff | 13062 | 27 | Wigan | 6114 | 22 | Peterborough | 4709 |
| 23 | Oxford | 11645 | 26 | Brentford | 6045 | 29 | Chesterfield | 4544 |
| 9 | QPR | 11619 | 18 | Wycombe | 6021 | 40 | Mansfield | 4471 |
| 33 | Barnsley | 8661 | 10 | Cheltenham | 5761 | 13 | Oldham | 4326 |
| 41 | Bristol City | 8629 | 1 | Barnsley | 5702 | 30 | Stockport | 4318 |
| 21 | Huddersfield | 8334 | 39 | Cheltenham | 5583 | 44 | Peterborough | 4310 |
| 24 | Plymouth | 8111 | 38 | Northampton | 5566 | 42 | Notts County | 4246 |
| 37 | QPR | 7716 | 6 | Stockport | 5456 | 20 | Huddersfield | 4210 |
| 4 | Cardiff | 7564 | 32 | Wigan | 5238 | 14 | Colchester | 4152 |
| 34 | Tranmere | 7181 | 19 | Tranmere | 5077 | 16 | Mansfield | 4136 |
| 48 | Oldham | 6873 | 47 | Plymouth | 5057 | 36 | Port Vale | 4085 |
| 49 | Luton | 6455 | 7 | Port Vale | 5029 | 43 | Colchester | 3787 |
| 3 | Blackpool | 6404 | 25 | Crewe | 4957 | 2 | Chesterfield | 3189 |
| 12 | Luton | 6393 | 17 | Notts County | 4797 | 8 | Wycombe | 2993 |
| 46 | Crewe | 6384 | 31 | Blackpool | 4787 | | | |
| 5 | Brentford | 6299 | 45 | Huddersfield | 4760 | | | |

■ Home □ Away ▒ Neutral

## KEY PLAYERS - GOALSCORERS

**1 Sam Parkin**

| | | | |
|---|---|---|---|
| Goals in the League | 25 | Player Strike Rate<br>Average number of minutes between League goals scored by player | 148 |
| Contribution to Attacking Power<br>Average number of minutes between League team goals while on pitch | 69 | Club Strike Rate<br>Average number of minutes between League goals scored by club | 70 |

| | PLAYER | LGE GOALS | POWER | STRIKE RATE |
|---|---|---|---|---|
| 2 | Danny Invincible | 7 | 68 | 457 mins |
| 3 | Andrew Gurney | 8 | 75 | 460 mins |
| 4 | Eric Sabin | 4 | 81 | 633 mins |
| 5 | Alan Reeves | 3 | 66 | 1049 mins |

## KEY PLAYERS - MIDFIELDERS

**1 Junior Lewis**

| | | | |
|---|---|---|---|
| Goals in the League | 0 | Contribution to Attacking Power<br>Average number of minutes between League team goals while on pitch | 72 |
| Defensive Rating<br>Average number of mins between League goals conceded while he was on the pitch | 87 | Scoring Difference<br>Defensive Rating minus Contribution to Attacking Power | 15 |

| | PLAYER | LGE GOALS | DEF RATE | POWER | SCORE DIFF |
|---|---|---|---|---|---|
| 2 | Steve Robinson | 2 | 69 | 66 | 3 mins |
| 3 | Danny Invincible | 7 | 70 | 68 | 2 mins |
| 4 | Matt Hewlett | 1 | 67 | 67 | 0 mins |
| 5 | Stefani Miglioranzi | 3 | 68 | 69 | -1 mins |

## KEY PLAYERS - DEFENDERS

**1 Matthew Heywood**

| | | | |
|---|---|---|---|
| Goals Conceded (GC)<br>The number of League goals conceded while he was on the pitch | 63 | Clean Sheets<br>In games when he played at least 70 minutes | 7 |
| Defensive Rating<br>Ave number of mins between League goals conceded while on the pitch | 66 | Club Defensive Rating<br>Average number of mins between League goals conceded by the club this season | 66 |

| | PLAYER | CON LGE | CLEAN SHEETS | DEF RATE |
|---|---|---|---|---|
| 2 | Alan Reeves | 48 | 5 | 66 mins |
| 3 | Andrew Gurney | 59 | 4 | 62 mins |

## KEY GOALKEEPER

**1 Bart Griemink**

| | |
|---|---|
| Goals Conceded in the League | 59 |
| Defensive Rating<br>Ave number of mins between League goals conceded while on the pitch | 67 |
| Counting Games<br>Games when he played at least 70 mins | 44 |
| Clean Sheets<br>In games when he played at least 70 mins | 6 |

## TOP POINT EARNERS

| | PLAYER | GAMES | AVE |
|---|---|---|---|
| 1 | Herring | 2 | 3.00 |
| 2 | Marney | 6 | 1.83 |
| 3 | Lewis | 9 | 1.56 |
| 4 | Farr | 2 | 1.50 |
| 5 | Invincible | 33 | 1.45 |
| 6 | Hewlett | 36 | 1.44 |
| 7 | Parkin | 40 | 1.40 |
| 8 | Robinson | 38 | 1.39 |
| 9 | Duke | 43 | 1.37 |
| 10 | Reeves | 35 | 1.34 |
| | CLUB AVERAGE: | | |

Ave = Average points per match in Counting Games

## DISCIPLINARY RECORDS

| | PLAYER | YELLOW | RED | AVE |
|---|---|---|---|---|
| 1 | Willis | 4 | 0 | 213 |
| 2 | Sabin | 10 | 0 | 253 |
| 3 | Gurney | 10 | 0 | 368 |
| 4 | Lewis | 2 | 0 | 393 |
| 5 | Robinson | 9 | 0 | 398 |
| 6 | Davis | 2 | 0 | 480 |
| 7 | Reeves | 5 | 0 | 629 |
| 8 | Marney | 1 | 0 | 684 |
| 9 | Edds | 1 | 0 | 824 |
| 10 | Heywood | 5 | 0 | 828 |
| 11 | Hewlett | 4 | 0 | 848 |
| 12 | Duke | 4 | 0 | 961 |
| 13 | Invincible | 2 | 0 | 1600 |
| | Other | 4 | 2 | |
| | TOTAL | 63 | 2 | |

## LEAGUE GOALS

| | PLAYER | MINS | GOALS | AVE |
|---|---|---|---|---|
| 1 | Parkin | 3693 | 25 | 148 |
| 2 | Gurney | 3681 | 8 | 460 |
| 3 | Invincible | 3200 | 7 | 457 |
| 4 | Sabin | 2532 | 4 | 633 |
| 5 | Miglioranzi | 3385 | 3 | 1128 |
| 6 | Reeves | 3146 | 3 | 1049 |
| 7 | Duke | 3847 | 2 | 1924 |
| 8 | Robinson | 3588 | 2 | 1794 |
| 9 | Davis | 961 | 2 | 481 |
| 10 | Jackson | 1103 | 1 | 1103 |
| 11 | Heywood | 4140 | 1 | 4140 |
| 12 | Hewlett | 3393 | 1 | 3393 |
| | Other | | 0 | |
| | TOTAL | | 59 | |

## MONTH BY MONTH GUIDE TO THE POINTS

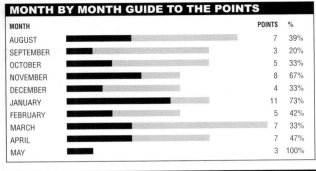

| MONTH | POINTS | % |
|---|---|---|
| AUGUST | 7 | 39% |
| SEPTEMBER | 3 | 20% |
| OCTOBER | 5 | 33% |
| NOVEMBER | 8 | 67% |
| DECEMBER | 4 | 33% |
| JANUARY | 11 | 73% |
| FEBRUARY | 5 | 42% |
| MARCH | 7 | 33% |
| APRIL | 7 | 47% |
| MAY | 3 | 100% |

## TEAM OF THE SEASON

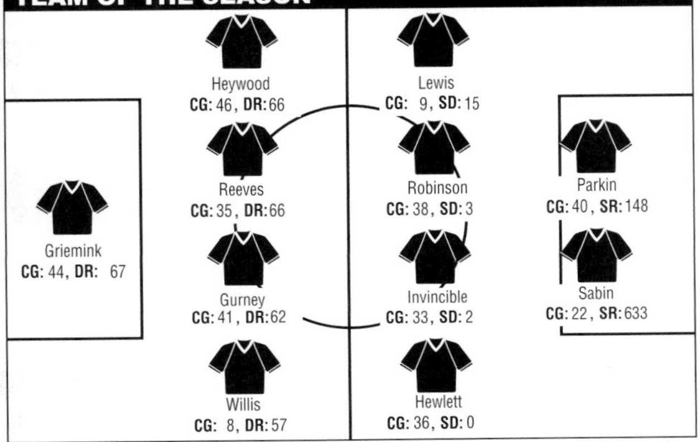

Griemink
CG: 44, DR: 67
Heywood
CG: 46, DR: 66
Reeves
CG: 35, DR: 66
Gurney
CG: 41, DR: 62
Willis
CG: 8, DR: 57
Lewis
CG: 9, SD: 15
Robinson
CG: 38, SD: 3
Invincible
CG: 33, SD: 2
Hewlett
CG: 36, SD: 0
Parkin
CG: 40, SR: 148
Sabin
CG: 22, SR: 633


KEY: DR = Defensive Rate, SD = Scoring Difference, S R = Strike Rate, CG = Counting Games – League games playing at least 70 minutes

## LEAGUE APPEARANCES, BOOKINGS AND CAPS

| | AGE | IN THE SQUAD | COUNTING GAMES | MINUTES ON PITCH | YELLOW CARDS | RED CARDS | THIS SEASON | HOME COUNTRY |
|---|---|---|---|---|---|---|---|---|
| **Goalkeepers** | | | | | | | | |
| Craig Farr | - | 41 | 2 | 180 | 0 | 0 | - | England |
| Bart Griemink | 31 | 46 | 44 | 3960 | 1 | 0 | - | Holland |
| Alan Judge | 43 | 2 | 0 | 0 | 0 | 0 | - | England |
| Steve Smith | - | 3 | 0 | 0 | 0 | 0 | - | England |
| **Defenders** | | | | | | | | |
| Dave Bampton | 18 | 5 | 0 | 11 | 0 | 0 | - | England |
| Jon Beswetherick | 25 | 5 | 3 | 244 | 0 | 1 | - | England |
| Juan Cobian | 27 | 3 | 0 | 0 | 0 | 0 | - | Argentina |
| Luke Garrard | - | 2 | 0 | 9 | 0 | 0 | - | England |
| Andrew Gurney | 29 | 41 | 41 | 3681 | 10 | 0 | - | England |
| Matthew Heywood | 23 | 46 | 46 | 4140 | 5 | 0 | - | England |
| Alan Reeves | 35 | 43 | 35 | 3146 | 5 | 0 | - | England |
| Chris Taylor | 17 | 10 | 0 | 64 | 0 | 0 | - | England |
| Adam Willis | 26 | 27 | 8 | 854 | 4 | 0 | - | England |
| **Midfielders** | | | | | | | | |
| David Duke | 24 | 44 | 43 | 3847 | 4 | 0 | - | Scotland |
| Darren Dykes | - | 15 | 0 | 85 | 0 | 0 | - | England |
| Gareth Edds | 22 | 31 | 8 | 824 | 1 | 0 | - | Australia |
| Nathan Edwards | 20 | 14 | 0 | 47 | 0 | 0 | - | England |
| Ian Herring | 19 | 5 | 2 | 236 | 1 | 0 | - | England |
| Matt Hewlett | 27 | 42 | 36 | 3393 | 4 | 0 | - | England |
| Jerel Ifil | 21 | 11 | 5 | 524 | 0 | 0 | - | England |
| Danny Invincible | 24 | 42 | 33 | 3200 | 2 | 0 | - | Australia |
| John Jackson | 20 | 13 | 12 | 1103 | 0 | 0 | - | England |
| Junior Lewis | 29 | 9 | 9 | 787 | 2 | 0 | - | England |
| Dean Marney | 19 | 10 | 6 | 684 | 1 | 0 | - | England |
| Stefani Miglioranzi | 25 | 45 | 36 | 3385 | 2 | 0 | - | Brazil |
| Steve Robinson | 27 | 45 | 38 | 3588 | 9 | 0 | - | England |
| Alan Young | 19 | 27 | 0 | 159 | 0 | 0 | - | England |
| **Forwards** | | | | | | | | |
| Jimmy Davis | 20 | 13 | 10 | 961 | 2 | 0 | - | England |
| Mark Draycott | - | 3 | 0 | 0 | 0 | 0 | - | England |
| Kevin Halliday | 19 | 2 | 0 | 0 | 0 | 0 | - | England |
| Luke Nightingale | 22 | 6 | 0 | 127 | 0 | 0 | - | England |
| Sam Parkin | 22 | 43 | 40 | 3693 | 0 | 1 | - | England |
| Eric Sabin | 28 | 41 | 22 | 2532 | 10 | 0 | - | France |
| John Sutton | 19 | 1 | 0 | 26 | 0 | 0 | - | England |

KEY: LEAGUE BOOKINGS CAPS

## SQUAD APPEARANCES

| Match | 1 | 2 | 3 | 4 | 5 | 6 | 7 | 8 | 9 | 10 | 11 | 12 | 13 | 14 | 15 | 16 | 17 | 18 | 19 | 20 | 21 | 22 | 23 | 24 | 25 |
|---|---|---|---|---|---|---|---|---|---|---|---|---|---|---|---|---|---|---|---|---|---|---|---|---|---|
| Venue | H | A | A | H | A | H | H | H | A | A | H | A | H | H | A | H | A | A | H | H | A | H | A | A | H |
| Competition | L | L | L | L | L | L | L | W | L | L | L | L | L | L | L | L | L | L | L | F | L | L | F | L | L |
| Result | W | W | D | L | L | L | L | D | L | L | W | L | L | D | L | W | D | W | D | W | W | D | L | D | L |

| Match | 26 | 27 | 28 | 29 | 30 | 31 | 32 | 33 | 34 | 35 | 36 | 37 | 38 | 39 | 40 | 41 | 42 | 43 | 44 | 45 | 46 | 47 | 48 | 49 |
|---|---|---|---|---|---|---|---|---|---|---|---|---|---|---|---|---|---|---|---|---|---|---|---|---|
| Venue | H | A | A | H | A | H | H | A | A | H | A | H | A | H | A | H | H | A | A | H | A | H | A | H |
| Competition | L | L | L | L | L | L | L | L | L | L | L | L | L | L | L | L | L | L | L | L | L | L | L | L |
| Result | W | L | D | W | W | D | W | D | W | L | D | W | L | L | L | D | W | L | D | L | W | W | L | W |

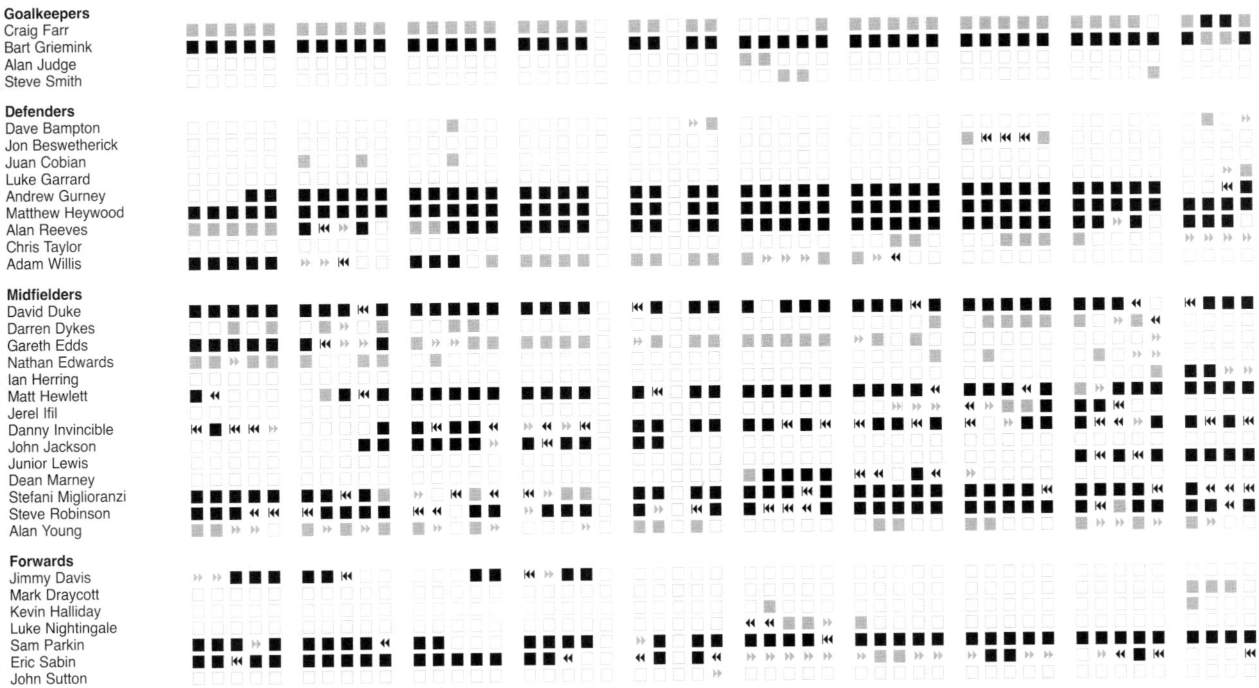

Goalkeepers
Craig Farr
Bart Griemink
Alan Judge
Steve Smith
Defenders
Dave Bampton
Jon Beswetherick
Juan Cobian
Luke Garrard
Andrew Gurney
Matthew Heywood
Alan Reeves
Chris Taylor
Adam Willis
Midfielders
David Duke
Darren Dykes
Gareth Edds
Nathan Edwards
Ian Herring
Matt Hewlett
Jerel Ifil
Danny Invincible
John Jackson
Junior Lewis
Dean Marney
Stefani Miglioranzi
Steve Robinson
Alan Young
Forwards
Jimmy Davis
Mark Draycott
Kevin Halliday
Luke Nightingale
Sam Parkin
Eric Sabin
John Sutton

# PETERBOROUGH UNITED

Final Position: **11th**

NICKNAME: THE POSH

| | | | | | | |
|---|---|---|---|---|---|---|
| 1 | div2 | Luton | A | W | 3-2 | Green 2; Clarke, A 31,69 |
| 2 | div2 | Oldham | H | L | 0-1 | |
| 3 | div2 | Huddersfield | H | L | 0-1 | |
| 4 | div2 | QPR | A | L | 0-2 | |
| 5 | div2 | Colchester | H | L | 0-1 | |
| 6 | div2 | Port Vale | A | L | 0-1 | |
| 7 | wcr1 | Portsmouth | A | L | 0-2 | |
| 8 | div2 | Crewe | H | D | 0-0 | |
| 9 | div2 | Plymouth | H | W | 2-0 | Clarke, A 57; Green 85 |
| 10 | div2 | Wigan | A | D | 2-2 | Newton 63; Clarke, A 75 |
| 11 | div2 | Brentford | H | W | 5-1 | Rea 1; Bullard 48 pen; Allen 67; Farrell 77; Clarke, A 89 |
| 12 | div2 | Notts County | A | D | 2-2 | Allen 45; Rea 54 |
| 13 | div2 | Stockport | A | L | 1-2 | Clarke, A 79 |
| 14 | div2 | Mansfield | H | D | 0-0 | |
| 15 | div2 | Wycombe | A | L | 2-3 | Allen 40; Bullard 90 |
| 16 | div2 | Bristol City | H | L | 1-3 | Clarke, A 43 |
| 17 | div2 | Tranmere | A | D | 1-1 | Farrell 88 |
| 18 | div2 | Cardiff | A | L | 0-3 | |
| 19 | div2 | Chesterfield | H | W | 1-0 | Clarke, A 82 |
| 20 | facr1 | Rochdale | A | L | 2-3 | Fenn 83; Clarke, A 88 |
| 21 | div2 | Barnsley | H | L | 1-3 | Lee 71 |
| 22 | div2 | Swindon | A | D | 1-1 | Bullard 73 |
| 23 | div2 | Cheltenham | H | W | 4-1 | Lee 19,37; Clarke, A 28,90 |
| 24 | div2 | Blackpool | A | L | 0-3 | |
| 25 | div2 | Colchester | A | D | 1-1 | Clarke, A 82 |
| 26 | div2 | Northampton | H | D | 0-0 | |
| 27 | div2 | QPR | H | L | 0-2 | |
| 28 | div2 | Oldham | A | D | 0-0 | |
| 29 | div2 | Huddersfield | A | W | 1-0 | Edwards 83 |
| 30 | div2 | Port Vale | H | L | 1-2 | Clarke, A 82 |
| 31 | div2 | Northampton | A | W | 1-0 | Clarke, A 55 |
| 32 | div2 | Luton | H | D | 1-1 | Fenn 39 |
| 33 | div2 | Chesterfield | A | D | 0-0 | |
| 34 | div2 | Stockport | H | W | 2-0 | Arber 53; Fotiadis 83 |
| 35 | div2 | Crewe | A | W | 1-0 | McKenzie 90 |
| 36 | div2 | Plymouth | A | L | 1-6 | McKenzie 70 |
| 37 | div2 | Wigan | H | D | 1-1 | McKenzie 70 |
| 38 | div2 | Bristol City | A | L | 0-1 | |
| 39 | div2 | Wycombe | H | L | 1-2 | Clarke, A 43 |
| 40 | div2 | Tranmere | H | D | 0-0 | |
| 41 | div2 | Mansfield | A | W | 5-1 | Rea 8; McKenzie 37; Hendon 44; Clarke, A 82; Fotiadis 90 |
| 42 | div2 | Swindon | H | D | 1-1 | Shields 35 |
| 43 | div2 | Barnsley | A | W | 2-1 | Arber 60 pen; Crooks 77 og |
| 44 | div2 | Cardiff | H | W | 2-0 | Gill 38; McKenzie 70 |
| 45 | div2 | Blackpool | H | W | 1-0 | Farrell 12 |
| 46 | div2 | Cheltenham | A | D | 1-1 | Clarke, A 64 |
| 47 | div2 | Notts County | H | W | 1-0 | Scott 73 |
| 48 | div2 | Brentford | A | D | 1-1 | Clarke, A 57 |

## ATTENDANCES

HOME GROUND: LONDON ROAD CAPACITY: 15500 AVERAGE LEAGUE AT HOME: 4950

| | | |
|---|---|---|
| 18 | Cardiff | 12918 |
| 4 | QPR | 11510 |
| 38 | Bristol City | 11231 |
| 29 | Huddersfield | 9022 |
| 43 | Barnsley | 8862 |
| 7 | Portsmouth | 8581 |
| 1 | Luton | 7860 |
| 26 | Northampton | 7767 |
| 36 | Plymouth | 6931 |
| 32 | Luton | 6760 |
| 48 | Brentford | 6687 |
| 12 | Notts County | 6548 |
| 27 | QPR | 6210 |
| 17 | Tranmere | 5980 |
| 28 | Oldham | 5922 |
| 31 | Northampton | 5906 |
| 10 | Wigan | 5797 |
| 35 | Crewe | 5704 |
| 41 | Mansfield | 5653 |
| 15 | Wycombe | 5539 |
| 47 | Notts County | 5381 |
| 16 | Bristol City | 5332 |
| 3 | Huddersfield | 5205 |
| 2 | Oldham | 5204 |
| 24 | Blackpool | 5068 |
| 14 | Mansfield | 5067 |
| 11 | Brentford | 5066 |
| 44 | Cardiff | 4984 |
| 37 | Wigan | 4970 |
| 46 | Cheltenham | 4809 |
| 30 | Port Vale | 4770 |
| 13 | Stockport | 4726 |
| 22 | Swindon | 4709 |
| 45 | Blackpool | 4587 |
| 23 | Cheltenham | 4522 |
| 21 | Barnsley | 4449 |
| 34 | Stockport | 4386 |
| 19 | Chesterfield | 4359 |
| 8 | Crewe | 4345 |
| 42 | Swindon | 4310 |
| 9 | Plymouth | 4208 |
| 5 | Colchester | 4203 |
| 40 | Tranmere | 4158 |
| 6 | Port Vale | 3862 |
| 25 | Colchester | 3760 |
| 39 | Wycombe | 3627 |
| 33 | Chesterfield | 3515 |
| 20 | Rochdale | 2566 |

Home / Away / Neutral

## KEY PLAYERS - GOALSCORERS

**1 Andy Clarke**

| | | | |
|---|---|---|---|
| Goals in the League | 17 | Player Strike Rate<br>Average number of minutes between League goals scored by player | 208 |
| Contribution to Attacking Power<br>Average number of minutes between League team goals while on pitch | 78 | Club Strike Rate<br>Average number of minutes between League goals scored by club | 81 |

| | PLAYER | LGE GOALS | POWER | STRIKE RATE |
|---|---|---|---|---|
| 2 | Dave Farrell | 3 | 65 | 703 mins |
| 3 | Jimmy Bullard | 3 | 80 | 774 mins |
| 4 | Simon Rea | 3 | 69 | 992 mins |
| 5 | Mark Arber | 2 | 88 | 1103 mins |

## KEY PLAYERS - MIDFIELDERS

**1 Matthew Gill**

| | | | |
|---|---|---|---|
| Goals in the League | 1 | Contribution to Attacking Power<br>Average number of minutes between League team goals while on pitch | 79 |
| Defensive Rating<br>Average number of mins between League goals conceded while he was on the pitch | 77 | Scoring Difference<br>Defensive Rating minus Contribution to Attacking Power | -2 |

| | PLAYER | LGE GOALS | DEF RATE | POWER | SCORE DIFF |
|---|---|---|---|---|---|
| 2 | Jimmy Bullard | 3 | 73 | 80 | -7 mins |
| 3 | Richard Scott | 1 | 74 | 84 | -10 mins |
| 4 | Helgi Danielsson | 0 | 80 | 116 | -36 mins |

## KEY PLAYERS - DEFENDERS

**1 Mark Arber**

| | | | |
|---|---|---|---|
| Goals Conceded (GC)<br>The number of League goals conceded while he was on the pitch | 22 | Clean Sheets<br>In games when he played at least 70 minutes | 11 |
| Defensive Rating<br>Ave number of mins between League goals conceded while on the pitch | 100 | Club Defensive Rating<br>Average number of mins between League goals conceded by the club this season | 77 |

| | PLAYER | CON LGE | CLEAN SHEETS | DEF RATE |
|---|---|---|---|---|
| 2 | Sagi Burton | 25 | 12 | 98 mins |
| 3 | Tony Shields | 28 | 10 | 92 mins |
| 4 | Gareth Jelleyman | 29 | 11 | 87 mins |
| 5 | Adam Newton | 36 | 9 | 79 mins |

## KEY GOALKEEPER

**1 Lee Harrison**

| | |
|---|---|
| Goals Conceded in the League | 12 |
| Defensive Rating<br>Ave number of mins between League goals conceded while on the pitch | 90 |
| Counting Games<br>Games when he played at least 70 mins | 12 |
| Clean Sheets<br>In games when he played at least 70 mins | 7 |

## TOP POINT EARNERS

| | PLAYER | GAMES | AVE |
|---|---|---|---|
| 1 | Fotiadis | 4 | 2.25 |
| 2 | McKenzie | 5 | 2.20 |
| 3 | Boucaud | 5 | 2.20 |
| 4 | Hendon | 7 | 2.00 |
| 5 | Burton | 26 | 1.58 |
| 6 | Arber | 24 | 1.54 |
| 7 | Rea | 31 | 1.52 |
| 8 | Jelleyman | 25 | 1.48 |
| 9 | Shields | 27 | 1.48 |
| 10 | Danielsson | 11 | 1.45 |
| | **CLUB AVERAGE:** | | **1.26** |

Ave = Average points per match in Counting Games

## DISCIPLINARY RECORDS

| | PLAYER | YELLOW | RED | AVE |
|---|---|---|---|---|
| 1 | MacDonald | 3 | 0 | 175 |
| 2 | McKenzie | 3 | 0 | 210 |
| 3 | Lee | 5 | 1 | 211 |
| 4 | Burton | 11 | 0 | 223 |
| 5 | Edwards | 7 | 1 | 244 |
| 6 | Green | 3 | 0 | 303 |
| 7 | Fenn | 2 | 0 | 394 |
| 8 | Joseph | 3 | 0 | 478 |
| 9 | Shields | 5 | 0 | 515 |
| 10 | Arber | 4 | 0 | 551 |
| 11 | Forsyth | 1 | 0 | 566 |
| 12 | Bullard | 4 | 0 | 580 |
| 13 | Hyde | 1 | 0 | 626 |
| | Other | 19 | 2 | |
| | TOTAL | 71 | 4 | |

## LEAGUE GOALS

| | PLAYER | MINS | GOALS | AVE |
|---|---|---|---|---|
| 1 | Clarke, A | 3531 | 17 | 208 |
| 2 | McKenzie | 632 | 5 | 126 |
| 3 | Farrell | 2109 | 3 | 703 |
| 4 | Rea | 2977 | 3 | 992 |
| 5 | Allen | 795 | 3 | 265 |
| 6 | Lee | 1271 | 3 | 424 |
| 7 | Bullard | 2322 | 3 | 774 |
| 8 | Green | 911 | 2 | 456 |
| 9 | Arber | 2205 | 2 | 1103 |
| 10 | Fotiadis | 541 | 2 | 271 |
| 11 | Gill | 3473 | 1 | 3473 |
| 12 | Fenn | 789 | 1 | 789 |
| 13 | Newton | 2848 | 1 | 2848 |
| | Other | | 5 | |
| | TOTAL | | 51 | |

## MONTH BY MONTH GUIDE TO THE POINTS

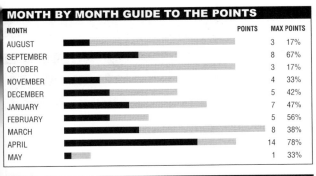

| MONTH | POINTS | MAX POINTS |
|---|---|---|
| AUGUST | 3 | 17% |
| SEPTEMBER | 8 | 67% |
| OCTOBER | 3 | 17% |
| NOVEMBER | 4 | 33% |
| DECEMBER | 5 | 42% |
| JANUARY | 7 | 47% |
| FEBRUARY | 5 | 56% |
| MARCH | 8 | 38% |
| APRIL | 14 | 78% |
| MAY | 1 | 33% |

## TEAM OF THE SEASON

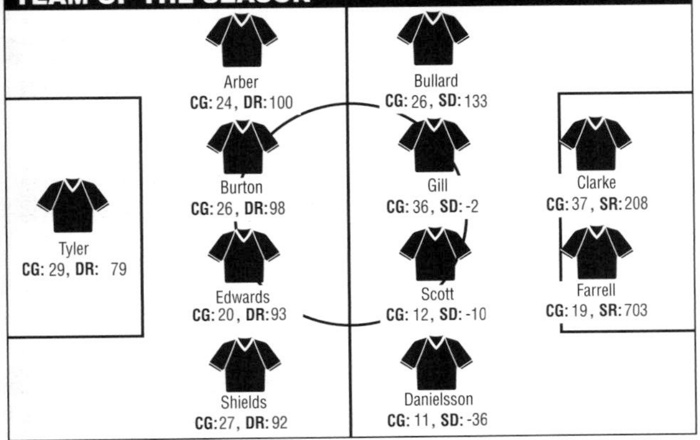
Arber
CG: 24, DR: 100
Bullard
CG: 26, SD: 133
Burton
CG: 26, DR: 98
Gill
CG: 36, SD: -2
Clarke
CG: 37, SR: 208
Tyler
CG: 29, DR: 79
Edwards
CG: 20, DR: 93
Scott
CG: 12, SD: -10
Farrell
CG: 19, SR: 703
Shields
CG: 27, DR: 92
Danielsson
CG: 11, SD: -36

KEY: DR = Defensive Rate, SD = Scoring Difference, SR = Strike Rate, CG = Counting Games – League games playing at least 70 minutes

## LEAGUE APPEARANCES, BOOKINGS AND CAPS

| | AGE | IN THE SQUAD | COUNTING GAMES | MINUTES ON PITCH | YELLOW CARDS | RED CARDS | THIS SEASON | HOME COUNTRY |
|---|---|---|---|---|---|---|---|---|
| **Goalkeepers** | | | | | | | | |
| Daniel Connor | 22 | 13 | 4 | 360 | 0 | 0 | - | Rep or Ireland |
| Lee Harrison | 31 | 15 | 12 | 1080 | 0 | 0 | - | |
| Brian Murphy | 20 | 1 | 1 | 90 | 0 | 0 | - | Rep of Ireland |
| Mark Tyler | 26 | 31 | 29 | 2610 | 0 | 0 | - | England |
| **Defenders** | | | | | | | | |
| Mark Arber | 25 | 26 | 24 | 2205 | 4 | 0 | - | South Africa |
| Sagi Burton | 25 | 31 | 26 | 2453 | 11 | 0 | - | England |
| Andrew Edwards | 31 | 26 | 20 | 1953 | 7 | 1 | - | England |
| Ian Hendon | 31 | 8 | 7 | 603 | 0 | 0 | - | England |
| Gareth Jelleyman | 22 | 35 | 25 | 2533 | 2 | 0 | - | England |
| Marc Joseph | 26 | 17 | 15 | 1435 | 3 | 0 | - | England |
| Steve Laurie | 20 | 4 | 0 | 0 | 0 | 0 | - | Australia |
| Gary MacDonald | - | 11 | 5 | 525 | 3 | 0 | - | |
| Brian McGovern | 23 | 1 | 0 | 45 | 0 | 0 | - | Rep of Ireland |
| Adam Newton | 22 | 42 | 29 | 2848 | 3 | 0 | - | England |
| Dennis Pearce | 28 | 4 | 1 | 144 | 0 | 0 | - | England |
| Simon Rea | 26 | 42 | 31 | 2977 | 2 | 1 | - | England |
| Tony Shields | 23 | 36 | 27 | 2577 | 5 | 0 | - | N Ireland |
| Sean St Ledger-Hall | 18 | 4 | 0 | 68 | 0 | 0 | - | England |
| Bradley Thomas | 19 | 2 | 0 | 0 | 0 | 0 | - | England |
| Roger Willis | 36 | 7 | 1 | 118 | 0 | 0 | - | |
| **Midfielders** | | | | | | | | |
| Andre Boucaud | 18 | 8 | 5 | 437 | 1 | 0 | - | England |
| Jimmy Bullard | 24 | 26 | 26 | 2322 | 4 | 0 | - | England |
| Helgi Danielsson | 21 | 28 | 11 | 1272 | 0 | 0 | - | Poland |
| Richard Forsyth | 32 | 9 | 6 | 566 | 1 | 0 | - | England |
| Matthew Gill | 22 | 43 | 36 | 3473 | 4 | 1 | - | England |
| Graham Hyde | 32 | 9 | 5 | 626 | 1 | 0 | - | England |
| Richard Scott | 28 | 24 | 12 | 1180 | 1 | 0 | - | England |
| Tony Scully | 27 | 4 | 0 | 63 | 0 | 0 | - | Rep of Ireland |
| Ryan Semple | 18 | 6 | 0 | 86 | 0 | 0 | - | England |
| Gavin Strachan | 24 | 3 | 1 | 124 | 0 | 0 | - | Scotland |
| **Forwards** | | | | | | | | |
| Bradley Allen | 31 | 12 | 6 | 795 | 0 | 0 | - | England |
| Andy Clarke | 35 | 45 | 37 | 3531 | 3 | 0 | - | England |
| Lee Clarke | 19 | 5 | 0 | 12 | 0 | 0 | - | England |
| Dave Farrell | 31 | 41 | 19 | 2109 | 3 | 0 | - | England |
| Neale Fenn | 26 | 35 | 7 | 789 | 2 | 0 | - | England |
| Andrew Fotiadis | 25 | 13 | 4 | 541 | 0 | 0 | - | England |
| Francis Green | 23 | 26 | 7 | 911 | 3 | 0 | - | England |
| Jason Lee | 32 | 30 | 10 | 1271 | 5 | 1 | - | England |
| Leon McKenzie | 25 | 11 | 5 | 632 | 3 | 0 | - | England |
| Shane Tolley | 18 | 2 | 0 | 0 | 0 | 0 | - | England |

## SQUAD APPEARANCES

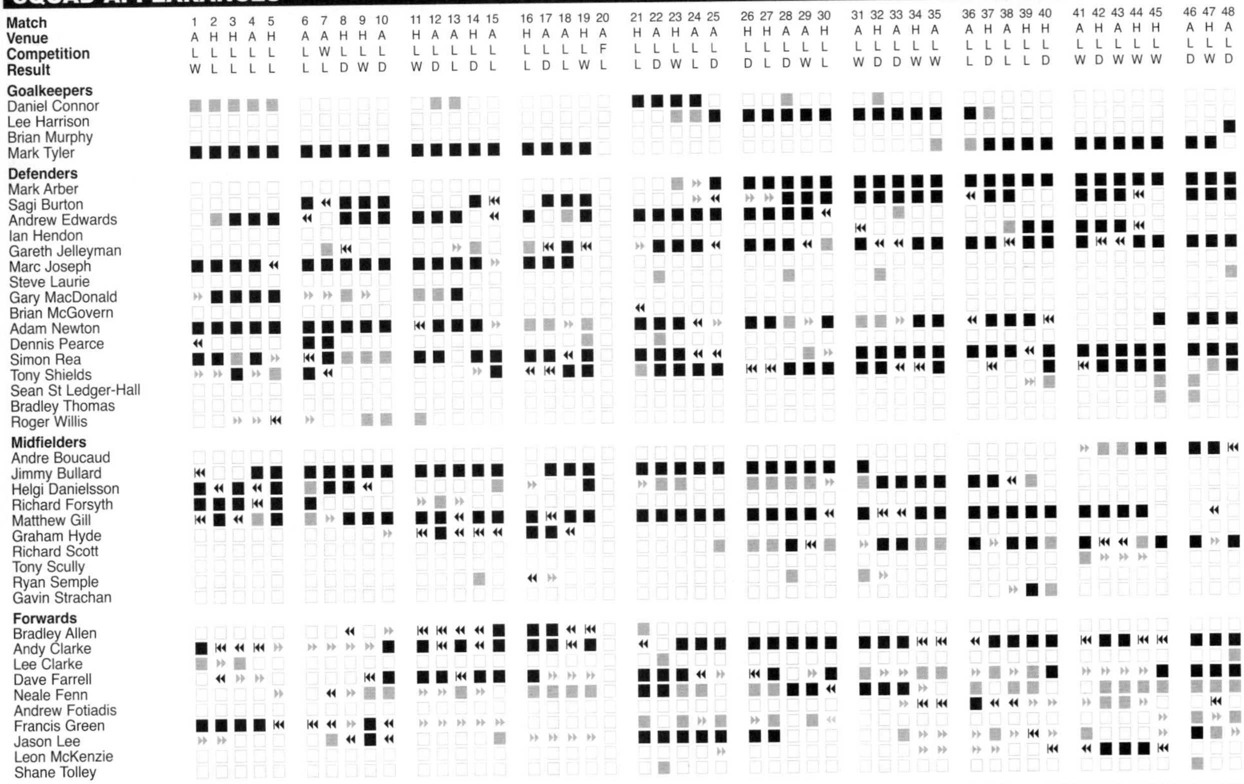
Match 1 2 3 4 5 6 7 8 9 10 11 12 13 14 15 16 17 18 19 20 21 22 23 24 25 26 27 28 29 30 31 32 33 34 35 36 37 38 39 40 41 42 43 44 45 46 47 48
Venue A H H A H A A H H A H A A H A H A A H A H A H A A H H A A H A H A H A A H A H H A H A H H A H A
Competition L L L L L L W L L L L L L L L L L L L F L L L L L L L L L L L L L L L L L L L L L L L L L L L L
Result W L L L L L L D W D W D L D L L D L W L L D W L D D L D W L W D D W W L D L L D W D W W W D W D
Goalkeepers
Daniel Connor
Lee Harrison
Brian Murphy
Mark Tyler
Defenders
Mark Arber
Sagi Burton
Andrew Edwards
Ian Hendon
Gareth Jelleyman
Marc Joseph
Steve Laurie
Gary MacDonald
Brian McGovern
Adam Newton
Dennis Pearce
Simon Rea
Tony Shields
Sean St Ledger-Hall
Bradley Thomas
Roger Willis
Midfielders
Andre Boucaud
Jimmy Bullard
Helgi Danielsson
Richard Forsyth
Matthew Gill
Graham Hyde
Richard Scott
Tony Scully
Ryan Semple
Gavin Strachan
Forwards
Bradley Allen
Andy Clarke
Lee Clarke
Dave Farrell
Neale Fenn
Andrew Fotiadis
Francis Green
Jason Lee
Leon McKenzie
Shane Tolley

# COLCHESTER UNITED

Final Position: **12th**

NICKNAME: THE U'S

| | | | | | | | |
|---|---|---|---|---|---|---|---|
| 1 | div2 | Stockport | H | W | 1-0 | Pinault 59 |
| 2 | div2 | Tranmere | A | D | 1-1 | Keith 53 |
| 3 | div2 | Crewe | A | L | 0-2 | |
| 4 | div2 | Brentford | H | L | 0-1 | |
| 5 | div2 | Peterborough | A | W | 1-0 | Keith 80 |
| 6 | div2 | Wigan | H | W | 1-0 | Morgan 41 |
| 7 | div2 | Cheltenham | H | D | 1-1 | Keith 58 pen |
| 8 | wcr1 | Coventry | A | L | 0-3 | |
| 9 | div2 | Port Vale | A | L | 0-1 | |
| 10 | div2 | Northampton | A | L | 1-4 | Sampson 36 og |
| 11 | div2 | Oldham | H | L | 0-1 | |
| 12 | div2 | QPR | A | L | 0-2 | |
| 13 | div2 | Wycombe | H | L | 0-1 | |
| 14 | div2 | Swindon | A | D | 2-2 | McGleish 2; Pinault 49 |
| 15 | div2 | Chesterfield | H | W | 2-0 | Izzet 58,72 |
| 16 | div2 | Huddersfield | A | D | 1-1 | Rapley 11 |
| 17 | div2 | Barnsley | H | D | 1-1 | Stockley 10 |
| 18 | div2 | Mansfield | A | L | 2-4 | Keith 25 pen; Rapley 31 |
| 19 | div2 | Bristol City | H | D | 2-2 | Pinault 55; Bowry 66 |
| 20 | facr1 | Chester | H | L | 0-1 | |
| 21 | div2 | Notts County | A | W | 3-2 | Morgan 7,35; McGleish 83 |
| 22 | div2 | Plymouth | H | D | 0-0 | |
| 23 | div2 | Luton | A | W | 2-1 | Duguid 45; Morgan 58 |
| 24 | div2 | Cardiff | H | L | 1-2 | Stockwell 52 |
| 25 | div2 | Peterborough | H | D | 1-1 | Izzet 45 |
| 26 | div2 | Blackpool | A | L | 1-3 | Izzet 71 |
| 27 | div2 | Tranmere | H | D | 2-2 | McGleish 12; Keith 69 pen |
| 28 | div2 | Crewe | H | L | 1-2 | Stockwell 41 |
| 29 | div2 | Wigan | A | L | 1-2 | Keith 90 pen |
| 30 | div2 | Blackpool | H | L | 0-2 | |
| 31 | div2 | Stockport | A | D | 1-1 | Keith 88 |
| 32 | div2 | Bristol City | A | W | 2-1 | McGleish 12; Pinault 82 |
| 33 | div2 | Mansfield | H | W | 1-0 | McGleish 88 |
| 34 | div2 | Cheltenham | A | D | 1-1 | Williams 44 |
| 35 | div2 | Port Vale | H | W | 4-1 | Williams 7,36,72; Keith 53 |
| 36 | div2 | Northampton | H | W | 2-0 | Williams 28; McGleish 76 |
| 37 | div2 | Oldham | A | L | 0-2 | |
| 38 | div2 | Brentford | A | D | 1-1 | Keith 84 pen |
| 39 | div2 | Huddersfield | H | W | 2-0 | Izzet 74; McGleish 81 |
| 40 | div2 | Chesterfield | A | W | 4-0 | Izzet 43; Williams 48; Payne 68 og; Morgan 81 |
| 41 | div2 | Barnsley | A | D | 1-1 | McGleish 38 |
| 42 | div2 | Swindon | H | W | 1-0 | Izzet 57 |
| 43 | div2 | Plymouth | A | D | 0-0 | |
| 44 | div2 | Notts County | H | D | 1-1 | Duguid 7 |
| 45 | div2 | Cardiff | A | W | 3-0 | Duguid 4; Izzet 61; Morgan 73 |
| 46 | div2 | Luton | H | L | 0-5 | |
| 47 | div2 | Wycombe | A | D | 0-0 | |
| 48 | div2 | QPR | H | L | 0-1 | |

## ATTENDANCES

HOME GROUND: LAYER ROAD CAPACITY: 6200 AVERAGE LEAGUE AT HOME: 3386

| | | | | | | | | |
|---|---|---|---|---|---|---|---|---|
| 12 | QPR | 12906 | 14 | Swindon | 4152 | 1 | Stockport | 3300 |
| 45 | Cardiff | 12633 | 31 | Stockport | 4011 | 13 | Wycombe | 3253 |
| 32 | Bristol City | 11107 | 38 | Brentford | 3990 | 33 | Mansfield | 3247 |
| 41 | Barnsley | 9154 | 46 | Luton | 3967 | 40 | Chesterfield | 3226 |
| 16 | Huddersfield | 8912 | 39 | Huddersfield | 3835 | 15 | Chesterfield | 3211 |
| 2 | Tranmere | 7499 | 42 | Swindon | 3787 | 4 | Brentford | 3135 |
| 43 | Plymouth | 7122 | 25 | Peterborough | 3760 | 24 | Cardiff | 3096 |
| 47 | Wycombe | 6283 | 22 | Plymouth | 3714 | 17 | Barnsley | 3096 |
| 8 | Coventry | 6075 | 10 | Northampton | 3663 | 11 | Oldham | 3021 |
| 26 | Blackpool | 6040 | 34 | Cheltenham | 3607 | 28 | Crewe | 2949 |
| 23 | Luton | 5890 | 35 | Port Vale | 3581 | 20 | Chester | 2901 |
| 29 | Wigan | 5792 | 44 | Notts County | 3435 | 27 | Tranmere | 2846 |
| 37 | Oldham | 5223 | 18 | Mansfield | 3414 | 7 | Cheltenham | 2845 |
| 3 | Crewe | 5138 | 36 | Northampton | 3408 | 6 | Wigan | 2721 |
| 48 | QPR | 5047 | 19 | Bristol City | 3338 | | | |
| 21 | Notts County | 4626 | 9 | Port Vale | 3325 | | | |
| 5 | Peterborough | 4203 | 30 | Blackpool | 3305 | | | |

■ Home □ Away ▨ Neutral

## KEY PLAYERS - GOALSCORERS

**1 Dean Morgan**

| | | | |
|---|---|---|---|
| Goals in the League | 6 | Player Strike Rate<br>Average number of minutes between League goals scored by player | 338 |
| Contribution to Attacking Power<br>Average number of minutes between League team goals while on pitch | 144 | Club Strike Rate<br>Average number of minutes between League goals scored by club | 80 |

| | PLAYER | LGE GOALS | POWER | STRIKE RATE |
|---|---|---|---|---|
| 2 | Joe Keith | 9 | 71 | 359 mins |
| 3 | Scott McGleish | 8 | 74 | 419 mins |
| 4 | Kemal Izzet | 8 | 77 | 493 mins |
| 5 | Thomas Pinault | 4 | 72 | 740 mins |

## KEY PLAYERS - MIDFIELDERS

**1 Thomas Pinault**

| | | | |
|---|---|---|---|
| Goals in the League | 4 | Contribution to Attacking Power<br>Average number of minutes between League team goals while on pitch | 72 |
| Defensive Rating<br>Average number of mins between League goals conceded while he was on the pitch | 93 | Scoring Difference<br>Defensive Rating minus Contribution to Attacking Power | 21 |

| | PLAYER | LGE GOALS | DEF RATE | POWER | SCORE DIFF |
|---|---|---|---|---|---|
| 2 | Karl Duguid | 3 | 77 | 72 | 5 mins |
| 3 | Kemal Izzet | 8 | 72 | 77 | -5 mins |
| 4 | Micky Stockwell | 2 | 70 | 84 | -14 mins |
| 5 | Pat Baldwin | 0 | 62 | 84 | -22 mins |

## KEY PLAYERS - DEFENDERS

**1 Sam Stockley**

| | | | |
|---|---|---|---|
| Goals Conceded (GC)<br>The number of League goals conceded while he was on the pitch | 30 | Clean Sheets<br>In games when he played at least 70 minutes | 9 |
| Defensive Rating<br>Ave number of mins between League goals conceded while on the pitch | 89 | Club Defensive Rating<br>Average number of mins between League goals conceded by the club this season | 74 |

| | PLAYER | CON LGE | CLEAN SHEETS | DEF RATE |
|---|---|---|---|---|
| 2 | Scott Fitzgerald | 30 | 8 | 78 mins |
| 3 | Joe Keith | 43 | 10 | 75 mins |
| 4 | Alan White | 49 | 12 | 74 mins |
| 5 | Mark Warren | 24 | 4 | 68 mins |

## KEY GOALKEEPER

**1 Richard McKinney**

| | |
|---|---|
| Goals Conceded in the League | 19 |
| Defensive Rating<br>Ave number of mins between League goals conceded while on the pitch | 95 |
| Counting Games<br>Games when he played at least 70 mins | 19 |
| Clean Sheets<br>In games when he played at least 70 mins | 9 |

## TOP POINT EARNERS

| | PLAYER | GAMES | AVE |
|---|---|---|---|
| 1 | Williams | 4 | 2.25 |
| 2 | Jackson | 6 | 2.00 |
| 3 | Chilvers | 6 | 1.83 |
| 4 | Pinault | 29 | 1.52 |
| 5 | Johnson, G | 8 | 1.50 |
| 6 | Stockley | 28 | 1.50 |
| 7 | McKinney | 19 | 1.42 |
| 8 | Morgan | 15 | 1.40 |
| 9 | Fitzgerald | 26 | 1.38 |
| 10 | Rapley | 11 | 1.36 |
| | **CLUB AVERAGE:** | | **1.26** |

Ave = Average points per match in Counting Games

## DISCIPLINARY RECORDS

| | PLAYER | YELLOW | RED | AVE |
|---|---|---|---|---|
| 1 | Warren | 6 | 2 | 204 |
| 2 | White | 14 | 2 | 227 |
| 3 | Chilvers | 2 | 0 | 261 |
| 4 | Duguid | 5 | 1 | 384 |
| 5 | Baldwin | 3 | 0 | 475 |
| 6 | Steele | 0 | 1 | 524 |
| 7 | Jackson | 1 | 0 | 559 |
| 8 | Rapley | 1 | 1 | 620 |
| 9 | Coote | 1 | 0 | 635 |
| 10 | Johnson, G | 1 | 0 | 753 |
| 11 | Bowry | 3 | 0 | 961 |
| 12 | Izzet | 4 | 0 | 986 |
| 13 | Pinault | 3 | 0 | 987 |
| | Other | 10 | 0 | |
| | TOTAL | 54 | 7 | |

## LEAGUE GOALS

| | PLAYER | MINS | GOALS | AVE |
|---|---|---|---|---|
| 1 | Keith | 3229 | 9 | 359 |
| 2 | McGleish | 3349 | 8 | 419 |
| 3 | Izzet | 3945 | 8 | 493 |
| 4 | Williams | 490 | 6 | 82 |
| 5 | Morgan | 2025 | 6 | 338 |
| 6 | Pinault | 2961 | 4 | 740 |
| 7 | Duguid | 2309 | 3 | 770 |
| 8 | Rapley | 1241 | 2 | 621 |
| 9 | Stockwell | 2509 | 2 | 1255 |
| 10 | Bowry | 2885 | 1 | 2885 |
| 11 | Stockley | 2683 | 1 | 2683 |
| | Other | | 2 | |
| | TOTAL | | 52 | |

## MONTH BY MONTH GUIDE TO THE POINTS

| MONTH | POINTS | % |
|---|---|---|
| AUGUST | 10 | 56% |
| SEPTEMBER | 1 | 7% |
| OCTOBER | 6 | 40% |
| NOVEMBER | 5 | 42% |
| DECEMBER | 4 | 33% |
| JANUARY | 1 | 8% |
| FEBRUARY | 8 | 67% |
| MARCH | 17 | 71% |
| APRIL | 6 | 40% |
| MAY | 0 | 0% |

## TEAM OF THE SEASON

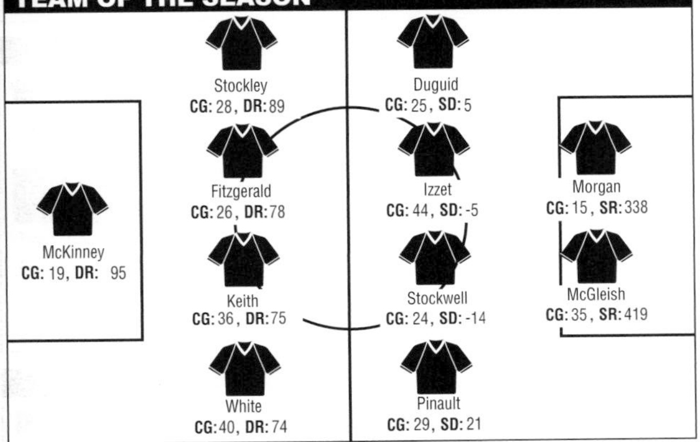
McKinney
CG: 19, DR: 95
Stockley
CG: 28, DR: 89
Fitzgerald
CG: 26, DR: 78
Keith
CG: 36, DR: 75
White
CG: 40, DR: 74
Duguid
CG: 25, SD: 5
Izzet
CG: 44, SD: -5
Stockwell
CG: 24, SD: -14
Pinault
CG: 29, SD: 21
Morgan
CG: 15, SR: 338
McGleish
CG: 35, SR: 419

**KEY:** DR = Defensive Rate, SD = Scoring Difference, SR = Strike Rate, CG=Counting Games – League games playing at least 70 minutes

## LEAGUE APPEARANCES, BOOKINGS AND CAPS

| | AGE | IN THE SQUAD | COUNTING GAMES | MINUTES ON PITCH | YELLOW CARDS | RED CARDS | THIS SEASON | HOME COUNTRY |
|---|---|---|---|---|---|---|---|---|
| **Goalkeepers** | | | | | | | | |
| Simon Brown | 26 | 35 | 25 | 2340 | 0 | 0 | - | England |
| Dean Gerken | - | 10 | 0 | 0 | 0 | 0 | - | England |
| Richard McKinney | 24 | 45 | 19 | 1800 | 1 | 0 | - | Rep or Ireland |
| **Defenders** | | | | | | | | |
| Liam Chilvers | 21 | 6 | 6 | 523 | 2 | 0 | - | England |
| Michael Edwards | 23 | 7 | 2 | 278 | 0 | 0 | - | England |
| Scott Fitzgerald | 33 | 27 | 26 | 2340 | 2 | 0 | - | England |
| Greg Halford | 18 | 4 | 1 | 77 | 0 | 0 | - | England |
| Joe Keith | 24 | 36 | 36 | 3229 | 0 | 0 | - | England |
| Daniel Steele | - | 15 | 5 | 524 | 0 | 1 | - | |
| Sam Stockley | 25 | 36 | 28 | 2683 | 2 | 0 | - | England |
| Mark Warren | 28 | 20 | 16 | 1632 | 6 | 2 | - | England |
| Alan White | 27 | 42 | 40 | 3636 | 14 | 2 | - | England |
| **Midfielders** | | | | | | | | |
| Pat Baldwin | 20 | 31 | 14 | 1426 | 3 | 0 | - | England |
| Bobby Bowry | 32 | 45 | 30 | 2885 | 3 | 0 | - | England |
| Marc Canham | 20 | 9 | 0 | 123 | 0 | 0 | - | England |
| Karl Duguid | 25 | 27 | 25 | 2309 | 5 | 1 | - | England |
| Dean Gerken | - | 2 | 0 | 0 | 0 | 0 | - | England |
| Kemal Izzet | 22 | 45 | 44 | 3945 | 4 | 0 | - | Turkey |
| Johnnie Jackson | 20 | 7 | 6 | 559 | 1 | 0 | - | England |
| Gavin Johnson | 32 | 9 | 8 | 753 | 1 | 0 | - | England |
| Chris Keeble | 24 | 6 | 0 | 49 | 0 | 0 | - | England |
| Ben May | 19 | 7 | 4 | 389 | 0 | 0 | - | England |
| Leke Odunsi | 22 | 15 | 2 | 303 | 1 | 0 | - | England |
| Thomas Pinault | 21 | 43 | 29 | 2961 | 3 | 0 | - | France |
| Micky Stockwell | 38 | 43 | 24 | 2509 | 1 | 0 | - | England |
| **Forwards** | | | | | | | | |
| Simon Atangana | - | 12 | 0 | 198 | 0 | 0 | - | |
| Adrian Coote | 24 | 24 | 3 | 635 | 1 | 0 | - | N Ireland |
| Scott McGleish | 29 | 43 | 35 | 3349 | 2 | 0 | - | England |
| Dean Morgan | 19 | 44 | 15 | 2025 | 0 | 0 | - | England |
| Lloyd Opara | 19 | 6 | 0 | 91 | 0 | 0 | - | England |
| Kevin Rapley | 25 | 23 | 11 | 1241 | 1 | 1 | - | England |
| Justin Richards | 22 | 4 | 0 | 34 | 1 | 0 | - | England |
| Gareth Williams | 20 | 8 | 4 | 490 | 0 | 0 | - | Wales |

**KEY:** LEAGUE BOOKINGS CAPS

## SQUAD APPEARANCES

| Match | 1 | 2 | 3 | 4 | 5 | 6 | 7 | 8 | 9 | 10 | 11 | 12 | 13 | 14 | 15 | 16 | 17 | 18 | 19 | 20 | 21 | 22 | 23 | 24 | 25 | 26 | 27 | 28 | 29 | 30 | 31 | 32 | 33 | 34 | 35 | 36 | 37 | 38 | 39 | 40 | 41 | 42 | 43 | 44 | 45 | 46 | 47 | 48 |
|---|---|---|---|---|---|---|---|---|---|---|---|---|---|---|---|---|---|---|---|---|---|---|---|---|---|---|---|---|---|---|---|---|---|---|---|---|---|---|---|---|---|---|---|---|---|---|---|---|
| Venue | H | A | A | H | A | H | H | A | A | A | H | A | H | A | H | A | H | A | H | H | A | H | A | H | H | A | H | H | A | H | A | A | H | A | H | H | A | A | H | A | A | H | A | H | A | H | A | H |
| Competition | L | L | L | L | L | L | L | W | L | L | L | L | L | L | L | L | L | L | L | F | L | L | L | L | L | L | L | L | L | L | L | L | L | L | L | L | L | L | L | L | L | L | L | L | L | L | L | L |
| Result | W | D | L | L | W | W | D | L | L | L | L | L | L | D | W | D | D | L | D | L | W | D | W | L | D | L | D | L | L | L | D | W | W | D | W | W | L | D | W | W | D | W | D | D | W | L | D | L |

**Goalkeepers**
Simon Brown
Dean Gerken
Richard McKinney

**Defenders**
Liam Chilvers
Michael Edwards
Scott Fitzgerald
Greg Halford
Joe Keith
Daniel Steele
Sam Stockley
Mark Warren
Alan White

**Midfielders**
Pat Baldwin
Bobby Bowry
Marc Canham
Karl Duguid
Dean Gerken
Kemal Izzet
Johnnie Jackson
Gavin Johnson
Chris Keeble
Ben May
Leke Odunsi
Thomas Pinault
Micky Stockwell

**Forwards**
Simon Atangana
Adrian Coote
Scott McGleish
Dean Morgan
Lloyd Opara
Kevin Rapley
Justin Richards
Gareth Williams

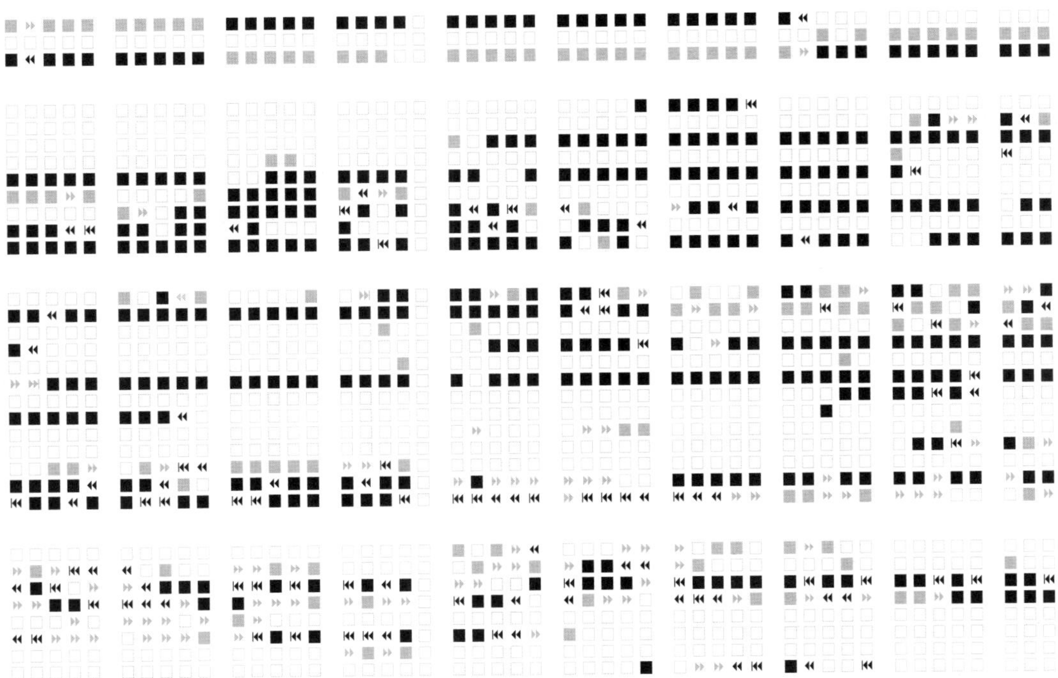

# BLACKPOOL

Final Position: **13th**

NICKNAME: THE SEASIDERS

| | | | | | | |
|---|---|---|---|---|---|---|
| 1 | div2 | Bristol City | A | L | 0-2 | |
| 2 | div2 | Luton | H | W | 5-2 | Clarke, P 19,24; Taylor 65,90; Dalglish 79 |
| 3 | div2 | Swindon | H | D | 0-0 | |
| 4 | div2 | Northampton | A | W | 1-0 | Murphy, J 90 |
| 5 | div2 | Oldham | H | D | 0-0 | |
| 6 | div2 | Huddersfield | A | D | 0-0 | |
| 7 | div2 | Tranmere | H | W | 3-0 | Southern 54; Hills 58 pen; Taylor 85 |
| 8 | wcr1 | Burnley | A | L | 0-3 | |
| 9 | div2 | Wycombe | A | W | 2-1 | Hills 14 pen,28 |
| 10 | div2 | Barnsley | A | L | 1-2 | Murphy, J 12 |
| 11 | div2 | Port Vale | H | W | 3-2 | Murphy, J 62,65; Clarke, P 81 |
| 12 | div2 | Chesterfield | A | L | 0-1 | |
| 13 | div2 | Cheltenham | H | W | 3-1 | Spencer 41 og; Wellens 65; Walker 83 |
| 14 | div2 | QPR | A | L | 1-2 | Taylor 63 |
| 15 | div2 | Cardiff | H | W | 1-0 | Hills 54 |
| 16 | div2 | Plymouth | A | W | 3-1 | Taylor 16,40; Murphy 87 |
| 17 | div2 | Stockport | H | L | 1-3 | Milligan 90 |
| 18 | div2 | Brentford | A | L | 0-5 | |
| 19 | div2 | Wigan | H | L | 0-2 | |
| 20 | facr1 | Barnsley | A | W | 4-1 | Hills 37; Murphy 49; Dalglish 50; Taylor 70 |
| 21 | div2 | Crewe | A | L | 0-3 | |
| 22 | div2 | Notts County | H | D | 1-1 | Clarke, C 21 |
| 23 | facr2 | Torquay | H | W | 3-1 | Hazell 21 og; Taylor 56; Murphy 90 |
| 24 | div2 | Mansfield | A | L | 0-4 | |
| 25 | div2 | Peterborough | H | W | 3-0 | Grayson 17; Bullock 21; Walker 62 |
| 26 | div2 | Oldham | A | D | 1-1 | Murphy 17 |
| 27 | div2 | Colchester | H | W | 3-1 | Walker 34; Grayson 45; Murphy 59 |
| 28 | div2 | Huddersfield | H | D | 1-1 | Hills 89 pen |
| 29 | facr3 | Crystal Palace | H | L | 1-2 | Popovic 10 og |
| 30 | div2 | Northampton | H | W | 2-1 | Walker 77 pen; Murphy 90 |
| 31 | div2 | Swindon | A | D | 1-1 | Taylor 61 |
| 32 | div2 | Colchester | A | W | 2-0 | Murphy 52; Coid 70 |
| 33 | div2 | Bristol City | H | D | 0-0 | |
| 34 | div2 | Wigan | A | D | 1-1 | Taylor 85 |
| 35 | div2 | Luton | A | W | 3-1 | Murphy 10,52,74 |
| 36 | div2 | Brentford | H | W | 1-0 | Murphy 27 |
| 37 | div2 | Tranmere | A | L | 1-2 | Evans 59 |
| 38 | div2 | Wycombe | H | W | 1-0 | Murphy 20 |
| 39 | div2 | Barnsley | H | L | 1-2 | Murphy 56 |
| 40 | div2 | Port Vale | A | L | 0-1 | |
| 41 | div2 | Plymouth | H | D | 1-1 | Taylor 40 |
| 42 | div2 | Cardiff | A | L | 1-2 | Taylor 37 |
| 43 | div2 | Stockport | A | D | 2-2 | Murphy 32; Grayson 42 |
| 44 | div2 | QPR | H | L | 1-3 | Taylor 90 |
| 45 | div2 | Notts County | A | L | 1-3 | Robinson 35 |
| 46 | div2 | Crewe | H | L | 0-1 | |
| 47 | div2 | Peterborough | A | L | 0-1 | |
| 48 | div2 | Mansfield | H | D | 3-3 | Blinkhorn 30,43; Taylor 90 |
| 49 | div2 | Cheltenham | A | L | 0-3 | |
| 50 | div2 | Chesterfield | H | D | 1-1 | Robinson 64 |

## ATTENDANCES

HOME GROUND: BLOOMFIELD ROAD CAPACITY: 11295 AVERAGE LEAGUE AT HOME: 6989

| | | | | | | | | |
|---|---|---|---|---|---|---|---|---|
| 1 | Bristol City | 11891 | 46 | Crewe | 7623 | 27 | Colchester | 6040 |
| 42 | Cardiff | 11788 | 8 | Burnley | 7448 | 18 | Brentford | 5888 |
| 14 | QPR | 11335 | 33 | Bristol City | 7290 | 22 | Notts County | 5843 |
| 34 | Wigan | 10546 | 38 | Wycombe | 7266 | 9 | Wycombe | 5815 |
| 10 | Barnsley | 9619 | 28 | Huddersfield | 7148 | 30 | Northampton | 5646 |
| 6 | Huddersfield | 9506 | 17 | Stockport | 7047 | 4 | Northampton | 5556 |
| 26 | Oldham | 9415 | 21 | Crewe | 7019 | 45 | Notts County | 5551 |
| 37 | Tranmere | 9111 | 20 | Barnsley | 6857 | 49 | Cheltenham | 5150 |
| 29 | Crystal Palace | 9062 | 7 | Tranmere | 6834 | 25 | Peterborough | 5068 |
| 41 | Plymouth | 8772 | 39 | Barnsley | 6827 | 23 | Torquay | 5014 |
| 16 | Plymouth | 8717 | 13 | Cheltenham | 6649 | 31 | Swindon | 4787 |
| 5 | Oldham | 8201 | 43 | Stockport | 6599 | 47 | Peterborough | 4587 |
| 44 | QPR | 8162 | 35 | Luton | 6563 | 12 | Chesterfield | 4488 |
| 50 | Chesterfield | 7999 | 3 | Swindon | 6404 | 40 | Port Vale | 4394 |
| 11 | Port Vale | 7756 | 2 | Luton | 6377 | 24 | Mansfield | 4001 |
| 15 | Cardiff | 7744 | 36 | Brentford | 6203 | 32 | Colchester | 3305 |
| 19 | Wigan | 7676 | 48 | Mansfield | 6173 | | | |

■ Home □ Away ▒ Neutral

## KEY PLAYERS - GOALSCORERS

**1 John Murphy**

| | | | |
|---|---|---|---|
| Goals in the League | 16 | Player Strike Rate<br>Average number of minutes between League goals scored by player | 187 |
| Contribution to Attacking Power<br>Average number of minutes between League team goals while on pitch | 66 | Club Strike Rate<br>Average number of minutes between League goals scored by club | 74 |

| | PLAYER | LGE GOALS | POWER | STRIKE RATE |
|---|---|---|---|---|
| 2 | Scott Taylor | 12 | 67 | 237 mins |
| 3 | John Hills | 5 | 70 | 369 mins |
| 4 | Richard Walker | 4 | 87 | 437 mins |
| 5 | Peter Clarke | 3 | 62 | 480 mins |

## KEY PLAYERS - MIDFIELDERS

**1 Paul Evans**

| | | | |
|---|---|---|---|
| Goals in the League | 1 | Contribution to Attacking Power<br>Average number of minutes between League team goals while on pitch | 72 |
| Defensive Rating<br>Average number of mins between League goals conceded while he was on the pitch | 108 | Scoring Difference<br>Defensive Rating minus Contribution to Attacking Power | 36 |

| | PLAYER | LGE GOALS | DEF RATE | POWER | SCORE DIFF |
|---|---|---|---|---|---|
| 2 | Keith Southern | 1 | 71 | 68 | 3 mins |
| 3 | Richard Wellens | 1 | 66 | 69 | -3 mins |
| 4 | Martin Bullock | 1 | 60 | 71 | -11 mins |
| 5 | Simon Grayson | 3 | 62 | 74 | -12 mins |

## KEY PLAYERS - DEFENDERS

**1 Colin Hendry**

| | | | |
|---|---|---|---|
| Goals Conceded (GC)<br>The number of League goals conceded while he was on the pitch | 12 | Clean Sheets<br>In games when he played at least 70 minutes | 4 |
| Defensive Rating<br>Ave number of mins between League goals conceded while on the pitch | 101 | Club Defensive Rating<br>Average number of mins between League goals conceded by the club this season | 65 |

| | PLAYER | CON LGE | CLEAN SHEETS | DEF RATE |
|---|---|---|---|---|
| 2 | Leam Richardson | 23 | 5 | 76 mins |
| 3 | Tommy Jaszczun | 17 | 4 | 74 mins |
| 4 | Ian Hughes | 17 | 4 | 72 mins |
| 5 | Peter Clarke | 20 | 6 | 72 mins |

## KEY GOALKEEPER

**1 Philip Barnes**

| | |
|---|---|
| Goals Conceded in the League | 59 |
| Defensive Rating<br>Ave number of mins between League goals conceded while on the pitch | 67 |
| Counting Games<br>Games when he played at least 70 mins | 44 |
| Clean Sheets<br>In games when he played at least 70 mins | 11 |

## TOP POINT EARNERS

| | PLAYER | GAMES | AVE |
|---|---|---|---|
| 1 | Kay | 12 | 1.58 |
| 2 | Ward | 20 | 1.55 |
| 3 | Donovan | 16 | 1.44 |
| 4 | Mulligan | 27 | 1.30 |
| 5 | Ghent | 7 | 1.29 |
| 6 | Curle | 11 | 1.27 |
| 7 | Austin | 31 | 1.26 |
| 8 | Neil | 29 | 1.24 |
| 9 | Marriott | 36 | 1.19 |
| 10 | Morgan | 35 | 1.17 |
| | **CLUB AVERAGE:** | | **1.26** |

Ave = Average points per match in Counting Games

## DISCIPLINARY RECORDS

| | PLAYER | YELLOW | RED | AVE |
|---|---|---|---|---|
| 1 | Richardson | 8 | 0 | 219 |
| 2 | Wellens | 13 | 1 | 231 |
| 3 | Hendry | 4 | 1 | 241 |
| 4 | Hills | 6 | 1 | 263 |
| 5 | Flynn | 5 | 0 | 377 |
| 6 | Dalglish | 4 | 0 | 387 |
| 7 | Robinson | 1 | 0 | 469 |
| 8 | Walker | 3 | 0 | 582 |
| 9 | Thornley | 1 | 0 | 591 |
| 10 | Clarke, C | 1 | 1 | 593 |
| 11 | Jaszczun | 2 | 0 | 625 |
| 12 | Clarke, P | 2 | 0 | 720 |
| 13 | Bullock | 3 | 1 | 747 |
| | Other | 19 | 1 | |
| | TOTAL | 72 | 6 | |

## LEAGUE GOALS

| | PLAYER | MINS | GOALS | AVE |
|---|---|---|---|---|
| 1 | Murphy | 2999 | 16 | 187 |
| 2 | Taylor | 2839 | 12 | 237 |
| 3 | Hills | 1843 | 5 | 369 |
| 4 | Walker | 1746 | 4 | 437 |
| 5 | Clarke, P | 1440 | 3 | 480 |
| 6 | Grayson | 3989 | 3 | 1330 |
| 7 | Robinson | 469 | 2 | 235 |
| 8 | Blinkhorn | 260 | 2 | 130 |
| 9 | Milligan | 181 | 1 | 181 |
| 10 | Dalglish | 1548 | 1 | 1548 |
| 11 | Coid | 2682 | 1 | 2682 |
| 12 | Wellens | 3243 | 1 | 3243 |
| 13 | Bullock | 2988 | 1 | 2988 |
| | Other | | 4 | |
| | TOTAL | | 56 | |

## MONTH BY MONTH GUIDE TO THE POINTS

| MONTH | POINTS | % |
|---|---|---|
| AUGUST | 9 | 50% |
| SEPTEMBER | 9 | 60% |
| OCTOBER | 9 | 60% |
| NOVEMBER | 1 | 8% |
| DECEMBER | 7 | 58% |
| JANUARY | 8 | 67% |
| FEBRUARY | 8 | 53% |
| MARCH | 5 | 24% |
| APRIL | 1 | 7% |
| MAY | 1 | 33% |

## TEAM OF THE SEASON

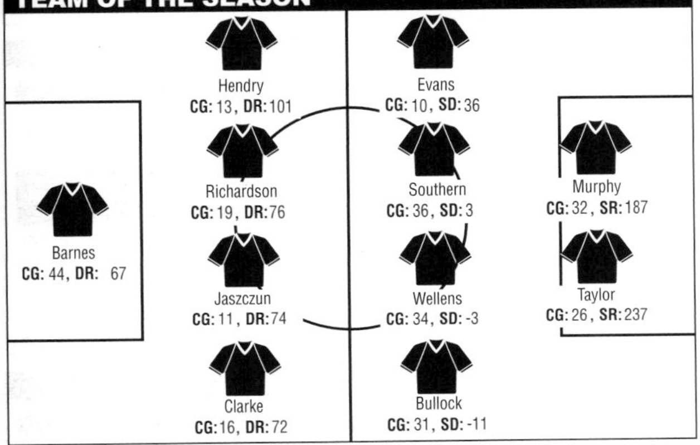
Hendry
CG: 13, DR: 101
Evans
CG: 10, SD: 36
Richardson
CG: 19, DR: 76
Southern
CG: 36, SD: 3
Murphy
CG: 32, SR: 187
Barnes
CG: 44, DR: 67
Jaszczun
CG: 11, DR: 74
Wellens
CG: 34, SD: -3
Taylor
CG: 26, SR: 237
Clarke
CG: 16, DR: 72
Bullock
CG: 31, SD: -11

KEY: DR = Defensive Rate, SD = Scoring Difference, SR = Strike Rate, CG = Counting Games – League games playing at least 70 minutes

## LEAGUE APPEARANCES, BOOKINGS AND CAPS

| | AGE | IN THE SQUAD | COUNTING GAMES | MINUTES ON PITCH | YELLOW CARDS | RED CARDS | THIS SEASON | HOME COUNTRY |
|---|---|---|---|---|---|---|---|---|
| **Goalkeepers** | | | | | | | | |
| Philip Barnes | 24 | 44 | 44 | 3960 | 1 | 0 | - | England |
| Andrew Lonergan | 19 | 8 | 0 | 0 | 0 | 0 | - | England |
| Michael Theoklitos | 22 | 16 | 2 | 180 | 1 | 0 | - | Australia |
| **Defenders** | | | | | | | | |
| Chris Clarke | 29 | 27 | 11 | 1187 | 1 | 1 | - | England |
| Peter Clarke | 21 | 16 | 16 | 1440 | 2 | 0 | - | England |
| Danny Coid | 21 | 36 | 28 | 2682 | 3 | 0 | - | England |
| Phil Doughty | 16 | 1 | 0 | 0 | 0 | 0 | - | England |
| Mike Flynn | 34 | 21 | 21 | 1889 | 5 | 0 | - | England |
| Phil Gulliver | 20 | 5 | 2 | 178 | 0 | 0 | - | |
| Colin Hendry | 37 | 14 | 13 | 1206 | 4 | 1 | - | Scotland |
| John Hills | 25 | 27 | 18 | 1843 | 6 | 1 | - | England |
| Ian Hughes | 28 | 26 | 11 | 1221 | 1 | 0 | - | Wales |
| Tommy Jaszczun | 25 | 25 | 11 | 1251 | 2 | 0 | - | England |
| John O'Kane | 28 | 27 | 5 | 744 | 0 | 0 | - | England |
| Brian Reid | 33 | 6 | 0 | 0 | 0 | 0 | - | Scotland |
| Leam Richardson | 23 | 20 | 19 | 1752 | 8 | 0 | - | England |
| **Midfielders** | | | | | | | | |
| Martin Bullock | 28 | 38 | 31 | 2988 | 3 | 1 | - | England |
| Jamie Burns | 19 | 9 | 2 | 336 | 0 | 0 | - | England |
| Lee Collins | 29 | 14 | 0 | 158 | 0 | 1 | - | Scotland |
| Paul Evans | 28 | 10 | 10 | 865 | 1 | 0 | 2 | Wales (50) |
| Simon Grayson | 33 | 45 | 44 | 3989 | 1 | 0 | - | England |
| Denny Herzig | 18 | 4 | 0 | 0 | 0 | 0 | - | England |
| Steve McMahon | 18 | 13 | 2 | 279 | 2 | 0 | - | England |
| Keith Southern | 19 | 38 | 36 | 3272 | 4 | 0 | - | England |
| Sean Thornton | 20 | 3 | 0 | 94 | 1 | 0 | - | Rep of Ireland |
| Richard Wellens | 23 | 40 | 34 | 3243 | 13 | 1 | - | England |
| **Forwards** | | | | | | | | |
| Matthew Blinkhorn | 18 | 11 | 2 | 260 | 0 | 0 | - | England |
| Paul Dalglish | 26 | 30 | 12 | 1548 | 4 | 0 | - | Scotland |
| Graham Fenton | 29 | 2 | 0 | 0 | 0 | 0 | - | England |
| Jamie Milligan | 23 | 10 | 0 | 181 | 0 | 0 | - | England |
| John Murphy | 26 | 35 | 32 | 2999 | 1 | 0 | - | England |
| Paul Robinson | 24 | 7 | 4 | 469 | 1 | 0 | - | England |
| Scott Taylor | 27 | 46 | 26 | 2839 | 3 | 0 | - | England |
| Ben Thornley | 28 | 16 | 5 | 591 | 1 | 0 | - | England |
| Richard Walker | 25 | 46 | 13 | 1746 | 3 | 0 | - | England |

KEY: LEAGUE BOOKINGS CAPS

## SQUAD APPEARANCES

| Match | 1 | 2 | 3 | 4 | 5 | 6 | 7 | 8 | 9 | 10 | 11 | 12 | 13 | 14 | 15 | 16 | 17 | 18 | 19 | 20 | 21 | 22 | 23 | 24 | 25 |
|---|---|---|---|---|---|---|---|---|---|---|---|---|---|---|---|---|---|---|---|---|---|---|---|---|---|
| Venue | A | H | H | A | H | A | H | A | A | A | H | A | H | A | H | A | H | A | H | A | A | H | H | A | H |
| Competition | L | L | L | L | L | L | L | W | L | L | L | L | L | L | L | L | L | L | L | F | L | L | F | L | L |
| Result | L | W | D | W | D | D | W | L | W | L | W | L | W | L | W | W | L | L | L | W | L | D | W | L | W |

| Match | 26 | 27 | 28 | 29 | 30 | 31 | 32 | 33 | 34 | 35 | 36 | 37 | 38 | 39 | 40 | 41 | 42 | 43 | 44 | 45 | 46 | 47 | 48 | 49 | 50 |
|---|---|---|---|---|---|---|---|---|---|---|---|---|---|---|---|---|---|---|---|---|---|---|---|---|---|
| Venue | A | H | H | H | H | A | A | H | A | A | H | A | H | H | A | H | A | A | H | A | H | A | H | A | H |
| Competition | L | L | L | F | L | L | L | L | L | L | L | L | L | L | L | L | L | L | L | L | L | L | L | L | L |
| Result | D | W | D | L | W | D | W | D | D | W | W | L | W | L | L | D | L | D | L | L | L | L | D | L | D |

**Goalkeepers**
Philip Barnes
Andrew Lonergan
Michael Theoklitos

**Defenders**
Chris Clarke
Peter Clarke
Danny Coid
Phil Doughty
Mike Flynn
Phil Gulliver
Colin Hendry
John Hills
Ian Hughes
Tommy Jaszczun
John O'Kane
Brian Reid
Leam Richardson

**Midfielders**
Martin Bullock
Jamie Burns
Lee Collins
Paul Evans
Simon Grayson
Denny Herzig
Steve McMahon
Keith Southern
Sean Thornton
Richard Wellens

**Forwards**
Matthew Blinkhorn
Paul Dalglish
Graham Fenton
Jamie Milligan
John Murphy
Paul Robinson
Scott Taylor
Ben Thornley
Richard Walker

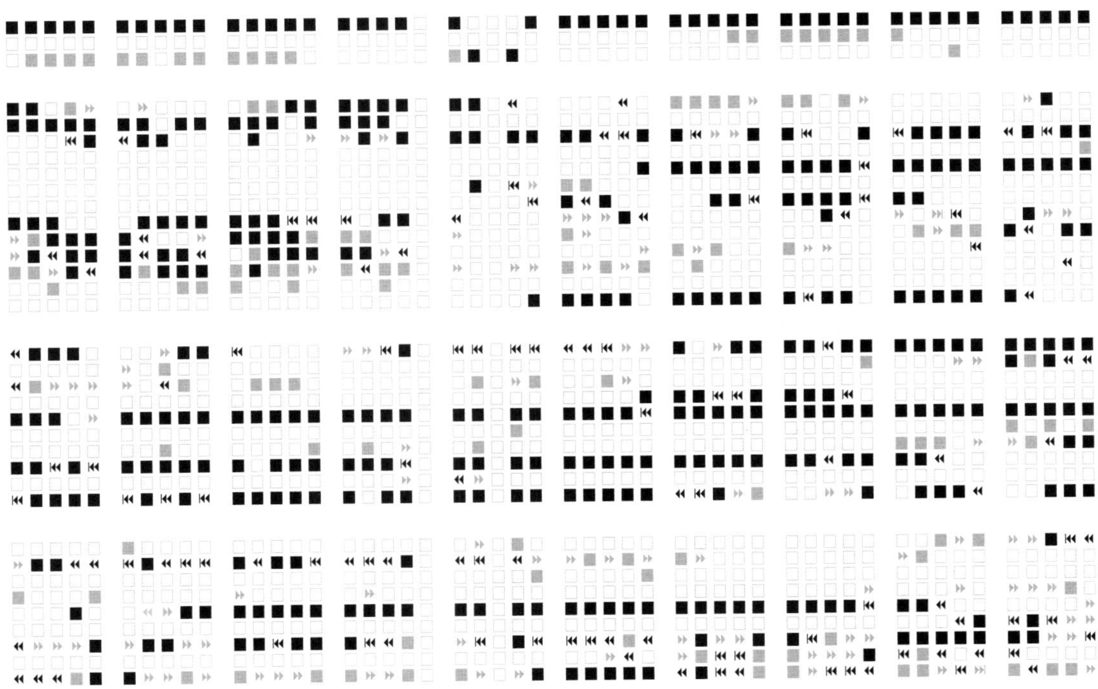

# STOCKPORT COUNTY

Final Position: **14th**

NICKNAME: COUNTY

| | | | | | | |
|---|---|---|---|---|---|---|
| 1 | div2 | Colchester | A | L | 0-1 | |
| 2 | div2 | QPR | H | D | 1-1 | Beckett 55 |
| 3 | div2 | Notts County | H | D | 0-0 | |
| 4 | div2 | Port Vale | A | W | 1-0 | Beckett 17 |
| 5 | div2 | Mansfield | H | W | 2-0 | Reddington 39 og; Beckett 55 |
| 6 | div2 | Swindon | A | W | 1-0 | Beckett 56 |
| 7 | wcr1 | Lincoln | A | W | 3-1 | Palmer 20; Beckett 54; Clare 83 |
| 8 | div2 | Cardiff | A | L | 1-2 | Beckett 16 |
| 9 | div2 | Chesterfield | A | L | 0-1 | |
| 10 | div2 | Barnsley | H | W | 4-1 | Goodwin 63,70; Beckett 65,75 |
| 11 | div2 | Tranmere | A | L | 0-1 | |
| 12 | wcr2 | Gillingham | H | L | 1-2 | Daley 8 |
| 13 | div2 | Luton | H | L | 2-3 | Beckett 18; Daley 45 |
| 14 | div2 | Peterborough | H | W | 2-1 | Beckett 13,61 |
| 15 | div2 | Crewe | H | L | 1-4 | Daley 65 |
| 16 | div2 | Wigan | A | L | 1-2 | Beckett 4 |
| 17 | div2 | Brentford | H | L | 2-3 | Beckett 45; Palmer 90 |
| 18 | div2 | Blackpool | A | W | 3-1 | Ellison 46; Gibb 74; Beckett 89 |
| 19 | div2 | Oldham | A | L | 0-2 | |
| 20 | div2 | Cheltenham | H | D | 1-1 | Burgess 40 |
| 21 | facr1 | St Albans City | H | W | 4-1 | Beckett 24; Fradin 42; Burgess 57 pen,80 |
| 22 | div2 | Plymouth | A | L | 1-4 | Wotton 11 og |
| 23 | div2 | Wycombe | H | W | 2-1 | Beckett 10; Ross 39 |
| 24 | facr2 | Plymouth | H | L | 0-3 | |
| 25 | div2 | Huddersfield | A | L | 1-2 | Briggs 74 |
| 26 | div2 | Northampton | H | W | 4-0 | Beckett 23,46,60; Burgess 77 |
| 27 | div2 | Mansfield | A | L | 2-4 | Day 3 og; Burgess 17 pen |
| 28 | div2 | Bristol City | H | L | 1-4 | Beckett 57 |
| 29 | div2 | Port Vale | H | D | 1-1 | Burgess 30 pen |
| 30 | div2 | QPR | A | L | 0-1 | |
| 31 | div2 | Swindon | H | L | 2-5 | Lescott 83; Lambert 89 |
| 32 | div2 | Notts County | A | L | 2-3 | Beckett 15,30 |
| 33 | div2 | Bristol City | A | D | 1-1 | Beckett 22 |
| 34 | div2 | Colchester | H | D | 1-1 | Beckett 36 |
| 35 | div2 | Cheltenham | A | W | 2-0 | Daly 76; Wild 90 |
| 36 | div2 | Oldham | H | L | 1-2 | Daly 46 |
| 37 | div2 | Peterborough | A | L | 0-2 | |
| 38 | div2 | Cardiff | H | D | 1-1 | Clarke 26 |
| 39 | div2 | Chesterfield | H | W | 2-1 | Beckett 40; Daly 84 |
| 40 | div2 | Barnsley | A | L | 0-1 | |
| 41 | div2 | Brentford | A | W | 2-1 | Beckett 51,54 |
| 42 | div2 | Wigan | H | D | 1-1 | Welsh 70 |
| 43 | div2 | Blackpool | H | D | 2-2 | Lambert 45 |
| 44 | div2 | Crewe | A | L | 0-1 | |
| 45 | div2 | Wycombe | A | W | 4-1 | Beckett 78; Greer 85; Wilbraham 88,90 |
| 46 | div2 | Plymouth | H | W | 2-1 | Wilbraham 40; Daly 86 pen |
| 47 | div2 | Northampton | A | W | 3-0 | Wilbraham 7,24; Goodwin 14 |
| 48 | div2 | Huddersfield | H | W | 2-1 | Daly 79; Wilbraham 81 |
| 49 | div2 | Luton | A | D | 1-1 | Challinor 83 |
| 50 | div2 | Tranmere | H | L | 2-3 | Wilbraham 7; Welsh 21 |

## ATTENDANCES

HOME GROUND: EDGELEY PARK CAPACITY: 12100 AVERAGE LEAGUE AT HOME: 5491

| | | | | | | | | |
|---|---|---|---|---|---|---|---|---|
| 8 | Cardiff | 11546 | 27 | Mansfield | 6434 | 17 | Brentford | 4601 |
| 33 | Bristol City | 10831 | 49 | Luton | 6010 | 20 | Cheltenham | 4531 |
| 30 | QPR | 10387 | 13 | Luton | 5932 | 26 | Northampton | 4516 |
| 40 | Barnsley | 9177 | 2 | QPR | 5881 | 39 | Chesterfield | 4428 |
| 19 | Oldham | 8251 | 47 | Northampton | 5873 | 32 | Notts County | 4392 |
| 36 | Oldham | 8168 | 10 | Barnsley | 5690 | 29 | Port Vale | 4390 |
| 25 | Huddersfield | 7978 | 45 | Wycombe | 5632 | 37 | Peterborough | 4386 |
| 22 | Plymouth | 7746 | 46 | Plymouth | 5484 | 31 | Swindon | 4318 |
| 11 | Tranmere | 7513 | 6 | Swindon | 5456 | 9 | Chesterfield | 4088 |
| 44 | Crewe | 7336 | 38 | Cardiff | 5385 | 4 | Port Vale | 4070 |
| 16 | Wigan | 7276 | 5 | Mansfield | 5190 | 34 | Colchester | 4011 |
| 50 | Tranmere | 7236 | 28 | Bristol City | 5100 | 24 | Plymouth | 3571 |
| 48 | Huddersfield | 7159 | 3 | Notts County | 5047 | 21 | St Albans City | 3303 |
| 18 | Blackpool | 7047 | 41 | Brentford | 4790 | 1 | Colchester | 3300 |
| 42 | Wigan | 6719 | 23 | Wycombe | 4731 | 12 | Gillingham | 2396 |
| 43 | Blackpool | 6599 | 14 | Peterborough | 4726 | 7 | Lincoln | 2084 |
| 15 | Crewe | 6468 | 35 | Cheltenham | 4692 | | | |

■ Home □ Away ▨ Neutral

## KEY PLAYERS - GOALSCORERS

**1 Luke Beckett**

| | | | |
|---|---|---|---|
| Goals in the League | 27 | Player Strike Rate<br>Average number of minutes between League goals scored by player | 135 |
| Contribution to Attacking Power<br>Average number of minutes between League team goals while on pitch | 66 | Club Strike Rate<br>Average number of minutes between League goals scored by club | 64 |

| | PLAYER | LGE GOALS | POWER | STRIKE RATE |
|---|---|---|---|---|
| 2 | John Daly | 7 | 61 | 315 mins |
| 3 | Ben Burgess | 4 | 70 | 354 mins |
| 4 | James Goodwin | 3 | 63 | 767 mins |
| 5 | Rickie Lambert | 2 | 61 | 982 mins |

## KEY PLAYERS - MIDFIELDERS

**1 Robert Clare**

| | | | |
|---|---|---|---|
| Goals in the League | 0 | Contribution to Attacking Power<br>Average number of minutes between League team goals while on pitch | 61 |
| Defensive Rating<br>Average number of mins between League goals conceded while he was on the pitch | 65 | Scoring Difference<br>Defensive Rating minus Contribution to Attacking Power | 4 |

| | PLAYER | LGE GOALS | DEF RATE | POWER | SCORE DIFF |
|---|---|---|---|---|---|
| 2 | Fraser McLachlan | 0 | 67 | 67 | 0 mins |
| 3 | Rickie Lambert | 2 | 61 | 61 | 0 mins |
| 4 | Aaron Lescott | 1 | 58 | 62 | -4 mins |
| 5 | Allistair Gibb | 1 | 58 | 64 | -6 mins |

## KEY PLAYERS - DEFENDERS

**1 Peter Clarke**

| | | | |
|---|---|---|---|
| Goals Conceded (GC)<br>The number of League goals conceded while he was on the pitch | 21 | Clean Sheets<br>In games when he played at least 70 minutes | 4 |
| Defensive Rating<br>Ave number of mins between League goals conceded while on the pitch | 86 | Club Defensive Rating<br>Average number of mins between League goals conceded by the club this season | 59 |

| | PLAYER | CON LGE | CLEAN SHEETS | DEF RATE |
|---|---|---|---|---|
| 2 | Keith Briggs | 20 | 5 | 67 mins |
| 3 | David Challinor | 67 | 6 | 60 mins |
| 4 | James Goodwin | 39 | 2 | 59 mins |
| 5 | Martin Pemberton | 22 | 2 | 58 mins |

## KEY GOALKEEPER

**1 Ola Tidman**

| | |
|---|---|
| Goals Conceded in the League | 21 |
| Defensive Rating<br>Ave number of mins between League goals conceded while on the pitch | 77 |
| Counting Games<br>Games when he played at least 70 mins | 18 |
| Clean Sheets<br>In games when he played at least70 mins | 2 |

## TOP POINT EARNERS

| | PLAYER | GAMES | AVE |
|---|---|---|---|
| 1 | Greer | 4 | 2.50 |
| 2 | Briggs | 12 | 1.75 |
| 3 | Wilbraham | 7 | 1.57 |
| 4 | Clarke | 19 | 1.53 |
| 5 | McLachlan | 14 | 1.50 |
| 6 | Tidman | 18 | 1.50 |
| 7 | Goodwin | 23 | 1.35 |
| 8 | Welsh | 6 | 1.33 |
| 9 | Blayney | 3 | 1.33 |
| 10 | Burgess | 15 | 1.27 |
| | CLUB AVERAGE: | | 1.20 |

Ave = Average points per match in Counting Games

## DISCIPLINARY RECORDS

| | PLAYER | YELLOW | RED | AVE |
|---|---|---|---|---|
| 1 | Palmer | 7 | 1 | 226 |
| 2 | Goodwin | 10 | 0 | 230 |
| 3 | McLachlan | 5 | 1 | 258 |
| 4 | Lescott | 8 | 1 | 356 |
| 5 | Clarke | 5 | 0 | 360 |
| 6 | Wilbraham | 2 | 0 | 415 |
| 7 | Hardiker | 3 | 0 | 550 |
| 8 | Ellison | 2 | 0 | 600 |
| 9 | Tonkin | 3 | 0 | 706 |
| 10 | Clare | 4 | 0 | 717 |
| 11 | Beckett | 5 | 0 | 731 |
| 12 | Fradin | 1 | 0 | 747 |
| 13 | Gibb | 5 | 0 | 769 |
| | Other | 10 | 1 | |
| | TOTAL | 70 | 4 | |

## LEAGUE GOALS

| | PLAYER | MINS | GOALS | AVE |
|---|---|---|---|---|
| 1 | Beckett | 3655 | 27 | 135 |
| 2 | Wilbraham | 830 | 7 | 119 |
| 3 | Daly | 2206 | 7 | 315 |
| 4 | Burgess | 1417 | 4 | 354 |
| 5 | Goodwin | 2300 | 3 | 767 |
| 6 | Lambert | 1963 | 2 | 982 |
| 7 | Welsh | 692 | 2 | 346 |
| 8 | Palmer | 1813 | 1 | 1813 |
| 9 | Briggs | 1336 | 1 | 1336 |
| 10 | Greer | 373 | 1 | 373 |
| 11 | Wild | 35 | 1 | 35 |
| 12 | Ross | 150 | 1 | 150 |
| 13 | Lescott | 3207 | 1 | 3207 |
| | Other | | 7 | |
| | TOTAL | | 65 | |

## MONTH BY MONTH GUIDE TO THE POINTS

| MONTH | POINTS | % |
|---|---|---|
| AUGUST | 11 | 61% |
| SEPTEMBER | 3 | 25% |
| OCTOBER | 6 | 33% |
| NOVEMBER | 4 | 33% |
| DECEMBER | 3 | 25% |
| JANUARY | 2 | 13% |
| FEBRUARY | 4 | 33% |
| MARCH | 9 | 43% |
| APRIL | 13 | 87% |
| MAY | 0 | 0% |

## TEAM OF THE SEASON

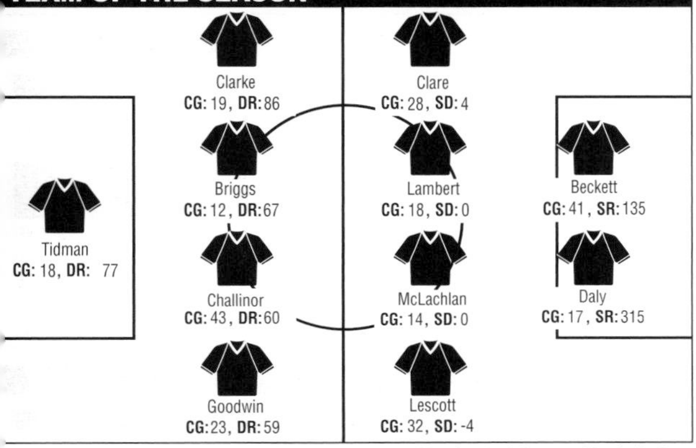
Tidman
CG: 18, DR: 77
Clarke
CG: 19, DR: 86
Briggs
CG: 12, DR: 67
Challinor
CG: 43, DR: 60
Goodwin
CG: 23, DR: 59
Clare
CG: 28, SD: 4
Lambert
CG: 18, SD: 0
McLachlan
CG: 14, SD: 0
Lescott
CG: 32, SD: -4
Beckett
CG: 41, SR: 135
Daly
CG: 17, SR: 315

**KEY:** DR = Defensive Rate, SD = Scoring Difference, SR = Strike Rate, CG = Counting Games – League games playing at least 70 minutes

## LEAGUE APPEARANCES, BOOKINGS AND CAPS

| | AGE | IN THE SQUAD | COUNTING GAMES | MINUTES ON PITCH | YELLOW CARDS | RED CARDS | THIS SEASON | HOME COUNTRY |
|---|---|---|---|---|---|---|---|---|
| **Goalkeepers** | | | | | | | | |
| Alan Blayney | 21 | 4 | 3 | 270 | 0 | 0 | - | N Ireland |
| Ben Coppinger | - | 1 | 0 | 0 | 0 | 0 | - | England |
| Michael Ingham | 22 | 10 | 0 | 0 | 0 | 0 | - | |
| Lee Jones | 32 | 44 | 24 | 2160 | 0 | 0 | - | Wales |
| James Spencer | 18 | 15 | 1 | 90 | 0 | 0 | - | England |
| Ola Tidman | - | 18 | 18 | 1620 | 1 | 0 | - | Sweden |
| **Defenders** | | | | | | | | |
| Keith Briggs | 21 | 23 | 12 | 1336 | 1 | 0 | - | England |
| David Challinor | 27 | 46 | 43 | 4006 | 4 | 1 | - | England |
| Peter Clarke | 23 | 21 | 19 | 1800 | 5 | 0 | - | England |
| James Goodwin | 21 | 37 | 23 | 2300 | 10 | 0 | 1 | Rep of Ireland (15) |
| Gordon Greer | 22 | 6 | 4 | 373 | 0 | 0 | - | Scotland |
| John Hardiker | 20 | 28 | 15 | 1652 | 3 | 0 | - | England |
| Martin Pemberton | 27 | 25 | 11 | 1269 | 0 | 0 | - | England |
| Andrew Thomas | 20 | 6 | 1 | 148 | 0 | 0 | - | England |
| Anthony Tonkin | 23 | 32 | 24 | 2119 | 3 | 0 | - | England |
| **Midfielders** | | | | | | | | |
| Jamie Baguley | 18 | 1 | 0 | 0 | 0 | 0 | - | England |
| Robert Clare | 20 | 40 | 28 | 2868 | 4 | 0 | - | England |
| Karim Fradin | 31 | 12 | 8 | 747 | 1 | 0 | - | France |
| Allistair Gibb | 27 | 45 | 42 | 3847 | 5 | 0 | - | England |
| Rickie Lambert | 21 | 39 | 18 | 1963 | 0 | 0 | - | England |
| Aaron Lescott | 24 | 41 | 32 | 3207 | 8 | 1 | - | England |
| Fraser McLachlan | 20 | 29 | 14 | 1552 | 5 | 1 | - | England |
| Carlton Palmer | 37 | 22 | 19 | 1813 | 7 | 1 | - | England |
| Andrew Welsh | 19 | 14 | 6 | 692 | 0 | 0 | - | England |
| **Forwards** | | | | | | | | |
| Luke Beckett | 26 | 42 | 41 | 3655 | 5 | 0 | - | England |
| Ben Burgess | 21 | 19 | 15 | 1417 | 1 | 0 | - | Rep of Ireland |
| John Daly | 20 | 45 | 17 | 2206 | 2 | 0 | - | Rep of Ireland |
| Kevin Ellison | 24 | 30 | 8 | 1200 | 2 | 0 | - | England |
| David Holt | 18 | 1 | 0 | 0 | 0 | 0 | - | England |
| Neil Ross | 20 | 16 | 1 | 150 | 1 | 0 | - | England |
| Aaron Wilbraham | 23 | 18 | 7 | 830 | 2 | 0 | - | England |
| Peter Wild | 20 | 6 | 0 | 35 | 0 | 0 | - | England |
| Chris Williams | 18 | 1 | 0 | 4 | 0 | 0 | - | England |

**KEY:** LEAGUE BOOKINGS CAPS

## SQUAD APPEARANCES

| Match | 1 | 2 | 3 | 4 | 5 | 6 | 7 | 8 | 9 | 10 | 11 | 12 | 13 | 14 | 15 | 16 | 17 | 18 | 19 | 20 | 21 | 22 | 23 | 24 | 25 | 26 | 27 | 28 | 29 | 30 | 31 | 32 | 33 | 34 | 35 | 36 | 37 | 38 | 39 | 40 | 41 | 42 | 43 | 44 | 45 | 46 | 47 | 48 | 49 | 50 |
|---|---|---|---|---|---|---|---|---|---|---|---|---|---|---|---|---|---|---|---|---|---|---|---|---|---|---|---|---|---|---|---|---|---|---|---|---|---|---|---|---|---|---|---|---|---|---|---|---|---|---|
| Venue | A | H | H | A | H | A | A | A | A | H | A | H | H | H | H | A | H | A | A | H | H | A | H | H | A | H | A | H | H | A | H | A | A | H | A | H | A | H | H | A | A | H | H | A | A | H | A | H | A | H |
| Competition | L | L | L | L | L | L | W | L | L | L | L | W | L | L | L | L | L | L | L | L | F | L | L | F | L | L | L | L | L | L | L | L | L | L | L | L | L | L | L | L | L | L | L | L | L | L | L | L | L | L |
| Result | L | D | D | W | W | W | W | L | L | W | L | D | L | W | L | L | L | W | L | D | W | L | W | L | L | W | L | L | D | L | L | L | D | D | W | L | L | D | W | L | W | D | D | L | W | W | W | W | D | L |

**Goalkeepers**
Alan Blayney
Ben Coppinger
Michael Ingham
Lee Jones
James Spencer
Ola Tidman

**Defenders**
Keith Briggs
David Challinor
Peter Clarke
James Goodwin
Gordon Greer
John Hardiker
Martin Pemberton
Andrew Thomas
Anthony Tonkin

**Midfielders**
Jamie Baguley
Robert Clare
Karim Fradin
Allistair Gibb
Rickie Lambert
Aaron Lescott
Fraser McLachlan
Carlton Palmer
Andrew Welsh

**Forwards**
Luke Beckett
Ben Burgess
John Daly
Kevin Ellison
David Holt
Neil Ross
Aaron Wilbraham
Peter Wild
Chris Williams

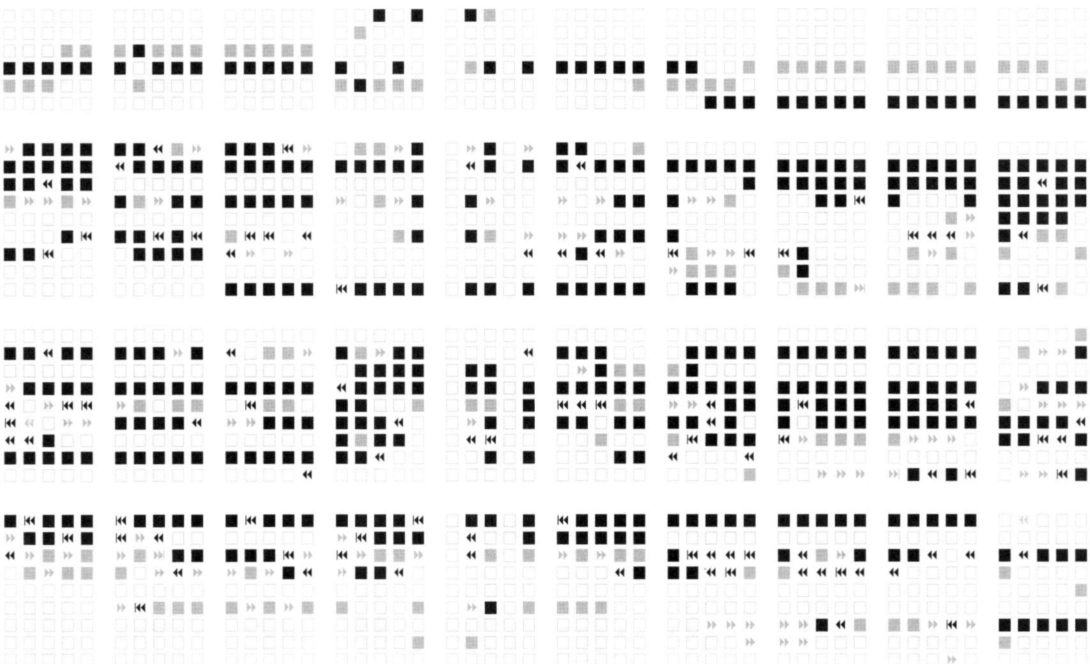

# NOTTS COUNTY

Final Position: **15th**

NICKNAME: THE MAGPIES

| | | | | | | |
|---|---|---|---|---|---|---|
| 1 | div2 | Wycombe | H | D | 1-1 | Cas 58 |
| 2 | div2 | Crewe | A | W | 3-0 | Allsopp 40,53; Stallard 41 |
| 3 | div2 | Stockport | A | D | 0-0 | |
| 4 | div2 | Wigan | H | L | 0-2 | |
| 5 | div2 | Barnsley | A | D | 0-0 | |
| 6 | div2 | Brentford | H | D | 2-2 | Stallard 10; Heffernan 46 |
| 7 | div2 | Oldham | H | L | 1-3 | Heffernan 27 |
| 8 | wcr1 | Oldham | A | L | 2-3 | Stallard 15; Heffernan 75 |
| 9 | div2 | Luton | A | D | 2-2 | Bolland 26; Allsopp 45 |
| 10 | div2 | Port Vale | A | L | 2-3 | Bolland 25; Allsopp 49 |
| 11 | div2 | Cardiff | H | L | 0-1 | |
| 12 | div2 | Cheltenham | A | W | 4-1 | Stallard 2,87; Allsopp 3,56 |
| 13 | div2 | Peterborough | H | D | 2-2 | Stallard 62; Cas 76 |
| 14 | div2 | Huddersfield | A | L | 0-3 | |
| 15 | div2 | Northampton | H | W | 2-1 | Stallard 51; Heffernan 83 |
| 16 | div2 | Chesterfield | A | D | 0-0 | |
| 17 | div2 | Swindon | H | D | 1-1 | Bolland 76 |
| 18 | div2 | Mansfield | H | D | 2-2 | Liburd 63; Caskey 85 |
| 19 | facr1 | Southport | A | L | 2-4 | Allsopp 8,41 |
| 20 | div2 | Colchester | H | L | 2-3 | Allsopp 16; Brough 18 |
| 21 | div2 | Blackpool | A | D | 1-1 | Baraclough 71 |
| 22 | div2 | Bristol City | A | L | 2-3 | Stallard 19,80 |
| 23 | div2 | QPR | H | W | 3-0 | Liburd 7; Fenton 14; Allsopp 83 |
| 24 | div2 | Tranmere | A | D | 2-2 | Stallard 27 pen,90 |
| 25 | div2 | Barnsley | H | W | 3-2 | Stallard 14 pen; Richardson 78; Baraclough 89 |
| 26 | div2 | Plymouth | A | L | 0-1 | |
| 27 | div2 | Wigan | A | L | 1-3 | Stallard 90 |
| 28 | div2 | Brentford | A | D | 1-1 | Fenton 45 |
| 29 | div2 | Stockport | H | W | 3-2 | Stallard 55; Heffernan 67; Caskey 75 |
| 30 | div2 | Plymouth | H | L | 0-2 | |
| 31 | div2 | Wycombe | A | L | 1-3 | Stallard 70 |
| 32 | div2 | Crewe | H | D | 2-2 | Caskey 61 pen; Allsopp 87 |
| 33 | div2 | Mansfield | A | L | 2-3 | Stallard 79,87 |
| 34 | div2 | Bristol City | H | W | 2-0 | Stallard 51 pen,51 pen; Heffernan 67 |
| 35 | div2 | Oldham | A | D | 1-1 | Heffernan 85 |
| 36 | div2 | Luton | H | W | 2-1 | Heffernan 79,84 |
| 37 | div2 | Port Vale | H | W | 1-0 | Stallard 59 |
| 38 | div2 | Cardiff | A | W | 2-0 | Stallard 62 pen,80 |
| 39 | div2 | Chesterfield | H | D | 1-1 | Stallard 79 |
| 40 | div2 | Northampton | A | L | 0-2 | |
| 41 | div2 | Swindon | A | L | 0-5 | |
| 42 | div2 | Huddersfield | H | W | 3-2 | Heffernan 31; Stallard 71 pen,90 |
| 43 | div2 | Blackpool | H | W | 3-1 | Heffernan 51; Ireland 72; Fenton 82 |
| 44 | div2 | Colchester | A | D | 1-1 | Stallard 45 |
| 45 | div2 | Tranmere | H | L | 0-1 | |
| 46 | div2 | QPR | A | L | 0-2 | |
| 47 | div2 | Peterborough | A | L | 0-1 | |
| 48 | div2 | Cheltenham | H | W | 1-0 | Allsopp 40 |

## ATTENDANCES

HOME GROUND: MEADOW LANE CAPACITY: 21300 AVERAGE LEAGUE AT HOME: 6153

| | | | | | | | | |
|---|---|---|---|---|---|---|---|---|
| 46 | QPR | 13585 | 4 | Wigan | 6302 | 47 | Peterborough | 5381 |
| 26 | Plymouth | 11901 | 37 | Port Vale | 6302 | 23 | QPR | 5343 |
| 38 | Cardiff | 11389 | 2 | Crewe | 6141 | 40 | Northampton | 5254 |
| 22 | Bristol City | 10690 | 11 | Cardiff | 6118 | 28 | Brentford | 5112 |
| 5 | Barnsley | 10431 | 1 | Wycombe | 6012 | 3 | Stockport | 5047 |
| 18 | Mansfield | 10302 | 27 | Wigan | 6009 | 17 | Swindon | 4797 |
| 14 | Huddersfield | 9984 | 15 | Northampton | 6009 | 20 | Colchester | 4626 |
| 48 | Cheltenham | 9710 | 42 | Huddersfield | 5872 | 12 | Cheltenham | 4565 |
| 24 | Tranmere | 8275 | 21 | Blackpool | 5843 | 16 | Chesterfield | 4539 |
| 33 | Mansfield | 8134 | 34 | Bristol City | 5754 | 29 | Stockport | 4392 |
| 25 | Barnsley | 7413 | 45 | Tranmere | 5715 | 41 | Swindon | 4246 |
| 39 | Chesterfield | 6801 | 31 | Wycombe | 5690 | 8 | Oldham | 4205 |
| 36 | Luton | 6778 | 35 | Oldham | 5657 | 32 | Crewe | 3875 |
| 13 | Peterborough | 6548 | 43 | Blackpool | 5551 | 19 | Southport | 3519 |
| 9 | Luton | 6456 | 6 | Brentford | 5551 | 10 | Port Vale | 3505 |
| 30 | Plymouth | 6329 | 7 | Oldham | 5435 | 44 | Colchester | 3435 |

■ Home □ Away ▒ Neutral

## KEY PLAYERS - GOALSCORERS

**1 Mark Stallard**

| | | | |
|---|---|---|---|
| Goals in the League | 24 | Player Strike Rate<br>Average number of minutes between League goals scored by player | 159 |
| Contribution to Attacking Power<br>Average number of minutes between League team goals while on pitch | 69 | Club Strike Rate<br>Average number of minutes between League goals scored by club | 67 |

| | PLAYER | LGE GOALS | POWER | STRIKE RATE |
|---|---|---|---|---|
| 2 | Paul Heffernan | 10 | 66 | 241 mins |
| 3 | Daniel Allsopp | 10 | 67 | 258 mins |
| 4 | Paul Bolland | 3 | 68 | 753 mins |
| 5 | Darren Caskey | 3 | 64 | 1005 mins |

## KEY PLAYERS - MIDFIELDERS

**1 Paul Bolland**

| | | | |
|---|---|---|---|
| Goals in the League | 3 | Contribution to Attacking Power<br>Average number of minutes between League team goals while on pitch | 68 |
| Defensive Rating<br>Average number of mins between League goals conceded while he was on the pitch | 75 | Scoring Difference<br>Defensive Rating minus Contribution to Attacking Power | 7 |

| | PLAYER | LGE GOALS | DEF RATE | POWER | SCORE DIFF |
|---|---|---|---|---|---|
| 2 | Ian Richardson | 1 | 64 | 64 | 0 mins |
| 3 | Jeff Whitley | 0 | 57 | 57 | 0 mins |
| 4 | Darren Caskey | 3 | 53 | 64 | -11 mins |
| 5 | Michael Brough | 1 | 58 | 80 | -22 mins |

## KEY PLAYERS - DEFENDERS

**1 Ian Baraclough**

| | | | |
|---|---|---|---|
| Goals Conceded (GC)<br>The number of League goals conceded while he was on the pitch | 46 | Clean Sheets<br>In games when he played at least 70 minutes | 7 |
| Defensive Rating<br>Ave number of mins between League goals conceded while on the pitch | 64 | Club Defensive Rating<br>Average number of mins between League goals conceded by the club this season | 59 |

| | PLAYER | CON LGE | CLEAN SHEETS | DEF RATE |
|---|---|---|---|---|
| 2 | Kevin Nicholson | 47 | 7 | 64 mins |
| 3 | Nicky Fenton | 56 | 8 | 62 mins |
| 4 | Craig Ireland | 52 | 7 | 59 mins |
| 5 | Danny Stone | 18 | 3 | 58 mins |

## KEY GOALKEEPER

**1 Stuart Garden**

| | |
|---|---|
| Goals Conceded in the League | 27 |
| Defensive Rating<br>Ave number of mins between League goals conceded while on the pitch | 60 |
| Counting Games<br>Games when he played at least 70 mins | 18 |
| Clean Sheets<br>In games when he played at least 70 mins | 4 |

## TOP POINT EARNERS

| | PLAYER | GAMES | AVE |
|---|---|---|---|
| 1 | Bolland | 24 | 1.46 |
| 2 | Deeney | 7 | 1.43 |
| 3 | Richardson | 29 | 1.38 |
| 4 | Heffernan | 25 | 1.32 |
| 5 | Nicholson | 32 | 1.31 |
| 6 | Mildenhall | 21 | 1.29 |
| 7 | Ireland | 34 | 1.26 |
| 8 | Jupp | 4 | 1.25 |
| 9 | Baraclough | 33 | 1.24 |
| 10 | Liburd | 22 | 1.23 |
| | CLUB AVERAGE: | | |

Ave = Average points per match in Counting Games

## DISCIPLINARY RECORDS

| | PLAYER | YELLOW | RED | AVE |
|---|---|---|---|---|
| 1 | Ramsden | 9 | 0 | 233 |
| 2 | Jupp | 2 | 0 | 260 |
| 3 | McCarthy | 2 | 0 | 270 |
| 4 | Fenton | 12 | 0 | 291 |
| 5 | Richardson | 8 | 1 | 303 |
| 6 | Brough | 7 | 0 | 306 |
| 7 | Whitley | 3 | 0 | 360 |
| 8 | Caskey | 6 | 0 | 502 |
| 9 | Ireland | 6 | 0 | 515 |
| 10 | Stallard | 7 | 0 | 545 |
| 11 | Liburd | 3 | 1 | 569 |
| 12 | Baraclough | 5 | 0 | 590 |
| 13 | Allsopp | 4 | 0 | 644 |
| | Other | 11 | 0 | |
| | TOTAL | 85 | 2 | |

## LEAGUE GOALS

| | PLAYER | MINS | GOALS | AVE |
|---|---|---|---|---|
| 1 | Stallard | 3816 | 24 | 159 |
| 2 | Heffernan | 2405 | 10 | 241 |
| 3 | Allsopp | 2576 | 10 | 258 |
| 4 | Fenton | 3495 | 3 | 1165 |
| 5 | Bolland | 2258 | 3 | 753 |
| 6 | Caskey | 3014 | 3 | 1005 |
| 7 | Liburd | 2278 | 2 | 1139 |
| 8 | Baraclough | 2953 | 2 | 1477 |
| 9 | Brough | 2147 | 1 | 2147 |
| 10 | Cas | 925 | 1 | 925 |
| 11 | Richardson | 2731 | 1 | 2731 |
| 12 | Ireland | 3093 | 1 | 3093 |
| | Other | | 1 | |
| | TOTAL | | 62 | |

## MONTH BY MONTH GUIDE TO THE POINTS

| MONTH | POINTS | % |
|---|---|---|
| AUGUST | 7 | 39% |
| SEPTEMBER | 4 | 27% |
| OCTOBER | 6 | 40% |
| NOVEMBER | 2 | 22% |
| DECEMBER | 7 | 47% |
| JANUARY | 4 | 33% |
| FEBRUARY | 5 | 33% |
| MARCH | 13 | 62% |
| APRIL | 4 | 27% |
| MAY | 3 | 100% |

## LEAGUE APPEARANCES, BOOKINGS AND CAPS

| | AGE | IN THE SQUAD | COUNTING GAMES | MINUTES ON PITCH | YELLOW CARDS | RED CARDS | THIS SEASON | HOME COUNTRY |
|---|---|---|---|---|---|---|---|---|
| **Goalkeepers** | | | | | | | | |
| Saul Deeney | 20 | 21 | 7 | 630 | 0 | 0 | - | N Ireland |
| Stuart Garden | 31 | 32 | 18 | 1620 | 0 | 0 | - | Scotland |
| Steve Mildenhall | 25 | 39 | 21 | 1890 | 0 | 0 | - | England |
| **Defenders** | | | | | | | | |
| Jon Ashton | 20 | 4 | 3 | 315 | 0 | 0 | - | England |
| Ian Baraclough | 32 | 34 | 33 | 2953 | 5 | 0 | - | England |
| Danny Bostock | 18 | 1 | 0 | 0 | 0 | 0 | - | England |
| Marcel Cas | 31 | 19 | 7 | 925 | 1 | 0 | - | Holland |
| Nicky Fenton | 23 | 41 | 37 | 3495 | 12 | 0 | - | England |
| Richard Holmes | 22 | 9 | 1 | 149 | 1 | 0 | - | England |
| Craig Ireland | 27 | 42 | 34 | 3093 | 6 | 0 | - | Scotland |
| Duncan Jupp | 28 | 9 | 4 | 520 | 2 | 0 | - | Scotland |
| Richard Liburd | 29 | 39 | 22 | 2278 | 3 | 1 | - | England |
| Patrick McCarthy | 20 | 6 | 6 | 540 | 2 | 0 | - | Rep of Ireland |
| Shane McFaul | - | 3 | 0 | 0 | 0 | 0 | - | England |
| Kevin Nicholson | 22 | 42 | 32 | 3006 | 1 | 0 | - | England |
| Simon Ramsden | 21 | 38 | 20 | 2105 | 9 | 0 | - | England |
| Paul Riley | 20 | 14 | 2 | 172 | 0 | 0 | - | England |
| Danny Stone | 20 | 28 | 10 | 1043 | 1 | 0 | - | England |
| **Midfielders** | | | | | | | | |
| Paul Bolland | 23 | 29 | 24 | 2258 | 3 | 0 | - | England |
| Michael Brough | 21 | 33 | 22 | 2147 | 7 | 0 | - | England |
| Darren Caskey | 28 | 39 | 31 | 3014 | 6 | 0 | - | England |
| Willis Francis | - | 14 | 2 | 267 | 1 | 0 | - | England |
| Shaun Harrard | - | 12 | 0 | 64 | 0 | 0 | - | England |
| Ian Richardson | 32 | 36 | 29 | 2731 | 8 | 1 | - | England |
| Jeff Whitley | 24 | 12 | 12 | 1080 | 3 | 0 | - | N Ireland |
| **Forwards** | | | | | | | | |
| Daniel Allsopp | 24 | 33 | 27 | 2576 | 4 | 0 | - | Australia |
| Tony Hackworth | 23 | 21 | 4 | 351 | 1 | 0 | - | England |
| Paul Heffernan | 21 | 41 | 25 | 2405 | 2 | 0 | - | Rep of Ireland |
| Mark Stallard | 28 | 45 | 42 | 3816 | 7 | 0 | - | England |

KEY: LEAGUE BOOKINGS CAPS

## TEAM OF THE SEASON

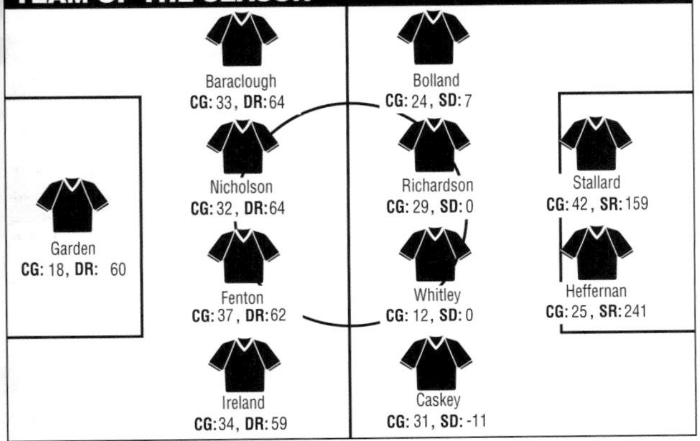

Baraclough
CG: 33, DR: 64
Bolland
CG: 24, SD: 7
Nicholson
CG: 32, DR: 64
Richardson
CG: 29, SD: 0
Stallard
CG: 42, SR: 159
Garden
CG: 18, DR: 60
Fenton
CG: 37, DR: 62
Whitley
CG: 12, SD: 0
Heffernan
CG: 25, SR: 241
Ireland
CG: 34, DR: 59
Caskey
CG: 31, SD: -11


KEY: DR = Defensive Rate, SD = Scoring Difference, SR = Strike Rate, CG = Counting Games – League games playing at least 70 minutes

## SQUAD APPEARANCES

| Match | 1 | 2 | 3 | 4 | 5 | 6 | 7 | 8 | 9 | 10 | 11 | 12 | 13 | 14 | 15 | 16 | 17 | 18 | 19 | 20 | 21 | 22 | 23 | 24 | 25 | 26 | 27 | 28 | 29 | 30 | 31 | 32 | 33 | 34 | 35 | 36 | 37 | 38 | 39 | 40 | 41 | 42 | 43 | 44 | 45 | 46 | 47 | 48 |
|---|---|---|---|---|---|---|---|---|---|---|---|---|---|---|---|---|---|---|---|---|---|---|---|---|---|---|---|---|---|---|---|---|---|---|---|---|---|---|---|---|---|---|---|---|---|---|---|---|
| Venue | H | A | A | H | A | H | H | A | A | A | H | A | H | A | H | A | H | H | A | H | A | A | H | A | H | A | A | A | H | H | A | H | A | H | A | H | H | A | H | A | A | H | H | A | H | A | A | H |
| Competition | L | L | L | L | L | L | L | W | L | L | L | L | L | L | L | L | L | L | F | L | L | L | L | L | L | L | L | L | L | L | L | L | L | L | L | L | L | L | L | L | L | L | L | L | L | L | L | L |
| Result | D | W | D | L | D | D | L | L | D | L | L | W | D | L | W | D | D | D | L | L | D | L | W | D | W | L | L | D | W | L | L | D | L | W | D | W | W | W | D | L | L | W | W | D | L | L | L | W |

Goalkeepers
Saul Deeney
Stuart Garden
Steve Mildenhall

Defenders
Jon Ashton
Ian Baraclough
Danny Bostock
Marcel Cas
Nicky Fenton
Richard Holmes
Craig Ireland
Duncan Jupp
Richard Liburd
Patrick McCarthy
Shane McFaul
Kevin Nicholson
Simon Ramsden
Paul Riley
Danny Stone

Midfielders
Paul Bolland
Michael Brough
Darren Caskey
Willis Francis
Shaun Harrard
Ian Richardson
Jeff Whitley

Forwards
Daniel Allsopp
Tony Hackworth
Paul Heffernan
Mark Stallard

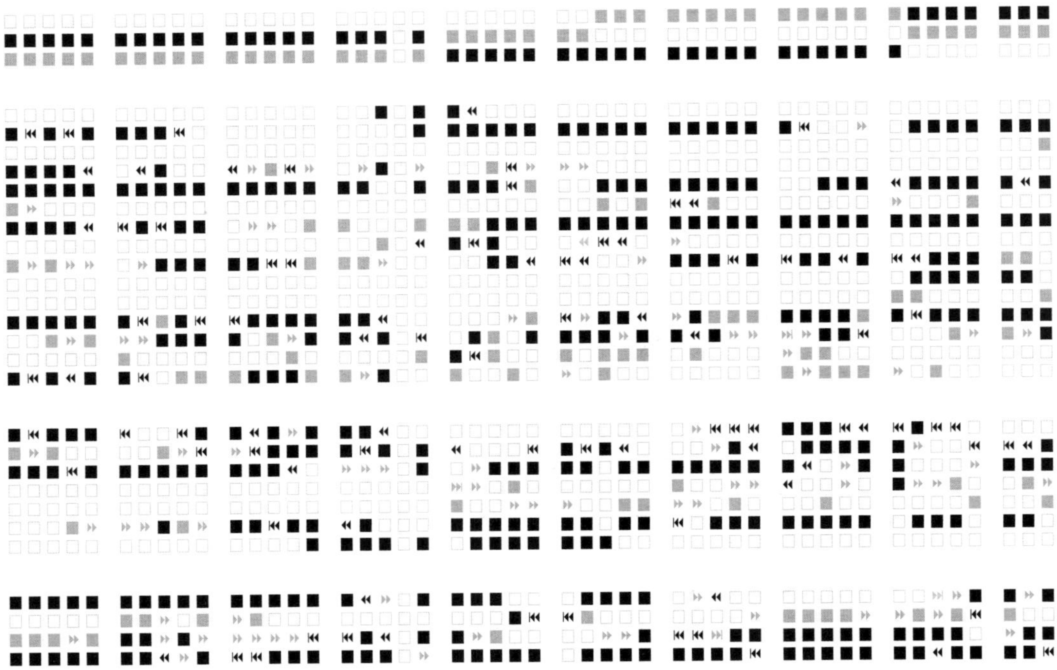

# BRENTFORD

Final Position: **16th**

NICKNAME: THE BEES

| | | | | | | |
|---|---|---|---|---|---|---|
| 1 | div2 | Huddersfield | A | W | 2-0 | Fullerton 26; Vine 39 |
| 2 | div2 | Bristol City | H | W | 1-0 | Hunt 68 pen |
| 3 | div2 | Oldham | H | D | 0-0 | |
| 4 | div2 | Colchester | A | W | 1-0 | Hunt 45 pen |
| 5 | div2 | Swindon | H | W | 3-1 | Vine 7,14; McCammon 77 |
| 6 | div2 | Notts County | A | D | 2-2 | McCammon 55; Williams 77 |
| 7 | div2 | Luton | H | D | 0-0 | |
| 8 | wcr1 | Bournemouth | A | W | 4-2* | O'Connor 6 pen,56 pen; Vine 72 (*on penalties) |
| 9 | div2 | Tranmere | A | L | 1-3 | O'Connor 89 |
| 10 | div2 | Cardiff | A | L | 0-2 | |
| 11 | div2 | Wycombe | H | W | 1-0 | Hunt 57 pen |
| 12 | div2 | Peterborough | A | L | 1-5 | Vine 85 |
| 13 | wcr2 | Middlesbrough | H | L | 1-4 | Sonko 90 |
| 14 | div2 | Barnsley | H | L | 1-2 | McCammon 26 |
| 15 | div2 | Northampton | A | W | 2-1 | Sonko 7; Vine 25 |
| 16 | div2 | Port Vale | H | D | 1-1 | Hunt 56 pen |
| 17 | div2 | Stockport | A | W | 3-2 | McCammon 8,52; Marshall 70 |
| 18 | div2 | Plymouth | H | D | 0-0 | |
| 19 | div2 | Blackpool | H | W | 5-0 | Vine 32; Evans 37,90; Sonko 60,86 |
| 20 | div2 | Crewe | A | L | 1-2 | Sonko 62 |
| 21 | facr1 | Wycombe | A | W | 4-2 | O'Connor 3; Somner 9; Vine 42,52 |
| 22 | div2 | Wigan | H | L | 0-1 | |
| 23 | div2 | Cheltenham | A | L | 0-1 | |
| 24 | facr2 | York | A | W | 2-1 | McCammon 35; Hunt 87 |
| 25 | div2 | Chesterfield | H | W | 2-1 | Hunt 6; Vine 48 |
| 26 | div2 | QPR | A | D | 1-1 | O'Connor 30 |
| 27 | div2 | Swindon | A | L | 1-2 | Vine 76 |
| 28 | div2 | Mansfield | H | W | 1-0 | O'Connor 58 |
| 29 | facr3 | Derby | H | W | 1-0 | Hunt 36 |
| 30 | div2 | Oldham | A | L | 1-2 | O'Connor 28 |
| 31 | div2 | Notts County | H | D | 1-1 | Vine 51 |
| 32 | facr4 | Burnley | H | L | 0-3 | |
| 33 | div2 | Mansfield | A | D | 0-0 | |
| 34 | div2 | Crewe | H | L | 1-2 | Hunt 11 |
| 35 | div2 | Bristol City | A | D | 0-0 | |
| 36 | div2 | Blackpool | A | L | 0-1 | |
| 37 | div2 | Luton | A | W | 1-0 | Vine 50 |
| 38 | div2 | Huddersfield | H | W | 1-0 | McCammon 56 |
| 39 | div2 | Tranmere | H | L | 1-2 | Sonko 90 |
| 40 | div2 | Cardiff | H | L | 0-2 | |
| 41 | div2 | Wycombe | A | L | 0-4 | |
| 42 | div2 | Colchester | H | D | 1-1 | McCammon 37 |
| 43 | div2 | Stockport | H | L | 1-2 | Antoine-Curier 39 |
| 44 | div2 | Port Vale | A | L | 0-1 | |
| 45 | div2 | Plymouth | A | L | 0-3 | |
| 46 | div2 | Northampton | H | W | 3-0 | Somner 52; Rowlands 77; Hunt 90 |
| 47 | div2 | Cheltenham | H | D | 2-2 | Dobson 63; O'Connor 78 |
| 48 | div2 | Wigan | A | L | 0-2 | |
| 49 | div2 | QPR | H | L | 1-2 | Peters 81 |
| 50 | div2 | Chesterfield | A | W | 2-0 | Antoine-Curier 36,55 |
| 51 | div2 | Barnsley | A | L | 0-1 | |
| 52 | div2 | Peterborough | H | D | 1-1 | Evans 67 |

## ATTENDANCES

HOME GROUND: GRIFFIN PARK CAPACITY: 12763 AVERAGE LEAGUE AT HOME: 5759

| | | | | | | | | |
|---|---|---|---|---|---|---|---|---|
| 26 | QPR | 15559 | 36 | Blackpool | 6203 | 25 | Chesterfield | 5151 |
| 10 | Cardiff | 12032 | 11 | Wycombe | 6172 | 31 | Notts County | 5112 |
| 1 | Huddersfield | 9635 | 27 | Swindon | 6045 | 12 | Peterborough | 5066 |
| 32 | Burnley | 9563 | 41 | Wycombe | 5930 | 30 | Oldham | 5039 |
| 49 | QPR | 9168 | 19 | Blackpool | 5888 | 23 | Cheltenham | 5013 |
| 35 | Bristol City | 9084 | 28 | Mansfield | 5844 | 47 | Cheltenham | 5011 |
| 51 | Barnsley | 9065 | 15 | Northampton | 5739 | 43 | Stockport | 4790 |
| 29 | Derby | 8709 | 40 | Cardiff | 5727 | 17 | Stockport | 4601 |
| 13 | Middlesbrough | 7558 | 21 | Wycombe | 5673 | 38 | Huddersfield | 4366 |
| 48 | Wigan | 7204 | 20 | Crewe | 5663 | 42 | Colchester | 3990 |
| 7 | Luton | 7145 | 6 | Notts County | 5551 | 33 | Mansfield | 3735 |
| 2 | Bristol City | 7130 | 22 | Wigan | 5454 | 24 | York | 3517 |
| 37 | Luton | 6940 | 34 | Crewe | 5424 | 8 | Bournemouth | 3302 |
| 45 | Plymouth | 6835 | 39 | Tranmere | 5396 | 50 | Chesterfield | 3296 |
| 52 | Peterborough | 6687 | 14 | Barnsley | 5394 | 44 | Port Vale | 3241 |
| 9 | Tranmere | 6626 | 3 | Oldham | 5356 | 4 | Colchester | 3135 |
| 18 | Plymouth | 6431 | 46 | Northampton | 5354 | | | |
| 5 | Swindon | 6299 | 16 | Port Vale | 5177 | | | |

■ Home □ Away ▒ Neutral

## KEY PLAYERS - GOALSCORERS

**1 Rowan Vine**

| | | | |
|---|---|---|---|
| Goals in the League | 10 | Player Strike Rate<br>Average number of minutes between League goals scored by player | 342 |
| Contribution to Attacking Power<br>Average number of minutes between League team goals while on pitch | 87 | Club Strike Rate<br>Average number of minutes between League goals scored by club | 88 |

| | PLAYER | LGE GOALS | POWER | STRIKE RATE |
|---|---|---|---|---|
| 2 | Mark McCammon | 7 | 88 | 381 mins |
| 3 | Stephen Hunt | 7 | 88 | 515 mins |
| 4 | Stephen Evans | 3 | 76 | 562 mins |
| 5 | Ibrahima Sonko | 5 | 92 | 666 mins |

## KEY PLAYERS - MIDFIELDERS

**1 Jamie Fullarton**

| | | | |
|---|---|---|---|
| Goals in the League | 1 | Contribution to Attacking Power<br>Average number of minutes between League team goals while on pitch | 75 |
| Defensive Rating<br>Average number of mins between League goals conceded while he was on the pitch | 89 | Scoring Difference<br>Defensive Rating minus Contribution to Attacking Power | 14 |

| | PLAYER | LGE GOALS | DEF RATE | POWER | SCORE DIFF |
|---|---|---|---|---|---|
| 2 | Stephen Hunt | 7 | 93 | 88 | 5 mins |
| 3 | Stephen Evans | 3 | 77 | 77 | 0 mins |
| 4 | Rowan Vine | 10 | 80 | 88 | -8 mins |
| 5 | Kevin O'Connor | 5 | 76 | 90 | -14 mins |

## KEY PLAYERS - DEFENDERS

**1 Michael Dobson**

| | | | |
|---|---|---|---|
| Goals Conceded (GC)<br>The number of League goals conceded while he was on the pitch | 50 | Clean Sheets<br>In games when he played at least 70 minutes | 14 |
| Defensive Rating<br>Ave number of mins between League goals conceded while on the pitch | 80 | Club Defensive Rating<br>Average number of mins between League goals conceded by the club this season | 74 |

| | PLAYER | CON LGE | CLEAN SHEETS | DEF RATE |
|---|---|---|---|---|
| 2 | Ibrahima Sonko | 42 | 11 | 79 mins |
| 3 | Leo Roget | 16 | 6 | 77 mins |
| 4 | Scott Marshall | 27 | 6 | 76 mins |
| 5 | Matt Somner | 47 | 14 | 75 mins |

## KEY GOALKEEPER

**1 Paul Smith**

| | |
|---|---|
| Goals Conceded in the League | 53 |
| Defensive Rating<br>Ave number of mins between League goals conceded while on the pitch | 73 |
| Counting Games<br>Games when he played at least 70 mins | 43 |
| Clean Sheets<br>In games when he played at least 70 mins | 14 |

## TOP POINT EARNERS

| | PLAYER | GAMES | AVE |
|---|---|---|---|
| 1 | Roget | 14 | 1.79 |
| 2 | Fieldwick | 6 | 1.67 |
| 3 | Hutchinson | 18 | 1.56 |
| 4 | Chorley | 2 | 1.50 |
| 5 | Peters | 2 | 1.50 |
| 6 | McCammon | 28 | 1.43 |
| 7 | Vine | 36 | 1.42 |
| 8 | Hunt | 38 | 1.39 |
| 9 | Smith, J | 18 | 1.33 |
| 10 | Evans | 16 | 1.31 |
| | CLUB AVERAGE: | | 1.17 |

Ave = Average points per match in Counting Games

## DISCIPLINARY RECORDS

| | PLAYER | YELLOW | RED | AVE |
|---|---|---|---|---|
| 1 | Rowlands | 7 | 1 | 151 |
| 2 | Fullarton | 5 | 2 | 278 |
| 3 | Vine | 10 | 1 | 311 |
| 4 | Roget | 2 | 1 | 412 |
| 5 | Frampton | 2 | 0 | 444 |
| 6 | Sonko | 6 | 0 | 555 |
| 7 | Evans | 3 | 0 | 562 |
| 8 | McCammon | 4 | 0 | 666 |
| 9 | Marshall | 2 | 1 | 681 |
| 10 | Hutchinson | 2 | 0 | 875 |
| 11 | Antoine-Curier | 1 | 0 | 898 |
| 12 | Hunt | 4 | 0 | 902 |
| 13 | Somner | 2 | 0 | 1764 |
| | Other | 4 | 0 | |
| | TOTAL | 54 | 6 | |

## LEAGUE GOALS

| | PLAYER | MINS | GOALS | AVE |
|---|---|---|---|---|
| 1 | Vine | 3422 | 10 | 342 |
| 2 | McCammon | 2667 | 7 | 381 |
| 3 | Hunt | 3608 | 7 | 515 |
| 4 | Sonko | 3330 | 5 | 666 |
| 5 | O'Connor | 3796 | 5 | 759 |
| 6 | Evans | 1686 | 3 | 562 |
| 7 | Antoine-Curier | 898 | 3 | 299 |
| 8 | Somner | 3529 | 1 | 3529 |
| 9 | Williams | 543 | 1 | 543 |
| 10 | Peters | 408 | 1 | 408 |
| 11 | Dobson | 3994 | 1 | 3994 |
| 12 | Rowlands | 1212 | 1 | 1212 |
| 13 | Fullarton | 1952 | 1 | 1952 |
| | Other | | 1 | |
| | TOTAL | | 47 | |

## MONTH BY MONTH GUIDE TO THE POINTS

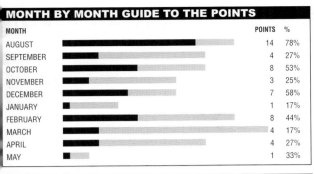

| MONTH | POINTS | % |
|---|---|---|
| AUGUST | 14 | 78% |
| SEPTEMBER | 4 | 27% |
| OCTOBER | 8 | 53% |
| NOVEMBER | 3 | 25% |
| DECEMBER | 7 | 58% |
| JANUARY | 1 | 17% |
| FEBRUARY | 8 | 44% |
| MARCH | 4 | 17% |
| APRIL | 4 | 27% |
| MAY | 1 | 33% |

## TEAM OF THE SEASON

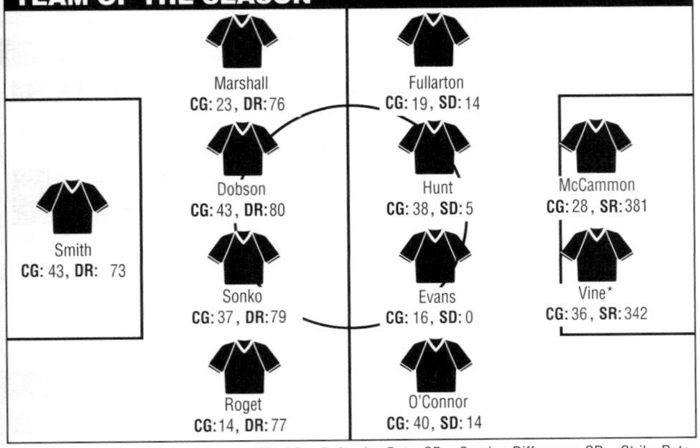
Marshall
CG: 23, DR: 76
Fullarton
CG: 19, SD: 14
Dobson
CG: 43, DR: 80
Hunt
CG: 38, SD: 5
McCammon
CG: 28, SR: 381
Smith
CG: 43, DR: 73
Sonko
CG: 37, DR: 79
Evans
CG: 16, SD: 0
Vine*
CG: 36, SR: 342
Roget
CG: 14, DR: 77
O'Connor
CG: 40, SD: 14

**KEY:** DR = Defensive Rate, SD = Scoring Difference, SR = Strike Rate, CG = Counting Games – League games playing at least 70 minutes

## LEAGUE APPEARANCES, BOOKINGS AND CAPS

| | AGE | IN THE SQUAD | COUNTING GAMES | MINUTES ON PITCH | YELLOW CARDS | RED CARDS | THIS SEASON | HOME COUNTRY |
|---|---|---|---|---|---|---|---|---|
| **Goalkeepers** | | | | | | | | |
| Olafur Gottskalksson | 35 | 1 | 0 | 0 | 0 | 0 | - | |
| Alan Julian | 27 | 43 | 3 | 270 | 0 | 0 | - | England |
| Barry Marchena | - | 3 | 0 | 0 | 0 | 0 | - | England |
| Paul Smith | 23 | 45 | 43 | 3870 | 1 | 0 | - | England |
| **Defenders** | | | | | | | | |
| Ijah Anderson | 27 | 10 | 9 | 810 | 0 | 0 | - | England |
| Ben Chorley | 20 | 9 | 2 | 180 | 0 | 0 | - | England |
| Michael Dobson | 22 | 46 | 43 | 3994 | 0 | 0 | - | England |
| Andrew Frampton | 23 | 23 | 9 | 889 | 2 | 0 | - | England |
| Jay Lovett | 25 | 3 | 0 | 55 | 0 | 0 | - | England |
| Scott Marshall | 30 | 30 | 23 | 2044 | 2 | 1 | - | Scotland |
| Leo Roget | 25 | 15 | 14 | 1238 | 2 | 1 | - | England |
| Matt Somner | 20 | 41 | 38 | 3529 | 2 | 0 | - | England |
| Ibrahima Sonko | 22 | 37 | 37 | 3330 | 6 | 0 | - | Senegal |
| **Midfielders** | | | | | | | | |
| Stephen Evans | 22 | 31 | 16 | 1686 | 3 | 0 | - | Wales |
| Lee Fieldwick | 21 | 17 | 6 | 555 | 0 | 0 | - | England |
| Jamie Fullarton | 28 | 27 | 19 | 1952 | 5 | 2 | - | Scotland |
| Stephen Hughes | 19 | 12 | 0 | 114 | 0 | 0 | - | England |
| Stephen Hunt | 21 | 42 | 38 | 3608 | 4 | 0 | - | Rep of Ireland |
| Eddie Hutchinson | 21 | 28 | 18 | 1751 | 2 | 0 | - | England |
| Kevin O'Connor | 21 | 45 | 40 | 3796 | 1 | 0 | - | England |
| Martin Rowlands | 24 | 19 | 11 | 1212 | 7 | 1 | - | England |
| Jay Smith | 21 | 30 | 18 | 1955 | 1 | 0 | - | England |
| Jay Tabb | 21 | 6 | 1 | 149 | 1 | 0 | - | England |
| Robert Traynor | 19 | 2 | 0 | 29 | 0 | 0 | - | England |
| Rowan Vine | 20 | 42 | 36 | 3422 | 10 | 1 | - | England |
| **Forwards** | | | | | | | | |
| Antoine-Curier | 20 | 11 | 8 | 898 | 1 | 0 | - | France |
| Lloyd Blackman | 19 | 1 | 1 | 90 | 0 | 0 | - | England |
| Leon Constantine | 25 | 26 | 2 | 369 | 0 | 0 | - | England |
| Mark McCammon | 24 | 37 | 28 | 2667 | 4 | 0 | - | England |
| Mark Peters | 19 | 16 | 2 | 408 | 0 | 0 | - | England |
| Mark Williams | 21 | 38 | 1 | 543 | 0 | 0 | - | England |

**KEY:** LEAGUE BOOKINGS CAPS

## SQUAD APPEARANCES

| | | | | | | | | | | | |
|---|---|---|---|---|---|---|---|---|---|---|---|
| **Match** | 1 2 3 4 5 | 6 7 8 9 10 | 11 12 13 14 15 | 16 17 18 19 20 | 21 22 23 24 25 | 26 27 28 29 30 | 31 32 33 34 35 | 36 37 38 39 40 | 41 42 43 44 45 | 46 47 48 49 50 | 51 52 |
| **Venue** | A H H A H | A H A A A | H A H H A | H A H H A | A H A A H | A A H H A | H H A H A | A A H H H | A H H A A | H H A H A | A H |
| **Competition** | L L L L L | L L W L L | L L W L L | L L L L L | F L L F L | L L L F L | L F L L L | L L L L L | L L L L L | L L L L L | L L |
| **Result** | W W D W W | D D W L L | W L L L W | D W D W L | W L L W W | D L W W L | D L D L D | L W W L L | L D L L L | W D L L W | L D |

**Goalkeepers**
Olafur Gottskalksson
Alan Julian
Barry Marchena
Paul Smith

**Defenders**
Ijah Anderson
Ben Chorley
Michael Dobson
Andrew Frampton
Jay Lovett
Scott Marshall
Leo Roget
Matt Somner
Ibrahima Sonko

**Midfielders**
Stephen Evans
Lee Fieldwick
Jamie Fullarton
Stephen Hughes
Stephen Hunt
Eddie Hutchinson
Kevin O'Connor
Martin Rowlands
Jay Smith
Jay Tabb
Robert Traynor
Rowan Vine

**Forwards**
Mickael Antoine-Curier
Lloyd Blackman
Leon Constantine
Mark McCammon
Mark Peters
Mark Williams

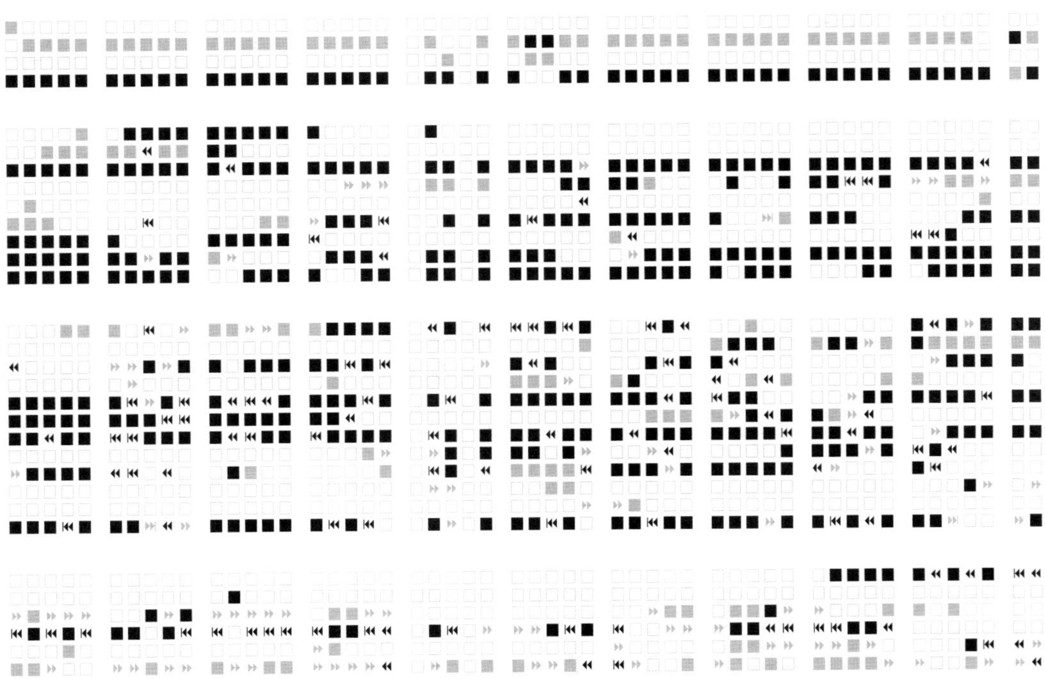

# PORT VALE

Final Position: **17th**

NICKNAME: THE VALIANTS

| No | Comp | Opponent | H/A | Res | Score | Scorers |
|---|---|---|---|---|---|---|
| 1 | div2 | Tranmere | H | L | 1-4 | Brooker 25 |
| 2 | div2 | Cardiff | A | L | 1-3 | Bridge-Wilkinson 38 pen |
| 3 | div2 | Chesterfield | A | L | 1-2 | Angell 90 pen |
| 4 | div2 | Stockport | H | L | 0-1 | |
| 5 | div2 | Wigan | A | W | 1-0 | Armstrong 45 |
| 6 | div2 | Peterborough | H | W | 1-0 | Angell 84 |
| 7 | div2 | Swindon | A | W | 2-1 | Bridge-Wilkinson 8,68 |
| 8 | wcr1 | Crewe | H | L | 0-2 | |
| 9 | div2 | Colchester | H | W | 1-0 | Collins 47 |
| 10 | div2 | Notts County | H | W | 3-2 | Angell 5,81; Paynter 58 |
| 11 | div2 | Blackpool | A | L | 2-3 | Collins 23; Bridge-Wilkinson 71 |
| 12 | div2 | Bristol City | H | L | 2-3 | Paynter 61; Cummins 89 |
| 13 | div2 | Huddersfield | A | D | 2-2 | Collins 5; Paynter 29 |
| 14 | div2 | Oldham | H | D | 1-1 | McPhee 65 |
| 15 | div2 | Brentford | A | D | 1-1 | Paynter 68 |
| 16 | div2 | Crewe | H | L | 1-2 | Angell 56 |
| 17 | div2 | Cheltenham | A | W | 1-0 | Bridge-Wilkinson 33 pen |
| 18 | div2 | QPR | H | D | 0-0 | |
| 19 | div2 | Luton | A | D | 0-0 | |
| 20 | facr1 | Crewe | H | L | 0-1 | |
| 21 | div2 | Northampton | A | L | 0-3 | |
| 22 | div2 | Mansfield | H | W | 4-2 | Cummins 30,33; Armstrong 50; Paynter 66 |
| 23 | div2 | Wycombe | A | L | 1-3 | Armstrong 49 |
| 24 | div2 | Plymouth | H | L | 1-2 | Brooker 26 |
| 25 | div2 | Wigan | H | L | 0-1 | |
| 26 | div2 | Barnsley | A | L | 1-2 | Bridge-Wilkinson 43 |
| 27 | div2 | Stockport | A | D | 1-1 | Brooker 71 |
| 28 | div2 | Peterborough | A | W | 2-1 | Brooker 73; Bridge-Wilkinson 90 |
| 29 | div2 | Barnsley | H | D | 0-0 | |
| 30 | div2 | Tranmere | A | L | 0-1 | |
| 31 | div2 | Luton | H | L | 1-2 | Boyd 87 |
| 32 | div2 | Chesterfield | H | W | 5-2 | McPhee 2; Boyd 10,66; Armstrong 14; Brooker 18 |
| 33 | div2 | QPR | A | L | 0-4 | |
| 34 | div2 | Swindon | H | D | 1-1 | Armstrong 46 |
| 35 | div2 | Cardiff | H | L | 0-2 | |
| 36 | div2 | Colchester | A | L | 1-4 | Bridge-Wilkinson 55 |
| 37 | div2 | Notts County | A | L | 0-1 | |
| 38 | div2 | Blackpool | H | W | 1-0 | Bridge-Wilkinson 49 pen |
| 39 | div2 | Crewe | A | D | 1-1 | Brisco 73 |
| 40 | div2 | Brentford | H | W | 1-0 | Collins 36 |
| 41 | div2 | Cheltenham | H | L | 1-2 | McPhee 74 |
| 42 | div2 | Oldham | A | D | 1-1 | Cummins 36 |
| 43 | div2 | Mansfield | A | W | 1-0 | Durnin 45 |
| 44 | div2 | Northampton | H | W | 3-2 | Walsh 11; Littlejohn 90; Clarke 90 |
| 45 | div2 | Plymouth | A | L | 0-3 | |
| 46 | div2 | Wycombe | H | D | 1-1 | Littlejohn 5 |
| 47 | div2 | Huddersfield | H | W | 5-1 | Armstrong 18,59; Littlejohn 31; Collins 82; Charnock 87 |
| 48 | div2 | Bristol City | A | L | 0-2 | |

## ATTENDANCES

HOME GROUND: VALE PARK CAPACITY: 22546 AVERAGE LEAGUE AT HOME: 4436

| | | | | | | | | |
|---|---|---|---|---|---|---|---|---|
| 33 | QPR | 13703 | 14 | Oldham | 5563 | 4 | Stockport | 4070 |
| 2 | Cardiff | 13296 | 20 | Crewe | 5507 | 29 | Barnsley | 4033 |
| 48 | Bristol City | 12410 | 23 | Wycombe | 5229 | 22 | Mansfield | 3880 |
| 26 | Barnsley | 9291 | 15 | Brentford | 5177 | 6 | Peterborough | 3862 |
| 13 | Huddersfield | 9091 | 7 | Swindon | 5029 | 17 | Cheltenham | 3852 |
| 39 | Crewe | 8146 | 24 | Plymouth | 4892 | 35 | Cardiff | 3831 |
| 45 | Plymouth | 7775 | 41 | Cheltenham | 4800 | 8 | Crewe | 3765 |
| 11 | Blackpool | 7756 | 28 | Peterborough | 4770 | 3 | Chesterfield | 3598 |
| 30 | Tranmere | 7461 | 31 | Luton | 4714 | 46 | Wycombe | 3590 |
| 42 | Oldham | 7209 | 43 | Mansfield | 4538 | 36 | Colchester | 3581 |
| 5 | Wigan | 6532 | 38 | Blackpool | 4394 | 10 | Notts County | 3505 |
| 25 | Wigan | 6395 | 18 | QPR | 4394 | 9 | Colchester | 3325 |
| 16 | Crewe | 6374 | 27 | Stockport | 4390 | 40 | Brentford | 3241 |
| 37 | Notts County | 6302 | 21 | Northampton | 4357 | 32 | Chesterfield | 3039 |
| 19 | Luton | 6112 | 12 | Bristol City | 4286 | | | |
| 47 | Huddersfield | 5925 | 44 | Northampton | 4209 | | | |
| 1 | Tranmere | 5629 | 34 | Swindon | 4085 | | | |

■ Home □ Away ▒ Neutral

## KEY PLAYERS - GOALSCORERS

**1 Brett Angell**

| | | | |
|---|---|---|---|
| Goals in the League | 5 | Player Strike Rate<br>Average number of minutes between League goals scored by player | 242 |
| Contribution to Attacking Power<br>Average number of minutes between League team goals while on pitch | 63 | Club Strike Rate<br>Average number of minutes between League goals scored by club | 77 |

| | PLAYER | LGE GOALS | POWER | STRIKE RATE |
|---|---|---|---|---|
| 2 | Ian Armstrong | 7 | 61 | 271 mins |
| 3 | Marc Bridge-Wilkinson | 9 | 92 | 288 mins |
| 4 | William Paynter | 5 | 73 | 366 mins |
| 5 | Stephen Brooker | 5 | 86 | 380 mins |

## KEY PLAYERS - MIDFIELDERS

**1 Peter Clarke**

| | | | |
|---|---|---|---|
| Goals in the League | 1 | Contribution to Attacking Power<br>Average number of minutes between League team goals while on pitch | 73 |
| Defensive Rating<br>Average number of mins between League goals conceded while he was on the pitch | 65 | Scoring Difference<br>Defensive Rating minus Contribution to Attacking Power | -8 |

| | PLAYER | LGE GOALS | DEF RATE | POWER | SCORE DIFF |
|---|---|---|---|---|---|
| 2 | Ian Brightwell | 0 | 64 | 73 | -9 mins |
| 3 | Michael Cummins | 4 | 59 | 68 | -9 mins |
| 4 | Sean McClare | 0 | 60 | 74 | -14 mins |
| 5 | Stephen McPhee | 3 | 67 | 83 | -16 mins |

## KEY PLAYERS - DEFENDERS

**1 Liam Burns**

| | | | |
|---|---|---|---|
| Goals Conceded (GC)<br>The number of League goals conceded while he was on the pitch | 16 | Clean Sheets<br>In games when he played at least 70 minutes | 4 |
| Defensive Rating<br>Ave number of mins between League goals conceded while on the pitch | 76 | Club Defensive Rating<br>Average number of mins between League goals conceded by the club this season | 59 |

| | PLAYER | CON LGE | CLEAN SHEETS | DEF RATE |
|---|---|---|---|---|
| 2 | Matthew Carragher | 44 | 10 | 69 mins |
| 3 | Michael Walsh | 21 | 4 | 69 mins |
| 4 | Steve Rowland | 32 | 6 | 61 mins |
| 5 | Sam Collins | 68 | 9 | 57 mins |

## KEY GOALKEEPER

**1 Mark Goodlad**

| | |
|---|---|
| Goals Conceded in the League | 54 |
| Defensive Rating<br>Ave number of mins between League goals conceded while on the pitch | 60 |
| Counting Games<br>Games when he played at least 70 mins | 36 |
| Clean Sheets<br>In games when he played at least 70 mins | 8 |

## TOP POINT EARNERS

| | PLAYER | GAMES | AVE |
|---|---|---|---|
| 1 | Littlejohn | 10 | 1.70 |
| 2 | Ingram | 2 | 1.50 |
| 3 | Carragher | 33 | 1.48 |
| 4 | Walsh | 15 | 1.40 |
| 5 | Brisco | 18 | 1.39 |
| 6 | Clarke | 13 | 1.38 |
| 7 | Durnin | 18 | 1.33 |
| 8 | Cummins | 28 | 1.32 |
| 9 | Bridge-Wilkinson | 28 | 1.29 |
| | CLUB AVERAGE: | | 1.15 |

Ave = Average points per match in Counting Games

## DISCIPLINARY RECORDS

| | PLAYER | YELLOW | RED | AVE |
|---|---|---|---|---|
| 1 | Boyd | 5 | 0 | 323 |
| 2 | Rowland | 5 | 1 | 325 |
| 3 | Charnock | 3 | 0 | 414 |
| 4 | Durnin | 5 | 0 | 417 |
| 5 | McCarthy | 1 | 0 | 460 |
| 6 | Collins | 7 | 1 | 488 |
| 7 | McPhee | 6 | 0 | 524 |
| 8 | Clarke | 2 | 0 | 585 |
| 9 | Carragher | 5 | 0 | 606 |
| 10 | Burns | 2 | 0 | 611 |
| 11 | Brisco | 3 | 0 | 619 |
| 12 | Bridge-Wilkinson | 4 | 0 | 649 |
| 13 | Cummins | 3 | 0 | 860 |
| | Other | 14 | 1 | |
| | TOTAL | 65 | 3 | |

## LEAGUE GOALS

| | PLAYER | MINS | GOALS | AVE |
|---|---|---|---|---|
| 1 | Bridge-Wilkinson | 2596 | 9 | 288 |
| 2 | Armstrong | 1899 | 7 | 271 |
| 3 | Angell | 1212 | 5 | 242 |
| 4 | Collins | 3907 | 5 | 781 |
| 5 | Brooker | 1900 | 5 | 380 |
| 6 | Paynter | 1829 | 5 | 366 |
| 7 | Cummins | 2581 | 4 | 645 |
| 8 | Boyd | 1618 | 3 | 539 |
| 9 | McPhee | 3148 | 3 | 1049 |
| 10 | Littlejohn | 1000 | 3 | 333 |
| 11 | Brisco | 1858 | 1 | 1858 |
| 12 | Durnin | 2089 | 1 | 2089 |
| 13 | Walsh | 1443 | 1 | 1443 |
| | Other | | 2 | |
| | TOTAL | | 54 | |

## MONTH BY MONTH GUIDE TO THE POINTS

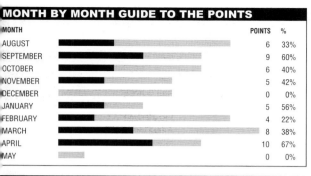

| MONTH | POINTS | % |
|---|---|---|
| AUGUST | 6 | 33% |
| SEPTEMBER | 9 | 60% |
| OCTOBER | 6 | 40% |
| NOVEMBER | 5 | 42% |
| DECEMBER | 0 | 0% |
| JANUARY | 5 | 56% |
| FEBRUARY | 4 | 22% |
| MARCH | 8 | 38% |
| APRIL | 10 | 67% |
| MAY | 0 | 0% |

## TEAM OF THE SEASON

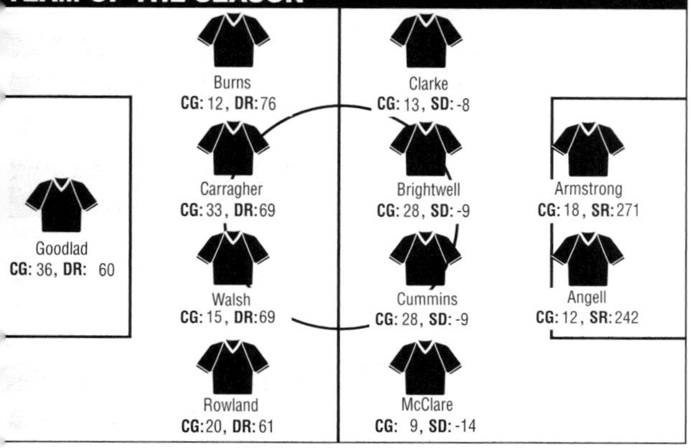
Burns
CG: 12, DR: 76
Clarke
CG: 13, SD: -8
Carragher
CG: 33, DR: 69
Brightwell
CG: 28, SD: -9
Armstrong
CG: 18, SR: 271
Goodlad
CG: 36, DR: 60
Walsh
CG: 15, DR: 69
Cummins
CG: 28, SD: -9
Angell
CG: 12, SR: 242
Rowland
CG: 20, DR: 61
McClare
CG: 9, SD: -14

KEY: DR = Defensive Rate, SD = Scoring Difference, SR = Strike Rate, CG = Counting Games – League games playing at least 70 minutes

## LEAGUE APPEARANCES, BOOKINGS AND CAPS

| | AGE | IN THE SQUAD | COUNTING GAMES | MINUTES ON PITCH | YELLOW CARDS | RED CARDS | THIS SEASON | HOME COUNTRY |
|---|---|---|---|---|---|---|---|---|
| **Goalkeepers** | | | | | | | | |
| Dean Delaney | 22 | 45 | 10 | 896 | 0 | 0 | - | Rep of Ireland |
| Mark Goodlad | 23 | 45 | 36 | 3244 | 1 | 0 | - | England |
| Joe Molloy | - | 2 | 0 | 0 | 0 | 0 | - | England |
| **Defenders** | | | | | | | | |
| Ryan Brown | - | 1 | 0 | 16 | 0 | 0 | - | England |
| Liam Burns | 24 | 32 | 12 | 1222 | 2 | 0 | - | N Ireland |
| Matthew Carragher | 27 | 35 | 33 | 3033 | 5 | 0 | - | England |
| Sam Collins | 26 | 44 | 43 | 3907 | 7 | 1 | - | England |
| Rae Ingram | 28 | 6 | 2 | 297 | 2 | 1 | - | England |
| Steve Rowland | 25 | 33 | 20 | 1950 | 5 | 1 | - | Wales |
| Michael Walsh | 25 | 19 | 15 | 1443 | 1 | 0 | - | England |
| **Midfielders** | | | | | | | | |
| Christopher Birchall | 19 | 8 | 0 | 24 | 0 | 0 | - | England |
| Mark Boyd | 21 | 31 | 17 | 1618 | 5 | 0 | - | England |
| Bridge-Wilkinson | - | 31 | 28 | 2596 | 4 | 0 | - | England |
| Ian Brightwell | 35 | 39 | 28 | 2862 | 3 | 0 | - | England |
| Neil Brisco | 25 | 25 | 18 | 1858 | 3 | 0 | - | England |
| Paul Byrne | 20 | 14 | 6 | 637 | 0 | 0 | - | South Africa |
| Phil Charnock | 28 | 25 | 11 | 1244 | 3 | 0 | - | England |
| Peter Clarke | 21 | 13 | 13 | 1170 | 2 | 0 | - | England |
| Michael Cummins | 25 | 30 | 28 | 2581 | 3 | 0 | - | Rep of Ireland |
| Jon McCarthy | 32 | 8 | 4 | 460 | 1 | 0 | - | N Ireland |
| Sean McClare | 25 | 23 | 9 | 967 | 1 | 0 | - | England |
| Stephen McPhee | 22 | 40 | 31 | 3148 | 6 | 0 | - | Scotland |
| Levi Reid | 20 | 4 | 0 | 26 | 0 | 0 | - | England |
| **Forwards** | | | | | | | | |
| Brett Angell | 34 | 16 | 12 | 1212 | 0 | 0 | - | England |
| Ian Armstrong | 21 | 40 | 18 | 1899 | 1 | 0 | - | England |
| Lee Ashcroft | 30 | 3 | 3 | 265 | 1 | 0 | - | England |
| Stephen Brooker | 22 | 27 | 17 | 1900 | 2 | 0 | - | England |
| John Durnin | 37 | 37 | 18 | 2089 | 5 | 0 | - | England |
| Simon Eldershaw | 19 | 4 | 0 | 19 | 0 | 0 | - | England |
| Adrian Littlejohn | 32 | 15 | 10 | 1000 | 0 | 0 | - | England |
| William Paynter | 18 | 41 | 17 | 1829 | 2 | 0 | - | England |

KEY: LEAGUE BOOKINGS CAPS

## SQUAD APPEARANCES

| | 1 | 2 | 3 | 4 | 5 | 6 | 7 | 8 | 9 | 10 | 11 | 12 | 13 | 14 | 15 | 16 | 17 | 18 | 19 | 20 | 21 | 22 | 23 | 24 | 25 | 26 | 27 | 28 | 29 | 30 | 31 | 32 | 33 | 34 | 35 | 36 | 37 | 38 | 39 | 40 | 41 | 42 | 43 | 44 | 45 | 46 | 47 | 48 |
|---|---|---|---|---|---|---|---|---|---|---|---|---|---|---|---|---|---|---|---|---|---|---|---|---|---|---|---|---|---|---|---|---|---|---|---|---|---|---|---|---|---|---|---|---|---|---|---|---|
| enue | H | A | A | H | A | H | A | H | H | H | A | H | A | H | A | H | A | H | A | H | A | H | A | H | H | A | A | A | H | A | H | H | A | H | H | A | A | H | A | H | H | A | A | H | A | H | H | A |
| ompetition | L | L | L | L | L | L | L | W | L | L | L | L | L | L | L | L | L | L | L | F | L | L | L | L | L | L | L | L | L | L | L | L | L | L | L | L | L | L | L | L | L | L | L | L | L | L | L | L |
| esult | L | L | L | L | W | W | W | L | W | W | L | L | D | D | D | L | W | D | D | L | L | W | L | L | L | L | D | W | D | L | L | W | L | D | L | L | L | W | D | W | L | D | W | W | L | D | W | L |

oalkeepers
ean Delaney
ark Goodlad
oe Molloy

efenders
yan Brown
am Burns
atthew Carragher
am Collins
ae Ingram
teve Rowland
ichael Walsh

idfielders
hristopher Birchall
ark Boyd
arc Bridge-Wilkinson
n Brightwell
eil Brisco
aul Byrne
hil Charnock
eter Clarke
ichael Cummins
on McCarthy
ean McClare
tephen McPhee
evi Reid

orwards
rett Angell
n Armstrong
ee Ashcroft
tephen Brooker
ohn Durnin
imon Eldershaw
drian Littlejohn
illiam Paynter

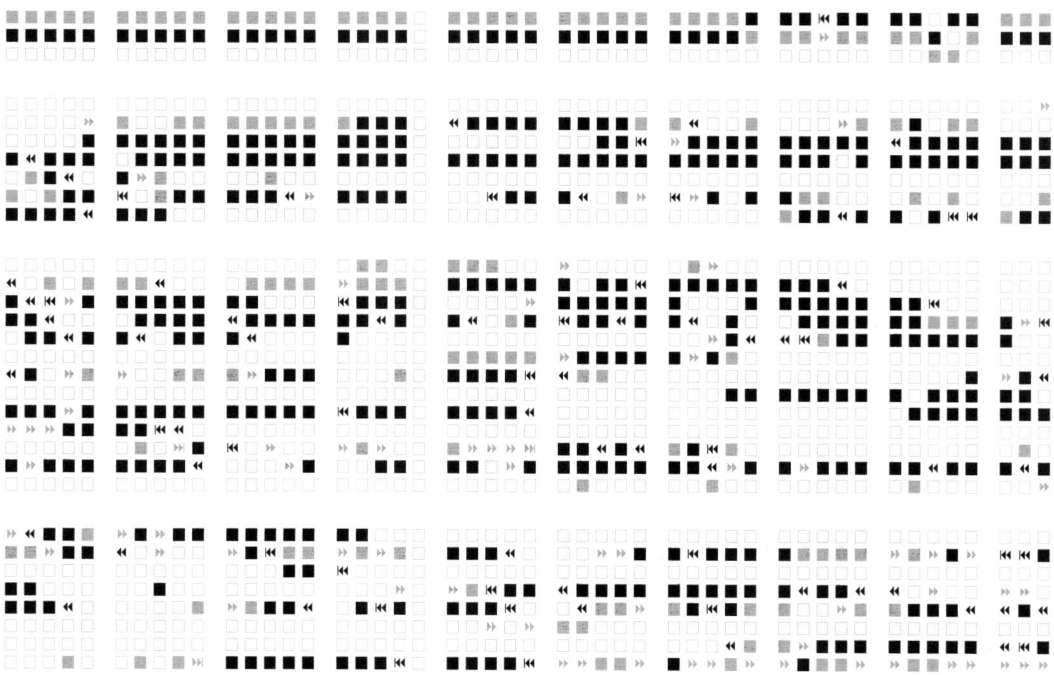

# WYCOMBE WANDERERS

Final Position: **18th**

NICKNAME: THE CHAIRBOYS

| | | | | | | |
|---|---|---|---|---|---|---|
| 1 | div2 | Notts County | A | D | 1-1 | Faulconbridge 89 |
| 2 | div2 | Northampton | H | D | 1-1 | Currie 48 |
| 3 | div2 | Mansfield | H | D | 3-3 | Devine 6; Faulconbridge 45; McCarthy 90 |
| 4 | div2 | Bristol City | A | L | 0-3 | |
| 5 | div2 | QPR | H | W | 4-1 | Faulconbridge 35; Rammell 47; Devine 61; Simpson 84 |
| 6 | div2 | Oldham | A | W | 2-0 | Bulman 5; Harris 85 |
| 7 | div2 | Wigan | A | L | 0-3 | |
| 8 | wcr1 | Swindon | A | W | 0-2 | Harris 91; McCarthy 109 |
| 9 | div2 | Blackpool | H | L | 1-2 | Faulconbridge 20 |
| 10 | div2 | Crewe | H | L | 1-2 | Devine 3 pen |
| 11 | div2 | Brentford | A | L | 0-1 | |
| 12 | div2 | Plymouth | H | W | 2-1 | Currie 27 pen,68 |
| 13 | wcr2 | Sheff Utd | A | L | 1-4 | McCarthy 89 |
| 14 | div2 | Colchester | A | W | 1-0 | Brown 3 pen |
| 15 | div2 | Cardiff | A | L | 0-1 | |
| 16 | div2 | Peterborough | H | W | 3-2 | Simpson 31; Brown 35 pen; Senda 85 |
| 17 | div2 | Barnsley | A | D | 1-1 | Ryan 44 |
| 18 | div2 | Chesterfield | H | W | 2-0 | Rammell 72,80 |
| 19 | div2 | Swindon | H | L | 2-3 | Faulconbridge 17; Rammell 72 |
| 20 | div2 | Huddersfield | A | D | 0-0 | |
| 21 | facr1 | Brentford | H | L | 2-4 | Rammell 12; Brown 26 |
| 22 | div2 | Tranmere | H | L | 1-3 | Simpson 71 |
| 23 | div2 | Stockport | A | L | 1-2 | Johnson 86 |
| 24 | div2 | Port Vale | H | W | 3-1 | Thomson 40; Devine 75 pen,90 |
| 25 | div2 | Cheltenham | A | D | 0-0 | |
| 26 | div2 | QPR | A | L | 1-2 | Dixon 79 |
| 27 | div2 | Luton | H | L | 1-2 | Dixon 65 |
| 28 | div2 | Bristol City | H | W | 2-1 | Johnson 49; Brown 68 pen |
| 29 | div2 | Northampton | A | W | 5-0 | Dixon 8; Simpson 45; Roberts 46,78,82 |
| 30 | div2 | Mansfield | A | D | 0-0 | |
| 31 | div2 | Oldham | H | D | 2-2 | Harris 71; Brown 83 pen |
| 32 | div2 | Luton | A | L | 0-1 | |
| 33 | div2 | Notts County | H | W | 3-1 | Harris 15,18; Roberts 59 |
| 34 | div2 | Huddersfield | H | D | 0-0 | |
| 35 | div2 | Swindon | A | W | 3-0 | Ryan 25; Bulman 57; Faulconbridge 73 |
| 36 | div2 | Wigan | H | L | 0-2 | |
| 37 | div2 | Blackpool | A | L | 0-1 | |
| 38 | div2 | Crewe | A | L | 2-4 | Dixon 9; Bulman 67 |
| 39 | div2 | Brentford | H | W | 4-0 | Dixon 16; Senda 17; Holligan 80; Currie 87 |
| 40 | div2 | Barnsley | H | D | 2-2 | McSporran 34; Johnson 82 |
| 41 | div2 | Peterborough | A | W | 2-1 | Rogers 37; Holligan 89 |
| 42 | div2 | Chesterfield | A | L | 0-4 | |
| 43 | div2 | Stockport | H | L | 1-4 | Simpson 65 |
| 44 | div2 | Cardiff | H | L | 0-4 | |
| 45 | div2 | Tranmere | A | L | 0-1 | |
| 46 | div2 | Cheltenham | H | D | 1-1 | Brown 4 pen |
| 47 | div2 | Port Vale | A | D | 1-1 | Harris 57 |
| 48 | div2 | Colchester | H | D | 0-0 | |
| 49 | div2 | Plymouth | A | L | 0-1 | |

## ATTENDANCES

HOME GROUND: ADAMS PARK CAPACITY: 10000 AVERAGE LEAGUE AT HOME: 6002

| | | | | | | | | |
|---|---|---|---|---|---|---|---|---|
| 26 | QPR | 14874 | 46 | Cheltenham | 6070 | 7 | Wigan | 5358 |
| 15 | Cardiff | 13130 | 36 | Wigan | 6052 | 24 | Port Vale | 5229 |
| 49 | Plymouth | 10129 | 19 | Swindon | 6021 | 3 | Mansfield | 5057 |
| 17 | Barnsley | 10044 | 1 | Notts County | 6012 | 10 | Crewe | 4909 |
| 4 | Bristol City | 9597 | 2 | Northampton | 5993 | 18 | Chesterfield | 4897 |
| 20 | Huddersfield | 8695 | 6 | Oldham | 5963 | 30 | Mansfield | 4811 |
| 5 | QPR | 8383 | 40 | Barnsley | 5931 | 23 | Stockport | 4731 |
| 27 | Luton | 7740 | 39 | Brentford | 5930 | 29 | Northampton | 4679 |
| 32 | Luton | 7351 | 44 | Cardiff | 5889 | 13 | Sheff Utd | 4389 |
| 37 | Blackpool | 7266 | 34 | Huddersfield | 5886 | 25 | Cheltenham | 4303 |
| 45 | Tranmere | 6814 | 9 | Blackpool | 5815 | 41 | Peterborough | 3627 |
| 28 | Bristol City | 6785 | 33 | Notts County | 5690 | 47 | Port Vale | 3590 |
| 12 | Plymouth | 6708 | 21 | Brentford | 5673 | 14 | Colchester | 3253 |
| 48 | Colchester | 6283 | 43 | Stockport | 5632 | 42 | Chesterfield | 3081 |
| 35 | Swindon | 6239 | 16 | Peterborough | 5539 | 8 | Swindon | 2993 |
| 31 | Oldham | 6226 | 38 | Crewe | 5398 | | | |
| 11 | Brentford | 6172 | 22 | Tranmere | 5386 | | | |

■ Home □ Away ▒ Neutral

## KEY PLAYERS - GOALSCORERS

**1 Jonathan Dixon**

| | | | |
|---|---|---|---|
| Goals in the League | 5 | Player Strike Rate<br>Average number of minutes between League goals scored by player | 259 |
| Contribution to Attacking Power<br>Average number of minutes between League team goals while on pitch | 92 | Club Strike Rate<br>Average number of minutes between League goals scored by club | 70 |

| | PLAYER | LGE GOALS | POWER | STRIKE RATE |
|---|---|---|---|---|
| 2 | Andy Rammell | 4 | 67 | 352 mins |
| 3 | Craig Faulconbridge | 6 | 62 | 425 mins |
| 4 | Darren Currie | 4 | 70 | 511 mins |
| 5 | Stephen Brown | 5 | 63 | 534 mins |

## KEY PLAYERS - MIDFIELDERS

**1 Stephen Brown**

| | | | |
|---|---|---|---|
| Goals in the League | 5 | Contribution to Attacking Power<br>Average number of minutes between League team goals while on pitch | 64 |
| Defensive Rating<br>Average number of mins between League goals conceded while he was on the pitch | 67 | Scoring Difference<br>Defensive Rating minus Contribution to Attacking Power | 3 |

| | PLAYER | LGE GOALS | DEF RATE | POWER | SCORE DIFF |
|---|---|---|---|---|---|
| 2 | Michael Simpson | 5 | 67 | 69 | -2 mins |
| 3 | Keith Ryan | 2 | 69 | 75 | -6 mins |
| 4 | Darren Currie | 4 | 55 | 70 | -15 mins |
| 5 | Chris Vinnicombe | 0 | 67 | 85 | -18 mins |

## KEY PLAYERS - DEFENDERS

**1 Andrew Thomson**

| | | | |
|---|---|---|---|
| Goals Conceded (GC)<br>The number of League goals conceded while he was on the pitch | 46 | Clean Sheets<br>In games when he played at least 70 minutes | 9 |
| Defensive Rating<br>Ave number of mins between League goals conceded while on the pitch | 67 | Club Defensive Rating<br>Average number of mins between League goals conceded by the club this season | 63 |

| | PLAYER | CON LGE | CLEAN SHEETS | DEF RATE |
|---|---|---|---|---|
| 2 | Roger Jonhnson | 37 | 7 | 66 mins |
| 3 | Paul McCarthy | 31 | 5 | 63 mins |
| 4 | Mark Rogers | 52 | 6 | 54 mins |

## KEY GOALKEEPER

**1 Martin Taylor**

| | |
|---|---|
| Goals Conceded in the League | 14 |
| Defensive Rating<br>Ave number of mins between League goals conceded while on the pitch | 71 |
| Counting Games<br>Games when he played at least 70 mins | 11 |
| Clean Sheets<br>In games when he played at least 70 mins | 2 |

## TOP POINT EARNERS

| | PLAYER | GAMES | AVE |
|---|---|---|---|
| 1 | Faulconbridge | 28 | 1.43 |
| 2 | Rammell | 13 | 1.31 |
| 3 | Currie | 18 | 1.28 |
| 4 | Thomson | 33 | 1.27 |
| 5 | Ryan | 26 | 1.23 |
| 6 | Bulman | 40 | 1.23 |
| 7 | Senda | 39 | 1.23 |
| 8 | Brown | 26 | 1.19 |
| 9 | Johnson | 26 | 1.19 |
| 10 | Taylor | 11 | 1.18 |
| | CLUB AVERAGE: | | 1.13 |

Ave = Average points per match in Counting Game

## DISCIPLINARY RECORDS

| | PLAYER | YELLOW | RED | AVE |
|---|---|---|---|---|
| 1 | Brown | 10 | 1 | 242 |
| 2 | McCarthy | 8 | 0 | 243 |
| 3 | Harris | 2 | 0 | 294 |
| 4 | Roberts | 4 | 0 | 335 |
| 5 | Rammell | 3 | 1 | 352 |
| 6 | Simpson | 9 | 0 | 415 |
| 7 | Devine | 2 | 0 | 523 |
| 8 | Cook | 1 | 0 | 574 |
| 9 | Dixon | 2 | 0 | 646 |
| 10 | Vinnicombe | 3 | 0 | 737 |
| 11 | Thomson | 4 | 0 | 767 |
| 12 | Johnson | 3 | 0 | 808 |
| 13 | Senda | 2 | 2 | 885 |
| | Other | 9 | 0 | |
| | TOTAL | 62 | 4 | |

## LEAGUE GOALS

| | PLAYER | MINS | GOALS | AVE |
|---|---|---|---|---|
| 1 | Faulconbridge | 2547 | 6 | 425 |
| 2 | Brown | 2668 | 5 | 534 |
| 3 | Devine | 1046 | 5 | 209 |
| 4 | Simpson | 3735 | 5 | 747 |
| 5 | Dixon | 1293 | 5 | 259 |
| 6 | Harris | 589 | 5 | 118 |
| 7 | Currie | 2043 | 4 | 511 |
| 8 | Rammell | 1409 | 4 | 352 |
| 9 | Roberts | 1340 | 4 | 335 |
| 10 | Johnson | 2425 | 3 | 808 |
| 11 | Bulman | 3707 | 3 | 1236 |
| 12 | Senda | 3542 | 2 | 1771 |
| 13 | Ryan | 2770 | 2 | 1385 |
| | Other | | 6 | |
| | TOTAL | | 59 | |

## MONTH BY MONTH GUIDE TO THE POINTS

| MONTH | POINTS | % |
|---|---|---|
| AUGUST | 9 | 50% |
| SEPTEMBER | 3 | 20% |
| OCTOBER | 10 | 67% |
| NOVEMBER | 1 | 8% |
| DECEMBER | 4 | 33% |
| JANUARY | 8 | 53% |
| FEBRUARY | 7 | 58% |
| MARCH | 7 | 39% |
| APRIL | 3 | 17% |
| MAY | 0 | 0% |

## TEAM OF THE SEASON

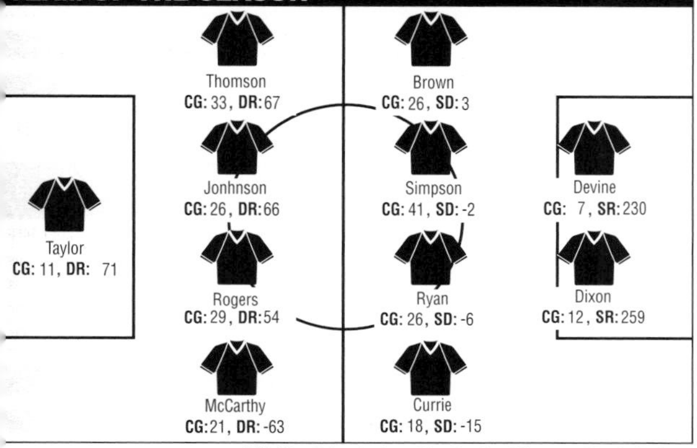
Thomson
CG: 33, DR: 67
Brown
CG: 26, SD: 3
Jonhnson
CG: 26, DR: 66
Simpson
CG: 41, SD: -2
Devine
CG: 7, SR: 230
Taylor
CG: 11, DR: 71
Rogers
CG: 29, DR: 54
Ryan
CG: 26, SD: -6
Dixon
CG: 12, SR: 259
McCarthy
CG: 21, DR: -63
Currie
CG: 18, SD: -15

**KEY:** DR = Defensive Rate, SD = Scoring Difference, SR = Strike Rate, CG=Counting Games – League games playing at least 70 minutes

## LEAGUE APPEARANCES, BOOKINGS AND CAPS

| | AGE | IN THE SQUAD | COUNTING GAMES | MINUTES ON PITCH | YELLOW CARDS | RED CARDS | THIS SEASON | HOME COUNTRY |
|---|---|---|---|---|---|---|---|---|
| **Goalkeepers** | | | | | | | | |
| Frank Talia | 30 | 38 | 35 | 3150 | 1 | 0 | - | Australia |
| Martin Taylor | 36 | 11 | 11 | 990 | 0 | 0 | - | England |
| Steve Williams | 20 | 2 | 0 | 0 | 0 | 0 | - | England |
| **Defenders** | | | | | | | | |
| Ijah Anderson | 27 | 5 | 5 | 450 | 2 | 0 | - | England |
| Richard Harris | 22 | 31 | 3 | 589 | 2 | 0 | - | England |
| Roger Jonhnson | 20 | 41 | 26 | 2425 | 3 | 0 | - | England |
| Paul McCarthy | 31 | 35 | 21 | 1950 | 8 | 0 | - | Rep of Ireland |
| Luke Oliver | - | 4 | 0 | 77 | 1 | 0 | - | England |
| Mark Rogers | 24 | 40 | 29 | 2796 | 0 | 0 | - | Canada |
| Andrew Thomson | 29 | 41 | 33 | 3071 | 4 | 0 | - | England |
| **Midfielders** | | | | | | | | |
| Stephen Brown | 37 | 42 | 26 | 2668 | 10 | 1 | - | England |
| Lewis Cook | 19 | 33 | 3 | 574 | 1 | 0 | - | England |
| Darren Currie | 28 | 44 | 18 | 2043 | 2 | 0 | - | England |
| Martyn Lee | 22 | 14 | 1 | 205 | 0 | 0 | - | England |
| Stuart Roberts | 22 | 31 | 8 | 1340 | 4 | 0 | - | Wales |
| Keith Ryan | 33 | 41 | 26 | 2770 | 1 | 0 | - | England |
| Ian Simpemba | 20 | 9 | 0 | 13 | 0 | 0 | - | Rep of Ireland |
| Michael Simpson | 29 | 42 | 41 | 3735 | 9 | 0 | - | England |
| Chris Vinnicombe | 32 | 25 | 24 | 2212 | 3 | 0 | - | England |
| **Forwards** | | | | | | | | |
| Dannie Bulman | 24 | 44 | 40 | 3707 | 2 | 0 | - | England |
| Sean Devine | 30 | 19 | 7 | 1046 | 2 | 0 | - | England |
| Jonathan Dixon | 19 | 25 | 12 | 1293 | 2 | 0 | - | England |
| Craig Faulconbridge | 25 | 35 | 28 | 2547 | 0 | 0 | - | England |
| Gavin Holligan | 23 | 11 | 1 | 284 | 0 | 0 | - | England |
| Jermaine McSporran | 26 | 9 | 6 | 621 | 0 | 0 | - | England |
| Andy Rammell | 36 | 23 | 13 | 1409 | 3 | 1 | - | England |
| Danny Senda | 22 | 41 | 39 | 3542 | 2 | 2 | - | England |

**KEY:** LEAGUE BOOKINGS CAPS

## SQUAD APPEARANCES

| Match | 1 | 2 | 3 | 4 | 5 | 6 | 7 | 8 | 9 | 10 | 11 | 12 | 13 | 14 | 15 | 16 | 17 | 18 | 19 | 20 | 21 | 22 | 23 | 24 | 25 | 26 | 27 | 28 | 29 | 30 | 31 | 32 | 33 | 34 | 35 | 36 | 37 | 38 | 39 | 40 | 41 | 42 | 43 | 44 | 45 | 46 | 47 | 48 | 49 |
|---|---|---|---|---|---|---|---|---|---|---|---|---|---|---|---|---|---|---|---|---|---|---|---|---|---|---|---|---|---|---|---|---|---|---|---|---|---|---|---|---|---|---|---|---|---|---|---|---|---|
| Venue | A | H | H | A | H | A | A | A | H | H | A | H | A | A | A | H | A | H | H | A | H | H | A | H | A | A | H | H | A | A | H | A | H | H | A | H | A | A | H | H | A | A | H | H | A | H | A | H | A |
| Competition | L | L | L | L | L | L | L | W | L | L | L | L | W | L | L | L | L | L | L | L | F | L | L | L | L | L | L | L | L | L | L | L | L | L | L | L | L | L | L | L | L | L | L | L | L | L | L | L | L |
| Result | D | D | D | L | W | W | L | D | L | L | L | W | L | W | L | W | D | W | L | D | L | L | L | W | D | L | L | W | W | D | D | L | W | D | W | L | L | L | W | D | W | L | L | L | L | D | D | D | L |

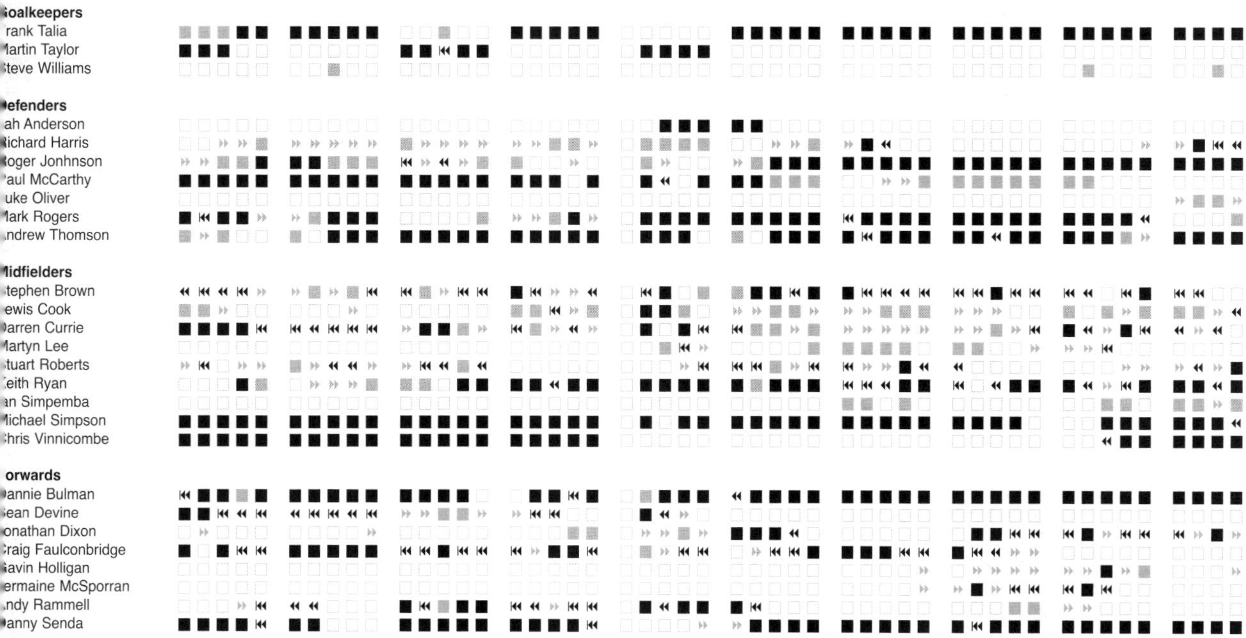
Goalkeepers
Frank Talia
Martin Taylor
Steve Williams
Defenders
Ijah Anderson
Richard Harris
Roger Jonhnson
Paul McCarthy
Luke Oliver
Mark Rogers
Andrew Thomson
Midfielders
Stephen Brown
Lewis Cook
Darren Currie
Martyn Lee
Stuart Roberts
Keith Ryan
Ian Simpemba
Michael Simpson
Chris Vinnicombe
Forwards
Dannie Bulman
Sean Devine
Jonathan Dixon
Craig Faulconbridge
Gavin Holligan
Jermaine McSporran
Andy Rammell
Danny Senda

KEY: ■ On all match | ⏮ Subbed or sent off (Counting game) | ⏭ Subbed on from bench (Counting Game) | Subbed on and then subbed or sent off (Counting Game) | Not in 16
■ On bench | « Subbed or sent off (playing less than 70 minutes) | » Subbed on (playing less than 70 minutes) | Subbed on and then subbed or sent off (playing less than 70 minutes)

# BARNSLEY

Final Position: **19th**

NICKNAME: THE TYKES

| | | | | | | |
|---|---|---|---|---|---|---|
| 1 | div2 | Swindon | A | L | 1-3 | Miglioranzi 30 pen |
| 2 | div2 | Cheltenham | H | D | 1-1 | Dyer 51 |
| 3 | div2 | QPR | H | W | 1-0 | Lumsdon 57 |
| 4 | div2 | Luton | A | W | 3-2 | Perrett 20 og; Sheron 43; Dyer 58 |
| 5 | div2 | Notts County | H | D | 0-0 | |
| 6 | div2 | Northampton | A | L | 0-1 | |
| 7 | div2 | Huddersfield | A | L | 0-1 | |
| 8 | wcr1 | Macclesfield | A | L | 1-4 | Rankin 84 |
| 9 | div2 | Plymouth | H | D | 1-1 | Dyer 10 |
| 10 | div2 | Blackpool | H | W | 2-1 | Sheron 31; Fallon 75 |
| 11 | div2 | Stockport | A | L | 1-4 | Fallon 26 |
| 12 | div2 | Wigan | H | L | 1-3 | Betsy 66 |
| 13 | div2 | Brentford | A | W | 2-1 | Betsy 13,81 |
| 14 | div2 | Bristol City | H | L | 1-4 | Bertos 49 |
| 15 | div2 | Tranmere | A | L | 0-1 | |
| 16 | div2 | Wycombe | H | D | 1-1 | Fallon 33 |
| 17 | div2 | Colchester | A | D | 1-1 | Dyer 15 |
| 18 | div2 | Chesterfield | A | L | 0-1 | |
| 19 | div2 | Cardiff | H | W | 3-2 | Morgan 22,64; Fallon 30 |
| 20 | facr1 | Blackpool | H | L | 1-4 | Dyer 17 |
| 21 | div2 | Peterborough | A | W | 3-1 | Sheron 35,38; Dyer 90 |
| 22 | div2 | Oldham | H | D | 2-2 | Sheron 28; Dyer 89 |
| 23 | div2 | Crewe | A | L | 0-2 | |
| 24 | div2 | Mansfield | H | L | 0-1 | |
| 25 | div2 | Notts County | A | L | 2-3 | Betsy 1; Dyer 62 |
| 26 | div2 | Port Vale | H | W | 2-1 | Fallon 12; Gibbs 79 pen |
| 27 | div2 | Northampton | H | L | 1-2 | Lumsdon 24 |
| 28 | div2 | QPR | A | L | 0-1 | |
| 29 | div2 | Luton | H | L | 2-3 | Betsy 1; Dyer 76 pen |
| 30 | div2 | Port Vale | A | D | 0-0 | |
| 31 | div2 | Swindon | H | D | 1-1 | Fallon 14 |
| 32 | div2 | Cardiff | A | D | 1-1 | Dyer 52 pen |
| 33 | div2 | Chesterfield | H | W | 2-1 | Fallon 20; Dyer 33 |
| 34 | div2 | Cheltenham | A | W | 3-1 | Sheron 18; Dyer 63; Jones, Gary 90 |
| 35 | div2 | Huddersfield | H | L | 0-1 | |
| 36 | div2 | Plymouth | A | D | 1-1 | Dyer 66 |
| 37 | div2 | Blackpool | A | W | 2-1 | Sheron 41,62 |
| 38 | div2 | Stockport | H | W | 1-0 | Dyer 10 |
| 39 | div2 | Wycombe | A | D | 2-2 | Sheron 76; Dyer 86 |
| 40 | div2 | Tranmere | H | D | 1-1 | Dyer 8 |
| 41 | div2 | Colchester | H | D | 1-1 | Betsy 36 |
| 42 | div2 | Bristol City | A | L | 0-2 | |
| 43 | div2 | Oldham | A | L | 1-2 | Mulligan 21 |
| 44 | div2 | Peterborough | H | L | 1-2 | Dyer 15 pen |
| 45 | div2 | Mansfield | A | W | 1-0 | O'Callaghan 31 |
| 46 | div2 | Crewe | H | L | 1-2 | Ince 33 og |
| 47 | div2 | Brentford | H | W | 1-0 | Rankin 90 |
| 48 | div2 | Wigan | A | L | 0-1 | |

## ATTENDANCES

HOME GROUND: OAKWELL CAPACITY: 22752 AVERAGE LEAGUE AT HOME: 9757

| | | | | | | | | |
|---|---|---|---|---|---|---|---|---|
| 32 | Cardiff | 12759 | 46 | Crewe | 9396 | 43 | Oldham | 6191 |
| 48 | Wigan | 12537 | 33 | Chesterfield | 9373 | 39 | Wycombe | 5931 |
| 35 | Huddersfield | 12474 | 26 | Port Vale | 9291 | 1 | Swindon | 5702 |
| 7 | Huddersfield | 11989 | 38 | Stockport | 9177 | 11 | Stockport | 5690 |
| 22 | Oldham | 11222 | 41 | Colchester | 9154 | 23 | Crewe | 5633 |
| 28 | QPR | 11217 | 9 | Plymouth | 9134 | 13 | Brentford | 5394 |
| 19 | Cardiff | 10894 | 29 | Luton | 9079 | 6 | Northampton | 5004 |
| 14 | Bristol City | 10495 | 47 | Brentford | 9065 | 45 | Mansfield | 4873 |
| 24 | Mansfield | 10495 | 44 | Peterborough | 8862 | 18 | Chesterfield | 4676 |
| 5 | Notts County | 10431 | 40 | Tranmere | 8786 | 21 | Peterborough | 4449 |
| 42 | Bristol City | 10232 | 31 | Swindon | 8661 | 30 | Port Vale | 4033 |
| 16 | Wycombe | 10044 | 36 | Plymouth | 8228 | 34 | Cheltenham | 3568 |
| 12 | Wigan | 9977 | 25 | Notts County | 7413 | 17 | Colchester | 3096 |
| 2 | Cheltenham | 9641 | 20 | Blackpool | 6857 | 8 | Macclesfield | 1720 |
| 3 | QPR | 9626 | 15 | Tranmere | 6855 | | | |
| 10 | Blackpool | 9619 | 37 | Blackpool | 6827 | | | |
| 27 | Northampton | 9531 | 4 | Luton | 6230 | | | |

■ Home □ Away ▩ Neutral

## KEY PLAYERS - GOALSCORERS

**1 Bruce Dyer**

| | | | |
|---|---|---|---|
| Goals in the League | 16 | Player Strike Rate<br>Average number of minutes between League goals scored by player | 211 |
| Contribution to Attacking Power<br>Average number of minutes between League team goals while on pitch | 78 | Club Strike Rate<br>Average number of minutes between League goals scored by club | 81 |

| | PLAYER | LGE GOALS | POWER | STRIKE RATE |
|---|---|---|---|---|
| 2 | Rory Fallon | 7 | 71 | 236 mins |
| 3 | Mike Sheron | 9 | 82 | 265 mins |
| 4 | Kevin Betsy | 6 | 80 | 511 mins |
| 5 | Chris Lumsdon | 3 | 87 | 609 mins |

## KEY PLAYERS - MIDFIELDERS

**1 Antony Kay**

| | | | |
|---|---|---|---|
| Goals in the League | 0 | Contribution to Attacking Power<br>Average number of minutes between League team goals while on pitch | 99 |
| Defensive Rating<br>Average number of mins between League goals conceded while he was on the pitch | 99 | Scoring Difference<br>Defensive Rating minus Contribution to Attacking Power | 0 |

| | PLAYER | LGE GOALS | DEF RATE | POWER | SCORE DIFF |
|---|---|---|---|---|---|
| 2 | Mitch Ward | 0 | 68 | 73 | -5 mins |
| 3 | Alex Neil | 0 | 71 | 80 | -9 mins |
| 4 | Kevin Donovan | 0 | 68 | 90 | -22 mins |
| 5 | Lee Crooks | 0 | 73 | 99 | -26 mins |

## KEY PLAYERS - DEFENDERS

**1 Neil Austin**

| | | | |
|---|---|---|---|
| Goals Conceded (GC)<br>The number of League goals conceded while he was on the pitch | 40 | Clean Sheets<br>In games when he played at least 70 minutes | 6 |
| Defensive Rating<br>Ave number of mins between League goals conceded while on the pitch | 72 | Club Defensive Rating<br>Average number of mins between League goals conceded by the club this season | 65 |

| | PLAYER | CON LGE | CLEAN SHEETS | DEF RATE |
|---|---|---|---|---|
| 2 | Dave Mulligan | 38 | 4 | 69 mins |
| 3 | Chris Morgan | 47 | 5 | 68 mins |
| 4 | Brian O'Callaghan | 15 | 1 | 67 mins |
| 5 | Paul Gibbs | 30 | 1 | 66 mins |

## KEY GOALKEEPER

**1 Andy Marriott**

| | |
|---|---|
| Goals Conceded in the League | 51 |
| Defensive Rating<br>Ave number of mins between League goals conceded while on the pitch | 64 |
| Counting Games<br>Games when he played at least 70 mins | 36 |
| Clean Sheets<br>In games when he played at least 70 mins | 4 |

## TOP POINT EARNERS

| | PLAYER | GAMES | AVE |
|---|---|---|---|
| 1 | Kay | 12 | 1.58 |
| 2 | Ward | 20 | 1.55 |
| 3 | Donovan | 16 | 1.44 |
| 4 | Mulligan | 27 | 1.30 |
| 5 | Ghent | 7 | 1.29 |
| 6 | Curle | 11 | 1.27 |
| 7 | Austin | 31 | 1.26 |
| 8 | Neil | 29 | 1.24 |
| 9 | Marriott | 36 | 1.19 |
| 10 | Morgan | 35 | 1.17 |
| | CLUB AVERAGE: | | 1.13 |

Ave = Average points per match in Counting Games

## DISCIPLINARY RECORDS

| | PLAYER | YELLOW | RED | AVE |
|---|---|---|---|---|
| 1 | Hayward | 3 | 0 | 169 |
| 2 | Ward | 8 | 2 | 190 |
| 3 | Morgan | 14 | 0 | 228 |
| 4 | Gibbs | 8 | 0 | 246 |
| 5 | Curle | 3 | 0 | 330 |
| 6 | Austin | 8 | 0 | 361 |
| 7 | Lumsdon | 5 | 0 | 365 |
| 8 | Kay | 3 | 0 | 396 |
| 9 | Flynn | 3 | 0 | 401 |
| 10 | Mulligan | 6 | 0 | 435 |
| 11 | Jones, Gary | 6 | 0 | 435 |
| 12 | Betsy | 6 | 0 | 511 |
| 13 | Williams | 1 | 0 | 647 |
| | Other | 15 | 1 | |
| | TOTAL | 89 | 3 | |

## LEAGUE GOALS

| | PLAYER | MINS | GOALS | AVE |
|---|---|---|---|---|
| 1 | Dyer | 3369 | 16 | 211 |
| 2 | Sheron | 2384 | 9 | 265 |
| 3 | Fallon | 1654 | 7 | 236 |
| 4 | Betsy | 3067 | 6 | 511 |
| 5 | Lumsdon | 1828 | 3 | 609 |
| 6 | Morgan | 3205 | 2 | 1603 |
| 7 | Rankin | 163 | 1 | 163 |
| 8 | Bertos | 236 | 1 | 236 |
| 9 | Jones, Gary | 2610 | 1 | 2610 |
| 10 | Mulligan | 2614 | 1 | 2614 |
| 11 | Gibbs | 1974 | 1 | 1974 |
| 12 | O'Callaghan | 999 | 1 | 999 |
| | Other | | 2 | |
| | TOTAL | | 51 | |

## MONTH BY MONTH GUIDE TO THE POINTS

| MONTH | POINTS | % |
|---|---|---|
| AUGUST | 8 | 44% |
| SEPTEMBER | 4 | 22% |
| OCTOBER | 5 | 33% |
| NOVEMBER | 7 | 39% |
| DECEMBER | 3 | 25% |
| JANUARY | 1 | 8% |
| FEBRUARY | 8 | 53% |
| MARCH | 10 | 48% |
| APRIL | 6 | 40% |
| MAY | 0 | 0% |

## TEAM OF THE SEASON

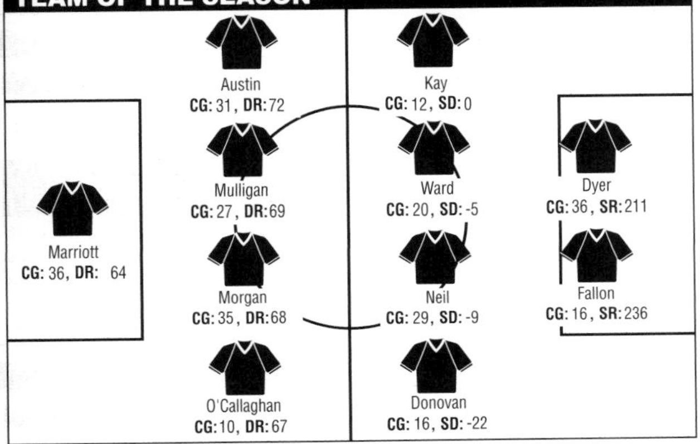

Austin
CG: 31, DR: 72
Kay
CG: 12, SD: 0
Mulligan
CG: 27, DR: 69
Ward
CG: 20, SD: -5
Dyer
CG: 36, SR: 211
Marriott
CG: 36, DR: 64
Morgan
CG: 35, DR: 68
Neil
CG: 29, SD: -9
Fallon
CG: 16, SR: 236
O'Callaghan
CG: 10, DR: 67
Donovan
CG: 16, SD: -22


KEY: DR = Defensive Rate, SD = Scoring Difference, SR = Strike Rate, CG = Counting Games – League games playing at least 70 minutes

## LEAGUE APPEARANCES, BOOKINGS AND CAPS

| | AGE | IN THE SQUAD | COUNTING GAMES | MINUTES ON PITCH | YELLOW CARDS | RED CARDS | THIS SEASON | HOME COUNTRY |
|---|---|---|---|---|---|---|---|---|
| **Goalkeepers** | | | | | | | | |
| Matthew Ghent | 22 | 44 | 7 | 630 | 0 | 0 | - | England |
| Andy Marriott | 32 | 36 | 36 | 3240 | 1 | 0 | - | Wales |
| Craig Parry | 19 | 8 | 0 | 0 | 0 | 0 | - | England |
| Martin Taylor | 36 | 4 | 3 | 270 | 0 | 0 | - | England |
| **Defenders** | | | | | | | | |
| Neil Austin | 20 | 42 | 31 | 2888 | 8 | 0 | - | England |
| Keith Curle | 39 | 11 | 11 | 990 | 3 | 0 | - | England |
| Mike Flynn | 34 | 18 | 13 | 1205 | 3 | 0 | - | England |
| Paul Gibbs | 30 | 31 | 21 | 1974 | 8 | 0 | - | England |
| Andy Holt | 25 | 7 | 4 | 399 | 0 | 1 | - | England |
| Chris Morgan | 25 | 36 | 35 | 3205 | 14 | 0 | - | England |
| Dave Mulligan | 21 | 37 | 27 | 2614 | 6 | 0 | - | England |
| Brian O'Callaghan | 22 | 27 | 10 | 999 | 1 | 0 | - | Rep of Ireland |
| Adam Oldham | 17 | 2 | 0 | 0 | 0 | 0 | - | England |
| Robbie Williams | 19 | 14 | 7 | 647 | 1 | 0 | - | England |
| **Midfielders** | | | | | | | | |
| Carl Barrowclough | 21 | 5 | 0 | 109 | 1 | 0 | - | England |
| Lee Crooks | 25 | 22 | 10 | 1089 | 1 | 0 | - | England |
| Kevin Donovan | 31 | 24 | 16 | 1703 | 2 | 0 | - | England |
| Dean Gorre | 32 | 37 | 17 | 1728 | 2 | 0 | - | Holland |
| Steve Hayward | 31 | 7 | 6 | 507 | 3 | 0 | - | England |
| Antony Kay | 20 | 24 | 12 | 1190 | 3 | 0 | - | England |
| Chris Lumsdon | 23 | 33 | 20 | 1828 | 5 | 0 | - | England |
| Alex Neil | 22 | 33 | 29 | 2706 | 4 | 0 | - | Scotland |
| Mitch Ward | 32 | 26 | 20 | 1901 | 8 | 2 | - | England |
| Nicky Wroe | - | 3 | 1 | 90 | 0 | 0 | - | England |
| **Forwards** | | | | | | | | |
| Leo Bertos | 21 | 10 | 1 | 236 | 1 | 0 | - | England |
| Kevin Betsy | 25 | 39 | 32 | 3067 | 6 | 0 | - | England |
| Bruce Dyer | 28 | 40 | 36 | 3369 | 1 | 0 | - | England |
| Rory Fallon | 21 | 28 | 16 | 1654 | 0 | 0 | - | New Zealand |
| Gary Jones | 34 | 31 | 26 | 2610 | 6 | 0 | - | England |
| Griff Jones | 19 | 6 | 0 | 51 | 0 | 0 | - | England |
| Isaiah Rankin | 25 | 14 | 1 | 163 | 0 | 0 | - | England |
| Mike Sheron | 31 | 36 | 23 | 2384 | 1 | 0 | - | England |

KEY: LEAGUE BOOKINGS CAPS

## SQUAD APPEARANCES

| Match | 1 | 2 | 3 | 4 | 5 | 6 | 7 | 8 | 9 | 10 | 11 | 12 | 13 | 14 | 15 | 16 |
|---|---|---|---|---|---|---|---|---|---|---|---|---|---|---|---|---|
| Venue | A | H | H | A | H | A | A | A | H | H | A | H | A | H | A | H |
| Competition | L | L | L | L | L | L | L | W | L | L | L | L | L | L | L | L |
| Result | L | D | W | W | D | L | L | D | D | W | L | L | W | L | L | D |

| Match | 17 | 18 | 19 | 20 | 21 | 22 | 23 | 24 | 25 | 26 | 27 | 28 | 29 | 30 | 31 | 32 |
|---|---|---|---|---|---|---|---|---|---|---|---|---|---|---|---|---|
| Venue | A | A | H | H | A | H | A | H | A | H | H | A | H | A | H | A |
| Competition | L | L | L | F | L | L | L | L | L | L | L | L | L | L | L | L |
| Result | D | L | W | L | W | D | L | L | L | W | L | L | L | D | D | D |

| Match | 33 | 34 | 35 | 36 | 37 | 38 | 39 | 40 | 41 | 42 | 43 | 44 | 45 | 46 | 47 | 48 |
|---|---|---|---|---|---|---|---|---|---|---|---|---|---|---|---|---|
| Venue | H | A | H | A | A | H | A | H | H | A | A | H | A | H | H | A |
| Competition | L | L | L | L | L | L | L | L | L | L | L | L | L | L | L | L |
| Result | W | W | L | D | W | W | D | D | D | L | L | L | W | L | W | L |

**Goalkeepers**
Matthew Ghent
Andy Marriott
Craig Parry
Martin Taylor

**Defenders**
Neil Austin
Keith Curle
Mike Flynn
Paul Gibbs
Andy Holt
Chris Morgan
Dave Mulligan
Brian O'Callaghan
Adam Oldham
Robbie Williams

**Midfielders**
Carl Barrowclough
Lee Crooks
Kevin Donovan
Dean Gorre
Steve Hayward
Antony Kay
Chris Lumsdon
Alex Neil
Mitch Ward
Nicky Wroe

**Forwards**
Leo Bertos
Kevin Betsy
Bruce Dyer
Rory Fallon
Gary Jones
Griff Jones
Isaiah Rankin
Mike Sheron

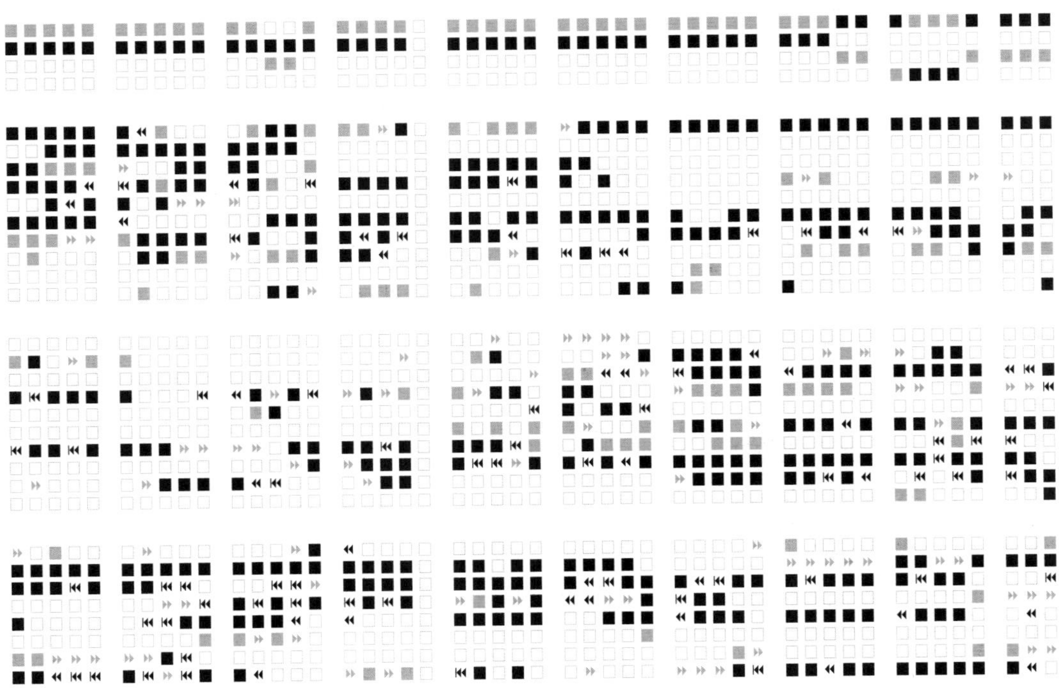

# CHESTERFIELD

Final Position: **20th**

NICKNAME: THE SPIREITES

| | | | | | | |
|---|---|---|---|---|---|---|
| 1 | div2 | QPR | A | L | 1-3 | Ebdon 55 pen |
| 2 | div2 | Swindon | H | L | 2-4 | Hurst 55 pen,74 |
| 3 | div2 | Port Vale | H | W | 2-1 | Edwards 46; Brandon 86 |
| 4 | div2 | Mansfield | A | W | 2-0 | Payne 39; Davies 54 |
| 5 | div2 | Northampton | H | W | 4-0 | Hurst 22,90; Hudson 28; Brandon 43 |
| 6 | div2 | Luton | A | L | 0-3 | |
| 7 | div2 | Crewe | A | D | 0-0 | |
| 8 | wcr1 | Grimsby | A | D | 0-0 | Allott 91 |
| 9 | div2 | Wigan | H | D | 0-0 | |
| 10 | div2 | Stockport | H | W | 1-0 | Brandon 44 |
| 11 | div2 | Plymouth | A | W | 1-0 | Ebdon 69 |
| 12 | div2 | Blackpool | H | W | 1-0 | Reeves 48 |
| 13 | wcr2 | West Ham | H | L | 4-5* | Brandon 52 (*on penalties) |
| 14 | div2 | Bristol City | A | L | 0-4 | |
| 15 | div2 | Tranmere | H | W | 1-0 | Howson 85 |
| 16 | div2 | Colchester | A | L | 0-2 | |
| 17 | div2 | Notts County | H | D | 0-0 | |
| 18 | div2 | Wycombe | A | L | 0-2 | |
| 19 | div2 | Barnsley | H | W | 1-0 | Burt 10 |
| 20 | div2 | Peterborough | A | L | 0-1 | |
| 21 | facr1 | Morecambe | H | L | 1-2 | Davies 74 |
| 22 | div2 | Cardiff | A | L | 0-1 | |
| 23 | div2 | Huddersfield | H | W | 1-0 | Dawson 33 |
| 24 | div2 | Brentford | A | L | 1-2 | Brandon 13 |
| 25 | div2 | Oldham | H | L | 0-1 | |
| 26 | div2 | Northampton | A | W | 1-0 | Bradley 88 |
| 27 | div2 | Cheltenham | H | D | 2-2 | Bradley 72; Howson 74 |
| 28 | div2 | Luton | H | W | 2-1 | Hurst 55; Reeves 60 |
| 29 | div2 | Swindon | A | L | 0-3 | |
| 30 | div2 | Mansfield | H | L | 1-2 | Ebdon 39 pen |
| 31 | div2 | Cheltenham | A | D | 0-0 | |
| 32 | div2 | QPR | H | L | 2-4 | Hurst 11; Brandon 90 |
| 33 | div2 | Peterborough | H | D | 0-0 | |
| 34 | div2 | Port Vale | A | L | 2-5 | Edwards 34; Ebdon 45 |
| 35 | div2 | Barnsley | A | L | 1-2 | Brandon 18 |
| 36 | div2 | Crewe | H | L | 0-2 | |
| 37 | div2 | Wigan | A | L | 1-3 | Reeves 66 pen |
| 38 | div2 | Stockport | A | L | 1-2 | Reeves 6 |
| 39 | div2 | Plymouth | H | W | 3-2 | Payne 10; Reeves 17,49 |
| 40 | div2 | Notts County | A | D | 1-1 | Folan 11 |
| 41 | div2 | Colchester | H | L | 0-4 | |
| 42 | div2 | Wycombe | H | W | 4-0 | Close 28; Reeves 53; Brandon 67; Hudson 86 |
| 43 | div2 | Tranmere | A | L | 1-2 | Reeves 78 |
| 44 | div2 | Huddersfield | A | L | 0-4 | |
| 45 | div2 | Cardiff | H | L | 0-3 | |
| 46 | div2 | Oldham | A | L | 0-4 | |
| 47 | div2 | Brentford | H | L | 0-2 | |
| 48 | div2 | Bristol City | H | W | 2-0 | Hurst 86; Hudson 90 |
| 49 | div2 | Blackpool | A | D | 1-1 | Douglas 39 |

## ATTENDANCES

HOME GROUND: SALTERGATE CAPACITY: 8880 AVERAGE LEAGUE AT HOME: 3917

| | | | | | | | | |
|---|---|---|---|---|---|---|---|---|
| 22 | Cardiff | 13331 | 26 | Northampton | 5282 | 10 | Stockport | 4088 |
| 45 | Cardiff | 13009 | 24 | Brentford | 5151 | 25 | Oldham | 4052 |
| 1 | QPR | 12603 | 18 | Wycombe | 4897 | 36 | Crewe | 3956 |
| 14 | Bristol City | 10107 | 48 | Bristol City | 4770 | 21 | Morecambe | 3703 |
| 35 | Barnsley | 9373 | 19 | Barnsley | 4676 | 39 | Plymouth | 3668 |
| 44 | Huddersfield | 9098 | 28 | Luton | 4638 | 3 | Port Vale | 3598 |
| 11 | Plymouth | 8547 | 29 | Swindon | 4544 | 5 | Northampton | 3585 |
| 43 | Tranmere | 8238 | 17 | Notts County | 4539 | 33 | Peterborough | 3515 |
| 49 | Blackpool | 7999 | 12 | Blackpool | 4488 | 47 | Brentford | 3296 |
| 4 | Mansfield | 7258 | 38 | Stockport | 4428 | 8 | Grimsby | 3248 |
| 13 | West Ham | 7102 | 31 | Cheltenham | 4423 | 41 | Colchester | 3226 |
| 46 | Oldham | 6885 | 32 | QPR | 4395 | 16 | Colchester | 3211 |
| 30 | Mansfield | 6813 | 20 | Peterborough | 4359 | 2 | Swindon | 3189 |
| 40 | Notts County | 6801 | 23 | Huddersfield | 4194 | 42 | Wycombe | 3081 |
| 37 | Wigan | 6384 | 9 | Wigan | 4124 | 34 | Port Vale | 3039 |
| 6 | Luton | 6060 | 15 | Tranmere | 4111 | | | |
| 7 | Crewe | 5837 | 27 | Cheltenham | 4092 | | | |

■ Home □ Away ▒ Neutral

## KEY PLAYERS - GOALSCORERS

**1 Glynn Hurst**

| | | | |
|---|---|---|---|
| Goals in the League | 7 | Player Strike Rate<br>Average number of minutes between League goals scored by player | 362 |
| Contribution to Attacking Power<br>Average number of minutes between League team goals while on pitch | 81 | Club Strike Rate<br>Average number of minutes between League goals scored by club | 96 |

| | PLAYER | LGE GOALS | POWER | STRIKE RATE |
|---|---|---|---|---|
| 2 | David Reeves | 8 | 85 | 383 mins |
| 3 | Chris Brandon | 7 | 92 | 434 mins |
| 4 | Marcus Ebdon | 4 | 99 | 473 mins |
| 5 | Mark Hudson | 3 | 98 | 686 mins |

## KEY PLAYERS - MIDFIELDERS

**1 Mark Hudson**

| | | | |
|---|---|---|---|
| Goals in the League | 3 | Contribution to Attacking Power<br>Average number of minutes between League team goals while on pitch | 98 |
| Defensive Rating<br>Average number of mins between League goals conceded while he was on the pitch | 69 | Scoring Difference<br>Defensive Rating minus Contribution to Attacking Power | -29 |

| | PLAYER | LGE GOALS | DEF RATE | POWER | SCORE DIFF |
|---|---|---|---|---|---|
| 2 | Chris Brandon | 7 | 61 | 92 | -31 mins |
| 3 | Glynn Hurst | 7 | 48 | 82 | -34 mins |
| 4 | Marcus Ebdon | 4 | 59 | 100 | -41 mins |
| 5 | Gareth Davies | 1 | 75 | 121 | -46 mins |

## KEY PLAYERS - DEFENDERS

**1 Kevin Dawson**

| | | | |
|---|---|---|---|
| Goals Conceded (GC)<br>The number of League goals conceded while he was on the pitch | 27 | Clean Sheets<br>In games when he played at least 70 minutes | 12 |
| Defensive Rating<br>Ave number of mins between League goals conceded while on the pitch | 81 | Club Defensive Rating<br>Average number of mins between League goals conceded by the club this season | 57 |

| | PLAYER | CON LGE | CLEAN SHEETS | DEF RATE |
|---|---|---|---|---|
| 2 | Steve Howson | 46 | 13 | 63 mins |
| 3 | Steve Payne | 51 | 11 | 57 mins |
| 4 | Martyn Booty | 54 | 10 | 57 mins |
| 5 | Steven Blatherwick | 49 | 7 | 54 mins |

## KEY GOALKEEPER

**1 Carl Muggleton**

| | |
|---|---|
| Goals Conceded in the League | 32 |
| Defensive Rating<br>Ave number of mins between League goals conceded while on the pitch | 71 |
| Counting Games<br>Games when he played at least 70 mins | 25 |
| Clean Sheets<br>In games when he played at least 70 mins | 12 |

## TOP POINT EARNERS

| | PLAYER | GAMES | AVE |
|---|---|---|---|
| 1 | Davies | 21 | 1.52 |
| 2 | Dawson | 23 | 1.48 |
| 3 | Reeves | 29 | 1.38 |
| 4 | Muggleton | 25 | 1.36 |
| 5 | Howson | 32 | 1.28 |
| 6 | Hudson | 22 | 1.27 |
| 7 | Rushbury | 21 | 1.19 |
| 8 | Close | 7 | 1.14 |
| 9 | Burt | 7 | 1.14 |
| | CLUB AVERAGE: | | 1.09 |

Ave = Average points per match in Counting Games

## DISCIPLINARY RECORDS

| | PLAYER | YELLOW | RED | AVE |
|---|---|---|---|---|
| 1 | Close | 5 | 0 | 137 |
| 2 | Burt | 5 | 0 | 206 |
| 3 | Innes | 2 | 0 | 245 |
| 4 | Blatherwick | 8 | 2 | 263 |
| 5 | Dawson | 8 | 0 | 273 |
| 6 | Brandon | 11 | 0 | 276 |
| 7 | Ebdon | 6 | 0 | 315 |
| 8 | Hurst | 8 | 0 | 317 |
| 9 | Folan | 2 | 0 | 385 |
| 10 | Edwards | 4 | 1 | 435 |
| 11 | Booty | 6 | 0 | 513 |
| 12 | Allott | 4 | 0 | 566 |
| 13 | Douglas | 1 | 0 | 630 |
| | Other | 15 | 1 | |
| | TOTAL | 85 | 4 | |

## LEAGUE GOALS

| | PLAYER | MINS | GOALS | AVE |
|---|---|---|---|---|
| 1 | Reeves | 3062 | 8 | 383 |
| 2 | Hurst | 2536 | 7 | 362 |
| 3 | Brandon | 3038 | 7 | 434 |
| 4 | Ebdon | 1891 | 4 | 473 |
| 5 | Hudson | 2059 | 3 | 686 |
| 6 | Howson | 2899 | 2 | 1450 |
| 7 | Bradley | 280 | 2 | 140 |
| 8 | Payne | 2904 | 2 | 1452 |
| 9 | Edwards | 2177 | 2 | 1089 |
| 10 | Burt | 1030 | 1 | 1030 |
| 11 | Douglas | 630 | 1 | 630 |
| 12 | Dawson | 2187 | 1 | 2187 |
| 13 | Davies | 2414 | 1 | 2414 |
| | Other | | 2 | |
| | TOTAL | | 43 | |

## MONTH BY MONTH GUIDE TO THE POINTS

| MONTH | POINTS | % |
|---|---|---|
| AUGUST | 9 | 50% |
| SEPTEMBER | 11 | 73% |
| OCTOBER | 4 | 27% |
| NOVEMBER | 6 | 50% |
| DECEMBER | 4 | 33% |
| JANUARY | 4 | 33% |
| FEBRUARY | 1 | 7% |
| MARCH | 7 | 33% |
| APRIL | 3 | 20% |
| MAY | 1 | 33% |

## TEAM OF THE SEASON

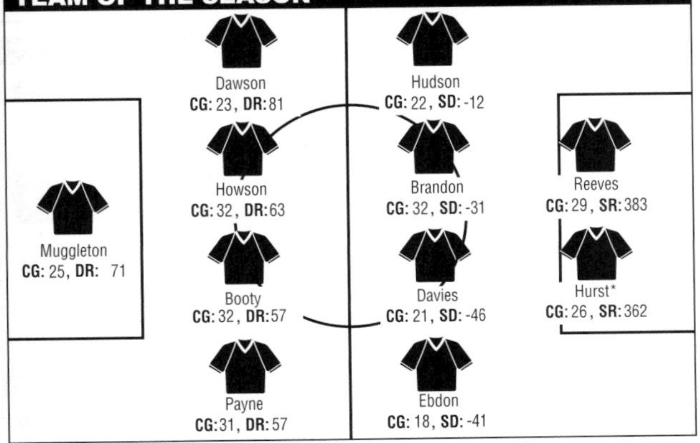

Muggleton
CG: 25, DR: 71
Dawson
CG: 23, DR: 81
Howson
CG: 32, DR: 63
Booty
CG: 32, DR: 57
Payne
CG: 31, DR: 57
Hudson
CG: 22, SD: -12
Brandon
CG: 32, SD: -31
Davies
CG: 21, SD: -46
Ebdon
CG: 18, SD: -41
Reeves
CG: 29, SR: 383
Hurst*
CG: 26, SR: 362


**KEY:** DR = Defensive Rate, SD = Scoring Difference, SR = Strike Rate, CG = Counting Games – League games playing at least 70 minutes

## LEAGUE APPEARANCES, BOOKINGS AND CAPS

| | AGE | IN THE SQUAD | COUNTING GAMES | MINUTES ON PITCH | YELLOW CARDS | RED CARDS | THIS SEASON | HOME COUNTRY |
|---|---|---|---|---|---|---|---|---|
| **Goalkeepers** | | | | | | | | |
| Sam Lancaster | - | 2 | 0 | 0 | 0 | 0 | - | England |
| Carl Muggleton | 34 | 27 | 25 | 2263 | 1 | 0 | - | England |
| Andy Richmond | 20 | 46 | 7 | 617 | 0 | 0 | - | England |
| Ben Williams | 20 | 16 | 14 | 1260 | 0 | 0 | - | England |
| **Defenders** | | | | | | | | |
| Steven Blatherwick | 29 | 33 | 28 | 2634 | 8 | 2 | - | England |
| Martyn Booty | 32 | 42 | 32 | 3081 | 6 | 0 | - | England |
| Kevin Dawson | 22 | 31 | 23 | 2187 | 8 | 0 | - | England |
| Rob Edwards | 33 | 29 | 22 | 2177 | 4 | 1 | - | England |
| Steve Howson | 21 | 33 | 32 | 2899 | 3 | 0 | - | England |
| Mark Innes | 24 | 13 | 3 | 490 | 2 | 0 | - | Scotland |
| Alan O'Hare | 20 | 30 | 16 | 1702 | 0 | 0 | - | Rep of Ireland |
| Steve Payne | 27 | 34 | 31 | 2904 | 3 | 0 | - | England |
| **Midfielders** | | | | | | | | |
| Chris Brandon | 27 | 36 | 32 | 3038 | 11 | 0 | - | England |
| Jamie Burt | 23 | 22 | 7 | 1030 | 5 | 0 | - | England |
| Brian Close | 21 | 8 | 7 | 687 | 5 | 0 | - | N Ireland |
| Gareth Davies | 20 | 37 | 21 | 2414 | 2 | 0 | - | England |
| John Douglas | 21 | 7 | 7 | 630 | 1 | 0 | - | Rep of Ireland |
| Marcus Ebdon | 32 | 29 | 18 | 1891 | 6 | 0 | - | England |
| Mark Hudson | 22 | 24 | 22 | 2059 | 1 | 0 | - | England |
| Glynn Hurst | 27 | 33 | 26 | 2536 | 8 | 0 | - | England |
| Lee Richardson | 34 | 4 | 0 | 0 | 0 | 0 | - | England |
| Keith Rowland | 31 | 5 | 0 | 79 | 0 | 0 | - | |
| Andy Rushbury | 20 | 40 | 21 | 2217 | 1 | 0 | - | England |
| Stephen Warne | | 16 | 0 | 124 | 0 | 0 | - | England |
| Shaun Wilkinson | 21 | 3 | 0 | 36 | 0 | 0 | - | England |
| **Forwards** | | | | | | | | |
| Mark Allott | 25 | 44 | 23 | 2264 | 4 | 0 | - | England |
| Shayne Bradley | 23 | 11 | 1 | 280 | 0 | 1 | - | England |
| Caleb Folan | 17 | 14 | 7 | 771 | 2 | 0 | - | England |
| Jonathan Howard | 31 | 21 | 0 | 146 | 1 | 0 | - | England |
| David Reeves | 35 | 41 | 29 | 3062 | 3 | 0 | - | England |
| Adam Smith | | 5 | 0 | 0 | 0 | 0 | - | England |

**KEY:** LEAGUE BOOKINGS CAPS

## SQUAD APPEARANCES

| Match | 1 | 2 | 3 | 4 | 5 | 6 | 7 | 8 | 9 | 10 | 11 | 12 | 13 | 14 | 15 | 16 | 17 | 18 | 19 | 20 | 21 | 22 | 23 | 24 | 25 | 26 | 27 | 28 | 29 | 30 | 31 | 32 | 33 | 34 | 35 | 36 | 37 | 38 | 39 | 40 | 41 | 42 | 43 | 44 | 45 | 46 | 47 | 48 | 49 |
|---|---|---|---|---|---|---|---|---|---|---|---|---|---|---|---|---|---|---|---|---|---|---|---|---|---|---|---|---|---|---|---|---|---|---|---|---|---|---|---|---|---|---|---|---|---|---|---|---|---|
| Venue | A | H | H | A | H | A | A | A | H | H | A | H | H | A | H | A | H | A | H | A | H | A | H | A | H | A | H | H | A | H | A | H | H | A | A | H | A | A | H | A | H | H | A | A | H | A | H | H | A |
| Competition | L | L | L | L | L | L | L | W | L | L | L | L | W | L | L | L | L | L | L | L | F | L | L | L | L | L | L | L | L | L | L | L | L | L | L | L | L | L | L | L | L | L | L | L | L | L | L | L | L |
| Result | L | L | W | W | W | L | D | D | D | W | W | W | L | L | W | L | D | L | W | L | L | L | W | L | L | W | D | W | L | L | D | L | D | L | L | L | L | L | W | D | L | W | L | L | L | L | L | W | D |

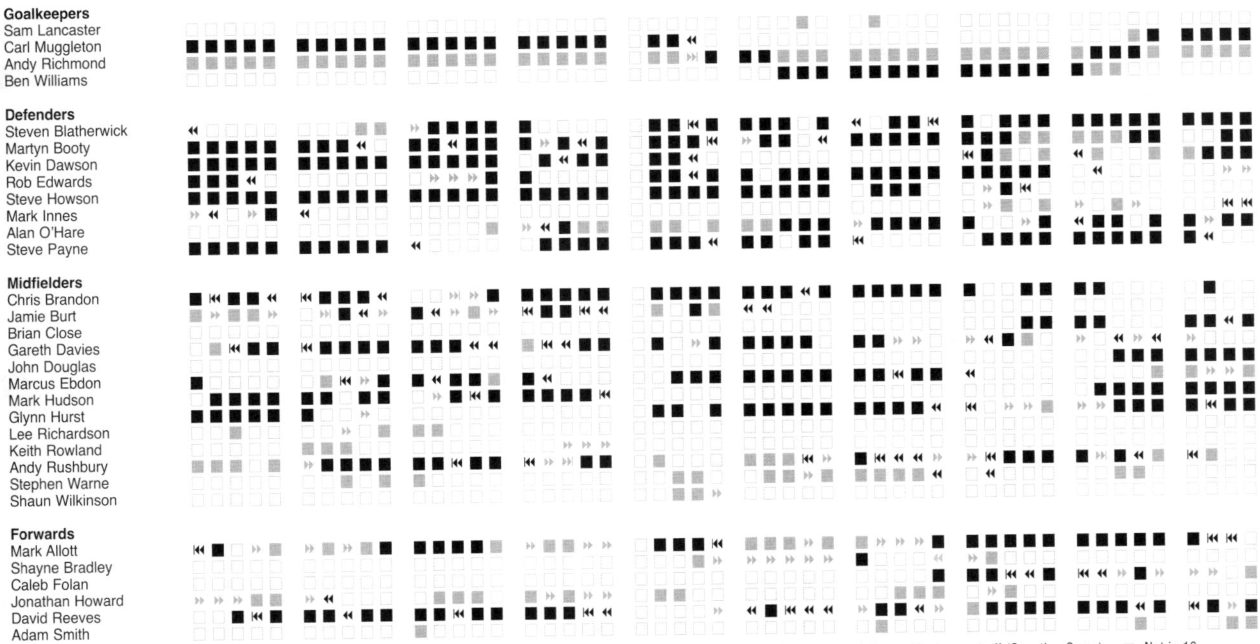

Goalkeepers
Sam Lancaster
Carl Muggleton
Andy Richmond
Ben Williams
Defenders
Steven Blatherwick
Martyn Booty
Kevin Dawson
Rob Edwards
Steve Howson
Mark Innes
Alan O'Hare
Steve Payne
Midfielders
Chris Brandon
Jamie Burt
Brian Close
Gareth Davies
John Douglas
Marcus Ebdon
Mark Hudson
Glynn Hurst
Lee Richardson
Keith Rowland
Andy Rushbury
Stephen Warne
Shaun Wilkinson
Forwards
Mark Allott
Shayne Bradley
Caleb Folan
Jonathan Howard
David Reeves
Adam Smith


**KEY:** ■ On all match ■ On bench ⏮ Subbed or sent off (Counting game) « Subbed or sent off (playing less than 70 minutes) » Subbed on from bench (Counting Game) » Subbed on (playing less than 70 minutes) » Subbed on and then subbed or sent off (Counting Game) » Subbed on and then subbed or sent off (playing less than 70 minutes) □ Not in 16

# CHELTENHAM

Final Position: **21st**

NICKNAME: THE ROBINS

| | | | | | | |
|---|---|---|---|---|---|---|
| 1 | div2 | Wigan | H | L | 0-2 | |
| 2 | div2 | Barnsley | A | D | 1-1 | Naylor 85 |
| 3 | div2 | Tranmere | A | L | 0-1 | |
| 4 | div2 | Plymouth | H | L | 1-2 | Spencer 33 |
| 5 | div2 | Crewe | A | L | 0-1 | |
| 6 | div2 | Cardiff | H | D | 1-1 | Howarth 32 |
| 7 | div2 | Colchester | A | D | 1-1 | Naylor 45 |
| 8 | wcr1 | Norwich | A | W | 3-0 | Naylor 30,45; McAuley 84 |
| 9 | div2 | Bristol City | H | L | 2-3 | Alsop 1,22 |
| 10 | div2 | Swindon | H | W | 2-0 | McAuley 29; Milton 65 |
| 11 | div2 | Mansfield | A | W | 2-0 | Victory 71; McAuley 83 |
| 12 | div2 | Notts County | H | L | 1-4 | Alsop 65 |
| 13 | wcr2 | Crystal Palace | A | L | 0-7 | |
| 14 | div2 | Blackpool | A | L | 1-3 | Spencer 30 |
| 15 | div2 | Luton | A | L | 1-2 | Milton 11 |
| 16 | div2 | QPR | H | D | 1-1 | Devaney 64 |
| 17 | div2 | Northampton | A | W | 2-1 | Alsop 31; Forsyth 62 |
| 18 | div2 | Port Vale | H | L | 0-1 | |
| 19 | div2 | Huddersfield | H | W | 1-0 | Brayson 71 |
| 20 | div2 | Stockport | A | D | 1-1 | Alsop 31 |
| 21 | facr1 | Yeovil | A | W | 2-0 | Alsop 8; Devaney 64 |
| 22 | div2 | Oldham | A | D | 0-0 | |
| 23 | div2 | Brentford | H | W | 1-0 | Alsop 90 |
| 24 | facr2 | Oldham | A | W | 2-1 | Yates 17; Brayson 20 |
| 25 | div2 | Peterborough | A | L | 1-4 | Forsyth 46 |
| 26 | div2 | Wycombe | H | D | 0-0 | |
| 27 | div2 | Crewe | H | L | 0-4 | |
| 28 | div2 | Chesterfield | A | D | 2-2 | Spencer 55,70 |
| 29 | div2 | Plymouth | A | L | 1-3 | Worrell 13 og |
| 30 | facr3 | Sheff Utd | A | L | 0-4 | |
| 31 | div2 | Cardiff | A | L | 1-2 | Finnigan 19 |
| 32 | div2 | Chesterfield | H | D | 0-0 | |
| 33 | div2 | Wigan | A | D | 0-0 | |
| 34 | div2 | Tranmere | H | W | 3-1 | Brown, M 8; Naylor 64; Devaney 72 |
| 35 | div2 | Stockport | H | L | 0-2 | |
| 36 | div2 | Huddersfield | A | D | 3-3 | McCann 37,71; Alsop 40 |
| 37 | div2 | Barnsley | H | L | 1-3 | Naylor 2 |
| 38 | div2 | Colchester | H | D | 1-1 | Alsop 2 |
| 39 | div2 | Bristol City | A | L | 1-3 | McCann 45 |
| 40 | div2 | Mansfield | H | W | 3-1 | Devaney 2; Brown, M 38; Spencer 90 |
| 41 | div2 | Swindon | A | W | 3-0 | Devaney 32; Brough 40; Spencer 90 |
| 42 | div2 | Northampton | H | D | 1-1 | Yates 60 |
| 43 | div2 | QPR | A | L | 1-4 | Devaney 5 |
| 44 | div2 | Port Vale | A | W | 2-1 | McCann 43; Alsop 81 |
| 45 | div2 | Brentford | A | D | 2-2 | McCann 23 pen; Devaney 29 |
| 46 | div2 | Luton | H | D | 2-2 | McCann 27 pen; Alsop 81 |
| 47 | div2 | Oldham | H | D | 1-1 | Yates 2 |
| 48 | div2 | Wycombe | A | D | 1-1 | Naylor 89 |
| 49 | div2 | Peterborough | H | D | 1-1 | Duff, M 86 |
| 50 | div2 | Blackpool | H | W | 3-0 | Victory 37; Duff, M 40; Naylor 65 |
| 51 | div2 | Notts County | A | L | 0-1 | |

## ATTENDANCES

HOME GROUND: WHADDON ROAD  CAPACITY: 6114  AVERAGE LEAGUE AT HOME: 4655

| | | | | | | | | |
|---|---|---|---|---|---|---|---|---|
| 8 | Norwich | 13285 | 10 | Swindon | 5761 | 47 | Oldham | 4439 |
| 39 | Bristol City | 11711 | 41 | Swindon | 5583 | 32 | Chesterfield | 4423 |
| 31 | Cardiff | 11605 | 27 | Crewe | 5548 | 24 | Oldham | 4416 |
| 43 | QPR | 11370 | 5 | Crewe | 5488 | 6 | Cardiff | 4395 |
| 29 | Plymouth | 10927 | 17 | Northampton | 5354 | 19 | Huddersfield | 4322 |
| 51 | Notts County | 9710 | 50 | Blackpool | 5150 | 26 | Wycombe | 4303 |
| 2 | Barnsley | 9641 | 1 | Wigan | 5138 | 11 | Mansfield | 4116 |
| 36 | Huddersfield | 9309 | 23 | Brentford | 5013 | 28 | Chesterfield | 4092 |
| 30 | Sheff Utd | 9166 | 45 | Brentford | 5011 | 34 | Tranmere | 3936 |
| 3 | Tranmere | 6807 | 42 | Northampton | 4917 | 40 | Mansfield | 3881 |
| 14 | Blackpool | 6649 | 13 | Crystal Palace | 4901 | 18 | Port Vale | 3852 |
| 22 | Oldham | 6575 | 49 | Peterborough | 4809 | 46 | Luton | 3762 |
| 21 | Yeovil | 6455 | 44 | Port Vale | 4800 | 38 | Colchester | 3607 |
| 15 | Luton | 6447 | 4 | Plymouth | 4713 | 37 | Barnsley | 3568 |
| 16 | QPR | 6382 | 35 | Stockport | 4692 | 7 | Colchester | 2845 |
| 33 | Wigan | 6171 | 12 | Notts County | 4565 | | | |
| 48 | Wycombe | 6070 | 20 | Stockport | 4531 | | | |
| 9 | Bristol City | 5895 | 25 | Peterborough | 4522 | | | |

■ Home □ Away ▨ Neutral

## KEY PLAYERS - GOALSCORERS

**1 Julian Alsop**

| | | | |
|---|---|---|---|
| Goals in the League | 10 | Player Strike Rate<br>Average number of minutes between League goals scored by player | 301 |
| Contribution to Attacking Power<br>Average number of minutes between League team goals while on pitch | 88 | Club Strike Rate<br>Average number of minutes between League goals scored by club | 78 |

| | PLAYER | LGE GOALS | POWER | STRIKE RATE |
|---|---|---|---|---|
| 2 | Tony Naylor | 6 | 63 | 306 mins |
| 3 | Grant McCann | 6 | 69 | 393 mins |
| 4 | Martin Devaney | 6 | 79 | 515 mins |
| 5 | Richard Forsyth | 2 | 108 | 540 mins |

## KEY PLAYERS - MIDFIELDERS

**1 David Bird**

| | | | |
|---|---|---|---|
| Goals in the League | 0 | Contribution to Attacking Power<br>Average number of minutes between League team goals while on pitch | 54 |
| Defensive Rating<br>Average number of mins between League goals conceded while he was on the pitch | 79 | Scoring Difference<br>Defensive Rating minus Contribution to Attacking Power | 25 |

| | PLAYER | LGE GOALS | DEF RATE | POWER | SCORE DIFF |
|---|---|---|---|---|---|
| 2 | Grant McCann | 6 | 72 | 69 | 3 mins |
| 3 | Mark Yates | 2 | 55 | 67 | -12 mins |
| 4 | Russell Milton | 2 | 68 | 82 | -14 mins |
| 5 | Martin Devaney | 6 | 64 | 79 | -15 mins |

## KEY PLAYERS - DEFENDERS

**1 Shane Duff**

| | | | |
|---|---|---|---|
| Goals Conceded (GC)<br>The number of League goals conceded while he was on the pitch | 22 | Clean Sheets<br>In games when he played at least 70 minutes | 3 |
| Defensive Rating<br>Ave number of mins between League goals conceded while on the pitch | 69 | Club Defensive Rating<br>Average number of mins between League goals conceded by the club this season | 61 |

| | PLAYER | CON LGE | CLEAN SHEETS | DEF RATE |
|---|---|---|---|---|
| 2 | John Brough | 27 | 6 | 68 mins |
| 3 | Mike Duff | 60 | 10 | 63 mins |
| 4 | Neil Howarth | 37 | 5 | 61 mins |
| 5 | Richard Walker | 23 | 2 | 56 mins |

## KEY GOALKEEPER

**1 Shane Higgs**

| | |
|---|---|
| Goals Conceded in the League | 12 |
| Defensive Rating<br>Ave number of mins between League goals conceded while on the pitch | 75 |
| Counting Games<br>Games when he played at least 70 mins | 10 |
| Clean Sheets<br>In games when he played at least 70 mins | 2 |

## TOP POINT EARNERS

| | PLAYER | GAMES | AVE |
|---|---|---|---|
| 1 | Brown, M | 8 | 1.88 |
| 2 | Bird | 9 | 1.56 |
| 3 | Higgs | 10 | 1.40 |
| 4 | Griffin | 8 | 1.38 |
| 5 | McCann | 24 | 1.33 |
| 6 | Brayson | 9 | 1.33 |
| 7 | Duff, S | 16 | 1.25 |
| 8 | Milton | 10 | 1.20 |
| 9 | Devaney | 32 | 1.19 |
| 10 | Brough | 17 | 1.12 |
| | **CLUB AVERAGE:** | | **1.04** |

Ave = Average points per match in Counting Games

## DISCIPLINARY RECORDS

| | PLAYER | YELLOW | RED | AVE |
|---|---|---|---|---|
| 1 | Forsyth | 4 | 0 | 270 |
| 2 | McCann | 6 | 1 | 337 |
| 3 | Spencer | 3 | 0 | 385 |
| 4 | Finnigan | 7 | 0 | 439 |
| 5 | Duff, M | 7 | 1 | 472 |
| 6 | Yates | 6 | 0 | 492 |
| 7 | Alsop | 4 | 1 | 602 |
| 8 | McAuley | 2 | 0 | 631 |
| 9 | Howarth | 2 | 1 | 756 |
| 10 | Devaney | 4 | 0 | 773 |
| 11 | Victory | 5 | 0 | 790 |
| 12 | Walker | 1 | 0 | 1294 |
| 13 | Brough | 1 | 0 | 1824 |
| | Other | 2 | 0 | |
| | TOTAL | 54 | 4 | |

## LEAGUE GOALS

| | PLAYER | MINS | GOALS | AVE |
|---|---|---|---|---|
| 1 | Alsop | 3014 | 10 | 301 |
| 2 | McCann | 2360 | 6 | 393 |
| 3 | Spencer | 1156 | 6 | 193 |
| 4 | Devaney | 3092 | 6 | 515 |
| 5 | Naylor | 1836 | 6 | 306 |
| 6 | Victory | 3954 | 2 | 1977 |
| 7 | Brown, M | 956 | 2 | 478 |
| 8 | McAuley | 1263 | 2 | 632 |
| 9 | Duff, M | 3779 | 2 | 1890 |
| 10 | Yates | 2954 | 2 | 1477 |
| 11 | Forsyth | 1080 | 2 | 540 |
| 12 | Milton | 1231 | 2 | 616 |
| 13 | Finnigan | 3075 | 1 | 3075 |
| | Other | | 4 | |
| | TOTAL | | 53 | |

## MONTH BY MONTH GUIDE TO THE POINTS

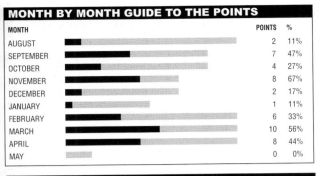

| MONTH | POINTS | % |
|---|---|---|
| AUGUST | 2 | 11% |
| SEPTEMBER | 7 | 47% |
| OCTOBER | 4 | 27% |
| NOVEMBER | 8 | 67% |
| DECEMBER | 2 | 17% |
| JANUARY | 1 | 11% |
| FEBRUARY | 6 | 33% |
| MARCH | 10 | 56% |
| APRIL | 8 | 44% |
| MAY | 0 | 0% |

## TEAM OF THE SEASON

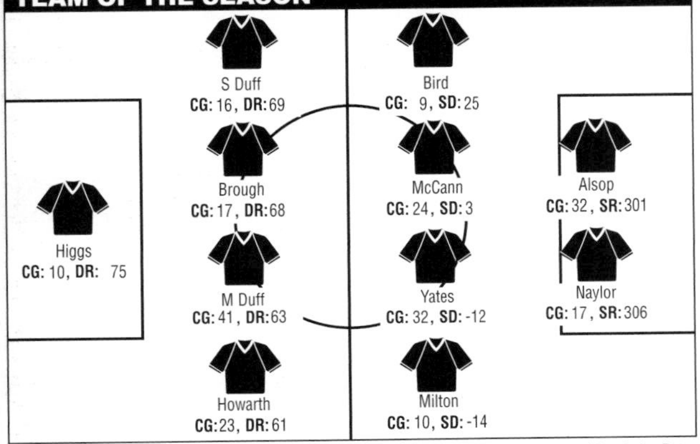

S Duff
CG: 16, DR: 69
Bird
CG: 9, SD: 25
Brough
CG: 17, DR: 68
McCann
CG: 24, SD: 3
Alsop
CG: 32, SR: 301
Higgs
CG: 10, DR: 75
M Duff
CG: 41, DR: 63
Yates
CG: 32, SD: -12
Naylor
CG: 17, SR: 306
Howarth
CG: 23, DR: 61
Milton
CG: 10, SD: -14


KEY: DR = Defensive Rate, SD = Scoring Difference, SR = Strike Rate, CG = Counting Games – League games playing at least 70 minutes

## LEAGUE APPEARANCES, BOOKINGS AND CAPS

| | AGE | IN THE SQUAD | COUNTING GAMES | MINUTES ON PITCH | YELLOW CARDS | RED CARDS | THIS SEASON | HOME COUNTRY |
|---|---|---|---|---|---|---|---|---|
| **Goalkeepers** | | | | | | | | |
| Steve Book | 34 | 40 | 36 | 3240 | 0 | 0 | - | England |
| Shane Higgs | 26 | 46 | 10 | 900 | 0 | 0 | - | England |
| **Defenders** | | | | | | | | |
| John Brough | 30 | 39 | 17 | 1824 | 1 | 0 | - | England |
| Mike Duff | 25 | 43 | 41 | 3779 | 7 | 1 | 4 | N Ireland (111) |
| Shane Duff | 21 | 25 | 16 | 1522 | 0 | 0 | - | England |
| Tony Griffin | 24 | 20 | 8 | 772 | 0 | 0 | - | England |
| Neil Howarth | 31 | 30 | 23 | 2269 | 2 | 1 | - | England |
| Lee Howells | 34 | 2 | 0 | 0 | 0 | 0 | - | Australia |
| Stephen Jones | 32 | 12 | 3 | 380 | 0 | 0 | - | England |
| Michael Simpkins | 24 | 3 | 2 | 180 | 0 | 0 | - | England |
| Greg Strong | 27 | 4 | 3 | 330 | 1 | 0 | - | England |
| Richard Walker | 31 | 15 | 14 | 1294 | 1 | 0 | - | England |
| Lee Williams | 30 | 20 | 7 | 743 | 0 | 0 | - | England |
| **Midfielders** | | | | | | | | |
| David Bird | 18 | 15 | 9 | 1029 | 0 | 0 | - | England |
| Martin Devaney | 23 | 41 | 32 | 3092 | 4 | 0 | - | England |
| John Finnigan | 27 | 41 | 33 | 3075 | 7 | 0 | - | England |
| Richard Forsyth | 32 | 13 | 12 | 1080 | 4 | 0 | - | England |
| Grant McCann | 23 | 27 | 24 | 2360 | 6 | 1 | - | Scotland |
| Russell Milton | 34 | 31 | 10 | 1231 | 0 | 0 | - | England |
| Jamie Victory | 27 | 44 | 44 | 3954 | 5 | 0 | - | England |
| Mark Yates | 33 | 42 | 32 | 2954 | 6 | 0 | - | England |
| **Forwards** | | | | | | | | |
| Julian Alsop | 30 | 37 | 32 | 3014 | 4 | 1 | - | England |
| Paul Brayson | 25 | 31 | 9 | 1212 | 0 | 0 | - | England |
| Marvin Brown | 20 | 16 | 8 | 956 | 0 | 0 | - | England |
| Hugh McAuley | 26 | 22 | 12 | 1263 | 2 | 0 | - | England |
| Tony Naylor | 36 | 35 | 17 | 1836 | 1 | 0 | - | England |
| Damian Spencer | 21 | 41 | 7 | 1156 | 3 | 0 | - | England |

KEY: LEAGUE BOOKINGS CAPS

## SQUAD APPEARANCES

| Match | 1 | 2 | 3 | 4 | 5 | 6 | 7 | 8 | 9 | 10 | 11 | 12 | 13 | 14 | 15 | 16 | 17 | 18 | 19 | 20 | 21 | 22 | 23 | 24 | 25 | 26 | 27 | 28 | 29 | 30 | 31 | 32 | 33 | 34 | 35 | 36 | 37 | 38 | 39 | 40 | 41 | 42 | 43 | 44 | 45 | 46 | 47 | 48 | 49 | 50 | 51 |
|---|---|---|---|---|---|---|---|---|---|---|---|---|---|---|---|---|---|---|---|---|---|---|---|---|---|---|---|---|---|---|---|---|---|---|---|---|---|---|---|---|---|---|---|---|---|---|---|---|---|---|---|
| Venue | H | A | A | H | A | H | A | A | H | H | A | H | A | A | A | H | A | H | H | A | A | A | H | A | A | H | H | A | A | A | A | H | A | H | H | A | H | H | A | H | A | H | A | A | A | H | H | A | H | H | A |
| Competition | L | L | L | L | L | L | L | W | L | L | L | L | W | L | L | L | L | L | L | L | F | L | L | F | L | L | L | L | L | F | L | L | L | L | L | L | L | L | L | L | L | L | L | L | L | L | L | L | L | L | L |
| Result | L | D | L | L | L | D | D | W | L | W | W | L | L | L | L | D | W | L | W | D | W | D | W | W | L | D | L | D | L | L | L | D | D | W | L | D | L | D | L | W | W | D | L | W | D | D | D | D | D | W | L |

**Goalkeepers**
Steve Book
Shane Higgs

**Defenders**
John Brough
Mike Duff
Shane Duff
Tony Griffin
Neil Howarth
Lee Howells
Stephen Jones
Michael Simpkins
Greg Strong
Richard Walker
Lee Williams

**Midfielders**
David Bird
Martin Devaney
John Finnigan
Richard Forsyth
Grant McCann
Russell Milton
Jamie Victory
Mark Yates

**Forwards**
Julian Alsop
Paul Brayson
Marvin Brown
Hugh McAuley
Tony Naylor
Damian Spencer

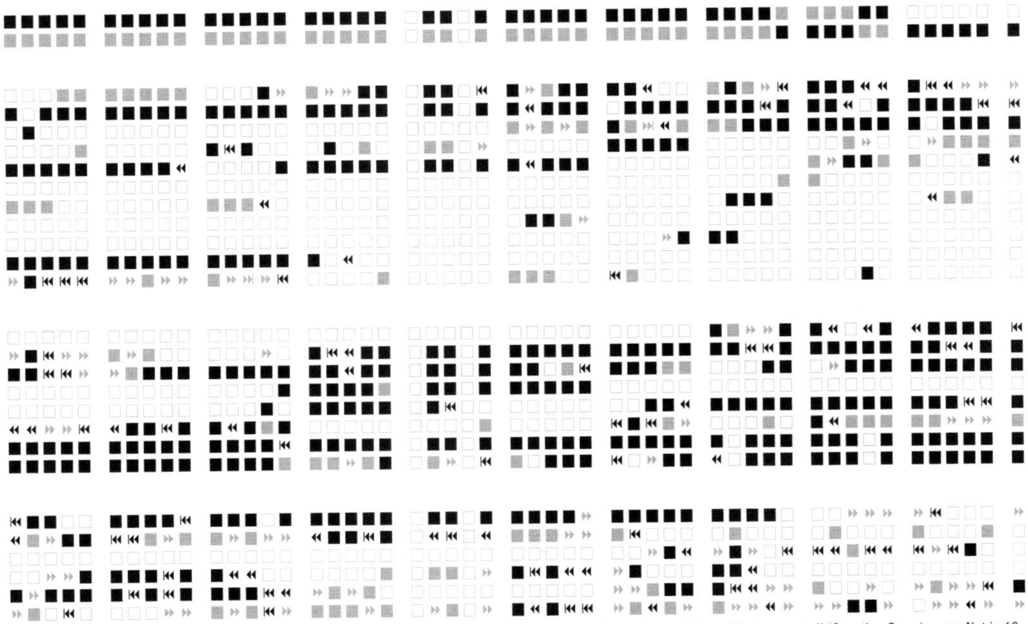

KEY: ■ On all match ■ On bench
⏮ Subbed or sent off (Counting game)
« Subbed or sent off (playing less than 70 minutes)
⏭ Subbed on from bench (Counting Game)
» Subbed on (playing less than 70 minutes)
Subbed on and then subbed or sent off (Counting Game)
Subbed on and then subbed or sent off (playing less than 70 minutes)
□ Not in 16

# HUDDERSFIELD TOWN

Final Position: **22nd**

NICKNAME: THE TERRIERS

| | | | | | | |
|---|---|---|---|---|---|---|
| 1 | div2 | Brentford | H | L | 0-2 | |
| 2 | div2 | Plymouth | A | L | 1-2 | Thorington 89 |
| 3 | div2 | Peterborough | A | W | 1-0 | Mattis 10 |
| 4 | div2 | Crewe | H | D | 1-1 | Booth 26 |
| 5 | div2 | Tranmere | A | L | 1-2 | McDonald 44 |
| 6 | div2 | Blackpool | H | D | 0-0 | |
| 7 | div2 | Barnsley | H | W | 1-0 | Smith 59 |
| 8 | wcr1 | Darlington | H | W | 2-0 | Baldry 3; Clarke, M 15 og |
| 9 | div2 | Northampton | A | D | 0-0 | |
| 10 | div2 | QPR | A | L | 0-3 | |
| 11 | div2 | Luton | H | L | 0-1 | |
| 12 | div2 | Oldham | A | L | 0-4 | |
| 13 | wcr2 | Burnley | H | L | 0-1 | |
| 14 | div2 | Port Vale | H | D | 2-2 | Smith 12; Baldry 17 |
| 15 | div2 | Notts County | H | W | 3-0 | Stead 15,72; Moses 25 |
| 16 | div2 | Mansfield | A | W | 2-0 | Smith 53,61 |
| 17 | div2 | Colchester | H | D | 1-1 | Stead 90 |
| 18 | div2 | Bristol City | A | L | 0-1 | |
| 19 | div2 | Cheltenham | A | L | 0-1 | |
| 20 | div2 | Wycombe | H | D | 0-0 | |
| 21 | facr1 | Swindon | A | L | 0-1 | |
| 22 | div2 | Swindon | H | L | 2-3 | Smith 36; Stead 90 |
| 23 | div2 | Chesterfield | A | L | 0-1 | |
| 24 | div2 | Stockport | H | W | 2-1 | Smith 27,83 |
| 25 | div2 | Wigan | A | L | 0-1 | |
| 26 | div2 | Tranmere | H | L | 1-2 | Smith 78 |
| 27 | div2 | Cardiff | A | L | 0-4 | |
| 28 | div2 | Blackpool | A | D | 1-1 | Booth 75 |
| 29 | div2 | Peterborough | H | L | 0-1 | |
| 30 | div2 | Crewe | A | L | 0-1 | |
| 31 | div2 | Cardiff | H | W | 1-0 | Booth 80 |
| 32 | div2 | Plymouth | H | W | 1-0 | Smith 82 pen |
| 33 | div2 | Wycombe | A | D | 0-0 | |
| 34 | div2 | Cheltenham | H | D | 3-3 | Irons 54; Smith 56,59 |
| 35 | div2 | Barnsley | A | W | 1-0 | Booth 26 |
| 36 | div2 | Brentford | A | L | 0-1 | |
| 37 | div2 | Northampton | H | W | 2-0 | Baldry 44; Smith 45 |
| 38 | div2 | QPR | H | L | 0-3 | |
| 39 | div2 | Luton | A | L | 0-3 | |
| 40 | div2 | Colchester | A | L | 0-2 | |
| 41 | div2 | Mansfield | H | D | 1-1 | Smith 51 |
| 42 | div2 | Bristol City | H | L | 1-2 | Smith 20 pen |
| 43 | div2 | Notts County | A | L | 2-3 | Booth 19; Schofield 37 |
| 44 | div2 | Chesterfield | H | W | 4-0 | Smith 17,53; Stead 23,66 |
| 45 | div2 | Swindon | A | W | 1-0 | Smith 87 |
| 46 | div2 | Wigan | H | D | 0-0 | |
| 47 | div2 | Stockport | A | L | 1-2 | Booth 3 |
| 48 | div2 | Port Vale | A | L | 1-5 | Gavin 45 |
| 49 | div2 | Oldham | H | D | 1-1 | Schofield 26 |

## ATTENDANCES

HOME GROUND: MCALPINE STADIUM CAPACITY: 24500 AVERAGE LEAGUE AT HOME: 9506

| | | | | | | | | |
|---|---|---|---|---|---|---|---|---|
| 46 | Wigan | 13769 | 14 | Port Vale | 9091 | 48 | Port Vale | 5925 |
| 27 | Cardiff | 13703 | 29 | Peterborough | 9022 | 13 | Burnley | 5887 |
| 35 | Barnsley | 12474 | 2 | Plymouth | 8953 | 33 | Wycombe | 5886 |
| 7 | Barnsley | 11989 | 17 | Colchester | 8912 | 43 | Notts County | 5872 |
| 18 | Bristol City | 11494 | 41 | Mansfield | 8756 | 30 | Crewe | 5819 |
| 49 | Oldham | 11271 | 20 | Wycombe | 8695 | 3 | Peterborough | 5205 |
| 10 | QPR | 11010 | 38 | QPR | 8695 | 16 | Mansfield | 4998 |
| 26 | Tranmere | 11002 | 4 | Crewe | 8467 | 45 | Swindon | 4760 |
| 15 | Notts County | 9984 | 22 | Swindon | 8334 | 9 | Northampton | 4679 |
| 37 | Northampton | 9651 | 24 | Stockport | 7978 | 36 | Brentford | 4366 |
| 1 | Brentford | 9635 | 12 | Oldham | 7643 | 19 | Cheltenham | 4322 |
| 6 | Blackpool | 9506 | 5 | Tranmere | 7534 | 21 | Swindon | 4210 |
| 42 | Bristol City | 9477 | 32 | Plymouth | 7294 | 23 | Chesterfield | 4194 |
| 31 | Cardiff | 9462 | 47 | Stockport | 7159 | 40 | Colchester | 3835 |
| 34 | Cheltenham | 9309 | 28 | Blackpool | 7148 | 8 | Darlington | 3810 |
| 11 | Luton | 9249 | 39 | Luton | 6122 | | | |
| 44 | Chesterfield | 9098 | 25 | Wigan | 6013 | | | |

■ Home □ Away ▨ Neutral

## KEY PLAYERS - GOALSCORERS

**1 Martin Smith**

| | | | |
|---|---|---|---|
| Goals in the League | 17 | Player Strike Rate<br>Average number of minutes between League goals scored by player | 184 |
| Contribution to Attacking Power<br>Average number of minutes between League team goals while on pitch | 92 | Club Strike Rate<br>Average number of minutes between League goals scored by club | 106 |

| | PLAYER | LGE GOALS | POWER | STRIKE RATE |
|---|---|---|---|---|
| 2 | John Stead | 6 | 88 | 428 mins |
| 3 | Andy Booth | 6 | 105 | 457 mins |
| 4 | Danny Schofield | 2 | 109 | 1152 mins |
| 5 | John Thorrington | 1 | 89 | 1609 mins |

## KEY PLAYERS - MIDFIELDERS

**1 John Thorrington**

| | | | |
|---|---|---|---|
| Goals in the League | 1 | Contribution to Attacking Power<br>Average number of minutes between League team goals while on pitch | 89 |
| Defensive Rating<br>Average number of mins between League goals conceded while he was on the pitch | 85 | Scoring Difference<br>Defensive Rating minus Contribution to Attacking Power | -4 |

| | PLAYER | LGE GOALS | DEF RATE | POWER | SCORE DIFF |
|---|---|---|---|---|---|
| 2 | Simon Baldry | 2 | 76 | 92 | -16 mins |
| 3 | Chris Holland | 0 | 68 | 102 | -34 mins |
| 4 | Dwayne Mattis | 1 | 85 | 126 | -41 mins |
| 5 | Kenny Irons | 1 | 74 | 148 | -74 mins |

## KEY PLAYERS - DEFENDERS

**1 Eddie Youds**

| | | | |
|---|---|---|---|
| Goals Conceded (GC)<br>The number of League goals conceded while he was on the pitch | 32 | Clean Sheets<br>In games when he played at least 70 minutes | 9 |
| Defensive Rating<br>Ave number of mins between League goals conceded while on the pitch | 71 | Club Defensive Rating<br>Average number of mins between League goals conceded by the club this season | 68 |

| | PLAYER | CON LGE | CLEAN SHEETS | DEF RATE |
|---|---|---|---|---|
| 2 | Adrian Moses | 51 | 12 | 70 mins |
| 3 | Kevin Sharp | 49 | 12 | 69 mins |
| 4 | Stephen Jenkins | 32 | 6 | 69 mins |
| 5 | Thomas Heary | 23 | 5 | 63 mins |

## KEY GOALKEEPER

**1 Scott Bevan**

| | |
|---|---|
| Goals Conceded in the League | 36 |
| Defensive Rating<br>Ave number of mins between League goals conceded while on the pitch | 73 |
| Counting Games<br>Games when he played at least 70 mins | 28 |
| Clean Sheets<br>In games when he played at least 70 mins | 9 |

## TOP POINT EARNERS

| | PLAYER | GAMES | AVE |
|---|---|---|---|
| 1 | Clarke | 3 | 1.67 |
| 2 | Ashcroft | 2 | 1.50 |
| 3 | Baldry | 11 | 1.36 |
| 4 | Gallacher | 3 | 1.33 |
| 5 | Stead | 25 | 1.20 |
| 6 | Thorrington | 12 | 1.17 |
| 7 | Heary | 14 | 1.14 |
| 8 | Senior, P | 16 | 1.13 |
| 9 | Smith | 33 | 1.09 |
| 10 | Irons | 22 | 1.09 |
| | CLUB AVERAGE: | | 0.98 |

Ave = Average points per match in Counting Games

## DISCIPLINARY RECORDS

| | PLAYER | YELLOW | RED | AVE |
|---|---|---|---|---|
| 1 | Worthington | 4 | 0 | 225 |
| 2 | Schofield | 7 | 1 | 288 |
| 3 | Stead | 8 | 0 | 320 |
| 4 | Heary | 3 | 1 | 360 |
| 5 | Sharp | 8 | 1 | 373 |
| 6 | Baldry | 3 | 0 | 429 |
| 7 | Moses | 7 | 0 | 507 |
| 8 | Youds | 4 | 0 | 566 |
| 9 | Smith | 5 | 0 | 626 |
| 10 | Holland | 4 | 0 | 711 |
| 11 | Jenkins | 3 | 0 | 732 |
| 12 | Brown | 4 | 0 | 790 |
| 13 | Irons | 3 | 0 | 791 |
| | Other | 5 | 1 | |
| | TOTAL | 68 | 4 | |

## LEAGUE GOALS

| | PLAYER | MINS | GOALS | AVE |
|---|---|---|---|---|
| 1 | Smith | 3133 | 17 | 184 |
| 2 | Booth | 2742 | 6 | 457 |
| 3 | Stead | 2566 | 6 | 428 |
| 4 | Baldry | 1289 | 2 | 645 |
| 5 | Schofield | 2304 | 2 | 1152 |
| 6 | Gavin | 900 | 1 | 900 |
| 7 | Mattis | 2392 | 1 | 2392 |
| 8 | Irons | 2374 | 1 | 2374 |
| 9 | Moses | 3552 | 1 | 3552 |
| 10 | Thorrington | 1609 | 1 | 1609 |
| 11 | McDonald | 602 | 1 | 602 |
| | Other | | 0 | |
| | TOTAL | | 39 | |

## MONTH BY MONTH GUIDE TO THE POINTS

| MONTH | POINTS | % |
|---|---|---|
| AUGUST | 5 | 28% |
| SEPTEMBER | 4 | 27% |
| OCTOBER | 8 | 53% |
| NOVEMBER | 1 | 8% |
| DECEMBER | 3 | 25% |
| JANUARY | 4 | 33% |
| FEBRUARY | 8 | 53% |
| MARCH | 4 | 19% |
| APRIL | 7 | 47% |
| MAY | 1 | 33% |

## TEAM OF THE SEASON

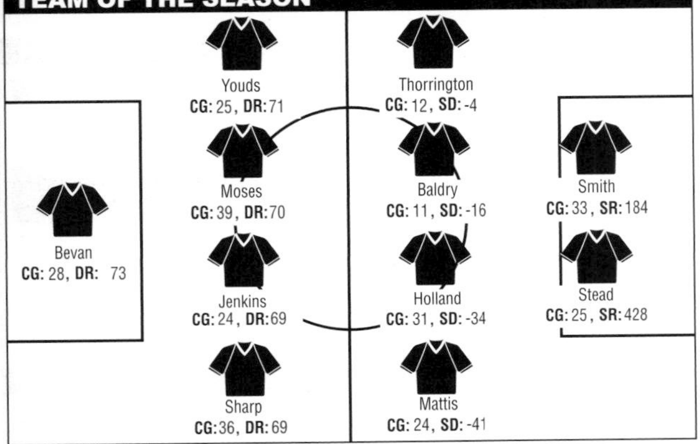

Youds
CG: 25, DR: 71
Thorrington
CG: 12, SD: -4
Moses
CG: 39, DR: 70
Baldry
CG: 11, SD: -16
Smith
CG: 33, SR: 184
Bevan
CG: 28, DR: 73
Jenkins
CG: 24, DR: 69
Holland
CG: 31, SD: -34
Stead
CG: 25, SR: 428
Sharp
CG: 36, DR: 69
Mattis
CG: 24, SD: -41


**KEY:** DR = Defensive Rate, SD = Scoring Difference, SR = Strike Rate, CG = Counting Games – League games playing at least 70 minutes

## LEAGUE APPEARANCES, BOOKINGS AND CAPS

| | AGE | IN THE SQUAD | COUNTING GAMES | MINUTES ON PITCH | YELLOW CARDS | RED CARDS | THIS SEASON | HOME COUNTRY |
|---|---|---|---|---|---|---|---|---|
| **Goalkeepers** | | | | | | | | |
| Scott Bevan | 23 | 30 | 28 | 2624 | 0 | 1 | - | England |
| Andy Jeffrey | - | 16 | 0 | 0 | 0 | 0 | - | England |
| Phil Senior | 20 | 46 | 16 | 1516 | 0 | 0 | - | England |
| **Defenders** | | | | | | | | |
| Nathaniel Brown | 22 | 40 | 34 | 3161 | 4 | 0 | - | England |
| Nathan Clarke | 19 | 4 | 3 | 315 | 0 | 0 | - | England |
| Jon Dyson | 31 | 9 | 2 | 189 | 0 | 0 | - | England |
| Jason Gavin | 23 | 10 | 10 | 900 | 0 | 0 | - | Rep of Ireland |
| Thomas Heary | 24 | 27 | 14 | 1442 | 3 | 1 | - | Rep of Ireland |
| Stephen Jenkins | 30 | 26 | 24 | 2198 | 3 | 0 | - | Wales |
| Anthony Lloyd | 19 | 1 | 0 | 0 | 0 | 0 | - | England |
| John McCombe | 18 | 1 | 0 | 1 | 0 | 0 | - | England |
| David Mirfin | 18 | 1 | 0 | 7 | 0 | 0 | - | England |
| Adrian Moses | 28 | 40 | 39 | 3552 | 7 | 0 | - | England |
| Kevin Sharp | 28 | 41 | 36 | 3365 | 8 | 1 | - | Canada |
| Eddie Youds | 33 | 27 | 25 | 2266 | 4 | 0 | - | England |
| **Midfielders** | | | | | | | | |
| Ben Austin | - | 3 | 0 | 0 | 0 | 0 | - | England |
| Simon Baldry | 27 | 23 | 11 | 1289 | 3 | 0 | - | England |
| Andy Holdsworth | 19 | 1 | 0 | 0 | 0 | 0 | - | England |
| Chris Holland | 27 | 34 | 31 | 2845 | 4 | 0 | - | England |
| Kenny Irons | 32 | 38 | 22 | 2374 | 3 | 0 | - | England |
| Dwayne Mattis | 21 | 38 | 24 | 2392 | 2 | 0 | - | England |
| Paul Scott | 23 | 24 | 2 | 367 | 0 | 0 | - | England |
| John Thorrington | 23 | 41 | 12 | 1609 | 1 | 0 | - | South Africa |
| John Worthington | 20 | 31 | 6 | 900 | 4 | 0 | - | England |
| **Forwards** | | | | | | | | |
| Lee Ashcroft | 30 | 4 | 2 | 259 | 0 | 0 | - | England |
| Andy Booth | 29 | 32 | 30 | 2742 | 2 | 0 | - | England |
| Kevin Gallacher | 36 | 7 | 3 | 394 | 0 | 0 | - | Scotland |
| Gianfranco Labarthe | 18 | 8 | 0 | 29 | 0 | 0 | - | Peru |
| Paul Macari | 26 | 9 | 0 | 69 | 0 | 0 | - | England |
| Scott McDonald | 19 | 14 | 6 | 602 | 0 | 0 | - | Australia |
| Danny Schofield | 23 | 30 | 24 | 2304 | 7 | 1 | - | England |
| Martin Smith | 28 | 38 | 33 | 3133 | 5 | 0 | - | England |
| John Stead | 20 | 43 | 25 | 2566 | 8 | 0 | - | England |

**KEY:** LEAGUE BOOKINGS CAPS

## SQUAD APPEARANCES

| Match | 1 | 2 | 3 | 4 | 5 | 6 | 7 | 8 | 9 | 10 | 11 | 12 | 13 | 14 | 15 | 16 | 17 | 18 | 19 | 20 | 21 | 22 | 23 | 24 | 25 |
|---|---|---|---|---|---|---|---|---|---|---|---|---|---|---|---|---|---|---|---|---|---|---|---|---|---|
| Venue | H | A | A | H | A | H | H | H | A | A | H | A | H | H | H | A | H | A | A | H | A | H | A | H | A |
| Competition | L | L | L | L | L | L | L | W | L | L | L | L | W | L | L | L | L | L | L | L | F | L | L | L | L |
| Result | L | L | W | D | L | D | W | W | D | L | L | L | D | D | W | W | D | L | L | D | L | L | L | W | L |

| Match | 26 | 27 | 28 | 29 | 30 | 31 | 32 | 33 | 34 | 35 | 36 | 37 | 38 | 39 | 40 | 41 | 42 | 43 | 44 | 45 | 46 | 47 | 48 | 49 |
|---|---|---|---|---|---|---|---|---|---|---|---|---|---|---|---|---|---|---|---|---|---|---|---|---|
| Venue | H | A | A | H | A | H | H | A | H | A | A | H | H | A | A | H | H | A | H | A | H | A | A | H |
| Competition | L | L | L | L | L | L | L | L | L | L | L | L | L | L | L | L | L | L | L | L | L | L | L | L |
| Result | L | L | D | L | L | W | W | D | D | W | L | W | L | L | L | D | L | L | W | W | D | L | L | D |

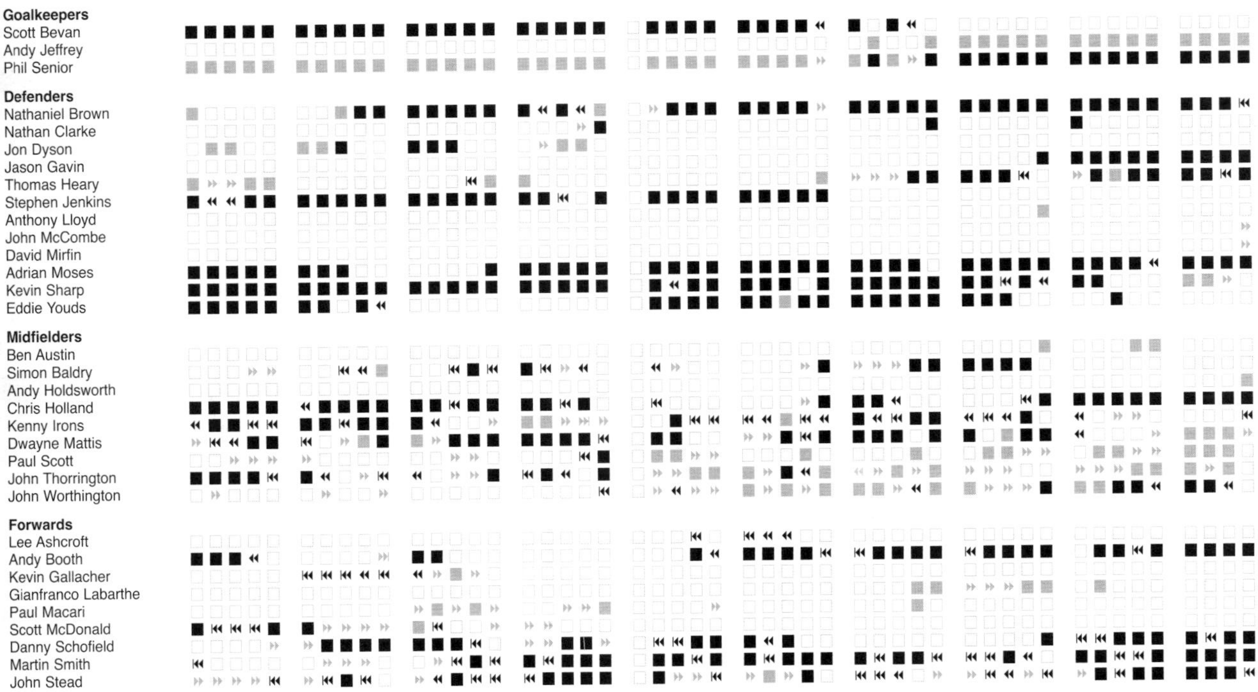

Goalkeepers
Scott Bevan
Andy Jeffrey
Phil Senior
Defenders
Nathaniel Brown
Nathan Clarke
Jon Dyson
Jason Gavin
Thomas Heary
Stephen Jenkins
Anthony Lloyd
John McCombe
David Mirfin
Adrian Moses
Kevin Sharp
Eddie Youds
Midfielders
Ben Austin
Simon Baldry
Andy Holdsworth
Chris Holland
Kenny Irons
Dwayne Mattis
Paul Scott
John Thorrington
John Worthington
Forwards
Lee Ashcroft
Andy Booth
Kevin Gallacher
Gianfranco Labarthe
Paul Macari
Scott McDonald
Danny Schofield
Martin Smith
John Stead

# MANSFIELD TOWN

Final Position: **23rd**

NICKNAME: THE STAGS

| | | | | | | |
|---|---|---|---|---|---|---|
| 1 | div2 | Plymouth | H | W | 4-3 | White, A 32,67; Disley 51; Larkin 56 |
| 2 | div2 | Wigan | A | L | 2-3 | Larkin 45,53 |
| 3 | div2 | Wycombe | A | D | 3-3 | Corden 5,86; Christie 74 |
| 4 | div2 | Chesterfield | H | L | 0-2 | |
| 5 | div2 | Stockport | A | L | 0-2 | |
| 6 | div2 | Crewe | H | L | 0-5 | |
| 7 | div2 | QPR | H | L | 0-4 | |
| 8 | wcr1 | Derby | H | L | 1-3 | Moore, N 8 |
| 9 | div2 | Oldham | A | L | 1-6 | Corden 19 |
| 10 | div2 | Luton | A | W | 3-2 | Lawrence 9; Sellars 24; Christie 50 |
| 11 | div2 | Cheltenham | H | L | 0-2 | |
| 12 | div2 | Northampton | A | L | 0-2 | |
| 13 | div2 | Tranmere | H | W | 6-1 | MacKenzie 46; Sellars 52; Lawrence 61; Christie 69,78; Larkin 75 |
| 14 | div2 | Peterborough | A | D | 0-0 | |
| 15 | div2 | Huddersfield | H | L | 0-2 | |
| 16 | div2 | Swindon | A | L | 1-2 | Lawrence 2 |
| 17 | div2 | Cardiff | H | L | 0-1 | |
| 18 | div2 | Colchester | H | W | 4-2 | Christie 19,25,29,64 |
| 19 | div2 | Notts County | A | D | 2-2 | Lawrence 43; Christie 90 |
| 20 | facr1 | Team Bath | A | W | 4-2 | Lawrence 19,36; Tisdale 43 og; Christie 56 |
| 21 | div2 | Bristol City | H | L | 4-5 | Corden 38,68 pen; Christie 62,76 |
| 22 | div2 | Port Vale | A | L | 2-4 | Corden 1; Christie 67 |
| 23 | facr2 | Crewe | A | L | 0-3 | |
| 24 | div2 | Blackpool | H | W | 4-0 | Christie 9; Lawrence 56; Larkin 74,76 |
| 25 | div2 | Barnsley | A | W | 1-0 | White, A 50 |
| 26 | div2 | Stockport | H | W | 4-2 | Christie 6; Corden 48 pen,79; Disley 54 |
| 27 | div2 | Brentford | A | L | 0-1 | |
| 28 | div2 | Crewe | A | L | 0-2 | |
| 29 | div2 | Wycombe | H | D | 0-0 | |
| 30 | div2 | Chesterfield | A | W | 2-1 | Disley 43; Lawrence 90 |
| 31 | div2 | Wigan | H | L | 1-2 | Christie 50 |
| 32 | div2 | Plymouth | A | L | 1-3 | Lawrence 11 |
| 33 | div2 | Brentford | H | D | 0-0 | |
| 34 | div2 | Notts County | H | W | 3-2 | White, A 52; Mitchell 65; Corden 71 |
| 35 | div2 | Colchester | A | L | 0-1 | |
| 36 | div2 | QPR | A | D | 2-2 | Christie 25,50 |
| 37 | div2 | Oldham | H | L | 0-1 | |
| 38 | div2 | Luton | H | W | 3-2 | Day 9; Christie 29; Corden 79 |
| 39 | div2 | Cheltenham | A | L | 1-3 | Lawrence 83 |
| 40 | div2 | Swindon | H | W | 2-1 | Junior Mendes 15; Corden 39 pen |
| 41 | div2 | Huddersfield | A | D | 1-1 | Gavin 79 pen |
| 42 | div2 | Cardiff | A | L | 0-1 | |
| 43 | div2 | Peterborough | H | L | 1-5 | Corden 17 pen |
| 44 | div2 | Port Vale | H | L | 0-1 | |
| 45 | div2 | Bristol City | A | L | 2-5 | Disley 37; Butler 61 og |
| 46 | div2 | Barnsley | H | L | 0-1 | |
| 47 | div2 | Blackpool | A | D | 3-3 | Clarke, J 13; Larkin 46; White, A 86 |
| 48 | div2 | Tranmere | A | L | 1-3 | Lawrence 54 pen |
| 49 | div2 | Northampton | H | W | 2-1 | White, A 62; Lawrence 77 |

## ATTENDANCES

HOME GROUND: FIELD MILL CAPACITY: 9990 AVERAGE LEAGUE AT HOME: 4887

| | | | | | | | | |
|---|---|---|---|---|---|---|---|---|
| 42 | Cardiff | 13009 | 8 | Derby | 5788 | 23 | Crewe | 4563 |
| 45 | Bristol City | 12013 | 37 | Oldham | 5712 | 44 | Port Vale | 4538 |
| 36 | QPR | 11942 | 43 | Peterborough | 5653 | 40 | Swindon | 4471 |
| 25 | Barnsley | 10495 | 12 | Northampton | 5594 | 6 | Crewe | 4183 |
| 48 | Tranmere | 10418 | 31 | Wigan | 5524 | 16 | Swindon | 4136 |
| 19 | Notts County | 10302 | 9 | Oldham | 5490 | 11 | Cheltenham | 4116 |
| 41 | Huddersfield | 8756 | 20 | Team Bath | 5469 | 24 | Blackpool | 4001 |
| 34 | Notts County | 8134 | 1 | Plymouth | 5309 | 49 | Northampton | 3928 |
| 32 | Plymouth | 8030 | 5 | Stockport | 5190 | 39 | Cheltenham | 3881 |
| 4 | Chesterfield | 7258 | 14 | Peterborough | 5067 | 22 | Port Vale | 3880 |
| 28 | Crewe | 6931 | 3 | Wycombe | 5057 | 33 | Brentford | 3735 |
| 30 | Chesterfield | 6813 | 15 | Huddersfield | 4998 | 13 | Tranmere | 3668 |
| 26 | Stockport | 6434 | 46 | Barnsley | 4873 | 17 | Cardiff | 3441 |
| 47 | Blackpool | 6173 | 38 | Luton | 4829 | 18 | Colchester | 3414 |
| 10 | Luton | 6004 | 29 | Wycombe | 4811 | 35 | Colchester | 3247 |
| 27 | Brentford | 5844 | 21 | Bristol City | 4801 | | | |
| 2 | Wigan | 5837 | 7 | QPR | 4581 | | | |

■ Home □ Away ▒ Neutral

## KEY PLAYERS - GOALSCORERS

**1 Iyseden Christie**

| | | | |
|---|---|---|---|
| Goals in the League | 18 | Player Strike Rate<br>Average number of minutes between League goals scored by player | 157 |
| Contribution to Attacking Power<br>Average number of minutes between League team goals while on pitch | 62 | Club Strike Rate<br>Average number of minutes between League goals scored by club | 63 |

| | PLAYER | LGE GOALS | POWER | STRIKE RATE |
|---|---|---|---|---|
| 2 | Wayne Corden | 13 | 60 | 250 mins |
| 3 | Liam Lawrence | 10 | 70 | 353 mins |
| 4 | Craig Disley | 4 | 60 | 858 mins |
| 5 | Junior Mendes | 1 | 73 | 1396 mins |

## KEY PLAYERS - MIDFIELDERS

**1 Colin Larkin**

| | | | |
|---|---|---|---|
| Goals in the League | 7 | Contribution to Attacking Power<br>Average number of minutes between League team goals while on pitch | 47 |
| Defensive Rating<br>Average number of mins between League goals conceded while he was on the pitch | 61 | Scoring Difference<br>Defensive Rating minus Contribution to Attacking Power | 14 |

| | PLAYER | LGE GOALS | DEF RATE | POWER | SCORE DIFF |
|---|---|---|---|---|---|
| 2 | Neil MacKenzie | 1 | 39 | 49 | -10 mins |
| 3 | Wayne Corden | 13 | 42 | 60 | -18 mins |
| 4 | Jamie Clarke | 1 | 38 | 57 | -19 mins |
| 5 | Craig Disley | 4 | 40 | 60 | -20 mins |

## KEY PLAYERS - DEFENDERS

**1 Adam Eaton**

| | | | |
|---|---|---|---|
| Goals Conceded (GC)<br>The number of League goals conceded while he was on the pitch | 28 | Clean Sheets<br>In games when he played at least 70 minutes | 4 |
| Defensive Rating<br>Ave number of mins between League goals conceded while on the pitch | 62 | Club Defensive Rating<br>Average number of mins between League goals conceded by the club this season | 43 |

| | PLAYER | CON LGE | CLEAN SHEETS | DEF RATE |
|---|---|---|---|---|
| 2 | Ben Doane | 18 | 1 | 54 mins |
| 3 | Rhys Day | 37 | 4 | 54 mins |
| 4 | Keith Curle | 21 | 2 | 50 mins |
| 5 | Bobby Hassell | 35 | 2 | 48 mins |

## KEY GOALKEEPER

**1 Kevin Pilkington**

| | |
|---|---|
| Goals Conceded in the League | 59 |
| Defensive Rating<br>Ave number of mins between League goals conceded while on the pitch | 39 |
| Counting Games<br>Games when he played at least 70 mins | 32 |
| Clean Sheets<br>In games when he played at least 70 mins | 4 |

## TOP POINT EARNERS

| | PLAYER | GAMES | AVE |
|---|---|---|---|
| 1 | MacKenzie | 13 | 1.54 |
| 2 | White, A | 11 | 1.36 |
| 3 | Buxton | 3 | 1.33 |
| 4 | Curle | 10 | 1.30 |
| 5 | Day | 21 | 1.19 |
| 6 | Hassell | 18 | 1.17 |
| 7 | Eaton | 19 | 1.16 |
| 8 | Corden | 32 | 1.03 |
| 9 | Pilkington | 32 | 1.00 |
| 10 | Doane | 11 | 1.00 |
| | CLUB AVERAGE: | | 0.96 |

Ave = Average points per match in Counting Games

## DISCIPLINARY RECORDS

| | PLAYER | YELLOW | RED | AVE |
|---|---|---|---|---|
| 1 | White, A | 8 | 0 | 197 |
| 2 | Curle | 3 | 1 | 262 |
| 3 | Sellars | 2 | 1 | 273 |
| 4 | Williamson | 8 | 1 | 306 |
| 5 | Curtis | 6 | 0 | 322 |
| 6 | Christie | 8 | 0 | 352 |
| 7 | Moore | 4 | 0 | 405 |
| 8 | Reddington | 1 | 0 | 467 |
| 9 | Day | 3 | 1 | 497 |
| 10 | Lawrence | 7 | 0 | 503 |
| 11 | Eaton | 3 | 0 | 580 |
| 12 | Gadsby | 2 | 0 | 599 |
| 13 | Delaney | 1 | 0 | 630 |
| | Other | 24 | 1 | |
| | TOTAL | 80 | 5 | |

## LEAGUE GOALS

| | PLAYER | MINS | GOALS | AVE |
|---|---|---|---|---|
| 1 | Christie | 2818 | 18 | 157 |
| 2 | Corden | 3248 | 13 | 250 |
| 3 | Lawrence | 3527 | 10 | 353 |
| 4 | Larkin | 1225 | 7 | 175 |
| 5 | White, A | 1583 | 6 | 264 |
| 6 | Disley | 3430 | 4 | 858 |
| 7 | Sellars | 819 | 2 | 410 |
| 8 | Junior Mendes | 1396 | 1 | 1396 |
| 9 | Day | 1991 | 1 | 1991 |
| 10 | Clarke, J | 1652 | 1 | 1652 |
| 11 | MacKenzie | 1555 | 1 | 1555 |
| 12 | Mitchell | 348 | 1 | 348 |
| | Other | | 1 | |
| | TOTAL | | 66 | |

## MONTH BY MONTH GUIDE TO THE POINTS

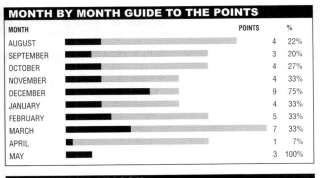

| MONTH | POINTS | % |
|---|---|---|
| AUGUST | 4 | 22% |
| SEPTEMBER | 3 | 20% |
| OCTOBER | 4 | 27% |
| NOVEMBER | 4 | 33% |
| DECEMBER | 9 | 75% |
| JANUARY | 4 | 33% |
| FEBRUARY | 5 | 33% |
| MARCH | 7 | 33% |
| APRIL | 1 | 7% |
| MAY | 3 | 100% |

## TEAM OF THE SEASON

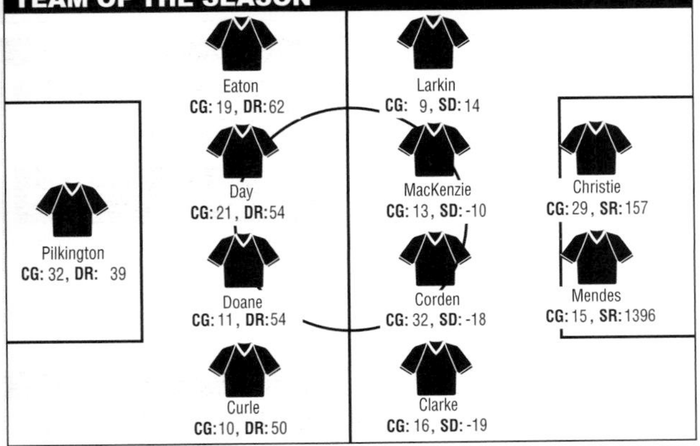
Eaton
CG: 19, DR: 62
Larkin
CG: 9, SD: 14
Day
CG: 21, DR: 54
MacKenzie
CG: 13, SD: -10
Christie
CG: 29, SR: 157
Pilkington
CG: 32, DR: 39
Doane
CG: 11, DR: 54
Corden
CG: 32, SD: -18
Mendes
CG: 15, SR: 1396
Curle
CG: 10, DR: 50
Clarke
CG: 16, SD: -19

**KEY:** DR = Defensive Rate, SD = Scoring Difference, SR = Strike Rate, CG=Counting Games – League games playing at least 70 minutes

## LEAGUE APPEARANCES, BOOKINGS AND CAPS

| | AGE | IN THE SQUAD | COUNTING GAMES | MINS ON PITCH | YELLOW CARDS | RED CARDS | THIS SEASON | HOME COUNTRY |
|---|---|---|---|---|---|---|---|---|
| **Goalkeepers** | | | | | | | | |
| Michael Bingham | - | 2 | 0 | 0 | 0 | 0 | - | |
| Kevin Pilkington | 29 | 36 | 32 | 2874 | 1 | 0 | - | England |
| Arjan Van Heusden | 30 | 5 | 5 | 450 | 1 | 0 | - | Holland |
| Keith Welch | 34 | 15 | 9 | 810 | 0 | 0 | - | England |
| Jason White | 17 | 34 | 0 | 6 | 0 | 0 | - | England |
| **Defenders** | | | | | | | | |
| Alex Baptiste | - | 7 | 4 | 355 | 0 | 0 | - | England |
| Jake Buxton | - | 6 | 3 | 270 | 0 | 0 | - | England |
| Mark Carter | - | 1 | 0 | 0 | 0 | 0 | - | England |
| Peter Clarke | 23 | 3 | 2 | 181 | 0 | 0 | - | England |
| Keith Curle | 39 | 14 | 10 | 1049 | 3 | 1 | - | England |
| Rhys Day | 20 | 23 | 21 | 1991 | 3 | 1 | - | Wales |
| Damien Delaney | 21 | 7 | 7 | 630 | 1 | 0 | - | Rep of Ireland |
| Ben Doane | 23 | 12 | 11 | 970 | 1 | 0 | - | England |
| Adam Eaton | 23 | 20 | 19 | 1741 | 3 | 0 | - | England |
| Matthew Gadsby | 23 | 25 | 12 | 1198 | 2 | 0 | - | England |
| Bobby Hassell | 23 | 22 | 18 | 1682 | 1 | 0 | - | England |
| Danny Holyoak | - | 11 | 0 | 40 | 0 | 0 | - | |
| David Jervis | - | 5 | 4 | 371 | 1 | 0 | - | |
| Mark Lever | 33 | 15 | 14 | 1305 | 2 | 0 | - | England |
| Neil Moore | 30 | 19 | 18 | 1620 | 4 | 0 | - | England |
| Stuart Reddington | 25 | 11 | 5 | 467 | 1 | 0 | - | England |
| Dion Scott | 22 | 1 | 0 | 0 | 0 | 0 | - | England |
| Allen Tankard | 34 | 1 | 0 | 0 | 0 | 0 | - | England |
| Tony Vaughan | 27 | 4 | 3 | 304 | 0 | 0 | - | England |
| **Midfielders** | | | | | | | | |
| Jamie Clarke | 20 | 29 | 16 | 1652 | 2 | 0 | - | England |
| Wayne Corden | 27 | 46 | 32 | 3248 | 5 | 0 | - | England |
| Tom Curtis | 30 | 24 | 20 | 1933 | 6 | 0 | - | England |
| Craig Disley | 21 | 44 | 35 | 3430 | 4 | 0 | - | England |
| Andy Jones | - | 1 | 0 | 9 | 2 | 1 | - | England |
| Colin Larkin | 21 | 23 | 9 | 1225 | 0 | 0 | - | Rep of Ireland |
| Liam Lawrence | 21 | 43 | 36 | 3527 | 7 | 0 | - | England |
| Neil MacKenzie | 27 | 27 | 13 | 1555 | 2 | 0 | - | England |
| Scott Sellars | 37 | 15 | 7 | 819 | 2 | 1 | - | England |
| Lee Williamson | 21 | 41 | 26 | 2762 | 8 | 1 | - | England |
| **Forwards** | | | | | | | | |
| Daniel Bacon | 22 | 13 | 0 | 23 | 0 | 0 | - | England |
| Chris Beardsley | | 10 | 1 | 161 | 0 | 0 | - | England |
| Shayne Bradley | 23 | 2 | 0 | 0 | 0 | 0 | - | England |
| Iyseden Christie | 26 | 37 | 29 | 2818 | 8 | 0 | - | England |
| Lee Glover | 33 | 2 | 0 | 35 | 0 | 0 | - | England |
| Dean Hankey | | 1 | 0 | 26 | 0 | 0 | - | England |
| Paul Hurst | | 2 | 1 | 90 | 0 | 0 | - | England |
| Junior Mendes | 26 | 18 | 15 | 1396 | 1 | 0 | - | England |
| Colin Little | 30 | 5 | 4 | 403 | 1 | 0 | - | England |
| Craig Mitchell | | 19 | 1 | 348 | 0 | 0 | - | England |
| Andy White | 21 | 33 | 11 | 1583 | 8 | 0 | - | England |

## SQUAD APPEARANCES

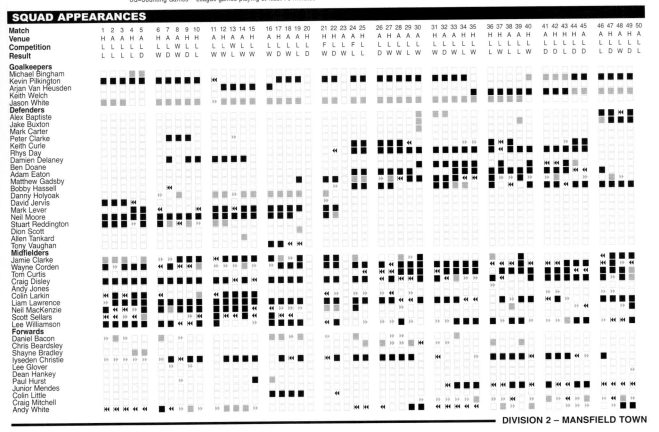

| Match | 1 | 2 | 3 | 4 | 5 | 6 | 7 | 8 | 9 | 10 | 11 | 12 | 13 | 14 | 15 | 16 | 17 | 18 | 19 | 20 | 21 | 22 | 23 | 24 | 25 |
|---|---|---|---|---|---|---|---|---|---|---|---|---|---|---|---|---|---|---|---|---|---|---|---|---|---|
| Venue | H | A | A | H | A | H | A | A | H | H | A | H | A | A | H | A | H | A | A | H | H | H | A | A | H |
| Competition | L | L | L | L | L | L | L | W | L | L | L | L | W | L | L | L | L | L | L | L | F | L | L | F | L |
| Result | L | L | L | L | D | W | D | W | D | L | W | W | L | W | W | W | D | W | L | D | W | D | W | L | L |

| Match | 26 | 27 | 28 | 29 | 30 | 31 | 32 | 33 | 34 | 35 | 36 | 37 | 38 | 39 | 40 | 41 | 42 | 43 | 44 | 45 | 46 | 47 | 48 | 49 | 50 |
|---|---|---|---|---|---|---|---|---|---|---|---|---|---|---|---|---|---|---|---|---|---|---|---|---|---|
| Venue | A | H | A | A | A | H | A | A | H | H | H | H | A | A | H | A | H | H | H | A | A | H | A | H | A |
| Competition | L | L | L | L | L | L | L | L | L | L | L | L | L | L | L | L | L | L | L | L | L | L | L | L | L |
| Result | D | W | W | L | W | W | D | W | L | W | L | W | L | L | W | D | D | L | D | D | L | D | W | D | L |

**Goalkeepers**
Michael Bingham
Kevin Pilkington
Arjan Van Heusden
Keith Welch
Jason White
**Defenders**
Alex Baptiste
Jake Buxton
Mark Carter
Peter Clarke
Keith Curle
Rhys Day
Damien Delaney
Ben Doane
Adam Eaton
Matthew Gadsby
Bobby Hassell
Danny Holyoak
David Jervis
Mark Lever
Neil Moore
Stuart Reddington
Dion Scott
Allen Tankard
Tony Vaughan
**Midfielders**
Jamie Clarke
Wayne Corden
Tom Curtis
Craig Disley
Andy Jones
Colin Larkin
Liam Lawrence
Neil MacKenzie
Scott Sellars
Lee Williamson
**Forwards**
Daniel Bacon
Chris Beardsley
Shayne Bradley
Iyseden Christie
Lee Glover
Dean Hankey
Paul Hurst
Junior Mendes
Colin Little
Craig Mitchell
Andy White

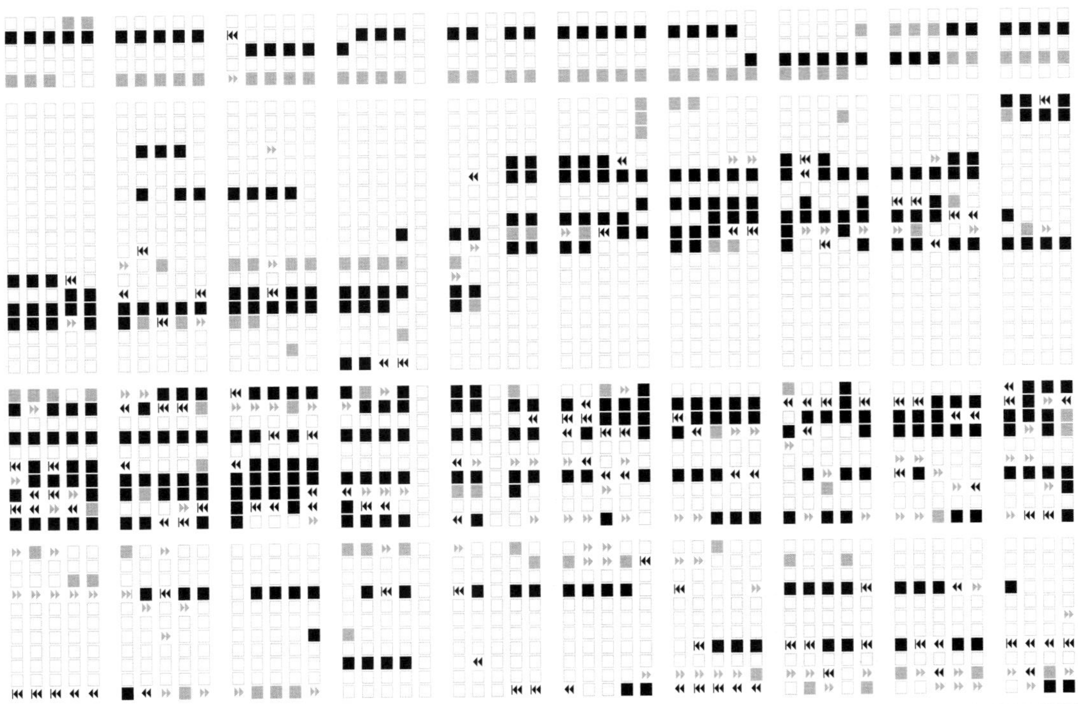

# NORTHAMPTON TOWN

Final Position: **24th**

NICKNAME: THE COBBLERS

| | | | | | | | |
|---|---|---|---|---|---|---|---|
| 1 | div2 | Crewe | H | D | 1-1 | Gabbiadini 87 |
| 2 | div2 | Wycombe | A | D | 1-1 | Forrester 69 |
| 3 | div2 | Cardiff | A | W | 2-1 | Gabbiadini 10,50 |
| 4 | div2 | Blackpool | H | L | 0-1 | |
| 5 | div2 | Chesterfield | A | L | 0-4 | |
| 6 | div2 | Barnsley | H | W | 1-0 | McGregor 74 |
| 7 | div2 | Bristol City | A | L | 0-3 | |
| 8 | wcr1 | Wigan | H | L | 0-1 | |
| 9 | div2 | Huddersfield | H | D | 0-0 | |
| 10 | div2 | Colchester | H | W | 4-1 | Gabbiadini 15,45,61; One 23 |
| 11 | div2 | Swindon | A | L | 0-2 | |
| 12 | div2 | Mansfield | H | W | 2-0 | Gabbiadini 3 pen; Trollope 80 |
| 13 | div2 | Plymouth | A | D | 0-0 | |
| 14 | div2 | Brentford | H | L | 1-2 | Asamoah 90 |
| 15 | div2 | Notts County | A | L | 1-2 | Asamoah 79 |
| 16 | div2 | Cheltenham | H | L | 1-2 | Forrester 24 |
| 17 | div2 | Oldham | A | L | 0-4 | |
| 18 | div2 | Luton | H | W | 3-0 | Forrester 9,19; Gabbiadini 50 |
| 19 | div2 | QPR | A | W | 1-0 | Trollope 61 |
| 20 | facr1 | Boston | H | W | 3-2 | Harsley 10; Gabbiadini 35; Asamoah 68 |
| 21 | div2 | Port Vale | H | W | 3-0 | Gabbiadini 38,56; Forrester 89 |
| 22 | div2 | Wigan | A | L | 0-1 | |
| 23 | facr2 | Cambridge | A | D | 2-2 | Stamp 55; Hargreaves 83 |
| 24 | div2 | Tranmere | H | L | 0-4 | |
| 25 | facr2r | Cambridge | H | L | 0-1 | |
| 26 | div2 | Stockport | A | L | 0-4 | |
| 27 | div2 | Chesterfield | H | L | 0-1 | |
| 28 | div2 | Peterborough | A | D | 0-0 | |
| 29 | div2 | Barnsley | A | W | 2-1 | Lumsdon 45 og; Stamp 70 |
| 30 | div2 | Wycombe | H | L | 0-5 | |
| 31 | div2 | Blackpool | A | L | 1-2 | Stamp 33 |
| 32 | div2 | Peterborough | H | L | 0-1 | |
| 33 | div2 | Crewe | A | D | 3-3 | Gabbiadini 45 pen; Hope 63; Asamoah 81 |
| 34 | div2 | Cardiff | H | L | 0-1 | |
| 35 | div2 | QPR | H | D | 1-1 | Rahim 16 |
| 36 | div2 | Luton | A | L | 2-3 | Burgess 23; Johnson 71 pen,71 pen |
| 37 | div2 | Bristol City | H | L | 1-2 | McGregor 45 |
| 38 | div2 | Huddersfield | A | L | 0-2 | |
| 39 | div2 | Colchester | A | L | 0-2 | |
| 40 | div2 | Swindon | H | W | 1-0 | Harsley 61 |
| 41 | div2 | Cheltenham | A | D | 1-1 | Harsley 75 |
| 42 | div2 | Notts County | H | W | 2-0 | Asamoah 24; Sampson 82 |
| 43 | div2 | Oldham | H | L | 0-2 | |
| 44 | div2 | Brentford | A | L | 0-3 | |
| 45 | div2 | Wigan | H | L | 0-2 | |
| 46 | div2 | Port Vale | A | L | 2-3 | Gabbiadini 62; Dudfield 89 |
| 47 | div2 | Stockport | H | L | 0-3 | |
| 48 | div2 | Tranmere | A | L | 0-4 | |
| 49 | div2 | Plymouth | H | D | 2-2 | Stamp 66; Morison 72 |
| 50 | div2 | Mansfield | A | L | 1-2 | Stamp 1 |

## ATTENDANCES

HOME GROUND: SIXFIELDS STADIUM   CAPACITY: 7653   AVERAGE LEAGUE AT HOME: 5210

| | | | | | | | | |
|---|---|---|---|---|---|---|---|---|
| 3 | Cardiff | 13321 | 18 | **Luton** | **5750** | 11 | Swindon | 4719 |
| 19 | QPR | 11947 | 14 | **Brentford** | **5739** | 37 | **Bristol City** | **4688** |
| 7 | Bristol City | 11104 | 1 | **Crewe** | **5694** | 30 | **Wycombe** | **4679** |
| 38 | Huddersfield | 9651 | 43 | **Oldham** | **5646** | 9 | **Huddersfield** | **4679** |
| 29 | Barnsley | 9531 | 31 | Blackpool | 5646 | 25 | **Cambridge** | **4591** |
| 13 | Plymouth | 8530 | 12 | **Mansfield** | **5594** | 34 | **Cardiff** | **4553** |
| 28 | Peterborough | 7767 | 40 | **Swindon** | **5566** | 26 | Stockport | 4516 |
| 48 | Tranmere | 7348 | 4 | **Blackpool** | **5556** | 20 | **Boston** | **4373** |
| 36 | Luton | 7048 | 17 | Oldham | 5512 | 21 | **Port Vale** | **4357** |
| 33 | Crewe | 6164 | 44 | Brentford | 5354 | 24 | **Tranmere** | **4268** |
| 22 | Wigan | 6032 | 16 | **Cheltenham** | **5354** | 46 | Port Vale | 4209 |
| 15 | Notts County | 6009 | 27 | **Chesterfield** | **5282** | 50 | Mansfield | 3928 |
| 2 | Wycombe | 5993 | 42 | **Notts County** | **5254** | 10 | **Colchester** | **3663** |
| 32 | **Peterborough** | **5906** | 23 | Cambridge | 5076 | 5 | Chesterfield | 3585 |
| 47 | **Stockport** | **5873** | 49 | **Plymouth** | **5063** | 39 | Colchester | 3408 |
| 35 | **QPR** | **5859** | 6 | **Barnsley** | **5004** | 8 | **Wigan** | **2336** |
| 45 | **Wigan** | **5822** | 41 | Cheltenham | 4917 | | | |

■ Home □ Away ▒ Neutral

## KEY PLAYERS - GOALSCORERS

**1 Marco Gabbiadini**

| | | | |
|---|---|---|---|
| Goals in the League | 12 | **Player Strike Rate** Average number of minutes between League goals scored by player | 255 |
| **Contribution to Attacking Power** Average number of minutes between League team goals while on pitch | 95 | **Club Strike Rate** Average number of minutes between League goals scored by club | 104 |

| | PLAYER | LGE GOALS | POWER | STRIKE RATE |
|---|---|---|---|---|
| 2 | Jamie Forrester | 5 | 105 | 316 mins |
| 3 | Derek Asamoah | 4 | 94 | 518 mins |
| 4 | Paul McGregor | 2 | 119 | 720 mins |
| 5 | Richard Hope | 1 | 103 | 1648 mins |

## KEY PLAYERS - MIDFIELDERS

**1 Chris Carruthers**

| | | | |
|---|---|---|---|
| Goals in the League | 0 | **Contribution to Attacking Power** Average number of minutes between League team goals while on pitch | 92 |
| **Defensive Rating** Average number of mins between League goals conceded while he was on the pitch | 57 | **Scoring Difference** Defensive Rating minus Contribution to Attacking Power | -35 |

| | PLAYER | LGE GOALS | DEF RATE | POWER | SCORE DIFF |
|---|---|---|---|---|---|
| 2 | Paul Trollope | 2 | 53 | 95 | -42 mins |
| 3 | Chris Hargreaves | 0 | 53 | 108 | -55 mins |
| 4 | Paul Harsley | 2 | 54 | 111 | -57 mins |
| 5 | John Frain | 0 | 41 | 133 | -92 mins |

## KEY PLAYERS - DEFENDERS

**1 Daryl Burgess**

| | | | |
|---|---|---|---|
| **Goals Conceded (GC)** The number of League goals conceded while he was on the pitch | 31 | **Clean Sheets** In games when he played at least 70 minutes | 7 |
| **Defensive Rating** Ave number of mins between League goals conceded while on the pitch | 64 | **Club Defensive Rating** Average number of mins between League goals conceded by the club this season | 52 |

| | PLAYER | CON LGE | CLEAN SHEETS | DEF RATE |
|---|---|---|---|---|
| 2 | Jeremy Gill | 63 | 10 | 58 mins |
| 3 | Ian Sampson | 57 | 7 | 49 mins |
| 4 | Christopher Marsh | 27 | 1 | 48 mins |
| 5 | Duncan Spedding | 17 | 1 | 47 mins |

## KEY GOALKEEPER

**1 Lee Harper**

| | |
|---|---|
| Goals Conceded in the League | 48 |
| **Defensive Rating** Ave number of mins between League goals conceded while on the pitch | 58 |
| **Counting Games** Games when he played at least 70 mins | 31 |
| **Clean Sheets** In games when he played at least 70 mins | 8 |

## TOP POINT EARNERS

| | PLAYER | GAMES | AVE |
|---|---|---|---|
| 1 | One | 5 | 1.60 |
| 2 | Rickers | 5 | 1.60 |
| 3 | Lincoln | 4 | 1.25 |
| 4 | Burgess | 20 | 1.20 |
| 5 | Harper | 31 | 1.03 |
| 6 | Harsley | 37 | 1.03 |
| 7 | Gabbiadini | 33 | 1.00 |
| 8 | Johnson | 4 | 1.00 |
| 9 | Sampson | 30 | 1.00 |
| 10 | Gill | 39 | 0.97 |
| | **CLUB AVERAGE:** | | **0.85** |

Ave = Average points per match in Counting Games

## DISCIPLINARY RECORDS

| | PLAYER | YELLOW | RED | AVE |
|---|---|---|---|---|
| 1 | Stamp | 4 | 1 | 219 |
| 2 | Burgess | 5 | 1 | 328 |
| 3 | Hope | 5 | 0 | 329 |
| 4 | Gabbiadini | 7 | 1 | 382 |
| 5 | Sampson | 6 | 1 | 399 |
| 6 | Spedding | 2 | 0 | 403 |
| 7 | Hargreaves | 8 | 0 | 420 |
| 8 | Rahim | 1 | 0 | 487 |
| 9 | Reid | 3 | 0 | 547 |
| 10 | Trollope | 6 | 0 | 586 |
| 11 | Rickers | 1 | 0 | 638 |
| 12 | Marsh | 2 | 0 | 653 |
| 13 | Asamoah | 2 | 0 | 1036 |
| | Other | 7 | 1 | |
| | TOTAL | 59 | 5 | |

## LEAGUE GOALS

| | PLAYER | MINS | GOALS | AVE |
|---|---|---|---|---|
| 1 | Gabbiadini | 3056 | 12 | 255 |
| 2 | Forrester | 1580 | 5 | 316 |
| 3 | Asamoah | 2072 | 4 | 518 |
| 4 | Stamp | 1098 | 4 | 275 |
| 5 | Trollope | 3518 | 2 | 1759 |
| 6 | Harsley | 3661 | 2 | 1831 |
| 7 | McGregor | 1439 | 2 | 720 |
| 8 | Hope | 1648 | 1 | 1648 |
| 9 | Burgess | 1971 | 1 | 1971 |
| 10 | Johnson | 449 | 1 | 449 |
| 11 | Dudfield | 675 | 1 | 675 |
| 12 | Rahim | 487 | 1 | 487 |
| 13 | Morison | 449 | 1 | 449 |
| | Other | | 3 | |
| | TOTAL | | 40 | |

## MONTH BY MONTH GUIDE TO THE POINTS

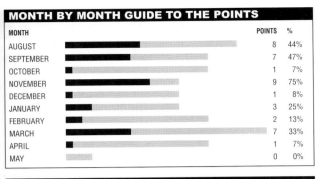

| MONTH | POINTS | % |
|---|---|---|
| AUGUST | 8 | 44% |
| SEPTEMBER | 7 | 47% |
| OCTOBER | 1 | 7% |
| NOVEMBER | 9 | 75% |
| DECEMBER | 1 | 8% |
| JANUARY | 3 | 25% |
| FEBRUARY | 2 | 13% |
| MARCH | 7 | 33% |
| APRIL | 1 | 7% |
| MAY | 0 | 0% |

## TEAM OF THE SEASON

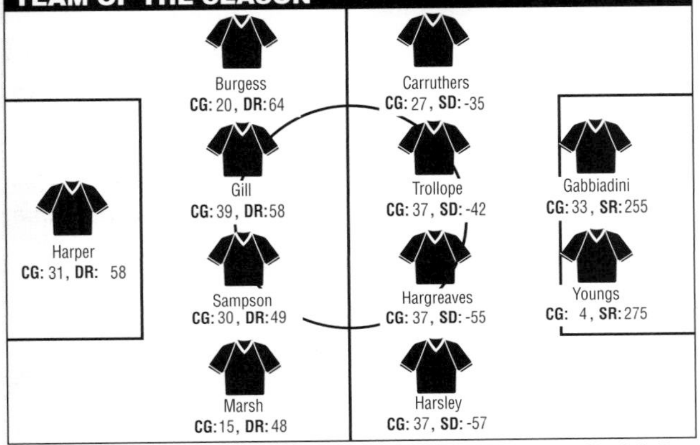
Burgess
CG: 20, DR: 64
Carruthers
CG: 27, SD: -35
Gill
CG: 39, DR: 58
Trollope
CG: 37, SD: -42
Gabbiadini
CG: 33, SR: 255
Harper
CG: 31, DR: 58
Sampson
CG: 30, DR: 49
Hargreaves
CG: 37, SD: -55
Youngs
CG: 4, SR: 275
Marsh
CG: 15, DR: 48
Harsley
CG: 37, SD: -57

KEY: DR = Defensive Rate, SD = Scoring Difference, SR = Strike Rate, CG = Counting Games – League games playing at least 70 minutes

## LEAGUE APPEARANCES, BOOKINGS AND CAPS

| | AGE | IN THE SQUAD | COUNTING GAMES | MINUTES ON PITCH | YELLOW CARDS | RED CARDS | THIS SEASON | HOME COUNTRY |
|---|---|---|---|---|---|---|---|---|
| **Goalkeepers** | | | | | | | | |
| Nathan Abbey | 24 | 34 | 4 | 373 | 0 | 0 | - | England |
| Mark Bunn | 18 | 6 | 0 | 0 | 0 | 0 | - | England |
| Lee Harper | 31 | 33 | 31 | 2777 | 0 | 1 | - | England |
| Glyn Thompson | 22 | 19 | 11 | 990 | 0 | 0 | - | England |
| **Defenders** | | | | | | | | |
| Daryl Burgess | 32 | 28 | 20 | 1971 | 5 | 1 | - | England |
| Luke Chambers | 17 | 2 | 0 | 30 | 0 | 0 | - | England |
| Jeremy Gill | 32 | 41 | 39 | 3629 | 3 | 0 | - | England |
| Richard Hope | 25 | 31 | 17 | 1648 | 5 | 0 | - | England |
| Christopher Marsh | 33 | 21 | 15 | 1306 | 2 | 0 | - | England |
| Paul Reid | 21 | 19 | 18 | 1643 | 3 | 0 | - | England |
| Ian Sampson | 34 | 37 | 30 | 2799 | 6 | 1 | - | England |
| Duncan Spedding | 25 | 13 | 9 | 806 | 2 | 0 | - | England |
| **Midfielders** | | | | | | | | |
| Chris Carruthers | - | 39 | 27 | 2566 | 0 | 0 | - | England |
| Aaron Cavill | 19 | 4 | 0 | 0 | 0 | 0 | - | England |
| John Frain | 34 | 16 | 11 | 1066 | 0 | 0 | - | England |
| Chris Hargreaves | 31 | 39 | 37 | 3362 | 8 | 0 | - | England |
| Paul Harsley | 25 | 46 | 37 | 3661 | 1 | 0 | - | England |
| Richard Johnson | 29 | 6 | 4 | 449 | 2 | 0 | - | Australia |
| Greg Lincoln | 23 | 33 | 4 | 473 | 0 | 0 | - | England |
| Daniel Lowe | 19 | 2 | 0 | 0 | 0 | 0 | - | England |
| Brent Rahim | 24 | 6 | 4 | 487 | 1 | 0 | - | Trinidad & Tobago |
| Paul Rickers | 28 | 12 | 5 | 638 | 1 | 0 | - | England |
| Paul Trollope | 31 | 41 | 37 | 3518 | 6 | 0 | 3 | Wales (50) |
| Andy Turner | 28 | 3 | 0 | 57 | 0 | 0 | - | |
| **Forwards** | | | | | | | | |
| Derek Asamoah | - | 42 | 19 | 2072 | 2 | 0 | - | Ghana |
| Lawrie Dudfield | 23 | 10 | 6 | 675 | 0 | 0 | - | England |
| Jamie Forrester | 28 | 27 | 15 | 1580 | 0 | 0 | - | England |
| Marco Gabbiadini | 35 | 41 | 33 | 3056 | 7 | 1 | - | England |
| Paul McGregor | 28 | 28 | 13 | 1439 | 1 | 0 | - | England |
| Steve Morison | 19 | 20 | 3 | 449 | 0 | 0 | - | England |
| Armand One | - | 6 | 5 | 442 | 0 | 0 | - | |
| Darryn Stamp | 24 | 26 | 10 | 1098 | 4 | 1 | - | England |
| Tom Youngs | 23 | 5 | 4 | 344 | 0 | 0 | - | England |

KEY: LEAGUE BOOKINGS CAPS

## SQUAD APPEARANCES

| Match | 1 | 2 | 3 | 4 | 5 | 6 | 7 | 8 | 9 | 10 | 11 | 12 | 13 | 14 | 15 | 16 | 17 | 18 | 19 | 20 | 21 | 22 | 23 | 24 | 25 |
|---|---|---|---|---|---|---|---|---|---|---|---|---|---|---|---|---|---|---|---|---|---|---|---|---|---|
| Venue | H | A | A | H | A | H | A | H | H | H | A | H | A | H | A | H | A | H | A | H | H | A | A | H | H |
| Competition | L | L | L | L | L | L | L | W | L | L | L | L | L | L | L | L | L | L | L | F | L | L | F | L | F |
| Result | D | D | W | L | L | W | L | L | D | W | L | W | D | L | L | L | L | W | W | W | W | L | D | L | L |

| Match | 26 | 27 | 28 | 29 | 30 | 31 | 32 | 33 | 34 | 35 | 36 | 37 | 38 | 39 | 40 | 41 | 42 | 43 | 44 | 45 | 46 | 47 | 48 | 49 | 50 |
|---|---|---|---|---|---|---|---|---|---|---|---|---|---|---|---|---|---|---|---|---|---|---|---|---|---|
| Venue | A | H | A | A | H | A | H | A | H | H | A | H | A | A | H | A | H | H | A | H | A | H | A | H | A |
| Competition | L | L | L | L | L | L | L | L | L | L | L | L | L | L | L | L | L | L | L | L | L | L | L | L | L |
| Result | L | L | D | W | L | L | L | D | L | D | L | L | L | L | W | D | W | L | L | L | L | L | L | D | L |

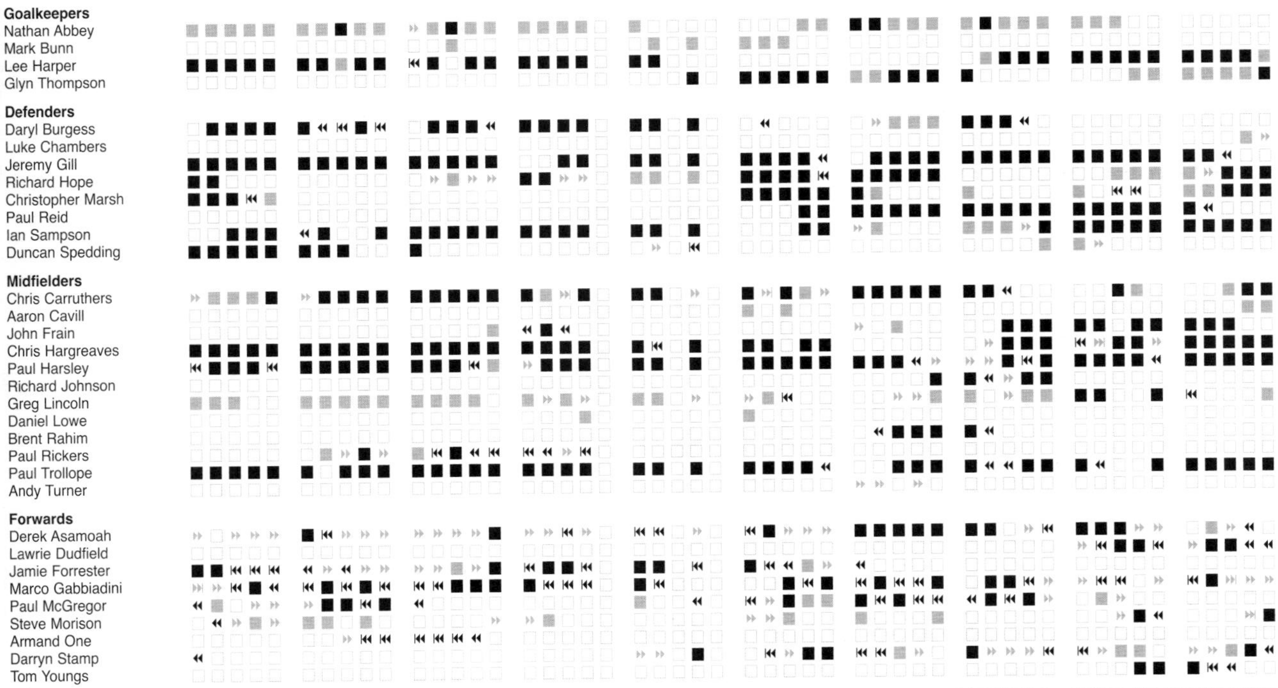
Goalkeepers
Nathan Abbey
Mark Bunn
Lee Harper
Glyn Thompson
Defenders
Daryl Burgess
Luke Chambers
Jeremy Gill
Richard Hope
Christopher Marsh
Paul Reid
Ian Sampson
Duncan Spedding
Midfielders
Chris Carruthers
Aaron Cavill
John Frain
Chris Hargreaves
Paul Harsley
Richard Johnson
Greg Lincoln
Daniel Lowe
Brent Rahim
Paul Rickers
Paul Trollope
Andy Turner
Forwards
Derek Asamoah
Lawrie Dudfield
Jamie Forrester
Marco Gabbiadini
Paul McGregor
Steve Morison
Armand One
Darryn Stamp
Tom Youngs

# DIVISION TWO ROUND-UP

## STADIUM CAPACITY AND HOME CROWDS

| | TEAM | CAPACITY | AVE(%) | HIGH | LOW |
|---|---|---|---|---|---|
| 1 | Cheltenham | 6400 | 76.14 | 6382 | 3568 |
| 2 | QPR | 19148 | 68.97 | 16921 | 10387 |
| 3 | Northampton | 7653 | 68.09 | 5906 | 3663 |
| 4 | Luton | 9970 | 67.67 | 9477 | 5890 |
| 5 | Crewe | 10118 | 66.82 | 9562 | 5138 |
| 6 | Blackpool | 11295 | 61.88 | 8772 | 5068 |
| 7 | Wycombe | 10000 | 60.02 | 8383 | 4897 |
| 8 | Cardiff | 22000 | 59.32 | 15245 | 11389 |
| 9 | Bristol City | 21500 | 55.3 | 18085 | 9084 |
| 10 | Colchester | 6200 | 54.63 | 5047 | 2721 |
| 11 | Mansfield | 9990 | 48.92 | 8134 | 3414 |
| 12 | Oldham | 13700 | 48.9 | 9415 | 5039 |
| 13 | Plymouth | 18600 | 48.28 | 11922 | 6835 |
| 14 | Tranmere | 16789 | 46.92 | 10418 | 5980 |
| 15 | Chesterfield | 8880 | 46.26 | 6813 | 3081 |
| 16 | Stockport | 12100 | 45.39 | 8168 | 4011 |
| 17 | Brentford | 12763 | 45.12 | 9168 | 3990 |
| 18 | Barnsley | 22752 | 42.89 | 12474 | 8661 |
| 19 | Huddersfield | 24500 | 38.8 | 13769 | 7294 |
| 20 | Swindon | 16000 | 34 | 8629 | 4136 |
| 21 | Peterborough | 15500 | 31.94 | 7767 | 3627 |
| 22 | Wigan | 25000 | 29.15 | 12783 | 5358 |
| 23 | Notts County | 21300 | 28.89 | 10302 | 3875 |
| 24 | Port Vale | 22546 | 19.68 | 6395 | 3039 |

**Key:** Average. The percentage of each stadium filled in League games over the season (AVE), the stadium capacity and the highest and lowest crowds recorded.

## AWAY ATTENDANCE

| | TEAM | AVE(%) | HIGH | LOW |
|---|---|---|---|---|
| 1 | QPR | 57.62 | 15245 | 4394 |
| 2 | Wigan | 55.57 | 14703 | 2721 |
| 3 | Oldham | 54.03 | 15491 | 3021 |
| 4 | Bristol City | 53.32 | 15239 | 3338 |
| 5 | Cardiff | 53.25 | 15615 | 3096 |
| 6 | Luton | 52.63 | 15786 | 3762 |
| 7 | Plymouth | 52.23 | 18085 | 3668 |
| 8 | Notts County | 50.5 | 13585 | 3435 |
| 9 | Blackpool | 50.48 | 11891 | 3305 |
| 10 | Huddersfield | 49.72 | 13703 | 3835 |
| 11 | Crewe | 49.71 | 16921 | 2949 |
| 12 | Mansfield | 49.58 | 13009 | 3247 |
| 13 | Port Vale | 49.03 | 13703 | 3581 |
| 14 | Swindon | 48.73 | 13205 | 3189 |
| 15 | Barnsley | 48.39 | 12759 | 3096 |
| 16 | Stockport | 48.39 | 11546 | 3300 |
| 17 | Chesterfield | 48.07 | 13331 | 3039 |
| 18 | Peterborough | 47.96 | 12918 | 3515 |
| 19 | Tranmere | 47.01 | 12249 | 2846 |
| 20 | Wycombe | 46.69 | 14874 | 3081 |
| 21 | Northampton | 46.62 | 13321 | 3408 |
| 22 | Brentford | 46.52 | 15559 | 3135 |
| 23 | Cheltenham | 46.44 | 11711 | 2845 |
| 24 | Colchester | 41.51 | 12906 | 3226 |

**Key:** Average. How close each club has come to filling grounds in its away league matches (AVE) and the highest and lowest crowds recorded.

## CLUB STRIKE FORCE

Murray - a scorer for City

| | |
|---|---|
| Goals scored in the League | 79 |
| Goals scored in all competions | 103 |
| Shots on target (SoT) Shots on target hit by the team recorded in League games | 264 |

**1 Bristol City**

| | |
|---|---|
| Club Strike Rate (CSR) Average number of minutes between League goals scored by club | 52 |

| | CLUB | LGE | ALL | SoT | CSR |
|---|---|---|---|---|---|
| 2 | Crewe | 76 | 90 | 299 | **54** |
| 3 | QPR | 69 | 74 | 261 | **60** |
| 4 | Cardiff | 68 | 87 | 272 | **61** |
| 5 | Oldham | 68 | 80 | 262 | **61** |
| 6 | Wigan | 68 | 79 | 317 | **61** |
| 7 | Luton | 67 | 77 | 217 | **62** |
| 8 | Mansfield | 66 | 71 | 273 | **63** |
| 9 | Tranmere | 66 | 74 | 280 | **63** |
| 10 | Stockport | 65 | 73 | 226 | **64** |
| 11 | Plymouth | 63 | 72 | 307 | **66** |
| 12 | Notts County | 62 | 66 | 214 | **67** |
| 13 | Swindon | 59 | 63 | 240 | **70** |
| 14 | Wycombe | 59 | 66 | 243 | **70** |
| 15 | Blackpool | 56 | 64 | 244 | **74** |
| 16 | Port Vale | 54 | 55 | 216 | **77** |
| 17 | Cheltenham | 53 | 61 | 246 | **78** |
| 18 | Colchester | 52 | 52 | 243 | **80** |
| 19 | Barnsley | 51 | 53 | 284 | **81** |
| 20 | Peterborough | 51 | 53 | 252 | **81** |
| 21 | Brentford | 47 | 60 | 187 | **88** |
| 22 | Chesterfield | 43 | 47 | 210 | **96** |
| 23 | Northampton | 40 | 47 | 192 | **104** |
| 24 | Huddersfield | 39 | 41 | 241 | **106** |

## CLUB DEFENCES

**1 Wigan**

| | |
|---|---|
| Club Defensive Rate (CDR) Average number of minutes between League goals conceded by club | 166 |

| | CLUB | LGE | ALL | CS | SoT | CDR |
|---|---|---|---|---|---|---|
| 2 | Oldham | 38 | 51 | 20 | 232 | **109** |
| 3 | Crewe | 40 | 49 | 17 | 270 | **104** |
| 4 | Cardiff | 43 | 53 | 18 | 194 | **96** |
| 5 | QPR | 45 | 51 | 19 | 192 | **92** |
| 6 | Bristol City | 48 | 57 | 16 | 213 | **86** |
| 7 | Plymouth | 52 | 59 | 14 | 213 | **80** |
| 8 | Peterborough | 54 | 59 | 15 | 267 | **77** |
| 9 | Brentford | 56 | 71 | 15 | 273 | **74** |
| 10 | Colchester | 56 | 60 | 13 | 266 | **74** |
| 11 | Tranmere | 57 | 69 | 13 | 248 | **73** |
| 12 | Huddersfield | 61 | 63 | 15 | 240 | **68** |
| 13 | Luton | 62 | 72 | 15 | 193 | **67** |
| 14 | Swindon | 63 | 69 | 7 | 228 | **66** |
| 15 | Barnsley | 64 | 73 | 6 | 245 | **65** |
| 16 | Blackpool | 64 | 73 | 11 | 232 | **65** |
| 17 | Wycombe | 66 | 76 | 11 | 275 | **63** |
| 18 | Cheltenham | 68 | 82 | 10 | 239 | **61** |
| 19 | Notts County | 70 | 77 | 9 | 323 | **59** |
| 20 | Port Vale | 70 | 74 | 10 | 286 | **59** |
| 21 | Stockport | 70 | 78 | 7 | 272 | **59** |
| 22 | Chesterfield | 73 | 77 | 16 | 341 | **57** |
| 23 | Northampton | 79 | 89 | 10 | 270 | **52** |
| 24 | Mansfield | 97 | 105 | 5 | 319 | **43** |

Eaden of Wigan

| | |
|---|---|
| Goals conceded in the League | 25 |
| Goals conceded in all competions | 33 |
| Clean Sheets (CS) Number of league games where no goals were conceded | 25 |
| Shots on Target Against (SoT) Shots on Target conceded by team in League games | 159 |

## CLUB GOAL ATTEMPTS

### GOAL ATTEMPTS – FOR

**KEY:** Shots on Target (SoT), Shots Off Target (SO) Total shots (Tot) Ratio of shots on target to goals (SG) Accuracy Rating (AR)

| | CLUB | SoT | SO | Tot | SG | AR |
|---|---|---|---|---|---|---|
| 1 | Wigan | 317 | 320 | **637** | 4.7 | 49.8 |
| 2 | Plymouth | 307 | 322 | **629** | 4.9 | 48.8 |
| 3 | Cardiff | 272 | 280 | **552** | 4 | 49.3 |
| 4 | Barnsley | 284 | 264 | **548** | 5.6 | 51.8 |
| 5 | Crewe | 299 | 225 | **524** | 3.9 | 57.1 |
| 6 | QPR | 261 | 262 | **523** | 3.8 | 49.9 |
| 7 | Oldham | 262 | 253 | **515** | 3.9 | 50.9 |
| 8 | Tranmere | 280 | 232 | **512** | 4.2 | 54.7 |
| 9 | Mansfield | 273 | 238 | **511** | 4.1 | 53.4 |
| 10 | Bristol City | 264 | 239 | **503** | 3.3 | 52.5 |
| 11 | Peterborough | 252 | 227 | **479** | 4.9 | 52.6 |
| 12 | Cheltenham | 246 | 230 | **476** | 4.6 | 51.7 |
| 13 | Swindon | 240 | 234 | **474** | 4.1 | 50.6 |
| 14 | Blackpool | 244 | 227 | **471** | 4.4 | 51.8 |
| 15 | Huddersfield | 241 | 230 | **471** | 6.2 | 51.2 |
| 16 | Wycombe | 243 | 195 | **438** | 4.1 | 55.5 |
| 17 | Colchester | 243 | 185 | **428** | 4.7 | 56.8 |
| 18 | Luton | 217 | 211 | **428** | 3.2 | 50.7 |
| 19 | Stockport | 226 | 196 | **422** | 3.5 | 53.6 |
| 20 | Port Vale | 216 | 201 | **417** | 4 | 51.8 |
| 21 | Notts County | 214 | 188 | **402** | 3.5 | 53.2 |
| 22 | Chesterfield | 210 | 188 | **398** | 4.9 | 52.8 |
| 23 | Northampton | 192 | 190 | **382** | 4.8 | 50.3 |
| 24 | Brentford | 187 | 183 | **370** | 4 | 50.5 |

### GOAL ATTEMPTS – AGAINST

**KEY:** Shots on Target (SoT), Shots Off Target (SO) Total shots (Tot) Ratio of shots on target to goals (SG) Accuracy Rating (AR)

| | CLUB | SoT | SO | Tot | SG | AR |
|---|---|---|---|---|---|---|
| 1 | Wigan | 159 | 196 | **355** | 6.4 | 44.8 |
| 2 | Luton | 193 | 179 | **372** | 3.1 | 51.9 |
| 3 | Cardiff | 194 | 190 | **384** | 4.5 | 50.5 |
| 4 | Bristol City | 213 | 185 | **398** | 4.4 | 53.5 |
| 5 | QPR | 192 | 213 | **405** | 4.3 | 47.4 |
| 6 | Swindon | 228 | 196 | **424** | 3.6 | 53.8 |
| 7 | Blackpool | 232 | 199 | **431** | 3.6 | 53.8 |
| 8 | Plymouth | 213 | 220 | **433** | 4.1 | 49.2 |
| 9 | Brentford | 273 | 174 | **447** | 4.9 | 61.1 |
| 10 | Northampton | 270 | 177 | **447** | 3.4 | 60.4 |
| 11 | Huddersfield | 240 | 214 | **454** | 3.9 | 52.9 |
| 12 | Stockport | 272 | 196 | **468** | 3.9 | 58.1 |
| 13 | Tranmere | 248 | 223 | **471** | 4.4 | 52.7 |
| 14 | Cheltenham | 239 | 234 | **473** | 3.5 | 50.5 |
| 15 | Oldham | 232 | 241 | **473** | 6.1 | 49 |
| 16 | Barnsley | 245 | 230 | **475** | 3.8 | 51.6 |
| 17 | Peterborough | 267 | 218 | **485** | 4.9 | 55.1 |
| 18 | Port Vale | 286 | 205 | **491** | 4.1 | 58.2 |
| 19 | Colchester | 266 | 227 | **493** | 4.8 | 54 |
| 20 | Wycombe | 275 | 251 | **526** | 4.2 | 52.3 |
| 21 | Notts County | 323 | 215 | **538** | 4.6 | 60 |
| 22 | Crewe | 270 | 269 | **539** | 6.8 | 50.1 |
| 23 | Chesterfield | 341 | 200 | **541** | 4.7 | 63 |
| 24 | Mansfield | 319 | 225 | **544** | 3.3 | 58.6 |

## CLUB DISCIPLINARY RECORDS

iSOFT

Barnsley defender Morgan

| | |
|---|---|
| League Yellow | 89 |
| League Red | 3 |
| League Total | 92 |
| All Comps Yellow | 91 |
| All Comps Red | 3 |
| TOTAL | 94 |

**1 Barnsley**

| | |
|---|---|
| Cards Average in League Average number of minutes between a card being shown of either colour | 45 |

| | PLAYER | LEAGUE | | TOTAL | | AVE |
|---|---|---|---|---|---|---|
| 2 | Luton | 87Y | 6R | 91Y | 6R | **45** |
| 3 | Chesterfield | 85 | 4 | 88 | 4 | **47** |
| 4 | Notts County | 85 | 2 | 88 | 2 | **48** |
| 5 | Mansfield | 80 | 5 | 81 | 6 | **49** |
| 6 | Oldham | 74 | 9 | 85 | 10 | **50** |
| 7 | QPR | 71 | 8 | 84 | 9 | **52** |
| 8 | Blackpool | 72 | 6 | 74 | 6 | **53** |
| 9 | Peterborough | 71 | 4 | 72 | 5 | **55** |
| 10 | Stockport | 70 | 4 | 72 | 4 | **56** |
| 11 | Huddersfield | 68 | 4 | 69 | 4 | **58** |
| 12 | Tranmere | 64 | 5 | 70 | 5 | **60** |
| 13 | Port Vale | 65 | 3 | 68 | 3 | **61** |
| 14 | Wigan | 64 | 3 | 68 | 3 | **62** |
| 15 | Wycombe | 62 | 4 | 68 | 5 | **63** |
| 16 | Bristol City | 59 | 6 | 62 | 6 | **64** |
| 17 | Swindon | 63 | 2 | 67 | 2 | **64** |
| 18 | Northampton | 59 | 5 | 60 | 5 | **65** |
| 19 | Cardiff | 60 | 2 | 73 | 2 | **67** |
| 20 | Colchester | 54 | 7 | 55 | 7 | **68** |
| 21 | Brentford | 54 | 6 | 62 | 7 | **69** |
| 22 | Cheltenham | 54 | 4 | 55 | 4 | **71** |
| 23 | Plymouth | 51 | 2 | 56 | 2 | **78** |
| 24 | Crewe | 34 | 3 | 36 | 3 | **112** |

## CHART-TOPPING MIDFIELDERS

JJB

| 1 Jimmy Bullard - Wigan | |
|---|---|
| Goals scored in the League | 1 |
| Defensive Rating<br>Av number of mins between League goals conceded while on the pitch | 217 |
| Contribution to Attacking Power<br>Average number of minutes between League team goals while on pitch | 84 |
| **Scoring Difference<br>Defensive Rating minus Contribution to Attacking Power** | **133** |

| | PLAYER | CLUB | GOALS | DEF R | POWER | SCORE DIFF |
|---|---|---|---|---|---|---|
| 2 | Low | Oldham | 3 | 136 | 45 | **91 mins** |
| 3 | Sheridan, D | Oldham | 1 | 139 | 52 | **87 mins** |
| 4 | Green | Wigan | 2 | 138 | 52 | **86 mins** |
| 5 | Appleby | Oldham | 0 | 142 | 62 | **80 mins** |
| 6 | Tierney | Crewe | 1 | 105 | 36 | **69 mins** |
| 7 | Vaughan | Crewe | 3 | 109 | 53 | **56 mins** |
| 8 | Brammer | Crewe | 1 | 108 | 52 | **56 mins** |
| 9 | Walker | Crewe | 2 | 105 | 56 | **49 mins** |
| 10 | Lunt | Crewe | 7 | 102 | 54 | **48 mins** |
| 11 | Carss | Oldham | 2 | 113 | 69 | **44 mins** |
| 12 | Tinnion | Bristol City | 9 | 90 | 50 | **40 mins** |
| 13 | Sorvel | Crewe | 3 | 97 | 57 | **40 mins** |
| 14 | Langley | QPR | 9 | 93 | 56 | **37 mins** |
| 15 | Evans | Blackpool | 1 | 108 | 72 | **36 mins** |
| 16 | Bent | Plymouth | 1 | 91 | 55 | **36 mins** |
| 17 | Doherty | Bristol City | 0 | 92 | 57 | **35 mins** |
| 18 | Murray | Oldham | 1 | 101 | 67 | **34 mins** |
| 19 | Kavanagh | Cardiff | 5 | 94 | 61 | **33 mins** |
| 20 | Whalley | Cardiff | 0 | 89 | 57 | **32 mins** |

The Divisional Round-up charts combine the records of chart-topping keepers, defenders, midfield players and forwards, from every club in the division. The one above is for **the Chart-topping Midfielders**. The players are ranked by their Scoring Difference although other attributes are shown for you to compare.

## CHART-TOPPING GOALSCORERS

Herald

| 1 Robert Earnshaw - Cardiff City | |
|---|---|
| Goals scored in the League (GL) | 31 |
| Goals scored in all competitions (GA) | 35 |
| Contribution to Attacking Power (AP)<br>Average number of minutes between League team goals while on pitch | 61 |
| **Player Strike Rate (SR)<br>Average number of minutes between League goals scored by player** | **116** |
| Club Strike Rate (CSR)<br>Average minutes between League goals scored by club | 61 |

| | PLAYER | CLUB | GOALS: LGE | ALL | POWER | CSR | S RATE |
|---|---|---|---|---|---|---|---|
| 2 | Beckett | Stockport | 27 | 28 | 66 | 64 | **135 mins** |
| 3 | Hulse | Crewe | 22 | 23 | 56 | 54 | **142 mins** |
| 4 | Parkin | Swindon | 25 | 25 | 69 | 70 | **148 mins** |
| 5 | Christie | Mansfield | 18 | 18 | 62 | 63 | **157 mins** |
| 6 | Stallard | Notts County | 24 | 25 | 69 | 67 | **159 mins** |
| 7 | Howard | Luton | 22 | 23 | 61 | 62 | **164 mins** |
| 8 | Liddell | Wigan | 16 | 16 | 60 | 61 | **178 mins** |
| 9 | Keith | Plymouth | 11 | 11 | 63 | 66 | **179 mins** |
| 10 | Smith | Huddersfield | 17 | 17 | 92 | 106 | **184 mins** |
| 11 | Murphy | Blackpool | 16 | 16 | 66 | 74 | **187 mins** |
| 12 | Thorpe | Luton | 13 | 13 | 66 | 62 | **189 mins** |
| 13 | Furlong | QPR | 13 | 14 | 51 | 60 | **189 mins** |
| 14 | Jones | Crewe | 9 | 10 | 64 | 54 | **194 mins** |
| 15 | Haworth | Tranmere | 19 | 20 | 60 | 63 | **196 mins** |
| 16 | Clarke, A | Peterborough | 17 | 17 | 78 | 81 | **208 mins** |
| 17 | Murray | Bristol City | 19 | 19 | 53 | 52 | **210 mins** |
| 18 | Dyer | Barnsley | 16 | 16 | 78 | 81 | **211 mins** |
| 19 | Wijnhard | Oldham | 10 | 12 | 62 | 61 | **211 mins** |
| 20 | Roberts | Bristol City | 13 | 13 | 51 | 52 | **212 mins** |

**The Chart-topping Goalscorers** measures the players by Strike Rate. They are most likely to be Forwards but Midfield players and even Defenders do come through the club tables. It is not a measure of the number of League goals scored - although that is also noted - but how often on average they have scored.

## CHART-TOPPING DEFENDERS

JJB

| 1 Peter Kennedy - Wigan | |
|---|---|
| Goals Conceded in the League<br>The number of League goals conceded while he was on the pitch | 9 |
| Goals Conceded in all competitions<br>The number of goals conceded while he was on the pitch in all competitions | 14 |
| Clean Sheets<br>In games when he played at least 70 mins | 13 |
| **Defensive Rating (DR)<br>Average number of minutes between League goals conceded while on pitch** | **211** |
| Club Defensive Rating<br>Average mins between League goals conceded by the club this season | 166 |

| | PLAYER | CLUB | CON: LGE | ALL | CS | CDR | DEF RATE |
|---|---|---|---|---|---|---|---|
| 2 | Mitchell | Wigan | 7 | 11 | 6 | 166 | **201 mins** |
| 3 | McMillan | Wigan | 15 | 17 | 14 | 166 | **169 mins** |
| 4 | Dinning | Wigan | 19 | 22 | 16 | 166 | **163 mins** |
| 5 | De Vos | Wigan | 24 | 28 | 23 | 166 | **161 mins** |
| 6 | Eaden | Wigan | 21 | 28 | 19 | 166 | **159 mins** |
| 7 | Jackson | Wigan | 25 | 32 | 24 | 166 | **157 mins** |
| 8 | Jarrett | Wigan | 15 | 22 | 13 | 166 | **151 mins** |
| 9 | Hill | Oldham | 10 | 15 | 9 | 109 | **149 mins** |
| 10 | Foster | Crewe | 26 | 29 | 15 | 104 | **120 mins** |
| 11 | Padula | QPR | 13 | 13 | 7 | 92 | **116 mins** |
| 12 | Walton | Crewe | 22 | 24 | 10 | 104 | **113 mins** |
| 13 | Hall, F | Oldham | 31 | 38 | 16 | 109 | **113 mins** |
| 14 | Weston | Cardiff | 31 | 38 | 16 | 96 | **109 mins** |
| 15 | Croft | Cardiff | 33 | 39 | 17 | 96 | **107 mins** |
| 16 | Carey | Bristol City | 19 | 20 | 7 | 86 | **102 mins** |
| 17 | Carlisle | QPR | 29 | 32 | 14 | 92 | **102 mins** |
| 18 | Loran | Tranmere | 13 | 13 | 6 | 73 | **102 mins** |
| 19 | Hendry | Blackpool | 12 | 12 | 4 | 65 | **101 mins** |
| 20 | Prior | Cardiff | 31 | 33 | 15 | 96 | **101 mins** |

**The Chart-topping Defenders** are resolved by their Defensive Rating, how often their team concedes a goal while they are playing. All these rightly favour players at the best performing clubs because good players win matches. However, good players in lower-table clubs will chart where they have lifted the team's performance.

## CHART-TOPPING GOALKEEPERS

| 1 Chris Day - QPR | |
|---|---|
| Goals conceded in the League (CL) | 5 |
| Goals conceded in all comps (CA) | 7 |
| Counting Games<br>League games when he played at least 70 minutes | 12 |
| Clean Sheets<br>In games when he played at least 70 mins | 7 |
| Goals to Shots Ratio (GSR)<br>The average number of shots on target per each League goal conceded | 10 |
| **Defensive Rating (DR)<br>Average number of minutes between League goals conceded while on pitch** | **216** |

| | PLAYER | CLUB | CG | CON: LGE | ALL | CS | GSR | DEF RATE |
|---|---|---|---|---|---|---|---|---|
| 2 | Filan | Wigan | 46 | 25 | 32 | 25 | 6.4 | **166 mins** |
| 3 | Pogliacomi | Oldham | 36 | 28 | 31 | 18 | 6 | **117 mins** |
| 4 | Ince | Crewe | 43 | 35 | 39 | 16 | 7.2 | **110 mins** |
| 5 | Alexander | Cardiff | 40 | 36 | 42 | 15 | 4.6 | **100 mins** |
| 6 | McKinney | Colchester | 19 | 19 | 22 | 9 | 4.6 | **95 mins** |
| 7 | Berthelin | Luton | 9 | 9 | 9 | 3 | 3.8 | **90 mins** |
| 8 | Harrison | Peterborough | 12 | 12 | 12 | 7 | 7.1 | **90 mins** |
| 9 | Miskelly | Oldham | 9 | 10 | 14 | 2 | 5.9 | **88 mins** |
| 10 | Phillips | Bristol City | 46 | 48 | 52 | 16 | 4.4 | **86 mins** |
| 11 | Royce | QPR | 15 | 17 | 17 | 6 | 3.8 | **81 mins** |
| 12 | Larrieu | Plymouth | 43 | 48 | 54 | 13 | 4.2 | **81 mins** |
| 13 | Tyler | Peterborough | 29 | 33 | 35 | 8 | 4.6 | **79 mins** |
| 14 | Tidman | Stockport | 18 | 21 | 21 | 2 | 4.3 | **77 mins** |
| 15 | Higgs | Cheltenham | 10 | 12 | 12 | 2 | 4.4 | **75 mins** |
| 16 | Achterberg | Tranmere | 37 | 45 | 46 | 9 | 4.4 | **75 mins** |
| 17 | Culkin | QPR | 17 | 21 | 21 | 5 | 3.2 | **73 mins** |
| 18 | Bevan | Huddersfield | 28 | 36 | 37 | 9 | 3.9 | **73 mins** |
| 19 | Smith, P | Brentford | 43 | 53 | 63 | 14 | 4.7 | **73 mins** |
| 20 | Muggleton | Chesterfield | 25 | 32 | 33 | 12 | 5.6 | **71 mins** |

**The Chart-topping Goalkeepers** are positioned by their Defensive Rating. We also show Clean Sheets where the team has not conceded and the Keeper has played all or most (at least 70 minutes) of the game. Now teams use several keepers in a season, not every team will necessarily chart on this page.

## FINAL LEAGUE TABLE

| | | HOME | | | | | AWAY | | | | | TOTAL | | | |
|---|---|---|---|---|---|---|---|---|---|---|---|---|---|---|---|
| | P | W | D | L | F | A | W | D | L | F | A | F | A | DIF | PTS |
| Wigan | 46 | 14 | 7 | 2 | 37 | 16 | 15 | 6 | 2 | 31 | 9 | 68 | 25 | 43 | 100 |
| Crewe | 46 | 11 | 5 | 7 | 29 | 19 | 14 | 6 | 3 | 47 | 21 | 76 | 40 | 36 | 86 |
| Bristol City | 46 | 15 | 5 | 3 | 43 | 15 | 9 | 6 | 8 | 36 | 33 | 79 | 48 | 31 | 83 |
| QPR | 46 | 14 | 4 | 5 | 38 | 19 | 10 | 7 | 6 | 31 | 26 | 69 | 45 | 24 | 83 |
| Oldham | 46 | 11 | 6 | 6 | 39 | 18 | 11 | 10 | 2 | 29 | 20 | 68 | 38 | 30 | 82 |
| Cardiff | 46 | 12 | 6 | 5 | 33 | 20 | 11 | 6 | 6 | 35 | 23 | 68 | 43 | 25 | 81 |
| Tranmere | 46 | 14 | 5 | 4 | 38 | 23 | 9 | 6 | 8 | 28 | 34 | 66 | 57 | 9 | 80 |
| Plymouth | 46 | 11 | 6 | 6 | 39 | 24 | 6 | 8 | 9 | 24 | 28 | 63 | 52 | 11 | 65 |
| Luton | 46 | 8 | 8 | 7 | 32 | 28 | 9 | 6 | 8 | 35 | 34 | 67 | 62 | 5 | 65 |
| Swindon | 46 | 10 | 5 | 8 | 34 | 27 | 6 | 7 | 10 | 25 | 36 | 59 | 63 | -4 | 60 |
| Peterborough | 46 | 8 | 7 | 8 | 25 | 20 | 6 | 9 | 8 | 26 | 34 | 51 | 54 | -3 | 58 |
| Colchester | 46 | 8 | 7 | 8 | 24 | 24 | 6 | 9 | 8 | 28 | 32 | 52 | 56 | -4 | 58 |
| Blackpool | 46 | 10 | 8 | 5 | 35 | 25 | 5 | 5 | 13 | 21 | 39 | 56 | 64 | -8 | 58 |
| Stockport | 46 | 8 | 8 | 7 | 39 | 38 | 7 | 2 | 14 | 26 | 32 | 65 | 70 | -5 | 55 |
| Notts County | 46 | 10 | 7 | 6 | 37 | 32 | 3 | 9 | 11 | 25 | 38 | 62 | 70 | -8 | 55 |
| Brentford | 46 | 8 | 8 | 7 | 28 | 21 | 6 | 4 | 13 | 19 | 35 | 47 | 56 | -9 | 54 |
| Port Vale | 46 | 9 | 5 | 9 | 34 | 31 | 5 | 6 | 12 | 20 | 39 | 54 | 70 | -16 | 53 |
| Wycombe | 46 | 8 | 7 | 8 | 39 | 38 | 5 | 6 | 12 | 20 | 28 | 59 | 66 | -7 | 52 |
| Barnsley | 46 | 7 | 8 | 8 | 27 | 31 | 6 | 5 | 12 | 24 | 33 | 51 | 64 | -13 | 52 |
| Chesterfield | 46 | 11 | 4 | 8 | 29 | 28 | 3 | 4 | 16 | 14 | 45 | 43 | 73 | -30 | 50 |
| Cheltenham | 46 | 6 | 9 | 8 | 26 | 31 | 4 | 9 | 10 | 27 | 37 | 53 | 68 | -15 | 48 |
| Huddersfield | 46 | 7 | 9 | 7 | 27 | 24 | 4 | 3 | 16 | 12 | 37 | 39 | 61 | -22 | 45 |
| Mansfield | 46 | 9 | 2 | 12 | 38 | 45 | 3 | 6 | 14 | 28 | 52 | 66 | 97 | -31 | 44 |
| Northampton | 46 | 7 | 4 | 12 | 23 | 31 | 3 | 5 | 15 | 17 | 48 | 40 | 79 | -39 | 39 |

## PLAYER DISCIPLINARY RECORD

GMB
11

| | |
|---|---|
| League Yellow | 7 |
| League Red | 1 |
| TOTAL | 8 |

**1 Martin Rowlands - Brentford**

| Cards Average<br>Average number of minutes between a card being shown of either colour | 151 |
|---|---|

| | PLAYER | | LY | LR | TOT | AVE |
|---|---|---|---|---|---|---|
| 2 | Ward | Barnsley | 8 | 2 | 10 | 190 |
| 3 | Bayliss | Luton | 4 | 0 | 4 | 197 |
| 4 | White, A | Mansfield | 8 | 0 | 8 | 197 |
| 5 | Appleby | Oldham | 4 | 1 | 5 | 198 |
| 6 | Warren | Colchester | 6 | 2 | 8 | 204 |
| 7 | Burt | Chesterfield | 5 | 0 | 5 | 206 |
| 8 | Lee | Peterborough | 5 | 1 | 6 | 211 |
| 9 | Willis | Swindon | 4 | 0 | 4 | 213 |
| 10 | Baudet | Oldham | 6 | 2 | 8 | 214 |
| 11 | Nicholls | Luton | 13 | 1 | 14 | 218 |
| 12 | Richardson | Blackpool | 8 | 0 | 8 | 219 |
| 13 | Stamp | Northampton | 4 | 1 | 5 | 219 |
| 14 | Burton | Peterborough | 11 | 0 | 11 | 223 |
| 15 | Worthington | Huddersfield | 4 | 0 | 4 | 225 |
| 16 | Palmer | Stockport | 7 | 1 | 8 | 226 |
| 17 | White | Colchester | 14 | 2 | 16 | 227 |
| 18 | McGlinchey | Plymouth | 4 | 1 | 5 | 227 |
| 19 | Morgan | Barnsley | 14 | 0 | 14 | 228 |
| 20 | Goodwin | Stockport | 10 | 0 | 10 | 230 |

## PREMIERSHIP CHART-TOPPING POINT EARNERS

| | PLAYER | TEAM | GAMES | POINTS | AVE |
|---|---|---|---|---|---|
| 2 | Day | QPR | 12 | 29 | 2.42 |
| 3 | Tierney | Crewe | 14 | 33 | 2.36 |
| 4 | Roberts | Wigan | 22 | 52 | 2.36 |
| 5 | Padula | QPR | 15 | 35 | 2.33 |
| 6 | Teale | Wigan | 22 | 51 | 2.32 |
| 7 | Jarrett | Wigan | 22 | 51 | 2.32 |
| 8 | Ellington | Wigan | 40 | 90 | 2.25 |
| 9 | Dinning | Wigan | 33 | 74 | 2.24 |
| 10 | Jackson | Wigan | 42 | 94 | 2.24 |
| 11 | Green | Wigan | 13 | 29 | 2.23 |
| 12 | Eaden | Wigan | 37 | 81 | 2.19 |
| 13 | Low | Oldham | 17 | 37 | 2.18 |
| 14 | Filan | Wigan | 46 | 100 | 2.17 |
| 15 | Corazzin | Oldham | 19 | 41 | 2.16 |
| 16 | De Vos | Wigan | 43 | 93 | 2.16 |
| 17 | Loran | Tranmere | 14 | 30 | 2.14 |
| 18 | Roberts | Bristol City | 26 | 55 | 2.12 |
| 19 | Appleby | Oldham | 11 | 23 | 2.09 |
| 20 | Eyre, J | Oldham | 22 | 46 | 2.09 |

JJB

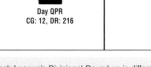

**1 Peter Kennedy - Wigan**

| | |
|---|---|
| Counting Games<br>League games where he played at least 70 minutes | 20 |
| Total League Points<br>Taken in Counting Games | 51 |
| Average League Points<br>Taken in Counting Games | 2.55 |

Nationwide

## TEAM OF THE SEASON

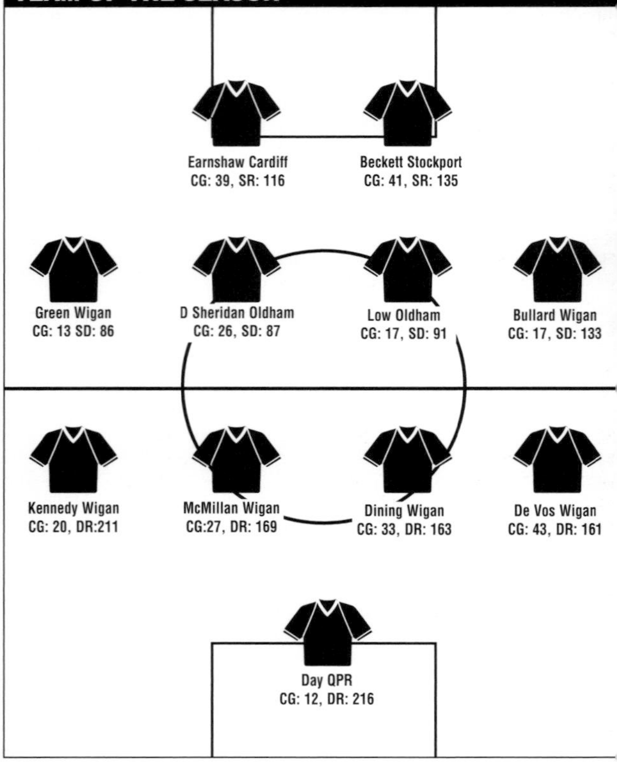
Earnshaw Cardiff
CG: 39, SR: 116
Beckett Stockport
CG: 41, SR: 135
Green Wigan
CG: 13 SD: 86
D Sheridan Oldham
CG: 26, SD: 87
Low Oldham
CG: 17, SD: 91
Bullard Wigan
CG: 17, SD: 133
Kennedy Wigan
CG: 20, DR:211
McMillan Wigan
CG:27, DR: 169
Dining Wigan
CG: 33, DR: 163
De Vos Wigan
CG: 43, DR: 161
Day QPR
CG: 12, DR: 216

**The Team of the Season** in each League's Divisional Round-up is different to those at club level. It doesn't just mirror the Chart-topping performances but highlights Keepers, Defenders, Midfield players and Forwards who are dramatically out-performing their team-mates. We compare their key rating to the club average see below: -

- **The Division Team's goalkeeper** has to be the player with the highest Defensive Rating as he often plays most or all the games in a league season.
- **The Division Team's defenders** are also tested by Defensive Rating but against their co-defender's Ratings. We weight it to take into account the fact that differences can fluctuate wildly at the bottom of a division.
- **The Division Team's midfield** all have good Scoring Differences compared to the average Ratings of their colleagues. In all cases these players must have played at least a minimum of Counting Games.
- **The Divisional Team strikeforce** is made up of the two players who have the biggest gap in Strike Rate between themselves and their next forward. These are weighted again, as lower sides may not even have a second charting forward.

## NATIONWIDE FOOTBALL DIVISION THREE CHAMPIONS

# RUSHDEN & DIAMONDS

Final Position: **1st**

NICKNAME: THE DIAMONDS

| | | | | | | |
|---|---|---|---|---|---|---|
| 1 | div3 | Swansea | A | D | 2-2 | Lowe 13; Underwood 90 |
| 2 | div3 | Torquay | H | W | 3-0 | Darby 5; Wardley 56; Hall 74 |
| 3 | div3 | Kidderminster | H | W | 3-1 | Flynn 14 og; Gray 64 pen; Darby 80 |
| 4 | div3 | Shrewsbury | A | D | 1-1 | Darby 72 |
| 5 | div3 | Scunthorpe | H | W | 2-0 | Lowe 9; Burgess 50 |
| 6 | div3 | Cambridge | A | L | 1-4 | Wardley 83 |
| 7 | div3 | Southend | H | W | 3-0 | Gray 9 pen,33; Hall 83 |
| 8 | wcr1 | Millwall | H | W | 5-4* | (*on penalties) |
| 9 | div3 | York | A | D | 0-0 | |
| 10 | div3 | Bournemouth | A | L | 1-3 | Dempster 31 |
| 11 | div3 | Wrexham | H | D | 2-2 | Hall 42,79 |
| 12 | div3 | Hartlepool | A | W | 2-1 | Peters 48; Hall 83 |
| 13 | wcr2 | Coventry | A | L | 0-8 | |
| 14 | div3 | Leyton Orient | H | W | 2-0 | Darby 79,86 |
| 15 | div3 | Exeter | A | D | 1-1 | Darby 28 |
| 16 | div3 | Bury | H | L | 0-1 | |
| 17 | div3 | Hull City | A | D | 1-1 | Gray 38 |
| 18 | div3 | Boston | H | W | 1-0 | Lowe 10 |
| 19 | div3 | Rochdale | A | W | 1-0 | Darby 64 |
| 20 | div3 | Darlington | H | W | 2-0 | Lowe 79; Clarke, M 87 og |
| 21 | facr1 | Kidderminster | A | D | 2-2 | Duffy 45,71 |
| 22 | div3 | Lincoln | A | W | 2-1 | Bell 27; Wardley 56 |
| 23 | facr1r | Kidderminster | H | W | 2-1 | Duffy 36; Wardley 67 |
| 24 | div3 | Bristol Rovers | H | W | 2-1 | Lowe 22; Hall 72 |
| 25 | facr2 | Exeter | A | L | 1-3 | Lowe 71 |
| 26 | div3 | Macclesfield | A | W | 1-0 | Lowe 81 |
| 27 | div3 | Carlisle | H | D | 1-1 | Lowe 16 |
| 28 | div3 | Scunthorpe | A | D | 0-0 | |
| 29 | div3 | Oxford | H | L | 0-2 | |
| 30 | div3 | Shrewsbury | H | W | 5-1 | Darby 9,39; Gray 41; Lowe 61; Hall 70 |
| 31 | div3 | Torquay | A | D | 1-1 | Darby 57 |
| 32 | div3 | Kidderminster | A | W | 2-0 | Hall 15,69 |
| 33 | div3 | Cambridge | H | W | 4-1 | Gray 39; Bell 59; Hall 85,90 |
| 34 | div3 | Oxford | A | L | 0-3 | |
| 35 | div3 | Swansea | H | D | 1-1 | Hall 71 |
| 36 | div3 | Darlington | A | D | 2-2 | Burgess 56 pen; Hall 84 |
| 37 | div3 | Southend | A | L | 1-2 | Hunter 38 |
| 38 | div3 | York | H | W | 2-1 | Wardley 45; Brass 75 og |
| 39 | div3 | Bournemouth | H | W | 2-1 | Darby 20; Lowe 84 pen |
| 40 | div3 | Wrexham | A | L | 0-3 | |
| 41 | div3 | Hull City | H | W | 4-2 | Delaney 2 og; Hall 68; Lowe 87; Wardley 90 |
| 42 | div3 | Bury | A | W | 1-0 | Darby 67 |
| 43 | div3 | Boston | A | D | 1-1 | Darby 79 |
| 44 | div3 | Rochdale | H | D | 3-3 | Hall 49; Lowe 65,73 |
| 45 | div3 | Exeter | H | W | 1-0 | Darby 58 |
| 46 | div3 | Bristol Rovers | A | W | 2-1 | Lowe 37,68 |
| 47 | div3 | Lincoln | H | W | 1-0 | Lowe 18 |
| 48 | div3 | Carlisle | A | W | 2-1 | Wardley 55; Edwards 63 |
| 49 | div3 | Macclesfield | H | W | 3-0 | Holdsworth, Dean 43,70; Bell 66 |
| 50 | div3 | Leyton Orient | A | D | 0-0 | |
| 51 | div3 | Hartlepool | H | D | 1-1 | Hall 29 |

■ Home □ Away ▨ Neutral

## ATTENDANCES

HOME GROUND: NENE PARK CAPACITY: 6441 AVERAGE LEAGUE AT HOME: 4223

| | | | | | | | | | | | |
|---|---|---|---|---|---|---|---|---|---|---|---|
| 17 | Hull City | 10659 | 29 | Oxford | 4891 | 28 | Scunthorpe | 4096 | 23 | Kidderminster | 3391 |
| 13 | Coventry | 8570 | 5 | Scunthorpe | 4849 | 11 | Wrexham | 4090 | 3 | Kidderminster | 3329 |
| 46 | Bristol Rovers | 6736 | 41 | Hull City | 4713 | 18 | Boston | 4079 | 22 | Lincoln | 3198 |
| 34 | Oxford | 6508 | 6 | Cambridge | 4598 | 35 | Swansea | 4046 | 21 | Kidderminster | 3079 |
| 37 | Southend | 6453 | 10 | Bournemouth | 4527 | 24 | Bristol Rovers | 3960 | 15 | Exeter | 2884 |
| 1 | Swansea | 6327 | 49 | Macclesfield | 4494 | 16 | Bury | 3925 | 36 | Darlington | 2742 |
| 51 | Hartlepool | 6291 | 38 | York | 4463 | 20 | Darlington | 3911 | 8 | Millwall | 2731 |
| 12 | Hartlepool | 5502 | 14 | Leyton Orient | 4381 | 2 | Torquay | 3602 | 31 | Torquay | 2651 |
| 48 | Carlisle | 5468 | 27 | Carlisle | 4355 | 4 | Shrewsbury | 3548 | 19 | Rochdale | 2628 |
| 33 | Cambridge | 5206 | 39 | Bournemouth | 4353 | 43 | Boston | 3504 | 42 | Bury | 2291 |
| 50 | Leyton Orient | 5180 | 7 | Southend | 4176 | 44 | Rochdale | 3444 | 25 | Exeter | 2277 |
| 47 | Lincoln | 4962 | 30 | Shrewsbury | 4144 | 40 | Wrexham | 3441 | 26 | Macclesfield | 1839 |
| 45 | Exeter | 4921 | 9 | York | 4109 | 32 | Kidderminster | 3417 | | | |

## KEY PLAYER APPEARANCES

| | PLAYER | POS | AGE | APP | MINS ON | GOALS | CARDS(Y/R) | | HOME COUNTRY |
|---|---|---|---|---|---|---|---|---|---|
| 1 | Billy Turley | GK | 29 | 45 | 3977 | 0 | 0 | 0 | England |
| 2 | Paul Hall | ATT | 31 | 45 | 3941 | 16 | 2 | 0 | England |
| 3 | Paul Underwood | DEF | 29 | 40 | 3513 | 1 | 4 | 0 | England |
| 4 | Barry Hunter | DEF | 34 | 41 | 3483 | 1 | 11 | 2 | N Ireland |
| 5 | Onandi Lowe | ATT | 28 | 39 | 3397 | 15 | 12 | 0 | Jamaica |
| 6 | Stuart Wardley | MID | 28 | 40 | 3237 | 6 | 3 | 0 | England |
| 7 | Stuart Gray | DEF | 29 | 39 | 3013 | 6 | 4 | 0 | England |
| 8 | Marcus Bignot | DEF | 28 | 35 | 2870 | 0 | 6 | 0 | England |
| 9 | Duane Darby | ATT | 39 | 37 | 2835 | 14 | 5 | 0 | England |
| 10 | Mark Peters | DEF | 31 | 36 | 2223 | 1 | 1 | 0 | Wales |
| 11 | David Bell | MID | 19 | 36 | 2221 | 3 | 3 | 0 | England |
| 12 | Gary Mills | MID | 22 | 37 | 2040 | 0 | 7 | 0 | England |
| 13 | Andrew Burgess | MID | 21 | 29 | 1906 | 2 | 1 | 0 | England |
| 14 | John Dempster | DEF | 20 | 43 | 1086 | 1 | 1 | 0 | England |
| 15 | Andrew Edwards | DEF | 31 | 12 | 1021 | 1 | 3 | 0 | England |
| 16 | Tarkan Mustafa | MID | 29 | 16 | 912 | 0 | 1 | 0 | |
| 17 | Andy Sambrook | MID | 23 | 29 | 743 | 0 | 2 | 1 | England |
| 18 | Gary Setchell | MID | 28 | 16 | 666 | 0 | 2 | 0 | England |

## KEY PLAYERS - GOALSCORERS

**1 Duane Darby**

| | | | |
|---|---|---|---|
| Goals in the League | 14 | Player Strike Rate<br>Average number of minutes between League goals scored by player | 203 |
| Contribution to Attacking Power<br>Average number of minutes between League team goals while on pitch | 57 | Club Strike Rate<br>Average number of minutes between League goals scored by club | 57 |

| | PLAYER | LGE GOALS | POWER | STRIKE RATE |
|---|---|---|---|---|
| 2 | Onandi Lowe | 15 | 57 | 226 mins |
| 3 | Paul Hall | 16 | 57 | 246 mins |
| 4 | Stuart Gray | 6 | 54 | 502 mins |
| 5 | Stuart Wardley | 6 | 54 | 540 mins |

## KEY PLAYERS - MIDFIELDERS

**1 Stuart Wardley**

| | | | |
|---|---|---|---|
| Goals in the League | 6 | Contribution to Attacking Power<br>Average number of minutes between League team goals while on pitch | 55 |
| Defensive Rating<br>Average number of mins between League goals conceded while he was on the pitch | 90 | Scoring Difference<br>Defensive Rating minus Contribution to Attacking Power | 35 |

| | PLAYER | LGE GOALS | DEF RATE | POWER | SCORE DIFF |
|---|---|---|---|---|---|
| 2 | David Bell | 3 | 93 | 58 | 35 mins |
| 3 | Gary Mills | 0 | 93 | 62 | 31 mins |
| 4 | Andrew Burgess | 2 | 71 | 54 | 17 mins |
| 5 | Tarkan Mustafa | 0 | 76 | 65 | 11 mins |

## KEY PLAYERS - DEFENDERS

**1 Marcus Bignot**

| | | | |
|---|---|---|---|
| Goals Conceded when he was on pitch | 29 | Clean Sheets<br>In games when he played at least 70 minutes | 11 |
| Defensive Rating<br>Ave number of mins between League goals conceded while on the pitch | 99 | Club Defensive Rating<br>Average number of mins between League goals conceded by the club this season. | 88 |

| | PLAYER | CON LGE | CLN SHEETS | DEF RATE |
|---|---|---|---|---|
| 2 | Mark Peters | 23 | 9 | 97 mins |
| 3 | Stuart Gray | 32 | 12 | 94 mins |
| 4 | Andrew Edwards | 11 | 5 | 93 mins |
| 5 | John Dempster | 12 | 4 | 91 mins |

## KEY GOALKEEPER

**1 Billy Turley**

| | |
|---|---|
| Goals Conceded in the League | 46 |
| Defensive Rating<br>Ave number of mins between League goals conceded while on the pitch. | 86 |
| Counting Games<br>Games when he played at least 70 mins | 44 |
| Clean Sheets<br>In games when he played at least 70 mins | 15 |

## TEAM OF THE SEASON

| GOALKEEPER | GAMES | DEF RATE |
|---|---|---|
| Billy Turley | 44 | 86 |
| **DEFENDERS** | **GAMES** | **DEF RATE** |
| Marcus Bignot | 31 | 99 |
| Mark Peters | 23 | 97 |
| Stuart Gray | 32 | 94 |
| Andrew Edwards | 11 | 93 |
| **MIDFIELDERS** | **GAMES** | **SCORE DIFF** |
| David Bell | 23 | 35 |
| Stuart Wardley | 35 | 35 |
| Gary Mills | 21 | 31 |
| Andrew Burgess | 19 | 17 |
| **FORWARDS** | **GAMES** | **STRIKE RATE** |
| Duane Darby | 27 | 203 |
| Onandi Lowe | 36 | 226 |

# HARTLEPOOL

Final Position: **2nd**

NICKNAME: THE POOL

| | | | | | | |
|---|---|---|---|---|---|---|
| 1 | div3 | Carlisle | A | W | 3-1 | Tinkler 33,72; Humphreys 47 |
| 2 | div3 | Boston | H | W | 2-0 | Watson 53; Tinkler 76 pen |
| 3 | div3 | Macclesfield | H | L | 0-2 | |
| 4 | div3 | Torquay | A | D | 1-1 | Humphreys 47 |
| 5 | div3 | Hull City | H | W | 2-0 | Williams, E 31; Watson 63 |
| 6 | div3 | Oxford | A | W | 1-0 | Watson 38 |
| 7 | div3 | Swansea | A | D | 2-2 | Tinkler 14; Watson 44 |
| 8 | wcr1 | Tranmere | H | L | 1-2 | Williams, E 78 |
| 9 | div3 | Darlington | H | W | 4-1 | Williams, E 2,34; Humphreys 58; Tinkler 82 |
| 10 | div3 | Lincoln | H | W | 2-1 | Boyd 62; Williams, E 65 |
| 11 | div3 | Bury | A | D | 1-1 | Boyd 81 |
| 12 | div3 | Rushden & D | H | L | 1-2 | Boyd 30 |
| 13 | div3 | Shrewsbury | A | W | 1-0 | Williams, E 55 |
| 14 | div3 | Bournemouth | A | L | 1-2 | Williams, E 17 |
| 15 | div3 | Wrexham | H | W | 4-3 | Tinkler 13,41,51; Richardson 18 |
| 16 | div3 | Southend | A | W | 1-0 | Williams, E 1 |
| 17 | div3 | Bristol Rovers | H | W | 2-0 | Arnison 41; Williams, E 64 |
| 18 | div3 | York | H | D | 0-0 | |
| 19 | div3 | Exeter | A | W | 2-1 | Tinkler 63; Richardson 66 |
| 20 | facr1 | Southend | A | D | 1-1 | Barron 23 |
| 21 | div3 | Leyton Orient | A | W | 2-1 | Williams, E 26,72 |
| 22 | facr1r | Southend | H | L | 1-2 | Richardson 63 |
| 23 | div3 | Kidderminster | H | W | 2-1 | Humphreys 3; Tinkler 15 |
| 24 | div3 | Rochdale | A | L | 0-4 | |
| 25 | div3 | Scunthorpe | H | D | 2-2 | McCombe 45 og; Henderson 89 |
| 26 | div3 | Hull City | A | L | 0-2 | |
| 27 | div3 | Cambridge | H | W | 3-0 | Williams, E 45; Tinkler 83; Clarke 87 pen |
| 28 | div3 | Carlisle | H | W | 2-1 | Lee 50; Williams, E 80 |
| 29 | div3 | Boston | A | W | 1-0 | Clarke 70 |
| 30 | div3 | Oxford | H | W | 3-1 | Humphreys 24; Richardson 43,90 |
| 31 | div3 | Macclesfield | A | W | 1-0 | Williams, E 16 |
| 32 | div3 | Cambridge | A | D | 0-0 | |
| 33 | div3 | Torquay | H | W | 3-2 | Clarke 56,69; Richardson 79 |
| 34 | div3 | Exeter | H | W | 2-1 | Humphreys 79; Boyd 80 |
| 35 | div3 | York | A | D | 0-0 | |
| 36 | div3 | Swansea | H | W | 4-0 | Humphreys 11,40,69; Widdrington 72 |
| 37 | div3 | Darlington | A | D | 2-2 | Boyd 48 pen; Clarke 53 |
| 38 | div3 | Lincoln | A | L | 0-3 | |
| 39 | div3 | Bury | H | D | 0-0 | |
| 40 | div3 | Southend | H | W | 2-1 | Humphreys 36,49 |
| 41 | div3 | Wrexham | A | L | 0-2 | |
| 42 | div3 | Bristol Rovers | A | L | 0-1 | |
| 43 | div3 | Bournemouth | H | D | 0-0 | |
| 44 | div3 | Kidderminster | A | D | 2-2 | Clarke 63; Williams, E 90 |
| 45 | div3 | Leyton Orient | H | W | 4-1 | Tinkler 10,66 pen; Lee 61; Clarke 90 |
| 46 | div3 | Scunthorpe | A | L | 0-4 | |
| 47 | div3 | Rochdale | H | D | 2-2 | Widdrington 42,52 |
| 48 | div3 | Shrewsbury | H | W | 3-0 | Williams, E 36; Tinkler 45; Henderson 79 |
| 49 | div3 | Rushden & D | A | D | 1-1 | Westwood 90 |

■ Home □ Away □ Neutral

## ATTENDANCES

HOME GROUND: VICTORIA GROUND CAPACITY: 7629 AVERAGE LEAGUE AT HOME: 4943

| | | | | | | | | | | | |
|---|---|---|---|---|---|---|---|---|---|---|---|
| 26 | Hull City | 22319 | 48 | Shrewsbury | 5384 | 3 | Macclesfield | 4684 | 38 | Lincoln | 3409 |
| 1 | Carlisle | 10684 | 46 | Scunthorpe | 5280 | 41 | Wrexham | 4658 | 7 | Swansea | 3370 |
| 42 | Bristol Rovers | 6557 | 16 | Southend | 5168 | 32 | Cambridge | 4543 | 13 | Shrewsbury | 3142 |
| 9 | Darlington | 6360 | 28 | Carlisle | 5071 | 15 | Wrexham | 4506 | 29 | Boston | 3081 |
| 49 | Rushden & D | 6291 | 34 | Exeter | 5058 | 36 | Swansea | 4486 | 24 | Rochdale | 3059 |
| 14 | Bournemouth | 5998 | 30 | Oxford | 5049 | 23 | Kidderminster | 4296 | 44 | Kidderminster | 2900 |
| 35 | York | 5953 | 20 | Southend | 4984 | 10 | Lincoln | 4248 | 8 | Tranmere | 2778 |
| 37 | Darlington | 5832 | 33 | Torquay | 4975 | 5 | Hull City | 4236 | 19 | Exeter | 2778 |
| 18 | York | 5789 | 40 | Southend | 4868 | 25 | Scunthorpe | 4089 | 4 | Torquay | 2403 |
| 39 | Bury | 5734 | 2 | Boston | 4841 | 22 | Southend | 4080 | 31 | Macclesfield | 1576 |
| 43 | Bournemouth | 5625 | 27 | Cambridge | 4805 | 21 | Leyton Orient | 4009 | | | |
| 12 | Rushden & D | 5502 | 45 | Leyton Orient | 4795 | 17 | Bristol Rovers | 3889 | | | |
| 47 | Rochdale | 5408 | 6 | Oxford | 4768 | 11 | Bury | 3547 | | | |

## KEY PLAYER APPEARANCES

| | PLAYER | POS | AGE | APP | MINS ON | GOALS | CARDS(Y/R) | | HOME COUNTRY |
|---|---|---|---|---|---|---|---|---|---|
| 1 | Anthony Williams | GK | 25 | 46 | 4140 | 0 | 1 | 0 | Wales |
| 2 | Chris Westwood | DEF | 26 | 46 | 4140 | 1 | 3 | 0 | England |
| 3 | Richie Humphreys | MID | 25 | 46 | 4124 | 11 | 3 | 0 | England |
| 4 | Graeme Lee | MID | 25 | 45 | 4050 | 2 | 10 | 0 | England |
| 5 | Mark Tinkler | ATT | 28 | 45 | 4045 | 14 | 8 | 0 | England |
| 6 | Darrell Clarke | DEF | 25 | 45 | 3931 | 7 | 6 | 0 | England |
| 7 | Eifion Williams, E | ATT | 27 | 45 | 3605 | 15 | 5 | 0 | Wales |
| 8 | Michael Barron | DEF | 28 | 43 | 3573 | 0 | 7 | 1 | England |
| 9 | Mark Robinson | DEF | 21 | 39 | 3347 | 0 | 1 | 0 | England |
| 10 | Tommy Widdrington | MID | 31 | 41 | 2378 | 3 | 2 | 0 | England |
| 11 | Marcus Richardson | ATT | 25 | 27 | 1665 | 5 | 2 | 0 | England |
| 12 | Paul Smith | MID | 27 | 29 | 1391 | 0 | 0 | 0 | England |
| 13 | Adam Boyd | ATT | 21 | 30 | 1085 | 5 | 0 | 0 | England |
| 14 | Gordon Watson | ATT | 32 | 18 | 1024 | 4 | 2 | 0 | England |
| 15 | Paul Arnison | DEF | 25 | 38 | 931 | 1 | 0 | 0 | England |
| 16 | Kevin Henderson | ATT | 29 | 40 | 819 | 2 | 1 | 0 | England |
| 17 | Brian Barry-Murphy | DEF | 24 | 8 | 630 | 0 | 0 | 0 | Rep of Ireland |
| 18 | Jonathan Bass | DEF | 27 | 9 | 212 | 0 | 1 | 0 | England |

## KEY PLAYERS - GOALSCORERS

**1 Eifion Williams**

| | | | |
|---|---|---|---|
| Goals in the League | 15 | Player Strike Rate<br>Average number of minutes between League goals scored by player | 240 |
| Contribution to Attacking Power<br>Average number of minutes between League team goals while on pitch | 58 | Club Strike Rate<br>Average number of minutes between League goals scored by club | 58 |

| | PLAYER | LGE GOALS | POWER | STRIKE RATE |
|---|---|---|---|---|
| 2 | Mark Tinkler | 14 | 59 | 289 mins |
| 3 | Marcus Richardson | 5 | 59 | 333 mins |
| 4 | Richie Humphreys | 11 | 58 | 375 mins |
| 5 | Darrell Clarke | 7 | 56 | 562 mins |

## KEY PLAYERS - MIDFIELDERS

**1 Paul Smith**

| | | | |
|---|---|---|---|
| Goals in the League | 0 | Contribution to Attacking Power<br>Average number of minutes between League team goals while on pitch | 58 |
| Defensive Rating<br>Average number of mins between League goals conceded while he was on the pitch | 93 | Scoring Difference<br>Defensive Rating minus Contribution to Attacking Power | 35 |

| | PLAYER | LGE GOALS | DEF RATE | POWER | SCORE DIFF |
|---|---|---|---|---|---|
| 2 | Richie Humphreys | 11 | 81 | 58 | 23 mins |
| 3 | Graeme Lee | 2 | 81 | 60 | 21 mins |
| 4 | Tommy Widdrington | 3 | 72 | 61 | 11 mins |

## KEY PLAYERS - DEFENDERS

**1 Mark Robinson**

| | | | |
|---|---|---|---|
| Goals Conceded when he was on pitch | 36 | Clean Sheets<br>In games when he played at least 70 minutes | 15 |
| Defensive Rating<br>Ave number of mins between League goals conceded while on the pitch | 93 | Club Defensive Rating<br>Average number of mins between League goals conceded by the club this season. | 81 |

| | PLAYER | CON LGE | CLN SHEETS | DEF RATE |
|---|---|---|---|---|
| 2 | Darrell Clarke | 47 | 15 | 84 mins |
| 3 | Michael Barron | 43 | 12 | 83 mins |
| 4 | Chris Westwood | 51 | 16 | 81 mins |

## KEY GOALKEEPER

**1 Anthony Williams**

| | |
|---|---|
| Goals Conceded in the League | 51 |
| Defensive Rating<br>Ave number of mins between League goals conceded while on the pitch. | 81 |
| Counting Games<br>Games when he played at least 70 mins | 46 |
| Clean Sheets<br>In games when he played at least 70 mins | 16 |

## TEAM OF THE SEASON

| GOALKEEPER | GAMES | DEF RATE |
|---|---|---|
| Anthony Williams | 46 | 81 |
| **DEFENDERS** | **GAMES** | **DEF RATE** |
| Mark Robinson | 37 | 93 |
| Darrell Clarke | 43 | 84 |
| Michael Barron | 38 | 83 |
| Chris Westwood | 46 | 81 |
| **MIDFIELDERS** | **GAMES** | **SCORE DIFF** |
| Paul Smith | 14 | 35 |
| Richie Humphreys | 46 | 23 |
| Graeme Lee | 45 | 21 |
| Tommy Widdrington | 24 | 11 |
| **FORWARDS** | **GAMES** | **STRIKE RATE** |
| Eifion Williams | 38 | 240 |
| Mark Tinkler | 45 | 289 |

# WREXHAM

Final Position: **3rd**

NICKNAME: THE ROBINS

| | | | | | | |
|---|---|---|---|---|---|---|
| 1 | div3 | Scunthorpe | A | D | 1-1 | Morrell 65 |
| 2 | div3 | Oxford | H | W | 1-0 | Sam 87 |
| 3 | div3 | Boston | H | D | 1-1 | Trundle 27 |
| 4 | div3 | Macclesfield | A | W | 1-0 | Sam 68 |
| 5 | div3 | Rochdale | H | L | 2-5 | Thomas 13; Morrell 37 |
| 6 | div3 | Torquay | A | L | 1-2 | Morrell 14 pen |
| 7 | wcr1 | Bradford | H | W | 2-1 | Morrell 89; Edwards, C 90 |
| 8 | div3 | Swansea | H | W | 4-0 | Morrell 9,12; Sam 29; Edwards, C 55 |
| 9 | div3 | Exeter | H | W | 4-0 | Morrell 37,39,80; Ferguson 47 |
| 10 | div3 | Rushden & D | A | D | 2-2 | Edwards, C 8; Morrell 65 |
| 11 | div3 | Darlington | A | W | 1-0 | Morrell 34 |
| 12 | div3 | Bury | H | D | 2-2 | Morrell 22,24 pen |
| 13 | wcr2 | Everton | H | L | 0-3 | |
| 14 | div3 | Cambridge | A | D | 2-2 | Whitley 26; Morgan 90 |
| 15 | div3 | Leyton Orient | H | D | 0-0 | |
| 16 | div3 | Hartlepool | A | L | 3-4 | Jones, L 20; Trundle 68; Sam 86 pen |
| 17 | div3 | Lincoln | H | L | 0-2 | |
| 18 | div3 | York | A | D | 1-1 | Roberts 8 |
| 19 | div3 | Southend | A | W | 1-0 | Thomas 41 |
| 20 | div3 | Bournemouth | H | W | 3-2 | Trundle 5; Morrell 69; Edwards, P 86 |
| 21 | facr1 | Darlington | H | L | 0-2 | |
| 22 | div3 | Bristol Rovers | A | W | 3-0 | Morrell 18,43; Trundle 75 |
| 23 | div3 | Hull City | H | D | 0-0 | |
| 24 | div3 | Carlisle | A | W | 2-1 | Jones, L 33; Sam 87 |
| 25 | div3 | Kidderminster | H | L | 0-2 | |
| 26 | div3 | Rochdale | A | D | 2-2 | Morrell 23,75 |
| 27 | div3 | Macclesfield | H | L | 1-3 | Trundle 29 |
| 28 | div3 | Torquay | H | W | 2-1 | Morrell 21; Edwards, C 76 |
| 29 | div3 | Scunthorpe | H | W | 2-1 | Morrell 39 pen; Trundle 80 |
| 30 | div3 | Oxford | A | W | 2-0 | Morrell 63; Lawrence 74 |
| 31 | div3 | Bournemouth | A | L | 0-2 | |
| 32 | div3 | Southend | H | W | 3-0 | Edwards, C 15; Morrell 50; Edwards, P 75 |
| 33 | div3 | Darlington | H | D | 0-0 | |
| 34 | div3 | Swansea | A | D | 0-0 | |
| 35 | div3 | Exeter | A | L | 0-1 | |
| 36 | div3 | Rushden & D | H | W | 3-0 | Edwards, C 15; Morrell 62,79 |
| 37 | div3 | Shrewsbury | H | D | 3-3 | Trundle 31; Morrell 58; Edwards, P 72 |
| 38 | div3 | Lincoln | A | D | 1-1 | Morrell 58 |
| 39 | div3 | Hartlepool | H | W | 2-0 | Green 3,66 |
| 40 | div3 | York | H | D | 1-1 | Morrell 89 |
| 41 | div3 | Boston | A | D | 3-3 | Trundle 12,76; Carey 64 |
| 42 | div3 | Hull City | A | W | 2-1 | Morrell 67 pen,80 |
| 43 | div3 | Shrewsbury | A | W | 2-1 | Morrell 24; Jones, L 90 |
| 44 | div3 | Bristol Rovers | H | W | 3-2 | Green 23; Morrell 43 pen; Edwards, C 88 |
| 45 | div3 | Kidderminster | A | W | 2-0 | Trundle 37,64 |
| 46 | div3 | Carlisle | H | W | 6-1 | Morrell 22 pen,32,85; Carey 39,54; Edwards, C 89 |
| 47 | div3 | Cambridge | H | W | 5-0 | Barrett 16; Carey 20; Roberts 23; Edwards, P 60; Jones, L 62 |
| 48 | div3 | Leyton Orient | A | W | 1-0 | Morrell 25 pen |
| 49 | div3 | Bury | A | W | 3-0 | Edwards, C 7; Swailes 57 og; Ferguson 61 |

■ Home □ Away ▨ Neutral

## ATTENDANCES

HOME GROUND: RACECOURSE GROUND CAPACITY: 15000 AVERAGE LEAGUE AT HOME: 4265

| | | | | | | | | | | | |
|---|---|---|---|---|---|---|---|---|---|---|---|
| 42 | Hull City | 15002 | 39 | Hartlepool | 4658 | 19 | Southend | 3727 | 20 | Bournemouth | 3105 |
| 13 | Everton | 13420 | 16 | Hartlepool | 4506 | 26 | Rochdale | 3727 | 28 | Torquay | 3006 |
| 47 | Cambridge | 9960 | 24 | Carlisle | 4480 | 45 | Kidderminster | 3689 | 18 | York | 2970 |
| 37 | Shrewsbury | 7024 | 40 | York | 4425 | 2 | Oxford | 3591 | 9 | Exeter | 2968 |
| 46 | Carlisle | 6746 | 23 | Hull City | 4412 | 8 | Swansea | 3555 | 4 | Macclesfield | 2592 |
| 34 | Swansea | 6463 | 5 | Rochdale | 4340 | 15 | Leyton Orient | 3495 | 11 | Darlington | 2573 |
| 22 | Bristol Rovers | 6328 | 10 | Rushden & D | 4090 | 27 | Macclesfield | 3445 | 35 | Exeter | 2537 |
| 14 | Cambridge | 6044 | 33 | Darlington | 4079 | 21 | Darlington | 3442 | 6 | Torquay | 2283 |
| 30 | Oxford | 5532 | 12 | Bury | 3949 | 36 | Rushden & D | 3441 | 7 | Bradford | 2232 |
| 43 | Shrewsbury | 5451 | 38 | Lincoln | 3916 | 17 | Lincoln | 3312 | 41 | Boston | 1919 |
| 31 | Bournemouth | 5445 | 1 | Scunthorpe | 3879 | 3 | Boston | 3293 | | | |
| 44 | Bristol Rovers | 5330 | 48 | Leyton Orient | 3766 | 29 | Scunthorpe | 3129 | | | |
| 49 | Bury | 5186 | 25 | Kidderminster | 3734 | 32 | Southend | 3109 | | | |

## KEY PLAYER APPEARANCES

| | PLAYER | POS | AGE | APP | MINS ON | GOALS | CARDS(Y/R) | | HOME COUNTRY |
|---|---|---|---|---|---|---|---|---|---|
| 1 | Andy Morrell | ATT | 28 | 45 | 3962 | 34 | 3 | 0 | England |
| 2 | Carlos Edwards, C | MID | 24 | 44 | 3892 | 8 | 1 | 1 | Trinidad & Tobago |
| 3 | Jim Whitley | MID | 28 | 44 | 3884 | 1 | 4 | 0 | England |
| 4 | Darren Ferguson | MID | 31 | 41 | 3564 | 2 | 7 | 1 | Scotland |
| 5 | Stephen Roberts | MID | 23 | 39 | 3280 | 2 | 3 | 0 | Wales |
| 6 | Lee Trundle | ATT | 23 | 44 | 2964 | 10 | 3 | 0 | |
| 7 | Andy Dibble | GK | 38 | 34 | 2910 | 0 | 0 | 0 | Wales |
| 8 | Paul Edwards | MID | 23 | 42 | 2785 | 4 | 6 | 0 | England |
| 9 | Brian Carey | DEF | 35 | 35 | 2701 | 4 | 4 | 0 | Rep or Ireland |
| 10 | Dennis Lawrence | DEF | 29 | 39 | 2685 | 1 | 4 | 0 | Trinidad & Tobago |
| 11 | Shaun Pejic | DEF | 20 | 36 | 2034 | 0 | 0 | 0 | England |
| 12 | Paul Barrett | MID | 25 | 35 | 1935 | 1 | 0 | 0 | England |
| 13 | Stephen Thomas | MID | 24 | 32 | 1554 | 2 | 4 | 0 | England |
| 14 | Dan Bennett | DEF | 25 | 21 | 1440 | 0 | 1 | 0 | England |
| 15 | Shaun Holmes | DEF | 22 | 45 | 1339 | 0 | 4 | 0 | N Ireland |
| 16 | Scott Green | MID | 33 | 16 | 1120 | 3 | 3 | 0 | England |
| 17 | Lee Jones | ATT | 30 | 32 | 958 | 4 | 1 | 0 | Wales |
| 18 | Hector Sam | ATT | 25 | 28 | 864 | 5 | 2 | 0 | Trinidad & Tobago |

## KEY PLAYERS - GOALSCORERS

**1 Andy Morrell**

| | |
|---|---|
| Goals in the League | 34 |
| Contribution to Attacking Power<br>Average number of minutes between League team goals while on pitch | 48 |
| Player Strike Rate<br>Average number of minutes between League goals scored by player | 117 |
| Club Strike Rate<br>Average number of minutes between League goals scored by club | 49 |

| | PLAYER | LGE GOALS | POWER | STRIKE RATE |
|---|---|---|---|---|
| 2 | Lee Trundle | 10 | 47 | 296 mins |
| 3 | Carlos Edwards | 8 | 48 | 487 mins |
| 4 | Brian Carey | 4 | 46 | 675 mins |
| 5 | Paul Edwards | 4 | 47 | 696 mins |

## KEY PLAYERS - MIDFIELDERS

**1 Scott Green**

| | |
|---|---|
| Goals in the League | 3 |
| Defensive Rating<br>Average number of mins between League goals conceded while he was on the pitch | 112 |
| Contribution to Attacking Power<br>Average number of minutes between League team goals while on pitch | 45 |
| Scoring Difference<br>Defensive Rating minus Contribution to Attacking Power | 67 |

| | PLAYER | LGE GOALS | DEF RATE | POWER | SCORE DIFF |
|---|---|---|---|---|---|
| 2 | Paul Edwards | 4 | 93 | 47 | 46 mins |
| 3 | Stephen Roberts | 2 | 89 | 48 | 41 mins |
| 4 | Carlos Edwards | 8 | 86 | 48 | 38 mins |
| 5 | Paul Barrett | 1 | 84 | 48 | 36 mins |

## KEY PLAYERS - DEFENDERS

**1 Dennis Lawrence**

| | |
|---|---|
| Goals Conceded when he was on pitch | 28 |
| Defensive Rating<br>Ave number of mins between League goals conceded while on the pitch | 96 |
| Clean Sheets<br>In games when he played at least 70 minutes | 11 |
| Club Defensive Rating<br>Average number of mins between League goals conceded by the club this season. | 83 |

| | PLAYER | CON LGE | CLN SHEETS | DEF RATE |
|---|---|---|---|---|
| 2 | Brian Carey | 29 | 11 | 93 mins |
| 3 | Dan Bennett | 19 | 7 | 76 mins |
| 4 | Shaun Pejic | 33 | 7 | 62 mins |

## KEY GOALKEEPER

**1 Andy Dibble**

| | |
|---|---|
| Goals Conceded in the League | 35 |
| Defensive Rating<br>Ave number of mins between League goals conceded while on the pitch. | 83 |
| Counting Games<br>Games when he played at least 70 mins | 32 |
| Clean Sheets<br>In games when he played at least 70 mins | 13 |

## TEAM OF THE SEASON

| GOALKEEPER | GAMES | DEF RATE |
|---|---|---|
| Andy Dibble | 32 | 83 |
| **DEFENDERS** | **GAMES** | **DEF RATE** |
| Dennis Lawrence | 29 | 96 |
| Brian Carey | 28 | 93 |
| Dan Bennett | 16 | 76 |
| Shaun Pejic | 20 | 62 |
| **MIDFIELDERS** | **GAMES** | **SCORE DIFF** |
| Scott Green | 10 | 67 |
| Paul Edwards | 27 | 46 |
| Stephen Roberts | 36 | 41 |
| Carlos Edwards | 43 | 38 |
| **FORWARDS** | **GAMES** | **STRIKE RATE** |
| Andy Morrell | 43 | 117 |
| Lee Trundle | 30 | 296 |

# BOURNEMOUTH

Final Position: **4th**

NICKNAME: THE CHERRIES

| | | | | | | |
|---|---|---|---|---|---|---|
| 1 | div3 | Boston | A | D | 2-2 | Maher 9; Stock 54 |
| 2 | div3 | Kidderminster | H | D | 0-0 | |
| 3 | div3 | Cambridge | H | D | 1-1 | Feeney 64 |
| 4 | div3 | Swansea | A | L | 0-2 | |
| 5 | div3 | Oxford | H | D | 1-1 | Holmes 41 |
| 6 | div3 | Macclesfield | A | W | 1-0 | Connell 39 |
| 7 | div3 | Exeter | A | W | 3-1 | Connell 35; Elliott 38 pen; O'Connor 73 |
| 8 | wcr1 | Brentford | H | L | 2-4* | Browning 2; Connell 15; Thomas 39 (*on penalties) |
| 9 | div3 | Bury | H | L | 1-2 | O'Connor 70 |
| 10 | div3 | Rushden & D | H | W | 3-1 | Purches 22; Maher 58; Connell 85 |
| 11 | div3 | Darlington | A | D | 2-2 | Holmes 27; Connell 82 |
| 12 | div3 | Carlisle | H | W | 3-1 | Tindall 61; Connell 76 pen; Stock 86 |
| 13 | div3 | Lincoln | A | W | 2-1 | Purches 13; Connell 64 |
| 14 | div3 | Hartlepool | H | W | 2-1 | Elliott 61; Widdrington 84 og |
| 15 | div3 | Leyton Orient | A | D | 0-0 | |
| 16 | div3 | York | H | W | 1-0 | Fletcher, C 78 |
| 17 | div3 | Torquay | A | L | 0-4 | |
| 18 | div3 | Bristol Rovers | H | W | 1-0 | Fletcher, S 16 |
| 19 | div3 | Wrexham | A | L | 2-3 | Thomas 30; Hayter 54 |
| 20 | facr1 | Doncaster | H | W | 2-1 | Thomas 38; Elliott 73 |
| 21 | div3 | Southend | A | W | 1-0 | O'Connor 71 pen |
| 22 | div3 | Scunthorpe | H | W | 2-1 | Broadhurst 59; Hayter 66 |
| 23 | facr2 | Southend | A | D | 1-1 | Broadhurst 41 |
| 24 | div3 | Shrewsbury | A | D | 0-0 | |
| 25 | facr2r | Southend | H | W | 3-2 | Fletcher, S 39; Holmes 80; Browning 89 |
| 26 | div3 | Hull City | H | D | 0-0 | |
| 27 | div3 | Oxford | A | L | 0-3 | |
| 28 | div3 | Rochdale | H | D | 3-3 | Browning 6; Fletcher, S 45; O'Connor 87 pen |
| 29 | facr3 | Crewe | H | D | 0-0 | |
| 30 | facr3r | Crewe | A | W | 3-1* | Hayter 38; Fletcher, S 98 (*on penalties) |
| 31 | div3 | Macclesfield | H | D | 2-2 | Elliott 68; Hayter 73 |
| 32 | facr4 | Stoke | A | L | 0-3 | |
| 33 | div3 | Boston | H | W | 2-1 | Redfearn 90 og; Feeney 90 |
| 34 | div3 | Kidderminster | A | L | 0-1 | |
| 35 | div3 | Wrexham | H | W | 2-0 | Feeney 52,55 |
| 36 | div3 | Swansea | H | W | 3-0 | Hayter 45; O'Connor 89,90 pen |
| 37 | div3 | Bristol Rovers | A | D | 0-0 | |
| 38 | div3 | Exeter | H | W | 2-0 | Holmes 36; O'Connor 80 |
| 39 | div3 | Bury | A | L | 1-2 | Feeney 12 |
| 40 | div3 | Rushden & D | A | L | 1-2 | Feeney 43 |
| 41 | div3 | Darlington | H | W | 2-0 | O'Connor 28; Hayter 67 |
| 42 | div3 | Rochdale | A | D | 1-1 | Fletcher, C 31 |
| 43 | div3 | York | A | L | 0-1 | |
| 44 | div3 | Leyton Orient | H | W | 3-1 | Jones, B 9 og; Joseph 17 og; Feeney 60 |
| 45 | div3 | Torquay | H | D | 1-1 | Clist 90 og |
| 46 | div3 | Cambridge | A | L | 1-2 | Fletcher, S 42 |
| 47 | div3 | Hartlepool | A | D | 0-0 | |
| 48 | div3 | Scunthorpe | A | W | 2-0 | Hayter 49; Thomas 77 |
| 49 | div3 | Southend | H | W | 1-0 | Purches, S 9 |
| 50 | div3 | Hull City | A | L | 1-3 | Fletcher, S 5 |
| 51 | div3 | Shrewsbury | H | W | 2-1 | McDonald 22; Elliott 45 |
| 52 | div3 | Lincoln | H | L | 0-1 | |
| 53 | div3 | Carlisle | A | W | 2-0 | Hayter 86,90 |
| 54 | d3po1 | Bury | A | D | 0-0 | |
| 55 | d3po2 | Bury | H | W | 3-1 | O'Connor 21; Hayter 38,60 |
| 56 | d3pof | Lincoln | N | W | 5-2 | Fletcher, S 29; Fletcher, C 45,77; Purches, S 56; O'Connor 60 |

■ Home □ Away ▨ Neutral

## ATTENDANCES

HOME GROUND: THE FITNESS FIRST STADIUM CAPACITY: 10770 AVERAGE LEAGUE AT HOME: 5828

| | | | | | | | | | | | |
|---|---|---|---|---|---|---|---|---|---|---|---|
| 56 | Lincoln | 32148 | 37 | Bristol Rovers | 6347 | 20 | Doncaster | 5371 | 21 | Southend | 4221 |
| 50 | Hull City | 15816 | 28 | Rochdale | 6240 | 33 | Boston | 5180 | 1 | Boston | 4184 |
| 32 | Stoke | 12004 | 26 | Hull City | 6098 | 12 | Carlisle | 5103 | 43 | York | 3642 |
| 27 | Oxford | 8349 | 14 | Hartlepool | 5998 | 44 | Leyton Orient | 5078 | 17 | Torquay | 3543 |
| 55 | Bury | 7945 | 31 | Macclesfield | 5840 | 9 | Bury | 4851 | 8 | Brentford | 3302 |
| 52 | Lincoln | 7578 | 54 | Bury | 5782 | 5 | Oxford | 4842 | 13 | Lincoln | 3273 |
| 53 | Carlisle | 7402 | 41 | Darlington | 5758 | 2 | Kidderminster | 4771 | 19 | Wrexham | 3105 |
| 29 | Crewe | 7252 | 16 | York | 5755 | 30 | Crewe | 4540 | 11 | Darlington | 2950 |
| 45 | Torquay | 7181 | 23 | Southend | 5721 | 10 | Rushden & D | 4527 | 39 | Bury | 2914 |
| 51 | Shrewsbury | 7102 | 47 | Hartlepool | 5625 | 48 | Scunthorpe | 4488 | 46 | Cambridge | 2885 |
| 18 | Bristol Rovers | 6924 | 15 | Leyton Orient | 5622 | 7 | Exeter | 4466 | 24 | Shrewsbury | 2869 |
| 49 | Southend | 6767 | 36 | Swansea | 5511 | 40 | Rushden & D | 4353 | 34 | Kidderminster | 2157 |
| 38 | Exeter | 6674 | 25 | Southend | 5456 | 4 | Swansea | 4325 | 42 | Rochdale | 1958 |
| 22 | Scunthorpe | 6527 | 35 | Wrexham | 5445 | 3 | Cambridge | 4315 | 6 | Macclesfield | 1795 |

## KEY PLAYER APPEARANCES

| | PLAYER | POS | AGE | APP | MINS ON | GOALS | CARDS(Y/R) | | HOME COUNTRY |
|---|---|---|---|---|---|---|---|---|---|
| 1 | Carl Fletcher | MID | 23 | 42 | 3755 | 2 | 7 | 0 | England |
| 2 | Marcus Browning | MID | 32 | 43 | 3518 | 1 | 7 | 1 | Wales |
| 3 | Wade Elliott | MID | 24 | 45 | 3379 | 4 | 3 | 1 | England |
| 4 | Stephen Purches | MID | 23 | 38 | 3258 | 3 | 2 | 0 | England |
| 5 | James Hayter | ATT | 24 | 46 | 3186 | 8 | 1 | 0 | Wales |
| 6 | Neil Moss | GK | 28 | 33 | 2925 | 0 | 1 | 0 | England |
| 7 | Garreth O'Connor | MID | 24 | 43 | 2649 | 8 | 3 | 0 | Rep of Ireland |
| 8 | Steve Fletcher | ATT | 31 | 35 | 2617 | 4 | 5 | 0 | England |
| 9 | Danny Thomas | DEF | 22 | 44 | 2527 | 2 | 0 | 0 | England |
| 10 | Neil Young | DEF | 29 | 35 | 2516 | 0 | 5 | 1 | England |
| 11 | Jason Tindall | DEF | 25 | 28 | 2193 | 1 | 5 | 0 | England |
| 12 | Warren Cummings | DEF | 22 | 20 | 1758 | 0 | 5 | 0 | Scotland |
| 13 | Karl Broadhurst | DEF | 23 | 24 | 1750 | 1 | 4 | 0 | England |
| 14 | Brian Stock | ATT | 21 | 38 | 1408 | 2 | 5 | 0 | England |
| 15 | Lewis Buxton | DEF | 19 | 18 | 1335 | 0 | 0 | 0 | Wales |
| 16 | Warren Feeney | ATT | 22 | 21 | 1112 | 7 | 3 | 0 | N Ireland |
| 17 | Derek Holmes | ATT | 24 | 38 | 1082 | 3 | 1 | 0 | Scotland |
| 18 | Alan Connell | ATT | 20 | 14 | 866 | 6 | 1 | 0 | England |

## KEY PLAYERS - GOALSCORERS

**1 Garreth O'Connor**

| | | | |
|---|---|---|---|
| Goals in the League | 8 | Player Strike Rate<br>Average number of minutes between League goals scored by player | 331 |
| Contribution to Attacking Power<br>Average number of minutes between League team goals while on pitch | 71 | Club Strike Rate<br>Average number of minutes between League goals scored by club | 69 |

| | PLAYER | LGE GOALS | POWER | STRIKE RATE |
|---|---|---|---|---|
| 2 | James Hayter | 8 | 75 | 398 mins |
| 3 | Steve Fletcher | 4 | 67 | 654 mins |
| 4 | Wade Elliott | 4 | 70 | 845 mins |
| 5 | Stephen Purches | 3 | 74 | 1086 mins |

## KEY PLAYERS - MIDFIELDERS

**1 Wade Elliott**

| | | | |
|---|---|---|---|
| Goals in the League | 4 | Contribution to Attacking Power<br>Average number of minutes between League team goals while on pitch | 70 |
| Defensive Rating<br>Average number of mins between League goals conceded while he was on the pitch | 97 | Scoring Difference<br>Defensive Rating minus Contribution to Attacking Power | 27 |

| | PLAYER | LGE GOALS | DEF RATE | POWER | SCORE DIFF |
|---|---|---|---|---|---|
| 2 | Marcus Browning | 1 | 93 | 66 | 27 mins |
| 3 | Carl Fletcher | 2 | 87 | 68 | 19 mins |
| 4 | Garreth O'Connor | 8 | 85 | 72 | 13 mins |
| 5 | Stephen Purches | 3 | 76 | 74 | 2 mins |

## KEY PLAYERS - DEFENDERS

**1 Lewis Buxton**

| | | | |
|---|---|---|---|
| Goals Conceded when he was on pitch | 9 | Clean Sheets<br>In games when he played at least 70 minutes | 8 |
| Defensive Rating<br>Ave number of mins between League goals conceded while on the pitch | 148 | Club Defensive Rating<br>Average number of mins between League goals conceded by the club this season. | 86 |

| | PLAYER | CON LGE | CLN SHEETS | DEF RATE |
|---|---|---|---|---|
| 2 | Warren Cummings | 16 | 9 | 110 mins |
| 3 | Karl Broadhurst | 18 | 8 | 97 mins |
| 4 | Danny Thomas | 30 | 7 | 84 mins |
| 5 | Neil Young | 31 | 11 | 81 mins |

## KEY GOALKEEPER

**1 Neil Moss**

| | |
|---|---|
| Goals Conceded in the League | 31 |
| Defensive Rating<br>Ave number of mins between League goals conceded while on the pitch. | 94 |
| Counting Games<br>Games when he played at least 70 mins | 32 |
| Clean Sheets<br>In games when he played at least 70 mins | 13 |

## TEAM OF THE SEASON

| GOALKEEPER | GAMES | DEF RATE |
|---|---|---|
| Neil Moss | 32 | 94 |
| **DEFENDERS** | **GAMES** | **DEF RATE** |
| Lewis Buxton | 14 | 148 |
| Warren Cummings | 19 | 110 |
| Karl Broadhurst | 19 | 97 |
| Danny Thomas | 21 | 84 |
| **MIDFIELDERS** | **GAMES** | **SCORE DIFF** |
| Marcus Browning | 37 | 27 |
| Wade Elliott | 34 | 27 |
| Carl Fletcher | 41 | 19 |
| Garreth O'Connor | 24 | 13 |
| **FORWARDS** | **GAMES** | **STRIKE RATE** |
| James Hayter | 33 | 398 |
| Steve Fletcher | 27 | 654 |

# SCUNTHORPE UNITED

Final Position: **5th**

NICKNAME: THE IRON

| | | | | | | |
|---|---|---|---|---|---|---|
| 1 | div3 | Wrexham | H | D | 1-1 | Calvo-Garcia 14 |
| 2 | div3 | Exeter | A | D | 1-1 | Carruthers 80 |
| 3 | div3 | Leyton Orient | A | L | 0-2 | |
| 4 | div3 | York | H | W | 2-1 | Smith 1 og; Carruthers 40 |
| 5 | div3 | Rushden & D | A | L | 0-2 | |
| 6 | div3 | Bristol Rovers | H | D | 2-2 | Dawson 16; Carruthers 25 |
| 7 | div3 | Lincoln | A | L | 0-1 | |
| 8 | wcr1 | Preston | A | L | 1-2 | Torpey 9 |
| 9 | div3 | Kidderminster | H | D | 1-1 | Brough 70 |
| 10 | div3 | Carlisle | H | W | 3-1 | Torpey 13,75; Carruthers 73 |
| 11 | div3 | Macclesfield | A | W | 3-2 | Carruthers 29; Torpey 44,59 |
| 12 | div3 | Shrewsbury | H | D | 1-1 | Sparrow 53 |
| 13 | div3 | Oxford | A | W | 1-0 | Beagrie 58 pen |
| 14 | div3 | Cambridge | H | L | 1-2 | Sparrow 30 |
| 15 | div3 | Rochdale | A | W | 2-1 | Carruthers 49,72 |
| 16 | div3 | Torquay | H | W | 5-1 | Carruthers 39; Torpey 45,82,90; McCombe 73 |
| 17 | div3 | Darlington | A | D | 1-1 | Carruthers 5 |
| 18 | div3 | Hull City | A | L | 0-2 | |
| 19 | div3 | Boston | H | W | 2-0 | Beagrie 16 pen; Torpey 66 |
| 20 | facr1 | Northwich | A | W | 3-0 | Torpey 38,48,72 pen |
| 21 | div3 | Swansea | H | W | 2-0 | Carruthers 23 pen; Sparrow 45 |
| 22 | div3 | Bournemouth | A | L | 1-2 | Torpey 25 |
| 23 | facr2 | Carlisle | H | D | 0-0 | |
| 24 | div3 | Bury | H | L | 0-1 | |
| 25 | div3 | Hartlepool | A | D | 2-2 | Brough 25; Carruthers 49 |
| 26 | facr2r | Carlisle | A | W | 1-0 | Carruthers 25 |
| 27 | div3 | Rushden & D | H | D | 0-0 | |
| 28 | div3 | Southend | A | W | 2-1 | Carruthers 75; Torpey 81 |
| 29 | div3 | York | A | W | 3-1 | Torpey 14 pen; Carruthers 37; Graves 50 |
| 30 | facr3 | Leeds | H | L | 0-2 | |
| 31 | div3 | Leyton Orient | H | W | 2-1 | Sparrow 27; Kilford 67 |
| 32 | div3 | Bristol Rovers | A | L | 1-2 | Carruthers 64 |
| 33 | div3 | Exeter | H | D | 1-1 | Carruthers 28 |
| 34 | div3 | Southend | H | W | 4-1 | Carruthers 11; Kilford 36; Calvo-Garcia 43; Hayes 70 |
| 35 | div3 | Wrexham | A | L | 1-2 | Sparrow 83 |
| 36 | div3 | Boston | A | L | 0-1 | |
| 37 | div3 | Hull City | H | W | 3-1 | Hayes 50; Sparrow 76,82 |
| 38 | div3 | Lincoln | H | D | 0-0 | |
| 39 | div3 | Kidderminster | A | W | 3-1 | Beagrie 32,73 pen; Carruthers 33 |
| 40 | div3 | Macclesfield | H | D | 1-1 | Hayes 53 |
| 41 | div3 | Carlisle | A | W | 2-1 | Beagrie 18; Dawson 67 |
| 42 | div3 | Torquay | A | D | 1-1 | Sparrow 8 |
| 43 | div3 | Rochdale | H | W | 3-1 | Hayes 10,66; Kilford 31 |
| 44 | div3 | Darlington | H | L | 0-1 | |
| 45 | div3 | Cambridge | A | D | 1-1 | Hayes 67 |
| 46 | div3 | Bournemouth | H | L | 0-2 | |
| 47 | div3 | Swansea | A | D | 1-1 | Carruthers 75 |
| 48 | div3 | Hartlepool | H | W | 4-0 | Hayes 32; Carruthers 72,82; Calvo-Garcia 86 |
| 49 | div3 | Bury | A | D | 0-0 | |
| 50 | div3 | Oxford | H | W | 2-0 | Hayes 30; Dalglish 90 |
| 51 | div3 | Shrewsbury | A | W | 2-1 | Dalglish 50,81 |
| 52 | d3po1 | Lincoln | A | L | 3-5 | Calvo-Garcia 26,69; Stanton 70 |
| 53 | d3po2 | Lincoln | H | L | 0-1 | |

■ Home □ Away ▨ Neutral

## ATTENDANCES

HOME GROUND: GLANFORD PARK CAPACITY: 9183 AVERAGE LEAGUE AT HOME: 3690

| | | | | | | | | | | | |
|---|---|---|---|---|---|---|---|---|---|---|---|
| 18 | Hull City | 11885 | 5 | Rushden & D | 4849 | 2 | Exeter | 3722 | 24 | Bury | 3011 |
| 52 | Lincoln | 8902 | 29 | York | 4554 | 43 | Rochdale | 3616 | 12 | Shrewsbury | 2988 |
| 30 | Leeds | 8329 | 46 | Bournemouth | 4488 | 23 | Carlisle | 3590 | 16 | Torquay | 2911 |
| 53 | Lincoln | 8295 | 28 | Southend | 4248 | 4 | York | 3504 | 21 | Swansea | 2886 |
| 26 | Carlisle | 6809 | 7 | Lincoln | 4204 | 15 | Rochdale | 3442 | 39 | Kidderminster | 2834 |
| 32 | Bristol Rovers | 6617 | 51 | Shrewsbury | 4127 | 40 | Macclesfield | 3398 | 9 | Kidderminster | 2676 |
| 22 | Bournemouth | 6527 | 27 | Rushden & D | 4096 | 36 | Boston | 3358 | 42 | Torquay | 2486 |
| 37 | Hull City | 6284 | 25 | Hartlepool | 4089 | 31 | Leyton Orient | 3242 | 33 | Exeter | 2461 |
| 47 | Swansea | 6014 | 3 | Leyton Orient | 4028 | 6 | Bristol Rovers | 3178 | 10 | Carlisle | 2342 |
| 13 | Oxford | 5658 | 45 | Cambridge | 3951 | 14 | Cambridge | 3140 | 11 | Macclesfield | 1929 |
| 50 | Oxford | 5629 | 44 | Darlington | 3904 | 35 | Wrexham | 3129 | 20 | Northwich | 1724 |
| 8 | Preston | 5594 | 49 | Bury | 3898 | 41 | Carlisle | 3124 | | | |
| 48 | Hartlepool | 5280 | 1 | Wrexham | 3879 | 34 | Southend | 3096 | | | |
| 38 | Lincoln | 5141 | 19 | Boston | 3730 | 17 | Darlington | 3059 | | | |

## KEY PLAYER APPEARANCES

| | PLAYER | POS | AGE | APP | MINS ON | GOALS | CARDS(Y/R) | | HOME COUNTRY |
|---|---|---|---|---|---|---|---|---|---|
| 1 | Tom Evans | GK | 26 | 46 | 4140 | 0 | 0 | 0 | England |
| 2 | Andrew Dawson | DEF | 24 | 43 | 3717 | 2 | 8 | 1 | England |
| 3 | Nathan Stanton | DEF | 22 | 42 | 3704 | 0 | 4 | 1 | England |
| 4 | Martin Carruthers | ATT | 30 | 46 | 3686 | 20 | 7 | 0 | England |
| 5 | Matthew Sparrow | DEF | 19 | 42 | 3669 | 8 | 6 | 1 | England |
| 6 | Wayne Graves | MID | 22 | 41 | 3038 | 1 | 9 | 1 | England |
| 7 | Mark Jackson | DEF | 25 | 35 | 2910 | 0 | 5 | 0 | England |
| 8 | Alex Calvo-Garcia | MID | 31 | 45 | 2601 | 3 | 3 | 0 | Spain |
| 9 | Peter Beagrie | MID | 37 | 34 | 2498 | 5 | 9 | 1 | England |
| 10 | Steve Torpey | ATT | 32 | 28 | 2373 | 11 | 4 | 0 | England |
| 11 | Ian Kilford | MID | 29 | 29 | 2321 | 3 | 6 | 0 | England |
| 12 | Jamie McCombe | DEF | 20 | 40 | 2205 | 1 | 6 | 0 | England |
| 13 | Paul Hayes | ATT | 19 | 18 | 1375 | 8 | 2 | 0 | England |
| 14 | Clifford Byrne | DEF | 21 | 13 | 1102 | 0 | 2 | 1 | Rep of Ireland |
| 15 | Scott Brough | MID | 20 | 30 | 1082 | 2 | 1 | 0 | England |
| 16 | Lee Featherstone | MID | 20 | 21 | 968 | 0 | 0 | 1 | England |
| 17 | Lee Ridley | DEF | 20 | 33 | 829 | 0 | 0 | 0 | England |
| 18 | Greg Strong | DEF | 27 | 7 | 630 | 0 | 0 | 0 | England |

## KEY PLAYERS - GOALSCORERS

**1 Paul Hayes**

Goals in the League **8**

Contribution to Attacking Power
Average number of minutes between League team goals while on pitch **55**

**Player Strike Rate**
**Average number of minutes between League goals scored by player** **172**

Club Strike Rate
Average number of minutes between League goals scored by club **61**

| | PLAYER | LGE GOALS | POWER | STRIKE RATE |
|---|---|---|---|---|
| 2 | Martin Carruthers | 20 | 60 | 184 mins |
| 3 | Steve Torpey | 11 | 59 | 216 mins |
| 4 | Matthew Sparrow | 8 | 62 | 459 mins |
| 5 | Peter Beagrie | 5 | 71 | 500 mins |

## KEY PLAYERS - MIDFIELDERS

**1 Alex Calvo-Garcia**

Goals in the League **3**

Defensive Rating
Average number of mins between League goals conceded while he was on the pitch **93**

Contribution to Attacking Power
Average number of minutes between League team goals while on pitch **60**

**Scoring Difference**
**Defensive Rating minus Contribution to Attacking Power** **33**

| | PLAYER | LGE GOALS | DEF RATE | POWER | SCORE DIFF |
|---|---|---|---|---|---|
| 2 | Wayne Graves | 1 | 87 | 57 | 30 mins |
| 3 | Ian Kilford | 3 | 89 | 60 | 29 mins |
| 4 | Peter Beagrie | 5 | 93 | 71 | 22 mins |

## KEY PLAYERS - DEFENDERS

**1 Mark Jackson**

Goals Conceded when he was on pitch **33**

**Defensive Rating**
**Ave number of mins between League goals conceded while on the pitch** **88**

Clean Sheets
In games when he played at least 70 minutes **6**

Club Defensive Rating
Average number of mins between League goals conceded by the club this season. **84**

| | PLAYER | CON LGE | CLN SHEETS | DEF RATE |
|---|---|---|---|---|
| 2 | Clifford Byrne | 13 | 2 | 85 mins |
| 3 | Matthew Sparrow | 44 | 7 | 83 mins |
| 4 | Andrew Dawson | 45 | 6 | 83 mins |
| 5 | Nathan Stanton | 45 | 6 | 82 mins |

## KEY GOALKEEPER

**1 Tom Evans**

Goals Conceded in the League **49**

**Defensive Rating**
**Ave number of mins between League goals conceded while on the pitch.** **84**

Counting Games
Games when he played at least 70 mins **46**

Clean Sheets
In games when he played at least 70 mins **8**

## TEAM OF THE SEASON

| GOALKEEPER | GAMES | DEF RATE |
|---|---|---|
| Tom Evans | 46 | 84 |
| **DEFENDERS** | **GAMES** | **DEF RATE** |
| Mark Jackson | 32 | 88 |
| Clifford Byrne | 11 | 85 |
| Andrew Dawson | 40 | 83 |
| Matthew Sparrow | 39 | 83 |
| **MIDFIELDERS** | **GAMES** | **SCORE DIFF** |
| Alex Calvo-Garcia | 28 | 33 |
| Wayne Graves | 31 | 30 |
| Ian Kilford | 26 | 29 |
| Peter Beagrie | 26 | 22 |
| **FORWARDS** | **GAMES** | **STRIKE RATE** |
| Paul Hayes | 12 | 172 |
| Martin Carruthers | 39 | 184 |

# LINCOLN CITY

Final Position: **6th**

NICKNAME: THE RED IMPS

| | | | | | | |
|---|---|---|---|---|---|---|
| 1 | div3 | Kidderminster | A | D | 1-1 | Weaver 11 |
| 2 | div3 | Rochdale | H | W | 2-0 | Yeo 58; Cropper 81 |
| 3 | div3 | Carlisle | H | L | 0-1 | |
| 4 | div3 | Boston | A | L | 0-2 | |
| 5 | div3 | Macclesfield | H | W | 3-0 | Yeo 42,83; Willis 51 |
| 6 | div3 | Shrewsbury | A | W | 2-1 | Mike 68; Sedgemore 80 pen |
| 7 | div3 | Scunthorpe | H | W | 1-0 | Futcher 43 |
| 8 | wcr1 | Stockport | H | L | 1-3 | Mike 58 |
| 9 | div3 | Leyton Orient | A | D | 1-1 | Futcher 75 |
| 10 | div3 | Hartlepool | A | L | 1-2 | Mike 1 |
| 11 | div3 | Southend | H | W | 2-1 | Gain 62; Yeo 71 |
| 12 | div3 | Torquay | A | D | 0-0 | |
| 13 | div3 | Bournemouth | H | L | 1-2 | Cropper 17 |
| 14 | div3 | Bristol Rovers | A | L | 0-2 | |
| 15 | div3 | Exeter | H | W | 1-0 | Willis 75 |
| 16 | div3 | Wrexham | A | W | 2-0 | Cropper 48; Smith, P 77 |
| 17 | div3 | Bury | H | D | 1-1 | Sedgemore 24 pen |
| 18 | div3 | Darlington | A | D | 0-0 | |
| 19 | div3 | Hull City | H | D | 1-1 | Futcher 7 |
| 20 | facr1 | Carlisle | A | L | 1-2 | Futcher 87 |
| 21 | div3 | Rushden & D | H | L | 1-2 | Gain 83 |
| 22 | div3 | Oxford | A | L | 0-1 | |
| 23 | div3 | Cambridge | H | D | 2-2 | Butcher 34; Weaver 67 |
| 24 | div3 | York | A | D | 1-1 | Watts 8 |
| 25 | div3 | Macclesfield | A | W | 1-0 | Gain 83 |
| 26 | div3 | Swansea | H | W | 1-0 | O'Leary 90 og |
| 27 | div3 | Boston | H | D | 1-1 | Weaver 10 |
| 28 | div3 | Shrewsbury | H | D | 1-1 | Butcher 33 |
| 29 | div3 | Rochdale | A | W | 1-0 | Futcher 83 |
| 30 | div3 | Swansea | A | L | 0-2 | |
| 31 | div3 | Carlisle | A | W | 4-1 | Ward 6; Willis 34; Gain 67; Smith, P 71 |
| 32 | div3 | Hull City | A | W | 1-0 | Bimson 65 pen |
| 33 | div3 | Darlington | H | D | 1-1 | Ward 31 |
| 34 | div3 | Scunthorpe | A | D | 0-0 | |
| 35 | div3 | Leyton Orient | H | D | 1-1 | Futcher 88 |
| 36 | div3 | Hartlepool | H | W | 3-0 | Pearce 44; Gain 83; Bloomer 88 |
| 37 | div3 | Southend | A | W | 1-0 | Futcher 10 |
| 38 | div3 | Wrexham | H | D | 1-1 | Weaver 51 |
| 39 | div3 | Exeter | A | L | 0-2 | |
| 40 | div3 | Bury | A | L | 0-2 | |
| 41 | div3 | Kidderminster | H | W | 1-0 | Bradley 15 |
| 42 | div3 | Bristol Rovers | H | W | 2-1 | Webb 21; Futcher 29 |
| 43 | div3 | Oxford | H | L | 0-1 | |
| 44 | div3 | Rushden & D | A | L | 0-1 | |
| 45 | div3 | York | H | W | 1-0 | Futcher 41 |
| 46 | div3 | Cambridge | A | D | 0-0 | |
| 47 | div3 | Bournemouth | A | W | 1-0 | Butcher 28 |
| 48 | div3 | Torquay | H | D | 1-1 | Yeo 86 |
| 49 | d3po1 | Scunthorpe | H | W | 5-3 | Weaver 15; Mayo 18; Smith, P 55; Yeo 82,90 |
| 50 | d3po2 | Scunthorpe | A | W | 1-0 | Yeo 88 |
| 51 | d3pof | Bournemouth | N | L | 2-5 | Futcher 35; Bailey 75 |

■ Home □ Away ▨ Neutral

## ATTENDANCES

HOME GROUND: SINCIL BANK CAPACITY: 11729 AVERAGE LEAGUE AT HOME: 3923

| | | | | | | | | | | | |
|---|---|---|---|---|---|---|---|---|---|---|---|
| 51 | Bournemouth | 32148 | 22 | Oxford | 4923 | 31 | Carlisle | 3567 | 3 | Carlisle | 3034 |
| 32 | Hull City | 13728 | 45 | York | 4653 | 42 | Bristol Rovers | 3550 | 15 | Exeter | 2979 |
| 49 | Scunthorpe | 8902 | 9 | Leyton Orient | 4579 | 12 | Torquay | 3428 | 2 | Rochdale | 2894 |
| 50 | Scunthorpe | 8295 | 26 | Swansea | 4553 | 24 | York | 3411 | 28 | Shrewsbury | 2885 |
| 48 | Torquay | 7906 | 20 | Carlisle | 4388 | 36 | Hartlepool | 3409 | 23 | Cambridge | 2845 |
| 27 | Boston | 7846 | 10 | Hartlepool | 4248 | 16 | Wrexham | 3312 | 17 | Bury | 2830 |
| 47 | Bournemouth | 7578 | 7 | Scunthorpe | 4204 | 18 | Darlington | 3277 | 40 | Bury | 2776 |
| 19 | Hull City | 6271 | 41 | Kidderminster | 4092 | 13 | Bournemouth | 3273 | 1 | Kidderminster | 2687 |
| 14 | Bristol Rovers | 6135 | 46 | Cambridge | 4013 | 21 | Rushden & D | 3198 | 5 | Macclesfield | 2444 |
| 4 | Boston | 5159 | 39 | Exeter | 4009 | 33 | Darlington | 3193 | 25 | Macclesfield | 2187 |
| 34 | Scunthorpe | 5141 | 43 | Oxford | 3990 | 6 | Shrewsbury | 3168 | 29 | Rochdale | 2122 |
| 30 | Swansea | 5099 | 38 | Wrexham | 3916 | 11 | Southend | 3151 | 8 | Stockport | 2084 |
| 44 | Rushden & D | 4962 | 37 | Southend | 3912 | 35 | Leyton Orient | 3130 | | | |

## KEY PLAYER APPEARANCES

| | PLAYER | POS | AGE | APP | MINS ON | GOALS | CARDS(Y/R) | | HOME COUNTRY |
|---|---|---|---|---|---|---|---|---|---|
| 1 | Alan Marriott | GK | 24 | 46 | 4140 | 0 | 1 | 0 | England |
| 2 | Paul Morgan | ATT | 24 | 45 | 3905 | 0 | 2 | 1 | England |
| 3 | Peter Gain | MID | 26 | 43 | 3847 | 5 | 9 | 0 | England |
| 4 | Mark Bailey | MID | 26 | 45 | 3846 | 0 | 5 | 0 | England |
| 5 | Simon Weaver | DEF | 25 | 44 | 3658 | 4 | 3 | 1 | England |
| 6 | Stuart Bimson | DEF | 33 | 44 | 3647 | 1 | 3 | 0 | England |
| 7 | Ben Futcher | DEF | 22 | 42 | 3633 | 8 | 9 | 0 | England |
| 8 | Simon Yeo | ATT | 29 | 40 | 2185 | 5 | 9 | 1 | England |
| 9 | Richard Butcher | DEF | 22 | 27 | 2157 | 3 | 5 | 0 | England |
| 10 | Paul Smith | ATT | 27 | 40 | 2131 | 2 | 7 | 0 | England |
| 11 | Dean Cropper | ATT | 20 | 31 | 2085 | 3 | 3 | 1 | England |
| 12 | Scott Willis | MID | 21 | 33 | 1976 | 3 | 8 | 1 | England |
| 13 | Ben Sedgemore | MID | 27 | 42 | 1954 | 2 | 3 | 0 | England |
| 14 | Allan Pearce | ATT | 20 | 18 | 770 | 1 | 2 | 0 | England |
| 15 | Chris Cornelly | ATT | 27 | 25 | 767 | 0 | 2 | 1 | England |
| 16 | Richard Logan | MID | 34 | 11 | 727 | 0 | 4 | 0 | |
| 17 | Paul Mayo | DEF | 21 | 22 | 625 | 0 | 4 | 0 | England |
| 18 | Adie Mike | ATT | 29 | 17 | 623 | 2 | 0 | 0 | England |

## KEY PLAYERS - GOALSCORERS

**1 Simon Yeo**

| | |
|---|---|
| Goals in the League | 5 |
| Contribution to Attacking Power<br>Average number of minutes between League team goals while on pitch | 95 |
| Player Strike Rate<br>Average number of minutes between League goals scored by player | 437 |
| Club Strike Rate<br>Average number of minutes between League goals scored by club | 90 |

| | PLAYER | LGE GOALS | POWER | STRIKE RATE |
|---|---|---|---|---|
| 2 | Ben Futcher | 8 | 86 | 454 mins |
| 3 | Scott Willis | 3 | 70 | 659 mins |
| 4 | Dean Cropper | 3 | 115 | 695 mins |
| 5 | Richard Butcher | 3 | 93 | 719 mins |

## KEY PLAYERS - MIDFIELDERS

**1 Scott Willis**

| | |
|---|---|
| Goals in the League | 3 |
| Defensive Rating<br>Average number of mins between League goals conceded while he was on the pitch | 110 |
| Contribution to Attacking Power<br>Average number of minutes between League team goals while on pitch | 71 |
| Scoring Difference<br>Defensive Rating minus Contribution to Attacking Power | 39 |

| | PLAYER | LGE GOALS | DEF RATE | POWER | SCORE DIFF |
|---|---|---|---|---|---|
| 2 | Peter Gain | 5 | 124 | 87 | 37 mins |
| 3 | Ben Sedgemore | 2 | 115 | 85 | 30 mins |
| 4 | Mark Bailey | 0 | 113 | 94 | 19 mins |

## KEY PLAYERS - DEFENDERS

**1 Ben Futcher**

| | |
|---|---|
| Goals Conceded when he was on pitch | 32 |
| Defensive Rating<br>Ave number of mins between League goals conceded while on the pitch | 114 |
| Clean Sheets<br>In games when he played at least 70 minutes | 16 |
| Club Defensive Rating<br>Average number of mins between League goals conceded by the club this season. | 112 |

| | PLAYER | CON LGE | CLN SHEETS | DEF RATE |
|---|---|---|---|---|
| 2 | Richard Butcher | 20 | 8 | 108 mins |
| 3 | Stuart Bimson | 34 | 15 | 107 mins |
| 4 | Simon Weaver | 35 | 17 | 105 mins |

## KEY GOALKEEPER

**1 Alan Marriott**

| | |
|---|---|
| Goals Conceded in the League | 37 |
| Defensive Rating<br>Ave number of mins between League goals conceded while on the pitch. | 112 |
| Counting Games<br>Games when he played at least 70 mins | 46 |
| Clean Sheets<br>In games when he played at least 70 mins | 18 |

## TEAM OF THE SEASON

| GOALKEEPER | GAMES | DEF RATE |
|---|---|---|
| Alan Marriott | 46 | 112 |
| **DEFENDERS** | **GAMES** | **DEF RATE** |
| Ben Futcher | 40 | 114 |
| Richard Butcher | 23 | 108 |
| Stuart Bimson | 40 | 107 |
| Simon Weaver | 37 | 105 |
| **MIDFIELDERS** | **GAMES** | **SCORE DIFF** |
| Scott Willis | 19 | 39 |
| Peter Gain | 42 | 37 |
| Ben Sedgemore | 20 | 30 |
| Mark Bailey | 40 | 19 |
| **FORWARDS** | **GAMES** | **STRIKE RATE** |
| Simon Yeo | 17 | 437 |
| Dean Cropper | 21 | 695 |

# BURY

Final Position: **7th**

NICKNAME: THE SHAKERS

| | | | | | | |
|---|---|---|---|---|---|---|
| 1 | div3 | Oxford | A | L | 1-2 | Clegg 87 |
| 2 | div3 | Cambridge | H | L | 0-1 | |
| 3 | div3 | Swansea | H | W | 3-2 | Clegg 9; Newby 36; Swailes 80 |
| 4 | div3 | Hull City | A | D | 1-1 | Abbott 64 |
| 5 | div3 | Shrewsbury | H | W | 4-3 | Newby 20,56; Dunfield 46; Abbott 53 |
| 6 | div3 | Boston | A | D | 1-1 | Newby 48 |
| 7 | div3 | York | H | W | 2-1 | Newby 20; Abbott 26 |
| 8 | wcr1 | Stoke | H | W | 1-0 | Stuart 56 |
| 9 | div3 | Bournemouth | A | W | 2-1 | Forrest 44 pen; Unsworth 56 |
| 10 | div3 | Bristol Rovers | A | L | 1-2 | Abbott 90 |
| 11 | div3 | Hartlepool | H | D | 1-1 | Abbott 20 |
| 12 | div3 | Wrexham | A | D | 2-2 | Newby 31,59 |
| 13 | wcr2 | Bolton | A | W | 1-0 | Mendy 48 og |
| 14 | div3 | Southend | H | L | 1-3 | Nelson 3 |
| 15 | div3 | Darlington | H | D | 2-2 | Nugent 87; Nelson 90 |
| 16 | div3 | Rushden & D | A | W | 1-0 | Billy 45 |
| 17 | div3 | Macclesfield | H | W | 2-1 | Preece 12; Swailes 84 |
| 18 | div3 | Lincoln | A | D | 1-1 | Preece 77 pen |
| 19 | div3 | Leyton Orient | A | W | 2-1 | Preece 45; Dunfield 85 |
| 20 | wcr3 | Fulham | A | L | 1-3 | Newby 90 |
| 21 | div3 | Torquay | H | L | 0-1 | |
| 22 | facr1 | Plymouth | H | L | 0-3 | |
| 23 | div3 | Carlisle | A | W | 2-1 | Preece 73; Unsworth 75 |
| 24 | div3 | Exeter | H | W | 1-0 | George 82 |
| 25 | div3 | Scunthorpe | A | W | 1-0 | Swailes 73 |
| 26 | div3 | Rochdale | H | D | 1-1 | Newby 62 |
| 27 | div3 | Shrewsbury | A | L | 1-4 | Nugent 87 |
| 28 | div3 | Kidderminster | H | D | 1-1 | Newby 77 |
| 29 | div3 | Hull City | H | W | 1-0 | Lawson 72 |
| 30 | div3 | Swansea | A | W | 3-2 | Billy 2; Nelson 28; Lawson 29 |
| 31 | div3 | Boston | H | D | 0-0 | |
| 32 | div3 | Kidderminster | A | L | 2-3 | Lawson 80; Redmond 89 |
| 33 | div3 | Cambridge | A | W | 2-1 | Nugent 78; Cramb 84 |
| 34 | div3 | Torquay | A | D | 1-1 | Billy 44 |
| 35 | div3 | Leyton Orient | H | L | 0-1 | |
| 36 | div3 | York | A | D | 1-1 | Clegg 60 |
| 37 | div3 | Bournemouth | H | W | 2-1 | Redmond 33; Cramb 84 |
| 38 | div3 | Bristol Rovers | H | L | 0-1 | |
| 39 | div3 | Hartlepool | A | D | 0-0 | |
| 40 | div3 | Macclesfield | A | D | 0-0 | |
| 41 | div3 | Rushden & D | H | L | 0-1 | |
| 42 | div3 | Lincoln | H | W | 2-0 | Clegg 33,42 |
| 43 | div3 | Oxford | H | D | 1-1 | Abbott 23 |
| 44 | div3 | Darlington | A | L | 1-3 | Connell 11 |
| 45 | div3 | Exeter | A | W | 2-1 | Billy 23; Newby 30 |
| 46 | div3 | Carlisle | H | D | 1-1 | Nugent 33 |
| 47 | div3 | Rochdale | A | W | 2-1 | Nelson 23; Cramb 71 pen |
| 48 | div3 | Scunthorpe | H | D | 0-0 | |
| 49 | div3 | Southend | A | W | 2-1 | Nelson 10; Connell 48 |
| 50 | div3 | Wrexham | H | L | 0-3 | |
| 51 | d3po1 | Bournemouth | H | D | 0-0 | |
| 52 | d3po2 | Bournemouth | A | L | 1-3 | Preece 67 |

■ Home □ Away □ Neutral

## ATTENDANCES

HOME GROUND: GIGG LANE CAPACITY: 11840 AVERAGE LEAGUE AT HOME: 3226

| | | | | | | | | | | | |
|---|---|---|---|---|---|---|---|---|---|---|---|
| 13 | Bolton | 12621 | 47 | Rochdale | 4513 | 14 | Southend | 3301 | 5 | Shrewsbury | 2866 |
| 4 | Hull City | 8804 | 29 | Hull City | 4290 | 7 | York | 3294 | 18 | Lincoln | 2830 |
| 52 | Bournemouth | 7945 | 19 | Leyton Orient | 4234 | 21 | Torquay | 3210 | 6 | Boston | 2790 |
| 20 | Fulham | 6700 | 27 | Shrewsbury | 4175 | 28 | Kidderminster | 3202 | 42 | Lincoln | 2776 |
| 26 | Rochdale | 5827 | 36 | York | 4115 | 34 | Torquay | 3123 | 32 | Kidderminster | 2736 |
| 51 | Bournemouth | 5782 | 12 | Wrexham | 3949 | 31 | Boston | 3024 | 35 | Leyton Orient | 2707 |
| 39 | Hartlepool | 5734 | 16 | Rushden & D | 3925 | 25 | Scunthorpe | 3011 | 2 | Cambridge | 2650 |
| 10 | Bristol Rovers | 5493 | 48 | Scunthorpe | 3898 | 22 | Plymouth | 2987 | 8 | Stoke | 2581 |
| 1 | Oxford | 5309 | 30 | Swansea | 3555 | 15 | Darlington | 2944 | 43 | Oxford | 2578 |
| 50 | Wrexham | 5186 | 11 | Hartlepool | 3547 | 40 | Macclesfield | 2920 | 38 | Bristol Rovers | 2425 |
| 9 | Bournemouth | 4851 | 17 | Macclesfield | 3506 | 37 | Bournemouth | 2914 | 3 | Swansea | 2348 |
| 49 | Southend | 4707 | 46 | Carlisle | 3384 | 44 | Darlington | 2879 | 41 | Rushden & D | 2291 |
| 23 | Carlisle | 4678 | 45 | Exeter | 3338 | 33 | Cambridge | 2875 | 24 | Exeter | 2039 |

## KEY PLAYER APPEARANCES

| | PLAYER | POS | AGE | APP | MINS ON | GOALS | CARDS(Y/R) | | HOME COUNTRY |
|---|---|---|---|---|---|---|---|---|---|
| 1 | Glyn Garner | GK | 26 | 46 | 4140 | 0 | 0 | 0 | Wales |
| 2 | Jon Newby | ATT | 24 | 46 | 4121 | 10 | 3 | 0 | England |
| 3 | Micheal Nelson | DEF | 21 | 45 | 3454 | 5 | 3 | 0 | England |
| 4 | Danny Swailes | DEF | 24 | 41 | 3308 | 3 | 9 | 1 | England |
| 5 | Lee Unsworth | DEF | 30 | 38 | 2996 | 2 | 3 | 0 | England |
| 6 | Chris Billy | MID | 30 | 38 | 2933 | 4 | 5 | 0 | England |
| 7 | Jamie Stuart | DEF | 26 | 42 | 2860 | 0 | 4 | 1 | England |
| 8 | Colin Woodthorpe | DEF | 34 | 41 | 2693 | 0 | 7 | 0 | England |
| 9 | George Clegg | ATT | 22 | 33 | 2460 | 5 | 4 | 0 | England |
| 10 | Terry Dunfield | MID | 21 | 38 | 2366 | 2 | 4 | 1 | Canada |
| 11 | Stephen Redmond | DEF | 35 | 33 | 2226 | 2 | 2 | 0 | England |
| 12 | Martyn Forrest | MID | 24 | 35 | 2018 | 1 | 0 | 0 | England |
| 13 | Pawel Abbott | ATT | 21 | 17 | 1497 | 6 | 4 | 0 | Poland |
| 14 | David Nugent | ATT | 18 | 34 | 1366 | 4 | 1 | 0 | England |
| 15 | Colin Cramb | ATT | 29 | 18 | 1350 | 3 | 1 | 0 | England |
| 16 | Matthew Barrass | MID | 23 | 19 | 1292 | 0 | 5 | 0 | England |
| 17 | Andy Preece | MID | 36 | 45 | 1170 | 4 | 0 | 0 | England |
| 18 | Lee Connell | DEF | 22 | 18 | 1119 | 2 | 3 | 0 | England |

## KEY PLAYERS - GOALSCORERS

**1 Pawel Abbott**

| | |
|---|---|
| Goals in the League | 6 |
| Contribution to Attacking Power<br>Average number of minutes between League team goals while on pitch | 59 |
| Player Strike Rate<br>Average number of minutes between League goals scored by player | 250 |
| Club Strike Rate<br>Average number of minutes between League goals scored by club | 73 |

| | PLAYER | LGE GOALS | POWER | STRIKE RATE |
|---|---|---|---|---|
| 2 | Jon Newby | 10 | 72 | 412 mins |
| 3 | Colin Cramb | 3 | 71 | 450 mins |
| 4 | George Clegg | 5 | 79 | 492 mins |
| 5 | Micheal Nelson | 5 | 71 | 691 mins |

## KEY PLAYERS - MIDFIELDERS

**1 Chris Billy**

| | |
|---|---|
| Goals in the League | 4 |
| Defensive Rating<br>Average number of mins between League goals conceded while he was on the pitch | 75 |
| Contribution to Attacking Power<br>Average number of minutes between League team goals while on pitch | 68 |
| Scoring Difference<br>Defensive Rating minus Contribution to Attacking Power | 7 |

| | PLAYER | LGE GOALS | DEF RATE | POWER | SCORE DIFF |
|---|---|---|---|---|---|
| 2 | Martyn Forrest | 1 | 78 | 72 | 6 mins |
| 3 | Matthew Barrass | 0 | 72 | 72 | 0 mins |
| 4 | Terry Dunfield | 2 | 62 | 66 | -4 mins |
| 5 | Andy Preece | 4 | 73 | 90 | -17 mins |

## KEY PLAYERS - DEFENDERS

**1 Lee Connell**

| | |
|---|---|
| Goals Conceded when he was on pitch | 13 |
| Defensive Rating<br>Ave number of mins between League goals conceded while on the pitch | 86 |
| Clean Sheets<br>In games when he played at least 70 minutes | 2 |
| Club Defensive Rating<br>Average number of mins between League goals conceded by the club this season. | 74 |

| | PLAYER | CON LGE | CLN SHEETS | DEF RATE |
|---|---|---|---|---|
| 2 | Stephen Redmond | 27 | 6 | 82 mins |
| 3 | Micheal Nelson | 43 | 9 | 80 mins |
| 4 | Colin Woodthorpe | 35 | 7 | 77 mins |
| 5 | Danny Swailes | 44 | 7 | 75 mins |

## KEY GOALKEEPER

**1 Glyn Garner**

| | |
|---|---|
| Goals Conceded in the League | 56 |
| Defensive Rating<br>Ave number of mins between League goals conceded while on the pitch. | 74 |
| Counting Games<br>Games when he played at least 70 mins | 46 |
| Clean Sheets<br>In games when he played at least 70 mins | 9 |

## TEAM OF THE SEASON

| | | |
|---|---|---|
| **GOALKEEPER** | **GAMES** | **DEF RATE** |
| Glyn Garner | 46 | 74 |
| **DEFENDERS** | **GAMES** | **DEF RATE** |
| Lee Connell | 11 | 86 |
| Stephen Redmond | 23 | 82 |
| Micheal Nelson | 38 | 80 |
| Colin Woodthorpe | 29 | 77 |
| **MIDFIELDERS** | **GAMES** | **SCORE DIFF** |
| Chris Billy | 31 | 7 |
| Martyn Forrest | 19 | 6 |
| Matthew Barrass | 13 | 0 |
| Terry Dunfield | 26 | -4 |
| **FORWARDS** | **GAMES** | **STRIKE RATE** |
| Pawel Abbott | 17 | 250 |
| Jon Newby | 46 | 412 |

# OXFORD UNITED

Final Position: **8th**

NICKNAME: THE U'S

| | | | | | | |
|---|---|---|---|---|---|---|
| 1 | div3 | Bury | H | W | 2-1 | Crosby 30 pen; Omoyimni 34 |
| 2 | div3 | Wrexham | A | L | 0-1 | |
| 3 | div3 | Darlington | A | W | 1-0 | Basham 44 |
| 4 | div3 | Southend | H | L | 0-1 | |
| 5 | div3 | Bournemouth | A | D | 1-1 | Basham 47 |
| 6 | div3 | Hartlepool | H | L | 0-1 | |
| 7 | div3 | Torquay | H | D | 2-2 | Omoyimni 81; Powell 88 |
| 8 | wcr1 | Bristol City | A | W | 1-0 | Hunt 17 |
| 9 | div3 | Boston | A | W | 3-1 | Powell 16; Scott 24,36 |
| 10 | div3 | Leyton Orient | A | W | 2-1 | Scott 8; Crosby 55 pen |
| 11 | div3 | Hull City | H | D | 0-0 | |
| 12 | div3 | York | A | W | 1-0 | Gordon 60 |
| 13 | wcr2 | Charlton | A | W | 6-5* | (*on penalties) |
| 14 | div3 | Scunthorpe | H | L | 0-1 | |
| 15 | div3 | Swansea | H | W | 1-0 | Louis 73 |
| 16 | div3 | Cambridge | A | D | 1-1 | Scott 80 |
| 17 | div3 | Shrewsbury | H | D | 2-2 | Scott 7; Louis 16 |
| 18 | div3 | Macclesfield | A | L | 1-2 | Louis 90 |
| 19 | div3 | Carlisle | A | L | 0-1 | |
| 20 | wcr3 | Aston Villa | H | L | 0-3 | |
| 21 | div3 | Rochdale | H | W | 2-0 | Hunt 17; Basham 70 |
| 22 | facr1 | Dover | A | W | 1-0 | Oldfield 22 |
| 23 | div3 | Lincoln | H | W | 1-0 | Crosby 90 pen |
| 24 | facr2 | Swindon | H | W | 1-0 | Louis 65 |
| 25 | div3 | Bristol Rovers | A | W | 2-0 | Robinson 12; Louis 49 |
| 26 | div3 | Exeter | H | D | 2-2 | Steele 78; Bound 83 |
| 27 | div3 | Bournemouth | H | W | 3-0 | Whitehead 30; Hunter 74; Oldfield 76 |
| 28 | div3 | Rushden & D | A | W | 2-0 | Savage 13; Oldfield 30 |
| 29 | facr3 | Arsenal | A | L | 0-2 | |
| 30 | div3 | Darlington | H | D | 1-1 | Basham 49 |
| 31 | div3 | Hartlepool | A | L | 1-3 | Barron 36 og |
| 32 | div3 | Southend | A | L | 1-2 | Basham 89 |
| 33 | div3 | Rushden & D | H | W | 3-0 | Crosby 51 pen; Savage 84,87 |
| 34 | div3 | Kidderminster | A | W | 3-1 | Basham 21; Hinton 29 og; Scott 61 |
| 35 | div3 | Wrexham | H | L | 0-2 | |
| 36 | div3 | Rochdale | A | L | 1-2 | Savage 71 |
| 37 | div3 | Torquay | A | W | 3-2 | Scott 56; Steele 81,90 |
| 38 | div3 | Boston | H | W | 2-1 | Crosby 16; Ford, B 54 |
| 39 | div3 | Leyton Orient | H | L | 0-2 | |
| 40 | div3 | Hull City | A | D | 0-0 | |
| 41 | div3 | Shrewsbury | A | W | 2-1 | Waterman 21; Louis 46 |
| 42 | div3 | Cambridge | H | D | 1-1 | Louis 65 |
| 43 | div3 | Macclesfield | H | L | 0-1 | |
| 44 | div3 | Bury | A | D | 1-1 | McNiven 35 |
| 45 | div3 | Swansea | A | L | 2-3 | Scott 25,82 |
| 46 | div3 | Carlisle | H | D | 0-0 | |
| 47 | div3 | Lincoln | A | W | 1-0 | Scott 4 |
| 48 | div3 | Kidderminster | H | W | 2-1 | McCarthy 38; Omoyimni 88 |
| 49 | div3 | Exeter | A | D | 2-2 | Crosby 10; Scott 68 |
| 50 | div3 | Bristol Rovers | H | L | 0-1 | |
| 51 | div3 | Scunthorpe | A | L | 0-2 | |
| 52 | div3 | York | H | W | 2-0 | Basham 3,63 |

Home / Away / Neutral

## ATTENDANCES

HOME GROUND: KASSAM STADIUM CAPACITY: 12400 AVERAGE LEAGUE AT HOME: 5862

| | | | | | | | | | | | |
|---|---|---|---|---|---|---|---|---|---|---|---|
| 29 | Arsenal | 35432 | 25 | Bristol Rovers | 5864 | 39 | Leyton Orient | 5013 | 47 | Lincoln | 3990 |
| 40 | Hull City | 17404 | 43 | Macclesfield | 5691 | 42 | Cambridge | 4983 | 12 | York | 3962 |
| 20 | Aston Villa | 12177 | 14 | Scunthorpe | 5658 | 30 | Darlington | 4968 | 10 | Leyton Orient | 3758 |
| 24 | Swindon | 11645 | 51 | Scunthorpe | 5629 | 23 | Lincoln | 4923 | 2 | Wrexham | 3591 |
| 13 | Charlton | 9494 | 17 | Shrewsbury | 5559 | 49 | Exeter | 4900 | 3 | Darlington | 3533 |
| 50 | Bristol Rovers | 8732 | 35 | Wrexham | 5532 | 28 | Rushden & D | 4891 | 41 | Shrewsbury | 3520 |
| 27 | Bournemouth | 8349 | 11 | Hull City | 5445 | 5 | Bournemouth | 4842 | 37 | Torquay | 3372 |
| 38 | Boston | 7157 | 15 | Swansea | 5440 | 6 | Hartlepool | 4768 | 32 | Southend | 3203 |
| 26 | Exeter | 7057 | 1 | Bury | 5309 | 16 | Cambridge | 4621 | 34 | Kidderminster | 2991 |
| 52 | York | 6905 | 7 | Torquay | 5260 | 21 | Rochdale | 4547 | 36 | Rochdale | 2764 |
| 48 | Kidderminster | 6820 | 4 | Southend | 5162 | 22 | Dover | 4186 | 9 | Boston | 2685 |
| 33 | Rushden & D | 6508 | 31 | Hartlepool | 5049 | 8 | Bristol City | 4065 | 44 | Bury | 2578 |
| 45 | Swansea | 5982 | 46 | Carlisle | 5044 | 19 | Carlisle | 4039 | 18 | Macclesfield | 1583 |

## KEY PLAYER APPEARANCES

| | PLAYER | POS | AGE | APP | MINS ON | GOALS | CARDS(Y/R) | | HOME COUNTRY |
|---|---|---|---|---|---|---|---|---|---|
| 1 | Andrew Crosby | DEF | 30 | 46 | 4095 | 6 | 6 | 0 | England |
| 2 | Andy Woodman | GK | 31 | 45 | 4005 | 0 | 2 | 0 | England |
| 3 | Scott McNiven | DEF | 25 | 44 | 3873 | 1 | 7 | 0 | England |
| 4 | Matthew Robinson | MID | 28 | 43 | 3759 | 1 | 5 | 0 | England |
| 5 | Matthew Bound | MID | 30 | 46 | 3539 | 1 | 2 | 0 | England |
| 6 | James Hunt | MID | 26 | 41 | 3358 | 1 | 8 | 1 | England |
| 7 | Dave Savage | MID | 29 | 42 | 3230 | 4 | 6 | 0 | Rep of Ireland |
| 8 | Bobby Ford | MID | 28 | 38 | 2890 | 1 | 5 | 1 | England |
| 9 | Andy Scott | ATT | 30 | 40 | 2616 | 11 | 3 | 0 | England |
| 10 | David Waterman | DEF | 26 | 40 | 2395 | 1 | 5 | 1 | England |
| 11 | Steve Basham | ATT | 25 | 31 | 2031 | 8 | 0 | 0 | England |
| 12 | David Oldfield | MID | 35 | 33 | 1646 | 2 | 0 | 0 | Australia |
| 13 | Jefferson Louis | ATT | 24 | 37 | 1276 | 6 | 4 | 0 | England |
| 14 | Roy Hunter | MID | 29 | 31 | 1179 | 1 | 0 | 0 | England |
| 15 | Adrian Viveash | DEF | 33 | 11 | 990 | 0 | 2 | 0 | England |
| 16 | Dean Whitehead | MID | 21 | 38 | 944 | 1 | 1 | 0 | England |
| 17 | Emmanuel Omoyimni | MID | 25 | 24 | 722 | 3 | 2 | 0 | Nigeria |
| 18 | Paul McCarthy | DEF | 31 | 6 | 540 | 1 | 2 | 0 | Rep of Ireland |

## KEY PLAYERS - GOALSCORERS

**1 Andy Scott**

Goals in the League: 11

Contribution to Attacking Power: Average number of minutes between League team goals while on pitch: 81

Player Strike Rate: Average number of minutes between League goals scored by player: 238

Club Strike Rate: Average number of minutes between League goals scored by club: 73

| | PLAYER | LGE GOALS | POWER | STRIKE RATE |
|---|---|---|---|---|
| 2 | Steve Basham | 8 | 65 | 254 mins |
| 3 | Andrew Crosby | 6 | 71 | 683 mins |
| 4 | Dave Savage | 4 | 78 | 808 mins |
| 5 | David Oldfield | 2 | 86 | 823 mins |

## KEY PLAYERS - MIDFIELDERS

**1 David Oldfield**

Goals in the League: 2

Defensive Rating: Average number of mins between League goals conceded while he was on the pitch: 127

Contribution to Attacking Power: Average number of minutes between League team goals while on pitch: 87

Scoring Difference: Defensive Rating minus Contribution to Attacking Power: 40

| | PLAYER | LGE GOALS | DEF RATE | POWER | SCORE DIFF |
|---|---|---|---|---|---|
| 2 | Roy Hunter | 1 | 84 | 56 | 28 mins |
| 3 | Matthew Bound | 1 | 88 | 71 | 17 mins |
| 4 | Matthew Robinson | 1 | 87 | 72 | 15 mins |
| 5 | Bobby Ford | 1 | 83 | 72 | 11 mins |

## KEY PLAYERS - DEFENDERS

**1 David Waterman**

Goals Conceded when he was on pitch: 23

Defensive Rating: Ave number of mins between League goals conceded while on the pitch: 104

Clean Sheets: In games when he played at least 70 minutes: 8

Club Defensive Rating: Average number of mins between League goals conceded by the club this season: 88

| | PLAYER | CON LGE | CLN SHEETS | DEF RATE |
|---|---|---|---|---|
| 2 | Scott McNiven | 43 | 14 | 90 mins |
| 3 | Adrian Viveash | 11 | 3 | 90 mins |
| 4 | Andrew Crosby | 47 | 14 | 87 mins |

## KEY GOALKEEPER

**1 Andy Woodman**

Goals Conceded in the League: 46

Defensive Rating: Ave number of mins between League goals conceded while on the pitch: 87

Counting Games: Games when he played at least 70 mins: 44

Clean Sheets: In games when he played at least 70 mins: 14

## TEAM OF THE SEASON

| GOALKEEPER | GAMES | DEF RATE |
|---|---|---|
| Andy Woodman | 44 | 87 |
| **DEFENDERS** | **GAMES** | **DEF RATE** |
| David Waterman | 26 | 104 |
| Scott McNiven | 42 | 90 |
| Adrian Viveash | 11 | 90 |
| Andrew Crosby | 45 | 87 |
| **MIDFIELDERS** | **GAMES** | **SCORE DIFF** |
| David Oldfield | 13 | 40 |
| Roy Hunter | 12 | 28 |
| Matthew Bound | 39 | 17 |
| Matthew Robinson | 42 | 15 |
| **FORWARDS** | **GAMES** | **STRIKE RATE** |
| Andy Scott | 26 | 238 |
| Steve Basham | 20 | 254 |

# TORQUAY UNITED

Final Position: **9th**

ICKNAME: THE GULLS

| | | | | | | | |
|---|---|---|---|---|---|---|---|
| 1 | div3 | Bristol Rovers | H | W | 2-1 | Gritton 45; Russell, A 73 pen |
| 2 | div3 | Rushden & D | A | L | 0-3 | |
| 3 | div3 | York | A | L | 3-4 | Hankin 55; Richardson 63; Hockley 65 |
| 4 | div3 | Hartlepool | H | D | 1-1 | Richardson 51 |
| 5 | div3 | Exeter | A | W | 2-1 | Graham, D 26; Bedeau 45 |
| 6 | div3 | Wrexham | H | W | 2-1 | Hill 20; Graham, D 29 |
| 7 | div3 | Oxford | A | D | 2-2 | Graham 48; Bedeau 79 |
| 8 | wcr1 | Gillingham | H | L | 0-1 | |
| 9 | div3 | Cambridge | H | W | 3-2 | Graham 41,70; Hill 62 |
| 10 | div3 | Shrewsbury | H | W | 2-1 | Fowler 18; Graham 77 |
| 11 | div3 | Swansea | A | W | 1-0 | Graham 31 |
| 12 | div3 | Lincoln | H | D | 0-0 | |
| 13 | div3 | Carlisle | A | W | 2-1 | Graham 2; Gritton 90 |
| 14 | div3 | Boston | A | L | 1-2 | Hockley 6 |
| 15 | div3 | Hull City | H | L | 1-4 | Hill 65 |
| 16 | div3 | Scunthorpe | A | L | 1-5 | Graham 30 |
| 17 | div3 | Bournemouth | H | W | 4-0 | Gritton 30; Graham 34,77; Russell, A 47 |
| 18 | div3 | Bury | A | W | 1-0 | Graham 57 |
| 19 | facr1 | Boreham W | H | W | 5-0 | Russell, A 6 pen; Gritton 43,62; Osei-Kuffour 76; Fowler 89 |
| 20 | div3 | Kidderminster | H | D | 2-2 | Russell, A 23; Gritton 32 |
| 21 | div3 | Macclesfield | A | D | 3-3 | Graham 2; Fowler 7; Woozley 10 |
| 22 | div3 | Rochdale | H | D | 2-2 | Gritton 52; Hazell 90 |
| 23 | facr2 | Blackpool | A | L | 1-3 | Gritton 8 |
| 24 | div3 | Leyton Orient | A | L | 0-2 | |
| 25 | div3 | Southend | H | W | 3-1 | Osei-Kuffour 21; Dunning 65; Bedeau 78 |
| 26 | div3 | Darlington | A | D | 1-1 | Fowler 74 |
| 27 | div3 | Rushden & D | H | D | 1-1 | Fowler 39 pen |
| 28 | div3 | York | H | W | 3-1 | Gritton 6,21; Bedeau 24 |
| 29 | div3 | Bristol Rovers | A | D | 1-1 | Russell, A 6 |
| 30 | div3 | Wrexham | A | L | 1-2 | Bedeau 18 |
| 31 | div3 | Darlington | H | W | 3-1 | Gritton 22; Russell, A 31 pen; Woozley 38 |
| 32 | div3 | Hartlepool | A | L | 2-3 | Graham 8; Gritton 58 |
| 33 | div3 | Bury | H | D | 1-1 | Russell, A 13 pen |
| 34 | div3 | Exeter | H | W | 1-0 | Gritton 28 |
| 35 | div3 | Kidderminster | A | L | 0-2 | |
| 36 | div3 | Oxford | H | L | 2-3 | Russell, A 70 pen; Wills 75 |
| 37 | div3 | Cambridge | A | W | 1-0 | Osei-Kuffour 4 |
| 38 | div3 | Swansea | H | D | 0-0 | |
| 39 | div3 | Scunthorpe | H | D | 1-1 | Clist 83 |
| 40 | div3 | Hull City | A | D | 1-1 | Hill 90 |
| 41 | div3 | Bournemouth | A | D | 1-1 | Bedeau 68 |
| 42 | div3 | Shrewsbury | A | W | 3-2 | Gritton 20; Russell, A 57; Woozley 90 |
| 43 | div3 | Boston | H | D | 1-1 | Russell, A 68 |
| 44 | div3 | Rochdale | A | W | 2-0 | Griffiths 18 og; Clist 52 |
| 45 | div3 | Macclesfield | H | D | 2-2 | Osei-Kuffour 4; Gritton 61 |
| 46 | div3 | Southend | A | L | 0-3 | |
| 47 | div3 | Leyton Orient | H | D | 2-2 | Killoughery 26; Graham 65 |
| 48 | div3 | Carlisle | H | L | 2-3 | Murphy 69 og; Osei-Kuffour 77 |
| 49 | div3 | Lincoln | A | D | 1-1 | Gritton 31 |

Home / Away / Neutral

## ATTENDANCES

HOME GROUND: PLAINMOOR CAPACITY: 6117 AVERAGE LEAGUE AT HOME: 3131

| | | | | | | | | | | | |
|---|---|---|---|---|---|---|---|---|---|---|---|
| 40 | Hull City | 13310 | 11 | Swansea | 3872 | 33 | Bury | 3123 | 9 | Cambridge | 2557 |
| 49 | Lincoln | 7906 | 48 | Carlisle | 3761 | 43 | Boston | 3039 | 10 | Shrewsbury | 2528 |
| 41 | Bournemouth | 7181 | 15 | Hull City | 3607 | 35 | Kidderminster | 3039 | 14 | Boston | 2514 |
| 29 | Bristol Rovers | 6196 | 2 | Rushden & D | 3602 | 30 | Wrexham | 3006 | 39 | Scunthorpe | 2486 |
| 5 | Exeter | 6065 | 46 | Southend | 3594 | 45 | Macclesfield | 2970 | 4 | Hartlepool | 2403 |
| 34 | Exeter | 5761 | 17 | Bournemouth | 3543 | 16 | Scunthorpe | 2911 | 6 | Wrexham | 2283 |
| 7 | Oxford | 5260 | 26 | Darlington | 3506 | 22 | Rochdale | 2754 | 25 | Southend | 2244 |
| 23 | Blackpool | 5014 | 12 | Lincoln | 3428 | 19 | Boreham W | 2739 | 44 | Rochdale | 2216 |
| 32 | Hartlepool | 4975 | 47 | Leyton Orient | 3379 | 42 | Shrewsbury | 2694 | 8 | Gillingham | 1981 |
| 1 | Bristol Rovers | 4937 | 36 | Oxford | 3372 | 28 | York | 2663 | 21 | Macclesfield | 1835 |
| 24 | Leyton Orient | 4443 | 38 | Swansea | 3287 | 27 | Rushden & D | 2651 | | | |
| 37 | Cambridge | 4280 | 18 | Bury | 3210 | 20 | Kidderminster | 2629 | | | |
| 13 | Carlisle | 4014 | 3 | York | 3203 | 31 | Darlington | 2628 | | | |

## KEY PLAYER APPEARANCES

| | PLAYER | POS | AGE | APP | MINS ON | GOALS | CARDS(Y/R) | | HOME COUNTRY |
|---|---|---|---|---|---|---|---|---|---|
| 1 | Reuben Hazell | DEF | 24 | 46 | 4140 | 1 | 7 | 0 | England |
| 2 | David Woozley | DEF | 23 | 46 | 4074 | 3 | 5 | 0 | England |
| 3 | Alex Russell | MID | 30 | 39 | 3464 | 9 | 5 | 0 | England |
| 4 | Jason Fowler | MID | 28 | 40 | 3420 | 4 | 9 | 1 | England |
| 5 | Martin Gritton | ATT | 25 | 43 | 3334 | 13 | 5 | 0 | Scotland |
| 6 | Kevin Hill | ATT | 27 | 40 | 3138 | 4 | 7 | 0 | England |
| 7 | Anthony Bedeau | ATT | 24 | 40 | 3091 | 6 | 9 | 1 | England |
| 8 | Lee Canoville | DEF | 22 | 36 | 3066 | 0 | 5 | 0 | England |
| 9 | Matt Hockley | DEF | 21 | 46 | 2392 | 2 | 3 | 0 | England |
| 10 | Kevin Dearden | GK | 33 | 41 | 2317 | 0 | 0 | 0 | England |
| 11 | David Graham | ATT | 24 | 35 | 2305 | 15 | 1 | 0 | Scotland |
| 12 | Jo Osei-Kuffour | ATT | 21 | 33 | 1803 | 4 | 2 | 0 | England |
| 13 | Sean Hankin | DEF | 22 | 22 | 1451 | 1 | 5 | 0 | Wales |
| 14 | Arjan Van Heusden | GK | 30 | 22 | 1170 | 0 | 0 | 0 | Holland |
| 15 | Simon Clist | MID | 22 | 11 | 917 | 2 | 1 | 0 | England |
| 16 | Kevin Wills | ATT | 22 | 23 | 666 | 1 | 1 | 0 | England |
| 17 | Paul Holmes | DEF | 35 | 10 | 588 | 0 | 0 | 0 | England |
| 18 | Stephen Woods | DEF | 26 | 14 | 543 | 0 | 2 | 0 | England |

## KEY PLAYERS - GOALSCORERS

**1 David Graham**

Goals in the League: 15

Contribution to Attacking Power — Average number of minutes between League team goals while on pitch: 60

Player Strike Rate — Average number of minutes between League goals scored by player: 154

Club Strike Rate — Average number of minutes between League goals scored by club: 58

| | PLAYER | LGE GOALS | POWER | STRIKE RATE |
|---|---|---|---|---|
| 2 | Martin Gritton | 13 | 61 | 256 mins |
| 3 | Alex Russell | 9 | 56 | 385 mins |
| 4 | Jo Osei-Kuffour | 4 | 66 | 451 mins |
| 5 | Anthony Bedeau | 6 | 53 | 515 mins |

## KEY PLAYERS - MIDFIELDERS

**1 Simon Clist**

Goals in the League: 2

Defensive Rating — Average number of mins between League goals conceded while he was on the pitch: 71

Contribution to Attacking Power — Average number of minutes between League team goals while on pitch: 66

Scoring Difference — Defensive Rating minus Contribution to Attacking Power: 5

| | PLAYER | LGE GOALS | DEF RATE | POWER | SCORE DIFF |
|---|---|---|---|---|---|
| 2 | Alex Russell | 9 | 60 | 57 | 3 mins |
| 3 | Jason Fowler | 4 | 53 | 58 | -5 mins |

## KEY PLAYERS - DEFENDERS

**1 Lee Canoville**

Goals Conceded when he was on pitch: 49

Defensive Rating — Ave number of mins between League goals conceded while on the pitch: 63

Clean Sheets — In games when he played at least 70 minutes: 6

Club Defensive Rating — Average number of mins between League goals conceded by the club this season.: 58

| | PLAYER | CON LGE | CLN SHEETS | DEF RATE |
|---|---|---|---|---|
| 2 | Sean Hankin | 24 | 1 | 60 mins |
| 3 | David Woozley | 68 | 8 | 60 mins |
| 4 | Matt Hockley | 40 | 5 | 60 mins |
| 5 | Reuben Hazell | 71 | 8 | 58 mins |

## KEY GOALKEEPER

**1 Arjan Van Heusden**

Goals Conceded in the League: 16

Defensive Rating — Ave number of mins between League goals conceded while on the pitch.: 73

Counting Games — Games when he played at least 70 mins: 12

Clean Sheets — In games when he played at least 70 mins: 3

## TEAM OF THE SEASON

| GOALKEEPER | GAMES | DEF RATE |
|---|---|---|
| Arjan Van Heusden | 12 | 73 |
| **DEFENDERS** | **GAMES** | **DEF RATE** |
| Lee Canoville | 33 | 63 |
| Sean Hankin | 14 | 60 |
| Matt Hockley | 20 | 60 |
| David Woozley | 45 | 60 |
| **MIDFIELDERS** | **GAMES** | **SCORE DIFF** |
| Simon Clist | 10 | 5 |
| Alex Russell | 38 | 3 |
| Jason Fowler | 37 | -5 |
| Reuben Hazell* | 46 | 58DR |
| **FORWARDS** | **GAMES** | **STRIKE RATE** |
| David Graham | 20 | 154 |
| Martin Gritton | 34 | 256 |

# YORK CITY

**Final Position: 10th**

NICKNAME: THE MINSTERMEN

| | | | | | | |
|---|---|---|---|---|---|---|
| 1 | div3 | Macclesfield | A | D | 1-1 | Duffield 90 |
| 2 | div3 | Shrewsbury | H | W | 2-1 | Duffield 46; Parkin 72 |
| 3 | div3 | Torquay | H | W | 4-3 | Duffield 14; Nogan 49; Parkin 53,73 |
| 4 | div3 | Scunthorpe | A | L | 1-2 | Duffield 25 |
| 5 | div3 | Boston | H | W | 2-0 | Duffield 22; Nogan 51 |
| 6 | div3 | Swansea | A | W | 2-1 | Bullock 31; Duffield 80 pen |
| 7 | div3 | Bury | A | L | 1-2 | Cowan 51 |
| 8 | wcr1 | Sheff Utd | A | L | 0-1 | |
| 9 | div3 | Rushden & D | H | D | 0-0 | |
| 10 | div3 | Darlington | H | W | 1-0 | Parkin 73 |
| 11 | div3 | Cambridge | A | L | 0-3 | |
| 12 | div3 | Oxford | H | L | 0-1 | |
| 13 | div3 | Exeter | A | W | 1-0 | Cook 42 |
| 14 | div3 | Southend | A | L | 0-1 | |
| 15 | div3 | Bristol Rovers | H | D | 2-2 | Duffield 39 pen; Brackston 90 |
| 16 | div3 | Bournemouth | A | L | 0-1 | |
| 17 | div3 | Wrexham | H | D | 1-1 | Duffield 75 |
| 18 | div3 | Hartlepool | A | D | 0-0 | |
| 19 | div3 | Leyton Orient | H | W | 3-2 | Brass 28; Parkin 80; Bullock 87 |
| 20 | div3 | Rochdale | A | W | 1-0 | Duffield 71 |
| 21 | facr1 | Swansea | H | W | 2-1 | Duffield 21,88 |
| 22 | div3 | Carlisle | H | W | 2-1 | Reddy 44; Duffield 79 |
| 23 | facr2 | Brentford | H | L | 1-2 | Bullock 63 |
| 24 | div3 | Kidderminster | A | W | 2-1 | Brackstone 23; Nogan 86 |
| 25 | div3 | Lincoln | H | D | 1-1 | Cooper 81 |
| 26 | div3 | Boston | A | L | 0-3 | |
| 27 | div3 | Hull City | H | D | 1-1 | Edmondson 33 |
| 28 | div3 | Scunthorpe | H | L | 1-3 | Edmondson 26 |
| 29 | div3 | Torquay | A | L | 1-3 | Duffield 5 pen |
| 30 | div3 | Swansea | H | W | 3-1 | Duffield 9 pen,41; Reddy 82 |
| 31 | div3 | Hull City | A | D | 0-0 | |
| 32 | div3 | Macclesfield | H | W | 2-1 | Parkin 5; Bullock 52 |
| 33 | div3 | Leyton Orient | A | W | 1-0 | Shandran 70 |
| 34 | div3 | Shrewsbury | A | D | 2-2 | Potter 60; Parkin 62 |
| 35 | div3 | Hartlepool | H | D | 0-0 | |
| 36 | div3 | Bury | H | D | 1-1 | Parkin 53 pen |
| 37 | div3 | Rushden & D | A | L | 1-2 | Bullock 90 |
| 38 | div3 | Darlington | A | L | 1-2 | Bullock 48 |
| 39 | div3 | Cambridge | H | W | 3-1 | Parkin 48; Nogan 49; Shandran 90 |
| 40 | div3 | Bournemouth | H | W | 1-0 | Parkin 49 |
| 41 | div3 | Bristol Rovers | A | W | 1-0 | Edmondson 42 |
| 42 | div3 | Wrexham | A | D | 1-1 | Edmondson 6 |
| 43 | div3 | Southend | H | W | 2-0 | Nogan 18; Bullock 45 |
| 44 | div3 | Rochdale | H | D | 2-2 | Graydon 35 pen; Edmondson 63 |
| 45 | div3 | Carlisle | A | D | 1-1 | Shandran 75 |
| 46 | div3 | Lincoln | A | L | 0-1 | |
| 47 | div3 | Kidderminster | H | D | 0-0 | |
| 48 | div3 | Exeter | H | L | 0-2 | |
| 49 | div3 | Oxford | A | L | 0-2 | |

■ Home □ Away □ Neutral

## ATTENDANCES

HOME GROUND: BOOTHAM CRESCENT CAPACITY: 9534 AVERAGE LEAGUE AT HOME: 3997

| | | | | | | | | | | | |
|---|---|---|---|---|---|---|---|---|---|---|---|
| 31 | Hull City | 18437 | 37 | Rushden & D | 4463 | 32 | Macclesfield | 4009 | 7 | Bury | 3294 |
| 41 | Bristol Rovers | 8248 | 42 | Wrexham | 4425 | 44 | Rochdale | 3966 | 3 | Torquay | 3203 |
| 27 | Hull City | 7856 | 14 | Southend | 4411 | 12 | Oxford | 3962 | 13 | Exeter | 3187 |
| 49 | Oxford | 6905 | 22 | Carlisle | 4335 | 26 | Boston | 3864 | 20 | Rochdale | 3056 |
| 35 | Hartlepool | 5953 | 43 | Southend | 4312 | 40 | Bournemouth | 3642 | 17 | Wrexham | 2970 |
| 18 | Hartlepool | 5789 | 33 | Leyton Orient | 4260 | 15 | Bristol Rovers | 3616 | 21 | Swansea | 2948 |
| 16 | Bournemouth | 5755 | 5 | Boston | 4228 | 23 | Brentford | 3517 | 29 | Torquay | 2663 |
| 45 | Carlisle | 4935 | 11 | Cambridge | 4204 | 4 | Scunthorpe | 3504 | 34 | Shrewsbury | 2599 |
| 48 | Exeter | 4840 | 10 | Darlington | 4128 | 2 | Shrewsbury | 3463 | 1 | Macclesfield | 2586 |
| 8 | Sheff Utd | 4675 | 36 | Bury | 4115 | 38 | Darlington | 3434 | 24 | Kidderminster | 2304 |
| 46 | Lincoln | 4653 | 9 | Rushden & D | 4109 | 25 | Lincoln | 3411 | | | |
| 30 | Swansea | 4611 | 6 | Swansea | 4086 | 39 | Cambridge | 3394 | | | |
| 28 | Scunthorpe | 4554 | 47 | Kidderminster | 4069 | 19 | Leyton Orient | 3304 | | | |

## KEY PLAYER APPEARANCES

| | PLAYER | POS | AGE | APP | MINS ON | GOALS | CARDS(Y/R) | | HOME COUNTRY |
|---|---|---|---|---|---|---|---|---|---|
| 1 | Chris Brass | DEF | 27 | 40 | 3496 | 1 | 4 | 0 | England |
| 2 | Lee Nogan | ATT | 34 | 46 | 3433 | 5 | 4 | 0 | England |
| 3 | Lee Bullock | MID | 22 | 39 | 3358 | 6 | 6 | 0 | England |
| 4 | Darren Edmondson | DEF | 31 | 39 | 3309 | 5 | 7 | 0 | England |
| 5 | Graham Potter | DEF | 28 | 42 | 3280 | 1 | 2 | 0 | England |
| 6 | Jonathan Parkin | DEF | 21 | 41 | 3183 | 10 | 11 | 0 | England |
| 7 | Chris Smith | DEF | 22 | 38 | 3043 | 0 | 7 | 1 | England |
| 8 | Thomas Cowan | DEF | 33 | 36 | 2681 | 1 | 9 | 0 | Scotland |
| 9 | Peter Duffield | ATT | 34 | 28 | 2453 | 13 | 1 | 0 | England |
| 10 | Gary Hobson | DEF | 31 | 34 | 2016 | 0 | 3 | 0 | England |
| 11 | Stephen Brackstone | MID | 20 | 31 | 1972 | 2 | 1 | 0 | England |
| 12 | Alan Fettis | GK | 32 | 24 | 1890 | 0 | 2 | 0 | N Ireland |
| 13 | Richard Cooper | DEF | 23 | 27 | 1882 | 1 | 4 | 0 | England |
| 14 | Scott Jones | DEF | 28 | 29 | 1737 | 0 | 6 | 0 | England |
| 15 | Michael Ingham | GK | 22 | 17 | 1485 | 0 | 1 | 0 | |
| 16 | Anthony Shandran | ATT | 21 | 18 | 1041 | 3 | 1 | 0 | England |
| 17 | Michael Reddy | ATT | 23 | 11 | 945 | 2 | 4 | 0 | Rep of Ireland |
| 18 | Leigh Wood | MID | 20 | 38 | 907 | 0 | 2 | 0 | England |

## KEY PLAYERS - GOALSCORERS

**1 Peter Duffield**

| | | | |
|---|---|---|---|
| Goals in the League | 13 | Player Strike Rate<br>Average number of minutes between League goals scored by player | 189 |
| Contribution to Attacking Power<br>Average number of minutes between League team goals while on pitch | 74 | Club Strike Rate<br>Average number of minutes between League goals scored by club | 80 |

| | PLAYER | LGE GOALS | POWER | STRIKE RAT |
|---|---|---|---|---|
| 2 | Jonathan Parkin | 10 | 74 | 318 mir |
| 3 | Lee Bullock | 6 | 83 | 560 min |
| 4 | Darren Edmondson | 5 | 78 | 662 mir |
| 5 | Lee Nogan | 5 | 74 | 687 mir |

## KEY PLAYERS - MIDFIELDERS

**1 Stephen Brackstone**

| | | | |
|---|---|---|---|
| Goals in the League | 2 | Contribution to Attacking Power<br>Average number of minutes between League team goals while on pitch | 82 |
| Defensive Rating<br>Average number of mins between League goals conceded while he was on the pitch | 76 | Scoring Difference<br>Defensive Rating minus Contribution to Attacking Power | -6 |

| | PLAYER | LGE GOALS | DEF RATE | POWER | SCORE DIF |
|---|---|---|---|---|---|
| 2 | Lee Bullock | 6 | 76 | 84 | -8 min |
| 3 | Leigh Wood | 0 | 82 | 113 | -31 min |

## KEY PLAYERS - DEFENDERS

**1 Richard Cooper**

| | | | |
|---|---|---|---|
| Goals Conceded when he was on pitch | 21 | Clean Sheets<br>In games when he played at least 70 minutes | 7 |
| Defensive Rating<br>Ave number of mins between League goals conceded while on the pitch | 90 | Club Defensive Rating<br>Average number of mins between League goals conceded by the club this season. | 78 |

| | PLAYER | CON LGE | CLN SHEETS | DEF RAT |
|---|---|---|---|---|
| 2 | Chris Brass | 41 | 12 | 85 mins |
| 3 | Scott Jones | 21 | 6 | 83 mins |
| 4 | Chris Smith | 38 | 10 | 80 mins |
| 5 | Graham Potter | 41 | 10 | 80 mins |

## KEY GOALKEEPER

**1 Michael Ingham**

| | |
|---|---|
| Goals Conceded in the League | 15 |
| Defensive Rating<br>Ave number of mins between League goals conceded while on the pitch. | 99 |
| Counting Games<br>Games when he played at least 70 mins | 16 |
| Clean Sheets<br>In games when he played at least 70 mins | 7 |

## TEAM OF THE SEASON

| GOALKEEPER | GAMES | DEF RAT |
|---|---|---|
| Michael Ingham | 16 | 9 |
| **DEFENDERS** | **GAMES** | **DEF RAT** |
| Richard Cooper | 19 | 9 |
| Chris Brass | 39 | 8 |
| Scott Jones | 18 | 8 |
| Graham Potter | 35 | 8 |
| **MIDFIELDERS** | **GAMES** | **SCORE DIF** |
| Stephen Brackstone | 21 | - |
| Lee Bullock | 37 | - |
| Leigh Wood | 9 | -3 |
| Chris Smith* | 42 | 80DF |
| **FORWARDS** | **GAMES** | **STRIKE RAT** |
| Peter Duffield | 27 | 18 |
| Lee Nogan | 36 | 68 |

# KIDDERMINSTER

**Final Position: 11th**

NICKNAME: THE HARRIERS

| | | | | | | |
|---|---|---|---|---|---|---|
| 1 | div3 | Lincoln | H | D | 1-1 | Henriksen 59 |
| 2 | div3 | Bournemouth | A | D | 0-0 | |
| 3 | div3 | Rushden & D | A | L | 1-3 | Williams 77 |
| 4 | div3 | Exeter | H | W | 4-3 | Henriksen 29,53; Ayres 35,68 |
| 5 | div3 | Leyton Orient | A | D | 0-0 | |
| 6 | div3 | Darlington | H | D | 1-1 | Foster 53 pen |
| 7 | div3 | Boston | H | D | 0-0 | |
| 8 | wcr1 | Nottm Forest | A | L | 0-4 | |
| 9 | div3 | Scunthorpe | A | D | 1-1 | Shilton 45 |
| 10 | div3 | Southend | A | W | 2-0 | Flynn 45; Melligan 49 |
| 11 | div3 | Rochdale | H | D | 0-0 | |
| 12 | div3 | Bristol Rovers | A | W | 2-1 | Melligan 27; Henriksen 75 |
| 13 | div3 | Hull City | H | W | 1-0 | Henriksen 60 |
| 14 | div3 | Macclesfield | H | L | 0-2 | |
| 15 | div3 | Shrewsbury | A | W | 3-2 | Henriksen 5; Williams 45; Artell 55 og |
| 16 | div3 | Cambridge | H | W | 2-1 | Melligan 4,27 |
| 17 | div3 | Swansea | A | W | 4-0 | Shilton 28; Henriksen 52; Broughton 57; Melligan 62 |
| 18 | div3 | Carlisle | H | L | 1-2 | Flynn 66 |
| 19 | facr1 | Rushden & D | H | D | 2-2 | Setchell 58 og; Broughton 77 |
| 20 | div3 | Torquay | A | D | 2-2 | Henriksen 61; Bishop 72 |
| 21 | facr1r | Rushden & D | A | L | 1-2 | Broughton 73 |
| 22 | div3 | Hartlepool | A | L | 1-2 | Parrish 47 |
| 23 | div3 | York | H | L | 1-2 | Bishop 40 |
| 24 | div3 | Wrexham | A | W | 2-0 | Parrish 44; Melligan 89 |
| 25 | div3 | Leyton Orient | H | W | 3-2 | Bennett 39; Shilton 78; Henriksen 84 |
| 26 | div3 | Bury | A | D | 1-1 | Henriksen 49 pen |
| 27 | div3 | Rushden & D | H | L | 0-2 | |
| 28 | div3 | Darlington | A | L | 1-2 | Henriksen 50 |
| 29 | div3 | Bury | H | W | 3-2 | Parrish 21; Bishop 45,62 |
| 30 | div3 | Oxford | H | L | 1-3 | Parrish 52 |
| 31 | div3 | Bournemouth | H | W | 1-0 | Henriksen 83 |
| 32 | div3 | Carlisle | A | D | 2-2 | Henriksen 30; Scott 83 |
| 33 | div3 | Torquay | H | W | 2-0 | Melligan 20; Henriksen 69 |
| 34 | div3 | Exeter | A | W | 5-2 | Henriksen 25,45 pen,56; Whitbread 39 og; Broughton 57 |
| 35 | div3 | Boston | A | L | 0-3 | |
| 36 | div3 | Scunthorpe | H | L | 1-3 | Henriksen 49 |
| 37 | div3 | Southend | H | W | 1-0 | Melligan 76 |
| 38 | div3 | Cambridge | A | W | 2-0 | Melligan 66; Morgan 73 |
| 39 | div3 | Shrewsbury | H | D | 2-2 | Broughton 62,68 |
| 40 | div3 | Swansea | H | D | 2-2 | Shilton 8; Smith 32 |
| 41 | div3 | Lincoln | A | L | 0-1 | |
| 42 | div3 | Macclesfield | A | L | 0-2 | |
| 43 | div3 | Hartlepool | H | D | 2-2 | Henriksen 22; Bishop 27 |
| 44 | div3 | Oxford | A | L | 1-2 | Henriksen 45 |
| 45 | div3 | Rochdale | A | W | 1-0 | Shilton 83 |
| 46 | div3 | Wrexham | H | L | 0-2 | |
| 47 | div3 | York | A | D | 0-0 | |
| 48 | div3 | Hull City | A | L | 1-4 | Parrish 60 |
| 49 | div3 | Bristol Rovers | H | D | 1-1 | Melligan 15 |

Home / Away / Neutral

## ATTENDANCES

HOME GROUND: AGGBOROUGH CAPACITY: 6293 AVERAGE LEAGUE AT HOME: 2895

| | | | | | | | | | | | |
|---|---|---|---|---|---|---|---|---|---|---|---|
| 48 | Hull City | 14544 | 24 | Wrexham | 3734 | 18 | Carlisle | 3009 | 6 | Darlington | 2488 |
| 12 | Bristol Rovers | 9447 | 38 | Cambridge | 3705 | 30 | Oxford | 2991 | 35 | Boston | 2485 |
| 44 | Oxford | 6820 | 46 | Wrexham | 3689 | 10 | Southend | 2959 | 23 | York | 2304 |
| 2 | Bournemouth | 4771 | 15 | Shrewsbury | 3507 | 43 | Hartlepool | 2900 | 7 | Boston | 2222 |
| 8 | Nottm Forest | 4498 | 17 | Swansea | 3421 | 36 | Scunthorpe | 2834 | 4 | Exeter | 2195 |
| 22 | Hartlepool | 4296 | 27 | Rushden & D | 3417 | 16 | Cambridge | 2779 | 31 | Bournemouth | 2157 |
| 5 | Leyton Orient | 4147 | 21 | Rushden & D | 3391 | 29 | Bury | 2736 | 42 | Macclesfield | 2069 |
| 41 | Lincoln | 4092 | 3 | Rushden & D | 3329 | 1 | Lincoln | 2687 | 37 | Southend | 2006 |
| 47 | York | 4069 | 39 | Shrewsbury | 3284 | 11 | Rochdale | 2685 | 34 | Exeter | 1957 |
| 32 | Carlisle | 3882 | 26 | Bury | 3202 | 9 | Scunthorpe | 2676 | 45 | Rochdale | 1810 |
| 49 | Bristol Rovers | 3872 | 40 | Swansea | 3172 | 28 | Darlington | 2630 | | | |
| 25 | Leyton Orient | 3821 | 19 | Rushden & D | 3079 | 20 | Torquay | 2629 | | | |
| 13 | Hull City | 3787 | 33 | Torquay | 3039 | 14 | Macclesfield | 2521 | | | |

## KEY PLAYER APPEARANCES

| | PLAYER | POS | AGE | APP | MINS ON | GOALS | CARDS(Y/R) | | HOME COUNTRY |
|---|---|---|---|---|---|---|---|---|---|
| 1 | Sean Flynn | MID | 35 | 45 | 4050 | 2 | 6 | 1 | England |
| 2 | Craig Hinton | DEF | 25 | 44 | 3892 | 0 | 6 | 0 | England |
| 3 | Danny Williams | MID | 23 | 45 | 3822 | 2 | 11 | 0 | Wales |
| 4 | Sam Shilton | MID | 24 | 43 | 3384 | 5 | 0 | 0 | England |
| 5 | Stuart Brock | GK | 26 | 46 | 3150 | 0 | 1 | 0 | England |
| 6 | Bo Henriksen | ATT | 28 | 41 | 3063 | 20 | 10 | 0 | Denmark |
| 7 | Drew Broughton | ATT | 24 | 39 | 2485 | 4 | 11 | 2 | England |
| 8 | John Melligan | MID | 22 | 30 | 2442 | 10 | 2 | 0 | Rep of Ireland |
| 9 | Dean Bennett | MID | 25 | 35 | 2412 | 1 | 3 | 0 | England |
| 10 | Adrian Smith | DEF | 29 | 31 | 2384 | 1 | 3 | 0 | England |
| 11 | Lee Ayres | DEF | 20 | 36 | 2163 | 2 | 4 | 0 | England |
| 12 | Sean Parrish | MID | 31 | 37 | 1960 | 5 | 4 | 0 | Wales |
| 13 | Andrew Bishop | ATT | 20 | 29 | 1934 | 5 | 2 | 0 | England |
| 14 | Scott Stamps | DEF | 28 | 27 | 1721 | 0 | 9 | 1 | England |
| 15 | Dion Scott | DEF | 22 | 19 | 1665 | 1 | 1 | 0 | England |
| 16 | Kenny Coleman | DEF | 20 | 17 | 1172 | 0 | 1 | 0 | Rep of Ireland |
| 17 | Ian Foster | ATT | 26 | 40 | 1006 | 1 | 0 | 0 | England |
| 18 | Fraser Digby | GK | 36 | 12 | 990 | 0 | 0 | 0 | England |

## KEY PLAYERS - GOALSCORERS

**1 Bo Henriksen**

| | |
|---|---|
| Goals in the League | 20 |
| Contribution to Attacking Power: Average number of minutes between League team goals while on pitch | 58 |
| Player Strike Rate: Average number of minutes between League goals scored by player | 153 |
| Club Strike Rate: Average number of minutes between League goals scored by club | 67 |

| | PLAYER | LGE GOALS | POWER | STRIKE RATE |
|---|---|---|---|---|
| 2 | John Melligan | 10 | 54 | 244 mins |
| 3 | Andrew Bishop | 5 | 71 | 387 mins |
| 4 | Sean Parrish | 5 | 81 | 392 mins |
| 5 | Drew Broughton | 4 | 62 | 621 mins |

## KEY PLAYERS - MIDFIELDERS

**1 John Melligan**

| | |
|---|---|
| Goals in the League | 10 |
| Defensive Rating: Average number of mins between League goals conceded while he was on the pitch | 74 |
| Contribution to Attacking Power: Average number of minutes between League team goals while on pitch | 54 |
| Scoring Difference: Defensive Rating minus Contribution to Attacking Power | 20 |

| | PLAYER | LGE GOALS | DEF RATE | POWER | SCORE DIFF |
|---|---|---|---|---|---|
| 2 | Sam Shilton | 5 | 71 | 64 | 7 mins |
| 3 | Sean Flynn | 2 | 64 | 65 | -1 mins |
| 4 | Danny Williams | 2 | 65 | 68 | -3 mins |
| 5 | Dean Bennett | 1 | 56 | 67 | -11 mins |

## KEY PLAYERS - DEFENDERS

**1 Scott Stamps**

| | |
|---|---|
| Goals Conceded when he was on pitch | 24 |
| Defensive Rating: Ave number of mins between League goals conceded while on the pitch | 72 |
| Clean Sheets: In games when he played at least 70 minutes | 7 |
| Club Defensive Rating: Average number of mins between League goals conceded by the club this season. | 66 |

| | PLAYER | CON LGE | CLN SHEETS | DEF RATE |
|---|---|---|---|---|
| 2 | Lee Ayres | 31 | 7 | 70 mins |
| 3 | Craig Hinton | 60 | 12 | 65 mins |
| 4 | Dion Scott | 26 | 6 | 64 mins |
| 5 | Adrian Smith | 39 | 7 | 61 mins |

## KEY GOALKEEPER

**1 Stuart Brock**

| | |
|---|---|
| Goals Conceded in the League | 48 |
| Defensive Rating: Ave number of mins between League goals conceded while on the pitch. | 66 |
| Counting Games: Games when he played at least 70 mins | 35 |
| Clean Sheets: In games when he played at least 70 mins | 10 |

## TEAM OF THE SEASON

| GOALKEEPER | GAMES | DEF RATE |
|---|---|---|
| Stuart Brock | 35 | 66 |
| **DEFENDERS** | **GAMES** | **DEF RATE** |
| Scott Stamps | 17 | 72 |
| Lee Ayres | 22 | 70 |
| Craig Hinton | 43 | 65 |
| Dion Scott | 18 | 64 |
| **MIDFIELDERS** | **GAMES** | **SCORE DIFF** |
| John Melligan | 26 | 20 |
| Sam Shilton | 36 | 7 |
| Sean Flynn | 45 | -1 |
| Danny Williams | 40 | -3 |
| **FORWARDS** | **GAMES** | **STRIKE RATE** |
| Bo Henriksen | 34 | 153 |
| Andrew Bishop | 20 | 387 |

# CAMBRIDGE UNITED

Final Position: **12th**

NICKNAME: THE U'S

| | | | | | | |
|---|---|---|---|---|---|---|
| 1 | div3 | Darlington | H | L | 1-2 | Kitson 6 |
| 2 | div3 | Bury | A | W | 1-0 | Riza 53 |
| 3 | div3 | Bournemouth | A | D | 1-1 | Fleming 35 |
| 4 | div3 | Leyton Orient | H | W | 2-1 | Kitson 5; Warner 55 |
| 5 | div3 | Southend | A | L | 1-2 | Riza 28 |
| 6 | div3 | Rushden & D | H | W | 4-1 | Youngs 21,77; Riza 64; Kitson 90 |
| 7 | div3 | Hull City | H | L | 1-2 | Kitson 90 |
| 8 | wcr1 | Reading | H | W | 3-1 | Duncan 23; Kitson 38; Tudor 71 |
| 9 | div3 | Torquay | A | L | 2-3 | Tudor 89,90 |
| 10 | div3 | Rochdale | A | L | 3-4 | Riza 18; Tudor 38; Wanless 50 pen |
| 11 | div3 | York | H | W | 3-0 | Kitson 13; Tann 82; Bridges 84 |
| 12 | div3 | Boston | A | W | 3-1 | Kitson 2,90; Redfearn 22 og |
| 13 | wcr2 | Sunderland | H | L | 0-7 | |
| 14 | div3 | Wrexham | H | D | 2-2 | Youngs 84; Riza 85 |
| 15 | div3 | Scunthorpe | A | W | 2-1 | Riza 53; Tudor 80 |
| 16 | div3 | Oxford | H | D | 1-1 | Tudor 28 |
| 17 | div3 | Kidderminster | A | L | 1-2 | Kitson 8 |
| 18 | div3 | Carlisle | H | W | 2-1 | Tudor 25,63 |
| 19 | div3 | Swansea | H | W | 1-0 | Kitson 53 |
| 20 | div3 | Shrewsbury | A | L | 1-3 | Youngs 53 |
| 21 | facr1 | Scarborough | A | D | 0-0 | |
| 22 | div3 | Exeter | A | W | 2-1 | Tudor 34; Kitson 81 |
| 23 | facr1r | Scarborough | H | L | 2-1 | Wanless 31; Hotte 97 og |
| 24 | div3 | Macclesfield | H | W | 3-1 | Wanless 29; Kitson 70; Riza 74 pen |
| 25 | facr2 | Northampton | H | D | 2-2 | Tann 5,45 |
| 26 | div3 | Lincoln | A | D | 2-2 | Guttridge 4; Wanless 78 |
| 27 | facr2r | Northampton | A | W | 1-0 | Riza 79 |
| 28 | div3 | Bristol Rovers | H | W | 3-1 | Parker 17 og; Youngs 49; Kitson 66 |
| 29 | div3 | Southend | H | D | 1-1 | Fleming 63 |
| 30 | div3 | Hartlepool | A | L | 0-3 | |
| 31 | facr3 | Millwall | H | D | 1-1 | Youngs 49 |
| 32 | facr3r | Millwall | A | L | 2-3 | Kitson 58; Youngs 61 |
| 33 | div3 | Rushden & D | A | L | 1-4 | Wanless 87 |
| 34 | div3 | Hartlepool | H | D | 0-0 | |
| 35 | div3 | Leyton Orient | A | D | 1-1 | Youngs 35 |
| 36 | div3 | Bury | H | L | 1-2 | Youngs 39 |
| 37 | div3 | Shrewsbury | H | W | 5-0 | Kitson 4,59; Riza 45; Youngs 47,81 |
| 38 | div3 | Swansea | A | L | 0-2 | |
| 39 | div3 | Hull City | A | D | 1-1 | Youngs 38 |
| 40 | div3 | Torquay | H | L | 0-1 | |
| 41 | div3 | Rochdale | H | D | 2-2 | Kitson 4; Tudor 45 |
| 42 | div3 | York | A | L | 1-3 | Iriekpen 6 |
| 43 | div3 | Darlington | A | W | 2-1 | Riza 38,85 |
| 44 | div3 | Kidderminster | H | L | 0-2 | |
| 45 | div3 | Oxford | A | D | 1-1 | Guttridge 59 |
| 46 | div3 | Carlisle | A | W | 1-0 | Kitson 26 |
| 47 | div3 | Bournemouth | H | W | 2-1 | Kitson 12; Guttridge 83 |
| 48 | div3 | Scunthorpe | H | D | 1-1 | Kitson 14 |
| 49 | div3 | Macclesfield | A | D | 1-1 | Riza 67 |
| 50 | div3 | Exeter | H | W | 2-1 | Wanless 69 pen; Turner 90 |
| 51 | div3 | Bristol Rovers | A | L | 1-3 | Kitson 90 pen |
| 52 | div3 | Lincoln | H | D | 0-0 | |
| 53 | div3 | Wrexham | A | L | 0-5 | |
| 54 | div3 | Boston | H | L | 1-2 | Riza 72 |

■ Home □ Away ▨ Neutral

## ATTENDANCES

HOME GROUND: ABBEY STADIUM CAPACITY: 8200 AVERAGE LEAGUE AT HOME: 4172

| | | | | | | | | | | | |
|---|---|---|---|---|---|---|---|---|---|---|---|
| 39 | Hull City | 15607 | 30 | Hartlepool | 4805 | 19 | Swansea | 3956 | 36 | Bury | 2875 |
| 53 | Wrexham | 9960 | 16 | Oxford | 4621 | 35 | Leyton Orient | 3953 | 26 | Lincoln | 2845 |
| 13 | Sunderland | 8175 | 6 | Rushden & D | 4598 | 48 | Scunthorpe | 3951 | 17 | Kidderminster | 2779 |
| 51 | Bristol Rovers | 7563 | 27 | Northampton | 4591 | 24 | Macclesfield | 3834 | 22 | Exeter | 2722 |
| 32 | Millwall | 7031 | 34 | Hartlepool | 4543 | 37 | Shrewsbury | 3755 | 8 | Reading | 2696 |
| 31 | Millwall | 6864 | 54 | Boston | 4488 | 44 | Kidderminster | 3705 | 2 | Bury | 2650 |
| 29 | Southend | 6237 | 5 | Southend | 4462 | 28 | Bristol Rovers | 3701 | 41 | Rochdale | 2586 |
| 14 | Wrexham | 6044 | 3 | Bournemouth | 4315 | 42 | York | 3394 | 9 | Torquay | 2557 |
| 50 | Exeter | 5218 | 40 | Torquay | 4280 | 23 | Scarborough | 3373 | 10 | Rochdale | 2392 |
| 33 | Rushden & D | 5206 | 7 | Hull City | 4258 | 18 | Carlisle | 3334 | 21 | Scarborough | 2084 |
| 25 | Northampton | 5076 | 11 | York | 4204 | 15 | Scunthorpe | 3140 | 43 | Darlington | 2076 |
| 45 | Oxford | 4983 | 1 | Darlington | 4079 | 12 | Boston | 3090 | 49 | Macclesfield | 2053 |
| 38 | Swansea | 4903 | 52 | Lincoln | 4013 | 20 | Shrewsbury | 2928 | | | |
| 4 | Leyton Orient | 4807 | 46 | Carlisle | 3992 | 47 | Bournemouth | 2885 | | | |

## KEY PLAYER APPEARANCES

| | PLAYER | POS | AGE | APP | MINS ON | GOALS | CARDS(Y/R) | | HOME COUNTRY |
|---|---|---|---|---|---|---|---|---|---|
| 1 | Shaun Marshall | GK | 24 | 45 | 4050 | 0 | 0 | 0 | England |
| 2 | David Kitson | ATT | 23 | 44 | 3892 | 19 | 4 | 0 | England |
| 3 | Terry Fleming | DEF | 30 | 43 | 3708 | 2 | 8 | 1 | England |
| 4 | Omer Riza | ATT | 23 | 46 | 3612 | 12 | 7 | 0 | England |
| 5 | Stevland Angus | DEF | 22 | 40 | 3468 | 0 | 7 | 0 | England |
| 6 | Luke Guttridge | MID | 21 | 43 | 3357 | 3 | 8 | 1 | England |
| 7 | Warren Goodhind | DEF | 25 | 37 | 3055 | 0 | 10 | 2 | South Africa |
| 8 | Tom Youngs | ATT | 23 | 37 | 2754 | 10 | 1 | 1 | England |
| 9 | Paul Wanless | MID | 29 | 43 | 2579 | 5 | 2 | 0 | England |
| 10 | Shane Tudor | MID | 21 | 28 | 2250 | 9 | 6 | 1 | England |
| 11 | Fred Murray | DEF | 21 | 30 | 2180 | 0 | 4 | 0 | Rep of Ireland |
| 12 | Andrew Duncan | DEF | 25 | 25 | 1926 | 0 | 6 | 1 | England |
| 13 | Adam Tann | DEF | 21 | 34 | 1908 | 1 | 2 | 1 | England |
| 14 | Daniel Chillingworth | ATT | 21 | 37 | 1153 | 0 | 0 | 0 | England |
| 15 | Ezomo Iriekpen | DEF | 21 | 13 | 1125 | 1 | 3 | 0 | England |
| 16 | Stephen Jordan | MID | 21 | 12 | 954 | 0 | 1 | 0 | England |
| 17 | Franco Nacca | DEF | 21 | 33 | 771 | 0 | 0 | 0 | Venezuela |
| 18 | David Bridges | MID | 20 | 24 | 719 | 1 | 2 | 0 | England |

## KEY PLAYERS - GOALSCORERS

**1 David Kitson**

| | | | |
|---|---|---|---|
| Goals in the League | 19 | Player Strike Rate<br>Average number of minutes between League goals scored by player | 204 |
| Contribution to Attacking Power<br>Average number of minutes between League team goals while on pitch | 21 | Club Strike Rate<br>Average number of minutes between League goals scored by club | 62 |

| | PLAYER | LGE GOALS | POWER | STRIKE RATE |
|---|---|---|---|---|
| 2 | Shane Tudor | 9 | 57 | 250 mins |
| 3 | Tom Youngs | 10 | 56 | 275 mins |
| 4 | Omer Riza | 12 | 65 | 301 mins |
| 5 | Paul Wanless | 5 | 59 | 516 mins |

## KEY PLAYERS - MIDFIELDERS

**1 Stephen Jordan**

| | | | |
|---|---|---|---|
| Goals in the League | 0 | Contribution to Attacking Power<br>Average number of minutes between League team goals while on pitch | 56 |
| Defensive Rating<br>Average number of mins between League goals conceded while he was on the pitch | 64 | Scoring Difference<br>Defensive Rating minus Contribution to Attacking Power | 8 |

| | PLAYER | LGE GOALS | DEF RATE | POWER | SCORE DIFF |
|---|---|---|---|---|---|
| 2 | Luke Guttridge | 3 | 63 | 61 | 2 mins |
| 3 | Paul Wanless | 5 | 61 | 60 | 1 mins |
| 4 | Shane Tudor | 9 | 56 | 58 | -2 mins |
| 5 | David Kitson | 19 | 60 | 63 | -3 mins |

## KEY PLAYERS - DEFENDERS

**1 Fred Murray**

| | | | |
|---|---|---|---|
| Goals Conceded when he was on pitch | 29 | Clean Sheets<br>In games when he played at least 70 minutes | 6 |
| Defensive Rating<br>Ave number of mins between League goals conceded while on the pitch | 75 | Club Defensive Rating<br>Average number of mins between League goals conceded by the club this season. | 58 |

| | PLAYER | CON LGE | CLN SHEETS | DEF RATE |
|---|---|---|---|---|
| 2 | Ezomo Iriekpen | 17 | 1 | 66 mins |
| 3 | Terry Fleming | 60 | 7 | 62 mins |
| 4 | Adam Tann | 31 | 4 | 62 mins |
| 5 | Stevland Angus | 60 | 5 | 58 mins |

## KEY GOALKEEPER

**1 Shaun Marshall**

| | |
|---|---|
| Goals Conceded in the League | 71 |
| Defensive Rating<br>Ave number of mins between League goals conceded while on the pitch. | 57 |
| Counting Games<br>Games when he played at least 70 mins | 45 |
| Clean Sheets<br>In games when he played at least 70 mins | 6 |

## TEAM OF THE SEASON

| | | |
|---|---|---|
| **GOALKEEPER** | **GAMES** | **DEF RATE** |
| Shaun Marshall | 45 | 57 |
| **DEFENDERS** | **GAMES** | **DEF RATE** |
| Fred Murray | 22 | 75 |
| Ezomo Iriekpen | 13 | 66 |
| Terry Fleming | 40 | 62 |
| Adam Tann | 20 | 62 |
| **MIDFIELDERS** | **GAMES** | **SCORE DIFF** |
| Stephen Jordan | 11 | 8 |
| Luke Guttridge | 35 | 2 |
| Paul Wanless | 26 | 1 |
| Shane Tudor | 23 | -2 |
| **FORWARDS** | **GAMES** | **STRIKE RATE** |
| David Kitson | 44 | 204 |
| Tom Youngs | 29 | 275 |

# HULL CITY

Final Position: **13th**

NICKNAME: THE TIGERS

| | | | | | | |
|---|---|---|---|---|---|---|
| 1 | div3 | Southend | H | D | 2-2 | Green 7; Elliott 68 |
| 2 | div3 | Bristol Rovers | A | D | 1-1 | Johnson 85 |
| 3 | div3 | Exeter | A | L | 1-3 | Green 10 |
| 4 | div3 | Bury | H | D | 1-1 | Johnson 36 |
| 5 | div3 | Hartlepool | A | L | 0-2 | |
| 6 | div3 | Leyton Orient | H | D | 1-1 | Keates 38 |
| 7 | div3 | Cambridge | A | W | 2-1 | Whittle 70; Smith 73 |
| 8 | wcr1 | Leicester | H | L | 2-4 | Alexander 31; Ashbee 117 |
| 9 | div3 | Carlisle | H | W | 4-0 | Alexander 20,49,73; Dudfield 78 |
| 10 | div3 | Macclesfield | H | L | 1-3 | Green 16 |
| 11 | div3 | Oxford | A | D | 0-0 | |
| 12 | div3 | Swansea | H | D | 1-1 | Jevons 27 |
| 13 | div3 | Kidderminster | A | L | 0-1 | |
| 14 | div3 | Rochdale | H | W | 3-0 | Jevons 28; Branch 45,84 |
| 15 | div3 | Torquay | A | W | 4-1 | Ashbee 45; Jevons 47; Anderson 68; Green 85 |
| 16 | div3 | Rushden & D | H | D | 1-1 | Green 1 |
| 17 | div3 | Shrewsbury | A | D | 1-1 | Elliott 59 |
| 18 | div3 | Scunthorpe | H | W | 2-0 | Branch 85; Alexander 90 |
| 19 | div3 | Lincoln | A | D | 1-1 | Alexander 22 |
| 20 | facr1 | Macclesfield | H | L | 0-3 | |
| 21 | div3 | Boston | H | W | 1-0 | Delaney 49 |
| 22 | div3 | Wrexham | A | D | 0-0 | |
| 23 | div3 | Darlington | H | L | 0-1 | |
| 24 | div3 | Bournemouth | A | D | 0-0 | |
| 25 | div3 | Hartlepool | H | W | 2-0 | Keates 21; Green 75 |
| 26 | div3 | York | A | D | 1-1 | Keates 51 |
| 27 | div3 | Bury | A | L | 0-1 | |
| 28 | div3 | Bristol Rovers | H | W | 1-0 | Alexander 25 |
| 29 | div3 | Exeter | H | D | 2-2 | Elliott 61,67 |
| 30 | div3 | Leyton Orient | A | L | 0-2 | |
| 31 | div3 | York | H | D | 0-0 | |
| 32 | div3 | Southend | A | L | 0-3 | |
| 33 | div3 | Lincoln | H | L | 0-1 | |
| 34 | div3 | Scunthorpe | A | L | 1-3 | Forrester 65 |
| 35 | div3 | Cambridge | H | D | 1-1 | Forrester 51 pen |
| 36 | div3 | Carlisle | A | W | 5-1 | Walters 20,67; Elliott 39,48; Forrester 45 |
| 37 | div3 | Macclesfield | A | W | 1-0 | Elliott 45 |
| 38 | div3 | Oxford | H | D | 0-0 | |
| 39 | div3 | Rushden & D | A | L | 2-4 | Otsemobor 59; Walters 63 |
| 40 | div3 | Torquay | H | D | 1-1 | Elliott 54 |
| 41 | div3 | Shrewsbury | H | W | 2-0 | Otsemobor 81; Keates 90 pen |
| 42 | div3 | Wrexham | H | L | 1-2 | Otsemobor 55 |
| 43 | div3 | Boston | A | W | 1-0 | Elliott 73 |
| 44 | div3 | Bournemouth | H | W | 3-1 | Walters 31; Elliott 35,46 |
| 45 | div3 | Darlington | A | L | 0-2 | |
| 46 | div3 | Kidderminster | H | W | 4-1 | Burgess 6 pen,38,88; Walters 80 |
| 47 | div3 | Rochdale | A | L | 1-2 | Burgess 65 |
| 48 | div3 | Swansea | A | L | 2-4 | Elliott 9; Reeves 25 |

■ Home □ Away ▨ Neutral

## ATTENDANCES

HOME GROUND: KC STADIUM CAPACITY: 25404 AVERAGE LEAGUE AT HOME: 12843

| | | | | | | | | | | | |
|---|---|---|---|---|---|---|---|---|---|---|---|
| 25 | Hartlepool | 22319 | 41 | Shrewsbury | 13253 | 20 | Macclesfield | 7803 | 22 | Wrexham | 4412 |
| 31 | York | 18437 | 18 | Scunthorpe | 11885 | 6 | Leyton Orient | 7684 | 27 | Bury | 4290 |
| 38 | Oxford | 17404 | 16 | Rushden & D | 10659 | 2 | Bristol Rovers | 7501 | 7 | Cambridge | 4258 |
| 44 | Bournemouth | 15816 | 1 | Southend | 10449 | 8 | Leicester | 7061 | 3 | Exeter | 4257 |
| 35 | Cambridge | 15607 | 48 | Swansea | 9585 | 34 | Scunthorpe | 6284 | 5 | Hartlepool | 4236 |
| 42 | Wrexham | 15002 | 21 | Boston | 9460 | 19 | Lincoln | 6271 | 13 | Kidderminster | 3787 |
| 28 | Bristol Rov | 14913 | 14 | Rochdale | 9057 | 24 | Bournemouth | 6098 | 43 | Boston | 3782 |
| 46 | Kidderminster | 14544 | 4 | Bury | 8804 | 11 | Oxford | 5445 | 15 | Torquay | 3607 |
| 23 | Darlington | 14162 | 10 | Macclesfield | 8703 | 30 | Leyton Orient | 5125 | 45 | Darlington | 3487 |
| 33 | Lincoln | 13728 | 9 | Carlisle | 8461 | 39 | Rushden & D | 4713 | 17 | Shrewsbury | 3086 |
| 29 | Exeter | 13667 | 12 | Swansea | 8070 | 36 | Carlisle | 4678 | 37 | Macclesfield | 2229 |
| 40 | Torquay | 13310 | 26 | York | 7856 | 32 | Southend | 4534 | 47 | Rochdale | 2225 |

## KEY PLAYER APPEARANCES

| | PLAYER | POS | AGE | APP | MINS ON | GOALS | CARDS(Y/R) | | HOME COUNTRY |
|---|---|---|---|---|---|---|---|---|---|
| 1 | John Anderson | DEF | 30 | 44 | 3745 | 1 | 5 | 0 | Scotland |
| 2 | Dean Keates | MID | 25 | 37 | 3083 | 4 | 8 | 0 | England |
| 3 | Justin Whittle | DEF | 32 | 41 | 3081 | 1 | 5 | 1 | England |
| 4 | Carl Regan | DEF | 23 | 42 | 3005 | 0 | 2 | 0 | England |
| 5 | Ian Ashbee | DEF | 26 | 31 | 2780 | 1 | 11 | 1 | England |
| 6 | Stuart Elliott | MID | 24 | 37 | 2615 | 12 | 5 | 0 | N Ireland |
| 7 | Damien Delaney | DEF | 21 | 29 | 2600 | 1 | 8 | 0 | Rep of Ireland |
| 8 | Stuart Green | MID | 22 | 28 | 2379 | 6 | 2 | 1 | England |
| 9 | Marc Joseph | DEF | 26 | 24 | 1873 | 0 | 5 | 0 | England |
| 10 | Paul Musselwhite | GK | 34 | 46 | 1800 | 0 | 0 | 0 | England |
| 11 | Stephen Melton | MID | 24 | 26 | 1698 | 0 | 2 | 0 | England |
| 12 | Gary Alexander | ATT | 23 | 25 | 1652 | 6 | 2 | 0 | England |
| 13 | Shaun Smith | DEF | 32 | 27 | 1604 | 1 | 2 | 0 | England |
| 14 | Alan Fettis | GK | 32 | 18 | 1530 | 0 | 0 | 0 | N Ireland |
| 15 | Ryan Williams | MID | 24 | 27 | 1358 | 0 | 2 | 0 | England |
| 16 | Phil Jevons | MID | 23 | 30 | 1198 | 3 | 3 | 0 | England |
| 17 | Jonathan Walters | ATT | 19 | 11 | 920 | 5 | 0 | 0 | England |
| 18 | Jamie Forrester | ATT | 28 | 11 | 899 | 3 | 0 | 0 | England |

## KEY PLAYERS - GOALSCORERS

**1 Stuart Elliott**

Goals in the League: 12

Contribution to Attacking Power
Average number of minutes between League team goals while on pitch: 63

Player Strike Rate
Average number of minutes between League goals scored by player: 218

Club Strike Rate
Average number of minutes between League goals scored by club: 71

| | PLAYER | LGE GOALS | POWER | STRIKE RATE |
|---|---|---|---|---|
| 2 | Gary Alexander | 6 | 75 | 275 mins |
| 3 | Stuart Green | 6 | 79 | 397 mins |
| 4 | Dean Keates | 4 | 61 | 771 mins |
| 5 | Shaun Smith | 1 | 57 | 1604 mins |

## KEY PLAYERS - MIDFIELDERS

**1 Dean Keates**

Goals in the League: 4

Defensive Rating
Average number of mins between League goals conceded while he was on the pitch: 88

Contribution to Attacking Power
Average number of minutes between League team goals while on pitch: 62

Scoring Difference
Defensive Rating minus Contribution to Attacking Power: 26

| | PLAYER | LGE GOALS | DEF RATE | POWER | SCORE DIFF |
|---|---|---|---|---|---|
| 2 | Stuart Green | 6 | 95 | 79 | 16 mins |
| 3 | Stuart Elliott | 12 | 77 | 64 | 13 mins |
| 4 | Ryan Williams | 0 | 85 | 85 | 0 mins |
| 5 | Stephen Melton | 0 | 71 | 81 | -10 mins |

## KEY PLAYERS - DEFENDERS

**1 Ian Ashbee**

Goals Conceded when he was on pitch: 28

Defensive Rating
Ave number of mins between League goals conceded while on the pitch: 99

Clean Sheets
In games when he played at least 70 minutes: 12

Club Defensive Rating
Average number of mins between League goals conceded by the club this season.: 78

| | PLAYER | CON LGE | CLN SHEETS | DEF RATE |
|---|---|---|---|---|
| 2 | John Anderson | 42 | 13 | 89 mins |
| 3 | Carl Regan | 35 | 10 | 86 mins |
| 4 | Justin Whittle | 37 | 9 | 83 mins |
| 5 | Marc Joseph | 23 | 7 | 81 mins |

## KEY GOALKEEPER

**1 Paul Musselwhite**

Goals Conceded in the League: 13

Defensive Rating
Ave number of mins between League goals conceded while on the pitch.: 138

Counting Games
Games when he played at least 70 mins: 20

Clean Sheets
In games when he played at least 70 mins: 9

## TEAM OF THE SEASON

| GOALKEEPER | GAMES | DEF RATE |
|---|---|---|
| Paul Musselwhite | 20 | 138 |
| **DEFENDERS** | **GAMES** | **DEF RATE** |
| Ian Ashbee | 31 | 99 |
| John Anderson | 41 | 89 |
| Carl Regan | 31 | 86 |
| Justin Whittle | 31 | 83 |
| **MIDFIELDERS** | **GAMES** | **SCORE DIFF** |
| Dean Keates | 33 | 26 |
| Stuart Green | 25 | 16 |
| Stuart Elliott | 24 | 13 |
| Ryan Williams | 10 | 0 |
| **FORWARDS** | **GAMES** | **STRIKE RATE** |
| Gary Alexander | 22 | 275 |
| Jonathan Walters | 10 | 184 |

# DARLINGTON

Final Position: **14th**

NICKNAME: THE QUAKERS

| | | | | | | |
|---|---|---|---|---|---|---|
| 1 | div3 | Cambridge | A | W | 2-1 | Clarke, M 44; Nicolls 76 |
| 2 | div3 | Swansea | H | D | 2-2 | Clark 65; Liddle, C 70 |
| 3 | div3 | Oxford | H | L | 0-1 | |
| 4 | div3 | Rochdale | A | D | 1-1 | Nicolls 14 |
| 5 | div3 | Carlisle | H | W | 2-0 | Naylor 56,81 |
| 6 | div3 | Kidderminster | A | D | 1-1 | Clarke, M 61 |
| 7 | wcr1 | Huddersfield | A | L | 0-2 | |
| 8 | div3 | Hartlepool | A | L | 1-4 | Clark 25 |
| 9 | div3 | York | A | L | 0-1 | |
| 10 | div3 | Bournemouth | H | D | 2-2 | Fenton 34; Conlon 73 |
| 11 | div3 | Wrexham | H | L | 0-1 | |
| 12 | div3 | Leyton Orient | A | L | 1-2 | Conlon 45 |
| 13 | div3 | Bristol Rovers | H | W | 1-0 | Conlon 19 |
| 14 | div3 | Bury | A | D | 2-2 | Valentine 33; Clark 72 pen |
| 15 | div3 | Boston | H | L | 2-3 | Clark 83; Conlon 86 |
| 16 | div3 | Exeter | A | W | 4-0 | Liddle, C 35; Clarke, M 42; Conlon 68; Nicholls 90 |
| 17 | div3 | Scunthorpe | H | D | 1-1 | Clark 28 pen |
| 18 | div3 | Lincoln | H | D | 0-0 | |
| 19 | div3 | Rushden & D | A | L | 0-2 | |
| 20 | facr1 | Wrexham | A | W | 2-0 | Conlon 59; Liddle, C 70 |
| 21 | div3 | Shrewsbury | A | D | 2-2 | Conlon 63; Keltie 82 |
| 22 | div3 | Southend | H | W | 2-1 | Conlon 37; Nicholls 87 |
| 23 | facr2 | Stevenage | H | W | 4-1 | Hodgson 2; Offiong 38,63; Conlon 46 |
| 24 | div3 | Hull City | A | W | 1-0 | Betts 45 |
| 25 | div3 | Macclesfield | H | D | 0-0 | |
| 26 | div3 | Carlisle | A | D | 2-2 | Offiong 19,63 pen |
| 27 | div3 | Torquay | H | D | 1-1 | Nicholls 34 |
| 28 | facr3 | Farnborough | H | L | 2-3 | Nicolls 13; Clark 37 |
| 29 | div3 | Oxford | A | D | 1-1 | Hodgson 87 |
| 30 | div3 | Kidderminster | H | W | 2-1 | Clarke, M 61,83 |
| 31 | div3 | Torquay | A | L | 1-3 | Conlon 18 |
| 32 | div3 | Swansea | A | L | 0-1 | |
| 33 | div3 | Rushden & D | H | D | 2-2 | Hodgson 51; Clark 69 |
| 34 | div3 | Rochdale | H | L | 0-1 | |
| 35 | div3 | Lincoln | A | D | 1-1 | Conlon 22 |
| 36 | div3 | Wrexham | A | D | 0-0 | |
| 37 | div3 | Hartlepool | H | D | 2-2 | Conlon 36; Liddle, C 60 |
| 38 | div3 | York | H | W | 2-1 | Mellanby 30; Conlon 87 |
| 39 | div3 | Bournemouth | A | L | 0-2 | |
| 40 | div3 | Cambridge | H | L | 1-2 | Mellanby 82 |
| 41 | div3 | Exeter | H | D | 2-2 | Mellanby 47,52 |
| 42 | div3 | Boston | A | L | 0-1 | |
| 43 | div3 | Scunthorpe | A | W | 1-0 | Keltie 81 |
| 44 | div3 | Bury | H | W | 3-1 | Corbett 20; Naylor 87; Liddle, C 90 pen |
| 45 | div3 | Southend | A | L | 0-2 | |
| 46 | div3 | Shrewsbury | H | W | 5-1 | Nicolls 20; Conlon 33,88; Maddison 37; Pearson 74 |
| 47 | div3 | Macclesfield | A | L | 0-1 | |
| 48 | div3 | Hull City | H | W | 2-0 | Newey 56; Conlon 90 |
| 49 | div3 | Bristol Rovers | A | L | 1-2 | Keltie 67 |
| 50 | div3 | Leyton Orient | H | D | 2-2 | Corbett 44; Wainwright 76 |

■ Home □ Away ▒ Neutral

## ATTENDANCES

HOME GROUND: NEASHAM ROAD CAPACITY: 24000 AVERAGE LEAGUE AT HOME: 3312

| | | | | | | | | | | | |
|---|---|---|---|---|---|---|---|---|---|---|---|
| 24 | Hull City | 14162 | 36 | Wrexham | 4079 | 35 | Lincoln | 3193 | 33 | Rushden & D | 2742 |
| 49 | Bristol Rovers | 9835 | 12 | Leyton Orient | 3975 | 25 | Macclesfield | 3079 | 46 | Shrewsbury | 2660 |
| 8 | Hartlepool | 6360 | 2 | Swansea | 3914 | 17 | Scunthorpe | 3059 | 30 | Kidderminster | 2630 |
| 26 | Carlisle | 6016 | 19 | Rushden & D | 3911 | 45 | Southend | 3053 | 31 | Torquay | 2628 |
| 37 | Hartlepool | 5832 | 43 | Scunthorpe | 3904 | 15 | Boston | 3033 | 11 | Wrexham | 2573 |
| 39 | Bournemouth | 5758 | 7 | Huddersfield | 3810 | 10 | Bournemouth | 2950 | 6 | Kidderminster | 2488 |
| 50 | Leyton Orient | 5723 | 3 | Oxford | 3533 | 14 | Bury | 2944 | 34 | Rochdale | 2479 |
| 32 | Swansea | 5553 | 27 | Torquay | 3506 | 44 | Bury | 2879 | 41 | Exeter | 2476 |
| 5 | Carlisle | 5163 | 48 | Hull City | 3487 | 13 | Bristol Rovers | 2849 | 42 | Boston | 2186 |
| 29 | Oxford | 4968 | 20 | Wrexham | 3442 | 4 | Rochdale | 2834 | 40 | Cambridge | 2076 |
| 28 | Farnborough | 4260 | 38 | York | 3434 | 22 | Southend | 2830 | 47 | Macclesfield | 1967 |
| 9 | York | 4128 | 23 | Stevenage | 3351 | 16 | Exeter | 2757 | | | |
| 1 | Cambridge | 4079 | 18 | Lincoln | 3277 | 21 | Shrewsbury | 2755 | | | |

## KEY PLAYER APPEARANCES

| | PLAYER | POS | AGE | APP | MINS ON | GOALS | CARDS(Y/R) | | HOME COUNTRY |
|---|---|---|---|---|---|---|---|---|---|
| 1 | Ryan Valentine | DEF | 20 | 45 | 3789 | 1 | 6 | 1 | England |
| 2 | Craig Liddle | MID | 31 | 42 | 3679 | 4 | 6 | 1 | England |
| 3 | Barry Conlon | ATT | 24 | 41 | 3639 | 14 | 11 | 2 | Rep of Ireland |
| 4 | Simon Betts | DEF | 30 | 42 | 3576 | 1 | 6 | 0 | England |
| 5 | Ashley Nicholls | MID | 21 | 45 | 3489 | 6 | 2 | 0 | England |
| 6 | Andrew Collett | GK | 29 | 39 | 3375 | 0 | 0 | 0 | England |
| 7 | Matthew Clarke | ATT | 22 | 38 | 3161 | 5 | 7 | 0 | England |
| 8 | Neil Maddison | MID | 33 | 32 | 2258 | 1 | 0 | 0 | England |
| 9 | Clark Keltie | MID | 19 | 26 | 2202 | 3 | 12 | 0 | England |
| 10 | Ian Clark | ATT | 28 | 46 | 2164 | 6 | 0 | 0 | England |
| 11 | Neil Wainwright | MID | 25 | 41 | 2026 | 1 | 5 | 0 | England |
| 12 | Richard Hodgson | MID | 23 | 32 | 1951 | 2 | 4 | 0 | England |
| 13 | Stuart Whitehead | DEF | 26 | 23 | 1901 | 0 | 5 | 1 | England |
| 14 | Gary Pearson | MID | 26 | 26 | 1698 | 1 | 9 | 1 | England |
| 15 | Mark Ford | MID | 27 | 17 | 904 | 0 | 5 | 0 | England |
| 16 | Jim Corbett | ATT | 23 | 11 | 829 | 2 | 0 | 0 | England |
| 17 | Tom Newey | MID | 20 | 7 | 589 | 1 | 3 | 0 | England |
| 18 | Richard Offiong | ATT | 19 | 8 | 550 | 2 | 0 | 0 | England |

## KEY PLAYERS - GOALSCORERS

**1 Barry Conlon**

| | |
|---|---|
| Goals in the League | 14 |
| Contribution to Attacking Power<br>Average number of minutes between League team goals while on pitch | 71 |
| Player Strike Rate<br>Average number of minutes between League goals scored by player | 260 |
| Club Strike Rate<br>Average number of minutes between League goals scored by club | 71 |

| | PLAYER | LGE GOALS | POWER | STRIKE RATE |
|---|---|---|---|---|
| 2 | Ian Clark | 6 | 74 | 361 mins |
| 3 | Ashley Nicholls | 6 | 69 | 582 mins |
| 4 | Matthew Clarke | 5 | 67 | 632 mins |
| 5 | Clark Keltie | 3 | 64 | 734 mins |

## KEY PLAYERS - MIDFIELDERS

**1 Clark Keltie**

| | |
|---|---|
| Goals in the League | 3 |
| Defensive Rating<br>Average number of mins between League goals conceded while he was on the pitch | 73 |
| Contribution to Attacking Power<br>Average number of minutes between League team goals while on pitch | 65 |
| Scoring Difference<br>Defensive Rating minus Contribution to Attacking Power | 8 |

| | PLAYER | LGE GOALS | DEF RATE | POWER | SCORE DIFF |
|---|---|---|---|---|---|
| 2 | Gary Pearson | 1 | 65 | 59 | 6 mins |
| 3 | Ashley Nicholls | 6 | 73 | 70 | 3 mins |
| 4 | Craig Liddle | 4 | 74 | 72 | 2 mins |
| 5 | Richard Hodgson | 2 | 81 | 85 | -4 mins |

## KEY PLAYERS - DEFENDERS

**1 Stuart Whitehead**

| | |
|---|---|
| Goals Conceded when he was on pitch | 23 |
| Defensive Rating<br>Ave number of mins between League goals conceded while on the pitch | 83 |
| Clean Sheets<br>In games when he played at least 70 minutes | 5 |
| Club Defensive Rating<br>Average number of mins between League goals conceded by the club this season. | 70 |

| | PLAYER | CON LGE | CLN SHEETS | DEF RATE |
|---|---|---|---|---|
| 2 | Simon Betts | 51 | 8 | 70 mins |
| 3 | Ryan Valentine | 54 | 9 | 70 mins |

## KEY GOALKEEPER

**1 Andrew Collett**

| | |
|---|---|
| Goals Conceded in the League | 51 |
| Defensive Rating<br>Ave number of mins between League goals conceded while on the pitch. | 66 |
| Counting Games<br>Games when he played at least 70 mins | 37 |
| Clean Sheets<br>In games when he played at least 70 mins | 6 |

## TEAM OF THE SEASON

| GOALKEEPER | GAMES | DEF RATE |
|---|---|---|
| Andrew Collett | 37 | 66 |
| **DEFENDERS** | **GAMES** | **DEF RATE** |
| Stuart Whitehead | 20 | 83 |
| Simon Betts | 39 | 70 |
| Ryan Valentine | 41 | 70 |
| Richard Hodgson* | 27 | 81 |
| **MIDFIELDERS** | **GAMES** | **SCORE DIFF** |
| Clark Keltie | 24 | 8 |
| Gary Pearson | 18 | 6 |
| Ashley Nicholls | 38 | 3 |
| Craig Liddle | 39 | 2 |
| **FORWARDS** | **GAMES** | **STRIKE RATE** |
| Barry Conlon | 40 | 260 |
| Ian Clark | 20 | 361 |

# BOSTON UNITED

Final Position: **15th**

NICKNAME: THE PILGRIMS

| | | | | | | |
|---|---|---|---|---|---|---|
| 1 | div3 | Bournemouth | H | D | 2-2 | Young 51 og; Gould 54 |
| 2 | div3 | Hartlepool | A | L | 0-2 | |
| 3 | div3 | Wrexham | A | D | 1-1 | Rusk 63 |
| 4 | div3 | Lincoln | H | W | 2-0 | Weatherstone, S 30; Clare 89 |
| 5 | div3 | York | A | L | 0-2 | |
| 6 | div3 | Bury | H | D | 1-1 | Weatherstone, S 90 |
| 7 | div3 | Kidderminster | A | D | 0-0 | |
| 8 | wcr1 | Cardiff | H | L | 1-5 | Ellender 52 |
| 9 | div3 | Oxford | H | L | 1-3 | Redfearn 55 |
| 10 | div3 | Swansea | H | W | 1-0 | Weatherstone, S 36 |
| 11 | div3 | Carlisle | A | L | 2-4 | Cook 40; Douglas 69 |
| 12 | div3 | Cambridge | H | L | 1-3 | Weatherstone, S 43 |
| 13 | div3 | Macclesfield | A | L | 0-2 | |
| 14 | div3 | Torquay | H | W | 2-1 | Cook 55; Thompson, Lee 63 |
| 15 | div3 | Darlington | A | W | 3-2 | Thompson, Lee 25,66,79 |
| 16 | div3 | Rochdale | H | W | 3-1 | Weatherstone, R 20; Battersby 64; Douglas 90 |
| 17 | div3 | Rushden & D | A | L | 0-1 | |
| 18 | div3 | Exeter | H | L | 0-3 | |
| 19 | div3 | Scunthorpe | A | L | 0-2 | |
| 20 | facr1 | Northampton | A | L | 2-3 | Battersby 56; Higgins 82 |
| 21 | div3 | Hull City | A | L | 0-1 | |
| 22 | div3 | Leyton Orient | H | L | 0-1 | |
| 23 | div3 | Southend | A | L | 2-4 | Logan 57; Angel 64 |
| 24 | div3 | Shrewsbury | H | W | 6-0 | Logan 13,29; Van Blerk 21 og; Douglas 41; Redfearn 56; Gould 90 |
| 25 | div3 | York | H | W | 3-0 | Douglas 30,90; Logan 52 |
| 26 | div3 | Bristol Rovers | A | D | 1-1 | Logan 8 |
| 27 | div3 | Lincoln | A | D | 1-1 | Logan 56 |
| 28 | div3 | Hartlepool | H | L | 0-1 | |
| 29 | div3 | Bury | A | D | 0-0 | |
| 30 | div3 | Bristol Rovers | H | D | 0-0 | |
| 31 | div3 | Bournemouth | A | L | 1-2 | Angel 78 |
| 32 | div3 | Scunthorpe | H | W | 1-0 | Logan 90 |
| 33 | div3 | Exeter | A | W | 2-0 | Redfearn 44; Douglas 90 |
| 34 | div3 | Kidderminster | H | W | 3-0 | Logan 24,83; Weatherstone, R 44 |
| 35 | div3 | Oxford | A | L | 1-2 | Douglas 69 |
| 36 | div3 | Swansea | A | D | 0-0 | |
| 37 | div3 | Carlisle | H | D | 0-0 | |
| 38 | div3 | Rochdale | A | L | 0-1 | |
| 39 | div3 | Darlington | H | W | 1-0 | Greaves 5 |
| 40 | div3 | Rushden & D | H | D | 1-1 | Jones 67 |
| 41 | div3 | Torquay | A | D | 1-1 | Angel 82 pen |
| 42 | div3 | Wrexham | H | D | 3-3 | Duffield 27,62; Redfearn 49 pen |
| 43 | div3 | Leyton Orient | A | L | 2-3 | Logan 28; Redfearn 53 |
| 44 | div3 | Hull City | H | L | 0-1 | |
| 45 | div3 | Shrewsbury | A | W | 2-1 | Duffield 44; Redfearn 48 |
| 46 | div3 | Southend | H | W | 1-0 | Angel 85 pen |
| 47 | div3 | Macclesfield | H | W | 2-1 | Duffield 20 pen; Hocking 51 |
| 48 | div3 | Cambridge | A | W | 2-1 | Angel 37; Rusk 82 |

■ Home □ Away □ Neutral

## ATTENDANCES

HOME GROUND: YORK STREET STADIUM CAPACITY: 5184 AVERAGE LEAGUE AT HOME: 3048

| | | | | | | | | | | | |
|---|---|---|---|---|---|---|---|---|---|---|---|
| 21 | Hull City | 9460 | 1 | Bournemouth | 4184 | 23 | Southend | 3245 | 22 | Leyton Orient | 2616 |
| 26 | Bristol Rovers | 8311 | 17 | Rushden & D | 4079 | 30 | Bristol Rovers | 3209 | 38 | Rochdale | 2538 |
| 27 | Lincoln | 7846 | 43 | Leyton Orient | 3939 | 37 | Carlisle | 3131 | 14 | Torquay | 2514 |
| 35 | Oxford | 7157 | 25 | York | 3864 | 12 | Cambridge | 3090 | 34 | Kidderminster | 2485 |
| 36 | Swansea | 6642 | 47 | Macclesfield | 3825 | 28 | Hartlepool | 3081 | 18 | Exeter | 2474 |
| 31 | Bournemouth | 5180 | 44 | Hull City | 3782 | 41 | Torquay | 3039 | 8 | Cardiff | 2280 |
| 4 | Lincoln | 5159 | 19 | Scunthorpe | 3730 | 15 | Darlington | 3033 | 7 | Kidderminster | 2222 |
| 2 | Hartlepool | 4841 | 11 | Carlisle | 3623 | 29 | Bury | 3024 | 10 | Swansea | 2209 |
| 48 | Cambridge | 4488 | 40 | Rushden & D | 3504 | 33 | Exeter | 2834 | 39 | Darlington | 2186 |
| 20 | Northampton | 4373 | 32 | Scunthorpe | 3358 | 6 | Bury | 2790 | 24 | Shrewsbury | 2155 |
| 45 | Shrewsbury | 4373 | 3 | Wrexham | 3293 | 9 | Oxford | 2685 | 13 | Macclesfield | 1941 |
| 5 | York | 4228 | 46 | Southend | 3247 | 16 | Rochdale | 2653 | 42 | Wrexham | 1919 |

## KEY PLAYER APPEARANCES

| | PLAYER | POS | AGE | APP | MINS ON | GOALS | CARDS(Y/R) | | HOME COUNTRY |
|---|---|---|---|---|---|---|---|---|---|
| 1 | Paul Bastock | GK | 33 | 46 | 4140 | 0 | 3 | 0 | England |
| 2 | Matthew Hocking | DEF | 25 | 45 | 3922 | 1 | 3 | 0 | England |
| 3 | Simon Weatherstone | ATT | 23 | 43 | 3575 | 4 | 7 | 0 | England |
| 4 | Ben Chapman | DEF | 24 | 37 | 3308 | 0 | 6 | 0 | England |
| 5 | Tom Bennett | DEF | 33 | 33 | 2696 | 0 | 5 | 1 | Scotland |
| 6 | Neil Redfearn | MID | 38 | 37 | 2481 | 6 | 7 | 0 | England |
| 7 | Mark Angel | ATT | 27 | 35 | 2257 | 5 | 5 | 0 | England |
| 8 | Paul Ellender | DEF | 28 | 27 | 2159 | 0 | 6 | 0 | England |
| 9 | Richard Logan | ATT | 21 | 27 | 2079 | 10 | 3 | 0 | England |
| 10 | Stuart Balmer | DEF | 33 | 23 | 1953 | 0 | 4 | 0 | Scotland |
| 11 | Mark Greaves | DEF | 28 | 29 | 1879 | 1 | 8 | 2 | England |
| 12 | Stuart Douglas | ATT | 25 | 32 | 1538 | 7 | 5 | 1 | England |
| 13 | Raymond Warburton | DEF | 35 | 17 | 1413 | 0 | 5 | 1 | England |
| 14 | Peter Costello | MID | 33 | 21 | 1225 | 0 | 2 | 0 | England |
| 15 | Simon Rusk | MID | 21 | 18 | 1134 | 2 | 2 | 0 | England |
| 16 | Peter Duffield | ATT | 34 | 18 | 1109 | 4 | 1 | 0 | England |
| 17 | Lee Thompson | MID | 20 | 18 | 1084 | 4 | 2 | 0 | England |
| 18 | James Gould | MID | 21 | 28 | 1023 | 2 | 0 | 0 | England |

## KEY PLAYERS - GOALSCORERS

**1 Richard Logan**

Goals in the League: **10**

Contribution to Attacking Power
Average number of minutes between League team goals while on pitch: **71**

**Player Strike Rate**
**Average number of minutes between League goals scored by player: 208**

Club Strike Rate
Average number of minutes between League goals scored by club: **75**

| | PLAYER | LGE GOALS | POWER | STRIKE RATE |
|---|---|---|---|---|
| 2 | Stuart Douglas | 7 | 64 | 220 mins |
| 3 | Lee Thompson | 4 | 98 | 271 mins |
| 4 | Neil Redfearn | 6 | 75 | 414 mins |
| 5 | Mark Angel | 5 | 68 | 451 mins |

## KEY PLAYERS - MIDFIELDERS

**1 Alex Higgins**

Goals in the League: **0**

Defensive Rating
Average number of mins between League goals conceded while he was on the pitch: **64**

Contribution to Attacking Power
Average number of minutes between League team goals while on pitch: **54**

**Scoring Difference**
**Defensive Rating minus Contribution to Attacking Power: 10**

| | PLAYER | LGE GOALS | DEF RATE | POWER | SCORE DIFF |
|---|---|---|---|---|---|
| 2 | Neil Redfearn | 6 | 73 | 75 | -2 mins |
| 3 | Peter Costello | 0 | 64 | 68 | -4 mins |
| 4 | Simon Rusk | 2 | 76 | 87 | -11 mins |
| 5 | Lee Thompson | 4 | 60 | 99 | -39 mins |

## KEY PLAYERS - DEFENDERS

**1 Patrick McCarthy**

Goals Conceded when he was on pitch: **7**

**Defensive Rating**
**Ave number of mins between League goals conceded while on the pitch: 134**

Clean Sheets
In games when he played at least 70 minutes: **5**

Club Defensive Rating
Average number of mins between League goals conceded by the club this season: **74**

| | PLAYER | CON LGE | CLN SHEETS | DEF RATE |
|---|---|---|---|---|
| 2 | Stuart Balmer | 19 | 11 | 103 mins |
| 3 | Ben Chapman | 41 | 11 | 81 mins |
| 4 | Tom Bennett | 36 | 6 | 75 mins |
| 5 | Paul Ellender | 29 | 8 | 74 mins |

## KEY GOALKEEPER

**1 Paul Bastock**

Goals Conceded in the League: **56**

**Defensive Rating**
**Ave number of mins between League goals conceded while on the pitch: 74**

Counting Games
Games when he played at least 70 mins: **46**

Clean Sheets
In games when he played at least 70 mins: **14**

## TEAM OF THE SEASON

| GOALKEEPER | GAMES | DEF RATE |
|---|---|---|
| Paul Bastock | 46 | 74 |
| **DEFENDERS** | **GAMES** | **DEF RATE** |
| Patrick McCarthy | 9 | 134 |
| Stuart Balmer | 22 | 103 |
| Ben Chapman | 37 | 81 |
| Tom Bennett | 28 | 75 |
| **MIDFIELDERS** | **GAMES** | **SCORE DIFF** |
| Alex Higgins | 10 | 10 |
| Neil Redfearn | 27 | -2 |
| Peter Costello | 13 | -4 |
| Simon Rusk | 10 | -11 |
| **FORWARDS** | **GAMES** | **STRIKE RATE** |
| Peter Duffield | 11 | 189 |
| Richard Logan | 20 | 208 |

# MACCLESFIELD

Final Position: **16th**

NICKNAME: THE SILKMEN

| | | | | | | |
|---|---|---|---|---|---|---|
| 1 | div3 | York | H | D | 1-1 | Tipton 18 |
| 2 | div3 | Leyton Orient | A | L | 2-3 | Glover 49; Lightbourne 78 |
| 3 | div3 | Hartlepool | A | W | 2-0 | Adams 82; Whitaker 83 |
| 4 | div3 | Wrexham | H | L | 0-1 | |
| 5 | div3 | Lincoln | A | L | 0-3 | |
| 6 | div3 | Bournemouth | H | L | 0-1 | |
| 7 | div3 | Bristol Rovers | H | W | 2-1 | Tipton 10 pen; Byrne 17 |
| 8 | wcr1 | Barnsley | H | W | 4-1 | Lightbourne 30; Whitaker 106,108,120 |
| 9 | div3 | Southend | A | L | 0-1 | |
| 10 | div3 | Hull City | A | W | 3-1 | Welch 47; Lightbourne 50; Askey 89 |
| 11 | div3 | Scunthorpe | H | L | 2-3 | Whitaker 79 pen; Lightbourne 86 |
| 12 | div3 | Rochdale | A | L | 1-3 | Welsh 39 |
| 13 | ccR2 | Preston | H | L | 1-2 | Tipton 7 |
| 14 | div3 | Boston | H | W | 2-0 | Whitaker 6; Welsh 73 |
| 15 | div3 | Kidderminster | A | W | 2-0 | Welch 31; Eaton 71 |
| 16 | div3 | Carlisle | H | D | 2-2 | Eaton 29; Priest 59 |
| 17 | div3 | Bury | A | L | 1-2 | Lightbourne 52 |
| 18 | div3 | Oxford | H | W | 2-1 | Lightbourne 66; Whitaker 88 |
| 19 | div3 | Shrewsbury | H | L | 1-2 | Whitaker 80 |
| 20 | div3 | Swansea | A | L | 0-1 | |
| 21 | facr1 | Hull City | A | W | 3-0 | Tipton 12; Lightbourne 27; Whitaker 76 |
| 22 | div3 | Torquay | H | D | 3-3 | Eaton 31; Macauley 75; Lightbourne 87 |
| 23 | div3 | Cambridge | A | L | 1-3 | Tipton 44 |
| 24 | facr2 | Vaux Motors | H | W | 2-0 | Lightbourne 82; Tipton 90 |
| 25 | div3 | Rushden & D | H | L | 0-1 | |
| 26 | div3 | Darlington | A | D | 0-0 | |
| 27 | div3 | Lincoln | H | L | 0-1 | |
| 28 | div3 | Exeter | A | D | 1-1 | Lightbourne 27 |
| 29 | div3 | Wrexham | A | W | 3-1 | Pejic 10 og; Tipton 46; Eaton 88 |
| 30 | facr3 | Watford | H | L | 0-2 | |
| 31 | div3 | Bournemouth | A | D | 2-2 | Whitaker 27; Priest 43 |
| 32 | div3 | Hartlepool | H | L | 0-1 | |
| 33 | div3 | Exeter | H | D | 1-1 | Whitaker 56 |
| 34 | div3 | York | A | L | 1-2 | Welch 60 |
| 35 | div3 | Swansea | H | L | 1-3 | O'Leary 45 og |
| 36 | div3 | Bristol Rovers | A | D | 1-1 | Lightbourne 77 |
| 37 | div3 | Southend | H | W | 2-1 | Eaton 69; Lightbourne 80 |
| 38 | div3 | Hull City | H | L | 0-1 | |
| 39 | div3 | Scunthorpe | A | D | 1-1 | Tipton 71 |
| 40 | div3 | Leyton Orient | H | W | 3-1 | Whitaker 18; Tipton 54,67 |
| 41 | div3 | Bury | H | D | 0-0 | |
| 42 | div3 | Carlisle | A | L | 0-1 | |
| 43 | div3 | Oxford | A | W | 1-0 | Tipton 39 |
| 44 | div3 | Kidderminster | H | W | 2-0 | Miles 52; Whitaker 54 |
| 45 | div3 | Cambridge | H | D | 1-1 | Lightbourne 41 |
| 46 | div3 | Torquay | A | D | 2-2 | Miles 10; Lightbourne 26 |
| 47 | div3 | Shrewsbury | A | W | 3-2 | Abbey, G 6; Miles 40,90 |
| 48 | div3 | Darlington | H | W | 1-0 | Whitaker 13 |
| 49 | div3 | Rushden & D | A | L | 0-3 | |
| 50 | div3 | Boston | A | L | 1-2 | Little 61 |
| 51 | div3 | Rochdale | H | W | 3-2 | Hockenhull 48 og; Askey 88; Tipton 90 |

■ Home □ Away ▨ Neutral

## ATTENDANCES

HOME GROUND: MOSS ROSE   CAPACITY: 6028   AVERAGE LEAGUE AT HOME: 2110

| | | | | | | | | | | | |
|---|---|---|---|---|---|---|---|---|---|---|---|
| 10 | Hull City | 8703 | 42 | Carlisle | 3773 | 4 | Wrexham | 2592 | 48 | Darlington | 1967 |
| 21 | Hull City | 7803 | 20 | Swansea | 3526 | 1 | York | 2586 | 14 | Boston | 1941 |
| 36 | Bristol Rovers | 6005 | 17 | Bury | 3506 | 15 | Kidderminster | 2521 | 11 | Scunthorpe | 1929 |
| 31 | Bournemouth | 5840 | 29 | Wrexham | 3445 | 35 | Swansea | 2515 | 37 | Southend | 1917 |
| 43 | Oxford | 5691 | 39 | Scunthorpe | 3398 | 5 | Lincoln | 2444 | 25 | Rushden & D | 1839 |
| 3 | Hartlepool | 4684 | 9 | Southend | 3249 | 16 | Carlisle | 2383 | 22 | Torquay | 1835 |
| 49 | Rushden & D | 4494 | 12 | Rochdale | 3090 | 38 | Hull City | 2229 | 7 | Bristol Rovers | 1814 |
| 30 | Watford | 4244 | 26 | Darlington | 3079 | 19 | Shrewsbury | 2218 | 6 | Bournemouth | 1795 |
| 47 | Shrewsbury | 4100 | 28 | Exeter | 3017 | 27 | Lincoln | 2187 | 8 | Barnsley | 1720 |
| 34 | York | 4009 | 24 | Vaux Motors | 2972 | 44 | Kidderminster | 2069 | 40 | Leyton Orient | 1676 |
| 2 | Leyton Orient | 3880 | 46 | Torquay | 2970 | 45 | Cambridge | 2053 | 18 | Oxford | 1583 |
| 23 | Cambridge | 3834 | 41 | Bury | 2920 | 13 | Preston | 2036 | 32 | Hartlepool | 1576 |
| 50 | Boston | 3825 | 51 | Rochdale | 2873 | 33 | Exeter | 2035 | | | |

## KEY PLAYER APPEARANCES

| | PLAYER | POS | AGE | APP | MINS ON | GOALS | CARDS(Y/R) | | HOME COUNTRY |
|---|---|---|---|---|---|---|---|---|---|
| 1 | Darren Tinson | DEF | 33 | 45 | 4050 | 0 | 5 | 0 | England |
| 2 | Daniel Adams | DEF | 27 | 45 | 4032 | 1 | 5 | 0 | England |
| 3 | Steve Wilson | GK | 29 | 43 | 3870 | 0 | 1 | 0 | England |
| 4 | Danny Whitaker | MID | 22 | 41 | 3543 | 10 | 0 | 1 | England |
| 5 | Kyle Lightbourne | ATT | 34 | 44 | 3526 | 11 | 5 | 0 | Bermuda |
| 6 | Michael Welch | ATT | 20 | 40 | 3250 | 3 | 9 | 0 | |
| 7 | Chris Priest | MID | 29 | 39 | 3039 | 2 | 10 | 0 | |
| 8 | Steve Hitchen | DEF | 26 | 37 | 2804 | 0 | 3 | 0 | England |
| 9 | Matthew Tipton | ATT | 23 | 43 | 2479 | 9 | 8 | 0 | England |
| 10 | Karl Munroe | MID | 23 | 33 | 1790 | 0 | 6 | 0 | England |
| 11 | Steven Macauley | DEF | 34 | 20 | 1733 | 1 | 2 | 0 | England |
| 12 | George Abbey | DEF | 24 | 24 | 1551 | 1 | 3 | 0 | England |
| 13 | David Ridler | DEF | 27 | 19 | 1473 | 0 | 1 | 0 | England |
| 14 | Darren Dunning | MID | 22 | 17 | 1428 | 0 | 3 | 0 | England |
| 15 | David Eaton | ATT | 21 | 27 | 1030 | 5 | 1 | 0 | England |
| 16 | Paul O'Neil | DEF | 21 | 18 | 951 | 0 | 1 | 0 | England |
| 17 | Lee Hardy | MID | 31 | 29 | 820 | 0 | 3 | 0 | England |

## KEY PLAYERS - GOALSCORERS

**1 Matthew Tipton**

| | | | |
|---|---|---|---|
| Goals in the League | 9 | Player Strike Rate<br>Average number of minutes between League goals scored by player | 275 |
| Contribution to Attacking Power<br>Average number of minutes between League team goals while on pitch | 75 | Club Strike Rate<br>Average number of minutes between League goals scored by club | 73 |

| | PLAYER | LGE GOALS | POWER | STRIKE RATE |
|---|---|---|---|---|
| 2 | Kyle Lightbourne | 11 | 70 | 321 mins |
| 3 | Danny Whitaker | 10 | 65 | 354 mins |
| 4 | Michael Welch | 3 | 83 | 1083 mins |
| 5 | Chris Priest | 2 | 75 | 1520 mins |

## KEY PLAYERS - MIDFIELDERS

**1 Darren Dunning**

| | | | |
|---|---|---|---|
| Goals in the League | 0 | Contribution to Attacking Power<br>Average number of minutes between League team goals while on pitch | 68 |
| Defensive Rating<br>Average number of mins between League goals conceded while he was on the pitch | 75 | Scoring Difference<br>Defensive Rating minus Contribution to Attacking Power | 7 |

| | PLAYER | LGE GOALS | DEF RATE | POWER | SCORE DIFF |
|---|---|---|---|---|---|
| 2 | Danny Whitaker | 10 | 68 | 66 | 2 mins |
| 3 | Chris Priest | 2 | 68 | 76 | -8 mins |
| 4 | Karl Munroe | 0 | 60 | 81 | -21 mins |

## KEY PLAYERS - DEFENDERS

**1 George Abbey**

| | | | |
|---|---|---|---|
| Goals Conceded when he was on pitch | 21 | Clean Sheets<br>In games when he played at least 70 minutes | 5 |
| Defensive Rating<br>Ave number of mins between League goals conceded while on the pitch | 74 | Club Defensive Rating<br>Average number of mins between League goals conceded by the club this season. | 66 |

| | PLAYER | CON LGE | CLN SHEETS | DEF RATE |
|---|---|---|---|---|
| 2 | Paul O'Neil | 13 | 3 | 73 mins |
| 3 | Darren Tinson | 60 | 8 | 68 mins |
| 4 | Daniel Adams | 62 | 8 | 65 mins |
| 5 | Steve Hitchen | 45 | 3 | 62 mins |

## KEY GOALKEEPER

**1 Steve Wilson**

| | |
|---|---|
| Goals Conceded in the League | 59 |
| Defensive Rating<br>Ave number of mins between League goals conceded while on the pitch. | 66 |
| Counting Games<br>Games when he played at least 70 mins | 43 |
| Clean Sheets<br>In games when he played at least 70 mins | 7 |

## TEAM OF THE SEASON

| GOALKEEPER | GAMES | DEF RATE |
|---|---|---|
| Steve Wilson | 43 | 66 |
| **DEFENDERS** | **GAMES** | **DEF RATE** |
| George Abbey | 16 | 74 |
| Paul O'Neil | 9 | 73 |
| Darren Tinson | 45 | 68 |
| Daniel Adams | 45 | 65 |
| **MIDFIELDERS** | **GAMES** | **SCORE DIFF** |
| Danny Whitaker | 37 | 2 |
| Chris Priest | 32 | -8 |
| Karl Munroe | 17 | -21 |
| Darren Dunning | 20 | 7 |
| **FORWARDS** | **GAMES** | **STRIKE RATE** |
| Matthew Tipton | 24 | 275 |
| Kyle Lightbourne | 36 | 321 |

# SOUTHEND UNITED

Final Position: **17th**

ICKNAME: THE SHRIMPERS

| | | | | | | |
|---|---|---|---|---|---|---|
| 1 | div3 | Hull City | A | D | 2-2 | Jenkins 63; Bramble 90 |
| 2 | div3 | Carlisle | H | L | 0-1 | |
| 3 | div3 | Shrewsbury | H | L | 2-3 | Jenkins 9; Bramble 81 pen |
| 4 | div3 | Oxford | A | W | 1-0 | Rawle 20 |
| 5 | div3 | Cambridge | H | W | 2-1 | Broad 7; Smith 30 |
| 6 | div3 | Rochdale | A | W | 2-1 | Rawle 35; Bramble 82 |
| 7 | div3 | Rushden & D | A | L | 0-3 | |
| 8 | wcr1 | Wimbledon | H | L | 1-4 | Rawle 82 |
| 9 | div3 | Macclesfield | H | W | 1-0 | Cort 26 |
| 10 | div3 | Kidderminster | H | L | 0-2 | |
| 11 | div3 | Lincoln | A | L | 1-2 | Jenkins 75 |
| 12 | div3 | Exeter | H | W | 1-0 | Jones 43 |
| 13 | div3 | Bury | A | W | 3-1 | Jones 66; Jenkins 79; Bramble 84 |
| 14 | div3 | York | H | W | 1-0 | Belgrave 90 |
| 15 | div3 | Swansea | A | L | 0-1 | |
| 16 | div3 | Hartlepool | H | L | 0-1 | |
| 17 | div3 | Leyton Orient | A | L | 1-2 | Belgrave 73 |
| 18 | div3 | Wrexham | H | L | 0-1 | |
| 19 | div3 | Bristol Rovers | A | W | 1-0 | Bramble 78 |
| 20 | facr1 | Hartlepool | H | D | 1-1 | Lee 3 og |
| 21 | div3 | Bournemouth | H | L | 0-1 | |
| 22 | facr1r | Hartlepool | A | W | 2-1 | Bramble 88; Cort 89 |
| 23 | div3 | Darlington | A | L | 1-2 | Bramble 90 |
| 24 | facr2 | Bournemouth | H | D | 1-1 | Rawle 53 |
| 25 | div3 | Boston | H | W | 4-2 | Cort 7,23,88; Rawle 39 |
| 26 | facr2r | Bournemouth | A | L | 2-3 | Bramble 42; Rawle 45 |
| 27 | div3 | Torquay | A | L | 1-3 | Bramble 60 |
| 28 | div3 | Cambridge | A | D | 1-1 | Rawle 10 |
| 29 | div3 | Scunthorpe | H | L | 1-2 | Cort 39 |
| 30 | div3 | Carlisle | A | L | 0-1 | |
| 31 | div3 | Shrewsbury | A | W | 1-0 | Smith 20 |
| 32 | div3 | Rochdale | H | W | 1-0 | Bramble 89 |
| 33 | div3 | Oxford | H | W | 2-1 | Rawle 45; Bramble 70 |
| 34 | div3 | Scunthorpe | A | L | 1-4 | Smith 17 |
| 35 | div3 | Hull City | H | W | 3-0 | Smith 22,45 pen; Rawle 41 |
| 36 | div3 | Bristol Rovers | H | D | 2-2 | Belgrave 36; Maher 76 |
| 37 | div3 | Wrexham | A | L | 0-3 | |
| 38 | div3 | Rushden & D | H | W | 2-1 | Rawle 4; Searle 6 |
| 39 | div3 | Macclesfield | A | L | 1-2 | Jenkins 88 |
| 40 | div3 | Kidderminster | A | L | 0-1 | |
| 41 | div3 | Lincoln | H | L | 0-1 | |
| 42 | div3 | Hartlepool | A | L | 1-2 | Sutch 74 |
| 43 | div3 | Swansea | H | L | 0-2 | |
| 44 | div3 | Leyton Orient | H | W | 1-0 | Salter 5 |
| 45 | div3 | York | A | L | 0-2 | |
| 46 | div3 | Darlington | H | W | 2-0 | Maher 40; Jenkins 42 |
| 47 | div3 | Bournemouth | A | L | 0-1 | |
| 48 | div3 | Torquay | H | W | 3-0 | Rawle 2,40; Jenkins 88 |
| 49 | div3 | Boston | A | L | 0-1 | |
| 50 | div3 | Bury | H | L | 1-2 | Cort 13 |
| 51 | div3 | Exeter | A | L | 0-1 | |

■ Home □ Away □ Neutral

## ATTENDANCES

HOME GROUND: ROOTS HALL CAPACITY: 12306 AVERAGE LEAGUE AT HOME: 3951

| | | | | | | | | | | | |
|---|---|---|---|---|---|---|---|---|---|---|---|
| 1 | Hull City | 10449 | 36 | Bristol Rovers | 4708 | 2 | Carlisle | 3881 | 37 | Wrexham | 3109 |
| 51 | Exeter | 9036 | 50 | Bury | 4707 | 18 | Wrexham | 3727 | 34 | Scunthorpe | 3096 |
| 47 | Bournemouth | 6767 | 35 | Hull City | 4534 | 32 | Rochdale | 3645 | 46 | Darlington | 3053 |
| 38 | Rushden & D | 6453 | 5 | Cambridge | 4462 | 15 | Swansea | 3623 | 10 | Kidderminster | 2959 |
| 28 | Cambridge | 6237 | 14 | York | 4411 | 48 | Torquay | 3594 | 6 | Rochdale | 2852 |
| 24 | Bournemouth | 5721 | 45 | York | 4312 | 12 | Exeter | 3364 | 43 | Swansea | 2832 |
| 19 | Bristol Rovers | 5691 | 29 | Scunthorpe | 4248 | 13 | Bury | 3301 | 23 | Darlington | 2830 |
| 26 | Bournemouth | 5456 | 21 | Bournemouth | 4221 | 9 | Macclesfield | 3249 | 31 | Shrewsbury | 2699 |
| 17 | Leyton Orient | 5343 | 7 | Rushden & D | 4176 | 49 | Boston | 3247 | 8 | Wimbledon | 2634 |
| 16 | Hartlepool | 5168 | 44 | Leyton Orient | 4148 | 25 | Boston | 3245 | 27 | Torquay | 2244 |
| 4 | Oxford | 5162 | 22 | Hartlepool | 4080 | 33 | Oxford | 3203 | 40 | Kidderminster | 2006 |
| 20 | Hartlepool | 4984 | 30 | Carlisle | 4016 | 11 | Lincoln | 3151 | 39 | Macclesfield | 1917 |
| 42 | Hartlepool | 4868 | 41 | Lincoln | 3912 | 3 | Shrewsbury | 3150 | | | |

## KEY PLAYER APPEARANCES

| | PLAYER | POS | AGE | APP | MINS ON | GOALS | CARDS(Y) | CARDS(R) | HOME COUNTRY |
|---|---|---|---|---|---|---|---|---|---|
| 1 | Leon Cort | DEF | 23 | 46 | 4140 | 6 | 3 | 0 | England |
| 2 | Darryl Flahavan | GK | 24 | 41 | 3690 | 0 | 3 | 0 | England |
| 3 | Kevin Maher | MID | 26 | 41 | 3690 | 2 | 11 | 0 | England |
| 4 | Damon Searle | DEF | 31 | 45 | 3643 | 1 | 4 | 0 | Wales |
| 5 | Tesfaye Bramble | ATT | 22 | 34 | 2775 | 9 | 4 | 1 | England |
| 6 | Mark Rawle | ATT | 24 | 34 | 2739 | 9 | 3 | 0 | England |
| 7 | Jay Smith | MID | 21 | 31 | 2709 | 5 | 7 | 0 | England |
| 8 | Mark Beard | DEF | 28 | 43 | 2594 | 0 | 7 | 0 | England |
| 9 | Neil Jenkins | DEF | 21 | 40 | 2522 | 7 | 3 | 0 | England |
| 10 | Anthony Clark | MID | 18 | 33 | 1692 | 0 | 4 | 0 | England |
| 11 | Graeme Jones | ATT | 33 | 22 | 1626 | 2 | 7 | 0 | England |
| 12 | Steve Broad | DEF | 23 | 21 | 1430 | 1 | 4 | 0 | England |
| 13 | David McSweeney | DEF | 21 | 22 | 1400 | 0 | 4 | 0 | England |
| 14 | Daryl Sutch | MID | 31 | 16 | 1387 | 1 | 0 | 0 | England |
| 15 | Daniel Marney | ATT | 21 | 17 | 1158 | 0 | 0 | 0 | England |
| 16 | Phil Whelan | DEF | 30 | 19 | 1049 | 0 | 4 | 0 | England |
| 17 | Stuart Thurgood | MID | 21 | 39 | 927 | 0 | 2 | 0 | England |
| 18 | Stephen Kelly | DEF | 19 | 10 | 900 | 0 | 1 | 0 | Rep of Ireland |

## KEY PLAYERS - GOALSCORERS

**1 Mark Rawle**

Goals in the League: **9**

Contribution to Attacking Power: Average number of minutes between League team goals while on pitch: **83**

Player Strike Rate: Average number of minutes between League goals scored by player: **304**

Club Strike Rate: Average number of minutes between League goals scored by club: **88**

| | PLAYER | LGE GOALS | POWER | STRIKE RATE |
|---|---|---|---|---|
| 2 | Tesfaye Bramble | 9 | 81 | 308 mins |
| 3 | Neil Jenkins | 7 | 93 | 360 mins |
| 4 | Jay Smith | 5 | 90 | 542 mins |
| 5 | Leon Cort | 6 | 88 | 690 mins |

## KEY PLAYERS - MIDFIELDERS

**1 Anthony Clark**

Goals in the League: **0**

Defensive Rating: Average number of mins between League goals conceded while he was on the pitch: **74**

Contribution to Attacking Power: Average number of minutes between League team goals while on pitch: **77**

Scoring Difference: Defensive Rating minus Contribution to Attacking Power: **-3**

| | PLAYER | LGE GOALS | DEF RATE | POWER | SCORE DIFF |
|---|---|---|---|---|---|
| 2 | Jay Smith | 5 | 75 | 90 | -15 mins |
| 3 | Kevin Maher | 2 | 66 | 86 | -20 mins |
| 4 | Daryl Sutch | 1 | 63 | 92 | -29 mins |

## KEY PLAYERS - DEFENDERS

**1 Neil Jenkins**

Goals Conceded when he was on pitch: **32**

Defensive Rating: Ave number of mins between League goals conceded while on the pitch: **79**

Clean Sheets: In games when he played at least 70 minutes: **8**

Club Defensive Rating: Average number of mins between League goals conceded by the club this season: **70**

| | PLAYER | CON LGE | CLN SHEETS | DEF RATE |
|---|---|---|---|---|
| 2 | Steve Broad | 18 | 4 | 79 mins |
| 3 | David McSweeney | 18 | 3 | 78 mins |
| 4 | Mark Beard | 36 | 6 | 72 mins |
| 5 | Damon Searle | 51 | 9 | 71 mins |

## KEY GOALKEEPER

**1 Darryl Flahavan**

Goals Conceded in the League: **53**

Defensive Rating: Ave number of mins between League goals conceded while on the pitch: **70**

Counting Games: Games when he played at least 70 mins: **41**

Clean Sheets: In games when he played at least 70 mins: **9**

## TEAM OF THE SEASON

| GOALKEEPER | GAMES | DEF RATE |
|---|---|---|
| Darryl Flahavan | 41 | 70 |
| **DEFENDERS** | **GAMES** | **DEF RATE** |
| Steve Broad | 15 | 79 |
| Neil Jenkins | 25 | 79 |
| David McSweeney | 14 | 78 |
| Mark Beard | 26 | 72 |
| **MIDFIELDERS** | **GAMES** | **SCORE DIFF** |
| Anthony Clark | 16 | -3 |
| Jay Smith | 30 | -15 |
| Kevin Maher | 41 | -20 |
| Daryl Sutch | 15 | -29 |
| **FORWARDS** | **GAMES** | **STRIKE RATE** |
| Mark Rawle | 27 | 304 |
| Tesfaye Bramble | 29 | 308 |

# LEYTON ORIENT

Final Position: **18th**

NICKNAME: THE O'S

| | | | | | | |
|---|---|---|---|---|---|---|
| 1 | div3 | Rochdale | A | L | 0-1 | |
| 2 | div3 | Macclesfield | H | W | 3-2 | Smith 17; Thorpe 29; Lockwood 43 pen |
| 3 | div3 | Scunthorpe | H | W | 2-0 | Martin 37; Lockwood 81 pen |
| 4 | div3 | Cambridge | A | L | 1-2 | Guttridge 50 og |
| 5 | div3 | Kidderminster | H | D | 0-0 | |
| 6 | div3 | Hull City | A | D | 1-1 | Toner 19 |
| 7 | div3 | Shrewsbury | A | L | 1-2 | Lockwood 5 |
| 8 | wcr1 | QPR | H | W | 3-2 | Campbell-Ryce 33; Thorpe 44; Fletcher 76 |
| 9 | div3 | Lincoln | H | D | 1-1 | Thorpe 89 |
| 10 | div3 | Oxford | H | L | 1-2 | Crosby 90 og |
| 11 | div3 | Exeter | A | L | 0-1 | |
| 12 | div3 | Darlington | H | W | 2-1 | Hutchings 59; Nugent 72 |
| 13 | wcr2 | Birmingham | H | L | 2-3 | Nugent 60; Ibehre 81 |
| 14 | div3 | Rushden & D | A | L | 0-2 | |
| 15 | div3 | Wrexham | A | D | 0-0 | |
| 16 | div3 | Bournemouth | H | D | 0-0 | |
| 17 | div3 | Bristol Rovers | A | W | 2-1 | Campbell-Ryce 57; Nugent 67 |
| 18 | div3 | Southend | H | W | 2-1 | Iriekpen 2; Whelan 45 og |
| 19 | div3 | Bury | H | L | 1-2 | Thorpe 83 |
| 20 | div3 | York | A | L | 2-3 | Nugent 9; Martin 58 |
| 21 | facr1 | Margate | H | D | 1-1 | Martin 25 |
| 22 | div3 | Hartlepool | H | L | 1-2 | Canham 69 |
| 23 | facr1r | Margate | A | L | 0-1 | |
| 24 | div3 | Boston | A | W | 1-0 | Tate 5 |
| 25 | div3 | Torquay | H | W | 2-0 | Canham 3; Tate 17 |
| 26 | div3 | Swansea | A | W | 1-0 | Tate 54 |
| 27 | div3 | Kidderminster | A | L | 2-3 | Ibehre 19,60 |
| 28 | div3 | Carlisle | H | W | 2-1 | Ibehre 25; Smith 34 |
| 29 | div3 | Scunthorpe | A | L | 1-2 | Smith 39 |
| 30 | div3 | Hull City | H | W | 2-0 | Thorpe 24; Ibehre 27 |
| 31 | div3 | Carlisle | A | L | 0-3 | |
| 32 | div3 | Cambridge | H | D | 1-1 | Ibehre 76 |
| 33 | div3 | York | H | L | 0-1 | |
| 34 | div3 | Bury | A | W | 1-0 | Martin 88 |
| 35 | div3 | Shrewsbury | H | L | 0-2 | |
| 36 | div3 | Rochdale | H | L | 0-1 | |
| 37 | div3 | Lincoln | A | D | 1-1 | Brazier 65 |
| 38 | div3 | Oxford | A | W | 2-0 | Tate 17; Harris 54 |
| 39 | div3 | Exeter | H | D | 1-1 | Thorpe 45 |
| 40 | div3 | Macclesfield | A | L | 1-3 | Thorpe 22 |
| 41 | div3 | Bristol Rovers | H | L | 1-2 | Lockwood 42 pen |
| 42 | div3 | Bournemouth | A | L | 1-3 | Thorpe 90 |
| 43 | div3 | Southend | A | L | 0-1 | |
| 44 | div3 | Boston | H | W | 3-2 | Purser 2,33,79 |
| 45 | div3 | Hartlepool | A | L | 1-4 | Heald 63 |
| 46 | div3 | Swansea | H | W | 3-1 | Tate 10,65; Turner 52 |
| 47 | div3 | Torquay | A | D | 2-2 | Alexander 41; Fletcher 73 |
| 48 | div3 | Rushden & D | H | D | 0-0 | |
| 49 | div3 | Wrexham | H | L | 0-1 | |
| 50 | div3 | Darlington | A | D | 2-2 | Lockwood 26; Alexander 37 |

■ Home □ Away ▨ Neutral

## ATTENDANCES

HOME GROUND: LONDON MATCHROOM STADIUM CAPACITY: 13842 AVERAGE LEAGUE AT HOME: 4257

| | | | | | | | | | | | |
|---|---|---|---|---|---|---|---|---|---|---|---|
| 6 | Hull City | 7684 | 9 | Lincoln | 4579 | 12 | Darlington | 3975 | 20 | York | 3304 |
| 17 | Bristol Rovers | 6625 | 46 | Swansea | 4480 | 32 | Cambridge | 3953 | 1 | Rochdale | 3252 |
| 50 | Darlington | 5723 | 25 | Torquay | 4443 | 44 | Boston | 3939 | 29 | Scunthorpe | 3242 |
| 16 | Bournemouth | 5622 | 14 | Rushden & D | 4381 | 35 | Shrewsbury | 3939 | 37 | Lincoln | 3130 |
| 18 | Southend | 5343 | 31 | Carlisle | 4269 | 2 | Macclesfield | 3880 | 11 | Exeter | 2784 |
| 48 | Rushden & D | 5180 | 33 | York | 4260 | 27 | Kidderminster | 3821 | 7 | Shrewsbury | 2756 |
| 30 | Hull City | 5125 | 19 | Bury | 4234 | 49 | Wrexham | 3766 | 34 | Bury | 2707 |
| 42 | Bournemouth | 5078 | 43 | Southend | 4148 | 10 | Oxford | 3758 | 36 | Rochdale | 2633 |
| 38 | Oxford | 5013 | 5 | Kidderminster | 4147 | 39 | Exeter | 3667 | 24 | Boston | 2616 |
| 8 | QPR | 4981 | 26 | Swansea | 4120 | 13 | Birmingham | 3615 | 23 | Margate | 2048 |
| 28 | Carlisle | 4879 | 41 | Bristol Rovers | 4081 | 21 | Margate | 3605 | 40 | Macclesfield | 1676 |
| 4 | Cambridge | 4807 | 3 | Scunthorpe | 4028 | 15 | Wrexham | 3495 | | | |
| 45 | Hartlepool | 4795 | 22 | Hartlepool | 4009 | 47 | Torquay | 3379 | | | |

## KEY PLAYER APPEARANCES

| | PLAYER | POS | AGE | APP | MINS ON | GOALS | CARDS(Y/R) | | HOME COUNTRY |
|---|---|---|---|---|---|---|---|---|---|
| 1 | Andy Harris | DEF | 26 | 45 | 3953 | 1 | 9 | 0 | England |
| 2 | Matthew Lockwood | MID | 26 | 43 | 3822 | 5 | 3 | 0 | England |
| 3 | Matthew Joseph | DEF | 30 | 38 | 3094 | 0 | 2 | 1 | England |
| 4 | Matthew Brazier | MID | 27 | 35 | 2745 | 1 | 4 | 0 | England |
| 5 | Dean Smith | DEF | 32 | 27 | 2403 | 3 | 6 | 1 | England |
| 6 | Lee Thorpe | ATT | 27 | 39 | 2337 | 7 | 10 | 1 | England |
| 7 | Glenn Morris | GK | 19 | 40 | 2025 | 0 | 0 | 0 | England |
| 8 | Carl Hutchings | MID | 28 | 27 | 2023 | 1 | 3 | 0 | England |
| 9 | John Martin | DEF | 21 | 42 | 2009 | 3 | 4 | 0 | England |
| 10 | Billy Jones | DEF | 20 | 29 | 1985 | 0 | 3 | 0 | England |
| 11 | Donny Barnard | DEF | 19 | 36 | 1956 | 0 | 3 | 0 | England |
| 12 | Ciaran Toner | MID | 22 | 32 | 1795 | 1 | 3 | 0 | N Ireland |
| 13 | Chris Tate | ATT | 25 | 24 | 1704 | 6 | 5 | 1 | England |
| 14 | Justin Miller | MID | 22 | 20 | 1600 | 0 | 3 | 1 | South Africa |
| 15 | Jamal Campbell-Ryce | MID | 20 | 17 | 1374 | 1 | 3 | 0 | England |
| 16 | Jabo Ibehre | MID | 20 | 28 | 1283 | 5 | 3 | 0 | England |
| 17 | Gary Alexander | ATT | 23 | 16 | 1075 | 2 | 2 | 0 | England |
| 18 | Scott Barrett | GK | 40 | 33 | 990 | 0 | 0 | 0 | England |

## KEY PLAYERS - GOALSCORERS

**1 Chris Tate**

| | |
|---|---|
| Goals in the League | 6 |
| Contribution to Attacking Power<br>Average number of minutes between League team goals while on pitch | 65 |
| Player Strike Rate<br>Average number of minutes between League goals scored by player | 284 |
| Club Strike Rate<br>Average number of minutes between League goals scored by club | 81 |

| | PLAYER | LGE GOALS | POWER | STRIKE RATE |
|---|---|---|---|---|
| 2 | Lee Thorpe | 7 | 86 | 334 mins |
| 3 | John Martin | 3 | 80 | 670 mins |
| 4 | Matthew Lockwood | 5 | 79 | 764 mins |
| 5 | Dean Smith | 3 | 80 | 801 mins |

## KEY PLAYERS - MIDFIELDERS

**1 Jamal Campbell-Ryce**

| | |
|---|---|
| Goals in the League | 1 |
| Defensive Rating<br>Average number of mins between League goals conceded while he was on the pitch | 92 |
| Contribution to Attacking Power<br>Average number of minutes between League team goals while on pitch | 92 |
| Scoring Difference<br>Defensive Rating minus Contribution to Attacking Power | 0 |

| | PLAYER | LGE GOALS | DEF RATE | POWER | SCORE DIFF |
|---|---|---|---|---|---|
| 2 | Matthew Brazier | 1 | 74 | 76 | -2 mins |
| 3 | Justin Miller | 0 | 73 | 80 | -7 mins |
| 4 | Matthew Lockwood | 5 | 68 | 80 | -12 mins |
| 5 | Ciaran Toner | 1 | 62 | 78 | -16 mins |

## KEY PLAYERS - DEFENDERS

**1 Dean Smith**

| | |
|---|---|
| Goals Conceded when he was on pitch | 29 |
| Defensive Rating<br>Ave number of mins between League goals conceded while on the pitch | 83 |
| Clean Sheets<br>In games when he played at least 70 minutes | 8 |
| Club Defensive Rating<br>Average number of mins between League goals conceded by the club this season. | 68 |

| | PLAYER | CON LGE | CLN SHEETS | DEF RATE |
|---|---|---|---|---|
| 2 | Donny Barnard | 29 | 7 | 67 mins |
| 3 | Andy Harris | 59 | 10 | 67 mins |
| 4 | Matthew Joseph | 46 | 8 | 67 mins |
| 5 | Billy Jones | 34 | 4 | 58 mins |

## KEY GOALKEEPER

**1 Scott Barrett**

| | |
|---|---|
| Goals Conceded in the League | 13 |
| Defensive Rating<br>Ave number of mins between League goals conceded while on the pitch. | 76 |
| Counting Games<br>Games when he played at least 70 mins | 11 |
| Clean Sheets<br>In games when he played at least 70 mins | 4 |

## TEAM OF THE SEASON

| GOALKEEPER | GAMES | DEF RATE |
|---|---|---|
| Scott Barrett | 11 | 76 |
| **DEFENDERS** | **GAMES** | **DEF RATE** |
| Dean Smith | 26 | 83 |
| Donny Barnard | 20 | 67 |
| Andy Harris | 43 | 67 |
| Matthew Joseph | 31 | 67 |
| **MIDFIELDERS** | **GAMES** | **SCORE DIFF** |
| Jamal Campbell-Ryce | 14 | 0 |
| Matthew Brazier | 28 | -2 |
| Justin Miller | 17 | -7 |
| Matthew Lockwood | 42 | -12 |
| **FORWARDS** | **GAMES** | **STRIKE RATE** |
| Kevin Nugent | 8 | 253 |
| Chris Tate | 18 | 284 |

# ROCHDALE

Final Position: **19th**

**NICKNAME: THE DALE**

| | | | | | | |
|---|---|---|---|---|---|---|
| 1 | div3 | Leyton Orient | H | W | 1-0 | Connor 90 |
| 2 | div3 | Lincoln | A | L | 0-2 | |
| 3 | div3 | Bristol Rovers | A | W | 2-1 | Platt 36; Simpson 78 |
| 4 | div3 | Darlington | H | D | 1-1 | McEvilly 8 |
| 5 | div3 | Wrexham | A | W | 5-2 | McEvilly 17; Simpson 22,41 pen,59 pen; Griffiths 24 |
| 6 | div3 | Southend | H | L | 1-2 | Griffiths 83 |
| 7 | div3 | Carlisle | A | W | 2-0 | Platt 11; Simpson 21 |
| 8 | wcr1 | Sheff Wed | A | L | 0-1 | |
| 9 | div3 | Shrewsbury | H | D | 1-1 | Simpson 79 pen |
| 10 | div3 | Cambridge | H | W | 4-3 | Bridges 5 og; Simpson 59; Townson 89; Oliver 90 |
| 11 | div3 | Kidderminster | A | D | 0-0 | |
| 12 | div3 | Macclesfield | H | W | 3-1 | Connor 20,67; Platt 81 |
| 13 | div3 | Swansea | A | D | 1-1 | Connor 70 |
| 14 | div3 | Hull City | A | L | 0-3 | |
| 15 | div3 | Scunthorpe | H | L | 1-2 | Simpson 85 |
| 16 | div3 | Boston | A | L | 1-3 | Flitcroft 81 |
| 17 | div3 | Exeter | H | D | 3-3 | Beech 41; Simpson 59; Griffiths 86 |
| 18 | div3 | Rushden & D | H | L | 0-1 | |
| 19 | div3 | Oxford | A | L | 0-2 | |
| 20 | facr1 | Peterborough | H | W | 3-2 | Connor 3; Platt 12; Beech 61 |
| 21 | div3 | York | H | L | 0-1 | |
| 22 | div3 | Torquay | A | D | 2-2 | Connor 74; Griffiths 78 |
| 23 | facr2 | Bristol Rovers | A | D | 1-1 | Platt 6 |
| 24 | div3 | Hartlepool | H | W | 4-0 | Platt 24; McEvilly 43,62; Connor 56 |
| 25 | facr2r | Bristol Rovers | H | W | 3-2 | Platt 34; Connor 48; McCourt 80 |
| 26 | div3 | Bury | A | D | 1-1 | McEvilly 66 |
| 27 | div3 | Wrexham | H | D | 2-2 | Connor 2,18 |
| 28 | div3 | Bournemouth | A | D | 3-3 | Flitcroft 16; McEvilly 45 pen; Platt 73 |
| 29 | facr3 | Preston | A | W | 2-1 | McEvilly 35; Simpson 54 |
| 30 | div3 | Southend | A | L | 0-1 | |
| 31 | div3 | Lincoln | H | L | 0-1 | |
| 32 | facr4 | Coventry | H | W | 2-0 | Connor 33; Griffiths 47 |
| 33 | div3 | Oxford | H | W | 2-1 | Oliver 44; Melaugh 89 |
| 34 | div3 | Darlington | A | W | 1-0 | Platt 21 |
| 35 | facr5 | Wolves | A | L | 1-3 | Melaugh 52 |
| 36 | div3 | Carlisle | H | L | 0-1 | |
| 37 | div3 | Leyton Orient | A | W | 1-0 | McEvilly 45 pen |
| 38 | div3 | Shrewsbury | A | L | 1-3 | McEvilly 84 |
| 39 | div3 | Cambridge | A | D | 2-2 | McEvilly 2; McCourt 51 |
| 40 | div3 | Bournemouth | H | D | 1-1 | Griffiths 49 |
| 41 | div3 | Boston | H | W | 1-0 | McEvilly 75 pen |
| 42 | div3 | Scunthorpe | A | L | 1-3 | McCourt 13 |
| 43 | div3 | Exeter | A | D | 1-1 | Coleman 30 pen |
| 44 | div3 | Rushden & D | A | D | 3-3 | Simpson 27; Grand 63; McCourt 87 |
| 45 | div3 | Torquay | H | L | 0-2 | |
| 46 | div3 | Bristol Rovers | H | D | 1-1 | Connor 21 |
| 47 | div3 | York | A | D | 2-2 | Connor 3; McEvilly 70 pen |
| 48 | div3 | Kidderminster | H | L | 0-1 | |
| 49 | div3 | Bury | H | L | 1-2 | Stuart 34 og |
| 50 | div3 | Hartlepool | A | D | 2-2 | Grand 23; McEvilly 45 |
| 51 | div3 | Swansea | H | L | 1-2 | Griffiths 43 |
| 52 | div3 | Hull City | H | W | 2-1 | McEvilly 6; Hockenhull 18 |
| 53 | div3 | Macclesfield | A | L | 2-3 | McEvilly 36 pen; Hill 70 |

■ Home □ Away □ Neutral

## ATTENDANCES

**HOME GROUND: SPOTLAND CAPACITY: 9223 AVERAGE LEAGUE AT HOME: 2739**

| | | | | | | | | | | | |
|---|---|---|---|---|---|---|---|---|---|---|---|
| 35 | Wolverhampton | 23921 | 5 | Wrexham | 4340 | 9 | Shrewsbury | 2914 | 41 | Boston | 2538 |
| 32 | Coventry | 9156 | 43 | Exeter | 4003 | 2 | Lincoln | 2894 | 34 | Darlington | 2479 |
| 14 | Hull City | 9057 | 47 | York | 3966 | 53 | Macclesfield | 2873 | 10 | Cambridge | 2392 |
| 8 | Sheff Wed | 8815 | 13 | Swansea | 3732 | 6 | Southend | 2852 | 52 | Hull City | 2225 |
| 29 | Preston | 8762 | 27 | Wrexham | 3727 | 4 | Darlington | 2834 | 45 | Torquay | 2216 |
| 3 | Bristol Rovers | 6478 | 30 | Southend | 3645 | 51 | Swansea | 2777 | 25 | Bristol Rovers | 2206 |
| 28 | Bournemouth | 6240 | 42 | Scunthorpe | 3616 | 33 | Oxford | 2764 | 31 | Lincoln | 2122 |
| 26 | Bury | 5827 | 44 | Rushden & D | 3444 | 22 | Torquay | 2754 | 40 | Bournemouth | 1958 |
| 50 | Hartlepool | 5408 | 38 | Shrewsbury | 3423 | 11 | Kidderminster | 2685 | 17 | Exeter | 1944 |
| 19 | Oxford | 4547 | 1 | Leyton Orient | 3252 | 16 | Boston | 2653 | 48 | Kidderminster | 1810 |
| 49 | Bury | 4513 | 36 | Carlisle | 3247 | 37 | Leyton Orient | 2633 | 46 | Bristol Rovers | 1658 |
| 7 | Carlisle | 4501 | 12 | Macclesfield | 3090 | 18 | Rushden & D | 2628 | | | |
| 23 | Bristol Rovers | 4369 | 24 | Hartlepool | 3059 | 39 | Cambridge | 2586 | | | |
| | | | 21 | York | 3056 | 20 | Peterborough | 2566 | | | |

## KEY PLAYER APPEARANCES

| | PLAYER | POS | AGE | APP | MINS ON | GOALS | CARDS(Y/R) | | HOME COUNTRY |
|---|---|---|---|---|---|---|---|---|---|
| 1 | Gareth Griffiths | DEF | 33 | 44 | 3656 | 6 | 8 | 1 | England |
| 2 | David Flitcroft | MID | 29 | 41 | 3548 | 2 | 13 | 0 | England |
| 3 | Wayne Evans | DEF | 31 | 43 | 3488 | 0 | 4 | 0 | Wales |
| 4 | Matt Doughty | DEF | 21 | 45 | 3483 | 0 | 2 | 0 | England |
| 5 | Clive Platt | ATT | 25 | 43 | 3471 | 6 | 2 | 1 | England |
| 6 | Paul Simpson | MID | 36 | 42 | 2738 | 10 | 2 | 0 | England |
| 7 | Paul Connor | ATT | 24 | 41 | 2671 | 10 | 1 | 0 | England |
| 8 | Lee McEvilly | ATT | 21 | 39 | 2466 | 14 | 6 | 0 | England |
| 9 | Neil Edwards | GK | 32 | 26 | 2324 | 0 | 0 | 0 | Wales |
| 10 | Simon Grand | DEF | 19 | 25 | 1972 | 2 | 4 | 0 | England |
| 11 | Lee Duffy | DEF | 20 | 26 | 1679 | 0 | 7 | 0 | England |
| 12 | Mathew Gilkes | GK | 21 | 45 | 1654 | 0 | 0 | 0 | England |
| 13 | Michael Oliver | MID | 27 | 23 | 1597 | 2 | 4 | 0 | England |
| 14 | Gavin Melaugh | MID | 21 | 23 | 1407 | 1 | 4 | 0 | N Ireland |
| 15 | Pat McCourt | MID | 19 | 28 | 1384 | 3 | 3 | 0 | N Ireland |
| 16 | Richard Jobson | DEF | 40 | 25 | 1280 | 0 | 3 | 0 | England |
| 17 | Chris Beech | MID | 28 | 21 | 1248 | 1 | 1 | 0 | England |
| 18 | Stephen Hill | DEF | 20 | 12 | 732 | 1 | 0 | 0 | England |

## KEY PLAYERS - GOALSCORERS

**1 Lee McEvilly**

| | |
|---|---|
| **Goals in the League** | 14 |
| **Contribution to Attacking Power** Average number of minutes between League team goals while on pitch | 54 |
| **Player Strike Rate** Average number of minutes between League goals scored by player | 176 |
| **Club Strike Rate** Average number of minutes between League goals scored by club | 66 |

| | PLAYER | LGE GOALS | POWER | STRIKE RATE |
|---|---|---|---|---|
| 2 | Paul Connor | 10 | 68 | 267 mins |
| 3 | Paul Simpson | 10 | 72 | 274 mins |
| 4 | Clive Platt | 6 | 66 | 579 mins |
| 5 | Gareth Griffiths | 6 | 68 | 609 mins |

## KEY PLAYERS - MIDFIELDERS

**1 Michael Oliver**

| | |
|---|---|
| **Goals in the League** | 2 |
| **Defensive Rating** Average number of mins between League goals conceded while he was on the pitch | 67 |
| **Contribution to Attacking Power** Average number of minutes between League team goals while on pitch | 61 |
| **Scoring Difference** Defensive Rating minus Contribution to Attacking Power | 6 |

| | PLAYER | LGE GOALS | DEF RATE | POWER | SCORE DIFF |
|---|---|---|---|---|---|
| 2 | Pat McCourt | 3 | 60 | 58 | 2 mins |
| 3 | Gavin Melaugh | 1 | 59 | 64 | -5 mins |
| 4 | David Flitcroft | 2 | 59 | 66 | -7 mins |
| 5 | Paul Simpson | 10 | 60 | 72 | -12 mins |

## KEY PLAYERS - DEFENDERS

**1 Wayne Evans**

| | |
|---|---|
| **Goals Conceded when he was on pitch** | 54 |
| **Defensive Rating** Ave number of mins between League goals conceded while on the pitch | 65 |
| **Clean Sheets** In games when he played at least 70 minutes | 6 |
| **Club Defensive Rating** Average number of mins between League goals conceded by the club this season. | 59 |

| | PLAYER | CON LGE | CLN SHEETS | DEF RATE |
|---|---|---|---|---|
| 2 | Simon Grand | 33 | 3 | 60 mins |
| 3 | Gareth Griffiths | 62 | 6 | 59 mins |
| 4 | Lee Duffy | 29 | 2 | 58 mins |
| 5 | Matt Doughty | 62 | 5 | 56 mins |

## KEY GOALKEEPER

**1 Neil Edwards**

| | |
|---|---|
| **Goals Conceded in the League** | 38 |
| **Defensive Rating** Ave number of mins between League goals conceded while on the pitch. | 61 |
| **Counting Games** Games when he played at least 70 mins | 26 |
| **Clean Sheets** In games when he played at least 70 mins | 4 |

## TEAM OF THE SEASON

| | | |
|---|---|---|
| **GOALKEEPER** | **GAMES** | **DEF RATE** |
| Neil Edwards | 26 | 61 |
| **DEFENDERS** | **GAMES** | **DEF RATE** |
| Wayne Evans | 37 | 65 |
| Simon Grand | 22 | 60 |
| Gareth Griffiths | 41 | 59 |
| Lee Duffy | 16 | 58 |
| **MIDFIELDERS** | **GAMES** | **SCORE DIFF** |
| Michael Oliver | 16 | 6 |
| Pat McCourt | 10 | 2 |
| Gavin Melaugh | 13 | -5 |
| David Flitcroft | 39 | -7 |
| **FORWARDS** | **GAMES** | **STRIKE RATE** |
| Lee McEvilly | 22 | 176 |
| Paul Connor | 26 | 267 |

# BRISTOL ROVERS

Final Position: **20th**

NICKNAME: THE PIRATES

| | | | | | | | |
|---|---|---|---|---|---|---|---|
| 1 | div3 | Torquay | A | L | 1-2 | Grazioli 4 |
| 2 | div3 | Hull City | H | D | 1-1 | Grazioli 30 |
| 3 | div3 | Rochdale | H | L | 1-2 | Bryant 44 |
| 4 | div3 | Carlisle | A | D | 0-0 | |
| 5 | div3 | Swansea | H | W | 3-1 | Grazioli 33; Tait 52; Astafjevs 84 |
| 6 | div3 | Scunthorpe | A | D | 2-2 | Quinn 48; Carlisle 90 pen |
| 7 | div3 | Macclesfield | A | L | 1-2 | Carlisle 72 |
| 8 | div3 | Exeter | H | D | 1-1 | Tait 39 |
| 9 | div3 | Bury | H | W | 2-1 | Tait 7; Grazioli 45 |
| 10 | div3 | Shrewsbury | A | W | 5-2 | Grazioli 35,52,65; Astafjevs 56; Carlisle 80 |
| 11 | div3 | Kidderminster | H | L | 1-2 | Tait 74 |
| 12 | div3 | Darlington | A | L | 0-1 | |
| 13 | div3 | Lincoln | H | W | 2-0 | Futcher 17 og; Grazioli 51 pen |
| 14 | div3 | York | A | D | 2-2 | Uddin 40; Astafjevs 44 |
| 15 | div3 | Leyton Orient | H | L | 1-2 | Coote 54 |
| 16 | div3 | Hartlepool | A | L | 0-2 | |
| 17 | div3 | Bournemouth | A | L | 0-1 | |
| 18 | div3 | Southend | H | L | 0-1 | |
| 19 | facr1 | Runcorn | H | D | 0-0 | |
| 20 | div3 | Wrexham | H | L | 0-3 | |
| 21 | facr1r | Runcorn | A | W | 3-1 | Grazioli 17; Carlisle 108; Gilroy 118 |
| 22 | div3 | Rushden & D | A | L | 1-2 | Grazioli 14 pen |
| 23 | facr2 | Rochdale | H | D | 1-1 | Allen 73 |
| 24 | div3 | Oxford | H | L | 0-2 | |
| 25 | facr2r | Rochdale | A | L | 2-3 | Barrett 19; Tait 51 |
| 26 | div3 | Cambridge | A | L | 1-3 | Allen 45 |
| 27 | div3 | Swansea | A | W | 1-0 | Tait 30 |
| 28 | div3 | Boston | H | D | 1-1 | Carlisle 87 pen |
| 29 | div3 | Hull City | A | L | 0-1 | |
| 30 | div3 | Torquay | H | D | 1-1 | Carlisle 18 pen |
| 31 | div3 | Scunthorpe | H | W | 2-1 | Astafjevs 85; Carlisle 88 |
| 32 | div3 | Boston | A | D | 0-0 | |
| 33 | div3 | Carlisle | H | L | 1-2 | Grazioli 33 |
| 34 | div3 | Southend | A | D | 2-2 | Barrett 51; Street 56 |
| 35 | div3 | Bournemouth | H | D | 0-0 | |
| 36 | div3 | Macclesfield | H | D | 1-1 | Llewellyn 80 |
| 37 | div3 | Exeter | A | D | 0-0 | |
| 38 | div3 | Bury | A | W | 1-0 | Quinn 65 |
| 39 | div3 | Shrewsbury | H | D | 0-0 | |
| 40 | div3 | Leyton Orient | A | W | 2-1 | Grazioli 13; Tait 72 |
| 41 | div3 | York | H | L | 0-1 | |
| 42 | div3 | Hartlepool | H | W | 1-0 | Hyde 7 |
| 43 | div3 | Lincoln | A | L | 1-2 | Astafjevs 23 |
| 44 | div3 | Rushden & D | H | L | 1-2 | Astafjevs 3 |
| 45 | div3 | Rochdale | A | D | 1-1 | Astafjevs 44 |
| 46 | div3 | Wrexham | A | L | 2-3 | Llewellyn 44,82 |
| 47 | div3 | Cambridge | H | W | 3-1 | Rammell 29,65; Astafjevs 82 |
| 48 | div3 | Oxford | A | W | 1-0 | Rammell 54 |
| 49 | div3 | Darlington | H | W | 2-1 | Rammell 23; Carlisle 75 |
| 50 | div3 | Kidderminster | A | D | 1-1 | Tait 71 |

■ Home □ Away ▒ Neutral

## ATTENDANCES

HOME GROUND: MEMORIAL STADIUM CAPACITY: 12000 AVERAGE LEAGUE AT HOME: 6934

| | | | | | | | | | | | |
|---|---|---|---|---|---|---|---|---|---|---|---|
| 29 | Hull City | 14913 | 15 | Leyton Orient | 6625 | 37 | Exeter | 5759 | 14 | York | 3616 |
| 49 | Darlington | 9835 | 31 | Scunthorpe | 6617 | 18 | Southend | 5691 | 43 | Lincoln | 3550 |
| 11 | Kidderminster | 9447 | 42 | Hartlepool | 6557 | 9 | Bury | 5493 | 10 | Shrewsbury | 3510 |
| 48 | Oxford | 8732 | 8 | Exeter | 6498 | 46 | Wrexham | 5330 | 32 | Boston | 3209 |
| 28 | Boston | 8311 | 3 | Rochdale | 6478 | 1 | Torquay | 4937 | 6 | Scunthorpe | 3178 |
| 41 | York | 8248 | 4 | Carlisle | 6475 | 34 | Southend | 4708 | 12 | Darlington | 2849 |
| 47 | Cambridge | 7563 | 35 | Bournemouth | 6347 | 23 | Rochdale | 4369 | 21 | Runcorn | 2444 |
| 33 | Carlisle | 7527 | 20 | Wrexham | 6328 | 19 | Runcorn | 4135 | 38 | Bury | 2425 |
| 2 | Hull City | 7501 | 30 | Torquay | 6196 | 40 | Leyton Orient | 4081 | 25 | Rochdale | 2206 |
| 17 | Bournemouth | 6924 | 13 | Lincoln | 6135 | 22 | Rushden & D | 3960 | 7 | Macclesfield | 1814 |
| 39 | Shrewsbury | 6839 | 36 | Macclesfield | 6005 | 16 | Hartlepool | 3889 | 45 | Rochdale | 1658 |
| 44 | Rushden & D | 6736 | 27 | Swansea | 5879 | 50 | Kidderminster | 3872 | | | |
| 5 | Swansea | 6644 | 24 | Oxford | 5864 | 26 | Cambridge | 3701 | | | |

## KEY PLAYER APPEARANCES

| | PLAYER | POS | AGE | APP | MINS ON | GOALS | CARDS(Y/R) | | HOME COUNTRY |
|---|---|---|---|---|---|---|---|---|---|
| 1 | Adam Barrett | DEF | 23 | 45 | 4043 | 1 | 5 | 0 | England |
| 2 | Scott Howie | GK | 31 | 46 | 3960 | 0 | 0 | 0 | Scotland |
| 3 | Robert Quinn | DEF | 26 | 44 | 3822 | 2 | 8 | 0 | England |
| 4 | Daniel Boxall | DEF | 25 | 42 | 3136 | 0 | 3 | 0 | England |
| 5 | Wayne Carlisle | MID | 23 | 44 | 3027 | 7 | 1 | 0 | N Ireland |
| 6 | Paul Tait | ATT | 28 | 43 | 2963 | 7 | 7 | 1 | England |
| 7 | Kevin Austin | DEF | 30 | 33 | 2666 | 0 | 1 | 0 | England |
| 8 | Guiliano Grazioli | ATT | 28 | 42 | 2389 | 11 | 4 | 0 | England |
| 9 | Vitalijs Astafjevs | MID | 32 | 34 | 2336 | 8 | 4 | 0 | Latvia |
| 10 | Graham Hyde | MID | 32 | 22 | 1712 | 1 | 3 | 1 | England |
| 11 | Anwar Uddin | DEF | 21 | 19 | 1542 | 1 | 0 | 0 | England |
| 12 | Simon Bryant | MID | 20 | 31 | 1463 | 1 | 2 | 0 | England |
| 13 | Trevor Challis | DEF | 27 | 16 | 1273 | 0 | 6 | 0 | England |
| 14 | Sonny Parker | MID | | 23 | 1258 | 0 | 2 | 0 | England |
| 15 | Ijah Anderson | DEF | 27 | 14 | 1243 | 0 | 1 | 0 | England |
| 16 | Chris Llewellyn | ATT | 23 | 14 | 1229 | 3 | 1 | 0 | Wales |
| 17 | Kevin Street | MID | 25 | 26 | 1176 | 1 | 0 | 0 | England |
| 18 | Lewis Hogg | MID | 20 | 29 | 809 | 0 | 2 | 0 | England |

## KEY PLAYERS - GOALSCORERS

**1 Guiliano Grazioli**

| | | | |
|---|---|---|---|
| Goals in the League | 11 | Player Strike Rate<br>Average number of minutes between League goals scored by player | 217 |
| Contribution to Attacking Power<br>Average number of minutes between League team goals while on pitch | 82 | Club Strike Rate<br>Average number of minutes between League goals scored by club | 83 |

| | PLAYER | LGE GOALS | POWER | STRIKE RATE |
|---|---|---|---|---|
| 2 | Vitalijs Astafjevs | 8 | 70 | 292 mins |
| 3 | Chris Llewellyn | 3 | 76 | 410 mins |
| 4 | Paul Tait | 7 | 84 | 423 mins |
| 5 | Wayne Carlisle | 7 | 84 | 432 mins |

## KEY PLAYERS - MIDFIELDERS

**1 Sonny Parker**

| | | | |
|---|---|---|---|
| Goals in the League | 0 | Contribution to Attacking Power<br>Average number of minutes between League team goals while on pitch | 74 |
| Defensive Rating<br>Average number of mins between League goals conceded while he was on the pitch | 74 | Scoring Difference<br>Defensive Rating minus Contribution to Attacking Power | 0 |

| | PLAYER | LGE GOALS | DEF RATE | POWER | SCORE DIFF |
|---|---|---|---|---|---|
| 2 | Vitalijs Astafjevs | 8 | 69 | 71 | -2 mins |
| 3 | Wayne Carlisle | 7 | 80 | 84 | -4 mins |
| 4 | Graham Hyde | 1 | 82 | 90 | -8 mins |
| 5 | Simon Bryant | 1 | 56 | 73 | -17 mins |

## KEY PLAYERS - DEFENDERS

**1 Ijah Anderson**

| | | | |
|---|---|---|---|
| Goals Conceded when he was on pitch | 10 | Clean Sheets<br>In games when he played at least 70 minutes | 6 |
| Defensive Rating<br>Ave number of mins between League goals conceded while on the pitch | 124 | Club Defensive Rating<br>Average number of mins between League goals conceded by the club this season. | 73 |

| | PLAYER | CON LGE | CLN SHEETS | DEF RATE |
|---|---|---|---|---|
| 2 | Kevin Austin | 31 | 9 | 86 mins |
| 3 | Robert Quinn | 51 | 10 | 75 mins |
| 4 | Richard Rose | 11 | 2 | 73 mins |
| 5 | Adam Barrett | 57 | 9 | 71 mins |

## KEY GOALKEEPER

**1 Scott Howie**

| | |
|---|---|
| Goals Conceded in the League | 55 |
| Defensive Rating<br>Ave number of mins between League goals conceded while on the pitch. | 72 |
| Counting Games<br>Games when he played at least 70 mins | 44 |
| Clean Sheets<br>In games when he played at least 70 mins | 9 |

## TEAM OF THE SEASON

| GOALKEEPER | GAMES | DEF RATE |
|---|---|---|
| Scott Howie | 44 | 72 |
| **DEFENDERS** | **GAMES** | **DEF RATE** |
| Ijah Anderson | 14 | 124 |
| Kevin Austin | 28 | 86 |
| Robert Quinn | 43 | 75 |
| Richard Rose | 9 | 73 |
| **MIDFIELDERS** | **GAMES** | **SCORE DIFF** |
| Sonny Parker | 13 | 0 |
| Vitalijs Astafjevs | 23 | -2 |
| Wayne Carlisle | 28 | -4 |
| Graham Hyde | 18 | -8 |
| **FORWARDS** | **GAMES** | **STRIKE RATE** |
| Guiliano Grazioli | 23 | 217 |
| Chris Llewellyn | 13 | 410 |

# SWANSEA

Final Position: **21st**

NICKNAME: THE SWANS

| | | | | | | |
|---|---|---|---|---|---|---|
| 1 | div3 | Rushden & D | H | D | 2-2 | Thomas 15; Reid 64 |
| 2 | div3 | Darlington | A | D | 2-2 | Smith 61; Watkin 89 |
| 3 | div3 | Bury | A | L | 2-3 | Thomas 63; Swailes 78 og |
| 4 | div3 | Bournemouth | H | W | 2-0 | Wood 1; Mumford 82 |
| 5 | div3 | Bristol Rovers | A | L | 1-3 | Moss 80 |
| 6 | div3 | York | H | L | 1-2 | Moss 77 |
| 7 | div3 | Hartlepool | H | D | 2-2 | Cusack 28; Wood 41 pen |
| 8 | wcr1 | Wolverhampton | H | L | 2-3 | Thomas 7; Wood 22 |
| 9 | div3 | Wrexham | A | L | 0-4 | |
| 10 | div3 | Boston | A | L | 0-1 | |
| 11 | div3 | Torquay | H | L | 0-1 | |
| 12 | div3 | Hull City | A | D | 1-1 | Thomas 52 |
| 13 | div3 | Rochdale | H | D | 1-1 | Thomas 32 |
| 14 | div3 | Oxford | A | L | 0-1 | |
| 15 | div3 | Southend | H | W | 1-0 | Thomas 52 pen |
| 16 | div3 | Carlisle | A | D | 2-2 | Thomas 8,65 |
| 17 | div3 | Kidderminster | H | L | 0-4 | |
| 18 | div3 | Cambridge | A | L | 0-1 | |
| 19 | div3 | Macclesfield | H | W | 1-0 | Murphy 84 |
| 20 | div3 | Scunthorpe | A | L | 0-2 | |
| 21 | facr1 | York | A | L | 1-2 | Murphy 80 |
| 22 | div3 | Shrewsbury | H | W | 2-0 | Murphy 42; Richards 70 |
| 23 | div3 | Exeter | A | L | 0-1 | |
| 24 | div3 | Leyton Orient | H | L | 0-1 | |
| 25 | div3 | Bristol Rovers | H | L | 0-1 | |
| 26 | div3 | Lincoln | A | L | 0-1 | |
| 27 | div3 | Bury | H | L | 2-3 | Smith, J 68; Smith, D 78 |
| 28 | div3 | York | A | L | 1-3 | Parkin 14 og |
| 29 | div3 | Lincoln | H | W | 2-0 | Nugent 44; Williams 67 |
| 30 | div3 | Rushden & D | A | D | 1-1 | Nugent 16 |
| 31 | div3 | Darlington | H | W | 1-0 | Nugent 37 |
| 32 | div3 | Macclesfield | A | W | 3-1 | Watkin 41; Smith, J 52; Martinez 67 |
| 33 | div3 | Bournemouth | A | L | 0-3 | |
| 34 | div3 | Cambridge | H | W | 2-0 | Richards 58,82 |
| 35 | div3 | Hartlepool | A | L | 0-4 | |
| 36 | div3 | Wrexham | H | D | 0-0 | |
| 37 | div3 | Boston | H | D | 0-0 | |
| 38 | div3 | Torquay | A | D | 0-0 | |
| 39 | div3 | Carlisle | H | L | 1-2 | Williams 90 |
| 40 | div3 | Southend | A | W | 2-0 | Thomas 60 pen; Nugent 64 |
| 41 | div3 | Kidderminster | A | D | 2-2 | Johnrose 22; Martinez 35 |
| 42 | div3 | Oxford | H | W | 3-2 | Richards 35,62 pen; Johnrose 55 |
| 43 | div3 | Shrewsbury | A | D | 0-0 | |
| 44 | div3 | Scunthorpe | H | D | 1-1 | Richards 14 |
| 45 | div3 | Leyton Orient | A | L | 1-3 | Thomas 8 |
| 46 | div3 | Exeter | H | L | 0-1 | |
| 47 | div3 | Rochdale | A | W | 2-1 | Nugent 18; Richards 68 |
| 48 | div3 | Hull City | H | W | 4-2 | Thomas 8 pen,45 pen,57; Johnrose 48 |

■ Home □ Away □ Neutral

## ATTENDANCES

HOME GROUND: VETCH FIELD CAPACITY: 12000 AVERAGE LEAGUE AT HOME: 5159

| | | | | | | | | | | | |
|---|---|---|---|---|---|---|---|---|---|---|---|
| 48 | Hull City | 9585 | 33 | Bournemouth | 5511 | 6 | York | 4086 | 17 | Kidderminster | 3421 |
| 46 | Exeter | 9115 | 14 | Oxford | 5440 | 30 | Rushden & D | 4046 | 7 | Hartlepool | 3370 |
| 12 | Hull City | 8070 | 29 | Lincoln | 5099 | 18 | Cambridge | 3956 | 38 | Torquay | 3287 |
| 5 | Bristol Rovers | 6644 | 34 | Cambridge | 4903 | 16 | Carlisle | 3940 | 41 | Kidderminster | 3172 |
| 37 | Boston | 6642 | 8 | Wolves | 4799 | 2 | Darlington | 3914 | 21 | York | 2948 |
| 36 | Wrexham | 6463 | 43 | Shrewsbury | 4645 | 11 | Torquay | 3872 | 20 | Scunthorpe | 2886 |
| 1 | Rushden & D | 6327 | 28 | York | 4611 | 13 | Rochdale | 3732 | 40 | Southend | 2832 |
| 44 | Scunthorpe | 6014 | 26 | Lincoln | 4553 | 22 | Shrewsbury | 3638 | 47 | Rochdale | 2777 |
| 42 | Oxford | 5982 | 35 | Hartlepool | 4486 | 15 | Southend | 3623 | 23 | Exeter | 2625 |
| 25 | Bristol Rovers | 5879 | 45 | Leyton Orient | 4480 | 9 | Wrexham | 3555 | 32 | Macclesfield | 2515 |
| 39 | Carlisle | 5845 | 4 | Bournemouth | 4325 | 27 | Bury | 3555 | 3 | Bury | 2348 |
| 31 | Darlington | 5553 | 24 | Leyton Orient | 4120 | 19 | Macclesfield | 3526 | 10 | Boston | 2209 |

## KEY PLAYER APPEARANCES

| | PLAYER | POS | AGE | APP | MINS ON | GOALS | CARDS(Y/R) | | HOME COUNTRY |
|---|---|---|---|---|---|---|---|---|---|
| 1 | Michael Howard | DEF | 24 | 42 | 3243 | 0 | 8 | 0 | England |
| 2 | James Thomas | ATT | 24 | 39 | 2967 | 12 | 1 | 0 | Wales |
| 3 | Roger Freestone | GK | 34 | 39 | 2949 | 0 | 4 | 0 | Wales |
| 4 | Kristian O'Leary | DEF | 25 | 42 | 2550 | 0 | 2 | 1 | Wales |
| 5 | Lee Jenkins | MID | 24 | 36 | 2438 | 0 | 5 | 1 | Wales |
| 6 | Alan Tate | DEF | 20 | 27 | 2430 | 0 | 9 | 0 | England |
| 7 | Jason Smith | DEF | 28 | 28 | 2226 | 2 | 8 | 0 | England |
| 8 | Terry Evans | DEF | 27 | 28 | 2168 | 0 | 4 | 0 | Wales |
| 9 | Leon Britton | MID | 20 | 25 | 2157 | 0 | 2 | 0 | England |
| 10 | Gareth Phillips | MID | 23 | 36 | 1890 | 0 | 3 | 0 | Wales |
| 11 | Roberto Martinez | MID | 29 | 19 | 1710 | 2 | 5 | 0 | Spain |
| 12 | Paul Reid | MID | 35 | 20 | 1607 | 1 | 6 | 0 | England |
| 13 | Andrew Mumford | DEF | 22 | 38 | 1540 | 1 | 2 | 0 | Wales |
| 14 | Steve Watkin | ATT | 32 | 37 | 1359 | 2 | 2 | 1 | Wales |
| 15 | Lenny Johnrose | MID | 33 | 15 | 1302 | 3 | 1 | 0 | England |
| 16 | John Williams | ATT | 35 | 38 | 1292 | 2 | 0 | 0 | England |
| 17 | Kevin Nugent | ATT | 34 | 15 | 1266 | 5 | 2 | 1 | England |
| 18 | Marc Richards | MID | 20 | 21 | 1205 | 7 | 1 | 1 | England |

## KEY PLAYERS - GOALSCORERS

**1 Marc Richards**

| | |
|---|---|
| Goals in the League | 7 |
| **Contribution to Attacking Power** Average number of minutes between League team goals while on pitch | 120 |
| **Player Strike Rate** Average number of minutes between League goals scored by player | 172 |
| **Club Strike Rate** Average number of minutes between League goals scored by club | 86 |

| | PLAYER | LGE GOALS | POWER | STRIKE RATE |
|---|---|---|---|---|
| 2 | James Thomas | 12 | 82 | 247 mins |
| 3 | Kevin Nugent | 5 | 70 | 253 mins |
| 4 | Lenny Johnrose | 3 | 56 | 434 mins |
| 5 | Roberto Martinez | 2 | 74 | 855 mins |

## KEY PLAYERS - MIDFIELDERS

**1 Lenny Johnrose**

| | |
|---|---|
| Goals in the League | 3 |
| **Defensive Rating** Average number of mins between League goals conceded while he was on the pitch | 81 |
| **Contribution to Attacking Power** Average number of minutes between League team goals while on pitch | 57 |
| **Scoring Difference** Defensive Rating minus Contribution to Attacking Power | 24 |

| | PLAYER | LGE GOALS | DEF RATE | POWER | SCORE DIFF |
|---|---|---|---|---|---|
| 2 | Roberto Martinez | 2 | 74 | 74 | 0 mins |
| 3 | Leon Britton | 0 | 70 | 86 | -16 mins |
| 4 | Lee Jenkins | 0 | 64 | 84 | -20 mins |
| 5 | Paul Reid | 1 | 47 | 85 | -38 mins |

## KEY PLAYERS - DEFENDERS

**1 Andrew Mumford**

| | |
|---|---|
| Goals Conceded when he was on pitch | 16 |
| **Defensive Rating** Ave number of mins between League goals conceded while on the pitch | 96 |
| **Clean Sheets** In games when he played at least 70 minutes | 8 |
| **Club Defensive Rating** Average number of mins between League goals conceded by the club this season. | 64 |

| | PLAYER | CON LGE | CLN SHEETS | DEF RATE |
|---|---|---|---|---|
| 2 | Alan Tate | 34 | 9 | 71 mins |
| 3 | Kristian O'Leary | 37 | 6 | 69 mins |
| 4 | David Theobald | 13 | 1 | 64 mins |
| 5 | Michael Howard | 52 | 8 | 62 mins |

## KEY GOALKEEPER

**1 Neil Cutler**

| | |
|---|---|
| Goals Conceded in the League | 14 |
| **Defensive Rating** Ave number of mins between League goals conceded while on the pitch. | 84 |
| **Counting Games** Games when he played at least 70 mins | 13 |
| **Clean Sheets** In games when he played at least 70 mins | 5 |

## TEAM OF THE SEASON

| GOALKEEPER | GAMES | DEF RATE |
|---|---|---|
| Neil Cutler | 13 | 84 |
| **DEFENDERS** | **GAMES** | **DEF RATE** |
| Andrew Mumford | 12 | 96 |
| Alan Tate | 27 | 71 |
| Kristian O'Leary | 26 | 69 |
| David Theobald | 9 | 64 |
| **MIDFIELDERS** | **GAMES** | **SCORE DIFF** |
| Lenny Johnrose | 14 | 24 |
| Roberto Martinez | 19 | 0 |
| Leon Britton | 24 | -16 |
| Lee Jenkins | 25 | -20 |
| **FORWARDS** | **GAMES** | **STRIKE RATE** |
| James Thomas | 29 | 247 |
| Kevin Nugent | 12 | 253 |

# CARLISLE UNITED

Final Position: **22nd**

NICKNAME: THE FOXES

| | | | | | | |
|---|---|---|---|---|---|---|
| 1 | div3 | Hartlepool | H | L | 1-3 | Wake 80 |
| 2 | div3 | Southend | A | W | 1-0 | McDonagh 85 |
| 3 | div3 | Lincoln | A | W | 1-0 | Molloy 66 pen |
| 4 | div3 | Bristol Rovers | H | D | 0-0 | |
| 5 | div3 | Darlington | A | L | 0-2 | |
| 6 | div3 | Exeter | H | L | 0-2 | |
| 7 | div3 | Rochdale | H | L | 0-2 | |
| 8 | wcr1 | Rotherham | A | L | 1-3 | McGill 83 |
| 9 | div3 | Hull City | A | L | 0-4 | |
| 10 | div3 | Scunthorpe | A | L | 1-3 | Foran 24 |
| 11 | div3 | Boston | H | W | 4-2 | Wake 14,34,45; Foran 22 pen |
| 12 | div3 | Bournemouth | A | L | 1-3 | Murphy 89 |
| 13 | div3 | Torquay | H | L | 1-2 | Farrell 30 |
| 14 | div3 | Shrewsbury | H | L | 1-2 | Redmile 56 og |
| 15 | div3 | Macclesfield | A | D | 2-2 | Osman 2; McGill 80 |
| 16 | div3 | Swansea | H | D | 2-2 | Magennis 3; Farrell 46 pen |
| 17 | div3 | Cambridge | A | L | 1-2 | Sutton 20 |
| 18 | div3 | Oxford | H | W | 1-0 | McGill 33 |
| 19 | div3 | Kidderminster | A | W | 2-1 | Farrell 15 pen; McDonagh 84 |
| 20 | facr1 | Lincoln | H | W | 2-1 | Foran 56; Farrell 67 |
| 21 | div3 | Bury | H | L | 1-2 | Murphy 61 |
| 22 | div3 | York | A | L | 1-2 | Robinson 73 |
| 23 | facr2 | Scunthorpe | A | D | 0-0 | |
| 24 | div3 | Wrexham | H | L | 1-2 | Foran 5 |
| 25 | div3 | Rushden & D | A | D | 1-1 | Farrell 12 |
| 26 | facr2r | Scunthorpe | H | L | 0-1 | |
| 27 | div3 | Darlington | H | D | 2-2 | Farrell 9 pen; Hudson 37 |
| 28 | div3 | Leyton Orient | A | L | 1-2 | Shelley 22 |
| 29 | div3 | Hartlepool | A | L | 1-2 | Burt 10 |
| 30 | div3 | Southend | H | W | 1-0 | McCarthy 32 |
| 31 | div3 | Exeter | A | L | 0-1 | |
| 32 | div3 | Leyton Orient | H | W | 3-0 | Farrell 53,70; Maddison 56 |
| 33 | div3 | Bristol Rovers | A | W | 2-1 | Farrell 45; Foran 51 |
| 34 | div3 | Lincoln | H | L | 1-4 | Farrell 90 |
| 35 | div3 | Kidderminster | H | D | 2-2 | Foran 7; Rundle 41 |
| 36 | div3 | Rochdale | A | W | 1-0 | Green 62 |
| 37 | div3 | Hull City | H | L | 1-5 | Farrell 90 |
| 38 | div3 | Boston | A | D | 0-0 | |
| 39 | div3 | Scunthorpe | H | L | 1-2 | Foran 14 |
| 40 | div3 | Swansea | A | W | 2-1 | Farrell 73 pen; McGill 89 |
| 41 | div3 | Macclesfield | H | W | 1-0 | Birch 8 |
| 42 | div3 | Cambridge | H | L | 0-1 | |
| 43 | div3 | Oxford | A | D | 0-0 | |
| 44 | div3 | Bury | A | D | 1-1 | Foran 80 |
| 45 | div3 | York | H | D | 1-1 | Kelly 79 |
| 46 | div3 | Rushden & D | H | L | 1-2 | Green 80 |
| 47 | div3 | Wrexham | A | L | 1-6 | Wake 68 |
| 48 | div3 | Torquay | A | W | 3-2 | Russell 30; Wake 37; Summerbell 45 |
| 49 | div3 | Shrewsbury | A | W | 3-2 | Wake 36,37,50 |
| 50 | div3 | Bournemouth | H | L | 0-2 | |

■ Home □ Away ▒ Neutral

## ATTENDANCES

HOME GROUND: BRUNTON PARK CAPACITY: 16651 AVERAGE LEAGUE AT HOME: 4775

| | | | | | | | | | | | |
|---|---|---|---|---|---|---|---|---|---|---|---|
| 1 | Hartlepool | 10684 | 29 | Hartlepool | 5071 | 18 | Oxford | 4039 | 44 | Bury | 3384 |
| 9 | Hull City | 8461 | 43 | Oxford | 5044 | 30 | Southend | 4016 | 17 | Cambridge | 3334 |
| 33 | Bristol Rovers | 7527 | 45 | York | 4935 | 13 | Torquay | 4014 | 31 | Exeter | 3333 |
| 50 | Bournemouth | 7402 | 28 | Leyton Orient | 4879 | 42 | Cambridge | 3992 | 36 | Rochdale | 3247 |
| 49 | Shrewsbury | 7236 | 6 | Exeter | 4806 | 16 | Swansea | 3940 | 38 | Boston | 3131 |
| 26 | Scunthorpe | 6809 | 21 | Bury | 4678 | 35 | Kidderminster | 3882 | 39 | Scunthorpe | 3124 |
| 47 | Wrexham | 6746 | 37 | Hull City | 4678 | 2 | Southend | 3881 | 3 | Lincoln | 3034 |
| 4 | Bristol Rovers | 6475 | 7 | Rochdale | 4501 | 41 | Macclesfield | 3773 | 19 | Kidderminster | 3009 |
| 27 | Darlington | 6016 | 24 | Wrexham | 4480 | 48 | Torquay | 3761 | 8 | Rotherham | 2902 |
| 40 | Swansea | 5845 | 20 | Lincoln | 4388 | 11 | Boston | 3623 | 15 | Macclesfield | 2383 |
| 46 | Rushden & D | 5468 | 25 | Rushden & D | 4355 | 23 | Scunthorpe | 3590 | 10 | Scunthorpe | 2342 |
| 5 | Darlington | 5163 | 22 | York | 4335 | 34 | Lincoln | 3567 | | | |
| 12 | Bournemouth | 5103 | 32 | Leyton Orient | 4269 | 14 | Shrewsbury | 3484 | | | |

## KEY PLAYER APPEARANCES

| | PLAYER | POS | AGE | APP | MINS ON | GOALS | CARDS(Y) | CARDS(R) | HOME COUNTRY |
|---|---|---|---|---|---|---|---|---|---|
| 1 | Peter Murphy | DEF | 22 | 41 | 3458 | 2 | 6 | 0 | Rep of Ireland |
| 2 | Mark Summerbell | MID | 32 | 39 | 3429 | 1 | 17 | 2 | England |
| 3 | Brian Shelley | DEF | 21 | 41 | 2928 | 1 | 4 | 1 | Rep of Ireland |
| 4 | Mathew Glennon | GK | 24 | 32 | 2790 | 0 | 1 | 0 | England |
| 5 | Darren Kelly | DEF | 24 | 35 | 2728 | 1 | 9 | 0 | N Ireland |
| 6 | Craig Farrell | ATT | 20 | 34 | 2556 | 11 | 2 | 0 | England |
| 7 | Ritchie Foran | ATT | 23 | 31 | 2305 | 7 | 7 | 2 | Rep of Ireland |
| 8 | Brendan McGill | MID | 22 | 41 | 2145 | 3 | 1 | 0 | Rep of Ireland |
| 9 | Mark Birch | DEF | 26 | 36 | 1701 | 1 | 5 | 1 | England |
| 10 | Adam Rundle | ATT | 18 | 21 | 1632 | 1 | 0 | 0 | England |
| 11 | Jon McCarthy | MID | 32 | 22 | 1556 | 1 | 6 | 1 | N Ireland |
| 12 | Lee Maddison | DEF | 30 | 25 | 1509 | 1 | 5 | 0 | England |
| 13 | William McDonagh | MID | 20 | 36 | 1206 | 2 | 4 | 1 | Rep of Ireland |
| 14 | Mark Hudson | MID | 22 | 15 | 1205 | 1 | 1 | 0 | England |
| 15 | Brian Wake | ATT | 20 | 35 | 1170 | 9 | 2 | 0 | England |
| 16 | Peter Keen | GK | 26 | 25 | 1170 | 0 | 1 | 0 | England |
| 17 | Lee Andrews | MID | 20 | 24 | 1101 | 0 | 1 | 0 | England |
| 18 | Leon Osman | MID | 22 | 12 | 960 | 1 | 0 | 0 | England |

## KEY PLAYERS - GOALSCORERS

**1 Craig Farrell**

| | |
|---|---|
| Goals in the League | 11 |
| Contribution to Attacking Power<br>Average number of minutes between League team goals while on pitch | 77 |
| Player Strike Rate<br>Average number of minutes between League goals scored by player | 232 |
| Club Strike Rate<br>Average number of minutes between League goals scored by club | 80 |

| | PLAYER | LGE GOALS | POWER | STRIKE RATE |
|---|---|---|---|---|
| 2 | Ritchie Foran | 7 | 67 | 329 mins |
| 3 | Brendan McGill | 3 | 73 | 715 mins |
| 4 | Mark Hudson | 1 | 75 | 1205 mins |
| 5 | Lee Maddison | 1 | 65 | 1509 mins |

## KEY PLAYERS - MIDFIELDERS

**1 Mark Hudson**

| | |
|---|---|
| Goals in the League | 1 |
| Defensive Rating<br>Average number of mins between League goals conceded while he was on the pitch | 63 |
| Contribution to Attacking Power<br>Average number of minutes between League team goals while on pitch | 75 |
| Scoring Difference<br>Defensive Rating minus Contribution to Attacking Power | -12 |

| | PLAYER | LGE GOALS | DEF RATE | POWER | SCORE DIFF |
|---|---|---|---|---|---|
| 2 | Leon Osman | 1 | 53 | 74 | -21 mins |
| 3 | Brendan McGill | 3 | 50 | 74 | -24 mins |
| 4 | Lee Andrews | 0 | 48 | 73 | -25 mins |
| 5 | Mark Summerbell | 1 | 51 | 78 | -27 mins |

## KEY PLAYERS - DEFENDERS

**1 Paul Raven**

| | |
|---|---|
| Goals Conceded when he was on pitch | 11 |
| Defensive Rating<br>Ave number of mins between League goals conceded while on the pitch | 80 |
| Clean Sheets<br>In games when he played at least 70 minutes | 4 |
| Club Defensive Rating<br>Average number of mins between League goals conceded by the club this season. | 53 |

| | PLAYER | CON LGE | CLN SHEETS | DEF RATE |
|---|---|---|---|---|
| 2 | Des Byrne | 13 | 2 | 61 mins |
| 3 | Mark Birch | 29 | 6 | 59 mins |
| 4 | Peter Murphy | 61 | 7 | 57 mins |
| 5 | Lee Maddison | 27 | 4 | 56 mins |

## KEY GOALKEEPER

**1 Mathew Glennon**

| | |
|---|---|
| Goals Conceded in the League | 50 |
| Defensive Rating<br>Ave number of mins between League goals conceded while on the pitch. | 56 |
| Counting Games<br>Games when he played at least 70 mins | 31 |
| Clean Sheets<br>In games when he played at least 70 mins | 7 |

## TEAM OF THE SEASON

| GOALKEEPER | GAMES | DEF RATE |
|---|---|---|
| Mathew Glennon | 31 | 56 |
| **DEFENDERS** | **GAMES** | **DEF RATE** |
| Paul Raven | 9 | 80 |
| Des Byrne | 9 | 61 |
| Mark Birch | 16 | 59 |
| Peter Murphy | 36 | 57 |
| **MIDFIELDERS** | **GAMES** | **SCORE DIFF** |
| Mark Hudson | 12 | -12 |
| Leon Osman | 10 | -21 |
| Brendan McGill | 15 | -24 |
| Mark Summerbell | 38 | -27 |
| **FORWARDS** | **GAMES** | **STRIKE RATE** |
| Craig Farrell | 25 | 232 |
| Ritchie Foran | 22 | 329 |

# EXETER CITY

Final Position: **23rd**

NICKNAME: THE GRECIANS

| | | | | | | |
|---|---|---|---|---|---|---|
| 1 | div3 | Shrewsbury | A | L | 0-1 | |
| 2 | div3 | Scunthorpe | H | D | 1-1 | Thomas 90 |
| 3 | div3 | Hull City | H | W | 3-1 | Sharpe 20; Flack 45,46 |
| 4 | div3 | Kidderminster | A | L | 3-4 | Flack 3; Thomas 14; Roscoe 78 |
| 5 | div3 | Torquay | H | L | 1-2 | Coppinger 41 |
| 6 | div3 | Carlisle | A | W | 2-0 | Goodman 42; Gaia 45 |
| 7 | div3 | Bournemouth | H | L | 1-3 | Roscoe 6 |
| 8 | wcr1 | Brighton | A | D | 1-3 | McConnell 5 pen |
| 9 | div3 | Bristol Rovers | A | D | 1-1 | Flack 27 |
| 10 | div3 | Wrexham | A | L | 0-4 | |
| 11 | div3 | Leyton Orient | H | W | 1-0 | Walker 69 pen |
| 12 | div3 | Southend | A | L | 0-1 | |
| 13 | div3 | York | H | L | 0-1 | |
| 14 | div3 | Rushden & D | H | D | 1-1 | Flack 5 |
| 15 | div3 | Lincoln | A | L | 0-1 | |
| 16 | div3 | Darlington | H | L | 0-4 | |
| 17 | div3 | Rochdale | A | D | 3-3 | Flack 1,75; Thomas 79 |
| 18 | div3 | Boston | A | W | 3-0 | Hocking 35 og; Moor 54,81 |
| 19 | div3 | Hartlepool | H | L | 1-2 | Moor 49 |
| 20 | facr1 | Forest Green | A | D | 0-0 | |
| 21 | div3 | Cambridge | H | L | 1-2 | Flack 11 |
| 22 | facr1r | Forest Green | H | W | 2-1 | Sheldon 25; Lock 85 |
| 23 | div3 | Bury | A | L | 0-1 | |
| 24 | facr2 | Rushden & D | H | W | 3-1 | McConnell 20; Walker 62 pen; Moor 85 |
| 25 | div3 | Swansea | H | W | 1-0 | Roscoe 73 |
| 26 | div3 | Oxford | A | D | 2-2 | Flack 58; Walker 89 pen |
| 27 | div3 | Macclesfield | H | D | 1-1 | Coppinger 63 |
| 28 | facr3 | Charlton | A | L | 1-3 | Gaia 49 |
| 29 | div3 | Hull City | A | D | 2-2 | Partridge 68; Flack 90 |
| 30 | div3 | Carlisle | H | W | 1-0 | Partridge 60 |
| 31 | div3 | Scunthorpe | A | D | 1-1 | Devine 75 |
| 32 | div3 | Macclesfield | A | D | 1-1 | Devine 90 |
| 33 | div3 | Shrewsbury | H | D | 1-1 | Devine 19 |
| 34 | div3 | Hartlepool | A | L | 1-2 | Walker 83 pen |
| 35 | div3 | Torquay | A | L | 0-1 | |
| 36 | div3 | Boston | H | L | 0-2 | |
| 37 | div3 | Kidderminster | H | L | 2-5 | Devine 3; Coppinger 47 |
| 38 | div3 | Bournemouth | A | L | 0-2 | |
| 39 | div3 | Bristol Rovers | H | D | 0-0 | |
| 40 | div3 | Wrexham | H | W | 1-0 | Flack 73 |
| 41 | div3 | Leyton Orient | A | D | 1-1 | Devine 90 |
| 42 | div3 | Darlington | A | D | 2-2 | Pettefer 19; Devine 70 |
| 43 | div3 | Lincoln | H | W | 2-0 | Coppinger 22; Sheldon 37 |
| 44 | div3 | Rochdale | H | D | 1-1 | Walker 15 pen |
| 45 | div3 | Rushden & D | A | L | 0-1 | |
| 46 | div3 | Bury | H | L | 1-2 | Flack 52 |
| 47 | div3 | Cambridge | A | L | 1-2 | Iriekpen 1 og |
| 48 | div3 | Oxford | H | D | 2-2 | Devine 10; Walker 24 |
| 49 | div3 | Swansea | A | W | 1-0 | Devine 69 |
| 50 | div3 | York | A | W | 2-0 | Flack 5; Coppinger 55 |
| 51 | div3 | Southend | H | W | 1-0 | Flack 90 |

■ Home □ Away ▢ Neutral

## ATTENDANCES

HOME GROUND: ST JAMES PARK CAPACITY: 10570 AVERAGE LEAGUE AT HOME: 3763

| | | | | | | | | | | | |
|---|---|---|---|---|---|---|---|---|---|---|---|
| 28 | Charlton | 18107 | 45 | Rushden & D | 4921 | 46 | Bury | 3338 | 25 | Swansea | 2625 |
| 29 | Hull City | 13667 | 48 | Oxford | 4900 | 30 | Carlisle | 3333 | 40 | Wrexham | 2537 |
| 49 | Swansea | 9115 | 50 | York | 4840 | 13 | York | 3187 | 42 | Darlington | 2476 |
| 51 | Southend | 9036 | 6 | Carlisle | 4806 | 27 | Macclesfield | 3017 | 18 | Boston | 2474 |
| 26 | Oxford | 7057 | 7 | Bournemouth | 4466 | 15 | Lincoln | 2979 | 31 | Scunthorpe | 2461 |
| 38 | Bournemouth | 6674 | 3 | Hull City | 4257 | 10 | Wrexham | 2968 | 24 | Rushden & D | 2277 |
| 9 | Bristol Rovers | 6498 | 43 | Lincoln | 4009 | 22 | Forest Green | 2951 | 4 | Kidderminster | 2195 |
| 5 | Torquay | 6065 | 44 | Rochdale | 4003 | 14 | Rushden & D | 2884 | 20 | Forest Green | 2147 |
| 35 | Torquay | 5761 | 1 | Shrewsbury | 3781 | 36 | Boston | 2834 | 23 | Bury | 2039 |
| 39 | Bristol Rovers | 5759 | 2 | Scunthorpe | 3722 | 11 | Leyton Orient | 2784 | 32 | Macclesfield | 2035 |
| 47 | Cambridge | 5218 | 41 | Leyton Orient | 3667 | 19 | Hartlepool | 2778 | 37 | Kidderminster | 1957 |
| 8 | Brighton | 5200 | 33 | Shrewsbury | 3587 | 16 | Darlington | 2757 | 17 | Rochdale | 1944 |
| 34 | Hartlepool | 5058 | 12 | Southend | 3364 | 21 | Cambridge | 2722 | | | |

## KEY PLAYER APPEARANCES

| | PLAYER | POS | AGE | APP | MINS ON | GOALS | CARDS(Y) | CARDS(R) | HOME COUNTRY |
|---|---|---|---|---|---|---|---|---|---|
| 1 | Kevin Miller | GK | 34 | 46 | 4140 | 0 | 1 | 1 | England |
| 2 | Steven Flack | ATT | 32 | 40 | 3359 | 14 | 11 | 1 | England |
| 3 | Scott Hiley | DEF | 34 | 37 | 3287 | 0 | 2 | 0 | England |
| 4 | James Coppinger | ATT | 22 | 44 | 3121 | 5 | 4 | 0 | England |
| 5 | Justin Walker | MID | 27 | 39 | 3034 | 5 | 12 | 0 | England |
| 6 | Marcio dos Santos Gaia | DEF | 24 | 35 | 2795 | 1 | 9 | 2 | Brazil |
| 7 | Glenn Cronin | DEF | 21 | 40 | 2731 | 0 | 11 | 2 | Rep of Ireland |
| 8 | Carl Pettefer | MID | 22 | 31 | 2670 | 1 | 6 | 0 | England |
| 9 | Graeme Power | DEF | 26 | 33 | 2401 | 0 | 8 | 1 | England |
| 10 | Andrew Roscoe | MID | 30 | 39 | 1910 | 3 | 2 | 0 | England |
| 11 | Martin Thomas | ATT | 29 | 27 | 1889 | 3 | 9 | 0 | England |
| 12 | Sean Devine | ATT | 30 | 23 | 1837 | 8 | 2 | 0 | England |
| 13 | Kwame Ampadu | MID | 32 | 27 | 1597 | 0 | 5 | 0 | England |
| 14 | Barry McConnell | ATT | 26 | 34 | 1277 | 0 | 3 | 0 | England |
| 15 | Chris Todd | DEF | 21 | 17 | 1080 | 0 | 2 | 0 | Wales |
| 16 | Chris Curran | DEF | 31 | 20 | 935 | 0 | 4 | 1 | England |
| 17 | Don Goodman | ATT | 37 | 14 | 906 | 1 | 3 | 0 | England |
| 18 | Adam Virgo | DEF | 20 | 10 | 746 | 0 | 0 | 0 | England |

## KEY PLAYERS - GOALSCORERS

**1 Sean Devine**

| | |
|---|---|
| Goals in the League | 8 |
| Contribution to Attacking Power<br>Average number of minutes between League team goals while on pitch | 87 |
| Player Strike Rate<br>Average number of minutes between League goals scored by player | 230 |
| Club Strike Rate<br>Average number of minutes between League goals scored by club | 83 |

| | PLAYER | LGE GOALS | POWER | STRIKE RATE |
|---|---|---|---|---|
| 2 | Steven Flack | 14 | 76 | 240 mins |
| 3 | Justin Walker | 5 | 94 | 607 mins |
| 4 | James Coppinger | 5 | 78 | 624 mins |
| 5 | Martin Thomas | 3 | 67 | 630 mins |

## KEY PLAYERS - MIDFIELDERS

**1 Kwame Ampadu**

| | |
|---|---|
| Goals in the League | 0 |
| Defensive Rating<br>Average number of mins between League goals conceded while he was on the pitch | 114 |
| Contribution to Attacking Power<br>Average number of minutes between League team goals while on pitch | 89 |
| Scoring Difference<br>Defensive Rating minus Contribution to Attacking Power | 25 |

| | PLAYER | LGE GOALS | DEF RATE | POWER | SCORE DIFF |
|---|---|---|---|---|---|
| 2 | Carl Pettefer | 1 | 67 | 79 | -12 mins |
| 3 | Andrew Roscoe | 3 | 66 | 80 | -14 mins |
| 4 | Justin Walker | 5 | 62 | 95 | -33 mins |

## KEY PLAYERS - DEFENDERS

**1 Chris Todd**

| | |
|---|---|
| Goals Conceded when he was on pitch | 11 |
| Defensive Rating<br>Ave number of mins between League goals conceded while on the pitch | 98 |
| Clean Sheets<br>In games when he played at least 70 minutes | 5 |
| Club Defensive Rating<br>Average number of mins between League goals conceded by the club this season. | 65 |

| | PLAYER | CON LGE | CLN SHEETS | DEF RATE |
|---|---|---|---|---|
| 2 | Scott Hiley | 47 | 10 | 70 mins |
| 3 | Graeme Power | 35 | 6 | 69 mins |
| 4 | Marcio dos Santos Gaia | 41 | 8 | 68 mins |
| 5 | Glenn Cronin | 44 | 4 | 62 mins |

## KEY GOALKEEPER

**1 Kevin Miller**

| | |
|---|---|
| Goals Conceded in the League | 64 |
| Defensive Rating<br>Ave number of mins between League goals conceded while on the pitch. | 65 |
| Counting Games<br>Games when he played at least 70 mins | 46 |
| Clean Sheets<br>In games when he played at least 70 mins | 11 |

## TEAM OF THE SEASON

| GOALKEEPER | GAMES | DEF RATE |
|---|---|---|
| Kevin Miller | 46 | 65 |
| **DEFENDERS** | **GAMES** | **DEF RATE** |
| Chris Todd | 12 | 98 |
| Scott Hiley | 36 | 70 |
| Graeme Power | 25 | 69 |
| Marcio Gaia | 30 | 68 |
| **MIDFIELDERS** | **GAMES** | **SCORE DIFF** |
| Kwame Ampadu | 15 | 25 |
| Carl Pettefer | 29 | -12 |
| Andrew Roscoe | 13 | -14 |
| Justin Walker | 32 | -33 |
| **FORWARDS** | **GAMES** | **STRIKE RATE** |
| Sean Devine | 18 | 230 |
| Steven Flack | 35 | 240 |

# SHREWSBURY TOWN

Final Position: **24th**

NICKNAME: THE SHREWS

| | | | | | | |
|---|---|---|---|---|---|---|
| 1 | div3 | Exeter | H | W | 1-0 | Rodgers 43 |
| 2 | div3 | York | A | L | 1-2 | Moss 12 |
| 3 | div3 | Southend | A | W | 3-2 | Rodgers 40,57; Atkins 77 |
| 4 | div3 | Rushden & D | H | D | 1-1 | Rodgers 70 |
| 5 | div3 | Bury | A | L | 3-4 | Jemson 65,71,72 |
| 6 | div3 | Lincoln | H | L | 1-2 | Rodgers 3 |
| 7 | div3 | Leyton Orient | H | W | 2-1 | Rodgers 46; Jemson 75 |
| 8 | wcr1 | Walsall | A | L | 0-1 | |
| 9 | div3 | Rochdale | A | D | 1-1 | van Blerk 37 |
| 10 | div3 | Torquay | A | L | 1-2 | Jemson 53 |
| 11 | div3 | Bristol Rovers | H | L | 2-5 | Murray 47; Rodgers 72 |
| 12 | div3 | Scunthorpe | A | D | 1-1 | Rodgers 18 |
| 13 | div3 | Hartlepool | H | L | 0-1 | |
| 14 | div3 | Carlisle | A | W | 2-1 | Murray 1; Artell 78 |
| 15 | div3 | Kidderminster | H | L | 2-3 | Lowe 18,44 |
| 16 | div3 | Oxford | A | D | 2-2 | Woan 21; Drysdale 27 |
| 17 | div3 | Hull City | H | D | 1-1 | Stevens, I 89 |
| 18 | div3 | Macclesfield | A | W | 2-1 | Lowe 33; Woan 63 |
| 19 | div3 | Cambridge | H | W | 3-1 | Jemson 67,88; Woan 77 |
| 20 | facr1 | Stafford | H | W | 4-0 | Jemson 32; Wilding 39,74; Tolley, J 89 |
| 21 | div3 | Darlington | H | D | 2-2 | Rodgers 2; Stevens, I 25 |
| 22 | div3 | Swansea | A | L | 0-2 | |
| 23 | facr2 | Barrow | H | W | 3-1 | van Blerk 7; Jemson 19,76 |
| 24 | div3 | Bournemouth | H | D | 0-0 | |
| 25 | div3 | Boston | A | L | 0-6 | |
| 26 | div3 | Bury | H | W | 4-1 | Wilding 12; Lowe 69,83,90 |
| 27 | div3 | Rushden & D | A | L | 1-5 | Rodgers 46 |
| 28 | facr3 | Everton | H | W | 2-1 | Jemson 39,89 |
| 29 | div3 | Southend | H | L | 0-1 | |
| 30 | div3 | Lincoln | A | D | 1-1 | Jagielka 73 |
| 31 | facr4 | Chelsea | H | L | 0-4 | |
| 32 | div3 | Exeter | A | D | 1-1 | Jemson 55 pen |
| 33 | div3 | Cambridge | A | L | 0-5 | |
| 34 | div3 | York | H | D | 2-2 | Rodgers 31,74 |
| 35 | div3 | Leyton Orient | A | W | 2-0 | Moss 65; Redmile 70 |
| 36 | div3 | Rochdale | H | W | 3-1 | Jagielka 5,40; Lowe 67 |
| 37 | div3 | Bristol Rovers | A | D | 0-0 | |
| 38 | div3 | Wrexham | A | D | 3-3 | Woan 3; Tolley, J 33; Jemson 67 |
| 39 | div3 | Oxford | H | L | 1-2 | Tolley, J 45 |
| 40 | div3 | Kidderminster | A | D | 2-2 | Wilding 7; Rodgers 15 |
| 41 | div3 | Hull City | A | L | 0-2 | |
| 42 | div3 | Torquay | H | L | 2-3 | Wilding 76; Rodgers 83 pen |
| 43 | div3 | Swansea | H | D | 0-0 | |
| 44 | div3 | Wrexham | H | L | 1-2 | Tolley, J 59 |
| 45 | div3 | Darlington | A | L | 1-5 | Lowe 53 |
| 46 | div3 | Macclesfield | H | L | 2-3 | Aiston 15; Jemson 42 |
| 47 | div3 | Boston | H | L | 1-2 | Lowe 72 |
| 48 | div3 | Bournemouth | A | L | 1-2 | Aiston 6 |
| 49 | div3 | Hartlepool | A | L | 0-3 | |
| 50 | div3 | Carlisle | H | L | 2-3 | Jemson 31; Rodgers 84 |
| 51 | div3 | Scunthorpe | H | L | 1-2 | Rodgers 43 |

■ Home □ Away □ Neutral

## ATTENDANCES

HOME GROUND: GAY MEADOW CAPACITY: 8000 AVERAGE LEAGUE AT HOME: 3543

| | | | | | | | | | | | |
|---|---|---|---|---|---|---|---|---|---|---|---|
| 41 | Hull City | 13253 | 23 | Barrow | 4210 | 11 | Bristol Rovers | 3510 | 30 | Lincoln | 2885 |
| 31 | Chelsea | 7950 | 26 | Bury | 4175 | 15 | Kidderminster | 3507 | 24 | Bournemouth | 2869 |
| 28 | Everton | 7800 | 27 | Rushden & D | 4144 | 14 | Carlisle | 3484 | 5 | Bury | 2866 |
| 50 | Carlisle | 7236 | 51 | Scunthorpe | 4127 | 2 | York | 3463 | 7 | Leyton Orient | 2756 |
| 48 | Bournemouth | 7102 | 46 | Macclesfield | 4100 | 36 | Rochdale | 3423 | 21 | Darlington | 2755 |
| 38 | Wrexham | 7024 | 35 | Leyton Orient | 3939 | 40 | Kidderminster | 3284 | 29 | Southend | 2699 |
| 37 | Bristol Rovers | 6839 | 8 | Walsall | 3847 | 6 | Lincoln | 3168 | 42 | Torquay | 2694 |
| 16 | Oxford | 5559 | 1 | Exeter | 3781 | 3 | Southend | 3150 | 45 | Darlington | 2660 |
| 44 | Wrexham | 5451 | 33 | Cambridge | 3755 | 13 | Hartlepool | 3142 | 34 | York | 2599 |
| 49 | Hartlepool | 5384 | 22 | Swansea | 3638 | 17 | Hull City | 3086 | 10 | Torquay | 2528 |
| 20 | Stafford | 5114 | 32 | Exeter | 3587 | 12 | Scunthorpe | 2988 | 18 | Macclesfield | 2218 |
| 43 | Swansea | 4645 | 4 | Rushden & D | 3548 | 19 | Cambridge | 2928 | 25 | Boston | 2155 |
| 47 | Boston | 4373 | 39 | Oxford | 3520 | 9 | Rochdale | 2914 | | | |

## KEY PLAYER APPEARANCES

| | PLAYER | POS | AGE | APP | MINS ON | GOALS | CARDS(Y/R) | | HOME COUNTRY |
|---|---|---|---|---|---|---|---|---|---|
| 1 | Matthew Redmile | DEF | 26 | 43 | 3510 | 1 | 7 | 0 | England |
| 2 | Nigel Jemson | ATT | 33 | 40 | 3224 | 11 | 11 | 0 | England |
| 3 | Darren Moss | DEF | 22 | 40 | 3160 | 2 | 12 | 0 | Wales |
| 4 | Luke Rodgers | ATT | 30 | 37 | 3052 | 16 | 9 | 1 | England |
| 5 | Ian Dunbavin | GK | 23 | 37 | 2970 | 0 | 1 | 0 | England |
| 6 | Ian Woan | MID | 35 | 38 | 2907 | 4 | 5 | 1 | England |
| 7 | Jamie Tolley | MID | 20 | 33 | 2641 | 3 | 9 | 0 | England |
| 8 | Peter Wilding | DEF | 34 | 40 | 2600 | 3 | 4 | 0 | England |
| 9 | Mark Atkins | DEF | 34 | 33 | 2575 | 1 | 1 | 0 | England |
| 10 | Ryan Lowe | ATT | 24 | 42 | 2409 | 9 | 6 | 0 | England |
| 11 | David Artell | DEF | 22 | 35 | 2369 | 1 | 3 | 0 | England |
| 12 | Karl Murray | MID | 20 | 38 | 1717 | 2 | 5 | 0 | England |
| 13 | Andy Thompson | DEF | 35 | 18 | 1284 | 0 | 3 | 0 | Wales |
| 14 | Steve Jagielka | ATT | 25 | 25 | 1273 | 3 | 2 | 0 | England |
| 15 | Leon Drysdale | DEF | 22 | 26 | 1213 | 1 | 6 | 0 | England |
| 16 | Jason van Blerk | DEF | 35 | 29 | 1212 | 1 | 3 | 0 | Australia |
| 17 | Mark Cartwright | GK | 30 | 14 | 1170 | 0 | 0 | 0 | England |
| 18 | Sam Aiston | ATT | 26 | 24 | 1140 | 2 | 5 | 0 | England |

## KEY PLAYERS - GOALSCORERS

**1 Luke Rodgers**

| | |
|---|---|
| Goals in the League | 16 |
| Contribution to Attacking Power<br>Average number of minutes between League team goals while on pitch | 61 |
| Player Strike Rate<br>Average number of minutes between League goals scored by player | 191 |
| Club Strike Rate<br>Average number of minutes between League goals scored by club | 67 |

| | PLAYER | LGE GOALS | POWER | STRIKE RATE |
|---|---|---|---|---|
| 2 | Ryan Lowe | 9 | 60 | 268 mins |
| 3 | Nigel Jemson | 11 | 65 | 293 mins |
| 4 | Ian Woan | 4 | 60 | 727 mins |
| 5 | Karl Murray | 2 | 71 | 859 mins |

## KEY PLAYERS - MIDFIELDERS

**1 Ian Woan**

| | |
|---|---|
| Goals in the League | 4 |
| Defensive Rating<br>Average number of mins between League goals conceded while he was on the pitch | 43 |
| Contribution to Attacking Power<br>Average number of minutes between League team goals while on pitch | 61 |
| Scoring Difference<br>Defensive Rating minus Contribution to Attacking Power | -18 |

| | PLAYER | LGE GOALS | DEF RATE | POWER | SCORE DIFF |
|---|---|---|---|---|---|
| 2 | Jamie Tolley | 3 | 51 | 70 | -19 mins |
| 3 | Karl Murray | 2 | 43 | 72 | -29 mins |

## KEY PLAYERS - DEFENDERS

**1 David Artell**

| | |
|---|---|
| Goals Conceded when he was on pitch | 48 |
| Defensive Rating<br>Ave number of mins between League goals conceded while on the pitch | 49 |
| Clean Sheets<br>In games when he played at least 70 minutes | 4 |
| Club Defensive Rating<br>Average number of mins between League goals conceded by the club this season. | 45 |

| | PLAYER | CON LGE | CLN SHEETS | DEF RATE |
|---|---|---|---|---|
| 2 | Darren Moss | 68 | 4 | 46 mins |
| 3 | Peter Wilding | 57 | 3 | 46 mins |
| 4 | Andy Thompson | 28 | 1 | 46 mins |
| 5 | Matthew Redmile | 76 | 5 | 46 mins |

## KEY GOALKEEPER

**1 Ian Dunbavin**

| | |
|---|---|
| Goals Conceded in the League | 66 |
| Defensive Rating<br>Ave number of mins between League goals conceded while on the pitch. | 45 |
| Counting Games<br>Games when he played at least 70 mins | 33 |
| Clean Sheets<br>In games when he played at least 70 mins | 2 |

## TEAM OF THE SEASON

| | | |
|---|---|---|
| **GOALKEEPER** | **GAMES** | **DEF RATE** |
| Ian Dunbavin | 33 | 45 |
| **DEFENDERS** | **GAMES** | **DEF RATE** |
| David Artell | 25 | 49 |
| Darren Moss | 33 | 46 |
| Matthew Redmile | 39 | 46 |
| Andy Thompson | 13 | 46 |
| **MIDFIELDERS** | **GAMES** | **SCORE DIFF** |
| Ian Woan | 30 | -18 |
| Jamie Tolley | 28 | -19 |
| Karl Murray | 16 | -29 |
| Nigel Jemson* | 42 | 293SR |
| **FORWARDS** | **GAMES** | **STRIKE RATE** |
| Luke Rodgers | 32 | 191 |
| Ryan Lowe | 21 | 268 |

# DIVISION THREE ROUND-UP

## STADIUM CAPACITY AND HOME CROWDS

| | TEAM | CAPACITY | AVE (%) | HIGH | LOW |
|---|---|---|---|---|---|
| 1 | Rushden & D | 6441 | 67.89 | 6291 | 3329 |
| 2 | Hartlepool | 7629 | 64.79 | 6360 | 3889 |
| 3 | Boston | 5184 | 58.82 | 5159 | 1919 |
| 4 | Bristol Rovers | 12000 | 57.78 | 9835 | 5493 |
| 5 | Cambridge | 7400 | 56.39 | 6237 | 2586 |
| 6 | Bournemouth | 10770 | 54.12 | 7578 | 4315 |
| 7 | Torquay | 6117 | 51.2 | 5761 | 2244 |
| 8 | Hull City | 25404 | 50.56 | 22319 | 7684 |
| 9 | Oxford | 12400 | 47.27 | 8732 | 4547 |
| 10 | Kidderminster | 6293 | 46 | 3872 | 2006 |
| 11 | Shrewsbury | 8000 | 45.7 | 7236 | 2599 |
| 12 | York | 9534 | 43.8 | 7856 | 2970 |
| 13 | Swansea | 12000 | 43 | 9585 | 3370 |
| 14 | Scunthorpe | 9183 | 40.18 | 6284 | 2342 |
| 15 | Exeter | 10570 | 35.6 | 9036 | 1957 |
| 16 | Macclesfield | 6028 | 35 | 2920 | 1576 |
| 17 | Lincoln | 11729 | 33.46 | 7906 | 2444 |
| 18 | Southend | 12306 | 32.11 | 6453 | 2832 |
| 19 | Leyton Orient | 13842 | 30.75 | 5622 | 2633 |
| 20 | Rochdale | 9223 | 29.71 | 4513 | 1658 |
| 21 | Carlisle | 16651 | 28.68 | 10684 | 3124 |
| 22 | Wrexham | 15000 | 28.43 | 9960 | 2968 |
| 23 | Bury | 11840 | 27.25 | 5827 | 2039 |
| 24 | Darlington | 24000 | 13.8 | 5832 | 2076 |

## AWAY ATTENDANCE

| | TEAM | AVE (%) | HIGH | LOW |
|---|---|---|---|---|
| 1 | Hull City | 49.9 | 9585 | 2225 |
| 2 | Hartlepool | 46.21 | 22319 | 1576 |
| 3 | Carlisle | 45.09 | 8461 | 2342 |
| 4 | Bristol Rovers | 44.9 | 14913 | 1658 |
| 5 | Exeter | 44.69 | 13667 | 1944 |
| 6 | York | 44.59 | 18437 | 2304 |
| 7 | Wrexham | 44.32 | 15002 | 1919 |
| 8 | Lincoln | 44.22 | 13728 | 2122 |
| 9 | Bournemouth | 43.17 | 15816 | 1795 |
| 10 | Oxford | 43.15 | 17404 | 1583 |
| 11 | Darlington | 42.61 | 14162 | 1967 |
| 12 | Scunthorpe | 42.59 | 11885 | 1929 |
| 13 | Southend | 42.53 | 10449 | 1917 |
| 14 | Boston | 42.17 | 9460 | 1941 |
| 15 | Rushden & D | 42.04 | 10659 | 1839 |
| 16 | Torquay | 41.16 | 13310 | 1835 |
| 17 | Bury | 40.77 | 8804 | 2736 |
| 18 | Cambridge | 40.76 | 15607 | 2053 |
| 19 | Shrewsbury | 40.17 | 13253 | 2155 |
| 20 | Leyton Orient | 39.98 | 7684 | 1676 |
| 21 | Swansea | 39.84 | 8070 | 2209 |
| 22 | Macclesfield | 39.78 | 8703 | 2444 |
| 23 | Rochdale | 39.64 | 9057 | 2479 |
| 24 | Kidderminster | 38.09 | 14544 | 1810 |

## CLUB STRIKE FORCE

18

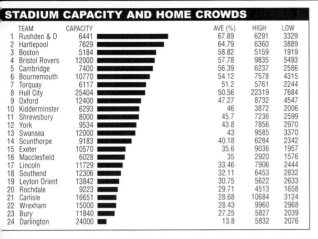

Pejic shoots for Wrexham

| | |
|---|---|
| Goals scored in the League | 84 |
| Goals scored in all competions | 90 |
| Shots on target (SoT) Shots on target hit by the team recorded in League games | 326 |

**1 Wrexham**

| | |
|---|---|
| Club Strike Rate (CSR) Average number of minutes between League goals scored by club | 49 |

| | CLUB | LGE | ALL | SoT | CSR |
|---|---|---|---|---|---|
| 2 | Rushden & D | 73 | 78 | 279 | **57** |
| 3 | Hartlepool | 71 | 74 | 308 | **58** |
| 4 | Torquay | 71 | 77 | 292 | **58** |
| 5 | Scunthorpe | 68 | 76 | 284 | **61** |
| 6 | Cambridge | 67 | 86 | 258 | **62** |
| 7 | Rochdale | 63 | 75 | 272 | **66** |
| 8 | Kidderminster | 62 | 68 | 233 | **67** |
| 9 | Shrewsbury | 62 | 77 | 216 | **67** |
| 10 | Bournemouth | 60 | 81 | 266 | **69** |
| 11 | Darlington | 58 | 66 | 217 | **71** |
| 12 | Hull City | 58 | 60 | 261 | **71** |
| 13 | Bury | 57 | 64 | 269 | **73** |
| 14 | Macclesfield | 57 | 68 | 217 | **73** |
| 15 | Oxford | 57 | 60 | 243 | **73** |
| 16 | Boston | 55 | 59 | 242 | **75** |
| 17 | Carlisle | 52 | 60 | 246 | **80** |
| 18 | York | 52 | 55 | 225 | **80** |
| 19 | Leyton Orient | 51 | 57 | 221 | **81** |
| 20 | Bristol Rovers | 50 | 56 | 207 | **83** |
| 21 | Exeter | 50 | 57 | 237 | **83** |
| 22 | Swansea | 48 | 51 | 189 | **86** |
| 23 | Southend | 47 | 54 | 224 | **88** |
| 24 | Lincoln | 46 | 57 | 194 | **90** |

## CLUB DEFENCES

**1 Lincoln**

| | |
|---|---|
| Club Defensive Rate (CDR) Average number of minutes between League goals conceded by club | 112 |

| | CLUB | LGE | ALL | CS | SoT | CDR |
|---|---|---|---|---|---|---|
| 2 | Oxford | 47 | 52 | 14 | 261 | **88** |
| 3 | Rushden & D | 47 | 61 | 16 | 245 | **88** |
| 4 | Bournemouth | 48 | 66 | 17 | 196 | **86** |
| 5 | Scunthorpe | 49 | 59 | 8 | 264 | **84** |
| 6 | Wrexham | 50 | 59 | 19 | 198 | **83** |
| 7 | Hartlepool | 51 | 56 | 16 | 232 | **81** |
| 8 | Hull City | 53 | 60 | 14 | 237 | **78** |
| 9 | York | 53 | 57 | 13 | 249 | **78** |
| 10 | Boston | 56 | 66 | 14 | 251 | **74** |
| 11 | Bury | 56 | 68 | 9 | 204 | **74** |
| 12 | Bristol Rovers | 57 | 62 | 10 | 258 | **73** |
| 13 | Darlington | 59 | 65 | 9 | 231 | **70** |
| 14 | Southend | 59 | 69 | 11 | 272 | **70** |
| 15 | Leyton Orient | 61 | 69 | 11 | 253 | **68** |
| 16 | Kidderminster | 63 | 73 | 14 | 227 | **66** |
| 17 | Macclesfield | 63 | 70 | 8 | 258 | **66** |
| 18 | Exeter | 64 | 74 | 11 | 256 | **65** |
| 19 | Swansea | 65 | 70 | 12 | 221 | **64** |
| 20 | Cambridge | 70 | 95 | 7 | 314 | **59** |
| 21 | Rochdale | 70 | 80 | 7 | 291 | **59** |
| 22 | Torquay | 71 | 75 | 8 | 255 | **58** |
| 23 | Carlisle | 78 | 87 | 10 | 269 | **53** |
| 24 | Shrewsbury | 92 | 103 | 5 | 261 | **45** |

EMENS

Brimson - Lincoln City

| | |
|---|---|
| Goals conceded in the League | 37 |
| Goals conceded in all competions | 52 |
| Clean Sheets (CS) Number of league games where no goals were conceded | 18 |
| Shots on Target Against (SoT) Shots on Target conceded by team in League games | 223 |

## CLUB GOAL ATTEMPTS

### GOAL ATTEMPTS – FOR

**KEY:** Shots on Target (SoT), Shots Off Target (SO) Total shots (Tot) Ratio of shots on target to goals (SG) Accuracy Rating (AR)

| | CLUB | SoT | SO | Tot | SG | AR |
|---|---|---|---|---|---|---|
| 1 | Wrexham | 326 | 260 | **586** | 3.9 | 55.6 |
| 2 | Hartlepool | 308 | 270 | **578** | 4.3 | 53.3 |
| 3 | Torquay | 292 | 255 | **547** | 4.1 | 53.4 |
| 4 | Hull City | 261 | 267 | **528** | 4.5 | 49.4 |
| 5 | Rushden & D | 279 | 249 | **528** | 3.8 | 52.8 |
| 6 | Bournemouth | 266 | 234 | **500** | 4.4 | 53.2 |
| 7 | Rochdale | 272 | 228 | **500** | 4.3 | 54.4 |
| 8 | Darlington | 217 | 282 | **499** | 3.7 | 43.5 |
| 9 | Bury | 269 | 220 | **489** | 4.7 | 55.0 |
| 10 | Southend | 224 | 262 | **486** | 4.8 | 46.1 |
| 11 | Macclesfield | 217 | 258 | **475** | 3.8 | 45.7 |
| 12 | Oxford | 243 | 228 | **471** | 4.3 | 51.6 |
| 13 | Scunthorpe | 284 | 181 | **465** | 4.2 | 61.1 |
| 14 | Cambridge | 258 | 203 | **461** | 3.9 | 56.0 |
| 15 | Boston | 242 | 202 | **444** | 4.4 | 54.5 |
| 16 | Kidderminster | 233 | 210 | **443** | 3.8 | 52.6 |
| 17 | Carlisle | 246 | 195 | **441** | 4.7 | 55.8 |
| 18 | Leyton Orient | 221 | 217 | **438** | 4.3 | 50.5 |
| 19 | Exeter | 237 | 192 | **429** | 4.7 | 55.2 |
| 20 | York | 225 | 201 | **426** | 4.3 | 52.8 |
| 21 | Shrewsbury | 216 | 197 | **413** | 3.5 | 52.3 |
| 22 | Bristol Rovers | 207 | 199 | **406** | 4.1 | 51.0 |
| 23 | Lincoln | 194 | 204 | **398** | 4.2 | 48.7 |
| 24 | Swansea | 189 | 200 | **389** | 3.9 | 48.6 |

### GOAL ATTEMPTS – AGAINST

**KEY:** Shots on Target (SoT), Shots Off Target (SO) Total shots (Tot) Ratio of shots on target to goals (SG) Accuracy Rating (AR)

| | CLUB | SoT | SO | Tot | SG | AR |
|---|---|---|---|---|---|---|
| 1 | Bournemouth | 196 | 188 | **384** | 4.1 | 51.0 |
| 2 | Lincoln | 223 | 173 | **396** | 6.0 | 56.3 |
| 3 | Swansea | 221 | 175 | **396** | 3.4 | 55.8 |
| 4 | Darlington | 231 | 177 | **408** | 3.9 | 56.6 |
| 5 | Wrexham | 198 | 225 | **423** | 4.0 | 46.8 |
| 6 | Bury | 204 | 221 | **425** | 3.6 | 48.0 |
| 7 | Kidderminster | 227 | 204 | **431** | 3.6 | 52.7 |
| 8 | Boston | 251 | 194 | **445** | 4.5 | 56.4 |
| 9 | Leyton Orient | 253 | 196 | **449** | 4.1 | 56.3 |
| 10 | Hartlepool | 232 | 226 | **458** | 4.5 | 50.7 |
| 11 | Rushden & D | 245 | 219 | **464** | 5.2 | 52.8 |
| 12 | Torquay | 255 | 209 | **464** | 3.6 | 55.0 |
| 13 | Scunthorpe | 264 | 202 | **466** | 5.4 | 56.7 |
| 14 | Shrewsbury | 261 | 206 | **467** | 2.8 | 55.9 |
| 15 | York | 249 | 218 | **467** | 4.7 | 53.3 |
| 16 | Southend | 272 | 197 | **469** | 4.6 | 58.0 |
| 17 | Exeter | 256 | 214 | **470** | 4.0 | 54.5 |
| 18 | Hull City | 237 | 233 | **470** | 4.5 | 50.4 |
| 19 | Macclesfield | 258 | 212 | **470** | 4.1 | 54.9 |
| 20 | Oxford | 261 | 220 | **481** | 5.6 | 54.3 |
| 21 | Bristol Rovers | 258 | 224 | **482** | 4.5 | 53.5 |
| 22 | Carlisle | 269 | 234 | **503** | 3.4 | 53.5 |
| 23 | Rochdale | 291 | 227 | **518** | 4.2 | 56.2 |
| 24 | Cambridge | 314 | 206 | **520** | 4.5 | 60.4 |

## CLUB DISCIPLINARY RECORDS

JEWSON
4

Walker bites in the tackle

| | |
|---|---|
| League Yellow | 100 |
| League Red | 10 |
| League Total | 110 |
| All Comps Yellow | 104 |
| All Comps Red | 10 |
| TOTAL IN ALL COMPETITIONS | 114 |

**1 Exeter**

| | |
|---|---|
| Cards Average in League Average number of minutes between a card being shown of either colour | 38 |

| | PLAYER | LEAGUE | | TOTAL | | AVE |
|---|---|---|---|---|---|---|
| 2 | Shrewsbury | 97Y | 2R | 100Y | 2R | **42** |
| 3 | Carlisle | 88 | 9 | 89 | 9 | **43** |
| 4 | Darlington | 90 | 6 | 93 | 6 | **43** |
| 5 | Boston | 88 | 6 | 90 | 6 | **44** |
| 6 | Lincoln | 84 | 6 | 90 | 7 | **46** |
| 7 | Leyton Orient | 80 | 6 | 85 | 6 | **48** |
| 8 | Swansea | 80 | 7 | 82 | 7 | **48** |
| 9 | York | 86 | 1 | 88 | 1 | **48** |
| 10 | Scunthorpe | 76 | 8 | 86 | 8 | **49** |
| 11 | Cambridge | 73 | 9 | 79 | 9 | **50** |
| 12 | Hull City | 79 | 4 | 81 | 4 | **50** |
| 13 | Kidderminster | 77 | 4 | 78 | 4 | **51** |
| 14 | Southend | 79 | 2 | 80 | 2 | **51** |
| 15 | Macclesfield | 74 | 2 | 79 | 2 | **54** |
| 16 | Rushden & D | 73 | 4 | 76 | 6 | **54** |
| 17 | Rochdale | 72 | 2 | 78 | 2 | **56** |
| 18 | Torquay | 69 | 2 | 69 | 2 | **58** |
| 19 | Bury | 67 | 3 | 74 | 4 | **59** |
| 20 | Oxford | 64 | 4 | 72 | 5 | **61** |
| 21 | Bournemouth | 61 | 3 | 67 | 4 | **65** |
| 22 | Bristol Rovers | 61 | 2 | 61 | 2 | **66** |
| 23 | Hartlepool | 52 | 1 | 53 | 1 | **78** |
| 24 | Wrexham | 50 | 2 | 52 | 2 | **80** |

## CHART-TOPPING MIDFIELDERS

Pictured: 2 Edwards - Wrexham

| 1 Scott Green - Wrexham | |
|---|---|
| Goals scored in the League | 3 |
| Defensive Rating<br>Av number of mins between League goals conceded while on the pitch | 112 |
| Contribution to Attacking Power<br>Average number of minutes between League team goals while on pitch | 45 |
| Scoring Difference<br>Defensive Rating minus Contribution to Attacking Power | 67 |

| | PLAYER | CLUB | GOALS | DEF R | POWER | SCORE DIFF |
|---|---|---|---|---|---|---|
| 2 | Edwards, P | Wrexham | 4 | 93 | 47 | 46 mins |
| 3 | Roberts | Wrexham | 2 | 89 | 48 | 41 mins |
| 4 | Oldfield | Oxford | 2 | 127 | 87 | 40 mins |
| 5 | Willis | Lincoln | 3 | 110 | 71 | 39 mins |
| 6 | Edwards, C | Wrexham | 8 | 86 | 48 | 38 mins |
| 7 | Gain | Lincoln | 5 | 124 | 87 | 37 mins |
| 8 | Barrett | Wrexham | 1 | 84 | 48 | 36 mins |
| 9 | Whitley | Wrexham | 1 | 83 | 47 | 36 mins |
| 10 | Smith | Hartlepool | 0 | 93 | 58 | 35 mins |
| 11 | Wardley | Rushden & D | 6 | 90 | 55 | 35 mins |
| 12 | Bell | Rushden & D | 3 | 93 | 58 | 35 mins |
| 13 | Calvo-Garcia | Scunthorpe | 3 | 93 | 60 | 33 mins |
| 14 | Mills | Rushden & D | 0 | 93 | 62 | 31 mins |
| 15 | Sedgemore | Lincoln | 2 | 115 | 85 | 30 mins |
| 16 | Graves | Scunthorpe | 1 | 87 | 57 | 30 mins |
| 17 | Kilford | Scunthorpe | 3 | 89 | 60 | 29 mins |
| 18 | Ferguson | Wrexham | 2 | 79 | 50 | 29 mins |
| 19 | Hunter | Oxford | 1 | 84 | 56 | 28 mins |
| 20 | Elliott | Bournemouth | 4 | 97 | 70 | 27 mins |

The Divisional Round-up charts combine the records of chart-topping keepers, defenders, midfield players and forwards, from every club in the division.. The one above is for **the Chart-topping Midfielders**. The players are ranked by their Scoring Difference although other attributes are shown for you to compare.

## CHART-TOPPING GOALSCORERS

gap

| 1 Andy Morrell - Wrexham | |
|---|---|
| Goals scored in the League (GL) | 34 |
| Goals scored in all competitions (GA) | 35 |
| Contribution to Attacking Power (AP)<br>Average number of minutes between League team goals while on pitch | 48 |
| Player Strike Rate (SR)<br>Average number of minutes between League goals scored by player | 117 |
| Club Strike Rate (CSR)<br>Average minutes between League goals scored by club | 49 |

| | PLAYER | CLUB | GOALS: LGE | ALL | POWER | CSR | S RATE |
|---|---|---|---|---|---|---|---|
| 2 | Henriksen | Kidderminster | 20 | 20 | 58 | 67 | 153 mins |
| 3 | Graham | Torquay | 15 | 15 | 60 | 58 | 154 mins |
| 4 | Hayes | Scunthorpe | 8 | 8 | 55 | 61 | 172 mins |
| 5 | Richards | Swansea | 7 | 7 | 120 | 86 | 172 mins |
| 6 | McEvilly | Rochdale | 14 | 15 | 54 | 66 | 176 mins |
| 7 | Carruthers | Scunthorpe | 20 | 20 | 60 | 61 | 184 mins |
| 8 | Duffield | York | 13 | 15 | 74 | 80 | 189 mins |
| 9 | Rodgers | Shrewsbury | 16 | 16 | 61 | 67 | 191 mins |
| 10 | Darby | Rushden & D | 14 | 14 | 57 | 57 | 203 mins |
| 11 | Kitson | Cambridge | 19 | 21 | 62 | 62 | 205 mins |
| 12 | Logan | Boston | 10 | 10 | 71 | 75 | 208 mins |
| 13 | Torpey | Scunthorpe | 11 | 12 | 59 | 61 | 216 mins |
| 14 | Grazioli | Bristol Rovers | 11 | 11 | 82 | 83 | 217 mins |
| 15 | Elliott | Hull City | 12 | 12 | 63 | 71 | 218 mins |
| 16 | Douglas | Boston | 7 | 7 | 64 | 75 | 220 mins |
| 17 | Lowe | Rushden & D | 15 | 15 | 57 | 57 | 226 mins |
| 18 | Devine | Exeter | 8 | 8 | 87 | 83 | 230 mins |
| 19 | Farrell | Carlisle | 11 | 11 | 77 | 80 | 232 mins |
| 20 | Scott | Oxford | 11 | 11 | 81 | 73 | 238 mins |

**The Chart-topping Goalscorers** measures the players by Strike Rate. They are most likely to be Forwards but Midfield players and even Defenders do come through the club tables. It is not a measure of the number of League goals scored - although that is also noted - but how often on average they have scored.

## CHART-TOPPING DEFENDERS

Seward
SAAB

| 1 Lewis Buxton - Bournemouth | |
|---|---|
| Goals Conceded in the League<br>The number of League goals conceded while he was on the pitch | 9 |
| Goals Conceded in all competitions<br>The number of goals conceded while he was on the pitch in all competitions | 12 |
| Clean Sheets<br>In games when he played at least 70 mins | 8 |
| Defensive Rating (DR)<br>Average number of minutes between League goals conceded while on pitch | 148 |
| Club Defensive Rating<br>Average mins between League goals conceded by the club this season | 86 |

| | PLAYER | CLUB | CON: LGE | ALL | CS | CDR | DEF RATE |
|---|---|---|---|---|---|---|---|
| 2 | McCarthy | Boston | 7 | 7 | 5 | 74 | 134 mins |
| 3 | Anderson | Bristol Rovers | 10 | 10 | 6 | 73 | 124 mins |
| 4 | Futcher | Lincoln | 32 | 40 | 16 | 112 | 114 mins |
| 5 | Cummings | Bournemouth | 16 | 19 | 9 | 86 | 110 mins |
| 6 | Butcher | Lincoln | 20 | 28 | 8 | 112 | 108 mins |
| 7 | Bimson | Lincoln | 34 | 45 | 15 | 112 | 107 mins |
| 8 | Weaver | Lincoln | 35 | 41 | 17 | 112 | 105 mins |
| 9 | Waterman | Oxford | 23 | 25 | 8 | 88 | 104 mins |
| 10 | Balmer | Boston | 19 | 19 | 11 | 74 | 103 mins |
| 11 | Ashbee | Hull City | 28 | 32 | 12 | 78 | 99 mins |
| 12 | Bignot | Rushden & D | 29 | 31 | 11 | 88 | 99 mins |
| 13 | Todd | Exeter | 11 | 11 | 5 | 65 | 98 mins |
| 14 | Broadhurst | Bournemouth | 18 | 19 | 8 | 86 | 97 mins |
| 15 | Peters | Rushden & D | 23 | 31 | 9 | 88 | 97 mins |
| 16 | Mumford | Swansea | 16 | 18 | 8 | 64 | 96 mins |
| 17 | Lawrence | Wrexham | 28 | 31 | 11 | 83 | 96 mins |
| 18 | Gray | Rushden & D | 32 | 40 | 12 | 88 | 94 mins |
| 19 | Robinson | Hartlepool | 36 | 38 | 15 | 81 | 93 mins |
| 20 | Edwards | Rushden & D | 11 | 11 | 5 | 88 | 93 mins |

**The Chart-topping Defenders** are resolved by their Defensive Rating, how often their team concedes a goal while they are playing. All these rightly favour players at the best performing clubs because good players win matches. However, good players in lower-table clubs will chart where they have lifted the team's performance.

## CHART-TOPPING GOALKEEPERS

BONUS
ELECTRICAL

| 1 Paul Musselwhite - Hull City | |
|---|---|
| Goals conceded in the League (CL) | 13 |
| Goals conceded in all comps (CA) | 13 |
| Counting Games<br>League games when he played at least 70 minutes | 20 |
| Clean Sheets<br>In games when he played at least 70 mins | 9 |
| Goals to Shots Ratio (GSR)<br>The average number of shots on target per each League goal conceded | 7.7 |
| Defensive Rating (DR)<br>Average number of minutes between League goals conceded while on pitch | 138 |

| | | | CG | CL | CA | CS | GSR | DR |
|---|---|---|---|---|---|---|---|---|
| 2 | Marriott | Lincoln | 46 | 37 | 48 | 18 | 6.0 | 112 mins |
| 3 | Ingham | York | 16 | 15 | 15 | 7 | 5.8 | 99 mins |
| 4 | Moss | Bournemouth | 32 | 31 | 34 | 13 | 4.5 | 94 mins |
| 5 | Woodman | Oxford | 44 | 46 | 51 | 14 | 5.4 | 87 mins |
| 6 | Turley | Rushden & D | 44 | 46 | 54 | 15 | 5.2 | 86 mins |
| 7 | Cutler | Swansea | 13 | 14 | 14 | 5 | 4.6 | 84 mins |
| 8 | Evans | Scunthorpe | 46 | 49 | 59 | 8 | 5.4 | 84 mins |
| 9 | Dibble | Wrexham | 32 | 35 | 36 | 13 | 3.7 | 83 mins |
| 10 | Williams, A | Hartlepool | 46 | 51 | 53 | 16 | 4.5 | 81 mins |
| 11 | Barrett | Leyton Orient | 11 | 13 | 13 | 4 | 4.8 | 76 mins |
| 12 | Morris | Leyton Orient | 22 | 27 | 32 | 5 | 4.4 | 75 mins |
| 13 | Tardif | Bournemouth | 8 | 10 | 15 | 1 | 3.7 | 74 mins |
| 14 | Bastock | Boston | 46 | 56 | 61 | 14 | 4.5 | 74 mins |
| 15 | Garner | Bury | 46 | 56 | 62 | 9 | 3.6 | 74 mins |
| 16 | Van Heusden | Torquay | 12 | 16 | 16 | 3 | 4.6 | 73 mins |
| 17 | Howie | Bristol Rovers | 44 | 55 | 55 | 9 | 4.5 | 72 mins |
| 18 | Fettis | York | 21 | 27 | 29 | 5 | 4.7 | 70 mins |
| 19 | Flahavan | Southend | 41 | 53 | 57 | 9 | 4.5 | 70 mins |
| 20 | Wilson | Macclesfield | 43 | 59 | 64 | 7 | 4.1 | 66 mins |

**The Chart-topping Goalkeepers** are positioned by their Defensive Rating. We also show Clean Sheets where the team has not conceded and the Keeper has played all or most (at least 70 minutes) of the game. Now teams use several keepers in a season, not every team will necessarily chart on this page.

## FINAL LEAGUE TABLE

| | HOME | | | | | | AWAY | | | | | TOTAL | | | |
|---|---|---|---|---|---|---|---|---|---|---|---|---|---|---|---|
| | P | W | D | L | F | A | W | D | L | F | A | F | A | DIF | PTS |
| Rushden & D | 46 | 16 | 5 | 2 | 48 | 19 | 8 | 10 | 5 | 25 | 28 | 73 | 47 | 26 | 87 |
| Hartlepool | 46 | 16 | 5 | 2 | 49 | 21 | 8 | 8 | 7 | 22 | 30 | 71 | 51 | 20 | 85 |
| Wrexham | 46 | 12 | 7 | 4 | 48 | 26 | 11 | 8 | 4 | 36 | 24 | 84 | 50 | 34 | 84 |
| Bournemouth | 46 | 14 | 7 | 2 | 38 | 18 | 6 | 7 | 10 | 22 | 30 | 60 | 48 | 12 | 74 |
| Scunthorpe | 46 | 11 | 8 | 4 | 40 | 20 | 8 | 7 | 8 | 28 | 29 | 68 | 49 | 19 | 72 |
| Lincoln | 46 | 10 | 9 | 4 | 29 | 18 | 8 | 7 | 8 | 17 | 19 | 46 | 37 | 9 | 70 |
| Bury | 46 | 8 | 8 | 7 | 25 | 26 | 10 | 8 | 5 | 32 | 30 | 57 | 56 | 1 | 70 |
| Oxford | 46 | 9 | 7 | 7 | 26 | 20 | 10 | 5 | 8 | 31 | 27 | 57 | 47 | 10 | 69 |
| Torquay | 46 | 9 | 11 | 3 | 41 | 31 | 7 | 7 | 9 | 30 | 40 | 71 | 71 | 0 | 66 |
| York | 46 | 11 | 9 | 3 | 34 | 24 | 6 | 6 | 11 | 18 | 29 | 52 | 53 | -1 | 66 |
| Kidderminster | 46 | 8 | 8 | 7 | 30 | 33 | 8 | 7 | 8 | 32 | 30 | 62 | 63 | -1 | 63 |
| Cambridge | 46 | 10 | 7 | 6 | 38 | 25 | 6 | 6 | 11 | 29 | 45 | 67 | 70 | -3 | 61 |
| Hull City | 46 | 9 | 10 | 4 | 34 | 19 | 5 | 7 | 11 | 24 | 34 | 58 | 53 | 5 | 59 |
| Darlington | 46 | 8 | 10 | 5 | 36 | 27 | 4 | 8 | 11 | 22 | 32 | 58 | 59 | -1 | 54 |
| Boston | 46 | 11 | 6 | 6 | 34 | 22 | 4 | 7 | 12 | 21 | 34 | 55 | 56 | -1 | 54 |
| Macclesfield | 46 | 8 | 6 | 9 | 29 | 28 | 6 | 6 | 11 | 28 | 35 | 57 | 63 | -6 | 54 |
| Southend | 46 | 12 | 1 | 10 | 29 | 23 | 5 | 2 | 16 | 18 | 36 | 47 | 59 | -12 | 54 |
| Leyton Orient | 46 | 9 | 6 | 8 | 28 | 24 | 5 | 5 | 13 | 23 | 37 | 51 | 61 | -10 | 53 |
| Rochdale | 46 | 7 | 6 | 10 | 30 | 30 | 5 | 10 | 8 | 33 | 40 | 63 | 70 | -7 | 52 |
| Bristol Rovers | 46 | 7 | 7 | 9 | 25 | 27 | 5 | 8 | 10 | 25 | 30 | 50 | 57 | -7 | 51 |
| Swansea | 46 | 9 | 6 | 8 | 28 | 25 | 3 | 7 | 13 | 20 | 40 | 48 | 65 | -17 | 49 |
| Carlisle | 46 | 5 | 5 | 13 | 26 | 40 | 8 | 5 | 10 | 26 | 38 | 52 | 78 | -26 | 49 |
| Exeter | 46 | 7 | 7 | 9 | 24 | 31 | 4 | 8 | 11 | 26 | 33 | 50 | 64 | -14 | 48 |
| Shrewsbury | 46 | 5 | 6 | 12 | 34 | 39 | 4 | 8 | 11 | 28 | 53 | 62 | 92 | -30 | 41 |

## PLAYER DISCIPLINARY RECORD

| | |
|---|---|
| League Yellow | 4 |
| League Red | 1 |
| TOTAL | 5 |

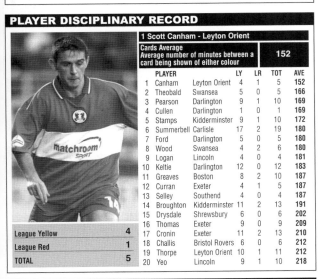

**1 Scott Canham - Leyton Orient**

| Cards Average<br>Average number of minutes between a card being shown of either colour | 152 |
|---|---|

| | PLAYER | | LY | LR | TOT | AVE |
|---|---|---|---|---|---|---|
| 1 | Canham | Leyton Orient | 4 | 1 | 5 | 152 |
| 2 | Theobald | Swansea | 5 | 0 | 5 | 166 |
| 3 | Pearson | Darlington | 9 | 1 | 10 | 169 |
| 4 | Cullen | Darlington | 1 | 0 | 1 | 169 |
| 5 | Stamps | Kidderminster | 9 | 1 | 10 | 172 |
| 6 | Summerbell | Carlisle | 17 | 2 | 19 | 180 |
| 7 | Ford | Darlington | 5 | 0 | 5 | 180 |
| 8 | Wood | Swansea | 4 | 2 | 6 | 180 |
| 9 | Logan | Lincoln | 4 | 0 | 4 | 181 |
| 10 | Keltie | Darlington | 12 | 0 | 12 | 183 |
| 11 | Greaves | Boston | 8 | 2 | 10 | 187 |
| 12 | Curran | Exeter | 4 | 1 | 5 | 187 |
| 13 | Selley | Southend | 4 | 0 | 4 | 187 |
| 14 | Broughton | Kidderminster | 11 | 2 | 13 | 191 |
| 15 | Drysdale | Shrewsbury | 6 | 0 | 6 | 202 |
| 16 | Thomas | Exeter | 9 | 0 | 9 | 209 |
| 17 | Cronin | Exeter | 11 | 2 | 13 | 210 |
| 18 | Challis | Bristol Rovers | 6 | 0 | 6 | 212 |
| 19 | Thorpe | Leyton Orient | 10 | 1 | 11 | 212 |
| 20 | Yeo | Lincoln | 9 | 1 | 10 | 218 |

## PREMIERSHIP CHART-TOPPING POINT EARNERS

| | PLAYER | TEAM | GAMES | POINTS | AVE |
|---|---|---|---|---|---|
| 2 | Smith | Hartlepool | 14 | 32 | 2.29 |
| 3 | Edwards | Rushden & D | 11 | 25 | 2.27 |
| 4 | Wardley | Rushden & D | 35 | 73 | 2.09 |
| 5 | Darby | Rushden & D | 27 | 55 | 2.04 |
| 6 | Hunter | Rushden & D | 38 | 77 | 2.03 |
| 7 | Bignot | Rushden & D | 31 | 62 | 2.00 |
| 8 | Buxton | Bournemouth | 14 | 28 | 2.00 |
| 9 | Carey | Wrexham | 28 | 55 | 1.96 |
| 10 | Mills | Rushden & D | 21 | 41 | 1.95 |
| 11 | Clarke | Hartlepool | 43 | 83 | 1.93 |
| 12 | Whitley | Wrexham | 43 | 83 | 1.93 |
| 13 | Trundle | Wrexham | 30 | 58 | 1.93 |
| 14 | Lawrence | Wrexham | 29 | 56 | 1.93 |
| 15 | Barron | Hartlepool | 38 | 73 | 1.92 |
| 16 | Lowe | Rushden & D | 36 | 69 | 1.92 |
| 17 | Barrass | Bury | 13 | 25 | 1.92 |
| 18 | Hayes | Scunthorpe | 12 | 23 | 1.92 |
| 19 | Edwards, C | Wrexham | 43 | 82 | 1.91 |
| 20 | Gray | Rushden & D | 32 | 61 | 1.91 |

**1 Marcus Richardson**

| | |
|---|---|
| Counting Games<br>League games where he played at least 70 minutes | 15 |
| Total League Points<br>Taken in Counting Games | 41 |
| Average League Points<br>Taken in Counting Games | 2.73 |

## TEAM OF THE SEASON

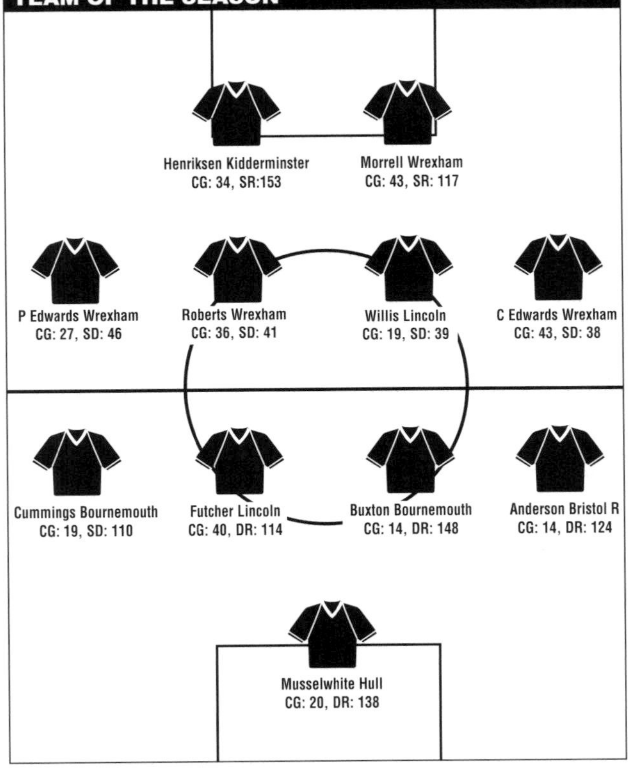

Henriksen Kidderminster
CG: 34, SR:153
Morrell Wrexham
CG: 43, SR: 117
P Edwards Wrexham
CG: 27, SD: 46
Roberts Wrexham
CG: 36, SD: 41
Willis Lincoln
CG: 19, SD: 39
C Edwards Wrexham
CG: 43, SD: 38
Cummings Bournemouth
CG: 19, SD: 110
Futcher Lincoln
CG: 40, DR: 114
Buxton Bournemouth
CG: 14, DR: 148
Anderson Bristol R
CG: 14, DR: 124
Musselwhite Hull
CG: 20, DR: 138


**The Team of the Season** in each League's Divisional Round-up is different to those at club level. It doesn't just mirror the Chart-topping performances but highlights Keepers, Defenders, Midfield players and Forwards who are dramatically out-performing their team-mates. We compare their key rating to the club average see below: -

- **The Division Team's goalkeeper** has to be the player with the highest Defensive Rating as he often plays most or all the games in a league season.
- **The Division Team's defenders** are also tested by Defensive Rating but against their co-defender's Ratings. We weight it to take into account the fact that differences can fluctuate wildly at the bottom of a division.
- **The Division Team's midfield** all have good Scoring Differences compared to the average Ratings of their colleagues. In all cases these players must have played at least a minimum of Counting Games.
- **The Divisional Team strikeforce** is made up of the two players who have the biggest gap in Strike Rate between themselves and their next forward. These are weighted again, as lower sides may not even have a second charting forward.

# LYON

Final Position: **1st**

| | | | | | | |
|---|---|---|---|---|---|---|
| 1 | lge | Guingamp | A | D | 3-3 | Juninho 3; Chanelet 38; Anderson 51 |
| 2 | lge | Sedan | H | W | 6-1 | Juninho 43,68; Cacapa 45; Anderson 59,81; Luyindula 90 |
| 3 | lge | Marseille | A | D | 1-1 | Govou 13 |
| 4 | lge | Bastia | H | W | 4-1 | Anderson 16,35,62; Carriere 85 |
| 5 | lge | Sochaux | A | D | L-L | Saveljic 88 og |
| 6 | lge | Lens | H | W | 1-0 | Juninho 32 |
| 7 | lge | Nantes | A | L | 0-1 | |
| 8 | ecgd | Ajax | A | L | 1-2 | Anderson 83 |
| 9 | lge | Monaco | H | L | 1-3 | Laville 54 |
| 10 | ecgd | Rosenborg BK | H | W | 5-0 | Carriere 6; Vairelles 26,45; Anderson 34; Luyindula 75 |
| 11 | lge | Troyes | A | D | 1-1 | Dhorasoo 73 |
| 12 | ecgd | Inter Milan | A | W | 2-1 | Govou 21; Anderson 62 |
| 13 | lge | Rennes | A | W | 1-0 | Govou 49 |
| 14 | lge | Auxerre | H | W | 3-0 | Juninho 36,50,74 |
| 15 | ecgd | Inter Milan | H | D | 3-3 | Anderson 21,75; Carriere 44 |
| 16 | lge | AC Ajaccio | A | W | 1-0 | Vairelles 30 |
| 17 | ecgd | Ajax | H | L | 0-2 | |
| 18 | lge | Nice | H | D | 2-2 | Anderson 47; Delmotte 66 |
| 19 | lge | Le Havre | A | W | 2-1 | Carriere 11; Cacapa 86 |
| 20 | ecgd | Rosenborg BK | A | D | 1-1 | Govou 83 |
| 21 | lge | Bordeaux | H | W | 4-2 | Govou 1; Luyindula 46,49; Vairelles 53 |
| 22 | lge | Lille | A | L | 1-2 | Nee 90 |
| 23 | uc3rl1 | Denizlispor | A | D | 0-0 | |
| 24 | lge | Strasbourg | H | W | 2-1 | Luyindula 33; Diarra 48 |
| 25 | lge | Paris SG | A | L | 0-2 | |
| 26 | uc3rl2 | Denizlispor | H | L | 0-1 | |
| 27 | lge | Montpellier | H | D | 1-1 | Carriere 55 |
| 28 | lge | Sedan | A | D | 1-1 | Anderson 47 |
| 29 | lge | Marseille | H | W | 1-0 | Luyindula 41 |
| 30 | lge | Bastia | A | L | 0-2 | |
| 31 | lge | Sochaux | H | W | 4-1 | Luyindula 27,43; Juninho 38,48 |
| 32 | lge | Lens | A | D | 2-2 | Dhorasoo 26; Carriere 44 |
| 33 | lge | Nantes | H | D | 0-0 | |
| 34 | lge | Monaco | A | L | 0-2 | |
| 35 | lge | Troyes | H | D | 0-0 | |
| 36 | lge | Rennes | H | W | 4-1 | Juninho 16; Luyindula 44,72; Govou 61 |
| 37 | lge | Auxerre | A | W | 2-1 | Govou 5; Luyindula 37 |
| 38 | lge | AC Ajaccio | H | W | 3-1 | Juninho 8,38; Anderson 84 |
| 39 | lge | Nice | A | W | 1-0 | Juninho 83 |
| 40 | lge | Le Havre | H | W | 2-1 | Govou 37; Carriere 84 |
| 41 | lge | Bordeaux | A | W | 1-0 | Anderson 61 |
| 42 | lge | Lille | H | D | 0-0 | |
| 43 | lge | Strasbourg | A | W | 4-0 | Anderson 4; Carriere 59; Luyindula 64; Violeau 79 |
| 44 | lge | Paris SG | H | W | 1-0 | Anderson 25 |
| 45 | lge | Montpellier | A | D | 1-1 | Juninho 25 |
| 46 | lge | Guingamp | H | L | 1-4 | Govou 65 |

## ATTENDANCES

HOME GROUND: STADE DE GERLAND CAPACITY: 42000 AVERAGE LEAGUE AT HOME: 35222

| | | | | | | | | |
|---|---|---|---|---|---|---|---|---|
| 3 | Marseille | 56652 | **46** | **Guingamp** | **36000** | **31** | **Sochaux** | **20000** |
| **21** | **Bordeaux** | **49300** | 19 | Le Havre | 35000 | 13 | Rennes | 20000 |
| **42** | **Lille** | **46025** | 41 | Bordeaux | 35000 | 22 | Lille | 20000 |
| 25 | Paris SG | 44000 | 7 | Nantes | 35000 | 1 | Guingamp | 20000 |
| **10** | **Rosenborg BK** | **40000** | **18** | **Nice** | **35000** | 45 | Montpellier | 19764 |
| **15** | **Inter Milan** | **40000** | **14** | **Auxerre** | **35000** | 28 | Sedan | 19240 |
| **33** | **Nantes** | **40000** | **24** | **Strasbourg** | **34235** | 5 | Sochaux | 18000 |
| **29** | **Marseille** | **40000** | **2** | **Sedan** | **32225** | 39 | Nice | 15544 |
| **6** | **Lens** | **40000** | 12 | Inter Milan | 31448 | 23 | Denizlispor | 15000 |
| **38** | **AC Ajaccio** | **40000** | **4** | **Bastia** | **30000** | 11 | Troyes | 13000 |
| 32 | Lens | 40000 | **9** | **Monaco** | **30000** | 37 | Auxerre | 12000 |
| **17** | **Ajax** | **39000** | **26** | **Denizlispor** | **29000** | 16 | AC Ajaccio | 10000 |
| **36** | **Rennes** | **38500** | 20 | Rosenborg BK | 28000 | 30 | Bastia | 6516 |
| **44** | **Paris SG** | **37823** | **35** | **Troyes** | **26114** | 34 | Monaco | 4000 |
| 8 | Ajax | 37455 | 43 | Strasbourg | 26000 | | | |
| **40** | **Le Havre** | **36000** | **27** | **Montpellier** | **23000** | | | |

Home / Away / Neutral

## KEY PLAYERS - GOALSCORERS

**1 Sonny Anderson**

| | | | |
|---|---|---|---|
| Goals in the League | 12 | Player Strike Rate<br>Average number of minutes between League goals scored by player | 138 |
| Contribution to Attacking Power<br>Average number of minutes between League team goals while on pitch | 45 | Club Strike Rate<br>Average number of minutes between League goals scored by club | 54 |

| | PLAYER | LGE GOALS | POWER | STRIKE RATE |
|---|---|---|---|---|
| 2 | Pernambucano Juninho | 14 | 45 | 166 mins |
| 3 | Pegguy Luyindula | 11 | 55 | 172 mins |
| 4 | Phillipe Govou | 7 | 54 | 337 mins |
| 5 | Eric Carriere | 6 | 51 | 452 mins |

## KEY PLAYERS - MIDFIELDERS

**1 Eric Carriere**

| | | | |
|---|---|---|---|
| Goals in the League | 6 | Contribution to Attacking Power<br>Average number of minutes between League team goals while on pitch | 51 |
| Defensive Rating<br>Average number of mins between League goals conceded while he was on the pitch | 90 | Scoring Difference<br>Defensive Rating minus Contribution to Attacking Power | 39 |

| | PLAYER | LGE GOALS | DEF RATE | POWER | SCORE DIFF |
|---|---|---|---|---|---|
| 2 | Philippe Violeau | 1 | 92 | 57 | 35 mins |
| 3 | Pernambucano Juninho | 14 | 80 | 46 | 34 mins |
| 4 | Vikash Dhorasoo | 2 | 84 | 55 | 29 mins |
| 5 | Patrick Muller | 0 | 82 | 53 | 29 mins |

## KEY PLAYERS - DEFENDERS

**1 Eric Deflandre**

| | | | |
|---|---|---|---|
| Goals Conceded (GC)<br>The number of League goals conceded while he was on the pitch | 16 | Clean Sheets<br>In games when he played at least 70 minutes | 7 |
| Defensive Rating<br>Ave number of mins between League goals conceded while on the pitch | 101 | Club Defensive Rating<br>Average number of mins between League goals conceded by the club this season | 83 |

| | PLAYER | CON LGE | CLEAN SHEETS | DEF RATE |
|---|---|---|---|---|
| 2 | Jose Gomes Edmilson | 20 | 7 | 90 mins |
| 3 | Jean-Marc Chanelet | 14 | 3 | 86 mins |
| 4 | Claudio Roberto Cacapa | 37 | 10 | 85 mins |
| 5 | Jeremie Brechet | 30 | 10 | 85 mins |

## KEY GOALKEEPER

**1 Gregory Coupet**

| | |
|---|---|
| Goals Conceded in the League | 39 |
| Defensive Rating<br>Ave number of mins between League goals conceded while on the pitch | 80 |
| Counting Games<br>Games when he played at least 70 minutes | 34 |
| Clean Sheets<br>In games when he played at least 70 minutes | 10 |

## TOP POINT EARNERS

| | PLAYER | GAMES | AVE |
|---|---|---|---|
| 1 | Brechet | 26 | 2.12 |
| 2 | Violeau | 25 | 2.08 |
| 3 | Carriere | 27 | 2.04 |
| 4 | Govou | 26 | 2.04 |
| 5 | Juninho | 25 | 1.96 |
| 6 | Luyindula | 18 | 1.94 |
| 7 | Dhorasoo | 32 | 1.94 |
| 8 | Deflandre | 18 | 1.89 |
| 9 | Coupet | 34 | 1.88 |
| 10 | Cacapa | 34 | 1.88 |
| | CLUB AVERAGE: | | 1.79 |

Ave = Average points per match in Counting Games

## DISCIPLINARY RECORDS

| | PLAYER | YELLOW | RED | AVE |
|---|---|---|---|---|
| 1 | Edmilson | 6 | 1 | 258 |
| 2 | Chanelet | 4 | 0 | 300 |
| 3 | Brechet | 8 | 0 | 317 |
| 4 | Deflandre | 5 | 0 | 323 |
| 5 | Diarra | 4 | 1 | 350 |
| 6 | Juninho | 5 | 0 | 464 |
| 7 | Govou | 5 | 0 | 471 |
| 8 | Delmotte | 2 | 0 | 516 |
| 9 | Dhorasoo | 6 | 0 | 517 |
| 10 | Muller | 4 | 0 | 757 |
| 11 | Violeau | 2 | 0 | 1198 |
| 12 | Cacapa | 2 | 0 | 1575 |
| 13 | Anderson | 1 | 0 | 1650 |
| | Other | 2 | 1 | |
| | TOTAL | 56 | 3 | |

## LEAGUE GOALS

| | PLAYER | MINS | GOALS | AVE |
|---|---|---|---|---|
| 1 | Juninho | 2323 | 14 | 166 |
| 2 | Anderson | 1650 | 12 | 138 |
| 3 | Luyindula | 1889 | 11 | 172 |
| 4 | Govou | 2358 | 7 | 337 |
| 5 | Carriere | 2714 | 6 | 452 |
| 6 | Vairelles | 734 | 2 | 367 |
| 7 | Cacapa | 3150 | 2 | 1575 |
| 8 | Dhorasoo | 3102 | 2 | 1551 |
| 9 | Laville | 252 | 1 | 252 |
| 10 | Violeau | 2396 | 1 | 2396 |
| 11 | Diarra | 1751 | 1 | 1751 |
| 12 | Chanelet | 1200 | 1 | 1200 |
| 13 | Nee | 171 | 1 | 171 |
| | Other | | 2 | |
| | TOTAL | | 63 | |

## MONTH BY MONTH GUIDE TO THE POINTS

| MONTH | POINTS | % |
|---|---|---|
| AUGUST | 8 | 67% |
| SEPTEMBER | 4 | 33% |
| OCTOBER | 9 | 100% |
| NOVEMBER | 7 | 58% |
| DECEMBER | 5 | 42% |
| JANUARY | 7 | 58% |
| FEBRUARY | 5 | 42% |
| MARCH | 9 | 100% |
| APRIL | 7 | 78% |
| MAY | 7 | 58% |

## TEAM OF THE SEASON

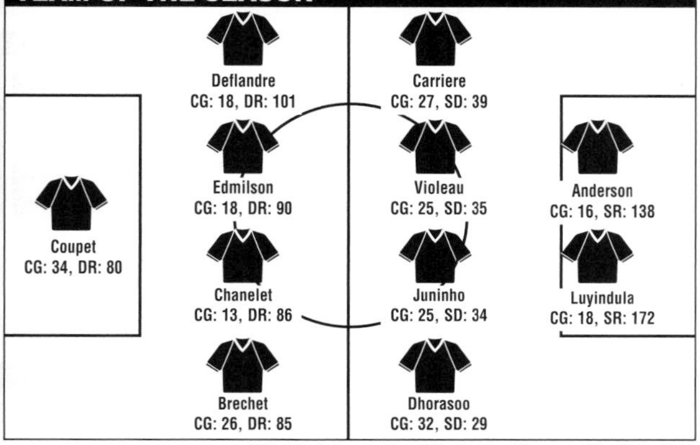

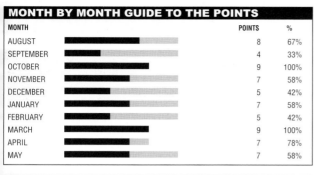

Deflandre
CG: 18, DR: 101
Carriere
CG: 27, SD: 39
Edmilson
CG: 18, DR: 90
Violeau
CG: 25, SD: 35
Anderson
CG: 16, SR: 138
Coupet
CG: 34, DR: 80
Chanelet
CG: 13, DR: 86
Juninho
CG: 25, SD: 34
Luyindula
CG: 18, SR: 172
Brechet
CG: 26, DR: 85
Dhorasoo
CG: 32, SD: 29


**KEY:** DR = Defensive Rate, SD = Scoring Difference, SR = Strike Rate, CG = Counting Games – League games playing at least 70 minutes

## LEAGUE APPEARANCES, BOOKINGS AND CAPS

| | AGE (on 01/07/03) | IN THE SQUAD | COUNTING GAMES | MINUTES ON PITCH | YELLOW CARDS | RED CARDS | THIS SEASON | HOME COUNTRY |
|---|---|---|---|---|---|---|---|---|
| **Goalkeepers** | | | | | | | | |
| Gregory Coupet | 30 | 35 | 34 | 3107 | 1 | 0 | 7 | France (2) |
| Nicolas Puydebois | 22 | 8 | 1 | 133 | 0 | 0 | - | France |
| Remi Vercoutre | 23 | 31 | 2 | 180 | 0 | 0 | - | France |
| **Defenders** | | | | | | | | |
| Jeremie Brechet | 23 | 31 | 26 | 2539 | 8 | 0 | 2 | France (2) |
| Claudio Cacapa | 27 | 37 | 34 | 3150 | 2 | 0 | - | Brazil |
| Jean-Marc Chanelet | 34 | 17 | 13 | 1200 | 4 | 0 | - | France |
| Eric Deflandre | 29 | 25 | 18 | 1616 | 5 | 0 | 4 | Belgium (16) |
| Edmilson Moraes | 26 | 30 | 18 | 1807 | 6 | 1 | 4 | Brazil (1) |
| Yohann Gomez | 21 | 3 | 0 | 0 | 0 | 0 | - | France |
| Florent Laville | 29 | 11 | 1 | 252 | 0 | 1 | - | France |
| Laurent Montoya | 22 | 2 | 0 | 45 | 0 | 0 | - | France |
| **Midfielders** | | | | | | | | |
| Florent Balmont | 23 | 12 | 1 | 318 | 0 | 0 | - | France |
| Eric Carriere | 30 | 37 | 27 | 2714 | 1 | 0 | 4 | France (2) |
| Christophe Delmotte | 34 | 21 | 8 | 1033 | 2 | 0 | - | France |
| Vikash Dhorasoo | 29 | 37 | 32 | 3102 | 6 | 0 | - | France |
| Mahamadou Diarra | 22 | 30 | 17 | 1751 | 4 | 1 | - | Mali |
| Alexandre Hauw | 21 | 4 | 0 | 4 | 0 | 0 | - | France |
| Perna'cano Juninho | 28 | 33 | 25 | 2323 | 5 | 0 | 2 | Brazil (1) |
| Patrick Muller | 26 | 35 | 33 | 3029 | 4 | 0 | - | Switzerland |
| Philippe Violeau | 32 | 35 | 25 | 2396 | 2 | 0 | - | France |
| **Forwards** | | | | | | | | |
| Sonny Anderson | 32 | 24 | 16 | 1650 | 1 | 0 | - | Brazil |
| Sydney Govou | 23 | 29 | 26 | 2358 | 5 | 0 | 6 | France (2) |
| Pegguy Luyindula | 24 | 36 | 18 | 1889 | 0 | 0 | - | France |
| Frederic Nee | 28 | 16 | 0 | 171 | 0 | 0 | - | France |
| Demba Toure | 18 | 6 | 0 | 29 | 0 | 0 | - | Senegal |
| Tony Vairelles | 30 | 22 | 6 | 734 | 0 | 0 | - | France |
| Julien Viale | 21 | 1 | 0 | 0 | 0 | 0 | - | France |

**KEY:** LEAGUE BOOKINGS CAPS (FIFA RANKING)

## SQUAD APPEARANCES

| Match | 1 | 2 | 3 | 4 | 5 | 6 | 7 | 8 | 9 | 10 | 11 | 12 | 13 | 14 | 15 | 16 | 17 | 18 | 19 | 20 | 21 | 22 | 23 | 24 | 25 | 26 | 27 | 28 | 29 | 30 | 31 | 32 | 33 | 34 | 35 | 36 | 37 | 38 | 39 | 40 | 41 | 42 | 43 | 44 | 45 | 46 |
|---|---|---|---|---|---|---|---|---|---|---|---|---|---|---|---|---|---|---|---|---|---|---|---|---|---|---|---|---|---|---|---|---|---|---|---|---|---|---|---|---|---|---|---|---|---|---|
| Venue | A | H | A | H | A | H | A | A | H | H | A | A | A | H | H | A | H | H | A | A | H | A | A | H | A | H | H | A | H | A | H | A | H | A | H | H | A | H | A | H | A | H | A | H | A | H |
| Competition | L | L | L | L | L | L | L | C | L | C | L | C | L | L | C | L | C | L | L | C | L | L | E | L | L | E | L | L | L | L | L | L | L | L | L | L | L | L | L | L | L | L | L | L | L | L |
| Result | D | W | D | W | D | W | L | L | L | W | D | W | W | W | D | W | L | D | W | D | W | L | D | W | L | L | D | D | W | L | W | D | D | L | D | W | W | W | W | W | W | D | W | W | D | L |

**Goalkeepers**
Gregory Coupet
Nicolas Puydebois
Remi Vercoutre

**Defenders**
Jeremie Brechet
Claudio Roberto Cacapa
Jean-Marc Chanelet
Eric Deflandre
Jose Gomes Edmilson
Yohann Gomez
Florent Laville
Laurent Montoya

**Midfielders**
Florent Balmont
Eric Carriere
Christophe Delmotte
Vikash Dhorasoo
Mahamadou Diarra
Alexandre Hauw
Pernambucano Juninho
Patrick Muller
Philippe Violeau

**Forwards**
Sonny Anderson
Phillipe Govou
Pegguy Luyindula
Frederic Nee
Demba Toure
Tony Vairelles
Julien Viale

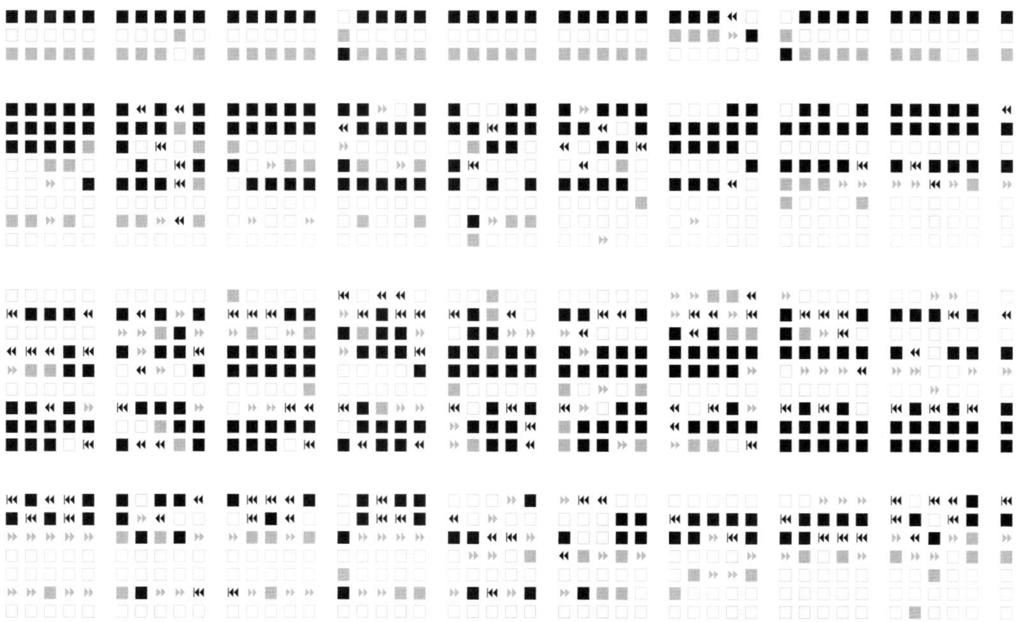

**KEY:** ■ On all match; ▒ On bench; ⏮ Subbed or sent off (Counting game); ◀◀ Subbed or sent off (playing less than 70 minutes); ⏭ Subbed on from bench (Counting Game); ▶▶ Subbed on (playing less than 70 minutes); Subbed on and then subbed or sent off (Counting Game); Subbed on and then subbed or sent off (playing less than 70 minutes); □ Not in 16

# MONACO

Final Position: **2nd**

| | | | | | | |
|---|---|---|---|---|---|---|
| 1 | lge | Troyes | A | W | 4-0 | Nonda 38,63; Giuly 41; Gallardo 86 |
| 2 | lge | Marseille | H | L | 0-1 | |
| 3 | lge | Bastia | A | L | 0-1 | |
| 4 | lge | Sochaux | H | W | 1-0 | Rothen 40 |
| 5 | lge | Lens | A | L | 0-1 | |
| 6 | lge | Nantes | H | W | 2-1 | Pierre-Fanfan 12; Camara 72 |
| 7 | lge | Sedan | A | D | 2-2 | Nonda 15,84 |
| 8 | lge | Lyon | A | W | 3-1 | Nonda 14; Giuly 52; Camara 90 |
| 9 | lge | Rennes | H | W | 2-1 | Camara 9; Evra 77 |
| 10 | lge | Auxerre | A | D | 1-1 | Nonda 67 |
| 11 | lge | Lille | H | D | 1-1 | Giuly 66 |
| 12 | lge | Bordeaux | A | D | 2-2 | Giuly 20; Givet 45 |
| 13 | lge | Le Havre | H | D | 1-1 | Giuly 30 |
| 14 | lge | Nice | A | L | 0-1 | |
| 15 | lge | AC Ajaccio | H | W | 3-2 | Nonda 63; Camara 84; Givet 90 |
| 16 | lge | Strasbourg | A | L | 0-1 | |
| 17 | lge | Paris SG | H | W | 3-1 | Nonda 39,69; Marquez 79 |
| 18 | lge | Montpellier | A | W | 2-1 | Giuly 12,90 |
| 19 | lge | Guingamp | H | W | 4-0 | Nonda 39; Rothen 53,68; Prso 75 |
| 20 | lge | Marseille | A | D | 1-1 | Prso 44 |
| 21 | lge | Bastia | H | D | 0-0 | |
| 22 | lge | Sochaux | A | D | 0-0 | |
| 23 | lge | Lens | H | D | 1-1 | Squillaci 53 |
| 24 | lge | Nantes | A | W | 2-0 | Giuly 3; Nonda 72 |
| 25 | lge | Sedan | H | W | 3-0 | Charpenet 34 og; Squillaci 39; Prso 85 |
| 26 | lge | Lyon | H | W | 2-0 | Prso 30; Nonda 64 |
| 27 | lge | Rennes | A | D | 0-0 | |
| 28 | lge | Auxerre | H | W | 3-1 | Prso 13; Giuly 49; Nonda 72 |
| 29 | lge | Lille | A | W | 3-1 | Giuly 46; Bernardi 85; Nonda 90 |
| 30 | lge | Bordeaux | H | L | 0-1 | |
| 31 | lge | Le Havre | A | W | 3-0 | Nonda 23 pen; Prso 27; Evra 29 |
| 32 | lge | Nice | H | L | 0-1 | |
| 33 | lge | AC Ajaccio | A | W | 4-2 | Giuly 5; Prso 14,18; Nonda 25 pen |
| 34 | lge | Strasbourg | H | W | 2-0 | Prso 18; Nonda 67 |
| 35 | lge | Paris SG | A | L | 1-2 | Nonda 39 |
| 36 | lge | Montpellier | H | W | 3-1 | Nonda 53,86; Prso 73 |
| 37 | lge | Guingamp | A | L | 1-3 | Nonda 55 |
| 38 | lge | Troyes | H | W | 6-0 | Prso 3,20; Nonda 12,89,90; Rothen 81 |

## KEY PLAYERS - GOALSCORERS

**1 Dado Prso**

| | | | |
|---|---|---|---|
| Goals in the League | 12 | Player Strike Rate: Average number of minutes between League goals scored by player | 118 |
| Contribution to Attacking Power: Average number of minutes between League team goals while on pitch | 45 | Club Strike Rate: Average number of minutes between League goals scored by club | 52 |

| | PLAYER | LGE GOALS | POWER | STRIKE RATE |
|---|---|---|---|---|
| 2 | Shabani Nonda | 24 | 49 | 126 mins |
| 3 | Ludovic Giuly | 11 | 52 | 283 mins |
| 4 | Gael Givet | 2 | 54 | 623 mins |
| 5 | Jerome Rothen | 4 | 51 | 768 mins |

## KEY PLAYERS - MIDFIELDERS

**1 Patrice Evra**

| | | | |
|---|---|---|---|
| Goals in the League | 2 | Contribution to Attacking Power: Average number of minutes between League team goals while on pitch | 49 |
| Defensive Rating: Average number of mins between League goals conceded while he was on the pitch | 118 | Scoring Difference: Defensive Rating minus Contribution to Attacking Power | 69 |

| | PLAYER | LGE GOALS | DEF RATE | POWER | SCORE DIFF |
|---|---|---|---|---|---|
| 2 | Jerome Rothen | 4 | 102 | 51 | 51 mins |
| 3 | Lucas Ademar Bernardi | 1 | 95 | 44 | 51 mins |
| 4 | Marcelo Gallardo | 1 | 97 | 52 | 45 mins |
| 5 | Ludovic Giuly | 11 | 94 | 53 | 41 mins |

## KEY PLAYERS - DEFENDERS

**1 Rafael Marquez**

| | | | |
|---|---|---|---|
| Goals Conceded (GC): The number of League goals conceded while he was on the pitch | 20 | Clean Sheets: In games when he played at least 70 minutes | 12 |
| Defensive Rating: Ave number of mins between League goals conceded while on the pitch | 130 | Club Defensive Rating: Average number of mins between League goals conceded by the club this season | 104 |

| | PLAYER | CON LGE | CLEAN SHEETS | DEF RATE |
|---|---|---|---|---|
| 2 | Eric Cubilier | 11 | 4 | 117 mins |
| 3 | Sebastien Squillaci | 28 | 12 | 112 mins |
| 4 | Julien Rodriguez | 22 | 7 | 98 mins |
| 5 | Gael Givet | 13 | 4 | 96 mins |

## GOALS SCORED

**AT HOME**

| | | |
|---|---|---|
| MOST | Lyon | 40 |
| | | 37 |
| LEAST | AC Ajaccio | 14 |

**AWAY**

| | | |
|---|---|---|
| MOST | Monaco | 29 |
| | | 29 |
| LEAST | Troyes | 7 |

## GOALS CONCEDED

**AT HOME**

| | | |
|---|---|---|
| LEAST | Sochaux & Auxerre | 8 |
| | | 13 |
| MOST | Strasbourg | 23 |

**AWAY**

| | | |
|---|---|---|
| LEAST | Lens | 15 |
| | | 20 |
| MOST | Sedan | 39 |

## KEY GOALKEEPER

**1 Tony Sylva**

| | |
|---|---|
| Goals Conceded in the League | 9 |
| Defensive Rating: Ave number of mins between League goals conceded while on the pitch | 116 |
| Counting Games: Games when he played at least 70 minutes | 11 |
| Clean Sheets: In games when he played at least 70 minutes | 3 |

## TOP POINT EARNERS

| | PLAYER | GAMES | AVE |
|---|---|---|---|
| 1 | Bernardi | 21 | 1.95 |
| 2 | Givet | 12 | 1.92 |
| 3 | Roma | 26 | 1.88 |
| 4 | Rodriguez | 23 | 1.87 |
| 5 | Marquez | 29 | 1.86 |
| 6 | Evra | 29 | 1.86 |
| 7 | Rothen | 33 | 1.79 |
| 8 | Cubilier | 13 | 1.77 |
| 9 | Nonda | 33 | 1.76 |
| 10 | Giuly | 34 | 1.74 |
| | CLUB AVERAGE: | | 1.76 |

Ave = Average points per match in Counting Games

## ATTENDANCES

HOME GROUND: STADE LOUIS II CAPACITY: 18520 AVERAGE LEAGUE AT HOME: 6660

| | | |
|---|---|---|
| 20 | Marseille | 58000 |
| 35 | Paris SG | 48450 |
| 5 | Lens | 35000 |
| 12 | Bordeaux | 33000 |
| 24 | Nantes | 30000 |
| 8 | Lyon | 30000 |
| 16 | Strasbourg | 25000 |
| 10 | Auxerre | 20000 |
| 2 | Marseille | 18500 |
| 37 | Guingamp | 18000 |
| 31 | Le Havre | 16000 |
| 14 | Nice | 15000 |
| 27 | Rennes | 15000 |
| 1 | Troyes | 15000 |
| 7 | Sedan | 14000 |
| 32 | Nice | 12045 |
| 30 | Bordeaux | 12000 |
| 29 | Lille | 12000 |
| 22 | Sochaux | 11655 |
| 33 | AC Ajaccio | 10000 |
| 3 | Bastia | 9165 |
| 34 | Strasbourg | 9000 |
| 36 | Montpellier | 8360 |
| 18 | Montpellier | 8000 |
| 38 | Troyes | 7148 |
| 23 | Lens | 6000 |
| 28 | Auxerre | 5502 |
| 19 | Guingamp | 5000 |
| 17 | Paris SG | 5000 |
| 13 | Le Havre | 5000 |
| 9 | Rennes | 5000 |
| 25 | Sedan | 5000 |
| 11 | Lille | 5000 |
| 26 | Lyon | 4000 |
| 21 | Bastia | 4000 |
| 15 | AC Ajaccio | 4000 |
| 4 | Sochaux | 3000 |
| 6 | Nantes | 3000 |

Home Away Neutral

## DISCIPLINARY RECORDS

| | PLAYER | YELLOW | RED | AVE |
|---|---|---|---|---|
| 1 | Givet | 7 | 1 | 155 |
| 2 | Bernardi | 10 | 0 | 209 |
| 3 | Cubilier | 4 | 1 | 256 |
| 4 | Pierre-Fanfan | 2 | 1 | 258 |
| 5 | Zikos | 6 | 0 | 321 |
| 6 | Marquez | 7 | 1 | 324 |
| 7 | Gallardo | 3 | 1 | 337 |
| 8 | El Fakiri | 2 | 0 | 436 |
| 9 | Giuly | 7 | 0 | 445 |
| 10 | Camara | 2 | 0 | 447 |
| 11 | Rothen | 5 | 0 | 614 |
| 12 | Rodriguez | 3 | 0 | 719 |
| 13 | Squillaci | 4 | 0 | 786 |
| | Other | 12 | 2 | |
| | TOTAL | 74 | 7 | |

## LEAGUE GOALS

| | PLAYER | MINS | GOALS | AVE |
|---|---|---|---|---|
| 1 | Nonda | 3029 | 24 | 126 |
| 2 | Prso | 1414 | 12 | 118 |
| 3 | Giuly | 3118 | 11 | 283 |
| 4 | Rothen | 3073 | 4 | 768 |
| 5 | Camara | 894 | 4 | 224 |
| 6 | Squillaci | 3145 | 2 | 1573 |
| 7 | Givet | 1246 | 2 | 623 |
| 8 | Evra | 2830 | 2 | 1415 |
| 9 | Pierre-Fanfan | 776 | 1 | 776 |
| 10 | Bernardi | 2095 | 1 | 2095 |
| 11 | Gallardo | 1351 | 1 | 1351 |
| 12 | Marquez | 2595 | 1 | 2595 |
| | Other | | 1 | |
| | TOTAL | | 66 | |

## MONTH BY MONTH GUIDE TO THE POINTS

| MONTH | POINTS | % |
|---|---|---|
| AUGUST | 6 | 40% |
| SEPTEMBER | 10 | 83% |
| OCTOBER | 3 | 33% |
| NOVEMBER | 7 | 47% |
| DECEMBER | 7 | 78% |
| JANUARY | 6 | 50% |
| FEBRUARY | 10 | 83% |
| MARCH | 6 | 67% |
| APRIL | 6 | 67% |
| MAY | 6 | 50% |

## TEAM OF THE SEASON

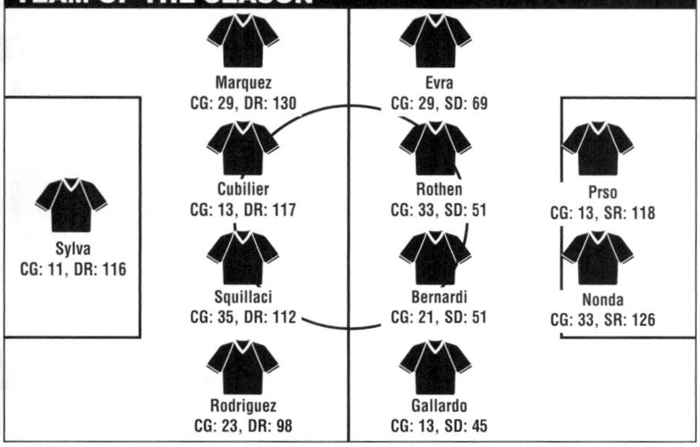
Marquez
CG: 29, DR: 130
Evra
CG: 29, SD: 69
Cubilier
CG: 13, DR: 117
Rothen
CG: 33, SD: 51
Prso
CG: 13, SR: 118
Sylva
CG: 11, DR: 116
Squillaci
CG: 35, DR: 112
Bernardi
CG: 21, SD: 51
Nonda
CG: 33, SR: 126
Rodriguez
CG: 23, DR: 98
Gallardo
CG: 13, SD: 45

**KEY:** DR = Defensive Rate, SD = Scoring Difference, SR = Strike Rate, CG = Counting Games – League games playing at least 70 minutes

## LEAGUE APPEARANCES, BOOKINGS AND CAPS

| | AGE | IN THE SQUAD | COUNTING GAMES | MINUTES ON PITCH | YELLOW CARDS | RED CARDS | THIS SEASON | HOME COUNTRY |
|---|---|---|---|---|---|---|---|---|
| **Goalkeepers** | | | | | | | | |
| Andre Biancarelli | 33 | 10 | 0 | 0 | 0 | 0 | - | France |
| Flavio Roma | 29 | 28 | 26 | 2374 | 1 | 1 | - | Italy |
| Tony Mario Sylva | 28 | 37 | 11 | 1045 | 0 | 0 | 3 | Senegal (29) |
| **Defenders** | | | | | | | | |
| Eric Abidal | 23 | 1 | 1 | 90 | 0 | 0 | - | |
| Eric Cubilier | 24 | 22 | 13 | 1283 | 4 | 1 | - | France |
| Gael Givet | 21 | 34 | 12 | 1246 | 7 | 1 | - | France |
| Franck Jurietti | 28 | 8 | 5 | 483 | 0 | 0 | - | France |
| Philippe Leonard | 29 | 7 | 3 | 287 | 2 | 0 | - | Belgium |
| Rafael Marquez | 24 | 31 | 29 | 2595 | 7 | 1 | 3 | Mexico (9) |
| Jose Pierre-Fanfan | 27 | 14 | 7 | 776 | 2 | 1 | - | France |
| Julien Rodriguez | 25 | 27 | 23 | 2157 | 3 | 0 | - | France |
| Sebastien Squillaci | 22 | 35 | 35 | 3145 | 4 | 0 | - | France |
| **Midfielders** | | | | | | | | |
| Lucas Bernardi | 25 | 35 | 21 | 2095 | 10 | 0 | - | Argentina |
| Sebastien Carole | 20 | 3 | 1 | 182 | 0 | 0 | - | France |
| Hassan El Fakiri | 26 | 20 | 8 | 873 | 2 | 0 | - | Norway |
| Patrice Evra | 22 | 36 | 29 | 2830 | 3 | 0 | - | France |
| Pontus Farnerud | 23 | 16 | 5 | 553 | 0 | 0 | 5 | Sweden (20) |
| Marcelo Gallardo | 27 | 30 | 11 | 1351 | 3 | 1 | 1 | Argentina (5) |
| Ludovic Giuly | 26 | 36 | 34 | 3118 | 7 | 0 | 1 | France (2) |
| Hislen2004 | 1 | 0 | 1 | 0 | 0 | - | | |
| Jimmy Juan | 20 | 3 | 0 | 18 | 0 | 0 | - | France |
| Laurent Lanteri | 18 | 5 | 0 | 0 | 0 | 0 | - | France |
| Jaroslav Plasil | 21 | 7 | 0 | 63 | 0 | 0 | - | Czech Republic |
| Jerome Rothen | 25 | 37 | 33 | 3073 | 5 | 0 | 2 | France (2) |
| Vassilis Zikos | 29 | 22 | 21 | 1931 | 6 | 0 | - | Greece |
| **Forwards** | | | | | | | | |
| Souleymane Camara | 20 | 27 | 6 | 894 | 2 | 0 | 2 | Senegal (29) |
| Sebastien Grax | 19 | 5 | 0 | 26 | 2 | 0 | - | France |
| Abdelrahmane Mazhar | 26 | 7 | 1 | 177 | 2 | 1 | - | Egypt |
| Shabani Nonda | 26 | 35 | 33 | 3029 | 2 | 0 | - | Burundi |
| Dado Prso | 28 | 20 | 13 | 1414 | 0 | 0 | - | France |
| Marco Simone | 34 | 6 | 2 | 217 | 0 | 0 | - | Italy |

KEY: LEAGUE BOOKINGS CAPS (FIFA RANKING)

## SQUAD APPEARANCES

| Match | 1 | 2 | 3 | 4 | 5 | 6 | 7 | 8 | 9 | 10 | 11 | 12 | 13 | 14 | 15 | 16 | 17 | 18 | 19 | 20 | 21 | 22 | 23 | 24 | 25 | 26 | 27 | 28 | 29 | 30 | 31 | 32 | 33 | 34 | 35 | 36 | 37 | 38 |
|---|---|---|---|---|---|---|---|---|---|---|---|---|---|---|---|---|---|---|---|---|---|---|---|---|---|---|---|---|---|---|---|---|---|---|---|---|---|---|
| **Venue** | A | H | A | H | A | H | A | A | H | A | H | A | H | A | H | A | H | A | H | A | H | A | H | A | H | H | A | H | A | H | A | H | A | H | A | H | A | H |
| **Competition** | L | L | L | L | L | L | L | L | L | L | L | L | L | L | L | L | L | L | L | L | L | L | L | L | L | L | L | L | L | L | L | L | L | L | L | L | L | L |
| **Result** | W | L | L | W | L | W | D | W | W | D | D | D | D | L | W | L | W | W | W | D | D | D | D | W | W | W | D | W | W | L | W | L | W | W | L | W | L | W |

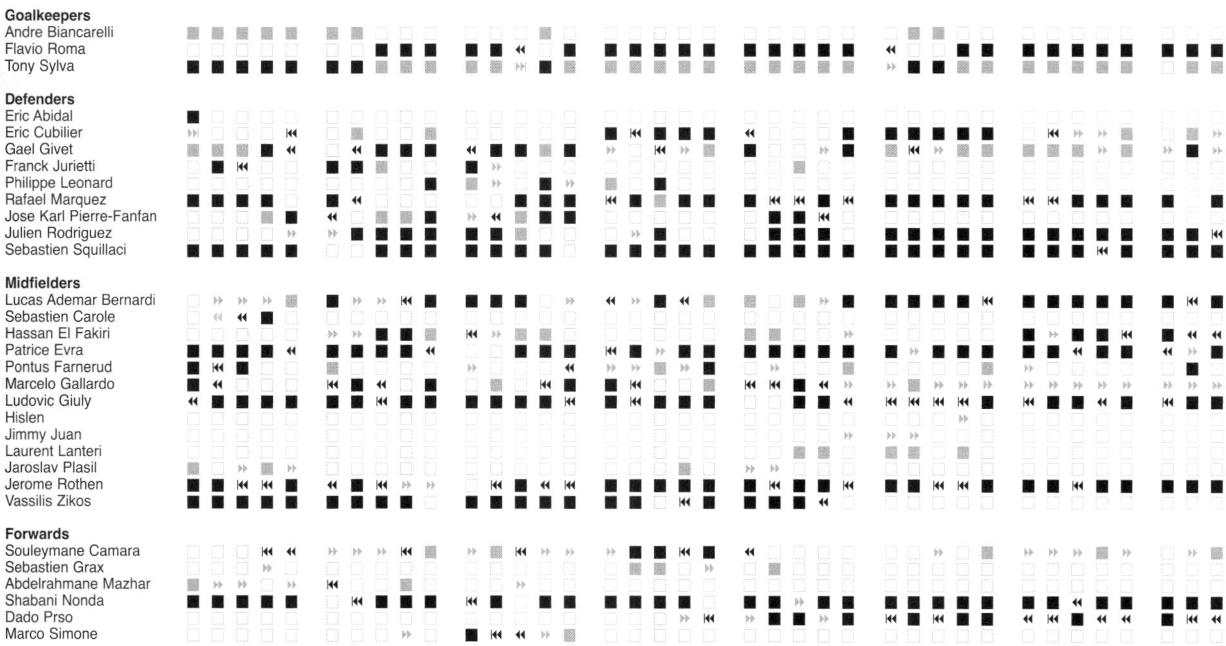
Goalkeepers
Andre Biancarelli
Flavio Roma
Tony Sylva
Defenders
Eric Abidal
Eric Cubilier
Gael Givet
Franck Jurietti
Philippe Leonard
Rafael Marquez
Jose Karl Pierre-Fanfan
Julien Rodriguez
Sebastien Squillaci
Midfielders
Lucas Ademar Bernardi
Sebastien Carole
Hassan El Fakiri
Patrice Evra
Pontus Farnerud
Marcelo Gallardo
Ludovic Giuly
Hislen
Jimmy Juan
Laurent Lanteri
Jaroslav Plasil
Jerome Rothen
Vassilis Zikos
Forwards
Souleymane Camara
Sebastien Grax
Abdelrahmane Mazhar
Shabani Nonda
Dado Prso
Marco Simone

KEY: ■ On all match ⏮ Subbed or sent off (Counting game) ⏭ Subbed on from bench (Counting Game) Subbed on and then subbed or sent off (Counting Game) Not in 16
■ On bench « Subbed or sent off (playing less than 70 minutes) » Subbed on (playing less than 70 minutes) Subbed on and then subbed or sent off (playing less than 70 minutes)

# MARSEILLE

Final Position: **3rd**

| | | | | | | |
|---|---|---|---|---|---|---|
| 1 | lge | Nantes | H | L | 0-2 | |
| 2 | lge | Monaco | A | W | 1-0 | Fernandao 54 |
| 3 | lge | Lyon | H | D | 1-1 | Bakayoko 29 |
| 4 | lge | Rennes | A | W | 3-1 | Chapuis 34,69; Sahko 90 |
| 5 | lge | Auxerre | H | D | 0-0 | |
| 6 | lge | Nice | A | L | 0-2 | |
| 7 | lge | Bordeaux | H | W | 2-1 | Leboeuf 15 pen; Bakayoko 74 |
| 8 | lge | Le Havre | A | W | 3-1 | Sahko 45; Johansen 56; Celestini 89 |
| 9 | lge | AC Ajaccio | H | W | 3-1 | Van Buyten 40; Chapuis 45; Bakayoko 76 pen |
| 10 | lge | Lille | A | L | 0-3 | |
| 11 | lge | Strasbourg | H | W | 1-0 | Fernandao 23 |
| 12 | lge | Paris SG | A | L | 0-3 | |
| 13 | lge | Montpellier | H | W | 2-0 | Bakayoko 31,60 |
| 14 | lge | Guingamp | A | D | 0-0 | |
| 15 | lge | Troyes | H | D | 0-0 | |
| 16 | lge | Lens | H | W | 1-0 | Olembe 11 |
| 17 | lge | Bastia | A | L | 0-2 | |
| 18 | lge | Sochaux | H | W | 1-0 | Fernandao 38 |
| 19 | lge | Sedan | A | W | 2-1 | Dos Santos 38; Bakayoko 48 |
| 20 | lge | Monaco | H | D | 1-1 | Marquez 62 og |
| 21 | lge | Lyon | A | L | 0-1 | |
| 22 | lge | Rennes | H | W | 2-0 | Bakayoko 6; Van Buyten 19 |
| 23 | lge | Auxerre | A | D | 0-0 | |
| 24 | lge | Nice | H | W | 2-0 | Van Buyten 45; Sychev 86 |
| 25 | lge | Bordeaux | A | L | 1-3 | Van Buyten 88 |
| 26 | lge | Le Havre | H | W | 2-0 | Sychev 16; Van Buyten 53 |
| 27 | lge | AC Ajaccio | A | W | 2-0 | Bakayoko 34; Sahko 78 pen |
| 28 | lge | Lille | H | W | 2-0 | Bakayoko 12; Johansen 74 |
| 29 | lge | Strasbourg | A | D | 0-0 | |
| 30 | lge | Paris SG | H | L | 0-3 | |
| 31 | lge | Montpellier | A | W | 2-1 | Sahko 22; Van Buyten 82 |
| 32 | lge | Guingamp | H | L | 0-2 | |
| 33 | lge | Troyes | A | D | 0-0 | |
| 34 | lge | Lens | A | W | 1-0 | Leboeuf 32 pen |
| 35 | lge | Bastia | H | W | 2-1 | Sychev 45; Van Buyten 86 |
| 36 | lge | Sochaux | A | L | 0-3 | |
| 37 | lge | Sedan | H | W | 4-2 | Perez 9; Chapuis 43; Hemdani 82; Sahko 90 |
| 38 | lge | Nantes | A | L | 0-1 | |

## KEY PLAYERS - GOALSCORERS

**1 Ibrahim Bakayoko**

| | | | |
|---|---|---|---|
| Goals in the League | 9 | Player Strike Rate<br>Average number of minutes between League goals scored by player | 253 |
| Contribution to Attacking Power<br>Average number of minutes between League team goals while on pitch | 81 | Club Strike Rate<br>Average number of minutes between League goals scored by club | 83 |

| | PLAYER | LGE GOALS | POWER | STRIKE RATE |
|---|---|---|---|---|
| 2 | Daniel Van Buyten | 7 | 87 | 439 mins |
| 3 | Cyril Chapuis | 4 | 76 | 519 mins |
| 4 | Frank Leboeuf | 2 | 83 | 1091 mins |
| 5 | Pascal Johansen | 2 | 77 | 1203 mins |

## KEY PLAYERS - MIDFIELDERS

**1 Pascal Johansen**

| | | | |
|---|---|---|---|
| Goals in the League | 2 | Contribution to Attacking Power<br>Average number of minutes between League team goals while on pitch | 78 |
| Defensive Rating<br>Average number of mins between League goals conceded while he was on the pitch | 105 | Scoring Difference<br>Defensive Rating minus Contribution to Attacking Power | 27 |

| | PLAYER | LGE GOALS | DEF RATE | POWER | SCORE DIFF |
|---|---|---|---|---|---|
| 2 | Fabio Celestini | 1 | 87 | 82 | 5 mins |
| 3 | Ibrahim Hemdani | 1 | 88 | 86 | 2 mins |
| 4 | Lamine Sahko | 5 | 79 | 88 | -9 mins |
| 5 | Salomon Olembe | 1 | 91 | 109 | -18 mins |

## KEY PLAYERS - DEFENDERS

**1 Frank Leboeuf**

| | | | |
|---|---|---|---|
| Goals Conceded (GC)<br>The number of League goals conceded while he was on the pitch | 20 | Clean Sheets<br>In games when he played at least 70 minutes | 11 |
| Defensive Rating<br>Ave number of mins between League goals conceded while on the pitch | 109 | Club Defensive Rating<br>Average number of mins between League goals conceded by the club this season | 95 |

| | PLAYER | CON LGE | CLEAN SHEETS | DEF RATE |
|---|---|---|---|---|
| 2 | Daniel Van Buyten | 29 | 16 | 106 mins |
| 3 | Manuel Dos Santos | 28 | 15 | 103 mins |
| 4 | Abdoulaye Meite | 22 | 10 | 99 mins |
| 5 | Johnny Ecker | 29 | 16 | 97 mins |

## GOALS SCORED

AT HOME

| | | |
|---|---|---|
| MOST | Lyon | 40 |
| | | 26 |
| LEAST | AC Ajaccio | 14 |

AWAY

| | | |
|---|---|---|
| MOST | Monaco | 29 |
| | | 15 |
| LEAST | Troyes | 7 |

## GOALS CONCEDED

AT HOME

| | | |
|---|---|---|
| LEAST | Sochaux & Auxerre | 8 |
| | | 14 |
| MOST | Strasbourg | 23 |

AWAY

| | | |
|---|---|---|
| LEAST | Lens | 15 |
| | | 22 |
| MOST | Sedan | 39 |

## KEY GOALKEEPER

**1 Vedran Runje**

| | |
|---|---|
| Goals Conceded in the League | 36 |
| Defensive Rating<br>Ave number of mins between League goals conceded while on the pitch | 90 |
| Counting Games<br>Games when he played at least 70 minutes | 36 |
| Clean Sheets<br>In games when he played at least 70 minutes | 15 |

## TOP POINT EARNERS

| | PLAYER | GAMES | AVE |
|---|---|---|---|
| 1 | Chapuis | 20 | 1.90 |
| 2 | Bakayoko | 20 | 1.90 |
| 3 | Johansen | 25 | 1.88 |
| 4 | Leboeuf | 23 | 1.87 |
| 5 | Meite | 21 | 1.81 |
| 6 | Ecker | 30 | 1.80 |
| 7 | Van Buyten | 34 | 1.74 |
| 8 | Celestini | 31 | 1.71 |
| 9 | Olembe | 14 | 1.71 |
| 10 | Runje | 36 | 1.69 |
| | CLUB AVERAGE: | | 1.71 |

Ave = Average points per match in Counting Games

## ATTENDANCES

HOME GROUND: STADE VELODROME CAPACITY: 60000 AVERAGE LEAGUE AT HOME: 45998

| | | | | | | | | |
|---|---|---|---|---|---|---|---|---|
| 30 | Paris SG | 60000 | 12 | Paris SG | 45000 | 23 | Auxerre | 20000 |
| 20 | Monaco | 58000 | 21 | Lyon | 40000 | 36 | Sochaux | 19910 |
| 7 | Bordeaux | 57000 | 9 | AC Ajaccio | 40000 | 2 | Monaco | 18500 |
| 3 | Lyon | 56652 | 34 | Lens | 40000 | 14 | Guingamp | 17000 |
| 37 | Sedan | 55442 | 11 | Strasbourg | 40000 | 8 | Le Havre | 16000 |
| 18 | Sochaux | 55000 | 22 | Rennes | 39885 | 19 | Sedan | 16000 |
| 32 | Guingamp | 55000 | 38 | Nantes | 36411 | 6 | Nice | 15000 |
| 35 | Bastia | 55000 | 26 | Le Havre | 35000 | 1 | Nantes | 15000 |
| 16 | Lens | 50000 | 31 | Montpellier | 30000 | 33 | Troyes | 12500 |
| 5 | Auxerre | 50000 | 29 | Strasbourg | 28000 | 13 | Montpellier | 10000 |
| 28 | Lille | 50000 | 25 | Bordeaux | 26000 | 17 | Bastia | 9500 |
| 24 | Nice | 47000 | 4 | Rennes | 23700 | 27 | AC Ajaccio | 7000 |
| 15 | Troyes | 45000 | 10 | Lille | 20000 | | | |

■ Home □ Away ▒ Neutral

## DISCIPLINARY RECORDS

| | PLAYER | YELLOW | RED | AVE |
|---|---|---|---|---|
| 1 | Givet | 7 | 1 | 155 |
| 2 | Bernardi | 10 | 0 | 209 |
| 3 | Cubilier | 4 | 1 | 256 |
| 4 | Pierre-Fanfan | 2 | 1 | 258 |
| 5 | Zikos | 6 | 0 | 321 |
| 6 | Marquez | 7 | 1 | 324 |
| 7 | Gallardo | 3 | 1 | 337 |
| 8 | El Fakiri | 2 | 0 | 436 |
| 9 | Giuly | 7 | 0 | 445 |
| 10 | Camara | 2 | 0 | 447 |
| 11 | Rothen | 5 | 0 | 614 |
| 12 | Rodriguez | 3 | 0 | 719 |
| 13 | Squillaci | 4 | 0 | 786 |
| | Other | 12 | 2 | |
| | TOTAL | 74 | 7 | |

## LEAGUE GOALS

| | PLAYER | MINS | GOALS | AVE |
|---|---|---|---|---|
| 1 | Bakayoko | 2280 | 9 | 253 |
| 2 | Van Buyten | 3075 | 7 | 439 |
| 3 | Sahko | 1582 | 5 | 316 |
| 4 | Chapuis | 2076 | 4 | 519 |
| 5 | Sychev | 877 | 3 | 292 |
| 6 | Fernandao | 1188 | 3 | 396 |
| 7 | Johansen | 2406 | 2 | 1203 |
| 8 | Leboeuf | 2181 | 2 | 1091 |
| 9 | Celestini | 2877 | 1 | 2877 |
| 10 | Dos Santos | 2894 | 1 | 2894 |
| 11 | Perez, S | 802 | 1 | 802 |
| 12 | Hemdani | 2994 | 1 | 2994 |
| 13 | Olembe | 1635 | 1 | 1635 |
| | Other | | 1 | |
| | TOTAL | | 41 | |

## MONTH BY MONTH GUIDE TO THE POINTS

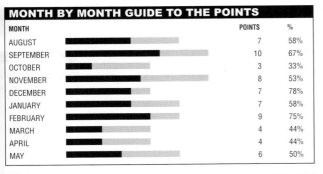

| MONTH | POINTS | % |
|---|---|---|
| AUGUST | 7 | 58% |
| SEPTEMBER | 10 | 67% |
| OCTOBER | 3 | 33% |
| NOVEMBER | 8 | 53% |
| DECEMBER | 7 | 78% |
| JANUARY | 7 | 58% |
| FEBRUARY | 9 | 75% |
| MARCH | 4 | 44% |
| APRIL | 4 | 44% |
| MAY | 6 | 50% |

## TEAM OF THE SEASON

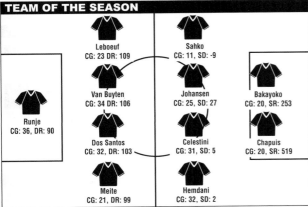

Leboeuf CG: 23 DR: 109
Sahko CG: 11, SD: -9
Van Buyten CG: 34 DR: 106
Johansen CG: 25, SD: 27
Bakayoko CG: 20, SR: 253
Runje CG: 36, DR: 90
Dos Santos CG: 32, DR: 103
Celestini CG: 31, SD: 5
Chapuis CG: 20, SR: 519
Meite CG: 21, DR: 99
Hemdani CG: 32, SD: 2

KEY: DR = Defensive Rate, SD = Scoring Difference, SR = Strike Rate, CG = Counting Games – League games playing at least 70 minutes

## LEAGUE APPEARANCES, BOOKINGS AND CAPS

| | AGE | IN THE SQUAD | COUNTING GAMES | MINUTES ON PITCH | YELLOW CARDS | RED CARDS | THIS SEASON | HOME COUNTRY |
|---|---|---|---|---|---|---|---|---|
| **Goalkeepers** | | | | | | | | |
| Cedric Carasso | 21 | 37 | 2 | 180 | 0 | 0 | - | France |
| Vedran Runje | 28 | 38 | 36 | 3240 | 3 | 0 | - | Croatia |
| **Defenders** | | | | | | | | |
| Elhadji Khalifa Ba | | 2 | 0 | 0 | 0 | 0 | - | Senegal |
| Manuel Dos Santos | 29 | 33 | 32 | 2894 | 7 | 0 | - | France |
| Johnny Ecker | 30 | 34 | 30 | 2810 | 7 | 0 | - | France |
| Benjamin Gavanon | 22 | 1 | 0 | 0 | 0 | 0 | - | France |
| Fabien Laurenti | 20 | 19 | 5 | 603 | 0 | 0 | - | France |
| Frank Leboeuf | 35 | 26 | 23 | 2181 | 9 | 1 | - | France |
| Abdoulaye Meite | 22 | 32 | 21 | 2171 | 7 | 2 | - | France |
| Sebastien Perez | 29 | 14 | 6 | 802 | 4 | 0 | - | France |
| Eduardo Tuzzio | 28 | 8 | 2 | 238 | 1 | 0 | - | Argentina |
| Daniel Van Buyten | 25 | 35 | 34 | 3075 | 4 | 1 | 8 | Belgium (16) |
| **Midfielders** | | | | | | | | |
| Djamel Belmadi | 27 | 17 | 4 | 599 | 1 | 0 | - | France |
| Fabio Celestini | 27 | 33 | 31 | 2877 | 11 | 1 | - | Switzerland |
| Nicolas Cicut | 19 | 1 | 0 | 0 | 0 | 0 | - | France |
| Jose Teixeira Delfim | 26 | 1 | 0 | 14 | 0 | 0 | - | Portugal |
| Michel Gafour | 21 | 7 | 1 | 206 | 0 | 0 | - | France |
| Sebastien Gregori | | 1 | 0 | 0 | 0 | 0 | - | |
| Ibrahim Hemdani | 25 | 35 | 32 | 2994 | 5 | 0 | - | France |
| Pascal Johansen | 24 | 29 | 25 | 2406 | 15 | 1 | - | France |
| Mickael Marsiglia | 27 | 5 | 0 | 23 | 0 | 0 | - | France |
| Laurent Merlin | 18 | 4 | 0 | 16 | 0 | 0 | - | France |
| Salomon Olembe | 22 | 28 | 14 | 1635 | 1 | 0 | 2 | Cameroon (18) |
| Lamine Sahko | 25 | 29 | 11 | 1582 | 2 | 0 | - | France |
| Piotr Swierczewski | 31 | 19 | 3 | 474 | 2 | 0 | 3 | Poland (29) |
| Dmitri Sychev | 19 | 17 | 7 | 877 | 4 | 0 | - | Russia |
| **Forwards** | | | | | | | | |
| Ibrahim Bakayoko | 26 | 37 | 20 | 2280 | 1 | 1 | - | Ivory Coast |
| Cyril Chapuis | 24 | 36 | 20 | 2076 | 6 | 0 | - | France |
| Lucio Fernandao | 25 | 25 | 5 | 1188 | 2 | 0 | - | Brazil |
| Papis M'Bodji | | 3 | 0 | 40 | 0 | 0 | - | France |

KEY: LEAGUE BOOKINGS CAPS (FIFA RANKING)

## SQUAD APPEARANCES

| Match | 1 | 2 | 3 | 4 | 5 | 6 | 7 | 8 | 9 | 10 | 11 | 12 | 13 | 14 | 15 | 16 | 17 | 18 | 19 | 20 | 21 | 22 | 23 | 24 | 25 | 26 | 27 | 28 | 29 | 30 | 31 | 32 | 33 | 34 | 35 | 36 | 37 | 38 |
|---|---|---|---|---|---|---|---|---|---|---|---|---|---|---|---|---|---|---|---|---|---|---|---|---|---|---|---|---|---|---|---|---|---|---|---|---|---|---|
| Venue | H | A | H | A | H | A | H | A | H | A | H | A | H | A | H | H | A | H | A | H | A | H | A | H | A | H | A | H | A | H | A | H | A | A | H | A | H | A |
| Competition | L | L | L | L | L | L | L | L | L | L | L | L | L | L | L | L | L | L | L | L | L | L | L | L | L | L | L | L | L | L | L | L | L | L | L | L | L | L |
| Result | L | W | D | W | D | L | W | W | W | L | W | L | W | D | D | W | L | W | W | D | L | W | D | W | L | W | W | W | D | L | W | L | D | W | W | L | W | L |

**Goalkeepers**
Cedric Carasso
Vedran Runje

**Defenders**
Elhadji Khalifa Ba
Manuel Dos Santos
Johnny Ecker
Benjamin Gavanon
Fabien Laurenti
Frank Leboeuf
Abdoulaye Meite
Sebastien Perez
Eduardo Tuzzio
Daniel Van Buyten

**Midfielders**
Djamel Belmadi
Fabio Celestini
Nicolas Cicut
Jose Rola Teixeira Delfim
Michel Gafour
Sebastien Gregori
Ibrahim Hemdani
Pascal Johansen
Mickael Marsiglia
Laurent Merlin
Salomon Olembe
Lamine Sahko
Piotr Swierczewski
Dmitri Sychev

**Forwards**
Ibrahim Bakayoko
Cyril Chapuis
Lucio Da Costa Fernandao
Papis M'Bodji

KEY: On all match | On bench | Subbed or sent off (Counting game) | Subbed or sent off (playing less than 70 minutes) | Subbed on from bench (Counting Game) | Subbed on (playing less than 70 minutes) | Subbed on and then subbed or sent off (Counting Game) | Subbed on and then subbed or sent off (playing less than 70 minutes) | Not in 16

# BORDEAUX

Final Position: **4th**

| | | | | | | |
|---|---|---|---|---|---|---|
| 1 | lge | Lille | A | W | 3-0 | Pauleta 23; Smertin 54; Costa 56 |
| 2 | lge | Paris SG | H | D | 0-0 | |
| 3 | lge | Montpellier | A | W | 1-0 | Smertin 19 |
| 4 | lge | Strasbourg | H | L | 1-2 | Pauleta 60 |
| 5 | lge | Guingamp | A | D | 0-0 | |
| 6 | lge | Troyes | H | W | 1-0 | Darcheville 39 |
| 7 | lge | Marseille | A | L | 1-2 | Pauleta 51 |
| 8 | uc1rl1 | Puchov | H | W | 6-0 | Sommeil 23; Dugarry 35; Feindouno 62; Pauleta 67 pen; Vavrik 78 og; Darcheville 89 |
| 9 | lge | Lens | H | W | 1-0 | Jemmali 75 |
| 10 | lge | Bastia | A | L | 1-2 | Pauleta 84 |
| 11 | uc1rl2 | Puchov | A | W | 4-1 | Savio 40; Darcheville 41,88; Feindouno 67 |
| 12 | lge | Sedan | H | D | 2-2 | Pauleta 5,61 |
| 13 | lge | Sochaux | A | L | 0-2 | |
| 14 | lge | Monaco | H | D | 2-2 | Darcheville 30; Savio 65 |
| 15 | uc2rl1 | Djurgarden | A | W | 1-0 | Feindouno 63 |
| 16 | lge | Nantes | A | D | 0-0 | |
| 17 | lge | Rennes | H | W | 2-0 | Pauleta 30,76 |
| 18 | uc2rl2 | Djurgarden | H | W | 2-1 | Feindouno 37,50 |
| 19 | lge | Lyon | A | L | 2-4 | Sahnoun 17; Sommeil 31 |
| 20 | lge | AC Ajaccio | H | W | 1-0 | Pauleta 35 |
| 21 | uc3rl1 | Anderlecht | H | L | 0-2 | |
| 22 | lge | Auxerre | A | L | 0-1 | |
| 23 | lge | Le Havre | A | L | 0-1 | |
| 24 | uc3rl2 | Anderlecht | A | D | 2-2 | Darcheville 82,89 |
| 25 | lge | Nice | H | W | 4-0 | Savio 27,43; Pauleta 59; Costa 90 |
| 26 | lge | Paris SG | A | D | 1-1 | Feindouno 40 |
| 27 | lge | Montpellier | H | W | 3-1 | Savio 24; Jemmali 47; Pauleta 89 |
| 28 | lge | Guingamp | H | W | 4-2 | Pauleta 17,67; Savio 41; Darcheville 49 |
| 29 | lge | Troyes | A | W | 1-0 | Feindouno 16 |
| 30 | lge | Marseille | H | W | 3-1 | Feindouno 56; Darcheville 62 pen; Savio 90 |
| 31 | lge | Lens | A | D | 3-3 | Pauleta 16,79; Afanou 49 |
| 32 | lge | Bastia | H | L | 0-2 | |
| 33 | lge | Sedan | A | W | 1-0 | Feindouno 37 |
| 34 | lge | Sochaux | H | W | 2-0 | Pauleta 10; Darcheville 34 |
| 35 | lge | Monaco | A | W | 1-0 | Darcheville 73 |
| 36 | lge | Strasbourg | A | D | 1-1 | Darcheville 90 pen |
| 37 | lge | Nantes | H | D | 0-0 | |
| 38 | lge | Rennes | A | W | 4-3 | Darcheville 58,80; Jay 63 og; Pauleta 81 |
| 39 | lge | Lyon | H | L | 0-1 | |
| 40 | lge | AC Ajaccio | A | W | 6-1 | Pauleta 38,61,82; Savio 73; Darcheville 80; Meriem 88 |
| 41 | lge | Auxerre | H | L | 0-1 | |
| 42 | lge | Le Havre | H | W | 2-0 | Pauleta 9; Darcheville 44 |
| 43 | lge | Nice | A | D | 1-1 | Chamakh 90 |
| 44 | lge | Lille | H | W | 2-0 | Pauleta 15,90 pen |

## ATTENDANCES

HOME GROUND: PARK LESCURE CAPACITY: 35200 AVERAGE LEAGUE AT HOME: 28234

| | | | | | | | | |
|---|---|---|---|---|---|---|---|---|
| 7 | Marseille | 57000 | 6 | Troyes | 30000 | 22 | Auxerre | 15000 |
| 19 | Lyon | 49300 | 41 | Auxerre | 30000 | 5 | Guingamp | 15000 |
| 26 | Paris SG | 40000 | 44 | Lille | 28695 | 27 | Montpellier | 15000 |
| 15 | Djurgarden | 40000 | 42 | Le Havre | 26824 | 1 | Lille | 14145 |
| 4 | Strasbourg | 36819 | 34 | Sochaux | 26000 | 36 | Strasbourg | 12939 |
| 31 | Lens | 36765 | 30 | Marseille | 26000 | 21 | Anderlecht | 12180 |
| 9 | Lens | 35000 | 28 | Guingamp | 20114 | 35 | Monaco | 12000 |
| 2 | Paris SG | 35000 | 25 | Nice | 20000 | 33 | Sedan | 11000 |
| 39 | Lyon | 35000 | 3 | Montpellier | 20000 | 18 | Djurgarden | 10653 |
| 37 | Nantes | 34000 | 38 | Rennes | 18156 | 10 | Bastia | 10000 |
| 14 | Monaco | 33000 | 8 | Puchov | 18000 | 29 | Troyes | 10000 |
| 16 | Nantes | 30000 | 13 | Sochaux | 18000 | 23 | Le Havre | 9000 |
| 17 | Rennes | 30000 | 24 | Anderlecht | 17721 | 40 | AC Ajaccio | 7500 |
| 32 | Bastia | 30000 | 43 | Nice | 17000 | 11 | Puchov | 3000 |
| 20 | AC Ajaccio | 30000 | 12 | Sedan | 15000 | | | |

■ Home □ Away ▒ Neutral

## KEY PLAYERS - GOALSCORERS

**1 Pedro Pauleta**

| | | | |
|---|---|---|---|
| Goals in the League | 23 | Player Strike Rate<br>Average number of minutes between League goals scored by player | 143 |
| Contribution to Attacking Power<br>Average number of minutes between League team goals while on pitch | 61 | Club Strike Rate<br>Average number of minutes between League goals scored by club | 60 |

| | PLAYER | LGE GOALS | POWER | STRIKE RATE |
|---|---|---|---|---|
| 2 | Jean-Claude Darcheville | 11 | 56 | 226 mins |
| 3 | Savio | 7 | 58 | 308 mins |
| 4 | Pascal Feindouno | 4 | 53 | 688 mins |
| 5 | David Jemmali | 2 | 58 | 1224 mins |

## KEY PLAYERS - MIDFIELDERS

**1 Camel Meriem**

| | | | |
|---|---|---|---|
| Goals in the League | 1 | Contribution to Attacking Power<br>Average number of minutes between League team goals while on pitch | 57 |
| Defensive Rating<br>Average number of mins between League goals conceded while he was on the pitch | 106 | Scoring Difference<br>Defensive Rating minus Contribution to Attacking Power | 49 |

| | PLAYER | LGE GOALS | DEF RATE | POWER | SCORE DIFF |
|---|---|---|---|---|---|
| 2 | Eduardo Costa | 2 | 107 | 63 | 44 mins |
| 3 | Alexei Smertin | 2 | 114 | 73 | 41 mins |

## KEY PLAYERS - DEFENDERS

**1 Marc Planus**

| | | | |
|---|---|---|---|
| Goals Conceded (GC)<br>The number of League goals conceded while he was on the pitch | 12 | Clean Sheets<br>In games when he played at least 70 minutes | 6 |
| Defensive Rating<br>Ave number of mins between League goals conceded while on the pitch | 106 | Club Defensive Rating<br>Average number of mins between League goals conceded by the club this season | 95 |

| | PLAYER | CON LGE | CLEAN SHEETS | DEF RATE |
|---|---|---|---|---|
| 2 | David Jemmali | 25 | 12 | 98 mins |
| 3 | Bruno Basto | 28 | 12 | 94 mins |
| 4 | Nicolas Sahnoun | 12 | 4 | 88 mins |
| 5 | Jerome Bonnissel | 10 | 5 | 85 mins |

## KEY GOALKEEPER

**1 Frederick Roux**

| | |
|---|---|
| Goals Conceded in the League | 9 |
| Defensive Rating<br>Ave number of mins between League goals conceded while on the pitch | 101 |
| Counting Games<br>Games when he played at least 70 minutes | 10 |
| Clean Sheets<br>In games when he played at least 70 minutes | 4 |

## TOP POINT EARNERS

| | PLAYER | GAMES | AVE |
|---|---|---|---|
| 1 | Planus | 13 | 2.15 |
| 2 | Basto | 28 | 1.89 |
| 3 | Darcheville | 25 | 1.88 |
| 4 | Meriem | 14 | 1.86 |
| 5 | Smertin | 26 | 1.85 |
| 6 | Jemmali | 25 | 1.84 |
| 7 | Feindouno | 29 | 1.76 |
| 8 | Pauleta | 37 | 1.70 |
| 9 | Rame | 28 | 1.68 |
| 10 | Costa | 30 | 1.67 |
| | CLUB AVERAGE: | | 1.68 |

Ave = Average points per match in Counting Games

## DISCIPLINARY RECORDS

| | PLAYER | YELLOW | RED | AVE |
|---|---|---|---|---|
| 1 | Dugarry | 4 | 2 | 156 |
| 2 | Jemmali | 10 | 4 | 174 |
| 3 | Sahnoun | 6 | 0 | 175 |
| 4 | Sommeil | 6 | 1 | 217 |
| 5 | Costa | 10 | 1 | 252 |
| 6 | Smertin | 8 | 0 | 327 |
| 7 | Basto | 8 | 0 | 327 |
| 8 | Caneira | 5 | 1 | 409 |
| 9 | Planus | 3 | 0 | 425 |
| 10 | Afanou | 6 | 0 | 435 |
| 11 | Roux | 2 | 0 | 456 |
| 12 | Pauleta | 7 | 0 | 470 |
| 13 | Savio | 3 | 1 | 539 |
| | Other | 13 | 0 | |
| | TOTAL | 91 | 10 | |

## LEAGUE GOALS

| | PLAYER | MINS | GOALS | AVE |
|---|---|---|---|---|
| 1 | Pauleta | 3296 | 23 | 143 |
| 2 | Darcheville | 2484 | 11 | 226 |
| 3 | Savio | 2159 | 7 | 308 |
| 4 | Feindouno | 2750 | 4 | 688 |
| 5 | Smertin | 2623 | 2 | 1312 |
| 6 | Costa | 2775 | 2 | 1388 |
| 7 | Jemmali | 2447 | 2 | 1224 |
| 8 | Sahnoun | 1050 | 1 | 1050 |
| 9 | Meriem | 1587 | 1 | 1587 |
| 10 | Sommeil | 1525 | 1 | 1525 |
| 11 | Chamakh | 90 | 1 | 90 |
| 12 | Afanou | 2610 | 1 | 2610 |
| | Other | | 1 | |
| | TOTAL | | 57 | |

## MONTH BY MONTH GUIDE TO THE POINTS

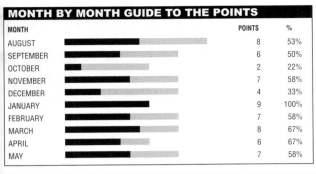

| MONTH | POINTS | % |
|---|---|---|
| AUGUST | 8 | 53% |
| SEPTEMBER | 6 | 50% |
| OCTOBER | 2 | 22% |
| NOVEMBER | 7 | 58% |
| DECEMBER | 4 | 33% |
| JANUARY | 9 | 100% |
| FEBRUARY | 7 | 58% |
| MARCH | 8 | 67% |
| APRIL | 6 | 67% |
| MAY | 7 | 58% |

## TEAM OF THE SEASON

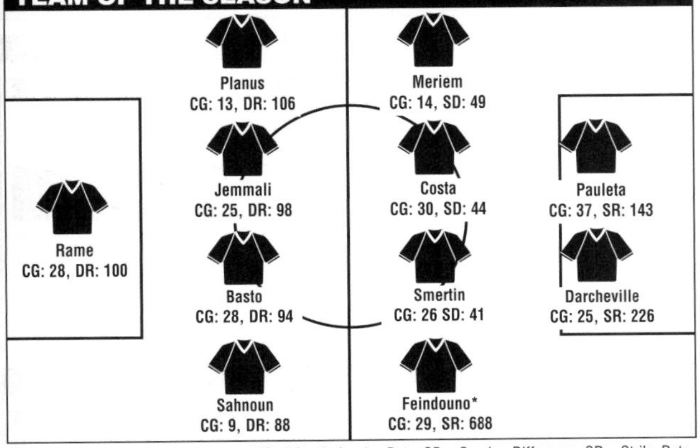

Rame
CG: 28, DR: 100
Planus
CG: 13, DR: 106
Jemmali
CG: 25, DR: 98
Basto
CG: 28, DR: 94
Sahnoun
CG: 9, DR: 88
Meriem
CG: 14, SD: 49
Costa
CG: 30, SD: 44
Smertin
CG: 26 SD: 41
Feindouno*
CG: 29, SR: 688
Pauleta
CG: 37, SR: 143
Darcheville
CG: 25, SR: 226


KEY: DR = Defensive Rate, SD = Scoring Difference, SR = Strike Rate, CG = Counting Games – League games playing at least 70 minutes

## LEAGUE APPEARANCES, BOOKINGS AND CAPS

| | AGE | IN THE SQUAD | COUNTING GAMES | MINUTES ON PITCH | YELLOW CARDS | RED CARDS | THIS SEASON | HOME COUNTRY |
|---|---|---|---|---|---|---|---|---|
| **Goalkeepers** | | | | | | | | |
| Ulrich Rame | 30 | 28 | 28 | 2508 | 2 | 0 | 1 | France (2) |
| Frederick Roux | 30 | 36 | 10 | 912 | 2 | 0 | - | France |
| Mathieu Valverde | 20 | 10 | 0 | 0 | 0 | 0 | - | France |
| **Defenders** | | | | | | | | |
| Kodjo Afanou | 31 | 30 | 29 | 2610 | 6 | 0 | - | France |
| Bruno Basto | 25 | 39 | 28 | 2620 | 8 | 0 | - | Portugal |
| Mathieu Beda | 21 | 18 | 3 | 299 | 1 | 0 | - | France |
| Jerome Bonnissel | 30 | 11 | 9 | 850 | 0 | 0 | - | France |
| Marco Caneira | 24 | 31 | 26 | 2455 | 5 | 1 | - | Portugal |
| David Jemmali | 28 | 29 | 25 | 2447 | 10 | 4 | - | France |
| Patrick Leugueun | 22 | 3 | 0 | 17 | 0 | 0 | - | France |
| Marc Planus | 21 | 28 | 13 | 1277 | 3 | 0 | - | France |
| Nicolas Sahnoun | 22 | 35 | 9 | 1050 | 6 | 0 | - | France |
| David Sommeil | 28 | 17 | 17 | 1525 | 6 | 1 | - | France |
| Ivan Vukomanovic | 26 | 1 | 1 | 90 | 0 | 0 | - | Serbia & Montenegro |
| **Midfielders** | | | | | | | | |
| Olivier Auriac | 19 | 10 | 0 | 7 | 0 | 0 | - | France |
| Maromane Chamakh | 19 | 14 | 0 | 90 | 1 | 0 | - | France |
| Eduardo Costa | 20 | 32 | 30 | 2775 | 10 | 1 | 1 | Brazil (1) |
| Cedric Fiston | 22 | 3 | 0 | 1 | 0 | 0 | - | France |
| Leonardo Lopez | | 0 | 0 | 0 | 0 | 0 | - | |
| Camel Meriem | 23 | 37 | 14 | 1587 | 1 | 0 | - | France |
| Paulo Miranda | 29 | 1 | 0 | 0 | 0 | 0 | - | |
| Alexei Smertin | 28 | 32 | 26 | 2623 | 8 | 0 | 6 | Russia (25) |
| **Forwards** | | | | | | | | |
| Jean-C Darcheville | 27 | 36 | 25 | 2484 | 4 | 0 | - | France |
| Christophe Dugarry | 31 | 13 | 8 | 940 | 4 | 2 | - | France |
| Pascal Feindouno | 22 | 36 | 29 | 2750 | 4 | 0 | - | Guinea |
| Pedro Pauleta | 30 | 37 | 37 | 3296 | 7 | 0 | 9 | Portugal (14) |
| Christophe Sanchez | 30 | 9 | 0 | 34 | 0 | 0 | - | France |
| Savio29 | 27 | 24 | 2159 | 3 | 1 | - | Brazil | |

KEY: LEAGUE BOOKINGS CAPS (FIFA RANKING)

## SQUAD APPEARANCES

| Match | 1 | 2 | 3 | 4 | 5 | 6 | 7 | 8 | 9 | 10 | 11 | 12 | 13 | 14 | 15 | 16 | 17 | 18 | 19 | 20 | 21 | 22 | 23 | 24 | 25 | 26 | 27 | 28 | 29 | 30 | 31 | 32 | 33 | 34 | 35 | 36 | 37 | 38 | 39 | 40 | 41 | 42 | 43 | 44 |
|---|---|---|---|---|---|---|---|---|---|---|---|---|---|---|---|---|---|---|---|---|---|---|---|---|---|---|---|---|---|---|---|---|---|---|---|---|---|---|---|---|---|---|---|---|
| Venue | A | H | A | H | A | H | A | H | H | A | A | H | A | H | A | A | H | H | A | H | H | A | A | A | H | A | H | H | A | H | A | H | A | H | A | A | H | A | H | A | H | H | A | H |
| Competition | L | L | L | L | L | L | L | E | L | L | E | L | L | L | E | L | L | E | L | L | E | L | L | E | L | L | L | L | L | L | L | L | L | L | L | L | L | L | L | L | L | L | L | L |
| Result | W | D | W | L | D | W | L | W | W | L | W | D | L | D | W | D | W | W | L | W | L | L | L | D | W | D | W | W | W | W | D | L | W | W | W | D | D | W | L | W | L | W | D | W |

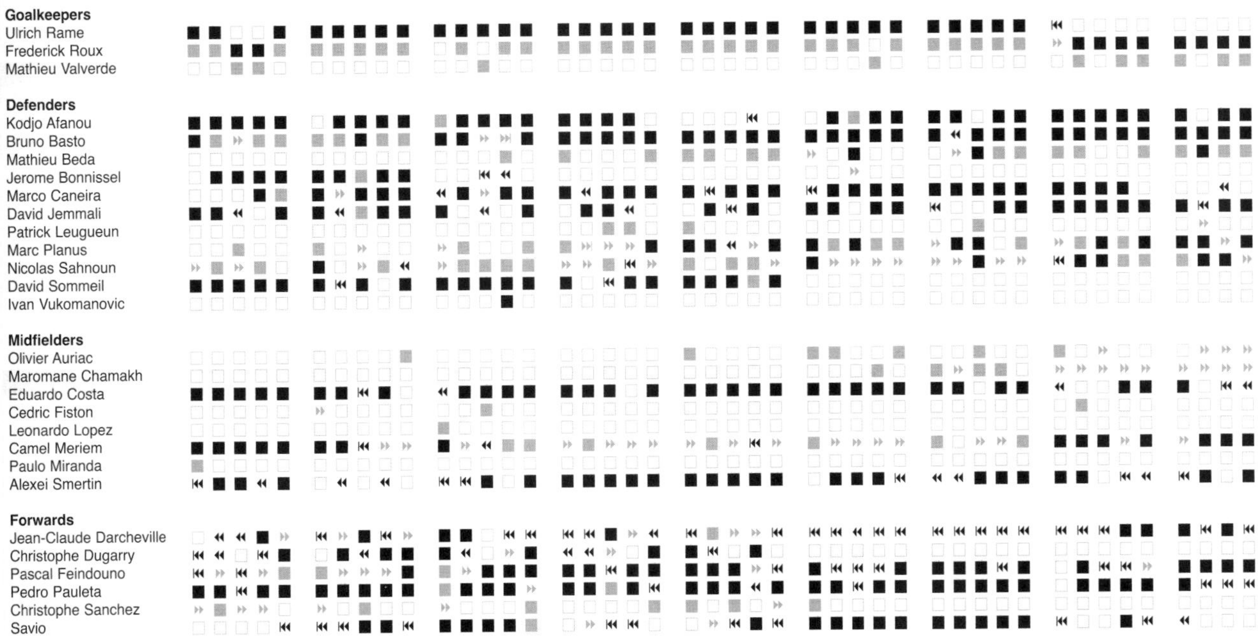

Goalkeepers
Ulrich Rame
Frederick Roux
Mathieu Valverde
Defenders
Kodjo Afanou
Bruno Basto
Mathieu Beda
Jerome Bonnissel
Marco Caneira
David Jemmali
Patrick Leugueun
Marc Planus
Nicolas Sahnoun
David Sommeil
Ivan Vukomanovic
Midfielders
Olivier Auriac
Maromane Chamakh
Eduardo Costa
Cedric Fiston
Leonardo Lopez
Camel Meriem
Paulo Miranda
Alexei Smertin
Forwards
Jean-Claude Darcheville
Christophe Dugarry
Pascal Feindouno
Pedro Pauleta
Christophe Sanchez
Savio


KEY: ■ On all match; ■ On bench; ⏮ Subbed or sent off (Counting game); ◀◀ Subbed or sent off (playing less than 70 minutes); ⏭ Subbed on from bench (Counting Game); ▶▶ Subbed on (playing less than 70 minutes); Subbed on and then subbed or sent off (Counting Game); Subbed on and then subbed or sent off (playing less than 70 minutes); □ Not in 16

# SOCHAUX

Final Position: **5th**

| | | | | | | |
|---|---|---|---|---|---|---|
| 1 | lge | Sedan | A | D | 0-0 | |
| 2 | lge | Lens | A | D | 1-1 | Raschke 33 |
| 3 | lge | Nantes | H | W | 4-2 | Pedretti 2 pen,76; Santos 84; Oruma 90 |
| 4 | lge | Monaco | A | L | 0-1 | |
| 5 | lge | Lyon | H | D | L-L | Monsoreau 68; Pagis 84 |
| 6 | lge | Rennes | A | D | 2-2 | Frau 31; Mathieu 72 |
| 7 | lge | Auxerre | H | D | 1-1 | Santos 44 |
| 8 | lge | AC Ajaccio | A | W | 1-0 | Santos 30 |
| 9 | lge | Nice | H | W | 1-0 | Boudarene 85 |
| 10 | lge | Le Havre | A | L | 0-1 | |
| 11 | lge | Bordeaux | H | W | 2-0 | Pagis 33,49 |
| 12 | lge | Lille | A | L | 0-1 | |
| 13 | lge | Strasbourg | H | W | 2-0 | Santos 6; Ismael 47 og |
| 14 | lge | Paris SG | A | D | 1-1 | Mathieu 84 |
| 15 | lge | Montpellier | H | D | 0-0 | |
| 16 | lge | Guingamp | A | L | 0-2 | |
| 17 | lge | Troyes | H | W | 1-0 | Oruma 65 |
| 18 | lge | Marseille | A | L | 0-1 | |
| 19 | lge | Bastia | H | W | 2-0 | Pagis 15; Frau 29 |
| 20 | lge | Lens | H | W | 3-0 | Santos 58,73; Frau 79 |
| 21 | lge | Monaco | H | D | 0-0 | |
| 22 | lge | Lyon | A | L | 1-4 | Pagis 71 |
| 23 | lge | Rennes | H | W | 1-0 | Oruma 22 |
| 24 | lge | Auxerre | A | L | 0-2 | |
| 25 | lge | Nice | A | D | 2-2 | Pagis 39; Frau 79 pen |
| 26 | lge | Nantes | A | W | 1-0 | Mathieu 53 |
| 27 | lge | Le Havre | H | W | 1-0 | Mathieu 90 |
| 28 | lge | Bordeaux | A | L | 0-2 | |
| 29 | lge | Lille | H | D | 2-2 | Saveljic 21; Flachez 28 |
| 30 | lge | AC Ajaccio | H | D | 1-1 | Saveljic 42 |
| 31 | lge | Strasbourg | A | W | 3-1 | Frau 34; Pagis 49; Ismael 86 og |
| 32 | lge | Paris SG | H | D | 0-0 | |
| 33 | lge | Montpellier | A | W | 2-0 | Frau 36; Santos 53 |
| 34 | lge | Guingamp | H | D | 0-0 | |
| 35 | lge | Troyes | A | W | 2-0 | Monsoreau 48; Frau 60 |
| 36 | lge | Marseille | H | W | 3-0 | Santos 28; Frau 64; Isabey 86 |
| 37 | lge | Bastia | A | D | 2-2 | Saveljic 5 pen; Frau 31 |
| 38 | lge | Sedan | H | W | 2-1 | Pedretti 20; Santos 76 |

## KEY PLAYERS - GOALSCORERS

**1 Pierre-Alain Frau**

| | | | |
|---|---|---|---|
| Goals in the League | 9 | **Player Strike Rate** Average number of minutes between League goals scored by player | 210 |
| **Contribution to Attacking Power** Average number of minutes between League team goals while on pitch | 65 | **Club Strike Rate** Average number of minutes between League goals scored by club | 74 |

| | PLAYER | LGE GOALS | POWER | STRIKE RATE |
|---|---|---|---|---|
| 2 | Francileudo Santos | 9 | 84 | 245 mins |
| 3 | Jeremy Mathieu | 4 | 77 | 348 mins |
| 4 | Michael Pagis | 7 | 68 | 392 mins |
| 5 | Wilson Oruma | 3 | 54 | 525 mins |

## KEY PLAYERS - MIDFIELDERS

**1 Wilson Oruma**

| | | | |
|---|---|---|---|
| Goals in the League | 3 | **Contribution to Attacking Power** Average number of minutes between League team goals while on pitch | 54 |
| **Defensive Rating** Average number of mins between League goals conceded while he was on the pitch | 158 | **Scoring Difference** Defensive Rating minus Contribution to Attacking Power | 104 |

| | PLAYER | LGE GOALS | DEF RATE | POWER | SCORE DIFF |
|---|---|---|---|---|---|
| 2 | Mickael Isabey | 1 | 140 | 79 | 61 mins |
| 3 | Benoit Pedretti | 3 | 116 | 77 | 39 mins |
| 4 | Jeremy Mathieu | 4 | 116 | 77 | 39 mins |
| 5 | Ibrahim Tall | 0 | 85 | 79 | 6 mins |

## KEY PLAYERS - DEFENDERS

**1 Jean-Jacques Domoraud**

| | | | |
|---|---|---|---|
| **Goals Conceded (GC)** The number of League goals conceded while he was on the pitch | 5 | **Clean Sheets** In games when he played at least 70 minutes | 8 |
| **Defensive Rating** Ave number of mins between League goals conceded while on the pitch | 196 | **Club Defensive Rating** Average number of mins between League goals conceded by the club this season | 110 |

| | PLAYER | CON LGE | CLEAN SHEETS | DEF RATE |
|---|---|---|---|---|
| 2 | Phillipe Raschke | 11 | 7 | 135 mins |
| 3 | Omar Daf | 8 | 3 | 123 mins |
| 4 | Maxence Flachez | 27 | 17 | 120 mins |
| 5 | Sylvain Monsoreau | 29 | 17 | 109 mins |

## GOALS SCORED

**AT HOME**

| | | |
|---|---|---|
| MOST | Lyon | 40 |
| | | 28 |
| LEAST | AC Ajaccio | 14 |

**AWAY**

| | | |
|---|---|---|
| MOST | Monaco | 29 |
| | | 18 |
| LEAST | Troyes | 7 |

## GOALS CONCEDED

**AT HOME**

| | | |
|---|---|---|
| LEAST | Sochaux & Auxerre | 8 |
| | | 8 |
| MOST | Strasbourg | 23 |

**AWAY**

| | | |
|---|---|---|
| LEAST | Lens | 15 |
| | | 23 |
| MOST | Sedan | 39 |

## KEY GOALKEEPER

**1 Teddy Richert**

| | |
|---|---|
| Goals Conceded in the League | 28 |
| **Defensive Rating** Ave number of mins between League goals conceded while on the pitch | 109 |
| **Counting Games** Games when he played at least 70 minutes | 34 |
| **Clean Sheets** In games when he played at least 70 minutes | 16 |

## TOP POINT EARNERS

| | PLAYER | GAMES | AVE |
|---|---|---|---|
| 1 | Oruma | 15 | 2.40 |
| 2 | Frau | 17 | 2.00 |
| 3 | Mathieu | 12 | 1.92 |
| 4 | Lonfat | 20 | 1.70 |
| 5 | Monsoreau | 35 | 1.69 |
| 6 | Flachez | 36 | 1.67 |
| 7 | Santos | 21 | 1.62 |
| 8 | Isabey | 13 | 1.62 |
| 9 | Pedretti | 35 | 1.60 |
| 10 | Richert | 34 | 1.59 |
| | **CLUB AVERAGE:** | | **1.68** |

Ave = Average points per match in Counting Games

## ATTENDANCES

HOME GROUND: AUGUSTE-BONAL CAPACITY: 20000 AVERAGE LEAGUE AT HOME: 14763

| | | | | | | | | |
|---|---|---|---|---|---|---|---|---|
| 18 | Marseille | 55000 | 12 | Lille | 19000 | **17** | **Troyes** | **11000** |
| 1 | Sedan | 45000 | **5** | **Lyon** | **18000** | 25 | Nice | 11000 |
| 14 | Paris SG | 40000 | **11** | **Bordeaux** | **18000** | **29** | **Lille** | **10000** |
| 2 | Lens | 35000 | 33 | Montpellier | 15000 | **19** | **Bastia** | **10000** |
| 28 | Bordeaux | 26000 | 6 | Rennes | 15000 | 24 | Auxerre | 10000 |
| 26 | Nantes | 25000 | **13** | **Strasbourg** | **15000** | 10 | Le Havre | 9000 |
| **9** | **Nice** | **20000** | **34** | **Guingamp** | **15000** | 35 | Troyes | 8000 |
| 22 | Lyon | 20000 | **15** | **Montpellier** | **15000** | **30** | **AC Ajaccio** | **5500** |
| **27** | **Le Havre** | **20000** | **3** | **Nantes** | **15000** | 8 | AC Ajaccio | 5000 |
| **7** | **Auxerre** | **20000** | 31 | Strasbourg | 13500 | **23** | **Rennes** | **5000** |
| **36** | **Marseille** | **19910** | **20** | **Lens** | **12686** | 37 | Bastia | 4500 |
| **32** | **Paris SG** | **19682** | **21** | **Monaco** | **11655** | 4 | Monaco | 3000 |
| **38** | **Sedan** | **19078** | 16 | Guingamp | 11000 | | | |

■ Home □ Away ▨ Neutral

## DISCIPLINARY RECORDS

| | PLAYER | YELLOW | RED | AVE |
|---|---|---|---|---|
| 1 | Trapasso | 4 | 0 | 131 |
| 2 | Mathieu | 6 | 0 | 231 |
| 3 | Tall | 4 | 1 | 238 |
| 4 | Chedli | 2 | 0 | 241 |
| 5 | Domoraud | 4 | 0 | 245 |
| 6 | Pagis | 11 | 0 | 249 |
| 7 | Saveljic | 10 | 0 | 297 |
| 8 | Daf | 3 | 0 | 327 |
| 9 | Pedretti | 8 | 0 | 392 |
| 10 | Boudarene | 3 | 0 | 591 |
| 11 | Raschke | 2 | 0 | 741 |
| 12 | Monsoreau | 4 | 0 | 791 |
| 13 | Isabey | 2 | 0 | 910 |
| | Other | 8 | 0 | |
| | **TOTAL** | **71** | **1** | |

## LEAGUE GOALS

| | PLAYER | MINS | GOALS | AVE |
|---|---|---|---|---|
| 1 | Santos | 2203 | 9 | 245 |
| 2 | Frau | 1887 | 9 | 210 |
| 3 | Pagis | 2746 | 7 | 392 |
| 4 | Mathieu | 1391 | 4 | 348 |
| 5 | Oruma | 1576 | 3 | 525 |
| 6 | Pedretti | 3142 | 3 | 1047 |
| 7 | Saveljic | 2970 | 3 | 990 |
| 8 | Monsoreau | 3167 | 2 | 1584 |
| 9 | Isabey | 1821 | 1 | 1821 |
| 10 | Flachez | 3238 | 1 | 3238 |
| 11 | Boudarene | 1774 | 1 | 1774 |
| 12 | Raschke | 1483 | 1 | 1483 |
| | Other | | 2 | |
| | **TOTAL** | | **46** | |

## MONTH BY MONTH GUIDE TO THE POINTS

| MONTH | POINTS | % |
|---|---|---|
| AUGUST | 5 | 42% |
| SEPTEMBER | 8 | 67% |
| OCTOBER | 3 | 33% |
| NOVEMBER | 8 | 53% |
| DECEMBER | 6 | 67% |
| JANUARY | 4 | 44% |
| FEBRUARY | 7 | 58% |
| MARCH | 5 | 42% |
| APRIL | 5 | 56% |
| MAY | 10 | 83% |

## TEAM OF THE SEASON

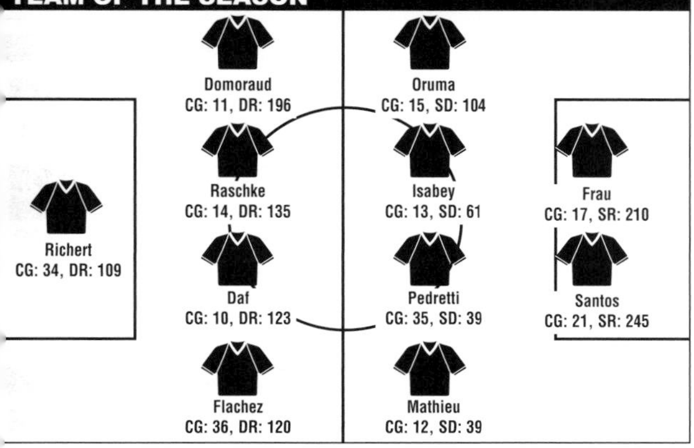
Domoraud
CG: 11, DR: 196
Oruma
CG: 15, SD: 104
Raschke
CG: 14, DR: 135
Isabey
CG: 13, SD: 61
Frau
CG: 17, SR: 210
Richert
CG: 34, DR: 109
Daf
CG: 10, DR: 123
Pedretti
CG: 35, SD: 39
Santos
CG: 21, SR: 245
Flachez
CG: 36, DR: 120
Mathieu
CG: 12, SD: 39

**KEY:** DR = Defensive Rate, SD = Scoring Difference, SR = Strike Rate, CG = Counting Games – League games playing at least 70 minutes

## LEAGUE APPEARANCES, BOOKINGS AND CAPS

| | AGE | IN THE SQUAD | COUNTING GAMES | MINUTES ON PITCH | YELLOW CARDS | RED CARDS | THIS SEASON | HOME COUNTRY |
|---|---|---|---|---|---|---|---|---|
| **Goalkeepers** | | | | | | | | |
| Jean-Baptiste Daguet | 23 | 3 | 0 | 0 | 0 | 0 | - | France |
| Gerard Gnanhouan | 24 | 36 | 4 | 360 | 0 | 0 | - | Ivory Coast |
| Alexandre Martinovic | 28 | 1 | 0 | 0 | 0 | 0 | - | France |
| Teddy Richert | 28 | 34 | 34 | 3060 | 1 | 0 | - | France |
| **Defenders** | | | | | | | | |
| Laurent Charvet | 30 | 3 | 1 | 124 | 0 | 0 | - | France |
| Omar Daf | 26 | 12 | 10 | 983 | 3 | 0 | - | Senegal |
| Jean-J Domoraud | 22 | 17 | 11 | 982 | 4 | 0 | - | Ivory Coast |
| Maxence Flachez | 30 | 36 | 36 | 3238 | 3 | 0 | - | France |
| Johan Lonfat | 29 | 33 | 20 | 1919 | 1 | 0 | - | Switzerland |
| Sylvain Monsoreau | 22 | 36 | 35 | 3167 | 4 | 0 | - | France |
| William Quevedo | 32 | 3 | 0 | 0 | 0 | 0 | - | France |
| Phillipe Raschke | 35 | 23 | 14 | 1483 | 2 | 0 | - | France |
| Nisa Saveljic | 33 | 33 | 33 | 2970 | 10 | 0 | - | Serbia & Montenegro |
| **Midfielders** | | | | | | | | |
| Fabien Boudarene | 24 | 32 | 17 | 1774 | 3 | 0 | - | France |
| Boumelaha | 19 | 3 | 1 | 94 | 0 | 0 | - | France |
| Adel Chedli | 26 | 16 | 5 | 482 | 2 | 0 | - | France |
| Mickael Isabey | 28 | 33 | 13 | 1821 | 2 | 0 | - | France |
| Jeremy Mathieu | 19 | 24 | 12 | 1391 | 6 | 0 | - | France |
| Guirane N'Daw | | 1 | 0 | 2 | 0 | 0 | - | |
| Wilson Oruma | 26 | 30 | 15 | 1576 | 1 | 0 | - | Nigeria |
| Benoit Pedretti | 22 | 36 | 35 | 3142 | 8 | 0 | 5 | France (2) |
| Ibrahim Tall | 27 | 28 | 11 | 1190 | 4 | 1 | 1 | Senegal (29) |
| Kamal Tassali | 22 | 1 | 0 | 8 | 0 | 0 | - | France |
| **Forwards** | | | | | | | | |
| Stephane Crucet | 32 | 2 | 0 | 64 | 0 | 0 | - | France |
| Basile De Carvalho | 22 | 3 | 0 | 34 | 0 | 0 | - | Senegal |
| Pierre-Alain Frau | 23 | 26 | 17 | 1887 | 1 | 0 | - | France |
| Michael Pagis | 29 | 34 | 28 | 2746 | 11 | 0 | - | France |
| Francileudo Santos | 24 | 34 | 21 | 2203 | 1 | 0 | - | Brazil |
| Marcelo Trapasso | 27 | 14 | 5 | 527 | 4 | 0 | - | Argentina |
| Jaouad Zairi | 21 | 17 | 0 | 385 | 0 | 0 | - | Morocco |

KEY: LEAGUE BOOKINGS CAPS (FIFA RANKING)

## SQUAD APPEARANCES

| **Match** | 1 | 2 | 3 | 4 | 5 | 6 | 7 | 8 | 9 | 10 | 11 | 12 | 13 | 14 | 15 | 16 | 17 | 18 | 19 | 20 | 21 | 22 | 23 | 24 | 25 | 26 | 27 | 28 | 29 | 30 | 31 | 32 | 33 | 34 | 35 | 36 | 37 | 38 |
|---|---|---|---|---|---|---|---|---|---|---|---|---|---|---|---|---|---|---|---|---|---|---|---|---|---|---|---|---|---|---|---|---|---|---|---|---|---|---|
| **Venue** | A | A | H | A | H | A | H | A | H | A | H | A | H | A | H | A | H | A | H | H | H | A | H | A | A | A | H | A | H | H | A | H | A | H | A | H | A | H |
| **Competition** | L | L | L | L | L | L | L | L | L | L | L | L | L | L | L | L | L | L | L | L | L | L | L | L | L | L | L | L | L | L | L | L | L | L | L | L | L | L |
| **Result** | D | D | W | L | D | D | D | W | W | L | W | L | W | D | D | L | W | L | W | W | D | L | W | L | D | W | W | L | D | D | W | D | W | D | W | W | D | W |

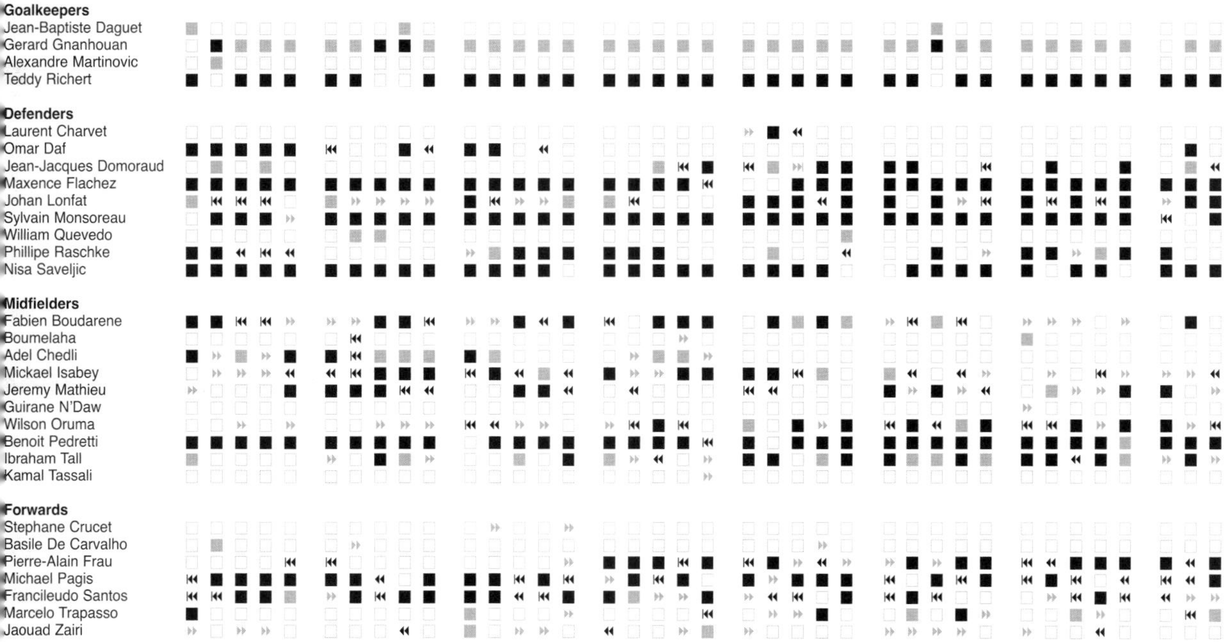
Goalkeepers
Jean-Baptiste Daguet
Gerard Gnanhouan
Alexandre Martinovic
Teddy Richert
Defenders
Laurent Charvet
Omar Daf
Jean-Jacques Domoraud
Maxence Flachez
Johan Lonfat
Sylvain Monsoreau
William Quevedo
Phillipe Raschke
Nisa Saveljic
Midfielders
Fabien Boudarene
Boumelaha
Adel Chedli
Mickael Isabey
Jeremy Mathieu
Guirane N'Daw
Wilson Oruma
Benoit Pedretti
Ibraham Tall
Kamal Tassali
Forwards
Stephane Crucet
Basile De Carvalho
Pierre-Alain Frau
Michael Pagis
Francileudo Santos
Marcelo Trapasso
Jaouad Zairi

KEY: ■ On all match ■ On bench
⏮ Subbed or sent off (Counting game)
◀◀ Subbed or sent off (playing less than 70 minutes)
⏭ Subbed on from bench (Counting Game)
▶▶ Subbed on (playing less than 70 minutes)
Subbed on and then subbed or sent off (Counting Game)
Subbed on and then subbed or sent off (playing less than 70 minutes)
□ Not in 16

# AUXERRE

Final Position: **6th**

| | | | | | | |
|---|---|---|---|---|---|---|
| 1 | lge | Paris SG | A | L | 0-1 | |
| 2 | lge | Montpellier | H | W | 2-0 | Cisse 72; Mwaruwari 89 |
| 3 | ecql1 | Boavista | A | W | 1-0 | Cisse 71 |
| 4 | lge | Troyes | A | W | 2-1 | Boumsong 62; Cisse 83 |
| 5 | lge | Guingamp | H | W | 2-1 | Kapo Obou 33; Cisse 73 |
| 6 | ecql2 | Boavista | H | D | 0-0 | |
| 7 | lge | Marseille | A | D | 0-0 | |
| 8 | lge | Bastia | H | W | 1-0 | Mwaruwari 78 |
| 9 | lge | Sochaux | A | D | 1-1 | Mwaruwari 64 |
| 10 | ecga | PSV Eindhoven | H | D | 0-0 | |
| 11 | ecga | B Dortmund | A | L | 1-2 | Mwaruwari 83 |
| 12 | lge | Nantes | A | W | 4-1 | Mwaruwari 23; Gonzalez 26; Lachuer 32,78 |
| 13 | ecga | Arsenal | H | L | 0-1 | |
| 14 | lge | Monaco | H | D | 1-1 | Mwaruwari 16 |
| 15 | lge | Lyon | A | L | 0-3 | |
| 16 | ecga | Arsenal | A | W | 2-1 | Kapo Obou 7; Fadiga 27 |
| 17 | lge | Rennes | H | W | 1-0 | Kapo Obou 66 |
| 18 | ecga | PSV Eindhoven | A | L | 0-3 | |
| 19 | lge | Lens | A | L | 1-3 | Faye 5 |
| 20 | lge | AC Ajaccio | A | L | 0-1 | |
| 21 | ecga | B Dortmund | H | W | 1-0 | Mwaruwari 75 |
| 22 | lge | Nice | H | L | 0-2 | |
| 23 | lge | Le Havre | A | W | 1-0 | Tainio 60 |
| 24 | uc3rl1 | Real Betis | A | L | 0-1 | |
| 25 | lge | Bordeaux | H | W | 1-0 | Cisse 35 |
| 26 | lge | Lille | A | D | 2-2 | Cisse 26,72 |
| 27 | uc3rl2 | Real Betis | H | W | 2-0 | Tainio 19; Lachuer 47 pen |
| 28 | lge | Strasbourg | H | D | 0-0 | |
| 29 | lge | Troyes | H | W | 1-0 | Faye 4 |
| 30 | lge | Guingamp | A | W | 2-0 | Cisse 7,90 |
| 31 | lge | Montpellier | A | D | 0-0 | |
| 32 | lge | Marseille | H | D | 0-0 | |
| 33 | lge | Bastia | A | L | 0-2 | |
| 34 | lge | Sochaux | H | W | 2-0 | Cisse 34; Mexes 54 |
| 35 | lge | Sedan | A | W | 2-1 | Cisse 62; Lachuer 87 |
| 36 | lge | Nantes | H | L | 0-1 | |
| 37 | uc4rl1 | Liverpool | H | L | 0-1 | |
| 38 | lge | Monaco | A | L | 1-3 | Cisse 55 |
| 39 | uc4rl2 | Liverpool | A | L | 0-2 | |
| 40 | lge | Lyon | H | L | 1-2 | Cisse 90 |
| 41 | lge | Rennes | A | D | 0-0 | |
| 42 | lge | Lens | H | D | 0-0 | |
| 43 | lge | AC Ajaccio | H | W | 1-0 | Fadiga 84 |
| 44 | lge | Sedan | H | W | 3-1 | Mwaruwari 32,84; Cisse 90 |
| 45 | lge | Nice | A | L | 0-1 | |
| 46 | lge | Le Havre | H | W | 1-0 | Kapo Obou 14 |
| 47 | lge | Bordeaux | A | W | 1-0 | Cisse 75 |
| 48 | lge | Lille | H | D | 0-0 | |
| 49 | lge | Strasbourg | A | W | 2-1 | Lachuer 45; Kapo Obou 69 |
| 50 | lge | Paris SG | H | W | 2-0 | Kapo Obou 8,27 |

## ATTENDANCES

HOME GROUND: ABBE DESCHAMPS CAPACITY: 23550 AVERAGE LEAGUE AT HOME: 12396

| | | | | | | | | |
|---|---|---|---|---|---|---|---|---|
| 7 | Marseille | 50000 | 14 | Monaco | 20000 | 44 | Sedan | 11000 |
| 11 | B Dortmund | 48000 | 6 | Boavista | 18000 | 31 | Montpellier | 10500 |
| 1 | Paris SG | 45000 | 22 | Nice | 17000 | 2 | Montpellier | 10000 |
| 19 | Lens | 39700 | 25 | Bordeaux | 15000 | 42 | Lens | 10000 |
| 24 | Real Betis | 37800 | 45 | Nice | 15000 | 46 | Le Havre | 10000 |
| 16 | Arsenal | 35206 | 27 | Real Betis | 15000 | 34 | Sochaux | 10000 |
| 15 | Lyon | 35000 | 36 | Nantes | 15000 | 17 | Rennes | 10000 |
| 39 | Liverpool | 34252 | 8 | Bastia | 15000 | 35 | Sedan | 10000 |
| 12 | Nantes | 30000 | 5 | Guingamp | 15000 | 50 | Paris SG | 10000 |
| 47 | Bordeaux | 30000 | 49 | Strasbourg | 14932 | 23 | Le Havre | 10000 |
| 18 | PSV Eindhoven | 27500 | 3 | Boavista | 14500 | 43 | AC Ajaccio | 9000 |
| 10 | PSV Eindhoven | 23550 | 41 | Rennes | 14000 | 20 | AC Ajaccio | 8500 |
| 13 | Arsenal | 23000 | 26 | Lille | 13000 | 28 | Strasbourg | 8000 |
| 37 | Liverpool | 20452 | 40 | Lyon | 12000 | 29 | Troyes | 7000 |
| 32 | Marseille | 20000 | 48 | Lille | 11537 | 33 | Bastia | 6000 |
| 21 | B Dortmund | 20000 | 30 | Guingamp | 11195 | 38 | Monaco | 5502 |
| 9 | Sochaux | 20000 | 4 | Troyes | 11000 | | | |

■ Home □ Away ▨ Neutral

## KEY PLAYERS - GOALSCORERS

**1 Djibril Cisse**

| | | | |
|---|---|---|---|
| Goals in the League | 14 | Player Strike Rate: Average number of minutes between League goals scored by player | 190 |
| Contribution to Attacking Power: Average number of minutes between League team goals while on pitch | 102 | Club Strike Rate: Average number of minutes between League goals scored by club | 90 |

| | PLAYER | LGE GOALS | POWER | STRIKE RATE |
|---|---|---|---|---|
| 2 | Narcisse Kapo Obou | 6 | 84 | 280 mins |
| 3 | Yann Lachuer | 4 | 89 | 849 mins |
| 4 | Amdy Faye | 2 | 84 | 1438 mins |
| 5 | Teemu Tainio | 1 | 107 | 2142 mins |

## KEY PLAYERS - MIDFIELDERS

**1 Teemu Tainio**

| | | | |
|---|---|---|---|
| Goals in the League | 1 | Contribution to Attacking Power: Average number of minutes between League team goals while on pitch | 107 |
| Defensive Rating: Average number of mins between League goals conceded while he was on the pitch | 153 | Scoring Difference: Defensive Rating minus Contribution to Attacking Power | 46 |

| | PLAYER | LGE GOALS | DEF RATE | POWER | SCORE DIFF |
|---|---|---|---|---|---|
| 2 | Yann Lachuer | 4 | 126 | 89 | 37 mins |
| 3 | Lionel Mathis | 0 | 105 | 85 | 20 mins |

## KEY PLAYERS - DEFENDERS

**1 Perrier Ndoumbe**

| | | | |
|---|---|---|---|
| Goals Conceded (GC): The number of League goals conceded while he was on the pitch | 11 | Clean Sheets: In games when he played at least 70 minutes | 10 |
| Defensive Rating: Ave number of mins between League goals conceded while on the pitch | 146 | Club Defensive Rating: Average number of mins between League goals conceded by the club this season | 118 |

| | PLAYER | CON LGE | CLEAN SHEETS | DEF RATE |
|---|---|---|---|---|
| 2 | Johan Radet | 23 | 17 | 122 mins |
| 3 | Amdy Faye | 26 | 15 | 111 mins |
| 4 | Jean-Alain Boumsong | 27 | 15 | 107 mins |
| 5 | Philippe Mexes | 29 | 15 | 104 mins |

## KEY GOALKEEPER

**1 Fabien Cool**

| | |
|---|---|
| Goals Conceded in the League | 29 |
| Defensive Rating: Ave number of mins between League goals conceded while on the pitch | 118 |
| Counting Games: Games when he played at least 70 minutes | 38 |
| Clean Sheets: In games when he played at least 70 minutes | 19 |

## TOP POINT EARNERS

| | PLAYER | GAMES | AVE |
|---|---|---|---|
| 1 | Kapo Obou | 18 | 2.00 |
| 2 | Ndoumbe | 18 | 1.89 |
| 3 | Fadiga | 29 | 1.86 |
| 4 | Mexes | 33 | 1.76 |
| 5 | Faye | 32 | 1.75 |
| 6 | Lachuer | 37 | 1.73 |
| 7 | Radet | 31 | 1.71 |
| 8 | Cool | 38 | 1.68 |
| 9 | Mathis | 25 | 1.68 |
| 10 | Cisse | 28 | 1.68 |
| | CLUB AVERAGE: | | 1.68 |

Ave = Average points per match in Counting Games

## DISCIPLINARY RECORDS

| | PLAYER | YELLOW | RED | AVE |
|---|---|---|---|---|
| 1 | Mathis | 9 | 1 | 230 |
| 2 | Jaures | 5 | 1 | 337 |
| 3 | Fadiga | 8 | 0 | 348 |
| 4 | Mexes | 7 | 1 | 378 |
| 5 | Faye | 7 | 0 | 410 |
| 6 | Kapo Obou | 3 | 0 | 560 |
| 7 | Radet | 4 | 0 | 701 |
| 8 | Tainio | 3 | 0 | 714 |
| 9 | Boumsong | 3 | 1 | 719 |
| 10 | Ndoumbe | 2 | 0 | 801 |
| 11 | Grichting | 1 | 0 | 813 |
| 12 | Mwaruwari | 1 | 0 | 1194 |
| 13 | Cisse | 2 | 0 | 1331 |
| | Other | 4 | 0 | |
| | TOTAL | 59 | 4 | |

## LEAGUE GOALS

| | PLAYER | MINS | GOALS | AVE |
|---|---|---|---|---|
| 1 | Cisse | 2662 | 14 | 190 |
| 2 | Mwaruwari | 1194 | 6 | 199 |
| 3 | Kapo Obou | 1680 | 6 | 280 |
| 4 | Lachuer | 3394 | 4 | 849 |
| 5 | Faye | 2875 | 2 | 1438 |
| 6 | Mexes | 3028 | 1 | 3028 |
| 7 | Tainio | 2142 | 1 | 2142 |
| 8 | Fadiga | 2790 | 1 | 2790 |
| 9 | Boumsong | 2877 | 1 | 2877 |
| 10 | Gonzalez | 781 | 1 | 781 |
| | Other | | 1 | |
| | TOTAL | | 38 | |

## MONTH BY MONTH GUIDE TO THE POINTS

| MONTH | POINTS | % |
|---|---|---|
| AUGUST | 9 | 75% |
| SEPTEMBER | 8 | 67% |
| OCTOBER | 4 | 44% |
| NOVEMBER | 3 | 25% |
| DECEMBER | 5 | 56% |
| JANUARY | 8 | 53% |
| FEBRUARY | 6 | 50% |
| MARCH | 2 | 22% |
| APRIL | 9 | 75% |
| MAY | 10 | 83% |

## TEAM OF THE SEASON

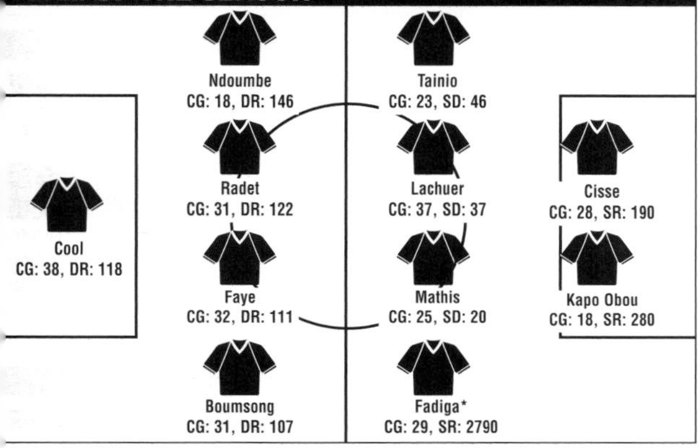
Ndoumbe
CG: 18, DR: 146
Tainio
CG: 23, SD: 46
Radet
CG: 31, DR: 122
Lachuer
CG: 37, SD: 37
Cisse
CG: 28, SR: 190
Cool
CG: 38, DR: 118
Faye
CG: 32, DR: 111
Mathis
CG: 25, SD: 20
Kapo Obou
CG: 18, SR: 280
Boumsong
CG: 31, DR: 107
Fadiga*
CG: 29, SR: 2790

KEY: DR = Defensive Rate, SD = Scoring Difference, SR = Strike Rate, CG = Counting Games – League games playing at least 70 minutes

## LEAGUE APPEARANCES, BOOKINGS AND CAPS

| | AGE | IN THE SQUAD | COUNTING GAMES | MINUTES ON PITCH | YELLOW CARDS | RED CARDS | THIS SEASON | HOME COUNTRY |
|---|---|---|---|---|---|---|---|---|
| **Goalkeepers** | | | | | | | | |
| Fabien Cool | 30 | 38 | 38 | 3420 | 0 | 0 | - | France |
| Sebastien Hamel | 27 | 26 | 0 | 0 | 0 | 0 | - | France |
| Baptiste Chabert | 20 | 12 | 0 | 0 | 0 | 0 | - | France |
| **Defenders** | | | | | | | | |
| Joseph Assati | 28 | 6 | 2 | 226 | 0 | 0 | - | France |
| Jean-Alain Boumsong | 23 | 33 | 31 | 2877 | 3 | 1 | - | France |
| Amdy Faye | 26 | 36 | 32 | 2875 | 7 | 0 | 2 | Senegal (29) |
| Stephane Grichting | 24 | 26 | 8 | 813 | 1 | 0 | - | Switzerland |
| Jean-Sebastien Jaures | 25 | 24 | 22 | 2025 | 5 | 1 | - | France |
| Frederic Jay | 26 | 5 | 1 | 112 | 0 | 0 | - | France |
| Philippe Mexes | 21 | 34 | 33 | 3028 | 7 | 1 | 6 | France (2) |
| Jean Pascal Mignot | 22 | 11 | 2 | 214 | 0 | 0 | - | France |
| Perrier Ndoumbe | 24 | 28 | 18 | 1603 | 2 | 0 | 2 | Cameroon (18) |
| Johan Radet | 26 | 32 | 31 | 2807 | 4 | 0 | - | France |
| **Midfielders** | | | | | | | | |
| Kuami Agboh | 25 | 3 | 2 | 180 | 0 | 0 | - | Togo |
| Kanga Akale | 22 | 13 | 2 | 203 | 0 | 0 | - | Ivory Coast |
| Ferdinand Benjani | 19 | 1 | 0 | 12 | 0 | 0 | - | Cameroon |
| Pierre Deblock | 30 | 10 | 1 | 125 | 1 | 0 | - | France |
| Pedro Kamata | 22 | 1 | 0 | 0 | 0 | 0 | - | France |
| Yann Lachuer | 31 | 38 | 37 | 3394 | 2 | 0 | - | France |
| Lionel Mathis | 21 | 33 | 25 | 2301 | 9 | 1 | - | France |
| Francois Sirieix | 22 | 19 | 0 | 77 | 1 | 0 | - | France |
| Teemu Tainio | 23 | 25 | 23 | 2142 | 3 | 0 | - | Finland |
| **Forwards** | | | | | | | | |
| Djibril Cisse | 21 | 33 | 28 | 2662 | 2 | 0 | 6 | France (2) |
| Khalilou Fadiga | 28 | 34 | 29 | 2790 | 8 | 0 | 3 | Senegal (29) |
| Arnaud Gonzalez | 25 | 24 | 7 | 781 | 0 | 0 | - | France |
| Narcisse Kapo Obou | 22 | 21 | 18 | 1680 | 3 | 0 | 3 | France (2) |
| Nicolas Marin | 22 | 5 | 0 | 6 | 0 | 0 | - | France |
| Benjamin Mwaruwari | 24 | 35 | 9 | 1194 | 1 | 0 | - | Zimbabwe |
| David Vandenbossche | 22 | 4 | 0 | 28 | 0 | 0 | - | France |

KEY: LEAGUE BOOKINGS CAPS (FIFA RANKING)

## SQUAD APPEARANCES

| Match | Venue | Competition | Result |
|---|---|---|---|
| 1 | A | L | L |
| 2 | H | L | W |
| 3 | A | C | W |
| 4 | A | L | W |
| 5 | H | L | W |
| 6 | A | L | D |
| 7 | H | L | W |
| 8 | A | L | D |
| 9 | H | C | D |
| 10 | H | L | W |
| 11 | A | C | L |
| 12 | A | L | W |
| 13 | H | C | L |
| 14 | H | L | D |
| 15 | A | L | L |
| 16 | A | C | W |
| 17 | H | L | W |
| 18 | A | C | L |
| 19 | A | L | L |
| 20 | A | L | L |
| 21 | H | C | W |
| 22 | H | L | L |
| 23 | A | L | W |
| 24 | A | E | L |
| 25 | H | L | W |
| 26 | A | L | D |
| 27 | H | E | W |
| 28 | H | L | D |
| 29 | H | L | W |
| 30 | A | L | W |
| 31 | A | L | D |
| 32 | H | L | D |
| 33 | A | L | L |
| 34 | H | L | W |
| 35 | A | L | W |
| 36 | H | L | L |
| 37 | H | E | L |
| 38 | A | L | L |
| 39 | A | E | L |
| 40 | H | L | L |
| 41 | A | L | D |
| 42 | H | L | D |
| 43 | H | L | W |
| 44 | H | L | W |
| 45 | A | L | L |
| 46 | H | L | W |
| 47 | A | L | W |
| 48 | H | L | D |
| 49 | A | L | W |
| 50 | H | L | W |

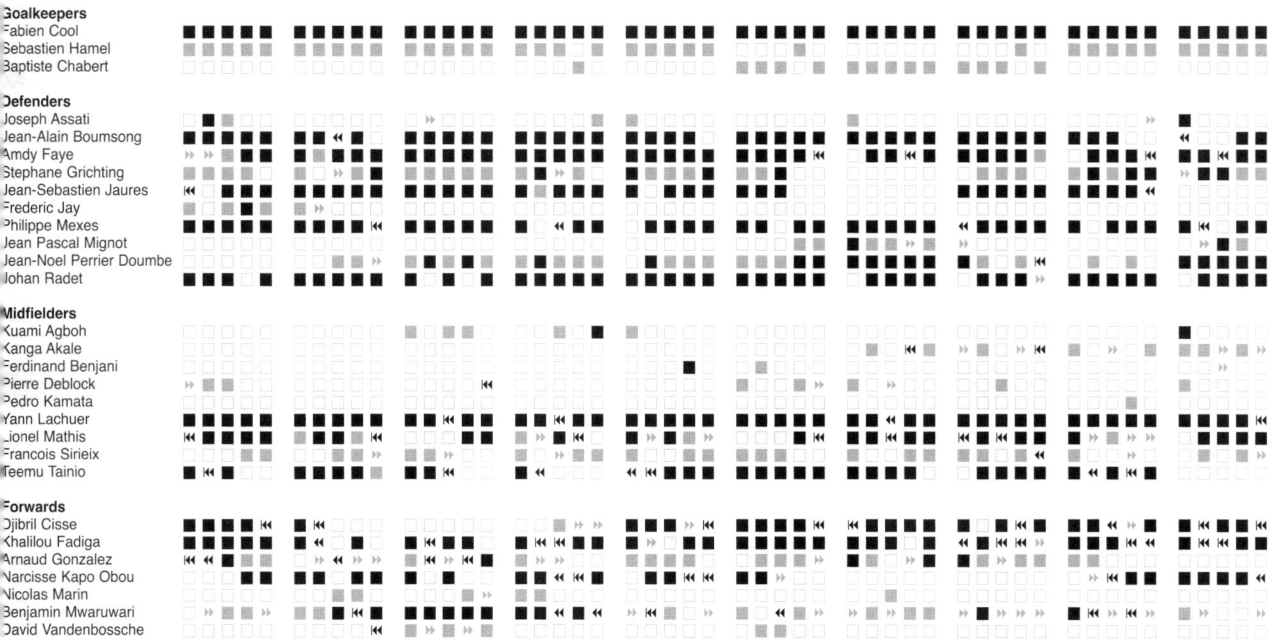
Goalkeepers
Fabien Cool
Sebastien Hamel
Baptiste Chabert
Defenders
Joseph Assati
Jean-Alain Boumsong
Amdy Faye
Stephane Grichting
Jean-Sebastien Jaures
Frederic Jay
Philippe Mexes
Jean Pascal Mignot
Jean-Noel Perrier Doumbe
Johan Radet
Midfielders
Kuami Agboh
Kanga Akale
Ferdinand Benjani
Pierre Deblock
Pedro Kamata
Yann Lachuer
Lionel Mathis
Francois Sirieix
Teemu Tainio
Forwards
Djibril Cisse
Khalilou Fadiga
Arnaud Gonzalez
Narcisse Kapo Obou
Nicolas Marin
Benjamin Mwaruwari
David Vandenbossche

KEY: On all match; On bench; Subbed or sent off (Counting game); Subbed or sent off (playing less than 70 minutes); Subbed on from bench (Counting Game); Subbed on (playing less than 70 minutes); Subbed on and then subbed or sent off (Counting Game); Subbed on and then subbed or sent off (playing less than 70 minutes); Not in 16

# GUINGAMP

Final Position: **7th**

| | | | | | | |
|---|---|---|---|---|---|---|
| 1 | lge | Lyon | H | D | 3-3 | Carnot 22; Bardon 88; Drogba 90 |
| 2 | lge | AC Ajaccio | A | W | 2-0 | Drogba 1; Bardon 69 pen |
| 3 | lge | Rennes | H | W | 3-0 | Malouda 33,86; Le Roux 66 |
| 4 | lge | Auxerre | A | L | 1-2 | Carnot 54 |
| 5 | lge | Bordeaux | H | D | 0-0 | |
| 6 | lge | Le Havre | A | W | 2-1 | Malouda 45; Eloi 70 |
| 7 | lge | Nice | H | D | 0-0 | |
| 8 | lge | Lille | A | L | 1-2 | Eloi 71 |
| 9 | lge | Strasbourg | H | L | 2-3 | Eloi 69; Carnot 90 |
| 10 | lge | Paris SG | A | L | 0-5 | |
| 11 | lge | Montpellier | H | W | 3-1 | Moullec 39 og; Le Roux 59; Eloi 68 |
| 12 | lge | Sedan | H | L | 0-1 | |
| 13 | lge | Troyes | A | W | 2-0 | Drogba 29; Eloi 58 |
| 14 | lge | Marseille | H | D | 0-0 | |
| 15 | lge | Bastia | A | W | 2-0 | Malouda 18; Drogba 46 |
| 16 | lge | Sochaux | H | W | 2-0 | Drogba 48; Flachez 67 og |
| 17 | lge | Lens | A | W | 3-1 | Saci 30; Malouda 53; Le Roux 90 pen |
| 18 | lge | Nantes | H | W | 2-0 | Drogba 66; Saci 90 |
| 19 | lge | Monaco | A | L | 0-4 | |
| 20 | lge | AC Ajaccio | H | W | 3-1 | Bardon 31 pen; Drogba 33,35 |
| 21 | lge | Rennes | A | L | 1-2 | Carnot 90 |
| 22 | lge | Auxerre | H | L | 0-2 | |
| 23 | lge | Bordeaux | A | L | 2-4 | Carnot 60,69 |
| 24 | lge | Le Havre | H | L | 1-2 | Fabbri 60 |
| 25 | lge | Nice | A | L | 0-1 | |
| 26 | lge | Strasbourg | A | L | 1-3 | Carnot 68 |
| 27 | lge | Paris SG | H | W | 3-2 | Guillaume 60; Drogba 67,89 |
| 28 | lge | Montpellier | A | L | 0-2 | |
| 29 | lge | Sedan | A | L | 0-2 | |
| 30 | lge | Lille | H | W | 1-0 | Bardon 31 |
| 31 | lge | Troyes | H | W | 2-0 | Drogba 66; Malouda 90 |
| 32 | lge | Marseille | A | W | 2-0 | Bah 11; Drogba 15 |
| 33 | lge | Bastia | H | W | 3-0 | Drogba 7,51; Le Roux 39 |
| 34 | lge | Sochaux | A | D | 0-0 | |
| 35 | lge | Lens | H | W | 1-0 | Malouda 16 |
| 36 | lge | Nantes | A | W | 4-0 | Le Roux 21 pen,37; Carnot 47; Drogba 53 pen |
| 37 | lge | Monaco | H | W | 3-1 | Carnot 23,51; Malouda 89 |
| 38 | lge | Lyon | A | W | 4-1 | Drogba 18,67; Malouda 19,46 |

## KEY PLAYERS - GOALSCORERS

**1 Didier Drogba**

| | | | |
|---|---|---|---|
| Goals in the League | 17 | Player Strike Rate<br>Average number of minutes between League goals scored by player | 138 |
| Contribution to Attacking Power<br>Average number of minutes between League team goals while on pitch | 54 | Club Strike Rate<br>Average number of minutes between League goals scored by club | 58 |

| | PLAYER | LGE GOALS | POWER | STRIKE RATE |
|---|---|---|---|---|
| 2 | Stephane Carnot | 9 | 59 | 230 mins |
| 3 | Florent Malouda | 10 | 55 | 320 mins |
| 4 | Christophe Le Roux | 6 | 53 | 491 mins |
| 5 | Hakim Saci | 2 | 63 | 796 mins |

## KEY PLAYERS - MIDFIELDERS

**1 Lionel Bah**

| | | | |
|---|---|---|---|
| Goals in the League | 1 | Contribution to Attacking Power<br>Average number of minutes between League team goals while on pitch | 38 |
| Defensive Rating<br>Average number of mins between League goals conceded while he was on the pitch | 202 | Scoring Difference<br>Defensive Rating minus Contribution to Attacking Power | 164 |

| | PLAYER | LGE GOALS | DEF RATE | POWER | SCORE DIFF |
|---|---|---|---|---|---|
| 2 | Claude Michel | 0 | 74 | 60 | 14 mins |
| 3 | Christophe Le Roux | 6 | 67 | 54 | 13 mins |
| 4 | Stephane Carnot | 9 | 65 | 59 | 6 mins |

## KEY PLAYERS - DEFENDERS

**1 Blaise Kouassi**

| | | | |
|---|---|---|---|
| Goals Conceded (GC)<br>The number of League goals conceded while he was on the pitch | 17 | Clean Sheets<br>In games when he played at least 70 minutes | 11 |
| Defensive Rating<br>Ave number of mins between League goals conceded while on the pitch | 109 | Club Defensive Rating<br>Average number of mins between League goals conceded by the club this season | 74 |

| | PLAYER | CON LGE | CLEAN SHEETS | DEF RATE |
|---|---|---|---|---|
| 2 | Alledine Yahia | 13 | 6 | 98 mins |
| 3 | Jean-Louis Montero | 33 | 15 | 84 mins |
| 4 | Nestor Fabbri | 36 | 16 | 82 mins |
| 5 | Romain Ferrier | 26 | 9 | 81 mins |

## GOALS SCORED

AT HOME

| | | |
|---|---|---|
| MOST | Lyon | 40 |
| | | 32 |
| LEAST | AC Ajaccio | 14 |

AWAY

| | | |
|---|---|---|
| MOST | Monaco | 29 |
| | | 27 |
| LEAST | Troyes | 7 |

## GOALS CONCEDED

AT HOME

| | | |
|---|---|---|
| LEAST | Sochaux & Auxerre | 8 |
| | | 16 |
| MOST | Strasbourg | 23 |

AWAY

| | | |
|---|---|---|
| LEAST | Lens | 15 |
| | | 30 |
| MOST | Sedan | 39 |

## KEY GOALKEEPER

**1 Ronan Le Crom**

| | |
|---|---|
| Goals Conceded in the League | 46 |
| Defensive Rating<br>Ave number of mins between League goals conceded while on the pitch | 74 |
| Counting Games<br>Games when he played at least 70 minutes | 38 |
| Clean Sheets<br>In games when he played at least 70 minutes | 16 |

## TOP POINT EARNERS

| | PLAYER | GAMES | AVE |
|---|---|---|---|
| 1 | Kouassi | 20 | 1.95 |
| 2 | Carnot | 14 | 1.93 |
| 3 | Saci | 13 | 1.85 |
| 4 | Yahia | 13 | 1.77 |
| 5 | Montero | 31 | 1.71 |
| 6 | Ferrier | 21 | 1.71 |
| 7 | Drogba | 23 | 1.70 |
| 8 | Le Roux | 33 | 1.67 |
| 9 | Malouda | 35 | 1.66 |
| 10 | Le Crom | 38 | 1.63 |
| | CLUB AVERAGE: | | 1.63 |

Ave = Average points per match in Counting Games

## ATTENDANCES

HOME GROUND: STADE DE ROUDOUROU CAPACITY: 18016 AVERAGE LEAGUE AT HOME: 14685

| | | | | | | | | |
|---|---|---|---|---|---|---|---|---|
| 32 | Marseille | 55000 | 35 | **Lens** | **15500** | 30 | **Lille** | **12000** |
| 38 | Lyon | 36000 | 5 | **Bordeaux** | **15000** | 22 | **Auxerre** | **11195** |
| 10 | Paris SG | 35000 | 24 | **Le Havre** | **15000** | 26 | Strasbourg | 11000 |
| 36 | Nantes | 34919 | 34 | Sochaux | 15000 | 16 | **Sochaux** | **11000** |
| 17 | Lens | 33500 | 4 | Auxerre | 15000 | 13 | Troyes | 10000 |
| 21 | Rennes | 23525 | 7 | **Nice** | **15000** | 25 | Nice | 10000 |
| 23 | Bordeaux | 20114 | 9 | **Strasbourg** | **15000** | 12 | **Sedan** | **10000** |
| 1 | **Lyon** | **20000** | 11 | **Montpellier** | **15000** | 28 | Montpellier | 10000 |
| 3 | **Rennes** | **18500** | 8 | Lille | 15000 | 27 | **Paris SG** | **9500** |
| 37 | **Monaco** | **18000** | 31 | **Troyes** | **14000** | 15 | Bastia | 5000 |
| 18 | **Nantes** | **18000** | 6 | Le Havre | 14000 | 19 | Monaco | 5000 |
| 14 | **Marseille** | **17000** | 33 | **Bastia** | **13000** | 2 | AC Ajaccio | 1000 |
| 20 | **AC Ajaccio** | **16336** | 29 | Sedan | 13000 | | | |

■ Home □ Away ▒ Neutral

## DISCIPLINARY RECORDS

| | PLAYER | YELLOW | RED | AVE |
|---|---|---|---|---|
| 1 | Kouassi | 5 | 3 | 232 |
| 2 | Sikimic | 4 | 1 | 244 |
| 3 | Fabbri | 10 | 2 | 245 |
| 4 | Michel | 10 | 0 | 311 |
| 5 | Yahia | 4 | 0 | 317 |
| 6 | Guillaume | 5 | 0 | 364 |
| 7 | Saci | 4 | 0 | 398 |
| 8 | Malouda | 7 | 1 | 400 |
| 9 | Le Roux | 6 | 1 | 420 |
| 10 | Bardon | 4 | 0 | 439 |
| 11 | Drogba | 5 | 0 | 469 |
| 12 | Danic | 0 | 1 | 598 |
| 13 | Montero | 3 | 0 | 925 |
| | Other | 7 | 0 | |
| | TOTAL | 74 | 9 | |

## LEAGUE GOALS

| | PLAYER | MINS | GOALS | AVE |
|---|---|---|---|---|
| 1 | Drogba | 2348 | 17 | 138 |
| 2 | Malouda | 3201 | 10 | 320 |
| 3 | Carnot | 2070 | 9 | 230 |
| 4 | Le Roux | 2945 | 6 | 491 |
| 5 | Eloi | 765 | 5 | 153 |
| 6 | Bardon | 1756 | 4 | 439 |
| 7 | Saci | 1592 | 2 | 796 |
| 8 | Fabbri | 2947 | 1 | 2947 |
| 9 | Guillaume | 1824 | 1 | 1824 |
| 10 | Bah | 807 | 1 | 807 |
| | Other | | 3 | |
| | TOTAL | | 59 | |

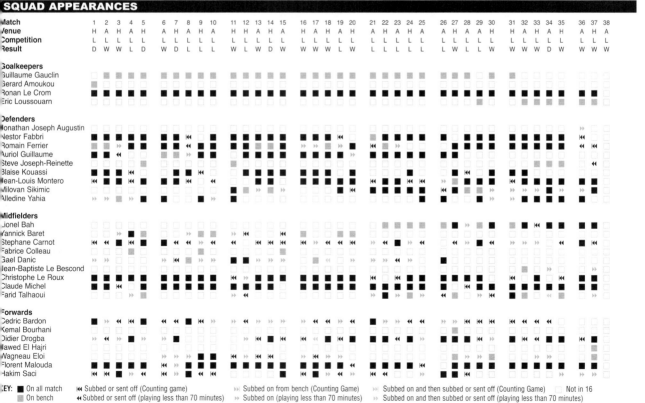

## MONTH BY MONTH GUIDE TO THE POINTS

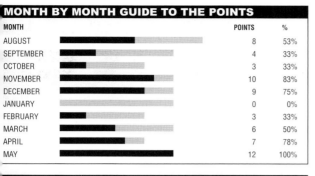

| MONTH | POINTS | % |
|---|---|---|
| AUGUST | 8 | 53% |
| SEPTEMBER | 4 | 33% |
| OCTOBER | 3 | 33% |
| NOVEMBER | 10 | 83% |
| DECEMBER | 9 | 75% |
| JANUARY | 0 | 0% |
| FEBRUARY | 3 | 33% |
| MARCH | 6 | 50% |
| APRIL | 7 | 78% |
| MAY | 12 | 100% |

## TEAM OF THE SEASON

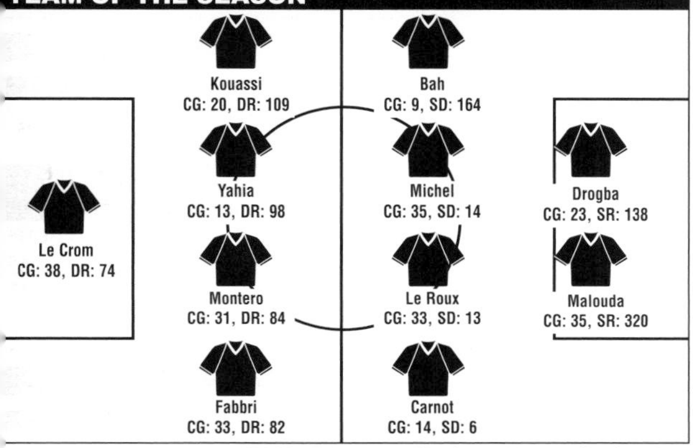
Kouassi
CG: 20, DR: 109
Bah
CG: 9, SD: 164
Yahia
CG: 13, DR: 98
Michel
CG: 35, SD: 14
Drogba
CG: 23, SR: 138
Le Crom
CG: 38, DR: 74
Montero
CG: 31, DR: 84
Le Roux
CG: 33, SD: 13
Malouda
CG: 35, SR: 320
Fabbri
CG: 33, DR: 82
Carnot
CG: 14, SD: 6

KEY: DR = Defensive Rate, SD = Scoring Difference, SR = Strike Rate, CG = Counting Games – League games playing at least 70 minutes

## LEAGUE APPEARANCES, BOOKINGS AND CAPS

| | AGE | IN THE SQUAD | COUNTING GAMES | MINUTES ON PITCH | YELLOW CARDS | RED CARDS | THIS SEASON | HOME COUNTRY |
|---|---|---|---|---|---|---|---|---|
| **Goalkeepers** | | | | | | | | |
| Guillaume Gauclin | 22 | 29 | 0 | 0 | 0 | 0 | - | France |
| Gerard Amoukou | 24 | 1 | 0 | 0 | 0 | 0 | - | |
| Ronan Le Crom | 28 | 38 | 38 | 3420 | 2 | 0 | - | France |
| Eric Loussouarn | 28 | 8 | 0 | 0 | 0 | 0 | - | France |
| **Defenders** | | | | | | | | |
| Jonathan Augustin | 22 | 1 | 0 | 3 | 0 | 0 | - | France |
| Nestor Fabbri | 35 | 34 | 33 | 2947 | 10 | 2 | - | Argentina |
| Romain Ferrier | 27 | 34 | 21 | 2093 | 2 | 0 | - | France |
| Auriol Guillaume | 23 | 24 | 19 | 1824 | 5 | 0 | - | France |
| Steve Joseph-Reinette | 19 | 7 | 0 | 65 | 0 | 0 | - | France |
| Blaise Kouassi | 28 | 21 | 20 | 1859 | 5 | 3 | - | France |
| Jean-Louis Montero | 32 | 34 | 31 | 2777 | 3 | 0 | - | France |
| Milovan Sikimic | 22 | 25 | 13 | 1223 | 4 | 1 | - | Serbia & Montenegro |
| Alledine Yahia | 21 | 20 | 13 | 1269 | 4 | 0 | - | France |
| **Midfielders** | | | | | | | | |
| Lionel Bah | 23 | 17 | 9 | 807 | 0 | 0 | - | France |
| Yannick Baret | 30 | 12 | 3 | 278 | 1 | 0 | - | |
| Stephane Carnot | 30 | 35 | 14 | 2070 | 2 | 0 | - | France |
| Fabrice Colleau | 26 | 3 | 0 | 0 | 0 | 0 | - | |
| Gael Danic | 21 | 20 | 4 | 598 | 0 | 1 | - | France |
| Jean-B Le Bescond | 23 | 4 | 0 | 27 | 0 | 0 | - | France |
| Christophe Le Roux | 34 | 34 | 33 | 2945 | 6 | 1 | - | France |
| Claude Michel | 32 | 35 | 35 | 3119 | 10 | 0 | - | France |
| Farid Talhaoui | 21 | 19 | 3 | 558 | 0 | 0 | - | France |
| **Forwards** | | | | | | | | |
| Cedric Bardon | 26 | 34 | 9 | 1756 | 4 | 0 | - | France |
| Kemal Bourhani | 21 | 1 | 0 | 0 | 0 | 0 | - | France |
| Didier Drogba | 25 | 34 | 23 | 2348 | 5 | 0 | - | Ivory Coast |
| Jawed El Hajri | 23 | 1 | 0 | 0 | 0 | 0 | - | France |
| Wagneau Eloi | 29 | 20 | 6 | 765 | 0 | 0 | - | France |
| Florent Malouda | 23 | 37 | 35 | 3201 | 7 | 1 | - | France |
| Hakim Saci | 26 | 26 | 13 | 1592 | 4 | 0 | - | Algeria |

KEY: LEAGUE BOOKINGS CAPS (FIFA RANKING)

## SQUAD APPEARANCES

| Match | 1 | 2 | 3 | 4 | 5 | 6 | 7 | 8 | 9 | 10 | 11 | 12 | 13 | 14 | 15 | 16 | 17 | 18 | 19 | 20 | 21 | 22 | 23 | 24 | 25 | 26 | 27 | 28 | 29 | 30 | 31 | 32 | 33 | 34 | 35 | 36 | 37 | 38 |
|---|---|---|---|---|---|---|---|---|---|---|---|---|---|---|---|---|---|---|---|---|---|---|---|---|---|---|---|---|---|---|---|---|---|---|---|---|---|---|
| Venue | H | A | H | A | H | A | H | A | H | A | H | H | A | H | A | H | A | H | A | H | A | H | A | H | A | A | H | A | A | H | H | A | H | A | H | A | H | A |
| Competition | L | L | L | L | L | L | L | L | L | L | L | L | L | L | L | L | L | L | L | L | L | L | L | L | L | L | L | L | L | L | L | L | L | L | L | L | L | L |
| Result | D | W | W | L | D | W | D | L | L | L | W | L | W | D | W | W | W | W | L | W | L | L | L | L | L | L | W | L | L | W | W | W | W | D | W | W | W | W |

**Goalkeepers**
Guillaume Gauclin
Gerard Amoukou
Ronan Le Crom
Eric Loussouarn

**Defenders**
Jonathan Joseph Augustin
Nestor Fabbri
Romain Ferrier
Auriol Guillaume
Steve Joseph-Reinette
Blaise Kouassi
Jean-Louis Montero
Milovan Sikimic
Alledine Yahia

**Midfielders**
Lionel Bah
Yannick Baret
Stephane Carnot
Fabrice Colleau
Gael Danic
Jean-Baptiste Le Bescond
Christophe Le Roux
Claude Michel
Farid Talhaoui

**Forwards**
Cedric Bardon
Kemal Bourhani
Didier Drogba
Jawed El Hajri
Wagneau Eloi
Florent Malouda
Hakim Saci

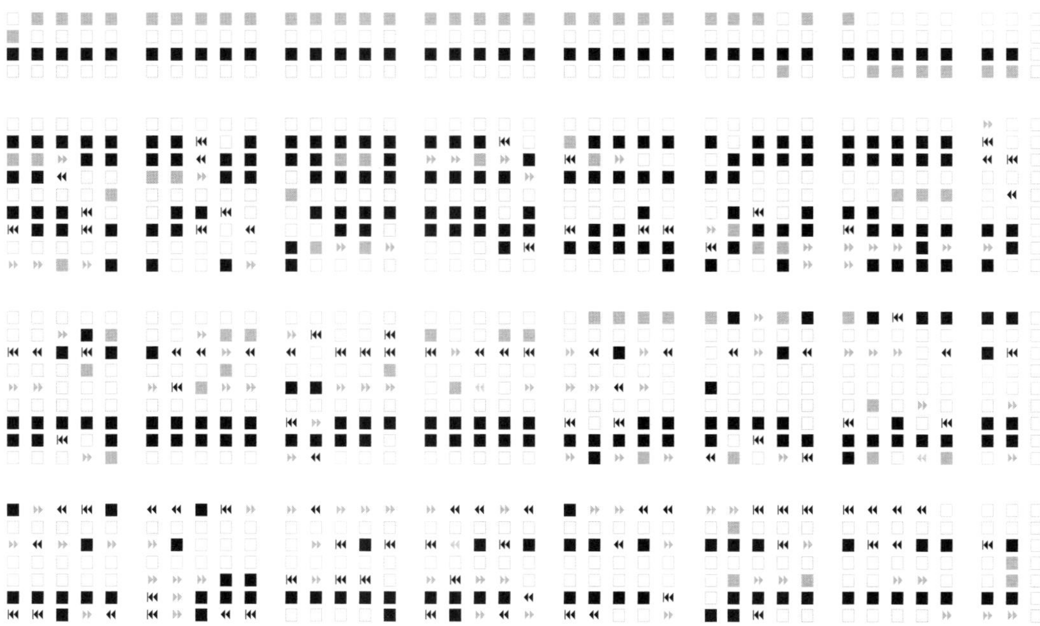

KEY: ■ On all match | ⏮ Subbed or sent off (Counting game) | ⏭ Subbed on from bench (Counting Game) | Subbed on and then subbed or sent off (Counting Game) | Not in 16
On bench | « Subbed or sent off (playing less than 70 minutes) | » Subbed on (playing less than 70 minutes) | Subbed on and then subbed or sent off (playing less than 70 minutes)

# LENS

Final Position: **8th**

| | | | | | | |
|---|---|---|---|---|---|---|
| 1 | lge | Bastia | A | D | 1-1 | Sibierski 75 |
| 2 | lge | Sochaux | H | D | 1-1 | Keita 61 |
| 3 | lge | Sedan | A | W | 1-0 | Song 45 |
| 4 | lge | Nantes | A | D | 2-2 | Utaka 61; Diop 71 |
| 5 | lge | Monaco | H | W | 1-0 | Diop 36 pen |
| 6 | lge | Lyon | A | L | 0-1 | |
| 7 | lge | Rennes | H | W | 1-0 | Utaka 90 |
| 8 | ecgg | AC Milan | A | L | 1-2 | Moreira 75 |
| 9 | lge | Bordeaux | A | L | 0-1 | |
| 10 | ecgg | Bayern Munich | H | D | 1-1 | Utaka 76 |
| 11 | lge | Lille | H | D | 0-0 | |
| 12 | ecgg | Deportivo | A | L | 1-3 | Moreira 10 |
| 13 | lge | Montpellier | A | W | 2-0 | Moreira 40; Utaka 88 |
| 14 | lge | AC Ajaccio | H | D | 1-1 | Sibierski 83 pen |
| 15 | ecgg | Deportivo | H | W | 3-1 | Coulibaly 61; Moreira 79; Thomert 84 |
| 16 | lge | Nice | A | D | 0-0 | |
| 17 | ecgg | AC Milan | H | W | 2-1 | Moreira 41; Utaka 49 |
| 18 | lge | Auxerre | H | W | 3-1 | Song 35; Sibierski 45; Sikora 90 |
| 19 | lge | Strasbourg | A | L | 0-2 | |
| 20 | ecgg | Bayern Munich | A | D | 3-3 | Fink 21 og; Bakari 54; Blanchard 90 |
| 21 | lge | Paris SG | H | W | 3-2 | Sibierski 29; Moreira 60; Utaka 68 |
| 22 | lge | Marseille | A | L | 0-1 | |
| 23 | uc3rl1 | Porto | A | L | 0-3 | |
| 24 | lge | Guingamp | H | L | 1-3 | Sibierski 20 |
| 25 | lge | Troyes | A | D | 0-0 | |
| 26 | uc3rl2 | Porto | H | W | 1-0 | Song 27 |
| 27 | lge | Le Havre | H | W | 1-0 | Utaka 35 |
| 28 | lge | Sochaux | A | L | 0-3 | |
| 29 | lge | Sedan | H | W | 4-0 | Moreira 20; Utaka 38; Keita 42; Sibierski 89 |
| 30 | lge | Monaco | A | D | 1-1 | Coridon 14 |
| 31 | lge | Lyon | H | D | 2-2 | Sibierski 19 pen,44 |
| 32 | lge | Rennes | A | D | 1-1 | Utaka 39 |
| 33 | lge | Bordeaux | H | D | 3-3 | Utaka 2; Moreira 8; Sibierski 31 |
| 34 | lge | Lille | A | W | 2-0 | Song 41; Vairelles 75 |
| 35 | lge | Montpellier | H | W | 4-0 | Sibierski 9; Vairelles 19; Moreira 63,66 |
| 36 | lge | AC Ajaccio | A | D | 0-0 | |
| 37 | lge | Nice | H | D | 0-0 | |
| 38 | lge | Nantes | H | L | 0-1 | |
| 39 | lge | Auxerre | A | D | 0-0 | |
| 40 | lge | Strasbourg | H | D | 1-1 | Moreira 90 |
| 41 | lge | Paris SG | A | W | 1-0 | Moreira 47 |
| 42 | lge | Marseille | H | L | 0-1 | |
| 43 | lge | Guingamp | A | L | 0-1 | |
| 44 | lge | Troyes | H | W | 1-0 | Moreira 81 |
| 45 | lge | Le Havre | A | W | 3-1 | Sibierski 8; Diop 86; Bakari 90 |
| 46 | lge | Bastia | H | W | 2-0 | Sibierski 31; Bakari 74 |

## ATTENDANCES

HOME GROUND: STADE BOLLEART CAPACITY: 41649 AVERAGE LEAGUE AT HOME: 36318

| | | | | | | | | |
|---|---|---|---|---|---|---|---|---|
| 8 | AC Milan | 70259 | 44 | Troyes | 37703 | 16 | Nice | 17500 |
| 23 | Porto | 60000 | 33 | Bordeaux | 36765 | 34 | Lille | 16500 |
| 22 | Marseille | 50000 | 35 | Montpellier | 35000 | 19 | Strasbourg | 16500 |
| 26 | Porto | 44505 | 21 | Paris SG | 35000 | 43 | Guingamp | 15500 |
| 11 | Lille | 40500 | 5 | Monaco | 35000 | 13 | Montpellier | 15000 |
| 42 | Marseille | 40000 | 4 | Nantes | 35000 | 45 | Le Havre | 13583 |
| 31 | Lyon | 40000 | 46 | Bastia | 35000 | 28 | Sochaux | 12686 |
| 41 | Paris SG | 40000 | 15 | Deportivo | 35000 | 3 | Sedan | 12000 |
| 38 | Nantes | 40000 | 9 | Bordeaux | 35000 | 36 | AC Ajaccio | 10000 |
| 17 | AC Milan | 40000 | 2 | Sochaux | 35000 | 32 | Rennes | 10000 |
| 6 | Lyon | 40000 | 29 | Sedan | 34000 | 39 | Auxerre | 10000 |
| 18 | Auxerre | 39700 | 24 | Guingamp | 33500 | 25 | Troyes | 9500 |
| 40 | Strasbourg | 38500 | 7 | Rennes | 33500 | 1 | Bastia | 7000 |
| 37 | Nice | 38124 | 27 | Le Havre | 24758 | 30 | Monaco | 6000 |
| 10 | Bayern Munich | 38000 | 20 | Bayern Munich | 22000 | | | |
| 14 | AC Ajaccio | 38000 | 12 | Deportivo | 18156 | | | |

Home / Away / Neutral

## KEY PLAYERS - GOALSCORERS

**1 Antoine Sibierski**

| | | | |
|---|---|---|---|
| Goals in the League | 12 | Player Strike Rate<br>Average number of minutes between League goals scored by player | 240 |
| Contribution to Attacking Power<br>Average number of minutes between League team goals while on pitch | 75 | Club Strike Rate<br>Average number of minutes between League goals scored by club | 80 |

| | PLAYER | LGE GOALS | POWER | STRIKE RATE |
|---|---|---|---|---|
| 2 | John Utaka | 8 | 69 | 303 mins |
| 3 | Daniel Moreira | 9 | 74 | 346 mins |
| 4 | Rigobert Song | 3 | 75 | 1005 mins |
| 5 | Seyadou Keita | 2 | 78 | 1065 mins |

## KEY PLAYERS - MIDFIELDERS

**1 Papa Bouba Diop**

| | | | |
|---|---|---|---|
| Goals in the League | 3 | Contribution to Attacking Power<br>Average number of minutes between League team goals while on pitch | 74 |
| Defensive Rating<br>Average number of mins between League goals conceded while he was on the pitch | 208 | Scoring Difference<br>Defensive Rating minus Contribution to Attacking Power | 134 |

| | PLAYER | LGE GOALS | DEF RATE | POWER | SCORE DIFF |
|---|---|---|---|---|---|
| 2 | Charles-Edouard Coridon | 1 | 130 | 89 | 41 mins |
| 3 | Daniel Moreira | 9 | 104 | 74 | 30 mins |
| 4 | Seyadou Keita | 2 | 107 | 79 | 28 mins |
| 5 | Antoine Sibierski | 12 | 99 | 76 | 23 mins |

## KEY PLAYERS - DEFENDERS

**1 Yoan Lachor**

| | | | |
|---|---|---|---|
| Goals Conceded (GC)<br>The number of League goals conceded while he was on the pitch | 9 | Clean Sheets<br>In games when he played at least 70 minutes | 7 |
| Defensive Rating<br>Ave number of mins between League goals conceded while on the pitch | 127 | Club Defensive Rating<br>Average number of mins between League goals conceded by the club this season | 110 |

| | PLAYER | CON LGE | CLEAN SHEETS | DEF RATE |
|---|---|---|---|---|
| 2 | Rigobert Song | 25 | 16 | 121 mins |
| 3 | Jacek Bak | 20 | 11 | 115 mins |
| 4 | Daouda Jabi | 10 | 5 | 109 mins |
| 5 | Zoumana Camara | 12 | 5 | 99 mins |

## KEY GOALKEEPER

**1 Guillaume Warmuz**

| | |
|---|---|
| Goals Conceded in the League | 13 |
| Defensive Rating<br>Ave number of mins between League goals conceded while on the pitch | 111 |
| Counting Games<br>Games when he played at least 70 minutes | 16 |
| Clean Sheets<br>In games when he played at least 70 minutes | 6 |

## TOP POINT EARNERS

| | PLAYER | GAMES | AVE |
|---|---|---|---|
| 1 | Camara | 13 | 1.69 |
| 2 | Moreira | 34 | 1.65 |
| 3 | Utaka | 22 | 1.64 |
| 4 | Song | 33 | 1.61 |
| 5 | Bak | 25 | 1.56 |
| 6 | Warmuz | 16 | 1.50 |
| 7 | Itandje | 22 | 1.50 |
| 8 | Coulibaly | 21 | 1.48 |
| 9 | Sibierski | 31 | 1.48 |
| 10 | Rool | 13 | 1.46 |
| | CLUB AVERAGE: | | 1.50 |

Ave = Average points per match in Counting Games

## DISCIPLINARY RECORDS

| | PLAYER | YELLOW | RED | AVE |
|---|---|---|---|---|
| 1 | Rool | 9 | 1 | 121 |
| 2 | Coly | 4 | 0 | 153 |
| 3 | Jabi | 6 | 1 | 155 |
| 4 | Diop | 6 | 0 | 173 |
| 5 | Faye | 5 | 1 | 178 |
| 6 | Fanni | 3 | 0 | 221 |
| 7 | Bakari | 2 | 0 | 377 |
| 8 | Lachor | 3 | 0 | 382 |
| 9 | Bak | 5 | 0 | 461 |
| 10 | Coridon | 4 | 0 | 488 |
| 11 | Keita | 4 | 0 | 532 |
| 12 | Moreira | 5 | 0 | 623 |
| 13 | Blanchard | 4 | 0 | 678 |
| | Other | 12 | 1 | |
| | TOTAL | 72 | 4 | |

## LEAGUE GOALS

| | PLAYER | MINS | GOALS | AVE |
|---|---|---|---|---|
| 1 | Sibierski | 2880 | 12 | 240 |
| 2 | Moreira | 3116 | 9 | 346 |
| 3 | Utaka | 2426 | 8 | 303 |
| 4 | Song | 3016 | 3 | 1005 |
| 5 | Diop | 1041 | 3 | 347 |
| 6 | Vairelles | 760 | 2 | 380 |
| 7 | Keita | 2130 | 2 | 1065 |
| 8 | Bakari | 755 | 2 | 378 |
| 9 | Sikora | 145 | 1 | 145 |
| 10 | Coridon | 1954 | 1 | 1954 |
| | Other | | 0 | |
| | TOTAL | | 43 | |

## MONTH BY MONTH GUIDE TO THE POINTS

| MONTH | POINTS | % |
|---|---|---|
| AUGUST | 9 | 60% |
| SEPTEMBER | 4 | 33% |
| OCTOBER | 5 | 56% |
| NOVEMBER | 6 | 50% |
| DECEMBER | 4 | 33% |
| JANUARY | 5 | 56% |
| FEBRUARY | 8 | 67% |
| MARCH | 3 | 25% |
| APRIL | 4 | 44% |
| MAY | 9 | 75% |

## TEAM OF THE SEASON

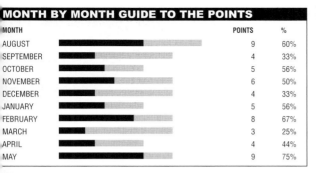

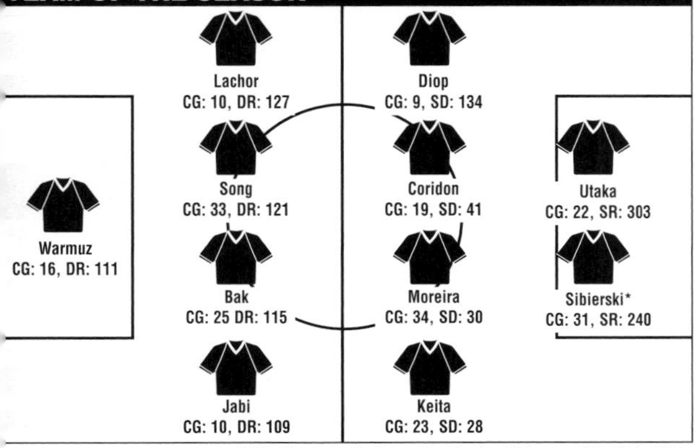
Lachor
CG: 10, DR: 127
Diop
CG: 9, SD: 134
Song
CG: 33, DR: 121
Coridon
CG: 19, SD: 41
Utaka
CG: 22, SR: 303
Warmuz
CG: 16, DR: 111
Bak
CG: 25 DR: 115
Moreira
CG: 34, SD: 30
Sibierski*
CG: 31, SR: 240
Jabi
CG: 10, DR: 109
Keita
CG: 23, SD: 28

KEY: DR = Defensive Rate, SD = Scoring Difference, SR = Strike Rate, CG = Counting Games – League games playing at least 70 minutes

## LEAGUE APPEARANCES, BOOKINGS AND CAPS

| | AGE | IN THE SQUAD | COUNTING GAMES | MINUTES ON PITCH | YELLOW CARDS | RED CARDS | THIS SEASON | HOME COUNTRY |
|---|---|---|---|---|---|---|---|---|
| **Goalkeepers** | | | | | | | | |
| Joe Cannon | 28 | 12 | 0 | 0 | 0 | 0 | 1 | United States (10) |
| Sebastien Chabbert | 24 | 14 | 0 | 0 | 0 | 0 | - | France |
| Guillaume Cherreau | 20 | 2 | 0 | 0 | 0 | 0 | - | France |
| Charles-Hubert Itandje | 20 | 32 | 22 | 1980 | 1 | 0 | - | France |
| Guillaume Warmuz | 32 | 16 | 16 | 1440 | 0 | 0 | - | France |
| **Defenders** | | | | | | | | |
| Jacek Bak | 30 | 28 | 25 | 2305 | 5 | 0 | 6 | Poland (29) |
| Zoumana Camara | 24 | 16 | 13 | 1193 | 1 | 0 | - | France |
| Ferdinand Coly | 29 | 11 | 6 | 614 | 4 | 0 | 2 | Senegal (29) |
| Adama Coulibaly | 22 | 26 | 21 | 2021 | 2 | 0 | - | Mali |
| Rod Fanni | 21 | 16 | 5 | 665 | 3 | 0 | - | France |
| Daouda Jabi | 21 | 16 | 10 | 1087 | 6 | 1 | - | France |
| Yoan Lachor | 27 | 22 | 10 | 1146 | 3 | 0 | - | France |
| Ibrahima N'Diaye | 28 | 2 | 0 | 5 | 0 | 0 | 1 | Senegal (29) |
| Eric Sikora | 35 | 11 | 1 | 145 | 0 | 0 | - | France |
| Rigobert Song | 27 | 34 | 33 | 3016 | 2 | 1 | 2 | Cameroon (18) |
| **Midfielders** | | | | | | | | |
| Jocelyn Blanchard | 31 | 35 | 29 | 2712 | 4 | 0 | - | France |
| Charles-Ed Coridon | 30 | 27 | 19 | 1954 | 4 | 0 | - | France |
| Papa Bouba Diop | 25 | 17 | 9 | 1041 | 6 | 0 | - | Senegal |
| Abd'laye Diagne Faye | 25 | 19 | 9 | 1068 | 5 | 1 | 1 | Senegal (29) |
| Seyadou Keita | 23 | 30 | 23 | 2130 | 4 | 0 | - | Mali |
| Daniel Moreira | 25 | 38 | 34 | 3116 | 5 | 0 | 2 | France (2) |
| Stephane Pedron | 32 | 21 | 6 | 804 | 0 | 0 | - | France |
| Cyril Rool | 28 | 15 | 13 | 1217 | 9 | 1 | - | France |
| Pape Sarr | 25 | 5 | 0 | 45 | 1 | 0 | 2 | Senegal (29) |
| Antoine Sibierski | 28 | 37 | 31 | 2880 | 3 | 0 | - | France |
| **Forwards** | | | | | | | | |
| Dagui Bakari | 28 | 29 | 5 | 755 | 2 | 0 | - | France |
| Olivier Thomert | 23 | 26 | 7 | 977 | 0 | 0 | - | France |
| John Utaka | 21 | 37 | 22 | 2426 | 2 | 0 | - | Nigeria |
| Tony Vairelles | 30 | 13 | 7 | 760 | 0 | 0 | - | France |

KEY: LEAGUE BOOKINGS CAPS (FIFA RANKING)

## SQUAD APPEARANCES

| Match | 1 | 2 | 3 | 4 | 5 | 6 | 7 | 8 | 9 | 10 | 11 | 12 | 13 | 14 | 15 | 16 | 17 | 18 | 19 | 20 | 21 | 22 | 23 | 24 | 25 | 26 | 27 | 28 | 29 | 30 | 31 | 32 | 33 | 34 | 35 | 36 | 37 | 38 | 39 | 40 | 41 | 42 | 43 | 44 | 45 | 46 |
|---|---|---|---|---|---|---|---|---|---|---|---|---|---|---|---|---|---|---|---|---|---|---|---|---|---|---|---|---|---|---|---|---|---|---|---|---|---|---|---|---|---|---|---|---|---|---|
| Venue | A | H | A | A | H | A | H | A | A | H | H | A | A | H | H | A | H | H | A | A | H | A | A | H | A | H | H | A | H | A | H | A | H | A | H | A | H | H | A | H | A | H | A | H | A | H |
| Competition | L | L | L | L | L | L | L | C | L | C | L | C | L | L | C | L | C | L | L | C | L | L | E | L | L | E | L | L | L | L | L | L | L | L | L | L | L | L | L | L | L | L | L | L | L | L |
| Result | D | D | W | D | W | L | W | L | L | D | D | L | W | D | W | D | W | W | L | D | W | L | L | L | D | W | W | L | W | D | D | D | D | W | W | D | D | L | D | D | W | L | L | W | W | W |

**Goalkeepers**
Joe Cannon
Sebastien Chabbert
Guillaume Cherreau
Charles-Hubert Itandje
Guillaume Warmuz

**Defenders**
Jacek Bak
Zoumana Camara
Ferdinand Coly
Adama Coulibaly
Rod Fanni
Daouda Jabi
Yoan Lachor
Ibrahima N'Diaye
Eric Sikora
Rigobert Song

**Midfielders**
Jocelyn Blanchard
Charles-Edouard Coridon
Papa Bouba Diop
Abdoulaye Faye
Seyadou Keita
Daniel Moreira
Stephane Pedron
Cyril Rool
Elhadji Sarr
Antoine Sibierski

**Forwards**
Dagui Bakari
Olivier Thomert
John Utaka
Tony Vairelles

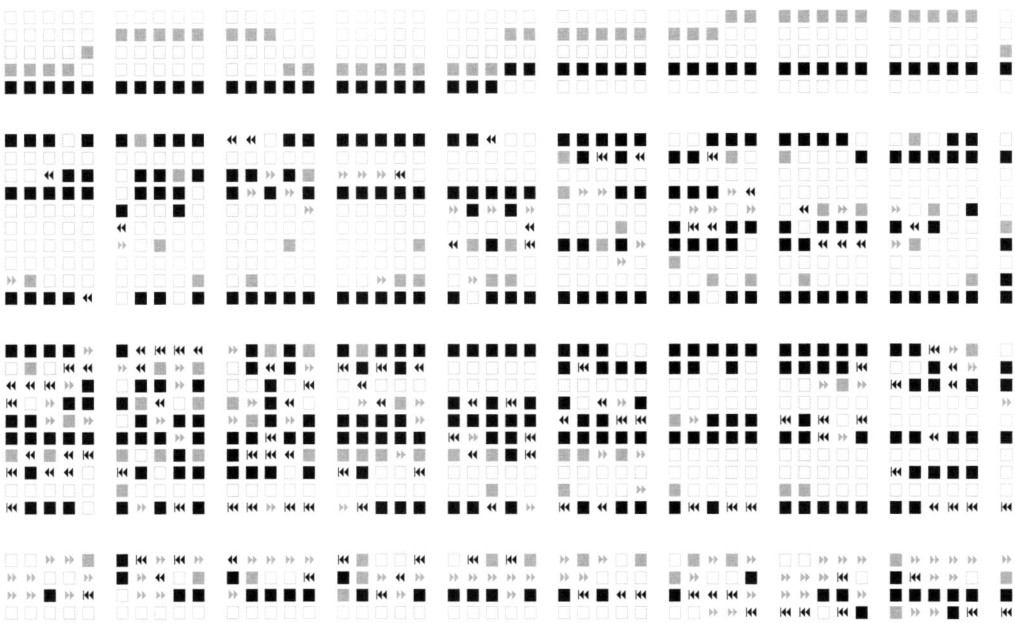

KEY: On all match; On bench; Subbed or sent off (Counting game); Subbed or sent off (playing less than 70 minutes); Subbed on from bench (Counting Game); Subbed on (playing less than 70 minutes); Subbed on and then subbed or sent off (Counting Game); Subbed on and then subbed or sent off (playing less than 70 minutes); Not in 16

# NANTES

Final Position: **9th**

| | | | | | | |
|---|---|---|---|---|---|---|
| 1 | lge | Marseille | A | W | 2-0 | Yepes 61; Berson 90 |
| 2 | lge | Bastia | H | W | 1-0 | Berson 85 |
| 3 | lge | Sochaux | A | L | 2-4 | Moldovan 18; Djemba-Djemba 62 |
| 4 | lge | Lens | H | D | 2-2 | Yepes 5; Da Rocha 26 |
| 5 | lge | Sedan | A | L | 0-1 | |
| 6 | lge | Monaco | A | L | 1-2 | Makukula 41 |
| 7 | lge | Lyon | H | W | 1-0 | Vahirua 19 |
| 8 | lge | Rennes | A | L | 0-1 | |
| 9 | lge | Auxerre | H | L | 1-4 | Moldovan 34 |
| 10 | lge | AC Ajaccio | A | L | 0-1 | |
| 11 | lge | Nice | H | D | 0-0 | |
| 12 | lge | Le Havre | A | D | 1-1 | Gillet 11 |
| 13 | lge | Bordeaux | H | D | 0-0 | |
| 14 | lge | Lille | A | W | 1-0 | Ziani 49 |
| 15 | lge | Strasbourg | H | W | 4-1 | Vahirua 18,59; Dalmat 78,88 |
| 16 | lge | Paris SG | A | W | 1-0 | Armand 30 |
| 17 | lge | Montpellier | H | W | 3-1 | Vahirua 32; Da Rocha 57; Gillet 89 pen |
| 18 | lge | Guingamp | A | L | 0-2 | |
| 19 | lge | Troyes | H | W | 2-1 | Pujol 11; Gillet 13 |
| 20 | lge | Bastia | A | L | 1-3 | Vahirua 63 |
| 21 | lge | Sedan | H | W | 4-1 | Pujol 50; Ziani 52; Savinaud 62; Moldovan 86 |
| 22 | lge | Monaco | H | L | 0-2 | |
| 23 | lge | Lyon | A | D | 0-0 | |
| 24 | lge | Rennes | H | W | 1-0 | Pujol 78 |
| 25 | lge | Auxerre | A | W | 1-0 | Moldovan 2 |
| 26 | lge | Sochaux | H | L | 0-1 | |
| 27 | lge | AC Ajaccio | H | W | 1-0 | Gillet 66 pen |
| 28 | lge | Nice | A | D | 1-1 | Vahirua 73 |
| 29 | lge | Le Havre | H | W | 2-0 | Pujol 28; Vahirua 90 |
| 30 | lge | Lens | A | W | 1-0 | Savinaud 62 |
| 31 | lge | Bordeaux | A | D | 0-0 | |
| 32 | lge | Lille | H | W | 1-0 | Gillet 48 pen |
| 33 | lge | Strasbourg | A | L | 0-2 | |
| 34 | lge | Paris SG | H | D | 1-1 | Gillet 48 |
| 35 | lge | Montpellier | A | L | 0-1 | |
| 36 | lge | Guingamp | H | L | 0-4 | |
| 37 | lge | Troyes | A | L | 0-2 | |
| 38 | lge | Marseille | H | W | 1-0 | Quint 82 |

## KEY PLAYERS - GOALSCORERS

**1 Marama Vahirua**

| | | | |
|---|---|---|---|
| Goals in the League | 7 | Player Strike Rate<br>Average number of minutes between League goals scored by player | 243 |
| Contribution to Attacking Power<br>Average number of minutes between League team goals while on pitch | 94 | Club Strike Rate<br>Average number of minutes between League goals scored by club | 92 |

| | PLAYER | LGE GOALS | POWER | STRIKE RATE |
|---|---|---|---|---|
| 2 | Gregory Pujol | 4 | 96 | 409 mins |
| 3 | Nicholas Gillet | 6 | 96 | 483 mins |
| 4 | Nicolas Savinaud | 2 | 90 | 1136 mins |
| 5 | Mathieu Berson | 2 | 100 | 1202 mins |

## KEY PLAYERS - MIDFIELDERS

**1 Eric Djemba-Djemba**

| | | | |
|---|---|---|---|
| Goals in the League | 1 | Contribution to Attacking Power<br>Average number of minutes between League team goals while on pitch | 84 |
| Defensive Rating<br>Average number of mins between League goals conceded while he was on the pitch | 99 | Scoring Difference<br>Defensive Rating minus Contribution to Attacking Power | 15 |

| | PLAYER | LGE GOALS | DEF RATE | POWER | SCORE DIFF |
|---|---|---|---|---|---|
| 2 | Mathieu Berson | 2 | 109 | 100 | 9 mins |
| 3 | Olivier Quint | 1 | 94 | 99 | -5 mins |

## KEY PLAYERS - DEFENDERS

**1 Mario Yepes**

| | | | |
|---|---|---|---|
| Goals Conceded (GC)<br>The number of League goals conceded while he was on the pitch | 29 | Clean Sheets<br>In games when he played at least 70 minutes | 14 |
| Defensive Rating<br>Ave number of mins between League goals conceded while on the pitch | 101 | Club Defensive Rating<br>Average number of mins between League goals conceded by the club this season | 88 |

| | PLAYER | CON LGE | CLEAN SHEETS | DEF RATE |
|---|---|---|---|---|
| 2 | Pascal Delhommeau | 23 | 12 | 88 mins |
| 3 | Nicholas Gillet | 35 | 12 | 83 mins |
| 4 | Mauro Cetto | 17 | 5 | 82 mins |
| 5 | Sylvain Armand | 33 | 13 | 82 mins |

## GOALS SCORED

AT HOME

| | | |
|---|---|---|
| MOST | Lyon | 40 |
| | | 25 |
| LEAST | AC Ajaccio | 14 |

AWAY

| | | |
|---|---|---|
| MOST | Monaco | 29 |
| | | 12 |
| LEAST | Troyes | 7 |

## GOALS CONCEDED

AT HOME

| | | |
|---|---|---|
| LEAST | Sochaux & Auxerre | 8 |
| | | 18 |
| MOST | Strasbourg | 23 |

AWAY

| | | |
|---|---|---|
| LEAST | Lens | 15 |
| | | 21 |
| MOST | Sedan | 39 |

## KEY GOALKEEPER

**1 Mickael Landreau**

| | |
|---|---|
| Goals Conceded in the League | 33 |
| Defensive Rating<br>Ave number of mins between League goals conceded while on the pitch | 98 |
| Counting Games<br>Games when he played at least 70 minutes | 36 |
| Clean Sheets<br>In games when he played at least 70 minutes | 16 |

## TOP POINT EARNERS

| | PLAYER | GAMES | AVE |
|---|---|---|---|
| 1 | Delhommeau | 21 | 1.95 |
| 2 | Da Rocha | 27 | 1.70 |
| 3 | Djemba-Djemba | 22 | 1.64 |
| 4 | Berson | 26 | 1.62 |
| 5 | Ziani | 28 | 1.61 |
| 6 | Pujol | 15 | 1.60 |
| 7 | Landreau | 36 | 1.56 |
| 8 | Armand | 30 | 1.53 |
| 9 | Yepes | 33 | 1.52 |
| 10 | Vahirua | 14 | 1.50 |
| | CLUB AVERAGE: | | 1.47 |

Ave = Average points per match in Counting Games

## ATTENDANCES

HOME GROUND: BEAUJOIRE CAPACITY: 38486 AVERAGE LEAGUE AT HOME: 30938

| | | | | | | | | |
|---|---|---|---|---|---|---|---|---|
| 16 | Paris SG | 40000 | 17 | Montpellier | 30000 | 3 | Sochaux | 15000 |
| 30 | Lens | 40000 | 15 | Strasbourg | 30000 | 35 | Montpellier | 15000 |
| 23 | Lyon | 40000 | 9 | Auxerre | 30000 | 14 | Lille | 15000 |
| 34 | Paris SG | 38000 | 11 | Nice | 30000 | 25 | Auxerre | 15000 |
| 38 | Marseille | 36411 | 13 | Bordeaux | 30000 | 33 | Strasbourg | 12928 |
| 24 | Rennes | 35000 | 27 | AC Ajaccio | 28000 | 20 | Bastia | 11500 |
| 7 | Lyon | 35000 | 19 | Troyes | 28000 | 28 | Nice | 11000 |
| 4 | Lens | 35000 | 26 | Sochaux | 25000 | 37 | Troyes | 11000 |
| 36 | Guingamp | 34919 | 29 | Le Havre | 25000 | 5 | Sedan | 10000 |
| 31 | Bordeaux | 34000 | 32 | Lille | 25000 | 10 | AC Ajaccio | 9000 |
| 2 | Bastia | 31500 | 8 | Rennes | 23625 | 12 | Le Havre | 9000 |
| 21 | Sedan | 31000 | 18 | Guingamp | 18000 | 6 | Monaco | 3000 |
| 22 | Monaco | 30000 | 1 | Marseille | 15000 | | | |

■ Home □ Away ▒ Neutral

## DISCIPLINARY RECORDS

| | PLAYER | YELLOW | RED | AVE |
|---|---|---|---|---|
| 1 | Cetto | 6 | 1 | 198 |
| 2 | Djemba-Djemba | 10 | 1 | 198 |
| 3 | Moldovan | 4 | 0 | 212 |
| 4 | Berson | 10 | 1 | 218 |
| 5 | Toulalan | 2 | 0 | 249 |
| 6 | Delhommeau | 5 | 2 | 288 |
| 7 | Makukula | 3 | 0 | 300 |
| 8 | Da Rocha | 8 | 0 | 304 |
| 9 | Ateba | 2 | 1 | 315 |
| 10 | Yepes | 6 | 2 | 366 |
| 11 | Savinaud | 6 | 0 | 378 |
| 12 | Gillet | 6 | 1 | 414 |
| 13 | Quint | 4 | 0 | 447 |
| | Other | 14 | 1 | |
| | **TOTAL** | **86** | **10** | |

## LEAGUE GOALS

| | PLAYER | MINS | GOALS | AVE |
|---|---|---|---|---|
| 1 | Vahirua | 1703 | 7 | 243 |
| 2 | Gillet | 2899 | 6 | 483 |
| 3 | Pujol | 1635 | 4 | 409 |
| 4 | Moldovan | 851 | 4 | 213 |
| 5 | Berson | 2404 | 2 | 1202 |
| 6 | Yepes | 2935 | 2 | 1468 |
| 7 | Dalmat | 442 | 2 | 221 |
| 8 | Da Rocha | 2437 | 2 | 1219 |
| 9 | Ziani | 2558 | 2 | 1279 |
| 10 | Savinaud | 2271 | 2 | 1136 |
| 11 | Quint | 1789 | 1 | 1789 |
| 12 | Armand | 2697 | 1 | 2697 |
| 13 | Djemba-Dj. | 2179 | 1 | 2179 |
| | Other | | 1 | |
| | **TOTAL** | | **37** | |

## MONTH BY MONTH GUIDE TO THE POINTS

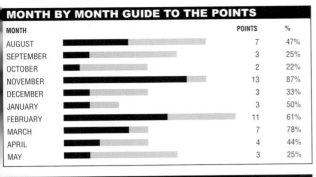

| MONTH | POINTS | % |
|---|---|---|
| AUGUST | 7 | 47% |
| SEPTEMBER | 3 | 25% |
| OCTOBER | 2 | 22% |
| NOVEMBER | 13 | 87% |
| DECEMBER | 3 | 33% |
| JANUARY | 3 | 50% |
| FEBRUARY | 11 | 61% |
| MARCH | 7 | 78% |
| APRIL | 4 | 44% |
| MAY | 3 | 25% |

## TEAM OF THE SEASON

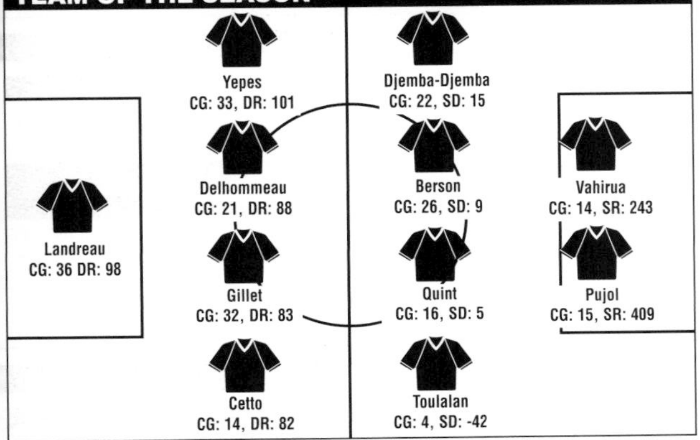
Yepes
CG: 33, DR: 101
Djemba-Djemba
CG: 22, SD: 15
Delhommeau
CG: 21, DR: 88
Berson
CG: 26, SD: 9
Vahirua
CG: 14, SR: 243
Landreau
CG: 36 DR: 98
Gillet
CG: 32, DR: 83
Quint
CG: 16, SD: 5
Pujol
CG: 15, SR: 409
Cetto
CG: 14, DR: 82
Toulalan
CG: 4, SD: -42

KEY: DR = Defensive Rate, SD = Scoring Difference, SR = Strike Rate, CG = Counting Games – League games playing at least 70 minutes

## LEAGUE APPEARANCES, BOOKINGS AND CAPS

| | AGE | IN THE SQUAD | COUNTING GAMES | MINUTES ON PITCH | YELLOW CARDS | RED CARDS | THIS SEASON | HOME COUNTRY |
|---|---|---|---|---|---|---|---|---|
| **Goalkeepers** | | | | | | | | |
| Willy Grondin | 28 | 38 | 2 | 180 | 0 | 0 | - | France |
| Mickael Landreau | 24 | 37 | 36 | 3240 | 1 | 0 | - | France |
| Sebastien Pauvert | 25 | 1 | 0 | 0 | 0 | 0 | - | |
| **Defenders** | | | | | | | | |
| Sylvain Armand | 22 | 30 | 30 | 2697 | 5 | 1 | - | France |
| Jean-Hughes Ateba | 21 | 19 | 8 | 946 | 2 | 1 | - | Cameroon |
| Mauro Cetto | 21 | 22 | 13 | 1388 | 6 | 1 | - | Argentina |
| Pascal Delhommeau | 24 | 37 | 21 | 2017 | 5 | 2 | - | France |
| Stephen Drouin | 19 | 3 | 1 | 90 | 0 | 0 | - | France |
| Emerse Fae | 19 | 1 | 0 | 0 | 0 | 0 | - | France |
| Nicholas Gillet | 26 | 33 | 32 | 2899 | 6 | 1 | - | France |
| Nicolas Laspalles | 31 | 7 | 6 | 507 | 0 | 0 | - | |
| Nicolas Savinaud | 27 | 30 | 24 | 2271 | 6 | 0 | - | France |
| Mario Yepes | 27 | 33 | 33 | 2935 | 6 | 2 | - | Columbia |
| **Midfielders** | | | | | | | | |
| Mathieu Berson | 23 | 30 | 26 | 2404 | 10 | 1 | - | France |
| Charles Devineau | 23 | 1 | 0 | 0 | 0 | 0 | - | |
| Eric Djemba-Djemba | 22 | 33 | 22 | 2179 | 10 | 1 | 2 | Cameroon (18) |
| Luigi Glombard | 18 | 5 | 0 | 46 | 0 | 0 | - | France |
| Loic Guillon | 21 | 2 | 0 | 0 | 0 | 0 | - | France |
| Loic Pailleres | 23 | 5 | 0 | 16 | 0 | 0 | - | France |
| Olivier Quint | 31 | 32 | 16 | 1789 | 4 | 0 | - | France |
| Goran Rubil | 22 | 6 | 2 | 356 | 1 | 0 | - | Croatia |
| Jeremy Toulalan | 19 | 19 | 4 | 499 | 2 | 0 | - | France |
| **Forwards** | | | | | | | | |
| Pierre-Yves Andre | 29 | 7 | 1 | 188 | 0 | 0 | - | France |
| Frederic Da Rocha | 28 | 28 | 27 | 2437 | 8 | 0 | - | France |
| Wilfried Dalmat | 20 | 17 | 2 | 442 | 1 | 0 | - | France |
| Ariza Makukula | 22 | 20 | 6 | 902 | 3 | 0 | - | Portugal |
| Dinu Viorel Moldovan | 31 | 18 | 5 | 851 | 4 | 0 | 3 | Romania (27) |
| Shiva N'Zigou | 19 | 6 | 2 | 221 | 0 | 0 | - | Gambia |
| Gregory Pujol | 23 | 24 | 15 | 1635 | 0 | 0 | - | France |
| Marama Vahirua | 23 | 33 | 14 | 1703 | 1 | 0 | - | France |
| Stephane Ziani | 30 | 30 | 28 | 2558 | 5 | 0 | - | France |

KEY: LEAGUE BOOKINGS CAPS (FIFA RANKING)

## SQUAD APPEARANCES

| Match | 1 | 2 | 3 | 4 | 5 | 6 | 7 | 8 | 9 | 10 | 11 | 12 | 13 | 14 | 15 | 16 | 17 | 18 | 19 | 20 | 21 | 22 | 23 | 24 | 25 | 26 | 27 | 28 | 29 | 30 | 31 | 32 | 33 | 34 | 35 | 36 | 37 | 38 |
|---|---|---|---|---|---|---|---|---|---|---|---|---|---|---|---|---|---|---|---|---|---|---|---|---|---|---|---|---|---|---|---|---|---|---|---|---|---|---|
| Venue | A | H | A | H | A | A | H | A | H | A | H | A | H | A | H | A | H | A | H | A | H | H | A | H | A | H | H | A | H | A | A | H | A | H | A | H | A | H |
| Competition | L | L | L | L | L | L | L | L | L | L | L | L | L | L | L | L | L | L | L | L | L | L | L | L | L | L | L | L | L | L | L | L | L | L | L | L | L | L |
| Result | W | W | L | D | L | L | W | L | L | L | D | D | D | W | W | W | W | L | W | L | W | L | D | W | W | L | W | D | W | W | D | W | L | D | L | L | L | W |

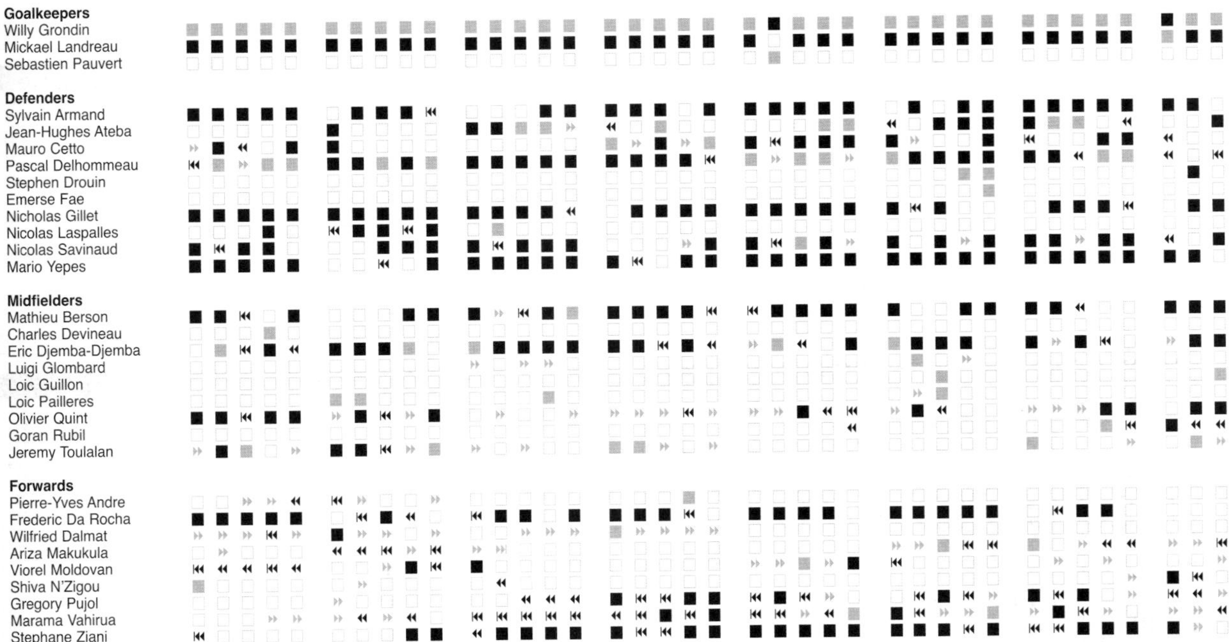
Goalkeepers
Willy Grondin
Mickael Landreau
Sebastien Pauvert
Defenders
Sylvain Armand
Jean-Hughes Ateba
Mauro Cetto
Pascal Delhommeau
Stephen Drouin
Emerse Fae
Nicholas Gillet
Nicolas Laspalles
Nicolas Savinaud
Mario Yepes
Midfielders
Mathieu Berson
Charles Devineau
Eric Djemba-Djemba
Luigi Glombard
Loic Guillon
Loic Pailleres
Olivier Quint
Goran Rubil
Jeremy Toulalan
Forwards
Pierre-Yves Andre
Frederic Da Rocha
Wilfried Dalmat
Ariza Makukula
Viorel Moldovan
Shiva N'Zigou
Gregory Pujol
Marama Vahirua
Stephane Ziani

KEY: ■ On all match; ▒ On bench; ⏮ Subbed or sent off (Counting game); « Subbed or sent off (playing less than 70 minutes); » Subbed on from bench (Counting Game); » Subbed on (playing less than 70 minutes); » Subbed on and then subbed or sent off (Counting Game); » Subbed on and then subbed or sent off (playing less than 70 minutes); □ Not in 16

# NICE

Final Position: **10th**

| | | | | | | |
|---|---|---|---|---|---|---|
| 1 | lge | Le Havre | H | L | 1-2 | Diawara 63 |
| 2 | lge | Strasbourg | H | W | 4-0 | Diawara 10,37,52; Cobos 90 |
| 3 | lge | Lille | A | W | 3-0 | Cobos 16; Varrault 39; Bigne 72 |
| 4 | lge | Montpellier | H | W | 2-1 | Diawara 45; Roy 62 |
| 5 | lge | Paris SG | A | D | 1-1 | Everson 61 |
| 6 | lge | Marseille | H | W | 2-0 | Everson 57; Olufade 86 |
| 7 | lge | Guingamp | A | D | 0-0 | |
| 8 | lge | Troyes | H | W | 1-0 | Meslin 39 |
| 9 | lge | Sochaux | A | L | 0-1 | |
| 10 | lge | Bastia | H | W | 2-0 | Cherrad 75; Diawara 87 |
| 11 | lge | Nantes | A | D | 0-0 | |
| 12 | lge | Lens | H | D | 0-0 | |
| 13 | lge | Lyon | A | D | 2-2 | Diawara 40; Abardonado 90 |
| 14 | lge | Monaco | H | W | 1-0 | Everson 24 |
| 15 | lge | Auxerre | A | W | 2-0 | Olufade 87; Traore 90 |
| 16 | lge | Rennes | H | D | 0-0 | |
| 17 | lge | Sedan | A | L | 0-3 | |
| 18 | lge | AC Ajaccio | H | W | 3-0 | Everson 25; Ayeli 35; Diawara 82 |
| 19 | lge | Bordeaux | A | L | 0-4 | |
| 20 | lge | Strasbourg | A | D | 0-0 | |
| 21 | lge | Lille | H | W | 2-0 | Cherrad 56; Diawara 78 |
| 22 | lge | Montpellier | A | D | 2-2 | Cherrad 20; Diawara 65 |
| 23 | lge | Paris SG | H | D | 0-0 | |
| 24 | lge | Marseille | A | L | 0-2 | |
| 25 | lge | Guingamp | H | W | 1-0 | Pamarot 42 |
| 26 | lge | Troyes | A | L | 0-1 | |
| 27 | lge | Sochaux | H | D | 2-2 | Everson 54; Mionnet 63 |
| 28 | lge | Bastia | A | D | 1-1 | Cherrad 72 |
| 29 | lge | Nantes | H | D | 1-1 | Cherrad 31 |
| 30 | lge | Lens | A | D | 0-0 | |
| 31 | lge | Lyon | H | L | 0-1 | |
| 32 | lge | Monaco | A | W | 1-0 | Diawara 78 |
| 33 | lge | Auxerre | H | W | 1-0 | Everson 47 |
| 34 | lge | Rennes | A | D | 2-2 | Bign? 15; Mionnet 68 |
| 35 | lge | Sedan | H | D | 0-0 | |
| 36 | lge | AC Ajaccio | A | L | 0-2 | |
| 37 | lge | Bordeaux | H | D | 1-1 | Roy 13 |
| 38 | lge | Le Havre | A | L | 1-2 | Diawara 76 |

## KEY PLAYERS - GOALSCORERS

**1 Kaba Diawara**

| | | | |
|---|---|---|---|
| Goals in the League | 12 | Player Strike Rate<br>Average number of minutes between League goals scored by player | 251 |
| Contribution to Attacking Power<br>Average number of minutes between League team goals while on pitch | 86 | Club Strike Rate<br>Average number of minutes between League goals scored by club | 88 |

| | PLAYER | LGE GOALS | POWER | STRIKE RATE |
|---|---|---|---|---|
| 2 | Pereira da Silva Everson | 6 | 83 | 474 mins |
| 3 | Sammy Traore | 1 | 99 | 1191 mins |
| 4 | Yohann Bigne | 2 | 82 | 1369 mins |
| 5 | Jose Cobos | 2 | 90 | 1448 mins |

## KEY PLAYERS - MIDFIELDERS

**1 Romain Pitau**

| | | | |
|---|---|---|---|
| Goals in the League | 0 | Contribution to Attacking Power<br>Average number of minutes between League team goals while on pitch | 85 |
| Defensive Rating<br>Average number of mins between League goals conceded while he was on the pitch | 118 | Scoring Difference<br>Defensive Rating minus Contribution to Attacking Power | 33 |

| | PLAYER | LGE GOALS | DEF RATE | POWER | SCORE DIFF |
|---|---|---|---|---|---|
| 2 | Yohann Bigne | 2 | 110 | 83 | 27 mins |
| 3 | Pereira da Silva Everson | 6 | 105 | 84 | 21 mins |
| 4 | Eric Roy | 2 | 117 | 96 | 21 mins |
| 5 | Sammy Traore | 1 | 92 | 99 | -7 mins |

## KEY PLAYERS - DEFENDERS

**1 Jose Cobos**

| | | | |
|---|---|---|---|
| Goals Conceded (GC)<br>The number of League goals conceded while he was on the pitch | 22 | Clean Sheets<br>In games when he played at least 70 minutes | 19 |
| Defensive Rating<br>Ave number of mins between League goals conceded while on the pitch | 132 | Club Defensive Rating<br>Average number of mins between League goals conceded by the club this season | 110 |

| | PLAYER | CON LGE | CLEAN SHEETS | DEF RATE |
|---|---|---|---|---|
| 2 | Louis Pamarot | 26 | 18 | 116 mins |
| 3 | Jacques Abardonado | 31 | 20 | 110 mins |
| 4 | Cedric Varrault | 28 | 15 | 105 mins |

## GOALS SCORED

**AT HOME**

| | | |
|---|---|---|
| MOST | Lyon | 40 |
| | | 24 |
| LEAST | AC Ajaccio | 14 |

**AWAY**

| | | |
|---|---|---|
| MOST | Monaco | 29 |
| | | 15 |
| LEAST | Troyes | 7 |

## GOALS CONCEDED

**AT HOME**

| | | |
|---|---|---|
| LEAST | Sochaux & Auxerre | 8 |
| | | 8 |
| MOST | Strasbourg | 23 |

**AWAY**

| | | |
|---|---|---|
| LEAST | Lens | 15 |
| | | 23 |
| MOST | Sedan | 39 |

## KEY GOALKEEPER

**1 Damien Gregorini**

| | |
|---|---|
| Goals Conceded in the League | 29 |
| Defensive Rating<br>Ave number of mins between League goals conceded while on the pitch | 115 |
| Counting Games<br>Games when he played at least 70 minutes | 37 |
| Clean Sheets<br>In games when he played at least 70 minutes | 20 |

## TOP POINT EARNERS

| | PLAYER | GAMES | AVE |
|---|---|---|---|
| 1 | Bigne | 31 | 1.65 |
| 2 | Cobos | 31 | 1.61 |
| 3 | Everson | 30 | 1.53 |
| 4 | Gregorini | 37 | 1.49 |
| 5 | Diawara | 31 | 1.48 |
| 6 | Roy | 35 | 1.46 |
| 7 | Varrault | 31 | 1.45 |
| 8 | Abardonado | 38 | 1.45 |
| 9 | Pitau | 34 | 1.44 |
| 10 | Pamarot | 33 | 1.42 |
| | CLUB AVERAGE: | | 1.45 |

Ave = Average points per match in Counting Games

## ATTENDANCES

HOME GROUND: STADE DU RAY CAPACITY: 17800 AVERAGE LEAGUE AT HOME: 13797

| | | | | | | | | |
|---|---|---|---|---|---|---|---|---|
| 24 | Marseille | 47000 | 18 | AC Ajaccio | 15000 | 32 | Monaco | 12045 |
| 5 | Paris SG | 45000 | 3 | Lille | 15000 | 1 | Le Havre | 12000 |
| 30 | Lens | 38124 | 33 | Auxerre | 15000 | 8 | Troyes | 12000 |
| 13 | Lyon | 35000 | 7 | Guingamp | 15000 | 2 | Strasbourg | 12000 |
| 11 | Nantes | 30000 | 14 | Monaco | 15000 | 17 | Sedan | 11000 |
| 9 | Sochaux | 20000 | 4 | Montpellier | 15000 | 21 | Lille | 11000 |
| 19 | Bordeaux | 20000 | 6 | Marseille | 15000 | 27 | Sochaux | 11000 |
| 34 | Rennes | 19000 | 35 | Sedan | 14115 | 29 | Nantes | 11000 |
| 12 | Lens | 17500 | 38 | Le Havre | 14000 | 26 | Troyes | 10000 |
| 15 | Auxerre | 17000 | 16 | Rennes | 14000 | 25 | Guingamp | 10000 |
| 37 | Bordeaux | 17000 | 20 | Strasbourg | 13652 | 28 | Bastia | 9000 |
| 23 | Paris SG | 17000 | 10 | Bastia | 13000 | 36 | AC Ajaccio | 4397 |
| 31 | Lyon | 15544 | 22 | Montpellier | 12392 | | | |

Home / Away / Neutral

## DISCIPLINARY RECORDS

| | PLAYER | YELLOW | RED | AVE |
|---|---|---|---|---|
| 1 | Barul | 3 | 0 | 178 |
| 2 | Everson | 13 | 0 | 218 |
| 3 | Olufade | 2 | 0 | 247 |
| 4 | Pamarot | 9 | 0 | 335 |
| 5 | Bigne | 8 | 0 | 342 |
| 6 | Traore | 3 | 0 | 397 |
| 7 | Cobos | 6 | 1 | 413 |
| 8 | Pitau | 6 | 1 | 436 |
| 9 | Varrault | 5 | 1 | 492 |
| 10 | Diawara | 6 | 0 | 502 |
| 11 | Roy | 5 | 0 | 634 |
| 12 | Cherrad | 2 | 0 | 661 |
| 13 | Ayeli | 1 | 0 | 663 |
| | Other | 10 | 1 | |
| | TOTAL | 79 | 4 | |

## LEAGUE GOALS

| | PLAYER | MINS | GOALS | AVE |
|---|---|---|---|---|
| 1 | Diawara | 3014 | 12 | 251 |
| 2 | Everson | 2845 | 6 | 474 |
| 3 | Cherrad | 1323 | 5 | 265 |
| 4 | Cobos | 2895 | 2 | 1448 |
| 5 | Olufade | 495 | 2 | 248 |
| 6 | Roy | 3172 | 2 | 1586 |
| 7 | Mionnet | 550 | 2 | 275 |
| 8 | Bigne | 2738 | 2 | 1369 |
| 9 | Ayeli | 663 | 1 | 663 |
| 10 | Varrault | 2952 | 1 | 2952 |
| 11 | Meslin | 503 | 1 | 503 |
| 12 | Pamarot | 3019 | 1 | 3019 |
| 13 | Abardonado | 3420 | 1 | 3420 |
| | Other | | 1 | |
| | TOTAL | | 39 | |

## MONTH BY MONTH GUIDE TO THE POINTS

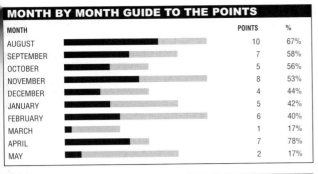

| MONTH | POINTS | % |
|---|---|---|
| AUGUST | 10 | 67% |
| SEPTEMBER | 7 | 58% |
| OCTOBER | 5 | 56% |
| NOVEMBER | 8 | 53% |
| DECEMBER | 4 | 44% |
| JANUARY | 5 | 42% |
| FEBRUARY | 6 | 40% |
| MARCH | 1 | 17% |
| APRIL | 7 | 78% |
| MAY | 2 | 17% |

## TEAM OF THE SEASON

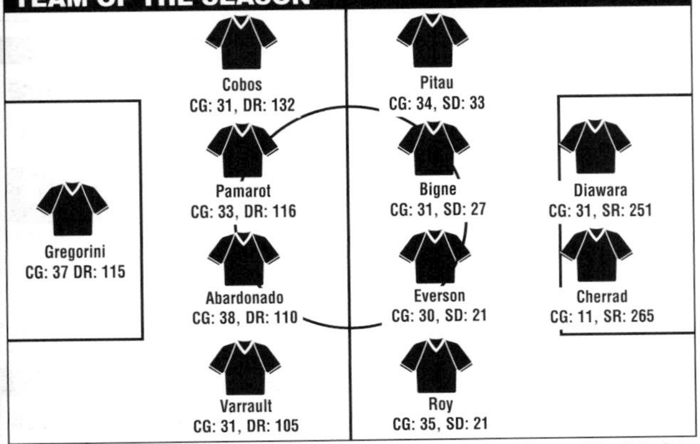

Cobos
CG: 31, DR: 132
Pitau
CG: 34, SD: 33
Pamarot
CG: 33, DR: 116
Bigne
CG: 31, SD: 27
Diawara
CG: 31, SR: 251
Gregorini
CG: 37 DR: 115
Abardonado
CG: 38, DR: 110
Everson
CG: 30, SD: 21
Cherrad
CG: 11, SR: 265
Varrault
CG: 31, DR: 105
Roy
CG: 35, SD: 21


KEY: DR = Defensive Rate, SD = Scoring Difference, SR = Strike Rate, CG = Counting Games – League games playing at least 70 minutes

## LEAGUE APPEARANCES, BOOKINGS AND CAPS

| | AGE | IN THE SQUAD | COUNTING GAMES | MINUTES ON PITCH | YELLOW CARDS | RED CARDS | THIS SEASON | HOME COUNTRY |
|---|---|---|---|---|---|---|---|---|
| **Goalkeepers** | | | | | | | | |
| Damien Gregorini | 24 | 38 | 38 | 3420 | 0 | 0 | - | France |
| Hilaire Munoz | 20 | 1 | 0 | 0 | 0 | 0 | - | France |
| Jean Padovani | 23 | 1 | 0 | 0 | 0 | 0 | - | France |
| Bruno Valencony | 35 | 36 | 0 | 0 | 0 | 0 | - | France |
| **Defenders** | | | | | | | | |
| Jacques Abardonado | 25 | 38 | 38 | 3420 | 5 | 0 | - | France |
| Patrick Barul | 25 | 26 | 4 | 536 | 3 | 0 | - | France |
| Kelly Berville | 25 | 4 | 0 | 46 | 1 | 0 | - | France |
| Alcaly Camara | 22 | 1 | 1 | 90 | 0 | 0 | - | Senegal |
| Jean-Charles Cirilli | 20 | 7 | 0 | 20 | 0 | 0 | - | France |
| Jose Cobos | 35 | 33 | 31 | 2895 | 6 | 1 | - | France |
| Serge Die | 25 | 4 | 0 | 96 | 0 | 0 | - | Ivory Coast |
| Louis Pamarot | 24 | 34 | 33 | 3019 | 9 | 0 | - | France |
| Cedric Varrault | 23 | 35 | 31 | 2952 | 5 | 1 | - | France |
| **Midfielders** | | | | | | | | |
| Dominique Aulanier | 29 | 7 | 1 | 273 | 1 | 1 | - | France |
| Oumar Bakari | 23 | 6 | 0 | 113 | 1 | 0 | - | France |
| Yohann Bigne | 25 | 34 | 31 | 2738 | 8 | 0 | - | France |
| Pereira Everson | 27 | 33 | 30 | 2845 | 13 | 0 | - | Brazil |
| Cedric Mionnet | 29 | 15 | 4 | 550 | 0 | 0 | - | France |
| Romain Pitau | 25 | 35 | 34 | 3057 | 6 | 1 | - | France |
| Pablo Rodriguez | 26 | 4 | 2 | 182 | 0 | 0 | - | Argentina |
| Eric Roy | 35 | 36 | 35 | 3172 | 5 | 0 | - | France |
| Thibault Di Porfirio | 24 | 17 | 7 | 790 | 1 | 0 | - | France |
| Janik Tamazout | 24 | 3 | 0 | 5 | 0 | 0 | - | France |
| Sammy Traore | 21 | 28 | 12 | 1191 | 3 | 0 | - | Ivory Coast |
| **Forwards** | | | | | | | | |
| Johan Audel | 19 | 1 | 0 | 0 | 0 | 0 | - | France |
| Sergi Ayeli | 21 | 23 | 4 | 663 | 1 | 0 | - | Ivory Coast |
| Abdelmalek Cherrad | 22 | 30 | 11 | 1323 | 2 | 0 | - | Algeria |
| Kaba Diawara | 27 | 37 | 31 | 3014 | 6 | 0 | - | France |
| Laurent Gagnier | 24 | 8 | 1 | 127 | 1 | 0 | - | France |
| Christophe Meslin | 25 | 9 | 5 | 503 | 0 | 0 | - | France |
| Adekamni Olufade | 23 | 26 | 2 | 495 | 2 | 0 | - | Togo |

KEY: LEAGUE BOOKINGS CAPS (FIFA RANKING)

## SQUAD APPEARANCES

| Match | 1 | 2 | 3 | 4 | 5 | 6 | 7 | 8 | 9 | 10 | 11 | 12 | 13 | 14 | 15 | 16 | 17 | 18 | 19 | 20 | 21 | 22 | 23 | 24 | 25 | 26 | 27 | 28 | 29 | 30 | 31 | 32 | 33 | 34 | 35 | 36 | 37 | 38 |
|---|---|---|---|---|---|---|---|---|---|---|---|---|---|---|---|---|---|---|---|---|---|---|---|---|---|---|---|---|---|---|---|---|---|---|---|---|---|---|
| Venue | H | H | A | H | A | H | H | H | A | H | A | H | A | H | A | H | A | H | A | A | H | A | H | A | H | A | H | A | H | A | H | A | H | A | H | A | H | A |
| Competition | L | L | L | L | L | L | L | L | L | L | L | L | L | L | L | L | L | L | L | L | L | L | L | L | L | L | L | L | L | L | L | L | L | L | L | L | L | L |
| Result | L | W | W | W | D | W | D | W | L | W | D | D | D | W | W | D | L | W | L | D | W | D | D | L | W | L | D | D | D | D | L | W | W | D | D | L | D | L |

**Goalkeepers**
Damien Gregorini
Hilaire Munoz
Jean Padovani
Bruno Valencony

**Defenders**
Jacques Abardonado
Patrick Barul
Kelly Berville
Alcaly Camara
Jean-Charles Cirilli
Jose Cobos
Serge Die
Louis Pamarot
Cedric Varrault

**Midfielders**
Dominique Aulanier
Oumar Bakari
Yohann Bigne
Pereira da Silva Everson
Cedric Mionnet
Romain Pitau
Pablo Rodriguez
Eric Roy
Thibault Scotto Di Porfirio
Janik Belgacem Tamazout
Sammy Traore

**Forwards**
Johan Audel
Sergi Ayeli
Abdelmalek Cherrad
Kaba Diawara
Laurent Gagnier
Christophe Meslin
Adekamni Olufade

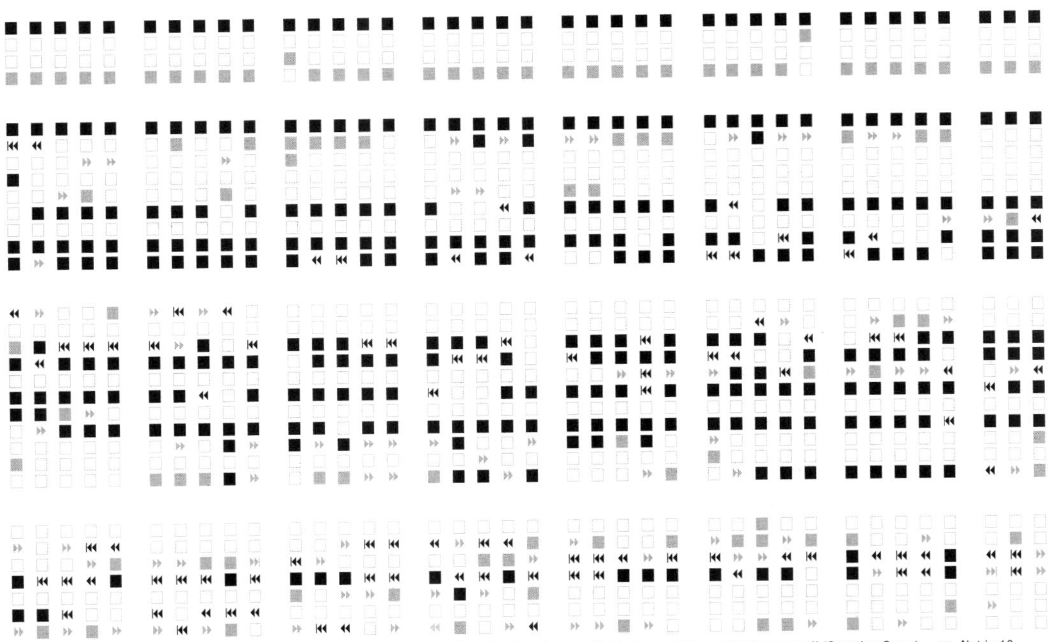

KEY: ■ On all match ■ On bench ⏮ Subbed or sent off (Counting game) ◀◀ Subbed or sent off (playing less than 70 minutes) ⏭ Subbed on from bench (Counting Game) ▶▶ Subbed on (playing less than 70 minutes) Subbed on and then subbed or sent off (Counting Game) Subbed on and then subbed or sent off (playing less than 70 minutes) □ Not in 16

# PARIS St GERMAIN

Final Position: **11th**

| | | | | | | |
|---|---|---|---|---|---|---|
| 1 | lge | Auxerre | H | W | 1-0 | Aloisio 50 |
| 2 | lge | Bordeaux | A | D | 0-0 | |
| 3 | lge | AC Ajaccio | H | D | 2-2 | Cardetti 43; Aloisio 45 |
| 4 | lge | Le Havre | A | W | 1-0 | Aloisio 90 |
| 5 | lge | Nice | H | D | 1-1 | Cardetti 73 |
| 6 | lge | Lille | A | L | 1-2 | Ronaldinho 48 pen |
| 7 | lge | Strasbourg | H | W | 3-0 | Fiorese 7; Cardetti 14,47 |
| 8 | uc1rl1 | Ujpesti | H | W | 3-0 | Ronaldinho 12; Pochettino 23; Cardetti 43 |
| 9 | lge | Bastia | H | D | 1-1 | Paulo Cesar 77 |
| 10 | lge | Montpellier | A | D | 1-1 | Paulo Cesar 65 |
| 11 | uc1rl2 | Ujpesti | A | W | 1-0 | Benachour 58 |
| 12 | lge | Guingamp | H | W | 5-0 | Paulo Cesar 9,62; Aloisio 14,23; Cardetti 29 |
| 13 | lge | Troyes | A | W | 2-1 | Cardetti 3; Ronaldinho 8 |
| 14 | lge | Marseille | H | W | 3-0 | Ronaldinho 15,36 pen; Cardetti 81 |
| 15 | uc2rl1 | Nat Bucharest | A | W | 2-0 | Leroy, L 5; Andre Luiz 68 |
| 16 | lge | Sedan | A | L | 1-3 | Dehu 33 |
| 17 | lge | Sochaux | H | D | 1-1 | Ogbeche 64 |
| 18 | uc2rl2 | Nat Bucharest | H | W | 1-0 | Leroy, L 57 |
| 19 | lge | Lens | A | L | 2-3 | Heinze 39; Andre Luiz 48 |
| 20 | lge | Nantes | H | L | 0-1 | |
| 21 | uc3rl1 | Boavista | H | W | 2-1 | Nyarko 17; Fiorese 44 |
| 22 | lge | Monaco | A | L | 1-3 | Ronaldinho 25 |
| 23 | lge | Lyon | H | W | 2-0 | Heinze 37; El Karkouri 52 |
| 24 | uc3rl2 | Boavista | A | L | 0-1 | |
| 25 | lge | Rennes | A | L | 0-1 | |
| 26 | lge | Bordeaux | H | D | 1-1 | Fiorese 12 |
| 27 | lge | AC Ajaccio | A | D | 0-0 | |
| 28 | lge | Le Havre | H | W | 1-0 | Aloisio 35 |
| 29 | lge | Nice | A | D | 0-0 | |
| 30 | lge | Lille | H | W | 1-0 | Pochettino 46 |
| 31 | lge | Strasbourg | A | W | 1-0 | Devaux 60 og |
| 32 | lge | Bastia | A | L | 0-1 | |
| 33 | lge | Montpellier | H | L | 1-3 | Leroy, J 3 |
| 34 | lge | Guingamp | A | L | 2-3 | Ronaldinho 20; Leroy, J 57 |
| 35 | lge | Troyes | H | W | 4-2 | Pedron 34; Aloisio 57; Fiorese 68; Leroy, J 90 |
| 36 | lge | Marseille | A | W | 3-0 | Leroy, J 27,83; Ronaldinho 55 |
| 37 | lge | Sedan | H | W | 2-0 | Pochettino 68; Pedron 85 |
| 38 | lge | Sochaux | A | D | 0-0 | |
| 39 | lge | Lens | H | L | 0-1 | |
| 40 | lge | Nantes | A | D | 1-1 | Toure 66 |
| 41 | lge | Monaco | H | W | 2-1 | Fiorese 58; Ronaldinho 76 pen |
| 42 | lge | Lyon | A | L | 0-1 | |
| 43 | lge | Rennes | H | D | 0-0 | |
| 44 | lge | Auxerre | A | L | 0-2 | |

## ATTENDANCES

HOME GROUND: PARC DES PRINCES CAPACITY: 48712 AVERAGE LEAGUE AT HOME: 37839

| | | | | | | | |
|---|---|---|---|---|---|---|---|
| 36 | Marseille | 60000 | 12 | Guingamp | 35000 | 4 | Le Havre | 16500 |
| 41 | Monaco | 48450 | 9 | Bastia | 35000 | 18 | Nat Bucharest | 15000 |
| 5 | Nice | 45000 | 2 | Bordeaux | 35000 | 31 | Strasbourg | 14765 |
| 14 | Marseille | 45000 | 3 | AC Ajaccio | 35000 | 15 | Nat Bucharest | 14000 |
| 1 | Auxerre | 45000 | 28 | Le Havre | 33438 | 24 | Boavista | 14000 |
| 23 | Lyon | 44000 | 35 | Troyes | 30000 | 44 | Auxerre | 10000 |
| 17 | Sochaux | 40000 | 37 | Sedan | 30000 | 13 | Troyes | 10000 |
| 20 | Nantes | 40000 | 21 | Boavista | 30000 | 27 | AC Ajaccio | 10000 |
| 39 | Lens | 40000 | 16 | Sedan | 23000 | 34 | Guingamp | 9500 |
| 26 | Bordeaux | 40000 | 25 | Rennes | 23000 | 32 | Bastia | 8000 |
| 7 | Strasbourg | 39000 | 30 | Lille | 22015 | 11 | Ujpesti | 6000 |
| 40 | Nantes | 38000 | 8 | Ujpesti | 22000 | 22 | Monaco | 5000 |
| 42 | Lyon | 37823 | 10 | Montpellier | 20000 | | | |
| 43 | Rennes | 37052 | 6 | Lille | 20000 | | | |
| 33 | Montpellier | 35000 | 38 | Sochaux | 19682 | | | |
| 19 | Lens | 35000 | 29 | Nice | 17000 | | | |

■ Home □ Away ▨ Neutral

## KEY PLAYERS - GOALSCORERS

**1 De Assis Moreira Ronaldinho**

| | | | |
|---|---|---|---|
| Goals in the League | 8 | **Player Strike Rate** Average number of minutes between League goals scored by player | 237 |
| **Contribution to Attacking Power** Average number of minutes between League team goals while on pitch | 55 | **Club Strike Rate** Average number of minutes between League goals scored by club | 73 |

| | PLAYER | LGE GOALS | POWER | STRIKE RATE |
|---|---|---|---|---|
| 2 | Arruda Parente Paulo Cesar | 4 | 54 | 378 mins |
| 3 | Jerome Leroy | 5 | 73 | 562 mins |
| 4 | Fabrice Fiorese | 4 | 67 | 621 mins |
| 5 | Mauricio Pochettino | 2 | 77 | 1542 mins |

## KEY PLAYERS - MIDFIELDERS

**1 Moreiras Andre Luiz**

| | | | |
|---|---|---|---|
| Goals in the League | 1 | **Contribution to Attacking Power** Average number of minutes between League team goals while on pitch | 90 |
| **Defensive Rating** Average number of mins between League goals conceded while he was on the pitch | 126 | **Scoring Difference** Defensive Rating minus Contribution to Attacking Power | 36 |

| | PLAYER | LGE GOALS | DEF RATE | POWER | SCORE DIFF |
|---|---|---|---|---|---|
| 2 | Frederic Dehu | 1 | 92 | 72 | 20 mins |
| 3 | Jerome Leroy | 5 | 85 | 74 | 11 mins |
| 4 | Stephane Pedron | 2 | 90 | 83 | 7 mins |
| 5 | Alex Nyarko | 0 | 69 | 65 | 4 mins |

## KEY PLAYERS - DEFENDERS

**1 Parralo Aquilera Cristobal**

| | | | |
|---|---|---|---|
| **Goals Conceded (GC)** The number of League goals conceded while he was on the pitch | 25 | **Clean Sheets** In games when he played at least 70 minutes | 13 |
| **Defensive Rating** Ave number of mins between League goals conceded while on the pitch | 108 | **Club Defensive Rating** Average number of mins between League goals conceded by the club this season | 95 |

| | PLAYER | CON LGE | CLEAN SHEETS | DEF RATE |
|---|---|---|---|---|
| 2 | Gabriel Ivan Heinze | 29 | 15 | 107 mins |
| 3 | Mauricio Pochettino | 31 | 14 | 99 mins |
| 4 | Lionel Potillon | 21 | 10 | 96 mins |
| 5 | Arruda Parente Paulo Cesar | 19 | 6 | 80 mins |

## KEY GOALKEEPER

**1 Jerome Alonzo**

| | |
|---|---|
| Goals Conceded in the League | 10 |
| **Defensive Rating** Ave number of mins between League goals conceded while on the pitch | 108 |
| **Counting Games** Games when he played at least 70 minutes | 12 |
| **Clean Sheets** In games when he played at least 70 minutes | 4 |

## TOP POINT EARNERS

| | PLAYER | GAMES | AVE |
|---|---|---|---|
| 1 | Potillon | 19 | 1.68 |
| 2 | Fiorese | 26 | 1.62 |
| 3 | Paulo Cesar | 16 | 1.56 |
| 4 | Cristobal | 30 | 1.53 |
| 5 | Heinze | 34 | 1.47 |
| 6 | Letizi | 26 | 1.46 |
| 7 | Leroy | 29 | 1.45 |
| 8 | Dehu | 29 | 1.45 |
| 9 | Ronaldinho | 18 | 1.44 |
| 10 | Nyarko | 12 | 1.42 |
| | CLUB AVERAGE: | | 1.42 |

Ave = Average points per match in Counting Games

## DISCIPLINARY RECORDS

| | PLAYER | YELLOW | RED | AVE |
|---|---|---|---|---|
| 1 | Nyarko | 6 | 2 | 162 |
| 2 | Ogbeche | 4 | 1 | 166 |
| 3 | Aloisio | 8 | 1 | 169 |
| 4 | Andre Luiz | 5 | 1 | 210 |
| 5 | Leal | 3 | 1 | 241 |
| 6 | Paulo Cesar | 5 | 1 | 252 |
| 7 | Leroy | 10 | 1 | 255 |
| 8 | Heinze | 10 | 0 | 310 |
| 9 | Dehu | 8 | 0 | 333 |
| 10 | Potillon | 5 | 0 | 404 |
| 11 | Pocchettino | 6 | 1 | 440 |
| 12 | El Karkouri | 2 | 0 | 450 |
| 13 | Ronaldinho | 3 | 1 | 474 |
| | Other | 21 | 2 | |
| | TOTAL | 96 | 12 | |

## LEAGUE GOALS

| | PLAYER | MINS | GOALS | AVE |
|---|---|---|---|---|
| 1 | Ronaldinho | 1898 | 8 | 237 |
| 2 | Cardetti | 1238 | 7 | 177 |
| 3 | Aloisio | 1526 | 7 | 218 |
| 4 | Leroy | 2811 | 5 | 562 |
| 5 | Paulo Cesar | 1512 | 4 | 378 |
| 6 | Fiorese | 2485 | 4 | 621 |
| 7 | Pocchettino | 3083 | 2 | 1542 |
| 8 | Pedron | 993 | 2 | 497 |
| 9 | Heinze | 3105 | 2 | 1553 |
| 10 | Andre Luiz | 1264 | 1 | 1264 |
| 11 | El Karkouri | 901 | 1 | 901 |
| 12 | Toure | 513 | 1 | 513 |
| 13 | Dehu | 2670 | 1 | 2670 |
| | Other | | 2 | |
| | TOTAL | | 47 | |

## MONTH BY MONTH GUIDE TO THE POINTS

| MONTH | POINTS | % |
|---|---|---|
| AUGUST | 9 | 60% |
| SEPTEMBER | 5 | 42% |
| OCTOBER | 9 | 100% |
| NOVEMBER | 1 | 7% |
| DECEMBER | 4 | 44% |
| JANUARY | 8 | 67% |
| FEBRUARY | 3 | 25% |
| MARCH | 9 | 100% |
| APRIL | 2 | 22% |
| MAY | 4 | 33% |

## TEAM OF THE SEASON

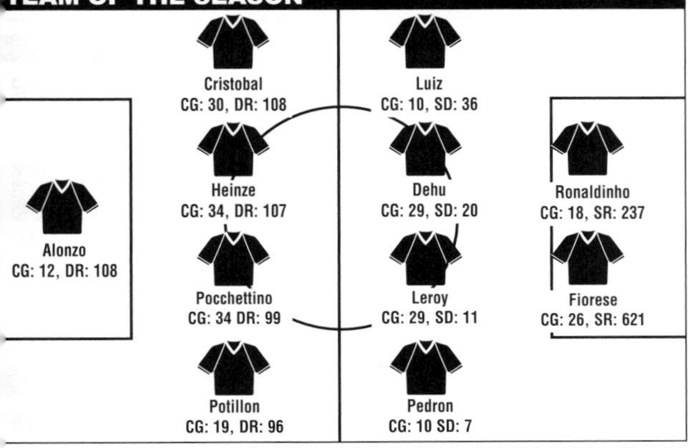

Cristobal
CG: 30, DR: 108
Luiz
CG: 10, SD: 36
Heinze
CG: 34, DR: 107
Dehu
CG: 29, SD: 20
Ronaldinho
CG: 18, SR: 237
Alonzo
CG: 12, DR: 108
Pocchettino
CG: 34 DR: 99
Leroy
CG: 29, SD: 11
Fiorese
CG: 26, SR: 621
Potillon
CG: 19, DR: 96
Pedron
CG: 10 SD: 7


KEY: DR = Defensive Rate, SD = Scoring Difference, SR = Strike Rate, CG = Counting Games – League games playing at least 70 minutes

## LEAGUE APPEARANCES, BOOKINGS AND CAPS

| | AGE | IN THE SQUAD | COUNTING GAMES | MINUTES ON PITCH | YELLOW CARDS | RED CARDS | THIS SEASON | HOME COUNTRY |
|---|---|---|---|---|---|---|---|---|
| **Goalkeepers** | | | | | | | | |
| Jerome Alonzo | 30 | 38 | 12 | 1080 | 2 | 0 | - | France |
| Stephane Gillet | 25 | 8 | 0 | 0 | 0 | 0 | - | Luxembourg |
| Lionel Letizi | 30 | 28 | 26 | 2340 | 1 | 0 | - | France |
| **Defenders** | | | | | | | | |
| Parralo Cristobal | 35 | 31 | 30 | 2709 | 4 | 1 | - | Spain |
| Didier Domi | 25 | 12 | 3 | 424 | 3 | 0 | - | France |
| Talal El Karkouri | 26 | 18 | 9 | 901 | 2 | 0 | - | Morocco |
| Gabriel Ivan Heinze | 25 | 35 | 34 | 3105 | 10 | 0 | 2 | Argentina (5) |
| Francis Llacer | 31 | 25 | 3 | 421 | 1 | 1 | - | France |
| Arruda Paulo Cesar | 30 | 24 | 16 | 1512 | 5 | 1 | - | Brazil |
| Mauricio Pocchettino | 31 | 35 | 34 | 3083 | 6 | 1 | 1 | Argentina (5) |
| Lionel Potillon | 29 | 29 | 19 | 2022 | 5 | 0 | - | France |
| **Midfielders** | | | | | | | | |
| Moreiras Andre Luiz | 29 | 18 | 10 | 1264 | 5 | 1 | - | Brazil |
| Lorik Cana | 19 | 4 | 2 | 225 | 1 | 0 | - | Bosnia |
| Frederic Dehu | 30 | 31 | 29 | 2670 | 8 | 0 | - | France |
| Hugo Leal | 23 | 18 | 8 | 965 | 3 | 1 | - | Portugal |
| Jerome Leroy | 28 | 33 | 29 | 2811 | 10 | 1 | - | France |
| Alex Nyarko | 29 | 19 | 12 | 1302 | 6 | 2 | - | Ghana |
| Stephane Pedron | 32 | 13 | 10 | 993 | 1 | 0 | - | France |
| Samuel Pietre | 19 | 0 | 0 | 0 | 0 | 0 | - | France |
| Romain Rocchi | 21 | 10 | 2 | 279 | 3 | 0 | - | France |
| Felipe Teixeira | 22 | 11 | 1 | 262 | 1 | 0 | - | France |
| **Forwards** | | | | | | | | |
| Jose Da Silva Aloisio | 28 | 27 | 9 | 1526 | 8 | 1 | - | Brazil |
| Selim Benachour | | 12 | 2 | 335 | 0 | 0 | - | Tunisia |
| Alejandro Cardetti | 27 | 21 | 8 | 1238 | 1 | 0 | - | Argentina |
| Fabrice Fiorese | 27 | 32 | 26 | 2485 | 3 | 0 | - | France |
| Laurent Leroy | 27 | 9 | 0 | 188 | 0 | 0 | - | France |
| Chigury Lucau | 18 | 2 | 0 | 25 | 0 | 0 | - | Congo |
| Pato Ogbeche | 19 | 19 | 4 | 831 | 4 | 1 | - | Nigeria |
| De Assis Ronaldinho | 23 | 28 | 18 | 1898 | 3 | 1 | 6 | Brazil (1) |
| Alioune Toure | 24 | 19 | 3 | 513 | 0 | 0 | - | France |

KEY: LEAGUE BOOKINGS CAPS (FIFA RANKING)

## SQUAD APPEARANCES

| Match | 1 | 2 | 3 | 4 | 5 | 6 | 7 | 8 | 9 | 10 | 11 | 12 | 13 | 14 | 15 | 16 | 17 | 18 | 19 | 20 | 21 | 22 | 23 | 24 | 25 | 26 | 27 | 28 | 29 | 30 | 31 | 32 | 33 | 34 | 35 | 36 | 37 | 38 | 39 | 40 | 41 | 42 | 43 | 44 |
|---|---|---|---|---|---|---|---|---|---|---|---|---|---|---|---|---|---|---|---|---|---|---|---|---|---|---|---|---|---|---|---|---|---|---|---|---|---|---|---|---|---|---|---|---|
| Venue | H | A | H | A | H | A | H | H | H | A | A | H | A | H | A | A | H | H | A | H | H | A | H | A | A | H | A | H | A | H | A | A | H | A | H | A | H | A | H | A | H | A | H | A |
| Competition | L | L | L | L | L | L | L | E | L | L | E | L | L | L | E | L | L | E | L | L | E | L | L | E | L | L | L | L | L | L | L | L | L | L | L | L | L | L | L | L | L | L | L | L |
| Result | W | D | D | W | D | L | W | W | D | D | W | W | W | W | W | L | D | W | L | L | W | L | W | L | L | D | D | W | D | W | W | L | L | L | W | W | W | D | L | D | W | L | D | L |

**Goalkeepers**
Jerome Alonzo
Stephane Gillet
Lionel Letizi

**Defenders**
Parralo Aquilera Cristobal
Didier Domi
Talal El Karkouri
Gabriel Ivan Heinze
Francis Llacer
Arruda Parente Paulo Cesar
Mauricio Pochettino
Lionel Potillon

**Midfielders**
Moreiras Andre Luiz
Lorik Cana
Frederic Dehu
Hugo Leal
Jerome Leroy
Alex Nyarko
Stephane Pedron
Samuel Pietre
Romain Rocchi
Felipe Teixeira

**Forwards**
Jose Da Silva Aloisio
Selim Benachour
Alejandro Cardetti
Fabrice Fiorese
Laurent Leroy
Chigury Lucau
Pato Ogbeche
De Assis Moreira Ronaldinho
Alioune Toure

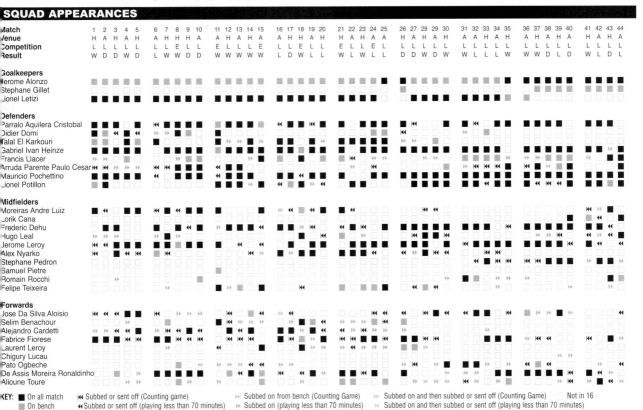

KEY: ■ On all match ■ On bench ⏮ Subbed or sent off (Counting game) ◀◀ Subbed or sent off (playing less than 70 minutes) ⏭ Subbed on from bench (Counting Game) ▶▶ Subbed on (playing less than 70 minutes) Subbed on and then subbed or sent off (Counting Game) Subbed on and then subbed or sent off (playing less than 70 minutes) Not in 16

# BASTIA

Final Position: **12th**

| | | | | | | |
|---|---|---|---|---|---|---|
| 1 | lge | Lens | H | D | 1-1 | Essien 60 |
| 2 | lge | Nantes | A | L | 0-1 | |
| 3 | lge | Monaco | H | W | 1-0 | Prince 67 |
| 4 | lge | Lyon | A | L | 1-4 | Ahamada 21 |
| 5 | lge | Rennes | H | W | 3-1 | Gourvennec 12; Ahamada 21; Maurice 70 |
| 6 | lge | Auxerre | A | L | 0-1 | |
| 7 | lge | AC Ajaccio | H | L | 1-2 | Laslandes 26 |
| 8 | lge | Paris SG | A | D | 1-1 | Laslandes 57 |
| 9 | lge | Bordeaux | H | W | 2-1 | Maurice 13 pen; Laslandes 62 |
| 10 | lge | Nice | A | L | 0-2 | |
| 11 | lge | Le Havre | H | W | 3-1 | Mendy 1; Maurice 4; Gourvennec 56 |
| 12 | lge | Strasbourg | A | L | 0-2 | |
| 13 | lge | Lille | H | W | 1-0 | Laslandes 23 |
| 14 | lge | Troyes | A | L | 0-3 | |
| 15 | lge | Guingamp | H | L | 0-2 | |
| 16 | lge | Montpellier | A | D | 2-2 | Essien 51; Uras 81 |
| 17 | lge | Marseille | H | W | 2-0 | Saada 74,87 |
| 18 | lge | Sedan | H | L | 0-1 | |
| 19 | lge | Sochaux | A | L | 0-2 | |
| 20 | lge | Nantes | H | W | 3-1 | Battles 33; Essien 72; Laslandes 85 |
| 21 | lge | Monaco | A | D | 0-0 | |
| 22 | lge | Lyon | H | W | 2-0 | Essien 65; Maurice 80 |
| 23 | lge | Rennes | A | W | 1-0 | Saada 58 |
| 24 | lge | Auxerre | H | W | 2-0 | Silvestre 69; Maurice 79 |
| 25 | lge | AC Ajaccio | A | D | 1-1 | Silvestre 76 |
| 26 | lge | Paris SG | H | W | 1-0 | Maurice 37 |
| 27 | lge | Bordeaux | A | W | 2-0 | Essien 20; Laslandes 51 |
| 28 | lge | Nice | H | D | 1-1 | Maurice 45 |
| 29 | lge | Le Havre | A | L | 0-2 | |
| 30 | lge | Strasbourg | H | D | 1-1 | Battles 13 |
| 31 | lge | Lille | A | D | 1-1 | Essien 90 |
| 32 | lge | Troyes | H | D | 1-1 | Maurice 38 |
| 33 | lge | Guingamp | A | L | 0-3 | |
| 34 | lge | Montpellier | H | L | 1-2 | Maurice 67 |
| 35 | lge | Marseille | A | L | 1-2 | Battles 90 |
| 36 | lge | Sedan | A | D | 2-2 | Battles 8; Maurice 35 |
| 37 | lge | Sochaux | H | D | 2-2 | Laslandes 18,60 |
| 38 | lge | Lens | A | L | 0-2 | |

## KEY PLAYERS - GOALSCORERS

**1 Florian Maurice**

| | | | |
|---|---|---|---|
| **Goals in the League** | 10 | **Player Strike Rate** Average number of minutes between League goals scored by player | 239 |
| **Contribution to Attacking Power** Average number of minutes between League team goals while on pitch | 74 | **Club Strike Rate** Average number of minutes between League goals scored by club | 86 |

| | PLAYER | LGE GOALS | POWER | STRIKE RATE |
|---|---|---|---|---|
| 2 | Lilian Laslandes | 8 | 90 | 305 mins |
| 3 | Laurent Battles | 4 | 74 | 408 mins |
| 4 | Michael Essien | 6 | 81 | 422 mins |
| 5 | Franck Silvestre | 2 | 84 | 720 mins |

## KEY PLAYERS - MIDFIELDERS

**1 Sebastien Piocelle**

| | | | |
|---|---|---|---|
| **Goals in the League** | 0 | **Contribution to Attacking Power** Average number of minutes between League team goals while on pitch | 74 |
| **Defensive Rating** Average number of mins between League goals conceded while he was on the pitch | 86 | **Scoring Difference** Defensive Rating minus Contribution to Attacking Power | 12 |

| | PLAYER | LGE GOALS | DEF RATE | POWER | SCORE DIFF |
|---|---|---|---|---|---|
| 2 | Laurent Battles | 4 | 82 | 74 | 8 mins |
| 3 | Frederic Mendy | 1 | 75 | 84 | -9 mins |
| 4 | Franck Silvestre | 2 | 76 | 85 | -9 mins |
| 5 | Jocelyn Gourvennec | 2 | 62 | 88 | -26 mins |

## KEY PLAYERS - DEFENDERS

**1 Michael Essien**

| | | | |
|---|---|---|---|
| **Goals Conceded (GC)** The number of League goals conceded while he was on the pitch | 33 | **Clean Sheets** In games when he played at least 70 minutes | 8 |
| **Defensive Rating** Ave number of mins between League goals conceded while on the pitch | 77 | **Club Defensive Rating** Average number of mins between League goals conceded by the club this season | 71 |

| | PLAYER | CON LGE | CLEAN SHEETS | DEF RATE |
|---|---|---|---|---|
| 2 | Gregory Vignal | 17 | 5 | 76 mins |
| 3 | Cedric Uras | 41 | 9 | 75 mins |
| 4 | Anthar Yahia | 23 | 3 | 73 mins |
| 5 | Demetrius Ferreira | 40 | 8 | 70 mins |

## GOALS SCORED

**AT HOME**

| | | |
|---|---|---|
| MOST | Lyon | 40 |
| | | 28 |
| LEAST | AC Ajaccio | 14 |

**AWAY**

| | | |
|---|---|---|
| MOST | Monaco | 29 |
| | | 12 |
| LEAST | Troyes | 7 |

## GOALS CONCEDED

**AT HOME**

| | | |
|---|---|---|
| LEAST | Sochaux & Auxerre | 8 |
| | | 17 |
| MOST | Strasbourg | 23 |

**AWAY**

| | | |
|---|---|---|
| LEAST | Lens | 15 |
| | | 31 |
| MOST | Sedan | 39 |

## KEY GOALKEEPER

**1 Nicolas Penneteau**

| | |
|---|---|
| **Goals Conceded in the League** | 39 |
| **Defensive Rating** Ave number of mins between League goals conceded while on the pitch | 77 |
| **Counting Games** Games when he played at least 70 minutes | 33 |
| **Clean Sheets** In games when he played at least 70 minutes | 9 |

## TOP POINT EARNERS

| | PLAYER | GAMES | AVE |
|---|---|---|---|
| 1 | Piocelle | 24 | 1.54 |
| 2 | Mendy | 14 | 1.43 |
| 3 | Vignal | 14 | 1.43 |
| 4 | Battles | 19 | 1.37 |
| 5 | Essien | 27 | 1.37 |
| 6 | Maurice | 24 | 1.33 |
| 7 | Uras | 34 | 1.32 |
| 8 | Penneteau | 33 | 1.27 |
| 9 | Ferreira | 31 | 1.26 |
| 10 | Yahia | 16 | 1.25 |
| | **CLUB AVERAGE:** | | **1.24** |

Ave = Average points per match in Counting Games

## ATTENDANCES

**HOME GROUND: FURIANI CAPACITY: 10660 AVERAGE LEAGUE AT HOME: 7562**

| | | | | | | | | |
|---|---|---|---|---|---|---|---|---|
| 35 | Marseille | 55000 | 20 | Nantes | 11500 | 30 | Strasbourg | 7000 |
| 8 | Paris SG | 35000 | 19 | Sochaux | 10000 | 1 | Lens | 7000 |
| 38 | Lens | 35000 | 29 | Le Havre | 10000 | 34 | Montpellier | 7000 |
| 2 | Nantes | 31500 | 7 | AC Ajaccio | 10000 | 22 | Lyon | 6516 |
| 27 | Bordeaux | 30000 | 9 | Bordeaux | 10000 | 32 | Troyes | 6000 |
| 4 | Lyon | 30000 | 14 | Troyes | 10000 | 24 | Auxerre | 6000 |
| 12 | Strasbourg | 25000 | 5 | Rennes | 9500 | 18 | Sedan | 6000 |
| 36 | Sedan | 21982 | 17 | Marseille | 9500 | 11 | Le Havre | 6000 |
| 31 | Lille | 15000 | 3 | Monaco | 9165 | 13 | Lille | 6000 |
| 6 | Auxerre | 15000 | 25 | AC Ajaccio | 9000 | 15 | Guingamp | 5000 |
| 23 | Rennes | 14624 | 28 | Nice | 9000 | 37 | Sochaux | 4500 |
| 10 | Nice | 13000 | 26 | Paris SG | 8000 | 21 | Monaco | 4000 |
| 33 | Guingamp | 13000 | 16 | Montpellier | 8000 | | | |

■ Home □ Away ▨ Neutral

## DISCIPLINARY RECORDS

| | PLAYER | YELLOW | RED | AVE |
|---|---|---|---|---|
| 1 | Mendy | 8 | 0 | 179 |
| 2 | Ahamada | 4 | 1 | 185 |
| 3 | Jeunechamp | 6 | 1 | 188 |
| 4 | Essien | 10 | 1 | 229 |
| 5 | Uras | 12 | 1 | 235 |
| 6 | Yahia | 5 | 1 | 278 |
| 7 | Piocelle | 7 | 0 | 318 |
| 8 | Ferreira | 8 | 0 | 350 |
| 9 | Maurice | 4 | 2 | 398 |
| 10 | Gourvennec | 5 | 0 | 459 |
| 11 | Ben Saada | 2 | 0 | 470 |
| 12 | Matingou | 1 | 0 | 471 |
| 13 | Alnoudji | 1 | 0 | 534 |
| | Other | 19 | 1 | |
| | **TOTAL** | **92** | **8** | |

## LEAGUE GOALS

| | PLAYER | MINS | GOALS | AVE |
|---|---|---|---|---|
| 1 | Maurice | 2392 | 10 | 239 |
| 2 | Laslandes | 2443 | 8 | 305 |
| 3 | Essien | 2529 | 6 | 422 |
| 4 | Battles | 1633 | 4 | 408 |
| 5 | Ben Saada | 941 | 3 | 314 |
| 6 | Silvestre | 1440 | 2 | 720 |
| 7 | Ahamada | 926 | 2 | 463 |
| 8 | Gourvennec | 2297 | 2 | 1149 |
| 9 | Mendy | 1432 | 1 | 1432 |
| 10 | Uras | 3060 | 1 | 3060 |
| 11 | Prince | 333 | 1 | 333 |
| | Other | | 0 | |
| | **TOTAL** | | **40** | |

## MONTH BY MONTH GUIDE TO THE POINTS

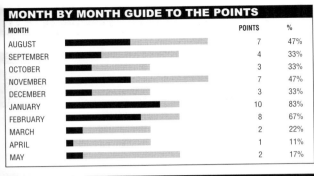

| MONTH | POINTS | % |
|---|---|---|
| AUGUST | 7 | 47% |
| SEPTEMBER | 4 | 33% |
| OCTOBER | 3 | 33% |
| NOVEMBER | 7 | 47% |
| DECEMBER | 3 | 33% |
| JANUARY | 10 | 83% |
| FEBRUARY | 8 | 67% |
| MARCH | 2 | 22% |
| APRIL | 1 | 11% |
| MAY | 2 | 17% |

## LEAGUE APPEARANCES, BOOKINGS AND CAPS

| | AGE | IN THE SQUAD | COUNTING GAMES | MINUTES ON PITCH | YELLOW CARDS | RED CARDS | THIS SEASON | HOME COUNTRY |
|---|---|---|---|---|---|---|---|---|
| **Goalkeepers** | | | | | | | | |
| Ali Boumnijel | 38 | 34 | 4 | 422 | 0 | 0 | - | Turkey |
| Arnoud Paoli | 24 | 4 | 0 | 0 | 0 | 0 | - | France |
| Nicolas Penneteau | 22 | 35 | 33 | 2998 | 2 | 1 | - | France |
| Julien Vanni | | 2 | 0 | 0 | 0 | 0 | - | France |
| **Defenders** | | | | | | | | |
| Samir Beloufa | 23 | 5 | 0 | 11 | 0 | 0 | - | France |
| Michael Essien | 20 | 29 | 27 | 2529 | 10 | 1 | - | Ghana |
| Demetrius Ferreira | 29 | 33 | 31 | 2806 | 8 | 0 | - | Brazil |
| Adel Guemari | 19 | 6 | 0 | 103 | 0 | 0 | - | France |
| Franck Matingou | 23 | 10 | 5 | 471 | 1 | 0 | - | France |
| Morlaye Soumah | 31 | 18 | 18 | 1608 | 3 | 0 | - | Guinea |
| Cedric Uras | 25 | 35 | 34 | 3060 | 12 | 1 | - | France |
| Greg Vanney | 29 | 19 | 5 | 685 | 1 | 0 | 2 | United States (10) |
| Gregory Vignal | 21 | 15 | 14 | 1289 | 2 | 0 | - | France |
| Anthar Yahia | 21 | 28 | 16 | 1673 | 5 | 1 | - | France |
| **Midfielders** | | | | | | | | |
| Nicolas Alnoudji | 23 | 23 | 5 | 534 | 1 | 0 | - | Cameroon |
| Laurent Battles | 27 | 19 | 19 | 1633 | 3 | 0 | - | France |
| Philippe Billy | 21 | 7 | 3 | 265 | 0 | 0 | - | France |
| Paul Essola | 21 | 3 | 1 | 90 | 0 | 0 | - | Cameroon |
| Jocelyn Gourvennec | 31 | 36 | 22 | 2297 | 5 | 0 | - | France |
| Herve Guy | | 3 | 0 | 8 | 0 | 0 | - | France |
| Fabrice Jau | | 10 | 3 | 354 | 1 | 0 | - | |
| Cyril Jeunechamp | 27 | 15 | 15 | 1316 | 6 | 1 | - | |
| Mathieu Jolibois | | 10 | 4 | 398 | 0 | 0 | - | France |
| Jean-C Lamberti | 21 | 1 | 1 | 90 | 0 | 0 | - | |
| Longue | | 3 | 0 | 14 | 0 | 0 | - | |
| Frederic Mendy | 29 | 20 | 14 | 1432 | 8 | 0 | - | France |
| Reynald Pedros | 31 | 12 | 2 | 395 | 0 | 0 | - | France |
| Sebastien Piocelle | 24 | 29 | 24 | 2232 | 7 | 0 | - | France |
| Franck Silvestre | 36 | 16 | 16 | 1440 | 1 | 0 | - | France |
| **Forwards** | | | | | | | | |
| Hassan Ahamada | 22 | 16 | 9 | 926 | 4 | 1 | - | France |
| Chaouki Ben Saada | 19 | 23 | 6 | 941 | 2 | 0 | - | France |
| Samir D'Avesnes | | 1 | 0 | 4 | 0 | 0 | - | France |
| Nicolas Dieuze | 24 | 10 | 1 | 197 | 1 | 0 | - | |
| Lilian Laslandes | 31 | 30 | 27 | 2443 | 3 | 0 | - | France |
| Florian Maurice | 29 | 32 | 24 | 2392 | 4 | 2 | - | France |
| Daye Prince | 25 | 11 | 3 | 333 | 2 | 0 | - | Liberia |

KEY: LEAGUE BOOKINGS CAPS (FIFA RANKING)

## TEAM OF THE SEASON

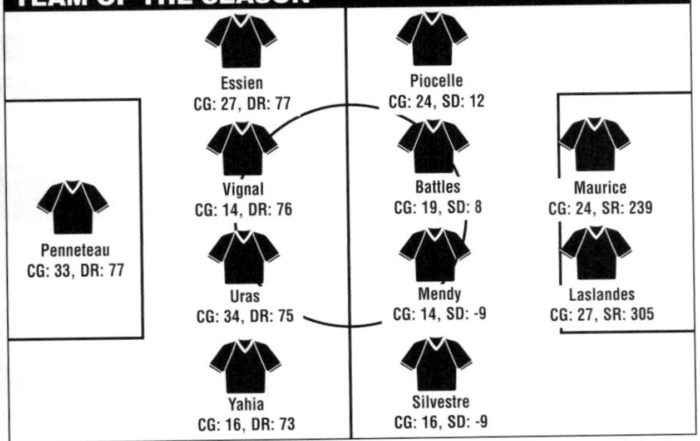
Essien
CG: 27, DR: 77
Piocelle
CG: 24, SD: 12
Vignal
CG: 14, DR: 76
Battles
CG: 19, SD: 8
Maurice
CG: 24, SR: 239
Penneteau
CG: 33, DR: 77
Uras
CG: 34, DR: 75
Mendy
CG: 14, SD: -9
Laslandes
CG: 27, SR: 305
Yahia
CG: 16, DR: 73
Silvestre
CG: 16, SD: -9

KEY: DR = Defensive Rate, SD = Scoring Difference, SR = Strike Rate, CG = Counting Games – League games playing at least 70 minutes

## SQUAD APPEARANCES

| Match | 1 | 2 | 3 | 4 | 5 | 6 | 7 | 8 | 9 | 10 | 11 | 12 | 13 | 14 | 15 | 16 | 17 | 18 | 19 | 20 | 21 | 22 | 23 | 24 | 25 | 26 | 27 | 28 | 29 | 30 | 31 | 32 | 33 | 34 | 35 | 36 | 37 | 38 |
|---|---|---|---|---|---|---|---|---|---|---|---|---|---|---|---|---|---|---|---|---|---|---|---|---|---|---|---|---|---|---|---|---|---|---|---|---|---|---|
| Venue | H | A | H | A | H | A | H | A | H | A | H | A | H | A | H | A | H | H | A | H | A | H | A | H | A | H | A | H | A | H | A | H | A | H | A | A | H | A |
| Competition | L | L | L | L | L | L | L | L | L | L | L | L | L | L | L | L | L | L | L | L | L | L | L | L | L | L | L | L | L | L | L | L | L | L | L | L | L | L |
| Result | D | L | W | L | W | L | L | D | W | L | W | L | W | L | L | D | W | L | L | W | D | W | W | W | D | W | W | D | L | D | D | D | L | L | L | D | D | L |

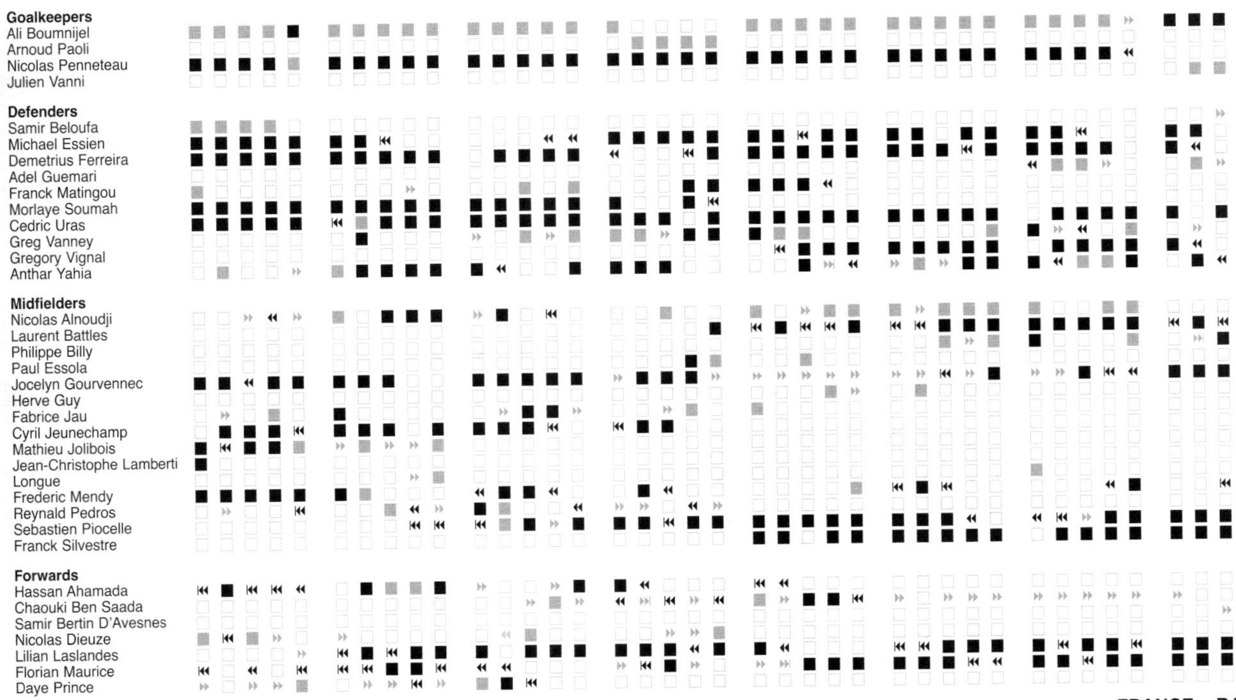
Goalkeepers
Ali Boumnijel
Arnoud Paoli
Nicolas Penneteau
Julien Vanni
Defenders
Samir Beloufa
Michael Essien
Demetrius Ferreira
Adel Guemari
Franck Matingou
Morlaye Soumah
Cedric Uras
Greg Vanney
Gregory Vignal
Anthar Yahia
Midfielders
Nicolas Alnoudji
Laurent Battles
Philippe Billy
Paul Essola
Jocelyn Gourvennec
Herve Guy
Fabrice Jau
Cyril Jeunechamp
Mathieu Jolibois
Jean-Christophe Lamberti
Longue
Frederic Mendy
Reynald Pedros
Sebastien Piocelle
Franck Silvestre
Forwards
Hassan Ahamada
Chaouki Ben Saada
Samir Bertin D'Avesnes
Nicolas Dieuze
Lilian Laslandes
Florian Maurice
Daye Prince

# STRASBOURG

Final Position: **13th**

| | | | | | | |
|---|---|---|---|---|---|---|
| 1 | lge | AC Ajaccio | H | D | 1-1 | Robin 6 og |
| 2 | lge | Nice | A | L | 0-4 | |
| 3 | lge | Le Havre | H | D | 1-1 | Martins 40 |
| 4 | lge | Bordeaux | A | W | 2-1 | Bertin 4 pen; Ljuboja 71 |
| 5 | lge | Lille | H | D | 2-2 | Le Pen 37; Martins 52 |
| 6 | lge | Sedan | H | D | 1-1 | Martins 28 |
| 7 | lge | Paris SG | A | L | 0-3 | |
| 8 | lge | Montpellier | H | W | 3-2 | Ljuboja 24,84; Bertin 90 |
| 9 | lge | Guingamp | A | W | 3-2 | Martins 43; Ljuboja 72; Ehret 75 |
| 10 | lge | Troyes | H | W | 2-1 | Ehret 19; Ismael 49 |
| 11 | lge | Marseille | A | L | 0-1 | |
| 12 | lge | Bastia | H | W | 2-0 | Beye 23; Laurent 69 |
| 13 | lge | Sochaux | A | L | 0-2 | |
| 14 | lge | Lens | H | W | 2-0 | Fischer 43; Bassila 80 |
| 15 | lge | Nantes | A | L | 1-4 | Ljuboja 30 pen |
| 16 | lge | Monaco | H | W | 1-0 | Bassila 35 |
| 17 | lge | Lyon | A | L | 1-2 | Le Pen 22 |
| 18 | lge | Rennes | H | L | 1-3 | Bagayoko 89 |
| 19 | lge | Auxerre | A | D | 0-0 | |
| 20 | lge | Nice | H | D | 0-0 | |
| 21 | lge | Le Havre | A | D | 1-1 | Laurent 20 |
| 22 | lge | Lille | A | W | 1-0 | Bagayoko 87 |
| 23 | lge | Sedan | A | L | 1-2 | Laurent 90 |
| 24 | lge | Paris SG | H | L | 0-1 | |
| 25 | lge | Montpellier | A | L | 1-2 | Le Pen 49 |
| 26 | lge | Guingamp | H | W | 3-1 | Bassila 51; Ljuboja 54; Martins 57 |
| 27 | lge | Troyes | A | L | 0-1 | |
| 28 | lge | Marseille | H | D | 0-0 | |
| 29 | lge | Bastia | A | D | 1-1 | Ismael 78 |
| 30 | lge | Bordeaux | H | D | 1-1 | Ljuboja 64 |
| 31 | lge | Sochaux | H | L | 1-3 | Pena 74 |
| 32 | lge | Lens | A | D | 1-1 | Ljuboja 90 |
| 33 | lge | Nantes | H | W | 2-0 | Deroff 42; Martins 84 |
| 34 | lge | Monaco | A | L | 0-2 | |
| 35 | lge | Lyon | H | L | 0-4 | |
| 36 | lge | Rennes | A | W | 3-2 | Cech 8 og; Martins 71; Ljuboja 84 |
| 37 | lge | Auxerre | H | L | 1-2 | Drobny 17 |
| 38 | lge | AC Ajaccio | A | D | 0-0 | |

## KEY PLAYERS - GOALSCORERS

**1 Danijel Ljuboja**

| | | | |
|---|---|---|---|
| Goals in the League | 9 | Player Strike Rate: Average number of minutes between League goals scored by player | 319 |
| Contribution to Attacking Power: Average number of minutes between League team goals while on pitch | 89 | Club Strike Rate: Average number of minutes between League goals scored by club | 86 |

| | PLAYER | LGE GOALS | POWER | STRIKE RATE |
|---|---|---|---|---|
| 2 | Corentin Martins | 7 | 83 | 406 mins |
| 3 | Teddy Bertin | 2 | 63 | 536 mins |
| 4 | Ulrich Le Pen | 3 | 95 | 540 mins |
| 5 | Christian Bassila | 3 | 88 | 828 mins |

## KEY PLAYERS - MIDFIELDERS

**1 Teddy Bertin**

| | | | |
|---|---|---|---|
| Goals in the League | 2 | Contribution to Attacking Power: Average number of minutes between League team goals while on pitch | 63 |
| Defensive Rating: Average number of mins between League goals conceded while he was on the pitch | 56 | Scoring Difference: Defensive Rating minus Contribution to Attacking Power | -7 |

| | PLAYER | LGE GOALS | DEF RATE | POWER | SCORE DIFF |
|---|---|---|---|---|---|
| 2 | Guillaume Lacour | 0 | 50 | 65 | -15 mins |
| 3 | Corentin Martins | 7 | 68 | 84 | -16 mins |
| 4 | Pascal Camadini | 0 | 68 | 88 | -20 mins |
| 5 | Yannick Fischer | 1 | 58 | 82 | -24 mins |

## KEY PLAYERS - DEFENDERS

**1 Vaclav Drobny**

| | | | |
|---|---|---|---|
| Goals Conceded (GC): The number of League goals conceded while he was on the pitch | 18 | Clean Sheets: In games when he played at least 70 minutes | 6 |
| Defensive Rating: Ave number of mins between League goals conceded while on the pitch | 90 | Club Defensive Rating: Average number of mins between League goals conceded by the club this season | 63 |

| | PLAYER | CON LGE | CLEAN SHEETS | DEF RATE |
|---|---|---|---|---|
| 2 | Jean-Christophe Devaux | 30 | 8 | 73 mins |
| 3 | Christian Bassila | 37 | 8 | 67 mins |
| 4 | Habib Beye | 36 | 7 | 65 mins |
| 5 | Valerien Ismael | 38 | 7 | 62 mins |

## GOALS SCORED

**AT HOME**

| | | |
|---|---|---|
| MOST | Lyon | 40 |
| | | 24 |
| LEAST | AC Ajaccio | 14 |

**AWAY**

| | | |
|---|---|---|
| MOST | Monaco | 29 |
| | | 16 |
| LEAST | Troyes | 7 |

## GOALS CONCEDED

**AT HOME**

| | | |
|---|---|---|
| LEAST | Sochaux & Auxerre | 8 |
| | | 23 |
| MOST | Strasbourg | 23 |

**AWAY**

| | | |
|---|---|---|
| LEAST | Lens | 15 |
| | | 31 |
| MOST | Sedan | 39 |

## KEY GOALKEEPER

**1 Vincent Fernandez**

| | |
|---|---|
| Goals Conceded in the League | 40 |
| Defensive Rating: Ave number of mins between League goals conceded while on the pitch | 59 |
| Counting Games: Games when he played at least 70 minutes | 26 |
| Clean Sheets: In games when he played at least 70 minutes | 3 |

## TOP POINT EARNERS

| | PLAYER | GAMES | AVE |
|---|---|---|---|
| 1 | Bertin | 12 | 1.50 |
| 2 | Ljuboja | 27 | 1.44 |
| 3 | Ehret | 25 | 1.40 |
| 4 | Beye | 26 | 1.38 |
| 5 | Martins | 29 | 1.38 |
| 6 | Pena | 12 | 1.33 |
| 7 | Ismael | 26 | 1.23 |
| 8 | Fernandez | 26 | 1.23 |
| 9 | Bassila | 26 | 1.23 |
| 10 | Camadini | 27 | 1.19 |
| | **CLUB AVERAGE:** | | **1.18** |

Ave = Average points per match in Counting Games

## ATTENDANCES

HOME GROUND: LA MEINAU CAPACITY: 43247 AVERAGE LEAGUE AT HOME: 16353

| | | | | | | | | |
|---|---|---|---|---|---|---|---|---|
| 11 | Marseille | 40000 | 23 | Sedan | 17000 | 5 | Lille | 11000 |
| 7 | Paris SG | 39000 | 14 | Lens | 16500 | 26 | Guingamp | 11000 |
| 32 | Lens | 38500 | 13 | Sochaux | 15000 | 1 | AC Ajaccio | 10000 |
| 4 | Bordeaux | 36819 | 9 | Guingamp | 15000 | 21 | Le Havre | 10000 |
| 17 | Lyon | 34235 | 37 | Auxerre | 14932 | 27 | Troyes | 10000 |
| 15 | Nantes | 30000 | 24 | Paris SG | 14765 | 8 | Montpellier | 9500 |
| 28 | Marseille | 28000 | 20 | Nice | 13652 | 34 | Monaco | 9000 |
| 35 | Lyon | 26000 | 31 | Sochaux | 13500 | 6 | Sedan | 9000 |
| 10 | Troyes | 25000 | 30 | Bordeaux | 12939 | 25 | Montpellier | 8500 |
| 16 | Monaco | 25000 | 33 | Nantes | 12928 | 19 | Auxerre | 8000 |
| 12 | Bastia | 25000 | 2 | Nice | 12000 | 38 | AC Ajaccio | 7200 |
| 18 | Rennes | 20000 | 3 | Le Havre | 12000 | 29 | Bastia | 7000 |
| 36 | Rennes | 18302 | 22 | Lille | 11000 | | | |

■ Home □ Away ▨ Neutral

## DISCIPLINARY RECORDS

| | PLAYER | YELLOW | RED | AVE |
|---|---|---|---|---|
| 1 | Bassila | 13 | 1 | 177 |
| 2 | Pena | 5 | 0 | 233 |
| 3 | Fischer | 7 | 0 | 246 |
| 4 | Devaux | 7 | 0 | 311 |
| 5 | Beye | 6 | 0 | 388 |
| 6 | Camadini | 6 | 0 | 408 |
| 7 | Ismael | 5 | 0 | 468 |
| 8 | Deroff | 5 | 0 | 506 |
| 9 | Bertin | 1 | 1 | 535 |
| 10 | Le Pen | 3 | 0 | 540 |
| 11 | Ljuboja | 5 | 0 | 575 |
| 12 | Njanka | 1 | 0 | 749 |
| 13 | Martins | 3 | 0 | 946 |
| | Other | 12 | 0 | |
| | TOTAL | 79 | 2 | |

## LEAGUE GOALS

| | PLAYER | MINS | GOALS | AVE |
|---|---|---|---|---|
| 1 | Ljuboja | 2875 | 9 | 319 |
| 2 | Martins | 2840 | 7 | 406 |
| 3 | Bassila | 2485 | 3 | 828 |
| 4 | Le Pen | 1621 | 3 | 540 |
| 5 | Laurent | 427 | 2 | 214 |
| 6 | Ismael | 2340 | 2 | 1170 |
| 7 | Bagayoko | 539 | 2 | 270 |
| 8 | Ehret | 2357 | 2 | 1179 |
| 9 | Bertin | 1071 | 2 | 536 |
| 10 | Fischer | 1728 | 1 | 1728 |
| 11 | Drobny | 1620 | 1 | 1620 |
| 12 | Pena | 1167 | 1 | 1167 |
| 13 | Deroff | 2532 | 1 | 2532 |
| | Other | | 4 | |
| | TOTAL | | 40 | |

## MONTH BY MONTH GUIDE TO THE POINTS

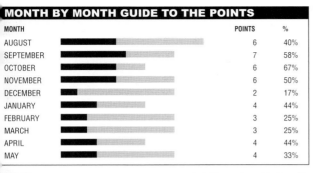

| MONTH | POINTS | % |
|---|---|---|
| AUGUST | 6 | 40% |
| SEPTEMBER | 7 | 58% |
| OCTOBER | 6 | 67% |
| NOVEMBER | 6 | 50% |
| DECEMBER | 2 | 17% |
| JANUARY | 4 | 44% |
| FEBRUARY | 3 | 25% |
| MARCH | 3 | 25% |
| APRIL | 4 | 44% |
| MAY | 4 | 33% |

## TEAM OF THE SEASON

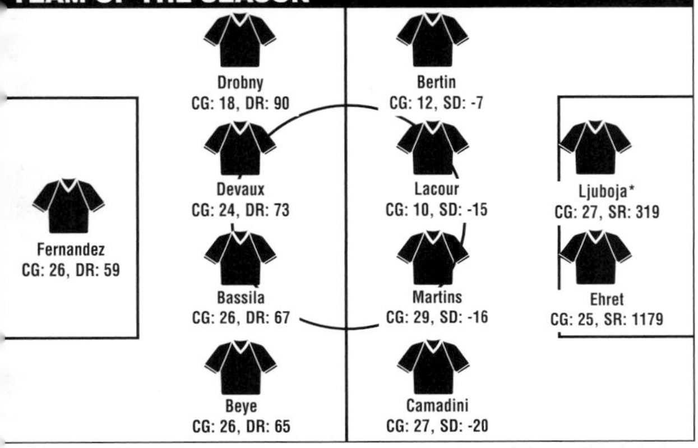
Drobny
CG: 18, DR: 90
Bertin
CG: 12, SD: -7
Devaux
CG: 24, DR: 73
Lacour
CG: 10, SD: -15
Ljuboja*
CG: 27, SR: 319
Fernandez
CG: 26, DR: 59
Bassila
CG: 26, DR: 67
Martins
CG: 29, SD: -16
Ehret
CG: 25, SR: 1179
Beye
CG: 26, DR: 65
Camadini
CG: 27, SD: -20

KEY: DR = Defensive Rate, SD = Scoring Difference, SR = Strike Rate, CG = Counting Games – League games playing at least 70 minutes

## LEAGUE APPEARANCES, BOOKINGS AND CAPS

| | AGE | IN THE SQUAD | COUNTING GAMES | MINUTES ON PITCH | YELLOW CARDS | RED CARDS | THIS SEASON | HOME COUNTRY |
|---|---|---|---|---|---|---|---|---|
| **Goalkeepers** | | | | | | | | |
| Nicolas Bonis | 21 | 19 | 9 | 810 | 0 | 0 | - | France |
| Benjamin Delin | 20 | 3 | 0 | 0 | 0 | 0 | - | France |
| Christophe Eggimann | 26 | 25 | 3 | 270 | 0 | 0 | - | France |
| Vincent Fernandez | 28 | 27 | 26 | 2340 | 2 | 0 | - | France |
| Jean-F Kornetsky | 20 | 1 | 0 | 0 | 0 | 0 | - | France |
| **Defenders** | | | | | | | | |
| Christian Bassila | 25 | 32 | 26 | 2485 | 13 | 1 | - | France |
| Habib Beye | 26 | 27 | 26 | 2333 | 6 | 0 | - | France |
| Jean-C Devaux | 28 | 26 | 24 | 2183 | 7 | 0 | - | France |
| Vaclav Drobny | 22 | 20 | 18 | 1620 | 1 | 0 | - | Czech Republic |
| Claude Ficheaux | 34 | 2 | 2 | 180 | 0 | 0 | - | France |
| Valerien Ismael | 27 | 26 | 26 | 2340 | 5 | 0 | - | France |
| Jacques Momha | 20 | 7 | 1 | 222 | 1 | 0 | - | Cameroon |
| Pierre Beaka Njanka | 28 | 12 | 8 | 749 | 1 | 0 | 1 | Cameroon (18) |
| **Midfielders** | | | | | | | | |
| Teddy Bertin | 33 | 13 | 12 | 1071 | 1 | 1 | - | France |
| Pascal Camadini | 31 | 32 | 27 | 2451 | 6 | 0 | - | France |
| Yves Deroff | 24 | 35 | 28 | 2532 | 5 | 0 | - | France |
| Yannick Fischer | 28 | 31 | 17 | 1728 | 7 | 0 | - | France |
| David Kobylik | 22 | 20 | 0 | 316 | 0 | 0 | - | Czech Republic |
| Guillaume Lacour | 22 | 24 | 10 | 1103 | 1 | 0 | - | France |
| Ulrich Le Pen | 29 | 26 | 13 | 1621 | 3 | 0 | - | France |
| Danijel Ljuboja | 25 | 37 | 27 | 2875 | 5 | 0 | - | Serbia & Montenegro |
| Nicolas Loison | | 1 | 0 | 13 | 0 | 0 | - | France |
| Corentin Martins | 33 | 37 | 29 | 2840 | 3 | 0 | - | France |
| Cedric Moukouri | 23 | 2 | 0 | 27 | 0 | 0 | - | France |
| Stephane Roda | 30 | 14 | 0 | 124 | 0 | 0 | - | France |
| Nordine Sam | 21 | 1 | 1 | 90 | 0 | 0 | - | France |
| Cedric Stoll | 20 | 2 | 0 | 0 | 0 | 0 | - | France |
| Fabrice Viau | | 2 | 1 | 106 | 0 | 0 | - | France |
| **Forwards** | | | | | | | | |
| Mamadou Bagayoko | 24 | 22 | 2 | 539 | 0 | 0 | - | Mali |
| Fabrice Ehret | 23 | 29 | 25 | 2357 | 2 | 0 | - | France |
| Pascal Johansen | | 3 | 3 | 270 | 0 | 0 | - | |
| Yannick Kamanan | 20 | 4 | 0 | 74 | 0 | 0 | - | France |
| Pierre Laurent | 32 | 17 | 2 | 427 | 3 | 0 | - | France |
| Eric Mouloungui | 19 | 13 | 1 | 296 | 2 | 0 | - | Gabon |
| Renivaldo Pena | 29 | 20 | 12 | 1167 | 5 | 0 | - | Brazil |

KEY: LEAGUE BOOKINGS CAPS (FIFA RANKING)

## SQUAD APPEARANCES

| Match | 1 | 2 | 3 | 4 | 5 | 6 | 7 | 8 | 9 | 10 | 11 | 12 | 13 | 14 | 15 | 16 | 17 | 18 | 19 | 20 | 21 | 22 | 23 | 24 | 25 | 26 | 27 | 28 | 29 | 30 | 31 | 32 | 33 | 34 | 35 | 36 | 37 | 38 |
|---|---|---|---|---|---|---|---|---|---|---|---|---|---|---|---|---|---|---|---|---|---|---|---|---|---|---|---|---|---|---|---|---|---|---|---|---|---|---|
| Venue | H | A | H | A | H | H | A | H | A | H | A | H | A | H | A | H | A | H | A | H | A | A | A | H | A | H | A | H | A | H | H | A | H | A | H | A | H | A |
| Competition | L | L | L | L | L | L | L | L | L | L | L | L | L | L | L | L | L | L | L | L | L | L | L | L | L | L | L | L | L | L | L | L | L | L | L | L | L | L |
| Result | D | L | D | W | D | D | L | W | W | W | L | W | L | W | L | W | L | L | D | D | D | W | L | L | L | W | L | D | D | D | L | D | W | L | L | W | L | D |

**Goalkeepers**
Nicolas Bonis
Benjamin Delin
Christophe Eggimann
Vincent Fernandez
Jean-Francois Kornetsky

**Defenders**
Christian Bassila
Habib Beye
Jean-Christophe Devaux
Vaclav Drobny
Claude Ficheaux
Valerien Ismael
Jacques Momha
Pierre Njanka

**Midfielders**
Teddy Bertin
Pascal Camadini
Yves Deroff
Yannick Fischer
David Kobylik
Guillaume Lacour
Ulrich Le Pen
Danijel Ljuboja
Nicolas Loison
Corentin Martins
Cedric Moukouri
Stephane Roda
Cedric Stoll
Fabrice Viau

**Forwards**
Mamadou Bagayoko
Fabrice Ehret
Pascal Johansen
Yannick Kamanan
Pierre Laurent
Eric Mouloungui
Renivaldo Pereira Pena

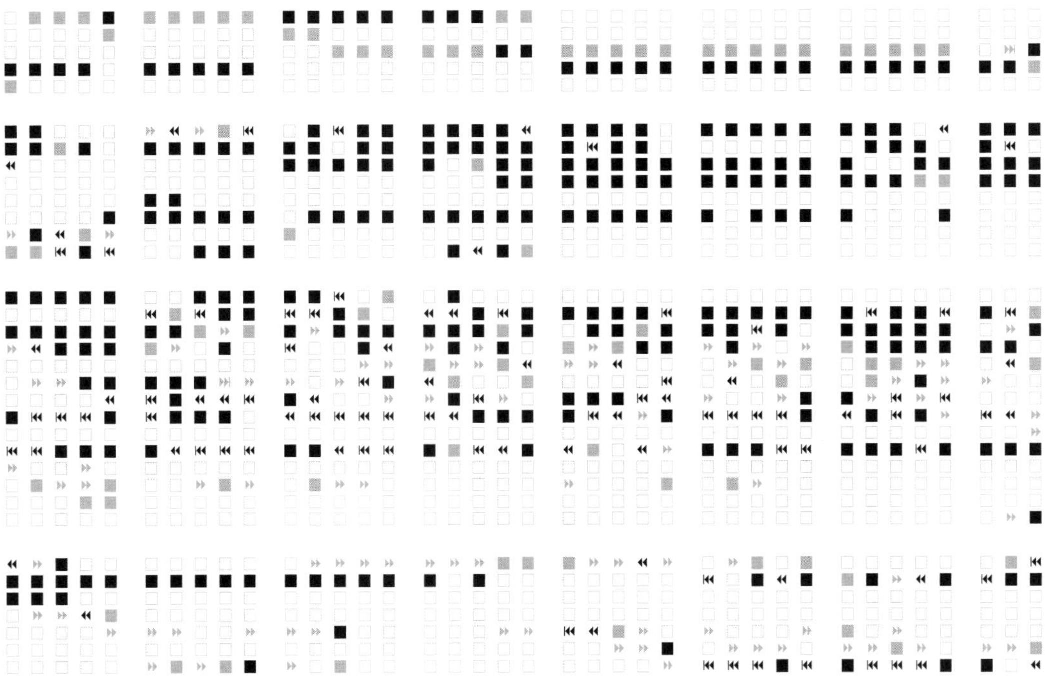

# LILLE

Final Position: **14th**

| | | | | | | |
|---|---|---|---|---|---|---|
| 1 | lge | Bordeaux | H | L | 0-3 | |
| 2 | lge | Le Havre | A | D | 0-0 | |
| 3 | lge | Nice | H | L | 0-3 | |
| 4 | lge | Troyes | H | D | 0-0 | |
| 5 | lge | Strasbourg | A | D | 2-2 | Delpierre 51; Tapia 85 |
| 6 | lge | Paris SG | H | W | 2-1 | Manchev 28,74 |
| 7 | lge | Montpellier | A | L | 0-1 | |
| 8 | lge | Guingamp | H | W | 2-1 | Tapia 49; Sterjovski 87 |
| 9 | lge | Lens | A | D | 0-0 | |
| 10 | lge | Marseille | H | W | 3-0 | Tapia 15; Brunel 54; Cheyrou, Be 64 |
| 11 | lge | Monaco | A | D | 1-1 | Moussilou 69 |
| 12 | lge | Sochaux | H | W | 1-0 | Sterjovski 54 pen |
| 13 | lge | Bastia | A | L | 0-1 | |
| 14 | lge | Nantes | H | L | 0-1 | |
| 15 | lge | Sedan | A | W | 1-0 | Landrin 77 |
| 16 | lge | Lyon | H | W | 2-1 | Manchev 68; Landrin 73 |
| 17 | lge | Rennes | A | L | 1-5 | Manchev 64 |
| 18 | lge | Auxerre | H | D | 2-2 | Manchev 3; Jaures 25 og |
| 19 | lge | AC Ajaccio | A | D | 2-2 | Manchev 22; Landrin 35 |
| 20 | lge | Le Havre | H | W | 1-0 | Delpierre 83 |
| 21 | lge | Nice | A | L | 0-2 | |
| 22 | lge | Strasbourg | H | L | 0-1 | |
| 23 | lge | Paris SG | A | L | 0-1 | |
| 24 | lge | Lens | H | L | 0-2 | |
| 25 | lge | Troyes | A | L | 0-2 | |
| 26 | lge | Marseille | A | L | 0-2 | |
| 27 | lge | Monaco | H | L | 1-3 | Landrin 86 |
| 28 | lge | Sochaux | A | D | 2-2 | Brunel 56; Manchev 59 |
| 29 | lge | Montpellier | H | W | 2-0 | Landrin 59; Sterjovski 77 pen |
| 30 | lge | Guingamp | A | L | 0-1 | |
| 31 | lge | Bastia | H | D | 1-1 | Brunel 32 pen |
| 32 | lge | Nantes | A | L | 0-1 | |
| 33 | lge | Sedan | H | D | 0-0 | |
| 34 | lge | Lyon | A | D | 0-0 | |
| 35 | lge | Rennes | H | W | 1-0 | Sterjovski 30 |
| 36 | lge | Auxerre | A | D | 0-0 | |
| 37 | lge | AC Ajaccio | H | W | 2-0 | Delpierre 58; Sterjovski 70 |
| 38 | lge | Bordeaux | A | L | 0-2 | |

## KEY PLAYERS - GOALSCORERS

**1 Vladimir Manchev**

| | | | |
|---|---|---|---|
| Goals in the League | 7 | Player Strike Rate: Average number of minutes between League goals scored by player | 365 |
| Contribution to Attacking Power: Average number of minutes between League team goals while on pitch | 111 | Club Strike Rate: Average number of minutes between League goals scored by club | 114 |

| | PLAYER | LGE GOALS | POWER | STRIKE RATE |
|---|---|---|---|---|
| 2 | Christophe Landrin | 5 | 111 | 513 mins |
| 3 | Mathieu Delpierre | 3 | 120 | 885 mins |
| 4 | Phillipe Brunel | 3 | 104 | 943 mins |
| 5 | Benoit Cheyrou | 1 | 107 | 1833 mins |

## KEY PLAYERS - MIDFIELDERS

**1 Fernando D'Amico**

| | | | |
|---|---|---|---|
| Goals in the League | 0 | Contribution to Attacking Power: Average number of minutes between League team goals while on pitch | 94 |
| Defensive Rating: Average number of mins between League goals conceded while he was on the pitch | 72 | Scoring Difference: Defensive Rating minus Contribution to Attacking Power | -22 |

| | PLAYER | LGE GOALS | DEF RATE | POWER | SCORE DIFF |
|---|---|---|---|---|---|
| 2 | Benoit Cheyrou | 1 | 83 | 108 | -25 mins |
| 3 | Christophe Landrin | 5 | 89 | 117 | -28 mins |
| 4 | Sylvain Ndiaye | 0 | 76 | 125 | -49 mins |

## KEY PLAYERS - DEFENDERS

**1 Eric Abidal**

| | | | |
|---|---|---|---|
| Goals Conceded (GC): The number of League goals conceded while he was on the pitch | 22 | Clean Sheets: In games when he played at least 70 minutes | 10 |
| Defensive Rating: Ave number of mins between League goals conceded while on the pitch | 106 | Club Defensive Rating: Average number of mins between League goals conceded by the club this season | 78 |

| | PLAYER | CON LGE | CLEAN SHEETS | DEF RATE |
|---|---|---|---|---|
| 2 | Marius Achim Baciu | 17 | 8 | 90 mins |
| 3 | Stephane Pichot | 28 | 11 | 87 mins |
| 4 | Mathieu Delpierre | 35 | 10 | 76 mins |
| 5 | Gregory Tafforeau | 38 | 9 | 73 mins |

## GOALS SCORED

**AT HOME**

| | | |
|---|---|---|
| MOST | Lyon | 40 |
| | | 20 |
| LEAST | AC Ajaccio | 14 |

**AWAY**

| | | |
|---|---|---|
| MOST | Monaco | 29 |
| | | 9 |
| LEAST | Troyes | 7 |

## GOALS CONCEDED

**AT HOME**

| | | |
|---|---|---|
| LEAST | Sochaux & Auxerre | 8 |
| | | 19 |
| MOST | Strasbourg | 23 |

**AWAY**

| | | |
|---|---|---|
| LEAST | Lens | 15 |
| | | 25 |
| MOST | Sedan | 39 |

## KEY GOALKEEPER

**1 Gregory Wimbee**

| | |
|---|---|
| Goals Conceded in the League | 36 |
| Defensive Rating: Ave number of mins between League goals conceded while on the pitch | 78 |
| Counting Games: Games when he played at least 70 minutes | 31 |
| Clean Sheets: In games when he played at least 70 minutes | 11 |

## TOP POINT EARNERS

| | PLAYER | GAMES | AVE |
|---|---|---|---|
| 1 | Baciu | 16 | 1.50 |
| 2 | D'Amico | 21 | 1.43 |
| 3 | Abidal | 25 | 1.40 |
| 4 | Pichot | 26 | 1.38 |
| 5 | Brunel | 29 | 1.28 |
| 6 | Manchev | 26 | 1.15 |
| 7 | Landrin | 26 | 1.15 |
| 8 | Delpierre | 29 | 1.07 |
| 9 | Cheyrou | 16 | 1.06 |
| 10 | Tafforeau | 31 | 1.06 |
| | CLUB AVERAGE: | | 1.11 |

Ave = Average points per match in Counting Games

## ATTENDANCES

HOME GROUND: STADE GRIMONPREZ CAPACITY: 21128 AVERAGE LEAGUE AT HOME: 14784

| | | | | | | | | |
|---|---|---|---|---|---|---|---|---|
| 26 | Marseille | 50000 | 24 | Lens | 16500 | 36 | Auxerre | 11537 |
| 34 | Lyon | 46025 | 29 | Montpellier | 15000 | 21 | Nice | 11000 |
| 9 | Lens | 40500 | 31 | Bastia | 15000 | 5 | Strasbourg | 11000 |
| 38 | Bordeaux | 28695 | 8 | Guingamp | 15000 | 22 | Strasbourg | 11000 |
| 7 | Montpellier | 28000 | 3 | Nice | 15000 | 25 | Troyes | 10177 |
| 32 | Nantes | 25000 | 14 | Nantes | 15000 | 4 | Troyes | 10000 |
| 23 | Paris SG | 22015 | 2 | Le Havre | 14750 | 35 | Rennes | 10000 |
| 10 | Marseille | 20000 | 1 | Bordeaux | 14145 | 28 | Sochaux | 10000 |
| 16 | Lyon | 20000 | 20 | Le Havre | 13525 | 33 | Sedan | 10000 |
| 6 | Paris SG | 20000 | 15 | Sedan | 13500 | 13 | Bastia | 6000 |
| 12 | Sochaux | 19000 | 18 | Auxerre | 13000 | 11 | Monaco | 5000 |
| 37 | AC Ajaccio | 16729 | 27 | Monaco | 12000 | 19 | AC Ajaccio | 5000 |
| 17 | Rennes | 16500 | 30 | Guingamp | 12000 | | | |

Home / Away / Neutral

## DISCIPLINARY RECORDS

| | PLAYER | YELLOW | RED | AVE |
|---|---|---|---|---|
| 1 | D'Amico | 13 | 1 | 154 |
| 2 | Bonnal | 3 | 1 | 169 |
| 3 | Baciu | 5 | 1 | 254 |
| 4 | Chalme | 3 | 0 | 292 |
| 5 | Delpierre | 8 | 1 | 294 |
| 6 | Sterjovski | 2 | 1 | 319 |
| 7 | Pichot | 6 | 0 | 406 |
| 8 | Cheyrou | 4 | 0 | 458 |
| 9 | Tapia | 2 | 0 | 490 |
| 10 | Tafforeau | 5 | 0 | 552 |
| 11 | Ndiaye | 3 | 1 | 685 |
| 12 | Brunel | 4 | 0 | 707 |
| 13 | Abidal | 2 | 1 | 780 |
| | Other | 10 | 1 | |
| | TOTAL | 70 | 8 | |

## LEAGUE GOALS

| | PLAYER | MINS | GOALS | AVE |
|---|---|---|---|---|
| 1 | Manchev | 2556 | 7 | 365 |
| 2 | Landrin | 2567 | 5 | 513 |
| 3 | Sterjovski | 957 | 5 | 191 |
| 4 | Delpierre | 2654 | 3 | 885 |
| 5 | Tapia | 981 | 3 | 327 |
| 6 | Brunel | 2828 | 3 | 943 |
| 7 | Moussilou | 469 | 1 | 469 |
| 8 | Cheyrou | 1833 | 1 | 1833 |
| | Other | | 1 | |
| | TOTAL | | 29 | |

## MONTH BY MONTH GUIDE TO THE POINTS

| MONTH | POINTS | % |
|---|---|---|
| AUGUST | 3 | 20% |
| SEPTEMBER | 7 | 58% |
| OCTOBER | 7 | 78% |
| NOVEMBER | 6 | 40% |
| DECEMBER | 5 | 56% |
| JANUARY | 0 | 0% |
| FEBRUARY | 0 | 0% |
| MARCH | 5 | 33% |
| APRIL | 2 | 22% |
| MAY | 7 | 58% |

## TEAM OF THE SEASON

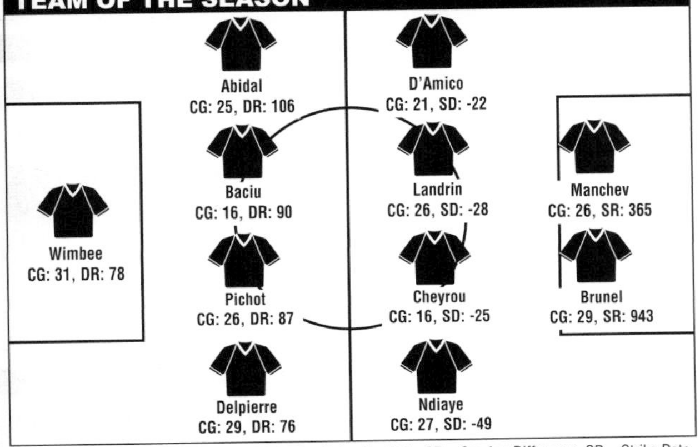

Abidal
CG: 25, DR: 106
D'Amico
CG: 21, SD: -22
Baciu
CG: 16, DR: 90
Landrin
CG: 26, SD: -28
Manchev
CG: 26, SR: 365
Wimbee
CG: 31, DR: 78
Pichot
CG: 26, DR: 87
Cheyrou
CG: 16, SD: -25
Brunel
CG: 29, SR: 943
Delpierre
CG: 29, DR: 76
Ndiaye
CG: 27, SD: -49


**KEY:** DR = Defensive Rate, SD = Scoring Difference, SR = Strike Rate, CG = Counting Games – League games playing at least 70 minutes

## LEAGUE APPEARANCES, BOOKINGS AND CAPS

| | AGE | IN THE SQUAD | COUNTING GAMES | MINUTES ON PITCH | YELLOW CARDS | RED CARDS | THIS SEASON | HOME COUNTRY |
|---|---|---|---|---|---|---|---|---|
| **Goalkeepers** | | | | | | | | |
| Gregory Malicki | 29 | 35 | 6 | 594 | 0 | 0 | - | France |
| Laurent Pichon | 22 | 7 | 0 | 0 | 0 | 0 | - | France |
| Gregory Wimbee | 31 | 32 | 31 | 2823 | 2 | 1 | - | France |
| **Defenders** | | | | | | | | |
| Eric Abidal | 23 | 27 | 25 | 2342 | 2 | 1 | - | France |
| Marius Achim Baciu | 28 | 26 | 16 | 1529 | 5 | 1 | - | Romania |
| Mathieu Delpierre | 22 | 32 | 29 | 2654 | 8 | 1 | - | France |
| Abdelilah Fahmi | 29 | 23 | 16 | 1571 | 2 | 0 | - | Morocco |
| Stephane Pichot | 26 | 28 | 26 | 2439 | 6 | 0 | - | France |
| Rafael Schmitz | 22 | 8 | 2 | 180 | 0 | 0 | - | Brazil |
| Gregory Tafforeau | 26 | 32 | 31 | 2764 | 5 | 0 | - | France |
| **Midfielders** | | | | | | | | |
| Nicolas Aubriot | 18 | 1 | 0 | 0 | 0 | 0 | - | France |
| Mathieu Chalme | 22 | 30 | 6 | 877 | 3 | 0 | - | France |
| Benoit Cheyrou | 22 | 33 | 16 | 1833 | 4 | 0 | - | France |
| Fernando D'Amico | 28 | 28 | 21 | 2164 | 13 | 1 | - | Argentina |
| Stephane Dumont | 20 | 1 | 0 | 0 | 0 | 0 | - | France |
| Christophe Landrin | 26 | 36 | 26 | 2567 | 3 | 0 | - | France |
| Sylvain Ndiaye | 27 | 36 | 27 | 2741 | 3 | 1 | 3 | Senegal (29) |
| **Forwards** | | | | | | | | |
| Nicholas Bonnal | 26 | 19 | 4 | 679 | 3 | 1 | - | France |
| Djezon Boutoille | 27 | 16 | 8 | 902 | 0 | 0 | - | France |
| Phillipe Brunel | 30 | 36 | 29 | 2828 | 4 | 0 | - | France |
| Gregory Campi | 27 | 2 | 0 | 6 | 0 | 0 | - | Italy |
| Marc-Antoine Fortune | 22 | 16 | 3 | 601 | 0 | 0 | - | France |
| Jean Makoun | 20 | 12 | 3 | 355 | 0 | 0 | - | Cameroon |
| Vladimir Manchev | 25 | 36 | 26 | 2556 | 3 | 0 | - | Bulgaria |
| Matt Moussilou | 21 | 19 | 1 | 469 | 0 | 0 | - | France |
| Mike Sterjovski | 24 | 25 | 9 | 957 | 2 | 1 | - | Australia |
| Hector Tapia | 25 | 16 | 6 | 981 | 2 | 0 | - | Chile |

**KEY:** LEAGUE BOOKINGS CAPS (FIFA RANKING)

## SQUAD APPEARANCES

| Match | 1 | 2 | 3 | 4 | 5 | 6 | 7 | 8 | 9 | 10 | 11 | 12 | 13 | 14 | 15 | 16 | 17 | 18 | 19 | 20 | 21 | 22 | 23 | 24 | 25 | 26 | 27 | 28 | 29 | 30 | 31 | 32 | 33 | 34 | 35 | 36 | 37 | 38 |
|---|---|---|---|---|---|---|---|---|---|---|---|---|---|---|---|---|---|---|---|---|---|---|---|---|---|---|---|---|---|---|---|---|---|---|---|---|---|---|
| Venue | H | A | H | H | A | H | A | H | A | H | A | H | A | H | A | H | A | H | A | H | A | H | A | H | A | A | H | A | H | A | H | A | H | A | H | A | H | A |
| Competition | L | L | L | L | L | L | L | L | L | L | L | L | L | L | L | L | L | L | L | L | L | L | L | L | L | L | L | L | L | L | L | L | L | L | L | L | L | L |
| Result | L | D | L | D | D | W | L | W | D | W | D | W | L | L | W | W | L | D | D | W | L | L | L | L | L | L | L | D | W | L | D | L | D | D | W | D | W | L |

**Goalkeepers**
Gregory Malicki
Laurent Pichon
Gregory Wimbee

**Defenders**
Eric Abidal
Marius Achim Baciu
Mathieu Delpierre
Abdelilah Fahmi
Stephane Pichot
Rafael Schmitz
Gregory Tafforeau

**Midfielders**
Nicolas Aubriot
Mathieu Chalme
Benoit Cheyrou
Fernando D'Amico
Stephane Dumont
Christophe Landrin
Sylvain N'Diaye

**Forwards**
Nicholas Bonnal
Djezon Boutoille
Phillipe Brunel
Gregory Campi
Marc-Antoine Fortune
Jean Makoun
Vladimir Manchev
Matt Moussilou
Mike Sterjovski
Hector Tapia

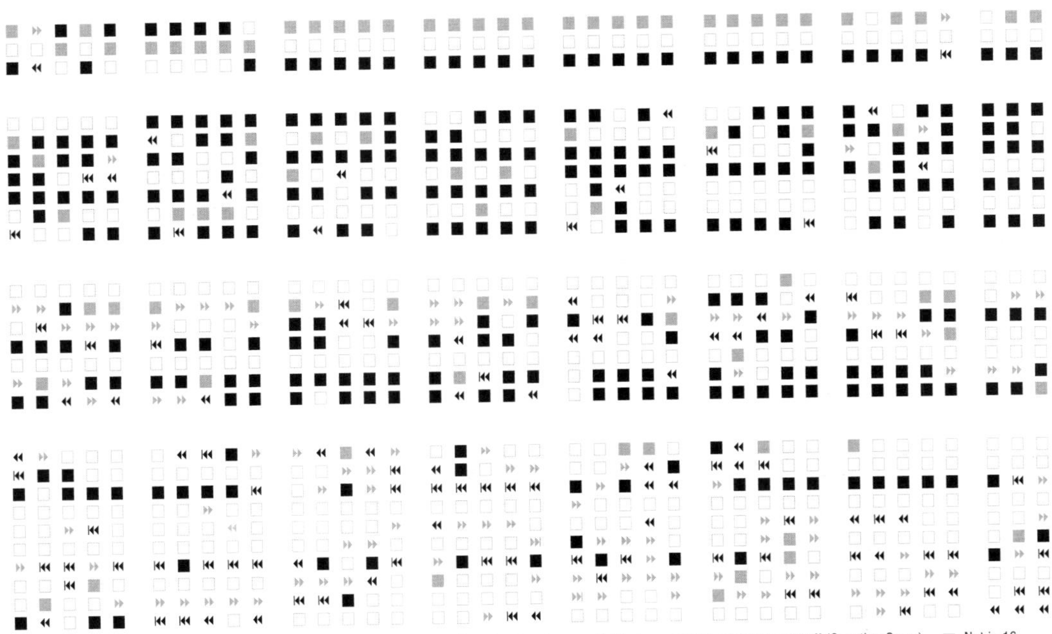

**KEY:** ■ On all match ■ On bench ⏮ Subbed or sent off (Counting game) « Subbed or sent off (playing less than 70 minutes) ⏭ Subbed on from bench (Counting Game) » Subbed on (playing less than 70 minutes) Subbed on and then subbed or sent off (Counting Game) Subbed on and then subbed or sent off (playing less than 70 minutes) □ Not in 16

# RENNES

Final Position: **15th**

| | | | | | | |
|---|---|---|---|---|---|---|
| 1 | lge | Montpellier | A | L | 0-1 | |
| 2 | lge | Troyes | H | D | 0-0 | |
| 3 | lge | Guingamp | A | L | 0-3 | |
| 4 | lge | Marseille | H | L | 1-3 | Piquionne 8 |
| 5 | lge | Bastia | A | L | 1-3 | Piquionne 16 |
| 6 | lge | Sochaux | H | D | 2-2 | Monterrubio 83 pen,90 pen |
| 7 | lge | Lens | A | L | 0-1 | |
| 8 | lge | Nantes | H | W | 1-0 | Arribage 75 |
| 9 | lge | Monaco | A | L | 1-2 | Reveillere 33 |
| 10 | lge | Lyon | H | L | 0-1 | |
| 11 | lge | Sedan | A | W | 3-1 | Piquionne 40; Maoulida 71; N'Diaye 77 |
| 12 | lge | Auxerre | A | L | 0-1 | |
| 13 | lge | AC Ajaccio | H | D | 0-0 | |
| 14 | lge | Bordeaux | A | L | 0-2 | |
| 15 | lge | Le Havre | H | D | 0-0 | |
| 16 | lge | Nice | A | D | 0-0 | |
| 17 | lge | Lille | H | W | 5-1 | Monterrubio 22 pen; Echouafni 29; Piquionne 35,49,63 |
| 18 | lge | Strasbourg | A | W | 3-1 | Monterrubio 46 pen; Beye 63 og; Maoulida 90 |
| 19 | lge | Paris SG | H | W | 1-0 | Arribage 69 |
| 20 | lge | Troyes | A | W | 1-0 | Piquionne 89 |
| 21 | lge | Guingamp | H | W | 2-1 | Michel 16 og; Arribage 83 |
| 22 | lge | Marseille | A | L | 0-2 | |
| 23 | lge | Bastia | H | L | 0-1 | |
| 24 | lge | Sochaux | A | L | 0-1 | |
| 25 | lge | Lens | H | D | 1-1 | Jeunechamp 45 |
| 26 | lge | Nantes | A | L | 0-1 | |
| 27 | lge | Monaco | H | D | 0-0 | |
| 28 | lge | Lyon | A | L | 1-4 | Delaye 22 |
| 29 | lge | Sedan | H | W | 1-0 | Maoulida 87 |
| 30 | lge | Auxerre | H | D | 0-0 | |
| 31 | lge | AC Ajaccio | A | L | 0-1 | |
| 32 | lge | Bordeaux | H | L | 3-4 | Piquionne 45; Delaye 84; Frei 86 |
| 33 | lge | Le Havre | A | W | 1-0 | Piquionne 24 |
| 34 | lge | Nice | H | D | 2-2 | Delaye 23; Arribage 53 |
| 35 | lge | Lille | A | L | 0-1 | |
| 36 | lge | Strasbourg | H | L | 2-3 | Arribage 23; Devaux 75 og |
| 37 | lge | Paris SG | A | D | 0-0 | |
| 38 | lge | Montpellier | H | W | 3-1 | Monterrubio 5,47 pen; Piquionne 67 |

## KEY PLAYERS - GOALSCORERS

**1 Frederic Piquionne**

| | | | |
|---|---|---|---|
| Goals in the League | 10 | Player Strike Rate<br>Average number of minutes between League goals scored by player | 243 |
| Contribution to Attacking Power<br>Average number of minutes between League team goals while on pitch | 89 | Club Strike Rate<br>Average number of minutes between League goals scored by club | 98 |

| | PLAYER | LGE GOALS | POWER | STRIKE RATE |
|---|---|---|---|---|
| 2 | Olivier Monterrubio | 6 | 77 | 321 mins |
| 3 | Phillipe Delaye | 3 | 82 | 549 mins |
| 4 | Dominique Arribage | 5 | 95 | 666 mins |
| 5 | Cyril Jeunechamp | 1 | 188 | 1133 mins |

## KEY PLAYERS - MIDFIELDERS

**1 Francois Grenet**

| | | | |
|---|---|---|---|
| Goals in the League | 0 | Contribution to Attacking Power<br>Average number of minutes between League team goals while on pitch | 72 |
| Defensive Rating<br>Average number of mins between League goals conceded while he was on the pitch | 89 | Scoring Difference<br>Defensive Rating minus Contribution to Attacking Power | 17 |

| | PLAYER | LGE GOALS | DEF RATE | POWER | SCORE DIFF |
|---|---|---|---|---|---|
| 2 | Etienne Didot | 0 | 80 | 80 | 0 mins |
| 3 | Olivier Echouafni | 1 | 88 | 88 | 0 mins |
| 4 | Phillipe Delaye | 3 | 69 | 82 | -13 mins |
| 5 | Oliver Sorlin | 0 | 72 | 100 | -28 mins |

## KEY PLAYERS - DEFENDERS

**1 Anthony Reveillere**

| | | | |
|---|---|---|---|
| Goals Conceded (GC)<br>The number of League goals conceded while he was on the pitch | 18 | Clean Sheets<br>In games when he played at least 70 minutes | 7 |
| Defensive Rating<br>Ave number of mins between League goals conceded while on the pitch | 99 | Club Defensive Rating<br>Average number of mins between League goals conceded by the club this season | 76 |

| | PLAYER | CON LGE | CLEAN SHEETS | DEF RATE |
|---|---|---|---|---|
| 2 | Gregory Bourillon | 16 | 6 | 99 mins |
| 3 | Julien Escude | 30 | 9 | 88 mins |
| 4 | Lamine Diatta | 20 | 7 | 86 mins |
| 5 | Dominique Arribage | 44 | 12 | 76 mins |

## GOALS SCORED

AT HOME

| | | |
|---|---|---|
| MOST | Lyon | 40 |
| | | 24 |
| LEAST | AC Ajaccio | 14 |

AWAY

| | | |
|---|---|---|
| MOST | Monaco | 29 |
| | | 11 |
| LEAST | Troyes | 7 |

## GOALS CONCEDED

AT HOME

| | | |
|---|---|---|
| LEAST | Sochaux & Auxerre | 8 |
| | | 20 |
| MOST | Strasbourg | 23 |

AWAY

| | | |
|---|---|---|
| LEAST | Lens | 15 |
| | | 25 |
| MOST | Sedan | 39 |

## KEY GOALKEEPER

**1 Petr Cech**

| | |
|---|---|
| Goals Conceded in the League | 41 |
| Defensive Rating<br>Ave number of mins between League goals conceded while on the pitch | 81 |
| Counting Games<br>Games when he played at least 70 minutes | 37 |
| Clean Sheets<br>In games when he played at least 70 minutes | 12 |

## TOP POINT EARNERS

| | PLAYER | GAMES | AVE |
|---|---|---|---|
| 1 | Echouafni | 18 | 1.50 |
| 2 | Monterrubio | 15 | 1.40 |
| 3 | Bourillon | 16 | 1.25 |
| 4 | Didot | 14 | 1.21 |
| 5 | Escude | 29 | 1.17 |
| 6 | Piquionne | 26 | 1.15 |
| 7 | Reveillere | 20 | 1.15 |
| 8 | Delaye | 17 | 1.12 |
| 9 | Cech | 37 | 1.08 |
| 10 | Arribage | 37 | 1.08 |
| | CLUB AVERAGE: | | 1.05 |

Ave = Average points per match in Counting Games

## ATTENDANCES

HOME GROUND: ROUTE DE LORIENT  CAPACITY: 31716  AVERAGE LEAGUE AT HOME: 17666

| | | | | | | | | |
|---|---|---|---|---|---|---|---|---|
| 22 | Marseille | 39885 | 13 | AC Ajaccio | 20000 | 16 | Nice | 14000 |
| 28 | Lyon | 38500 | 34 | Nice | 19000 | 20 | Troyes | 13000 |
| 37 | Paris SG | 37052 | 3 | Guingamp | 18500 | 11 | Sedan | 12000 |
| 26 | Nantes | 35000 | 36 | Strasbourg | 18302 | 33 | Le Havre | 11000 |
| 7 | Lens | 33500 | 38 | Montpellier | 18237 | 12 | Auxerre | 10000 |
| 14 | Bordeaux | 30000 | 32 | Bordeaux | 18156 | 35 | Lille | 10000 |
| 4 | Marseille | 23700 | 29 | Sedan | 18000 | 2 | Troyes | 10000 |
| 8 | Nantes | 23625 | 17 | Lille | 16500 | 31 | AC Ajaccio | 10000 |
| 21 | Guingamp | 23525 | 15 | Le Havre | 15000 | 25 | Lens | 10000 |
| 19 | Paris SG | 23000 | 6 | Sochaux | 15000 | 5 | Bastia | 9500 |
| 10 | Lyon | 20000 | 27 | Monaco | 15000 | 9 | Monaco | 5000 |
| 1 | Montpellier | 20000 | 23 | Bastia | 14624 | 24 | Sochaux | 5000 |
| 18 | Strasbourg | 20000 | 30 | Auxerre | 14000 | | | |

■ Home □ Away ▨ Neutral

## DISCIPLINARY RECORDS

| | PLAYER | YELLOW | RED | AVE |
|---|---|---|---|---|
| 1 | Battles | 8 | 1 | 119 |
| 2 | Fleurquin | 6 | 0 | 138 |
| 3 | Delaye | 7 | 1 | 206 |
| 4 | Jeunechamp | 4 | 1 | 226 |
| 5 | Diatta | 6 | 0 | 286 |
| 6 | Maoulida | 3 | 1 | 289 |
| 7 | Echouafni | 4 | 1 | 336 |
| 8 | Grenet | 2 | 1 | 384 |
| 9 | Faty | 2 | 0 | 389 |
| 10 | Piquionne | 6 | 0 | 404 |
| 11 | Jay | 2 | 0 | 453 |
| 12 | Monterrubio | 4 | 0 | 482 |
| 13 | Ivanov | 1 | 0 | 497 |
| | Other | 28 | 2 | |
| | TOTAL | 83 | 8 | |

## LEAGUE GOALS

| | PLAYER | MINS | GOALS | AVE |
|---|---|---|---|---|
| 1 | Piquionne | 2426 | 10 | 243 |
| 2 | Monterrubio | 1928 | 6 | 321 |
| 3 | Arribage | 3330 | 5 | 666 |
| 4 | Maoulida | 1159 | 3 | 386 |
| 5 | Delaye | 1648 | 3 | 549 |
| 6 | Echouafni | 1681 | 1 | 1681 |
| 7 | Reveillere | 1788 | 1 | 1788 |
| 8 | N'Diaye | 998 | 1 | 998 |
| 9 | Frei | 437 | 1 | 437 |
| 10 | Jeunechamp | 1133 | 1 | 1133 |
| | Other | | 3 | |
| | TOTAL | | 35 | |

## MONTH BY MONTH GUIDE TO THE POINTS

| MONTH | POINTS | % |
|---|---|---|
| AUGUST | 1 | 7% |
| SEPTEMBER | 4 | 33% |
| OCTOBER | 3 | 33% |
| NOVEMBER | 6 | 40% |
| DECEMBER | 9 | 100% |
| JANUARY | 3 | 25% |
| FEBRUARY | 2 | 17% |
| MARCH | 4 | 44% |
| APRIL | 4 | 44% |
| MAY | 4 | 33% |

## TEAM OF THE SEASON

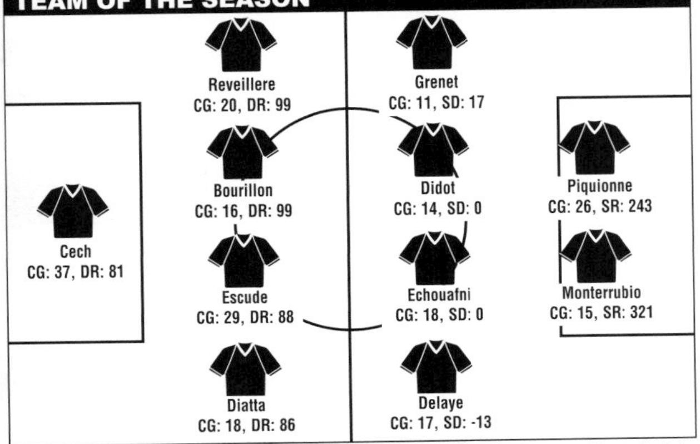
Reveillere
CG: 20, DR: 99
Grenet
CG: 11, SD: 17
Bourillon
CG: 16, DR: 99
Didot
CG: 14, SD: 0
Piquionne
CG: 26, SR: 243
Cech
CG: 37, DR: 81
Escude
CG: 29, DR: 88
Echouafni
CG: 18, SD: 0
Monterrubio
CG: 15, SR: 321
Diatta
CG: 18, DR: 86
Delaye
CG: 17, SD: -13

**KEY:** DR = Defensive Rate, SD = Scoring Difference, SR = Strike Rate, CG = Counting Games – League games playing at least 70 minutes

## LEAGUE APPEARANCES, BOOKINGS AND CAPS

| | AGE | IN THE SQUAD | COUNTING GAMES | MINUTES ON PITCH | YELLOW CARDS | RED CARDS | THIS SEASON | HOME COUNTRY |
|---|---|---|---|---|---|---|---|---|
| **Goalkeepers** | | | | | | | | |
| Boubacar Barry | 24 | 8 | 0 | 0 | 0 | 0 | - | Ivory Coast |
| Petr Cech | 21 | 37 | 37 | 3330 | 0 | 0 | 10 | Czech Republic (13) |
| Eric Durand | 37 | 31 | 1 | 90 | 0 | 0 | - | France |
| **Defenders** | | | | | | | | |
| Dominique Arribage | 32 | 37 | 37 | 3330 | 4 | 0 | - | France |
| Gregory Bourillon | 19 | 20 | 16 | 1578 | 2 | 1 | - | France |
| Lamine Diatta | 28 | 24 | 18 | 1716 | 6 | 0 | 2 | Senegal (29) |
| Julien Escude | 23 | 30 | 29 | 2644 | 5 | 0 | - | France |
| Jacques Faty | 19 | 10 | 8 | 779 | 2 | 0 | - | France |
| Frederic Jay | 26 | 13 | 10 | 907 | 2 | 0 | - | France |
| Arnaud le Lan | 25 | 25 | 17 | 1565 | 2 | 0 | - | France |
| Gabriel Loeschbor | 26 | 8 | 3 | 333 | 3 | 1 | - | Argentina |
| Sebastien Puygrenier | 21 | 7 | 1 | 96 | 0 | 0 | - | France |
| Anthony Reveillere | 23 | 20 | 20 | 1788 | 3 | 0 | - | France |
| **Midfielders** | | | | | | | | |
| Laurent Battles | 27 | 15 | 11 | 1074 | 8 | 1 | - | France |
| Mickael Citony | | 4 | 1 | 110 | 0 | 0 | - | |
| Phillipe Delaye | 28 | 25 | 17 | 1648 | 7 | 1 | - | France |
| Etienne Didot | 19 | 24 | 14 | 1366 | 2 | 0 | - | France |
| Olivier Echouafni | 30 | 22 | 18 | 1681 | 4 | 1 | - | France |
| Andres Fleurquin | 28 | 15 | 7 | 833 | 6 | 0 | - | Uruguay |
| Francois Grenet | 28 | 20 | 11 | 1154 | 2 | 1 | - | France |
| Cyril Jeunechamp | 27 | 14 | 12 | 1133 | 4 | 1 | - | France |
| Stephane N'Guema | 18 | 7 | 2 | 207 | 1 | 0 | - | Gabon |
| Oliver Sorlin | 24 | 33 | 24 | 2292 | 4 | 0 | - | France |
| Syril Yapi | 23 | 7 | 4 | 385 | 0 | 0 | - | France |
| **Forwards** | | | | | | | | |
| Alexander Frei | 23 | 14 | 4 | 437 | 0 | 0 | - | Switzerland |
| Gueorgui Ivanov | 27 | 15 | 4 | 497 | 1 | 0 | - | Bulgaria |
| Benoit Le Bris | 26 | 1 | 0 | 0 | 0 | 0 | - | France |
| Toifilou Maoulida | 24 | 28 | 10 | 1159 | 3 | 1 | - | France |
| Olivier Monterrubio | 26 | 37 | 15 | 1928 | 4 | 0 | - | France |
| Makhtar N'Diaye | 21 | 24 | 9 | 998 | 2 | 0 | 3 | Senegal (29) |
| Frederic Piquionne | 24 | 31 | 26 | 2426 | 6 | 0 | - | France |

**KEY:** LEAGUE BOOKINGS CAPS (FIFA RANKING)

## SQUAD APPEARANCES

| Match | 1 | 2 | 3 | 4 | 5 | 6 | 7 | 8 | 9 | 10 | 11 | 12 | 13 | 14 | 15 | 16 | 17 | 18 | 19 | 20 | 21 | 22 | 23 | 24 | 25 | 26 | 27 | 28 | 29 | 30 | 31 | 32 | 33 | 34 | 35 | 36 | 37 | 38 |
|---|---|---|---|---|---|---|---|---|---|---|---|---|---|---|---|---|---|---|---|---|---|---|---|---|---|---|---|---|---|---|---|---|---|---|---|---|---|---|
| Venue | A | H | A | H | A | H | A | H | A | H | A | A | H | A | H | A | H | A | H | A | H | A | H | A | H | A | H | A | H | H | A | H | A | H | A | H | A | H |
| Competition | L | L | L | L | L | L | L | L | L | L | L | L | L | L | L | L | L | L | L | L | L | L | L | L | L | L | L | L | L | L | L | L | L | L | L | L | L | L |
| Result | L | D | L | L | L | D | L | W | L | L | W | L | D | L | D | D | W | W | W | W | W | L | L | L | D | L | D | L | W | D | L | L | W | D | L | L | D | W |

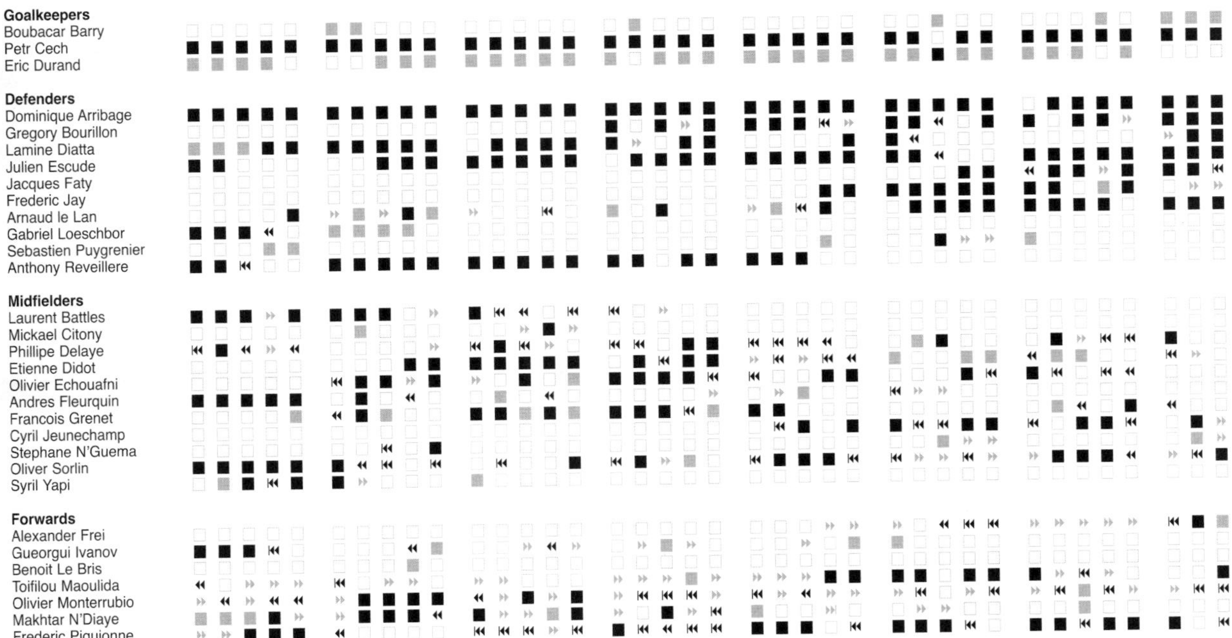
Goalkeepers
Boubacar Barry
Petr Cech
Eric Durand
Defenders
Dominique Arribage
Gregory Bourillon
Lamine Diatta
Julien Escude
Jacques Faty
Frederic Jay
Arnaud le Lan
Gabriel Loeschbor
Sebastien Puygrenier
Anthony Reveillere
Midfielders
Laurent Battles
Mickael Citony
Phillipe Delaye
Etienne Didot
Olivier Echouafni
Andres Fleurquin
Francois Grenet
Cyril Jeunechamp
Stephane N'Guema
Oliver Sorlin
Syril Yapi
Forwards
Alexander Frei
Gueorgui Ivanov
Benoit Le Bris
Toifilou Maoulida
Olivier Monterrubio
Makhtar N'Diaye
Frederic Piquionne

**KEY:** On all match | On bench | Subbed or sent off (Counting game) | Subbed or sent off (playing less than 70 minutes) | Subbed on from bench (Counting Game) | Subbed on (playing less than 70 minutes) | Subbed on and then subbed or sent off (Counting Game) | Subbed on and then subbed or sent off (playing less than 70 minutes) | Not in 16

# MONTPELLIER

Final Position: **16th**

| | | | | | | |
|---|---|---|---|---|---|---|
| 1 | lge | Rennes | H | W | 1-0 | Silvestre 87 |
| 2 | lge | Auxerre | A | L | 0-2 | |
| 3 | lge | Bordeaux | H | L | 0-1 | |
| 4 | lge | Nice | A | L | 1-2 | Mezague 40 |
| 5 | lge | Le Havre | H | D | 0-0 | |
| 6 | lge | AC Ajaccio | A | D | 0-0 | |
| 7 | lge | Lille | H | W | 1-0 | Mansare 68 |
| 8 | lge | Strasbourg | A | L | 2-3 | Mezague 55,68 |
| 9 | lge | Paris SG | H | D | 1-1 | Bamago 12 |
| 10 | lge | Lens | H | L | 0-2 | |
| 11 | lge | Guingamp | A | L | 1-3 | Rouviere 53 |
| 12 | lge | Troyes | H | D | 2-2 | Silvestre 43,76 |
| 13 | lge | Marseille | A | L | 0-2 | |
| 14 | lge | Sedan | H | W | 2-0 | Bamago 30; Guei 53 |
| 15 | lge | Sochaux | A | D | 0-0 | |
| 16 | lge | Bastia | H | D | 2-2 | Guei 2,15 |
| 17 | lge | Nantes | A | L | 1-3 | Carotti 78 |
| 18 | lge | Monaco | H | L | 1-2 | Squillaci 17 og |
| 19 | lge | Lyon | A | D | 1-1 | Cisse 90 |
| 20 | lge | Bordeaux | A | L | 1-3 | Robert 10 |
| 21 | lge | Nice | H | D | 2-2 | Barbosa 3,22 |
| 22 | lge | Auxerre | H | D | 0-0 | |
| 23 | lge | Le Havre | A | L | 0-1 | |
| 24 | lge | AC Ajaccio | H | L | 0-1 | |
| 25 | lge | Strasbourg | H | W | 2-1 | Robert 30; Barbosa 56 |
| 26 | lge | Paris SG | A | W | 3-1 | Mezague 14,19; Mansare 74 |
| 27 | lge | Lens | A | L | 0-4 | |
| 28 | lge | Guingamp | H | W | 2-0 | Mansare 5; Mezague 72 |
| 29 | lge | Troyes | A | W | 2-0 | Barbosa 37; Doumeng 89 |
| 30 | lge | Lille | A | L | 0-2 | |
| 31 | lge | Marseille | H | L | 1-2 | Rouviere 70 |
| 32 | lge | Sedan | A | W | 2-1 | Bamago 9; Carotti 78 |
| 33 | lge | Sochaux | H | L | 0-2 | |
| 34 | lge | Bastia | A | W | 2-1 | Robert 9; Doumeng 75 |
| 35 | lge | Nantes | H | W | 1-0 | Mansare 27 pen |
| 36 | lge | Monaco | A | L | 1-3 | Assoumani 49 |
| 37 | lge | Lyon | H | D | 1-1 | Bamago 14 |
| 38 | lge | Rennes | A | L | 1-3 | Diatta 18 og |

## KEY PLAYERS - GOALSCORERS

**1 Valery Mezague**

| | | | |
|---|---|---|---|
| Goals in the League | 6 | Player Strike Rate<br>Average number of minutes between League goals scored by player | 341 |
| Contribution to Attacking Power<br>Average number of minutes between League team goals while on pitch | 78 | Club Strike Rate<br>Average number of minutes between League goals scored by club | 92 |

| | PLAYER | LGE GOALS | POWER | STRIKE RATE |
|---|---|---|---|---|
| 2 | Franck Silvestre | 3 | 117 | 510 mins |
| 3 | Fode Mansare | 4 | 78 | 529 mins |
| 4 | Bertrand Robert | 3 | 82 | 552 mins |
| 5 | Habib Bamago | 4 | 97 | 660 mins |

## KEY PLAYERS - MIDFIELDERS

**1 Geoffrey Doumeng**

| | | | |
|---|---|---|---|
| Goals in the League | 2 | Contribution to Attacking Power<br>Average number of minutes between League team goals while on pitch | 69 |
| Defensive Rating<br>Average number of mins between League goals conceded while he was on the pitch | 59 | Scoring Difference<br>Defensive Rating minus Contribution to Attacking Power | -10 |

| | PLAYER | LGE GOALS | DEF RATE | POWER | SCORE DIFF |
|---|---|---|---|---|---|
| 2 | Valery Mezague | 6 | 64 | 79 | -15 mins |
| 3 | Bruno Carotti | 2 | 65 | 88 | -23 mins |
| 4 | Cedric Barbosa | 4 | 64 | 92 | -28 mins |
| 5 | Jean Christophe Rouviere | 2 | 57 | 89 | -32 mins |

## KEY PLAYERS - DEFENDERS

**1 Bill Tchato**

| | | | |
|---|---|---|---|
| Goals Conceded (GC)<br>The number of League goals conceded while he was on the pitch | 12 | Clean Sheets<br>In games when he played at least 70 minutes | 4 |
| Defensive Rating<br>Ave number of mins between League goals conceded while on the pitch | 80 | Club Defensive Rating<br>Average number of mins between League goals conceded by the club this season | 63 |

| | PLAYER | CON LGE | CLEAN SHEETS | DEF RATE |
|---|---|---|---|---|
| 2 | Serge Blanc | 18 | 4 | 73 mins |
| 3 | Nenad Dzodic | 24 | 5 | 71 mins |
| 4 | Sebastien Michalowski | 21 | 5 | 68 mins |
| 5 | Cyril Ramond | 25 | 3 | 58 mins |

## GOALS SCORED

**AT HOME**

| | | |
|---|---|---|
| MOST | Lyon | 40 |
| | | 19 |
| LEAST | AC Ajaccio | 14 |

**AWAY**

| | | |
|---|---|---|
| MOST | Monaco | 29 |
| | | 18 |
| LEAST | Troyes | 7 |

## GOALS CONCEDED

**AT HOME**

| | | |
|---|---|---|
| LEAST | Sochaux & Auxerre | 8 |
| | | 19 |
| MOST | Strasbourg | 23 |

**AWAY**

| | | |
|---|---|---|
| LEAST | Lens | 15 |
| | | 35 |
| MOST | Sedan | 39 |

## KEY GOALKEEPER

**1 Rudy Riou**

| | |
|---|---|
| Goals Conceded in the League | 34 |
| Defensive Rating<br>Ave number of mins between League goals conceded while on the pitch | 72 |
| Counting Games<br>Games when he played at least 70 minutes | 27 |
| Clean Sheets<br>In games when he played at least 70 minutes | 9 |

## TOP POINT EARNERS

| | PLAYER | GAMES | AVE |
|---|---|---|---|
| 1 | Blanc | 14 | 1.50 |
| 2 | Mezague | 19 | 1.37 |
| 3 | Robert | 15 | 1.33 |
| 4 | Bamago | 26 | 1.15 |
| 5 | Mansare | 20 | 1.15 |
| 6 | Riou | 27 | 1.11 |
| 7 | Barbosa | 30 | 1.10 |
| 8 | Carotti | 32 | 1.06 |
| 9 | Dzodic | 18 | 1.06 |
| 10 | Michalowski | 14 | 1.00 |
| | **CLUB AVERAGE:** | | **1.05** |

Ave = Average points per match in Counting Games

## ATTENDANCES

**HOME GROUND: STADE DE LA MOSSON CAPACITY: 31250 AVERAGE LEAGUE AT HOME: 14534**

| | | | | | | | | |
|---|---|---|---|---|---|---|---|---|
| 26 | Paris SG | 35000 | 20 | Bordeaux | 15000 | 2 | Auxerre | 10000 |
| 27 | Lens | 35000 | 4 | Nice | 15000 | **24** | **AC Ajaccio** | **10000** |
| 17 | Nantes | 30000 | **35** | **Nantes** | **15000** | 8 | Strasbourg | 9500 |
| **31** | **Marseille** | **30000** | 11 | Guingamp | 15000 | **25** | **Strasbourg** | **8500** |
| **7** | **Lille** | **28000** | **10** | **Lens** | **15000** | 36 | Monaco | 8360 |
| 19 | Lyon | 23000 | 15 | Sochaux | 15000 | **12** | **Troyes** | **8000** |
| **3** | **Bordeaux** | **20000** | 32 | Sedan | 15000 | 6 | AC Ajaccio | 8000 |
| **1** | **Rennes** | **20000** | **33** | **Sochaux** | **15000** | **16** | **Bastia** | **8000** |
| **9** | **Paris SG** | **20000** | **21** | **Nice** | **12392** | **18** | **Monaco** | **8000** |
| **37** | **Lyon** | **19764** | **22** | **Auxerre** | **10500** | **14** | **Sedan** | **8000** |
| 38 | Rennes | 18237 | **28** | **Guingamp** | **10000** | 23 | Le Havre | 8000 |
| 30 | Lille | 15000 | 13 | Marseille | 10000 | 34 | Bastia | 7000 |
| 29 | Troyes | 15000 | **5** | **Le Havre** | **10000** | | | |

■ Home □ Away ▨ Neutral

## DISCIPLINARY RECORDS

| | PLAYER | YELLOW | RED | AVE |
|---|---|---|---|---|
| 1 | Gathuessi | 3 | 0 | 198 |
| 2 | Michalowski | 6 | 1 | 202 |
| 3 | Mezague | 8 | 2 | 204 |
| 4 | Blanc | 6 | 0 | 218 |
| 5 | Dzodic | 6 | 1 | 243 |
| 6 | Colombo | 2 | 0 | 257 |
| 7 | Mansare | 8 | 0 | 264 |
| 8 | Barbosa | 9 | 0 | 305 |
| 9 | Tchato | 3 | 0 | 319 |
| 10 | Carotti | 9 | 0 | 323 |
| 11 | Bonilla | 3 | 0 | 327 |
| 12 | Bamago | 6 | 2 | 329 |
| 13 | Rouviere | 6 | 1 | 344 |
| | Other | 22 | 2 | |
| | **TOTAL** | **97** | **9** | |

## LEAGUE GOALS

| | PLAYER | MINS | GOALS | AVE |
|---|---|---|---|---|
| 1 | Mezague | 2047 | 6 | 341 |
| 2 | Barbosa | 2746 | 4 | 687 |
| 3 | Mansare | 2116 | 4 | 529 |
| 4 | Bamago | 2639 | 4 | 660 |
| 5 | Guei | 1289 | 3 | 430 |
| 6 | Robert | 1657 | 3 | 552 |
| 7 | Silvestre | 1530 | 3 | 510 |
| 8 | Doumeng | 1170 | 2 | 585 |
| 9 | Rouviere | 2414 | 2 | 1207 |
| 10 | Carotti | 2908 | 2 | 1454 |
| 11 | Cisse | 79 | 1 | 79 |
| 12 | Assoumani | 1162 | 1 | 1162 |
| | Other | | 2 | |
| | **TOTAL** | | **37** | |

## MONTH BY MONTH GUIDE TO THE POINTS

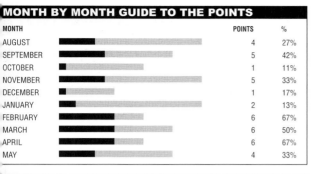

| MONTH | POINTS | % |
|---|---|---|
| AUGUST | 4 | 27% |
| SEPTEMBER | 5 | 42% |
| OCTOBER | 1 | 11% |
| NOVEMBER | 5 | 33% |
| DECEMBER | 1 | 17% |
| JANUARY | 2 | 13% |
| FEBRUARY | 6 | 67% |
| MARCH | 6 | 50% |
| APRIL | 6 | 67% |
| MAY | 4 | 33% |

## TEAM OF THE SEASON

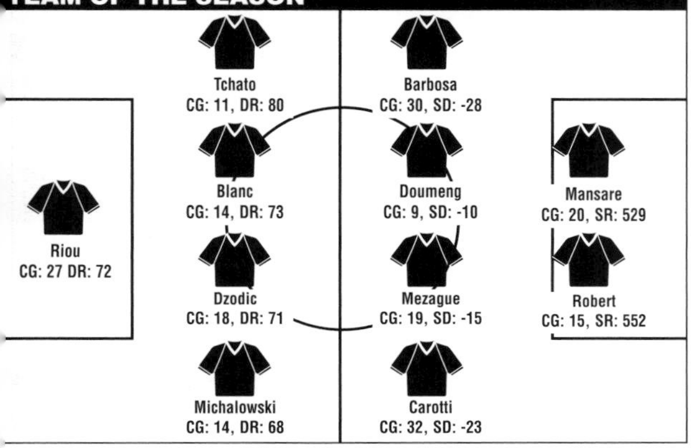
Tchato
CG: 11, DR: 80
Barbosa
CG: 30, SD: -28
Riou
CG: 27 DR: 72
Blanc
CG: 14, DR: 73
Doumeng
CG: 9, SD: -10
Mansare
CG: 20, SR: 529
Dzodic
CG: 18, DR: 71
Mezague
CG: 19, SD: -15
Robert
CG: 15, SR: 552
Michalowski
CG: 14, DR: 68
Carotti
CG: 32, SD: -23

KEY: DR = Defensive Rate, SD = Scoring Difference, SR = Strike Rate, CG = Counting Games – League games playing at least 70 minutes

## LEAGUE APPEARANCES, BOOKINGS AND CAPS

| | AGE | IN THE SQUAD | COUNTING GAMES | MINUTES ON PITCH | YELLOW CARDS | RED CARDS | THIS SEASON | HOME COUNTRY |
|---|---|---|---|---|---|---|---|---|
| **Goalkeepers** | | | | | | | | |
| Laurent Pionnier | 21 | 20 | 8 | 783 | 1 | 0 | - | France |
| Rudy Riou | 23 | 28 | 27 | 2439 | 0 | 1 | - | France |
| Jodi Viviani | 21 | 28 | 2 | 198 | 0 | 0 | - | France |
| **Defenders** | | | | | | | | |
| Mansour Assoumani | 20 | 16 | 12 | 1162 | 2 | 0 | - | France |
| Serge Blanc | 30 | 19 | 14 | 1309 | 6 | 0 | - | France |
| Julio Colombo | 19 | 14 | 5 | 514 | 2 | 0 | - | France |
| Nenad Dzodic | 26 | 21 | 18 | 1704 | 6 | 1 | - | Serbia & Montenegro |
| Pascal Fugier | 34 | 8 | 1 | 232 | 1 | 0 | - | France |
| Theirry Gathuessi | 21 | 11 | 6 | 594 | 3 | 0 | - | France |
| Seb Michalowski | 25 | 23 | 14 | 1418 | 6 | 1 | - | France |
| Cyril Ramond | 23 | 21 | 15 | 1457 | 2 | 0 | - | France |
| Bill Tchato | 28 | 11 | 11 | 958 | 3 | 0 | 2 | Cameroon (18) |
| **Midfielders** | | | | | | | | |
| Cedric Barbosa | 27 | 33 | 30 | 2746 | 9 | 0 | - | France |
| Bruno Carotti | 30 | 33 | 32 | 2908 | 9 | 0 | - | France |
| Mathijs Descamps | 20 | 9 | 0 | 125 | 0 | 0 | - | France |
| Geoffrey Doumeng | 22 | 27 | 9 | 1170 | 0 | 0 | - | France |
| Pierre Laigle | 32 | 23 | 7 | 1006 | 2 | 0 | - | France |
| Fabien Lefevre | 31 | 3 | 0 | 0 | 0 | 0 | - | France |
| Mickael Llorente | 20 | 5 | 1 | 76 | 1 | 0 | - | France |
| Valery Mezague | 19 | 31 | 19 | 2047 | 8 | 2 | 1 | Cameroon (18) |
| Guillaume Moullec | 23 | 24 | 18 | 1780 | 2 | 0 | - | France |
| Almeida Sergio | 27 | 1 | 0 | 22 | 0 | 0 | - | Portugal |
| Jean C Rouviere | 28 | 35 | 24 | 2414 | 6 | 1 | - | France |
| Franck Silvestre | 36 | 17 | 17 | 1530 | 4 | 0 | - | France |
| **Forwards** | | | | | | | | |
| Habib Bamago | 21 | 33 | 26 | 2639 | 6 | 2 | - | France |
| Victor Bonilla | 32 | 14 | 8 | 982 | 3 | 0 | - | Colombia |
| Abdoulaye Cisse | 19 | 9 | 0 | 79 | 1 | 0 | - | France |
| Eric Guei | 22 | 28 | 11 | 1289 | 2 | 1 | - | Ivory Coast |
| Fode Mansare | 21 | 30 | 20 | 2116 | 8 | 0 | - | Guinea |
| Bertrand Robert | 19 | 25 | 15 | 1657 | 4 | 0 | - | France |
| Carlos Jorge Pataca | 30 | 7 | 0 | 86 | 0 | 0 | - | Portugal |

KEY: LEAGUE BOOKINGS CAPS (FIFA RANKING)

## SQUAD APPEARANCES

| Match | 1 | 2 | 3 | 4 | 5 | 6 | 7 | 8 | 9 | 10 | 11 | 12 | 13 | 14 | 15 | 16 | 17 | 18 | 19 | 20 | 21 | 22 | 23 | 24 | 25 | 26 | 27 | 28 | 29 | 30 | 31 | 32 | 33 | 34 | 35 | 36 | 37 | 38 |
|---|---|---|---|---|---|---|---|---|---|---|---|---|---|---|---|---|---|---|---|---|---|---|---|---|---|---|---|---|---|---|---|---|---|---|---|---|---|---|
| Venue | H | A | H | A | H | A | H | A | H | H | A | H | A | H | A | H | A | H | A | A | H | A | A | H | H | A | A | H | A | A | H | A | H | A | H | A | H | A |
| Competition | L | L | L | L | L | L | L | L | L | L | L | L | L | L | L | L | L | L | L | L | L | L | L | L | L | L | L | L | L | L | L | L | L | L | L | L | L | L |
| Result | W | L | L | L | D | D | W | L | D | L | L | D | L | W | D | D | L | L | D | L | D | D | L | L | W | W | L | W | W | L | L | W | L | W | W | L | D | L |

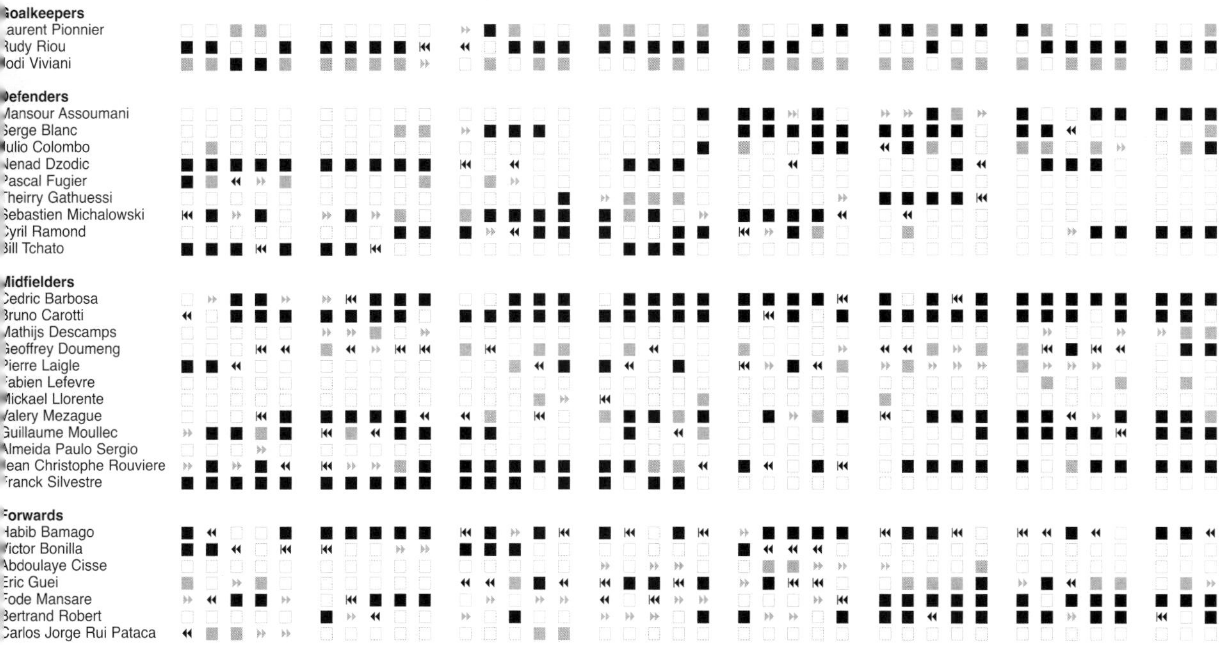
Goalkeepers
aurent Pionnier
Rudy Riou
odi Viviani
Defenders
Mansour Assoumani
Serge Blanc
Julio Colombo
Nenad Dzodic
Pascal Fugier
Thierry Gathuessi
Sebastien Michalowski
Cyril Ramond
Bill Tchato
Midfielders
Cedric Barbosa
Bruno Carotti
Mathijs Descamps
Geoffrey Doumeng
Pierre Laigle
Fabien Lefevre
Mickael Llorente
Valery Mezague
Guillaume Moullec
Almeida Paulo Sergio
Jean Christophe Rouviere
Franck Silvestre
Forwards
Habib Bamago
Victor Bonilla
Abdoulaye Cisse
Eric Guei
Fode Mansare
Bertrand Robert
Carlos Jorge Rui Pataca

KEY: ■ On all match ■ On bench ⏮ Subbed or sent off (Counting game) « Subbed or sent off (playing less than 70 minutes) ⏭ Subbed on from bench (Counting Game) » Subbed on (playing less than 70 minutes) ⏭ Subbed on and then subbed or sent off (Counting Game) » Subbed on and then subbed or sent off (playing less than 70 minutes) □ Not in 16

# AJACCIO

Final Position: **17th**

| | | | | | | |
|---|---|---|---|---|---|---|
| 1 | lge | Strasbourg | A | D | 1-1 | Collin 27 |
| 2 | lge | Guingamp | H | L | 0-2 | |
| 3 | lge | Paris SG | A | D | 2-2 | Granon 69; Alicarte 90 |
| 4 | lge | Sedan | H | W | 1-0 | Guglielmone 27 |
| 5 | lge | Troyes | A | L | 0-1 | |
| 6 | lge | Montpellier | H | D | 0-0 | |
| 7 | lge | Bastia | A | W | 2-1 | Rodriguez 35; Faderne 87 |
| 8 | lge | Sochaux | H | L | 0-1 | |
| 9 | lge | Marseille | A | L | 1-3 | Destruhaut 14 |
| 10 | lge | Nantes | H | W | 1-0 | Rodriguez 85 |
| 11 | lge | Lens | A | D | 1-1 | Alicarte 39 |
| 12 | lge | Lyon | H | L | 0-1 | |
| 13 | lge | Rennes | A | D | 0-0 | |
| 14 | lge | Auxerre | H | W | 1-0 | Regragui 88 |
| 15 | lge | Monaco | A | L | 2-3 | Marquez 79 og; Rodriguez 86 pen |
| 16 | lge | Bordeaux | A | L | 0-1 | |
| 17 | lge | Le Havre | H | L | 1-2 | Faderne 43 |
| 18 | lge | Nice | A | L | 0-3 | |
| 19 | lge | Lille | H | D | 2-2 | Seck 45; Rodriguez 86 |
| 20 | lge | Guingamp | A | L | 1-3 | Bezzaz 23 |
| 21 | lge | Paris SG | H | D | 0-0 | |
| 22 | lge | Sedan | A | D | 1-1 | Demont 29 |
| 23 | lge | Troyes | H | W | 1-0 | Diomede 27 |
| 24 | lge | Montpellier | A | W | 1-0 | Lacombe 65 |
| 25 | lge | Bastia | H | D | 1-1 | Rodriguez 39 |
| 26 | lge | Marseille | H | L | 0-2 | |
| 27 | lge | Nantes | A | L | 0-1 | |
| 28 | lge | Lens | H | D | 0-0 | |
| 29 | lge | Lyon | A | L | 1-3 | Lacombe 32 |
| 30 | lge | Sochaux | A | D | 1-1 | Lacombe 64 |
| 31 | lge | Rennes | H | W | 1-0 | Lacombe 48 |
| 32 | lge | Auxerre | A | L | 0-1 | |
| 33 | lge | Monaco | H | L | 2-4 | Robin 57; Lacombe 66 |
| 34 | lge | Bordeaux | H | L | 1-6 | Diomede 60 |
| 35 | lge | Le Havre | A | W | 1-0 | Rodriguez 75 |
| 36 | lge | Nice | H | W | 2-0 | Seck 7; Bezzaz 80 |
| 37 | lge | Lille | A | L | 0-2 | |
| 38 | lge | Strasbourg | H | D | 0-0 | |

## KEY PLAYERS - GOALSCORERS

**1 Bruno Rodriguez**

| | | | |
|---|---|---|---|
| Goals in the League | 6 | Player Strike Rate<br>Average number of minutes between League goals scored by player | 411 |
| Contribution to Attacking Power<br>Average number of minutes between League team goals while on pitch | 129 | Club Strike Rate<br>Average number of minutes between League goals scored by club | 118 |

| | PLAYER | LGE GOALS | POWER | STRIKE RATE |
|---|---|---|---|---|
| 2 | Bernard Diomede | 2 | 99 | 550 mins |
| 3 | Mamadou Seck | 2 | 111 | 891 mins |
| 4 | Herve Alicarte | 2 | 108 | 975 mins |
| 5 | Christophe Destruhaut | 1 | 166 | 1333 mins |

## KEY PLAYERS - MIDFIELDERS

**1 Abdelnasser Ouadah**

| | | | |
|---|---|---|---|
| Goals in the League | 0 | Contribution to Attacking Power<br>Average number of minutes between League team goals while on pitch | 106 |
| Defensive Rating<br>Average number of mins between League goals conceded while he was on the pitch | 95 | Scoring Difference<br>Defensive Rating minus Contribution to Attacking Power | -11 |

| | PLAYER | LGE GOALS | DEF RATE | POWER | SCORE DIFF |
|---|---|---|---|---|---|
| 2 | Martial Robin | 1 | 74 | 113 | -39 mins |
| 3 | Bernard Diomede | 2 | 61 | 100 | -39 mins |
| 4 | Stephane Gregoire | 0 | 69 | 114 | -45 mins |
| 5 | Dimitri Ananko | 0 | 90 | 136 | -46 mins |

## KEY PLAYERS - DEFENDERS

**1 Mamadou Seck**

| | | | |
|---|---|---|---|
| Goals Conceded (GC)<br>The number of League goals conceded while he was on the pitch | 20 | Clean Sheets<br>In games when he played at least 70 minutes | 8 |
| Defensive Rating<br>Ave number of mins between League goals conceded while on the pitch | 89 | Club Defensive Rating<br>Average number of mins between League goals conceded by the club this season | 70 |

| | PLAYER | CON LGE | CLEAN SHEETS | DEF RATE |
|---|---|---|---|---|
| 2 | David Terrier | 22 | 6 | 76 mins |
| 3 | Xavier Collin | 45 | 13 | 72 mins |
| 4 | Christophe Destruhaut | 22 | 4 | 61 mins |
| 5 | Herve Alicarte | 32 | 6 | 61 mins |

## GOALS SCORED

**AT HOME**

| | | |
|---|---|---|
| MOST | Lyon | 40 |
| | | 14 |
| LEAST | AC Ajaccio | 14 |

**AWAY**

| | | |
|---|---|---|
| MOST | Monaco | 29 |
| | | 15 |
| LEAST | Troyes | 7 |

## GOALS CONCEDED

**AT HOME**

| | | |
|---|---|---|
| LEAST | Sochaux & Auxerre | 8 |
| | | 21 |
| MOST | Strasbourg | 23 |

**AWAY**

| | | |
|---|---|---|
| LEAST | Lens | 15 |
| | | 28 |
| MOST | Sedan | 39 |

## KEY GOALKEEPER

**1 Stephane Trevisan**

| | |
|---|---|
| Goals Conceded in the League | 43 |
| Defensive Rating<br>Ave number of mins between League goals conceded while on the pitch | 67 |
| Counting Games<br>Games when he played at least 70 minutes | 32 |
| Clean Sheets<br>In games when he played at least 70 minutes | 11 |

## TOP POINT EARNERS

| | PLAYER | GAMES | AVE |
|---|---|---|---|
| 1 | Ananko | 12 | 1.33 |
| 2 | Diomede | 12 | 1.25 |
| 3 | Seck | 20 | 1.20 |
| 4 | Regragui | 29 | 1.14 |
| 5 | Collin | 35 | 1.09 |
| 6 | Robin | 18 | 1.06 |
| 7 | Gregoire | 37 | 1.05 |
| 8 | Rodriguez | 25 | 1.04 |
| 9 | Alicarte | 21 | 1.00 |
| 10 | Trevisan | 32 | 1.00 |
| | CLUB AVERAGE: | | 1.03 |

Ave = Average points per match in Counting Games

## ATTENDANCES

HOME GROUND: STADE FRANCOIS COTY CAPACITY: 10660 AVERAGE LEAGUE AT HOME: 7268

| | | | | | | | | |
|---|---|---|---|---|---|---|---|---|
| 9 | Marseille | 40000 | 28 | Lens | 10000 | 38 | Strasbourg | 7200 |
| 29 | Lyon | 40000 | 24 | Montpellier | 10000 | 26 | Marseille | 7000 |
| 11 | Lens | 38000 | 5 | Troyes | 10000 | 22 | Sedan | 7000 |
| 3 | Paris SG | 35000 | 7 | Bastia | 10000 | 4 | Sedan | 6000 |
| 16 | Bordeaux | 30000 | 33 | Monaco | 10000 | 17 | Le Havre | 5500 |
| 27 | Nantes | 28000 | 12 | Lyon | 10000 | 30 | Sochaux | 5500 |
| 13 | Rennes | 20000 | 25 | Bastia | 9000 | 8 | Sochaux | 5000 |
| 37 | Lille | 16729 | 32 | Auxerre | 9000 | 19 | Lille | 5000 |
| 20 | Guingamp | 16336 | 10 | Nantes | 9000 | 23 | Troyes | 5000 |
| 18 | Nice | 15000 | 14 | Auxerre | 8500 | 36 | Nice | 4397 |
| 31 | Rennes | 10000 | 6 | Montpellier | 8000 | 15 | Monaco | 4000 |
| 1 | Strasbourg | 10000 | 35 | Le Havre | 8000 | 2 | Guingamp | 1000 |
| 21 | Paris SG | 10000 | 34 | Bordeaux | 7500 | | | |

## DISCIPLINARY RECORDS

| | PLAYER | YELLOW | RED | AVE |
|---|---|---|---|---|
| 1 | Destruhaut | 8 | 0 | 166 |
| 2 | Wuillot | 3 | 0 | 180 |
| 3 | Connen | 7 | 0 | 190 |
| 4 | Moracchini | 2 | 1 | 224 |
| 5 | Demont | 4 | 0 | 252 |
| 6 | Lacombe | 5 | 1 | 260 |
| 7 | Rodriguez | 8 | 1 | 274 |
| 8 | Alicarte | 6 | 1 | 278 |
| 9 | Ouadah | 6 | 0 | 299 |
| 10 | Faderne | 2 | 0 | 318 |
| 11 | Guglielmone | 3 | 0 | 330 |
| 12 | Regragui | 5 | 2 | 396 |
| 13 | Terrier | 4 | 0 | 419 |
| | Other | 27 | 0 | |
| | TOTAL | 90 | 6 | |

## LEAGUE GOALS

| | PLAYER | GAMES | MINS | AVE |
|---|---|---|---|---|
| 1 | Rodriguez | 2468 | 6 | 411 |
| 2 | Lacombe | 1560 | 5 | 312 |
| 3 | Faderne | 636 | 2 | 318 |
| 4 | Diomede | 1099 | 2 | 550 |
| 5 | Bezzaz | 252 | 2 | 126 |
| 6 | Seck | 1781 | 2 | 891 |
| 7 | Alicarte | 1950 | 2 | 975 |
| 8 | Collin | 3244 | 1 | 3244 |
| 9 | Guglielmone | 992 | 1 | 992 |
| 10 | Destruhaut | 1333 | 1 | 1333 |
| 11 | Granon | 703 | 1 | 703 |
| 12 | Regragui | 2777 | 1 | 2777 |
| 13 | Demont | 1011 | 1 | 1011 |
| | Other | | 2 | |
| | TOTAL | | 29 | |

## MONTH BY MONTH GUIDE TO THE POINTS

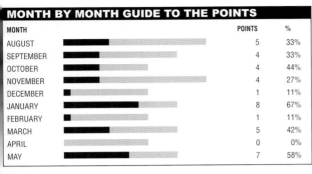

| MONTH | POINTS | % |
|---|---|---|
| AUGUST | 5 | 33% |
| SEPTEMBER | 4 | 33% |
| OCTOBER | 4 | 44% |
| NOVEMBER | 4 | 27% |
| DECEMBER | 1 | 11% |
| JANUARY | 8 | 67% |
| FEBRUARY | 1 | 11% |
| MARCH | 5 | 42% |
| APRIL | 0 | 0% |
| MAY | 7 | 58% |

## TEAM OF THE SEASON

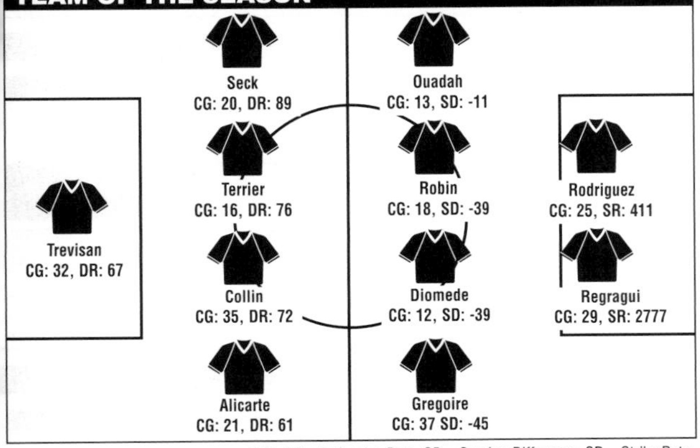
Seck
CG: 20, DR: 89
Ouadah
CG: 13, SD: -11
Terrier
CG: 16, DR: 76
Robin
CG: 18, SD: -39
Rodriguez
CG: 25, SR: 411
Trevisan
CG: 32, DR: 67
Collin
CG: 35, DR: 72
Diomede
CG: 12, SD: -39
Regragui
CG: 29, SR: 2777
Alicarte
CG: 21, DR: 61
Gregoire
CG: 37 SD: -45

KEY: DR = Defensive Rate, SD = Scoring Difference, SR = Strike Rate, CG = Counting Games – League games playing at least 70 minutes

## LEAGUE APPEARANCES, BOOKINGS AND CAPS

| | AGE | IN THE SQUAD | COUNTING GAMES | MINUTES ON PITCH | YELLOW CARDS | RED CARDS | THIS SEASON | HOME COUNTRY |
|---|---|---|---|---|---|---|---|---|
| **Goalkeepers** | | | | | | | | |
| Florian Lucchini | 22 | 7 | 4 | 360 | 1 | 0 | - | France |
| Herve Sekli | 25 | 29 | 2 | 180 | 0 | 0 | - | France |
| Stephane Trevisan | 30 | 33 | 32 | 2880 | 1 | 0 | - | France |
| **Defenders** | | | | | | | | |
| Herve Alicarte | 28 | 22 | 21 | 1950 | 6 | 1 | - | France |
| Xavier Collin | 28 | 37 | 35 | 3244 | 7 | 0 | - | France |
| Christophe Destruhaut | 30 | 24 | 12 | 1333 | 8 | 0 | - | France |
| David Jaureguiberry | 27 | 4 | 0 | 17 | 0 | 0 | - | France |
| Mamadou Seck | 23 | 22 | 20 | 1781 | 3 | 0 | - | Senegal |
| David Terrier | 29 | 22 | 16 | 1678 | 4 | 0 | - | France |
| Laurent Wuillot | 27 | 9 | 5 | 542 | 3 | 0 | - | Belgium |
| **Midfielders** | | | | | | | | |
| Dimitri Ananko | 29 | 18 | 12 | 1357 | 1 | 0 | - | Russia |
| Yacine Bezzaz | 21 | 6 | 2 | 252 | 0 | 0 | - | Algeria |
| Renaud Connen | 23 | 24 | 9 | 1330 | 7 | 0 | - | France |
| Yohan Demont | 25 | 19 | 7 | 1011 | 4 | 0 | - | France |
| Bernard Diomede | 29 | 14 | 12 | 1099 | 2 | 0 | - | France |
| Juan Esnaider | 30 | 5 | 4 | 389 | 1 | 0 | - | Argentina |
| Cyril Granon | 31 | 22 | 2 | 703 | 0 | 0 | - | France |
| Stephane Gregoire | 35 | 37 | 37 | 3309 | 4 | 0 | - | France |
| Fabrice Levrat | 23 | 12 | 1 | 214 | 0 | 0 | - | France |
| Laurent Moracchini | 35 | 14 | 4 | 672 | 2 | 1 | - | France |
| Ousman Nyan | 27 | 3 | 0 | 113 | 1 | 0 | - | Gambia |
| Abdelnasser Ouadah | 27 | 32 | 13 | 1798 | 6 | 0 | - | France |
| Martial Robin | 25 | 31 | 18 | 1919 | 4 | 0 | - | France |
| **Forwards** | | | | | | | | |
| Xavier Becas | 24 | 21 | 3 | 652 | 1 | 0 | - | France |
| David Faderne | 33 | 21 | 0 | 636 | 2 | 0 | - | France |
| Walter Guglielmone | 25 | 27 | 8 | 992 | 3 | 0 | - | Uruguay |
| Gregory Lacombe | 21 | 30 | 10 | 1560 | 5 | 1 | - | France |
| Mickael Marquet | 21 | 6 | 0 | 179 | 1 | 0 | - | France |
| Hoalid Regragui | 27 | 32 | 29 | 2777 | 5 | 2 | - | France |
| Bruno Rodriguez | 30 | 31 | 25 | 2468 | 8 | 1 | - | France |

KEY: LEAGUE BOOKINGS CAPS (FIFA RANKING)

## SQUAD APPEARANCES

| Match | 1 | 2 | 3 | 4 | 5 | 6 | 7 | 8 | 9 | 10 | 11 | 12 | 13 | 14 | 15 | 16 | 17 | 18 | 19 | 20 | 21 | 22 | 23 | 24 | 25 | 26 | 27 | 28 | 29 | 30 | 31 | 32 | 33 | 34 | 35 | 36 | 37 | 38 |
|---|---|---|---|---|---|---|---|---|---|---|---|---|---|---|---|---|---|---|---|---|---|---|---|---|---|---|---|---|---|---|---|---|---|---|---|---|---|---|
| Venue | A | H | A | H | A | H | A | H | A | H | A | H | A | H | A | A | H | A | H | A | H | A | H | A | H | H | A | H | A | A | H | A | H | H | A | H | A | H |
| Competition | L | L | L | L | L | L | L | L | L | L | L | L | L | L | L | L | L | L | L | L | L | L | L | L | L | L | L | L | L | L | L | L | L | L | L | L | L | L |
| Result | D | L | D | W | L | D | W | L | L | W | D | L | D | W | L | L | L | L | D | L | D | D | W | W | D | L | L | D | L | D | W | L | L | L | W | W | L | D |

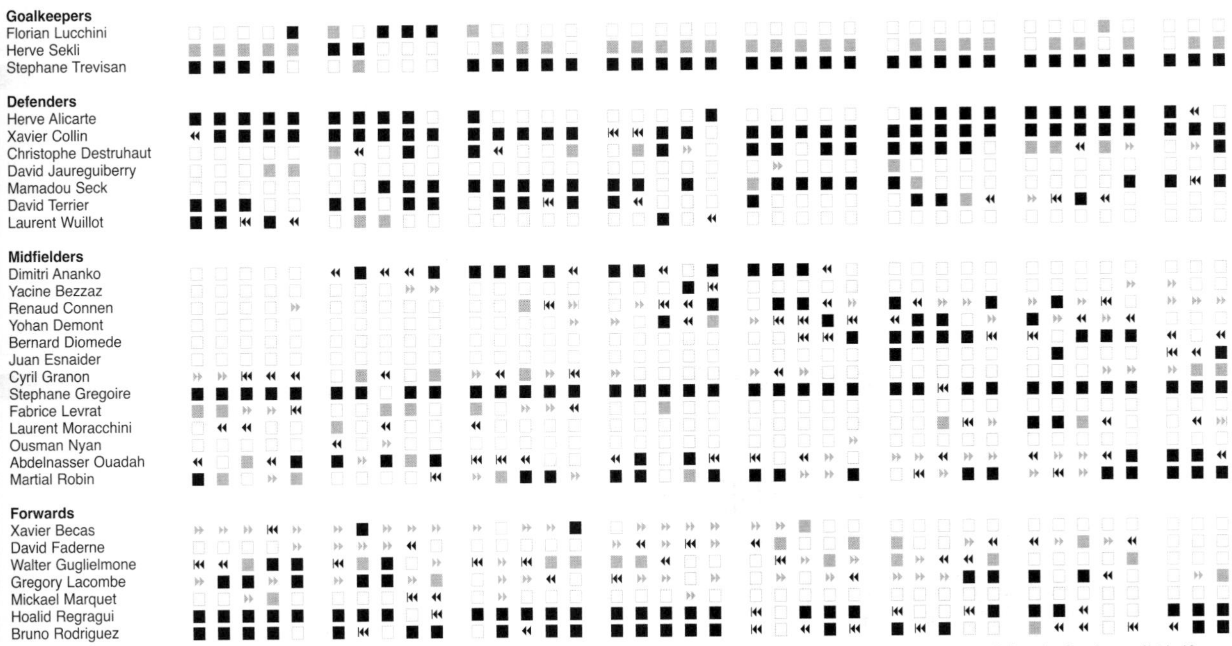
Goalkeepers
Florian Lucchini
Herve Sekli
Stephane Trevisan
Defenders
Herve Alicarte
Xavier Collin
Christophe Destruhaut
David Jaureguiberry
Mamadou Seck
David Terrier
Laurent Wuillot
Midfielders
Dimitri Ananko
Yacine Bezzaz
Renaud Connen
Yohan Demont
Bernard Diomede
Juan Esnaider
Cyril Granon
Stephane Gregoire
Fabrice Levrat
Laurent Moracchini
Ousman Nyan
Abdelnasser Ouadah
Martial Robin
Forwards
Xavier Becas
David Faderne
Walter Guglielmone
Gregory Lacombe
Mickael Marquet
Hoalid Regragui
Bruno Rodriguez

KEY: ■ On all match
■ On bench
⏮ Subbed or sent off (Counting game)
« Subbed or sent off (playing less than 70 minutes)
⏭ Subbed on from bench (Counting Game)
» Subbed on (playing less than 70 minutes)
Subbed on and then subbed or sent off (Counting Game)
Subbed on and then subbed or sent off (playing less than 70 minutes)
Not in 16

# LE HAVRE

Final Position: **18th**

| | | | | | | |
|---|---|---|---|---|---|---|
| 1 | lge | Nice | A | W | 2-1 | Ciechelski 7; Fauconnier 81 |
| 2 | lge | Lille | H | D | 0-0 | |
| 3 | lge | Strasbourg | A | D | 1-1 | Sinama-Pongolle 43 pen |
| 4 | lge | Paris SG | H | L | 0-1 | |
| 5 | lge | Montpellier | A | D | 0-0 | |
| 6 | lge | Guingamp | H | L | 1-2 | Fauconnier 24 |
| 7 | lge | Troyes | A | D | 1-1 | Henin 46 pen |
| 8 | lge | Marseille | H | L | 1-3 | Fauconnier 65 |
| 9 | lge | Sedan | A | L | 0-4 | |
| 10 | lge | Sochaux | H | W | 1-0 | Fauconnier 49 |
| 11 | lge | Bastia | A | L | 1-3 | Fauconnier 62 |
| 12 | lge | Nantes | H | D | 1-1 | Sinama-Pongolle 74 |
| 13 | lge | Monaco | A | D | 1-1 | Sinama-Pongolle 58 |
| 14 | lge | Lyon | H | L | 1-2 | Le Tallec 58 |
| 15 | lge | Rennes | A | D | 0-0 | |
| 16 | lge | Auxerre | H | L | 0-1 | |
| 17 | lge | AC Ajaccio | A | W | 2-1 | Fauconnier 53; Lesage 78 |
| 18 | lge | Bordeaux | H | W | 1-0 | Diawara 56 |
| 19 | lge | Lens | A | L | 0-1 | |
| 20 | lge | Lille | A | L | 0-1 | |
| 21 | lge | Paris SG | A | L | 0-1 | |
| 22 | lge | Strasbourg | H | D | 1-1 | Chimbonda 50 |
| 23 | lge | Montpellier | H | W | 1-0 | Chimbonda 90 |
| 24 | lge | Guingamp | A | W | 2-1 | Beuzelin 67; Martot 82 |
| 25 | lge | Troyes | H | W | 1-0 | Henin 84 pen |
| 26 | lge | Marseille | A | L | 0-2 | |
| 27 | lge | Sedan | H | W | 2-1 | Martot 34; Lesage 75 |
| 28 | lge | Sochaux | A | L | 0-1 | |
| 29 | lge | Bastia | H | W | 2-0 | Sinama-Pongolle 41; Ciechelski 90 |
| 30 | lge | Nantes | A | L | 0-2 | |
| 31 | lge | Monaco | H | L | 0-3 | |
| 32 | lge | Lyon | A | L | 1-2 | Lesage 42 |
| 33 | lge | Rennes | H | L | 0-1 | |
| 34 | lge | Auxerre | A | L | 0-1 | |
| 35 | lge | AC Ajaccio | H | L | 0-1 | |
| 36 | lge | Bordeaux | A | L | 0-2 | |
| 37 | lge | Lens | H | L | 1-3 | Ciechelski 65 |
| 38 | lge | Nice | H | W | 2-1 | Le Tallec 25; Sinama-Pongolle 90 |

## KEY PLAYERS - GOALSCORERS

**1 Olivier Fauconnier**

| | | | |
|---|---|---|---|
| **Goals in the League** | 6 | **Player Strike Rate** Average number of minutes between League goals scored by player | 230 |
| **Contribution to Attacking Power** Average number of minutes between League team goals while on pitch | 106 | **Club Strike Rate** Average number of minutes between League goals scored by club | 127 |

| | PLAYER | LGE GOALS | POWER | STRIKE RATE |
|---|---|---|---|---|
| 2 | Florent Sinama-Pongolle | 5 | 121 | 412 mins |
| 3 | Laurent Ciechelski | 3 | 120 | 561 mins |
| 4 | Jean-Michel Lesage | 3 | 119 | 715 mins |
| 5 | David Martot | 2 | 157 | 867 mins |

## KEY PLAYERS - MIDFIELDERS

**1 Pierre Ducrocq**

| | | | |
|---|---|---|---|
| **Goals in the League** | 0 | **Contribution to Attacking Power** Average number of minutes between League team goals while on pitch | 117 |
| **Defensive Rating** Average number of mins between League goals conceded while he was on the pitch | 77 | **Scoring Difference** Defensive Rating minus Contribution to Attacking Power | -40 |

| | PLAYER | LGE GOALS | DEF RATE | POWER | SCORE DIFF |
|---|---|---|---|---|---|
| 2 | Guillaume Beuzelin | 1 | 79 | 127 | -48 mins |
| 3 | Jean-Michel Lesage | 3 | 69 | 119 | -50 mins |
| 4 | Yazid Mansouri | 0 | 70 | 122 | -52 mins |
| 5 | Anthony Le Tallec | 2 | 79 | 152 | -73 mins |

## KEY PLAYERS - DEFENDERS

**1 Souleymane Diawara**

| | | | |
|---|---|---|---|
| **Goals Conceded (GC)** The number of League goals conceded while he was on the pitch | 34 | **Clean Sheets** In games when he played at least 70 minutes | 6 |
| **Defensive Rating** Ave number of mins between League goals conceded while on the pitch | 80 | **Club Defensive Rating** Average number of mins between League goals conceded by the club this season | 73 |

| | PLAYER | CON LGE | CLEAN SHEETS | DEF RATE |
|---|---|---|---|---|
| 2 | Pascal Chimbonda | 25 | 4 | 73 mins |
| 3 | Jeremy Henin | 47 | 8 | 73 mins |
| 4 | Gregory Paisley | 45 | 8 | 71 mins |
| 5 | Laurent Ciechelski | 24 | 4 | 70 mins |

## GOALS SCORED

**AT HOME**

| | | |
|---|---|---|
| MOST | Lyon | 40 |
| | | 16 |
| LEAST | AC Ajaccio | 14 |

**AWAY**

| | | |
|---|---|---|
| MOST | Monaco | 29 |
| | | 11 |
| LEAST | Troyes | 7 |

## GOALS CONCEDED

**AT HOME**

| | | |
|---|---|---|
| LEAST | Sochaux & Auxerre | 8 |
| | | 21 |
| MOST | Strasbourg | 23 |

**AWAY**

| | | |
|---|---|---|
| LEAST | Lens | 15 |
| | | 26 |
| MOST | Sedan | 39 |

## KEY GOALKEEPER

**1 Alexander Vencel**

| | |
|---|---|
| **Goals Conceded in the League** | 47 |
| **Defensive Rating** Ave number of mins between League goals conceded while on the pitch | 73 |
| **Counting Games** Games when he played at least 70 minutes | 38 |
| **Clean Sheets** In games when he played at least 70 minutes | 8 |

## TOP POINT EARNERS

| | PLAYER | GAMES | AVE |
|---|---|---|---|
| 1 | Sinama-Pongolle | 17 | 1.35 |
| 2 | Beuzelin | 26 | 1.27 |
| 3 | Martot | 18 | 1.22 |
| 4 | Lesage | 22 | 1.14 |
| 5 | Chimbonda | 19 | 1.11 |
| 6 | Ducrocq | 29 | 1.07 |
| 7 | Diawara | 30 | 1.03 |
| 8 | Henin | 38 | 1.00 |
| 9 | Vencel | 38 | 1.00 |
| 10 | Paisley | 34 | 1.00 |
| | **CLUB AVERAGE:** | | **1.00** |

Ave = Average points per match in Counting Games

## ATTENDANCES

HOME GROUND: JULES DESCHASEAUX CAPACITY: 18000 AVERAGE LEAGUE AT HOME: 12622

| | | | | | | | | |
|---|---|---|---|---|---|---|---|---|
| 32 | Lyon | 36000 | 24 | Guingamp | 15000 | 5 | Montpellier | 10000 |
| 26 | Marseille | 35000 | 2 | Lille | 14750 | 10 | Sochaux | 9000 |
| 14 | Lyon | 35000 | 38 | Nice | 14000 | 9 | Sedan | 9000 |
| 21 | Paris SG | 33438 | 6 | Guingamp | 14000 | 18 | Bordeaux | 9000 |
| 36 | Bordeaux | 26824 | 37 | Lens | 13583 | 12 | Nantes | 9000 |
| 30 | Nantes | 25000 | 20 | Lille | 13525 | 27 | Sedan | 9000 |
| 19 | Lens | 24758 | 1 | Nice | 12000 | 35 | AC Ajaccio | 8000 |
| 28 | Sochaux | 20000 | 3 | Strasbourg | 12000 | 23 | Montpellier | 8000 |
| 4 | Paris SG | 16500 | 33 | Rennes | 11000 | 25 | Troyes | 7000 |
| 8 | Marseille | 16000 | 16 | Auxerre | 10000 | 11 | Bastia | 6000 |
| 31 | Monaco | 16000 | 29 | Bastia | 10000 | 17 | AC Ajaccio | 5500 |
| 7 | Troyes | 15000 | 34 | Auxerre | 10000 | 13 | Monaco | 5000 |
| 15 | Rennes | 15000 | 22 | Strasbourg | 10000 | | | |

Home / Away / Neutral

## DISCIPLINARY RECORDS

| | PLAYER | YELLOW | RED | AVE |
|---|---|---|---|---|
| 1 | Diawara | 11 | 3 | 195 |
| 2 | Ciechelski | 6 | 2 | 210 |
| 3 | Ducrocq | 11 | 1 | 224 |
| 4 | Sinama-Pongolle | 8 | 1 | 228 |
| 5 | Chimbonda | 6 | 0 | 303 |
| 6 | Mansouri | 7 | 0 | 332 |
| 7 | Diarra | 3 | 0 | 509 |
| 8 | Paisley | 6 | 0 | 535 |
| 9 | Henin | 6 | 0 | 570 |
| 10 | Beuzelin | 4 | 0 | 635 |
| 11 | Fauconnier | 2 | 0 | 690 |
| 12 | Lesage | 2 | 1 | 715 |
| 13 | Bertin | 1 | 0 | 787 |
| | Other | 10 | 1 | |
| | TOTAL | 83 | 9 | |

## LEAGUE GOALS

| | PLAYER | MINS | MINS | AVE |
|---|---|---|---|---|
| 1 | Fauconnier | 1381 | 6 | 230 |
| 2 | S-Pongolle | 2060 | 5 | 412 |
| 3 | Ciechelski | 1684 | 3 | 561 |
| 4 | Lesage | 2145 | 3 | 715 |
| 5 | Martot | 1734 | 2 | 867 |
| 6 | Le Tallec | 1970 | 2 | 985 |
| 7 | Chimbonda | 1819 | 2 | 910 |
| 8 | Henin | 3420 | 2 | 1710 |
| 9 | Diawara | 2736 | 1 | 2736 |
| 10 | Beuzelin | 2541 | 1 | 2541 |
| | Other | | 0 | |
| | TOTAL | | 27 | |

## MONTH BY MONTH GUIDE TO THE POINTS

| MONTH | POINTS | % |
|---|---|---|
| AUGUST | 6 | 40% |
| SEPTEMBER | 1 | 8% |
| OCTOBER | 4 | 44% |
| NOVEMBER | 5 | 33% |
| DECEMBER | 3 | 33% |
| JANUARY | 7 | 58% |
| FEBRUARY | 6 | 50% |
| MARCH | 3 | 33% |
| APRIL | 0 | 0% |
| MAY | 3 | 25% |

## TEAM OF THE SEASON

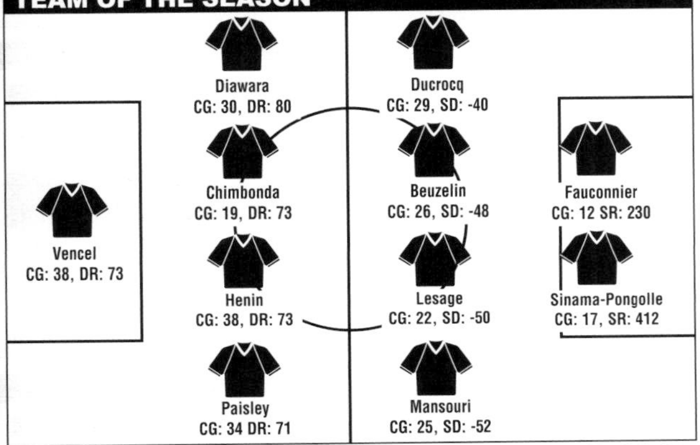
Vencel
CG: 38, DR: 73
Diawara
CG: 30, DR: 80
Chimbonda
CG: 19, DR: 73
Henin
CG: 38, DR: 73
Paisley
CG: 34 DR: 71
Ducrocq
CG: 29, SD: -40
Beuzelin
CG: 26, SD: -48
Lesage
CG: 22, SD: -50
Mansouri
CG: 25, SD: -52
Fauconnier
CG: 12 SR: 230
Sinama-Pongolle
CG: 17, SR: 412

KEY: DR = Defensive Rate, SD = Scoring Difference, SR = Strike Rate,
CG = Counting Games – League games playing at least 70 minutes

## LEAGUE APPEARANCES, BOOKINGS AND CAPS

| | AGE | IN THE SQUAD | COUNTING GAMES | MINUTES ON PITCH | YELLOW CARDS | RED CARDS | THIS SEASON | HOME COUNTRY |
|---|---|---|---|---|---|---|---|---|
| **Goalkeepers** | | | | | | | | |
| Olivier Blondel | 23 | 11 | 0 | 0 | 0 | 0 | - | France |
| Nicolas Douchez | 23 | 26 | 0 | 0 | 0 | 0 | - | France |
| Alexander Vencel | 36 | 38 | 38 | 3420 | 0 | 0 | - | Slovakia |
| **Defenders** | | | | | | | | |
| Pascal Chimbonda | 24 | 27 | 19 | 1819 | 6 | 0 | - | France |
| Laurent Ciechelski | 32 | 23 | 19 | 1684 | 6 | 2 | - | France |
| Alou Diarra | 21 | 30 | 13 | 1528 | 3 | 0 | - | France |
| Souleymane Diawara | 24 | 33 | 30 | 2736 | 11 | 3 | 2 | Senegal (29) |
| Jeremy Henin | 25 | 38 | 38 | 3420 | 6 | 0 | - | France |
| Cyril N'Diba | 22 | 10 | 1 | 132 | 0 | 0 | - | Cameroon |
| Gregory Paisley | 26 | 37 | 34 | 3212 | 6 | 0 | - | France |
| **Midfielders** | | | | | | | | |
| Jamel Ait Ben Idir | | 1 | 0 | 15 | 0 | 0 | - | |
| Alexis Bertin | 23 | 18 | 8 | 787 | 1 | 0 | - | France |
| Guillaume Beuzelin | 24 | 38 | 26 | 2541 | 4 | 0 | - | France |
| Davidas | | 2 | 1 | 147 | 0 | 0 | - | |
| Pierre Ducrocq | 26 | 31 | 29 | 2697 | 11 | 1 | - | France |
| Jean-J Ebentsi | 22 | 13 | 4 | 374 | 0 | 0 | - | France |
| Anthony Le Tallec | 18 | 34 | 19 | 1970 | 2 | 0 | - | France |
| Thomas Lecossais | 21 | 16 | 4 | 386 | 1 | 0 | - | France |
| Jean-Michel Lesage | 26 | 31 | 22 | 2145 | 2 | 1 | - | France |
| Yazid Mansouri | 25 | 30 | 25 | 2326 | 7 | 0 | - | France |
| David Martot | 22 | 30 | 18 | 1734 | 1 | 0 | - | France |
| Mohamed Said | 19 | 1 | 0 | 9 | 0 | 0 | - | Morocco |
| Khalid Souhayli | | 2 | 0 | 0 | 0 | 0 | - | France |
| **Forwards** | | | | | | | | |
| Fadel Brahami | 24 | 13 | 0 | 75 | 0 | 0 | - | France |
| Olivier Fauconnier | 27 | 24 | 12 | 1381 | 2 | 0 | - | France |
| William Mocquet | 20 | 7 | 3 | 412 | 5 | 1 | - | France |
| Milan Osterc | 28 | 9 | 3 | 421 | 1 | 0 | - | Slovenia |
| F Sinama-Pongolle | 18 | 31 | 17 | 2060 | 8 | 1 | - | France |

KEY: LEAGUE BOOKINGS CAPS (FIFA RANKING)

## SQUAD APPEARANCES

| Match | 1 | 2 | 3 | 4 | 5 | 6 | 7 | 8 | 9 | 10 | 11 | 12 | 13 | 14 | 15 | 16 | 17 | 18 | 19 | 20 | 21 | 22 | 23 | 24 | 25 | 26 | 27 | 28 | 29 | 30 | 31 | 32 | 33 | 34 | 35 | 36 | 37 | 38 |
|---|---|---|---|---|---|---|---|---|---|---|---|---|---|---|---|---|---|---|---|---|---|---|---|---|---|---|---|---|---|---|---|---|---|---|---|---|---|---|
| Venue | A | H | A | H | A | H | A | H | A | H | A | H | A | H | A | H | A | H | A | A | A | H | H | A | H | A | H | A | H | A | H | A | H | A | H | A | H | H |
| Competition | L | L | L | L | L | L | L | L | L | L | L | L | L | L | L | L | L | L | L | L | L | L | L | L | L | L | L | L | L | L | L | L | L | L | L | L | L | L |
| Result | W | D | D | L | D | L | D | L | L | W | L | D | D | L | D | L | W | W | L | L | L | D | W | W | W | L | W | L | W | L | L | L | L | L | L | L | L | W |

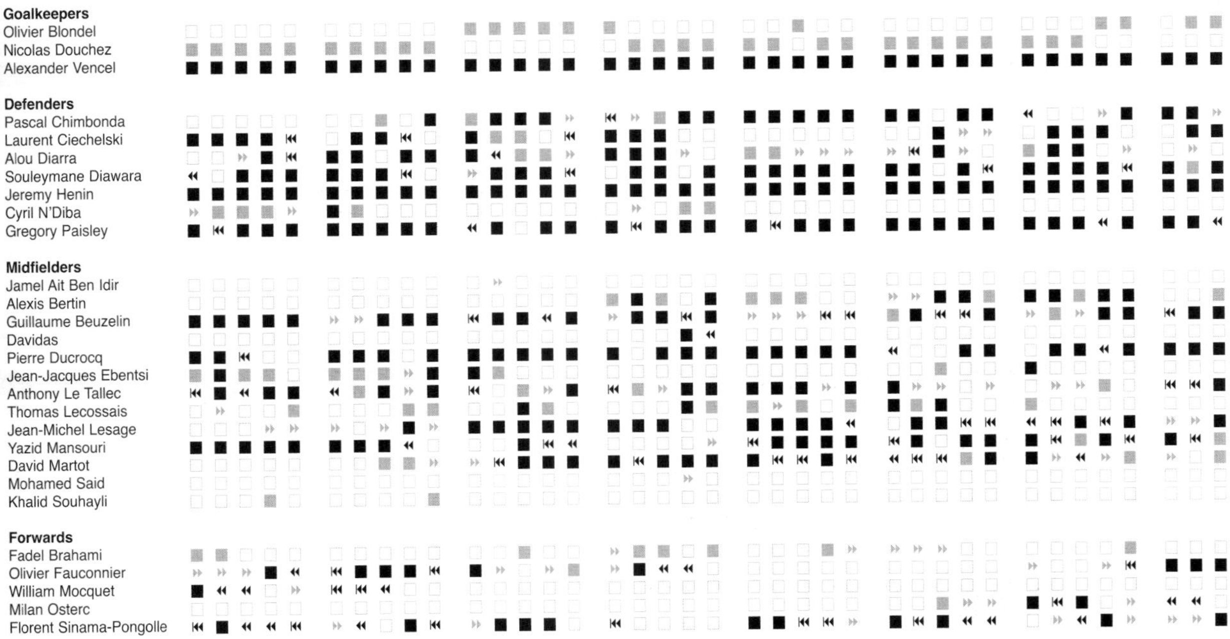
Goalkeepers
Olivier Blondel
Nicolas Douchez
Alexander Vencel
Defenders
Pascal Chimbonda
Laurent Ciechelski
Alou Diarra
Souleymane Diawara
Jeremy Henin
Cyril N'Diba
Gregory Paisley
Midfielders
Jamel Ait Ben Idir
Alexis Bertin
Guillaume Beuzelin
Davidas
Pierre Ducrocq
Jean-Jacques Ebentsi
Anthony Le Tallec
Thomas Lecossais
Jean-Michel Lesage
Yazid Mansouri
David Martot
Mohamed Said
Khalid Souhayli
Forwards
Fadel Brahami
Olivier Fauconnier
William Mocquet
Milan Osterc
Florent Sinama-Pongolle

KEY: ■ On all match ■ On bench ⏮ Subbed or sent off (Counting game) ◀◀ Subbed or sent off (playing less than 70 minutes) ⏭ Subbed on from bench (Counting Game) ▶▶ Subbed on (playing less than 70 minutes) Subbed on and then subbed or sent off (Counting Game) Subbed on and then subbed or sent off (playing less than 70 minutes) □ Not in 16

# SEDAN

Final Position: **19th**

| | | | | | | |
|---|---|---|---|---|---|---|
| 1 | lge | Sochaux | H | D | 0-0 | |
| 2 | lge | Lyon | A | L | 1-6 | Camara 7 |
| 3 | lge | Lens | H | L | 0-1 | |
| 4 | lge | AC Ajaccio | A | L | 0-1 | |
| 5 | lge | Nantes | H | W | 1-0 | Noro 27 |
| 6 | lge | Strasbourg | A | D | 1-1 | Asuar 11 |
| 7 | lge | Monaco | H | D | 2-2 | Djurisic 55; Mionnet 88 |
| 8 | lge | Le Havre | H | W | 4-0 | Camara, H 1; Noro 47,83; Liri 73 |
| 9 | lge | Bordeaux | A | D | 2-2 | Di Tommaso 10; Liri 76 |
| 10 | lge | Rennes | H | L | 1-3 | Oulida 89 |
| 11 | lge | Guingamp | A | W | 1-0 | Liri 75 |
| 12 | lge | Paris SG | H | W | 3-1 | Noro 8; Asuar 50,67 |
| 13 | lge | Montpellier | A | L | 0-2 | |
| 14 | lge | Lille | H | L | 0-1 | |
| 15 | lge | Troyes | A | L | 0-2 | |
| 16 | lge | Nice | H | W | 3-0 | Camara, H 34,46; Liri 88 |
| 17 | lge | Bastia | A | W | 1-0 | N'Diaye 21 |
| 18 | lge | Marseille | H | L | 1-2 | Camara, H 68 |
| 19 | lge | Lyon | H | D | 1-1 | Camara, H 89 |
| 20 | lge | AC Ajaccio | H | D | 1-1 | Camara, H 42 |
| 21 | lge | Lens | A | L | 0-4 | |
| 22 | lge | Nantes | A | L | 1-4 | Camara, H 85 |
| 23 | lge | Strasbourg | H | W | 2-1 | Camara, H 26 pen; N'Diaye 43 |
| 24 | lge | Monaco | A | L | 0-3 | |
| 25 | lge | Auxerre | H | L | 1-2 | N'Diefi 3 |
| 26 | lge | Le Havre | A | L | 1-2 | Camara, H 45 |
| 27 | lge | Bordeaux | H | L | 0-1 | |
| 28 | lge | Rennes | A | L | 0-1 | |
| 29 | lge | Guingamp | H | W | 2-0 | Asuar 78; Liri 90 |
| 30 | lge | Paris SG | A | L | 0-2 | |
| 31 | lge | Montpellier | H | L | 1-2 | Asuar 43 |
| 32 | lge | Auxerre | A | L | 1-3 | N'Diefi 61 |
| 33 | lge | Lille | A | D | 0-0 | |
| 34 | lge | Troyes | H | W | 4-0 | Camara, H 54,62,71; Asuar 65 |
| 35 | lge | Nice | A | D | 0-0 | |
| 36 | lge | Bastia | H | D | 2-2 | Noro 37,76 |
| 37 | lge | Marseille | A | L | 2-4 | N'Diefi 56; Perez 60 og |
| 38 | lge | Sochaux | A | L | 1-2 | Camara, H 66 pen |

## KEY PLAYERS - GOALSCORERS

**1 Henri Camara**

| | | | |
|---|---|---|---|
| Goals in the League | 14 | Player Strike Rate<br>Average number of minutes between League goals scored by player | 189 |
| Contribution to Attacking Power<br>Average number of minutes between League team goals while on pitch | 80 | Club Strike Rate<br>Average number of minutes between League goals scored by club | 83 |

| | PLAYER | LGE GOALS | POWER | STRIKE RATE |
|---|---|---|---|---|
| 2 | Stephane Noro | 6 | 65 | 349 mins |
| 3 | Ludovic Asuar | 6 | 87 | 394 mins |
| 4 | Pius N'Diefi | 3 | 93 | 776 mins |
| 5 | Moussa N'Diaye | 2 | 82 | 911 mins |

## KEY PLAYERS - MIDFIELDERS

**1 Stephane Noro**

| | | | |
|---|---|---|---|
| Goals in the League | 6 | Contribution to Attacking Power<br>Average number of minutes between League team goals while on pitch | 65 |
| Defensive Rating<br>Average number of mins between League goals conceded while he was on the pitch | 77 | Scoring Difference<br>Defensive Rating minus Contribution to Attacking Power | 12 |

| | PLAYER | LGE GOALS | DEF RATE | POWER | SCORE DIFF |
|---|---|---|---|---|---|
| 2 | Tarik Oulida | 1 | 64 | 78 | -14 mins |
| 3 | Modeste Mbami | 0 | 55 | 89 | -34 mins |
| 4 | Ludovic Asuar | 6 | 52 | 87 | -35 mins |

## KEY PLAYERS - DEFENDERS

**1 David Ducourtioux**

| | | | |
|---|---|---|---|
| Goals Conceded (GC)<br>The number of League goals conceded while he was on the pitch | 19 | Clean Sheets<br>In games when he played at least 70 minutes | 4 |
| Defensive Rating<br>Ave number of mins between League goals conceded while on the pitch | 73 | Club Defensive Rating<br>Average number of mins between League goals conceded by the club this season | 58 |

| | PLAYER | CON LGE | CLEAN SHEETS | DEF RATE |
|---|---|---|---|---|
| 2 | David Di Tommaso | 19 | 4 | 61 mins |
| 3 | Richard Jezierski | 43 | 10 | 60 mins |
| 4 | Eddy Capron | 51 | 9 | 59 mins |
| 5 | Hamada Jambay | 38 | 6 | 53 mins |

## GOALS SCORED

AT HOME

| | | |
|---|---|---|
| MOST | Lyon | 40 |
| | | 29 |
| LEAST | AC Ajaccio | 14 |

AWAY

| | | |
|---|---|---|
| MOST | Monaco | 29 |
| | | 12 |
| LEAST | Troyes | 7 |

## GOALS CONCEDED

AT HOME

| | | |
|---|---|---|
| LEAST | Sochaux & Auxerre | 8 |
| | | 20 |
| MOST | Strasbourg | 23 |

AWAY

| | | |
|---|---|---|
| LEAST | Lens | 15 |
| | | 39 |
| MOST | Sedan | 39 |

## KEY GOALKEEPER

**1 Patrick Regnault**

| | |
|---|---|
| Goals Conceded in the League | 59 |
| Defensive Rating<br>Ave number of mins between League goals conceded while on the pitch | 58 |
| Counting Games<br>Games when he played at least 70 minutes | 38 |
| Clean Sheets<br>In games when he played at least 70 minutes | 10 |

## TOP POINT EARNERS

| | PLAYER | GAMES | AVE |
|---|---|---|---|
| 1 | Noro | 18 | 1.44 |
| 2 | Ducourtioux | 13 | 1.31 |
| 3 | Oulida | 18 | 1.28 |
| 4 | Ndiaye | 17 | 1.24 |
| 5 | Jezierski | 28 | 1.11 |
| 6 | Capron | 33 | 0.97 |
| 7 | Regnault | 38 | 0.95 |
| 8 | Camara, H | 27 | 0.93 |
| 9 | Mbami | 30 | 0.90 |
| 10 | Ndiefi | 22 | 0.82 |
| | **CLUB AVERAGE:** | | **0.95** |

Ave = Average points per match in Counting Games

## ATTENDANCES

HOME GROUND: STADE LOUIS DUGUAGUEZ CAPACITY: 24000 AVERAGE LEAGUE AT HOME: 15511

| | | | | | | | | |
|---|---|---|---|---|---|---|---|---|
| 37 | Marseille | 55442 | 34 | Troyes | 15000 | 33 | Lille | 10000 |
| 1 | Sochaux | 45000 | 31 | Montpellier | 15000 | 5 | Nantes | 10000 |
| 21 | Lens | 34000 | 9 | Bordeaux | 15000 | 11 | Guingamp | 10000 |
| 2 | Lyon | 32225 | 35 | Nice | 14115 | 25 | Auxerre | 10000 |
| 22 | Nantes | 31000 | 7 | Monaco | 14000 | 8 | Le Havre | 9000 |
| 30 | Paris SG | 30000 | 14 | Lille | 13500 | 6 | Strasbourg | 9000 |
| 12 | Paris SG | 23000 | 29 | Guingamp | 13000 | 26 | Le Havre | 9000 |
| 36 | Bastia | 21982 | 15 | Troyes | 12000 | 13 | Montpellier | 8000 |
| 19 | Lyon | 19240 | 3 | Lens | 12000 | 20 | AC Ajaccio | 7000 |
| 38 | Sochaux | 19078 | 10 | Rennes | 12000 | 4 | AC Ajaccio | 6000 |
| 28 | Rennes | 18000 | 27 | Bordeaux | 11000 | 17 | Bastia | 6000 |
| 23 | Strasbourg | 17000 | 16 | Nice | 11000 | 24 | Monaco | 5000 |
| 18 | Marseille | 16000 | 32 | Auxerre | 11000 | | | |

## DISCIPLINARY RECORDS

| | PLAYER | YELLOW | RED | AVE |
|---|---|---|---|---|
| 1 | Trapasso | 4 | 0 | 131 |
| 2 | Mathieu | 6 | 0 | 231 |
| 3 | Tall | 4 | 1 | 238 |
| 4 | Chedli | 2 | 0 | 241 |
| 5 | Domoraud | 4 | 0 | 245 |
| 6 | Pagis | 11 | 0 | 249 |
| 7 | Saveljic | 10 | 0 | 297 |
| 8 | Daf | 3 | 0 | 327 |
| 9 | Pedretti | 8 | 0 | 392 |
| 10 | Boudarene | 3 | 0 | 591 |
| 11 | Raschke | 2 | 0 | 741 |
| 12 | Monsoreau | 4 | 0 | 791 |
| 13 | Isabey | 2 | 0 | 910 |
| | Other | 8 | 0 | |
| | **TOTAL** | **71** | **1** | |

## LEAGUE GOALS

| | PLAYER | MINS | GOALS | AVE |
|---|---|---|---|---|
| 1 | Camara, H | 2648 | 14 | 189 |
| 2 | Asuar | 2361 | 6 | 394 |
| 3 | Noro | 2091 | 6 | 349 |
| 4 | Liri | 739 | 5 | 148 |
| 5 | Ndiefi | 2328 | 3 | 776 |
| 6 | Ndiaye | 1822 | 2 | 911 |
| 7 | Di Tommaso | 1153 | 1 | 1153 |
| 8 | Mionnet | 619 | 1 | 619 |
| 9 | Djurisic | 1112 | 1 | 1112 |
| 10 | Oulida | 1796 | 1 | 1796 |
| | Other | | 1 | |
| | **TOTAL** | | **41** | |

## MONTH BY MONTH GUIDE TO THE POINTS

| MONTH | POINTS | % |
|---|---|---|
| AUGUST | 4 | 27% |
| SEPTEMBER | 5 | 56% |
| OCTOBER | 4 | 44% |
| NOVEMBER | 6 | 40% |
| DECEMBER | 4 | 44% |
| JANUARY | 4 | 33% |
| FEBRUARY | 0 | 0% |
| MARCH | 3 | 33% |
| APRIL | 4 | 33% |
| MAY | 2 | 17% |

## TEAM OF THE SEASON

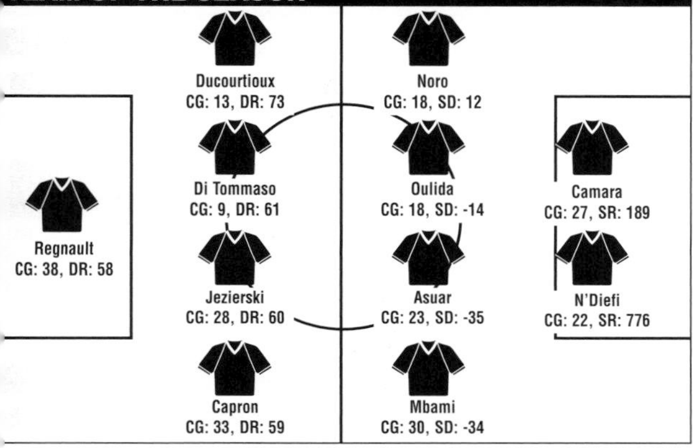
Ducourtioux
CG: 13, DR: 73
Noro
CG: 18, SD: 12
Di Tommaso
CG: 9, DR: 61
Oulida
CG: 18, SD: -14
Camara
CG: 27, SR: 189
Regnault
CG: 38, DR: 58
Jezierski
CG: 28, DR: 60
Asuar
CG: 23, SD: -35
N'Diefi
CG: 22, SR: 776
Capron
CG: 33, DR: 59
Mbami
CG: 30, SD: -34

**KEY:** DR = Defensive Rate, SD = Scoring Difference, SR = Strike Rate, CG = Counting Games – League games playing at least 70 minutes

## LEAGUE APPEARANCES, BOOKINGS AND CAPS

| | AGE | IN THE SQUAD | COUNTING GAMES | MINUTES ON PITCH | YELLOW CARDS | RED CARDS | THIS SEASON | HOME COUNTRY |
|---|---|---|---|---|---|---|---|---|
| **Goalkeepers** | | | | | | | | |
| Fabrice Catherine | 30 | 37 | 0 | 0 | 0 | 0 | - | France |
| Patrick Regnault | 29 | 38 | 38 | 3420 | 1 | 0 | - | France |
| **Defenders** | | | | | | | | |
| Alcaly Camara | 22 | 8 | 2 | 249 | 2 | 0 | - | Senegal |
| Eddy Capron | 32 | 35 | 33 | 2986 | 7 | 1 | - | France |
| Johan Charpenet | 26 | 12 | 2 | 201 | 0 | 1 | - | France |
| David Di Tommaso | 23 | 28 | 9 | 1153 | 2 | 0 | - | France |
| Dusko Djurisic | 25 | 16 | 11 | 1112 | 0 | 0 | - | Serbia & Montenegro |
| David Ducourtioux | 25 | 25 | 13 | 1379 | 4 | 0 | - | France |
| Cedric Elzeard | 28 | 21 | 15 | 1512 | 4 | 0 | - | France |
| Hamada Jambay | 28 | 26 | 21 | 2005 | 8 | 0 | - | France |
| Richard Jezierski | 32 | 31 | 28 | 2585 | 10 | 1 | - | France |
| Pierre Beaka Njanka | 28 | 10 | 9 | 801 | 4 | 1 | 1 | Cameroon (18) |
| Pascal Pedemonte | 23 | 2 | 1 | 76 | 0 | 0 | - | France |
| **Midfielders** | | | | | | | | |
| Ludovic Asuar | 26 | 31 | 23 | 2361 | 3 | 0 | - | France |
| Sophiane Baghdad | 22 | 2 | 0 | 21 | 0 | 0 | - | France |
| Frederic Brando | 29 | 11 | 4 | 489 | 2 | 1 | - | France |
| Lukas Jarolim | 26 | 13 | 8 | 931 | 0 | 0 | - | Czech Republic |
| Modeste Mbami | 20 | 34 | 30 | 2861 | 10 | 1 | 1 | Cameroon (18) |
| Stephane Noro | 23 | 34 | 18 | 2091 | 8 | 0 | - | France |
| Tarik Oulida | 29 | 26 | 18 | 1796 | 4 | 1 | - | Holland |
| Patrick Vaz | 24 | 6 | 3 | 329 | 1 | 0 | - | France |
| Mathieu Verschuere | 31 | 15 | 6 | 731 | 0 | 0 | - | France |
| **Forwards** | | | | | | | | |
| Henri Camara | 26 | 35 | 27 | 2648 | 1 | 0 | 2 | Senegal (29) |
| Cedric Collet | | 2 | 0 | 6 | 0 | 0 | - | France |
| Alain Liri | 24 | 26 | 5 | 739 | 2 | 0 | - | France |
| Julien Lorthioir | 19 | 4 | 1 | 100 | 0 | 0 | - | France |
| Cedric Mionnet | 29 | 14 | 4 | 619 | 0 | 0 | - | France |
| Moussa Ndiaye | 24 | 27 | 17 | 1822 | 4 | 0 | 2 | Senegal (29) |
| Pius Ndiefi | 28 | 31 | 22 | 2328 | 1 | 0 | 1 | Cameroon (18) |
| Julien Puoeys | 23 | 8 | 0 | 93 | 0 | 0 | - | France |

**KEY:** LEAGUE BOOKINGS CAPS (FIFA RANKING)

## SQUAD APPEARANCES

| Match | 1 | 2 | 3 | 4 | 5 | 6 | 7 | 8 | 9 | 10 | 11 | 12 | 13 | 14 | 15 | 16 | 17 | 18 | 19 | 20 | 21 | 22 | 23 | 24 | 25 | 26 | 27 | 28 | 29 | 30 | 31 | 32 | 33 | 34 | 35 | 36 | 37 | 38 |
|---|---|---|---|---|---|---|---|---|---|---|---|---|---|---|---|---|---|---|---|---|---|---|---|---|---|---|---|---|---|---|---|---|---|---|---|---|---|---|
| Venue | H | A | H | A | H | A | H | H | A | H | A | H | A | H | A | H | A | H | H | H | A | A | H | A | H | A | H | A | H | A | H | A | A | H | A | H | A | A |
| Competition | L | L | L | L | L | L | L | L | L | L | L | L | L | L | L | L | L | L | L | L | L | L | L | L | L | L | L | L | L | L | L | L | L | L | L | L | L | L |
| Result | D | L | L | L | W | D | D | W | D | L | W | W | L | L | L | W | W | L | D | D | L | L | W | L | L | L | L | L | W | L | L | L | D | W | D | D | L | L |

**Goalkeepers**
Fabrice Catherine
Patrick Regnault

**Defenders**
Alcaly Camara
Eddy Capron
Johan Charpenet
David Di Tommaso
Dusko Djurisic
David Ducourtioux
Cedric Elzeard
Hamada Jambay
Richard Jezierski
Pierre Beaka Njanka
Pascal Pedemonte

**Midfielders**
Ludovic Asuar
Sophiane Baghdad
Frederic Brando
Lukas Jarolim
Modeste Mbami
Stephane Noro
Tarik Oulida
Patrick Vaz
Mathieu Verschuere

**Forwards**
Henri Camara
Cedric Collet
Alain Liri
Julien Lorthioir
Cedric Mionnet
Moussa Ndiaye
Pius Ndiefi
Julien Puoeys

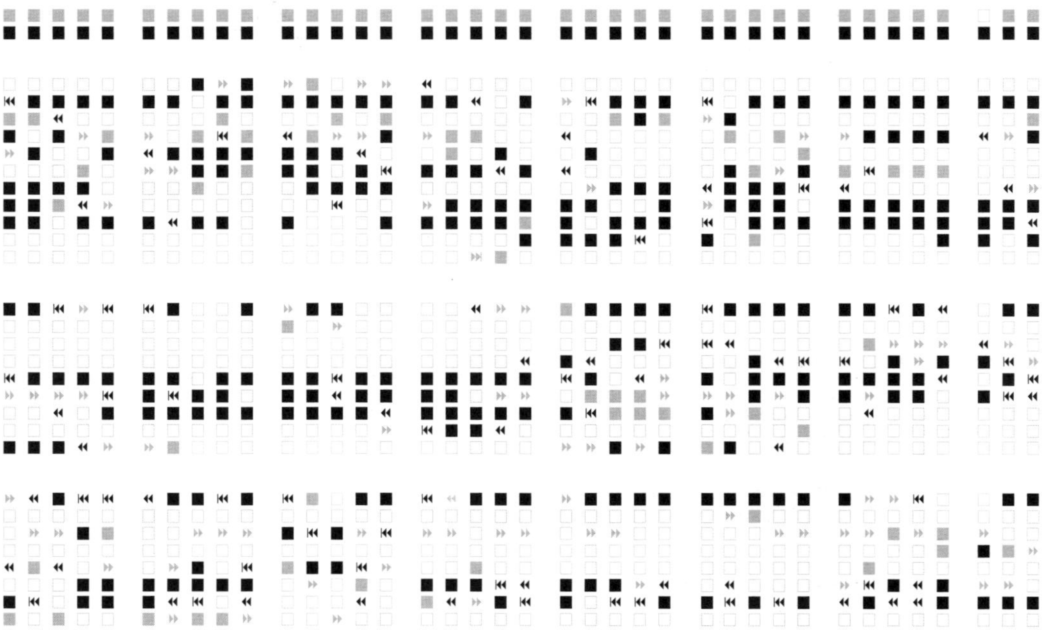

KEY: ■ On all match ⏮ Subbed or sent off (Counting game) ⏭ Subbed on from bench (Counting Game) Subbed on and then subbed or sent off (Counting Game) □ Not in 16
■ On bench « Subbed or sent off (playing less than 70 minutes) » Subbed on (playing less than 70 minutes) Subbed on and then subbed or sent off (playing less than 70 minutes)

# TROYES

Final Position: **20th**

| | | | | | | |
|---|---|---|---|---|---|---|
| 1 | lge | Monaco | H | L | 0-4 | |
| 2 | lge | Rennes | A | D | 0-0 | |
| 3 | lge | Auxerre | H | L | 1-2 | Gousse 3 |
| 4 | lge | Lille | A | D | 0-0 | |
| 5 | lge | AC Ajaccio | H | W | 1-0 | Niang 4 |
| 6 | lge | Bordeaux | A | L | 0-1 | |
| 7 | lge | Le Havre | H | D | 1-1 | Nivet 39 |
| 8 | lge | Nice | A | L | 0-1 | |
| 9 | lge | Lyon | H | D | 1-1 | Niang 83 |
| 10 | lge | Strasbourg | A | L | 1-2 | Gousse 28 |
| 11 | lge | Paris SG | H | L | 1-2 | Saifi 18 |
| 12 | lge | Montpellier | A | D | 2-2 | Baticle 22; Gousse 62 |
| 13 | lge | Guingamp | H | L | 0-2 | |
| 14 | lge | Bastia | H | W | 3-0 | Gousse 22 pen,71; Niang 90 |
| 15 | lge | Marseille | A | D | 0-0 | |
| 16 | lge | Sedan | H | W | 2-0 | Adam 29; Hamed 70 |
| 17 | lge | Sochaux | A | L | 0-1 | |
| 18 | lge | Lens | H | D | 0-0 | |
| 19 | lge | Nantes | A | L | 1-2 | Saifi 32 |
| 20 | lge | Rennes | H | L | 0-1 | |
| 21 | lge | Auxerre | A | L | 0-1 | |
| 22 | lge | AC Ajaccio | A | L | 0-1 | |
| 23 | lge | Bordeaux | H | L | 0-1 | |
| 24 | lge | Le Havre | A | L | 0-1 | |
| 25 | lge | Nice | H | W | 1-0 | Saifi 3 |
| 26 | lge | Lyon | A | D | 0-0 | |
| 27 | lge | Lille | H | W | 2-0 | Gousse 3 pen; Saifi 58 |
| 28 | lge | Strasbourg | H | W | 1-0 | Benachour 6 |
| 29 | lge | Paris SG | A | L | 2-4 | Adam 10; Benachour 28 |
| 30 | lge | Montpellier | H | L | 0-2 | |
| 31 | lge | Guingamp | A | L | 0-2 | |
| 32 | lge | Bastia | A | D | 1-1 | Nivet 85 |
| 33 | lge | Marseille | H | D | 0-0 | |
| 34 | lge | Sedan | A | L | 0-4 | |
| 35 | lge | Sochaux | H | L | 0-2 | |
| 36 | lge | Lens | A | L | 0-1 | |
| 37 | lge | Nantes | H | W | 2-0 | Nade 51; Akrour 69 |
| 38 | lge | Monaco | A | L | 0-6 | |

## KEY PLAYERS - GOALSCORERS

**1 Nicolas Gousse**

| | | | |
|---|---|---|---|
| Goals in the League | 6 | Player Strike Rate<br>Average number of minutes between League goals scored by player | 412 |
| Contribution to Attacking Power<br>Average number of minutes between League team goals while on pitch | 154 | Club Strike Rate<br>Average number of minutes between League goals scored by club | 149 |

| | PLAYER | LGE GOALS | POWER | STRIKE RATE |
|---|---|---|---|---|
| 2 | Rafik Saifi | 4 | 113 | 456 mins |
| 3 | Frederic Adam | 2 | 129 | 839 mins |
| 4 | Gerald Baticle | 1 | 115 | 1495 mins |
| 5 | David Hamed | 1 | 148 | 2674 mins |

## KEY PLAYERS - MIDFIELDERS

**1 Olivier Thomas**

| | | | |
|---|---|---|---|
| Goals in the League | 0 | Contribution to Attacking Power<br>Average number of minutes between League team goals while on pitch | 115 |
| Defensive Rating<br>Average number of mins between League goals conceded while he was on the pitch | 88 | Scoring Difference<br>Defensive Rating minus Contribution to Attacking Power | -27 |

| | PLAYER | LGE GOALS | DEF RATE | POWER | SCORE DIFF |
|---|---|---|---|---|---|
| 2 | David Hamed | 1 | 86 | 149 | -63 mins |
| 3 | Benjamin Nivet | 2 | 67 | 133 | -66 mins |
| 4 | David Linares | 0 | 68 | 158 | -90 mins |
| 5 | Karim Ziani | 0 | 74 | 167 | -93 mins |

## KEY PLAYERS - DEFENDERS

**1 Mohamed Bradja**

| | | | |
|---|---|---|---|
| Goals Conceded (GC)<br>The number of League goals conceded while he was on the pitch | 32 | Clean Sheets<br>In games when he played at least 70 minutes | 10 |
| Defensive Rating<br>Ave number of mins between League goals conceded while on the pitch | 78 | Club Defensive Rating<br>Average number of mins between League goals conceded by the club this season | 70 |

| | PLAYER | CON LGE | CLEAN SHEETS | DEF RATE |
|---|---|---|---|---|
| 2 | Mehdi Meniri | 22 | 4 | 77 mins |
| 3 | Frederic Adam | 25 | 6 | 67 mins |
| 4 | David Regis | 23 | 6 | 64 mins |
| 5 | Frederic Danjou | 27 | 6 | 64 mins |

## GOALS SCORED

**AT HOME**

| | | |
|---|---|---|
| MOST | Lyon | 40 |
| | | 16 |
| LEAST | AC Ajaccio | 14 |

**AWAY**

| | | |
|---|---|---|
| MOST | Monaco | 29 |
| | | 7 |
| LEAST | Troyes | 7 |

## GOALS CONCEDED

**AT HOME**

| | | |
|---|---|---|
| LEAST | Sochaux & Auxerre | 8 |
| | | 18 |
| MOST | Strasbourg | 23 |

**AWAY**

| | | |
|---|---|---|
| LEAST | Lens | 15 |
| | | 30 |
| MOST | Sedan | 39 |

## KEY GOALKEEPER

**1 Tony Heurtebis**

| | |
|---|---|
| Goals Conceded in the League | 43 |
| Defensive Rating<br>Ave number of mins between League goals conceded while on the pitch | 69 |
| Counting Games<br>Games when he played at least 70 minutes | 33 |
| Clean Sheets<br>In games when he played at least 70 minutes | 12 |

## TOP POINT EARNERS

| | PLAYER | GAMES | AVE |
|---|---|---|---|
| 1 | Baticle | 13 | 1.15 |
| 2 | Saifi | 18 | 1.06 |
| 3 | Regis | 15 | 1.00 |
| 4 | Bradja | 26 | 1.00 |
| 5 | Hamed | 28 | 0.96 |
| 6 | Heurtebis | 33 | 0.94 |
| 7 | Linares | 20 | 0.90 |
| 8 | Thomas | 16 | 0.88 |
| 9 | Gousse | 26 | 0.85 |
| 10 | Ziani | 19 | 0.84 |
| | CLUB AVERAGE: | | 0.82 |

Ave = Average points per match in Counting Game

## ATTENDANCES

HOME GROUND: STADE DE L'AUBE CAPACITY: 18240 AVERAGE LEAGUE AT HOME: 11325

| | | | | | | | | |
|---|---|---|---|---|---|---|---|---|
| 15 | Marseille | 45000 | 9 | Lyon | 13000 | 14 | Bastia | 10000 |
| 36 | Lens | 37703 | 33 | Marseille | 12500 | 13 | Guingamp | 10000 |
| 6 | Bordeaux | 30000 | 16 | Sedan | 12000 | 23 | Bordeaux | 10000 |
| 29 | Paris SG | 30000 | 8 | Nice | 12000 | 5 | AC Ajaccio | 10000 |
| 19 | Nantes | 28000 | 37 | Nantes | 11000 | 18 | Lens | 9500 |
| 26 | Lyon | 26114 | 3 | Auxerre | 11000 | 35 | Sochaux | 8000 |
| 10 | Strasbourg | 25000 | 17 | Sochaux | 11000 | 12 | Montpellier | 8000 |
| 1 | Monaco | 15000 | 27 | Lille | 10177 | 38 | Monaco | 7148 |
| 30 | Montpellier | 15000 | 28 | Strasbourg | 10000 | 21 | Auxerre | 7000 |
| 34 | Sedan | 15000 | 11 | Paris SG | 10000 | 24 | Le Havre | 7000 |
| 7 | Le Havre | 15000 | 2 | Rennes | 10000 | 32 | Bastia | 6000 |
| 31 | Guingamp | 14000 | 25 | Nice | 10000 | 22 | AC Ajaccio | 5000 |
| 20 | Rennes | 13000 | 4 | Lille | 10000 | | | |

Home / Away / Neutral

## DISCIPLINARY RECORDS

| | PLAYER | YELLOW | RED | AVE |
|---|---|---|---|---|
| 1 | Nivet | 7 | 1 | 149 |
| 2 | Meniri | 8 | 0 | 212 |
| 3 | Benachour | 3 | 0 | 214 |
| 4 | Saifi | 8 | 0 | 227 |
| 5 | Adam | 7 | 0 | 239 |
| 6 | Leroy | 3 | 0 | 309 |
| 7 | Berthe | 1 | 1 | 343 |
| 8 | Amzine | 6 | 0 | 348 |
| 9 | Ziani | 5 | 0 | 368 |
| 10 | Regis | 3 | 1 | 369 |
| 11 | Linares | 5 | 0 | 379 |
| 12 | Niang | 2 | 0 | 545 |
| 13 | Tourenne | 4 | 1 | 554 |
| | Other | 16 | 0 | |
| | TOTAL | 78 | 4 | |

## LEAGUE GOALS

| | PLAYER | MINS | GOALS | AVE |
|---|---|---|---|---|
| 1 | Gousse | 2470 | 6 | 412 |
| 2 | Saifi | 1822 | 4 | 456 |
| 3 | Niang | 1091 | 3 | 364 |
| 4 | Benachour | 642 | 2 | 321 |
| 5 | Nivet | 1197 | 2 | 599 |
| 6 | Adam | 1677 | 2 | 839 |
| 7 | Baticle | 1495 | 1 | 1495 |
| 8 | Hamed | 2674 | 1 | 2674 |
| 9 | Akrour | 602 | 1 | 602 |
| 10 | Nade | 170 | 1 | 170 |
| | Other | | 0 | |
| | TOTAL | | 23 | |

## MONTH BY MONTH GUIDE TO THE POINTS

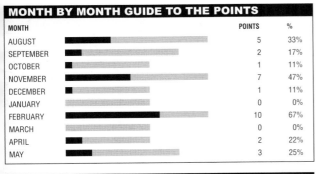

| MONTH | POINTS | % |
|---|---|---|
| AUGUST | 5 | 33% |
| SEPTEMBER | 2 | 17% |
| OCTOBER | 1 | 11% |
| NOVEMBER | 7 | 47% |
| DECEMBER | 1 | 11% |
| JANUARY | 0 | 0% |
| FEBRUARY | 10 | 67% |
| MARCH | 0 | 0% |
| APRIL | 2 | 22% |
| MAY | 3 | 25% |

## TEAM OF THE SEASON

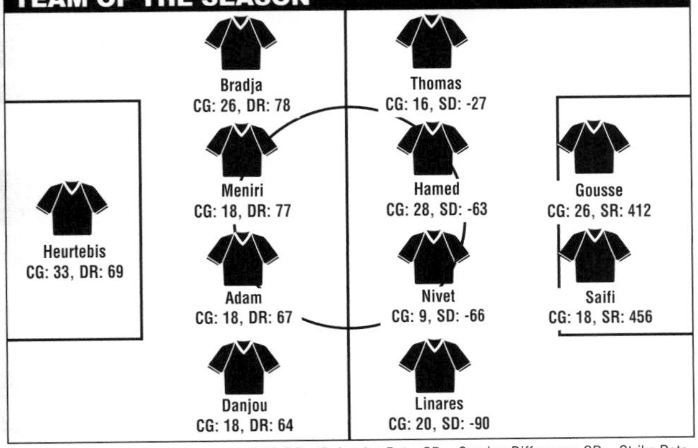
Bradja
CG: 26, DR: 78
Thomas
CG: 16, SD: -27
Meniri
CG: 18, DR: 77
Hamed
CG: 28, SD: -63
Gousse
CG: 26, SR: 412
Heurtebis
CG: 33, DR: 69
Adam
CG: 18, DR: 67
Nivet
CG: 9, SD: -66
Saifi
CG: 18, SR: 456
Danjou
CG: 18, DR: 64
Linares
CG: 20, SD: -90

**KEY:** DR = Defensive Rate, SD = Scoring Difference, SR = Strike Rate, CG = Counting Games – League games playing at least 70 minutes

## LEAGUE APPEARANCES, BOOKINGS AND CAPS

| | AGE | IN THE SQUAD | COUNTING GAMES | MINUTES ON PITCH | YELLOW CARDS | RED CARDS | THIS SEASON | HOME COUNTRY |
|---|---|---|---|---|---|---|---|---|
| **Goalkeepers** | | | | | | | | |
| Stephane Cassard | 30 | 37 | 5 | 450 | 1 | 0 | - | France |
| Eddy Heurlie | 25 | 1 | 0 | 0 | 0 | 0 | - | France |
| Tony Heurtebis | 28 | 37 | 33 | 2970 | 1 | 0 | - | France |
| **Defenders** | | | | | | | | |
| Frederic Adam | 29 | 24 | 18 | 1677 | 7 | 0 | - | France |
| Sekou Berthe | 25 | 10 | 7 | 687 | 1 | 1 | - | Mali |
| Mohamed Bradja | 33 | 35 | 26 | 2497 | 1 | 0 | - | France |
| Frederic Danjou | 28 | 20 | 18 | 1732 | 2 | 0 | - | France |
| Mehdi Meniri | 26 | 21 | 18 | 1703 | 8 | 0 | - | France |
| Yannick Nomede | 19 | 1 | 0 | 18 | 0 | 0 | - | France |
| David Regis | 34 | 21 | 15 | 1476 | 3 | 1 | - | United States |
| Gael Sanz | 26 | 12 | 2 | 208 | 1 | 0 | - | France |
| Carl Tourenne | 31 | 33 | 29 | 2770 | 4 | 1 | - | France |
| **Midfielders** | | | | | | | | |
| Nassim Akrour | 28 | 15 | 4 | 602 | 0 | 0 | - | France |
| Gharib Amzine | 30 | 35 | 20 | 2090 | 6 | 0 | - | Morocco |
| Selim Benachour | 21 | 10 | 6 | 642 | 3 | 0 | - | Tunisia |
| Nabil Berkak | 19 | 2 | 0 | 41 | 0 | 0 | - | France |
| Nick Carle | 21 | 1 | 0 | 0 | 0 | 0 | - | Australia |
| David Hamed | 29 | 33 | 28 | 2674 | 3 | 0 | - | France |
| Medhi Leroy | 25 | 12 | 9 | 928 | 3 | 0 | - | France |
| David Linares | 27 | 26 | 20 | 1897 | 5 | 0 | - | France |
| Badile Lubamba | 27 | 1 | 0 | 0 | 0 | 0 | - | Switzerland |
| Christian Nade | 18 | 6 | 0 | 170 | 1 | 0 | - | France |
| Benjamin Nivet | 26 | 29 | 9 | 1197 | 7 | 1 | - | France |
| Damien Perquis | 19 | 1 | 0 | 0 | 0 | 0 | - | France |
| Olivier Thomas | 26 | 17 | 16 | 1498 | 2 | 0 | - | France |
| Karim Ziani | 20 | 27 | 19 | 1841 | 5 | 0 | - | France |
| **Forwards** | | | | | | | | |
| Ibrahima Bangoura | 20 | 6 | 0 | 75 | 0 | 0 | - | France |
| Gerald Baticle | 33 | 31 | 13 | 1495 | 0 | 0 | - | France |
| Nicolas Florentin | 25 | 20 | 4 | 574 | 0 | 0 | - | France |
| Farid Ghazi | 29 | 4 | 0 | 122 | 0 | 0 | - | Algeria |
| Nicolas Gousse | 27 | 33 | 26 | 2470 | 3 | 0 | - | France |
| Nordin Jbari | 28 | 2 | 0 | 33 | 0 | 0 | - | Belgium |
| Laurent Leroy | 27 | 1 | 0 | 58 | 1 | 0 | - | France |
| Eric Marester | 19 | 1 | 0 | 14 | 0 | 0 | - | France |
| Mamadou Niang | 23 | 20 | 8 | 1091 | 2 | 0 | 1 | Senegal (29) |
| Rafik Saifi | 28 | 25 | 18 | 1822 | 8 | 0 | - | Algeria |

## SQUAD APPEARANCES

| Match | 1 | 2 | 3 | 4 | 5 | 6 | 7 | 8 | 9 | 10 | 11 | 12 | 13 | 14 | 15 | 16 | 17 | 18 | 19 | 20 | 21 | 22 | 23 | 24 | 25 | 26 | 27 | 28 | 29 | 30 | 31 | 32 | 33 | 34 | 35 | 36 | 37 | 38 |
|---|---|---|---|---|---|---|---|---|---|---|---|---|---|---|---|---|---|---|---|---|---|---|---|---|---|---|---|---|---|---|---|---|---|---|---|---|---|---|
| Venue | H | A | H | A | H | A | H | A | H | A | H | A | H | H | A | H | A | H | A | H | A | A | H | A | H | A | H | H | A | H | A | A | H | A | H | A | H | A |
| Competition | L | L | L | L | L | L | L | L | L | L | L | L | L | L | L | L | L | L | L | L | L | L | L | L | L | L | L | L | L | L | L | L | L | L | L | L | L | L |
| Result | L | D | L | D | W | L | D | L | D | L | L | D | L | W | D | W | L | D | L | L | L | L | L | L | W | D | W | W | L | L | L | D | D | L | L | L | W | L |

**Goalkeepers**
Stephane Cassard
Eddy Heurlie
Tony Heurtebis

**Defenders**
Frederic Adam
Sekou Berthe
Mohamed Bradja
Frederic Danjou
Mehdi Meniri
David Regis
Gael Sanz
Carl Tourenne

**Midfielders**
Nassim Akrour
Gharib Amzine
Selim Benachour
Nabil Berkak
Nick Carle
David Hamed
Medhi Leroy
David Linares
Badile Lubamba
Christian Nade
Benjamin Nivet
Damien Perquis
Olivier Thomas
Karim Ziani

**Forwards**
Ibrahima Bangoura
Gerald Baticle
Nicolas Florentin
Farid Ghazi
Nicolas Gousse
Nordin Jbari
Laurent Leroy
Mamadou Niang
Rafik Saifi

**KEY:** ■ On all match · On bench · ⏮ Subbed or sent off (Counting game) · ◀◀ Subbed or sent off (playing less than 70 minutes) · ⏭ Subbed on from bench (Counting Game) · ▶▶ Subbed on (playing less than 70 minutes) · Subbed on and then subbed or sent off (Counting Game) · Subbed on and then subbed or sent off (playing less than 70 minutes) · Not in 16

# FRENCH LEAGUE ROUND-UP

## FINAL LEAGUE TABLE

| | | HOME | | | | | AWAY | | | | | TOTAL | | | |
|---|---|---|---|---|---|---|---|---|---|---|---|---|---|---|---|
| | P | W | D | L | F | A | W | D | L | F | A | F | A | DIF | PTS |
| Lyon | 38 | 12 | 5 | 2 | 40 | 19 | 7 | 6 | 6 | 23 | 22 | 63 | 41 | 22 | 68 |
| Monaco | 38 | 12 | 4 | 3 | 37 | 13 | 7 | 6 | 6 | 29 | 20 | 66 | 33 | 33 | 67 |
| Marseille | 38 | 12 | 4 | 3 | 26 | 14 | 7 | 4 | 8 | 15 | 22 | 41 | 36 | 5 | 65 |
| Bordeaux | 38 | 11 | 4 | 4 | 30 | 14 | 7 | 6 | 6 | 27 | 22 | 57 | 36 | 21 | 64 |
| Sochaux | 38 | 12 | 7 | 0 | 28 | 8 | 5 | 6 | 8 | 18 | 23 | 46 | 31 | 15 | 64 |
| Auxerre | 38 | 11 | 5 | 3 | 19 | 8 | 7 | 5 | 7 | 19 | 21 | 38 | 29 | 9 | 64 |
| Guingamp | 38 | 11 | 4 | 4 | 32 | 16 | 8 | 1 | 10 | 27 | 30 | 59 | 46 | 13 | 62 |
| Lens | 38 | 9 | 7 | 3 | 29 | 16 | 5 | 8 | 6 | 14 | 15 | 43 | 31 | 12 | 57 |
| Nantes | 38 | 11 | 4 | 4 | 25 | 18 | 5 | 4 | 10 | 12 | 21 | 37 | 39 | -2 | 56 |
| Nice | 38 | 10 | 7 | 2 | 24 | 8 | 3 | 9 | 7 | 15 | 23 | 39 | 31 | 8 | 55 |
| Paris SG | 38 | 10 | 6 | 3 | 31 | 14 | 4 | 6 | 9 | 16 | 22 | 47 | 36 | 11 | 54 |
| Bastia | 38 | 10 | 5 | 4 | 28 | 17 | 2 | 6 | 11 | 12 | 31 | 40 | 48 | -8 | 47 |
| Strasbourg | 38 | 7 | 7 | 5 | 24 | 23 | 4 | 5 | 10 | 16 | 31 | 40 | 54 | -14 | 45 |
| Lille | 38 | 9 | 4 | 6 | 20 | 19 | 1 | 8 | 10 | 9 | 25 | 29 | 44 | -15 | 42 |
| Rennes | 38 | 6 | 8 | 5 | 24 | 20 | 4 | 2 | 13 | 11 | 25 | 35 | 45 | -10 | 40 |
| Montpellier | 38 | 6 | 7 | 6 | 19 | 19 | 4 | 3 | 12 | 18 | 35 | 37 | 54 | -17 | 40 |
| AC Ajaccio | 38 | 6 | 6 | 7 | 14 | 21 | 3 | 6 | 10 | 15 | 28 | 29 | 49 | -20 | 39 |
| Le Havre | 38 | 7 | 3 | 9 | 16 | 21 | 3 | 5 | 11 | 11 | 26 | 27 | 47 | -20 | 38 |
| Sedan | 38 | 7 | 5 | 7 | 29 | 20 | 2 | 4 | 13 | 12 | 39 | 41 | 59 | -18 | 36 |
| Troyes | 38 | 7 | 4 | 8 | 16 | 18 | 0 | 6 | 13 | 7 | 30 | 23 | 48 | -25 | 31 |

## TEAM OF THE SEASON

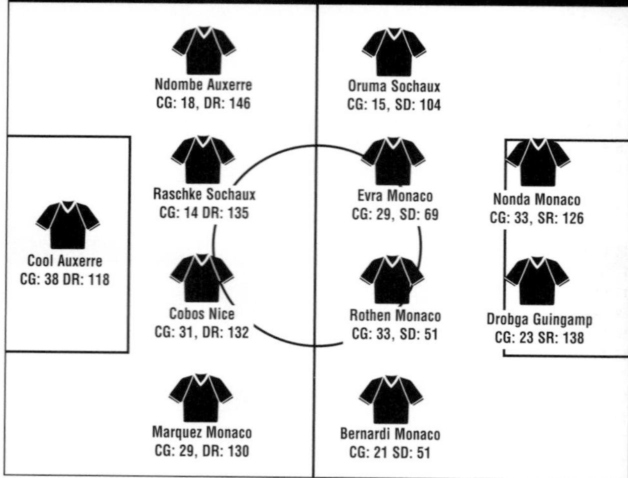
Cool Auxerre
CG: 38 DR: 118
Ndombe Auxerre
CG: 18, DR: 146
Raschke Sochaux
CG: 14 DR: 135
Cobos Nice
CG: 31, DR: 132
Marquez Monaco
CG: 29, DR: 130
Oruma Sochaux
CG: 15, SD: 104
Evra Monaco
CG: 29, SD: 69
Rothen Monaco
CG: 33, SD: 51
Bernardi Monaco
CG: 21 SD: 51
Nonda Monaco
CG: 33, SR: 126
Drobga Guingamp
CG: 23 SR: 138

KEY: DR = Defensive Rate, SD = Scoring Difference AP = Attacking Power SR = Strike Rate, CG=Counting Games – League games playing at least 70 minutes

## CLUB STRIKE FORCE

KEY: Goals: Total number of goals scored in League.
Club Strike Rate (CSR): Average number of mins between goals scored

| | CLUB | GOALS | CSR |
|---|---|---|---|
| 1 | Monaco | 66 | 52 mins |
| 2 | Lyon | 62 | 55 mins |
| 3 | Guingamp | 59 | 58 mins |
| 4 | Bordeaux | 57 | 60 mins |
| 5 | Paris SG | 47 | 73 mins |
| 6 | Sochaux | 44 | 78 mins |
| 7 | Lens | 43 | 80 mins |
| 8 | Marseille | 41 | 83 mins |
| 9 | Sedan | 41 | 83 mins |
| 10 | Bastia | 40 | 86 mins |
| 11 | Strasbourg | 40 | 86 mins |
| 12 | Nice | 39 | 88 mins |
| 13 | Auxerre | 38 | 90 mins |
| 14 | Montpellier | 37 | 92 mins |
| 15 | Nantes | 37 | 92 mins |
| 16 | Rennes | 35 | 98 mins |
| 17 | AC Ajaccio | 29 | 118 mins |
| 18 | Lille | 29 | 118 mins |
| 19 | Le Havre | 27 | 127 mins |
| 20 | Troyes | 23 | 149 mins |
| TOTAL | | 834 | |

## CLUB DEFENCES

KEY: Defensive Rating: Average number of mins between goals conceded. CS: Clean Sheets - Games where no goals were conceded.

| | CLUB | CONCEDED | CLEAN SH | DEF RATE |
|---|---|---|---|---|
| 1 | Auxerre | 29 | 19 | 118 mins |
| 2 | Sochaux | 30 | 19 | 114 mins |
| 3 | Lens | 31 | 17 | 110 mins |
| 4 | Nice | 31 | 20 | 110 mins |
| 5 | Monaco | 33 | 12 | 104 mins |
| 6 | Bordeaux | 36 | 17 | 95 mins |
| 7 | Marseille | 36 | 17 | 95 mins |
| 8 | Paris SG | 36 | 16 | 95 mins |
| 9 | Lyon | 39 | 13 | 88 mins |
| 10 | Nantes | 39 | 16 | 88 mins |
| 11 | Lille | 44 | 13 | 78 mins |
| 12 | Rennes | 45 | 12 | 76 mins |
| 13 | Guingamp | 46 | 16 | 74 mins |
| 14 | Le Havre | 47 | 8 | 73 mins |
| 15 | Bastia | 48 | 9 | 71 mins |
| 16 | Troyes | 48 | 13 | 71 mins |
| 17 | AC Ajaccio | 49 | 13 | 70 mins |
| 18 | Montpellier | 54 | 10 | 63 mins |
| 19 | Strasbourg | 54 | 9 | 63 mins |
| 20 | Sedan | 59 | 10 | 58 mins |
| TOTAL | | 834 | 279 | |

## CLUB DISCIPLINARY RECORDS

KEY: AVE: Average number of mins between cards

| | CLUB | YELL | RED | TOT | AVE |
|---|---|---|---|---|---|
| 1 | Montpellier | 97 | 9 | 106 | 32 mins |
| 2 | Paris SG | 96 | 12 | 108 | 32 mins |
| 3 | Bastia | 92 | 8 | 100 | 34 mins |
| 4 | Bordeaux | 91 | 10 | 101 | 34 mins |
| 5 | Marseille | 92 | 7 | 99 | 35 mins |
| 6 | AC Ajaccio | 90 | 6 | 96 | 36 mins |
| 7 | Nantes | 86 | 10 | 96 | 36 mins |
| 8 | Le Havre | 83 | 9 | 92 | 37 mins |
| 9 | Rennes | 83 | 8 | 91 | 38 mins |
| 10 | Sedan | 78 | 7 | 85 | 40 mins |
| 11 | Guingamp | 74 | 9 | 83 | 41 mins |
| 12 | Nice | 79 | 4 | 83 | 41 mins |
| 13 | Monaco | 74 | 7 | 81 | 42 mins |
| 14 | Strasbourg | 79 | 2 | 81 | 42 mins |
| 15 | Troyes | 78 | 4 | 82 | 42 mins |
| 16 | Lille | 70 | 8 | 78 | 44 mins |
| 17 | Lens | 72 | 4 | 76 | 45 mins |
| 18 | Sochaux | 71 | 1 | 72 | 48 mins |
| 19 | Auxerre | 59 | 4 | 63 | 54 mins |
| 20 | Lyon | 56 | 3 | 59 | 58 mins |
| | TOTAL | 1600 | 132 | 1732 | |

## STADIUM CAPACITY AND HOME CROWDS

| | TEAM | CAPACITY | AVE | HIGH | LOW |
|---|---|---|---|---|---|
| 1 | Lens | 41810 | 86.86 | 40500 | 24758 |
| 2 | Nice | 15761 | 85.88 | 15544 | 10000 |
| 3 | Bordeaux | 34088 | 81.93 | 34000 | 15000 |
| 4 | Lyon | 43000 | 80.77 | 43000 | 20000 |
| 5 | Nantes | 38486 | 80.39 | 38000 | 25000 |
| 6 | Guingamp | 17990 | 79.73 | 17000 | 9500 |
| 7 | Paris SG | 48712 | 77.68 | 48450 | 22015 |
| 8 | Marseille | 60000 | 76.67 | 60000 | 10000 |
| 9 | Bastia | 10080 | 74.24 | 10000 | 4500 |
| 10 | Sochaux | 20000 | 73.82 | 20000 | 5000 |
| 11 | Lille | 21128 | 69.97 | 20000 | 10000 |
| 12 | AC Ajaccio | 10660 | 68.18 | 10000 | 1000 |
| 13 | Le Havre | 18000 | 65.16 | 18000 | 7000 |
| 14 | Troyes | 18240 | 62.09 | 15000 | 8000 |
| 15 | Sedan | 24000 | 57.40 | 23000 | 7000 |
| 16 | Rennes | 31716 | 55.70 | 23700 | 10000 |
| 17 | Auxerre | 23550 | 52.64 | 20000 | 7000 |
| 18 | Montpellier | 31250 | 46.51 | 30000 | 8000 |
| 19 | Strasbourg | 43247 | 37.81 | 28000 | 9000 |
| 20 | Monaco | 18520 | 35.97 | 18500 | 3000 |

## AWAY ATTENDANCE

| | TEAM | AVE | HIGH | LOW |
|---|---|---|---|---|
| 1 | Marseille | 86.32 | 45000 | 7000 |
| 2 | Lyon | 79.88 | 56652 | 4000 |
| 3 | Paris SG | 77.37 | 60000 | 5000 |
| 4 | Monaco | 76.79 | 58000 | 8000 |
| 5 | Bordeaux | 72.71 | 57000 | 7500 |
| 6 | Nice | 69.03 | 47000 | 4397 |
| 7 | Lens | 68.87 | 50000 | 6000 |
| 8 | Rennes | 68.26 | 39885 | 5000 |
| 9 | Auxerre | 67.14 | 50000 | 5502 |
| 10 | Nantes | 67.04 | 40000 | 3000 |
| 11 | Strasbourg | 66.76 | 40000 | 7000 |
| 12 | Bastia | 66.52 | 55000 | 4000 |
| 13 | Lille | 63.39 | 50000 | 5000 |
| 14 | AC Ajaccio | 62.18 | 40000 | 4000 |
| 15 | Montpellier | 61.73 | 35000 | 7000 |
| 16 | Guingamp | 60.77 | 55000 | 1000 |
| 17 | Le Havre | 60.23 | 36000 | 5000 |
| 18 | Sedan | 59.53 | 55442 | 5000 |
| 19 | Troyes | 57.66 | 45000 | 5000 |
| 20 | Sochaux | 57.19 | 55000 | 3000 |

## TOP GOALSCORERS

**KEY: Strike Rate:** Average number of minutes between League goals scored by player. **Club Strike Rate (CSR):** Average minutes between League goals scored by club. **Contribution to Attacking Power (PWR):** Average mins between League goals scored by club while on pitch.

| | PLAYER | CLUB | GOALS | PWR | CSR | S RATE |
|---|---|---|---|---|---|---|
| 1 | Prso | Monaco | 12 | 45 | 52 | 118 |
| 2 | Nonda | Monaco | 24 | 49 | 52 | 126 |
| 3 | Drogba | Guingamp | 17 | 54 | 58 | 138 |
| 4 | Anderson | Lyon | 12 | 45 | 54 | 138 |
| 5 | Pauleta | Bordeaux | 23 | 61 | 60 | 143 |
| 6 | Juninho | Lyon | 14 | 45 | 54 | 166 |
| 7 | Luyindula | Lyon | 11 | 55 | 54 | 172 |
| 8 | Camara, H | Sedan | 14 | 80 | 83 | 189 |
| 9 | Cisse | Auxerre | 14 | 102 | 90 | 190 |
| 10 | Frau | Sochaux | 9 | 65 | 74 | 210 |
| 11 | Darcheville | Bordeaux | 11 | 56 | 60 | 226 |
| 12 | Carnot | Guingamp | 9 | 59 | 58 | 230 |
| 13 | Fauconnier | Le Havre | 6 | 106 | 127 | 230 |
| 14 | Ronaldinho | Paris SG | 8 | 55 | 73 | 237 |
| 15 | Maurice | Bastia | 10 | 74 | 86 | 239 |
| 16 | Sibierski | Lens | 12 | 75 | 80 | 240 |
| 17 | Vahirua | Nantes | 7 | 94 | 92 | 243 |
| 18 | Piquionne | Rennes | 10 | 89 | 98 | 243 |
| 19 | Santos | Sochaux | 9 | 84 | 74 | 245 |
| 20 | Diawara | Nice | 12 | 86 | 88 | 251 |
| 21 | Bakayoko | Marseille | 9 | 81 | 83 | 253 |
| 22 | Kapo Obou | Auxerre | 6 | 84 | 90 | 280 |
| 23 | Giuly | Monaco | 11 | 52 | 52 | 283 |
| 24 | Utaka | Lens | 8 | 69 | 80 | 303 |
| 25 | Laslandes | Bastia | 8 | 90 | 86 | 305 |
| 26 | Savio | Bordeaux | 7 | 58 | 60 | 308 |
| 27 | Ljuboja | Strasbourg | 9 | 89 | 86 | 319 |
| 28 | Malouda | Guingamp | 10 | 55 | 58 | 320 |
| 29 | Monterrubio | Rennes | 6 | 77 | 98 | 321 |
| 30 | Govou | Lyon | 7 | 54 | 54 | 337 |

## TOP DEFENDERS

**KEY: Defensive Rating (DR)** Average mins between League goals conceded while on pitch. **Club Defensive Rating (CDR):** Average minutes between League goals conceded by club. **Clean Sheets (CS)** - Games where no goals were conceded.

| | PLAYER | CLUB | CONC | CS | CDR | DR |
|---|---|---|---|---|---|---|
| 1 | Domoraud | Sochaux | 5 | 8 | 110 | 196 |
| 2 | Ndoumbe | Auxerre | 11 | 10 | 118 | 146 |
| 3 | Raschke | Sochaux | 11 | 7 | 110 | 135 |
| 4 | Cobos | Nice | 22 | 19 | 110 | 132 |
| 5 | Marquez | Monaco | 20 | 12 | 104 | 130 |
| 6 | Lachor | Lens | 9 | 7 | 110 | 127 |
| 7 | Daf | Sochaux | 8 | 3 | 110 | 123 |
| 8 | Radet | Auxerre | 23 | 17 | 118 | 122 |
| 9 | Song | Lens | 25 | 16 | 110 | 121 |
| 10 | Flachez | Sochaux | 27 | 17 | 110 | 120 |
| 11 | Cubilier | Monaco | 11 | 4 | 104 | 117 |
| 12 | Pamarot | Nice | 26 | 18 | 110 | 116 |
| 13 | Bak | Lens | 20 | 11 | 110 | 115 |
| 14 | Squillaci | Monaco | 28 | 12 | 104 | 112 |
| 15 | Faye | Auxerre | 26 | 15 | 118 | 111 |
| 16 | Abardonado | Nice | 31 | 20 | 110 | 110 |
| 17 | Kouassi | Guingamp | 17 | 11 | 74 | 109 |
| 18 | Jabi | Lens | 10 | 5 | 110 | 109 |
| 19 | Leboeuf | Marseille | 20 | 11 | 95 | 109 |
| 20 | Monsoreau | Sochaux | 29 | 17 | 110 | 109 |
| 21 | Cristobal | Paris SG | 25 | 13 | 95 | 108 |
| 22 | Boumsong | Auxerre | 27 | 15 | 118 | 107 |
| 23 | Heinze | Paris SG | 29 | 15 | 95 | 107 |
| 24 | Planus | Bordeaux | 12 | 6 | 95 | 106 |
| 25 | Abidal | Lille | 22 | 10 | 78 | 106 |
| 26 | Van Buyten | Marseille | 29 | 16 | 95 | 106 |
| 27 | Varrault | Nice | 28 | 15 | 110 | 105 |
| 28 | Mexes | Auxerre | 29 | 15 | 118 | 104 |
| 29 | Dos Santos | Marseille | 28 | 15 | 95 | 103 |
| 30 | Saveljic | Sochaux | 29 | 14 | 110 | 10 |

## TOP MIDFIELDERS

**KEY: Scoring Difference (SD)** Team goals scored while on the pitch minus team goals conceded. **Contribution to Attacking Power:** Average mins between League goals scored by club while on pitch. **Defensive Rating (DR)** Average mins between League goals conceded while on pitch.

| | PLAYER | TEAM | GOALS | DR | PWR | SD |
|---|---|---|---|---|---|---|
| 1 | Bah | Guingamp | 1 | 202 | 38 | 164 |
| 2 | Diop | Lens | 3 | 208 | 74 | 134 |
| 3 | Oruma | Sochaux | 3 | 158 | 54 | 104 |
| 4 | Evra | Monaco | 2 | 118 | 49 | 69 |
| 5 | Isabey | Sochaux | 1 | 140 | 79 | 61 |
| 6 | Rothen | Monaco | 4 | 102 | 51 | 51 |
| 7 | Bernardi | Monaco | 1 | 95 | 44 | 51 |
| 8 | Meriem | Bordeaux | 1 | 106 | 57 | 49 |
| 9 | Tainio | Auxerre | 1 | 153 | 107 | 46 |
| 10 | Gallardo | Monaco | 1 | 97 | 52 | 45 |
| 11 | Costa | Bordeaux | 2 | 107 | 63 | 44 |
| 12 | Smertin | Bordeaux | 2 | 114 | 73 | 41 |
| 13 | Coridon | Lens | 1 | 130 | 89 | 41 |
| 14 | Giuly | Monaco | 11 | 94 | 53 | 41 |
| 15 | Zikos | Monaco | 0 | 102 | 62 | 40 |
| 16 | Carriere | Lyon | 6 | 90 | 51 | 39 |
| 17 | Pedretti | Sochaux | 3 | 116 | 77 | 39 |
| 18 | Mathieu | Sochaux | 4 | 116 | 77 | 39 |
| 19 | Lachuer | Auxerre | 4 | 126 | 89 | 37 |
| 20 | Andre Luiz | Paris SG | 1 | 126 | 90 | 36 |
| 21 | Violeau | Lyon | 1 | 92 | 57 | 35 |
| 22 | Juninho | Lyon | 14 | 80 | 46 | 34 |
| 23 | Pitau | Nice | 0 | 118 | 85 | 33 |
| 24 | Moreira | Lens | 9 | 104 | 74 | 30 |
| 25 | Dhorasoo | Lyon | 2 | 84 | 55 | 29 |
| 26 | Muller | Lyon | 0 | 82 | 53 | 29 |
| 27 | Keita | Lens | 2 | 107 | 79 | 28 |
| 28 | Johansen | Marseille | 2 | 105 | 78 | 27 |
| 29 | Bigne | Nice | 2 | 110 | 83 | 27 |
| 30 | Sibierski | Lens | 12 | 99 | 76 | 23 |

## PLAYER DISCIPLINARY RECORDS

**KEY: AVE:** Average number of mins between cards

| | PLAYER | TEAM | YELL | RED | TOTAL | AVE |
|---|---|---|---|---|---|---|
| 1 | Battles | Rennes | 8 | 1 | 9 | 119 |
| 2 | Rool | Lens | 9 | 1 | 10 | 121 |
| 3 | Fleurquin | Rennes | 6 | 0 | 6 | 138 |
| 4 | Nivet | Troyes | 7 | 1 | 8 | 149 |
| 5 | Johansen | Marseille | 15 | 1 | 16 | 150 |
| 6 | Coly | Lens | 4 | 0 | 4 | 153 |
| 7 | D'Amico | Lille | 13 | 1 | 14 | 154 |
| 8 | Jabi | Lens | 6 | 1 | 7 | 155 |
| 9 | Givet | Monaco | 7 | 1 | 8 | 155 |
| 10 | Dugarry | Bordeaux | 4 | 2 | 6 | 156 |
| 11 | Njanka | Sedan | 4 | 1 | 5 | 160 |
| 12 | Nyarko | Paris SG | 6 | 2 | 8 | 162 |
| 13 | Destruhaut | AC Ajaccio | 8 | 0 | 8 | 166 |
| 14 | Ogbeche | Paris SG | 4 | 1 | 5 | 166 |
| 15 | Bonnal | Lille | 3 | 1 | 4 | 169 |
| 16 | Aloisio | Paris SG | 8 | 1 | 9 | 169 |
| 17 | Diop | Lens | 6 | 0 | 6 | 173 |
| 18 | Jemmali | Bordeaux | 10 | 4 | 14 | 174 |
| 19 | Sahnoun | Bordeaux | 6 | 0 | 6 | 175 |
| 20 | Bassila | Strasbourg | 13 | 1 | 14 | 177 |
| 21 | Faye | Lens | 5 | 1 | 6 | 178 |
| 22 | Mendy | Bastia | 8 | 0 | 8 | 179 |
| 23 | Ahamada | Bastia | 4 | 1 | 5 | 185 |
| 24 | Jeunechamp | Bastia | 6 | 1 | 7 | 188 |
| 25 | Connen | AC Ajaccio | 7 | 0 | 7 | 190 |
| 26 | Diawara | Le Havre | 11 | 3 | 14 | 195 |
| 27 | Gathuessi | Montpellier | 3 | 0 | 3 | 198 |
| 28 | Cetto | Nantes | 6 | 1 | 7 | 198 |
| 29 | Djemba-Djemba | Nantes | 10 | 1 | 11 | 198 |
| 30 | Perez, S | Marseille | 4 | 0 | 4 | 200 |

## CHART TOPPING GOALKEEPERS

**KEY: Defensive Rating (DR)** Average mins between League goals conceded while on pitch. **Clean Sheets (CS)** - Games where no goals were conceded.

| | PLAYER | TEAM | CON | CS | DR |
|---|---|---|---|---|---|
| 1 | Cool | Auxerre | 29 | 19 | 118 |
| 2 | Sylva | Monaco | 9 | 3 | 116 |
| 3 | Gregorini | Nice | 29 | 20 | 115 |
| 4 | Warmuz | Lens | 13 | 6 | 111 |
| 5 | Itandje | Lens | 18 | 11 | 110 |
| 6 | Richert | Sochaux | 28 | 16 | 109 |
| 7 | Alonzo | Paris SG | 10 | 4 | 108 |
| 8 | Roux | Bordeaux | 9 | 4 | 101 |
| 9 | Roma | Monaco | 24 | 8 | 99 |
| 10 | Landreau | Nantes | 33 | 16 | 98 |
| 11 | Rame | Bordeaux | 27 | 13 | 93 |
| 12 | Runje | Marseille | 36 | 15 | 90 |
| 13 | Letizi | Paris SG | 26 | 12 | 90 |
| 14 | Cech | Rennes | 41 | 12 | 81 |
| 15 | Coupet | Lyon | 39 | 10 | 80 |
| 16 | Wimbee | Lille | 36 | 11 | 78 |
| 17 | Penneteau | Bastia | 39 | 9 | 77 |
| 18 | Le Crom | Guingamp | 46 | 16 | 74 |
| 19 | Vencel | Le Havre | 47 | 8 | 73 |
| 20 | Riou | Montpellier | 34 | 9 | 72 |
| 21 | Heurtebis | Troyes | 43 | 12 | 69 |
| 22 | Trevisan | AC Ajaccio | 43 | 11 | 67 |
| 23 | Fernandez | Strasbourg | 40 | 3 | 59 |
| 24 | Regnault | Sedan | 59 | 10 | 58 |
| 25 | Bonis | Strasbourg | 14 | 3 | 58 |
| 26 | Pionnier | Montpellier | 16 | 1 | 49 |

## TOP POINT EARNERS

**KEY: Counting Games** League games where he played more than 70 minutes. **Total League Points** Taken in Counting Games. **Average League Points** Taken in Counting Games.

| | PLAYER | TEAM | GAMES | POINTS | AVE |
|---|---|---|---|---|---|
| 1 | Oruma | Sochaux | 15 | 36 | 2.40 |
| 2 | Planus | Bordeaux | 13 | 28 | 2.15 |
| 3 | Violeau | Lyon | 25 | 52 | 2.08 |
| 4 | Mathieu | Sochaux | 12 | 25 | 2.08 |
| 5 | Carriere | Lyon | 27 | 55 | 2.04 |
| 6 | Brechet | Lyon | 26 | 53 | 2.04 |
| 7 | Kapo Obou | Auxerre | 18 | 36 | 2.00 |
| 8 | Frau | Sochaux | 17 | 34 | 2.00 |
| 9 | Govou | Lyon | 26 | 51 | 1.96 |
| 10 | Juninho | Lyon | 25 | 49 | 1.96 |
| 11 | Bernardi | Monaco | 21 | 41 | 1.95 |
| 12 | Delhommeau | Nantes | 21 | 41 | 1.95 |
| 13 | Kouassi | Guingamp | 20 | 39 | 1.95 |
| 14 | Dhorasoo | Lyon | 32 | 62 | 1.94 |
| 15 | Edmilson | Lyon | 18 | 35 | 1.94 |
| 16 | Luyindula | Lyon | 18 | 35 | 1.94 |
| 17 | Carnot | Guingamp | 14 | 27 | 1.93 |
| 18 | Givet | Monaco | 12 | 23 | 1.92 |
| 19 | Chapuis | Marseille | 20 | 38 | 1.90 |
| 20 | Bakayoko | Marseille | 20 | 38 | 1.90 |
| 21 | Basto | Bordeaux | 28 | 53 | 1.89 |
| 22 | Ndoumbe | Auxerre | 18 | 34 | 1.89 |
| 23 | Deflandre | Lyon | 18 | 34 | 1.89 |
| 24 | Cacapa | Lyon | 34 | 64 | 1.88 |
| 25 | Roma | Monaco | 26 | 49 | 1.88 |
| 26 | Darcheville | Bordeaux | 25 | 47 | 1.88 |
| 27 | Johansen | Marseille | 25 | 47 | 1.88 |
| 28 | Leboeuf | Marseille | 23 | 43 | 1.87 |
| 29 | Rodriguez | Monaco | 23 | 43 | 1.87 |
| 30 | Fadiga | Auxerre | 29 | 54 | 1.86 |

# BAYERN MUNICH

Final Position: **1st**

| | | | | | | |
|---|---|---|---|---|---|---|
| 1 | lge | B M'gladbach | A | D | 0-0 | |
| 2 | ecql1 | Partizan | A | W | 3-0 | Tarnat 22; Jeremies 71; Pizarro 78 |
| 3 | lge | Arminia B | H | W | 6-2 | Elber 18,41,65,85; Ballack 26; Pizarro 81 |
| 4 | lge | Hamburg | A | W | 3-0 | Pizarro 25,85; Zickler 90 |
| 5 | ecql2 | Partizan | H | W | 3-1 | Ballack 26; Elber 71; Salihamidzic 73 pen |
| 6 | lge | 1860 Munich | H | W | 3-1 | Salihamidzic 41; Pizarro 53; Elber 76 |
| 7 | lge | Nurnberg | A | W | 2-1 | Ballack 13,52 |
| 8 | ecgg | Deportivo | H | L | 2-3 | Salihamidzic 57; Elber 64 |
| 9 | lge | Cottbus | H | W | 3-1 | Zickler 45; Ballack 47; Elber 76 |
| 10 | ecgg | Lens | A | D | 1-1 | Linke 23 |
| 11 | lge | B Leverkusen | A | L | 1-2 | Salihamidzic 88 |
| 12 | ecgg | AC Milan | H | L | 1-2 | Pizarro 54 |
| 13 | lge | Bochum | H | W | 4-1 | Elber 27,90; Pizarro 39,66 |
| 14 | lge | Hansa Rostock | A | W | 1-0 | Ze Roberto 73 |
| 15 | ecgg | AC Milan | A | L | 1-2 | Tarnat 23 |
| 16 | lge | Hannover 96 | H | D | 3-3 | Elber 4,80; Scholl 75 |
| 17 | ecgg | Deportivo | A | L | 1-2 | Santa Cruz 77 |
| 18 | lge | W Bremen | A | L | 0-2 | |
| 19 | lge | B Dortmund | H | W | 2-1 | Santa Cruz 62; Pizarro 65 |
| 20 | ecgg | Lens | H | D | 3-3 | Kovac, N 6; Salihamidzic 19; Feulner 87 |
| 21 | lge | Wolfsburg | H | W | 1-0 | Santa Cruz 27 |
| 22 | lge | Kaiserslautern | A | W | 2-0 | Ballack 9; Santa Cruz 16 |
| 23 | lge | Hertha Berlin | H | W | 2-0 | Ballack 40,72 pen |
| 24 | lge | Stuttgart | A | W | 3-0 | Zickler 30; Santa Cruz 34,69 |
| 25 | lge | Schalke | H | D | 0-0 | |
| 26 | lge | B M'gladbach | H | W | 3-0 | Hargreaves 25; Zickler 85; Elber 90 |
| 27 | lge | Arminia B | A | D | 0-0 | |
| 28 | lge | Hamburg | H | D | 1-1 | Pizarro 11 |
| 29 | lge | 1860 Munich | A | W | 5-0 | Scholl 58,68,80; Lizarazu 72; Pizarro 78 |
| 30 | lge | Nurnberg | H | W | 2-0 | Lizarazu 18; Elber 59 |
| 31 | lge | Cottbus | A | W | 2-0 | Ballack 33,58 |
| 32 | lge | B Leverkusen | H | W | 3-0 | Pizarro 2; Elber 22,76 |
| 33 | lge | Bochum | A | W | 4-1 | Pizarro 19; Van Duijnhoven 37 og; Kovac, N 49; Sagnol 89 |
| 34 | lge | Hansa Rostock | H | W | 1-0 | Kovar 60 og |
| 35 | lge | Hannover 96 | A | D | 2-2 | Sagnol 77; Pizarro 85 |
| 36 | lge | W Bremen | H | L | 0-1 | |
| 37 | lge | B Dortmund | A | L | 0-1 | |
| 38 | lge | Wolfsburg | A | W | 2-0 | Elber 59; Pizarro 83 |
| 39 | lge | Kaiserslautern | H | W | 1-0 | Kuffour 85 |
| 40 | lge | Hertha Berlin | A | W | 6-3 | Elber 19,33,45; Pizarro 23,24; Ballack 86 |
| 41 | lge | Stuttgart | H | W | 2-1 | Elber 46,76 |
| 42 | lge | Schalke | A | L | 0-1 | |

## GOALS SCORED

AT HOME

| | | |
|---|---|---|
| MOST | B Munich | 37 |
| | | 37 |
| LEAST | Nurnberg | 16 |

AWAY

| | | |
|---|---|---|
| MOST | B Munich | 33 |
| | | 33 |
| LEAST | B M'gladbach & Arminia B | 12 |

## GOALS CONCEDED

AT HOME

| | | |
|---|---|---|
| LEAST | Hamburg & B M'gladbach | 11 |
| | | 12 |
| MOST | Hannover 96 | 33 |

AWAY

| | | |
|---|---|---|
| LEAST | B Munich | 13 |
| | | 13 |
| MOST | Nurnberg | 36 |

## ATTENDANCES

HOME GROUND: OLYMPIASTADION CAPACITY: 69060 AVERAGE LEAGUE AT HOME: 49823

| | | |
|---|---|---|
| 15 | AC Milan | 70000 |
| 6 | 1860 Munich | 69000 |
| 37 | B Dortmund | 68600 |
| 29 | 1860 Munich | 64000 |
| 39 | Kaiserslautern | 63000 |
| 19 | B Dortmund | 63000 |
| 36 | W Bremen | 63000 |
| 41 | Stuttgart | 63000 |
| 42 | Schalke | 60886 |
| 40 | Hertha Berlin | 59200 |
| 12 | AC Milan | 59000 |
| 13 | Bochum | 58000 |
| 4 | Hamburg | 55400 |
| 24 | Stuttgart | 53700 |
| 25 | Schalke | 51000 |
| 16 | Hannover 96 | 50000 |
| 3 | Arminia B | 50000 |
| 32 | B Leverkusen | 45000 |
| 7 | Nurnberg | 44600 |
| 21 | Wolfsburg | 44000 |
| 18 | W Bremen | 40200 |
| 22 | Kaiserslautern | 40010 |
| 30 | Nurnberg | 40000 |
| 26 | B M'gladbach | 40000 |
| 8 | Deportivo | 40000 |
| 5 | Partizan | 40000 |
| 23 | Hertha Berlin | 40000 |
| 10 | Lens | 38000 |
| 9 | Cottbus | 38000 |
| 34 | Hansa Rostock | 35000 |
| 28 | Hamburg | 35000 |
| 1 | B M'gladbach | 34500 |
| 17 | Deportivo | 33000 |
| 33 | Bochum | 32645 |
| 2 | Partizan | 32000 |
| 35 | Hannover 96 | 31878 |
| 38 | Wolfsburg | 30000 |
| 14 | Hansa Rostock | 30000 |
| 27 | Arminia B | 26601 |
| 11 | B Leverkusen | 22500 |
| 20 | Lens | 22000 |
| 31 | Cottbus | 18250 |

■ Home □ Away ▒ Neutral

## KEY PLAYERS - GOALSCORERS

**1 Giovane Elber**

| | | | |
|---|---|---|---|
| Goals in the League | 20 | Player Strike Rate<br>Average number of minutes between League goals scored by player | 142 |
| Contribution to Attacking Power<br>Average number of minutes between League team goals while on pitch | 42 | Club Strike Rate<br>Average number of minutes between League goals scored by club | 44 |

| | PLAYER | LGE GOALS | POWER | STRIKE RATE |
|---|---|---|---|---|
| 2 | Claudio Pizarro | 15 | 43 | 152 mins |
| 3 | Michael Ballack | 10 | 37 | 225 mins |
| 4 | Willy Sagnol | 2 | 41 | 871 mins |
| 5 | Bixente Lizarazu | 2 | 46 | 1109 mins |

## KEY PLAYERS - MIDFIELDERS

**1 Jens Jeremies**

| | | | |
|---|---|---|---|
| Goals in the League | 0 | Contribution to Attacking Power<br>Average number of minutes between League team goals while on pitch | 42 |
| Defensive Rating<br>Average number of mins between League goals conceded while he was on the pitch | 162 | Scoring Difference<br>Defensive Rating minus Contribution to Attacking Power | 120 |

| | PLAYER | LGE GOALS | DEF RATE | POWER | SCORE DIFF |
|---|---|---|---|---|---|
| 2 | Michael Ballack | 10 | 141 | 38 | 103 mins |
| 3 | Owen Hargreaves | 1 | 122 | 47 | 75 mins |
| 4 | Bixente Lizarazu | 2 | 117 | 46 | 71 mins |
| 5 | Nico Kovac | 1 | 117 | 58 | 59 mins |

## KEY PLAYERS - DEFENDERS

**1 Robert Kovac**

| | | | |
|---|---|---|---|
| Goals Conceded (GC)<br>The number of League goals conceded while he was on the pitch | 11 | Clean Sheets<br>In games when he played at least 70 minutes | 15 |
| Defensive Rating<br>Ave number of mins between League goals conceded while on the pitch | 191 | Club Defensive Rating<br>Average number of mins between League goals conceded by the club this season | 122 |

| | PLAYER | CON LGE | CLEAN SHEETS | DEF RATE |
|---|---|---|---|---|
| 2 | Thomas Linke | 21 | 15 | 129 mins |
| 3 | Willy Sagnol | 18 | 6 | 97 mins |
| 4 | Samuel Osei Kuffour | 19 | 7 | 88 mins |

## KEY GOALKEEPER

**1 Oliver Kahn**

| | |
|---|---|
| Goals Conceded in the League | 22 |
| Defensive Rating<br>Ave number of mins between League goals conceded while on the pitch | 135 |
| Counting Games<br>Games when he played at least 70 minutes | 33 |
| Clean Sheets<br>In games when he played at least 70 minutes | 17 |

## TOP POINT EARNERS

| | PLAYER | GAMES | AVE |
|---|---|---|---|
| 1 | Ballack | 25 | 2.52 |
| 2 | Elber | 32 | 2.34 |
| 3 | Jeremies | 25 | 2.32 |
| 4 | Ze Roberto | 24 | 2.25 |
| 5 | Kahn | 33 | 2.24 |
| 6 | Pizarro | 23 | 2.22 |
| 7 | Kuffour | 18 | 2.22 |
| 8 | Lizarazu | 24 | 2.17 |
| 9 | Linke | 30 | 2.17 |
| 10 | Kovac, R | 23 | 2.17 |
| | CLUB AVERAGE: | | 2.21 |

Ave = Average points per match in Counting Games

## DISCIPLINARY RECORDS

| | PLAYER | YELLOW | RED | AVE |
|---|---|---|---|---|
| 1 | Kovac, N | 5 | 0 | 210 |
| 2 | Ballack | 7 | 0 | 321 |
| 3 | Jeremies | 6 | 0 | 378 |
| 4 | Kovac, R | 5 | 0 | 419 |
| 5 | Salihamidzic | 2 | 0 | 486 |
| 6 | Scholl | 2 | 0 | 512 |
| 7 | Sagnol | 3 | 0 | 580 |
| 8 | Linke | 4 | 0 | 678 |
| 9 | Schweinsteiger | 1 | 0 | 688 |
| 10 | Tarnat | 1 | 0 | 690 |
| 11 | Elber | 4 | 0 | 708 |
| 12 | Lizarazu | 3 | 0 | 739 |
| 13 | Pizarro | 3 | 0 | 761 |
| | Other | 4 | 0 | |
| | TOTAL | 50 | 0 | |

## LEAGUE GOALS

| | PLAYER | MINS | GOALS | AVE |
|---|---|---|---|---|
| 1 | Elber | 2834 | 20 | 142 |
| 2 | Pizarro | 2285 | 15 | 152 |
| 3 | Ballack | 2251 | 10 | 225 |
| 4 | Santa Cruz | 768 | 5 | 154 |
| 5 | Zickler | 345 | 4 | 86 |
| 6 | Scholl | 1025 | 4 | 256 |
| 7 | Lizarazu | 2217 | 2 | 1109 |
| 8 | Sagnol | 1741 | 2 | 871 |
| 9 | Salihamidzic | 972 | 2 | 486 |
| 10 | Ze Roberto | 2336 | 1 | 2336 |
| 11 | Kovac, N | 1050 | 1 | 1050 |
| 12 | Hargreaves | 1701 | 1 | 1701 |
| 13 | Kuffour | 1672 | 1 | 1672 |
| | Other | | 2 | |
| | TOTAL | | 70 | |

## MONTH BY MONTH GUIDE TO THE POINTS

| Month | Points | % |
|---|---|---|
| AUGUST | 7 | 78% |
| SEPTEMBER | 9 | 75% |
| OCTOBER | 7 | 78% |
| NOVEMBER | 12 | 80% |
| DECEMBER | 4 | 67% |
| JANUARY | 3 | 100% |
| FEBRUARY | 8 | 67% |
| MARCH | 12 | 100% |
| APRIL | 4 | 33% |
| MAY | 9 | 75% |

## TEAM OF THE SEASON

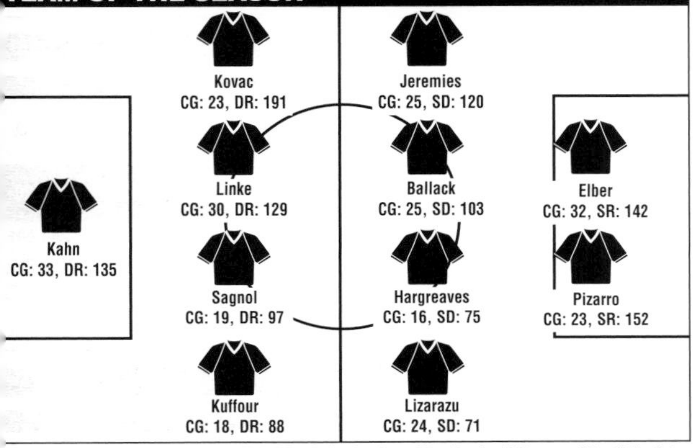

Kahn
CG: 33, DR: 135
Kovac
CG: 23, DR: 191
Linke
CG: 30, DR: 129
Sagnol
CG: 19, DR: 97
Kuffour
CG: 18, DR: 88
Jeremies
CG: 25, SD: 120
Ballack
CG: 25, SD: 103
Hargreaves
CG: 16, SD: 75
Lizarazu
CG: 24, SD: 71
Elber
CG: 32, SR: 142
Pizarro
CG: 23, SR: 152


KEY: DR = Defensive Rate, SD = Scoring Difference, SR = Strike Rate,
CG = Counting Games – League games playing at least 70 minutes

## LEAGUE APPEARANCES, BOOKINGS AND CAPS

| | AGE | IN THE SQUAD | COUNTING GAMES | MINUTES ON PITCH | YELLOW CARDS | RED CARDS | THIS SEASON | HOME COUNTRY |
|---|---|---|---|---|---|---|---|---|
| **Goalkeepers** | | | | | | | | |
| Bernd Dreher | 38 | 6 | 0 | 0 | 0 | 0 | - | Germany |
| Oliver Kahn | 34 | 33 | 33 | 2970 | 2 | 0 | 8 | Germany (4) |
| Stefan Wessels | 24 | 7 | 1 | 90 | 0 | 0 | - | Germany |
| **Defenders** | | | | | | | | |
| Robert Kovac | 29 | 26 | 23 | 2098 | 5 | 0 | 6 | Croatia (26) |
| Samuel Kuffour | 26 | 24 | 18 | 1672 | 0 | 0 | - | Ghana |
| Thomas Linke | 33 | 32 | 30 | 2712 | 4 | 0 | 1 | Germany (4) |
| Willy Sagnol | 26 | 24 | 19 | 1741 | 3 | 0 | 6 | France (2) |
| **Midfielders** | | | | | | | | |
| Michael Ballack | 26 | 26 | 25 | 2251 | 7 | 0 | 5 | Germany (4) |
| Sebastian Deisler | 23 | 8 | 1 | 260 | 0 | 0 | - | Germany |
| Markus Feulner | 21 | 13 | 0 | 223 | 0 | 0 | - | Germany |
| Thorsten Fink | 35 | 14 | 1 | 178 | 1 | 0 | - | Germany |
| Owen Hargreaves | 22 | 26 | 16 | 1701 | 0 | 0 | 6 | England (7) |
| Jens Jeremies | 29 | 29 | 25 | 2270 | 6 | 0 | 8 | Germany (4) |
| Nico Kovac | 31 | 22 | 10 | 1050 | 5 | 0 | 6 | Croatia (26) |
| Bixente Lizarazu | 33 | 27 | 24 | 2217 | 3 | 0 | 4 | France (2) |
| Zvjezdan Misimovic | 21 | 4 | 0 | 11 | 0 | 0 | - | Serbia & Montenegro |
| Hazan Salihamidzic | 26 | 12 | 10 | 972 | 2 | 0 | - | Bosnia |
| Mehmet Scholl | 32 | 20 | 8 | 1025 | 2 | 0 | - | Germany |
| B'n Schweinsteiger | 18 | 15 | 5 | 688 | 1 | 0 | - | Germany |
| Michael Tarnat | 33 | 16 | 7 | 690 | 1 | 0 | - | Germany |
| Pablo Thiam | 29 | 7 | 2 | 197 | 0 | 0 | - | Guinea |
| Piotr Trochowski | 19 | 4 | 0 | 76 | 0 | 0 | - | Germany |
| **Forwards** | | | | | | | | |
| Giovane Elber | 30 | 33 | 32 | 2834 | 4 | 0 | - | Brazil |
| Claudio Pizarro | 24 | 31 | 23 | 2285 | 3 | 0 | - | Peru |
| Roque Santa Cruz | 21 | 14 | 6 | 768 | 0 | 0 | 1 | Paraguay (19) |
| Jose Ze Roberto | 29 | 31 | 24 | 2336 | 1 | 0 | 4 | Brazil (1) |
| Alexander Zickler | 29 | 17 | 3 | 345 | 0 | 0 | 3 | Germany (4) |

KEY: LEAGUE BOOKINGS CAPS (FIFA RANKING)

## SQUAD APPEARANCES

| Match | 1 | 2 | 3 | 4 | 5 | 6 | 7 | 8 | 9 | 10 | 11 | 12 | 13 | 14 | 15 | 16 | 17 | 18 | 19 | 20 | 21 | 22 | 23 | 24 | 25 | 26 | 27 | 28 | 29 | 30 | 31 | 32 | 33 | 34 | 35 | 36 | 37 | 38 | 39 | 40 | 41 | 42 |
|---|---|---|---|---|---|---|---|---|---|---|---|---|---|---|---|---|---|---|---|---|---|---|---|---|---|---|---|---|---|---|---|---|---|---|---|---|---|---|---|---|---|---|
| Venue | A | A | H | A | H | H | A | H | H | A | A | H | H | A | A | H | A | A | H | H | H | A | H | A | H | H | A | H | A | H | A | H | A | H | A | H | A | A | H | A | H | A |
| Competition | L | C | L | L | C | L | L | C | L | C | L | C | L | L | C | L | C | L | L | C | L | L | L | L | L | L | L | L | L | L | L | L | L | L | L | L | L | L | L | L | L | L |
| Result | D | W | W | W | W | W | W | L | W | D | L | L | W | W | L | D | L | L | W | D | W | W | W | W | D | W | D | D | W | W | W | W | W | W | D | L | L | W | W | W | W | L |

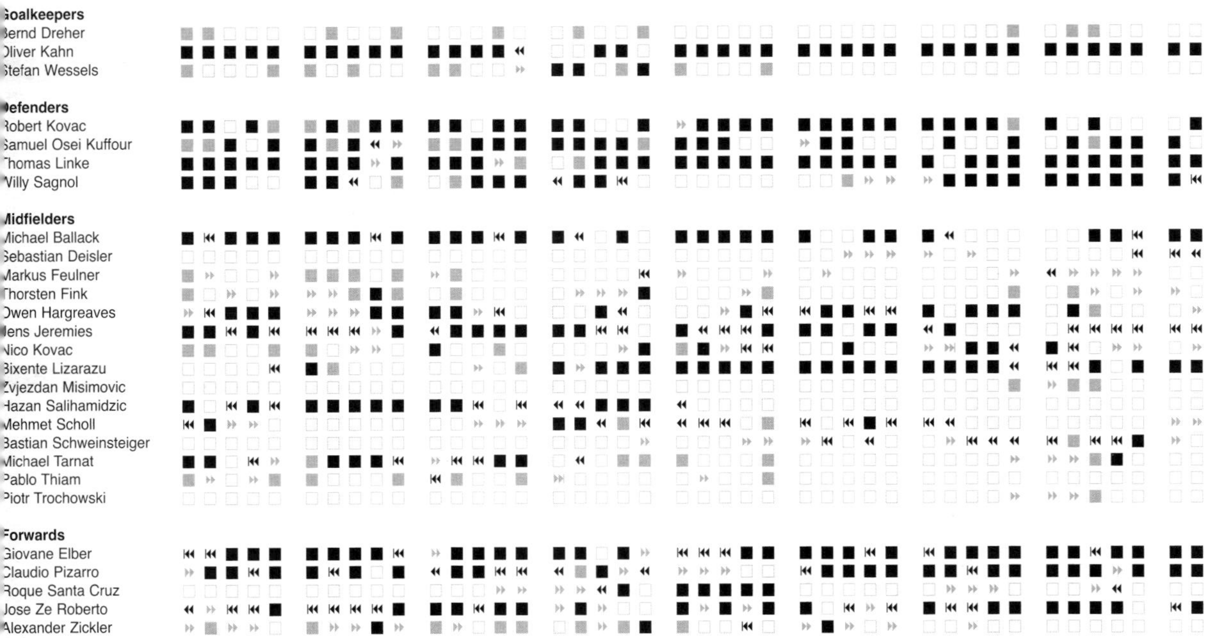

Goalkeepers
Bernd Dreher
Oliver Kahn
Stefan Wessels
Defenders
Robert Kovac
Samuel Osei Kuffour
Thomas Linke
Willy Sagnol
Midfielders
Michael Ballack
Sebastian Deisler
Markus Feulner
Thorsten Fink
Owen Hargreaves
Jens Jeremies
Nico Kovac
Bixente Lizarazu
Zvjezdan Misimovic
Hazan Salihamidzic
Mehmet Scholl
Bastian Schweinsteiger
Michael Tarnat
Pablo Thiam
Piotr Trochowski
Forwards
Giovane Elber
Claudio Pizarro
Roque Santa Cruz
Jose Ze Roberto
Alexander Zickler


KEY: ■ On all match ■ On bench ⏮ Subbed or sent off (Counting game) ◀ Subbed or sent off (playing less than 70 minutes) ⏭ Subbed on from bench (Counting Game) ▶ Subbed on (playing less than 70 minutes) Subbed on and then subbed or sent off (Counting Game) Subbed on and then subbed or sent off (playing less than 70 minutes) □ Not in 16

# STUTTGART

Final Position: **2nd**

| | | | | | | |
|---|---|---|---|---|---|---|
| 1 | lge | Kaiserslautern | H | D | 1-1 | Dundee 45 |
| 2 | lge | Hertha Berlin | A | D | 1-1 | Dundee 14 |
| 3 | lge | B Dortmund | A | L | 1-3 | Dundee 77 pen |
| 4 | lge | Schalke | H | D | 1-1 | Bordon 33 |
| 5 | lge | B M'gladbach | A | D | 1-1 | Kuranyi 71 |
| 6 | uc1rl1 | FK Ventspils | H | W | 4-1 | Amanatidis 22; Kuranyi 33,40; Hleb 59 pen |
| 7 | lge | Arminia B | H | W | 3-0 | Kuranyi 5,64,69 |
| 8 | lge | Hamburg | A | L | 2-3 | Seitz 9; Hleb 26 |
| 9 | uc1rl2 | FK Ventspils | A | W | 4-1 | Tiffert 22,90; Ganea 52; Amanatidis 87 |
| 10 | lge | 1860 Munich | H | W | 4-1 | Kuranyi 47,48; Ganea 50,90 |
| 11 | lge | Nurnberg | A | W | 2-1 | Kuranyi 80; Amanatidis 84 |
| 12 | lge | Cottbus | H | D | 0-0 | |
| 13 | uc2rl1 | Ferencvaros | A | D | 0-0 | |
| 14 | lge | B Leverkusen | A | W | 1-0 | Meissner 19 |
| 15 | lge | Bochum | H | W | 3-2 | Ganea 73,86 pen,90 |
| 16 | uc2rl2 | Ferencvaros | H | W | 2-0 | Amanatidis 65; Meira 90 pen |
| 17 | lge | Hansa Rostock | A | D | 1-1 | Kuranyi 46 |
| 18 | lge | Hannover 96 | H | W | 3-0 | Amanatidis 35; Hleb 54; Stefulj 73 og |
| 19 | uc3rl1 | Club Brugge | A | W | 2-1 | Balakov 72; Kuranyi 89 |
| 20 | lge | W Bremen | A | L | 1-3 | Kuranyi 55 |
| 21 | lge | Bayern Munich | H | L | 0-3 | |
| 22 | uc3rl2 | Club Brugge | H | W | 1-0 | Hleb 90 |
| 23 | lge | Wolfsburg | A | W | 2-1 | Schneider 36; Meira 55 |
| 24 | lge | Kaiserslautern | A | W | 2-1 | Kuranyi 29; Balakov 70 |
| 25 | lge | Hertha Berlin | H | W | 3-1 | Amanatidis 29; Hleb 69; Ganea 90 |
| 26 | lge | B Dortmund | H | W | 1-0 | Soldo 77 |
| 27 | lge | Schalke | A | L | 0-2 | |
| 28 | uc4rl1 | Celtic | A | L | 1-3 | Kuranyi 27 |
| 29 | lge | B M'gladbach | H | W | 4-0 | Kuranyi 8,88; Amanatidis 24; Ganea 86 |
| 30 | uc4rl2 | Celtic | H | W | 3-2 | Tiffert 37; Hleb 75; Mutzel 87 |
| 31 | lge | Arminia B | A | W | 1-0 | Meissner 15 |
| 32 | lge | Hamburg | H | D | 1-1 | Kuranyi 20 |
| 33 | lge | 1860 Munich | A | W | 1-0 | Bordon 40 |
| 34 | lge | Nurnberg | H | L | 0-2 | |
| 35 | lge | Cottbus | A | W | 3-2 | Meissner 2; Heldt 75; Ganea 90 pen |
| 36 | lge | B Leverkusen | H | W | 3-0 | Amanatidis 9; Hleb 16; Ganea 51 |
| 37 | lge | Bochum | A | L | 1-3 | Kuranyi 25 |
| 38 | lge | Hansa Rostock | H | D | 1-1 | Meissner 27 |
| 39 | lge | Hannover 96 | A | W | 2-1 | Dundee 19,37 |
| 40 | lge | W Bremen | H | L | 0-1 | |
| 41 | lge | Bayern Munich | A | L | 1-2 | Dundee 83 |
| 42 | lge | Wolfsburg | H | W | 2-0 | Kuranyi 11; Balakov 23 pen |

## GOALS SCORED

AT HOME

| | | |
|---|---|---|
| MOST | B Munich | 37 |
| | | 30 |
| LEAST | Nurnberg | 16 |

AWAY

| | | |
|---|---|---|
| MOST | B Munich | 33 |
| | | 23 |
| LEAST | B M'gladbach &Arminia B | 12 |

## GOALS CONCEDED

AT HOME

| | | |
|---|---|---|
| LEAST | Hamburg & B M'gladbach | 11 |
| | | 12 |
| MOST | Hannover 96 | 33 |

AWAY

| | | |
|---|---|---|
| LEAST | B Munich | 13 |
| | | 25 |
| MOST | Nurnberg | 36 |

## ATTENDANCES

HOME GROUND: GOTTLIEB-DAIMLER-STADION CAPACITY: 54267 AVERAGE LEAGUE AT HOME: 32321

| | | | | | | | | |
|---|---|---|---|---|---|---|---|---|
| 3 | B Dortmund | 66000 | 22 | Club Brugge | 34000 | 33 | 1860 Munich | 20000 |
| 41 | Bayern Munich | 63000 | 25 | Hertha Berlin | 32000 | 7 | Arminia B | 20000 |
| 27 | Schalke | 60672 | 39 | Hannover 96 | 31000 | 23 | Wolfsburg | 20000 |
| 28 | Celtic | 59000 | 11 | Nurnberg | 29500 | 15 | Bochum | 19000 |
| 40 | W Bremen | 54267 | 34 | Nurnberg | 28000 | 19 | Club Brugge | 18000 |
| 21 | Bayern Munich | 53700 | 20 | W Bremen | 28000 | 13 | Ferencvaros | 16000 |
| 2 | Hertha Berlin | 49202 | 5 | B M'gladbach | 27000 | 16 | Ferencvaros | 15000 |
| 42 | Wolfsburg | 49000 | 4 | Schalke | 26500 | 17 | Hansa Rostock | 15000 |
| 30 | Celtic | 45000 | 38 | Hansa Rostock | 23000 | 35 | Cottbus | 12000 |
| 26 | B Dortmund | 40000 | 37 | Bochum | 23000 | 6 | FK Ventspils | 10000 |
| 18 | Hannover 96 | 40000 | 12 | Cottbus | 23000 | 31 | Arminia B | 2000 |
| 36 | B Leverkusen | 40000 | 1 | Kaiserslautern | 23000 | 9 | FK Ventspils | 2000 |
| 8 | Hamburg | 38000 | 14 | B Leverkusen | 22500 | | | |
| 24 | Kaiserslautern | 36692 | 29 | B M'gladbach | 22000 | | | |
| 32 | Hamburg | 35000 | 10 | 1860 Munich | 21000 | | | |

■ Home □ Away ▨ Neutral

## KEY PLAYERS - GOALSCORERS

**1 Kevin Kuranyi**

| | | | |
|---|---|---|---|
| Goals in the League | 15 | Player Strike Rate<br>Average number of minutes between League goals scored by player | 167 |
| Contribution to Attacking Power<br>Average number of minutes between League team goals while on pitch | 53 | Club Strike Rate<br>Average number of minutes between League goals scored by club | 58 |

| | PLAYER | LGE GOALS | POWER | STRIKE RATE |
|---|---|---|---|---|
| 2 | Silvio Meissner | 4 | 77 | 429 mins |
| 3 | Alexander Hleb | 4 | 57 | 652 mins |
| 4 | Marcelo Jose Bordon | 2 | 60 | 1155 mins |
| 5 | Krasimir Balakov | 2 | 59 | 1185 mins |

## KEY PLAYERS - MIDFIELDERS

**1 Zvonimir Soldo**

| | | | |
|---|---|---|---|
| Goals in the League | 1 | Contribution to Attacking Power<br>Average number of minutes between League team goals while on pitch | 53 |
| Defensive Rating<br>Average number of mins between League goals conceded while he was on the pitch | 91 | Scoring Difference<br>Defensive Rating minus Contribution to Attacking Power | 38 |

| | PLAYER | LGE GOALS | DEF RATE | POWER | SCORE DIFF |
|---|---|---|---|---|---|
| 2 | Alexander Hleb | 4 | 87 | 58 | 29 mins |
| 3 | Heiko Gerber | 0 | 86 | 59 | 27 mins |
| 4 | Andreas Hinkel | 0 | 82 | 56 | 26 mins |
| 5 | Krasimir Balakov | 2 | 74 | 59 | 15 mins |

## KEY PLAYERS - DEFENDERS

**1 Rui Manuel Marques**

| | | | |
|---|---|---|---|
| Goals Conceded (GC)<br>The number of League goals conceded while he was on the pitch | 10 | Clean Sheets<br>In games when he played at least 70 minutes | 2 |
| Defensive Rating<br>Ave number of mins between League goals conceded while on the pitch | 86 | Club Defensive Rating<br>Average number of mins between League goals conceded by the club this season | 78 |

| | PLAYER | CON LGE | CLEAN SHEETS | DEF RATE |
|---|---|---|---|---|
| 2 | Marcelo Jose Bordon | 28 | 8 | 82 mins |
| 3 | Fernando Jose da Silva Meira | 37 | 9 | 75 mins |

## KEY GOALKEEPER

**1 Thomas Ernst**

| | |
|---|---|
| Goals Conceded in the League | 15 |
| Defensive Rating<br>Ave number of mins between League goals conceded while on the pitch | 84 |
| Counting Games<br>Games when he played at least 70 minutes | 14 |
| Clean Sheets<br>In games when he played at least 70 minutes | 6 |

## TOP POINT EARNERS

| | PLAYER | GAMES | AVE |
|---|---|---|---|
| 1 | Soldo | 24 | 2.04 |
| 2 | Gerber | 23 | 2.00 |
| 3 | Ernst | 14 | 1.93 |
| 4 | Kuranyi | 27 | 1.85 |
| 5 | Hinkel | 32 | 1.81 |
| 6 | Fernando Meira | 30 | 1.73 |
| 7 | Hleb | 26 | 1.65 |
| 8 | Bordon | 26 | 1.65 |
| 9 | Balakov | 24 | 1.63 |
| 10 | Hildebrand | 20 | 1.60 |
| | CLUB AVERAGE: | | 1.74 |

Ave = Average points per match in Counting Games

## DISCIPLINARY RECORDS

| | PLAYER | YELLOW | RED | AVE |
|---|---|---|---|---|
| 1 | Meissner | 9 | 1 | 171 |
| 2 | Marques | 3 | 0 | 287 |
| 3 | Bordon | 8 | 0 | 288 |
| 4 | Gerber | 7 | 0 | 319 |
| 5 | Soldo | 5 | 0 | 474 |
| 6 | Dundee | 1 | 0 | 486 |
| 7 | Ganea | 2 | 0 | 515 |
| 8 | Fernando Meira | 4 | 1 | 558 |
| 9 | Hinkel | 5 | 0 | 574 |
| 10 | Seitz | 2 | 0 | 590 |
| 11 | Balakov | 4 | 0 | 592 |
| 12 | Tiffert | 1 | 0 | 670 |
| 13 | Mutzel | 1 | 0 | 716 |
| | Other | 12 | 0 | |
| | TOTAL | 64 | 2 | |

## LEAGUE GOALS

| | PLAYER | MINS | GOALS | AVE |
|---|---|---|---|---|
| 1 | Kuranyi | 2510 | 15 | 167 |
| 2 | Ganea | 1031 | 9 | 115 |
| 3 | Dundee | 486 | 6 | 81 |
| 4 | Amanatidis | 1342 | 5 | 268 |
| 5 | Meissner | 1714 | 4 | 429 |
| 6 | Hleb | 2608 | 4 | 652 |
| 7 | Balakov | 2370 | 2 | 1185 |
| 8 | Bordon | 2309 | 2 | 1155 |
| 9 | Schneider | 352 | 1 | 352 |
| 10 | Soldo | 2374 | 1 | 2374 |
| 11 | Seitz | 1181 | 1 | 1181 |
| 12 | Meira | 2792 | 1 | 2792 |
| 13 | Heldt | 153 | 1 | 153 |
| | Other | | 1 | |
| | TOTAL | | 53 | |

## MONTH BY MONTH GUIDE TO THE POINTS

| | | |
|---|---|---|
| AUGUST | 2 | 22% |
| SEPTEMBER | 5 | 42% |
| OCTOBER | 7 | 78% |
| NOVEMBER | 10 | 83% |
| DECEMBER | 3 | 33% |
| JANUARY | 3 | 100% |
| FEBRUARY | 9 | 75% |
| MARCH | 7 | 58% |
| APRIL | 7 | 58% |
| MAY | 6 | 50% |

## TEAM OF THE SEASON

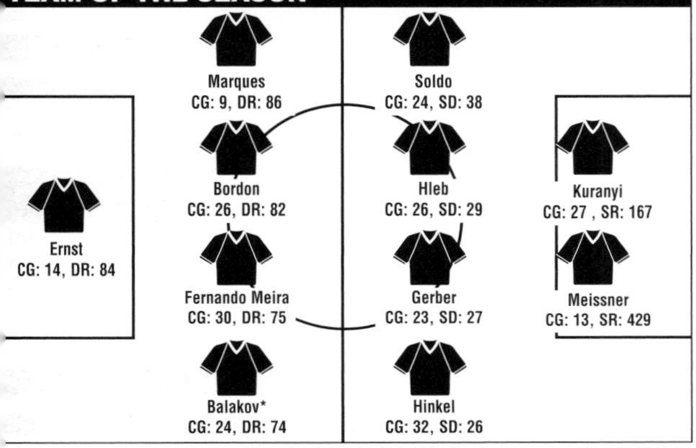

Marques
CG: 9, DR: 86
Soldo
CG: 24, SD: 38
Bordon
CG: 26, DR: 82
Hleb
CG: 26, SD: 29
Kuranyi
CG: 27 , SR: 167
Ernst
CG: 14, DR: 84
Fernando Meira
CG: 30, DR: 75
Gerber
CG: 23, SD: 27
Meissner
CG: 13, SR: 429
Balakov*
CG: 24, DR: 74
Hinkel
CG: 32, SD: 26


KEY: DR = Defensive Rate, SD = Scoring Difference, SR = Strike Rate, CG = Counting Games – League games playing at least 70 minutes

## LEAGUE APPEARANCES, BOOKINGS AND CAPS

| | AGE | IN THE SQUAD | COUNTING GAMES | MINUTES ON PITCH | YELLOW CARDS | RED CARDS | THIS SEASON | HOME COUNTRY |
|---|---|---|---|---|---|---|---|---|
| **Goalkeepers** | | | | | | | | |
| Diego Benaglio | 19 | 6 | 0 | 0 | 0 | 0 | - | Switzerland |
| Thomas Ernst | 35 | 20 | 14 | 1260 | 0 | 0 | - | Germany |
| Timo Hildebrand | 24 | 20 | 20 | 1800 | 0 | 0 | - | Germany |
| **Defenders** | | | | | | | | |
| Marcelo Jose Bordon | 27 | 26 | 26 | 2309 | 8 | 0 | - | Brazil |
| Steffen Dangelmayr | 24 | 5 | 4 | 348 | 0 | 0 | - | Germany |
| Jose Fernando Meira | 25 | 32 | 30 | 2792 | 4 | 1 | 9 | Portugal (14) |
| Rui Manuel Marques | 25 | 15 | 9 | 863 | 3 | 0 | - | Angola |
| Michael Rundio | 20 | 3 | 1 | 120 | 1 | 0 | - | Germany |
| Thomas Schneider | 30 | 11 | 4 | 352 | 3 | 0 | - | Germany |
| Timo Wenzel | 25 | 25 | 8 | 962 | 0 | 0 | - | Germany |
| **Midfielders** | | | | | | | | |
| Krasimir Balakov | 37 | 28 | 24 | 2370 | 4 | 0 | - | Bulgaria |
| Bradley Carnell | 26 | 11 | 2 | 358 | 2 | 0 | - | South Africa |
| Heiko Gerber | 30 | 28 | 23 | 2233 | 7 | 0 | - | Germany |
| Horst Heldt | 33 | 6 | 0 | 153 | 0 | 0 | - | Germany |
| Andreas Hinkel | 21 | 33 | 32 | 2871 | 5 | 0 | 5 | Germany (4) |
| Alexander Hleb | 22 | 33 | 26 | 2608 | 2 | 0 | - | Belarus |
| Michael Mutzel | 23 | 19 | 4 | 716 | 1 | 0 | - | Germany |
| Zvonimir Soldo | 35 | 28 | 24 | 2374 | 5 | 0 | - | Croatia |
| Jens Todt | 33 | 4 | 2 | 208 | 1 | 0 | - | Germany |
| **Forwards** | | | | | | | | |
| Ioannis Amanatidis | 21 | 29 | 7 | 1342 | 0 | 0 | - | Greece |
| Sean Dundee | 30 | 11 | 4 | 486 | 1 | 0 | - | Germany |
| Ioan Vlorel Ganea | 29 | 29 | 4 | 1031 | 2 | 0 | 8 | Romania (27) |
| Kevin Kuranyi | 21 | 32 | 27 | 2510 | 3 | 0 | - | Brazil |
| Silvio Meissner | 30 | 27 | 13 | 1714 | 9 | 1 | - | Germany |
| Jochen Seitz | 26 | 24 | 8 | 1181 | 2 | 0 | - | Germany |
| Christian Tiffert | 21 | 23 | 2 | 670 | 1 | 0 | - | Germany |

KEY: LEAGUE BOOKINGS CAPS (FIFA RANKING)

## SQUAD APPEARANCES

| Match | 1 | 2 | 3 | 4 | 5 | 6 | 7 | 8 | 9 | 10 | 11 | 12 | 13 | 14 | 15 | 16 | 17 | 18 | 19 | 20 | 21 | 22 | 23 | 24 | 25 | 26 | 27 | 28 | 29 | 30 | 31 | 32 | 33 | 34 | 35 | 36 | 37 | 38 | 39 | 40 | 41 | 42 |
|---|---|---|---|---|---|---|---|---|---|---|---|---|---|---|---|---|---|---|---|---|---|---|---|---|---|---|---|---|---|---|---|---|---|---|---|---|---|---|---|---|---|---|
| Venue | H | A | A | H | A | H | H | A | A | H | A | H | A | A | H | H | A | H | A | A | H | H | A | A | H | H | A | A | H | H | A | H | A | H | A | H | A | H | A | H | A | H |
| Competition | L | L | L | L | L | E | L | L | E | L | L | L | E | L | L | E | L | L | E | L | L | E | L | L | L | L | L | E | L | E | L | L | L | L | L | L | L | L | L | L | L | L |
| Result | D | D | L | D | D | W | W | L | W | W | W | D | D | W | W | W | D | W | W | L | L | W | W | W | W | W | L | L | W | W | W | D | W | L | W | W | L | D | W | L | L | W |

Goalkeepers: Diego Benaglio, Thomas Ernst, Timo Hildebrand
Defenders: Marcelo Jose Bordon, Steffen Dangelmayr, Rui Manuel Marques, Fernando Meira, Michael Rundio, Thomas Schneider, Timo Wenzel
Midfielders: Krasimir Balakov, Bradley Carnell, Heiko Gerber, Horst Heldt, Andreas Hinkel, Alexander Hleb, Michael Mutzel, Zvonimir Soldo, Jens Todt
Forwards: Ioannis Amanatidis, Sean Dundee, Ioan Vlorel Ganea, Kevin Kuranyi, Silvio Meissner, Jochen Seitz, Christian Tiffert

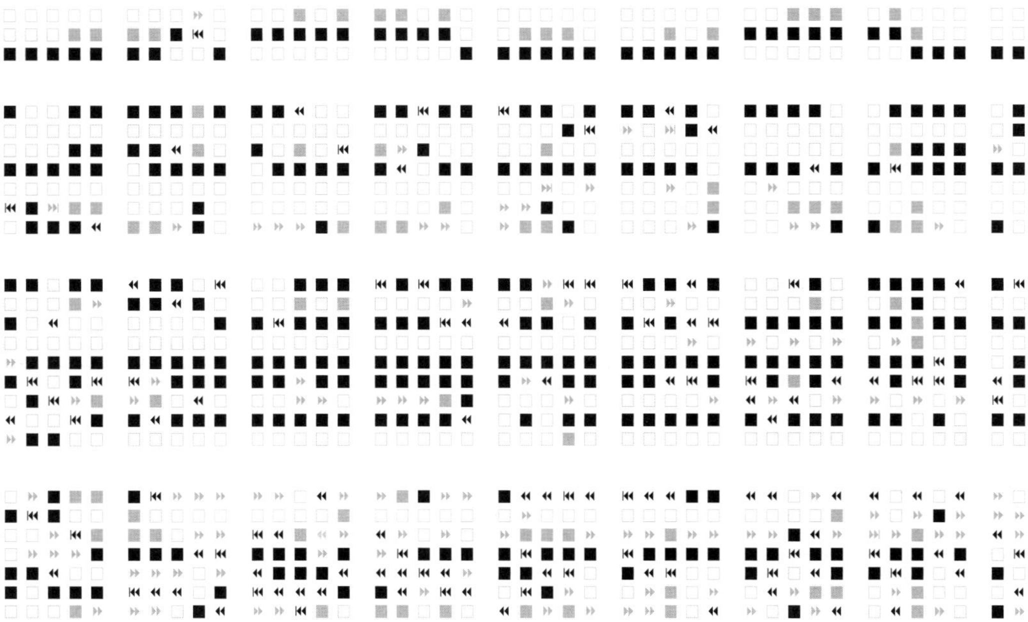

KEY: ■ On all match ⏮ Subbed or sent off (Counting game) ⏭ Subbed on from bench (Counting Game) Subbed on and then subbed or sent off (Counting Game) Not in 16
On bench « Subbed or sent off (playing less than 70 minutes) » Subbed on (playing less than 70 minutes) Subbed on and then subbed or sent off (playing less than 70 minutes)

# BORUSSIA DORTMUND

Final Position: **3rd**

| | | | | | | | |
|---|---|---|---|---|---|---|---|
| 1 | lge | Hertha Berlin | H | D | 2-2 | Frings 4; Ewerthon 36 |
| 2 | lge | B Leverkusen | A | D | 1-1 | Koller 61 |
| 3 | lge | Stuttgart | H | W | 3-1 | Koller 39; Dede 66; Ewerthon 87 |
| 4 | lge | Bochum | A | D | 0-0 | |
| 5 | lge | Schalke | H | D | 1-1 | Ewerthon 71 |
| 6 | ecga | Arsenal | A | L | 0-2 | |
| 7 | lge | Hansa Rostock | A | W | 1-0 | Koller 12 |
| 8 | ecga | Auxerre | H | W | 2-1 | Koller 6; Amoroso 78 |
| 9 | lge | B M'gladbach | H | W | 1-0 | Ewerthon 85 |
| 10 | ecga | PSV Eindhoven | A | W | 3-1 | Koller 21; Rosicky 69; Amoroso 90 |
| 11 | lge | Hannover 96 | A | W | 3-0 | Frings 42 pen; Koller 63; Amoroso 87 |
| 12 | lge | Arminia B | H | D | 0-0 | |
| 13 | ecga | PSV Eindhoven | H | D | 1-1 | Koller 10 |
| 14 | lge | W Bremen | A | W | 4-1 | Frings 2; Dede 71; Ewerthon 74,85 |
| 15 | ecga | Arsenal | H | W | 2-1 | Gilberto 38 og; Rosicky 63 pen |
| 16 | lge | Hamburg | H | D | 1-1 | Rosicky 67 |
| 17 | lge | Bayern Munich | A | L | 1-2 | Amoroso 7 |
| 18 | ecga | Auxerre | A | L | 0-1 | |
| 19 | lge | 1860 Munich | H | W | 1-0 | Ewerthon 5 |
| 20 | lge | Wolfsburg | A | L | 0-2 | |
| 21 | ecgc | L Moscow | A | W | 2-1 | Frings 33; Koller 43 |
| 22 | lge | Nurnberg | A | W | 2-1 | Ricken 54; Ewerthon 78 |
| 23 | lge | Kaiserslautern | H | W | 3-1 | Klos, T 22 og; Amoroso 73,78 |
| 24 | ecgc | AC Milan | H | L | 0-1 | |
| 25 | lge | Cottbus | A | W | 4-0 | Koller 8,90; Ewerthon 47; Amoroso 83 |
| 26 | lge | Hertha Berlin | A | L | 1-2 | Koller 80 |
| 27 | lge | B Leverkusen | H | W | 2-0 | Ewerthon 3; Koller 26 |
| 28 | lge | Stuttgart | A | L | 0-1 | |
| 29 | lge | Bochum | H | W | 4-1 | Reina 33; Koller 43; Frings 45 pen,68 pen |
| 30 | ecgc | Real Madrid | A | L | 1-2 | Koller 30 |
| 31 | lge | Schalke | A | D | 2-2 | Koller 52; Ewerthon 58 |
| 32 | ecgc | Real Madrid | H | D | 1-1 | Koller 21 |
| 33 | lge | Hansa Rostock | H | W | 2-0 | Dede 43; Madouni 82 |
| 34 | lge | B M'gladbach | A | L | 0-1 | |
| 35 | ecgc | L Moscow | H | W | 3-0 | Frings 39; Koller 58; Amoroso 66 |
| 36 | lge | Hannover 96 | H | W | 2-0 | Frings 33; Leandro 76 |
| 37 | ecgc | AC Milan | A | W | 1-0 | Koller 80 |
| 38 | lge | Arminia B | A | D | 0-0 | |
| 39 | lge | W Bremen | H | L | 1-2 | Amoroso 29 |
| 40 | lge | Hamburg | A | D | 1-1 | Koller 69 |
| 41 | lge | Bayern Munich | H | W | 1-0 | Amoroso 61 pen |
| 42 | lge | 1860 Munich | A | D | 0-0 | |
| 43 | lge | Wolfsburg | H | D | 2-2 | Ricken 16; Rosicky 67 |
| 44 | lge | Nurnberg | H | W | 4-1 | Ricken 27,54; Reina 65; Koller 67 |
| 45 | lge | Kaiserslautern | A | D | 0-0 | |
| 46 | lge | Cottbus | H | D | 1-1 | Rosicky 26 |

## GOALS SCORED

AT HOME

| | | |
|---|---|---|
| MOST | B Munich | 37 |
| | | 31 |
| LEAST | Nurnberg | 16 |

AWAY

| | | |
|---|---|---|
| MOST | B Munich | 33 |
| | | 20 |
| LEAST | B M'gladbach &Arminia B | 12 |

## GOALS CONCEDED

AT HOME

| | | |
|---|---|---|
| LEAST | Hamburg & B M'gladbach | 11 |
| | | 13 |
| MOST | Hannover 96 | 33 |

AWAY

| | | |
|---|---|---|
| LEAST | B Munich | 13 |
| | | 14 |
| MOST | Nurnberg | 36 |

## ATTENDANCES

HOME GROUND: WESTFALENSTADION CAPACITY: 68600 AVERAGE LEAGUE AT HOME: 67382

| | | | | | | | |
|---|---|---|---|---|---|---|---|
| 5 | Schalke | 68800 | 33 | Hansa Rostock | 64000 | 22 | Nurnberg | 40000 |
| 12 | Arminia B | 68600 | 17 | Bayern Munich | 63000 | 28 | Stuttgart | 40000 |
| 19 | 1860 Munich | 68600 | 31 | Schalke | 60878 | 42 | 1860 Munich | 35000 |
| 9 | B M'gladbach | 68600 | 40 | Hamburg | 55400 | 6 | Arsenal | 34907 |
| 41 | Bayern Munich | 68600 | 24 | AC Milan | 52000 | 34 | B M'gladbach | 33000 |
| 39 | W Bremen | 68500 | 15 | Arsenal | 52000 | 4 | Bochum | 32645 |
| 16 | Hamburg | 68000 | 26 | Hertha Berlin | 50547 | 10 | PSV Eindhoven | 30000 |
| 23 | Kaiserslautern | 68000 | 13 | PSV Eindhoven | 50000 | 7 | Hansa Rostock | 29000 |
| 46 | Cottbus | 68000 | 32 | Real Madrid | 50000 | 38 | Arminia B | 26601 |
| 36 | Hannover 96 | 67000 | 30 | Real Madrid | 50000 | 2 | B Leverkusen | 22500 |
| 43 | Wolfsburg | 67000 | 11 | Hannover 96 | 49800 | 18 | Auxerre | 20000 |
| 29 | Bochum | 67000 | 8 | Auxerre | 48000 | 20 | Wolfsburg | 18000 |
| 27 | B Leverkusen | 67000 | 35 | Lokomotiv Moscow | 48000 | 21 | Lokomotiv Moscow | 17000 |
| 44 | Nurnberg | 66000 | 37 | AC Milan | 45000 | 25 | Cottbus | 15000 |
| 3 | Stuttgart | 66000 | 14 | W Bremen | 40200 | | | |
| 1 | Hertha Berlin | 65800 | 45 | Kaiserslautern | 40160 | | | |

■ Home □ Away ▨ Neutral

## KEY PLAYERS - GOALSCORERS

**1 Henrique da Souza Ewerthon**

| | | | |
|---|---|---|---|
| Goals in the League | 11 | Player Strike Rate<br>Average number of minutes between League goals scored by player | 215 |
| Contribution to Attacking Power<br>Average number of minutes between League team goals while on pitch | 63 | Club Strike Rate<br>Average number of minutes between League goals scored by club | 60 |

| | PLAYER | LGE GOALS | POWER | STRIKE RATE |
|---|---|---|---|---|
| 2 | Jan Koller | 12 | 59 | 251 mins |
| 3 | Torsten Frings | 6 | 58 | 432 mins |
| 4 | Tomas Rosicky | 3 | 61 | 839 mins |
| 5 | Leonardo De Deus Santos | 3 | 61 | 846 mins |

## KEY PLAYERS - MIDFIELDERS

**1 Ferreira Evanilson**

| | | | |
|---|---|---|---|
| Goals in the League | 0 | Contribution to Attacking Power<br>Average number of minutes between League team goals while on pitch | 65 |
| Defensive Rating<br>Average number of mins between League goals conceded while he was on the pitch | 130 | Scoring Difference<br>Defensive Rating minus Contribution to Attacking Power | 65 |

| | PLAYER | LGE GOALS | DEF RATE | POWER | SCORE DIFF |
|---|---|---|---|---|---|
| 2 | Leonardo De Deus Santos | 3 | 121 | 62 | 59 mins |
| 3 | Torsten Frings | 6 | 113 | 59 | 54 mins |
| 4 | Lars Ricken | 4 | 103 | 58 | 45 mins |
| 5 | Tomas Rosicky | 3 | 105 | 61 | 44 mins |

## KEY PLAYERS - DEFENDERS

**1 Ahmed Reda Madouni**

| | | | |
|---|---|---|---|
| Goals Conceded (GC)<br>The number of League goals conceded while he was on the pitch | 13 | Clean Sheets<br>In games when he played at least 70 minutes | 8 |
| Defensive Rating<br>Ave number of mins between League goals conceded while on the pitch | 126 | Club Defensive Rating<br>Average number of mins between League goals conceded by the club this season | 113 |

| | PLAYER | CON LGE | CLEAN SHEETS | DEF RATE |
|---|---|---|---|---|
| 2 | Christian Worns | 21 | 12 | 123 mins |
| 3 | Stefan Reuter | 21 | 10 | 116 mins |
| 4 | Sebastian Kehl | 20 | 11 | 108 mins |
| 5 | Christoph Metzelder | 19 | 8 | 108 mins |

## KEY GOALKEEPER

**1 Roman Weidenfeller**

| | |
|---|---|
| Goals Conceded in the League | 7 |
| Defensive Rating<br>Ave number of mins between League goals conceded while on the pitch | 130 |
| Counting Games<br>Games when he played at least 70 minutes | 10 |
| Clean Sheets<br>In games when he played at least 70 minutes | 5 |

## TOP POINT EARNERS

| | PLAYER | GAMES | AVE |
|---|---|---|---|
| 1 | Metzelder | 21 | 1.90 |
| 2 | Lehmann | 23 | 1.78 |
| 3 | Reuter | 25 | 1.76 |
| 4 | Dede | 28 | 1.75 |
| 5 | Madouni | 14 | 1.71 |
| 6 | Koller | 34 | 1.71 |
| 7 | Worns | 28 | 1.71 |
| 8 | Heinrich | 12 | 1.67 |
| 9 | Kehl | 23 | 1.65 |
| 10 | Evanilson | 18 | 1.61 |
| | CLUB AVERAGE: | | 1.71 |

Ave = Average points per match in Counting Games

## DISCIPLINARY RECORDS

| | PLAYER | YELLOW | RED | AVE |
|---|---|---|---|---|
| 1 | Amoroso | 5 | 1 | 163 |
| 2 | Kehl | 10 | 0 | 216 |
| 3 | Frings | 9 | 2 | 235 |
| 4 | Dede | 6 | 0 | 422 |
| 5 | Lehmann | 3 | 2 | 425 |
| 6 | Ricken | 3 | 0 | 446 |
| 7 | Ewerthon | 4 | 0 | 591 |
| 8 | Heinrich | 2 | 0 | 597 |
| 9 | Reuter | 4 | 0 | 611 |
| 10 | Rosicky | 4 | 0 | 629 |
| 11 | Evanilson | 3 | 0 | 651 |
| 12 | Metzelder | 3 | 0 | 686 |
| 13 | Koller | 4 | 0 | 754 |
| | Other | 7 | 0 | |
| | TOTAL | 67 | 5 | |

## LEAGUE GOALS

| | PLAYER | MINS | GOALS | AVE |
|---|---|---|---|---|
| 1 | Koller | 3016 | 12 | 251 |
| 2 | Ewerthon | 2365 | 11 | 215 |
| 3 | Amoroso | 982 | 7 | 140 |
| 4 | Frings | 2594 | 6 | 432 |
| 5 | Ricken | 1339 | 4 | 335 |
| 6 | Rosicky | 2518 | 3 | 839 |
| 7 | Dede | 2537 | 3 | 846 |
| 8 | Reina | 464 | 2 | 232 |
| 9 | Leandro | 57 | 1 | 57 |
| 10 | Madouni | 1639 | 1 | 163 |
| | Other | | 1 | |
| | TOTAL | | 51 | |

## MONTH BY MONTH GUIDE TO THE POINTS

| | | |
|---|---|---|
| AUGUST | 5 | 56% |
| SEPTEMBER | 8 | 67% |
| OCTOBER | 7 | 78% |
| NOVEMBER | 7 | 47% |
| DECEMBER | 6 | 100% |
| JANUARY | 0 | 0% |
| FEBRUARY | 7 | 58% |
| MARCH | 7 | 58% |
| APRIL | 5 | 42% |
| MAY | 6 | 50% |

## TEAM OF THE SEASON

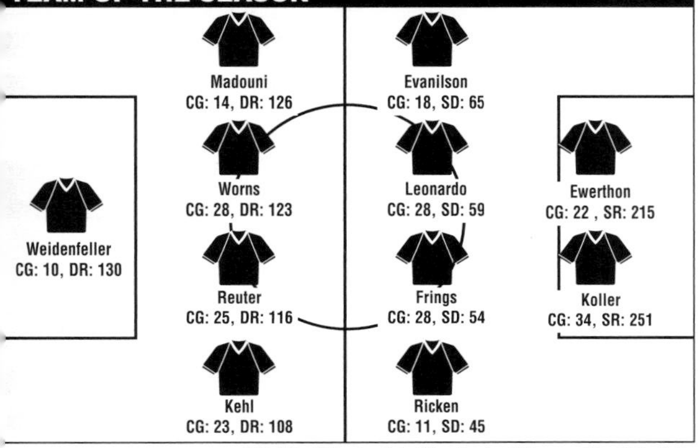
Weidenfeller
CG: 10, DR: 130
Madouni
CG: 14, DR: 126
Worns
CG: 28, DR: 123
Reuter
CG: 25, DR: 116
Kehl
CG: 23, DR: 108
Evanilson
CG: 18, SD: 65
Leonardo
CG: 28, SD: 59
Frings
CG: 28, SD: 54
Ricken
CG: 11, SD: 45
Ewerthon
CG: 22 , SR: 215
Koller
CG: 34, SR: 251

KEY: DR = Defensive Rate, SD = Scoring Difference, SR = Strike Rate, CG = Counting Games – League games playing at least 70 minutes

## LEAGUE APPEARANCES, BOOKINGS AND CAPS

| | AGE | IN THE SQUAD | COUNTING GAMES | MINUTES ON PITCH | YELLOW CARDS | RED CARDS | THIS SEASON | HOME COUNTRY |
|---|---|---|---|---|---|---|---|---|
| **Goalkeepers** | | | | | | | | |
| Jens Lehmann | 33 | 24 | 23 | 2126 | 3 | 2 | 5 | Germany (4) |
| Michael Ratajczak | 21 | 4 | 0 | 0 | 0 | 0 | - | Germany |
| Roman Weidenfeller | 22 | 17 | 10 | 909 | 0 | 0 | - | Germany |
| **Defenders** | | | | | | | | |
| Juan Fernandez | 23 | 9 | 2 | 226 | 1 | 0 | - | Argentina |
| Sebastian Kehl | 23 | 28 | 23 | 2167 | 10 | 0 | 10 | Germany (4) |
| Juergen Kohler | 37 | 0 | 0 | 0 | 0 | 0 | - | Germany |
| Ahmed Madouni | 22 | 30 | 14 | 1639 | 1 | 0 | - | France |
| Christoph Metzelder | 22 | 24 | 21 | 2059 | 3 | 0 | 3 | Germany (4) |
| Stefan Reuter | 36 | 32 | 25 | 2446 | 4 | 0 | - | Germany |
| Florian Thorwart | 21 | 1 | 0 | 1 | 0 | 0 | - | Germany |
| Christian Worns | 31 | 31 | 28 | 2579 | 2 | 0 | 8 | Germany (4) |
| **Midfielders** | | | | | | | | |
| Otto Addo | 28 | 4 | 2 | 177 | 2 | 0 | - | Ghana |
| Leonardo Santos | 25 | 30 | 28 | 2537 | 6 | 0 | - | Brazil |
| Guy Demel | 22 | 5 | 0 | 89 | 0 | 0 | - | France |
| Ferreira Evanilson | 27 | 25 | 18 | 1953 | 3 | 0 | - | Brazil |
| Torsten Frings | 26 | 31 | 28 | 2594 | 9 | 2 | 8 | Germany (4) |
| Jorg Heinrich | 33 | 17 | 12 | 1195 | 2 | 0 | - | Germany |
| De Deus Leandro | 26 | 9 | 0 | 57 | 0 | 0 | - | Brazil |
| Sunday Oliseh | 28 | 4 | 0 | 21 | 0 | 0 | - | Nigeria |
| Lars Ricken | 26 | 24 | 11 | 1339 | 3 | 0 | - | Germany |
| Tomas Rosicky | 22 | 30 | 27 | 2518 | 4 | 0 | 9 | Czech Republic (13) |
| Sahr Senesie | 18 | 0 | 0 | 0 | 0 | 0 | - | Sierra Leone |
| **Forwards** | | | | | | | | |
| Marcio Amoroso | 29 | 24 | 6 | 982 | 5 | 1 | 4 | Brazil (1) |
| Fredi Bobic | 31 | 1 | 0 | 0 | 0 | 0 | 7 | Germany (4) |
| Henrique Ewerthon | 22 | 34 | 22 | 2365 | 4 | 0 | - | Brazil |
| Heiko Herrlich | 31 | 12 | 0 | 28 | 1 | 0 | - | Germany |
| Jan Koller | 30 | 34 | 34 | 3016 | 4 | 0 | 9 | Czech Republic (13) |
| David Odonkor | 19 | 9 | 0 | 76 | 0 | 0 | - | Germany |
| Guiseppe Reina | 31 | 16 | 2 | 464 | 0 | 0 | - | Germany |

KEY: LEAGUE BOOKINGS CAPS (FIFA RANKING)

## SQUAD APPEARANCES

| Match | 1 | 2 | 3 | 4 | 5 | 6 | 7 | 8 | 9 | 10 | 11 | 12 | 13 | 14 | 15 | 16 | 17 | 18 | 19 | 20 | 21 | 22 | 23 | 24 | 25 | 26 | 27 | 28 | 29 | 30 | 31 | 32 | 33 | 34 | 35 | 36 | 37 | 38 | 39 | 40 | 41 | 42 | 43 | 44 | 45 | 46 |
|---|---|---|---|---|---|---|---|---|---|---|---|---|---|---|---|---|---|---|---|---|---|---|---|---|---|---|---|---|---|---|---|---|---|---|---|---|---|---|---|---|---|---|---|---|---|---|
| Venue | H | A | H | A | H | A | A | H | H | A | A | H | H | A | H | H | A | A | H | A | A | A | H | H | A | A | H | A | H | A | A | H | H | A | H | H | A | A | H | A | H | A | H | H | A | H |
| Competition | L | L | L | L | L | C | L | C | L | C | L | L | C | L | C | L | L | C | L | L | C | L | L | C | L | L | L | L | L | C | L | C | L | L | C | L | C | L | L | L | L | L | L | L | L | L |
| Result | D | D | W | D | D | L | W | W | W | W | W | D | D | W | W | D | L | L | W | L | W | W | W | L | W | L | W | L | W | L | D | D | W | L | W | W | W | D | L | D | W | D | D | W | D | D |

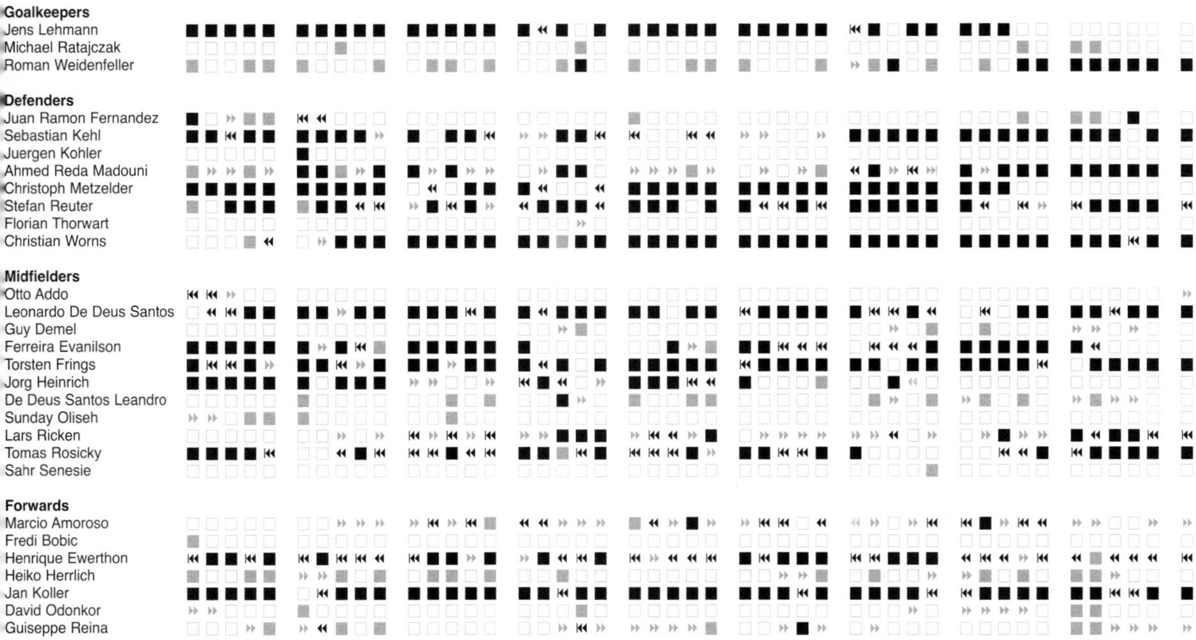
Goalkeepers
Jens Lehmann
Michael Ratajczak
Roman Weidenfeller
Defenders
Juan Ramon Fernandez
Sebastian Kehl
Juergen Kohler
Ahmed Reda Madouni
Christoph Metzelder
Stefan Reuter
Florian Thorwart
Christian Worns
Midfielders
Otto Addo
Leonardo De Deus Santos
Guy Demel
Ferreira Evanilson
Torsten Frings
Jorg Heinrich
De Deus Santos Leandro
Sunday Oliseh
Lars Ricken
Tomas Rosicky
Sahr Senesie
Forwards
Marcio Amoroso
Fredi Bobic
Henrique Ewerthon
Heiko Herrlich
Jan Koller
David Odonkor
Guiseppe Reina

KEY: ■ On all match ■ On bench ⏮ Subbed or sent off (Counting game) « Subbed or sent off (playing less than 70 minutes) ⏭ Subbed on from bench (Counting Game) » Subbed on (playing less than 70 minutes) Subbed on and then subbed or sent off (Counting Game) Subbed on and then subbed or sent off (playing less than 70 minutes) ☐ Not in 16

# HAMBURG

Final Position: **4th**

| | | | | | | |
|---|---|---|---|---|---|---|
| 1 | lge | Hannover 96 | H | W | 2-1 | Albertz 82 pen,85 |
| 2 | lge | W Bremen | A | L | 1-2 | Ujfalusi 20 |
| 3 | lge | Bayern Munich | H | L | 0-3 | |
| 4 | lge | Wolfsburg | A | L | 1-2 | Antar 71 |
| 5 | lge | Kaiserslautern | H | W | 2-0 | Romeo 66,77 |
| 6 | lge | Hertha Berlin | A | L | 0-2 | |
| 7 | lge | Stuttgart | H | W | 3-2 | Romeo 14,86; Barbarez 23 |
| 8 | lge | Schalke | A | L | 0-3 | |
| 9 | lge | B M'gladbach | H | W | 1-0 | Meijer 47 |
| 10 | lge | Arminia B | A | L | 1-2 | Meijer 66 |
| 11 | lge | B Dortmund | A | D | 1-1 | Christensen 89 |
| 12 | lge | 1860 Munich | H | W | 1-0 | Romeo 29 |
| 13 | lge | Nurnberg | A | W | 3-1 | Barbarez 26; Maltritz 51; Romeo 66 |
| 14 | lge | Cottbus | H | D | 1-1 | Cardoso 47 |
| 15 | lge | B Leverkusen | A | W | 3-2 | Romeo 3,52; Barbarez 77 |
| 16 | lge | Bochum | H | D | 1-1 | Barbarez 56 |
| 17 | lge | Hansa Rostock | A | D | 0-0 | |
| 18 | lge | Hannover 96 | A | D | 2-2 | Ujfalusi 63; Meijer 78 |
| 19 | lge | W Bremen | H | W | 1-0 | Barbarez 56 |
| 20 | lge | Bayern Munich | A | D | 1-1 | Takahara 90 |
| 21 | lge | Wolfsburg | H | W | 2-0 | Cardoso 39; Benjamin 90 |
| 22 | lge | Kaiserslautern | A | L | 0-2 | |
| 23 | lge | Hertha Berlin | H | W | 1-0 | Hoogma 55 |
| 24 | lge | Stuttgart | A | D | 1-1 | Mahdavikia 43 |
| 25 | lge | Schalke | H | W | 3-1 | Romeo 30,90; Takahara 87 |
| 26 | lge | B M'gladbach | A | L | 0-2 | |
| 27 | lge | Arminia B | H | W | 1-0 | Reinhardt 10 og |
| 28 | lge | B Dortmund | H | D | 1-1 | Romeo 67 |
| 29 | lge | 1860 Munich | A | D | 1-1 | Fukal 65 |
| 30 | lge | Nurnberg | H | W | 4-0 | Fukal 36; Romeo 44; Mahdavikia 55; Takahara 77 |
| 31 | lge | Cottbus | A | D | 0-0 | |
| 32 | lge | B Leverkusen | H | W | 4-1 | Barbarez 18; Romeo 56; Meijer 90; Jacobsen 90 |
| 33 | lge | Bochum | A | D | 1-1 | Rahn 82 |
| 34 | lge | Hansa Rostock | H | W | 2-0 | Cardoso 45; Romeo 53 |

## KEY PLAYERS - GOALSCORERS

**1 Bernado Romeo**

| | | | |
|---|---|---|---|
| Goals in the League | 14 | Player Strike Rate<br>Average number of minutes between League goals scored by player | 162 |
| Contribution to Attacking Power<br>Average number of minutes between League team goals while on pitch | 64 | Club Strike Rate<br>Average number of minutes between League goals scored by club | 67 |

| | PLAYER | LGE GOALS | POWER | STRIKE RATE |
|---|---|---|---|---|
| 2 | Sergei Barbarez | 6 | 60 | 341 mins |
| 3 | Mehdi Mahdavikia | 2 | 60 | 1153 mins |
| 4 | Milan Fukal | 2 | 62 | 1223 mins |
| 5 | Tomas Ujfalusi | 2 | 68 | 1376 mins |

## KEY PLAYERS - MIDFIELDERS

**1 Rodolfo Esteban Cardoso**

| | | | |
|---|---|---|---|
| Goals in the League | 3 | Contribution to Attacking Power<br>Average number of minutes between League team goals while on pitch | 76 |
| Defensive Rating<br>Average number of mins between League goals conceded while he was on the pitch | 144 | Scoring Difference<br>Defensive Rating minus Contribution to Attacking Power | 68 |

| | PLAYER | LGE GOALS | DEF RATE | POWER | SCORE DIFF |
|---|---|---|---|---|---|
| 2 | Naohiro Takahara | 3 | 110 | 68 | 42 mins |
| 3 | Sergei Barbarez | 6 | 85 | 60 | 25 mins |
| 4 | Bernd Hollerbach | 0 | 94 | 74 | 20 mins |
| 5 | Raul Ledesma | 0 | 77 | 61 | 16 mins |

## KEY PLAYERS - DEFENDERS

**1 Marcel Maltritz**

| | | | |
|---|---|---|---|
| Goals Conceded (GC)<br>The number of League goals conceded while he was on the pitch | 16 | Clean Sheets<br>In games when he played at least 70 minutes | 9 |
| Defensive Rating<br>Ave number of mins between League goals conceded while on the pitch | 123 | Club Defensive Rating<br>Average number of mins between League goals conceded by the club this season | 85 |

| | PLAYER | CON LGE | CLEAN SHEETS | DEF RATE |
|---|---|---|---|---|
| 2 | Milan Fukal | 25 | 10 | 98 mins |
| 3 | Tomas Ujfalusi | 32 | 10 | 86 mins |
| 4 | Nico Hoogma | 29 | 9 | 83 mins |
| 5 | Ingo Hertzsch | 19 | 3 | 66 mins |

## GOALS SCORED

**AT HOME**

| | | |
|---|---|---|
| MOST | B Munich | 37 |
| | | 30 |
| LEAST | Nurnberg | 16 |

**AWAY**

| | | |
|---|---|---|
| MOST | B Munich | 33 |
| | | 16 |
| LEAST | B M'gladbach &Arminia B | 12 |

## GOALS CONCEDED

**AT HOME**

| | | |
|---|---|---|
| LEAST | Hamburg & B M'gladbach | 11 |
| | | 11 |
| MOST | Hannover 96 | 33 |

**AWAY**

| | | |
|---|---|---|
| LEAST | B Munich | 13 |
| | | 25 |
| MOST | Nurnberg | 36 |

## KEY GOALKEEPER

**1 Martin Pieckenhagen**

| | |
|---|---|
| Goals Conceded in the League | 36 |
| Defensive Rating<br>Ave number of mins between League goals conceded while on the pitch | 85 |
| Counting Games<br>Games when he played at least 70 minutes | 34 |
| Clean Sheets<br>In games when he played at least 70 minutes | 11 |

## TOP POINT EARNERS

| | PLAYER | GAMES | AVE |
|---|---|---|---|
| 1 | Maltritz | 21 | 2.00 |
| 2 | Mahdavikia | 26 | 1.88 |
| 3 | Wicky | 13 | 1.85 |
| 4 | Barbarez | 23 | 1.74 |
| 5 | Fukal | 27 | 1.74 |
| 6 | Hollerbach | 20 | 1.65 |
| 7 | Romeo | 26 | 1.65 |
| 8 | Pieckenhagen | 34 | 1.65 |
| 9 | Hoogma | 27 | 1.63 |
| 10 | Ujfalusi | 30 | 1.63 |
| | CLUB AVERAGE: | | 1.65 |

Ave = Average points per match in Counting Games

## ATTENDANCES

HOME GROUND: AOL-ARENA CAPACITY: 55500 AVERAGE LEAGUE AT HOME: 44790

| | | | | | | | | |
|---|---|---|---|---|---|---|---|---|
| 11 | B Dortmund | 68000 | 5 | Kaiserslautern | 42000 | 2 | W Bremen | 31000 |
| 8 | Schalke | 60601 | 30 | Nurnberg | 41000 | 26 | B M'gladbach | 30000 |
| 34 | Hansa Rostock | 55500 | 6 | Hertha Berlin | 40000 | 21 | Wolfsburg | 30000 |
| 28 | B Dortmund | 55400 | 22 | Kaiserslautern | 39000 | 10 | Arminia B | 26500 |
| 3 | Bayern Munich | 55400 | 16 | Bochum | 38000 | 13 | Nurnberg | 26000 |
| 1 | Hannover 96 | 55000 | 7 | Stuttgart | 38000 | 15 | B Leverkusen | 22500 |
| 25 | Schalke | 55000 | 23 | Hertha Berlin | 37000 | 29 | 1860 Munich | 22000 |
| 32 | B Leverkusen | 52000 | 14 | Cottbus | 35000 | 17 | Hansa Rostock | 21400 |
| 9 | B M'gladbach | 49000 | 24 | Stuttgart | 35000 | 4 | Wolfsburg | 17546 |
| 27 | Arminia B | 46140 | 20 | Bayern Munich | 35000 | 31 | Cottbus | 15000 |
| 19 | W Bremen | 45000 | 33 | Bochum | 32645 | | | |
| 18 | Hannover 96 | 43183 | 12 | 1860 Munich | 32000 | | | |

Home / Away / Neutral

## DISCIPLINARY RECORDS

| | PLAYER | YELLOW | RED | AVE |
|---|---|---|---|---|
| 1 | Ledesma | 6 | 1 | 121 |
| 2 | Baur | 4 | 1 | 128 |
| 3 | Hollerbach | 13 | 0 | 159 |
| 4 | Barbarez | 9 | 2 | 186 |
| 5 | Meijer | 3 | 1 | 204 |
| 6 | Wicky | 4 | 0 | 374 |
| 7 | Benjamin | 4 | 0 | 375 |
| 8 | Ujfalusi | 6 | 1 | 393 |
| 9 | Maltritz | 5 | 0 | 394 |
| 10 | Fukal | 6 | 0 | 407 |
| 11 | Hertzsch | 3 | 0 | 420 |
| 12 | Cardoso | 3 | 0 | 480 |
| 13 | Jacobsen | 1 | 0 | 541 |
| | Other | 12 | 0 | |
| | TOTAL | 79 | 6 | |

## LEAGUE GOALS

| | PLAYER | MINS | GOALS | AVE |
|---|---|---|---|---|
| 1 | Romeo | 2263 | 14 | 162 |
| 2 | Barbarez | 2047 | 6 | 341 |
| 3 | Meijer | 816 | 4 | 204 |
| 4 | Cardoso | 1440 | 3 | 480 |
| 5 | Takahara | 878 | 3 | 293 |
| 6 | Mahdavikia | 2305 | 2 | 1153 |
| 7 | Ujfalusi | 2752 | 2 | 1376 |
| 8 | Albertz | 360 | 2 | 180 |
| 9 | Fukal | 2446 | 2 | 1223 |
| 10 | Maltritz | 1971 | 1 | 1971 |
| 11 | Hoogma | 2406 | 1 | 2406 |
| 12 | Antar | 267 | 1 | 267 |
| 13 | Jacobsen | 541 | 1 | 541 |
| | Other | | 4 | |
| | TOTAL | | 46 | |

## MONTH BY MONTH GUIDE TO THE POINTS

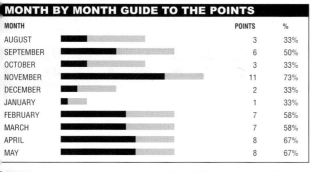

| MONTH | POINTS | % |
|---|---|---|
| AUGUST | 3 | 33% |
| SEPTEMBER | 6 | 50% |
| OCTOBER | 3 | 33% |
| NOVEMBER | 11 | 73% |
| DECEMBER | 2 | 33% |
| JANUARY | 1 | 33% |
| FEBRUARY | 7 | 58% |
| MARCH | 7 | 58% |
| APRIL | 8 | 67% |
| MAY | 8 | 67% |

## TEAM OF THE SEASON

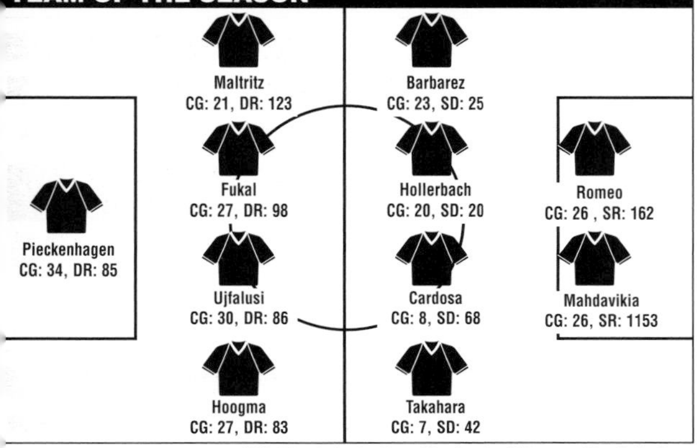
Maltritz
CG: 21, DR: 123
Barbarez
CG: 23, SD: 25
Fukal
CG: 27, DR: 98
Hollerbach
CG: 20, SD: 20
Romeo
CG: 26 , SR: 162
Pieckenhagen
CG: 34, DR: 85
Ujfalusi
CG: 30, DR: 86
Cardosa
CG: 8, SD: 68
Mahdavikia
CG: 26, SR: 1153
Hoogma
CG: 27, DR: 83
Takahara
CG: 7, SD: 42

KEY: DR = Defensive Rate, SD = Scoring Difference, SR = Strike Rate,
CG = Counting Games – League games playing at least 70 minutes

## LEAGUE APPEARANCES, BOOKINGS AND CAPS

| | AGE | IN THE SQUAD | COUNTING GAMES | MINUTES ON PITCH | YELLOW CARDS | RED CARDS | THIS SEASON | HOME COUNTRY |
|---|---|---|---|---|---|---|---|---|
| **Goalkeepers** | | | | | | | | |
| Martin Pieckenhagen | 31 | 34 | 34 | 3060 | 0 | 0 | - | Germany |
| Stefan Wachter | 25 | 12 | 0 | 0 | 0 | 0 | - | Germany |
| Carsten Wehlmann | 31 | 1 | 0 | 0 | 0 | 0 | - | Germany |
| **Defenders** | | | | | | | | |
| Michael Baur | 34 | 14 | 5 | 644 | 4 | 1 | - | Austria |
| Milan Fukal | 28 | 31 | 27 | 2446 | 6 | 0 | 2 | Czech Republic (13) |
| Ingo Hertzsch | 25 | 22 | 13 | 1262 | 3 | 0 | 2 | Germany (4) |
| Nico Hoogma | 34 | 27 | 27 | 2406 | 4 | 0 | - | Holland |
| Jacobsen | 23 | 19 | 4 | 541 | 1 | 0 | - | Denmark |
| Stephan Kling | 22 | 7 | 4 | 445 | 1 | 0 | - | Germany |
| Marcel Maltritz | 24 | 28 | 21 | 1971 | 5 | 0 | - | Germany |
| Tomas Ujfalusi | 25 | 31 | 30 | 2752 | 6 | 1 | 10 | Czech Republic (13) |
| **Midfielders** | | | | | | | | |
| Jorg Albertz | 32 | 5 | 4 | 360 | 0 | 0 | - | Germany |
| Roda Antar | 22 | 10 | 1 | 267 | 0 | 0 | - | Liberia |
| Sergei Barbarez | 31 | 24 | 23 | 2047 | 9 | 2 | - | Bosnia |
| Collin Benjamin | 24 | 23 | 16 | 1500 | 4 | 0 | - | Namibia |
| Rodolfo Cardoso | 34 | 22 | 8 | 1440 | 3 | 0 | - | Argentina |
| Martin Groth | 33 | 2 | 0 | 55 | 0 | 0 | - | Germany |
| Bernd Hollerbach | 33 | 26 | 20 | 2069 | 13 | 0 | - | Germany |
| Richard Kitzbichler | 29 | 14 | 1 | 227 | 1 | 0 | - | Austria |
| Raul Ledesma | 24 | 20 | 7 | 937 | 6 | 1 | - | Argentina |
| Christian Rahn | 24 | 15 | 3 | 419 | 1 | 0 | - | Germany |
| Naohiro Takahara | 24 | 16 | 7 | 878 | 1 | 0 | 4 | Japan (23) |
| Raphael Wicky | 26 | 27 | 13 | 1498 | 4 | 0 | - | Switzerland |
| **Forwards** | | | | | | | | |
| Kim Christensen | 23 | 13 | 2 | 289 | 0 | 0 | - | Denmark |
| Marek Heinz | 25 | 12 | 5 | 599 | 1 | 0 | - | Czech Republic |
| Mehdi Mahdavikia | 25 | 26 | 26 | 2305 | 0 | 0 | - | Iran |
| Erik Meijer | 33 | 23 | 6 | 816 | 3 | 1 | - | Holland |
| Bernardo Romeo | 25 | 26 | 26 | 2263 | 3 | 0 | 2 | Argentina (5) |

KEY: LEAGUE BOOKINGS CAPS (FIFA RANKING)

## SQUAD APPEARANCES

| Match | 1 | 2 | 3 | 4 | 5 | 6 | 7 | 8 | 9 | 10 | 11 | 12 | 13 | 14 | 15 | 16 | 17 | 18 | 19 | 20 | 21 | 22 | 23 | 24 | 25 | 26 | 27 | 28 | 29 | 30 | 31 | 32 | 33 | 34 |
|---|---|---|---|---|---|---|---|---|---|---|---|---|---|---|---|---|---|---|---|---|---|---|---|---|---|---|---|---|---|---|---|---|---|---|
| Venue | H | A | H | A | H | A | H | A | H | A | A | H | A | H | A | H | A | A | H | A | H | A | H | A | H | A | H | H | A | H | A | H | A | H |
| Competition | L | L | L | L | L | L | L | L | L | L | L | L | L | L | L | L | L | L | L | L | L | L | L | L | L | L | L | L | L | L | L | L | L | L |
| Result | W | L | L | L | W | L | W | L | W | L | D | W | W | D | W | D | D | D | W | D | W | L | W | D | W | L | W | D | D | W | D | W | D | W |

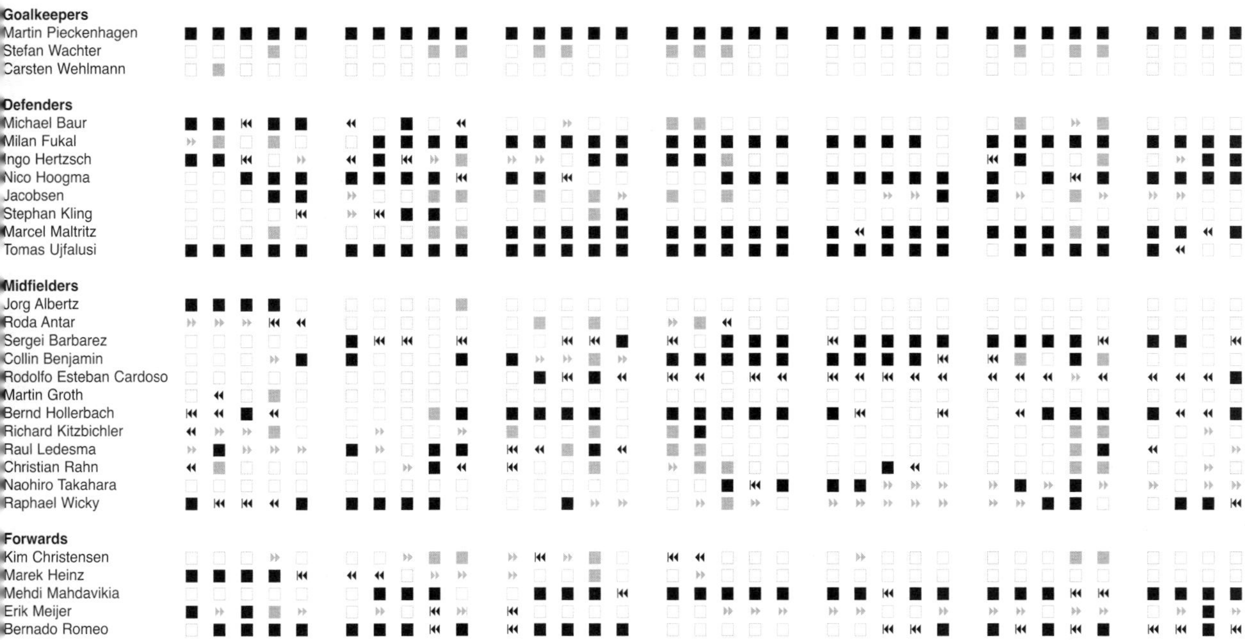
Goalkeepers
Martin Pieckenhagen
Stefan Wachter
Carsten Wehlmann
Defenders
Michael Baur
Milan Fukal
Ingo Hertzsch
Nico Hoogma
Jacobsen
Stephan Kling
Marcel Maltritz
Tomas Ujfalusi
Midfielders
Jorg Albertz
Roda Antar
Sergei Barbarez
Collin Benjamin
Rodolfo Esteban Cardoso
Martin Groth
Bernd Hollerbach
Richard Kitzbichler
Raul Ledesma
Christian Rahn
Naohiro Takahara
Raphael Wicky
Forwards
Kim Christensen
Marek Heinz
Mehdi Mahdavikia
Erik Meijer
Bernado Romeo

KEY: ■ On all match ■ On bench
⏮ Subbed or sent off (Counting game) ⏪ Subbed or sent off (playing less than 70 minutes)
⏭ Subbed on from bench (Counting Game) ⏩ Subbed on (playing less than 70 minutes)
Subbed on and then subbed or sent off (Counting Game) Subbed on and then subbed or sent off (playing less than 70 minutes)
□ Not in 16

# HERTHA BERLIN

Final Position: **5th**

| | | | | | | |
|---|---|---|---|---|---|---|
| 1 | lge | B Dortmund | A | D | 2-2 | Goor 1; Neuendorf 85 |
| 2 | lge | Stuttgart | H | D | 1-1 | Friedrich 85 |
| 3 | lge | Schalke | A | D | 0-0 | |
| 4 | lge | B M'gladbach | H | L | 1-2 | Preetz 80 |
| 5 | lge | Arminia B | A | W | 1-0 | Marcelinho 52 |
| 6 | uc1rl1 | Aberdeen | A | D | 0-0 | |
| 7 | lge | Hamburg | H | W | 2-0 | Marcelinho 51; Goor 53 |
| 8 | lge | 1860 Munich | A | L | 0-1 | |
| 9 | uc1rl2 | Aberdeen | H | W | 1-0 | Preetz 88 |
| 10 | lge | Nurnberg | H | W | 2-1 | Marcelinho 75,83 |
| 11 | lge | Cottbus | A | W | 2-0 | Marcelinho 22; Alves 44 |
| 12 | lge | B Leverkusen | H | D | 1-1 | Friedrich 20 |
| 13 | uc2rl1 | Apoel Nicosia | A | W | 1-0 | Karwan 90 |
| 14 | lge | Bochum | A | L | 0-3 | |
| 15 | uc2rl2 | Apoel Nicosia | H | W | 4-0 | Preetz 8; Marcelinho 13; Beinlich 62; Luizao 67 |
| 16 | lge | Hansa Rostock | H | W | 3-1 | Goor 8; Alves 10; Friedrich 58 |
| 17 | lge | Hannover 96 | A | W | 1-0 | Goor 17 |
| 18 | lge | W Bremen | H | L | 0-1 | |
| 19 | uc3rl1 | Fulham | H | W | 2-1 | Beinlich 28; Sava 68 og |
| 20 | lge | Bayern Munich | A | L | 0-2 | |
| 21 | lge | Wolfsburg | H | D | 2-2 | Simunic 25; Goor 47 |
| 22 | uc3rl2 | Fulham | A | D | 0-0 | |
| 23 | lge | Kaiserslautern | A | L | 1-2 | Dardai 64 |
| 24 | lge | B Dortmund | H | W | 2-1 | Dardai 69; Marcelinho 90 |
| 25 | lge | Stuttgart | A | L | 1-3 | Marcelinho 81 |
| 26 | lge | Schalke | H | W | 4-2 | Preetz 28; Alves 39; Simunic 51; Marcelinho 88 |
| 27 | lge | B M'gladbach | A | W | 2-0 | Alves 9,14 |
| 28 | uc4rl1 | Boavista | H | W | 3-2 | Alves 15,42; Van Burik 90 |
| 29 | lge | Arminia B | H | D | 0-0 | |
| 30 | uc4rl2 | Boavista | A | L | 0-1 | |
| 31 | lge | Hamburg | A | L | 0-1 | |
| 32 | lge | 1860 Munich | H | W | 6-0 | Marcelinho 7 pen,35; Preetz 26,55; Luizao 62 pen; Jentzsch 79 og |
| 33 | lge | Nurnberg | A | W | 3-0 | Preetz 15; Marx 40; Marcelinho 85 |
| 34 | lge | Cottbus | H | W | 3-1 | Dardai 72; Alves 85; Preetz 86 |
| 35 | lge | B Leverkusen | A | L | 1-4 | Preetz 76 |
| 36 | lge | Bochum | H | W | 1-0 | Dardai 63 |
| 37 | lge | Hansa Rostock | A | W | 1-0 | Friedrich 50 |
| 38 | lge | Hannover 96 | H | W | 2-0 | Luizao 10; Marcelinho 44 pen |
| 39 | lge | W Bremen | A | L | 2-4 | Friedrich 21; Marx 80 |
| 40 | lge | Bayern Munich | H | L | 3-6 | Ballack 5 og; Marcelinho 60 pen,89 |
| 41 | lge | Wolfsburg | A | L | 0-2 | |
| 42 | lge | Kaiserslautern | H | W | 2-0 | Rafael 45,84 |

## KEY PLAYERS - GOALSCORERS

**1 Marcelo dos Santos Marcelinho**

| | | | |
|---|---|---|---|
| Goals in the League | 14 | Player Strike Rate: Average number of minutes between League goals scored by player | 210 |
| Contribution to Attacking Power: Average number of minutes between League team goals while on pitch | 61 | Club Strike Rate: Average number of minutes between League goals scored by club | 59 |

| | PLAYER | LGE GOALS | POWER | STRIKE RATE |
|---|---|---|---|---|
| 2 | Alex Alves | 6 | 54 | 227 mins |
| 3 | Michael Preetz | 6 | 56 | 328 mins |
| 4 | Bart Goor | 5 | 62 | 512 mins |
| 5 | Pal Dardai | 4 | 56 | 555 mins |

## KEY PLAYERS - MIDFIELDERS

**1 Michael Hartmann**

| | | | |
|---|---|---|---|
| Goals in the League | 0 | Contribution to Attacking Power: Average number of minutes between League team goals while on pitch | 56 |
| Defensive Rating: Average number of mins between League goals conceded while he was on the pitch | 79 | Scoring Difference: Defensive Rating minus Contribution to Attacking Power | 23 |

| | PLAYER | LGE GOALS | DEF RATE | POWER | SCORE DIFF |
|---|---|---|---|---|---|
| 2 | Bart Goor | 5 | 78 | 62 | 16 mins |
| 3 | Thorben Marx | 2 | 68 | 53 | 15 mins |
| 4 | Pal Dardai | 4 | 65 | 57 | 8 mins |
| 5 | Andreas Schmidt | 0 | 74 | 74 | 0 mins |

## KEY PLAYERS - DEFENDERS

**1 Dick Van Burik**

| | | | |
|---|---|---|---|
| Goals Conceded (GC): The number of League goals conceded while he was on the pitch | 10 | Clean Sheets: In games when he played at least 70 minutes | 6 |
| Defensive Rating: Ave number of mins between League goals conceded while on the pitch | 122 | Club Defensive Rating: Average number of mins between League goals conceded by the club this season | 71 |

| | PLAYER | CON LGE | CLEAN SHEETS | DEF RATE |
|---|---|---|---|---|
| 2 | Arne Friedrich | 42 | 12 | 69 mins |
| 3 | Josip Simunic | 31 | 8 | 62 mins |
| 4 | Marko Rehmer | 27 | 4 | 59 mins |

## GOALS SCORED

**AT HOME**

| | | |
|---|---|---|
| MOST | B Munich | 37 |
| | | 35 |
| LEAST | Nurnberg | 16 |

**AWAY**

| | | |
|---|---|---|
| MOST | B Munich | 33 |
| | | 17 |
| LEAST | B M'gladbach &Arminia B | 12 |

## GOALS CONCEDED

**AT HOME**

| | | |
|---|---|---|
| LEAST | Hamburg & B M'gladbach | 11 |
| | | 19 |
| MOST | Hannover 96 | 33 |

**AWAY**

| | | |
|---|---|---|
| LEAST | B Munich | 13 |
| | | 24 |
| MOST | Nurnberg | 36 |

## KEY GOALKEEPER

**1 Gabor Kiraly**

| | |
|---|---|
| Goals Conceded in the League | 42 |
| Defensive Rating: Ave number of mins between League goals conceded while on the pitch | 71 |
| Counting Games: Games when he played at least 70 minutes | 33 |
| Clean Sheets: In games when he played at least 70 minutes | 13 |

## TOP POINT EARNERS

| | PLAYER | GAMES | AVE |
|---|---|---|---|
| 1 | Hartmann | 26 | 1.96 |
| 2 | Alves | 14 | 1.93 |
| 3 | Goor | 26 | 1.69 |
| 4 | Dardai | 22 | 1.68 |
| 5 | Marx | 21 | 1.67 |
| 6 | Rehmer | 14 | 1.64 |
| 7 | Preetz | 19 | 1.63 |
| 8 | Friedrich | 32 | 1.59 |
| 9 | Kiraly | 33 | 1.55 |
| 10 | Marcelinho | 33 | 1.55 |
| | CLUB AVERAGE: | | 1.59 |

Ave = Average points per match in Counting Games

## ATTENDANCES

HOME GROUND: OLYMPIASTADION CAPACITY: 76243 AVERAGE LEAGUE AT HOME: 39183

| | | | | | | | | |
|---|---|---|---|---|---|---|---|---|
| 1 | B Dortmund | 65800 | 31 | Hamburg | 37000 | 35 | B Leverkusen | 22500 |
| 3 | Schalke | 60500 | 39 | W Bremen | 36000 | 14 | Bochum | 22009 |
| 40 | Bayern Munich | 59200 | 4 | B M'gladbach | 35000 | 37 | Hansa Rostock | 22000 |
| 24 | B Dortmund | 50547 | 23 | Kaiserslautern | 33000 | 5 | Arminia B | 20000 |
| 42 | Kaiserslautern | 50000 | 25 | Stuttgart | 32000 | 28 | Boavista | 18000 |
| 2 | Stuttgart | 49202 | 9 | Aberdeen | 30770 | 22 | Fulham | 15161 |
| 38 | Hannover 96 | 45031 | 32 | 1860 Munich | 30000 | 19 | Fulham | 14477 |
| 12 | B Leverkusen | 43146 | 10 | Nurnberg | 30000 | 11 | Cottbus | 13000 |
| 7 | Hamburg | 40000 | 21 | Wolfsburg | 28000 | 6 | Aberdeen | 10180 |
| 34 | Cottbus | 40000 | 27 | B M'gladbach | 26000 | 15 | Apoel Nicosia | 10083 |
| 18 | W Bremen | 40000 | 36 | Bochum | 25000 | 13 | Apoel Nicosia | 10000 |
| 20 | Bayern Munich | 40000 | 29 | Arminia B | 25000 | 30 | Boavista | 5500 |
| 17 | Hannover 96 | 38795 | 8 | 1860 Munich | 25000 | | | |
| 16 | Hansa Rostock | 38000 | 41 | Wolfsburg | 25000 | | | |
| 26 | Schalke | 38000 | 33 | Nurnberg | 23000 | | | |

■ Home □ Away ▒ Neutral

## DISCIPLINARY RECORDS

| | PLAYER | YELLOW | RED | AVE |
|---|---|---|---|---|
| 1 | Neuendorf | 4 | 0 | 167 |
| 2 | Madlung | 2 | 0 | 227 |
| 3 | Van Burik | 4 | 1 | 243 |
| 4 | Marx | 6 | 0 | 329 |
| 5 | Beinlich | 4 | 0 | 346 |
| 6 | Marcelinho | 8 | 0 | 367 |
| 7 | Nene | 2 | 0 | 390 |
| 8 | Hartmann | 6 | 0 | 419 |
| 9 | Dardai | 5 | 0 | 444 |
| 10 | Pinto | 1 | 0 | 477 |
| 11 | Karwan | 1 | 0 | 552 |
| 12 | Simunic | 3 | 0 | 638 |
| 13 | Rehmer | 2 | 0 | 798 |
| | Other | 11 | 0 | |
| | TOTAL | 59 | 1 | |

## LEAGUE GOALS

| | PLAYER | MINS | GOALS | AVE |
|---|---|---|---|---|
| 1 | Marcelinho | 2939 | 14 | 210 |
| 2 | Preetz | 1970 | 6 | 328 |
| 3 | Alves | 1359 | 6 | 227 |
| 4 | Friedrich | 2894 | 5 | 579 |
| 5 | Goor | 2560 | 5 | 512 |
| 6 | Dardai | 2221 | 4 | 555 |
| 7 | Luizao | 1204 | 2 | 602 |
| 8 | Rafael | 239 | 2 | 120 |
| 9 | Marx | 1976 | 2 | 988 |
| 10 | Simunic | 1916 | 2 | 958 |
| 11 | Neuendorf | 668 | 1 | 668 |
| | Other | | 3 | |
| | TOTAL | | 52 | |

## MONTH BY MONTH GUIDE TO THE POINTS

| | | |
|---|---|---|
| AUGUST | 3 | 33% |
| SEPTEMBER | 6 | 50% |
| OCTOBER | 7 | 78% |
| NOVEMBER | 6 | 40% |
| DECEMBER | 1 | 17% |
| JANUARY | 3 | 100% |
| FEBRUARY | 7 | 58% |
| MARCH | 9 | 75% |
| APRIL | 9 | 75% |
| MAY | 3 | 25% |

## TEAM OF THE SEASON

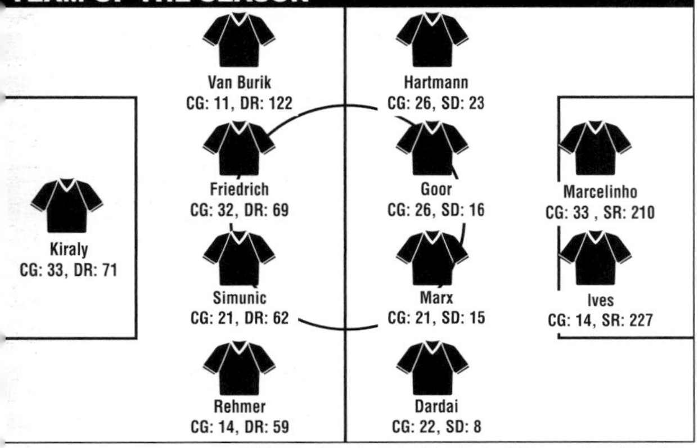
Van Burik
CG: 11, DR: 122
Hartmann
CG: 26, SD: 23
Friedrich
CG: 32, DR: 69
Goor
CG: 26, SD: 16
Marcelinho
CG: 33 , SR: 210
Kiraly
CG: 33, DR: 71
Simunic
CG: 21, DR: 62
Marx
CG: 21, SD: 15
Ives
CG: 14, SR: 227
Rehmer
CG: 14, DR: 59
Dardai
CG: 22, SD: 8

KEY: DR = Defensive Rate, SD = Scoring Difference, SR = Strike Rate, CG = Counting Games – League games playing at least 70 minutes

## LEAGUE APPEARANCES, BOOKINGS AND CAPS

| | AGE | IN THE SQUAD | COUNTING GAMES | MINUTES ON PITCH | YELLOW CARDS | RED CARDS | THIS SEASON | HOME COUNTRY |
|---|---|---|---|---|---|---|---|---|
| **Goalkeepers** | | | | | | | | |
| Christian Fiedler | 28 | 17 | 1 | 90 | 0 | 0 | - | Germany |
| Gabor Kiraly | 27 | 33 | 33 | 2970 | 3 | 0 | - | Hungary |
| Tomasz Kuszczak | 21 | 1 | 0 | 0 | 0 | 0 | - | Poland |
| **Defenders** | | | | | | | | |
| Arne Friedrich | 24 | 33 | 32 | 2894 | 2 | 0 | 10 | Germany (4) |
| Kostas Konstantinidis | 30 | 3 | 0 | 13 | 0 | 0 | - | Greece |
| Denis Lapaczinski | 21 | 6 | 0 | 101 | 0 | 0 | - | Germany |
| Alexander Madlung | 20 | 10 | 3 | 454 | 2 | 0 | - | Germany |
| Nene28 | 13 | 8 | 781 | 2 | 0 | - | Brazil | |
| Marko Rehmer | 31 | 21 | 14 | 1597 | 2 | 0 | 6 | Germany (4) |
| Josip Simunic | 25 | 22 | 21 | 1916 | 3 | 0 | - | Australia |
| Eyolfur Sverrisson | 34 | 11 | 2 | 261 | 1 | 0 | - | Iceland |
| Dick Van Burik | 29 | 18 | 11 | 1218 | 4 | 1 | - | Holland |
| **Midfielders** | | | | | | | | |
| Stefan Beinlich | 31 | 26 | 12 | 1387 | 4 | 0 | - | Germany |
| Pal Dardai | 27 | 31 | 22 | 2221 | 5 | 0 | - | Hungary |
| Bart Goor | 30 | 34 | 26 | 2560 | 3 | 0 | 9 | Belgium (16) |
| Michael Hartmann | 28 | 31 | 26 | 2518 | 6 | 0 | 3 | Germany (4) |
| Bartosz Karwan | 27 | 23 | 3 | 552 | 1 | 0 | 3 | Poland (29) |
| Rob Maas | 33 | 6 | 0 | 21 | 0 | 0 | - | Holland |
| Thorben Marx | 22 | 26 | 21 | 1976 | 6 | 0 | - | Germany |
| Alexander Mladenov | 21 | 3 | 0 | 30 | 0 | 0 | - | Bulgaria |
| Andreas Neuendorf | 28 | 14 | 4 | 668 | 4 | 0 | - | Germany |
| Roberto Pinto | 24 | 18 | 2 | 477 | 1 | 0 | - | Portugal |
| Andreas Schmidt | 29 | 19 | 10 | 1041 | 1 | 0 | - | Germany |
| Rene Tretschok | 34 | 9 | 1 | 154 | 0 | 0 | - | Germany |
| **Forwards** | | | | | | | | |
| Alex Alves | 28 | 24 | 14 | 1359 | 0 | 0 | - | Brazil |
| Luiz Carlos Goulart | 27 | 24 | 10 | 1204 | 1 | 0 | - | Brazil |
| Marcelo Marcelinho | 28 | 33 | 33 | 2939 | 8 | 0 | - | Brazil |
| Michael Preetz | 35 | 31 | 19 | 1970 | 0 | 0 | - | Germany |
| Nando Rafael | 19 | 7 | 2 | 239 | 0 | 0 | - | Angola |

KEY: LEAGUE BOOKINGS CAPS (FIFA RANKING)

## SQUAD APPEARANCES

| Match | 1 | 2 | 3 | 4 | 5 | 6 | 7 | 8 | 9 | 10 | 11 | 12 | 13 | 14 | 15 | 16 | 17 | 18 | 19 | 20 | 21 | 22 | 23 | 24 | 25 | 26 | 27 | 28 | 29 | 30 | 31 | 32 | 33 | 34 | 35 | 36 | 37 | 38 | 39 | 40 | 41 | 42 |
|---|---|---|---|---|---|---|---|---|---|---|---|---|---|---|---|---|---|---|---|---|---|---|---|---|---|---|---|---|---|---|---|---|---|---|---|---|---|---|---|---|---|---|
| Venue | A | H | A | H | A | A | H | A | H | H | A | H | A | A | H | H | A | H | H | A | H | A | A | H | A | H | A | H | H | A | A | H | A | H | A | H | A | H | A | H | A | H |
| Competition | L | L | L | L | L | E | L | L | E | L | L | L | E | L | E | L | L | L | E | L | L | E | L | L | L | L | L | E | L | E | L | L | L | L | L | L | L | L | L | L | L | L |
| Result | D | D | D | L | W | D | W | L | W | W | W | D | W | L | W | W | W | L | W | L | D | D | L | W | L | W | W | W | D | L | L | W | W | W | L | W | W | W | L | L | L | W |

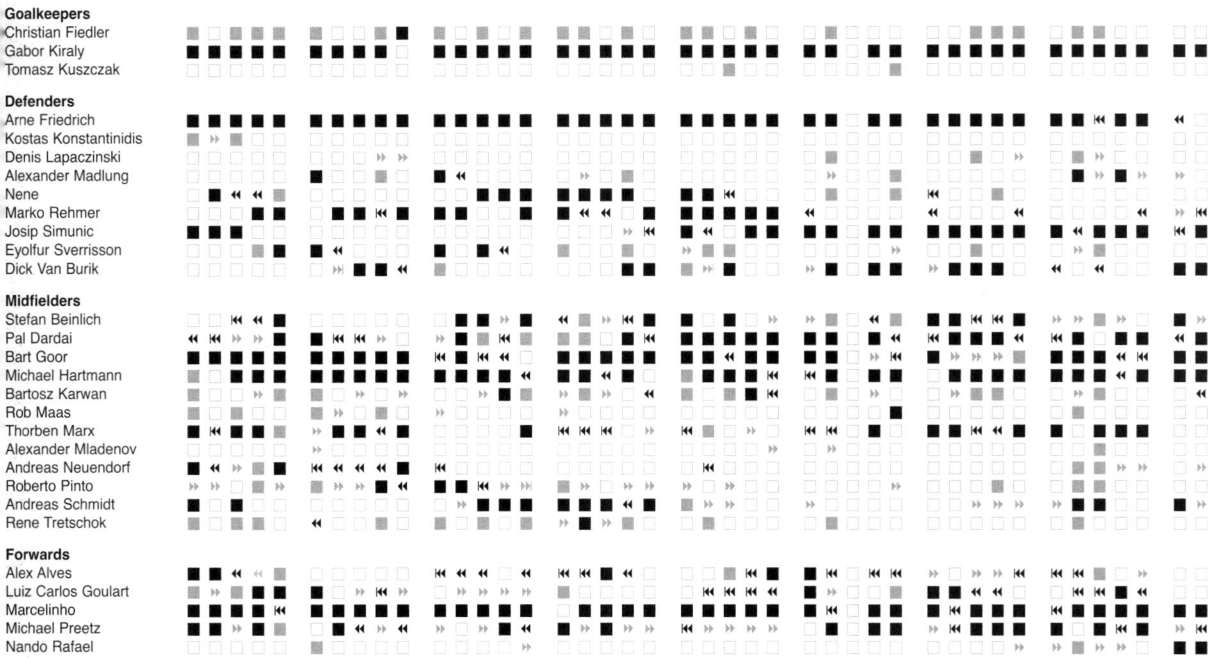
Goalkeepers
Christian Fiedler
Gabor Kiraly
Tomasz Kuszczak
Defenders
Arne Friedrich
Kostas Konstantinidis
Denis Lapaczinski
Alexander Madlung
Nene
Marko Rehmer
Josip Simunic
Eyolfur Sverrisson
Dick Van Burik
Midfielders
Stefan Beinlich
Pal Dardai
Bart Goor
Michael Hartmann
Bartosz Karwan
Rob Maas
Thorben Marx
Alexander Mladenov
Andreas Neuendorf
Roberto Pinto
Andreas Schmidt
Rene Tretschok
Forwards
Alex Alves
Luiz Carlos Goulart
Marcelinho
Michael Preetz
Nando Rafael

# WERDER BREMEN

Final Position: **6th**

| | | | | | | |
|---|---|---|---|---|---|---|
| 1 | lge | Arminia B | A | L | 0-3 | |
| 2 | lge | Hamburg | H | W | 2-1 | Charisteas 9; Wehlage 50 |
| 3 | lge | 1860 Munich | A | L | 0-3 | |
| 4 | lge | Nurnberg | H | W | 4-1 | Ailton 30 pen,65,78; Micoud 59 |
| 5 | lge | Cottbus | A | W | 1-0 | Piplica 51 og |
| 6 | uc1rl1 | Metalurgs | A | D | 2-2 | Lisztes 10; Verlaat 12 |
| 7 | lge | B Leverkusen | H | W | 3-2 | Ailton 26 pen; Charisteas 27,31 |
| 8 | lge | Bochum | A | W | 4-1 | Ailton 16,49; Charisteas 36; Krstajic 87 |
| 9 | uc1rl2 | Metalurgs | H | W | 8-0 | Verlaat 14; Micoud 43,47; Borowski 45,79; Charisteas 51; Klasnic 66,90 |
| 10 | lge | Hansa Rostock | H | D | 0-0 | |
| 11 | lge | Hannover 96 | A | D | 4-4 | Verlaat 10; Ailton 52; Charisteas 60; Micoud 67 |
| 12 | lge | B Dortmund | H | L | 1-4 | Ernst 35 |
| 13 | uc2rl1 | Vitesse Arnhem | A | L | 1-2 | Verlaat 43 |
| 14 | lge | Bayern Munich | H | W | 2-0 | Daun 17; Krstajic 80 |
| 15 | lge | Wolfsburg | A | L | 1-3 | Micoud 70 |
| 16 | uc2rl2 | Vitesse Arnhem | H | D | 3-3 | Baumann 25; Krstajic 49; Charisteas 77 |
| 17 | lge | Kaiserslautern | H | W | 5-3 | Verlaat 14; Klose, M 61 og; Ailton 77,88; Klasnic 90 |
| 18 | lge | Hertha Berlin | A | W | 1-0 | Ailton 10 |
| 19 | lge | Stuttgart | H | W | 3-1 | Ailton 27,89 pen; Krstajic 80 |
| 20 | lge | Schalke | A | D | 1-1 | Daun 3 |
| 21 | lge | B M'gladbach | H | W | 2-0 | Daun 14; Ailton 58 |
| 22 | lge | Arminia B | H | D | 2-2 | Skrypnyk 3; Ailton 36 pen |
| 23 | lge | Hamburg | A | L | 0-1 | |
| 24 | lge | 1860 Munich | H | L | 1-2 | Klasnic 45 |
| 25 | lge | Nurnberg | A | L | 0-1 | |
| 26 | lge | Cottbus | H | L | 0-1 | |
| 27 | lge | B Leverkusen | A | L | 0-3 | |
| 28 | lge | Bochum | H | W | 2-0 | Ailton 52; Banovic 56 |
| 29 | lge | Hansa Rostock | A | L | 0-1 | |
| 30 | lge | Hannover 96 | H | L | 1-2 | Ailton 10 |
| 31 | lge | B Dortmund | A | W | 2-1 | Charisteas 54; Ernst 86 |
| 32 | lge | Bayern Munich | A | W | 1-0 | Micoud 13 |
| 33 | lge | Wolfsburg | H | L | 0-1 | |
| 34 | lge | Kaiserslautern | A | L | 0-1 | |
| 35 | lge | Hertha Berlin | H | W | 4-2 | Krstajic 23; Magnin 27; Charisteas 36,77 |
| 36 | lge | Stuttgart | A | W | 1-0 | Marques 51 og |
| 37 | lge | Schalke | H | W | 2-1 | Charisteas 23; Micoud 57 |
| 38 | lge | B M'gladbach | A | L | 1-4 | Korzynietz 84 og |

## KEY PLAYERS - GOALSCORERS

**1 Da Silva Gonclaves Ailton**

| | | | |
|---|---|---|---|
| Goals in the League | 16 | Player Strike Rate<br>Average number of minutes between League goals scored by player | 147 |
| Contribution to Attacking Power<br>Average number of minutes between League team goals while on pitch | 57 | Club Strike Rate<br>Average number of minutes between League goals scored by club | 60 |

| | PLAYER | LGE GOALS | POWER | STRIKE RATE |
|---|---|---|---|---|
| 2 | Angelos Charisteas | 9 | 68 | 252 mins |
| 3 | Markus Daun | 3 | 61 | 451 mins |
| 4 | Johan Micoud | 5 | 56 | 489 mins |
| 5 | Mladen Krstajic | 4 | 55 | 681 mins |

## KEY PLAYERS - MIDFIELDERS

**1 Ludovic Magnin**

| | | | |
|---|---|---|---|
| Goals in the League | 1 | Contribution to Attacking Power<br>Average number of minutes between League team goals while on pitch | 51 |
| Defensive Rating<br>Average number of mins between League goals conceded while he was on the pitch | 80 | Scoring Difference<br>Defensive Rating minus Contribution to Attacking Power | 29 |

| | PLAYER | LGE GOALS | DEF RATE | POWER | SCORE DIFF |
|---|---|---|---|---|---|
| 2 | Krisztian Lisztes | 0 | 70 | 62 | 8 mins |
| 3 | Johan Micoud | 5 | 64 | 57 | 7 mins |
| 4 | Paul Stalteri | 0 | 62 | 57 | 5 mins |
| 5 | Fabian Ernst | 2 | 62 | 58 | 4 mins |

## KEY PLAYERS - DEFENDERS

**1 Mladen Krstajic**

| | | | |
|---|---|---|---|
| Goals Conceded (GC)<br>The number of League goals conceded while he was on the pitch | 42 | Clean Sheets<br>In games when he played at least 70 minutes | 8 |
| Defensive Rating<br>Ave number of mins between League goals conceded while on the pitch | 65 | Club Defensive Rating<br>Average number of mins between League goals conceded by the club this season | 61 |

| | PLAYER | CON LGE | CLEAN SHEETS | DEF RATE |
|---|---|---|---|---|
| 2 | Frank Verlaat | 39 | 6 | 63 mins |
| 3 | Frank Baumann | 35 | 7 | 61 mins |
| 4 | Victor Skrypnyk | 33 | 4 | 58 mins |

## GOALS SCORED

**AT HOME**

| | | |
|---|---|---|
| MOST | B Munich | 37 |
| | | 34 |
| LEAST | Nurnberg | 16 |

**AWAY**

| | | |
|---|---|---|
| MOST | B Munich | 33 |
| | | 17 |
| LEAST | B M'gladbach &Arminia B | 12 |

## GOALS CONCEDED

**AT HOME**

| | | |
|---|---|---|
| LEAST | Hamburg & B M'gladbach | 11 |
| | | 23 |
| MOST | Hannover 96 | 33 |

**AWAY**

| | | |
|---|---|---|
| LEAST | B Munich | 13 |
| | | 27 |
| MOST | Nurnberg | 36 |

## KEY GOALKEEPER

**1 Pascal Borel**

| | |
|---|---|
| Goals Conceded in the League | 45 |
| Defensive Rating<br>Ave number of mins between League goals conceded while on the pitch | 62 |
| Counting Games<br>Games when he played at least 70 minutes | 31 |
| Clean Sheets<br>In games when he played at least 70 minutes | 8 |

## TOP POINT EARNERS

| | PLAYER | GAMES | AVE |
|---|---|---|---|
| 1 | Lisztes | 22 | 1.77 |
| 2 | Daun | 13 | 1.77 |
| 3 | Baumann | 23 | 1.74 |
| 4 | Krstajic | 30 | 1.70 |
| 5 | Borel | 31 | 1.68 |
| 6 | Ailton | 24 | 1.67 |
| 7 | Micoud | 26 | 1.65 |
| 8 | Stalteri | 32 | 1.63 |
| 9 | Verlaat | 26 | 1.54 |
| 10 | Ernst | 30 | 1.53 |
| | CLUB AVERAGE: | | 1.53 |

Ave = Average points per match in Counting Games

## ATTENDANCES

HOME GROUND: WESERSTADION CAPACITY: 40200 AVERAGE LEAGUE AT HOME: 32517

| | | | | | | | | |
|---|---|---|---|---|---|---|---|---|
| 31 | B Dortmund | 68500 | 38 | B M'gladbach | 34500 | 27 | B Leverkusen | 22500 |
| 32 | Bayern Munich | 63000 | 24 | 1860 Munich | 34000 | 8 | Bochum | 22000 |
| 20 | Schalke | 60600 | 33 | Wolfsburg | 33300 | 3 | 1860 Munich | 21000 |
| 36 | Stuttgart | 54267 | 10 | Hansa Rostock | 32300 | 13 | Vitesse Arnhem | 20000 |
| 23 | Hamburg | 45000 | 21 | B M'gladbach | 32188 | 16 | Vitesse Arnhem | 20000 |
| 11 | Hannover 96 | 45000 | 26 | Cottbus | 32000 | 25 | Nurnberg | 20000 |
| 12 | B Dortmund | 40200 | 7 | B Leverkusen | 32000 | 1 | Arminia B | 20000 |
| 14 | Bayern Munich | 40200 | 2 | Hamburg | 31000 | 6 | Metalurgs | 18000 |
| 18 | Hertha Berlin | 40000 | 22 | Arminia B | 29604 | 9 | Metalurgs | 18000 |
| 34 | Kaiserslautern | 40000 | 19 | Stuttgart | 28000 | 29 | Hansa Rostock | 16000 |
| 37 | Schalke | 39000 | 4 | Nurnberg | 27000 | 15 | Wolfsburg | 16000 |
| 30 | Hannover 96 | 36000 | 28 | Bochum | 26000 | 5 | Cottbus | 15000 |
| 35 | Hertha Berlin | 36000 | 17 | Kaiserslautern | 24000 | | | |

■ Home □ Away ▨ Neutral

## DISCIPLINARY RECORDS

| | PLAYER | YELLOW | RED | AVE |
|---|---|---|---|---|
| 1 | Tjikuzu | 3 | 1 | 130 |
| 2 | Banovic | 5 | 0 | 198 |
| 3 | Barten | 3 | 0 | 202 |
| 4 | Micoud | 8 | 2 | 244 |
| 5 | Ernst | 9 | 1 | 273 |
| 6 | Krstajic | 9 | 0 | 302 |
| 7 | Baumann | 6 | 0 | 357 |
| 8 | Lisztes | 5 | 1 | 363 |
| 9 | Skrypnyk | 5 | 0 | 384 |
| 10 | Verlaat | 5 | 1 | 411 |
| 11 | Stalteri | 7 | 0 | 418 |
| 12 | Daun | 2 | 1 | 451 |
| 13 | Ailton | 5 | 0 | 470 |
| | Other | 4 | 1 | |
| | TOTAL | 76 | 8 | |

## LEAGUE GOALS

| | PLAYER | MINS | GOALS | AVE |
|---|---|---|---|---|
| 1 | Ailton | 2352 | 16 | 147 |
| 2 | Charisteas | 2264 | 9 | 252 |
| 3 | Micoud | 2445 | 5 | 489 |
| 4 | Krstajic | 2724 | 4 | 681 |
| 5 | Daun | 1353 | 3 | 451 |
| 6 | Ernst | 2738 | 2 | 1369 |
| 7 | Klasnic | 270 | 2 | 135 |
| 8 | Verlaat | 2466 | 2 | 1233 |
| 9 | Banovic | 992 | 1 | 992 |
| 10 | Wehlage | 98 | 1 | 98 |
| 11 | Magnin | 719 | 1 | 719 |
| 12 | Skrypnyk | 1923 | 1 | 1923 |
| | Other | | 4 | |
| | TOTAL | | 51 | |

## MONTH BY MONTH GUIDE TO THE POINTS

| Month | Points | % |
|---|---|---|
| AUGUST | 3 | 33% |
| SEPTEMBER | 12 | 100% |
| OCTOBER | 2 | 22% |
| NOVEMBER | 9 | 75% |
| DECEMBER | 7 | 78% |
| JANUARY | 1 | 33% |
| FEBRUARY | 0 | 0% |
| MARCH | 3 | 25% |
| APRIL | 6 | 50% |
| MAY | 9 | 75% |

## TEAM OF THE SEASON

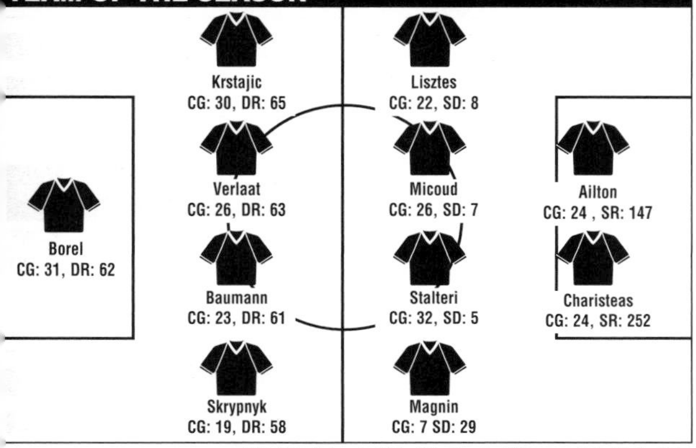

Krstajic
CG: 30, DR: 65
Lisztes
CG: 22, SD: 8
Verlaat
CG: 26, DR: 63
Micoud
CG: 26, SD: 7
Ailton
CG: 24 , SR: 147
Borel
CG: 31, DR: 62
Baumann
CG: 23, DR: 61
Stalteri
CG: 32, SD: 5
Charisteas
CG: 24, SR: 252
Skrypnyk
CG: 19, DR: 58
Magnin
CG: 7 SD: 29


KEY: DR = Defensive Rate, SD = Scoring Difference, SR = Strike Rate,
CG = Counting Games – League games playing at least 70 minutes

## LEAGUE APPEARANCES, BOOKINGS AND CAPS

| | AGE | IN THE SQUAD | COUNTING GAMES | MINUTES ON PITCH | YELLOW CARDS | RED CARDS | THIS SEASON | HOME COUNTRY |
|---|---|---|---|---|---|---|---|---|
| **Goalkeepers** | | | | | | | | |
| Pascal Borel | 23 | 31 | 31 | 2790 | 0 | 0 | - | Germany |
| Michael Jurgen | | 1 | 0 | 0 | 0 | 0 | - | Germany |
| Jacub Wierzchowski | 26 | 12 | 3 | 270 | 0 | 0 | - | Poland |
| **Defenders** | | | | | | | | |
| Mike Barten | 29 | 7 | 6 | 606 | 3 | 0 | - | Germany |
| Frank Baumann | 27 | 25 | 23 | 2142 | 6 | 0 | 5 | Germany (4) |
| Stefan Blank | 26 | 1 | 0 | 0 | 0 | 0 | - | Germany |
| Tim Borowski | 23 | 21 | 4 | 642 | 1 | 0 | 3 | Germany (4) |
| Mladen Krstajic | 29 | 32 | 30 | 2724 | 9 | 0 | - | Serbia & Montenegro |
| Victor Skrypnyk | 33 | 25 | 19 | 1923 | 5 | 0 | - | Ukraine |
| Razundara Tjikuzu | 23 | 13 | 5 | 523 | 3 | 1 | - | Namibia |
| Frank Verlaat | 35 | 29 | 26 | 2466 | 5 | 1 | - | Holland |
| **Midfielders** | | | | | | | | |
| Ivica Banovic | 22 | 16 | 8 | 992 | 5 | 0 | - | Croatia |
| Stefan Beckert | 21 | 1 | 0 | 0 | 0 | 0 | - | Germany |
| Fabian Ernst | 24 | 32 | 30 | 2738 | 9 | 1 | 2 | Germany (4) |
| Krisztian Lisztes | 27 | 31 | 22 | 2179 | 5 | 1 | - | Hungary |
| Ludovic Magnin | 24 | 17 | 7 | 719 | 1 | 0 | - | Switzerland |
| Johan Micoud | 29 | 28 | 26 | 2445 | 8 | 2 | - | France |
| Simon Rolfes | 21 | 0 | 0 | 0 | 0 | 0 | - | Germany |
| Christian Schulz | 20 | 11 | 7 | 693 | 1 | 0 | - | Germany |
| Paul Stalteri | 25 | 33 | 32 | 2928 | 7 | 0 | - | Canada |
| Holger Wehlage | 27 | 5 | 1 | 98 | 0 | 0 | - | Germany |
| **Forwards** | | | | | | | | |
| Gonclaves Ailton | 29 | 31 | 24 | 2352 | 5 | 0 | - | Brazil |
| Angelos Charisteas | 23 | 31 | 24 | 2264 | 1 | 1 | - | Greece |
| Markus Daun | 22 | 28 | 13 | 1353 | 2 | 1 | - | Germany |
| Nelson Haedo Valdez | 19 | 5 | 0 | 29 | 0 | 0 | - | Paraguay |
| Ivan Klasnic | 23 | 14 | 2 | 270 | 0 | 0 | - | Croatia |
| Christian Lenze | 26 | 4 | 0 | 0 | 0 | 0 | - | Germany |
| Marco Reich | 25 | 19 | 0 | 289 | 0 | 0 | - | Germany |

KEY: LEAGUE BOOKINGS CAPS (FIFA RANKING)

## SQUAD APPEARANCES

| Match | 1 | 2 | 3 | 4 | 5 | 6 | 7 | 8 | 9 | 10 | 11 | 12 | 13 | 14 | 15 | 16 | 17 | 18 | 19 | 20 | 21 | 22 | 23 | 24 | 25 | 26 | 27 | 28 | 29 | 30 | 31 | 32 | 33 | 34 | 35 | 36 | 37 | 38 |
|---|---|---|---|---|---|---|---|---|---|---|---|---|---|---|---|---|---|---|---|---|---|---|---|---|---|---|---|---|---|---|---|---|---|---|---|---|---|---|
| Venue | A | H | A | H | A | A | H | A | H | H | A | H | A | H | A | H | H | A | H | A | H | H | A | H | A | H | A | H | A | H | A | A | H | A | H | A | H | A |
| Competition | L | L | L | L | L | E | L | L | E | L | L | L | E | L | L | E | L | L | L | L | L | L | L | L | L | L | L | L | L | L | L | L | L | L | L | L | L | L |
| Result | L | W | L | W | W | D | W | W | W | D | D | L | L | W | L | D | W | W | W | D | W | D | L | L | L | L | L | W | L | L | W | W | L | L | W | W | W | L |

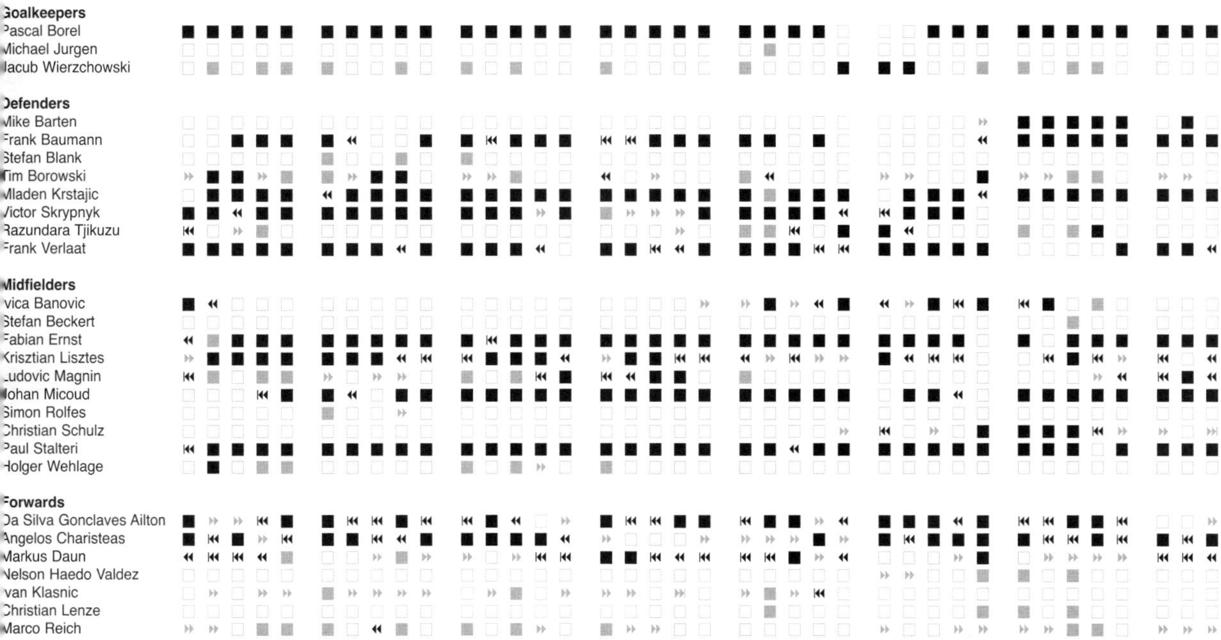

Goalkeepers
Pascal Borel
Michael Jurgen
Jacub Wierzchowski
Defenders
Mike Barten
Frank Baumann
Stefan Blank
Tim Borowski
Mladen Krstajic
Victor Skrypnyk
Razundara Tjikuzu
Frank Verlaat
Midfielders
Ivica Banovic
Stefan Beckert
Fabian Ernst
Krisztian Lisztes
Ludovic Magnin
Johan Micoud
Simon Rolfes
Christian Schulz
Paul Stalteri
Holger Wehlage
Forwards
Da Silva Gonclaves Ailton
Angelos Charisteas
Markus Daun
Nelson Haedo Valdez
Ivan Klasnic
Christian Lenze
Marco Reich


KEY: ■ On all match ■ On bench ⏮ Subbed or sent off (Counting game) « Subbed or sent off (playing less than 70 minutes) Subbed on from bench (Counting Game) » Subbed on (playing less than 70 minutes) Subbed on and then subbed or sent off (Counting Game) Subbed on and then subbed or sent off (playing less than 70 minutes) □ Not in 16

# SCHALKE

Final Position: **7th**

| | | | | | | |
|---|---|---|---|---|---|---|
| 1 | lge | Wolfsburg | H | W | 1-0 | Vermant 90 |
| 2 | lge | Kaiserslautern | A | W | 3-1 | Bohme 48 pen; Agali 57; Sand 90 |
| 3 | lge | Hertha Berlin | H | D | 0-0 | |
| 4 | lge | Stuttgart | A | D | 1-1 | Hajto 87 pen |
| 5 | lge | B Dortmund | A | D | 1-1 | Agali 70 |
| 6 | uc1rl1 | Gomel | A | W | 4-1 | Sand 58,73; Poulsen 66; Rodriguez 73 |
| 7 | lge | B M'gladbach | H | W | 2-1 | Poulsen 15; Agali 45 |
| 8 | lge | Arminia B | A | L | 1-2 | Varela 19 |
| 9 | uc1rl2 | Gomel | H | W | 4-0 | Wilmots 10; Hanke 62,72; Kmetsch 66 |
| 10 | lge | Hamburg | H | W | 3-0 | Agali 9; Sand 15; Asamoah 45 |
| 11 | lge | 1860 Munich | A | L | 0-3 | |
| 12 | lge | Nurnberg | H | D | 1-1 | Vermant 90 |
| 13 | uc2rl1 | Legia Warsaw | A | W | 3-2 | Varela 50,54; Sand 90 |
| 14 | lge | Cottbus | A | W | 1-0 | Moller 79 |
| 15 | lge | B Leverkusen | H | L | 0-1 | |
| 16 | uc2rl2 | Legia Warsaw | H | D | 0-0 | |
| 17 | lge | Bochum | A | W | 2-0 | Kalla 48 og; Asamoah 86 |
| 18 | lge | Hansa Rostock | H | D | 2-2 | Sand 5; Mpenza 39 |
| 19 | uc3rl1 | Wisla Krakow | A | D | 1-1 | Mpenza 81 |
| 20 | lge | Hannover 96 | A | W | 2-0 | Bohme 16 pen; Mpenza 19 |
| 21 | lge | W Bremen | H | D | 1-1 | Sand 8 |
| 22 | uc3rl2 | Wisla Krakow | H | L | 1-4 | Hajto 42 |
| 23 | lge | Bayern Munich | A | D | 0-0 | |
| 24 | lge | Wolfsburg | A | W | 2-1 | Kmetsch 47; Varela 50 |
| 25 | lge | Kaiserslautern | H | D | 2-2 | Agali 6,70 |
| 26 | lge | Hertha Berlin | A | L | 2-4 | Mpenza 1; Oude Kamphuis 68 |
| 27 | lge | Stuttgart | H | W | 2-0 | Mpenza 4; Hajto 45 |
| 28 | lge | B Dortmund | H | D | 2-2 | Vermant 13; Van Kerckhoven 16 |
| 29 | lge | B M'gladbach | A | D | 2-2 | Waldoch 27; Hajto 65 |
| 30 | lge | Arminia B | H | D | 1-1 | Vermant 90 |
| 31 | lge | Hamburg | A | L | 1-3 | Van Hoogdalem 58 |
| 32 | lge | 1860 Munich | H | D | 1-1 | Mpenza 38 |
| 33 | lge | Nurnberg | A | D | 0-0 | |
| 34 | lge | Cottbus | H | W | 3-0 | Bohme 45 pen,61 pen; Sand 54 |
| 35 | lge | B Leverkusen | A | W | 3-1 | Bohme 12; Sand 61; Asamoah 90 |
| 36 | lge | Bochum | H | L | 1-2 | Varela 29 |
| 37 | lge | Hansa Rostock | A | L | 1-3 | Varela 17 |
| 38 | lge | Hannover 96 | H | L | 0-2 | |
| 39 | lge | W Bremen | A | L | 1-2 | Agali 36 |
| 40 | lge | Bayern Munich | H | W | 1-0 | Oude Kamphuis 39 |

## KEY PLAYERS - GOALSCORERS

**1 Jorg Bohme**

| | | | |
|---|---|---|---|
| Goals in the League | 5 | Player Strike Rate<br>Average number of minutes between League goals scored by player | 392 |
| Contribution to Attacking Power<br>Average number of minutes between League team goals while on pitch | 61 | Club Strike Rate<br>Average number of minutes between League goals scored by club | 67 |

| | PLAYER | LGE GOALS | POWER | STRIKE RATE |
|---|---|---|---|---|
| 2 | Gustavo Antonio Varela | 4 | 63 | 398 mins |
| 3 | Sven Vermant | 4 | 75 | 416 mins |
| 4 | Ebbe Sand | 6 | 68 | 433 mins |
| 5 | Gerald Asamoah | 3 | 69 | 530 mins |

## KEY PLAYERS - MIDFIELDERS

**1 Andreas Moller**

| | | | |
|---|---|---|---|
| Goals in the League | 1 | Contribution to Attacking Power<br>Average number of minutes between League team goals while on pitch | 67 |
| Defensive Rating<br>Average number of mins between League goals conceded while he was on the pitch | 107 | Scoring Difference<br>Defensive Rating minus Contribution to Attacking Power | 40 |

| | PLAYER | LGE GOALS | DEF RATE | POWER | SCORE DIFF |
|---|---|---|---|---|---|
| 2 | Sven Kmetsch | 1 | 104 | 68 | 36 mins |
| 3 | Jorg Bohme | 5 | 82 | 61 | 21 mins |
| 4 | Christian Poulsen | 1 | 82 | 63 | 19 mins |
| 5 | Niels Oude Kamphuis | 2 | 67 | 61 | 6 mins |

## KEY PLAYERS - DEFENDERS

**1 Dario Rodriguez**

| | | | |
|---|---|---|---|
| Goals Conceded (GC)<br>The number of League goals conceded while he was on the pitch | 9 | Clean Sheets<br>In games when he played at least 70 minutes | 4 |
| Defensive Rating<br>Ave number of mins between League goals conceded while on the pitch | 106 | Club Defensive Rating<br>Average number of mins between League goals conceded by the club this season | 77 |

| | PLAYER | CON LGE | CLEAN SHEETS | DEF RATE |
|---|---|---|---|---|
| 2 | Anibal Matellan | 16 | 6 | 87 mins |
| 3 | Marco van Hoogdalem | 24 | 8 | 84 mins |
| 4 | Tomasz Hajto | 31 | 8 | 81 mins |
| 5 | Tomasz Waldoch | 17 | 4 | 69 mins |

## GOALS SCORED

**AT HOME**

| | | |
|---|---|---|
| MOST | B Munich | 37 |
| | | 23 |
| LEAST | Nurnberg | 16 |

**AWAY**

| | | |
|---|---|---|
| MOST | B Munich | 33 |
| | | 23 |
| LEAST | B M'gladbach &Arminia B | 12 |

## GOALS CONCEDED

**AT HOME**

| | | |
|---|---|---|
| LEAST | Hamburg & B M'gladbach | 11 |
| | | 16 |
| MOST | Hannover 96 | 33 |

**AWAY**

| | | |
|---|---|---|
| LEAST | B Munich | 13 |
| | | 24 |
| MOST | Nurnberg | 36 |

## KEY GOALKEEPER

**1 Frank Rost**

| | |
|---|---|
| Goals Conceded in the League | 39 |
| Defensive Rating<br>Ave number of mins between League goals conceded while on the pitch | 76 |
| Counting Games<br>Games when he played at least 70 minutes | 33 |
| Clean Sheets<br>In games when he played at least 70 minutes | 10 |

## TOP POINT EARNERS

| | PLAYER | GAMES | AVE |
|---|---|---|---|
| 1 | Kmetsch | 14 | 1.71 |
| 2 | Matellan | 13 | 1.69 |
| 3 | Moller | 16 | 1.63 |
| 4 | Hajto | 27 | 1.56 |
| 5 | Bohme | 20 | 1.55 |
| 6 | Poulsen | 24 | 1.54 |
| 7 | van Hoogdalem | 20 | 1.50 |
| 8 | Sand | 26 | 1.50 |
| 9 | Varela | 14 | 1.43 |
| 10 | Asamoah | 14 | 1.43 |
| | **CLUB AVERAGE:** | | **1.44** |

Ave = Average points per match in Counting Games

## ATTENDANCES

HOME GROUND: AUFSCHALKE ARENA  CAPACITY: 61000  AVERAGE LEAGUE AT HOME: 60632

| | | | | | | | | |
|---|---|---|---|---|---|---|---|---|
| 5 | B Dortmund | 68800 | 21 | W Bremen | 60600 | 29 | B M'gladbach | 33000 |
| 36 | Bochum | 60886 | 3 | Hertha Berlin | 60500 | 17 | Bochum | 32645 |
| 34 | Cottbus | 60886 | 1 | Wolfsburg | 60000 | 8 | Arminia B | 26601 |
| 38 | Hannover 96 | 60886 | 32 | 1860 Munich | 60000 | 4 | Stuttgart | 26500 |
| 40 | Bayern Munich | 60886 | 31 | Hamburg | 55000 | 24 | Wolfsburg | 26174 |
| 28 | B Dortmund | 60878 | 9 | Gomel | 52828 | 37 | Hansa Rostock | 25000 |
| 30 | Arminia B | 60878 | 16 | Legia Warsaw | 52265 | 11 | 1860 Munich | 25000 |
| 25 | Kaiserslautern | 60672 | 23 | Bayern Munich | 51000 | 35 | B Leverkusen | 22500 |
| 27 | Stuttgart | 60672 | 22 | Wisla Krakow | 50000 | 13 | Legia Warsaw | 15000 |
| 15 | B Leverkusen | 60601 | 20 | Hannover 96 | 48696 | 14 | Cottbus | 13340 |
| 18 | Hansa Rostock | 60601 | 33 | Nurnberg | 41100 | 19 | Wisla Krakow | 10300 |
| 12 | Nurnberg | 60601 | 39 | W Bremen | 39000 | 6 | Gomel | 6000 |
| 10 | Hamburg | 60601 | 2 | Kaiserslautern | 38000 | | | |
| 7 | B M'gladbach | 60601 | 26 | Hertha Berlin | 38000 | | | |

■ Home □ Away ▒ Neutral

## DISCIPLINARY RECORDS

| | PLAYER | YELLOW | RED | AVE |
|---|---|---|---|---|
| 1 | Varela | 8 | 2 | 159 |
| 2 | Hajto | 13 | 1 | 180 |
| 3 | Bohme | 8 | 0 | 245 |
| 4 | Kmetsch | 6 | 0 | 258 |
| 5 | Poulsen | 7 | 1 | 267 |
| 6 | Waldoch | 3 | 1 | 291 |
| 7 | Rodriguez | 3 | 0 | 316 |
| 8 | Asamoah | 5 | 0 | 318 |
| 9 | Agali | 3 | 1 | 322 |
| 10 | Vermant | 4 | 1 | 332 |
| 11 | Wilmots | 1 | 0 | 459 |
| 12 | van Hoogdalem | 4 | 0 | 501 |
| 13 | Oude Kamphuis | 4 | 0 | 520 |
| | Other | 14 | 2 | |
| | TOTAL | 83 | 9 | |

## LEAGUE GOALS

| | PLAYER | MINS | GOALS | AVE |
|---|---|---|---|---|
| 1 | Agali | 1290 | 7 | 184 |
| 2 | Sand | 2595 | 6 | 433 |
| 3 | Mpenza | 1312 | 5 | 262 |
| 4 | Bohme | 1961 | 5 | 392 |
| 5 | Varela | 1592 | 4 | 398 |
| 6 | Vermant | 1662 | 4 | 416 |
| 7 | Hajto | 2523 | 3 | 841 |
| 8 | Asamoah | 1590 | 3 | 530 |
| 9 | Oude Kamphuis | 2080 | 2 | 1040 |
| 10 | Poulsen | 2142 | 1 | 2142 |
| 11 | van Hoogdalem | 2006 | 1 | 2006 |
| 12 | Waldoch | 1166 | 1 | 1166 |
| 13 | Kmetsch | 1553 | 1 | 1553 |
| | Other | | 3 | |
| | TOTAL | | 46 | |

## MONTH BY MONTH GUIDE TO THE POINTS

| Month | Points | % |
|---|---|---|
| AUGUST | 7 | 78% |
| SEPTEMBER | 5 | 42% |
| OCTOBER | 4 | 44% |
| NOVEMBER | 7 | 58% |
| DECEMBER | 5 | 56% |
| JANUARY | 3 | 100% |
| FEBRUARY | 5 | 42% |
| MARCH | 3 | 25% |
| APRIL | 7 | 58% |
| MAY | 3 | 25% |

## TEAM OF THE SEASON

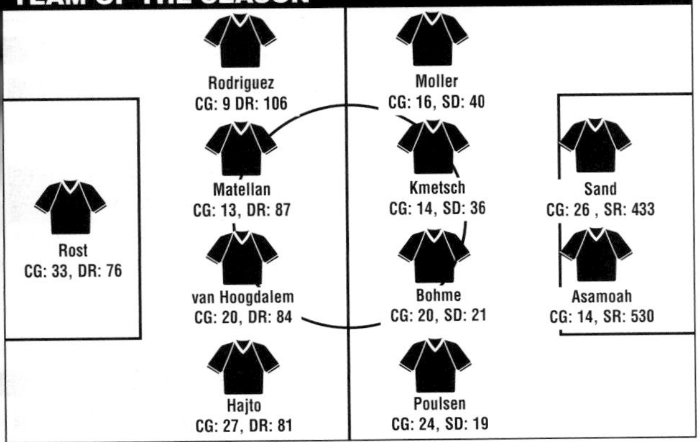
Rodriguez
CG: 9 DR: 106
Moller
CG: 16, SD: 40
Matellan
CG: 13, DR: 87
Kmetsch
CG: 14, SD: 36
Sand
CG: 26 , SR: 433
Rost
CG: 33, DR: 76
van Hoogdalem
CG: 20, DR: 84
Bohme
CG: 20, SD: 21
Asamoah
CG: 14, SR: 530
Hajto
CG: 27, DR: 81
Poulsen
CG: 24, SD: 19

KEY: DR = Defensive Rate, SD = Scoring Difference, SR = Strike Rate, CG = Counting Games – League games playing at least 70 minutes

## LEAGUE APPEARANCES, BOOKINGS AND CAPS

| | AGE | IN THE SQUAD | COUNTING GAMES | MINUTES ON PITCH | YELLOW CARDS | RED CARDS | THIS SEASON | HOME COUNTRY |
|---|---|---|---|---|---|---|---|---|
| **Goalkeepers** | | | | | | | | |
| Oliver Reck | 38 | 16 | 1 | 91 | 0 | 0 | - | Germany |
| Frank Rost | 30 | 33 | 33 | 2969 | 2 | 1 | 4 | Germany (4) |
| **Defenders** | | | | | | | | |
| Tomasz Hajto | 30 | 29 | 27 | 2523 | 13 | 1 | 3 | Poland (29) |
| Anibal Matellan | 26 | 25 | 13 | 1389 | 1 | 1 | - | Argentina |
| Dario Rodriguez | 28 | 19 | 9 | 950 | 3 | 0 | 2 | Uruguay (28) |
| Marco v Hoogdalem | 31 | 28 | 20 | 2006 | 4 | 0 | - | Holland |
| Tomasz Waldoch | 32 | 14 | 13 | 1166 | 3 | 1 | - | Poland |
| **Midfielders** | | | | | | | | |
| Jorg Bohme | 29 | 26 | 20 | 1961 | 8 | 0 | 4 | Germany (4) |
| Michael Buskens | 35 | 1 | 0 | 0 | 0 | 0 | - | Germany |
| Kristijan Djordjevic | 27 | 4 | 0 | 0 | 0 | 0 | - | Serbia & Montenegro |
| Sven Kmetsch | 32 | 24 | 14 | 1553 | 6 | 0 | - | Germany |
| Andreas Moller | 33 | 24 | 16 | 1605 | 2 | 0 | - | Germany |
| Niels Oude Kamphuis | 25 | 26 | 21 | 2080 | 4 | 0 | - | Holland |
| Christian Pander | 19 | 5 | 0 | 0 | 0 | 0 | - | Germany |
| Christian Poulsen | 23 | 24 | 24 | 2142 | 7 | 1 | 6 | Denmark (10) |
| Filip Trojan | 20 | 13 | 0 | 73 | 1 | 0 | - | Czech Republic |
| Nico van Kerckhoven | 32 | 16 | 13 | 1274 | 2 | 0 | 1 | Belgium (16) |
| Gustavo Varela | 25 | 23 | 14 | 1592 | 8 | 2 | - | Uruguay |
| Sven Vermant | 30 | 26 | 16 | 1662 | 4 | 1 | - | Belgium |
| Marc Wilmots | 34 | 11 | 4 | 459 | 1 | 0 | - | Belgium |
| **Forwards** | | | | | | | | |
| Victor Agali | 24 | 22 | 11 | 1290 | 3 | 1 | - | Nigeria |
| Gerald Asamoah | 24 | 28 | 14 | 1590 | 5 | 0 | 6 | Germany (4) |
| Michael Hanke | 19 | 15 | 2 | 289 | 0 | 0 | - | Germany |
| Abdul Iyodo | 23 | 7 | 1 | 126 | 0 | 0 | - | Nigeria |
| Emile Mpenza | 25 | 24 | 11 | 1312 | 2 | 0 | 6 | Belgium (16) |
| Sergio Pinto | 22 | 9 | 8 | 704 | 1 | 0 | - | Portugal |
| Ebbe Sand | 30 | 33 | 26 | 2595 | 3 | 0 | 8 | Denmark (10) |

KEY: LEAGUE BOOKINGS CAPS (FIFA RANKING)

## SQUAD APPEARANCES

| Match | 1 | 2 | 3 | 4 | 5 | 6 | 7 | 8 | 9 | 10 | 11 | 12 | 13 | 14 | 15 | 16 | 17 | 18 | 19 | 20 | 21 | 22 | 23 | 24 | 25 | 26 | 27 | 28 | 29 | 30 | 31 | 32 | 33 | 34 | 35 | 36 | 37 | 38 | 39 | 40 |
|---|---|---|---|---|---|---|---|---|---|---|---|---|---|---|---|---|---|---|---|---|---|---|---|---|---|---|---|---|---|---|---|---|---|---|---|---|---|---|---|---|
| Venue | H | A | H | A | A | A | H | A | H | H | A | H | A | A | H | H | A | H | A | A | H | H | A | A | H | A | H | H | A | H | A | H | A | H | A | H | A | H | A | H |
| Competition | L | L | L | L | L | E | L | L | E | L | L | L | E | L | L | E | L | L | E | L | L | E | L | L | L | L | L | L | L | L | L | L | L | L | L | L | L | L | L | L |
| Result | W | W | D | D | D | W | W | L | W | W | L | D | W | W | L | D | W | D | D | W | D | L | D | W | D | L | W | D | D | D | L | D | D | W | W | L | L | L | L | W |

**Goalkeepers**
Oliver Reck
Frank Rost

**Defenders**
Tomasz Hajto
Anibal Matellan
Dario Rodriguez
Marco van Hoogdalem
Tomasz Waldoch

**Midfielders**
Jorg Bohme
Michael Buskens
Kristijan Djordjevic
Sven Kmetsch
Andreas Moller
Niels Oude Kamphuis
Christian Pander
Christian Poulsen
Filip Trojan
Nico van Kerckhoven
Gustavo Antonio Varela
Sven Vermant
Marc Wilmots

**Forwards**
Victor Agali
Gerald Asamoah
Michael Hanke
Abdul Iyodo
Emile Mpenza
Sergio Pinto
Ebbe Sand

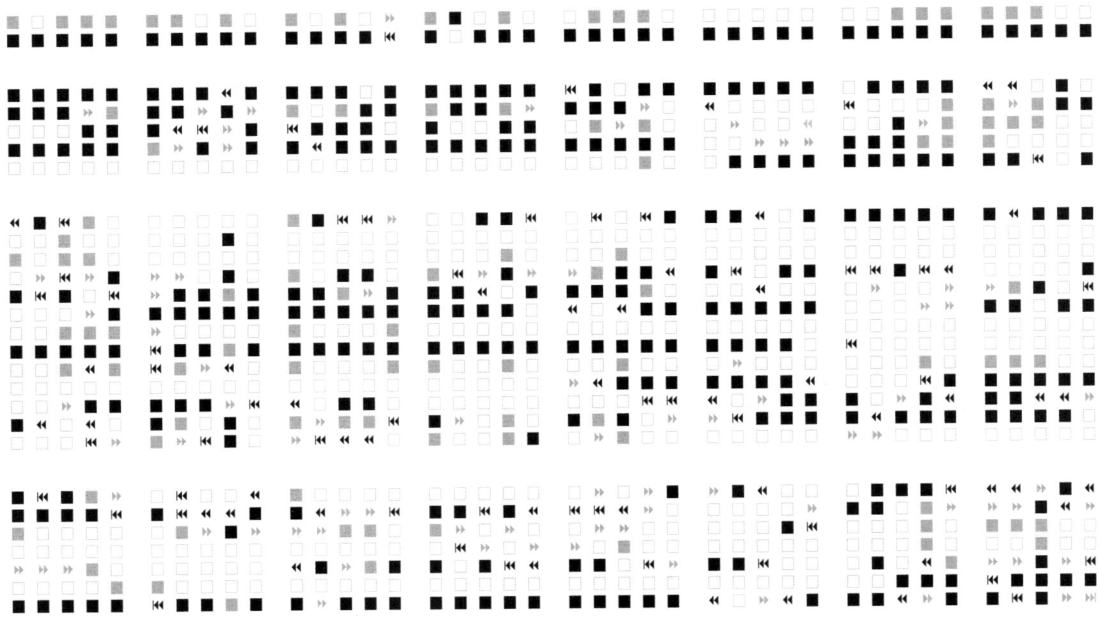

KEY: ■ On all match ■ On bench ⏮ Subbed or sent off (Counting game) « Subbed or sent off (playing less than 70 minutes) ⏭ Subbed on from bench (Counting Game) » Subbed on (playing less than 70 minutes) » Subbed on and then subbed or sent off (Counting Game) » Subbed on and then subbed or sent off (playing less than 70 minutes) □ Not in 16

# WOLFSBURG

**Final Position: 8th**

| | | | | | | |
|---|---|---|---|---|---|---|
| 1 | lge | Schalke | A | L | 0-1 | |
| 2 | lge | B M'gladbach | H | W | 1-0 | Petrov 67 |
| 3 | lge | Arminia B | A | L | 0-1 | |
| 4 | lge | Hamburg | H | W | 2-1 | Effenberg 51 pen; Sarpei 83 |
| 5 | lge | 1860 Munich | A | D | 2-2 | Ponte 77; Klimowicz 87 |
| 6 | lge | Nurnberg | H | L | 0-2 | |
| 7 | lge | Cottbus | A | W | 1-0 | Maric 55 |
| 8 | lge | B Leverkusen | H | W | 2-0 | Maric 6; Effenberg 74 |
| 9 | lge | Bochum | A | L | 2-4 | Klimowicz 6; Ponte 37 |
| 10 | lge | Hansa Rostock | H | W | 1-0 | Klimowicz 29 |
| 11 | lge | Hannover 96 | A | L | 1-3 | Munteanu 76 |
| 12 | lge | W Bremen | H | W | 3-1 | Petrov 28; Ponte 66; Effenberg 84 |
| 13 | lge | Bayern Munich | A | L | 0-1 | |
| 14 | lge | B Dortmund | H | W | 2-0 | Klimowicz 19,55 |
| 15 | lge | Kaiserslautern | A | L | 0-2 | |
| 16 | lge | Hertha Berlin | A | D | 2-2 | Ponte 63; Madsen, K 90 |
| 17 | lge | Stuttgart | H | L | 1-2 | Maric 76 pen |
| 18 | lge | Schalke | H | L | 1-2 | Maric 71 |
| 19 | lge | Arminia B | H | W | 2-0 | Schnoor 24; Maric 51 |
| 20 | lge | Hamburg | A | L | 0-2 | |
| 21 | lge | B M'gladbach | A | L | 0-2 | |
| 22 | lge | 1860 Munich | H | D | 1-1 | Klimowicz 71 |
| 23 | lge | Nurnberg | A | D | 1-1 | Maric 90 |
| 24 | lge | Cottbus | H | W | 3-2 | Maric 7; Prager 30; Ponte 62 |
| 25 | lge | B Leverkusen | A | D | 1-1 | Maric 81 |
| 26 | lge | Bochum | H | W | 2-0 | Maric 21; Prager 31 |
| 27 | lge | Hansa Rostock | A | L | 0-1 | |
| 28 | lge | Hannover 96 | H | W | 1-0 | Klimowicz 55 |
| 29 | lge | W Bremen | A | W | 1-0 | Biliskov 86 |
| 30 | lge | Bayern Munich | H | L | 0-2 | |
| 31 | lge | B Dortmund | A | D | 2-2 | Thiam 59,62 |
| 32 | lge | Kaiserslautern | H | D | 2-2 | Maric 19,57 |
| 33 | lge | Hertha Berlin | H | W | 2-0 | Maric 5 pen; Munteanu 58 |
| 34 | lge | Stuttgart | A | L | 0-2 | |

## KEY PLAYERS - GOALSCORERS

**1 Tomislav Maric**

| | | | |
|---|---|---|---|
| Goals in the League | 12 | Player Strike Rate<br>Average number of minutes between League goals scored by player | 162 |
| Contribution to Attacking Power<br>Average number of minutes between League team goals while on pitch | 66 | Club Strike Rate<br>Average number of minutes between League goals scored by club | 78 |

| | PLAYER | LGE GOALS | POWER | STRIKE RATE |
|---|---|---|---|---|
| 2 | Diego Fernando Klimowicz | 7 | 85 | 244 mins |
| 3 | Robson Ponte | 5 | 71 | 441 mins |
| 4 | Stefan Effenberg | 3 | 76 | 561 mins |
| 5 | Pablo Thiam | 2 | 80 | 686 mins |

## KEY PLAYERS - MIDFIELDERS

**1 Tobias Rau**

| | | | |
|---|---|---|---|
| Goals in the League | 0 | Contribution to Attacking Power<br>Average number of minutes between League team goals while on pitch | 70 |
| Defensive Rating<br>Average number of mins between League goals conceded while he was on the pitch | 70 | Scoring Difference<br>Defensive Rating minus Contribution to Attacking Power | 0 |

| | PLAYER | LGE GOALS | DEF RATE | POWER | SCORE DIFF |
|---|---|---|---|---|---|
| 2 | Pablo Thiam | 2 | 76 | 81 | -5 mins |
| 3 | Stefan Effenberg | 3 | 65 | 77 | -12 mins |
| 4 | Hans Sarpei | 1 | 67 | 79 | -12 mins |
| 5 | Charles Akonnor | 0 | 71 | 84 | -13 mins |

## KEY PLAYERS - DEFENDERS

**1 Maik Franz**

| | | | |
|---|---|---|---|
| Goals Conceded (GC)<br>The number of League goals conceded while he was on the pitch | 12 | Clean Sheets<br>In games when he played at least 70 minutes | 4 |
| Defensive Rating<br>Ave number of mins between League goals conceded while on the pitch | 85 | Club Defensive Rating<br>Average number of mins between League goals conceded by the club this season | 73 |

| | PLAYER | CON LGE | CLEAN SHEETS | DEF RATE |
|---|---|---|---|---|
| 2 | Stefan Schnoor | 34 | 10 | 77 mins |
| 3 | Miroslav Karhan | 36 | 9 | 75 mins |
| 4 | Thomas Rytter | 28 | 9 | 74 mins |
| 5 | Marino Biliskov | 22 | 4 | 73 mins |

## GOALS SCORED

**AT HOME**

| | | |
|---|---|---|
| MOST | B Munich | 37 |
| | | 26 |
| LEAST | Nurnberg | 16 |

**AWAY**

| | | |
|---|---|---|
| MOST | B Munich | 33 |
| | | 13 |
| LEAST | B M'gladbach &Arminia B | 12 |

## GOALS CONCEDED

**AT HOME**

| | | |
|---|---|---|
| LEAST | Hamburg & B M'gladbach | 11 |
| | | 15 |
| MOST | Hannover 96 | 33 |

**AWAY**

| | | |
|---|---|---|
| LEAST | B Munich | 13 |
| | | 27 |
| MOST | Nurnberg | 36 |

## KEY GOALKEEPER

**1 Sead Ramovic**

| | |
|---|---|
| Goals Conceded in the League | 7 |
| Defensive Rating<br>Ave number of mins between League goals conceded while on the pitch | 77 |
| Counting Games<br>Games when he played at least 70 minutes | 6 |
| Clean Sheets<br>In games when he played at least 70 minutes | 2 |

## TOP POINT EARNERS

| | PLAYER | GAMES | AVE |
|---|---|---|---|
| 1 | Klimowicz | 16 | 1.88 |
| 2 | Rau | 21 | 1.71 |
| 3 | Rytter | 22 | 1.55 |
| 4 | Schnoor | 28 | 1.54 |
| 5 | Thiam | 14 | 1.50 |
| 6 | Karhan | 28 | 1.43 |
| 7 | Ponte | 22 | 1.41 |
| 8 | Reitmaier | 28 | 1.39 |
| 9 | Maric | 19 | 1.37 |
| 10 | Biliskov | 17 | 1.35 |
| | **CLUB AVERAGE:** | | **1.35** |

Ave = Average points per match in Counting Games

## ATTENDANCES

HOME GROUND: VOLKSWAGEN ARENA CAPACITY: 30000 AVERAGE LEAGUE AT HOME: 19508

| | | | | | | | | |
|---|---|---|---|---|---|---|---|---|
| 31 | B Dortmund | 67000 | 33 | Hertha Berlin | 25000 | 12 | W Bremen | 16000 |
| 1 | Schalke | 60000 | 3 | Arminia B | 25000 | 22 | 1860 Munich | 16000 |
| 34 | Stuttgart | 49000 | 5 | 1860 Munich | 23000 | 19 | Arminia B | 15976 |
| 13 | Bayern Munich | 44000 | 21 | B M'gladbach | 22900 | 2 | B M'gladbach | 15000 |
| 11 | Hannover 96 | 40000 | 25 | B Leverkusen | 22500 | 23 | Nurnberg | 15000 |
| 29 | W Bremen | 33300 | 32 | Kaiserslautern | 21136 | 8 | B Leverkusen | 14234 |
| 15 | Kaiserslautern | 31000 | 26 | Bochum | 20973 | 6 | Nurnberg | 14000 |
| 28 | Hannover 96 | 30000 | 24 | Cottbus | 20000 | 7 | Cottbus | 12000 |
| 20 | Hamburg | 30000 | 17 | Stuttgart | 20000 | 10 | Hansa Rostock | 11600 |
| 30 | Bayern Munich | 30000 | 9 | Bochum | 18858 | 27 | Hansa Rostock | 9000 |
| 16 | Hertha Berlin | 28000 | 14 | B Dortmund | 18000 | | | |
| 18 | Schalke | 26174 | 4 | Hamburg | 17546 | | | |

■ Home □ Away ▨ Neutral

## DISCIPLINARY RECORDS

| | PLAYER | YELLOW | RED | AVE |
|---|---|---|---|---|
| 1 | Prager | 7 | 0 | 174 |
| 2 | Petrov | 7 | 1 | 228 |
| 3 | Sarpei | 3 | 1 | 235 |
| 4 | Schnoor | 11 | 0 | 237 |
| 5 | Franz | 4 | 0 | 255 |
| 6 | Maric | 6 | 1 | 277 |
| 7 | Effenberg | 6 | 0 | 280 |
| 8 | Ponte | 6 | 1 | 314 |
| 9 | Karhan | 8 | 0 | 337 |
| 10 | Thiam | 4 | 0 | 343 |
| 11 | Rytter | 6 | 0 | 344 |
| 12 | Biliskov | 4 | 0 | 401 |
| 13 | Rau | 5 | 0 | 408 |
| | Other | 15 | 0 | |
| | TOTAL | 92 | 4 | |

## LEAGUE GOALS

| | PLAYER | MINS | GOALS | AVE |
|---|---|---|---|---|
| 1 | Maric | 1939 | 12 | 162 |
| 2 | Klimowicz | 1710 | 7 | 244 |
| 3 | Ponte | 2203 | 5 | 441 |
| 4 | Effenberg | 1683 | 3 | 561 |
| 5 | Petrov | 1824 | 2 | 912 |
| 6 | Prager | 1222 | 2 | 611 |
| 7 | Thiam | 1372 | 2 | 686 |
| 8 | Munteanu | 875 | 2 | 438 |
| 9 | Madsen, K | 1081 | 1 | 1081 |
| 10 | Schnoor | 2613 | 1 | 2613 |
| 11 | Biliskov | 1604 | 1 | 1604 |
| 12 | Sarpei | 943 | 1 | 943 |
| | Other | | 0 | |
| | TOTAL | | 39 | |

## MONTH BY MONTH GUIDE TO THE POINTS

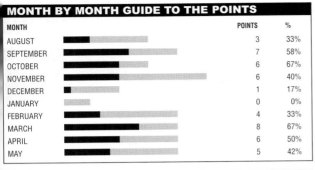

| MONTH | POINTS | % |
|---|---|---|
| AUGUST | 3 | 33% |
| SEPTEMBER | 7 | 58% |
| OCTOBER | 6 | 67% |
| NOVEMBER | 6 | 40% |
| DECEMBER | 1 | 17% |
| JANUARY | 0 | 0% |
| FEBRUARY | 4 | 33% |
| MARCH | 8 | 67% |
| APRIL | 6 | 50% |
| MAY | 5 | 42% |

## TEAM OF THE SEASON

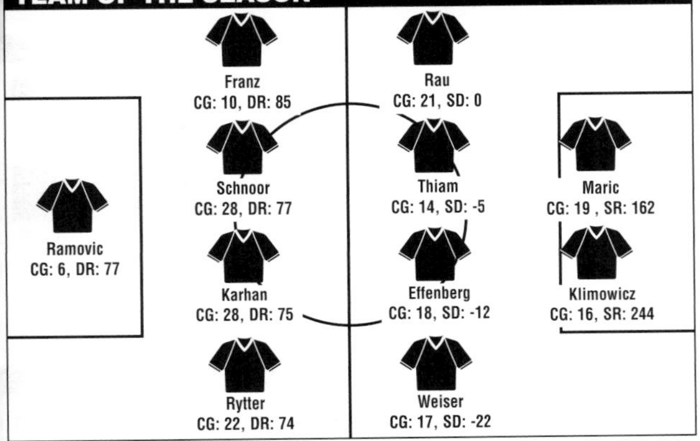
Franz
CG: 10, DR: 85
Rau
CG: 21, SD: 0
Schnoor
CG: 28, DR: 77
Thiam
CG: 14, SD: -5
Maric
CG: 19 , SR: 162
Ramovic
CG: 6, DR: 77
Karhan
CG: 28, DR: 75
Effenberg
CG: 18, SD: -12
Klimowicz
CG: 16, SR: 244
Rytter
CG: 22, DR: 74
Weiser
CG: 17, SD: -22

KEY: DR = Defensive Rate, SD = Scoring Difference, SR = Strike Rate, CG = Counting Games – League games playing at least 70 minutes

## LEAGUE APPEARANCES, BOOKINGS AND CAPS

| | AGE | IN THE SQUAD | COUNTING GAMES | MINUTES ON PITCH | YELLOW CARDS | RED CARDS | THIS SEASON | HOME COUNTRY |
|---|---|---|---|---|---|---|---|---|
| **Goalkeepers** | | | | | | | | |
| Patrick Platins | 20 | 2 | 0 | 0 | 0 | 0 | - | Germany |
| Sead Ramovic | 24 | 17 | 6 | 540 | 0 | 0 | - | Germany |
| Claus Reitmaier | 39 | 30 | 28 | 2520 | 1 | 0 | - | Germany |
| **Defenders** | | | | | | | | |
| Marino Biliskov | 27 | 25 | 17 | 1604 | 4 | 0 | - | Croatia |
| Karsten Fischer | | 2 | 0 | 0 | 0 | 0 | - | Germany |
| Maik Franz | 21 | 16 | 10 | 1020 | 4 | 0 | - | Germany |
| Frank Greiner | 37 | 9 | 0 | 27 | 0 | 0 | - | Germany |
| Miroslav Karhan | 27 | 32 | 28 | 2700 | 8 | 0 | - | Slovakia |
| Stefan Lorenz | 21 | 2 | 0 | 1 | 0 | 0 | - | Germany |
| Kim Madsen | 29 | 15 | 10 | 1081 | 1 | 0 | - | Denmark |
| Sven Muller | 23 | 21 | 3 | 489 | 1 | 0 | - | Germany |
| Pablo Quattrocchi | 29 | 10 | 4 | 405 | 1 | 0 | - | Argentina |
| Thomas Rytter | 29 | 27 | 22 | 2069 | 6 | 0 | 2 | Denmark (10) |
| Stefan Schnoor | 32 | 32 | 28 | 2613 | 11 | 0 | - | Germany |
| **Midfielders** | | | | | | | | |
| Charles Akonnor | 29 | 14 | 8 | 928 | 2 | 0 | - | Ghana |
| Stefan Effenberg | 34 | 19 | 18 | 1683 | 6 | 0 | - | Germany |
| Michael Habryka | 21 | 2 | 0 | 0 | 0 | 0 | - | Germany |
| Dorinel Munteanu | 35 | 21 | 5 | 875 | 2 | 0 | 7 | Romania (27) |
| Tobias Rau | 21 | 27 | 21 | 2043 | 5 | 0 | 5 | Germany (4) |
| Bartos Romanczuk | | 1 | 0 | 0 | 0 | 0 | - | |
| Hans Sarpei | 27 | 23 | 7 | 943 | 3 | 1 | - | Germany |
| Pablo Thiam | 29 | 16 | 14 | 1372 | 4 | 0 | - | Guinea |
| Patrick Weiser | 31 | 21 | 17 | 1610 | 3 | 0 | - | Germany |
| **Forwards** | | | | | | | | |
| Michal Janicki | 20 | 2 | 0 | 39 | 0 | 0 | - | Germany |
| Diego Klimowicz | 29 | 25 | 16 | 1710 | 4 | 0 | - | Argentina |
| Peter Madsen | 25 | 6 | 1 | 134 | 0 | 0 | 1 | Denmark (10) |
| Tomislav Maric | 30 | 29 | 19 | 1939 | 6 | 1 | 7 | Croatia (26) |
| Martin Petrov | 24 | 28 | 17 | 1824 | 7 | 1 | - | Bulgaria |
| Robson Ponte | 26 | 30 | 22 | 2203 | 6 | 1 | - | Brazil |
| Roy Prager | 31 | 29 | 8 | 1222 | 7 | 0 | - | Germany |

KEY: LEAGUE BOOKINGS CAPS (FIFA RANKING)

## SQUAD APPEARANCES

| Match | 1 | 2 | 3 | 4 | 5 | 6 | 7 | 8 | 9 | 10 | 11 | 12 | 13 | 14 | 15 | 16 | 17 | 18 | 19 | 20 | 21 | 22 | 23 | 24 | 25 | 26 | 27 | 28 | 29 | 30 | 31 | 32 | 33 | 34 |
|---|---|---|---|---|---|---|---|---|---|---|---|---|---|---|---|---|---|---|---|---|---|---|---|---|---|---|---|---|---|---|---|---|---|---|
| Venue | A | H | A | H | A | H | A | H | A | H | A | H | A | H | A | A | H | H | H | A | A | H | A | H | A | H | A | H | A | H | A | H | H | A |
| Competition | L | L | L | L | L | L | L | L | L | L | L | L | L | L | L | L | L | L | L | L | L | L | L | L | L | L | L | L | L | L | L | L | L | L |
| Result | L | W | L | W | D | L | W | W | L | W | L | W | L | W | L | D | L | L | W | L | L | D | D | W | D | W | L | W | W | L | D | D | W | L |

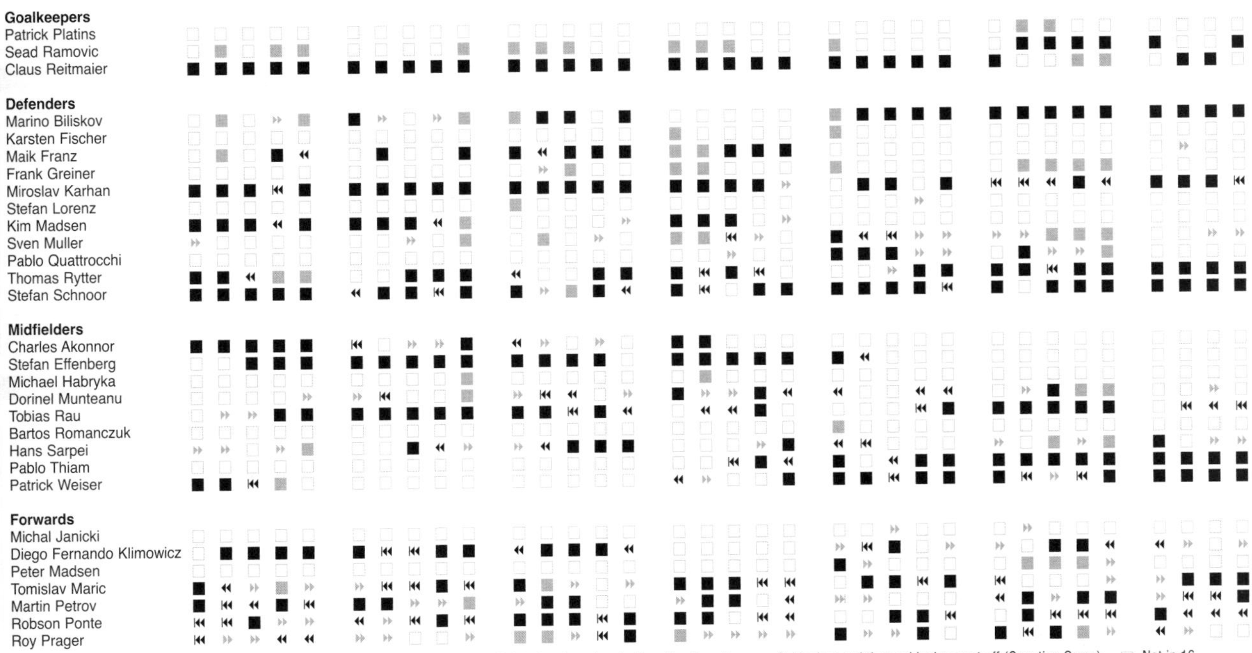
Goalkeepers
Patrick Platins
Sead Ramovic
Claus Reitmaier
Defenders
Marino Biliskov
Karsten Fischer
Maik Franz
Frank Greiner
Miroslav Karhan
Stefan Lorenz
Kim Madsen
Sven Muller
Pablo Quattrocchi
Thomas Rytter
Stefan Schnoor
Midfielders
Charles Akonnor
Stefan Effenberg
Michael Habryka
Dorinel Munteanu
Tobias Rau
Bartos Romanczuk
Hans Sarpei
Pablo Thiam
Patrick Weiser
Forwards
Michal Janicki
Diego Fernando Klimowicz
Peter Madsen
Tomislav Maric
Martin Petrov
Robson Ponte
Roy Prager

KEY: ■ On all match ■ On bench ⏮ Subbed or sent off (Counting game) « Subbed or sent off (playing less than 70 minutes) ⏭ Subbed on from bench (Counting Game) » Subbed on (playing less than 70 minutes) ⏭ Subbed on and then subbed or sent off (Counting Game) ⏭ Subbed on and then subbed or sent off (playing less than 70 minutes) □ Not in 16

# VFL BOCHUM

Final Position: **9th**

| | | | | | | |
|---|---|---|---|---|---|---|
| 1 | lge | Nurnberg | A | W | 3-1 | Christiansen 6,20; Hashemian 83 |
| 2 | lge | Cottbus | H | W | 5-0 | Christiansen 26,35,84; Freier 33; Hashemian 64 |
| 3 | lge | B Leverkusen | A | W | 4-2 | Gudjonsson 13; Wosz 33; Fahrenhorst 43; Christiansen 60 |
| 4 | lge | B Dortmund | H | D | 0-0 | |
| 5 | lge | Hansa Rostock | H | L | 0-1 | |
| 6 | lge | Hannover 96 | A | D | 2-2 | Fahrenhorst 24; Tapalovic, F 89 |
| 7 | lge | W Bremen | H | L | 1-4 | Freier 21 |
| 8 | lge | Bayern Munich | A | L | 1-4 | Schindzielorz 77 |
| 9 | lge | Wolfsburg | H | W | 4-2 | Christiansen 4; Fahrenhorst 56; Freier 56; Hashemian 82 |
| 10 | lge | Hertha Berlin | H | W | 3-0 | Wosz 49; Freier 79; Gudjonsson 90 |
| 11 | lge | Stuttgart | A | L | 2-3 | Christiansen 58; Schindzielorz 84 |
| 12 | lge | Kaiserslautern | A | W | 2-0 | Christiansen 7,21 |
| 13 | lge | Schalke | H | L | 0-2 | |
| 14 | lge | B M'gladbach | A | D | 2-2 | Hashemian 86; Graulund 90 |
| 15 | lge | Arminia B | H | L | 0-3 | |
| 16 | lge | Hamburg | A | D | 1-1 | Graulund 90 |
| 17 | lge | 1860 Munich | H | D | 1-1 | Christiansen 76 |
| 18 | lge | Nurnberg | H | W | 2-1 | Christiansen 27; Freier 33 |
| 19 | lge | Cottbus | A | L | 1-2 | Gudjonsson 90 |
| 20 | lge | B Leverkusen | H | W | 2-1 | Hashemian 68,84 |
| 21 | lge | B Dortmund | A | L | 1-4 | Buckley 8 |
| 22 | lge | Hansa Rostock | A | D | 1-1 | Hashemian 61 |
| 23 | lge | Hannover 96 | H | L | 1-2 | Christiansen 62 |
| 24 | lge | W Bremen | A | L | 0-2 | |
| 25 | lge | Bayern Munich | H | L | 1-4 | Christiansen 90 |
| 26 | lge | Wolfsburg | A | L | 0-2 | |
| 27 | lge | Kaiserslautern | H | D | 1-1 | Christiansen 82 |
| 28 | lge | Hertha Berlin | A | L | 0-1 | |
| 29 | lge | Stuttgart | H | W | 3-1 | Hashemian 40,66; Christiansen 68 |
| 30 | lge | Schalke | A | W | 2-1 | Christiansen 25; Buckley 90 |
| 31 | lge | B M'gladbach | H | D | 1-1 | Christiansen 21 |
| 32 | lge | Arminia B | A | W | 3-1 | Freier 23; Christiansen 71 pen; Buckley 90 |
| 33 | lge | Hamburg | H | D | 1-1 | Christiansen 31 |
| 34 | lge | 1860 Munich | A | W | 4-2 | Freier 1; Hashemian 64; Christiansen 73; Reis 89 |

## KEY PLAYERS - GOALSCORERS

**1 Thomas Christiansen**

| | | | |
|---|---|---|---|
| Goals in the League | 21 | Player Strike Rate<br>Average number of minutes between League goals scored by player | 116 |
| Contribution to Attacking Power<br>Average number of minutes between League team goals while on pitch | 52 | Club Strike Rate<br>Average number of minutes between League goals scored by club | 56 |

| | PLAYER | LGE GOALS | POWER | STRIKE RATE |
|---|---|---|---|---|
| 2 | Paul Freier | 7 | 54 | 397 mins |
| 3 | Thordur Gudjonsson | 3 | 56 | 640 mins |
| 4 | Frank Fahrenhorst | 3 | 52 | 698 mins |
| 5 | Delron Buckley | 3 | 65 | 724 mins |

## KEY PLAYERS - MIDFIELDERS

**1 Sunday Oliseh**

| | | | |
|---|---|---|---|
| Goals in the League | 0 | Contribution to Attacking Power<br>Average number of minutes between League team goals while on pitch | 48 |
| Defensive Rating<br>Average number of mins between League goals conceded while he was on the pitch | 72 | Scoring Difference<br>Defensive Rating minus Contribution to Attacking Power | 24 |

| | PLAYER | LGE GOALS | DEF RATE | POWER | SCORE DIFF |
|---|---|---|---|---|---|
| 2 | Paul Freier | 7 | 56 | 54 | 2 mins |
| 3 | Sebastian Schindzielorz | 2 | 57 | 57 | 0 mins |
| 4 | Thordur Gudjonsson | 3 | 56 | 56 | 0 mins |
| 5 | Dariusz Wosz | 2 | 53 | 56 | -3 mins |

## KEY PLAYERS - DEFENDERS

**1 Raymond Kalla**

| | | | |
|---|---|---|---|
| Goals Conceded (GC)<br>The number of League goals conceded while he was on the pitch | 35 | Clean Sheets<br>In games when he played at least 70 minutes | 4 |
| Defensive Rating<br>Ave number of mins between League goals conceded while on the pitch | 66 | Club Defensive Rating<br>Average number of mins between League goals conceded by the club this season | 55 |

| | PLAYER | CON LGE | CLEAN SHEETS | DEF RATE |
|---|---|---|---|---|
| 2 | Martin Meichelbeck | 28 | 4 | 58 mins |
| 3 | Frank Fahrenhorst | 38 | 4 | 55 mins |
| 4 | Soren Colding | 56 | 4 | 54 mins |
| 5 | Filip Tapalovic | 32 | 1 | 45 mins |

## GOALS SCORED

**AT HOME**

| | | |
|---|---|---|
| MOST | B Munich | 37 |
| | | 26 |
| LEAST | Nurnberg | 16 |

**AWAY**

| | | |
|---|---|---|
| MOST | B Munich | 33 |
| | | 29 |
| LEAST | B M'gladbach &Arminia B | 12 |

## GOALS CONCEDED

**AT HOME**

| | | |
|---|---|---|
| LEAST | Hamburg & B M'gladbach | 11 |
| | | 25 |
| MOST | Hannover 96 | 33 |

**AWAY**

| | | |
|---|---|---|
| LEAST | B Munich | 13 |
| | | 31 |
| MOST | Nurnberg | 36 |

## KEY GOALKEEPER

**1 Rein Van Duijnhoven**

| | |
|---|---|
| Goals Conceded in the League | 41 |
| Defensive Rating<br>Ave number of mins between League goals conceded while on the pitch | 60 |
| Counting Games<br>Games when he played at least 70 minutes | 27 |
| Clean Sheets<br>In games when he played at least 70 minutes | 4 |

## TOP POINT EARNERS

| | PLAYER | GAMES | AVE |
|---|---|---|---|
| 1 | Meichelbeck | 15 | 1.67 |
| 2 | Kalla | 25 | 1.64 |
| 3 | Gudjonsson | 18 | 1.50 |
| 4 | Schindzielorz | 20 | 1.45 |
| 5 | Van Duijnhoven | 27 | 1.44 |
| 6 | Wosz | 27 | 1.44 |
| 7 | Christiansen | 23 | 1.43 |
| 8 | Freier | 30 | 1.37 |
| 9 | Fahrenhorst | 22 | 1.36 |
| 10 | Colding | 34 | 1.32 |
| | CLUB AVERAGE: | | 1.32 |

Ave = Average points per match in Counting Games

## ATTENDANCES

HOME GROUND: RUHRSTADION CAPACITY: 32645 AVERAGE LEAGUE AT HOME: 23854

| | | | | | | | | |
|---|---|---|---|---|---|---|---|---|
| 21 | B Dortmund | 67000 | 14 | B M'gladbach | 29000 | 26 | Wolfsburg | 20973 |
| 30 | Schalke | 60886 | 24 | W Bremen | 26000 | 18 | Nurnberg | 20280 |
| 8 | Bayern Munich | 58000 | 32 | Arminia B | 26000 | 2 | Cottbus | 20000 |
| 6 | Hannover 96 | 40000 | 34 | 1860 Munich | 25000 | 11 | Stuttgart | 19000 |
| 16 | Hamburg | 38000 | 28 | Hertha Berlin | 25000 | 9 | Wolfsburg | 18858 |
| 12 | Kaiserslautern | 34000 | 27 | Kaiserslautern | 23146 | 20 | B Leverkusen | 18000 |
| 25 | Bayern Munich | 32645 | 29 | Stuttgart | 23000 | 17 | 1860 Munich | 18000 |
| 31 | B M'gladbach | 32645 | 3 | B Leverkusen | 22500 | 23 | Hannover 96 | 15000 |
| 33 | Hamburg | 32645 | 10 | Hertha Berlin | 22009 | 22 | Hansa Rostock | 13000 |
| 13 | Schalke | 32645 | 7 | W Bremen | 22000 | 19 | Cottbus | 12000 |
| 4 | B Dortmund | 32645 | 15 | Arminia B | 21000 | | | |
| 1 | Nurnberg | 30000 | 5 | Hansa Rostock | 21000 | | | |

■ Home □ Away ▨ Neutral

## DISCIPLINARY RECORDS

| | PLAYER | YELLOW | RED | AVE |
|---|---|---|---|---|
| 1 | Vriesde | 5 | 0 | 211 |
| 2 | Wosz | 8 | 0 | 315 |
| 3 | Kalla | 6 | 0 | 386 |
| 4 | Buckley | 5 | 0 | 434 |
| 5 | Tapalovic, F | 3 | 0 | 475 |
| 6 | Hashemian | 3 | 0 | 481 |
| 7 | Schindzielorz | 4 | 0 | 486 |
| 8 | Fahrenhorst | 4 | 0 | 523 |
| 9 | Bemben | 2 | 0 | 546 |
| 10 | Freier | 5 | 0 | 555 |
| 11 | Colding | 4 | 0 | 759 |
| 12 | Meichelbeck | 2 | 0 | 816 |
| 13 | Oliseh | 1 | 0 | 859 |
| | Other | 6 | 0 | |
| | TOTAL | 58 | 0 | |

## LEAGUE GOALS

| | PLAYER | MINS | GOALS | AVE |
|---|---|---|---|---|
| 1 | Christiansen | 2428 | 21 | 116 |
| 2 | Hashemian | 1444 | 10 | 144 |
| 3 | Freier | 2777 | 7 | 397 |
| 4 | Buckley | 2172 | 3 | 724 |
| 5 | Gudjonsson | 1919 | 3 | 640 |
| 6 | Fahrenhorst | 2095 | 3 | 698 |
| 7 | Graulund | 232 | 2 | 116 |
| 8 | Schindzielorz | 1947 | 2 | 974 |
| 9 | Wosz | 2525 | 2 | 1263 |
| 10 | Tapalovic, F | 1425 | 1 | 1425 |
| 11 | Reis | 886 | 1 | 886 |
| | Other | | 0 | |
| | TOTAL | | 55 | |

## MONTH BY MONTH GUIDE TO THE POINTS

| MONTH | POINTS | % |
|---|---|---|
| AUGUST | 9 | 100% |
| SEPTEMBER | 2 | 17% |
| OCTOBER | 3 | 50% |
| NOVEMBER | 7 | 39% |
| DECEMBER | 2 | 33% |
| JANUARY | 3 | 100% |
| FEBRUARY | 4 | 33% |
| MARCH | 0 | 0% |
| APRIL | 7 | 58% |
| MAY | 8 | 67% |

## LEAGUE APPEARANCES, BOOKINGS AND CAPS

| | AGE | IN THE SQUAD | COUNTING GAMES | MINUTES ON PITCH | YELLOW CARDS | RED CARDS | THIS SEASON | HOME COUNTRY |
|---|---|---|---|---|---|---|---|---|
| **Goalkeepers** | | | | | | | | |
| Rein V Duijnhoven | 35 | 28 | 27 | 2475 | 1 | 0 | - | Holland |
| Christian Vander | 22 | 17 | 6 | 585 | 0 | 0 | - | Germany |
| **Defenders** | | | | | | | | |
| Soren Colding | 30 | 34 | 34 | 3036 | 4 | 0 | - | Denmark |
| Mirko Dickhaut | 32 | 4 | 0 | 5 | 0 | 0 | - | |
| Frank Fahrenhorst | 25 | 26 | 22 | 2095 | 4 | 0 | - | Germany |
| Bjorn Joppe | 24 | 7 | 0 | 0 | 0 | 0 | - | Germany |
| Raymond Kalla | 28 | 26 | 25 | 2317 | 6 | 0 | - | Cameroon |
| Martin Meichelbeck | 26 | 23 | 15 | 1633 | 2 | 0 | - | Germany |
| Filip Tapalovic | 26 | 21 | 13 | 1425 | 3 | 0 | 3 | Croatia (26) |
| **Midfielders** | | | | | | | | |
| Michael Bemben | 27 | 26 | 9 | 1093 | 2 | 0 | - | Germany |
| Christian Fiel | 23 | 7 | 0 | 152 | 0 | 0 | - | Germany |
| Marcus Fischer | | 2 | 1 | 86 | 0 | 0 | - | Germany |
| Paul Freier | 23 | 32 | 30 | 2777 | 5 | 0 | 10 | Germany (4) |
| Thordur Gudjonsson | 29 | 32 | 18 | 1919 | 2 | 0 | - | Iceland |
| Serjei Mandreko | 31 | 10 | 4 | 440 | 0 | 0 | - | Russia |
| Sunday Oliseh | 28 | 11 | 9 | 859 | 1 | 0 | - | Nigeria |
| Thomas Reis | 29 | 21 | 8 | 886 | 0 | 0 | - | Germany |
| Seb Schindzielorz | 24 | 25 | 20 | 1947 | 4 | 0 | - | Germany |
| Alexander Tamm | | 2 | 0 | 9 | 0 | 0 | - | Germany |
| Luciano Velardi | 21 | 2 | 0 | 42 | 0 | 0 | - | Italy |
| Anton Vriesde | 34 | 20 | 10 | 1057 | 5 | 0 | - | Holland |
| Dariusz Wosz | 34 | 30 | 27 | 2525 | 8 | 0 | - | Germany |
| David Zajas | | 1 | 0 | 12 | 0 | 0 | - | Germany |
| **Forwards** | | | | | | | | |
| Delron Buckley | 25 | 31 | 21 | 2172 | 5 | 0 | - | South Africa |
| Thomas Christiansen | 30 | 34 | 23 | 2428 | 1 | 0 | - | Spain |
| Peter Graulund | 26 | 13 | 0 | 232 | 2 | 0 | - | Denmark |
| Vahid Hashemian | 26 | 34 | 9 | 1444 | 3 | 0 | - | Iran |

KEY: LEAGUE BOOKINGS CAPS (FIFA RANKING)

## TEAM OF THE SEASON

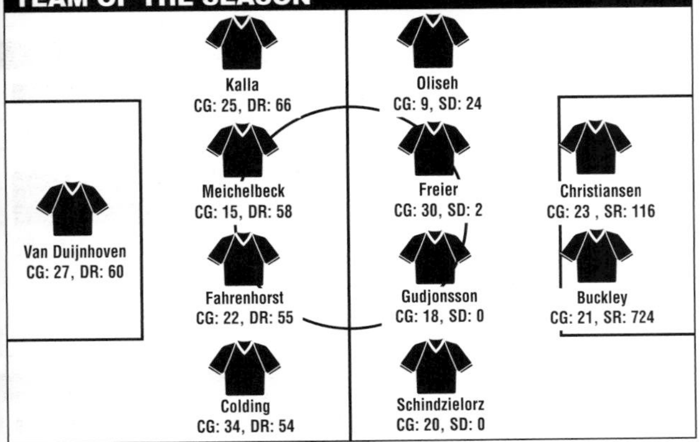

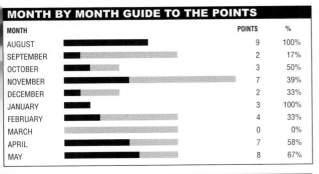

Kalla
CG: 25, DR: 66
Oliseh
CG: 9, SD: 24
Meichelbeck
CG: 15, DR: 58
Freier
CG: 30, SD: 2
Christiansen
CG: 23 , SR: 116
Van Duijnhoven
CG: 27, DR: 60
Fahrenhorst
CG: 22, DR: 55
Gudjonsson
CG: 18, SD: 0
Buckley
CG: 21, SR: 724
Colding
CG: 34, DR: 54
Schindzielorz
CG: 20, SD: 0


KEY: DR = Defensive Rate, SD = Scoring Difference, SR = Strike Rate, CG = Counting Games – League games playing at least 70 minutes

## SQUAD APPEARANCES

| Match | 1 | 2 | 3 | 4 | 5 | 6 | 7 | 8 | 9 | 10 | 11 | 12 | 13 | 14 | 15 | 16 | 17 | 18 | 19 | 20 | 21 | 22 | 23 | 24 | 25 | 26 | 27 | 28 | 29 | 30 | 31 | 32 | 33 | 34 |
|---|---|---|---|---|---|---|---|---|---|---|---|---|---|---|---|---|---|---|---|---|---|---|---|---|---|---|---|---|---|---|---|---|---|---|
| Venue | A | H | A | H | H | A | H | A | H | H | A | A | H | A | H | A | H | H | A | H | A | A | H | A | H | A | H | A | H | A | H | A | H | A |
| Competition | L | L | L | L | L | L | L | L | L | L | L | L | L | L | L | L | L | L | L | L | L | L | L | L | L | L | L | L | L | L | L | L | L | L |
| Result | W | W | W | D | L | D | L | L | W | W | L | W | L | D | L | D | D | W | L | W | L | D | L | L | L | L | D | L | W | W | D | W | D | W |

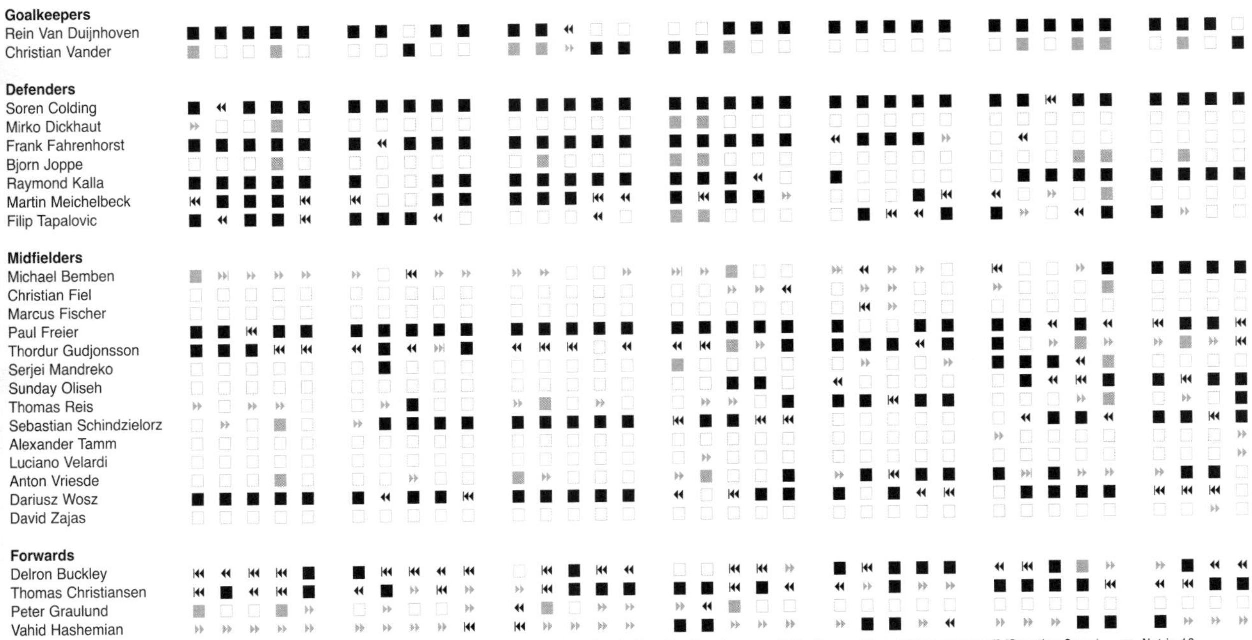

Goalkeepers
Rein Van Duijnhoven
Christian Vander
Defenders
Soren Colding
Mirko Dickhaut
Frank Fahrenhorst
Bjorn Joppe
Raymond Kalla
Martin Meichelbeck
Filip Tapalovic
Midfielders
Michael Bemben
Christian Fiel
Marcus Fischer
Paul Freier
Thordur Gudjonsson
Serjei Mandreko
Sunday Oliseh
Thomas Reis
Sebastian Schindzielorz
Alexander Tamm
Luciano Velardi
Anton Vriesde
Dariusz Wosz
David Zajas
Forwards
Delron Buckley
Thomas Christiansen
Peter Graulund
Vahid Hashemian


KEY: On all match; On bench; Subbed or sent off (Counting game); Subbed or sent off (playing less than 70 minutes); Subbed on from bench (Counting Game); Subbed on (playing less than 70 minutes); Subbed on and then subbed or sent off (Counting Game); Subbed on and then subbed or sent off (playing less than 70 minutes); Not in 16

# 1860 MUNICH

Final Position: **10th**

| | | | | | | | |
|---|---|---|---|---|---|---|---|
| 1 | lge | Hansa Rostock | H | L | 0-2 | |
| 2 | lge | Hannover 96 | A | W | 3-1 | Borimirov 5; Max 41; Lauth 90 |
| 3 | lge | W Bremen | H | W | 3-0 | Schroth 33; Cerny 62; Max 68 |
| 4 | lge | Bayern Munich | A | L | 1-3 | Max 15 |
| 5 | lge | Wolfsburg | H | D | 2-2 | Wiesinger 48; Schroth 64 |
| 6 | lge | Kaiserslautern | A | D | 0-0 | |
| 7 | lge | Hertha Berlin | H | W | 1-0 | Schroth 15 |
| 8 | lge | Stuttgart | A | L | 1-4 | Schroth 22 |
| 9 | lge | Schalke | H | W | 3-0 | Lauth 60,76; Schroth 80 |
| 10 | lge | B M'gladbach | A | W | 1-0 | Schroth 46 |
| 11 | lge | Arminia B | H | W | 3-1 | Suker 14; Lauth 30,38 |
| 12 | lge | Hamburg | A | L | 0-1 | |
| 13 | lge | B Dortmund | A | L | 0-1 | |
| 14 | lge | Nurnberg | H | D | 2-2 | Lauth 39,71 |
| 15 | lge | Cottbus | A | W | 4-3 | Lauth 38; Schroth 54,63; Weissenberger 61 |
| 16 | lge | B Leverkusen | H | L | 0-3 | |
| 17 | lge | Bochum | A | D | 1-1 | Lauth 15 |
| 18 | lge | Hansa Rostock | A | W | 4-1 | Schroth 6,20,71; Costa 21 |
| 19 | lge | Hannover 96 | H | L | 0-1 | |
| 20 | lge | W Bremen | A | W | 2-1 | Lauth 53; Borimirov 82 |
| 21 | lge | Bayern Munich | H | L | 0-5 | |
| 22 | lge | Wolfsburg | A | D | 1-1 | Lauth 55 |
| 23 | lge | Kaiserslautern | H | D | 0-0 | |
| 24 | lge | Hertha Berlin | A | L | 0-6 | |
| 25 | lge | Stuttgart | H | L | 0-1 | |
| 26 | lge | Schalke | A | D | 1-1 | Van Hoogdalem 43 og |
| 27 | lge | B M'gladbach | H | W | 2-0 | Schroth 79; Max 89 |
| 28 | lge | Arminia B | A | L | 1-2 | Stranzl 20 |
| 29 | lge | Hamburg | H | D | 1-1 | Max 36 |
| 30 | lge | B Dortmund | H | D | 0-0 | |
| 31 | lge | Nurnberg | A | W | 2-1 | Lauth 56,73 |
| 32 | lge | Cottbus | H | W | 3-0 | Shao 6; Schroth 34,65 |
| 33 | lge | B Leverkusen | A | L | 0-3 | |
| 34 | lge | Bochum | H | L | 2-4 | Stranzl 37; Max 78 |

## KEY PLAYERS - GOALSCORERS

**1 Benjamin Lauth**

| | | | |
|---|---|---|---|
| Goals in the League | 13 | Player Strike Rate<br>Average number of minutes between League goals scored by player | 187 |
| Contribution to Attacking Power<br>Average number of minutes between League team goals while on pitch | 71 | Club Strike Rate<br>Average number of minutes between League goals scored by club | 70 |

| | PLAYER | LGE GOALS | POWER | STRIKE RATE |
|---|---|---|---|---|
| 2 | Markus Schroth | 14 | 67 | 197 mins |
| 3 | Martin Stranzl | 2 | 67 | 771 mins |
| 4 | Markus Weissenberger | 1 | 74 | 1777 mins |
| 5 | Rodrigo Costa | 1 | 71 | 2294 mins |

## KEY PLAYERS - MIDFIELDERS

**1 Marcus Purk**

| | | | |
|---|---|---|---|
| Goals in the League | 0 | Contribution to Attacking Power<br>Average number of minutes between League team goals while on pitch | 46 |
| Defensive Rating<br>Average number of mins between League goals conceded while he was on the pitch | 60 | Scoring Difference<br>Defensive Rating minus Contribution to Attacking Power | 14 |

| | PLAYER | LGE GOALS | DEF RATE | POWER | SCORE DIFF |
|---|---|---|---|---|---|
| 2 | Thomas Hassler | 0 | 67 | 58 | 9 mins |
| 3 | Rodrigo Costa | 1 | 70 | 72 | -2 mins |
| 4 | Remo Meyer | 0 | 62 | 70 | -8 mins |
| 5 | Harald Cerny | 1 | 57 | 65 | -8 mins |

## KEY PLAYERS - DEFENDERS

**1 Marco Kurz**

| | | | |
|---|---|---|---|
| Goals Conceded (GC)<br>The number of League goals conceded while he was on the pitch | 31 | Clean Sheets<br>In games when he played at least 70 minutes | 6 |
| Defensive Rating<br>Ave number of mins between League goals conceded while on the pitch | 62 | Club Defensive Rating<br>Average number of mins between League goals conceded by the club this season | 59 |

| | PLAYER | CON LGE | CLEAN SHEETS | DEF RATE |
|---|---|---|---|---|
| 2 | Torben Hoffmann | 39 | 6 | 58 mins |
| 3 | Tomas Votava | 28 | 3 | 58 mins |
| 4 | Martin Stranzl | 32 | 3 | 48 mins |

## GOALS SCORED

**AT HOME**

| | | |
|---|---|---|
| MOST | B Munich | 37 |
| | | 22 |
| LEAST | Nurnberg | 16 |

**AWAY**

| | | |
|---|---|---|
| MOST | B Munich | 33 |
| | | 22 |
| LEAST | B M'gladbach &Arminia B | 12 |

## GOALS CONCEDED

**AT HOME**

| | | |
|---|---|---|
| LEAST | Hamburg & B M'gladbach | 11 |
| | | 22 |
| MOST | Hannover 96 | 33 |

**AWAY**

| | | |
|---|---|---|
| LEAST | B Munich | 13 |
| | | 30 |
| MOST | Nurnberg | 36 |

## KEY GOALKEEPER

**1 Simon Jentzsch**

| | |
|---|---|
| Goals Conceded in the League | 50 |
| Defensive Rating<br>Ave number of mins between League goals conceded while on the pitch | 58 |
| Counting Games<br>Games when he played at least 70 minutes | 32 |
| Clean Sheets<br>In games when he played at least 70 minutes | 9 |

## TOP POINT EARNERS

| | PLAYER | GAMES | AVE |
|---|---|---|---|
| 1 | Cerny | 31 | 1.42 |
| 2 | Meyer | 23 | 1.39 |
| 3 | Jentzsch | 32 | 1.38 |
| 4 | Costa | 25 | 1.36 |
| 5 | Hoffmann, T | 25 | 1.36 |
| 6 | Schroth | 31 | 1.35 |
| 7 | Votava | 17 | 1.35 |
| 8 | Lauth | 24 | 1.33 |
| 9 | Kurz | 19 | 1.26 |
| 10 | Weissenberger | 17 | 1.24 |
| | **CLUB AVERAGE:** | | **1.32** |

Ave = Average points per match in Counting Games

## ATTENDANCES

HOME GROUND: OLYMPIASTADION CAPACITY: 69060 AVERAGE LEAGUE AT HOME: 24782

| | | | | | | | | |
|---|---|---|---|---|---|---|---|---|
| 4 | Bayern Munich | 69000 | 10 | B M'gladbach | 26000 | 8 | Stuttgart | 21000 |
| 13 | B Dortmund | 68600 | 7 | Hertha Berlin | 25000 | 3 | W Bremen | 21000 |
| 21 | Bayern Munich | 64000 | 34 | Bochum | 25000 | 16 | B Leverkusen | 20000 |
| 26 | Schalke | 60000 | 9 | Schalke | 25000 | 25 | Stuttgart | 20000 |
| 2 | Hannover 96 | 47000 | 5 | Wolfsburg | 23000 | 17 | Bochum | 18000 |
| 6 | Kaiserslautern | 38000 | 1 | Hansa Rostock | 22800 | 22 | Wolfsburg | 16000 |
| 30 | B Dortmund | 35000 | 11 | Arminia B | 22500 | 18 | Hansa Rostock | 15000 |
| 31 | Nurnberg | 35000 | 33 | B Leverkusen | 22500 | 27 | B M'gladbach | 12000 |
| 20 | W Bremen | 34000 | 29 | Hamburg | 22000 | 15 | Cottbus | 11000 |
| 12 | Hamburg | 32000 | 28 | Arminia B | 21070 | 32 | Cottbus | 10000 |
| 14 | Nurnberg | 32000 | 23 | Kaiserslautern | 21000 | | | |
| 24 | Hertha Berlin | 30000 | 19 | Hannover 96 | 21000 | | | |

■ Home □ Away ▒ Neutral

## DISCIPLINARY RECORDS

| | PLAYER | YELLOW | RED | AVE |
|---|---|---|---|---|
| 1 | Kurz | 10 | 2 | 159 |
| 2 | Stranzl | 6 | 1 | 220 |
| 3 | Suker | 2 | 0 | 236 |
| 4 | Max | 4 | 0 | 238 |
| 5 | Costa | 7 | 1 | 286 |
| 6 | Wiesinger | 3 | 0 | 345 |
| 7 | Meyer | 6 | 0 | 360 |
| 8 | Purk | 2 | 0 | 389 |
| 9 | Cerny | 7 | 0 | 397 |
| 10 | Borimirov | 3 | 0 | 460 |
| 11 | Votava | 3 | 0 | 543 |
| 12 | Tyce | 1 | 0 | 608 |
| 13 | Ehlers | 1 | 0 | 657 |
| | Other | 18 | 0 | |
| | TOTAL | 73 | 4 | |

## LEAGUE GOALS

| | PLAYER | MINS | GOALS | AVE |
|---|---|---|---|---|
| 1 | Schroth | 2754 | 14 | 197 |
| 2 | Lauth | 2430 | 13 | 187 |
| 3 | Max | 954 | 6 | 159 |
| 4 | Borimirov | 1381 | 2 | 691 |
| 5 | Stranzl | 1541 | 2 | 771 |
| 6 | Suker | 472 | 1 | 472 |
| 7 | Weissenberger | 1777 | 1 | 1777 |
| 8 | Wiesinger | 1036 | 1 | 1036 |
| 9 | Costa | 2294 | 1 | 2294 |
| 10 | Cerny | 2779 | 1 | 2779 |
| 11 | Shao | 419 | 1 | 419 |
| | Other | | 1 | |
| | TOTAL | | 44 | |

## MONTH BY MONTH GUIDE TO THE POINTS

| MONTH | POINTS | % |
|---|---|---|
| AUGUST | 6 | 67% |
| SEPTEMBER | 5 | 42% |
| OCTOBER | 6 | 67% |
| NOVEMBER | 7 | 47% |
| DECEMBER | 1 | 17% |
| JANUARY | 3 | 100% |
| FEBRUARY | 4 | 33% |
| MARCH | 2 | 17% |
| APRIL | 5 | 42% |
| MAY | 6 | 50% |

## TEAM OF THE SEASON

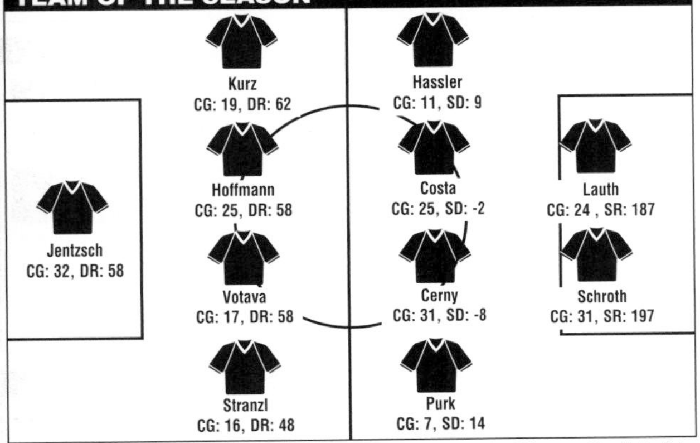
Kurz
CG: 19, DR: 62
Hassler
CG: 11, SD: 9
Hoffmann
CG: 25, DR: 58
Costa
CG: 25, SD: -2
Lauth
CG: 24 , SR: 187
Jentzsch
CG: 32, DR: 58
Votava
CG: 17, DR: 58
Cerny
CG: 31, SD: -8
Schroth
CG: 31, SR: 197
Stranzl
CG: 16, DR: 48
Purk
CG: 7, SD: 14

KEY: DR = Defensive Rate, SD = Scoring Difference, SR = Strike Rate,
CG = Counting Games – League games playing at least 70 minutes

## LEAGUE APPEARANCES, BOOKINGS AND CAPS

| | AGE | IN THE SQUAD | COUNTING GAMES | MINUTES ON PITCH | YELLOW CARDS | RED CARDS | THIS SEASON | HOME COUNTRY |
|---|---|---|---|---|---|---|---|---|
| **Goalkeepers** | | | | | | | | |
| Michael Hofmann | 30 | 16 | 2 | 180 | 1 | 0 | - | Germany |
| Simon Jentzsch | 27 | 32 | 32 | 2880 | 3 | 0 | - | Germany |
| Jurgen Wittmann | 36 | 1 | 0 | 0 | 0 | 0 | - | Germany |
| **Defenders** | | | | | | | | |
| Uwe Ehlers | 28 | 19 | 5 | 657 | 1 | 0 | - | Germany |
| Torben Hoffmann | 28 | 27 | 25 | 2255 | 3 | 0 | - | Germany |
| Marco Kurz | 34 | 27 | 19 | 1919 | 10 | 2 | - | Germany |
| Achim Pfuderer | 27 | 9 | 0 | 89 | 0 | 0 | - | Germany |
| Vidar Riseth | 31 | 5 | 0 | 140 | 2 | 0 | 1 | Norway (24) |
| Martin Stranzl | 23 | 21 | 16 | 1541 | 6 | 1 | - | Austria |
| Tomas Votava | 29 | 24 | 17 | 1629 | 3 | 0 | - | Czech Republic |
| **Midfielders** | | | | | | | | |
| Daniel Borimirov | 33 | 27 | 10 | 1381 | 3 | 0 | - | Bulgaria |
| Harald Cerny | 29 | 31 | 31 | 2779 | 7 | 0 | - | Austria |
| Rodrigo Costa | 27 | 27 | 25 | 2294 | 7 | 1 | - | Brazil |
| Andreas Gorlitz | 21 | 2 | 0 | 18 | 0 | 0 | - | Germany |
| Thomas Hassler | 37 | 22 | 11 | 1403 | 1 | 0 | - | Germany |
| Remo Meyer | 22 | 29 | 23 | 2162 | 6 | 0 | - | Switzerland |
| Marcus Purk | 28 | 12 | 7 | 779 | 2 | 0 | - | Austria |
| Da Silva Rafael | 24 | 8 | 2 | 302 | 2 | 0 | - | Brazil |
| Danny Schwarz | 28 | 16 | 1 | 247 | 0 | 0 | - | Germany |
| Jiayi Shao | 23 | 12 | 1 | 419 | 0 | 0 | - | China |
| Roman Tyce | 26 | 7 | 7 | 608 | 1 | 0 | 2 | Czech Republic (13) |
| Markus Weissenberger | 28 | 27 | 17 | 1777 | 1 | 0 | - | Austria |
| Micheal Wiesinger | 30 | 22 | 9 | 1036 | 3 | 0 | - | Germany |
| **Forwards** | | | | | | | | |
| Paul Agostino | 28 | 20 | 2 | 441 | 0 | 0 | - | Australia |
| Benjamin Lauth | 21 | 34 | 24 | 2430 | 3 | 0 | 5 | Germany (4) |
| Martin Max | 34 | 22 | 8 | 954 | 4 | 0 | - | Germany |
| Markus Schroth | 28 | 31 | 31 | 2754 | 2 | 0 | - | Germany |
| Davor Suker | 35 | 16 | 2 | 472 | 2 | 0 | - | Croatia |

KEY: LEAGUE BOOKINGS CAPS (FIFA RANKING)

## SQUAD APPEARANCES

| Match | 1 | 2 | 3 | 4 | 5 | 6 | 7 | 8 | 9 | 10 | 11 | 12 | 13 | 14 | 15 | 16 | 17 | 18 | 19 | 20 | 21 | 22 | 23 | 24 | 25 | 26 | 27 | 28 | 29 | 30 | 31 | 32 | 33 | 34 |
|---|---|---|---|---|---|---|---|---|---|---|---|---|---|---|---|---|---|---|---|---|---|---|---|---|---|---|---|---|---|---|---|---|---|---|
| Venue | H | A | H | A | H | A | H | A | H | A | H | A | A | H | A | H | A | A | H | A | H | A | H | A | H | A | H | A | H | H | A | H | A | H |
| Competition | L | L | L | L | L | L | L | L | L | L | L | L | L | L | L | L | L | L | L | L | L | L | L | L | L | L | L | L | L | L | L | L | L | L |
| Result | L | W | W | L | D | D | W | L | W | W | W | L | L | D | W | L | D | W | L | W | L | D | D | L | L | D | W | L | D | D | W | W | L | L |

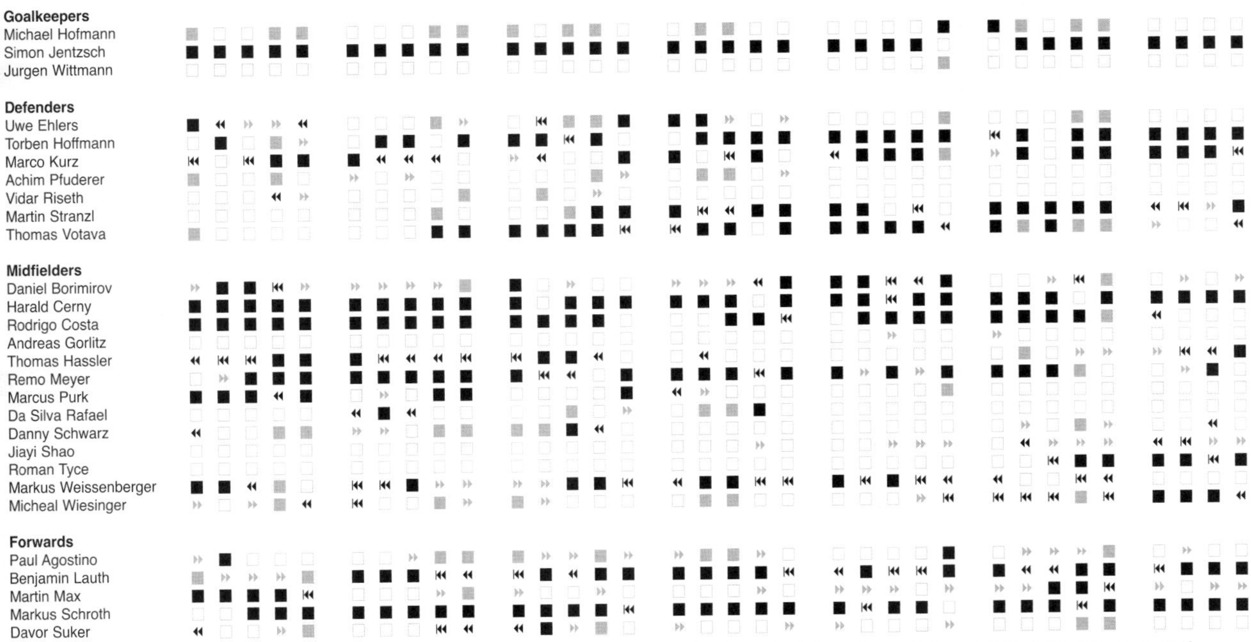

KEY: On all match · On bench · Subbed or sent off (Counting game) · Subbed or sent off (playing less than 70 minutes) · Subbed on from bench (Counting Game) · Subbed on (playing less than 70 minutes) · Subbed on and then subbed or sent off (Counting Game) · Subbed on and then subbed or sent off (playing less than 70 minutes) · Not in 16

# HANNOVER 96

Final Position: **11th**

| | | | | | | |
|---|---|---|---|---|---|---|
| 1 | lge | Hamburg | A | L | 1-2 | Zuraw 6 |
| 2 | lge | 1860 Munich | H | L | 1-3 | Stajner 27 |
| 3 | lge | Nurnberg | A | L | 1-3 | N'Diaye 83 |
| 4 | lge | Cottbus | H | L | 1-3 | Idrissou 25 |
| 5 | lge | B Leverkusen | A | W | 3-1 | Bobic 41,81; Idrissou 83 |
| 6 | lge | Bochum | H | D | 2-2 | Bobic 44; Linke 72 |
| 7 | lge | Hansa Rostock | A | W | 2-1 | Idrissou 32; Bobic 43 |
| 8 | lge | B Dortmund | H | L | 0-3 | |
| 9 | lge | W Bremen | H | D | 4-4 | Krupnikovic 6; Idrissou 39; Bobic 81,83 |
| 10 | lge | Bayern Munich | A | D | 3-3 | Zuraw 16; Stendel 44,83 |
| 11 | lge | Wolfsburg | H | W | 3-1 | Stendel 23; Bobic 28; Konstantinidis 81 |
| 12 | lge | Kaiserslautern | A | W | 1-0 | Bobic 41 |
| 13 | lge | Hertha Berlin | H | L | 0-1 | |
| 14 | lge | Stuttgart | A | L | 0-3 | |
| 15 | lge | Schalke | H | L | 0-2 | |
| 16 | lge | B M'gladbach | A | L | 0-1 | |
| 17 | lge | Arminia B | H | D | 0-0 | |
| 18 | lge | Hamburg | H | D | 2-2 | Bobic 40; Idrissou 50 |
| 19 | lge | 1860 Munich | A | W | 1-0 | Krupnikovic 26 |
| 20 | lge | Nurnberg | H | W | 4-2 | Idrissou 10,22,25; Stefulj 72 |
| 21 | lge | Cottbus | A | L | 0-3 | |
| 22 | lge | B Leverkusen | H | L | 1-2 | Popescu 14 |
| 23 | lge | Bochum | A | W | 2-1 | Vinicius 6; Bobic 36 |
| 24 | lge | Hansa Rostock | H | W | 3-1 | Bobic 41; Idrissou 45; Konstantinidis 67 |
| 25 | lge | B Dortmund | A | L | 0-2 | |
| 26 | lge | W Bremen | A | W | 2-1 | Bobic 44,76 |
| 27 | lge | Bayern Munich | H | D | 2-2 | Stajner 35; Vinicius 44 |
| 28 | lge | Wolfsburg | A | L | 0-1 | |
| 29 | lge | Kaiserslautern | H | W | 2-1 | Krupnikovic 49; Bobic 61 |
| 30 | lge | Hertha Berlin | A | L | 0-2 | |
| 31 | lge | Stuttgart | H | L | 1-2 | Kaufman 85 |
| 32 | lge | Schalke | A | W | 2-0 | Krupnikovic 60; Stajner 74 |
| 33 | lge | B M'gladbach | H | D | 2-2 | Krupnikovic 10; Stajner 90 |
| 34 | lge | Arminia B | A | W | 1-0 | Casey 85 |

## KEY PLAYERS - GOALSCORERS

**1 Fredi Bobic**

| | | | |
|---|---|---|---|
| Goals in the League | 14 | Player Strike Rate<br>Average number of minutes between League goals scored by player | 171 |
| Contribution to Attacking Power<br>Average number of minutes between League team goals while on pitch | 63 | Club Strike Rate<br>Average number of minutes between League goals scored by club | 65 |

| | PLAYER | LGE GOALS | POWER | STRIKE RATE |
|---|---|---|---|---|
| 2 | Mohamadou Idrissou | 9 | 58 | 267 mins |
| 3 | Nebosja Krupnikovic | 5 | 64 | 513 mins |
| 4 | Jiri Stajner | 4 | 66 | 548 mins |
| 5 | Dariusz Zuraw | 2 | 70 | 599 mins |

## KEY PLAYERS - MIDFIELDERS

**1 Julian De Guzman**

| | | | |
|---|---|---|---|
| Goals in the League | 0 | Contribution to Attacking Power<br>Average number of minutes between League team goals while on pitch | 61 |
| Defensive Rating<br>Average number of mins between League goals conceded while he was on the pitch | 55 | Scoring Difference<br>Defensive Rating minus Contribution to Attacking Power | -6 |

| | PLAYER | LGE GOALS | DEF RATE | POWER | SCORE DIFF |
|---|---|---|---|---|---|
| 2 | Nebosja Krupnikovic | 5 | 53 | 64 | -11 mins |
| 3 | Altin Lala | 0 | 51 | 63 | -12 mins |
| 4 | Sanchez Fernandez Jaime | 0 | 60 | 73 | -13 mins |
| 5 | Danijel Stefulj | 1 | 46 | 75 | -29 mins |

## KEY PLAYERS - DEFENDERS

**1 Kostas Konstantinidis**

| | | | |
|---|---|---|---|
| Goals Conceded (GC)<br>The number of League goals conceded while he was on the pitch | 26 | Clean Sheets<br>In games when he played at least 70 minutes | 4 |
| Defensive Rating<br>Ave number of mins between League goals conceded while on the pitch | 68 | Club Defensive Rating<br>Average number of mins between League goals conceded by the club this season | 54 |

| | PLAYER | CON LGE | CLEAN SHEETS | DEF RATE |
|---|---|---|---|---|
| 2 | Bergantin Vinicius | 24 | 3 | 64 mins |
| 3 | Steven Cherundolo | 49 | 5 | 59 mins |
| 4 | Gheorghe Popescu | 21 | 1 | 57 mins |
| 5 | Dariusz Zuraw | 21 | 3 | 57 mins |

## GOALS SCORED

AT HOME

| | | |
|---|---|---|
| MOST | B Munich | 37 |
| | | 28 |
| LEAST | Nurnberg | 16 |

AWAY

| | | |
|---|---|---|
| MOST | B Munich | 33 |
| | | 19 |
| LEAST | B M'gladbach &Arminia B | 12 |

## GOALS CONCEDED

AT HOME

| | | |
|---|---|---|
| LEAST | Hamburg & B M'gladbach | 11 |
| | | 33 |
| MOST | Hannover 96 | 33 |

AWAY

| | | |
|---|---|---|
| LEAST | B Munich | 13 |
| | | 24 |
| MOST | Nurnberg | 36 |

## KEY GOALKEEPER

**1 Gerd Tremmel**

| | |
|---|---|
| Goals Conceded in the League | 24 |
| Defensive Rating<br>Ave number of mins between League goals conceded while on the pitch | 67 |
| Counting Games<br>Games when he played at least 70 minutes | 18 |
| Clean Sheets<br>In games when he played at least 70 minutes | 4 |

## TOP POINT EARNERS

| | PLAYER | GAMES | AVE |
|---|---|---|---|
| 1 | Vinicius | 17 | 1.59 |
| 2 | Tremmel | 18 | 1.56 |
| 3 | Idrissou | 23 | 1.52 |
| 4 | Konstantinidis | 18 | 1.44 |
| 5 | Bobic | 26 | 1.42 |
| 6 | Cherundolo | 30 | 1.33 |
| 7 | Jaime | 18 | 1.33 |
| 8 | Lala | 28 | 1.32 |
| 9 | Popescu | 13 | 1.31 |
| 10 | Zuraw | 13 | 1.23 |
| | **CLUB AVERAGE:** | | **1.26** |

Ave = Average points per match in Counting Games

## ATTENDANCES

HOME GROUND: AWD-ARENA CAPACITY: 50418 AVERAGE LEAGUE AT HOME: 37547

| | | | | | | | | |
|---|---|---|---|---|---|---|---|---|
| 25 | B Dortmund | 67000 | 11 | Wolfsburg | 40000 | 20 | Nurnberg | 28000 |
| 32 | Schalke | 60886 | 22 | B Leverkusen | 39000 | 24 | Hansa Rostock | 28000 |
| 1 | Hamburg | 55000 | 13 | Hertha Berlin | 38795 | 34 | Arminia B | 26601 |
| 10 | Bayern Munich | 50000 | 26 | W Bremen | 36000 | 7 | Hansa Rostock | 25000 |
| 8 | B Dortmund | 49800 | 4 | Cottbus | 35506 | 16 | B M'gladbach | 24000 |
| 15 | Schalke | 48696 | 12 | Kaiserslautern | 34000 | 5 | B Leverkusen | 22500 |
| 2 | 1860 Munich | 47000 | 33 | B M'gladbach | 31878 | 3 | Nurnberg | 22000 |
| 30 | Hertha Berlin | 45031 | 27 | Bayern Munich | 31878 | 19 | 1860 Munich | 21000 |
| 9 | W Bremen | 45000 | 31 | Stuttgart | 31000 | 23 | Bochum | 15000 |
| 18 | Hamburg | 43183 | 29 | Kaiserslautern | 30573 | 21 | Cottbus | 14000 |
| 6 | Bochum | 40000 | 28 | Wolfsburg | 30000 | | | |
| 14 | Stuttgart | 40000 | 17 | Arminia B | 30000 | | | |

Home / Away / Neutral

## DISCIPLINARY RECORDS

| | PLAYER | YELLOW | RED | AVE |
|---|---|---|---|---|
| 1 | van Hintum | 4 | 1 | 158 |
| 2 | Jaime | 6 | 0 | 268 |
| 3 | Lala | 9 | 0 | 299 |
| 4 | Popescu | 4 | 0 | 301 |
| 5 | Schuler | 3 | 0 | 325 |
| 6 | Bobic | 6 | 1 | 342 |
| 7 | Konstantinidis | 5 | 0 | 351 |
| 8 | Cherundolo | 8 | 0 | 358 |
| 9 | Zuraw | 3 | 0 | 399 |
| 10 | Linke | 2 | 0 | 419 |
| 11 | Krupnikovic | 6 | 0 | 427 |
| 12 | Stefulj | 3 | 0 | 475 |
| 13 | Sievers | 3 | 0 | 480 |
| | Other | 16 | 1 | |
| | TOTAL | 78 | 3 | |

## LEAGUE GOALS

| | PLAYER | MINS | GOALS | AVE |
|---|---|---|---|---|
| 1 | Bobic | 2398 | 14 | 171 |
| 2 | Idrissou | 2400 | 9 | 267 |
| 3 | Krupnikovic | 2563 | 5 | 513 |
| 4 | Stajner | 2191 | 4 | 548 |
| 5 | Stendel | 1376 | 3 | 459 |
| 6 | Zuraw | 1198 | 2 | 599 |
| 7 | Konstantinidis | 1755 | 2 | 878 |
| 8 | Vinicius | 1530 | 2 | 765 |
| 9 | Kaufman | 357 | 1 | 357 |
| 10 | Stefulj | 1426 | 1 | 1426 |
| 11 | N'Diaye | 73 | 1 | 73 |
| 12 | Linke | 838 | 1 | 838 |
| 13 | Popescu | 1206 | 1 | 1206 |
| | Other | | 1 | |
| | TOTAL | | 47 | |

## MONTH BY MONTH GUIDE TO THE POINTS

| MONTH | POINTS | % |
|---|---|---|
| AUGUST | 0 | 0% |
| SEPTEMBER | 7 | 58% |
| OCTOBER | 2 | 22% |
| NOVEMBER | 6 | 50% |
| DECEMBER | 1 | 11% |
| JANUARY | 1 | 33% |
| FEBRUARY | 6 | 50% |
| MARCH | 9 | 75% |
| APRIL | 4 | 33% |
| MAY | 7 | 58% |

## TEAM OF THE SEASON

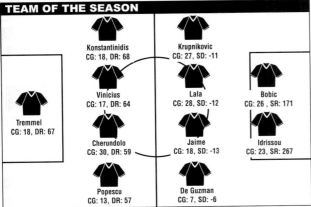

- Tremmel CG: 18, DR: 67
- Konstantinidis CG: 18, DR: 68
- Vinicius CG: 17, DR: 64
- Cherundolo CG: 30, DR: 59
- Popescu CG: 13, DR: 57
- Krupnikovic CG: 27, SD: -11
- Lala CG: 28, SD: -12
- Jaime CG: 18, SD: -13
- De Guzman CG: 7, SD: -6
- Bobic CG: 26 , SR: 171
- Idrissou CG: 23, SR: 267

KEY: DR = Defensive Rate, SD = Scoring Difference, SR = Strike Rate, CG = Counting Games – League games playing at least 70 minutes

## LEAGUE APPEARANCES, BOOKINGS AND CAPS

| | AGE | IN THE SQUAD | COUNTING GAMES | MINUTES ON PITCH | YELLOW CARDS | RED CARDS | THIS SEASON | HOME COUNTRY |
|---|---|---|---|---|---|---|---|---|
| **Goalkeepers** | | | | | | | | |
| Timo Ochs | 21 | 2 | 0 | 0 | 0 | 0 | - | Germany |
| Jorg Sievers | 37 | 26 | 16 | 1442 | 3 | 0 | - | Germany |
| Gerd Tremmel | 24 | 26 | 18 | 1618 | 0 | 0 | - | Germany |
| **Defenders** | | | | | | | | |
| Steve Cherundolo | 24 | 33 | 30 | 2870 | 8 | 0 | 3 | United States (10) |
| Dame Diouf | 25 | 7 | 4 | 439 | 3 | 1 | - | Senegal |
| Kostas Konstantinidis | 30 | 22 | 18 | 1755 | 5 | 0 | - | Greece |
| Carsten Linke | 37 | 25 | 8 | 838 | 2 | 0 | - | Germany |
| Kai Oswald | 25 | 13 | 1 | 135 | 1 | 0 | - | Germany |
| Gheorghe Popescu | 35 | 14 | 13 | 1206 | 4 | 0 | 3 | Romania (27) |
| Markus Schuler | 25 | 24 | 8 | 976 | 3 | 0 | - | Germany |
| Marc van Hintum | 36 | 15 | 7 | 791 | 4 | 1 | - | Holland |
| Bergantin Vinicius | 22 | 17 | 17 | 1530 | 1 | 0 | - | Brazil |
| Dariusz Zuraw | 30 | 17 | 13 | 1198 | 3 | 0 | - | Poland |
| **Midfielders** | | | | | | | | |
| Julian De Guzman | 22 | 22 | 7 | 983 | 2 | 0 | - | Canada |
| Guido Gorges | | 2 | 0 | 12 | 0 | 0 | - | |
| Sanchez Jaime | 30 | 21 | 18 | 1613 | 6 | 0 | - | Spain |
| Colmenero Manuel | | 1 | 0 | 21 | 0 | 0 | - | |
| Nebosja Krupnikovic | 29 | 32 | 27 | 2563 | 6 | 0 | - | Serbia & Montenegro |
| Altin Lala | 27 | 32 | 28 | 2695 | 9 | 0 | - | Albania |
| Babacar N'Diaye | 29 | 9 | 0 | 73 | 0 | 0 | - | Senegal |
| Thorsten Nehrbauer | 25 | 5 | 0 | 4 | 0 | 0 | - | Germany |
| Sanchez Cipitra | | 2 | 1 | 135 | 1 | 0 | - | |
| Sanchez Fernandez | | 2 | 1 | 90 | 1 | 0 | - | |
| Danijel Stefulj | 30 | 23 | 13 | 1426 | 3 | 0 | - | Croatia |
| **Forwards** | | | | | | | | |
| Fredi Bobic | 31 | 27 | 26 | 2398 | 6 | 1 | 7 | Germany (4) |
| Connor Casey | 21 | 8 | 0 | 68 | 0 | 0 | - | United States |
| Mohamadou Idrissou | 23 | 31 | 23 | 2400 | 4 | 0 | 1 | Cameroon (18) |
| Jiri Kaufman | 23 | 21 | 2 | 357 | 0 | 0 | - | Czech Republic |
| Blaise N'Kufo | 28 | 14 | 3 | 429 | 1 | 0 | - | Switzerland |
| Jiri Stajner | 27 | 33 | 23 | 2191 | 2 | 0 | 6 | Czech Republic (13) |
| Daniel Stendel | 29 | 31 | 11 | 1376 | 0 | 0 | - | Germany |

KEY: LEAGUE BOOKINGS CAPS (FIFA RANKING)

## SQUAD APPEARANCES

| Match | 1 | 2 | 3 | 4 | 5 | 6 | 7 | 8 | 9 | 10 | 11 | 12 | 13 | 14 | 15 | 16 | 17 | 18 | 19 | 20 | 21 | 22 | 23 | 24 | 25 | 26 | 27 | 28 | 29 | 30 | 31 | 32 | 33 | 34 |
|---|---|---|---|---|---|---|---|---|---|---|---|---|---|---|---|---|---|---|---|---|---|---|---|---|---|---|---|---|---|---|---|---|---|---|
| Venue | A | H | A | H | A | H | A | H | H | A | H | A | H | A | H | A | H | H | A | H | A | H | A | H | A | A | H | A | H | A | H | A | H | A |
| Competition | L | L | L | L | L | L | L | L | L | L | L | L | L | L | L | L | L | L | L | L | L | L | L | L | L | L | L | L | L | L | L | L | L | L |
| Result | L | L | L | L | W | D | W | L | D | D | W | W | L | L | L | L | D | D | W | W | L | L | W | W | L | W | D | L | W | L | L | W | D | W |
| **Goalkeepers** | | | | | | | | | | | | | | | | | | | | | | | | | | | | | | | | | | |
| Timo Ochs | | | ▒ | | | | | | | | | | | | | | | | | | ▒ | | | | | | | | | | | | | |
| Jorg Sievers | ■ | ■ | ■ | ■ | ■ | ■ | ■ | ■ | ■ | ■ | ■ | ■ | ■ | ■ | ■ | ■ | ▒ | ▒ | | | | | | ▒ | | ▒ | ▒ | ▒ | ▒ | ▒ | | ▒ | | » |
| Gerd Tremmel | | | | ▒ | ▒ | | | | | | ▒ | ▒ | ▒ | | | ▒ | ■ | ■ | ■ | ■ | ■ | ■ | ■ | ■ | ■ | ■ | ■ | ■ | ■ | ■ | ■ | ■ | ■ | ⏮ |
| **Defenders** | | | | | | | | | | | | | | | | | | | | | | | | | | | | | | | | | | |
| Steven Cherundolo | ⏮ | ■ | ■ | ■ | ■ | ■ | ■ | ■ | ■ | ■ | « | ■ | ■ | « | ■ | ■ | ■ | ■ | ■ | ■ | | ■ | ■ | ■ | « | ■ | ■ | ■ | ■ | ■ | ■ | ■ | ■ | ■ |
| Dame Diouf | | | » | ■ | ■ | | | ⏮ | | | | | ▒ | » | ■ | | | | | | | | | | | | | | | | | | | |
| Kostas Konstantinidis | | | | | | | | | | ■ | ■ | ■ | ■ | « | | ■ | ■ | ■ | ■ | « | | ■ | ■ | ■ | ■ | ■ | ■ | ■ | ▒ | ■ | « | ■ | ■ | |
| Carsten Linke | ■ | ■ | « | ■ | ■ | ■ | ■ | ■ | ⏮ | | ▒ | | | | | ▒ | ▒ | ▒ | » | | ▒ | | » | ▒ | | ▒ | ▒ | ▒ | » | ▒ | | » | » | » |
| Kai Oswald | | | ■ | ▒ | | | | | | | | ▒ | ▒ | | | « | | ▒ | | | | | | ▒ | | ▒ | | ▒ | ▒ | ▒ | | | | |
| Gheorghe Popescu | | | | | | | | | | | | | | | | | | | | » | ■ | ■ | ■ | ■ | ■ | ■ | ■ | ⏮ | ■ | ■ | ■ | ■ | ■ | |
| Markus Schuler | » | » | ■ | ▒ | » | ■ | « | | ▒ | | » | | ▒ | | » | » | ■ | ■ | ■ | ■ | ⏮ | ■ | | » | » | » | » | | ▒ | » | | | | |
| Marc van Hintum | ⏮ | « | ▒ | ▒ | | | | | ▒ | | | ▒ | | | | | | | | | | | ■ | ■ | ⏮ | ■ | « | ■ | ⏮ | | | ▒ | ⏮ | |
| Bergantin Vinicius | | | | | | | | | | | | | | | | | | ■ | ■ | ■ | ■ | ■ | ■ | ■ | ■ | ■ | ■ | ■ | ■ | ■ | ■ | ■ | ■ | ■ |
| Dariusz Zuraw | ■ | ■ | ▒ | ▒ | | ■ | ■ | | ■ | ■ | ■ | ■ | ■ | « | ■ | ■ | ■ | | | | ▒ | | | | | | | | | | | | | ⏮ |
| **Midfielders** | | | | | | | | | | | | | | | | | | | | | | | | | | | | | | | | | | |
| Julian De Guzman | | | » | ▒ | ■ | | | ⏮ | » | » | ■ | ■ | « | » | | « | ▒ | ▒ | » | ■ | » | ■ | | | | » | » | | « | « | | | | ■ |
| Guido Gorges | | | | » | ▒ | | | | | | | | | | | | | | | | | | | | | | | | | | | | | |
| Sanchez Fernandez Jaime | | | | | | ■ | ■ | | ⏮ | ■ | ■ | ■ | ⏮ | ■ | ■ | ■ | ⏮ | ■ | « | | ⏮ | | | | | | ▒ | | ⏮ | » | ⏮ | ■ | ⏮ | ■ |
| Colmenero Jose Manuel | | | | | | | | | | | | | | | | | » | | | | | | | | | | | | | | | | | |
| Nebosja Krupnikovic | ■ | ■ | ■ | ■ | ■ | ⏮ | ⏮ | ■ | ■ | ⏮ | ■ | ⏮ | ■ | ■ | ■ | ■ | ⏮ | ⏮ | ⏮ | « | ■ | | » | « | ■ | ⏮ | ⏮ | ⏮ | » | ■ | ■ | ⏮ | « | |
| Altin Lala | ■ | ■ | ■ | ⏮ | ■ | ■ | ■ | ■ | ■ | ■ | | » | » | ■ | « | | ■ | ■ | ■ | ■ | ■ | ■ | ■ | ■ | ■ | ■ | ■ | ■ | ■ | « | ■ | ■ | ■ | ■ |
| Thorsten Nehrbauer | | | | ▒ | ▒ | | » | | ▒ | | | | | | | | | | | | | | | | | | | | | | | | | |
| Sanchez Cipitra | | | | ■ | « | | | | | | | | | | | | | | | | | | | | | | | | | | | | | |
| Sanchez Fernandez | | | | ■ | | | | | | | ▒ | | | | | | | | | | | | | | | | | | | | | | | |
| Danijel Stefulj | ■ | ■ | « | | » | » | » | ■ | ■ | ■ | ■ | ■ | ■ | ■ | ■ | | ■ | | | » | ■ | | ⏮ | » | | | | » | » | ▒ | « | | | |
| **Forwards** | | | | | | | | | | | | | | | | | | | | | | | | | | | | | | | | | | |
| Fredi Bobic | | | | ⏮ | ⏮ | ■ | ■ | | ■ | ■ | ⏮ | ⏮ | ■ | ■ | ■ | ■ | ■ | ■ | ■ | | ⏮ | | ■ | ■ | ■ | ■ | ■ | ■ | ■ | ■ | ■ | ⏮ | ■ | |
| Connor Casey | | | | | | | | » | | | | | | | | | | | | » | | » | | | | | | ▒ | ▒ | ▒ | | ▒ | | » |
| Mohamadou Idrissou | » | | | ■ | ■ | ■ | ■ | ■ | ■ | ■ | ■ | ■ | ■ | ■ | « | ■ | | ■ | ■ | ■ | ■ | ■ | « | ⏮ | ■ | ⏮ | ■ | « | ▒ | « | » | ■ | » | ■ |
| Jiri Kaufman | | » | ▒ | | | | | » | | | | | | | | » | | ▒ | | ⏮ | » | « | | ▒ | » | ▒ | ▒ | » | ▒ | ▒ | » | » | » | ⏮ |
| Blaise N'Kufo | « | ⏮ | ■ | ▒ | | | | | ▒ | | » | » | » | | » | ▒ | ▒ | ⏮ | « | | ▒ | | | | | | | | | | | | | |
| Jiri Stajner | ■ | ■ | ■ | ⏮ | ⏮ | ⏮ | « | ⏮ | » | » | » | ▒ | » | ■ | » | ⏮ | » | » | | ■ | ⏮ | ■ | ⏮ | ⏮ | ⏮ | » | ⏮ | ■ | ■ | ■ | ■ | ⏮ | ■ | ■ |
| Daniel Stendel | ■ | ⏮ | ⏮ | » | » | » | » | ■ | ■ | ⏮ | ⏮ | ■ | « | » | « | » | « | » | » | | » | | » | » | » | ⏮ | » | » | ⏮ | » | » | » | | ■ |

KEY: ■ On all match ▒ On bench ⏮ Subbed or sent off (Counting game) « Subbed or sent off (playing less than 70 minutes) ⏭ Subbed on from bench (Counting Game) » Subbed on (playing less than 70 minutes) Subbed on and then subbed or sent off (Counting Game) Subbed on and then subbed or sent off (playing less than 70 minutes) ☐ Not in 16

# BORUSSIA MONCHENGLADBACH

Final Position: **12th**

| | | | | | | |
|---|---|---|---|---|---|---|
| 1 | lge | Bayern Munich | H | D | 0-0 | |
| 2 | lge | Wolfsburg | A | L | 0-1 | |
| 3 | lge | Kaiserslautern | H | W | 3-0 | Van Hout 23,48; Munch 36 |
| 4 | lge | Hertha Berlin | A | W | 2-1 | Munch 10 pen; Van Hout 58 |
| 5 | lge | Stuttgart | H | D | 1-1 | Munch 50 |
| 6 | lge | Schalke | A | L | 1-2 | Van Hout 31 |
| 7 | lge | B Dortmund | A | L | 0-1 | |
| 8 | lge | Arminia B | H | W | 3-0 | Aidoo 32,60; van Houdt 45 |
| 9 | lge | Hamburg | A | L | 0-1 | |
| 10 | lge | 1860 Munich | H | L | 0-1 | |
| 11 | lge | Nurnberg | A | L | 1-2 | Strasser 75 |
| 12 | lge | Cottbus | H | W | 3-0 | Felgenhauer 2; Ulich 6; Van Hout 22 |
| 13 | lge | B Leverkusen | A | D | 2-2 | Demo 25; Korzynietz 70 |
| 14 | lge | Bochum | H | D | 2-2 | Demo 57; Van Hout 60 |
| 15 | lge | Hansa Rostock | A | L | 1-3 | Demo 38 pen |
| 16 | lge | Hannover 96 | H | W | 1-0 | Demo 15 |
| 17 | lge | W Bremen | A | L | 0-2 | |
| 18 | lge | Bayern Munich | A | L | 0-3 | |
| 19 | lge | Kaiserslautern | A | L | 0-2 | |
| 20 | lge | Hertha Berlin | H | L | 0-2 | |
| 21 | lge | Wolfsburg | H | W | 2-0 | Schnoor 34 og; Aidoo 71 |
| 22 | lge | Stuttgart | A | L | 0-4 | |
| 23 | lge | Schalke | H | D | 2-2 | Kluge 58; Demo 69 |
| 24 | lge | B Dortmund | H | W | 1-0 | Forssell 63 |
| 25 | lge | Arminia B | A | L | 1-4 | van Houdt 75 |
| 26 | lge | Hamburg | H | W | 2-0 | Pletsch 51; Forssell 61 |
| 27 | lge | 1860 Munich | A | L | 0-2 | |
| 28 | lge | Nurnberg | H | W | 2-0 | Ulich 12; Forssell 56 |
| 29 | lge | Cottbus | A | D | 1-1 | Pletsch 83 |
| 30 | lge | B Leverkusen | H | D | 2-2 | Demo 6; Skoubo 89 |
| 31 | lge | Bochum | A | D | 1-1 | Forssell 20 |
| 32 | lge | Hansa Rostock | H | W | 3-0 | Demo 37; Forssell 63; Skoubo 77 |
| 33 | lge | Hannover 96 | A | D | 2-2 | Forssell 62; Asanin 66 |
| 34 | lge | W Bremen | H | W | 4-1 | Kluge 61; Skoubo 73,76; Forssell 90 |

## KEY PLAYERS - GOALSCORERS

**1 Mikael Forssell**

| | | | |
|---|---|---|---|
| Goals in the League | 7 | Player Strike Rate<br>Average number of minutes between League goals scored by player | 199 |
| Contribution to Attacking Power<br>Average number of minutes between League team goals while on pitch | 60 | Club Strike Rate<br>Average number of minutes between League goals scored by club | 71 |

| | PLAYER | LGE GOALS | POWER | STRIKE RATE |
|---|---|---|---|---|
| 2 | Joris Van Hout | 6 | 72 | 229 mins |
| 3 | Igor Demo | 7 | 61 | 300 mins |
| 4 | Markus Munch | 3 | 86 | 463 mins |
| 5 | Lawrence Aidoo | 3 | 65 | 590 mins |

## KEY PLAYERS - MIDFIELDERS

**1 Peer Kluge**

| | | | |
|---|---|---|---|
| Goals in the League | 2 | Contribution to Attacking Power<br>Average number of minutes between League team goals while on pitch | 63 |
| Defensive Rating<br>Average number of mins between League goals conceded while he was on the pitch | 80 | Scoring Difference<br>Defensive Rating minus Contribution to Attacking Power | 17 |

| | PLAYER | LGE GOALS | DEF RATE | POWER | SCORE DIFF |
|---|---|---|---|---|---|
| 2 | Igor Demo | 7 | 78 | 62 | 16 mins |
| 3 | Ivo Ulich | 2 | 76 | 69 | 7 mins |
| 4 | Bernd Korzynietz | 1 | 70 | 63 | 7 mins |
| 5 | Markus Munch | 3 | 82 | 87 | -5 mins |

## KEY PLAYERS - DEFENDERS

**1 Slajdan Asanin**

| | | | |
|---|---|---|---|
| Goals Conceded (GC)<br>The number of League goals conceded while he was on the pitch | 11 | Clean Sheets<br>In games when he played at least 70 minutes | 3 |
| Defensive Rating<br>Ave number of mins between League goals conceded while on the pitch | 84 | Club Defensive Rating<br>Average number of mins between League goals conceded by the club this season | 68 |

| | PLAYER | CON LGE | CLEAN SHEETS | DEF RATE |
|---|---|---|---|---|
| 2 | Steffan Korell | 19 | 5 | 78 mins |
| 3 | Jeff Strasser | 35 | 8 | 69 mins |
| 4 | Markus Hausweiler | 22 | 3 | 62 mins |
| 5 | Max Eberl | 34 | 8 | 61 mins |

## GOALS SCORED

**AT HOME**

| | | |
|---|---|---|
| MOST | B Munich | 37 |
| | | 31 |
| LEAST | Nurnberg | 16 |

**AWAY**

| | | |
|---|---|---|
| MOST | B Munich | 33 |
| | | 12 |
| LEAST | B M'gladbach &Arminia B | 12 |

## GOALS CONCEDED

**AT HOME**

| | | |
|---|---|---|
| LEAST | Hamburg & B M'gladbach | 11 |
| | | 11 |
| MOST | Hannover 96 | 33 |

**AWAY**

| | | |
|---|---|---|
| LEAST | B Munich | 13 |
| | | 34 |
| MOST | Nurnberg | 36 |

## KEY GOALKEEPER

**1 Jorg Stiel**

| | |
|---|---|
| Goals Conceded in the League | 40 |
| Defensive Rating<br>Ave number of mins between League goals conceded while on the pitch | 70 |
| Counting Games<br>Games when he played at least 70 minutes | 31 |
| Clean Sheets<br>In games when he played at least 70 minutes | 9 |

## TOP POINT EARNERS

| | PLAYER | GAMES | AVE |
|---|---|---|---|
| 1 | Demo | 20 | 1.65 |
| 2 | Ulich | 23 | 1.57 |
| 3 | Forssell | 16 | 1.44 |
| 4 | Kluge | 22 | 1.41 |
| 5 | Pletsch | 23 | 1.35 |
| 6 | Eberl | 21 | 1.33 |
| 7 | Strasser | 26 | 1.31 |
| 8 | Korzynietz | 13 | 1.31 |
| 9 | Stiel | 31 | 1.26 |
| 10 | Van Hout | 15 | 1.20 |
| | CLUB AVERAGE: | | **1.24** |

Ave = Average points per match in Counting Games

## ATTENDANCES

HOME GROUND: BOKELBERGSTADION CAPACITY: 34500 AVERAGE LEAGUE AT HOME: 28717

| | | | | | | | | |
|---|---|---|---|---|---|---|---|---|
| 7 | B Dortmund | 68600 | 17 | W Bremen | 32188 | 16 | Hannover 96 | 24000 |
| 6 | Schalke | 60601 | 33 | Hannover 96 | 31878 | 8 | Arminia B | 24000 |
| 9 | Hamburg | 49000 | 32 | Hansa Rostock | 31300 | 21 | Wolfsburg | 22900 |
| 18 | Bayern Munich | 40000 | 26 | Hamburg | 30000 | 13 | B Leverkusen | 22500 |
| 19 | Kaiserslautern | 36000 | 28 | Nurnberg | 29000 | 22 | Stuttgart | 22000 |
| 4 | Hertha Berlin | 35000 | 14 | Bochum | 29000 | 12 | Cottbus | 22000 |
| 1 | Bayern Munich | 34500 | 3 | Kaiserslautern | 28000 | 2 | Wolfsburg | 15000 |
| 34 | W Bremen | 34500 | 5 | Stuttgart | 27000 | 15 | Hansa Rostock | 14000 |
| 30 | B Leverkusen | 34000 | 10 | 1860 Munich | 26000 | 29 | Cottbus | 13241 |
| 23 | Schalke | 33000 | 20 | Hertha Berlin | 26000 | 27 | 1860 Munich | 12000 |
| 24 | B Dortmund | 33000 | 25 | Arminia B | 26000 | | | |
| 31 | Bochum | 32645 | 11 | Nurnberg | 25000 | | | |

■ Home □ Away ▨ Neutral

## DISCIPLINARY RECORDS

| | PLAYER | YELLOW | RED | AVE |
|---|---|---|---|---|
| 1 | Korell | 6 | 2 | 186 |
| 2 | Eberl | 7 | 1 | 260 |
| 3 | Hausweiler | 5 | 0 | 271 |
| 4 | Embers | 2 | 0 | 302 |
| 5 | van Houdt | 3 | 0 | 313 |
| 6 | Strasser | 7 | 0 | 345 |
| 7 | Aidoo | 4 | 0 | 442 |
| 8 | Kluge | 4 | 0 | 501 |
| 9 | Demo | 4 | 0 | 525 |
| 10 | Felgenhauer | 1 | 0 | 569 |
| 11 | Korzynietz | 2 | 0 | 666 |
| 12 | Munch | 2 | 0 | 694 |
| 13 | Skoubo | 1 | 0 | 879 |
| | Other | 7 | 1 | |
| | TOTAL | 55 | 4 | |

## LEAGUE GOALS

| | PLAYER | MINS | GOALS | AVE |
|---|---|---|---|---|
| 1 | Forssell | 1395 | 7 | 199 |
| 2 | Demo | 2103 | 7 | 300 |
| 3 | Van Hout | 1376 | 6 | 229 |
| 4 | Skoubo | 879 | 4 | 220 |
| 5 | Munch | 1389 | 3 | 463 |
| 6 | Aidoo | 1769 | 3 | 590 |
| 7 | Ulich | 2285 | 2 | 1143 |
| 8 | Pletsch | 2162 | 2 | 1081 |
| 9 | van Houdt | 940 | 2 | 470 |
| 10 | Kluge | 2004 | 2 | 1002 |
| 11 | Felgenhauer | 569 | 1 | 569 |
| 12 | Strasser | 2420 | 1 | 2420 |
| 13 | Korzynietz | 1332 | 1 | 1332 |
| | Other | | 2 | |
| | TOTAL | | 43 | |

## MONTH BY MONTH GUIDE TO THE POINTS

| MONTH | POINTS | % |
|---|---|---|
| AUGUST | 4 | 44% |
| SEPTEMBER | 4 | 33% |
| OCTOBER | 3 | 33% |
| NOVEMBER | 5 | 33% |
| DECEMBER | 3 | 50% |
| JANUARY | 0 | 0% |
| FEBRUARY | 3 | 25% |
| MARCH | 7 | 58% |
| APRIL | 5 | 42% |
| MAY | 8 | 67% |

## TEAM OF THE SEASON

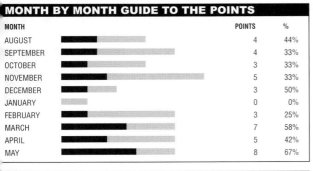

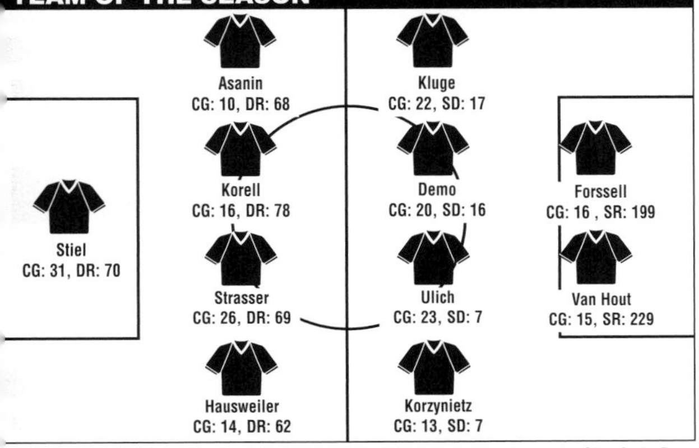
Asanin
CG: 10, DR: 68
Kluge
CG: 22, SD: 17
Korell
CG: 16, DR: 78
Demo
CG: 20, SD: 16
Forssell
CG: 16 , SR: 199
Stiel
CG: 31, DR: 70
Strasser
CG: 26, DR: 69
Ulich
CG: 23, SD: 7
Van Hout
CG: 15, SR: 229
Hausweiler
CG: 14, DR: 62
Korzynietz
CG: 13, SD: 7

**KEY:** DR = Defensive Rate, SD = Scoring Difference, SR = Strike Rate, CG = Counting Games – League games playing at least 70 minutes

## LEAGUE APPEARANCES, BOOKINGS AND CAPS

| | AGE | IN THE SQUAD | COUNTING GAMES | MINUTES ON PITCH | YELLOW CARDS | RED CARDS | THIS SEASON | HOME COUNTRY |
|---|---|---|---|---|---|---|---|---|
| **Goalkeepers** | | | | | | | | |
| Otto Fredrikson | 21 | 6 | 0 | 0 | 0 | 0 | - | Finland |
| Uwe Kamps | 39 | 2 | 0 | 0 | 0 | 0 | - | Germany |
| Michael Melka | 24 | 13 | 3 | 270 | 0 | 0 | - | Germany |
| Jorg Stiel | 35 | 31 | 31 | 2790 | 2 | 0 | - | Switzerland |
| **Defenders** | | | | | | | | |
| Slajdan Asanin | 31 | 12 | 10 | 926 | 1 | 0 | - | Croatia |
| Max Eberl | 29 | 29 | 21 | 2081 | 7 | 1 | - | Germany |
| Markus Hausweiler | 27 | 19 | 14 | 1357 | 5 | 0 | - | Germany |
| Steffan Korell | 31 | 20 | 16 | 1491 | 6 | 2 | - | Germany |
| Marcello Pletsch | 27 | 28 | 23 | 2162 | 0 | 0 | - | Brazil |
| Stephan Schulz-Winge | 28 | 2 | 1 | 108 | 0 | 0 | - | Germany |
| Stephane Stassin | 26 | 18 | 3 | 428 | 2 | 1 | - | Belgium |
| Jeff Strasser | 28 | 30 | 26 | 2420 | 7 | 0 | - | Luxembourg |
| **Midfielders** | | | | | | | | |
| Igor Demo | 27 | 30 | 20 | 2103 | 4 | 0 | - | Slovakia |
| Daniel Embers | 21 | 11 | 6 | 604 | 2 | 0 | - | Germany |
| Enrico Gaede | 21 | 1 | 0 | 21 | 0 | 0 | - | Germany |
| Peer Kluge | 22 | 24 | 22 | 2004 | 4 | 0 | - | Germany |
| Bernd Korzynietz | 23 | 25 | 13 | 1332 | 2 | 0 | - | Germany |
| Markus Munch | 30 | 17 | 15 | 1389 | 2 | 0 | - | Germany |
| Sebastian Plate | 23 | 1 | 0 | 12 | 0 | 0 | - | Germany |
| Jan Schlaudraff | 19 | 5 | 0 | 23 | 0 | 0 | - | Germany |
| Benjamin Schussler | 22 | 2 | 0 | 0 | 0 | 0 | - | Germany |
| Andreas Spann | 19 | 2 | 0 | 58 | 0 | 0 | - | Germany |
| Berthil ter Avest | 32 | 1 | 0 | 0 | 0 | 0 | - | Holland |
| Ivo Ulich | 28 | 29 | 23 | 2285 | 0 | 0 | - | Czech Republic |
| Marcel Witeczek | 34 | 20 | 11 | 1156 | 1 | 0 | - | Germany |
| **Forwards** | | | | | | | | |
| Lawrence Aidoo | 21 | 30 | 15 | 1769 | 4 | 0 | - | Ghana |
| Benjamin Auer | 22 | 1 | 0 | 0 | 0 | 0 | - | Germany |
| Daniel Felgenhauer | 27 | 16 | 4 | 569 | 1 | 0 | - | Germany |
| Mikael Forssell | 22 | 16 | 16 | 1395 | 0 | 0 | - | Finland |
| Marcel Ketelaer | 25 | 26 | 9 | 1033 | 0 | 0 | - | Germany |
| Marco Kuntzel | 27 | 12 | 0 | 104 | 0 | 0 | - | Germany |
| Morten Skoubo | 23 | 22 | 6 | 879 | 1 | 0 | 2 | Denmark (10) |
| Peter van Houdt | 26 | 20 | 9 | 940 | 3 | 0 | 3 | Belgium (16) |
| Joris Van Hout | 26 | 16 | 15 | 1376 | 1 | 0 | - | Belgium |
| Ari Van Lent | 31 | 13 | 2 | 454 | 0 | 0 | - | Holland |

**KEY:** LEAGUE BOOKINGS CAPS (FIFA RANKING)

## SQUAD APPEARANCES

| Match | 1 | 2 | 3 | 4 | 5 | 6 | 7 | 8 | 9 | 10 | 11 | 12 | 13 | 14 | 15 | 16 | 17 | 18 | 19 | 20 | 21 | 22 | 23 | 24 | 25 | 26 | 27 | 28 | 29 | 30 | 31 | 32 | 33 | 34 |
|---|---|---|---|---|---|---|---|---|---|---|---|---|---|---|---|---|---|---|---|---|---|---|---|---|---|---|---|---|---|---|---|---|---|---|
| Venue | H | A | H | A | H | A | A | A | A | H | A | H | A | H | A | H | A | A | A | H | H | A | H | H | A | H | A | H | A | H | A | H | A | H |
| Competition | L | L | L | L | L | L | L | L | L | L | L | L | L | L | L | L | L | L | L | L | L | L | L | L | L | L | L | L | L | L | L | L | L | L |
| Result | D | L | W | W | D | L | L | W | L | L | L | W | D | D | L | W | L | L | L | L | W | L | D | W | L | W | L | W | D | D | D | W | D | W |

**Goalkeepers**
Otto Fredrikson
Uwe Kamps
Michael Melka
Jorg Stiel

**Defenders**
Slajdan Asanin
Max Eberl
Markus Hausweiler
Steffan Korell
Marcello Pletsch
Stephan Schulz-Winge
Stephane Stassin
Jeff Strasser

**Midfielders**
Igor Demo
Daniel Embers
Enrico Gaede
Peer Kluge
Bernd Korzynietz
Markus Munch
Sebastian Plate
Jan Schlaudraff
Benjamin Schussler
Andreas Spann
Berthil ter Avest
Ivo Ulich
Marcel Witeczek

**Forwards**
Lawrence Aidoo
Benjamin Auer
Daniel Felgenhauer
Mikael Forssell
Marcel Ketelaer
Marco Kuntzel
Morten Skoubo
Peter van Houdt
Joris Van Hout
Ari Van Lent

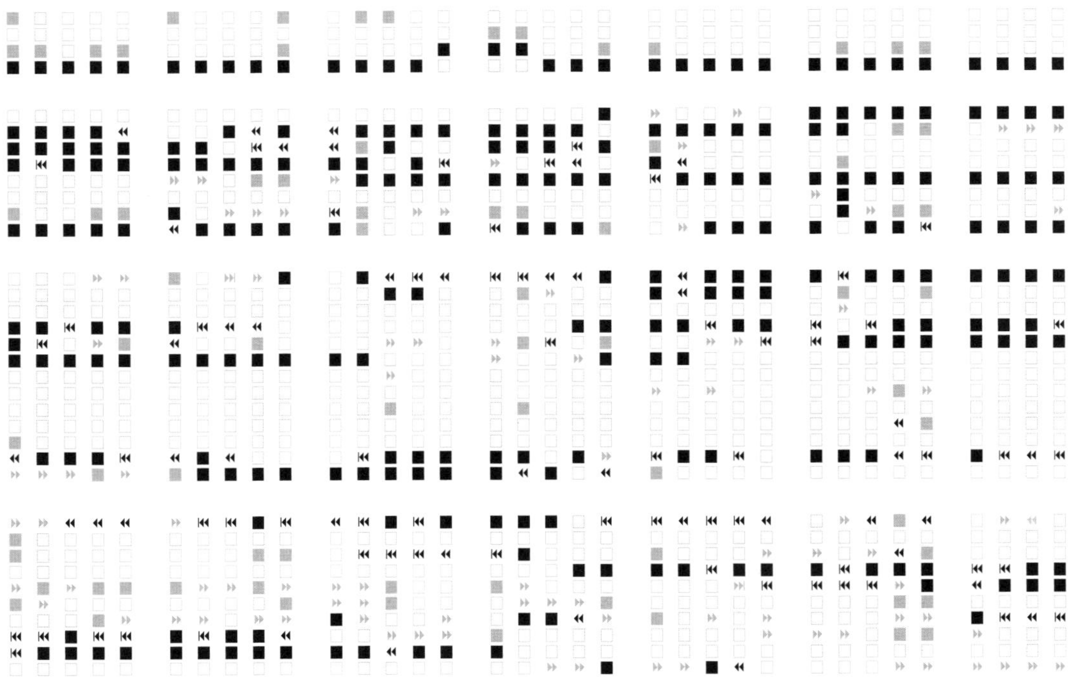

# HANSA ROSTOCK

Final Position: **13th**

| | | | | | | |
|---|---|---|---|---|---|---|
| 1 | lge | 1860 Munich | A | W | 2-0 | Vorbeck 44; Lantz 54 |
| 2 | lge | Nurnberg | H | W | 2-0 | Rydlewicz 37,83 |
| 3 | lge | Cottbus | A | W | 4-0 | Rydlewicz 17,64; Prica 27; Wibran 47 |
| 4 | lge | B Leverkusen | H | L | 1-3 | Kientz 75 |
| 5 | lge | Bochum | A | W | 1-0 | Salou 32 |
| 6 | lge | B Dortmund | H | L | 0-1 | |
| 7 | lge | Hannover 96 | H | L | 1-2 | Wibran 10 |
| 8 | lge | W Bremen | A | D | 0-0 | |
| 9 | lge | Bayern Munich | H | L | 0-1 | |
| 10 | lge | Wolfsburg | A | L | 0-1 | |
| 11 | lge | Kaiserslautern | H | D | 2-2 | Rydlewicz 17; Vorbeck 71 |
| 12 | lge | Hertha Berlin | A | L | 1-3 | Salou 15 |
| 13 | lge | Stuttgart | H | D | 1-1 | Prica 5 |
| 14 | lge | Schalke | A | D | 2-2 | Wibran 51; Prica 86 |
| 15 | lge | B M'gladbach | H | W | 3-1 | Vorbeck 19; Prica 53,64 |
| 16 | lge | Arminia B | A | L | 0-3 | |
| 17 | lge | Hamburg | H | D | 0-0 | |
| 18 | lge | 1860 Munich | H | L | 1-4 | Jakobsson 57 |
| 19 | lge | Nurnberg | A | W | 1-0 | Prica 42 |
| 20 | lge | Cottbus | H | D | 0-0 | |
| 21 | lge | B Leverkusen | A | W | 2-1 | Salou 35,41 |
| 22 | lge | Bochum | H | D | 1-1 | Di Salvo 32 |
| 23 | lge | B Dortmund | A | L | 0-2 | |
| 24 | lge | Hannover 96 | A | L | 1-3 | Meggle 40 |
| 25 | lge | W Bremen | H | W | 1-0 | Hirsch 72 |
| 26 | lge | Bayern Munich | A | L | 0-1 | |
| 27 | lge | Wolfsburg | H | W | 1-0 | Hill 3 |
| 28 | lge | Kaiserslautern | A | L | 0-1 | |
| 29 | lge | Hertha Berlin | H | L | 0-1 | |
| 30 | lge | Stuttgart | A | D | 1-1 | Hill 59 |
| 31 | lge | Schalke | H | W | 3-1 | Prica 65; Arvidsson 79; Rydlewicz 84 pen |
| 32 | lge | B M'gladbach | A | L | 0-3 | |
| 33 | lge | Arminia B | H | W | 3-0 | Aduobe 8; Vorbeck 56; Di Salvo 86 |
| 34 | lge | Hamburg | A | L | 0-2 | |

## KEY PLAYERS - GOALSCORERS

**1 Rade Prica**

| | | | |
|---|---|---|---|
| Goals in the League | 7 | Player Strike Rate<br>Average number of minutes between League goals scored by player | 261 |
| Contribution to Attacking Power<br>Average number of minutes between League team goals while on pitch | 70 | Club Strike Rate<br>Average number of minutes between League goals scored by club | 87 |

| | PLAYER | LGE GOALS | POWER | STRIKE RATE |
|---|---|---|---|---|
| 2 | Rene Rydlewicz | 6 | 73 | 280 mins |
| 3 | Bachirou Salou | 4 | 124 | 373 mins |
| 4 | Peter Wibran | 3 | 109 | 582 mins |
| 5 | Delano Hill | 2 | 92 | 829 mins |

## KEY PLAYERS - MIDFIELDERS

**1 Rene Rydlewicz**

| | | | |
|---|---|---|---|
| Goals in the League | 6 | Contribution to Attacking Power<br>Average number of minutes between League team goals while on pitch | 73 |
| Defensive Rating<br>Average number of mins between League goals conceded while he was on the pitch | 73 | Scoring Difference<br>Defensive Rating minus Contribution to Attacking Power | 0 |

| | PLAYER | LGE GOALS | DEF RATE | POWER | SCORE DIFF |
|---|---|---|---|---|---|
| 2 | Marcus Lantz | 1 | 80 | 82 | -2 mins |
| 3 | Gerd Wimmer | 0 | 79 | 90 | -11 mins |
| 4 | Ronald Maul | 0 | 80 | 94 | -14 mins |
| 5 | Dietmar Hirsch | 1 | 72 | 86 | -14 mins |

## KEY PLAYERS - DEFENDERS

**1 Delano Hill**

| | | | |
|---|---|---|---|
| Goals Conceded (GC)<br>The number of League goals conceded while he was on the pitch | 20 | Clean Sheets<br>In games when he played at least 70 minutes | 6 |
| Defensive Rating<br>Ave number of mins between League goals conceded while on the pitch | 83 | Club Defensive Rating<br>Average number of mins between League goals conceded by the club this season | 75 |

| | PLAYER | CON LGE | CLEAN SHEETS | DEF RATE |
|---|---|---|---|---|
| 2 | Michal Kovar | 24 | 6 | 75 mins |
| 3 | Andreas Jakobsson | 40 | 10 | 73 mins |
| 4 | Jochen Kientz | 15 | 4 | 70 mins |

## GOALS SCORED

**AT HOME**

| | | |
|---|---|---|
| MOST | B Munich | 37 |
| | | 20 |
| LEAST | Nurnberg | 16 |

**AWAY**

| | | |
|---|---|---|
| MOST | B Munich | 33 |
| | | 15 |
| LEAST | B M'gladbach &Arminia B | 12 |

## GOALS CONCEDED

**AT HOME**

| | | |
|---|---|---|
| LEAST | Hamburg & B M'gladbach | 11 |
| | | 18 |
| MOST | Hannover 96 | 33 |

**AWAY**

| | | |
|---|---|---|
| LEAST | B Munich | 13 |
| | | 23 |
| MOST | Nurnberg | 36 |

## KEY GOALKEEPER

**1 Matthias Schober**

| | |
|---|---|
| Goals Conceded in the League | 41 |
| Defensive Rating<br>Ave number of mins between League goals conceded while on the pitch | 75 |
| Counting Games<br>Games when he played at least 70 minutes | 34 |
| Clean Sheets<br>In games when he played at least 70 minutes | 11 |

## TOP POINT EARNERS

| | PLAYER | GAMES | AVE |
|---|---|---|---|
| 1 | Prica | 17 | 1.53 |
| 2 | Lantz | 27 | 1.37 |
| 3 | Hill | 17 | 1.35 |
| 4 | Hirsch | 13 | 1.31 |
| 5 | Meggle | 13 | 1.31 |
| 6 | Wimmer | 20 | 1.30 |
| 7 | Jakobsson | 32 | 1.25 |
| 8 | Maul | 22 | 1.23 |
| 9 | Schober | 34 | 1.21 |
| 10 | Rydlewicz | 17 | 1.18 |
| | **CLUB AVERAGE:** | | **1.21** |

Ave = Average points per match in Counting Games

## ATTENDANCES

HOME GROUND: OSSEESTADION CAPACITY: 30000 AVERAGE LEAGUE AT HOME: 19764

| | | | | | | | | |
|---|---|---|---|---|---|---|---|---|
| 23 | B Dortmund | 64000 | 7 | Hannover 96 | 25000 | 25 | W Bremen | 16000 |
| 14 | Schalke | 60601 | 4 | B Leverkusen | 25000 | 13 | Stuttgart | 15000 |
| 34 | Hamburg | 55500 | 31 | Schalke | 25000 | 19 | Nurnberg | 15000 |
| 28 | Kaiserslautern | 38000 | 30 | Stuttgart | 23000 | 18 | 1860 Munich | 15000 |
| 12 | Hertha Berlin | 38000 | 1 | 1860 Munich | 22800 | 15 | B M'gladbach | 14000 |
| 26 | Bayern Munich | 35000 | 21 | B Leverkusen | 22500 | 20 | Cottbus | 13000 |
| 8 | W Bremen | 32300 | 29 | Hertha Berlin | 22000 | 3 | Cottbus | 13000 |
| 32 | B M'gladbach | 31300 | 17 | Hamburg | 21400 | 22 | Bochum | 13000 |
| 9 | Bayern Munich | 30000 | 5 | Bochum | 21000 | 10 | Wolfsburg | 11600 |
| 6 | B Dortmund | 29000 | 2 | Nurnberg | 19600 | 27 | Wolfsburg | 9000 |
| 33 | Arminia B | 28000 | 16 | Arminia B | 19109 | | | |
| 24 | Hannover 96 | 28000 | 11 | Kaiserslautern | 16000 | | | |

■ Home □ Away ▒ Neutral

## DISCIPLINARY RECORDS

| | PLAYER | YELLOW | RED | AVE |
|---|---|---|---|---|
| 1 | Meggle | 5 | 0 | 246 |
| 2 | Prica | 6 | 1 | 261 |
| 3 | Vorbeck | 4 | 0 | 292 |
| 4 | Lantz | 6 | 1 | 352 |
| 5 | Kientz | 3 | 0 | 352 |
| 6 | Di Salvo | 2 | 0 | 371 |
| 7 | Aduobe | 4 | 1 | 431 |
| 8 | Persson | 4 | 0 | 478 |
| 9 | Wimmer | 4 | 0 | 494 |
| 10 | Hill | 3 | 0 | 552 |
| 11 | Rydlewicz | 3 | 0 | 560 |
| 12 | Hirsch | 2 | 0 | 645 |
| 13 | Maul | 3 | 0 | 689 |
| | Other | 8 | 2 | |
| | TOTAL | 57 | 5 | |

## LEAGUE GOALS

| | PLAYER | MINS | GOALS | AVE |
|---|---|---|---|---|
| 1 | Prica | 1829 | 7 | 261 |
| 2 | Rydlewicz | 1682 | 6 | 280 |
| 3 | Salou | 1491 | 4 | 373 |
| 4 | Vorbeck | 1170 | 4 | 293 |
| 5 | Wibran | 1746 | 3 | 582 |
| 6 | Hill | 1657 | 2 | 829 |
| 7 | Di Salvo | 743 | 2 | 372 |
| 8 | Jakobsson | 2939 | 1 | 2939 |
| 9 | Aduobe | 2157 | 1 | 2157 |
| 10 | Meggle | 1232 | 1 | 1232 |
| 11 | Arvidsson | 811 | 1 | 811 |
| 12 | Kientz | 1056 | 1 | 1056 |
| 13 | Hirsch | 1291 | 1 | 1291 |
| | Other | | 1 | |
| | TOTAL | | 35 | |

## MONTH BY MONTH GUIDE TO THE POINTS

| MONTH | POINTS | % |
|---|---|---|
| AUGUST | 9 | 100% |
| SEPTEMBER | 3 | 25% |
| OCTOBER | 1 | 11% |
| NOVEMBER | 6 | 40% |
| DECEMBER | 1 | 17% |
| JANUARY | 0 | 0% |
| FEBRUARY | 8 | 67% |
| MARCH | 3 | 25% |
| APRIL | 4 | 33% |
| MAY | 6 | 50% |

## TEAM OF THE SEASON

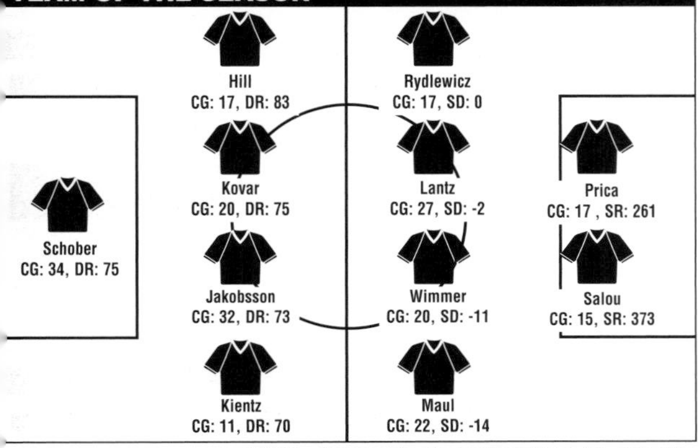
Hill
CG: 17, DR: 83
Rydlewicz
CG: 17, SD: 0
Kovar
CG: 20, DR: 75
Lantz
CG: 27, SD: -2
Prica
CG: 17 , SR: 261
Schober
CG: 34, DR: 75
Jakobsson
CG: 32, DR: 73
Wimmer
CG: 20, SD: -11
Salou
CG: 15, SR: 373
Kientz
CG: 11, DR: 70
Maul
CG: 22, SD: -14

KEY: DR = Defensive Rate, SD = Scoring Difference, SR = Strike Rate, CG = Counting Games – League games playing at least 70 minutes

## LEAGUE APPEARANCES, BOOKINGS AND CAPS

| | AGE | IN THE SQUAD | COUNTING GAMES | MINUTES ON PITCH | YELLOW CARDS | RED CARDS | THIS SEASON | HOME COUNTRY |
|---|---|---|---|---|---|---|---|---|
| **Goalkeepers** | | | | | | | | |
| Daniel Klewer | 26 | 14 | 0 | 0 | 0 | 0 | - | Germany |
| Matthias Schober | 27 | 34 | 34 | 3060 | 1 | 0 | - | Germany |
| **Defenders** | | | | | | | | |
| Delano Hill | 28 | 25 | 17 | 1657 | 3 | 0 | - | Holland |
| Andreas Jakobsson | 30 | 33 | 32 | 2939 | 3 | 1 | 9 | Sweden (20) |
| Jochen Kientz | 30 | 15 | 11 | 1056 | 3 | 0 | - | Germany |
| Michal Kovar | 29 | 24 | 20 | 1790 | 2 | 0 | - | Czech Republic |
| Uwe Mohrle | 23 | 7 | 0 | 28 | 0 | 0 | - | Germany |
| **Midfielders** | | | | | | | | |
| Godfried Aduobe | 27 | 29 | 21 | 2157 | 4 | 1 | - | Ghana |
| Kevin Hansen | 23 | 9 | 1 | 297 | 1 | 0 | - | Germany |
| Dietmar Hirsch | 31 | 23 | 13 | 1291 | 2 | 0 | - | Germany |
| Timo Lange | 35 | 10 | 1 | 138 | 0 | 0 | - | Germany |
| Marcus Lantz | 27 | 29 | 27 | 2466 | 6 | 1 | 3 | Sweden (20) |
| Ronald Maul | 30 | 27 | 22 | 2068 | 3 | 0 | - | Germany |
| Thomas Meggle | 28 | 24 | 13 | 1232 | 5 | 0 | - | Germany |
| Joakim Persson | 28 | 29 | 20 | 1913 | 4 | 0 | - | Sweden |
| Rene Rydlewicz | 29 | 22 | 17 | 1682 | 3 | 0 | - | Germany |
| Peter Wibran | 34 | 30 | 17 | 1746 | 0 | 0 | - | Sweden |
| Gerd Wimmer | 26 | 29 | 20 | 1977 | 4 | 0 | - | Austria |
| **Forwards** | | | | | | | | |
| Magnus Arvidsson | 29 | 23 | 6 | 811 | 0 | 0 | - | Sweden |
| Markus Beierle | 31 | 1 | 0 | 0 | 0 | 0 | - | Germany |
| Antonio Di Salvo | 24 | 18 | 5 | 743 | 2 | 0 | - | Italy |
| Rade Prica | 23 | 28 | 17 | 1829 | 6 | 1 | 3 | Sweden (20) |
| Bachirou Salou | 32 | 26 | 15 | 1491 | 1 | 1 | - | Germany |
| Marcel Schied | 19 | 1 | 0 | 0 | 0 | 0 | - | Germany |
| Marco Vorbeck | 22 | 24 | 8 | 1170 | 4 | 0 | - | Germany |

KEY: LEAGUE BOOKINGS CAPS (FIFA RANKING)

## SQUAD APPEARANCES

| Match | 1 | 2 | 3 | 4 | 5 | 6 | 7 | 8 | 9 | 10 | 11 | 12 | 13 | 14 | 15 | 16 | 17 | 18 | 19 | 20 | 21 | 22 | 23 | 24 | 25 | 26 | 27 | 28 | 29 | 30 | 31 | 32 | 33 | 34 |
|---|---|---|---|---|---|---|---|---|---|---|---|---|---|---|---|---|---|---|---|---|---|---|---|---|---|---|---|---|---|---|---|---|---|---|
| Venue | A | H | A | H | A | H | H | A | H | A | H | A | H | A | H | A | H | H | A | H | A | H | A | A | H | A | H | A | H | A | H | A | H | A |
| Competition | L | L | L | L | L | L | L | L | L | L | L | L | L | L | L | L | L | L | L | L | L | L | L | L | L | L | L | L | L | L | L | L | L | L |
| Result | W | W | W | L | W | L | L | D | L | L | D | L | D | D | W | L | D | L | W | D | W | D | L | L | W | L | W | L | L | D | W | L | W | L |

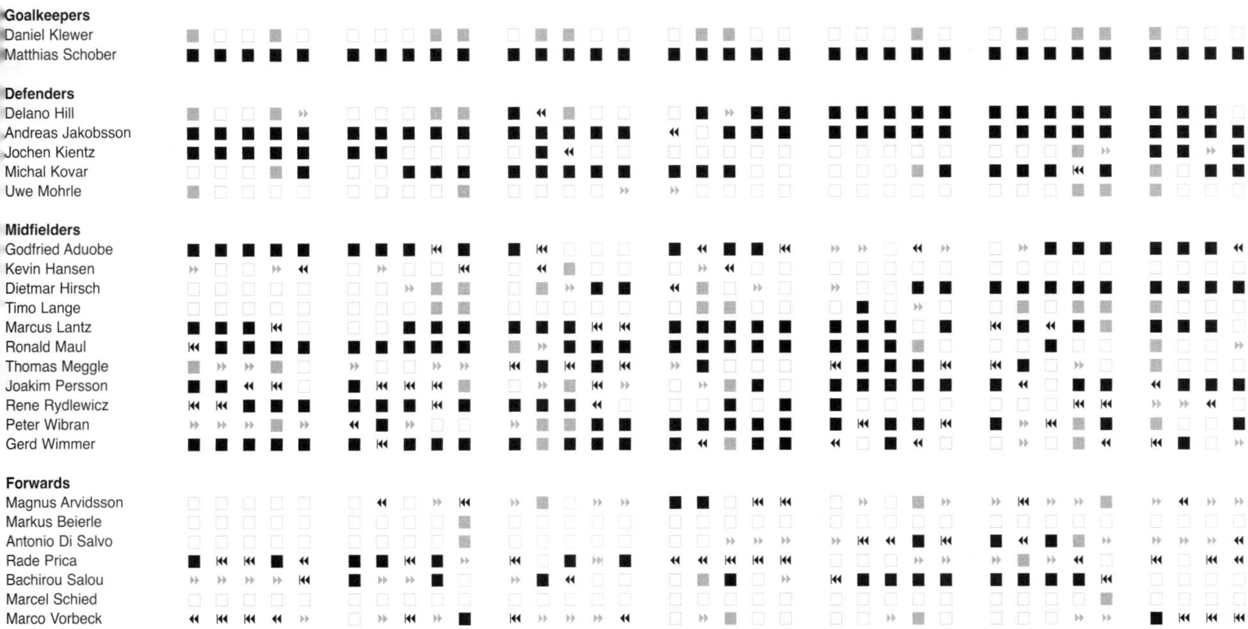
Goalkeepers
Daniel Klewer
Matthias Schober
Defenders
Delano Hill
Andreas Jakobsson
Jochen Kientz
Michal Kovar
Uwe Mohrle
Midfielders
Godfried Aduobe
Kevin Hansen
Dietmar Hirsch
Timo Lange
Marcus Lantz
Ronald Maul
Thomas Meggle
Joakim Persson
Rene Rydlewicz
Peter Wibran
Gerd Wimmer
Forwards
Magnus Arvidsson
Markus Beierle
Antonio Di Salvo
Rade Prica
Bachirou Salou
Marcel Schied
Marco Vorbeck

KEY: ■ On all match ■ On bench ⏮ Subbed or sent off (Counting game) ◀◀ Subbed or sent off (playing less than 70 minutes) ▶▶ Subbed on from bench (Counting Game) ▶▶ Subbed on (playing less than 70 minutes) ▶▶ Subbed on and then subbed or sent off (Counting Game) ▶▶ Subbed on and then subbed or sent off (playing less than 70 minutes) □ Not in 16

# KAISERSLAUTERN

Final Position: **14th**

| | | | | | | |
|---|---|---|---|---|---|---|
| 1 | lge | Stuttgart | A | D | 1-1 | Klose, M 51 |
| 2 | lge | Schalke | H | L | 1-3 | Riedl 35 |
| 3 | lge | B M'gladbach | A | L | 0-3 | |
| 4 | lge | Arminia B | H | D | 1-1 | Basler 56 |
| 5 | lge | Hamburg | A | L | 0-2 | |
| 6 | lge | 1860 Munich | H | D | 0-0 | |
| 7 | lge | Nurnberg | A | L | 0-1 | |
| 8 | lge | Cottbus | H | W | 4-0 | Klose, M 18,72; Knavs 49; Hujdurovic 77 og |
| 9 | lge | B Leverkusen | A | L | 0-1 | |
| 10 | lge | Hansa Rostock | A | D | 2-2 | Lokvenc 22; Mifsud 78 |
| 11 | lge | Hannover 96 | H | L | 0-1 | |
| 12 | lge | Bochum | H | L | 0-2 | |
| 13 | lge | W Bremen | A | L | 3-5 | Lincoln 10; Koch, H 18 pen; Timm 54 |
| 14 | lge | Bayern Munich | H | L | 0-2 | |
| 15 | lge | Wolfsburg | H | W | 2-0 | Lokvenc 15; Lincoln 66 |
| 16 | lge | B Dortmund | A | L | 1-3 | Dominguez 24 |
| 17 | lge | Hertha Berlin | H | W | 2-1 | Lokvenc 28; Koch, H 87 pen |
| 18 | lge | Stuttgart | H | L | 1-2 | Lokvenc 34 |
| 19 | lge | Schalke | A | D | 2-2 | Klos, T 31; Koch, H 90 |
| 20 | lge | B M'gladbach | H | W | 2-0 | Knavs 35; Klose, M 88 pen |
| 21 | lge | Arminia B | A | D | 1-1 | Lokvenc 26 |
| 22 | lge | Hamburg | H | W | 2-0 | Lokvenc 51; Klose, M 58 |
| 23 | lge | 1860 Munich | A | D | 0-0 | |
| 24 | lge | Nurnberg | H | W | 5-0 | Lokvenc 19; Klose, M 25 pen; Dominguez 62; Timm 64; Bjelica 88 |
| 25 | lge | Cottbus | A | W | 3-1 | Klose, M 39; Hristov 71; Lokvenc 90 |
| 26 | lge | B Leverkusen | H | W | 1-0 | Klose, M 40 |
| 27 | lge | Bochum | A | D | 1-1 | Ramzy 90 |
| 28 | lge | Hansa Rostock | H | W | 1-0 | Dominguez 72 |
| 29 | lge | Hannover 96 | A | L | 1-2 | Klos, T 11 |
| 30 | lge | W Bremen | H | W | 1-0 | Klose, M 66 pen |
| 31 | lge | Bayern Munich | A | L | 0-1 | |
| 32 | lge | Wolfsburg | A | D | 2-2 | Sforza 5; Mifsud 69 |
| 33 | lge | B Dortmund | H | D | 0-0 | |
| 34 | lge | Hertha Berlin | A | L | 0-2 | |

## KEY PLAYERS - GOALSCORERS

**1 Miroslav Klose**

| | | | |
|---|---|---|---|
| Goals in the League | 9 | **Player Strike Rate** Average number of minutes between League goals scored by player | 297 |
| **Contribution to Attacking Power** Average number of minutes between League team goals while on pitch | 74 | **Club Strike Rate** Average number of minutes between League goals scored by club | 77 |

| | PLAYER | LGE GOALS | POWER | STRIKE RATE |
|---|---|---|---|---|
| 2 | Vratislav Lokvenc | 8 | 73 | 320 mins |
| 3 | Aleksander Knavs | 2 | 61 | 673 mins |
| 4 | Harry Koch | 3 | 80 | 674 mins |
| 5 | Hany Ramzy | 1 | 63 | 1405 mins |

## KEY PLAYERS - MIDFIELDERS

**1 Jose Dominguez**

| | | | |
|---|---|---|---|
| Goals in the League | 3 | **Contribution to Attacking Power** Average number of minutes between League team goals while on pitch | 66 |
| **Defensive Rating** Average number of mins between League goals conceded while he was on the pitch | 114 | **Scoring Difference** Defensive Rating minus Contribution to Attacking Power | 48 |

| | PLAYER | LGE GOALS | DEF RATE | POWER | SCORE DIFF |
|---|---|---|---|---|---|
| 2 | Ciriaco Sforza | 1 | 86 | 63 | 23 mins |
| 3 | Markus Anfang | 0 | 82 | 82 | 0 mins |
| 4 | Marian Hristov | 1 | 101 | 101 | 0 mins |
| 5 | Mario Basler | 1 | 74 | 78 | -4 mins |

## KEY PLAYERS - DEFENDERS

**1 Bill Tchato**

| | | | |
|---|---|---|---|
| **Goals Conceded (GC)** The number of League goals conceded while he was on the pitch | 12 | **Clean Sheets** In games when he played at least 70 minutes | 6 |
| **Defensive Rating** Ave number of mins between League goals conceded while on the pitch | 116 | **Club Defensive Rating** Average number of mins between League goals conceded by the club this season | 73 |

| | PLAYER | CON LGE | CLEAN SHEETS | DEF RATE |
|---|---|---|---|---|
| 2 | Aleksander Knavs | 14 | 6 | 96 mins |
| 3 | Hany Ramzy | 18 | 5 | 78 mins |
| 4 | Harry Koch | 35 | 4 | 58 mins |
| 5 | Thomas Hengen | 17 | 2 | 56 mins |

## GOALS SCORED

**AT HOME**

| | | |
|---|---|---|
| MOST | B Munich | 37 |
| | | 23 |
| LEAST | Nurnberg | 16 |

**AWAY**

| | | |
|---|---|---|
| MOST | B Munich | 33 |
| | | 17 |
| LEAST | B M'gladbach &Arminia B | 12 |

## GOALS CONCEDED

**AT HOME**

| | | |
|---|---|---|
| LEAST | Hamburg & B M'gladbach | 11 |
| | | 12 |
| MOST | Hannover 96 | 33 |

**AWAY**

| | | |
|---|---|---|
| LEAST | B Munich | 13 |
| | | 30 |
| MOST | Nurnberg | 36 |

## KEY GOALKEEPER

**1 Tim Wiese**

| | |
|---|---|
| Goals Conceded in the League | 25 |
| **Defensive Rating** Ave number of mins between League goals conceded while on the pitch | 76 |
| **Counting Games** Games when he played at least 70 minutes | 21 |
| **Clean Sheets** In games when he played at least 70 minutes | 8 |

## TOP POINT EARNERS

| | PLAYER | GAMES | AVE |
|---|---|---|---|
| 1 | Tchato | 14 | 1.64 |
| 2 | Sforza | 19 | 1.53 |
| 3 | Ramzy | 15 | 1.53 |
| 4 | Knavs | 14 | 1.43 |
| 5 | Lokvenc | 27 | 1.41 |
| 6 | Anfang | 15 | 1.40 |
| 7 | Wiese | 21 | 1.33 |
| 8 | Basler | 14 | 1.29 |
| 9 | Klose, M | 28 | 1.18 |
| 10 | Grammozis | 27 | 1.00 |
| | **CLUB AVERAGE:** | | **1.18** |

Ave = Average points per match in Counting Games

## ATTENDANCES

HOME GROUND: FRITZ-WALTER STADION CAPACITY: 40600 AVERAGE LEAGUE AT HOME: 36329

| | | | | | | | | |
|---|---|---|---|---|---|---|---|---|
| 16 | B Dortmund | 68000 | 6 | 1860 Munich | 38000 | 13 | W Bremen | 24000 |
| 31 | Bayern Munich | 63000 | 18 | Stuttgart | 36692 | 27 | Bochum | 23146 |
| 19 | Schalke | 60672 | 20 | B M'gladbach | 36000 | 1 | Stuttgart | 23000 |
| 34 | Hertha Berlin | 50000 | 11 | Hannover 96 | 34000 | 9 | B Leverkusen | 22500 |
| 5 | Hamburg | 42000 | 12 | Bochum | 34000 | 7 | Nurnberg | 22000 |
| 26 | B Leverkusen | 40500 | 8 | Cottbus | 33246 | 32 | Wolfsburg | 21136 |
| 33 | B Dortmund | 40160 | 24 | Nurnberg | 33000 | 23 | 1860 Munich | 21000 |
| 14 | Bayern Munich | 40010 | 4 | Arminia B | 33000 | 21 | Arminia B | 19237 |
| 30 | W Bremen | 40000 | 17 | Hertha Berlin | 33000 | 10 | Hansa Rostock | 16000 |
| 22 | Hamburg | 39000 | 15 | Wolfsburg | 31000 | 25 | Cottbus | 13000 |
| 2 | Schalke | 38000 | 29 | Hannover 96 | 30573 | | | |
| 28 | Hansa Rostock | 38000 | 3 | B M'gladbach | 28000 | | | |

■ Home □ Away ▒ Neutral

## DISCIPLINARY RECORDS

| | PLAYER | YELLOW | RED | AVE |
|---|---|---|---|---|
| 1 | Nzelo-Lembi | 3 | 0 | 176 |
| 2 | Bjelica | 5 | 0 | 179 |
| 3 | Sforza | 9 | 1 | 181 |
| 4 | Hristov | 3 | 0 | 201 |
| 5 | Basler | 8 | 0 | 203 |
| 6 | Tchato | 5 | 0 | 278 |
| 7 | Teber | 2 | 0 | 307 |
| 8 | Lembi | 2 | 0 | 307 |
| 9 | Koch, H | 5 | 0 | 404 |
| 10 | Dominguez | 3 | 0 | 418 |
| 11 | Knavs | 3 | 0 | 448 |
| 12 | Anfang | 3 | 0 | 463 |
| 13 | Riedl | 3 | 0 | 470 |
| | Other | 20 | 0 | |
| | TOTAL | 74 | 1 | |

## LEAGUE GOALS

| | PLAYER | MINS | GOALS | AVE |
|---|---|---|---|---|
| 1 | Klose, M | 2672 | 9 | 297 |
| 2 | Lokvenc | 2558 | 8 | 320 |
| 3 | Dominguez | 1255 | 3 | 418 |
| 4 | Koch, H | 2023 | 3 | 674 |
| 5 | Mifsud | 463 | 2 | 232 |
| 6 | Knavs | 1346 | 2 | 673 |
| 7 | Klos, T | 1154 | 2 | 577 |
| 8 | Timm | 1081 | 2 | 541 |
| 9 | Lincoln | 1417 | 2 | 709 |
| 10 | Riedl | 1412 | 1 | 1412 |
| 11 | Hristov | 604 | 1 | 604 |
| 12 | Bjelica | 898 | 1 | 898 |
| 13 | Sforza | 1815 | 1 | 1815 |
| | Other | | 3 | |
| | TOTAL | | 40 | |

## MONTH BY MONTH GUIDE TO THE POINTS

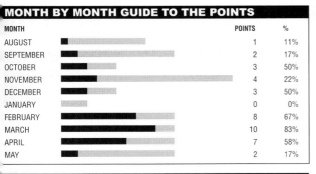

| MONTH | POINTS | % |
|---|---|---|
| AUGUST | 1 | 11% |
| SEPTEMBER | 2 | 17% |
| OCTOBER | 3 | 50% |
| NOVEMBER | 4 | 22% |
| DECEMBER | 3 | 50% |
| JANUARY | 0 | 0% |
| FEBRUARY | 8 | 67% |
| MARCH | 10 | 83% |
| APRIL | 7 | 58% |
| MAY | 2 | 17% |

## TEAM OF THE SEASON

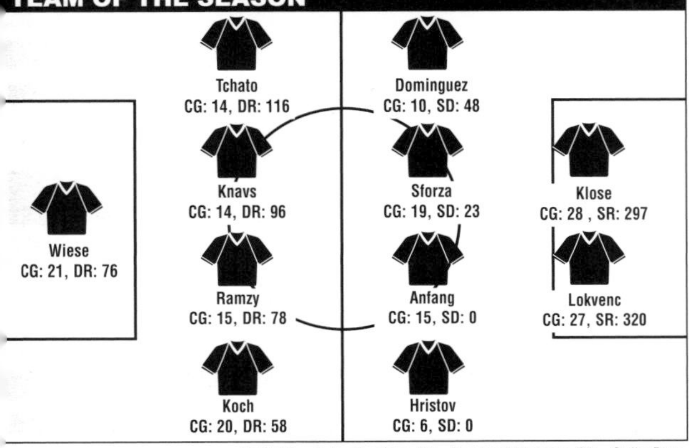
Wiese
CG: 21, DR: 76
Tchato
CG: 14, DR: 116
Knavs
CG: 14, DR: 96
Ramzy
CG: 15, DR: 78
Koch
CG: 20, DR: 58
Dominguez
CG: 10, SD: 48
Sforza
CG: 19, SD: 23
Anfang
CG: 15, SD: 0
Hristov
CG: 6, SD: 0
Klose
CG: 28 , SR: 297
Lokvenc
CG: 27, SR: 320

KEY: DR = Defensive Rate, SD = Scoring Difference, SR = Strike Rate, CG = Counting Games – League games playing at least 70 minutes

## LEAGUE APPEARANCES, BOOKINGS AND CAPS

| | AGE | IN THE SQUAD | COUNTING GAMES | MINUTES ON PITCH | YELLOW CARDS | RED CARDS | THIS SEASON | HOME COUNTRY |
|---|---|---|---|---|---|---|---|---|
| **Goalkeepers** | | | | | | | | |
| Jens Kern | 20 | 2 | 0 | 0 | 0 | 0 | - | Germany |
| Georg Koch | 31 | 16 | 13 | 1170 | 1 | 0 | - | Germany |
| Tim Wiese | 21 | 26 | 21 | 1890 | 1 | 0 | - | Germany |
| **Defenders** | | | | | | | | |
| Thomas Hengen | 28 | 11 | 10 | 945 | 2 | 0 | - | Germany |
| Tomasz Klos | 30 | 20 | 11 | 1154 | 1 | 0 | 3 | Poland (29) |
| Aleksander Knavs | 27 | 16 | 14 | 1346 | 3 | 0 | - | Slovenia |
| Harry Koch | 33 | 30 | 20 | 2023 | 5 | 0 | - | Germany |
| Nzelo Lembi | 27 | 7 | 7 | 614 | 2 | 0 | - | Congo DR |
| Hervi Nzelo-Lembi | 27 | 9 | 3 | 529 | 3 | 0 | - | Belgium |
| Hany Ramzy | 34 | 17 | 15 | 1405 | 1 | 0 | - | Egypt |
| Torsten Reuter | 20 | 10 | 2 | 280 | 0 | 0 | - | Germany |
| Bill Tchato | 28 | 16 | 14 | 1390 | 5 | 0 | 2 | Cameroon (18) |
| **Midfielders** | | | | | | | | |
| Markus Anfang | 29 | 21 | 15 | 1389 | 3 | 0 | - | Germany |
| Mario Basler | 34 | 24 | 14 | 1628 | 8 | 0 | - | Germany |
| Nenad Bjelica | 31 | 22 | 5 | 898 | 5 | 0 | - | Croatia |
| Jose Dominguez | 29 | 21 | 10 | 1255 | 3 | 0 | - | Portugal |
| Dimitrios Grammozis | 24 | 29 | 27 | 2415 | 4 | 0 | - | Greece |
| Marian Hristov | 29 | 8 | 6 | 604 | 3 | 0 | - | Bulgaria |
| Cassio Lincoln | 24 | 21 | 11 | 1417 | 3 | 0 | - | Brazil |
| Stefan Malz | 31 | 6 | 2 | 228 | 1 | 0 | - | Germany |
| Rodriguez Ratinho | 32 | 11 | 1 | 245 | 0 | 0 | - | Brazil |
| Thomas Riedl | 27 | 20 | 14 | 1412 | 3 | 0 | - | Germany |
| Ciriaco Sforza | 33 | 23 | 19 | 1815 | 9 | 1 | - | Switzerland |
| **Forwards** | | | | | | | | |
| Silvio Adzic | 22 | 5 | 1 | 166 | 0 | 0 | - | Germany |
| Miroslav Klose | 25 | 32 | 28 | 2672 | 4 | 0 | 10 | Germany (4) |
| Vratislav Lokvenc | 29 | 31 | 27 | 2558 | 2 | 0 | 6 | Czech Republic (13) |
| Michael Mifsud | 22 | 16 | 1 | 463 | 0 | 0 | - | Malta |
| Selim Teber | 22 | 20 | 2 | 615 | 2 | 0 | - | Turkey |
| Christian Timm | 24 | 19 | 6 | 1081 | 0 | 0 | - | Germany |

KEY: LEAGUE BOOKINGS CAPS (FIFA RANKING)

## SQUAD APPEARANCES

| Match | 1 | 2 | 3 | 4 | 5 | 6 | 7 | 8 | 9 | 10 | 11 | 12 | 13 | 14 | 15 | 16 | 17 | 18 | 19 | 20 | 21 | 22 | 23 | 24 | 25 | 26 | 27 | 28 | 29 | 30 | 31 | 32 | 33 | 34 |
|---|---|---|---|---|---|---|---|---|---|---|---|---|---|---|---|---|---|---|---|---|---|---|---|---|---|---|---|---|---|---|---|---|---|---|
| Venue | A | H | A | H | A | H | A | H | A | A | H | H | A | H | H | A | H | H | A | H | A | H | A | H | A | H | A | H | A | H | A | A | H | A |
| Competition | L | L | L | L | L | L | L | L | L | L | L | L | L | L | L | L | L | L | L | L | L | L | L | L | L | L | L | L | L | L | L | L | L | L |
| Result | D | L | L | D | L | D | L | W | L | D | L | L | L | L | W | L | W | L | D | W | D | W | D | W | W | W | D | W | L | W | L | D | D | L |

**Goalkeepers**
Jens Kern
Georg Koch
Tim Wiese

**Defenders**
Thomas Hengen
Tomasz Klos
Aleksander Knavs
Harry Koch
Nzelo Lembi
Hervi Nzelo-Lembi
Hany Ramzy
Torsten Reuter
Bill Tchato

**Midfielders**
Markus Anfang
Mario Basler
Nenad Bjelica
Jose Dominguez
Dimitrios Grammozis
Marian Hristov
Cassio de Souza Lincoln
Stefan Malz
Rodriguez Ratinho
Thomas Riedl
Ciriaco Sforza

**Forwards**
Silvio Adzic
Miroslav Klose
Vratislav Lokvenc
Michael Mifsud
Selim Teber
Christian Timm

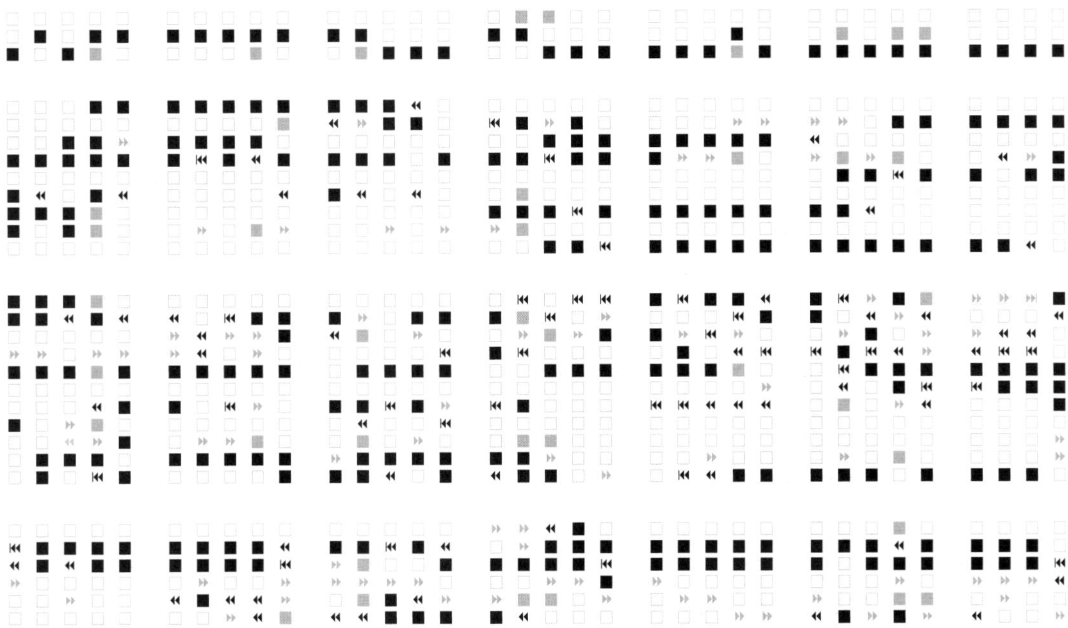

KEY: On all match; On bench; Subbed or sent off (Counting game); Subbed or sent off (playing less than 70 minutes); Subbed on from bench (Counting Game); Subbed on (playing less than 70 minutes); Subbed on and then subbed or sent off (Counting Game); Subbed on and then subbed or sent off (playing less than 70 minutes); Not in 16

# BAYER LEVERKUSEN

Final Position: **15th**

| | | | | | | |
|---|---|---|---|---|---|---|
| 1 | lge | Cottbus | A | D | 1-1 | Simak 64 |
| 2 | lge | B Dortmund | H | D | 1-1 | Placente 23 |
| 3 | lge | Bochum | H | L | 2-4 | Simak 10; Franca 75 |
| 4 | lge | Hansa Rostock | A | W | 3-1 | Neuville 5; Brdaric 22; Wimmer 87 og |
| 5 | lge | Hannover 96 | H | L | 1-3 | Basturk 11 |
| 6 | ecgf | Olympiakos | A | L | 2-6 | Eleftheropoulos 22 og; Schneider 78 pen |
| 7 | lge | W Bremen | A | L | 2-3 | Brdaric 11; Stalteri 42 og |
| 8 | ecgf | Man Utd | H | L | 1-2 | Berbatov 52 |
| 9 | lge | Bayern Munich | H | W | 2-1 | Lucio 9; Bierofka 63 |
| 10 | ecgf | Maccabi Haifa | A | W | 2-0 | Babic 31,64 |
| 11 | lge | Wolfsburg | A | L | 0-2 | |
| 12 | lge | Kaiserslautern | H | W | 1-0 | Brdaric 20 |
| 13 | ecgf | Maccabi Haifa | H | W | 2-1 | Babic 45; Juan 67 |
| 14 | lge | Hertha Berlin | A | D | 1-1 | Juan 55 |
| 15 | ecgf | Olympiakos | H | W | 2-0 | Juan 14; Schneider 89 pen |
| 16 | lge | Stuttgart | H | L | 0-1 | |
| 17 | lge | Schalke | A | W | 1-0 | Schneider 90 pen |
| 18 | ecgf | Man Utd | A | L | 0-2 | |
| 19 | lge | B M'gladbach | H | D | 2-2 | Bierofka 29,87 |
| 20 | lge | Arminia B | A | D | 2-2 | Brdaric 17; Zivkovic 69 |
| 21 | ecga | Barcelona | H | L | 1-2 | Berbatov 39 |
| 22 | lge | Hamburg | H | L | 2-3 | Balitsch 11; Basturk 22 |
| 23 | lge | 1860 Munich | A | W | 3-0 | Bierofka 9; Berbatov 52; Neuville 89 |
| 24 | ecga | Inter Milan | A | L | 2-3 | Zivkovic 63; Franca 90 |
| 25 | lge | Nurnberg | H | L | 0-2 | |
| 26 | lge | Cottbus | H | L | 0-3 | |
| 27 | lge | B Dortmund | A | L | 0-2 | |
| 28 | lge | Bochum | A | L | 1-2 | Babic 78 |
| 29 | lge | Hansa Rostock | H | L | 1-2 | Babic 38 |
| 30 | ecga | Newcastle | H | L | 1-3 | Franca 25 |
| 31 | lge | Hannover 96 | A | W | 2-1 | Schoof 80; Simak 90 |
| 32 | ecga | Newcastle | A | L | 1-3 | Babic 73 |
| 33 | lge | W Bremen | H | W | 3-0 | Bierofka 11; Schoof 50; Juan 61 |
| 34 | lge | Bayern Munich | A | L | 0-3 | |
| 35 | ecga | Barcelona | A | L | 0-2 | |
| 36 | lge | Wolfsburg | H | D | 1-1 | Ramelow 69 |
| 37 | ecga | Inter Milan | H | L | 0-2 | |
| 38 | lge | Kaiserslautern | A | L | 0-1 | |
| 39 | lge | Hertha Berlin | H | W | 4-1 | Butt 14 pen; Schneider 31; Neuville 40,69 |
| 40 | lge | Stuttgart | A | L | 0-3 | |
| 41 | lge | Schalke | H | L | 1-3 | Berbatov 9 |
| 42 | lge | B M'gladbach | A | D | 2-2 | Bierofka 17; Berbatov 48 |
| 43 | lge | Arminia B | H | W | 3-1 | Lucio 38,69; Balitsch 71 |
| 44 | lge | Hamburg | A | L | 1-4 | Balitsch 88 |
| 45 | lge | 1860 Munich | H | W | 3-0 | Bierofka 8; Berbatov 44; Babic 48 |
| 46 | lge | Nurnberg | A | W | 1-0 | Basturk 36 |

## GOALS SCORED

**AT HOME**

| | | |
|---|---|---|
| MOST | B Munich | 37 |
| | | 27 |
| LEAST | Nurnberg | 16 |

**AWAY**

| | | |
|---|---|---|
| MOST | B Munich | 33 |
| | | 20 |
| LEAST | B M'gladbach &Arminia B | 12 |

## GOALS CONCEDED

**AT HOME**

| | | |
|---|---|---|
| LEAST | Hamburg & B M'gladbach | 11 |
| | | 28 |
| MOST | Hannover 96 | 33 |

**AWAY**

| | | |
|---|---|---|
| LEAST | B Munich | 13 |
| | | 28 |
| MOST | Nurnberg | 36 |

## ATTENDANCES

HOME GROUND: BAYARENA LEVERKUSEN CAPACITY: 25500 AVERAGE LEAGUE AT HOME: 22500

| | | | | | | | | |
|---|---|---|---|---|---|---|---|---|
| 27 | B Dortmund | 67000 | 21 | Barcelona | 25500 | 13 | Maccabi Haifa | 22500 |
| 18 | Man Utd | 66185 | 4 | Hansa Rostock | 25000 | 22 | Hamburg | 22500 |
| 35 | Barcelona | 62228 | 15 | Olympiakos | 23500 | 26 | Cottbus | 22500 |
| 17 | Schalke | 60601 | 5 | Hannover 96 | 22500 | 8 | Man Utd | 22500 |
| 44 | Hamburg | 52000 | 45 | 1860 Munich | 22500 | 25 | Nurnberg | 22500 |
| 34 | Bayern Munich | 45000 | 29 | Hansa Rostock | 22500 | 41 | Schalke | 22500 |
| 14 | Hertha Berlin | 43146 | 30 | Newcastle | 22500 | 9 | Bayern Munich | 22500 |
| 37 | Inter Milan | 43000 | 36 | Wolfsburg | 22500 | 20 | Arminia B | 20000 |
| 32 | Newcastle | 40508 | 2 | B Dortmund | 22500 | 23 | 1860 Munich | 20000 |
| 38 | Kaiserslautern | 40500 | 3 | Bochum | 22500 | 28 | Bochum | 18000 |
| 40 | Stuttgart | 40000 | 33 | W Bremen | 22500 | 6 | Olympiakos | 15000 |
| 24 | Inter Milan | 40000 | 39 | Hertha Berlin | 22500 | 1 | Cottbus | 15000 |
| 31 | Hannover 96 | 39000 | 19 | B M'gladbach | 22500 | 11 | Wolfsburg | 14234 |
| 42 | B M'gladbach | 34000 | 43 | Arminia B | 22500 | 10 | Maccabi Haifa | 5000 |
| 7 | W Bremen | 32000 | 12 | Kaiserslautern | 22500 | | | |
| 46 | Nurnberg | 30000 | 16 | Stuttgart | 22500 | | | |

■ Home □ Away ▒ Neutral

## KEY PLAYERS - GOALSCORERS

**1 Daniel Bierofka**

| | | | |
|---|---|---|---|
| Goals in the League | 7 | Player Strike Rate<br>Average number of minutes between League goals scored by player | 259 |
| Contribution to Attacking Power<br>Average number of minutes between League team goals while on pitch | 62 | Club Strike Rate<br>Average number of minutes between League goals scored by club | 65 |

| | PLAYER | LGE GOALS | POWER | STRIKE RATE |
|---|---|---|---|---|
| 2 | Dimitar Berbatov | 4 | 66 | 413 mins |
| 3 | Marco Babic | 3 | 56 | 487 mins |
| 4 | Da Silva Ferreira Lucio | 3 | 57 | 611 mins |
| 5 | Oliver Neuville | 4 | 62 | 623 mins |

## KEY PLAYERS - MIDFIELDERS

**1 Marco Babic**

| | | | |
|---|---|---|---|
| Goals in the League | 3 | Contribution to Attacking Power<br>Average number of minutes between League team goals while on pitch | 56 |
| Defensive Rating<br>Average number of mins between League goals conceded while he was on the pitch | 61 | Scoring Difference<br>Defensive Rating minus Contribution to Attacking Power | 5 |

| | PLAYER | LGE GOALS | DEF RATE | POWER | SCORE DIFF |
|---|---|---|---|---|---|
| 2 | Daniel Bierofka | 7 | 62 | 62 | 0 mins |
| 3 | Jan Simak | 3 | 50 | 55 | -5 mins |
| 4 | Hanno Balitsch | 3 | 54 | 62 | -8 mins |
| 5 | Carsten Ramelow | 1 | 54 | 64 | -10 mins |

## KEY PLAYERS - DEFENDERS

**1 Juan**

| | | | |
|---|---|---|---|
| Goals Conceded (GC)<br>The number of League goals conceded while he was on the pitch | 33 | Clean Sheets<br>In games when he played at least 70 minutes | 4 |
| Defensive Rating<br>Ave number of mins between League goals conceded while on the pitch | 58 | Club Defensive Rating<br>Average number of mins between League goals conceded by the club this season | 55 |

| | PLAYER | CON LGE | CLEAN SHEETS | DEF RATE |
|---|---|---|---|---|
| 2 | Diego Placente | 33 | 5 | 58 mins |
| 3 | Da Silva Ferreira Lucio | 32 | 4 | 57 mins |
| 4 | Boris Zivkovic | 45 | 5 | 56 mins |

## KEY GOALKEEPER

**1 Hans-Jorg Butt**

| | |
|---|---|
| Goals Conceded in the League | 53 |
| Defensive Rating<br>Ave number of mins between League goals conceded while on the pitch | 56 |
| Counting Games<br>Games when he played at least 70 minutes | 33 |
| Clean Sheets<br>In games when he played at least 70 minutes | 6 |

## TOP POINT EARNERS

| | PLAYER | GAMES | AV |
|---|---|---|---|
| 1 | Babic | 12 | 1.5 |
| 2 | Bierofka | 14 | 1.5 |
| 3 | Balitsch | 21 | 1.3 |
| 4 | Lucio | 20 | 1.3 |
| 5 | Juan | 20 | 1.3 |
| 6 | Ramelow | 31 | 1.2 |
| 7 | Zivkovic | 27 | 1.2 |
| 8 | Neuville | 24 | 1.2 |
| 9 | Butt | 33 | 1.2 |
| 10 | Placente | 19 | 1.1 |
| | CLUB AVERAGE: | | 1.1 |

Ave = Average points per match in Counting Gam

## DISCIPLINARY RECORDS

| | PLAYER | YELLOW | RED | AVE |
|---|---|---|---|---|
| 1 | Brdaric | 3 | 1 | 170 |
| 2 | Placente | 8 | 1 | 210 |
| 3 | Zivkovic | 11 | 1 | 211 |
| 4 | Schneider | 7 | 1 | 303 |
| 5 | Balitsch | 7 | 0 | 309 |
| 6 | Simak | 3 | 0 | 349 |
| 7 | Basturk | 4 | 1 | 377 |
| 8 | Berbatov | 3 | 1 | 412 |
| 9 | Sebescen | 1 | 0 | 452 |
| 10 | Ramelow | 6 | 0 | 468 |
| 11 | Juan | 4 | 0 | 475 |
| 12 | Babic | 3 | 0 | 486 |
| 13 | Neuville | 5 | 0 | 498 |
| | Other | 10 | 0 | |
| | TOTAL | 75 | 6 | |

## LEAGUE GOALS

| | PLAYER | MINS | GOALS | AV |
|---|---|---|---|---|
| 1 | Bierofka | 1811 | 7 | 25 |
| 2 | Neuville | 2490 | 4 | 62 |
| 3 | Berbatov | 1651 | 4 | 41 |
| 4 | Brdaric | 682 | 4 | 17 |
| 5 | Lucio | 1834 | 3 | 61 |
| 6 | Balitsch | 2169 | 3 | 72 |
| 7 | Babic | 1460 | 3 | 48 |
| 8 | Simak | 1048 | 3 | 34 |
| 9 | Basturk | 1886 | 3 | 62 |
| 10 | Schoof | 214 | 2 | 10 |
| 11 | Juan | 1900 | 2 | 95 |
| 12 | Schneider | 2428 | 2 | 121 |
| 13 | Franca | 647 | 1 | 64 |
| | Other | | 6 | |
| | TOTAL | | 47 | |

## MONTH BY MONTH GUIDE TO THE POINTS

| Month | Points | % |
|---|---|---|
| AUGUST | 2 | 22% |
| SEPTEMBER | 6 | 50% |
| OCTOBER | 4 | 44% |
| NOVEMBER | 5 | 33% |
| DECEMBER | 3 | 50% |
| JANUARY | 0 | 0% |
| FEBRUARY | 3 | 25% |
| MARCH | 4 | 33% |
| APRIL | 4 | 33% |
| MAY | 9 | 75% |

## TEAM OF THE SEASON

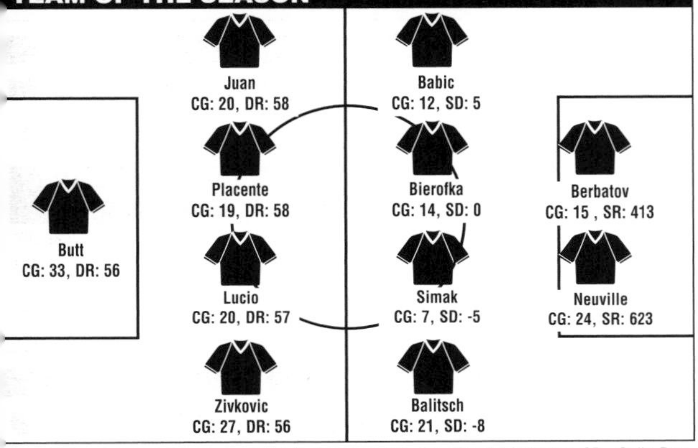

Butt
CG: 33, DR: 56
Juan
CG: 20, DR: 58
Placente
CG: 19, DR: 58
Lucio
CG: 20, DR: 57
Zivkovic
CG: 27, DR: 56
Babic
CG: 12, SD: 5
Bierofka
CG: 14, SD: 0
Simak
CG: 7, SD: -5
Balitsch
CG: 21, SD: -8
Berbatov
CG: 15 , SR: 413
Neuville
CG: 24, SR: 623


KEY: DR = Defensive Rate, SD = Scoring Difference, SR = Strike Rate, CG = Counting Games – League games playing at least 70 minutes

## LEAGUE APPEARANCES, BOOKINGS AND CAPS

| | AGE | IN THE SQUAD | COUNTING GAMES | MINUTES ON PITCH | YELLOW CARDS | RED CARDS | THIS SEASON | HOME COUNTRY |
|---|---|---|---|---|---|---|---|---|
| **Goalkeepers** | | | | | | | | |
| Hans-Jorg Butt | 29 | 33 | 33 | 2970 | 1 | 0 | 2 | Germany (4) |
| Frank Juric | 29 | 9 | 1 | 135 | 0 | 0 | - | Australia |
| Tom Starke | 22 | 3 | 0 | 0 | 0 | 0 | - | Germany |
| **Defenders** | | | | | | | | |
| Mile Bozic | 21 | 0 | 0 | 0 | 0 | 0 | - | Croatia |
| Jan-I Callsen-Bracker | 18 | 1 | 0 | 0 | 0 | 0 | - | Germany |
| Cristiano Cris | 26 | 4 | 3 | 270 | 0 | 0 | 1 | Brazil (1) |
| Silveira Juan | 24 | 24 | 20 | 1900 | 4 | 0 | 2 | Brazil (1) |
| Thomas Kleine | 25 | 11 | 1 | 266 | 0 | 0 | - | Germany |
| Lucimar Lucio | 25 | 21 | 20 | 1834 | 3 | 0 | 2 | Brazil (1) |
| Jens Nowotny | 29 | 1 | 1 | 90 | 0 | 0 | - | Germany |
| Diego Placente | 26 | 25 | 19 | 1898 | 8 | 1 | 2 | Argentina (5) |
| Boris Zivkovic | 27 | 31 | 27 | 2537 | 11 | 1 | 9 | Croatia (26) |
| **Midfielders** | | | | | | | | |
| Marko Babic | 22 | 28 | 12 | 1460 | 3 | 0 | 9 | Croatia (26) |
| Hanno Balitsch | 22 | 28 | 21 | 2169 | 7 | 0 | 1 | Germany (4) |
| Yildiray Basturk | 24 | 26 | 19 | 1886 | 4 | 1 | 8 | Turkey (8) |
| Daniel Bierofka | 24 | 31 | 14 | 1811 | 3 | 0 | 1 | Germany (4) |
| Anel Dzaka | 22 | 2 | 0 | 45 | 0 | 0 | - | Germany |
| Nasir El Kasmi | 20 | 0 | 0 | 0 | 0 | 0 | - | Germany |
| Frankie Hejduk | 28 | 1 | 0 | 0 | 0 | 0 | - | America |
| Radoslaw Kaluzny | 29 | 5 | 3 | 284 | 0 | 0 | 4 | Poland (29) |
| Pascal Ojigwe | 26 | 19 | 10 | 1161 | 2 | 0 | - | Nigeria |
| Christoph Preuss | 22 | 7 | 0 | 66 | 0 | 0 | - | Germany |
| Carsten Ramelow | 29 | 32 | 31 | 2811 | 6 | 0 | 10 | Germany (4) |
| Bernd Schneider | 29 | 28 | 27 | 2428 | 7 | 1 | 10 | Germany (4) |
| Zoltan Sebescen | 27 | 8 | 4 | 452 | 1 | 0 | - | Germany |
| Jan Simak | 24 | 23 | 7 | 1048 | 3 | 0 | 3 | Czech Republic (13) |
| Jurica Vranjes | 23 | 9 | 0 | 76 | 1 | 0 | 1 | Croatia (26) |
| **Forwards** | | | | | | | | |
| Dimitar Berbatov | 22 | 26 | 15 | 1651 | 3 | 1 | - | Bulgaria |
| Thomas Brdaric | 28 | 19 | 4 | 682 | 3 | 1 | - | Germany |
| Huzeyfe Dogan | 22 | 0 | 0 | 0 | 0 | 0 | - | Germany |
| Franca | 27 | 18 | 2 | 647 | 0 | 0 | - | Brazil |
| Ulf Kirsten | 37 | 9 | 1 | 98 | 0 | 0 | - | Germany |
| Oliver Neuville | 30 | 34 | 24 | 2490 | 5 | 0 | 7 | Germany (4) |
| Sebastian Schoof | 23 | 8 | 0 | 214 | 0 | 0 | - | Germany |

KEY: LEAGUE BOOKINGS CAPS (FIFA RANKING)

## SQUAD APPEARANCES

| Match | 1 | 2 | 3 | 4 | 5 | 6 | 7 | 8 | 9 | 10 | 11 | 12 | 13 | 14 | 15 | 16 | 17 | 18 | 19 | 20 | 21 | 22 | 23 |
|---|---|---|---|---|---|---|---|---|---|---|---|---|---|---|---|---|---|---|---|---|---|---|---|
| Venue | A | H | H | A | H | A | A | H | H | A | A | H | H | A | H | H | A | A | H | A | H | H | A |
| Competition | L | L | L | L | L | C | L | C | L | C | L | L | C | L | C | L | L | C | L | L | C | L | L |
| Result | D | D | L | W | L | L | L | L | W | W | L | W | W | D | W | L | W | L | D | D | L | L | W |

| Match | 24 | 25 | 26 | 27 | 28 | 29 | 30 | 31 | 32 | 33 | 34 | 35 | 36 | 37 | 38 | 39 | 40 | 41 | 42 | 43 | 44 | 45 | 46 |
|---|---|---|---|---|---|---|---|---|---|---|---|---|---|---|---|---|---|---|---|---|---|---|---|
| Venue | A | H | H | A | A | H | H | A | A | H | A | A | H | H | A | H | A | H | A | H | A | H | A |
| Competition | C | L | L | L | L | L | C | L | C | L | L | C | L | C | L | L | L | L | L | L | L | L | L |
| Result | L | L | L | L | L | L | L | W | L | W | L | L | D | L | L | W | L | L | D | W | L | W | W |

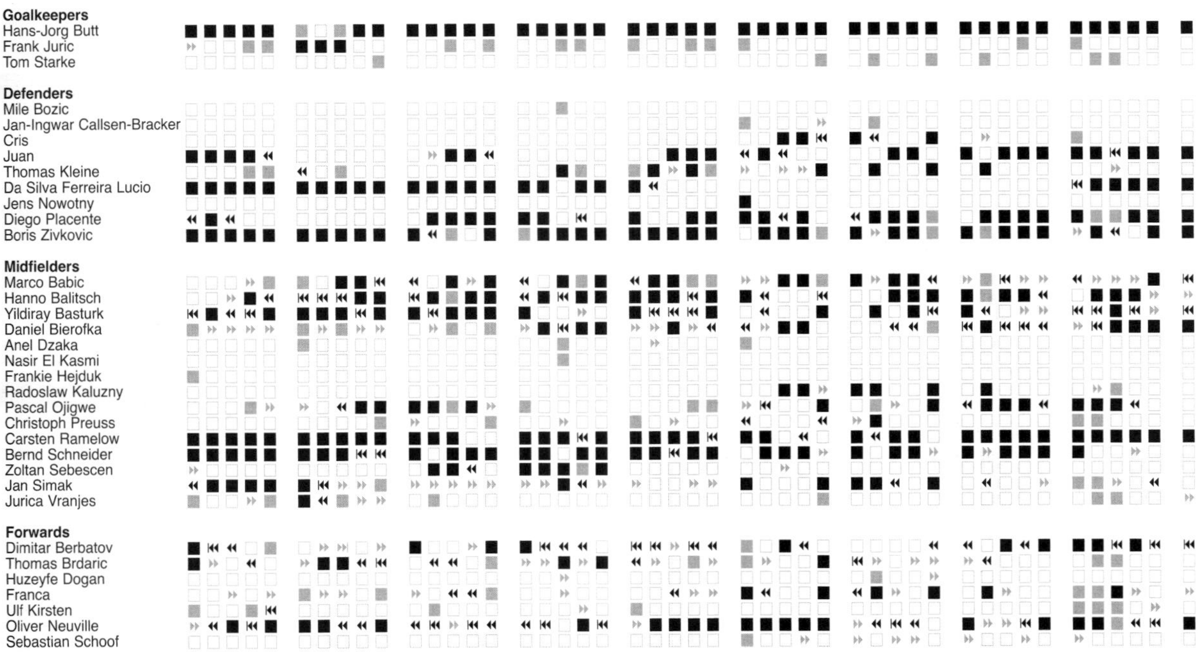

KEY: On all match / On bench / Subbed or sent off (Counting game) / Subbed or sent off (playing less than 70 minutes) / Subbed on from bench (Counting Game) / Subbed on (playing less than 70 minutes) / Subbed on and then subbed or sent off (Counting Game) / Subbed on and then subbed or sent off (playing less than 70 minutes) / Not in 16

# ARMINIA BIELEFELD

Final Position: **16th**

| | | | | | | |
|---|---|---|---|---|---|---|
| 1 | lge | W Bremen | H | W | 3-0 | Reina 17; Wichinarek 90; Porcello 90 |
| 2 | lge | Bayern Munich | A | L | 2-6 | Wichinarek 51; Diabang 89 |
| 3 | lge | Wolfsburg | H | W | 1-0 | Brinkmann 43 |
| 4 | lge | Kaiserslautern | A | D | 1-1 | Diabang 59 |
| 5 | lge | Hertha Berlin | H | L | 0-1 | |
| 6 | lge | Stuttgart | A | L | 0-3 | |
| 7 | lge | Schalke | H | W | 2-1 | Albayrak 7 pen; Diabang 69 |
| 8 | lge | B M'gladbach | A | L | 0-3 | |
| 9 | lge | B Dortmund | A | D | 0-0 | |
| 10 | lge | Hamburg | H | W | 2-1 | Diabang 14,57 |
| 11 | lge | 1860 Munich | A | L | 1-3 | Wichinarek 15 |
| 12 | lge | Nurnberg | H | L | 0-1 | |
| 13 | lge | Cottbus | A | L | 1-2 | Kauf 72 |
| 14 | lge | B Leverkusen | H | D | 2-2 | Wichinarek 26,85 |
| 15 | lge | Bochum | A | W | 3-0 | Lenze 3; Vander 54 og; Diabang 86 |
| 16 | lge | Hansa Rostock | H | W | 3-0 | Wichinarek 45,55; Reinhardt 81 |
| 17 | lge | Hannover 96 | A | D | 0-0 | |
| 18 | lge | W Bremen | A | D | 2-2 | Diabang 11; Cha 40 |
| 19 | lge | Bayern Munich | H | D | 0-0 | |
| 20 | lge | Wolfsburg | A | L | 0-2 | |
| 21 | lge | Kaiserslautern | H | D | 1-1 | Reinhardt 35 |
| 22 | lge | Hertha Berlin | A | D | 0-0 | |
| 23 | lge | Stuttgart | H | L | 0-1 | |
| 24 | lge | Schalke | A | D | 1-1 | Waldoch 57 og |
| 25 | lge | B M'gladbach | H | W | 4-1 | Diabang 14,46,82; Wichinarek 54 |
| 26 | lge | B Dortmund | H | D | 0-0 | |
| 27 | lge | Hamburg | A | L | 0-1 | |
| 28 | lge | 1860 Munich | H | W | 2-1 | Wichinarek 14 pen,42 |
| 29 | lge | Nurnberg | A | D | 0-0 | |
| 30 | lge | Cottbus | H | D | 2-2 | Dabrowski 56; Wichinarek 58 |
| 31 | lge | B Leverkusen | A | L | 1-3 | Brinkmann 34 pen |
| 32 | lge | Bochum | H | L | 1-3 | Wichinarek 43 |
| 33 | lge | Hansa Rostock | A | L | 0-3 | |
| 34 | lge | Hannover 96 | H | L | 0-1 | |

## KEY PLAYERS - GOALSCORERS

**1 Artur Wichinarek**

| | | | |
|---|---|---|---|
| Goals in the League | 12 | Player Strike Rate<br>Average number of minutes between League goals scored by player | 200 |
| Contribution to Attacking Power<br>Average number of minutes between League team goals while on pitch | 82 | Club Strike Rate<br>Average number of minutes between League goals scored by club | 87 |

| | PLAYER | LGE GOALS | POWER | STRIKE RATE |
|---|---|---|---|---|
| 2 | Mamadou Lamine Diabang | 10 | 84 | 212 mins |
| 3 | Ansgar Brinkmann | 2 | 90 | 1091 mins |
| 4 | Erhan Albayrak | 1 | 72 | 1165 mins |
| 5 | Bastian Reinhardt | 2 | 92 | 1485 mins |

## KEY PLAYERS - MIDFIELDERS

**1 Ansgar Brinkmann**

| | | | |
|---|---|---|---|
| Goals in the League | 2 | Contribution to Attacking Power<br>Average number of minutes between League team goals while on pitch | 91 |
| Defensive Rating<br>Average number of mins between League goals conceded while he was on the pitch | 84 | Scoring Difference<br>Defensive Rating minus Contribution to Attacking Power | -7 |

| | PLAYER | LGE GOALS | DEF RATE | POWER | SCORE DIFF |
|---|---|---|---|---|---|
| 2 | Christophe Dabrowski | 1 | 74 | 87 | -13 mins |
| 3 | Ruediger Kauf | 1 | 68 | 89 | -21 mins |
| 4 | Detlev Dammeier | 0 | 61 | 90 | -29 mins |
| 5 | Fatmir Vata | 0 | 58 | 88 | -30 mins |

## KEY PLAYERS - DEFENDERS

**1 Marcio Borges**

| | | | |
|---|---|---|---|
| Goals Conceded (GC)<br>The number of League goals conceded while he was on the pitch | 11 | Clean Sheets<br>In games when he played at least 70 minutes | 3 |
| Defensive Rating<br>Ave number of mins between League goals conceded while on the pitch | 84 | Club Defensive Rating<br>Average number of mins between League goals conceded by the club this season | 67 |

| | PLAYER | CON LGE | CLEAN SHEETS | DEF RATE |
|---|---|---|---|---|
| 2 | Torjus Hansen | 36 | 8 | 74 mins |
| 3 | Benjamin Lenze | 14 | 4 | 65 mins |
| 4 | Bastian Reinhardt | 46 | 9 | 65 mins |
| 5 | Daniel Bogusz | 17 | 4 | 62 mins |

## GOALS SCORED

**AT HOME**

| | | |
|---|---|---|
| MOST | B Munich | 37 |
| | | 23 |
| LEAST | Nurnberg | 16 |

**AWAY**

| | | |
|---|---|---|
| MOST | B Munich | 33 |
| | | 12 |
| LEAST | B M'gladbach &Arminia B | 12 |

## GOALS CONCEDED

**AT HOME**

| | | |
|---|---|---|
| LEAST | Hamburg & B M'gladbach | 11 |
| | | 16 |
| MOST | Hannover 96 | 33 |

**AWAY**

| | | |
|---|---|---|
| LEAST | B Munich | 13 |
| | | 30 |
| MOST | Nurnberg | 36 |

## KEY GOALKEEPER

**1 Mathias Hain**

| | |
|---|---|
| Goals Conceded in the League | 46 |
| Defensive Rating<br>Ave number of mins between League goals conceded while on the pitch | 67 |
| Counting Games<br>Games when he played at least 70 minutes | 34 |
| Clean Sheets<br>In games when he played at least 70 minutes | 10 |

## TOP POINT EARNERS

| | PLAYER | GAMES | AVE |
|---|---|---|---|
| 1 | Brinkmann | 19 | 1.42 |
| 2 | Dammeier | 26 | 1.23 |
| 3 | Dabrowski | 27 | 1.19 |
| 4 | Wichinarek | 26 | 1.15 |
| 5 | Hain | 34 | 1.06 |
| 6 | Kauf | 31 | 1.06 |
| 7 | Vata | 20 | 1.00 |
| 8 | Hansen | 29 | 1.00 |
| 9 | Diabang | 20 | 1.00 |
| 10 | Reinhardt | 33 | 1.00 |
| | **CLUB AVERAGE:** | | **1.06** |

Ave = Average points per match in Counting Games

## ATTENDANCES

HOME GROUND: ALM CAPACITY: 26601 AVERAGE LEAGUE AT HOME: 21724

| | | | | | | | | |
|---|---|---|---|---|---|---|---|---|
| 9 | B Dortmund | 68600 | 10 | Hamburg | 26500 | 6 | Stuttgart | 20000 |
| 24 | Schalke | 60878 | 32 | Bochum | 26000 | 5 | Hertha Berlin | 20000 |
| 2 | Bayern Munich | 50000 | 25 | B M'gladbach | 26000 | 14 | B Leverkusen | 20000 |
| 27 | Hamburg | 46140 | 22 | Hertha Berlin | 25000 | 30 | Cottbus | 20000 |
| 4 | Kaiserslautern | 33000 | 3 | Wolfsburg | 25000 | 21 | Kaiserslautern | 19237 |
| 17 | Hannover 96 | 30000 | 8 | B M'gladbach | 24000 | 16 | Hansa Rostock | 19109 |
| 18 | W Bremen | 29604 | 29 | Nurnberg | 23500 | 12 | Nurnberg | 18000 |
| 33 | Hansa Rostock | 28000 | 11 | 1860 Munich | 22500 | 20 | Wolfsburg | 15976 |
| 34 | Hannover 96 | 26601 | 31 | B Leverkusen | 22500 | 13 | Cottbus | 12628 |
| 26 | B Dortmund | 26601 | 28 | 1860 Munich | 21070 | 23 | Stuttgart | 2000 |
| 19 | Bayern Munich | 26601 | 15 | Bochum | 21000 | | | |
| 7 | Schalke | 26601 | 1 | W Bremen | 20000 | | | |

■ Home □ Away ▒ Neutral

## DISCIPLINARY RECORDS

| | PLAYER | YELLOW | RED | AVE |
|---|---|---|---|---|
| 1 | Bogusz | 6 | 1 | 149 |
| 2 | Kauf | 10 | 0 | 277 |
| 3 | Albayrak | 4 | 0 | 291 |
| 4 | Lenze | 2 | 1 | 301 |
| 5 | Borges | 3 | 0 | 307 |
| 6 | Brinkmann | 4 | 1 | 436 |
| 7 | Cha | 2 | 0 | 459 |
| 8 | Dammeier | 4 | 0 | 628 |
| 9 | Diabang | 3 | 0 | 706 |
| 10 | Hain | 4 | 0 | 765 |
| 11 | Wichinarek | 2 | 1 | 800 |
| 12 | Dabrowski | 2 | 1 | 810 |
| 13 | Murawski | 1 | 0 | 826 |
| | Other | 7 | 0 | |
| | TOTAL | 54 | 5 | |

## LEAGUE GOALS

| | PLAYER | MINS | GOALS | AVE |
|---|---|---|---|---|
| 1 | Wichinarek | 2402 | 12 | 200 |
| 2 | Diabang | 2119 | 10 | 212 |
| 3 | Reinhardt | 2970 | 2 | 1485 |
| 4 | Brinkmann | 2181 | 2 | 1091 |
| 5 | Reina | 90 | 1 | 90 |
| 6 | Lenze | 904 | 1 | 904 |
| 7 | Porcello | 362 | 1 | 362 |
| 8 | Kauf | 2774 | 1 | 2774 |
| 9 | Cha | 918 | 1 | 918 |
| 10 | Albayrak | 1165 | 1 | 1165 |
| 11 | Dabrowski | 2430 | 1 | 2430 |
| | Other | | 2 | |
| | TOTAL | | 35 | |

## MONTH BY MONTH GUIDE TO THE POINTS

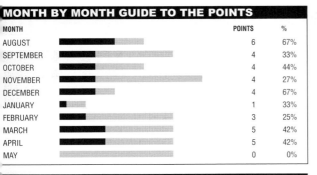

| MONTH | POINTS | % |
|---|---|---|
| AUGUST | 6 | 67% |
| SEPTEMBER | 4 | 33% |
| OCTOBER | 4 | 44% |
| NOVEMBER | 4 | 27% |
| DECEMBER | 4 | 67% |
| JANUARY | 1 | 33% |
| FEBRUARY | 3 | 25% |
| MARCH | 5 | 42% |
| APRIL | 5 | 42% |
| MAY | 0 | 0% |

## TEAM OF THE SEASON

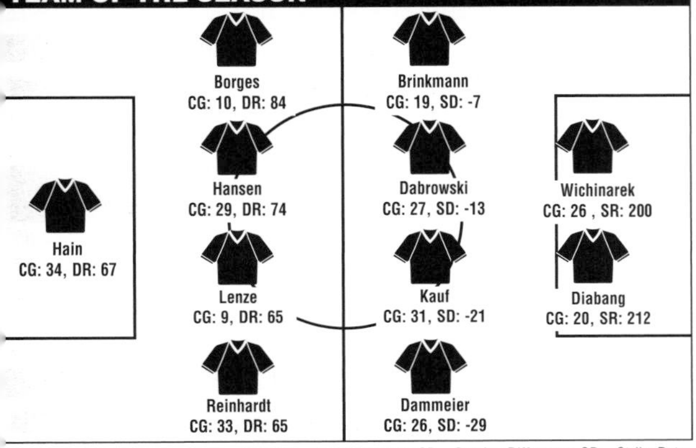
Borges
CG: 10, DR: 84
Brinkmann
CG: 19, SD: -7
Hain
CG: 34, DR: 67
Hansen
CG: 29, DR: 74
Dabrowski
CG: 27, SD: -13
Wichinarek
CG: 26 , SR: 200
Lenze
CG: 9, DR: 65
Kauf
CG: 31, SD: -21
Diabang
CG: 20, SR: 212
Reinhardt
CG: 33, DR: 65
Dammeier
CG: 26, SD: -29

KEY: DR = Defensive Rate, SD = Scoring Difference, SR = Strike Rate, CG = Counting Games – League games playing at least 70 minutes

## LEAGUE APPEARANCES, BOOKINGS AND CAPS

| | AGE | IN THE SQUAD | COUNTING GAMES | MINUTES ON PITCH | YELLOW CARDS | RED CARDS | THIS SEASON | HOME COUNTRY |
|---|---|---|---|---|---|---|---|---|
| **Goalkeepers** | | | | | | | | |
| Dennis Eilhoff | 20 | 7 | 0 | 0 | 0 | 0 | - | Germany |
| Mathias Hain | 30 | 34 | 34 | 3060 | 4 | 0 | - | Germany |
| Simon Henzler | 30 | 2 | 0 | 0 | 0 | 0 | - | Germany |
| **Defenders** | | | | | | | | |
| Martin Amedick | 20 | 2 | 0 | 0 | 0 | 0 | - | Germany |
| Daniel Bogusz | 28 | 19 | 11 | 1046 | 6 | 1 | - | Portugal |
| Marcio Borges | 30 | 12 | 10 | 922 | 3 | 0 | - | Brazil |
| Torjus Hansen | 29 | 31 | 29 | 2669 | 1 | 0 | 6 | Norway (24) |
| Benjamin Lenze | 24 | 18 | 9 | 904 | 2 | 1 | - | Germany |
| Maciej Murawski | 29 | 19 | 8 | 826 | 1 | 0 | 3 | Poland (29) |
| Bastian Reinhardt | 27 | 33 | 33 | 2970 | 2 | 0 | - | Germany |
| **Midfielders** | | | | | | | | |
| Ansgar Brinkmann | 34 | 31 | 19 | 2181 | 4 | 1 | - | Germany |
| Christophe Dabrowski | 25 | 27 | 27 | 2430 | 2 | 1 | - | Germany |
| Detlev Dammeier | 34 | 30 | 26 | 2514 | 4 | 0 | - | Germany |
| Dirk Flock | 31 | 4 | 0 | 0 | 0 | 0 | - | Germany |
| Sasa Janic | 28 | 4 | 0 | 13 | 1 | 0 | - | Croatia |
| Ruediger Kauf | 28 | 31 | 31 | 2774 | 10 | 0 | - | Germany |
| Heinz MŸller | | 5 | 0 | 0 | 0 | 0 | - | |
| Massimiliano Porcello | 23 | 23 | 1 | 362 | 1 | 0 | - | Italy |
| Bernd Gerd Rauw | 23 | 19 | 13 | 1221 | 1 | 0 | - | Belgium |
| Jesus Sinisterra | 27 | 4 | 0 | 8 | 0 | 0 | - | Colombia |
| Van der Ven | 33 | 1 | 0 | 14 | 0 | 0 | - | Holland |
| Fatmir Vata | 31 | 30 | 20 | 2018 | 1 | 0 | - | Albania |
| **Forwards** | | | | | | | | |
| Erhan Albayrak | 26 | 16 | 12 | 1165 | 4 | 0 | - | Turkey |
| Rade Bogdanovic | 33 | 23 | 0 | 314 | 0 | 0 | - | Serbia & Montenegro |
| Doo-Ri Cha | 22 | 24 | 6 | 918 | 2 | 0 | 4 | South Korea (21) |
| Mamadou Diabang | 24 | 34 | 20 | 2119 | 3 | 0 | 2 | Senegal (29) |
| Marek Heinz | 25 | 15 | 3 | 518 | 0 | 0 | - | Czech Republic |
| Artur Wichinarek | 26 | 30 | 26 | 2402 | 2 | 1 | 6 | Poland (29) |

KEY: LEAGUE BOOKINGS CAPS (FIFA RANKING)

## SQUAD APPEARANCES

| Match | 1 | 2 | 3 | 4 | 5 | 6 | 7 | 8 | 9 | 10 | 11 | 12 | 13 | 14 | 15 | 16 | 17 | 18 | 19 | 20 | 21 | 22 | 23 | 24 | 25 | 26 | 27 | 28 | 29 | 30 | 31 | 32 | 33 | 34 |
|---|---|---|---|---|---|---|---|---|---|---|---|---|---|---|---|---|---|---|---|---|---|---|---|---|---|---|---|---|---|---|---|---|---|---|
| Venue | H | A | H | A | H | A | H | A | A | H | A | H | A | H | A | H | A | A | H | A | H | A | H | A | H | H | A | H | A | H | A | H | A | H |
| Competition | L | L | L | L | L | L | L | L | L | L | L | L | L | L | L | L | L | L | L | L | L | L | L | L | L | L | L | L | L | L | L | L | L | L |
| Result | W | L | W | D | L | L | W | L | D | W | L | L | L | D | W | W | D | D | D | L | D | D | L | D | W | D | L | W | D | D | L | L | L | L |

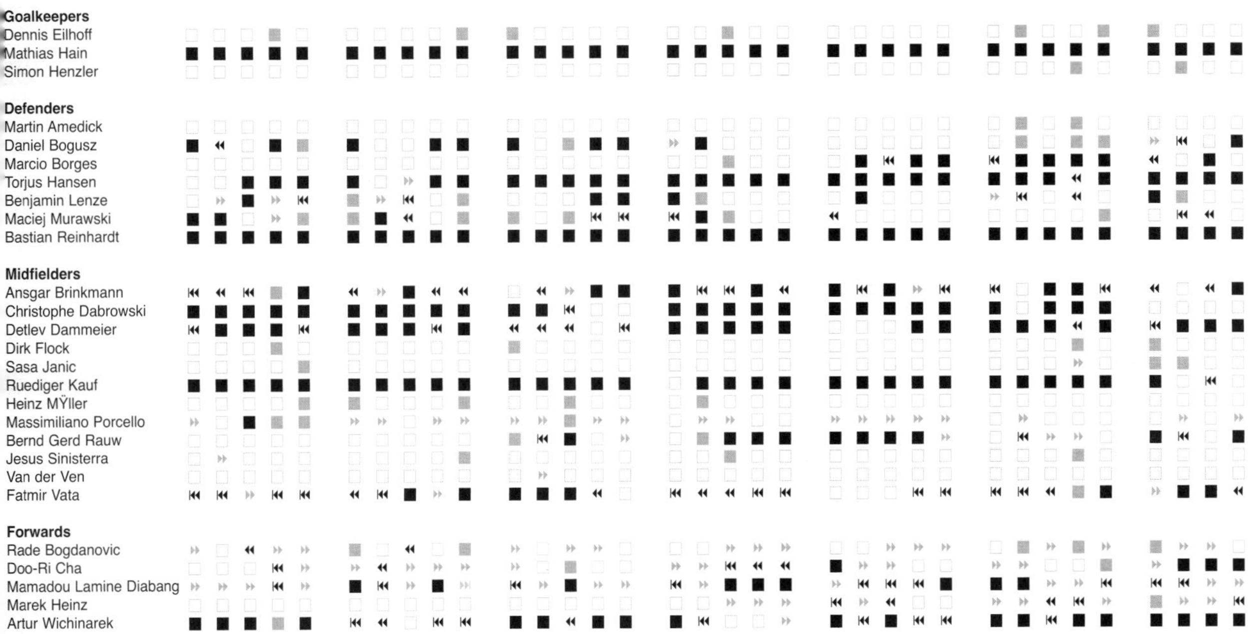
Goalkeepers
Dennis Eilhoff
Mathias Hain
Simon Henzler
Defenders
Martin Amedick
Daniel Bogusz
Marcio Borges
Torjus Hansen
Benjamin Lenze
Maciej Murawski
Bastian Reinhardt
Midfielders
Ansgar Brinkmann
Christophe Dabrowski
Detlev Dammeier
Dirk Flock
Sasa Janic
Ruediger Kauf
Heinz MŸller
Massimiliano Porcello
Bernd Gerd Rauw
Jesus Sinisterra
Van der Ven
Fatmir Vata
Forwards
Rade Bogdanovic
Doo-Ri Cha
Mamadou Lamine Diabang
Marek Heinz
Artur Wichinarek

KEY: ■ On all match ■ On bench | ⏮ Subbed or sent off (Counting game) « Subbed or sent off (playing less than 70 minutes) | ⏭ Subbed on from bench (Counting Game) » Subbed on (playing less than 70 minutes) | » Subbed on and then subbed or sent off (Counting Game) » Subbed on and then subbed or sent off (playing less than 70 minutes) | □ Not in 16

# NURNBERG

Final Position: **17th**

| | | | | | | |
|---|---|---|---|---|---|---|
| 1 | lge | Bochum | H | L | 1-3 | Ciric 51 |
| 2 | lge | Hansa Rostock | A | L | 0-2 | |
| 3 | lge | Hannover 96 | H | W | 3-1 | Ciric 16 pen,36; Cacau 49 |
| 4 | lge | W Bremen | A | L | 1-4 | Ciric 54 |
| 5 | lge | Bayern Munich | H | L | 1-2 | Ciric 36 pen |
| 6 | lge | Wolfsburg | A | W | 2-0 | Petkovic 68; Sanneh 69 |
| 7 | lge | Kaiserslautern | H | W | 1-0 | Sanneh 69 |
| 8 | lge | Hertha Berlin | A | L | 1-2 | Ciric 42 |
| 9 | lge | Stuttgart | H | L | 1-2 | Ciric 44 |
| 10 | lge | Schalke | A | D | 1-1 | Ciric 12 |
| 11 | lge | B M'gladbach | H | W | 2-1 | Nikl 8; Ciric 22 pen |
| 12 | lge | Arminia B | A | W | 1-0 | Driller 56 |
| 13 | lge | Hamburg | H | L | 1-3 | Ciric 40 |
| 14 | lge | 1860 Munich | A | D | 2-2 | Stehle 12,42 |
| 15 | lge | B Dortmund | H | L | 1-2 | Jarolim 3 |
| 16 | lge | Cottbus | H | D | 2-2 | Nikl 42; Petkovic 53 pen |
| 17 | lge | B Leverkusen | A | W | 2-0 | Ciric 58; Junior 88 |
| 18 | lge | Bochum | A | L | 1-2 | Cacau 25 |
| 19 | lge | Hansa Rostock | H | L | 0-1 | |
| 20 | lge | Hannover 96 | A | L | 2-4 | Junior 33; Ciric 54 |
| 21 | lge | W Bremen | H | W | 1-0 | Muller 41 |
| 22 | lge | Bayern Munich | A | L | 0-2 | |
| 23 | lge | Wolfsburg | H | D | 1-1 | Muller 25 pen |
| 24 | lge | Kaiserslautern | A | L | 0-5 | |
| 25 | lge | Hertha Berlin | H | L | 0-3 | |
| 26 | lge | Stuttgart | A | W | 2-0 | Jarolim 28; Junior 88 |
| 27 | lge | Schalke | H | D | 0-0 | |
| 28 | lge | B M'gladbach | A | L | 0-2 | |
| 29 | lge | Arminia B | H | D | 0-0 | |
| 30 | lge | Hamburg | A | L | 0-4 | |
| 31 | lge | 1860 Munich | H | L | 1-2 | Driller 1 |
| 32 | lge | B Dortmund | A | L | 1-4 | Ciric 89 |
| 33 | lge | Cottbus | A | L | 1-2 | Krzynowek 22 |
| 34 | lge | B Leverkusen | H | L | 0-1 | |

## KEY PLAYERS - GOALSCORERS

**1 Sasa Ciric**

| | | | |
|---|---|---|---|
| Goals in the League | 13 | Player Strike Rate<br>Average number of minutes between League goals scored by player | 150 |
| Contribution to Attacking Power<br>Average number of minutes between League team goals while on pitch | 81 | Club Strike Rate<br>Average number of minutes between League goals scored by club | 93 |

| | PLAYER | LGE GOALS | POWER | STRIKE RATE |
|---|---|---|---|---|
| 2 | Tony Sanneh | 2 | 68 | 620 mins |
| 3 | Jeronimo Cacau Baretto | 2 | 78 | 900 mins |
| 4 | Dusan Petkovic | 2 | 76 | 918 mins |
| 5 | Marek Nikl | 2 | 93 | 1118 mins |

## KEY PLAYERS - MIDFIELDERS

**1 Tommy Svindal Larsen**

| | | | |
|---|---|---|---|
| Goals in the League | 0 | Contribution to Attacking Power<br>Average number of minutes between League team goals while on pitch | 87 |
| Defensive Rating<br>Average number of mins between League goals conceded while he was on the pitch | 55 | Scoring Difference<br>Defensive Rating minus Contribution to Attacking Power | -32 |

| | PLAYER | LGE GOALS | DEF RATE | POWER | SCORE DIFF |
|---|---|---|---|---|---|
| 2 | Lars Muller | 2 | 55 | 91 | -36 mins |
| 3 | David Jarolim | 2 | 55 | 92 | -37 mins |
| 4 | Dieter Frey | 0 | 41 | 84 | -43 mins |
| 5 | Jose Carlos de Jesus Junior | 3 | 57 | 109 | -52 mins |

## KEY PLAYERS - DEFENDERS

**1 Milorad Popovic**

| | | | |
|---|---|---|---|
| Goals Conceded (GC)<br>The number of League goals conceded while he was on the pitch | 35 | Clean Sheets<br>In games when he played at least 70 minutes | 5 |
| Defensive Rating<br>Ave number of mins between League goals conceded while on the pitch | 57 | Club Defensive Rating<br>Average number of mins between League goals conceded by the club this season | 51 |

| | PLAYER | CON LGE | CLEAN SHEETS | DEF RATE |
|---|---|---|---|---|
| 2 | Andreas Wolf | 22 | 5 | 57 mins |
| 3 | Tony Sanneh | 23 | 3 | 54 mins |
| 4 | Tomasz Kos | 43 | 6 | 52 mins |
| 5 | Marek Nikl | 46 | 5 | 49 mins |

## GOALS SCORED

| AT HOME | | |
|---|---|---|
| MOST | B Munich | 37 |
| | | 16 |
| LEAST | Nurnberg | 16 |

| AWAY | | |
|---|---|---|
| MOST | B Munich | 33 |
| | | 17 |
| LEAST | B M'gladbach &Arminia B | 12 |

## GOALS CONCEDED

| AT HOME | | |
|---|---|---|
| LEAST | Hamburg & B M'gladbach | 11 |
| | | 24 |
| MOST | Hannover 96 | 33 |

| AWAY | | |
|---|---|---|
| LEAST | B Munich | 13 |
| | | 36 |
| MOST | Nurnberg | 36 |

## KEY GOALKEEPER

**1 Darius Kampa**

| | |
|---|---|
| Goals Conceded in the League | 58 |
| Defensive Rating<br>Ave number of mins between League goals conceded while on the pitch | 52 |
| Counting Games<br>Games when he played at least 70 minutes | 33 |
| Clean Sheets<br>In games when he played at least 70 minutes | 8 |

## TOP POINT EARNERS

| | PLAYER | GAMES | AVE |
|---|---|---|---|
| 1 | Sanneh | 14 | 1.21 |
| 2 | Larsen | 28 | 1.07 |
| 3 | Cacau | 17 | 1.06 |
| 4 | Petkovic | 20 | 1.05 |
| 5 | Frey | 12 | 1.00 |
| 6 | Popovic | 22 | 1.00 |
| 7 | Muller | 31 | 0.97 |
| 8 | Jarolim | 31 | 0.94 |
| 9 | Wolf | 14 | 0.93 |
| 10 | Nikl | 23 | 0.91 |
| | **CLUB AVERAGE:** | | **0.88** |

Ave = Average points per match in Counting Games

## ATTENDANCES

HOME GROUND: FRANKENSTADION CAPACITY: 44600 AVERAGE LEAGUE AT HOME: 27452

| | | | | | | | | |
|---|---|---|---|---|---|---|---|---|
| 32 | B Dortmund | 66000 | 8 | Hertha Berlin | 30000 | 7 | Kaiserslautern | 22000 |
| 10 | Schalke | 60601 | 9 | Stuttgart | 29500 | 3 | Hannover 96 | 22000 |
| 5 | Bayern Munich | 44600 | 28 | B M'gladbach | 29000 | 18 | Bochum | 20280 |
| 27 | Schalke | 41100 | 20 | Hannover 96 | 28000 | 21 | W Bremen | 20000 |
| 30 | Hamburg | 41000 | 26 | Stuttgart | 28000 | 2 | Hansa Rostock | 19600 |
| 22 | Bayern Munich | 40000 | 4 | W Bremen | 27000 | 12 | Arminia B | 18000 |
| 15 | B Dortmund | 40000 | 13 | Hamburg | 26000 | 23 | Wolfsburg | 15000 |
| 31 | 1860 Munich | 35000 | 11 | B M'gladbach | 25000 | 19 | Hansa Rostock | 15000 |
| 24 | Kaiserslautern | 33000 | 16 | Cottbus | 25000 | 6 | Wolfsburg | 14000 |
| 14 | 1860 Munich | 32000 | 29 | Arminia B | 23500 | 33 | Cottbus | 10000 |
| 34 | B Leverkusen | 30000 | 25 | Hertha Berlin | 23000 | | | |
| 1 | Bochum | 30000 | 17 | B Leverkusen | 22500 | | | |

Home Away Neutral

## DISCIPLINARY RECORDS

| | PLAYER | YELLOW | RED | AVE |
|---|---|---|---|---|
| 1 | Passlack | 4 | 1 | 138 |
| 2 | Stehle | 7 | 0 | 144 |
| 3 | Cacau | 7 | 0 | 257 |
| 4 | Jarolim | 8 | 1 | 306 |
| 5 | Larsen | 8 | 0 | 324 |
| 6 | Kos | 6 | 0 | 373 |
| 7 | Frey | 3 | 0 | 393 |
| 8 | Wolf | 3 | 0 | 420 |
| 9 | Driller | 2 | 0 | 443 |
| 10 | Petkovic | 4 | 0 | 458 |
| 11 | Michalke | 1 | 0 | 593 |
| 12 | Junior | 2 | 0 | 600 |
| 13 | Sanneh | 2 | 0 | 619 |
| | Other | 14 | 1 | |
| | TOTAL | 71 | 3 | |

## LEAGUE GOALS

| | PLAYER | MINS | GOALS | AVE |
|---|---|---|---|---|
| 1 | Ciric | 1945 | 13 | 150 |
| 2 | Junior | 1201 | 3 | 400 |
| 3 | Stehle | 1008 | 2 | 504 |
| 4 | Jarolim | 2762 | 2 | 1381 |
| 5 | Nikl | 2236 | 2 | 1118 |
| 6 | Cacau | 1800 | 2 | 900 |
| 7 | Petkovic | 1835 | 2 | 918 |
| 8 | Muller | 2921 | 2 | 1461 |
| 9 | Driller | 886 | 2 | 443 |
| 10 | Sanneh | 1239 | 2 | 620 |
| 11 | Krzynowek | 913 | 1 | 913 |
| | Other | | 0 | |
| | TOTAL | | 33 | |

## MONTH BY MONTH GUIDE TO THE POINTS

| MONTH | POINTS | MAX POINTS |
|---|---|---|
| AUGUST | 3 | 33% |
| SEPTEMBER | 6 | 50% |
| OCTOBER | 1 | 11% |
| NOVEMBER | 7 | 47% |
| DECEMBER | 4 | 67% |
| JANUARY | 0 | 0% |
| FEBRUARY | 3 | 25% |
| MARCH | 4 | 33% |
| APRIL | 2 | 17% |
| MAY | 0 | 0% |

## TEAM OF THE SEASON

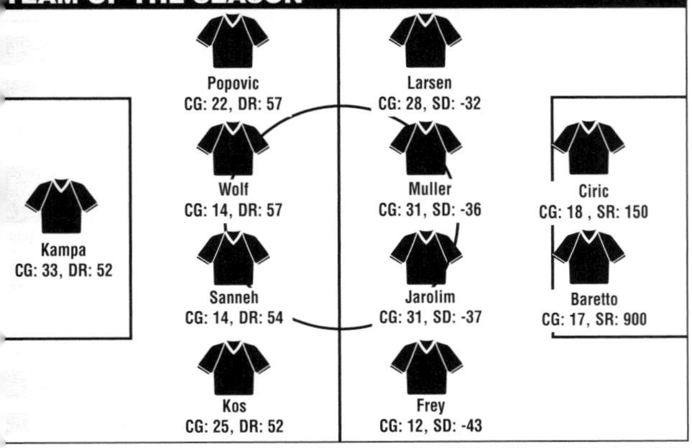
Popovic
CG: 22, DR: 57
Larsen
CG: 28, SD: -32
Wolf
CG: 14, DR: 57
Muller
CG: 31, SD: -36
Ciric
CG: 18 , SR: 150
Kampa
CG: 33, DR: 52
Sanneh
CG: 14, DR: 54
Jarolim
CG: 31, SD: -37
Baretto
CG: 17, SR: 900
Kos
CG: 25, DR: 52
Frey
CG: 12, SD: -43

**KEY:** DR = Defensive Rate, SD = Scoring Difference, SR = Strike Rate, CG = Counting Games – League games playing at least 70 minutes

## LEAGUE APPEARANCES, BOOKINGS AND CAPS

| | AGE | IN THE SQUAD | COUNTING GAMES | MINUTES ON PITCH | YELLOW CARDS | RED CARDS | THIS SEASON | HOME COUNTRY |
|---|---|---|---|---|---|---|---|---|
| **Goalkeepers** | | | | | | | | |
| Darius Kampa | 26 | 34 | 33 | 3015 | 0 | 0 | - | Germany |
| Raphael Schafer | 24 | 17 | 0 | 45 | 0 | 0 | - | Germany |
| **Defenders** | | | | | | | | |
| Tomasz Kos | 29 | 28 | 25 | 2243 | 6 | 0 | 2 | Poland (29) |
| Marek Nikl | 27 | 31 | 23 | 2236 | 3 | 0 | - | Czech Republic |
| Stephan Passlack | 32 | 18 | 4 | 691 | 4 | 1 | - | Germany |
| Dusan Petkovic | 29 | 26 | 20 | 1835 | 4 | 0 | - | Serbia & Montenegro |
| Milorad Popovic | 32 | 25 | 22 | 2005 | 1 | 0 | - | Serbia & Montenegro |
| Dominik Reinhardt | | 1 | 0 | 63 | 0 | 0 | - | Germany |
| Anthony Sanneh | 32 | 14 | 14 | 1239 | 2 | 0 | - | United States |
| Thomas Stehle | 22 | 22 | 7 | 1008 | 7 | 0 | - | Germany |
| Andreas Wolf | 21 | 15 | 14 | 1260 | 3 | 0 | - | Germany |
| **Midfielders** | | | | | | | | |
| Baretto Baretto | | 1 | 0 | 29 | 0 | 0 | - | |
| Pavel David | 24 | 5 | 1 | 154 | 0 | 0 | - | Czech Republic |
| Dieter Frey | 30 | 21 | 12 | 1181 | 3 | 0 | - | Germany |
| David Jarolim | 24 | 32 | 31 | 2762 | 8 | 1 | - | Czech Republic |
| Jose Carlos Junior | 25 | 20 | 11 | 1201 | 2 | 0 | - | Brazil |
| Stefan Kiessling | | 1 | 0 | 10 | 0 | 0 | - | Germany |
| Jacek Krzynowek | 27 | 17 | 7 | 913 | 1 | 0 | 4 | Poland (29) |
| Michael Kugler | 21 | 5 | 2 | 166 | 0 | 0 | - | Germany |
| Tommy Larsen | 29 | 31 | 28 | 2596 | 8 | 0 | - | Norway |
| Lars Muller | 27 | 33 | 31 | 2921 | 4 | 0 | - | Germany |
| Rade Todorovic | 29 | 15 | 3 | 335 | 1 | 0 | - | Serbia & Montenegro |
| **Forwards** | | | | | | | | |
| Milan Belic | 25 | 12 | 2 | 292 | 2 | 0 | - | Serbia & Montenegro |
| Jeronimo Baretto | 22 | 26 | 17 | 1800 | 7 | 0 | - | Brazil |
| Sasa Ciric | 35 | 29 | 18 | 1945 | 2 | 1 | - | Marcedonia |
| Martin Driller | 33 | 25 | 6 | 886 | 2 | 0 | - | Germany |
| Kai Michalke | 27 | 17 | 4 | 593 | 1 | 0 | - | Germany |
| Marco Villa | 24 | 7 | 0 | 116 | 0 | 0 | - | Germany |

**KEY:** LEAGUE BOOKINGS CAPS (FIFA RANKING)

## SQUAD APPEARANCES

| Match | 1 | 2 | 3 | 4 | 5 | 6 | 7 | 8 | 9 | 10 | 11 | 12 | 13 | 14 | 15 | 16 | 17 | 18 | 19 | 20 | 21 | 22 | 23 | 24 | 25 | 26 | 27 | 28 | 29 | 30 | 31 | 32 | 33 | 34 |
|---|---|---|---|---|---|---|---|---|---|---|---|---|---|---|---|---|---|---|---|---|---|---|---|---|---|---|---|---|---|---|---|---|---|---|
| Venue | H | A | H | A | H | A | H | A | H | A | H | A | H | A | H | H | A | A | H | A | H | A | H | A | H | A | H | A | H | A | H | A | A | H |
| Competition | L | L | L | L | L | L | L | L | L | L | L | L | L | L | L | L | L | L | L | L | L | L | L | L | L | L | L | L | L | L | L | L | L | L |
| Result | L | L | W | L | L | W | W | L | L | D | W | W | L | D | L | D | W | L | L | L | W | L | D | L | L | W | D | L | D | L | L | L | L | L |

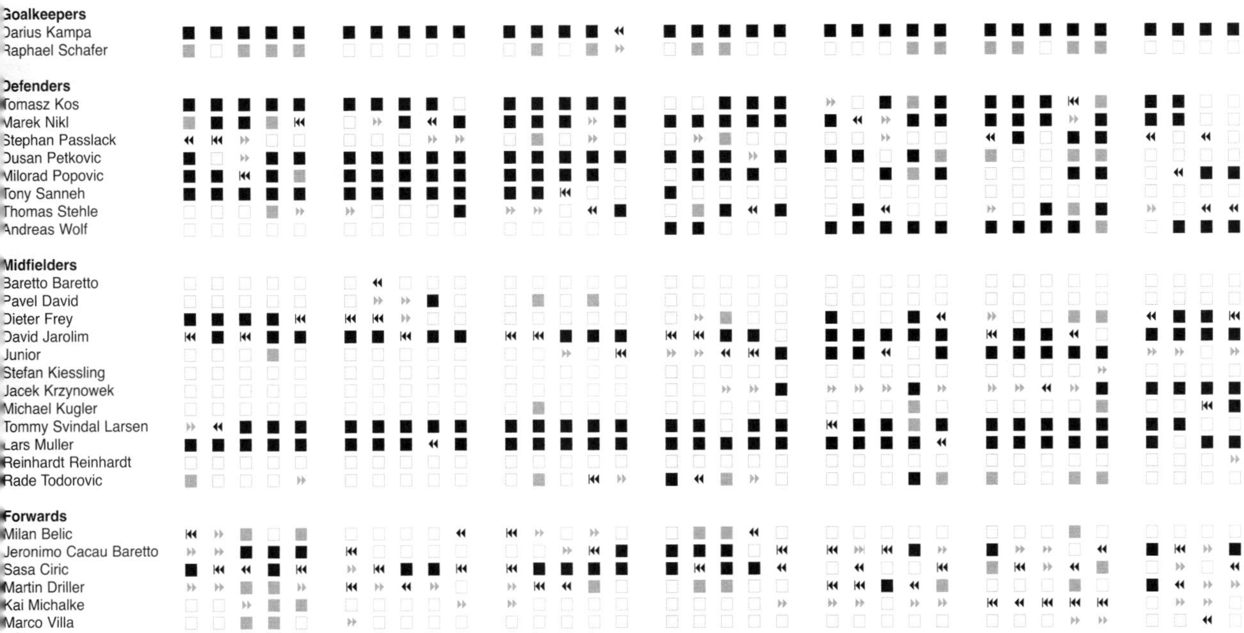
Goalkeepers
Darius Kampa
Raphael Schafer
Defenders
Tomasz Kos
Marek Nikl
Stephan Passlack
Dusan Petkovic
Milorad Popovic
Tony Sanneh
Thomas Stehle
Andreas Wolf
Midfielders
Baretto Baretto
Pavel David
Dieter Frey
David Jarolim
Junior
Stefan Kiessling
Jacek Krzynowek
Michael Kugler
Tommy Svindal Larsen
Lars Muller
Reinhardt Reinhardt
Rade Todorovic
Forwards
Milan Belic
Jeronimo Cacau Baretto
Sasa Ciric
Martin Driller
Kai Michalke
Marco Villa

KEY: On all match; On bench; Subbed or sent off (Counting game); Subbed or sent off (playing less than 70 minutes); Subbed on from bench (Counting Game); Subbed on (playing less than 70 minutes); Subbed on and then subbed or sent off (Counting Game); Subbed on and then subbed or sent off (playing less than 70 minutes); Not in 16

# ENERGIE COTTBUS

Final Position: **18th**

| | | | | | | |
|---|---|---|---|---|---|---|
| 1 | lge | B Leverkusen | H | D | 1-1 | Sebok 79 |
| 2 | lge | Bochum | A | L | 0-5 | |
| 3 | lge | Hansa Rostock | H | L | 0-4 | |
| 4 | lge | Hannover 96 | A | W | 3-1 | Topic 8; Idrissou 67 og; Jungnickel 90 |
| 5 | lge | W Bremen | H | L | 0-1 | |
| 6 | lge | Bayern Munich | A | L | 1-3 | Rink 20 |
| 7 | lge | Wolfsburg | H | L | 0-1 | |
| 8 | lge | Kaiserslautern | A | L | 0-4 | |
| 9 | lge | Hertha Berlin | H | L | 0-2 | |
| 10 | lge | Stuttgart | A | D | 0-0 | |
| 11 | lge | Schalke | H | L | 0-1 | |
| 12 | lge | B M'gladbach | A | L | 0-3 | |
| 13 | lge | Arminia B | H | W | 2-1 | Kobylanski 8; Beeck 66 |
| 14 | lge | Hamburg | A | D | 1-1 | Juskowiak 90 |
| 15 | lge | 1860 Munich | H | L | 3-4 | Topic 80; Kaluzny 85; Rink 86 |
| 16 | lge | Nurnberg | A | D | 2-2 | Kaluzny 15; Jungnickel 87 |
| 17 | lge | B Dortmund | H | L | 0-4 | |
| 18 | lge | B Leverkusen | A | W | 3-0 | Gebhardt 15; Topic 32; Juskowiak 85 |
| 19 | lge | Bochum | H | W | 2-1 | Reghecampf 2; Juskowiak 82 |
| 20 | lge | Hansa Rostock | A | D | 0-0 | |
| 21 | lge | Hannover 96 | H | W | 3-0 | da Silva 74; Reghecampf 77; Topic 81 |
| 22 | lge | W Bremen | A | W | 1-0 | Topic 5 |
| 23 | lge | Bayern Munich | H | L | 0-2 | |
| 24 | lge | Wolfsburg | A | L | 2-3 | Rink 8; Reghecampf 17 pen |
| 25 | lge | Kaiserslautern | H | L | 1-3 | Rost 43 |
| 26 | lge | Hertha Berlin | A | L | 1-3 | Vagner 10 |
| 27 | lge | Stuttgart | H | L | 2-3 | Vagner 7; Juskowiak 84 |
| 28 | lge | Schalke | A | L | 0-3 | |
| 29 | lge | B M'gladbach | H | D | 1-1 | Latoundji 5 |
| 30 | lge | Arminia B | A | D | 2-2 | Gebhardt 1,40 |
| 31 | lge | Hamburg | H | D | 0-0 | |
| 32 | lge | 1860 Munich | A | L | 0-3 | |
| 33 | lge | Nurnberg | H | W | 2-1 | Topic 13; Juskowiak 74 |
| 34 | lge | B Dortmund | A | D | 1-1 | Rost 75 |

## GOALS SCORED

**AT HOME**

| | | |
|---|---|---|
| MOST | B Munich | 37 |
| | | 17 |
| LEAST | Nurnberg | 16 |

**AWAY**

| | | |
|---|---|---|
| MOST | B Munich | 33 |
| | | 17 |
| LEAST | B M'gladbach &Arminia B | 12 |

## GOALS CONCEDED

**AT HOME**

| | | |
|---|---|---|
| LEAST | Hamburg & B M'gladbach | 11 |
| | | 30 |
| MOST | Hannover 96 | 33 |

**AWAY**

| | | |
|---|---|---|
| LEAST | B Munich | 13 |
| | | 34 |
| MOST | Nurnberg | 36 |

## ATTENDANCES

**HOME GROUND: STADION DER FREUNDSCHAFT CAPACITY: 20500 AVERAGE LEAGUE AT HOME: 13379**

| | | |
|---|---|---|
| 34 | B Dortmund | 68000 |
| 28 | Schalke | 60886 |
| 26 | Hertha Berlin | 40000 |
| 6 | Bayern Munich | 38000 |
| 4 | Hannover 96 | 35506 |
| 14 | Hamburg | 35000 |
| 8 | Kaiserslautern | 33246 |
| 22 | W Bremen | 32000 |
| 16 | Nurnberg | 25000 |
| 10 | Stuttgart | 23000 |
| 18 | B Leverkusen | 22500 |
| 12 | B M'gladbach | 22000 |
| 30 | Arminia B | 20000 |
| 2 | Bochum | 20000 |
| 24 | Wolfsburg | 20000 |
| 23 | Bayern Munich | 18250 |
| 31 | Hamburg | 15000 |
| 5 | W Bremen | 15000 |
| 1 | B Leverkusen | 15000 |
| 17 | B Dortmund | 15000 |
| 21 | Hannover 96 | 14000 |
| 11 | Schalke | 13340 |
| 29 | B M'gladbach | 13241 |
| 9 | Hertha Berlin | 13000 |
| 3 | Hansa Rostock | 13000 |
| 20 | Hansa Rostock | 13000 |
| 25 | Kaiserslautern | 13000 |
| 13 | Arminia B | 12628 |
| 19 | Bochum | 12000 |
| 27 | Stuttgart | 12000 |
| 7 | Wolfsburg | 12000 |
| 15 | 1860 Munich | 11000 |
| 33 | Nurnberg | 10000 |
| 32 | 1860 Munich | 10000 |

■ Home □ Away ▒ Neutral

## KEY PLAYERS - GOALSCORERS

**1 Marko Topic**

| | | | |
|---|---|---|---|
| Goals in the League | 6 | Player Strike Rate<br>Average number of minutes between League goals scored by player | 394 |
| Contribution to Attacking Power<br>Average number of minutes between League team goals while on pitch | 91 | Club Strike Rate<br>Average number of minutes between League goals scored by club | 90 |

| | PLAYER | LGE GOALS | POWER | STRIKE RATE |
|---|---|---|---|---|
| 2 | Marco Gebhardt | 3 | 89 | 445 mins |
| 3 | Radoslaw Kaluzny | 2 | 89 | 629 mins |
| 4 | Robert Vagner | 2 | 78 | 667 mins |
| 5 | Laurentiu Reghecampf | 3 | 82 | 689 mins |

## KEY PLAYERS - MIDFIELDERS

**1 Robert Vagner**

| | | | |
|---|---|---|---|
| Goals in the League | 2 | Contribution to Attacking Power<br>Average number of minutes between League team goals while on pitch | 78 |
| Defensive Rating<br>Average number of mins between League goals conceded while he was on the pitch | 64 | Scoring Difference<br>Defensive Rating minus Contribution to Attacking Power | -14 |

| | PLAYER | LGE GOALS | DEF RATE | POWER | SCORE DIFF |
|---|---|---|---|---|---|
| 2 | Moussa Latoundji | 1 | 54 | 79 | -25 mins |
| 3 | Silvio Schroter | 0 | 52 | 79 | -27 mins |
| 4 | Timo Rost | 2 | 53 | 81 | -28 mins |
| 5 | Laurentiu Reghecampf | 3 | 45 | 83 | -38 mins |

## KEY PLAYERS - DEFENDERS

**1 Greg Berhalter**

| | | | |
|---|---|---|---|
| Goals Conceded (GC)<br>The number of League goals conceded while he was on the pitch | 38 | Clean Sheets<br>In games when he played at least 70 minutes | 4 |
| Defensive Rating<br>Ave number of mins between League goals conceded while on the pitch | 52 | Club Defensive Rating<br>Average number of mins between League goals conceded by the club this season | 48 |

| | PLAYER | CON LGE | CLEAN SHEETS | DEF RATE |
|---|---|---|---|---|
| 2 | Zsolt Low | 51 | 6 | 52 mins |
| 3 | Vragel da Silva | 49 | 5 | 51 mins |
| 4 | Marcel Rozgony | 22 | 2 | 49 mins |
| 5 | Christian Beeck | 34 | 1 | 40 mins |

## KEY GOALKEEPER

**1 Andre Lenz**

| | |
|---|---|
| Goals Conceded in the League | 40 |
| Defensive Rating<br>Ave number of mins between League goals conceded while on the pitch | 52 |
| Counting Games<br>Games when he played at least 70 minutes | 23 |
| Clean Sheets<br>In games when he played at least 70 minutes | 6 |

## TOP POINT EARNERS

| | PLAYER | GAMES | AVE |
|---|---|---|---|
| 1 | Vagner | 12 | 1.17 |
| 2 | Gebhardt | 13 | 1.08 |
| 3 | Latoundji | 20 | 1.05 |
| 4 | Schroter | 22 | 1.05 |
| 5 | Rost | 24 | 1.04 |
| 6 | Berhalter | 22 | 1.00 |
| 7 | Lenz | 23 | 0.96 |
| 8 | da Silva | 27 | 0.93 |
| 9 | Low | 28 | 0.93 |
| 10 | Topic | 24 | 0.92 |
| | CLUB AVERAGE: | | 0.88 |

Ave = Average points per match in Counting Game

## DISCIPLINARY RECORDS

| | PLAYER | YELLOW | RED | AVE |
|---|---|---|---|---|
| 1 | Akrapovic | 4 | 1 | 111 |
| 2 | Hujdurovic | 5 | 0 | 123 |
| 3 | Kaluzny | 8 | 0 | 157 |
| 4 | Beeck | 7 | 1 | 168 |
| 5 | Reghecampf | 7 | 0 | 295 |
| 6 | Miriuta | 2 | 0 | 308 |
| 7 | da Silva | 8 | 0 | 311 |
| 8 | Rink | 2 | 0 | 324 |
| 9 | Berhalter | 6 | 0 | 331 |
| 10 | Gebhardt | 4 | 0 | 333 |
| 11 | Topic | 7 | 0 | 338 |
| 12 | Schroter | 6 | 0 | 340 |
| 13 | Jungnickel | 2 | 0 | 373 |
| | Other | 22 | 3 | |
| | TOTAL | 90 | 5 | |

## LEAGUE GOALS

| | PLAYER | MINS | GOALS | AVE |
|---|---|---|---|---|
| 1 | Topic | 2366 | 6 | 394 |
| 2 | Juskowiak | 1167 | 5 | 233 |
| 3 | Reghecampf | 2068 | 3 | 689 |
| 4 | Gebhardt | 1335 | 3 | 445 |
| 5 | Vagner | 1334 | 2 | 667 |
| 6 | Rost | 2264 | 2 | 1132 |
| 7 | Jungnickel | 747 | 2 | 374 |
| 8 | Rink | 648 | 2 | 324 |
| 9 | Kaluzny | 1257 | 2 | 629 |
| 10 | Sebok | 206 | 1 | 206 |
| 11 | Latoundji | 1900 | 1 | 1900 |
| 12 | Beeck | 1349 | 1 | 1349 |
| 13 | Kobylanski | 750 | 1 | 750 |
| | Other | | 3 | |
| | TOTAL | | 34 | |

## MONTH BY MONTH GUIDE TO THE POINTS

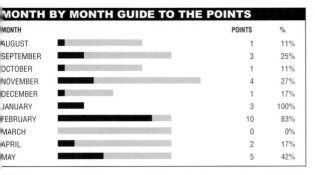

| MONTH | POINTS | % |
|---|---|---|
| AUGUST | 1 | 11% |
| SEPTEMBER | 3 | 25% |
| OCTOBER | 1 | 11% |
| NOVEMBER | 4 | 27% |
| DECEMBER | 1 | 17% |
| JANUARY | 3 | 100% |
| FEBRUARY | 10 | 83% |
| MARCH | 0 | 0% |
| APRIL | 2 | 17% |
| MAY | 5 | 42% |

## TEAM OF THE SEASON

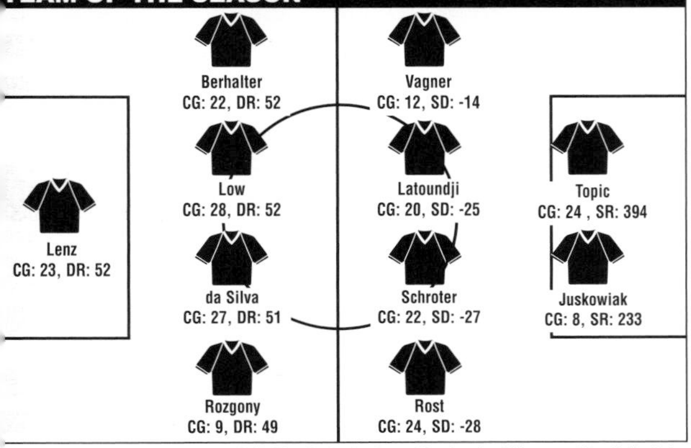
Berhalter
CG: 22, DR: 52
Vagner
CG: 12, SD: -14
Low
CG: 28, DR: 52
Latoundji
CG: 20, SD: -25
Topic
CG: 24 , SR: 394
Lenz
CG: 23, DR: 52
da Silva
CG: 27, DR: 51
Schroter
CG: 22, SD: -27
Juskowiak
CG: 8, SR: 233
Rozgony
CG: 9, DR: 49
Rost
CG: 24, SD: -28

KEY: DR = Defensive Rate, SD = Scoring Difference, SR = Strike Rate, CG = Counting Games – League games playing at least 70 minutes

## LEAGUE APPEARANCES, BOOKINGS AND CAPS

| | AGE | IN THE SQUAD | COUNTING GAMES | MINUTES ON PITCH | YELLOW CARDS | RED CARDS | THIS SEASON | HOME COUNTRY |
|---|---|---|---|---|---|---|---|---|
| **Goalkeepers** | | | | | | | | |
| Gunnar Bernsten | 25 | 3 | 2 | 180 | 0 | 0 | - | Germany |
| Andre Lenz | 29 | 27 | 23 | 2070 | 2 | 0 | - | Germany |
| Tomislav Piplica | 34 | 20 | 9 | 810 | 0 | 0 | - | Bosnia |
| **Defenders** | | | | | | | | |
| Christian Beeck | 31 | 18 | 13 | 1349 | 7 | 1 | - | Germany |
| Greg Berhalter | 29 | 25 | 22 | 1988 | 6 | 0 | 1 | United States (10) |
| Vragel da Silva | 29 | 30 | 27 | 2494 | 8 | 0 | - | Brazil |
| Faruk Hujdurovic | 33 | 17 | 3 | 617 | 5 | 0 | - | Bosnia |
| Patrick Jahn | 20 | 2 | 0 | 9 | 0 | 0 | - | Germany |
| Zsolt Low | 24 | 32 | 28 | 2640 | 3 | 1 | - | Hungary |
| Marcel Rozgony | 27 | 20 | 9 | 1069 | 1 | 0 | - | Germany |
| Vilmos Sebok | 30 | 4 | 2 | 206 | 0 | 0 | - | Hungary |
| **Midfielders** | | | | | | | | |
| Bruno Akrapovic | 35 | 7 | 5 | 555 | 4 | 1 | - | Croatian |
| Marco Gebhardt | 30 | 19 | 13 | 1335 | 4 | 0 | - | Germany |
| Radoslaw Kaluzny | 29 | 16 | 13 | 1257 | 8 | 0 | 4 | Poland (29) |
| Moussa Latoundji | 24 | 29 | 20 | 1900 | 5 | 0 | - | Benin |
| Torsten Mattuschka | 22 | 6 | 1 | 130 | 0 | 0 | - | Germany |
| Vasile Miriuta | 34 | 7 | 7 | 616 | 2 | 0 | - | Hungary |
| Laurentiu Reghecampf | 27 | 30 | 21 | 2068 | 7 | 0 | 1 | Romania (27) |
| Timo Rost | 24 | 28 | 24 | 2264 | 4 | 1 | - | Germany |
| Silvio Schroter | 24 | 25 | 22 | 2044 | 6 | 0 | - | Germany |
| Ronny Thielemann | 29 | 8 | 2 | 285 | 4 | 1 | - | Germany |
| Robert Vagner | 29 | 23 | 12 | 1334 | 2 | 0 | - | Czech Republic |
| **Forwards** | | | | | | | | |
| Markus Feldhoff | 28 | 3 | 0 | 78 | 0 | 0 | - | Germany |
| Bitencourt Franklin | 34 | 5 | 0 | 54 | 0 | 0 | - | Brazil |
| Lara Jungnickel | 21 | 27 | 2 | 747 | 2 | 0 | - | Germany |
| Andrzej Juskowiak | 32 | 29 | 8 | 1167 | 0 | 0 | - | Poland |
| Andrzei Kobylanski | 32 | 21 | 4 | 750 | 1 | 0 | - | Poland |
| Thomas Reichenberger | 28 | 14 | 4 | 505 | 0 | 0 | - | Germany |
| Paolo Roberto Rink | 30 | 17 | 5 | 648 | 2 | 0 | - | Germany |
| Marko Topic | 27 | 30 | 24 | 2366 | 7 | 0 | - | Bosnia |

KEY: LEAGUE BOOKINGS CAPS (FIFA RANKING)

## SQUAD APPEARANCES

| Match | 1 | 2 | 3 | 4 | 5 | 6 | 7 | 8 | 9 | 10 | 11 | 12 | 13 | 14 | 15 | 16 | 17 | 18 | 19 | 20 | 21 | 22 | 23 | 24 | 25 | 26 | 27 | 28 | 29 | 30 | 31 | 32 | 33 | 34 |
|---|---|---|---|---|---|---|---|---|---|---|---|---|---|---|---|---|---|---|---|---|---|---|---|---|---|---|---|---|---|---|---|---|---|---|
| Venue | H | A | H | A | H | A | H | A | H | A | H | A | H | A | H | A | H | A | H | A | H | A | H | A | H | A | H | A | H | A | H | A | H | A |
| Competition | L | L | L | L | L | L | L | L | L | L | L | L | L | L | L | L | L | L | L | L | L | L | L | L | L | L | L | L | L | L | L | L | L | L |
| Result | D | L | L | W | L | L | L | L | L | D | L | L | W | D | L | D | L | W | W | D | W | W | L | L | L | L | L | L | D | D | D | L | W | D |

**Goalkeepers**
Gunnar Bernsten
Andre Lenz
Tomislav Piplica

**Defenders**
Christian Beeck
Greg Berhalter
Vragel da Silva
Faruk Hujdurovic
Patrick Jahn
Zsolt Low
Marcel Rozgony
Vilmos Sebok

**Midfielders**
Bruno Akrapovic
Marco Gebhardt
Radoslaw Kaluzny
Moussa Latoundji
Torsten Mattuschka
Vasile Miriuta
Laurentiu Reghecampf
Timo Rost
Silvio Schroter
Ronny Thielemann
Robert Vagner

**Forwards**
Markus Feldhoff
Bitencourt Franklin
Lara Jungnickel
Andrzej Juskowiak
Andrzei Kobylanski
Thomas Reichenberger
Paolo Roberto Rink
Marko Topic

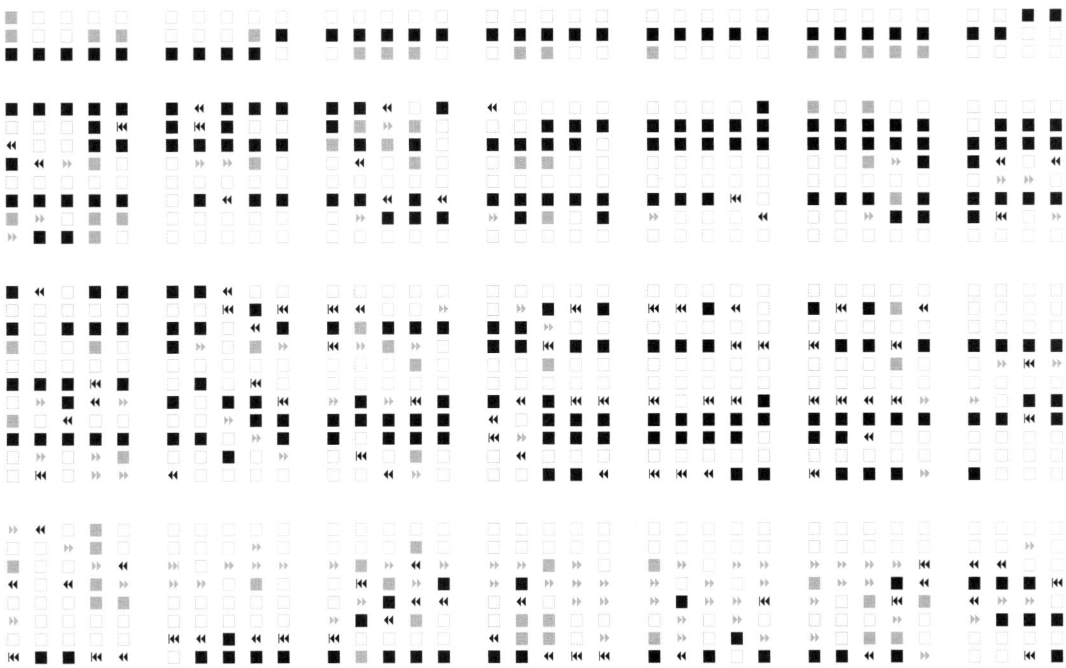

# GERMAN LEAGUE ROUND-UP

## FINAL LEAGUE TABLE

| | | HOME | | | | | AWAY | | | | | TOTAL | | | |
|---|---|---|---|---|---|---|---|---|---|---|---|---|---|---|---|
| | P | W | D | L | F | A | W | D | L | F | A | F | A | DIF | PTS |
| Bayern Munich | 34 | 13 | 3 | 1 | 37 | 12 | 10 | 3 | 4 | 33 | 13 | 70 | 25 | 45 | 75 |
| Stuttgart | 34 | 9 | 5 | 3 | 30 | 14 | 8 | 3 | 6 | 23 | 25 | 53 | 39 | 14 | 59 |
| B Dortmund | 34 | 10 | 6 | 1 | 31 | 13 | 5 | 7 | 5 | 20 | 14 | 51 | 27 | 24 | 58 |
| Hamburg | 34 | 13 | 3 | 1 | 30 | 11 | 2 | 8 | 7 | 16 | 25 | 46 | 36 | 10 | 56 |
| Hertha Berlin | 34 | 10 | 4 | 3 | 35 | 19 | 6 | 2 | 9 | 17 | 24 | 52 | 43 | 9 | 54 |
| W Bremen | 34 | 10 | 2 | 5 | 34 | 23 | 6 | 2 | 9 | 17 | 27 | 51 | 50 | 1 | 52 |
| Schalke | 34 | 6 | 8 | 3 | 23 | 16 | 6 | 5 | 6 | 23 | 24 | 46 | 40 | 6 | 49 |
| Wolfsburg | 34 | 11 | 2 | 4 | 26 | 15 | 2 | 5 | 10 | 13 | 27 | 39 | 42 | -3 | 46 |
| Bochum | 34 | 6 | 5 | 6 | 26 | 25 | 6 | 4 | 7 | 29 | 31 | 55 | 56 | -1 | 45 |
| 1860 Munich | 34 | 6 | 5 | 6 | 22 | 22 | 6 | 4 | 7 | 22 | 30 | 44 | 52 | -8 | 45 |
| Hannover 96 | 34 | 4 | 6 | 7 | 28 | 33 | 8 | 1 | 8 | 19 | 24 | 47 | 57 | -10 | 43 |
| B M'gladbach | 34 | 10 | 5 | 2 | 31 | 11 | 1 | 4 | 12 | 12 | 34 | 43 | 45 | -2 | 42 |
| Hansa Rostock | 34 | 6 | 5 | 6 | 20 | 18 | 5 | 3 | 9 | 15 | 23 | 35 | 41 | -6 | 41 |
| Kaiserslautern | 34 | 9 | 3 | 5 | 23 | 12 | 1 | 7 | 9 | 17 | 30 | 40 | 42 | -2 | 40 |
| B Leverkusen | 34 | 6 | 3 | 8 | 27 | 28 | 5 | 4 | 8 | 20 | 28 | 47 | 56 | -9 | 40 |
| Arminia B | 34 | 7 | 5 | 5 | 23 | 16 | 1 | 7 | 9 | 12 | 30 | 35 | 46 | -11 | 36 |
| Nurnberg | 34 | 4 | 4 | 9 | 16 | 24 | 4 | 2 | 11 | 17 | 36 | 33 | 60 | -27 | 30 |
| Cottbus | 34 | 4 | 3 | 10 | 17 | 30 | 3 | 6 | 8 | 17 | 34 | 34 | 64 | -30 | 30 |

## TEAM OF THE SEASON

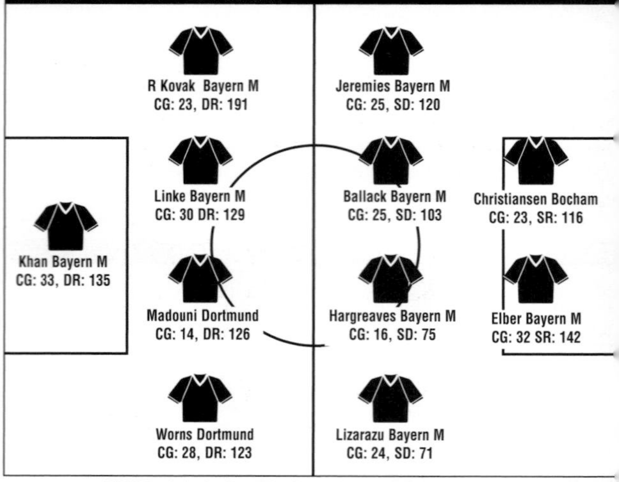

R Kovak Bayern M
CG: 23, DR: 191
Jeremies Bayern M
CG: 25, SD: 120
Linke Bayern M
CG: 30 DR: 129
Ballack Bayern M
CG: 25, SD: 103
Christiansen Bocham
CG: 23, SR: 116
Khan Bayern M
CG: 33, DR: 135
Madouni Dortmund
CG: 14, DR: 126
Hargreaves Bayern M
CG: 16, SD: 75
Elber Bayern M
CG: 32 SR: 142
Worns Dortmund
CG: 28, DR: 123
Lizarazu Bayern M
CG: 24, SD: 71


**KEY:** DR = Defensive Rate, SD = Scoring Difference AP = Attacking Power SR = Strike Ra
CG=Counting Games – League games playing at least 70 minut

## CLUB STRIKE FORCE

**KEY:** Goals: Total number of goals scored in League.
Club Strike Rate (CSR): Average number of mins between goals scored

| | CLUB | GOALS | CSR |
|---|---|---|---|
| 1 | Bayern Munich | 70 | 44 mins |
| 2 | Bochum | 55 | 56 mins |
| 3 | Stuttgart | 53 | 58 mins |
| 4 | Hertha Berlin | 52 | 59 mins |
| 5 | B Dortmund | 51 | 60 mins |
| 6 | W Bremen | 51 | 60 mins |
| 7 | B Leverkusen | 47 | 65 mins |
| 8 | Hannover 96 | 47 | 65 mins |
| 9 | Hamburg | 46 | 67 mins |
| 10 | Schalke | 46 | 67 mins |
| 11 | 1860 Munich | 44 | 70 mins |
| 12 | B M'gladbach | 43 | 71 mins |
| 13 | Kaiserslautern | 40 | 77 mins |
| 14 | Wolfsburg | 39 | 78 mins |
| 15 | Arminia B | 35 | 87 mins |
| 16 | Hansa Rostock | 35 | 87 mins |
| 17 | Cottbus | 34 | 90 mins |
| 18 | Nurnberg | 33 | 93 mins |
| | TOTAL | 821 | |

## CLUB DEFENCES

**KEY:** Defensive Rating: Average number of mins between goals conceded. CS: Clean Sheets - Games where no goals were conceded.

| | CLUB | CONCEDED | CLEAN SH | DEF RATE |
|---|---|---|---|---|
| 1 | Bayern Munich | 25 | 17 | 122 mins |
| 2 | B Dortmund | 27 | 14 | 113 mins |
| 3 | Hamburg | 36 | 11 | 85 mins |
| 4 | Stuttgart | 39 | 10 | 78 mins |
| 5 | Schalke | 40 | 11 | 77 mins |
| 6 | Hansa Rostock | 41 | 11 | 75 mins |
| 7 | Kaiserslautern | 42 | 11 | 73 mins |
| 8 | Wolfsburg | 42 | 10 | 73 mins |
| 9 | Hertha Berlin | 43 | 13 | 71 mins |
| 10 | B M'gladbach | 45 | 10 | 68 mins |
| 11 | Arminia B | 46 | 10 | 67 mins |
| 12 | W Bremen | 50 | 8 | 61 mins |
| 13 | 1860 Munich | 52 | 9 | 59 mins |
| 14 | B Leverkusen | 56 | 6 | 55 mins |
| 15 | Bochum | 56 | 4 | 55 mins |
| 16 | Hannover 96 | 57 | 5 | 54 mins |
| 17 | Nurnberg | 60 | 8 | 51 mins |
| 18 | Cottbus | 64 | 6 | 48 mins |
| | TOTAL | 821 | 174 | |

## CLUB DISCIPLINARY RECORDS

**KEY:** AVE: Average number of mins between cards

| | CLUB | YELL | RED | TOT | AVE |
|---|---|---|---|---|---|
| 1 | Wolfsburg | 92 | 4 | 96 | 32 mins |
| 2 | Cottbus | 90 | 5 | 95 | 32 mins |
| 3 | Schalke | 83 | 9 | 92 | 33 mins |
| 4 | W Bremen | 76 | 8 | 84 | 36 mins |
| 5 | Hamburg | 79 | 6 | 85 | 36 mins |
| 6 | Hannover 96 | 78 | 3 | 81 | 38 mins |
| 7 | B Leverkusen | 75 | 6 | 81 | 38 mins |
| 8 | 1860 Munich | 73 | 4 | 77 | 40 mins |
| 9 | Nurnberg | 71 | 3 | 74 | 41 mins |
| 10 | Kaiserslautern | 74 | 1 | 75 | 41 mins |
| 11 | B Dortmund | 67 | 5 | 72 | 43 mins |
| 12 | Stuttgart | 64 | 2 | 66 | 46 mins |
| 13 | Hansa Rostock | 57 | 5 | 62 | 49 mins |
| 14 | Hertha Berlin | 59 | 1 | 60 | 51 mins |
| 15 | B M'gladbach | 55 | 4 | 59 | 52 mins |
| 16 | Arminia B | 54 | 5 | 59 | 52 mins |
| 17 | Bochum | 58 | 0 | 58 | 53 mins |
| 18 | Bayern Munich | 50 | 0 | 50 | 61 mins |
| TOTAL | | 1255 | 71 | 1326 | |

## STADIUM CAPACITY AND HOME CROWDS

| | TEAM | CAPACITY | AVE | HIGH | LOW |
|---|---|---|---|---|---|
| 1 | B Leverkusen | 22500 | 100 | 22500 | 22500 |
| 2 | Schalke | 60890 | 99.58 | 60886 | 60000 |
| 3 | Kaiserslautern | 40600 | 89.48 | 40500 | 31000 |
| 4 | W Bremen | 35800 | 88.79 | 35800 | 24000 |
| 5 | Arminia B | 26601 | 86.11 | 26601 | 18000 |
| 6 | B M'gladbach | 34500 | 83.24 | 34500 | 22000 |
| 7 | Hamburg | 55000 | 81.44 | 55500 | 30000 |
| 8 | B Dortmund | 83100 | 81.07 | 68600 | 64000 |
| 9 | Hannover 96 | 50418 | 74.47 | 49800 | 28000 |
| 10 | Bochum | 32645 | 73.07 | 32645 | 15000 |
| 11 | Bayern Munich | 69060 | 72.15 | 69000 | 35000 |
| 12 | Hansa Rostock | 30000 | 67.16 | 30000 | 13000 |
| 13 | Cottbus | 20500 | 65.27 | 18250 | 10000 |
| 14 | Wolfsburg | 30000 | 65.03 | 30000 | 11600 |
| 15 | Nurnberg | 44600 | 61.55 | 44600 | 15000 |
| 16 | Stuttgart | 54267 | 59.56 | 54267 | 19000 |
| 17 | Hertha Berlin | 76243 | 51.39 | 59200 | 25000 |
| 18 | 1860 Munich | 69060 | 35.88 | 64000 | 10000 |

## AWAY ATTENDANCE

| | TEAM | AVE | HIGH | LOW |
|---|---|---|---|---|
| 1 | Bayern Munich | 94.31 | 68600 | 18250 |
| 2 | B Dortmund | 87.97 | 63000 | 15000 |
| 3 | Schalke | 82.64 | 68600 | 13340 |
| 4 | Hannover 96 | 77.44 | 67000 | 14000 |
| 5 | Hamburg | 76.30 | 68000 | 15000 |
| 6 | W Bremen | 76.05 | 68500 | 15000 |
| 7 | B Leverkusen | 74.45 | 67000 | 14234 |
| 8 | Hertha Berlin | 73.34 | 65800 | 13000 |
| 9 | 1860 Munich | 73.19 | 69000 | 11000 |
| 10 | Stuttgart | 72.71 | 66000 | 12000 |
| 11 | Bochum | 70.64 | 67000 | 12000 |
| 12 | B M'gladbach | 69.99 | 68600 | 12000 |
| 13 | Kaiserslautern | 69.18 | 68000 | 13000 |
| 14 | Wolfsburg | 68.34 | 67000 | 12000 |
| 15 | Arminia B | 68.19 | 68600 | 12628 |
| 16 | Hansa Rostock | 67.96 | 64000 | 11600 |
| 17 | Nurnberg | 66.80 | 66000 | 10000 |
| 18 | Cottbus | 65.75 | 68000 | 10000 |

## TOP GOALSCORERS

**KEY: Strike Rate:** Average number of minutes between League goals scored by player. **Club Strike Rate (CSR):** Average minutes between League goals scored by club. **Contribution to Attacking Power (PWR):** Average mins between League goals scored by club while on pitch.

| | PLAYER | CLUB | GOALS | PWR | CSR | S RATE |
|---|---|---|---|---|---|---|
| 1 | Christiansen | Bochum | 21 | 52 | 56 | 116 |
| 2 | Elber | Bayern Munich | 20 | 42 | 44 | 142 |
| 3 | Ailton | W Bremen | 16 | 57 | 60 | 147 |
| 4 | Ciric | Nurnberg | 13 | 81 | 93 | 150 |
| 5 | Pizarro | Bayern Munich | 15 | 43 | 44 | 152 |
| 6 | Romeo | Hamburg | 14 | 64 | 67 | 162 |
| 7 | Maric | Wolfsburg | 12 | 66 | 78 | 162 |
| 8 | Kuranyi | Stuttgart | 15 | 53 | 58 | 167 |
| 9 | Bobic | Hannover 96 | 14 | 63 | 65 | 171 |
| 10 | Lauth | 1860 Munich | 13 | 71 | 70 | 187 |
| 11 | Schroth | 1860 Munich | 14 | 67 | 70 | 197 |
| 12 | Forssell | B M'gladbach | 7 | 60 | 71 | 199 |
| 13 | Wichinarek | Arminia B | 12 | 82 | 87 | 200 |
| 14 | Marcelinho | Hertha Berlin | 14 | 61 | 59 | 210 |
| 15 | Diabang | Arminia B | 10 | 84 | 87 | 212 |
| 16 | Ewerthon | B Dortmund | 11 | 63 | 60 | 215 |
| 17 | Ballack | Bayern Munich | 10 | 37 | 44 | 225 |
| 18 | Alves | Hertha Berlin | 6 | 54 | 59 | 227 |
| 19 | Van Hout | B M'gladbach | 6 | 72 | 71 | 229 |
| 20 | Klimowicz | Wolfsburg | 7 | 85 | 78 | 244 |
| 21 | Koller | B Dortmund | 12 | 59 | 60 | 251 |
| 22 | Charisteas | W Bremen | 9 | 68 | 60 | 252 |
| 23 | Bierofka | B Leverkusen | 7 | 62 | 65 | 259 |
| 24 | Prica | Hansa Rostock | 7 | 70 | 87 | 261 |
| 25 | Idrissou | Hannover 96 | 9 | 58 | 65 | 267 |
| 26 | Rydlewicz | Hansa Rostock | 6 | 73 | 87 | 280 |
| 27 | Klose, M | Kaiserslautern | 9 | 74 | 77 | 297 |
| 28 | Demo | B M'gladbach | 7 | 61 | 71 | 300 |
| 29 | Lokvenc | Kaiserslautern | 8 | 73 | 77 | 320 |
| 30 | Preetz | Hertha Berlin | 6 | 56 | 59 | 328 |

## TOP DEFENDERS

**KEY: Defensive Rating (DR)** Average mins between League goals conceded while on pitch. **Club Defensive Rating (CDR):** Average minutes between League goals conceded by club. **Clean Sheets (CS)** - Games where no goals were conceded.

| | PLAYER | CLUB | CONC | CS | CDR | DR |
|---|---|---|---|---|---|---|
| 1 | Kovac, R | Bayern Munich | 11 | 15 | 122 | 191 |
| 2 | Linke | Bayern Munich | 21 | 15 | 122 | 129 |
| 3 | Madouni | B Dortmund | 13 | 8 | 113 | 126 |
| 4 | Worns | B Dortmund | 21 | 12 | 113 | 123 |
| 5 | Maltritz | Hamburg | 16 | 9 | 85 | 123 |
| 6 | Van Burik | Hertha Berlin | 10 | 6 | 71 | 122 |
| 7 | Reuter | B Dortmund | 21 | 10 | 113 | 116 |
| 8 | Tchato | Kaiserslautern | 12 | 6 | 73 | 116 |
| 9 | Kehl | B Dortmund | 20 | 11 | 113 | 108 |
| 10 | Metzelder | B Dortmund | 19 | 8 | 113 | 108 |
| 11 | Rodriguez | Schalke | 9 | 4 | 77 | 106 |
| 12 | Fukal | Hamburg | 25 | 10 | 85 | 98 |
| 13 | Sagnol | Bayern Munich | 18 | 6 | 122 | 97 |
| 14 | Knavs | Kaiserslautern | 14 | 6 | 73 | 96 |
| 15 | Kuffour | Bayern Munich | 19 | 7 | 122 | 88 |
| 16 | Matellan | Schalke | 16 | 6 | 77 | 87 |
| 17 | Ujfalusi | Hamburg | 32 | 10 | 85 | 86 |
| 18 | Marques | Stuttgart | 10 | 2 | 78 | 86 |
| 19 | Franz | Wolfsburg | 12 | 4 | 73 | 85 |
| 20 | Borges | Arminia B | 11 | 3 | 67 | 84 |
| 21 | Asanin | B M'gladbach | 11 | 3 | 68 | 84 |
| 22 | van Hoogdalem | Schalke | 24 | 8 | 77 | 84 |
| 23 | Hoogma | Hamburg | 29 | 9 | 85 | 83 |
| 24 | Hill | Hansa Rostock | 20 | 6 | 75 | 83 |
| 25 | Bordon | Stuttgart | 28 | 8 | 78 | 82 |
| 26 | Hajto | Schalke | 31 | 8 | 77 | 81 |
| 27 | Korell | B M'gladbach | 19 | 5 | 68 | 78 |
| 28 | Ramzy | Kaiserslautern | 18 | 5 | 73 | 78 |
| 29 | Schnoor | Wolfsburg | 34 | 10 | 73 | 77 |
| 30 | Kovar | Hansa Rostock | 24 | 6 | 75 | 75 |

## TOP MIDFIELDERS

**KEY: Scoring Difference (SD)** Team goals scored while on the pitch minus team goals conceded. **Contribution to Attacking Power:** Average mins between League goals scored by club while on pitch. **Defensive Rating (DR)** Average mins between League goals conceded while on pitch.

| | PLAYER | TEAM | GOALS | DR | PWR | SD |
|---|---|---|---|---|---|---|
| 1 | Jeremies | Bayern Munich | 0 | 162 | 42 | 120 |
| 2 | Ballack | Bayern Munich | 10 | 141 | 38 | 103 |
| 3 | Hargreaves | Bayern Munich | 1 | 122 | 47 | 75 |
| 4 | Lizarazu | Bayern Munich | 2 | 117 | 46 | 71 |
| 5 | Evanilson | B Dortmund | 0 | 130 | 65 | 65 |
| 6 | Dede | B Dortmund | 3 | 121 | 62 | 59 |
| 7 | Kovac, N | Bayern Munich | 1 | 117 | 58 | 59 |
| 8 | Salihamidzic | Bayern Munich | 2 | 97 | 42 | 55 |
| 9 | Frings | B Dortmund | 6 | 113 | 59 | 54 |
| 10 | Dominguez | Kaiserslautern | 3 | 114 | 66 | 48 |
| 11 | Ricken | B Dortmund | 4 | 103 | 58 | 45 |
| 12 | Rosicky | B Dortmund | 3 | 105 | 61 | 44 |
| 13 | Heinrich | B Dortmund | 0 | 100 | 57 | 43 |
| 14 | Moller | Schalke | 1 | 107 | 67 | 40 |
| 15 | Soldo | Stuttgart | 1 | 91 | 53 | 38 |
| 16 | Kmetsch | Schalke | 1 | 104 | 68 | 36 |
| 17 | Hleb | Stuttgart | 4 | 87 | 58 | 29 |
| 18 | Gerber | Stuttgart | 0 | 86 | 59 | 27 |
| 19 | Hinkel | Stuttgart | 0 | 82 | 56 | 26 |
| 20 | Barbarez | Hamburg | 6 | 85 | 60 | 25 |
| 21 | Oliseh | Bochum | 0 | 72 | 48 | 24 |
| 22 | Hartmann | Hertha Berlin | 0 | 79 | 56 | 23 |
| 23 | Sforza | Kaiserslautern | 1 | 86 | 63 | 23 |
| 24 | Bohme | Schalke | 5 | 82 | 61 | 21 |
| 25 | Hollerbach | Hamburg | 0 | 94 | 74 | 20 |
| 26 | Poulsen | Schalke | 1 | 82 | 63 | 19 |
| 27 | Kluge | B M'gladbach | 2 | 80 | 63 | 17 |
| 28 | Demo | B M'gladbach | 7 | 78 | 62 | 16 |
| 29 | Goor | Hertha Berlin | 5 | 78 | 62 | 16 |
| 30 | Wicky | Hamburg | 0 | 75 | 60 | 15 |

## PLAYER DISCIPLINARY RECORDS

**KEY: AVE:** Average number of mins between cards

| | PLAYER | TEAM | YELL | RED | TOTAL | AVE |
|---|---|---|---|---|---|---|
| 1 | Akrapovic | Cottbus | 4 | 1 | 5 | 111 |
| 2 | Ledesma | Hamburg | 6 | 1 | 7 | 121 |
| 3 | Hujdurovic | Cottbus | 5 | 0 | 5 | 123 |
| 4 | Baur | Hamburg | 4 | 1 | 5 | 128 |
| 5 | Passlack | Nurnberg | 4 | 1 | 5 | 138 |
| 6 | Stehle | Nurnberg | 7 | 0 | 7 | 144 |
| 7 | Bogusz | Arminia B | 6 | 1 | 7 | 149 |
| 8 | Kaluzny | Cottbus | 8 | 0 | 8 | 157 |
| 9 | van Hintum | Hannover 96 | 4 | 1 | 5 | 158 |
| 10 | Kurz | 1860 Munich | 10 | 2 | 12 | 159 |
| 11 | Hollerbach | Hamburg | 13 | 0 | 13 | 159 |
| 12 | Varela | Schalke | 8 | 2 | 10 | 159 |
| 13 | Amoroso | B Dortmund | 5 | 1 | 6 | 163 |
| 14 | Neuendorf | Hertha Berlin | 4 | 0 | 4 | 167 |
| 15 | Beeck | Cottbus | 7 | 1 | 8 | 168 |
| 16 | Brdaric | B Leverkusen | 3 | 1 | 4 | 170 |
| 17 | Meissner | Stuttgart | 9 | 1 | 10 | 171 |
| 18 | Prager | Wolfsburg | 7 | 0 | 7 | 174 |
| 19 | Nzelo-Lembi | Kaiserslautern | 3 | 0 | 3 | 176 |
| 20 | Bjelica | Kaiserslautern | 5 | 0 | 5 | 179 |
| 21 | Hajto | Schalke | 13 | 1 | 14 | 180 |
| 22 | Sforza | Kaiserslautern | 9 | 1 | 10 | 181 |
| 23 | Korell | B M'gladbach | 6 | 2 | 8 | 186 |
| 24 | Barbarez | Hamburg | 9 | 2 | 11 | 186 |
| 25 | Banovic | W Bremen | 5 | 0 | 5 | 198 |
| 26 | Hristov | Kaiserslautern | 3 | 0 | 3 | 201 |
| 27 | Barten | W Bremen | 3 | 0 | 3 | 202 |
| 28 | Basler | Kaiserslautern | 8 | 0 | 8 | 203 |
| 29 | Meijer | Hamburg | 3 | 1 | 4 | 204 |
| 30 | Placente | B Leverkusen | 8 | 1 | 9 | 210 |

## CHART TOPPING GOALKEEPERS

**KEY: Defensive Rating (DR)** Average mins between League goals conceded while on pitch. **Clean Sheets (CS)** - Games where no goals were conceded.

| | PLAYER | TEAM | CON | CS | DR |
|---|---|---|---|---|---|
| 1 | Kahn | Bayern Munich | 22 | 17 | 135 |
| 2 | Weidenfeller | B Dortmund | 7 | 5 | 130 |
| 3 | Lehmann | B Dortmund | 20 | 9 | 106 |
| 4 | Pieckenhagen | Hamburg | 36 | 11 | 85 |
| 5 | Ernst | Stuttgart | 15 | 6 | 84 |
| 6 | Ramovic | Wolfsburg | 7 | 2 | 77 |
| 7 | Wiese | Kaiserslautern | 25 | 8 | 76 |
| 8 | Rost | Schalke | 39 | 10 | 76 |
| 9 | Schober | Hansa Rostock | 41 | 11 | 75 |
| 10 | Hildebrand | Stuttgart | 24 | 4 | 75 |
| 11 | Reitmaier | Wolfsburg | 35 | 8 | 72 |
| 12 | Kiraly | Hertha Berlin | 42 | 13 | 71 |
| 13 | Stiel | B M'gladbach | 40 | 9 | 70 |
| 14 | Koch, G | Kaiserslautern | 17 | 3 | 69 |
| 15 | Hain | Arminia B | 46 | 10 | 67 |
| 16 | Tremmel | Hannover 96 | 24 | 4 | 67 |
| 17 | Borel | W Bremen | 45 | 8 | 62 |
| 18 | Van Duijnhoven | Bochum | 41 | 4 | 60 |
| 19 | Jentzsch | 1860 Munich | 50 | 9 | 58 |
| 20 | Butt | B Leverkusen | 53 | 6 | 56 |
| 21 | Lenz | Cottbus | 40 | 6 | 52 |
| 22 | Kampa | Nurnberg | 58 | 8 | 52 |
| 23 | Sievers | Hannover 96 | 33 | 1 | 44 |
| 24 | Vander | Bochum | 15 | 0 | 39 |
| 25 | Piplica | Cottbus | 22 | 0 | 37 |

## TOP POINT EARNERS

**KEY: Counting Games** League games where he played more than 70 minutes. **Total League Points** Taken in Counting Games. **Average League Points** Taken in Counting Games.

| | PLAYER | TEAM | GAMES | POINTS | AVE |
|---|---|---|---|---|---|
| 1 | Ballack | Bayern Munich | 25 | 63 | 2.52 |
| 2 | Elber | Bayern Munich | 32 | 75 | 2.34 |
| 3 | Jeremies | Bayern Munich | 25 | 58 | 2.32 |
| 4 | Ze Roberto | Bayern Munich | 24 | 54 | 2.25 |
| 5 | Kahn | Bayern Munich | 33 | 74 | 2.24 |
| 6 | Pizarro | Bayern Munich | 23 | 51 | 2.22 |
| 7 | Kuffour | Bayern Munich | 18 | 40 | 2.22 |
| 8 | Salihamidzic | Bayern Munich | 10 | 22 | 2.20 |
| 9 | Linke | Bayern Munich | 30 | 65 | 2.17 |
| 10 | Kovac, R | Bayern Munich | 23 | 50 | 2.17 |
| 11 | Lizarazu | Bayern Munich | 24 | 52 | 2.17 |
| 12 | Sagnol | Bayern Munich | 19 | 41 | 2.16 |
| 13 | Dominguez | Kaiserslautern | 10 | 21 | 2.10 |
| 14 | Soldo | Stuttgart | 24 | 49 | 2.04 |
| 15 | Maltritz | Hamburg | 21 | 42 | 2.00 |
| 16 | Agali | Schalke | 11 | 22 | 2.00 |
| 17 | Gerber | Stuttgart | 23 | 46 | 2.00 |
| 18 | Hartmann | Hertha Berlin | 26 | 51 | 1.96 |
| 19 | Hargreaves | Bayern Munich | 16 | 31 | 1.94 |
| 20 | Alves | Hertha Berlin | 14 | 27 | 1.93 |
| 21 | Ernst | Stuttgart | 14 | 27 | 1.93 |
| 22 | Metzelder | B Dortmund | 21 | 40 | 1.90 |
| 23 | Mahdavikia | Hamburg | 26 | 49 | 1.88 |
| 24 | Klimowicz | Wolfsburg | 16 | 30 | 1.88 |
| 25 | Wicky | Hamburg | 13 | 24 | 1.85 |
| 26 | Kuranyi | Stuttgart | 27 | 50 | 1.85 |
| 27 | Hinkel | Stuttgart | 32 | 58 | 1.81 |
| 28 | Luizao | Hertha Berlin | 10 | 18 | 1.80 |
| 29 | Lehmann | B Dortmund | 23 | 41 | 1.78 |
| 30 | Lisztes | W Bremen | 22 | 39 | 1.77 |

## HOLLAND CASINO EREDIVISIE CHAMPIONS

# PSV EINDHOVEN

Final Position: **1st**

| | | | | | | |
|---|---|---|---|---|---|---|
| 1 | lge | Excelsior | A | W | 2-0 | Van Bommel 3; Bruggink 17 |
| 2 | lge | Groningen | H | W | 1-0 | Vogel 82 |
| 3 | lge | AZ Alkmaar | A | W | 4-0 | Ooijer 14; Kezman 36,45; Vennegoor 85 |
| 4 | lge | RKC Waalwijk | H | W | 4-0 | Kezman 8,63,73; Bruggink 53 |
| 5 | ecga | Auxerre | A | D | 0-0 | |
| 6 | lge | Zwolle | A | W | 3-1 | Kezman 10,66; Vennegoor 85 |
| 7 | ecga | Arsenal | H | L | 0-4 | |
| 8 | lge | De Graafschap | H | W | 4-0 | Rommedahl 21; Kezman 29,62; Robben 34 |
| 9 | ecga | B Dortmund | H | L | 1-3 | van der Schaaf 74 |
| 10 | lge | NAC Breda | A | D | 2-2 | Kezman 57; Rommedahl 90 |
| 11 | lge | Roda JC Kerk | H | D | 0-0 | |
| 12 | ecga | B Dortmund | A | D | 1-1 | Bruggink 47 |
| 13 | lge | NEC Nijmegen | A | W | 5-0 | Bruggink 3,36; Rommedahl 68; Kezman 71; Robben 85 |
| 14 | ecga | Auxerre | H | W | 3-0 | Bruggink 34; Rommedahl 48; Robben 64 |
| 15 | lge | Twente | A | D | 0-0 | |
| 16 | lge | Heerenveen | H | W | 3-1 | Kezman 63,78; Van Bommel 86 |
| 17 | ecga | Arsenal | A | D | 0-0 | |
| 18 | lge | Feyenoord | H | L | 1-2 | Rommedahl 54 |
| 19 | lge | Roosendaal | A | W | 3-0 | Kezman 45; Ooijer 49; Rommedahl 53 |
| 20 | lge | Willem II Tilb | H | W | 2-1 | Vennegoor 14; Kezman 45 |
| 21 | lge | Utrecht | H | W | 3-1 | Kezman 2,66; Ooijer 5 |
| 22 | lge | Ajax | A | W | 4-2 | Robben 14; Kezman 48; Vennegoor 57,78 |
| 23 | lge | Vitesse Arnhem | H | W | 1-0 | Bouma 42 |
| 24 | lge | Roosendaal | H | W | 3-0 | Robben 37; Kezman 53; Gakhokidze 79 |
| 25 | lge | RKC Waalwijk | A | W | 1-0 | Robben 40 |
| 26 | lge | Zwolle | H | W | 6-0 | Vennegoor 1; Kezman 3,9,25; Van Bommel 12; Robben 59 |
| 27 | lge | NAC Breda | H | W | 1-0 | Vennegoor 9 |
| 28 | lge | Heerenveen | A | W | 1-0 | Robben 90 |
| 29 | lge | NEC Nijmegen | H | W | 2-1 | Kezman 33 pen; Van Bommel 66 |
| 30 | lge | Vitesse Arnhem | A | W | 5-0 | Van Halst 2 og; Robben 34; Van Bommel 37; Bruggink 79,87 |
| 31 | lge | Ajax | H | W | 2-0 | Kezman 10 pen,88 |
| 32 | lge | Willem II Tilb | A | D | 1-1 | Robben 55 |
| 33 | lge | Roda JC Kerk | A | W | 3-2 | Kezman 21,60; Robben 42 |
| 34 | lge | Twente | H | W | 2-0 | Vennegoor 31; Kezman 60 pen |
| 35 | lge | De Graafschap | A | W | 6-1 | Kezman 6,15,84; Rommedahl 19; Robben 60; Leandro 90 |
| 36 | lge | AZ Alkmaar | H | D | 2-2 | Bruggink 69,80 |
| 37 | lge | Excelsior | H | W | 7-0 | Van Bommel 32,45,47,90; Kezman 46,70; Robben 85 |
| 38 | lge | Feyenoord | A | L | 1-3 | Kezman 52 |
| 39 | lge | Utrecht | H | W | 2-0 | Bruggink 3; Kezman 30 pen |
| 40 | lge | Groningen | A | D | 0-0 | |

## KEY PLAYERS - GOALSCORERS

**1 Mateja Kezman**

| | | | |
|---|---|---|---|
| Goals in the League | 35 | Player Strike Rate<br>Average number of minutes between League goals scored by player | 81 |
| Contribution to Attacking Power<br>Average number of minutes between League team goals while on pitch | 35 | Club Strike Rate<br>Average number of minutes between League goals scored by club | 35 |

| | PLAYER | LGE GOALS | POWER | STRIKE RATE |
|---|---|---|---|---|
| 2 | Jan Vennegoor of Hesselink | 8 | 33 | 221 mins |
| 3 | Arjen Robben | 12 | 34 | 223 mins |
| 4 | Mark Van Bommel | 9 | 35 | 275 mins |
| 5 | Dennis Rommedahl | 6 | 38 | 437 mins |

## KEY PLAYERS - MIDFIELDERS

**1 Mark Van Bommel**

| | | | |
|---|---|---|---|
| Goals in the League | 9 | Contribution to Attacking Power<br>Average number of minutes between League team goals while on pitch | 35 |
| Defensive Rating<br>Average number of mins between League goals conceded while he was on the pitch | 177 | Scoring Difference<br>Defensive Rating minus Contribution to Attacking Power | 142 |

| | PLAYER | LGE GOALS | DEF RATE | POWER | SCORE DIFF |
|---|---|---|---|---|---|
| 2 | Johann Vogel | 1 | 140 | 39 | 101 mins |
| 3 | Young Pyo Lee | 0 | 131 | 36 | 95 mins |
| 4 | Remco van der Schaaf | 0 | 106 | 28 | 78 mins |

## KEY PLAYERS - DEFENDERS

**1 Kasper Bogelund**

| | | | |
|---|---|---|---|
| Goals Conceded (GC)<br>The number of League goals conceded while he was on the pitch | 12 | Clean Sheets<br>In games when he played at least 70 minutes | 12 |
| Defensive Rating<br>Ave number of mins between League goals conceded while on the pitch | 144 | Club Defensive Rating<br>Average number of mins between League goals conceded by the club this season | 153 |

| | PLAYER | CON LGE | CLEAN SHEETS | DEF RATE |
|---|---|---|---|---|
| 2 | Andre Ooijer | 20 | 17 | 139 mins |
| 3 | Ernest Faber | 13 | 10 | 134 mins |

## GOALS SCORED

**AT HOME**

| | | |
|---|---|---|
| MOST | Ajax | 57 |
| | | 43 |
| LEAST | Twente | 18 |

**AWAY**

| | | |
|---|---|---|
| MOST | PSV | 44 |
| | | 44 |
| LEAST | Roosendaal & Groningen | 9 |

## GOALS CONCEDED

**AT HOME**

| | | |
|---|---|---|
| LEAST | PSV | 7 |
| | | 7 |
| MOST | Excelsior | 38 |

**AWAY**

| | | |
|---|---|---|
| LEAST | PSV | 13 |
| | | 13 |
| MOST | De G'schap | 50 |

## KEY GOALKEEPER

**1 Ronald Waterreus**

| | |
|---|---|
| Goals Conceded in the League | 13 |
| Defensive Rating<br>Ave number of mins between League goals conceded while on the pitch | 187 |
| Counting Games<br>Games when he played at least 70 mins | 27 |
| Clean Sheets<br>In games when he played at least 70 mins | 18 |

## TOP POINT EARNERS

| | PLAYER | GAMES | AVE |
|---|---|---|---|
| 1 | Bouma | 26 | 2.58 |
| 2 | Ooijer | 29 | 2.52 |
| 3 | Waterreus | 27 | 2.52 |
| 4 | Rommedahl | 27 | 2.48 |
| 5 | Faber | 17 | 2.47 |
| 6 | Vennegoor | 13 | 2.46 |
| 7 | Robben | 28 | 2.43 |
| 8 | Vogel | 28 | 2.43 |
| 9 | Kezman | 31 | 2.42 |
| 10 | Lee | 14 | 2.36 |
| | CLUB AVERAGE: | | 2.47 |

Ave = Average points per match in Counting Games

## ATTENDANCES

HOME GROUND: PHILIPS STADION CAPACITY: 35270 AVERAGE LEAGUE AT HOME: 33217

| | | | | | | | | |
|---|---|---|---|---|---|---|---|---|
| 12 | B Dortmund | 50000 | 24 | Roosendaal | 33000 | 10 | NAC Breda | 15259 |
| 22 | Ajax | 49871 | 26 | Zwolle | 33000 | 28 | Heerenveen | 14700 |
| 38 | Feyenoord | 45000 | 29 | NEC Nijmegen | 33000 | 32 | Willem II Tilb | 13820 |
| 17 | Arsenal | 35274 | 36 | AZ Alkmaar | 33000 | 15 | Twente | 13250 |
| 18 | Feyenoord | 35200 | 4 | RKC Waalwijk | 32000 | 40 | Groningen | 12500 |
| 31 | Ajax | 35000 | 8 | De Graafschap | 31000 | 13 | NEC Nijmegen | 12500 |
| 2 | Groningen | 34000 | 11 | Roda JC Kerk | 31000 | 35 | De Graafschap | 11000 |
| 39 | Utrecht | 34000 | 9 | B Dortmund | 30000 | 25 | RKC Waalwijk | 7500 |
| 16 | Heerenveen | 33500 | 14 | Auxerre | 27500 | 3 | AZ Alkmaar | 7480 |
| 27 | NAC Breda | 33500 | 5 | Auxerre | 25000 | 6 | Zwolle | 6800 |
| 34 | Twente | 33500 | 7 | Arsenal | 24000 | 19 | Roosendaal | 5000 |
| 20 | Willem II Tilb | 33500 | 30 | Vitesse Arnhem | 23900 | 1 | Excelsior | 3150 |
| 23 | Vitesse Arnhem | 33500 | 21 | Utrecht | 18500 | | | |
| 37 | Excelsior | 33000 | 33 | Roda JC Kerk | 16000 | | | |

Home / Away / Neutral

## DISCIPLINARY RECORDS

| | PLAYER | YELLOW | RED | AVE |
|---|---|---|---|---|
| 1 | Hofland | 2 | 0 | 282 |
| 2 | Kezman | 5 | 1 | 471 |
| 3 | Van Bommel | 5 | 0 | 495 |
| 4 | Bruggink | 2 | 0 | 564 |
| 5 | van der Schaaf | 2 | 0 | 583 |
| 6 | Ooijer | 4 | 0 | 696 |
| 7 | Vennegoor | 2 | 0 | 882 |
| 8 | Robben | 3 | 0 | 892 |
| 9 | Lee | 1 | 0 | 1305 |
| 10 | Vogel | 2 | 0 | 1327 |
| 11 | Faber | 1 | 0 | 1736 |
| 12 | Rommedahl | 1 | 0 | 2619 |
| | Other | 2 | 0 | |
| | TOTAL | 32 | 1 | |

## LEAGUE GOALS

| | PLAYER | MINS | GOALS | AVE |
|---|---|---|---|---|
| 1 | Kezman | 2828 | 35 | 81 |
| 2 | Robben | 2676 | 12 | 223 |
| 3 | Van Bommel | 2479 | 9 | 275 |
| 4 | Bruggink | 1128 | 9 | 125 |
| 5 | Vennegoor | 1764 | 8 | 221 |
| 6 | Rommedahl | 2619 | 6 | 437 |
| 7 | Ooijer | 2785 | 3 | 928 |
| 8 | Gakhokidze | 265 | 1 | 265 |
| 9 | Leandro | 626 | 1 | 626 |
| 10 | Vogel | 2655 | 1 | 2655 |
| 11 | Bouma | 2393 | 1 | 239 |
| | Other | | 1 | |
| | TOTAL | | 87 | |

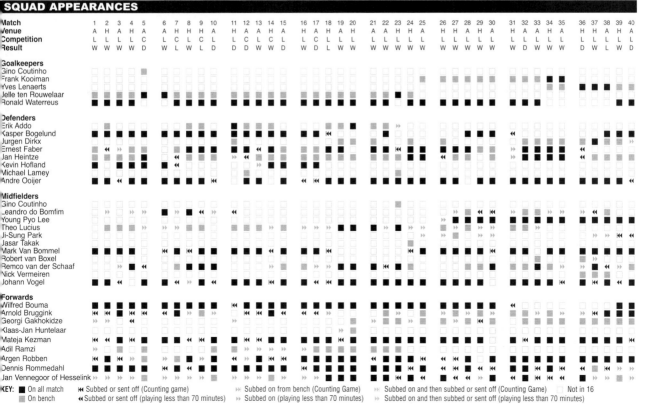

## MONTH BY MONTH GUIDE TO THE POINTS

| MONTH | POINTS | % |
|---|---|---|
| AUGUST | 6 | 100% |
| SEPTEMBER | 12 | 100% |
| OCTOBER | 5 | 56% |
| NOVEMBER | 10 | 67% |
| DECEMBER | 9 | 100% |
| JANUARY | 3 | 100% |
| FEBRUARY | 9 | 100% |
| MARCH | 12 | 100% |
| APRIL | 10 | 83% |
| MAY | 8 | 53% |

## TEAM OF THE SEASON

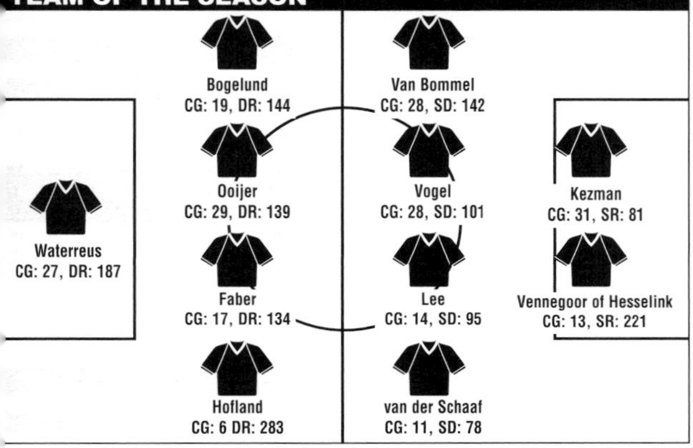
Waterreus
CG: 27, DR: 187
Bogelund
CG: 19, DR: 144
Ooijer
CG: 29, DR: 139
Faber
CG: 17, DR: 134
Hofland
CG: 6 DR: 283
Van Bommel
CG: 28, SD: 142
Vogel
CG: 28, SD: 101
Lee
CG: 14, SD: 95
van der Schaaf
CG: 11, SD: 78
Kezman
CG: 31, SR: 81
Vennegoor of Hesselink
CG: 13, SR: 221

KEY: DR = Defensive Rate, SD = Scoring Difference, SR = Strike Rate, CG = Counting Games – League games playing at least 70 minutes

## LEAGUE APPEARANCES, BOOKINGS AND CAPS

| | AGE (on 01/07/03) | IN THE SQUAD | COUNTING GAMES | MINUTES ON PITCH | YELLOW CARDS | RED CARDS | THIS SEASON | HOME COUNTRY |
|---|---|---|---|---|---|---|---|---|
| **Goalkeepers** | | | | | | | | |
| Gino Coutinho | | 0 | 0 | 0 | 0 | 0 | - | |
| Frank Kooiman | 33 | 11 | 2 | 180 | 0 | 0 | - | Holland |
| Yves Lenaerts | 20 | 7 | 3 | 270 | 0 | 0 | - | Holland |
| Jelle ten Rouwelaar | 22 | 18 | 2 | 180 | 0 | 0 | - | Holland |
| Ronald Waterreus | 32 | 27 | 27 | 2430 | 0 | 0 | 6 | Holland (6) |
| **Defenders** | | | | | | | | |
| Erik Addo | 24 | 10 | 2 | 193 | 0 | 0 | - | Holland |
| Kasper Bogelund | 22 | 20 | 19 | 1723 | 0 | 0 | 5 | Denmark (10) |
| Jurgen Dirkx | 27 | 15 | 1 | 122 | 0 | 0 | - | Holland |
| Ernest Faber | 31 | 28 | 17 | 1736 | 1 | 0 | - | Holland |
| Jan Heintze | 39 | 32 | 6 | 686 | 0 | 0 | - | Denmark |
| Kevin Hofland | 24 | 7 | 6 | 565 | 2 | 0 | - | Holland |
| Michael Lamey | 23 | 1 | 0 | 0 | 0 | 0 | - | Holland |
| Andre Ooijer | 28 | 32 | 29 | 2785 | 4 | 0 | 3 | Holland (6) |
| **Midfielders** | | | | | | | | |
| Gino Coutinho | | 1 | 0 | 0 | 0 | 0 | - | |
| Leandro do Bomfim | 19 | 18 | 3 | 626 | 0 | 0 | - | Brazil |
| Young Pyo Lee | 26 | 15 | 14 | 1305 | 1 | 0 | - | South Korea |
| Theo Lucius | 26 | 25 | 4 | 441 | 1 | 0 | - | Holland |
| Ji-Sung Park | 22 | 9 | 1 | 321 | 0 | 0 | 2 | South Korea (21) |
| Jasar Takak | | 1 | 0 | 0 | 0 | 0 | - | |
| Mark Van Bommel | 26 | 28 | 28 | 2479 | 5 | 0 | 7 | Holland (6) |
| Robert van Boxel | 20 | 3 | 0 | 18 | 0 | 0 | - | Holland |
| Remco v d Schaaf | 24 | 26 | 11 | 1166 | 2 | 0 | - | Holland |
| Nick Vermeiren | | 3 | 0 | 0 | 0 | 0 | - | Holland |
| Johann Vogel | 26 | 32 | 28 | 2655 | 2 | 0 | - | Switzerland |
| **Forwards** | | | | | | | | |
| Wilfred Bouma | 25 | 27 | 26 | 2393 | 0 | 0 | 2 | Holland (6) |
| Arnold Bruggink | 25 | 29 | 9 | 1128 | 2 | 0 | - | Holland |
| Georgi Gakhokidze | 27 | 24 | 1 | 265 | 1 | 0 | - | Georgia |
| Klaas-Jan Huntelaar | 19 | 2 | 0 | 15 | 0 | 0 | - | Holland |
| Mateja Kezman | 24 | 33 | 31 | 2828 | 5 | 1 | - | Serbia & Montenegro |
| Adil Ramzi | 25 | 13 | 0 | 79 | 0 | 0 | - | Morocco |
| Argen Robben | 19 | 33 | 28 | 2676 | 3 | 0 | 1 | Holland (6) |
| Dennis Rommedahl | 24 | 34 | 27 | 2619 | 1 | 0 | 10 | Denmark (10) |
| Jan V Hesselink | 24 | 34 | 13 | 1764 | 2 | 0 | - | Holland |

KEY: LEAGUE BOOKINGS CAPS (FIFA RANKING)

## SQUAD APPEARANCES

| Match | 1 | 2 | 3 | 4 | 5 | 6 | 7 | 8 | 9 | 10 | 11 | 12 | 13 | 14 | 15 | 16 | 17 | 18 | 19 | 20 | 21 | 22 | 23 | 24 | 25 | 26 | 27 | 28 | 29 | 30 | 31 | 32 | 33 | 34 | 35 | 36 | 37 | 38 | 39 | 40 |
|---|---|---|---|---|---|---|---|---|---|---|---|---|---|---|---|---|---|---|---|---|---|---|---|---|---|---|---|---|---|---|---|---|---|---|---|---|---|---|---|---|
| Venue | A | H | A | H | A | A | H | H | H | A | H | A | A | H | A | H | A | H | A | H | A | A | H | H | A | H | H | A | H | A | H | A | A | H | A | H | H | A | H | A |
| Competition | L | L | L | L | C | L | C | L | C | L | L | C | L | C | L | L | C | L | L | L | L | L | L | L | L | L | L | L | L | L | L | L | L | L | L | L | L | L | L | L |
| Result | W | W | W | W | D | W | L | W | L | D | D | D | W | W | D | W | D | L | W | W | W | W | W | W | W | W | W | W | W | W | W | D | W | W | W | D | W | L | W | D |

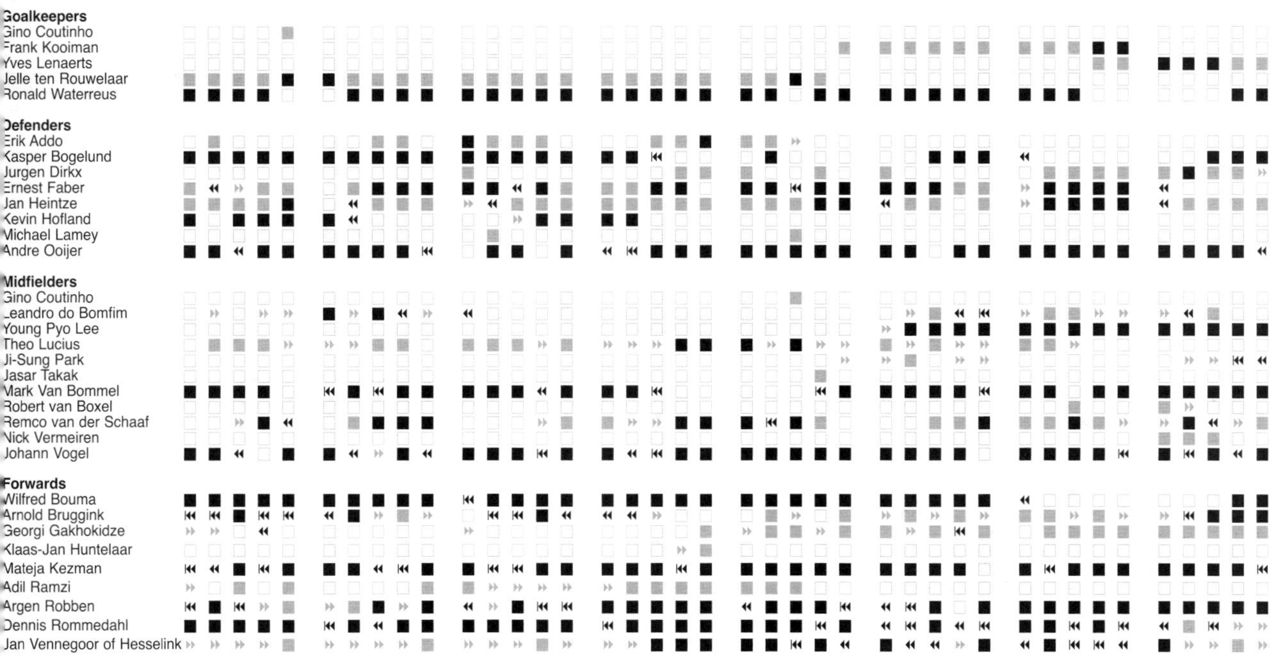
Goalkeepers
Gino Coutinho
Frank Kooiman
Yves Lenaerts
Jelle ten Rouwelaar
Ronald Waterreus
Defenders
Erik Addo
Kasper Bogelund
Jurgen Dirkx
Ernest Faber
Jan Heintze
Kevin Hofland
Michael Lamey
Andre Ooijer
Midfielders
Gino Coutinho
Leandro do Bomfim
Young Pyo Lee
Theo Lucius
Ji-Sung Park
Jasar Takak
Mark Van Bommel
Robert van Boxel
Remco van der Schaaf
Nick Vermeiren
Johann Vogel
Forwards
Wilfred Bouma
Arnold Bruggink
Georgi Gakhokidze
Klaas-Jan Huntelaar
Mateja Kezman
Adil Ramzi
Argen Robben
Dennis Rommedahl
Jan Vennegoor of Hesselink

KEY: ■ On all match ■ On bench ⏮ Subbed or sent off (Counting game) « Subbed or sent off (playing less than 70 minutes) ⏭ Subbed on from bench (Counting Game) » Subbed on (playing less than 70 minutes) ⏭ Subbed on and then subbed or sent off (Counting Game) » Subbed on and then subbed or sent off (playing less than 70 minutes) □ Not in 16

# AJAX

Final Position: **2nd**

| | | | | | | |
|---|---|---|---|---|---|---|
| 1 | lge | Utrecht | H | W | 3-1 | Galasek 4; Mido 77; Pienaar 84 |
| 2 | lge | Vitesse Arnhem | A | W | 2-1 | Pasanen 51; Chivu 77 |
| 3 | lge | Groningen | A | W | 3-1 | van der Vaart 13,40; van der Meyde 50 |
| 4 | lge | Zwolle | H | W | 2-0 | Witschge 59; Chivu 78 pen |
| 5 | ecgd | Lyon | H | W | 2-1 | Ibrahimovic 11,33 |
| 6 | lge | Roosendaal | A | W | 3-2 | Ibrahimovic 58; Galasek 66; Chivu 75 pen |
| 7 | ecgd | Inter Milan | A | L | 0-1 | |
| 8 | lge | NAC Breda | H | D | 2-2 | Ibrahimovic 48; Mido 56 |
| 9 | ecgd | Rosenborg BK | A | D | 0-0 | |
| 10 | lge | Feyenoord | A | W | 2-1 | Wamberto 23; Litmanen 43 |
| 11 | lge | AZ Alkmaar | H | W | 6-2 | Mido 10,12; Litmanen 22,48; Boukhari 79,83 |
| 12 | ecgd | Rosenborg BK | H | D | 1-1 | Ibrahimovic 41 |
| 13 | lge | RKC Waalwijk | A | D | 1-1 | Maxwell 72 |
| 14 | ecgd | Lyon | A | W | 2-0 | Pienaar 7; van der Vaart 90 |
| 15 | lge | Willem II Tilb | H | W | 3-0 | Mido 9; van der Vaart 72; Pienaar 87 |
| 16 | lge | Roda JC Kerk | A | D | 1-1 | van der Vaart 72 |
| 17 | ecgd | Inter Milan | H | L | 1-2 | van der Vaart 90 |
| 18 | lge | NEC Nijmegen | H | W | 6-0 | Mido 16,47; van der Meyde 52; van der Vaart 72; Bergdolmo 76 pen; Boukhari 90 |
| 19 | lge | Heerenveen | A | W | 3-0 | van der Meyde 6,76; Galasek 38 |
| 20 | ecgb | Valencia | A | D | 1-1 | Ibrahimovic 88 |
| 21 | lge | Twente | H | W | 2-1 | van der Vaart 18,90 |
| 22 | lge | De Graafschap | A | D | 1-1 | Mido 17 |
| 23 | ecgb | Roma | H | W | 2-1 | Ibrahimovic 11; Litmanen 66 |
| 24 | lge | PSV Eindhoven | H | L | 2-4 | Ibrahimovic 26; van der Meyde 55 |
| 25 | lge | Excelsior | A | W | 2-0 | Ibrahimovic 2; Pasanen 48 |
| 26 | lge | Willem II Tilb | A | W | 6-0 | van der Meyde 8; Ibrahimovic 13,64; Chivu 29 pen; Galasek 46; Mido 78 |
| 27 | lge | Feyenoord | H | D | 1-1 | Ibrahimovic 28 |
| 28 | lge | Groningen | H | W | 2-1 | van der Meyde 38; Ibrahimovic 59 |
| 29 | ecgb | Arsenal | A | D | 1-1 | de Jong 17 |
| 30 | lge | Utrecht | A | L | 0-1 | |
| 31 | ecgb | Arsenal | H | D | 0-0 | |
| 32 | lge | Vitesse Arnhem | H | W | 2-0 | Pienaar 27,90 |
| 33 | lge | Zwolle | A | W | 5-0 | van der Vaart 14,58; Ibrahimovic 30,65; van der Haar 32 og |
| 34 | ecgb | Valencia | H | D | 1-1 | Pasanen 57 |
| 35 | lge | Excelsior | H | W | 2-1 | Ibrahimovic 25,81 |
| 36 | ecgb | Roma | A | D | 1-1 | van der Meyde 1 |
| 37 | lge | PSV Eindhoven | A | L | 0-2 | |
| 38 | lge | Roosendaal | H | W | 4-1 | van der Vaart 34; Maxwell 40; van der Meyde 45; Boukhari 90 |
| 39 | ecqfl1 | AC Milan | H | D | 0-0 | |
| 40 | lge | NAC Breda | A | W | 3-0 | Sneijder 43; van der Meyde 75,84 |
| 41 | lge | Roda JC Kerk | H | W | 4-2 | Ibrahimovic 16; van der Vaart 18; Sneijder 27; Boukhari 82 |
| 42 | ecqfl2 | AC Milan | A | L | 2-3 | Litmanen 63; Pienaar 78 |
| 43 | lge | AZ Alkmaar | A | W | 3-1 | van der Vaart 21; Litmanen 48; van der Meyde 64 |
| 44 | lge | RKC Waalwijk | H | W | 6-1 | Sneijder 17; van der Vaart 19,45,82; Pasanen 53; Trabelsi 76 |
| 45 | lge | NEC Nijmegen | A | W | 2-1 | Litmanen 64; Maxwell 78 |
| 46 | lge | De Graafschap | H | W | 7-1 | van der Vaart 16,44; Sneijder 63; Galasek 67 pen; Pienaar 71; Maxwell 76; Boukhari 88 |
| 47 | lge | Twente | A | W | 2-1 | Chivu 63 pen; van der Vaart 82 |
| 48 | lge | Heerenveen | H | W | 3-0 | Sikora 44,86; Chivu 63 |

## ATTENDANCES

HOME GROUND: AMSTERDAM ARENA CAPACITY: 51342 AVERAGE LEAGUE AT HOME: 46927

| | | | | | | | | |
|---|---|---|---|---|---|---|---|---|
| 42 | AC Milan | 76079 | 11 | AZ Alkmaar | 47481 | 30 | Utrecht | 18000 |
| 36 | Roma | 54502 | 28 | Groningen | 47215 | 16 | Roda JC Kerk | 17500 |
| 31 | Arsenal | 51025 | 35 | Excelsior | 47192 | 40 | NAC Breda | 15700 |
| 39 | AC Milan | 50967 | 21 | Twente | 47044 | 26 | Willem II Tilb | 14700 |
| 27 | Feyenoord | 50777 | 18 | NEC Nijmegen | 46084 | 19 | Heerenveen | 14400 |
| 17 | Inter Milan | 50272 | 7 | Inter Milan | 45748 | 47 | Twente | 13400 |
| 48 | Heerenveen | 50272 | 10 | Feyenoord | 42200 | 3 | Groningen | 12400 |
| 23 | Roma | 50148 | 12 | Rosenborg BK | 42000 | 45 | NEC Nijmegen | 12250 |
| 24 | PSV Eindhoven | 49871 | 20 | Valencia | 40000 | 22 | De Graafschap | 11000 |
| 41 | Roda JC Kerk | 49421 | 14 | Lyon | 39000 | 43 | AZ Alkmaar | 7735 |
| 46 | De Graafschap | 49300 | 5 | Lyon | 37455 | 13 | RKC Waalwijk | 7300 |
| 38 | Roosendaal | 49182 | 29 | Arsenal | 35427 | 33 | Zwolle | 6865 |
| 44 | RKC Waalwijk | 49076 | 8 | NAC Breda | 35000 | 6 | Roosendaal | 5000 |
| 4 | Zwolle | 49003 | 37 | PSV Eindhoven | 35000 | 25 | Excelsior | 3478 |
| 34 | Valencia | 48633 | 1 | Utrecht | 34434 | | | |
| 15 | Willem II Tilb | 48248 | 2 | Vitesse Arnhem | 24200 | | | |
| 32 | Vitesse Arnhem | 48162 | 9 | Rosenborg BK | 21300 | | | |

■ Home □ Away ▒ Neutral

## KEY PLAYERS - GOALSCORERS

**1 Rafael van der Vaart**

| | | | |
|---|---|---|---|
| Goals in the League | 18 | Player Strike Rate<br>Average number of minutes between League goals scored by player | 95 |
| Contribution to Attacking Power<br>Average number of minutes between League team goals while on pitch | 27 | Club Strike Rate<br>Average number of minutes between League goals scored by club | 32 |

| | PLAYER | LGE GOALS | POWER | STRIKE RATE |
|---|---|---|---|---|
| 2 | Zlatan Ibrahimovic | 13 | 41 | 139 mins |
| 3 | Andy van der Meyde | 11 | 31 | 215 mins |
| 4 | Wesley Sneijder | 4 | 28 | 323 mins |
| 5 | Christian Chivu | 6 | 33 | 352 mins |

## KEY PLAYERS - MIDFIELDERS

**1 Scherrer Cabelino Andrade Maxw**

| | | | |
|---|---|---|---|
| Goals in the League | 4 | Contribution to Attacking Power<br>Average number of minutes between League team goals while on pitch | 32 |
| Defensive Rating<br>Average number of mins between League goals conceded while he was on the pitch | 132 | Scoring Difference<br>Defensive Rating minus Contribution to Attacking Power | 100 |

| | PLAYER | LGE GOALS | DEF RATE | POWER | SCORE DIFF |
|---|---|---|---|---|---|
| 2 | Rafael van der Vaart | 18 | 115 | 28 | 87 mins |
| 3 | Victor Sikora | 2 | 113 | 27 | 86 mins |
| 4 | Wesley Sneijder | 4 | 108 | 29 | 79 mins |
| 5 | Andy van der Meyde | 11 | 103 | 31 | 72 mins |

## KEY PLAYERS - DEFENDERS

**1 John O'Brien**

| | | | |
|---|---|---|---|
| Goals Conceded (GC)<br>The number of League goals conceded while he was on the pitch | 9 | Clean Sheets<br>In games when he played at least 70 minutes | 4 |
| Defensive Rating<br>Ave number of mins between League goals conceded while on the pitch | 118 | Club Defensive Rating<br>Average number of mins between League goals conceded by the club this season | 96 |

| | PLAYER | CON LGE | CLEAN SHEETS | DEF RATE |
|---|---|---|---|---|
| 2 | Christian Chivu | 18 | 8 | 117 mins |
| 3 | Nigel de Jong | 13 | 5 | 101 mins |
| 4 | Tomas Galasek | 26 | 8 | 99 mins |
| 5 | Hatem Trabelsi | 22 | 6 | 98 mins |

## KEY GOALKEEPER

**1 Bogdan Lonut Lobont**

| | |
|---|---|
| Goals Conceded in the League | 14 |
| Defensive Rating<br>Ave number of mins between League goals conceded while on the pitch | 109 |
| Counting Games<br>Games when he played at least 70 mins | 17 |
| Clean Sheets<br>In games when he played at least 70 mins | 5 |

## TOP POINT EARNERS

| | PLAYER | GAMES | AVE |
|---|---|---|---|
| 1 | O'Brien | 12 | 2.75 |
| 2 | van der Vaart | 18 | 2.72 |
| 3 | Chivu | 22 | 2.64 |
| 4 | Sneijder | 13 | 2.62 |
| 5 | Lobont | 17 | 2.53 |
| 6 | Maxwell | 21 | 2.43 |
| 7 | de Jong | 12 | 2.42 |
| 8 | van der Meyde | 24 | 2.38 |
| 9 | Trabelsi | 22 | 2.36 |
| 10 | Galasek | 26 | 2.35 |
| | CLUB AVERAGE: | | 2.44 |

Ave = Average points per match in Counting Games

## DISCIPLINARY RECORDS

| | PLAYER | YELLOW | RED | AVE |
|---|---|---|---|---|
| 1 | Boukhari | 3 | 0 | 259 |
| 2 | Chivu | 4 | 2 | 352 |
| 3 | Van Damme | 2 | 0 | 393 |
| 4 | Galasek | 5 | 0 | 517 |
| 5 | Witschge | 2 | 0 | 522 |
| 6 | Yakubu | 2 | 0 | 567 |
| 7 | Sneijder | 2 | 0 | 645 |
| 8 | Trabelsi | 3 | 0 | 721 |
| 9 | Mido | 0 | 1 | 823 |
| 10 | Sikora | 1 | 0 | 1014 |
| 11 | van der Meyde | 1 | 1 | 1180 |
| 12 | de Jong | 1 | 0 | 1311 |
| 13 | Lobont | 1 | 0 | 1530 |
| | Other | 5 | 0 | |
| | TOTAL | 32 | 4 | |

## LEAGUE GOALS

| | PLAYER | MINS | GOALS | AVE |
|---|---|---|---|---|
| 1 | van der Vaart | 1718 | 18 | 95 |
| 2 | Ibrahimovic | 1804 | 13 | 139 |
| 3 | van der Meyde | 2360 | 11 | 215 |
| 4 | Mido | 823 | 9 | 91 |
| 5 | Boukhari | 777 | 6 | 130 |
| 6 | Chivu | 2113 | 6 | 352 |
| 7 | Galasek | 2585 | 5 | 517 |
| 8 | Pienaar | 2232 | 5 | 446 |
| 9 | Litmanen | 744 | 5 | 149 |
| 10 | Sneijder | 1290 | 4 | 323 |
| 11 | Maxwell | 2239 | 4 | 560 |
| 12 | Pasanen | 1647 | 3 | 549 |
| 13 | Sikora | 1014 | 2 | 507 |
| | Other | | 5 | |
| | TOTAL | | 96 | |

## MONTH BY MONTH GUIDE TO THE POINTS

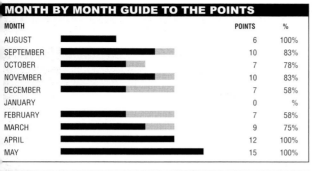

| MONTH | POINTS | % |
|---|---|---|
| AUGUST | 6 | 100% |
| SEPTEMBER | 10 | 83% |
| OCTOBER | 7 | 78% |
| NOVEMBER | 10 | 83% |
| DECEMBER | 7 | 58% |
| JANUARY | 0 | % |
| FEBRUARY | 7 | 58% |
| MARCH | 9 | 75% |
| APRIL | 12 | 100% |
| MAY | 15 | 100% |

## TEAM OF THE SEASON

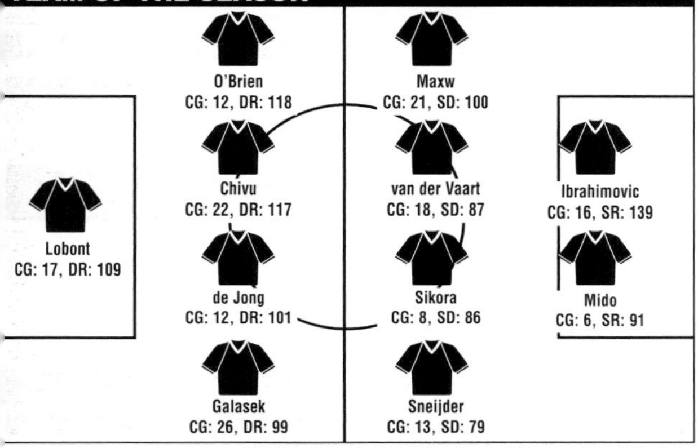
O'Brien
CG: 12, DR: 118
Maxw
CG: 21, SD: 100
Chivu
CG: 22, DR: 117
van der Vaart
CG: 18, SD: 87
Ibrahimovic
CG: 16, SR: 139
Lobont
CG: 17, DR: 109
de Jong
CG: 12, DR: 101
Sikora
CG: 8, SD: 86
Mido
CG: 6, SR: 91
Galasek
CG: 26, DR: 99
Sneijder
CG: 13, SD: 79

KEY: DR = Defensive Rate, SD = Scoring Difference, SR = Strike Rate,
CG = Counting Games – League games playing at least 70 minutes

## LEAGUE APPEARANCES, BOOKINGS AND CAPS

| | AGE | IN THE SQUAD | COUNTING GAMES | MINUTES ON PITCH | YELLOW CARDS | RED CARDS | THIS SEASON | HOME COUNTRY |
|---|---|---|---|---|---|---|---|---|
| **Goalkeepers** | | | | | | | | |
| Joe Dudilica | 25 | 24 | 6 | 570 | 0 | 0 | - | Australia |
| Fred Grim | 37 | 0 | 0 | 0 | 0 | 0 | - | |
| Bogdan L Lobont | 25 | 18 | 17 | 1530 | 1 | 0 | 5 | Romania (27) |
| Maarten Stekelenburg | 20 | 13 | 7 | 735 | 0 | 0 | - | Holland |
| Henk Timmer | 31 | 11 | 1 | 135 | 0 | 0 | - | Holland |
| **Defenders** | | | | | | | | |
| Andre Bergdolmo | 31 | 28 | 13 | 1238 | 0 | 0 | 8 | Norway (24) |
| Christian Chivu | 22 | 26 | 22 | 2113 | 4 | 2 | 8 | Romania (27) |
| Nigel de Jong | 18 | 25 | 12 | 1311 | 1 | 0 | - | Holland |
| Tomas Galasek | 30 | 31 | 26 | 2585 | 5 | 0 | 9 | Czech Republic (13) |
| John Heitinga | 19 | 1 | 0 | 45 | 1 | 0 | - | Holland |
| David Mendes | 20 | 5 | 0 | 0 | 0 | 0 | - | Holland |
| John O'Brien | 25 | 16 | 12 | 1060 | 0 | 0 | 1 | United States (10) |
| Petri Pasanen | 22 | 24 | 17 | 1647 | 1 | 0 | - | Finland |
| Hatem Trabelsi | 24 | 26 | 22 | 2165 | 3 | 0 | - | Tunisia |
| Jelle Van Damme | 19 | 17 | 8 | 786 | 2 | 0 | 1 | Belgium (16) |
| Abubakarl Yakubu | 21 | 29 | 11 | 1135 | 2 | 0 | - | Ghana |
| **Midfielders** | | | | | | | | |
| Michael Kron Delhi | 20 | 1 | 0 | 0 | 0 | 0 | - | Denmark |
| Scherrer Maxw | 21 | 29 | 21 | 2239 | 1 | 0 | - | Brazil |
| Steven Pienaar | 21 | 33 | 21 | 2232 | 1 | 0 | - | South Africa |
| Stephano Seedorf | 21 | 8 | 0 | 81 | 0 | 0 | - | Holland |
| Victor Sikora | 25 | 19 | 8 | 1014 | 1 | 0 | - | Holland |
| Wesley Sneijder | 19 | 18 | 13 | 1290 | 2 | 0 | 1 | Holland (6) |
| Andy van der Meyde | 23 | 29 | 24 | 2360 | 1 | 1 | 3 | Holland (6) |
| Rafael van der Vaart | 20 | 21 | 18 | 1718 | 0 | 0 | 6 | Holland (6) |
| Jan van Halst | 34 | 12 | 0 | 43 | 1 | 0 | - | |
| Aron Winter | 36 | 2 | 0 | 0 | 0 | 0 | - | Holland |
| Richard Witschge | 33 | 29 | 5 | 1044 | 2 | 0 | - | Holland |
| **Forwards** | | | | | | | | |
| Jamal Akachar | 20 | 1 | 0 | 33 | 0 | 0 | - | Morocco |
| Nourdin Boukhari | 23 | 30 | 5 | 777 | 3 | 0 | - | Morocco |
| Zlatan Ibrahimovic | 21 | 27 | 16 | 1804 | 0 | 0 | 4 | Sweden (20) |
| Jari Litmanen | 32 | 14 | 5 | 744 | 0 | 0 | - | Finland |
| Nikos Machlas | 30 | 6 | 1 | 90 | 0 | 0 | - | Greece |
| Ahmed Mido | 20 | 18 | 6 | 823 | 0 | 1 | - | Egypt |
| Wamberto | 28 | 10 | 1 | 246 | 0 | 0 | - | Brazil |

KEY: LEAGUE BOOKINGS CAPS (FIFA RANKING)

## SQUAD APPEARANCES

| Match | 1 | 2 | 3 | 4 | 5 | 6 | 7 | 8 | 9 | 10 | 11 | 12 | 13 | 14 | 15 | 16 | 17 | 18 | 19 | 20 | 21 | 22 | 23 | 24 | 25 | 26 | 27 | 28 | 29 | 30 | 31 | 32 | 33 | 34 | 35 | 36 | 37 | 38 | 39 | 40 | 41 | 42 | 43 | 44 | 45 | 46 | 47 | 48 |
|---|---|---|---|---|---|---|---|---|---|---|---|---|---|---|---|---|---|---|---|---|---|---|---|---|---|---|---|---|---|---|---|---|---|---|---|---|---|---|---|---|---|---|---|---|---|---|---|---|
| Venue | H | A | A | H | H | A | A | H | A | A | H | H | A | A | H | A | H | H | A | A | H | A | H | H | A | A | H | H | A | A | H | H | A | H | H | A | A | H | H | A | H | A | A | H | A | H | A | H |
| Competition | L | L | L | L | C | L | C | L | C | L | L | C | L | C | L | L | C | L | L | C | L | L | C | L | L | L | L | L | C | L | C | L | L | C | L | C | L | L | C | L | L | C | L | L | L | L | L | L |
| Result | W | W | W | W | W | W | L | D | D | W | W | D | D | W | W | D | L | W | W | D | W | D | W | L | W | W | D | W | D | L | D | W | W | D | W | D | L | W | D | W | W | L | W | W | W | W | W | W |

**Goalkeepers**
Joe Dudilica
Fred Grim
Bogdan Lobont
Maarten Stekelenburg
Henk Timmer

**Defenders**
Andre Bergdolmo
Christian Chivu
Nigel de Jong
John Heitinga
David Mendes Da Silva
John O'Brien
Petri Pasanen
Hatem Trabelsi
Jelle Van Damme
Abubakarl Yakubu

**Midfielders**
Tomas Galasek
Michael Kron Delhi
Scherrer Cabelino Maxw
Steven Pienaar
Stephano Seedorf
Victor Sikora
Wesley Sneijder
Andy van der Meyde
Rafael van der Vaart
Jan van Halst
Aron Winter
Richard Witschge

**Forwards**
Jamal Akachar
Nourdin Boukhari
Zlatan Ibrahimovic
Jari Litmanen
Nikos Machlas
Ahmed Hossam Mido
Wamberto

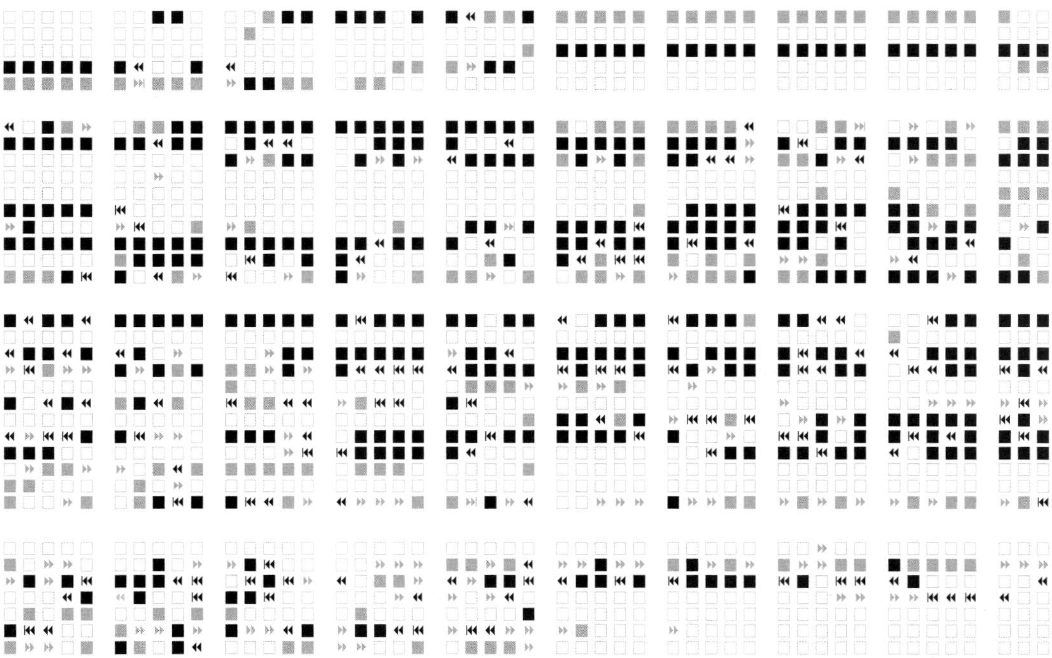

# FEYENOORD

Final Position: **3rd**

| | | | | | | |
|---|---|---|---|---|---|---|
| 1 | ecql1 | Fenerbahce | H | W | 1-0 | Ono 64 |
| 2 | lge | NEC Nijmegen | H | W | 2-0 | Kalou 77; Emerton 80 |
| 3 | lge | Roda JC Kerk | A | D | 2-2 | Paauwe 13; van Hooijdonk 81 |
| 4 | ecqll2 | Fenerbahce | A | W | 2-0 | Ono 48; Buffel 88 |
| 5 | escup | Real Madrid | A | L | 1-3 | van Hooijdonk 56 |
| 6 | lge | Excelsior | H | W | 4-1 | van Hooijdonk 11 pen,14; Pardo 53; Bombarda 90 |
| 7 | lge | Twente | A | W | 5-1 | Ono 24,45; Buffel 40,76; van Hooijdonk 70 |
| 8 | ecge | Juventus | H | D | 1-1 | van Hooijdonk 75 |
| 9 | lge | De Graafschap | H | W | 2-0 | van Hooijdonk 6; Buffel 56 |
| 10 | ecge | Newcastle | H | W | 1-0 | Pardo 4 |
| 11 | lge | Roosendaal | A | L | 2-4 | Buffel 30; van Hooijdonk 78 |
| 12 | ecge | Dinamo Kiev | H | D | 0-0 | |
| 13 | lge | Ajax | H | L | 1-2 | van Hooijdonk 56 |
| 14 | lge | Vitesse Arnhem | A | D | 1-1 | Buffel 57 |
| 15 | ecge | Dinamo Kiev | A | L | 0-2 | |
| 16 | lge | Willem II Tilb | H | W | 5-1 | Bosvelt 14; Kalou 45; Lurling 47,67; Song 51 |
| 17 | ecge | Juventus | A | L | 0-2 | |
| 18 | lge | Groningen | A | W | 2-0 | Buffel 50; Ono 64 |
| 19 | lge | Zwolle | H | W | 2-0 | Ono 65 pen; Bombarda 67 |
| 20 | ecge | Newcastle | H | L | 2-3 | Bombarda 65; Lurling 71 |
| 21 | lge | PSV Eindhoven | A | W | 2-1 | Ono 28; Buffel 43 |
| 22 | lge | RKC Waalwijk | A | L | 0-1 | |
| 23 | lge | Utrecht | H | W | 2-1 | Emerton 32; Bosvelt 90 |
| 24 | lge | Heerenveen | A | L | 1-3 | Bosvelt 57 |
| 25 | lge | AZ Alkmaar | H | W | 6-1 | Ono 2,86; van Hooijdonk 17,62; Pardo 26; Bombarda 89 |
| 26 | lge | NAC Breda | A | D | 1-1 | Pardo 6 |
| 27 | lge | Twente | H | W | 4-2 | Kalou 10,66; Buffel 70; van Persie 88 |
| 28 | lge | Ajax | A | D | 1-1 | van Persie 44 |
| 29 | lge | AZ Alkmaar | A | W | 4-1 | van Persie 12; van Hooijdonk 15,30; Kalou 18 |
| 30 | lge | Groningen | H | W | 4-1 | van Hooijdonk 32,35; Emerton 39; Buffel 52 |
| 31 | lge | NAC Breda | H | W | 2-1 | Buffel 14; van Hooijdonk 86 |
| 32 | lge | Excelsior | A | W | 6-2 | van Persie 13; Buffel 25,87; van Hooijdonk 35,90 pen; Kalou 50 |
| 33 | lge | NEC Nijmegen | A | W | 2-1 | van Hooijdonk 37,87 |
| 34 | lge | Heerenveen | H | W | 5-0 | Buffel 10; van Persie 50; van Hooijdonk 58,62,66 pen |
| 35 | lge | De Graafschap | A | W | 4-3 | van Persie 25; Buffel 40; Kalou 77; van Hooijdonk 84 pen |
| 36 | lge | Vitesse Arnhem | H | W | 2-1 | van Persie 19; Lurling 90 |
| 37 | lge | Zwolle | A | W | 3-1 | Buffel 4; van Hooijdonk 14,89 |
| 38 | lge | Roosendaal | H | W | 1-0 | Paauwe 90 |
| 39 | lge | Utrecht | A | W | 2-1 | van Persie 3; Buffel 71 |
| 40 | lge | RKC Waalwijk | H | W | 2-1 | Kalou 38; van Hooijdonk 77 |
| 41 | lge | PSV Eindhoven | H | W | 3-1 | van Hooijdonk 34 pen,45,66 pen |
| 42 | lge | Willem II Tilb | A | D | 1-1 | Kalou 73 |
| 43 | lge | Roda JC Kerk | H | W | 3-1 | Kalou 29; van Persie 38; Buffel 78 |

## KEY PLAYERS - GOALSCORERS

**1 Pierre van Hooijdonk**

| | | | |
|---|---|---|---|
| Goals in the League | 28 | Player Strike Rate<br>Average number of minutes between League goals scored by player | 85 |
| Contribution to Attacking Power<br>Average number of minutes between League team goals while on pitch | 33 | Club Strike Rate<br>Average number of minutes between League goals scored by club | 34 |

| | PLAYER | LGE GOALS | POWER | STRIKE RATE |
|---|---|---|---|---|
| 2 | Thomas Buffel | 17 | 34 | 149 mins |
| 3 | Bonaventure Kalou | 10 | 34 | 208 mins |
| 4 | Shinji Ono | 7 | 33 | 345 mins |
| 5 | Paul Bosvelt | 3 | 33 | 925 mins |

## KEY PLAYERS - MIDFIELDERS

**1 Anthony Lurling**

| | | | |
|---|---|---|---|
| Goals in the League | 3 | Contribution to Attacking Power<br>Average number of minutes between League team goals while on pitch | 41 |
| Defensive Rating<br>Average number of mins between League goals conceded while he was on the pitch | 109 | Scoring Difference<br>Defensive Rating minus Contribution to Attacking Power | 68 |

| | PLAYER | LGE GOALS | DEF RATE | POWER | SCORE DIFF |
|---|---|---|---|---|---|
| 2 | Patrick Paauwe | 2 | 87 | 33 | 54 mins |
| 3 | Thomas Buffel | 17 | 84 | 35 | 49 mins |
| 4 | Shinji Ono | 7 | 83 | 34 | 49 mins |
| 5 | Brett Emerton | 3 | 80 | 34 | 46 mins |

## KEY PLAYERS - DEFENDERS

**1 Gerard de Nooijer**

| | | | |
|---|---|---|---|
| Goals Conceded (GC)<br>The number of League goals conceded while he was on the pitch | 13 | Clean Sheets<br>In games when he played at least 70 minutes | 2 |
| Defensive Rating<br>Ave number of mins between League goals conceded while on the pitch | 92 | Club Defensive Rating<br>Average number of mins between League goals conceded by the club this season | 78 |

| | PLAYER | CON LGE | CLEAN SHEETS | DEF RATE |
|---|---|---|---|---|
| 2 | Kees van Wonderen | 31 | 6 | 83 mins |

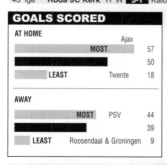

## GOALS SCORED

**AT HOME**

| | | |
|---|---|---|
| MOST | Ajax | 57 |
| | | 50 |
| LEAST | Twente | 18 |

**AWAY**

| | | |
|---|---|---|
| MOST | PSV | 44 |
| | | 39 |
| LEAST | Roosendaal & Groningen | 9 |

## GOALS CONCEDED

**AT HOME**

| | | |
|---|---|---|
| LEAST | PSV | 7 |
| | | 14 |
| MOST | Excelsior | 38 |

**AWAY**

| | | |
|---|---|---|
| LEAST | PSV | 13 |
| | | 25 |
| MOST | De G'schap | 50 |

## KEY GOALKEEPER

**1 Patrick Lodewijks**

| | |
|---|---|
| Goals Conceded in the League | 22 |
| Defensive Rating<br>Ave number of mins between League goals conceded while on the pitch | 90 |
| Counting Games<br>Games when he played at least 70 mins | 22 |
| Clean Sheets<br>In games when he played at least 70 mins | 4 |

## TOP POINT EARNERS

| | PLAYER | GAMES | AVE |
|---|---|---|---|
| 1 | Lodewijks | 22 | 2.73 |
| 2 | de Nooijer | 12 | 2.67 |
| 3 | Kalou | 19 | 2.47 |
| 4 | Paauwe | 30 | 2.43 |
| 5 | van Wonderen | 28 | 2.43 |
| 6 | Buffel | 27 | 2.37 |
| 7 | van Hooijdonk | 26 | 2.35 |
| 8 | Emerton | 33 | 2.33 |
| 9 | Bosvelt | 31 | 2.29 |
| 10 | Ono | 26 | 2.23 |
| | **CLUB AVERAGE:** | | **2.35** |

Ave = Average points per match in Counting Games

## ATTENDANCES

**HOME GROUND: DE KUIP CAPACITY: 51177 AVERAGE LEAGUE AT HOME: 44035**

| | | | | | | | | |
|---|---|---|---|---|---|---|---|---|
| 28 | Ajax | 50777 | 4 | Fenerbahce | 43000 | 26 | NAC Breda | 15340 |
| 15 | Dinamo Kiev | 50000 | 13 | Ajax | 42200 | 42 | Willem II Tilb | 14600 |
| 9 | De Graafschap | 50000 | 23 | Utrecht | 42000 | 24 | Heerenveen | 14400 |
| 40 | RKC Waalwijk | 47000 | 8 | Juventus | 42000 | 3 | Roda JC Kerk | 13000 |
| 34 | Heerenveen | 46200 | 27 | Twente | 42000 | 18 | Groningen | 12800 |
| 36 | Vitesse Arnhem | 46000 | 10 | Newcastle | 40540 | 33 | NEC Nijmegen | 12500 |
| 43 | Roda JC Kerk | 45000 | 31 | NAC Breda | 40100 | 7 | Twente | 12000 |
| 20 | Newcastle | 45000 | 12 | Dinamo Kiev | 40000 | 35 | De Graafschap | 11000 |
| 41 | PSV Eindhoven | 45000 | 2 | NEC Nijmegen | 40000 | 29 | AZ Alkmaar | 8072 |
| 19 | Zwolle | 44000 | 17 | Juventus | 35789 | 37 | Zwolle | 6865 |
| 16 | Willem II Tilb | 44000 | 21 | PSV Eindhoven | 35200 | 22 | RKC Waalwijk | 6000 |
| 25 | AZ Alkmaar | 44000 | 14 | Vitesse Arnhem | 26000 | 11 | Roosendaal | 5000 |
| 38 | Roosendaal | 44000 | 1 | Fenerbahce | 25500 | 32 | Excelsior | 3500 |
| 30 | Groningen | 44000 | 5 | Real Madrid | 20000 | | | |
| 6 | Excelsior | 43100 | 39 | Utrecht | 18925 | | | |

■ Home □ Away ▨ Neutral

## DISCIPLINARY RECORDS

| | PLAYER | YELLOW | RED | AVE |
|---|---|---|---|---|
| 1 | de Nooijer | 3 | 1 | 299 |
| 2 | van Persie | 3 | 1 | 350 |
| 3 | Lurling | 3 | 0 | 436 |
| 4 | Buffel | 4 | 1 | 505 |
| 5 | van Wonderen | 4 | 0 | 644 |
| 6 | Loovens | 1 | 0 | 644 |
| 7 | Bosvelt | 4 | 0 | 693 |
| 8 | Rzasa | 1 | 0 | 883 |
| 9 | Paauwe | 3 | 0 | 932 |
| 10 | Song | 1 | 0 | 1305 |
| 11 | Lodewijks | 1 | 0 | 1980 |
| 12 | Kalou | 1 | 0 | 2077 |
| 13 | van Hooijdonk | 1 | 0 | 2384 |
| | Other | 1 | 0 | |
| | TOTAL | 31 | 3 | |

## LEAGUE GOALS

| | PLAYER | MINS | GOALS | AVE |
|---|---|---|---|---|
| 1 | van Hooijdonk | 2384 | 28 | 85 |
| 2 | Buffel | 2526 | 17 | 149 |
| 3 | Kalou | 2077 | 10 | 208 |
| 4 | van Persie | 1402 | 9 | 156 |
| 5 | Ono | 2412 | 7 | 345 |
| 6 | Lurling | 1308 | 3 | 436 |
| 7 | Emerton | 2953 | 3 | 984 |
| 8 | Pardo | 703 | 3 | 234 |
| 9 | Bombarda | 486 | 3 | 162 |
| 10 | Bosvelt | 2775 | 3 | 925 |
| 11 | Paauwe | 2796 | 2 | 1398 |
| 12 | Song | 1305 | 1 | 1305 |
| | Other | | 0 | |
| | TOTAL | | 89 | |

## MONTH BY MONTH GUIDE TO THE POINTS

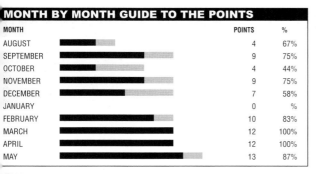

| MONTH | POINTS | % |
|---|---|---|
| AUGUST | 4 | 67% |
| SEPTEMBER | 9 | 75% |
| OCTOBER | 4 | 44% |
| NOVEMBER | 9 | 75% |
| DECEMBER | 7 | 58% |
| JANUARY | 0 | % |
| FEBRUARY | 10 | 83% |
| MARCH | 12 | 100% |
| APRIL | 12 | 100% |
| MAY | 13 | 87% |

## TEAM OF THE SEASON

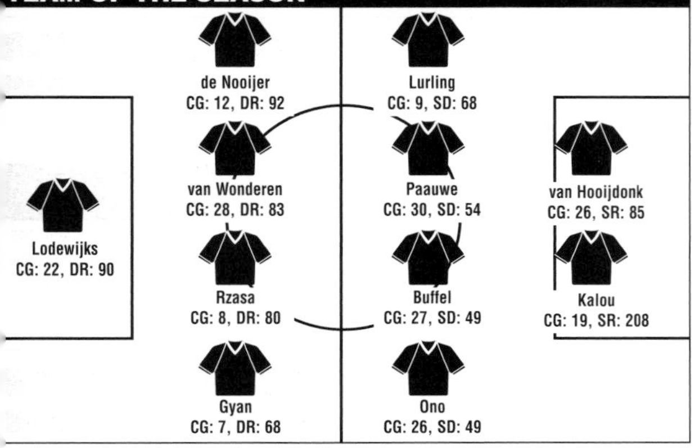
de Nooijer
CG: 12, DR: 92
Lurling
CG: 9, SD: 68
van Wonderen
CG: 28, DR: 83
Paauwe
CG: 30, SD: 54
van Hooijdonk
CG: 26, SR: 85
Lodewijks
CG: 22, DR: 90
Rzasa
CG: 8, DR: 80
Buffel
CG: 27, SD: 49
Kalou
CG: 19, SR: 208
Gyan
CG: 7, DR: 68
Ono
CG: 26, SD: 49

KEY: DR = Defensive Rate, SD = Scoring Difference, SR = Strike Rate, CG = Counting Games – League games playing at least 70 minutes

## LEAGUE APPEARANCES, BOOKINGS AND CAPS

| | AGE | IN THE SQUAD | COUNTING GAMES | MINUTES ON PITCH | YELLOW CARDS | RED CARDS | THIS SEASON | HOME COUNTRY |
|---|---|---|---|---|---|---|---|---|
| **Goalkeepers** | | | | | | | | |
| Carlo L'Ami | 36 | 6 | 2 | 188 | 0 | 0 | - | Holland |
| Patrick Lodewijks | 36 | 30 | 22 | 1980 | 1 | 0 | - | Holland |
| Edwin Zoetebier | 33 | 27 | 9 | 810 | 0 | 0 | - | Holland |
| **Defenders** | | | | | | | | |
| Pieter Collen | 23 | 3 | 0 | 0 | 0 | 0 | - | Belgium |
| Gerard de Nooijer | 34 | 16 | 12 | 1199 | 3 | 1 | - | Holland |
| Christian Gyan | 24 | 27 | 7 | 813 | 0 | 0 | - | Ghana |
| Glenn Loovens | 19 | 23 | 6 | 644 | 1 | 0 | - | Holland |
| Tomasz Rzasa | 30 | 30 | 8 | 883 | 1 | 0 | 1 | Poland (29) |
| Civard Sprockel | 20 | 1 | 0 | 0 | 0 | 0 | - | Holland |
| Ramon van Haaren | 30 | 6 | 6 | 523 | 0 | 0 | - | Holland |
| Kees van Wonderen | 34 | 29 | 28 | 2578 | 4 | 0 | - | Holland |
| Yue-Ting-Chiung | 18 | 1 | 0 | 0 | 0 | 0 | - | China |
| **Midfielders** | | | | | | | | |
| Jorge Acuna | 24 | 15 | 3 | 567 | 0 | 0 | - | Chile |
| Paul Bosvelt | 33 | 32 | 31 | 2775 | 4 | 0 | 39 | Feyenoord (0) |
| Thomas Buffel | 22 | 32 | 27 | 2526 | 4 | 1 | 7 | Belgium (16) |
| Ferry de Haan | 30 | 15 | 1 | 81 | 0 | 0 | - | Holland |
| Brett Emerton | 24 | 34 | 33 | 2953 | 1 | 0 | - | Australia |
| Jesper Hogedoorn | | 2 | 1 | 82 | 0 | 0 | - | |
| Leonardo dos Santos | 26 | 3 | 0 | 7 | 0 | 0 | - | Brazil |
| Anthony Lurling | 26 | 33 | 9 | 1308 | 3 | 0 | - | Holland |
| Shinji Ono | 23 | 30 | 26 | 2412 | 0 | 0 | 2 | Japan (23) |
| Patrick Paauwe | 27 | 32 | 30 | 2796 | 3 | 0 | 1 | Holland (6) |
| Sebastien Pardo | 21 | 29 | 3 | 703 | 0 | 0 | - | Chile |
| Ferne Snojil | 18 | 1 | 0 | 0 | 0 | 0 | - | Holland |
| Chong- Gug Song | 24 | 21 | 12 | 1305 | 1 | 0 | - | South Korea |
| Bas Van Wegen | | 2 | 0 | 0 | 0 | 0 | - | |
| **Forwards** | | | | | | | | |
| Mariano Bombarda | 30 | 30 | 2 | 486 | 0 | 0 | - | Argentina |
| Johan Elmander | 22 | 2 | 0 | 2 | 0 | 0 | - | |
| Bonaventure Kalou | 25 | 33 | 19 | 2077 | 1 | 0 | - | Ivory Coast |
| Leonardo Santiago | 20 | 4 | 0 | 45 | 0 | 0 | - | Brazil |
| Euzebiusz Smolarek | 22 | 1 | 0 | 0 | 0 | 0 | - | Poland |
| Pierre van Hooijdonk | 33 | 28 | 26 | 2384 | 1 | 0 | 6 | Holland (6) |
| Robin van Persie | 19 | 28 | 11 | 1402 | 3 | 1 | - | Holland |

KEY: LEAGUE BOOKINGS CAPS (FIFA RANKING)

## SQUAD APPEARANCES

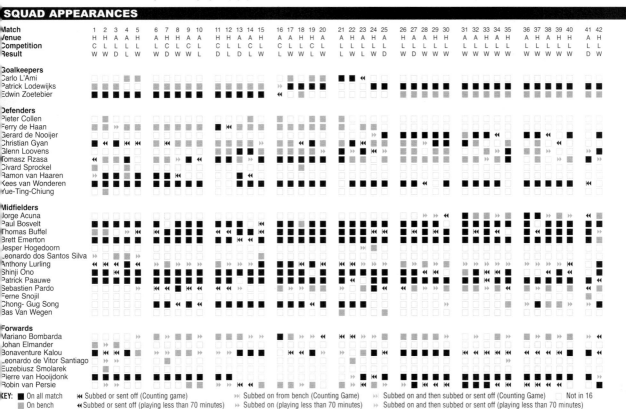

| Match | 1 | 2 | 3 | 4 | 5 | 6 | 7 | 8 | 9 | 10 | 11 | 12 | 13 | 14 | 15 | 16 | 17 | 18 | 19 | 20 | 21 | 22 | 23 | 24 | 25 | 26 | 27 | 28 | 29 | 30 | 31 | 32 | 33 | 34 | 35 | 36 | 37 | 38 | 39 | 40 | 41 | 42 |
|---|---|---|---|---|---|---|---|---|---|---|---|---|---|---|---|---|---|---|---|---|---|---|---|---|---|---|---|---|---|---|---|---|---|---|---|---|---|---|---|---|---|---|
| Venue | H | H | A | A | H | A | H | H | A | A | H | H | A | A | H | A | A | H | H | A | A | H | A | H | A | H | A | A | H | H | A | A | H | A | H | A | H | A | H | H | A | H |
| Competition | C | L | L | L | L | L | C | L | C | L | C | L | L | C | L | C | L | L | C | L | L | L | L | L | L | L | L | L | L | L | L | L | L | L | L | L | L | L | L | L | L | L |
| Result | W | W | D | L | W | W | D | W | W | L | D | L | D | L | W | L | W | W | L | W | L | W | L | W | D | W | D | W | W | W | W | W | W | W | W | W | W | W | W | W | D | W |

**Goalkeepers**
Carlo L'Ami
Patrick Lodewijks
Edwin Zoetebier

**Defenders**
Pieter Collen
Ferry de Haan
Gerard de Nooijer
Christian Gyan
Glenn Loovens
Tomasz Rzasa
Civard Sprockel
Ramon van Haaren
Kees van Wonderen
Yue-Ting-Chiung

**Midfielders**
Jorge Acuna
Paul Bosvelt
Thomas Buffel
Brett Emerton
Jesper Hogedoorn
Leonardo dos Santos Silva
Anthony Lurling
Shinji Ono
Patrick Paauwe
Sebastien Pardo
Ferne Snojil
Chong- Gug Song
Bas Van Wegen

**Forwards**
Mariano Bombarda
Johan Elmander
Bonaventure Kalou
Leonardo de Vitor Santiago
Euzebiusz Smolarek
Pierre van Hooijdonk
Robin van Persie

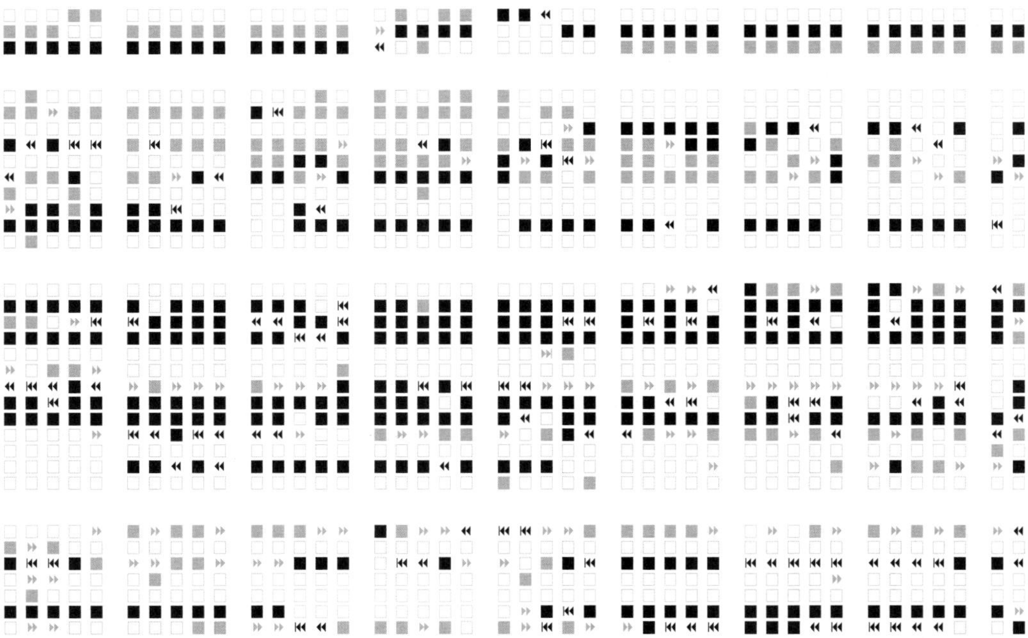

KEY: On all match | On bench | Subbed or sent off (Counting game) | Subbed or sent off (playing less than 70 minutes) | Subbed on from bench (Counting Game) | Subbed on (playing less than 70 minutes) | Subbed on and then subbed or sent off (Counting Game) | Subbed on and then subbed or sent off (playing less than 70 minutes) | Not in 16

# NAC BREDA

Final Position: **4th**

| | | | | | | |
|---|---|---|---|---|---|---|
| 1 | lge | Roda JC Kerk | H | D | 2-2 | Slot 24; Feher 52 |
| 2 | lge | Willem II Tilb | A | D | 1-1 | Van den Eede 24 |
| 3 | lge | NEC Nijmegen | H | D | 0-0 | |
| 4 | lge | Heerenveen | A | W | 2-0 | Engelaar 12,23 |
| 5 | lge | Twente | H | W | 2-0 | Bobson 35; Stewart 79 |
| 6 | lge | Ajax | A | D | 2-2 | Bobson 3; Stewart 21 |
| 7 | lge | PSV Eindhoven | H | D | 2-2 | Engelaar 31,77 |
| 8 | lge | Zwolle | A | W | 3-0 | Engelaar 23; Feher 35; Penders 49 |
| 9 | lge | Vitesse Arnhem | H | D | 0-0 | |
| 10 | lge | Utrecht | A | L | 0-1 | |
| 11 | lge | Groningen | H | D | 0-0 | |
| 12 | lge | Excelsior | A | W | 3-0 | Engelaar 29; Boussaboun 51; Penders 60 |
| 13 | lge | De Graafschap | A | L | 2-3 | Feher 18; Boussaboun 24 |
| 14 | lge | Roosendaal | H | W | 1-0 | Bobson 71 |
| 15 | lge | RKC Waalwijk | H | W | 1-0 | Engelaar 26 |
| 16 | lge | Feyenoord | H | D | 1-1 | Feher 86 |
| 17 | lge | Heerenveen | H | D | 1-1 | Feher 40 |
| 18 | lge | NEC Nijmegen | A | L | 0-2 | |
| 19 | lge | Excelsior | H | W | 2-1 | Engelaar 21; Schreuder 77 |
| 20 | lge | AZ Alkmaar | A | L | 1-3 | Van den Eede 54 |
| 21 | lge | PSV Eindhoven | A | L | 0-1 | |
| 22 | lge | Feyenoord | A | L | 1-2 | Boussaboun 5 |
| 23 | lge | De Graafschap | H | W | 1-0 | Bobson 32 |
| 24 | lge | Roda JC Kerk | A | D | 0-0 | |
| 25 | lge | Willem II Tilb | H | D | 0-0 | |
| 26 | lge | Twente | A | D | 0-0 | |
| 27 | lge | Ajax | H | L | 0-3 | |
| 28 | lge | Groningen | A | D | 0-0 | |
| 29 | lge | Vitesse Arnhem | A | L | 1-3 | Engelaar 49 |
| 30 | lge | Zwolle | H | W | 2-0 | Slot 2,78 |
| 31 | lge | Utrecht | H | W | 2-0 | Engelaar 31; Bobson 68 |
| 32 | lge | RKC Waalwijk | A | W | 3-2 | Engelaar 51; Boussaboun 60; Diba 87 |
| 33 | lge | AZ Alkmaar | H | W | 4-0 | Penders 31; Schreuder 44; Engelaar 52 pen; Koning 90 |
| 34 | lge | Roosendaal | A | W | 2-1 | Slot 8; Bobson 51 |

## KEY PLAYERS - GOALSCORERS

**1 Orlando Engelaar**

| | | | |
|---|---|---|---|
| Goals in the League | 12 | Player Strike Rate<br>Average number of minutes between League goals scored by player | 224 |
| Contribution to Attacking Power<br>Average number of minutes between League team goals while on pitch | 72 | Club Strike Rate<br>Average number of minutes between League goals scored by club | 73 |

| | PLAYER | LGE GOALS | POWER | STRIKE RATE |
|---|---|---|---|---|
| 2 | Arne Slot | 4 | 88 | 464 mins |
| 3 | Ali Boussaboun | 4 | 79 | 478 mins |
| 4 | Kevin Bobson | 6 | 73 | 479 mins |
| 5 | Csaba Feher | 5 | 71 | 604 mins |

## KEY PLAYERS - MIDFIELDERS

**1 Nebosja Gudelj**

| | | | |
|---|---|---|---|
| Goals in the League | 0 | Contribution to Attacking Power<br>Average number of minutes between League team goals while on pitch | 70 |
| Defensive Rating<br>Average number of mins between League goals conceded while he was on the pitch | 106 | Scoring Difference<br>Defensive Rating minus Contribution to Attacking Power | 36 |

| | PLAYER | LGE GOALS | DEF RATE | POWER | SCORE DIFF |
|---|---|---|---|---|---|
| 2 | Alfred Schreuder | 2 | 102 | 73 | 29 mins |
| 3 | Arne Slot | 4 | 109 | 88 | 21 mins |

## KEY PLAYERS - DEFENDERS

**1 Rob Penders**

| | | | |
|---|---|---|---|
| Goals Conceded (GC)<br>The number of League goals conceded while he was on the pitch | 21 | Clean Sheets<br>In games when he played at least 70 minutes | 16 |
| Defensive Rating<br>Ave number of mins between League goals conceded while on the pitch | 118 | Club Defensive Rating<br>Average number of mins between League goals conceded by the club this season | 99 |

| | PLAYER | CON LGE | CLEAN SHEETS | DEF RATE |
|---|---|---|---|---|
| 2 | Jurgen Colin | 28 | 15 | 101 mins |
| 3 | Csaba Feher | 31 | 16 | 97 mins |
| 4 | Mark Schenning | 24 | 12 | 93 mins |

## GOALS SCORED

AT HOME

| | | |
|---|---|---|
| MOST | Ajax | 57 |
| | | 21 |
| LEAST | Twente | 18 |

AWAY

| | | |
|---|---|---|
| MOST | PSV | 44 |
| | | 21 |
| LEAST | Roosendaal & Groningen | 9 |

## GOALS CONCEDED

AT HOME

| | | |
|---|---|---|
| LEAST | PSV | 7 |
| | | 10 |
| MOST | Excelsior | 38 |

AWAY

| | | |
|---|---|---|
| LEAST | PSV | 13 |
| | | 21 |
| MOST | De G'schap | 50 |

## KEY GOALKEEPER

**1 Gabor Babos**

| | |
|---|---|
| Goals Conceded in the League | 31 |
| Defensive Rating<br>Ave number of mins between League goals conceded while on the pitch | 99 |
| Counting Games<br>Games when he played at least 70 mins | 34 |
| Clean Sheets<br>In games when he played at least 70 mins | 17 |

## TOP POINT EARNERS

| | PLAYER | GAMES | AVE |
|---|---|---|---|
| 1 | Penders | 27 | 1.74 |
| 2 | Engelaar | 29 | 1.59 |
| 3 | Boussaboun | 18 | 1.56 |
| 4 | Feher | 33 | 1.55 |
| 5 | Colin | 31 | 1.55 |
| 6 | Babos | 34 | 1.53 |
| 7 | Gudelj | 30 | 1.53 |
| 8 | Schreuder | 34 | 1.53 |
| 9 | Bobson | 32 | 1.53 |
| 10 | Slot | 19 | 1.47 |
| | CLUB AVERAGE: | | 1.53 |

Ave = Average points per match in Counting Games

## ATTENDANCES

HOME GROUND: FUJIFILM-STADION CAPACITY: 16400 AVERAGE LEAGUE AT HOME: 13646

| | | | | | | | | |
|---|---|---|---|---|---|---|---|---|
| 22 | Feyenoord | 40100 | 33 | AZ Alkmaar | 14268 | 19 | Excelsior | 12153 |
| 6 | Ajax | 35000 | 2 | Willem II Tilb | 13910 | 17 | Heerenveen | 12123 |
| 21 | PSV Eindhoven | 33500 | 11 | Groningen | 13874 | 13 | De Graafschap | 11000 |
| 29 | Vitesse Arnhem | 22130 | 15 | RKC Waalwijk | 13585 | 18 | NEC Nijmegen | 11000 |
| 27 | Ajax | 15700 | 3 | NEC Nijmegen | 13440 | 30 | Zwolle | 9912 |
| 16 | Feyenoord | 15340 | 24 | Roda JC Kerk | 13300 | 20 | AZ Alkmaar | 7152 |
| 7 | PSV Eindhoven | 15259 | 26 | Twente | 13250 | 32 | RKC Waalwijk | 7100 |
| 14 | Roosendaal | 14872 | 5 | Twente | 13246 | 8 | Zwolle | 6250 |
| 9 | Vitesse Arnhem | 14858 | 1 | Roda JC Kerk | 13104 | 34 | Roosendaal | 5000 |
| 10 | Utrecht | 14500 | 23 | De Graafschap | 13024 | 12 | Excelsior | 2948 |
| 25 | Willem II Tilb | 14325 | 28 | Groningen | 13000 | | | |
| 4 | Heerenveen | 14300 | 31 | Utrecht | 12915 | | | |

■ Home □ Away ▒ Neutral

## DISCIPLINARY RECORDS

| | PLAYER | YELLOW | RED | AVE |
|---|---|---|---|---|
| 1 | Mensah | 2 | 0 | 310 |
| 2 | Van den Eede | 3 | 0 | 357 |
| 3 | Penders | 6 | 0 | 413 |
| 4 | Diba | 1 | 0 | 459 |
| 5 | Koning | 1 | 0 | 503 |
| 6 | Schenning | 4 | 0 | 556 |
| 7 | Engelaar | 3 | 0 | 897 |
| 8 | Gudelj | 2 | 1 | 916 |
| 9 | Bobson | 3 | 0 | 958 |
| 10 | Feher | 3 | 0 | 1006 |
| 11 | Schreuder | 3 | 0 | 1016 |
| 12 | Colin | 2 | 0 | 1411 |
| 13 | Boussaboun | 1 | 0 | 1910 |
| | Other | 4 | 0 | |
| | TOTAL | 38 | 1 | |

## LEAGUE GOALS

| | PLAYER | MINS | GOALS | AVE |
|---|---|---|---|---|
| 1 | Engelaar | 2691 | 12 | 224 |
| 2 | Bobson | 2875 | 6 | 479 |
| 3 | Feher | 3019 | 5 | 604 |
| 4 | Slot | 1854 | 4 | 464 |
| 5 | Boussaboun | 1910 | 4 | 478 |
| 6 | Penders | 2483 | 3 | 828 |
| 7 | Schreuder | 3050 | 2 | 1525 |
| 8 | Stewart | 837 | 2 | 419 |
| 9 | Van den Eede | 1071 | 2 | 536 |
| 10 | Diba | 459 | 1 | 459 |
| 11 | Koning | 503 | 1 | 503 |
| | Other | | 0 | |
| | TOTAL | | 42 | |

## MONTH BY MONTH GUIDE TO THE POINTS

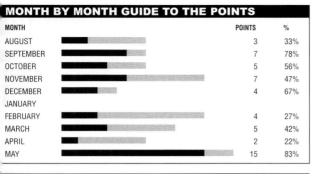

| MONTH | POINTS | % |
|---|---|---|
| AUGUST | 3 | 33% |
| SEPTEMBER | 7 | 78% |
| OCTOBER | 5 | 56% |
| NOVEMBER | 7 | 47% |
| DECEMBER | 4 | 67% |
| JANUARY | | |
| FEBRUARY | 4 | 27% |
| MARCH | 5 | 42% |
| APRIL | 2 | 22% |
| MAY | 15 | 83% |

## TEAM OF THE SEASON

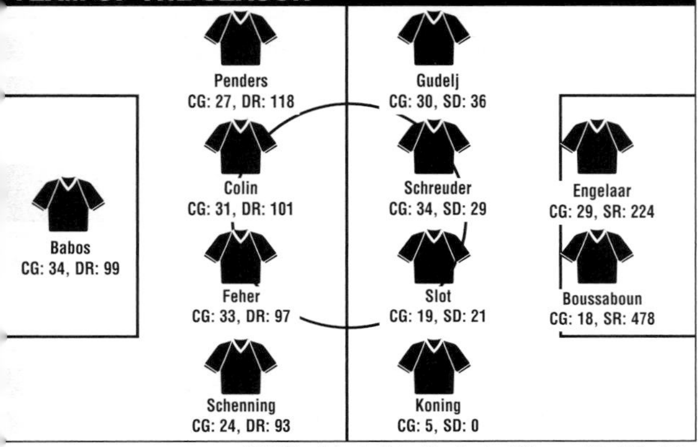
Penders
CG: 27, DR: 118
Gudelj
CG: 30, SD: 36
Colin
CG: 31, DR: 101
Schreuder
CG: 34, SD: 29
Engelaar
CG: 29, SR: 224
Babos
CG: 34, DR: 99
Feher
CG: 33, DR: 97
Slot
CG: 19, SD: 21
Boussaboun
CG: 18, SR: 478
Schenning
CG: 24, DR: 93
Koning
CG: 5, SD: 0

KEY: DR = Defensive Rate, SD = Scoring Difference, SR = Strike Rate,
CG = Counting Games – League games playing at least 70 minutes

## LEAGUE APPEARANCES, BOOKINGS AND CAPS

| | AGE | IN THE SQUAD | COUNTING GAMES | MINUTES ON PITCH | YELLOW CARDS | RED CARDS | THIS SEASON | HOME COUNTRY |
|---|---|---|---|---|---|---|---|---|
| **Goalkeepers** | | | | | | | | |
| Gabor Babos | 28 | 34 | 34 | 3060 | 1 | 0 | - | Hungary |
| Arjan Cristianen | 20 | 14 | 0 | 0 | 0 | 0 | - | Holland |
| Peter Zois | 25 | 20 | 0 | 0 | 0 | 0 | - | Australia |
| **Defenders** | | | | | | | | |
| Jurgen Colin | 22 | 33 | 31 | 2823 | 2 | 0 | - | Holland |
| Csaba Feher | 27 | 34 | 33 | 3019 | 3 | 0 | - | Hungary |
| Kofi Mensah | 25 | 27 | 7 | 621 | 2 | 0 | - | Ghana |
| Rob Penders | 27 | 28 | 27 | 2483 | 6 | 0 | - | Holland |
| Levi Risamasu | 20 | 10 | 0 | 37 | 0 | 0 | - | Holland |
| Mark Schenning | 32 | 26 | 24 | 2224 | 4 | 0 | - | Holland |
| **Midfielders** | | | | | | | | |
| Adnan Barakat | 20 | 21 | 3 | 389 | 0 | 0 | - | Holland |
| Pieter Collen | 23 | 2 | 1 | 127 | 0 | 0 | - | Belgium |
| Nebosja Gudelj | 33 | 31 | 30 | 2749 | 2 | 1 | - | Serbia & Montenegro |
| Rob Haemhouts | 19 | 18 | 0 | 22 | 0 | 0 | - | Belgium |
| Benny Kerstens | | 16 | 0 | 0 | 0 | 0 | - | Holland |
| Marcel Koning | 28 | 11 | 5 | 503 | 1 | 0 | - | Holland |
| Igor Korneev | 25 | 15 | 0 | 184 | 0 | 0 | - | |
| Tamas Peto | 29 | 1 | 0 | 43 | 0 | 0 | - | Hungary |
| Alfred Schreuder | 30 | 34 | 34 | 3050 | 3 | 0 | - | Holland |
| Cedric Seedorf | 20 | 13 | 0 | 0 | 0 | 0 | - | Holland |
| Arne Slot | 24 | 34 | 19 | 1854 | 0 | 0 | - | Holland |
| Ronnie Stam | | 5 | 0 | 7 | 0 | 0 | - | Holland |
| Rick Versteeg | 26 | 13 | 2 | 377 | 2 | 0 | - | Holland |
| **Forwards** | | | | | | | | |
| Yassine Abdellaoui | 28 | 14 | 1 | 208 | 1 | 0 | - | Morocco |
| Kevin Bobson | 22 | 34 | 32 | 2875 | 3 | 0 | - | Holland |
| Ali Boussaboun | 24 | 28 | 18 | 1910 | 1 | 0 | - | Morocco |
| Anouar Diba | 20 | 12 | 4 | 459 | 1 | 0 | - | Holland |
| Orlando Engelaar | 23 | 33 | 29 | 2691 | 3 | 0 | - | Holland |
| Ernie Stewart | 34 | 15 | 6 | 837 | 0 | 0 | 4 | United States (10) |
| Bart Van den Eede | 29 | 24 | 6 | 1071 | 3 | 0 | - | Belgium |

KEY: LEAGUE BOOKINGS CAPS (FIFA RANKING)

## SQUAD APPEARANCES

| Match | 1 | 2 | 3 | 4 | 5 | 6 | 7 | 8 | 9 | 10 | 11 | 12 | 13 | 14 | 15 | 16 | 17 | 18 | 19 | 20 | 21 | 22 | 23 | 24 | 25 | 26 | 27 | 28 | 29 | 30 | 31 | 32 | 33 | 34 |
|---|---|---|---|---|---|---|---|---|---|---|---|---|---|---|---|---|---|---|---|---|---|---|---|---|---|---|---|---|---|---|---|---|---|---|
| Venue | H | A | H | A | H | A | H | A | H | A | H | A | A | H | H | H | H | A | H | A | A | A | H | A | H | A | H | A | A | H | H | A | H | A |
| Competition | L | L | L | L | L | L | L | L | L | L | L | L | L | L | L | L | L | L | L | L | L | L | L | L | L | L | L | L | L | L | L | L | L | L |
| Result | D | D | D | W | W | D | D | W | D | L | D | W | L | W | W | D | D | L | W | L | L | L | W | D | D | D | L | D | L | W | W | W | W | W |

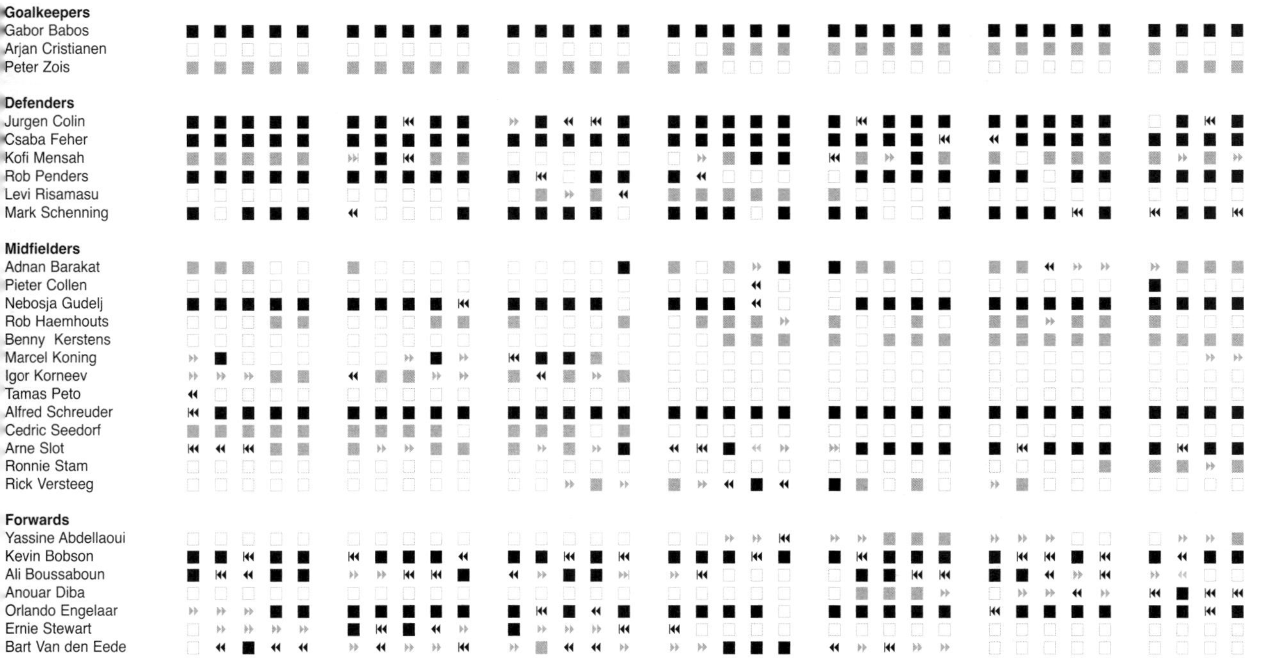
Goalkeepers
Gabor Babos
Arjan Cristianen
Peter Zois
Defenders
Jurgen Colin
Csaba Feher
Kofi Mensah
Rob Penders
Levi Risamasu
Mark Schenning
Midfielders
Adnan Barakat
Pieter Collen
Nebosja Gudelj
Rob Haemhouts
Benny Kerstens
Marcel Koning
Igor Korneev
Tamas Peto
Alfred Schreuder
Cedric Seedorf
Arne Slot
Ronnie Stam
Rick Versteeg
Forwards
Yassine Abdellaoui
Kevin Bobson
Ali Boussaboun
Anouar Diba
Orlando Engelaar
Ernie Stewart
Bart Van den Eede

# NEC NIMEGEN

Final Position: **5th**

| | | | | | | |
|---|---|---|---|---|---|---|
| 1 | lge | Feyenoord | A | L | 0-2 | |
| 2 | lge | AZ Alkmaar | H | W | 2-0 | Hesp 3 pen; de Nooijer 80 |
| 3 | lge | NAC Breda | A | D | 0-0 | |
| 4 | lge | Roda JC Kerk | H | L | 2-4 | de Nooijer 20; Hersi 45 |
| 5 | lge | Willem II Tilb | A | D | 1-1 | Hesp 28 pen |
| 6 | lge | Heerenveen | H | W | 4-2 | Wielaert 14; Simr 27; Hersi 55; de Nooijer 72 |
| 7 | lge | Groningen | H | W | 2-0 | Hersi 32; de Nooijer 76 |
| 8 | lge | De Graafschap | A | W | 3-1 | Ax 62; Hristov 70; Hesp 90 pen |
| 9 | lge | PSV Eindhoven | H | L | 0-5 | |
| 10 | lge | Excelsior | A | D | 0-0 | |
| 11 | lge | Twente | H | L | 1-2 | Tumba 76 |
| 12 | lge | Ajax | A | L | 0-6 | |
| 13 | lge | Utrecht | A | L | 2-3 | Demouge 87; Hesp 89 |
| 14 | lge | Vitesse Arnhem | H | W | 2-0 | Hristov 31; Wisgerhof 61 |
| 15 | lge | Zwolle | A | D | 0-0 | |
| 16 | lge | Roosendaal | H | W | 3-0 | Hersi 57,66; Zonneveld 69 |
| 17 | lge | RKC Waalwijk | H | D | 0-0 | |
| 18 | lge | AZ Alkmaar | A | D | 0-0 | |
| 19 | lge | NAC Breda | H | W | 2-0 | Zonneveld 47; Demouge 70 |
| 20 | lge | Twente | A | W | 2-1 | Hesp 19 pen; Hersi 34 |
| 21 | lge | De Graafschap | H | W | 1-0 | Hersi 63 |
| 22 | lge | Willem II Tilb | H | W | 1-0 | Ax 45 |
| 23 | lge | PSV Eindhoven | A | L | 1-2 | Schuurman 53 |
| 24 | lge | Feyenoord | H | L | 1-2 | Wielaert 11 pen |
| 25 | lge | Roda JC Kerk | A | L | 1-2 | Demouge 1 |
| 26 | lge | Excelsior | H | W | 1-0 | Tumba 82 |
| 27 | lge | Heerenveen | A | W | 3-2 | Hersi 44; Demouge 54; Govedarica 58 |
| 28 | lge | Vitesse Arnhem | A | D | 1-1 | Schuurman 49 |
| 29 | lge | Utrecht | H | L | 1-2 | Hesp 34 pen |
| 30 | lge | Groningen | A | D | 0-0 | |
| 31 | lge | Ajax | H | L | 1-2 | Hersi 11 |
| 32 | lge | Roosendaal | A | W | 2-0 | Zonneveld 45; Wielaert 64 |
| 33 | lge | Zwolle | H | D | 0-0 | |
| 34 | lge | RKC Waalwijk | A | W | 1-0 | Simr 90 |

## KEY PLAYERS - GOALSCORERS

**1 Youssef Hersi**

| | | | |
|---|---|---|---|
| Goals in the League | 9 | **Player Strike Rate** Average number of minutes between League goals scored by player | 279 |
| **Contribution to Attacking Power** Average number of minutes between League team goals while on pitch | 67 | **Club Strike Rate** Average number of minutes between League goals scored by club | 75 |

| | PLAYER | LGE GOALS | POWER | STRIKE RATE |
|---|---|---|---|---|
| 2 | Danny Hesp | 6 | 70 | 444 mins |
| 3 | Dennis de Nooijer | 4 | 64 | 471 mins |
| 4 | Frank Demouge | 4 | 73 | 555 mins |
| 5 | Mike Zonneveld | 3 | 67 | 882 mins |

## KEY PLAYERS - MIDFIELDERS

**1 Jarda Simr**

| | | | |
|---|---|---|---|
| Goals in the League | 2 | **Contribution to Attacking Power** Average number of minutes between League team goals while on pitch | 75 |
| **Defensive Rating** Average number of mins between League goals conceded while he was on the pitch | 98 | **Scoring Difference** Defensive Rating minus Contribution to Attacking Power | 23 |

| | PLAYER | LGE GOALS | DEF RATE | POWER | SCORE DIFF |
|---|---|---|---|---|---|
| 2 | Jeffrey Leiwakabessy | 0 | 92 | 78 | 14 mins |
| 3 | Mike Zonneveld | 3 | 80 | 68 | 12 mins |
| 4 | Youssef Hersi | 9 | 76 | 68 | 8 mins |
| 5 | Dejan Govedarica | 1 | 74 | 76 | -2 mins |

## KEY PLAYERS - DEFENDERS

**1 Danny Hesp**

| | | | |
|---|---|---|---|
| **Goals Conceded (GC)** The number of League goals conceded while he was on the pitch | 28 | **Clean Sheets** In games when he played at least 70 minutes | 16 |
| **Defensive Rating** Ave number of mins between League goals conceded while on the pitch | 95 | **Club Defensive Rating** Average number of mins between League goals conceded by the club this season | 77 |

| | PLAYER | CON LGE | CLEAN SHEETS | DEF RATE |
|---|---|---|---|---|
| 2 | Resit Schuurman | 40 | 17 | 77 mins |
| 3 | Rob Wielaert | 38 | 16 | 76 mins |
| 4 | Peter Wisgerhof | 40 | 15 | 72 mins |

## GOALS SCORED

**AT HOME**

| | | |
|---|---|---|
| MOST | Ajax | 57 |
| | | 24 |
| LEAST | Twente | 18 |

**AWAY**

| | | |
|---|---|---|
| MOST | PSV | 44 |
| | | 17 |
| LEAST | Roosendaal & Groningen | 9 |

## GOALS CONCEDED

**AT HOME**

| | | |
|---|---|---|
| LEAST | PSV | 7 |
| | | 19 |
| MOST | Excelsior | 38 |

**AWAY**

| | | |
|---|---|---|
| LEAST | PSV | 13 |
| | | 21 |
| MOST | De G'schap | 50 |

## KEY GOALKEEPER

**1 Dennis Gentenaar**

| | |
|---|---|
| Goals Conceded in the League | 40 |
| **Defensive Rating** Ave number of mins between League goals conceded while on the pitch | 77 |
| **Counting Games** Games when he played at least 70 mins | 34 |
| **Clean Sheets** In games when he played at least 70 mins | 17 |

## TOP POINT EARNERS

| | PLAYER | GAMES | AVE |
|---|---|---|---|
| 1 | Hesp | 29 | 1.66 |
| 2 | de Nooijer | 16 | 1.63 |
| 3 | Hersi | 27 | 1.63 |
| 4 | Leiwakabessy | 22 | 1.59 |
| 5 | Wielaert | 32 | 1.56 |
| 6 | Govedarica | 33 | 1.52 |
| 7 | Gentenaar | 34 | 1.50 |
| 8 | Schuurman | 34 | 1.50 |
| 9 | Zonneveld | 29 | 1.48 |
| 10 | Wisgerhof | 32 | 1.41 |
| | CLUB AVERAGE: | | 1.50 |

Ave = Average points per match in Counting Games

## ATTENDANCES

HOME GROUND: DE GOFFERT CAPACITY: 12500 AVERAGE LEAGUE AT HOME: 11185

| | | | | | | | | |
|---|---|---|---|---|---|---|---|---|
| 12 | Ajax | 46084 | 31 | Ajax | 12250 | 7 | Groningen | 10500 |
| 1 | Feyenoord | 40000 | 14 | Vitesse Arnhem | 12250 | 22 | Willem II Tilb | 10250 |
| 23 | PSV Eindhoven | 33000 | 29 | Utrecht | 12000 | 26 | Excelsior | 10150 |
| 28 | Vitesse Arnhem | 24196 | 33 | Zwolle | 12000 | 16 | Roosendaal | 10000 |
| 13 | Utrecht | 15000 | 30 | Groningen | 11704 | 17 | RKC Waalwijk | 10000 |
| 27 | Heerenveen | 14400 | 21 | De Graafschap | 11250 | 34 | RKC Waalwijk | 7500 |
| 3 | NAC Breda | 13440 | 4 | Roda JC Kerk | 11000 | 18 | AZ Alkmaar | 6939 |
| 20 | Twente | 13250 | 6 | Heerenveen | 11000 | 15 | Zwolle | 6100 |
| 5 | Willem II Tilb | 13000 | 2 | AZ Alkmaar | 11000 | 32 | Roosendaal | 5000 |
| 25 | Roda JC Kerk | 12500 | 19 | NAC Breda | 11000 | 10 | Excelsior | 3356 |
| 9 | PSV Eindhoven | 12500 | 8 | De Graafschap | 11000 | | | |
| 24 | Feyenoord | 12500 | 11 | Twente | 10500 | | | |

■ Home □ Away ▨ Neutral

## DISCIPLINARY RECORDS

| | PLAYER | YELLOW | RED | AVE |
|---|---|---|---|---|
| 1 | Hristov | 3 | 1 | 182 |
| 2 | Zonneveld | 9 | 1 | 264 |
| 3 | Simr | 4 | 0 | 318 |
| 4 | Hersi | 6 | 1 | 358 |
| 5 | Demouge | 6 | 0 | 369 |
| 6 | Ax | 2 | 1 | 451 |
| 7 | Hesp | 5 | 0 | 533 |
| 8 | Wisgerhof | 5 | 0 | 572 |
| 9 | Govedarica | 5 | 0 | 592 |
| 10 | Tumba | 1 | 0 | 691 |
| 11 | Wielaert | 4 | 0 | 720 |
| 12 | Leiwakabessy | 2 | 0 | 1015 |
| 13 | Schuurman | 3 | 0 | 1020 |
| | Other | 0 | 0 | |
| | TOTAL | 55 | 4 | |

## LEAGUE GOALS

| | PLAYER | MINS | GOALS | AVE |
|---|---|---|---|---|
| 1 | Hersi | 2509 | 9 | 279 |
| 2 | Hesp | 2666 | 6 | 444 |
| 3 | de Nooijer | 1883 | 4 | 471 |
| 4 | Demouge | 2218 | 4 | 555 |
| 5 | Wielaert | 2880 | 3 | 960 |
| 6 | Zonneveld | 2645 | 3 | 882 |
| 7 | Simr | 1274 | 2 | 637 |
| 8 | Schuurman | 3060 | 2 | 1530 |
| 9 | Hristov | 731 | 2 | 366 |
| 10 | Tumba | 691 | 2 | 346 |
| 11 | Ax | 1355 | 2 | 678 |
| 12 | Wisgerhof | 2860 | 1 | 2860 |
| 13 | Govedarica | 2960 | 1 | 2960 |
| | Other | | 0 | |
| | TOTAL | | 41 | |

## MONTH BY MONTH GUIDE TO THE POINTS

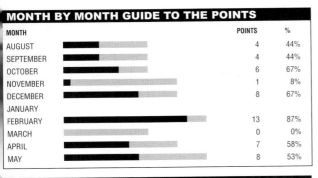

| MONTH | POINTS | % |
|---|---|---|
| AUGUST | 4 | 44% |
| SEPTEMBER | 4 | 44% |
| OCTOBER | 6 | 67% |
| NOVEMBER | 1 | 8% |
| DECEMBER | 8 | 67% |
| JANUARY | | |
| FEBRUARY | 13 | 87% |
| MARCH | 0 | 0% |
| APRIL | 7 | 58% |
| MAY | 8 | 53% |

## TEAM OF THE SEASON

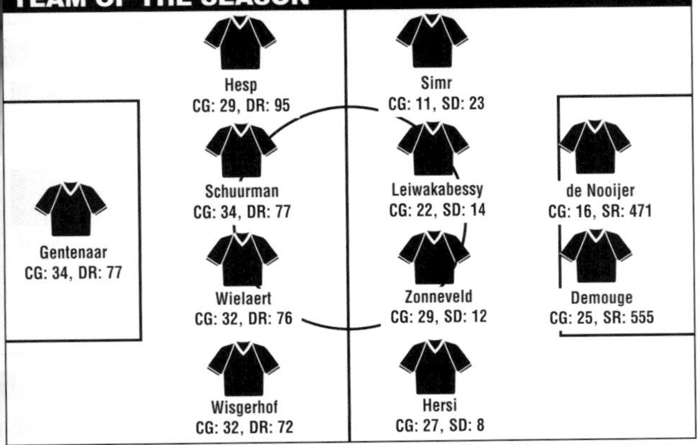
Gentenaar
CG: 34, DR: 77
Hesp
CG: 29, DR: 95
Schuurman
CG: 34, DR: 77
Wielaert
CG: 32, DR: 76
Wisgerhof
CG: 32, DR: 72
Simr
CG: 11, SD: 23
Leiwakabessy
CG: 22, SD: 14
Zonneveld
CG: 29, SD: 12
Hersi
CG: 27, SD: 8
de Nooijer
CG: 16, SR: 471
Demouge
CG: 25, SR: 555

KEY: DR = Defensive Rate, SD = Scoring Difference, SR = Strike Rate, CG = Counting Games – League games playing at least 70 minutes

## LEAGUE APPEARANCES, BOOKINGS AND CAPS

| | AGE | IN THE SQUAD | COUNTING GAMES | MINUTES ON PITCH | YELLOW CARDS | RED CARDS | THIS SEASON | HOME COUNTRY |
|---|---|---|---|---|---|---|---|---|
| **Goalkeepers** | | | | | | | | |
| Dennis Gentenaar | 27 | 34 | 34 | 3060 | 0 | 0 | - | Holland |
| Henri Timmer | 22 | 7 | 0 | 0 | 0 | 0 | - | Holland |
| Albert Van der Sleen | 40 | 24 | 0 | 0 | 0 | 0 | - | Holland |
| **Defenders** | | | | | | | | |
| Danny Hesp | 33 | 30 | 29 | 2666 | 5 | 0 | - | Holland |
| Mike Owusu | 26 | 18 | 0 | 14 | 0 | 0 | - | Sweden |
| Resit Schuurman | 24 | 34 | 34 | 3060 | 3 | 0 | - | Holland |
| Rob Wielaert | 24 | 32 | 32 | 2880 | 4 | 0 | - | Holland |
| Peter Wisgerhof | 23 | 32 | 32 | 2860 | 5 | 0 | - | Holland |
| **Midfielders** | | | | | | | | |
| Patrick Ax | 23 | 28 | 10 | 1355 | 2 | 1 | - | Holland |
| Wilfried Brookhuis | | 3 | 0 | 0 | 0 | 0 | - | Holland |
| Dejan Govedarica | 33 | 33 | 33 | 2960 | 5 | 0 | - | Serbia & Montenegro |
| Youssef Hersi | 20 | 30 | 27 | 2509 | 6 | 1 | - | Holland |
| Jeffrey Leiwakabessy | 22 | 33 | 22 | 2031 | 2 | 0 | - | Holland |
| Marc Peters | 24 | 1 | 0 | 0 | 0 | 0 | - | Holland |
| Ivo Rossen | 20 | 10 | 0 | 0 | 0 | 0 | - | Holland |
| Jarda Simr | 24 | 34 | 11 | 1274 | 4 | 0 | - | Czech Republic |
| Gary Spier | 19 | 1 | 0 | 0 | 0 | 0 | - | Holland |
| Erik Wegh | 23 | 29 | 1 | 113 | 0 | 0 | - | Holland |
| Mike Zonneveld | 22 | 31 | 29 | 2645 | 9 | 1 | - | Holland |
| **Forwards** | | | | | | | | |
| Dennis de Nooijer | 34 | 25 | 16 | 1883 | 0 | 0 | - | Holland |
| Frank Demouge | 21 | 29 | 25 | 2218 | 6 | 0 | - | Holland |
| Georgi Hristov | 27 | 30 | 3 | 731 | 3 | 1 | - | Macedonia |
| Zico Tumba | 26 | 31 | 3 | 691 | 1 | 0 | - | Congo |
| Rene van Rijswijk | 32 | 32 | 4 | 647 | 0 | 0 | - | Holland |

KEY: LEAGUE BOOKINGS CAPS (FIFA RANKING)

## SQUAD APPEARANCES

| Match | 1 | 2 | 3 | 4 | 5 | 6 | 7 | 8 | 9 | 10 | 11 | 12 | 13 | 14 | 15 | 16 | 17 | 18 | 19 | 20 | 21 | 22 | 23 | 24 | 25 | 26 | 27 | 28 | 29 | 30 | 31 | 32 | 33 | 34 |
|---|---|---|---|---|---|---|---|---|---|---|---|---|---|---|---|---|---|---|---|---|---|---|---|---|---|---|---|---|---|---|---|---|---|---|
| Venue | A | H | A | H | A | H | H | A | H | A | H | A | A | H | A | H | H | A | H | A | H | H | A | H | A | H | A | A | H | A | H | A | H | A |
| Competition | L | L | L | L | L | L | L | L | L | L | L | L | L | L | L | L | L | L | L | L | L | L | L | L | L | L | L | L | L | L | L | L | L | L |
| Result | L | W | D | L | D | W | W | W | L | D | L | L | L | W | D | W | D | D | W | W | W | W | L | L | L | W | W | D | L | D | L | W | D | W |

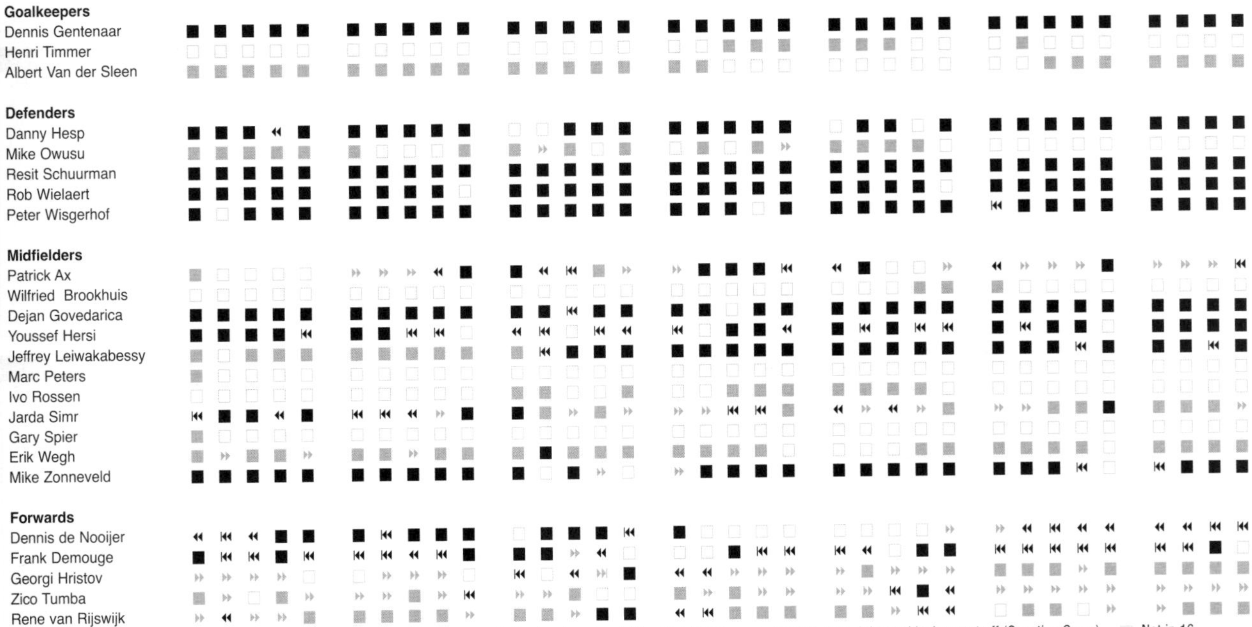
Goalkeepers
Dennis Gentenaar
Henri Timmer
Albert Van der Sleen
Defenders
Danny Hesp
Mike Owusu
Resit Schuurman
Rob Wielaert
Peter Wisgerhof
Midfielders
Patrick Ax
Wilfried Brookhuis
Dejan Govedarica
Youssef Hersi
Jeffrey Leiwakabessy
Marc Peters
Ivo Rossen
Jarda Simr
Gary Spier
Erik Wegh
Mike Zonneveld
Forwards
Dennis de Nooijer
Frank Demouge
Georgi Hristov
Zico Tumba
Rene van Rijswijk

KEY: ■ On all match ■ On bench ⏮ Subbed or sent off (Counting game) « Subbed or sent off (playing less than 70 minutes) ⏭ Subbed on from bench (Counting Game) » Subbed on (playing less than 70 minutes) Subbed on and then subbed or sent off (Counting Game) Subbed on and then subbed or sent off (playing less than 70 minutes) □ Not in 16

# RODA JC KERK

Final Position: **6th**

| | | | | | | |
|---|---|---|---|---|---|---|
| 1 | lge | NAC Breda | A | D | 2-2 | Nygaard 56; van Dessel 85 |
| 2 | lge | Feyenoord | H | D | 2-2 | Soetaers 37,87 |
| 3 | lge | Willem II Tilb | H | W | 1-0 | Anastasiou 87 |
| 4 | lge | NEC Nijmegen | A | W | 4-2 | Soetaers 42,90; Cristiano 56,61 |
| 5 | lge | Heerenveen | H | W | 1-0 | Soetaers 23 |
| 6 | lge | Twente | A | D | 3-3 | Sonko 56; Anastasiou 70; Berglund 80 |
| 7 | lge | Excelsior | H | L | 2-3 | Berglund 62; Sonko 90 |
| 8 | lge | PSV Eindhoven | A | D | 0-0 | |
| 9 | lge | Vitesse Arnhem | A | W | 2-0 | Sonko 43; Sergio 62 pen |
| 10 | lge | De Graafschap | H | W | 5-0 | Cristiano 39; Anastasiou 44 pen,69; Soetaers 45; Sonko 76 |
| 11 | lge | Ajax | H | D | 1-1 | Sonko 63 |
| 12 | lge | Roosendaal | A | L | 0-4 | |
| 13 | lge | AZ Alkmaar | H | L | 1-3 | Filipovic 77 |
| 14 | lge | Zwolle | H | W | 2-0 | Cristiano 58; Sonko 63 |
| 15 | lge | RKC Waalwijk | A | L | 1-2 | Jongen 73 |
| 16 | lge | Groningen | A | L | 2-3 | Cristiano 16; Vicelich 25 |
| 17 | lge | Utrecht | H | W | 1-0 | Sonko 39 |
| 18 | lge | Vitesse Arnhem | H | W | 2-0 | Anastasiou 9; Sonkaya, F 79 |
| 19 | lge | Willem II Tilb | A | L | 0-5 | |
| 20 | lge | Excelsior | A | W | 2-0 | Soetaers 4; Anastasiou 33 |
| 21 | lge | Twente | H | W | 2-0 | Sonko 39; Soetaers 90 |
| 22 | lge | De Graafschap | A | D | 1-1 | Soetaers 57 |
| 23 | lge | AZ Alkmaar | A | L | 0-1 | |
| 24 | lge | NAC Breda | H | D | 0-0 | |
| 25 | lge | NEC Nijmegen | H | W | 2-1 | Filipovic 31; Anastasiou 61 |
| 26 | lge | Heerenveen | A | L | 2-3 | Vicelich 28; Soetaers 38 |
| 27 | lge | PSV Eindhoven | H | L | 2-3 | Anastasiou 4; Sergio 23 |
| 28 | lge | Ajax | A | L | 2-4 | Sergio 32,80 |
| 29 | lge | Zwolle | A | L | 1-3 | Vicelich 71 |
| 30 | lge | Roosendaal | H | W | 1-0 | Sergio 12 |
| 31 | lge | Groningen | H | W | 5-1 | Sergio 31,60; Cristiano 68,85; Anastasiou 84 |
| 32 | lge | Utrecht | A | D | 4-4 | Cristiano 19; Anastasiou 58,86; Zwaanswijk 63 og |
| 33 | lge | RKC Waalwijk | H | W | 1-0 | Cornelisse 20 og |
| 34 | lge | Feyenoord | A | L | 1-3 | Cristiano 50 |

## KEY PLAYERS - GOALSCORERS

**1 Edrissa Sonko**

| | | | |
|---|---|---|---|
| **Goals in the League** | 8 | **Player Strike Rate** Average number of minutes between League goals scored by player | 184 |
| **Contribution to Attacking Power** Average number of minutes between League team goals while on pitch | 50 | **Club Strike Rate** Average number of minutes between League goals scored by club | 53 |

| | PLAYER | LGE GOALS | POWER | STRIKE RATE |
|---|---|---|---|---|
| 2 | Tom Soetaers | 10 | 56 | 241 mins |
| 3 | Ioannis Anastasiou | 11 | 50 | 247 mins |
| 4 | Dos Santos Rodriquez Cristiano | 9 | 48 | 276 mins |
| 5 | Sergio | 7 | 57 | 293 mins |

## KEY PLAYERS - MIDFIELDERS

**1 Edrissa Sonko**

| | | | |
|---|---|---|---|
| **Goals in the League** | 8 | **Contribution to Attacking Power** Average number of minutes between League team goals while on pitch | 51 |
| **Defensive Rating** Average number of mins between League goals conceded while he was on the pitch | 64 | **Scoring Difference** Defensive Rating minus Contribution to Attacking Power | 13 |

| | PLAYER | LGE GOALS | DEF RATE | POWER | SCORE DIFF |
|---|---|---|---|---|---|
| 2 | Dos Santos Rodriquez Cristiano | 9 | 55 | 49 | 6 mins |
| 3 | Ivan Vicelich | 3 | 52 | 50 | 2 mins |
| 4 | Kevin van Dessel | 1 | 61 | 60 | 1 mins |
| 5 | Gregoor van Dijk | 0 | 55 | 55 | 0 mins |

## KEY PLAYERS - DEFENDERS

**1 Roel Brouwers**

| | | | |
|---|---|---|---|
| **Goals Conceded (GC)** The number of League goals conceded while he was on the pitch | 8 | **Clean Sheets** In games when he played at least 70 minutes | 8 |
| **Defensive Rating** Ave number of mins between League goals conceded while on the pitch | 131 | **Club Defensive Rating** Average number of mins between League goals conceded by the club this season | 56 |

| | PLAYER | CON LGE | CLEAN SHEETS | DEF RATE |
|---|---|---|---|---|
| 2 | Fatih Sonkaya | 38 | 11 | 61 mins |
| 3 | Ger Senden | 21 | 4 | 55 mins |
| 4 | Mark Luijpers | 46 | 9 | 53 mins |
| 5 | Eric Addo | 26 | 5 | 51 mins |

## GOALS SCORED

**AT HOME**

| | | |
|---|---|---|
| MOST | Ajax | 57 |
| | | 31 |
| LEAST | Twente | 18 |

**AWAY**

| | | |
|---|---|---|
| MOST | PSV | 44 |
| | | 27 |
| LEAST | Roosendaal & Groningen | 9 |

## GOALS CONCEDED

**AT HOME**

| | | |
|---|---|---|
| LEAST | PSV | 7 |
| | | 14 |
| MOST | Excelsior | 38 |

**AWAY**

| | | |
|---|---|---|
| LEAST | PSV | 13 |
| | | 40 |
| MOST | De G'schap | 50 |

## KEY GOALKEEPER

**1 Vladan Kujovic**

| | |
|---|---|
| **Goals Conceded in the League** | 34 |
| **Defensive Rating** Ave number of mins between League goals conceded while on the pitch | 56 |
| **Counting Games** Games when he played at least 70 mins | 21 |
| **Clean Sheets** In games when he played at least 70 mins | 8 |

## TOP POINT EARNERS

| | PLAYER | GAMES | AVE |
|---|---|---|---|
| 1 | Sonko | 14 | 1.71 |
| 2 | Sonkaya, F | 24 | 1.63 |
| 3 | Sergio | 20 | 1.60 |
| 4 | Kujovic | 21 | 1.57 |
| 5 | Vicelich | 22 | 1.55 |
| 6 | van Dijk | 19 | 1.53 |
| 7 | Soetaers | 25 | 1.48 |
| 8 | Cristiano | 25 | 1.48 |
| 9 | van Dessel | 25 | 1.44 |
| 10 | Luijpers | 26 | 1.42 |
| | **CLUB AVERAGE:** | | **1.47** |

Ave = Average points per match in Counting Games

## ATTENDANCES

HOME GROUND: PARKSTAD LIMBURG CAPACITY: 19500 AVERAGE LEAGUE AT HOME: 13697

| | | | | | | | | |
|---|---|---|---|---|---|---|---|---|
| 28 | Ajax | 49421 | 19 | Willem II Tilb | 13250 | 30 | Roosendaal | 12000 |
| 34 | Feyenoord | 45000 | 5 | Heerenveen | 13250 | 18 | Vitesse Arnhem | 12000 |
| 8 | PSV Eindhoven | 31000 | 6 | Twente | 13200 | 16 | Groningen | 11600 |
| 9 | Vitesse Arnhem | 22000 | 1 | NAC Breda | 13104 | 4 | NEC Nijmegen | 11000 |
| 11 | Ajax | 17500 | 2 | Feyenoord | 13000 | 22 | De Graafschap | 10700 |
| 33 | RKC Waalwijk | 17400 | 3 | Willem II Tilb | 13000 | 23 | AZ Alkmaar | 6871 |
| 27 | PSV Eindhoven | 16000 | 7 | Excelsior | 13000 | 29 | Zwolle | 6450 |
| 10 | De Graafschap | 16000 | 25 | NEC Nijmegen | 12500 | 15 | RKC Waalwijk | 6000 |
| 32 | Utrecht | 15500 | 21 | Twente | 12500 | 12 | Roosendaal | 5000 |
| 26 | Heerenveen | 14300 | 17 | Utrecht | 12500 | 20 | Excelsior | 2258 |
| 14 | Zwolle | 14000 | 13 | AZ Alkmaar | 12500 | | | |
| 24 | NAC Breda | 13300 | 31 | Groningen | 12400 | | | |

■ Home □ Away ▒ Neutral

## DISCIPLINARY RECORDS

| | PLAYER | YELLOW | RED | AVE |
|---|---|---|---|---|
| 1 | Brouwers | 6 | 1 | 149 |
| 2 | Addo | 5 | 1 | 219 |
| 3 | Sonkaya, F | 6 | 0 | 388 |
| 4 | Luijpers | 6 | 0 | 407 |
| 5 | van Dijk | 3 | 1 | 452 |
| 6 | Soetaers | 5 | 0 | 482 |
| 7 | Filipovic | 4 | 0 | 596 |
| 8 | Sergio | 3 | 0 | 684 |
| 9 | Rudge | 1 | 0 | 705 |
| 10 | Roorda | 1 | 0 | 1150 |
| 11 | van Dessel | 2 | 0 | 1220 |
| 12 | Anastasiou | 2 | 0 | 1361 |
| 13 | Sonko | 1 | 0 | 1475 |
| | Other | 1 | 0 | |
| | TOTAL | 46 | 3 | |

## LEAGUE GOALS

| | PLAYER | MINS | GOALS | AVE |
|---|---|---|---|---|
| 1 | Anastasiou | 2722 | 11 | 247 |
| 2 | Soetaers | 2411 | 10 | 241 |
| 3 | Cristiano | 2484 | 9 | 276 |
| 4 | Sonko | 1475 | 8 | 184 |
| 5 | Sergio | 2053 | 7 | 293 |
| 6 | Vicelich | 2139 | 3 | 713 |
| 7 | Filipovic | 2385 | 2 | 1193 |
| 8 | Berglund | 365 | 2 | 183 |
| 9 | Jongen | 211 | 1 | 211 |
| 10 | Nygaard | 223 | 1 | 223 |
| 11 | van Dessel | 2441 | 1 | 2441 |
| 12 | Sonkaya, F | 2333 | 1 | 2333 |
| | Other | | 2 | |
| | TOTAL | | 58 | |

## MONTH BY MONTH GUIDE TO THE POINTS

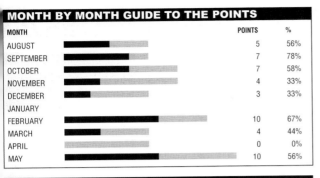

| MONTH | POINTS | % |
|---|---|---|
| AUGUST | 5 | 56% |
| SEPTEMBER | 7 | 78% |
| OCTOBER | 7 | 58% |
| NOVEMBER | 4 | 33% |
| DECEMBER | 3 | 33% |
| JANUARY | | |
| FEBRUARY | 10 | 67% |
| MARCH | 4 | 44% |
| APRIL | 0 | 0% |
| MAY | 10 | 56% |

## TEAM OF THE SEASON

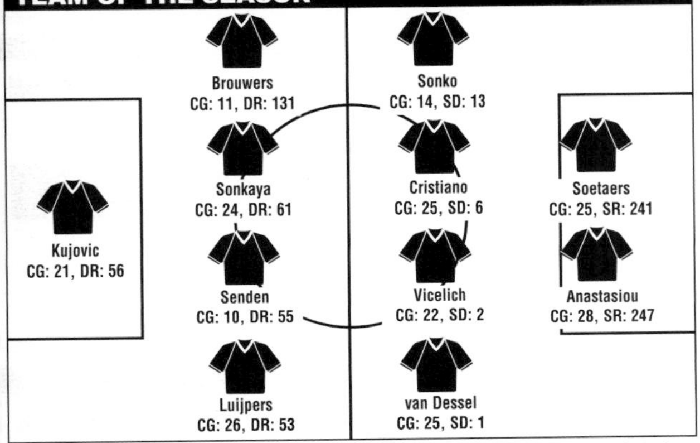
Brouwers
CG: 11, DR: 131
Sonko
CG: 14, SD: 13
Kujovic
CG: 21, DR: 56
Sonkaya
CG: 24, DR: 61
Cristiano
CG: 25, SD: 6
Soetaers
CG: 25, SR: 241
Senden
CG: 10, DR: 55
Vicelich
CG: 22, SD: 2
Anastasiou
CG: 28, SR: 247
Luijpers
CG: 26, DR: 53
van Dessel
CG: 25, SD: 1

KEY: DR = Defensive Rate, SD = Scoring Difference, SR = Strike Rate, CG = Counting Games – League games playing at least 70 minutes

## LEAGUE APPEARANCES, BOOKINGS AND CAPS

| | AGE | IN THE SQUAD | COUNTING GAMES | MINUTES ON PITCH | YELLOW CARDS | RED CARDS | THIS SEASON | HOME COUNTRY |
|---|---|---|---|---|---|---|---|---|
| **Goalkeepers** | | | | | | | | |
| Taylon Aydagon | 20 | 3 | 0 | 0 | 0 | 0 | - | Turkey |
| Vladan Kujovic | 24 | 34 | 21 | 1910 | 0 | 0 | - | Serbia & Montenegro |
| Bas Roorda | 30 | 29 | 13 | 1150 | 1 | 0 | - | Holland |
| **Defenders** | | | | | | | | |
| Eric Addo | 24 | 16 | 13 | 1315 | 5 | 1 | - | Ghana |
| Roel Brouwers | 21 | 29 | 11 | 1044 | 6 | 1 | - | Holland |
| Vincent Lachambre | 22 | 10 | 0 | 0 | 0 | 0 | - | Belgium |
| Mark Luijpers | 32 | 28 | 26 | 2442 | 6 | 0 | - | Holland |
| Humphrey Rudge | 25 | 22 | 7 | 705 | 1 | 0 | - | Holland |
| Ger Senden | 32 | 31 | 10 | 1147 | 0 | 0 | - | Holland |
| Fatih Sonkaya | 22 | 31 | 24 | 2333 | 6 | 0 | 3 | Turkey (8) |
| **Midfielders** | | | | | | | | |
| Seydihan Baslanti | 19 | 4 | 0 | 3 | 0 | 0 | - | Holland |
| Jerome Collinet | 20 | 7 | 0 | 0 | 0 | 0 | - | Belgium |
| Rodriquez Cristiano | 22 | 32 | 25 | 2484 | 0 | 0 | - | Brazil |
| Predrag Filipovic | 28 | 33 | 29 | 2835 | 4 | 0 | - | Serbia & Montenegro |
| Donovan Maury | 22 | 3 | 1 | 90 | 0 | 0 | - | Belgium |
| Marc Nygaard | 27 | 12 | 3 | 362 | 0 | 0 | - | Denmark |
| Sergio | 22 | 30 | 20 | 2053 | 3 | 0 | - | Brazil |
| Edrissa Sonko | 23 | 23 | 14 | 1475 | 1 | 0 | - | Gambia |
| Kevin van Dessel | 24 | 31 | 25 | 2441 | 2 | 0 | - | Belgium |
| Gregoor van Dijk | 21 | 24 | 19 | 1811 | 3 | 1 | - | Holland |
| Alain van Mieghem | 21 | 12 | 0 | 81 | 0 | 0 | - | Belgium |
| Sven Vandenbroeck | 23 | 24 | 1 | 122 | 0 | 0 | - | Belgium |
| Ivan Vicelich | 27 | 29 | 22 | 2139 | 1 | 0 | - | New Zealand |
| **Forwards** | | | | | | | | |
| Ioannis Anastasiou | 30 | 34 | 28 | 2722 | 2 | 0 | - | Greece |
| Fredrik Berglund | 24 | 17 | 1 | 365 | 0 | 0 | - | Sweden |
| Diego Jongen | 20 | 21 | 0 | 211 | 0 | 0 | - | Holland |
| Tom Soetaers | 22 | 30 | 25 | 2411 | 5 | 0 | 6 | Belgium (16) |

KEY: LEAGUE BOOKINGS CAPS (FIFA RANKING)

## SQUAD APPEARANCES

| Match | 1 | 2 | 3 | 4 | 5 | 6 | 7 | 8 | 9 | 10 | 11 | 12 | 13 | 14 | 15 | 16 | 17 | 18 | 19 | 20 | 21 | 22 | 23 | 24 | 25 | 26 | 27 | 28 | 29 | 30 | 31 | 32 | 33 | 34 |
|---|---|---|---|---|---|---|---|---|---|---|---|---|---|---|---|---|---|---|---|---|---|---|---|---|---|---|---|---|---|---|---|---|---|---|
| Venue | A | H | H | A | H | A | H | A | A | H | H | A | H | H | A | A | H | H | A | A | H | A | A | H | H | A | H | A | A | H | H | A | H | A |
| Competition | L | L | L | L | L | L | L | L | L | L | L | L | L | L | L | L | L | L | L | L | L | L | L | L | L | L | L | L | L | L | L | L | L | L |
| Result | D | D | W | W | W | D | L | D | W | W | D | L | L | W | L | L | W | W | L | W | W | D | L | D | W | L | L | L | L | W | W | D | W | L |

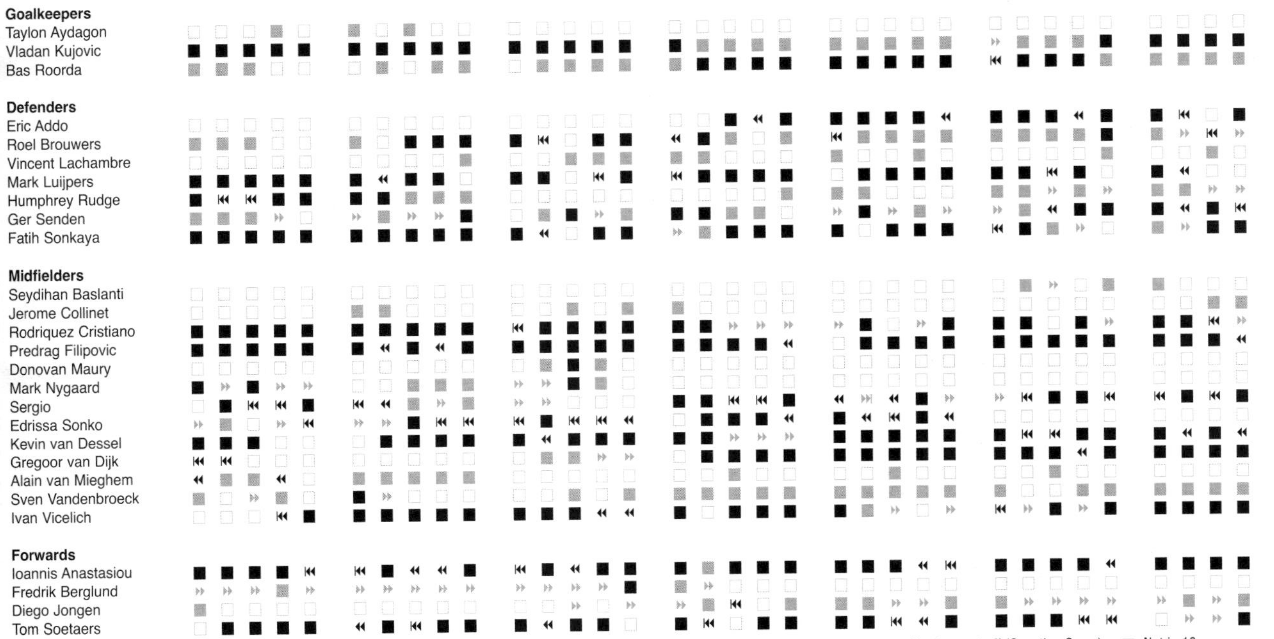
Goalkeepers
Taylon Aydagon
Vladan Kujovic
Bas Roorda
Defenders
Eric Addo
Roel Brouwers
Vincent Lachambre
Mark Luijpers
Humphrey Rudge
Ger Senden
Fatih Sonkaya
Midfielders
Seydihan Baslanti
Jerome Collinet
Rodriquez Cristiano
Predrag Filipovic
Donovan Maury
Mark Nygaard
Sergio
Edrissa Sonko
Kevin van Dessel
Gregoor van Dijk
Alain van Mieghem
Sven Vandenbroeck
Ivan Vicelich
Forwards
Ioannis Anastasiou
Fredrik Berglund
Diego Jongen
Tom Soetaers

KEY: ■ On all match ■ On bench
⏮ Subbed or sent off (Counting game)
◀◀ Subbed or sent off (playing less than 70 minutes)
⏭ Subbed on from bench (Counting Game)
▶▶ Subbed on (playing less than 70 minutes)
⏭ Subbed on and then subbed or sent off (Counting Game)
▶▶ Subbed on and then subbed or sent off (playing less than 70 minutes)
□ Not in 16

# HEERENVEEN

Final Position: **7th**

| | | | | | | |
|---|---|---|---|---|---|---|
| 1 | lge | AZ Alkmaar | A | D | 3-3 | Denneboom 12,54; Venema 28 |
| 2 | lge | RKC Waalwijk | H | L | 1-2 | de Nooijer 11 |
| 3 | lge | Roosendaal | A | L | 0-3 | |
| 4 | lge | NAC Breda | H | L | 0-2 | |
| 5 | uc1rl1 | Nat Bucharest | A | L | 0-3 | |
| 6 | lge | Roda JC Kerk | A | L | 0-1 | |
| 7 | lge | NEC Nijmegen | A | L | 2-4 | Selakovic 65; De Jong 73 |
| 8 | uc1rl2 | Nat Bucharest | H | W | 2-0 | Hansson 53; Denneboom 65 |
| 9 | lge | Willem II Tilb | H | D | 1-1 | Nurmela 37 pen |
| 10 | lge | Twente | A | D | 1-1 | Nurmela 69 pen |
| 11 | lge | Excelsior | H | W | 2-0 | Vayrynen 67,88 |
| 12 | lge | De Graafschap | H | W | 3-1 | Hansson 14,53; Denneboom 55 |
| 13 | lge | PSV Eindhoven | A | L | 1-3 | Hansson 52 |
| 14 | lge | Vitesse Arnhem | A | W | 2-1 | Vayrynen 35; Hansma 40 |
| 15 | lge | Ajax | H | L | 0-3 | |
| 16 | lge | Groningen | A | D | 1-1 | Samaras 77 |
| 17 | lge | Feyenoord | H | W | 3-1 | Vayrynen 63; Denneboom 69; Nurmela 88 |
| 18 | lge | Utrecht | H | D | 2-2 | De Jong 41; Denneboom 60 |
| 19 | lge | Zwolle | H | W | 2-0 | Denneboom 6; Samaras 85 |
| 20 | lge | NAC Breda | A | D | 1-1 | Nurmela 22 |
| 21 | lge | AZ Alkmaar | H | W | 5-0 | Fortes Rodriguez 2 og; De Jong 8; Hansma 44; Venema 64; Samaras 86 |
| 22 | lge | De Graafschap | A | W | 5-1 | Denneboom 39,63; De Jong 47; Sibon 50; Selakovic 90 |
| 23 | lge | Utrecht | A | D | 2-2 | Sibon 13; Nurmela 40 pen |
| 24 | lge | PSV Eindhoven | H | L | 0-1 | |
| 25 | lge | RKC Waalwijk | A | L | 0-3 | |
| 26 | lge | Twente | H | W | 3-0 | Nurmela 60 pen; Selakovic 71,79 |
| 27 | lge | Feyenoord | A | L | 0-5 | |
| 28 | lge | Roda JC Kerk | H | W | 3-2 | Jensen, D 47,61; Denneboom 56 |
| 29 | lge | NEC Nijmegen | H | L | 2-3 | Nurmela 40; Samaras 74 |
| 30 | lge | Excelsior | A | L | 0-1 | |
| 31 | lge | Vitesse Arnhem | H | D | 2-2 | Jensen, D 15; Selakovic 89 |
| 32 | lge | Willem II Tilb | A | W | 5-1 | De Jong 12,17; Selakovic 31,64; Nurmela 55 |
| 33 | lge | Groningen | H | W | 2-1 | Sibon 45; de Jong 90 pen |
| 34 | lge | Zwolle | A | W | 1-0 | Selakovic 34 |
| 35 | lge | Roosendaal | H | W | 6-0 | Nurmela 1; Sibon 8; Denneboom 12; De Jong 25,51; Jensen, D 55 |
| 36 | lge | Ajax | A | L | 0-3 | |

## KEY PLAYERS - GOALSCORERS

**1 Stefan Selakovic**

| | | | |
|---|---|---|---|
| Goals in the League | 8 | Player Strike Rate<br>Average number of minutes between League goals scored by player | 212 |
| Contribution to Attacking Power<br>Average number of minutes between League team goals while on pitch | 48 | Club Strike Rate<br>Average number of minutes between League goals scored by club | 50 |

| | PLAYER | LGE GOALS | POWER | STRIKE RATE |
|---|---|---|---|---|
| 2 | John de Jong | 9 | 43 | 253 mins |
| 3 | Romano Denneboom | 10 | 46 | 258 mins |
| 4 | Mike Nurmela | 9 | 49 | 286 mins |
| 5 | Mika Vayrynen | 4 | 49 | 393 mins |

## KEY PLAYERS - MIDFIELDERS

**1 John de Jong**

| | | | |
|---|---|---|---|
| Goals in the League | 9 | Contribution to Attacking Power<br>Average number of minutes between League team goals while on pitch | 44 |
| Defensive Rating<br>Average number of mins between League goals conceded while he was on the pitch | 60 | Scoring Difference<br>Defensive Rating minus Contribution to Attacking Power | 16 |

| | PLAYER | LGE GOALS | DEF RATE | POWER | SCORE DIFF |
|---|---|---|---|---|---|
| 2 | Daniel Jensen | 4 | 56 | 47 | 9 mins |
| 3 | Petter Hansson | 3 | 56 | 48 | 8 mins |
| 4 | Arek Radomski | 0 | 55 | 56 | -1 mins |

## KEY PLAYERS - DEFENDERS

**1 Erik Edman**

| | | | |
|---|---|---|---|
| Goals Conceded (GC)<br>The number of League goals conceded while he was on the pitch | 49 | Clean Sheets<br>In games when he played at least 70 minutes | 6 |
| Defensive Rating<br>Ave number of mins between League goals conceded while on the pitch | 55 | Club Defensive Rating<br>Average number of mins between League goals conceded by the club this season | 56 |

| | PLAYER | CON LGE | CLEAN SHEETS | DEF RATE |
|---|---|---|---|---|
| 2 | Ronnie Venema | 40 | 3 | 52 mins |
| 3 | Johan Hansma | 37 | 3 | 52 mins |

## GOALS SCORED

**AT HOME**

| | | |
|---|---|---|
| MOST | Ajax | 57 |
| | | 37 |
| LEAST | Twente | 18 |

**AWAY**

| | | |
|---|---|---|
| MOST | PSV | 44 |
| | | 24 |
| LEAST | Roosendaal & Groningen | 9 |

## GOALS CONCEDED

**AT HOME**

| | | |
|---|---|---|
| LEAST | PSV | 7 |
| | | 21 |
| MOST | Excelsior | 38 |

**AWAY**

| | | |
|---|---|---|
| LEAST | PSV | 13 |
| | | 34 |
| MOST | De G'schap | 50 |

## KEY GOALKEEPER

**1 Hans Vonk**

| | |
|---|---|
| Goals Conceded in the League | 55 |
| Defensive Rating<br>Ave number of mins between League goals conceded while on the pitch | 56 |
| Counting Games<br>Games when he played at least 70 mins | 34 |
| Clean Sheets<br>In games when he played at least 70 mins | 6 |

## TOP POINT EARNERS

| | PLAYER | GAMES | AVE |
|---|---|---|---|
| 1 | Vayrynen | 14 | 2.07 |
| 2 | Jensen, D | 30 | 1.57 |
| 3 | de Jong | 25 | 1.56 |
| 4 | Hansma | 19 | 1.53 |
| 5 | Denneboom | 27 | 1.48 |
| 6 | Hansson | 32 | 1.47 |
| 7 | Selakovic | 16 | 1.44 |
| 8 | Vonk | 34 | 1.38 |
| 9 | Venema | 22 | 1.36 |
| 10 | Radomski | 28 | 1.32 |
| | **CLUB AVERAGE:** | | **1.38** |

Ave = Average points per match in Counting Games

## ATTENDANCES

HOME GROUND: ABE LENSTRA STADION CAPACITY: 14700 AVERAGE LEAGUE AT HOME: 14335

| | | |
|---|---|---|
| 36 | Ajax | 50272 |
| 27 | Feyenoord | 46200 |
| 13 | PSV Eindhoven | 33500 |
| 14 | Vitesse Arnhem | 22000 |
| 23 | Utrecht | 16300 |
| 24 | PSV Eindhoven | 14700 |
| 15 | Ajax | 14400 |
| 31 | Vitesse Arnhem | 14400 |
| 33 | Groningen | 14400 |
| 17 | Feyenoord | 14400 |
| 26 | Twente | 14400 |
| 29 | NEC Nijmegen | 14400 |
| 18 | Utrecht | 14400 |
| 21 | AZ Alkmaar | 14300 |
| 19 | Zwolle | 14300 |
| 28 | Roda JC Kerk | 14300 |
| 4 | NAC Breda | 14300 |
| 35 | Roosendaal | 14200 |
| 12 | De Graafschap | 14200 |
| 11 | Excelsior | 14200 |
| 2 | RKC Waalwijk | 14200 |
| 9 | Willem II Tilb | 14200 |
| 6 | Roda JC Kerk | 13250 |
| 10 | Twente | 13250 |
| 16 | Groningen | 12500 |
| 20 | NAC Breda | 12123 |
| 8 | Nat Bucharest | 12000 |
| 32 | Willem II Tilb | 11000 |
| 22 | De Graafschap | 11000 |
| 7 | NEC Nijmegen | 11000 |
| 1 | AZ Alkmaar | 7025 |
| 5 | Nat Bucharest | 7000 |
| 25 | RKC Waalwijk | 7000 |
| 34 | Zwolle | 6000 |
| 3 | Roosendaal | 5000 |
| 30 | Excelsior | 3164 |

■ Home □ Away ▒ Neutral

## DISCIPLINARY RECORDS

| | PLAYER | YELLOW | RED | AVE |
|---|---|---|---|---|
| 1 | Klompe | 1 | 1 | 229 |
| 2 | Venema | 5 | 0 | 412 |
| 3 | Vayrynen | 3 | 0 | 523 |
| 4 | Sibon | 2 | 0 | 526 |
| 5 | Radomski | 5 | 0 | 536 |
| 6 | de Jong | 4 | 0 | 568 |
| 7 | Denneboom | 4 | 0 | 645 |
| 8 | Edman | 4 | 0 | 672 |
| 9 | Nurmela | 3 | 0 | 858 |
| 10 | Jensen, D | 3 | 0 | 900 |
| 11 | Hansma | 2 | 0 | 955 |
| 12 | Hansson | 2 | 0 | 1459 |
| 13 | Vonk | 2 | 0 | 1530 |
| | Other | 7 | 0 | |
| | TOTAL | 47 | 1 | |

## LEAGUE GOALS

| | PLAYER | MINS | GOALS | AVE |
|---|---|---|---|---|
| 1 | Denneboom | 2583 | 10 | 258 |
| 2 | Nurmela | 2575 | 9 | 286 |
| 3 | de Jong | 2274 | 9 | 253 |
| 4 | Selakovic | 1699 | 8 | 212 |
| 5 | Samaras | 362 | 4 | 91 |
| 6 | Sibon | 1052 | 4 | 263 |
| 7 | Vayrynen | 1571 | 4 | 393 |
| 8 | Jensen, D | 2702 | 4 | 676 |
| 9 | Hansson | 2918 | 3 | 973 |
| 10 | Venema | 2061 | 2 | 1031 |
| 11 | Hansma | 1911 | 2 | 956 |
| 12 | de Nooijer | 360 | 1 | 360 |
| | Other | | 1 | |
| | TOTAL | | 61 | |

## MONTH BY MONTH GUIDE TO THE POINTS

| MONTH | POINTS | % |
|---|---|---|
| AUGUST | 1 | 17% |
| SEPTEMBER | 0 | 0% |
| OCTOBER | 5 | 56% |
| NOVEMBER | 6 | 50% |
| DECEMBER | 8 | 67% |
| JANUARY | | |
| FEBRUARY | 8 | 67% |
| MARCH | 3 | 25% |
| APRIL | 4 | 33% |
| MAY | 12 | 80% |

## LEAGUE APPEARANCES, BOOKINGS AND CAPS

| | AGE | IN THE SQUAD | COUNTING GAMES | MINUTES ON PITCH | YELLOW CARDS | RED CARDS | THIS SEASON | HOME COUNTRY |
|---|---|---|---|---|---|---|---|---|
| **Goalkeepers** | | | | | | | | |
| Jacob De Vries | 23 | 29 | 0 | 0 | 0 | 0 | - | Holland |
| Hans Vonk | 33 | 34 | 34 | 3060 | 2 | 0 | - | South Africa |
| **Defenders** | | | | | | | | |
| Said Bakkati | 21 | 28 | 7 | 830 | 0 | 0 | - | Holland |
| Gerard de Nooijer | 34 | 6 | 4 | 360 | 0 | 0 | - | Holland |
| Arjan Ebbinge | 28 | 23 | 2 | 381 | 1 | 0 | - | Holland |
| Erik Edman | 24 | 30 | 30 | 2689 | 4 | 0 | 8 | Sweden (20) |
| Johan Hansma | 34 | 24 | 19 | 1911 | 2 | 0 | - | Holland |
| Marc Hegeman | 27 | 5 | 1 | 164 | 2 | 0 | - | Holland |
| Tieme Klompe | 27 | 22 | 3 | 458 | 1 | 1 | - | Holland |
| Ronnie Venema | 28 | 29 | 22 | 2061 | 5 | 0 | - | Holland |
| **Midfielders** | | | | | | | | |
| Abgar Barsom | 25 | 15 | 2 | 349 | 1 | 0 | - | Sweden |
| Antonio Correia | | 3 | 0 | 19 | 0 | 0 | - | |
| John de Jong | 26 | 26 | 25 | 2274 | 4 | 0 | - | Holland |
| Mark Jan Flederus | | 6 | 0 | 21 | 0 | 0 | - | Holland |
| Jesper Hakansson | 22 | 2 | 0 | 0 | 0 | 0 | - | Denmark |
| Petter Hansson | 26 | 34 | 32 | 2918 | 2 | 0 | - | Sweden |
| Thomas Holm | 22 | 1 | 0 | 0 | 0 | 0 | - | |
| Jos Hooiveld | | 10 | 0 | 5 | 0 | 0 | - | Holland |
| Daniel Jensen | 24 | 33 | 30 | 2702 | 3 | 0 | - | Denmark |
| Arek Radomski | 26 | 31 | 28 | 2680 | 5 | 0 | 1 | Poland (29) |
| Georgios Samaras | 18 | 23 | 2 | 362 | 0 | 0 | - | Holland |
| Marcel Seip | 21 | 13 | 4 | 412 | 1 | 0 | - | Holland |
| Stephan van Hoving | | 1 | 0 | 0 | 0 | 0 | - | Holland |
| **Forwards** | | | | | | | | |
| Romano Denneboom | 22 | 33 | 27 | 2583 | 4 | 0 | - | Holland |
| Niels Kokmeijer | 23 | 1 | 0 | 0 | 0 | 0 | - | Holland |
| Santi Kolk | 21 | 20 | 0 | 126 | 1 | 0 | - | Holland |
| Mike Nurmela | 31 | 32 | 26 | 2575 | 3 | 0 | - | Finland |
| Radoslav Samardzic | 33 | 12 | 3 | 333 | 0 | 0 | - | Serbia & Montenegro |
| Stefan Selakovic | 26 | 32 | 16 | 1699 | 1 | 0 | 2 | Sweden (20) |
| Gerald Sibon | 29 | 13 | 10 | 1052 | 2 | 0 | - | Holland |
| Jeffrey Talan | 31 | 6 | 0 | 58 | 0 | 0 | - | Holland |
| Mika Vayrynen | 21 | 25 | 14 | 1571 | 3 | 0 | - | Finland |

**KEY:** LEAGUE BOOKINGS CAPS (FIFA RANKING)

## TEAM OF THE SEASON

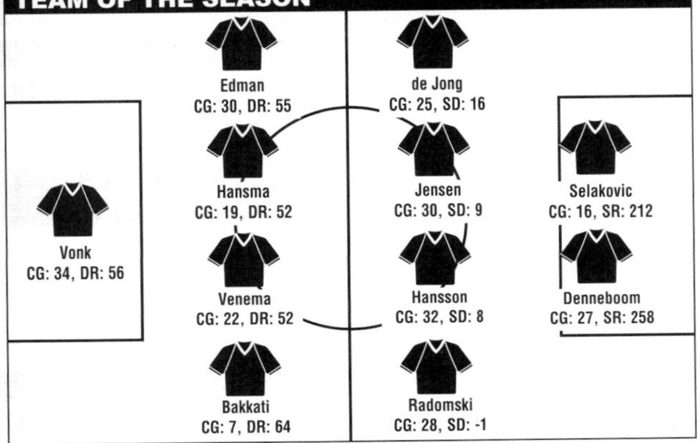

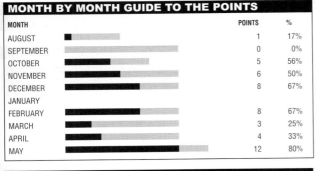

Vonk
CG: 34, DR: 56
Edman
CG: 30, DR: 55
Hansma
CG: 19, DR: 52
Venema
CG: 22, DR: 52
Bakkati
CG: 7, DR: 64
de Jong
CG: 25, SD: 16
Jensen
CG: 30, SD: 9
Hansson
CG: 32, SD: 8
Radomski
CG: 28, SD: -1
Selakovic
CG: 16, SR: 212
Denneboom
CG: 27, SR: 258


**KEY:** DR = Defensive Rate, SD = Scoring Difference, SR = Strike Rate, CG = Counting Games – League games playing at least 70 minutes

## SQUAD APPEARANCES

| Match | 1 | 2 | 3 | 4 | 5 | 6 | 7 | 8 | 9 | 10 | 11 | 12 | 13 | 14 | 15 | 16 | 17 | 18 | 19 | 20 | 21 | 22 | 23 | 24 | 25 | 26 | 27 | 28 | 29 | 30 | 31 | 32 | 33 | 34 | 35 | 36 |
|---|---|---|---|---|---|---|---|---|---|---|---|---|---|---|---|---|---|---|---|---|---|---|---|---|---|---|---|---|---|---|---|---|---|---|---|---|
| Venue | A | H | A | H | A | A | A | H | H | A | H | H | A | A | H | A | H | H | H | A | H | A | A | H | A | H | A | H | H | A | H | A | H | A | H | A |
| Competition | L | L | L | L | E | L | L | E | L | L | L | L | L | L | L | L | L | L | L | L | L | L | L | L | L | L | L | L | L | L | L | L | L | L | L | L |
| Result | D | L | L | L | L | L | L | W | D | D | W | W | L | W | L | D | W | D | W | D | W | W | D | L | L | W | L | W | L | L | D | W | W | W | W | L |

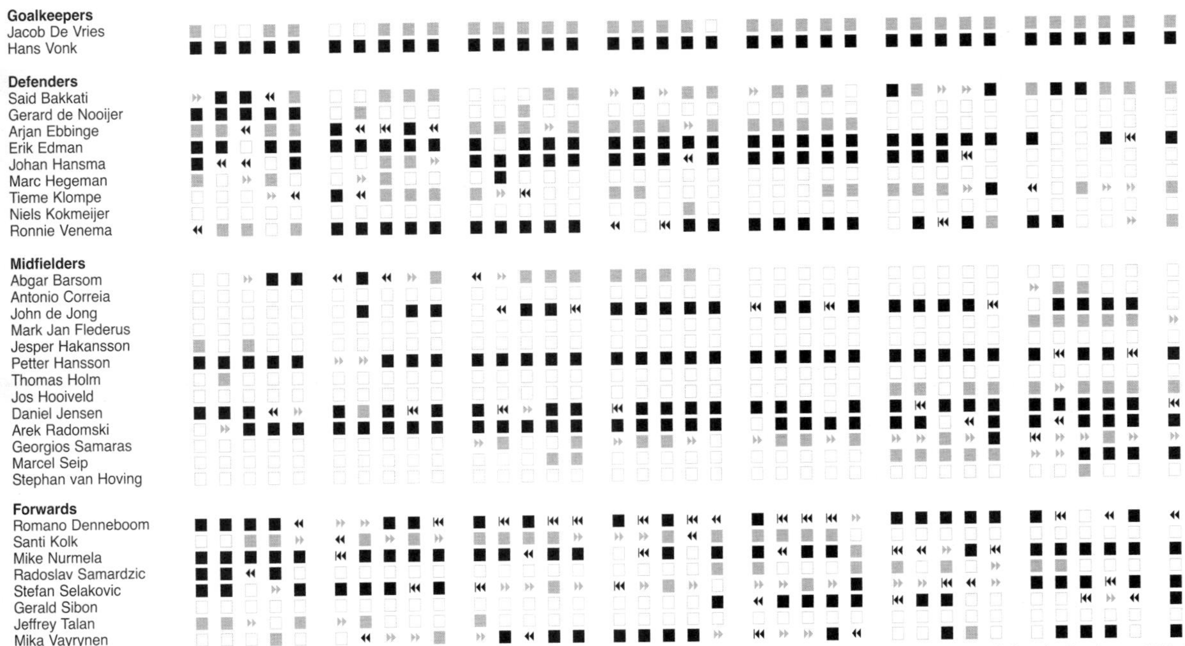

Goalkeepers
Jacob De Vries
Hans Vonk
Defenders
Said Bakkati
Gerard de Nooijer
Arjan Ebbinge
Erik Edman
Johan Hansma
Marc Hegeman
Tieme Klompe
Niels Kokmeijer
Ronnie Venema
Midfielders
Abgar Barsom
Antonio Correia
John de Jong
Mark Jan Flederus
Jesper Hakansson
Petter Hansson
Thomas Holm
Jos Hooiveld
Daniel Jensen
Arek Radomski
Georgios Samaras
Marcel Seip
Stephan van Hoving
Forwards
Romano Denneboom
Santi Kolk
Mike Nurmela
Radoslav Samardzic
Stefan Selakovic
Gerald Sibon
Jeffrey Talan
Mika Vayrynen


**KEY:** On all match · On bench · Subbed or sent off (Counting game) · Subbed or sent off (playing less than 70 minutes) · Subbed on from bench (Counting Game) · Subbed on (playing less than 70 minutes) · Subbed on and then subbed or sent off (Counting Game) · Subbed on and then subbed or sent off (playing less than 70 minutes) · Not in 16

# UTRECHT

Final Position: **8th**

| | | | | | | |
|---|---|---|---|---|---|---|
| 1 | lge | Ajax | A | L | 1-3 | Chivu 31 og |
| 2 | lge | Twente | A | D | 1-1 | Kuijt 27 |
| 3 | lge | De Graafschap | H | W | 4-0 | Kuijt 2 pen,75,75; Gluscevic 27; Tanghe 52 |
| 4 | lge | Willem II Tilb | A | L | 0-2 | |
| 5 | uc1rl1 | Legia Warsaw | A | L | 1-4 | Kuijt 48 og |
| 6 | lge | Groningen | A | D | 0-0 | |
| 7 | lge | Vitesse Arnhem | H | W | 1-0 | Van den Bergh 28 |
| 8 | uc1rl2 | Legia Warsaw | H | L | 1-3 | Amelianchyuk 44 og |
| 9 | lge | Roosendaal | H | D | 2-2 | Kuijt 39; Schut 90 |
| 10 | lge | Excelsior | A | D | 1-1 | Van den Bergh 31 |
| 11 | lge | NAC Breda | H | W | 1-0 | Van den Bergh 80 |
| 12 | lge | RKC Waalwijk | A | W | 1-0 | Roiha 56 |
| 13 | lge | Zwolle | H | W | 2-0 | Tanghe 2; Van den Bergh 10 |
| 14 | lge | AZ Alkmaar | H | D | 2-2 | Tanghe 71; Kuijt 90 |
| 15 | lge | NEC Nijmegen | H | W | 3-2 | Tanghe 13; Gluscevic 46; Bosschaart 65 |
| 16 | lge | Feyenoord | A | L | 1-2 | Tanghe 78 |
| 17 | lge | PSV Eindhoven | H | L | 1-3 | Van den Bergh 45 |
| 18 | lge | Heerenveen | A | D | 2-2 | Kuijt 54,58 pen |
| 19 | lge | Roda JC Kerk | A | L | 0-1 | |
| 20 | lge | Excelsior | H | D | 2-2 | Roiha 58; Kuijt 71 |
| 21 | lge | Roosendaal | A | W | 1-0 | Kuijt 20 |
| 22 | lge | Ajax | H | W | 1-0 | Kuijt 71 |
| 23 | lge | Heerenveen | H | D | 2-2 | Schut 29; Kuijt 35 pen |
| 24 | lge | Vitesse Arnhem | A | W | 4-1 | Kuijt 22,51; Vreven 30; Roiha 82 |
| 25 | lge | De Graafschap | A | L | 0-1 | |
| 26 | lge | AZ Alkmaar | A | L | 0-2 | |
| 27 | lge | Groningen | H | D | 0-0 | |
| 28 | lge | Zwolle | A | L | 1-3 | Kuijt 80 |
| 29 | lge | Willem II Tilb | H | D | 1-1 | Gluscevic 83 |
| 30 | lge | RKC Waalwijk | H | W | 4-3 | Kuijt 26,32 pen,87 pen; Jochemsen 90 |
| 31 | lge | NEC Nijmegen | A | W | 2-1 | Tanghe 19,79 |
| 32 | lge | Feyenoord | H | L | 1-2 | Gluscevic 12 |
| 33 | lge | NAC Breda | A | L | 0-2 | |
| 34 | lge | Roda JC Kerk | H | D | 4-4 | Gluscevic 2,41; Kuijt 9 pen; Chaiat 82 |
| 35 | lge | PSV Eindhoven | A | L | 0-2 | |
| 36 | lge | Twente | H | W | 3-2 | Kuijt 56,83; Chaiat 77 |

## KEY PLAYERS - GOALSCORERS

**1 Dirk Kuijt**

| | | | |
|---|---|---|---|
| Goals in the League | 21 | Player Strike Rate<br>Average number of minutes between League goals scored by player | 145 |
| Contribution to Attacking Power<br>Average number of minutes between League team goals while on pitch | 62 | Club Strike Rate<br>Average number of minutes between League goals scored by club | 61 |

| | PLAYER | LGE GOALS | POWER | STRIKE RATE |
|---|---|---|---|---|
| 2 | Igor Gluscevic | 6 | 64 | 247 mins |
| 3 | Stefaan Tanghe | 7 | 64 | 405 mins |
| 4 | Dave Van den Bergh | 5 | 56 | 544 mins |
| 5 | Alje Schut | 2 | 63 | 1209 mins |

## KEY PLAYERS - MIDFIELDERS

**1 Karim Touzani**

| | | | |
|---|---|---|---|
| Goals in the League | 0 | Contribution to Attacking Power<br>Average number of minutes between League team goals while on pitch | 60 |
| Defensive Rating<br>Average number of mins between League goals conceded while he was on the pitch | 92 | Scoring Difference<br>Defensive Rating minus Contribution to Attacking Power | 32 |

| | PLAYER | LGE GOALS | DEF RATE | POWER | SCORE DIFF |
|---|---|---|---|---|---|
| 2 | Tom van Mol | 0 | 87 | 62 | 25 mins |
| 3 | Arco Jochemsen | 1 | 62 | 58 | 4 mins |
| 4 | Jordy Zuidam | 0 | 60 | 57 | 3 mins |
| 5 | Stefaan Tanghe | 7 | 63 | 64 | -1 mins |

## KEY PLAYERS - DEFENDERS

**1 Stijn Vreven**

| | | | |
|---|---|---|---|
| Goals Conceded (GC)<br>The number of League goals conceded while he was on the pitch | 35 | Clean Sheets<br>In games when he played at least 70 minutes | 9 |
| Defensive Rating<br>Ave number of mins between League goals conceded while on the pitch | 66 | Club Defensive Rating<br>Average number of mins between League goals conceded by the club this season | 62 |

| | PLAYER | CON LGE | CLEAN SHEETS | DEF RATE |
|---|---|---|---|---|
| 2 | Pascal Bosschaart | 48 | 8 | 63 mins |
| 3 | Alje Schut | 40 | 6 | 60 mins |
| 4 | Patrick Zwaanswijk | 42 | 6 | 58 mins |
| 5 | Ettiene Shew-Atjon | 28 | 1 | 51 mins |

## GOALS SCORED

**AT HOME**

| | | |
|---|---|---|
| MOST | Ajax | 57 |
| | | 34 |
| LEAST | Twente | 18 |

**AWAY**

| | | |
|---|---|---|
| MOST | PSV | 44 |
| | | 15 |
| LEAST | Roosendaal & Groningen | 9 |

## GOALS CONCEDED

**AT HOME**

| | | |
|---|---|---|
| LEAST | PSV | 7 |
| | | 25 |
| MOST | Excelsior | 38 |

**AWAY**

| | | |
|---|---|---|
| LEAST | PSV | 13 |
| | | 24 |
| MOST | De G'schap | 50 |

## KEY GOALKEEPER

**1 Harald Wapenaar**

| | |
|---|---|
| Goals Conceded in the League | 48 |
| Defensive Rating<br>Ave number of mins between League goals conceded while on the pitch | 56 |
| Counting Games<br>Games when he played at least 70 mins | 30 |
| Clean Sheets<br>In games when he played at least 70 mins | 6 |

## TOP POINT EARNERS

| | PLAYER | GAMES | AVE |
|---|---|---|---|
| 1 | van Mol | 16 | 1.63 |
| 2 | Vreven | 25 | 1.48 |
| 3 | Van den Bergh | 31 | 1.45 |
| 4 | Bosschaart | 33 | 1.39 |
| 5 | Kuijt | 34 | 1.38 |
| 6 | Schut | 26 | 1.38 |
| 7 | Tanghe | 32 | 1.34 |
| 8 | Wapenaar | 30 | 1.23 |
| 9 | Shew-Atjon | 15 | 1.20 |
| 10 | Zwaanswijk | 26 | 1.19 |
| | **CLUB AVERAGE:** | | **1.38** |

Ave = Average points per match in Counting Games

## ATTENDANCES

HOME GROUND: NEIUW GALGEWAARD CAPACITY: 18925 AVERAGE LEAGUE AT HOME: 16285

| | | | | | | | | |
|---|---|---|---|---|---|---|---|---|
| 16 | Feyenoord | 42000 | 36 | Twente | 16200 | 19 | Roda JC Kerk | 12500 |
| 1 | Ajax | 34434 | 34 | Roda JC Kerk | 15500 | 31 | NEC Nijmegen | 12000 |
| 35 | PSV Eindhoven | 34000 | 7 | Vitesse Arnhem | 15331 | 6 | Groningen | 12000 |
| 24 | Vitesse Arnhem | 22800 | 15 | NEC Nijmegen | 15000 | 25 | De Graafschap | 11000 |
| 32 | Feyenoord | 18925 | 30 | RKC Waalwijk | 15000 | 5 | Legia Warsaw | 8000 |
| 17 | PSV Eindhoven | 18500 | 13 | Zwolle | 14700 | 26 | AZ Alkmaar | 7103 |
| 22 | Ajax | 18000 | 11 | NAC Breda | 14500 | 12 | RKC Waalwijk | 6000 |
| 3 | De Graafschap | 18000 | 18 | Heerenveen | 14400 | 21 | Roosendaal | 5000 |
| 14 | AZ Alkmaar | 17500 | 8 | Legia Warsaw | 14000 | 28 | Zwolle | 5000 |
| 9 | Roosendaal | 17500 | 4 | Willem II Tilb | 13400 | 10 | Excelsior | 3000 |
| 29 | Willem II Tilb | 16500 | 2 | Twente | 13300 | | | |
| 27 | Groningen | 16400 | 20 | Excelsior | 13000 | | | |
| 23 | Heerenveen | 16300 | 33 | NAC Breda | 12915 | | | |

■ Home □ Away ▒ Neutral

## DISCIPLINARY RECORDS

| | PLAYER | YELLOW | RED | AVE |
|---|---|---|---|---|
| 1 | de Jong | 8 | 1 | 274 |
| 2 | Vreven | 7 | 0 | 331 |
| 3 | Touzani | 3 | 0 | 338 |
| 4 | Zuidam | 3 | 0 | 382 |
| 5 | Tanghe | 6 | 0 | 472 |
| 6 | Shew-Atjon | 3 | 0 | 475 |
| 7 | Zwaanswijk | 2 | 1 | 810 |
| 8 | Van den Bergh | 2 | 1 | 907 |
| 9 | Jochemsen | 1 | 0 | 1110 |
| 10 | Bosschaart | 2 | 0 | 1501 |
| 11 | Kuijt | 2 | 0 | 1519 |
| 12 | Schut | 1 | 0 | 2417 |
| | Other | 0 | 0 | |
| | TOTAL | 40 | 3 | |

## LEAGUE GOALS

| | PLAYER | MINS | GOALS | AVE |
|---|---|---|---|---|
| 1 | Kuijt | 3039 | 20 | 152 |
| 2 | Tanghe | 2833 | 7 | 405 |
| 3 | Gluscevic | 1479 | 6 | 247 |
| 4 | Van den Bergh | 2722 | 5 | 544 |
| 5 | Roiha | 772 | 3 | 257 |
| 6 | Schut | 2417 | 2 | 1209 |
| 7 | Chaiat | 253 | 2 | 127 |
| 8 | Jochemsen | 1110 | 1 | 1110 |
| 9 | Vreven | 2321 | 1 | 2321 |
| 10 | Bosschaart | 3002 | 1 | 3002 |
| | Other | | 1 | |
| | TOTAL | | 49 | |

## MONTH BY MONTH GUIDE TO THE POINTS

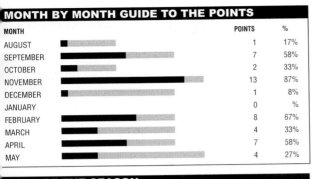

| MONTH | POINTS | % |
|---|---|---|
| AUGUST | 1 | 17% |
| SEPTEMBER | 7 | 58% |
| OCTOBER | 2 | 33% |
| NOVEMBER | 13 | 87% |
| DECEMBER | 1 | 8% |
| JANUARY | 0 | % |
| FEBRUARY | 8 | 67% |
| MARCH | 4 | 33% |
| APRIL | 7 | 58% |
| MAY | 4 | 27% |

## LEAGUE APPEARANCES, BOOKINGS AND CAPS

| | AGE | IN THE SQUAD | COUNTING GAMES | MINUTES ON PITCH | YELLOW CARDS | RED CARDS | THIS SEASON | HOME COUNTRY |
|---|---|---|---|---|---|---|---|---|
| **Goalkeepers** | | | | | | | | |
| Rene Ponk | 31 | 30 | 4 | 360 | 0 | 0 | - | Holland |
| Harald Wapenaar | 33 | 30 | 30 | 2700 | 0 | 0 | - | Holland |
| **Defenders** | | | | | | | | |
| Pascal Bosschaart | 23 | 34 | 33 | 3002 | 2 | 0 | - | Holland |
| Robert Roest | 33 | 33 | 1 | 250 | 0 | 0 | - | Holland |
| Alje Schut | 22 | 34 | 26 | 2417 | 1 | 0 | - | Holland |
| Ettiene Shew-Atjon | 23 | 34 | 15 | 1426 | 3 | 0 | - | Holland |
| Stijn Vreven | 29 | 27 | 25 | 2321 | 7 | 0 | 2 | Belgium (16) |
| Patrick Zwaanswijk | 28 | 33 | 26 | 2430 | 2 | 1 | - | Holland |
| **Midfielders** | | | | | | | | |
| Arno Arts | 34 | 33 | 2 | 298 | 0 | 0 | - | Holland |
| Ergun Cakir | | 2 | 0 | 0 | 0 | 0 | - | Turkey |
| Abdelhali Chaiat | | 17 | 2 | 253 | 0 | 0 | - | |
| Jean-Paul de Jong | 32 | 31 | 26 | 2466 | 8 | 1 | - | Holland |
| Arco Jochemsen | 32 | 32 | 8 | 1110 | 1 | 0 | - | Holland |
| Richal Leitoe | | 1 | 0 | 0 | 0 | 0 | - | |
| Stefaan Tanghe | 31 | 32 | 32 | 2833 | 6 | 0 | - | Belgium |
| Joost Terol | | 6 | 0 | 0 | 0 | 0 | - | Holland |
| Karim Touzani | 22 | 12 | 11 | 1014 | 3 | 0 | - | Holland |
| Bas Van den Brink | | 3 | 0 | 0 | 0 | 0 | - | Holland |
| Tom van Mol | 30 | 19 | 16 | 1562 | 0 | 0 | - | Belgium |
| Jordy Zuidam | 22 | 32 | 9 | 1148 | 3 | 0 | - | Holland |
| **Forwards** | | | | | | | | |
| Igor Gluscevic | 29 | 22 | 13 | 1479 | 0 | 0 | - | Serbia & Montenegro |
| Frank Karreman | 19 | 1 | 0 | 0 | 0 | 0 | - | Holland |
| Dirk Kuijt | 22 | 34 | 34 | 3039 | 2 | 0 | 1 | Holland (6) |
| Paulus Roiha | 22 | 27 | 5 | 772 | 0 | 0 | - | Finland |
| Dave Van den Bergh | 27 | 31 | 31 | 2722 | 2 | 1 | - | Holland |

**KEY:** LEAGUE BOOKINGS CAPS (FIFA RANKING)

## TEAM OF THE SEASON

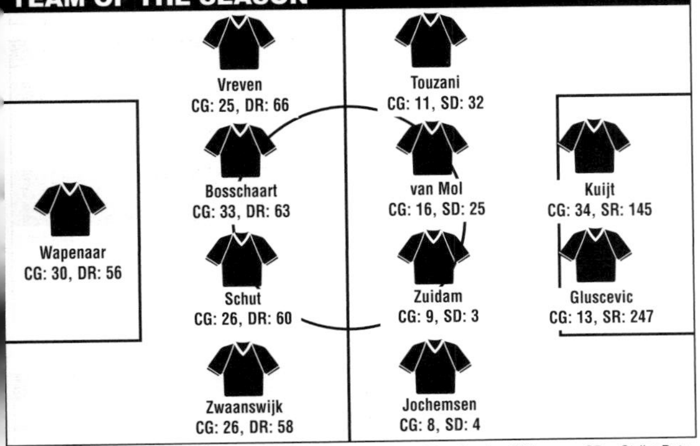
Vreven
CG: 25, DR: 66
Touzani
CG: 11, SD: 32
Bosschaart
CG: 33, DR: 63
van Mol
CG: 16, SD: 25
Kuijt
CG: 34, SR: 145
Wapenaar
CG: 30, DR: 56
Schut
CG: 26, DR: 60
Zuidam
CG: 9, SD: 3
Gluscevic
CG: 13, SR: 247
Zwaanswijk
CG: 26, DR: 58
Jochemsen
CG: 8, SD: 4

**KEY:** DR = Defensive Rate, SD = Scoring Difference, SR = Strike Rate, CG = Counting Games – League games playing at least 70 minutes

## SQUAD APPEARANCES

| Match | 1 | 2 | 3 | 4 | 5 | 6 | 7 | 8 | 9 | 10 | 11 | 12 | 13 | 14 | 15 | 16 | 17 | 18 | 19 | 20 | 21 | 22 | 23 | 24 | 25 | 26 | 27 | 28 | 29 | 30 | 31 | 32 | 33 | 34 | 35 | 36 |
|---|---|---|---|---|---|---|---|---|---|---|---|---|---|---|---|---|---|---|---|---|---|---|---|---|---|---|---|---|---|---|---|---|---|---|---|---|
| Venue | A | A | H | A | A | A | H | H | H | A | H | A | H | H | H | A | H | A | A | H | A | H | H | A | A | A | H | A | H | H | A | H | A | H | A | H |
| Competition | L | L | L | L | E | L | L | E | L | L | L | L | L | L | L | L | L | L | L | L | L | L | L | L | L | L | L | L | L | L | L | L | L | L | L | L |
| Result | L | D | W | L | L | D | W | L | D | D | W | W | W | D | W | L | L | D | L | D | W | W | D | W | L | L | D | L | D | W | W | L | L | D | L | W |

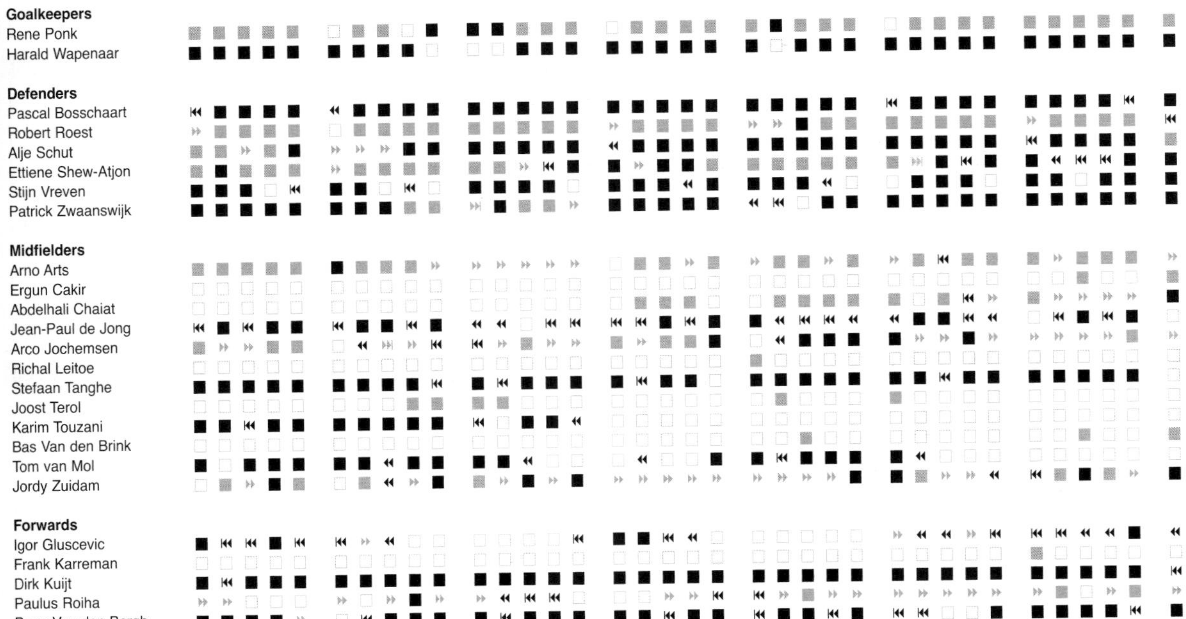
Goalkeepers
Rene Ponk
Harald Wapenaar
Defenders
Pascal Bosschaart
Robert Roest
Alje Schut
Ettiene Shew-Atjon
Stijn Vreven
Patrick Zwaanswijk
Midfielders
Arno Arts
Ergun Cakir
Abdelhali Chaiat
Jean-Paul de Jong
Arco Jochemsen
Richal Leitoe
Stefaan Tanghe
Joost Terol
Karim Touzani
Bas Van den Brink
Tom van Mol
Jordy Zuidam
Forwards
Igor Gluscevic
Frank Karreman
Dirk Kuijt
Paulus Roiha
Dave Van den Bergh

**KEY:** ■ On all match ■ On bench ⏮ Subbed or sent off (Counting game) ◀◀ Subbed or sent off (playing less than 70 minutes) ⏭ Subbed on from bench (Counting Game) ▶▶ Subbed on (playing less than 70 minutes) Subbed on and then subbed or sent off (Counting Game) Subbed on and then subbed or sent off (playing less than 70 minutes) □ Not in 16

# RKC WAALWIJK

Final Position: **9th**

| | | | | | | |
|---|---|---|---|---|---|---|
| 1 | lge | De Graafschap | H | W | 4-2 | Hoogendorp 28,61; Oost 62; Cornelisse 68 |
| 2 | lge | Heerenveen | A | W | 2-1 | Cornelisse 59; Hoogendorp 69 |
| 3 | lge | Twente | H | W | 3-2 | Hoogendorp 42,79; Putter 89 |
| 4 | lge | PSV Eindhoven | A | L | 0-4 | |
| 5 | lge | Vitesse Arnhem | A | D | 1-1 | van Diemen 90 |
| 6 | lge | Excelsior | H | L | 0-3 | |
| 7 | lge | Zwolle | H | L | 0-2 | |
| 8 | lge | Groningen | A | W | 3-2 | Cornelisse 7,57; van den Berg 47 |
| 9 | lge | Ajax | H | D | 1-1 | Hoogendorp 57 |
| 10 | lge | Roosendaal | A | D | 0-0 | |
| 11 | lge | Utrecht | H | L | 0-1 | |
| 12 | lge | Willem II Tilb | A | W | 1-0 | Cornelisse 4 |
| 13 | lge | Feyenoord | H | W | 1-0 | Oost 82 |
| 14 | lge | AZ Alkmaar | A | L | 0-2 | |
| 15 | lge | Roda JC Kerk | H | W | 2-1 | Petrovic 33; Janssen 60; Hoogendorp 90 |
| 16 | lge | NAC Breda | A | L | 0-1 | |
| 17 | lge | NEC Nijmegen | A | D | 0-0 | |
| 18 | lge | Groningen | H | W | 1-0 | Janssen 68 |
| 19 | lge | PSV Eindhoven | H | L | 0-1 | |
| 20 | lge | Vitesse Arnhem | H | W | 1-0 | van Diemen 44 |
| 21 | lge | Zwolle | A | L | 1-2 | Janssen 59 |
| 22 | lge | Excelsior | A | W | 2-1 | Hoogendorp 32,58 |
| 23 | lge | Heerenveen | H | W | 3-0 | Hoogendorp 14; Cornelisse 49; Oost 78 |
| 24 | lge | De Graafschap | A | W | 4-2 | Fuchs 6; van den Berg 10; Hoogendorp 67; Cornelisse 90 |
| 25 | lge | Twente | A | L | 1-2 | Janssen 16 |
| 26 | lge | AZ Alkmaar | H | W | 2-0 | Cornelisse 34; van Diemen 37 |
| 27 | lge | Roosendaal | H | L | 1-2 | Hoogendorp 44 pen |
| 28 | lge | Utrecht | A | L | 3-4 | Cornelisse 28; Hoogendorp 46,49 |
| 29 | lge | Willem II Tilb | H | W | 3-1 | Nikiforov 5; Putter 90; Hoogendorp 90 |
| 30 | lge | Ajax | A | L | 1-6 | Janssen 89 |
| 31 | lge | Feyenoord | A | L | 1-2 | van Diemen 5 |
| 32 | lge | NAC Breda | H | L | 2-3 | Hoogendorp 74 pen,77 pen |
| 33 | lge | Roda JC Kerk | A | L | 0-1 | |
| 34 | lge | NEC Nijmegen | H | L | 0-1 | |

## KEY PLAYERS - GOALSCORERS

**1 Rick Hoogendorp**

| | | | |
|---|---|---|---|
| Goals in the League | 16 | Player Strike Rate<br>Average number of minutes between League goals scored by player | 152 |
| Contribution to Attacking Power<br>Average number of minutes between League team goals while on pitch | 67 | Club Strike Rate<br>Average number of minutes between League goals scored by club | 70 |

| | PLAYER | LGE GOALS | POWER | STRIKE RATE |
|---|---|---|---|---|
| 2 | Youri Cornelisse | 9 | 65 | 298 mins |
| 3 | Jochen Janssen | 5 | 61 | 419 mins |
| 4 | Patrick van Diemen | 4 | 71 | 737 mins |
| 5 | Peter van den Berg | 2 | 66 | 1304 mins |

## KEY PLAYERS - MIDFIELDERS

**1 Zeljko Petrovic**

| | | | |
|---|---|---|---|
| Goals in the League | 1 | Contribution to Attacking Power<br>Average number of minutes between League team goals while on pitch | 51 |
| Defensive Rating<br>Average number of mins between League goals conceded while he was on the pitch | 67 | Scoring Difference<br>Defensive Rating minus Contribution to Attacking Power | 16 |

| | PLAYER | LGE GOALS | DEF RATE | POWER | SCORE DIFF |
|---|---|---|---|---|---|
| 2 | Robert Fuchs | 1 | 54 | 62 | -8 mins |
| 3 | Rogier Molhoek | 0 | 97 | 106 | -9 mins |
| 4 | Garry de Graef | 0 | 71 | 82 | -11 mins |
| 5 | Patrick van Diemen | 4 | 59 | 72 | -13 mins |

## KEY PLAYERS - DEFENDERS

**1 Peter van den Berg**

| | | | |
|---|---|---|---|
| Goals Conceded (GC)<br>The number of League goals conceded while he was on the pitch | 39 | Clean Sheets<br>In games when he played at least 70 minutes | 7 |
| Defensive Rating<br>Ave number of mins between League goals conceded while on the pitch | 67 | Club Defensive Rating<br>Average number of mins between League goals conceded by the club this season | 61 |

| | PLAYER | CON LGE | CLEAN SHEETS | DEF RATE |
|---|---|---|---|---|
| 2 | Khalid Boulahrouz | 39 | 6 | 63 mins |
| 3 | Yuri Nikiforov | 42 | 6 | 58 mins |
| 4 | Virgilio Teixeira | 17 | 3 | 52 mins |

## GOALS SCORED

| | | | |
|---|---|---|---|
| AT HOME | MOST | Ajax | 57 |
| | | | 24 |
| | LEAST | Twente | 18 |
| AWAY | MOST | PSV | 44 |
| | | | 20 |
| | LEAST | Roosendaal & Groningen | 9 |

## GOALS CONCEDED

| | | | |
|---|---|---|---|
| AT HOME | LEAST | PSV | 7 |
| | | | 20 |
| | MOST | Excelsior | 38 |
| AWAY | LEAST | PSV | 13 |
| | | | 31 |
| | MOST | De G'schap | 50 |

## KEY GOALKEEPER

**1 Rob van Dijk**

| | |
|---|---|
| Goals Conceded in the League | 33 |
| Defensive Rating<br>Ave number of mins between League goals conceded while on the pitch | 61 |
| Counting Games<br>Games when he played at least 70 mins | 22 |
| Clean Sheets<br>In games when he played at least 70 mins | 6 |

## TOP POINT EARNERS

| | PLAYER | GAMES | AVE |
|---|---|---|---|
| 1 | Fuchs | 16 | 1.75 |
| 2 | de Graef | 22 | 1.68 |
| 3 | Molhoek | 13 | 1.62 |
| 4 | Janssen | 18 | 1.61 |
| 5 | Nikiforov | 25 | 1.60 |
| 6 | Boulahrouz | 25 | 1.56 |
| 7 | Cornelisse | 30 | 1.50 |
| 8 | van den Berg | 29 | 1.48 |
| 9 | Hoogendorp | 26 | 1.27 |
| 10 | van Diemen | 32 | 1.25 |
| | CLUB AVERAGE: | | 1.35 |

Ave = Average points per match in Counting Games

## ATTENDANCES

HOME GROUND: SPORTPARK OLYMPIA CAPACITY: 7500 AVERAGE LEAGUE AT HOME: 6667

| | | | | | | | | |
|---|---|---|---|---|---|---|---|---|
| 30 | Ajax | 49076 | 17 | NEC Nijmegen | 10000 | 21 | Zwolle | 6148 |
| 31 | Feyenoord | 47000 | 14 | AZ Alkmaar | 7551 | 26 | AZ Alkmaar | 6141 |
| 4 | PSV Eindhoven | 32000 | 7 | Zwolle | 7500 | 13 | Feyenoord | 6000 |
| 5 | Vitesse Arnhem | 21812 | 19 | PSV Eindhoven | 7500 | 15 | Roda JC Kerk | 6000 |
| 33 | Roda JC Kerk | 17400 | 34 | NEC Nijmegen | 7500 | 11 | Utrecht | 6000 |
| 28 | Utrecht | 15000 | 29 | Willem II Tilb | 7500 | 27 | Roosendaal | 6000 |
| 2 | Heerenveen | 14200 | 9 | Ajax | 7300 | 18 | Groningen | 5950 |
| 12 | Willem II Tilb | 13800 | 6 | Excelsior | 7200 | 1 | De Graafschap | 5500 |
| 16 | NAC Breda | 13585 | 32 | NAC Breda | 7100 | 10 | Roosendaal | 5000 |
| 25 | Twente | 13200 | 23 | Heerenveen | 7000 | 22 | Excelsior | 2368 |
| 8 | Groningen | 12500 | 3 | Twente | 6900 | | | |
| 24 | De Graafschap | 10500 | 20 | Vitesse Arnhem | 6249 | | | |

■ Home □ Away ▒ Neutral

## DISCIPLINARY RECORDS

| | PLAYER | YELLOW | RED | AVE |
|---|---|---|---|---|
| 1 | Van der Leegte | 3 | 0 | 236 |
| 2 | Peppinck | 3 | 0 | 266 |
| 3 | Greene | 4 | 0 | 276 |
| 4 | Boulahrouz | 6 | 1 | 353 |
| 5 | van Wanrooy | 2 | 0 | 380 |
| 6 | Hoogendorp | 5 | 1 | 405 |
| 7 | van den Berg | 5 | 1 | 434 |
| 8 | Teixeira | 2 | 0 | 438 |
| 9 | Nikiforov | 4 | 1 | 486 |
| 10 | de Graef | 4 | 0 | 531 |
| 11 | Molhoek | 2 | 0 | 633 |
| 12 | Putter | 0 | 1 | 706 |
| 13 | van Dijk | 1 | 1 | 1005 |
| | Other | 7 | 1 | |
| | TOTAL | 48 | 7 | |

## LEAGUE GOALS

| | PLAYER | MINS | GOALS | AVE |
|---|---|---|---|---|
| 1 | Hoogendorp | 2435 | 16 | 152 |
| 2 | Cornelisse | 2683 | 9 | 298 |
| 3 | Janssen | 2097 | 5 | 419 |
| 4 | van Diemen | 2948 | 4 | 737 |
| 5 | Oost | 1253 | 3 | 418 |
| 6 | Putter | 706 | 2 | 353 |
| 7 | van den Berg | 2608 | 2 | 1304 |
| 8 | Nikiforov | 2432 | 1 | 2432 |
| 9 | Fuchs | 1662 | 1 | 1662 |
| 10 | Petrovic | 1268 | 1 | 1268 |
| | Other | | 0 | |
| | TOTAL | | 44 | |

## MONTH BY MONTH GUIDE TO THE POINTS

| MONTH | POINTS | % |
|---|---|---|
| AUGUST | 9 | 100% |
| SEPTEMBER | 1 | 11% |
| OCTOBER | 4 | 44% |
| NOVEMBER | 7 | 47% |
| DECEMBER | 4 | 44% |
| JANUARY | | |
| FEBRUARY | 6 | 50% |
| MARCH | 9 | 75% |
| APRIL | 6 | 50% |
| MAY | 0 | 0% |

## TEAM OF THE SEASON

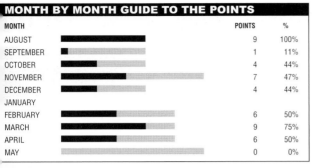

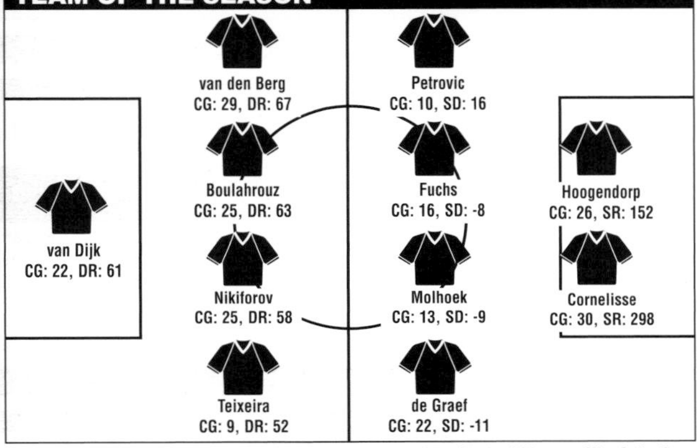
van den Berg
CG: 29, DR: 67
Petrovic
CG: 10, SD: 16
Boulahrouz
CG: 25, DR: 63
Fuchs
CG: 16, SD: -8
Hoogendorp
CG: 26, SR: 152
van Dijk
CG: 22, DR: 61
Nikiforov
CG: 25, DR: 58
Molhoek
CG: 13, SD: -9
Cornelisse
CG: 30, SR: 298
Teixeira
CG: 9, DR: 52
de Graef
CG: 22, SD: -11

**KEY:** DR = Defensive Rate, SD = Scoring Difference, SR = Strike Rate,
CG = Counting Games – League games playing at least 70 minutes

## LEAGUE APPEARANCES, BOOKINGS AND CAPS

| | AGE | IN THE SQUAD | COUNTING GAMES | MINUTES ON PITCH | YELLOW CARDS | RED CARDS | THIS SEASON | HOME COUNTRY |
|---|---|---|---|---|---|---|---|---|
| **Goalkeepers** | | | | | | | | |
| Kris Ottoy | 18 | 1 | 0 | 0 | 0 | 0 | - | Belgium |
| Khalid Sinouh | 28 | 33 | 11 | 1050 | 0 | 0 | - | Morocco |
| Rob van Dijk | 34 | 28 | 22 | 2010 | 1 | 1 | - | Holland |
| **Defenders** | | | | | | | | |
| Khalid Boulahrouz | 21 | 31 | 25 | 2475 | 6 | 1 | - | Holland |
| Serginho Greene | 21 | 31 | 8 | 1104 | 4 | 0 | - | Holland |
| Yuri Nikiforov | 32 | 30 | 25 | 2432 | 4 | 1 | - | |
| Emanuel Nwakire | 24 | 3 | 0 | 0 | 0 | 0 | - | Nigeria |
| Virgilio Teixeira | 29 | 28 | 9 | 877 | 2 | 0 | - | Portugal |
| Peter van den Berg | 31 | 29 | 29 | 2608 | 5 | 1 | - | Holland |
| Carlos van Wanrooy | 36 | 17 | 8 | 761 | 2 | 0 | - | Holland |
| **Midfielders** | | | | | | | | |
| Jean Brustolin | 21 | 1 | 0 | 0 | 0 | 0 | - | Brazil |
| Garry de Graef | 28 | 32 | 22 | 2126 | 4 | 0 | - | Belgium |
| Robert Fuchs | 28 | 30 | 16 | 1662 | 0 | 1 | - | Holland |
| Rogier Molhoek | 21 | 20 | 13 | 1266 | 2 | 0 | - | Holland |
| Kris Ottoy | 18 | 5 | 0 | 0 | 0 | 0 | - | Belgium |
| Fabian Peppinck | 25 | 19 | 8 | 798 | 3 | 0 | - | Holland |
| Zeljko Petrovic | 37 | 31 | 10 | 1268 | 1 | 0 | - | Serbia & Montenegro |
| Michael Vd Heijden | 21 | 9 | 0 | 0 | 0 | 0 | - | Holland |
| Tommy Vd Leegte | 26 | 13 | 6 | 710 | 3 | 0 | - | Holland |
| Patrick van Diemen | 31 | 33 | 32 | 2948 | 2 | 0 | - | Holland |
| Ivar van Dinteren | 26 | 1 | 0 | 0 | 0 | 0 | - | |
| John van Loenhout | 26 | 11 | 0 | 26 | 0 | 0 | - | Holland |
| **Forwards** | | | | | | | | |
| Tim Aelbrecht | 21 | 4 | 0 | 0 | 0 | 0 | - | Belgium |
| Youri Cornelisse | 28 | 32 | 30 | 2683 | 2 | 0 | - | Holland |
| Rick Hoogendorp | 28 | 31 | 26 | 2435 | 5 | 1 | - | Holland |
| Jochen Janssen | 27 | 32 | 18 | 2097 | 1 | 0 | - | Belgium |
| Jason Oost | 20 | 34 | 6 | 1253 | 1 | 0 | - | Holland |
| Yuri Petrov | 28 | 3 | 0 | 21 | 0 | 0 | - | Ukraine |
| Eddy Putter | 21 | 29 | 5 | 706 | 0 | 1 | - | Holland |
| Iwan Redan | 22 | 9 | 1 | 218 | 0 | 0 | - | Holland |

**KEY:** LEAGUE BOOKINGS CAPS (FIFA RANKING)

## SQUAD APPEARANCES

| Match | 1 | 2 | 3 | 4 | 5 | 6 | 7 | 8 | 9 | 10 | 11 | 12 | 13 | 14 | 15 | 16 | 17 | 18 | 19 | 20 | 21 | 22 | 23 | 24 | 25 | 26 | 27 | 28 | 29 | 30 | 31 | 32 | 33 | 34 |
|---|---|---|---|---|---|---|---|---|---|---|---|---|---|---|---|---|---|---|---|---|---|---|---|---|---|---|---|---|---|---|---|---|---|---|
| Venue | H | A | H | A | A | H | H | A | H | A | H | A | H | A | H | A | A | H | H | H | A | A | H | A | A | H | H | A | H | A | A | H | A | H |
| Competition | L | L | L | L | L | L | L | L | L | L | L | L | L | L | L | L | L | L | L | L | L | L | L | L | L | L | L | L | L | L | L | L | L | L |
| Result | W | W | W | L | D | L | L | W | D | D | L | W | W | L | W | L | D | W | L | W | L | W | W | W | L | W | L | L | W | L | L | L | L | L |

**Goalkeepers**
Kris Ottoy
Khalid Sinouh
Rob van Dijk

**Defenders**
Khalid Boulahrouz
Serginho Greene
Yuri Nikiforov
Emanuel Nwakire
Virgilio Teixeira
Peter van den Berg
Carlos van Wanrooy

**Midfielders**
Jean Brustolin
Garry de Graef
Robert Fuchs
Robert Fuchs
Rogier Molhoek
Kris Ottoy
Fabian Peppinck
Zeljko Petrovic
Michael Van der Heijden
Tommy Van der Leegte
Patrick van Diemen
Ivar van Dinteren
John van Loenhout

**Forwards**
Tim Aelbrecht
Youri Cornelisse
Rick Hoogendorp
Jochen Janssen
Jason Oost
Jason Oost
Yuri Petrov
Eddy Putter
Iwan Redan

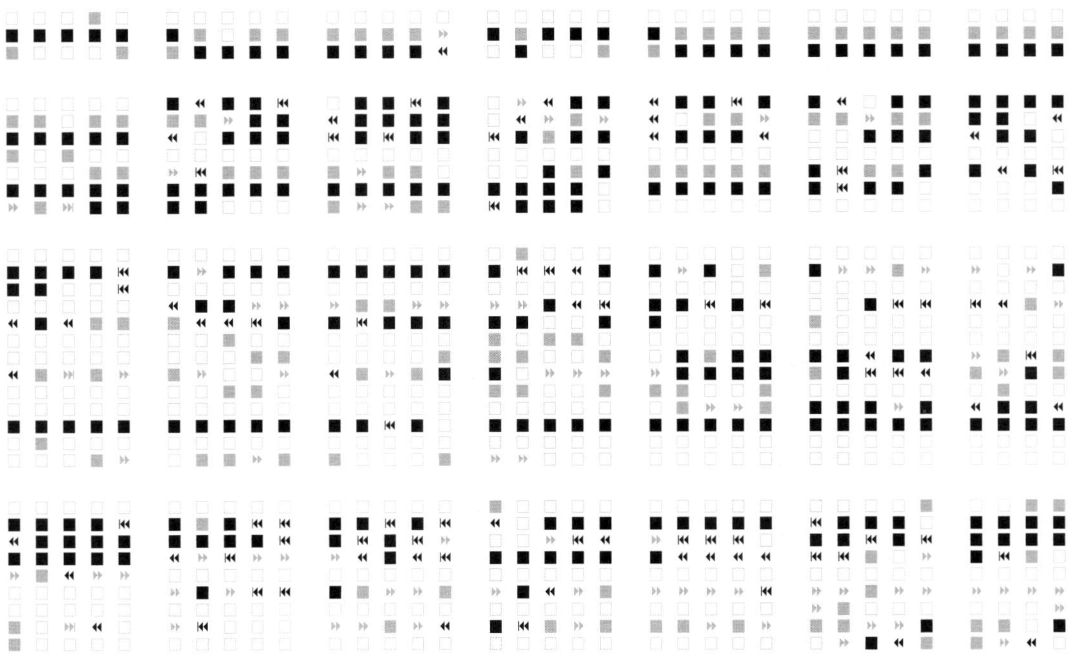

# AZ ALKMAAR

Final Position: **10th**

| | | | | | | |
|---|---|---|---|---|---|---|
| 1 | lge | Heerenveen | H | D | 3-3 | van Galen 26; El Khattabi 48; Perez 71 |
| 2 | lge | NEC Nijmegen | A | L | 0-2 | |
| 3 | lge | PSV Eindhoven | H | L | 0-4 | |
| 4 | lge | De Graafschap | A | W | 2-1 | Meerdink 40; van Galen 44 |
| 5 | lge | Excelsior | A | W | 2-1 | van Galen 33; Nelisse 44 |
| 6 | lge | Groningen | H | W | 4-1 | Perez 3,33,60; Nelisse 20 |
| 7 | lge | Vitesse Arnhem | H | L | 1-3 | van Galen 45 |
| 8 | lge | Ajax | A | L | 2-6 | Perez 3,61 |
| 9 | lge | Twente | H | L | 1-2 | Meerdink 64 |
| 10 | lge | Zwolle | A | L | 1-5 | Perez 53 |
| 11 | lge | Roosendaal | H | W | 2-0 | van Galen 18; Buskermolen 68 |
| 12 | lge | Utrecht | A | D | 2-2 | Nelisse 26; Meerdink 85 |
| 13 | lge | Roda JC Kerk | A | W | 3-1 | van Galen 3,43; Tobiassen 20 |
| 14 | lge | RKC Waalwijk | H | W | 2-0 | Buskermolen 63; Kromkamp 86 |
| 15 | lge | Willem II Tilb | A | L | 1-3 | Meerdink 69 |
| 16 | lge | Feyenoord | A | L | 1-6 | Perez 69 |
| 17 | lge | NEC Nijmegen | H | D | 0-0 | |
| 18 | lge | Heerenveen | A | L | 0-5 | |
| 19 | lge | Feyenoord | H | L | 1-4 | Kromkamp 85 |
| 20 | lge | NAC Breda | H | W | 3-1 | Lamey 8; Perez 19; El Khattabi 85 |
| 21 | lge | Vitesse Arnhem | A | D | 2-2 | Perez 34; Buskermolen 72 |
| 22 | lge | Twente | A | D | 0-0 | |
| 23 | lge | Roda JC Kerk | H | W | 1-0 | El Khattabi 52 |
| 24 | lge | Utrecht | H | W | 2-0 | Buskermolen 12; van Galen 26 |
| 25 | lge | De Graafschap | H | W | 3-1 | van Galen 40; Nelisse 45; Buskermolen 59 |
| 26 | lge | RKC Waalwijk | A | L | 0-2 | |
| 27 | lge | Zwolle | H | D | 1-1 | Perez 23 |
| 28 | lge | Roosendaal | A | D | 0-0 | |
| 29 | lge | Ajax | H | L | 1-3 | Buskermolen 86 |
| 30 | lge | PSV Eindhoven | A | D | 2-2 | de Cler 25; El Khattabi 43 |
| 31 | lge | Willem II Tilb | H | W | 3-2 | de Cler 64 pen; El Khattabi 77; Nelisse 88 |
| 32 | lge | Groningen | A | L | 0-1 | |
| 33 | lge | NAC Breda | A | L | 0-4 | |
| 34 | lge | Excelsior | H | W | 3-1 | El Khattabi 21,37; Swerts 58 og |

## KEY PLAYERS - GOALSCORERS

**1 Kenneth Perez**

| | | | |
|---|---|---|---|
| Goals in the League | 11 | Player Strike Rate<br>Average number of minutes between League goals scored by player | 184 |
| Contribution to Attacking Power<br>Average number of minutes between League team goals while on pitch | 72 | Club Strike Rate<br>Average number of minutes between League goals scored by club | 62 |

| | PLAYER | LGE GOALS | POWER | STRIKE RATE |
|---|---|---|---|---|
| 2 | Ali El Khattabi | 7 | 65 | 207 mins |
| 3 | Barry van Galen | 9 | 55 | 241 mins |
| 4 | Michael Buskermolen | 6 | 69 | 324 mins |
| 5 | Robin Nelisse | 5 | 56 | 484 mins |

## KEY PLAYERS - MIDFIELDERS

**1 Barry van Galen**

| | | | |
|---|---|---|---|
| Goals in the League | 9 | Contribution to Attacking Power<br>Average number of minutes between League team goals while on pitch | 56 |
| Defensive Rating<br>Average number of mins between League goals conceded while he was on the pitch | 56 | Scoring Difference<br>Defensive Rating minus Contribution to Attacking Power | 0 |

| | PLAYER | LGE GOALS | DEF RATE | POWER | SCORE DIFF |
|---|---|---|---|---|---|
| 2 | Ole Tobiassen | 1 | 41 | 46 | -5 mins |
| 3 | Reinier Robbemond | 0 | 43 | 48 | -5 mins |
| 4 | Martijn Meerdink | 4 | 36 | 54 | -18 mins |
| 5 | Barry Opdam | 0 | 43 | 61 | -18 mins |

## KEY PLAYERS - DEFENDERS

**1 Michael Lamey**

| | | | |
|---|---|---|---|
| Goals Conceded (GC)<br>The number of League goals conceded while he was on the pitch | 18 | Clean Sheets<br>In games when he played at least 70 minutes | 5 |
| Defensive Rating<br>Ave number of mins between League goals conceded while on the pitch | 68 | Club Defensive Rating<br>Average number of mins between League goals conceded by the club this season | 44 |

| | PLAYER | CON LGE | CLEAN SHEETS | DEF RATE |
|---|---|---|---|---|
| 2 | Michael Buskermolen | 36 | 7 | 54 mins |
| 3 | Jose Fortes Rodriguez | 24 | 4 | 54 mins |
| 4 | Tim de Cler | 51 | 6 | 50 mins |
| 5 | Olaf Lindenbergh | 67 | 6 | 42 mins |

## GOALS SCORED

**AT HOME**

| | | |
|---|---|---|
| MOST | Ajax | 57 |
| | | 31 |
| LEAST | Twente | 18 |

**AWAY**

| | | |
|---|---|---|
| MOST | PSV | 44 |
| | | 18 |
| LEAST | Roosendaal & Groningen | 9 |

## GOALS CONCEDED

**AT HOME**

| | | |
|---|---|---|
| LEAST | PSV | 7 |
| | | 26 |
| MOST | Excelsior | 38 |

**AWAY**

| | | |
|---|---|---|
| LEAST | PSV | 13 |
| | | 43 |
| MOST | De G'schap | 50 |

## KEY GOALKEEPER

**1 Theo Zwarthoed**

| | |
|---|---|
| Goals Conceded in the League | 23 |
| Defensive Rating<br>Ave number of mins between League goals conceded while on the pitch | 63 |
| Counting Games<br>Games when he played at least 70 mins | 16 |
| Clean Sheets<br>In games when he played at least 70 mins | 4 |

## TOP POINT EARNERS

| | PLAYER | GAMES | AVE |
|---|---|---|---|
| 1 | Robbemond | 12 | 1.67 |
| 2 | Lamey | 13 | 1.54 |
| 3 | Buskermolen | 20 | 1.50 |
| 4 | El Khattabi | 13 | 1.46 |
| 5 | de Cler | 27 | 1.44 |
| 6 | Zwarthoed | 16 | 1.44 |
| 7 | Wijker | 18 | 1.39 |
| 8 | van Galen | 22 | 1.32 |
| 9 | Opdam | 33 | 1.30 |
| 10 | Lindenbergh | 31 | 1.29 |
| | CLUB AVERAGE: | | 1.29 |

Ave = Average points per match in Counting Games

## ATTENDANCES

HOME GROUND: ALKMAARDERHOUT CAPACITY: 8419 AVERAGE LEAGUE AT HOME: 7180

| | | | | | | | |
|---|---|---|---|---|---|---|---|
| 8 | Ajax | 47481 | 2 | NEC Nijmegen | 11000 | 7 Vitesse Arnhem | 7000 |
| 16 | Feyenoord | 44000 | 19 | Feyenoord | 8072 | 17 NEC Nijmegen | 6939 |
| 30 | PSV Eindhoven | 33000 | 29 | Ajax | 7735 | 9 Twente | 6937 |
| 21 | Vitesse Arnhem | 22284 | 14 | RKC Waalwijk | 7551 | 23 Roda JC Kerk | 6871 |
| 12 | Utrecht | 17500 | 3 | PSV Eindhoven | 7480 | 11 Roosendaal | 6823 |
| 18 | Heerenveen | 14300 | 31 | Willem II Tilb | 7326 | 6 Groningen | 6758 |
| 33 | NAC Breda | 14268 | 20 | NAC Breda | 7152 | 10 Zwolle | 6500 |
| 22 | Twente | 13101 | 34 | Excelsior | 7144 | 26 RKC Waalwijk | 6141 |
| 15 | Willem II Tilb | 12700 | 25 | De Graafschap | 7105 | 28 Roosendaal | 5000 |
| 13 | Roda JC Kerk | 12500 | 24 | Utrecht | 7103 | 5 Excelsior | 3100 |
| 32 | Groningen | 11820 | 27 | Zwolle | 7041 | | |
| 4 | De Graafschap | 11000 | 1 | Heerenveen | 7025 | | |

Home / Away / Neutral

## DISCIPLINARY RECORDS

| | PLAYER | YELLOW | RED | AVE |
|---|---|---|---|---|
| 1 | van Galen | 10 | 1 | 197 |
| 2 | Fortes Rodriguez | 6 | 0 | 215 |
| 3 | Lamey | 4 | 1 | 245 |
| 4 | Wijker | 6 | 0 | 300 |
| 5 | Meerdink | 6 | 0 | 341 |
| 6 | Lindenbergh | 7 | 1 | 355 |
| 7 | de Cler | 4 | 2 | 425 |
| 8 | Buskermolen | 4 | 0 | 485 |
| 9 | Mans | 1 | 0 | 503 |
| 10 | El Khattabi | 2 | 0 | 723 |
| 11 | Opdam | 4 | 0 | 742 |
| 12 | Kromkamp | 2 | 0 | 941 |
| 13 | Perez | 2 | 0 | 1010 |
| | Other | 2 | 0 | |
| | TOTAL | 60 | 5 | |

## LEAGUE GOALS

| | PLAYER | MINS | GOALS | AVE |
|---|---|---|---|---|
| 1 | Perez | 2021 | 11 | 184 |
| 2 | van Galen | 2173 | 9 | 241 |
| 3 | El Khattabi | 1447 | 7 | 207 |
| 4 | Buskermolen | 1943 | 6 | 324 |
| 5 | Nelisse | 2422 | 5 | 484 |
| 6 | Meerdink | 2046 | 4 | 512 |
| 7 | de Cler | 2553 | 2 | 1277 |
| 8 | Kromkamp | 1883 | 2 | 942 |
| 9 | Tobiassen | 1053 | 1 | 1053 |
| 10 | Lamey | 1227 | 1 | 1227 |
| | Other | | 1 | |
| | TOTAL | | 49 | |

## MONTH BY MONTH GUIDE TO THE POINTS

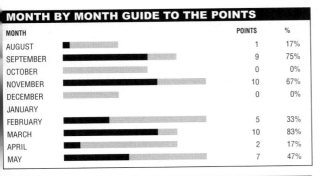

| MONTH | POINTS | % |
|---|---|---|
| AUGUST | 1 | 17% |
| SEPTEMBER | 9 | 75% |
| OCTOBER | 0 | 0% |
| NOVEMBER | 10 | 67% |
| DECEMBER | 0 | 0% |
| JANUARY | | |
| FEBRUARY | 5 | 33% |
| MARCH | 10 | 83% |
| APRIL | 2 | 17% |
| MAY | 7 | 47% |

## TEAM OF THE SEASON

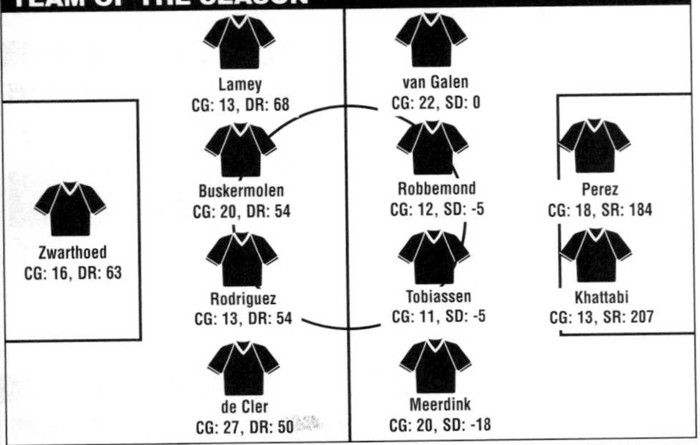
Zwarthoed
CG: 16, DR: 63
Lamey
CG: 13, DR: 68
Buskermolen
CG: 20, DR: 54
Rodriguez
CG: 13, DR: 54
de Cler
CG: 27, DR: 50
van Galen
CG: 22, SD: 0
Robbemond
CG: 12, SD: -5
Tobiassen
CG: 11, SD: -5
Meerdink
CG: 20, SD: -18
Perez
CG: 18, SR: 184
Khattabi
CG: 13, SR: 207

**KEY:** DR = Defensive Rate, SD = Scoring Difference, SR = Strike Rate,
CG = Counting Games – League games playing at least 70 minutes

## LEAGUE APPEARANCES, BOOKINGS AND CAPS

| | AGE | IN THE SQUAD | COUNTING GAMES | MINUTES ON PITCH | YELLOW CARDS | RED CARDS | THIS SEASON | HOME COUNTRY |
|---|---|---|---|---|---|---|---|---|
| **Goalkeepers** | | | | | | | | |
| Kris Mampaey | 32 | 11 | 0 | 0 | 0 | 0 | - | Belgium |
| Oscar Moens | 30 | 18 | 18 | 1620 | 0 | 0 | - | Holland |
| Beau Molenaar | | 4 | 0 | 0 | 0 | 0 | - | Holland |
| Theo Zwarthoed | 20 | 34 | 16 | 1440 | 0 | 0 | - | Holland |
| **Defenders** | | | | | | | | |
| Michael Buskermolen | 31 | 32 | 20 | 1943 | 4 | 0 | - | Holland |
| Tim de Cler | 24 | 30 | 27 | 2553 | 4 | 2 | - | Holland |
| Abdelkrim El Hadrioui | 31 | 4 | 0 | 0 | 0 | 0 | - | |
| Jose Rodriguez | 31 | 20 | 13 | 1294 | 6 | 0 | - | Spain |
| Michael Lamey | 23 | 14 | 13 | 1227 | 4 | 1 | - | Holland |
| Olaf Lindenbergh | 29 | 32 | 31 | 2843 | 7 | 1 | - | Holland |
| Juha Reini | 28 | 26 | 5 | 605 | 0 | 0 | - | Finland |
| Joost Volmer | 29 | 30 | 3 | 300 | 1 | 0 | - | Holland |
| Peter Wijker | 31 | 32 | 18 | 1805 | 6 | 0 | - | Holland |
| Jannes Wolters | 24 | 28 | 2 | 180 | 0 | 0 | - | Holland |
| **Midfielders** | | | | | | | | |
| Alair Cruz Vicente | 22 | 14 | 0 | 44 | 0 | 0 | - | Brazil |
| Christy Janga | | 1 | 0 | 0 | 0 | 0 | - | |
| Jan Kromkamp | 22 | 27 | 20 | 1883 | 2 | 0 | - | Holland |
| Miel Mans | 25 | 26 | 4 | 503 | 1 | 0 | - | Holland |
| Martijn Meerdink | 26 | 31 | 20 | 2046 | 6 | 0 | - | Holland |
| Deivsion Vagner | | 1 | 0 | 0 | 0 | 0 | - | |
| Barry Opdam | 27 | 33 | 33 | 2970 | 4 | 0 | - | Holland |
| Reinier Robbemond | 31 | 14 | 12 | 1194 | 0 | 0 | - | Holland |
| Ole Tobiassen | | 15 | 11 | 1053 | 1 | 0 | - | |
| Ramon Van der Pal | | 1 | 0 | 0 | 0 | 0 | - | |
| Barry van Galen | 33 | 28 | 22 | 2173 | 10 | 1 | - | Holland |
| **Forwards** | | | | | | | | |
| Nascimento Canigia | 24 | 2 | 0 | 5 | 0 | 0 | - | Brazil |
| Ali El Khattabi | 26 | 31 | 13 | 1447 | 2 | 0 | - | Morocco |
| Robin Nelisse | 25 | 34 | 24 | 2422 | 0 | 0 | - | Holland |
| Kenneth Perez | 28 | 33 | 18 | 2021 | 2 | 0 | - | Denmark |

**KEY:** LEAGUE BOOKINGS CAPS (FIFA RANKING)

## SQUAD APPEARANCES

| Match | 1 | 2 | 3 | 4 | 5 | 6 | 7 | 8 | 9 | 10 | 11 | 12 | 13 | 14 | 15 | 16 | 17 | 18 | 19 | 20 | 21 | 22 | 23 | 24 | 25 | 26 | 27 | 28 | 29 | 30 | 31 | 32 | 33 | 34 |
|---|---|---|---|---|---|---|---|---|---|---|---|---|---|---|---|---|---|---|---|---|---|---|---|---|---|---|---|---|---|---|---|---|---|---|
| **Venue** | H | A | H | A | A | H | H | A | H | A | H | A | A | H | A | A | H | A | H | H | A | A | H | H | H | A | H | A | H | A | H | A | A | H |
| **Competition** | L | L | L | L | L | L | L | L | L | L | L | L | L | L | L | L | L | L | L | L | L | L | L | L | L | L | L | L | L | L | L | L | L | L |
| **Result** | D | L | L | W | W | W | L | L | L | L | W | D | W | W | L | L | D | L | L | W | D | D | W | W | W | L | D | D | L | D | W | L | L | W |

**Goalkeepers**
Kris Mampaey
Oscar Moens
Beau Molenaar
Theo Zwarthoed

**Defenders**
Michael Buskermolen
Tim de Cler
Abdelkrim El Hadrioui
Jose Fortes Rodriguez
Michael Lamey
Olaf Lindenbergh
Juha Reini
Joost Volmer
Peter Wijker
Jannes Wolters

**Midfielders**
Alair Cruz Vicente
Christy Janga
Jan Kromkamp
Miel Mans
Martijn Meerdink
D Nascimento Vagner
Barry Opdam
Reinier Robbemond
Ole Tobiassen
Ramon Van der Pal
Barry van Galen

**Forwards**
Nascimento Canigia
Ali El Khattabi
Robin Nelisse
Kenneth Perez

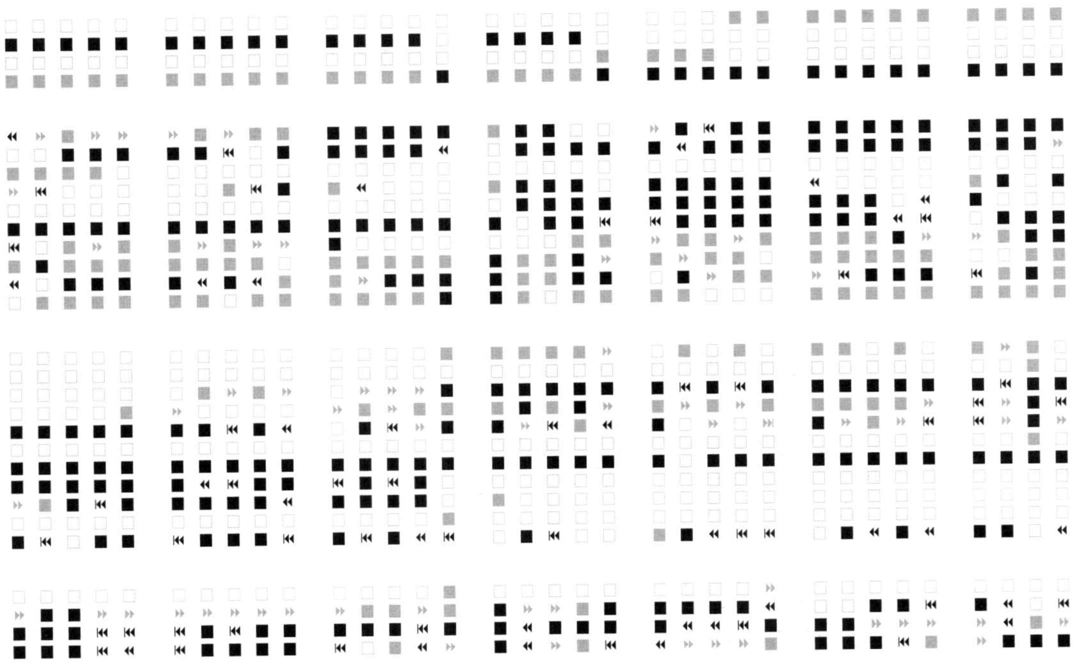

# WILLEM II TILB

Final Position: **11th**

| | | | | | | |
|---|---|---|---|---|---|---|
| 1 | lge | Twente | A | W | 2-0 | Sektioui 61; Shoukov 69 |
| 2 | lge | NAC Breda | H | D | 1-1 | Mghizrat 39 |
| 3 | lge | Roda JC Kerk | A | L | 0-1 | |
| 4 | lge | Utrecht | H | W | 2-0 | Landzaat 42; Sektioui 77 |
| 5 | lge | NEC Nijmegen | H | D | 1-1 | Ceesay 59 |
| 6 | lge | Zwolle | H | W | 5-2 | Sektioui 8; Van der Gun 11; Mathijsen, J 40; Ceesay 56; Shoukov 57 |
| 7 | lge | Heerenveen | A | D | 1-1 | Van der Gun 69 |
| 8 | lge | Roosendaal | H | W | 3-1 | Keller 14 og; Shoukov 28; Ceesay 57 |
| 9 | lge | Feyenoord | A | L | 1-5 | Van der Gun 41 |
| 10 | lge | Ajax | A | L | 0-3 | |
| 11 | lge | Vitesse Arnhem | H | L | 1-3 | Janssens 32 |
| 12 | lge | RKC Waalwijk | H | L | 0-1 | |
| 13 | lge | Excelsior | A | W | 3-0 | Shoukov 24; Mghizrat 82; Ceesay 90 |
| 14 | lge | PSV Eindhoven | A | L | 1-2 | Van der Gun 47 |
| 15 | lge | AZ Alkmaar | H | W | 3-1 | Quinn 21; Landzaat 50 pen; Shoukov 80 |
| 16 | lge | De Graafschap | A | D | 1-1 | Van der Gun 1 |
| 17 | lge | Groningen | H | W | 1-0 | Landzaat 48 |
| 18 | lge | Ajax | H | L | 0-6 | |
| 19 | lge | Zwolle | A | W | 3-0 | Quinn 13; Van der Gun 44; Ceesay 76 |
| 20 | lge | Roda JC Kerk | H | W | 5-0 | Ceesay 20; Quinn 26; Landzaat 48; Shoukov 66,75 |
| 21 | lge | NEC Nijmegen | A | L | 0-1 | |
| 22 | lge | Roosendaal | A | L | 0-1 | |
| 23 | lge | Twente | H | L | 1-2 | Shoukov 90 |
| 24 | lge | Groningen | A | D | 1-1 | Mghizrat 78 |
| 25 | lge | NAC Breda | A | D | 0-0 | |
| 26 | lge | PSV Eindhoven | H | D | 1-1 | Sektioui 62 |
| 27 | lge | Utrecht | A | D | 1-1 | Landzaat 31 |
| 28 | lge | De Graafschap | H | W | 3-0 | Ceesay 4; Jaliens 22; Shoukov 50 |
| 29 | lge | RKC Waalwijk | A | L | 1-3 | Sektioui 74 |
| 30 | lge | Heerenveen | H | L | 1-5 | Sektioui 66 |
| 31 | lge | AZ Alkmaar | A | L | 2-3 | Sektioui 16; van Nieuwstadt 75 |
| 32 | lge | Excelsior | H | W | 2-1 | Sektioui 63; Quinn 89 |
| 33 | lge | Feyenoord | H | D | 1-1 | Quinn 6 |
| 34 | lge | Vitesse Arnhem | A | L | 0-2 | |

## KEY PLAYERS - GOALSCORERS

**1 Tarik Sektioui**

| | | | |
|---|---|---|---|
| Goals in the League | 8 | **Player Strike Rate** Average number of minutes between League goals scored by player | 239 |
| **Contribution to Attacking Power** Average number of minutes between League team goals while on pitch | 61 | **Club Strike Rate** Average number of minutes between League goals scored by club | 64 |

| | PLAYER | LGE GOALS | POWER | STRIKE RATE |
|---|---|---|---|---|
| 2 | Dmitri Shoukov | 9 | 54 | 244 mins |
| 3 | Jattoo Ceesay | 7 | 60 | 317 mins |
| 4 | Cedric Van der Gun | 6 | 64 | 323 mins |
| 5 | Danny Landzaat | 5 | 63 | 612 mins |

## KEY PLAYERS - MIDFIELDERS

**1 Dmitri Shoukov**

| | | | |
|---|---|---|---|
| Goals in the League | 9 | **Contribution to Attacking Power** Average number of minutes between League team goals while on pitch | 55 |
| **Defensive Rating** Average number of mins between League goals conceded while he was on the pitch | 69 | **Scoring Difference** Defensive Rating minus Contribution to Attacking Power | 14 |

| | PLAYER | LGE GOALS | DEF RATE | POWER | SCORE DIFF |
|---|---|---|---|---|---|
| 2 | Danny Landzaat | 5 | 60 | 64 | -4 mins |
| 3 | Tarik Sektioui | 8 | 58 | 62 | -4 mins |
| 4 | Christiaan Janssens | 1 | 54 | 59 | -5 mins |
| 5 | Youssef Mariana | 0 | 66 | 74 | -8 mins |

## KEY PLAYERS - DEFENDERS

**1 Nuelson Wau**

| | | | |
|---|---|---|---|
| **Goals Conceded (GC)** The number of League goals conceded while he was on the pitch | 24 | **Clean Sheets** In games when he played at least 70 minutes | 6 |
| **Defensive Rating** Ave number of mins between League goals conceded while on the pitch | 77 | **Club Defensive Rating** Average number of mins between League goals conceded by the club this season | 60 |

| | PLAYER | CON LGE | CLEAN SHEETS | DEF RATE |
|---|---|---|---|---|
| 2 | Kew Jaliens | 48 | 8 | 60 mins |
| 3 | Joris Mathijssen, J | 51 | 8 | 60 mins |
| 4 | Raymond Victoria | 34 | 2 | 53 mins |

## GOALS SCORED

**AT HOME**

| | | |
|---|---|---|
| MOST | Ajax | 57 |
| | | 31 |
| LEAST | Twente | 18 |

**AWAY**

| | | |
|---|---|---|
| MOST | PSV | 44 |
| | | 17 |
| LEAST | Roosendaal & Groningen | 9 |

## GOALS CONCEDED

**AT HOME**

| | | |
|---|---|---|
| LEAST | PSV | 7 |
| | | 26 |
| MOST | Excelsior | 38 |

**AWAY**

| | | |
|---|---|---|
| LEAST | PSV | 13 |
| | | 25 |
| MOST | De G'schap | 50 |

## KEY GOALKEEPER

**1 Geert De Vlieger**

| | |
|---|---|
| Goals Conceded in the League | 48 |
| **Defensive Rating** Ave number of mins between League goals conceded while on the pitch | 58 |
| **Counting Games** Games when he played at least 70 mins | 31 |
| **Clean Sheets** In games when he played at least 70 mins | 8 |

## TOP POINT EARNERS

| | PLAYER | GAMES | AVE |
|---|---|---|---|
| 1 | Ceesay | 20 | 1.55 |
| 2 | Shoukov | 24 | 1.42 |
| 3 | Wau | 19 | 1.37 |
| 4 | Jaliens | 32 | 1.31 |
| 5 | De Vlieger | 31 | 1.29 |
| 6 | Mathijssen, J | 34 | 1.24 |
| 7 | Landzaat | 34 | 1.24 |
| 8 | Janssens | 21 | 1.24 |
| 9 | Van der Gun | 18 | 1.22 |
| 10 | Victoria | 17 | 1.18 |
| | **CLUB AVERAGE:** | | **1.24** |

Ave = Average points per match in Counting Games

## ATTENDANCES

HOME GROUND: WILLEM II STADION CAPACITY: 14700 AVERAGE LEAGUE AT HOME: 13328

| | | | | | | | | |
|---|---|---|---|---|---|---|---|---|
| 10 | Ajax | 48248 | 28 | De Graafschap | 13500 | 24 | Groningen | 12444 |
| 9 | Feyenoord | 44000 | 8 | Roosendaal | 13500 | 6 | Zwolle | 12300 |
| 14 | PSV Eindhoven | 33500 | 23 | Twente | 13450 | 30 | Heerenveen | 11000 |
| 34 | Vitesse Arnhem | 28000 | 4 | Utrecht | 13400 | 16 | De Graafschap | 10400 |
| 27 | Utrecht | 16500 | 11 | Vitesse Arnhem | 13400 | 21 | NEC Nijmegen | 10250 |
| 18 | Ajax | 14700 | 32 | Excelsior | 13400 | 29 | RKC Waalwijk | 7500 |
| 33 | Feyenoord | 14600 | 20 | Roda JC Kerk | 13250 | 31 | AZ Alkmaar | 7326 |
| 25 | NAC Breda | 14325 | 1 | Twente | 13200 | 19 | Zwolle | 5745 |
| 7 | Heerenveen | 14200 | 3 | Roda JC Kerk | 13000 | 22 | Roosendaal | 5000 |
| 2 | NAC Breda | 13910 | 5 | NEC Nijmegen | 13000 | 13 | Excelsior | 3358 |
| 26 | PSV Eindhoven | 13820 | 17 | Groningen | 12850 | | | |
| 12 | RKC Waalwijk | 13800 | 15 | AZ Alkmaar | 12700 | | | |

■ Home □ Away ▨ Neutral

## DISCIPLINARY RECORDS

| | PLAYER | YELLOW | RED | AVE |
|---|---|---|---|---|
| 1 | Janssens | 7 | 0 | 285 |
| 2 | Mariana | 3 | 0 | 371 |
| 3 | Victoria | 4 | 0 | 446 |
| 4 | Wau | 4 | 0 | 462 |
| 5 | Sektioui | 4 | 0 | 478 |
| 6 | Quinn | 1 | 1 | 504 |
| 7 | Ceesay | 2 | 2 | 555 |
| 8 | Jaliens | 5 | 0 | 571 |
| 9 | Mathijssen, D | 2 | 0 | 682 |
| 10 | van Nieuwstadt | 2 | 0 | 780 |
| 11 | Caluwe | 1 | 0 | 1057 |
| 12 | Shoukov | 1 | 1 | 1098 |
| 13 | Landzaat | 2 | 0 | 1530 |
| | Other | 3 | 0 | |
| | TOTAL | 41 | 4 | |

## LEAGUE GOALS

| | PLAYER | MINS | GOALS | AVE |
|---|---|---|---|---|
| 1 | Shoukov | 2196 | 9 | 244 |
| 2 | Sektioui | 1912 | 8 | 239 |
| 3 | Ceesay | 2222 | 7 | 317 |
| 4 | Van der Gun | 1935 | 6 | 323 |
| 5 | Landzaat | 3060 | 5 | 612 |
| 6 | Quinn | 1009 | 5 | 202 |
| 7 | Mghizrat | 700 | 3 | 233 |
| 8 | Mathijssen, J | 3059 | 1 | 3059 |
| 9 | van Nieuwstadt | 1561 | 1 | 1561 |
| 10 | Janssens | 2000 | 1 | 2000 |
| 11 | Jaliens | 2856 | 1 | 2856 |
| | Other | | 1 | |
| | TOTAL | | 48 | |

## MONTH BY MONTH GUIDE TO THE POINTS

| MONTH | POINTS | % |
|---|---|---|
| AUGUST | 4 | 44% |
| SEPTEMBER | 7 | 78% |
| OCTOBER | 4 | 44% |
| NOVEMBER | 3 | 20% |
| DECEMBER | 7 | 78% |
| JANUARY | | |
| FEBRUARY | 6 | 40% |
| MARCH | 2 | 22% |
| APRIL | 5 | 42% |
| MAY | 4 | 27% |

## LEAGUE APPEARANCES, BOOKINGS AND CAPS

| | AGE | IN THE SQUAD | COUNTING GAMES | MINUTES ON PITCH | YELLOW CARDS | RED CARDS | THIS SEASON | HOME COUNTRY |
|---|---|---|---|---|---|---|---|---|
| **Goalkeepers** | | | | | | | | |
| Geert De Vlieger | 31 | 31 | 31 | 2790 | 1 | 0 | 8 | Belgium (16) |
| Christophe Martin | 28 | 34 | 3 | 270 | 1 | 0 | - | Belgium |
| **Defenders** | | | | | | | | |
| Kew Jaliens | 24 | 33 | 32 | 2856 | 5 | 0 | - | Holland |
| Joris Mathijssen, J | 23 | 34 | 34 | 3059 | 0 | 0 | - | Holland |
| Guy Veldeman | 24 | 8 | 0 | 0 | 0 | 0 | - | Belgium |
| Raymond Victoria | 30 | 32 | 17 | 1787 | 4 | 0 | - | Holland |
| Nuelson Wau | 22 | 33 | 19 | 1850 | 4 | 0 | - | Holland |
| **Midfielders** | | | | | | | | |
| Tom Caluwe | 28 | 25 | 5 | 1057 | 1 | 0 | - | Belgium |
| Tim Gorris | | 1 | 0 | 0 | 0 | 0 | - | |
| Christiaan Janssens | 34 | 29 | 21 | 2000 | 7 | 0 | - | Belgium |
| Danny Landzaat | 27 | 34 | 34 | 3060 | 2 | 0 | - | Holland |
| Youssef Mariana | 29 | 23 | 10 | 1114 | 3 | 0 | - | Morocco |
| Danny Mathijssen | 20 | 27 | 11 | 1365 | 2 | 0 | - | Holland |
| Marcel Meeuwes | 22 | 1 | 0 | 0 | 0 | 0 | - | Holland |
| Mourad Mghizrat | 28 | 33 | 0 | 700 | 0 | 0 | - | Morocco |
| Ozcan Ozkaya | 22 | 1 | 0 | 5 | 0 | 0 | - | Holland |
| Joost Peijnenburg | | 3 | 0 | 0 | 0 | 0 | - | Holland |
| Tarik Sektioui | 26 | 26 | 20 | 1912 | 4 | 0 | - | Morocco |
| Dmitri Shoukov | 27 | 29 | 24 | 2196 | 1 | 1 | - | Russia |
| Regillio Simons | 30 | 33 | 1 | 462 | 0 | 0 | - | Holland |
| Cedric Van der Gun | 24 | 32 | 18 | 1935 | 1 | 0 | - | Holland |
| Emile Vd Meerakker | 22 | 9 | 2 | 234 | 0 | 0 | - | Holland |
| Frank Van Kouwen | 23 | 10 | 0 | 0 | 0 | 0 | - | Holland |
| Jos van Nieuwstadt | 23 | 25 | 16 | 1561 | 2 | 0 | - | Holland |
| Sharon van Zon | | 4 | 0 | 0 | 0 | 0 | - | Holland |
| **Forwards** | | | | | | | | |
| Jattoo Ceesay | 28 | 30 | 20 | 2222 | 2 | 2 | - | Gambia |
| Anouar Hadouir | 20 | 9 | 0 | 78 | 0 | 0 | - | Holland |
| James Quinn | 28 | 26 | 7 | 1009 | 1 | 1 | 4 | N Ireland (111) |

KEY: LEAGUE BOOKINGS CAPS (FIFA RANKING)

## TEAM OF THE SEASON

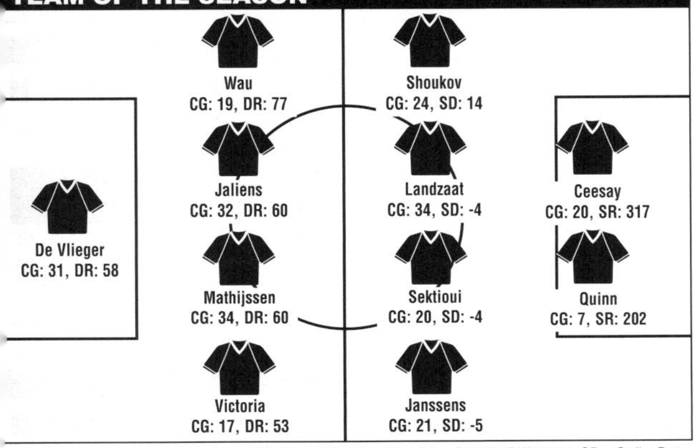
Wau
CG: 19, DR: 77
Shoukov
CG: 24, SD: 14
Jaliens
CG: 32, DR: 60
Landzaat
CG: 34, SD: -4
Ceesay
CG: 20, SR: 317
De Vlieger
CG: 31, DR: 58
Mathijssen
CG: 34, DR: 60
Sektioui
CG: 20, SD: -4
Quinn
CG: 7, SR: 202
Victoria
CG: 17, DR: 53
Janssens
CG: 21, SD: -5

KEY: DR = Defensive Rate, SD = Scoring Difference, SR = Strike Rate,
CG = Counting Games – League games playing at least 70 minutes

## SQUAD APPEARANCES

| Match | 1 | 2 | 3 | 4 | 5 | 6 | 7 | 8 | 9 | 10 | 11 | 12 | 13 | 14 | 15 | 16 | 17 | 18 | 19 | 20 | 21 | 22 | 23 | 24 | 25 | 26 | 27 | 28 | 29 | 30 | 31 | 32 | 33 | 34 |
|---|---|---|---|---|---|---|---|---|---|---|---|---|---|---|---|---|---|---|---|---|---|---|---|---|---|---|---|---|---|---|---|---|---|---|
| Venue | A | H | A | H | H | H | A | H | A | A | H | H | A | A | H | A | H | H | A | H | A | A | H | A | A | H | A | H | A | H | A | H | H | A |
| Competition | L | L | L | L | L | L | L | L | L | L | L | L | L | L | L | L | L | L | L | L | L | L | L | L | L | L | L | L | L | L | L | L | L | L |
| Result | W | D | L | W | D | W | D | W | L | L | L | L | W | L | W | D | W | L | W | W | L | L | L | D | D | D | D | W | L | L | L | W | D | L |

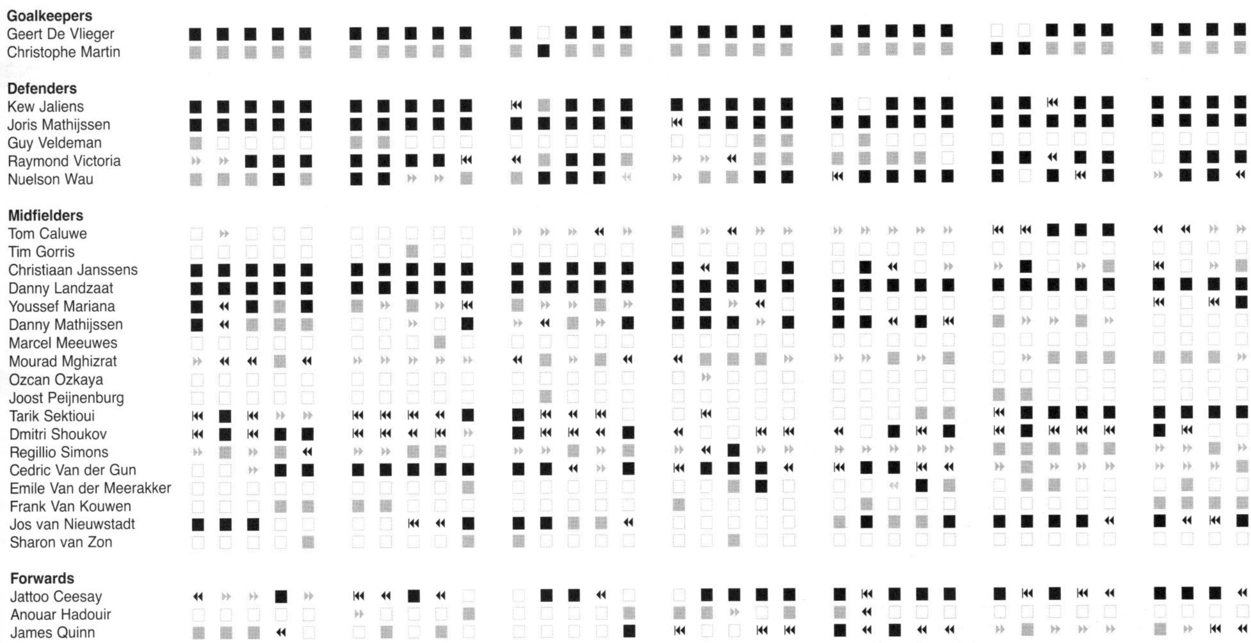
Goalkeepers
Geert De Vlieger
Christophe Martin
Defenders
Kew Jaliens
Joris Mathijssen
Guy Veldeman
Raymond Victoria
Nuelson Wau
Midfielders
Tom Caluwe
Tim Gorris
Christiaan Janssens
Danny Landzaat
Youssef Mariana
Danny Mathijssen
Marcel Meeuwes
Mourad Mghizrat
Ozcan Ozkaya
Joost Peijnenburg
Tarik Sektioui
Dmitri Shoukov
Regillio Simons
Cedric Van der Gun
Emile Van der Meerakker
Frank Van Kouwen
Jos van Nieuwstadt
Sharon van Zon
Forwards
Jattoo Ceesay
Anouar Hadouir
James Quinn

KEY: ■ On all match ■ On bench ⏮ Subbed or sent off (Counting game) ◀◀ Subbed or sent off (playing less than 70 minutes) ▶▶ Subbed on from bench (Counting Game) ▶▶ Subbed on (playing less than 70 minutes) ▶▶ Subbed on and then subbed or sent off (Counting Game) ▶▶ Subbed on and then subbed or sent off (playing less than 70 minutes) □ Not in 16

# TWENTE ENSCHEDE

Final Position: **12th**

| | | | | | | |
|---|---|---|---|---|---|---|
| 1 | lge | Willem II Tilb | H | L | 0-2 | |
| 2 | lge | Utrecht | H | D | 1-1 | Houwing 20 |
| 3 | lge | RKC Waalwijk | A | L | 2-3 | Cairo 43; Cavens 86 |
| 4 | lge | Feyenoord | H | L | 1-5 | Booth 25 |
| 5 | lge | NAC Breda | A | L | 0-2 | |
| 6 | lge | Roda JC Kerk | H | D | 3-3 | Booth 71; Cavens 85; Cairo 89 |
| 7 | lge | De Graafschap | A | W | 1-0 | Cairo 90 |
| 8 | lge | Heerenveen | H | D | 1-1 | El Brazi 89 |
| 9 | lge | AZ Alkmaar | A | W | 2-1 | Cziommer 24; Cairo 35 |
| 10 | lge | PSV Eindhoven | H | D | 0-0 | |
| 11 | lge | NEC Nijmegen | A | W | 2-1 | Polak 16; Zonneveld 38 og |
| 12 | lge | Zwolle | A | D | 1-1 | Cavens 47 |
| 13 | lge | Vitesse Arnhem | H | W | 1-0 | van de Paar 12 |
| 14 | lge | Ajax | A | L | 1-2 | Polak 42 pen |
| 15 | lge | Groningen | H | D | 0-0 | |
| 16 | lge | Excelsior | A | D | 2-2 | Cairo 6; Cavens 82 |
| 17 | lge | Roosendaal | H | W | 3-0 | Cavens 21; Houwing 71; John 75 |
| 18 | lge | Feyenoord | A | L | 2-4 | Cavens 39; Cziommer 72 |
| 19 | lge | Groningen | A | D | 0-0 | |
| 20 | lge | NEC Nijmegen | H | L | 1-2 | Polak 78 |
| 21 | lge | Roda JC Kerk | A | L | 0-2 | |
| 22 | lge | AZ Alkmaar | H | D | 0-0 | |
| 23 | lge | Willem II Tilb | A | W | 2-1 | Polak 8; Cairo 32 |
| 24 | lge | Heerenveen | A | L | 0-3 | |
| 25 | lge | RKC Waalwijk | H | W | 2-1 | Houwing 45; Polak 90 |
| 26 | lge | NAC Breda | H | D | 0-0 | |
| 27 | lge | De Graafschap | H | W | 3-0 | Cziommer 34; El Brazi 43; Cairo 66 |
| 28 | lge | PSV Eindhoven | A | L | 0-2 | |
| 29 | lge | Excelsior | H | W | 1-0 | Polak 26 |
| 30 | lge | Roosendaal | A | L | 0-1 | |
| 31 | lge | Zwolle | H | D | 0-0 | |
| 32 | lge | Vitesse Arnhem | A | W | 1-0 | Houwing 79 |
| 33 | lge | Ajax | H | L | 1-2 | John 90 |
| 34 | lge | Utrecht | A | L | 2-3 | Cziommer 26,68 |

## KEY PLAYERS - GOALSCORERS

**1 Jurgen Cavens**

| | | | |
|---|---|---|---|
| Goals in the League | 6 | Player Strike Rate<br>Average number of minutes between League goals scored by player | 260 |
| Contribution to Attacking Power<br>Average number of minutes between League team goals while on pitch | 64 | Club Strike Rate<br>Average number of minutes between League goals scored by club | 85 |

| | PLAYER | LGE GOALS | POWER | STRIKE RATE |
|---|---|---|---|---|
| 2 | Ellery Cairo | 7 | 88 | 381 mins |
| 3 | Sjaak Polak | 6 | 88 | 457 mins |
| 4 | Simon Cziommer | 5 | 88 | 546 mins |
| 5 | Abdelkader El Brazi | 2 | 81 | 1432 mins |

## KEY PLAYERS - MIDFIELDERS

**1 Thijs Houwing**

| | | | |
|---|---|---|---|
| Goals in the League | 4 | Contribution to Attacking Power<br>Average number of minutes between League team goals while on pitch | 71 |
| Defensive Rating<br>Average number of mins between League goals conceded while he was on the pitch | 75 | Scoring Difference<br>Defensive Rating minus Contribution to Attacking Power | 4 |

| | PLAYER | LGE GOALS | DEF RATE | POWER | SCORE DIFF |
|---|---|---|---|---|---|
| 2 | Jurgen Cavens | 6 | 62 | 65 | -3 mins |
| 3 | Kurt van de Paar | 1 | 76 | 90 | -14 mins |
| 4 | Scott Booth | 2 | 76 | 96 | -20 mins |
| 5 | Simon Cziommer | 5 | 64 | 88 | -24 mins |

## KEY PLAYERS - DEFENDERS

**1 Patrick Pothuizen**

| | | | |
|---|---|---|---|
| Goals Conceded (GC)<br>The number of League goals conceded while he was on the pitch | 26 | Clean Sheets<br>In games when he played at least 70 minutes | 11 |
| Defensive Rating<br>Ave number of mins between League goals conceded while on the pitch | 91 | Club Defensive Rating<br>Average number of mins between League goals conceded by the club this season | 68 |

| | PLAYER | CON LGE | CLEAN SHEETS | DEF RATE |
|---|---|---|---|---|
| 2 | Sjaak Polak | 35 | 11 | 78 mins |
| 3 | Rahim Ouedraogo | 30 | 8 | 76 mins |
| 4 | Spira Grujic | 40 | 11 | 70 mins |
| 5 | Abdelkader El Brazi | 44 | 11 | 65 mins |

## GOALS SCORED

AT HOME

| | | |
|---|---|---|
| MOST | Ajax | 57 |
| | | 18 |
| LEAST | Twente | 18 |

AWAY

| | | |
|---|---|---|
| MOST | PSV | 44 |
| | | 18 |
| LEAST | Roosendaal & Groningen | 9 |

## GOALS CONCEDED

AT HOME

| | | |
|---|---|---|
| LEAST | PSV | 7 |
| | | 17 |
| MOST | Excelsior | 38 |

AWAY

| | | |
|---|---|---|
| LEAST | PSV | 13 |
| | | 28 |
| MOST | De G'schap | 50 |

## KEY GOALKEEPER

**1 Sander Boschker**

| | |
|---|---|
| Goals Conceded in the League | 38 |
| Defensive Rating<br>Ave number of mins between League goals conceded while on the pitch | 75 |
| Counting Games<br>Games when he played at least 70 mins | 31 |
| Clean Sheets<br>In games when he played at least 70 mins | 12 |

## TOP POINT EARNERS

| | PLAYER | GAMES | AVE |
|---|---|---|---|
| 1 | van de Paar | 15 | 1.53 |
| 2 | Pothuizen | 26 | 1.42 |
| 3 | Cavens | 16 | 1.31 |
| 4 | Polak | 31 | 1.29 |
| 5 | Boschker | 31 | 1.29 |
| 6 | El Brazi | 32 | 1.25 |
| 7 | Cairo | 30 | 1.23 |
| 8 | Heubach | 28 | 1.18 |
| 9 | Cziommer | 30 | 1.17 |
| 10 | Ouedraogo | 24 | 1.13 |
| | **CLUB AVERAGE:** | | **1.21** |

Ave = Average points per match in Counting Games

## ATTENDANCES

HOME GROUND: ARKE CAPACITY: 13250 AVERAGE LEAGUE AT HOME: 13145

| | | | | | | | | |
|---|---|---|---|---|---|---|---|---|
| 14 | Ajax | 47044 | 26 | NAC Breda | 13250 | 21 | Roda JC Kerk | 12500 |
| 18 | Feyenoord | 42000 | 8 | Heerenveen | 13250 | 4 | Feyenoord | 12000 |
| 28 | PSV Eindhoven | 33500 | 10 | PSV Eindhoven | 13250 | 19 | Groningen | 11700 |
| 32 | Vitesse Arnhem | 23600 | 5 | NAC Breda | 13246 | 7 | De Graafschap | 11000 |
| 34 | Utrecht | 16200 | 25 | RKC Waalwijk | 13200 | 11 | NEC Nijmegen | 10500 |
| 24 | Heerenveen | 14400 | 1 | Willem II Tilb | 13200 | 9 | AZ Alkmaar | 6937 |
| 23 | Willem II Tilb | 13450 | 6 | Roda JC Kerk | 13200 | 3 | RKC Waalwijk | 6900 |
| 33 | Ajax | 13400 | 17 | Roosendaal | 13200 | 12 | Zwolle | 6350 |
| 13 | Vitesse Arnhem | 13300 | 27 | De Graafschap | 13175 | 30 | Roosendaal | 5000 |
| 2 | Utrecht | 13300 | 22 | AZ Alkmaar | 13101 | 16 | Excelsior | 2764 |
| 31 | Zwolle | 13300 | 15 | Groningen | 13100 | | | |
| 20 | NEC Nijmegen | 13250 | 29 | Excelsior | 13000 | | | |

Home / Away / Neutral

## DISCIPLINARY RECORDS

| | PLAYER | YELLOW | RED | AVE |
|---|---|---|---|---|
| 1 | Ouedraogo | 9 | 0 | 253 |
| 2 | Heubach | 7 | 1 | 327 |
| 3 | van de Paar | 4 | 0 | 359 |
| 4 | Cziommer | 7 | 0 | 390 |
| 5 | van der Doelen | 2 | 0 | 404 |
| 6 | Pothuizen | 5 | 0 | 473 |
| 7 | Houwing | 2 | 0 | 601 |
| 8 | van der Weerden | 1 | 0 | 683 |
| 9 | Polak | 3 | 1 | 685 |
| 10 | Grujic | 3 | 1 | 698 |
| 11 | Cavens | 2 | 0 | 779 |
| 12 | El Brazi | 3 | 0 | 954 |
| 13 | Cairo | 0 | 1 | 2667 |
| | Other | 5 | 0 | |
| | TOTAL | 53 | 4 | |

## LEAGUE GOALS

| | PLAYER | MINS | GOALS | AVE |
|---|---|---|---|---|
| 1 | Cairo | 2667 | 7 | 381 |
| 2 | Cavens | 1559 | 6 | 260 |
| 3 | Polak | 2740 | 6 | 457 |
| 4 | Cziommer | 2731 | 5 | 546 |
| 5 | Houwing | 1203 | 4 | 301 |
| 6 | Booth | 1440 | 2 | 720 |
| 7 | El Brazi | 2863 | 2 | 1432 |
| 8 | John | 605 | 2 | 303 |
| 9 | van de Paar | 1438 | 1 | 1438 |
| | Other | | 1 | |
| | TOTAL | | 36 | |

## MONTH BY MONTH GUIDE TO THE POINTS

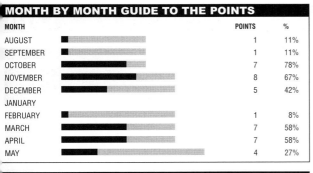

| MONTH | POINTS | % |
|---|---|---|
| AUGUST | 1 | 11% |
| SEPTEMBER | 1 | 11% |
| OCTOBER | 7 | 78% |
| NOVEMBER | 8 | 67% |
| DECEMBER | 5 | 42% |
| JANUARY | | |
| FEBRUARY | 1 | 8% |
| MARCH | 7 | 58% |
| APRIL | 7 | 58% |
| MAY | 4 | 27% |

## TEAM OF THE SEASON

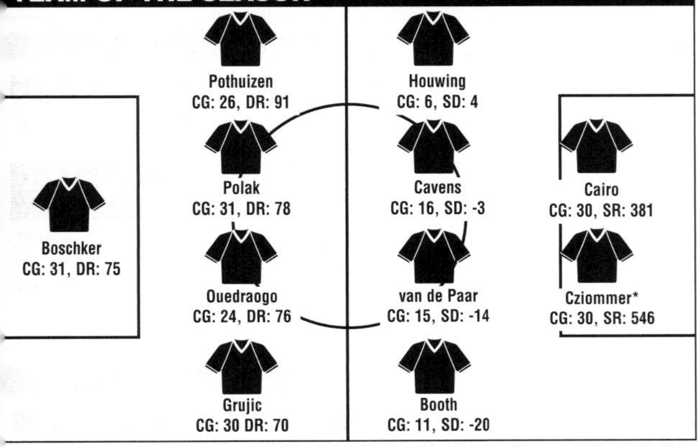
Boschker
CG: 31, DR: 75
Pothuizen
CG: 26, DR: 91
Polak
CG: 31, DR: 78
Ouedraogo
CG: 24, DR: 76
Grujic
CG: 30 DR: 70
Houwing
CG: 6, SD: 4
Cavens
CG: 16, SD: -3
van de Paar
CG: 15, SD: -14
Booth
CG: 11, SD: -20
Cairo
CG: 30, SR: 381
Cziommer*
CG: 30, SR: 546

KEY: DR = Defensive Rate, SD = Scoring Difference, SR = Strike Rate, CG = Counting Games – League games playing at least 70 minutes

## LEAGUE APPEARANCES, BOOKINGS AND CAPS

| | AGE | IN THE SQUAD | COUNTING GAMES | MINUTES ON PITCH | YELLOW CARDS | RED CARDS | THIS SEASON | HOME COUNTRY |
|---|---|---|---|---|---|---|---|---|
| **Goalkeepers** | | | | | | | | |
| Sander Boschker | 32 | 32 | 31 | 2835 | 0 | 0 | - | Holland |
| Cees Paauwe | 25 | 34 | 2 | 225 | 0 | 0 | - | Holland |
| Mikko Rahkamaa | 22 | 3 | 0 | 0 | 0 | 0 | - | Finland |
| **Defenders** | | | | | | | | |
| Abdelkader El Brazi | 26 | 33 | 32 | 2863 | 3 | 0 | - | Morocco |
| Spira Grujic | 31 | 32 | 30 | 2793 | 3 | 1 | - | Serbia & Montenegro |
| Jeroen Heubach | 28 | 31 | 28 | 2619 | 7 | 1 | - | Holland |
| Rahim Ouedraogo | 22 | 27 | 24 | 2279 | 9 | 0 | - | Burkino Faso |
| Sjaak Polak | 27 | 33 | 31 | 2740 | 3 | 1 | - | Holland |
| Patrick Pothuizen | 31 | 28 | 26 | 2368 | 5 | 0 | - | Holland |
| Chris Vd Weerden | 30 | 12 | 6 | 683 | 1 | 0 | - | Holland |
| **Midfielders** | | | | | | | | |
| Scott Booth | 31 | 25 | 11 | 1440 | 0 | 0 | - | Scotland |
| Jurgen Cavens | 24 | 30 | 16 | 1559 | 2 | 0 | - | Belgium |
| Simon Cziommer | 22 | 31 | 30 | 2731 | 7 | 0 | - | Germany |
| Jeffrey De Visscher | 22 | 31 | 1 | 276 | 0 | 0 | - | Holland |
| Thijs Houwing | 22 | 31 | 6 | 1203 | 2 | 0 | - | Holland |
| John Collins | 18 | 3 | 605 | 0 | 0 | - | | |
| Peter Niemeyer | 19 | 5 | 0 | 111 | 0 | 0 | - | Holland |
| Kurt van de Paar | 25 | 24 | 15 | 1438 | 4 | 0 | - | Belgium |
| Tom van der Leegte | 26 | 6 | 2 | 235 | 1 | 0 | - | Holland |
| Jan Verlinden | 26 | 24 | 2 | 202 | 0 | 0 | - | Belgium |
| Ramon Zomer | 20 | 34 | 2 | 385 | 3 | 0 | - | Holland |
| **Forwards** | | | | | | | | |
| Ellery Cairo | 24 | 30 | 30 | 2667 | 0 | 1 | - | Holland |
| Jack de Gier | 34 | 7 | 1 | 157 | 0 | 0 | - | Holland |
| Chris de Witte | 25 | 24 | 2 | 387 | 1 | 0 | - | Belgium |
| Nelson Goncalves | 20 | 5 | 0 | 0 | 0 | 0 | - | Germany |
| Bjorn van der Doelen | 26 | 22 | 8 | 808 | 2 | 0 | - | Holland |

KEY: LEAGUE BOOKINGS CAPS (FIFA RANKING)

## SQUAD APPEARANCES

| Match | 1 | 2 | 3 | 4 | 5 | 6 | 7 | 8 | 9 | 10 | 11 | 12 | 13 | 14 | 15 | 16 | 17 | 18 | 19 | 20 | 21 | 22 | 23 | 24 | 25 | 26 | 27 | 28 | 29 | 30 | 31 | 32 | 33 | 34 |
|---|---|---|---|---|---|---|---|---|---|---|---|---|---|---|---|---|---|---|---|---|---|---|---|---|---|---|---|---|---|---|---|---|---|---|
| Venue | H | H | A | H | A | H | A | H | A | H | A | A | H | A | H | A | H | A | A | H | A | H | A | A | H | H | H | A | H | A | H | A | H | A |
| Competition | L | L | L | L | L | L | L | L | L | L | L | L | L | L | L | L | L | L | L | L | L | L | L | L | L | L | L | L | L | L | L | L | L | L |
| Result | L | D | L | L | L | D | W | D | W | D | W | D | W | L | D | D | W | L | D | L | L | D | W | L | W | D | W | L | W | L | D | W | L | L |

**Goalkeepers**
Sander Boschker
Cees Paauwe
Mikko Rahkamaa

**Defenders**
Abdelkader El Brazi
Spira Grujic
Jeroen Heubach
Rahim Ouedraogo
Sjaak Polak
Patrick Pothuizen
Chris van der Weerden

**Midfielders**
Scott Booth
Jurgen Cavens
Simon Cziommer
Jeffrey De Visscher
Thijs Houwing
Collins John
Peter Niemeyer
Kurt van de Paar
Tom van der Leegte
Jan Verlinden
Ramon Zomer

**Forwards**
Ellery Cairo
Jack de Gier
Chris de Witte
Nelson da Costa Goncalves
Bjorn van der Doelen

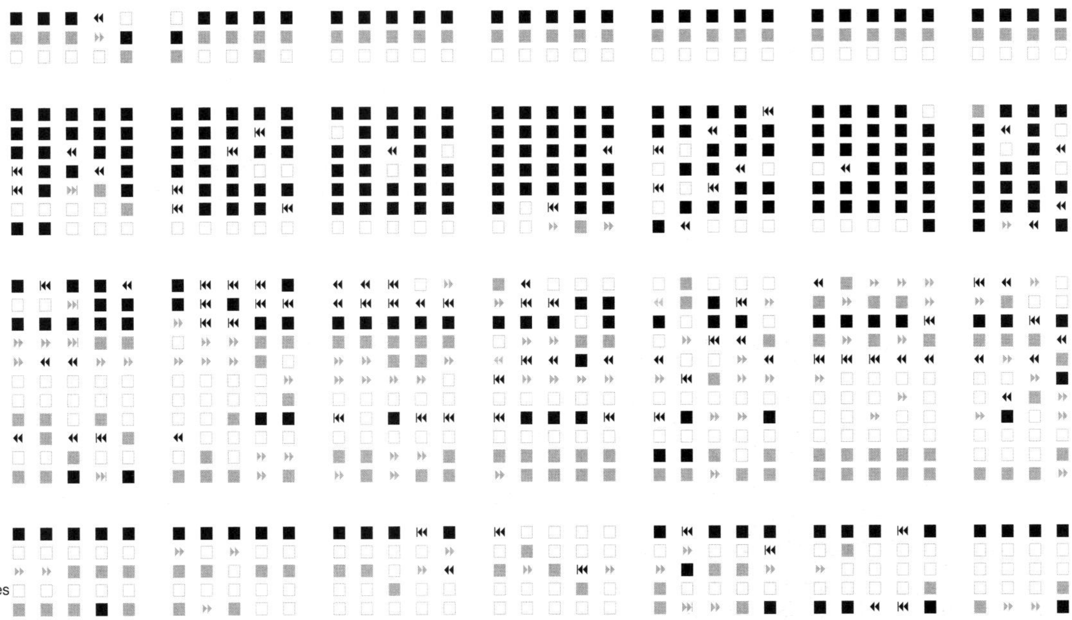

KEY: ■ On all match ■ On bench ⏮ Subbed or sent off (Counting game) ◀◀ Subbed or sent off (playing less than 70 minutes) ⏭ Subbed on from bench (Counting Game) ▶▶ Subbed on (playing less than 70 minutes) Subbed on and then subbed or sent off (Counting Game) Subbed on and then subbed or sent off (playing less than 70 minutes) □ Not in 16

# RBC ROOSENDAAL

Final Position: **13th**

| | | | | | | |
|---|---|---|---|---|---|---|
| 1 | lge | Zwolle | H | D | 1-1 | Maseland 8 |
| 2 | lge | De Graafschap | A | L | 0-2 | |
| 3 | lge | Heerenveen | H | W | 3-0 | Vos 2; Wooter 38; Sillah 66 |
| 4 | lge | Vitesse Arnhem | A | L | 0-3 | |
| 5 | lge | Ajax | H | L | 2-3 | Wooter 82; den Ouden 88 |
| 6 | lge | Feyenoord | H | W | 4-2 | Nascimento 45; den Ouden 51; Vos 60; Daelemans 94 |
| 7 | lge | Utrecht | A | D | 2-2 | den Ouden 43; de Graaf 53 |
| 8 | lge | Willem II Tilb | A | L | 1-3 | den Ouden 77 |
| 9 | lge | RKC Waalwijk | H | D | 0-0 | |
| 10 | lge | AZ Alkmaar | A | L | 0-2 | |
| 11 | lge | Groningen | H | W | 2-0 | Hellemons 53,88 |
| 12 | lge | Roda JC Kerk | H | W | 4-0 | den Ouden 31,53; Vos 85 pen; Fleur 88 |
| 13 | lge | PSV Eindhoven | H | L | 0-3 | |
| 14 | lge | NAC Breda | A | L | 0-1 | |
| 15 | lge | Excelsior | H | D | 1-1 | Vos 44 |
| 16 | lge | NEC Nijmegen | A | L | 0-3 | |
| 17 | lge | Twente | A | L | 0-3 | |
| 18 | lge | PSV Eindhoven | A | L | 0-3 | |
| 19 | lge | De Graafschap | H | W | 1-0 | Vos 42 pen |
| 20 | lge | Utrecht | H | L | 0-1 | |
| 21 | lge | Excelsior | A | W | 2-1 | Hellemons 47; Keller 88 |
| 22 | lge | Willem II Tilb | H | W | 1-0 | Sillah 61 |
| 23 | lge | Groningen | A | L | 0-1 | |
| 24 | lge | Zwolle | A | D | 1-1 | den Ouden 85 |
| 25 | lge | Vitesse Arnhem | H | W | 3-1 | Vos 11 pen; de Graaf 30; den Ouden 61 |
| 26 | lge | Ajax | A | L | 1-4 | Daelemans 77 |
| 27 | lge | RKC Waalwijk | A | W | 2-1 | den Ouden 14; Vos 74 pen |
| 28 | lge | AZ Alkmaar | H | D | 0-0 | |
| 29 | lge | Feyenoord | A | L | 0-1 | |
| 30 | lge | Twente | H | W | 1-0 | de Graaf 70 |
| 31 | lge | Roda JC Kerk | A | L | 0-1 | |
| 32 | lge | NEC Nijmegen | H | L | 0-2 | |
| 33 | lge | Heerenveen | A | L | 0-6 | |
| 34 | lge | NAC Breda | H | L | 1-2 | Sillah 80 |

## KEY PLAYERS - GOALSCORERS

**1 Geert den Ouden**

| | | | |
|---|---|---|---|
| **Goals in the League** | 9 | **Player Strike Rate** Average number of minutes between League goals scored by player | 195 |
| **Contribution to Attacking Power** Average number of minutes between League team goals while on pitch | 79 | **Club Strike Rate** Average number of minutes between League goals scored by club | 93 |

| | PLAYER | LGE GOALS | POWER | STRIKE RATE |
|---|---|---|---|---|
| 2 | Henk Vos | 7 | 85 | 366 mins |
| 3 | Eric Hellemons | 3 | 103 | 656 mins |
| 4 | Ebou Sillah | 3 | 126 | 674 mins |
| 5 | Edwin de Graaf | 3 | 92 | 805 mins |

## KEY PLAYERS - MIDFIELDERS

**1 Edwin de Graaf**

| | | | |
|---|---|---|---|
| **Goals in the League** | 3 | **Contribution to Attacking Power** Average number of minutes between League team goals while on pitch | 93 |
| **Defensive Rating** Average number of mins between League goals conceded while he was on the pitch | 76 | **Scoring Difference** Defensive Rating minus Contribution to Attacking Power | -17 |

| | PLAYER | LGE GOALS | DEF RATE | POWER | SCORE DIFF |
|---|---|---|---|---|---|
| 2 | Peter Maseland | 1 | 46 | 96 | -50 mins |
| 3 | Juan Jose Viedma | 0 | 70 | 125 | -55 mins |
| 4 | Ebou Sillah | 3 | 65 | 126 | -61 mins |
| 5 | Carlos Van Wanrooy | 0 | 47 | 113 | -66 mins |

## KEY PLAYERS - DEFENDERS

**1 Ronildo Tininho**

| | | | |
|---|---|---|---|
| **Goals Conceded (GC)** The number of League goals conceded while he was on the pitch | 29 | **Clean Sheets** In games when he played at least 70 minutes | 8 |
| **Defensive Rating** Ave number of mins between League goals conceded while on the pitch | 78 | **Club Defensive Rating** Average number of mins between League goals conceded by the club this season | 57 |

| | PLAYER | CON LGE | CLEAN SHEETS | DEF RATE |
|---|---|---|---|---|
| 2 | Eric Hellemons | 30 | 5 | 66 mins |
| 3 | Sander Keller | 35 | 5 | 58 mins |
| 4 | Azubuike Oliseh | 51 | 8 | 56 mins |
| 5 | Pascal Heije | 31 | 5 | 56 mins |

## GOALS SCORED

**AT HOME**

| | | |
|---|---|---|
| MOST | Ajax | 57 |
| | | 24 |
| LEAST | Twente | 18 |

**AWAY**

| | | |
|---|---|---|
| MOST | PSV | 44 |
| | | 9 |
| LEAST | Roosendaal & Groningen | 9 |

## GOALS CONCEDED

**AT HOME**

| | | |
|---|---|---|
| LEAST | PSV | 7 |
| | | 16 |
| MOST | Excelsior | 38 |

**AWAY**

| | | |
|---|---|---|
| LEAST | PSV | 13 |
| | | 38 |
| MOST | De G'schap | 50 |

## KEY GOALKEEPER

**1 Wim de Ron**

| | |
|---|---|
| **Goals Conceded in the League** | 23 |
| **Defensive Rating** Ave number of mins between League goals conceded while on the pitch | 65 |
| **Counting Games** Games when he played at least 70 mins | 16 |
| **Clean Sheets** In games when he played at least 70 mins | 4 |

## TOP POINT EARNERS

| | PLAYER | GAMES | AVE |
|---|---|---|---|
| 1 | Tininho | 24 | 1.46 |
| 2 | de Graaf | 24 | 1.33 |
| 3 | de Ron | 16 | 1.25 |
| 4 | den Ouden | 13 | 1.23 |
| 5 | Hellemons | 21 | 1.19 |
| 6 | Oliseh | 32 | 1.09 |
| 7 | Keller | 22 | 1.05 |
| 8 | Vos | 28 | 1.04 |
| 9 | Fleur | 24 | 1.04 |
| 10 | Heije | 18 | 1.00 |
| | **CLUB AVERAGE:** | | **1.06** |

Ave = Average points per match in Counting Games

## ATTENDANCES

HOME GROUND: VAST & GOED STADION CAPACITY: 5000 AVERAGE LEAGUE AT HOME: 4985

| | | | | | | | | |
|---|---|---|---|---|---|---|---|---|
| 26 | Ajax | 49182 | 2 | De Graafschap | 7500 | 6 | Feyenoord | 5000 |
| 29 | Feyenoord | 44000 | 10 | AZ Alkmaar | 6823 | 13 | PSV Eindhoven | 5000 |
| 18 | PSV Eindhoven | 33000 | 27 | RKC Waalwijk | 6000 | 11 | Groningen | 5000 |
| 4 | Vitesse Arnhem | 21600 | 24 | Zwolle | 6000 | 12 | Roda JC Kerk | 5000 |
| 7 | Utrecht | 17500 | 25 | Vitesse Arnhem | 5000 | 20 | Utrecht | 5000 |
| 14 | NAC Breda | 14872 | 3 | Heerenveen | 5000 | 22 | Willem II Tilb | 5000 |
| 33 | Heerenveen | 14200 | 1 | Zwolle | 5000 | 19 | De Graafschap | 5000 |
| 8 | Willem II Tilb | 13500 | 32 | NEC Nijmegen | 5000 | 5 | Ajax | 5000 |
| 17 | Twente | 13200 | 30 | Twente | 5000 | 15 | Excelsior | 4750 |
| 31 | Roda JC Kerk | 12000 | 28 | AZ Alkmaar | 5000 | 21 | Excelsior | 2638 |
| 23 | Groningen | 11934 | 34 | NAC Breda | 5000 | | | |
| 16 | NEC Nijmegen | 10000 | 9 | RKC Waalwijk | 5000 | | | |

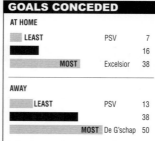

■ Home □ Away ▨ Neutral

## DISCIPLINARY RECORDS

| | PLAYER | YELLOW | RED | AVE |
|---|---|---|---|---|
| 1 | de Graaf | 5 | 0 | 483 |
| 2 | Sillah | 4 | 0 | 505 |
| 3 | Nascimento | 4 | 0 | 544 |
| 4 | Fleur | 4 | 0 | 567 |
| 5 | Viedma | 0 | 1 | 626 |
| 6 | Vos | 2 | 2 | 639 |
| 7 | Keller | 3 | 0 | 674 |
| 8 | Oliseh | 4 | 0 | 718 |
| 9 | den Ouden | 2 | 0 | 878 |
| 10 | Van Wanrooy | 1 | 0 | 901 |
| 11 | Hellemons | 2 | 0 | 984 |
| 12 | de Ron | 1 | 0 | 1485 |
| 13 | Heije | 1 | 0 | 1745 |
| | Other | 3 | 0 | |
| | TOTAL | 36 | 3 | |

## LEAGUE GOALS

| | PLAYER | MINS | GOALS | AVE |
|---|---|---|---|---|
| 1 | den Ouden | 1756 | 9 | 195 |
| 2 | Vos | 2559 | 7 | 366 |
| 3 | Hellemons | 1968 | 3 | 656 |
| 4 | Sillah | 2023 | 3 | 674 |
| 5 | de Graaf | 2416 | 3 | 805 |
| 6 | Wooter | 2218 | 2 | 1109 |
| 7 | Daelemans | 579 | 2 | 290 |
| 8 | Fleur | 2269 | 1 | 2269 |
| 9 | Maseland | 1154 | 1 | 1154 |
| 10 | Keller | 2024 | 1 | 2024 |
| 11 | Nascimento | 2178 | 1 | 2178 |
| | Other | | 0 | |
| | TOTAL | | 33 | |

## MONTH BY MONTH GUIDE TO THE POINTS

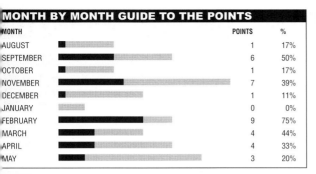

| MONTH | POINTS | % |
|---|---|---|
| AUGUST | 1 | 17% |
| SEPTEMBER | 6 | 50% |
| OCTOBER | 1 | 17% |
| NOVEMBER | 7 | 39% |
| DECEMBER | 1 | 11% |
| JANUARY | 0 | 0% |
| FEBRUARY | 9 | 75% |
| MARCH | 4 | 44% |
| APRIL | 4 | 33% |
| MAY | 3 | 20% |

## LEAGUE APPEARANCES, BOOKINGS AND CAPS

| | AGE | IN THE SQUAD | COUNTING GAMES | MINUTES ON PITCH | YELLOW CARDS | RED CARDS | THIS SEASON | HOME COUNTRY |
|---|---|---|---|---|---|---|---|---|
| **Goalkeepers** | | | | | | | | |
| Maikel Aerts | 26 | 17 | 17 | 1530 | 0 | 0 | - | Holland |
| Wim de Ron | 33 | 33 | 16 | 1485 | 1 | 0 | - | Holland |
| Wilko de Vogt | 27 | 15 | 0 | 45 | 0 | 0 | - | Holland |
| Erwin Friebel | 20 | 1 | 0 | 0 | 0 | 0 | - | Holland |
| **Defenders** | | | | | | | | |
| Fleur | 21 | 29 | 24 | 2269 | 4 | 0 | - | Holland |
| Pascal Heije | 23 | 25 | 18 | 1745 | 1 | 0 | - | Holland |
| Eric Hellemons | 32 | 26 | 21 | 1968 | 2 | 0 | - | Holland |
| Sander Keller | 23 | 24 | 22 | 2024 | 3 | 0 | - | Holland |
| Sampo Koskinen | 24 | 11 | 0 | 0 | 0 | 0 | - | Finland |
| David Nascimento | 37 | 27 | 23 | 2178 | 4 | 0 | - | Portugal |
| Azubuike Oliseh | 24 | 32 | 32 | 2873 | 4 | 0 | - | Nigeria |
| Mitchell Pique | 22 | 28 | 4 | 744 | 0 | 0 | - | Holland |
| Sebastien Stassin | 25 | 1 | 0 | 0 | 0 | 0 | - | |
| Ronildo Tininho | 25 | 29 | 24 | 2269 | 1 | 0 | - | Brazil |
| **Midfielders** | | | | | | | | |
| Edwin de Graaf | 23 | 29 | 24 | 2416 | 5 | 0 | - | Holland |
| Ramon Luijten | 21 | 1 | 0 | 0 | 0 | 0 | - | Holland |
| Peter Maseland | 24 | 31 | 8 | 1154 | 0 | 0 | - | Holland |
| Ebou Sillah | 23 | 25 | 22 | 2023 | 4 | 0 | - | Gambia |
| Marcel van der Sloot | 23 | 21 | 1 | 181 | 1 | 0 | - | Holland |
| Carlos Van Wanrooy | 36 | 12 | 9 | 901 | 1 | 0 | - | Holland |
| Juan Jose Viedma | 28 | 10 | 7 | 626 | 0 | 1 | - | Holland |
| **Forwards** | | | | | | | | |
| Bjorn Daelemans | 25 | 30 | 3 | 579 | 0 | 0 | - | Belgium |
| Geert den Ouden | 26 | 31 | 13 | 1756 | 2 | 0 | - | Holland |
| Jeroen van Wetten | 23 | 17 | 0 | 17 | 0 | 0 | - | Holland |
| Henk Vos | 35 | 29 | 28 | 2559 | 2 | 2 | - | Holland |
| Nordin Wooter | 26 | 29 | 22 | 2218 | 1 | 0 | - | Holland |

**KEY:** LEAGUE BOOKINGS CAPS (FIFA RANKING)

## TEAM OF THE SEASON

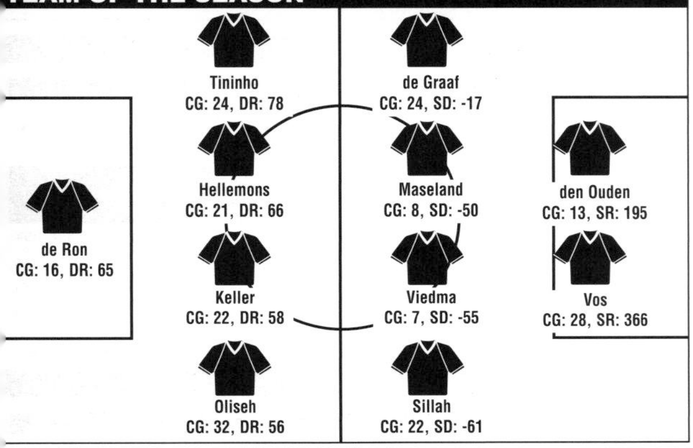

Tininho
CG: 24, DR: 78
de Graaf
CG: 24, SD: -17
Hellemons
CG: 21, DR: 66
Maseland
CG: 8, SD: -50
den Ouden
CG: 13, SR: 195
de Ron
CG: 16, DR: 65
Keller
CG: 22, DR: 58
Viedma
CG: 7, SD: -55
Vos
CG: 28, SR: 366
Oliseh
CG: 32, DR: 56
Sillah
CG: 22, SD: -61


**KEY:** DR = Defensive Rate, SD = Scoring Difference, SR = Strike Rate, CG = Counting Games – League games playing at least 70 minutes

## SQUAD APPEARANCES

| Match | 1 | 2 | 3 | 4 | 5 | 6 | 7 | 8 | 9 | 10 | 11 | 12 | 13 | 14 | 15 | 16 | 17 | 18 | 19 | 20 | 21 | 22 | 23 | 24 | 25 | 26 | 27 | 28 | 29 | 30 | 31 | 32 | 33 | 34 |
|---|---|---|---|---|---|---|---|---|---|---|---|---|---|---|---|---|---|---|---|---|---|---|---|---|---|---|---|---|---|---|---|---|---|---|
| Venue | H | A | H | A | H | H | A | A | H | A | H | H | H | A | H | A | A | A | H | H | A | H | A | A | H | A | A | H | A | H | A | H | A | H |
| Competition | L | L | L | L | L | L | L | L | L | L | L | L | L | L | L | L | L | L | L | L | L | L | L | L | L | L | L | L | L | L | L | L | L | L |
| Result | D | L | W | L | L | W | D | L | D | L | W | W | L | L | D | L | L | L | W | L | W | W | L | D | W | L | W | D | L | W | L | L | L | L |

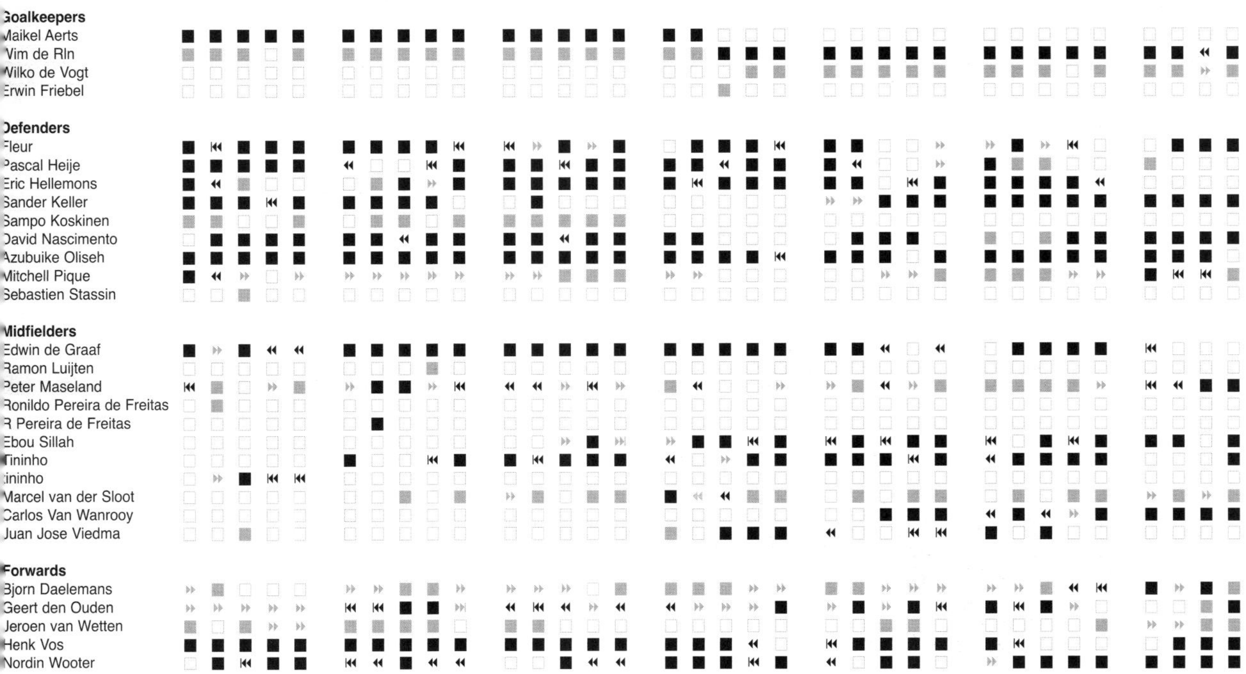

Goalkeepers
Maikel Aerts
Vim de Rln
Wilko de Vogt
Erwin Friebel
Defenders
Fleur
Pascal Heije
Eric Hellemons
Sander Keller
Sampo Koskinen
David Nascimento
Azubuike Oliseh
Mitchell Pique
Sebastien Stassin
Midfielders
Edwin de Graaf
Ramon Luijten
Peter Maseland
Ronildo Pereira de Freitas
R Pereira de Freitas
Ebou Sillah
Tininho
ininho
Marcel van der Sloot
Carlos Van Wanrooy
Juan Jose Viedma
Forwards
Bjorn Daelemans
Geert den Ouden
Jeroen van Wetten
Henk Vos
Nordin Wooter

# VITESSE ARNHEM

Final Position: **14th**

| | | | | | | | |
|---|---|---|---|---|---|---|---|
| 1 | lge | Groningen | A | W | 2-1 | Amoah 26,67 |
| 2 | lge | Ajax | H | L | 1-2 | Amoah 16 |
| 3 | lge | Zwolle | A | L | 0-1 | |
| 4 | lge | Roosendaal | H | W | 3-0 | Peeters 11; Hofs 68; Sone 90 |
| 5 | uc1rl1 | Rapid Bucharest | H | | 1-1 | Peeters 62 |
| 6 | lge | RKC Waalwijk | H | D | 1-1 | Rankovic 70 |
| 7 | lge | Utrecht | A | L | 0-1 | |
| 8 | uc1rl2 | Rapid Bucharest | A | | 1-0 | Peeters 62 |
| 9 | lge | AZ Alkmaar | A | W | 3-1 | Claessens 5; Amoah 67; Hofs 90 |
| 10 | lge | Feyenoord | H | D | 1-1 | Amoah 31 |
| 11 | lge | Roda JC Kerk | H | L | 0-2 | |
| 12 | lge | NAC Breda | A | D | 0-0 | |
| 13 | uc2rl1 | W Bremen | H | W | 2-1 | Amoah 37; Verlaat 62 og |
| 14 | lge | Willem II Tilb | A | W | 3-1 | Levchenko 21 pen; Zeman 37; Amoah 90 |
| 15 | uc2rl2 | W Bremen | A | D | 3-3 | Levchenko 51 pen; Claessens 73; Mbamba 90 |
| 16 | lge | Heerenveen | H | L | 1-2 | Sone 83 |
| 17 | lge | Twente | A | L | 0-1 | |
| 18 | uc3rl1 | Liverpool | H | L | 0-1 | |
| 19 | lge | De Graafschap | H | D | 1-1 | Sone 66 |
| 20 | lge | NEC Nijmegen | A | L | 0-2 | |
| 21 | uc3rl2 | Liverpool | A | L | 0-1 | |
| 22 | lge | Excelsior | H | L | 1-2 | Claessens 17 |
| 23 | lge | PSV Eindhoven | A | L | 0-1 | |
| 24 | lge | Roda JC Kerk | A | L | 0-2 | |
| 25 | lge | RKC Waalwijk | A | L | 0-1 | |
| 26 | lge | Zwolle | H | W | 2-1 | Jansen, M 32; Peeters 61 |
| 27 | lge | AZ Alkmaar | H | D | 2-2 | Amoah 75 pen; Jansen, M 85 |
| 28 | lge | Ajax | A | L | 0-2 | |
| 29 | lge | Utrecht | H | L | 1-4 | Peeters 76 |
| 30 | lge | PSV Eindhoven | H | L | 0-5 | |
| 31 | lge | Roosendaal | A | L | 1-3 | Amoah 89 |
| 32 | lge | Groningen | H | D | 0-0 | |
| 33 | lge | Feyenoord | A | L | 1-2 | Peeters 23 |
| 34 | lge | NEC Nijmegen | H | D | 1-1 | Peeters 12 |
| 35 | lge | Heerenveen | A | D | 2-2 | Peeters 30; Amoah 40 |
| 36 | lge | NAC Breda | H | W | 3-1 | Amoah 20,56; Peeters 69 |
| 37 | lge | De Graafschap | A | W | 1-0 | Amoah 39 |
| 38 | lge | Twente | H | L | 0-1 | |
| 39 | lge | Excelsior | A | D | 4-4 | Amoah 14,44,78; Claessens 76 |
| 40 | lge | Willem II Tilb | H | W | 2-0 | Mghizrat 61 og; Amoah 90 |

## KEY PLAYERS - GOALSCORERS

**1 Matthew Amoah**

| | | | |
|---|---|---|---|
| Goals in the League | 16 | Player Strike Rate<br>Average number of minutes between League goals scored by player | 167 |
| Contribution to Attacking Power<br>Average number of minutes between League team goals while on pitch | 83 | Club Strike Rate<br>Average number of minutes between League goals scored by club | 83 |

| | PLAYER | LGE GOALS | POWER | STRIKE RATE |
|---|---|---|---|---|
| 2 | Bob Peeters | 7 | 71 | 287 mins |
| 3 | Gert Claessens | 3 | 80 | 808 mins |
| 4 | Serhiy Levchenko | 1 | 81 | 1546 mins |
| 5 | Aleksandar Rankovic | 1 | 75 | 2043 mins |

## KEY PLAYERS - MIDFIELDERS

**1 Didier Martel**

| | | | |
|---|---|---|---|
| Goals in the League | 0 | Contribution to Attacking Power<br>Average number of minutes between League team goals while on pitch | 71 |
| Defensive Rating<br>Average number of mins between League goals conceded while he was on the pitch | 68 | Scoring Difference<br>Defensive Rating minus Contribution to Attacking Power | -3 |

| | PLAYER | LGE GOALS | DEF RATE | POWER | SCORE DIFF |
|---|---|---|---|---|---|
| 2 | Gert Claessens | 3 | 61 | 81 | -20 mins |
| 3 | Aleksandar Rankovic | 1 | 55 | 76 | -21 mins |
| 4 | Theo Janssen | 0 | 55 | 106 | -51 mins |
| 5 | Jan Van Halst | 0 | 59 | 117 | -58 mins |

## KEY PLAYERS - DEFENDERS

**1 Marian Zeman**

| | | | |
|---|---|---|---|
| Goals Conceded (GC)<br>The number of League goals conceded while he was on the pitch | 14 | Clean Sheets<br>In games when he played at least 70 minutes | 3 |
| Defensive Rating<br>Ave number of mins between League goals conceded while on the pitch | 76 | Club Defensive Rating<br>Average number of mins between League goals conceded by the club this season | 60 |

| | PLAYER | CON LGE | CLEAN SHEETS | DEF RATE |
|---|---|---|---|---|
| 2 | Tim Cornelisse | 46 | 5 | 65 mins |
| 3 | Dejan Stefanovic | 37 | 4 | 64 mins |
| 4 | Serhiy Levchenko | 25 | 2 | 62 mins |
| 5 | Purrel Frankel | 45 | 5 | 60 mins |

## GOALS SCORED

**AT HOME**

| | | |
|---|---|---|
| MOST | Ajax | 57 |
| | | 20 |
| LEAST | Twente | 18 |

**AWAY**

| | | |
|---|---|---|
| MOST | PSV | 44 |
| | | 17 |
| LEAST | Roosendaal & Groningen | 9 |

## GOALS CONCEDED

**AT HOME**

| | | |
|---|---|---|
| LEAST | PSV | 7 |
| | | 26 |
| MOST | Excelsior | 38 |

**AWAY**

| | | |
|---|---|---|
| LEAST | PSV | 13 |
| | | 25 |
| MOST | De G'schap | 50 |

## KEY GOALKEEPER

**1 Dragoslav Jevric**

| | |
|---|---|
| Goals Conceded in the League | 51 |
| Defensive Rating<br>Ave number of mins between League goals conceded while on the pitch | 60 |
| Counting Games<br>Games when he played at least 70 mins | 34 |
| Clean Sheets<br>In games when he played at least 70 mins | 5 |

## TOP POINT EARNERS

| | PLAYER | GAMES | AVE |
|---|---|---|---|
| 1 | Peeters | 20 | 1.20 |
| 2 | Rankovic | 18 | 1.17 |
| 3 | Martel | 15 | 1.13 |
| 4 | Levchenko | 14 | 1.07 |
| 5 | Claessens | 25 | 1.04 |
| 6 | Cornelisse | 33 | 1.00 |
| 7 | Frankel | 30 | 0.97 |
| 8 | Amoah | 30 | 0.97 |
| 9 | Jevric | 34 | 0.97 |
| 10 | Stefanovic | 25 | 0.92 |
| | **CLUB AVERAGE:** | | **0.97** |

Ave = Average points per match in Counting Games

## ATTENDANCES

HOME GROUND: GELREDOME CAPACITY: 29000 AVERAGE LEAGUE AT HOME: 23071

| | | | | | | | | |
|---|---|---|---|---|---|---|---|---|
| 28 | Ajax | 48162 | 27 | AZ Alkmaar | 22284 | 17 | Twente | 13300 |
| 33 | Feyenoord | 46000 | 36 | NAC Breda | 22130 | 20 | NEC Nijmegen | 12250 |
| 23 | PSV Eindhoven | 33500 | 11 | Roda JC Kerk | 22000 | 8 | Rapid Bucharest | 12000 |
| 40 | Willem II Tilb | 28000 | 16 | Heerenveen | 22000 | 24 | Roda JC Kerk | 12000 |
| 18 | Liverpool | 27000 | 6 | RKC Waalwijk | 21812 | 1 | Groningen | 11558 |
| 10 | Feyenoord | 26000 | 4 | Roosendaal | 21600 | 37 | De Graafschap | 11000 |
| 2 | Ajax | 24200 | 22 | Excelsior | 21000 | 5 | Rapid Bucharest | 10850 |
| 34 | NEC Nijmegen | 24196 | 26 | Zwolle | 21000 | 9 | AZ Alkmaar | 7000 |
| 30 | PSV Eindhoven | 23900 | 13 | W Bremen | 20000 | 25 | RKC Waalwijk | 6249 |
| 38 | Twente | 23600 | 15 | W Bremen | 20000 | 3 | Zwolle | 5200 |
| 21 | Liverpool | 23576 | 7 | Utrecht | 15331 | 31 | Roosendaal | 5000 |
| 32 | Groningen | 23200 | 12 | NAC Breda | 14858 | 39 | Excelsior | 3124 |
| 29 | Utrecht | 22800 | 35 | Heerenveen | 14400 | | | |
| 19 | De Graafschap | 22500 | 14 | Willem II Tilb | 13400 | | | |

■ Home □ Away ▒ Neutral

## DISCIPLINARY RECORDS

| | PLAYER | YELLOW | RED | AVE |
|---|---|---|---|---|
| 1 | Zeman | 4 | 1 | 212 |
| 2 | Stefanovic | 8 | 2 | 235 |
| 3 | Hofs | 3 | 0 | 260 |
| 4 | Claessens | 7 | 0 | 346 |
| 5 | Mbamba | 3 | 0 | 444 |
| 6 | Janssen | 4 | 0 | 505 |
| 7 | Frankel | 4 | 0 | 671 |
| 8 | Van Halst | 1 | 0 | 938 |
| 9 | Cornelisse | 3 | 0 | 990 |
| 10 | Rankovic | 2 | 0 | 1021 |
| 11 | Amoah | 2 | 0 | 1336 |
| 12 | Jevric | 2 | 0 | 1530 |
| 13 | Levchenko | 1 | 0 | 1546 |
| | Other | 1 | 0 | |
| | TOTAL | 45 | 3 | |

## LEAGUE GOALS

| | PLAYER | MINS | GOALS | AVE |
|---|---|---|---|---|
| 1 | Amoah | 2672 | 16 | 167 |
| 2 | Peeters | 2007 | 7 | 287 |
| 3 | Claessens | 2424 | 3 | 808 |
| 4 | Sone | 444 | 3 | 148 |
| 5 | Jansen, M | 862 | 2 | 431 |
| 6 | Hofs | 782 | 2 | 391 |
| 7 | Levchenko | 1546 | 1 | 1546 |
| 8 | Rankovic | 2043 | 1 | 2043 |
| 9 | Zeman | 1062 | 1 | 1062 |
| | Other | | 1 | |
| | TOTAL | | 37 | |

## MONTH BY MONTH GUIDE TO THE POINTS

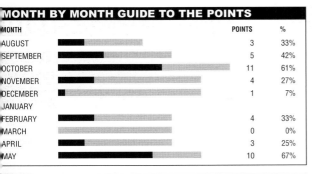

| MONTH | POINTS | % |
|---|---|---|
| AUGUST | 3 | 33% |
| SEPTEMBER | 5 | 42% |
| OCTOBER | 11 | 61% |
| NOVEMBER | 4 | 27% |
| DECEMBER | 1 | 7% |
| JANUARY | | |
| FEBRUARY | 4 | 33% |
| MARCH | 0 | 0% |
| APRIL | 3 | 25% |
| MAY | 10 | 67% |

## TEAM OF THE SEASON

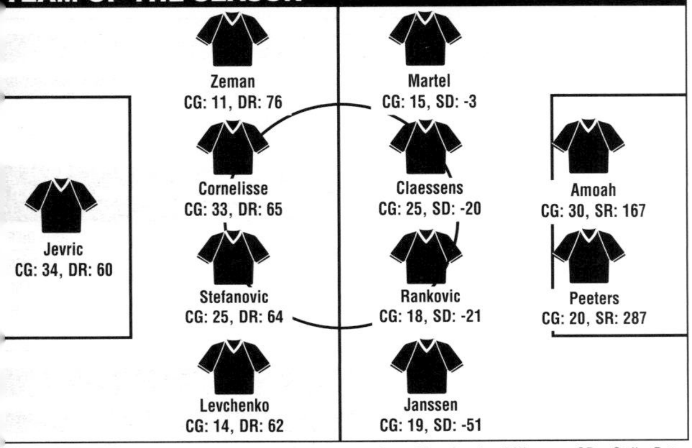

Zeman
CG: 11, DR: 76
Martel
CG: 15, SD: -3
Cornelisse
CG: 33, DR: 65
Claessens
CG: 25, SD: -20
Amoah
CG: 30, SR: 167
Jevric
CG: 34, DR: 60
Stefanovic
CG: 25, DR: 64
Rankovic
CG: 18, SD: -21
Peeters
CG: 20, SR: 287
Levchenko
CG: 14, DR: 62
Janssen
CG: 19, SD: -51


KEY: DR = Defensive Rate, SD = Scoring Difference, SR = Strike Rate, CG = Counting Games – League games playing at least 70 minutes

## LEAGUE APPEARANCES, BOOKINGS AND CAPS

| | AGE | IN THE SQUAD | COUNTING GAMES | MINUTES ON PITCH | YELLOW CARDS | RED CARDS | THIS SEASON | HOME COUNTRY |
|---|---|---|---|---|---|---|---|---|
| **Goalkeepers** | | | | | | | | |
| Dragoslav Jevric | 29 | 34 | 34 | 3060 | 2 | 0 | - | Serbia & Montenegro |
| Jimmy van Fessem | 27 | 33 | 0 | 58 | 0 | 0 | - | Holland |
| **Defenders** | | | | | | | | |
| Tim Cornelisse | 25 | 33 | 33 | 2970 | 3 | 0 | - | Holland |
| Michael Dingsdag | 20 | 32 | 8 | 763 | 0 | 0 | - | Holland |
| Purrel Frankel | 26 | 33 | 30 | 2687 | 4 | 0 | - | Holland |
| Michael Jansen | 19 | 21 | 9 | 862 | 0 | 0 | - | Holland |
| Ruud Knol | 22 | 2 | 2 | 180 | 0 | 0 | - | Holland |
| Serhiy Levchenko | 25 | 32 | 14 | 1546 | 1 | 0 | - | Ukraine |
| Stefan Nanu | 34 | 1 | 0 | 0 | 0 | 0 | - | |
| Francisco Rojas | 28 | 12 | 1 | 300 | 0 | 0 | - | |
| Dejan Stefanovic | 28 | 28 | 25 | 2352 | 8 | 2 | - | Serbia & Montenegro |
| Marian Zeman | 29 | 18 | 11 | 1062 | 4 | 1 | - | Slovakia |
| **Midfielders** | | | | | | | | |
| Ricky Bochem | 20 | 6 | 1 | 91 | 0 | 0 | - | Holland |
| Gert Claessens | 31 | 29 | 25 | 2424 | 7 | 0 | - | Belgium |
| Raymond Fafiani | | 3 | 0 | 0 | 0 | 0 | - | Holland |
| Theo Groeneveld | 20 | 1 | 0 | 0 | 0 | 0 | - | Holland |
| Nick Hofs | 20 | 14 | 4 | 782 | 3 | 0 | - | Holland |
| Theo Janssen | 21 | 30 | 19 | 2020 | 4 | 0 | - | Holland |
| Louis Laros | 30 | 1 | 0 | 0 | 0 | 0 | - | Holland |
| Didier Martel | 31 | 26 | 15 | 1628 | 0 | 0 | - | France |
| Aleksandar Rankovic | 24 | 34 | 18 | 2043 | 2 | 0 | - | Serbia & Montenegro |
| Stijn Schaars | 19 | 12 | 0 | 34 | 0 | 0 | - | Holland |
| Richard Terpstra | 21 | 1 | 0 | 45 | 0 | 0 | - | Holland |
| Jan Van Halst | | 14 | 10 | 938 | 1 | 0 | - | |
| **Forwards** | | | | | | | | |
| Matthew Amoah | 22 | 30 | 30 | 2672 | 2 | 0 | - | Ghana |
| Emile Mbamba | 20 | 34 | 9 | 1332 | 3 | 0 | - | Cameroon |
| Rahamat Riga | 21 | 21 | 9 | 1037 | 0 | 0 | - | Ghana |
| Bob Peeters | 29 | 30 | 20 | 2007 | 1 | 0 | - | Belgium |
| Kalle Sone | 20 | 22 | 1 | 444 | 0 | 0 | - | Cameroon |
| John van Beukering | 15 | 1 | 204 | 0 | 0 | - Holland | | |

KEY: LEAGUE BOOKINGS CAPS (FIFA RANKING)

## SQUAD APPEARANCES

| Match | 1 | 2 | 3 | 4 | 5 | 6 | 7 | 8 | 9 | 10 | 11 | 12 | 13 | 14 | 15 | 16 | 17 | 18 | 19 | 20 | 21 | 22 | 23 | 24 | 25 | 26 | 27 | 28 | 29 | 30 | 31 | 32 | 33 | 34 | 35 | 36 | 37 | 38 | 39 | 40 |
|---|---|---|---|---|---|---|---|---|---|---|---|---|---|---|---|---|---|---|---|---|---|---|---|---|---|---|---|---|---|---|---|---|---|---|---|---|---|---|---|---|
| Venue | A | H | A | H | H | H | A | A | A | H | H | A | H | A | A | H | A | H | H | A | A | H | A | A | A | H | H | A | H | H | A | H | A | H | A | H | A | H | A | H |
| Competition | L | L | L | L | E | L | L | E | L | L | L | L | E | L | E | L | L | E | L | L | E | L | L | L | L | L | L | L | L | L | L | L | L | L | L | L | L | L | L | L |
| Result | W | L | L | W | D | D | L | W | W | D | L | D | W | W | D | L | L | L | D | L | L | L | L | L | L | W | D | L | L | L | L | D | L | D | D | W | W | L | D | W |

**Goalkeepers**
Dragoslav Jevric
Jimmy van Fessem

**Defenders**
Tim Cornelisse
Michael Dingsdag
Purrel Frankel
Michael Jansen
Ruud Knol
Serhiy Levchenko
Stefan Nanu
Francisco Rojas
Dejan Stefanovic
Marian Zeman

**Midfielders**
Ricky Bochem
Gert Claessens
Raymond Fafiani
Theo Groeneveld
Nick Hofs
Theo Janssen
Louis Laros
Didier Martel
Aleksandar Rankovic
Stijn Schaars
Richard Terpstra
Jan Van Halst

**Forwards**
Matthew Amoah
Emile Mbamba
Rahamat Mustapha Riga
Bob Peeters
Kalle Sone
John van Beukering

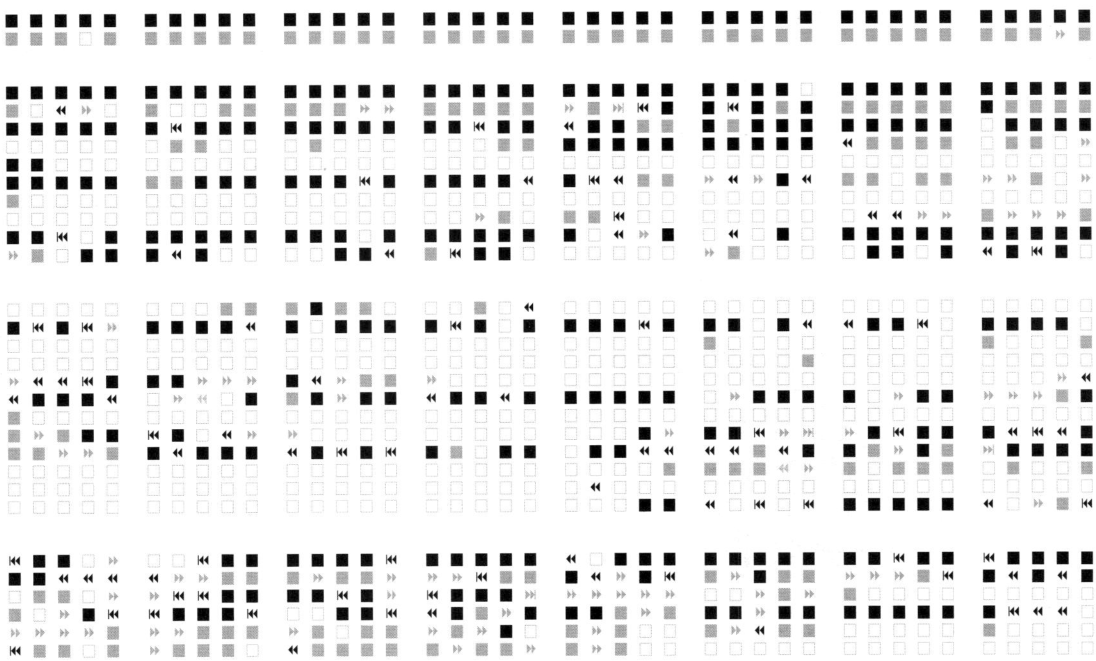

# FC GRONINGEN

Final Position: **15th**

| | | | | | | |
|---|---|---|---|---|---|---|
| 1 | lge | Vitesse Arnhem | H | L | 1-2 | Drent 25 |
| 2 | lge | PSV Eindhoven | A | L | 0-1 | |
| 3 | lge | Ajax | H | L | 1-3 | Hugo 75 |
| 4 | lge | Excelsior | A | L | 2-4 | Matthijs 36; Broerse 57 |
| 5 | lge | Utrecht | H | D | 0-0 | |
| 6 | lge | AZ Alkmaar | A | L | 1-4 | Bronkhorst 90 |
| 7 | lge | NEC Nijmegen | A | L | 0-2 | |
| 8 | lge | RKC Waalwijk | H | L | 2-3 | Drent 85; Salmon 90 |
| 9 | lge | Feyenoord | H | L | 0-2 | |
| 10 | lge | NAC Breda | A | D | 0-0 | |
| 11 | lge | Roosendaal | A | L | 0-2 | |
| 12 | lge | De Graafschap | H | W | 3-1 | Salmon 64; Landerl 80; Drent 83 |
| 13 | lge | Zwolle | A | W | 2-0 | Drent 64,89 |
| 14 | lge | Heerenveen | H | D | 1-1 | Salmon 60 |
| 15 | lge | Twente | A | D | 0-0 | |
| 16 | lge | Roda JC Kerk | H | W | 3-2 | Van Gessel 40; Hugo 63; Matthijs 75 |
| 17 | lge | Willem II Tilb | A | L | 0-1 | |
| 18 | lge | RKC Waalwijk | A | L | 0-1 | |
| 19 | lge | Twente | H | D | 0-0 | |
| 20 | lge | Ajax | A | L | 1-2 | Schoenmakers 73 |
| 21 | lge | Feyenoord | A | L | 1-4 | Van Gessel 85 |
| 22 | lge | Zwolle | H | W | 4-0 | Tuhuteru 16; Drent 46; Krstev 71,80 |
| 23 | lge | Roosendaal | H | W | 1-0 | Drent 63 |
| 24 | lge | Willem II Tilb | H | D | 1-1 | Matthijs 90 |
| 25 | lge | Utrecht | A | D | 0-0 | |
| 26 | lge | Vitesse Arnhem | A | D | 0-0 | |
| 27 | lge | Excelsior | H | W | 1-0 | Van Gessel 77 |
| 28 | lge | NAC Breda | H | D | 0-0 | |
| 29 | lge | NEC Nijmegen | H | D | 0-0 | |
| 30 | lge | Heerenveen | A | L | 1-2 | Salmon 72 |
| 31 | lge | Roda JC Kerk | A | L | 1-5 | Ikedia 64 |
| 32 | lge | AZ Alkmaar | H | W | 1-0 | Salmon 86 |
| 33 | lge | De Graafschap | A | L | 0-1 | |
| 34 | lge | PSV Eindhoven | H | D | 0-0 | |

## KEY PLAYERS - GOALSCORERS

**1 Martin Drent**

| | | | |
|---|---|---|---|
| Goals in the League | 7 | Player Strike Rate<br>Average number of minutes between League goals scored by player | 231 |
| Contribution to Attacking Power<br>Average number of minutes between League team goals while on pitch | 85 | Club Strike Rate<br>Average number of minutes between League goals scored by club | 109 |

| | PLAYER | LGE GOALS | POWER | STRIKE RATE |
|---|---|---|---|---|
| 2 | Glen Salmon | 5 | 128 | 410 mins |
| 3 | Sander Van Gessel | 3 | 108 | 724 mins |
| 4 | Paul Matthijs | 3 | 107 | 751 mins |
| 5 | Mile Krstev | 2 | 116 | 932 mins |

## KEY PLAYERS - MIDFIELDERS

**1 Rolf Landerl**

| | | | |
|---|---|---|---|
| Goals in the League | 1 | Contribution to Attacking Power<br>Average number of minutes between League team goals while on pitch | 106 |
| Defensive Rating<br>Average number of mins between League goals conceded while he was on the pitch | 116 | Scoring Difference<br>Defensive Rating minus Contribution to Attacking Power | 10 |

| | PLAYER | LGE GOALS | DEF RATE | POWER | SCORE DIFF |
|---|---|---|---|---|---|
| 2 | Alves Velame Hugo | 2 | 92 | 92 | 0 mins |
| 3 | Sander Van Gessel | 3 | 87 | 109 | -22 mins |
| 4 | Paul Matthijs | 3 | 61 | 107 | -46 mins |

## KEY PLAYERS - DEFENDERS

**1 Mile Krstev**

| | | | |
|---|---|---|---|
| Goals Conceded (GC)<br>The number of League goals conceded while he was on the pitch | 23 | Clean Sheets<br>In games when he played at least 70 minutes | 8 |
| Defensive Rating<br>Ave number of mins between League goals conceded while on the pitch | 81 | Club Defensive Rating<br>Average number of mins between League goals conceded by the club this season | 70 |

| | PLAYER | CON LGE | CLEAN SHEETS | DEF RATE |
|---|---|---|---|---|
| 2 | Arnold Kruiswijk | 21 | 8 | 79 mins |
| 3 | Joost Broerse | 34 | 13 | 79 mins |
| 4 | Claus Boekweg | 26 | 8 | 71 mins |
| 5 | Mathias Floren | 40 | 14 | 71 mins |

## GOALS SCORED

**AT HOME**

| | | |
|---|---|---|
| MOST | Ajax | 57 |
| | | 19 |
| LEAST | Twente | 18 |

**AWAY**

| | | |
|---|---|---|
| MOST | PSV | 44 |
| | | 9 |
| LEAST | Roosendaal & Groningen | 9 |

## GOALS CONCEDED

**AT HOME**

| | | |
|---|---|---|
| LEAST | PSV | 7 |
| | | 15 |
| MOST | Excelsior | 38 |

**AWAY**

| | | |
|---|---|---|
| LEAST | PSV | 13 |
| | | 29 |
| MOST | De G'schap | 50 |

## KEY GOALKEEPER

**1 Roy Beukenkamp**

| | |
|---|---|
| Goals Conceded in the League | 37 |
| Defensive Rating<br>Ave number of mins between League goals conceded while on the pitch | 72 |
| Counting Games<br>Games when he played at least 70 mins | 29 |
| Clean Sheets<br>In games when he played at least 70 mins | 12 |

## TOP POINT EARNERS

| | PLAYER | GAMES | AVE |
|---|---|---|---|
| 1 | Krstev | 16 | 1.25 |
| 2 | Van Gessel | 23 | 1.22 |
| 3 | Kruiswijk | 16 | 1.19 |
| 4 | Tuhuteru | 17 | 1.06 |
| 5 | Floren | 32 | 1.00 |
| 6 | Drent | 14 | 1.00 |
| 7 | Broerse | 29 | 1.00 |
| 8 | Beukenkamp | 29 | 0.97 |
| 9 | Salmon | 19 | 0.89 |
| 10 | Elshot | 27 | 0.85 |
| | CLUB AVERAGE: | | 0.94 |

Ave = Average points per match in Counting Games

## ATTENDANCES

HOME GROUND: OOSTERPARK CAPACITY: 13000 AVERAGE LEAGUE AT HOME: 12187

| | | | | | | | | |
|---|---|---|---|---|---|---|---|---|
| 20 | Ajax | 47215 | 8 | RKC Waalwijk | 12500 | 19 | Twente | 11700 |
| 21 | Feyenoord | 44000 | 34 | PSV Eindhoven | 12500 | 16 | Roda JC Kerk | 11600 |
| 2 | PSV Eindhoven | 34000 | 12 | De Graafschap | 12500 | 1 | Vitesse Arnhem | 11558 |
| 26 | Vitesse Arnhem | 23200 | 24 | Willem II Tilb | 12444 | 33 | De Graafschap | 11000 |
| 25 | Utrecht | 16400 | 27 | Excelsior | 12400 | 7 | NEC Nijmegen | 10500 |
| 30 | Heerenveen | 14400 | 31 | Roda JC Kerk | 12400 | 6 | AZ Alkmaar | 6758 |
| 10 | NAC Breda | 13874 | 3 | Ajax | 12400 | 18 | RKC Waalwijk | 5950 |
| 15 | Twente | 13100 | 5 | Utrecht | 12000 | 13 | Zwolle | 5600 |
| 28 | NAC Breda | 13000 | 23 | Roosendaal | 11934 | 11 | Roosendaal | 5000 |
| 17 | Willem II Tilb | 12850 | 22 | Zwolle | 11829 | 4 | Excelsior | 3142 |
| 9 | Feyenoord | 12800 | 32 | AZ Alkmaar | 11820 | | | |
| 14 | Heerenveen | 12500 | 29 | NEC Nijmegen | 11704 | | | |

■ Home □ Away ▒ Neutral

## DISCIPLINARY RECORDS

| | PLAYER | YELLOW | RED | AVE |
|---|---|---|---|---|
| 1 | Boekweg | 6 | 0 | 307 |
| 2 | Hoogstrate | 3 | 0 | 351 |
| 3 | Krstev | 5 | 0 | 372 |
| 4 | Elshot | 5 | 0 | 486 |
| 5 | Schoenmakers | 1 | 0 | 555 |
| 6 | Landerl | 2 | 0 | 638 |
| 7 | Broerse | 4 | 0 | 671 |
| 8 | Matthijs | 3 | 0 | 751 |
| 9 | Kruiswijk | 2 | 0 | 827 |
| 10 | Floren | 3 | 0 | 949 |
| 11 | Van Gessel | 2 | 0 | 1086 |
| 12 | Salmon | 1 | 0 | 2050 |
| 13 | Beukenkamp | 1 | 0 | 2646 |
| | Other | 1 | 0 | |
| | TOTAL | 39 | 0 | |

## LEAGUE GOALS

| | PLAYER | MINS | GOALS | AVE |
|---|---|---|---|---|
| 1 | Drent | 1620 | 7 | 231 |
| 2 | Salmon | 2050 | 5 | 410 |
| 3 | Matthijs | 2254 | 3 | 751 |
| 4 | Van Gessel | 2173 | 3 | 724 |
| 5 | Krstev | 1863 | 2 | 932 |
| 6 | Hugo | 1103 | 2 | 552 |
| 7 | Ikedia | 2065 | 1 | 2065 |
| 8 | Landerl | 1277 | 1 | 1277 |
| 9 | Bronkhorst | 307 | 1 | 307 |
| 10 | Broerse | 2687 | 1 | 2687 |
| 11 | Schoenmakers | 555 | 1 | 555 |
| 12 | Tuhuteru | 1941 | 1 | 1941 |
| | Other | | 0 | |
| | TOTAL | | 28 | |

## MONTH BY MONTH GUIDE TO THE POINTS

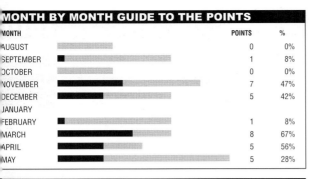

| MONTH | POINTS | % |
|---|---|---|
| AUGUST | 0 | 0% |
| SEPTEMBER | 1 | 8% |
| OCTOBER | 0 | 0% |
| NOVEMBER | 7 | 47% |
| DECEMBER | 5 | 42% |
| JANUARY | | |
| FEBRUARY | 1 | 8% |
| MARCH | 8 | 67% |
| APRIL | 5 | 56% |
| MAY | 5 | 28% |

## TEAM OF THE SEASON

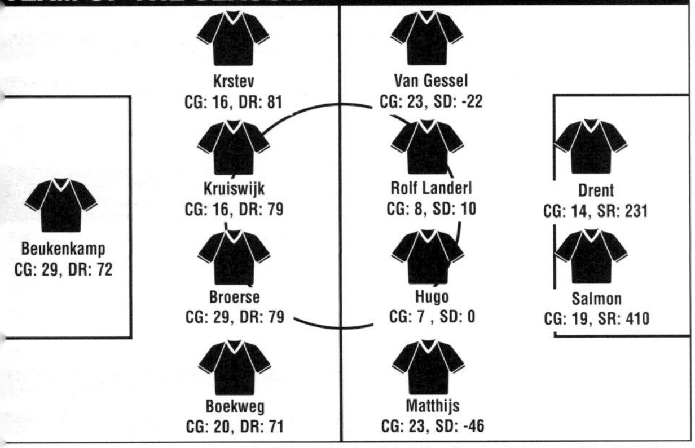
Krstev
CG: 16, DR: 81
Van Gessel
CG: 23, SD: -22
Kruiswijk
CG: 16, DR: 79
Rolf Landerl
CG: 8, SD: 10
Drent
CG: 14, SR: 231
Beukenkamp
CG: 29, DR: 72
Broerse
CG: 29, DR: 79
Hugo
CG: 7 , SD: 0
Salmon
CG: 19, SR: 410
Boekweg
CG: 20, DR: 71
Matthijs
CG: 23, SD: -46

**KEY:** DR = Defensive Rate, SD = Scoring Difference, SR = Strike Rate, CG = Counting Games – League games playing at least 70 minutes

## LEAGUE APPEARANCES, BOOKINGS AND CAPS

| | AGE | IN THE SQUAD | COUNTING GAMES | MINUTES ON PITCH | YELLOW CARDS | RED CARDS | THIS SEASON | HOME COUNTRY |
|---|---|---|---|---|---|---|---|---|
| **Goalkeepers** | | | | | | | | |
| Roy Beukenkamp | 35 | 30 | 29 | 2646 | 1 | 0 | - | Holland |
| Egbert Darwinkel | 37 | 21 | 0 | 54 | 0 | 0 | - | Holland |
| Jelle Ten Rouwelaar | 22 | 16 | 4 | 360 | 0 | 0 | - | Holland |
| **Defenders** | | | | | | | | |
| Claus Boekweg | 37 | 26 | 20 | 1845 | 6 | 0 | - | Holland |
| Joost Broerse | 24 | 34 | 29 | 2687 | 4 | 0 | - | Holland |
| Kurt Elshot | 26 | 27 | 27 | 2430 | 5 | 0 | - | Surinam |
| Mathias Floren | 26 | 33 | 32 | 2847 | 3 | 0 | - | Sweden |
| Magnus Johansson | 31 | 19 | 1 | 249 | 0 | 0 | - | Sweden |
| Mile Krstev | 24 | 32 | 16 | 1863 | 5 | 0 | - | Macedonia |
| Arnold Kruiswijk | 18 | 27 | 16 | 1655 | 2 | 0 | - | Holland |
| Melchior Schoenmakers | 27 | 25 | 5 | 555 | 1 | 0 | - | Holland |
| **Midfielders** | | | | | | | | |
| Mohammed Allach | 29 | 7 | 5 | 462 | 0 | 0 | - | Holland |
| Raymond Bronkhorst | 24 | 27 | 1 | 307 | 1 | 0 | - | Holland |
| Harold de Vries | | 2 | 0 | 0 | 0 | 0 | - | |
| Johannes Hardarson | 26 | 13 | 0 | 0 | 0 | 0 | - | Iceland |
| Jordi Hoogstrate | 20 | 17 | 8 | 1054 | 3 | 0 | - | Holland |
| Alves Velame Hugo | 28 | 30 | 7 | 1103 | 0 | 0 | - | Brazil |
| Anton Jongsma | 20 | 8 | 0 | 11 | 0 | 0 | - | Holland |
| Pedro Kamata | 22 | 1 | 1 | 90 | 0 | 0 | - | France |
| Rolf Landerl | 27 | 26 | 8 | 1277 | 2 | 0 | - | Austria |
| Paul Matthijs | 26 | 30 | 23 | 2254 | 3 | 0 | - | Holland |
| Peter Van de Slot | | 2 | 0 | 0 | 0 | 0 | - | Holland |
| Sander Van Gessel | 26 | 26 | 23 | 2173 | 2 | 0 | - | Holland |
| Christiaan Westerveld | | 1 | 0 | 0 | 0 | 0 | - | Holland |
| Angelo Zimmerman | | 2 | 0 | 0 | 0 | 0 | - | Holland |
| **Forwards** | | | | | | | | |
| Dejan Curovic | 34 | 9 | 0 | 62 | 0 | 0 | - | Serbia & Montenegro |
| Martin Drent | 33 | 29 | 14 | 1620 | 0 | 0 | - | Holland |
| Pius Ikedia | 22 | 27 | 20 | 2065 | 0 | 0 | - | Nigeria |
| Glen Salmon | 25 | 30 | 19 | 2050 | 1 | 0 | - | South Africa |
| Ignacio Tuhuteru | 29 | 30 | 17 | 1941 | 0 | 0 | - | Holland |

**KEY:** LEAGUE BOOKINGS CAPS (FIFA RANKING)

## SQUAD APPEARANCES

| Match | 1 | 2 | 3 | 4 | 5 | 6 | 7 | 8 | 9 | 10 | 11 | 12 | 13 | 14 | 15 | 16 | 17 | 18 | 19 | 20 | 21 | 22 | 23 | 24 | 25 | 26 | 27 | 28 | 29 | 30 | 31 | 32 | 33 | 34 |
|---|---|---|---|---|---|---|---|---|---|---|---|---|---|---|---|---|---|---|---|---|---|---|---|---|---|---|---|---|---|---|---|---|---|---|
| Venue | H | A | H | A | H | A | A | H | H | A | A | H | A | H | A | H | A | A | H | A | A | H | H | H | A | A | H | H | H | A | A | H | A | H |
| Competition | L | L | L | L | L | L | L | L | L | L | L | L | L | L | L | L | L | L | L | L | L | L | L | L | L | L | L | L | L | L | L | L | L | L |
| Result | L | L | L | L | D | L | L | L | L | D | L | W | W | D | D | W | L | L | D | L | L | W | W | D | D | D | W | D | D | L | L | W | L | D |

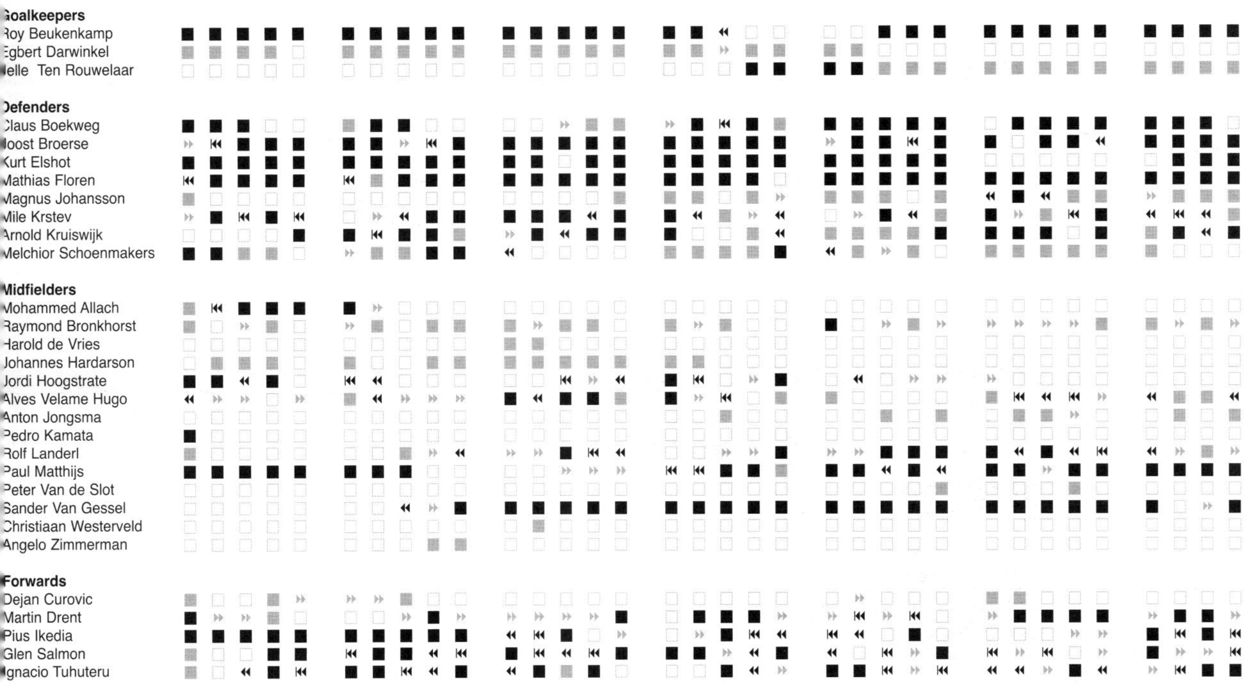
Goalkeepers
Roy Beukenkamp
Egbert Darwinkel
Jelle Ten Rouwelaar
Defenders
Claus Boekweg
Joost Broerse
Kurt Elshot
Mathias Floren
Magnus Johansson
Mile Krstev
Arnold Kruiswijk
Melchior Schoenmakers
Midfielders
Mohammed Allach
Raymond Bronkhorst
Harold de Vries
Johannes Hardarson
Jordi Hoogstrate
Alves Velame Hugo
Anton Jongsma
Pedro Kamata
Rolf Landerl
Paul Matthijs
Peter Van de Slot
Sander Van Gessel
Christiaan Westerveld
Angelo Zimmerman
Forwards
Dejan Curovic
Martin Drent
Pius Ikedia
Glen Salmon
Ignacio Tuhuteru

# FC ZWOLLE

Final Position: **16th**

| | | | | | | |
|---|---|---|---|---|---|---|
| 1 | lge | Roosendaal | A | D | 1-1 | Lim-Duan 73 |
| 2 | lge | Excelsior | H | D | 1-1 | Roelofsen, M 9 |
| 3 | lge | Vitesse Arnhem | H | W | 1-0 | Roelofsen, R 57 |
| 4 | lge | Ajax | A | L | 0-2 | |
| 5 | lge | PSV Eindhoven | H | L | 1-3 | Promes 52 |
| 6 | lge | Willem II Tilb | A | L | 2-5 | Cvetkov 52; Lim-Duan 89 |
| 7 | lge | RKC Waalwijk | A | W | 2-0 | Bosschaart 11; van der Haar 29 |
| 8 | lge | NAC Breda | H | L | 0-3 | |
| 9 | lge | AZ Alkmaar | H | W | 5-1 | Schops 1; Promes 10,29,45; Bosschaart 44 |
| 10 | lge | Feyenoord | A | L | 0-2 | |
| 11 | lge | Utrecht | A | L | 0-2 | |
| 12 | lge | Twente | H | D | 1-1 | Roelofsen, R 83 |
| 13 | lge | Groningen | H | L | 0-2 | |
| 14 | lge | Roda JC Kerk | A | L | 0-2 | |
| 15 | lge | NEC Nijmegen | H | D | 0-0 | |
| 16 | lge | Heerenveen | A | L | 0-2 | |
| 17 | lge | De Graafschap | A | L | 2-3 | Bosschaart 17; van der Haar 53 |
| 18 | lge | Willem II Tilb | H | L | 0-3 | |
| 19 | lge | PSV Eindhoven | A | L | 0-6 | |
| 20 | lge | Vitesse Arnhem | A | L | 1-2 | Van Beukering 59 |
| 21 | lge | RKC Waalwijk | H | W | 2-1 | Promes 30; Van Beukering 62 |
| 22 | lge | Groningen | A | L | 0-4 | |
| 23 | lge | Ajax | H | L | 0-5 | |
| 24 | lge | Roosendaal | H | D | 1-1 | de Ridder 27 |
| 25 | lge | Excelsior | A | W | 1-0 | Lim-Duan 89 |
| 26 | lge | Utrecht | H | W | 3-1 | Roelofsen, R 56,74,75 |
| 27 | lge | AZ Alkmaar | A | D | 1-1 | Promes 81 |
| 28 | lge | Feyenoord | H | L | 1-3 | Bosschaart 49 |
| 29 | lge | Roda JC Kerk | H | W | 3-1 | Roelofsen, R 10; Promes 15; Karlsen 90 |
| 30 | lge | NAC Breda | A | L | 0-2 | |
| 31 | lge | Twente | A | D | 0-0 | |
| 32 | lge | Heerenveen | H | L | 0-1 | |
| 33 | lge | NEC Nijmegen | A | D | 0-0 | |
| 34 | lge | De Graafschap | H | W | 2-1 | Roelofsen, R 3; Bosschaart 20 |

## KEY PLAYERS - GOALSCORERS

**1 Arjan Bosschaart**

| | | | |
|---|---|---|---|
| Goals in the League | 5 | Player Strike Rate<br>Average number of minutes between League goals scored by player | 284 |
| Contribution to Attacking Power<br>Average number of minutes between League team goals while on pitch | 88 | Club Strike Rate<br>Average number of minutes between League goals scored by club | 99 |

| | PLAYER | LGE GOALS | POWER | STRIKE RATE |
|---|---|---|---|---|
| 2 | Marino Promes | 7 | 100 | 360 mins |
| 3 | Richard Roelofsen | 7 | 93 | 372 mins |
| 4 | Dominggus Lim-Duan | 3 | 86 | 893 mins |
| 5 | Albert van der Haar | 2 | 98 | 1372 mins |

## KEY PLAYERS - MIDFIELDERS

**1 Remco Schol**

| | | | |
|---|---|---|---|
| Goals in the League | 0 | Contribution to Attacking Power<br>Average number of minutes between League team goals while on pitch | 81 |
| Defensive Rating<br>Average number of mins between League goals conceded while he was on the pitch | 48 | Scoring Difference<br>Defensive Rating minus Contribution to Attacking Power | -33 |

| | PLAYER | LGE GOALS | DEF RATE | POWER | SCORE DIFF |
|---|---|---|---|---|---|
| 2 | Marco Roelofsen | 1 | 46 | 95 | -49 mins |
| 3 | Maarten Schops | 1 | 57 | 109 | -52 mins |
| 4 | Andre de Ridder | 1 | 47 | 109 | -62 mins |
| 5 | Morten Karlsen | 1 | 49 | 114 | -65 mins |

## KEY PLAYERS - DEFENDERS

**1 Michael Doesburg**

| | | | |
|---|---|---|---|
| Goals Conceded (GC)<br>The number of League goals conceded while he was on the pitch | 39 | Clean Sheets<br>In games when he played at least 70 minutes | 5 |
| Defensive Rating<br>Ave number of mins between League goals conceded while on the pitch | 54 | Club Defensive Rating<br>Average number of mins between League goals conceded by the club this season | 49 |

| | PLAYER | CON LGE | CLEAN SHEETS | DEF RATE |
|---|---|---|---|---|
| 2 | Ruud Kras | 49 | 6 | 54 mins |
| 3 | Albert van der Haar | 58 | 5 | 47 mins |

## GOALS SCORED

**AT HOME**

| | | |
|---|---|---|
| MOST | Ajax | 57 |
| | | 21 |
| LEAST | Twente | 18 |

**AWAY**

| | | |
|---|---|---|
| MOST | PSV | 44 |
| | | 10 |
| LEAST | Roosendaal & Groningen | 9 |

## GOALS CONCEDED

**AT HOME**

| | | |
|---|---|---|
| LEAST | PSV | 7 |
| | | 28 |
| MOST | Excelsior | 38 |

**AWAY**

| | | |
|---|---|---|
| LEAST | PSV | 13 |
| | | 29 |
| MOST | De G'schap | 50 |

## KEY GOALKEEPER

**1 van der Werff**

| | |
|---|---|
| Goals Conceded in the League | 57 |
| Defensive Rating<br>Ave number of mins between League goals conceded while on the pitch | 52 |
| Counting Games<br>Games when he played at least 70 mins | 33 |
| Clean Sheets<br>In games when he played at least 70 mins | 6 |

## TOP POINT EARNERS

| | PLAYER | GAMES | AVE |
|---|---|---|---|
| 1 | Doesburg | 22 | 1.23 |
| 2 | Roelofsen, M | 21 | 1.14 |
| 3 | Promes | 26 | 1.08 |
| 4 | Kras | 29 | 1.07 |
| 5 | Roelofsen, R | 28 | 1.00 |
| 6 | Bosschaart | 12 | 1.00 |
| 7 | van der Werff | 33 | 0.97 |
| 8 | Lim-Duan | 27 | 0.96 |
| 9 | de Ridder | 23 | 0.91 |
| 10 | Karlsen | 20 | 0.90 |
| | CLUB AVERAGE: | | 0.94 |

Ave = Average points per match in Counting Games

## ATTENDANCES

HOME GROUND: OOSTERENK STADION CAPACITY: 6865 AVERAGE LEAGUE AT HOME: 6171

| | | | | | | | | |
|---|---|---|---|---|---|---|---|---|
| 4 | Ajax | 49003 | 30 | NAC Breda | 9912 | 21 | RKC Waalwijk | 6148 |
| 10 | Feyenoord | 44000 | 7 | RKC Waalwijk | 7500 | 15 | NEC Nijmegen | 6100 |
| 19 | PSV Eindhoven | 33000 | 27 | AZ Alkmaar | 7041 | 24 | Roosendaal | 6000 |
| 20 | Vitesse Arnhem | 21000 | 28 | Feyenoord | 6865 | 32 | Heerenveen | 6000 |
| 11 | Utrecht | 14700 | 23 | Ajax | 6865 | 18 | Willem II Tilb | 5745 |
| 16 | Heerenveen | 14300 | 5 | PSV Eindhoven | 6800 | 13 | Groningen | 5600 |
| 14 | Roda JC Kerk | 14000 | 34 | De Graafschap | 6800 | 3 | Vitesse Arnhem | 5200 |
| 31 | Twente | 13300 | 9 | AZ Alkmaar | 6500 | 1 | Roosendaal | 5000 |
| 6 | Willem II Tilb | 12300 | 29 | Roda JC Kerk | 6450 | 26 | Utrecht | 5000 |
| 33 | NEC Nijmegen | 12000 | 12 | Twente | 6350 | 25 | Excelsior | 2500 |
| 22 | Groningen | 11829 | 8 | NAC Breda | 6250 | | | |
| 17 | De Graafschap | 10900 | 2 | Excelsior | 6250 | | | |

■ Home □ Away ▨ Neutral

## DISCIPLINARY RECORDS

| | PLAYER | YELLOW | RED | AVE |
|---|---|---|---|---|
| 1 | van Steeg | 4 | 0 | 262 |
| 2 | Kras | 5 | 1 | 441 |
| 3 | Karlsen | 3 | 0 | 686 |
| 4 | Doesburg | 3 | 0 | 702 |
| 5 | Bosschaart | 2 | 0 | 709 |
| 6 | Roelofsen, M | 3 | 0 | 759 |
| 7 | Promes | 3 | 0 | 839 |
| 8 | de Ridder | 2 | 0 | 1146 |
| 9 | Roelofsen, R | 2 | 0 | 1303 |
| 10 | Lim-Duan | 2 | 0 | 1340 |
| 11 | van der Haar | 2 | 0 | 1372 |
| 12 | Schol | 1 | 0 | 1772 |
| | Other | 4 | 1 | |
| | TOTAL | 36 | 2 | |

## LEAGUE GOALS

| | PLAYER | MINS | GOALS | AVE |
|---|---|---|---|---|
| 1 | Roelofsen, R | 2607 | 7 | 372 |
| 2 | Promes | 2519 | 7 | 360 |
| 3 | Bosschaart | 1419 | 5 | 284 |
| 4 | Lim-Duan | 2680 | 3 | 893 |
| 5 | Van Beukering | 542 | 2 | 271 |
| 6 | van der Haar | 2744 | 2 | 1372 |
| 7 | Roelofsen, M | 2277 | 1 | 2277 |
| 8 | Schops | 1203 | 1 | 1203 |
| 9 | de Ridder | 2293 | 1 | 2293 |
| 10 | Karlsen | 2058 | 1 | 2058 |
| 11 | Cvetkov | 1314 | 1 | 1314 |
| | Other | | 0 | |
| | TOTAL | | 31 | |

## MONTH BY MONTH GUIDE TO THE POINTS

| MONTH | POINTS | % |
|---|---|---|
| AUGUST | 5 | 56% |
| SEPTEMBER | 0 | 0% |
| OCTOBER | 3 | 50% |
| NOVEMBER | 4 | 22% |
| DECEMBER | 1 | 11% |
| JANUARY | | |
| FEBRUARY | 3 | 25% |
| MARCH | 4 | 33% |
| APRIL | 4 | 44% |
| MAY | 8 | 44% |

## TEAM OF THE SEASON

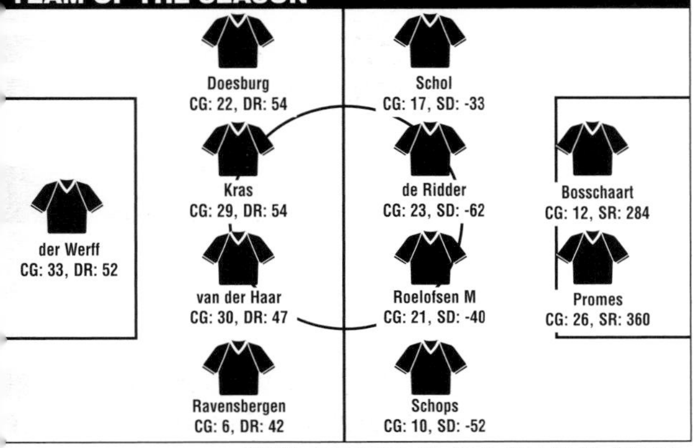
Doesburg
CG: 22, DR: 54
Schol
CG: 17, SD: -33
Kras
CG: 29, DR: 54
de Ridder
CG: 23, SD: -62
Bosschaart
CG: 12, SR: 284
der Werff
CG: 33, DR: 52
van der Haar
CG: 30, DR: 47
Roelofsen M
CG: 21, SD: -40
Promes
CG: 26, SR: 360
Ravensbergen
CG: 6, DR: 42
Schops
CG: 10, SD: -52

KEY: DR = Defensive Rate, SD = Scoring Difference, SR = Strike Rate, CG = Counting Games – League games playing at least 70 minutes

## LEAGUE APPEARANCES, BOOKINGS AND CAPS

| | AGE | IN THE SQUAD | COUNTING GAMES | MINUTES ON PITCH | YELLOW CARDS | RED CARDS | THIS SEASON | HOME COUNTRY |
|---|---|---|---|---|---|---|---|---|
| **Goalkeepers** | | | | | | | | |
| Diederik Boer | 22 | 17 | 1 | 90 | 0 | 0 | - | Holland |
| Henry Louwdijk | 25 | 16 | 0 | 21 | 0 | 0 | - | Holland |
| van der Werff | 28 | 33 | 33 | 2949 | 0 | 0 | - | Holland |
| **Defenders** | | | | | | | | |
| Michael Doesburg | 34 | 26 | 22 | 2107 | 3 | 0 | - | Holland |
| Ruud Kras | 21 | 30 | 29 | 2648 | 5 | 1 | - | Holland |
| R-Jan Ravensbergen | 24 | 24 | 6 | 762 | 0 | 0 | - | Holland |
| Albert van der Haar | 27 | 32 | 30 | 2744 | 2 | 0 | - | Holland |
| Robert Wijnands | 31 | 16 | 0 | 83 | 0 | 0 | - | Holland |
| **Midfielders** | | | | | | | | |
| Marcel Boudesteijn | 31 | 10 | 1 | 120 | 1 | 0 | - | Holland |
| Andre de Ridder | 29 | 31 | 23 | 2293 | 2 | 0 | - | Holland |
| Thijs Heuvink | | 2 | 0 | 0 | 0 | 0 | - | Holland |
| Morten Karlsen | 24 | 29 | 20 | 2058 | 3 | 0 | - | Denmark |
| Tjeerd Korf | 20 | 7 | 0 | 21 | 0 | 0 | - | Holland |
| Marco Roelofsen | 34 | 33 | 21 | 2277 | 3 | 0 | - | Holland |
| Richard Roelofsen | 33 | 31 | 28 | 2607 | 2 | 0 | - | Holland |
| Remco Schol | 30 | 30 | 17 | 1772 | 1 | 0 | - | Holland |
| Maarten Schops | 27 | 25 | 10 | 1203 | 0 | 0 | - | Holland |
| Remco Snippe | | 1 | 0 | 0 | 0 | 0 | - | |
| Henk van Steeg | 28 | 33 | 8 | 1051 | 4 | 0 | - | Holland |
| **Forwards** | | | | | | | | |
| Peter  Blom | 20 | 12 | 0 | 33 | 0 | 0 | - | Holland |
| Arjan Bosschaart | 31 | 27 | 12 | 1419 | 2 | 0 | - | Holland |
| Ivan Cvetkov | 23 | 31 | 10 | 1314 | 0 | 0 | - | Bulgaria |
| Dom  Lim-Duan | 20 | 34 | 27 | 2680 | 2 | 0 | - | Holland |
| Marino Promes | 26 | 32 | 26 | 2519 | 3 | 0 | - | Holland |
| Jhonny V Beukering | 19 | 7 | 6 | 542 | 0 | 0 | - | Holland |
| Bert Zuurman | 30 | 31 | 1 | 295 | 3 | 1 | - | Holland |

KEY: LEAGUE   BOOKINGS   CAPS (FIFA RANKING)

## SQUAD APPEARANCES

| Match | 1 | 2 | 3 | 4 | 5 | 6 | 7 | 8 | 9 | 10 | 11 | 12 | 13 | 14 | 15 | 16 | 17 | 18 | 19 | 20 | 21 | 22 | 23 | 24 | 25 | 26 | 27 | 28 | 29 | 30 | 31 | 32 | 33 | 34 |
|---|---|---|---|---|---|---|---|---|---|---|---|---|---|---|---|---|---|---|---|---|---|---|---|---|---|---|---|---|---|---|---|---|---|---|
| Venue | A | H | H | A | H | A | A | H | H | A | A | H | H | A | H | A | A | H | A | A | H | A | H | H | A | H | A | H | H | A | A | H | A | H |
| Competition | L | L | L | L | L | L | L | L | L | L | L | L | L | L | L | L | L | L | L | L | L | L | L | L | L | L | L | L | L | L | L | L | L | L |
| Result | D | D | W | L | L | L | W | L | W | L | L | D | L | L | D | L | L | L | L | L | W | L | L | D | W | W | D | L | W | L | D | L | D | W |

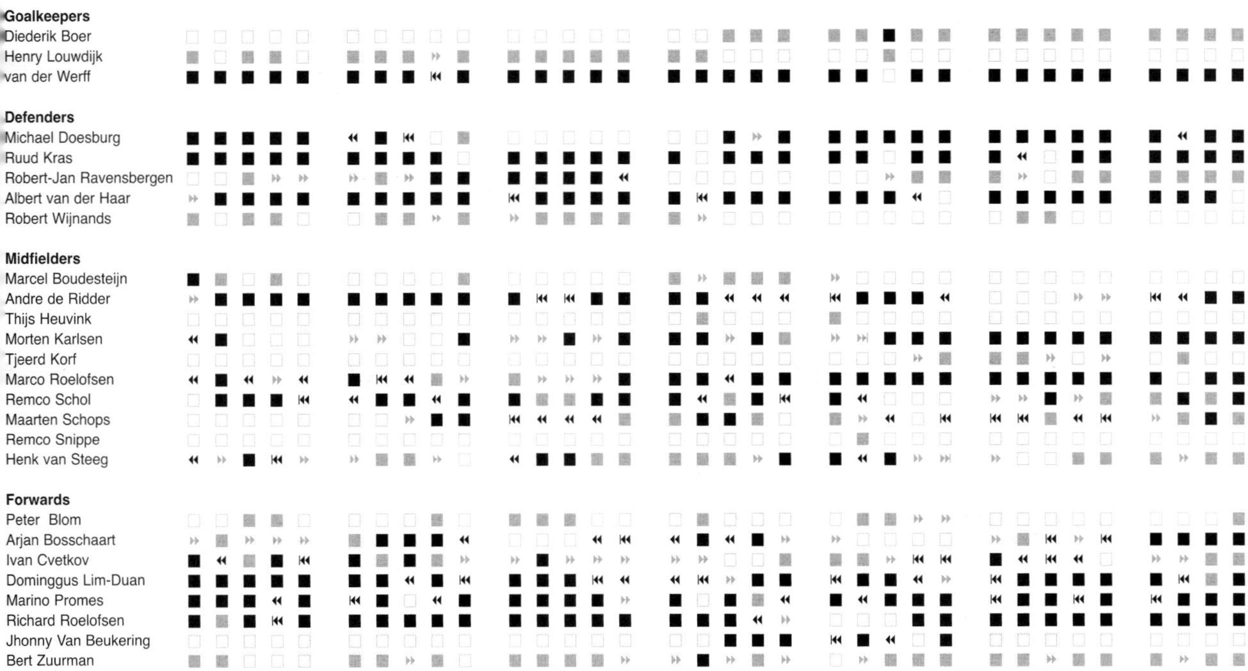
Goalkeepers
Diederik Boer
Henry Louwdijk
van der Werff
Defenders
Michael Doesburg
Ruud Kras
Robert-Jan Ravensbergen
Albert van der Haar
Robert Wijnands
Midfielders
Marcel Boudesteijn
Andre de Ridder
Thijs Heuvink
Morten Karlsen
Tjeerd Korf
Marco Roelofsen
Remco Schol
Maarten Schops
Remco Snippe
Henk van Steeg
Forwards
Peter  Blom
Arjan Bosschaart
Ivan Cvetkov
Dominggus Lim-Duan
Marino Promes
Richard Roelofsen
Jhonny Van Beukering
Bert Zuurman

# EXCELSIOR

Final Position: **17th**

| | | | | | | |
|---|---|---|---|---|---|---|
| 1 | lge | PSV Eindhoven | H | L | 0-2 | |
| 2 | lge | Zwolle | A | D | 1-1 | Boutahar 88 |
| 3 | lge | Feyenoord | A | L | 1-4 | Pinas 24 |
| 4 | lge | Groningen | H | W | 4-2 | Pinas 37; Olfers 40; Lopes 68; Boutahar 75 |
| 5 | lge | AZ Alkmaar | H | L | 1-2 | Mtiliga 85 |
| 6 | lge | RKC Waalwijk | A | W | 3-0 | Mtiliga 45; Koswal 77; Holman 90 |
| 7 | lge | Roda JC Kerk | A | W | 3-2 | Lopes 19,68; Koswal 83 |
| 8 | lge | Utrecht | H | D | 1-1 | Lopes 3 |
| 9 | lge | Heerenveen | A | L | 0-2 | |
| 10 | lge | NEC Nijmegen | H | D | 0-0 | |
| 11 | lge | De Graafschap | A | D | 1-1 | El Hamdaoui 89 |
| 12 | lge | NAC Breda | H | L | 0-3 | |
| 13 | lge | Willem II Tilb | H | L | 0-3 | |
| 14 | lge | Roosendaal | A | D | 1-1 | Boutahar 66 |
| 15 | lge | Twente | H | D | 2-2 | Boutahar 26; Olfers 90 |
| 16 | lge | Vitesse Arnhem | A | W | 2-1 | Pinas 28; Boutahar 41 |
| 17 | lge | Ajax | H | L | 0-2 | |
| 18 | lge | Utrecht | A | D | 2-2 | Mtiliga 21; van Dieren 66 |
| 19 | lge | NAC Breda | A | L | 1-2 | Holman 72 |
| 20 | lge | Roda JC Kerk | H | L | 0-2 | |
| 21 | lge | Roosendaal | H | L | 1-2 | Holman 72 |
| 22 | lge | RKC Waalwijk | H | L | 1-2 | Holman 71 |
| 23 | lge | Feyenoord | H | L | 2-6 | Swerts 31; Holman 86 |
| 24 | lge | Ajax | A | L | 1-2 | Lopes 4 |
| 25 | lge | Zwolle | H | L | 0-1 | |
| 26 | lge | NEC Nijmegen | A | L | 0-1 | |
| 27 | lge | Groningen | A | L | 0-1 | |
| 28 | lge | Heerenveen | H | W | 1-0 | Boutahar 66 |
| 29 | lge | Twente | A | L | 0-1 | |
| 30 | lge | De Graafschap | H | L | 3-4 | Boutahar 44; Pinas 47; Holman 60 |
| 31 | lge | PSV Eindhoven | A | L | 0-7 | |
| 32 | lge | Willem II Tilb | A | L | 1-2 | Boutahar 43 |
| 33 | lge | Vitesse Arnhem | H | D | 4-4 | Boutahar 3; Pinas 37; Olfers 58; El Hamdaoui 86 |
| 34 | lge | AZ Alkmaar | A | L | 1-3 | Nygaard 59 |

## KEY PLAYERS - GOALSCORERS

**1 Said Boutahar**

| | | | |
|---|---|---|---|
| Goals in the League | 9 | **Player Strike Rate** Average number of minutes between League goals scored by player | 280 |
| **Contribution to Attacking Power** Average number of minutes between League team goals while on pitch | 76 | **Club Strike Rate** Average number of minutes between League goals scored by club | 81 |

| | PLAYER | LGE GOALS | POWER | STRIKE RATE |
|---|---|---|---|---|
| 2 | Cecilio Lopes | 5 | 87 | 455 mins |
| 3 | Brian Pinas | 5 | 77 | 494 mins |
| 4 | Leo Koswal | 2 | 74 | 821 mins |
| 5 | Patrick Mtiliga | 3 | 72 | 850 mins |

## KEY PLAYERS - MIDFIELDERS

**1 Civard Sprockel**

| | | | |
|---|---|---|---|
| Goals in the League | 0 | **Contribution to Attacking Power** Average number of minutes between League team goals while on pitch | 77 |
| **Defensive Rating** Average number of mins between League goals conceded while he was on the pitch | 53 | **Scoring Difference** Defensive Rating minus Contribution to Attacking Power | -24 |

| | PLAYER | LGE GOALS | DEF RATE | POWER | SCORE DIFF |
|---|---|---|---|---|---|
| 2 | Said Boutahar | 9 | 45 | 76 | -31 mins |
| 3 | Gill Swerts | 1 | 43 | 78 | -35 mins |
| 4 | Marc Nygaard | 1 | 43 | 92 | -49 mins |
| 5 | Ferry de Haan | 0 | 40 | 95 | -55 mins |

## KEY PLAYERS - DEFENDERS

**1 Michel Fernandes Bastos**

| | | | |
|---|---|---|---|
| **Goals Conceded (GC)** The number of League goals conceded while he was on the pitch | 45 | **Clean Sheets** In games when he played at least 70 minutes | 3 |
| **Defensive Rating** Ave number of mins between League goals conceded while on the pitch | 49 | **Club Defensive Rating** Average number of mins between League goals conceded by the club this season | 43 |

| | PLAYER | CON LGE | CLEAN SHEETS | DEF RATE |
|---|---|---|---|---|
| 2 | Michel Breuer | 44 | 3 | 44 mins |
| 3 | Steve Olfers | 70 | 3 | 43 mins |
| 4 | Danny Buijs | 46 | 2 | 41 mins |

## GOALS SCORED

**AT HOME**

| | | |
|---|---|---|
| MOST | Ajax | 57 |
| | | 20 |
| LEAST | Twente | 18 |

**AWAY**

| | | |
|---|---|---|
| MOST | PSV | 44 |
| | | 18 |
| LEAST | Roosendaal & Groningen | 9 |

## GOALS CONCEDED

**AT HOME**

| | | |
|---|---|---|
| LEAST | PSV | 7 |
| | | 38 |
| MOST | Excelsior | 38 |

**AWAY**

| | | |
|---|---|---|
| LEAST | PSV | 13 |
| | | 33 |
| MOST | De G'schap | 50 |

## KEY GOALKEEPER

**1 Zbigniew Malkowski**

| | |
|---|---|
| Goals Conceded in the League | 48 |
| **Defensive Rating** Ave number of mins between League goals conceded while on the pitch | 44 |
| **Counting Games** Games when he played at least 70 mins | 23 |
| **Clean Sheets** In games when he played at least 70 mins | 2 |

## TOP POINT EARNERS

| | PLAYER | GAMES | AVE |
|---|---|---|---|
| 1 | Koswal | 16 | 1.19 |
| 2 | Bastos | 22 | 0.86 |
| 3 | Boutahar | 26 | 0.85 |
| 4 | Malkowski | 23 | 0.83 |
| 5 | Breuer | 21 | 0.81 |
| 6 | Buijs | 14 | 0.79 |
| 7 | Lopes | 22 | 0.77 |
| 8 | Mtiliga | 28 | 0.71 |
| 9 | Olfers | 33 | 0.70 |
| 10 | Swerts | 33 | 0.70 |
| | **CLUB AVERAGE:** | | **0.68** |

Ave = Average points per match in Counting Games

## ATTENDANCES

HOME GROUND: ROTTERDAM VERZEKERINGEN CAPACITY: 3500 AVERAGE LEAGUE AT HOME: 3018

| | | | | | | | | |
|---|---|---|---|---|---|---|---|---|
| 24 | Ajax | 47192 | 26 | NEC Nijmegen | 10150 | 4 | Groningen | 3142 |
| 3 | Feyenoord | 43100 | 6 | RKC Waalwijk | 7200 | 33 | Vitesse Arnhem | 3124 |
| 31 | PSV Eindhoven | 33000 | 34 | AZ Alkmaar | 7144 | 5 | AZ Alkmaar | 3100 |
| 16 | Vitesse Arnhem | 21000 | 2 | Zwolle | 6250 | 8 | Utrecht | 3000 |
| 9 | Heerenveen | 14200 | 14 | Roosendaal | 4750 | 12 | NAC Breda | 2948 |
| 32 | Willem II Tilb | 13400 | 23 | Feyenoord | 3500 | 15 | Twente | 2764 |
| 18 | Utrecht | 13000 | 17 | Ajax | 3478 | 21 | Roosendaal | 2638 |
| 29 | Twente | 13000 | 30 | De Graafschap | 3468 | 25 | Zwolle | 2500 |
| 7 | Roda JC Kerk | 13000 | 13 | Willem II Tilb | 3358 | 22 | RKC Waalwijk | 2368 |
| 27 | Groningen | 12400 | 10 | NEC Nijmegen | 3356 | 20 | Roda JC Kerk | 2258 |
| 19 | NAC Breda | 12153 | 28 | Heerenveen | 3164 | | | |
| 11 | De Graafschap | 11000 | 1 | PSV Eindhoven | 3150 | | | |

■ Home □ Away ▒ Neutral

## DISCIPLINARY RECORDS

| | PLAYER | YELLOW | RED | AVE |
|---|---|---|---|---|
| 1 | Buijs | 3 | 1 | 466 |
| 2 | Sprockel | 2 | 0 | 499 |
| 3 | Mtiliga | 4 | 1 | 510 |
| 4 | van Dieren | 1 | 0 | 563 |
| 5 | Martis | 1 | 0 | 618 |
| 6 | Nygaard | 1 | 0 | 647 |
| 7 | Swerts | 4 | 0 | 739 |
| 8 | de Haan | 1 | 0 | 1330 |
| 9 | Olfers | 2 | 0 | 1507 |
| 10 | Koswal | 1 | 0 | 1642 |
| 11 | Breuer | 1 | 0 | 1919 |
| 12 | Bastos | 1 | 0 | 2187 |
| 13 | Pinas | 1 | 0 | 2472 |
| | Other | 0 | 0 | |
| | TOTAL | 23 | 2 | |

## LEAGUE GOALS

| | PLAYER | MINS | GOALS | AVE |
|---|---|---|---|---|
| 1 | Boutahar | 2519 | 9 | 280 |
| 2 | Holman | 1263 | 6 | 211 |
| 3 | Pinas | 2472 | 5 | 494 |
| 4 | Lopes | 2276 | 5 | 455 |
| 5 | Mtiliga | 2551 | 3 | 850 |
| 6 | Olfers | 3015 | 3 | 1005 |
| 7 | Koswal | 1642 | 2 | 821 |
| 8 | Swerts | 2957 | 1 | 2957 |
| 9 | El Hamdaoui | 697 | 1 | 697 |
| 10 | van Dieren | 563 | 1 | 563 |
| 11 | Nygaard | 647 | 1 | 647 |
| | Other | | 1 | |
| | TOTAL | | 38 | |

## MONTH BY MONTH GUIDE TO THE POINTS

| MONTH | POINTS | % |
|---|---|---|
| AUGUST | 1 | 17% |
| SEPTEMBER | 6 | 50% |
| OCTOBER | 4 | 44% |
| NOVEMBER | 2 | 17% |
| DECEMBER | 5 | 42% |
| JANUARY | | |
| FEBRUARY | 1 | 8% |
| MARCH | 0 | 0% |
| APRIL | 3 | 25% |
| MAY | 1 | 7% |

## TEAM OF THE SEASON

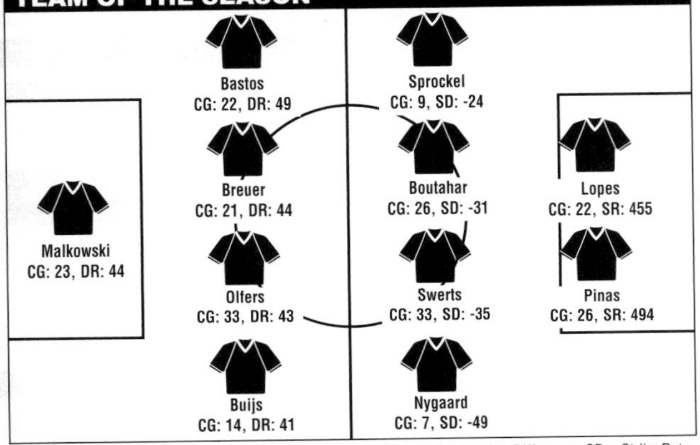
Malkowski
CG: 23, DR: 44
Bastos
CG: 22, DR: 49
Breuer
CG: 21, DR: 44
Olfers
CG: 33, DR: 43
Buijs
CG: 14, DR: 41
Sprockel
CG: 9, SD: -24
Boutahar
CG: 26, SD: -31
Swerts
CG: 33, SD: -35
Nygaard
CG: 7, SD: -49
Lopes
CG: 22, SR: 455
Pinas
CG: 26, SR: 494

KEY: DR = Defensive Rate, SD = Scoring Difference, SR = Strike Rate, CG = Counting Games – League games playing at least 70 minutes

## LEAGUE APPEARANCES, BOOKINGS AND CAPS

| | AGE | IN THE SQUAD | COUNTING GAMES | MINUTES ON PITCH | YELLOW CARDS | RED CARDS | THIS SEASON | HOME COUNTRY |
|---|---|---|---|---|---|---|---|---|
| **Goalkeepers** | | | | | | | | |
| Zbigniew Malkowski | 25 | 32 | 23 | 2115 | 0 | 0 | - | Poland |
| Jorg V Nieuwenhuijzen | 24 | 7 | 0 | 0 | 0 | 0 | - | Holland |
| Cor Varkevisser | 21 | 28 | 10 | 945 | 0 | 0 | - | Holland |
| **Defenders** | | | | | | | | |
| Michel Bastos | 19 | 32 | 22 | 2187 | 1 | 0 | - | Brazil |
| Michel Breuer | 23 | 23 | 21 | 1919 | 1 | 0 | - | Holland |
| Danny Buijs | 21 | 29 | 14 | 1867 | 3 | 1 | - | Holland |
| Pascal de Nijs | 23 | 16 | 0 | 0 | 0 | 0 | - | Holland |
| Jan Frederiksen | 21 | 9 | 0 | 2 | 0 | 0 | - | Denmark |
| Dennis Jos | 22 | 3 | 0 | 0 | 0 | 0 | - | Holland |
| Shelton Martis | 20 | 26 | 5 | 618 | 1 | 0 | - | Holland |
| Steve Olfers | 21 | 34 | 33 | 3015 | 2 | 0 | - | Holland |
| Rene van Dieren | 22 | 22 | 4 | 563 | 1 | 0 | - | Holland |
| **Midfielders** | | | | | | | | |
| Said Boutahar | 20 | 30 | 26 | 2519 | 0 | 0 | - | Holland |
| Ferry de Haan | 30 | 17 | 14 | 1330 | 1 | 0 | - | Holland |
| Nam-Il Kim | 26 | 12 | 5 | 568 | 0 | 0 | 5 | South Korea (21) |
| Ronnie Nouwen | 20 | 26 | 0 | 97 | 0 | 0 | - | Holland |
| Marc Nygaard | 26 | 8 | 7 | 647 | 1 | 0 | - | Denmark |
| Civard Sprockel | 20 | 19 | 9 | 998 | 2 | 0 | - | Holland |
| Gill Swerts | 20 | 33 | 33 | 2957 | 4 | 0 | - | Belgium |
| Dick Tijdeman | 19 | 2 | 0 | 0 | 0 | 0 | - | Holland |
| **Forwards** | | | | | | | | |
| Dries Boussatta | 30 | 15 | 1 | 355 | 0 | 0 | - | Holland |
| Mounir El Hamdaoui | 18 | 25 | 2 | 697 | 0 | 0 | - | Holland |
| Bart Fiegel | 22 | 2 | 0 | 0 | 0 | 0 | - | Holland |
| Brett Holman | 19 | 34 | 9 | 1263 | 0 | 0 | - | Australia |
| Leo Koswal | 27 | 26 | 16 | 1642 | 1 | 0 | - | Holland |
| Cecilio Lopes | 24 | 34 | 22 | 2276 | 0 | 0 | - | Holland |
| Patrick Mtiliga | 22 | 29 | 28 | 2551 | 4 | 1 | - | Denmark |
| Brian Pinas | 24 | 31 | 26 | 2472 | 1 | 0 | - | Holland |

KEY: LEAGUE BOOKINGS CAPS (FIFA RANKING)

## SQUAD APPEARANCES

| Match | 1 | 2 | 3 | 4 | 5 | 6 | 7 | 8 | 9 | 10 | 11 | 12 | 13 | 14 | 15 | 16 | 17 | 18 | 19 | 20 | 21 | 22 | 23 | 24 | 25 | 26 | 27 | 28 | 29 | 30 | 31 | 32 | 33 | 34 |
|---|---|---|---|---|---|---|---|---|---|---|---|---|---|---|---|---|---|---|---|---|---|---|---|---|---|---|---|---|---|---|---|---|---|---|
| Venue | H | A | A | H | H | A | A | H | A | H | A | H | H | A | H | A | H | A | A | H | H | H | H | A | H | A | A | H | A | H | A | A | H | A |
| Competition | L | L | L | L | L | L | L | L | L | L | L | L | L | L | L | L | L | L | L | L | L | L | L | L | L | L | L | L | L | L | L | L | L | L |
| Result | L | D | L | W | L | W | W | D | L | D | D | L | L | D | D | W | L | D | L | L | L | L | L | L | L | L | L | W | L | L | L | L | D | L |

**Goalkeepers**
Zbigniew Malkowski
Jorg van Nieuwenhuijzen
Cor Varkevisser

**Defenders**
Michel Fernandes Bastos
Michel Breuer
Danny Buijs
Pascal de Nijs
Jan Frederiksen
Dennis Jos
Shelton Martis
Steve Olfers
Rene van Dieren

**Midfielders**
Said Boutahar
Ferry de Haan
Nam-Il Kim
Marc Nygaard
Civard Sprockel
Gill Swerts
Dick Tijdeman

**Forwards**
Dries Boussatta
Mounir El Hamdaoui
Bart Fiegel
Brett Holman
Leo Koswal
Cecilio Lopes
Patrick Mtiliga
Ronnie Nouwen
Brian Pinas

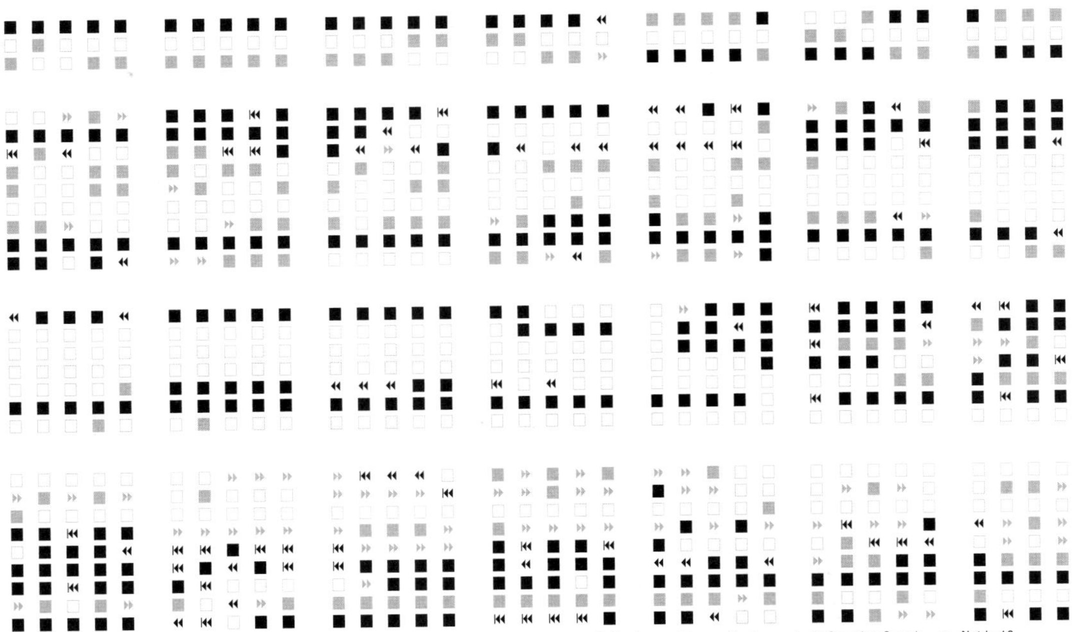

KEY: On all match / On bench / Subbed or sent off (Counting game) / Subbed or sent off (playing less than 70 minutes) / Subbed on from bench (Counting Game) / Subbed on (playing less than 70 minutes) / Subbed on and then subbed or sent off (Counting Game) / Subbed on and then subbed or sent off (playing less than 70 minutes) / Not in 16

# DE GRAAFSCHAP

Final Position: **18th**

| | | | | | | |
|---|---|---|---|---|---|---|
| 1 | lge | RKC Waalwijk | A | L | 2-4 | Van Leerdam 47; van der Haar 74 |
| 2 | lge | Roosendaal | H | W | 2-0 | Van Vossen 22; Valeev 72 |
| 3 | lge | Utrecht | A | L | 0-4 | |
| 4 | lge | AZ Alkmaar | H | L | 1-2 | Culina 28 |
| 5 | lge | Feyenoord | A | L | 0-2 | |
| 6 | lge | PSV Eindhoven | A | L | 0-4 | |
| 7 | lge | Twente | H | L | 0-1 | |
| 8 | lge | NEC Nijmegen | H | L | 1-3 | Smit 88 |
| 9 | lge | Roda JC Kerk | A | L | 0-5 | |
| 10 | lge | Heerenveen | A | L | 1-3 | van der Haar 43 |
| 11 | lge | Excelsior | H | D | 1-1 | Bakens 47 |
| 12 | lge | Groningen | A | L | 1-3 | Turpijn 85 |
| 13 | lge | NAC Breda | H | W | 3-2 | van der Haar 61; Van Vossen 86; Bakens 88 |
| 14 | lge | Vitesse Arnhem | A | D | 1-1 | van der Haar 61 |
| 15 | lge | Ajax | H | D | 1-1 | Zafarin 47 |
| 16 | lge | Willem II Tilb | H | D | 1-1 | Zafarin 74 |
| 17 | lge | Zwolle | H | W | 3-2 | Smit 8; van der Haar 77 pen; Bakens 90 |
| 18 | lge | Roosendaal | A | L | 0-1 | |
| 19 | lge | Heerenveen | H | L | 1-5 | Smit 18 |
| 20 | lge | NEC Nijmegen | A | L | 0-1 | |
| 21 | lge | Roda JC Kerk | H | D | 1-1 | van Gastel 21 |
| 22 | lge | NAC Breda | A | L | 0-1 | |
| 23 | lge | Utrecht | H | W | 1-0 | van der Haar 90 |
| 24 | lge | RKC Waalwijk | H | L | 2-4 | van der Haar 36,77 |
| 25 | lge | AZ Alkmaar | A | L | 1-3 | Duits 52 |
| 26 | lge | Feyenoord | H | L | 3-4 | Van Leerdam 52; van Gastel 61; van der Haar 63 |
| 27 | lge | Twente | A | L | 0-3 | |
| 28 | lge | Willem II Tilb | A | L | 0-3 | |
| 29 | lge | PSV Eindhoven | H | L | 1-6 | Bakens 26 |
| 30 | lge | Excelsior | A | W | 4-3 | Bakens 8; Schulp 16; Hertog 21; Smit 90 |
| 31 | lge | Vitesse Arnhem | H | L | 0-1 | |
| 32 | lge | Ajax | A | L | 1-7 | van der Haar 4 |
| 33 | lge | Groningen | H | W | 1-0 | Zafarin 45 |
| 34 | lge | Zwolle | A | L | 1-2 | van der Haar 90 |

## KEY PLAYERS - GOALSCORERS

**1 Hans van der Haar**

| | | | |
|---|---|---|---|
| Goals in the League | 11 | Player Strike Rate<br>Average number of minutes between League goals scored by player | 198 |
| Contribution to Attacking Power<br>Average number of minutes between League team goals while on pitch | 77 | Club Strike Rate<br>Average number of minutes between League goals scored by club | 87 |

| | PLAYER | LGE GOALS | POWER | STRIKE RATE |
|---|---|---|---|---|
| 2 | Tim Bakens | 5 | 65 | 341 mins |
| 3 | Arvid Smit | 4 | 83 | 418 mins |
| 4 | Dave Zafarin | 3 | 91 | 517 mins |
| 5 | Peter Van Vossen | 2 | 93 | 654 mins |

## KEY PLAYERS - MIDFIELDERS

**1 Arvid Smit**

| | | | |
|---|---|---|---|
| Goals in the League | 4 | Contribution to Attacking Power<br>Average number of minutes between League team goals while on pitch | 84 |
| Defensive Rating<br>Average number of mins between League goals conceded while he was on the pitch | 41 | Scoring Difference<br>Defensive Rating minus Contribution to Attacking Power | -43 |

| | PLAYER | LGE GOALS | DEF RATE | POWER | SCORE DIFF |
|---|---|---|---|---|---|
| 2 | Dami'n Hertog | 1 | 33 | 80 | -47 mins |
| 3 | Leonardo Dos Santos Silva Leon | 0 | 30 | 79 | -49 mins |
| 4 | Ilja Van Leerdam | 2 | 36 | 87 | -51 mins |
| 5 | Jean-Paul van Gastel | 2 | 44 | 116 | -72 mins |

## KEY PLAYERS - DEFENDERS

**1 Tim Bakens**

| | | | |
|---|---|---|---|
| Goals Conceded (GC)<br>The number of League goals conceded while he was on the pitch | 46 | Clean Sheets<br>In games when he played at least 70 minutes | 1 |
| Defensive Rating<br>Ave number of mins between League goals conceded while on the pitch | 37 | Club Defensive Rating<br>Average number of mins between League goals conceded by the club this season | 36 |

| | PLAYER | CON LGE | CLEAN SHEETS | DEF RATE |
|---|---|---|---|---|
| 2 | Edwin Hermans | 56 | 2 | 37 mins |
| 3 | Milan Berck-Beelenkamp | 56 | 2 | 37 mins |
| 4 | Rene Bot | 69 | 2 | 36 mins |
| 5 | Michaerl van der Kruis | 56 | 1 | 33 mins |

## GOALS SCORED

**AT HOME**

| | | |
|---|---|---|
| MOST | Ajax | 57 |
| | | 23 |
| LEAST | Twente | 18 |

**AWAY**

| | | |
|---|---|---|
| MOST | PSV | 44 |
| | | 12 |
| LEAST | Roosendaal & Groningen | 9 |

## GOALS CONCEDED

**AT HOME**

| | | |
|---|---|---|
| LEAST | PSV | 7 |
| | | 34 |
| MOST | Excelsior | 38 |

**AWAY**

| | | |
|---|---|---|
| LEAST | PSV | 13 |
| | | 50 |
| MOST | De G'schap | 50 |

## KEY GOALKEEPER

**1 Jurgen Wevers**

| | |
|---|---|
| Goals Conceded in the League | 85 |
| Defensive Rating<br>Ave number of mins between League goals conceded while on the pitch | 36 |
| Counting Games<br>Games when he played at least 70 mins | 34 |
| Clean Sheets<br>In games when he played at least 70 mins | 3 |

## TOP POINT EARNERS

| | PLAYER | GAMES | AVE |
|---|---|---|---|
| 1 | Bakens | 17 | 0.94 |
| 2 | Smit | 15 | 0.87 |
| 3 | Van Vossen | 13 | 0.85 |
| 4 | van der Haar | 20 | 0.80 |
| 5 | Hermans | 22 | 0.77 |
| 6 | Berck-Beelenkamp | 21 | 0.76 |
| 7 | Van Leerdam | 29 | 0.76 |
| 8 | Hertog | 19 | 0.74 |
| 9 | Wevers | 34 | 0.68 |
| 10 | Zafarin | 13 | 0.62 |
| | **CLUB AVERAGE:** | | **0.68** |

Ave = Average points per match in Counting Games

## ATTENDANCES

HOME GROUND: DE VIJVERBERG CAPACITY: 11000 AVERAGE LEAGUE AT HOME: 10705

| | | | | | | | | |
|---|---|---|---|---|---|---|---|---|
| 5 | Feyenoord | 50000 | 4 | AZ Alkmaar | 11000 | 17 | Zwolle | 10900 |
| 32 | Ajax | 49300 | 19 | Heerenveen | 11000 | 21 | Roda JC Kerk | 10700 |
| 6 | PSV Eindhoven | 31000 | 26 | Feyenoord | 11000 | 24 | RKC Waalwijk | 10500 |
| 14 | Vitesse Arnhem | 22500 | 23 | Utrecht | 11000 | 16 | Willem II Tilb | 10400 |
| 3 | Utrecht | 18000 | 33 | Groningen | 11000 | 2 | Roosendaal | 7500 |
| 9 | Roda JC Kerk | 16000 | 7 | Twente | 11000 | 25 | AZ Alkmaar | 7105 |
| 10 | Heerenveen | 14200 | 8 | NEC Nijmegen | 11000 | 34 | Zwolle | 6800 |
| 28 | Willem II Tilb | 13500 | 13 | NAC Breda | 11000 | 1 | RKC Waalwijk | 5500 |
| 27 | Twente | 13175 | 11 | Excelsior | 11000 | 18 | Roosendaal | 5000 |
| 22 | NAC Breda | 13024 | 29 | PSV Eindhoven | 11000 | 30 | Excelsior | 3468 |
| 12 | Groningen | 12500 | 31 | Vitesse Arnhem | 11000 | | | |
| 20 | NEC Nijmegen | 11250 | 15 | Ajax | 11000 | | | |

Home / Away / Neutral

## DISCIPLINARY RECORDS

| | PLAYER | YELLOW | RED | AVE |
|---|---|---|---|---|
| 1 | van der Kruis | 6 | 0 | 311 |
| 2 | Bot | 7 | 1 | 314 |
| 3 | Leonardo | 3 | 0 | 342 |
| 4 | Culina | 3 | 1 | 349 |
| 5 | Schulp | 3 | 0 | 353 |
| 6 | Berck-Beelenkamp | 4 | 1 | 416 |
| 7 | van Gastel | 2 | 0 | 463 |
| 8 | Hermans | 4 | 0 | 520 |
| 9 | van der Haar | 3 | 0 | 726 |
| 10 | Smit | 2 | 0 | 836 |
| 11 | Van Leerdam | 3 | 0 | 902 |
| 12 | Van Vossen | 1 | 0 | 1308 |
| 13 | Zafarin | 1 | 0 | 1551 |
| | Other | 7 | 0 | |
| | TOTAL | 49 | 3 | |

## LEAGUE GOALS

| | PLAYER | MINS | GOALS | AVE |
|---|---|---|---|---|
| 1 | van der Haar | 2178 | 11 | 198 |
| 2 | Bakens | 1707 | 5 | 341 |
| 3 | Smit | 1672 | 4 | 418 |
| 4 | Zafarin | 1551 | 3 | 517 |
| 5 | Van Vossen | 1308 | 2 | 654 |
| 6 | Van Leerdam | 2706 | 2 | 1353 |
| 7 | van Gastel | 927 | 2 | 464 |
| 8 | Turpijn | 494 | 1 | 494 |
| 9 | Valeev | 1254 | 1 | 1254 |
| 10 | Culina | 1398 | 1 | 1398 |
| 11 | Hertog | 1992 | 1 | 1992 |
| 12 | Duits | 404 | 1 | 404 |
| 13 | Schulp | 1061 | 1 | 1061 |
| | Other | | 0 | |
| | TOTAL | | 35 | |

## MONTH BY MONTH GUIDE TO THE POINTS

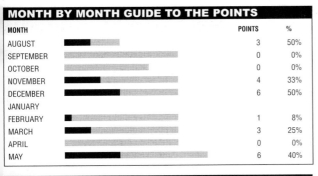

| MONTH | POINTS | % |
|---|---|---|
| AUGUST | 3 | 50% |
| SEPTEMBER | 0 | 0% |
| OCTOBER | 0 | 0% |
| NOVEMBER | 4 | 33% |
| DECEMBER | 6 | 50% |
| JANUARY | | |
| FEBRUARY | 1 | 8% |
| MARCH | 3 | 25% |
| APRIL | 0 | 0% |
| MAY | 6 | 40% |

## TEAM OF THE SEASON

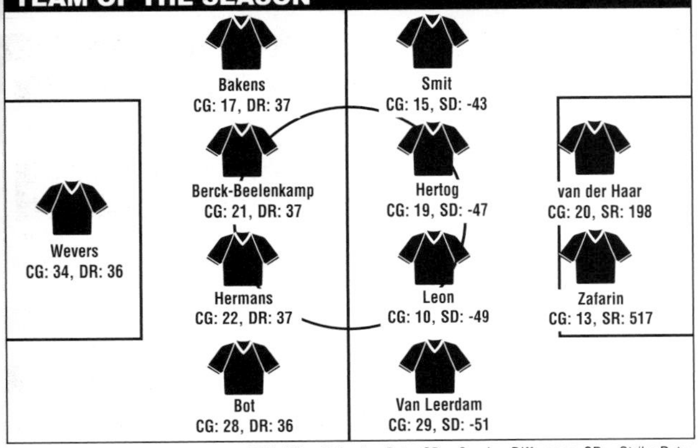

Bakens
CG: 17, DR: 37
Smit
CG: 15, SD: -43
Berck-Beelenkamp
CG: 21, DR: 37
Hertog
CG: 19, SD: -47
van der Haar
CG: 20, SR: 198
Wevers
CG: 34, DR: 36
Hermans
CG: 22, DR: 37
Leon
CG: 10, SD: -49
Zafarin
CG: 13, SR: 517
Bot
CG: 28, DR: 36
Van Leerdam
CG: 29, SD: -51


**KEY:** DR = Defensive Rate, SD = Scoring Difference, SR = Strike Rate, CG = Counting Games – League games playing at least 70 minutes

## LEAGUE APPEARANCES, BOOKINGS AND CAPS

| | AGE | IN THE SQUAD | COUNTING GAMES | MINUTES ON PITCH | YELLOW CARDS | RED CARDS | THIS SEASON | HOME COUNTRY |
|---|---|---|---|---|---|---|---|---|
| **Goalkeepers** | | | | | | | | |
| Martijn Besselink | 28 | 34 | 0 | 0 | 0 | 0 | - | Holland |
| Jurgen Wevers | 24 | 34 | 34 | 3060 | 1 | 0 | - | Holland |
| **Defenders** | | | | | | | | |
| Tim Bakens | 20 | 21 | 17 | 1707 | 1 | 0 | - | Holland |
| Milan Berck-Beelenkamp | 25 | 31 | 21 | 2081 | 4 | 1 | - | Holland |
| Harald Berendsen | 22 | 1 | 0 | 0 | 0 | 0 | - | Holland |
| Rene Bot | 25 | 28 | 28 | 2514 | 7 | 1 | - | Holland |
| Edwin Hermans | 29 | 26 | 22 | 2080 | 4 | 0 | - | Holland |
| Michaerl Vd Kruis | 24 | 30 | 17 | 1868 | 6 | 0 | - | Holland |
| Jan Vreman | 37 | 20 | 5 | 554 | 0 | 0 | - | Holland |
| Cihan Yalcin | 18 | 4 | 0 | 15 | 0 | 0 | - | Turkey |
| **Midfielders** | | | | | | | | |
| Jason Culina | 22 | 27 | 11 | 1398 | 3 | 1 | - | Australia |
| Sander Duits | | 22 | 2 | 404 | 4 | 0 | - | Holland |
| Dami'n Hertog | 28 | 28 | 19 | 1992 | 0 | 0 | - | Holland |
| Klaas-Jan Huntelaar | 19 | 15 | 1 | 279 | 0 | 0 | - | Holland |
| Leonardo Leon | 26 | 14 | 10 | 1026 | 3 | 0 | - | Brazil |
| Kevin Nicolai | 22 | 2 | 0 | 45 | 0 | 0 | - | Belgium |
| Arvid Smit | 22 | 33 | 15 | 1672 | 2 | 0 | - | Holland |
| Arno Splinter | 25 | 8 | 0 | 0 | 0 | 0 | - | |
| Bertil Ter Avest | 32 | 19 | 9 | 1173 | 0 | 0 | - | Holland |
| John Van den Brom | 36 | 15 | 1 | 195 | 1 | 0 | - | Holland |
| Jean-Paul van Gastel | 31 | 13 | 11 | 927 | 2 | 0 | - | Holland |
| Ilja Van Leerdam | 24 | 32 | 29 | 2706 | 3 | 0 | - | Holland |
| **Forwards** | | | | | | | | |
| Yasin Karaca | 19 | 5 | 0 | 23 | 0 | 0 | - | Belgium |
| Dennis Schulp | 25 | 26 | 8 | 1061 | 3 | 0 | - | Holland |
| Rody Turpijn | 25 | 14 | 2 | 494 | 0 | 0 | - | Holland |
| Ruslan Valeev | 21 | 26 | 10 | 1254 | 0 | 0 | - | Ukraine |
| Hans van der Haar | 28 | 33 | 20 | 2178 | 3 | 0 | - | Holland |
| Peter Van Vossen | 35 | 17 | 13 | 1308 | 1 | 0 | - | Holland |
| Dave Zafarin | 25 | 29 | 13 | 1551 | 1 | 0 | - | Holland |

**KEY:** LEAGUE BOOKINGS CAPS (FIFA RANKING)

## SQUAD APPEARANCES

| Match | 1 | 2 | 3 | 4 | 5 | 6 | 7 | 8 | 9 | 10 | 11 | 12 | 13 | 14 | 15 | 16 | 17 | 18 | 19 | 20 | 21 | 22 | 23 | 24 | 25 | 26 | 27 | 28 | 29 | 30 | 31 | 32 | 33 | 34 |
|---|---|---|---|---|---|---|---|---|---|---|---|---|---|---|---|---|---|---|---|---|---|---|---|---|---|---|---|---|---|---|---|---|---|---|
| Venue | A | H | A | H | A | A | H | H | A | A | H | A | H | A | H | H | H | A | H | A | H | A | H | H | A | H | A | A | H | A | H | A | H | A |
| Competition | L | L | L | L | L | L | L | L | L | L | L | L | L | L | L | L | L | L | L | L | L | L | L | L | L | L | L | L | L | L | L | L | L | L |
| Result | L | W | L | L | L | L | L | L | L | L | D | L | W | D | D | D | W | L | L | L | D | L | W | L | L | L | L | L | L | W | L | L | W | L |

**Goalkeepers**
Martijn Besselink
Jurgen Wevers

**Defenders**
Tim Bakens
Milan Berck-Beelenkamp
Harald Berendsen
Rene Bot
Edwin Hermans
Michaerl van der Kruis
Jan Vreman
Cihan Yalcin

**Midfielders**
Jason Culina
Sander Duits
Dami'n Hertog
Klaas-Jan Huntelaar
L Dos Santos Silva Leon
Kevin Nicolai
Arvid Smit
Arno Splinter
Bertil Ter Avest
John Van den Brom
Jean-Paul van Gastel
Ilja Van Leerdam

**Forwards**
Yasin Karaca
Dennis Schulp
Rody Turpijn
Ruslan Valeev
Hans van der Haar
Peter Van Vossen
Dave Zafarin

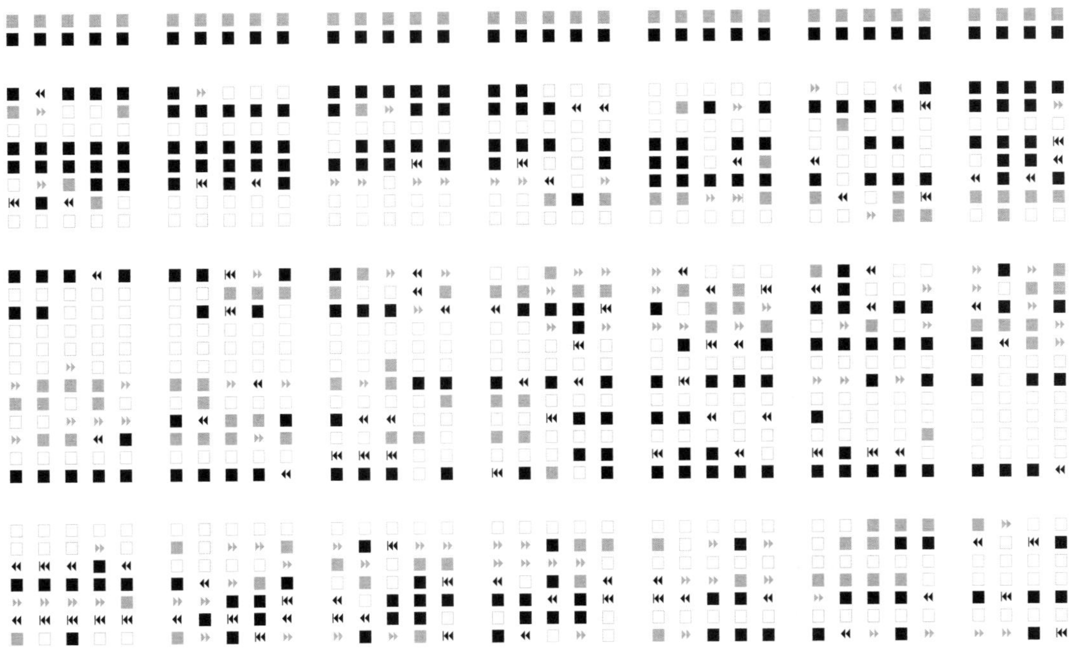

**KEY:** ■ On all match ■ On bench □ Not in 16 ◂◂ Subbed off ▸▸ Subbed on from bench

# DUTCH LEAGUE ROUND-UP

## FINAL LEAGUE TABLE

| | | HOME | | | | | AWAY | | | | | TOTAL | | | |
|---|---|---|---|---|---|---|---|---|---|---|---|---|---|---|---|
| | P | W | D | L | F | A | W | D | L | F | A | F | A | DIF | PTS |
| PSV Eindhoven | 34 | 14 | 2 | 1 | 43 | 7 | 12 | 4 | 1 | 44 | 13 | 87 | 20 | 67 | 84 |
| Ajax | 34 | 14 | 2 | 1 | 57 | 18 | 12 | 3 | 2 | 39 | 14 | 96 | 32 | 64 | 83 |
| Feyenoord | 34 | 16 | 0 | 1 | 50 | 14 | 9 | 5 | 3 | 39 | 25 | 89 | 39 | 50 | 80 |
| NAC Breda | 34 | 8 | 8 | 1 | 21 | 10 | 5 | 5 | 7 | 21 | 21 | 42 | 31 | 11 | 52 |
| NEC Nijmegen | 34 | 9 | 2 | 6 | 24 | 19 | 5 | 7 | 5 | 17 | 21 | 41 | 40 | 1 | 51 |
| Roda JC Kerk | 34 | 11 | 3 | 3 | 31 | 14 | 3 | 5 | 9 | 27 | 40 | 58 | 54 | 4 | 50 |
| Heerenveen | 34 | 9 | 3 | 5 | 37 | 21 | 4 | 5 | 8 | 24 | 34 | 61 | 55 | 6 | 47 |
| Utrecht | 34 | 8 | 7 | 2 | 34 | 25 | 4 | 4 | 9 | 15 | 24 | 49 | 49 | 0 | 47 |
| RKC Waalwijk | 34 | 9 | 1 | 7 | 24 | 20 | 5 | 3 | 9 | 20 | 31 | 44 | 51 | -7 | 46 |
| AZ Alkmaar | 34 | 9 | 3 | 5 | 31 | 26 | 3 | 5 | 9 | 18 | 43 | 49 | 69 | -20 | 44 |
| Willem II Tilb | 34 | 8 | 4 | 5 | 31 | 26 | 3 | 5 | 9 | 17 | 25 | 48 | 51 | -3 | 42 |
| Twente | 34 | 5 | 8 | 4 | 18 | 17 | 5 | 3 | 9 | 18 | 28 | 36 | 45 | -9 | 41 |
| Roosendaal | 34 | 8 | 4 | 5 | 24 | 16 | 2 | 2 | 13 | 9 | 38 | 33 | 54 | -21 | 36 |
| Vitesse Arnhem | 34 | 4 | 6 | 7 | 20 | 26 | 4 | 3 | 10 | 17 | 25 | 37 | 51 | -14 | 33 |
| Groningen | 34 | 6 | 7 | 4 | 19 | 15 | 1 | 4 | 12 | 9 | 29 | 28 | 44 | -16 | 32 |
| Zwolle | 34 | 6 | 4 | 7 | 21 | 28 | 2 | 4 | 11 | 10 | 34 | 31 | 62 | -31 | 32 |
| Excelsior | 34 | 2 | 4 | 11 | 20 | 38 | 3 | 4 | 10 | 18 | 33 | 38 | 71 | -33 | 23 |
| De Graafschap | 34 | 5 | 4 | 8 | 23 | 34 | 1 | 1 | 15 | 12 | 50 | 35 | 84 | -49 | 23 |

## TEAM OF THE SEASON

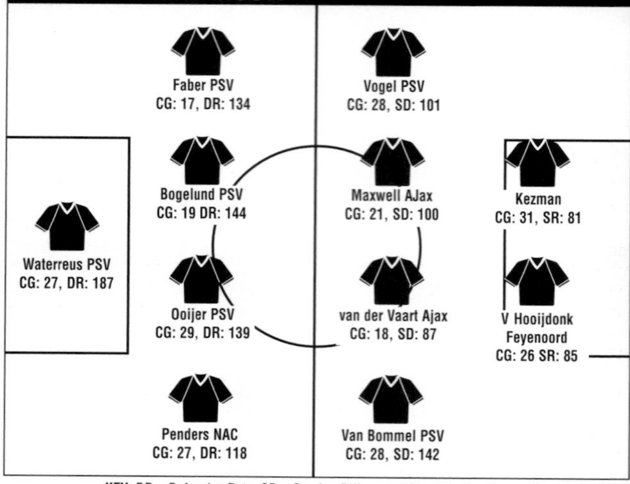

Faber PSV
CG: 17, DR: 134
Vogel PSV
CG: 28, SD: 101
Bogelund PSV
CG: 19 DR: 144
Maxwell AJax
CG: 21, SD: 100
Kezman
CG: 31, SR: 81
Waterreus PSV
CG: 27, DR: 187
Ooijer PSV
CG: 29, DR: 139
van der Vaart Ajax
CG: 18, SD: 87
V Hooijdonk
Feyenoord
CG: 26 SR: 85
Penders NAC
CG: 27, DR: 118
Van Bommel PSV
CG: 28, SD: 142


**KEY:** DR = Defensive Rate, SD = Scoring Difference AP = Attacking Power SR = Strike Rate, CG=Counting Games – League games playing at least 70 minutes

## CLUB STRIKE FORCE

**KEY:** Goals: Total number of goals scored in League. Club Strike Rate (CSR): Average number of mins between goals scored

| | CLUB | GOALS | CSR |
|---|---|---|---|
| 1 | Ajax | 96 | 32 mins |
| 2 | Feyenoord | 89 | 34 mins |
| 3 | PSV Eindhoven | 87 | 35 mins |
| 4 | Heerenveen | 61 | 50 mins |
| 5 | Roda JC Kerk | 58 | 53 mins |
| 6 | AZ Alkmaar | 49 | 62 mins |
| 7 | Utrecht | 49 | 62 mins |
| 8 | Willem II Tilb | 48 | 64 mins |
| 9 | RKC Waalwijk | 44 | 70 mins |
| 10 | NAC Breda | 42 | 73 mins |
| 11 | NEC Nijmegen | 41 | 75 mins |
| 12 | Excelsior | 38 | 81 mins |
| 13 | Vitesse Arnhem | 37 | 83 mins |
| 14 | Twente | 36 | 85 mins |
| 15 | De Graafschap | 35 | 87 mins |
| 16 | Roosendaal | 33 | 93 mins |
| 17 | Zwolle | 31 | 99 mins |
| 18 | Groningen | 28 | 109 mins |
| | TOTAL | 902 | |

## CLUB DEFENCES

**KEY:** Defensive Rating: Average number of mins between goals conceded. CS: Clean Sheets - Games where no goals were conceded.

| | CLUB | CONCEDED | CLEAN SH | DEF RATE |
|---|---|---|---|---|
| 1 | PSV Eindhoven | 20 | 21 | 153 mins |
| 2 | NAC Breda | 31 | 17 | 99 mins |
| 3 | Ajax | 32 | 10 | 96 mins |
| 4 | Feyenoord | 39 | 6 | 78 mins |
| 5 | NEC Nijmegen | 40 | 17 | 77 mins |
| 6 | Groningen | 44 | 14 | 70 mins |
| 7 | Twente | 45 | 12 | 68 mins |
| 8 | Utrecht | 49 | 9 | 62 mins |
| 9 | RKC Waalwijk | 51 | 8 | 60 mins |
| 10 | Vitesse Arnhem | 51 | 5 | 60 mins |
| 11 | Willem II Tilb | 51 | 8 | 60 mins |
| 12 | Roda JC Kerk | 54 | 13 | 57 mins |
| 13 | Roosendaal | 54 | 8 | 57 mins |
| 14 | Heerenveen | 55 | 6 | 56 mins |
| 15 | Zwolle | 62 | 6 | 49 mins |
| 16 | AZ Alkmaar | 69 | 7 | 44 mins |
| 17 | Excelsior | 71 | 3 | 43 mins |
| 18 | De Graafschap | 84 | 3 | 36 mins |
| TOTAL | | 902 | 173 | |

## CLUB DISCIPLINARY RECORDS

**KEY:** AVE: Average number of mins between cards

| | CLUB | YELL | RED | TOT | AVE |
|---|---|---|---|---|---|
| 1 | AZ Alkmaar | 60 | 5 | 65 | 47 mins |
| 2 | NEC Nijmegen | 55 | 4 | 59 | 52 mins |
| 3 | Twente | 53 | 4 | 57 | 54 mins |
| 4 | RKC Waalwijk | 48 | 7 | 55 | 56 mins |
| 5 | De Graafschap | 49 | 3 | 52 | 59 mins |
| 6 | Roda JC Kerk | 46 | 3 | 49 | 62 mins |
| 7 | Heerenveen | 47 | 1 | 48 | 64 mins |
| 8 | Vitesse Arnhem | 45 | 3 | 48 | 64 mins |
| 9 | Willem II Tilb | 41 | 4 | 45 | 68 mins |
| 10 | Utrecht | 40 | 3 | 43 | 71 mins |
| 11 | Groningen | 39 | 0 | 39 | 78 mins |
| 12 | NAC Breda | 38 | 1 | 39 | 78 mins |
| 13 | Roosendaal | 36 | 3 | 39 | 78 mins |
| 14 | Zwolle | 36 | 2 | 38 | 81 mins |
| 15 | Ajax | 32 | 4 | 36 | 85 mins |
| 16 | Feyenoord | 31 | 3 | 34 | 90 mins |
| 17 | PSV Eindhoven | 32 | 1 | 33 | 93 mins |
| 18 | Excelsior | 23 | 2 | 25 | 122 mins |
| TOTAL | | 751 | 53 | 804 | |

## STADIUM CAPACITY AND HOME CROWDS

| | TEAM | CAPACITY | AVE | HIGH | LOW |
|---|---|---|---|---|---|
| 1 | Roosendaal | 5000 | 99.70 | 5000 | 4750 |
| 2 | Twente | 13300 | 98.80 | 13300 | 12000 |
| 3 | Heerenveen | 14700 | 97.52 | 14700 | 14200 |
| 4 | De Graafschap | 11000 | 97.33 | 11000 | 7500 |
| 5 | Groningen | 13000 | 93.75 | 13000 | 11558 |
| 6 | Ajax | 51324 | 91.43 | 50777 | 34434 |
| 7 | PSV Eindhoven | 36500 | 91.01 | 35200 | 31000 |
| 8 | Willem II Tilb | 14700 | 90.67 | 14700 | 11000 |
| 9 | Zwolle | 6865 | 89.91 | 6865 | 5000 |
| 10 | NEC Nijmegen | 12500 | 89.48 | 12500 | 10000 |
| 11 | RKC Waalwijk | 7500 | 88.89 | 7500 | 5500 |
| 12 | Excelsior | 3500 | 86.26 | 3500 | 2258 |
| 13 | Utrecht | 18925 | 86.06 | 18925 | 13000 |
| 14 | Feyenoord | 51180 | 86.04 | 50000 | 40000 |
| 15 | AZ Alkmaar | 8419 | 85.28 | 8072 | 6758 |
| 16 | NAC Breda | 16400 | 83.21 | 15700 | 9912 |
| 17 | Vitesse Arnhem | 29000 | 79.56 | 28000 | 21000 |
| 18 | Roda JC Kerk | 19500 | 70.24 | 17500 | 12000 |

## AWAY ATTENDANCE

| | TEAM | AVE | HIGH | LOW |
|---|---|---|---|---|
| 1 | Ajax | 95.43 | 42200 | 3478 |
| 2 | PSV Eindhoven | 94.59 | 49871 | 3150 |
| 3 | Feyenoord | 94.53 | 50777 | 3500 |
| 4 | Willem II Tilb | 90.84 | 48248 | 3358 |
| 5 | De Graafschap | 90.73 | 50000 | 3468 |
| 6 | Vitesse Arnhem | 89.19 | 48162 | 3124 |
| 7 | AZ Alkmaar | 89.15 | 47481 | 3100 |
| 8 | NEC Nijmegen | 88.84 | 46084 | 3356 |
| 9 | RKC Waalwijk | 88.82 | 49076 | 2368 |
| 10 | Heerenveen | 88.06 | 50272 | 3164 |
| 11 | NAC Breda | 87.88 | 40100 | 2948 |
| 12 | Roda JC Kerk | 87.53 | 49421 | 2258 |
| 13 | Twente | 87.45 | 47044 | 2764 |
| 14 | Groningen | 87.34 | 47215 | 3142 |
| 15 | Excelsior | 86.91 | 47192 | 4750 |
| 16 | Zwolle | 86.84 | 49003 | 2500 |
| 17 | Utrecht | 86.12 | 42000 | 3000 |
| 18 | Roosendaal | 84.87 | 49182 | 2638 |

## TOP GOALSCORERS

**KEY: Strike Rate:** Average number of minutes between League goals scored by player. **Club Strike Rate (CSR):** Average minutes between League goals scored by club. **Contribution to Attacking Power (PWR):** Average mins between League goals scored by club while on pitch.

| | PLAYER | CLUB | GOALS | PWR | CSR | S RATE |
|---|---|---|---|---|---|---|
| 1 | Kezman | PSV Eindhoven | 35 | 35 | 35 | 81 |
| 2 | van Hooijdonk | Feyenoord | 28 | 33 | 34 | 85 |
| 3 | van der Vaart | Ajax | 18 | 27 | 32 | 95 |
| 4 | Ibrahimovic | Ajax | 13 | 41 | 32 | 139 |
| 5 | Buffel | Feyenoord | 17 | 34 | 34 | 149 |
| 6 | Hoogendorp | RKC Waalwijk | 16 | 67 | 70 | 152 |
| 7 | Kuijt | Utrecht | 20 | 63 | 62 | 152 |
| 8 | Amoah | Vitesse Arnhem | 16 | 83 | 83 | 167 |
| 9 | Perez | AZ Alkmaar | 11 | 72 | 62 | 184 |
| 10 | Sonko | Roda JC Kerk | 8 | 50 | 53 | 184 |
| 11 | den Ouden | Roosendaal | 9 | 79 | 93 | 195 |
| 12 | van der Haar | De Graafschap | 11 | 77 | 87 | 198 |
| 13 | El Khattabi | AZ Alkmaar | 7 | 65 | 62 | 207 |
| 14 | Kalou | Feyenoord | 10 | 34 | 34 | 208 |
| 15 | Selakovic | Heerenveen | 8 | 48 | 50 | 212 |
| 16 | van der Meyde | Ajax | 11 | 31 | 32 | 215 |
| 17 | Vennegoor | PSV Eindhoven | 8 | 33 | 35 | 221 |
| 18 | Robben | PSV Eindhoven | 12 | 34 | 35 | 223 |
| 19 | Engelaar | NAC Breda | 12 | 72 | 73 | 224 |
| 20 | Drent | Groningen | 7 | 85 | 109 | 231 |
| 21 | Sektioui | Willem II Tilb | 8 | 61 | 64 | 239 |
| 22 | van Galen | AZ Alkmaar | 9 | 55 | 62 | 241 |
| 23 | Soetaers | Roda JC Kerk | 10 | 56 | 53 | 241 |
| 24 | Shoukov | Willem II Tilb | 9 | 54 | 64 | 244 |
| 25 | Anastasiou | Roda JC Kerk | 11 | 50 | 53 | 247 |
| 26 | Gluscevic | Utrecht | 6 | 67 | 62 | 247 |
| 27 | de Jong | Heerenveen | 9 | 43 | 50 | 253 |
| 28 | Denneboom | Heerenveen | 10 | 46 | 50 | 258 |
| 29 | Cavens | Twente | 6 | 64 | 85 | 260 |
| 30 | Van Bommel | PSV Eindhoven | 9 | 35 | 35 | 275 |

## TOP DEFENDERS

**KEY: Defensive Rating (DR)** Average mins between League goals conceded while on pitch. **Club Defensive Rating (CDR):** Average minutes between League goals conceded by club. **Clean Sheets (CS)** - Games where no goals were conceded.

| | PLAYER | CLUB | CONC | CS | CDR | DR |
|---|---|---|---|---|---|---|
| 1 | Bogelund | PSV Eindhoven | 12 | 12 | 153 | 144 |
| 2 | Ooijer | PSV Eindhoven | 20 | 17 | 153 | 139 |
| 3 | Faber | PSV Eindhoven | 13 | 10 | 153 | 134 |
| 4 | Brouwers | Roda JC Kerk | 8 | 8 | 56 | 131 |
| 5 | O'Brien | Ajax | 9 | 4 | 96 | 118 |
| 6 | Penders | NAC Breda | 21 | 16 | 99 | 118 |
| 7 | Chivu | Ajax | 18 | 8 | 96 | 117 |
| 8 | de Jong | Ajax | 13 | 5 | 96 | 101 |
| 9 | Colin | NAC Breda | 28 | 15 | 99 | 101 |
| 10 | Galasek | Ajax | 26 | 8 | 96 | 99 |
| 11 | Trabelsi | Ajax | 22 | 6 | 96 | 98 |
| 12 | Feher | NAC Breda | 31 | 16 | 99 | 97 |
| 13 | Hesp | NEC Nijmegen | 28 | 16 | 77 | 95 |
| 14 | Schenning | NAC Breda | 24 | 12 | 99 | 93 |
| 15 | de Nooijer | Feyenoord | 13 | 2 | 78 | 92 |
| 16 | Pothuizen | Twente | 26 | 11 | 68 | 91 |
| 17 | Bergdolmo | Ajax | 14 | 5 | 96 | 88 |
| 18 | van Wonderen | Feyenoord | 31 | 6 | 78 | 83 |
| 19 | Krstev | Groningen | 23 | 8 | 70 | 81 |
| 20 | Kruiswijk | Groningen | 21 | 8 | 70 | 79 |
| 21 | Broerse | Groningen | 34 | 13 | 70 | 79 |
| 22 | Pasanen | Ajax | 21 | 5 | 96 | 78 |
| 23 | Tininho | Roosendaal | 29 | 8 | 57 | 78 |
| 24 | Polak | Twente | 35 | 11 | 68 | 78 |
| 25 | Schuurman | NEC Nijmegen | 40 | 17 | 77 | 77 |
| 26 | Wau | Willem II Tilb | 24 | 6 | 60 | 77 |
| 27 | Wielaert | NEC Nijmegen | 38 | 16 | 77 | 76 |
| 28 | Ouedraogo | Twente | 30 | 8 | 68 | 76 |
| 29 | Zeman | Vitesse Arnhem | 14 | 3 | 60 | 76 |
| 30 | Wisgerhof | NEC Nijmegen | 40 | 15 | 77 | 72 |

## TOP MIDFIELDERS

**KEY: Scoring Difference (SD)** Team goals scored while on the pitch minus team goals conceded. **Contribution to Attacking Power:** Average mins between League goals scored by club while on pitch. **Defensive Rating (DR)** Average mins between League goals conceded while on pitch.

| | PLAYER | TEAM | GOALS | DR | PWR | SD |
|---|---|---|---|---|---|---|
| 1 | Van Bommel | PSV Eindhoven | 9 | 177 | 35 | 142 |
| 2 | Vogel | PSV Eindhoven | 1 | 140 | 39 | 101 |
| 3 | Maxwell | Ajax | 4 | 132 | 32 | 100 |
| 4 | Lee | PSV Eindhoven | 0 | 131 | 36 | 95 |
| 5 | van der Vaart | Ajax | 18 | 115 | 28 | 87 |
| 6 | Sneijder | Ajax | 4 | 108 | 29 | 79 |
| 7 | van der Schaaf | PSV Eindhoven | 0 | 106 | 28 | 78 |
| 8 | van der Meyde | Ajax | 11 | 103 | 31 | 72 |
| 9 | Lurling | Feyenoord | 3 | 109 | 41 | 68 |
| 10 | Pienaar | Ajax | 5 | 101 | 34 | 67 |
| 11 | Paauwe | Feyenoord | 2 | 87 | 33 | 54 |
| 12 | Buffel | Feyenoord | 17 | 84 | 35 | 49 |
| 13 | Ono | Feyenoord | 7 | 83 | 34 | 49 |
| 14 | Emerton | Feyenoord | 3 | 80 | 34 | 46 |
| 15 | Song | Feyenoord | 1 | 87 | 42 | 45 |
| 16 | Bosvelt | Feyenoord | 3 | 75 | 33 | 42 |
| 17 | Gudelj | NAC Breda | 0 | 106 | 70 | 36 |
| 18 | Schreuder | NAC Breda | 2 | 102 | 73 | 29 |
| 19 | Touzani | Utrecht | 0 | 92 | 63 | 29 |
| 20 | Simr | NEC Nijmegen | 2 | 98 | 75 | 23 |
| 21 | van Mol | Utrecht | 0 | 87 | 65 | 22 |
| 22 | Slot | NAC Breda | 4 | 109 | 88 | 21 |
| 23 | de Jong | Heerenveen | 9 | 60 | 44 | 16 |
| 24 | Petrovic | RKC Waalwijk | 1 | 67 | 51 | 16 |
| 25 | Leiwakabessy | NEC Nijmegen | 0 | 92 | 78 | 14 |
| 26 | Shoukov | Willem II Tilb | 9 | 69 | 55 | 14 |
| 27 | Sonko | Roda JC Kerk | 8 | 64 | 51 | 13 |
| 28 | Zonneveld | NEC Nijmegen | 3 | 80 | 68 | 12 |
| 29 | Jensen, D | Heerenveen | 4 | 56 | 47 | 9 |
| 30 | Hansson | Heerenveen | 3 | 56 | 48 | 8 |

## PLAYER DISCIPLINARY RECORDS

**KEY: AVE:** Average number of mins between cards

| | PLAYER | TEAM | YELL | RED | TOTAL | AVE |
|---|---|---|---|---|---|---|
| 1 | Brouwers | Roda JC Kerk | 6 | 1 | 7 | 149 |
| 2 | van Galen | AZ Alkmaar | 10 | 1 | 11 | 197 |
| 3 | Zeman | Vitesse Arnhem | 4 | 1 | 5 | 212 |
| 4 | Fortes Rodriguez | AZ Alkmaar | 6 | 0 | 6 | 215 |
| 5 | Addo | Roda JC Kerk | 5 | 1 | 6 | 219 |
| 6 | Stefanovic | Vitesse Arnhem | 8 | 2 | 10 | 235 |
| 7 | Van der Leegte | RKC Waalwijk | 3 | 0 | 3 | 236 |
| 8 | Lamey | AZ Alkmaar | 4 | 1 | 5 | 245 |
| 9 | Ouedraogo | Twente | 9 | 0 | 9 | 253 |
| 10 | Boukhari | Ajax | 3 | 0 | 3 | 259 |
| 11 | Hofs | Vitesse Arnhem | 3 | 0 | 3 | 260 |
| 12 | van Steeg | Zwolle | 4 | 0 | 4 | 262 |
| 13 | Zonneveld | NEC Nijmegen | 9 | 1 | 10 | 264 |
| 14 | Peppinck | RKC Waalwijk | 3 | 0 | 3 | 266 |
| 15 | de Jong | Utrecht | 8 | 1 | 9 | 274 |
| 16 | Greene | RKC Waalwijk | 4 | 0 | 4 | 276 |
| 17 | Janssens | Willem II Tilb | 7 | 0 | 7 | 285 |
| 18 | de Nooijer | Feyenoord | 3 | 1 | 4 | 299 |
| 19 | Wijker | AZ Alkmaar | 6 | 0 | 6 | 300 |
| 20 | Boekweg | Groningen | 6 | 0 | 6 | 307 |
| 21 | van der Kruis | De Graafschap | 6 | 0 | 6 | 311 |
| 22 | Bot | De Graafschap | 7 | 1 | 8 | 314 |
| 23 | Simr | NEC Nijmegen | 4 | 0 | 4 | 318 |
| 24 | Heubach | Twente | 7 | 1 | 8 | 327 |
| 25 | Vreven | Utrecht | 7 | 0 | 7 | 331 |
| 26 | Touzani | Utrecht | 3 | 0 | 3 | 338 |
| 27 | Meerdink | AZ Alkmaar | 6 | 0 | 6 | 341 |
| 28 | Leonardo | De Graafschap | 3 | 0 | 3 | 342 |
| 29 | Claessens | Vitesse Arnhem | 7 | 0 | 7 | 346 |
| 30 | Culina | De Graafschap | 3 | 1 | 4 | 349 |

## CHART TOPPING GOALKEEPERS

**KEY: Defensive Rating (DR)** Average mins between League goals conceded while on pitch. **Clean Sheets (CS)** - Games where no goals were conceded.

| | PLAYER | TEAM | CON | CS | DR |
|---|---|---|---|---|---|
| 1 | Waterreus | PSV Eindhoven | 13 | 18 | 187 |
| 2 | Lobont | Ajax | 14 | 5 | 109 |
| 3 | Babos | NAC Breda | 31 | 17 | 99 |
| 4 | Lodewijks | Feyenoord | 22 | 4 | 90 |
| 5 | Gentenaar | NEC Nijmegen | 40 | 17 | 77 |
| 6 | Boschker | Twente | 38 | 12 | 75 |
| 7 | Beukenkamp | Groningen | 37 | 12 | 72 |
| 8 | de Ron | Roosendaal | 23 | 4 | 65 |
| 9 | Zwarthoed | AZ Alkmaar | 23 | 4 | 63 |
| 10 | van Dijk | RKC Waalwijk | 33 | 6 | 61 |
| 11 | Jevric | Vitesse Arnhem | 51 | 5 | 60 |
| 12 | Sinouh | RKC Waalwijk | 18 | 2 | 58 |
| 13 | De Vlieger | Willem II Tilb | 48 | 8 | 58 |
| 14 | Vonk | Heerenveen | 55 | 6 | 56 |
| 15 | Kujovic | Roda JC Kerk | 34 | 8 | 56 |
| 16 | Wapenaar | Utrecht | 48 | 6 | 56 |
| 17 | Roorda | Roda JC Kerk | 21 | 5 | 55 |
| 18 | Aerts | Roosendaal | 29 | 4 | 53 |
| 19 | van der Werff | Zwolle | 57 | 6 | 52 |
| 20 | Malkowski | Excelsior | 48 | 2 | 44 |
| 21 | Varkevisser | Excelsior | 23 | 1 | 41 |
| 22 | Wevers | De Graafschap | 85 | 3 | 36 |
| 23 | Moens | AZ Alkmaar | 46 | 3 | 35 |

## TOP POINT EARNERS

**KEY: Counting Games** League games where he played more than 70 minutes. **Total League Points** Taken in Counting Games. **Average League Points** Taken in Counting Games.

| | PLAYER | TEAM | GAMES | POINTS | AVE |
|---|---|---|---|---|---|
| 1 | O'Brien | Ajax | 12 | 33 | 2.75 |
| 2 | Lodewijks | Feyenoord | 22 | 60 | 2.73 |
| 3 | van der Vaart | Ajax | 18 | 49 | 2.72 |
| 4 | de Nooijer | Feyenoord | 12 | 32 | 2.67 |
| 5 | Chivu | Ajax | 22 | 58 | 2.64 |
| 6 | Sneijder | Ajax | 13 | 34 | 2.62 |
| 7 | Bouma | PSV Eindhoven | 26 | 67 | 2.58 |
| 8 | Lobont | Ajax | 17 | 43 | 2.53 |
| 9 | Ooijer | PSV Eindhoven | 29 | 73 | 2.52 |
| 10 | Waterreus | PSV Eindhoven | 27 | 68 | 2.52 |
| 11 | Rommedahl | PSV Eindhoven | 27 | 67 | 2.48 |
| 12 | Kalou | Feyenoord | 19 | 47 | 2.47 |
| 13 | Faber | PSV Eindhoven | 17 | 42 | 2.47 |
| 14 | Vennegoor | PSV Eindhoven | 13 | 32 | 2.46 |
| 15 | Paauwe | Feyenoord | 30 | 73 | 2.43 |
| 16 | van Wonderen | Feyenoord | 28 | 68 | 2.43 |
| 17 | Vogel | PSV Eindhoven | 28 | 68 | 2.43 |
| 18 | Robben | PSV Eindhoven | 28 | 68 | 2.43 |
| 19 | Maxwell | Ajax | 21 | 51 | 2.43 |
| 20 | Kezman | PSV Eindhoven | 31 | 75 | 2.42 |
| 21 | de Jong | Ajax | 12 | 29 | 2.42 |
| 22 | van der Meyde | Ajax | 24 | 57 | 2.38 |
| 23 | Buffel | Feyenoord | 27 | 64 | 2.37 |
| 24 | Van Bommel | PSV Eindhoven | 28 | 66 | 2.36 |
| 25 | Trabelsi | Ajax | 22 | 52 | 2.36 |
| 26 | Lee | PSV Eindhoven | 14 | 33 | 2.36 |
| 27 | Galasek | Ajax | 26 | 61 | 2.35 |
| 28 | van Hooijdonk | Feyenoord | 26 | 61 | 2.35 |
| 29 | Emerton | Feyenoord | 33 | 77 | 2.33 |
| 30 | Bergdolmo | Ajax | 13 | 30 | 2.31 |

# JUVENTUS

Final Position: **1st**

| | | | | | | |
|---|---|---|---|---|---|---|
| 1 | lge | Atalanta | H | W | 3-0 | Del Piero 27 pen,34; Fresi 90 |
| 2 | ecge | Feyenoord | A | D | 1-1 | Camoranesi 32 |
| 3 | lge | Empoli | A | W | 2-0 | Del Piero 5 pen,73 |
| 4 | ecge | Dinamo Kiev | H | W | 5-0 | Di Vaio 14,52; Del Piero 22; Davids 67; Nedved 79 |
| 5 | lge | Parma | H | D | 2-2 | Tudor 87; Del Piero 90 |
| 6 | ecge | Newcastle | H | W | 2-0 | Del Piero 66,81 |
| 7 | lge | Como | H | D | 1-1 | Zalayeta 88 |
| 8 | lge | Inter Milan | A | D | 1-1 | Del Piero 88 pen |
| 9 | ecge | Newcastle | A | L | 0-1 | |
| 10 | lge | Udinese | H | W | 1-0 | Salas 50 |
| 11 | ecge | Feyenoord | H | W | 2-0 | Di Vaio 4,69 |
| 12 | lge | Modena | A | W | 1-0 | Del Piero 74 |
| 13 | lge | Piacenza | A | W | 1-0 | Nedved 70 |
| 14 | lge | AC Milan | H | W | 2-1 | Di Vaio 8; Thuram 21 |
| 15 | ecge | Dinamo Kiev | A | W | 2-1 | Salas 53; Zalayeta 61 |
| 16 | lge | Torino | A | W | 4-0 | Del Piero 6; Di Vaio 34; Nedved 52; Davids 89 |
| 17 | lge | Bologna | H | D | 1-1 | Iuliano 87 |
| 18 | ecgd | Deportivo | A | D | 2-2 | Birindelli 38; Nedved 57 |
| 19 | lge | Roma | A | D | 2-2 | Del Piero 45; Nedved 85 |
| 20 | lge | Brescia | A | L | 0-2 | |
| 21 | ecgd | Basel | H | W | 4-0 | Trezeguet 3; Montero 34; Tacchinardi 43; Del Piero 51 pen |
| 22 | lge | Lazio | H | L | 1-2 | Nedved 33 |
| 23 | lge | Perugia | A | W | 1-0 | Camoranesi 90 |
| 24 | lge | Reggina | H | W | 5-0 | Conte 22; Trezeguet 35; Cozza 65 og; Del Piero 72 pen; Di Vaio 85 |
| 25 | lge | Chievo | A | W | 4-1 | Trezeguet 11,68,86 pen; Del Piero 20 pen |
| 26 | lge | Piacenza | H | W | 2-0 | Del Piero 10; Nedved 43 |
| 27 | lge | Atalanta | A | D | 1-1 | Di Vaio 50 |
| 28 | lge | Empoli | H | W | 1-0 | Trezeguet 6 pen |
| 29 | lge | Parma | A | W | 2-1 | Di Vaio 13; Tacchinardi 29 |
| 30 | ecgd | Man Utd | A | L | 1-2 | Nedved 90 |
| 31 | lge | Como | A | W | 3-1 | Juarez 11 og; Di Vaio 22; Camoranesi 43 |
| 32 | ecgd | Man Utd | H | L | 0-3 | |
| 33 | lge | Inter Milan | H | W | 3-0 | Guly 4 og; Nedved 34; Camoranesi 83 |
| 34 | lge | Udinese | A | W | 1-0 | Trezeguet 84 |
| 35 | ecgd | Deportivo | H | W | 3-2 | Ferrara 12; Trezeguet 63; Tudor 90 |
| 36 | lge | Modena | H | W | 3-0 | Nedved 54,83; Trezeguet 85 |
| 37 | ecgd | Basel | A | L | 1-2 | Tacchinardi 10 |
| 38 | lge | AC Milan | A | L | 1-2 | Nedved 10 |
| 39 | lge | Torino | H | W | 2-0 | Comotto 6 og; Tacchinardi 88 |
| 40 | ecqfl1 | Barcelona | H | D | 1-1 | Montero 16 |
| 41 | lge | Bologna | A | D | 2-2 | Zambrotta 86; Camoranesi 90 |
| 42 | lge | Roma | H | W | 2-1 | Del Piero 31 pen,40 |
| 43 | ecqfl2 | Barcelona | A | W | 2-1 | Nedved 53; Zalayeta 114 |
| 44 | lge | Brescia | H | W | 2-1 | Del Piero 9,86 |
| 45 | lge | Lazio | A | D | 0-0 | |
| 46 | ecsfl1 | Real Madrid | A | L | 1-2 | Trezeguet 45 |
| 47 | lge | Perugia | H | D | 2-2 | Trezeguet 23 pen; Di Vaio 46 |
| 48 | ecsfl2 | Real Madrid | H | W | 3-1 | Trezeguet 12; Del Piero 42; Nedved 73 |
| 49 | lge | Reggina | A | L | 1-2 | Zalayeta 25 |
| 50 | lge | Chievo | H | W | 4-3 | Zalayeta 16,58; Trezeguet 70; Zenoni 86 |
| 51 | ecfin | AC Milan | N | L | 2-3* | (*on penalties) |

## ATTENDANCES

HOME GROUND: DELLE ALPI CAPACITY: 69041 AVERAGE LEAGUE AT HOME: 41025

| | | | | | | | | |
|---|---|---|---|---|---|---|---|---|
| 43 | Barcelona | 98000 | 42 | Roma | 42592 | 34 | Udinese | 28000 |
| 38 | AC Milan | 78871 | 2 | Feyenoord | 42000 | 18 | Deportivo | 27500 |
| 8 | Inter Milan | 76166 | 44 | Brescia | 40880 | 4 | Dinamo Kiev | 26876 |
| 19 | Roma | 75000 | 7 | Como | 40000 | 49 | Reggina | 26500 |
| 46 | Real Madrid | 74773 | 5 | Parma | 40000 | 27 | Atalanta | 25500 |
| 30 | Man Utd | 66073 | 1 | Atalanta | 40000 | 29 | Parma | 25393 |
| 14 | AC Milan | 65000 | 47 | Perugia | 40000 | 35 | Deportivo | 25070 |
| 45 | Lazio | 65000 | 50 | Chievo | 39400 | 20 | Brescia | 25000 |
| 51 | AC Milan | 63215 | 41 | Bologna | 37000 | 39 | Torino | 25000 |
| 48 | Real Madrid | 60253 | 36 | Modena | 36921 | 21 | Basel | 22639 |
| 32 | Man Utd | 59111 | 17 | Bologna | 36544 | 23 | Perugia | 20000 |
| 22 | Lazio | 58000 | 11 | Feyenoord | 35789 | 13 | Piacenza | 20000 |
| 33 | Inter Milan | 57393 | 25 | Chievo | 35544 | 3 | Empoli | 19000 |
| 6 | Newcastle | 49700 | 26 | Piacenza | 35539 | 12 | Modena | 17000 |
| 40 | Barcelona | 48500 | 10 | Udinese | 35168 | 31 | Como | 12500 |
| 9 | Newcastle | 48370 | 28 | Empoli | 35000 | | | |
| 16 | Torino | 45000 | 37 | Basel | 31500 | | | |
| 15 | Dinamo Kiev | 44000 | 24 | Reggina | 30000 | | | |

■ Home □ Away ▨ Neutral

## KEY PLAYERS - GOALSCORERS

**1 Alessandro Del Piero**

| | | | |
|---|---|---|---|
| **Goals in the League** | 16 | **Player Strike Rate** Average number of minutes between League goals scored by player | 117 |
| **Contribution to Attacking Power** Average number of minutes between League team goals while on pitch | 49 | **Club Strike Rate** Average number of minutes between League goals scored by club | 48 |

| | PLAYER | LGE GOALS | POWER | STRIKE RATE |
|---|---|---|---|---|
| 2 | Marco Di Vaio | 7 | 45 | 221 mins |
| 3 | Pavel Nedved | 9 | 45 | 254 mins |
| 4 | Mauro Camoranesi | 4 | 44 | 529 mins |
| 5 | Alessio Tacchinardi | 2 | 48 | 1016 mins |

## KEY PLAYERS - MIDFIELDERS

**1 Pavel Nedved**

| | | | |
|---|---|---|---|
| **Goals in the League** | 9 | **Contribution to Attacking Power** Average number of minutes between League team goals while on pitch | 46 |
| **Defensive Rating** Average number of mins between League goals conceded while he was on the pitch | 120 | **Scoring Difference** Defensive Rating minus Contribution to Attacking Power | 74 |

| | PLAYER | LGE GOALS | DEF RATE | POWER | SCORE DIFF |
|---|---|---|---|---|---|
| 2 | Edgar Davids | 1 | 125 | 53 | 72 mins |
| 3 | Gianluca Zambrotta | 1 | 113 | 49 | 64 mins |
| 4 | Mauro Camoranesi | 4 | 101 | 44 | 57 mins |
| 5 | Alessio Tacchinardi | 2 | 102 | 48 | 54 mins |

## KEY PLAYERS - DEFENDERS

**1 Lilian Thuram**

| | | | |
|---|---|---|---|
| **Goals Conceded (GC)** The number of League goals conceded while he was on the pitch | 19 | **Clean Sheets** In games when he played at least 70 minutes | 12 |
| **Defensive Rating** Ave number of mins between League goals conceded while on the pitch | 121 | **Club Defensive Rating** Average number of mins between League goals conceded by the club this season | 106 |

| | PLAYER | CON LGE | CLEAN SHEETS | DEF RATE |
|---|---|---|---|---|
| 2 | Ciro Ferrara | 19 | 9 | 109 mins |
| 3 | Alessandro Birindelli | 11 | 5 | 108 mins |
| 4 | Paolo Montero | 17 | 8 | 105 mins |
| 5 | Mark Iuliano | 17 | 8 | 99 mins |

## KEY GOALKEEPER

**1 Gianluigi Buffon**

| | |
|---|---|
| **Goals Conceded in the League** | 23 |
| **Defensive Rating** Ave number of mins between League goals conceded while on the pitch | 123 |
| **Counting Games** Games when he played at least 70 minutes | 31 |
| **Clean Sheets** In games when he played at least 70 minutes | 15 |

## TOP POINT EARNERS

| | PLAYER | GAMES | AVE |
|---|---|---|---|
| 1 | Nedved | 24 | 2.33 |
| 2 | Camoranesi | 19 | 2.26 |
| 3 | Zambrotta | 18 | 2.22 |
| 4 | Ferrara | 20 | 2.20 |
| 5 | Del Piero | 20 | 2.15 |
| 6 | Buffon | 31 | 2.13 |
| 7 | Thuram | 25 | 2.08 |
| 8 | Di Vaio | 12 | 2.08 |
| 9 | Davids | 22 | 2.05 |
| 10 | Iuliano | 17 | 2.00 |
| | **CLUB AVERAGE:** | | **2.12** |

Ave = Average points per match in Counting Games

## DISCIPLINARY RECORDS

| | PLAYER | YELLOW | RED | AVE |
|---|---|---|---|---|
| 1 | Tudor | 2 | 1 | 251 |
| 2 | Camoranesi | 7 | 0 | 302 |
| 3 | Moretti | 1 | 0 | 471 |
| 4 | Ferrara | 4 | 0 | 520 |
| 5 | Conte | 1 | 1 | 542 |
| 6 | Salas | 1 | 0 | 549 |
| 7 | Iuliano | 3 | 0 | 560 |
| 8 | Zalayeta | 2 | 0 | 560 |
| 9 | Birindelli | 2 | 0 | 594 |
| 10 | Zambrotta | 3 | 0 | 642 |
| 11 | Tacchinardi | 3 | 0 | 677 |
| 12 | Davids | 3 | 0 | 706 |
| 13 | Nedved | 3 | 0 | 762 |
| | Other | 6 | 0 | |
| | TOTAL | 41 | 2 | |

## LEAGUE GOALS

| | PLAYER | MINS | GOALS | AVE |
|---|---|---|---|---|
| 1 | Del Piero | 1866 | 16 | 117 |
| 2 | Trezeguet | 1155 | 9 | 128 |
| 3 | Nedved | 2286 | 9 | 254 |
| 4 | Di Vaio | 1549 | 7 | 221 |
| 5 | Camoranesi | 2116 | 4 | 529 |
| 6 | Zalayeta | 1121 | 4 | 280 |
| 7 | Tacchinardi | 2032 | 2 | 1016 |
| 8 | Tudor | 755 | 1 | 755 |
| 9 | Iuliano | 1682 | 1 | 1682 |
| 10 | Zenoni | 622 | 1 | 622 |
| 11 | Davids | 2120 | 1 | 2120 |
| 12 | Zambrotta | 1928 | 1 | 1928 |
| 13 | Conte | 1085 | 1 | 1085 |
| | Other | | 7 | |
| | TOTAL | | 64 | |

## MONTH BY MONTH GUIDE TO THE POINTS

| Month | Points | % |
|---|---|---|
| SEPTEMBER | 7 | 78% |
| OCTOBER | 5 | 56% |
| NOVEMBER | 13 | 87% |
| DECEMBER | 4 | 33% |
| JANUARY | 9 | 100% |
| FEBRUARY | 10 | 83% |
| MARCH | 9 | 75% |
| APRIL | 10 | 83% |
| MAY | 5 | 42% |

## TEAM OF THE SEASON

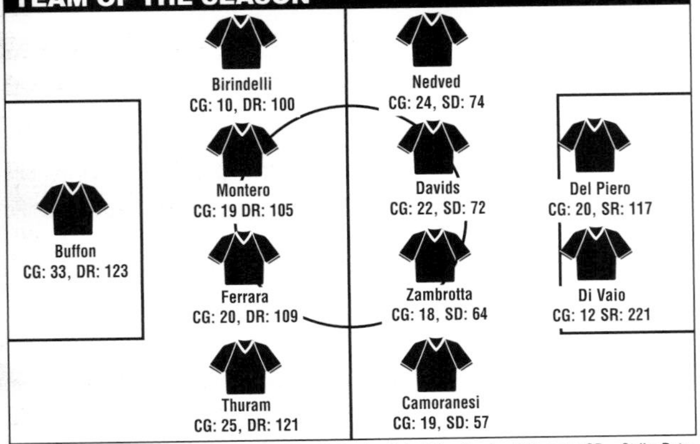
Birindelli
CG: 10, DR: 100
Nedved
CG: 24, SD: 74
Montero
CG: 19 DR: 105
Davids
CG: 22, SD: 72
Del Piero
CG: 20, SR: 117
Buffon
CG: 33, DR: 123
Ferrara
CG: 20, DR: 109
Zambrotta
CG: 18, SD: 64
Di Vaio
CG: 12 SR: 221
Thuram
CG: 25, DR: 121
Camoranesi
CG: 19, SD: 57

**KEY:** DR = Defensive Rate, SD = Scoring Difference, SR = Strike Rate, CG = Counting Games – League games playing at least 70 minutes

## LEAGUE APPEARANCES, BOOKINGS AND CAPS

| | AGE (on 01/07/03) | IN THE SQUAD | COUNTING GAMES | MINUTES ON PITCH | YELLOW CARDS | RED CARDS | THIS SEASON | HOME COUNTRY |
|---|---|---|---|---|---|---|---|---|
| **Goalkeepers** | | | | | | | | |
| Landry Bonnefoi | 19 | 2 | 0 | 0 | 0 | 0 | - | France |
| Gianluigi Buffon | 25 | 32 | 31 | 2826 | 1 | 0 | 8 | Italy (12) |
| Antonio Chimenti | 33 | 33 | 2 | 234 | 0 | 0 | - | Italy |
| Emiliano Moretti | 22 | 9 | 3 | 471 | 1 | 0 | - | Italy |
| **Defenders** | | | | | | | | |
| Davide Baiocco | 28 | 14 | 0 | 332 | 0 | 0 | - | Italy |
| Alessandro Birindelli | 28 | 30 | 10 | 1189 | 2 | 0 | 4 | Italy (12) |
| Mattia Cassani | 19 | 0 | 0 | 0 | 0 | 0 | - | Italy |
| Ciro Ferrara | 36 | 30 | 20 | 2080 | 4 | 0 | - | Italy |
| Salvatore Fresi | 30 | 18 | 4 | 448 | 0 | 0 | - | Italy |
| Daniele Gastaldello | 20 | 2 | 0 | 0 | 0 | 0 | - | Italy |
| Mark Iuliano | 29 | 25 | 17 | 1682 | 3 | 0 | 4 | Italy (12) |
| Paolo Montero | 31 | 26 | 19 | 1788 | 2 | 0 | - | Uruguay |
| Gianluca Pessotto | 32 | 24 | 8 | 863 | 1 | 0 | - | Italy |
| Lilian Thuram | 31 | 27 | 25 | 2307 | 0 | 0 | 8 | France (2) |
| Igor Tudor | 25 | 17 | 5 | 755 | 2 | 1 | 4 | Croatia (26) |
| Cristiano Zenoni | 26 | 19 | 4 | 622 | 0 | 0 | - | Italy |
| **Midfielders** | | | | | | | | |
| Mauro Camoranesi | 26 | 31 | 19 | 2116 | 7 | 0 | - | Argentina |
| Antonio Conte | 33 | 21 | 10 | 1085 | 1 | 1 | - | Italy |
| Edgar Davids | 30 | 28 | 22 | 2120 | 3 | 0 | 8 | Holland (6) |
| Pavel Nedved | 30 | 30 | 24 | 2286 | 3 | 0 | 8 | Czech Republic (13) |
| Ruben Olivera | 20 | 6 | 1 | 137 | 0 | 0 | - | Uruguay |
| Matteo Paro | 20 | 3 | 1 | 70 | 0 | 0 | - | Italy |
| Alex Pederzoli | 19 | 1 | 0 | 0 | 0 | 0 | - | Italy |
| Alessio Tacchinardi | 27 | 27 | 21 | 2032 | 3 | 0 | - | Italy |
| Gianluca Zambrotta | 26 | 29 | 18 | 1928 | 3 | 0 | 3 | Italy (12) |
| **Forwards** | | | | | | | | |
| Alessandro Del Piero | 28 | 25 | 20 | 1866 | 0 | 0 | 6 | Italy (12) |
| Marco Di Vaio | 26 | 30 | 12 | 1549 | 2 | 0 | 5 | Italy (12) |
| Marcelo Salas | 28 | 21 | 2 | 549 | 1 | 0 | - | Chile |
| Ivano Sorrentino | 20 | 0 | 0 | 0 | 0 | 0 | - | Italy |
| David Trezeguet | 25 | 18 | 10 | 1155 | 0 | 0 | 3 | France (2) |
| Marcelo Zalayeta | 24 | 30 | 8 | 1121 | 2 | 0 | - | Uruguay |

**KEY:** LEAGUE BOOKINGS CAPS (FIFA RANKING)

## SQUAD APPEARANCES

| Match | 1 | 2 | 3 | 4 | 5 | 6 | 7 | 8 | 9 | 10 |
|---|---|---|---|---|---|---|---|---|---|---|
| Venue | H | A | A | H | H | H | H | A | A | H |
| Competition | L | C | L | C | L | C | L | L | C | L |
| Result | W | D | W | W | D | W | D | D | L | W |

| Match | 11 | 12 | 13 | 14 | 15 | 16 | 17 | 18 | 19 | 20 |
|---|---|---|---|---|---|---|---|---|---|---|
| Venue | H | A | A | H | A | A | H | A | A | A |
| Competition | C | L | L | L | C | L | L | C | L | L |
| Result | W | W | W | W | W | W | D | D | D | L |

| Match | 21 | 22 | 23 | 24 | 25 | 26 | 27 | 28 | 29 | 30 |
|---|---|---|---|---|---|---|---|---|---|---|
| Venue | H | H | A | H | A | H | A | H | A | A |
| Competition | C | L | L | L | L | L | L | L | L | C |
| Result | W | L | W | W | W | W | D | W | W | L |

| Match | 31 | 32 | 33 | 34 | 35 | 36 | 37 | 38 | 39 | 40 |
|---|---|---|---|---|---|---|---|---|---|---|
| Venue | A | H | H | A | H | H | A | A | H | H |
| Competition | L | C | L | L | C | L | C | L | L | C |
| Result | W | L | W | W | W | W | L | L | W | D |

| Match | 41 | 42 | 43 | 44 | 45 | 46 | 47 | 48 | 49 | 50 | 51 |
|---|---|---|---|---|---|---|---|---|---|---|---|
| Venue | A | H | A | H | A | A | H | H | A | H | N |
| Competition | L | L | C | L | L | C | L | C | L | L | C |
| Result | D | W | W | W | D | L | D | W | L | W | L |

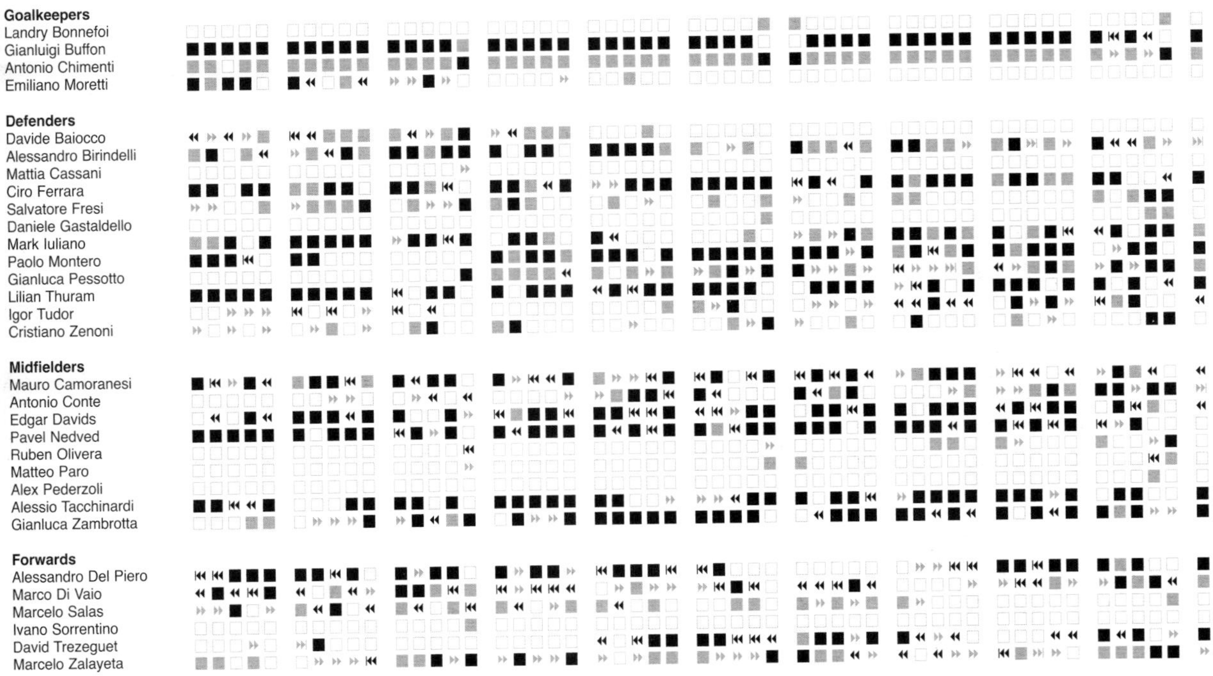
Goalkeepers
Landry Bonnefoi
Gianluigi Buffon
Antonio Chimenti
Emiliano Moretti
Defenders
Davide Baiocco
Alessandro Birindelli
Mattia Cassani
Ciro Ferrara
Salvatore Fresi
Daniele Gastaldello
Mark Iuliano
Paolo Montero
Gianluca Pessotto
Lilian Thuram
Igor Tudor
Cristiano Zenoni
Midfielders
Mauro Camoranesi
Antonio Conte
Edgar Davids
Pavel Nedved
Ruben Olivera
Matteo Paro
Alex Pederzoli
Alessio Tacchinardi
Gianluca Zambrotta
Forwards
Alessandro Del Piero
Marco Di Vaio
Marcelo Salas
Ivano Sorrentino
David Trezeguet
Marcelo Zalayeta

# INTER MILAN

Final Position: **2nd**

| | | | | | | |
|---|---|---|---|---|---|---|
| 1 | ecql1 | Sp Lisbon | A | D | 0-0 | |
| 2 | ecql2 | Sp Lisbon | H | W | 2-0 | Di Biagio 32; Recoba 45 |
| 3 | lge | Torino | H | W | 1-0 | Vieri 22 |
| 4 | ecgd | Rosenborg BK | A | D | 2-2 | Crespo 33,79 |
| 5 | lge | Reggina | A | W | 2-1 | Vieri 6; Recoba 90 |
| 6 | ecgd | Ajax | H | W | 1-0 | Crespo 75 |
| 7 | lge | Chievo | H | W | 2-1 | Vieri 15,77 pen |
| 8 | ecgd | Lyon | H | L | 1-2 | Cannavaro 73 |
| 9 | lge | Piacenza | A | W | 4-1 | Di Biagio 35,50; Recoba 68; Crespo 85 |
| 10 | lge | Juventus | H | D | 1-1 | Vieri 90 |
| 11 | ecgd | Lyon | A | D | 3-3 | Cacapa 31 og; Crespo 56,66 |
| 12 | lge | Bologna | H | W | 2-0 | Materazzi 66; Vieri 90 |
| 13 | ecgd | Rosenborg BK | H | W | 3-0 | Recoba 31; Saarinen 52 og; Crespo 72 |
| 14 | lge | Como | A | W | 2-0 | Vieri 59; Recoba 66 |
| 15 | lge | Empoli | A | W | 4-3 | Crespo 5; Zanetti, J 11; Recoba 50; Adani 85 |
| 16 | lge | Udinese | H | L | 1-2 | Vieri 3 |
| 17 | ecgd | Ajax | A | W | 2-1 | Crespo 48,50 |
| 18 | lge | Roma | A | D | 2-2 | Morfeo 58; Okan 89 |
| 19 | lge | AC Milan | A | L | 0-1 | |
| 20 | ecga | Newcastle | A | W | 4-1 | Morfeo 2; Almeyda 35; Crespo 45; Recoba 81 |
| 21 | lge | Brescia | H | W | 4-0 | Vieri 3,12,57,82 |
| 22 | lge | Lazio | A | D | 3-3 | Couto 38 og; Emre 67,76 |
| 23 | ecga | B Leverkusen | H | W | 3-2 | Di Biagio 15,27; Crespo 80 |
| 24 | lge | Atalanta | H | W | 1-0 | Kallon 71 |
| 25 | lge | Parma | A | W | 2-1 | Di Biagio 37; Recoba 75 pen |
| 26 | lge | Modena | H | W | 2-0 | Recoba 6; Crespo 22 |
| 27 | lge | Perugia | A | L | 1-4 | Vieri 79 pen |
| 28 | lge | Empoli | H | W | 3-0 | Vieri 70,73,85 |
| 29 | lge | Torino | A | W | 2-0 | Vieri 47; Okan 57 |
| 30 | lge | Reggina | H | W | 3-0 | Vieri 10; Kallon 39,42 |
| 31 | lge | Chievo | A | L | 1-2 | Vieri 70 |
| 32 | ecga | Barcelona | A | L | 0-3 | |
| 33 | lge | Piacenza | H | W | 3-1 | Batistuta 64; Vieri 66,68 |
| 34 | ecga | Barcelona | H | D | 0-0 | |
| 35 | lge | Juventus | A | L | 0-3 | |
| 36 | lge | Bologna | A | W | 2-1 | Recoba 9,40 |
| 37 | ecga | Newcastle | H | D | 2-2 | Vieri 47; Cordoba 61 |
| 38 | lge | Como | H | W | 4-0 | Batistuta 14; Di Biagio 25; Vieri 55,76 |
| 39 | ecga | B Leverkusen | A | W | 2-0 | Martins 36; Emre 89 |
| 40 | lge | Udinese | A | L | 1-2 | Cordoba 73 |
| 41 | lge | Roma | H | D | 3-3 | Vieri 52; Recoba 59; Emre 77 |
| 42 | ecqfl1 | Valencia | H | W | 1-0 | Vieri 14 |
| 43 | lge | AC Milan | H | L | 0-1 | |
| 44 | lge | Brescia | A | W | 1-0 | Crespo 90 |
| 45 | ecqfl2 | Valencia | A | L | 1-2 | Vieri 5 |
| 46 | lge | Lazio | H | D | 1-1 | Crespo 43 |
| 47 | lge | Atalanta | A | D | 1-1 | Martins 13 |
| 48 | ecsfl1 | AC Milan | A | D | 0-0 | |
| 49 | lge | Parma | H | D | 1-1 | Kallon 37 |
| 50 | ecsfl2 | AC Milan | H | D | 1-1 | Martins 84 |
| 51 | lge | Modena | A | W | 2-0 | Pavan 29 og; Kallon 35 |
| 52 | lge | Perugia | H | D | 2-2 | Crespo 10,56 |

## ATTENDANCES

HOME GROUND: SAN SIRO CAPACITY: 85700 AVERAGE LEAGUE AT HOME: 58866

| | | | | | | | | |
|---|---|---|---|---|---|---|---|---|
| 50 | AC Milan | 83679 | 33 | Piacenza | 56000 | 40 | Udinese | 32000 |
| 32 | Barcelona | 82717 | 24 | Atalanta | 55000 | 26 | Modena | 32000 |
| 22 | Lazio | 80000 | 21 | Brescia | 55000 | 8 | Lyon | 31448 |
| 48 | AC Milan | 78175 | 18 | Roma | 55000 | 15 | Empoli | 30000 |
| 43 | AC Milan | 78000 | 37 | Newcastle | 53459 | 47 | Atalanta | 30000 |
| 10 | Juventus | 76166 | 42 | Valencia | 52623 | 49 | Parma | 30000 |
| 19 | AC Milan | 75000 | 17 | Ajax | 50272 | 5 | Reggina | 30000 |
| 46 | Lazio | 75000 | 20 | Newcastle | 50108 | 25 | Parma | 26000 |
| 34 | Barcelona | 71740 | 2 | Sp Lisbon | 50000 | 1 | Sp Lisbon | 25650 |
| 41 | Roma | 70000 | 45 | Valencia | 49290 | 29 | Torino | 25000 |
| 3 | Torino | 65000 | 6 | Ajax | 45748 | 44 | Brescia | 23000 |
| 30 | Reggina | 65000 | 52 | Perugia | 45000 | 4 | Rosenborg BK | 21040 |
| 38 | Como | 60000 | 39 | B Leverkusen | 43000 | 27 | Perugia | 20000 |
| 7 | Chievo | 60000 | 23 | B Leverkusen | 40000 | 9 | Piacenza | 17000 |
| 12 | Bologna | 60000 | 11 | Lyon | 40000 | 51 | Modena | 15000 |
| 28 | Empoli | 59600 | 36 | Bologna | 35000 | 14 | Como | 14000 |
| 16 | Udinese | 58962 | 31 | Chievo | 34634 | | | |
| 35 | Juventus | 57393 | 13 | Rosenborg BK | 33686 | | | |

Home / Away / Neutral

## KEY PLAYERS - GOALSCORERS

**1 Christian Vieri**

| | | | |
|---|---|---|---|
| Goals in the League | 24 | Player Strike Rate<br>Average number of minutes between League goals scored by player | 78 |
| Contribution to Attacking Power<br>Average number of minutes between League team goals while on pitch | 49 | Club Strike Rate<br>Average number of minutes between League goals scored by club | 48 |

| | PLAYER | LGE GOALS | POWER | STRIKE RATE |
|---|---|---|---|---|
| 2 | Hernan Crespo | 7 | 40 | 187 mins |
| 3 | Alvaro Recoba | 9 | 48 | 231 mins |
| 4 | Luigi Di Biagio | 4 | 54 | 425 mins |
| 5 | Belozoglu Emre | 3 | 43 | 657 mins |

## KEY PLAYERS - MIDFIELDERS

**1 Matias Almeyda**

| | | | |
|---|---|---|---|
| Goals in the League | 0 | Contribution to Attacking Power<br>Average number of minutes between League team goals while on pitch | 45 |
| Defensive Rating<br>Average number of mins between League goals conceded while he was on the pitch | 90 | Scoring Difference<br>Defensive Rating minus Contribution to Attacking Power | 45 |

| | PLAYER | LGE GOALS | DEF RATE | POWER | SCORE DIFF |
|---|---|---|---|---|---|
| 2 | Cristiano Zanetti | 0 | 87 | 50 | 37 mins |
| 3 | Javier Zanetti | 1 | 78 | 46 | 32 mins |
| 4 | Emre Belozoglu | 3 | 73 | 44 | 29 mins |
| 5 | Francesco Coco | 0 | 71 | 50 | 21 mins |

## KEY PLAYERS - DEFENDERS

**1 Giovanni Pasquale**

| | | | |
|---|---|---|---|
| Goals Conceded (GC)<br>The number of League goals conceded while he was on the pitch | 13 | Clean Sheets<br>In games when he played at least 70 minutes | 6 |
| Defensive Rating<br>Ave number of mins between League goals conceded while on the pitch | 97 | Club Defensive Rating<br>Average number of mins between League goals conceded by the club this season | 78 |

| | PLAYER | CON LGE | CLEAN SHEETS | DEF RATE |
|---|---|---|---|---|
| 2 | Marco Materazzi | 17 | 6 | 88 mins |
| 3 | Fabio Cannavaro | 30 | 9 | 81 mins |
| 4 | Ivan Cordoba | 36 | 8 | 67 mins |

## KEY GOALKEEPER

**1 Francesco Toldo**

| | |
|---|---|
| Goals Conceded in the League | 38 |
| Defensive Rating<br>Ave number of mins between League goals conceded while on the pitch | 76 |
| Counting Games<br>Games when he played at least 70 minutes | 32 |
| Clean Sheets<br>In games when he played at least 70 minutes | 11 |

## TOP POINT EARNERS

| | PLAYER | GAMES | AVE |
|---|---|---|---|
| 1 | Pasquale | 12 | 2.08 |
| 2 | Zanetti, J | 31 | 2.03 |
| 3 | Crespo | 12 | 2.00 |
| 4 | Materazzi | 16 | 1.94 |
| 5 | Cannavaro | 26 | 1.92 |
| 6 | Emre Belozoglu | 20 | 1.90 |
| 7 | Recoba | 21 | 1.86 |
| 8 | Di Biagio | 14 | 1.86 |
| 9 | Toldo | 32 | 1.84 |
| 10 | Cordoba | 26 | 1.77 |
| | CLUB AVERAGE: | | 1.91 |

Ave = Average points per match in Counting Games

## DISCIPLINARY RECORDS

| | PLAYER | YELLOW | RED | AVE |
|---|---|---|---|---|
| 1 | Di Biagio | 9 | 1 | 169 |
| 2 | Conceicao | 5 | 1 | 202 |
| 3 | Zanetti, C | 5 | 1 | 218 |
| 4 | Morfeo | 3 | 1 | 236 |
| 5 | Cordoba | 9 | 1 | 242 |
| 6 | Okan | 2 | 1 | 270 |
| 7 | Pasquale | 4 | 0 | 316 |
| 8 | Gamarra | 2 | 0 | 383 |
| 9 | Emre Belozoglu | 4 | 0 | 492 |
| 10 | Kallon | 1 | 0 | 535 |
| 11 | Cannavaro | 4 | 0 | 606 |
| 12 | Vieri | 2 | 1 | 625 |
| 13 | Dalmat | 1 | 0 | 849 |
| | Other | 11 | 0 | |
| | TOTAL | 62 | 7 | |

## LEAGUE GOALS

| | PLAYER | MINS | GOALS | AVE |
|---|---|---|---|---|
| 1 | Vieri | 1877 | 24 | 78 |
| 2 | Recoba | 2078 | 9 | 231 |
| 3 | Crespo | 1308 | 7 | 187 |
| 4 | Kallon | 535 | 5 | 107 |
| 5 | Di Biagio | 1698 | 4 | 425 |
| 6 | Emre Belozoglu | 1971 | 3 | 657 |
| 7 | Okan | 810 | 2 | 405 |
| 8 | Batistuta | 859 | 2 | 430 |
| 9 | Martins | 249 | 1 | 249 |
| 10 | Cordoba | 2429 | 1 | 2429 |
| 11 | Adani | 334 | 1 | 334 |
| 12 | Materazzi | 1489 | 1 | 1489 |
| 13 | Zanetti, J | 2880 | 1 | 2880 |
| | Other | | 3 | |
| | TOTAL | | 64 | |

## MONTH BY MONTH GUIDE TO THE POINTS

| Month | Points | % |
|---|---|---|
| SEPTEMBER | 9 | 100% |
| OCTOBER | 7 | 78% |
| NOVEMBER | 7 | 47% |
| DECEMBER | 10 | 83% |
| JANUARY | 6 | 67% |
| FEBRUARY | 9 | 75% |
| MARCH | 6 | 50% |
| APRIL | 5 | 42% |
| MAY | 6 | 50% |

## TEAM OF THE SEASON

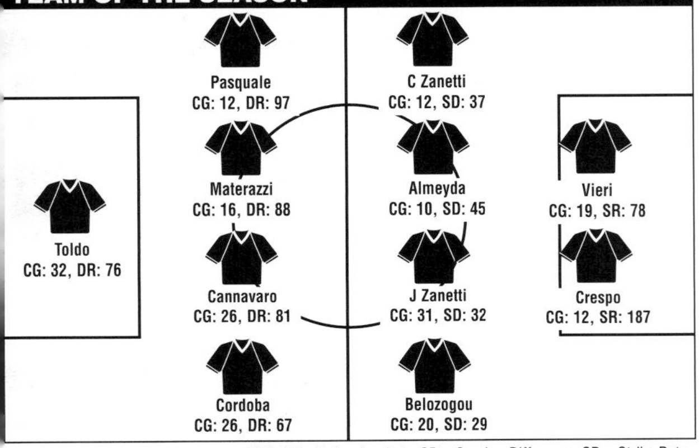
Pasquale
CG: 12, DR: 97
C Zanetti
CG: 12, SD: 37
Materazzi
CG: 16, DR: 88
Almeyda
CG: 10, SD: 45
Vieri
CG: 19, SR: 78
Toldo
CG: 32, DR: 76
Cannavaro
CG: 26, DR: 81
J Zanetti
CG: 31, SD: 32
Crespo
CG: 12, SR: 187
Cordoba
CG: 26, DR: 67
Belozogou
CG: 20, SD: 29

**KEY:** DR = Defensive Rate, SD = Scoring Difference, SR = Strike Rate, CG = Counting Games – League games playing at least 70 minutes

## LEAGUE APPEARANCES, BOOKINGS AND CAPS

| | AGE | IN THE SQUAD | COUNTING GAMES | MINUTES ON PITCH | YELLOW CARDS | RED CARDS | THIS SEASON | HOME COUNTRY |
|---|---|---|---|---|---|---|---|---|
| **Goalkeepers** | | | | | | | | |
| Alberto Fontana | 36 | 32 | 2 | 180 | 0 | 0 | - | Italy |
| Mathieu Moreau | 20 | 3 | 0 | 0 | 0 | 0 | - | France |
| Enrico Rossi | 19 | 1 | 0 | 0 | 0 | 0 | - | Italy |
| Francesco Toldo | 31 | 32 | 32 | 2880 | 1 | 0 | 5 | Italy (12) |
| **Defenders** | | | | | | | | |
| Daniele Adani | 28 | 14 | 2 | 334 | 0 | 0 | 2 | Italy (12) |
| Fabio Cannavaro | 29 | 29 | 26 | 2425 | 4 | 0 | 9 | Italy (12) |
| Ivan Cordoba | 26 | 30 | 26 | 2429 | 9 | 1 | - | Colombia |
| Luca Franchini | 19 | 4 | 0 | 45 | 0 | 0 | - | Italy |
| Carlos Gamarra | 32 | 20 | 7 | 766 | 2 | 0 | 2 | Paraguay (19) |
| Marco Materazzi | 29 | 25 | 16 | 1489 | 1 | 0 | 2 | Italy (12) |
| Giovanni Pasquale | 21 | 33 | 12 | 1267 | 4 | 0 | 1 | Italy (12) |
| Nelson Vivas | 33 | 18 | 1 | 239 | 2 | 0 | - | Argentina |
| **Midfielders** | | | | | | | | |
| Matias Almeyda | 29 | 17 | 10 | 1078 | 1 | 0 | 1 | Argentina (5) |
| Nicola Beati | 20 | 12 | 0 | 34 | 0 | 0 | - | Italy |
| Francesco Coco | 26 | 21 | 12 | 1354 | 1 | 0 | 2 | Italy (12) |
| Sergio Conceicao | 28 | 25 | 12 | 1217 | 5 | 1 | 9 | Portugal (14) |
| Stephane Dalmat | 24 | 17 | 8 | 849 | 1 | 0 | - | France |
| Luigi Di Biagio | 32 | 27 | 14 | 1698 | 9 | 1 | 4 | Italy (12) |
| Emre Belozoglu | 22 | 25 | 20 | 1971 | 4 | 0 | 7 | Turkey (8) |
| Francisco Zampata | 25 | 3 | 1 | 82 | 0 | 0 | - | Spain |
| A Guglielminpietro | 29 | 14 | 0 | 220 | 0 | 0 | - | Argentina |
| Domenico Morfeo | 27 | 21 | 7 | 944 | 3 | 1 | - | Italy |
| Nicola Napolitano | 20 | 5 | 0 | 75 | 0 | 0 | - | Italy |
| Buruk Okan | 29 | 23 | 7 | 810 | 2 | 1 | 10 | Turkey (8) |
| Cristiano Zanetti | 26 | 18 | 12 | 1309 | 5 | 1 | 4 | Italy (12) |
| Javier Zanetti | 29 | 33 | 31 | 2880 | 2 | 0 | 4 | Argentina (5) |
| **Forwards** | | | | | | | | |
| Mattia Altobelli | 19 | 0 | 0 | 0 | 0 | 0 | - | Italy |
| Gabriel Batistuta | 34 | 12 | 9 | 859 | 0 | 0 | - | Argentina |
| Bernardo Corradi | 27 | 0 | 0 | 0 | 0 | 0 | 5 | Italy (12) |
| Hernan Crespo | 28 | 22 | 12 | 1308 | 1 | 0 | 1 | Argentina (5) |
| Mohammed Kallon | 23 | 14 | 4 | 535 | 1 | 0 | - | Sierra Leone |
| Obafemi Martins | 18 | 10 | 2 | 249 | 0 | 0 | - | Nigeria |
| Alvaro Recoba | 27 | 29 | 21 | 2078 | 2 | 0 | 2 | Uruguay (28) |
| Nicola Ventola | 25 | 1 | 0 | 0 | 0 | 0 | - | Italy |
| Christian Vieri | 29 | 23 | 19 | 1877 | 2 | 1 | 3 | Italy (12) |

**KEY:** LEAGUE — BOOKINGS — CAPS (FIFA RANKING)

## SQUAD APPEARANCES

| Match | 1 | 2 | 3 | 4 | 5 | 6 | 7 | 8 | 9 | 10 | 11 | 12 | 13 | 14 | 15 | 16 | 17 | 18 | 19 | 20 | 21 | 22 | 23 | 24 | 25 | 26 | 27 | 28 | 29 | 30 | 31 | 32 | 33 | 34 | 35 | 36 | 37 | 38 | 39 | 40 | 41 | 42 | 43 | 44 | 45 | 46 | 47 | 48 | 49 | 50 | 51 | 52 |
|---|---|---|---|---|---|---|---|---|---|---|---|---|---|---|---|---|---|---|---|---|---|---|---|---|---|---|---|---|---|---|---|---|---|---|---|---|---|---|---|---|---|---|---|---|---|---|---|---|---|---|---|---|
| Venue | A | H | H | A | A | H | H | H | A | H | A | H | H | A | A | H | A | A | A | A | H | A | H | H | A | H | A | H | A | H | A | A | H | H | A | A | H | H | A | A | H | H | H | A | A | H | A | A | H | H | A | H |
| Competition | C | C | L | C | L | C | L | C | L | L | C | L | C | L | L | L | C | L | L | C | L | L | C | L | L | L | L | L | L | L | L | C | L | C | L | L | C | L | C | L | L | C | L | L | C | L | L | C | L | C | L | L |
| Result | D | W | W | D | W | W | W | L | W | D | D | W | W | W | W | L | W | D | L | W | W | D | W | W | W | W | L | W | W | W | L | L | W | D | L | W | D | W | W | L | D | W | L | W | L | D | D | D | D | D | W | D |

**Goalkeepers**
Alberto Fontana
Mathieu Moreau
Chauvenet Enrico Rossi
Francesco Toldo

**Defenders**
Daniele Adani
Fabio Cannavaro
Ivan Cordoba
Luca Franchini
Carlos Alberto Gamarra
Marco Materazzi
Giovanni Pasquale
Nelson Vivas

**Midfielders**
Matias Almeyda
Nicola Beati
Francesco Coco
Sergio Conceicao
Stephane Dalmat
Luigi Di Biagio
Emre Belozoglu
Francisco Zampata Farin
Andreas Guglielminpietro
Domenico Morfeo
Nicola Napolitano
Buruk Okan
Cristiano Zanetti
Javier Zanetti

**Forwards**
Mattia Altobelli
Gabriel Batistuta
Bernardo Corradi
Hernan Crespo
Mohammed Kallon
Obafemi Martins
Alvaro Recoba
Nicola Ventola
Christian Vieri

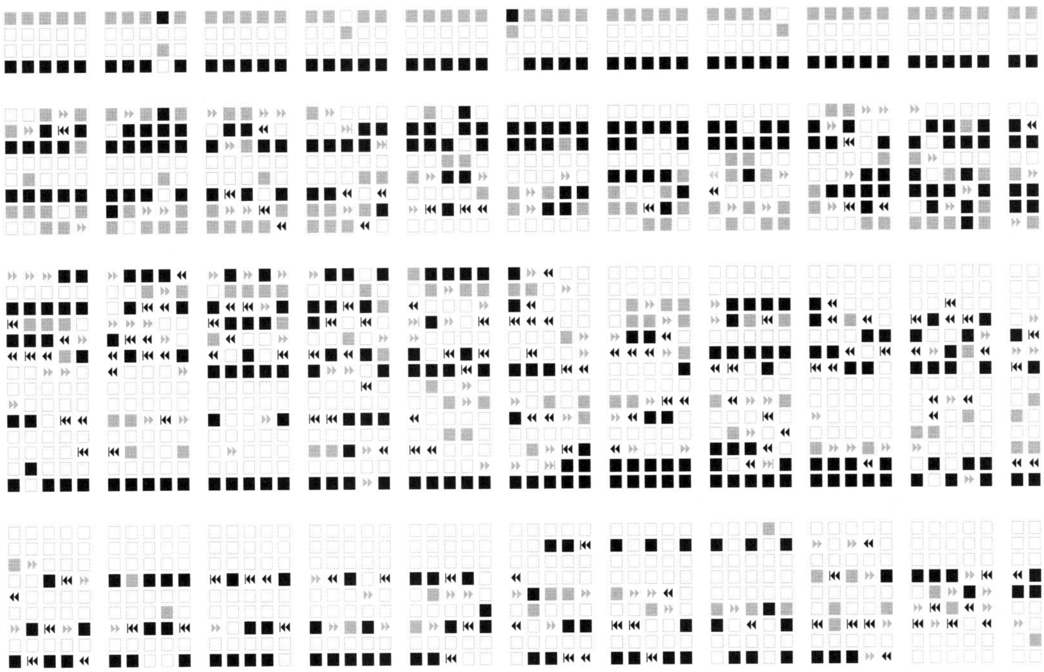

# AC MILAN

Final Position: **3rd**

| | | | | | | |
|---|---|---|---|---|---|---|
| 1 | ecql1 | S Liberec | H | W | 1-0 | Inzaghi 68 |
| 2 | ecql2 | Slovan Liberec | A | L | 1-2 | Inzaghi 20 |
| 3 | lge | Modena | A | W | 3-0 | Inzaghi 17,90; Simic 54 |
| 4 | ecgg | Lens | H | W | 2-1 | Inzaghi 57,61 |
| 5 | lge | Perugia | H | W | 3-0 | Maldini 40; Inzaghi 49; Seedorf 65 |
| 6 | ecgg | Deportivo | A | W | 4-0 | Seedorf 17; Inzaghi 33,55,62 |
| 7 | lge | Lazio | A | D | 1-1 | Maldini 7 |
| 8 | ecgg | B Munich | A | W | 2-1 | Inzaghi 52,84 |
| 9 | lge | Torino | H | W | 6-0 | Pirlo 21 pen; Inzaghi 31,79,86; Serginho 41; Fattori 84 og |
| 10 | lge | Atalanta | A | W | 4-1 | Rivaldo 15; Tomasson 40; Pirlo 66 pen,79 |
| 11 | ecgg | B Munich | H | W | 2-1 | Serginho 11; Inzaghi 64 |
| 12 | lge | Chievo | A | L | 2-3 | Shevchenko 60; Tomasson 90 |
| 13 | ecgg | Lens | A | L | 1-2 | Shevchenko 31 |
| 14 | lge | Reggina | H | W | 2-0 | Inzaghi 20; Rivaldo 64 |
| 15 | lge | Udinese | H | W | 1-0 | Rivaldo 89 |
| 16 | lge | Juventus | A | L | 1-2 | Pirlo 31 pen |
| 17 | ecgg | Deportivo | H | L | 1-2 | Tomasson 34 |
| 18 | lge | Parma | H | W | 2-1 | Pirlo 47 pen,69 pen |
| 19 | lge | Inter Milan | H | W | 1-0 | Serginho 13 |
| 20 | ecgc | Real Madrid | H | W | 1-0 | Shevchenko 40 |
| 21 | lge | Empoli | A | D | 1-1 | Shevchenko 51 |
| 22 | lge | Roma | H | W | 1-0 | Inzaghi 73 |
| 23 | ecgc | B Dortmund | A | W | 1-0 | Inzaghi 49 |
| 24 | lge | Como | A | W | 2-1 | Ambrosini 19; Shevchenko 42 |
| 25 | lge | Brescia | H | D | 0-0 | |
| 26 | lge | Bologna | A | W | 2-0 | Shevchenko 51; Serginho 78 |
| 27 | lge | Piacenza | H | W | 2-1 | Pirlo 54 pen; Rivaldo 69 |
| 28 | lge | Udinese | A | L | 0-1 | |
| 29 | lge | Modena | H | W | 2-1 | Pirlo 77 pen; Inzaghi 80 |
| 30 | lge | Perugia | A | L | 0-1 | |
| 31 | lge | Lazio | H | D | 2-2 | Inzaghi 62; Rivaldo 70 |
| 32 | ecgc | Lokomotiv M | H | W | 1-0 | Tomasson 62 |
| 33 | lge | Torino | A | W | 3-0 | Inzaghi 2; Seedorf 43,45 |
| 34 | ecgc | Lokomotiv M | A | W | 1-0 | Rivaldo 34 |
| 35 | lge | Atalanta | H | D | 3-3 | Inzaghi 34,79; Tomasson 70 |
| 36 | lge | Chievo | H | D | 0-0 | |
| 37 | ecgc | Real Madrid | A | L | 1-3 | Rivaldo 81 |
| 38 | lge | Reggina | A | D | 0-0 | |
| 39 | ecgc | B Dortmund | H | L | 0-1 | |
| 40 | lge | Juventus | H | W | 2-1 | Shevchenko 4; Inzaghi 25 |
| 41 | lge | Parma | A | L | 0-1 | |
| 42 | ecqfl1 | Ajax | A | D | 0-0 | |
| 43 | lge | Inter Milan | A | W | 1-0 | Inzaghi 63 |
| 44 | lge | Empoli | H | L | 0-1 | |
| 45 | ecqfl2 | Ajax | H | W | 3-2 | Inzaghi 30; Shevchenko 65; Tomasson 90 |
| 46 | lge | Roma | A | L | 1-2 | Tomasson 81 |
| 47 | lge | Como | H | W | 2-0 | Inzaghi 11 pen; Nesta 59 |
| 48 | ecsfl1 | Inter Milan | H | D | 0-0 | |
| 49 | lge | Brescia | A | L | 0-1 | |
| 50 | ecsfl2 | Inter Milan | A | D | 1-1 | Shevchenko 45 |
| 51 | lge | Bologna | H | W | 3-1 | Pirlo 23 pen; Seedorf 51; Inzaghi 67 |
| 52 | lge | Piacenza | A | L | 2-4 | Brocchi 30 pen,90 |
| 53 | ecfin | Juventus | N | W | 3-2* | (*on penalties) |

## ATTENDANCES

HOME GROUND: SAN SIRO CAPACITY: 85700 AVERAGE LEAGUE AT HOME: 57051

| | | | | | | | | |
|---|---|---|---|---|---|---|---|---|
| 50 | Inter Milan | 83679 | 9 | Torino | 60000 | 47 | Como | 35000 |
| 40 | Juventus | 78871 | 18 | Parma | 60000 | 6 | Deportivo | 32000 |
| 48 | Inter Milan | 78175 | 8 | Bayern Munich | 59000 | 12 | Chievo | 30000 |
| 37 | Real Madrid | 78000 | 17 | Deportivo | 56294 | 38 | Reggina | 26000 |
| 43 | Inter Milan | 78000 | 25 | Brescia | 55000 | 41 | Parma | 25603 |
| 45 | Ajax | 76079 | 7 | Lazio | 55000 | 33 | Torino | 22000 |
| 20 | Real Madrid | 75777 | 44 | Empoli | 55000 | 49 | Brescia | 20000 |
| 19 | Inter Milan | 75000 | 23 | B Dortmund | 52000 | 30 | Perugia | 20000 |
| 32 | Lokomotiv Moscow | 72028 | 42 | Ajax | 50967 | 10 | Atalanta | 20000 |
| 22 | Roma | 72000 | 51 | Bologna | 50000 | 34 | Lokomotiv Moscow | 20000 |
| 4 | Lens | 70259 | 29 | Modena | 50000 | 21 | Empoli | 17600 |
| 11 | Bayern Munich | 70000 | 27 | Piacenza | 50000 | 3 | Modena | 17300 |
| 14 | Reggina | 66000 | 36 | Chievo | 48000 | 24 | Como | 14000 |
| 16 | Juventus | 65000 | 39 | B Dortmund | 45000 | 28 | Udinese | 14000 |
| 31 | Lazio | 65000 | 15 | Udinese | 45000 | 1 | Slovan Liberec | 12000 |
| 53 | Juventus | 63215 | 5 | Perugia | 45000 | 2 | Slovan Liberec | 9090 |
| 35 | Atalanta | 60000 | 13 | Lens | 40000 | 52 | Piacenza | 6100 |
| 46 | Roma | 60000 | 26 | Bologna | 37000 | | | |

■ Home □ Away ▒ Neutral

## KEY PLAYERS - GOALSCORERS

**1 Filippo Inzaghi**

| | | | |
|---|---|---|---|
| Goals in the League | 17 | Player Strike Rate<br>Average number of minutes between League goals scored by player | 143 |
| Contribution to Attacking Power<br>Average number of minutes between League team goals while on pitch | 51 | Club Strike Rate<br>Average number of minutes between League goals scored by club | 56 |

| | PLAYER | LGE GOALS | POWER | STRIKE RATE |
|---|---|---|---|---|
| 2 | Andrea Pirlo | 9 | 50 | 209 mins |
| 3 | Vitor Barbosa Ferreira Rivaldo | 5 | 52 | 303 mins |
| 4 | Andriy Shevchenko | 5 | 79 | 319 mins |
| 5 | Clarence Seedorf | 4 | 53 | 573 mins |

## KEY PLAYERS - MIDFIELDERS

**1 Gennaro Gattuso**

| | | | |
|---|---|---|---|
| Goals in the League | 0 | Contribution to Attacking Power<br>Average number of minutes between League team goals while on pitch | 58 |
| Defensive Rating<br>Average number of mins between League goals conceded while he was on the pitch | 143 | Scoring Difference<br>Defensive Rating minus Contribution to Attacking Power | 85 |

| | PLAYER | LGE GOALS | DEF RATE | POWER | SCORE DIFF |
|---|---|---|---|---|---|
| 2 | Manuel Rui Costa | 0 | 113 | 56 | 57 mins |
| 3 | Andrea Pirlo | 9 | 105 | 51 | 54 mins |
| 4 | Clarence Seedorf | 4 | 104 | 53 | 51 mins |
| 5 | Massimo Ambrosini | 1 | 109 | 73 | 36 mins |

## KEY PLAYERS - DEFENDERS

**1 Dario Simic**

| | | | |
|---|---|---|---|
| Goals Conceded (GC)<br>The number of League goals conceded while he was on the pitch | 16 | Clean Sheets<br>In games when he played at least 70 minutes | 14 |
| Defensive Rating<br>Ave number of mins between League goals conceded while on the pitch | 149 | Club Defensive Rating<br>Average number of mins between League goals conceded by the club this season | 102 |

| | PLAYER | CON LGE | CLEAN SHEETS | DEF RATE |
|---|---|---|---|---|
| 2 | Alessandro Costacurta | 11 | 5 | 116 mins |
| 3 | Alessandro Nesta | 22 | 12 | 114 mins |
| 4 | Paolo Maldini | 22 | 12 | 114 mins |
| 5 | Kakha Kaladze | 20 | 9 | 103 mins |

## KEY GOALKEEPER

**1 Nelson Dida**

| | |
|---|---|
| Goals Conceded in the League | 23 |
| Defensive Rating<br>Ave number of mins between League goals conceded while on the pitch | 117 |
| Counting Games<br>Games when he played at least 70 minutes | 30 |
| Clean Sheets<br>In games when he played at least 70 minutes | 13 |

## TOP POINT EARNERS

| | PLAYER | GAMES | AVE |
|---|---|---|---|
| 1 | Gattuso | 19 | 2.26 |
| 2 | Kaladze | 20 | 2.20 |
| 3 | Pirlo | 16 | 2.19 |
| 4 | Shevchenko | 15 | 2.07 |
| 5 | Simic | 23 | 2.04 |
| 6 | Seedorf | 24 | 2.00 |
| 7 | Rivaldo | 14 | 1.93 |
| 8 | Inzaghi | 25 | 1.92 |
| 9 | Costacurta | 13 | 1.92 |
| 10 | Maldini | 27 | 1.89 |
| | CLUB AVERAGE: | | 1.79 |

Ave = Average points per match in Counting Games

## DISCIPLINARY RECORDS

| | PLAYER | YELLOW | RED | AVE |
|---|---|---|---|---|
| 1 | Pirlo | 5 | 1 | 313 |
| 2 | Brocchi | 2 | 0 | 332 |
| 3 | Gattuso | 5 | 0 | 371 |
| 4 | Nesta | 5 | 0 | 501 |
| 5 | Ambrosini | 2 | 1 | 510 |
| 6 | Laursen | 1 | 0 | 539 |
| 7 | Simic | 4 | 0 | 596 |
| 8 | Maldini | 4 | 0 | 628 |
| 9 | Kaladze | 3 | 0 | 686 |
| 10 | Rui Costa | 2 | 0 | 958 |
| 11 | Serginho | 1 | 0 | 984 |
| 12 | Inzaghi | 2 | 0 | 1212 |
| 13 | Costacurta | 1 | 0 | 1277 |
| | Other | 7 | 0 | |
| | TOTAL | 44 | 2 | |

## LEAGUE GOALS

| | PLAYER | MINS | GOALS | AVE |
|---|---|---|---|---|
| 1 | Inzaghi | 2424 | 17 | 143 |
| 2 | Pirlo | 1881 | 9 | 209 |
| 3 | Shevchenko | 1593 | 5 | 319 |
| 4 | Rivaldo | 1514 | 5 | 303 |
| 5 | Tomasson | 787 | 4 | 197 |
| 6 | Seedorf | 2290 | 4 | 573 |
| 7 | Serginho | 984 | 3 | 328 |
| 8 | Brocchi | 665 | 2 | 333 |
| 9 | Maldini | 2514 | 2 | 1257 |
| 10 | Simic | 2387 | 1 | 2387 |
| 11 | Nesta | 2507 | 1 | 2507 |
| 12 | Ambrosini | 1531 | 1 | 1531 |
| | Other | | 1 | |
| | TOTAL | | 55 | |

## MONTH BY MONTH GUIDE TO THE POINTS

| | | |
|---|---|---|
| SEPTEMBER | 7 | 78% |
| OCTOBER | 6 | 67% |
| NOVEMBER | 12 | 80% |
| DECEMBER | 8 | 67% |
| JANUARY | 6 | 67% |
| FEBRUARY | 7 | 58% |
| MARCH | 6 | 50% |
| APRIL | 3 | 25% |
| MAY | 6 | 50% |

## TEAM OF THE SEASON

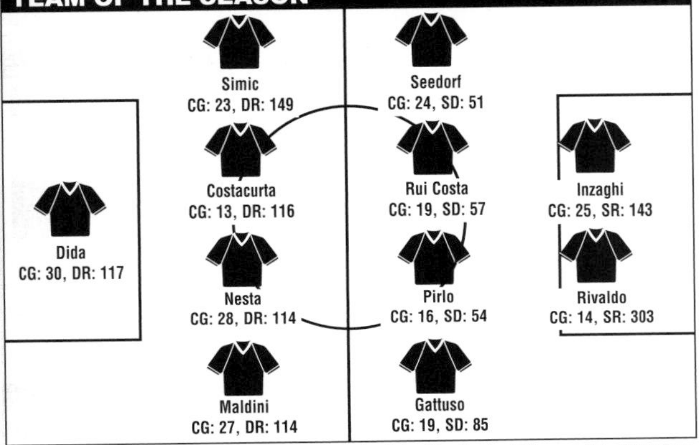
Simic
CG: 23, DR: 149
Seedorf
CG: 24, SD: 51
Costacurta
CG: 13, DR: 116
Rui Costa
CG: 19, SD: 57
Inzaghi
CG: 25, SR: 143
Dida
CG: 30, DR: 117
Nesta
CG: 28, DR: 114
Pirlo
CG: 16, SD: 54
Rivaldo
CG: 14, SR: 303
Maldini
CG: 27, DR: 114
Gattuso
CG: 19, SD: 85

**KEY:** DR = Defensive Rate, SD = Scoring Difference, SR = Strike Rate, CG = Counting Games – League games playing at least 70 minutes

## LEAGUE APPEARANCES, BOOKINGS AND CAPS

| | AGE | IN THE SQUAD | COUNTING GAMES | MINUTES ON PITCH | YELLOW CARDS | RED CARDS | THIS SEASON | HOME COUNTRY |
|---|---|---|---|---|---|---|---|---|
| **Goalkeepers** | | | | | | | | |
| Christian Abbiati | 25 | 30 | 3 | 270 | 0 | 0 | 5 | Italy (12) |
| Simone Brunelli | 20 | 1 | 0 | 0 | 0 | 0 | - | Italy |
| Nelson Dida | 29 | 30 | 30 | 2700 | 0 | 0 | 5 | Brazil (1) |
| Valerio Fiori | 34 | 6 | 1 | 90 | 0 | 0 | - | Italy |
| **Defenders** | | | | | | | | |
| Jose Antonio Chamot | 34 | 6 | 1 | 88 | 0 | 0 | - | Argentina |
| Dos Santos Clayton | 18 | 1 | 0 | 0 | 0 | 0 | - | Brazil |
| Cosmin Contra | 27 | 0 | 0 | 0 | 0 | 0 | 9 | Romania (27) |
| Alessandro Costacurta | 37 | 24 | 13 | 1277 | 1 | 0 | - | Italy |
| Matteo Giordano | 18 | 1 | 0 | 0 | 0 | 0 | - | Italy |
| Kakha Kaladze | 25 | 27 | 20 | 2058 | 3 | 0 | - | Georgia |
| Martin Laursen | 25 | 25 | 4 | 539 | 1 | 0 | 7 | Denmark (10) |
| Paolo Maldini | 35 | 29 | 27 | 2514 | 4 | 0 | - | Italy |
| Alessandro Nesta | 27 | 29 | 28 | 2507 | 5 | 0 | 7 | Italy (12) |
| Jose Roque Junior | 26 | 6 | 2 | 231 | 2 | 0 | - | Brazil |
| Dario Simic | 27 | 32 | 23 | 2387 | 4 | 0 | 7 | Croatia (26) |
| Mirko Stefani | 19 | 1 | 0 | 45 | 0 | 0 | - | Italy |
| **Midfielders** | | | | | | | | |
| Massimo Ambrosini | 26 | 26 | 15 | 1531 | 2 | 1 | 8 | Italy (12) |
| Catilina Aubameyang | 19 | 1 | 0 | 60 | 0 | 0 | - | Gabon |
| Ibrahim Ba | 29 | 6 | 1 | 148 | 0 | 0 | - | France |
| Christian Brocchi | 27 | 21 | 6 | 665 | 2 | 0 | - | Italy |
| Mauro Calvi | 19 | 0 | 0 | 0 | 0 | 0 | - | Italy |
| Mattia Dal Bello | 19 | 1 | 0 | 45 | 0 | 0 | - | Italy |
| Samuelle Dalla Bona | 22 | 13 | 1 | 142 | 1 | 0 | - | Italy |
| Gennaro Gattuso | 25 | 27 | 19 | 1859 | 5 | 0 | 4 | Italy (12) |
| Thomas Helveg | 32 | 21 | 1 | 329 | 2 | 0 | 4 | Denmark (10) |
| Patrick Kalambay | 19 | 1 | 0 | 0 | 0 | 0 | - | Italy |
| Stefano Pastrello | 19 | 1 | 0 | 30 | 0 | 0 | - | Italy |
| Andrea Pirlo | 24 | 28 | 16 | 1881 | 5 | 1 | 4 | Italy (12) |
| Fernando Redondo | 34 | 16 | 4 | 490 | 0 | 0 | - | Argentina |
| Manuel Rui Costa | 31 | 30 | 19 | 1916 | 2 | 0 | 9 | Portugal (14) |
| Clarence Seedorf | 27 | 29 | 24 | 2290 | 1 | 0 | 6 | Holland (6) |
| Serginho | 32 | 23 | 6 | 984 | 1 | 0 | - | Brazil |
| Jon Dahl Tomasson | 26 | 29 | 5 | 787 | 0 | 0 | 8 | Denmark (10) |
| **Forwards** | | | | | | | | |
| Marco Borriello | 21 | 6 | 0 | 63 | 0 | 0 | - | Italy |
| Roberto Bortolotto | 18 | 1 | 0 | 20 | 0 | 0 | - | Italy |
| Filippo Inzaghi | 29 | 31 | 25 | 2424 | 2 | 0 | 5 | Italy (12) |
| Nascimento Leonardo | 33 | 1 | 0 | 22 | 0 | 0 | - | Brazil |
| Allessandro Matri | 18 | 1 | 1 | 70 | 0 | 0 | - | Italy |
| Michele Piccolo | 17 | 1 | 1 | 90 | 0 | 0 | - | Italy |
| Rivaldo Vitor Ferreira | 31 | 26 | 14 | 1514 | 1 | 0 | 3 | Brazil (1) |
| Andriy Shevchenko | 26 | 26 | 15 | 1593 | 0 | 0 | - | Ukraine |

## SQUAD APPEARANCES

| Match | 1 | 2 | 3 | 4 | 5 | 6 | 7 | 8 | 9 | 10 | 11 | 12 | 13 | 14 | 15 | 16 | 17 | 18 | 19 | 20 | 21 | 22 | 23 | 24 | 25 | 26 | 27 | 28 | 29 | 30 | 31 | 32 | 33 | 34 | 35 | 36 | 37 | 38 | 39 | 40 | 41 | 42 | 43 | 44 | 45 | 46 | 47 | 48 | 49 | 50 | 51 | 52 | 53 |
|---|---|---|---|---|---|---|---|---|---|---|---|---|---|---|---|---|---|---|---|---|---|---|---|---|---|---|---|---|---|---|---|---|---|---|---|---|---|---|---|---|---|---|---|---|---|---|---|---|---|---|---|---|---|
| Venue | H | A | A | H | H | A | A | A | H | A | H | A | A | H | H | A | H | H | H | H | A | H | A | A | H | A | H | A | H | A | H | H | A | A | H | H | A | A | H | H | A | A | A | H | H | A | H | H | A | A | H | A | N |
| Competition | C | C | L | C | L | C | L | C | L | L | C | L | C | L | L | L | C | L | L | C | L | L | C | L | L | L | L | L | L | L | L | C | L | C | L | L | C | L | C | L | L | C | L | L | C | L | L | C | L | C | L | L | C |
| Result | W | L | W | W | W | W | D | W | W | W | W | L | L | W | W | L | L | W | W | W | D | W | W | W | D | W | W | L | W | L | D | W | W | W | D | D | L | D | L | W | L | D | W | L | W | L | W | D | L | D | W | L | W |

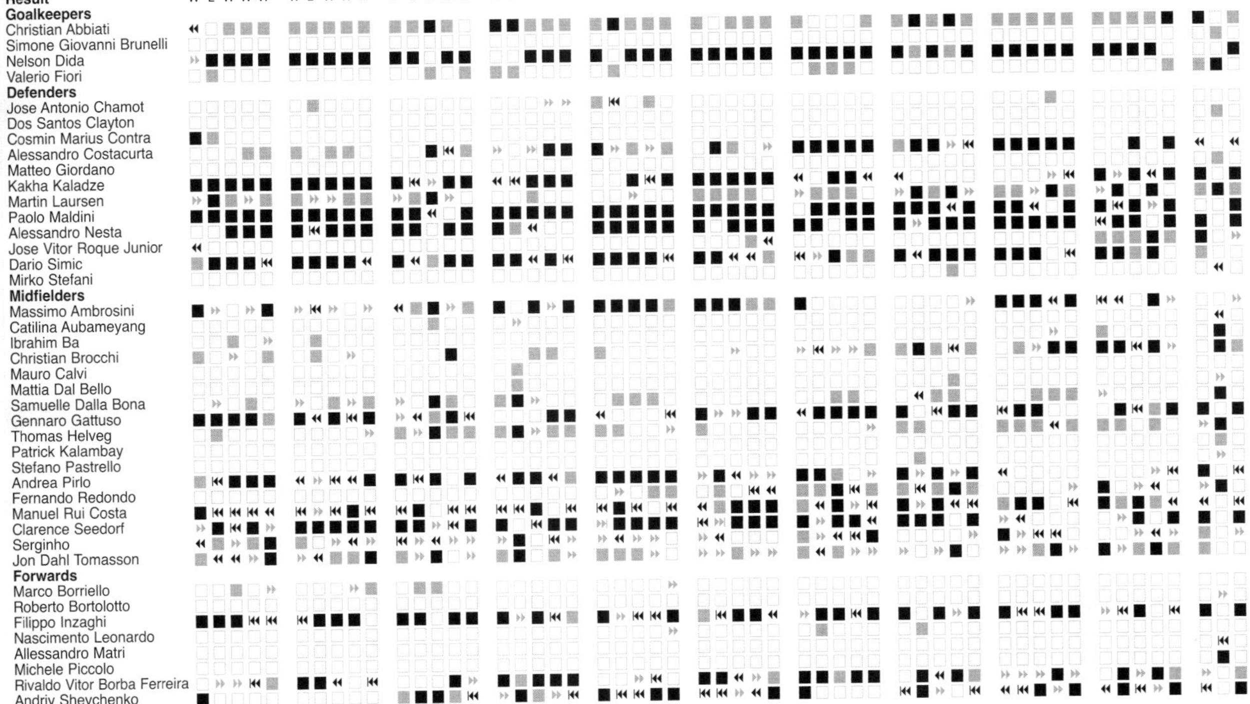
Goalkeepers
Christian Abbiati
Simone Giovanni Brunelli
Nelson Dida
Valerio Fiori
Defenders
Jose Antonio Chamot
Dos Santos Clayton
Cosmin Marius Contra
Alessandro Costacurta
Matteo Giordano
Kakha Kaladze
Martin Laursen
Paolo Maldini
Alessandro Nesta
Jose Vitor Roque Junior
Dario Simic
Mirko Stefani
Midfielders
Massimo Ambrosini
Catilina Aubameyang
Ibrahim Ba
Christian Brocchi
Mauro Calvi
Mattia Dal Bello
Samuelle Dalla Bona
Gennaro Gattuso
Thomas Helveg
Patrick Kalambay
Stefano Pastrello
Andrea Pirlo
Fernando Redondo
Manuel Rui Costa
Clarence Seedorf
Serginho
Jon Dahl Tomasson
Forwards
Marco Borriello
Roberto Bortolotto
Filippo Inzaghi
Nascimento Leonardo
Allessandro Matri
Michele Piccolo
Rivaldo Vitor Borba Ferreira
Andriy Shevchenko

# LAZIO

Final Position: **4th**

| | | | | | | |
|---|---|---|---|---|---|---|
| 1 | lge | Chievo | H | L | 2-3 | Simeone 6; Corradi 64 |
| 2 | uc1rl1 | Xanthi | H | W | 4-0 | Manfredini 44; Lopez 52; Inzaghi 67; Cesar 68 |
| 3 | lge | Torino | A | W | 1-0 | Simeone 86 |
| 4 | lge | AC Milan | H | D | 1-1 | Lopez 51 |
| 5 | uc1rl2 | Xanthi | A | D | 0-0 | |
| 6 | lge | Atalanta | A | W | 1-0 | Cesar 24 |
| 7 | lge | Perugia | H | W | 3-0 | Inzaghi 11; Chiesa 84,90 |
| 8 | lge | Roma | H | D | 2-2 | Fiore 50; Stankovic 74 |
| 9 | uc2rl1 | Crvena Zvezda | H | W | 1-0 | Fiore 10 |
| 10 | lge | Empoli | A | W | 2-1 | Corradi 44; Stankovic 81 |
| 11 | lge | Reggina | A | W | 3-0 | Pierini 17 og; Stankovic 32; Corradi 53 |
| 12 | lge | Parma | H | D | 0-0 | |
| 13 | uc2rl2 | Crvena Zvezda | A | D | 1-1 | Chiesa 78 |
| 14 | lge | Como | A | W | 3-1 | Simeone 18; Lopez 55,63 |
| 15 | lge | Modena | H | W | 4-0 | Corradi 24,90; Lopez 31; Cesar 71 |
| 16 | uc3rl1 | Sturm Graz | A | W | 3-1 | Chiesa 47; Inzaghi 56,87 |
| 17 | lge | Piacenza | A | W | 3-2 | Simeone 41; Lopez 45; Corradi 90 |
| 18 | lge | Inter Milan | H | D | 3-3 | Lopez 9 pen,31,36 |
| 19 | uc3rl2 | Sturm Graz | H | L | 0-1 | |
| 20 | lge | Juventus | A | W | 2-1 | Fiore 34,51 |
| 21 | lge | Bologna | H | D | 1-1 | Lopez 45 |
| 22 | lge | Brescia | A | D | 0-0 | |
| 23 | lge | Udinese | H | W | 2-1 | Lopez 27; Fiore 45 |
| 24 | lge | Reggina | H | L | 0-1 | |
| 25 | lge | Chievo | A | D | 1-1 | Simeone 88 |
| 26 | lge | Torino | H | D | 1-1 | Simeone 35 |
| 27 | lge | AC Milan | A | D | 2-2 | Stankovic 21; Lopez 30 pen |
| 28 | uc4rl1 | Wisla Krakow | H | D | 3-3 | Lazetic 22; Job 45 og; Chiesa 71 |
| 29 | lge | Atalanta | H | D | 0-0 | |
| 30 | lge | Perugia | A | D | 2-2 | Corradi 16; Favalli 85 |
| 31 | uc4rl2 | Wisla Krakow | A | W | 2-1 | Couto 21; Chiesa 54 |
| 32 | lge | Roma | A | D | 1-1 | Stankovic 8 |
| 33 | ucqfl1 | Besiktas | H | W | 1-0 | Inzaghi 55 |
| 34 | lge | Empoli | H | W | 4-1 | Lopez 8; Corradi 41; Simeone 71; Castroman 85 |
| 35 | ucqfl2 | Besiktas | A | W | 2-1 | Fiore 5; Castroman 9 |
| 36 | lge | Parma | A | L | 1-2 | Stankovic 49 |
| 37 | lge | Como | H | W | 3-0 | Fiore 7; Corradi 11; Lopez 66 pen |
| 38 | ucsfl1 | Porto | A | L | 1-4 | Lopez 5 |
| 39 | lge | Modena | A | D | 0-0 | |
| 40 | lge | Piacenza | H | W | 2-1 | Inzaghi 61; Corradi 74 |
| 41 | ucsfl2 | Porto | H | D | 0-0 | |
| 42 | lge | Inter Milan | A | D | 1-1 | Inzaghi 77 |
| 43 | lge | Juventus | H | D | 0-0 | |
| 44 | lge | Bologna | A | W | 2-0 | Inzaghi 45; Favalli 59 |
| 45 | lge | Brescia | H | W | 3-1 | Mihajlovic 40 pen; Cesar 45; Lopez 81 |
| 46 | lge | Udinese | A | L | 1-2 | Lopez 86 pen |

## ATTENDANCES

HOME GROUND: STADIO OLIMPICO CAPACITY: 82307 AVERAGE LEAGUE AT HOME: 48411

| | | | | | | | | |
|---|---|---|---|---|---|---|---|---|
| 8 | Roma | 80000 | 15 | Modena | 45000 | 44 | Bologna | 15000 |
| 18 | Inter Milan | 80000 | 37 | Como | 40000 | 16 | Sturm Graz | 15000 |
| 42 | Inter Milan | 75000 | 12 | Parma | 40000 | 28 | Wisla Krakow | 15000 |
| 45 | Brescia | 68000 | 1 | Chievo | 40000 | 25 | Chievo | 14921 |
| 43 | Juventus | 65000 | 29 | Atalanta | 40000 | 39 | Modena | 13800 |
| 27 | AC Milan | 65000 | 34 | Empoli | 35000 | 3 | Torino | 12000 |
| 41 | Porto | 65000 | 7 | Perugia | 35000 | 9 | Crvena Zvezda | 12000 |
| 20 | Juventus | 58000 | 35 | Besiktas | 28000 | 10 | Empoli | 10000 |
| 4 | AC Milan | 55000 | 11 | Reggina | 28000 | 19 | Sturm Graz | 10000 |
| 13 | Crvena Zvezda | 50000 | 33 | Besiktas | 25000 | 31 | Wisla Krakow | 10000 |
| 32 | Roma | 50000 | 40 | Piacenza | 20000 | 5 | Xanthi | 8500 |
| 38 | Porto | 45518 | 46 | Udinese | 20000 | 17 | Piacenza | 7000 |
| 21 | Bologna | 45000 | 36 | Parma | 20000 | 30 | Perugia | 7000 |
| 26 | Torino | 45000 | 22 | Brescia | 16000 | 14 | Como | 7000 |
| 24 | Reggina | 45000 | 6 | Atalanta | 15000 | | | |
| 23 | Udinese | 45000 | 2 | Xanthi | 15000 | | | |

■ Home □ Away ▨ Neutral

## KEY PLAYERS - GOALSCORERS

**1 Claudio Lopez**

| | | | |
|---|---|---|---|
| Goals in the League | 15 | Player Strike Rate<br>Average number of minutes between League goals scored by player | 186 |
| Contribution to Attacking Power<br>Average number of minutes between League team goals while on pitch | 53 | Club Strike Rate<br>Average number of minutes between League goals scored by club | 54 |

| | PLAYER | LGE GOALS | POWER | STRIKE RATE |
|---|---|---|---|---|
| 2 | Diego Simeone | 7 | 47 | 231 mins |
| 3 | Bernardo Corradi | 10 | 52 | 264 mins |
| 4 | Dejan Stankovic | 6 | 54 | 418 mins |
| 5 | Stefano Fiore | 5 | 55 | 477 mins |

## KEY PLAYERS - MIDFIELDERS

**1 Fabio Liverani**

| | | | |
|---|---|---|---|
| Goals in the League | 0 | Contribution to Attacking Power<br>Average number of minutes between League team goals while on pitch | 52 |
| Defensive Rating<br>Average number of mins between League goals conceded while he was on the pitch | 98 | Scoring Difference<br>Defensive Rating minus Contribution to Attacking Power | 46 |

| | PLAYER | LGE GOALS | DEF RATE | POWER | SCORE DIFF |
|---|---|---|---|---|---|
| 2 | Dejan Stankovic | 6 | 96 | 54 | 42 mins |
| 3 | Claudio Lopez | 15 | 93 | 54 | 39 mins |
| 4 | Stefano Fiore | 5 | 92 | 55 | 37 mins |
| 5 | Diego Simeone | 7 | 85 | 48 | 37 mins |

## KEY PLAYERS - DEFENDERS

**1 Sinisa Mihajlovic**

| | | | |
|---|---|---|---|
| Goals Conceded (GC)<br>The number of League goals conceded while he was on the pitch | 11 | Clean Sheets<br>In games when he played at least 70 minutes | 9 |
| Defensive Rating<br>Ave number of mins between League goals conceded while on the pitch | 151 | Club Defensive Rating<br>Average number of mins between League goals conceded by the club this season | 96 |

| | PLAYER | CON LGE | CLEAN SHEETS | DEF RATE |
|---|---|---|---|---|
| 2 | Massimo Oddo | 13 | 6 | 116 mins |
| 3 | Guiseppi Favalli | 21 | 7 | 101 mins |
| 4 | Rodriguez Cesar | 22 | 10 | 98 mins |
| 5 | Paolo Negro | 17 | 8 | 97 mins |

## KEY GOALKEEPER

**1 Angelo Peruzzi**

| | |
|---|---|
| Goals Conceded in the League | 28 |
| Defensive Rating<br>Ave number of mins between League goals conceded while on the pitch | 90 |
| Counting Games<br>Games when he played at least 70 minutes | 26 |
| Clean Sheets<br>In games when he played at least 70 minutes | 8 |

## TOP POINT EARNERS

| | PLAYER | GAMES | AVE |
|---|---|---|---|
| 1 | Mihajlovic | 17 | 2.18 |
| 2 | Favalli | 24 | 2.00 |
| 3 | Negro | 18 | 1.89 |
| 4 | Cesar | 23 | 1.87 |
| 5 | Fiore | 22 | 1.82 |
| 6 | Stankovic | 27 | 1.78 |
| 7 | Oddo | 16 | 1.75 |
| 8 | Simeone | 15 | 1.73 |
| 9 | Lopez | 30 | 1.73 |
| 10 | Corradi | 27 | 1.70 |
| | CLUB AVERAGE: | | 1.76 |

Ave = Average points per match in Counting Games

## DISCIPLINARY RECORDS

| | PLAYER | YELLOW | RED | AVE |
|---|---|---|---|---|
| 1 | Castroman | 3 | 0 | 169 |
| 2 | Negro | 6 | 0 | 276 |
| 3 | Giannichedda | 5 | 0 | 318 |
| 4 | Oddo | 4 | 0 | 376 |
| 5 | Couto | 2 | 1 | 390 |
| 6 | Simeone | 4 | 0 | 404 |
| 7 | Mihajlovic | 4 | 0 | 416 |
| 8 | Stankovic | 5 | 1 | 417 |
| 9 | Corradi | 6 | 0 | 440 |
| 10 | Liverani | 1 | 1 | 441 |
| 11 | Inzaghi | 1 | 0 | 531 |
| 12 | Pancaro | 2 | 0 | 534 |
| 13 | Stam | 3 | 0 | 870 |
| | Other | 10 | 0 | |
| | TOTAL | 56 | 3 | |

## LEAGUE GOALS

| | PLAYER | MINS | GOALS | AVE |
|---|---|---|---|---|
| 1 | Lopez | 2790 | 15 | 186 |
| 2 | Corradi | 2640 | 10 | 264 |
| 3 | Simeone | 1617 | 7 | 231 |
| 4 | Stankovic | 2505 | 6 | 418 |
| 5 | Fiore | 2384 | 5 | 477 |
| 6 | Inzaghi | 531 | 4 | 133 |
| 7 | Cesar | 2164 | 3 | 721 |
| 8 | Favalli | 2119 | 2 | 1060 |
| 9 | Chiesa | 341 | 2 | 171 |
| 10 | Mihajlovic | 1665 | 1 | 1665 |
| 11 | Castroman | 508 | 1 | 508 |
| | Other | | 1 | |
| | TOTAL | | 57 | |

## MONTH BY MONTH GUIDE TO THE POINTS

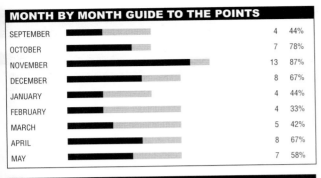

| Month | Points | % |
|---|---|---|
| SEPTEMBER | 4 | 44% |
| OCTOBER | 7 | 78% |
| NOVEMBER | 13 | 87% |
| DECEMBER | 8 | 67% |
| JANUARY | 4 | 44% |
| FEBRUARY | 4 | 33% |
| MARCH | 5 | 42% |
| APRIL | 8 | 67% |
| MAY | 7 | 58% |

## TEAM OF THE SEASON

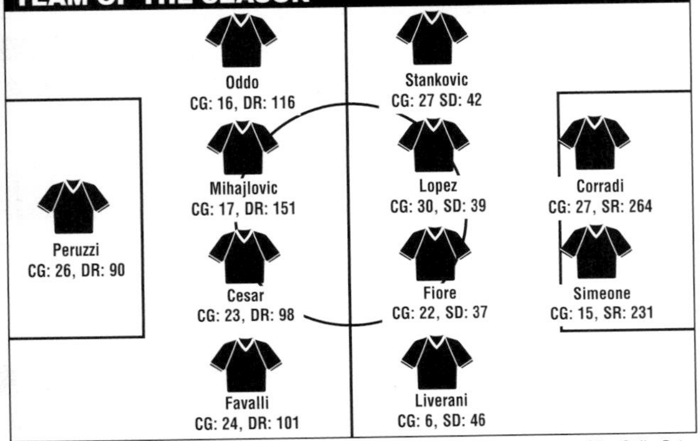
Peruzzi
CG: 26, DR: 90
Oddo
CG: 16, DR: 116
Mihajlovic
CG: 17, DR: 151
Cesar
CG: 23, DR: 98
Favalli
CG: 24, DR: 101
Stankovic
CG: 27 SD: 42
Lopez
CG: 30, SD: 39
Fiore
CG: 22, SD: 37
Liverani
CG: 6, SD: 46
Corradi
CG: 27, SR: 264
Simeone
CG: 15, SR: 231

KEY: DR = Defensive Rate, SD = Scoring Difference, SR = Strike Rate, CG = Counting Games – League games playing at least 70 minutes

## LEAGUE APPEARANCES, BOOKINGS AND CAPS

| | AGE | IN THE SQUAD | COUNTING GAMES | MINUTES ON PITCH | YELLOW CARDS | RED CARDS | THIS SEASON | HOME COUNTRY |
|---|---|---|---|---|---|---|---|---|
| **Goalkeepers** | | | | | | | | |
| Alessandro Boccolini | 18 | 1 | 0 | 0 | 0 | 0 | - | Italy |
| Emanuele Concetti | 25 | 12 | 0 | 102 | 0 | 0 | - | Italy |
| Luca Marchegiani | 37 | 24 | 4 | 433 | 0 | 0 | - | Italy |
| Angelo Peruzzi | 33 | 31 | 26 | 2525 | 0 | 0 | - | Italy |
| **Defenders** | | | | | | | | |
| Rodriguez Cesar | 28 | 27 | 23 | 2164 | 1 | 0 | - | Brazil |
| Francesco Colonnese | 31 | 6 | 0 | 0 | 0 | 0 | - | Italy |
| Manuel Couto | 33 | 29 | 13 | 1170 | 2 | 1 | 9 | Portugal (14) |
| Guiseppi Favalli | 31 | 30 | 24 | 2119 | 2 | 0 | - | Italy |
| Sinisa Mihajlovic | 34 | 25 | 17 | 1665 | 4 | 0 | - | Serbia & Montenegro |
| Paolo Negro | 31 | 24 | 18 | 1657 | 6 | 0 | - | Italy |
| Massimo Oddo | 27 | 26 | 16 | 1507 | 4 | 0 | 6 | Italy (12) |
| Guiseppe Pancaro | 31 | 25 | 9 | 1068 | 2 | 0 | 1 | Italy (12) |
| Juan Pablo Sorin | 27 | 10 | 3 | 384 | 0 | 0 | 2 | Argentina (5) |
| Jaap Stam | 30 | 29 | 29 | 2610 | 3 | 0 | 7 | Holland (6) |
| **Midfielders** | | | | | | | | |
| Dino Baggio | 31 | 7 | 0 | 63 | 1 | 0 | - | Italy |
| Lucas Castroman | 22 | 21 | 3 | 508 | 3 | 0 | 2 | Argentina (5) |
| Stefano Fiore | 28 | 34 | 22 | 2384 | 2 | 0 | 5 | Italy (12) |
| Alessandro Gazzi | 20 | 1 | 0 | 0 | 0 | 0 | - | Italy |
| Guiliano Giannichedda | 28 | 27 | 17 | 1591 | 5 | 0 | - | Italy |
| Guerino Gottardi | 32 | 2 | 0 | 20 | 0 | 0 | - | Italy |
| Nikola Lazetic | 25 | 9 | 2 | 237 | 0 | 0 | - | Serbia & Montenegro |
| Fabio Liverani | 27 | 26 | 6 | 883 | 1 | 1 | - | Italy |
| Claudio Lopez | 28 | 34 | 30 | 2790 | 3 | 0 | 2 | Argentina (5) |
| Christian Manfredini | 28 | 7 | 0 | 91 | 0 | 0 | - | Italy |
| Diego Simeone | 33 | 31 | 15 | 1617 | 4 | 0 | 1 | Argentina (5) |
| Dejan Stankovic | 24 | 30 | 27 | 2505 | 5 | 1 | - | Serbia & Montenegro |
| **Forwards** | | | | | | | | |
| Enrico Chiesa | 32 | 28 | 0 | 341 | 1 | 0 | - | Italy |
| Bernardo Corradi | 27 | 33 | 27 | 2640 | 6 | 0 | 5 | Italy (12) |
| Simone Inzaghi | 27 | 24 | 2 | 531 | 1 | 0 | - | Italy |

KEY: LEAGUE BOOKINGS CAPS (FIFA RANKING)

## SQUAD APPEARANCES

| Match | 1 | 2 | 3 | 4 | 5 | 6 | 7 | 8 | 9 | 10 | 11 | 12 | 13 | 14 | 15 | 16 | 17 | 18 | 19 | 20 | 21 | 22 | 23 | 24 | 25 | 26 | 27 | 28 | 29 | 30 | 31 | 32 | 33 | 34 | 35 | 36 | 37 | 38 | 39 | 40 | 41 | 42 | 43 | 44 | 45 | 46 |
|---|---|---|---|---|---|---|---|---|---|---|---|---|---|---|---|---|---|---|---|---|---|---|---|---|---|---|---|---|---|---|---|---|---|---|---|---|---|---|---|---|---|---|---|---|---|---|
| Venue | H | H | A | H | A | A | H | H | H | A | A | H | A | A | H | A | A | H | H | A | H | A | H | H | A | H | A | H | H | A | A | A | H | H | A | A | H | A | A | H | H | A | H | A | H | A |
| Competition | L | E | L | L | E | L | L | L | E | L | L | L | E | L | L | E | L | L | E | L | L | L | L | L | L | L | L | E | L | L | E | L | E | L | E | L | L | E | L | L | E | L | L | L | L | L |
| Result | L | W | W | D | D | W | W | D | W | W | W | D | D | W | W | W | W | D | L | W | D | D | W | L | D | D | D | D | D | D | W | D | W | W | W | L | W | L | D | W | D | D | D | W | W | L |

**Goalkeepers**
Alessandro Boccolini
Emanuele Concetti
Luca Marchegiani
Angelo Peruzzi

**Defenders**
Rodriguez Cesar
Francesco Colonnese
Fernando Couto
Guiseppi Favalli
Sinisa Mihajlovic
Paolo Negro
Massimo Oddo
Guiseppe Pancaro
Japp Stam

**Midfielders**
Dino Baggio
Lucas Castroman
Stefano Fiore
Gazzi
Guiliano Giannichedda
Guerino Gottardi
Nikola Lazetic
Fabio Liverani
Claudio Lopez
Christian Manfredini
Diego Simeone
Juan Pablo Sorin
Dejan Stankovic

**Forwards**
Enrico Chiesa
Bernardo Corradi
Simone Inzaghi

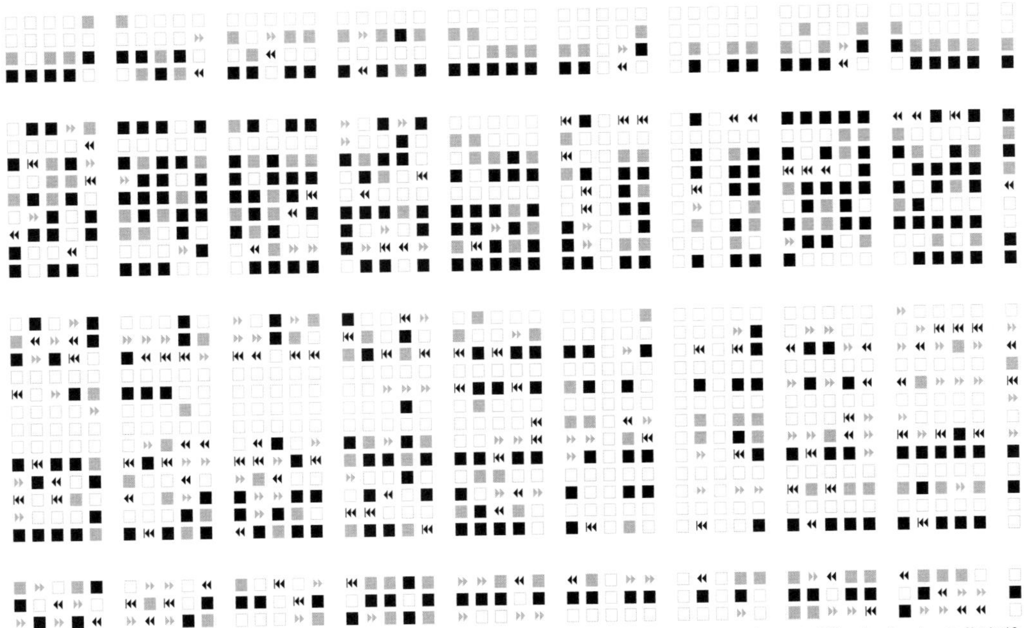

KEY: On all match · On bench · Subbed or sent off (Counting game) · Subbed or sent off (playing less than 70 minutes) · Subbed on from bench (Counting Game) · Subbed on (playing less than 70 minutes) · Subbed on and then subbed or sent off (Counting Game) · Subbed on and then subbed or sent off (playing less than 70 minutes) · Not in 16

# PARMA

Final Position: **5th**

| No | Comp | Opponent | Venue | Result | Score | Scorers |
|---|---|---|---|---|---|---|
| 1 | lge | Udinese | A | D | 1-1 | Adriano 24 |
| 2 | uc1rl1 | CSKA Moscow | A | D | 1-1 | Mutu 53 |
| 3 | lge | Como | H | W | 2-0 | Lamouchi 13; Adriano 46 |
| 4 | lge | Juventus | A | D | 2-2 | Nakata 65; Adriano 81 |
| 5 | uc1rl2 | CSKA Moscow | H | W | 3-2 | Adriano 8; Mutu 66,90 |
| 6 | lge | Perugia | H | D | 2-2 | Mutu 19; Donati 53 |
| 7 | lge | Modena | A | L | 1-2 | Mutu 40 |
| 8 | lge | Atalanta | H | W | 2-1 | Nakata 14; Mutu 71 |
| 9 | uc2rl1 | Wisla Krakow | H | W | 2-1 | Donati 26; Mutu 74 |
| 10 | lge | Chievo | H | L | 0-1 | |
| 11 | lge | Brescia | H | W | 4-3 | Ferrari 15; Mutu 26; Bonazzoli 52; Gilardino 74 |
| 12 | lge | Lazio | A | D | 0-0 | |
| 13 | uc2rl2 | Wisla Krakow | A | L | 0-0 | Adriano 6 |
| 14 | lge | AC Milan | A | L | 1-2 | Filippini, E 63 |
| 15 | lge | Roma | H | W | 3-0 | Bonazzoli 11,71; Mutu 22 pen |
| 16 | lge | Torino | A | W | 4-0 | Brighi 16; Mutu 25; Adriano 50,67 |
| 17 | lge | Reggina | H | W | 2-0 | Adriano 57,79 |
| 18 | lge | Bologna | A | L | 1-2 | Adriano 28 |
| 19 | lge | Inter Milan | H | L | 1-2 | Mutu 55 |
| 20 | lge | Piacenza | A | D | 1-1 | Mutu 29 |
| 21 | lge | Empoli | H | W | 2-0 | Gilardino 13; Adriano 81 |
| 22 | lge | Brescia | A | D | 1-1 | Bonera 33 |
| 23 | lge | Udinese | H | W | 3-2 | Adriano 11; Barone 55; Nakata 84 |
| 24 | lge | Como | A | D | 2-2 | Mutu 31,89 |
| 25 | lge | Juventus | H | L | 1-2 | Mutu 90 |
| 26 | lge | Perugia | A | W | 2-1 | Adriano 30; Ferrari 72 |
| 27 | lge | Modena | H | D | 1-1 | Adriano 26 |
| 28 | lge | Atalanta | A | D | 0-0 | |
| 29 | lge | Chievo | A | W | 4-0 | Mutu 6; Nakata 59; Lamouchi 67; Gilardino 90 |
| 30 | lge | Lazio | H | W | 2-1 | Cardone 4; Adriano 90 |
| 31 | lge | AC Milan | H | W | 1-0 | Adriano 77 |
| 32 | lge | Roma | A | L | 1-2 | Adriano 40 |
| 33 | lge | Torino | H | W | 1-0 | Mutu 70 pen |
| 34 | lge | Reggina | A | D | 0-0 | |
| 35 | lge | Bologna | H | L | 1-2 | Mutu 65 |
| 36 | lge | Inter Milan | A | D | 1-1 | Mutu 64 |
| 37 | lge | Piacenza | H | W | 3-2 | Gilardino 67; Adriano 70; Mutu 89 |
| 38 | lge | Empoli | A | W | 2-0 | Mutu 17; Filippini, E 86 |

## KEY PLAYERS - GOALSCORERS

**1 Leite Ribeiro Adriano**

| | | | |
|---|---|---|---|
| Goals in the League | 16 | Player Strike Rate<br>Average number of minutes between League goals scored by player | 144 |
| Contribution to Attacking Power<br>Average number of minutes between League team goals while on pitch | 57 | Club Strike Rate<br>Average number of minutes between League goals scored by club | 56 |

| | PLAYER | LGE GOALS | POWER | STRIKE RATE |
|---|---|---|---|---|
| 2 | Adrian Mutu | 17 | 53 | 154 mins |
| 3 | Hidetoshi Nakata | 4 | 59 | 592 mins |
| 4 | Sabri Lamouchi | 2 | 54 | 1227 mins |
| 5 | Emanuele Filippini | 2 | 58 | 1231 mins |

## KEY PLAYERS - MIDFIELDERS

**1 Simone Barone**

| | | | |
|---|---|---|---|
| Goals in the League | 1 | Contribution to Attacking Power<br>Average number of minutes between League team goals while on pitch | 60 |
| Defensive Rating<br>Average number of mins between League goals conceded while he was on the pitch | 92 | Scoring Difference<br>Defensive Rating minus Contribution to Attacking Power | 32 |

| | PLAYER | LGE GOALS | DEF RATE | POWER | SCORE DIFF |
|---|---|---|---|---|---|
| 2 | Sabri Lamouchi | 2 | 85 | 55 | 30 mins |
| 3 | Matteo Brighi | 1 | 74 | 50 | 24 mins |
| 4 | Emanuele Filippini | 2 | 79 | 59 | 20 mins |
| 5 | Hidetoshi Nakata | 4 | 74 | 59 | 15 mins |

## KEY PLAYERS - DEFENDERS

**1 Giuseppe Cardone**

| | | | |
|---|---|---|---|
| Goals Conceded (GC)<br>The number of League goals conceded while he was on the pitch | 11 | Clean Sheets<br>In games when he played at least 70 minutes | 4 |
| Defensive Rating<br>Ave number of mins between League goals conceded while on the pitch | 97 | Club Defensive Rating<br>Average number of mins between League goals conceded by the club this season | 85 |

| | PLAYER | CON LGE | CLEAN SHEETS | DEF RATE |
|---|---|---|---|---|
| 2 | Daniele Bonera | 30 | 12 | 93 mins |
| 3 | Junior Jenilson | 25 | 10 | 92 mins |
| 4 | Matteo Ferrari | 32 | 11 | 88 mins |
| 5 | Antonio Benarrivo | 19 | 5 | 76 mins |

## GOALS SCORED

| AT HOME | | |
|---|---|---|
| MOST | Juventus | 37 |
| | | 31 |
| LEAST | Torino | 10 |

| AWAY | | |
|---|---|---|
| MOST | Inter Milan | 30 |
| | | 24 |
| LEAST | Como | 9 |

## GOALS CONCEDED

| AT HOME | | |
|---|---|---|
| LEAST | AC Milan | 11 |
| | | 19 |
| MOST | Piacenza | 29 |

| AWAY | | |
|---|---|---|
| LEAST | Juventus | 15 |
| | | 17 |
| MOST | Perugia | 35 |

## KEY GOALKEEPER

**1 Sebastian Frey**

| | |
|---|---|
| Goals Conceded in the League | 36 |
| Defensive Rating<br>Ave number of mins between League goals conceded while on the pitch | 85 |
| Counting Games<br>Games when he played at least 70 minutes | 34 |
| Clean Sheets<br>In games when he played at least 70 minutes | 12 |

## TOP POINT EARNERS

| | PLAYER | GAMES | AVE |
|---|---|---|---|
| 1 | Junior Jenilson | 25 | 1.96 |
| 2 | Barone | 23 | 1.74 |
| 3 | Lamouchi | 25 | 1.72 |
| 4 | Adriano | 25 | 1.68 |
| 5 | Benarrivo | 15 | 1.67 |
| 6 | Frey | 34 | 1.65 |
| 7 | Bonera | 30 | 1.63 |
| 8 | Ferrari | 31 | 1.58 |
| 9 | Mutu | 28 | 1.57 |
| 10 | Nakata | 24 | 1.50 |
| | CLUB AVERAGE: | | 1.65 |

Ave = Average points per match in Counting Games

## ATTENDANCES

HOME GROUND: ENNIO TARDINI CAPACITY: 28783 AVERAGE LEAGUE AT HOME: 17172

| | | | | | | | | |
|---|---|---|---|---|---|---|---|---|
| 14 | AC Milan | 60000 | 3 | Como | 19000 | 10 | Chievo | 14929 |
| 32 | Roma | 55000 | 22 | Brescia | 17000 | 17 | Reggina | 14000 |
| 4 | Juventus | 40000 | 23 | Udinese | 16000 | 37 | Piacenza | 13000 |
| 12 | Lazio | 40000 | 21 | Empoli | 16000 | 33 | Torino | 12000 |
| 36 | Inter Milan | 30000 | 6 | Perugia | 16000 | 11 | Brescia | 12000 |
| 19 | Inter Milan | 26000 | 35 | Bologna | 16000 | 7 | Modena | 11000 |
| 31 | AC Milan | 25603 | 27 | Modena | 16000 | 13 | Wisla Krakow | 9000 |
| 25 | Juventus | 25393 | 8 | Atalanta | 15000 | 5 | CSKA Moscow | 8800 |
| 18 | Bologna | 25000 | 15 | Roma | 15000 | 9 | Wisla Krakow | 6936 |
| 34 | Reggina | 23500 | 26 | Perugia | 15000 | 20 | Piacenza | 6500 |
| 28 | Atalanta | 20000 | 1 | Udinese | 15000 | 38 | Empoli | 6400 |
| 30 | Lazio | 20000 | 16 | Torino | 15000 | 24 | Como | 5100 |
| 29 | Chievo | 20000 | 2 | CSKA Moscow | 15000 | | | |

■ Home □ Away ▨ Neutral

## DISCIPLINARY RECORDS

| | PLAYER | YELLOW | RED | AVE |
|---|---|---|---|---|
| 1 | Filippini, E | 9 | 0 | 273 |
| 2 | Benarrivo | 5 | 0 | 289 |
| 3 | Mutu | 8 | 1 | 290 |
| 4 | Bonera | 6 | 0 | 464 |
| 5 | Ferrari | 5 | 1 | 468 |
| 6 | Junior Jenilson | 4 | 0 | 576 |
| 7 | Lamouchi | 3 | 1 | 613 |
| 8 | Brighi | 2 | 0 | 627 |
| 9 | Barone | 3 | 0 | 738 |
| 10 | Cannavaro | 1 | 0 | 918 |
| 11 | Bresciano | 1 | 0 | 977 |
| 12 | Cardone | 1 | 0 | 1070 |
| 13 | Nakata | 1 | 0 | 2366 |
| | Other | 5 | 0 | |
| | TOTAL | 54 | 3 | |

## LEAGUE GOALS

| | PLAYER | MINS | GOALS | AVE |
|---|---|---|---|---|
| 1 | Mutu | 2617 | 17 | 154 |
| 2 | Adriano | 2301 | 16 | 144 |
| 3 | Nakata | 2366 | 4 | 592 |
| 4 | Gilardino | 636 | 4 | 159 |
| 5 | Bonazzoli | 379 | 3 | 126 |
| 6 | Filippini, E | 2462 | 2 | 1231 |
| 7 | Ferrari | 2812 | 2 | 1406 |
| 8 | Lamouchi | 2453 | 2 | 1227 |
| 9 | Brighi | 1254 | 1 | 1254 |
| 10 | Barone | 2214 | 1 | 2214 |
| 11 | Bonera | 2789 | 1 | 2789 |
| 12 | Donati | 329 | 1 | 329 |
| 13 | Cardone | 1070 | 1 | 1070 |
| | Other | | 0 | |
| | TOTAL | | 55 | |

## MONTH BY MONTH GUIDE TO THE POINTS

| Month | Points | % |
|---|---|---|
| SEPTEMBER | 5 | 56% |
| OCTOBER | 4 | 44% |
| NOVEMBER | 7 | 47% |
| DECEMBER | 6 | 50% |
| JANUARY | 5 | 56% |
| FEBRUARY | 7 | 58% |
| MARCH | 8 | 67% |
| APRIL | 7 | 58% |
| MAY | 7 | 58% |

## TEAM OF THE SEASON

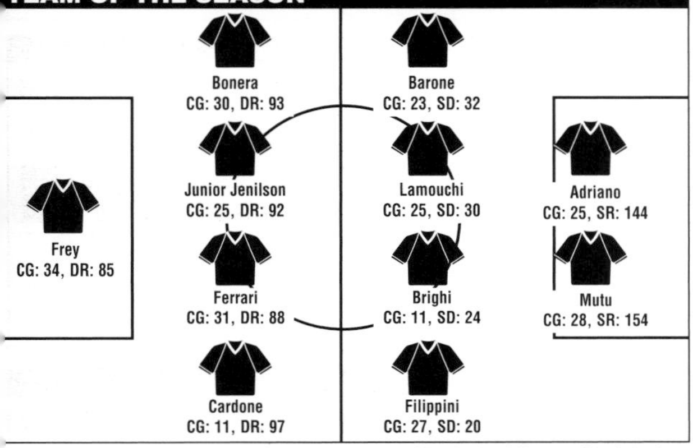

Frey
CG: 34, DR: 85
Bonera
CG: 30, DR: 93
Junior Jenilson
CG: 25, DR: 92
Ferrari
CG: 31, DR: 88
Cardone
CG: 11, DR: 97
Barone
CG: 23, SD: 32
Lamouchi
CG: 25, SD: 30
Brighi
CG: 11, SD: 24
Filippini
CG: 27, SD: 20
Adriano
CG: 25, SR: 144
Mutu
CG: 28, SR: 154


KEY: DR = Defensive Rate, SD = Scoring Difference, SR = Strike Rate, CG = Counting Games – League games playing at least 70 minutes

## LEAGUE APPEARANCES, BOOKINGS AND CAPS

| | AGE | IN THE SQUAD | COUNTING GAMES | MINUTES ON PITCH | YELLOW CARDS | RED CARDS | THIS SEASON | HOME COUNTRY |
|---|---|---|---|---|---|---|---|---|
| **Goalkeepers** | | | | | | | | |
| Alfonso De Lucia | 19 | 1 | 0 | 0 | 0 | 0 | - | Italy |
| Sebastian Frey | 23 | 34 | 34 | 3060 | 1 | 0 | - | France |
| Claudio Taffarel | 37 | 33 | 0 | 0 | 0 | 0 | - | Brazil |
| **Defenders** | | | | | | | | |
| Antonio Benarrivo | 34 | 28 | 15 | 1447 | 5 | 0 | - | Italy |
| Daniele Bonera | 22 | 32 | 30 | 2789 | 6 | 0 | 2 | Italy (12) |
| Paolo Cannavaro | 22 | 30 | 9 | 918 | 1 | 0 | - | Italy |
| Giuseppe Cardone | 29 | 13 | 11 | 1070 | 1 | 0 | - | Italy |
| Stefano Aimo Diana | 25 | 16 | 3 | 283 | 0 | 0 | - | Italy |
| Matteo Ferrari | 23 | 32 | 31 | 2812 | 5 | 1 | 4 | Italy (12) |
| Junior Jenilson | 30 | 29 | 25 | 2306 | 4 | 0 | 3 | Brazil (1) |
| Alessandro Pierini | 30 | 16 | 0 | 116 | 0 | 0 | - | Italy |
| Filippo Porcari | 19 | 11 | 0 | 45 | 0 | 0 | - | Italy |
| Sebastiano Siviglia | 30 | 5 | 1 | 83 | 0 | 0 | - | Italy |
| **Midfielders** | | | | | | | | |
| Simone Barone | 25 | 30 | 23 | 2214 | 3 | 0 | - | Italy |
| Matteo Brighi | 22 | 26 | 11 | 1254 | 2 | 0 | 1 | Italy (12) |
| Massimo Donati | 22 | 15 | 2 | 329 | 1 | 0 | - | Italy |
| Emanuele Filippini | 30 | 31 | 27 | 2462 | 9 | 0 | - | Italy |
| Vratislav Gresko | 25 | 11 | 3 | 318 | 2 | 0 | - | Slovakia |
| Sabri Lamouchi | 31 | 30 | 25 | 2453 | 3 | 1 | - | France |
| Hidetoshi Nakata | 26 | 32 | 24 | 2366 | 1 | 0 | 4 | Japan (23) |
| Gabriel Gaston Oyola | 20 | 2 | 0 | 0 | 0 | 0 | - | Argentina |
| Alessandro Rosina | 18 | 12 | 1 | 150 | 0 | 0 | - | Italy |
| Paulo Ruffini | 19 | 1 | 0 | 0 | 0 | 0 | - | Italy |
| **Forwards** | | | | | | | | |
| Leite Ribeiro Adriano | 21 | 29 | 25 | 2301 | 0 | 0 | 1 | Brazil (1) |
| Emiliano Bonazzoli | 24 | 11 | 4 | 379 | 0 | 0 | - | Italy |
| Mark Bresciano | 23 | 24 | 7 | 977 | 1 | 0 | - | Australia |
| Alberto Gilardino | 21 | 29 | 3 | 636 | 0 | 0 | - | Italy |
| Marco Marchionni | 22 | 13 | 0 | 146 | 1 | 0 | - | Italy |
| Johnnier Montano | 20 | 3 | 0 | 45 | 0 | 0 | - | Columbia |
| Adrian Mutu | 24 | 31 | 28 | 2617 | 8 | 1 | 8 | Romania (27) |

KEY: LEAGUE BOOKINGS CAPS (FIFA RANKING)

## SQUAD APPEARANCES

| Match | 1 | 2 | 3 | 4 | 5 | 6 | 7 | 8 | 9 | 10 | 11 | 12 | 13 | 14 | 15 | 16 | 17 | 18 | 19 | 20 | 21 | 22 | 23 | 24 | 25 | 26 | 27 | 28 | 29 | 30 | 31 | 32 | 33 | 34 | 35 | 36 | 37 | 38 |
|---|---|---|---|---|---|---|---|---|---|---|---|---|---|---|---|---|---|---|---|---|---|---|---|---|---|---|---|---|---|---|---|---|---|---|---|---|---|---|
| Venue | A | A | H | A | H | H | A | H | H | H | H | A | A | A | H | A | H | A | H | A | H | A | H | A | H | A | H | A | A | H | H | A | H | A | H | A | H | A |
| Competition | L | E | L | L | E | L | L | L | E | L | L | L | E | L | L | L | L | L | L | L | L | L | L | L | L | L | L | L | L | L | L | L | L | L | L | L | L | L |
| Result | D | D | W | D | W | D | L | W | W | L | W | D | L | L | W | W | W | L | L | D | W | D | W | D | L | W | D | D | W | W | W | L | W | D | L | D | W | W |

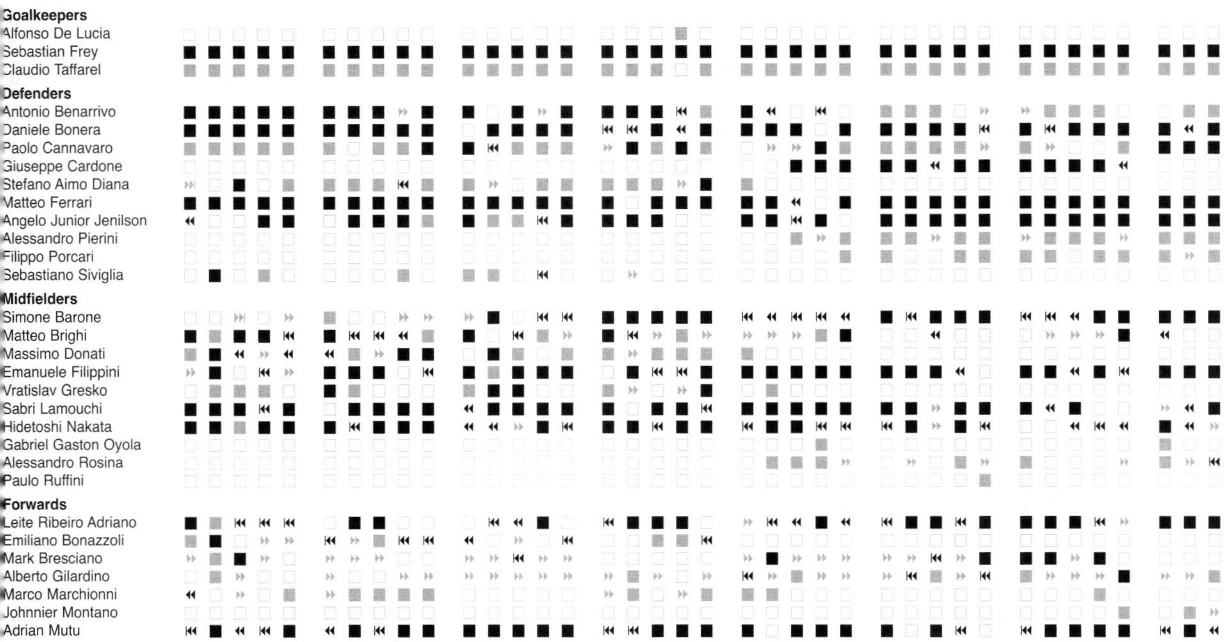

Goalkeepers
Alfonso De Lucia
Sebastian Frey
Claudio Taffarel
Defenders
Antonio Benarrivo
Daniele Bonera
Paolo Cannavaro
Giuseppe Cardone
Stefano Aimo Diana
Matteo Ferrari
Angelo Junior Jenilson
Alessandro Pierini
Filippo Porcari
Sebastiano Siviglia
Midfielders
Simone Barone
Matteo Brighi
Massimo Donati
Emanuele Filippini
Vratislav Gresko
Sabri Lamouchi
Hidetoshi Nakata
Gabriel Gaston Oyola
Alessandro Rosina
Paulo Ruffini
Forwards
Leite Ribeiro Adriano
Emiliano Bonazzoli
Mark Bresciano
Alberto Gilardino
Marco Marchionni
Johnnier Montano
Adrian Mutu


KEY: ■ On all match ■ On bench ⏮ Subbed or sent off (Counting game) ◂◂ Subbed or sent off (playing less than 70 minutes) ⏭ Subbed on from bench (Counting Game) ▸▸ Subbed on (playing less than 70 minutes) Subbed on and then subbed or sent off (Counting Game) Subbed on and then subbed or sent off (playing less than 70 minutes) □ Not in 16

# UDINESE

Final Position: **6th**

| | | | | | | |
|---|---|---|---|---|---|---|
| 1 | lge | Parma | H | D | 1-1 | Alberto 53 |
| 2 | lge | Piacenza | A | L | 0-2 | |
| 3 | lge | Atalanta | H | W | 1-0 | Sensini 59 |
| 4 | lge | Roma | A | L | 1-4 | Sensini 59 |
| 5 | lge | Reggina | H | W | 1-0 | Pizarro 51 pen |
| 6 | lge | Juventus | A | L | 0-1 | |
| 7 | lge | Bologna | H | D | 0-0 | |
| 8 | lge | AC Milan | A | L | 0-1 | |
| 9 | lge | Inter Milan | A | W | 2-1 | Jorgensen 25; Muzzi 54 |
| 10 | lge | Chievo | H | W | 2-1 | Jorgensen 12; Jancker 26 |
| 11 | lge | Brescia | A | D | 1-1 | Jorgensen 8 |
| 12 | lge | Empoli | H | W | 2-1 | Pizarro 15 pen; Iaquinta 90 pen |
| 13 | lge | Torino | H | D | 1-1 | Iaquinta 56 |
| 14 | lge | Como | A | W | 2-0 | (Awarded 2-0 to Udinese) |
| 15 | lge | Modena | A | W | 1-0 | Pinzi 24 |
| 16 | lge | Perugia | H | D | 0-0 | |
| 17 | lge | Lazio | A | L | 1-2 | Muzzi 40 |
| 18 | lge | AC Milan | H | W | 1-0 | Pizarro 37 pen |
| 19 | lge | Parma | A | L | 2-3 | Pizarro 57; Jankulovski 90 |
| 20 | lge | Piacenza | H | W | 2-1 | Jankulovski 18; Muzzi 84 |
| 21 | lge | Atalanta | A | D | 0-0 | |
| 22 | lge | Roma | H | W | 2-1 | Sensini 35; Iaquinta 72 |
| 23 | lge | Reggina | A | L | 2-3 | Pizarro 10; Iaquinta 45 |
| 24 | lge | Juventus | H | L | 0-1 | |
| 25 | lge | Bologna | A | L | 0-1 | |
| 26 | lge | Inter Milan | H | W | 2-1 | Jankulovski 48; Iaquinta 59 |
| 27 | lge | Chievo | A | L | 0-3 | |
| 28 | lge | Brescia | H | D | 0-0 | |
| 29 | lge | Como | H | W | 3-2 | Jankulovski 44; Iaquinta 68; Pinzi 72 |
| 30 | lge | Empoli | A | D | 1-1 | Pinzi 56 |
| 31 | lge | Torino | A | W | 1-0 | Iaquinta 81 |
| 32 | lge | Modena | H | W | 2-1 | Pizarro 42 pen; Muzzi 62 |
| 33 | lge | Perugia | A | W | 2-0 | Jankulovski 75; Jorgensen 88 |
| 34 | lge | Lazio | H | W | 2-1 | Pizarro 67 pen; Jankulovski 83 |

## KEY PLAYERS - GOALSCORERS

**1 Vincenzo Iaquinta**

| | | | |
|---|---|---|---|
| Goals in the League | 7 | Player Strike Rate<br>Average number of minutes between League goals scored by player | 215 |
| Contribution to Attacking Power<br>Average number of minutes between League team goals while on pitch | 75 | Club Strike Rate<br>Average number of minutes between League goals scored by club | 85 |

| | PLAYER | LGE GOALS | POWER | STRIKE RATE |
|---|---|---|---|---|
| 2 | Marek Jankulovski | 6 | 83 | 333 mins |
| 3 | David Marcelo Pizarro | 7 | 80 | 424 mins |
| 4 | Martin Jorgensen | 4 | 78 | 508 mins |
| 5 | Roberto Muzzi | 4 | 78 | 573 mins |

## KEY PLAYERS - MIDFIELDERS

**1 Martin Jorgensen**

| | | | |
|---|---|---|---|
| Goals in the League | 4 | Contribution to Attacking Power<br>Average number of minutes between League team goals while on pitch | 78 |
| Defensive Rating<br>Average number of mins between League goals conceded while he was on the pitch | 97 | Scoring Difference<br>Defensive Rating minus Contribution to Attacking Power | 19 |

| | PLAYER | LGE GOALS | DEF RATE | POWER | SCORE DIFF |
|---|---|---|---|---|---|
| 2 | Marek Jankulovski | 6 | 95 | 83 | 12 mins |
| 3 | David Marcelo Pizarro | 7 | 87 | 80 | 7 mins |
| 4 | Giampiero Pinzi | 3 | 85 | 85 | 0 mins |
| 5 | Giuseppe Gemiti | 0 | 79 | 104 | -25 mins |

## KEY PLAYERS - DEFENDERS

**1 Per Kroldrup**

| | | | |
|---|---|---|---|
| Goals Conceded (GC)<br>The number of League goals conceded while he was on the pitch | 20 | Clean Sheets<br>In games when he played at least 70 minutes | 9 |
| Defensive Rating<br>Ave number of mins between League goals conceded while on the pitch | 109 | Club Defensive Rating<br>Average number of mins between League goals conceded by the club this season | 87 |

| | PLAYER | CON LGE | CLEAN SHEETS | DEF RATE |
|---|---|---|---|---|
| 2 | Valentin Do Carmo Alberto | 18 | 5 | 91 mins |
| 3 | Roberto Nester Sensini | 29 | 8 | 90 mins |
| 4 | Valerio Bertotto | 21 | 5 | 89 mins |
| 5 | Mirko Pieri | 19 | 3 | 86 mins |

## GOALS SCORED

| AT HOME | | |
|---|---|---|
| MOST | Juventus | 37 |
| | | 22 |
| LEAST | Torino | 10 |

| AWAY | | |
|---|---|---|
| MOST | Inter Milan | 30 |
| | | 16 |
| LEAST | Como | 9 |

## GOALS CONCEDED

| AT HOME | | |
|---|---|---|
| LEAST | AC Milan | 11 |
| | | 12 |
| MOST | Piacenza | 29 |

| AWAY | | |
|---|---|---|
| LEAST | Juventus | 15 |
| | | 23 |
| MOST | Perugia | 35 |

## KEY GOALKEEPER

**1 Morgan De Sanctis**

| | |
|---|---|
| Goals Conceded in the League | 35 |
| Defensive Rating<br>Ave number of mins between League goals conceded while on the pitch | 85 |
| Counting Games<br>Games when he played at least 70 minutes | 33 |
| Clean Sheets<br>In games when he played at least 70 minutes | 10 |

## TOP POINT EARNERS

| | PLAYER | GAMES | AVE |
|---|---|---|---|
| 1 | Jankulovski | 21 | 1.86 |
| 2 | Jorgensen | 19 | 1.84 |
| 3 | Pinzi | 25 | 1.80 |
| 4 | Bertotto | 19 | 1.79 |
| 5 | Iaquinta | 14 | 1.79 |
| 6 | Kroldrup | 23 | 1.74 |
| 7 | Pizarro | 33 | 1.70 |
| 8 | Pieri | 16 | 1.63 |
| 9 | De Sanctis | 33 | 1.61 |
| 10 | Sensini | 28 | 1.61 |
| | CLUB AVERAGE: | | 1.65 |

Ave = Average points per match in Counting Games

## ATTENDANCES

HOME GROUND: COMUNALE FRIULI CAPACITY: 41705 AVERAGE LEAGUE AT HOME: 17378

| | | | | | | | | |
|---|---|---|---|---|---|---|---|---|
| 9 | Inter Milan | 58962 | 28 | Brescia | 16000 | 13 | Torino | 14000 |
| 4 | Roma | 55000 | 5 | Reggina | 15135 | 33 | Perugia | 13000 |
| 8 | AC Milan | 45000 | 27 | Chievo | 15100 | 15 | Modena | 13000 |
| 17 | Lazio | 45000 | 22 | Roma | 15000 | 21 | Atalanta | 13000 |
| 6 | Juventus | 35168 | 32 | Modena | 15000 | 11 | Brescia | 13000 |
| 26 | Inter Milan | 32000 | 29 | Como | 15000 | 10 | Chievo | 11000 |
| 24 | Juventus | 28000 | 12 | Empoli | 15000 | 2 | Piacenza | 9000 |
| 3 | Atalanta | 27000 | 20 | Piacenza | 15000 | 14 | Como | 8000 |
| 23 | Reggina | 26000 | 1 | Parma | 15000 | 30 | Empoli | 4450 |
| 34 | Lazio | 20000 | 16 | Perugia | 14300 | 31 | Torino | 300 |
| 25 | Bologna | 18000 | 7 | Bologna | 14000 | | | |
| 19 | Parma | 16000 | 18 | AC Milan | 14000 | | | |

Home / Away / Neutral

## DISCIPLINARY RECORDS

| | PLAYER | YELLOW | RED | AVE |
|---|---|---|---|---|
| 1 | Manfredini | 11 | 0 | 136 |
| 2 | Alberto | 6 | 1 | 233 |
| 3 | Rossitto | 3 | 0 | 248 |
| 4 | Pinzi | 6 | 1 | 338 |
| 5 | Iaquinta | 3 | 1 | 377 |
| 6 | Kroldrup | 4 | 1 | 435 |
| 7 | Bertotto | 4 | 0 | 466 |
| 8 | Sottil | 1 | 0 | 507 |
| 9 | Warley | 1 | 0 | 557 |
| 10 | Jankulovski | 3 | 0 | 665 |
| 11 | Pizarro | 4 | 0 | 742 |
| 12 | Pieri | 2 | 0 | 815 |
| 13 | Sensini | 2 | 1 | 874 |
| | Other | 10 | 1 | |
| | TOTAL | 60 | 6 | |

## LEAGUE GOALS

| | PLAYER | MINS | GOALS | AVE |
|---|---|---|---|---|
| 1 | Iaquinta | 1508 | 7 | 215 |
| 2 | Pizarro | 2970 | 7 | 424 |
| 3 | Jankulovski | 1996 | 6 | 333 |
| 4 | Muzzi | 2290 | 4 | 573 |
| 5 | Jorgensen | 2031 | 4 | 508 |
| 6 | Sensini | 2623 | 3 | 874 |
| 7 | Pinzi | 2369 | 3 | 790 |
| 8 | Jancker | 977 | 1 | 977 |
| 9 | Alberto | 1636 | 1 | 1636 |
| | Other | | 0 | |
| | TOTAL | | 36 | |

## MONTH BY MONTH GUIDE TO THE POINTS

| Month | Points | % |
|---|---|---|
| SEPTEMBER | 4 | 44% |
| OCTOBER | 3 | 33% |
| NOVEMBER | 8 | 53% |
| DECEMBER | 7 | 78% |
| JANUARY | 4 | 44% |
| FEBRUARY | 7 | 58% |
| MARCH | 3 | 25% |
| APRIL | 5 | 42% |
| MAY | 12 | 100% |

## TEAM OF THE SEASON

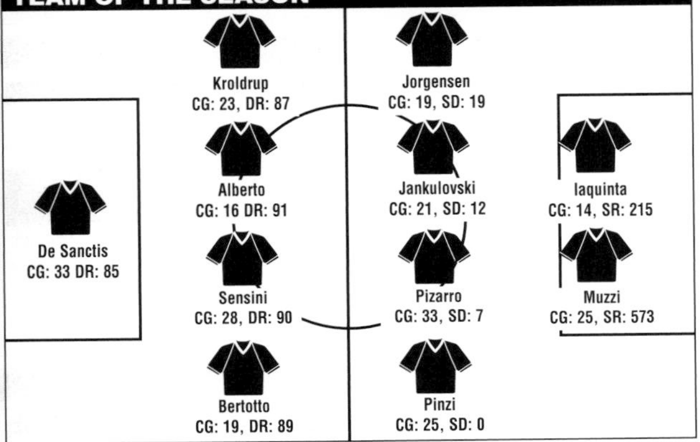
Kroldrup
CG: 23, DR: 87
Jorgensen
CG: 19, SD: 19
Alberto
CG: 16 DR: 91
Jankulovski
CG: 21, SD: 12
Iaquinta
CG: 14, SR: 215
De Sanctis
CG: 33 DR: 85
Sensini
CG: 28, DR: 90
Pizarro
CG: 33, SD: 7
Muzzi
CG: 25, SR: 573
Bertotto
CG: 19, DR: 89
Pinzi
CG: 25, SD: 0

**KEY:** DR = Defensive Rate, SD = Scoring Difference, SR = Strike Rate, CG = Counting Games – League games playing at least 70 minutes

## LEAGUE APPEARANCES, BOOKINGS AND CAPS

| | AGE | IN THE SQUAD | COUNTING GAMES | MINUTES ON PITCH | YELLOW CARDS | RED CARDS | THIS SEASON | HOME COUNTRY |
|---|---|---|---|---|---|---|---|---|
| **Goalkeepers** | | | | | | | | |
| Adriano Bonaiuti | 36 | 7 | 0 | 0 | 0 | 0 | - | Italy |
| Morgan De Sanctis | 26 | 33 | 33 | 2970 | 1 | 0 | - | Italy |
| Oliver Renard | | 26 | 0 | 0 | 0 | 0 | - | Belgium |
| **Defenders** | | | | | | | | |
| Valentin Alberto | 28 | 20 | 16 | 1636 | 6 | 1 | - | Brazil |
| Valerio Bertotto | 30 | 26 | 19 | 1864 | 4 | 0 | - | Italy |
| Jorge Caballero | 28 | 11 | 3 | 279 | 4 | 0 | - | Honduras |
| Dias Felipe Dal Belo | 18 | 15 | 0 | 45 | 0 | 0 | - | Brazil |
| Mohammed Gargo | 28 | 1 | 0 | 0 | 0 | 0 | - | Ghana |
| Per Kroldrup | 23 | 30 | 23 | 2179 | 4 | 1 | - | Denmark |
| Thomas Manfredini | 23 | 27 | 15 | 1504 | 11 | 0 | - | Italy |
| Gonzolo Martinez | 27 | 7 | 0 | 93 | 0 | 0 | - | |
| Mirko Pieri | 24 | 28 | 16 | 1631 | 2 | 0 | - | Italy |
| Giorgio Podimani | 20 | 2 | 0 | 0 | 0 | 0 | - | Italy |
| Roberto Sensini | 36 | 30 | 28 | 2623 | 2 | 1 | - | Argentina |
| Andrea Sottil | 29 | 14 | 5 | 507 | 1 | 0 | - | Italy |
| **Midfielders** | | | | | | | | |
| Sergio Almiron | 22 | 9 | 0 | 58 | 0 | 0 | - | Argentina |
| Maurizio Bedin | 24 | 5 | 1 | 99 | 2 | 1 | - | |
| Giuseppe Gemiti | 22 | 29 | 11 | 1350 | 1 | 0 | - | Germany |
| Marek Jankulovski | 26 | 26 | 21 | 1996 | 3 | 0 | 7 | Czech Republic (13) |
| Martin Jorgensen | 27 | 28 | 19 | 2031 | 0 | 0 | 7 | Denmark (10) |
| Alessandro Moro | 18 | 5 | 0 | 0 | 0 | 0 | - | Italy |
| Sulley Muntari | 18 | 21 | 0 | 259 | 1 | 0 | - | Ghana |
| Giampiero Pinzi | 22 | 28 | 25 | 2369 | 6 | 1 | - | Italy |
| David Marcelo Pizarro | 23 | 33 | 33 | 2970 | 4 | 0 | - | Chile |
| Fabio Rossitto | 23 | 21 | 5 | 746 | 3 | 0 | - | Italy |
| **Forwards** | | | | | | | | |
| Vincenzo Iaquinta | 23 | 28 | 14 | 1508 | 3 | 1 | - | Italy |
| Carsten Jancker | 28 | 24 | 9 | 977 | 1 | 0 | 4 | Germany (4) |
| Roberto Muzzi | 31 | 28 | 25 | 2290 | 0 | 0 | - | Italy |
| Siyabonga Nomvete | 25 | 3 | 0 | 0 | 0 | 0 | - | South Africa |
| Silva Warley | 25 | 26 | 2 | 557 | 1 | 0 | - | Brazil |

**KEY:** LEAGUE  BOOKINGS  CAPS (FIFA RANKING)

## SQUAD APPEARANCES

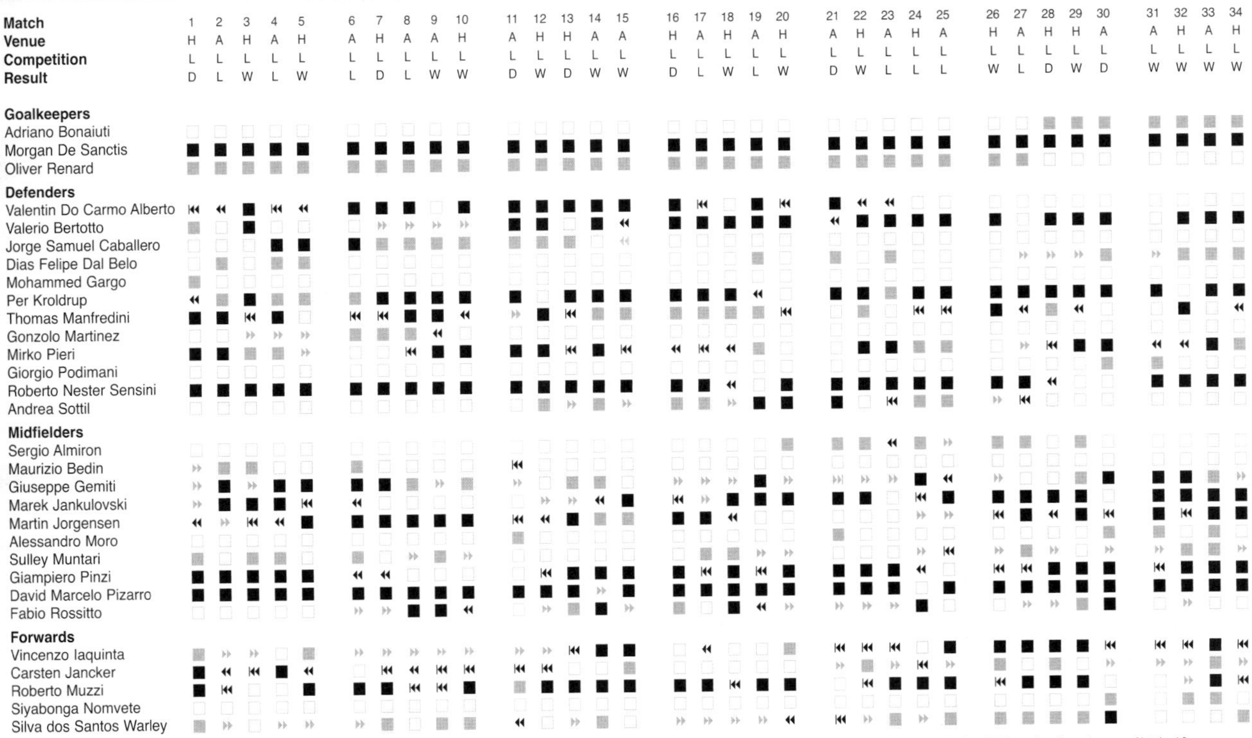
Match 1 2 3 4 5 6 7 8 9 10 11 12 13 14 15 16 17 18 19 20 21 22 23 24 25 26 27 28 29 30 31 32 33 34
Venue H A H A H A H A A H A H H A A H A H A H A H A H A H A H H A A H A H
Competition L L L L L L L L L L L L L L L L L L L L L L L L L L L L L L L L L L
Result D L W L W L D L W W D W D W W D L W L W D W L L L W L D W D W W W W
Goalkeepers
Adriano Bonaiuti
Morgan De Sanctis
Oliver Renard
Defenders
Valentin Do Carmo Alberto
Valerio Bertotto
Jorge Samuel Caballero
Dias Felipe Dal Belo
Mohammed Gargo
Per Kroldrup
Thomas Manfredini
Gonzolo Martinez
Mirko Pieri
Giorgio Podimani
Roberto Nester Sensini
Andrea Sottil
Midfielders
Sergio Almiron
Maurizio Bedin
Giuseppe Gemiti
Marek Jankulovski
Martin Jorgensen
Alessandro Moro
Sulley Muntari
Giampiero Pinzi
David Marcelo Pizarro
Fabio Rossitto
Forwards
Vincenzo Iaquinta
Carsten Jancker
Roberto Muzzi
Siyabonga Nomvete
Silva dos Santos Warley

**KEY:** On all match / On bench / Subbed or sent off (Counting game) / Subbed or sent off (playing less than 70 minutes) / Subbed on from bench (Counting Game) / Subbed on (playing less than 70 minutes) / Subbed on and then subbed or sent off (Counting Game) / Subbed on and then subbed or sent off (playing less than 70 minutes) / Not in 16

# CHIEVO

Final Position: **7th**

| | | | | | | |
|---|---|---|---|---|---|---|
| 1 | lge | Lazio | A | W | 3-2 | D'Anna 14; Bierhoff 48; Della Morte 70 |
| 2 | uc1rl1 | Crvena Zvezda | A | D | 0-0 | |
| 3 | lge | Brescia | H | L | 1-2 | Cossato 73 |
| 4 | lge | Inter Milan | A | L | 1-2 | Marazzina 2 |
| 5 | uc1rl2 | Crvena Zvezda | H | L | 0-2 | |
| 6 | lge | Modena | H | W | 2-0 | Franceschini 32; Corini 47 pen |
| 7 | lge | Torino | A | L | 0-1 | |
| 8 | lge | AC Milan | H | W | 3-2 | Marazzina 22; Bierhoff 50; Cossato 82 |
| 9 | lge | Parma | A | W | 1-0 | Pellissier 90 |
| 10 | lge | Perugia | H | W | 3-0 | Legrottaglie 24; Della Morte 27; Corini 50 pen |
| 11 | lge | Atalanta | H | W | 4-1 | Cossato 45,86; Franceschini 55; Perrotta 84 |
| 12 | lge | Udinese | A | L | 1-2 | Bierhoff 48 |
| 13 | lge | Empoli | H | W | 1-0 | Marazzina 26 |
| 14 | lge | Reggina | A | D | 1-1 | Legrottaglie 49 |
| 15 | lge | Bologna | H | D | 0-0 | |
| 16 | lge | Piacenza | A | W | 3-0 | Della Morte 50; Bierhoff 88; Pellissier 90 |
| 17 | lge | Como | H | W | 2-0 | Legrottaglie 66; Pellissier 73 |
| 18 | lge | Roma | A | W | 1-0 | Cossato 89 |
| 19 | lge | Juventus | H | L | 1-4 | Cossato 72 |
| 20 | lge | Perugia | A | L | 0-1 | |
| 21 | lge | Lazio | H | D | 1-1 | Corini 44 pen |
| 22 | lge | Brescia | A | D | 0-0 | |
| 23 | lge | Inter Milan | H | W | 2-1 | Corini 22 pen,36 pen |
| 24 | lge | Modena | A | L | 0-1 | |
| 25 | lge | Torino | H | W | 3-2 | Pellissier 30; Cossato 59; D'Anna 63 |
| 26 | lge | AC Milan | A | D | 0-0 | |
| 27 | lge | Parma | H | L | 0-4 | |
| 28 | lge | Atalanta | A | L | 0-1 | |
| 29 | lge | Udinese | H | W | 3-0 | Bjelanovic 10; Cossato 37; Pellissier 68 |
| 30 | lge | Empoli | A | L | 1-2 | Bjelanovic 8 |
| 31 | lge | Reggina | H | W | 2-1 | Cossato 24; Legrottaglie 74 |
| 32 | lge | Bologna | A | D | 1-1 | Della Morte 90 |
| 33 | lge | Piacenza | H | W | 3-1 | De Franceschi 65,69; Bjelanovic 80 |
| 34 | lge | Como | A | W | 4-2 | Franceschini 10,41; Luciano 21; Bjelanovic 48 |
| 35 | lge | Roma | H | D | 0-0 | |
| 36 | lge | Juventus | A | L | 3-4 | Bierhoff 62,75,81 |

## KEY PLAYERS - GOALSCORERS

**1 Federico Cossato**

| | | | |
|---|---|---|---|
| Goals in the League | 9 | Player Strike Rate<br>Average number of minutes between League goals scored by player | 224 |
| Contribution to Attacking Power<br>Average number of minutes between League team goals while on pitch | 59 | Club Strike Rate<br>Average number of minutes between League goals scored by club | 60 |

| | PLAYER | LGE GOALS | POWER | STRIKE RATE |
|---|---|---|---|---|
| 2 | Eugenio Corini | 5 | 59 | 535 mins |
| 3 | Daniele Franceschini | 4 | 62 | 623 mins |
| 4 | Nicola Legrottaglie | 4 | 55 | 675 mins |
| 5 | Lorenzo D'Anna | 2 | 57 | 1197 mins |

## KEY PLAYERS - MIDFIELDERS

**1 Daniele Franceschini**

| | | | |
|---|---|---|---|
| Goals in the League | 4 | Contribution to Attacking Power<br>Average number of minutes between League team goals while on pitch | 62 |
| Defensive Rating<br>Average number of mins between League goals conceded while he was on the pitch | 80 | Scoring Difference<br>Defensive Rating minus Contribution to Attacking Power | 18 |

| | PLAYER | LGE GOALS | DEF RATE | POWER | SCORE DIFF |
|---|---|---|---|---|---|
| 2 | Simone Perrotta | 1 | 79 | 64 | 15 mins |
| 3 | Eugenio Corini | 5 | 72 | 59 | 13 mins |
| 4 | Siqueira de Oliveira Luciano | 1 | 82 | 77 | 5 mins |

## KEY PLAYERS - DEFENDERS

**1 Salvatore Lanna**

| | | | |
|---|---|---|---|
| Goals Conceded (GC)<br>The number of League goals conceded while he was on the pitch | 28 | Clean Sheets<br>In games when he played at least 70 minutes | 10 |
| Defensive Rating<br>Ave number of mins between League goals conceded while on the pitch | 92 | Club Defensive Rating<br>Average number of mins between League goals conceded by the club this season | 78 |

| | PLAYER | CON LGE | CLEAN SHEETS | DEF RATE |
|---|---|---|---|---|
| 2 | Nicola Legrottaglie | 32 | 11 | 84 mins |
| 3 | Lorenzo D'Anna | 29 | 10 | 83 mins |
| 4 | Fabio Moro | 35 | 10 | 74 mins |

## GOALS SCORED

**AT HOME**

| | | |
|---|---|---|
| MOST | Juventus | 37 |
| | | 22 |
| LEAST | Torino | 10 |

**AWAY**

| | | |
|---|---|---|
| MOST | Inter Milan | 30 |
| | | 16 |
| LEAST | Como | 9 |

## GOALS CONCEDED

**AT HOME**

| | | |
|---|---|---|
| LEAST | AC Milan | 11 |
| | | 12 |
| MOST | Piacenza | 29 |

**AWAY**

| | | |
|---|---|---|
| LEAST | Juventus | 15 |
| | | 23 |
| MOST | Perugia | 35 |

## KEY GOALKEEPER

**1 Cristiano Lupatelli**

| | |
|---|---|
| Goals Conceded in the League | 28 |
| Defensive Rating<br>Ave number of mins between League goals conceded while on the pitch | 84 |
| Counting Games<br>Games when he played at least 70 minutes | 26 |
| Clean Sheets<br>In games when he played at least 70 minutes | 10 |

## TOP POINT EARNERS

| | PLAYER | GAMES | AVE |
|---|---|---|---|
| 1 | Franceschini | 22 | 2.09 |
| 2 | Legrottaglie | 30 | 1.80 |
| 3 | Cossato | 21 | 1.76 |
| 4 | D'Anna | 27 | 1.74 |
| 5 | Lanna | 27 | 1.67 |
| 6 | Corini | 29 | 1.66 |
| 7 | Moro | 29 | 1.59 |
| 8 | Lupatelli | 26 | 1.58 |
| 9 | Perrotta | 30 | 1.53 |
| | CLUB AVERAGE: | | 1.62 |

Ave = Average points per match in Counting Games

## ATTENDANCES

HOME GROUND: MARCANTONIO BENTEGODI CAPACITY: 44758 AVERAGE LEAGUE AT HOME: 18350

| | | | | | | | | |
|---|---|---|---|---|---|---|---|---|
| 4 | Inter Milan | 60000 | 27 | Parma | 20000 | 31 | Reggina | 11804 |
| 18 | Roma | 55000 | 29 | Udinese | 15100 | 10 | Perugia | 11556 |
| 26 | AC Milan | 48000 | 6 | Modena | 15000 | 17 | Como | 11527 |
| 1 | Lazio | 40000 | 24 | Modena | 15000 | 33 | Piacenza | 11400 |
| 36 | Juventus | 39400 | 9 | Parma | 14929 | 12 | Udinese | 11000 |
| 15 | Bologna | 36000 | 21 | Lazio | 14921 | 25 | Torino | 10000 |
| 19 | Juventus | 35544 | 35 | Roma | 14869 | 20 | Perugia | 10000 |
| 23 | Inter Milan | 34634 | 5 | Crvena Zvezda | 14807 | 16 | Piacenza | 6139 |
| 8 | AC Milan | 30000 | 28 | Atalanta | 14000 | 30 | Empoli | 5808 |
| 14 | Reggina | 23000 | 22 | Brescia | 14000 | 34 | Como | 4000 |
| 32 | Bologna | 21800 | 3 | Brescia | 13880 | | | |
| 2 | Crvena Zvezda | 20000 | 11 | Atalanta | 13200 | | | |
| 7 | Torino | 20000 | 13 | Empoli | 12530 | | | |

■ Home □ Away ▒ Neutral

## DISCIPLINARY RECORDS

| | PLAYER | YELLOW | RED | AVE |
|---|---|---|---|---|
| 1 | Mensah | 4 | 0 | 189 |
| 2 | Legrottaglie | 10 | 0 | 270 |
| 3 | Lazetic | 2 | 0 | 275 |
| 4 | Bjelanovic | 2 | 0 | 286 |
| 5 | Corini | 8 | 1 | 297 |
| 6 | Moro | 8 | 0 | 324 |
| 7 | Lorenzi | 2 | 0 | 351 |
| 8 | Perrotta | 7 | 0 | 394 |
| 9 | Cossato | 4 | 0 | 503 |
| 10 | Lanna | 4 | 1 | 517 |
| 11 | D'Anna | 3 | 1 | 598 |
| 12 | Luciano | 2 | 0 | 613 |
| 13 | Ambrosio | 1 | 0 | 720 |
| | Other | 12 | 2 | |
| | TOTAL | 69 | 5 | |

## LEAGUE GOALS

| | PLAYER | MINS | GOALS | AVE |
|---|---|---|---|---|
| 1 | Cossato | 2014 | 9 | 224 |
| 2 | Bierhoff | 1530 | 7 | 219 |
| 3 | Pellissier | 1171 | 5 | 234 |
| 4 | Corini | 2675 | 5 | 535 |
| 5 | Bjelanovic | 573 | 4 | 143 |
| 6 | Franceschini | 2493 | 4 | 623 |
| 7 | Della Morte | 917 | 4 | 229 |
| 8 | Legrottaglie | 2700 | 4 | 675 |
| 9 | Marazzina | 982 | 3 | 327 |
| 10 | D'Anna | 2394 | 2 | 1197 |
| 11 | De Franceschi | 119 | 2 | 60 |
| 12 | Luciano | 1227 | 1 | 1227 |
| 13 | Perrotta | 2764 | 1 | 2764 |
| | Other | | 0 | |
| | TOTAL | | 51 | |

## MONTH BY MONTH GUIDE TO THE POINTS

| | | |
|---|---|---|
| SEPTEMBER | 3 | 33% |
| OCTOBER | 6 | 67% |
| NOVEMBER | 13 | 72% |
| DECEMBER | 7 | 78% |
| JANUARY | 3 | 33% |
| FEBRUARY | 5 | 42% |
| MARCH | 4 | 33% |
| APRIL | 7 | 58% |
| MAY | 7 | 58% |

## TEAM OF THE SEASON

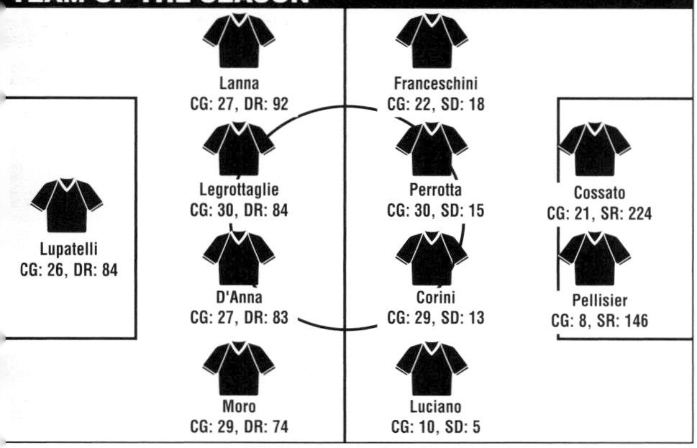
Lanna
CG: 27, DR: 92
Franceschini
CG: 22, SD: 18
Legrottaglie
CG: 30, DR: 84
Perrotta
CG: 30, SD: 15
Cossato
CG: 21, SR: 224
Lupatelli
CG: 26, DR: 84
D'Anna
CG: 27, DR: 83
Corini
CG: 29, SD: 13
Pellisier
CG: 8, SR: 146
Moro
CG: 29, DR: 74
Luciano
CG: 10, SD: 5

KEY: DR = Defensive Rate, SD = Scoring Difference, SR = Strike Rate, CG = Counting Games – League games playing at least 70 minutes

## LEAGUE APPEARANCES, BOOKINGS AND CAPS

| | AGE | IN THE SQUAD | COUNTING GAMES | MINUTES ON PITCH | YELLOW CARDS | RED CARDS | THIS SEASON | HOME COUNTRY |
|---|---|---|---|---|---|---|---|---|
| **Goalkeepers** | | | | | | | | |
| Marco Ambrosio | 30 | 34 | 8 | 720 | 1 | 0 | - | Italy |
| Cristiano Lupatelli | 25 | 27 | 26 | 2340 | 2 | 0 | - | Italy |
| Mattia Passarini | 22 | 7 | 0 | 0 | 0 | 0 | - | Italy |
| **Defenders** | | | | | | | | |
| Maurizio D'Angelo | 33 | 8 | 1 | 90 | 0 | 0 | - | |
| Lorenzo D'Anna | 31 | 27 | 27 | 2394 | 3 | 1 | - | Italy |
| Gianluca Grassadonia | 31 | 4 | 1 | 107 | 0 | 0 | - | Italy |
| Salvatore Lanna | 26 | 31 | 27 | 2585 | 4 | 1 | 1 | Italy (12) |
| Nicola Legrottaglie | 26 | 30 | 30 | 2700 | 10 | 0 | 6 | Italy (12) |
| Stefano Lorenzi | 26 | 23 | 7 | 702 | 2 | 0 | - | Italy |
| John Mensah | 20 | 23 | 7 | 756 | 4 | 0 | - | Ghana |
| Fabio Moro | 27 | 31 | 29 | 2594 | 8 | 0 | - | Italy |
| Emanuele Pesaresi | 26 | 19 | 2 | 267 | 1 | 0 | - | Italy |
| Fredrik Risp | 22 | 4 | 0 | 0 | 0 | 0 | - | Sweden |
| **Midfielders** | | | | | | | | |
| Daniel Andersson | 25 | 26 | 2 | 380 | 4 | 1 | - | Sweden |
| Eugenio Corini | 32 | 30 | 29 | 2675 | 8 | 1 | - | Italy |
| Ivone De Franceschi | 29 | 8 | 0 | 119 | 0 | 0 | - | Italy |
| Ivano Della Morte | 28 | 28 | 1 | 917 | 0 | 0 | - | Italy |
| Daniele Franceschini | 27 | 33 | 22 | 2493 | 2 | 0 | - | Italy |
| Nikola Lazetic | 25 | 14 | 1 | 551 | 2 | 0 | - | Serbia & Montenegro |
| Siqueira Luciano | 27 | 16 | 10 | 1227 | 2 | 0 | - | Brazil |
| Ariel De Paula Marcos | 19 | 8 | 0 | 32 | 0 | 0 | - | Brazil |
| Lilian Nalis | 31 | 10 | 1 | 288 | 1 | 0 | - | France |
| Dario Passoni | 29 | 7 | 2 | 251 | 0 | 0 | - | Italy |
| Simone Perrotta | 25 | 32 | 30 | 2764 | 7 | 0 | 6 | Italy (12) |
| **Forwards** | | | | | | | | |
| Luigi Beghetto | 30 | 21 | 2 | 339 | 1 | 0 | - | Italy |
| Oliver Bierhoff | 35 | 28 | 10 | 1530 | 1 | 1 | - | Germany |
| Sasa Bjelanovic | 24 | 15 | 1 | 573 | 2 | 0 | - | Croatia |
| Federico Cossato | 30 | 26 | 21 | 2014 | 4 | 0 | - | Italy |
| Massimo Marazzina | 28 | 15 | 9 | 982 | 0 | 0 | 3 | Italy (12) |
| Sergio Pellissier | 24 | 29 | 8 | 1171 | 0 | 0 | - | Italy |

KEY: LEAGUE BOOKINGS CAPS (FIFA RANKING)

## SQUAD APPEARANCES

| Match | 1 | 2 | 3 | 4 | 5 | 6 | 7 | 8 | 9 | 10 | 11 | 12 | 13 | 14 | 15 | 16 | 17 | 18 | 19 | 20 | 21 | 22 | 23 | 24 | 25 | 26 | 27 | 28 | 29 | 30 | 31 | 32 | 33 | 34 | 35 | 36 |
|---|---|---|---|---|---|---|---|---|---|---|---|---|---|---|---|---|---|---|---|---|---|---|---|---|---|---|---|---|---|---|---|---|---|---|---|---|
| Venue | A | A | H | A | H | H | A | H | A | H | H | A | H | A | H | A | H | A | H | A | H | A | H | A | H | A | H | A | H | A | H | A | H | A | H | A |
| Competition | L | E | L | L | E | L | L | L | L | L | L | L | L | L | L | L | L | L | L | L | L | L | L | L | L | L | L | L | L | L | L | L | L | L | L | L |
| Result | W | D | L | L | L | W | L | W | W | W | W | L | W | D | D | W | W | W | L | L | D | D | W | L | W | D | L | L | W | L | W | D | W | W | D | L |

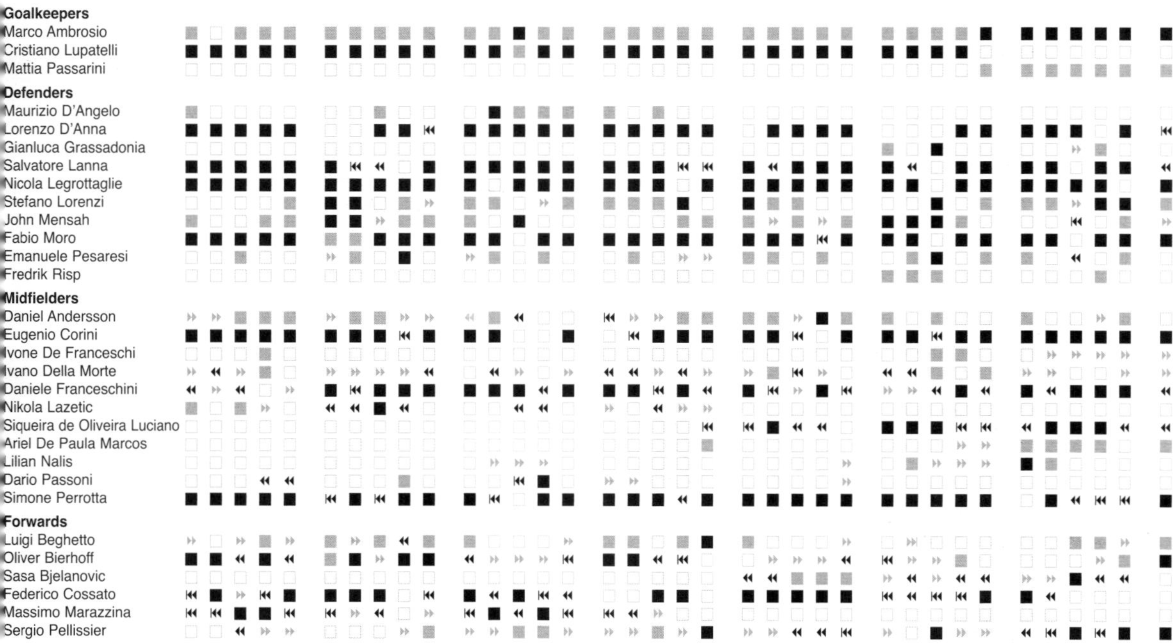
Goalkeepers
Marco Ambrosio
Cristiano Lupatelli
Mattia Passarini
Defenders
Maurizio D'Angelo
Lorenzo D'Anna
Gianluca Grassadonia
Salvatore Lanna
Nicola Legrottaglie
Stefano Lorenzi
John Mensah
Fabio Moro
Emanuele Pesaresi
Fredrik Risp
Midfielders
Daniel Andersson
Eugenio Corini
Ivone De Franceschi
Ivano Della Morte
Daniele Franceschini
Nikola Lazetic
Siqueira de Oliveira Luciano
Ariel De Paula Marcos
Lilian Nalis
Dario Passoni
Simone Perrotta
Forwards
Luigi Beghetto
Oliver Bierhoff
Sasa Bjelanovic
Federico Cossato
Massimo Marazzina
Sergio Pellissier

KEY: ■ On all match ■ On bench ⏮ Subbed or sent off (Counting game) « Subbed or sent off (playing less than 70 minutes) ⏭ Subbed on from bench (Counting Game) » Subbed on (playing less than 70 minutes) Subbed on and then subbed or sent off (Counting Game) Subbed on and then subbed or sent off (playing less than 70 minutes) □ Not in 16

# ROMA

Final Position: **8th**

| | | | | | | |
|---|---|---|---|---|---|---|
| 1 | lge | Bologna | A | L | 1-2 | Batistuta 43 pen |
| 2 | ecgc | Real Madrid | H | L | 0-3 | |
| 3 | lge | Modena | H | L | 1-2 | Totti 5 pen |
| 4 | ecgc | AEK Athens | A | D | 0-0 | |
| 5 | lge | Brescia | A | W | 3-2 | Totti 30 pen,40,81 |
| 6 | ecgc | Genk | A | W | 1-0 | Cassano 81 |
| 7 | lge | Udinese | H | W | 4-1 | Montella 24; Batistuta 76; Totti 81,90 |
| 8 | lge | Empoli | A | W | 3-1 | Emerson 31; Candela 34; Tommasi 90 |
| 9 | ecgc | Genk | H | D | 0-0 | |
| 10 | lge | Lazio | A | D | 2-2 | Delvecchio 57; Batistuta 66 |
| 11 | ecgc | Real Madrid | A | W | 1-0 | Totti 27 |
| 12 | lge | Perugia | H | D | 2-2 | Panucci 67; Totti 71 |
| 13 | lge | Como | H | W | 2-1 | Delvecchio 18; Totti 46 |
| 14 | lge | Piacenza | A | D | 1-1 | Cassano 26 |
| 15 | ecgc | AEK Athens | H | D | 1-1 | Delvecchio 40 |
| 16 | lge | Inter Milan | H | D | 2-2 | Montella 59; Batistuta 73 |
| 17 | lge | Parma | A | L | 0-3 | |
| 18 | ecgb | Arsenal | H | L | 1-3 | Cassano 4 |
| 19 | lge | Juventus | H | D | 2-2 | Totti 12; Cassano 44 |
| 20 | lge | AC Milan | A | L | 0-1 | |
| 21 | ecgb | Ajax | A | L | 1-2 | Batistuta 89 |
| 22 | lge | Reggina | H | W | 3-0 | Samuel 3; Totti 24; Montella 70 |
| 23 | lge | Torino | A | W | 1-0 | Samuel 46 |
| 24 | lge | Chievo | H | L | 0-1 | |
| 25 | lge | Atalanta | A | L | 1-2 | Totti 9 |
| 26 | lge | Como | A | L | 0-2 | |
| 27 | lge | Bologna | H | W | 3-1 | Montella 36; Delvecchio 52; Cassano 73 |
| 28 | lge | Modena | A | D | 1-1 | Dellas 90 |
| 29 | lge | Brescia | H | D | 0-0 | |
| 30 | ecgb | Valencia | H | L | 0-1 | |
| 31 | lge | Udinese | A | L | 1-2 | Montella 54 |
| 32 | ecgb | Valencia | A | W | 3-0 | Totti 24,30; Emerson 36 |
| 33 | lge | Empoli | H | W | 3-1 | Totti 31; Montella 49,68 |
| 34 | lge | Lazio | H | D | 1-1 | Cassano 90 |
| 35 | ecgb | Arsenal | A | D | 1-1 | Cassano 45 |
| 36 | lge | Perugia | A | L | 0-1 | |
| 37 | ecgb | Ajax | H | D | 1-1 | Cassano 24 |
| 38 | lge | Piacenza | H | W | 3-0 | Cassano 11; Delvecchio 30; Totti 43 |
| 39 | lge | Inter Milan | A | D | 3-3 | Cassano 46; Di Biagio 82 og; Montella 83 |
| 40 | lge | Parma | H | W | 2-1 | Totti 45; Guigou 73 |
| 41 | lge | Juventus | A | L | 1-2 | Montella 43 |
| 42 | lge | AC Milan | H | W | 2-1 | Cassano 61; Tommasi 76 |
| 43 | lge | Reggina | A | W | 3-2 | Tommasi 61; Emerson 63; Vargas 68 og |
| 44 | lge | Torino | H | W | 3-1 | Cassano 32,62; De Rossi 55 |
| 45 | lge | Chievo | A | D | 0-0 | |
| 46 | lge | Atalanta | H | L | 1-2 | De Rossi 30 |

## ATTENDANCES

HOME GROUND: STADIO OLIMPICO CAPACITY: 82307 AVERAGE LEAGUE AT HOME: 53982

| | | | | | | | | |
|---|---|---|---|---|---|---|---|---|
| 10 | Lazio | 80000 | **3** | **Modena** | **54000** | 43 | Reggina | 24000 |
| **2** | **Real Madrid** | **80000** | **22** | **Reggina** | **53000** | **15** | **AEK Athens** | **23734** |
| **19** | **Juventus** | **75000** | **44** | **Torino** | **52000** | 6 | Genk | 22989 |
| 20 | AC Milan | 72000 | **33** | **Empoli** | **51000** | 14 | Piacenza | 20000 |
| 11 | Real Madrid | 71722 | 21 | Ajax | 50148 | 5 | Brescia | 19000 |
| 39 | Inter Milan | 70000 | **38** | **Piacenza** | **50000** | 25 | Atalanta | 18000 |
| **18** | **Arsenal** | **70000** | **34** | **Lazio** | **50000** | 28 | Modena | 17500 |
| **42** | **AC Milan** | **60000** | **9** | **Genk** | **50000** | 23 | Torino | 15000 |
| **13** | **Como** | **55000** | **46** | **Atalanta** | **45000** | 17 | Parma | 15000 |
| **16** | **Inter Milan** | **55000** | **29** | **Brescia** | **43000** | 31 | Udinese | 15000 |
| **24** | **Chievo** | **55000** | 41 | Juventus | 42592 | 45 | Chievo | 14869 |
| **12** | **Perugia** | **55000** | 32 | Valencia | 38000 | 8 | Empoli | 13000 |
| **7** | **Udinese** | **55000** | 35 | Arsenal | 35472 | 36 | Perugia | 12000 |
| **40** | **Parma** | **55000** | 4 | AEK Athens | 33000 | 26 | Como | 3000 |
| **27** | **Bologna** | **54695** | 1 | Bologna | 32000 | | | |
| **37** | **Ajax** | **54502** | **30** | **Valencia** | **31000** | | | |

■ Home □ Away ▒ Neutral

## KEY PLAYERS - GOALSCORERS

**1 Francesco Totti**

| | | | |
|---|---|---|---|
| **Goals in the League** | 14 | **Player Strike Rate** Average number of minutes between League goals scored by player | 138 |
| **Contribution to Attacking Power** Average number of minutes between League team goals while on pitch | 52 | **Club Strike Rate** Average number of minutes between League goals scored by club | 56 |

| | PLAYER | LGE GOALS | POWER | STRIKE RATE |
|---|---|---|---|---|
| 2 | Vincenzo Montella | 9 | 65 | 195 mins |
| 3 | Ferreira da Rosa Emerson | 2 | 50 | 1360 mins |
| 4 | Walter Adrian Samuel | 2 | 52 | 1395 mins |
| 5 | Vincent Candela | 1 | 50 | 2019 mins |

## KEY PLAYERS - MIDFIELDERS

**1 Ferreira da Rosa Emerson**

| | | | |
|---|---|---|---|
| **Goals in the League** | 2 | **Contribution to Attacking Power** Average number of minutes between League team goals while on pitch | 50 |
| **Defensive Rating** Average number of mins between League goals conceded while he was on the pitch | 70 | **Scoring Difference** Defensive Rating minus Contribution to Attacking Power | 20 |

| | PLAYER | LGE GOALS | DEF RATE | POWER | SCORE DIFF |
|---|---|---|---|---|---|
| 2 | Francisco Lima | 0 | 70 | 50 | 20 mins |
| 3 | Damiano Tommasi | 3 | 72 | 61 | 11 mins |
| 4 | Olivier Dacourt | 0 | 74 | 74 | 0 mins |

## KEY PLAYERS - DEFENDERS

**1 Marcos Cafu**

| | | | |
|---|---|---|---|
| **Goals Conceded (GC)** The number of League goals conceded while he was on the pitch | 30 | **Clean Sheets** In games when he played at least 70 minutes | 3 |
| **Defensive Rating** Ave number of mins between League goals conceded while on the pitch | 70 | **Club Defensive Rating** Average number of mins between League goals conceded by the club this season | 67 |

| | PLAYER | CON LGE | CLEAN SHEETS | DEF RATE |
|---|---|---|---|---|
| 2 | Christian Panucci | 36 | 5 | 69 mins |
| 3 | Walter Adrian Samuel | 42 | 4 | 66 mins |
| 4 | Jonathan Zebina | 25 | 2 | 64 mins |
| 5 | Vincent Candela | 32 | 3 | 63 mins |

## KEY GOALKEEPER

**1 Ivan Pellizzoli**

| | |
|---|---|
| **Goals Conceded in the League** | 23 |
| **Defensive Rating** Ave number of mins between League goals conceded while on the pitch | 76 |
| **Counting Games** Games when he played at least 70 minutes | 18 |
| **Clean Sheets** In games when he played at least 70 minutes | 4 |

## TOP POINT EARNERS

| | PLAYER | GAMES | AVE |
|---|---|---|---|
| 1 | Lima | 27 | 1.67 |
| 2 | Zebina | 17 | 1.65 |
| 3 | Emerson | 30 | 1.63 |
| 4 | Candela | 22 | 1.59 |
| 5 | Samuel | 31 | 1.55 |
| 6 | Pellizzoli | 18 | 1.44 |
| 7 | Panucci | 26 | 1.42 |
| 8 | Antonioli | 14 | 1.36 |
| 9 | Totti | 20 | 1.35 |
| 10 | Cafu | 22 | 1.27 |
| | **CLUB AVERAGE:** | | **1.44** |

Ave = Average points per match in Counting Games

## DISCIPLINARY RECORDS

| | PLAYER | YELLOW | RED | AVE |
|---|---|---|---|---|
| 1 | Dellas | 5 | 2 | 103 |
| 2 | Cassano | 7 | 0 | 192 |
| 3 | Zebina | 6 | 1 | 229 |
| 4 | Sartor | 2 | 0 | 249 |
| 5 | Guigou | 2 | 0 | 310 |
| 6 | Samuel | 9 | 0 | 310 |
| 7 | Dacourt | 4 | 0 | 371 |
| 8 | Emerson | 6 | 1 | 388 |
| 9 | Totti | 3 | 1 | 482 |
| 10 | Lima | 5 | 0 | 488 |
| 11 | Candela | 3 | 1 | 504 |
| 12 | Delvecchio | 1 | 1 | 550 |
| 13 | Tommasi | 2 | 0 | 611 |
| | Other | 14 | 2 | |
| | TOTAL | 69 | 9 | |

## LEAGUE GOALS

| | PLAYER | MINS | GOALS | AVE |
|---|---|---|---|---|
| 1 | Totti | 1931 | 14 | 138 |
| 2 | Montella | 1757 | 9 | 195 |
| 3 | Cassano | 1345 | 9 | 149 |
| 4 | Batistuta | 662 | 4 | 166 |
| 5 | Delvecchio | 1101 | 4 | 275 |
| 6 | Tommasi | 1223 | 3 | 408 |
| 7 | Samuel | 2790 | 2 | 1395 |
| 8 | De Rossi | 278 | 2 | 139 |
| 9 | Emerson | 2720 | 2 | 1360 |
| 10 | Candela | 2019 | 1 | 2019 |
| 11 | Dellas | 727 | 1 | 727 |
| 12 | Guigou | 620 | 1 | 620 |
| 13 | Panucci | 2466 | 1 | 2466 |
| | Other | | 2 | |
| | TOTAL | | 55 | |

## MONTH BY MONTH GUIDE TO THE POINTS

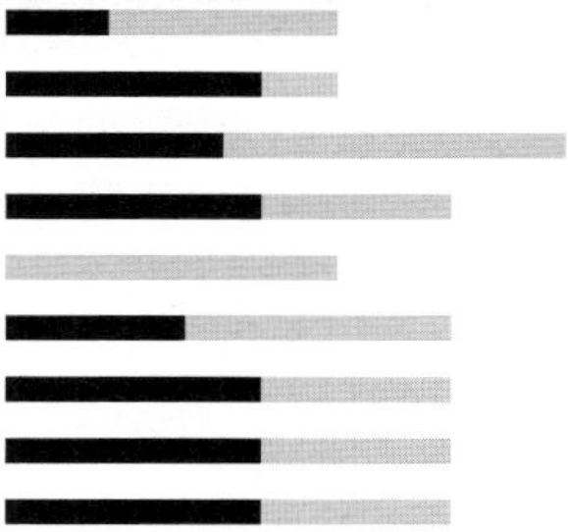

| | | |
|---|---|---|
| SEPTEMBER | 3 | 33% |
| OCTOBER | 7 | 78% |
| NOVEMBER | 6 | 40% |
| DECEMBER | 7 | 58% |
| JANUARY | 0 | 0% |
| FEBRUARY | 5 | 42% |
| MARCH | 7 | 58% |
| APRIL | 7 | 58% |
| MAY | 7 | 58% |

## TEAM OF THE SEASON

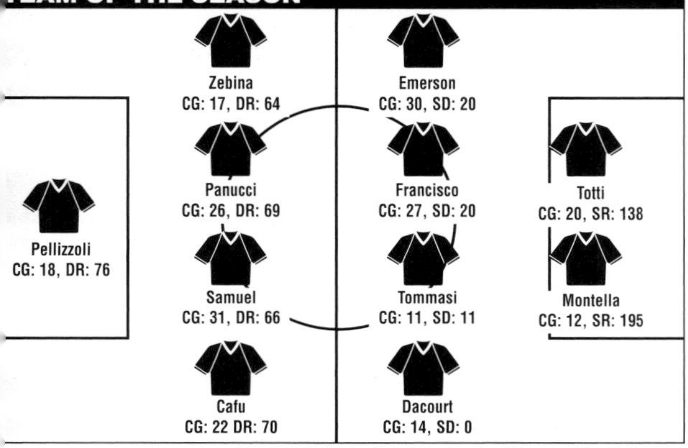
Zebina
CG: 17, DR: 64
Emerson
CG: 30, SD: 20
Panucci
CG: 26, DR: 69
Francisco
CG: 27, SD: 20
Totti
CG: 20, SR: 138
Pellizzoli
CG: 18, DR: 76
Samuel
CG: 31, DR: 66
Tommasi
CG: 11, SD: 11
Montella
CG: 12, SR: 195
Cafu
CG: 22 DR: 70
Dacourt
CG: 14, SD: 0

**KEY:** DR = Defensive Rate, SD = Scoring Difference, SR = Strike Rate, CG = Counting Games – League games playing at least 70 minutes

## LEAGUE APPEARANCES, BOOKINGS AND CAPS

| | AGE | IN THE SQUAD | COUNTING GAMES | MINUTES ON PITCH | YELLOW CARDS | RED CARDS | THIS SEASON | HOME COUNTRY |
|---|---|---|---|---|---|---|---|---|
| **Goalkeepers** | | | | | | | | |
| Francesco Antonioli | 33 | 25 | 14 | 1297 | 0 | 1 | - | Italy |
| Marco Paoloni | 19 | 1 | 0 | 0 | 0 | 0 | - | Italy |
| Ivan Pellizzoli | 22 | 28 | 18 | 1740 | 0 | 0 | 1 | Italy (12) |
| Carlo Zotti | 20 | 14 | 0 | 23 | 0 | 0 | - | Italy |
| **Defenders** | | | | | | | | |
| Aldair | 37 | 23 | 14 | 1329 | 1 | 0 | - | Brazil |
| Marcos Cafu | 33 | 27 | 22 | 2114 | 3 | 0 | 4 | Brazil (1) |
| Vincent Candela | 29 | 23 | 22 | 2019 | 3 | 1 | 1 | France (2) |
| Leandro Cufre | 25 | 24 | 4 | 469 | 0 | 0 | - | Argentina |
| Daniele De Rossi | 18 | 13 | 2 | 278 | 1 | 0 | - | Italy |
| Traianos Dellas | 27 | 22 | 7 | 727 | 5 | 2 | - | Greece |
| Damiano Ferronetti | 19 | 5 | 0 | 36 | 0 | 0 | - | Italy |
| Gianni Guigou | 28 | 21 | 4 | 620 | 2 | 0 | - | Uruguay |
| Christian Panucci | 30 | 29 | 26 | 2466 | 3 | 1 | 8 | Italy (12) |
| Walter Samuel | 25 | 32 | 31 | 2790 | 9 | 0 | 1 | Argentina (5) |
| Luigi Sartor | 28 | 17 | 3 | 499 | 2 | 0 | - | Italy |
| Jonathan Zebina | 24 | 20 | 17 | 1605 | 6 | 1 | - | France |
| **Midfielders** | | | | | | | | |
| Alberto Aguilani | 18 | 4 | 0 | 1 | 0 | 0 | - | Italy |
| Olasunkanmi Ajide | 17 | 1 | 0 | 0 | 0 | 0 | - | Nigeria |
| Davide Bombardini | 29 | 21 | 1 | 252 | 2 | 0 | - | Italy |
| Olivier Dacourt | 28 | 18 | 14 | 1486 | 4 | 0 | 3 | France (2) |
| Emerson Ferreira | 27 | 31 | 30 | 2720 | 6 | 1 | 5 | Brazil (1) |
| Diego Fuser | 34 | 8 | 0 | 88 | 0 | 0 | - | Italy |
| Josep Guardiola | 32 | 18 | 1 | 201 | 2 | 0 | - | Spain |
| Francisco Lima | 32 | 29 | 27 | 2440 | 5 | 0 | - | Brazil |
| Ivan Tomic | 27 | 6 | 0 | 53 | 1 | 0 | - | Serbia & Montenegro |
| Damiano Tommasi | 29 | 27 | 11 | 1223 | 2 | 0 | 8 | Italy (12) |
| **Forwards** | | | | | | | | |
| Gabriel Batistuta | 34 | 14 | 5 | 662 | 1 | 0 | - | Argentina |
| Antonio Cassano | 20 | 29 | 9 | 1345 | 7 | 0 | - | Italy |
| Marco Delvecchio | 30 | 18 | 9 | 1101 | 1 | 1 | 4 | Italy (12) |
| Massimo Marazzina | 28 | 8 | 0 | 180 | 0 | 0 | 3 | Italy (12) |
| Vincenzo Montella | 29 | 31 | 12 | 1757 | 0 | 0 | 3 | Italy (12) |
| Francesco Totti | 26 | 24 | 20 | 1931 | 3 | 1 | 2 | Italy (12) |

**KEY:** LEAGUE BOOKINGS CAPS (FIFA RANKING)

## SQUAD APPEARANCES

| latch | 1 | 2 | 3 | 4 | 5 | 6 | 7 | 8 | 9 | 10 | 11 | 12 | 13 | 14 | 15 | 16 | 17 | 18 | 19 | 20 | 21 | 22 | 23 | 24 | 25 | 26 | 27 | 28 | 29 | 30 | 31 | 32 | 33 | 34 | 35 | 36 | 37 | 38 | 39 | 40 | 41 | 42 | 43 | 44 | 45 | 46 |
|---|---|---|---|---|---|---|---|---|---|---|---|---|---|---|---|---|---|---|---|---|---|---|---|---|---|---|---|---|---|---|---|---|---|---|---|---|---|---|---|---|---|---|---|---|---|---|
| enue | A | H | H | A | A | A | H | A | H | A | A | H | H | A | H | H | A | H | H | A | A | H | A | H | A | A | H | A | H | H | A | A | H | H | A | A | H | H | A | H | A | H | A | H | A | H |
| ompetition | L | C | L | C | L | C | L | L | C | L | C | L | L | L | C | L | L | C | L | L | C | L | L | L | L | L | L | L | L | C | L | C | L | L | C | L | C | L | L | L | L | L | L | L | L | L |
| esult | L | L | L | D | W | W | W | W | D | D | W | D | W | D | D | D | L | L | D | L | L | W | W | L | L | L | W | D | D | L | L | W | W | D | D | L | D | W | D | W | L | W | W | W | D | L |

**oalkeepers**
rancesco Antonioli
larco Paoloni
van Pellizzoli
arlo Zotti

**efenders**
ldair
larcos Cafu
incent Candela
eandro Damian Cufre
aniele De Rossi
raianos Dellas
amiano Ferronetti
ianni Guigou
hristian Panucci
Valter Adrian Samuel
uigi Sartor
onathan Zebina

**lidfielders**
lberto Aguilani
jide
avide Bombardini
livier Dacourt
erreira da Rosa Emerson
iego Fuser
osep Guardiola
rancisco Lima
van Tomic
amiano Tommasi

**orwards**
abriel Batistuta
ntonio Cassano
larco Delvecchio
lassimo Marazzina
incenzo Montella
rancesco Totti

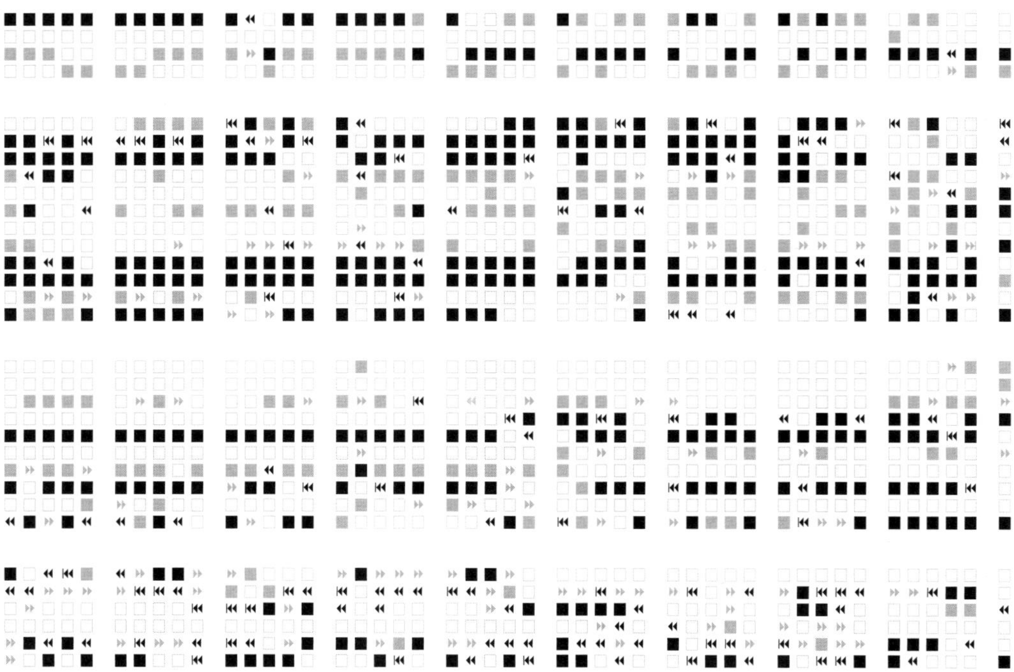

# BRESCIA

Final Position: **9th**

| | | | | | | |
|---|---|---|---|---|---|---|
| 1 | lge | Piacenza | H | L | 1-2 | Bachini 67 |
| 2 | lge | Chievo | A | W | 2-1 | Tare 57; Seric 88 |
| 3 | lge | Roma | H | L | 2-3 | Baggio 45 pen; Schopp 83 |
| 4 | lge | Reggina | A | D | 2-2 | Appiah 11; Baggio 45 pen |
| 5 | lge | Bologna | A | L | 0-3 | |
| 6 | lge | Como | H | D | 1-1 | Baggio 85 pen |
| 7 | lge | Torino | A | W | 2-0 | Tare 31; Appiah 82 |
| 8 | lge | Parma | A | L | 3-4 | Appiah 13; Baggio 24,58 pen |
| 9 | lge | Empoli | H | L | 0-2 | |
| 10 | lge | Atalanta | A | L | 0-2 | |
| 11 | lge | Udinese | H | D | 1-1 | Sensini 68 og |
| 12 | lge | Inter Milan | A | L | 0-4 | |
| 13 | lge | Juventus | H | W | 2-0 | Schopp 78; Tare 84 |
| 14 | lge | Perugia | H | W | 3-1 | Tare 24,40; Baggio 88 pen |
| 15 | lge | AC Milan | A | D | 0-0 | |
| 16 | lge | Lazio | H | D | 0-0 | |
| 17 | lge | Modena | A | D | 0-0 | |
| 18 | lge | Parma | H | D | 1-1 | Baggio 40 |
| 19 | lge | Piacenza | A | W | 4-1 | Appiah 7; Baggio 32; Toni 47; Tare 88 |
| 20 | lge | Chievo | H | D | 0-0 | |
| 21 | lge | Roma | A | D | 0-0 | |
| 22 | lge | Reggina | H | W | 2-1 | Baggio 61; Petruzzi 86 |
| 23 | lge | Bologna | H | D | 0-0 | |
| 24 | lge | Como | A | D | 1-1 | Toni 55 |
| 25 | lge | Torino | H | W | 1-0 | Guardiola 60 pen |
| 26 | lge | Empoli | A | D | 0-0 | |
| 27 | lge | Atalanta | H | W | 3-0 | Appiah 31; Baggio 45; Petruzzi 85 |
| 28 | lge | Udinese | A | D | 0-0 | |
| 29 | lge | Inter Milan | H | L | 0-1 | |
| 30 | lge | Juventus | A | L | 1-2 | Appiah 83 |
| 31 | lge | Perugia | A | D | 0-0 | |
| 32 | lge | AC Milan | H | W | 1-0 | Appiah 83 |
| 33 | lge | Lazio | A | L | 1-3 | Baggio 22 |
| 34 | lge | Modena | H | D | 2-2 | Filippini 69; Baggio 86 |

## KEY PLAYERS - GOALSCORERS

**1 Roberto Baggio**

| | | | |
|---|---|---|---|
| **Goals in the League** | 12 | **Player Strike Rate** Average number of minutes between League goals scored by player | 239 |
| **Contribution to Attacking Power** Average number of minutes between League team goals while on pitch | 82 | **Club Strike Rate** Average number of minutes between League goals scored by club | 85 |

| | PLAYER | LGE GOALS | POWER | STRIKE RATE |
|---|---|---|---|---|
| 2 | Igil Tare | 6 | 73 | 319 mins |
| 3 | Stephen Appiah | 7 | 80 | 403 mins |
| 4 | Luca Toni | 2 | 121 | 607 mins |
| 5 | Josep Guardiola | 1 | 86 | 1119 mins |

## KEY PLAYERS - MIDFIELDERS

**1 Josep Guardiola**

| | | | |
|---|---|---|---|
| **Goals in the League** | 1 | **Contribution to Attacking Power** Average number of minutes between League team goals while on pitch | 86 |
| **Defensive Rating** Average number of mins between League goals conceded while he was on the pitch | 124 | **Scoring Difference** Defensive Rating minus Contribution to Attacking Power | 38 |

| | PLAYER | LGE GOALS | DEF RATE | POWER | SCORE DIFF |
|---|---|---|---|---|---|
| 2 | Stephen Appiah | 7 | 85 | 81 | 4 mins |
| 3 | Francelino Da Silva Matuzalem | 0 | 85 | 94 | -9 mins |
| 4 | Anthony Seric | 1 | 79 | 91 | -12 mins |
| 5 | Jonathan Bachini | 1 | 70 | 82 | -12 mins |

## KEY PLAYERS - DEFENDERS

**1 Marco Pisano**

| | | | |
|---|---|---|---|
| **Goals Conceded (GC)** The number of League goals conceded while he was on the pitch | 8 | **Clean Sheets** In games when he played at least 70 minutes | 5 |
| **Defensive Rating** Ave number of mins between League goals conceded while on the pitch | 118 | **Club Defensive Rating** Average number of mins between League goals conceded by the club this season | 81 |

| | PLAYER | CON LGE | CLEAN SHEETS | DEF RATE |
|---|---|---|---|---|
| 2 | Dario Dainelli | 24 | 11 | 91 mins |
| 3 | Gilberto Martinez | 37 | 14 | 82 mins |
| 4 | Fabio Petruzzi | 37 | 12 | 75 mins |

## GOALS SCORED

| AT HOME | | |
|---|---|---|
| MOST | Juventus | 37 |
| | | 20 |
| LEAST | Torino | 10 |
| **AWAY** | | |
| MOST | Inter Milan | 30 |
| | | 16 |
| LEAST | Como | 9 |

## GOALS CONCEDED

| AT HOME | | |
|---|---|---|
| LEAST | AC Milan | 11 |
| | | 15 |
| MOST | Piacenza | 29 |
| **AWAY** | | |
| LEAST | Juventus | 15 |
| | | 23 |
| MOST | Perugia | 35 |

## KEY GOALKEEPER

**1 Matteo Sereni**

| | |
|---|---|
| **Goals Conceded in the League** | 17 |
| **Defensive Rating** Ave number of mins between League goals conceded while on the pitch | 121 |
| **Counting Games** Games when he played at least 70 minutes | 23 |
| **Clean Sheets** In games when he played at least 70 minutes | 13 |

## TOP POINT EARNERS

| | PLAYER | GAMES | AVE |
|---|---|---|---|
| 1 | Guardiola | 12 | 1.5 |
| 2 | Sereni | 23 | 1.4 |
| 3 | Dainelli | 24 | 1.38 |
| 4 | Toni | 13 | 1.3 |
| 5 | Filippini | 17 | 1.2 |
| 6 | Appiah | 31 | 1.29 |
| 7 | Matuzalem | 27 | 1.2 |
| 8 | Martinez | 34 | 1.24 |
| 9 | Tare | 18 | 1.22 |
| 10 | Seric | 25 | 1.20 |
| | **CLUB AVERAGE:** | | **1.24** |

Ave = Average points per match in Counting Games

## ATTENDANCES

HOME GROUND: MARIO RIGAMONTI CAPACITY: 27547 AVERAGE LEAGUE AT HOME: 17082

| | | | | | | | |
|---|---|---|---|---|---|---|---|
| 33 | Lazio | 68000 | 5 | Bologna | 19000 | 25 | Torino | 14000 |
| 12 | Inter Milan | 55000 | 22 | Reggina | 18000 | 20 | Chievo | 14000 |
| 15 | AC Milan | 55000 | 18 | Parma | 17000 | 2 | Chievo | 13880 |
| 21 | Roma | 43000 | 34 | Modena | 17000 | 11 | Udinese | 13000 |
| 30 | Juventus | 40880 | 23 | Bologna | 16000 | 14 | Perugia | 13000 |
| 4 | Reggina | 29302 | 6 | Como | 16000 | 8 | Parma | 12000 |
| 13 | Juventus | 25000 | 28 | Udinese | 16000 | 24 | Como | 8000 |
| 29 | Inter Milan | 23000 | 9 | Empoli | 16000 | 19 | Piacenza | 7705 |
| 7 | Torino | 20000 | 16 | Lazio | 16000 | 31 | Perugia | 6000 |
| 32 | AC Milan | 20000 | 17 | Modena | 14700 | 26 | Empoli | 4950 |
| 3 | Roma | 19000 | 1 | Piacenza | 14400 | | | |
| 27 | Atalanta | 19000 | 10 | Atalanta | 14000 | | | |

■ Home □ Away ▩ Neutral

## DISCIPLINARY RECORDS

| | PLAYER | YELLOW | RED | AVE |
|---|---|---|---|---|
| 1 | Filippini | 9 | 2 | 169 |
| 2 | Schopp | 5 | 0 | 224 |
| 3 | Matuzalem | 10 | 1 | 230 |
| 4 | Pisano | 4 | 0 | 235 |
| 5 | Bachini | 5 | 1 | 245 |
| 6 | Guardiola | 4 | 0 | 279 |
| 7 | Seric | 7 | 0 | 350 |
| 8 | Bilica | 0 | 2 | 424 |
| 9 | Dainelli | 5 | 0 | 435 |
| 10 | Petruzzi | 6 | 0 | 462 |
| 11 | Toni | 2 | 0 | 606 |
| 12 | Micillo | 1 | 0 | 623 |
| 13 | Appiah | 4 | 0 | 704 |
| | Other | 6 | 0 | |
| | TOTAL | 68 | 6 | |

## LEAGUE GOALS

| | PLAYER | MINS | GOALS | AVE |
|---|---|---|---|---|
| 1 | Baggio | 2870 | 12 | 239 |
| 2 | Appiah | 2818 | 7 | 403 |
| 3 | Tare | 1912 | 6 | 319 |
| 4 | Toni | 1213 | 2 | 607 |
| 5 | Petruzzi | 2774 | 2 | 1387 |
| 6 | Schopp | 1120 | 2 | 560 |
| 7 | Guardiola | 1119 | 1 | 1119 |
| 8 | Bachini | 1474 | 1 | 1474 |
| 9 | Seric | 2450 | 1 | 2450 |
| 10 | Filippini | 1865 | 1 | 1865 |
| | Other | | 1 | |
| | TOTAL | | 36 | |

## MONTH BY MONTH GUIDE TO THE POINTS

| MONTH | POINTS | % |
|---|---|---|
| SEPTEMBER | 3 | 33% |
| OCTOBER | 2 | 22% |
| NOVEMBER | 4 | 27% |
| DECEMBER | 7 | 58% |
| JANUARY | 3 | 33% |
| FEBRUARY | 8 | 67% |
| MARCH | 6 | 50% |
| APRIL | 4 | 33% |
| MAY | 5 | 42% |

## TEAM OF THE SEASON

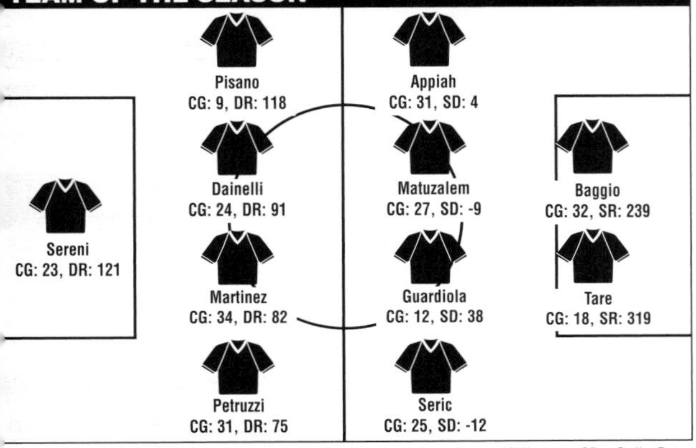

Pisano
CG: 9, DR: 118
Appiah
CG: 31, SD: 4
Dainelli
CG: 24, DR: 91
Matuzalem
CG: 27, SD: -9
Baggio
CG: 32, SR: 239
Sereni
CG: 23, DR: 121
Martinez
CG: 34, DR: 82
Guardiola
CG: 12, SD: 38
Tare
CG: 18, SR: 319
Petruzzi
CG: 31, DR: 75
Seric
CG: 25, SD: -12


KEY: DR = Defensive Rate, SD = Scoring Difference, SR = Strike Rate, CG = Counting Games – League games playing at least 70 minutes

## LEAGUE APPEARANCES, BOOKINGS AND CAPS

| | AGE | IN THE SQUAD | COUNTING GAMES | MINUTES ON PITCH | YELLOW CARDS | RED CARDS | THIS SEASON | HOME COUNTRY |
|---|---|---|---|---|---|---|---|---|
| **Goalkeepers** | | | | | | | | |
| Davide Micillo | 32 | 34 | 6 | 623 | 1 | 0 | - | Italy |
| Matteo Sereni | 28 | 24 | 23 | 2052 | 0 | 0 | - | Italy |
| Pavel Srnicek | 35 | 9 | 4 | 385 | 0 | 0 | - | Czech Republic |
| Michel Zanfretta | 19 | 2 | 0 | 0 | 0 | 0 | - | Italy |
| **Defenders** | | | | | | | | |
| Fabio Da Silva Bilica | 24 | 12 | 7 | 849 | 0 | 2 | - | Brazil |
| Dario Dainelli | 24 | 29 | 24 | 2176 | 5 | 0 | - | Italy |
| Simone Dallamano | 19 | 3 | 0 | 0 | 0 | 0 | - | Italy |
| Victor Hugo Mareco | 19 | 25 | 3 | 397 | 1 | 0 | - | Paraguay |
| Gilberto Martinez | 24 | 34 | 34 | 3029 | 0 | 0 | 4 | Costa Rica (17) |
| Fabio Petruzzi | 32 | 31 | 31 | 2774 | 6 | 0 | - | Italy |
| Marco Pisano | 21 | 30 | 9 | 942 | 4 | 0 | - | Italy |
| Marius Stankevicius | | 9 | 2 | 251 | 0 | 0 | - | Lithuania |
| **Midfielders** | | | | | | | | |
| Stephen Appiah | 22 | 32 | 31 | 2818 | 4 | 0 | - | Ghana |
| Jonathan Bachini | 28 | 20 | 16 | 1474 | 5 | 1 | - | Italy |
| Alejandro Rodriguez | 23 | 8 | 0 | 62 | 1 | 0 | - | |
| Antonio Filippini | 30 | 31 | 17 | 1865 | 9 | 2 | - | Italy |
| Stefano Fusari | 19 | 1 | 0 | 0 | 0 | 0 | - | Italy |
| Roberto Guana | 22 | 19 | 3 | 355 | 1 | 0 | - | Italy |
| Josep Guardiola | 32 | 14 | 12 | 1119 | 4 | 0 | - | Spain |
| Francelino Matuzalem | 23 | 30 | 27 | 2535 | 10 | 1 | - | Brazil |
| Markus Schopp | 29 | 33 | 8 | 1120 | 5 | 0 | - | Austria |
| Anthony Seric | 24 | 31 | 25 | 2450 | 7 | 0 | 2 | Croatia (26) |
| Andres Yllana | 28 | 1 | 0 | 0 | 0 | 0 | - | |
| **Forwards** | | | | | | | | |
| Andrea Alberti | 18 | 12 | 0 | 29 | 0 | 0 | - | Italy |
| Roberto Baggio | 36 | 32 | 32 | 2870 | 1 | 0 | - | Italy |
| Massimiliano Caputo | 22 | 6 | 0 | 13 | 0 | 0 | - | Italy |
| Simone Del Nero | 21 | 18 | 0 | 67 | 0 | 0 | - | Italy |
| Abderrazak Jadid | 20 | 26 | 0 | 157 | 0 | 0 | - | Morocco |
| Igil Tare | 29 | 34 | 18 | 1912 | 2 | 0 | - | Albania |
| Luca Toni | 26 | 18 | 13 | 1213 | 2 | 0 | - | Italy |

KEY: LEAGUE BOOKINGS CAPS (FIFA RANKING)

## SQUAD APPEARANCES

| Match | 1 | 2 | 3 | 4 | 5 | 6 | 7 | 8 | 9 | 10 | 11 | 12 | 13 | 14 | 15 | 16 | 17 | 18 | 19 | 20 | 21 | 22 | 23 | 24 | 25 | 26 | 27 | 28 | 29 | 30 | 31 | 32 | 33 | 34 |
|---|---|---|---|---|---|---|---|---|---|---|---|---|---|---|---|---|---|---|---|---|---|---|---|---|---|---|---|---|---|---|---|---|---|---|
| Venue | H | A | H | A | A | H | A | A | H | A | H | A | H | H | A | H | A | H | A | H | A | H | H | A | H | A | H | A | H | A | A | H | A | H |
| Competition | L | L | L | L | L | L | L | L | L | L | L | L | L | L | L | L | L | L | L | L | L | L | L | L | L | L | L | L | L | L | L | L | L | L |
| Result | L | W | L | D | L | D | W | L | L | L | D | L | W | W | D | D | D | D | W | D | D | W | D | D | W | D | W | D | L | L | D | W | L | D |

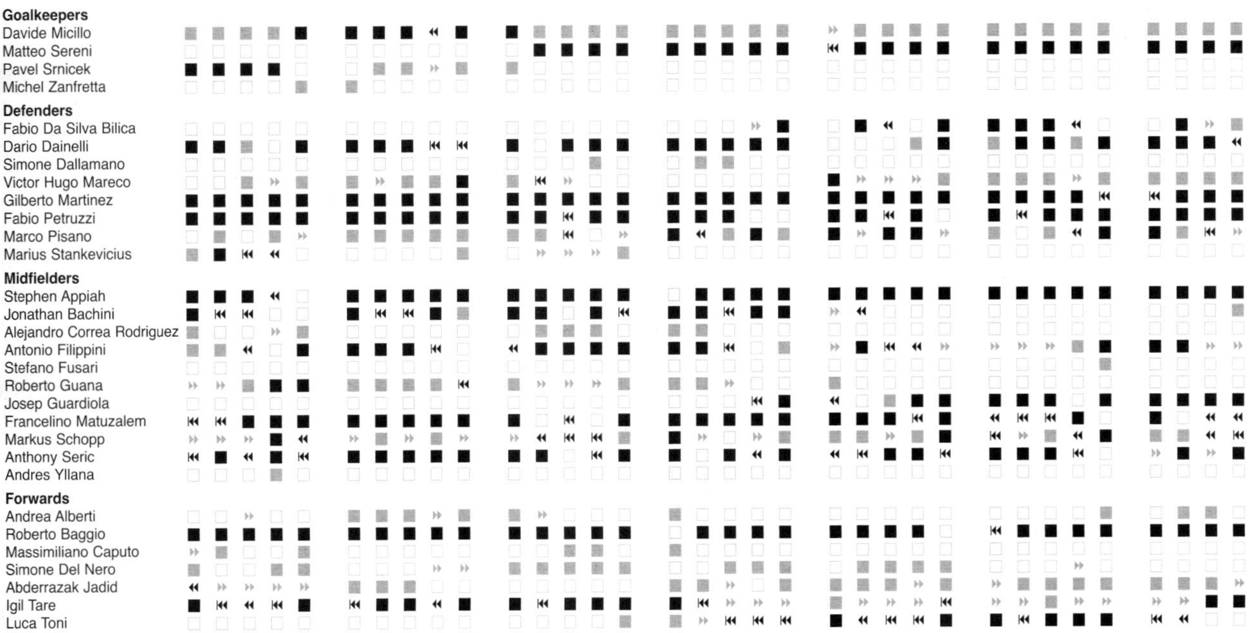

Goalkeepers
Davide Micillo
Matteo Sereni
Pavel Srnicek
Michel Zanfretta
Defenders
Fabio Da Silva Bilica
Dario Dainelli
Simone Dallamano
Victor Hugo Mareco
Gilberto Martinez
Fabio Petruzzi
Marco Pisano
Marius Stankevicius
Midfielders
Stephen Appiah
Jonathan Bachini
Alejandro Correa Rodriguez
Antonio Filippini
Stefano Fusari
Roberto Guana
Josep Guardiola
Francelino Matuzalem
Markus Schopp
Anthony Seric
Andres Yllana
Forwards
Andrea Alberti
Roberto Baggio
Massimiliano Caputo
Simone Del Nero
Abderrazak Jadid
Igil Tare
Luca Toni


KEY: On all match; On bench; Subbed or sent off (Counting game); Subbed or sent off (playing less than 70 minutes); Subbed on from bench (Counting Game); Subbed on (playing less than 70 minutes); Subbed on and then subbed or sent off (Counting Game); Subbed on and then subbed or sent off (playing less than 70 minutes); Not in 16

# PERUGIA

Final Position: **10th**

| | | | | | |
|---|---|---|---|---|---|
| 1 lge | Reggina | H | W | 2-0 | Miccoli 51; Tedesco 79 |
| 2 lge | AC Milan | A | L | 0-3 | |
| 3 lge | Empoli | H | L | 1-3 | Rezaei 8 |
| 4 lge | Parma | A | D | 2-2 | Tedesco 64,73 |
| 5 lge | Lazio | A | L | 0-3 | |
| 6 lge | Modena | H | W | 2-0 | Ze Maria 6 pen; Rezaei 27 |
| 7 lge | Roma | A | D | 2-2 | Ze Maria 39 pen; Miccoli 42 |
| 8 lge | Chievo | A | L | 0-3 | |
| 9 lge | Torino | H | W | 2-1 | Caracciolo 37; Ze Maria 87 pen |
| 10 lge | Bologna | A | L | 1-2 | Caracciolo 45 |
| 11 lge | Como | H | W | 3-0 | Fusani 14; Miccoli 47; Milanese 90 |
| 12 lge | Atalanta | A | W | 2-0 | Miccoli 22; Fusani 81 |
| 13 lge | Piacenza | H | D | 0-0 | |
| 14 lge | Brescia | A | L | 1-3 | Miccoli 64 |
| 15 lge | Juventus | H | L | 0-1 | |
| 16 lge | Udinese | A | D | 0-0 | |
| 17 lge | Inter Milan | H | W | 4-1 | Ze Maria 9 pen; Vryzas 34,64; Fusani 55 |
| 18 lge | Chievo | H | W | 1-0 | Di Loreto 37 |
| 19 lge | Reggina | A | L | 1-3 | Rezaei 2 |
| 20 lge | AC Milan | H | W | 1-0 | Miccoli 36 |
| 21 lge | Empoli | A | D | 1-1 | Vryzas 5 |
| 22 lge | Parma | H | L | 1-2 | Grosso 51 |
| 23 lge | Lazio | H | D | 2-2 | Ze Maria 13 pen; Grosso 43 |
| 24 lge | Modena | A | D | 1-1 | Vryzas 32 |
| 25 lge | Roma | H | W | 1-0 | Miccoli 53 |
| 26 lge | Torino | A | L | 1-2 | Grosso 41 |
| 27 lge | Bologna | H | D | 1-1 | Vryzas 33 |
| 28 lge | Como | A | D | 1-1 | Miccoli 90 |
| 29 lge | Atalanta | H | W | 1-0 | Pagliuca 79 |
| 30 lge | Piacenza | A | L | 1-5 | Ze Maria 51 |
| 31 lge | Brescia | H | D | 0-0 | |
| 32 lge | Juventus | A | D | 2-2 | Miccoli 36; Grosso 90 |
| 33 lge | Udinese | H | L | 0-2 | |
| 34 lge | Inter Milan | A | D | 2-2 | Obodo 48; Di Loreto 89 |

## KEY PLAYERS - GOALSCORERS

**1 Fabrizio Miccoli**

| | | | |
|---|---|---|---|
| Goals in the League | 9 | Player Strike Rate<br>Average number of minutes between League goals scored by player | 314 |
| Contribution to Attacking Power<br>Average number of minutes between League team goals while on pitch | 76 | Club Strike Rate<br>Average number of minutes between League goals scored by club | 77 |

| | PLAYER | LGE GOALS | POWER | STRIKE RATE |
|---|---|---|---|---|
| 2 | Zisis Vryzas | 5 | 78 | 376 mins |
| 3 | Massimilano Fusani | 3 | 70 | 445 mins |
| 4 | Jose Ferriera Ze Maria | 6 | 76 | 510 mins |
| 5 | Fabio Grosso | 4 | 75 | 642 mins |

## KEY PLAYERS - MIDFIELDERS

**1 Massimilano Fusani**

| | | | |
|---|---|---|---|
| Goals in the League | 3 | Contribution to Attacking Power<br>Average number of minutes between League team goals while on pitch | 70 |
| Defensive Rating<br>Average number of mins between League goals conceded while he was on the pitch | 79 | Scoring Difference<br>Defensive Rating minus Contribution to Attacking Power | 9 |

| | PLAYER | LGE GOALS | DEF RATE | POWER | SCORE DIFF |
|---|---|---|---|---|---|
| 2 | Christian Obodo | 1 | 58 | 66 | -8 mins |
| 3 | Giovanni Tedesco | 3 | 70 | 78 | -8 mins |
| 4 | Fabio Grosso | 4 | 60 | 75 | -15 mins |
| 5 | Manuele Blasi | 0 | 64 | 79 | -15 mins |

## KEY PLAYERS - DEFENDERS

**1 Sean Sogliano**

| | | | |
|---|---|---|---|
| Goals Conceded (GC)<br>The number of League goals conceded while he was on the pitch | 19 | Clean Sheets<br>In games when he played at least 70 minutes | 5 |
| Defensive Rating<br>Ave number of mins between League goals conceded while on the pitch | 81 | Club Defensive Rating<br>Average number of mins between League goals conceded by the club this season | 64 |

| | PLAYER | CON LGE | CLEAN SHEETS | DEF RATE |
|---|---|---|---|---|
| 2 | Mauro Milanese | 39 | 11 | 70 mins |
| 3 | Jose Ferriera Ze Maria | 48 | 11 | 64 mins |
| 4 | Williams Viali | 16 | 4 | 63 mins |
| 5 | Marco Di Loreto | 46 | 11 | 63 mins |

## GOALS SCORED

**AT HOME**

| | | |
|---|---|---|
| MOST | Juventus | 37 |
| | | 22 |
| LEAST | Torino | 10 |

**AWAY**

| | | |
|---|---|---|
| MOST | Inter Milan | 30 |
| | | 18 |
| LEAST | Como | 9 |

## GOALS CONCEDED

**AT HOME**

| | | |
|---|---|---|
| LEAST | AC Milan | 11 |
| | | 13 |
| MOST | Piacenza | 29 |

**AWAY**

| | | |
|---|---|---|
| LEAST | Juventus | 15 |
| | | 35 |
| MOST | Perugia | 35 |

## KEY GOALKEEPER

**1 Sebastiano Rossi**

| | |
|---|---|
| Goals Conceded in the League | 16 |
| Defensive Rating<br>Ave number of mins between League goals conceded while on the pitch | 67 |
| Counting Games<br>Games when he played at least 70 minutes | 12 |
| Clean Sheets<br>In games when he played at least 70 minutes | 5 |

## TOP POINT EARNERS

| | PLAYER | GAMES | AVE |
|---|---|---|---|
| 1 | Fusani | 13 | 1.77 |
| 2 | Obodo | 14 | 1.64 |
| 3 | Sogliano | 16 | 1.44 |
| 4 | Milanese | 30 | 1.40 |
| 5 | Rossi | 12 | 1.33 |
| 6 | Grosso | 28 | 1.29 |
| 7 | Vryzas | 14 | 1.29 |
| 8 | Blasi | 27 | 1.26 |
| 9 | Miccoli | 32 | 1.25 |
| 10 | Ze Maria | 34 | 1.24 |
| | CLUB AVERAGE: | | 1.24 |

Ave = Average points per match in Counting Games

## ATTENDANCES

HOME GROUND: RENATO CURI CAPACITY: 27663 AVERAGE LEAGUE AT HOME: 11694

| | | | | | | | |
|---|---|---|---|---|---|---|---|
| 7 | Roma | 55000 | 22 | Parma | 15000 | 27 | Bologna | 8000 |
| 2 | AC Milan | 45000 | 16 | Udinese | 14300 | 29 | Atalanta | 7000 |
| 34 | Inter Milan | 45000 | 24 | Modena | 14000 | 23 | Lazio | 7000 |
| 32 | Juventus | 40000 | 14 | Brescia | 13000 | 11 | Como | 7000 |
| 5 | Lazio | 35000 | 12 | Atalanta | 13000 | 30 | Piacenza | 6500 |
| 19 | Reggina | 23500 | 33 | Udinese | 13000 | 31 | Brescia | 6000 |
| 10 | Bologna | 20100 | 25 | Roma | 12000 | 13 | Piacenza | 6000 |
| 15 | Juventus | 20000 | 8 | Chievo | 11556 | 21 | Empoli | 5781 |
| 20 | AC Milan | 20000 | 18 | Chievo | 10000 | 26 | Torino | 5000 |
| 17 | Inter Milan | 20000 | 6 | Modena | 10000 | 28 | Como | 5000 |
| 1 | Reggina | 19800 | 9 | Torino | 10000 | | | |
| 4 | Parma | 16000 | 3 | Empoli | 8000 | | | |

■ Home □ Away ▒ Neutral

## DISCIPLINARY RECORDS

| | PLAYER | YELLOW | RED | AVE |
|---|---|---|---|---|
| 1 | Caracciolo | 6 | 1 | 134 |
| 2 | Obodo | 8 | 1 | 205 |
| 3 | Blasi | 12 | 0 | 211 |
| 4 | Sogliano | 7 | 0 | 220 |
| 5 | Grosso | 11 | 0 | 233 |
| 6 | Di Loreto | 9 | 0 | 320 |
| 7 | Milanese | 7 | 0 | 392 |
| 8 | Rezaei | 1 | 1 | 430 |
| 9 | Viali | 2 | 0 | 506 |
| 10 | Rossi | 2 | 0 | 538 |
| 11 | Vryzas | 3 | 0 | 626 |
| 12 | Pagliuca | 1 | 0 | 751 |
| 13 | Kalac | 2 | 0 | 887 |
| | Other | 6 | 0 | |
| | TOTAL | 77 | 3 | |

## LEAGUE GOALS

| | PLAYER | MINS | GOALS | AVE |
|---|---|---|---|---|
| 1 | Miccoli | 2823 | 9 | 314 |
| 2 | Ze Maria | 3060 | 6 | 510 |
| 3 | Vryzas | 1878 | 5 | 376 |
| 4 | Grosso | 2566 | 4 | 642 |
| 5 | Fusani | 1335 | 3 | 445 |
| 6 | Tedesco | 2180 | 3 | 727 |
| 7 | Caracciolo | 940 | 2 | 470 |
| 8 | Di Loreto | 2880 | 2 | 1440 |
| 9 | Rezaei | 861 | 2 | 431 |
| 10 | Obodo | 1845 | 1 | 1845 |
| 11 | Pagliuca | 751 | 1 | 751 |
| 12 | Milanese | 2745 | 1 | 2745 |
| | Other | | 1 | |
| | TOTAL | | 40 | |

## MONTH BY MONTH GUIDE TO THE POINTS

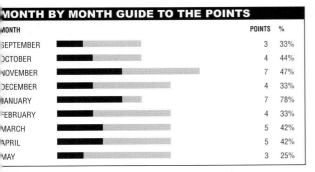

| MONTH | POINTS | % |
|---|---|---|
| SEPTEMBER | 3 | 33% |
| OCTOBER | 4 | 44% |
| NOVEMBER | 7 | 47% |
| DECEMBER | 4 | 33% |
| JANUARY | 7 | 78% |
| FEBRUARY | 4 | 33% |
| MARCH | 5 | 42% |
| APRIL | 5 | 42% |
| MAY | 3 | 25% |

## TEAM OF THE SEASON

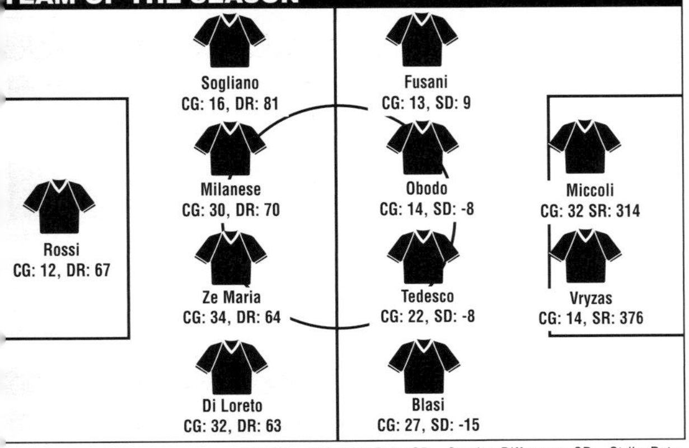
Sogliano
CG: 16, DR: 81
Fusani
CG: 13, SD: 9
Milanese
CG: 30, DR: 70
Obodo
CG: 14, SD: -8
Miccoli
CG: 32 SR: 314
Rossi
CG: 12, DR: 67
Ze Maria
CG: 34, DR: 64
Tedesco
CG: 22, SD: -8
Vryzas
CG: 14, SR: 376
Di Loreto
CG: 32, DR: 63
Blasi
CG: 27, SD: -15

KEY: DR = Defensive Rate, SD = Scoring Difference, SR = Strike Rate, CG = Counting Games – League games playing at least 70 minutes

## LEAGUE APPEARANCES, BOOKINGS AND CAPS

| | AGE | IN THE SQUAD | COUNTING GAMES | MINUTES ON PITCH | YELLOW CARDS | RED CARDS | THIS SEASON | HOME COUNTRY |
|---|---|---|---|---|---|---|---|---|
| **Goalkeepers** | | | | | | | | |
| Zajiko Kalac | 26 | 22 | 19 | 1774 | 2 | 0 | - | Australia |
| Sebastiano Rossi | 38 | 15 | 12 | 1076 | 2 | 0 | - | Italy |
| Michele Tardioli | 28 | 31 | 2 | 210 | 0 | 0 | - | Italy |
| **Defenders** | | | | | | | | |
| Luca Bisello Ragno | 20 | 2 | 0 | 0 | 0 | 0 | - | Italy |
| Marco Di Loreto | 28 | 32 | 32 | 2880 | 9 | 0 | - | Italy |
| Mauro Milanese | 31 | 31 | 30 | 2745 | 7 | 0 | - | Italy |
| Rahman Rezaei | | 21 | 9 | 861 | 1 | 1 | - | Iran |
| Sean Sogliano | 32 | 27 | 16 | 1543 | 7 | 0 | - | Italy |
| Williams Viali | 28 | 27 | 11 | 1013 | 2 | 0 | - | Italy |
| Jose Ferriera Ze Maria | 29 | 34 | 34 | 3060 | 1 | 0 | - | Brazil |
| **Midfielders** | | | | | | | | |
| Roberto Baronio | 25 | 23 | 1 | 409 | 1 | 0 | - | Italy |
| Manuele Blasi | 22 | 31 | 27 | 2540 | 12 | 0 | - | Italy |
| Massimilano Fusani | 23 | 33 | 13 | 1335 | 1 | 0 | - | Italy |
| Fabio Gatti | 21 | 2 | 0 | 2 | 0 | 0 | - | Italy |
| Fabio Grosso | 25 | 31 | 28 | 2566 | 11 | 0 | 2 | Italy (12) |
| K'tinos Loumpoutis | 24 | 15 | 4 | 392 | 0 | 0 | - | Greece |
| Christian Obodo | | 32 | 14 | 1845 | 8 | 1 | - | Nigeria |
| Luigi Pagliuca | 23 | 28 | 5 | 751 | 1 | 0 | - | Italy |
| Giovanni Sulcis | 28 | 14 | 0 | 62 | 0 | 0 | - | Italy |
| Giovanni Tedesco | 31 | 27 | 22 | 2180 | 0 | 0 | - | Italy |
| **Forwards** | | | | | | | | |
| Nicola Amoruso | 28 | 7 | 0 | 210 | 0 | 0 | - | Italy |
| Emanuele Berrettoni | 22 | 25 | 1 | 474 | 0 | 0 | - | Italy |
| Andrea Caracciolo | 21 | 28 | 5 | 940 | 6 | 1 | - | Italy |
| Antonio Criniti | 32 | 5 | 0 | 37 | 0 | 0 | - | Italy |
| Lorenzo Crocetti | 19 | 3 | 0 | 47 | 0 | 0 | - | Italy |
| Fabrizio Miccoli | 24 | 34 | 32 | 2823 | 3 | 0 | 5 | Italy (12) |
| Zisis Vryzas | 29 | 33 | 14 | 1878 | 3 | 0 | - | Greece |

KEY: LEAGUE BOOKINGS CAPS (FIFA RANKING)

## SQUAD APPEARANCES

| Match | 1 | 2 | 3 | 4 | 5 | 6 | 7 | 8 | 9 | 10 | 11 | 12 | 13 | 14 | 15 | 16 | 17 | 18 | 19 | 20 | 21 | 22 | 23 | 24 | 25 | 26 | 27 | 28 | 29 | 30 | 31 | 32 | 33 | 34 |
|---|---|---|---|---|---|---|---|---|---|---|---|---|---|---|---|---|---|---|---|---|---|---|---|---|---|---|---|---|---|---|---|---|---|---|
| Venue | H | A | H | A | A | H | A | A | H | A | H | A | H | A | H | A | H | H | A | H | A | H | H | A | H | A | H | A | H | A | H | A | H | A |
| Competition | L | L | L | L | L | L | L | L | L | L | L | L | L | L | L | L | L | L | L | L | L | L | L | L | L | L | L | L | L | L | L | L | L | L |
| Result | W | L | L | D | L | W | D | L | W | L | W | W | D | L | L | D | W | W | L | W | D | L | D | D | W | L | D | D | W | L | D | D | L | D |

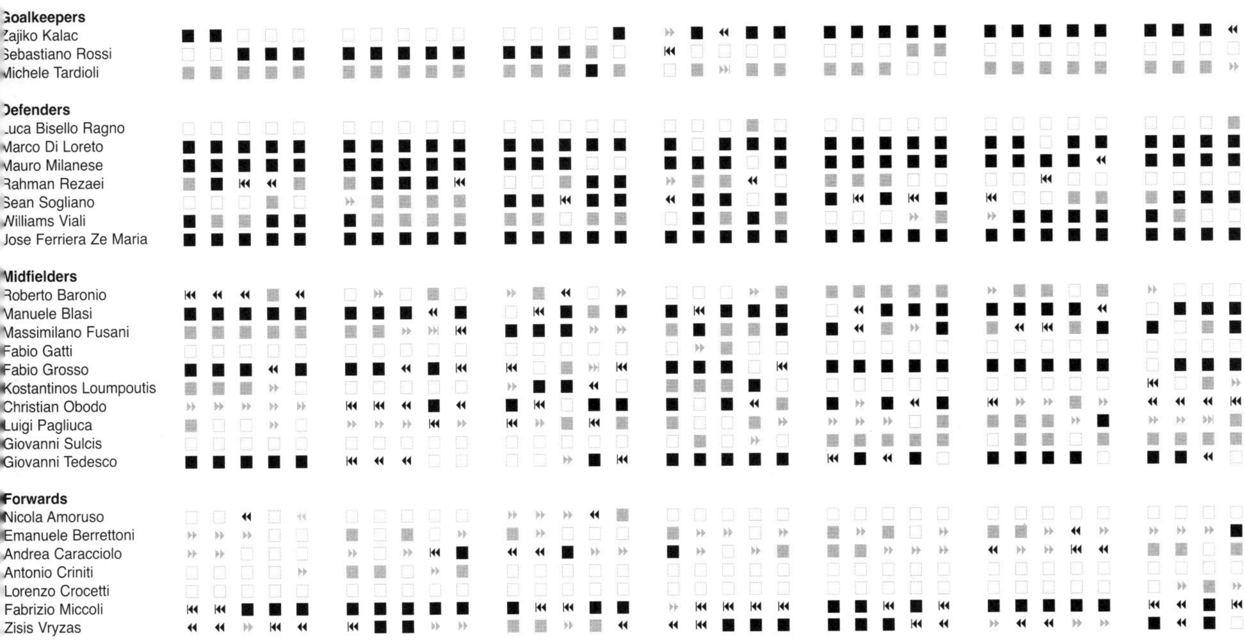
Goalkeepers
Zajiko Kalac
Sebastiano Rossi
Michele Tardioli
Defenders
Luca Bisello Ragno
Marco Di Loreto
Mauro Milanese
Rahman Rezaei
Sean Sogliano
Williams Viali
Jose Ferriera Ze Maria
Midfielders
Roberto Baronio
Manuele Blasi
Massimilano Fusani
Fabio Gatti
Fabio Grosso
Kostantinos Loumpoutis
Christian Obodo
Luigi Pagliuca
Giovanni Sulcis
Giovanni Tedesco
Forwards
Nicola Amoruso
Emanuele Berrettoni
Andrea Caracciolo
Antonio Criniti
Lorenzo Crocetti
Fabrizio Miccoli
Zisis Vryzas

KEY: ■ On all match ■ On bench ⏮ Subbed or sent off (Counting game) « Subbed or sent off (playing less than 70 minutes) ⏭ Subbed on from bench (Counting Game) » Subbed on (playing less than 70 minutes) Subbed on and then subbed or sent off (Counting Game) Subbed on and then subbed or sent off (playing less than 70 minutes) □ Not in 16

# BOLOGNA

Final Position: **11th**

| | | | | | | |
|---|---|---|---|---|---|---|
| 1 | lge | Roma | H | W | 2-1 | Cruz 60,90 |
| 2 | lge | Atalanta | A | D | 2-2 | Locatelli 13; Bellucci 75 pen |
| 3 | lge | Piacenza | H | W | 1-0 | Della Rocca 65 |
| 4 | lge | Empoli | A | D | 0-0 | |
| 5 | lge | Brescia | H | W | 3-0 | Locatelli 18; Cruz 75 pen,90 |
| 6 | lge | Inter Milan | A | L | 0-2 | |
| 7 | lge | Udinese | A | D | 0-0 | |
| 8 | lge | Torino | A | L | 1-2 | Vanoli 34 pen |
| 9 | lge | Como | H | W | 1-0 | Signori 73 pen |
| 10 | lge | Perugia | H | W | 2-1 | Cruz 31; Signori 38 |
| 11 | lge | Juventus | A | D | 1-1 | Signori 67 pen |
| 12 | lge | Modena | H | W | 3-0 | Locatelli 56; Cruz 80; Amoroso 81 |
| 13 | lge | Chievo | A | D | 0-0 | |
| 14 | lge | Parma | H | W | 2-1 | Cruz 42,43 |
| 15 | lge | Lazio | A | D | 1-1 | Zaccardo 65 |
| 16 | lge | AC Milan | H | L | 0-2 | |
| 17 | lge | Reggina | A | L | 0-1 | |
| 18 | lge | Torino | H | D | 2-2 | Signori 39 pen; Della Rocca 79 |
| 19 | lge | Roma | A | L | 1-3 | Signori 42 |
| 20 | lge | Atalanta | H | L | 2-3 | Signori 69 pen,72 pen |
| 21 | lge | Piacenza | A | L | 1-3 | Bellucci 84 |
| 22 | lge | Empoli | H | W | 2-0 | Bellucci 13; Vanoli 68 |
| 23 | lge | Brescia | A | D | 0-0 | |
| 24 | lge | Inter Milan | H | L | 1-2 | Cruz 23 |
| 25 | lge | Udinese | H | W | 1-0 | Signori 9 |
| 26 | lge | Como | A | L | 1-5 | Meghni 53 |
| 27 | lge | Perugia | A | D | 1-1 | Signori 67 |
| 28 | lge | Juventus | H | D | 2-2 | Cruz 15; Locatelli 74 |
| 29 | lge | Modena | A | L | 2-3 | Signori 19,46 |
| 30 | lge | Chievo | H | D | 1-1 | Signori 2 |
| 31 | lge | Parma | A | W | 2-1 | Paramatti 60; Locatelli 67 |
| 32 | lge | Lazio | H | L | 0-2 | |
| 33 | lge | AC Milan | A | L | 1-3 | Meghni 68 |
| 34 | lge | Reggina | H | L | 0-2 | |

## KEY PLAYERS - GOALSCORERS

**1 Guiseppe Signori**

| | | | |
|---|---|---|---|
| Goals in the League | 12 | Player Strike Rate<br>Average number of minutes between League goals scored by player | 140 |
| Contribution to Attacking Power<br>Average number of minutes between League team goals while on pitch | 83 | Club Strike Rate<br>Average number of minutes between League goals scored by club | 78 |

| | PLAYER | LGE GOALS | POWER | STRIKE RATI |
|---|---|---|---|---|
| 2 | Julio Cruz | 10 | 73 | 242 mins |
| 3 | Tomas Locatelli | 5 | 70 | 308 mins |
| 4 | Claudio Bellucci | 3 | 86 | 608 mins |
| 5 | Paolo Vanoli | 2 | 75 | 679 mins |

## KEY PLAYERS - MIDFIELDERS

**1 Carlo Nervo**

| | | | |
|---|---|---|---|
| Goals in the League | 0 | Contribution to Attacking Power<br>Average number of minutes between League team goals while on pitch | 80 |
| Defensive Rating<br>Average number of mins between League goals conceded while he was on the pitch | 75 | Scoring Difference<br>Defensive Rating minus Contribution to Attacking Power | -5 |

| | PLAYER | LGE GOALS | DEF RATE | POWER | SCORE DIFF |
|---|---|---|---|---|---|
| 2 | Renato Olive | 0 | 62 | 76 | -14 mins |
| 3 | Leonardo Colucci | 0 | 70 | 84 | -14 mins |
| 4 | Tomas Locatelli | 5 | 55 | 70 | -15 mins |
| 5 | Christian Amoroso | 1 | 61 | 78 | -17 mins |

## KEY PLAYERS - DEFENDERS

**1 Marco Zanchi**

| | | | |
|---|---|---|---|
| Goals Conceded (GC)<br>The number of League goals conceded while he was on the pitch | 16 | Clean Sheets<br>In games when he played at least 70 minutes | 8 |
| Defensive Rating<br>Ave number of mins between League goals conceded while on the pitch | 98 | Club Defensive Rating<br>Average number of mins between League goals conceded by the club this season | 64 |

| | PLAYER | CON LGE | CLEAN SHEETS | DEF RATE |
|---|---|---|---|---|
| 2 | Michele Paramatti | 34 | 8 | 74 mins |
| 3 | Marcello Castellini | 44 | 10 | 63 mins |
| 4 | Cristian Zaccardo | 39 | 4 | 61 mins |
| 5 | Paolo Vanoli | 27 | 1 | 50 mins |

## GOALS SCORED

AT HOME

| | | |
|---|---|---|
| MOST | Juventus | 37 |
| | | 25 |
| LEAST | Torino | 10 |

AWAY

| | | |
|---|---|---|
| MOST | Inter Milan | 30 |
| | | 14 |
| LEAST | Como | 9 |

## GOALS CONCEDED

AT HOME

| | | |
|---|---|---|
| LEAST | AC Milan | 11 |
| | | 19 |
| MOST | Piacenza | 29 |

AWAY

| | | |
|---|---|---|
| LEAST | Juventus | 15 |
| | | 28 |
| MOST | Perugia | 35 |

## KEY GOALKEEPER

**1 Gianluca Pagliuca**

| | |
|---|---|
| Goals Conceded in the League | 48 |
| Defensive Rating<br>Ave number of mins between League goals conceded while on the pitch | 64 |
| Counting Games<br>Games when he played at least 70 minutes | 34 |
| Clean Sheets<br>In games when he played at least 70 minutes | 10 |

## TOP POINT EARNERS

| | PLAYER | GAMES | AVE |
|---|---|---|---|
| 1 | Zanchi | 17 | 1.59 |
| 2 | Bellucci | 18 | 1.56 |
| 3 | Nervo | 23 | 1.39 |
| 4 | Locatelli | 12 | 1.33 |
| 5 | Cruz | 26 | 1.31 |
| 6 | Paramatti | 26 | 1.31 |
| 7 | Colucci | 27 | 1.22 |
| 8 | Pagliuca | 34 | 1.21 |
| 9 | Castellini | 31 | 1.19 |
| 10 | Olive | 23 | 1.17 |
| | CLUB AVERAGE: | | 1.21 |

Ave = Average points per match in Counting Games

## ATTENDANCES

HOME GROUND: RENATO DALL'ARA CAPACITY: 39300 AVERAGE LEAGUE AT HOME: 24082

| | | |
|---|---|---|
| 6 | Inter Milan | 60000 |
| 19 | Roma | 54695 |
| 33 | AC Milan | 50000 |
| 15 | Lazio | 45000 |
| 28 | Juventus | 37000 |
| 16 | AC Milan | 37000 |
| 11 | Juventus | 36544 |
| 13 | Chievo | 36000 |
| 12 | Modena | 35000 |
| 24 | Inter Milan | 35000 |
| 1 | Roma | 32000 |
| 14 | Parma | 25000 |
| 30 | Chievo | 21800 |
| 18 | Torino | 21000 |
| 10 | Perugia | 20100 |
| 3 | Piacenza | 20000 |
| 20 | Atalanta | 20000 |
| 9 | Como | 20000 |
| 5 | Brescia | 19000 |
| 34 | Reggina | 18500 |
| 17 | Reggina | 18500 |
| 25 | Udinese | 18000 |
| 29 | Modena | 17000 |
| 31 | Parma | 16000 |
| 2 | Atalanta | 16000 |
| 23 | Brescia | 16000 |
| 32 | Lazio | 15000 |
| 22 | Empoli | 15000 |
| 7 | Udinese | 14000 |
| 8 | Torino | 10000 |
| 4 | Empoli | 8500 |
| 27 | Perugia | 8000 |
| 21 | Piacenza | 6000 |
| 26 | Como | 6000 |

■ Home □ Away ▨ Neutral

## DISCIPLINARY RECORDS

| | PLAYER | YELLOW | RED | AVE |
|---|---|---|---|---|
| 1 | Falcone | 6 | 1 | 162 |
| 2 | Zanchi | 6 | 0 | 261 |
| 3 | Nervo | 6 | 2 | 289 |
| 4 | Paramatti | 8 | 0 | 313 |
| 5 | Vanoli | 4 | 0 | 339 |
| 6 | Colucci | 7 | 0 | 359 |
| 7 | Bellucci | 5 | 0 | 365 |
| 8 | Castellini | 7 | 0 | 398 |
| 9 | Olive | 5 | 0 | 458 |
| 10 | Zaccardo | 4 | 0 | 592 |
| 11 | Cruz | 4 | 0 | 604 |
| 12 | Frara | 1 | 0 | 778 |
| 13 | Pagliuca | 2 | 0 | 1530 |
| | Other | 6 | 0 | |
| | TOTAL | 71 | 3 | |

## LEAGUE GOALS

| | PLAYER | MINS | GOALS | AVE |
|---|---|---|---|---|
| 1 | Signori | 1676 | 12 | 140 |
| 2 | Cruz | 2418 | 10 | 242 |
| 3 | Locatelli | 1540 | 5 | 308 |
| 4 | Bellucci | 1825 | 3 | 608 |
| 5 | Meghni | 407 | 2 | 204 |
| 6 | Vanoli | 1357 | 2 | 679 |
| 7 | Della Rocca | 276 | 2 | 138 |
| 8 | Zaccardo | 2370 | 1 | 2370 |
| 9 | Amoroso | 1944 | 1 | 1944 |
| 10 | Paramatti | 2504 | 1 | 2504 |
| | Other | | 0 | |
| | TOTAL | | 39 | |

## ONTH BY MONTH GUIDE TO THE POINTS

| ONTH | POINTS | % |
|---|---|---|
| EPTEMBER | 7 | 78% |
| CTOBER | 4 | 44% |
| OVEMBER | 8 | 53% |
| ECEMBER | 8 | 67% |
| ANUARY | 1 | 11% |
| EBRUARY | 3 | 25% |
| ARCH | 4 | 33% |
| PRIL | 3 | 25% |
| AY | 3 | 25% |

## EAM OF THE SEASON

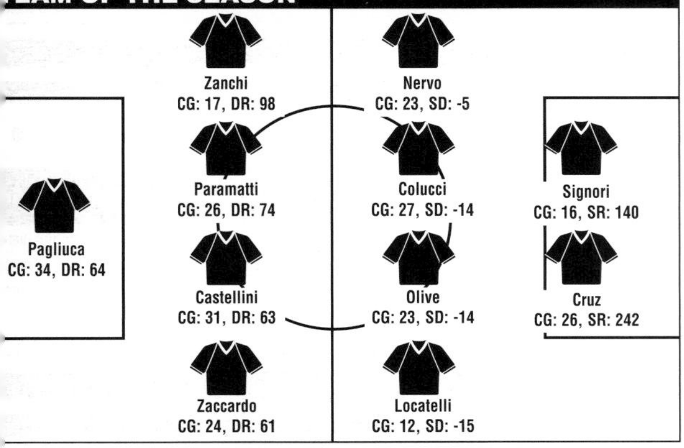
Zanchi
CG: 17, DR: 98
Nervo
CG: 23, SD: -5
Paramatti
CG: 26, DR: 74
Colucci
CG: 27, SD: -14
Signori
CG: 16, SR: 140
Pagliuca
CG: 34, DR: 64
Castellini
CG: 31, DR: 63
Olive
CG: 23, SD: -14
Cruz
CG: 26, SR: 242
Zaccardo
CG: 24, DR: 61
Locatelli
CG: 12, SD: -15

KEY: DR = Defensive Rate, SD = Scoring Difference, SR = Strike Rate, CG = Counting Games – League games playing at least 70 minutes

## LEAGUE APPEARANCES, BOOKINGS AND CAPS

| | AGE | IN THE SQUAD | COUNTING GAMES | MINUTES ON PITCH | YELLOW CARDS | RED CARDS | THIS SEASON | HOME COUNTRY |
|---|---|---|---|---|---|---|---|---|
| **Goalkeepers** | | | | | | | | |
| Ferdinando Coppola | 25 | 34 | 0 | 0 | 0 | 0 | - | Italy |
| Gianluca Pagliuca | 36 | 34 | 34 | 3060 | 2 | 0 | - | Italy |
| **Defenders** | | | | | | | | |
| Emanuele Brioschi | 28 | 1 | 0 | 0 | 0 | 0 | - | Italy |
| Marcello Castellini | 30 | 31 | 31 | 2789 | 7 | 0 | - | Italy |
| Guilio Falcone | 29 | 18 | 11 | 1136 | 6 | 1 | - | Italy |
| Steve Gohouri | 22 | 1 | 0 | 0 | 0 | 0 | - | France |
| Michele Paramatti | 35 | 32 | 26 | 2504 | 8 | 0 | - | Italy |
| Vlado Smit | 23 | 18 | 4 | 414 | 1 | 0 | - | Serbia & Montenegro |
| Claudio Terzi | 18 | 21 | 0 | 28 | 0 | 0 | - | Italy |
| Paolo Vanoli | 30 | 24 | 12 | 1357 | 4 | 0 | - | Italy |
| Cristian Zaccardo | 21 | 33 | 24 | 2370 | 4 | 0 | - | Italy |
| Marco Zanchi | 26 | 21 | 17 | 1571 | 6 | 0 | - | Italy |
| **Midfielders** | | | | | | | | |
| Christian Amoroso | 26 | 33 | 18 | 1944 | 1 | 0 | - | Italy |
| Leonardo Colucci | 30 | 32 | 27 | 2516 | 7 | 0 | - | Italy |
| Alessandro Frara | 20 | 29 | 4 | 778 | 1 | 0 | - | Italy |
| Roberto Goretti | 27 | 2 | 0 | 10 | 0 | 0 | - | |
| Tomas Locatelli | 27 | 27 | 12 | 1540 | 1 | 0 | - | Italy |
| Massimo Loviso | 19 | 1 | 0 | 0 | 0 | 0 | - | Italy |
| Mourad Meghni | 19 | 26 | 4 | 407 | 0 | 0 | - | France |
| Carlo Nervo | 31 | 31 | 23 | 2315 | 6 | 2 | 4 | Italy (12) |
| Renato Olive | 32 | 28 | 23 | 2290 | 5 | 0 | - | Italy |
| Emiliano Salvetti | 29 | 15 | 2 | 240 | 1 | 0 | - | Italy |
| **Forwards** | | | | | | | | |
| Claudio Bellucci | 28 | 33 | 18 | 1825 | 5 | 0 | - | Italy |
| Giacomo Cipriani | 22 | 3 | 0 | 112 | 0 | 0 | - | Italy |
| Julio Cruz | 28 | 28 | 26 | 2418 | 4 | 0 | - | Argentina |
| Luigi Della Rocca | 18 | 29 | 1 | 276 | 1 | 0 | - | Italy |
| Guiseppe Signori | 35 | 26 | 16 | 1676 | 1 | 0 | - | Italy |

KEY: LEAGUE BOOKINGS CAPS (FIFA RANKING)

## QUAD APPEARANCES

| atch | 1 | 2 | 3 | 4 | 5 | 6 | 7 | 8 | 9 | 10 | 11 | 12 | 13 | 14 | 15 | 16 | 17 | 18 | 19 | 20 | 21 | 22 | 23 | 24 | 25 | 26 | 27 | 28 | 29 | 30 | 31 | 32 | 33 | 34 |
|---|---|---|---|---|---|---|---|---|---|---|---|---|---|---|---|---|---|---|---|---|---|---|---|---|---|---|---|---|---|---|---|---|---|---|
| enue | H | A | H | A | H | A | A | A | H | H | A | H | A | H | A | H | A | H | A | H | A | H | A | H | H | A | A | H | A | H | A | H | A | H |
| ompetition | L | L | L | L | L | L | L | L | L | L | L | L | L | L | L | L | L | L | L | L | L | L | L | L | L | L | L | L | L | L | L | L | L | L |
| esult | W | D | W | D | W | L | D | L | W | W | D | W | D | W | D | L | L | D | L | L | L | W | D | L | W | L | D | D | L | D | W | L | L | L |

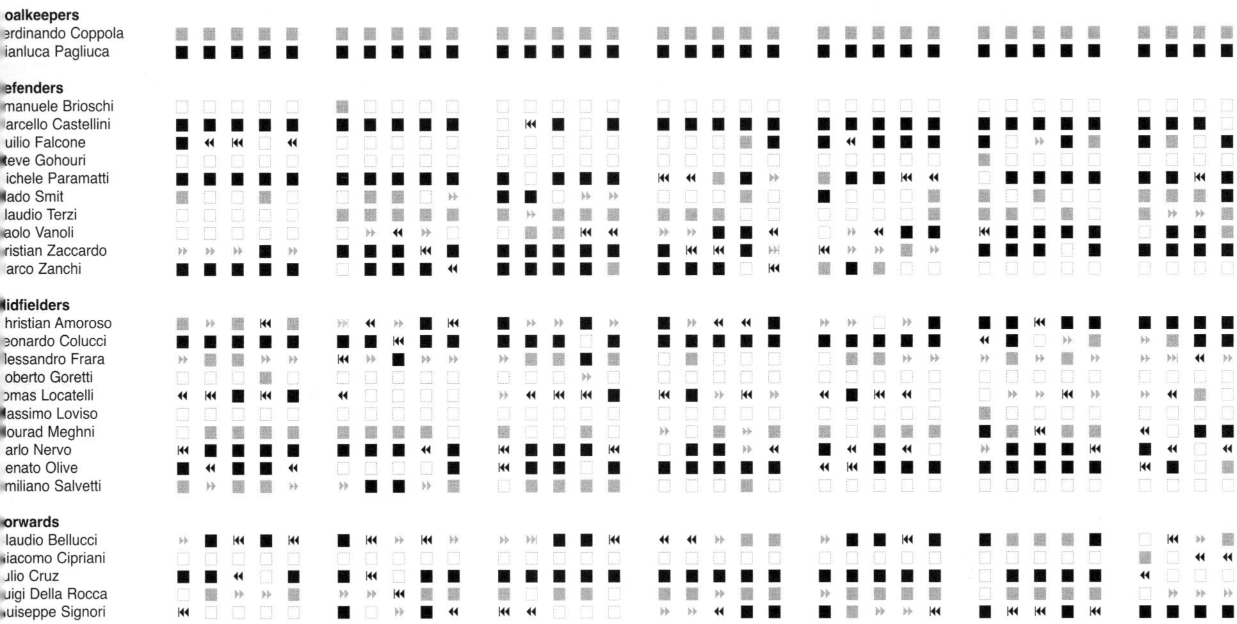
oalkeepers
erdinando Coppola
ianluca Pagliuca
efenders
manuele Brioschi
arcello Castellini
uilio Falcone
teve Gohouri
ichele Paramatti
ado Smit
laudio Terzi
aolo Vanoli
ristian Zaccardo
arco Zanchi
idfielders
hristian Amoroso
eonardo Colucci
lessandro Frara
oberto Goretti
omas Locatelli
assimo Loviso
ourad Meghni
arlo Nervo
enato Olive
miliano Salvetti
orwards
laudio Bellucci
iacomo Cipriani
ulio Cruz
uigi Della Rocca
uiseppe Signori

EY: ■ On all match ■ On bench ⏮ Subbed or sent off (Counting game) « Subbed or sent off (playing less than 70 minutes) » Subbed on from bench (Counting Game) » Subbed on (playing less than 70 minutes) » Subbed on and then subbed or sent off (Counting Game) » Subbed on and then subbed or sent off (playing less than 70 minutes) □ Not in 16

# EMPOLI

Final Position: **12th**

| | | | | | | |
|---|---|---|---|---|---|---|
| 1 | lge | Como | A | W | 2-0 | Saudati 14; Di Natale 59 |
| 2 | lge | Juventus | H | L | 0-2 | |
| 3 | lge | Perugia | A | W | 3-1 | Saudati 21; Di Natale 42; Rocchi 66 |
| 4 | lge | Bologna | H | D | 0-0 | |
| 5 | lge | Roma | H | L | 1-3 | Di Natale 74 |
| 6 | lge | Piacenza | A | W | 2-1 | Rocchi 31; Vannucchi 81 |
| 7 | lge | Lazio | H | L | 1-2 | Atzori 45 |
| 8 | lge | Inter Milan | H | L | 3-4 | Di Natale 16; Vannucchi 61; Tavano 90,90 |
| 9 | lge | Brescia | A | W | 2-0 | Busce 82; Di Natale 90 |
| 10 | lge | Reggina | H | W | 4-2 | Di Natale 3,39,90; Rocchi 51 pen |
| 11 | lge | Chievo | A | L | 0-1 | |
| 12 | lge | AC Milan | H | D | 1-1 | Rocchi 42 |
| 13 | lge | Udinese | A | L | 1-2 | Vannucchi 23 |
| 14 | lge | Modena | H | W | 1-0 | Rocchi 84 |
| 15 | lge | Atalanta | A | D | 2-2 | Grieco 85; Tavano 89 |
| 16 | lge | Torino | H | D | 1-1 | Rocchi 90 |
| 17 | lge | Parma | A | L | 0-2 | |
| 18 | lge | Inter Milan | A | L | 0-3 | |
| 19 | lge | Como | H | D | 0-0 | |
| 20 | lge | Juventus | A | L | 0-1 | |
| 21 | lge | Perugia | H | D | 1-1 | Carparelli 7 |
| 22 | lge | Bologna | A | L | 0-2 | |
| 23 | lge | Roma | A | L | 1-3 | Di Natale 11 |
| 24 | lge | Piacenza | H | W | 3-1 | Grella 56; Tavano 68; Borriello 81 |
| 25 | lge | Lazio | A | L | 1-4 | Oddo 4 og |
| 26 | lge | Brescia | H | D | 0-0 | |
| 27 | lge | Reggina | A | L | 0-1 | |
| 28 | lge | Chievo | H | W | 2-1 | Busce 23; Lucchini 61 |
| 29 | lge | AC Milan | A | W | 1-0 | Di Natale 12 |
| 30 | lge | Udinese | H | D | 1-1 | Di Natale 86 |
| 31 | lge | Modena | A | D | 1-1 | Di Natale 57 |
| 32 | lge | Atalanta | H | D | 0-0 | |
| 33 | lge | Torino | A | D | 1-1 | Di Natale 67 |
| 34 | lge | Parma | H | L | 0-2 | |

## KEY PLAYERS - GOALSCORERS

**1 Antonio Di Natale**

| | | | |
|---|---|---|---|
| **Goals in the League** | 13 | **Player Strike Rate** Average number of minutes between League goals scored by player | 14 |
| **Contribution to Attacking Power** Average number of minutes between League team goals while on pitch | 74 | **Club Strike Rate** Average number of minutes between League goals scored by club | 83 |

| | PLAYER | LGE GOALS | POWER | STRIKE RAT |
|---|---|---|---|---|
| 2 | Tommaso Rocchi | 6 | 88 | 456 min |
| 3 | Antonio Busce | 2 | 81 | 1094 min |
| 4 | Stefano Lucchini | 1 | 81 | 1549 min |
| 5 | Vincenzo Grella | 1 | 83 | 2582 min |

## KEY PLAYERS - MIDFIELDERS

**1 Flavio Giampieretti**

| | | | |
|---|---|---|---|
| **Goals in the League** | 0 | **Contribution to Attacking Power** Average number of minutes between League team goals while on pitch | 79 |
| **Defensive Rating** Average number of mins between League goals conceded while he was on the pitch | 69 | **Scoring Difference** Defensive Rating minus Contribution to Attacking Power | -1 |

| | PLAYER | LGE GOALS | DEF RATE | POWER | SCORE DIF |
|---|---|---|---|---|---|
| 2 | Antonio Busce | 2 | 71 | 84 | -13 min |
| 3 | Vincenzo Grella | 1 | 61 | 83 | -22 min |
| 4 | Ighli Vannucchi | 3 | 70 | 99 | -29 min |

## KEY PLAYERS - DEFENDERS

**1 Francesco Pratali**

| | | | |
|---|---|---|---|
| **Goals Conceded (GC)** The number of League goals conceded while he was on the pitch | 13 | **Clean Sheets** In games when he played at least 70 minutes | 5 |
| **Defensive Rating** Ave number of mins between League goals conceded while on the pitch | 93 | **Club Defensive Rating** Average number of mins between League goals conceded by the club this season | 67 |

| | PLAYER | CON LGE | CLEAN SHEETS | DEF RAT |
|---|---|---|---|---|
| 2 | Stefano Lucchini | 21 | 4 | 74 min |
| 3 | Manuel Belleri | 45 | 8 | 66 min |
| 4 | Emilson Sanchez Cribari | 41 | 6 | 66 min |
| 5 | Andrea Cupi | 38 | 6 | 63 min |

## GOALS SCORED

**AT HOME**

| | | |
|---|---|---|
| MOST | Juventus | 37 |
| | | 19 |
| LEAST | Torino | 10 |

**AWAY**

| | | |
|---|---|---|
| MOST | Inter Milan | 30 |
| | | 17 |
| LEAST | Como | 9 |

## GOALS CONCEDED

**AT HOME**

| | | |
|---|---|---|
| LEAST | AC Milan | 11 |
| | | 21 |
| MOST | Piacenza | 29 |

**AWAY**

| | | |
|---|---|---|
| LEAST | Juventus | 15 |
| | | 25 |
| MOST | Perugia | 35 |

## KEY GOALKEEPER

**1 Gianluca Berti**

| | |
|---|---|
| **Goals Conceded in the League** | 42 |
| **Defensive Rating** Ave number of mins between League goals conceded while on the pitch | 66 |
| **Counting Games** Games when he played at least 70 minutes | 31 |
| **Clean Sheets** In games when he played at least 70 minutes | 8 |

## TOP POINT EARNERS

| | PLAYER | GAMES | AV |
|---|---|---|---|
| 1 | Lucchini | 14 | 1.4 |
| 2 | Giampieretti | 29 | 1.3 |
| 3 | Di Natale | 20 | 1.3 |
| 4 | Pratali | 13 | 1.2 |
| 5 | Grella | 26 | 1.2 |
| 6 | Busce | 20 | 1.2 |
| 7 | Cupi | 26 | 1.1 |
| 8 | Berti | 31 | 1.1 |
| 9 | Rocchi | 28 | 1.1 |
| 10 | Cribari | 30 | 1.1 |
| | **CLUB AVERAGE:** | | **1.1** |

Ave = Average points per match in Counting Gam

## ATTENDANCES

HOME GROUND: CARLO CASTELLANI CAPACITY: 14000 AVERAGE LEAGUE AT HOME: 9632

| | | | | | | | | |
|---|---|---|---|---|---|---|---|---|
| 18 | Inter Milan | 59600 | 13 | Udinese | 15000 | 34 | Parma | 6400 |
| 29 | AC Milan | 55000 | 31 | Modena | 14000 | 24 | Piacenza | 6000 |
| 23 | Roma | 51000 | 5 | Roma | 13000 | 28 | Chievo | 5808 |
| 20 | Juventus | 35000 | 15 | Atalanta | 13000 | 21 | Perugia | 5781 |
| 25 | Lazio | 35000 | 11 | Chievo | 12530 | 14 | Modena | 5300 |
| 8 | Inter Milan | 30000 | 1 | Como | 10000 | 19 | Como | 5000 |
| 27 | Reggina | 23000 | 32 | Atalanta | 10000 | 16 | Torino | 4958 |
| 2 | Juventus | 19000 | 7 | Lazio | 10000 | 26 | Brescia | 4950 |
| 12 | AC Milan | 17600 | 4 | Bologna | 8500 | 30 | Udinese | 4450 |
| 17 | Parma | 16000 | 3 | Perugia | 8000 | 33 | Torino | 1000 |
| 9 | Brescia | 16000 | 6 | Piacenza | 7500 | | | |
| 22 | Bologna | 15000 | 10 | Reggina | 7000 | | | |

Home Away Neutral

## DISCIPLINARY RECORDS

| | PLAYER | YELLOW | RED | AVE |
|---|---|---|---|---|
| 1 | Ficini | 6 | 0 | 133 |
| 2 | Pratali | 6 | 1 | 173 |
| 3 | Atzori | 4 | 0 | 243 |
| 4 | Lucchini | 6 | 0 | 258 |
| 5 | Vannucchi | 6 | 0 | 279 |
| 6 | Giampieretti | 9 | 0 | 299 |
| 7 | Grella | 5 | 0 | 516 |
| 8 | Tavano | 2 | 0 | 545 |
| 9 | Borriello | 1 | 0 | 626 |
| 10 | Busce | 3 | 0 | 729 |
| 11 | Belleri | 4 | 0 | 742 |
| 12 | Cribari | 3 | 0 | 900 |
| 13 | Berti | 3 | 0 | 930 |
| | Other | 4 | 0 | |
| | TOTAL | 62 | 1 | |

## LEAGUE GOALS

| | PLAYER | MINS | GOALS | AV |
|---|---|---|---|---|
| 1 | Di Natale | 1927 | 13 | 14 |
| 2 | Rocchi | 2735 | 6 | 45 |
| 3 | Tavano | 1091 | 3 | 36 |
| 4 | Vannucchi | 1679 | 3 | 56 |
| 5 | Busce | 2188 | 2 | 109 |
| 6 | Saudati | 559 | 2 | 28 |
| 7 | Lucchini | 1549 | 1 | 154 |
| 8 | Grella | 2582 | 1 | 258 |
| 9 | Borriello | 626 | 1 | 62 |
| 10 | Grieco | 340 | 1 | 34 |
| 11 | Carparelli | 409 | 1 | 40 |
| 12 | Atzori | 975 | 1 | 97 |
| | Other | | 1 | |
| | TOTAL | | 36 | |

## MONTH BY MONTH GUIDE TO THE POINTS

| MONTH | POINTS | % |
|---|---|---|
| SEPTEMBER | 6 | 67% |
| OCTOBER | 4 | 44% |
| NOVEMBER | 6 | 40% |
| DECEMBER | 5 | 42% |
| JANUARY | 1 | 11% |
| FEBRUARY | 2 | 17% |
| MARCH | 4 | 33% |
| APRIL | 7 | 58% |
| MAY | 3 | 25% |

## TEAM OF THE SEASON

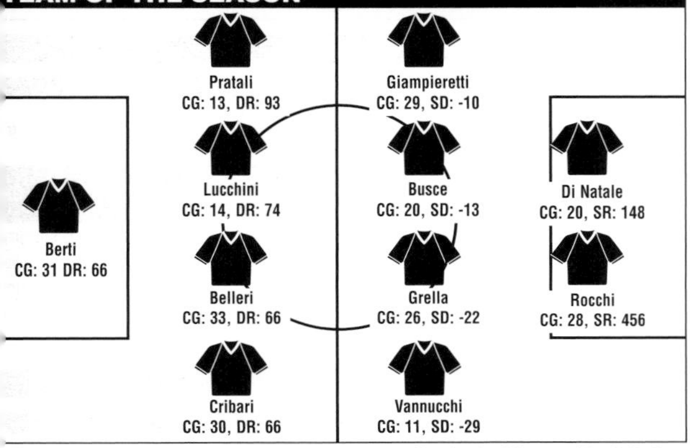

Pratali
CG: 13, DR: 93
Giampieretti
CG: 29, SD: -10
Lucchini
CG: 14, DR: 74
Busce
CG: 20, SD: -13
Di Natale
CG: 20, SR: 148
Berti
CG: 31 DR: 66
Belleri
CG: 33, DR: 66
Grella
CG: 26, SD: -22
Rocchi
CG: 28, SR: 456
Cribari
CG: 30, DR: 66
Vannucchi
CG: 11, SD: -29


KEY: DR = Defensive Rate, SD = Scoring Difference, SR = Strike Rate, CG = Counting Games – League games playing at least 70 minutes

## LEAGUE APPEARANCES, BOOKINGS AND CAPS

| | AGE | IN THE SQUAD | COUNTING GAMES | MINUTES ON PITCH | YELLOW CARDS | RED CARDS | THIS SEASON | HOME COUNTRY |
|---|---|---|---|---|---|---|---|---|
| **Goalkeepers** | | | | | | | | |
| Gianluca Berti | 36 | 33 | 31 | 2790 | 3 | 0 | - | Italy |
| David Bret | 19 | 1 | 0 | 0 | 0 | 0 | - | France |
| Mario Cassano | 19 | 33 | 3 | 270 | 0 | 0 | - | Italy |
| **Defenders** | | | | | | | | |
| Gianluca Atzori | 32 | 14 | 11 | 975 | 4 | 0 | - | Italy |
| Manuel Belleri | 25 | 33 | 33 | 2970 | 4 | 0 | - | Italy |
| Emilson Cribari | 23 | 32 | 30 | 2700 | 3 | 0 | - | Brazil |
| Andrea Cupi | 27 | 32 | 26 | 2398 | 2 | 0 | - | Italy |
| Simone Lonzi | 19 | 4 | 0 | 0 | 0 | 0 | - | Italy |
| Stefano Lucchini | 22 | 29 | 14 | 1549 | 6 | 0 | - | Italy |
| Roberto Mirri | 24 | 4 | 0 | 0 | 0 | 0 | - | |
| Francesco Pratali | | 25 | 13 | 1212 | 6 | 1 | - | Italy |
| Andrea Raggi | 19 | 2 | 0 | 0 | 0 | 0 | - | Italy |
| **Midfielders** | | | | | | | | |
| Alessandro Agostini | | 11 | 0 | 126 | 0 | 0 | - | |
| Marco Barollo | 30 | 1 | 0 | 0 | 0 | 0 | - | Italy |
| Antonio Busce | 27 | 34 | 20 | 2188 | 3 | 0 | - | Italy |
| Fabrizio Ficini | 29 | 31 | 6 | 798 | 6 | 0 | - | Italy |
| Flavio Giampieretti | 29 | 32 | 29 | 2691 | 9 | 0 | - | Italy |
| Vincenzo Grella | 23 | 33 | 26 | 2582 | 5 | 0 | - | Australia |
| Nicola Padoin | 24 | 10 | 0 | 13 | 0 | 0 | - | Italy |
| Vincenzo Pellecchia | 17 | 1 | 0 | 0 | 0 | 0 | - | Italy |
| Ighli Vannucchi | 26 | 31 | 11 | 1679 | 6 | 0 | - | Italy |
| **Forwards** | | | | | | | | |
| Marco Borriello | 21 | 14 | 5 | 626 | 1 | 0 | - | Italy |
| Massiliano Cappellini | 32 | 32 | 3 | 1012 | 0 | 0 | - | Italy |
| Marco Carparelli | 27 | 11 | 2 | 409 | 0 | 0 | - | Italy |
| Antonio Di Natale | 25 | 28 | 20 | 1927 | 1 | 0 | 3 | Italy (12) |
| Gaetano Grieco | 20 | 24 | 1 | 340 | 0 | 0 | - | Italy |
| Tommaso Rocchi | 25 | 34 | 28 | 2735 | 1 | 0 | - | Italy |
| Luca Saudati | 25 | 7 | 6 | 559 | 0 | 0 | - | Italy |
| Francesco Tavano | 24 | 28 | 7 | 1091 | 2 | 0 | - | Italy |

KEY: LEAGUE BOOKINGS CAPS (FIFA RANKING)

## SQUAD APPEARANCES

| | 1 | 2 | 3 | 4 | 5 | 6 | 7 | 8 | 9 | 10 | 11 | 12 | 13 | 14 | 15 | 16 | 17 | 18 | 19 | 20 | 21 | 22 | 23 | 24 | 25 | 26 | 27 | 28 | 29 | 30 | 31 | 32 | 33 | 34 |
|---|---|---|---|---|---|---|---|---|---|---|---|---|---|---|---|---|---|---|---|---|---|---|---|---|---|---|---|---|---|---|---|---|---|---|
| latch | | | | | | | | | | | | | | | | | | | | | | | | | | | | | | | | | | |
| enue | A | H | A | H | H | A | H | H | A | H | A | H | A | H | A | H | A | A | H | A | H | A | A | H | A | H | A | H | A | H | A | H | A | H |
| ompetition | L | L | L | L | L | L | L | L | L | L | L | L | L | L | L | L | L | L | L | L | L | L | L | L | L | L | L | L | L | L | L | L | L | L |
| esult | W | L | W | D | L | W | L | L | W | W | L | D | L | W | D | D | L | L | D | L | D | L | L | W | L | D | L | W | W | D | D | D | D | L |

oalkeepers
ianluca Berti
avid Bret
lario Cassano

efenders
ianluca Atzori
lanuel Belleri
milson Sanchez Cribari
ndrea Cupi
imone Lonzi
tefano Lucchini
oberto Mirri
rancesco Pratali
ndrea Raggi

lidfielders
lessandro Agostini
larco Barollo
ntonio Busce
abrizio Ficini
lavio Giampieretti
incenzo Grella
licola Padoin
incenzo Pellecchia
ghli Vannucchi

orwards
larco Borriello
lassiliano Cappellini
larco Carparelli
ntonio Di Natale
aetano Grieco
ommaso Rocchi
uca Saudati
rancesco Tavano

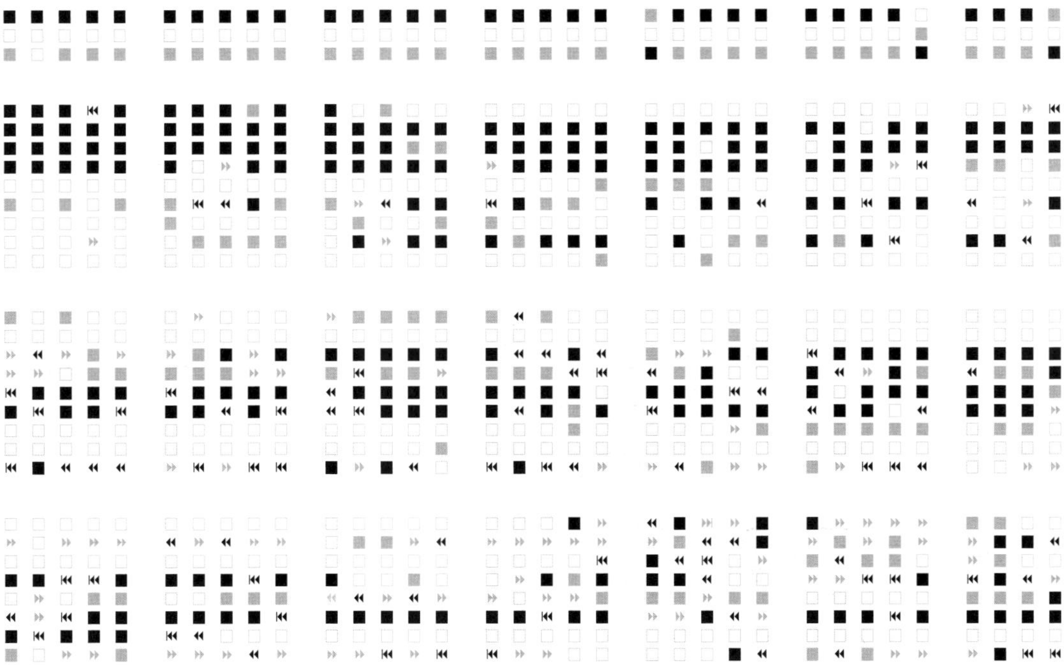

# ATALANTA

Final Position: **13th**

| | | | | | | |
|---|---|---|---|---|---|---|
| 1 | lge | Juventus | A | L | 0-3 | |
| 2 | lge | Bologna | H | D | 2-2 | Doni 17,51 pen |
| 3 | lge | Udinese | A | L | 0-1 | |
| 4 | lge | Lazio | H | L | 0-1 | |
| 5 | lge | AC Milan | H | L | 1-4 | Sala 29 |
| 6 | lge | Parma | A | L | 1-2 | Comandini 85 |
| 7 | lge | Piacenza | H | W | 2-0 | Sala 78; Comandini 87 |
| 8 | lge | Modena | H | L | 1-3 | Dabo 89 |
| 9 | lge | Chievo | A | L | 1-4 | Sala 41 |
| 10 | lge | Brescia | H | W | 2-0 | Dabo 69; Comandini 74 |
| 11 | lge | Reggina | A | D | 1-1 | Gautieri 34 |
| 12 | lge | Perugia | H | L | 0-2 | |
| 13 | lge | Inter Milan | A | L | 0-1 | |
| 14 | lge | Empoli | H | D | 2-2 | Doni 13; Zenoni 33 |
| 15 | lge | Torino | A | D | 1-1 | Natali 14 |
| 16 | lge | Como | A | D | 1-1 | Foglio 53 |
| 17 | lge | Roma | H | W | 2-1 | Doni 41; Tramezzani 87 |
| 18 | lge | Modena | A | W | 2-0 | Dabo 35; Pinardi 85 |
| 19 | lge | Juventus | H | D | 1-1 | Pinardi 40 |
| 20 | lge | Bologna | A | W | 3-2 | Pinardi 28,49; Rossini 90 |
| 21 | lge | Udinese | H | D | 0-0 | |
| 22 | lge | Lazio | A | D | 0-0 | |
| 23 | lge | AC Milan | A | D | 3-3 | Maldini 1 og; Rossini 29,31 |
| 24 | lge | Parma | H | D | 0-0 | |
| 25 | lge | Piacenza | A | L | 0-2 | |
| 26 | lge | Chievo | H | W | 1-0 | Dabo 52 |
| 27 | lge | Brescia | A | L | 0-3 | |
| 28 | lge | Reggina | H | D | 1-1 | Doni 9 |
| 29 | lge | Perugia | A | L | 0-1 | |
| 30 | lge | Torino | H | D | 2-2 | Doni 76,90 pen |
| 31 | lge | Inter Milan | H | D | 1-1 | Gautieri 70 |
| 32 | lge | Empoli | A | D | 0-0 | |
| 33 | lge | Como | H | W | 2-1 | Doni 63 pen,81 |
| 34 | lge | Roma | A | W | 2-1 | Doni 27; Gautieri 55 |

## KEY PLAYERS - GOALSCORERS

**1 Cristiano Doni**

| | | | |
|---|---|---|---|
| Goals in the League | 10 | **Player Strike Rate** Average number of minutes between League goals scored by player | 229 |
| **Contribution to Attacking Power** Average number of minutes between League team goals while on pitch | 91 | **Club Strike Rate** Average number of minutes between League goals scored by club | 87 |

| | PLAYER | LGE GOALS | POWER | STRIKE RATE |
|---|---|---|---|---|
| 2 | Ousmane Dabo | 4 | 83 | 628 mins |
| 3 | Fausto Rossini | 3 | 88 | 682 mins |
| 4 | Luigi Sala | 3 | 86 | 863 mins |
| 5 | Cesare Natali | 1 | 87 | 2370 mins |

## KEY PLAYERS - MIDFIELDERS

**1 Alex Pinardi**

| | | | |
|---|---|---|---|
| Goals in the League | 4 | **Contribution to Attacking Power** Average number of minutes between League team goals while on pitch | 68 |
| **Defensive Rating** Average number of mins between League goals conceded while he was on the pitch | 73 | **Scoring Difference** Defensive Rating minus Contribution to Attacking Power | 5 |

| | PLAYER | LGE GOALS | DEF RATE | POWER | SCORE DIFF |
|---|---|---|---|---|---|
| 2 | Carmine Gautieri | 3 | 57 | 65 | -8 mins |
| 3 | Ousmane Dabo | 4 | 72 | 84 | -12 mins |
| 4 | Damiano Zenoni | 1 | 65 | 86 | -21 mins |
| 5 | Cristiano Doni | 10 | 64 | 92 | -28 mins |

## KEY PLAYERS - DEFENDERS

**1 Sebastiano Siviglia**

| | | | |
|---|---|---|---|
| **Goals Conceded (GC)** The number of League goals conceded while he was on the pitch | 15 | **Clean Sheets** In games when he played at least 70 minutes | 6 |
| **Defensive Rating** Ave number of mins between League goals conceded while on the pitch | 95 | **Club Defensive Rating** Average number of mins between League goals conceded by the club this season | 65 |

| | PLAYER | CON LGE | CLEAN SHEETS | DEF RATE |
|---|---|---|---|---|
| 2 | Cesare Natali | 35 | 6 | 68 mins |
| 3 | Luigi Sala | 40 | 7 | 65 mins |
| 4 | Massimo Carrera | 21 | 2 | 57 mins |
| 5 | Paolo Foglio | 25 | 1 | 53 mins |

## GOALS SCORED

**AT HOME**

| | | |
|---|---|---|
| MOST | Juventus | 37 |
| | | 20 |
| LEAST | Torino | 10 |

**AWAY**

| | | |
|---|---|---|
| MOST | Inter Milan | 30 |
| | | 15 |
| LEAST | Como | 9 |

## GOALS CONCEDED

**AT HOME**

| | | |
|---|---|---|
| LEAST | AC Milan | 11 |
| | | 21 |
| MOST | Piacenza | 29 |

**AWAY**

| | | |
|---|---|---|
| LEAST | Juventus | 15 |
| | | 26 |
| MOST | Perugia | 35 |

## KEY GOALKEEPER

**1 Massimo Taibi**

| | |
|---|---|
| Goals Conceded in the League | 46 |
| **Defensive Rating** Ave number of mins between League goals conceded while on the pitch | 65 |
| **Counting Games** Games when he played at least 70 minutes | 33 |
| **Clean Sheets** In games when he played at least 70 minutes | 8 |

## TOP POINT EARNERS

| | PLAYER | GAMES | AVE |
|---|---|---|---|
| 1 | Siviglia | 15 | 1.53 |
| 2 | Sala | 28 | 1.21 |
| 3 | Rossini | 22 | 1.18 |
| 4 | Zenoni | 28 | 1.18 |
| 5 | Dabo | 27 | 1.15 |
| 6 | Natali | 26 | 1.12 |
| 7 | Taibi | 33 | 1.12 |
| 8 | Zauri | 31 | 1.06 |
| 9 | Doni | 26 | 1.04 |
| 10 | Carrera | 12 | 1.00 |
| | **CLUB AVERAGE:** | | **1.12** |

Ave = Average points per match in Counting Games

## ATTENDANCES

**HOME GROUND:** ATLETI AZZURI D'ITALIA **CAPACITY:** 30000 **AVERAGE LEAGUE AT HOME:** 16821

| | | | | | | | | |
|---|---|---|---|---|---|---|---|---|
| 23 | AC Milan | 60000 | 27 | Brescia | 19000 | 7 | Piacenza | 14000 |
| 13 | Inter Milan | 55000 | 17 | Roma | 18000 | 9 | Chievo | 13200 |
| 34 | Roma | 45000 | 28 | Reggina | 18000 | 12 | Perugia | 13000 |
| 22 | Lazio | 40000 | 2 | Bologna | 16000 | 14 | Empoli | 13000 |
| 1 | Juventus | 40000 | 30 | Torino | 15471 | 8 | Modena | 13000 |
| 31 | Inter Milan | 30000 | 15 | Torino | 15000 | 21 | Udinese | 13000 |
| 3 | Udinese | 27000 | 6 | Parma | 15000 | 32 | Empoli | 10000 |
| 19 | Juventus | 25500 | 18 | Modena | 15000 | 25 | Piacenza | 7000 |
| 11 | Reggina | 23000 | 4 | Lazio | 15000 | 29 | Perugia | 7000 |
| 20 | Bologna | 20000 | 26 | Chievo | 14000 | 16 | Como | 3000 |
| 5 | AC Milan | 20000 | 33 | Como | 14000 | | | |
| 24 | Parma | 20000 | 10 | Brescia | 14000 | | | |

■ Home □ Away ▒ Neutral

## DISCIPLINARY RECORDS

| | PLAYER | YELLOW | RED | AVE |
|---|---|---|---|---|
| 1 | Doni | 11 | 2 | 176 |
| 2 | Foglio | 5 | 0 | 264 |
| 3 | Zenoni | 9 | 1 | 266 |
| 4 | Zauri | 9 | 1 | 276 |
| 5 | Gautieri | 4 | 0 | 325 |
| 6 | Siviglia | 3 | 0 | 474 |
| 7 | Rossini | 4 | 0 | 511 |
| 8 | Berretta | 3 | 1 | 571 |
| 9 | Natali | 4 | 0 | 592 |
| 10 | Inacio Pia | 1 | 0 | 640 |
| 11 | Sala | 4 | 0 | 647 |
| 12 | Vugrinec | 1 | 0 | 662 |
| 13 | Bianchi | 1 | 0 | 813 |
| | Other | 7 | 0 | |
| | TOTAL | 66 | 5 | |

## LEAGUE GOALS

| | PLAYER | MINS | GOALS | AVE |
|---|---|---|---|---|
| 1 | Doni | 2291 | 10 | 229 |
| 2 | Dabo | 2512 | 4 | 628 |
| 3 | Pinardi | 1091 | 4 | 273 |
| 4 | Sala | 2589 | 3 | 863 |
| 5 | Gautieri | 1301 | 3 | 434 |
| 6 | Comandini | 804 | 3 | 268 |
| 7 | Rossini | 2045 | 3 | 682 |
| 8 | Natali | 2370 | 1 | 2370 |
| 9 | Tramezzani | 420 | 1 | 420 |
| 10 | Zenoni | 2667 | 1 | 2667 |
| 11 | Foglio | 1322 | 1 | 1322 |
| | Other | | 1 | |
| | TOTAL | | 35 | |

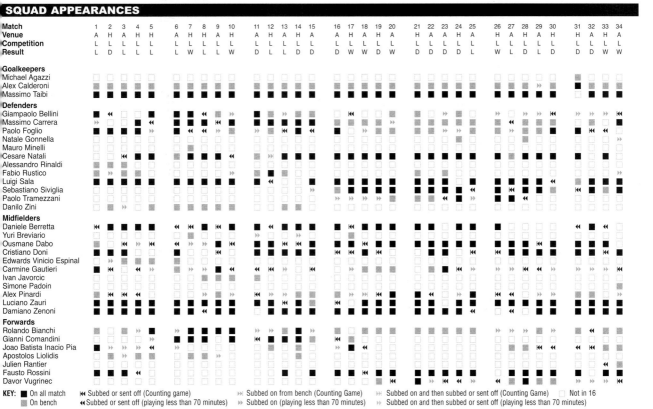

## MONTH BY MONTH GUIDE TO THE POINTS

| MONTH | POINTS | % |
|---|---|---|
| SEPTEMBER | 1 | 11% |
| OCTOBER | 0 | 0% |
| NOVEMBER | 7 | 47% |
| DECEMBER | 1 | 11% |
| JANUARY | 8 | 67% |
| FEBRUARY | 6 | 50% |
| MARCH | 5 | 42% |
| APRIL | 2 | 17% |
| MAY | 8 | 67% |

## TEAM OF THE SEASON

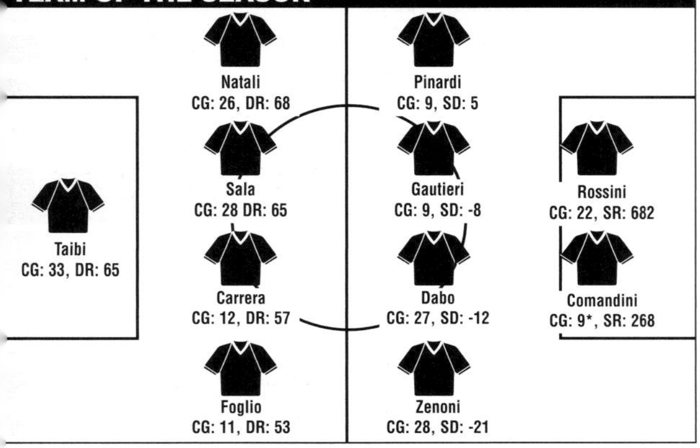

Natali
CG: 26, DR: 68
Pinardi
CG: 9, SD: 5
Sala
CG: 28 DR: 65
Gautieri
CG: 9, SD: -8
Rossini
CG: 22, SR: 682
Taibi
CG: 33, DR: 65
Carrera
CG: 12, DR: 57
Dabo
CG: 27, SD: -12
Comandini
CG: 9*, SR: 268
Foglio
CG: 11, DR: 53
Zenoni
CG: 28, SD: -21


KEY: DR = Defensive Rate, SD = Scoring Difference, SR = Strike Rate, CG = Counting Games – League games playing at least 70 minutes

## LEAGUE APPEARANCES, BOOKINGS AND CAPS

| | AGE | IN THE SQUAD | COUNTING GAMES | MINUTES ON PITCH | YELLOW CARDS | RED CARDS | THIS SEASON | HOME COUNTRY |
|---|---|---|---|---|---|---|---|---|
| **Goalkeepers** | | | | | | | | |
| Michael Agazzi | 19 | 1 | 0 | 0 | 0 | 0 | - | Italy |
| Alex Calderoni | 27 | 34 | 1 | 111 | 0 | 0 | - | Italy |
| Massimo Taibi | 33 | 33 | 33 | 2970 | 0 | 0 | - | Italy |
| **Defenders** | | | | | | | | |
| Giampaolo Bellini | 23 | 26 | 8 | 974 | 0 | 0 | - | Italy |
| Massimo Carrera | 39 | 30 | 12 | 1206 | 1 | 0 | - | Italy |
| Paolo Foglio | 27 | 32 | 11 | 1322 | 5 | 0 | - | Italy |
| Natale Gonnella | 27 | 3 | 0 | 3 | 0 | 0 | - | Italy |
| Mauro Minelli | 22 | 1 | 0 | 0 | 0 | 0 | - | Italy |
| Cesare Natali | 24 | 30 | 26 | 2370 | 4 | 0 | - | Italy |
| Alessandro Rinaldi | 28 | 3 | 0 | 0 | 0 | 0 | - | Italy |
| Fabio Rustico | 27 | 11 | 1 | 184 | 1 | 0 | - | Italy |
| Luigi Sala | 29 | 31 | 28 | 2589 | 4 | 0 | - | Italy |
| Sebastiano Siviglia | 30 | 20 | 15 | 1424 | 3 | 0 | - | Italy |
| Paolo Tramezzani | 32 | 13 | 3 | 420 | 1 | 0 | - | Italy |
| Danilo Zini | 25 | 10 | 0 | 2 | 0 | 0 | - | Italy |
| **Midfielders** | | | | | | | | |
| Daniele Berretta | 31 | 28 | 22 | 2287 | 3 | 1 | - | Italy |
| Yuri Breviario | 20 | 4 | 0 | 10 | 0 | 0 | - | Italy |
| Ousmane Dabo | 26 | 32 | 27 | 2512 | 3 | 0 | - | France |
| Cristiano Doni | 30 | 26 | 26 | 2291 | 11 | 2 | 3 | Italy (12) |
| Edwards Espinal | 20 | 5 | 0 | 8 | 0 | 0 | - | Dominican Republic |
| Carmine Gautieri | 32 | 30 | 9 | 1301 | 4 | 0 | - | Italy |
| Ivan Javorcic | 24 | 4 | 0 | 0 | 0 | 0 | - | Croatia |
| Simone Padoin | 19 | 1 | 0 | 0 | 0 | 0 | - | Italy |
| Alex Pinardi | 22 | 28 | 9 | 1091 | 1 | 0 | - | Italy |
| Luciano Zauri | 25 | 32 | 31 | 2767 | 9 | 1 | 4 | Italy (12) |
| Damiano Zenoni | 26 | 31 | 28 | 2667 | 9 | 1 | - | Italy |
| **Forwards** | | | | | | | | |
| Rolando Bianchi | 20 | 33 | 6 | 813 | 1 | 0 | - | Italy |
| Gianni Comandini | 26 | 12 | 9 | 804 | 0 | 0 | - | Italy |
| Joao Batista Pia | 21 | 19 | 4 | 640 | 1 | 0 | - | Brazil |
| Apostolos Liolidis | 25 | 8 | 0 | 19 | 0 | 0 | - | Greece |
| Julien Rantier | 19 | 2 | 0 | 54 | 0 | 0 | - | France |
| Fausto Rossini | 25 | 23 | 22 | 2045 | 4 | 0 | - | Italy |
| Davor Vugrinec | 28 | 16 | 5 | 662 | 1 | 0 | 3 | Croatia (26) |

KEY: LEAGUE BOOKINGS CAPS (FIFA RANKING)

## SQUAD APPEARANCES

| Match | 1 | 2 | 3 | 4 | 5 | 6 | 7 | 8 | 9 | 10 | 11 | 12 | 13 | 14 | 15 | 16 | 17 | 18 | 19 | 20 | 21 | 22 | 23 | 24 | 25 | 26 | 27 | 28 | 29 | 30 | 31 | 32 | 33 | 34 |
|---|---|---|---|---|---|---|---|---|---|---|---|---|---|---|---|---|---|---|---|---|---|---|---|---|---|---|---|---|---|---|---|---|---|---|
| Venue | A | H | A | H | H | A | H | H | A | H | A | H | A | H | A | A | H | A | H | A | H | A | A | H | A | H | A | H | A | H | H | A | H | A |
| Competition | L | L | L | L | L | L | L | L | L | L | L | L | L | L | L | L | L | L | L | L | L | L | L | L | L | L | L | L | L | L | L | L | L | L |
| Result | L | D | L | L | L | L | W | L | L | W | D | L | L | D | D | D | W | W | D | W | D | D | D | D | L | W | L | D | L | D | D | D | W | W |

**Goalkeepers**
Michael Agazzi
Alex Calderoni
Massimo Taibi

**Defenders**
Giampaolo Bellini
Massimo Carrera
Paolo Foglio
Natale Gonnella
Mauro Minelli
Cesare Natali
Alessandro Rinaldi
Fabio Rustico
Luigi Sala
Sebastiano Siviglia
Paolo Tramezzani
Danilo Zini

**Midfielders**
Daniele Berretta
Yuri Breviario
Ousmane Dabo
Cristiano Doni
Edwards Vinicio Espinal
Carmine Gautieri
Ivan Javorcic
Simone Padoin
Alex Pinardi
Luciano Zauri
Damiano Zenoni

**Forwards**
Rolando Bianchi
Gianni Comandini
Joao Batista Inacio Pia
Apostolos Liolidis
Julien Rantier
Fausto Rossini
Davor Vugrinec

KEY: ■ On all match · ■ On bench · ⏮ Subbed or sent off (Counting game) · « Subbed or sent off (playing less than 70 minutes) · ⏭ Subbed on from bench (Counting Game) · » Subbed on (playing less than 70 minutes) · Subbed on and then subbed or sent off (Counting Game) · Subbed on and then subbed or sent off (playing less than 70 minutes) · □ Not in 16

# REGGINA

Final Position: **14th**

| | | | | | | |
|---|---|---|---|---|---|---|
| 1 | lge | Perugia | A | L | 0-2 | |
| 2 | lge | Inter Milan | H | L | 1-2 | Nakamura 88 pen |
| 3 | lge | Como | A | D | 1-1 | Nakamura 63 pen |
| 4 | lge | Brescia | H | D | 2-2 | Pierini 43; Nakamura 81 |
| 5 | lge | Udinese | A | L | 0-1 | |
| 6 | lge | Torino | H | W | 2-1 | Bogdani 55; Paredes 81 |
| 7 | lge | AC Milan | A | L | 0-2 | |
| 8 | lge | Lazio | H | L | 0-3 | |
| 9 | lge | Modena | H | L | 0-1 | |
| 10 | lge | Empoli | A | L | 2-4 | Nakamura 7 pen; Vargas 80 |
| 11 | lge | Atalanta | H | D | 1-1 | Savoldi 55 |
| 12 | lge | Chievo | H | D | 1-1 | Nakamura 23 pen |
| 13 | lge | Parma | A | L | 0-2 | |
| 14 | lge | Roma | A | L | 0-3 | |
| 15 | lge | Piacenza | H | W | 3-1 | Savoldi 49,64; Di Michele 77 pen |
| 16 | lge | Juventus | A | L | 0-5 | |
| 17 | lge | Bologna | H | W | 1-0 | Savoldi 15 |
| 18 | lge | Lazio | A | W | 1-0 | Bonazzoli 46 |
| 19 | lge | Perugia | H | W | 3-1 | Di Michele 1; Cozza 27; Bonazzoli 47 |
| 20 | lge | Inter Milan | A | L | 0-3 | |
| 21 | lge | Como | H | W | 4-1 | Cozza 33,38; Diana 79; Mozart 88 |
| 22 | lge | Brescia | A | L | 1-2 | Di Michele 69 |
| 23 | lge | Udinese | H | W | 3-2 | Bonazzoli 3; Di Michele 12; Cozza 65 |
| 24 | lge | Torino | A | L | 0-1 | |
| 25 | lge | AC Milan | H | D | 0-0 | |
| 26 | lge | Modena | A | L | 1-2 | Savoldi 90 |
| 27 | lge | Empoli | H | W | 1-0 | Nakamura 54 pen |
| 28 | lge | Atalanta | A | D | 1-1 | Bonazzoli 52 |
| 29 | lge | Chievo | A | L | 1-2 | Cossato 41 og |
| 30 | lge | Parma | H | D | 0-0 | |
| 31 | lge | Roma | H | L | 2-3 | Bonazzoli 15; Nakamura 90 |
| 32 | lge | Piacenza | A | D | 2-2 | Di Michele 68; Mozart 77 |
| 33 | lge | Juventus | H | W | 2-1 | Di Michele 18; Bonazzoli 51 |
| 34 | lge | Bologna | A | W | 2-0 | Bonazzoli 13; Di Michele 68 |

## KEY PLAYERS - GOALSCORERS

**1 Emiliano Bonazzoli**

| | | | |
|---|---|---|---|
| **Goals in the League** | 7 | **Player Strike Rate** Average number of minutes between League goals scored by player | 212 |
| **Contribution to Attacking Power** Average number of minutes between League team goals while on pitch | 61 | **Club Strike Rate** Average number of minutes between League goals scored by club | 81 |

| | PLAYER | LGE GOALS | POWER | STRIKE RATE |
|---|---|---|---|---|
| 2 | Shunsuke Nakamura | 7 | 76 | 348 mins |
| 3 | David Di Michele | 7 | 76 | 384 mins |
| 4 | Francesco Cozza | 4 | 77 | 448 mins |
| 5 | Santos Batista Junior Mozart | 2 | 81 | 942 mins |

## KEY PLAYERS - MIDFIELDERS

**1 Jorge Vargas**

| | | | |
|---|---|---|---|
| **Goals in the League** | 1 | **Contribution to Attacking Power** Average number of minutes between League team goals while on pitch | 67 |
| **Defensive Rating** Average number of mins between League goals conceded while he was on the pitch | 69 | **Scoring Difference** Defensive Rating minus Contribution to Attacking Power | 2 |

| | PLAYER | LGE GOALS | DEF RATE | POWER | SCORE DIFF |
|---|---|---|---|---|---|
| 2 | Carlos Humberto Paredes | 0 | 67 | 86 | -19 mins |
| 3 | Shunsuke Nakamura | 7 | 54 | 76 | -22 mins |
| 4 | Santos Batista Junior Mozart | 2 | 57 | 82 | -25 mins |
| 5 | Francesco Cozza | 4 | 50 | 78 | -28 mins |

## KEY PLAYERS - DEFENDERS

**1 Stefano Aimo Diana**

| | | | |
|---|---|---|---|
| **Goals Conceded (GC)** The number of League goals conceded while he was on the pitch | 19 | **Clean Sheets** In games when he played at least 70 minutes | 4 |
| **Defensive Rating** Ave number of mins between League goals conceded while on the pitch | 70 | **Club Defensive Rating** Average number of mins between League goals conceded by the club this season | 58 |

| | PLAYER | CON LGE | CLEAN SHEETS | DEF RATE |
|---|---|---|---|---|
| 2 | Gianluca Falsini | 34 | 5 | 61 mins |
| 3 | Ivan Franceschini | 38 | 5 | 58 mins |
| 4 | Giovanni Morabito | 25 | 1 | 57 mins |
| 5 | Martin Jiranek | 38 | 4 | 56 mins |

## GOALS SCORED

| | | | |
|---|---|---|---|
| AT HOME | MOST | Juventus | 37 |
| | | | 26 |
| | LEAST | Torino | 10 |
| AWAY | MOST | Inter Milan | 30 |
| | | | 12 |
| | LEAST | Como | 9 |

## GOALS CONCEDED

| | | | |
|---|---|---|---|
| AT HOME | LEAST | AC Milan | 11 |
| | | | 20 |
| | MOST | Piacenza | 29 |
| AWAY | LEAST | Juventus | 15 |
| | | | 33 |
| | MOST | Perugia | 35 |

## KEY GOALKEEPER

**1 Emanuele Belardi**

| | |
|---|---|
| **Goals Conceded in the League** | 26 |
| **Defensive Rating** Ave number of mins between League goals conceded while on the pitch | 68 |
| **Counting Games** Games when he played at least 70 minutes | 19 |
| **Clean Sheets** In games when he played at least 70 minutes | 6 |

## TOP POINT EARNERS

| | PLAYER | GAMES | AVE |
|---|---|---|---|
| 1 | Belardi | 19 | 1.63 |
| 2 | Diana | 14 | 1.50 |
| 3 | Bonazzoli | 17 | 1.47 |
| 4 | Vargas | 25 | 1.44 |
| 5 | Falsini | 22 | 1.41 |
| 6 | Cozza | 15 | 1.40 |
| 7 | Jiranek | 22 | 1.27 |
| 8 | Paredes | 26 | 1.19 |
| 9 | Di Michele | 26 | 1.15 |
| 10 | Nakamura | 22 | 1.05 |
| | **CLUB AVERAGE:** | | **1.12** |

Ave = Average points per match in Counting Games

## ATTENDANCES

HOME GROUND: ORESTE GRANILLO CAPACITY: 30000 AVERAGE LEAGUE AT HOME: 24686

| | | | | | | | | |
|---|---|---|---|---|---|---|---|---|
| 7 | AC Milan | 66000 | 31 | Roma | 24000 | 28 | Atalanta | 18000 |
| 20 | Inter Milan | 65000 | 21 | Como | 24000 | 22 | Brescia | 18000 |
| 14 | Roma | 53000 | 19 | Perugia | 23500 | 5 | Udinese | 15135 |
| 18 | Lazio | 45000 | 30 | Parma | 23500 | 13 | Parma | 14000 |
| 16 | Juventus | 30000 | 9 | Modena | 23373 | 26 | Modena | 14000 |
| 2 | Inter Milan | 30000 | 12 | Chievo | 23000 | 29 | Chievo | 11804 |
| 4 | Brescia | 29302 | 11 | Atalanta | 23000 | 3 | Como | 10000 |
| 8 | Lazio | 28000 | 27 | Empoli | 23000 | 10 | Empoli | 7000 |
| 33 | Juventus | 26500 | 15 | Piacenza | 23000 | 32 | Piacenza | 6500 |
| 23 | Udinese | 26000 | 1 | Perugia | 19800 | 24 | Torino | 4500 |
| 25 | AC Milan | 26000 | 34 | Bologna | 18500 | | | |
| 6 | Torino | 25000 | 17 | Bologna | 18500 | | | |

Home / Away / Neutral

## DISCIPLINARY RECORDS

| | PLAYER | YELLOW | RED | AVE |
|---|---|---|---|---|
| 1 | Mamede | 5 | 0 | 182 |
| 2 | Cirillo | 4 | 0 | 193 |
| 3 | Rastelli | 2 | 0 | 251 |
| 4 | Franceschini | 7 | 0 | 314 |
| 5 | Vargas | 6 | 1 | 337 |
| 6 | Cozza | 5 | 0 | 358 |
| 7 | Mozart | 5 | 0 | 376 |
| 8 | Bonazzoli | 3 | 0 | 495 |
| 9 | Paredes | 5 | 0 | 496 |
| 10 | Savoldi | 2 | 0 | 499 |
| 11 | Belardi | 2 | 1 | 588 |
| 12 | Pierini | 2 | 0 | 591 |
| 13 | Jiranek | 3 | 0 | 703 |
| | Other | 7 | 0 | |
| | TOTAL | 58 | 2 | |

## LEAGUE GOALS

| | PLAYER | MINS | GOALS | AVE |
|---|---|---|---|---|
| 1 | Bonazzoli | 1486 | 7 | 212 |
| 2 | Di Michele | 2687 | 7 | 384 |
| 3 | Nakamura | 2436 | 7 | 348 |
| 4 | Savoldi | 999 | 5 | 200 |
| 5 | Cozza | 1793 | 4 | 448 |
| 6 | Mozart | 1884 | 2 | 942 |
| 7 | Bogdani | 307 | 1 | 307 |
| 8 | Vargas | 2359 | 1 | 2359 |
| 9 | Diana | 1322 | 1 | 1322 |
| 10 | Pierini | 1182 | 1 | 1182 |
| | Other | | 2 | |
| | TOTAL | | 38 | |

## MONTH BY MONTH GUIDE TO THE POINTS

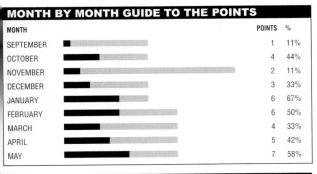

| MONTH | POINTS | % |
|---|---|---|
| SEPTEMBER | 1 | 11% |
| OCTOBER | 4 | 44% |
| NOVEMBER | 2 | 11% |
| DECEMBER | 3 | 33% |
| JANUARY | 6 | 67% |
| FEBRUARY | 6 | 50% |
| MARCH | 4 | 33% |
| APRIL | 5 | 42% |
| MAY | 7 | 58% |

## TEAM OF THE SEASON

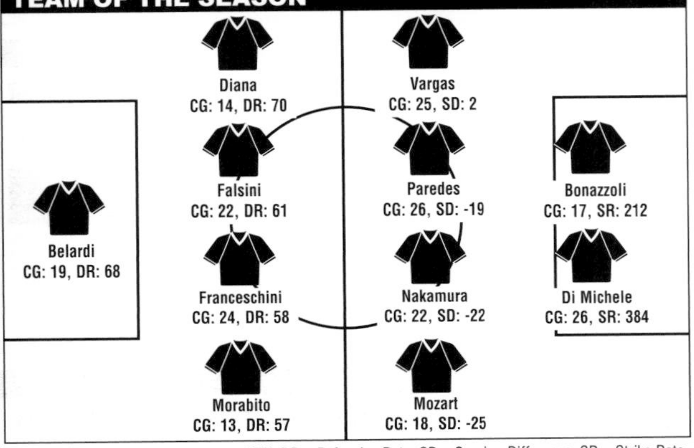
Diana
CG: 14, DR: 70
Vargas
CG: 25, SD: 2
Falsini
CG: 22, DR: 61
Paredes
CG: 26, SD: -19
Bonazzoli
CG: 17, SR: 212
Belardi
CG: 19, DR: 68
Franceschini
CG: 24, DR: 58
Nakamura
CG: 22, SD: -22
Di Michele
CG: 26, SR: 384
Morabito
CG: 13, DR: 57
Mozart
CG: 18, SD: -25

KEY: DR = Defensive Rate, SD = Scoring Difference, SR = Strike Rate, CG = Counting Games – League games playing at least 70 minutes

## LEAGUE APPEARANCES, BOOKINGS AND CAPS

| | AGE | IN THE SQUAD | COUNTING GAMES | MINUTES ON PITCH | YELLOW CARDS | RED CARDS | THIS SEASON | HOME COUNTRY |
|---|---|---|---|---|---|---|---|---|
| **Goalkeepers** | | | | | | | | |
| Emanuele Belardi | 25 | 31 | 19 | 1764 | 2 | 1 | - | Italy |
| Luca Castellazzi | 27 | 14 | 13 | 1197 | 0 | 0 | - | Italy |
| Martin Lejsal | 20 | 20 | 1 | 100 | 0 | 0 | - | Czech Republic |
| Graziano Tilaro | 18 | 1 | 0 | 0 | 0 | 0 | - | Italy |
| **Defenders** | | | | | | | | |
| Riccardo Alderuccio | 20 | 1 | 0 | 0 | 0 | 0 | - | Italy |
| Bruno Cirillo | | 16 | 7 | 775 | 4 | 0 | - | |
| Stefano Aimo Diana | 25 | 16 | 14 | 1322 | 1 | 0 | - | Italy |
| Gianluca Falsini | 27 | 28 | 22 | 2060 | 2 | 0 | - | Italy |
| Ivan Franceschini | 26 | 33 | 24 | 2200 | 7 | 0 | - | Italy |
| Martin Jiranek | 24 | 34 | 22 | 2110 | 3 | 0 | 5 | Czech Republic (13) |
| Giovanni Morabito | 24 | 29 | 13 | 1432 | 1 | 0 | - | Italy |
| Alessandro Pierini | 30 | 17 | 13 | 1182 | 2 | 0 | - | Italy |
| Stefano Torrisi | 32 | 12 | 6 | 621 | 0 | 0 | - | Italy |
| **Midfielders** | | | | | | | | |
| Francesco Cozza | 29 | 29 | 15 | 1793 | 5 | 0 | - | Italy |
| Julio Cesar Leon | 23 | 18 | 1 | 416 | 0 | 0 | - | Honduras |
| Jose Aleixo Mamede | 29 | 19 | 8 | 911 | 5 | 0 | - | Portugal |
| Giandomenico Mesto | 21 | 16 | 3 | 530 | 0 | 0 | - | Italy |
| Santos Batista Mozart | 23 | 33 | 18 | 1884 | 5 | 0 | - | Brazil |
| Shunsuke Nakamura | 25 | 34 | 22 | 2436 | 1 | 0 | 4 | Japan (23) |
| Carlos Paredes | 26 | 31 | 26 | 2482 | 5 | 0 | - | Paraguay |
| Tommaso Salvestroni | 18 | 2 | 0 | 0 | 0 | 0 | - | Italy |
| Jorge Vargas | 27 | 31 | 25 | 2359 | 6 | 1 | - | Chile |
| Ricardo Matias Veron | 22 | 19 | 0 | 24 | 0 | 0 | - | Argentina |
| **Forwards** | | | | | | | | |
| Erjon Bogdani | 26 | 16 | 1 | 307 | 0 | 0 | - | Albania |
| Emiliano Bonazzoli | 24 | 17 | 17 | 1486 | 3 | 0 | - | Italy |
| David Di Michele | 27 | 34 | 26 | 2687 | 2 | 0 | - | Italy |
| Roberto Maffucci | 18 | 1 | 0 | 0 | 0 | 0 | - | Italy |
| Massimo Rastelli | 34 | 28 | 1 | 502 | 2 | 0 | - | Italy |
| Gianluca Savoldi | 27 | 29 | 6 | 999 | 2 | 0 | - | Italy |

KEY: LEAGUE BOOKINGS CAPS (FIFA RANKING)

## SQUAD APPEARANCES

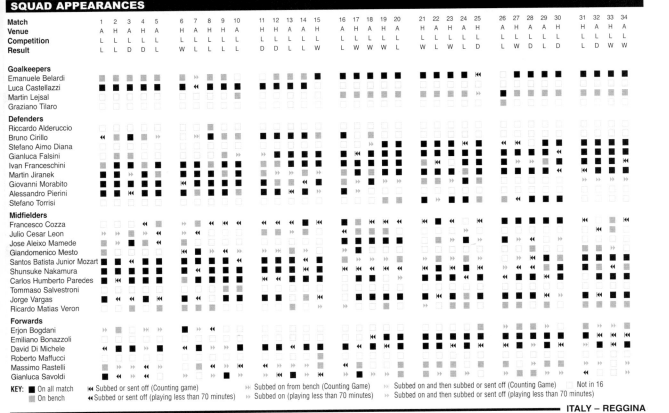

| Match | 1 | 2 | 3 | 4 | 5 | 6 | 7 | 8 | 9 | 10 | 11 | 12 | 13 | 14 | 15 | 16 | 17 | 18 | 19 | 20 | 21 | 22 | 23 | 24 | 25 | 26 | 27 | 28 | 29 | 30 | 31 | 32 | 33 | 34 |
|---|---|---|---|---|---|---|---|---|---|---|---|---|---|---|---|---|---|---|---|---|---|---|---|---|---|---|---|---|---|---|---|---|---|---|
| Venue | A | H | A | H | A | H | A | H | H | A | H | H | A | A | H | A | H | A | H | A | H | A | H | A | H | A | H | A | A | H | H | A | H | A |
| Competition | L | L | L | L | L | L | L | L | L | L | L | L | L | L | L | L | L | L | L | L | L | L | L | L | L | L | L | L | L | L | L | L | L | L |
| Result | L | L | D | D | L | W | L | L | L | L | D | D | L | L | W | L | W | W | W | L | W | L | W | L | D | L | W | D | L | D | L | D | W | W |

**Goalkeepers**
Emanuele Belardi
Luca Castellazzi
Martin Lejsal
Graziano Tilaro

**Defenders**
Riccardo Alderuccio
Bruno Cirillo
Stefano Aimo Diana
Gianluca Falsini
Ivan Franceschini
Martin Jiranek
Giovanni Morabito
Alessandro Pierini
Stefano Torrisi

**Midfielders**
Francesco Cozza
Julio Cesar Leon
Jose Aleixo Mamede
Giandomenico Mesto
Santos Batista Junior Mozart
Shunsuke Nakamura
Carlos Humberto Paredes
Tommaso Salvestroni
Jorge Vargas
Ricardo Matias Veron

**Forwards**
Erjon Bogdani
Emiliano Bonazzoli
David Di Michele
Roberto Maffucci
Massimo Rastelli
Gianluca Savoldi

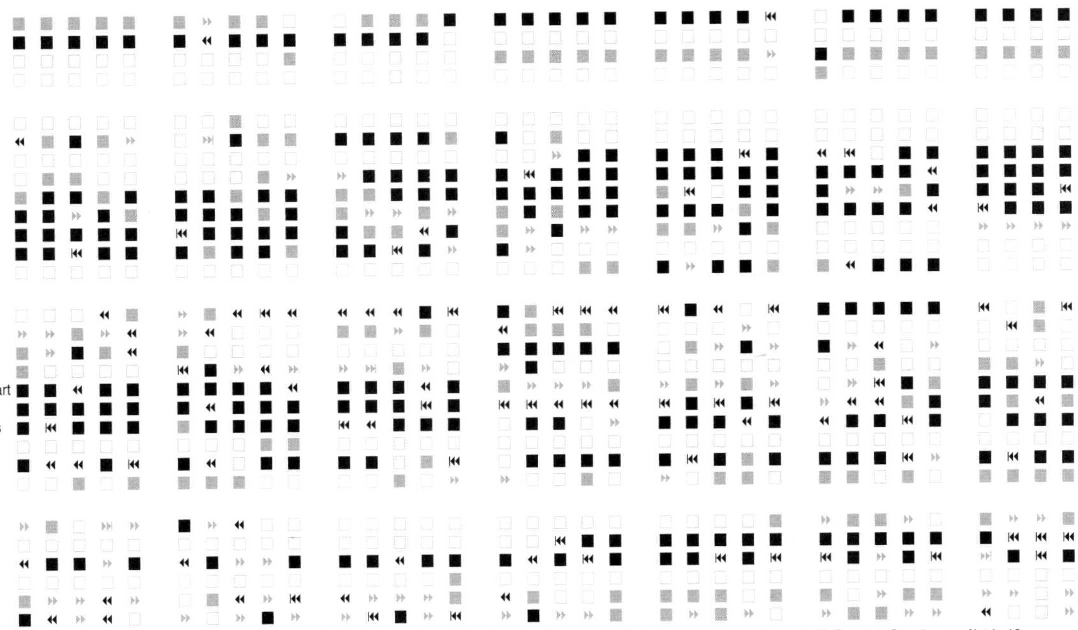

KEY: On all match / On bench / Subbed or sent off (Counting game) / Subbed or sent off (playing less than 70 minutes) / Subbed on from bench (Counting Game) / Subbed on (playing less than 70 minutes) / Subbed on and then subbed or sent off (Counting Game) / Subbed on and then subbed or sent off (playing less than 70 minutes) / Not in 16

# MODENA

Final Position: **15th**

| | | | | | | |
|---|---|---|---|---|---|---|
| 1 | lge | AC Milan | H | L | 0-3 | |
| 2 | lge | Roma | A | W | 2-1 | Milanetto 45 pen; Sculli 80 |
| 3 | lge | Torino | H | W | 2-1 | Sculli 27,53 |
| 4 | lge | Chievo | A | L | 0-2 | |
| 5 | lge | Parma | H | W | 2-1 | Fabbrini 67; Kamara 85 |
| 6 | lge | Perugia | A | L | 0-2 | |
| 7 | lge | Juventus | H | L | 0-1 | |
| 8 | lge | Atalanta | A | W | 3-1 | Colucci 13; Kamara 38; Mauri 75 |
| 9 | lge | Reggina | A | W | 1-0 | Pasino 79 |
| 10 | lge | Piacenza | H | W | 1-0 | Milanetto 33 pen |
| 11 | lge | Lazio | A | L | 0-4 | |
| 12 | lge | Bologna | A | L | 0-3 | |
| 13 | lge | Como | H | D | 1-1 | Sculli 73 |
| 14 | lge | Empoli | A | L | 0-1 | |
| 15 | lge | Udinese | H | L | 0-1 | |
| 16 | lge | Inter Milan | A | L | 0-2 | |
| 17 | lge | Brescia | H | D | 0-0 | |
| 18 | lge | Atalanta | H | L | 0-2 | |
| 19 | lge | AC Milan | A | L | 1-2 | Scoponi 90 |
| 20 | lge | Roma | H | D | 1-1 | Kamara 42 |
| 21 | lge | Torino | A | D | 1-1 | Milanetto 58 |
| 22 | lge | Chievo | H | W | 1-0 | Sculli 75 |
| 23 | lge | Parma | A | D | 1-1 | Scoponi 29 |
| 24 | lge | Perugia | H | D | 1-1 | Colucci 14 |
| 25 | lge | Juventus | A | L | 0-3 | |
| 26 | lge | Reggina | H | W | 2-1 | Balestri 61; Sculli 89 |
| 27 | lge | Piacenza | A | D | 3-3 | Milanetto 24 pen,26 pen; Vignaroli 86 |
| 28 | lge | Lazio | H | D | 0-0 | |
| 29 | lge | Bologna | H | W | 3-2 | Kamara 14; Sculli 74,86 |
| 30 | lge | Como | A | D | 0-0 | |
| 31 | lge | Empoli | H | D | 1-1 | Colucci 38 |
| 32 | lge | Udinese | A | L | 1-2 | Kamara 39 |
| 33 | lge | Inter Milan | H | L | 0-2 | |
| 34 | lge | Brescia | A | D | 2-2 | Colucci 4; Vignaroli 20 |

## KEY PLAYERS - GOALSCORERS

**1 Diomansy Mehdi Kamara**

| | | | |
|---|---|---|---|
| Goals in the League | 5 | Player Strike Rate<br>Average number of minutes between League goals scored by player | 377 |
| Contribution to Attacking Power<br>Average number of minutes between League team goals while on pitch | 104 | Club Strike Rate<br>Average number of minutes between League goals scored by club | 102 |

| | PLAYER | LGE GOALS | POWER | STRIKE RATE |
|---|---|---|---|---|
| 2 | Omar Milanetto | 5 | 111 | 559 mins |
| 3 | Giuseppe Colucci | 4 | 104 | 573 mins |
| 4 | Fabio Vignaroli | 2 | 79 | 636 mins |
| 5 | Stefano Mauri | 1 | 107 | 1719 mins |

## KEY PLAYERS - MIDFIELDERS

**1 Antonio Marasco**

| | | | |
|---|---|---|---|
| Goals in the League | 0 | Contribution to Attacking Power<br>Average number of minutes between League team goals while on pitch | 74 |
| Defensive Rating<br>Average number of mins between League goals conceded while he was on the pitch | 66 | Scoring Difference<br>Defensive Rating minus Contribution to Attacking Power | -8 |

| | PLAYER | LGE GOALS | DEF RATE | POWER | SCORE DIFF |
|---|---|---|---|---|---|
| 2 | Giuseppe Colucci | 4 | 79 | 104 | -25 mins |
| 3 | Paulo Ponzo | 0 | 60 | 91 | -31 mins |
| 4 | Jacopo Balestri | 1 | 67 | 101 | -34 mins |
| 5 | Stefano Mauri | 1 | 66 | 107 | -41 mins |

## KEY PLAYERS - DEFENDERS

**1 Roberto Cevoli**

| | | | |
|---|---|---|---|
| Goals Conceded (GC)<br>The number of League goals conceded while he was on the pitch | 39 | Clean Sheets<br>In games when he played at least 70 minutes | 6 |
| Defensive Rating<br>Ave number of mins between League goals conceded while on the pitch | 67 | Club Defensive Rating<br>Average number of mins between League goals conceded by the club this season | 64 |

| | PLAYER | CON LGE | CLEAN SHEETS | DEF RATE |
|---|---|---|---|---|
| 2 | Mauro Mayer | 39 | 5 | 64 mins |
| 3 | Luca Ungari | 23 | 3 | 62 mins |
| 4 | Simone Pavan | 29 | 2 | 61 mins |

## GOALS SCORED

| AT HOME | | |
|---|---|---|
| MOST | Juventus | 37 |
| | | 15 |
| LEAST | Torino | 10 |

| AWAY | | |
|---|---|---|
| MOST | Inter Milan | 30 |
| | | 15 |
| LEAST | Como | 9 |

## GOALS CONCEDED

| AT HOME | | |
|---|---|---|
| LEAST | AC Milan | 11 |
| | | 18 |
| MOST | Piacenza | 29 |

| AWAY | | |
|---|---|---|
| LEAST | Juventus | 15 |
| | | 30 |
| MOST | Perugia | 35 |

## KEY GOALKEEPER

**1 Marco Ballotta**

| | |
|---|---|
| Goals Conceded in the League | 48 |
| Defensive Rating<br>Ave number of mins between League goals conceded while on the pitch | 64 |
| Counting Games<br>Games when he played at least 70 minutes | 34 |
| Clean Sheets<br>In games when he played at least 70 minutes | 6 |

## TOP POINT EARNERS

| | PLAYER | GAMES | AVE |
|---|---|---|---|
| 1 | Ponzo | 21 | 1.43 |
| 2 | Mauri | 16 | 1.25 |
| 3 | Marasco | 14 | 1.21 |
| 4 | Mayer | 27 | 1.19 |
| 5 | Cevoli | 28 | 1.18 |
| 6 | Balestri | 33 | 1.15 |
| 7 | Colucci | 20 | 1.15 |
| 8 | Ballotta | 34 | 1.12 |
| 9 | Milanetto | 31 | 1.06 |
| 10 | Ungari | 16 | 1.06 |
| | **CLUB AVERAGE:** | | **1.12** |

Ave = Average points per match in Counting Games

## ATTENDANCES

HOME GROUND: ALBERTO BRAGLIA CAPACITY: 17000 AVERAGE LEAGUE AT HOME: 14747

| | | | | | | | | |
|---|---|---|---|---|---|---|---|---|
| 2 | Roma | 54000 | 29 | Bologna | 17000 | 24 | Perugia | 14000 |
| 19 | AC Milan | 50000 | 23 | Parma | 16000 | 28 | Lazio | 13800 |
| 11 | Lazio | 45000 | 3 | Torino | 15000 | 13 | Como | 13407 |
| 25 | Juventus | 36921 | 18 | Atalanta | 15000 | 8 | Atalanta | 13000 |
| 12 | Bologna | 35000 | 4 | Chievo | 15000 | 15 | Udinese | 13000 |
| 16 | Inter Milan | 32000 | 32 | Udinese | 15000 | 5 | Parma | 11000 |
| 9 | Reggina | 23373 | 22 | Chievo | 15000 | 6 | Perugia | 10000 |
| 21 | Torino | 20000 | 33 | Inter Milan | 15000 | 27 | Piacenza | 10000 |
| 20 | Roma | 17500 | 17 | Brescia | 14700 | 30 | Como | 6000 |
| 1 | AC Milan | 17300 | 26 | Reggina | 14000 | 14 | Empoli | 5300 |
| 7 | Juventus | 17000 | 10 | Piacenza | 14000 | | | |
| 34 | Brescia | 17000 | 31 | Empoli | 14000 | | | |

■ Home □ Away ▨ Neutral

## DISCIPLINARY RECORDS

| | PLAYER | YELLOW | RED | AVE |
|---|---|---|---|---|
| 1 | Mayer | 12 | 0 | 207 |
| 2 | Ungari | 6 | 0 | 238 |
| 3 | Scoponi | 3 | 0 | 250 |
| 4 | Cevoli | 8 | 2 | 259 |
| 5 | Sculli | 5 | 0 | 295 |
| 6 | Milanetto | 8 | 1 | 310 |
| 7 | Marasco | 4 | 0 | 315 |
| 8 | Pavan | 5 | 0 | 351 |
| 9 | Kamara | 5 | 0 | 377 |
| 10 | Mauri | 4 | 0 | 429 |
| 11 | Campedelli | 0 | 1 | 482 |
| 12 | Fabbrini | 2 | 0 | 540 |
| 13 | Ponzo | 4 | 0 | 543 |
| | Other | 10 | 1 | |
| | TOTAL | 76 | 5 | |

## LEAGUE GOALS

| | PLAYER | MINS | GOALS | AVE |
|---|---|---|---|---|
| 1 | Sculli | 1476 | 7 | 211 |
| 2 | Kamara | 1885 | 5 | 377 |
| 3 | Milanetto | 2794 | 5 | 559 |
| 4 | Colucci | 2293 | 4 | 573 |
| 5 | Vignaroli | 1272 | 2 | 636 |
| 6 | Scoponi | 750 | 2 | 375 |
| 7 | Balestri | 2935 | 1 | 2935 |
| 8 | Fabbrini | 1081 | 1 | 1081 |
| 9 | Mauri | 1719 | 1 | 1719 |
| 10 | Pasino | 359 | 1 | 359 |
| | Other | | 1 | |
| | TOTAL | | 30 | |

## MONTH BY MONTH GUIDE TO THE POINTS

| MONTH | POINTS | % |
|---|---|---|
| SEPTEMBER | 6 | 67% |
| OCTOBER | 3 | 33% |
| NOVEMBER | 9 | 60% |
| DECEMBER | 1 | 8% |
| JANUARY | 1 | 11% |
| FEBRUARY | 5 | 42% |
| MARCH | 5 | 42% |
| APRIL | 6 | 50% |
| MAY | 2 | 17% |

## TEAM OF THE SEASON

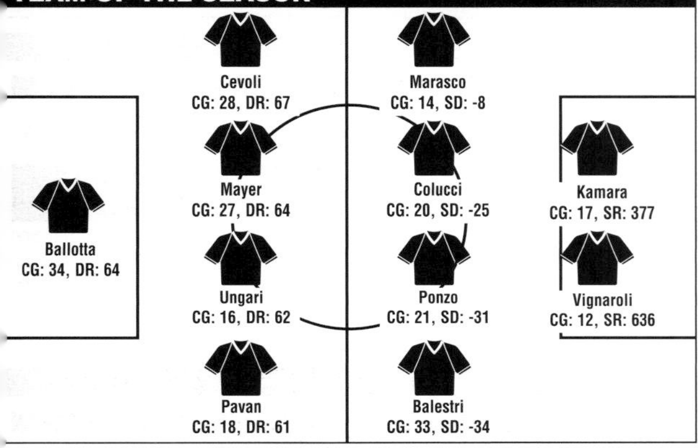
Cevoli
CG: 28, DR: 67
Marasco
CG: 14, SD: -8
Mayer
CG: 27, DR: 64
Colucci
CG: 20, SD: -25
Kamara
CG: 17, SR: 377
Ballotta
CG: 34, DR: 64
Ungari
CG: 16, DR: 62
Ponzo
CG: 21, SD: -31
Vignaroli
CG: 12, SR: 636
Pavan
CG: 18, DR: 61
Balestri
CG: 33, SD: -34

**KEY:** DR = Defensive Rate, SD = Scoring Difference, SR = Strike Rate, CG = Counting Games – League games playing at least 70 minutes

## LEAGUE APPEARANCES, BOOKINGS AND CAPS

| | AGE | IN THE SQUAD | COUNTING GAMES | MINUTES ON PITCH | YELLOW CARDS | RED CARDS | THIS SEASON | HOME COUNTRY |
|---|---|---|---|---|---|---|---|---|
| **Goalkeepers** | | | | | | | | |
| Marco Ballotta | 39 | 34 | 34 | 3060 | 1 | 0 | - | Italy |
| Emiliano Moretti | 22 | 15 | 4 | 490 | 0 | 0 | - | Italy |
| Adriano Zancope | 31 | 34 | 0 | 34 | 0 | 0 | - | Italy |
| **Defenders** | | | | | | | | |
| Roberto Cevoli | 34 | 31 | 28 | 2597 | 8 | 2 | - | Italy |
| Mauro Mayer | 32 | 30 | 27 | 2487 | 12 | 0 | - | Italy |
| Simone Pavan | 29 | 25 | 18 | 1755 | 5 | 0 | - | Italy |
| Andrea Quaglia | 31 | 4 | 0 | 20 | 0 | 0 | - | Italy |
| Luca Ungari | 28 | 29 | 16 | 1428 | 6 | 0 | - | Italy |
| Vincenzo Vado | 19 | 2 | 0 | 0 | 0 | 0 | - | Italy |
| Marco Zamboni | 25 | 8 | 1 | 149 | 1 | 0 | - | |
| Alessandro Zamperini | 20 | 1 | 0 | 0 | 0 | 0 | - | Italy |
| **Midfielders** | | | | | | | | |
| Marcello Albino | | 24 | 4 | 609 | 1 | 0 | - | Italy |
| Jacopo Balestri | 28 | 33 | 33 | 2935 | 4 | 1 | - | Italy |
| Nicola Campedelli | 24 | 28 | 3 | 482 | 0 | 1 | - | Italy |
| Giuseppe Colucci | 22 | 33 | 20 | 2293 | 2 | 0 | - | Italy |
| Antonio Marasco | 33 | 14 | 14 | 1260 | 4 | 0 | - | Italy |
| Stefano Mauri | 23 | 32 | 16 | 1719 | 4 | 0 | - | Italy |
| Omar Milanetto | 27 | 32 | 31 | 2794 | 8 | 1 | - | Italy |
| Rubens Pasino | 31 | 16 | 2 | 359 | 0 | 0 | - | Italy |
| Paulo Ponzo | 31 | 32 | 21 | 2175 | 4 | 0 | - | Italy |
| Massimo Scoponi | 29 | 27 | 4 | 750 | 3 | 0 | - | Italy |
| **Forwards** | | | | | | | | |
| Manuel De Luca | 19 | 1 | 0 | 0 | 0 | 0 | - | Italy |
| Andrea Fabbrini | 28 | 26 | 8 | 1081 | 2 | 0 | - | Italy |
| Giacomo Ferrari | 35 | 6 | 0 | 43 | 0 | 0 | - | Italy |
| Diomansy Kamara | 22 | 30 | 17 | 1885 | 5 | 0 | - | France |
| Giuseppe Sculli | 22 | 33 | 11 | 1476 | 5 | 0 | - | Italy |
| Carlo Taldo | 31 | 14 | 3 | 435 | 0 | 0 | - | |
| Fabio Vignaroli | 27 | 17 | 12 | 1272 | 1 | 0 | - | Italy |

**KEY:** LEAGUE BOOKINGS CAPS (FIFA RANKING)

## SQUAD APPEARANCES

| Match | 1 | 2 | 3 | 4 | 5 | 6 | 7 | 8 | 9 | 10 | 11 | 12 | 13 | 14 | 15 | 16 | 17 | 18 | 19 | 20 | 21 | 22 | 23 | 24 | 25 | 26 | 27 | 28 | 29 | 30 | 31 | 32 | 33 | 34 |
|---|---|---|---|---|---|---|---|---|---|---|---|---|---|---|---|---|---|---|---|---|---|---|---|---|---|---|---|---|---|---|---|---|---|---|
| Venue | H | A | H | A | H | A | H | A | A | H | A | A | H | A | H | A | H | H | A | H | A | H | A | H | A | H | A | H | H | A | H | A | H | A |
| Competition | L | L | L | L | L | L | L | L | L | L | L | L | L | L | L | L | L | L | L | L | L | L | L | L | L | L | L | L | L | L | L | L | L | L |
| Result | L | W | W | L | W | L | L | W | W | W | L | L | D | L | L | L | D | L | L | D | D | W | D | D | L | W | D | D | W | D | D | L | L | D |

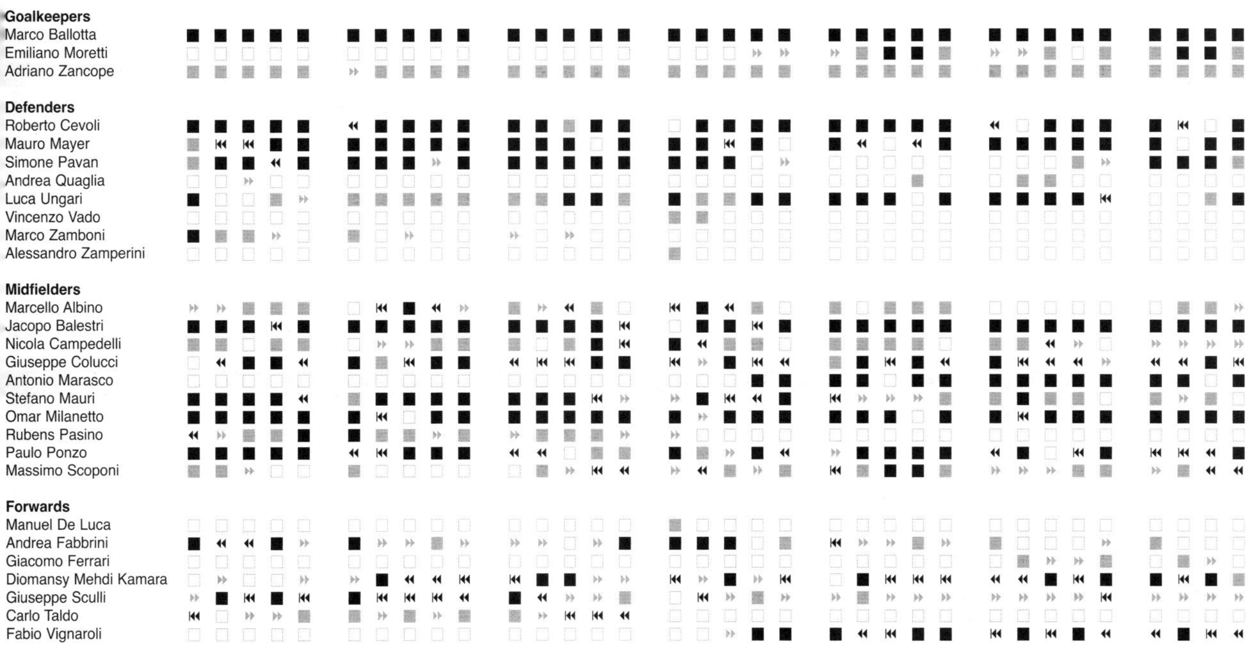
Goalkeepers
Marco Ballotta
Emiliano Moretti
Adriano Zancope
Defenders
Roberto Cevoli
Mauro Mayer
Simone Pavan
Andrea Quaglia
Luca Ungari
Vincenzo Vado
Marco Zamboni
Alessandro Zamperini
Midfielders
Marcello Albino
Jacopo Balestri
Nicola Campedelli
Giuseppe Colucci
Antonio Marasco
Stefano Mauri
Omar Milanetto
Rubens Pasino
Paulo Ponzo
Massimo Scoponi
Forwards
Manuel De Luca
Andrea Fabbrini
Giacomo Ferrari
Diomansy Mehdi Kamara
Giuseppe Sculli
Carlo Taldo
Fabio Vignaroli

**KEY:** On all match / On bench / Subbed or sent off (Counting game) / Subbed or sent off (playing less than 70 minutes) / Subbed on from bench (Counting Game) / Subbed on (playing less than 70 minutes) / Subbed on and then subbed or sent off (Counting Game) / Subbed on and then subbed or sent off (playing less than 70 minutes) / Not in 16

# PIACENZA

Final Position: **16th**

| | | | | | | |
|---|---|---|---|---|---|---|
| 1 | lge | Brescia | A | W | 2-1 | Montano 69; Hubner 77 |
| 2 | lge | Udinese | H | W | 2-0 | Hubner 26; Maresca 87 |
| 3 | lge | Bologna | A | L | 0-1 | |
| 4 | lge | Inter Milan | H | L | 1-4 | Maresca 73 |
| 5 | lge | Como | A | D | 1-1 | Caccia 30 |
| 6 | lge | Empoli | H | L | 1-2 | Cardone 6 |
| 7 | lge | Atalanta | A | L | 0-2 | |
| 8 | lge | Juventus | H | L | 0-1 | |
| 9 | lge | Roma | H | D | 1-1 | Maresca 74 |
| 10 | lge | Modena | A | L | 0-1 | |
| 11 | lge | Torino | H | W | 1-0 | Di Francesco 23 |
| 12 | lge | Lazio | H | L | 2-3 | Maresca 17; Caccia 26 |
| 13 | lge | Perugia | A | D | 0-0 | |
| 14 | lge | Chievo | H | L | 0-3 | |
| 15 | lge | Reggina | A | L | 1-3 | Boselli 13 |
| 16 | lge | Parma | H | D | 1-1 | Tosto 47 |
| 17 | lge | AC Milan | A | L | 1-2 | Gurenko 53 |
| 18 | lge | Juventus | A | L | 0-2 | |
| 19 | lge | Brescia | H | L | 1-4 | Hubner 17 |
| 20 | lge | Udinese | A | L | 1-2 | Hubner 77 |
| 21 | lge | Bologna | H | W | 3-1 | Hubner 19 pen; Maresca 40; De Cesare 62 |
| 22 | lge | Inter Milan | A | L | 1-3 | Hubner 89 |
| 23 | lge | Como | H | L | 0-1 | |
| 24 | lge | Empoli | A | L | 1-3 | Hubner 90 |
| 25 | lge | Atalanta | H | W | 2-0 | Hubner 41; De Cesare 89 |
| 26 | lge | Roma | A | L | 0-3 | |
| 27 | lge | Modena | H | D | 3-3 | Di Francesco 8,67; Maresca 90 |
| 28 | lge | Torino | A | W | 3-1 | Maresca 60; Di Francesco 83; Ferrarese 90 |
| 29 | lge | Lazio | A | L | 1-2 | De Cesare 45 |
| 30 | lge | Perugia | H | W | 5-1 | Di Francesco 6; Campagnaro 36,63; Hubner 41; Ferrarese 80 |
| 31 | lge | Chievo | A | L | 1-3 | Di Francesco 47 |
| 32 | lge | Reggina | H | D | 2-2 | Hubner 72,75 |
| 33 | lge | Parma | A | L | 2-3 | Maresca 34; Hubner 39 |
| 34 | lge | AC Milan | H | W | 4-2 | Hubner 6,82; Maresca 17 pen; Marchionni 31 |

## KEY PLAYERS - GOALSCORERS

**1 Dario Hubner**

| | | | |
|---|---|---|---|
| Goals in the League | 14 | Player Strike Rate<br>Average number of minutes between League goals scored by player | 161 |
| Contribution to Attacking Power<br>Average number of minutes between League team goals while on pitch | 60 | Club Strike Rate<br>Average number of minutes between League goals scored by club | 70 |

| | PLAYER | LGE GOALS | POWER | STRIKE RATE |
|---|---|---|---|---|
| 2 | Enzo Maresca | 9 | 64 | 294 mins |
| 3 | Eusebio Di Francesco | 6 | 67 | 436 mins |
| 4 | Giuseppe Cardone | 1 | 140 | 1260 mins |
| 5 | Marco Marchionni | 1 | 50 | 1322 mins |

## KEY PLAYERS - MIDFIELDERS

**1 Enzo Maresca**

| | | | |
|---|---|---|---|
| Goals in the League | 9 | Contribution to Attacking Power<br>Average number of minutes between League team goals while on pitch | 65 |
| Defensive Rating<br>Average number of mins between League goals conceded while he was on the pitch | 54 | Scoring Difference<br>Defensive Rating minus Contribution to Attacking Power | -11 |

| | PLAYER | LGE GOALS | DEF RATE | POWER | SCORE DIFF |
|---|---|---|---|---|---|
| 2 | Eusebio Di Francesco | 6 | 51 | 67 | -16 mins |
| 3 | Sergei Gurenko | 1 | 49 | 72 | -23 mins |
| 4 | Luigi Riccio | 0 | 53 | 110 | -57 mins |

## KEY PLAYERS - DEFENDERS

**1 Giuseppe Cardone**

| | | | |
|---|---|---|---|
| Goals Conceded (GC)<br>The number of League goals conceded while he was on the pitch | 21 | Clean Sheets<br>In games when he played at least 70 minutes | 2 |
| Defensive Rating<br>Ave number of mins between League goals conceded while on the pitch | 60 | Club Defensive Rating<br>Average number of mins between League goals conceded by the club this season | 49 |

| | PLAYER | CON LGE | CLEAN SHEETS | DEF RATE |
|---|---|---|---|---|
| 2 | Gianluca Lamacchi | 29 | 2 | 55 mins |
| 3 | Amedeo Mangone | 43 | 3 | 54 mins |
| 4 | Vittorio Tosto | 47 | 4 | 52 mins |
| 5 | Filipo Cristante | 47 | 2 | 46 mins |

## GOALS SCORED

**AT HOME**

| | | |
|---|---|---|
| MOST | Juventus | 37 |
| | | 29 |
| LEAST | Torino | 10 |

**AWAY**

| | | |
|---|---|---|
| MOST | Inter Milan | 30 |
| | | 15 |
| LEAST | Como | 9 |

## GOALS CONCEDED

**AT HOME**

| | | |
|---|---|---|
| LEAST | AC Milan | 11 |
| | | 29 |
| MOST | Piacenza | 29 |

**AWAY**

| | | |
|---|---|---|
| LEAST | Juventus | 15 |
| | | 33 |
| MOST | Perugia | 35 |

## KEY GOALKEEPER

**1 Matteo Guardalben**

| | |
|---|---|
| Goals Conceded in the League | 37 |
| Defensive Rating<br>Ave number of mins between League goals conceded while on the pitch | 52 |
| Counting Games<br>Games when he played at least 70 minutes | 21 |
| Clean Sheets<br>In games when he played at least 70 minutes | 3 |

## TOP POINT EARNERS

| | PLAYER | GAMES | AVE |
|---|---|---|---|
| 1 | Baiocco | 15 | 1.13 |
| 2 | Maresca | 29 | 1.00 |
| 3 | Marchionni | 13 | 1.00 |
| 4 | Di Francesco | 28 | 0.96 |
| 5 | Mangone | 24 | 0.92 |
| 6 | Tosto | 25 | 0.92 |
| 7 | Hubner | 22 | 0.86 |
| 8 | Lamacchi | 17 | 0.82 |
| 9 | Guardalben | 21 | 0.81 |
| 10 | Riccio | 15 | 0.80 |
| | CLUB AVERAGE: | | 0.88 |

Ave = Average points per match in Counting Games

## ATTENDANCES

HOME GROUND: LEONARDO GARILLI CAPACITY: 21608 AVERAGE LEAGUE AT HOME: 9173

| | | | | | | | | |
|---|---|---|---|---|---|---|---|---|
| 22 | Inter Milan | 56000 | 7 | Atalanta | 14000 | 32 | Reggina | 6500 |
| 17 | AC Milan | 50000 | 10 | Modena | 14000 | 30 | Perugia | 6500 |
| 26 | Roma | 50000 | 33 | Parma | 13000 | 16 | Parma | 6500 |
| 18 | Juventus | 35539 | 31 | Chievo | 11400 | 14 | Chievo | 6139 |
| 15 | Reggina | 23000 | 27 | Modena | 10000 | 34 | AC Milan | 6100 |
| 9 | Roma | 20000 | 2 | Udinese | 9000 | 24 | Empoli | 6000 |
| 29 | Lazio | 20000 | 23 | Como | 8000 | 21 | Bologna | 6000 |
| 3 | Bologna | 20000 | 5 | Como | 8000 | 13 | Perugia | 6000 |
| 8 | Juventus | 20000 | 19 | Brescia | 7705 | 11 | Torino | 5000 |
| 4 | Inter Milan | 17000 | 6 | Empoli | 7500 | 28 | Torino | 1000 |
| 20 | Udinese | 15000 | 25 | Atalanta | 7000 | | | |
| 1 | Brescia | 14400 | 12 | Lazio | 7000 | | | |

■ Home □ Away ▨ Neutral

## DISCIPLINARY RECORDS

| | PLAYER | YELLOW | RED | AVE |
|---|---|---|---|---|
| 1 | Cristante | 10 | 0 | 217 |
| 2 | Mangone | 10 | 0 | 234 |
| 3 | Caccia | 3 | 0 | 280 |
| 4 | Cardone | 4 | 0 | 315 |
| 5 | Lamacchi | 4 | 1 | 321 |
| 6 | Montano | 2 | 0 | 398 |
| 7 | Tosto | 6 | 0 | 405 |
| 8 | Baiocco | 3 | 0 | 466 |
| 9 | Riccio | 3 | 0 | 514 |
| 10 | Ferrarese | 1 | 0 | 562 |
| 11 | Hubner | 3 | 1 | 562 |
| 12 | Di Francesco | 3 | 0 | 871 |
| 13 | Maresca | 3 | 0 | 883 |
| | Other | 7 | 1 | |
| | TOTAL | 62 | 3 | |

## LEAGUE GOALS

| | PLAYER | MINS | GOALS | AVE |
|---|---|---|---|---|
| 1 | Hubner | 2251 | 14 | 161 |
| 2 | Maresca | 2650 | 9 | 294 |
| 3 | Di Francesco | 2613 | 6 | 436 |
| 4 | De Cesare | 1088 | 3 | 363 |
| 5 | Campagnaro | 734 | 2 | 367 |
| 6 | Caccia | 841 | 2 | 421 |
| 7 | Tosto | 2434 | 1 | 2434 |
| 8 | Marchionni | 1322 | 1 | 1322 |
| 9 | Montano | 796 | 1 | 796 |
| 10 | Boselli | 499 | 1 | 499 |
| 11 | Ferrarese | 562 | 1 | 562 |
| 12 | Gurenko | 1722 | 1 | 1722 |
| 13 | Cardone | 1260 | 1 | 1260 |
| | Other | | 1 | |
| | TOTAL | | 44 | |

## MONTH BY MONTH GUIDE TO THE POINTS

| MONTH | POINTS | % |
|---|---|---|
| SEPTEMBER | 6 | 67% |
| OCTOBER | 1 | 11% |
| NOVEMBER | 4 | 27% |
| DECEMBER | 1 | 8% |
| JANUARY | 1 | 11% |
| FEBRUARY | 3 | 25% |
| MARCH | 3 | 25% |
| APRIL | 7 | 58% |
| MAY | 4 | 33% |

## TEAM OF THE SEASON

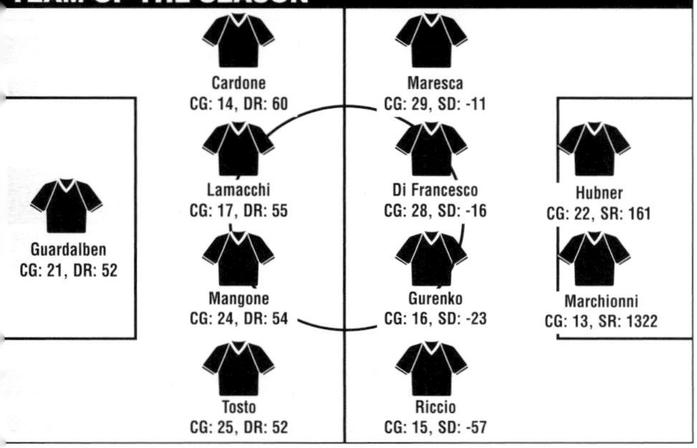

Cardone
CG: 14, DR: 60
Maresca
CG: 29, SD: -11
Lamacchi
CG: 17, DR: 55
Di Francesco
CG: 28, SD: -16
Hubner
CG: 22, SR: 161
Guardalben
CG: 21, DR: 52
Mangone
CG: 24, DR: 54
Gurenko
CG: 16, SD: -23
Marchionni
CG: 13, SR: 1322
Tosto
CG: 25, DR: 52
Riccio
CG: 15, SD: -57


KEY: DR = Defensive Rate, SD = Scoring Difference, SR = Strike Rate, CG = Counting Games – League games playing at least 70 minutes

## LEAGUE APPEARANCES, BOOKINGS AND CAPS

| | AGE | IN THE SQUAD | COUNTING GAMES | MINUTES ON PITCH | YELLOW CARDS | RED CARDS | THIS SEASON | HOME COUNTRY |
|---|---|---|---|---|---|---|---|---|
| **Goalkeepers** | | | | | | | | |
| Mauro Bertaccini | 19 | 2 | 0 | 0 | 0 | 0 | - | Italy |
| Maurizio Franzone | 34 | 10 | 1 | 90 | 0 | 0 | - | Italy |
| Matteo Guardalben | 29 | 23 | 21 | 1935 | 0 | 0 | - | Italy |
| Paolo Orlandoni | 30 | 30 | 11 | 1035 | 0 | 0 | - | Italy |
| Simone Paoletti | 19 | 2 | 0 | 0 | 0 | 0 | - | Italy |
| **Defenders** | | | | | | | | |
| Matteo Abbate | 19 | 19 | 6 | 590 | 0 | 0 | - | Italy |
| Davide Baiocco | 28 | 16 | 15 | 1399 | 3 | 0 | - | Italy |
| Nicola Boselli | 30 | 13 | 5 | 499 | 0 | 0 | - | Italy |
| Hugo Campagnaro | 23 | 25 | 7 | 734 | 0 | 0 | - | Italy |
| Giuseppe Cardone | 29 | 14 | 14 | 1260 | 4 | 0 | - | Italy |
| Filipo Cristante | 26 | 30 | 23 | 2178 | 10 | 0 | - | Italy |
| Gianluca Lamacchi | 31 | 21 | 17 | 1607 | 4 | 1 | - | Italy |
| Amedeo Mangone | 34 | 29 | 24 | 2340 | 10 | 0 | - | Italy |
| Alessandro Rinaldi | 28 | 6 | 0 | 120 | 2 | 1 | - | Italy |
| Vittorio Tosto | 29 | 31 | 25 | 2434 | 6 | 0 | - | Italy |
| Paolo Tramezzani | 32 | 8 | 2 | 308 | 1 | 0 | - | Italy |
| **Midfielders** | | | | | | | | |
| Olalekan Babatunde | 18 | 2 | 0 | 55 | 0 | 0 | - | Niger |
| Sandro Cois | 31 | 12 | 0 | 130 | 0 | 0 | - | Italy |
| Eusebio Di Francesco | 33 | 30 | 28 | 2613 | 3 | 0 | - | Italy |
| Claudio Ferrarese | 24 | 18 | 1 | 562 | 1 | 0 | - | Italy |
| Sergei Gurenko | 30 | 33 | 16 | 1722 | 1 | 0 | - | Belarus |
| Dario Marcolin | | 13 | 1 | 162 | 1 | 0 | - | |
| Enzo Maresca | 23 | 32 | 29 | 2650 | 3 | 0 | - | Italy |
| Salvatore Miceli | 29 | 11 | 1 | 244 | 1 | 0 | - | |
| Bogdan Patrascu | 24 | 28 | 1 | 360 | 0 | 0 | - | Romania |
| Marcello Premoli | 19 | 2 | 0 | 0 | 0 | 0 | - | Italy |
| Luigi Riccio | 25 | 22 | 15 | 1542 | 3 | 0 | - | Italy |
| Marco Stella | | 9 | 0 | 53 | 0 | 0 | - | |
| **Forwards** | | | | | | | | |
| Nicola Caccia | 33 | 13 | 8 | 841 | 3 | 0 | - | Italy |
| Ciro De Cesare | 31 | 19 | 9 | 1088 | 0 | 0 | - | Italy |
| Dario Hubner | 36 | 29 | 22 | 2251 | 3 | 1 | - | Italy |
| Marco Marchionni | 22 | 16 | 13 | 1322 | 0 | 0 | - | Italy |
| Johnnier Montano | 20 | 11 | 8 | 796 | 2 | 0 | - | Columbia |
| Mauro Ivan Obolo | 21 | 14 | 0 | 179 | 1 | 0 | - | Argentina |
| Francesco Zerbini | 23 | 19 | 3 | 476 | 0 | 0 | - | Italy |

KEY: LEAGUE BOOKINGS CAPS (FIFA RANKING)

## SQUAD APPEARANCES

| | 1 | 2 | 3 | 4 | 5 | 6 | 7 | 8 | 9 | 10 | 11 | 12 | 13 | 14 | 15 | 16 | 17 | 18 | 19 | 20 | 21 | 22 | 23 | 24 | 25 | 26 | 27 | 28 | 29 | 30 | 31 | 32 | 33 | 34 |
|---|---|---|---|---|---|---|---|---|---|---|---|---|---|---|---|---|---|---|---|---|---|---|---|---|---|---|---|---|---|---|---|---|---|---|
| **Venue** | A | H | A | H | A | H | A | H | H | A | H | H | A | H | A | H | A | A | H | A | H | A | H | A | H | A | H | A | A | H | A | H | A | H |
| **Competition** | L | L | L | L | L | L | L | L | L | L | L | L | L | L | L | L | L | L | L | L | L | L | L | L | L | L | L | L | L | L | L | L | L | L |
| **Result** | W | W | L | L | D | L | L | L | D | L | W | L | D | L | L | D | L | L | L | L | W | L | L | L | W | L | D | W | L | W | L | D | L | W |

**Goalkeepers**
Mauro Bertaccini
Maurizio Franzone
Matteo Guardalben
Paolo Orlandoni
Simone Paoletti

**Defenders**
Matteo Abbate
Davide Baiocco
Nicola Boselli
Hugo Campagnaro
Giuseppe Cardone
Filipo Cristante
Gianluca Lamacchi
Amedeo Mangone
Alessandro Rinaldi
Vittorio Tosto
Paolo Tramezzani

**Midfielders**
Olalekan Ibrahim Babatunde
Sandro Cois
Eusebio Di Francesco
Claudio Ferrarese
Sergei Gurenko
Dario Marcolin
Enzo Maresca
Salvatore Miceli
Bogdan Patrascu
Marcello Premoli
Luigi Riccio
Marco Stella

**Forwards**
Nicola Caccia
Ciro De Cesare
Dario Hubner
Marco Marchionni
Johnnier Montano
Mauro Ivan Obolo
Francesco Zerbini

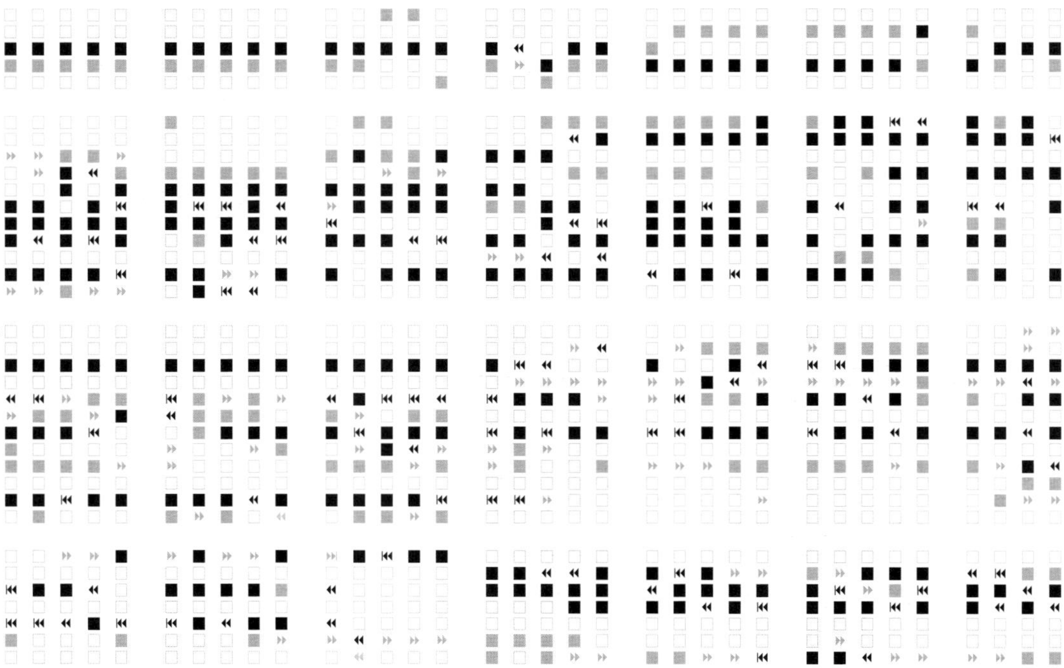

# COMO

Final Position: **17th**

| | | | | | | |
|---|---|---|---|---|---|---|
| 1 | lge | Empoli | H | L | 0-2 | |
| 2 | lge | Parma | A | L | 0-2 | |
| 3 | lge | Reggina | H | D | 1-1 | Carbone 18 pen |
| 4 | lge | Juventus | A | D | 1-1 | Pecchia 66 |
| 5 | lge | Piacenza | H | D | 1-1 | Cardone 45 og |
| 6 | lge | Brescia | A | D | 1-1 | Padalino 77 |
| 7 | lge | Inter Milan | H | L | 0-2 | |
| 8 | lge | Roma | A | L | 1-2 | Godeas 73 |
| 9 | lge | Bologna | A | L | 0-1 | |
| 10 | lge | Lazio | H | L | 1-3 | Corrent 37 |
| 11 | lge | Perugia | A | L | 0-3 | |
| 12 | lge | Modena | A | D | 1-1 | Bjelanovic 88 |
| 13 | lge | AC Milan | H | L | 1-2 | Pecchia 21 |
| 14 | lge | Udinese | H | L | 0-2 | (Awarded 2-0 to Udinese) |
| 15 | lge | Chievo | A | L | 0-2 | |
| 16 | lge | Atalanta | H | D | 1-1 | Bjelanovic 45 |
| 17 | lge | Torino | A | D | 0-0 | |
| 18 | lge | Roma | H | W | 2-0 | Music 83; Carbone 90 |
| 19 | lge | Empoli | A | D | 0-0 | |
| 20 | lge | Parma | H | D | 2-2 | Caccia 66; Amoruso 79 |
| 21 | lge | Reggina | A | L | 1-4 | Corrent 10 |
| 22 | lge | Juventus | H | L | 1-3 | Pecchia 80 |
| 23 | lge | Piacenza | A | W | 1-0 | Amoruso 7 |
| 24 | lge | Brescia | H | D | 1-1 | Pecchia 54 |
| 25 | lge | Inter Milan | A | L | 0-4 | |
| 26 | lge | Bologna | H | W | 5-1 | Caccia 18; Amoruso 50,89; Pecchia 57; Music 86 |
| 27 | lge | Lazio | A | L | 0-3 | |
| 28 | lge | Perugia | H | D | 1-1 | Amoruso 28 |
| 29 | lge | Udinese | A | L | 2-3 | Pecchia 59; Music 61 |
| 30 | lge | Modena | H | D | 0-0 | |
| 31 | lge | AC Milan | A | L | 0-2 | |
| 32 | lge | Chievo | H | L | 2-4 | Amoruso 51; Caccia 82 |
| 33 | lge | Atalanta | A | L | 1-2 | Caccia 17 |
| 34 | lge | Torino | H | W | 1-0 | Benin 83 |

## KEY PLAYERS - GOALSCORERS

**1 Fabio Pecchia**

| | | | |
|---|---|---|---|
| Goals in the League | 6 | Player Strike Rate<br>Average number of minutes between League goals scored by player | 295 |
| Contribution to Attacking Power<br>Average number of minutes between League team goals while on pitch | 84 | Club Strike Rate<br>Average number of minutes between League goals scored by club | 106 |

| | PLAYER | LGE GOALS | POWER | STRIKE RATE |
|---|---|---|---|---|
| 2 | Nicola Caccia | 4 | 82 | 332 mins |
| 3 | Vedin Music | 3 | 77 | 650 mins |
| 4 | Nicola Corrent | 2 | 90 | 726 mins |
| 5 | Pasquale Padalino | 1 | 96 | 1350 mins |

## KEY PLAYERS - MIDFIELDERS

**1 Fabio Pecchia**

| | | | |
|---|---|---|---|
| Goals in the League | 6 | Contribution to Attacking Power<br>Average number of minutes between League team goals while on pitch | 86 |
| Defensive Rating<br>Average number of mins between League goals conceded while he was on the pitch | 67 | Scoring Difference<br>Defensive Rating minus Contribution to Attacking Power | -19 |

| | PLAYER | LGE GOALS | DEF RATE | POWER | SCORE DIFF |
|---|---|---|---|---|---|
| 2 | Vedin Music | 3 | 56 | 78 | -22 mins |
| 3 | Nicola Corrent | 2 | 62 | 94 | -32 mins |
| 4 | Riccardo Allegretti | 0 | 56 | 115 | -59 mins |
| 5 | Benoit Cauet | 0 | 52 | 122 | -70 mins |

## KEY PLAYERS - DEFENDERS

**1 Juarez De Souza Texeira**

| | | | |
|---|---|---|---|
| Goals Conceded (GC)<br>The number of League goals conceded while he was on the pitch | 31 | Clean Sheets<br>In games when he played at least 70 minutes | 4 |
| Defensive Rating<br>Ave number of mins between League goals conceded while on the pitch | 57 | Club Defensive Rating<br>Average number of mins between League goals conceded by the club this season | 55 |

| | PLAYER | CON LGE | CLEAN SHEETS | DEF RATE |
|---|---|---|---|---|
| 2 | Pasquale Padalino | 24 | 1 | 56 mins |
| 3 | Cristian Stellini | 48 | 5 | 56 mins |
| 4 | Massimo Tarantino | 21 | 4 | 54 mins |
| 5 | Daniele Gregori | 24 | 2 | 49 mins |

## GOALS SCORED

**AT HOME**

| | | |
|---|---|---|
| MOST | Juventus | 37 |
| | | 20 |
| LEAST | Torino | 10 |

**AWAY**

| | | |
|---|---|---|
| MOST | Inter Milan | 30 |
| | | 9 |
| LEAST | Como | 9 |

## GOALS CONCEDED

**AT HOME**

| | | |
|---|---|---|
| LEAST | AC Milan | 11 |
| | | 26 |
| MOST | Piacenza | 29 |

**AWAY**

| | | |
|---|---|---|
| LEAST | Juventus | 15 |
| | | 31 |
| MOST | Perugia | 35 |

## KEY GOALKEEPER

**1 Alex Brunner**

| | |
|---|---|
| Goals Conceded in the League | 29 |
| Defensive Rating<br>Ave number of mins between League goals conceded while on the pitch | 61 |
| Counting Games<br>Games when he played at least 70 minutes | 19 |
| Clean Sheets<br>In games when he played at least 70 minutes | 4 |

## TOP POINT EARNERS

| | PLAYER | GAMES | AVE |
|---|---|---|---|
| 1 | Music | 19 | 1.00 |
| 2 | Juarez | 17 | 0.94 |
| 3 | Pecchia | 15 | 0.93 |
| 4 | Caccia | 13 | 0.92 |
| 5 | Tarantino | 12 | 0.92 |
| 6 | Corrent | 13 | 0.85 |
| 7 | Rossi | 12 | 0.83 |
| 8 | Padalino | 15 | 0.80 |
| 9 | Allegretti | 14 | 0.79 |
| 10 | Brunner | 18 | 0.78 |
| | CLUB AVERAGE: | | 0.71 |

Ave = Average points per match in Counting Games

## ATTENDANCES

HOME GROUND: SINIGAGLIA CAPACITY: 14000 AVERAGE LEAGUE AT HOME: 7505

| | | | | | | | | |
|---|---|---|---|---|---|---|---|---|
| 25 | Inter Milan | 60000 | 33 | Atalanta | 14000 | 11 | Perugia | 7000 |
| 8 | Roma | 55000 | 12 | Modena | 13407 | 30 | Modena | 6000 |
| 27 | Lazio | 40000 | 17 | Torino | 12927 | 26 | Bologna | 6000 |
| 4 | Juventus | 40000 | 22 | Juventus | 12500 | 20 | Parma | 5100 |
| 31 | AC Milan | 35000 | 15 | Chievo | 11527 | 28 | Perugia | 5000 |
| 21 | Reggina | 24000 | 3 | Reggina | 10000 | 19 | Empoli | 5000 |
| 9 | Bologna | 20000 | 1 | Empoli | 10000 | 32 | Chievo | 4000 |
| 2 | Parma | 19000 | 23 | Piacenza | 8000 | 34 | Torino | 4000 |
| 6 | Brescia | 16000 | 14 | Udinese | 8000 | 16 | Atalanta | 3000 |
| 29 | Udinese | 15000 | 5 | Piacenza | 8000 | 18 | Roma | 3000 |
| 13 | AC Milan | 14000 | 24 | Brescia | 8000 | | | |
| 7 | Inter Milan | 14000 | 10 | Lazio | 7000 | | | |

■ Home □ Away ▒ Neutral

## DISCIPLINARY RECORDS

| | PLAYER | YELLOW | RED | AVE |
|---|---|---|---|---|
| 1 | Corrent | 7 | 0 | 207 |
| 2 | Rossi | 4 | 0 | 313 |
| 3 | Allegretti | 5 | 0 | 326 |
| 4 | Bjelanovic | 2 | 0 | 351 |
| 5 | Binotto | 5 | 0 | 383 |
| 6 | Cauet | 6 | 0 | 430 |
| 7 | Stellini | 5 | 0 | 523 |
| 8 | Juarez | 3 | 0 | 558 |
| 9 | Gregori | 2 | 0 | 591 |
| 10 | Tomas | 3 | 0 | 596 |
| 11 | Carbone | 1 | 1 | 644 |
| 12 | Pecchia | 2 | 0 | 886 |
| 13 | Tarantino | 1 | 0 | 1127 |
| | Other | 4 | 0 | |
| | TOTAL | 50 | 1 | |

## LEAGUE GOALS

| | PLAYER | MINS | GOALS | AVE |
|---|---|---|---|---|
| 1 | Amoruso | 1156 | 6 | 193 |
| 2 | Pecchia | 1772 | 6 | 295 |
| 3 | Caccia | 1327 | 4 | 332 |
| 4 | Music | 1949 | 3 | 650 |
| 5 | Corrent | 1451 | 2 | 726 |
| 6 | Carbone | 1289 | 2 | 645 |
| 7 | Bjelanovic | 702 | 2 | 351 |
| 8 | Godeas | 855 | 1 | 855 |
| 9 | Benin | 470 | 1 | 470 |
| 10 | Padalino | 1350 | 1 | 1350 |
| | Other | | 1 | |
| | TOTAL | | 29 | |

## MONTH BY MONTH GUIDE TO THE POINTS

| MONTH | POINTS | % |
|---|---|---|
| SEPTEMBER | 1 | 11% |
| OCTOBER | 3 | 33% |
| NOVEMBER | 0 | 0% |
| DECEMBER | 1 | 11% |
| JANUARY | 5 | 56% |
| FEBRUARY | 2 | 17% |
| MARCH | 7 | 58% |
| APRIL | 2 | 17% |
| MAY | 3 | 25% |

## TEAM OF THE SEASON

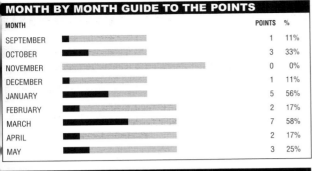

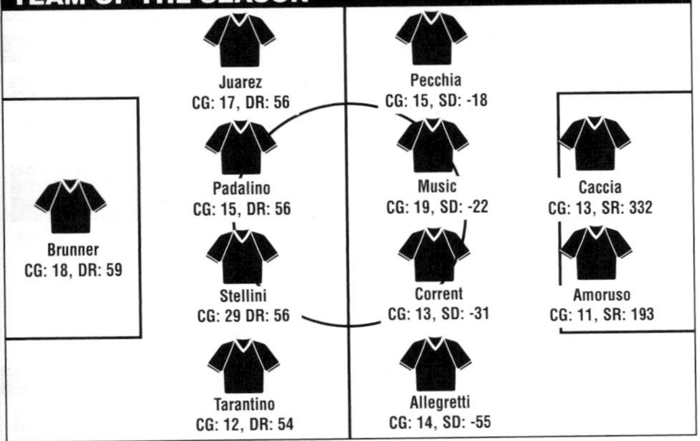
Brunner
CG: 18, DR: 59
Juarez
CG: 17, DR: 56
Padalino
CG: 15, DR: 56
Stellini
CG: 29 DR: 56
Tarantino
CG: 12, DR: 54
Pecchia
CG: 15, SD: -18
Music
CG: 19, SD: -22
Corrent
CG: 13, SD: -31
Allegretti
CG: 14, SD: -55
Caccia
CG: 13, SR: 332
Amoruso
CG: 11, SR: 193

KEY: DR = Defensive Rate, SD = Scoring Difference, SR = Strike Rate, CG = Counting Games – League games playing at least 70 minutes

## LEAGUE APPEARANCES, BOOKINGS AND CAPS

| | AGE | IN THE SQUAD | COUNTING GAMES | MINUTES ON PITCH | YELLOW CARDS | RED CARDS | THIS SEASON | HOME COUNTRY |
|---|---|---|---|---|---|---|---|---|
| **Goalkeepers** | | | | | | | | |
| Alex Brunner | 29 | 33 | 18 | 1665 | 0 | 0 | - | Italy |
| Fabrizio Ferron | 37 | 33 | 14 | 1305 | 0 | 0 | - | Italy |
| **Defenders** | | | | | | | | |
| Oscar Brevi | 25 | 14 | 8 | 798 | 0 | 0 | - | |
| Daniele Gregori | 27 | 28 | 11 | 1182 | 2 | 0 | - | Italy |
| Juarez Texeira | 28 | 27 | 17 | 1675 | 3 | 0 | - | Brazil |
| Pasquale Padalino | 30 | 18 | 15 | 1350 | 1 | 0 | - | Italy |
| Cristian Stellini | 29 | 32 | 29 | 2617 | 5 | 0 | - | Italy |
| Massimo Tarantino | 32 | 17 | 12 | 1127 | 1 | 0 | - | Italy |
| Stjepan Tomas | 27 | 32 | 18 | 1789 | 3 | 0 | 9 | Croatia (26) |
| **Midfielders** | | | | | | | | |
| Riccardo Allegretti | 25 | 31 | 14 | 1631 | 5 | 0 | - | Italy |
| Luca Belingheri | 20 | 6 | 1 | 103 | 0 | 0 | - | Italy |
| Mirko Benin | 25 | 19 | 2 | 470 | 0 | 0 | - | Italy |
| Jonatan Binotto | 28 | 32 | 17 | 1917 | 5 | 0 | - | Italy |
| Benoit Cauet | 34 | 30 | 28 | 2584 | 6 | 0 | - | France |
| Francesco Cigardi | 19 | 4 | 1 | 125 | 0 | 0 | - | Italy |
| Nicola Corrent | 24 | 28 | 13 | 1451 | 7 | 0 | - | Italy |
| Niccolo Guzzo | 20 | 3 | 0 | 6 | 0 | 0 | - | Italy |
| Vedin Music | 30 | 33 | 19 | 1949 | 0 | 0 | - | Bosnia |
| Fabio Pecchia | 29 | 29 | 15 | 1772 | 2 | 0 | - | Italy |
| Marco Rossi | 38 | 19 | 12 | 1254 | 4 | 0 | - | Italy |
| **Forwards** | | | | | | | | |
| Nicola Amoruso | 28 | 16 | 11 | 1156 | 0 | 0 | - | Italy |
| Luigi Anaclerio | 22 | 14 | 1 | 215 | 0 | 0 | - | Argentina |
| Robert Anderson | 20 | 1 | 1 | 90 | 0 | 0 | - | Brazil |
| Sasa Bjelanovic | 24 | 17 | 6 | 702 | 2 | 0 | - | Croatia |
| Nicola Caccia | 33 | 18 | 13 | 1327 | 1 | 0 | - | Italy |
| Benito Carbone | 31 | 26 | 10 | 1289 | 1 | 1 | - | Italy |
| Ciro De Cesare | 31 | 7 | 0 | 130 | 1 | 0 | - | Italy |
| Daniel Fonseca | 33 | 6 | 0 | 55 | 1 | 0 | - | Uruguay |
| Denis Godeas | 27 | 14 | 8 | 855 | 0 | 0 | - | |
| Giuseppe Greco | 19 | 3 | 0 | 45 | 0 | 0 | - | Italy |
| Jorge Horacio Serna | 23 | 4 | 0 | 33 | 0 | 0 | - | Colombia |

KEY: LEAGUE BOOKINGS CAPS (FIFA RANKING)

## SQUAD APPEARANCES

| Match | 1 | 2 | 3 | 4 | 5 | 6 | 7 | 8 | 9 | 10 | 11 | 12 | 13 | 14 | 15 | 16 | 17 | 18 | 19 | 20 | 21 | 22 | 23 | 24 | 25 | 26 | 27 | 28 | 29 | 30 | 31 | 32 | 33 | 34 |
|---|---|---|---|---|---|---|---|---|---|---|---|---|---|---|---|---|---|---|---|---|---|---|---|---|---|---|---|---|---|---|---|---|---|---|
| Venue | H | A | H | A | H | A | H | A | A | H | A | A | H | H | A | H | A | H | A | H | A | H | A | H | A | H | A | H | A | H | A | H | A | H |
| Competition | L | L | L | L | L | L | L | L | L | L | L | L | L | L | L | L | L | L | L | L | L | L | L | L | L | L | L | L | L | L | L | L | L | L |
| Result | L | L | D | D | D | D | L | L | L | L | L | D | L | L | L | D | D | W | D | D | L | L | W | D | L | W | L | D | L | D | L | L | L | W |

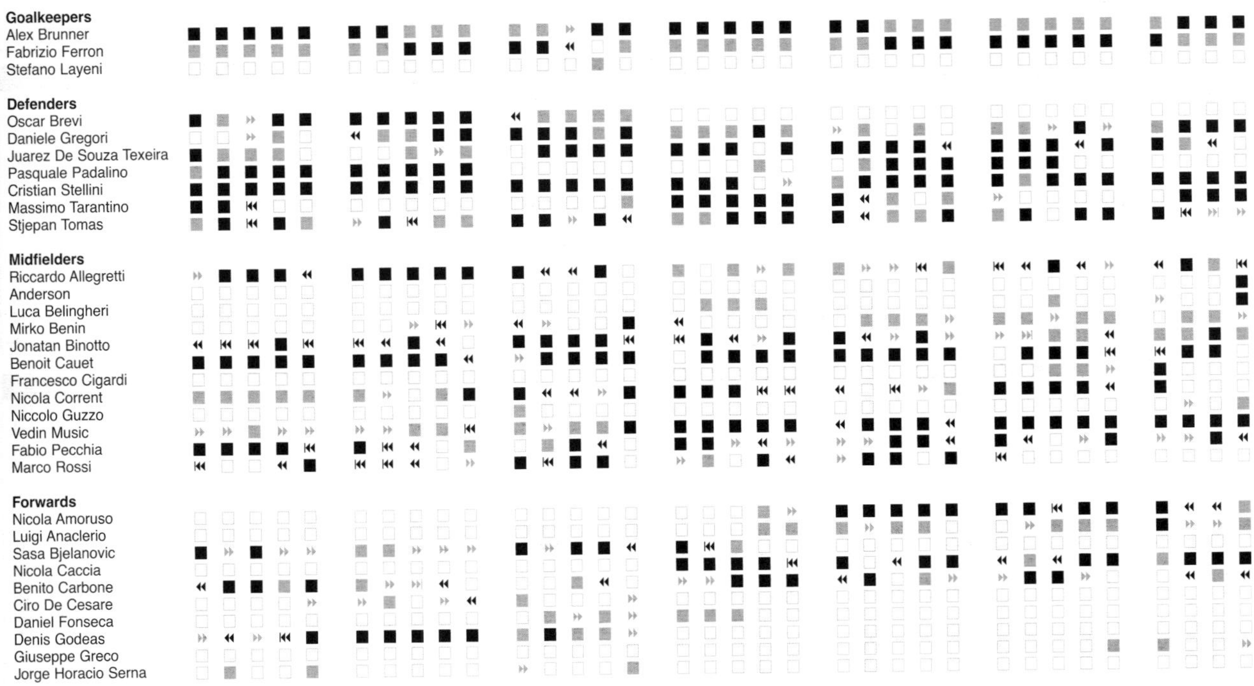
Goalkeepers
Alex Brunner
Fabrizio Ferron
Stefano Layeni
Defenders
Oscar Brevi
Daniele Gregori
Juarez De Souza Texeira
Pasquale Padalino
Cristian Stellini
Massimo Tarantino
Stjepan Tomas
Midfielders
Riccardo Allegretti
Anderson
Luca Belingheri
Mirko Benin
Jonatan Binotto
Benoit Cauet
Francesco Cigardi
Nicola Corrent
Niccolo Guzzo
Vedin Music
Fabio Pecchia
Marco Rossi
Forwards
Nicola Amoruso
Luigi Anaclerio
Sasa Bjelanovic
Nicola Caccia
Benito Carbone
Ciro De Cesare
Daniel Fonseca
Denis Godeas
Giuseppe Greco
Jorge Horacio Serna

# TORINO

Final Position: **18th**

| | | | | | | |
|---|---|---|---|---|---|---|
| 1 | lge | Inter Milan | A | L | 0-1 | |
| 2 | lge | Lazio | H | L | 0-1 | |
| 3 | lge | Modena | A | L | 1-2 | Ferrante 63 pen |
| 4 | lge | AC Milan | A | L | 0-6 | |
| 5 | lge | Chievo | H | W | 1-0 | Magallanes 18 |
| 6 | lge | Reggina | A | L | 1-2 | Conticchio 48 |
| 7 | lge | Brescia | H | L | 0-2 | |
| 8 | lge | Bologna | H | W | 2-1 | Conticchio 4; Castellini 89 |
| 9 | lge | Perugia | A | L | 1-2 | Ferrante 82 |
| 10 | lge | Juventus | H | L | 0-4 | |
| 11 | lge | Piacenza | A | L | 0-1 | |
| 12 | lge | Parma | H | L | 0-4 | |
| 13 | lge | Udinese | A | D | 1-1 | Lucarelli 59 |
| 14 | lge | Roma | H | L | 0-1 | |
| 15 | lge | Atalanta | H | D | 1-1 | Mezzano 61 pen |
| 16 | lge | Empoli | A | D | 1-1 | Cribari 90 og |
| 17 | lge | Como | H | D | 0-0 | |
| 18 | lge | Bologna | A | D | 2-2 | Vergassola 7; Franco 64; De Ascentis 83 |
| 19 | lge | Inter Milan | H | L | 0-2 | |
| 20 | lge | Lazio | A | D | 1-1 | Ferrante 70 |
| 21 | lge | Modena | H | D | 1-1 | Vergassola 65 |
| 22 | lge | AC Milan | H | L | 0-3 | |
| 23 | lge | Chievo | A | L | 2-3 | Sommese 16; Donati 38 |
| 24 | lge | Reggina | H | W | 1-0 | Ferrante 12 pen |
| 25 | lge | Brescia | A | L | 0-1 | |
| 26 | lge | Perugia | H | W | 2-1 | Ferrante 65,78 |
| 27 | lge | Juventus | A | L | 0-2 | |
| 28 | lge | Piacenza | H | L | 1-3 | Conticchio 58 |
| 29 | lge | Parma | A | L | 0-1 | |
| 30 | lge | Atalanta | A | D | 2-2 | Donati 22,90 |
| 31 | lge | Udinese | H | L | 0-1 | |
| 32 | lge | Roma | A | L | 1-3 | Frezza 78 |
| 33 | lge | Empoli | H | D | 1-1 | Donati 86 |
| 34 | lge | Como | A | L | 0-1 | |

## KEY PLAYERS - GOALSCORERS

**1 Marco Ferrante**

| | | | |
|---|---|---|---|
| Goals in the League | 6 | Player Strike Rate: Average number of minutes between League goals scored by player | 395 |
| Contribution to Attacking Power: Average number of minutes between League team goals while on pitch | 148 | Club Strike Rate: Average number of minutes between League goals scored by club | 128 |

| | PLAYER | LGE GOALS | POWER | STRIKE RATE |
|---|---|---|---|---|
| 2 | Alessandro Conticchio | 3 | 146 | 536 mins |
| 3 | Simone Vergassola | 2 | 145 | 1162 mins |
| 4 | Cristiano Lucarelli | 1 | 122 | 1720 mins |
| 5 | Luca Mezzano | 1 | 116 | 1870 mins |

## KEY PLAYERS - MIDFIELDERS

**1 Diego De Ascentis**

| | | | |
|---|---|---|---|
| Goals in the League | 0 | Contribution to Attacking Power: Average number of minutes between League team goals while on pitch | 127 |
| Defensive Rating: Average number of mins between League goals conceded while he was on the pitch | 52 | Scoring Difference: Defensive Rating minus Contribution to Attacking Power | -75 |

| | PLAYER | LGE GOALS | DEF RATE | POWER | SCORE DIFF |
|---|---|---|---|---|---|
| 2 | Alessandro Conticchio | 3 | 47 | 146 | -99 mins |
| 3 | Simone Vergassola | 2 | 54 | 155 | -101 mins |

## KEY PLAYERS - DEFENDERS

**1 Luca Mezzano**

| | | | |
|---|---|---|---|
| Goals Conceded (GC): The number of League goals conceded while he was on the pitch | 30 | Clean Sheets: In games when he played at least 70 minutes | 1 |
| Defensive Rating: Ave number of mins between League goals conceded while on the pitch | 62 | Club Defensive Rating: Average number of mins between League goals conceded by the club this season | 53 |

| | PLAYER | CON LGE | CLEAN SHEETS | DEF RATE |
|---|---|---|---|---|
| 2 | Paoli Castellini | 52 | 3 | 56 mins |
| 3 | Daniele Delli Carri | 42 | 2 | 52 mins |
| 4 | Stefano Fattori | 48 | 3 | 52 mins |
| 5 | Fabio Galante | 35 | 2 | 51 mins |

## GOALS SCORED

| | | | |
|---|---|---|---|
| AT HOME | MOST | Juventus | 37 |
| | | | 10 |
| | LEAST | Torino | 10 |
| AWAY | MOST | Inter Milan | 30 |
| | | | 13 |
| | LEAST | Como | 9 |

## GOALS CONCEDED

| | | | |
|---|---|---|---|
| AT HOME | LEAST | AC Milan | 11 |
| | | | 26 |
| | MOST | Piacenza | 29 |
| AWAY | LEAST | Juventus | 15 |
| | | | 32 |
| | MOST | Perugia | 35 |

## KEY GOALKEEPER

**1 Luca Bucci**

| | |
|---|---|
| Goals Conceded in the League | 40 |
| Defensive Rating: Ave number of mins between League goals conceded while on the pitch | 52 |
| Counting Games: Games when he played at least 70 minutes | 24 |
| Clean Sheets: In games when he played at least 70 minutes | 3 |

## TOP POINT EARNERS

| | PLAYER | GAMES | AVE |
|---|---|---|---|
| 1 | Vergassola | 25 | 0.80 |
| 2 | Bucci | 23 | 0.74 |
| 3 | Galante | 20 | 0.70 |
| 4 | Mezzano | 20 | 0.70 |
| 5 | Ferrante | 25 | 0.68 |
| 6 | Delli Carri | 24 | 0.67 |
| 7 | Castellini | 30 | 0.67 |
| 8 | Fattori | 27 | 0.63 |
| 9 | De Ascentis | 30 | 0.60 |
| 10 | Lucarelli | 15 | 0.60 |
| | CLUB AVERAGE: | | 0.62 |

Ave = Average points per match in Counting Games

## ATTENDANCES

HOME GROUND: STADIO DELLE ALPI CAPACITY: 69041 AVERAGE LEAGUE AT HOME: 14336

| | | | | | | | | |
|---|---|---|---|---|---|---|---|---|
| 1 | Inter Milan | 65000 | **5** | **Chievo** | **20000** | **8** | **Bologna** | **10000** |
| 4 | AC Milan | 60000 | 30 | Atalanta | 15471 | 23 | Chievo | 10000 |
| 32 | Roma | 52000 | **15** | **Atalanta** | **15000** | **26** | **Perugia** | **5000** |
| **10** | **Juventus** | **45000** | 3 | Modena | 15000 | 11 | Piacenza | 5000 |
| 20 | Lazio | 45000 | **12** | **Parma** | **15000** | 16 | Empoli | 4958 |
| **19** | **Inter Milan** | **25000** | **14** | **Roma** | **15000** | **24** | **Reggina** | **4500** |
| 27 | Juventus | 25000 | 25 | Brescia | 14000 | 34 | Como | 4000 |
| 6 | Reggina | 25000 | 13 | Udinese | 14000 | **33** | **Empoli** | **1000** |
| **22** | **AC Milan** | **22000** | **17** | **Como** | **12927** | **28** | **Piacenza** | **1000** |
| 18 | Bologna | 21000 | 29 | Parma | 12000 | **31** | **Udinese** | **300** |
| **21** | **Modena** | **20000** | **2** | **Lazio** | **12000** | | | |
| **7** | **Brescia** | **20000** | 9 | Perugia | 10000 | | | |

■ Home □ Away ▒ Neutral

## DISCIPLINARY RECORDS

| | PLAYER | YELLOW | RED | AVE |
|---|---|---|---|---|
| 1 | Conticchio | 8 | 0 | 201 |
| 2 | Lucarelli | 6 | 2 | 215 |
| 3 | Mezzano | 6 | 1 | 267 |
| 4 | Comotto | 4 | 1 | 273 |
| 5 | Fattori | 8 | 0 | 311 |
| 6 | Delli Carri | 7 | 0 | 313 |
| 7 | De Ascentis | 6 | 1 | 382 |
| 8 | Galante | 3 | 1 | 444 |
| 9 | Vergassola | 4 | 1 | 464 |
| 10 | Sommese | 2 | 0 | 640 |
| 11 | Ferrante | 3 | 0 | 790 |
| 12 | Magallanes | 1 | 0 | 923 |
| 13 | Donati | 1 | 0 | 1058 |
| | Other | 7 | 2 | |
| | TOTAL | 66 | 9 | |

## LEAGUE GOALS

| | PLAYER | MINS | GOALS | AVE |
|---|---|---|---|---|
| 1 | Ferrante | 2371 | 6 | 395 |
| 2 | Donati | 1058 | 4 | 265 |
| 3 | Conticchio | 1608 | 3 | 536 |
| 4 | Vergassola | 2324 | 2 | 1162 |
| 5 | Frezza | 305 | 1 | 305 |
| 6 | Franco Ramallo | 311 | 1 | 311 |
| 7 | Mezzano | 1870 | 1 | 1870 |
| 8 | Magallanes | 923 | 1 | 923 |
| 9 | Castellini | 2889 | 1 | 2889 |
| 10 | Sommese | 1281 | 1 | 1281 |
| 11 | Lucarelli | 1720 | 1 | 1720 |
| | Other | | 1 | |
| | TOTAL | | 23 | |

## MONTH BY MONTH GUIDE TO THE POINTS

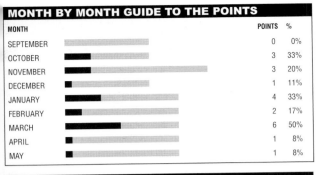

| MONTH | POINTS | % |
|---|---|---|
| SEPTEMBER | 0 | 0% |
| OCTOBER | 3 | 33% |
| NOVEMBER | 3 | 20% |
| DECEMBER | 1 | 11% |
| JANUARY | 4 | 33% |
| FEBRUARY | 2 | 17% |
| MARCH | 6 | 50% |
| APRIL | 1 | 8% |
| MAY | 1 | 8% |

## TEAM OF THE SEASON

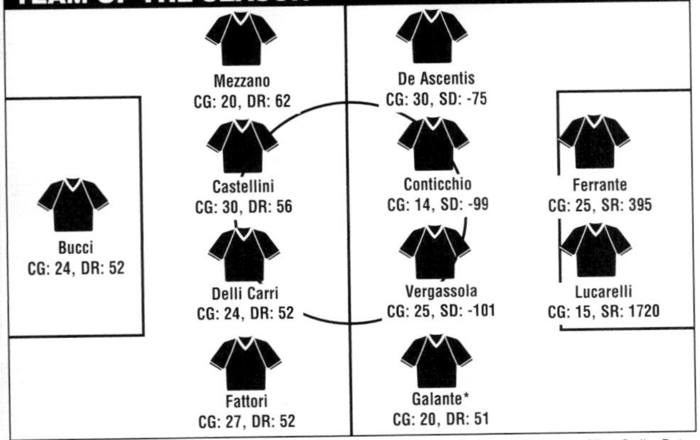
Mezzano
CG: 20, DR: 62
De Ascentis
CG: 30, SD: -75
Castellini
CG: 30, DR: 56
Conticchio
CG: 14, SD: -99
Ferrante
CG: 25, SR: 395
Bucci
CG: 24, DR: 52
Delli Carri
CG: 24, DR: 52
Vergassola
CG: 25, SD: -101
Lucarelli
CG: 15, SR: 1720
Fattori
CG: 27, DR: 52
Galante*
CG: 20, DR: 51

KEY: DR = Defensive Rate, SD = Scoring Difference, SR = Strike Rate, CG = Counting Games – League games playing at least 70 minutes

## LEAGUE APPEARANCES, BOOKINGS AND CAPS

| | AGE | IN THE SQUAD | COUNTING GAMES | MINUTES ON PITCH | YELLOW CARDS | RED CARDS | THIS SEASON | HOME COUNTRY |
|---|---|---|---|---|---|---|---|---|
| **Goalkeepers** | | | | | | | | |
| Luca Bucci | 34 | 24 | 23 | 2094 | 1 | 0 | - | Italy |
| Alberto Fontana | 28 | 4 | 0 | 0 | 0 | 0 | - | Italy |
| Alberto Fontano | 28 | 3 | 0 | 28 | 0 | 0 | - | Italy |
| Alex Manninger | 26 | 3 | 3 | 270 | 0 | 0 | - | Austria |
| Stefano Sorrentino | 24 | 34 | 6 | 668 | 0 | 0 | - | Italy |
| **Defenders** | | | | | | | | |
| Federico Balzaretti | 21 | 20 | 4 | 642 | 0 | 0 | - | Italy |
| Paoli Castellini | 24 | 34 | 30 | 2889 | 2 | 0 | - | Italy |
| Gianluca Comotto | 24 | 23 | 12 | 1367 | 4 | 1 | - | Italy |
| Daniele Delli Carri | 31 | 29 | 24 | 2197 | 7 | 0 | - | Italy |
| Stefano Fattori | 31 | 31 | 27 | 2489 | 8 | 0 | - | Italy |
| Fabio Galante | 29 | 24 | 20 | 1779 | 3 | 1 | - | Italy |
| Luigi Garzya | 34 | 17 | 5 | 480 | 0 | 0 | - | Italy |
| Giovanni Lopez | 36 | 9 | 0 | 0 | 0 | 0 | - | Italy |
| Andrea Mantovani | 19 | 16 | 4 | 416 | 0 | 0 | - | Italy |
| Giovanni Marchese | 18 | 1 | 0 | 0 | 0 | 0 | - | Italy |
| Luca Mezzano | 26 | 29 | 20 | 1870 | 6 | 1 | - | Italy |
| Claudio Pochint Patti | 19 | 1 | 1 | 90 | 0 | 0 | - | Italy |
| **Midfielders** | | | | | | | | |
| Alessandro Conticchio | 29 | 29 | 14 | 1608 | 8 | 0 | - | Italy |
| Diego De Ascentis | 26 | 32 | 30 | 2677 | 6 | 1 | - | Italy |
| Massimo Donati | 22 | 17 | 8 | 1058 | 1 | 0 | - | Italy |
| Gianmarco Frezza | 27 | 17 | 1 | 305 | 1 | 0 | - | Italy |
| Carlos Marinelli | 21 | 9 | 2 | 350 | 2 | 1 | - | Argentina |
| Riccardo Maspero | 33 | 7 | 0 | 72 | 1 | 0 | - | Italy |
| Alessio Scarchilli | 30 | 24 | 4 | 574 | 0 | 0 | - | Italy |
| Vincenzo Sommese | 24 | 25 | 4 | 1281 | 2 | 0 | - | Italy |
| Franscesco Statuto | 31 | 3 | 0 | 0 | 0 | 0 | - | Italy |
| Ronaldo Vanin | 20 | 7 | 0 | 110 | 0 | 0 | - | Italy |
| Simone Vergassola | 27 | 29 | 25 | 2324 | 4 | 1 | - | Italy |
| **Forwards** | | | | | | | | |
| Alessandro Campo | 19 | 3 | 0 | 0 | 0 | 0 | - | Italy |
| Marco Ferrante | 32 | 32 | 25 | 2371 | 3 | 0 | - | Italy |
| Jose Franco Ramallo | 24 | 9 | 2 | 311 | 0 | 0 | - | Uruguay |
| Cristiano Lucarelli | 27 | 27 | 15 | 1720 | 6 | 2 | - | Italy |
| Federico Magallanes | 26 | 18 | 3 | 923 | 1 | 0 | - | Uruguay |
| Akeem Omolade | 20 | 6 | 0 | 163 | 0 | 0 | - | Nigeria |
| Yksel Osmanovski | 26 | 20 | 1 | 339 | 0 | 1 | - | Sweden |

KEY: LEAGUE BOOKINGS CAPS (FIFA RANKING)

## SQUAD APPEARANCES

| Match | 1 | 2 | 3 | 4 | 5 | 6 | 7 | 8 | 9 | 10 | 11 | 12 | 13 | 14 | 15 | 16 | 17 | 18 | 19 | 20 | 21 | 22 | 23 | 24 | 25 | 26 | 27 | 28 | 29 | 30 | 31 | 32 | 33 | 34 |
|---|---|---|---|---|---|---|---|---|---|---|---|---|---|---|---|---|---|---|---|---|---|---|---|---|---|---|---|---|---|---|---|---|---|---|
| Venue | A | H | A | A | H | A | H | H | A | H | A | H | A | H | H | A | H | A | H | A | H | H | A | H | A | H | A | H | A | A | H | A | H | A |
| Competition | L | L | L | L | L | L | L | L | L | L | L | L | L | L | L | L | L | L | L | L | L | L | L | L | L | L | L | L | L | L | L | L | L | L |
| Result | L | L | L | L | W | L | L | W | L | L | L | L | D | L | D | D | D | D | L | D | D | L | L | W | L | W | L | L | L | D | L | L | D | L |

**Goalkeepers**
Luca Bucci
Alberto Fontana
Alberto Maria Fontano
Alex Manninger
Stefano Sorrentino

**Defenders**
Federico Balzaretti
Paoli Castellini
Gianluca Comotto
Daniele Delli Carri
Stefano Fattori
Fabio Galante
Luigi Garzya
Giovanni Lopez
Andrea Mantovani
Luca Mezzano

**Midfielders**
Alessandro Conticchio
Diego De Ascentis
Massimo Donati
Gianmarco Frezza
Marchese
Carlos Marinelli
Riccardo Maspero
Patti
Alessio Scarchilli
Vincenzo Sommese
Franscesco Statuto
Ronaldo Vanin
Simone Vergassola

**Forwards**
Alessandro Campo
Marco Ferrante
Jose Franco Ramallo
Cristiano Lucarelli
Federico Magallanes
Akeem Omolade
Yksel Osmanovski

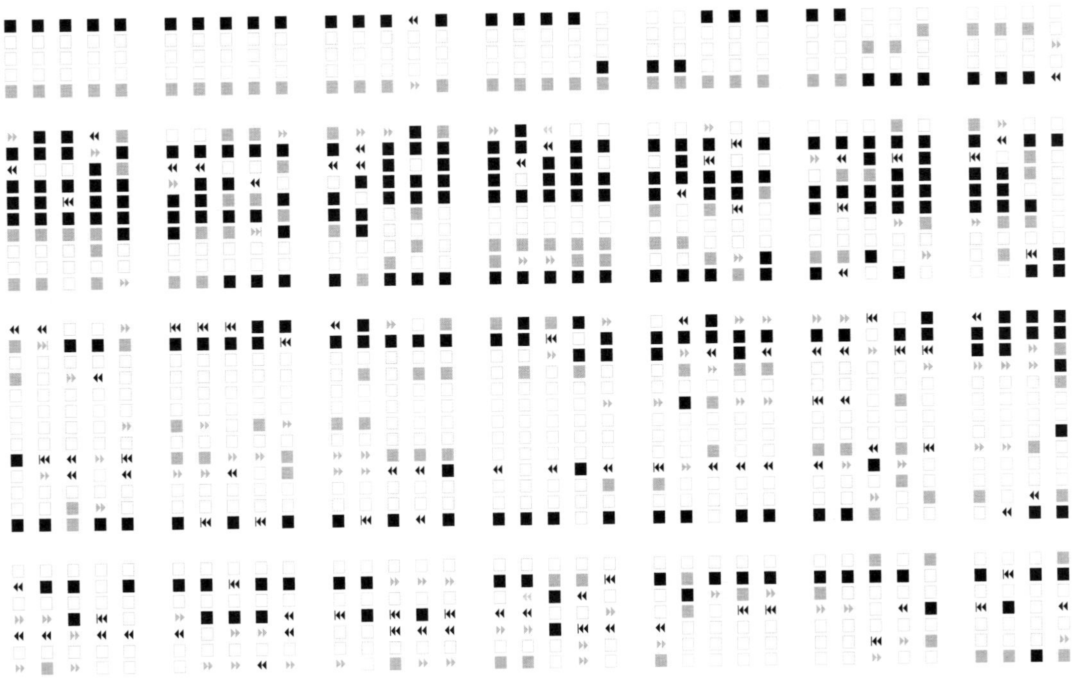

# ITALIAN LEAGUE ROUND-UP

## FINAL LEAGUE TABLE

| | | HOME | | | | | AWAY | | | | | TOTAL | | | |
|---|---|---|---|---|---|---|---|---|---|---|---|---|---|---|---|
| | P | W | D | L | F | A | W | D | L | F | A | F | A | DIF | PTS |
| Juventus | 34 | 12 | 4 | 1 | 37 | 14 | 9 | 5 | 3 | 27 | 15 | 64 | 29 | 35 | 72 |
| Inter Milan | 34 | 10 | 5 | 2 | 34 | 13 | 9 | 3 | 5 | 30 | 25 | 64 | 38 | 26 | 65 |
| AC Milan | 34 | 12 | 4 | 1 | 32 | 11 | 6 | 3 | 8 | 23 | 19 | 55 | 30 | 25 | 61 |
| Lazio | 34 | 7 | 8 | 2 | 31 | 16 | 8 | 7 | 2 | 26 | 16 | 57 | 32 | 25 | 60 |
| Parma | 34 | 11 | 2 | 4 | 31 | 19 | 4 | 9 | 4 | 24 | 17 | 55 | 36 | 19 | 56 |
| Udinese | 34 | 11 | 5 | 1 | 22 | 12 | 5 | 3 | 9 | 16 | 23 | 38 | 35 | 3 | 56 |
| Chievo | 34 | 11 | 3 | 3 | 31 | 19 | 5 | 4 | 8 | 20 | 20 | 51 | 39 | 12 | 55 |
| Roma | 34 | 9 | 5 | 3 | 34 | 19 | 4 | 5 | 8 | 21 | 27 | 55 | 46 | 9 | 49 |
| Brescia | 34 | 6 | 7 | 4 | 20 | 15 | 3 | 8 | 6 | 16 | 23 | 36 | 38 | -2 | 42 |
| Perugia | 34 | 9 | 4 | 4 | 22 | 13 | 1 | 8 | 8 | 18 | 35 | 40 | 48 | -8 | 42 |
| Bologna | 34 | 9 | 3 | 5 | 25 | 19 | 1 | 8 | 8 | 14 | 28 | 39 | 47 | -8 | 41 |
| Empoli | 34 | 4 | 8 | 5 | 19 | 21 | 5 | 3 | 9 | 17 | 25 | 36 | 46 | -10 | 38 |
| Atalanta | 34 | 5 | 8 | 4 | 20 | 21 | 3 | 6 | 8 | 15 | 26 | 35 | 47 | -12 | 38 |
| Reggina | 34 | 8 | 5 | 4 | 26 | 20 | 2 | 3 | 12 | 12 | 33 | 38 | 53 | -15 | 38 |
| Modena | 34 | 6 | 6 | 5 | 15 | 18 | 3 | 5 | 9 | 15 | 30 | 30 | 48 | -18 | 38 |
| Piacenza | 34 | 6 | 4 | 7 | 29 | 29 | 2 | 2 | 13 | 15 | 33 | 44 | 62 | -18 | 30 |
| Como | 34 | 3 | 7 | 7 | 20 | 26 | 1 | 5 | 11 | 9 | 31 | 29 | 57 | -28 | 24 |
| Torino | 34 | 4 | 4 | 9 | 10 | 26 | 0 | 5 | 12 | 13 | 32 | 23 | 58 | -35 | 21 |

## TEAM OF THE SEASON

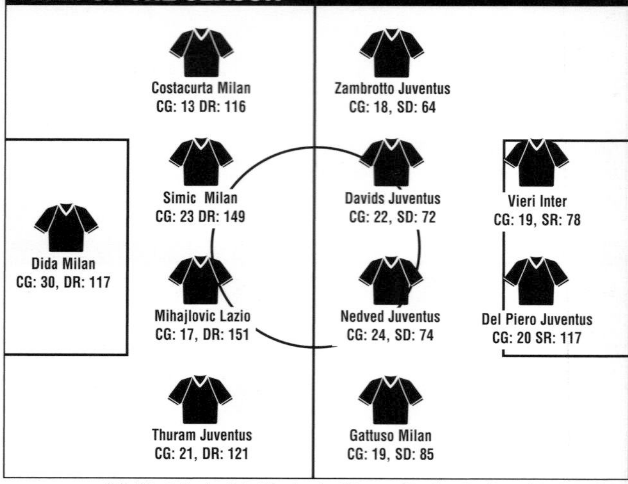
Dida Milan
CG: 30, DR: 117
Costacurta Milan
CG: 13 DR: 116
Simic Milan
CG: 23 DR: 149
Mihajlovic Lazio
CG: 17, DR: 151
Thuram Juventus
CG: 21, DR: 121
Zambrotto Juventus
CG: 18, SD: 64
Davids Juventus
CG: 22, SD: 72
Nedved Juventus
CG: 24, SD: 74
Gattuso Milan
CG: 19, SD: 85
Vieri Inter
CG: 19, SR: 78
Del Piero Juventus
CG: 20 SR: 117

**KEY:** DR = Defensive Rate, SD = Scoring Difference AP = Attacking Power SR = Strike Rate, CG=Counting Games – League games playing at least 70 minutes

## CLUB STRIKE FORCE

**KEY:** Goals: Total number of goals scored in League. Club Strike Rate (CSR): Average number of mins between goals scored

| | CLUB | GOALS | CSR |
|---|---|---|---|
| 1 | Inter Milan | 64 | 48 mins |
| 2 | Juventus | 64 | 48 mins |
| 3 | Lazio | 57 | 54 mins |
| 4 | AC Milan | 55 | 56 mins |
| 5 | Parma | 55 | 56 mins |
| 6 | Roma | 55 | 56 mins |
| 7 | Chievo | 51 | 60 mins |
| 8 | Piacenza | 44 | 70 mins |
| 9 | Perugia | 40 | 77 mins |
| 10 | Bologna | 39 | 78 mins |
| 11 | Reggina | 38 | 81 mins |
| 12 | Udinese | 36 | 83 mins |
| 13 | Brescia | 36 | 85 mins |
| 14 | Empoli | 36 | 85 mins |
| 15 | Atalanta | 35 | 87 mins |
| 16 | Como | 29 | 102 mins |
| 17 | Modena | 30 | 102 mins |
| 18 | Torino | 23 | 133 mins |
| | TOTAL | 787 | |

## CLUB DEFENCES

**KEY:** Defensive Rating: Average number of mins between goals conceded. CS: Clean Sheets - Games where no goals were conceded.

| | CLUB | CONCEDED | CLEAN SH | DEF RATE |
|---|---|---|---|---|
| 1 | Juventus | 29 | 15 | 106 mins |
| 2 | AC Milan | 30 | 14 | 102 mins |
| 3 | Lazio | 32 | 12 | 96 mins |
| 4 | Parma | 36 | 12 | 85 mins |
| 5 | Udinese | 35 | 10 | 85 mins |
| 6 | Brescia | 38 | 14 | 81 mins |
| 7 | Inter Milan | 38 | 12 | 81 mins |
| 8 | Chievo | 39 | 12 | 78 mins |
| 9 | Empoli | 46 | 8 | 67 mins |
| 10 | Roma | 46 | 5 | 67 mins |
| 11 | Atalanta | 47 | 8 | 65 mins |
| 12 | Bologna | 47 | 10 | 65 mins |
| 13 | Modena | 48 | 6 | 64 mins |
| 14 | Perugia | 48 | 11 | 64 mins |
| 15 | Reggina | 53 | 6 | 58 mins |
| 16 | Como | 55 | 6 | 54 mins |
| 17 | Torino | 58 | 3 | 53 mins |
| 18 | Piacenza | 62 | 4 | 49 mins |
| | TOTAL | 787 | 168 | |

## CLUB DISCIPLINARY RECORDS

**KEY:** AVE: Average number of mins between cards

| | CLUB | YELL | RED | TOT | AVE |
|---|---|---|---|---|---|
| 1 | Modena | 76 | 5 | 81 | 38 mins |
| 2 | Perugia | 77 | 3 | 80 | 38 mins |
| 3 | Roma | 69 | 9 | 78 | 39 mins |
| 4 | Bologna | 71 | 3 | 74 | 41 mins |
| 5 | Brescia | 68 | 6 | 74 | 41 mins |
| 6 | Chievo | 69 | 5 | 74 | 41 mins |
| 7 | Torino | 66 | 9 | 75 | 41 mins |
| 8 | Atalanta | 66 | 5 | 71 | 43 mins |
| 9 | Inter Milan | 62 | 7 | 69 | 44 mins |
| 10 | Udinese | 60 | 6 | 66 | 45 mins |
| 11 | Piacenza | 62 | 3 | 65 | 47 mins |
| 12 | Empoli | 62 | 1 | 63 | 49 mins |
| 13 | Reggina | 58 | 2 | 60 | 51 mins |
| 14 | Lazio | 56 | 3 | 59 | 52 mins |
| 15 | Parma | 54 | 3 | 57 | 54 mins |
| 16 | Como | 50 | 1 | 51 | 58 mins |
| 17 | AC Milan | 44 | 2 | 46 | 67 mins |
| 18 | Juventus | 41 | 2 | 43 | 71 mins |
| TOTAL | | 1111 | 75 | 1186 | |

## STADIUM CAPACITY AND HOME CROWDS

| | TEAM | CAPACITY | AVE | HIGH | LOW |
|---|---|---|---|---|---|
| 1 | Reggina | 27713 | 87.74 | 27000 | 18500 |
| 2 | Modena | 16875 | 86.42 | 16500 | 11000 |
| 3 | Inter Milan | 85700 | 68.69 | 78000 | 30000 |
| 4 | Como | 10230 | 66.66 | 10000 | 3000 |
| 5 | AC Milan | 85700 | 66.57 | 78871 | 35000 |
| 6 | Roma | 82307 | 65.59 | 75000 | 43000 |
| 7 | Atalanta | 26638 | 62.27 | 26000 | 13000 |
| 8 | Brescia | 27547 | 62.01 | 25000 | 13000 |
| 9 | Bologna | 39300 | 61.28 | 37000 | 15000 |
| 10 | Parma | 28783 | 59.66 | 26000 | 12000 |
| 11 | Juventus | 69041 | 59.42 | 65000 | 25000 |
| 12 | Lazio | 82307 | 58.82 | 80000 | 20000 |
| 13 | Empoli | 14000 | 58.46 | 14000 | 4450 |
| 14 | Piacenza | 21608 | 42.45 | 20000 | 5000 |
| 15 | Perugia | 27663 | 42.27 | 20000 | 6000 |
| 16 | Udinese | 41705 | 41.67 | 32000 | 11000 |
| 17 | Chievo | 44758 | 41.00 | 36000 | 10000 |
| 18 | Torino | 69041 | 20.77 | 45000 | 300 |

## AWAY ATTENDANCE

| | TEAM | AVE | HIGH | LOW |
|---|---|---|---|---|
| 1 | Juventus | 87.51 | 78871 | 10000 |
| 2 | Inter Milan | 83.56 | 80000 | 10000 |
| 3 | AC Milan | 75.18 | 78000 | 6100 |
| 4 | Roma | 66.36 | 80000 | 3000 |
| 5 | Lazio | 59.15 | 75000 | 7000 |
| 6 | Reggina | 55.62 | 66000 | 4500 |
| 7 | Bologna | 55.6 | 60000 | 6000 |
| 8 | Brescia | 54.05 | 68000 | 4950 |
| 9 | Atalanta | 53.75 | 60000 | 3000 |
| 10 | Parma | 53.59 | 60000 | 5100 |
| 11 | Modena | 52.14 | 54000 | 5300 |
| 12 | Empoli | 51.9 | 59600 | 1000 |
| 13 | Chievo | 51.86 | 60000 | 4000 |
| 14 | Torino | 51.34 | 65000 | 4000 |
| 15 | Udinese | 51.04 | 58962 | 300 |
| 16 | Como | 50.37 | 60000 | 5000 |
| 17 | Piacenza | 48.98 | 56000 | 1000 |
| 18 | Perugia | 48.85 | 55000 | 5000 |

## TOP GOALSCORERS

**KEY: Strike Rate:** Average number of minutes between League goals scored by player. **Club Strike Rate (CSR):** Average minutes between League goals scored by club. **Contribution to Attacking Power (PWR):** Average mins between League goals scored by club while on pitch.

| | PLAYER | CLUB | GOALS | PWR | CSR | S RATE |
|---|---|---|---|---|---|---|
| 1 | Vieri | Inter Milan | 24 | 49 | 48 | 78 |
| 2 | Del Piero | Juventus | 16 | 49 | 48 | 117 |
| 3 | Totti | Roma | 14 | 52 | 56 | 138 |
| 4 | Signori | Bologna | 12 | 83 | 78 | 140 |
| 5 | Inzaghi | AC Milan | 17 | 51 | 56 | 143 |
| 6 | Adriano | Parma | 16 | 57 | 56 | 144 |
| 7 | Di Natale | Empoli | 13 | 77 | 85 | 148 |
| 8 | Mutu | Parma | 17 | 53 | 56 | 154 |
| 9 | Hubner | Piacenza | 14 | 60 | 70 | 161 |
| 10 | Lopez | Lazio | 15 | 53 | 54 | 186 |
| 11 | Crespo | Inter Milan | 7 | 40 | 48 | 187 |
| 12 | Montella | Roma | 9 | 65 | 56 | 195 |
| 13 | Pirlo | AC Milan | 9 | 50 | 56 | 209 |
| 14 | Bonazzoli | Reggina | 7 | 61 | 81 | 212 |
| 15 | Iaquinta | Udinese | 7 | 75 | 85 | 215 |
| 16 | Di Vaio | Juventus | 7 | 45 | 48 | 221 |
| 17 | Cossato | Chievo | 9 | 59 | 60 | 224 |
| 18 | Doni | Atalanta | 10 | 91 | 87 | 229 |
| 19 | Recoba | Inter Milan | 9 | 48 | 48 | 231 |
| 20 | Simeone | Lazio | 7 | 47 | 54 | 231 |
| 21 | Baggio | Brescia | 12 | 82 | 85 | 239 |
| 22 | Cruz | Bologna | 10 | 73 | 78 | 242 |
| 23 | Nedved | Juventus | 9 | 45 | 48 | 254 |
| 24 | Corradi | Lazio | 10 | 52 | 54 | 264 |
| 25 | Maresca | Piacenza | 9 | 64 | 70 | 294 |
| 26 | Pecchia | Como | 6 | 84 | 106 | 295 |
| 27 | Rivaldo | AC Milan | 5 | 52 | 56 | 303 |
| 28 | Locatelli | Bologna | 5 | 70 | 78 | 308 |
| 29 | Miccoli | Perugia | 9 | 76 | 77 | 314 |
| 30 | Shevchenko | AC Milan | 5 | 79 | 56 | 319 |

## TOP DEFENDERS

**KEY: Defensive Rating (DR)** Average mins between League goals conceded while on pitch. **Club Defensive Rating (CDR):** Average minutes between League goals conceded by club. **Clean Sheets (CS)** - Games where no goals were conceded.

| | PLAYER | CLUB | CONC | CS | CDR | DR |
|---|---|---|---|---|---|---|
| 1 | Mihajlovic | Lazio | 11 | 9 | 96 | 151 |
| 2 | Simic | AC Milan | 16 | 14 | 102 | 149 |
| 3 | Thuram | Juventus | 19 | 12 | 106 | 121 |
| 4 | Pisano | Brescia | 8 | 5 | 81 | 118 |
| 5 | Costacurta | AC Milan | 11 | 5 | 102 | 116 |
| 6 | Oddo | Lazio | 13 | 6 | 96 | 116 |
| 7 | Nesta | AC Milan | 22 | 12 | 102 | 114 |
| 8 | Maldini | AC Milan | 22 | 12 | 102 | 114 |
| 9 | Ferrara | Juventus | 19 | 9 | 106 | 109 |
| 10 | Kroldrup | Udinese | 20 | 9 | 87 | 109 |
| 11 | Birindelli | Juventus | 11 | 5 | 106 | 108 |
| 12 | Montero | Juventus | 17 | 8 | 106 | 105 |
| 13 | Kaladze | AC Milan | 20 | 9 | 102 | 103 |
| 14 | Favalli | Lazio | 21 | 7 | 96 | 101 |
| 15 | Iuliano | Juventus | 17 | 8 | 106 | 99 |
| 16 | Zanchi | Bologna | 16 | 8 | 64 | 98 |
| 17 | Cesar | Lazio | 22 | 10 | 96 | 98 |
| 18 | Pasquale | Inter Milan | 13 | 6 | 78 | 97 |
| 19 | Negro | Lazio | 17 | 8 | 96 | 97 |
| 20 | Cardone | Parma | 11 | 4 | 85 | 97 |
| 21 | Siviglia | Atalanta | 15 | 6 | 65 | 95 |
| 22 | Pratali | Empoli | 13 | 5 | 67 | 93 |
| 23 | Bonera | Parma | 30 | 12 | 85 | 93 |
| 24 | Lanna | Chievo | 28 | 10 | 78 | 92 |
| 25 | Junior Jenilson | Parma | 25 | 10 | 85 | 92 |
| 26 | Dainelli | Brescia | 24 | 11 | 81 | 91 |
| 27 | Alberto | Udinese | 18 | 5 | 87 | 91 |
| 28 | Sensini | Udinese | 29 | 8 | 87 | 90 |
| 29 | Bertotto | Udinese | 21 | 5 | 87 | 89 |
| 30 | Materazzi | Inter Milan | 17 | 6 | 78 | 88 |

## TOP MIDFIELDERS

**KEY: Scoring Difference (SD)** Team goals scored while on the pitch minus team goals conceded. **Contribution to Attacking Power:** Average mins between League goals scored by club while on pitch. **Defensive Rating (DR)** Average mins between League goals conceded while on pitch.

| | PLAYER | TEAM | GOALS | DR | PWR | SD |
|---|---|---|---|---|---|---|
| 1 | Gattuso | AC Milan | 0 | 143 | 58 | 85 |
| 2 | Nedved | Juventus | 9 | 120 | 46 | 74 |
| 3 | Davids | Juventus | 1 | 125 | 53 | 72 |
| 4 | Zambrotta | Juventus | 1 | 113 | 49 | 64 |
| 5 | Rui Costa | AC Milan | 0 | 113 | 56 | 57 |
| 6 | Camoranesi | Juventus | 4 | 101 | 44 | 57 |
| 7 | Pirlo | AC Milan | 9 | 105 | 51 | 54 |
| 8 | Tacchinardi | Juventus | 2 | 102 | 48 | 54 |
| 9 | Seedorf | AC Milan | 4 | 104 | 53 | 51 |
| 10 | Almeyda | Inter Milan | 0 | 90 | 45 | 45 |
| 11 | Stankovic | Lazio | 6 | 96 | 54 | 42 |
| 12 | Conte | Juventus | 1 | 78 | 37 | 41 |
| 13 | Lopez | Lazio | 15 | 93 | 54 | 39 |
| 14 | Guardiola | Brescia | 1 | 124 | 86 | 38 |
| 15 | Zanetti, C | Inter Milan | 0 | 87 | 50 | 37 |
| 16 | Fiore | Lazio | 5 | 92 | 55 | 37 |
| 17 | Simeone | Lazio | 7 | 85 | 48 | 37 |
| 18 | Ambrosini | AC Milan | 1 | 109 | 73 | 36 |
| 19 | Zanetti, J | Inter Milan | 1 | 78 | 46 | 32 |
| 20 | Barone | Parma | 1 | 92 | 60 | 32 |
| 21 | Lamouchi | Parma | 2 | 85 | 55 | 30 |
| 22 | Emre Belozoglu | Inter Milan | 3 | 73 | 44 | 29 |
| 23 | Brighi | Parma | 1 | 74 | 50 | 24 |
| 24 | Coco | Inter Milan | 0 | 71 | 50 | 21 |
| 25 | Filippini, E | Parma | 2 | 79 | 59 | 20 |
| 26 | Emerson | Roma | 2 | 70 | 50 | 20 |
| 27 | Lima | Roma | 0 | 70 | 50 | 20 |
| 28 | Di Biagio | Inter Milan | 4 | 74 | 55 | 19 |
| 29 | Jorgensen | Udinese | 4 | 97 | 78 | 19 |
| 30 | Franceschini | Chievo | 4 | 80 | 62 | 18 |

## PLAYER DISCIPLINARY RECORDS

**KEY: AVE:** Average number of mins between cards

| | PLAYER | TEAM | YELL | RED | TOTAL | AVE |
|---|---|---|---|---|---|---|
| 1 | Ficini | Empoli | 6 | 0 | 6 | 133 |
| 2 | Caracciolo | Perugia | 6 | 1 | 7 | 134 |
| 3 | Manfredini | Udinese | 11 | 0 | 11 | 136 |
| 4 | Falcone | Bologna | 6 | 1 | 7 | 162 |
| 5 | Filippini | Brescia | 9 | 2 | 11 | 169 |
| 6 | Di Biagio | Inter Milan | 9 | 1 | 10 | 169 |
| 7 | Pratali | Empoli | 6 | 1 | 7 | 173 |
| 8 | Doni | Atalanta | 11 | 2 | 13 | 176 |
| 9 | Mamede | Reggina | 5 | 0 | 5 | 182 |
| 10 | Cassano | Roma | 7 | 0 | 7 | 192 |
| 11 | Conticchio | Torino | 8 | 0 | 8 | 201 |
| 12 | Conceicao | Inter Milan | 5 | 1 | 6 | 202 |
| 13 | Obodo | Perugia | 8 | 1 | 9 | 205 |
| 14 | Corrent | Como | 7 | 0 | 7 | 207 |
| 15 | Mayer | Modena | 12 | 0 | 12 | 207 |
| 16 | Blasi | Perugia | 12 | 0 | 12 | 211 |
| 17 | Lucarelli | Torino | 6 | 2 | 8 | 215 |
| 18 | Cristante | Piacenza | 10 | 0 | 10 | 217 |
| 19 | Zanetti, C | Inter Milan | 5 | 1 | 6 | 218 |
| 20 | Sogliano | Perugia | 7 | 0 | 7 | 220 |
| 21 | Schopp | Brescia | 5 | 0 | 5 | 224 |
| 22 | Zebina | Roma | 6 | 1 | 7 | 229 |
| 23 | Matuzalem | Brescia | 10 | 1 | 11 | 230 |
| 24 | Grosso | Perugia | 11 | 0 | 11 | 233 |
| 25 | Alberto | Udinese | 6 | 1 | 7 | 233 |
| 26 | Mangone | Piacenza | 10 | 0 | 10 | 234 |
| 27 | Pisano | Brescia | 4 | 0 | 4 | 235 |
| 28 | Morfeo | Inter Milan | 3 | 1 | 4 | 236 |
| 29 | Ungari | Modena | 6 | 0 | 6 | 238 |
| 30 | Cordoba | Inter Milan | 9 | 1 | 10 | 242 |

## CHART TOPPING GOALKEEPERS

**KEY: Defensive Rating (DR)** Average mins between League goals conceded while on pitch. **Clean Sheets (CS)** - Games where no goals were conceded.

| | PLAYER | TEAM | CON | CS | DR |
|---|---|---|---|---|---|
| 1 | Dida | AC Milan | 23 | 13 | 117 |
| 2 | Taibi | Atalanta | 46 | 8 | 65 |
| 3 | Pagliuca | Bologna | 48 | 10 | 64 |
| 4 | Sereni | Brescia | 17 | 13 | 121 |
| 5 | Lupatelli | Chievo | 28 | 10 | 84 |
| 6 | Ambrosio | Chievo | 11 | 2 | 65 |
| 7 | Brunner | Como | 28 | 4 | 59 |
| 8 | Ferron | Como | 27 | 2 | 48 |
| 9 | Berti | Empoli | 42 | 8 | 66 |
| 10 | Toldo | Inter Milan | 38 | 11 | 76 |
| 11 | Buffon | Juventus | 23 | 15 | 123 |
| 12 | Peruzzi | Lazio | 28 | 8 | 90 |
| 13 | Ballotta | Modena | 48 | 6 | 64 |
| 14 | Frey | Parma | 36 | 12 | 85 |
| 15 | Rossi | Perugia | 16 | 5 | 67 |
| 16 | Kalac | Perugia | 28 | 5 | 63 |
| 17 | Guardalben | Piacenza | 37 | 3 | 52 |
| 18 | Orlandoni | Piacenza | 24 | 1 | 43 |
| 19 | Belardi | Reggina | 26 | 6 | 68 |
| 20 | Castellazzi | Reggina | 25 | 0 | 48 |
| 21 | Pellizzoli | Roma | 23 | 4 | 76 |
| 22 | Antonioli | Roma | 22 | 1 | 59 |
| 23 | Bucci | Torino | 40 | 3 | 52 |
| 24 | De Sanctis | Udinese | 35 | 10 | 85 |

## TOP POINT EARNERS

**KEY: Counting Games** League games where he played more than 70 minutes. **Total League Points** Taken in Counting Games. **Average League Points** Taken in Counting Games.

| | PLAYER | TEAM | GAMES | POINTS | AVE |
|---|---|---|---|---|---|
| 1 | Nedved | Juventus | 24 | 56 | 2.33 |
| 2 | Gattuso | AC Milan | 19 | 43 | 2.26 |
| 3 | Camoranesi | Juventus | 19 | 43 | 2.26 |
| 4 | Zambrotta | Juventus | 18 | 40 | 2.22 |
| 5 | Kaladze | AC Milan | 20 | 44 | 2.20 |
| 6 | Ferrara | Juventus | 20 | 44 | 2.20 |
| 7 | Pirlo | AC Milan | 16 | 35 | 2.19 |
| 8 | Mihajlovic | Lazio | 17 | 37 | 2.18 |
| 9 | Del Piero | Juventus | 20 | 43 | 2.15 |
| 10 | Buffon | Juventus | 31 | 66 | 2.13 |
| 11 | Franceschini | Chievo | 22 | 46 | 2.09 |
| 12 | Thuram | Juventus | 25 | 52 | 2.08 |
| 13 | Pasquale | Inter Milan | 12 | 25 | 2.08 |
| 14 | Di Vaio | Juventus | 12 | 25 | 2.08 |
| 15 | Shevchenko | AC Milan | 15 | 31 | 2.07 |
| 16 | Davids | Juventus | 22 | 45 | 2.05 |
| 17 | Simic | AC Milan | 23 | 47 | 2.04 |
| 18 | Zanetti, J | Inter Milan | 31 | 63 | 2.03 |
| 19 | Seedorf | AC Milan | 24 | 48 | 2.00 |
| 20 | Favalli | Lazio | 24 | 48 | 2.00 |
| 21 | Tacchinardi | Juventus | 21 | 42 | 2.00 |
| 22 | Montero | Juventus | 19 | 38 | 2.00 |
| 23 | Iuliano | Juventus | 17 | 34 | 2.00 |
| 24 | Crespo | Inter Milan | 12 | 24 | 2.00 |
| 25 | Junior Jenilson | Parma | 25 | 49 | 1.96 |
| 26 | Materazzi | Inter Milan | 16 | 31 | 1.94 |
| 27 | Rivaldo | AC Milan | 14 | 27 | 1.93 |
| 28 | Cannavaro | Inter Milan | 26 | 50 | 1.92 |
| 29 | Inzaghi | AC Milan | 25 | 48 | 1.92 |
| 30 | Costacurta | AC Milan | 13 | 25 | 1.92 |

# REAL MADRID

Final Position: **1st**

| | | | | | | |
|---|---|---|---|---|---|---|
| 1 | escup | Feyenoord | H | W | 3-1 | Paauwe 14 og; Roberto Carlos 21; Guti 60 |
| 2 | lge | Espanyol | H | W | 2-0 | Helguera 35; McManaman 88 |
| 3 | ecgc | Roma | A | W | 3-0 | Guti 41,75; Raul 56 |
| 4 | lge | Osasuna | H | W | 4-1 | Helguera 11,79; Guti 52; Raul 53 |
| 5 | ecgc | Genk | H | W | 6-0 | Zokora 45 og; Salgado 46; Figo 55 pen; Guti 64; Celades 74; Raul 76 |
| 6 | lge | Valladolid | A | D | 1-1 | Raul 44 |
| 7 | ecgc | AEK Athens | A | D | 3-3 | Zidane 15,40; Guti 60 |
| 8 | lge | Alaves | H | W | 5-2 | Zidane 2; Figo 31 pen,72; Ronaldo 68,75 |
| 9 | lge | Real Betis | A | D | 1-1 | Raul 51 |
| 10 | lge | R Santander | A | L | 0-2 | |
| 11 | ecgc | AEK Athens | H | D | 2-2 | McManaman 24,43 |
| 12 | lge | Villarreal | H | D | 1-1 | Zidane 22 |
| 13 | ecgc | Roma | H | L | 0-1 | |
| 14 | lge | Deportivo | A | D | 0-0 | |
| 15 | lge | R Vallecano | A | W | 3-2 | Ronaldo 15; Figo 48; Roberto Carlos 58 |
| 16 | ecgc | Genk | A | D | 1-1 | Tote 21 |
| 17 | lge | Real Sociedad | H | D | 0-0 | |
| 18 | lge | Barcelona | A | D | 0-0 | |
| 19 | ecgc | AC Milan | A | L | 0-1 | |
| 20 | lge | Mallorca | A | W | 5-1 | Ronaldo 6,46; Raul 62,65; Guti 90 |
| 21 | ecgc | L Moscow | H | D | 2-2 | Raul 21,76 |
| 22 | lge | Recreativo | H | W | 4-2 | Raul Bravo 28; Helguera 64; Raul 70; Figo 90 pen |
| 23 | lge | Malaga | A | W | 3-2 | Zidane 46; Raul 72; Figo 78 pen |
| 24 | lge | Seville | H | W | 3-0 | Raul 9; Conceicao 28; Zidane 73 |
| 25 | lge | Valencia | H | W | 4-1 | Ronaldo 36; Zidane 67; Guti 85; Portillo 90 |
| 26 | lge | Celta Vigo | A | W | 1-0 | Ronaldo 6 |
| 27 | lge | Atl Madrid | H | D | 2-2 | Figo 32,44 pen |
| 28 | lge | Athl Bilbao | A | D | 1-1 | Ronaldo 57 |
| 29 | lge | Espanyol | A | D | 2-2 | Roberto Carlos 58; Figo 75 |
| 30 | lge | Real Betis | H | W | 4-1 | Raul 43; Figo 49 pen; Zidane 62; Ronaldo 88 |
| 31 | lge | Osasuna | A | L | 0-1 | |
| 32 | ecgc | B Dortmund | H | W | 2-1 | Raul 43; Ronaldo 55 |
| 33 | lge | Valladolid | H | W | 3-1 | Roberto Carlos 19; Ronaldo 22; Portillo 90 |
| 34 | ecgc | B Dortmund | A | D | 1-1 | Portillo 90 |
| 35 | lge | Alaves | A | W | 5-1 | Ronaldo 11,65,76; Raul 34,81 |
| 36 | lge | R Santander | H | W | 4-1 | Figo 13 pen; Zidane 43; Portillo 77; Guti 87 |
| 37 | ecgc | AC Milan | H | W | 3-1 | Raul 12,57; Guti 86 |
| 38 | lge | Villarreal | A | W | 1-0 | Helguera 89 |
| 39 | ecgc | L Moscow | A | W | 1-0 | Ronaldo 35 |
| 40 | lge | Deportivo | H | W | 2-0 | Zidane 44; Ronaldo 49 |
| 41 | lge | R Vallecano | H | W | 3-1 | Morientes 85,90; Portillo 89 |
| 42 | ecqfl1 | Man Utd | H | W | 3-1 | Figo 12; Raul 28,49 |
| 43 | lge | Real Sociedad | A | L | 2-4 | Ronaldo 32; Portillo 83 |
| 44 | lge | Barcelona | H | D | 1-1 | Ronaldo 15 |
| 45 | ecqfl2 | Man Utd | A | L | 3-4 | Ronaldo 12,50,59 |
| 46 | lge | Seville | A | W | 3-1 | Helguera 25; Zidane 53; Morientes 86 |
| 47 | lge | Mallorca | H | L | 1-5 | Ronaldo 9 |
| 48 | ecsfl1 | Juventus | H | W | 2-1 | Ronaldo 23; Roberto Carlos 73 |
| 49 | lge | Recreativo | A | D | 0-0 | |
| 50 | ecsfl2 | Juventus | A | L | 1-3 | Zidane 89 |
| 51 | lge | Malaga | H | W | 5-1 | Morientes 4,53; Raul 15,82; Roberto Carlos 18 |
| 52 | lge | Valencia | A | W | 2-1 | Ronaldo 25,64 |
| 53 | lge | Celta Vigo | H | D | 1-1 | Raul 67 |
| 54 | lge | Atl Madrid | A | W | 4-0 | Ronaldo 4,31; Raul 18,73 |
| 55 | lge | Athl Bilbao | H | W | 3-1 | Ronaldo 8,61; Roberto Carlos 45 |

## ATTENDANCES

HOME GROUND: SANTIAGO BERNABEU CAPACITY: 87000 AVERAGE LEAGUE AT HOME: 71193

| | | |
|---|---|---|
| 18 | Barcelona | 98000 |
| 3 | Roma | 80000 |
| 37 | AC Milan | 78000 |
| 22 | Recreativo Huelva | 76300 |
| 24 | Seville | 76300 |
| 17 | Real Sociedad | 76300 |
| 51 | Malaga | 76300 |
| 8 | Alaves | 76300 |
| 30 | Real Betis | 76300 |
| 40 | Deportivo | 76300 |
| 55 | Athl Bilbao | 76300 |
| 27 | Atl Madrid | 76300 |
| 44 | Barcelona | 76300 |
| 19 | AC Milan | 75777 |
| 25 | Valencia | 75537 |
| 48 | Juventus | 74773 |
| 2 | Espanyol | 72485 |
| 13 | Roma | 71722 |
| 53 | Celta Vigo | 68670 |
| 47 | Mallorca | 68670 |
| 5 | Genk | 68670 |
| 42 | Man Utd | 66708 |
| 45 | Man Utd | 66708 |
| 4 | Osasuna | 65000 |
| 12 | Villarreal | 64855 |
| 36 | R Santander | 61050 |
| 50 | Juventus | 60253 |
| 41 | R Vallecano | 60000 |
| 46 | Seville | 60000 |
| 21 | Lokomotiv Moscow | 60000 |
| 54 | Atl Madrid | 57000 |
| 33 | Valladolid | 53400 |
| 52 | Valencia | 53000 |
| 9 | Real Betis | 52500 |
| 32 | B Dortmund | 50000 |
| 34 | B Dortmund | 50000 |
| 29 | Espanyol | 49500 |
| 11 | AEK Athens | 40000 |
| 28 | Athl Bilbao | 38000 |
| 14 | Deportivo | 35600 |
| 23 | Malaga | 33390 |
| 43 | Real Sociedad | 32000 |
| 26 | Celta Vigo | 31164 |
| 6 | Valladolid | 25175 |
| 16 | Genk | 25000 |
| 7 | AEK Athens | 24800 |
| 20 | Mallorca | 23700 |
| 10 | R Santander | 22500 |
| 1 | Feyenoord | 20000 |
| 31 | Osasuna | 20000 |
| 49 | Recreativo Huelva | 20000 |
| 39 | Lokomotiv Moscow | 18000 |
| 38 | Villarreal | 15120 |
| 15 | R Vallecano | 14725 |
| 35 | Alaves | 11520 |

■ Home □ Away ▨ Neutral

## KEY PLAYERS - GOALSCORERS

**1 Luiz Nazario de Lima Ronaldo**

| | | | |
|---|---|---|---|
| Goals in the League | 23 | Player Strike Rate<br>Average number of minutes between League goals scored by player | 105 |
| Contribution to Attacking Power<br>Average number of minutes between League team goals while on pitch | 43 | Club Strike Rate<br>Average number of minutes between League goals scored by club | 40 |

| | PLAYER | LGE GOALS | POWER | STRIKE RATE |
|---|---|---|---|---|
| 2 | Gonzalez Blanco Raul | 16 | 37 | 168 mins |
| 3 | Luis Filipe Madeira Figo | 10 | 39 | 272 mins |
| 4 | Zinedine Zidane | 9 | 39 | 299 mins |
| 5 | Jose Maria Gutierrez Hernandez | 4 | 36 | 443 mins |

## KEY PLAYERS - MIDFIELDERS

**1 Jose Maria Gutierrez Hernandez (Guti)**

| | | | |
|---|---|---|---|
| Goals in the League | 4 | Contribution to Attacking Power<br>Average number of minutes between League team goals while on pitch | 36 |
| Defensive Rating<br>Average number of mins between League goals conceded while he was on the pitch | 84 | Scoring Difference<br>Defensive Rating minus Contribution to Attacking Power | 48 |

| | PLAYER | LGE GOALS | DEF RATE | POWER | SCORE DIFF |
|---|---|---|---|---|---|
| 2 | Ivan Bujia Helguera | 6 | 78 | 39 | 39 mins |
| 3 | Flavio Conceicao | 1 | 73 | 35 | 38 mins |
| 4 | Claude Makelele | 0 | 84 | 46 | 38 mins |
| 5 | Zinedine Zidane | 9 | 75 | 39 | 36 mins |

## KEY PLAYERS - DEFENDERS

**1 Francisco Pavon**

| | | | |
|---|---|---|---|
| Goals Conceded (GC)<br>The number of League goals conceded while he was on the pitch | 14 | Clean Sheets<br>In games when he played at least 70 minutes | 6 |
| Defensive Rating<br>Ave number of mins between League goals conceded while on the pitch | 113 | Club Defensive Rating<br>Average number of mins between League goals conceded by the club this season | 81 |

| | PLAYER | CON LGE | CLEAN SHEETS | DEF RATE |
|---|---|---|---|---|
| 2 | Roberto Carlos Da Silva | 40 | 10 | 83 mins |
| 3 | Miguel Angel Michel Fernandez | 37 | 9 | 81 mins |
| 4 | Fernando Ruiz Hierro | 32 | 5 | 69 mins |

## KEY GOALKEEPER

**1 Iker Fernandez Casillas**

| | |
|---|---|
| Goals Conceded in the League | 42 |
| Defensive Rating<br>Ave number of mins between League goals conceded while on the pitch | 81 |
| Counting Games<br>Games when he played at least 70 minutes | 38 |
| Clean Sheets<br>In games when he played at least 70 minutes | 10 |

## TOP POINT EARNERS

| | PLAYER | GAMES | AVE |
|---|---|---|---|
| 1 | Conceicao | 15 | 2.47 |
| 2 | Guti | 14 | 2.43 |
| 3 | Figo | 29 | 2.34 |
| 4 | Pavon | 17 | 2.24 |
| 5 | Raul | 30 | 2.20 |
| 6 | Helguera | 32 | 2.13 |
| 7 | Ronaldo | 26 | 2.08 |
| 8 | Cambiasso | 14 | 2.07 |
| 9 | Casillas | 38 | 2.05 |
| 10 | Roberto Carlos | 37 | 2.03 |
| | CLUB AVERAGE: | | 2.05 |

Ave = Average points per match in Counting Games

## DISCIPLINARY RECORDS

| | PLAYER | YELLOW | RED | AVE |
|---|---|---|---|---|
| 1 | Salgado | 12 | 2 | 214 |
| 2 | Hierro | 9 | 0 | 246 |
| 3 | Guti | 6 | 0 | 295 |
| 4 | Helguera | 8 | 1 | 321 |
| 5 | Solari | 2 | 0 | 408 |
| 6 | Makelele | 6 | 0 | 418 |
| 7 | Pavon | 3 | 0 | 526 |
| 8 | Figo | 4 | 1 | 543 |
| 9 | Conceicao | 3 | 0 | 556 |
| 10 | Roberto Carlos | 5 | 0 | 663 |
| 11 | Zidane | 4 | 0 | 673 |
| 12 | Cambiasso | 2 | 0 | 728 |
| 13 | Ronaldo | 1 | 0 | 2414 |
| | Other | 3 | 0 | |
| | TOTAL | 68 | 4 | |

## LEAGUE GOALS

| | PLAYER | MINS | GOALS | AVE |
|---|---|---|---|---|
| 1 | Ronaldo | 2414 | 23 | 105 |
| 2 | Raul | 2695 | 16 | 168 |
| 3 | Figo | 2717 | 10 | 272 |
| 4 | Zidane | 2692 | 9 | 299 |
| 5 | Helguera | 2890 | 6 | 482 |
| 6 | Morientes | 455 | 5 | 91 |
| 7 | R Carlos | 3319 | 5 | 664 |
| 8 | Portillo | 206 | 5 | 41 |
| 9 | Guti | 1771 | 4 | 443 |
| 10 | Conceicao | 1670 | 1 | 1670 |
| 11 | Raul Bravo | 122 | 1 | 122 |
| 12 | McManaman | 581 | 1 | 581 |
| | Other | | 0 | |
| | TOTAL | | 86 | |

## MONTH BY MONTH GUIDE TO THE POINTS

| MONTH | POINTS | % |
|---|---|---|
| SEPTEMBER | 7 | 78% |
| OCTOBER | 5 | 42% |
| NOVEMBER | 6 | 50% |
| DECEMBER | 9 | 100% |
| JANUARY | 11 | 73% |
| FEBRUARY | 7 | 58% |
| MARCH | 12 | 100% |
| APRIL | 7 | 58% |
| MAY | 8 | 53% |
| JUNE | 6 | 100% |

## TEAM OF THE SEASON

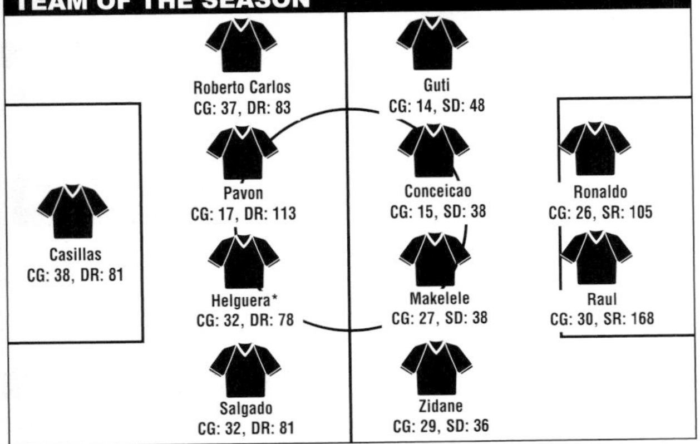
Roberto Carlos
CG: 37, DR: 83
Guti
CG: 14, SD: 48
Pavon
CG: 17, DR: 113
Conceicao
CG: 15, SD: 38
Ronaldo
CG: 26, SR: 105
Casillas
CG: 38, DR: 81
Helguera*
CG: 32, DR: 78
Makelele
CG: 27, SD: 38
Raul
CG: 30, SR: 168
Salgado
CG: 32, DR: 81
Zidane
CG: 29, SD: 36

**KEY:** DR = Defensive Rate, SD = Scoring Difference, SR = Strike Rate, CG = Counting Games – League games playing at least 70 minutes

## LEAGUE APPEARANCES, BOOKINGS AND CAPS

| | AGE (on 01/07/03) | IN THE SQUAD | COUNTING GAMES | MINUTES ON PITCH | YELLOW CARDS | RED CARDS | THIS SEASON | HOME COUNTRY |
|---|---|---|---|---|---|---|---|---|
| **Goalkeepers** | | | | | | | | |
| Casillas | 22 | 38 | 38 | 3420 | 0 | 0 | 10 | Spain (2) |
| Cesar | 31 | 37 | 0 | 0 | 0 | 0 | - | Spain |
| Sanchez | 25 | 1 | 0 | 0 | 0 | 0 | - | Spain |
| **Defenders** | | | | | | | | |
| Cesar Navas | 23 | 2 | 0 | 0 | 0 | 0 | - | Spain |
| Fernando Hierro | 35 | 27 | 25 | 2219 | 9 | 0 | - | Spain |
| Oscar Minambres | 22 | 32 | 4 | 690 | 0 | 0 | - | Spain |
| Francisco Pavon | 23 | 35 | 17 | 1580 | 3 | 0 | - | Spain |
| Roberto Carlos | 30 | 37 | 37 | 3319 | 5 | 0 | 4 | Brazil (1) |
| Gonzalez Ruben | 21 | 8 | 1 | 90 | 1 | 0 | - | Spain |
| Michel Salgado | 27 | 35 | 32 | 3008 | 12 | 2 | 10 | Spain (2) |
| **Midfielders** | | | | | | | | |
| Esteban Cambiasso | 22 | 32 | 14 | 1456 | 2 | 0 | 3 | Argentina (5) |
| Albert Celades | 27 | 15 | 0 | 69 | 1 | 0 | - | Spain |
| Flavio Conceicao | 29 | 31 | 15 | 1670 | 3 | 0 | 1 | Brazil (1) |
| Luis Figo | 30 | 33 | 29 | 2717 | 4 | 1 | 8 | Portugal (14) |
| Jose Maria Guti | 26 | 35 | 14 | 1771 | 6 | 0 | 9 | Spain (2) |
| Ivan Bujia Helguera | 28 | 35 | 32 | 2890 | 8 | 1 | 8 | Spain (2) |
| Claude Makelele | 30 | 30 | 27 | 2510 | 6 | 0 | 8 | France (2) |
| Steve McManaman | 31 | 32 | 3 | 581 | 0 | 0 | - | England |
| Sanfelix Raul Bravo | 22 | 10 | 1 | 122 | 0 | 0 | 10 | Spain (2) |
| Santiago Solari | 26 | 35 | 2 | 816 | 2 | 0 | 4 | Argentina (5) |
| Zinedine Zidane | 31 | 33 | 29 | 2692 | 4 | 0 | 7 | France (2) |
| **Forwards** | | | | | | | | |
| Fernando Morientes | 27 | 30 | 2 | 455 | 0 | 0 | 7 | Spain (2) |
| Javier Garcia Portillo | 21 | 34 | 0 | 206 | 0 | 0 | - | Spain |
| Raul | 26 | 31 | 30 | 2695 | 1 | 0 | 8 | Spain (2) |
| Ronaldo | 26 | 31 | 26 | 2414 | 1 | 0 | 5 | Brazil (1) |
| Savio | 29 | 1 | 0 | 0 | 0 | 0 | - | Brazil |
| Jorge Tote | 24 | 5 | 1 | 70 | 0 | 0 | - | Spain |

**KEY:** LEAGUE BOOKINGS CAPS (FIFA RANKING)

## SQUAD APPEARANCES

| Match | 1 2 3 4 5 | 6 7 8 9 10 | 11 12 13 14 15 | 16 17 18 19 20 | 21 22 23 24 25 | 26 27 28 29 30 | 31 32 33 34 35 | 36 37 38 39 40 | 41 42 43 44 45 | 46 47 48 49 50 | 51 52 53 54 55 |
|---|---|---|---|---|---|---|---|---|---|---|---|
| Venue | H H A H H | A A H A A | H H H A A | A H A A A | H H A H H | A H A A H | A H H A A | H H A A H | H H A H A | A H H A A | H A H A H |
| Competition | L L C L C | L C L L L | C L C L L | C L L C L | C L L L L | L L L L L | L C L C L | L C L C L | L C L L C | L L C L C | L L L L L |
| Result | W W W W W | D D W D L | D D L D W | D D D L W | D W W W W | W D D D W | L W W D W | W W W W W | W W L D L | W L W D L | W W D W W |

**Goalkeepers**
Iker Fernandez Casillas
Sanchez Dominguez Cesar
Carlos Garcia Sanchez

**Defenders**
Gonzalez Cesar Navas
Fernando Ruiz Hierro
Oscar Minambres
Francisco Pavon
Roberto Carlos Da Silva
Gonzalez Rocha Ruben
Michel Fernandez Salgado

**Midfielders**
Esteban Cambiasso
Albert Celades
Flavio Conceicao
Luis Madeira Caeira Figo
Jose Maria Guti
Ivan Bujia Helguera
Claude Makelele
Steve McManaman
Sanfelix Raul Bravo
Santiago Hernan Solari
Zinedine Zidane

**Forwards**
Fernando Morientes
Javier Garcia Portillo
Raul Gonzalez Blanco
Ronaldo Luiz de Lima
Bortolini Pimentel Savio
Jorge Lopez Marco Tote

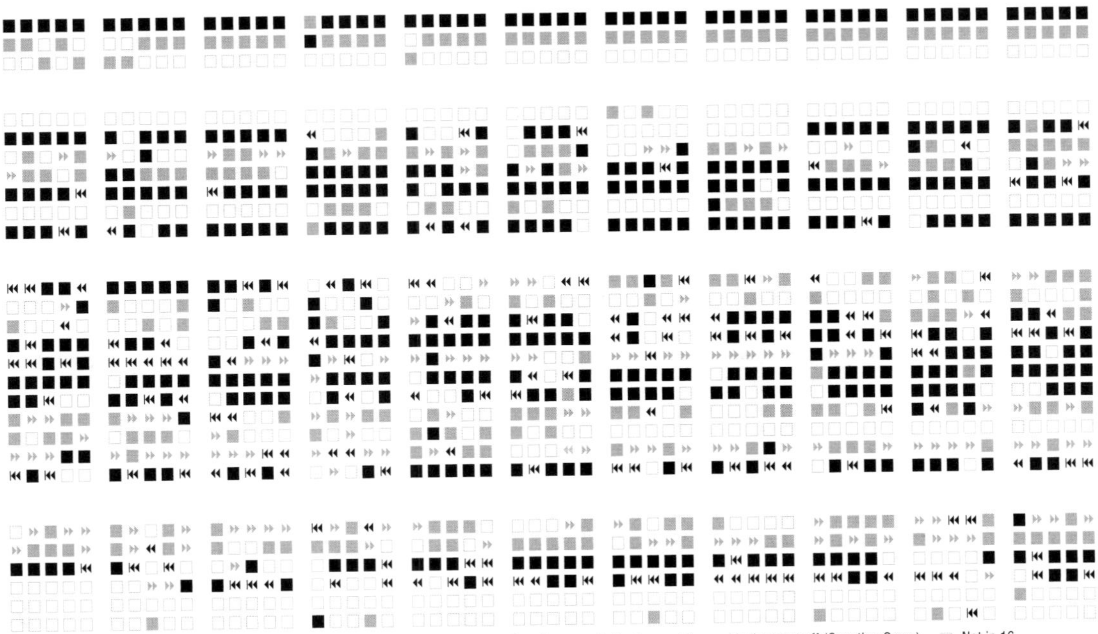

**KEY:** On all match | On bench | Subbed or sent off (Counting game) | Subbed or sent off (playing less than 70 minutes) | Subbed on from bench (Counting Game) | Subbed on (playing less than 70 minutes) | Subbed on and then subbed or sent off (Counting Game) | Subbed on and then subbed or sent off (playing less than 70 minutes) | Not in 16

# REAL SOCIEDAD

Final Position: **2nd**

| | | | | | | |
|---|---|---|---|---|---|---|
| 1 | lge | Athl Bilbao | H | W | 4-2 | Karpin 27; Nihat 33,62; Kovacevic 76 |
| 2 | lge | Espanyol | A | W | 3-1 | Kovacevic 41,90; Aramburu 55 |
| 3 | lge | Real Betis | H | D | 3-3 | Rivas 29 og; Kovacevic 58,79 |
| 4 | lge | Osasuna | A | W | 3-2 | Nihat 12; Jauregui 49; Khokhlov 83 |
| 5 | lge | Valladolid | H | W | 2-1 | Nihat 65; Karpin 67 |
| 6 | lge | Alaves | A | D | 2-2 | Nihat 34; Karpin 67 |
| 7 | lge | R Santander | H | W | 2-1 | Kovacevic 72; De Pedro 90 pen |
| 8 | lge | Villarreal | A | W | 1-0 | Nihat 36 |
| 9 | lge | Deportivo | H | D | 1-1 | Kovacevic 27 |
| 10 | lge | Real Madrid | A | D | 0-0 | |
| 11 | lge | R Vallecano | A | D | 0-0 | |
| 12 | lge | Barcelona | H | W | 2-1 | Kovacevic 39,53 |
| 13 | lge | Seville | A | W | 1-0 | Karpin 70 |
| 14 | lge | Mallorca | H | W | 2-1 | De Pedro 51; Aramburu 57 |
| 15 | lge | Recreativo | A | W | 3-1 | Nihat 42,57; Llorente 90 |
| 16 | lge | Malaga | H | D | 2-2 | Nihat 8; Khokhlov 24 |
| 17 | lge | Valencia | A | D | 2-2 | Kovacevic 68; Nihat 78 |
| 18 | lge | Celta Vigo | H | W | 1-0 | De Pedro 65 |
| 19 | lge | Atl Madrid | A | W | 2-1 | Tayfun 46; Kovacevic 62 |
| 20 | lge | Athl Bilbao | A | L | 0-3 | |
| 21 | lge | Espanyol | H | D | 0-0 | |
| 22 | lge | Real Betis | A | L | 2-3 | Nihat 72,77 |
| 23 | lge | Osasuna | H | W | 2-0 | Kovacevic 43; Mikel Alonso 63 |
| 24 | lge | Valladolid | A | L | 0-3 | |
| 25 | lge | Alaves | H | W | 3-1 | Kovacevic 16; Nihat 38; Karpin 43 |
| 26 | lge | R Santander | A | W | 2-1 | Nihat 22; Karpin 60 |
| 27 | lge | Villarreal | H | D | 2-2 | Kovacevic 26,73 pen |
| 28 | lge | Deportivo | A | L | 1-2 | Nihat 15 |
| 29 | lge | Real Madrid | H | W | 4-2 | Kovacevic 3,19; Nihat 31; Xabi Alonso 33 |
| 30 | lge | R Vallecano | H | W | 5-0 | De Pedro 45 pen; Karpin 50 pen; Nihat 59,87; Tayfun 90 |
| 31 | lge | Barcelona | A | L | 1-2 | Nihat 80 |
| 32 | lge | Seville | H | W | 1-0 | Xabi Alonso 30 |
| 33 | lge | Mallorca | A | W | 3-1 | De Pedro 10 pen; Karpin 25; Kovacevic 53 |
| 34 | lge | Recreativo | H | W | 1-0 | Nihat 8 |
| 35 | lge | Malaga | A | W | 2-0 | Gabilondo 78; Kovacevic 87 |
| 36 | lge | Valencia | H | D | 1-1 | Xabi Alonso 33 |
| 37 | lge | Celta Vigo | A | L | 2-3 | Nihat 65,82 |
| 38 | lge | Atl Madrid | H | W | 3-0 | Kovacevic 51; De Pedro 55; Nihat 73 |

## KEY PLAYERS - GOALSCORERS

**1 Kahveci Nihat**

| | | | |
|---|---|---|---|
| Goals in the League | 23 | Player Strike Rate<br>Average number of minutes between League goals scored by player | 130 |
| Contribution to Attacking Power<br>Average number of minutes between League team goals while on pitch | 42 | Club Strike Rate<br>Average number of minutes between League goals scored by club | 48 |

| | PLAYER | LGE GOALS | POWER | STRIKE RATE |
|---|---|---|---|---|
| 2 | Darko Kovacevic | 20 | 49 | 151 mins |
| 3 | Francisco Jose Falque De Pedro | 6 | 43 | 342 mins |
| 4 | Valeri Karpin | 8 | 47 | 397 mins |
| 5 | Xabier Alonso Olano | 3 | 48 | 920 mins |

## KEY PLAYERS - MIDFIELDERS

**1 Francisco Jose Falque De Pedro**

| | | | |
|---|---|---|---|
| Goals in the League | 6 | Contribution to Attacking Power<br>Average number of minutes between League team goals while on pitch | 44 |
| Defensive Rating<br>Average number of mins between League goals conceded while he was on the pitch | 86 | Scoring Difference<br>Defensive Rating minus Contribution to Attacking Power | 42 |

| | PLAYER | LGE GOALS | DEF RATE | POWER | SCORE DIFF |
|---|---|---|---|---|---|
| 2 | Xabier Alonso Olano | 3 | 86 | 48 | 38 mins |
| 3 | Miguel Eizaguirre Aramburu | 2 | 80 | 43 | 37 mins |
| 4 | Igor del Campo Gabilondo | 1 | 89 | 57 | 32 mins |
| 5 | Igor Iraola Jauregui | 1 | 77 | 48 | 29 mins |

## KEY PLAYERS - DEFENDERS

**1 Bjorn Tore Kvarme**

| | | | |
|---|---|---|---|
| Goals Conceded (GC)<br>The number of League goals conceded while he was on the pitch | 19 | Clean Sheets<br>In games when he played at least 70 minutes | 7 |
| Defensive Rating<br>Ave number of mins between League goals conceded while on the pitch | 88 | Club Defensive Rating<br>Average number of mins between League goals conceded by the club this season | 76 |

| | PLAYER | CON LGE | CLEAN SHEETS | DEF RATE |
|---|---|---|---|---|
| 2 | Aitor Lopez Rekarte | 44 | 12 | 76 mins |
| 3 | Sergio Gonz‡lez Monteagudo Bor | 19 | 5 | 75 mins |
| 4 | Gabriel Peralta Schurrer | 28 | 6 | 74 mins |
| 5 | Agustin Alkorta Aranzabal | 40 | 9 | 72 mins |

## GOALS SCORED

**AT HOME**

| | | |
|---|---|---|
| MOST | R Madrid | 52 |
| | | 41 |
| LEAST | R Vallecano | 17 |

**AWAY**

| | | |
|---|---|---|
| MOST | R Madrid | 34 |
| | | 30 |
| LEAST | Recreativo | 11 |

## GOALS CONCEDED

**AT HOME**

| | | |
|---|---|---|
| LEAST | C Vigo & Valencia | 15 |
| | | 18 |
| MOST | Mallorca | 33 |

**AWAY**

| | | |
|---|---|---|
| LEAST | R Madrid, Valencia & Seville | 20 |
| | | 27 |
| MOST | Alaves | 48 |

## KEY GOALKEEPER

**1 Sander Westerveld**

| | |
|---|---|
| Goals Conceded in the League | 45 |
| Defensive Rating<br>Ave number of mins between League goals conceded while on the pitch | 74 |
| Counting Games<br>Games when he played at least 70 minutes | 37 |
| Clean Sheets<br>In games when he played at least 70 minutes | 11 |

## TOP POINT EARNERS

| | PLAYER | GAMES | AVE |
|---|---|---|---|
| 1 | Aramburu | 25 | 2.36 |
| 2 | De Pedro | 22 | 2.32 |
| 3 | Kvarme | 18 | 2.17 |
| 4 | Nihat | 34 | 2.15 |
| 5 | Kovacevic | 33 | 2.09 |
| 6 | Schurrer | 23 | 2.04 |
| 7 | Xabier Alonso | 30 | 2.03 |
| 8 | Jauregui | 33 | 2.00 |
| 9 | Westerveld | 37 | 1.97 |
| 10 | Aranzabal | 32 | 1.97 |
| | **CLUB AVERAGE:** | | **2.00** |

Ave = Average points per match in Counting Games

## ATTENDANCES

HOME GROUND: ANOETA CAPACITY: 32000 AVERAGE LEAGUE AT HOME: 28680

| | | | | | | | | |
|---|---|---|---|---|---|---|---|---|
| 10 | Real Madrid | 76300 | **38** | **Atl Madrid** | **31400** | **16** | **Malaga** | **22400** |
| 31 | Barcelona | 65700 | **25** | **Alaves** | **31360** | **3** | **Real Betis** | **22400** |
| 17 | Valencia | 49290 | **9** | **Deportivo** | **30400** | **30** | **R Vallecano** | **22400** |
| 22 | Real Betis | 47800 | **34** | **Recreativo Huelva** | **30100** | 2 | Espanyol | 20300 |
| 19 | Atl Madrid | 45600 | **1** | **Athl Bilbao** | **30000** | 15 | Recreativo Huelva | 18600 |
| 20 | Athl Bilbao | 39600 | **14** | **Mallorca** | **29760** | 33 | Mallorca | 17780 |
| 35 | Malaga | 34503 | **21** | **Espanyol** | **29750** | 6 | Alaves | 17280 |
| 28 | Deportivo | 33108 | **27** | **Villarreal** | **28800** | 24 | Valladolid | 15900 |
| **12** | **Barcelona** | **32000** | **32** | **Seville** | **28800** | 26 | R Santander | 15750 |
| **23** | **Osasuna** | **32000** | **7** | **R Santander** | **28800** | 8 | Villarreal | 15120 |
| **36** | **Valencia** | **32000** | 13 | Seville | 27000 | 4 | Osasuna | 14129 |
| **29** | **Real Madrid** | **32000** | **5** | **Valladolid** | **26560** | 11 | R Vallecano | 5115 |
| 37 | Celta Vigo | 31800 | **18** | **Celta Vigo** | **24000** | | | |

■ Home □ Away ▒ Neutral

## DISCIPLINARY RECORDS

| | PLAYER | YELLOW | RED | AVE |
|---|---|---|---|---|
| 1 | Gabilondo | 4 | 0 | 200 |
| 2 | Jauregui | 8 | 1 | 349 |
| 3 | Aramburu | 7 | 0 | 354 |
| 4 | Xabier Alonso | 7 | 0 | 394 |
| 5 | Lopez Rekarte | 8 | 0 | 416 |
| 6 | Kovacevic | 6 | 1 | 431 |
| 7 | Karpin | 7 | 0 | 454 |
| 8 | Barkero | 1 | 0 | 579 |
| 9 | Nihat | 4 | 1 | 598 |
| 10 | Khokhlov | 1 | 0 | 607 |
| 11 | Schurrer | 3 | 0 | 686 |
| 12 | Aranzabal | 4 | 0 | 719 |
| 13 | Tayfun | 1 | 0 | 767 |
| | Other | 7 | 0 | |
| | **TOTAL** | **68** | **3** | |

## LEAGUE GOALS

| | PLAYER | MINS | GOALS | AVE |
|---|---|---|---|---|
| 1 | Nihat | 2992 | 23 | 130 |
| 2 | Kovacevic | 3019 | 20 | 151 |
| 3 | Karpin | 3179 | 8 | 397 |
| 4 | De Pedro | 2054 | 6 | 342 |
| 5 | Xabier Alonso | 2760 | 3 | 920 |
| 6 | Tayfun | 767 | 2 | 384 |
| 7 | Khokhlov | 607 | 2 | 304 |
| 8 | Aramburu | 2480 | 2 | 1240 |
| 9 | Llorente | 22 | 1 | 22 |
| 10 | Jauregui | 3146 | 1 | 3146 |
| 11 | Gabilondo | 803 | 1 | 803 |
| 12 | Mikel Alonso | 161 | 1 | 161 |
| | Other | | 1 | |
| | **TOTAL** | | **71** | |

## MONTH BY MONTH GUIDE TO THE POINTS

| MONTH | POINTS | % |
|---|---|---|
| SEPTEMBER | 10 | 83% |
| OCTOBER | 7 | 78% |
| NOVEMBER | 6 | 50% |
| DECEMBER | 12 | 100% |
| JANUARY | 8 | 67% |
| FEBRUARY | 4 | 33% |
| MARCH | 7 | 58% |
| APRIL | 6 | 50% |
| MAY | 12 | 100% |
| JUNE | 4 | 44% |

## TEAM OF THE SEASON

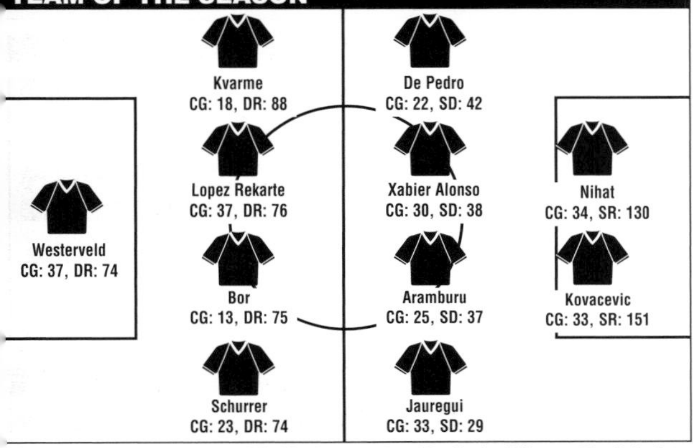
Kvarme
CG: 18, DR: 88
De Pedro
CG: 22, SD: 42
Lopez Rekarte
CG: 37, DR: 76
Xabier Alonso
CG: 30, SD: 38
Nihat
CG: 34, SR: 130
Westerveld
CG: 37, DR: 74
Bor
CG: 13, DR: 75
Aramburu
CG: 25, SD: 37
Kovacevic
CG: 33, SR: 151
Schurrer
CG: 23, DR: 74
Jauregui
CG: 33, SD: 29

KEY: DR = Defensive Rate, SD = Scoring Difference, SR = Strike Rate,
CG = Counting Games – League games playing at least 70 minutes

## LEAGUE APPEARANCES, BOOKINGS AND CAPS

| | AGE | IN THE SQUAD | COUNTING GAMES | MINUTES ON PITCH | YELLOW CARDS | RED CARDS | THIS SEASON | HOME COUNTRY |
|---|---|---|---|---|---|---|---|---|
| **Goalkeepers** | | | | | | | | |
| Lopez Alberto | 34 | 37 | 1 | 90 | 0 | 0 | - | Spain |
| Sander Westerveld | 28 | 38 | 37 | 3330 | 1 | 0 | 3 | Holland (6) |
| **Defenders** | | | | | | | | |
| Agustin Aranzabal | 30 | 32 | 32 | 2879 | 4 | 0 | 5 | Spain (2) |
| Sergio Bor | 23 | 34 | 13 | 1428 | 1 | 0 | - | Spain |
| Zuhaitz Gurrutxaga | 22 | 27 | 1 | 91 | 1 | 0 | - | Spain |
| Bjorn Tore Kvarme | 30 | 32 | 18 | 1669 | 2 | 0 | - | Norway |
| Aitor Lopez Rekarte | 27 | 37 | 37 | 3330 | 8 | 0 | - | Spain |
| Jose Pikabea | 32 | 2 | 0 | 0 | 0 | 0 | - | Spain |
| Gabriel Schurrer | 31 | 23 | 23 | 2060 | 3 | 0 | - | Argentina |
| **Midfielders** | | | | | | | | |
| Aitor Aldeondo | | 1 | 0 | 0 | 0 | 0 | - | |
| Miguel Aramburu | 24 | 37 | 25 | 2480 | 7 | 0 | - | Spain |
| Jose Javier Barkero | 24 | 23 | 5 | 579 | 1 | 0 | - | Spain |
| Francisco De Pedro | 29 | 30 | 22 | 2054 | 2 | 0 | 3 | Spain (2) |
| Igor Gabilondo | 24 | 35 | 6 | 803 | 4 | 0 | - | Spain |
| Jose Guerrero | | 1 | 0 | 0 | 0 | 0 | - | |
| Igor Iraola Jauregui | 29 | 36 | 33 | 3146 | 8 | 1 | - | Spain |
| Valeri Karpin | 34 | 36 | 36 | 3179 | 7 | 0 | 1 | Russia (25) |
| Dimitri Khokhlov | 27 | 38 | 4 | 607 | 1 | 0 | 3 | Russia (25) |
| Mikel Alonso Olano | 23 | 17 | 0 | 161 | 0 | 0 | - | Spain |
| Vangeneberg Llorca | 21 | 1 | 0 | 0 | 0 | 0 | - | Spain |
| Xavier Prieto | 19 | 1 | 0 | 0 | 0 | 0 | - | Spain |
| Korkut Tayfun | 29 | 37 | 6 | 767 | 1 | 0 | 2 | Turkey (8) |
| Olano Xabier Alonso | 21 | 33 | 30 | 2760 | 7 | 0 | 1 | Spain (2) |
| **Forwards** | | | | | | | | |
| Oscar De Paula | 28 | 27 | 0 | 148 | 0 | 0 | - | Spain |
| Darko Kovacevic | 29 | 36 | 33 | 3019 | 6 | 1 | - | Serbia & Montenegro |
| Joseba Llorente | 23 | 17 | 0 | 22 | 0 | 0 | - | Spain |
| Kahveci Nihat | 23 | 35 | 34 | 2992 | 4 | 1 | 8 | Turkey (8) |

KEY: LEAGUE BOOKINGS CAPS (FIFA RANKING)

## SQUAD APPEARANCES

| Match | 1 | 2 | 3 | 4 | 5 | 6 | 7 | 8 | 9 | 10 | 11 | 12 | 13 | 14 | 15 | 16 | 17 | 18 | 19 | 20 | 21 | 22 | 23 | 24 | 25 | 26 | 27 | 28 | 29 | 30 | 31 | 32 | 33 | 34 | 35 | 36 | 37 | 38 |
|---|---|---|---|---|---|---|---|---|---|---|---|---|---|---|---|---|---|---|---|---|---|---|---|---|---|---|---|---|---|---|---|---|---|---|---|---|---|---|
| Venue | H | A | H | A | H | A | H | A | H | A | A | H | A | H | A | H | A | H | A | A | H | A | H | A | H | A | H | A | H | H | A | H | A | H | A | H | A | H |
| Competition | L | L | L | L | L | L | L | L | L | L | L | L | L | L | L | L | L | L | L | L | L | L | L | L | L | L | L | L | L | L | L | L | L | L | L | L | L | L |
| Result | W | W | D | W | W | D | W | W | D | D | D | W | W | W | W | D | D | W | W | L | D | L | W | L | W | W | D | L | W | W | L | W | W | W | W | D | L | W |

**Goalkeepers**
Lopez Fernandez Alberto
Sander Westerveld

**Defenders**
Agustin Alkorta Aranzabal
Sergio Monteagudo Bor
Zuhaitz Loiola Gurrutxaga
Bjorn Tore Kvarme
Aitor Lopez Rekarte
Jose Antonio Pikabea
Gabriel Peralta Schurrer

**Midfielders**
Aitor Aldeondo
Miguel Eizaguirre Aramburu
Jose Javier Barkero
Francisco Javier De Pedro
Igor del Campo Gabilondo
Jose Felix Guerrero
Igor Iraola Jauregui
Valeri Karpin
Dimitri Khokhlov
Mikel Alonso Olano
Vangeneberg Pablo Llorca
Xavier Argarate Prieto
Korkut Tayfun
Olano Xabier Alonso

**Forwards**
Oscar Gamero De Paula
Darko Kovacevic
Joseba Etxarri Llorente
Kahveci Nihat

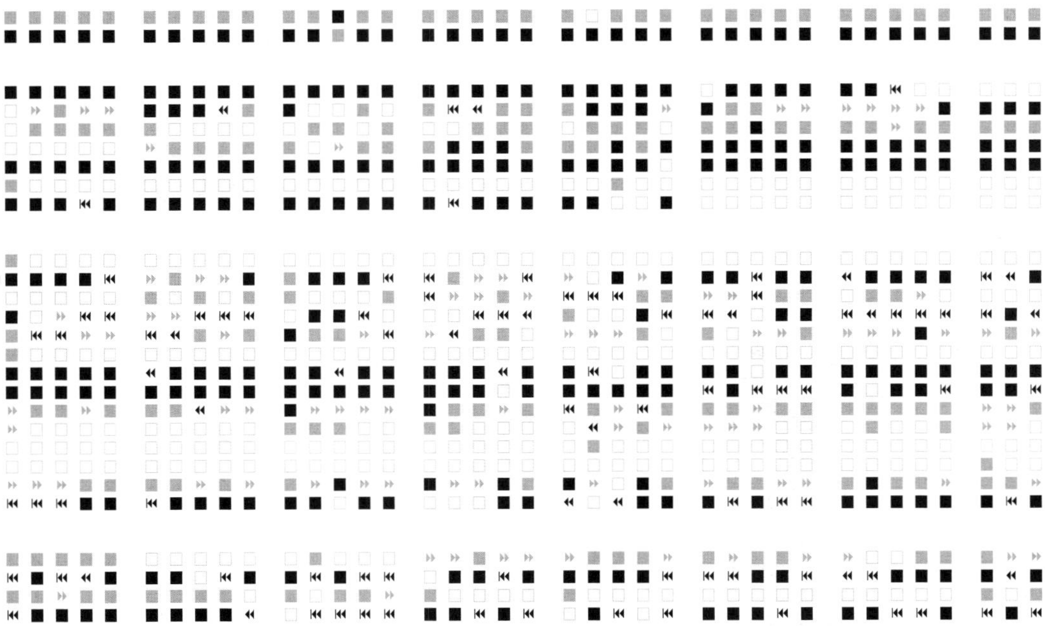

KEY: On all match | On bench | Subbed or sent off (Counting game) | Subbed or sent off (playing less than 70 minutes) | Subbed on from bench (Counting Game) | Subbed on (playing less than 70 minutes) | Subbed on and then subbed or sent off (Counting Game) | Subbed on and then subbed or sent off (playing less than 70 minutes) | Not in 16

# DEPORTIVO LA CORUNA

Final Position: **3rd**

| | | | | | | |
|---|---|---|---|---|---|---|
| 1 | lge | Real Betis | H | L | 2-4 | Makaay 32; Diego Tristan 75 pen |
| 2 | lge | Osasuna | A | W | 2-1 | Makaay 73,75 |
| 3 | ecgg | Bayern Munich | A | W | 3-2 | Makaay 12,45,77 |
| 4 | lge | Valladolid | H | W | 2-0 | Makaay 13,28 |
| 5 | ecgg | AC Milan | H | L | 0-4 | |
| 6 | lge | Alaves | A | W | 2-1 | Diego Tristan 68; Capdevila 88 |
| 7 | ecgg | Lens | H | W | 3-1 | Makaay 49; Capdevila 79; Cesar 84 |
| 8 | lge | R Santander | H | L | 0-2 | |
| 9 | lge | Villarreal | A | L | 1-3 | Victor 7 |
| 10 | ecgg | Lens | A | L | 1-3 | Makaay 15 |
| 11 | lge | R Vallecano | A | W | 2-1 | Makaay 24,50 |
| 12 | ecgg | Bayern Munich | H | W | 2-1 | Victor 55; Makaay 89 |
| 13 | lge | Real Madrid | H | D | 0-0 | |
| 14 | lge | Real Sociedad | A | D | 1-1 | Luque 40 |
| 15 | ecgg | AC Milan | A | W | 2-1 | Diego Tristan 58; Makaay 70 |
| 16 | lge | Barcelona | H | W | 2-0 | Scaloni 82; Luque 85 |
| 17 | lge | Seville | A | D | 1-1 | Makaay 48 |
| 18 | ecgd | Juventus | H | D | 2-2 | Tristan 9; Makaay 11 |
| 19 | lge | Mallorca | H | D | 2-2 | Makaay 13,70 |
| 20 | lge | Recreativo | A | D | 1-1 | Tristan 27 |
| 21 | ecgd | Man Utd | A | L | 0-2 | |
| 22 | lge | Malaga | H | W | 1-0 | Luque 86 |
| 23 | lge | Valencia | A | W | 1-0 | Makaay 20 |
| 24 | lge | Celta Vigo | H | W | 3-0 | Tristan 43; Sergio 48; Luque 90 |
| 25 | lge | Atl Madrid | A | L | 1-3 | Makaay 5 |
| 26 | lge | Athl Bilbao | H | W | 2-1 | Donato 50; Karanka 84 og |
| 27 | lge | Espanyol | A | L | 1-3 | Makaay 3 |
| 28 | lge | Real Betis | A | W | 2-0 | Tristan 60; Makaay 72 |
| 29 | lge | Osasuna | H | D | 1-1 | Makaay 63 |
| 30 | lge | Valladolid | A | W | 1-0 | Makaay 57 |
| 31 | ecgd | Basel | A | L | 0-1 | |
| 32 | lge | Alaves | H | W | 6-0 | Tristan 15,20,60; Makaay 34,52; Luque 62 |
| 33 | ecgpd | Basel | H | W | 1-0 | Tristan 4 |
| 34 | lge | R Santander | A | W | 2-1 | Makaay 3; Luque 80 |
| 35 | lge | Villarreal | H | W | 2-1 | Tristan 30 pen; Victor 40 |
| 36 | ecgd | Juventus | A | L | 2-3 | Tristan 34; Makaay 52 |
| 37 | lge | R Vallecano | H | W | 2-0 | Makaay 17 pen; Naybet 85 |
| 38 | ecgd | Man Utd | H | W | 2-0 | Victor 32; Lynch 47 og |
| 39 | lge | Real Madrid | A | L | 0-2 | |
| 40 | lge | Real Sociedad | H | W | 2-1 | Capdevila 43; Fran 83 |
| 41 | lge | Barcelona | A | W | 4-2 | Scaloni 15; Makaay 50,63; Sergio 74 |
| 42 | lge | Seville | H | W | 3-1 | Victor 40; Makaay 45 pen,69 |
| 43 | lge | Mallorca | A | L | 0-3 | |
| 44 | lge | Recreativo | H | W | 5-0 | Valeron 25; Victor 27; Makaay 32 pen,36,58 |
| 45 | lge | Malaga | A | W | 2-0 | Donato 13; Scaloni 90 |
| 46 | lge | Valencia | H | L | 1-2 | Donato 48 |
| 47 | lge | Celta Vigo | A | L | 0-3 | |
| 48 | lge | Atl Madrid | H | W | 3-2 | Romero 13; Makaay 77; Valeron 85 |
| 49 | lge | Athl Bilbao | A | L | 2-3 | Capdevila 66; Sergio 68 |
| 50 | lge | Espanyol | H | W | 2-1 | Makaay 74; Luque 75 |

## ATTENDANCES

HOME GROUND: RIAZOR CAPACITY: 35600 AVERAGE LEAGUE AT HOME: 29025

| | | | | | | | | |
|---|---|---|---|---|---|---|---|---|
| 41 | Barcelona | 91140 | **48** | **Atl Madrid** | **33820** | 36 | Juventus | 25070 |
| 39 | Real Madrid | 76300 | **40** | **Real Sociedad** | **33108** | **24** | **Celta Vigo** | **24480** |
| 21 | Man Utd | 67014 | **12** | **Bayern Munich** | **33000** | 47 | Celta Vigo | 22260 |
| 25 | Atl Madrid | 57000 | **42** | **Seville** | **32000** | **37** | **R Vallecano** | **21360** |
| 15 | AC Milan | 56294 | **5** | **AC Milan** | **32000** | **32** | **Alaves** | **21350** |
| 28 | Real Betis | 49875 | **1** | **Real Betis** | **32000** | 34 | R Santander | 19125 |
| 23 | Valencia | 45050 | 14 | Real Sociedad | 30400 | **7** | **Lens** | **18156** |
| 27 | Espanyol | 42350 | **35** | **Villarreal** | **30260** | 43 | Mallorca | 17775 |
| 17 | Seville | 41850 | **4** | **Valladolid** | **30000** | 6 | Alaves | 17664 |
| 3 | Bayern Munich | 40000 | **19** | **Mallorca** | **29904** | 20 | Recreativo Huelva | 16000 |
| 49 | Athl Bilbao | 39600 | 31 | Basel | 29031 | 2 | Osasuna | 16000 |
| 45 | Malaga | 37100 | **26** | **Athl Bilbao** | **28480** | 30 | Valladolid | 15900 |
| **13** | **Real Madrid** | **35600** | **22** | **Malaga** | **28480** | 11 | R Vallecano | 14725 |
| **16** | **Barcelona** | **35000** | **18** | **Juventus** | **27500** | **50** | **Espanyol** | **14240** |
| 10 | Lens | 35000 | **33** | **Basel** | **27000** | 9 | Villarreal | 12264 |
| **46** | **Valencia** | **34180** | **44** | **Recreativo Huelva** | **26700** | **38** | **Man Utd** | **7120** |
| **8** | **R Santander** | **33820** | **29** | **Osasuna** | **26700** | | | |

■ Home □ Away ▒ Neutral

## KEY PLAYERS - GOALSCORERS

**1 Roy Makaay**

| | | | |
|---|---|---|---|
| Goals in the League | 29 | Player Strike Rate<br>Average number of minutes between League goals scored by player | 111 |
| Contribution to Attacking Power<br>Average number of minutes between League team goals while on pitch | 52 | Club Strike Rate<br>Average number of minutes between League goals scored by club | 51 |

| | PLAYER | LGE GOALS | POWER | STRIKE RATE |
|---|---|---|---|---|
| 2 | Gama Da Silva Donato | 3 | 70 | 423 mins |
| 3 | Joan Mendez Capdevila | 3 | 41 | 459 mins |
| 4 | Sanchez del Amo Victor | 4 | 57 | 520 mins |
| 5 | Juan Carlos Valeron | 2 | 39 | 672 mins |

## KEY PLAYERS - MIDFIELDERS

**1 Jose Emilio Amavisca**

| | | | |
|---|---|---|---|
| Goals in the League | 0 | Contribution to Attacking Power<br>Average number of minutes between League team goals while on pitch | 63 |
| Defensive Rating<br>Average number of mins between League goals conceded while he was on the pitch | 221 | Scoring Difference<br>Defensive Rating minus Contribution to Attacking Power | 158 |

| | PLAYER | LGE GOALS | DEF RATE | POWER | SCORE DIFF |
|---|---|---|---|---|---|
| 2 | Aldo Pedro Duscher | 0 | 93 | 56 | 37 mins |
| 3 | Juan Carlos Valeron | 2 | 64 | 40 | 24 mins |
| 4 | Gonzalez Sergio | 3 | 70 | 51 | 19 mins |
| 5 | Mauro Gomes da Silva | 0 | 67 | 54 | 13 mins |

## KEY PLAYERS - DEFENDERS

**1 Joan Mendez Capdevila**

| | | | |
|---|---|---|---|
| Goals Conceded (GC)<br>The number of League goals conceded while he was on the pitch | 16 | Clean Sheets<br>In games when he played at least 70 minutes | 4 |
| Defensive Rating<br>Ave number of mins between League goals conceded while on the pitch | 86 | Club Defensive Rating<br>Average number of mins between League goals conceded by the club this season | 73 |

| | PLAYER | CON LGE | CLEAN SHEETS | DEF RATE |
|---|---|---|---|---|
| 2 | Hector Berenguel Del Pino | 20 | 5 | 84 mins |
| 3 | Noureddine Naybet | 26 | 9 | 80 mins |
| 4 | Lionel Scaloni | 32 | 8 | 75 mins |
| 5 | Martin Villar Cesar | 23 | 4 | 74 mins |

## KEY GOALKEEPER

**1 Juan Miguel Garcia Ingles**

| | |
|---|---|
| Goals Conceded in the League | 25 |
| Defensive Rating<br>Ave number of mins between League goals conceded while on the pitch | 96 |
| Counting Games<br>Games when he played at least 70 minutes | 27 |
| Clean Sheets<br>In games when he played at least 70 minutes | 11 |

## TOP POINT EARNERS

| | PLAYER | GAMES | AVE |
|---|---|---|---|
| 1 | Duscher | 12 | 2.33 |
| 2 | Hector | 16 | 2.25 |
| 3 | Sergio | 28 | 2.18 |
| 4 | Juanmi | 27 | 2.11 |
| 5 | Naybet | 23 | 2.04 |
| 6 | Romero | 29 | 1.90 |
| 7 | Makaay | 35 | 1.80 |
| 8 | Mauro Silva | 30 | 1.80 |
| 9 | Scaloni | 24 | 1.79 |
| 10 | Cesar | 18 | 1.78 |
| | **CLUB AVERAGE:** | | **1.89** |

Ave = Average points per match in Counting Games

## DISCIPLINARY RECORDS

| | PLAYER | YELLOW | RED | AVE |
|---|---|---|---|---|
| 1 | Duscher | 8 | 0 | 209 |
| 2 | Cesar | 6 | 1 | 242 |
| 3 | Mauro Silva | 10 | 0 | 281 |
| 4 | Victor | 7 | 0 | 297 |
| 5 | Hector | 5 | 0 | 336 |
| 6 | Naybet | 5 | 1 | 347 |
| 7 | Scaloni | 6 | 0 | 401 |
| 8 | Tristan | 2 | 1 | 418 |
| 9 | Amavisca | 2 | 0 | 442 |
| 10 | Andrade | 2 | 0 | 452 |
| 11 | Capdevila | 3 | 0 | 458 |
| 12 | Fran | 4 | 0 | 481 |
| 13 | Pablo | 1 | 0 | 594 |
| | Other | 9 | 1 | |
| | **TOTAL** | **70** | **4** | |

## LEAGUE GOALS

| | PLAYER | MINS | GOALS | AVE |
|---|---|---|---|---|
| 1 | Makaay | 3226 | 29 | 111 |
| 2 | Tristan | 1256 | 9 | 140 |
| 3 | Luque | 996 | 7 | 142 |
| 4 | Victor | 2081 | 4 | 520 |
| 5 | Scaloni | 2409 | 3 | 803 |
| 6 | Sergio | 2933 | 3 | 978 |
| 7 | Capdevila | 1376 | 3 | 459 |
| 8 | Donato | 1268 | 3 | 423 |
| 9 | Valeron | 1343 | 2 | 672 |
| 10 | Naybet | 2083 | 1 | 2083 |
| 11 | Romero | 2712 | 1 | 2712 |
| 12 | Fran | 1926 | 1 | 1926 |
| | Other | | 1 | |
| | **TOTAL** | | **67** | |

## MONTH BY MONTH GUIDE TO THE POINTS

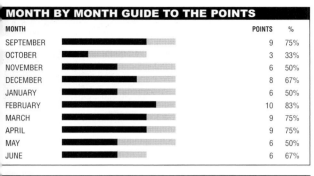

| MONTH | POINTS | % |
|---|---|---|
| SEPTEMBER | 9 | 75% |
| OCTOBER | 3 | 33% |
| NOVEMBER | 6 | 50% |
| DECEMBER | 8 | 67% |
| JANUARY | 6 | 50% |
| FEBRUARY | 10 | 83% |
| MARCH | 9 | 75% |
| APRIL | 9 | 75% |
| MAY | 6 | 50% |
| JUNE | 6 | 67% |

## TEAM OF THE SEASON

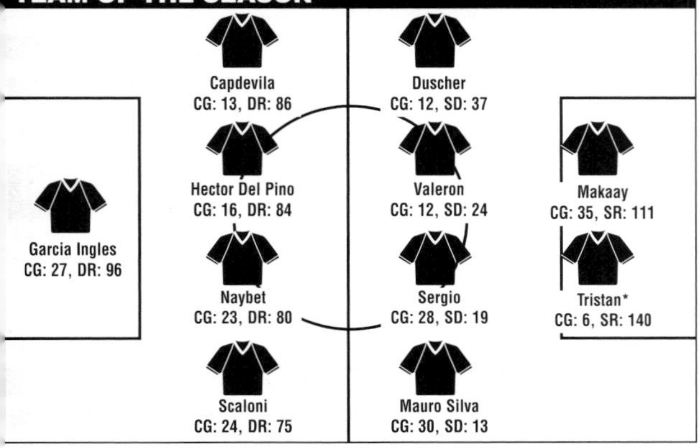

Capdevila
CG: 13, DR: 86
Duscher
CG: 12, SD: 37
Hector Del Pino
CG: 16, DR: 84
Valeron
CG: 12, SD: 24
Makaay
CG: 35, SR: 111
Garcia Ingles
CG: 27, DR: 96
Naybet
CG: 23, DR: 80
Sergio
CG: 28, SD: 19
Tristan*
CG: 6, SR: 140
Scaloni
CG: 24, DR: 75
Mauro Silva
CG: 30, SD: 13


KEY: DR = Defensive Rate, SD = Scoring Difference, SR = Strike Rate, CG = Counting Games – League games playing at least 70 minutes

## LEAGUE APPEARANCES, BOOKINGS AND CAPS

| | AGE | IN THE SQUAD | COUNTING GAMES | MINUTES ON PITCH | YELLOW CARDS | RED CARDS | THIS SEASON | HOME COUNTRY |
|---|---|---|---|---|---|---|---|---|
| **Goalkeepers** | | | | | | | | |
| Daniel Dani Mallo | 24 | 28 | 1 | 111 | 0 | 0 | - | Spain |
| Juan Miguel Ingles | 32 | 38 | 27 | 2409 | 0 | 0 | - | Spain |
| Francisco Molina | 32 | 10 | 10 | 900 | 0 | 0 | - | Spain |
| **Defenders** | | | | | | | | |
| Jorge Andrade | 25 | 15 | 9 | 905 | 2 | 0 | 4 | Portugal (14) |
| Joan Capdevila | 25 | 38 | 13 | 1376 | 3 | 0 | 3 | Spain (2) |
| Martin Villar Cesar | 26 | 24 | 18 | 1695 | 6 | 1 | 4 | Spain (2) |
| Goran Djorovic | 31 | 9 | 0 | 47 | 0 | 0 | - | Serbia & Montenegro |
| Gama Donato | 40 | 28 | 13 | 1268 | 1 | 0 | - | Brazil |
| Hector Del Pino | 28 | 36 | 16 | 1680 | 5 | 0 | - | Spain |
| Rodriques Helder | 32 | 1 | 0 | 0 | 0 | 0 | - | Portugal |
| Francisco Angeriz | 21 | 0 | 0 | 0 | 0 | 0 | - | Spain |
| Antonio Lopez | 21 | 0 | 0 | 0 | 0 | 0 | - | Spain |
| Noureddine Naybet | 33 | 26 | 23 | 2083 | 5 | 1 | - | Morocco |
| Manuel Garcia Diaz | 27 | 31 | 5 | 594 | 1 | 0 | - | Spain |
| Aguado Pablo Amo | 25 | 14 | 0 | 0 | 0 | 0 | - | Spain |
| Enrique Romero | 32 | 34 | 29 | 2712 | 2 | 1 | 1 | Spain (2) |
| Lionel Scaloni | 25 | 34 | 24 | 2409 | 6 | 0 | - | Argentina |
| **Midfielders** | | | | | | | | |
| Roberto Acuna | 31 | 14 | 0 | 150 | 0 | 0 | 2 | Paraguay (19) |
| Jose Amavisca | 32 | 29 | 6 | 884 | 2 | 0 | - | Spain |
| Djalma Djalminha | 32 | 1 | 0 | 0 | 0 | 0 | - | |
| Aldo Pedro Duscher | 24 | 37 | 12 | 1678 | 8 | 0 | - | Argentina |
| Francisco Gonazales | 33 | 31 | 15 | 1926 | 4 | 0 | - | Spain |
| Mauro Gomes | 35 | 35 | 30 | 2818 | 10 | 0 | - | Brazil |
| Gonzalez Sergio | 26 | 37 | 28 | 2933 | 4 | 0 | 4 | Spain (2) |
| Juan Carlos Valeron | 28 | 24 | 12 | 1343 | 1 | 0 | 7 | Spain (2) |
| Sanchez Victor | 27 | 31 | 18 | 2081 | 7 | 0 | - | Spain |
| **Forwards** | | | | | | | | |
| Alberto Luque | 25 | 37 | 3 | 996 | 1 | 0 | - | Spain |
| Roy Makaay | 28 | 38 | 35 | 3226 | 0 | 0 | 7 | Holland (6) |
| Diego Tristan | 27 | 28 | 6 | 1256 | 2 | 1 | 5 | Spain (2) |

KEY: LEAGUE BOOKINGS CAPS (FIFA RANKING)

## SQUAD APPEARANCES

| Match | 1 | 2 | 3 | 4 | 5 | 6 | 7 | 8 | 9 | 10 | 11 | 12 | 13 | 14 | 15 | 16 | 17 | 18 | 19 | 20 | 21 | 22 | 23 | 24 | 25 | 26 | 27 | 28 | 29 | 30 | 31 | 32 | 33 | 34 | 35 | 36 | 37 | 38 | 39 | 40 | 41 | 42 | 43 | 44 | 45 | 46 | 47 | 48 | 49 | 50 |
|---|---|---|---|---|---|---|---|---|---|---|---|---|---|---|---|---|---|---|---|---|---|---|---|---|---|---|---|---|---|---|---|---|---|---|---|---|---|---|---|---|---|---|---|---|---|---|---|---|---|---|
| Venue | H | A | A | H | H | A | H | H | A | A | A | H | H | A | A | H | A | H | H | A | A | H | A | H | A | H | A | A | H | A | A | H | H | A | H | A | H | H | A | H | A | H | A | H | A | H | A | H | A | H |
| Competition | L | L | C | L | C | L | C | L | L | C | L | C | L | L | C | L | L | C | L | L | C | L | L | L | L | L | L | L | L | L | C | L | C | L | L | C | L | C | L | L | L | L | L | L | L | L | L | L | L | L |
| Result | L | W | W | W | L | W | W | L | L | L | W | W | D | D | W | W | D | D | D | D | L | W | W | W | L | W | L | W | D | W | L | W | W | W | W | L | W | W | L | W | W | W | L | W | W | L | L | W | L | W |

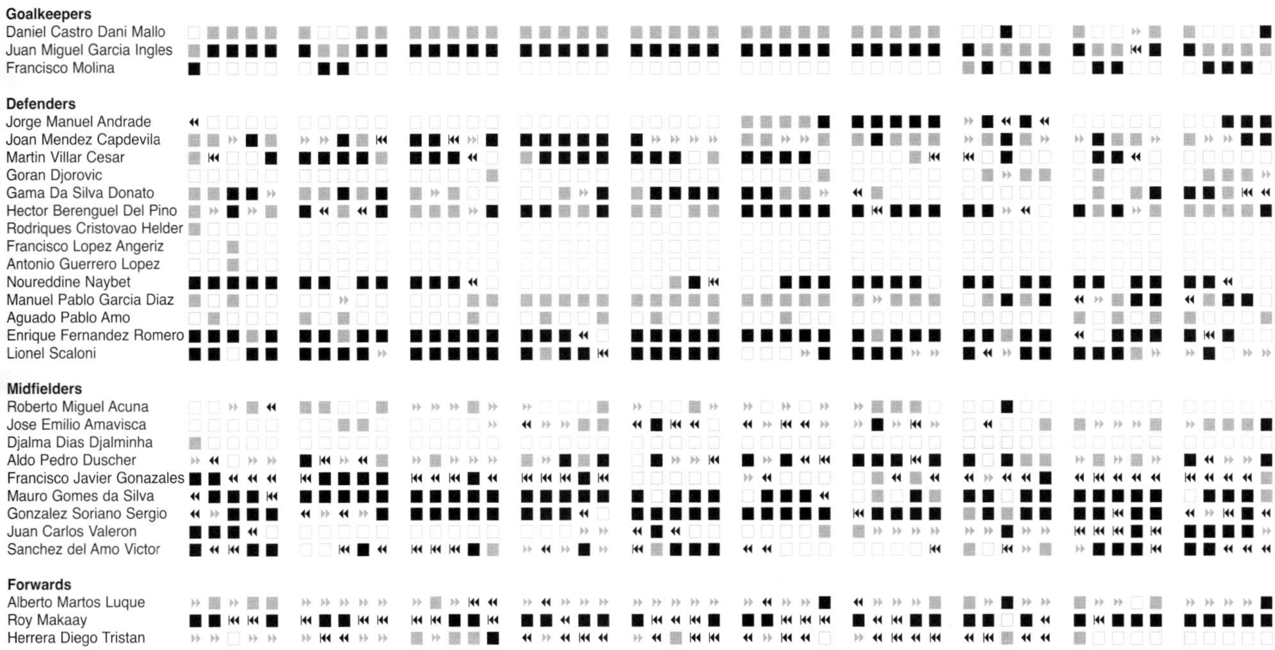

Goalkeepers
Daniel Castro Dani Mallo
Juan Miguel Garcia Ingles
Francisco Molina
Defenders
Jorge Manuel Andrade
Joan Mendez Capdevila
Martin Villar Cesar
Goran Djorovic
Gama Da Silva Donato
Hector Berenguel Del Pino
Rodriques Cristovao Helder
Francisco Lopez Angeriz
Antonio Guerrero Lopez
Noureddine Naybet
Manuel Pablo Garcia Diaz
Aguado Pablo Amo
Enrique Fernandez Romero
Lionel Scaloni
Midfielders
Roberto Miguel Acuna
Jose Emilio Amavisca
Djalma Dias Djalminha
Aldo Pedro Duscher
Francisco Javier Gonazales
Mauro Gomes da Silva
Gonzalez Soriano Sergio
Juan Carlos Valeron
Sanchez del Amo Victor
Forwards
Alberto Martos Luque
Roy Makaay
Herrera Diego Tristan


KEY: ■ On all match ■ On bench ⏮ Subbed or sent off (Counting game) « Subbed or sent off (playing less than 70 minutes) » Subbed on from bench (Counting Game) » Subbed on (playing less than 70 minutes) » Subbed on and then subbed or sent off (Counting Game) » Subbed on and then subbed or sent off (playing less than 70 minutes) □ Not in 16

# CELTA VIGO

Final Position: **4th**

| | | | | | | |
|---|---|---|---|---|---|---|
| 1 | lge | Seville | A | W | 1-0 | Gustavo Lopez 39 |
| 2 | lge | Mallorca | H | W | 3-1 | Catanha 28; Jesuli 40,82 |
| 3 | uc1rl1 | Odense | H | W | 2-0 | Catanha 70; McCarthy 76 |
| 4 | lge | Recreativo | A | W | 3-0 | Mostovoi 44,71; McCarthy 90 |
| 5 | lge | Malaga | H | D | 2-2 | Catanha 27 pen; Berizzo 39 |
| 6 | uc1rl2 | Odense | A | L | 0-1 | |
| 7 | lge | Valencia | A | W | 1-0 | Vagner 90 |
| 8 | lge | R Vallecano | H | L | 0-1 | |
| 9 | lge | Atl Madrid | H | D | 0-0 | |
| 10 | uc2rl1 | Viking | H | W | 3-0 | Jose Ignacio 35; Edu 38; McCarthy 75 |
| 11 | lge | Athl Bilbao | A | L | 1-2 | Edu 33 |
| 12 | lge | Espanyol | H | W | 1-0 | Jose Ignacio 17 |
| 13 | uc2rl2 | Viking | A | D | 1-1 | Mostovoi 75 |
| 14 | lge | Real Betis | A | L | 1-2 | Jose Ignacio 63 |
| 15 | lge | Osasuna | H | D | 0-0 | |
| 16 | uc3rl1 | Celtic | A | L | 0-1 | |
| 17 | lge | Valladolid | A | W | 2-0 | Catanha 10; Edu 52 |
| 18 | lge | Alaves | H | W | 2-1 | Karmona 22 og; Luccin 25 pen |
| 19 | uc3rl2 | Celtic | H | W | 2-1 | Jesuli 23; McCarthy 54 |
| 20 | lge | R Santander | A | L | 0-3 | |
| 21 | lge | Villarreal | H | W | 3-1 | Catanha 1; Edu 7; Jesuli 63 |
| 22 | lge | Deportivo | A | L | 0-3 | |
| 23 | lge | Real Madrid | H | L | 0-1 | |
| 24 | lge | Real Sociedad | A | L | 0-1 | |
| 25 | lge | Barcelona | H | W | 2-0 | Jesuli 47; Silvinho 71 |
| 26 | lge | Seville | H | L | 0-1 | |
| 27 | lge | Mallorca | A | W | 2-0 | Edu 9,64 |
| 28 | lge | Recreativo | H | W | 4-1 | Edu 38,56; Jesuli 62,70 |
| 29 | lge | Malaga | A | D | 1-1 | Jose Ignacio 4 |
| 30 | lge | Valencia | H | D | 1-1 | Edu 10 |
| 31 | lge | R Vallecano | A | L | 0-1 | |
| 32 | lge | Atl Madrid | A | W | 1-0 | Berizzo 87 |
| 33 | lge | Athl Bilbao | H | W | 2-1 | Mido 20; McCarthy 77 |
| 34 | lge | Espanyol | A | D | 0-0 | |
| 35 | lge | Real Betis | H | W | 1-0 | Mostovoi 45 |
| 36 | lge | Osasuna | A | W | 2-0 | Mido 14,50 |
| 37 | lge | Valladolid | H | D | 0-0 | |
| 38 | lge | Alaves | A | D | 0-0 | |
| 39 | lge | R Santander | H | D | 2-2 | Juanfran 35; Edu 82 pen |
| 40 | lge | Villarreal | A | L | 0-5 | |
| 41 | lge | Deportivo | H | W | 3-0 | Jesuli 58; Edu 63,79 |
| 42 | lge | Real Madrid | A | D | 1-1 | Mostovoi 34 |
| 43 | lge | Real Sociedad | H | W | 3-2 | Mostovoi 10,49; Mido 70 |
| 44 | lge | Barcelona | A | L | 0-2 | |

## KEY PLAYERS - GOALSCORERS

**1 Luis Eduardo Schmidt Edu**

| | | | |
|---|---|---|---|
| Goals in the League | 12 | Player Strike Rate<br>Average number of minutes between League goals scored by player | 229 |
| Contribution to Attacking Power<br>Average number of minutes between League team goals while on pitch | 78 | Club Strike Rate<br>Average number of minutes between League goals scored by club | 74 |

| | PLAYER | LGE GOALS | POWER | STRIKE RATE |
|---|---|---|---|---|
| 2 | Alexander Mostovoi | 6 | 59 | 338 mins |
| 3 | Henrique da Silva Catanha | 4 | 75 | 414 mins |
| 4 | Saenz Marin Jose Ignacio | 3 | 67 | 814 mins |
| 5 | Eduardo Berizzo | 2 | 66 | 1222 mins |

## KEY PLAYERS - MIDFIELDERS

**1 Alexander Mostovoi**

| | | | |
|---|---|---|---|
| Goals in the League | 6 | Contribution to Attacking Power<br>Average number of minutes between League team goals while on pitch | 60 |
| Defensive Rating<br>Average number of mins between League goals conceded while he was on the pitch | 156 | Scoring Difference<br>Defensive Rating minus Contribution to Attacking Power | 96 |

| | PLAYER | LGE GOALS | DEF RATE | POWER | SCORE DIFF |
|---|---|---|---|---|---|
| 2 | Pablo Gustavo Lopez | 1 | 116 | 71 | 45 mins |
| 3 | Peter Luccin | 1 | 100 | 72 | 28 mins |
| 4 | Saenz Marin Jose Ignacio | 3 | 94 | 68 | 26 mins |
| 5 | Luis Eduardo Schmidt Edu | 12 | 91 | 78 | 13 mins |

## KEY PLAYERS - DEFENDERS

**1 Juan Velasco Damas**

| | | | |
|---|---|---|---|
| Goals Conceded (GC)<br>The number of League goals conceded while he was on the pitch | 22 | Clean Sheets<br>In games when he played at least 70 minutes | 13 |
| Defensive Rating<br>Ave number of mins between League goals conceded while on the pitch | 115 | Club Defensive Rating<br>Average number of mins between League goals conceded by the club this season | 95 |

| | PLAYER | CON LGE | CLEAN SHEETS | DEF RATE |
|---|---|---|---|---|
| 2 | Juan Francisco Garcia | 14 | 7 | 110 mins |
| 3 | Eduardo Berizzo | 24 | 13 | 102 mins |
| 4 | Fernando Gabriel Caceres | 31 | 14 | 97 mins |
| 5 | Sylvio Mendes Campos Junior | 32 | 11 | 82 mins |

## GOALS SCORED

**AT HOME**

| | | |
|---|---|---|
| MOST | R Madrid | 52 |
| | | 29 |
| LEAST | R Vallecano | 17 |

**AWAY**

| | | |
|---|---|---|
| MOST | R Madrid | 34 |
| | | 16 |
| LEAST | Recreativo | 11 |

## GOALS CONCEDED

**AT HOME**

| | | |
|---|---|---|
| LEAST | C Vigo & Valencia | 15 |
| | | 15 |
| MOST | Mallorca | 33 |

**AWAY**

| | | |
|---|---|---|
| LEAST | R Madrid, Valencia & Seville | 20 |
| | | 21 |
| MOST | Alaves | 48 |

## KEY GOALKEEPER

**1 Pablo Rodriguez Cavallero**

| | |
|---|---|
| Goals Conceded in the League | 27 |
| Defensive Rating<br>Ave number of mins between League goals conceded while on the pitch | 117 |
| Counting Games<br>Games when he played at least 70 minutes | 34 |
| Clean Sheets<br>In games when he played at least 70 minutes | 15 |

## TOP POINT EARNERS

| | PLAYER | GAMES | AVE |
|---|---|---|---|
| 1 | Mostovoi | 20 | 2.05 |
| 2 | Berizzo | 27 | 1.89 |
| 3 | Velasco | 27 | 1.74 |
| 4 | Silvinho | 28 | 1.71 |
| 5 | Cavallero | 34 | 1.68 |
| 6 | Jose Ignacio | 24 | 1.67 |
| 7 | Caceres | 32 | 1.66 |
| 8 | Catanha | 14 | 1.64 |
| 9 | Luccin | 33 | 1.61 |
| 10 | Gustavo Lopez | 18 | 1.61 |
| | **CLUB AVERAGE:** | | **1.60** |

Ave = Average points per match in Counting Games

## ATTENDANCES

HOME GROUND: ESTADIO BALAIDOS CAPACITY: 31800 AVERAGE LEAGUE AT HOME: 25152

| | | |
|---|---|---|
| 42 | Real Madrid | 68670 |
| 32 | Atl Madrid | 57000 |
| 16 | Celtic | 53726 |
| 7 | Valencia | 49820 |
| 44 | Barcelona | 48507 |
| 14 | Real Betis | 39375 |
| 34 | Espanyol | 36850 |
| 1 | Seville | 32000 |
| 43 | Real Sociedad | 31800 |
| 29 | Malaga | 31550 |
| 11 | Athl Bilbao | 31200 |
| 21 | Villarreal | 31165 |
| 23 | Real Madrid | 31164 |
| 30 | Valencia | 30210 |
| 33 | Athl Bilbao | 29900 |
| 25 | Barcelona | 29574 |
| 15 | Osasuna | 28620 |
| 39 | R Santander | 28000 |
| 28 | Recreativo Huelva | 27700 |
| 9 | Atl Madrid | 27030 |
| 22 | Deportivo | 24480 |
| 24 | Real Sociedad | 24000 |
| 5 | Malaga | 23850 |
| 12 | Espanyol | 22260 |
| 18 | Alaves | 22260 |
| 41 | Deportivo | 22260 |
| 35 | Real Betis | 21625 |
| 27 | Mallorca | 20150 |
| 8 | R Vallecano | 19080 |
| 19 | Celtic | 19080 |
| 4 | Recreativo Huelva | 18000 |
| 2 | Mallorca | 18000 |
| 37 | Valladolid | 17500 |
| 17 | Valladolid | 15900 |
| 26 | Seville | 15900 |
| 40 | Villarreal | 14600 |
| 36 | Osasuna | 14530 |
| 10 | Viking | 14310 |
| 31 | R Vallecano | 12560 |
| 38 | Alaves | 11520 |
| 20 | R Santander | 11250 |
| 6 | Odense | 7051 |
| 3 | Odense | 7000 |
| 13 | Viking | 5555 |

Home Away Neutral

## DISCIPLINARY RECORDS

| | PLAYER | YELLOW | RED | AVE |
|---|---|---|---|---|
| 1 | Mido | 4 | 1 | 117 |
| 2 | Juanfran | 9 | 0 | 171 |
| 3 | Angel | 5 | 1 | 187 |
| 4 | Jose Ignacio | 12 | 0 | 203 |
| 5 | Luccin | 13 | 1 | 214 |
| 6 | Berizzo | 10 | 0 | 244 |
| 7 | Vagner | 4 | 0 | 253 |
| 8 | Mendez | 2 | 0 | 270 |
| 9 | Caceres | 11 | 0 | 272 |
| 10 | Mostovoi | 6 | 1 | 289 |
| 11 | Jesuli | 4 | 1 | 295 |
| 12 | Giovanella | 2 | 0 | 433 |
| 13 | Cavallero | 3 | 1 | 789 |
| | Other | 11 | 1 | |
| | **TOTAL** | **96** | **7** | |

## LEAGUE GOALS

| | PLAYER | MINS | GOALS | AVE |
|---|---|---|---|---|
| 1 | Edu | 2742 | 11 | 249 |
| 2 | Jesuli | 1479 | 7 | 211 |
| 3 | Mostovoi | 2025 | 6 | 338 |
| 4 | Mido | 589 | 4 | 147 |
| 5 | Catanha | 1657 | 4 | 414 |
| 6 | Jose Ignacio | 2441 | 3 | 814 |
| 7 | McCarthy | 337 | 2 | 169 |
| 8 | Berizzo | 2443 | 2 | 1222 |
| 9 | Silvinho | 2629 | 1 | 2629 |
| 10 | Juanfran | 1546 | 1 | 1546 |
| 11 | Luccin | 3008 | 1 | 3008 |
| 12 | G Lopez | 2204 | 1 | 2204 |
| 13 | Vagner | 1015 | 1 | 1015 |
| | Other | | 1 | |
| | **TOTAL** | | **45** | |

## MONTH BY MONTH GUIDE TO THE POINTS

| MONTH | POINTS | % |
|---|---|---|
| SEPTEMBER | 10 | 83% |
| OCTOBER | 4 | 44% |
| NOVEMBER | 4 | 33% |
| DECEMBER | 9 | 75% |
| JANUARY | 3 | 25% |
| FEBRUARY | 7 | 58% |
| MARCH | 7 | 58% |
| APRIL | 8 | 67% |
| MAY | 6 | 40% |
| JUNE | 3 | 50% |

## TEAM OF THE SEASON

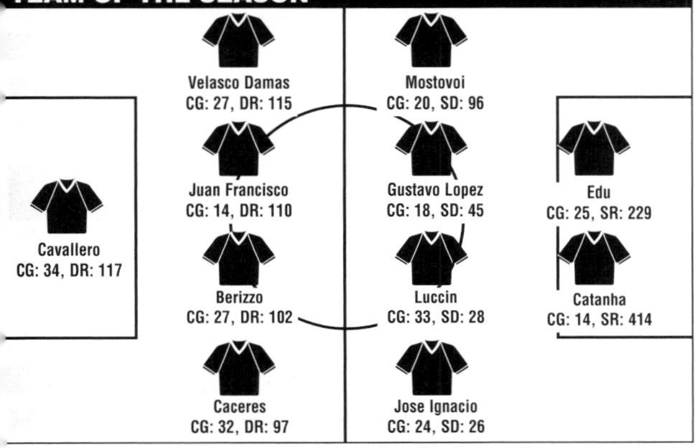

Velasco Damas
CG: 27, DR: 115
Mostovoi
CG: 20, SD: 96
Juan Francisco
CG: 14, DR: 110
Gustavo Lopez
CG: 18, SD: 45
Edu
CG: 25, SR: 229
Cavallero
CG: 34, DR: 117
Berizzo
CG: 27, DR: 102
Luccin
CG: 33, SD: 28
Catanha
CG: 14, SR: 414
Caceres
CG: 32, DR: 97
Jose Ignacio
CG: 24, SD: 26


KEY: DR = Defensive Rate, SD = Scoring Difference, SR = Strike Rate, CG = Counting Games – League games playing at least 70 minutes

## LEAGUE APPEARANCES, BOOKINGS AND CAPS

| | AGE | IN THE SQUAD | COUNTING GAMES | MINUTES ON PITCH | YELLOW CARDS | RED CARDS | THIS SEASON | HOME COUNTRY |
|---|---|---|---|---|---|---|---|---|
| **Goalkeepers** | | | | | | | | |
| Pablo Cavallero | 29 | 36 | 34 | 3159 | 3 | 1 | 4 | Argentina (5) |
| Jose Juan | 23 | 4 | 0 | 35 | 0 | 0 | - | Spain |
| Jose Manuel Pinto | 27 | 37 | 2 | 225 | 0 | 0 | - | Spain |
| **Defenders** | | | | | | | | |
| Eduardo Berizzo | 33 | 34 | 27 | 2443 | 10 | 0 | - | Argentina |
| Iago Bouzon | 20 | 1 | 0 | 0 | 0 | 0 | - | Spain |
| Fernando Caceres | 34 | 36 | 32 | 2998 | 11 | 0 | - | Argentina |
| Pablo Lojo Coira | 23 | 18 | 2 | 225 | 0 | 0 | - | Spain |
| Juan Francisco | 26 | 35 | 14 | 1546 | 9 | 0 | 2 | Spain (2) |
| Sebastien Mendez | 26 | 11 | 5 | 540 | 2 | 0 | - | Argentina |
| Fernandez Sergio | 26 | 20 | 10 | 988 | 1 | 0 | - | Spain |
| Sylvio Mendes | 29 | 34 | 28 | 2629 | 1 | 0 | - | Brazil |
| Juan Velasco Damas | 26 | 32 | 27 | 2523 | 3 | 0 | - | Spain |
| **Midfielders** | | | | | | | | |
| Eduardo Coudet | - | 12 | 1 | 335 | 0 | 0 | - | |
| Guidoni Doriva | 31 | 8 | 0 | 40 | 1 | 0 | - | Brazil |
| Everton Giovanella | 32 | 32 | 7 | 867 | 2 | 0 | - | Brazil |
| Gustavo Lopez | 30 | 34 | 18 | 2204 | 2 | 0 | 1 | Argentina (5) |
| Alejandro Jandro | - | 16 | 0 | 17 | 0 | 0 | - | |
| Jesuli | 25 | 31 | 11 | 1479 | 4 | 1 | - | Spain |
| Aspas Jonathan | 21 | 1 | 0 | 0 | 0 | 0 | - | Spain |
| Jorge Rodriguez | - | 9 | 1 | 90 | 0 | 0 | - | Spain |
| Jose Ignacio | 29 | 35 | 24 | 2441 | 12 | 0 | - | Spain |
| Peter Luccin | 24 | 35 | 33 | 3008 | 13 | 1 | - | France |
| Rodriguez Marcos | - | 1 | 0 | 0 | 0 | 0 | - | Spain |
| Alexander Mostovoi | 34 | 28 | 20 | 2025 | 6 | 1 | - | Russia |
| Rogerio Vagner | 24 | 24 | 7 | 1015 | 4 | 0 | - | Brazil |
| **Forwards** | | | | | | | | |
| Lopez Ruano Angel | 22 | 17 | 11 | 1127 | 5 | 1 | - | Spain |
| Henrique Catanha | 31 | 34 | 14 | 1657 | 2 | 0 | - | Brazil |
| Luis Eduardo Edu | 24 | 37 | 25 | 2742 | 0 | 0 | - | Brazil |
| Jaime Ivan Kaviedes | - | 5 | 0 | 36 | 0 | 0 | - | |
| Benni McCarthy | 25 | 30 | 1 | 337 | 1 | 1 | - | South Africa |
| Ahmed Mido | 20 | 8 | 7 | 589 | 4 | 1 | - | Egypt |

KEY: LEAGUE BOOKINGS CAPS (FIFA RANKING)

## SQUAD APPEARANCES

| Match | 1 | 2 | 3 | 4 | 5 | 6 | 7 | 8 | 9 | 10 | 11 | 12 | 13 | 14 | 15 | 16 | 17 | 18 | 19 | 20 | 21 | 22 | 23 | 24 | 25 | 26 | 27 | 28 | 29 | 30 | 31 | 32 | 33 | 34 | 35 | 36 | 37 | 38 | 39 | 40 | 41 | 42 | 43 | 44 |
|---|---|---|---|---|---|---|---|---|---|---|---|---|---|---|---|---|---|---|---|---|---|---|---|---|---|---|---|---|---|---|---|---|---|---|---|---|---|---|---|---|---|---|---|---|
| Venue | A | H | H | A | H | A | A | H | H | H | A | H | A | A | H | A | A | H | H | A | H | A | H | A | H | H | A | H | A | H | A | A | H | A | H | A | H | A | H | A | H | A | H | A |
| Competition | L | L | E | L | L | E | L | L | L | E | L | L | E | L | L | E | L | L | E | L | L | L | L | L | L | L | L | L | L | L | L | L | L | L | L | L | L | L | L | L | L | L | L | L |
| Result | W | W | W | W | D | L | W | L | D | W | L | W | D | L | D | L | W | W | W | L | W | L | L | L | W | L | W | W | D | D | L | W | W | D | W | W | D | D | D | L | W | D | W | L |

**Goalkeepers**
Pablo Rodriguez Cavallero
Figueiras Garcia Jose Juan
Jose Manuel Pinto Colorado

**Defenders**
Eduardo Berizzo
Iago Amoedo Bouzon
Fernando Gabriel Caceres
Pablo Lojo Coira
Juan Francisco Garcia
Sebastien Ariel Mendez
Fernandez Gonzalez Sergio
Sylvio Mendes Junior
Juan Velasco Damas

**Midfielders**
Eduardo Coudet
Guidoni Junior Doriva
Everton Giovanella
Pablo Gustavo Lopez
Alejandro Torres Jandro
Jesus Antonio Jesuli
Aspas Juncal Jonathan
Jorge Eugenio Rodriguez
Saenz Marin Jose Ignacio
Peter Luccin
Rodriguez Marcos
Alexander Mostovoi
Rogerio Nunes Vagner

**Forwards**
Lopez Ruano Angel
Henrique da Silva Catanha
Luis Eduardo Schmidt Edu
Jaime Ivan Kaviedes
Benni McCarthy
Ahmed Hossam Mido

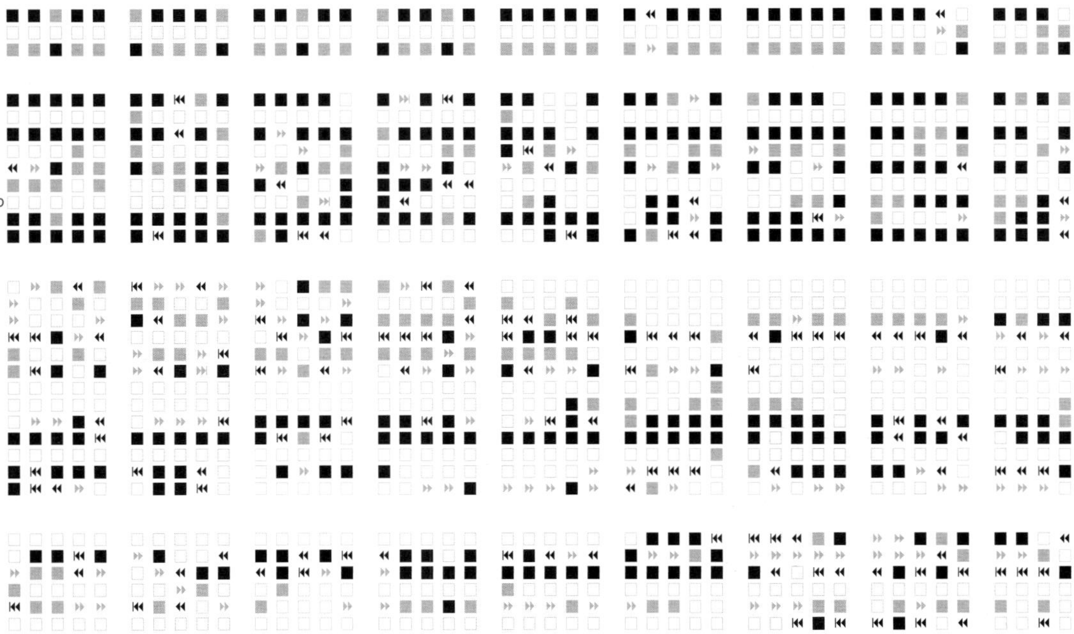

KEY: On all match; On bench; Subbed or sent off (Counting game); Subbed or sent off (playing less than 70 minutes); Subbed on from bench (Counting Game); Subbed on (playing less than 70 minutes); Subbed on and then subbed or sent off (Counting Game); Subbed on and then subbed or sent off (playing less than 70 minutes); Not in 16

# VALENCIA

Final Position: **5th**

| | | | | | | |
|---|---|---|---|---|---|---|
| 1 | lge | Mallorca | A | W | 2-0 | De Los Santos 10; Baraja 57 |
| 2 | lge | Recreativo | H | W | 3-0 | Vicente 10; Alieu Carew 87,90 |
| 3 | ecgb | Liverpool | H | W | 2-0 | Aimar 20; Baraja 39 |
| 4 | lge | Malaga | A | D | 2-2 | Mista 48; Angulo 90 |
| 5 | ecgb | S Moscow | A | W | 3-0 | Angulo 6; Mista 71; Sanchez 85 |
| 6 | lge | R Vallecano | H | W | 3-0 | Mista 34; Baraja 45 pen; Angulo 85 |
| 7 | ecgb | Basel | H | W | 6-2 | Carew 10,13; Aurelio 18; Baraja 28; Aimar 58; Mista 60 |
| 8 | lge | Celta Vigo | H | L | 0-1 | |
| 9 | lge | Atl Madrid | A | D | 1-1 | Baraja 40 |
| 10 | ecgb | Basel | A | D | 2-2 | Baraja 36; Curro Torres 72 |
| 11 | lge | Athl Bilbao | H | W | 5-1 | Aimar 6,28,43; Carew 8; Aurelio 48 pen |
| 12 | ecgb | Liverpool | A | W | 1-0 | Rufete 34 |
| 13 | lge | Espanyol | A | W | 1-0 | Aurelio 74 |
| 14 | lge | Real Betis | H | D | 1-1 | Aimar 82 |
| 15 | ecgb | S Moscow | H | W | 3-0 | Sanchez 38,46; Aurelio 76 |
| 16 | lge | Osasuna | A | L | 0-1 | |
| 17 | lge | Valladolid | H | W | 2-0 | Mista 10,31 |
| 18 | ecgb | Ajax | H | D | 1-1 | Angulo 90 |
| 19 | lge | Alaves | A | D | 0-0 | |
| 20 | lge | R Santander | H | W | 2-0 | Angulo 43; Carew 48 |
| 21 | ecgb | Arsenal | A | D | 0-0 | |
| 22 | lge | Villarreal | A | W | 2-0 | Carew 52,61 |
| 23 | lge | Deportivo | H | L | 0-1 | |
| 24 | lge | Real Madrid | A | L | 1-4 | Ayala 54 |
| 25 | lge | Real Sociedad | H | D | 2-2 | Aurelio 18; Aranzabal 60 og |
| 26 | lge | Barcelona | A | W | 4-2 | Aimar 12; Carew 25; Aurelio 83; Rufete 87 |
| 27 | lge | Seville | H | W | 1-0 | Aimar 34 |
| 28 | lge | Mallorca | H | W | 1-0 | Mista 79 |
| 29 | lge | Recreativo | A | D | 1-1 | Fabio Aurelio 85 |
| 30 | lge | Malaga | H | W | 2-0 | Pellegrino 54; Sanchez 74 |
| 31 | ecgb | Roma | A | W | 1-0 | Carew 78 |
| 32 | lge | R Vallecano | A | W | 4-0 | Angulo 10; Onopko 34 og; Baraja 43; Mista 58 |
| 33 | ecgb | Roma | H | L | 0-3 | |
| 34 | lge | Celta Vigo | A | D | 1-1 | Carew 7 |
| 35 | lge | Atl Madrid | H | L | 0-1 | |
| 36 | ecgb | Ajax | A | D | 1-1 | Kily Gonzalez 28 pen |
| 37 | lge | Athl Bilbao | A | L | 0-1 | |
| 38 | ecgb | Arsenal | H | W | 2-1 | Carew 35,57 |
| 39 | lge | Espanyol | H | D | 1-1 | Baraja 60 |
| 40 | lge | Real Betis | A | L | 0-2 | |
| 41 | ecqfl1 | Inter Milan | A | L | 0-1 | |
| 42 | lge | Osasuna | H | W | 1-0 | Mista 9 |
| 43 | lge | Valladolid | A | L | 0-1 | |
| 44 | ecqfl2 | Inter Milan | H | W | 2-1 | Aimar 7; Baraja 51 |
| 45 | lge | Alaves | H | W | 3-0 | Reveillere 31; Rufete 57; Aimar 67 |
| 46 | lge | R Santander | A | L | 1-2 | Rufete 11 |
| 47 | lge | Villarreal | H | L | 1-2 | Sanchez 79 pen |
| 48 | lge | Deportivo | A | W | 2-1 | Fabio Aurelio 13,63 |
| 49 | lge | Real Madrid | H | L | 1-2 | Fabio Aurelio 32 |
| 50 | lge | Real Sociedad | A | D | 1-1 | Reveillere 34 |
| 51 | lge | Barcelona | H | L | 1-3 | Sanchez 88 pen |
| 52 | lge | Seville | A | W | 3-0 | Aimar 20; Sanchez 29,53 |

## ATTENDANCES

**HOME GROUND: MESTALLA CAPACITY: 53000 AVERAGE LEAGUE AT HOME: 46974**

| | | |
|---|---|---|
| 26 | Barcelona | 93100 |
| 24 | Real Madrid | 75537 |
| 5 | Spartak Moscow | 58826 |
| 51 | Barcelona | 53000 |
| 49 | Real Madrid | 53000 |
| 47 | Villarreal | 53000 |
| 41 | Inter Milan | 52623 |
| 14 | Real Betis | 50880 |
| 39 | Espanyol | 50350 |
| 6 | R Vallecano | 50350 |
| 35 | Atl Madrid | 50350 |
| 9 | Atl Madrid | 50160 |
| 38 | Arsenal | 50000 |
| 8 | Celta Vigo | 49820 |
| 25 | Real Sociedad | 49290 |
| 44 | Inter Milan | 49290 |
| 36 | Ajax | 48633 |
| 11 | Athl Bilbao | 47700 |
| 28 | Mallorca | 47700 |
| 27 | Seville | 45580 |
| 42 | Osasuna | 45100 |
| 23 | Deportivo | 45050 |
| 2 | Recreativo Huelva | 45000 |
| 13 | Espanyol | 44000 |
| 3 | Liverpool | 43000 |
| 17 | Valladolid | 42400 |
| 40 | Real Betis | 42000 |
| 12 | Liverpool | 41831 |
| 7 | Basel | 40280 |
| 18 | Ajax | 40000 |
| 20 | R Santander | 39750 |
| 33 | Roma | 38000 |
| 45 | Alaves | 37100 |
| 30 | Malaga | 37100 |
| 4 | Malaga | 35000 |
| 15 | Spartak Moscow | 34980 |
| 21 | Arsenal | 34793 |
| 48 | Deportivo | 34180 |
| 37 | Athl Bilbao | 32400 |
| 50 | Real Sociedad | 32000 |
| 31 | Roma | 31000 |
| 34 | Celta Vigo | 30210 |
| 10 | Basel | 29500 |
| 52 | Seville | 27000 |
| 43 | Valladolid | 21200 |
| 1 | Mallorca | 20000 |
| 46 | R Santander | 18250 |
| 16 | Osasuna | 17711 |
| 22 | Villarreal | 16800 |
| 19 | Alaves | 15360 |
| 29 | Recreativo Huelva | 14000 |
| 32 | R Vallecano | 12400 |

Home / Away / Neutral

## KEY PLAYERS - GOALSCORERS

**1 John Alieu Carew**

| | | | |
|---|---|---|---|
| **Goals in the League** | 8 | **Player Strike Rate** Average number of minutes between League goals scored by player | 261 |
| **Contribution to Attacking Power** Average number of minutes between League team goals while on pitch | 63 | **Club Strike Rate** Average number of minutes between League goals scored by club | 61 |

| | PLAYER | LGE GOALS | POWER | STRIKE RATE |
|---|---|---|---|---|
| 2 | Fabio Aurelio | 8 | 64 | 268 mins |
| 3 | Pablo Aimar | 8 | 70 | 290 mins |
| 4 | Miguel Angel Valderrey Angulo | 4 | 65 | 363 mins |
| 5 | Ruben Vegas Baraja | 5 | 57 | 516 mins |

## KEY PLAYERS - MIDFIELDERS

**1 David Aliques Albelda**

| | | | |
|---|---|---|---|
| **Goals in the League** | 0 | **Contribution to Attacking Power** Average number of minutes between League team goals while on pitch | 55 |
| **Defensive Rating** Average number of mins between League goals conceded while he was on the pitch | 136 | **Scoring Difference** Defensive Rating minus Contribution to Attacking Power | 81 |

| | PLAYER | LGE GOALS | DEF RATE | POWER | SCORE DIFF |
|---|---|---|---|---|---|
| 2 | Rodriguez Guillen Vicente | 1 | 126 | 63 | 63 mins |
| 3 | Gonzalo da Rosa De Los Santos | 1 | 99 | 62 | 37 mins |
| 4 | Ruben Vegas Baraja | 5 | 86 | 57 | 29 mins |
| 5 | Francisco Joaquin Perez Rufete | 3 | 88 | 62 | 26 mins |

## KEY PLAYERS - DEFENDERS

**1 Curro Torres**

| | | | |
|---|---|---|---|
| **Goals Conceded (GC)** The number of League goals conceded while he was on the pitch | 12 | **Clean Sheets** In games when he played at least 70 minutes | 5 |
| **Defensive Rating** Ave number of mins between League goals conceded while on the pitch | 98 | **Club Defensive Rating** Average number of mins between League goals conceded by the club this season | 95 |

| | PLAYER | CON LGE | CLEAN SHEETS | DEF RATE |
|---|---|---|---|---|
| 2 | Carlos Marchena | 21 | 11 | 95 mins |
| 3 | Roberto Fabian Ayala | 31 | 9 | 87 mins |
| 4 | Anthony Reveillere | 17 | 4 | 86 mins |
| 5 | Fabio Aurelio | 25 | 9 | 86 mins |

## KEY GOALKEEPER

**1 Santiago Ruiz Canizares**

| | |
|---|---|
| **Goals Conceded in the League** | 28 |
| **Defensive Rating** Ave number of mins between League goals conceded while on the pitch | 95 |
| **Counting Games** Games when he played at least 70 minutes | 29 |
| **Clean Sheets** In games when he played at least 70 minutes | 10 |

## TOP POINT EARNERS

| | PLAYER | GAMES | AVE |
|---|---|---|---|
| 1 | Albelda | 22 | 1.91 |
| 2 | Marchena | 21 | 1.76 |
| 3 | Rufete | 20 | 1.70 |
| 4 | Vicente | 18 | 1.67 |
| 5 | Aurelio | 23 | 1.57 |
| 6 | Angulo | 12 | 1.50 |
| 7 | Canizares | 29 | 1.48 |
| 8 | Aimar | 23 | 1.48 |
| 9 | Carboni | 21 | 1.48 |
| 10 | Ayala | 28 | 1.46 |
| | **CLUB AVERAGE:** | | **1.58** |

Ave = Average points per match in Counting Games

## DISCIPLINARY RECORDS

| | PLAYER | YELLOW | RED | AVE |
|---|---|---|---|---|
| 1 | Baraja | 14 | 1 | 172 |
| 2 | Albelda | 11 | 0 | 185 |
| 3 | Mista | 5 | 1 | 190 |
| 4 | Ayala | 11 | 2 | 206 |
| 5 | Curro Torres | 5 | 0 | 236 |
| 6 | Carboni | 8 | 1 | 239 |
| 7 | Marchena | 7 | 1 | 250 |
| 8 | Vicente | 7 | 0 | 288 |
| 9 | Aimar | 7 | 1 | 289 |
| 10 | Pellegrino | 7 | 0 | 320 |
| 11 | Angulo | 4 | 0 | 362 |
| 12 | Reveillere | 4 | 0 | 366 |
| 13 | Garrido | 1 | 0 | 497 |
| | Other | 14 | 2 | |
| | **TOTAL** | **105** | **9** | |

## LEAGUE GOALS

| | PLAYER | MINS | GOALS | AVE |
|---|---|---|---|---|
| 1 | Carew | 2087 | 8 | 261 |
| 2 | Aurelio | 2141 | 8 | 268 |
| 3 | Aimar | 2318 | 8 | 290 |
| 4 | Mista | 1145 | 7 | 164 |
| 5 | Sanchez | 1030 | 5 | 206 |
| 6 | Baraja | 2581 | 5 | 516 |
| 7 | Angulo | 1450 | 4 | 363 |
| 8 | Rufete | 2108 | 3 | 703 |
| 9 | Reveillere | 1467 | 2 | 734 |
| 10 | De Los Santos | 993 | 1 | 993 |
| 11 | Pellegrino | 2241 | 1 | 2241 |
| 12 | Vicente | 2018 | 1 | 2018 |
| 13 | Ayala | 2683 | 1 | 2683 |
| | Other | | 2 | |
| | **TOTAL** | | **56** | |

## MONTH BY MONTH GUIDE TO THE POINTS

| MONTH | POINTS | % |
|---|---|---|
| SEPTEMBER | 10 | 83% |
| OCTOBER | 4 | 44% |
| NOVEMBER | 7 | 58% |
| DECEMBER | 7 | 58% |
| JANUARY | 7 | 58% |
| FEBRUARY | 10 | 83% |
| MARCH | 2 | 17% |
| APRIL | 6 | 50% |
| MAY | 3 | 25% |
| JUNE | 4 | 44% |

## LEAGUE APPEARANCES, BOOKINGS AND CAPS

| | AGE | IN THE SQUAD | COUNTING GAMES | MINUTES ON PITCH | YELLOW CARDS | RED CARDS | THIS SEASON | HOME COUNTRY |
|---|---|---|---|---|---|---|---|---|
| **Goalkeepers** | | | | | | | | |
| Santiago Canizares | 33 | 32 | 29 | 2666 | 2 | 1 | 7 | Spain (2) |
| Andres Palop | 29 | 38 | 8 | 753 | 1 | 0 | - | Spain |
| David Rangel Pastor | 23 | 4 | 0 | 0 | 0 | 0 | - | Spain |
| **Defenders** | | | | | | | | |
| Fabio Aurelio | 23 | 30 | 23 | 2141 | 4 | 0 | - | Brazil |
| Roberto Ayala | 30 | 34 | 28 | 2683 | 11 | 2 | 2 | Argentina (5) |
| Amadeo Carboni | 38 | 33 | 21 | 2159 | 8 | 1 | - | Italy |
| Curro Torres | 26 | 16 | 13 | 1180 | 5 | 0 | - | Spain |
| David Sanchez | 22 | 2 | 0 | 0 | 0 | 0 | - | Spain |
| Miroslav Djukic | 37 | 26 | 6 | 568 | 0 | 0 | - | Serbia & Montenegro |
| Jean-Felix Dorothee | 21 | 5 | 0 | 30 | 0 | 0 | - | France |
| Javier Garrido | 24 | 12 | 5 | 497 | 1 | 0 | - | Spain |
| Carlos Marchena | 24 | 34 | 21 | 2003 | 7 | 1 | 8 | Spain (2) |
| David Navarro | 23 | 7 | 3 | 249 | 0 | 0 | - | Spain |
| Mauricio Pellegrino | 31 | 35 | 22 | 2241 | 7 | 0 | - | Argentina |
| Anthony Reveillere | 23 | 19 | 15 | 1467 | 4 | 0 | - | France |
| **Midfielders** | | | | | | | | |
| Pablo Aimar | 23 | 32 | 23 | 2318 | 7 | 1 | 3 | Argentina (5) |
| David Albelda | 25 | 33 | 22 | 2045 | 11 | 0 | 6 | Spain (2) |
| Ruben Vegas Baraja | 27 | 35 | 25 | 2581 | 14 | 1 | 9 | Spain (2) |
| Garcia Carlos Perez | 19 | 1 | 0 | 0 | 0 | 0 | - | Spain |
| De Los Santos | 26 | 28 | 9 | 993 | 0 | 0 | - | Uruguay |
| Jaime Gavilan | 19 | 2 | 0 | 40 | 1 | 0 | - | Spain |
| Juanlu | 19 | 2 | 0 | 0 | 0 | 0 | - | Spain |
| Kily Gonzalez | 28 | 15 | 4 | 555 | 1 | 0 | 1 | Argentina (5) |
| Rangel | - | 1 | 0 | 0 | 0 | 0 | - | |
| Pablo Redondo | 21 | 3 | 0 | 23 | 0 | 0 | - | Spain |
| Francisco Rufete | 26 | 31 | 20 | 2108 | 2 | 0 | - | Spain |
| Denis Serban | 27 | 1 | 0 | 0 | 0 | 0 | - | Romania |
| Soriano | - | 1 | 0 | 26 | 0 | 0 | - | |
| Rodriguez Vicente | 21 | 31 | 18 | 2018 | 7 | 0 | 10 | Spain (2) |
| **Forwards** | | | | | | | | |
| Miguel Albiol | 21 | 2 | 0 | 14 | 0 | 0 | - | Spain |
| Angulo | 26 | 26 | 12 | 1450 | 4 | 0 | - | Spain |
| Eduardo Borja | 21 | 2 | 1 | 113 | 1 | 0 | - | Spain |
| John Alieu Carew | 23 | 38 | 17 | 2087 | 1 | 1 | 6 | Norway (24) |
| Miguel Angel Ferrer | 24 | 32 | 6 | 1145 | 5 | 1 | - | Spain |
| Ioan Ballesta Salva | 28 | 4 | 1 | 81 | 0 | 0 | - | Spain |
| Juan Sanchez | 31 | 36 | 8 | 1030 | 1 | 0 | - | Spain |

KEY: LEAGUE BOOKINGS CAPS (FIFA RANKING)

## TEAM OF THE SEASON

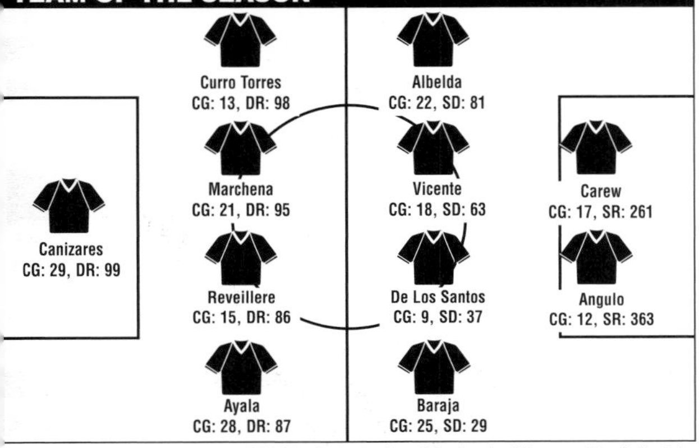

Curro Torres
CG: 13, DR: 98
Albelda
CG: 22, SD: 81
Marchena
CG: 21, DR: 95
Vicente
CG: 18, SD: 63
Carew
CG: 17, SR: 261
Canizares
CG: 29, DR: 99
Reveillere
CG: 15, DR: 86
De Los Santos
CG: 9, SD: 37
Angulo
CG: 12, SR: 363
Ayala
CG: 28, DR: 87
Baraja
CG: 25, SD: 29


KEY: DR = Defensive Rate, SD = Scoring Difference, SR = Strike Rate, CG = Counting Games – League games playing at least 70 minutes

## SQUAD APPEARANCES

| Match | 1 | 2 | 3 | 4 | 5 | 6 | 7 | 8 | 9 | 10 | 11 | 12 | 13 | 14 | 15 | 16 | 17 | 18 | 19 | 20 | 21 | 22 | 23 | 24 | 25 | 26 | 27 | 28 | 29 | 30 | 31 | 32 | 33 | 34 | 35 | 36 | 37 | 38 | 39 | 40 | 41 | 42 | 43 | 44 | 45 | 46 | 47 | 48 | 49 | 50 | 51 | 52 |
|---|---|---|---|---|---|---|---|---|---|---|---|---|---|---|---|---|---|---|---|---|---|---|---|---|---|---|---|---|---|---|---|---|---|---|---|---|---|---|---|---|---|---|---|---|---|---|---|---|---|---|---|---|
| Venue | A | H | H | A | A | H | H | H | A | A | H | A | A | H | H | A | H | H | A | H | A | A | H | A | H | A | H | H | A | H | A | A | H | A | H | A | A | H | H | A | A | H | A | H | H | A | H | A | H | A | H | A |
| Competition | L | L | C | L | C | L | C | L | L | C | L | C | L | L | C | L | L | C | L | L | C | L | L | L | L | L | L | L | L | L | C | L | C | L | L | C | L | C | L | L | C | L | L | C | L | L | L | L | L | L | L | L |
| Result | W | W | W | D | W | W | W | L | D | D | W | W | W | D | W | L | W | D | D | W | D | W | L | L | D | W | W | W | D | W | W | W | L | D | L | D | L | W | D | L | L | W | L | W | W | L | L | W | L | D | L | W |

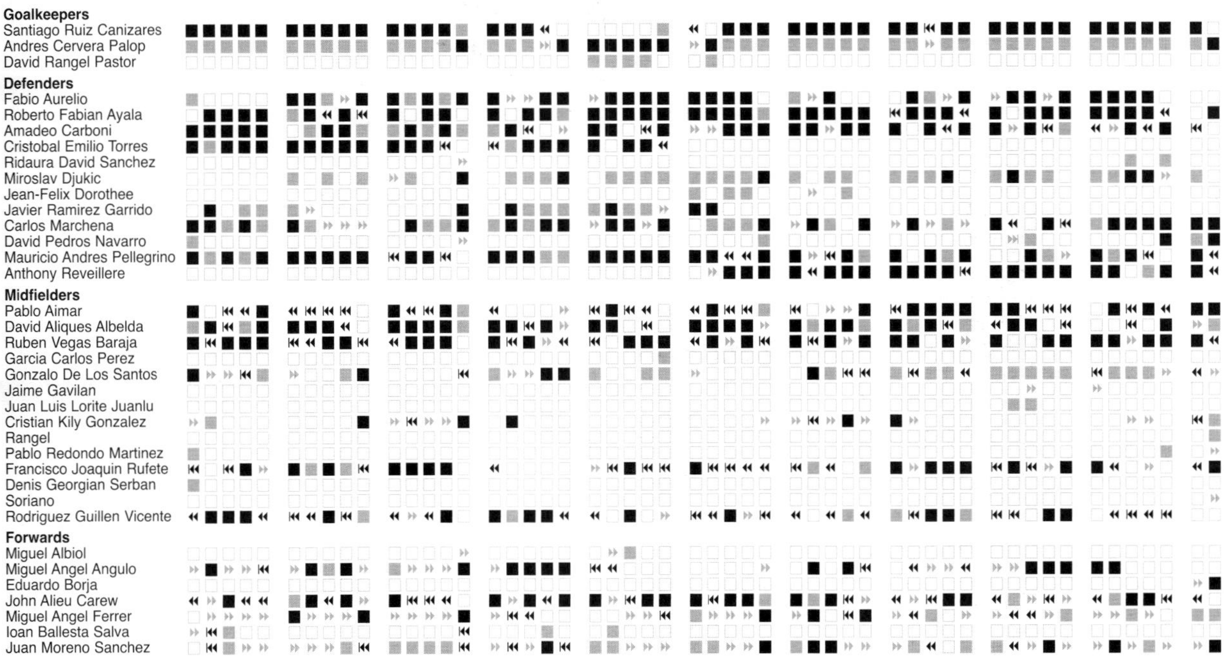

Goalkeepers
Santiago Ruiz Canizares
Andres Cervera Palop
David Rangel Pastor
Defenders
Fabio Aurelio
Roberto Fabian Ayala
Amadeo Carboni
Cristobal Emilio Torres
Ridaura David Sanchez
Miroslav Djukic
Jean-Felix Dorothee
Javier Ramirez Garrido
Carlos Marchena
David Pedros Navarro
Mauricio Andres Pellegrino
Anthony Reveillere
Midfielders
Pablo Aimar
David Aliques Albelda
Ruben Vegas Baraja
Garcia Carlos Perez
Gonzalo De Los Santos
Jaime Gavilan
Juan Luis Lorite Juanlu
Cristian Kily Gonzalez
Rangel
Pablo Redondo Martinez
Francisco Joaquin Rufete
Denis Georgian Serban
Soriano
Rodriguez Guillen Vicente
Forwards
Miguel Albiol
Miguel Angel Angulo
Eduardo Borja
John Alieu Carew
Miguel Angel Ferrer
Ioan Ballesta Salva
Juan Moreno Sanchez


KEY: On all match · On bench · Subbed or sent off (Counting game) · Subbed or sent off (playing less than 70 minutes) · Subbed on from bench (Counting Game) · Subbed on (playing less than 70 minutes) · Subbed on and then subbed or sent off (Counting Game) · Subbed on and then subbed or sent off (playing less than 70 minutes) · Not in 16

# BARCELONA

Final Position: **6th**

| | | | | | | |
|---|---|---|---|---|---|---|
| 1 | ecql1 | Legia Warsaw | H | W | 3-0 | de Boer 8; Riquelme 80; Cocu, P 90 |
| 2 | ecql2 | Legia Warsaw | A | W | 1-0 | Mendieta 68 pen |
| 3 | lge | Atl Madrid | H | D | 2-2 | Luis Enrique 4,53 |
| 4 | lge | Athl Bilbao | A | W | 2-0 | Luis Enrique 21; Saviola 36 |
| 5 | ecgh | Club Brugge | H | W | 3-2 | Luis Enrique 5; Mendieta 40; Saviola 44 |
| 6 | lge | Espanyol | H | W | 2-0 | Kluivert 58; Luis Enrique 71 |
| 7 | ecgh | Galatasaray | A | W | 2-0 | Kluivert 27; Luis Enrique 59 |
| 8 | lge | Real Betis | A | L | 0-3 | |
| 9 | ecgh | Lokomotiv M | A | W | 3-1 | Kluivert 29; Saviola 32,49 |
| 10 | lge | Osasuna | H | D | 2-2 | Motta 39; Kluivert 46 |
| 11 | lge | Valladolid | A | L | 1-2 | Saviola 89 |
| 12 | ecgh | Lokomotiv M | H | W | 1-0 | de Boer 76 |
| 13 | lge | Alaves | H | W | 6-1 | Kluivert 16,26,79; Mendieta 35 pen; Luis Enrique 40; Xavi 65 |
| 14 | ecgh | Club Brugge | A | W | 1-0 | Riquelme 64 |
| 15 | lge | R Santander | A | D | 1-1 | Navarro 83 |
| 16 | lge | Villarreal | H | W | 1-0 | Riquelme 75 pen |
| 17 | ecgh | Galatasaray | H | W | 3-1 | Dani 10; Gerard 44; Geovanni 56 |
| 18 | lge | Deportivo | A | L | 0-2 | |
| 19 | lge | Real Madrid | H | D | 0-0 | |
| 20 | ecga | B Leverkusen | A | W | 2-1 | Saviola 48; Overmars 88 |
| 21 | lge | Real Sociedad | A | L | 1-2 | Kluivert 33 |
| 22 | lge | R Vallecano | A | L | 0-1 | |
| 23 | ecga | Newcastle | H | W | 3-1 | Dani 7; Kluivert 35; Motta 58 |
| 24 | lge | Seville | H | L | 0-3 | |
| 25 | lge | Mallorca | A | W | 4-0 | Kluivert 26,48,52; Overmars 44 |
| 26 | lge | Recreativo | H | W | 3-0 | Rochemback 9; Loren 25 og; Cocu, P 80 |
| 27 | lge | Malaga | A | D | 0-0 | |
| 28 | lge | Valencia | H | L | 2-4 | Motta 38; Kluivert 89 |
| 29 | lge | Celta Vigo | A | L | 0-2 | |
| 30 | lge | Atl Madrid | A | L | 0-3 | |
| 31 | lge | Athl Bilbao | H | D | 2-2 | Saviola 5; Overmars 13 |
| 32 | lge | Espanyol | A | W | 2-0 | Cocu, P 40; Xavi 41 |
| 33 | ecga | Inter Milan | H | W | 3-0 | Saviola 7; Cocu, P 29; Kluivert 67 |
| 34 | lge | Real Betis | H | W | 4-0 | Saviola 1,40,53; Cocu, P 5 |
| 35 | ecga | Inter Milan | A | D | 0-0 | |
| 36 | lge | Osasuna | A | D | 2-2 | Luis Enrique 41; Saviola 61 |
| 37 | lge | Valladolid | H | D | 1-1 | Torres Gomez 29 og |
| 38 | ecga | B Leverkusen | H | W | 2-0 | Saviola 17; Kleine 49 og |
| 39 | lge | Alaves | A | D | 0-0 | |
| 40 | ecga | Newcastle | A | W | 2-0 | Kluivert 60; Motta 75 |
| 41 | lge | R Santander | H | W | 6-1 | Kluivert 1,30; Riquelme 7; Overmars 80,83; Mendieta 89 pen |
| 42 | lge | Villarreal | A | L | 0-2 | |
| 43 | ecqfl1 | Juventus | A | D | 1-1 | Saviola 78 |
| 44 | lge | Deportivo | H | L | 2-4 | Saviola 2; Motta 23 |
| 45 | lge | Real Madrid | A | D | 1-1 | Luis Enrique 31 |
| 46 | ecqfl2 | Juventus | H | L | 1-1 | Xavi 66 |
| 47 | lge | Real Sociedad | H | W | 2-1 | Saviola 13; Kluivert 24 |
| 48 | lge | R Vallecano | H | W | 3-0 | Luis Enrique 68; Overmars 76; Saviola 90 |
| 49 | lge | Seville | A | D | 0-0 | |
| 50 | lge | Mallorca | H | L | 1-2 | Kluivert 72 |
| 51 | lge | Recreativo | A | W | 3-1 | Saviola 43; Kluivert 53; Riquelme 84 |
| 52 | lge | Malaga | H | W | 2-1 | Saviola 24; Mendieta 67 pen |
| 53 | lge | Valencia | A | W | 3-1 | Mendieta 44 pen; Kluivert 72 pen; Overmars 79 |
| 54 | lge | Celta Vigo | H | W | 2-0 | Sorin 6; Saviola 50 |

## ATTENDANCES

HOME GROUND: NOU CAMP CAPACITY: 98600 AVERAGE LEAGUE AT HOME: 77900

| | | | | | | | | |
|---|---|---|---|---|---|---|---|---|
| 46 | Juventus | 98000 | 47 | Real Sociedad | 65700 | 14 | Club Brugge | 29773 |
| 19 | Real Madrid | 98000 | 12 | Lokomotiv Moscow | 62426 | 29 | Celta Vigo | 29574 |
| 16 | Villarreal | 96040 | 38 | B Leverkusen | 62228 | 20 | B Leverkusen | 25500 |
| 13 | Alaves | 94080 | 1 | Legia Warsaw | 60000 | 11 | Valladolid | 25175 |
| 28 | Valencia | 93100 | 30 | Atl Madrid | 57000 | 25 | Mallorca | 23700 |
| 44 | Deportivo | 91140 | 24 | Seville | 54257 | 2 | Legia Warsaw | 23000 |
| 41 | R Santander | 88200 | 53 | Valencia | 53000 | 15 | R Santander | 21375 |
| 6 | Espanyol | 85833 | 26 | Recreativo Huelva | 52920 | 4 | Athl Bilbao | 20000 |
| 3 | Atl Madrid | 85000 | 52 | Malaga | 51940 | 7 | Galatasaray | 20000 |
| 31 | Athl Bilbao | 83300 | 40 | Newcastle | 51883 | 36 | Osasuna | 19900 |
| 5 | Club Brugge | 83300 | 54 | Celta Vigo | 48507 | 51 | Recreativo Huelva | 19600 |
| 33 | Inter Milan | 82717 | 43 | Juventus | 48500 | 39 | Alaves | 18500 |
| 34 | Real Betis | 78500 | 32 | Espanyol | 48400 | 9 | Lokomotiv Moscow | 18000 |
| 10 | Osasuna | 78400 | 23 | Newcastle | 45100 | 8 | Real Betis | 18000 |
| 37 | Valladolid | 78400 | 17 | Galatasaray | 42928 | 22 | R Vallecano | 14725 |
| 48 | R Vallecano | 78400 | 18 | Deportivo | 35000 | 42 | Villarreal | 10080 |
| 50 | Mallorca | 78400 | 49 | Seville | 33750 | | | |
| 45 | Real Madrid | 76300 | 27 | Malaga | 33390 | | | |
| 35 | Inter Milan | 71740 | 21 | Real Sociedad | 32000 | | | |

■ Home □ Away ▒ Neutral

## KEY PLAYERS - GOALSCORERS

**1 Martinez Luis Enrique**

| | | | |
|---|---|---|---|
| Goals in the League | 8 | Player Strike Rate<br>Average number of minutes between League goals scored by player | 164 |
| Contribution to Attacking Power<br>Average number of minutes between League team goals while on pitch | 46 | Club Strike Rate<br>Average number of minutes between League goals scored by club | 54 |

| | PLAYER | LGE GOALS | POWER | STRIKE RATE |
|---|---|---|---|---|
| 2 | Javier Saviola | 13 | 47 | 186 mins |
| 3 | Patrick Kluivert | 16 | 55 | 196 mins |
| 4 | Marc Overmars | 6 | 48 | 289 mins |
| 5 | Thiago Motta | 3 | 72 | 506 mins |

## KEY PLAYERS - MIDFIELDERS

**1 Phillip Cocu**

| | | | |
|---|---|---|---|
| Goals in the League | 3 | Contribution to Attacking Power<br>Average number of minutes between League team goals while on pitch | 55 |
| Defensive Rating<br>Average number of mins between League goals conceded while he was on the pitch | 87 | Scoring Difference<br>Defensive Rating minus Contribution to Attacking Power | 32 |

| | PLAYER | LGE GOALS | DEF RATE | POWER | SCORE DIFF |
|---|---|---|---|---|---|
| 2 | Martinez Luis Enrique | 8 | 77 | 47 | 30 mins |
| 3 | Gaizka Mendieta | 4 | 73 | 47 | 26 mins |
| 4 | Marc Overmars | 6 | 72 | 48 | 24 mins |

## KEY PLAYERS - DEFENDERS

**1 Carlos Puyol**

| | | | |
|---|---|---|---|
| Goals Conceded (GC)<br>The number of League goals conceded while he was on the pitch | 38 | Clean Sheets<br>In games when he played at least 70 minutes | 11 |
| Defensive Rating<br>Ave number of mins between League goals conceded while on the pitch | 75 | Club Defensive Rating<br>Average number of mins between League goals conceded by the club this season | 73 |

| | PLAYER | CON LGE | CLEAN SHEETS | DEF RATE |
|---|---|---|---|---|
| 2 | Frank de Boer | 41 | 11 | 74 mins |
| 3 | Fernando Corbacho Navarro | 17 | 3 | 66 mins |
| 4 | Michael Reiziger | 25 | 5 | 62 mins |

## KEY GOALKEEPER

**1 Valdes Arribas Victor**

| | |
|---|---|
| Goals Conceded in the League | 15 |
| Defensive Rating<br>Ave number of mins between League goals conceded while on the pitch | 78 |
| Counting Games<br>Games when he played at least 70 minutes | 13 |
| Clean Sheets<br>In games when he played at least 70 minutes | 4 |

## TOP POINT EARNERS

| | PLAYER | GAMES | AVE |
|---|---|---|---|
| 1 | Victor | 13 | 1.85 |
| 2 | Luis Enrique | 12 | 1.83 |
| 3 | Mendieta | 21 | 1.62 |
| 4 | Cocu, P | 27 | 1.59 |
| 5 | Saviola | 22 | 1.59 |
| 6 | de Boer | 33 | 1.58 |
| 7 | Gabri | 18 | 1.56 |
| 8 | Puyol | 31 | 1.52 |
| 9 | Kluivert | 35 | 1.49 |
| 10 | Reiziger | 16 | 1.44 |
| | CLUB AVERAGE: | | 1.47 |

Ave = Average points per match in Counting Games

## DISCIPLINARY RECORDS

| | PLAYER | YELLOW | RED | AVE |
|---|---|---|---|---|
| 1 | Gabri | 12 | 1 | 147 |
| 2 | Navarro | 6 | 0 | 187 |
| 3 | Motta | 6 | 2 | 189 |
| 4 | Sorin | 5 | 1 | 189 |
| 5 | Gerard | 3 | 0 | 227 |
| 6 | Rochemback | 2 | 1 | 262 |
| 7 | de Boer | 10 | 0 | 303 |
| 8 | Reiziger | 5 | 0 | 310 |
| 9 | Cocu, P | 8 | 0 | 313 |
| 10 | Luis Enrique | 4 | 0 | 327 |
| 11 | Mendieta | 6 | 0 | 403 |
| 12 | Kluivert | 6 | 1 | 447 |
| 13 | Puyol | 6 | 0 | 472 |
| | Other | 11 | 2 | |
| | TOTAL | 90 | 8 | |

## LEAGUE GOALS

| | PLAYER | MINS | GOALS | AVE |
|---|---|---|---|---|
| 1 | Kluivert | 3129 | 16 | 196 |
| 2 | Saviola | 2414 | 13 | 186 |
| 3 | Luis Enrique | 1311 | 8 | 164 |
| 4 | Overmars | 1734 | 6 | 289 |
| 5 | Mendieta | 2422 | 4 | 606 |
| 6 | Motta | 1519 | 3 | 506 |
| 7 | Riquelme | 1614 | 3 | 538 |
| 8 | Cocu, P | 2511 | 3 | 837 |
| 9 | Xavi | 2507 | 2 | 1254 |
| 10 | Sorin | 1136 | 1 | 1136 |
| 11 | Navarro | 1124 | 1 | 1124 |
| 12 | Rochemback | 787 | 1 | 787 |
| | Other | | 2 | |
| | TOTAL | | 63 | |

## MONTH BY MONTH GUIDE TO THE POINTS

| MONTH | POINTS | % |
|---|---|---|
| SEPTEMBER | 7 | 58% |
| OCTOBER | 4 | 44% |
| NOVEMBER | 5 | 42% |
| DECEMBER | 3 | 25% |
| JANUARY | 4 | 33% |
| FEBRUARY | 7 | 58% |
| MARCH | 6 | 50% |
| APRIL | 4 | 33% |
| MAY | 7 | 58% |
| JUNE | 9 | 10 |

## TEAM OF THE SEASON

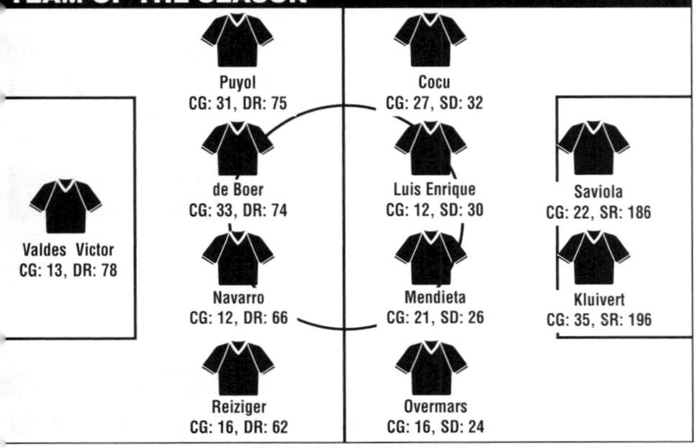
Puyol
CG: 31, DR: 75
Cocu
CG: 27, SD: 32
de Boer
CG: 33, DR: 74
Luis Enrique
CG: 12, SD: 30
Saviola
CG: 22, SR: 186
Valdes Victor
CG: 13, DR: 78
Navarro
CG: 12, DR: 66
Mendieta
CG: 21, SD: 26
Kluivert
CG: 35, SR: 196
Reiziger
CG: 16, DR: 62
Overmars
CG: 16, SD: 24

**KEY:** DR = Defensive Rate, SD = Scoring Difference, SR = Strike Rate, CG = Counting Games – League games playing at least 70 minutes

## LEAGUE APPEARANCES, BOOKINGS AND CAPS

| | AGE | IN THE SQUAD | COUNTING GAMES | MINUTES ON PITCH | YELLOW CARDS | RED CARDS | THIS SEASON | HOME COUNTRY |
|---|---|---|---|---|---|---|---|---|
| **Goalkeepers** | | | | | | | | |
| Roberto Bonano | 33 | 29 | 24 | 2139 | 1 | 0 | - | Argentina |
| Robert Enke | 25 | 28 | 0 | 21 | 0 | 0 | - | Germany |
| Valdes Victor | 21 | 18 | 13 | 1170 | 0 | 0 | - | Spain |
| **Defenders** | | | | | | | | |
| Patrik Andersson | 31 | 18 | 2 | 238 | 0 | 0 | - | Sweden |
| Philippe Christanval | 24 | 19 | 3 | 349 | 1 | 0 | 2 | France (2) |
| Daniel Dani Tortolero | 21 | 1 | 0 | 0 | 0 | 0 | - | Spain |
| Frank de Boer | 33 | 35 | 33 | 3038 | 10 | 0 | 9 | Holland (6) |
| Fernando Navarro | 21 | 13 | 12 | 1124 | 6 | 0 | - | Spain |
| Presas Oleguer | 23 | 7 | 3 | 238 | 0 | 0 | - | Spain |
| Oscar Lopez | 23 | 2 | 2 | 180 | 0 | 0 | - | Spain |
| Carlos Pena | - | 1 | 0 | 0 | 0 | 0 | - | Spain |
| Carlos Puyol | 25 | 32 | 31 | 2836 | 6 | 0 | 6 | Spain (2) |
| Michael Reiziger | 30 | 32 | 16 | 1553 | 5 | 0 | 7 | Holland (6) |
| Juan Pablo Sorin | 27 | 15 | 11 | 1136 | 5 | 1 | 2 | Argentina (5) |
| **Midfielders** | | | | | | | | |
| Phillip Cocu | 32 | 29 | 27 | 2511 | 8 | 0 | 7 | Holland (6) |
| Garcia Gabri | 24 | 29 | 18 | 1913 | 12 | 1 | 2 | Spain (2) |
| Deiberson Geovanni | - | 0 | 0 | 0 | 0 | 0 | - | |
| Lopez Segu Gerard | 24 | 29 | 3 | 683 | 3 | 0 | - | Spain |
| Andres Iniesta Lujan | 19 | 10 | 4 | 448 | 1 | 0 | - | Spain |
| Luis Enrique | 33 | 19 | 12 | 1311 | 4 | 0 | - | Spain |
| Gaizka Mendieta | 29 | 37 | 21 | 2422 | 6 | 0 | 5 | Spain (2) |
| Thiago Motta | 20 | 23 | 13 | 1519 | 6 | 2 | - | Brazil |
| Marc Overmars | 30 | 26 | 16 | 1734 | 2 | 1 | 2 | Holland (6) |
| Fabio Rochemback | 21 | 36 | 3 | 787 | 2 | 1 | - | Brazil |
| Sergio Garcia | 20 | 7 | 0 | 0 | 0 | 0 | - | Spain |
| Valdes | - | 1 | 1 | 90 | 0 | 0 | - | |
| Xavi Hernandez | 23 | 30 | 27 | 2507 | 0 | 0 | 8 | Spain (2) |
| **Forwards** | | | | | | | | |
| Dani | 28 | 26 | 0 | 228 | 0 | 0 | - | Spain |
| Sanchez David | 20 | 1 | 0 | 0 | 0 | 0 | - | Spain |
| Deiberson Geovanni | - | 15 | 0 | 79 | 0 | 0 | - | Brazil |
| Patrick Kluivert | 27 | 36 | 35 | 3129 | 6 | 1 | 9 | Holland (6) |
| Fernando Macedo | 21 | 7 | 0 | 43 | 0 | 0 | - | Spain |
| Juan Riquelme | 25 | 36 | 12 | 1614 | 2 | 0 | 2 | Argentina (5) |
| Javier Saviola | 21 | 36 | 22 | 2414 | 4 | 1 | 4 | Argentina (5) |

**KEY:** LEAGUE BOOKINGS CAPS (FIFA RANKING)

## SQUAD APPEARANCES

| Match | 1 | 2 | 3 | 4 | 5 | 6 | 7 | 8 | 9 | 10 | 11 | 12 | 13 | 14 | 15 | 16 | 17 | 18 | 19 | 20 | 21 | 22 | 23 | 24 | 25 | 26 | 27 |
|---|---|---|---|---|---|---|---|---|---|---|---|---|---|---|---|---|---|---|---|---|---|---|---|---|---|---|---|
| Venue | H | A | H | A | H | H | A | A | A | H | A | H | H | A | A | H | H | A | H | A | A | A | H | H | A | H | A |
| Competition | C | C | L | L | C | L | C | L | C | L | L | C | L | C | L | L | C | L | L | C | L | L | C | L | L | L | L |
| Result | W | W | D | W | W | W | W | L | W | D | L | W | W | W | D | W | W | L | D | W | L | L | W | L | W | W | D |

| Match | 28 | 29 | 30 | 31 | 32 | 33 | 34 | 35 | 36 | 37 | 38 | 39 | 40 | 41 | 42 | 43 | 44 | 45 | 46 | 47 | 48 | 49 | 50 | 51 | 52 | 53 | 54 |
|---|---|---|---|---|---|---|---|---|---|---|---|---|---|---|---|---|---|---|---|---|---|---|---|---|---|---|---|
| Venue | H | A | A | H | A | H | H | A | A | H | H | A | A | H | A | A | H | A | H | H | H | A | H | A | H | A | H |
| Competition | L | L | L | L | L | C | L | C | L | L | C | L | C | L | L | C | L | L | C | L | L | L | L | L | L | L | L |
| Result | L | L | L | D | W | W | W | D | D | D | W | D | W | W | L | D | L | D | L | W | W | D | L | W | W | W | W |

**Goalkeepers**
Roberto Bonano
Robert Enke
Valdes Arribas Victor

**Defenders**
Patrik Andersson
Philippe Christanval
Daniel Dani Tortolero
Frank de Boer
Fernando Navarro
Presas Oleguer
Hernandez Oscar Lopez
Carlos Gonzalez Pena
Carlos Puyol
Michael Reiziger
Juan Pablo Sorin

**Midfielders**
Phillip Cocu
Garcia de la Torre Gabri
Lopez Segu Gerard
Andres Iniesta Lujan
Martinez Luis Enrique
Gaizka Mendieta
Thiago Motta
Marc Overmars
Fabio Rochemback
de la Fuente Sergio Garcia
Vald?s
Xavi Hernandez

**Forwards**
Daniel Garcia Lara Dani
Sanchez David
Deiberson Geovanni
Patrick Kluivert
Fernando Macedo da Silva
Juan Riquelme
Javier Saviola

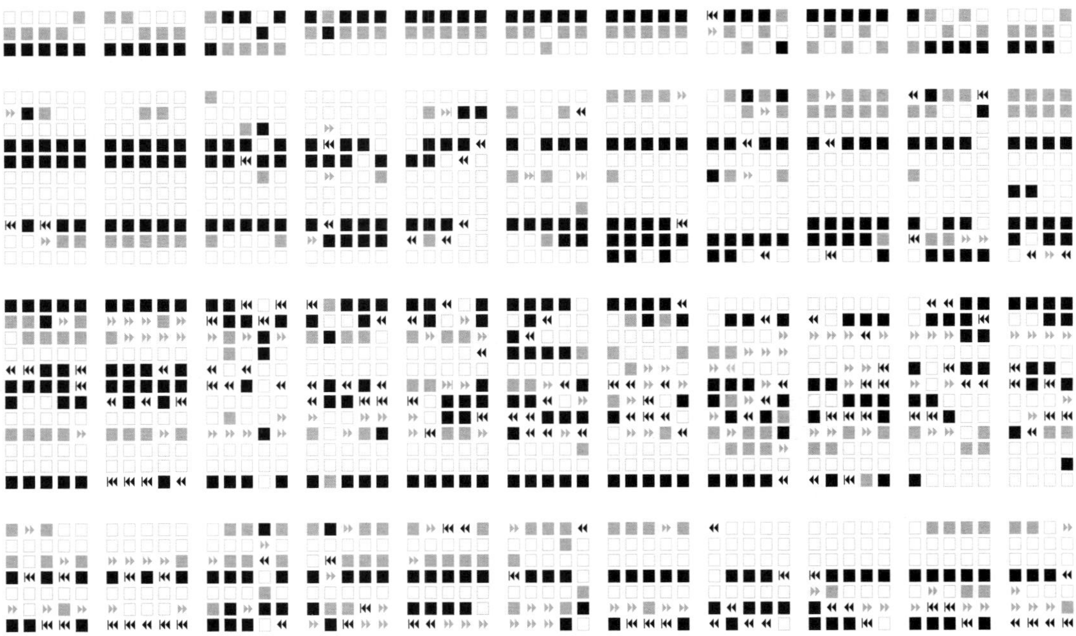

**KEY:** ■ On all match ■ On bench ⏮ Subbed or sent off (Counting game) « Subbed or sent off (playing less than 70 minutes) » Subbed on from bench (Counting Game) » Subbed on (playing less than 70 minutes) » Subbed on and then subbed or sent off (Counting Game) » Subbed on and then subbed or sent off (playing less than 70 minutes) □ Not in 16

# ATHLETIC BILBAO

Final Position: **7th**

| | | | | | | |
|---|---|---|---|---|---|---|
| 1 | lge | Real Sociedad | A | L | 2-4 | Gurpegui 29,74 |
| 2 | lge | Barcelona | H | L | 0-2 | |
| 3 | lge | Seville | A | D | 1-1 | Joseba Etxeberria 80 |
| 4 | lge | Mallorca | H | L | 0-2 | |
| 5 | lge | Recreativo | A | W | 2-1 | Gurpegui 62; Tiko 85 |
| 6 | lge | Malaga | H | D | 1-1 | Ezquerro 6 |
| 7 | lge | Valencia | A | L | 1-5 | Aitor Ocio 84 |
| 8 | lge | Celta Vigo | H | W | 2-1 | Joseba Etxeberria 80; Urzaiz 90 |
| 9 | lge | Atl Madrid | A | D | 3-3 | Urzaiz 48,52,82 |
| 10 | lge | R Vallecano | H | W | 2-1 | Urzaiz 76; Larrazabal 80 pen |
| 11 | lge | Espanyol | H | W | 4-1 | Larrazabal 19 pen; Gurpegui 48; Urzaiz 70; Joseba Etxeberria 78 |
| 12 | lge | Real Betis | A | L | 0-1 | |
| 13 | lge | Osasuna | H | L | 1-3 | Urzaiz 9 |
| 14 | lge | Valladolid | A | L | 0-2 | |
| 15 | lge | Alaves | H | W | 2-0 | Urzaiz 15; Joseba Etxeberria 30 |
| 16 | lge | R Santander | A | W | 4-3 | Mora 40 og; Urzaiz 52 pen; Joseba Etxeberria 61,87 |
| 17 | lge | Villarreal | H | L | 0-1 | |
| 18 | lge | Deportivo | A | L | 1-2 | Hector 48 og |
| 19 | lge | Real Madrid | H | D | 1-1 | Del Horno 70 |
| 20 | lge | Real Sociedad | H | W | 3-0 | Joseba Etxeberria 18,73; Ezquerro 90 |
| 21 | lge | Barcelona | A | D | 2-2 | Ezquerro 47 pen; Yeste 55 |
| 22 | lge | Seville | H | W | 2-0 | Joseba Etxeberria 60; Ezquerro 89 pen |
| 23 | lge | Mallorca | A | D | 1-1 | Ezquerro 5 |
| 24 | lge | Recreativo | H | L | 2-3 | Del Horno 58; Ezquerro 76 |
| 25 | lge | Malaga | A | L | 0-3 | |
| 26 | lge | Valencia | H | W | 1-0 | Joseba Etxeberria 38 |
| 27 | lge | Celta Vigo | A | L | 1-2 | Del Horno 7 |
| 28 | lge | Atl Madrid | H | W | 1-0 | Ezquerro 83 |
| 29 | lge | R Vallecano | A | D | 1-1 | Urzaiz 77 |
| 30 | lge | Espanyol | A | D | 3-3 | Ezquerro 2; Yeste 23,29; Urzaiz 36 |
| 31 | lge | Real Betis | H | W | 3-1 | Joseba Etxeberria 35; Urzaiz 41; Ezquerro 45 |
| 32 | lge | Osasuna | A | W | 5-1 | Aitor Ocio 15; Ezquerro 31; Yeste 41; Arriaga 65; Karanka 76 |
| 33 | lge | Valladolid | H | D | 0-0 | |
| 34 | lge | Alaves | A | W | 4-2 | Yeste 20; Urzaiz 57; Joseba Etxeberria 75,87 |
| 35 | lge | R Santander | H | W | 2-1 | Karanka 55; Urzaiz 90 pen |
| 36 | lge | Villarreal | A | D | 1-1 | Joseba Etxeberria 30 |
| 37 | lge | Deportivo | H | W | 3-2 | Del Horno 14; Yeste 43; Urzaiz 70 |
| 38 | lge | Real Madrid | A | L | 1-3 | Alkiza 35 |

## KEY PLAYERS - GOALSCORERS

**1 Ismael Urzaiz**

| | | | |
|---|---|---|---|
| **Goals in the League** | 15 | **Player Strike Rate** Average number of minutes between League goals scored by player | 176 |
| **Contribution to Attacking Power** Average number of minutes between League team goals while on pitch | 51 | **Club Strike Rate** Average number of minutes between League goals scored by club | 53 |

| | PLAYER | LGE GOALS | POWER | STRIKE RATE |
|---|---|---|---|---|
| 2 | Joseba Etxeberria Lizardi | 14 | 50 | 195 mins |
| 3 | Santiago Ezquerro Marin | 10 | 50 | 246 mins |
| 4 | Francisco Navaro Yeste | 6 | 47 | 282 mins |
| 5 | Asier Del Horno | 4 | 49 | 480 mins |

## KEY PLAYERS - MIDFIELDERS

**1 Luis Prieto**

| | | | |
|---|---|---|---|
| **Goals in the League** | 0 | **Contribution to Attacking Power** Average number of minutes between League team goals while on pitch | 42 |
| **Defensive Rating** Average number of mins between League goals conceded while he was on the pitch | 62 | **Scoring Difference** Defensive Rating minus Contribution to Attacking Power | 20 |

| | PLAYER | LGE GOALS | DEF RATE | POWER | SCORE DIFF |
|---|---|---|---|---|---|
| 2 | Bittor Alkiza Fernandez | 1 | 63 | 48 | 15 mins |
| 3 | Roberto Martinez Tiko | 1 | 69 | 55 | 14 mins |
| 4 | Francisco Navaro Yeste | 6 | 56 | 47 | 9 mins |
| 5 | Carlos Nausia Gurpegui | 4 | 51 | 63 | -12 mins |

## KEY PLAYERS - DEFENDERS

**1 Carrion Aitor Ocio**

| | | | |
|---|---|---|---|
| **Goals Conceded (GC)** The number of League goals conceded while he was on the pitch | 17 | **Clean Sheets** In games when he played at least 70 minutes | 3 |
| **Defensive Rating** Ave number of mins between League goals conceded while on the pitch | 64 | **Club Defensive Rating** Average number of mins between League goals conceded by the club this season | 56 |

| | PLAYER | CON LGE | CLEAN SHEETS | DEF RATE |
|---|---|---|---|---|
| 2 | Oscar Vales Varela | 27 | 3 | 60 mins |
| 3 | Asier Del Horno | 33 | 5 | 58 mins |
| 4 | Jesus Maria Lacruz Gomez | 33 | 2 | 56 mins |
| 5 | Aitor Larrazabal Bilbao | 27 | 1 | 55 mins |

## GOALS SCORED

**AT HOME**

| | | |
|---|---|---|
| MOST | R Madrid | 52 |
| | | 30 |
| LEAST | R Vallecano | 17 |

**AWAY**

| | | |
|---|---|---|
| MOST | R Madrid | 34 |
| | | 33 |
| LEAST | Recreativo | 11 |

## GOALS CONCEDED

**AT HOME**

| | | |
|---|---|---|
| LEAST | C Vigo & Valencia | 15 |
| | | 20 |
| MOST | Mallorca | 33 |

**AWAY**

| | | |
|---|---|---|
| LEAST | R Madrid, Valencia & Seville | 20 |
| | | 41 |
| MOST | Alaves | 48 |

## KEY GOALKEEPER

**1 Daniel Aranzubia Aguado**

| | |
|---|---|
| **Goals Conceded in the League** | 35 |
| **Defensive Rating** Ave number of mins between League goals conceded while on the pitch | 64 |
| **Counting Games** Games when he played at least 70 minutes | 25 |
| **Clean Sheets** In games when he played at least 70 minutes | 6 |

## TOP POINT EARNERS

| | PLAYER | GAMES | AVE |
|---|---|---|---|
| 1 | Prieto | 13 | 2.08 |
| 2 | Yeste | 15 | 1.67 |
| 3 | Alkiza | 28 | 1.64 |
| 4 | Joseba Etxeberria | 27 | 1.63 |
| 5 | Del Horno | 21 | 1.62 |
| 6 | Ezquerro | 25 | 1.60 |
| 7 | Aranzubia | 25 | 1.60 |
| 8 | Urzaiz | 29 | 1.59 |
| 9 | Karanka | 21 | 1.57 |
| 10 | Javi Gonzalez | 28 | 1.54 |
| | **CLUB AVERAGE:** | | **1.45** |

Ave = Average points per match in Counting Games

## ATTENDANCES

**HOME GROUND: SAN MAMES CAPACITY: 46500 AVERAGE LEAGUE AT HOME: 33642**

| | | | | | | | |
|---|---|---|---|---|---|---|---|
| 21 | Barcelona | 83300 | | | | | |
| 38 | Real Madrid | 76300 | | | | | |
| 7 | Valencia | 47700 | | | | | |
| 9 | Atl Madrid | 42750 | | | | | |
| 20 | Real Sociedad | 39600 | | | | | |
| 37 | Deportivo | 39600 | | | | | |
| 17 | Villarreal | 38400 | | | | | |
| 19 | Real Madrid | 38000 | | | | | |
| 28 | Atl Madrid | 38000 | | | | | |
| 35 | R Santander | 38000 | | | | | |
| 12 | Real Betis | 36750 | | | | | |
| 4 | Mallorca | 36000 | | | | | |
| 33 | Valladolid | 36000 | | | | | |
| 22 | Seville | 36000 | | | | | |
| 11 | Espanyol | 34000 | | | | | |
| 26 | Valencia | 32400 | | | | | |
| 6 | Malaga | 32000 | | | | | |
| 13 | Osasuna | 32000 | | | | | |
| 15 | Alaves | 32000 | | | | | |
| 10 | R Vallecano | 32000 | | | | | |
| 8 | Celta Vigo | 31200 | | | | | |
| 1 | Real Sociedad | 30000 | | | | | |
| 27 | Celta Vigo | 29900 | | | | | |
| 31 | Real Betis | 29600 | | | | | |
| 18 | Deportivo | 28480 | | | | | |
| 3 | Seville | 27000 | | | | | |
| 25 | Malaga | 26000 | | | | | |
| 24 | Recreativo Huelva | 24400 | | | | | |
| 16 | R Santander | 21150 | | | | | |
| 14 | Valladolid | 20935 | | | | | |
| 2 | Barcelona | 20000 | | | | | |
| 30 | Espanyol | 19250 | | | | | |
| 5 | Recreativo Huelva | 18000 | | | | | |
| 34 | Alaves | 16520 | | | | | |
| 32 | Osasuna | 15125 | | | | | |
| 36 | Villarreal | 13105 | | | | | |
| 29 | R Vallecano | 12100 | | | | | |
| 23 | Mallorca | 11850 | | | | | |

■ Home □ Away ▒ Neutral

## DISCIPLINARY RECORDS

| | PLAYER | YELLOW | RED | AVE |
|---|---|---|---|---|
| 1 | Cesar | 5 | 0 | 142 |
| 2 | Karanka | 9 | 0 | 208 |
| 3 | Del Horno | 8 | 1 | 213 |
| 4 | Prieto | 6 | 0 | 218 |
| 5 | Urzaiz | 9 | 1 | 264 |
| 6 | Gurpegui | 7 | 0 | 314 |
| 7 | Yeste | 5 | 0 | 338 |
| 8 | Aitor Ocio | 3 | 0 | 363 |
| 9 | Alkiza | 7 | 0 | 369 |
| 10 | Lacruz Gomez | 4 | 0 | 461 |
| 11 | Arriaga | 3 | 0 | 466 |
| 12 | Larrazabal | 3 | 0 | 492 |
| 13 | Ezquerro | 5 | 0 | 492 |
| | Other | 21 | 0 | |
| | **TOTAL** | **95** | **2** | |

## LEAGUE GOALS

| | PLAYER | MINS | GOALS | AVE |
|---|---|---|---|---|
| 1 | Urzaiz | 2642 | 14 | 189 |
| 2 | J Etxeberria | 2727 | 14 | 195 |
| 3 | Ezquerro | 2462 | 10 | 246 |
| 4 | Yeste | 1693 | 6 | 282 |
| 5 | Del Horno | 1918 | 4 | 480 |
| 6 | Gurpegui | 2203 | 4 | 551 |
| 7 | Aitor Ocio | 1091 | 2 | 546 |
| 8 | Karanka | 1878 | 2 | 939 |
| 9 | Larrazabal | 1478 | 2 | 739 |
| 10 | Alkiza | 2588 | 1 | 2588 |
| 11 | Arriaga | 1400 | 1 | 1400 |
| 12 | Tiko | 1719 | 1 | 1719 |
| | Other | | 2 | |
| | **TOTAL** | | **63** | |

## MONTH BY MONTH GUIDE TO THE POINTS

| MONTH | POINTS | % |
|---|---|---|
| SEPTEMBER | 1 | 8% |
| OCTOBER | 4 | 44% |
| NOVEMBER | 10 | 83% |
| DECEMBER | 3 | 25% |
| JANUARY | 4 | 33% |
| FEBRUARY | 8 | 67% |
| MARCH | 3 | 25% |
| APRIL | 8 | 67% |
| MAY | 10 | 83% |
| JUNE | 4 | 44% |

## TEAM OF THE SEASON

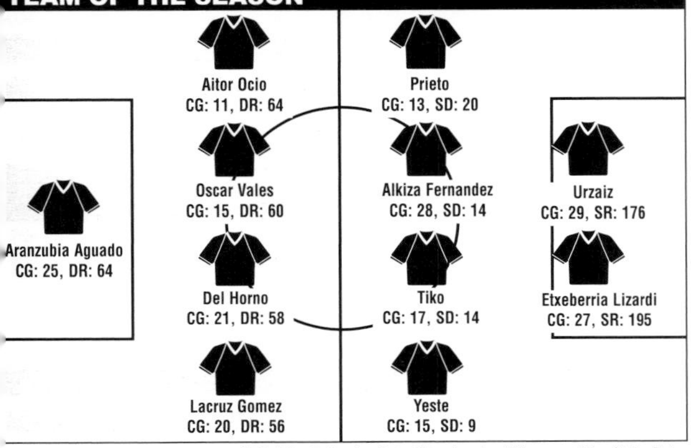
Aitor Ocio
CG: 11, DR: 64
Prieto
CG: 13, SD: 20
Oscar Vales
CG: 15, DR: 60
Alkiza Fernandez
CG: 28, SD: 14
Urzaiz
CG: 29, SR: 176
Aranzubia Aguado
CG: 25, DR: 64
Del Horno
CG: 21, DR: 58
Tiko
CG: 17, SD: 14
Etxeberria Lizardi
CG: 27, SR: 195
Lacruz Gomez
CG: 20, DR: 56
Yeste
CG: 15, SD: 9

KEY: DR = Defensive Rate, SD = Scoring Difference, SR = Strike Rate,
CG = Counting Games – League games playing at least 70 minutes

## LEAGUE APPEARANCES, BOOKINGS AND CAPS

| | AGE | IN THE SQUAD | COUNTING GAMES | MINUTES ON PITCH | YELLOW CARDS | RED CARDS | THIS SEASON | HOME COUNTRY |
|---|---|---|---|---|---|---|---|---|
| **Goalkeepers** | | | | | | | | |
| Daniel Aguado | 23 | 38 | 25 | 2250 | 1 | 0 | - | Spain |
| Miguel Escalona | 19 | 4 | 0 | 0 | 0 | 0 | - | Spain |
| Inaki Sancha | 27 | 35 | 13 | 1170 | 1 | 0 | - | Spain |
| **Defenders** | | | | | | | | |
| Carrion Aitor Ocio | 26 | 27 | 11 | 1091 | 3 | 0 | - | Spain |
| Ander Alana | 21 | 2 | 0 | 0 | 0 | 0 | - | Spain |
| Fernandez Cesar | 25 | 24 | 7 | 711 | 5 | 0 | - | Spain |
| Asier Del Horno | 22 | 28 | 21 | 1918 | 8 | 1 | - | Spain |
| Dias Felipe Dal Belo | 18 | 10 | 0 | 40 | 0 | 0 | - | Brazil |
| Jesus Lacruz Gomez | 25 | 30 | 20 | 1844 | 4 | 0 | - | Spain |
| Inigo Larrainzar | 32 | 19 | 3 | 335 | 0 | 0 | - | Spain |
| Larrazabal | 32 | 34 | 16 | 1478 | 3 | 0 | - | Spain |
| Ander Murillo | 19 | 28 | 12 | 1201 | 2 | 0 | - | Spain |
| Pablo Orbaiz Lesaca | 24 | 8 | 1 | 196 | 2 | 0 | 1 | Spain (2) |
| Oscar Vales Varela | 28 | 30 | 15 | 1614 | 2 | 0 | - | Spain |
| **Midfielders** | | | | | | | | |
| Bittor Alkiza | 32 | 32 | 28 | 2588 | 7 | 0 | - | Spain |
| Igor Aboniga Angulo | 19 | 3 | 0 | 3 | 0 | 0 | - | Spain |
| Gurendez Felipe | 27 | 6 | 0 | 5 | 1 | 0 | - | Spain |
| Carlos Garcia | 32 | 1 | 0 | 4 | 0 | 0 | - | Spain |
| Guerrero Lopez | 29 | 36 | 1 | 370 | 1 | 0 | - | Spain |
| Carlos Gurpegui | 22 | 27 | 23 | 2203 | 7 | 0 | - | Spain |
| Merino Gonzalez | 23 | 5 | 0 | 0 | 0 | 0 | - | Spain |
| Luis Prieto | 24 | 21 | 13 | 1310 | 6 | 0 | - | Spain |
| Roberto Tiko | 26 | 36 | 17 | 1719 | 3 | 0 | - | Spain |
| Jose Telleria Urrutia | 35 | 8 | 0 | 0 | 0 | 0 | - | Spain |
| Francisco Yeste | 23 | 30 | 15 | 1693 | 5 | 0 | - | Spain |
| **Forwards** | | | | | | | | |
| Aritz Aduriz | 22 | 7 | 0 | 53 | 0 | 0 | - | Spain |
| Joseba Arriaga | 20 | 35 | 11 | 1400 | 3 | 0 | - | Spain |
| Ezquerro Marin | 26 | 36 | 25 | 2462 | 5 | 0 | - | Spain |
| Javi Gonzalez | 29 | 36 | 28 | 2706 | 3 | 0 | - | Spain |
| Joseba Etxeberria | 25 | 33 | 27 | 2727 | 5 | 0 | 6 | Spain (2) |
| David Karanka | 29 | 31 | 21 | 1878 | 9 | 0 | - | Spain |
| Ismael Urzaiz | 31 | 33 | 29 | 2642 | 9 | 1 | - | Spain |

KEY: LEAGUE BOOKINGS CAPS (FIFA RANKING)

## SQUAD APPEARANCES

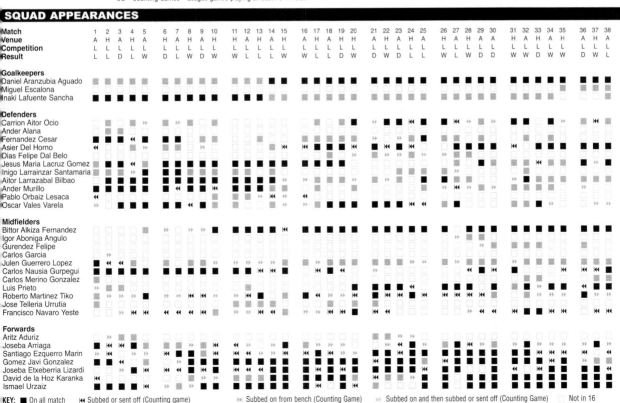

| Match | 1 | 2 | 3 | 4 | 5 | 6 | 7 | 8 | 9 | 10 | 11 | 12 | 13 | 14 | 15 | 16 | 17 | 18 | 19 | 20 | 21 | 22 | 23 | 24 | 25 | 26 | 27 | 28 | 29 | 30 | 31 | 32 | 33 | 34 | 35 | 36 | 37 | 38 |
|---|---|---|---|---|---|---|---|---|---|---|---|---|---|---|---|---|---|---|---|---|---|---|---|---|---|---|---|---|---|---|---|---|---|---|---|---|---|---|
| Venue | A | H | A | H | A | H | A | H | A | H | H | A | H | A | H | A | H | A | H | H | A | H | A | H | A | H | A | H | A | A | H | A | H | A | H | A | H | A |
| Competition | L | L | L | L | L | L | L | L | L | L | L | L | L | L | L | L | L | L | L | L | L | L | L | L | L | L | L | L | L | L | L | L | L | L | L | L | L | L |
| Result | L | L | D | L | W | D | L | W | D | W | W | L | L | L | W | W | L | L | D | W | D | W | D | L | L | W | L | W | D | D | W | W | D | W | W | D | W | L |

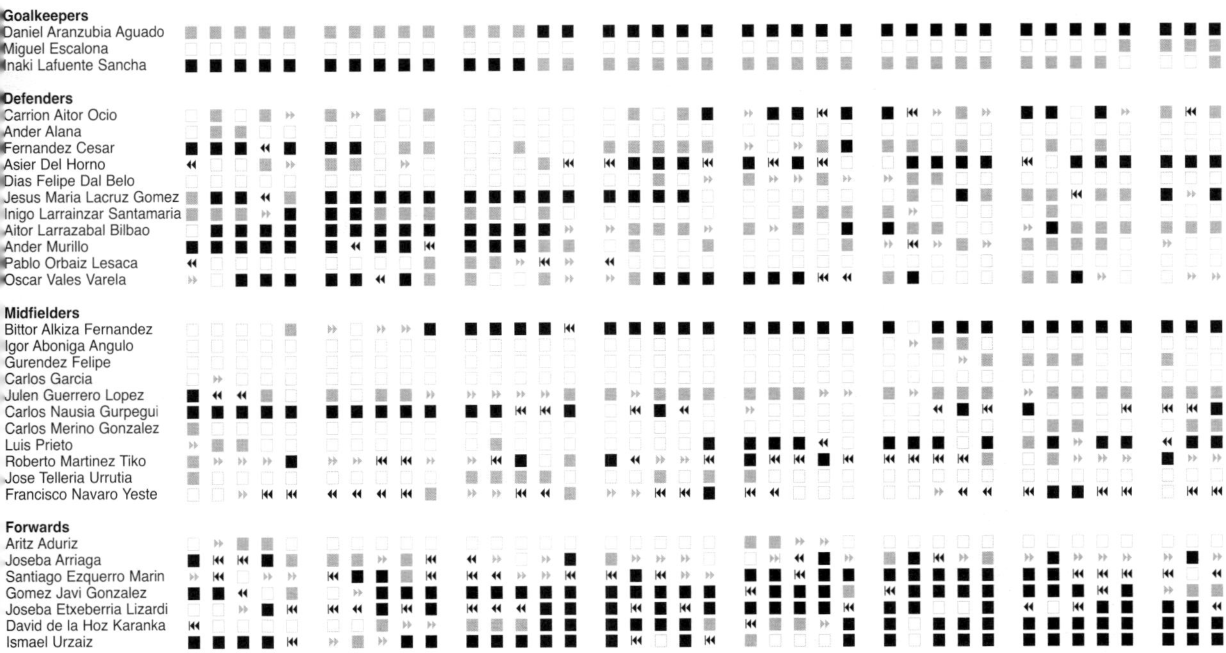
Goalkeepers
Daniel Aranzubia Aguado
Miguel Escalona
Inaki Lafuente Sancha
Defenders
Carrion Aitor Ocio
Ander Alana
Fernandez Cesar
Asier Del Horno
Dias Felipe Dal Belo
Jesus Maria Lacruz Gomez
Inigo Larrainzar Santamaria
Aitor Larrazabal Bilbao
Ander Murillo
Pablo Orbaiz Lesaca
Oscar Vales Varela
Midfielders
Bittor Alkiza Fernandez
Igor Aboniga Angulo
Gurendez Felipe
Carlos Garcia
Julen Guerrero Lopez
Carlos Nausia Gurpegui
Carlos Merino Gonzalez
Luis Prieto
Roberto Martinez Tiko
Jose Telleria Urrutia
Francisco Navaro Yeste
Forwards
Aritz Aduriz
Joseba Arriaga
Santiago Ezquerro Marin
Gomez Javi Gonzalez
Joseba Etxeberria Lizardi
David de la Hoz Karanka
Ismael Urzaiz

KEY: On all match; On bench; Subbed or sent off (Counting game); Subbed or sent off (playing less than 70 minutes); Subbed on from bench (Counting Game); Subbed on (playing less than 70 minutes); Subbed on and then subbed or sent off (Counting Game); Subbed on and then subbed or sent off (playing less than 70 minutes); Not in 16

# REAL BETIS

Final Position: **8th**

| | | | | | | |
|---|---|---|---|---|---|---|
| 1 | lge | Deportivo | A | W | 4-2 | Assuncao 22; Alfonso 25 pen; Arzu 39; Joaquin 52 |
| 2 | uc1rl1 | Zimbru | A | W | 2-0 | Alfonso 35; Dinu 45 og |
| 3 | lge | Real Sociedad | A | D | 3-3 | Capi 13,26; Alfonso 60 |
| 4 | lge | Barcelona | H | W | 3-0 | Alfonso 25 pen; Joaquin 66; Varela 84 |
| 5 | uc1rl2 | Zimbru | H | W | 2-1 | Tais 23; Casas 30 |
| 6 | lge | Seville | A | D | 1-1 | Joaquin 17 |
| 7 | lge | Real Madrid | H | D | 1-1 | Capi 34 |
| 8 | lge | Mallorca | H | L | 0-1 | |
| 9 | lge | Recreativo H | A | D | 1-1 | Casas 44 |
| 10 | uc2rl1 | Zizkov | A | W | 1-0 | Denilson 45 |
| 11 | lge | Malaga | H | W | 3-0 | Arzu 49; Fernando 57,76 pen |
| 12 | lge | Valencia | A | D | 1-1 | Assuncao 69 |
| 13 | uc2rl2 | Zizkov | H | W | 3-0 | Casas 45; Joaquin 57 pen; Tomas 87 |
| 14 | lge | Celta Vigo | H | W | 2-1 | Alfonso 69; Joaquin 87 |
| 15 | lge | Atl Madrid | A | L | 0-1 | |
| 16 | uc3rl1 | Auxerre | H | W | 1-0 | Alfonso 9 pen |
| 17 | lge | Athl Bilbao | H | W | 1-0 | Assuncao 75 |
| 18 | lge | Espanyol | A | W | 4-2 | Capi 12; Juanito 21; Fernando 72,86 |
| 19 | uc3rl2 | Auxerre | A | L | 0-2 | |
| 20 | lge | R Vallecano | H | L | 0-1 | |
| 21 | lge | Osasuna | H | W | 2-1 | Alfonso 18; Assuncao 90 |
| 22 | lge | Valladolid | A | L | 0-3 | |
| 23 | lge | Alaves | H | D | 2-2 | Fernando 44; Joaquin 90 |
| 24 | lge | R Santander | A | W | 1-0 | Joaquin 90 |
| 25 | lge | Villarreal | H | W | 2-1 | Denilson 19,77 |
| 26 | lge | Deportivo | H | L | 0-2 | |
| 27 | lge | Real Madrid | A | L | 1-4 | Fernando 36 |
| 28 | lge | Real Sociedad | H | W | 3-2 | Fernando 11,90 pen; Filipescu 86 |
| 29 | lge | Barcelona | A | L | 0-4 | |
| 30 | lge | Seville | H | L | 0-1 | |
| 31 | lge | Mallorca | A | L | 1-2 | Fernando 22 |
| 32 | lge | Recreativo | H | D | 1-1 | Capi 10 |
| 33 | lge | Malaga | A | D | 0-0 | |
| 34 | lge | Valencia | H | W | 2-0 | Fernando 36; Arzu 64 |
| 35 | lge | Celta Vigo | A | L | 0-1 | |
| 36 | lge | Atl Madrid | H | D | 2-2 | Alfonso 47; Arzu 84 |
| 37 | lge | Athl Bilbao | A | L | 1-3 | Fernando 26 |
| 38 | lge | Espanyol | H | D | 1-1 | Fernando 34 |
| 39 | lge | R Vallecano | A | D | 1-1 | Fernando 43 |
| 40 | lge | Osasuna | A | L | 1-2 | Juanito 27 |
| 41 | lge | Valladolid | H | D | 2-2 | Filipescu 64; Dani 88 |
| 42 | lge | Alaves | A | W | 1-0 | Fernando 56 |
| 43 | lge | R Santander | H | W | 4-2 | Fernando 12 pen; Joaquin 45; Dani 61; Assuncao 81 |
| 44 | lge | Villarreal | A | W | 4-1 | Dani 25,57; Joaquin 35,78 |

## KEY PLAYERS - GOALSCORERS

**1 Fernandez Escribano Fernando**

| | | | |
|---|---|---|---|
| **Goals in the League** | 15 | **Player Strike Rate** Average number of minutes between League goals scored by player | 163 |
| **Contribution to Attacking Power** Average number of minutes between League team goals while on pitch | 62 | **Club Strike Rate** Average number of minutes between League goals scored by club | 61 |

| | PLAYER | LGE GOALS | POWER | STRIKE RATE |
|---|---|---|---|---|
| 2 | Joaquin Sanchez Rodriguez | 9 | 62 | 349 mins |
| 3 | Zacarias Marcos Assuncao | 5 | 56 | 476 mins |
| 4 | Jesus Capitan Prada | 5 | 54 | 516 mins |
| 5 | Arturo Garcia Munoz | 4 | 61 | 664 mins |

## KEY PLAYERS - MIDFIELDERS

**1 Antonio Alvarez Ito**

| | | | |
|---|---|---|---|
| **Goals in the League** | 0 | **Contribution to Attacking Power** Average number of minutes between League team goals while on pitch | 62 |
| **Defensive Rating** Average number of mins between League goals conceded while he was on the pitch | 100 | **Scoring Difference** Defensive Rating minus Contribution to Attacking Power | 38 |

| | PLAYER | LGE GOALS | DEF RATE | POWER | SCORE DIFF |
|---|---|---|---|---|---|
| 2 | Jesus Capitan Prada | 5 | 63 | 55 | 8 mins |
| 3 | Zacarias Marcos Assuncao | 5 | 64 | 57 | 7 mins |
| 4 | Joaquin Sanchez Rodriguez | 9 | 68 | 63 | 5 mins |

## KEY PLAYERS - DEFENDERS

**1 Gutierrez Luis Fernandez**

| | | | |
|---|---|---|---|
| **Goals Conceded (GC)** The number of League goals conceded while he was on the pitch | 34 | **Clean Sheets** In games when he played at least 70 minutes | 5 |
| **Defensive Rating** Ave number of mins between League goals conceded while on the pitch | 74 | **Club Defensive Rating** Average number of mins between League goals conceded by the club this season | 65 |

| | PLAYER | CON LGE | CLEAN SHEETS | DEF RATE |
|---|---|---|---|---|
| 2 | Juan Jesus Juanito | 33 | 5 | 70 mins |
| 3 | Iulian Filipescu | 25 | 3 | 58 mins |
| 4 | David Rivas Rodriguez | 26 | 2 | 58 mins |

## GOALS SCORED

AT HOME

| | | |
|---|---|---|
| MOST | R Madrid | 52 |
| | | 31 |
| LEAST | R Vallecano | 17 |

AWAY

| | | |
|---|---|---|
| MOST | R Madrid | 34 |
| | | 25 |
| LEAST | Recreativo | 11 |

## GOALS CONCEDED

AT HOME

| | | |
|---|---|---|
| LEAST | C Vigo & Valencia | 15 |
| | | 21 |
| MOST | Mallorca | 33 |

AWAY

| | | |
|---|---|---|
| LEAST | R Madrid, Valencia & Seville | 20 |
| | | 32 |
| MOST | Alaves | 48 |

## KEY GOALKEEPER

**1 Antonio Prats**

| | |
|---|---|
| **Goals Conceded in the League** | 53 |
| **Defensive Rating** Ave number of mins between League goals conceded while on the pitch | 65 |
| **Counting Games** Games when he played at least 70 minutes | 38 |
| **Clean Sheets** In games when he played at least 70 minutes | 7 |

## TOP POINT EARNERS

| | PLAYER | GAMES | AVE |
|---|---|---|---|
| 1 | Assuncao | 24 | 1.71 |
| 2 | Ito | 19 | 1.68 |
| 3 | Filipescu | 13 | 1.54 |
| 4 | Capi | 25 | 1.48 |
| 5 | Juanito | 25 | 1.48 |
| 6 | Luis Fernandez | 27 | 1.48 |
| 7 | Prats | 38 | 1.42 |
| 8 | Joaquin | 33 | 1.39 |
| 9 | Arzu | 27 | 1.33 |
| 10 | Rivas | 15 | 1.27 |
| | **CLUB AVERAGE:** | | **1.42** |

Ave = Average points per match in Counting Games

## ATTENDANCES

HOME GROUND: RUIZ DE LOPERA CAPACITY: 52500 AVERAGE LEAGUE AT HOME: 41347

| | | |
|---|---|---|
| 29 | Barcelona | 78500 |
| 27 | Real Madrid | 76300 |
| 7 | Real Madrid | 52500 |
| 30 | Seville | 52500 |
| 12 | Valencia | 50880 |
| 26 | Deportivo | 49875 |
| 20 | R Vallecano | 48825 |
| 38 | Espanyol | 48300 |
| 28 | Real Sociedad | 47800 |
| 21 | Osasuna | 47250 |
| 11 | Malaga | 46200 |
| 6 | Seville | 45000 |
| 34 | Valencia | 42000 |
| 32 | Recreativo Huelva | 42000 |
| 15 | Atl Madrid | 41610 |
| 41 | Valladolid | 39400 |
| 14 | Celta Vigo | 39375 |
| 36 | Atl Madrid | 39375 |
| 25 | Villarreal | 39375 |
| 43 | R Santander | 39375 |
| 16 | Auxerre | 37800 |
| 23 | Alaves | 36750 |
| 17 | Athl Bilbao | 36750 |
| 18 | Espanyol | 33550 |
| 1 | Deportivo | 32000 |
| 33 | Malaga | 29700 |
| 37 | Athl Bilbao | 29600 |
| 3 | Real Sociedad | 22400 |
| 31 | Mallorca | 22280 |
| 35 | Celta Vigo | 21625 |
| 22 | Valladolid | 20935 |
| 9 | Recreativo Huelva | 20000 |
| 8 | Mallorca | 19950 |
| 40 | Osasuna | 18710 |
| 4 | Barcelona | 18000 |
| 5 | Zimbru | 15000 |
| 19 | Auxerre | 15000 |
| 44 | Villarreal | 12600 |
| 42 | Alaves | 11250 |
| 24 | R Santander | 11250 |
| 39 | R Vallecano | 10850 |
| 13 | Zizkov | 10000 |
| 2 | Zimbru | 8000 |
| 10 | Zizkov | 4461 |

Home / Away / Neutral

## DISCIPLINARY RECORDS

| | PLAYER | YELLOW | RED | AVE |
|---|---|---|---|---|
| 1 | Casas | 4 | 1 | 131 |
| 2 | Varela | 18 | 1 | 149 |
| 3 | Filipescu | 7 | 2 | 161 |
| 4 | Melli | 4 | 0 | 162 |
| 5 | Alfonso | 6 | 0 | 175 |
| 6 | Tais | 3 | 0 | 179 |
| 7 | Luis Fernandez | 10 | 1 | 227 |
| 8 | Ito | 8 | 0 | 238 |
| 9 | Assuncao | 8 | 0 | 297 |
| 10 | Denilson | 5 | 1 | 322 |
| 11 | Mingo | 2 | 0 | 341 |
| 12 | Fernando | 6 | 0 | 407 |
| 13 | Arzu | 6 | 0 | 442 |
| | Other | 20 | 1 | |
| | **TOTAL** | **107** | **7** | |

## LEAGUE GOALS

| | PLAYER | MINS | GOALS | AVE |
|---|---|---|---|---|
| 1 | Fernando | 2444 | 15 | 163 |
| 2 | Joaquin | 3137 | 9 | 349 |
| 3 | Alfonso | 1052 | 6 | 175 |
| 4 | Capi | 2580 | 5 | 516 |
| 5 | Assuncao | 2382 | 5 | 476 |
| 6 | Arzu | 2654 | 4 | 664 |
| 7 | Dani | 540 | 4 | 135 |
| 8 | Denilson | 1934 | 2 | 967 |
| 9 | Filipescu | 1457 | 2 | 729 |
| 10 | Juanito | 2312 | 2 | 1156 |
| 11 | Varela | 2835 | 1 | 2835 |
| 12 | Casas | 658 | 1 | 658 |
| | Other | | 0 | |
| | **TOTAL** | | **56** | |

## MONTH BY MONTH GUIDE TO THE POINTS

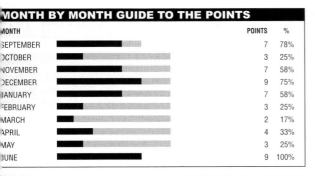

| MONTH | POINTS | % |
|---|---|---|
| SEPTEMBER | 7 | 78% |
| OCTOBER | 3 | 25% |
| NOVEMBER | 7 | 58% |
| DECEMBER | 9 | 75% |
| JANUARY | 7 | 58% |
| FEBRUARY | 3 | 25% |
| MARCH | 2 | 17% |
| APRIL | 4 | 33% |
| MAY | 3 | 25% |
| JUNE | 9 | 100% |

## TEAM OF THE SEASON

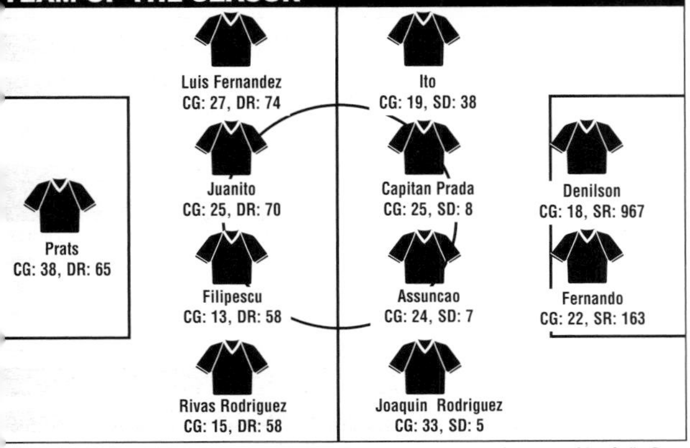
Luis Fernandez
CG: 27, DR: 74
Ito
CG: 19, SD: 38
Juanito
CG: 25, DR: 70
Capitan Prada
CG: 25, SD: 8
Denilson
CG: 18, SR: 967
Prats
CG: 38, DR: 65
Filipescu
CG: 13, DR: 58
Assuncao
CG: 24, SD: 7
Fernando
CG: 22, SR: 163
Rivas Rodriguez
CG: 15, DR: 58
Joaquin Rodriguez
CG: 33, SD: 5

KEY: DR = Defensive Rate, SD = Scoring Difference, SR = Strike Rate, CG = Counting Games – League games playing at least 70 minutes

## LEAGUE APPEARANCES, BOOKINGS AND CAPS

| | AGE | IN THE SQUAD | COUNTING GAMES | MINUTES ON PITCH | YELLOW CARDS | RED CARDS | THIS SEASON | HOME COUNTRY |
|---|---|---|---|---|---|---|---|---|
| **Goalkeepers** | | | | | | | | |
| Ronny Gaspercic | 34 | 38 | 0 | 0 | 0 | 0 | - | Belgium |
| Antonio Prats | 31 | 38 | 38 | 3420 | 2 | 0 | - | Spain |
| **Defenders** | | | | | | | | |
| David Belenguer | 30 | 16 | 3 | 270 | 0 | 0 | - | Spain |
| Iulian Filipescu | 29 | 22 | 13 | 1457 | 7 | 2 | 4 | Romania (27) |
| Juan Jesus Juanito | 26 | 26 | 25 | 2312 | 4 | 0 | 1 | Spain (2) |
| Luis Fernandez | 30 | 30 | 27 | 2507 | 10 | 1 | - | Spain |
| Carles Mingo | 26 | 24 | 6 | 682 | 2 | 0 | - | Spain |
| Rivas Rodriguez | 24 | 24 | 15 | 1510 | 2 | 0 | - | Spain |
| Washington Tais | 30 | 24 | 5 | 538 | 3 | 0 | - | Uruguay |
| **Midfielders** | | | | | | | | |
| Arturo Garcia Munoz | 22 | 36 | 27 | 2654 | 6 | 0 | - | Spain |
| Zacarias Assuncao | 26 | 30 | 24 | 2382 | 8 | 0 | - | Brazil |
| Benjamin Esono | 27 | 17 | 2 | 513 | 1 | 0 | - | Spain |
| Jose Antonio Calado | 29 | 20 | 0 | 142 | 2 | 0 | - | Portugal |
| Juan Jose Canas | 31 | 23 | 4 | 453 | 1 | 0 | - | Spain |
| Jesus Capitan Prada | 26 | 34 | 25 | 2580 | 3 | 0 | 3 | Spain (2) |
| Cesar Atienza | 27 | 14 | 0 | 143 | 1 | 0 | - | Spain |
| Daniel Gonzalez | 31 | 1 | 0 | 0 | 0 | 0 | - | Spain |
| Francisco Flores | 20 | 1 | 0 | 14 | 0 | 0 | - | Spain |
| Johannes Gudjonsson | 23 | 7 | 0 | 2 | 0 | 0 | - | Iceland |
| Antonio Alvarez Ito | 28 | 32 | 19 | 1907 | 8 | 0 | - | Spain |
| Joaquin Rodriguez | 22 | 37 | 33 | 3137 | 2 | 1 | 10 | Spain (2) |
| Juan Alvarado Melli | 19 | 16 | 7 | 649 | 4 | 0 | - | Spain |
| Fernando Varela | 23 | 34 | 30 | 2835 | 18 | 1 | - | Spain |
| **Forwards** | | | | | | | | |
| Perez Alfonso | 30 | 15 | 10 | 1052 | 6 | 0 | - | Spain |
| Gaston Casas | 25 | 28 | 1 | 658 | 4 | 1 | - | Argentina |
| Daniel Martin Dani | 21 | 13 | 3 | 540 | 1 | 0 | - | Spain |
| Denilson de Oliveira | 25 | 25 | 18 | 1934 | 5 | 1 | 2 | Brazil (1) |
| Fernandez Fernando | 29 | 36 | 22 | 2444 | 6 | 0 | - | Spain |
| Jose Maldonado | 22 | 7 | 1 | 116 | 0 | 0 | - | Spain |
| Pablo Nino Castellano | 25 | 2 | 0 | 0 | 0 | 0 | - | Spain |
| Joao Pataco Tomas | 28 | 19 | 3 | 555 | 1 | 0 | - | Portugal |

KEY: LEAGUE BOOKINGS CAPS (FIFA RANKING)

## SQUAD APPEARANCES

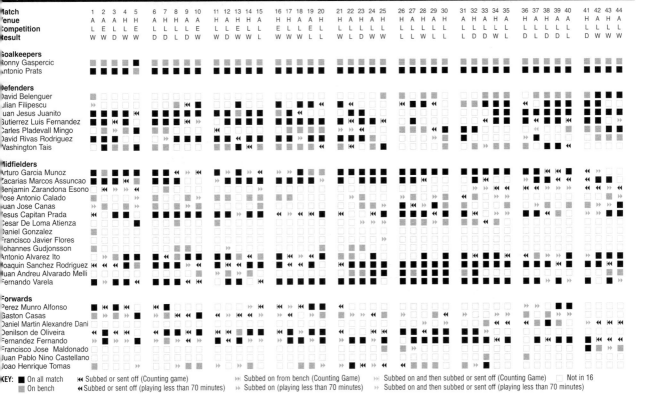

| Match | 1 | 2 | 3 | 4 | 5 | 6 | 7 | 8 | 9 | 10 | 11 | 12 | 13 | 14 | 15 | 16 | 17 | 18 | 19 | 20 | 21 | 22 | 23 | 24 | 25 | 26 | 27 | 28 | 29 | 30 | 31 | 32 | 33 | 34 | 35 | 36 | 37 | 38 | 39 | 40 | 41 | 42 | 43 | 44 |
|---|---|---|---|---|---|---|---|---|---|---|---|---|---|---|---|---|---|---|---|---|---|---|---|---|---|---|---|---|---|---|---|---|---|---|---|---|---|---|---|---|---|---|---|---|
| Venue | A | A | A | H | H | A | H | H | A | A | H | A | H | H | A | H | H | A | A | H | H | A | H | A | H | H | A | H | A | H | A | H | A | H | A | H | A | H | A | A | H | A | H | A |
| Competition | L | E | L | L | E | L | L | L | L | E | L | L | E | L | L | E | L | L | E | L | L | L | L | L | L | L | L | L | L | L | L | L | L | L | L | L | L | L | L | L | L | L | L | L |
| Result | W | W | D | W | W | D | D | L | D | W | W | D | W | W | L | W | W | W | L | L | W | L | D | W | W | L | L | W | L | L | L | D | D | W | L | D | L | D | D | L | D | W | W | W |

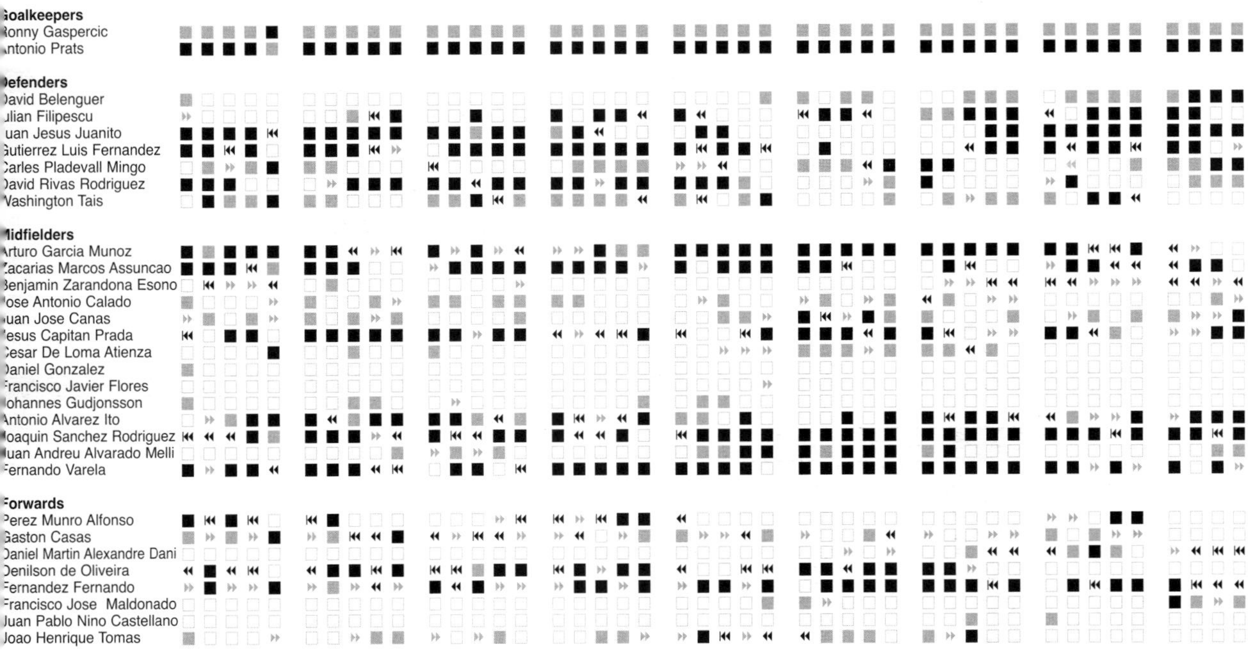
Goalkeepers
Ronny Gaspercic
Antonio Prats
Defenders
David Belenguer
Iulian Filipescu
Juan Jesus Juanito
Gutierrez Luis Fernandez
Carles Pladevall Mingo
David Rivas Rodriguez
Washington Tais
Midfielders
Arturo Garcia Munoz
Zacarias Marcos Assuncao
Benjamin Zarandona Esono
Jose Antonio Calado
Juan Jose Canas
Jesus Capitan Prada
Cesar De Loma Atienza
Daniel Gonzalez
Francisco Javier Flores
Johannes Gudjonsson
Antonio Alvarez Ito
Joaquin Sanchez Rodriguez
Juan Andreu Alvarado Melli
Fernando Varela
Forwards
Perez Munro Alfonso
Gaston Casas
Daniel Martin Alexandre Dani
Denilson de Oliveira
Fernandez Fernando
Francisco Jose Maldonado
Juan Pablo Nino Castellano
Joao Henrique Tomas

KEY: ■ On all match ■ On bench ⏮ Subbed or sent off (Counting game) ◀◀ Subbed or sent off (playing less than 70 minutes) ⏭ Subbed on from bench (Counting Game) ▶▶ Subbed on (playing less than 70 minutes) ▶▶ Subbed on and then subbed or sent off (Counting Game) ▶▶ Subbed on and then subbed or sent off (playing less than 70 minutes) □ Not in 16

# MALLORCA

Final Position: **9th**

| | | | | | | |
|---|---|---|---|---|---|---|
| 1 | lge | Valencia | H | L | 0-2 | |
| 2 | lge | Celta Vigo | A | L | 1-3 | Nino 78 |
| 3 | lge | Atl Madrid | H | L | 0-4 | |
| 4 | lge | Athl Bilbao | A | W | 2-0 | Robles 32; Larrainzar 74 og |
| 5 | lge | Espanyol | H | W | 2-0 | Lozano 58; Eto'o 86 pen |
| 6 | lge | Real Betis | A | W | 1-0 | Novo 32 |
| 7 | lge | Osasuna | H | W | 2-0 | Eto'o 58; Novo 69; Riera Ortega 70 |
| 8 | lge | Valladolid | A | W | 3-1 | Pandiani 26,56,69 |
| 9 | lge | Alaves | H | W | 3-1 | Pandiani 30,77 pen; Ibagaza 67 |
| 10 | lge | R Santander | A | W | 2-1 | Ibagaza 42; Pandiani 54 pen |
| 11 | lge | Villarreal | H | D | 1-1 | Pandiani 56 |
| 12 | lge | Deportivo | A | D | 2-2 | Pandiani 31; Eto'o 45 pen |
| 13 | lge | Real Madrid | H | L | 1-5 | Eto'o 17 |
| 14 | lge | Real Sociedad | A | L | 1-2 | Eto'o 47 |
| 15 | lge | Barcelona | H | L | 0-4 | |
| 16 | lge | Seville | A | L | 0-3 | |
| 17 | lge | R Vallecano | A | W | 2-1 | Pandiani 71; Carlos 85 |
| 18 | lge | Recreativo | H | D | 1-1 | Pandiani 71 pen |
| 19 | lge | Malaga | A | L | 0-1 | |
| 20 | lge | Valencia | A | L | 0-1 | |
| 21 | lge | Celta Vigo | H | L | 0-2 | |
| 22 | lge | Atl Madrid | A | L | 1-2 | Novo 21 |
| 23 | lge | Athl Bilbao | H | D | 1-1 | Robles 22 |
| 24 | lge | Espanyol | A | L | 0-2 | |
| 25 | lge | Real Betis | H | W | 2-1 | Pandiani 1 pen; Lozano 51 |
| 26 | lge | Osasuna | A | D | 0-0 | |
| 27 | lge | Valladolid | H | W | 2-1 | Pandiani 55; Riera Ortega 57 |
| 28 | lge | Alaves | A | D | 0-0 | |
| 29 | lge | R Santander | H | D | 3-3 | Riera Ortega 2; Eto'o 53,80 |
| 30 | lge | Villarreal | A | D | 1-1 | Eto'o 40 |
| 31 | lge | Deportivo | H | W | 3-0 | Eto'o 4,64; Riera Ortega 13 |
| 32 | lge | Real Madrid | A | W | 5-1 | Pandiani 48; Riera Ortega 51; Eto'o 62; Roberto Carlos 69 og; Carlos 90 |
| 33 | lge | Real Sociedad | H | L | 1-3 | Eto'o 60 |
| 34 | lge | Barcelona | A | W | 2-1 | Novo 22; Carlos 86 |
| 35 | lge | Seville | H | L | 1-3 | Eto'o 14 |
| 36 | lge | R Vallecano | H | D | 1-1 | Pandiani 80 pen |
| 37 | lge | Recreativo | A | D | 1-1 | Eto'o 5 pen |
| 38 | lge | Malaga | H | W | 1-0 | Tuni 89 |

## KEY PLAYERS - GOALSCORERS

**1 Samuel Fils Eto'o**

| | | | |
|---|---|---|---|
| Goals in the League | 14 | Player Strike Rate<br>Average number of minutes between League goals scored by player | 175 |
| Contribution to Attacking Power<br>Average number of minutes between League team goals while on pitch | 61 | Club Strike Rate<br>Average number of minutes between League goals scored by club | 68 |

| | PLAYER | LGE GOALS | POWER | STRIKE RATE |
|---|---|---|---|---|
| 2 | Walter Gerardo Pandiani | 14 | 66 | 200 mins |
| 3 | Albert Riera Ortega | 5 | 63 | 529 mins |
| 4 | Alvaro Ramirez Novo | 4 | 60 | 671 mins |
| 5 | John Harold Lozano | 2 | 71 | 1207 mins |

## KEY PLAYERS - MIDFIELDERS

**1 Alvaro Ramirez Novo**

| | | | |
|---|---|---|---|
| Goals in the League | 4 | Contribution to Attacking Power<br>Average number of minutes between League team goals while on pitch | 61 |
| Defensive Rating<br>Average number of mins between League goals conceded while he was on the pitch | 67 | Scoring Difference<br>Defensive Rating minus Contribution to Attacking Power | 6 |

| | PLAYER | LGE GOALS | DEF RATE | POWER | SCORE DIFF |
|---|---|---|---|---|---|
| 2 | Fernandez Poli | 0 | 65 | 69 | -4 mins |
| 3 | Ariel Miguel Santiago Ibagaza | 2 | 56 | 61 | -5 mins |
| 4 | John Harold Lozano | 2 | 59 | 71 | -12 mins |
| 5 | Martin de la Fuente Marcos | 0 | 57 | 79 | -22 mins |

## KEY PLAYERS - DEFENDERS

**1 David Cortez**

| | | | |
|---|---|---|---|
| Goals Conceded (GC)<br>The number of League goals conceded while he was on the pitch | 34 | Clean Sheets<br>In games when he played at least 70 minutes | 8 |
| Defensive Rating<br>Ave number of mins between League goals conceded while on the pitch | 79 | Club Defensive Rating<br>Average number of mins between League goals conceded by the club this season | 61 |

| | PLAYER | CON LGE | CLEAN SHEETS | DEF RATE |
|---|---|---|---|---|
| 2 | Fernando Bejarano Nino | 24 | 5 | 69 mins |
| 3 | Miguel Angel Homar Nadal | 35 | 5 | 57 mins |

## GOALS SCORED

AT HOME

| | | |
|---|---|---|
| MOST | R Madrid | 52 |
| | | 25 |
| LEAST | R Vallecano | 17 |

AWAY

| | | |
|---|---|---|
| MOST | R Madrid | 34 |
| | | 24 |
| LEAST | Recreativo | 11 |

## GOALS CONCEDED

AT HOME

| | | |
|---|---|---|
| LEAST | C Vigo & Valencia | 15 |
| | | 33 |
| MOST | Mallorca | 33 |

AWAY

| | | |
|---|---|---|
| LEAST | R Madrid, Valencia & Seville | 20 |
| | | 23 |
| MOST | Alaves | 48 |

## KEY GOALKEEPER

**1 Leonardo Franco**

| | |
|---|---|
| Goals Conceded in the League | 53 |
| Defensive Rating<br>Ave number of mins between League goals conceded while on the pitch | 61 |
| Counting Games<br>Games when he played at least 70 minutes | 36 |
| Clean Sheets<br>In games when he played at least 70 minutes | 8 |

## TOP POINT EARNERS

| | PLAYER | GAMES | AVE |
|---|---|---|---|
| 1 | Riera Ortega | 25 | 1.88 |
| 2 | Cortez | 30 | 1.60 |
| 3 | Nadal | 22 | 1.55 |
| 4 | Nino | 17 | 1.53 |
| 5 | Poli | 33 | 1.45 |
| 6 | Novo | 29 | 1.45 |
| 7 | Ibagaza | 29 | 1.41 |
| 8 | Lozano | 25 | 1.40 |
| 9 | Eto'o | 26 | 1.38 |
| 10 | Pandiani | 31 | 1.35 |
| | CLUB AVERAGE: | | 1.37 |

Ave = Average points per match in Counting Games

## ATTENDANCES

HOME GROUND: SON MOIX CAPACITY: 26500 AVERAGE LEAGUE AT HOME: 17212

| | | |
|---|---|---|
| 34 | Barcelona | 78400 |
| 32 | Real Madrid | 68670 |
| 22 | Atl Madrid | 55900 |
| 20 | Valencia | 47700 |
| 4 | Athl Bilbao | 36000 |
| 12 | Deportivo | 29904 |
| 14 | Real Sociedad | 29760 |
| 19 | Malaga | 28567 |
| 15 | Barcelona | 23700 |
| 13 | Real Madrid | 23700 |
| 25 | Real Betis | 22280 |
| 16 | Seville | 22000 |
| 21 | Celta Vigo | 20150 |
| 1 | Valencia | 20000 |
| 6 | Real Betis | 19950 |
| 24 | Espanyol | 19250 |
| 9 | Alaves | 19197 |
| 7 | Osasuna | 18960 |
| 2 | Celta Vigo | 18000 |
| 27 | Valladolid | 18000 |
| 33 | Real Sociedad | 17780 |
| 31 | Deportivo | 17775 |
| 11 | Villarreal | 17775 |
| 37 | Recreativo Huelva | 16800 |
| 28 | Alaves | 16705 |
| 5 | Espanyol | 16590 |
| 18 | Recreativo Huelva | 16590 |
| 3 | Atl Madrid | 16000 |
| 10 | R Santander | 14625 |
| 26 | Osasuna | 13950 |
| 8 | Valladolid | 13250 |
| 29 | R Santander | 12800 |
| 17 | R Vallecano | 12400 |
| 36 | R Vallecano | 11850 |
| 35 | Seville | 11850 |
| 23 | Athl Bilbao | 11850 |
| 38 | Malaga | 10191 |
| 30 | Villarreal | 9856 |

■ Home □ Away ▒ Neutral

## DISCIPLINARY RECORDS

| | PLAYER | YELLOW | RED | AVE |
|---|---|---|---|---|
| 1 | Lozano | 13 | 2 | 160 |
| 2 | Poli | 13 | 2 | 202 |
| 3 | Nino | 7 | 1 | 208 |
| 4 | Marcos | 8 | 0 | 257 |
| 5 | Lussenhof | 7 | 0 | 278 |
| 6 | Eto'o | 7 | 1 | 305 |
| 7 | Ibagaza | 7 | 1 | 322 |
| 8 | Pandiani | 6 | 1 | 400 |
| 9 | Novo | 4 | 1 | 536 |
| 10 | Nadal | 3 | 0 | 660 |
| 11 | Riera Ortega | 4 | 0 | 661 |
| 12 | Miquel Soler | 1 | 0 | 701 |
| 13 | Olaizola | 1 | 0 | 852 |
| | Other | 14 | 0 | |
| | TOTAL | 95 | 9 | |

## LEAGUE GOALS

| | PLAYER | MINS | GOALS | AVE |
|---|---|---|---|---|
| 1 | Pandiani | 2803 | 14 | 200 |
| 2 | Eto'o | 2443 | 14 | 175 |
| 3 | Novo | 2682 | 4 | 671 |
| 4 | Riera Ortega | 2647 | 4 | 662 |
| 5 | Carlos | 579 | 3 | 193 |
| 6 | Ibagaza | 2578 | 2 | 1289 |
| 7 | Robles | 385 | 2 | 193 |
| 8 | Lozano | 2414 | 2 | 1207 |
| 9 | Tuni | 66 | 1 | 66 |
| 10 | Nino | 1664 | 1 | 166 |
| | Other | | 2 | |
| | TOTAL | | 49 | |

## MONTH BY MONTH GUIDE TO THE POINTS

| MONTH | POINTS | % |
|---|---|---|
| SEPTEMBER | 3 | 25% |
| OCTOBER | 9 | 100% |
| NOVEMBER | 10 | 83% |
| DECEMBER | 1 | 8% |
| JANUARY | 4 | 33% |
| FEBRUARY | 1 | 8% |
| MARCH | 7 | 58% |
| APRIL | 6 | 50% |
| MAY | 6 | 50% |
| JUNE | 5 | 56% |

## TEAM OF THE SEASON

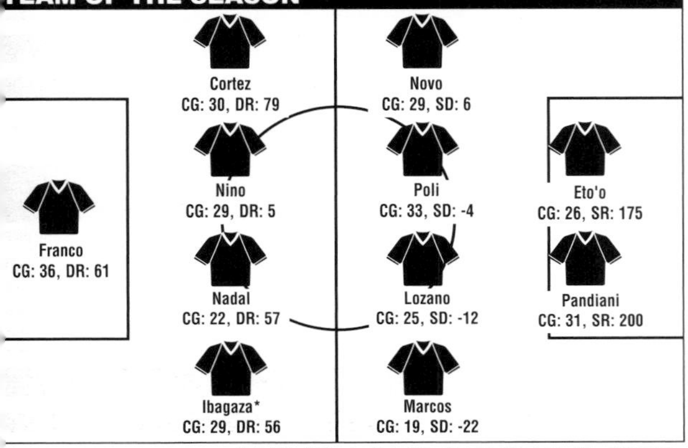
Cortez
CG: 30, DR: 79
Novo
CG: 29, SD: 6
Nino
CG: 29, DR: 5
Poli
CG: 33, SD: -4
Eto'o
CG: 26, SR: 175
Franco
CG: 36, DR: 61
Nadal
CG: 22, DR: 57
Lozano
CG: 25, SD: -12
Pandiani
CG: 31, SR: 200
Ibagaza*
CG: 29, DR: 56
Marcos
CG: 19, SD: -22

KEY: DR = Defensive Rate, SD = Scoring Difference, SR = Strike Rate, CG = Counting Games – League games playing at least 70 minutes

## LEAGUE APPEARANCES, BOOKINGS AND CAPS

| | AGE | IN THE SQUAD | COUNTING GAMES | MINUTES ON PITCH | YELLOW CARDS | RED CARDS | THIS SEASON | HOME COUNTRY |
|---|---|---|---|---|---|---|---|---|
| **Goalkeepers** | | | | | | | | |
| Cifuentes Alberto | 24 | 1 | 0 | 0 | 0 | 0 | - | Spain |
| Leonardo Franco | 26 | 36 | 36 | 3240 | 3 | 0 | - | Argentina |
| Miguel Garo Miki | 27 | 37 | 2 | 180 | 0 | 0 | - | Spain |
| Miquel Moya | 19 | 1 | 0 | 0 | 0 | 0 | - | Spain |
| **Defenders** | | | | | | | | |
| Luis Perez Angel | 22 | 15 | 1 | 90 | 0 | 0 | - | Spain |
| David Cortez | 23 | 32 | 30 | 2674 | 3 | 0 | - | Spain |
| Ariel Miguel Ibagaza | 26 | 34 | 29 | 2578 | 7 | 1 | - | Argentina |
| Miquel Soler | 38 | 24 | 5 | 701 | 1 | 0 | - | Spain |
| Miguel Angel Nadal | 36 | 23 | 22 | 1980 | 3 | 0 | - | Spain |
| Fernando Nino | 28 | 26 | 17 | 1664 | 7 | 1 | - | Spain |
| Xavier Olaizola | 33 | 13 | 8 | 852 | 1 | 0 | - | Spain |
| **Midfielders** | | | | | | | | |
| Alejandro Campano | 24 | 32 | 12 | 1320 | 0 | 0 | - | Spain |
| Atencia Cichi Soler | 33 | 31 | 1 | 130 | 1 | 0 | - | Spain |
| John Harold Lozano | 31 | 32 | 25 | 2414 | 13 | 2 | - | Colombia |
| Federico Lussenhof | 29 | 25 | 21 | 1952 | 7 | 0 | - | Argentina |
| Martin Marcos | 34 | 37 | 19 | 2059 | 8 | 0 | - | Spain |
| Alvaro Novo | 25 | 36 | 29 | 2682 | 4 | 1 | - | Spain |
| Fernandez Poli | 26 | 35 | 33 | 3041 | 13 | 2 | - | Spain |
| Raul Martin | 23 | 1 | 0 | 24 | 0 | 0 | - | Spain |
| Julian Robles | 22 | 26 | 2 | 385 | 3 | 0 | - | Spain |
| Manuel Viale | 22 | 1 | 0 | 0 | 0 | 0 | - | Argentina |
| Fernandez Vicente | 27 | 13 | 4 | 399 | 4 | 0 | - | Spain |
| **Forwards** | | | | | | | | |
| Leonardo Biagini | 26 | 14 | 0 | 103 | 0 | 0 | - | Argentina |
| Dominguez Carlos | 26 | 35 | 2 | 579 | 0 | 0 | - | Spain |
| Samuel Fils Eto'o | 22 | 31 | 26 | 2443 | 7 | 1 | 2 | Cameroon (18) |
| Daniel Guiza | 22 | 1 | 0 | 25 | 0 | 0 | - | Spain |
| Walter Pandiani | 27 | 34 | 31 | 2803 | 6 | 1 | - | Uruguay |
| Albert Riera Ortega | 21 | 35 | 25 | 2647 | 4 | 0 | - | Spain |
| Antoni Colom Tuni | 21 | 8 | 0 | 66 | 0 | 0 | - | Spain |
| Jose Turu Flores | 32 | 24 | 0 | 184 | 0 | 0 | - | Argentina |

KEY: LEAGUE BOOKINGS CAPS (FIFA RANKING)

## SQUAD APPEARANCES

| Match | 1 | 2 | 3 | 4 | 5 | 6 | 7 | 8 | 9 | 10 | 11 | 12 | 13 | 14 | 15 | 16 | 17 | 18 | 19 | 20 | 21 | 22 | 23 | 24 | 25 | 26 | 27 | 28 | 29 | 30 | 31 | 32 | 33 | 34 | 35 | 36 | 37 | 38 |
|---|---|---|---|---|---|---|---|---|---|---|---|---|---|---|---|---|---|---|---|---|---|---|---|---|---|---|---|---|---|---|---|---|---|---|---|---|---|---|
| Venue | H | A | H | A | H | A | A | H | A | A | H | A | H | A | H | A | A | H | A | A | H | A | H | A | H | A | H | A | H | A | H | A | H | A | H | H | A | H |
| Competition | L | L | L | L | L | L | L | L | L | L | L | L | L | L | L | L | L | L | L | L | L | L | L | L | L | L | L | L | L | L | L | L | L | L | L | L | L | L |
| Result | L | L | L | W | W | W | W | W | W | W | D | D | L | L | L | L | W | D | L | L | L | L | D | L | W | D | W | D | D | D | W | W | L | W | L | D | D | W |

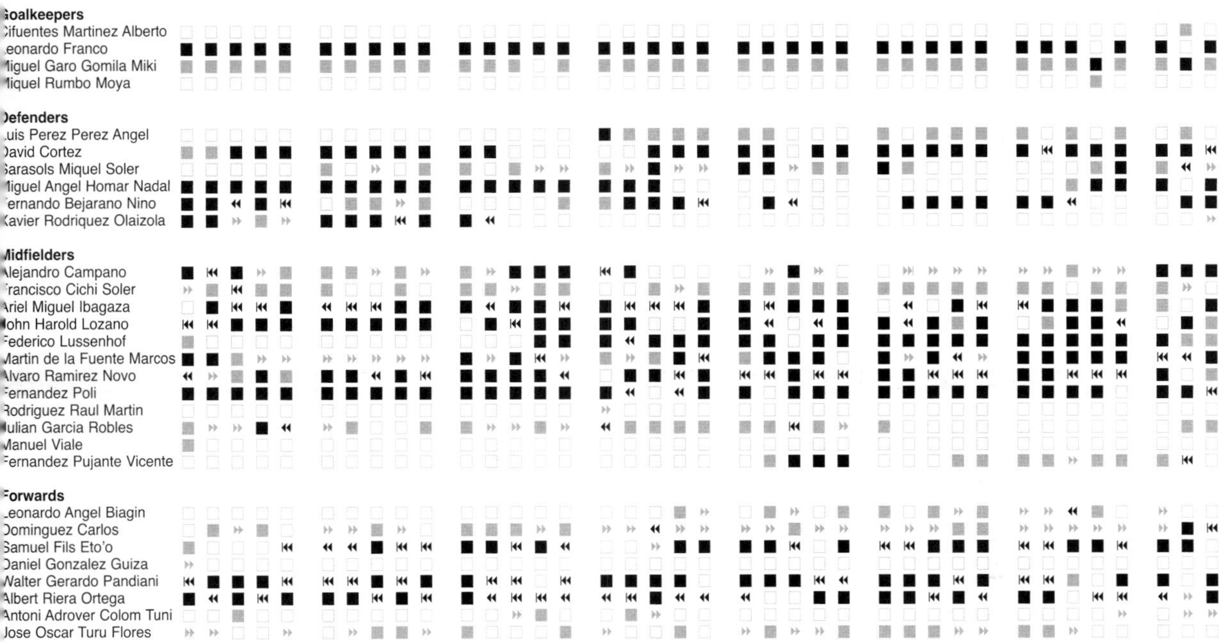
Goalkeepers
Cifuentes Martinez Alberto
Leonardo Franco
Miguel Garo Gomila Miki
Miquel Rumbo Moya
Defenders
Luis Perez Perez Angel
David Cortez
Sarasols Miquel Soler
Miguel Angel Homar Nadal
Fernando Bejarano Nino
Xavier Rodriquez Olaizola
Midfielders
Alejandro Campano
Francisco Cichi Soler
Ariel Miguel Ibagaza
John Harold Lozano
Federico Lussenhof
Martin de la Fuente Marcos
Alvaro Ramirez Novo
Fernandez Poli
Rodriguez Raul Martin
Julian Garcia Robles
Manuel Viale
Fernandez Pujante Vicente
Forwards
Leonardo Angel Biagin
Dominguez Carlos
Samuel Fils Eto'o
Daniel Gonzalez Guiza
Walter Gerardo Pandiani
Albert Riera Ortega
Antoni Adrover Colom Tuni
Jose Oscar Turu Flores

KEY: ■ On all match ■ On bench ⏮ Subbed or sent off (Counting game) « Subbed or sent off (playing less than 70 minutes) ⏭ Subbed on from bench (Counting Game) » Subbed on (playing less than 70 minutes) Subbed on and then subbed or sent off (Counting Game) Subbed on and then subbed or sent off (playing less than 70 minutes) Not in 16

# SEVILLE

Final Position: **10th**

| | | | | | | |
|---|---|---|---|---|---|---|
| 1 | lge | Celta Vigo | H | L | 0-1 | |
| 2 | lge | Atl Madrid | A | D | 1-1 | Moises 45 pen |
| 3 | lge | Athl Bilbao | H | D | 1-1 | Reyes 51 |
| 4 | lge | Espanyol | A | D | 0-0 | |
| 5 | lge | Real Betis | H | D | 1-1 | Juanito 68 og |
| 6 | lge | Osasuna | A | L | 1-2 | Pablo Alfaro 40 |
| 7 | lge | Valladolid | H | W | 2-1 | Antonito 11,23 |
| 8 | lge | Alaves | A | L | 0-1 | |
| 9 | lge | R Santander | H | W | 1-0 | Casquero 32 |
| 10 | lge | Villarreal | A | L | 0-1 | |
| 11 | lge | Deportivo | H | D | 1-1 | Antonito 4 |
| 12 | lge | Real Sociedad | H | L | 0-1 | |
| 13 | lge | Barcelona | A | W | 3-0 | Casquero 4 pen; Toedtli 77,88 |
| 14 | lge | R Vallecano | A | W | 1-0 | Marcos Vales 22 |
| 15 | lge | Real Madrid | A | L | 0-3 | |
| 16 | lge | Mallorca | H | W | 3-0 | Reyes 14; Toedtli 33,84 |
| 17 | lge | Recreativo | A | D | 0-0 | |
| 18 | lge | Malaga | H | D | 0-0 | |
| 19 | lge | Valencia | A | L | 0-1 | |
| 20 | lge | Celta Vigo | A | W | 1-0 | Casquero 75 |
| 21 | lge | Atl Madrid | H | D | 1-1 | Fredi 55 |
| 22 | lge | Athl Bilbao | A | L | 0-2 | |
| 23 | lge | Espanyol | H | W | 1-0 | Soldevilla 12 og |
| 24 | lge | Real Betis | A | W | 1-0 | Marcos Vales 76 |
| 25 | lge | Osasuna | H | W | 2-0 | Antonito 19; Reyes 36 |
| 26 | lge | Valladolid | A | D | 0-0 | |
| 27 | lge | Alaves | H | W | 3-2 | Casquero 21; Reyes 84 pen; Karmona 90 og |
| 28 | lge | R Santander | A | L | 0-1 | |
| 29 | lge | Villarreal | H | W | 3-1 | Reyes 9; Machlas 81,90 |
| 30 | lge | Deportivo | A | L | 1-3 | Antonito 55 |
| 31 | lge | Real Madrid | H | L | 1-3 | Gallardo 39 |
| 32 | lge | Real Sociedad | A | L | 0-1 | |
| 33 | lge | Barcelona | H | D | 0-0 | |
| 34 | lge | R Vallecano | H | D | 3-3 | Casquero 45; Reyes 49,79 pen |
| 35 | lge | Mallorca | A | W | 3-1 | Antonito 42,80; Reyes 55 |
| 36 | lge | Recreativo | H | W | 1-0 | Marcos Vales 50 |
| 37 | lge | Malaga | A | L | 2-3 | Reyes 33 pen; Navarro 60 |
| 38 | lge | Valencia | H | L | 0-3 | |

## KEY PLAYERS - GOALSCORERS

**1 Ramiro Perez Antonito**

| | | | |
|---|---|---|---|
| Goals in the League | 7 | Player Strike Rate<br>Average number of minutes between League goals scored by player | 258 |
| Contribution to Attacking Power<br>Average number of minutes between League team goals while on pitch | 75 | Club Strike Rate<br>Average number of minutes between League goals scored by club | 90 |

| | PLAYER | LGE GOALS | POWER | STRIKE RATE |
|---|---|---|---|---|
| 2 | Jose Antonio Reyes | 9 | 81 | 308 mins |
| 3 | Francisco Casquero | 5 | 105 | 571 mins |
| 4 | Llanes Marcos Vales | 3 | 74 | 723 mins |
| 5 | Alfredo Lobeiras Sanchez | 1 | 80 | 1612 mins |

## KEY PLAYERS - MIDFIELDERS

**1 Alfredo Lobeiras Sanchez**

| | | | |
|---|---|---|---|
| Goals in the League | 1 | Contribution to Attacking Power<br>Average number of minutes between League team goals while on pitch | 81 |
| Defensive Rating<br>Average number of mins between League goals conceded while he was on the pitch | 124 | Scoring Difference<br>Defensive Rating minus Contribution to Attacking Power | 43 |

| | PLAYER | LGE GOALS | DEF RATE | POWER | SCORE DIFF |
|---|---|---|---|---|---|
| 2 | Gerardo Torrado | 0 | 92 | 74 | 18 mins |
| 3 | Vinny Samways | 0 | 104 | 91 | 13 mins |
| 4 | Jean Luis Redondo | 0 | 113 | 106 | 7 mins |
| 5 | Zoran Njegus | 0 | 75 | 84 | -9 mins |

## KEY PLAYERS - DEFENDERS

**1 Javier Navarro**

| | | | |
|---|---|---|---|
| Goals Conceded (GC)<br>The number of League goals conceded while he was on the pitch | 28 | Clean Sheets<br>In games when he played at least 70 minutes | 12 |
| Defensive Rating<br>Ave number of mins between League goals conceded while on the pitch | 91 | Club Defensive Rating<br>Average number of mins between League goals conceded by the club this season | 86 |

| | PLAYER | CON LGE | CLEAN SHEETS | DEF RATE |
|---|---|---|---|---|
| 2 | Pablo Alfaro Armengot | 33 | 12 | 90 mins |
| 3 | David Castedo Escudero | 36 | 12 | 87 mins |
| 4 | Llanes Marcos Vales | 29 | 5 | 75 mins |
| 5 | Rodriguez Oscar | 18 | 4 | 74 mins |

## GOALS SCORED

**AT HOME**

| | | |
|---|---|---|
| MOST | R Madrid | 52 |
| | | 24 |
| LEAST | R Vallecano | 17 |

**AWAY**

| | | |
|---|---|---|
| MOST | R Madrid | 34 |
| | | 14 |
| LEAST | Recreativo | 11 |

## GOALS CONCEDED

**AT HOME**

| | | |
|---|---|---|
| LEAST | C Vigo & Valencia | 15 |
| | | 19 |
| MOST | Mallorca | 33 |

**AWAY**

| | | |
|---|---|---|
| LEAST | R Madrid, Valencia & Seville | 20 |
| | | 20 |
| MOST | Alaves | 48 |

## KEY GOALKEEPER

**1 Antonio Notario Caro**

| | |
|---|---|
| Goals Conceded in the League | 37 |
| Defensive Rating<br>Ave number of mins between League goals conceded while on the pitch | 90 |
| Counting Games<br>Games when he played at least 70 minutes | 37 |
| Clean Sheets<br>In games when he played at least 70 minutes | 14 |

## TOP POINT EARNERS

| | PLAYER | GAMES | AVE |
|---|---|---|---|
| 1 | Torrado | 19 | 1.74 |
| 2 | Fredi | 12 | 1.67 |
| 3 | Reyes | 30 | 1.53 |
| 4 | Redondo | 17 | 1.47 |
| 5 | Antonito | 14 | 1.43 |
| 6 | Navarro | 28 | 1.43 |
| 7 | Pablo Alfaro | 33 | 1.42 |
| 8 | Marcos Vales | 20 | 1.40 |
| 9 | Gallardo | 23 | 1.39 |
| 10 | Njegus | 13 | 1.38 |
| | CLUB AVERAGE: | | 1.32 |

Ave = Average points per match in Counting Games

## ATTENDANCES

HOME GROUND: SANCHEZ PIZJUAN CAPACITY: 45000 AVERAGE LEAGUE AT HOME: 34281

| | | | | | | | | |
|---|---|---|---|---|---|---|---|---|
| 15 | Real Madrid | 76300 | 21 | Atl Madrid | 36000 | 37 | Malaga | 23744 |
| 31 | Real Madrid | 60000 | 7 | Valladolid | 36000 | 16 | Mallorca | 22000 |
| 13 | Barcelona | 54257 | 29 | Villarreal | 33750 | 26 | Valladolid | 21200 |
| 24 | Real Betis | 52500 | 33 | Barcelona | 33750 | 28 | R Santander | 20250 |
| 2 | Atl Madrid | 47000 | 30 | Deportivo | 32000 | 20 | Celta Vigo | 15900 |
| 19 | Valencia | 45580 | 1 | Celta Vigo | 32000 | 18 | Malaga | 14000 |
| 5 | Real Betis | 45000 | 25 | Osasuna | 31500 | 17 | Recreativo Huelva | 14000 |
| 9 | R Santander | 42750 | 27 | Alaves | 31500 | 8 | Alaves | 13440 |
| 11 | Deportivo | 41850 | 36 | Recreativo Huelva | 29250 | 6 | Osasuna | 11940 |
| 4 | Espanyol | 40700 | 32 | Real Sociedad | 28800 | 35 | Mallorca | 11850 |
| 23 | Espanyol | 40500 | 3 | Athl Bilbao | 27000 | 14 | R Vallecano | 11780 |
| 34 | R Vallecano | 40500 | 38 | Valencia | 27000 | 10 | Villarreal | 11424 |
| 22 | Athl Bilbao | 36000 | 12 | Real Sociedad | 27000 | | | |

■ Home □ Away ▒ Neutral

## DISCIPLINARY RECORDS

| | PLAYER | YELLOW | RED | AVE |
|---|---|---|---|---|
| 1 | Samways | 4 | 0 | 181 |
| 2 | Reyes | 13 | 1 | 198 |
| 3 | Njegus | 6 | 0 | 224 |
| 4 | Fredi | 5 | 2 | 230 |
| 5 | Marcos Vales | 8 | 1 | 241 |
| 6 | Antonito | 7 | 0 | 258 |
| 7 | Oscar | 5 | 0 | 266 |
| 8 | Navarro | 7 | 2 | 284 |
| 9 | Redondo | 5 | 0 | 340 |
| 10 | Gallardo | 6 | 1 | 347 |
| 11 | Victor | 3 | 0 | 387 |
| 12 | Casquero | 7 | 0 | 407 |
| 13 | David Castedo | 6 | 1 | 446 |
| | Other | 18 | 2 | |
| | TOTAL | 100 | 10 | |

## LEAGUE GOALS

| | PLAYER | MINS | GOALS | AVE |
|---|---|---|---|---|
| 1 | Reyes | 2776 | 9 | 308 |
| 2 | Antonito | 1806 | 7 | 258 |
| 3 | Casquero | 2853 | 5 | 571 |
| 4 | Toedtli | 1212 | 4 | 303 |
| 5 | Marcos Vales | 2170 | 3 | 723 |
| 6 | Machlas | 364 | 2 | 182 |
| 7 | Fredi | 1612 | 1 | 1612 |
| 8 | Pablo Alfaro | 2968 | 1 | 2968 |
| 9 | Gallardo | 2433 | 1 | 2433 |
| 10 | Navarro | 2560 | 1 | 2560 |
| 11 | Moises | 404 | 1 | 404 |
| | Other | | 3 | |
| | TOTAL | | 38 | |

## MONTH BY MONTH GUIDE TO THE POINTS

| MONTH | POINTS | % |
|---|---|---|
| SEPTEMBER | 3 | 25% |
| OCTOBER | 4 | 44% |
| NOVEMBER | 4 | 33% |
| DECEMBER | 6 | 67% |
| JANUARY | 5 | 33% |
| FEBRUARY | 7 | 58% |
| MARCH | 10 | 83% |
| APRIL | 3 | 25% |
| MAY | 5 | 42% |
| JUNE | 3 | 33% |

## TEAM OF THE SEASON

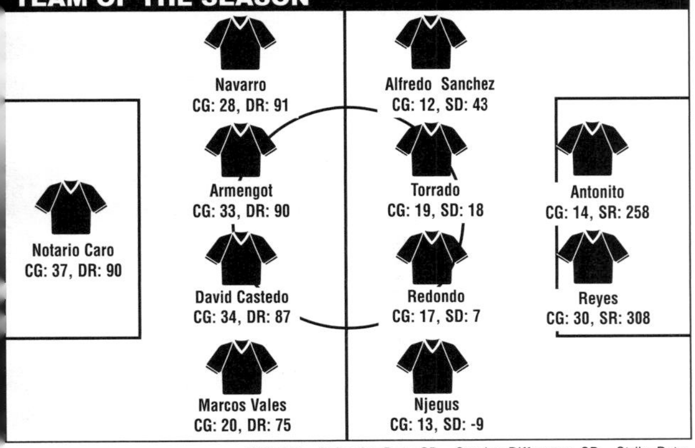
Notario Caro
CG: 37, DR: 90
Navarro
CG: 28, DR: 91
Armengot
CG: 33, DR: 90
David Castedo
CG: 34, DR: 87
Marcos Vales
CG: 20, DR: 75
Alfredo Sanchez
CG: 12, SD: 43
Torrado
CG: 19, SD: 18
Redondo
CG: 17, SD: 7
Njegus
CG: 13, SD: -9
Antonito
CG: 14, SR: 258
Reyes
CG: 30, SR: 308

**KEY:** DR = Defensive Rate, SD = Scoring Difference, SR = Strike Rate, CG = Counting Games – League games playing at least 70 minutes

## LEAGUE APPEARANCES, BOOKINGS AND CAPS

| | AGE | IN THE SQUAD | COUNTING GAMES | MINUTES ON PITCH | YELLOW CARDS | RED CARDS | THIS SEASON | HOME COUNTRY |
|---|---|---|---|---|---|---|---|---|
| **Goalkeepers** | | | | | | | | |
| Juan Caballero | 24 | 38 | 1 | 90 | 0 | 0 | - | Spain |
| Notario Caro | 30 | 38 | 37 | 3330 | 2 | 0 | - | Spain |
| **Defenders** | | | | | | | | |
| Carlos Perez | 23 | 1 | 0 | 0 | 0 | 0 | - | Spain |
| Daniel Alves | 20 | 14 | 0 | 252 | 0 | 0 | - | Brazil |
| David Castedo | 29 | 35 | 34 | 3125 | 6 | 1 | - | Spain |
| Juan Miguel | 23 | 20 | 3 | 287 | 4 | 1 | - | Spain |
| Llanes Marcos Vales | 28 | 35 | 20 | 2170 | 8 | 1 | - | Spain |
| Francisco Navarro | 29 | 30 | 28 | 2560 | 7 | 2 | 2 | Spain (2) |
| Rodriguez Oscar | 23 | 37 | 13 | 1331 | 5 | 0 | - | Spain |
| Pablo Alfaro | 34 | 33 | 33 | 2968 | 4 | 1 | - | Spain |
| Jose Miguel Prieto | 31 | 3 | 0 | 45 | 1 | 0 | - | Spain |
| **Midfielders** | | | | | | | | |
| Quintero Alfonso | 29 | 6 | 3 | 265 | 1 | 0 | - | Spain |
| David Perez Arteaga | 21 | 10 | 1 | 181 | 0 | 0 | - | Spain |
| Francisco Casquero | 26 | 36 | 28 | 2853 | 7 | 0 | - | Spain |
| Lama Diaz | 27 | 5 | 2 | 280 | 0 | 0 | - | |
| Fredi Lobeiras | 29 | 27 | 12 | 1612 | 5 | 2 | - | Spain |
| Zoran Njegus | 30 | 27 | 13 | 1344 | 6 | 0 | - | Serbia & Montenegro |
| Inti Podesta | 25 | 4 | 0 | 58 | 0 | 0 | - | Uruguay |
| Jean Luis Redondo | 26 | 34 | 17 | 1701 | 5 | 0 | - | Spain |
| Vinny Samways | 34 | 14 | 7 | 725 | 4 | 0 | - | England |
| Alberto Tomas | 32 | 14 | 2 | 243 | 2 | 0 | - | Spain |
| Gerardo Torrado | 24 | 23 | 19 | 1840 | 2 | 0 | - | Mexico |
| Victor Salas Banos | 23 | 38 | 8 | 1161 | 3 | 0 | - | Spain |
| **Forwards** | | | | | | | | |
| Ramiro Antonito | 25 | 38 | 14 | 1806 | 7 | 0 | - | Spain |
| Francisco Gallardo | 23 | 37 | 23 | 2433 | 6 | 1 | - | Spain |
| Nikos Machlas | 30 | 18 | 0 | 364 | 0 | 0 | - | Greece |
| Moises Garcia Leon | 31 | 14 | 2 | 404 | 1 | 0 | - | Spain |
| Jose Antonio Reyes | 19 | 34 | 30 | 2776 | 13 | 1 | - | Spain |
| Mariano Toedtli | 27 | 33 | 7 | 1212 | 1 | 0 | - | Argentina |

**KEY:** LEAGUE BOOKINGS CAPS (FIFA RANKING)

## SQUAD APPEARANCES

| Match | 1 | 2 | 3 | 4 | 5 | 6 | 7 | 8 | 9 | 10 | 11 | 12 | 13 | 14 | 15 | 16 | 17 | 18 | 19 | 20 | 21 | 22 | 23 | 24 | 25 | 26 | 27 | 28 | 29 | 30 | 31 | 32 | 33 | 34 | 35 | 36 | 37 | 38 |
|---|---|---|---|---|---|---|---|---|---|---|---|---|---|---|---|---|---|---|---|---|---|---|---|---|---|---|---|---|---|---|---|---|---|---|---|---|---|---|
| **Venue** | H | A | H | A | H | A | H | A | H | A | H | H | A | A | A | H | A | H | A | A | H | A | H | A | H | A | H | A | H | A | H | A | H | H | A | H | A | H |
| **Competition** | L | L | L | L | L | L | L | L | L | L | L | L | L | L | L | L | L | L | L | L | L | L | L | L | L | L | L | L | L | L | L | L | L | L | L | L | L | L |
| **Result** | L | D | D | D | D | L | W | L | W | L | D | L | W | W | L | W | D | D | L | W | D | L | W | W | W | D | W | L | W | L | L | L | D | D | W | W | L | L |

**Goalkeepers**
Juan Carlos Caballero
Antonio Notario Caro

**Defenders**
Vilagras Carlos Perez
Da Silva Daniel Alves
David Castedo Escudero
Juan Miguel Marguello
Llanes Marcos Vales
Francisco Javi Navarro
Rodriguez Oscar
Pablo Alfaro Armengot
Jose Miguel Prieto

**Midfielders**
Vera Quintero Alfonso
David Perez Arteaga
Francisco Casquero
Francisco Lama Diaz
Alfredo Lobeiras Sanchez
Zoran Njegus
Inti Podesta
Jean Luis Redondo
Vinny Samways
Alberto Hervas Giron Tomas
Gerardo Torrado
Victor Salas Banos

**Forwards**
Ramiro Perez Antonito
Francisco Gallardo
Nikos Machlas
Moises Garcia Leon
Jose Antonio Reyes
Mariano Ramon Toedtli

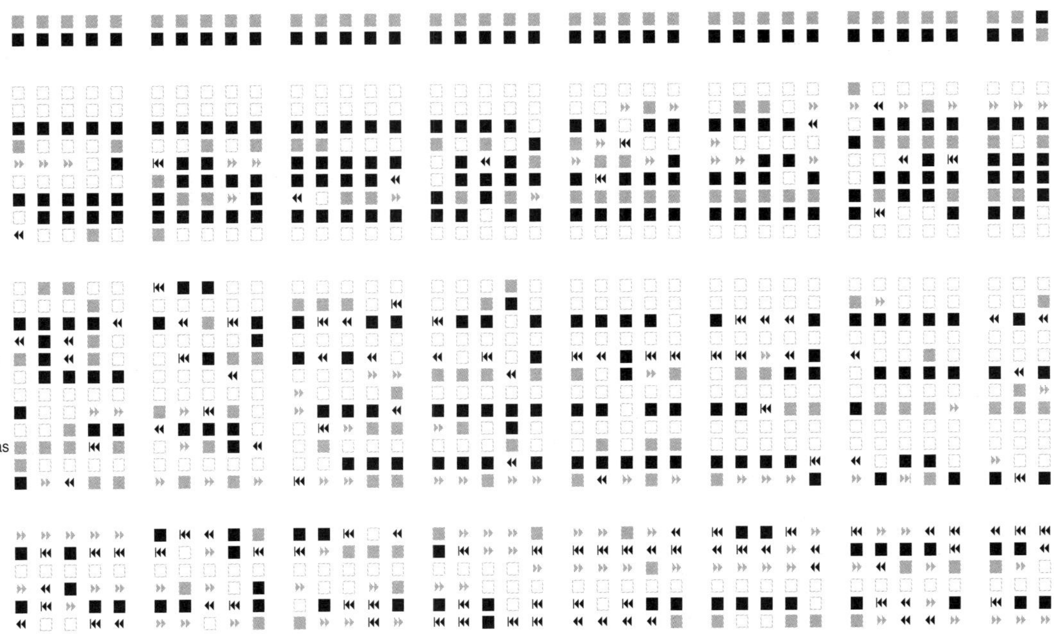

**KEY:** ■ On all match ▒ On bench ⏮ Subbed or sent off (Counting game) ◂◂ Subbed or sent off (playing less than 70 minutes) ⏭ Subbed on from bench (Counting Game) ▸▸ Subbed on (playing less than 70 minutes) Subbed on and then subbed or sent off (Counting Game) Subbed on and then subbed or sent off (playing less than 70 minutes) □ Not in 16

# ATLETICO MADRID

Final Position: **11th**

| | | | | | | |
|---|---|---|---|---|---|---|
| 1 | lge | Barcelona | A | D | 2-2 | Otero 45; Correa 86 |
| 2 | lge | Seville | H | D | 1-1 | Torres 57 |
| 3 | lge | Mallorca | A | W | 4-0 | Torres 9 pen,53; Correa 42; Jorge 66 |
| 4 | lge | Recreativo | H | D | 1-1 | Luis Garcia 32 |
| 5 | lge | Malaga | A | L | 1-3 | Jose Mari 95 |
| 6 | lge | Valencia | H | D | 1-1 | Javi Moreno 75 |
| 7 | lge | Celta Vigo | A | D | 0-0 | |
| 8 | lge | R Vallecano | H | W | 2-0 | Garcia Calvo 5; Torres 57 pen |
| 9 | lge | Athl Bilbao | H | D | 3-3 | Jose Mari 22,74,93 |
| 10 | lge | Espanyol | A | W | 2-1 | Garcia Calvo 44; Luis Garcia 74 |
| 11 | lge | Real Betis | H | W | 1-0 | Torres 13 |
| 12 | lge | Osasuna | A | L | 0-1 | |
| 13 | lge | Valladolid | H | W | 1-0 | Torres 61 |
| 14 | lge | Alaves | A | L | 0-2 | |
| 15 | lge | R Santander | H | L | 1-2 | Emerson 52 |
| 16 | lge | Villarreal | A | L | 3-4 | Torres 31,90; Santi 42 |
| 17 | lge | Deportivo | H | W | 3-1 | Jose Mari 2; Torres 78; Correa 80 |
| 18 | lge | Real Madrid | A | D | 2-2 | Javi Moreno 11 pen; Albertini 90 |
| 19 | lge | Real Sociedad | H | L | 1-2 | Luis Garcia 48 |
| 20 | lge | Barcelona | H | W | 3-0 | Torres 40; Emerson 69; Luis Garcia 87 |
| 21 | lge | Seville | A | D | 1-1 | Javi Moreno 49 |
| 22 | lge | Mallorca | H | W | 2-1 | Movilla 15; Luis Garcia 60 |
| 23 | lge | Recreativo | A | L | 0-3 | |
| 24 | lge | Malaga | H | W | 2-1 | Luis Garcia 13; Torres 47 |
| 25 | lge | Valencia | A | W | 1-0 | Aguilera 71 |
| 26 | lge | Celta Vigo | H | L | 0-1 | |
| 27 | lge | R Vallecano | A | D | 0-0 | |
| 28 | lge | Athl Bilbao | A | L | 0-1 | |
| 29 | lge | Espanyol | H | D | 3-3 | Luis Garcia 74; Hibic 86; Aguilera 90 |
| 30 | lge | Real Betis | A | D | 2-2 | Luis Garcia 26,75 |
| 31 | lge | Osasuna | H | L | 0-1 | |
| 32 | lge | Valladolid | A | L | 1-3 | Jose Mari 60 |
| 33 | lge | Alaves | H | L | 0-1 | |
| 34 | lge | R Santander | A | W | 2-0 | Javi Moreno 63,74 pen |
| 35 | lge | Villarreal | H | W | 3-2 | Reina 30 og; Torres 65,70 |
| 36 | lge | Deportivo | A | L | 2-3 | Albertini 6 pen; Correa 76 |
| 37 | lge | Real Madrid | H | L | 0-4 | |
| 38 | lge | Real Sociedad | A | L | 0-3 | |

## KEY PLAYERS - GOALSCORERS

**1 Fernando Torres**

| | | | |
|---|---|---|---|
| Goals in the League | 13 | Player Strike Rate<br>Average number of minutes between League goals scored by player | 181 |
| Contribution to Attacking Power<br>Average number of minutes between League team goals while on pitch | 71 | Club Strike Rate<br>Average number of minutes between League goals scored by club | 67 |

| | PLAYER | LGE GOALS | POWER | STRIKE RATE |
|---|---|---|---|---|
| 2 | Romero Jose Mari | 6 | 85 | 400 mins |
| 3 | Carlos Aguilera | 2 | 88 | 843 mins |
| 4 | Jose Antonio Garcia Calvo | 2 | 64 | 908 mins |
| 5 | Moises Costa Emerson | 2 | 64 | 1064 mins |

## KEY PLAYERS - MIDFIELDERS

**1 Txomin Arbizu Nagore**

| | | | |
|---|---|---|---|
| Goals in the League | 0 | Contribution to Attacking Power<br>Average number of minutes between League team goals while on pitch | 77 |
| Defensive Rating<br>Average number of mins between League goals conceded while he was on the pitch | 84 | Scoring Difference<br>Defensive Rating minus Contribution to Attacking Power | 7 |

| | PLAYER | LGE GOALS | DEF RATE | POWER | SCORE DIFF |
|---|---|---|---|---|---|
| 2 | Javier Sanz Luis Garcia | 9 | 60 | 56 | 4 mins |
| 3 | Moises Costa Emerson | 2 | 59 | 64 | -5 mins |
| 4 | Demetrio Albertini | 2 | 56 | 64 | -8 mins |
| 5 | Jose Maria Cubero Movilla | 1 | 66 | 84 | -18 mins |

## KEY PLAYERS - DEFENDERS

**1 Mirsad Hibic**

| | | | |
|---|---|---|---|
| Goals Conceded (GC)<br>The number of League goals conceded while he was on the pitch | 33 | Clean Sheets<br>In games when he played at least 70 minutes | 6 |
| Defensive Rating<br>Ave number of mins between League goals conceded while on the pitch | 71 | Club Defensive Rating<br>Average number of mins between League goals conceded by the club this season | 61 |

| | PLAYER | CON LGE | CLEAN SHEETS | DEF RATE |
|---|---|---|---|---|
| 2 | Sergi Barjuan | 36 | 6 | 64 mins |
| 3 | Fabricio Coloccini | 42 | 6 | 58 mins |
| 4 | Jose Antonio Garcia Calvo | 32 | 5 | 57 mins |

## GOALS SCORED

AT HOME

| | | |
|---|---|---|
| MOST | R Madrid | 52 |
| | | 28 |
| LEAST | R Vallecano | 17 |

AWAY

| | | |
|---|---|---|
| MOST | R Madrid | 34 |
| | | 23 |
| LEAST | Recreativo | 11 |

## GOALS CONCEDED

AT HOME

| | | |
|---|---|---|
| LEAST | C Vigo & Valencia | 15 |
| | | 25 |
| MOST | Mallorca | 33 |

AWAY

| | | |
|---|---|---|
| LEAST | R Madrid, Valencia & Seville | 20 |
| | | 31 |
| MOST | Alaves | 48 |

## KEY GOALKEEPER

**1 German Adrian Burgos**

| | |
|---|---|
| Goals Conceded in the League | 19 |
| Defensive Rating<br>Ave number of mins between League goals conceded while on the pitch | 63 |
| Counting Games<br>Games when he played at least 70 minutes | 13 |
| Clean Sheets<br>In games when he played at least 70 minutes | 3 |

## TOP POINT EARNERS

| | PLAYER | GAMES | AVE |
|---|---|---|---|
| 1 | Contra | 23 | 1.48 |
| 2 | Garcia Calvo | 18 | 1.39 |
| 3 | Esteban | 22 | 1.32 |
| 4 | Burgos | 13 | 1.31 |
| 5 | Torres | 24 | 1.29 |
| 6 | Hibic | 25 | 1.28 |
| 7 | Albertini | 23 | 1.26 |
| 8 | Sergi | 25 | 1.24 |
| 9 | Coloccini | 27 | 1.22 |
| 10 | Jose Mari | 22 | 1.18 |
| | CLUB AVERAGE: | | 1.24 |

Ave = Average points per match in Counting Games

## ATTENDANCES

HOME GROUND: VICENTE CALDERON CAPACITY: 57000 AVERAGE LEAGUE AT HOME: 48765

| | | | | | | | | |
|---|---|---|---|---|---|---|---|---|
| 1 | Barcelona | 85000 | 2 | Seville | 47000 | 33 | Alaves | 34200 |
| 18 | Real Madrid | 76300 | 19 | Real Sociedad | 45600 | 36 | Deportivo | 33820 |
| 20 | Barcelona | 57000 | 13 | Valladolid | 45600 | 38 | Real Sociedad | 31400 |
| 26 | Celta Vigo | 57000 | 24 | Malaga | 42750 | 7 | Celta Vigo | 27030 |
| 31 | Osasuna | 57000 | 9 | Athl Bilbao | 42750 | 34 | R Santander | 21150 |
| 37 | Real Madrid | 57000 | 11 | Real Betis | 41610 | 32 | Valladolid | 17500 |
| 17 | Deportivo | 57000 | 15 | R Santander | 39900 | 23 | Recreativo Huelva | 17200 |
| 22 | Mallorca | 55900 | 4 | Recreativo Huelva | 39900 | 12 | Osasuna | 16119 |
| 29 | Espanyol | 54150 | 30 | Real Betis | 39375 | 3 | Mallorca | 16000 |
| 35 | Villarreal | 53580 | 28 | Athl Bilbao | 38000 | 16 | Villarreal | 15120 |
| 25 | Valencia | 50350 | 10 | Espanyol | 37950 | 27 | R Vallecano | 14570 |
| 6 | Valencia | 50160 | 5 | Malaga | 37100 | 14 | Alaves | 13440 |
| 8 | R Vallecano | 48450 | 21 | Seville | 36000 | | | |

## DISCIPLINARY RECORDS

| | PLAYER | YELLOW | RED | AVE |
|---|---|---|---|---|
| 1 | Carreras | 7 | 0 | 72 |
| 2 | Emerson | 12 | 1 | 163 |
| 3 | Jose Mari | 13 | 1 | 171 |
| 4 | Contra | 13 | 1 | 175 |
| 5 | Otero | 5 | 1 | 182 |
| 6 | Correa | 5 | 0 | 193 |
| 7 | Nagore | 4 | 1 | 201 |
| 8 | Sergi | 11 | 0 | 210 |
| 9 | Jorge | 6 | 0 | 219 |
| 10 | Albertini | 9 | 1 | 225 |
| 11 | Stankovic | 4 | 0 | 264 |
| 12 | Aguilera | 6 | 0 | 281 |
| 13 | Coloccini | 8 | 0 | 303 |
| | Other | 25 | 4 | |
| | TOTAL | 128 | 10 | |

## LEAGUE GOALS

| | PLAYER | MINS | GOALS | AVE |
|---|---|---|---|---|
| 1 | Torres | 2357 | 13 | 181 |
| 2 | Luis Garcia | 1864 | 9 | 207 |
| 3 | Jose Mari | 2398 | 6 | 400 |
| 4 | Javi Moreno | 1136 | 5 | 227 |
| 5 | Correa | 968 | 3 | 323 |
| 6 | Aguilera | 1686 | 2 | 843 |
| 7 | Garcia Calvo | 1816 | 2 | 908 |
| 8 | Albertini | 2254 | 2 | 1127 |
| 9 | Emerson | 2128 | 2 | 1064 |
| 10 | Movilla | 1846 | 1 | 1846 |
| 11 | Jorge | 1319 | 1 | 1319 |
| 12 | Santi | 744 | 1 | 744 |
| 13 | Otero | 1095 | 1 | 1095 |
| | Other | | 3 | |
| | TOTAL | | 51 | |

## MONTH BY MONTH GUIDE TO THE POINTS

| MONTH | POINTS | % |
|---|---|---|
| SEPTEMBER | 6 | 50% |
| OCTOBER | 2 | 22% |
| NOVEMBER | 10 | 67% |
| DECEMBER | 3 | 33% |
| JANUARY | 4 | 33% |
| FEBRUARY | 7 | 58% |
| MARCH | 7 | 58% |
| APRIL | 2 | 17% |
| MAY | 6 | 50% |
| JUNE | 0 | 0% |

## LEAGUE APPEARANCES, BOOKINGS AND CAPS

| | AGE | IN THE SQUAD | COUNTING GAMES | MINUTES ON PITCH | YELLOW CARDS | RED CARDS | THIS SEASON | HOME COUNTRY |
|---|---|---|---|---|---|---|---|---|
| **Goalkeepers** | | | | | | | | |
| German Burgos | 34 | 22 | 13 | 1198 | 1 | 0 | - | Argentina |
| Ivan Cuellar | | 2 | 0 | 0 | 0 | 0 | - | Spain |
| Andres Esteban | 28 | 35 | 22 | 2042 | 0 | 1 | - | Spain |
| Ortiz Juanma | | 15 | 2 | 180 | 0 | 0 | - | Spain |
| **Defenders** | | | | | | | | |
| Alvarez Armando | 32 | 4 | 0 | 15 | 0 | 0 | - | Spain |
| Fabricio Coloccini | 21 | 28 | 27 | 2430 | 8 | 0 | 2 | Argentina (5) |
| Cosmin Contra | 27 | 31 | 23 | 2459 | 13 | 1 | 9 | Romania (27) |
| Jose Garcia Calvo | 28 | 26 | 18 | 1816 | 3 | 1 | 5 | Spain (2) |
| Mirsad Hibic | 29 | 30 | 25 | 2341 | 7 | 0 | - | Bosnia |
| Jorge Otero | 34 | 30 | 9 | 1095 | 5 | 1 | - | Spain |
| Denia Santi | 29 | 33 | 8 | 744 | 0 | 0 | - | Spain |
| Sergi Barjuan | 31 | 27 | 25 | 2312 | 11 | 0 | - | Spain |
| **Midfielders** | | | | | | | | |
| Carlos Aguilera | 34 | 33 | 13 | 1686 | 6 | 0 | - | Spain |
| Demetrio Albertini | 31 | 28 | 23 | 2254 | 9 | 1 | - | Italy |
| Luis Ferrer Carreras | 30 | 19 | 3 | 505 | 7 | 0 | - | Spain |
| Daniel Dani | 26 | 16 | 0 | 282 | 0 | 0 | - | Portugal |
| Moises Emerson | 31 | 32 | 19 | 2128 | 12 | 1 | - | Brazil |
| Jorge | 21 | 33 | 4 | 1319 | 6 | 0 | - | Spain |
| Javier Luis Garcia | 25 | 32 | 10 | 1864 | 3 | 1 | - | Spain |
| Jose Maria Movilla | 28 | 38 | 13 | 1846 | 4 | 0 | - | Spain |
| Txomin Nagore | 28 | 35 | 8 | 1005 | 4 | 1 | - | Spain |
| Jovan Stankovic | 32 | 20 | 7 | 1058 | 4 | 0 | - | Serbia & Montenegro |
| **Forwards** | | | | | | | | |
| Fernando Correa | 29 | 24 | 3 | 968 | 5 | 0 | - | Uruguay |
| Javi Moreno | 28 | 29 | 5 | 1136 | 1 | 0 | - | Spain |
| Romero Jose Mari | 24 | 32 | 22 | 2398 | 13 | 1 | 3 | Spain (2) |
| Fernando Torres | 19 | 29 | 24 | 2357 | 6 | 1 | - | Spain |

KEY: LEAGUE BOOKINGS CAPS (FIFA RANKING)

## TEAM OF THE SEASON

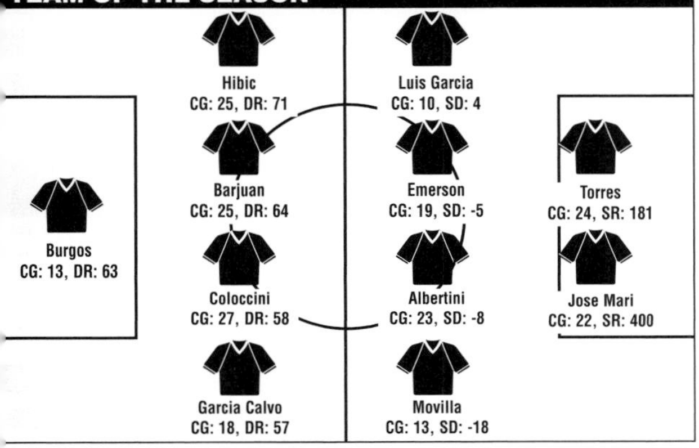

Hibic
CG: 25, DR: 71
Luis Garcia
CG: 10, SD: 4
Barjuan
CG: 25, DR: 64
Emerson
CG: 19, SD: -5
Torres
CG: 24, SR: 181
Burgos
CG: 13, DR: 63
Coloccini
CG: 27, DR: 58
Albertini
CG: 23, SD: -8
Jose Mari
CG: 22, SR: 400
Garcia Calvo
CG: 18, DR: 57
Movilla
CG: 13, SD: -18


KEY: DR = Defensive Rate, SD = Scoring Difference, SR = Strike Rate, CG = Counting Games – League games playing at least 70 minutes

## SQUAD APPEARANCES

| Match | 1 | 2 | 3 | 4 | 5 | 6 | 7 | 8 | 9 | 10 | 11 | 12 | 13 | 14 | 15 | 16 | 17 | 18 | 19 | 20 | 21 | 22 | 23 | 24 | 25 | 26 | 27 | 28 | 29 | 30 | 31 | 32 | 33 | 34 | 35 | 36 | 37 | 38 |
|---|---|---|---|---|---|---|---|---|---|---|---|---|---|---|---|---|---|---|---|---|---|---|---|---|---|---|---|---|---|---|---|---|---|---|---|---|---|---|
| Venue | A | H | A | H | A | H | A | H | H | A | H | A | H | A | H | A | H | A | H | H | A | H | A | H | A | H | A | A | H | A | H | A | H | A | H | A | H | A |
| Competition | L | L | L | L | L | L | L | L | L | L | L | L | L | L | L | L | L | L | L | L | L | L | L | L | L | L | L | L | L | L | L | L | L | L | L | L | L | L |
| Result | D | D | W | D | L | D | D | W | D | W | W | L | W | L | L | L | W | D | L | W | D | W | L | W | W | L | D | L | D | D | L | L | L | W | W | L | L | L |

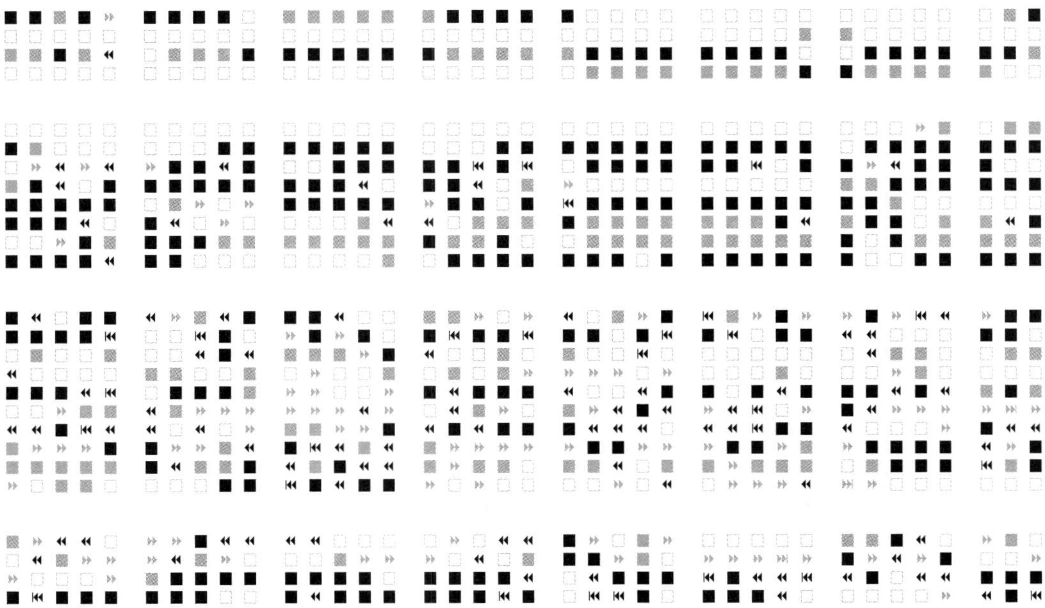

**Goalkeepers**
German Adrian Burgos
Ivan Cuellar
Andres Suarez Esteban
Ortiz Juanma

**Defenders**
Alvarez Armando
Fabricio Coloccini
Cosmin Marius Contra
Jose Antonio Garcia Calvo
Mirsad Hibic
Jorge Otero
Denia Santi
Sergi Barjuan

**Midfielders**
Carlos Aguilera
Demetrio Albertini
Luis Ferrer Carreras
Daniel Carvalho Dani
Moises Costa Emerson
Larena-Avellaneda Jorge
Javier Sanz Luis Garcia
Jose Maria Cubero Movilla
Txomin Arbizu Nagore
Jovan Stankovic

**Forwards**
Fernando Correa
Javi Moreno
Romero Jose Mari
Fernando Torres

KEY: On all match / On bench / Subbed or sent off (Counting game) / Subbed or sent off (playing less than 70 minutes) / Subbed on from bench (Counting Game) / Subbed on (playing less than 70 minutes) / Subbed on and then subbed or sent off (Counting Game) / Subbed on and then subbed or sent off (playing less than 70 minutes) / Not in 16

# OSASUNA

Final Position: **12th**

| | | | | | | |
|---|---|---|---|---|---|---|
| 1 | lge | Villarreal | A | D | 2-2 | Lopez 68; Garcia 81 |
| 2 | lge | Deportivo | H | L | 1-2 | Vidrio 12 |
| 3 | lge | Real Madrid | A | L | 1-4 | Rivero 58 pen |
| 4 | lge | Real Sociedad | H | L | 2-3 | Punal 21 pen; Rivero 48 |
| 5 | lge | Barcelona | A | D | 2-2 | Rivero 2; Gancedo 44 |
| 6 | lge | Seville | H | W | 2-1 | Aloisi 33 pen,45 |
| 7 | lge | Mallorca | A | L | 0-2 | |
| 8 | lge | Recreativo | H | L | 0-1 | |
| 9 | lge | Malaga | A | L | 0-1 | |
| 10 | lge | Valencia | H | W | 1-0 | Ivan Rosado 8 |
| 11 | lge | Celta Vigo | A | D | 0-0 | |
| 12 | lge | Atl Madrid | H | W | 1-0 | Rivero 61 |
| 13 | lge | Athl Bilbao | A | W | 3-1 | Aloisi 7 pen; Munoz 15; Ivan Rosado 43 |
| 14 | lge | Espanyol | H | W | 1-0 | Lopez 46 |
| 15 | lge | Real Betis | A | L | 1-2 | Ivan Rosado 83 |
| 16 | lge | R Vallecano | H | L | 0-1 | |
| 17 | lge | Valladolid | H | D | 1-1 | Mateo 58 |
| 18 | lge | Alaves | A | D | 1-1 | Aloisi 88 |
| 19 | lge | R Santander | H | W | 3-1 | Ivan Rosado 12; Rivero 45; Alfredo 52 |
| 20 | lge | Villarreal | H | L | 0-1 | |
| 21 | lge | Deportivo | A | D | 1-1 | Munoz 46 |
| 22 | lge | Real Madrid | H | W | 1-0 | Manfredini 38 |
| 23 | lge | Real Sociedad | A | L | 0-2 | |
| 24 | lge | Barcelona | H | D | 2-2 | Ivan Rosado 79; Rivero 90 |
| 25 | lge | Seville | A | L | 0-2 | |
| 26 | lge | Mallorca | H | D | 0-0 | |
| 27 | lge | Recreativo | A | D | 1-1 | Aloisi 51 |
| 28 | lge | Malaga | H | L | 0-1 | |
| 29 | lge | Valencia | A | L | 0-1 | |
| 30 | lge | Celta Vigo | H | L | 0-2 | |
| 31 | lge | Atl Madrid | A | W | 1-0 | Ivan Rosado 43 |
| 32 | lge | Athl Bilbao | H | L | 1-5 | Rivero 69 |
| 33 | lge | Espanyol | A | D | 0-0 | |
| 34 | lge | Real Betis | H | W | 2-1 | Moha 31; Punal 39 pen |
| 35 | lge | R Vallecano | A | D | 0-0 | |
| 36 | lge | Valladolid | A | W | 2-0 | Palacios 11; Valdo 44 |
| 37 | lge | Alaves | H | W | 4-2 | Aloisi 24 pen,78; Moha 68,84 |
| 38 | lge | R Santander | A | W | 3-2 | Munoz 20; Brit 35; Aloisi 73 |

## KEY PLAYERS - GOALSCORERS

**1 John Aloisi**

| | | | |
|---|---|---|---|
| Goals in the League | 8 | Player Strike Rate<br>Average number of minutes between League goals scored by player | 284 |
| Contribution to Attacking Power<br>Average number of minutes between League team goals while on pitch | 90 | Club Strike Rate<br>Average number of minutes between League goals scored by club | 86 |

| | PLAYER | LGE GOALS | POWER | STRIKE RATE |
|---|---|---|---|---|
| 2 | Gerald Damian Rivero | 7 | 69 | 346 mins |
| 3 | Mojarro Ivan Rosado | 6 | 90 | 439 mins |
| 4 | Francisco Martinez Punal | 2 | 82 | 1279 mins |
| 5 | Antonio Lopez | 2 | 83 | 1584 mins |

## KEY PLAYERS - MIDFIELDERS

**1 Mohamed El Yaagoubi Moha**

| | | | |
|---|---|---|---|
| Goals in the League | 3 | Contribution to Attacking Power<br>Average number of minutes between League team goals while on pitch | 68 |
| Defensive Rating<br>Average number of mins between League goals conceded while he was on the pitch | 71 | Scoring Difference<br>Defensive Rating minus Contribution to Attacking Power | 3 |

| | PLAYER | LGE GOALS | DEF RATE | POWER | SCORE DIFF |
|---|---|---|---|---|---|
| 2 | Gerald Damian Rivero | 7 | 71 | 69 | 2 mins |
| 3 | Inaki Oroz Munoz | 3 | 83 | 83 | 0 mins |
| 4 | Francisco Martinez Punal | 2 | 69 | 83 | -14 mins |
| 5 | Valmiro Lopes Rocha Valdo | 1 | 65 | 83 | -18 mins |

## KEY PLAYERS - DEFENDERS

**1 Jose Martinez Izquierdo**

| | | | |
|---|---|---|---|
| Goals Conceded (GC)<br>The number of League goals conceded while he was on the pitch | 11 | Clean Sheets<br>In games when he played at least 70 minutes | 6 |
| Defensive Rating<br>Ave number of mins between League goals conceded while on the pitch | 97 | Club Defensive Rating<br>Average number of mins between League goals conceded by the club this season | 70 |

| | PLAYER | CON LGE | CLEAN SHEETS | DEF RATE |
|---|---|---|---|---|
| 2 | Antonio Lopez | 43 | 10 | 74 mins |
| 3 | Jose Manuel Yanguas | 18 | 3 | 73 mins |
| 4 | Cesar Lasa Cruchaga | 44 | 9 | 73 mins |
| 5 | Jose Manuel Azcona Mateo | 34 | 6 | 69 mins |

## GOALS SCORED

AT HOME

| | | |
|---|---|---|
| MOST | R Madrid | 52 |
| | | 22 |
| LEAST | R Vallecano | 17 |

AWAY

| | | |
|---|---|---|
| MOST | R Madrid | 34 |
| | | 18 |
| LEAST | Recreativo | 11 |

## GOALS CONCEDED

AT HOME

| | | |
|---|---|---|
| LEAST | C Vigo & Valencia | 15 |
| | | 24 |
| MOST | Mallorca | 33 |

AWAY

| | | |
|---|---|---|
| LEAST | R Madrid, Valencia & Seville | 20 |
| | | 24 |
| MOST | Alaves | 48 |

## KEY GOALKEEPER

**1 Ricardo Goni Sanzol**

| | |
|---|---|
| Goals Conceded in the League | 37 |
| Defensive Rating<br>Ave number of mins between League goals conceded while on the pitch | 81 |
| Counting Games<br>Games when he played at least 70 minutes | 33 |
| Clean Sheets<br>In games when he played at least 70 minutes | 10 |

## TOP POINT EARNERS

| | PLAYER | GAMES | AVE |
|---|---|---|---|
| 1 | Alfredo | 18 | 1.67 |
| 2 | Josetxo | 20 | 1.40 |
| 3 | Rivero | 23 | 1.39 |
| 4 | Aloisi | 23 | 1.35 |
| 5 | Lopez | 35 | 1.34 |
| 6 | Punal | 25 | 1.32 |
| 7 | Sanzol | 33 | 1.30 |
| 8 | Cruchaga | 36 | 1.22 |
| 9 | Yanguas | 14 | 1.21 |
| 10 | Garcia | 16 | 1.19 |
| | **CLUB AVERAGE:** | | **1.24** |

Ave = Average points per match in Counting Games

## ATTENDANCES

**HOME GROUND: EL SADAR CAPACITY: 20000 AVERAGE LEAGUE AT HOME: 16338**

| | | | | | | | | |
|---|---|---|---|---|---|---|---|---|
| 5 | Barcelona | 78400 | 7 | Mallorca | 18960 | 32 | Athl Bilbao | 15125 |
| 3 | Real Madrid | 65000 | 34 | Real Betis | 18710 | 30 | Celta Vigo | 14530 |
| 31 | Atl Madrid | 57000 | 19 | R Santander | 18109 | 4 | Real Sociedad | 14129 |
| 15 | Real Betis | 47250 | 16 | R Vallecano | 17910 | 27 | Recreativo Huelva | 14000 |
| 29 | Valencia | 45100 | 20 | Villarreal | 17900 | 26 | Mallorca | 13950 |
| 13 | Athl Bilbao | 32000 | 10 | Valencia | 17711 | 37 | Alaves | 13930 |
| 23 | Real Sociedad | 32000 | 9 | Malaga | 16695 | 36 | Valladolid | 13250 |
| 25 | Seville | 31500 | 8 | Recreativo Huelva | 16517 | 28 | Malaga | 12935 |
| 11 | Celta Vigo | 28620 | 1 | Villarreal | 16500 | 6 | Seville | 11940 |
| 21 | Deportivo | 26700 | 12 | Atl Madrid | 16119 | 35 | R Vallecano | 11625 |
| 22 | Real Madrid | 20000 | 2 | Deportivo | 16000 | 33 | Espanyol | 9900 |
| 24 | Barcelona | 19900 | 18 | Alaves | 15936 | 38 | R Santander | 9601 |
| 17 | Valladolid | 19104 | 14 | Espanyol | 15920 | | | |

■ Home □ Away ▒ Neutral

## DISCIPLINARY RECORDS

| | PLAYER | YELLOW | RED | AVE |
|---|---|---|---|---|
| 1 | Garcia | 9 | 1 | 170 |
| 2 | Munoz | 4 | 1 | 181 |
| 3 | Punal | 11 | 1 | 213 |
| 4 | Josetxo | 7 | 0 | 266 |
| 5 | Morales | 2 | 0 | 266 |
| 6 | Alfredo | 7 | 0 | 273 |
| 7 | Cruchaga | 10 | 1 | 292 |
| 8 | Valdo | 3 | 0 | 305 |
| 9 | Rivero | 6 | 1 | 345 |
| 10 | Moha | 4 | 0 | 372 |
| 11 | Mateo | 6 | 0 | 388 |
| 12 | Yanguas | 3 | 0 | 440 |
| 13 | Lopez | 7 | 0 | 452 |
| | Other | 25 | 2 | |
| | **TOTAL** | **104** | **7** | |

## LEAGUE GOALS

| | PLAYER | MINS | GOALS | AVE |
|---|---|---|---|---|
| 1 | Aloisi | 2271 | 8 | 284 |
| 2 | Rivero | 2419 | 7 | 346 |
| 3 | Ivan Rosado | 2631 | 6 | 439 |
| 4 | Munoz | 909 | 3 | 303 |
| 5 | Moha | 1489 | 3 | 496 |
| 6 | Lopez | 3168 | 2 | 1584 |
| 7 | Punal | 2558 | 2 | 1279 |
| 8 | Valdo | 915 | 1 | 915 |
| 9 | Manfredini | 669 | 1 | 669 |
| 10 | Gancedo | 1497 | 1 | 1497 |
| 11 | Garcia | 1704 | 1 | 1704 |
| 12 | Brit | 324 | 1 | 324 |
| 13 | Palacios | 402 | 1 | 402 |
| | Other | | 3 | |
| | **TOTAL** | | **40** | |

## MONTH BY MONTH GUIDE TO THE POINTS

| MONTH | POINTS | % |
|---|---|---|
| SEPTEMBER | 1 | 8% |
| OCTOBER | 4 | 44% |
| NOVEMBER | 7 | 47% |
| DECEMBER | 6 | 67% |
| JANUARY | 5 | 42% |
| FEBRUARY | 4 | 33% |
| MARCH | 3 | 25% |
| APRIL | 3 | 25% |
| MAY | 5 | 42% |
| JUNE | 9 | 100% |

## TEAM OF THE SEASON

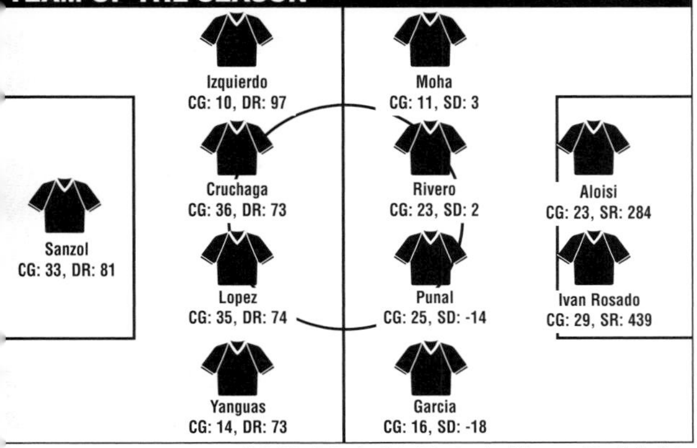
Sanzol
CG: 33, DR: 81
Izquierdo
CG: 10, DR: 97
Cruchaga
CG: 36, DR: 73
Lopez
CG: 35, DR: 74
Yanguas
CG: 14, DR: 73
Moha
CG: 11, SD: 3
Rivero
CG: 23, SD: 2
Punal
CG: 25, SD: -14
Garcia
CG: 16, SD: -18
Aloisi
CG: 23, SR: 284
Ivan Rosado
CG: 29, SR: 439

**KEY:** DR = Defensive Rate, SD = Scoring Difference, SR = Strike Rate, CG = Counting Games – League games playing at least 70 minutes

## LEAGUE APPEARANCES, BOOKINGS AND CAPS

| | AGE | IN THE SQUAD | COUNTING GAMES | MINUTES ON PITCH | YELLOW CARDS | RED CARDS | THIS SEASON | HOME COUNTRY |
|---|---|---|---|---|---|---|---|---|
| **Goalkeepers** | | | | | | | | |
| Ricardo Goni Sanzol | 27 | 38 | 33 | 2986 | 3 | 0 | - | Spain |
| Juan Carlos Unzue | 36 | 37 | 5 | 434 | 0 | 0 | - | Spain |
| **Defenders** | | | | | | | | |
| Cesar Cruchaga | 29 | 36 | 36 | 3219 | 10 | 1 | - | Spain |
| Jose Izquierdo | 22 | 16 | 10 | 1065 | 2 | 0 | - | Spain |
| Urtasun Josetxo | 28 | 26 | 20 | 1868 | 7 | 0 | - | Spain |
| Antonio Lopez | 21 | 37 | 35 | 3168 | 7 | 0 | - | Spain |
| Jose Mateo | 28 | 33 | 25 | 2332 | 6 | 0 | - | Spain |
| Francisco Paqui | 32 | 21 | 2 | 272 | 5 | 1 | - | Spain |
| Jose Yanguas | 31 | 34 | 14 | 1320 | 3 | 0 | - | Spain |
| **Midfielders** | | | | | | | | |
| Sanchez Alfredo | 30 | 36 | 18 | 1913 | 7 | 0 | - | Spain |
| Leonel Gancedo | 32 | 31 | 10 | 1497 | 3 | 0 | - | Argentina |
| Pablo Garcia | 26 | 23 | 16 | 1704 | 9 | 1 | - | Uruguay |
| Francisco Jusue | 23 | 5 | 0 | 0 | 0 | 0 | - | |
| Angel Lekumberri | | 3 | 0 | 8 | 0 | 0 | - | |
| Christian Manfredini | 28 | 13 | 5 | 669 | 1 | 0 | - | Italy |
| Mohamed Moha | 25 | 37 | 11 | 1489 | 4 | 0 | - | Spain |
| Inaki Oroz Munoz | 25 | 25 | 6 | 909 | 4 | 1 | - | Spain |
| Pagola | | 1 | 0 | 0 | 0 | 0 | - | |
| Cesar Palacios | 28 | 32 | 2 | 402 | 0 | 0 | - | Spain |
| Francisco Punal | 27 | 35 | 25 | 2558 | 11 | 1 | - | Spain |
| Gerald Rivero | 28 | 34 | 23 | 2419 | 6 | 1 | - | Argentina |
| Valmiro Valdo | 22 | 16 | 8 | 915 | 3 | 0 | - | Spain |
| Manuel Vidrio | | 9 | 5 | 450 | 2 | 0 | - | |
| **Forwards** | | | | | | | | |
| John Aloisi | 27 | 35 | 23 | 2271 | 4 | 1 | - | Australia |
| Gorka Gallego Brit | 25 | 12 | 0 | 324 | 0 | 0 | - | Spain |
| De Carlos Gorka | 25 | 4 | 0 | 30 | 0 | 0 | - | Spain |
| Ivan Rosado | 29 | 36 | 29 | 2631 | 5 | 0 | - | Spain |
| Richard Morales | 28 | 19 | 4 | 532 | 2 | 0 | 1 | Uruguay (28) |
| Carlos Ochoa | 25 | 7 | 0 | 67 | 0 | 0 | - | |

**KEY:** LEAGUE BOOKINGS CAPS (FIFA RANKING)

## SQUAD APPEARANCES

| Match | 1 | 2 | 3 | 4 | 5 | 6 | 7 | 8 | 9 | 10 | 11 | 12 | 13 | 14 | 15 | 16 | 17 | 18 | 19 | 20 | 21 | 22 | 23 | 24 | 25 | 26 | 27 | 28 | 29 | 30 | 31 | 32 | 33 | 34 | 35 | 36 | 37 | 38 |
|---|---|---|---|---|---|---|---|---|---|---|---|---|---|---|---|---|---|---|---|---|---|---|---|---|---|---|---|---|---|---|---|---|---|---|---|---|---|---|
| Venue | A | H | A | H | A | H | A | H | A | H | A | H | A | H | A | H | H | A | H | H | A | H | A | H | A | H | A | H | A | H | A | H | A | H | A | A | H | A |
| Competition | L | L | L | L | L | L | L | L | L | L | L | L | L | L | L | L | L | L | L | L | L | L | L | L | L | L | L | L | L | L | L | L | L | L | L | L | L | L |
| Result | D | L | L | L | D | W | L | L | L | W | D | W | W | W | L | L | D | D | W | L | D | W | L | D | L | D | D | L | L | L | W | L | D | W | D | W | W | W |

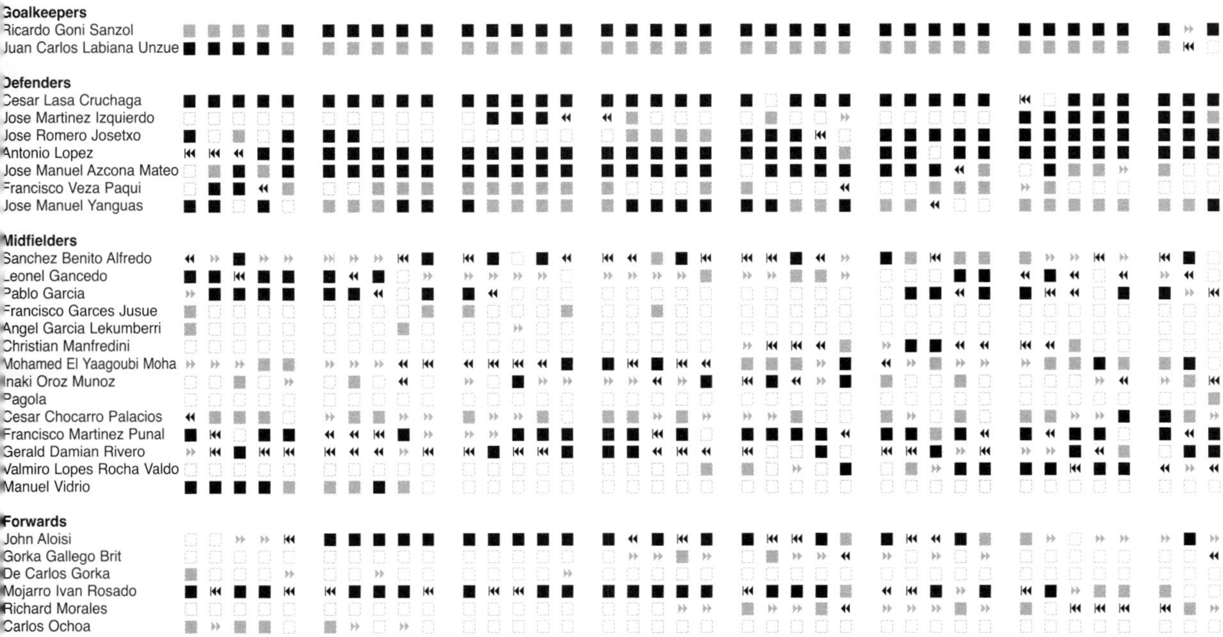
Goalkeepers
Ricardo Goni Sanzol
Juan Carlos Labiana Unzue
Defenders
Cesar Lasa Cruchaga
Jose Martinez Izquierdo
Jose Romero Josetxo
Antonio Lopez
Jose Manuel Azcona Mateo
Francisco Veza Paqui
Jose Manuel Yanguas
Midfielders
Sanchez Benito Alfredo
Leonel Gancedo
Pablo Garcia
Francisco Garces Jusue
Angel Garcia Lekumberri
Christian Manfredini
Mohamed El Yaagoubi Moha
Inaki Oroz Munoz
Pagola
Cesar Chocarro Palacios
Francisco Martinez Punal
Gerald Damian Rivero
Valmiro Lopes Rocha Valdo
Manuel Vidrio
Forwards
John Aloisi
Gorka Gallego Brit
De Carlos Gorka
Mojarro Ivan Rosado
Richard Morales
Carlos Ochoa

KEY: ■ On all match ■ On bench ⏮ Subbed or sent off (Counting game) « Subbed or sent off (playing less than 70 minutes) ⏭ Subbed on from bench (Counting Game) » Subbed on (playing less than 70 minutes) Subbed on and then subbed or sent off (Counting Game) Subbed on and then subbed or sent off (playing less than 70 minutes) □ Not in 16

# REAL VALLADOLID

Final Position: **13th**

| | | | | | | |
|---|---|---|---|---|---|---|
| 1 | lge | R Santander | A | W | 1-0 | Aganzo 90 |
| 2 | lge | Villarreal | H | W | 1-0 | Colsa 39 |
| 3 | lge | Deportivo | A | L | 0-2 | |
| 4 | lge | Real Madrid | H | D | 1-1 | Olivera 58 pen |
| 5 | lge | Real Sociedad | A | L | 1-2 | Colsa 71 |
| 6 | lge | Barcelona | H | W | 2-1 | Aganzo 53; Pachon 85 |
| 7 | lge | Seville | A | L | 1-2 | Colsa 50 |
| 8 | lge | Mallorca | H | L | 1-3 | Ibagaza 25 og |
| 9 | lge | Recreativo | A | W | 3-1 | Yago 21 og; Pachon 45; Mario 82 |
| 10 | lge | Malaga | H | D | 0-0 | |
| 11 | lge | Valencia | A | L | 0-2 | |
| 12 | lge | Celta Vigo | H | L | 0-2 | |
| 13 | lge | Atl Madrid | A | L | 0-1 | |
| 14 | lge | Athl Bilbao | H | W | 2-0 | Aganzo 62,72 |
| 15 | lge | Espanyol | A | L | 0-1 | |
| 16 | lge | Real Betis | H | W | 3-0 | Sales 49,64; Oscar 82 |
| 17 | lge | Osasuna | A | D | 1-1 | Aganzo 39 |
| 18 | lge | R Vallecano | A | W | 1-0 | Oscar 9 |
| 19 | lge | Alaves | H | L | 1-3 | Ciric 86 |
| 20 | lge | R Santander | H | W | 2-1 | Chema 18; Sales 82 |
| 21 | lge | Villarreal | A | L | 0-1 | |
| 22 | lge | Deportivo | H | L | 0-1 | |
| 23 | lge | Real Madrid | A | L | 1-3 | Sales 11 |
| 24 | lge | Real Sociedad | H | W | 3-0 | Olivera 1,8; Oscar 21 |
| 25 | lge | Barcelona | A | D | 1-1 | Bonano 46 og |
| 26 | lge | Seville | H | D | 0-0 | |
| 27 | lge | Mallorca | A | L | 1-2 | Jonathan 45 |
| 28 | lge | Recreativo | H | L | 0-1 | |
| 29 | lge | Malaga | A | L | 0-1 | |
| 30 | lge | Valencia | H | W | 1-0 | Antonio Lopez 75 |
| 31 | lge | Celta Vigo | A | D | 0-0 | |
| 32 | lge | Atl Madrid | H | W | 3-1 | Sales 31; Aganzo 50,75 |
| 33 | lge | Athl Bilbao | A | D | 0-0 | |
| 34 | lge | Espanyol | H | D | 1-1 | Sales 14 |
| 35 | lge | Real Betis | A | D | 2-2 | Colsa 46,71 |
| 36 | lge | Osasuna | H | L | 0-2 | |
| 37 | lge | R Vallecano | H | W | 2-0 | Aganzo 52; Antonio Lopez 82 pen |
| 38 | lge | Alaves | A | D | 1-1 | Aganzo 36 |

## KEY PLAYERS - GOALSCORERS

**1 David Mendez Aganzo**

| | | | |
|---|---|---|---|
| Goals in the League | 9 | Player Strike Rate<br>Average number of minutes between League goals scored by player | 229 |
| Contribution to Attacking Power<br>Average number of minutes between League team goals while on pitch | 103 | Club Strike Rate<br>Average number of minutes between League goals scored by club | 92 |

| | PLAYER | LGE GOALS | POWER | STRIKE RATE |
|---|---|---|---|---|
| 2 | Fernando de los Cobos Sales | 6 | 101 | 507 mins |
| 3 | Gonzalo Ruiz Abendea Colsa | 5 | 91 | 637 mins |
| 4 | Gonzalez Marcos Oscar | 3 | 86 | 691 mins |
| 5 | Pedro Alvarez Abrante Mario | 1 | 89 | 1342 mins |

## KEY PLAYERS - MIDFIELDERS

**1 Alvarez Antonio Lopez**

| | | | |
|---|---|---|---|
| Goals in the League | 2 | Contribution to Attacking Power<br>Average number of minutes between League team goals while on pitch | 71 |
| Defensive Rating<br>Average number of mins between League goals conceded while he was on the pitch | 98 | Scoring Difference<br>Defensive Rating minus Contribution to Attacking Power | 27 |

| | PLAYER | LGE GOALS | DEF RATE | POWER | SCORE DIFF |
|---|---|---|---|---|---|
| 2 | Gonzalez Marcos Oscar | 3 | 99 | 86 | 13 mins |
| 3 | Pedro Alvarez Abrante Mario | 1 | 89 | 89 | 0 mins |
| 4 | Jose Luis Perez Caminero | 0 | 88 | 88 | 0 mins |
| 5 | Gonzalo Ruiz Abendea Colsa | 5 | 82 | 91 | -9 mins |

## KEY PLAYERS - DEFENDERS

**1 Martin Carabias Jonathan**

| | | | |
|---|---|---|---|
| Goals Conceded (GC)<br>The number of League goals conceded while he was on the pitch | 10 | Clean Sheets<br>In games when he played at least 70 minutes | 5 |
| Defensive Rating<br>Ave number of mins between League goals conceded while on the pitch | 112 | Club Defensive Rating<br>Average number of mins between League goals conceded by the club this season | 83 |

| | PLAYER | CON LGE | CLEAN SHEETS | DEF RATE |
|---|---|---|---|---|
| 2 | Juan Manuel Montano Pena | 27 | 9 | 93 mins |
| 3 | Galvez Burgos Gaspar | 21 | 5 | 86 mins |
| 4 | Javier Torres Gomez | 38 | 10 | 83 mins |
| 5 | Alberto Rey Marcos | 32 | 6 | 75 mins |

## GOALS SCORED

**AT HOME**

| | | |
|---|---|---|
| MOST | R Madrid | 52 |
| | | 23 |
| LEAST | R Vallecano | 17 |

**AWAY**

| | | |
|---|---|---|
| MOST | R Madrid | 34 |
| | | 14 |
| LEAST | Recreativo | 11 |

## GOALS CONCEDED

**AT HOME**

| | | |
|---|---|---|
| LEAST | C Vigo & Valencia | 15 |
| | | 17 |
| MOST | Mallorca | 33 |

**AWAY**

| | | |
|---|---|---|
| LEAST | R Madrid, Valencia & Seville | 20 |
| | | 23 |
| MOST | Alaves | 48 |

## KEY GOALKEEPER

**1 Albano Benjamin Bizzarri**

| | |
|---|---|
| Goals Conceded in the League | 41 |
| Defensive Rating<br>Ave number of mins between League goals conceded while on the pitch | 83 |
| Counting Games<br>Games when he played at least 70 minutes | 38 |
| Clean Sheets<br>In games when he played at least 70 minutes | 11 |

## TOP POINT EARNERS

| | PLAYER | GAMES | AVE |
|---|---|---|---|
| 1 | Oscar Sanchez | 12 | 1.50 |
| 2 | Gaspar | 19 | 1.47 |
| 3 | Mario | 12 | 1.42 |
| 4 | Oscar | 20 | 1.40 |
| 5 | Pena | 27 | 1.33 |
| 6 | Colsa | 33 | 1.24 |
| 7 | Aganzo | 21 | 1.24 |
| 8 | Bizzarri | 38 | 1.21 |
| 9 | Torres Gomez | 35 | 1.14 |
| 10 | Marcos | 26 | 1.08 |
| | CLUB AVERAGE: | | 1.21 |

Ave = Average points per match in Counting Game

## ATTENDANCES

HOME GROUND: MUNICIPAL JOSE ZORRILLA CAPACITY: 26512 AVERAGE LEAGUE AT HOME: 18932

| | | | | | | | | |
|---|---|---|---|---|---|---|---|---|
| 25 | Barcelona | 78400 | **19** | **Alaves** | **23850** | 9 | Recreativo Huelva | 17400 |
| 23 | Real Madrid | 53400 | 29 | Malaga | 22260 | **2** | **Villarreal** | **16500** |
| 13 | Atl Madrid | 45600 | **10** | **Malaga** | **21200** | **24** | **Real Sociedad** | **15900** |
| 11 | Valencia | 42400 | **26** | **Seville** | **21200** | **12** | **Celta Vigo** | **15900** |
| 15 | Espanyol | 40700 | **30** | **Valencia** | **21200** | **22** | **Deportivo** | **15900** |
| 35 | Real Betis | 39400 | **16** | **Real Betis** | **20935** | 1 | R Santander | 14500 |
| 7 | Seville | 36000 | **14** | **Athl Bilbao** | **20935** | **8** | **Mallorca** | **13250** |
| 33 | Athl Bilbao | 36000 | **34** | **Espanyol** | **19900** | **36** | **Osasuna** | **13250** |
| 3 | Deportivo | 30000 | 17 | Osasuna | 19104 | 18 | R Vallecano | 12400 |
| 5 | Real Sociedad | 26560 | **28** | **Recreativo Huelva** | **18020** | 21 | Villarreal | 12265 |
| **4** | **Real Madrid** | **25175** | 27 | Mallorca | 18000 | 38 | Alaves | 9792 |
| **6** | **Barcelona** | **25175** | 31 | Celta Vigo | 17500 | **37** | **R Vallecano** | **9275** |
| **20** | **R Santander** | **24645** | **32** | **Atl Madrid** | **17500** | | | |

## DISCIPLINARY RECORDS

| | PLAYER | YELLOW | RED | AVE |
|---|---|---|---|---|
| 1 | Sousa | 3 | 1 | 148 |
| 2 | Mustafa | 5 | 1 | 162 |
| 3 | Richetti | 3 | 0 | 223 |
| 4 | Gaspar | 8 | 0 | 226 |
| 5 | Pena | 10 | 1 | 227 |
| 6 | Jesus | 4 | 0 | 227 |
| 7 | Caminero | 5 | 0 | 246 |
| 8 | Torres Gomez | 11 | 0 | 285 |
| 9 | Colsa | 7 | 1 | 398 |
| 10 | Aganzo | 4 | 1 | 412 |
| 11 | Oscar Sanchez | 3 | 0 | 426 |
| 12 | Marcos | 4 | 1 | 481 |
| 13 | Oscar | 4 | 0 | 518 |
| | Other | 14 | 1 | |
| | TOTAL | 85 | 7 | |

## LEAGUE GOALS

| | PLAYER | MINS | GOALS | AVE |
|---|---|---|---|---|
| 1 | Aganzo | 2062 | 9 | 229 |
| 2 | Sales | 3044 | 6 | 507 |
| 3 | Colsa | 3185 | 5 | 637 |
| 4 | Olivera | 1332 | 3 | 444 |
| 5 | Oscar | 2073 | 3 | 691 |
| 6 | Pachon | 1070 | 2 | 535 |
| 7 | Antonio Lopez | 781 | 2 | 391 |
| 8 | Jonathan | 1119 | 1 | 1119 |
| 9 | Ciric | 804 | 1 | 804 |
| 10 | Mario | 1342 | 1 | 1342 |
| 11 | Chema | 1200 | 1 | 1200 |
| | Other | | 3 | |
| | TOTAL | | 37 | |

## MONTH BY MONTH GUIDE TO THE POINTS

| MONTH | POINTS | % |
|---|---|---|
| SEPTEMBER | 4 | 44% |
| OCTOBER | 3 | 33% |
| NOVEMBER | 4 | 33% |
| DECEMBER | 3 | 25% |
| JANUARY | 7 | 58% |
| FEBRUARY | 3 | 25% |
| MARCH | 5 | 42% |
| APRIL | 4 | 33% |
| MAY | 6 | 50% |
| JUNE | 4 | 44% |

## LEAGUE APPEARANCES, BOOKINGS AND CAPS

| | AGE | IN THE SQUAD | COUNTING GAMES | MINUTES ON PITCH | YELLOW CARDS | RED CARDS | THIS SEASON | HOME COUNTRY |
|---|---|---|---|---|---|---|---|---|
| **Goalkeepers** | | | | | | | | |
| Albano Bizzarri | 25 | 38 | 38 | 3420 | 3 | 0 | - | Argentina |
| Jon Ander | 26 | 6 | 0 | 0 | 0 | 0 | - | Spain |
| Julio Iglesias | 30 | 32 | 0 | 0 | 0 | 0 | - | Spain |
| **Defenders** | | | | | | | | |
| Galvez Gaspar | 24 | 33 | 19 | 1810 | 8 | 0 | - | Spain |
| Martin Jonathan | 22 | 30 | 11 | 1119 | 1 | 1 | - | Spain |
| Alberto Rey Marcos | 29 | 28 | 26 | 2406 | 4 | 1 | - | Spain |
| Javier Mustafa | 25 | 26 | 10 | 975 | 5 | 1 | - | Argentina |
| Oscar Sanchez | 23 | 24 | 12 | 1280 | 3 | 0 | - | Spain |
| Juan Montano Pena | 30 | 30 | 27 | 2504 | 10 | 1 | - | Bolivia |
| Pablo Javier Richetti | 26 | 12 | 6 | 670 | 3 | 0 | - | Argentina |
| Jose Santamaria | 30 | 9 | 1 | 111 | 0 | 0 | - | Spain |
| Javier Torres Gomez | 33 | 35 | 35 | 3141 | 11 | 0 | - | Spain |
| **Midfielders** | | | | | | | | |
| Munoz Martin Abel | | 5 | 0 | 0 | 0 | 0 | - | Spain |
| Antonio Lopez | 23 | 15 | 8 | 847 | 1 | 0 | - | Spain |
| Jose Luis Caminero | 35 | 25 | 11 | 1230 | 5 | 0 | - | Spain |
| Sancho Che (Chema) | 27 | 36 | 8 | 1200 | 1 | 0 | - | Spain |
| Gonzalo Ruiz Colsa | 24 | 37 | 33 | 3185 | 7 | 1 | - | Spain |
| Pozo Javi Jimenez | 27 | 6 | 0 | 54 | 0 | 0 | - | Spain |
| Sanchez Jesus | 28 | 19 | 8 | 908 | 4 | 0 | - | Spain |
| Pedro Mario | 21 | 18 | 12 | 1342 | 0 | 0 | - | Spain |
| Javier Roca More | 21 | 5 | 1 | 200 | 0 | 0 | - | Spain |
| Gonzalez Oscar | 20 | 35 | 20 | 2073 | 4 | 0 | - | Spain |
| Francisco Sousa | 23 | 31 | 4 | 617 | 3 | 1 | - | Spain |
| **Forwards** | | | | | | | | |
| David Aganzo | 22 | 34 | 21 | 2062 | 4 | 1 | - | Spain |
| Dragan Ciric | 28 | 20 | 6 | 804 | 0 | 0 | - | Serbia & Montenegro |
| Nicolas Olivera | 25 | 31 | 11 | 1332 | 2 | 0 | 1 | Uruguay (28) |
| Valentin Pacho | 26 | 35 | 8 | 1070 | 2 | 0 | - | Spain |
| Fernando Sales | 25 | 35 | 35 | 3134 | 4 | 0 | - | Spain |

KEY: LEAGUE BOOKINGS CAPS (FIFA RANKING)

## TEAM OF THE SEASON

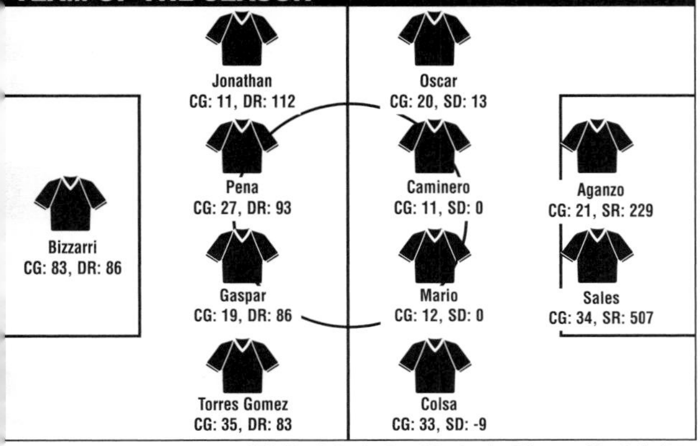
Bizzarri
CG: 83, DR: 86
Jonathan
CG: 11, DR: 112
Pena
CG: 27, DR: 93
Gaspar
CG: 19, DR: 86
Torres Gomez
CG: 35, DR: 83
Oscar
CG: 20, SD: 13
Caminero
CG: 11, SD: 0
Mario
CG: 12, SD: 0
Colsa
CG: 33, SD: -9
Aganzo
CG: 21, SR: 229
Sales
CG: 34, SR: 507

KEY: DR = Defensive Rate, SD = Scoring Difference, SR = Strike Rate, CG = Counting Games – League games playing at least 70 minutes

## SQUAD APPEARANCES

| Match | 1 | 2 | 3 | 4 | 5 | 6 | 7 | 8 | 9 | 10 | 11 | 12 | 13 | 14 | 15 | 16 | 17 | 18 | 19 | 20 | 21 | 22 | 23 | 24 | 25 | 26 | 27 | 28 | 29 | 30 | 31 | 32 | 33 | 34 | 35 | 36 | 37 | 38 |
|---|---|---|---|---|---|---|---|---|---|---|---|---|---|---|---|---|---|---|---|---|---|---|---|---|---|---|---|---|---|---|---|---|---|---|---|---|---|---|
| Venue | A | H | A | H | A | H | A | H | A | H | A | H | A | H | A | H | A | A | H | H | A | H | A | H | A | H | A | H | A | H | A | H | A | H | A | H | H | A |
| Competition | L | L | L | L | L | L | L | L | L | L | L | L | L | L | L | L | L | L | L | L | L | L | L | L | L | L | L | L | L | L | L | L | L | L | L | L | L | L |
| Result | W | W | L | D | L | W | L | L | W | D | L | L | L | W | L | W | D | W | L | W | L | L | L | W | D | D | L | L | L | W | D | W | D | D | D | L | W | D |

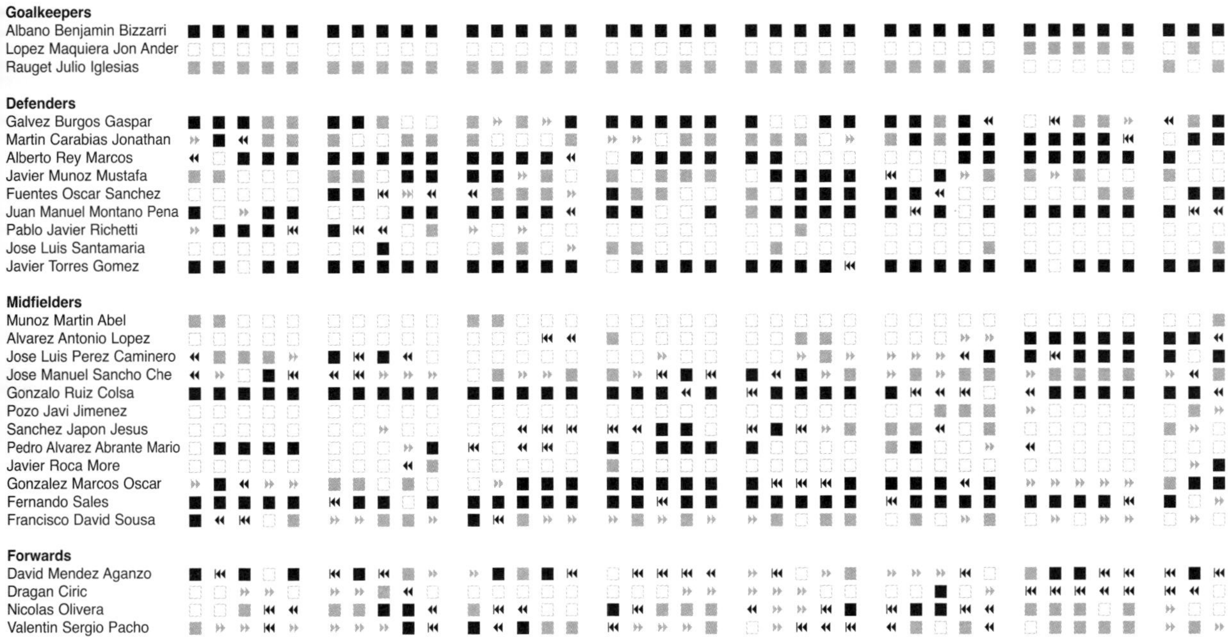
Goalkeepers
Albano Benjamin Bizzarri
Lopez Maquiera Jon Ander
Rauget Julio Iglesias
Defenders
Galvez Burgos Gaspar
Martin Carabias Jonathan
Alberto Rey Marcos
Javier Munoz Mustafa
Fuentes Oscar Sanchez
Juan Manuel Montano Pena
Pablo Javier Richetti
Jose Luis Santamaria
Javier Torres Gomez
Midfielders
Munoz Martin Abel
Alvarez Antonio Lopez
Jose Luis Perez Caminero
Jose Manuel Sancho Che
Gonzalo Ruiz Colsa
Pozo Javi Jimenez
Sanchez Japon Jesus
Pedro Alvarez Abrante Mario
Javier Roca More
Gonzalez Marcos Oscar
Fernando Sales
Francisco David Sousa
Forwards
David Mendez Aganzo
Dragan Ciric
Nicolas Olivera
Valentin Sergio Pacho

KEY: ■ On all match ▒ On bench
⏮ Subbed or sent off (Counting game)
« Subbed or sent off (playing less than 70 minutes)
⏭ Subbed on from bench (Counting Game)
» Subbed on (playing less than 70 minutes)
Subbed on and then subbed or sent off (Counting Game)
Subbed on and then subbed or sent off (playing less than 70 minutes)
□ Not in 16

# MALAGA

Final Position: **14th**

| | | | | | | |
|---|---|---|---|---|---|---|
| 1 | lge | Recreativo | A | W | 3-2 | Musampa 38,48,60 |
| 2 | lge | R Vallecano | H | W | 2-1 | Dely Valdes 52; Musampa 57 |
| 3 | uc1rl1 | Zeljeznicar | A | D | 0-0 | |
| 4 | lge | Valencia | H | D | 2-2 | Manu 26; Roteta 31 |
| 5 | lge | Celta Vigo | A | D | 2-2 | Musampa 15; Caceres 45 og |
| 6 | uc1rl2 | Zeljeznicar | H | W | 1-0 | Dely Valdes 5 pen |
| 7 | lge | Atl Madrid | H | W | 3-1 | Dely Valdes 43 pen; Fernando Sanz 65 pen; Manu 71 |
| 8 | lge | Athl Bilbao | A | D | 1-1 | Roteta 85 |
| 9 | lge | Espanyol | H | L | 3-4 | Dely Valdes 3 pen; Dario Silva 6,16 |
| 10 | uc2rl1 | Amica Wronki | H | W | 2-1 | Romero 39; Dely Valdes 68 |
| 11 | lge | Real Betis | A | L | 0-3 | |
| 12 | lge | Osasuna | H | W | 1-0 | Dario Silva 69 |
| 13 | uc2rl2 | Amica Wronki | A | W | 2-1 | Dario Silva 20; Musampa 72 |
| 14 | lge | Valladolid | A | D | 0-0 | |
| 15 | lge | Alaves | H | D | 0-0 | |
| 16 | uc3rl1 | Leeds | H | D | 0-0 | |
| 17 | lge | R Santander | A | L | 0-1 | |
| 18 | lge | Villarreal | H | D | 1-1 | Dario Silva 75 |
| 19 | uc3rl2 | Leeds | A | W | 2-1 | Dely Valdes 13,79 |
| 20 | lge | Deportivo | A | L | 0-1 | |
| 21 | lge | Real Madrid | H | L | 2-3 | Musampa 15; Dely Valdes 39 |
| 22 | lge | Real Sociedad | A | D | 2-2 | Musampa 19; Dario Silva 56 |
| 23 | lge | Barcelona | H | D | 0-0 | |
| 24 | lge | Seville | A | D | 0-0 | |
| 25 | lge | Mallorca | H | W | 1-0 | Musampa 64 |
| 26 | lge | Recreativo | H | W | 4-0 | Dely Valdes 49,80; Romero 68; Gerardo 70 |
| 27 | lge | R Vallecano | A | L | 1-2 | Dario Silva 86 |
| 28 | lge | Valencia | A | L | 0-2 | |
| 29 | uc4rl1 | AEK Athens | H | D | 0-0 | |
| 30 | lge | Celta Vigo | H | D | 1-1 | Koke 88 |
| 31 | uc4rl2 | AEK Athens | A | W | 1-0 | Manu 28 |
| 32 | lge | Atl Madrid | A | L | 1-2 | Dario Silva 62 |
| 33 | lge | Athl Bilbao | H | W | 3-0 | Dely Valdes 24; Manu 76,84 |
| 34 | ucqfl1 | Boavista | H | W | 1-0 | Dely Valdes 17 |
| 35 | lge | Espanyol | A | L | 1-2 | Manu 78 |
| 36 | ucqfl2 | Boavista | A | L | 1-4* | (*on penalties) |
| 37 | lge | Real Betis | H | D | 0-0 | |
| 38 | lge | Osasuna | A | W | 1-0 | Romero 59 |
| 39 | lge | Valladolid | H | W | 1-0 | Canabal 87 |
| 40 | lge | Alaves | A | W | 1-0 | Dario Silva 90 |
| 41 | lge | R Santander | H | D | 2-2 | Dely Valdes 61,71 |
| 42 | lge | Villarreal | A | D | 0-0 | |
| 43 | lge | Deportivo | H | L | 0-2 | |
| 44 | lge | Real Madrid | A | L | 1-5 | Manu 63 |
| 45 | lge | Real Sociedad | H | L | 0-2 | |
| 46 | lge | Barcelona | A | L | 1-2 | Dely Valdes 56 pen |
| 47 | lge | Seville | H | W | 3-2 | Dario Silva 18,88 pen; Canabal 77 |
| 48 | lge | Mallorca | A | L | 0-1 | |

## GOALS SCORED

**AT HOME**

| | | |
|---|---|---|
| MOST | R Madrid | 52 |
| | | 29 |
| LEAST | R Vallecano | 17 |

**AWAY**

| | | |
|---|---|---|
| MOST | R Madrid | 34 |
| | | 15 |
| LEAST | Recreativo | 11 |

## GOALS CONCEDED

**AT HOME**

| | | |
|---|---|---|
| LEAST | C Vigo & Valencia | 15 |
| | | 21 |
| MOST | Mallorca | 33 |

**AWAY**

| | | |
|---|---|---|
| LEAST | R Madrid, Valencia & Seville | 20 |
| | | 28 |
| MOST | Alaves | 48 |

## ATTENDANCES

HOME GROUND: LA ROSALEDA CAPACITY: 37151 AVERAGE LEAGUE AT HOME: 29229

| | | |
|---|---|---|
| 44 | Real Madrid | 76300 |
| 46 | Barcelona | 51940 |
| 11 | Real Betis | 46200 |
| 32 | Atl Madrid | 42750 |
| 35 | Espanyol | 38500 |
| 28 | Valencia | 37100 |
| 7 | Atl Madrid | 37100 |
| 43 | Deportivo | 37100 |
| 4 | Valencia | 35000 |
| 16 | Leeds | 35000 |
| 45 | Real Sociedad | 34503 |
| 19 | Leeds | 34123 |
| 23 | Barcelona | 33390 |
| 9 | Espanyol | 33390 |
| 21 | Real Madrid | 33390 |
| 8 | Athl Bilbao | 32000 |
| 30 | Celta Vigo | 31550 |
| 15 | Alaves | 30051 |
| 26 | Recreativo Huelva | 30050 |
| 37 | Real Betis | 29700 |
| 18 | Villarreal | 29309 |
| 41 | R Santander | 28570 |
| 25 | Mallorca | 28567 |
| 20 | Deportivo | 28480 |
| 33 | Athl Bilbao | 26000 |
| 5 | Celta Vigo | 23850 |
| 47 | Seville | 23744 |
| 22 | Real Sociedad | 22400 |
| 39 | Valladolid | 22260 |
| 14 | Valladolid | 21200 |
| 1 | Recreativo Huelva | 20000 |
| 10 | Amica Wronki | 19800 |
| 31 | AEK Athens | 18000 |
| 12 | Osasuna | 16695 |
| 2 | R Vallecano | 15000 |
| 29 | AEK Athens | 15000 |
| 3 | Zeljeznicar | 15000 |
| 6 | Zeljeznicar | 15000 |
| 34 | Boavista | 15000 |
| 27 | R Vallecano | 14100 |
| 24 | Seville | 14000 |
| 38 | Osasuna | 12935 |
| 40 | Alaves | 12865 |
| 42 | Villarreal | 11425 |
| 17 | R Santander | 11250 |
| 48 | Mallorca | 10191 |
| 36 | Boavista | 8500 |
| 13 | Amica Wronki | 3000 |

■ Home □ Away ▨ Neutral

## KEY PLAYERS - GOALSCORERS

**1 Debray Pereira Dario Silva**

| | | | |
|---|---|---|---|
| Goals in the League | 10 | Player Strike Rate<br>Average number of minutes between League goals scored by player | 241 |
| Contribution to Attacking Power<br>Average number of minutes between League team goals while on pitch | 75 | Club Strike Rate<br>Average number of minutes between League goals scored by club | 78 |

| | PLAYER | LGE GOALS | POWER | STRIKE RATE |
|---|---|---|---|---|
| 2 | Julio Cesar Dely Valdes | 10 | 76 | 260 mins |
| 3 | Kiki Musampa | 8 | 76 | 365 mins |
| 4 | Sanchez Manu | 6 | 87 | 379 mins |
| 5 | Clever Marcelo Gato Silva Rome | 2 | 92 | 1153 mins |

## KEY PLAYERS - MIDFIELDERS

**1 Carlos Alejandro Sierra Sandro**

| | | | |
|---|---|---|---|
| Goals in the League | 0 | Contribution to Attacking Power<br>Average number of minutes between League team goals while on pitch | 67 |
| Defensive Rating<br>Average number of mins between League goals conceded while he was on the pitch | 67 | Scoring Difference<br>Defensive Rating minus Contribution to Attacking Power | 0 |

| | PLAYER | LGE GOALS | DEF RATE | POWER | SCORE DIFF |
|---|---|---|---|---|---|
| 2 | Kiki Musampa | 8 | 75 | 77 | -2 mins |
| 3 | Clever Marcelo Gato Silva Rome | 2 | 89 | 92 | -3 mins |
| 4 | Sanchez Manu | 6 | 76 | 87 | -11 mins |

## KEY PLAYERS - DEFENDERS

**1 Garcia Moreno Leon Gerardo**

| | | | |
|---|---|---|---|
| Goals Conceded (GC)<br>The number of League goals conceded while he was on the pitch | 28 | Clean Sheets<br>In games when he played at least 70 minutes | 9 |
| Defensive Rating<br>Ave number of mins between League goals conceded while on the pitch | 81 | Club Defensive Rating<br>Average number of mins between League goals conceded by the club this season | 70 |

| | PLAYER | CON LGE | CLEAN SHEETS | DEF RATE |
|---|---|---|---|---|
| 2 | Vicente Cano Valcarce | 39 | 12 | 75 mins |
| 3 | Duran Fernando Sanz | 45 | 12 | 70 mins |
| 4 | Mikel Roteta | 42 | 11 | 70 mins |
| 5 | Miguel Gonzalez Rey Josemi | 41 | 9 | 68 mins |

## KEY GOALKEEPER

**1 Pedro Contreras**

| | |
|---|---|
| Goals Conceded in the League | 43 |
| Defensive Rating<br>Ave number of mins between League goals conceded while on the pitch | 73 |
| Counting Games<br>Games when he played at least 70 minutes | 34 |
| Clean Sheets<br>In games when he played at least 70 minutes | 12 |

## TOP POINT EARNERS

| | PLAYER | GAMES | AVE |
|---|---|---|---|
| 1 | Gerardo | 23 | 1.39 |
| 2 | Musampa | 31 | 1.32 |
| 3 | Dario Silva | 26 | 1.31 |
| 4 | Romero | 23 | 1.30 |
| 5 | Valcarce | 32 | 1.28 |
| 6 | Roteta | 33 | 1.27 |
| 7 | Contreras | 34 | 1.24 |
| 8 | Sandro | 13 | 1.23 |
| 9 | Dely Valdes | 26 | 1.12 |
| 10 | Fernando Sanz | 35 | 1.11 |
| | CLUB AVERAGE: | | 1.21 |

Ave = Average points per match in Counting Games

## DISCIPLINARY RECORDS

| | PLAYER | YELLOW | RED | AVE |
|---|---|---|---|---|
| 1 | Sandro | 12 | 1 | 149 |
| 2 | Dario Silva | 11 | 2 | 185 |
| 3 | Romero | 10 | 2 | 192 |
| 4 | Josemi | 13 | 1 | 198 |
| 5 | Rojas | 2 | 1 | 218 |
| 6 | Miguel Angel | 7 | 0 | 223 |
| 7 | Canabal | 3 | 0 | 224 |
| 8 | Roteta | 13 | 0 | 227 |
| 9 | Fernando Sanz | 11 | 1 | 262 |
| 10 | Litos | 2 | 0 | 275 |
| 11 | Iznata | 2 | 0 | 315 |
| 12 | Gerardo | 7 | 0 | 323 |
| 13 | Musampa | 7 | 0 | 416 |
| | Other | 15 | 2 | |
| | TOTAL | 115 | 10 | |

## LEAGUE GOALS

| | PLAYER | MINS | GOALS | AVE |
|---|---|---|---|---|
| 1 | Dario Silva | 2405 | 10 | 241 |
| 2 | Dely Valdes | 2596 | 10 | 260 |
| 3 | Musampa | 2917 | 8 | 365 |
| 4 | Manu | 2273 | 6 | 379 |
| 5 | Canabal | 672 | 2 | 336 |
| 6 | Roteta | 2959 | 2 | 1480 |
| 7 | Romero | 2306 | 2 | 1153 |
| 8 | Koke | 182 | 1 | 182 |
| 9 | Gerardo | 2263 | 1 | 2263 |
| 10 | Fernando Sanz | 3150 | 1 | 3150 |
| | Other | | 1 | |
| | TOTAL | | 44 | |

## MONTH BY MONTH GUIDE TO THE POINTS

| MONTH | POINTS | % |
|---|---|---|
| SEPTEMBER | 8 | 67% |
| OCTOBER | 4 | 44% |
| NOVEMBER | 5 | 42% |
| DECEMBER | 1 | 8% |
| JANUARY | 6 | 50% |
| FEBRUARY | 4 | 33% |
| MARCH | 4 | 33% |
| APRIL | 10 | 83% |
| MAY | 1 | 8% |
| JUNE | 3 | 33% |

## TEAM OF THE SEASON

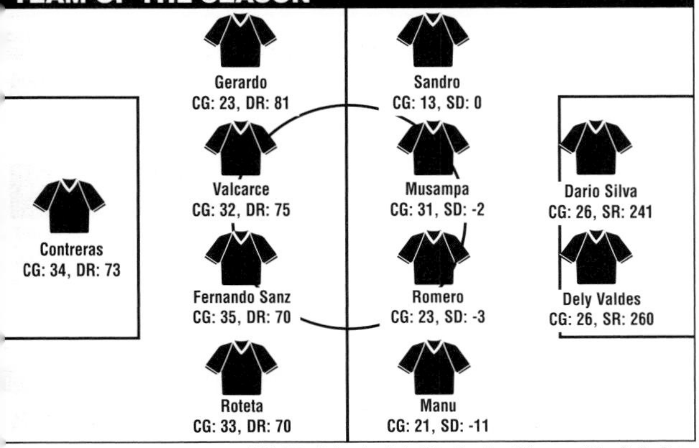
Gerardo
CG: 23, DR: 81
Sandro
CG: 13, SD: 0
Valcarce
CG: 32, DR: 75
Musampa
CG: 31, SD: -2
Dario Silva
CG: 26, SR: 241
Contreras
CG: 34, DR: 73
Fernando Sanz
CG: 35, DR: 70
Romero
CG: 23, SD: -3
Dely Valdes
CG: 26, SR: 260
Roteta
CG: 33, DR: 70
Manu
CG: 21, SD: -11

KEY: DR = Defensive Rate, SD = Scoring Difference, SR = Strike Rate, CG = Counting Games – League games playing at least 70 minutes

## LEAGUE APPEARANCES, BOOKINGS AND CAPS

| | AGE | IN THE SQUAD | COUNTING GAMES | MINUTES ON PITCH | YELLOW CARDS | RED CARDS | THIS SEASON | HOME COUNTRY |
|---|---|---|---|---|---|---|---|---|
| **Goalkeepers** | | | | | | | | |
| Arnau Grabalosa | 28 | 20 | 2 | 228 | 0 | 0 | - | Spain |
| Pedro Contreras | 31 | 36 | 34 | 3132 | 1 | 2 | 3 | Spain (2) |
| Rafael Rafa | 32 | 20 | 0 | 58 | 0 | 0 | - | Spain |
| **Defenders** | | | | | | | | |
| Ruano Alexis | 17 | 1 | 0 | 0 | 0 | 0 | - | Spain |
| Francisco Bravo | 29 | 7 | 1 | 217 | 1 | 0 | - | Spain |
| Duran Sanz | 29 | 35 | 35 | 3150 | 11 | 1 | - | Spain |
| Garcia Gerardo | 28 | 31 | 23 | 2263 | 7 | 0 | - | Spain |
| Raul Zabala Iznata | 25 | 28 | 5 | 631 | 2 | 0 | - | Spain |
| Miguel Josemi | 23 | 32 | 30 | 2775 | 13 | 1 | - | Spain |
| Carlos Litos | 29 | 37 | 6 | 551 | 2 | 0 | - | Portugal |
| Miguel Angel | 24 | 36 | 12 | 1562 | 7 | 0 | - | Spain |
| Roberto Rojas | 28 | 29 | 7 | 655 | 2 | 1 | - | Spain |
| Mikel Roteta | 33 | 34 | 33 | 2959 | 13 | 0 | - | Spain |
| Vicente Valcarce | 28 | 35 | 32 | 2933 | 7 | 0 | - | Spain |
| **Midfielders** | | | | | | | | |
| Ador | | 1 | 0 | 1 | 0 | 0 | - | |
| Alberto | | 1 | 0 | 26 | 0 | 0 | - | |
| Javier Dopico | 18 | 2 | 0 | 16 | 0 | 0 | - | Spain |
| Paco Esteban | | 2 | 0 | 18 | 0 | 0 | - | Spain |
| Juan Rodriguez | 21 | 1 | 0 | 0 | 0 | 0 | - | Spain |
| Ivan Leko | 25 | 38 | 0 | 572 | 0 | 0 | - | Croatia |
| Sanchez Manu | 24 | 37 | 21 | 2273 | 4 | 0 | - | Spain |
| Kiki Musampa | 25 | 35 | 31 | 2917 | 7 | 0 | - | Holland |
| Ignacio Perez Nacho | 23 | 6 | 1 | 141 | 0 | 0 | - | Spain |
| Perico | | 1 | 1 | 90 | 0 | 0 | - | |
| Clever Romero | 27 | 29 | 23 | 2306 | 10 | 2 | - | Uruguay |
| Francisco Ruano | 28 | 1 | 0 | 0 | 0 | 0 | - | |
| Carlos Sandro | 28 | 36 | 13 | 1938 | 12 | 1 | - | Spain |
| **Forwards** | | | | | | | | |
| Manuel Canabal | 28 | 22 | 3 | 672 | 3 | 0 | - | Spain |
| Debray Dario Silva | 30 | 29 | 26 | 2405 | 11 | 2 | - | Uruguay |
| Dely Valdes | 36 | 33 | 26 | 2596 | 2 | 0 | - | Panama |
| Patricio Edga | 25 | 9 | 0 | 87 | 0 | 0 | - | |
| Alexandre Geijo | 21 | 2 | 0 | 5 | 0 | 0 | - | Spain |
| Juanito | 23 | 7 | 0 | 36 | 0 | 0 | - | Spain |
| Sergio Pardo Koke | 20 | 11 | 0 | 182 | 0 | 0 | - | Spain |

KEY: LEAGUE BOOKINGS CAPS (FIFA RANKING)

## SQUAD APPEARANCES

| Match | 1 | 2 | 3 | 4 | 5 | 6 | 7 | 8 | 9 | 10 | 11 | 12 | 13 | 14 | 15 | 16 | 17 | 18 | 19 | 20 | 21 | 22 | 23 | 24 | 25 | 26 | 27 | 28 | 29 | 30 | 31 | 32 | 33 | 34 | 35 | 36 | 37 | 38 | 39 | 40 | 41 | 42 | 43 | 44 | 45 | 46 | 47 | 48 |
|---|---|---|---|---|---|---|---|---|---|---|---|---|---|---|---|---|---|---|---|---|---|---|---|---|---|---|---|---|---|---|---|---|---|---|---|---|---|---|---|---|---|---|---|---|---|---|---|---|
| Venue | A | H | A | H | A | H | H | A | H | H | A | H | A | A | H | H | A | H | A | A | H | A | H | A | H | H | A | A | H | H | A | A | H | H | A | A | H | A | H | A | H | A | H | A | H | A | H | A |
| Competition | L | L | E | L | L | E | L | L | L | E | L | L | E | L | L | E | L | L | E | L | L | L | L | L | L | L | L | L | E | L | E | L | L | E | L | E | L | L | L | L | L | L | L | L | L | L | L | L |
| Result | W | W | D | D | D | W | W | D | L | W | L | W | W | D | D | D | L | D | W | L | L | D | D | D | W | W | L | L | D | D | W | L | W | W | L | L | D | W | W | W | D | D | L | L | L | L | W | L |

**Goalkeepers**
Francesc Arnau Grabalosa
Pedro Contreras
Rafael Gonzalez Rafa

**Defenders**
Ruano Delgado Alexis
Francisco Lopez Bravo
Duran Fernando Sanz
Garcia Moreno Gerardo
Raul Zabala Iznata
Miguel Rey Josemi
Carlos Litos
Lozano Ayala Miguel Angel
Roberto Gonzalez Rojas
Mikel Roteta
Vicente Cano Valcarce

**Midfielders**
Ador
Alberto
Javier Morales Dopico
Francisco Paco Esteban
Juan Antonio Rodriguez
Ivan Leko
Sanchez Manu
Kiki Musampa
Ignacio Perez Nacho
Perico
Clever Marcelo Romero
Francisco Bausan Ruano
Carlos Sierra Sandro

**Forwards**
Manuel Canabal
Debray Dario Silva
Julio Cesar Dely Valdes
Patricio Pacheco Edga
Alexandre Geijo
Juanito
Sergio Contreras Koke

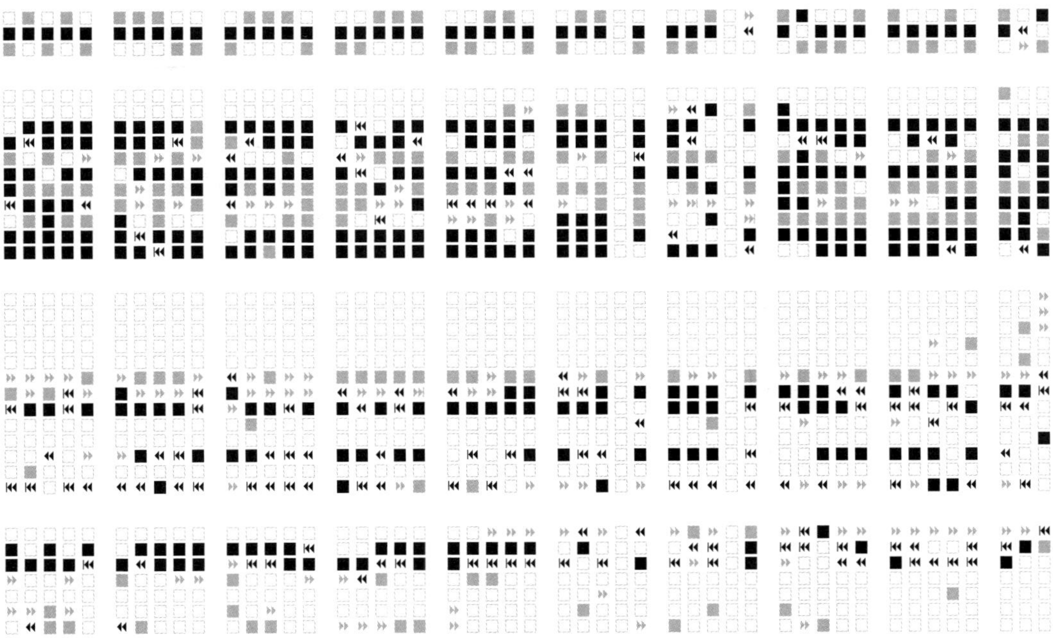

KEY: ■ On all match ■ On bench ⏮ Subbed or sent off (Counting game) « Subbed or sent off (playing less than 70 minutes) ⏭ Subbed on from bench (Counting Game) » Subbed on (playing less than 70 minutes) Subbed on and then subbed or sent off (Counting Game) Subbed on and then subbed or sent off (playing less than 70 minutes) □ Not in 16

# VILLARREAL

Final Position: **15th**

| | | | | | | |
|---|---|---|---|---|---|---|
| 1 | lge | Osasuna | H | D | 2-2 | Victor 11,14 |
| 2 | lge | Valladolid | A | L | 0-1 | |
| 3 | lge | Alaves | H | L | 0-1 | |
| 4 | lge | R Santander | A | D | 1-1 | Senna 64 |
| 5 | lge | R Vallecano | A | D | 2-2 | Belletti 20; Senna 21 |
| 6 | lge | Deportivo | H | W | 3-1 | Cesar 48 og; Victor 62 pen; Belletti 87 |
| 7 | lge | Real Madrid | A | D | 1-1 | Jorge Lopez 45 pen |
| 8 | lge | Real Sociedad | H | L | 0-1 | |
| 9 | lge | Barcelona | A | L | 0-1 | |
| 10 | lge | Seville | H | W | 1-0 | Belletti 88 |
| 11 | lge | Mallorca | A | D | 1-1 | Palermo 22 |
| 12 | lge | Recreativo | H | W | 1-0 | Victor 64 |
| 13 | lge | Malaga | A | D | 1-1 | Palermo 59 |
| 14 | lge | Valencia | H | L | 0-2 | |
| 15 | lge | Celta Vigo | A | L | 1-3 | Palermo 44 |
| 16 | lge | Atl Madrid | H | W | 4-3 | Unai 26; Palermo 28,90; Victor 45 |
| 17 | lge | Athl Bilbao | A | W | 1-0 | Farinos 5 |
| 18 | lge | Espanyol | H | D | 0-0 | |
| 19 | lge | Real Betis | A | L | 1-2 | Aranda 83 |
| 20 | lge | Osasuna | A | W | 1-0 | Josico 31 |
| 21 | lge | Valladolid | H | W | 1-0 | Jorge Lopez 24 pen |
| 22 | lge | Alaves | A | L | 0-1 | |
| 23 | lge | R Santander | H | L | 0-3 | |
| 24 | lge | R Vallecano | H | W | 2-1 | Guayre 22; De Nigris 89 |
| 25 | lge | Deportivo | A | L | 1-2 | Jorge Lopez 11 |
| 26 | lge | Real Madrid | H | L | 0-1 | |
| 27 | lge | Real Sociedad | A | D | 2-2 | Victor 90; Jorge Lopez 90 |
| 28 | lge | Barcelona | H | W | 2-0 | Jorge Lopez 56 pen; Calleja 90 pen |
| 29 | lge | Seville | A | L | 1-3 | Jorge Lopez 17 |
| 30 | lge | Mallorca | H | D | 1-1 | Palermo 23 |
| 31 | lge | Recreativo | A | L | 0-5 | |
| 32 | lge | Malaga | H | D | 0-0 | |
| 33 | lge | Valencia | A | W | 2-1 | Jorge Lopez 36 pen; Farinos 40 |
| 34 | lge | Celta Vigo | H | W | 5-0 | Guayre 48,88; Victor 53; Jorge Lopez 59; Palermo 62 |
| 35 | lge | Atl Madrid | A | L | 2-3 | Calleja 22; Josico 41 |
| 36 | lge | Athl Bilbao | H | D | 1-1 | Victor 4 |
| 37 | lge | Espanyol | A | D | 2-2 | De Nigris 53; Xisco Nadal 90 |
| 38 | lge | Real Betis | H | L | 1-4 | Guayre 13 |

## KEY PLAYERS - GOALSCORERS

**1 Manuel Fernandez Victor**

| | | | |
|---|---|---|---|
| Goals in the League | 8 | Player Strike Rate<br>Average number of minutes between League goals scored by player | 328 |
| Contribution to Attacking Power<br>Average number of minutes between League team goals while on pitch | 84 | Club Strike Rate<br>Average number of minutes between League goals scored by club | 78 |

| | PLAYER | LGE GOALS | POWER | STRIKE RATE |
|---|---|---|---|---|
| 2 | Martin Palermo | 7 | 81 | 373 mins |
| 3 | Montana Jorge Lopez | 8 | 76 | 385 mins |
| 4 | Antonio Guayre | 4 | 77 | 520 mins |
| 5 | Marcos Antonio da Silva Senna | 2 | 115 | 635 mins |

## KEY PLAYERS - MIDFIELDERS

**1 Marcos Antonio da Silva Senna**

| | | | |
|---|---|---|---|
| Goals in the League | 2 | Contribution to Attacking Power<br>Average number of minutes between League team goals while on pitch | 115 |
| Defensive Rating<br>Average number of mins between League goals conceded while he was on the pitch | 115 | Scoring Difference<br>Defensive Rating minus Contribution to Attacking Power | 0 |

| | PLAYER | LGE GOALS | DEF RATE | POWER | SCORE DIFF |
|---|---|---|---|---|---|
| 2 | Javier Revilla Calleja | 2 | 45 | 52 | -7 mins |
| 3 | Francisco Javier Zampata Farin | 2 | 62 | 71 | -9 mins |
| 4 | Montana Jorge Lopez | 8 | 66 | 77 | -11 mins |
| 5 | Jose Moreno Verdu Josico | 2 | 72 | 87 | -15 mins |

## KEY PLAYERS - DEFENDERS

**1 Juliano Haus Belletti**

| | | | |
|---|---|---|---|
| Goals Conceded (GC)<br>The number of League goals conceded while he was on the pitch | 36 | Clean Sheets<br>In games when he played at least 70 minutes | 8 |
| Defensive Rating<br>Ave number of mins between League goals conceded while on the pitch | 76 | Club Defensive Rating<br>Average number of mins between League goals conceded by the club this season | 65 |

| | PLAYER | CON LGE | CLEAN SHEETS | DEF RATE |
|---|---|---|---|---|
| 2 | Rodolfo Martin Arruabarrena | 37 | 6 | 73 mins |
| 3 | Sergio Martinez Ballesteros | 41 | 9 | 72 mins |
| 4 | Quique San Juan Alvarez | 43 | 5 | 60 mins |
| 5 | Vergara Diaz-Caballero Unai | 25 | 2 | 56 mins |

## GOALS SCORED

**AT HOME**

| | | |
|---|---|---|
| MOST | R Madrid | 52 |
| | | 24 |
| LEAST | R Vallecano | 17 |

**AWAY**

| | | |
|---|---|---|
| MOST | R Madrid | 34 |
| | | 20 |
| LEAST | Recreativo | 11 |

## GOALS CONCEDED

**AT HOME**

| | | |
|---|---|---|
| LEAST | C Vigo & Valencia | 15 |
| | | 21 |
| MOST | Mallorca | 33 |

**AWAY**

| | | |
|---|---|---|
| LEAST | R Madrid, Valencia & Seville | 20 |
| | | 32 |
| MOST | Alaves | 48 |

## KEY GOALKEEPER

**1 Jose Manuel Perez Reina**

| | |
|---|---|
| Goals Conceded in the League | 42 |
| Defensive Rating<br>Ave number of mins between League goals conceded while on the pitch | 69 |
| Counting Games<br>Games when he played at least 70 minutes | 32 |
| Clean Sheets<br>In games when he played at least 70 minutes | 9 |

## TOP POINT EARNERS

| | PLAYER | GAMES | AVE |
|---|---|---|---|
| 1 | Guayre | 16 | 1.56 |
| 2 | Belletti | 30 | 1.43 |
| 3 | Josico | 18 | 1.39 |
| 4 | Arruabarrena | 29 | 1.34 |
| 5 | Senna | 13 | 1.31 |
| 6 | Farinos | 20 | 1.30 |
| 7 | Ballesteros | 33 | 1.30 |
| 8 | Jorge Lopez | 32 | 1.28 |
| 9 | Reina | 32 | 1.25 |
| 10 | Victor | 25 | 1.20 |
| | **CLUB AVERAGE:** | | **1.18** |

Ave = Average points per match in Counting Games

## ATTENDANCES

HOME GROUND: EL MADRIGAL CAPACITY: 17000 AVERAGE LEAGUE AT HOME: 12991

| | | | | | | | | |
|---|---|---|---|---|---|---|---|---|
| 9 | Barcelona | 96040 | 22 | Alaves | 16900 | 38 | Real Betis | 12600 |
| 7 | Real Madrid | 64855 | 14 | Valencia | 16800 | 37 | Espanyol | 12400 |
| 35 | Atl Madrid | 53580 | 2 | Valladolid | 16500 | 21 | Valladolid | 12265 |
| 33 | Valencia | 53000 | 1 | Osasuna | 16500 | 6 | Deportivo | 12264 |
| 19 | Real Betis | 39375 | 31 | Recreativo Huelva | 16400 | 32 | Malaga | 11425 |
| 17 | Athl Bilbao | 38400 | 24 | R Vallecano | 15600 | 10 | Seville | 11424 |
| 29 | Seville | 33750 | 8 | Real Sociedad | 15120 | 4 | R Santander | 11250 |
| 15 | Celta Vigo | 31165 | 26 | Real Madrid | 15120 | 3 | Alaves | 11000 |
| 25 | Deportivo | 30260 | 16 | Atl Madrid | 15120 | 18 | Espanyol | 10920 |
| 13 | Malaga | 29309 | 34 | Celta Vigo | 14600 | 28 | Barcelona | 10080 |
| 27 | Real Sociedad | 28800 | 5 | R Vallecano | 13950 | 30 | Mallorca | 9856 |
| 20 | Osasuna | 17900 | 23 | R Santander | 13300 | 12 | Recreativo Huelva | 9744 |
| 11 | Mallorca | 17775 | 36 | Athl Bilbao | 13105 | | | |

■ Home □ Away ▨ Neutral

## DISCIPLINARY RECORDS

| | PLAYER | YELLOW | RED | AVE |
|---|---|---|---|---|
| 1 | Unai | 9 | 1 | 140 |
| 2 | Arruabarrena | 14 | 1 | 181 |
| 3 | Alvarez | 8 | 1 | 287 |
| 4 | Javi Venta | 2 | 0 | 296 |
| 5 | Ballesteros | 9 | 1 | 296 |
| 6 | De Nigris | 3 | 0 | 315 |
| 7 | Berruet | 2 | 0 | 316 |
| 8 | Guayre | 5 | 1 | 346 |
| 9 | Josico | 6 | 0 | 349 |
| 10 | Belletti | 6 | 1 | 389 |
| 11 | Senna | 3 | 0 | 423 |
| 12 | Jorge Lopez | 7 | 0 | 439 |
| 13 | Quique Medina | 2 | 0 | 463 |
| | Other | 20 | 0 | |
| | **TOTAL** | **96** | **6** | |

## LEAGUE GOALS

| | PLAYER | MINS | GOALS | AVE |
|---|---|---|---|---|
| 1 | Jorge Lopez | 3079 | 8 | 385 |
| 2 | Victor | 2622 | 8 | 328 |
| 3 | Palermo | 2612 | 7 | 373 |
| 4 | Guayre | 2079 | 4 | 520 |
| 5 | Belletti | 2724 | 3 | 908 |
| 6 | Josico | 2094 | 2 | 1047 |
| 7 | De Nigris | 947 | 2 | 474 |
| 8 | Calleja | 1041 | 2 | 521 |
| 9 | Senna | 1270 | 2 | 635 |
| 10 | Farinos | 1784 | 2 | 892 |
| 11 | Xisco Nadal | 56 | 1 | 56 |
| 12 | Aranda | 144 | 1 | 144 |
| 13 | Unai | 1409 | 1 | 1409 |
| | Other | | 1 | |
| | **TOTAL** | | **44** | |

## MONTH BY MONTH GUIDE TO THE POINTS

| MONTH | POINTS | % |
|---|---|---|
| SEPTEMBER | 2 | 17% |
| OCTOBER | 5 | 56% |
| NOVEMBER | 4 | 33% |
| DECEMBER | 4 | 33% |
| JANUARY | 7 | 58% |
| FEBRUARY | 6 | 50% |
| MARCH | 4 | 33% |
| APRIL | 4 | 33% |
| MAY | 7 | 58% |
| JUNE | 2 | 22% |

## TEAM OF THE SEASON

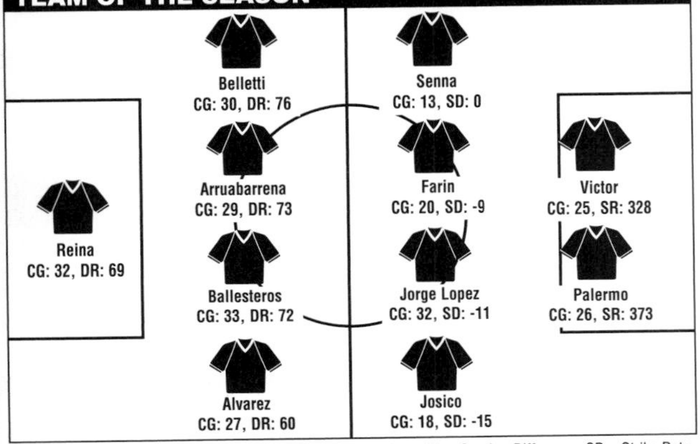

Belletti
CG: 30, DR: 76
Senna
CG: 13, SD: 0
Arruabarrena
CG: 29, DR: 73
Farin
CG: 20, SD: -9
Victor
CG: 25, SR: 328
Reina
CG: 32, DR: 69
Ballesteros
CG: 33, DR: 72
Jorge Lopez
CG: 32, SD: -11
Palermo
CG: 26, SR: 373
Alvarez
CG: 27, DR: 60
Josico
CG: 18, SD: -15


KEY: DR = Defensive Rate, SD = Scoring Difference, SR = Strike Rate, CG = Counting Games – League games playing at least 70 minutes

## LEAGUE APPEARANCES, BOOKINGS AND CAPS

| | AGE | IN THE SQUAD | COUNTING GAMES | MINUTES ON PITCH | YELLOW CARDS | RED CARDS | THIS SEASON | HOME COUNTRY |
|---|---|---|---|---|---|---|---|---|
| **Goalkeepers** | | | | | | | | |
| Javier Lopez Vallejo | 27 | 37 | 5 | 450 | 0 | 0 | - | Spain |
| Jose Manuel Reina | 20 | 37 | 32 | 2880 | 3 | 0 | - | Spain |
| Jesus Unanua | 34 | 3 | 1 | 90 | 0 | 0 | - | Spain |
| **Defenders** | | | | | | | | |
| Quique Alvarez | 27 | 32 | 27 | 2589 | 8 | 1 | - | Spain |
| Arruabarrena | 27 | 32 | 29 | 2738 | 14 | 1 | - | Argentina |
| Sergio Ballesteros | 27 | 33 | 33 | 2966 | 9 | 1 | - | Spain |
| Juliano Belletti | 27 | 32 | 30 | 2724 | 6 | 1 | - | Brazil |
| Michelena Berruet | | 16 | 6 | 632 | 2 | 0 | - | |
| Jesus Galvan | 28 | 34 | 7 | 778 | 1 | 0 | - | Spain |
| Javier Javi Venta | 27 | 29 | 4 | 683 | 2 | 0 | - | Spain |
| Quique Medina | 28 | 30 | 7 | 926 | 2 | 0 | - | Spain |
| Vergara Unai | 26 | 34 | 15 | 1409 | 9 | 1 | - | Spain |
| **Midfielders** | | | | | | | | |
| Javier Calleja | 25 | 37 | 6 | 1041 | 1 | 0 | - | Spain |
| Jose Maria Cases | 16 | 2 | 0 | 28 | 0 | 0 | - | Spain |
| Cesar Arzo | 17 | 5 | 0 | 90 | 0 | 0 | - | Spain |
| Francisco Farin(os) | 25 | 22 | 20 | 1784 | 3 | 0 | - | Spain |
| Constantin Galca | 31 | 14 | 2 | 246 | 0 | 0 | - | |
| Xavier Carlos Gracia | | 16 | 1 | 223 | 1 | 0 | - | |
| Hector Font | | 9 | 0 | 78 | 0 | 0 | - | Spain |
| Jorge Lopez | 24 | 36 | 32 | 3079 | 7 | 0 | - | Spain |
| Jose Moreno Josico | 28 | 30 | 18 | 2094 | 6 | 0 | - | Spain |
| Enrique Martin | 30 | 2 | 1 | 90 | 1 | 0 | - | |
| Diaz Ruben Reyes | 24 | 13 | 0 | 106 | 0 | 0 | - | Spain |
| Marcos Senna | 26 | 16 | 13 | 1270 | 3 | 0 | - | Brazil |
| Jose Garcia Verza | 16 | 2 | 0 | 0 | 0 | 0 | - | Spain |
| Xisco Nada | 17 | 7 | 0 | 56 | 0 | 0 | - | Spain |
| **Forwards** | | | | | | | | |
| Carlos Reina Aranda | 22 | 12 | 0 | 144 | 2 | 0 | - | Spain |
| Antonio De Nigris | 25 | 15 | 9 | 947 | 3 | 0 | - | Mexico |
| Antonio Guayre | 23 | 35 | 16 | 2079 | 5 | 1 | - | Spain |
| Martin Palermo | 29 | 37 | 26 | 2612 | 3 | 0 | - | Argentina |
| Manuel Victor | 29 | 34 | 25 | 2622 | 4 | 0 | - | Spain |

KEY: LEAGUE BOOKINGS CAPS (FIFA RANKING)

## SQUAD APPEARANCES

| Match | 1 | 2 | 3 | 4 | 5 | 6 | 7 | 8 | 9 | 10 | 11 | 12 | 13 | 14 | 15 | 16 | 17 | 18 | 19 | 20 | 21 | 22 | 23 | 24 | 25 | 26 | 27 | 28 | 29 | 30 | 31 | 32 | 33 | 34 | 35 | 36 | 37 | 38 |
|---|---|---|---|---|---|---|---|---|---|---|---|---|---|---|---|---|---|---|---|---|---|---|---|---|---|---|---|---|---|---|---|---|---|---|---|---|---|---|
| Venue | H | A | H | A | A | H | A | H | A | H | A | H | A | H | A | H | A | H | A | A | H | A | H | H | A | H | A | H | A | H | A | H | A | H | A | H | A | H |
| Competition | L | L | L | L | L | L | L | L | L | L | L | L | L | L | L | L | L | L | L | L | L | L | L | L | L | L | L | L | L | L | L | L | L | L | L | L | L | L |
| Result | D | L | L | D | D | W | D | L | L | W | D | W | D | L | L | W | W | D | L | W | W | L | L | W | L | L | D | W | L | D | L | D | W | W | L | D | D | L |

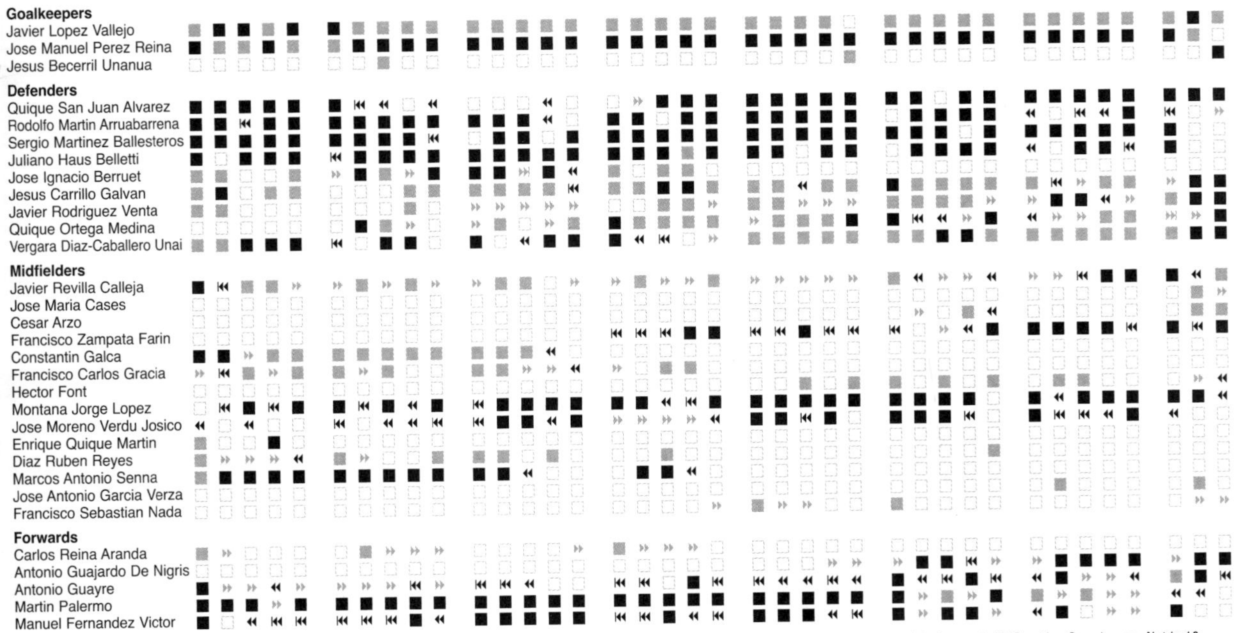

Goalkeepers
Javier Lopez Vallejo
Jose Manuel Perez Reina
Jesus Becerril Unanua
Defenders
Quique San Juan Alvarez
Rodolfo Martin Arruabarrena
Sergio Martinez Ballesteros
Juliano Haus Belletti
Jose Ignacio Berruet
Jesus Carrillo Galvan
Javier Rodriguez Venta
Quique Ortega Medina
Vergara Diaz-Caballero Unai
Midfielders
Javier Revilla Calleja
Jose Maria Cases
Cesar Arzo
Francisco Zampata Farin
Constantin Galca
Francisco Carlos Gracia
Hector Font
Montana Jorge Lopez
Jose Moreno Verdu Josico
Enrique Quique Martin
Diaz Ruben Reyes
Marcos Antonio Senna
Jose Antonio Garcia Verza
Francisco Sebastian Nada
Forwards
Carlos Reina Aranda
Antonio Guajardo De Nigris
Antonio Guayre
Martin Palermo
Manuel Fernandez Victor


KEY: ■ On all match ■ On bench ⏮ Subbed or sent off (Counting game) « Subbed or sent off (playing less than 70 minutes) ⏭ Subbed on from bench (Counting Game) » Subbed on (playing less than 70 minutes) Subbed on and then subbed or sent off (Counting Game) Subbed on and then subbed or sent off (playing less than 70 minutes) ☐ Not in 16

# RACING SANTANDER

Final Position: **16th**

| | | | | | | |
|---|---|---|---|---|---|---|
| 1 | lge | Valladolid | H | L | 0-1 | |
| 2 | lge | Alaves | A | W | 1-0 | Bodipo 31 |
| 3 | lge | R Vallecano | A | L | 1-3 | Munitis 45 |
| 4 | lge | Villarreal | H | D | 1-1 | Mora 83 |
| 5 | lge | Deportivo | A | W | 2-0 | Guerrero 27,71 |
| 6 | lge | Real Madrid | H | W | 2-0 | Regueiro 41; Munitis 51 |
| 7 | lge | Real Sociedad | A | L | 1-2 | Guerrero 22 |
| 8 | lge | Barcelona | H | D | 1-1 | Guerrero 1 |
| 9 | lge | Seville | A | L | 0-1 | |
| 10 | lge | Mallorca | H | L | 1-2 | Ismael 33 pen |
| 11 | lge | Recreativo | A | L | 1-2 | Pablo Sierra 3 |
| 12 | lge | Malaga | H | W | 1-0 | Munitis 33 |
| 13 | lge | Valencia | A | L | 0-2 | |
| 14 | lge | Celta Vigo | H | W | 3-0 | Mora 59; Benayoun 60,71 |
| 15 | lge | Atl Madrid | A | W | 2-1 | Munitis 43; Guerrero 65 |
| 16 | lge | Athl Bilbao | H | L | 3-4 | Munitis 9; Guerrero 18 pen; Regueiro 44 |
| 17 | lge | Espanyol | A | L | 0-3 | |
| 18 | lge | Real Betis | H | L | 0-1 | |
| 19 | lge | Osasuna | A | L | 1-3 | Juanma 37 |
| 20 | lge | Valladolid | A | L | 1-2 | Munitis 13 |
| 21 | lge | Alaves | H | W | 2-0 | Nafti 25; Munitis 87 |
| 22 | lge | R Vallecano | H | W | 2-0 | Guerrero 16; Benayoun 29 |
| 23 | lge | Villarreal | A | W | 3-0 | Mora 73; Bodipo 90; Regueiro 90 |
| 24 | lge | Deportivo | H | L | 1-2 | Bodipo 46 |
| 25 | lge | Real Madrid | A | L | 1-4 | Nafti 47 |
| 26 | lge | Real Sociedad | H | L | 1-2 | Benayoun 4 |
| 27 | lge | Barcelona | A | L | 1-6 | Guerrero 48 |
| 28 | lge | Seville | H | W | 1-0 | Guerrero 42 pen |
| 29 | lge | Mallorca | A | D | 3-3 | Bodipo 1,43; Guerrero 7 pen |
| 30 | lge | Recreativo | H | W | 1-0 | Pern'a 53 og |
| 31 | lge | Malaga | A | D | 2-2 | Guerrero 58; Regueiro 83 |
| 32 | lge | Valencia | H | W | 2-1 | Bodipo 10,25 |
| 33 | lge | Celta Vigo | A | D | 2-2 | Guerrero 56 pen; Diego Alonso 90 |
| 34 | lge | Atl Madrid | H | L | 0-2 | |
| 35 | lge | Athl Bilbao | A | L | 1-2 | Munitis 48 |
| 36 | lge | Espanyol | H | W | 5-2 | Bodipo 6,39; Guerrero 75; Casar 78,82 |
| 37 | lge | Real Betis | A | L | 2-4 | Munitis 75; Casar 83 |
| 38 | lge | Osasuna | H | L | 2-3 | Guerrero 28,88 |

## KEY PLAYERS - GOALSCORERS

**1 Javier Garcia Guerrero**

| | | | |
|---|---|---|---|
| Goals in the League | 15 | Player Strike Rate<br>Average number of minutes between League goals scored by player | 158 |
| Contribution to Attacking Power<br>Average number of minutes between League team goals while on pitch | 59 | Club Strike Rate<br>Average number of minutes between League goals scored by club | 63 |

| | PLAYER | LGE GOALS | POWER | STRIKE RATE |
|---|---|---|---|---|
| 2 | Pedro Munitis | 9 | 60 | 291 mins |
| 3 | Yossi Benayoun | 4 | 64 | 466 mins |
| 4 | Mario Regueiro | 4 | 49 | 497 mins |
| 5 | Jose Moraton Taeno Mora | 3 | 66 | 933 mins |

## KEY PLAYERS - MIDFIELDERS

**1 Yossi Benayoun**

| | | | |
|---|---|---|---|
| Goals in the League | 4 | Contribution to Attacking Power<br>Average number of minutes between League team goals while on pitch | 64 |
| Defensive Rating<br>Average number of mins between League goals conceded while he was on the pitch | 58 | Scoring Difference<br>Defensive Rating minus Contribution to Attacking Power | -6 |

| | PLAYER | LGE GOALS | DEF RATE | POWER | SCORE DIFF |
|---|---|---|---|---|---|
| 2 | Diego Mateo | 0 | 52 | 61 | -9 mins |
| 3 | Ruiz Salmon Ismael | 1 | 61 | 81 | -20 mins |
| 4 | Daniel Rodriguez Perez Txiki | 0 | 79 | 135 | -56 mins |

## KEY PLAYERS - DEFENDERS

**1 Jose Manuel Suarez Sietes**

| | | | |
|---|---|---|---|
| Goals Conceded (GC)<br>The number of League goals conceded while he was on the pitch | 20 | Clean Sheets<br>In games when he played at least 70 minutes | 5 |
| Defensive Rating<br>Ave number of mins between League goals conceded while on the pitch | 74 | Club Defensive Rating<br>Average number of mins between League goals conceded by the club this season | 53 |

| | PLAYER | CON LGE | CLEAN SHEETS | DEF RATE |
|---|---|---|---|---|
| 2 | Mehdi Nafti | 39 | 9 | 63 mins |
| 3 | Javier Pineda | 33 | 5 | 58 mins |
| 4 | Jose Moraton Taeno Mora | 54 | 9 | 52 mins |
| 5 | David Pararols Coromina | 28 | 5 | 51 mins |

## GOALS SCORED

**AT HOME**

| | | |
|---|---|---|
| MOST | R Madrid | 52 |
| | | 29 |
| LEAST | R Vallecano | 17 |

**AWAY**

| | | |
|---|---|---|
| MOST | R Madrid | 34 |
| | | 25 |
| LEAST | Recreativo | 11 |

## GOALS CONCEDED

**AT HOME**

| | | |
|---|---|---|
| LEAST | C Vigo & Valencia | 15 |
| | | 22 |
| MOST | Mallorca | 33 |

**AWAY**

| | | |
|---|---|---|
| LEAST | R Madrid, Valencia & Seville | 20 |
| | | 42 |
| MOST | Alaves | 48 |

## KEY GOALKEEPER

**1 Jose Maria Ceballos**

| | |
|---|---|
| Goals Conceded in the League | 13 |
| Defensive Rating<br>Ave number of mins between League goals conceded while on the pitch | 68 |
| Counting Games<br>Games when he played at least 70 minutes | 10 |
| Clean Sheets<br>In games when he played at least 70 minutes | 2 |

## TOP POINT EARNERS

| | PLAYER | GAMES | AVE |
|---|---|---|---|
| 1 | Mateo | 22 | 1.45 |
| 2 | Benayoun | 16 | 1.44 |
| 3 | Nafti | 26 | 1.42 |
| 4 | Coromina | 16 | 1.31 |
| 5 | Neru | 18 | 1.28 |
| 6 | Lemmens | 26 | 1.27 |
| 7 | Juanma | 23 | 1.26 |
| 8 | Regueiro | 17 | 1.18 |
| 9 | Munitis | 29 | 1.17 |
| 10 | Ismael | 16 | 1.13 |
| | CLUB AVERAGE: | | 1.15 |

Ave = Average points per match in Counting Games

## ATTENDANCES

HOME GROUND: EL SARDINERO   CAPACITY: 22500   AVERAGE LEAGUE AT HOME: 16439

| | | | | | | | | |
|---|---|---|---|---|---|---|---|---|
| 27 | Barcelona | 88200 | 6 | Real Madrid | 22500 | 2 | Alaves | 15000 |
| 25 | Real Madrid | 61050 | 22 | R Vallecano | 21600 | 10 | Mallorca | 14625 |
| 9 | Seville | 42750 | 8 | Barcelona | 21375 | 1 | Valladolid | 14500 |
| 15 | Atl Madrid | 39900 | 34 | Atl Madrid | 21150 | 30 | Recreativo Huelva | 13500 |
| 13 | Valencia | 39750 | 16 | Athl Bilbao | 21150 | 23 | Villarreal | 13300 |
| 37 | Real Betis | 39375 | 28 | Seville | 20250 | 29 | Mallorca | 12800 |
| 35 | Athl Bilbao | 38000 | 24 | Deportivo | 19125 | 14 | Celta Vigo | 11250 |
| 5 | Deportivo | 33820 | 32 | Valencia | 18250 | 18 | Real Betis | 11250 |
| 17 | Espanyol | 33000 | 19 | Osasuna | 18109 | 12 | Malaga | 11250 |
| 7 | Real Sociedad | 28800 | 21 | Alaves | 18000 | 4 | Villarreal | 11250 |
| 31 | Malaga | 28570 | 36 | Espanyol | 15975 | 38 | Osasuna | 9601 |
| 33 | Celta Vigo | 28000 | 26 | Real Sociedad | 15750 | 3 | R Vallecano | 9000 |
| 20 | Valladolid | 24645 | 11 | Recreativo Huelva | 15000 | | | |

■ Home □ Away ▨ Neutral

## DISCIPLINARY RECORDS

| | PLAYER | YELLOW | RED | AVE |
|---|---|---|---|---|
| 1 | Nafti | 14 | 1 | 164 |
| 2 | Coromina | 7 | 1 | 177 |
| 3 | Neru | 6 | 1 | 232 |
| 4 | Diego Alonso | 3 | 0 | 240 |
| 5 | Ismael | 7 | 0 | 243 |
| 6 | Regueiro | 7 | 0 | 283 |
| 7 | Sietes | 5 | 0 | 296 |
| 8 | Juanma | 6 | 0 | 345 |
| 9 | Mateo | 6 | 0 | 353 |
| 10 | Casar | 1 | 1 | 394 |
| 11 | Mora | 7 | 0 | 399 |
| 12 | Juanma | 2 | 0 | 405 |
| 13 | Munitis | 6 | 0 | 436 |
| | Other | 21 | 3 | |
| | TOTAL | 98 | 7 | |

## LEAGUE GOALS

| | PLAYER | MINS | GOALS | AVE |
|---|---|---|---|---|
| 1 | Guerrero | 2372 | 15 | 158 |
| 2 | Bodipo | 1359 | 9 | 151 |
| 3 | Munitis | 2618 | 9 | 291 |
| 4 | Regueiro | 1986 | 4 | 497 |
| 5 | Benayoun | 1865 | 4 | 466 |
| 6 | Mora | 2798 | 3 | 933 |
| 7 | Casar | 788 | 3 | 263 |
| 8 | Nafti | 2464 | 2 | 1232 |
| 9 | Diego Alonso | 722 | 1 | 722 |
| 10 | Pablo Sierra | 564 | 1 | 564 |
| 11 | Juanma | 2070 | 1 | 2070 |
| 12 | Ismael | 1706 | 1 | 1706 |
| | Other | | 1 | |
| | TOTAL | | 54 | |

## MONTH BY MONTH GUIDE TO THE POINTS

| MONTH | POINTS | % |
|---|---|---|
| SEPTEMBER | 4 | 44% |
| OCTOBER | 6 | 67% |
| NOVEMBER | 1 | 8% |
| DECEMBER | 9 | 75% |
| JANUARY | 0 | 0% |
| FEBRUARY | 9 | 75% |
| MARCH | 0 | 0% |
| APRIL | 8 | 67% |
| MAY | 4 | 33% |
| JUNE | 3 | 33% |

## TEAM OF THE SEASON

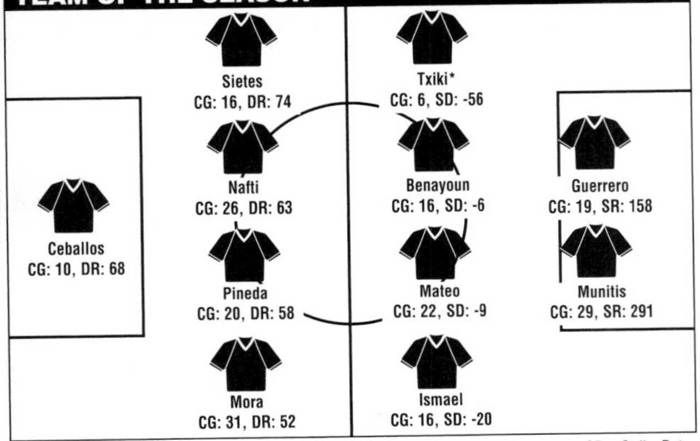

Sietes
CG: 16, DR: 74
Txiki*
CG: 6, SD: -56
Nafti
CG: 26, DR: 63
Benayoun
CG: 16, SD: -6
Guerrero
CG: 19, SR: 158
Ceballos
CG: 10, DR: 68
Pineda
CG: 20, DR: 58
Mateo
CG: 22, SD: -9
Munitis
CG: 29, SR: 291
Mora
CG: 31, DR: 52
Ismael
CG: 16, SD: -20


KEY: DR = Defensive Rate, SD = Scoring Difference, SR = Strike Rate, CG = Counting Games – League games playing at least 70 minutes

## LEAGUE APPEARANCES, BOOKINGS AND CAPS

| | AGE | IN THE SQUAD | COUNTING GAMES | MINUTES ON PITCH | YELLOW CARDS | RED CARDS | THIS SEASON | HOME COUNTRY |
|---|---|---|---|---|---|---|---|---|
| **Goalkeepers** | | | | | | | | |
| Francisco Borja | 25 | 5 | 2 | 180 | 0 | 0 | - | Spain |
| Jose Maria Ceballos | 34 | 36 | 10 | 882 | 0 | 0 | - | Spain |
| Erwin Lemmens | 27 | 34 | 26 | 2358 | 3 | 1 | - | Belgium |
| **Defenders** | | | | | | | | |
| Claudio Arzeno | 32 | 18 | 3 | 346 | 3 | 1 | - | Argentina |
| Ilan Bachar | 28 | 9 | 2 | 180 | 0 | 0 | - | Israel |
| Pablo Bustillo Casar | 24 | 19 | 8 | 788 | 1 | 1 | - | Spain |
| David Coromina | 28 | 17 | 16 | 1419 | 7 | 1 | - | Spain |
| Juan Ma Juan | 26 | 32 | 31 | 2880 | 8 | 0 | - | Spain |
| da Conceicao Messias | | 10 | 0 | 146 | 0 | 0 | - | |
| Jose Taeno Mora | 23 | 33 | 31 | 2798 | 7 | 0 | - | Spain |
| Jose Taeno Moraton | | 2 | 2 | 180 | 0 | 0 | - | |
| Mehdi Nafti | 24 | 35 | 27 | 2533 | 14 | 1 | - | France |
| Borja Enrique Neru | 29 | 35 | 18 | 1642 | 6 | 1 | - | Spain |
| Javier Pineda | 29 | 37 | 20 | 1915 | 4 | 0 | - | Spain |
| Jose Manuel Sietes | 29 | 21 | 16 | 1481 | 5 | 0 | - | Spain |
| **Midfielders** | | | | | | | | |
| Yossi Benayoun | 23 | 33 | 16 | 1865 | 1 | 0 | - | Israel |
| Ruiz Salmon Ismael | 26 | 29 | 16 | 1706 | 7 | 0 | - | Spain |
| Sergio Mata Buena | 24 | 25 | 3 | 344 | 2 | 0 | - | Spain |
| Diego Mateo | 24 | 25 | 22 | 2121 | 6 | 0 | - | Argentina |
| Fernando Moran | 27 | 19 | 2 | 401 | 1 | 0 | - | Spain |
| Ignacio Nacho | 20 | 3 | 0 | 37 | 0 | 0 | - | Spain |
| Pablo Lago | 28 | 21 | 2 | 475 | 1 | 0 | - | Spain |
| Mario Regueiro | 24 | 34 | 17 | 1986 | 7 | 0 | - | Uruguay |
| Daniel Perez Txiki | 26 | 36 | 6 | 947 | 0 | 0 | - | Spain |
| **Forwards** | | | | | | | | |
| Aguilar Leiva | 23 | 3 | 0 | 15 | 0 | 0 | - | Spain |
| Rodolfo Diaz Bodipo | 25 | 34 | 8 | 1359 | 2 | 1 | - | Spain |
| Martin Diego Alonso | 28 | 33 | 3 | 722 | 3 | 0 | - | Uruguay |
| Javier Guerrero | 26 | 38 | 19 | 2372 | 3 | 0 | - | Spain |
| Juan M Juan | | 23 | 23 | 2070 | 6 | 0 | - | Spain |
| Pedro Munitis | 28 | 30 | 29 | 2618 | 6 | 0 | - | Spain |
| Madrazo Sierra | | 13 | 5 | 564 | 0 | 0 | - | |
| Daniel Sarabia | 30 | 12 | 0 | 171 | 1 | 0 | - | Spain |

KEY: LEAGUE BOOKINGS CAPS (FIFA RANKING)

## SQUAD APPEARANCES

| Match | 1 | 2 | 3 | 4 | 5 | 6 | 7 | 8 | 9 | 10 | 11 | 12 | 13 | 14 | 15 | 16 | 17 | 18 | 19 | 20 | 21 | 22 | 23 | 24 | 25 | 26 | 27 | 28 | 29 | 30 | 31 | 32 | 33 | 34 | 35 | 36 | 37 | 38 |
|---|---|---|---|---|---|---|---|---|---|---|---|---|---|---|---|---|---|---|---|---|---|---|---|---|---|---|---|---|---|---|---|---|---|---|---|---|---|---|
| Venue | H | A | A | H | A | H | A | H | A | H | A | H | A | H | A | H | A | H | A | A | H | H | A | H | A | H | A | H | A | H | A | H | A | H | A | H | A | H |
| Competition | L | L | L | L | L | L | L | L | L | L | L | L | L | L | L | L | L | L | L | L | L | L | L | L | L | L | L | L | L | L | L | L | L | L | L | L | L | L |
| Result | L | W | L | D | W | W | L | D | L | L | L | W | L | W | W | L | L | L | L | L | W | W | W | L | L | L | L | W | D | W | D | W | D | L | L | W | L | L |

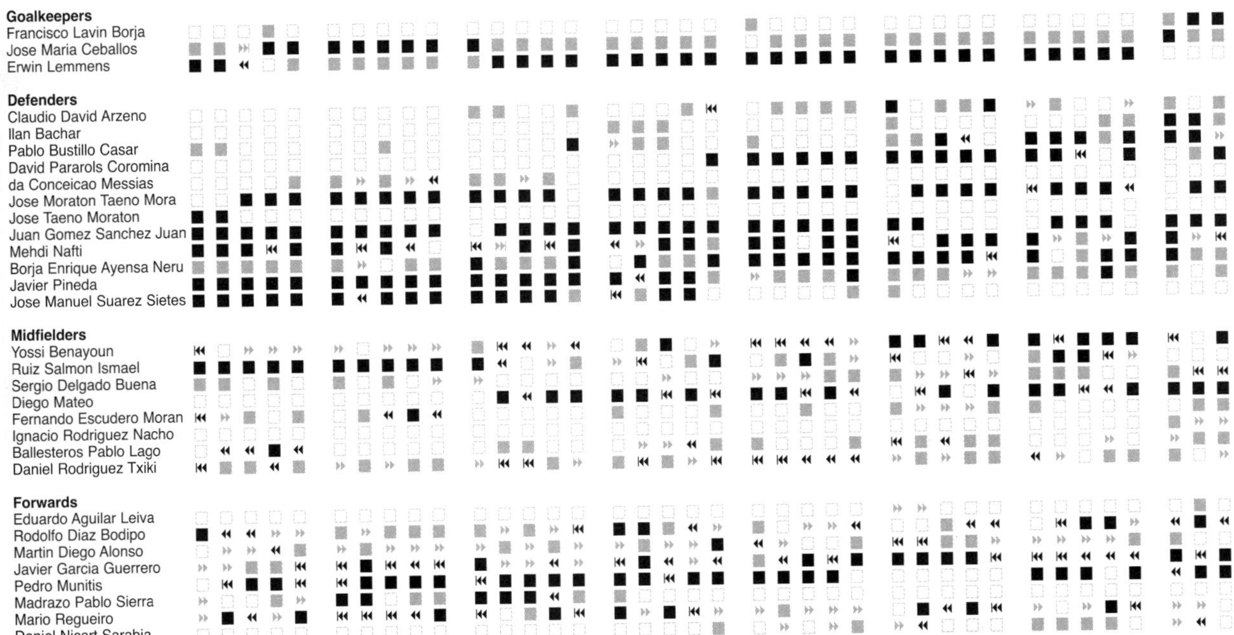

Goalkeepers
Francisco Lavin Borja
Jose Maria Ceballos
Erwin Lemmens
Defenders
Claudio David Arzeno
Ilan Bachar
Pablo Bustillo Casar
David Pararols Coromina
da Conceicao Messias
Jose Moraton Taeno Mora
Jose Taeno Moraton
Juan Gomez Sanchez Juan
Mehdi Nafti
Borja Enrique Ayensa Neru
Javier Pineda
Jose Manuel Suarez Sietes
Midfielders
Yossi Benayoun
Ruiz Salmon Ismael
Sergio Delgado Buena
Diego Mateo
Fernando Escudero Moran
Ignacio Rodriguez Nacho
Ballesteros Pablo Lago
Daniel Rodriguez Txiki
Forwards
Eduardo Aguilar Leiva
Rodolfo Diaz Bodipo
Martin Diego Alonso
Javier Garcia Guerrero
Pedro Munitis
Madrazo Pablo Sierra
Mario Regueiro
Daniel Nicart Sarabia


KEY: ■ On all match ■ On bench ⏮ Subbed or sent off (Counting game) ◂◂ Subbed or sent off (playing less than 70 minutes) ▸▸ Subbed on from bench (Counting Game) ▸▸ Subbed on (playing less than 70 minutes) Subbed on and then subbed or sent off (Counting Game) Subbed on and then subbed or sent off (playing less than 70 minutes) □ Not in 16

# ESPANYOL

Final Position: **17th**

| | | | | | | |
|---|---|---|---|---|---|---|
| 1 | lge | Real Madrid | A | L | 0-2 | |
| 2 | lge | Real Sociedad | H | L | 1-3 | Tamudo 79 |
| 3 | lge | Barcelona | A | L | 0-2 | |
| 4 | lge | Seville | H | D | 0-0 | |
| 5 | lge | Mallorca | A | L | 0-2 | |
| 6 | lge | Recreativo | H | W | 2-0 | Roger 61,72 |
| 7 | lge | Malaga | A | W | 4-3 | Domoraud 12; Milosevic 54; Tamudo 66 pen; Maxi 85 |
| 8 | lge | Valencia | H | L | 0-1 | |
| 9 | lge | Celta Vigo | A | L | 0-1 | |
| 10 | lge | Atl Madrid | H | L | 1-2 | Maxi 48 |
| 11 | lge | Athl Bilbao | A | L | 1-4 | Maxi 14 |
| 12 | lge | R Vallecano | H | W | 3-1 | Tamudo 9,69; Milosevic 90 |
| 13 | lge | Real Betis | H | L | 2-4 | Roger 62; Milosevic 71 |
| 14 | lge | Osasuna | A | L | 0-1 | |
| 15 | lge | Valladolid | H | W | 1-0 | Milosevic 7 |
| 16 | lge | Alaves | A | L | 1-2 | Milosevic 18 |
| 17 | lge | R Santander | H | W | 3-0 | Soldevilla 7; Tamudo 66 pen; Milosevic 77 |
| 18 | lge | Villarreal | A | D | 0-0 | |
| 19 | lge | Deportivo | H | W | 3-1 | Soldevilla 8; Roger 21; Morales 27 |
| 20 | lge | Real Madrid | H | D | 2-2 | Roger 40; Tamudo 45 |
| 21 | lge | Real Sociedad | A | D | 0-0 | |
| 22 | lge | Barcelona | H | L | 0-2 | |
| 23 | lge | Seville | A | L | 0-1 | |
| 24 | lge | Mallorca | H | W | 2-0 | Tamudo 32; Oscar 45 |
| 25 | lge | Recreativo | A | D | 0-0 | |
| 26 | lge | Malaga | H | W | 2-1 | Tamudo 52,90 pen |
| 27 | lge | Valencia | A | D | 1-1 | Garcia 9; Lopo 77 |
| 28 | lge | Celta Vigo | H | D | 0-0 | |
| 29 | lge | Atl Madrid | A | D | 3-3 | Tamudo 24 pen; Lopo 58; Domoraud 77 |
| 30 | lge | Athl Bilbao | H | D | 3-3 | Maxi 51; Milosevic 55; Roger 65 pen |
| 31 | lge | R Vallecano | A | W | 3-0 | Milosevic 37,47; Roger 56 |
| 32 | lge | Real Betis | A | D | 1-1 | Domoraud 86 |
| 33 | lge | Osasuna | H | D | 0-0 | |
| 34 | lge | Valladolid | A | D | 1-1 | Roger 16 |
| 35 | lge | Alaves | H | W | 3-1 | Milosevic 41,46 pen; Maxi 90 |
| 36 | lge | R Santander | A | L | 2-5 | Milosevic 63; Maxi 87 |
| 37 | lge | Villarreal | H | D | 2-2 | Maxi 23; Velamanzan 73 |
| 38 | lge | Deportivo | A | L | 1-2 | Roger 12 |

## KEY PLAYERS - GOALSCORERS

**1 Savo Milosevic**

| | | | |
|---|---|---|---|
| Goals in the League | 12 | Player Strike Rate<br>Average number of minutes between League goals scored by player | 193 |
| Contribution to Attacking Power<br>Average number of minutes between League team goals while on pitch | 64 | Club Strike Rate<br>Average number of minutes between League goals scored by club | 70 |

| | PLAYER | LGE GOALS | POWER | STRIKE RATE |
|---|---|---|---|---|
| 2 | Raul Tamudo | 10 | 80 | 218 mins |
| 3 | Garcia Junyent Roger | 9 | 68 | 259 mins |
| 4 | Maximillian Rodrigues Maxi | 7 | 68 | 440 mins |
| 5 | Cyril Domoraud | 3 | 73 | 957 mins |

## KEY PLAYERS - MIDFIELDERS

**1 Garcia Junyent Roger**

| | | | |
|---|---|---|---|
| Goals in the League | 9 | Contribution to Attacking Power<br>Average number of mins between League team goals while on pitch | 68 |
| Defensive Rating<br>Average number of mins between League goals conceded while he was on the pitch | 80 | Scoring Difference<br>Defensive Rating minus Contribution to Attacking Power | 12 |

| | PLAYER | LGE GOALS | DEF RATE | POWER | SCORE DIFF |
|---|---|---|---|---|---|
| 2 | Maximillian Rodrigues Maxi | 7 | 62 | 68 | -6 mins |
| 3 | Ivan De La Pena | 0 | 51 | 64 | -13 mins |
| 4 | Angel Morales | 1 | 57 | 73 | -16 mins |

## KEY PLAYERS - DEFENDERS

**1 Alberto Lopo**

| | | | |
|---|---|---|---|
| Goals Conceded (GC)<br>The number of League goals conceded while he was on the pitch | 25 | Clean Sheets<br>In games when he played at least 70 minutes | 9 |
| Defensive Rating<br>Ave number of mins between League goals conceded while on the pitch | 81 | Club Defensive Rating<br>Average number of mins between League goals conceded by the club this season | 62 |

| | PLAYER | CON LGE | CLEAN SHEETS | DEF RATE |
|---|---|---|---|---|
| 2 | Antoni Soldevilla | 40 | 11 | 73 mins |
| 3 | Cyril Domoraud | 42 | 11 | 68 mins |
| 4 | David Garcia | 43 | 9 | 63 mins |
| 5 | Mauro Esteban Navas | 21 | 3 | 56 mins |

## GOALS SCORED

**AT HOME**

| | | |
|---|---|---|
| MOST | R Madrid | 52 |
| | | 30 |
| LEAST | R Vallecano | 17 |

**AWAY**

| | | |
|---|---|---|
| MOST | R Madrid | 34 |
| | | 18 |
| LEAST | Recreativo | 11 |

## GOALS CONCEDED

**AT HOME**

| | | |
|---|---|---|
| LEAST | C Vigo & Valencia | 15 |
| | | 23 |
| MOST | Mallorca | 33 |

**AWAY**

| | | |
|---|---|---|
| LEAST | R Madrid, Valencia & Seville | 20 |
| | | 31 |
| MOST | Alaves | 48 |

## KEY GOALKEEPER

**1 Sergio Sanchez**

| | |
|---|---|
| Goals Conceded in the League | 5 |
| Defensive Rating<br>Ave number of mins between League goals conceded while on the pitch | 108 |
| Counting Games<br>Games when he played at least 70 minutes | 6 |
| Clean Sheets<br>In games when he played at least 70 minutes | 3 |

## TOP POINT EARNERS

| | PLAYER | GAMES | AVE |
|---|---|---|---|
| 1 | Lopo | 22 | 1.41 |
| 2 | Soldevilla | 32 | 1.31 |
| 3 | Toni | 20 | 1.30 |
| 4 | Garcia | 30 | 1.30 |
| 5 | Milosevic | 22 | 1.27 |
| 6 | Domoraud | 31 | 1.26 |
| 7 | Roger | 20 | 1.25 |
| 8 | Rodriguez | 34 | 1.24 |
| 9 | Tamudo | 22 | 1.14 |
| 10 | Torricelli | 18 | 1.11 |
| | CLUB AVERAGE: | | 1.13 |

Ave = Average points per match in Counting Games

## ATTENDANCES

HOME GROUND: LLUIS COMPANYS CAPACITY: 55000 AVERAGE LEAGUE AT HOME: 33013

| | | | | | | | | |
|---|---|---|---|---|---|---|---|---|
| 3 | Barcelona | 85833 | 26 | Malaga | 38500 | 25 | Recreativo Huelva | 19500 |
| 1 | Real Madrid | 72485 | 10 | Atl Madrid | 37950 | 30 | Athl Bilbao | 19250 |
| 29 | Atl Madrid | 54150 | 28 | Celta Vigo | 36850 | 24 | Mallorca | 19250 |
| 27 | Valencia | 50350 | 6 | Recreativo Huelva | 35750 | 16 | Alaves | 18240 |
| 20 | Real Madrid | 49500 | 11 | Athl Bilbao | 34000 | 5 | Mallorca | 16590 |
| 22 | Barcelona | 48400 | 13 | Real Betis | 33550 | 36 | R Santander | 15975 |
| 32 | Real Betis | 48300 | 7 | Malaga | 33390 | 14 | Osasuna | 15920 |
| 8 | Valencia | 44000 | 17 | R Santander | 33000 | 38 | Deportivo | 14240 |
| 35 | Alaves | 42900 | 21 | Real Sociedad | 29750 | 31 | R Vallecano | 12400 |
| 19 | Deportivo | 42350 | 9 | Celta Vigo | 22260 | 37 | Villarreal | 12400 |
| 15 | Valladolid | 40700 | 12 | R Vallecano | 22000 | 18 | Villarreal | 10920 |
| 4 | Seville | 40700 | 2 | Real Sociedad | 20300 | 33 | Osasuna | 9900 |
| 23 | Seville | 40500 | 34 | Valladolid | 19900 | | | |

## DISCIPLINARY RECORDS

| | PLAYER | YELLOW | RED | AVE |
|---|---|---|---|---|
| 1 | Lopo | 14 | 2 | 126 |
| 2 | Alex | 6 | 1 | 135 |
| 3 | Posse | 5 | 1 | 149 |
| 4 | Soldevilla | 15 | 1 | 182 |
| 5 | Amaya | 4 | 0 | 215 |
| 6 | Velamanzan | 3 | 0 | 248 |
| 7 | Roger | 7 | 2 | 258 |
| 8 | Torricelli | 5 | 1 | 263 |
| 9 | Tamudo | 8 | 0 | 272 |
| 10 | Domoraud | 7 | 1 | 359 |
| 11 | Morales | 6 | 0 | 363 |
| 12 | De La Pena | 4 | 0 | 370 |
| 13 | Garcia | 5 | 1 | 450 |
| | Other | 13 | 0 | |
| | TOTAL | 102 | 10 | |

## LEAGUE GOALS

| | PLAYER | MINS | GOALS | AVE |
|---|---|---|---|---|
| 1 | Milosevic | 2313 | 12 | 193 |
| 2 | Tamudo | 2178 | 10 | 218 |
| 3 | Roger | 2327 | 9 | 259 |
| 4 | Rodriguez | 3080 | 7 | 440 |
| 5 | Domoraud | 2872 | 3 | 957 |
| 6 | Soldevilla | 2914 | 2 | 1457 |
| 7 | Lopo | 2024 | 1 | 2024 |
| 8 | Garcia | 2700 | 1 | 2700 |
| 9 | Velamanzan | 744 | 1 | 744 |
| 10 | Oscar | 689 | 1 | 689 |
| 11 | Morales | 2181 | 1 | 2181 |
| | Other | | 0 | |
| | TOTAL | | 48 | |

## MONTH BY MONTH GUIDE TO THE POINTS

| MONTH | POINTS | % |
|---|---|---|
| SEPTEMBER | 1 | 8% |
| OCTOBER | 6 | 67% |
| NOVEMBER | 0 | 0% |
| DECEMBER | 6 | 50% |
| JANUARY | 7 | 58% |
| FEBRUARY | 2 | 17% |
| MARCH | 8 | 67% |
| APRIL | 6 | 50% |
| MAY | 6 | 50% |
| JUNE | 1 | 11% |

## TEAM OF THE SEASON

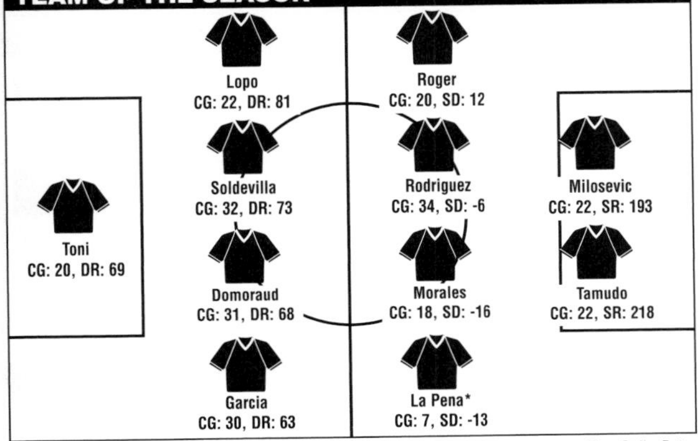

Lopo
CG: 22, DR: 81
Roger
CG: 20, SD: 12
Soldevilla
CG: 32, DR: 73
Rodriguez
CG: 34, SD: -6
Milosevic
CG: 22, SR: 193
Toni
CG: 20, DR: 69
Domoraud
CG: 31, DR: 68
Morales
CG: 18, SD: -16
Tamudo
CG: 22, SR: 218
Garcia
CG: 30, DR: 63
La Pena*
CG: 7, SD: -13


KEY: DR = Defensive Rate, SD = Scoring Difference, SR = Strike Rate, CG = Counting Games – League games playing at least 70 minutes

## LEAGUE APPEARANCES, BOOKINGS AND CAPS

| | AGE | IN THE SQUAD | COUNTING GAMES | MINUTES ON PITCH | YELLOW CARDS | RED CARDS | THIS SEASON | HOME COUNTRY |
|---|---|---|---|---|---|---|---|---|
| **Goalkeepers** | | | | | | | | |
| Alfredo Argenso | 28 | 14 | 12 | 1080 | 2 | 0 | - | |
| Gorka Iraioz | 22 | 5 | 0 | 0 | 0 | 0 | - | Spain |
| Sergio Sanchez | 26 | 36 | 6 | 540 | 0 | 0 | - | Spain |
| Antonio Toni | 32 | 20 | 20 | 1800 | 1 | 0 | - | Spain |
| **Defenders** | | | | | | | | |
| Ivan Amaya | 24 | 26 | 8 | 861 | 4 | 0 | - | Spain |
| Marc Bertran | 21 | 13 | 7 | 722 | 1 | 0 | - | Spain |
| David Catala | 22 | 2 | 0 | 0 | 0 | 0 | - | Spain |
| Cyril Domoraud | 31 | 33 | 31 | 2872 | 7 | 1 | - | France |
| David Garcia | 22 | 30 | 30 | 2700 | 5 | 1 | - | Spain |
| Daniel Jarque | 20 | 17 | 5 | 460 | 0 | 0 | - | Spain |
| Alberto Lopo | 24 | 28 | 22 | 2024 | 14 | 2 | - | Spain |
| Mauro Navas | 28 | 19 | 12 | 1186 | 1 | 0 | - | Argentina |
| Cavas Ricardo | | 5 | 1 | 155 | 1 | 0 | - | |
| Antoni Soldevilla | 24 | 33 | 32 | 2914 | 15 | 1 | - | Spain |
| Moreno Torricelli | 33 | 18 | 18 | 1583 | 5 | 1 | - | Italy |
| Xavier Mateo Roca | 29 | 2 | 0 | 29 | 0 | 0 | - | Spain |
| **Midfielders** | | | | | | | | |
| Alex Sanchez | 29 | 28 | 6 | 978 | 7 | 1 | - | Spain |
| Moises Arteag | 34 | 10 | 0 | 22 | 0 | 0 | - | Spain |
| Alain Boghossian | 32 | 8 | 1 | 182 | 0 | 0 | - | France |
| Albert Crusat | 21 | 5 | 1 | 139 | 1 | 0 | - | Spain |
| Ivan De La Pena | 27 | 32 | 7 | 1482 | 4 | 0 | - | Spain |
| Camara Fredson | 22 | 28 | 4 | 795 | 1 | 0 | - | Brazil |
| Edjogo Juvenal | 24 | 2 | 0 | 0 | 0 | 0 | - | Spain |
| Jose Juan Luque | 25 | 10 | 3 | 467 | 1 | 0 | - | |
| Hurtado Moises | 22 | 2 | 0 | 0 | 0 | 0 | - | Spain |
| Angel Morales | 27 | 36 | 18 | 2181 | 6 | 0 | - | Spain |
| Maxi Rodriguez | 22 | 37 | 34 | 3080 | 1 | 0 | - | Argentina |
| Garcia Roger | 26 | 32 | 20 | 2327 | 7 | 2 | - | Spain |
| Antonio Velamanzan | 26 | 30 | 2 | 744 | 3 | 0 | - | Spain |
| **Forwards** | | | | | | | | |
| Soriano Jonathan | 17 | 4 | 0 | 1 | 0 | 0 | - | Spain |
| Savo Milosevic | 29 | 37 | 22 | 2313 | 2 | 0 | - | Serbia & Montenegro |
| Garcia Oscar | 30 | 25 | 1 | 689 | 0 | 0 | - | Spain |
| Martin Posse | 27 | 29 | 6 | 895 | 5 | 1 | - | Argentina |
| Raul Tamudo | 25 | 29 | 22 | 2178 | 8 | 0 | 2 | Spain (2) |

KEY: LEAGUE BOOKINGS CAPS (FIFA RANKING)

## SQUAD APPEARANCES

| Match | 1 | 2 | 3 | 4 | 5 | 6 | 7 | 8 | 9 | 10 | 11 | 12 | 13 | 14 | 15 | 16 | 17 | 18 | 19 | 20 | 21 | 22 | 23 | 24 | 25 | 26 | 27 | 28 | 29 | 30 | 31 | 32 | 33 | 34 | 35 | 36 | 37 | 38 |
|---|---|---|---|---|---|---|---|---|---|---|---|---|---|---|---|---|---|---|---|---|---|---|---|---|---|---|---|---|---|---|---|---|---|---|---|---|---|---|
| Venue | A | H | A | H | A | H | A | H | A | H | A | H | H | A | H | A | H | A | H | H | A | H | A | H | A | H | A | H | A | H | A | A | H | A | H | A | H | A |
| Competition | L | L | L | L | L | L | L | L | L | L | L | L | L | L | L | L | L | L | L | L | L | L | L | L | L | L | L | L | L | L | L | L | L | L | L | L | L | L |
| Result | L | L | L | D | L | W | W | L | L | L | L | W | L | L | W | L | W | D | W | D | D | L | L | W | D | W | D | D | D | D | W | D | D | D | W | L | D | L |

**Goalkeepers**
Alfredo Argenso
Gorka Iraioz
Sergio Sanchez
Antonio Jimenez Toni

**Defenders**
Ivan Amaya
Marc Bertran
David Catala
Cyril Domoraud
David Garcia
Daniel Jarque
Alberto Lopo
Mauro Esteban Navas
Cavas Merino Ricardo
Antoni Soldevilla
Moreno Torricelli
Xavier Mateo Xavi Roca

**Midfielders**
Alejandro Fernandez Sanchez
Moises Garcia Arteag
Alain Boghossian
Albert Crusat
Ivan De La Pena
Camara Pereira Fredson
Edjogo Owono Juvenal
Jose Juan Luque
Hurtado Moises
Angel Morales
Maximilliano Rodriguez
Garcia Junyent Roger
Antonio Tejedor Velamanzan

**Forwards**
Soriano Jonathan
Savo Milosevic
Garcia Junyent Oscar
Martin Posse
Raul Tamudo

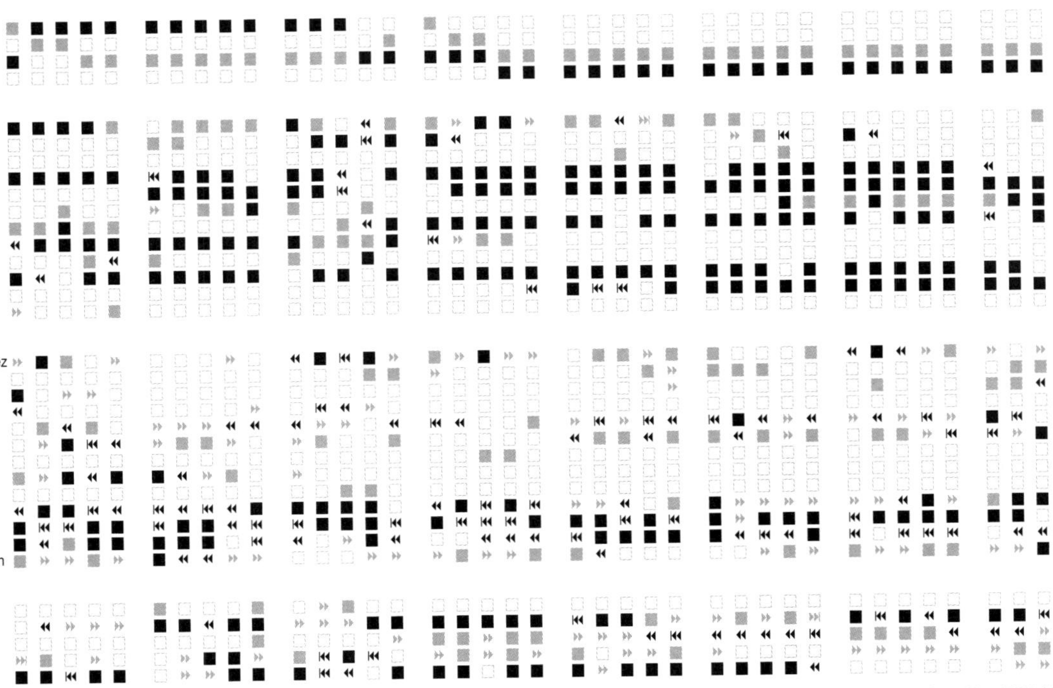

# RECREATIVO HUELVA

Final Position: **18th**

| | | | | | | |
|---|---|---|---|---|---|---|
| 1 | lge | Malaga | H | L | 2-3 | Raul Molina 17; Viqueira 33 |
| 2 | lge | Valencia | A | L | 0-3 | |
| 3 | lge | Celta Vigo | H | L | 0-3 | |
| 4 | lge | Atl Madrid | A | D | 1-1 | Raul Molina 27 |
| 5 | lge | Athl Bilbao | H | L | 1-2 | Xisco 88 |
| 6 | lge | Espanyol | A | L | 0-2 | |
| 7 | lge | Real Betis | H | D | 1-1 | Xisco 75 |
| 8 | lge | Osasuna | A | W | 1-0 | Cubillo 85 pen |
| 9 | lge | Valladolid | H | L | 1-3 | Loren 83 |
| 10 | lge | Alaves | A | L | 0-3 | |
| 11 | lge | R Santander | H | W | 2-1 | Raul Molina 86,90 |
| 12 | lge | Villarreal | A | L | 0-1 | |
| 13 | lge | Deportivo | H | D | 1-1 | Raul Molina 21 |
| 14 | lge | Real Madrid | A | L | 2-4 | Cubillo 3; Espinola 14 |
| 15 | lge | Real Sociedad | H | L | 1-3 | Raul Molina 40 |
| 16 | lge | Barcelona | A | L | 0-3 | |
| 17 | lge | Seville | H | D | 0-0 | |
| 18 | lge | Mallorca | A | D | 1-1 | Raul Molina 55 |
| 19 | lge | R Vallecano | H | W | 2-1 | Xisco 58; Loren 84 |
| 20 | lge | Malaga | A | L | 0-4 | |
| 21 | lge | Valencia | H | D | 1-1 | Raul Molina 31 |
| 22 | lge | Celta Vigo | A | L | 1-4 | Silvinho 90 og |
| 23 | lge | Atl Madrid | H | W | 3-0 | Romero 66; Xisco 81; Benitez 83 |
| 24 | lge | Athl Bilbao | A | W | 3-2 | Benitez 6; Romero 12; Xisco 19 |
| 25 | lge | Espanyol | H | D | 0-0 | |
| 26 | lge | Real Betis | A | D | 1-1 | Xisco 62 |
| 27 | lge | Osasuna | H | D | 1-1 | Pern'a 85 |
| 28 | lge | Valladolid | A | W | 1-0 | Raul Molina 21 |
| 29 | lge | Alaves | H | W | 1-0 | Garcia 4 |
| 30 | lge | R Santander | A | L | 0-1 | |
| 31 | lge | Villarreal | H | W | 5-0 | Raul Molina 33 pen; Viqueira 47,74; Pern'a 84; Romero 87 |
| 32 | lge | Deportivo | A | L | 0-5 | |
| 33 | lge | Real Madrid | H | D | 0-0 | |
| 34 | lge | Real Sociedad | A | L | 0-1 | |
| 35 | lge | Barcelona | H | L | 1-3 | Joaozinho 87 |
| 36 | lge | Seville | A | L | 0-1 | |
| 37 | lge | Mallorca | H | D | 1-1 | Joaozinho 46 |
| 38 | lge | R Vallecano | A | D | 0-0 | |

## KEY PLAYERS - GOALSCORERS

**1 Alcocer Raul Molina**

| | | | |
|---|---|---|---|
| Goals in the League | 10 | Player Strike Rate<br>Average number of minutes between League goals scored by player | 265 |
| Contribution to Attacking Power<br>Average number of minutes between League team goals while on pitch | 110 | Club Strike Rate<br>Average number of minutes between League goals scored by club | 98 |

| | PLAYER | LGE GOALS | POWER | STRIKE RATE |
|---|---|---|---|---|
| 2 | Emilio Jose Viqueira | 3 | 84 | 785 mins |
| 3 | Mariano Andres Pernia | 2 | 90 | 855 mins |
| 4 | Ignacio Benitez | 2 | 94 | 1084 mins |
| 5 | Lorenzo Moron Vizcaino Loren | 2 | 93 | 1362 mins |

## KEY PLAYERS - MIDFIELDERS

**1 Emilio Jose Viqueira**

| | | | |
|---|---|---|---|
| Goals in the League | 3 | Contribution to Attacking Power<br>Average number of minutes between League team goals while on pitch | 84 |
| Defensive Rating<br>Average number of mins between League goals conceded while he was on the pitch | 56 | Scoring Difference<br>Defensive Rating minus Contribution to Attacking Power | -28 |

| | PLAYER | LGE GOALS | DEF RATE | POWER | SCORE DIFF |
|---|---|---|---|---|---|
| 2 | Ignacio Benitez | 2 | 59 | 94 | -35 mins |
| 3 | Diego Camacho | 0 | 58 | 97 | -39 mins |
| 4 | David Cubillo | 2 | 44 | 86 | -42 mins |
| 5 | Juan Ruiz Merino | 0 | 79 | 127 | -48 mins |

## KEY PLAYERS - DEFENDERS

**1 Mariano Andres Pernia**

| | | | |
|---|---|---|---|
| Goals Conceded (GC)<br>The number of League goals conceded while he was on the pitch | 25 | Clean Sheets<br>In games when he played at least 70 minutes | 7 |
| Defensive Rating<br>Ave number of mins between League goals conceded while on the pitch | 68 | Club Defensive Rating<br>Average number of mins between League goals conceded by the club this season | 56 |

| | PLAYER | CON LGE | CLEAN SHEETS | DEF RATE |
|---|---|---|---|---|
| 2 | Javi Garcia | 46 | 7 | 59 mins |
| 3 | Lorenzo Moron Vizcaino Loren | 47 | 8 | 58 mins |
| 4 | Miguel Angel Espinola | 48 | 7 | 54 mins |
| 5 | Alejandro Perreira Alex | 25 | 1 | 47 mins |

## GOALS SCORED

AT HOME

| | | |
|---|---|---|
| MOST | R Madrid | 52 |
| | | 24 |
| LEAST | R Vallecano | 17 |

AWAY

| | | |
|---|---|---|
| MOST | R Madrid | 34 |
| | | 11 |
| LEAST | Recreativo | 11 |

## GOALS CONCEDED

AT HOME

| | | |
|---|---|---|
| LEAST | C Vigo & Valencia | 15 |
| | | 24 |
| MOST | Mallorca | 33 |

AWAY

| | | |
|---|---|---|
| LEAST | R Madrid, Valencia & Seville | 20 |
| | | 37 |
| MOST | Alaves | 48 |

## KEY GOALKEEPER

**1 Jose Antonio Luque**

| | |
|---|---|
| Goals Conceded in the League | 36 |
| Defensive Rating<br>Ave number of mins between League goals conceded while on the pitch | 65 |
| Counting Games<br>Games when he played at least 70 minutes | 26 |
| Clean Sheets<br>In games when he played at least 70 minutes | 8 |

## TOP POINT EARNERS

| | PLAYER | GAMES | AVE |
|---|---|---|---|
| 1 | Pernia | 19 | 1.16 |
| 2 | Luque | 26 | 1.15 |
| 3 | Benitez | 20 | 1.15 |
| 4 | Loren | 29 | 1.14 |
| 5 | Camacho | 29 | 1.14 |
| 6 | Viqueira | 24 | 1.13 |
| 7 | Merino | 12 | 1.08 |
| 8 | Garcia | 27 | 1.07 |
| 9 | Begona | 24 | 1.00 |
| 10 | Raul Molina | 23 | 0.87 |
| | **CLUB AVERAGE:** | | **0.95** |

Ave = Average points per match in Counting Games

## ATTENDANCES

HOME GROUND: COLOMBINO CAPACITY: 20000 AVERAGE LEAGUE AT HOME: 17384

| | | | | | | | | |
|---|---|---|---|---|---|---|---|---|
| 14 | Real Madrid | 76300 | 1 | Malaga | 20000 | 37 | Mallorca | 16800 |
| 16 | Barcelona | 52920 | 33 | Real Madrid | 20000 | 18 | Mallorca | 16590 |
| 2 | Valencia | 45000 | 35 | Barcelona | 19600 | 8 | Osasuna | 16517 |
| 26 | Real Betis | 42000 | 25 | Espanyol | 19500 | 31 | Villarreal | 16400 |
| 4 | Atl Madrid | 39900 | 10 | Alaves | 19200 | 13 | Deportivo | 16000 |
| 6 | Espanyol | 35750 | 19 | R Vallecano | 18800 | 11 | R Santander | 15000 |
| 34 | Real Sociedad | 30100 | 15 | Real Sociedad | 18600 | 21 | Valencia | 14000 |
| 20 | Malaga | 30050 | 28 | Valladolid | 18020 | 27 | Osasuna | 14000 |
| 36 | Seville | 29250 | 3 | Celta Vigo | 18000 | 17 | Seville | 14000 |
| 22 | Celta Vigo | 27700 | 5 | Athl Bilbao | 18000 | 30 | R Santander | 13500 |
| 32 | Deportivo | 26700 | 9 | Valladolid | 17400 | 12 | Villarreal | 9744 |
| 24 | Athl Bilbao | 24400 | 23 | Atl Madrid | 17200 | 38 | R Vallecano | 2550 |
| 7 | Real Betis | 20000 | 29 | Alaves | 17000 | | | |

■ Home □ Away ▒ Neutral

## DISCIPLINARY RECORDS

| | PLAYER | YELLOW | RED | AVE |
|---|---|---|---|---|
| 1 | Xisco | 6 | 1 | 168 |
| 2 | Yago | 3 | 0 | 173 |
| 3 | Loren | 12 | 2 | 194 |
| 4 | Romero | 3 | 0 | 238 |
| 5 | Camacho | 10 | 0 | 271 |
| 6 | Jose Mari | 2 | 0 | 274 |
| 7 | Bermejo | 5 | 0 | 289 |
| 8 | Alex | 4 | 0 | 295 |
| 9 | Cubillo | 4 | 0 | 299 |
| 10 | Galan | 1 | 1 | 312 |
| 11 | Espinola | 6 | 0 | 432 |
| 12 | Raul Molina | 6 | 0 | 441 |
| 13 | Begona | 4 | 1 | 463 |
| | Other | 20 | 3 | |
| | **TOTAL** | **86** | **8** | |

## LEAGUE GOALS

| | PLAYER | MINS | GOALS | AVE |
|---|---|---|---|---|
| 1 | Raul Molina | 2650 | 10 | 265 |
| 2 | Xisco | 1180 | 6 | 197 |
| 3 | Romero | 714 | 3 | 238 |
| 4 | Viqueira | 2354 | 3 | 785 |
| 5 | Benitez | 2168 | 2 | 1084 |
| 6 | Cubillo | 1199 | 2 | 600 |
| 7 | Loren | 2723 | 2 | 1362 |
| 8 | Joaozinho | 197 | 2 | 99 |
| 9 | Pernia | 1710 | 2 | 855 |
| 10 | Espinola | 2595 | 1 | 2595 |
| 11 | Garcia | 2714 | 1 | 2714 |
| | Other | | 1 | |
| | **TOTAL** | | **35** | |

## MONTH BY MONTH GUIDE TO THE POINTS

| MONTH | POINTS | % |
|---|---|---|
| SEPTEMBER | 1 | 8% |
| OCTOBER | 1 | 11% |
| NOVEMBER | 6 | 50% |
| DECEMBER | 1 | 8% |
| JANUARY | 5 | 42% |
| FEBRUARY | 4 | 33% |
| MARCH | 6 | 50% |
| APRIL | 9 | 75% |
| MAY | 1 | 8% |
| JUNE | 2 | 22% |

## TEAM OF THE SEASON

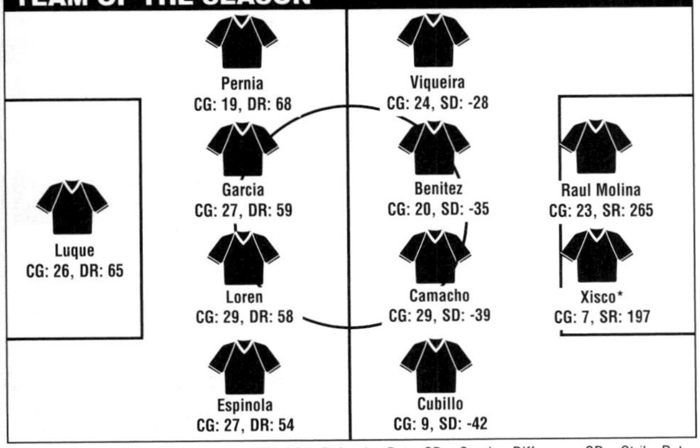
Pernia
CG: 19, DR: 68
Viqueira
CG: 24, SD: -28
Garcia
CG: 27, DR: 59
Benitez
CG: 20, SD: -35
Raul Molina
CG: 23, SR: 265
Luque
CG: 26, DR: 65
Loren
CG: 29, DR: 58
Camacho
CG: 29, SD: -39
Xisco*
CG: 7, SR: 197
Espinola
CG: 27, DR: 54
Cubillo
CG: 9, SD: -42

**KEY:** DR = Defensive Rate, SD = Scoring Difference, SR = Strike Rate, CG = Counting Games – League games playing at least 70 minutes

## LEAGUE APPEARANCES, BOOKINGS AND CAPS

| | AGE | IN THE SQUAD | COUNTING GAMES | MINUTES ON PITCH | YELLOW CARDS | RED CARDS | THIS SEASON | HOME COUNTRY |
|---|---|---|---|---|---|---|---|---|
| **Goalkeepers** | | | | | | | | |
| Manuel Almunia | 26 | 19 | 0 | 36 | 0 | 0 | - | Spain |
| Miguel Cesar | 34 | 26 | 11 | 1044 | 0 | 1 | - | Spain |
| Jose Antonio Luque | 29 | 32 | 26 | 2340 | 0 | 1 | - | Spain |
| **Defenders** | | | | | | | | |
| Alejandro Alex | 26 | 20 | 12 | 1183 | 4 | 0 | - | Venezuela |
| Miguel Espinola | 29 | 35 | 27 | 2595 | 6 | 0 | - | Spain |
| Jose Barba Galan | 29 | 16 | 6 | 624 | 1 | 1 | - | Spain |
| Javi Garcia | 25 | 35 | 27 | 2714 | 3 | 0 | - | Spain |
| Lorenzo Loren | 33 | 33 | 29 | 2723 | 12 | 2 | - | Spain |
| Mariano Pernia | 29 | 20 | 19 | 1710 | 3 | 0 | - | Argentina |
| Sergio Garcia Tejero | 24 | 5 | 3 | 295 | 0 | 0 | - | Spain |
| Alonso-Fueyo Yago | | 14 | 5 | 521 | 3 | 0 | - | |
| Nelson Zelaya | 29 | 10 | 0 | 51 | 0 | 1 | - | Paraguay |
| **Midfielders** | | | | | | | | |
| Oscar Ochoa Arpon | 28 | 38 | 14 | 1831 | 2 | 0 | - | Spain |
| Iker Begona | 26 | 34 | 24 | 2315 | 4 | 1 | - | Spain |
| Ignacio Benitez | 23 | 34 | 20 | 2168 | 3 | 0 | - | Spain |
| Diego Camacho | 26 | 35 | 29 | 2718 | 10 | 0 | - | Spain |
| David Cubillo | 25 | 36 | 9 | 1199 | 4 | 0 | - | Spain |
| David Galeggo | 31 | 12 | 1 | 208 | 0 | 0 | - | Spain |
| Jose Luis Gallego | 32 | 8 | 0 | 150 | 1 | 0 | - | Spain |
| Manuel Holgado | 21 | 1 | 0 | 0 | 0 | 0 | - | Spain |
| Juan Ruiz Merino | 32 | 24 | 12 | 1265 | 2 | 0 | - | Spain |
| Emilio Jose Viqueira | 28 | 36 | 24 | 2354 | 5 | 0 | - | Spain |
| **Forwards** | | | | | | | | |
| Mario Bermejo | 24 | 35 | 8 | 1447 | 5 | 0 | - | Spain |
| Daniel Guiza | 22 | 7 | 0 | 95 | 1 | 0 | - | Spain |
| Joao Joaozinho | 23 | 10 | 0 | 197 | 0 | 0 | - | Brazil |
| Garcia Jose Mari | 28 | 23 | 5 | 549 | 2 | 0 | - | Spain |
| Carlos Arceo Kaiku | 30 | 15 | 5 | 545 | 0 | 0 | - | Spain |
| Alcocer Raul Molina | 26 | 36 | 23 | 2650 | 6 | 0 | - | Spain |
| Quige Romero | 25 | 27 | 1 | 714 | 3 | 0 | - | Spain |
| Francisco Xisco | 22 | 24 | 7 | 1180 | 6 | 1 | - | Spain |

**KEY:** LEAGUE BOOKINGS CAPS (FIFA RANKING)

## SQUAD APPEARANCES

| Match | 1 | 2 | 3 | 4 | 5 | 6 | 7 | 8 | 9 | 10 | 11 | 12 | 13 | 14 | 15 | 16 | 17 | 18 | 19 | 20 | 21 | 22 | 23 | 24 | 25 | 26 | 27 | 28 | 29 | 30 | 31 | 32 | 33 | 34 | 35 | 36 | 37 | 38 |
|---|---|---|---|---|---|---|---|---|---|---|---|---|---|---|---|---|---|---|---|---|---|---|---|---|---|---|---|---|---|---|---|---|---|---|---|---|---|---|
| Venue | H | A | H | A | H | A | H | A | H | A | H | A | H | A | H | A | H | A | H | A | H | A | H | A | H | A | H | A | H | A | H | A | H | A | H | A | H | A |
| Competition | L | L | L | L | L | L | L | L | L | L | L | L | L | L | L | L | L | L | L | L | L | L | L | L | L | L | L | L | L | L | L | L | L | L | L | L | L | L |
| Result | L | L | L | D | L | L | D | W | L | L | W | L | D | L | L | L | D | D | W | L | D | L | W | W | D | D | D | W | W | L | W | L | D | L | L | L | D | D |

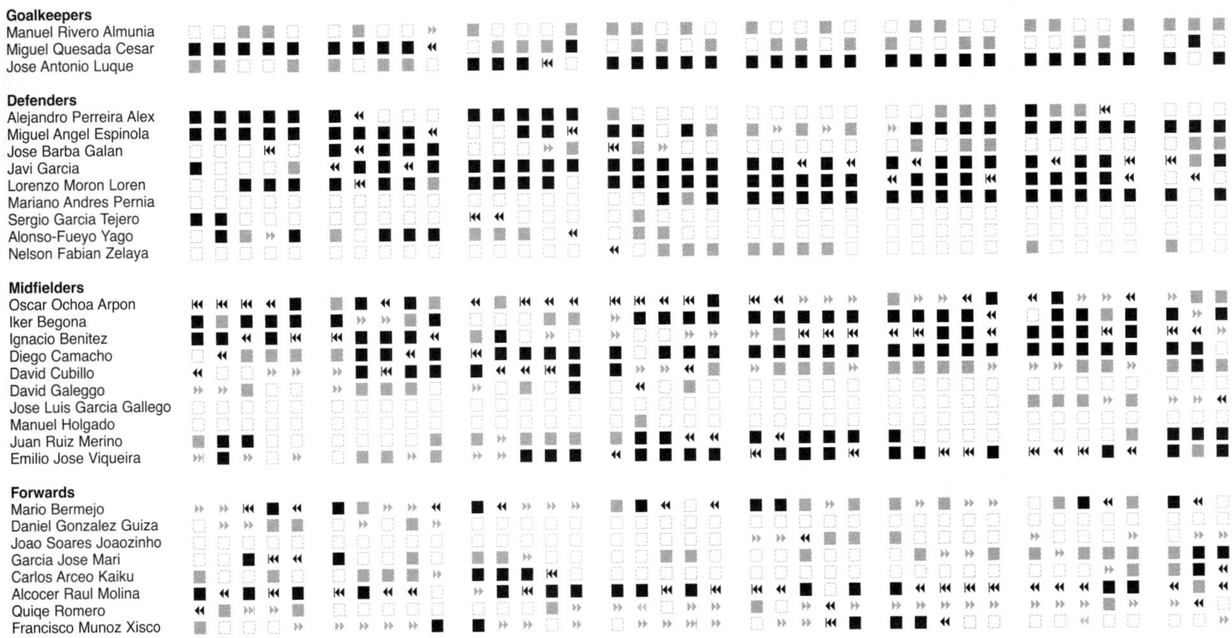
Goalkeepers
Manuel Rivero Almunia
Miguel Quesada Cesar
Jose Antonio Luque
Defenders
Alejandro Perreira Alex
Miguel Angel Espinola
Jose Barba Galan
Javi Garcia
Lorenzo Moron Loren
Mariano Andres Pernia
Sergio Garcia Tejero
Alonso-Fueyo Yago
Nelson Fabian Zelaya
Midfielders
Oscar Ochoa Arpon
Iker Begona
Ignacio Benitez
Diego Camacho
David Cubillo
David Galeggo
Jose Luis Garcia Gallego
Manuel Holgado
Juan Ruiz Merino
Emilio Jose Viqueira
Forwards
Mario Bermejo
Daniel Gonzalez Guiza
Joao Soares Joaozinho
Garcia Jose Mari
Carlos Arceo Kaiku
Alcocer Raul Molina
Quiqe Romero
Francisco Munoz Xisco

**KEY:** ■ On all match ▪ On bench ⏮ Subbed or sent off (Counting game) « Subbed or sent off (playing less than 70 minutes) ⏭ Subbed on from bench (Counting Game) » Subbed on (playing less than 70 minutes) Subbed on and then subbed or sent off (Counting Game) Subbed on and then subbed or sent off (playing less than 70 minutes) ☐ Not in 16

# ALAVES

Final Position: **19th**

| | | | | | | |
|---|---|---|---|---|---|---|
| 1 | lge | R Vallecano | A | D | 2-2 | Alonso 38; Magno 69 |
| 2 | lge | R Santander | H | L | 0-1 | |
| 3 | uc1rl1 | Ankaraguku | A | W | 2-1 | Desio 45; Navarro 81 |
| 4 | lge | Villarreal | A | W | 1-0 | Alonso 35 |
| 5 | lge | Deportivo | H | L | 1-2 | Alonso 55 |
| 6 | uc1rl2 | Ankaraguku | H | W | 3-0 | Alonso 6; Turiel 48,74 |
| 7 | lge | Real Madrid | A | L | 2-5 | Magno 37; Alonso 84 |
| 8 | lge | Real Sociedad | H | D | 2-2 | Astudillo 5; Navarro 89 |
| 9 | lge | Barcelona | A | L | 1-6 | Ibon Begona 53 |
| 10 | uc2rl1 | Besiktas | H | D | 1-1 | Abelardo 90 |
| 11 | lge | Seville | H | W | 1-0 | Navarro 90 |
| 12 | lge | Mallorca | A | L | 1-3 | Ilie 92 |
| 13 | uc2rl2 | Besiktas | A | L | 0-1 | |
| 14 | lge | Recreativo | H | W | 3-0 | Navarro 9; Magno 19; Ilie 56 |
| 15 | lge | Malaga | A | D | 0-0 | |
| 16 | lge | Valencia | H | D | 0-0 | |
| 17 | lge | Celta Vigo | A | L | 1-2 | Ilie 8 pen |
| 18 | lge | Atl Madrid | H | W | 2-0 | Navarro 11; Ilie 30 |
| 19 | lge | Athl Bilbao | A | L | 0-2 | |
| 20 | lge | Espanyol | H | W | 2-1 | Jordi 33; Soldevilla 76 og |
| 21 | lge | Real Betis | A | D | 2-2 | Magno 57; Turiel 90 |
| 22 | lge | Osasuna | H | D | 1-1 | Ilie 40 |
| 23 | lge | Valladolid | A | W | 3-1 | Navarro 20,73; Ivan Alonso 90 |
| 24 | lge | R Vallecano | H | D | 1-1 | Karmona 70 |
| 25 | lge | R Santander | A | L | 0-2 | |
| 26 | lge | Villarreal | H | W | 1-0 | Tomic 77 |
| 27 | lge | Deportivo | A | L | 0-6 | |
| 28 | lge | Real Madrid | H | L | 1-5 | Ivan Alonso 75 |
| 29 | lge | Real Sociedad | A | L | 1-3 | Navarro 83 pen |
| 30 | lge | Barcelona | H | D | 0-0 | |
| 31 | lge | Seville | A | L | 2-3 | Navarro 60; Astudillo 78; Abelardo 90 og |
| 32 | lge | Mallorca | H | D | 0-0 | |
| 33 | lge | Recreativo | A | L | 0-1 | |
| 34 | lge | Malaga | H | L | 0-1 | |
| 35 | lge | Valencia | A | L | 0-3 | |
| 36 | lge | Celta Vigo | H | D | 0-0 | |
| 37 | lge | Atl Madrid | A | W | 1-0 | Ilie 55 |
| 38 | lge | Athl Bilbao | H | L | 2-4 | Magno 27; Astudillo 29 |
| 39 | lge | Espanyol | A | L | 1-3 | Llorens 58 pen |
| 40 | lge | Real Betis | H | L | 0-1 | |
| 41 | lge | Osasuna | A | L | 2-4 | Navarro 35,84 |
| 42 | lge | Valladolid | H | D | 1-1 | Pablo 58 |

## KEY PLAYERS - GOALSCORERS

**1 Ruben Navarro**

| | | | |
|---|---|---|---|
| Goals in the League | 10 | **Player Strike Rate** Average number of minutes between League goals scored by player | 203 |
| **Contribution to Attacking Power** Average number of minutes between League team goals while on pitch | 77 | **Club Strike Rate** Average number of minutes between League goals scored by club | 88 |

| | PLAYER | LGE GOALS | POWER | STRIKE RATE |
|---|---|---|---|---|
| 2 | Daniel Ivan Alonso | 5 | 111 | 423 mins |
| 3 | Martin Mauricio Astudillo | 3 | 91 | 728 mins |
| 4 | Jordi Cruyff | 1 | 91 | 1733 mins |
| 5 | Zubiaur Ibon Begona | 1 | 85 | 1972 mins |

## KEY PLAYERS - MIDFIELDERS

**1 Ortiz de Guzman Pablo Gomez**

| | | | |
|---|---|---|---|
| Goals in the League | 0 | **Contribution to Attacking Power** Average number of minutes between League team goals while on pitch | 86 |
| **Defensive Rating** Average number of mins between League goals conceded while he was on the pitch | 71 | **Scoring Difference** Defensive Rating minus Contribution to Attacking Power | -15 |

| | PLAYER | LGE GOALS | DEF RATE | POWER | SCORE DIFF |
|---|---|---|---|---|---|
| 2 | Jesus Angel De La Cruz Turiel | 1 | 47 | 77 | -30 mins |
| 3 | Zubiaur Ibon Begona | 1 | 51 | 86 | -35 mins |
| 4 | Martin Mauricio Astudillo | 3 | 51 | 91 | -40 mins |
| 5 | Luis Helguera | 0 | 43 | 93 | -50 mins |

## KEY PLAYERS - DEFENDERS

**1 Oscar Gomez Tellez**

| | | | |
|---|---|---|---|
| **Goals Conceded (GC)** The number of League goals conceded while he was on the pitch | 37 | **Clean Sheets** In games when he played at least 70 minutes | 8 |
| **Defensive Rating** Ave number of mins between League goals conceded while on the pitch | 59 | **Club Defensive Rating** Average number of mins between League goals conceded by the club this season | 50 |

| | PLAYER | CON LGE | CLEAN SHEETS | DEF RATE |
|---|---|---|---|---|
| 2 | Antonio Herrera Karmona | 52 | 10 | 54 mins |
| 3 | Carlos Llorens | 57 | 10 | 52 mins |
| 4 | Delfi Geli Roura | 45 | 8 | 52 mins |
| 5 | Abelardo Fernandez | 58 | 6 | 43 mins |

## GOALS SCORED

**AT HOME**

| | | |
|---|---|---|
| MOST | R Madrid | 52 |
| | | 18 |
| LEAST | R Vallecano | 17 |

**AWAY**

| | | |
|---|---|---|
| MOST | R Madrid | 34 |
| | | 20 |
| LEAST | Recreativo | 11 |

## GOALS CONCEDED

**AT HOME**

| | | |
|---|---|---|
| LEAST | C Vigo & Valencia | 15 |
| | | 20 |
| MOST | Mallorca | 33 |

**AWAY**

| | | |
|---|---|---|
| LEAST | R Madrid, Valencia & Seville | 20 |
| | | 48 |
| MOST | Alaves | 48 |

## KEY GOALKEEPER

**1 Richard Dutruel**

| | |
|---|---|
| Goals Conceded in the League | 61 |
| **Defensive Rating** Ave number of mins between League goals conceded while on the pitch | 50 |
| **Counting Games** Games when he played at least 70 minutes | 34 |
| **Clean Sheets** In games when he played at least 70 minutes | 10 |

## TOP POINT EARNERS

| | PLAYER | GAMES | AVE |
|---|---|---|---|
| 1 | Begona | 18 | 1.22 |
| 2 | Pablo Gomez | 16 | 1.19 |
| 3 | Jordi | 17 | 1.06 |
| 4 | Edu Alonso | 13 | 1.00 |
| 5 | Helguera | 17 | 1.00 |
| 6 | Tellez | 24 | 1.00 |
| 7 | Dutruel | 34 | 0.97 |
| 8 | Karmona | 30 | 0.97 |
| 9 | Llorens | 30 | 0.97 |
| 10 | Navarro | 18 | 0.94 |
| | **CLUB AVERAGE:** | | **0.92** |

Ave = Average points per match in Counting Games

## ATTENDANCES

**HOME GROUND: MENDIZORROZA CAPACITY: 19500 AVERAGE LEAGUE AT HOME: 15220**

| | | |
|---|---|---|
| 9 | Barcelona | 94080 |
| 7 | Real Madrid | 76300 |
| 39 | Espanyol | 42900 |
| 35 | Valencia | 37100 |
| 21 | Real Betis | 36750 |
| 37 | Atl Madrid | 34200 |
| 19 | Athl Bilbao | 32000 |
| 31 | Seville | 31500 |
| 29 | Real Sociedad | 31360 |
| 15 | Malaga | 30051 |
| 13 | Besiktas | 28500 |
| 23 | Valladolid | 23850 |
| 17 | Celta Vigo | 22260 |
| 27 | Deportivo | 21350 |
| 3 | Ankaraguku | 20000 |
| 14 | Recreativo Huelva | 19200 |
| 12 | Mallorca | 19197 |
| 30 | Barcelona | 18500 |
| 20 | Espanyol | 18240 |
| 24 | R Vallecano | 18050 |
| 25 | R Santander | 18000 |
| 5 | Deportivo | 17664 |
| 8 | Real Sociedad | 17280 |
| 33 | Recreativo Huelva | 17000 |
| 26 | Villarreal | 16900 |
| 32 | Mallorca | 16705 |
| 38 | Athl Bilbao | 16520 |
| 22 | Osasuna | 15936 |
| 16 | Valencia | 15360 |
| 2 | R Santander | 15000 |
| 41 | Osasuna | 13930 |
| 11 | Seville | 13440 |
| 18 | Atl Madrid | 13440 |
| 34 | Malaga | 12865 |
| 1 | R Vallecano | 12500 |
| 28 | Real Madrid | 11520 |
| 36 | Celta Vigo | 11520 |
| 40 | Real Betis | 11250 |
| 4 | Villarreal | 11000 |
| 10 | Besiktas | 10373 |
| 42 | Valladolid | 9792 |
| 6 | Ankaraguku | 9476 |

■ Home □ Away ▒ Neutral

## DISCIPLINARY RECORDS

| | PLAYER | YELLOW | RED | AVE |
|---|---|---|---|---|
| 1 | Turiel | 8 | 1 | 136 |
| 2 | Desio | 5 | 2 | 156 |
| 3 | Helguera | 9 | 0 | 185 |
| 4 | Tomic | 4 | 0 | 192 |
| 5 | Tellez | 9 | 2 | 197 |
| 6 | Pablo Gomez | 7 | 1 | 205 |
| 7 | Ilie | 5 | 0 | 221 |
| 8 | Geli | 8 | 1 | 258 |
| 9 | Llorens | 11 | 0 | 269 |
| 10 | Begona | 7 | 0 | 281 |
| 11 | Magno | 4 | 1 | 314 |
| 12 | Abelardo | 7 | 0 | 357 |
| 13 | Jordi | 4 | 0 | 433 |
| | Other | 12 | 0 | |
| | **TOTAL** | **100** | **8** | |

## LEAGUE GOALS

| | PLAYER | MINS | GOALS | AVE |
|---|---|---|---|---|
| 1 | Navarro | 2025 | 10 | 203 |
| 2 | Ilie | 1109 | 6 | 185 |
| 3 | Magno | 1573 | 5 | 315 |
| 4 | Ivan Alonso | 2113 | 5 | 423 |
| 5 | Astudillo | 2184 | 3 | 728 |
| 6 | Karmona | 2808 | 1 | 2808 |
| 7 | Turiel | 1225 | 1 | 1225 |
| 8 | Llorens | 2965 | 1 | 2965 |
| 9 | Begona | 1972 | 1 | 1972 |
| 10 | Jordi | 1733 | 1 | 1733 |
| 11 | Pablo | 90 | 1 | 90 |
| 12 | Tomic | 770 | 1 | 770 |
| | Other | | 2 | |
| | **TOTAL** | | **38** | |

## MONTH BY MONTH GUIDE TO THE POINTS

| MONTH | POINTS | % |
|---|---|---|
| SEPTEMBER | 4 | 33% |
| OCTOBER | 1 | 11% |
| NOVEMBER | 7 | 58% |
| DECEMBER | 4 | 33% |
| JANUARY | 8 | 67% |
| FEBRUARY | 4 | 33% |
| MARCH | 1 | 8% |
| APRIL | 1 | 8% |
| MAY | 4 | 33% |
| JUNE | 1 | 11% |

## TEAM OF THE SEASON

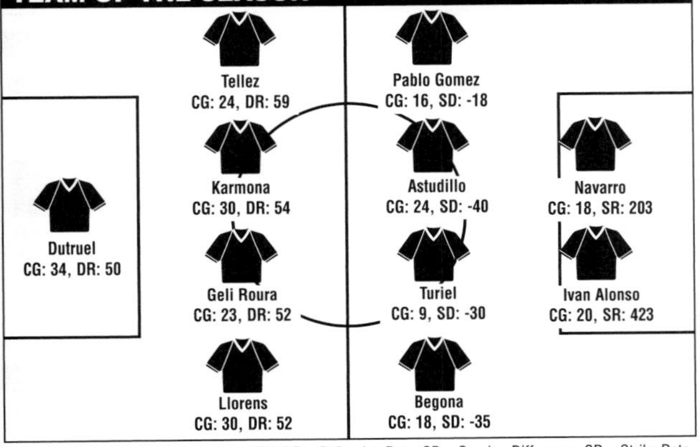

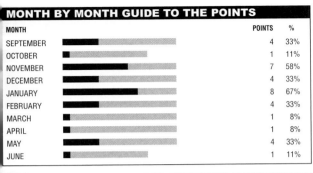

Dutruel
CG: 34, DR: 50
Tellez
CG: 24, DR: 59
Karmona
CG: 30, DR: 54
Geli Roura
CG: 23, DR: 52
Llorens
CG: 30, DR: 52
Pablo Gomez
CG: 16, SD: -18
Astudillo
CG: 24, SD: -40
Turiel
CG: 9, SD: -30
Begona
CG: 18, SD: -35
Navarro
CG: 18, SR: 203
Ivan Alonso
CG: 20, SR: 423


KEY: DR = Defensive Rate, SD = Scoring Difference, SR = Strike Rate, CG = Counting Games – League games playing at least 70 minutes

## LEAGUE APPEARANCES, BOOKINGS AND CAPS

| | AGE | IN THE SQUAD | COUNTING GAMES | MINUTES ON PITCH | YELLOW CARDS | RED CARDS | THIS SEASON | HOME COUNTRY |
|---|---|---|---|---|---|---|---|---|
| **Goalkeepers** | | | | | | | | |
| Richard Dutruel | 30 | 37 | 34 | 3060 | 0 | 0 | - | France |
| Colinas Juan Pablo | 24 | 38 | 4 | 360 | 0 | 0 | - | Spain |
| **Defenders** | | | | | | | | |
| Abelardo Fernandez | 33 | 36 | 28 | 2502 | 7 | 0 | - | Spain |
| Eduardo Edu Alonso | 29 | 19 | 13 | 1314 | 1 | 0 | - | Spain |
| Dan Eggen | 33 | 9 | 0 | 0 | 0 | 0 | - | Norway |
| Delfi Geli Roura | 34 | 35 | 23 | 2324 | 8 | 1 | - | Spain |
| Antonio Karmona | 35 | 38 | 30 | 2808 | 4 | 0 | - | Spain |
| Carlos Llorens | 33 | 35 | 30 | 2965 | 11 | 0 | - | Spain |
| Juan Cruz Ochoa | 24 | 24 | 1 | 214 | 1 | 0 | - | Spain |
| Oscar Gomez Tellez | 28 | 31 | 24 | 2170 | 9 | 2 | - | Spain |
| **Midfielders** | | | | | | | | |
| Martin Astudillo | 25 | 26 | 24 | 2184 | 5 | 0 | - | Argentina |
| Zubiaur Begona | 29 | 35 | 18 | 1972 | 7 | 0 | - | Spain |
| Hermes Aldo Desio | 33 | 30 | 9 | 1095 | 5 | 2 | - | Argentina |
| Luis Helguera | 27 | 35 | 17 | 1673 | 9 | 0 | - | Spain |
| Jordi Cruyff | 29 | 27 | 17 | 1733 | 4 | 0 | - | Holland |
| Fernandez Nacho | 23 | 8 | 0 | 88 | 0 | 0 | - | Spain |
| Pablo Gomez | 33 | 25 | 17 | 1730 | 7 | 1 | - | Spain |
| Ivan Tomic | 27 | 11 | 7 | 770 | 4 | 0 | - | Serbia & Montenegro |
| Jesus Angel Turiel | 29 | 35 | 9 | 1225 | 8 | 1 | - | Spain |
| **Forwards** | | | | | | | | |
| Adrian Ilie | 29 | 26 | 8 | 1109 | 5 | 0 | 5 | Romania (27) |
| Daniel Ivan Alonso | 24 | 38 | 20 | 2113 | 0 | 0 | - | Uruguay |
| Mocelin Magno | 29 | 33 | 11 | 1573 | 4 | 1 | - | Brazil |
| Ion Bogdan Mara | 25 | 27 | 1 | 474 | 0 | 0 | - | Romania |
| Ruben Navarro | 25 | 39 | 18 | 2025 | 1 | 0 | - | Spain |

KEY: LEAGUE BOOKINGS CAPS (FIFA RANKING)

## SQUAD APPEARANCES

| Match | 1 | 2 | 3 | 4 | 5 | 6 | 7 | 8 | 9 | 10 | 11 | 12 | 13 | 14 | 15 | 16 | 17 | 18 | 19 | 20 | 21 | 22 | 23 | 24 | 25 | 26 | 27 | 28 | 29 | 30 | 31 | 32 | 33 | 34 | 35 | 36 | 37 | 38 | 39 | 40 | 41 | 42 |
|---|---|---|---|---|---|---|---|---|---|---|---|---|---|---|---|---|---|---|---|---|---|---|---|---|---|---|---|---|---|---|---|---|---|---|---|---|---|---|---|---|---|---|
| Venue | A | H | A | A | H | H | A | H | A | H | H | A | A | H | A | H | A | H | A | H | A | H | A | H | A | H | A | H | A | H | A | H | A | H | A | H | A | H | A | H | A | H |
| Competition | L | L | E | L | L | E | L | L | L | E | L | L | E | L | L | L | L | L | L | L | L | L | L | L | L | L | L | L | L | L | L | L | L | L | L | L | L | L | L | L | L | L |
| Result | D | L | W | W | L | W | L | D | L | D | W | L | L | W | D | D | L | W | L | W | D | D | W | D | L | W | L | L | L | D | L | D | L | L | L | D | W | L | L | L | L | D |

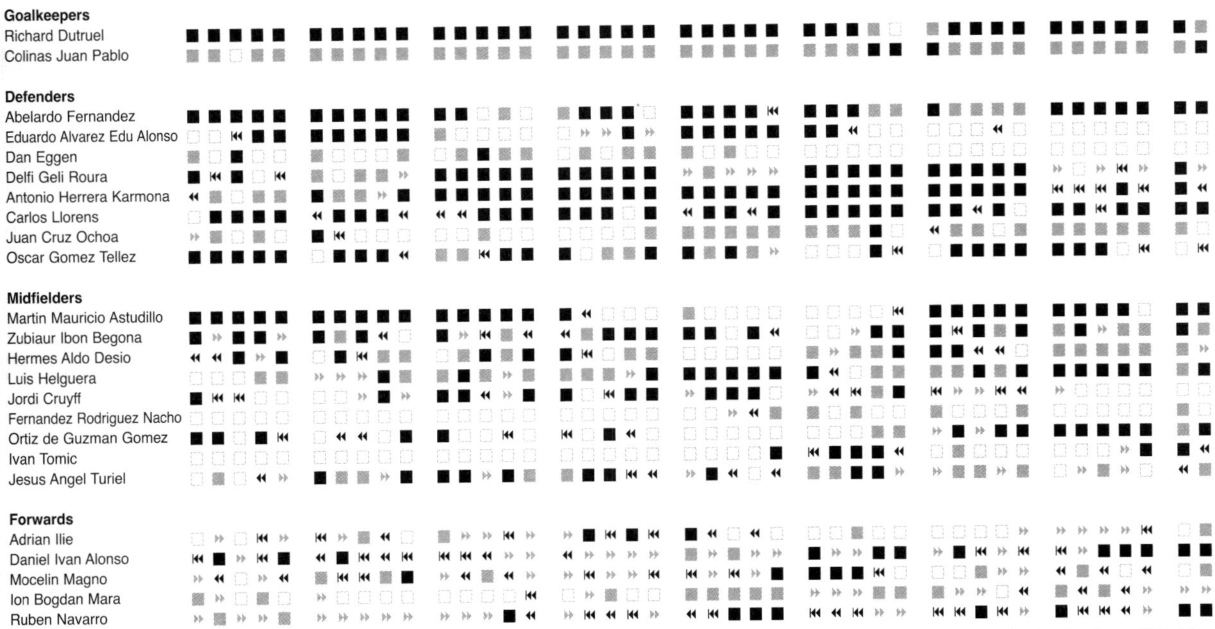

Goalkeepers
Richard Dutruel
Colinas Juan Pablo
Defenders
Abelardo Fernandez
Eduardo Alvarez Edu Alonso
Dan Eggen
Delfi Geli Roura
Antonio Herrera Karmona
Carlos Llorens
Juan Cruz Ochoa
Oscar Gomez Tellez
Midfielders
Martin Mauricio Astudillo
Zubiaur Ibon Begona
Hermes Aldo Desio
Luis Helguera
Jordi Cruyff
Fernandez Rodriguez Nacho
Ortiz de Guzman Gomez
Ivan Tomic
Jesus Angel Turiel
Forwards
Adrian Ilie
Daniel Ivan Alonso
Mocelin Magno
Ion Bogdan Mara
Ruben Navarro


KEY: ■ On all match ■ On bench
⏮ Subbed or sent off (Counting game)
« Subbed or sent off (playing less than 70 minutes)
⏭ Subbed on from bench (Counting Game)
» Subbed on (playing less than 70 minutes)
Subbed on and then subbed or sent off (Counting Game)
Subbed on and then subbed or sent off (playing less than 70 minutes)
Not in 16

# RAYO VALLECANO

Final Position: **20th**

| | | | | | | |
|---|---|---|---|---|---|---|
| 1 | lge | Alaves | H | D | 2-2 | Alvarez 21,64 pen |
| 2 | lge | Malaga | A | L | 1-2 | Bolic 38 |
| 3 | lge | R Santander | H | W | 3-1 | Alvarez 18 pen,52 pen,90 |
| 4 | lge | Valencia | A | L | 0-3 | |
| 5 | lge | Villarreal | H | D | 2-2 | Bolo 42; Alvarez 57 pen |
| 6 | lge | Celta Vigo | A | W | 1-0 | Bolo 6 |
| 7 | lge | Deportivo | H | L | 1-2 | Corino 90 |
| 8 | lge | Atl Madrid | A | L | 0-2 | |
| 9 | lge | Real Madrid | H | L | 2-3 | Azkoitia 28; Alvarez 75 pen |
| 10 | lge | Athl Bilbao | A | L | 1-2 | Bolo 43 |
| 11 | lge | Real Sociedad | H | D | 0-0 | |
| 12 | lge | Espanyol | A | L | 1-3 | Alex 87 og |
| 13 | lge | Barcelona | H | W | 1-0 | Azkoitia 65 |
| 14 | lge | Real Betis | A | W | 1-0 | Onopko 16 |
| 15 | lge | Seville | H | L | 0-1 | |
| 16 | lge | Osasuna | A | W | 1-0 | Alvarez 22 |
| 17 | lge | Mallorca | H | L | 1-2 | Bolic 56 |
| 18 | lge | Valladolid | H | L | 0-1 | |
| 19 | lge | Recreativo | A | L | 1-2 | De Quintana 3 |
| 20 | lge | Alaves | A | D | 1-1 | Peragon 19 |
| 21 | lge | Malaga | H | W | 2-1 | Michel I 4; Peragon 80 |
| 22 | lge | R Santander | A | L | 0-2 | |
| 23 | lge | Valencia | H | L | 0-4 | |
| 24 | lge | Villarreal | A | L | 1-2 | Luis Cembranos 67 pen |
| 25 | lge | Celta Vigo | H | W | 1-0 | De Quintana 87 |
| 26 | lge | Deportivo | A | L | 0-2 | |
| 27 | lge | Atl Madrid | H | D | 0-0 | |
| 28 | lge | Real Madrid | A | L | 1-3 | Luis Cembranos 9 |
| 29 | lge | Athl Bilbao | H | D | 1-1 | Bolic 85 |
| 30 | lge | Real Sociedad | A | L | 0-5 | |
| 31 | lge | Espanyol | H | L | 0-3 | |
| 32 | lge | Barcelona | A | L | 0-3 | |
| 33 | lge | Real Betis | H | D | 1-1 | Bolo 5 |
| 34 | lge | Seville | A | D | 3-3 | Luis Cembranos 62 pen; Michel I 84; Peragon 85 |
| 35 | lge | Osasuna | H | D | 0-0 | |
| 36 | lge | Mallorca | A | D | 1-1 | Peragon 70 |
| 37 | lge | Valladolid | A | L | 0-2 | |
| 38 | lge | Recreativo | H | D | 0-0 | |

## KEY PLAYERS - GOALSCORERS

**1 Julio Mosquera Alvarez**

| | | | |
|---|---|---|---|
| **Goals in the League** | 8 | **Player Strike Rate** Average number of minutes between League goals scored by player | 222 |
| **Contribution to Attacking Power** Average number of minutes between League team goals while on pitch | 93 | **Club Strike Rate** Average number of minutes between League goals scored by club | 110 |

| | PLAYER | LGE GOALS | POWER | STRIKE RATE |
|---|---|---|---|---|
| 2 | Juan Antonio Perez Alonso Bolo | 4 | 119 | 448 mins |
| 3 | Elvir Bolic | 3 | 93 | 655 mins |
| 4 | Roberto Lacalle Peragon | 4 | 109 | 686 mins |
| 5 | Jorge Azkoitia | 2 | 117 | 942 mins |

## KEY PLAYERS - MIDFIELDERS

**1 Julio Mosquera Alvarez**

| | | | |
|---|---|---|---|
| **Goals in the League** | 8 | **Contribution to Attacking Power** Average number of minutes between League team goals while on pitch | 93 |
| **Defensive Rating** Average number of mins between League goals conceded while he was on the pitch | 66 | **Scoring Difference** Defensive Rating minus Contribution to Attacking Power | -27 |

| | PLAYER | LGE GOALS | DEF RATE | POWER | SCORE DIFF |
|---|---|---|---|---|---|
| 2 | Jorge Azkoitia | 2 | 59 | 118 | -59 mins |
| 3 | Sergio Sanchez Mora | 0 | 54 | 114 | -60 mins |
| 4 | Jose Maria Garcia Quevedo | 0 | 49 | 116 | -67 mins |

## KEY PLAYERS - DEFENDERS

**1 Ramon Dalamau De Quintana**

| | | | |
|---|---|---|---|
| **Goals Conceded (GC)** The number of League goals conceded while he was on the pitch | 33 | **Clean Sheets** In games when he played at least 70 minutes | 7 |
| **Defensive Rating** Ave number of mins between League goals conceded while on the pitch | 62 | **Club Defensive Rating** Average number of mins between League goals conceded by the club this season | 54 |

| | PLAYER | CON LGE | CLEAN SHEETS | DEF RATE |
|---|---|---|---|---|
| 2 | Diego Garcia Mainz | 25 | 4 | 62 mins |
| 3 | Gomez Atanet Mario | 38 | 6 | 61 mins |
| 4 | Patricio Graff | 50 | 8 | 59 mins |
| 5 | Garcia Juncal Mauro | 16 | 1 | 52 mins |

## GOALS SCORED

**AT HOME**

| | | |
|---|---|---|
| MOST | R Madrid | 52 |
| | | 17 |
| LEAST | R Vallecano | 17 |

**AWAY**

| | | |
|---|---|---|
| MOST | R Madrid | 34 |
| | | 14 |
| LEAST | Recreativo | 11 |

## GOALS CONCEDED

**AT HOME**

| | | |
|---|---|---|
| LEAST | C Vigo & Valencia | 15 |
| | | 24 |
| MOST | Mallorca | 33 |

**AWAY**

| | | |
|---|---|---|
| LEAST | R Madrid, Valencia & Seville | 20 |
| | | 38 |
| MOST | Alaves | 48 |

## KEY GOALKEEPER

**1 Imanol Egana Exteberria**

| | |
|---|---|
| **Goals Conceded in the League** | 40 |
| **Defensive Rating** Ave number of mins between League goals conceded while on the pitch | 59 |
| **Counting Games** Games when he played at least 70 minutes | 25 |
| **Clean Sheets** In games when he played at least 70 minutes | 5 |

## TOP POINT EARNERS

| | PLAYER | GAMES | AVE |
|---|---|---|---|
| 1 | Mainz | 17 | 1.12 |
| 2 | Azkoitia | 18 | 1.11 |
| 3 | Etxeberria | 25 | 1.04 |
| 4 | Graff | 32 | 1.00 |
| 5 | Mario | 24 | 0.96 |
| 6 | De Quintana | 22 | 0.95 |
| 7 | Alvarez | 15 | 0.87 |
| 8 | Onopko | 25 | 0.84 |
| 9 | Corino | 17 | 0.82 |
| 10 | Michel I | 25 | 0.80 |
| | **CLUB AVERAGE:** | | **0.84** |

Ave = Average points per match in Counting Games

## ATTENDANCES

**HOME GROUND: VALLECAS CAPACITY: 15500 AVERAGE LEAGUE AT HOME: 11814**

| | | | | | | | | |
|---|---|---|---|---|---|---|---|---|
| 32 | Barcelona | 78400 | 20 | Alaves | 18050 | 18 | Valladolid | 12400 |
| 28 | Real Madrid | 60000 | 16 | Osasuna | 17910 | 23 | Valencia | 12400 |
| 4 | Valencia | 50350 | 24 | Villarreal | 15600 | 17 | Mallorca | 12400 |
| 14 | Real Betis | 48825 | 2 | Malaga | 15000 | 29 | Athl Bilbao | 12100 |
| 8 | Atl Madrid | 48450 | 9 | Real Madrid | 14725 | 36 | Mallorca | 11850 |
| 34 | Seville | 40500 | 7 | Deportivo | 14725 | 15 | Seville | 11780 |
| 10 | Athl Bilbao | 32000 | 13 | Barcelona | 14725 | 35 | Osasuna | 11625 |
| 30 | Real Sociedad | 22400 | 27 | Atl Madrid | 14570 | 33 | Real Betis | 10850 |
| 12 | Espanyol | 22000 | 21 | Malaga | 14100 | 37 | Valladolid | 9275 |
| 22 | R Santander | 21600 | 5 | Villarreal | 13950 | 3 | R Santander | 9000 |
| 26 | Deportivo | 21360 | 25 | Celta Vigo | 12560 | 11 | Real Sociedad | 5115 |
| 6 | Celta Vigo | 19080 | 1 | Alaves | 12500 | 38 | Recreativo Huelva | 2550 |
| 19 | Recreativo Huelva | 18800 | 31 | Espanyol | 12400 | | | |

■ Home □ Away ▒ Neutral

## DISCIPLINARY RECORDS

| | PLAYER | YELLOW | RED | AVE |
|---|---|---|---|---|
| 1 | Iriney | 6 | 2 | 148 |
| 2 | Azkoitia | 10 | 2 | 156 |
| 3 | Mauro | 5 | 0 | 167 |
| 4 | De Quintana | 10 | 0 | 205 |
| 5 | Graff | 13 | 1 | 209 |
| 6 | Mora | 5 | 0 | 228 |
| 7 | Corino | 6 | 1 | 233 |
| 8 | Pablo Sanz | 3 | 0 | 263 |
| 9 | Peragon | 9 | 0 | 304 |
| 10 | Luis Cembranos | 2 | 0 | 332 |
| 11 | Helder | 2 | 0 | 335 |
| 12 | Dorado | 2 | 0 | 361 |
| 13 | Onopko | 6 | 0 | 390 |
| | Other | 25 | 1 | |
| | **TOTAL** | **104** | **7** | |

## LEAGUE GOALS

| | PLAYER | MINS | GOALS | AVE |
|---|---|---|---|---|
| 1 | Alvarez | 1775 | 8 | 222 |
| 2 | Bolo | 1791 | 4 | 448 |
| 3 | Peragon | 2744 | 4 | 686 |
| 4 | Bolic | 1964 | 3 | 655 |
| 5 | L Cembranos | 665 | 3 | 222 |
| 6 | De Quintana | 2055 | 2 | 1028 |
| 7 | Azkoitia | 1883 | 2 | 942 |
| 8 | Michel I | 2329 | 1 | 2329 |
| 9 | Corino | 1635 | 1 | 1635 |
| 10 | Onopko | 2345 | 1 | 2345 |
| | Other | | 2 | |
| | **TOTAL** | | **31** | |

## MONTH BY MONTH GUIDE TO THE POINTS

| MONTH | POINTS | % |
|---|---|---|
| SEPTEMBER | 4 | 33% |
| OCTOBER | 4 | 44% |
| NOVEMBER | 1 | 8% |
| DECEMBER | 6 | 50% |
| JANUARY | 3 | 25% |
| FEBRUARY | 4 | 33% |
| MARCH | 4 | 33% |
| APRIL | 1 | 8% |
| MAY | 3 | 25% |
| JUNE | 2 | 22% |

## LEAGUE APPEARANCES, BOOKINGS AND CAPS

| | AGE | IN THE SQUAD | COUNTING GAMES | MINUTES ON PITCH | YELLOW CARDS | RED CARDS | THIS SEASON | HOME COUNTRY |
|---|---|---|---|---|---|---|---|---|
| **Goalkeepers** | | | | | | | | |
| Imanol Etxeberria | 30 | 38 | 25 | 2362 | 1 | 0 | - | Spain |
| Aparicio Oscar | 22 | 3 | 0 | 36 | 0 | 0 | - | Spain |
| Sergio Segura | 25 | 34 | 11 | 1022 | 0 | 0 | - | Spain |
| **Defenders** | | | | | | | | |
| Antonio Amaya | 20 | 2 | 0 | 0 | 0 | 0 | - | Spain |
| De La Vega Carlos | 23 | 2 | 0 | 5 | 0 | 0 | - | Spain |
| Sergio Corino | 28 | 33 | 17 | 1635 | 6 | 1 | - | Spain |
| Ramon De Quintana | 31 | 27 | 22 | 2055 | 10 | 0 | - | Spain |
| Javier Dorado | 25 | 28 | 6 | 722 | 2 | 0 | - | Spain |
| Patricio Graff | 27 | 34 | 32 | 2931 | 13 | 1 | - | Spain |
| Diego Garcia Mainz | 20 | 24 | 17 | 1560 | 4 | 0 | - | Spain |
| Gomez Atanet Mario | 22 | 32 | 24 | 2311 | 4 | 0 | - | Spain |
| Garcia Juncal Mauro | 32 | 19 | 9 | 837 | 5 | 0 | - | Spain |
| Viktor Onopko | 33 | 29 | 25 | 2345 | 6 | 0 | 5 | Russia (25) |
| Ruben Martin Pulido | | 3 | 0 | 0 | 0 | 0 | - | |
| **Midfielders** | | | | | | | | |
| Lopez Agustin | 21 | 1 | 0 | 0 | 0 | 0 | - | Spain |
| Julio Alvarez | 22 | 32 | 15 | 1775 | 1 | 0 | - | Spain |
| Jorge Azkoitia | 29 | 30 | 18 | 1883 | 10 | 2 | - | Spain |
| Javier Camunas | 22 | 27 | 1 | 381 | 2 | 0 | - | Spain |
| Manuel Elias Helder | 30 | 27 | 7 | 670 | 2 | 0 | - | Portugal |
| Santos Iriney | 22 | 15 | 13 | 1187 | 6 | 2 | - | Brazil |
| Luis Cembranos | 31 | 20 | 0 | 665 | 2 | 0 | - | Spain |
| Jose Marques | 18 | 17 | 0 | 229 | 2 | 0 | - | Spain |
| Miguel Angel Michel | 27 | 30 | 25 | 2329 | 0 | 0 | - | Spain |
| Sergio Mora | 23 | 31 | 8 | 1141 | 5 | 0 | - | Spain |
| Iniesta Pablo Sanz | 29 | 22 | 7 | 790 | 3 | 0 | - | Spain |
| Jose Maria Quevedo | 33 | 20 | 16 | 1620 | 3 | 1 | - | Spain |
| Idan Tal | 28 | 11 | 1 | 264 | 0 | 0 | - | Israel |
| **Forwards** | | | | | | | | |
| Elvir Bolic | 31 | 36 | 16 | 1964 | 4 | 0 | - | Bosnia |
| Juan Perez Bolo | 29 | 36 | 14 | 1791 | 4 | 0 | - | Spain |
| Carrilero Michel II | 25 | 7 | 1 | 215 | 0 | 0 | - | Spain |
| Roberto Peragon | 25 | 37 | 27 | 2744 | 9 | 0 | - | Spain |

KEY: LEAGUE BOOKINGS CAPS (FIFA RANKING)

## TEAM OF THE SEASON

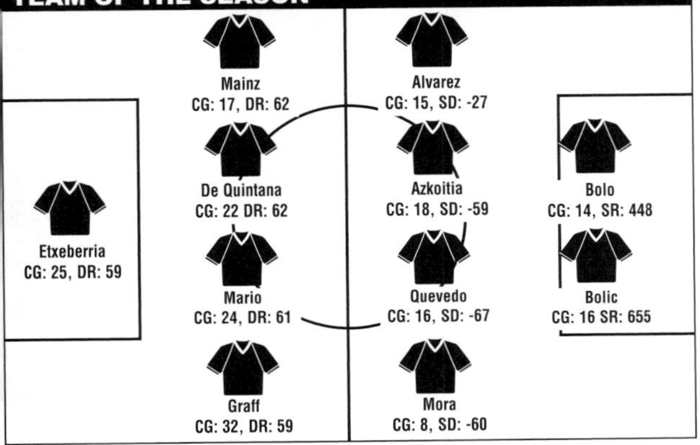
Etxeberria
CG: 25, DR: 59
Mainz
CG: 17, DR: 62
De Quintana
CG: 22 DR: 62
Mario
CG: 24, DR: 61
Graff
CG: 32, DR: 59
Alvarez
CG: 15, SD: -27
Azkoitia
CG: 18, SD: -59
Quevedo
CG: 16, SD: -67
Mora
CG: 8, SD: -60
Bolo
CG: 14, SR: 448
Bolic
CG: 16 SR: 655

KEY: DR = Defensive Rate, SD = Scoring Difference, SR = Strike Rate, CG = Counting Games – League games playing at least 70 minutes

## SQUAD APPEARANCES

| Match | 1 | 2 | 3 | 4 | 5 | 6 | 7 | 8 | 9 | 10 | 11 | 12 | 13 | 14 | 15 | 16 | 17 | 18 | 19 | 20 | 21 | 22 | 23 | 24 | 25 | 26 | 27 | 28 | 29 | 30 | 31 | 32 | 33 | 34 | 35 | 36 | 37 | 38 |
|---|---|---|---|---|---|---|---|---|---|---|---|---|---|---|---|---|---|---|---|---|---|---|---|---|---|---|---|---|---|---|---|---|---|---|---|---|---|---|
| Venue | H | A | H | A | H | A | H | A | H | A | H | A | H | A | H | A | H | H | A | A | H | A | H | A | H | A | H | A | H | A | H | A | H | A | H | A | A | H |
| Competition | L | L | L | L | L | L | L | L | L | L | L | L | L | L | L | L | L | L | L | L | L | L | L | L | L | L | L | L | L | L | L | L | L | L | L | L | L | L |
| Result | D | L | W | L | D | W | L | L | L | L | D | L | W | W | L | W | L | L | L | D | W | L | L | L | W | L | D | L | D | L | L | L | D | D | D | D | L | D |

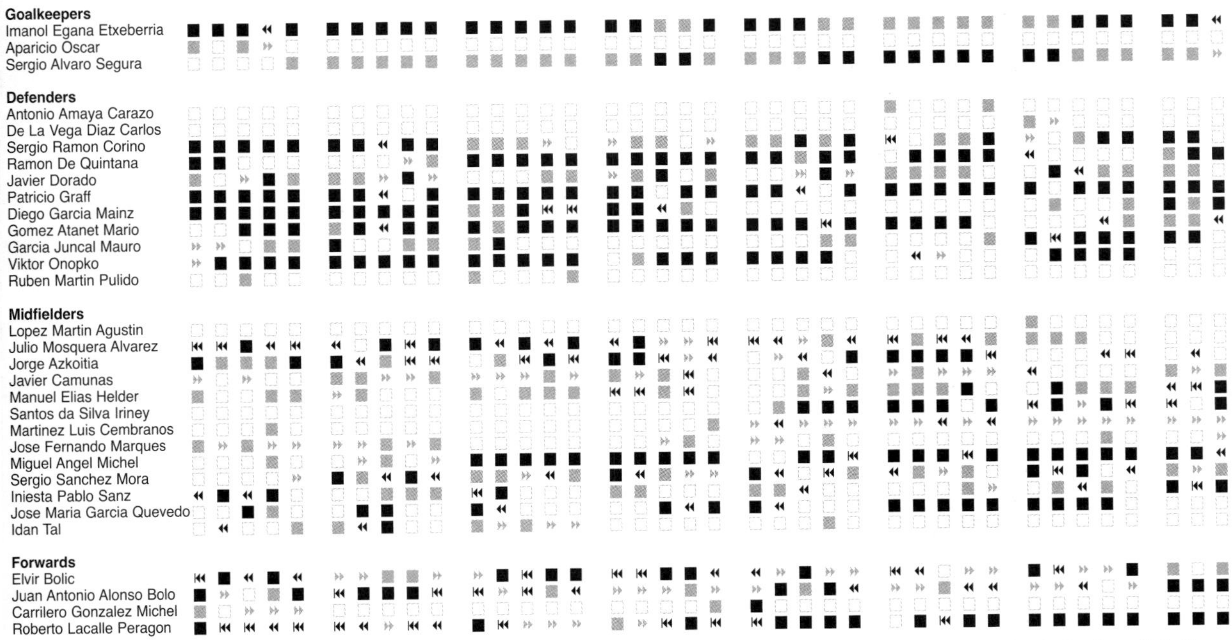
Goalkeepers
Imanol Egana Etxeberria
Aparicio Oscar
Sergio Alvaro Segura
Defenders
Antonio Amaya Carazo
De La Vega Diaz Carlos
Sergio Ramon Corino
Ramon De Quintana
Javier Dorado
Patricio Graff
Diego Garcia Mainz
Gomez Atanet Mario
Garcia Juncal Mauro
Viktor Onopko
Ruben Martin Pulido
Midfielders
Lopez Martin Agustin
Julio Mosquera Alvarez
Jorge Azkoitia
Javier Camunas
Manuel Elias Helder
Santos da Silva Iriney
Martinez Luis Cembranos
Jose Fernando Marques
Miguel Angel Michel
Sergio Sanchez Mora
Iniesta Pablo Sanz
Jose Maria Garcia Quevedo
Idan Tal
Forwards
Elvir Bolic
Juan Antonio Alonso Bolo
Carrilero Gonzalez Michel
Roberto Lacalle Peragon

KEY: On all match; On bench; Subbed or sent off (Counting game); Subbed or sent off (playing less than 70 minutes); Subbed on from bench (Counting Game); Subbed on (playing less than 70 minutes); Subbed on and then subbed or sent off (Counting Game); Subbed on and then subbed or sent off (playing less than 70 minutes); Not in 16

# SPANISH LEAGUE ROUND-UP

## FINAL LEAGUE TABLE

| | | HOME | | | | | AWAY | | | | | TOTAL | | | |
|---|---|---|---|---|---|---|---|---|---|---|---|---|---|---|---|
| | P | W | D | L | F | A | W | D | L | F | A | F | A | DIF | PTS |
| Real Madrid | 38 | 13 | 5 | 1 | 52 | 22 | 9 | 7 | 3 | 34 | 20 | 86 | 42 | 44 | 78 |
| Real Sociedad | 38 | 13 | 6 | 0 | 41 | 18 | 9 | 4 | 6 | 30 | 27 | 71 | 45 | 26 | 76 |
| Deportivo | 38 | 13 | 3 | 3 | 41 | 18 | 9 | 3 | 7 | 26 | 29 | 67 | 47 | 20 | 72 |
| Celta Vigo | 38 | 10 | 6 | 3 | 29 | 15 | 7 | 4 | 8 | 16 | 21 | 45 | 36 | 9 | 61 |
| Valencia | 38 | 10 | 3 | 6 | 30 | 15 | 7 | 6 | 6 | 26 | 20 | 56 | 35 | 21 | 60 |
| Barcelona | 38 | 10 | 5 | 4 | 43 | 24 | 5 | 6 | 8 | 20 | 23 | 63 | 47 | 16 | 56 |
| Athl Bilbao | 38 | 11 | 3 | 5 | 30 | 20 | 4 | 7 | 8 | 33 | 41 | 63 | 61 | 2 | 55 |
| Real Betis | 38 | 9 | 6 | 4 | 31 | 21 | 5 | 6 | 8 | 25 | 32 | 56 | 53 | 3 | 54 |
| Mallorca | 38 | 7 | 5 | 7 | 25 | 33 | 7 | 5 | 7 | 24 | 23 | 49 | 56 | -7 | 52 |
| Seville | 38 | 8 | 7 | 4 | 24 | 19 | 5 | 4 | 10 | 14 | 20 | 38 | 39 | -1 | 50 |
| Atl Madrid | 38 | 8 | 5 | 6 | 28 | 25 | 4 | 6 | 9 | 23 | 31 | 51 | 56 | -5 | 47 |
| Osasuna | 38 | 8 | 3 | 8 | 22 | 24 | 4 | 8 | 7 | 18 | 24 | 40 | 48 | -8 | 47 |
| Valladolid | 38 | 9 | 4 | 6 | 23 | 17 | 3 | 6 | 10 | 14 | 23 | 37 | 40 | -3 | 46 |
| Malaga | 38 | 8 | 7 | 4 | 29 | 21 | 3 | 6 | 10 | 15 | 28 | 44 | 49 | -5 | 46 |
| Villarreal | 38 | 8 | 5 | 6 | 24 | 21 | 3 | 7 | 9 | 20 | 32 | 44 | 53 | -9 | 45 |
| R Santander | 38 | 9 | 2 | 8 | 29 | 22 | 4 | 3 | 12 | 25 | 42 | 54 | 64 | -10 | 44 |
| Espanyol | 38 | 8 | 6 | 5 | 30 | 23 | 2 | 7 | 10 | 18 | 31 | 48 | 54 | -6 | 43 |
| Recreativo | 38 | 5 | 8 | 6 | 24 | 24 | 3 | 4 | 12 | 11 | 37 | 35 | 61 | -26 | 36 |
| Alaves | 38 | 5 | 8 | 6 | 18 | 20 | 3 | 3 | 13 | 20 | 48 | 38 | 68 | -30 | 35 |
| R Vallecano | 38 | 4 | 8 | 7 | 17 | 24 | 3 | 3 | 13 | 14 | 38 | 31 | 62 | -31 | 32 |

## TEAM OF THE SEASON

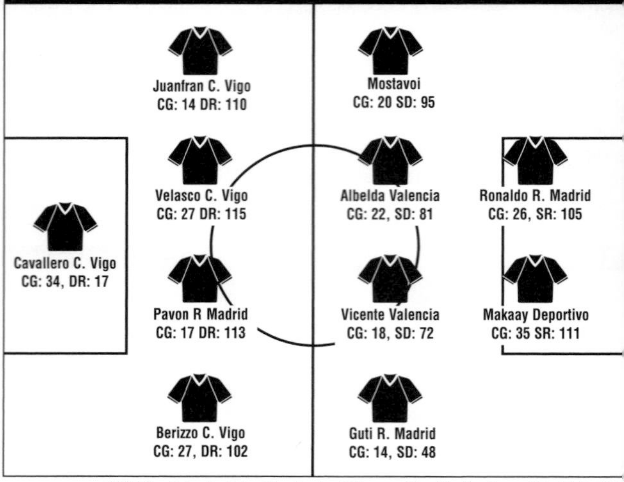

Cavallero C. Vigo
CG: 34, DR: 17
Juanfran C. Vigo
CG: 14 DR: 110
Velasco C. Vigo
CG: 27 DR: 115
Pavon R Madrid
CG: 17 DR: 113
Berizzo C. Vigo
CG: 27, DR: 102
Mostavoi
CG: 20 SD: 95
Albelda Valencia
CG: 22, SD: 81
Vicente Valencia
CG: 18, SD: 72
Guti R. Madrid
CG: 14, SD: 48
Ronaldo R. Madrid
CG: 26, SR: 105
Makaay Deportivo
CG: 35 SR: 111


**KEY:** DR = Defensive Rate, SD = Scoring Difference AP = Attacking Power SR = Strike Rate
CG=Counting Games – League games playing at least 70 minutes

## CLUB STRIKE FORCE

**KEY:** Goals: Total number of goals scored in League.
Club Strike Rate (CSR): Average number of mins between goals scored.

| | CLUB | GOALS | CSR |
|---|---|---|---|
| 1 | Real Madrid | 86 | 40 mins |
| 2 | Real Sociedad | 71 | 48 mins |
| 3 | Deportivo | 67 | 51 mins |
| 4 | Athl Bilbao | 63 | 54 mins |
| 5 | Barcelona | 63 | 54 mins |
| 6 | Real Betis | 56 | 61 mins |
| 7 | Valencia | 56 | 61 mins |
| 8 | R Santander | 54 | 63 mins |
| 9 | Atl Madrid | 51 | 67 mins |
| 10 | Mallorca | 49 | 70 mins |
| 11 | Espanyol | 48 | 71 mins |
| 12 | Celta Vigo | 45 | 76 mins |
| 13 | Malaga | 44 | 78 mins |
| 14 | Villarreal | 44 | 78 mins |
| 15 | Osasuna | 40 | 86 mins |
| 16 | Alaves | 38 | 90 mins |
| 17 | Seville | 38 | 90 mins |
| 18 | Valladolid | 37 | 92 mins |
| 19 | Recreativo Huelva | 35 | 98 mins |
| 20 | R Vallecano | 31 | 110 mins |
| | TOTAL | 1016 | |

## CLUB DEFENCES

**KEY:** Defensive Rating: Average number of mins between goals conceded. CS: Clean Sheets - Games where no goals were conceded.

| | CLUB | CONCEDED | CLEAN SH | DEF RATE |
|---|---|---|---|---|
| 1 | Valencia | 35 | 15 | 98 mins |
| 2 | Celta Vigo | 36 | 16 | 95 mins |
| 3 | Seville | 39 | 14 | 88 mins |
| 4 | Valladolid | 40 | 12 | 86 mins |
| 5 | Real Madrid | 42 | 10 | 81 mins |
| 6 | Real Sociedad | 45 | 12 | 76 mins |
| 7 | Barcelona | 47 | 13 | 73 mins |
| 8 | Deportivo | 47 | 12 | 73 mins |
| 9 | Osasuna | 48 | 10 | 71 mins |
| 10 | Malaga | 49 | 13 | 70 mins |
| 11 | Real Betis | 53 | 7 | 65 mins |
| 12 | Villarreal | 53 | 9 | 65 mins |
| 13 | Espanyol | 54 | 11 | 63 mins |
| 14 | Atl Madrid | 56 | 9 | 61 mins |
| 15 | Mallorca | 56 | 8 | 61 mins |
| 16 | Athl Bilbao | 61 | 6 | 56 mins |
| 17 | Recreativo Huelva | 61 | 9 | 56 mins |
| 18 | R Vallecano | 62 | 9 | 55 mins |
| 19 | R Santander | 64 | 10 | 53 mins |
| 20 | Alaves | 68 | 11 | 50 mins |
| | TOTAL | 1016 | 216 | |

## CLUB DISCIPLINARY RECORDS

**KEY:** AVE: Average number of mins between cards

| | CLUB | YELL | RED | TOT | AVE |
|---|---|---|---|---|---|
| 1 | Alaves | 128 | 10 | 138 | 25 mins |
| 2 | Athl Bilbao | 115 | 10 | 125 | 27 mins |
| 3 | Atl Madrid | 107 | 7 | 114 | 30 mins |
| 4 | Barcelona | 105 | 9 | 114 | 30 mins |
| 5 | Celta Vigo | 102 | 10 | 112 | 31 mins |
| 6 | Deportivo | 104 | 7 | 111 | 31 mins |
| 7 | Espanyol | 104 | 7 | 111 | 31 mins |
| 8 | Malaga | 100 | 10 | 110 | 31 mins |
| 9 | Mallorca | 100 | 8 | 108 | 32 mins |
| 10 | Osasuna | 96 | 7 | 103 | 33 mins |
| 11 | R Santander | 95 | 9 | 104 | 33 mins |
| 12 | R Vallecano | 98 | 7 | 105 | 33 mins |
| 13 | Real Betis | 96 | 6 | 102 | 34 mins |
| 14 | Real Madrid | 95 | 2 | 97 | 35 mins |
| 15 | Real Sociedad | 90 | 8 | 98 | 35 mins |
| 16 | Recreativo Huelva | 86 | 8 | 94 | 36 mins |
| 17 | Seville | 85 | 7 | 92 | 37 mins |
| 18 | Valencia | 70 | 4 | 74 | 46 mins |
| 19 | Valladolid | 68 | 4 | 72 | 48 mins |
| 20 | Villarreal | 68 | 3 | 71 | 48 mins |
| | TOTAL | 1255 | 71 | 1326 | |

## STADIUM CAPACITY AND HOME CROWDS

| | TEAM | CAPACITY | AVE | HIGH | LOW |
|---|---|---|---|---|---|
| 1 | Real Sociedad | 32000 | 89.63 | 32000 | 22400 |
| 2 | Valencia | 53000 | 88.63 | 53000 | 37100 |
| 3 | Recreativo Huelva | 20000 | 86.92 | 20000 | 14000 |
| 4 | Atl Madrid | 57000 | 85.55 | 57000 | 34200 |
| 5 | Real Madrid | 87000 | 81.83 | 76300 | 53400 |
| 6 | Osasuna | 20000 | 81.7 | 20000 | 11940 |
| 7 | Deportivo | 35800 | 81.08 | 35600 | 14240 |
| 8 | Celta Vigo | 31800 | 79.1 | 31800 | 15900 |
| 9 | Barcelona | 98800 | 78.85 | 98000 | 48507 |
| 10 | Real Betis | 52500 | 78.76 | 52500 | 18000 |
| 11 | Malaga | 37151 | 78.68 | 37100 | 15000 |
| 12 | Alaves | 19500 | 78.05 | 19200 | 9792 |
| 13 | R Vallecano | 15500 | 76.22 | 14725 | 2550 |
| 14 | Seville | 45000 | 74.43 | 45000 | 14000 |
| 15 | R Santander | 22500 | 73.07 | 22500 | 9601 |
| 16 | Athl Bilbao | 46500 | 72.35 | 39600 | 20000 |
| 17 | Valladolid | 26512 | 71.41 | 25175 | 9275 |
| 18 | Mallorca | 26500 | 64.95 | 23700 | 10191 |
| 19 | Espanyol | 55000 | 60.02 | 49500 | 9900 |
| 20 | Villarreal | 23000 | 56.49 | 16800 | 9744 |

## AWAY ATTENDANCE

| | TEAM | AVE | HIGH | LOW |
|---|---|---|---|---|
| 1 | Real Madrid | 92.76 | 98000 | 11520 |
| 2 | Barcelona | 85.22 | 76300 | 10080 |
| 3 | Deportivo | 83.73 | 91140 | 12264 |
| 4 | Valencia | 82.65 | 93100 | 12400 |
| 5 | Atl Madrid | 82.5 | 85000 | 13440 |
| 6 | Espanyol | 79.72 | 85833 | 10920 |
| 7 | Villarreal | 78.94 | 96040 | 11250 |
| 8 | R Santander | 77.12 | 88200 | 9000 |
| 9 | Real Betis | 76.69 | 78500 | 10850 |
| 10 | Athl Bilbao | 75.92 | 83300 | 11850 |
| 11 | Real Sociedad | 75.46 | 76300 | 5115 |
| 12 | Alaves | 75.46 | 94080 | 11000 |
| 13 | Seville | 73.41 | 76300 | 11424 |
| 14 | Valladolid | 73.02 | 78400 | 9792 |
| 15 | Celta Vigo | 72.78 | 68670 | 11250 |
| 16 | R Vallecano | 72.1 | 78400 | 9275 |
| 17 | Osasuna | 71.48 | 78400 | 9601 |
| 18 | Mallorca | 70.15 | 78400 | 9856 |
| 19 | Recreativo Huelva | 69.77 | 76300 | 2550 |
| 20 | Malaga | 68.81 | 76300 | 10191 |

## TOP GOALSCORERS

**KEY: Strike Rate:** Average number of minutes between League goals scored by player. **Club Strike Rate (CSR):** Average minutes between League goals scored by club. **Contribution to Attacking Power (PWR):** Average mins between League goals scored by club while on pitch.

| | PLAYER | CLUB | GOALS | PWR | CSR | S RATE |
|---|---|---|---|---|---|---|
| 1 | Ronaldo | Real Madrid | 23 | 43 | 40 | 105 |
| 2 | Makaay | Deportivo | 29 | 52 | 51 | 111 |
| 3 | Nihat | Real Sociedad | 23 | 42 | 48 | 130 |
| 4 | Kovacevic | Real Sociedad | 20 | 50 | 48 | 151 |
| 5 | Guerrero | R Santander | 15 | 59 | 63 | 158 |
| 6 | Fernando | Real Betis | 15 | 62 | 61 | 163 |
| 7 | Luis Enrique | Barcelona | 8 | 46 | 54 | 164 |
| 8 | Raul | Real Madrid | 16 | 37 | 40 | 168 |
| 9 | Eto'o | Mallorca | 14 | 61 | 70 | 175 |
| 10 | Torres | Atl Madrid | 13 | 71 | 67 | 181 |
| 11 | Saviola | Barcelona | 13 | 47 | 54 | 186 |
| 12 | Urzaiz | Athl Bilbao | 14 | 52 | 54 | 189 |
| 13 | Milosevic | Espanyol | 12 | 64 | 71 | 193 |
| 14 | Joseba Etxeberria | Athl Bilbao | 14 | 51 | 54 | 195 |
| 15 | Kluivert | Barcelona | 16 | 55 | 54 | 196 |
| 16 | Pandiani | Mallorca | 14 | 68 | 70 | 200 |
| 17 | Navarro | Alaves | 10 | 77 | 90 | 203 |
| 18 | Tamudo | Espanyol | 10 | 83 | 71 | 218 |
| 19 | Alvarez | R Vallecano | 8 | 93 | 110 | 222 |
| 20 | Aganzo | Valladolid | 9 | 103 | 92 | 229 |
| 21 | Dario Silva | Malaga | 10 | 75 | 78 | 241 |
| 22 | Ezquerro | Athl Bilbao | 10 | 51 | 54 | 246 |
| 23 | Edu | Celta Vigo | 11 | 78 | 76 | 249 |
| 24 | Antonito | Seville | 7 | 75 | 90 | 258 |
| 25 | Roger | Espanyol | 9 | 68 | 71 | 259 |
| 26 | Dely Valdes | Malaga | 10 | 76 | 78 | 260 |
| 27 | Carew | Valencia | 8 | 63 | 61 | 261 |
| 28 | Raul Molina | Recreativo Huelva | 10 | 110 | 98 | 265 |
| 29 | Aurelio | Valencia | 8 | 64 | 61 | 268 |
| 30 | Figo | Real Madrid | 10 | 39 | 40 | 272 |

## TOP DEFENDERS

**KEY: Defensive Rating (DR)** Average mins between League goals conceded while on pitch. **Club Defensive Rating (CDR):** Average minutes between League goals conceded by club. **Clean Sheets (CS)** - Games where no goals were conceded.

| | PLAYER | CLUB | CONC | CS | CDR | DR |
|---|---|---|---|---|---|---|
| 1 | Velasco | Celta Vigo | 22 | 13 | 95 | 115 |
| 2 | Pavon | Real Madrid | 14 | 6 | 81 | 113 |
| 3 | Jonathan | Valladolid | 10 | 5 | 86 | 112 |
| 4 | Juanfran | Celta Vigo | 14 | 7 | 95 | 110 |
| 5 | Sorin | Barcelona | 11 | 4 | 73 | 103 |
| 6 | Berizzo | Celta Vigo | 24 | 13 | 95 | 102 |
| 7 | Curro Torres | Valencia | 12 | 5 | 98 | 98 |
| 8 | Caceres | Celta Vigo | 31 | 14 | 95 | 97 |
| 9 | Izquierdo | Osasuna | 11 | 6 | 71 | 97 |
| 10 | Pena | Valladolid | 26 | 10 | 86 | 96 |
| 11 | Navarro | Seville | 27 | 12 | 88 | 95 |
| 12 | Marchena | Valencia | 21 | 11 | 98 | 95 |
| 13 | Pablo Alfaro | Seville | 32 | 12 | 88 | 93 |
| 14 | Reveillere | Valencia | 16 | 4 | 98 | 92 |
| 15 | Gaspar | Valladolid | 20 | 6 | 86 | 91 |
| 16 | David Castedo | Seville | 35 | 12 | 88 | 89 |
| 17 | Ayala | Valencia | 30 | 9 | 98 | 89 |
| 18 | Aurelio | Valencia | 24 | 9 | 98 | 89 |
| 19 | Kvarme | Real Sociedad | 19 | 7 | 76 | 88 |
| 20 | Capdevila | Deportivo | 16 | 4 | 73 | 86 |
| 21 | Pellegrino | Valencia | 26 | 7 | 98 | 86 |
| 22 | Carboni | Valencia | 25 | 7 | 98 | 86 |
| 23 | Torres Gomez | Valladolid | 37 | 11 | 86 | 85 |
| 24 | Hector | Deportivo | 20 | 5 | 73 | 84 |
| 25 | Lopo | Espanyol | 24 | 9 | 63 | 84 |
| 26 | Roberto Carlos | Real Madrid | 40 | 10 | 81 | 83 |
| 27 | Silvinho | Celta Vigo | 32 | 11 | 95 | 82 |
| 28 | Gerardo | Malaga | 28 | 9 | 70 | 81 |
| 29 | Salgado | Real Madrid | 37 | 9 | 81 | 81 |
| 30 | Naybet | Deportivo | 26 | 9 | 73 | 80 |

## TOP MIDFIELDERS

**KEY: Scoring Difference (SD)** Team goals scored while on the pitch minus team goals conceded. **Contribution to Attacking Power:** Average mins between League goals scored by club while on pitch. **Defensive Rating (DR)** Average mins between League goals conceded while on pitch.

| | PLAYER | TEAM | GOALS | DR | PWR | SD |
|---|---|---|---|---|---|---|
| 1 | Mostovoi | Celta Vigo | 6 | 156 | 61 | 95 |
| 2 | Albelda | Valencia | 0 | 136 | 55 | 81 |
| 3 | Vicente | Valencia | 1 | 135 | 63 | 72 |
| 4 | Guti | Real Madrid | 4 | 84 | 36 | 48 |
| 5 | Gustavo Lopez | Celta Vigo | 1 | 116 | 71 | 45 |
| 6 | Fredi | Seville | 1 | 124 | 81 | 43 |
| 7 | De Pedro | Real Sociedad | 6 | 86 | 45 | 41 |
| 8 | Ito | Real Betis | 0 | 100 | 62 | 38 |
| 9 | Conceicao | Real Madrid | 1 | 73 | 35 | 38 |
| 10 | Makelele | Real Madrid | 0 | 84 | 46 | 38 |
| 11 | Duscher | Deportivo | 0 | 93 | 56 | 37 |
| 12 | Xabier Alonso | Real Sociedad | 3 | 86 | 49 | 37 |
| 13 | De Los Santos | Valencia | 1 | 99 | 62 | 37 |
| 14 | Zidane | Real Madrid | 9 | 75 | 39 | 36 |
| 15 | Aramburu | Real Sociedad | 2 | 80 | 44 | 36 |
| 16 | Cambiasso | Real Madrid | 0 | 81 | 47 | 34 |
| 17 | Figo | Real Madrid | 10 | 73 | 39 | 34 |
| 18 | Cocu, P | Barcelona | 3 | 87 | 55 | 32 |
| 19 | Baraja | Valencia | 5 | 89 | 57 | 32 |
| 20 | Luis Enrique | Barcelona | 8 | 77 | 47 | 30 |
| 21 | Rufete | Valencia | 3 | 92 | 62 | 30 |
| 22 | Jauregui | Real Sociedad | 1 | 77 | 49 | 28 |
| 23 | Luccin | Celta Vigo | 1 | 100 | 73 | 27 |
| 24 | Mendieta | Barcelona | 4 | 73 | 47 | 26 |
| 25 | Karpin | Real Sociedad | 8 | 74 | 48 | 26 |
| 26 | Overmars | Barcelona | 6 | 72 | 48 | 24 |
| 27 | Gabri | Barcelona | 0 | 80 | 56 | 24 |
| 28 | Jose Ignacio | Celta Vigo | 3 | 94 | 70 | 24 |
| 29 | Valeron | Deportivo | 2 | 64 | 40 | 24 |
| 30 | Torrado | Seville | 0 | 97 | 74 | 23 |

## PLAYER DISCIPLINARY RECORDS

**KEY: AVE:** Average number of mins between cards

| | PLAYER | TEAM | YELL | RED | TOTAL | AVE |
|---|---|---|---|---|---|---|
| 1 | Lopo | Espanyol | 14 | 2 | 16 | 126 |
| 2 | Alex | Espanyol | 6 | 1 | 7 | 135 |
| 3 | Turiel | Alaves | 8 | 1 | 9 | 136 |
| 4 | Unai | Villarreal | 9 | 1 | 10 | 140 |
| 5 | Cesar | Athl Bilbao | 5 | 0 | 5 | 142 |
| 6 | Gabri | Barcelona | 12 | 1 | 13 | 147 |
| 7 | Iriney | R Vallecano | 6 | 2 | 8 | 148 |
| 8 | Sousa | Valladolid | 3 | 1 | 4 | 148 |
| 9 | Posse | Espanyol | 5 | 1 | 6 | 149 |
| 10 | Sandro | Malaga | 12 | 1 | 13 | 149 |
| 11 | Varela | Real Betis | 18 | 1 | 19 | 149 |
| 12 | Desio | Alaves | 5 | 2 | 7 | 156 |
| 13 | Azkoitia | R Vallecano | 10 | 2 | 12 | 156 |
| 14 | Lozano | Mallorca | 13 | 2 | 15 | 160 |
| 15 | Filipescu | Real Betis | 7 | 2 | 9 | 161 |
| 16 | Mustafa | Valladolid | 5 | 1 | 6 | 162 |
| 17 | Emerson | Atl Madrid | 12 | 1 | 13 | 163 |
| 18 | Nafti | R Santander | 14 | 1 | 15 | 164 |
| 19 | Mauro | R Vallecano | 5 | 0 | 5 | 167 |
| 20 | Xisco | Recreativo Huelva | 6 | 1 | 7 | 168 |
| 21 | Garcia | Osasuna | 9 | 1 | 10 | 170 |
| 22 | Jose Mari | Atl Madrid | 13 | 1 | 14 | 171 |
| 23 | Juanfran | Celta Vigo | 9 | 0 | 9 | 171 |
| 24 | Baraja | Valencia | 14 | 1 | 15 | 172 |
| 25 | Contra | Atl Madrid | 13 | 1 | 14 | 175 |
| 26 | Alfonso | Real Betis | 6 | 0 | 6 | 175 |
| 27 | Coromina | R Santander | 7 | 1 | 8 | 177 |
| 28 | Munoz | Osasuna | 4 | 1 | 5 | 181 |
| 29 | Samways | Seville | 4 | 0 | 4 | 181 |
| 30 | Arruabarrena | Villarreal | 14 | 1 | 15 | 181 |

## CHART TOPPING GOALKEEPERS

**KEY: Defensive Rating (DR)** Average mins between League goals conceded while on pitch. **Clean Sheets (CS)** - Games where no goals were conceded.

| | PLAYER | TEAM | CON | CS | DR |
|---|---|---|---|---|---|
| 1 | Cavallero | Celta Vigo | 27 | 15 | 117 |
| 2 | Canizares | Valencia | 27 | 10 | 99 |
| 3 | Juanmi | Deportivo | 25 | 11 | 96 |
| 4 | Notario | Seville | 36 | 14 | 93 |
| 5 | Miki | Mallorca | 2 | 0 | 90 |
| 6 | Sanzol | Osasuna | 36 | 10 | 83 |
| 7 | Casillas | Real Madrid | 42 | 10 | 81 |
| 8 | Victor | Barcelona | 15 | 4 | 78 |
| 9 | Westerveld | Real Sociedad | 45 | 11 | 74 |
| 10 | Contreras | Malaga | 43 | 12 | 73 |
| 11 | Bonano | Barcelona | 30 | 8 | 71 |
| 12 | Toni | Espanyol | 26 | 6 | 69 |
| 13 | Reina | Villarreal | 42 | 9 | 69 |
| 14 | Ceballos | R Santander | 13 | 2 | 68 |
| 15 | Prats | Real Betis | 53 | 7 | 65 |
| 16 | Luque | Recreativo Huelva | 36 | 8 | 65 |
| 17 | Aranzubia | Athl Bilbao | 35 | 6 | 64 |
| 18 | Burgos | Atl Madrid | 19 | 3 | 63 |
| 19 | Franco | Mallorca | 53 | 8 | 61 |
| 20 | Etxeberria | R Vallecano | 39 | 6 | 61 |
| 21 | Esteban | Atl Madrid | 34 | 6 | 60 |
| 22 | Lemmens | R Santander | 44 | 8 | 54 |
| 23 | Dutruel | Alaves | 61 | 10 | 50 |
| 24 | Lafuente | Athl Bilbao | 25 | 0 | 47 |
| 25 | Argenso | Espanyol | 23 | 2 | 47 |
| 26 | Segura | R Vallecano | 22 | 2 | 46 |
| 27 | Cesar | Recreativo Huelva | 24 | 1 | 44 |
| 28 | Molina | Deportivo | 21 | 1 | 43 |

## TOP POINT EARNERS

**KEY: Counting Games** League games where he played more than 70 minutes. **Total League Points** Taken in Counting Games. **Average League Points** Taken in Counting Games.

| | PLAYER | TEAM | GAMES | POINTS | AVE |
|---|---|---|---|---|---|
| 1 | Conceicao | Real Madrid | 15 | 37 | 2.47 |
| 2 | Guti | Real Madrid | 14 | 34 | 2.43 |
| 3 | Aramburu | Real Sociedad | 25 | 59 | 2.36 |
| 4 | Figo | Real Madrid | 29 | 68 | 2.34 |
| 5 | Duscher | Deportivo | 12 | 28 | 2.33 |
| 6 | De Pedro | Real Sociedad | 22 | 51 | 2.32 |
| 7 | Hector | Deportivo | 16 | 36 | 2.25 |
| 8 | Pavon | Real Madrid | 17 | 38 | 2.24 |
| 9 | Raul | Real Madrid | 30 | 66 | 2.20 |
| 10 | Sergio | Deportivo | 28 | 61 | 2.18 |
| 11 | Kvarme | Real Sociedad | 18 | 39 | 2.17 |
| 12 | Nihat | Real Sociedad | 34 | 73 | 2.15 |
| 13 | Helguera | Real Madrid | 32 | 68 | 2.13 |
| 14 | Juanmi | Deportivo | 27 | 57 | 2.11 |
| 15 | Kovacevic | Real Sociedad | 33 | 69 | 2.09 |
| 16 | Ronaldo | Real Madrid | 26 | 54 | 2.08 |
| 17 | Prieto | Athl Bilbao | 13 | 27 | 2.08 |
| 18 | Cambiasso | Real Madrid | 14 | 29 | 2.07 |
| 19 | Casillas | Real Madrid | 38 | 78 | 2.05 |
| 20 | Mostovoi | Celta Vigo | 20 | 41 | 2.05 |
| 21 | Naybet | Deportivo | 23 | 47 | 2.04 |
| 22 | Schurrer | Real Sociedad | 23 | 47 | 2.04 |
| 23 | Roberto Carlos | Real Madrid | 37 | 75 | 2.03 |
| 24 | Xabier Alonso | Real Sociedad | 30 | 61 | 2.03 |
| 25 | Jauregui | Real Sociedad | 33 | 66 | 2.00 |
| 26 | Westerveld | Real Sociedad | 37 | 73 | 1.97 |
| 27 | Lopez Rekarte | Real Sociedad | 37 | 73 | 1.97 |
| 28 | Aranzabal | Real Sociedad | 32 | 63 | 1.97 |
| 29 | Zidane | Real Madrid | 29 | 57 | 1.97 |
| 30 | Karpin | Real Sociedad | 36 | 70 | 1.94 |

# AC MILAN

ITALY
Winners

| | | | | | | |
|---|---|---|---|---|---|---|
| 1 | 3ql1 | **Slovan Liberec** | H | W | 1-0 | Inzaghi 68 |
| 2 | 3ql2 | **Slovan Liberec** | A | L | 1-2 | Inzaghi 20 |
| 3 | gpg | **Lens** | H | W | 2-1 | Inzaghi 57,61 |
| 4 | gpg | **Deportivo** | A | W | 4-0 | Seedorf 17; Inzaghi 33,55,62 |
| 5 | gpg | **Bayern Munich** | A | W | 2-1 | Inzaghi 52,84 |
| 6 | gpg | **Bayern Munich** | H | W | 2-1 | Serginho 11; Inzaghi 64 |
| 7 | gpg | **Lens** | A | L | 1-2 | Shevchenko 31 |
| 8 | gpg | **Deportivo** | H | L | 1-2 | Tomasson 34 |
| 9 | gpc | **Real Madrid** | H | W | 1-0 | Shevchenko 40 |
| 10 | gpc | **B Dortmund** | A | W | 1-0 | Inzaghi 49 |
| 11 | gpc | **Lokomotiv M** | H | W | 1-0 | Tomasson 62 |
| 12 | gpc | **Lokomotiv M** | A | W | 1-0 | Rivaldo 34 |
| 13 | gpc | **Real Madrid** | A | L | 1-3 | Rivaldo 81 |
| 14 | gpc | **B Dortmund** | H | L | 0-1 | |
| 15 | qfL1 | **Ajax** | A | D | 0-0 | |
| 16 | qfL2 | **Ajax** | H | W | 3-2 | Inzaghi 30; Shevchenko 65; Tomasson 90 |
| 17 | sfL1 | **Inter Milan** | H | D | 0-0 | |
| 18 | sfL2 | **Inter Milan** | A | D | 1-1 | Shevchenko 45 (won on away goals) |
| 19 | fin | **Juventus** | N | W | 3-2* | (*on penalties) |

**Phase 1 GROUP G**

| | P | W | D | L | F | A | DIF | PTS |
|---|---|---|---|---|---|---|---|---|
| **AC Milan** | **6** | **4** | **0** | **2** | **12** | **7** | **5** | **12** |
| Deportivo La Coruna | 6 | 4 | 0 | 2 | 11 | 12 | -1 | 12 |
| Lens | 6 | 2 | 2 | 2 | 11 | 11 | 0 | 8 |
| Bayern Munich | 6 | 0 | 2 | 4 | 9 | 13 | -4 | 2 |

**Phase 2 GROUP C**

| | P | W | D | L | F | A | DIF | PTS |
|---|---|---|---|---|---|---|---|---|
| **AC Milan** | **6** | **4** | **0** | **2** | **5** | **4** | **1** | **12** |
| Real Madrid | 6 | 3 | 2 | 1 | 9 | 6 | 3 | 11 |
| Borussia Dortmund | 6 | 3 | 1 | 2 | 8 | 5 | 3 | 10 |
| Lokomotiv Moscow | 6 | 0 | 1 | 5 | 3 | 10 | -7 | 1 |

## KEY PLAYER APPEARANCES

1 Paolo Maldini — Defender

| | |
|---|---|
| Age (on 01/07/03) | 35 |
| In the squad | 19 |
| Total minutes on the pitch | 1669 |
| Goals | 0 |
| Yellow cards | 1 |
| Red cards | 0 |
| Home Country | Italy |

| | PLAYER | POS | AGE | SQUAD | MINS ON | GOALS | CARDS(Y) | CARDS(R) | HOME COUNTRY |
|---|---|---|---|---|---|---|---|---|---|
| 1 | Paolo Maldini | DEF | 35 | 19 | 1669 | 0 | 1 | 0 | Italy |
| 2 | Manuel Rui Costa | MID | 31 | 18 | 1301 | 0 | 1 | 0 | Portugal |
| 3 | Kakha Kaladze | DEF | 25 | 15 | 1299 | 0 | 1 | 0 | Georgia |
| 4 | Filippo Inzaghi | ATT | 29 | 17 | 1277 | 12 | 1 | 0 | Italy |
| 5 | Nelson Dida | GK | 29 | 16 | 1245 | 0 | 0 | 0 | Brazil |
| 6 | Gennaro Gattuso | MID | 25 | 15 | 1232 | 0 | 6 | 0 | Italy |
| 7 | Alessandro Nesta | DEF | 27 | 15 | 1229 | 0 | 1 | 0 | Italy |
| 8 | Clarence Seedorf | MID | 27 | 16 | 1216 | 1 | 3 | 0 | Holland |
| 9 | Dario Simic | DEF | 27 | 17 | 1052 | 0 | 0 | 0 | Croatia |
| 10 | Andriy Shevchenko | ATT | 26 | 12 | 988 | 4 | 1 | 0 | Ukraine |
| 11 | Andrea Pirlo | MID | 24 | 15 | 938 | 0 | 2 | 0 | Italy |
| 12 | Alessandro Costacurta | DEF | 37 | 15 | 919 | 0 | 2 | 0 | Italy |
| 13 | Massimo Ambrosini | MID | 26 | 13 | 743 | 0 | 3 | 0 | Italy |
| 14 | Rivaldo | ATT | 31 | 16 | 741 | 2 | 0 | 0 | Brazil |
| 15 | Serginho | MID | 32 | 16 | 592 | 1 | 2 | 0 | Brazil |
| 16 | Christian Abbiati | GK | 25 | 16 | 495 | 0 | 0 | 0 | Italy |
| 17 | Jon Dahl Tomasson | MID | 26 | 17 | 458 | 3 | 1 | 0 | Denmark |
| 18 | Martin Laursen | DEF | 25 | 15 | 443 | 0 | 0 | 0 | Denmark |
| 19 | Christian Brocchi | MID | 27 | 10 | 429 | 0 | 0 | 0 | Italy |
| 20 | Fernando Redondo | MID | 34 | 6 | 262 | 0 | 0 | 0 | Argentina |
| 21 | Samuelle Dalla Bona | MID | 22 | 12 | 254 | 0 | 1 | 0 | Italy |
| 22 | Thomas Helveg | MID | 32 | 8 | 180 | 0 | 0 | 0 | Denmark |
| 23 | Cosmin Marius Contra | DEF | 27 | 2 | 90 | 0 | 0 | 0 | Romania |
| 24 | Jose Vitor Roque Junior | DEF | 26 | 4 | 80 | 0 | 0 | 0 | Brazil |
| 25 | Catilina Aubameyang | MID | 19 | 2 | 6 | 0 | 0 | 0 | Gabon |
| 26 | Jose Antonio Chamot | DEF | 34 | 1 | 2 | 0 | 0 | 0 | Argentina |

## KEY PLAYERS - GOALSCORERS

1 Filippo Inzaghi

| | |
|---|---|
| Goals in the Champions League | 12 |
| **Contribution to Attacking Power** Average number of minutes between team goals while on pitch | 67 |
| **Player Strike Rate** The total number of minutes he was on the pitch for every goal scored | 106 |
| **Club Strike Rate** Average number of minutes between goals scored by club | 76 |

| | PLAYER | GOALS | ATT POWER | STRIKE RATE |
|---|---|---|---|---|
| 2 | Andriy Shevchenko | 4 | 98 | 247 mins |
| 3 | Rivaldo Vitor Borba Ferreira | 2 | 61 | 371 mins |
| 4 | Serginho | 1 | 84 | 592 mins |
| 5 | Clarence Seedorf | 1 | 71 | 1216 mins |

## KEY PLAYERS - MIDFIELDERS

1 Gennaro Gattuso

| | |
|---|---|
| Goals in the Champions League | 0 |
| **Defensive Rating** Average number of mins between goals conceded while on the pitch | 205 |
| **Contribution to Attacking Power** Average number of minutes between team goals while on pitch | 82 |
| **Scoring Difference** Defensive Rating minus Contribution to attacking power | 123 |

| | PLAYER | GOALS | DEF RATE | ATT POWER | SCORE DIFF |
|---|---|---|---|---|---|
| 2 | Clarence Seedorf | 1 | 135 | 72 | 63 mins |
| 3 | Manuel Rui Costa | 0 | 130 | 68 | 62 mins |
| 4 | Andrea Pirlo | 0 | 94 | 59 | 35 mins |
| 5 | Massimo Ambrosini | 0 | 106 | 83 | 23 mins |

## KEY PLAYERS - DEFENDERS

1 Alessandro Nesta

| | |
|---|---|
| Goals Conceded in Champions League | 8 |
| **Clean Sheets** In League games when he played at least than 70 mins | 7 |
| **Defensive Rating** Ave number of mins between goals conceded while on the pitch | 154 |
| **Club Defensive Rating** Average number of mins between goals conceded by the club this season | 108 |

| | PLAYER | CONCEDED | CLEAN SHEETS | DEF RATE |
|---|---|---|---|---|
| 2 | Kakha Kaladze | 10 | 7 | 130 mins |
| 3 | Paolo Maldini | 15 | 9 | 111 mins |
| 4 | Alessandro Costacurta | 9 | 5 | 102 mins |
| 5 | Dario Simic | 12 | 4 | 88 mins |

## KEY GOALKEEPER

1 Nelson Dida

| | |
|---|---|
| Goals Conceded | 7 |
| Clean Sheets | 9 |
| Total minutes on the pitch | 1245 |
| **Defensive Rating** Ave number of mins between goals conceded while on the pitch | 178 |

## TOP POINT EARNERS

| | PLAYER | GAMES | AV PTS |
|---|---|---|---|
| 1 | Filippo Inzaghi | 7 | 3.00 |
| 2 | Nelson Dida | 8 | 3.00 |
| 3 | Alessandro Nesta | 8 | 2.63 |
| 4 | Kakha Kaladze | 8 | 2.63 |
| 5 | Clarence Seedorf | 8 | 2.63 |
| 6 | Gennaro Gattuso | 7 | 2.57 |
| 7 | Manuel Rui Costa | 7 | 2.57 |
| 8 | Paolo Maldini | 10 | 2.40 |
| 9 | Dario Simic | 8 | 2.25 |
| 10 | Rivaldo | 7 | 2.14 |
| | CLUB AVERAGE: | | 2.00 |

**Note:** Points awarded for league section only

# JUVENTUS

ITALY
Final

| | | | | | | |
|---|---|---|---|---|---|---|
| 1 | gpe | Feyenoord | A | D | 1-1 | Camoranesi 32 |
| 2 | gpe | Dinamo Kiev | H | W | 5-0 | Di Vaio 14,52; Del Piero 22; Davids 67; Nedved 79 |
| 3 | gpe | Newcastle | H | W | 2-0 | Del Piero 66,81 |
| 4 | gpe | Newcastle | A | L | 0-1 | |
| 5 | gpe | Feyenoord | H | W | 2-0 | Di Vaio 4,69 |
| 6 | gpe | Dinamo Kiev | A | W | 2-1 | Salas 53; Zalayeta 61 |
| 7 | gpd | Deportivo | A | D | 2-2 | Birindelli 38; Nedved 57 |
| 8 | gpd | Basel | H | W | 4-0 | Trezeguet 3; Montero 34; Tacchinardi 43; Del Piero 51 pen |
| 9 | gpd | Man Utd | A | L | 1-2 | Nedved 90 |
| 10 | gpd | Man Utd | H | L | 0-3 | |
| 11 | gpd | Deportivo | H | W | 3-2 | Ferrara 12; Trezeguet 63; Tudor 90 |
| 12 | gpd | Basel | A | L | 1-2 | Tacchinardi 10 |
| 13 | qfL1 | Barcelona | H | D | 1-1 | Montero 16 |
| 14 | qfL2 | Barcelona | A | W | 2-1 | Nedved 53; Zalayeta 114 |
| 15 | sfL1 | Real Madrid | A | L | 1-2 | Trezeguet 45 |
| 16 | sfL2 | Real Madrid | H | W | 3-1 | Trezeguet 12; Del Piero 42; Nedved 73 |
| 17 | fin | AC Milan | N | L | 2-3* | (*on penalties) |

**Phase 1 GROUP E**

| | P | W | D | L | F | A | DIF | PTS |
|---|---|---|---|---|---|---|---|---|
| Juventus | 6 | 4 | 1 | 1 | 12 | 3 | 9 | 13 |
| Newcastle | 6 | 3 | 0 | 3 | 6 | 8 | -2 | 9 |
| Dynamo Kiev | 6 | 2 | 1 | 3 | 6 | 9 | -3 | 7 |
| Feyenoord | 6 | 1 | 2 | 3 | 4 | 8 | -4 | 5 |

**Phase 2 GROUP D**

| | P | W | D | L | F | A | DIF | PTS |
|---|---|---|---|---|---|---|---|---|
| Manchester United | 6 | 4 | 1 | 1 | 11 | 5 | 6 | 13 |
| Juventus | 6 | 2 | 1 | 3 | 11 | 11 | 0 | 7 |
| FC Basel | 6 | 2 | 1 | 3 | 5 | 10 | -5 | 7 |
| Deportivo La Coruna | 6 | 2 | 1 | 3 | 7 | 8 | -1 | 7 |

## PLAYER APPEARANCES

**2 Pavel Nedved** Midfield

| | |
|---|---|
| Age (on 01/07/03) | 30 |
| In the squad | 15 |
| Total minutes on the pitch | 1362 |
| Goals | 5 |
| Yellow cards | 3 |
| Red cards | 0 |
| Home Country | Czech Republic |

| | PLAYER | POS | AGE | SQUAD | MINS ON | GOALS | CARDS(Y) | CARDS(R) | HOME COUNTRY |
|---|---|---|---|---|---|---|---|---|---|
| 1 | Gianluigi Buffon | GK | 25 | 16 | 1410 | 0 | 1 | 0 | Italy |
| 2 | Pavel Nedved | MID | 30 | 15 | 1362 | 5 | 3 | 0 | Czech Republic |
| 3 | Lilian Thuram | DEF | 31 | 15 | 1337 | 0 | 0 | 0 | France |
| 4 | Paolo Montero | DEF | 31 | 13 | 1215 | 2 | 4 | 0 | Uruguay |
| 5 | Alessio Tacchinardi | MID | 27 | 13 | 1193 | 2 | 9 | 0 | Italy |
| 6 | Edgar Davids | MID | 30 | 15 | 1165 | 1 | 5 | 1 | Holland |
| 7 | Ciro Ferrara | DEF | 36 | 15 | 1082 | 1 | 3 | 0 | Italy |
| 8 | Alessandro Del Piero | ATT | 28 | 13 | 1080 | 5 | 1 | 0 | Italy |
| 9 | Alessandro Birindelli | DEF | 28 | 16 | 970 | 1 | 2 | 0 | Italy |
| 10 | Gianluca Zambrotta | MID | 26 | 14 | 952 | 0 | 2 | 0 | Italy |
| 11 | Mauro Camoranesi | MID | 26 | 16 | 818 | 1 | 0 | 0 | Argentina |
| 12 | David Trezeguet | ATT | 25 | 10 | 730 | 4 | 0 | 0 | France |
| 13 | Igor Tudor | DEF | 25 | 11 | 606 | 1 | 0 | 0 | Croatia |
| 14 | Mark Iuliano | DEF | 29 | 14 | 605 | 0 | 3 | 0 | Italy |
| 15 | Marco Di Vaio | ATT | 26 | 14 | 550 | 4 | 0 | 0 | Italy |
| 16 | Marcelo Zalayeta | ATT | 24 | 15 | 457 | 2 | 0 | 0 | Uruguay |
| 17 | Gianluca Pessotto | DEF | 32 | 12 | 370 | 0 | 0 | 0 | Italy |
| 18 | Antonio Conte | MID | 33 | 9 | 302 | 0 | 1 | 0 | Italy |
| 19 | Marcelo Salas | ATT | 28 | 8 | 210 | 1 | 0 | 0 | Chile |
| 20 | Davide Baiocco | DEF | 28 | 7 | 200 | 0 | 0 | 0 | Italy |
| 21 | Emiliano Moretti | GK | 22 | 5 | 189 | 0 | 0 | 0 | Italy |
| 22 | Cristiano Zenoni | DEF | 26 | 2 | 180 | 0 | 0 | 0 | Italy |
| 23 | Antonio Chimenti | GK | 33 | 17 | 180 | 0 | 0 | 0 | Italy |
| 24 | Salvatore Fresi | DEF | 30 | 9 | 121 | 0 | 1 | 0 | Italy |
| 25 | Ruben Olivera | MID | 20 | 3 | 100 | 0 | 1 | 0 | Uruguay |
| 26 | Matteo Paro | MID | 20 | 2 | 64 | 0 | 0 | 0 | Italy |
| 27 | Mattia Cassani | DEF | 19 | 1 | 1 | 0 | 0 | 0 | Italy |

## KEY PLAYERS - GOALSCORERS

**1 Marco Di Vaio**

| | |
|---|---|
| Goals in the Champions League | 4 |
| Contribution to Attacking Power<br>Average number of minutes between team goals while on pitch | 55 |
| Player Strike Rate<br>The total number of minutes he was on the pitch for every goal scored | 138 |
| Club Strike Rate<br>Average number of minutes between goals scored by club | 52 |

| | PLAYER | GOALS | ATT POWER | STRIKE RATE |
|---|---|---|---|---|
| 2 | David Trezeguet | 4 | 48 | 183 mins |
| 3 | Alessandro Del Piero | 5 | 49 | 216 mins |
| 4 | Pavel Nedved | 5 | 48 | 272 mins |
| 5 | Alessio Tacchinardi | 2 | 51 | 597 mins |

## KEY PLAYERS - MIDFIELDERS

**1 Edgar Davids**

| | |
|---|---|
| Goals in the Champions League | 1 |
| Defensive Rating<br>Average number of mins between goals conceded while on the pitch | 106 |
| Contribution to Attacking Power<br>Average number of minutes between team goals while on pitch | 47 |
| Scoring Difference<br>Defensive Rating minus Contribution to attacking power | 59 |

| | PLAYER | GOALS | DEF RATE | ATT POWER | SCORE DIFF |
|---|---|---|---|---|---|
| 2 | Alessio Tacchinardi | 2 | 92 | 52 | 40 mins |
| 3 | Pavel Nedved | 5 | 76 | 49 | 27 mins |
| 4 | Gianluca Zambrotta | 0 | 79 | 56 | 23 mins |
| 5 | Mauro German Camoranesi | 1 | 74 | 63 | 11 mins |

## KEY PLAYERS - DEFENDERS

**1 Igor Tudor**

TAMOIL

| | |
|---|---|
| Goals Conceded in Champions League | 5 |
| Clean Sheets<br>In League games when he played at least than 70 mins | 2 |
| Defensive Rating<br>Ave number of mins between goals conceded while on the pitch | 121 |
| Club Defensive Rating<br>Average number of mins between goals conceded by the club this season | 80 |

| | PLAYER | CONCEDED | CLEAN SHEETS | DEF RATE |
|---|---|---|---|---|
| 2 | Lilian Thuram | 15 | 4 | 89 mins |
| 3 | Alessandro Birindelli | 11 | 3 | 88 mins |
| 4 | Mark Iuliano | 7 | 2 | 86 mins |
| 5 | Ciro Ferrara | 13 | 3 | 83 mins |

## KEY GOALKEEPER

**1 Gianluigi Buffon**

| | |
|---|---|
| Goals Conceded | 16 |
| Clean Sheets | 5 |
| Total minutes on the pitch | 1410 |
| Defensive Rating<br>Ave number of mins between goals conceded while on the pitch | 88 |

## TOP POINT EARNERS

| | PLAYER | GAMES | AV PTS |
|---|---|---|---|
| 1 | Emiliano Moretti | 2 | 3.00 |
| 2 | Igor Tudor | 2 | 3.00 |
| 3 | Davide Baiocco | 2 | 3.00 |
| 4 | Gianluca Zambrotta | 4 | 2.25 |
| 5 | Edgar Davids | 8 | 2.00 |
| 6 | Alessandro Del Piero | 7 | 2.00 |
| 7 | Marco Di Vaio | 4 | 2.00 |
| 8 | David Trezeguet | 3 | 2.00 |
| 9 | Gianluigi Buffon | 10 | 1.70 |
| 10 | Mark Iuliano | 6 | 1.67 |
| | CLUB AVERAGE: | | 1.67 |

**Note:** Points awarded for league section only

# INTER MILAN

ITALY
Semi-Final

| | | | | | | |
|---|---|---|---|---|---|---|
| 1 | 3ql1 | Sp Lisbon | A | D | 0-0 | |
| 2 | 3ql2 | Sp Lisbon | H | W | 2-0 | Di Biagio 32; Recoba 45 |
| 3 | gpd | Rosenborg BK | A | D | 2-2 | Crespo 33,79 |
| 4 | gpd | Ajax | H | W | 1-0 | Crespo 75 |
| 5 | gpd | Lyon | H | L | 1-2 | Cannavaro 73 |
| 6 | gpd | Lyon | A | D | 3-3 | Cacapa 31 og; Crespo 56,66 |
| 7 | gpd | Rosenborg BK | H | W | 3-0 | Recoba 31; Saarinen 52 og; Crespo 72 |
| 8 | gpd | Ajax | A | W | 2-1 | Crespo 48,50 |
| 9 | gpa | Newcastle | A | W | 4-1 | Morfeo 2; Almeyda 35; Crespo 45; Recoba 81 |
| 10 | gpa | B Leverkusen | H | W | 3-2 | Di Biagio 15,27; Crespo 80 |
| 11 | gpa | Barcelona | A | L | 0-3 | |
| 12 | gpa | Barcelona | H | D | 0-0 | |
| 13 | gpa | Newcastle | H | D | 2-2 | Vieri 47; Cordoba 61 |
| 14 | gpa | B Leverkusen | A | W | 2-0 | Martins 36; Emre 89 |
| 15 | qfL1 | Valencia | H | W | 1-0 | Vieri 14 |
| 16 | qfL2 | Valencia | A | L | 1-2 | Vieri 5 |
| 17 | sfL1 | AC Milan | A | D | 0-0 | |
| 18 | sfL2 | AC Milan | H | D | 1-1 | Martins 84 (lost on away goals) |

**Phase 1 GROUP D**

| | P | W | D | L | F | A | DIF | PTS |
|---|---|---|---|---|---|---|---|---|
| Inter Milan | 6 | 3 | 2 | 1 | 12 | 8 | 4 | 11 |
| Ajax | 6 | 2 | 2 | 2 | 6 | 5 | 1 | 8 |
| Lyon | 6 | 2 | 2 | 2 | 12 | 9 | 3 | 8 |
| Rosenborg | 6 | 0 | 4 | 2 | 4 | 12 | -8 | 4 |

**Phase 2 GROUP A**

| | P | W | D | L | F | A | DIF | PTS |
|---|---|---|---|---|---|---|---|---|
| Barcelona | 6 | 5 | 1 | 0 | 12 | 2 | 10 | 16 |
| Inter Milan | 6 | 3 | 2 | 1 | 11 | 8 | 3 | 11 |
| Newcastle | 6 | 2 | 1 | 3 | 10 | 13 | -3 | 7 |
| Bayer Leverkusen | 6 | 0 | 0 | 6 | 5 | 15 | -10 | 0 |

## PLAYER APPEARANCES

4 Christian Vieri — Attacker

| | |
|---|---|
| Age (on 01/07/03) | 29 |
| In the squad | 14 |
| Total minutes on the pitch | 1183 |
| Goals | 3 |
| Yellow cards | 4 |
| Red cards | 0 |
| Home Country | Italy |

| | PLAYER | POS | AGE | SQUAD | MINS ON | GOALS | CARDS(Y/R) | | HOME COUNTRY |
|---|---|---|---|---|---|---|---|---|---|
| 1 | Francesco Toldo | GK | 31 | 18 | 1620 | 0 | 2 | 0 | Italy |
| 2 | Javier Zanetti | MID | 29 | 17 | 1530 | 0 | 1 | 0 | Argentina |
| 3 | Ivan Cordoba | DEF | 26 | 17 | 1426 | 1 | 3 | 0 | Colombia |
| 4 | Christian Vieri | ATT | 29 | 14 | 1183 | 3 | 4 | 0 | Italy |
| 5 | Luigi Di Biagio | MID | 32 | 18 | 1138 | 3 | 3 | 0 | Italy |
| 6 | Marco Materazzi | DEF | 29 | 14 | 1094 | 0 | 2 | 0 | Italy |
| 7 | Hernan Crespo | ATT | 28 | 12 | 980 | 10 | 1 | 0 | Argentina |
| 8 | Fabio Cannavaro | DEF | 29 | 13 | 918 | 1 | 6 | 1 | Italy |
| 9 | Francesco Coco | MID | 26 | 14 | 914 | 0 | 1 | 0 | Italy |
| 10 | Emre Belozoglu | MID | 22 | 12 | 843 | 1 | 0 | 1 | Turkey |
| 11 | Domenico Morfeo | MID | 27 | 11 | 783 | 1 | 4 | 0 | Italy |
| 12 | Sergio Conceicao | MID | 28 | 16 | 774 | 0 | 1 | 0 | Portugal |
| 13 | Alvaro Recoba | ATT | 27 | 15 | 742 | 3 | 0 | 1 | Uruguay |
| 14 | Stephane Dalmat | MID | 24 | 11 | 703 | 0 | 0 | 0 | France |
| 15 | Cristiano Zanetti | MID | 26 | 7 | 612 | 0 | 3 | 0 | Italy |
| 16 | Matias Almeyda | MID | 29 | 10 | 600 | 1 | 1 | 0 | Argentina |
| 17 | Giovanni Pasquale | DEF | 21 | 17 | 511 | 0 | 2 | 0 | Italy |
| 18 | Carlos Alberto Gamarra | DEF | 32 | 10 | 360 | 0 | 0 | 0 | Paraguay |
| 19 | Buruk Okan | MID | 29 | 8 | 315 | 0 | 0 | 0 | Turkey |
| 20 | Andres Guly | MID | 29 | 8 | 225 | 0 | 0 | 0 | Argentina |
| 21 | Obafemi Martins | ATT | 18 | 7 | 210 | 2 | 1 | 0 | Nigeria |
| 22 | Mohammed Kallon | ATT | 23 | 6 | 166 | 0 | 0 | 0 | Sierra Leone |
| 23 | Daniele Adani | DEF | 28 | 8 | 88 | 0 | 0 | 0 | Italy |
| 24 | Nicola Beati | MID | 20 | 3 | 20 | 0 | 0 | 0 | Italy |
| 25 | Bernardo Corradi | ATT | 27 | 2 | 1 | 0 | 0 | 0 | Italy |

## KEY PLAYERS - GOALSCORERS

1 Hernan Crespo

| | |
|---|---|
| Goals in the Champions League | 10 |
| Contribution to Attacking Power<br>Average number of minutes between team goals while on pitch | 49 |
| Player Strike Rate<br>The total number of minutes he was on the pitch for every goal scored | 98 |
| Club Strike Rate<br>Average number of minutes between goals scored by club | 109 |

| | PLAYER | GOALS | ATT POWER | STRIKE RATE |
|---|---|---|---|---|
| 2 | Alvaro Recoba | 3 | 61 | 247 mins |
| 3 | Luigi Di Biagio | 3 | 75 | 379 mins |
| 4 | Christian Vieri | 3 | 51 | 394 mins |
| 5 | Matias Almeyda | 1 | 37 | 600 mins |

## KEY PLAYERS - MIDFIELDERS

1 Sergio Conceicao

| | |
|---|---|
| Goals in the Champions League | 0 |
| Defensive Rating<br>Average number of mins between goals conceded while on the pitch | 129 |
| Contribution to Attacking Power<br>Average number of minutes between team goals while on pitch | 48 |
| Scoring Difference<br>Defensive Rating minus Contribution to attacking power | 58 |

| | PLAYER | GOALS | DEF RATE | ATT POWER | SCORE DIFF |
|---|---|---|---|---|---|
| 2 | Francesco Coco | 0 | 91 | 51 | 40 mins |
| 3 | Emre Belozoglu | 1 | 77 | 42 | 35 mins |
| 4 | Domenico Morfeo | 1 | 87 | 56 | 31 mins |
| 5 | Javier Zanetti | 0 | 81 | 59 | 22 mins |

## KEY PLAYERS - DEFENDERS

1 Giovanni Pasquale

| | |
|---|---|
| Goals Conceded in Champions League | 4 |
| Clean Sheets<br>In League games when he played at least than 70 mins | 2 |
| Defensive Rating<br>Ave number of mins between goals conceded while on the pitch | 128 |
| Club Defensive Rating<br>Average number of mins between goals conceded by the club this season | 85 |

| | PLAYER | CONCEDED | CLEAN SHEETS | DEF RATE |
|---|---|---|---|---|
| 2 | Marco Materazzi | 11 | 6 | 99 mins |
| 3 | Fabio Cannavaro | 11 | 4 | 83 mins |
| 4 | Ivan Cordoba | 19 | 6 | 75 mins |

## KEY GOALKEEPER

1 Francesco Toldo

| | |
|---|---|
| Goals Conceded | 19 |
| Clean Sheets | 8 |
| Total minutes on the pitch | 1620 |
| Defensive Rating<br>Ave number of mins between goals conceded while on the pitch | 85 |

## TOP POINT EARNERS

| | PLAYER | GAMES | AV PTS |
|---|---|---|---|
| 1 | Luigi Di Biagio | 5 | 2.60 |
| 2 | Giovanni Pasquale | 4 | 2.50 |
| 3 | Emre Belozoglu | 6 | 2.33 |
| 4 | Sergio Conceicao | 5 | 2.20 |
| 5 | Domenico Morfeo | 6 | 2.00 |
| 6 | Matias Almeyda | 5 | 2.00 |
| 7 | Hernan Crespo | 7 | 2.00 |
| 8 | Christian Vieri | 10 | 1.90 |
| 9 | Francesco Toldo | 12 | 1.83 |
| 10 | Marco Materazzi | 6 | 1.83 |
| | CLUB AVERAGE: | | 1.83 |

**Note:** Points awarded for league section only

# REAL MADRID

SPAIN
Semi-Final

| | | | | | | |
|---|---|---|---|---|---|---|
| 1 | gpc | Roma | A | W | 3-0 | Guti 41,75; Raul 56 |
| 2 | gpc | Genk | H | W | 6-0 | Zokora 45 og; Salgado 46; Figo 55 pen; Guti 64; Celades 74; Raul 76 |
| 3 | gpc | AEK Athens | A | D | 3-3 | Zidane 15,40; Guti 60 |
| 4 | gpc | AEK Athens | H | D | 2-2 | McManaman 24,43 |
| 5 | gpc | Roma | H | L | 0-1 | |
| 6 | gpc | Genk | A | D | 1-1 | Tote 21 |
| 7 | gpc | AC Milan | A | L | 0-1 | |
| 8 | gpc | Lokomotiv M | H | D | 2-2 | Raul 21,76 |
| 9 | gpc | B Dortmund | H | W | 2-1 | Raul 43; Ronaldo 55 |
| 10 | gpc | B Dortmund | A | D | 1-1 | Portillo 90 |
| 11 | gpc | AC Milan | H | W | 3-1 | Raul 12,57; Guti 86 |
| 12 | gpc | Lokomotiv M | A | W | 1-0 | Ronaldo 35 |
| 13 | qfL1 | Man Utd | H | W | 3-1 | Figo 12; Raul 28,49 |
| 14 | qfL2 | Man Utd | A | L | 3-4 | Ronaldo 12,50,59 |
| 15 | sfL1 | Juventus | H | W | 2-1 | Ronaldo 23; Roberto Carlos 73 |
| 16 | sfL2 | Juventus | A | L | 1-3 | Zidane 89 |

Phase 1
**GROUP C**

| | P | W | D | L | F | A | DIF | PTS |
|---|---|---|---|---|---|---|---|---|
| **Real Madrid** | **6** | **2** | **3** | **1** | **15** | **7** | **8** | **9** |
| Roma | 6 | 2 | 3 | 1 | 3 | 4 | -1 | 9 |
| AEK Athens | 6 | 0 | 6 | 0 | 7 | 7 | 0 | 6 |
| Genk | 6 | 0 | 4 | 2 | 2 | 9 | -7 | 4 |

Phase 2
**GROUP C**

| | P | W | D | L | F | A | DIF | PTS |
|---|---|---|---|---|---|---|---|---|
| AC Milan | 6 | 4 | 0 | 2 | 5 | 4 | 1 | 12 |
| **Real Madrid** | **6** | **3** | **2** | **1** | **9** | **6** | **3** | **11** |
| Borussia Dortmund | 6 | 3 | 1 | 2 | 8 | 5 | 3 | 10 |
| Lokomotiv Moscow | 6 | 0 | 1 | 5 | 3 | 10 | -7 | 1 |

## PLAYER APPEARANCES

5 Figo — Midfielder

| | |
|---|---|
| Age (on 01/07/03) | 30 |
| In the squad | 15 |
| Total minutes on the pitch | 1303 |
| Goals | 2 |
| Yellow cards | 2 |
| Red cards | 0 |
| Home Country | Portugal |

| | PLAYER | POS | AGE | SQUAD | MINS ON | GOALS | CARDS(Y/R) | | HOME COUNTRY |
|---|---|---|---|---|---|---|---|---|---|
| 1 | M Fernandez Salgado | DEF | 27 | 16 | 1350 | 1 | 2 | 0 | Spain |
| 2 | Iker Fernandez Casillas | GK | 22 | 16 | 1350 | 0 | 0 | 0 | Spain |
| 3 | Ivan Bujia Helguera | MID | 28 | 15 | 1321 | 0 | 3 | 0 | Spain |
| 4 | Roberto Carlos Da Silva | DEF | 30 | 15 | 1313 | 1 | 3 | 0 | Brazil |
| 5 | Figo | MID | 30 | 15 | 1303 | 2 | 2 | 0 | Portugal |
| 6 | Zinedine Zidane | MID | 31 | 14 | 1174 | 3 | 0 | 0 | France |
| 7 | Raul Gonzalez Blanco | ATT | 26 | 12 | 1054 | 9 | 0 | 0 | Spain |
| 8 | Claude Makelele | MID | 30 | 11 | 918 | 0 | 1 | 0 | France |
| 9 | Jose Maria Guti | MID | 26 | 15 | 848 | 5 | 0 | 0 | Spain |
| 10 | Fernando Ruiz Hierro | DEF | 35 | 10 | 839 | 0 | 2 | 0 | Spain |
| 11 | Ronaldo | ATT | 26 | 11 | 755 | 6 | 0 | 0 | Brazil |
| 12 | Francisco Pavon | DEF | 23 | 15 | 722 | 0 | 1 | 0 | Spain |
| 13 | Esteban Cambiasso | MID | 22 | 14 | 647 | 0 | 0 | 0 | Argentina |
| 14 | Flavio Conceicao | MID | 29 | 10 | 627 | 0 | 2 | 0 | Brazil |
| 15 | Albert Celades | MID | 27 | 5 | 360 | 1 | 0 | 0 | Spain |
| 16 | Santiago Hernan Solari | MID | 26 | 16 | 323 | 0 | 0 | 0 | Argentina |
| 17 | Morientes | ATT | 27 | 14 | 277 | 0 | 1 | 0 | Spain |
| 18 | Steve McManaman | MID | 31 | 12 | 207 | 2 | 0 | 0 | England |
| 19 | Oscar Minambres | DEF | 22 | 9 | 118 | 0 | 0 | 0 | Spain |
| 20 | Javier Garcia Portillo | ATT | 21 | 14 | 117 | 1 | 0 | 0 | Spain |
| 21 | Cesar | GK | 31 | 12 | 90 | 0 | 0 | 0 | Spain |
| 22 | Jorge Lopez Marco Tote | ATT | 24 | 2 | 90 | 1 | 0 | 0 | Spain |
| 23 | Sanfelix Raul Bravo | MID | 22 | 6 | 37 | 0 | 0 | 0 | Spain |

## KEY PLAYERS - GOALSCORERS

1 Raul Gonzalez Blanco

| | |
|---|---|
| Goals in the Champions League | 9 |
| Contribution to Attacking Power<br>Average number of minutes between team goals while on pitch | 43 |
| Player Strike Rate<br>The total number of minutes he was on the pitch for every goal scored | 117 |
| Club Strike Rate<br>Average number of minutes between goals scored by club | 44 |

| | PLAYER | GOALS | ATT POWER | STRIKE RATE |
|---|---|---|---|---|
| 2 | Ronaldo Luiz Nazario de Lima | 6 | 44 | 126 mins |
| 3 | Jose Maria Guti | 5 | 35 | 170 mins |
| 4 | Zinedine Zidane | 3 | 46 | 391 mins |
| 5 | Luis Madeira Caeira Figo | 2 | 43 | 652 mins |

## KEY PLAYERS - MIDFIELDERS

1 Claude Makelele

| | |
|---|---|
| Goals in the Champions League | 0 |
| Defensive Rating<br>Average number of mins between goals conceded while on the pitch | 71 |
| Contribution to Attacking Power<br>Average number of minutes between team goals while on pitch | 42 |
| Scoring Difference<br>Defensive Rating minus Contribution to attacking power | 29 |

| | PLAYER | GOALS | DEF RATE | ATT POWER | SCORE DIFF |
|---|---|---|---|---|---|
| 2 | Luis Madeira Caeira Figo | 2 | 69 | 43 | 26 mins |
| 3 | Jose Maria Guti | 5 | 50 | 35 | 15 mins |
| 4 | Zinedine Zidane | 3 | 62 | 47 | 15 mins |
| 5 | Flavio Conceicao | 0 | 70 | 57 | 13 mins |

## KEY PLAYERS - DEFENDERS

1 Francisco Pavon

| | |
|---|---|
| Goals Conceded in Champions League | 10 |
| Clean Sheets<br>In League games when he played at least than 70 mins | 1 |
| Defensive Rating<br>Ave number of mins between goals conceded while on the pitch | 72 |
| Club Defensive Rating<br>Average number of mins between goals conceded by the club this season | 65 |

| | PLAYER | CONCEDED | CLEAN SHEETS | DEF RATE |
|---|---|---|---|---|
| 2 | Ivan Bujia Helguera | 20 | 3 | 66 mins |
| 3 | Michel Fernandez Salgado | 21 | 3 | 64 mins |
| 4 | Roberto Carlos Da Silva | 21 | 2 | 63 mins |
| 5 | Fernando Ruiz Hierro | 14 | 2 | 60 mins |

## KEY GOALKEEPER

1 Iker Fernandez Casillas

| | |
|---|---|
| Goals Conceded | 21 |
| Clean Sheets | 3 |
| Total minutes on the pitch | 1350 |
| Defensive Rating<br>Ave number of mins between goals conceded while on the pitch | 64 |

## TOP POINT EARNERS

| | PLAYER | GAMES | AV PTS |
|---|---|---|---|
| 1 | Santiago Hernan Solari | 2 | 3.00 |
| 2 | Flavio Conceicao | 4 | 2.50 |
| 3 | Claude Makelele | 7 | 2.00 |
| 4 | Jose Maria Guti | 5 | 1.80 |
| 5 | Raul Gonzalez Blanco | 10 | 1.80 |
| 6 | Ivan Bujia Helguera | 10 | 1.80 |
| 7 | Figo | 10 | 1.80 |
| 8 | M Fernandez Salgado | 11 | 1.73 |
| 9 | Iker Fernandez Casillas | 11 | 1.73 |
| 10 | Zinedine Zidane | 9 | 1.67 |
| | **CLUB AVERAGE:** | | **1.67** |

**Note:** Points awarded for league section only

# AJAX

HOLLAND
Quarter-Final

| | | | | | | |
|---|---|---|---|---|---|---|
| 1 | gpd | **Lyon** | H | W | 2-1 | Ibrahimovic 11,33 |
| 2 | gpd | **Inter Milan** | A | L | 0-1 | |
| 3 | gpd | **Rosenborg BK** | A | D | 0-0 | |
| 4 | gpd | **Rosenborg BK** | H | D | 1-1 | Ibrahimovic 41 |
| 5 | gpd | **Lyon** | A | W | 2-0 | Pienaar 7; van der Vaart 90 |
| 6 | gpd | **Inter Milan** | H | L | 1-2 | van der Vaart 90 |
| 7 | gpb | **Valencia** | A | D | 1-1 | Ibrahimovic 88 |
| 8 | gpb | **Roma** | H | W | 2-1 | Ibrahimovic 11; Litmanen 66 |
| 9 | gpb | **Arsenal** | A | D | 1-1 | de Jong 17 |
| 10 | gpb | **Arsenal** | H | D | 0-0 | |
| 11 | gpb | **Valencia** | H | D | 1-1 | Pasanen 57 |
| 12 | gpb | **Roma** | A | D | 1-1 | van der Meyde 1 |
| 13 | qfL1 | **AC Milan** | H | D | 0-0 | |
| 14 | qfL2 | **AC Milan** | A | L | 2-3 | Litmanen 63; Pienaar 78 |

**Phase 1 GROUP D**

| | P | W | D | L | F | A | DIF | PTS |
|---|---|---|---|---|---|---|---|---|
| Inter Milan | 6 | 3 | 2 | 1 | 12 | 8 | 4 | 11 |
| **Ajax** | **6** | **2** | **2** | **2** | **6** | **5** | **1** | **8** |
| Lyon | 6 | 2 | 2 | 2 | 12 | 9 | 3 | 8 |
| Rosenborg | 6 | 0 | 4 | 2 | 4 | 12 | -8 | 4 |

**Phase 2 GROUP B**

| | P | W | D | L | F | A | DIF | PTS |
|---|---|---|---|---|---|---|---|---|
| Valencia | 6 | 2 | 3 | 1 | 5 | 6 | -1 | 9 |
| **Ajax** | **6** | **1** | **5** | **0** | **6** | **5** | **1** | **8** |
| Arsenal | 6 | 1 | 4 | 1 | 6 | 5 | 1 | 7 |
| Roma | 6 | 1 | 2 | 3 | 7 | 8 | -1 | 5 |

## PLAYER APPEARANCES

7 Steven Pienaar — Midfield

ABN·AMRO

| | |
|---|---|
| Age (on 01/07/03) | 21 |
| In the squad | 14 |
| Total minutes on the pitch | 875 |
| Goals | 2 |
| Yellow cards | 2 |
| Red cards | 0 |
| Home Country | South Africa |

| | PLAYER | POS | AGE | SQUAD | MINS ON | GOALS | CARDS(Y) | (R) | HOME COUNTRY |
|---|---|---|---|---|---|---|---|---|---|
| 1 | Hatem Trabelsi | DEF | 24 | 14 | 1202 | 0 | 2 | 0 | Tunisia |
| 2 | Christian Chivu | DEF | 22 | 12 | 1052 | 0 | 4 | 1 | Romania |
| 3 | Zlatan Ibrahimovic | ATT | 21 | 13 | 1005 | 5 | 2 | 0 | Sweden |
| 4 | Maxwell | MID | 21 | 12 | 1003 | 0 | 0 | 0 | Brazil |
| 5 | Tomas Galasek | DEF | 30 | 12 | 981 | 0 | 3 | 0 | Czech Republic |
| 6 | Andy van der Meyde | MID | 23 | 13 | 936 | 1 | 3 | 0 | Holland |
| 7 | Steven Pienaar | MID | 21 | 14 | 875 | 2 | 2 | 0 | South Africa |
| 8 | Petri Pasanen | DEF | 22 | 9 | 691 | 1 | 2 | 0 | Finland |
| 9 | Andre Bergdolmo | DEF | 31 | 13 | 552 | 0 | 1 | 0 | Norway |
| 10 | Nigel de Jong | DEF | 18 | 11 | 548 | 1 | 1 | 0 | Holland |
| 11 | Bogdan Lonut Lobont | GK | 25 | 6 | 540 | 0 | 2 | 0 | Romania |
| 12 | Rafael van der Vaart | MID | 20 | 6 | 486 | 2 | 2 | 0 | Holland |
| 13 | John O'Brien | DEF | 25 | 5 | 449 | 0 | 0 | 0 | United States |
| 14 | Jelle Van Damme | DEF | 19 | 9 | 442 | 0 | 0 | 1 | Belgium |
| 15 | Jari Litmanen | ATT | 32 | 7 | 426 | 2 | 0 | 0 | Finland |
| 16 | Ahmed Hossam Mido | ATT | 20 | 8 | 411 | 0 | 2 | 0 | Egypt |
| 17 | Richard Witschge | MID | 33 | 14 | 390 | 0 | 0 | 0 | Holland |
| 18 | Abubakarl Yakubu | DEF | 21 | 12 | 390 | 0 | 2 | 1 | Ghana |
| 19 | Joe Dudilica | GK | 25 | 11 | 360 | 0 | 1 | 0 | Australia |
| 20 | Victor Sikora | MID | 25 | 7 | 240 | 0 | 1 | 0 | Holland |
| 21 | Maarten Stekelenburg | GK | 20 | 4 | 200 | 0 | 1 | 0 | Holland |
| 22 | Henk Timmer | GK | 31 | 6 | 160 | 0 | 0 | 0 | Holland |
| 23 | Wamberto | ATT | 28 | 7 | 124 | 0 | 0 | 0 | Brazil |
| 24 | Nourdin Boukhari | ATT | 23 | 9 | 119 | 0 | 1 | 0 | Morocco |
| 25 | Wesley Sneijder | MID | 19 | 5 | 115 | 0 | 0 | 0 | Holland |
| 26 | Jan van Halst | MID | 34 | 5 | 101 | 0 | 1 | 0 | Holland |
| 27 | Aron Winter | MID | 36 | 2 | 23 | 0 | 0 | 0 | Holland |

## KEY PLAYERS - GOALSCORERS

1 Zlatan Ibrahimovic

| | |
|---|---|
| **Goals in the Champions League** | 5 |
| **Contribution to Attacking Power** Average number of minutes between team goals while on pitch | 83 |
| **Player Strike Rate** The total number of minutes he was on the pitch for every goal scored | 201 |
| **Club Strike Rate** Average number of minutes between goals scored by club | 90 |

| | PLAYER | GOALS | ATT POWER | STRIKE RATE |
|---|---|---|---|---|
| 2 | Steven Pienaar | 2 | 97 | 438 mins |
| 3 | Nigel de Jong | 1 | 78 | 548 mins |
| 4 | Petri Pasanen | 1 | 98 | 691 mins |
| 5 | Andy van der Meyde | 1 | 72 | 936 mins |

## KEY PLAYERS - MIDFIELDERS

1 Andy van der Meyde

| | |
|---|---|
| **Goals in the Champions League** | 1 |
| **Defensive Rating** Average number of mins between goals conceded while on the pitch | 94 |
| **Contribution to Attacking Power** Average number of minutes between team goals while on pitch | 72 |
| **Scoring Difference** Defensive Rating minus Contribution to attacking power | 22 |

| | PLAYER | GOALS | DEF RATE | ATT POWER | SCORE DIFF |
|---|---|---|---|---|---|
| 2 | Scherrer Cabelino Andrade Maxw | 0 | 111 | 91 | 20 mins |
| 3 | Steven Pienaar | 2 | 97 | 97 | 0 mins |

## KEY PLAYERS - DEFENDERS

1 Tomas Galasek

ABN·AM

| | |
|---|---|
| **Goals Conceded in Champions League** | 8 |
| **Clean Sheets** In League games when he played at least than 70 mins | 3 |
| **Defensive Rating** Ave number of mins between goals conceded while on the pitch | 123 |
| **Club Defensive Rating** Average number of mins between goals conceded by the club this season | 96 |

| | PLAYER | CONCEDED | CLEAN SHEETS | DEF RATE |
|---|---|---|---|---|
| 2 | Christian Chivu | 10 | 3 | 105 mins |
| 3 | Hatem Trabelsi | 12 | 4 | 100 mins |
| 4 | Petri Pasanen | 8 | 2 | 86 mins |
| 5 | Andre Bergdolmo | 7 | 2 | 79 mins |

## KEY GOALKEEPER

1 Bogdan Lonut Lobont

| | |
|---|---|
| **Goals Conceded** | 6 |
| **Clean Sheets** | 2 |
| **Total minutes on the pitch** | 540 |
| **Defensive Rating** Ave number of mins between goals conceded while on the pitch | 90 |

## TOP POINT EARNERS

| | PLAYER | GAMES | AV PTS |
|---|---|---|---|
| 1 | Maarten Stekelenburg | 2 | 3.00 |
| 2 | John O'Brien | 3 | 1.67 |
| 3 | Nigel de Jong | 5 | 1.60 |
| 4 | Steven Pienaar | 7 | 1.57 |
| 5 | Zlatan Ibrahimovic | 9 | 1.56 |
| 6 | Andre Bergdolmo | 6 | 1.50 |
| 7 | Richard Witschge | 4 | 1.50 |
| 8 | Maxwell | 10 | 1.40 |
| 9 | Jari Litmanen | 3 | 1.33 |
| 10 | Joe Dudilica | 4 | 1.25 |
| | CLUB AVERAGE: | | 1.33 |

**Note:** Points awarded for league section only

# BARCELONA

SPAIN
Quarter-Final

| | | | | | | |
|---|---|---|---|---|---|---|
| 1 | 3ql1 | Legia Warsaw | H | W | 3-0 | de Boer 8; Riquelme 80; Cocu, P 90 |
| 2 | 3ql2 | Legia Warsaw | A | W | 1-0 | Mendieta 68 pen |
| 3 | gph | Club Brugge | H | W | 3-2 | Luis Enrique 5; Mendieta 40; Saviola 44 |
| 4 | gph | Galatasaray | A | W | 2-0 | Kluivert 27; Luis Enrique 59 |
| 5 | gph | Lokomotiv M | A | W | 3-1 | Kluivert 29; Saviola 32,49 |
| 6 | gph | Lokomotiv M | H | W | 1-0 | de Boer 76 |
| 7 | gph | Club Brugge | A | W | 1-0 | Riquelme 64 |
| 8 | gph | Galatasaray | H | W | 3-1 | Dani 10; Gerard 44; Geovanni 56 |
| 9 | gpa | B Leverkusen | A | W | 2-1 | Saviola 48; Overmars 88 |
| 10 | gpa | Newcastle | H | W | 3-1 | Dani 7; Kluivert 35; Motta 58 |
| 11 | gpa | Inter Milan | H | W | 3-0 | Saviola 7; Cocu, P 29; Kluivert 67 |
| 12 | gpa | Inter Milan | A | D | 0-0 | |
| 13 | gpa | B Leverkusen | H | W | 2-0 | Saviola 17; Kleine 49 og |
| 14 | gpa | Newcastle | A | W | 2-0 | Kluivert 60; Motta 75 |
| 15 | qfL1 | Juventus | A | D | 1-1 | Saviola 78 |
| 16 | qfL2 | Juventus | H | L | 1-2 | Xavi 66 |

Phase 1
**GROUP H**

| | P | W | D | L | F | A | DIF | PTS |
|---|---|---|---|---|---|---|---|---|
| Barcelona | 6 | 6 | 0 | 0 | 13 | 4 | 9 | 18 |
| Lokomotiv Moscow | 6 | 2 | 1 | 3 | 5 | 7 | -2 | 7 |
| Club Brugge | 6 | 1 | 2 | 3 | 5 | 7 | -2 | 5 |
| Galatasaray | 6 | 1 | 1 | 4 | 5 | 10 | -5 | 4 |

Phase 2
**GROUP A**

| | P | W | D | L | F | A | DIF | PTS |
|---|---|---|---|---|---|---|---|---|
| Barcelona | 6 | 5 | 1 | 0 | 12 | 2 | 10 | 16 |
| Inter Milan | 6 | 3 | 2 | 1 | 11 | 8 | 3 | 11 |
| Newcastle | 6 | 2 | 1 | 3 | 10 | 13 | -3 | 7 |
| Bayer Leverkusen | 6 | 0 | 0 | 6 | 5 | 15 | -10 | 0 |

## PLAYER APPEARANCES

1 Frank de Boer — Defender

| | |
|---|---|
| Age (on 01/07/03) | 33 |
| In the squad | 14 |
| Total minutes on the pitch | 1256 |
| Goals | 2 |
| Yellow cards | 1 |
| Red cards | 0 |
| Home Country | Holland |

| | PLAYER | POS | AGE | SQUAD | MINS ON | GOALS | CARDS(Y) | CARDS(R) | HOME COUNTRY |
|---|---|---|---|---|---|---|---|---|---|
| 1 | Frank de Boer | DEF | 33 | 14 | 1256 | 2 | 1 | 0 | Holland |
| 2 | Patrick Kluivert | ATT | 27 | 15 | 1242 | 5 | 2 | 0 | Holland |
| 3 | Carlos Puyol | DEF | 25 | 14 | 1240 | 0 | 1 | 0 | Spain |
| 4 | Xavi Hernandez | MID | 23 | 15 | 1211 | 1 | 1 | 0 | Spain |
| 5 | Thiago Motta | MID | 20 | 13 | 1120 | 2 | 3 | 0 | Brazil |
| 6 | Javier Saviola | ATT | 21 | 14 | 1100 | 7 | 0 | 0 | Argentina |
| 7 | Gaizka Mendieta | MID | 29 | 15 | 1004 | 2 | 1 | 0 | Spain |
| 8 | Navarro | DEF | 21 | 9 | 810 | 0 | 3 | 0 | Spain |
| 9 | Phillip Cocu | MID | 32 | 11 | 793 | 2 | 2 | 0 | Holland |
| 10 | Roberto Bonano | GK | 33 | 12 | 750 | 0 | 0 | 0 | Argentina |
| 11 | Michael Reiziger | DEF | 30 | 12 | 733 | 0 | 0 | 0 | Holland |
| 12 | Garcia de la Torre Gabri | MID | 24 | 14 | 719 | 0 | 6 | 0 | Spain |
| 13 | Juan Riquelme | ATT | 25 | 13 | 669 | 2 | 0 | 0 | Argentina |
| 14 | Valdes Arribas Victor | GK | 21 | 11 | 540 | 0 | 0 | 0 | Spain |
| 15 | Martinez Luis Enrique | MID | 33 | 8 | 486 | 2 | 2 | 0 | Spain |
| 16 | Marc Overmars | MID | 30 | 8 | 408 | 1 | 1 | 0 | Holland |
| 17 | Fabio Rochemback | MID | 21 | 15 | 404 | 0 | 1 | 0 | Brazil |
| 18 | Lopez Segu Gerard | MID | 24 | 11 | 290 | 1 | 1 | 0 | Spain |
| 19 | Daniel Garcia Lara Dani | ATT | 28 | 9 | 276 | 2 | 0 | 0 | Spain |
| 20 | Patrik Andersson | DEF | 31 | 6 | 253 | 0 | 0 | 0 | Sweden |
| 21 | Deiberson Geovanni | ATT | 23 | 10 | 198 | 1 | 1 | 0 | Brazil |
| 22 | Robert Enke | GK | 25 | 9 | 180 | 0 | 0 | 0 | Germany |
| 23 | Philippe Christanval | DEF | 24 | 8 | 174 | 0 | 0 | 0 | France |
| 24 | Andres Iniesta Lujan | MID | 19 | 5 | 137 | 0 | 0 | 0 | Spain |
| 25 | Daniel Dani Tortolero | DEF | 21 | 2 | 120 | 0 | 1 | 0 | Spain |
| 26 | Presas Oleguer | DEF | 23 | 6 | 34 | 0 | 0 | 0 | Spain |
| 27 | Sergio Garcia | MID | 20 | 2 | 21 | 0 | 0 | 0 | Spain |
| 28 | Sanchez David | ATT | 20 | 1 | 2 | 0 | 0 | 0 | Spain |

## KEY PLAYERS - GOALSCORERS

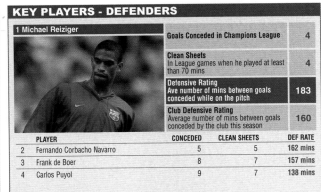

1 Javier Saviola

| | |
|---|---|
| Goals in the Champions League | 7 |
| Contribution to Attacking Power<br>Average number of minutes between team goals while on pitch | 45 |
| Player Strike Rate<br>The total number of minutes he was on the pitch for every goal scored | 157 |
| Club Strike Rate<br>Average number of minutes between goals scored by club | 46 |

| | PLAYER | GOALS | ATT POWER | STRIKE RATE |
|---|---|---|---|---|
| 2 | Patrick Kluivert | 5 | 47 | 248 mins |
| 3 | Juan Riquelme | 2 | 51 | 335 mins |
| 4 | Phillip Cocu | 2 | 41 | 397 mins |
| 5 | Gaizka Mendieta | 2 | 45 | 502 mins |

## KEY PLAYERS - MIDFIELDERS

1 Garcia de la Torre Gabri

| | |
|---|---|
| Goals in the Champions League | 0 |
| Defensive Rating<br>Average number of mins between goals conceded while on the pitch | 360 |
| Contribution to Attacking Power<br>Average number of minutes between team goals while on pitch | 65 |
| Scoring Difference<br>Defensive Rating minus Contribution to attacking power | 295 |

| | PLAYER | GOALS | DEF RATE | ATT POWER | SCORE DIFF |
|---|---|---|---|---|---|
| 2 | Phillip Cocu | 2 | 198 | 42 | 156 mins |
| 3 | Gaizka Mendieta | 2 | 167 | 46 | 121 mins |
| 4 | Xavi Hernandez | 1 | 151 | 50 | 101 mins |
| 5 | Thiago Motta | 2 | 124 | 43 | 81 mins |

## KEY PLAYERS - DEFENDERS

1 Michael Reiziger

| | |
|---|---|
| Goals Conceded in Champions League | 4 |
| Clean Sheets<br>In League games when he played at least than 70 mins | 4 |
| Defensive Rating<br>Ave number of mins between goals conceded while on the pitch | 183 |
| Club Defensive Rating<br>Average number of mins between goals conceded by the club this season | 160 |

| | PLAYER | CONCEDED | CLEAN SHEETS | DEF RATE |
|---|---|---|---|---|
| 2 | Fernando Corbacho Navarro | 5 | 5 | 162 mins |
| 3 | Frank de Boer | 8 | 7 | 157 mins |
| 4 | Carlos Puyol | 9 | 7 | 138 mins |

## KEY GOALKEEPER

1 Valdes Arribas Victor

| | |
|---|---|
| Goals Conceded | 3 |
| Clean Sheets | 4 |
| Total minutes on the pitch | 540 |
| Defensive Rating<br>Ave number of mins between goals conceded while on the pitch | 180 |

## TOP POINT EARNERS

| | PLAYER | GAMES | AV PTS |
|---|---|---|---|
| 1 | Juan Riquelme | 5 | 3.00 |
| 2 | Lopez Segu Gerard | 2 | 3.00 |
| 3 | Daniel Garcia Lara Dani | 3 | 3.00 |
| 4 | Valdes Arribas Victor | 4 | 3.00 |
| 5 | Navarro | 7 | 3.00 |
| 6 | Fabio Rochemback | 3 | 3.00 |
| 7 | Gaizka Mendieta | 6 | 3.00 |
| 8 | Martinez Luis Enrique | 2 | 3.00 |
| 9 | Patrik Andersson | 2 | 3.00 |
| 10 | Phillip Cocu | 6 | 3.00 |
| | CLUB AVERAGE: | | 2.83 |

**Note:** Points awarded for league section only

# MANCHESTER UNITED

ENGLAND
Quarter-Final

| | | | | | | |
|---|---|---|---|---|---|---|
| 1 | 3ql1 | Zalaegerszeg | A | L | 0-1 | |
| 2 | 3ql2 | Zalaegerszeg | H | W | 5-0 | van Nistelrooy 6,77 pen; Beckham 15; Scholes 21; Solskjaer 83 |
| 3 | gpf | Maccabi Haifa | H | W | 5-2 | Giggs 11; Solskjaer 35; Veron 46; van Nistelrooy 54; Forlan 89 pen |
| 4 | gpf | B Leverkusen | A | W | 2-1 | van Nistelrooy 31,42 |
| 5 | gpf | Olympiakos | H | W | 4-0 | Giggs 19,66; Veron 26; Solskjaer 77 |
| 6 | gpf | Olympiakos | A | W | 3-2 | Blanc 21; Veron 59; Scholes 84 |
| 7 | gpf | Maccabi Haifa | A | L | 0-3 | |
| 8 | gpf | B Leverkusen | H | W | 2-0 | Veron 42; van Nistelrooy 69 |
| 9 | gpd | Basel | A | W | 3-1 | van Nistelrooy 62,63; Solskjaer 68 |
| 10 | gpd | Deportivo | H | W | 2-0 | van Nistelrooy 8,55 |
| 11 | gpd | Juventus | H | W | 2-1 | Brown 4; van Nistelrooy 85 |
| 12 | gpd | Juventus | A | W | 3-0 | Giggs 15,41; van Nistelrooy 63 |
| 13 | gpd | Basel | H | D | 1-1 | Neville, G 53 |
| 14 | gpd | Deportivo | A | L | 0-2 | |
| 15 | qfL1 | Real Madrid | A | L | 1-3 | van Nistelrooy 52 |
| 16 | qfL2 | Real Madrid | H | W | 4-3 | van Nistelrooy 43; Helguera 53 og; Beckham 71,84 |

**Phase 1 GROUP F**

| | P | W | D | L | F | A | DIF | PTS |
|---|---|---|---|---|---|---|---|---|
| Manchester United | 6 | 5 | 0 | 1 | 16 | 8 | 8 | 15 |
| Bayer Leverkusen | 6 | 3 | 0 | 3 | 9 | 11 | -2 | 9 |
| Maccabi Haifa | 6 | 2 | 1 | 3 | 12 | 12 | 0 | 7 |
| Olympiakos | 6 | 1 | 1 | 4 | 11 | 17 | -6 | 4 |

**Phase 2 GROUP D**

| | P | W | D | L | F | A | DIF | PTS |
|---|---|---|---|---|---|---|---|---|
| Manchester United | 6 | 4 | 1 | 1 | 11 | 5 | 6 | 13 |
| Juventus | 6 | 2 | 1 | 3 | 11 | 11 | 0 | 7 |
| FC Basel | 6 | 2 | 1 | 3 | 5 | 10 | -5 | 7 |
| Deportivo La Coruna | 6 | 2 | 1 | 3 | 7 | 8 | -1 | 7 |

## PLAYER APPEARANCES

1 Ryan Giggs — Midfielder

vodafone

| | |
|---|---|
| Age (on 01/07/03) | 29 |
| In the squad | 15 |
| Total minutes on the pitch | 1141 |
| Goals | 5 |
| Yellow cards | 0 |
| Red cards | 0 |
| Home Country | Wales |

| | PLAYER | POS | AGE | SQUAD | MINS ON | GOALS | CARDS(Y | R) | HOME COUNTRY |
|---|---|---|---|---|---|---|---|---|---|
| 1 | Ryan Giggs | MID | 29 | 15 | 1141 | 5 | 0 | 0 | Wales |
| 2 | John O'Shea | DEF | 22 | 16 | 1112 | 0 | 1 | 0 | Rep of Ireland |
| 3 | Mikael Silvestre | DEF | 25 | 13 | 1084 | 0 | 1 | 0 | France |
| 4 | Phil Neville | MID | 26 | 15 | 987 | 0 | 3 | 0 | England |
| 5 | Rio Ferdinand | DEF | 24 | 11 | 967 | 0 | 2 | 0 | England |
| 6 | Juan Sebastian Veron | MID | 28 | 11 | 955 | 4 | 4 | 0 | Argentina |
| 7 | David Beckham | MID | 28 | 13 | 895 | 3 | 1 | 0 | England |
| 8 | Fabien Barthez | GK | 32 | 10 | 876 | 0 | 0 | 0 | France |
| 9 | Ole Gunnar Solskjaer | ATT | 30 | 15 | 870 | 4 | 1 | 0 | Norway |
| 10 | Ruud van Nistelrooy | ATT | 27 | 12 | 863 | 14 | 1 | 0 | Holland |
| 11 | Gary Neville | DEF | 28 | 11 | 774 | 1 | 3 | 0 | England |
| 12 | Paul Scholes | ATT | 28 | 11 | 761 | 2 | 3 | 0 | England |
| 13 | Laurent Blanc | DEF | 37 | 11 | 756 | 1 | 0 | 0 | France |
| 14 | Nicky Butt | MID | 28 | 9 | 720 | 0 | 1 | 0 | England |
| 15 | Roy Keane | MID | 31 | 6 | 531 | 0 | 2 | 0 | Rep of Ireland |
| 16 | Diego Forlan | ATT | 24 | 16 | 489 | 1 | 0 | 0 | Uruguay |
| 17 | Wes Brown | DEF | 23 | 6 | 454 | 1 | 0 | 0 | England |
| 18 | Quinton Fortune | MID | 26 | 7 | 329 | 0 | 2 | 0 | South Africa |
| 19 | Ricardo Lopez Felipe | GK | 31 | 14 | 294 | 0 | 2 | 0 | Spain |
| 20 | Roy Carroll | GK | 25 | 6 | 270 | 0 | 0 | 0 | N Ireland |
| 21 | Darren Fletcher | MID | 19 | 6 | 163 | 0 | 0 | 0 | Scotland |
| 22 | Danny Pugh | MID | 20 | 9 | 137 | 0 | 0 | 0 | England |
| 23 | Keiron Richardson | MID | 18 | 7 | 130 | 0 | 0 | 0 | England |
| 24 | Mark Lynch | DEF | 21 | 2 | 90 | 0 | 0 | 0 | England |
| 25 | Michael Stewart | MID | 22 | 8 | 45 | 0 | 0 | 0 | England |
| 26 | Lee Roche | DEF | 22 | 4 | 45 | 0 | 0 | 0 | England |
| 27 | Luke Chadwick | MID | 22 | 6 | 40 | 0 | 0 | 0 | England |
| 28 | Daniel Nardiello | ATT | 20 | 3 | 30 | 0 | 0 | 0 | England |
| 29 | Danny Webber | ATT | 21 | 2 | 19 | 0 | 0 | 0 | England |
| 30 | Mads Timms | MID | 18 | 1 | 12 | 0 | 0 | 0 | Denmark |
| 31 | David May | DEF | 33 | 7 | 1 | 0 | 0 | 0 | England |

## KEY PLAYERS - GOALSCORERS

1 Ruud van Nistelrooy

| | |
|---|---|
| Goals in the Champions League | 14 |
| Contribution to Attacking Power<br>Average number of minutes between team goals while on pitch | 33 |
| Player Strike Rate<br>The total number of minutes he was on the pitch for every goal scored | 62 |
| Club Strike Rate<br>Average number of minutes between goals scored by club | 39 |

| | PLAYER | GOALS | ATT POWER | STRIKE RATE |
|---|---|---|---|---|
| 2 | Ole Gunnar Solskjaer | 4 | 34 | 218 mins |
| 3 | Ryan Giggs | 5 | 34 | 228 mins |
| 4 | Juan Sebastian Veron | 4 | 30 | 239 mins |
| 5 | David Beckham | 3 | 34 | 298 mins |

## KEY PLAYERS - MIDFIELDERS

1 David Beckham

| | |
|---|---|
| Goals in the Champions League | 3 |
| Defensive Rating<br>Average number of mins between goals conceded while on the pitch | 112 |
| Contribution to Attacking Power<br>Average number of minutes between team goals while on pitch | 34 |
| Scoring Difference<br>Defensive Rating minus Contribution to attacking power | 78 |

| | PLAYER | GOALS | DEF RATE | ATT POWER | SCORE DIFF |
|---|---|---|---|---|---|
| 2 | Juan Sebastian Veron | 4 | 96 | 31 | 65 mins |
| 3 | Ryan Giggs | 5 | 95 | 35 | 60 mins |
| 4 | Phil Neville | 0 | 76 | 39 | 37 mins |
| 5 | Roy Keane | 0 | 66 | 38 | 28 mins |

## KEY PLAYERS - DEFENDERS

1 Laurent Blanc

vodafone

| | |
|---|---|
| Goals Conceded in Champions League | 9 |
| Clean Sheets<br>In League games when he played at least than 70 mins | 2 |
| Defensive Rating<br>Ave number of mins between goals conceded while on the pitch | 84 |
| Club Defensive Rating<br>Average number of mins between goals conceded by the club this season | 72 |

| | PLAYER | CONCEDED | CLEAN SHEETS | DEF RATE |
|---|---|---|---|---|
| 2 | Gary Neville | 11 | 3 | 70 mins |
| 3 | John O'Shea | 16 | 2 | 70 mins |
| 4 | Rio Ferdinand | 14 | 3 | 69 mins |
| 5 | Mikael Silvestre | 16 | 4 | 68 mins |

## KEY GOALKEEPER

1 Fabien Barthez

| | |
|---|---|
| Goals Conceded | 12 |
| Clean Sheets | 3 |
| Total minutes on the pitch | 876 |
| Defensive Rating<br>Ave number of mins between goals conceded while on the pitch | 73 |

## TOP POINT EARNERS

| | PLAYER | GAMES | AV PTS |
|---|---|---|---|
| 1 | Ruud van Nistelrooy | 5 | 3.00 |
| 2 | Fabien Barthez | 7 | 3.00 |
| 3 | Juan Sebastian Veron | 8 | 3.00 |
| 4 | Wes Brown | 3 | 3.00 |
| 5 | David Beckham | 6 | 3.00 |
| 6 | Roy Keane | 2 | 3.00 |
| 7 | Mikael Silvestre | 8 | 2.63 |
| 8 | Paul Scholes | 7 | 2.57 |
| 9 | Ryan Giggs | 6 | 2.50 |
| 10 | Rio Ferdinand | 8 | 2.38 |
| | CLUB AVERAGE: | | 2.33 |

**Note:** Points awarded for league section only

# VALENCIA

SPAIN
Quarter-Final

| | | | | | | |
|---|---|---|---|---|---|---|
| 1 | gpb | Liverpool | H | W | 2-0 | Aimar 20; Baraja 39 |
| 2 | gpb | S Moscow | A | W | 3-0 | Angulo 6; Mista 71; Sanchez 85 |
| 3 | gpb | Basel | H | W | 6-2 | Carew 10,13; Aurelio 18; Baraja 28; Aimar 58; Mista 60 |
| 4 | gpb | Basel | A | D | 2-2 | Baraja 36; Curro Torres 72 |
| 5 | gpb | Liverpool | A | W | 1-0 | Rufete 34 |
| 6 | gpb | S Moscow | H | W | 3-0 | Sanchez 38,46; Aurelio 76 |
| 7 | gpb | Ajax | H | D | 1-1 | Angulo 90 |
| 8 | gpb | Arsenal | A | D | 0-0 | |
| 9 | gpb | Roma | A | W | 1-0 | Carew 78 |
| 10 | gpb | Roma | H | L | 0-3 | |
| 11 | gpb | Ajax | A | D | 1-1 | Kily Gonzalez 28 pen |
| 12 | gpb | Arsenal | H | W | 2-1 | Carew 35,57 |
| 13 | qfL1 | Inter Milan | A | L | 0-1 | |
| 14 | qfL2 | Inter Milan | H | W | 2-1 | Aimar 7; Baraja 51 |

Phase 1
**GROUP B**

| | P | W | D | L | F | A | DIF | PTS |
|---|---|---|---|---|---|---|---|---|
| Valencia | 6 | 5 | 1 | 0 | 17 | 4 | 13 | 16 |
| FC Basel | 6 | 2 | 3 | 1 | 12 | 12 | 0 | 9 |
| Liverpool | 6 | 2 | 2 | 2 | 12 | 8 | 4 | 8 |
| Spartak Moscow | 6 | 0 | 0 | 6 | 1 | 18 | -17 | 0 |

Phase 2
**GROUP B**

| | P | W | D | L | F | A | DIF | PTS |
|---|---|---|---|---|---|---|---|---|
| Valencia | 6 | 2 | 3 | 1 | 5 | 6 | -1 | 9 |
| Ajax | 6 | 1 | 5 | 0 | 6 | 5 | 1 | 8 |
| Arsenal | 6 | 1 | 4 | 1 | 6 | 5 | 1 | 7 |
| Roma | 6 | 1 | 2 | 3 | 7 | 8 | -1 | 5 |

## PLAYER APPEARANCES

3 Ruben Vegas Baraja — Midfielder

| | |
|---|---|
| Age (on 01/07/03) | 27 |
| In the squad | 12 |
| Total minutes on the pitch | 1016 |
| Goals | 4 |
| Yellow cards | 4 |
| Red cards | 0 |
| Home Country | Spain |

| | PLAYER | POS | AGE | SQUAD | MINS ON | GOALS | CARDS(Y) | CARDS(R) | HOME COUNTRY |
|---|---|---|---|---|---|---|---|---|---|
| 1 | Roberto Fabian Ayala | DEF | 30 | 12 | 1075 | 0 | 3 | 1 | Argentina |
| 2 | Santiago Ruiz Canizares | GK | 33 | 13 | 1061 | 0 | 2 | 0 | Spain |
| 3 | Ruben Vegas Baraja | MID | 27 | 12 | 1016 | 4 | 4 | 0 | Spain |
| 4 | Mauricio Pellegrino | DEF | 31 | 12 | 976 | 0 | 3 | 0 | Argentina |
| 5 | John Alieu Carew | ATT | 23 | 13 | 974 | 5 | 0 | 0 | Norway |
| 6 | David Aliques Albelda | MID | 25 | 12 | 943 | 0 | 2 | 1 | Spain |
| 7 | Amadeo Carboni | DEF | 38 | 14 | 886 | 0 | 1 | 0 | Italy |
| 8 | Pablo Aimar | MID | 23 | 12 | 838 | 3 | 2 | 0 | Argentina |
| 9 | Vicente | MID | 21 | 13 | 751 | 0 | 0 | 0 | Spain |
| 10 | Francisco Rufete | MID | 26 | 12 | 692 | 1 | 2 | 0 | Spain |
| 11 | Curro Torres | DEF | 26 | 7 | 630 | 1 | 0 | 0 | Spain |
| 12 | Miguel Angulo | ATT | 26 | 11 | 612 | 2 | 1 | 1 | Spain |
| 13 | Anthony Reveillere | DEF | 23 | 6 | 540 | 0 | 0 | 0 | France |
| 14 | Juan Sanchez | ATT | 31 | 14 | 481 | 3 | 0 | 0 | Spain |
| 15 | Kily Gonzalez | MID | 28 | 6 | 425 | 1 | 2 | 0 | Argentina |
| 16 | Miguel Angel Ferrer | ATT | 24 | 12 | 419 | 2 | 3 | 0 | Spain |
| 17 | Fabio Aurelio | DEF | 23 | 11 | 398 | 2 | 0 | 0 | Brazil |
| 18 | Carlos Marchena | DEF | 24 | 14 | 393 | 0 | 1 | 0 | Spain |
| 19 | Andres Cervera Palop | GK | 29 | 14 | 199 | 0 | 0 | 0 | Spain |
| 20 | Gonzalo De Los Santos | MID | 26 | 11 | 190 | 0 | 0 | 0 | Uruguay |
| 21 | Javier Ramirez Garrido | DEF | 24 | 5 | 121 | 0 | 1 | 0 | Spain |
| 22 | Miroslav Djukic | DEF | 37 | 10 | 90 | 0 | 0 | 0 | Serbia & Mont |
| 23 | Ioan Ballesta Salva | ATT | 28 | 2 | 70 | 0 | 1 | 0 | Spain |
| 24 | Miguel Albiol | ATT | 21 | 1 | 20 | 0 | 0 | 0 | Spain |
| 25 | Ridaura David Sanchez | DEF | 22 | 1 | 4 | 0 | 0 | 0 | Spain |
| 26 | David Pedros Navarro | DEF | 23 | 1 | 3 | 0 | 0 | 0 | Spain |

## KEY PLAYERS - GOALSCORERS

1 John Alieu Carew

| | |
|---|---|
| Goals in the Champions League | 5 |
| Contribution to Attacking Power<br>Average number of minutes between team goals while on pitch | 57 |
| Player Strike Rate<br>The total number of minutes he was on the pitch for every goal scored | 195 |
| Club Strike Rate<br>Average number of minutes between goals scored by club | 53 |

| | PLAYER | GOALS | ATT POWER | STRIKE RATE |
|---|---|---|---|---|
| 2 | Ruben Vegas Baraja | 4 | 59 | 254 mins |
| 3 | Pablo Aimar | 3 | 46 | 279 mins |
| 4 | Miguel Angel Valderrey Angulo | 2 | 40 | 306 mins |
| 5 | Cristobal Emilio Curro Torres | 1 | 42 | 630 mins |

## KEY PLAYERS - MIDFIELDERS

1 Pablo Aimar

| | |
|---|---|
| Goals in the Champions League | 3 |
| Defensive Rating<br>Average number of mins between goals conceded while on the pitch | 168 |
| Contribution to Attacking Power<br>Average number of minutes between team goals while on pitch | 47 |
| Scoring Difference<br>Defensive Rating minus Contribution to attacking power | 121 |

| | PLAYER | GOALS | DEF RATE | ATT POWER | SCORE DIFF |
|---|---|---|---|---|---|
| 2 | Ruben Vegas Baraja | 4 | 127 | 60 | 67 mins |
| 3 | David Aliques Albelda | 0 | 118 | 59 | 59 mins |
| 4 | Rodriguez Guillen Vicente | 0 | 94 | 58 | 36 mins |
| 5 | Francisco Joaquin Perez Rufete | 1 | 99 | 77 | 22 mins |

## KEY PLAYERS - DEFENDERS

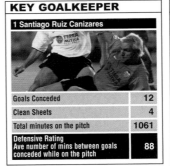

1 Amadeo Carboni

| | |
|---|---|
| Goals Conceded in Champions League | 4 |
| Clean Sheets<br>In League games when he played at least than 70 minutes | 5 |
| Defensive Rating<br>Ave number of mins between goals conceded while on the pitch | 222 |
| Club Defensive Rating<br>Average number of mins between goals conceded by the club this season | 105 |

| | PLAYER | CONCEDED | CLEAN SHEETS | DEF RATE |
|---|---|---|---|---|
| 2 | Cristobal Emilio Curro Torres | 5 | 4 | 126 mins |
| 3 | Mauricio Andres Pellegrino | 10 | 5 | 98 mins |
| 4 | Roberto Fabian Ayala | 11 | 4 | 98 mins |
| 5 | Anthony Reveillere | 7 | 1 | 77 mins |

## KEY GOALKEEPER

1 Santiago Ruiz Canizares

| | |
|---|---|
| Goals Conceded | 12 |
| Clean Sheets | 4 |
| Total minutes on the pitch | 1061 |
| Defensive Rating<br>Ave number of mins between goals conceded while on the pitch | 88 |

## TOP POINT EARNERS

| | PLAYER | GAMES | AV PTS |
|---|---|---|---|
| 1 | Carlos Marchena | 2 | 3.00 |
| 2 | Pablo Aimar | 7 | 2.43 |
| 3 | Francisco Rufete | 6 | 2.33 |
| 4 | Vicente | 3 | 2.33 |
| 5 | Amadeo Carboni | 8 | 2.25 |
| 6 | Miguel Angulo | 5 | 2.20 |
| 7 | Curro Torres | 7 | 2.14 |
| 8 | John Alieu Carew | 8 | 2.13 |
| 9 | David Aliques Albelda | 10 | 2.10 |
| 10 | S Ruiz Canizares | 10 | 2.10 |
| | CLUB AVERAGE: | | 2.08 |

**Note:** Points awarded for league section only

# NEWCASTLE UNITED

ENGLAND
Phase 2 - 3rd Group A

| | | | | | | |
|---|---|---|---|---|---|---|
| 1 | 3ql1 | Zeljeznicar | A | W | 1-0 | Dyer 56 |
| 2 | 3ql2 | Zeljeznicar | H | W | 4-0 | Dyer 24; Lua Lua 37; Viana 74; Shearer 80 |
| 3 | gpe | Dinamo Kiev | A | L | 0-2 | |
| 4 | gpe | Feyenoord | H | L | 0-1 | |
| 5 | gpe | Juventus | A | L | 0-2 | |
| 6 | gpe | Juventus | H | W | 1-0 | Griffin 62 |
| 7 | gpe | Dinamo Kiev | H | W | 2-1 | Speed 58; Shearer 69 pen |
| 8 | gpe | Feyenoord | A | W | 3-2 | Bellamy 45,90; Viana 49 |
| 9 | gpa | Inter Milan | H | L | 1-4 | Solano 72 |
| 10 | gpa | Barcelona | A | L | 1-3 | Ameobi 24 |
| 11 | gpa | B Leverkusen | A | W | 3-1 | Ameobi 5,15; LuaLua 32 |
| 12 | gpa | B Leverkusen | H | W | 3-1 | Shearer 5,11,36 pen |
| 13 | gpa | Inter Milan | A | D | 2-2 | Shearer 42,49 |
| 14 | gpa | Barcelona | H | L | 0-2 | |

## KEY GOALSCORERS

1 Alan Shearer

| Goals in the Champions League | 7 | Player Strike Rate | 151 |
|---|---|---|---|
| Contribution to Attacking Power | 62 | Club Strike Rate | 60 |

| | PLAYER | GOALS | POWER | S RATE |
|---|---|---|---|---|
| 2 | Kieron Dyer | 2 | 60 | 485 mins |
| 3 | Nolberto Solano | 1 | 74 | 892 mins |
| 4 | Andrew Griffin | 1 | 75 | 978 mins |
| 5 | Gary Speed | 1 | 54 | 1080 mins |

**Phase 1 GROUP E**

| | P | W | D | L | F | A | DIF | PTS |
|---|---|---|---|---|---|---|---|---|
| Juventus | 6 | 4 | 1 | 1 | 12 | 3 | 9 | 13 |
| **Newcastle** | **6** | **3** | **0** | **3** | **6** | **8** | **-2** | **9** |
| Dynamo Kiev | 6 | 2 | 1 | 3 | 6 | 9 | -3 | 7 |
| Feyenoord | 6 | 1 | 2 | 3 | 4 | 8 | -4 | 5 |

**Phase 2 GROUP A**

| | P | W | D | L | F | A | DIF | PTS |
|---|---|---|---|---|---|---|---|---|
| Barcelona | 6 | 5 | 1 | 0 | 12 | 2 | 10 | 16 |
| Inter Milan | 6 | 3 | 2 | 1 | 11 | 8 | 3 | 11 |
| **Newcastle** | **6** | **2** | **1** | **3** | **10** | **13** | **-3** | **7** |
| Bayer Leverkusen | 6 | 0 | 0 | 6 | 5 | 15 | -10 | 0 |

## KEY PLAYER APPEARANCES

6 Kieron Dyer — Midfielder

| | |
|---|---|
| Age (on 01/07/03) | 24 |
| In the squad | 12 |
| Total minutes on the pitch | 969 |
| Goals | 2 |
| Yellow cards | 0 |
| Red cards | 0 |
| Home Country | England |

| | PLAYER | POS | AGE | SQUAD | MINS ON | GOALS | CARDS(Y/R) | | HOME COUNTRY |
|---|---|---|---|---|---|---|---|---|---|
| 1 | Shay Given | GK | 27 | 14 | 1080 | 0 | 0 | 0 | Rep of Ireland |
| 2 | Gary Speed | MID | 33 | 12 | 1080 | 1 | 0 | 0 | Wales |
| 3 | Alan Shearer | ATT | 33 | 12 | 1058 | 7 | 1 | 0 | England |
| 4 | Aaron Hughes | DEF | 23 | 14 | 993 | 0 | 1 | 0 | N Ireland |
| 5 | Andrew Griffin | DEF | 24 | 14 | 978 | 1 | 1 | 0 | England |
| 6 | Kieron Dyer | MID | 24 | 12 | 969 | 2 | 0 | 0 | England |
| 7 | Andy O'Brien | DEF | 24 | 14 | 933 | 0 | 0 | 0 | Rep of Ireland |
| 8 | Nolberto Solano | MID | 28 | 13 | 892 | 1 | 0 | 0 | Peru |
| 9 | Laurent Robert | MID | 28 | 11 | 841 | 0 | 0 | 0 | France |
| 10 | Oliver Bernard | DEF | 23 | 13 | 747 | 0 | 1 | 0 | France |
| 11 | Jermaine Jenas | MID | 20 | 13 | 709 | 0 | 0 | 0 | England |
| 12 | Nikos Dabizas | DEF | 29 | 9 | 674 | 0 | 3 | 0 | Greece |
| 13 | Titus Bramble | DEF | 21 | 11 | 656 | 0 | 1 | 0 | England |
| 14 | Lomana Tresor LuaLua | ATT | 22 | 14 | 465 | 2 | 2 | 0 | Congo DR |
| 15 | Hugo Viana | MID | 20 | 12 | 462 | 2 | 0 | 0 | Portugal |
| 16 | Craig Bellamy | ATT | 23 | 6 | 440 | 2 | 2 | 1 | Wales |
| 17 | Shola Ameobi | ATT | 21 | 14 | 416 | 3 | 2 | 0 | England |
| 18 | Steve Harper | GK | 29 | 14 | 180 | 0 | 0 | 0 | England |
| 19 | Stephen Caldwell | DEF | 22 | 7 | 95 | 0 | 0 | 0 | Scotland |
| 20 | Brian Kerr | MID | 21 | 6 | 81 | 0 | 0 | 0 | Scotland |
| 21 | Michael Chopra | ATT | 19 | 2 | 14 | 0 | 0 | 0 | England |

# BAYER LEVERKUSEN

GERMANY
Phase 2 - 4th Group A

| | | | | | | |
|---|---|---|---|---|---|---|
| 1 | gpf | Olympiakos | A | L | 2-6 | Eleftheropoulos 22 og; Schneider 78 pen |
| 2 | gpf | Man Utd | H | L | 1-2 | Berbatov 52 |
| 3 | gpf | Maccabi Haifa | A | W | 2-0 | Babic 31,64 |
| 4 | gpf | Maccabi Haifa | H | W | 2-1 | Babic 45; Juan 67 |
| 5 | gpf | Olympiakos | H | W | 2-0 | Juan 14; Schneider 89 pen |
| 6 | gpf | Man Utd | A | L | 0-2 | |
| 7 | gpa | Barcelona | H | L | 1-2 | Berbatov 39 |
| 8 | gpa | Inter Milan | A | L | 2-3 | Zivkovic 63; Franca 90 |
| 9 | gpa | Newcastle | H | L | 1-3 | Franca 25 |
| 10 | gpa | Newcastle | A | L | 1-3 | Babic 73 |
| 11 | gpa | Barcelona | A | L | 0-2 | |
| 12 | gpa | Inter Milan | H | L | 0-2 | |

## KEY GOALSCORERS

1 Marko Babic

| Goals in the Champions League | 4 | Player Strike Rate | 145 |
|---|---|---|---|
| Contribution to Attacking Power | 64 | Club Strike Rate | 77 |

| | PLAYER | GOALS | POWER | S RATE |
|---|---|---|---|---|
| 2 | Bernd Schneider | 2 | 60 | 366 mins |
| 3 | Boris Zivkovic | 1 | 62 | 692 mins |

**Note:** Must have played at least 500 mins to qualify for tables

**Phase 1 GROUP F**

| | P | W | D | L | F | A | DIF | PTS |
|---|---|---|---|---|---|---|---|---|
| Manchester United | 6 | 5 | 0 | 1 | 16 | 8 | 8 | 15 |
| **Bayer Leverkusen** | **6** | **3** | **0** | **3** | **9** | **11** | **-2** | **9** |
| Maccabi Haifa | 6 | 2 | 1 | 3 | 12 | 12 | 0 | 7 |
| Olympiakos | 6 | 1 | 1 | 4 | 11 | 17 | -6 | 4 |

**Phase 2 GROUP A**

| | P | W | D | L | F | A | DIF | PTS |
|---|---|---|---|---|---|---|---|---|
| Barcelona | 6 | 5 | 1 | 0 | 12 | 2 | 10 | 16 |
| Inter Milan | 6 | 3 | 2 | 1 | 11 | 8 | 3 | 11 |
| Newcastle | 6 | 2 | 1 | 3 | 10 | 13 | -3 | 7 |
| **Bayer Leverkusen** | **6** | **0** | **0** | **6** | **5** | **15** | **-10** | **0** |

## KEY PLAYER APPEARANCES

1 Yildiray Basturk — Midfielder

| | |
|---|---|
| Age (on 01/07/03) | 24 |
| In the squad | 11 |
| Total minutes on the pitch | 920 |
| Goals | 0 |
| Yellow cards | 4 |
| Red cards | 0 |
| Home Country | Turkey |

| | PLAYER | POS | AGE | SQUAD | MINS ON | GOALS | CARDS(Y/R) | | HOME COUNTRY |
|---|---|---|---|---|---|---|---|---|---|
| 1 | Yildiray Basturk | MID | 24 | 11 | 920 | 0 | 4 | 0 | Turkey |
| 2 | Hans-Jorg Butt | GK | 29 | 12 | 900 | 0 | 1 | 0 | Germany |
| 3 | Carsten Ramelow | MID | 29 | 9 | 765 | 0 | 1 | 0 | Germany |
| 4 | Hanno Balitsch | MID | 22 | 11 | 746 | 0 | 3 | 0 | Germany |
| 5 | Bernd Schneider | MID | 29 | 10 | 731 | 2 | 1 | 0 | Germany |
| 6 | Boris Zivkovic | DEF | 27 | 12 | 692 | 1 | 0 | 0 | Croatia |
| 7 | Oliver Neuville | ATT | 30 | 10 | 628 | 0 | 1 | 0 | Germany |
| 8 | Jan Simak | MID | 24 | 12 | 616 | 0 | 1 | 0 | Czech Republic |
| 9 | Thomas Kleine | DEF | 25 | 9 | 590 | 0 | 3 | 0 | Germany |
| 10 | Thomas Brdaric | ATT | 28 | 12 | 586 | 0 | 1 | 0 | Germany |
| 11 | Marko Babic | MID | 22 | 12 | 578 | 4 | 0 | 0 | Croatia |
| 12 | Diego Placente | DEF | 26 | 7 | 540 | 0 | 2 | 0 | Argentina |
| 13 | Lucimar da Silva Lucio | DEF | 25 | 6 | 540 | 0 | 0 | 0 | Brazil |
| 14 | Pascal Ojigwe | MID | 26 | 10 | 487 | 0 | 1 | 0 | Nigeria |
| 15 | Franca | ATT | 27 | 11 | 473 | 2 | 0 | 0 | Brazil |
| 16 | Dimitar Berbatov | ATT | 22 | 7 | 454 | 2 | 0 | 0 | Bulgaria |
| 17 | Radoslaw Kaluzny | MID | 29 | 4 | 282 | 0 | 1 | 0 | Poland |
| 18 | Silveira dos Santos Juan | DEF | 24 | 3 | 225 | 2 | 0 | 0 | Brazil |
| 19 | Cristiano Gomez Cris | DEF | 26 | 4 | 217 | 0 | 2 | 0 | Brazil |
| 20 | Daniel Bierofka | MID | 24 | 10 | 211 | 0 | 0 | 0 | Germany |
| 21 | Frank Juric | GK | 29 | 7 | 180 | 0 | 0 | 0 | Australia |
| 22 | Zoltan Sebescen | MID | 27 | 2 | 180 | 0 | 1 | 0 | Germany |

# ARSENAL

ENGLAND
Phase 2 - 3rd Group B

| | | | | | | |
|---|---|---|---|---|---|---|
| 1 | gpa | B Dortmund | H | W | 2-0 | Bergkamp 61; Ljungberg 77 |
| 2 | gpa | PSV Eindhoven | A | W | 4-0 | Silva 1; Ljungberg 66; Henry 81,90 |
| 3 | gpa | Auxerre | A | W | 1-0 | Silva 48 |
| 4 | gpa | Auxerre | H | L | 1-2 | Kanu 53 |
| 5 | gpa | B Dortmund | A | L | 1-2 | Henry 18 |
| 6 | gpa | PSV Eindhoven | H | D | 0-0 | |
| 7 | gpb | Roma | A | W | 3-1 | Henry 6,70,75 |
| 8 | gpb | Valencia | H | D | 0-0 | |
| 9 | gpb | Ajax | H | D | 1-1 | Wiltord 5 |
| 10 | gpb | Ajax | A | D | 0-0 | |
| 11 | gpb | Roma | H | D | 1-1 | Vieira 12 |
| 12 | gpb | Valencia | A | L | 1-2 | Henry 49 |

## KEY GOALSCORERS

1 Thierry Henry

| | | | |
|---|---|---|---|
| Goals in the Champions League | 7 | Player Strike Rate | 146 |
| Contribution to Attacking Power | 68 | Club Strike Rate | 72 |

| | PLAYER | GOALS | POWER | S RATE |
|---|---|---|---|---|
| 2 | Fredrik Ljungberg | 2 | 56 | 312 mins |
| 3 | Gilberto Silva | 2 | 63 | 477 mins |
| 4 | Dennis Bergkamp | 1 | 86 | 521 mins |
| 5 | Sylvain Wiltord | 1 | 57 | 864 mins |

Phase 1 GROUP A

| | P | W | D | L | F | A | DIF | PTS |
|---|---|---|---|---|---|---|---|---|
| **Arsenal** | **6** | **3** | **1** | **2** | **9** | **4** | **5** | **10** |
| Borussia Dortmund | 6 | 3 | 1 | 2 | 8 | 6 | 2 | 10 |
| Auxerre | 6 | 2 | 1 | 3 | 4 | 7 | -3 | 7 |
| PSV Eindhoven | 6 | 1 | 2 | 3 | 5 | 9 | -4 | 6 |

Phase 2 GROUP B

| | P | W | D | L | F | A | DIF | PTS |
|---|---|---|---|---|---|---|---|---|
| Valencia | 6 | 2 | 3 | 1 | 5 | 6 | -1 | 9 |
| Ajax | 6 | 1 | 5 | 0 | 6 | 5 | 1 | 8 |
| **Arsenal** | **6** | **1** | **4** | **1** | **6** | **5** | **1** | **7** |
| Roma | 6 | 1 | 2 | 3 | 7 | 8 | -1 | 5 |

## KEY PLAYER APPEARANCES

4 Sol Campbell — Defender

| | |
|---|---|
| Age (on 01/07/03) | 28 |
| In the squad | 10 |
| Total minutes on the pitch | 900 |
| Goals | 0 |
| Yellow cards | 1 |
| Red cards | 0 |
| Home Country | England |

| | PLAYER | POS | AGE | SQUAD | MINS ON | GOALS | CARDS(Y/R) | | HOME COUNTRY |
|---|---|---|---|---|---|---|---|---|---|
| 1 | Thierry Henry | ATT | 25 | 12 | 1020 | 7 | 0 | 0 | France |
| 2 | Patrick Vieira | MID | 27 | 12 | 1013 | 1 | 3 | 0 | France |
| 3 | Gilberto Silva | MID | 26 | 12 | 954 | 2 | 0 | 0 | Brazil |
| 4 | Sol Campbell | DEF | 28 | 10 | 900 | 0 | 1 | 0 | England |
| 5 | Pascal Cygan | DEF | 29 | 12 | 898 | 0 | 0 | 0 | France |
| 6 | Sylvain Wiltord | ATT | 29 | 12 | 864 | 1 | 0 | 0 | France |
| 7 | Lauren | DEF | 26 | 10 | 811 | 0 | 1 | 0 | Cameroon |
| 8 | Ashley Cole | DEF | 22 | 10 | 810 | 0 | 1 | 0 | England |
| 9 | David Seaman | GK | 39 | 9 | 765 | 0 | 0 | 0 | England |
| 10 | Robert Pires | MID | 29 | 9 | 692 | 0 | 2 | 0 | France |
| 11 | Fredrik Ljungberg | MID | 26 | 10 | 623 | 2 | 0 | 0 | Sweden |
| 12 | Dennis Bergkamp | ATT | 34 | 7 | 521 | 1 | 0 | 0 | Holland |
| 13 | Martin Keown | DEF | 36 | 6 | 285 | 0 | 0 | 0 | England |
| 14 | Oleg Luzhny | DEF | 34 | 8 | 259 | 0 | 0 | 0 | Ukraine |
| 15 | Nwankwo Kanu | ATT | 26 | 9 | 225 | 1 | 0 | 0 | Nigeria |
| 16 | Habib Kolo Toure | MID | 22 | 9 | 224 | 0 | 2 | 1 | Ivory Coast |
| 17 | Van Bronckhorst | MID | 28 | 6 | 196 | 0 | 1 | 0 | Holland |
| 18 | Rami Shaaban | GK | 28 | 4 | 180 | 0 | 0 | 0 | Sweden |
| 19 | Stuart Taylor | GK | 22 | 10 | 135 | 0 | 0 | 0 | England |
| 20 | Edu | MID | 25 | 9 | 133 | 0 | 0 | 0 | Brazil |
| 21 | Francis Jeffers | ATT | 22 | 10 | 130 | 0 | 0 | 0 | England |
| 22 | Igors Stepanovs | DEF | 27 | 8 | 90 | 0 | 0 | 0 | Latvia |

# ROMA

ITALY
Phase 2 - 4th Group B

| | | | | | | |
|---|---|---|---|---|---|---|
| 1 | gpc | Real Madrid | H | L | 0-3 | |
| 2 | gpc | AEK Athens | A | D | 0-0 | |
| 3 | gpc | Genk | A | W | 1-0 | Cassano 81 |
| 4 | gpc | Genk | H | D | 0-0 | |
| 5 | gpc | Real Madrid | A | W | 1-0 | Totti 27 |
| 6 | gpc | AEK Athens | H | D | 1-1 | Delvecchio 40 |
| 7 | gpb | Arsenal | H | L | 1-3 | Cassano 4 |
| 8 | gpb | Ajax | A | L | 1-2 | Batistuta 89 |
| 9 | gpb | Valencia | H | L | 0-1 | |
| 10 | gpb | Valencia | A | W | 3-0 | Totti 24,30; Emerson 36 |
| 11 | gpb | Arsenal | A | D | 1-1 | Cassano 45 |
| 12 | gpb | Ajax | H | D | 1-1 | Cassano 24 |

## KEY GOALSCORERS

1 Antonio Cassano

| | | | |
|---|---|---|---|
| Goals in the Champions League | 4 | Player Strike Rate | 160 |
| Contribution to Attacking Power | 79 | Club Strike Rate | 108 |

| | PLAYER | GOALS | POWER | S RATE |
|---|---|---|---|---|
| 2 | Emerson | 1 | 99 | 990 mins |

**Note:** Must have played at least 500 mins to qualify for tables

Phase 1 GROUP C

| | P | W | D | L | F | A | DIF | PTS |
|---|---|---|---|---|---|---|---|---|
| Real Madrid | 6 | 2 | 3 | 1 | 15 | 7 | 8 | 9 |
| **Roma** | **6** | **2** | **3** | **1** | **3** | **4** | **-1** | **9** |
| AEK Athens | 6 | 0 | 6 | 0 | 7 | 7 | 0 | 6 |
| Genk | 6 | 0 | 4 | 2 | 2 | 9 | -7 | 4 |

Phase 2 GROUP B

| | P | W | D | L | F | A | DIF | PTS |
|---|---|---|---|---|---|---|---|---|
| Valencia | 6 | 2 | 3 | 1 | 5 | 6 | -1 | 9 |
| Ajax | 6 | 1 | 5 | 0 | 6 | 5 | 1 | 8 |
| Arsenal | 6 | 1 | 4 | 1 | 6 | 5 | 1 | 7 |
| **Roma** | **6** | **1** | **2** | **3** | **7** | **8** | **-1** | **5** |

## KEY PLAYER APPEARANCES

12 Francesco Totti — Attacker

| | |
|---|---|
| Age (on 01/07/03) | 26 |
| In the squad | 6 |
| Total minutes on the pitch | 469 |
| Goals | 3 |
| Yellow cards | 1 |
| Red cards | 1 |
| Home Country | Italy |

| | PLAYER | POS | AGE | SQUAD | MINS ON | GOALS | CARDS(Y/R) | | HOME COUNTRY |
|---|---|---|---|---|---|---|---|---|---|
| 1 | Marcos de Moraes Cafu | DEF | 33 | 12 | 1015 | 0 | 0 | 0 | Brazil |
| 2 | Christian Panucci | DEF | 30 | 11 | 990 | 0 | 1 | 0 | Italy |
| 3 | Emerson | MID | 27 | 11 | 990 | 1 | 4 | 0 | Brazil |
| 4 | Walter Adrian Samuel | DEF | 25 | 10 | 900 | 0 | 5 | 0 | Argentina |
| 5 | Vincent Candela | DEF | 29 | 10 | 900 | 0 | 2 | 0 | France |
| 6 | Francisco Lima | MID | 32 | 11 | 849 | 0 | 0 | 0 | Brazil |
| 7 | Damiano Tommasi | MID | 29 | 10 | 820 | 0 | 2 | 0 | Italy |
| 8 | Francesco Antonioli | GK | 33 | 12 | 810 | 0 | 0 | 0 | Italy |
| 9 | Antonio Cassano | ATT | 20 | 12 | 638 | 4 | 1 | 0 | Italy |
| 10 | Jonathan Zebina | DEF | 24 | 10 | 603 | 0 | 2 | 0 | France |
| 11 | Vincenzo Montella | ATT | 29 | 11 | 565 | 0 | 1 | 0 | Italy |
| 12 | Francesco Totti | ATT | 26 | 6 | 469 | 3 | 1 | 1 | Italy |
| 13 | Aldair | DEF | 37 | 7 | 449 | 0 | 3 | 0 | Brazil |
| 14 | Marco Delvecchio | ATT | 30 | 6 | 402 | 1 | 2 | 0 | Italy |
| 15 | Leandro Damian Cufre | DEF | 25 | 9 | 317 | 0 | 1 | 0 | Argentina |
| 16 | Gabriel Batistuta | ATT | 34 | 6 | 302 | 1 | 2 | 0 | Argentina |
| 17 | Ivan Pellizzoli | GK | 22 | 8 | 270 | 0 | 0 | 0 | Italy |
| 18 | Traianos Dellas | DEF | 27 | 7 | 202 | 0 | 0 | 0 | Greece |
| 19 | Gianni Guigou | DEF | 28 | 9 | 177 | 0 | 1 | 0 | Uruguay |
| 20 | Davide Bombardini | MID | 29 | 6 | 47 | 0 | 0 | 0 | Italy |
| 21 | Josep Guardiola | MID | 32 | 7 | 45 | 0 | 0 | 0 | Spain |
| 22 | Ivan Tomic | MID | 27 | 2 | 38 | 0 | 0 | 0 | Serbia & Mont |

# BORUSSIA DORTMUND

GERMANY
Phase 2 - 3rd Group C

| | | | | | | |
|---|---|---|---|---|---|---|
| 1 | gpa | Arsenal | A | L | 0-2 | |
| 2 | gpa | Auxerre | H | W | 2-1 | Koller 6; Amoroso 78 |
| 3 | gpa | PSV Eindhoven | A | W | 3-1 | Koller 21; Rosicky 69; Amoroso 90 |
| 4 | gpa | PSV Eindhoven | H | D | 1-1 | Koller 10 |
| 5 | gpa | Arsenal | H | W | 2-1 | Gilberto 38 og; Rosicky 63 pen |
| 6 | gpa | Auxerre | A | L | 0-1 | |
| 7 | gpc | Lokomotiv M | A | W | 2-1 | Frings 33; Koller 43 |
| 8 | gpc | AC Milan | H | L | 0-1 | |
| 9 | gpc | Real Madrid | A | L | 1-2 | Koller 30 |
| 10 | gpc | Real Madrid | H | D | 1-1 | Koller 21 |
| 11 | gpc | Lokomotiv M | H | W | 3-0 | Frings 39; Koller 58; Amoroso 66 |
| 12 | gpc | AC Milan | A | W | 1-0 | Koller 80 |

## KEY GOALSCORERS

1 Jan Koller

e-on

| Goals in the Champions League | 8 | Player Strike Rate | 121 |
|---|---|---|---|
| Contribution to Attacking Power | 60 | Club Strike Rate | 68 |

| | PLAYER | GOALS | POWER | S RATE |
|---|---|---|---|---|
| 2 | Tomas Rosicky | 2 | 65 | 296 mins |
| 3 | Torsten Frings | 2 | 70 | 493 mins |

**Note:** Must have played at least 500 mins to qualify for tables

**Phase 1 GROUP A**

| | P | W | D | L | F | A | DIF | PTS |
|---|---|---|---|---|---|---|---|---|
| Arsenal | 6 | 3 | 1 | 2 | 9 | 4 | 5 | 10 |
| **Borussia Dortmund** | **6** | **3** | **1** | **2** | **8** | **6** | **2** | **10** |
| Auxerre | 6 | 2 | 1 | 3 | 4 | 7 | -3 | 7 |
| PSV Eindhoven | 6 | 1 | 2 | 3 | 5 | 9 | -4 | 6 |

**Phase 2 GROUP C**

| | P | W | D | L | F | A | DIF | PTS |
|---|---|---|---|---|---|---|---|---|
| AC Milan | 6 | 4 | 0 | 2 | 5 | 4 | 1 | 12 |
| Real Madrid | 6 | 3 | 2 | 1 | 9 | 6 | 3 | 11 |
| **Borussia Dortmund** | **6** | **3** | **1** | **2** | **8** | **5** | **3** | **10** |
| Lokomotiv Moscow | 6 | 0 | 1 | 5 | 3 | 10 | -7 | 1 |

## KEY PLAYER APPEARANCES

11 Tomas Rosicky — Midfielder

| | |
|---|---|
| Age (on 01/07/03) | 22 |
| In the squad | 8 |
| Total minutes on the pitch | 591 |
| Goals | 2 |
| Yellow cards | 0 |
| Red cards | 0 |
| Home Country | Czech Republic |

| | PLAYER | POS | AGE | SQUAD | MINS ON | GOALS | CARDS(Y | /R) | HOME COUNTRY |
|---|---|---|---|---|---|---|---|---|---|
| 1 | Jens Lehmann | GK | 33 | 12 | 1080 | 0 | 1 | 0 | Germany |
| 2 | Torsten Frings | MID | 26 | 12 | 986 | 2 | 2 | 0 | Germany |
| 3 | Jan Koller | ATT | 30 | 11 | 965 | 8 | 1 | 0 | Czech Republic |
| 4 | Ewerthon | ATT | 22 | 12 | 947 | 0 | 1 | 0 | Brazil |
| 5 | De Deus Santos | MID | 25 | 12 | 915 | 0 | 2 | 0 | Brazil |
| 6 | Christian Worns | DEF | 31 | 11 | 900 | 0 | 2 | 0 | Germany |
| 7 | Christoph Metzelder | DEF | 22 | 10 | 900 | 0 | 0 | 0 | Germany |
| 8 | Sebastian Kehl | DEF | 23 | 12 | 894 | 0 | 1 | 0 | Germany |
| 9 | Stefan Reuter | DEF | 36 | 11 | 762 | 0 | 2 | 0 | Germany |
| 10 | Ferreira Evanilson | MID | 27 | 10 | 718 | 0 | 1 | 0 | Brazil |
| 11 | Tomas Rosicky | MID | 22 | 8 | 591 | 2 | 0 | 0 | Czech Republic |
| 12 | Ahmed Reda Madouni | DEF | 22 | 12 | 533 | 0 | 1 | 0 | France |
| 13 | Jorg Heinrich | MID | 33 | 8 | 464 | 0 | 1 | 0 | Germany |
| 14 | Marcio Amoroso | ATT | 29 | 11 | 424 | 3 | 0 | 0 | Brazil |
| 15 | Lars Ricken | MID | 26 | 11 | 373 | 0 | 0 | 0 | Germany |
| 16 | Juergen Kohler | DEF | 37 | 1 | 90 | 0 | 0 | 0 | Germany |
| 17 | Juan Ramon Fernandez | DEF | 23 | 2 | 71 | 0 | 0 | 0 | Argentina |
| 18 | Guiseppe Reina | ATT | 31 | 8 | 68 | 0 | 0 | 0 | Germany |
| 19 | Guy Demel | MID | 22 | 3 | 65 | 0 | 1 | 0 | France |
| 20 | Heiko Herrlich | ATT | 31 | 10 | 27 | 0 | 0 | 0 | Germany |
| 21 | David Odonkor | ATT | 19 | 2 | 17 | 0 | 0 | 0 | Germany |

# LOKOMOTIV MOSCOW

RUSSIA
Phase 2 - 4th Group C

| | | | | | | |
|---|---|---|---|---|---|---|
| 1 | 3ql1 | Grazer AK | A | W | 2-0 | Lekseto 6; Loskov 41 |
| 2 | 3ql2 | Grazer AK | H | D | 3-3 | Ignashevitch 6; Evseev 32; Cesar 45 |
| 3 | gph | Galatasaray | H | L | 0-2 | |
| 4 | gph | Club Brugge | A | D | 0-0 | |
| 5 | gph | Barcelona | H | L | 1-3 | Obiorah 56 |
| 6 | gph | Barcelona | A | L | 0-1 | |
| 7 | gph | Galatasaray | A | W | 2-1 | Loskov 70; Evseev 75 |
| 8 | gph | Club Brugge | H | W | 2-0 | Cesar 44; Loskov 90 |
| 9 | gpc | B Dortmund | H | L | 1-2 | Ignashevitch 31 |
| 10 | gpc | Real Madrid | A | D | 2-2 | Obiorah 47; Mnguni 74 |
| 11 | gpc | AC Milan | A | L | 0-1 | |
| 12 | gpc | AC Milan | H | L | 0-1 | |
| 13 | gpc | B Dortmund | A | L | 0-3 | |
| 14 | gpc | Real Madrid | H | L | 0-1 | |

## KEY GOALSCORERS

1 Julio Cesar

| Goals in the Champions League | 2 | Player Strike Rate | 311 |
|---|---|---|---|
| Contribution to Attacking Power | 155 | Club Strike Rate | 96 |

| | PLAYER | GOALS | POWER | S RATE |
|---|---|---|---|---|
| 2 | Dmitri Loskov | 3 | 85 | 343 mins |
| 3 | Vadim Evseev | 2 | 87 | 567 mins |
| 4 | Sergei Ignashevitch | 2 | 96 | 627 mins |
| 5 | Jacob Lekseto | 1 | 76 | 990 mins |

**Phase 1 GROUP H**

| | P | W | D | L | F | A | DIF | PTS |
|---|---|---|---|---|---|---|---|---|
| Barcelona | 6 | 6 | 0 | 0 | 13 | 4 | 9 | 18 |
| **Lokomotiv Moscow** | **6** | **2** | **1** | **3** | **5** | **7** | **-2** | **7** |
| Club Brugge | 6 | 1 | 2 | 3 | 5 | 7 | -2 | 5 |
| Galatasaray | 6 | 1 | 1 | 4 | 5 | 10 | -5 | 4 |

**Phase 2 GROUP C**

| | P | W | D | L | F | A | DIF | PTS |
|---|---|---|---|---|---|---|---|---|
| AC Milan | 6 | 4 | 0 | 2 | 5 | 4 | 1 | 12 |
| Real Madrid | 6 | 3 | 2 | 1 | 9 | 6 | 3 | 11 |
| Borussia Dortmund | 6 | 3 | 1 | 2 | 8 | 5 | 3 | 10 |
| **Lokomotiv Moscow** | **6** | **0** | **1** | **5** | **3** | **10** | **-7** | **1** |

## KEY PLAYER APPEARANCES

14 James Obiorah — Attacker

| | |
|---|---|
| Age (on 01/07/03) | 24 |
| In the squad | 8 |
| Total minutes on the pitch | 383 |
| Goals | 2 |
| Yellow cards | 2 |
| Red cards | 0 |
| Home Country | Nigeria |

| | PLAYER | POS | AGE | SQUAD | MINS ON | GOALS | CARDS(Y | /R) | HOME COUNTRY |
|---|---|---|---|---|---|---|---|---|---|
| 1 | Sergei Ovchinnikov | GK | 32 | 16 | 1260 | 0 | 1 | 0 | Russia |
| 2 | Sergei Ignashevitch | DEF | 23 | 14 | 1253 | 2 | 1 | 0 | Russia |
| 3 | Vladimir Maminov | MID | 28 | 14 | 1160 | 0 | 0 | 0 | Russia |
| 4 | Vadim Evseev | MID | 27 | 13 | 1133 | 2 | 4 | 0 | Russia |
| 5 | Gennadi Nizhergorodov | DEF | 26 | 12 | 1080 | 0 | 3 | 0 | Russia |
| 6 | Dmitri Loskov | MID | 29 | 12 | 1028 | 3 | 5 | 1 | Russia |
| 7 | Jacob Lekseto | DEF | 29 | 12 | 990 | 1 | 5 | 0 | South Africa |
| 8 | Dmitri Sennikov | MID | 27 | 12 | 968 | 0 | 3 | 0 | Russia |
| 9 | Oleg Pashinin | DEF | 28 | 12 | 959 | 0 | 2 | 0 | Russia |
| 10 | Rouslan Pimenov | ATT | 21 | 12 | 940 | 0 | 1 | 0 | Russia |
| 11 | Julio Cesar | MID | 23 | 13 | 621 | 2 | 0 | 0 | Brazil |
| 12 | Maxim Buznikin | ATT | 26 | 12 | 422 | 0 | 0 | 0 | Russia |
| 13 | Milan Orbradovic | DEF | 25 | 12 | 405 | 0 | 1 | 0 | Serbia & Mont |
| 14 | James Obiorah | ATT | 24 | 8 | 383 | 2 | 2 | 0 | Nigeria |
| 15 | Thabo Mnguni | MID | 29 | 11 | 341 | 1 | 1 | 0 | South Africa |
| 16 | Marat Izmailov | MID | 20 | 4 | 315 | 0 | 0 | 0 | Russia |
| 17 | Yuriy Drozdov | MID | 31 | 14 | 306 | 0 | 0 | 0 | Russia |
| 18 | Narvik Sirkhaev | MID | 29 | 9 | 202 | 0 | 0 | 0 | Azerbaijan |
| 19 | Armando Adamu | ATT | 23 | 8 | 36 | 0 | 0 | 0 | Ghana |
| 20 | Nemanja Vucicevic | ATT | 23 | 11 | 35 | 0 | 0 | 0 | Serbia & Mont |

# FC BASEL

SWITZERLAND
Phase 2 - 3rd Group D

| | | | | | | |
|---|---|---|---|---|---|---|
| 1 | 3ql1 | Celtic | A | L | 1-3 | Gimenez 2 |
| 2 | 3ql2 | Celtic | H | W | 2-0 | Gimenez 8; Yakin, H 22 |
| 3 | gpb | S Moscow | H | W | 2-0 | Yakin, H 50; Rossi 55 |
| 4 | gpb | Liverpool | A | D | 1-1 | Rossi 42 |
| 5 | gpb | Valencia | A | L | 2-6 | Rossi 46; Yakin, H 90 |
| 6 | gpb | Valencia | H | D | 2-2 | Ergic 32,90 |
| 7 | gpb | S Moscow | A | W | 2-0 | Rossi 18; Gimenez 89 |
| 8 | gpb | Liverpool | H | D | 3-3 | Rossi 2; Gimenez 22; Atouba 29 |
| 9 | gpd | Man Utd | H | L | 1-3 | Gimenez 1 |
| 10 | gpd | Juventus | A | L | 0-4 | |
| 11 | gpd | Deportivo | H | W | 1-0 | Yakin, H 30 |
| 12 | gpd | Deportivo | A | L | 0-1 | |
| 13 | gpd | Man Utd | A | D | 1-1 | Gimenez 14 |
| 14 | gpd | Juventus | H | W | 2-1 | Cantaluppi 38; Gimenez 90 |

## KEY GOALSCORERS

1 Christian Gimenez

| | | | |
|---|---|---|---|
| Goals in the Champions League | 7 | Player Strike Rate | 147 |
| Contribution to Attacking Power | 64 | Club Strike Rate | 63 |

| | PLAYER | GOALS | POWER | S RATE |
|---|---|---|---|---|
| 2 | Julio Rossi | 5 | 54 | 186 mins |
| 3 | Ivan Ergic | 2 | 44 | 266 mins |
| 4 | Hakan Yakin | 4 | 63 | 301 mins |
| 5 | Timothee Atouba | 1 | 65 | 975 mins |

**Phase 1 GROUP B**

| | P | W | D | L | F | A | DIF | PTS |
|---|---|---|---|---|---|---|---|---|
| Valencia | 6 | 5 | 1 | 0 | 17 | 4 | 13 | 16 |
| **FC Basel** | **6** | **2** | **3** | **1** | **12** | **12** | **0** | **9** |
| Liverpool | 6 | 2 | 2 | 2 | 12 | 8 | 4 | 8 |
| Spartak Moscow | 6 | 0 | 0 | 6 | 1 | 18 | -17 | 0 |

**Phase 2 GROUP D**

| | P | W | D | L | F | A | DIF | PTS |
|---|---|---|---|---|---|---|---|---|
| Manchester United | 6 | 4 | 1 | 1 | 11 | 5 | 6 | 13 |
| Juventus | 6 | 2 | 1 | 3 | 11 | 11 | 0 | 7 |
| **FC Basel** | **6** | **2** | **1** | **3** | **5** | **10** | **-5** | **7** |
| Deportivo La Coruna | 6 | 2 | 1 | 3 | 7 | 8 | -1 | 7 |

## KEY PLAYER APPEARANCES

2 Hakan Yakin — Attacker

| | |
|---|---|
| Age (on 01/07/03) | 26 |
| In the squad | 14 |
| Total minutes on the pitch | 1205 |
| Goals | 4 |
| Yellow cards | 2 |
| Red cards | 0 |
| Home Country | Switzerland |

| | PLAYER | POS | AGE | SQUAD | MINS ON | GOALS | CARDS(Y/R) | | HOME COUNTRY |
|---|---|---|---|---|---|---|---|---|---|
| 1 | Pascal Zuberbuhler | GK | 32 | 14 | 1260 | 0 | 0 | 0 | Switzerland |
| 2 | Hakan Yakin | ATT | 26 | 14 | 1205 | 4 | 2 | 0 | Switzerland |
| 3 | Mario Cantaluppi | MID | 29 | 13 | 1170 | 1 | 2 | 0 | Switzerland |
| 4 | Murat Yakin | DEF | 28 | 13 | 1164 | 0 | 0 | 0 | Switzerland |
| 5 | Christian Gimenez | ATT | 28 | 14 | 1028 | 7 | 1 | 0 | Argentina |
| 6 | Bernt Haas | DEF | 25 | 11 | 990 | 0 | 2 | 0 | Switzerland |
| 7 | Timothee Atouba | MID | 21 | 14 | 975 | 1 | 1 | 0 | Cameroon |
| 8 | Julio Rossi | ATT | 26 | 14 | 928 | 5 | 1 | 0 | Argentina |
| 9 | Sebastien Barberis | MID | 31 | 14 | 878 | 0 | 0 | 0 | Switzerland |
| 10 | Marco Zwyssig | DEF | 31 | 12 | 851 | 0 | 1 | 0 | Switzerland |
| 11 | Antonio Esposito | MID | 30 | 8 | 627 | 0 | 2 | 0 | Switzerland |
| 12 | Ivan Ergic | MID | 22 | 7 | 532 | 2 | 0 | 0 | Serbia & Mont |
| 13 | Scott Chipperfield | MID | 27 | 6 | 475 | 0 | 0 | 0 | Australia |
| 14 | Alexander Quennoz | DEF | 24 | 13 | 470 | 0 | 0 | 0 | Switzerland |
| 15 | Gregory Duruz | DEF | 26 | 14 | 449 | 0 | 0 | 0 | Switzerland |
| 16 | Carlos Varela | MID | 25 | 13 | 320 | 0 | 3 | 0 | Spain |
| 17 | Herve Tum | ATT | 24 | 14 | 299 | 0 | 0 | 0 | Cameroon |
| 18 | Benjamin Huggel | MID | 26 | 7 | 193 | 0 | 0 | 0 | Switzerland |
| 19 | Philip Degem | DEF | 20 | 8 | 29 | 0 | 0 | 0 | Switzerland |
| 20 | George Koumantarakis | ATT | 29 | 8 | 13 | 0 | 0 | 0 | South Africa |
| 21 | Nenad Savic | MID | 22 | 2 | 4 | 0 | 0 | 0 | Switzerland |

# DEPORTIVO LA CORUNA

SPAIN
Phase 2 - 4th Group D

| | | | | | | |
|---|---|---|---|---|---|---|
| 1 | gpg | Bayern Munich | A | W | 3-2 | Makaay 12,45,77 |
| 2 | gpg | AC Milan | H | L | 0-4 | |
| 3 | gpg | Lens | H | W | 3-1 | Makaay 49; Capdevila 79; Cesar 84 |
| 4 | gpg | Lens | A | L | 1-3 | Makaay 15 |
| 5 | gpg | Bayern Munich | H | W | 2-1 | Victor 55; Makaay 89 |
| 6 | gpg | AC Milan | A | W | 2-1 | Diego Tristan 58; Makaay 70 |
| 7 | gpd | Juventus | H | D | 2-2 | Tristan 9; Makaay 11 |
| 8 | gpd | Man Utd | A | L | 0-2 | |
| 9 | gpd | Basel | A | L | 0-1 | |
| 10 | gpd | Basel | H | W | 1-0 | Tristan 4 |
| 11 | gpd | Juventus | A | L | 2-3 | Tristan 34; Makaay 52 |
| 12 | gpd | Man Utd | H | W | 2-0 | Victor 32; Lynch 47 og |

## KEY GOALSCORERS

1 Roy Makaay

| | | | |
|---|---|---|---|
| Goals in the Champions League | 9 | Player Strike Rate | 101 |
| Contribution to Attacking Power | 56 | Club Strike Rate | 60 |

| | PLAYER | GOALS | POWER | S RATE |
|---|---|---|---|---|
| 2 | Herrera Diego Tristan | 4 | 56 | 127 mins |
| 3 | Martin Villar Cesar | 1 | 55 | 610 mins |
| 4 | Joan Mendez Capdevila | 1 | 47 | 623 mins |

**Phase 1 GROUP G**

| | P | W | D | L | F | A | DIF | PTS |
|---|---|---|---|---|---|---|---|---|
| AC Milan | 6 | 4 | 0 | 2 | 12 | 7 | 5 | 12 |
| **Deportivo La Coruna** | **6** | **4** | **0** | **2** | **11** | **12** | **-1** | **12** |
| Lens | 6 | 2 | 2 | 2 | 11 | 11 | 0 | 8 |
| Bayern Munich | 6 | 0 | 2 | 4 | 9 | 13 | -4 | 2 |

**Phase 2 GROUP D**

| | P | W | D | L | F | A | DIF | PTS |
|---|---|---|---|---|---|---|---|---|
| Manchester United | 6 | 4 | 1 | 1 | 11 | 5 | 6 | 13 |
| Juventus | 6 | 2 | 1 | 3 | 11 | 11 | 0 | 7 |
| FC Basel | 6 | 2 | 1 | 3 | 5 | 10 | -5 | 7 |
| **Deportivo La Coruna** | **6** | **2** | **1** | **3** | **7** | **8** | **-1** | **7** |

## KEY PLAYER APPEARANCES

13 Herrera Diego Tristan — Attacker

| | |
|---|---|
| Age (on 01/07/03) | 27 |
| In the squad | 11 |
| Total minutes on the pitch | 508 |
| Goals | 4 |
| Yellow cards | 0 |
| Red cards | 0 |
| Home Country | Spain |

| | PLAYER | POS | AGE | SQUAD | MINS ON | GOALS | CARDS(Y/R) | | HOME COUNTRY |
|---|---|---|---|---|---|---|---|---|---|
| 1 | Romero | DEF | 32 | 12 | 990 | 0 | 0 | 0 | Spain |
| 2 | Roy Makaay | ATT | 28 | 11 | 909 | 9 | 0 | 0 | Holland |
| 3 | Juanmi | GK | 32 | 13 | 900 | 0 | 0 | 0 | Spain |
| 4 | Lionel Scaloni | DEF | 25 | 11 | 875 | 0 | 0 | 0 | Argentina |
| 5 | Gonzalez Soriano Sergio | MID | 26 | 12 | 845 | 0 | 0 | 0 | Spain |
| 6 | Mauro Gomes da Silva | MID | 35 | 9 | 798 | 0 | 2 | 0 | Brazil |
| 7 | Noureddine Naybet | DEF | 33 | 8 | 720 | 0 | 2 | 0 | Morocco |
| 8 | Francisco J Gonazales | MID | 33 | 10 | 666 | 0 | 0 | 0 | Spain |
| 9 | Joan Mendez Capdevila | DEF | 25 | 12 | 623 | 1 | 1 | 0 | Spain |
| 10 | Martin Villar Cesar | DEF | 26 | 8 | 610 | 1 | 1 | 0 | Spain |
| 11 | Hector | DEF | 28 | 12 | 598 | 0 | 0 | 0 | Spain |
| 12 | Aldo Pedro Duscher | MID | 24 | 10 | 561 | 0 | 1 | 0 | Argentina |
| 13 | Herrera Diego Tristan | ATT | 27 | 11 | 508 | 4 | 0 | 0 | Spain |
| 14 | Sanchez del Amo Victor | MID | 27 | 9 | 487 | 2 | 2 | 0 | Spain |
| 15 | Juan Carlos Valeron | MID | 28 | 6 | 291 | 0 | 0 | 0 | Spain |
| 16 | Alberto Martos Luque | ATT | 25 | 12 | 290 | 0 | 2 | 0 | Spain |
| 17 | Andrade | DEF | 25 | 4 | 263 | 0 | 0 | 0 | Portugal |
| 18 | Roberto Miguel Acuna | MID | 31 | 10 | 258 | 0 | 1 | 0 | Paraguay |
| 19 | Gama Da Silva Donato | DEF | 40 | 8 | 238 | 0 | 1 | 0 | Brazil |
| 20 | Jose Emilio Amavisca | MID | 32 | 5 | 153 | 0 | 0 | 0 | Spain |

# AUXERRE

FRANCE
Phase 1 - 3rd Group A

| | | | | | | |
|---|---|---|---|---|---|---|
| 1 | 3ql1 | Boavista | A | W | 1-0 | Cisse 71 |
| 2 | 3ql2 | Boavista | H | D | 0-0 | |
| 3 | gpa | PSV Eindhoven | H | D | 0-0 | |
| 4 | gpa | B Dortmund | A | L | 1-2 | Mwaruwari 83 |
| 5 | gpa | Arsenal | H | L | 0-1 | |
| 6 | gpa | Arsenal | A | W | 2-1 | Kapo Obou 7; Fadiga 27 |
| 7 | gpa | PSV Eindhoven | A | L | 0-3 | |
| 8 | gpa | B Dortmund | H | W | 1-0 | Mwaruwari 75 |

## KEY PLAYER APPEARANCES

2 Jean-Alain Boumsong — Defender

| | |
|---|---|
| Age (on 01/07/03) | 23 |
| In the squad | 8 |
| Total minutes on the pitch | 720 |
| Goals | 0 |
| Yellow cards | 1 |
| Red cards | 0 |
| Home country | France |

| | PLAYER | POS | AGE | SQUAD | MINS ON | GOALS | CARDS(Y/R) | | HOME COUNTRY |
|---|---|---|---|---|---|---|---|---|---|
| 1 | Jean-Sebastien Jaures | DEF | 25 | 8 | 720 | 0 | 1 | 0 | France |
| 2 | Jean-Alain Boumsong | DEF | 23 | 8 | 720 | 0 | 1 | 0 | France |
| 3 | Johan Radet | DEF | 26 | 8 | 720 | 0 | 0 | 0 | France |
| 4 | Fabien Cool | GK | 30 | 8 | 720 | 0 | 0 | 0 | France |
| 5 | Khalilou Fadiga | ATT | 28 | 8 | 716 | 1 | 1 | 0 | Senegal |
| 6 | Yann Lachuer | MID | 31 | 8 | 692 | 0 | 0 | 0 | France |
| 7 | Amdy Faye | DEF | 26 | 8 | 630 | 0 | 2 | 0 | Senegal |
| 8 | Philippe Mexes | DEF | 21 | 7 | 566 | 0 | 2 | 1 | France |
| 9 | Teemu Tainio | MID | 23 | 7 | 508 | 0 | 2 | 0 | Finland |
| 10 | Olivier Kapo | ATT | 22 | 6 | 501 | 1 | 0 | 1 | France |
| 11 | Benjamin Mwaruwari | ATT | 24 | 8 | 425 | 2 | 0 | 0 | Zimbabwe |
| 12 | Lionel Mathis | MID | 21 | 6 | 346 | 0 | 1 | 0 | France |
| 13 | Djibril Cisse | ATT | 21 | 4 | 270 | 1 | 2 | 0 | France |
| 14 | Stephane Grichting | DEF | 24 | 8 | 153 | 0 | 0 | 0 | Switzerland |
| 15 | Arnaud Gonzalez | ATT | 25 | 8 | 119 | 0 | 0 | 0 | France |

# PSV EINDHOVEN

HOLLAND
Phase 1 - 4th GroupA

| | | | | | | |
|---|---|---|---|---|---|---|
| 1 | gpa | Auxerre | A | D | 0-0 | |
| 2 | gpa | Arsenal | H | L | 0-4 | |
| 3 | gpa | B Dortmund | H | L | 1-3 | van der Schaaf 74 |
| 4 | gpa | B Dortmund | A | D | 1-1 | Bruggink 47 |
| 5 | gpa | Auxerre | H | W | 3-0 | Bruggink 34; Rommedahl 48; Robben 64 |
| 6 | gpa | Arsenal | A | D | 0-0 | |

## KEY PLAYER APPEARANCES

1 Dennis Rommedahl — Attacker

PHILIPS

| | |
|---|---|
| Age (on 01/07/03) | 24 |
| In the squad | 6 |
| Total minutes on the pitch | 540 |
| Goals | 1 |
| Yellow cards | 0 |
| Red cards | 0 |
| Home country | Denmark |

| | PLAYER | POS | AGE | SQUAD | MINS ON | GOALS | CARDS(Y/R) | | HOME COUNTRY |
|---|---|---|---|---|---|---|---|---|---|
| 1 | Dennis Rommedahl | ATT | 24 | 6 | 540 | 1 | 0 | 0 | Denmark |
| 2 | Wilfred Bouma | ATT | 25 | 6 | 540 | 0 | 0 | 0 | Holland |
| 3 | Kasper Bogelund | DEF | 22 | 6 | 540 | 0 | 1 | 0 | Denmark |
| 4 | Mateja Kezman | ATT | 24 | 6 | 518 | 0 | 0 | 0 | Serbia & Mont |
| 5 | Ronald Waterreus | GK | 32 | 5 | 450 | 0 | 0 | 0 | Holland |
| 6 | Andre Ooijer | DEF | 28 | 5 | 439 | 0 | 4 | 0 | Holland |
| 7 | Mark Van Bommel | MID | 26 | 5 | 424 | 0 | 3 | 0 | Holland |
| 8 | Johann Vogel | MID | 26 | 6 | 414 | 0 | 2 | 0 | Switzerland |
| 9 | Arnold Bruggink | ATT | 25 | 6 | 411 | 2 | 1 | 0 | Holland |
| 10 | Kevin Hofland | DEF | 24 | 4 | 315 | 0 | 1 | 0 | Holland |
| 11 | Ernest Faber | DEF | 31 | 6 | 270 | 0 | 1 | 0 | Holland |
| 12 | Argen Robben | ATT | 19 | 6 | 240 | 1 | 0 | 0 | Holland |
| 13 | Jan Heintze | DEF | 39 | 6 | 196 | 0 | 0 | 0 | Denmark |
| 14 | Remco van der Schaaf | MID | 24 | 5 | 178 | 1 | 1 | 0 | Holland |
| 15 | Theo Lucius | MID | 26 | 6 | 142 | 0 | 0 | 0 | Holland |
| 16 | Leandro do Bomfim | MID | 19 | 3 | 123 | 0 | 0 | 0 | Brazil |

# LIVERPOOL

ENGLAND
Phase 1 - 3rd Group B

| | | | | | | |
|---|---|---|---|---|---|---|
| 1 | gpb | Valencia | A | L | 0-2 | |
| 2 | gpb | Basel | H | D | 1-1 | Baros 34 |
| 3 | gpb | S Moscow | H | W | 5-0 | Heskey 7,89; Cheyrou 13; Hyypia 27; Diao 80 |
| 4 | gpb | S Moscow | A | W | 3-1 | Owen 29,70,90 |
| 5 | gpb | Valencia | H | L | 0-1 | |
| 6 | gpb | Basel | A | D | 3-3 | Murphy 61; Smicer 64; Owen 85 |

## KEY PLAYER APPEARANCES

6 Michael Owen — Attacker

| | |
|---|---|
| Age (on 01/07/03) | 23 |
| In the squad | 6 |
| Total minutes on the pitch | 483 |
| Goals | 4 |
| Yellow cards | 0 |
| Red cards | 0 |
| Home country | England |

| | PLAYER | POS | AGE | SQUAD | MINS ON | GOALS | CARDS(Y/R) | | HOME COUNTRY |
|---|---|---|---|---|---|---|---|---|---|
| 1 | Sami Hyypia | DEF | 29 | 6 | 540 | 1 | 0 | 0 | Finland |
| 2 | Jerzy Dudek | GK | 30 | 6 | 540 | 0 | 0 | 0 | Poland |
| 3 | John Arne Riise | MID | 22 | 6 | 540 | 0 | 0 | 0 | Norway |
| 4 | Jamie Carragher | DEF | 25 | 6 | 519 | 0 | 0 | 0 | England |
| 5 | Danny Murphy | MID | 26 | 6 | 495 | 1 | 1 | 0 | England |
| 6 | Michael Owen | ATT | 23 | 6 | 483 | 4 | 0 | 0 | England |
| 7 | Dietmar Hamann | MID | 29 | 5 | 437 | 0 | 2 | 1 | Germany |
| 8 | Emile Heskey | ATT | 25 | 6 | 426 | 2 | 0 | 0 | England |
| 9 | Steven Gerrard | MID | 23 | 5 | 390 | 0 | 0 | 0 | England |
| 10 | Djimi Traore | DEF | 23 | 6 | 384 | 0 | 1 | 0 | France |
| 11 | Salif Diao | MID | 26 | 6 | 285 | 1 | 0 | 0 | Senegal |
| 12 | Milan Baros | ATT | 21 | 6 | 234 | 1 | 0 | 0 | Czech Republic |
| 13 | Bruno Cheyrou | MID | 25 | 5 | 225 | 1 | 0 | 0 | France |
| 14 | Stephane Henchoz | DEF | 28 | 2 | 156 | 0 | 1 | 0 | Switzerland |
| 15 | Vladimir Smicer | MID | 30 | 3 | 120 | 1 | 1 | 0 | Czech Republic |
| 16 | El Hadji Diouf | ATT | 22 | 6 | 106 | 0 | 1 | 0 | Senegal |

# SPARTAK MOSCOW

RUSSIA
Phase 1 - 4th Group B

| | | | | | | |
|---|---|---|---|---|---|---|
| 1 | gpb | Basel | A | L | 0-2 | |
| 2 | gpb | Valencia | H | L | 0-3 | |
| 3 | gpb | Liverpool | A | L | 0-5 | |
| 4 | gpb | Liverpool | H | L | 1-3 | Danishevskiy 23 |
| 5 | gpb | Basel | H | L | 0-2 | |
| 6 | gpb | Valencia | A | L | 0-3 | |

## KEY PLAYER APPEARANCES

4 Moises — Defender

| | |
|---|---|
| Age (on 01/07/03) | 23 |
| In the squad | 5 |
| Total minutes on the pitch | 450 |
| Goals | 0 |
| Yellow cards | 3 |
| Red cards | 0 |
| Home country | Brazil |

| | PLAYER | POS | AGE | SQUAD | MINS ON | GOALS | CARDS(Y/R) | | HOME COUNTRY |
|---|---|---|---|---|---|---|---|---|---|
| 1 | Vladimir Beschastnykh | ATT | 29 | 6 | 540 | 0 | 0 | 0 | Russia |
| 2 | Maksym Kalinichenko | MID | 24 | 6 | 497 | 0 | 0 | 0 | Ukraine |
| 3 | Alexander Danishevskiy | ATT | 19 | 6 | 458 | 1 | 0 | 0 | Forward |
| 4 | Moises | DEF | 23 | 5 | 450 | 0 | 3 | 0 | Brazil |
| 5 | Yuri Kovtun | DEF | 33 | 6 | 413 | 0 | 3 | 0 | Russia |
| 6 | Baye Aly Jbra Kebe | DEF | 24 | 5 | 400 | 0 | 2 | 0 | Senegal |
| 7 | Dmitri Khlestov | DEF | 32 | 6 | 384 | 0 | 1 | 0 | Russia |
| 8 | Igor Mitreski | DEF | 24 | 6 | 370 | 0 | 3 | 0 | Macedonia |
| 9 | Olexandr Pavelenko | MID | 18 | 5 | 360 | 0 | 0 | 0 | Russia |
| 10 | Dmitri Koudriashov | MID | 20 | 6 | 346 | 0 | 2 | 0 | Russia |
| 11 | Valeri Abramidze | DEF | 23 | 5 | 298 | 0 | 1 | 0 | Georgia |
| 12 | Stanislav Cherchessov | GK | 39 | 6 | 270 | 0 | 0 | 0 | Russia |
| 13 | Maxym Levytsky | GK | 30 | 5 | 270 | 0 | 0 | 0 | Ukraine |
| 14 | Artem Bezrodny | MID | 24 | 6 | 246 | 0 | 0 | 0 | Russia |
| 15 | Jerry-Christian Tchuisse | DEF | 28 | 4 | 180 | 0 | 0 | 0 | Cameroon |
| 16 | Marcelo Silva | MID | 27 | 6 | 121 | 0 | 0 | 0 | Brazil |

## AEK ATHENS

GREECE
Phase 1 - 3rd Group C

| | | | | | | |
|---|---|---|---|---|---|---|
| 1 | 3ql1 | Apoel Nicosia | A | W | 3-2 | Borbokis 43,47; Nikolaidis 90 |
| 2 | 3ql2 | Apoel Nicosia | H | W | 1-0 | Wright 56 |
| 3 | gpc | Genk | A | D | 0-0 | |
| 4 | gpc | Roma | H | D | 0-0 | |
| 5 | gpc | Real Madrid | H | D | 3-3 | Tsartas 6; Maladenis 25; Nikolaidis 28 |
| 6 | gpc | Real Madrid | A | D | 2-2 | Katsouranis 74; Centeno 86 |
| 7 | gpc | Genk | H | D | 1-1 | Lakis 30 |
| 8 | gpc | Roma | A | D | 1-1 | Centeno 90 |

### KEY PLAYER APPEARANCES

2 Mauricio Wright — Defender

| | |
|---|---|
| Age (on 01/07/03) | 32 |
| In the squad | 8 |
| Total minutes on the pitch | 720 |
| Goals | 1 |
| Yellow cards | 1 |
| Red cards | 0 |
| Home country | Costa Rica |

| | PLAYER | POS | AGE | SQUAD | MINS ON | GOALS | CARDS(Y) | CARDS(R) | HOME COUNTRY |
|---|---|---|---|---|---|---|---|---|---|
| 1 | Dionisios Chiotis | GK | 26 | 8 | 720 | 0 | 0 | 0 | Greece |
| 2 | Mauricio Wright | DEF | 32 | 8 | 720 | 1 | 1 | 0 | Costa Rica |
| 3 | Themistoklis Nikolaidis | ATT | 29 | 8 | 683 | 2 | 0 | 0 | Greece |
| 4 | Konstantinos Katsouranis | MID | 24 | 8 | 649 | 1 | 1 | 0 | Greece |
| 5 | Theodoros Zagorakis | MID | 31 | 7 | 623 | 0 | 4 | 0 | Greece |
| 6 | Vassilios Lakis | MID | 26 | 8 | 595 | 1 | 1 | 0 | Greece |
| 7 | Michalis Kapsis | DEF | 29 | 7 | 585 | 0 | 0 | 0 | Greece |
| 8 | Mihalis Kassapis | DEF | 32 | 8 | 585 | 0 | 1 | 0 | Greece |
| 9 | Vassilios Tsartas | MID | 30 | 8 | 581 | 1 | 1 | 0 | Greece |
| 10 | Nikos Kostenoglou | DEF | 32 | 7 | 517 | 0 | 2 | 0 | Greece |
| 11 | Grigorious Georgatos | DEF | 30 | 7 | 352 | 0 | 1 | 0 | Greece |
| 12 | Vassilios Borbokis | DEF | 34 | 5 | 297 | 2 | 1 | 0 | Greece |
| 13 | Ilija Ivic | ATT | 32 | 8 | 213 | 0 | 0 | 0 | Serbia & Mont |
| 14 | Christos Maladenis | MID | 29 | 7 | 211 | 1 | 0 | 0 | Greece |
| 15 | Walter Centeno | MID | 28 | 7 | 148 | 2 | 0 | 0 | Costa Rica |
| 16 | Dimitrious Nalitzis | ATT | 27 | 3 | 136 | 0 | 0 | 0 | Greece |

## GENK

BELGIUM
Phase 1 - 4th Group C

| | | | | | | |
|---|---|---|---|---|---|---|
| 1 | 3ql1 | Sparta Prague | H | W | 2-0 | Thijs 33; Beslija 40 |
| 2 | 3ql2 | Sparta Prague | A | L | 2-4 | Dagano 25; Sonck 57 |
| 3 | gpc | AEK Athens | H | D | 0-0 | |
| 4 | gpc | Real Madrid | A | L | 0-6 | |
| 5 | gpc | Roma | H | L | 0-1 | |
| 6 | gpc | Roma | A | D | 0-0 | |
| 7 | gpc | AEK Athens | A | D | 1-1 | Sonck 22 |
| 8 | gpc | Real Madrid | H | D | 1-1 | Sonck 85 |

### KEY PLAYER APPEARANCES

1 Wesley Sonck — Attacker

| | |
|---|---|
| Age (on 01/07/03) | 24 |
| In the squad | 8 |
| Total minutes on the pitch | 720 |
| Goals | 3 |
| Yellow cards | 3 |
| Red cards | 0 |
| Home country | Belgium |

| | PLAYER | POS | AGE | SQUAD | MINS ON | GOALS | CARDS(Y) | CARDS(R) | HOME COUNTRY |
|---|---|---|---|---|---|---|---|---|---|
| 1 | Wesley Sonck | ATT | 24 | 8 | 720 | 3 | 3 | 0 | Belgium |
| 2 | Josip Skoko | MID | 27 | 8 | 720 | 0 | 1 | 0 | Australia |
| 3 | Didier Zokora | DEF | 22 | 8 | 720 | 0 | 1 | 0 | Ivory Coast |
| 4 | Akran Roumani | DEF | 25 | 7 | 621 | 0 | 0 | 0 | Morocco |
| 5 | Mirsad Beslija | MID | 24 | 8 | 602 | 1 | 0 | 0 | Bosnia and Herz |
| 6 | Koen Daerden | MID | 21 | 7 | 594 | 0 | 3 | 0 | Belgium |
| 7 | Igor Tomasic | DEF | 26 | 8 | 561 | 0 | 0 | 0 | Croatia |
| 8 | Jan Moons | GK | 32 | 7 | 550 | 0 | 0 | 1 | Belgium |
| 9 | Bernd Thijs | MID | 25 | 6 | 540 | 1 | 2 | 0 | Belgium |
| 10 | Bell-Moumouni Dagano | ATT | 22 | 6 | 506 | 1 | 0 | 0 | Burkina Faso |
| 11 | Justice Wamfor | DEF | 21 | 8 | 478 | 0 | 1 | 0 | Cameroon |
| 12 | Kevin Vanbeuren | DEF | 22 | 8 | 302 | 0 | 0 | 0 | Belgium |
| 13 | Davy Schollen | GK | 25 | 8 | 169 | 0 | 1 | 0 | Belgium |
| 14 | Takayuki Suzuki | ATT | 27 | 8 | 167 | 0 | 0 | 0 | Japan |
| 15 | Marco Ingrao | MID | 20 | 8 | 158 | 0 | 0 | 0 | Belgium |
| 16 | Soley Seyfo | DEF | 23 | 7 | 145 | 0 | 1 | 0 | Gambia |

## LYON

FRANCE
Phase 1 - 3rd Group D

| | | | | | | |
|---|---|---|---|---|---|---|
| 1 | gpd | Ajax | A | L | 1-2 | Anderson 83 |
| 2 | gpd | Rosenborg BK | H | W | 5-0 | Carriere 6; Vairelles 26,45; Anderson 34; Luyindula 75 |
| 3 | gpd | Inter Milan | A | W | 2-1 | Govou 21; Anderson 62 |
| 4 | gpd | Inter Milan | H | D | 3-3 | Anderson 21,75; Carriere 44 |
| 5 | gpd | Ajax | H | L | 0-2 | |
| 6 | gpd | Rosenborg BK | A | D | 1-1 | Govou 83 |

### KEY PLAYER APPEARANCES

6 Sonny Anderson — Brazil

| | |
|---|---|
| Age (on 01/07/03) | 32 |
| In the squad | 6 |
| Total minutes on the pitch | 503 |
| Goals | 5 |
| Yellow cards | 0 |
| Red cards | 0 |
| Home country | Brazil |

| | PLAYER | POS | AGE | SQUAD | MINS ON | GOALS | CARDS(Y) | CARDS(R) | HOME COUNTRY |
|---|---|---|---|---|---|---|---|---|---|
| 1 | Gregory Coupet | GK | 30 | 6 | 540 | 0 | 0 | 0 | France |
| 2 | Jeremie Brechet | DEF | 23 | 6 | 540 | 0 | 1 | 0 | France |
| 3 | Claudio Roberto Cacapa | DEF | 27 | 6 | 540 | 0 | 1 | 0 | Brazil |
| 4 | Vikash Dhorasoo | MID | 29 | 6 | 508 | 0 | 0 | 0 | France |
| 5 | Eric Carriere | MID | 30 | 6 | 507 | 2 | 0 | 0 | France |
| 6 | Sonny Anderson | ATT | 32 | 6 | 503 | 5 | 0 | 0 | Brazil |
| 7 | Patrick Muller | MID | 26 | 6 | 450 | 0 | 0 | 0 | Switzerland |
| 8 | Edmilson Moraes | DEF | 26 | 6 | 450 | 0 | 0 | 0 | Brazil |
| 9 | Philippe Violeau | MID | 32 | 6 | 416 | 0 | 0 | 0 | France |
| 10 | Mahamadou Diarra | MID | 22 | 5 | 372 | 0 | 1 | 0 | Mali |
| 11 | Sydney Govou | ATT | 23 | 4 | 309 | 2 | 1 | 0 | France |
| 12 | Pernambucano Juninho | MID | 28 | 6 | 289 | 0 | 1 | 0 | Brazil |
| 13 | Tony Vairelles | ATT | 30 | 6 | 175 | 2 | 0 | 0 | France |
| 14 | Florent Laville | DEF | 29 | 6 | 92 | 0 | 1 | 0 | France |
| 15 | Eric Deflandre | DEF | 29 | 4 | 90 | 0 | 0 | 0 | Belgium |
| 16 | Jean-Marc Chanelet | DEF | 34 | 2 | 78 | 0 | 0 | 0 | France |
| 17 | Pegguy Luyindula | ATT | 24 | 6 | 49 | 1 | 0 | 0 | France |

## ROSENBORG BK

NORWAY
Phase 1 - 4th Group D

| | | | | | | |
|---|---|---|---|---|---|---|
| 1 | 3ql1 | Brondby | H | W | 1-0 | Brattbakk 53 |
| 2 | 3ql2 | Brondby | A | W | 3-2 | Johnsen, F 28,71; Brattbakk 79 |
| 3 | gpd | Inter Milan | H | D | 2-2 | Karadas 52,65 |
| 4 | gpd | Lyon | A | L | 0-5 | |
| 5 | gpd | Ajax | H | D | 0-0 | |
| 6 | gpd | Ajax | A | D | 1-1 | Enerly 86 pen |
| 7 | gpd | Inter Milan | A | L | 0-3 | |
| 8 | gpd | Lyon | H | D | 1-1 | Brattbakk 68 |

### KEY PLAYER APPEARANCES

7 Frode Johnsen — Attacker

| | |
|---|---|
| Age (on 01/07/03) | 29 |
| In the squad | 8 |
| Total minutes on the pitch | 663 |
| Goals | 2 |
| Yellow cards | 0 |
| Red cards | 0 |
| Home country | Norway |

| | PLAYER | POS | AGE | SQUAD | MINS ON | GOALS | CARDS(Y) | CARDS(R) | HOME COUNTRY |
|---|---|---|---|---|---|---|---|---|---|
| 1 | Christer Basma | DEF | 30 | 8 | 720 | 0 | 0 | 0 | Norway |
| 2 | Arni Gautur Arason | GK | 28 | 8 | 720 | 0 | 0 | 0 | Iceland |
| 3 | Erik Hoftun | DEF | 34 | 8 | 720 | 0 | 0 | 0 | Norway |
| 4 | Janne Saarinen | DEF | 26 | 8 | 708 | 0 | 0 | 0 | Finland |
| 5 | Orjan Berg | MID | 34 | 8 | 708 | 0 | 2 | 0 | Norway |
| 6 | Bent Skammelsrud | MID | 37 | 8 | 669 | 0 | 0 | 0 | Norway |
| 7 | Frode Johnsen | ATT | 29 | 8 | 663 | 2 | 0 | 0 | Norway |
| 8 | Azar Karadas | DEF | 21 | 8 | 659 | 2 | 2 | 0 | Norway |
| 9 | Harald Brattbakk | ATT | 32 | 8 | 618 | 3 | 1 | 0 | Norway |
| 10 | Roar Strand | MID | 33 | 7 | 614 | 0 | 2 | 0 | Norway |
| 11 | Odd Inge Olsen | MID | 33 | 8 | 460 | 0 | 0 | 0 | Norway |
| 12 | Dagfinn Enerly | ATT | 30 | 8 | 400 | 1 | 0 | 0 | Norway |
| 13 | Stale Stensaas | DEF | 32 | 8 | 90 | 0 | 0 | 0 | Norway |
| 14 | Trond Ludvigsen | ATT | 21 | 8 | 73 | 0 | 0 | 0 | Norway |
| 15 | Christa George | ATT | 23 | 8 | 51 | 0 | 0 | 0 | Norway |

# DINAMO KIEV

RUSSIA
Phase 1 - 3rd Group E

| | | | | | | |
|---|---|---|---|---|---|---|
| 1 | 3ql1 | **Levski Sofia** | A | W | 1-0 | Cernat 60 |
| 2 | 3ql2 | **Levski Sofia** | H | W | 1-0 | Cernat 42 |
| 3 | gpe | **Newcastle** | H | W | 2-0 | Shatskikh 16; Khatskevitch 62 |
| 4 | gpe | **Juventus** | A | L | 0-5 | |
| 5 | gpe | **Feyenoord** | A | D | 0-0 | |
| 6 | gpe | **Feyenoord** | H | W | 2-0 | Khatskevitch 16; Belkevich 47 |
| 7 | gpe | **Newcastle** | A | L | 1-2 | Shatskikh 47 |
| 8 | gpe | **Juventus** | H | L | 1-2 | Shatskikh 50 |

## KEY PLAYER APPEARANCES

1 Maksim Shatskikh — Attacker

| | |
|---|---|
| Age (on 01/07/03) | 24 |
| In the squad | 8 |
| Total minutes on the pitch | 720 |
| Goals | 3 |
| Yellow cards | 1 |
| Red cards | 0 |
| Home country | Uzbekistan |

| | PLAYER | POS | AGE | SQUAD | MINS ON | GOALS | CARDS(Y | /R) | HOME COUNTRY |
|---|---|---|---|---|---|---|---|---|---|
| 1 | Maksim Shatskikh | ATT | 24 | 8 | 720 | 3 | 1 | 0 | Uzbekistan |
| 2 | Tiberiu Ghioane | MID | 22 | 8 | 720 | 0 | 0 | 0 | Romania |
| 3 | Vitalii Reva | GK | 28 | 8 | 720 | 0 | 0 | 0 | Ukraine |
| 4 | Georgi Pejev | ATT | 24 | 7 | 595 | 0 | 0 | 0 | Bulgaria |
| 5 | Andrii Nesmachnyi | DEF | 24 | 7 | 574 | 0 | 0 | 0 | Ukraine |
| 6 | Andriy Husin | MID | 30 | 7 | 559 | 0 | 1 | 0 | Ukraine |
| 7 | Goran Gavrancic | DEF | 24 | 7 | 556 | 0 | 1 | 0 | Serbia & Mont |
| 8 | Alexandre Khatskevitch | MID | 29 | 7 | 534 | 2 | 0 | 0 | Belarus |
| 9 | Florin Cernat | MID | 23 | 8 | 480 | 2 | 0 | 0 | Romania |
| 10 | Yuri Dmitrulin | DEF | 28 | 5 | 436 | 0 | 1 | 0 | Ukraine |
| 11 | Jerko Leko | MID | 23 | 6 | 310 | 0 | 1 | 0 | Croatia |
| 12 | Goran Sablic | DEF | 23 | 7 | 284 | 0 | 0 | 0 | Ukraine |
| 13 | Valentin Belkevich | ATT | 30 | 3 | 270 | 1 | 0 | 0 | Belarus |
| 14 | Laszlo Bodnar | DEF | 24 | 7 | 270 | 0 | 0 | 0 | Hungary |
| 15 | Badr El Kaddouri | MID | 22 | 8 | 256 | 0 | 1 | 0 | Morocco |
| 16 | Olexsandr Melashchenko | ATT | 24 | 8 | 236 | 0 | 0 | 0 | Ukraine |
| 17 | Olexandr Radchenko | DEF | 26 | 2 | 180 | 0 | 1 | 0 | Ukraine |

# FEYENOORD

HOLLAND
Phase 1 - 4th Group E

| | | | | | | |
|---|---|---|---|---|---|---|
| 1 | 3ql1 | **Fenerbahce** | H | W | 1-0 | Ono 64 |
| 2 | 3ql2 | **Fenerbahce** | A | W | 2-0 | Ono 48; Buffel 88 |
| 3 | gpe | **Juventus** | H | D | 1-1 | van Hooijdonk 75 |
| 4 | gpe | **Newcastle** | A | W | 1-0 | Pardo 4 |
| 5 | gpe | **Dinamo Kiev** | H | D | 0-0 | |
| 6 | gpe | **Dinamo Kiev** | A | L | 0-2 | |
| 7 | gpe | **Juventus** | A | L | 0-2 | |
| 8 | gpe | **Newcastle** | H | L | 2-3 | Bombarda 65; Lurling 71 |

## KEY PLAYER APPEARANCES

1 Patrick Paauwe — Midfielder

| | |
|---|---|
| Age (on 01/07/03) | 27 |
| In the squad | 8 |
| Total minutes on the pitch | 720 |
| Goals | 0 |
| Yellow cards | 2 |
| Red cards | 0 |
| Home country | Holland |

| | PLAYER | POS | AGE | SQUAD | MINS ON | GOALS | CARDS(Y | /R) | HOME COUNTRY |
|---|---|---|---|---|---|---|---|---|---|
| 1 | Patrick Paauwe | MID | 27 | 8 | 720 | 0 | 2 | 0 | Holland |
| 2 | Brett Emerton | MID | 24 | 8 | 691 | 0 | 2 | 0 | Australia |
| 3 | Shinji Ono | MID | 23 | 7 | 630 | 2 | 3 | 0 | Japan |
| 4 | Kees van Wonderen | DEF | 34 | 7 | 630 | 0 | 2 | 0 | Holland |
| 5 | Edwin Zoetebier | GK | 33 | 7 | 585 | 0 | 0 | 0 | Holland |
| 6 | Paul Bosvelt | MID | 33 | 6 | 540 | 0 | 2 | 0 | Feyenoord |
| 7 | Thomas Buffel | MID | 22 | 8 | 532 | 1 | 0 | 0 | Belgium |
| 8 | Tomasz Rzasa | DEF | 30 | 8 | 530 | 0 | 2 | 0 | Poland |
| 9 | Chong- Gug Song | MID | 24 | 6 | 501 | 0 | 0 | 0 | South Korea |
| 10 | Pierre van Hooijdonk | ATT | 33 | 5 | 450 | 1 | 1 | 0 | Holland |
| 11 | Bonaventure Kalou | ATT | 25 | 7 | 421 | 0 | 3 | 0 | Ivory Coast |
| 12 | Anthony Lurling | MID | 26 | 8 | 371 | 1 | 1 | 0 | Holland |
| 13 | Christian Gyan | DEF | 24 | 8 | 339 | 0 | 0 | 0 | Ghana |
| 14 | Ramon van Haaren | DEF | 30 | 3 | 190 | 0 | 0 | 0 | Holland |
| 15 | Sebastien Pardo | MID | 21 | 5 | 190 | 1 | 0 | 0 | Chile |
| 16 | Mariano Bombarda | ATT | 30 | 6 | 179 | 1 | 2 | 0 | Argentina |

# MACCABI HAIFA

ISRAEL
Phase 1 - 3rd Group F

| | | | | | | |
|---|---|---|---|---|---|---|
| 1 | 3ql1 | **Sturm Graz** | H | W | 2-0 | Ayegbeni 17,90 |
| 2 | 3ql2 | **Sturm Graz** | A | D | 3-3 | Rosso 27; Keise 77; Badir 90 |
| 3 | gpf | **Man Utd** | A | L | 2-5 | Katan 8; Cohen 85 |
| 4 | gpf | **Olympiakos** | H | W | 3-0 | Ayegbeni 27 pen,60,86 |
| 5 | gpf | **B Leverkusen** | H | L | 0-2 | |
| 6 | gpf | **B Leverkusen** | A | L | 1-2 | Pralija 53 |
| 7 | gpf | **Man Utd** | H | W | 3-0 | Katan 40; Zatuttas 56; Ayegbeni 77 pen |
| 8 | gpf | **Olympiakos** | A | D | 3-3 | Badir 9; Ayegbeni 10; Katan 41 |

## KEY PLAYER APPEARANCES

4 Dovani Rosso — Midfielder

| | |
|---|---|
| Age (on 01/07/03) | 30 |
| In the squad | 8 |
| Total minutes on the pitch | 720 |
| Goals | 1 |
| Yellow cards | 1 |
| Red cards | 0 |
| Home country | Croatia |

| | PLAYER | POS | AGE | SQUAD | MINS ON | GOALS | CARDS(Y | /R) | HOME COUNTRY |
|---|---|---|---|---|---|---|---|---|---|
| 1 | Adoram Keise | DEF | 31 | 8 | 720 | 1 | 0 | 0 | Israel |
| 2 | Arik Benado | DEF | 29 | 8 | 720 | 0 | 0 | 0 | Israel |
| 3 | Dudu Awat | GK | 25 | 8 | 720 | 0 | 0 | 0 | Israel |
| 4 | Dovani Rosso | MID | 30 | 8 | 720 | 1 | 1 | 0 | Croatia |
| 5 | Walid Badir | MID | 29 | 8 | 674 | 2 | 2 | 0 | Israel |
| 6 | Yakubu Ayegbeni | ATT | 20 | 7 | 602 | 7 | 1 | 1 | Nigeria |
| 7 | Nenad Pralija | MID | 32 | 7 | 576 | 1 | 2 | 0 | Croatia |
| 8 | Alon Harazi | DEF | 32 | 7 | 573 | 0 | 0 | 0 | Israel |
| 9 | Eric Ejiofor | DEF | 23 | 6 | 540 | 0 | 2 | 0 | Nigeria |
| 10 | Yaniv Katan | ATT | 22 | 8 | 531 | 3 | 2 | 0 | Israel |
| 11 | Raimondas Zatuttas | DEF | 30 | 6 | 530 | 1 | 1 | 0 | Lithuania |
| 12 | Avishay Zano | DEF | 32 | 8 | 470 | 0 | 0 | 0 | Israel |
| 13 | Michael Zandberg | ATT | 23 | 6 | 212 | 0 | 0 | 0 | Israel |
| 14 | Pralija | ATT | | 1 | 90 | 0 | 0 | 0 | |
| 15 | Eyal Almoshnino | MID | 27 | 9 | 74 | 0 | 0 | 0 | Israel |
| 16 | Guillermo Israilevich | MID | 20 | 8 | 69 | 0 | 0 | 0 | Israel |
| 17 | Rafi Cohen | ATT | 28 | 8 | 67 | 1 | 0 | 0 | Israel |

# OLYMPIAKOS

GREECE
Phase 1 - 4th Group F

| | | | | | | |
|---|---|---|---|---|---|---|
| 1 | gpf | **B Leverkusen** | H | W | 6-2 | Kleine 27 og; Giannakopoulos 38; Djordjevic 44,64 pen,73; Zetterberg 87 |
| 2 | gpf | **Maccabi Haifa** | A | L | 0-3 | |
| 3 | gpf | **Man Utd** | A | L | 0-4 | |
| 4 | gpf | **Man Utd** | H | L | 2-3 | Choutos 70; Djordjevic 74 |
| 5 | gpf | **B Leverkusen** | A | L | 0-2 | |
| 6 | gpf | **Maccabi Haifa** | H | D | 3-3 | Alexandris 37; Niniadis 51; Antzas 79 |

## KEY PLAYER APPEARANCES

1 Stelios Venetidis — Defender

SIEMENS
mobile

| | |
|---|---|
| Age (on 01/07/03) | 26 |
| In the squad | 6 |
| Total minutes on the pitch | 540 |
| Goals | 0 |
| Yellow cards | 1 |
| Red cards | 0 |
| Home country | Greece |

| | PLAYER | POS | AGE | SQUAD | MINS ON | GOALS | CARDS(Y | /R) | HOME COUNTRY |
|---|---|---|---|---|---|---|---|---|---|
| 1 | Stelios Venetidis | DEF | 26 | 6 | 540 | 0 | 1 | 0 | Greece |
| 2 | Christian Karembeu | MID | 32 | 6 | 540 | 0 | 2 | 0 | France |
| 3 | D Eleftheropoulos | GK | 26 | 6 | 540 | 0 | 0 | 0 | Greece |
| 4 | Predrag Djordjevic | MID | 30 | 6 | 539 | 4 | 2 | 0 | Serbia & Mont |
| 5 | Pareskevas Antzas | MID | 26 | 6 | 512 | 1 | 1 | 0 | Greece |
| 6 | S Giannakopoulos | MID | 28 | 6 | 473 | 1 | 1 | 0 | Greece |
| 7 | Christos Patsatzoglou | MID | 24 | 6 | 468 | 0 | 1 | 0 | Greece |
| 8 | Par Zetterberg | MID | 32 | 6 | 410 | 1 | 1 | 0 | Sweden |
| 9 | Georgios Anatolakis | DEF | 29 | 5 | 405 | 0 | 2 | 0 | Greece |
| 10 | Silva Giovanni | MID | 30 | 6 | 357 | 0 | 1 | 0 | Brazil |
| 11 | Edu Dracena | DEF | 22 | 6 | 316 | 0 | 2 | 0 | Greece |
| 12 | Jose Ze Elias | MID | 26 | 3 | 189 | 0 | 1 | 1 | Brazil |
| 13 | Alexios Alexandris | ATT | 34 | 4 | 163 | 1 | 0 | 0 | Greece |
| 14 | Peter Oforiquaye | ATT | 23 | 6 | 145 | 0 | 0 | 0 | Ghana |
| 15 | Dimitrios Mavrogenidis | DEF | 26 | 5 | 93 | 0 | 1 | 0 | Greece |
| 16 | Georgios Amanatidis | DEF | 33 | 6 | 72 | 0 | 0 | 0 | Greece |
| 17 | Lampros Choutos | ATT | 23 | 2 | 68 | 1 | 0 | 0 | Greece |
| 18 | Andreas Niniadis | MID | 32 | 6 | 65 | 1 | 0 | 0 | Greece |

# LENS

FRANCE
Phase 1 - 3rd Group G

| | | | | | | |
|---|---|---|---|---|---|---|
| 1 | gpg | AC Milan | A | L | 1-2 | Moreira 75 |
| 2 | gpg | Bayern Munich | H | D | 1-1 | Utaka 76 |
| 3 | gpg | Deportivo | A | L | 1-3 | Moreira 10 |
| 4 | gpg | Deportivo | H | W | 3-1 | Coulibaly 61; Moreira 79; Thomert 84 |
| 5 | gpg | AC Milan | H | W | 2-1 | Moreira 41; Utaka 49 |
| 6 | gpg | Bayern Munich | A | D | 3-3 | Fink 21 og; Bakari 54; Blanchard 90 |

## KEY PLAYER APPEARANCES

3 Guillaume Warmuz — Goalkeeper

| | |
|---|---|
| Age (on 01/07/03) | 32 |
| In the squad | 6 |
| Total minutes on the pitch | 540 |
| Goals | 0 |
| Yellow cards | 0 |
| Red cards | 0 |
| Home country | France |

| | PLAYER | POS | AGE | SQUAD | MINS ON | GOALS | CARDS(Y | /R) | HOME COUNTRY |
|---|---|---|---|---|---|---|---|---|---|
| 1 | Daniel Moreira | MID | 25 | 6 | 540 | 4 | 0 | 0 | France |
| 2 | Rigobert Song | DEF | 27 | 6 | 540 | 0 | 0 | 0 | Cameroon |
| 3 | Guillaume Warmuz | GK | 32 | 6 | 540 | 0 | 0 | 0 | France |
| 4 | Jacek Bak | DEF | 30 | 6 | 514 | 0 | 0 | 0 | Poland |
| 5 | Antoine Sibierski | MID | 28 | 6 | 511 | 0 | 0 | 0 | France |
| 6 | John Utaka | ATT | 21 | 6 | 477 | 2 | 0 | 0 | Nigeria |
| 7 | Cyril Rool | MID | 28 | 5 | 428 | 0 | 1 | 0 | France |
| 8 | Adama Coulibaly | DEF | 22 | 5 | 386 | 1 | 0 | 0 | Mali |
| 9 | Jocelyn Blanchard | MID | 31 | 6 | 330 | 1 | 1 | 0 | France |
| 10 | Papa Bouba Diop | MID | 25 | 4 | 325 | 0 | 2 | 0 | Senegal |
| 11 | Seyadou Keita | MID | 23 | 6 | 319 | 0 | 1 | 0 | Mali |
| 12 | Ferdinand Coly | DEF | 29 | 5 | 304 | 0 | 1 | 0 | Senegal |
| 13 | Charles-Edouard Coridon | MID | 30 | 6 | 209 | 0 | 1 | 0 | France |
| 14 | Olivier Thomert | ATT | 23 | 6 | 164 | 1 | 0 | 0 | France |
| 15 | Abdoulaye Diagne Faye | MID | 25 | 5 | 144 | 0 | 0 | 0 | Senegal |
| 16 | Dagui Bakari | ATT | 28 | 6 | 130 | 1 | 0 | 0 | France |

# BAYERN MUNICH

GERMANY
Phase 1 - 4th Group G

| | | | | | | |
|---|---|---|---|---|---|---|
| 1 | 3ql1 | Partizan | A | W | 3-0 | Tarnat 22; Jeremies 71; Pizarro 78 |
| 2 | 3ql2 | Partizan | H | W | 3-1 | Ballack 26; Elber 71; Salihamidzic 73 pen |
| 3 | gpg | Deportivo | H | L | 2-3 | Salihamidzic 57; Elber 64 |
| 4 | gpg | Lens | A | D | 1-1 | Linke 23 |
| 5 | gpg | AC Milan | H | L | 1-2 | Pizarro 54 |
| 6 | gpg | AC Milan | A | L | 1-2 | Tarnat 23 |
| 7 | gpg | Deportivo | A | L | 1-2 | Santa Cruz 77 |
| 8 | gpg | Lens | H | D | 3-3 | Kovac, N 6; Salihamidzic 19; Feulner 87 |

## KEY PLAYER APPEARANCES

3 Michael Ballack — Midfielder

| | |
|---|---|
| Age (on 01/07/03) | 26 |
| In the squad | 7 |
| Total minutes on the pitch | 579 |
| Goals | 1 |
| Yellow cards | 1 |
| Red cards | 0 |
| Home country | Germany |

| | PLAYER | POS | AGE | SQUAD | MINS ON | GOALS | CARDS(Y | /R) | HOME COUNTRY |
|---|---|---|---|---|---|---|---|---|---|
| 1 | Giovane Elber | ATT | 30 | 8 | 638 | 2 | 1 | 0 | Brazil |
| 2 | Jens Jeremies | MID | 29 | 7 | 601 | 1 | 1 | 0 | Germany |
| 3 | Michael Ballack | MID | 26 | 7 | 579 | 1 | 1 | 0 | Germany |
| 4 | Claudio Pizarro | ATT | 24 | 8 | 566 | 2 | 1 | 0 | Peru |
| 5 | Hazan Salihamidzic | MID | 26 | 7 | 552 | 3 | 2 | 0 | Bosnia |
| 6 | Jose Ze Roberto | ATT | 29 | 7 | 550 | 0 | 0 | 0 | Brazil |
| 7 | Thomas Linke | DEF | 33 | 8 | 540 | 1 | 1 | 0 | Germany |
| 8 | Robert Kovac | DEF | 29 | 8 | 540 | 0 | 2 | 0 | Croatia |
| 9 | Michael Tarnat | MID | 33 | 8 | 507 | 2 | 0 | 0 | Germany |
| 10 | Oliver Kahn | GK | 34 | 6 | 500 | 0 | 0 | 0 | Germany |
| 11 | Owen Hargreaves | MID | 22 | 5 | 396 | 0 | 1 | 0 | England |
| 12 | Samuel Osei Kuffour | DEF | 26 | 8 | 374 | 0 | 1 | 0 | Ghana |
| 13 | Willy Sagnol | DEF | 26 | 6 | 315 | 0 | 1 | 0 | France |
| 14 | Mehmet Scholl | MID | 32 | 4 | 276 | 0 | 1 | 0 | Germany |
| 15 | Stefan Wessels | GK | 24 | 6 | 220 | 0 | 0 | 0 | Germany |
| 16 | Bixente Lizarazu | MID | 33 | 4 | 195 | 0 | 0 | 0 | France |

# CLUB BRUGGE

BELGIUM
Phase 1 - 3rd Group H

| | | | | | | |
|---|---|---|---|---|---|---|
| 1 | 3ql1 | S Donetsk | A | D | 1-1 | Simons 86 pen |
| 2 | 3ql2 | S Donetsk | H | W | 4-1* | Ceh 75 (*on penalties) |
| 3 | gph | Barcelona | A | L | 2-3 | Simons 21 pen; Englebert 84 |
| 4 | gph | Lokomotiv M | H | D | 0-0 | |
| 5 | gph | Galatasaray | A | D | 0-0 | |
| 6 | gph | Galatasaray | H | W | 3-1 | Martens 45; Verheyen 72; Saeternes 90 |
| 7 | gph | Barcelona | H | L | 0-1 | |
| 8 | gph | Lokomotiv M | A | L | 0-2 | |

## KEY PLAYER APPEARANCES

5 Peter van der Heyden — Defender

| | |
|---|---|
| Age (on 01/07/03) | 26 |
| In the squad | 7 |
| Total minutes on the pitch | 572 |
| Goals | 0 |
| Yellow cards | 3 |
| Red cards | 0 |
| Home country | Belgium |

| | PLAYER | POS | AGE | SQUAD | MINS ON | GOALS | CARDS(Y | /R) | HOME COUNTRY |
|---|---|---|---|---|---|---|---|---|---|
| 1 | Gaetan Englebert | MID | 27 | 7 | 630 | 1 | 0 | 0 | Belgium |
| 2 | Timmy Simons | MID | 27 | 7 | 630 | 2 | 1 | 0 | Belgium |
| 3 | Bierger Maertens | MID | 23 | 7 | 630 | 0 | 1 | 0 | Belgium |
| 4 | Dany Verlinden | GK | 39 | 7 | 630 | 0 | 0 | 0 | Belgium |
| 5 | Peter van der Heyden | DEF | 26 | 7 | 572 | 0 | 3 | 0 | Belgium |
| 6 | Olivier De Cock | DEF | 27 | 7 | 564 | 0 | 2 | 0 | Belgium |
| 7 | Gert Verheyen | ATT | 32 | 6 | 538 | 1 | 2 | 0 | Belgium |
| 8 | Philippe Clement | MID | 29 | 7 | 403 | 0 | 0 | 0 | Belgium |
| 9 | Alin Stoica | MID | 23 | 6 | 402 | 0 | 1 | 0 | Romania |
| 10 | Andres Mendoza | ATT | 25 | 5 | 353 | 0 | 0 | 0 | Peru |
| 11 | Sandy Martens | MID | 30 | 7 | 350 | 1 | 2 | 0 | Belgium |
| 12 | Sergei Serebrennikov | MID | 26 | 4 | 315 | 0 | 2 | 0 | Ukraine |
| 13 | Marek Spilar | DEF | 28 | 5 | 300 | 0 | 1 | 0 | Slovakia |
| 14 | Rune Lange | ATT | 26 | 4 | 223 | 0 | 0 | 0 | Norway |
| 15 | Milan Lesnjak | DEF | 26 | 4 | 143 | 0 | 1 | 0 | Serbia & Mont |
| 16 | Nastja Ceh | ATT | 25 | 6 | 95 | 0 | 1 | 0 | Slovenia |
| 17 | Jose Duarte Filho | ATT | 23 | 3 | 80 | 0 | 0 | 0 | Brazil |
| 18 | Bengt Saeternes | ATT | 28 | 2 | 38 | 1 | 0 | 0 | Norway |

# GALATASARAY

TURKEY
Phase 1 - 4th Group H

| | | | | | | |
|---|---|---|---|---|---|---|
| 1 | gph | Lokomotiv M | A | W | 2-0 | Sarr 72; Arif 81 |
| 2 | gph | Barcelona | H | L | 0-2 | |
| 3 | gph | Club Brugge | H | D | 0-0 | |
| 4 | gph | Club Brugge | A | L | 1-3 | Pinto 56 |
| 5 | gph | Lokomotiv M | H | L | 1-2 | Hasan Sas 73 |
| 6 | gph | Barcelona | A | L | 1-3 | Haspolatli 20 |

## KEY PLAYER APPEARANCES

10 Gokhan Hasan Sas — Midfielder

| | |
|---|---|
| Age (on 01/07/03) | 26 |
| In the squad | 6 |
| Total minutes on the pitch | 294 |
| Goals | 1 |
| Yellow cards | 1 |
| Red cards | 0 |
| Home country | Turkey |

| | PLAYER | POS | AGE | SQUAD | MINS ON | GOALS | CARDS(Y | /R) | HOME COUNTRY |
|---|---|---|---|---|---|---|---|---|---|
| 1 | Hakan Unsal | DEF | 30 | 6 | 540 | 0 | 0 | 0 | Turkey |
| 2 | Faryd Mondragon | GK | 32 | 6 | 540 | 0 | 0 | 0 | Colombia |
| 3 | Bulent Korkmaz | DEF | 34 | 6 | 532 | 0 | 1 | 0 | Turkey |
| 4 | Umit Davala | MID | 29 | 5 | 450 | 0 | 0 | 0 | Turkey |
| 5 | Penbe Ergun | MID | 31 | 5 | 439 | 0 | 0 | 0 | Turkey |
| 6 | Joao Batista | MID | 28 | 5 | 375 | 0 | 1 | 0 | Brazil |
| 7 | Erden Arif | ATT | 31 | 6 | 362 | 1 | 0 | 0 | Turkey |
| 8 | Jorge Felipe | MID | | 5 | 315 | 0 | 0 | 0 | |
| 9 | Fabio Pinto | ATT | 22 | 4 | 315 | 1 | 0 | 0 | Brazil |
| 10 | Gokhan Hasan Sas | MID | 26 | 6 | 294 | 1 | 1 | 0 | Turkey |
| 11 | Sergio Almaguer | MID | | 5 | 270 | 0 | 0 | 0 | |
| 12 | Emre Asik | DEF | 29 | 5 | 268 | 0 | 1 | 0 | Turkey |
| 13 | Elvir Baljic | ATT | 29 | 5 | 254 | 0 | 0 | 0 | Boznia-Herz |
| 14 | Cihan Haspolatli | MID | | 5 | 204 | 1 | 1 | 0 | |
| 15 | Christian Correa Dionisio | MID | | 6 | 184 | 0 | 0 | 0 | |
| 16 | Suat Kaya | MID | 35 | 3 | 156 | 0 | 1 | 0 | Turkey |
| 17 | Hohamed Sarr | MID | | 4 | 156 | 1 | 0 | 0 | |
| 18 | Akman Ayhan | MID | 26 | 5 | 132 | 0 | 1 | 0 | Turkey |

# THE CHAMPIONS LEAGUE

**PHASE 2**

| MATCHDAY 1 | MATCHDAY 2 | MATCHDAY 3 | MATCHDAY 4 | MATCHDAY 5 | MATCHDAY 6 |
|---|---|---|---|---|---|
| Aimar supreme and Valencia are home before Hamann sees red | Gilberto nets in 20.07 seconds, to set a UEFA Champions League record | Heskey weighs in with two as Spartak tumble | McManaman puts Madrid two goals up but AEK level at the last | Totti slams in for Roma win at the Bernabéu but Madrid are through | Yakin inspires Basle on the break to win through with 3 before half-time |

| | MATCHDAY 1 | MATCHDAY 2 | MATCHDAY 3 | MATCHDAY 4 | MATCHDAY 5 | MATCHDAY 6 |
|---|---|---|---|---|---|---|
| **GROUP A** | Arsenal 2 Dortmund 0<br>Auxerre 0 PSV 0 | Dortmund 2 Auxerre 1<br>**PSV 0 Arsenal 4** | Auxerre 0 Arsenal 1<br>PSV 1 Dortmund 3 | Dortmund 1 PSV 1<br>Arsenal 1 Auxerre 2 | Dortmund 2 Arsenal 1<br>PSV 3 Auxerre 0 | Arsenal 0 PSV 0<br>Auxerre 1 Dortmund 0 |
| **GROUP B** | **Valencia 2 Liverpool 0**<br>Basle 2 Spartak 0 | Liverpool 1 Basle 1<br>Spartak 0 Valencia 3 | **Liverpool 5 Spartak 0**<br>Valencia 6 Basle 2 | Basle 2 Valencia 2<br>Spartak 1 Liverpool 3 | Liverpool 0 Valencia 1<br>Spartak 0 Basle 2 | **Basle 3 Liverpool 3**<br>Valencia 3 Spartak 0 |
| **GROUP C** | Genk 0 AEK 0<br>Roma 0 Madrid 3 | AEK 0 Roma 0<br>Madrid 6 Genk 0 | AEK 3 Madrid 3<br>Genk 0 Roma 1 | Roma 0 Genk 0<br>**Madrid 2 AEK 2** | AEK 1 Genk 1<br>**Madrid 0 Roma 1** | Genk 1 Madrid 1<br>Roma 1 AEK 1 |
| **GROUP D** | Ajax 2 Lyon 1<br>Rosenborg 2 Inter 2 | Inter Milan 1 Ajax 0<br>Lyon 5 Rosenborg 0 | Inter Milan 1 Lyon 2<br>Rosenborg 0 Ajax 0 | Ajax 1 Rosenborg 1<br>Lyon 3 Inter Milan 3 | Inter Milan 3 Rosenborg 0<br>Lyon 0 Ajax 2 | Ajax 1 Inter Milan 2<br>Rosenborg 1 Lyon 1 |

| MATCHDAY 1 | MATCHDAY 2 | MATCHDAY 3 | MATCHDAY 4 | MATCHDAY 5 | MATCHDAY 6 |
|---|---|---|---|---|---|
| Mendieta back on Champions League form with goal for Barca | Filippo Inzaghi slams a hat-trick to crush Deportivo away | Del Piero double claims points in a pulsating contest | Buffon error helps turn Griffin cross into first goal for Robson | Deportivo oust 2001 winners Bayern with a game to go | Bellamy shoots Newcastle into second phase in stoppage time |

| | MATCHDAY 1 | MATCHDAY 2 | MATCHDAY 3 | MATCHDAY 4 | MATCHDAY 5 | MATCHDAY 6 |
|---|---|---|---|---|---|---|
| **GROUP E** | Feyenoord 1 Juventus 1<br>Dynamo 2 Newcastle 0 | Newcastle 0 Feyenoord 1<br>Juventus 5 Dynamo 0 | Feyenoord 0 Dynamo 0<br>**Juventus 2 Newcastle 0** | Dynamo 2 Feyenoord 0<br>**Newcastle 1 Juventus 0** | Juventus 2 Feyenoord 0<br>Newcastle 2 Dynamo 0 | Dynamo 1 Juventus 2<br>**Feyenoord 2 Newcastle 3** |
| **GROUP F** | Olympiakos 6 Leverkusen 2<br>Man Utd 5 M Haifa 2 | Leverkusen 1 Man Utd 2<br>M Haifa 3 Olympiakos 0 | Man U 4 Olympiakos 0<br>M Haifa 0 Leverkusen 2 | Leverkusen 2 M Haifa 1<br>Olympiakos 2 Man U 3 | Leverkusen 2 Olymp 0<br>M Haifa 3 Man United 0 | Man U 2 Leverkusen 0<br>Olympiakos 3 M Haifa 3 |
| **GROUP G** | Bayern 2 Deportivo 3<br>AC Milan 2 Lens 1 | Lens 1 Bayern 1<br>**Deportivo 0 AC Milan 4** | Bayern 1 AC Milan 2<br>Deportivo 3 Lens 1 | Lens 3 Deportivo 1<br>AC Milan 2 Bayern 1 | Lens 2 AC Milan 1<br>**Deportivo 2 Bayern 1** | Bayern 3 Lens 3<br>AC Milan 1 Deportivo 2 |
| **GROUP H** | **Barcelona 3 Brugge 2**<br>Lokomotiv 0 Galatasaray 2 | Brugge 0 Lokomotiv 0<br>Galatasaray 0 Barcelona 2 | Galatasaray 0 Brugge 0<br>Lokomotiv 1 Barcelona 3 | Barcelona 1 Lokomotiv 0<br>Brugge 3 Galatasaray 1 | Brugge 0 Barcelona 1<br>Galatasaray 1 Lokomotiv 2 | Barcelona 3 Galatasaray 1<br>Lokomotiv 2 Brugge 0 |

## STADIUM CAPACITY AND HOME CROWDS

| | TEAM | CAPACITY | AVE (%) | HIGH | LOW |
|---|---|---|---|---|---|
| 1 | B Leverkusen | 22500 | 100.00 | 22500 | 22500 |
| 2 | Man Utd | 67750 | 97.67 | 67014 | 63439 |
| 3 | Basel | 31539 | 94.61 | 31500 | 29031 |
| 4 | Ajax | 51324 | 91.99 | 51025 | 37455 |
| 5 | Arsenal | 38500 | 91.38 | 35472 | 34793 |
| 6 | Newcastle | 52200 | 86.72 | 51883 | 40185 |
| 7 | Valencia | 53000 | 79.66 | 50000 | 34980 |
| 8 | AC Milan | 85700 | 79.29 | 78175 | 45000 |
| 9 | Real Madrid | 87000 | 73.26 | 78000 | 40000 |
| 10 | Barcelona | 98800 | 68.93 | 98000 | 42928 |
| 11 | Deportivo | 35800 | 67.4 | 33000 | 7120 |
| 12 | Roma | 82307 | 62.62 | 80000 | 23734 |
| 13 | Lokomotiv Mos | 30000 | 62.61 | 20000 | 17000 |
| 14 | B Dortmund | 83100 | 60.17 | 52000 | 48000 |
| 15 | Inter Milan | 85700 | 60.15 | 83679 | 31448 |
| 16 | Juventus | 69041 | 59.37 | 60253 | 22639 |

**Key:** Average. The percentage of each stadium filled in League games over the season (AVE), the stadium capacity and the highest and lowest crowds recorded.

## AWAY ATTENDANCE

| | TEAM | AVE (%) | HIGH | LOW |
|---|---|---|---|---|
| 1 | Inter Milan | 91.26 | 82717 | 21040 |
| 2 | Roma | 89.85 | 71722 | 22989 |
| 3 | Barcelona | 85.94 | 71740 | 18000 |
| 4 | Juventus | 85.87 | 98000 | 27500 |
| 5 | AC Milan | 85.79 | 83679 | 20000 |
| 6 | Arsenal | 84.13 | 70000 | 23000 |
| 7 | Real Madrid | 83.63 | 80000 | 18000 |
| 8 | Man Utd | 82.25 | 66708 | 7120 |
| 9 | Lokomotiv Moscow | 79.38 | 72028 | 23000 |
| 10 | Ajax | 77.52 | 76079 | 21300 |
| 11 | Valencia | 73.8 | 52623 | 15000 |
| 12 | Deportivo | 72.43 | 67014 | 25070 |
| 13 | B Dortmund | 70.74 | 50000 | 17000 |
| 14 | Newcastle | 69.84 | 53459 | 22500 |
| 15 | B Leverkusen | 67.86 | 66185 | 5000 |
| 16 | Basel | 63.64 | 66870 | 5000 |

**Key:** Average. How close each club has come to filling grounds in its away league matches (AVE) and the highest and lowest crowds recorded.

**A**

| | P | W | D | L | DIF | PTS |
|---|---|---|---|---|---|---|
| **Arsenal** | **6** | **3** | **1** | **2** | **5** | **10** |
| **B Dortmund** | **6** | **3** | **1** | **2** | **2** | **10** |
| Auxerre | 6 | 2 | 1 | 3 | -3 | 7 |
| PSV | 6 | 1 | 2 | 3 | -4 | 6 |

**E**

| | P | W | D | L | DIF | PTS |
|---|---|---|---|---|---|---|
| **Juventus** | **6** | **4** | **1** | **1** | **9** | **13** |
| **Newcastle** | **6** | **3** | **0** | **3** | **-2** | **9** |
| Dynamo Kiev | 6 | 2 | 1 | 3 | -3 | 7 |
| Feyenoord | 6 | 1 | 2 | 3 | -4 | 5 |

**B**

| | P | W | D | L | DIF | PTS |
|---|---|---|---|---|---|---|
| **Valencia** | **6** | **5** | **1** | **0** | **13** | **16** |
| **FC Basel** | **6** | **2** | **3** | **1** | **0** | **9** |
| Liverpool | 6 | 2 | 2 | 2 | 4 | 8 |
| S Moscow | 6 | 0 | 0 | 6 | -17 | 0 |

**F**

| | P | W | D | L | DIF | PTS |
|---|---|---|---|---|---|---|
| **Man Utd** | **6** | **5** | **0** | **1** | **8** | **15** |
| **B Leverkusen** | **6** | **3** | **0** | **3** | **-2** | **9** |
| M Haifa | 6 | 2 | 1 | 3 | 0 | 7 |
| Olympiakos | 6 | 1 | 1 | 4 | -6 | 4 |

**C**

| | P | W | D | L | DIF | PTS |
|---|---|---|---|---|---|---|
| **Real Madrid** | **6** | **2** | **3** | **1** | **8** | **9** |
| **Roma** | **6** | **2** | **3** | **1** | **-1** | **9** |
| AEK Athens | 6 | 0 | 6 | 0 | 0 | 6 |
| Genk | 6 | 0 | 4 | 2 | -7 | 4 |

**G**

| CLUB | P | W | D | L | DIF | PTS |
|---|---|---|---|---|---|---|
| **AC Milan** | **6** | **4** | **0** | **2** | **5** | **12** |
| **Deportivo** | **6** | **4** | **0** | **2** | **-1** | **12** |
| Lens | 6 | 2 | 2 | 2 | 0 | 8 |
| B Munich | 6 | 0 | 2 | 4 | -4 | 2 |

**D**

| | P | W | D | L | DIF | PTS |
|---|---|---|---|---|---|---|
| **Inter Milan** | **6** | **3** | **2** | **1** | **4** | **11** |
| **Ajax** | **6** | **2** | **2** | **2** | **1** | **8** |
| Lyon | 6 | 2 | 2 | 2 | 3 | 8 |
| Rosenborg | 6 | 0 | 4 | 2 | -8 | 4 |

**H**

| CLUB | P | W | D | L | DIF | PTS |
|---|---|---|---|---|---|---|
| **Barcelona** | **6** | **6** | **0** | **0** | **9** | **18** |
| **Lokomotiv** | **6** | **2** | **1** | **3** | **-2** | **7** |
| Club Brugge | 6 | 1 | 2 | 3 | -2 | 5 |
| Galatasaray | 6 | 1 | 1 | 4 | -5 | 4 |

## CLUB STRIKE FORCE

**1 Manchester United**

| | |
|---|---|
| Goals in the Champions League | 37 |
| Club Strike Rate (CSR) Average number of minutes between League goals scored by club | 39 |

| | CLUB | GOALS | CSR |
|---|---|---|---|
| 2 | Real Madrid | 33 | 44 mins |
| 3 | Barcelona | 31 | 47 mins |
| 4 | Juventus | 30 | 53 mins |
| 5 | Valencia | 24 | 53 mins |
| 6 | Inter Milan | 28 | 58 mins |
| 7 | Deportivo | 18 | 60 mins |
| 8 | Newcastle | 21 | 60 mins |
| 9 | Basel | 20 | 63 mins |
| 10 | B Dortmund | 16 | 68 mins |
| 11 | Arsenal | 15 | 72 mins |
| 12 | AC Milan | 23 | 76 mins |
| 13 | B Leverkusen | 14 | 77 mins |
| 14 | Ajax | 14 | 90 mins |
| 15 | Lokomotiv Moscow | 13 | 97 mins |
| 16 | Roma | 10 | 108 mins |

## CLUB DISCIPLINARY RECORD

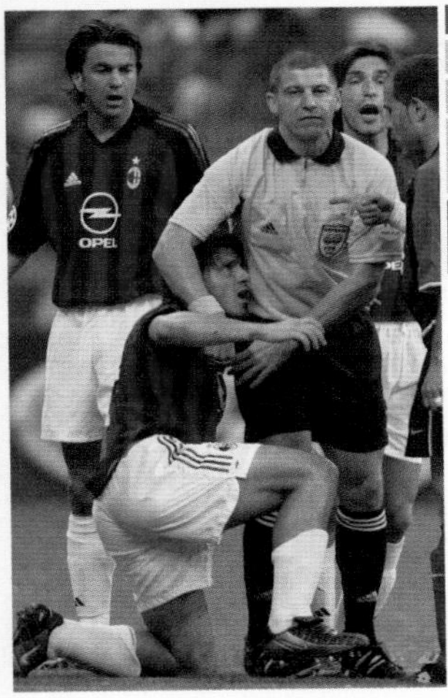

**1 AC Milan**

| | |
|---|---|
| Yellow Card | 33 |
| Red Card | 3 |
| Total | 36 |
| Cards Average Average number of minutes between a card being shown of either colour | 35 |

| | TEAM | YELL | RED | TOT | AVE |
|---|---|---|---|---|---|
| 2 | Ajax | 28 | 1 | 29 | 37 mins |
| 3 | Arsenal | 28 | 3 | 31 | 41 mins |
| 4 | B Dortmund | 29 | 1 | 30 | 42 mins |
| 5 | B Leverkusen | 35 | 3 | 38 | 43 mins |
| 6 | Barcelona | 36 | 1 | 37 | 43 mins |
| 7 | Basel | 23 | 0 | 23 | 47 mins |
| 8 | Deportivo | 27 | 0 | 27 | 53 mins |
| 9 | Inter Milan | 27 | 0 | 27 | 54 mins |
| 10 | Juventus | 17 | 0 | 17 | 64 mins |
| 11 | Lokomotiv Moscow | 26 | 0 | 26 | 67 mins |
| 12 | Man Utd | 13 | 0 | 13 | 83 mins |
| 13 | Newcastle | 15 | 0 | 15 | 84 mins |
| 14 | Real Madrid | 14 | 1 | 15 | 84 mins |
| 15 | Roma | 17 | 0 | 17 | 85 mins |
| 16 | Valencia | 11 | 1 | 12 | 90 mins |

## CLUB DEFENCE

**1 Barcelona**

| | |
|---|---|
| Goals conceded in the Champions League | 9 |
| Clean Sheets (CS) | 9 |
| Club Defensive Rate (CSR) Average number of minutes between goals conceded by club | 163 |

| | CLUB | CONCEDED | CS | CDR |
|---|---|---|---|---|
| 2 | Arsenal | 9 | 6 | 120 mins |
| 3 | AC Milan | 16 | 9 | 109 mins |
| 4 | Valencia | 12 | 6 | 105 mins |
| 5 | Ajax | 13 | 4 | 97 mins |
| 6 | B Dortmund | 12 | 2 | 90 mins |
| 7 | Roma | 12 | 5 | 90 mins |
| 8 | Inter Milan | 19 | 8 | 85 mins |
| 9 | Juventus | 19 | 5 | 84 mins |
| 10 | Man Utd | 20 | 5 | 72 mins |
| 11 | Real Madrid | 22 | 3 | 65 mins |
| 12 | Lokomotiv Moscow | 20 | 3 | 63 mins |
| 13 | Newcastle | 21 | 3 | 60 mins |
| 14 | Deportivo | 20 | 2 | 54 mins |
| 15 | Basel | 25 | 4 | 50 mins |
| 16 | B Leverkusen | 26 | 2 | 42 mins |

## PLAYER DISCIPLINARY RECORD

**1 Gabri - Barcelona**

| | |
|---|---|
| Yellow | 6 |
| Red | 0 |
| TOTAL | 6 |
| Cards Average Average number of minutes between a card being shown of either colour | 119 |

| | PLAYER | TEAM | YELL | RED | TOT | AVE |
|---|---|---|---|---|---|---|
| 2 | Cannavaro | Inter Milan | 6 | 1 | 7 | 131 |
| 3 | Tacchinardi | Juventus | 9 | 0 | 9 | 132 |
| 4 | Loskov | Lokomotiv M | 5 | 1 | 6 | 171 |
| 5 | Morfeo | Inter Milan | 4 | 0 | 4 | 195 |
| 6 | Kleine | B Leverkusen | 3 | 0 | 3 | 196 |
| 7 | Lekseto | Lokomotiv M | 5 | 0 | 5 | 198 |
| 8 | Iuliano | Juventus | 3 | 0 | 3 | 201 |
| 9 | Zanetti, C | Inter Milan | 3 | 0 | 3 | 204 |
| 10 | Gattuso | AC Milan | 6 | 0 | 6 | 205 |
| 11 | Chivu | Ajax | 4 | 1 | 5 | 210 |
| 12 | Dabizas | Newcastle | 3 | 0 | 3 | 224 |
| 13 | Basturk | B Leverkusen | 4 | 0 | 4 | 230 |
| 14 | LuaLua | Newcastle | 2 | 0 | 2 | 232 |
| 15 | Totti | Roma | 1 | 1 | 2 | 234 |
| 16 | Veron | Man Utd | 4 | 0 | 4 | 238 |
| 17 | van der Vaart | Ajax | 2 | 0 | 2 | 243 |
| 18 | Luis Enrique | Barcelona | 2 | 0 | 2 | 243 |
| 19 | Victor | Deportivo | 2 | 0 | 2 | 243 |
| 20 | Ambrosini | AC Milan | 3 | 0 | 3 | 247 |

## KEY GOALSCORERS

**1 Ruud van Nistelrooy - Manchester Utd**

| | |
|---|---|
| Goals in Chapions League | 14 |
| Contribution to Attacking Power (AP) Average number of minutes between League team goals while on pitch | 33 |
| Player Strike Rate (SR) Average number of minutes between League goals scored by player | 62 |

| | PLAYER | TEAM | G | AP | SR |
|---|---|---|---|---|---|
| 2 | Crespo | Inter Milan | 10 | 49 | 98 |
| 3 | Makaay | Deportivo | 9 | 56 | 101 |
| 4 | Inzaghi | AC Milan | 12 | 67 | 106 |
| 5 | Raul | Real Madrid | 9 | 43 | 117 |
| 6 | Koller | B Dortmund | 8 | 60 | 121 |
| 7 | Ronaldo | Real Madrid | 6 | 44 | 126 |
| 8 | Tristan | Deportivo | 4 | 56 | 127 |
| 9 | Di Vaio | Juventus | 4 | 55 | 138 |
| 10 | Babic | B Leverkusen | 4 | 64 | 145 |
| 11 | Henry | Arsenal | 7 | 68 | 146 |
| 12 | Gimenez | Basel | 7 | 64 | 147 |
| 13 | Shearer | Newcastle | 7 | 62 | 151 |
| 14 | Saviola | Barcelona | 7 | 45 | 157 |
| 15 | Cassano | Roma | 4 | 79 | 160 |

## PHASE 2

### MATCHDAY 7

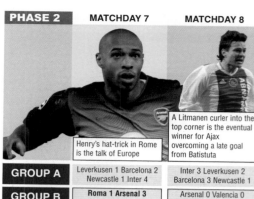

Henry's hat-trick in Rome is the talk of Europe

### MATCHDAY 8

A Litmanen curler into the top corner is the eventual winner for Ajax overcoming a late goal from Batistuta

### MATCHDAY 9

New manager Antic off to a record-breaking start as Barca notch 11th straight Champions League win

### MATCHDAY 10

Totti does the damage to make Roma the first team to beat Valencia at the Mestalla stadium in this competition

### MATCHDAY 11

Five in two games for Shearer but Inter level each time to keep a narrow advantage

### MATCHDAY 12

Carew brace fires Valencia through to possible third final in four years as Arsenal go out

| | MATCHDAY 7 | MATCHDAY 8 | MATCHDAY 9 | MATCHDAY 10 | MATCHDAY 11 | MATCHDAY 12 |
|---|---|---|---|---|---|---|
| GROUP A | Leverkusen 1 Barcelona 2<br>Newcastle 1 Inter 4 | Inter 3 Leverkusen 2<br>Barcelona 3 Newcastle 1 | **Barcelona 3 Inter Milan 0**<br>Leverkusen 1 Newcastle 3 | Inter 0 Barcelona 0<br>Newcastle 3 Leverkusen 1 | Barcelona 2 Leverkusen 0<br>**Inter 2 Newcastle 2** | Leverkusen 0 Inter 2<br>Newcastle 0 Barcelona 2 |
| GROUP B | **Roma 1 Arsenal 3**<br>Valencia 1 Ajax 1 | Arsenal 0 Valencia 0<br>**Ajax 2 Roma 1** | Arsenal 1 Ajax 1<br>Roma 0 Valencia 1 | Ajax 0 Arsenal 0<br>**Valencia 0 Roma 3** | Ajax 1 Valencia 1<br>Arsenal 1 Roma 1 | Roma 1 Ajax 1<br>**Valencia 2 Arsenal 1** |

Van Nistlerooy helps United overcome nerves and overturn Basle's early lead

Trezeguet returns from injury with a goal after three minutes – the first of four from Juvé

Zidane runs the midfield and Ronaldo delivers to get Madrid back on track

Giggs hits two to put Utd into the quarters with a compelling win in Italy

Raul fires home twice as Real turn it on against Milan to keep ahead of Dortmund's pressure

Koller gives Dortmund win in Milan but ten points is not enough as Madrid beat Lokomotiv

| | MATCHDAY 7 | MATCHDAY 8 | MATCHDAY 9 | MATCHDAY 10 | MATCHDAY 11 | MATCHDAY 12 |
|---|---|---|---|---|---|---|
| GROUP C | Lokomotiv 1 Dortmund 2<br>AC Milan 1 Madrid 0 | Dortmund 0 AC Milan 1<br>Madrid 2 Lokomotiv 2 | **Madrid 2 Dortmund 1**<br>AC Milan 1 Lokomotiv 0 | Dortmund 1 Madrid 1<br>Lokomotiv 0 AC Milan 1 | Dortmund 3 Lokomotiv 0<br>**Madrid 3 AC Milan 1** | Locomotiv 0 Madrid 1<br>**AC Milan 0 Dortmund 1** |
| GROUP D | **Basel 1 Man United 3**<br>Deportivo 2 Juventus 2 | **Juventus 4 Basel 0**<br>Man United 2 Deportivo 0 | Basle 1 Deportivo 0<br>Man United 2 Juventus 1 | Deportivo 1 Basle 0<br>**Juventus 0 Man United 3** | Juventus 3 Deportivo 2<br>Man United 1 Basel 1 | Basle 2 Juventus 1<br>Deportivo 2 Man United 0 |

## CHART-TOPPING MIDFIELDERS

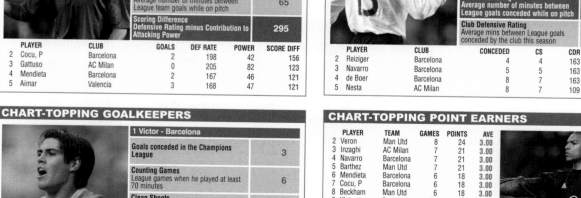

**1 Gabri - Barcelona**

| | |
|---|---|
| **Goals scored in the Champions League** | 0 |
| **Defensive Rating**<br>Av number of mins between League goals conceded while on the pitch | 360 |
| **Contribution to Attacking Power**<br>Average number of minutes between League team goals while on pitch | 65 |
| **Scoring Difference**<br>Defensive Rating minus Contribution to Attacking Power | 295 |

| | PLAYER | CLUB | GOALS | DEF RATE | POWER | SCORE DIFF |
|---|---|---|---|---|---|---|
| 2 | Cocu, P | Barcelona | 2 | 198 | 42 | 156 |
| 3 | Gattuso | AC Milan | 0 | 205 | 82 | 123 |
| 4 | Mendieta | Barcelona | 2 | 167 | 46 | 121 |
| 5 | Aimar | Valencia | 3 | 168 | 47 | 121 |

## CHART-TOPPING DEFENDERS

**1 Carboni - Valencia**

| | |
|---|---|
| **Goals Conceded in the League**<br>The number of League goals conceded while he was on the pitch | 4 |
| **Clean Sheets**<br>In games when he played at least 70 mins | 5 |
| **Defensive Rating**<br>Average number of minutes between League goals conceded while on pitch | 222 |
| **Club Defensive Rating**<br>Average mins between League goals conceded by the club this season | 105 |

| | PLAYER | CLUB | CONCEDED | CS | CDR | DEF RATE |
|---|---|---|---|---|---|---|
| 2 | Reiziger | Barcelona | 4 | 4 | 163 | 183 |
| 3 | Navarro | Barcelona | 5 | 5 | 163 | 162 |
| 4 | de Boer | Barcelona | 8 | 7 | 163 | 157 |
| 5 | Nesta | AC Milan | 8 | 7 | 109 | 154 |

## CHART-TOPPING GOALKEEPERS

**1 Victor - Barcelona**

| | |
|---|---|
| **Goals conceded in the Champions League** | 3 |
| **Counting Games**<br>League games when he played at least 70 minutes | 6 |
| **Clean Sheets**<br>In games when he played at least 70 mins | 4 |
| **Defensive Rating**<br>Average number of minutes between League goals conceded while on pitch | 180 |

| | PLAYER | CLUB | CG | CL | CS | DR |
|---|---|---|---|---|---|---|
| 2 | Dida | AC Milan | 14 | 7 | 9 | 178 mins |
| 3 | Bonano | Barcelona | 8 | 5 | 4 | 150 mins |
| 4 | Seaman | Arsenal | 9 | 6 | 5 | 128 mins |
| 5 | Lobont | Ajax | 6 | 6 | 2 | 90 mins |

## CHART-TOPPING POINT EARNERS

| | PLAYER | TEAM | GAMES | POINTS | AVE |
|---|---|---|---|---|---|
| 2 | Veron | Man Utd | 8 | 24 | 3.00 |
| 3 | Inzaghi | AC Milan | 7 | 21 | 3.00 |
| 4 | Navarro | Barcelona | 7 | 21 | 3.00 |
| 5 | Barthez | Man Utd | 7 | 21 | 3.00 |
| 6 | Mendieta | Barcelona | 6 | 18 | 3.00 |
| 7 | Cocu, P | Barcelona | 6 | 18 | 3.00 |
| 8 | Beckham | Man Utd | 6 | 18 | 3.00 |
| 9 | Kluivert | Barcelona | 10 | 28 | 2.80 |
| 10 | de Boer | Barcelona | 9 | 25 | 2.78 |
| 11 | Motta | Barcelona | 9 | 25 | 2.78 |
| 12 | Xavi | Barcelona | 9 | 25 | 2.78 |
| 13 | Puyol | Barcelona | 9 | 25 | 2.78 |
| 14 | Saviola | Barcelona | 7 | 19 | 2.71 |
| 15 | Bonano | Barcelona | 6 | 16 | 2.67 |
| 16 | Gabri | Barcelona | 6 | 16 | 2.67 |
| 17 | Reiziger | Barcelona | 6 | 16 | 2.67 |
| 18 | Nesta | AC Milan | 8 | 21 | 2.63 |
| 19 | Kaladze | AC Milan | 8 | 21 | 2.63 |
| 20 | Seedorf | AC Milan | 8 | 21 | 2.63 |

**1 Dida - AC Milan**

| | |
|---|---|
| **Counting Games**<br>League games where he played at least 70 minutes | 8 |
| **Total League Points**<br>Taken in Counting Games | 24 |
| **Average League Points**<br>Taken in Counting Games | 3.00 |

| A | P | W | D | L | DIF | PTS |
|---|---|---|---|---|---|---|
| Barcelona | 6 | 5 | 1 | 0 | 10 | 16 |
| Inter Milan | 6 | 3 | 2 | 1 | 3 | 11 |
| Newcastle | 6 | 2 | 2 | 2 | –3 | 7 |
| BLeverkusen | 6 | 0 | 0 | 6 | –10 | 0 |

| B | P | W | D | L | DIF | PTS |
|---|---|---|---|---|---|---|
| Valencia | 6 | 2 | 3 | 1 | –1 | 9 |
| Ajax | 6 | 1 | 5 | 0 | 1 | 8 |
| Arsenal | 6 | 1 | 4 | 1 | 1 | 7 |
| Roma | 6 | 1 | 2 | 3 | –1 | 5 |

| C | P | W | D | L | DIF | PTS |
|---|---|---|---|---|---|---|
| AC Milan | 6 | 4 | 0 | 2 | 1 | 12 |
| Real Madrid | 6 | 3 | 2 | 1 | 3 | 11 |
| B Dortmund | 6 | 3 | 1 | 2 | 3 | 10 |
| Lokomotiv | 6 | 0 | 1 | 5 | –7 | 1 |

| D | P | W | D | L | DIF | PTS |
|---|---|---|---|---|---|---|
| Man Utd | 6 | 4 | 1 | 1 | 6 | 13 |
| Juventus | 6 | 2 | 1 | 3 | 0 | 7 |
| Deportivo | 6 | 2 | 1 | 3 | –1 | 7 |
| Basle | 6 | 2 | 1 | 3 | –5 | 7 |

**Hat-rick of wins** for Clarence Seedorf makes Champions League history. Milan's Dutch midfielder Seedorf, competing against his International colleague Davids, becomes the first player ever to win Champions League titles with 3 different clubs

## QUARTER FINALS

Ajax 0 AC Milan 0
AC Milan 3 Ajax 2

**All to play for** as Milan resist Ajax pressure in Amsterdam before Jon Dahl Tomasson scores in extra time to nudge Milan into the semies despite a battling Ajax performance

Inter Milan 1 Valencia 0
Valencia 2 Inter Milan 1

**Vieri nets in each leg** to help Inter manager Cúper beat the Spanish side he twice coached to Champions League finals. And it's the Italian striker's second away goal that provides the narrow margin of victory.

Juventus 1 Barcelona 1
Barcelona 1 Juventus 2

**Saviola gives Barca the edge** with a late equaliser of Montero's 16th minute goal in Turin but Juvé turn the tables despite losing Davids to two yellows when Zalayeta nets winner in extra time in Spain.

Madrid 3 Man United 1
Man United 4 Madrid 3

SIEMENS

**Real give United the run around** with Raul scoring 2 although Van Nistlerooy away goal offers hope. That is extinguished as Ronaldo hat-trick leaves United with too big a mountain to climb.

## SEMI FINALS

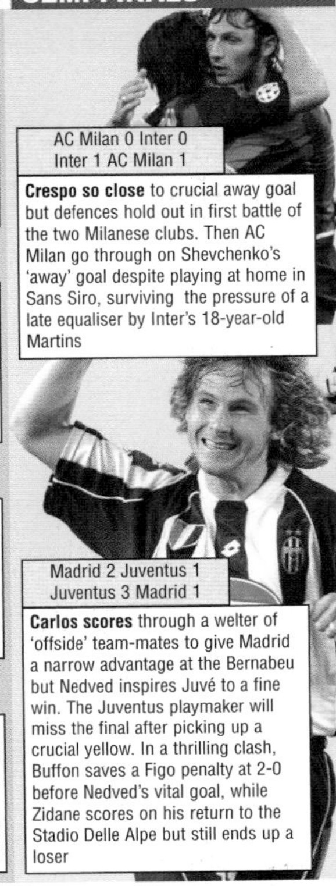

AC Milan 0 Inter 0
Inter 1 AC Milan 1

**Crespo so close** to crucial away goal but defences hold out in first battle of the two Milanese clubs. Then AC Milan go through on Shevchenko's 'away' goal despite playing at home in Sans Siro, surviving the pressure of a late equaliser by Inter's 18-year-old Martins

Madrid 2 Juventus 1
Juventus 3 Madrid 1

**Carlos scores** through a welter of 'offside' team-mates to give Madrid a narrow advantage at the Bernabeu but Nedved inspires Juvé to a fine win. The Juventus playmaker will miss the final after picking up a crucial yellow. In a thrilling clash, Buffon saves a Figo penalty at 2-0 before Nedved's vital goal, while Zidane scores on his return to the Stadio Delle Alpe but still ends up a loser

## FINAL

AC Milan 0 Juventus 0
(Milan win 3-2 on penalties)

**Italian defences rule in Europe** – even in penalty shoot-outs! AC Milan win the all-Italian final with Shevchenko scoring the final penalty of only five converted.

Stalwart defenders such as Milan's Maldini and Costacurta and Juvé's Thuram and Montero keep the strikers quiet over 120 minutes of normal and extra-time. Then it comes down to the keepers - Buffon against Dida.

Dida's three saves edge it for Milan to take their sixth European title. Juventus, who had beaten both Milan teams to the Italian Scudetto, are second best in the final at Old Trafford until Roque Junior's injury effectively reduces Milan to ten men in extra time.

**The Team of the Season** in each League's Divisional Round-up is different to those at club level. It doesn't just mirror the Chart-topping performances but highlights Keepers, Defenders, Midfield players and Forwards who are dramatically out-performing their team-mates. We compare their key rating to the club average see below: -

- **The Division Team's goalkeeper** has to be the player with the highest Defensive Rating as he often plays most or all the games in a league season.
- **The Division Team's defenders** are also tested by Defensive Rating but against their co-defender's Ratings. We weight it to take into account the fact that differences can fluctuate wildly at the bottom of a division.
- **The Division Team's midfield** all have good Scoring Differences compared to the average Ratings of their colleagues. In all cases these players must have played at least a minimum of Counting Games.
- **The Divisional Team strikeforce** is made up of the two players who have the biggest gap in Strike Rate between themselves and their next forward. These are weighted again, as lower sides may not even have a second charting forward.

## TEAM OF THE SEASON

Victor
Barcelona
M 540 DR 180
Carboni
Valencia
M 886 DR 222
Nesta
AC Milan
M 1229 DR 154
Tudor
Juventus
M 606 DR 121
Galasek
Ajax
M 981 DR 123
Gattuso
AC Milan
M 1233 SD 123
Davids
Juventus
M 1165 SD 59
Aimar
Valencia
M 838 SD 121
Gabri
Barcelona
M 719 SD 295
Crespo
Inter Milan
M 980 SR 98
van Nistlerooy
Man Utd
M 863 SR 62

**KEY:** DR = Defensive Rate, SD = Scoring Difference AP = Attacking Power SR = Strike Rate, M = Minutes played in Champions League proper.

# THE UEFA CUP

## 1ST ROUND

| | AGG | | 1ST | 2ND |
|---|---|---|---|---|
| Aberdeen | 0-1 | **Hertha Berlin** | 0-0 | 0-1 |
| AIK Solna | 4-6 | **Fenerbahce** | 3-3 | 1-3 |
| **Anderlecht** | 2-2 | Stabaek | 0-1 | 2-1 |
| Ankaraguku | 1-5 | **Alaves** | 1-2 | 0-3 |
| **Apoel Nicosia** | 3-1 | Grazer AK | 2-0 | 1-1 |
| **A Vienna** | 5-2 | Shakhtar Donetsk | 5-1 | 0-1 |
| **Besiktas** | 7-2 | Sarajevo | 2-2 | 5-0 |
| **Blackburn** | 4-4 | CSKA Sofia | 1-1 | 3-3 |
| Blackburn win on away goals rule | | | | |
| **Bordeaux** | 10-1 | Puchov | 6-0 | 4-1 |
| **Celta Vigo** | 2-1 | Odense | 2-0 | 0-1 |
| **Celtic** | 10-1 | FK Suduva | 8-1 | 2-0 |
| Chelsea | 4-5 | **Viking** | 2-1 | 2-4 |
| **Crvena Z** | 2-0 | Chievo | 0-0 | 2-0 |
| CSKA Mos | 3-4 | **Parma** | 1-1 | 2-3 |
| **Denizlispor** | 3-3 | Lorient | 2-0 | 1-3 |
| Denizlispor win on away goals rule | | | | |
| **D Zagreb** | 9-1 | Zalaegerszeg | 6-0 | 3-1 |
| Copenhagen | 1-3 | **Djurgarden** | 0-0 | 1-3 |
| **Ferencvaros** | 5-0 | Kocaelispor | 4-0 | 1-0 |
| Gomel | 1-8 | **Schalke** | 1-4 | 0-4 |
| **Grasshoppers** | 4-3 | Zenit St Petersburg | 3-1 | 1-2 |
| Hajduk Split | 2-3 | **Fulham** | 0-1 | 2-2 |
| **Ipswich** | 2-1 | FK Sartid | 1-1 | 1-0 |
| Iraklis | 5-5 | **Anorthosis F** | 4-2 | 1-3 |
| Anorthosis win on away goals rule | | | | |
| Karnten | 1-4 | **Hapoel Tel-Aviv** | 0-4 | 1-0 |
| **Lazio** | 4-0 | Xanthi | 4-0 | 0-0 |
| **Leeds** | 2-1 | Zaporizhya | 1-0 | 1-1 |
| **L Warsaw** | 7-2 | Utrecht | 4-1 | 3-1 |
| Leixoes | 3-5 | **PAOK Salonika** | 2-1 | 1-4 |
| **Levski Sofia** | 5-2 | Brondby | 4-1 | 1-1 |
| Liteks Lovetch | 1-3 | **Panathinaikos** | 0-1 | 1-2 |
| M Tel-Aviv | 2-4 | **Boavista** | 1-0 | 1-4 |
| Metalurgs | 2-10 | **W Bremen** | 2-2 | 0-8 |
| **Midtjylland** | 2-1 | Varteks | 1-0 | 1-1 |
| Mouscron | 3-7 | **Slavia Prague** | 2-2 | 1-5 |
| **N Bucharest** | 3-2 | Heerenveen | 3-0 | 0-2 |
| **Paris SG** | 4-0 | Ujpesti | 3-0 | 1-0 |
| **Porto** | 6-2 | Polonia Warsaw | 6-0 | 0-2 |
| Primorje | 1-8 | **Wisla Krakow** | 0-2 | 1-6 |
| Servette | 4-4 | **Amica Wronki** | 2-3 | 2-1 |
| **Slovan L** | 4-2 | Dinamo Tbilisi | 3-2 | 1-0 |
| Sp Lisbon | 4-6 | **Partizan** | 1-3 | 3-3 |
| **S Prague** | 4-0 | Siroki Brijeg | 3-0 | 1-0 |
| **Sturm Graz** | 8-6 | Livingston | 5-2 | 3-4 |
| **Stuttgart** | 8-2 | FK Ventspils | 4-1 | 4-1 |
| **V Arnhem** | 2-1 | Rapid Bucharest | 1-1 | 1-0 |
| Zeljeznicar | 0-1 | **Malaga** | 0-0 | 0-1 |
| Zimbru | 1-4 | **Real Betis** | 0-2 | 1-2 |
| **Zizkov** | 3-3 | Rangers | 2-0 | 1-3 |
| Zizkov win on away goals rule | | | | |

## 2ND ROUND

| | AGG | | 1ST | 2ND |
|---|---|---|---|---|
| Alaves | **1-2** | **Besiktas** | **1-1** | **0-1** |
| **Anderlecht** | 6-1 | Midtjylland | 3-1 | 3-0 |
| Apoel Nicosia | 0-5 | **Hertha Berlin** | 0-1 | 0-4 |
| A Vienna | 0-3 | **Porto** | 0-1 | 0-2 |
| **Boavista** | 3-1 | Anorthosis F | 2-1 | 1-0 |
| **Celta Vigo** | 4-1 | Viking | 3-0 | 1-1 |
| **Celtic** | 3-0 | Blackburn | 1-0 | 2-0 |
| Djurgarden | 1-3 | **Bordeaux** | 0-1 | 1-2 |
| D Zagreb | 1-5 | **Fulham** | 0-3 | 1-2 |
| Fenerbahce | 2-5 | **Panathinaikos** | 1-1 | 1-4 |
| Ferencvaros | 0-2 | **Stuttgart** | 0-0 | 0-2 |
| Ipswich | 1-1 | **Slovan Liberec** | 1-0 | 0-1 |
| Slovan Liberec win 4-2 on penalties | | | | |
| **Lazio** | 2-1 | Crvena Zvezda | 1-0 | 1-1 |
| **Leeds** | 5-1 | Hapoel Tel-Aviv | 1-0 | 4-1 |
| Legia Warsaw | 2-3 | **Schalke** | 2-3 | 0-0 |
| **Malaga** | 4-2 | Amica Wronki | 2-1 | 2-1 |
| Nat Bucharest | 0-3 | **Paris SG** | 0-2 | 0-1 |
| **PAOK S'nika** | 3-2 | Grasshoppers | 2-1 | 1-1 |
| Parma | 3-5 | **Wisla Krakow** | 2-1 | 1-4 |
| Partizan | 4-6 | **Slavia Prague** | 3-1 | 1-5 |
| S Prague | 1-2 | **Denizlispor** | 1-0 | 0-2 |
| **Sturm Graz** | 1-1 | Levski Sofia | 1-0 | 0-1 |
| Sturm Graz win 8-7 on penalties | | | | |
| **V Arnhem** | 5-4 | W Bremen | 2-1 | 3-3 |
| Zizkov | 0-4 | **Real Betis** | 0-1 | 0-3 |

## 3RD ROUND

**AEK Athens** 4 **Maccabi Haifa** 0
Georgatos 13, Nikolaidis 24, Petkov 31, Zagorakis 36 — 19,000

**Maccabi Haifa** 1 **AEK Athens** 4
Badir 5 — Katsouranis 56, Lakis 79,89, Nalitzis 90
11,209

**Besiktas** 3 **Dinamo Kiev** 1
Pancu 31, Ronaldo 71, Nouma 82 — Rincon 30
28,000

**Dinamo Kiev** 0 **Besiktas** 0
35,000

**Bordeaux** 0 **Anderlecht** 2
12,180 — Jestrovic 9, Hasi 90

**Anderlecht** 2 **Bordeaux** 2
Dindane 28, Jestrovic 68 — Darcheville 82,89
17,721

**A vital away goal** by Hartson helped Celtic beat powerful Spanish outfit Celta Vigo and go beyond Xmas in European competition for the first time in 23 years.

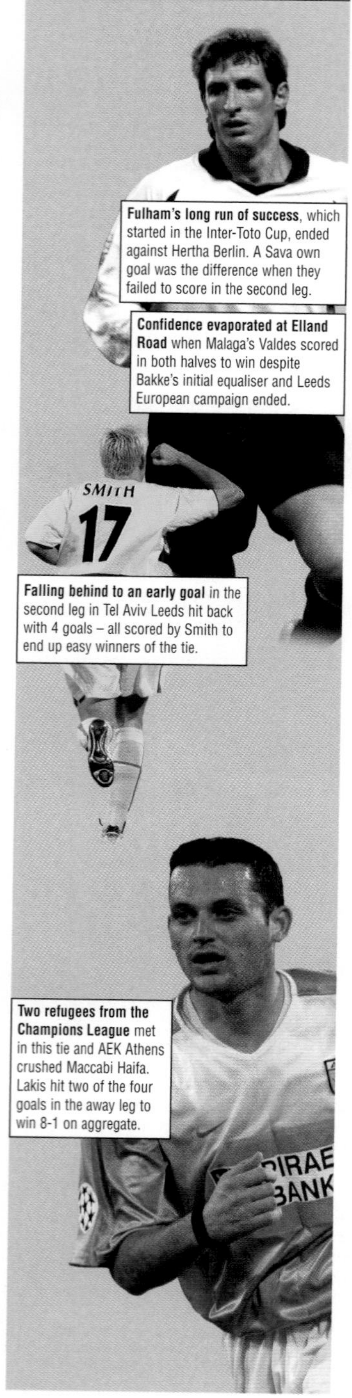
SMITH
17

**Fulham's long run of success**, which started in the Inter-Toto Cup, ended against Hertha Berlin. A Sava own goal was the difference when they failed to score in the second leg.

**Confidence evaporated at Elland Road** when Malaga's Valdes scored in both halves to win despite Bakke's initial equaliser and Leeds European campaign ended.

**Falling behind to an early goal** in the second leg in Tel Aviv Leeds hit back with 4 goals – all scored by Smith to end up easy winners of the tie.

**Two refugees from the Champions League** met in this tie and AEK Athens crushed Maccabi Haifa. Lakis hit two of the four goals in the away leg to win 8-1 on aggregate.

**Celtic** 1 **Celta Vigo** 0
Larsson 52 — 53,726

**Celta Vigo** 2 **Celtic** 1
Jesuli 23, McCarthy 54 — Hartson 37
19,080
Celtic win on the away goals rule

**Club Brugge** 1 **Stuttgart** 2
van der Heyden 42 — Balakov 72, Kuranyi 89
18,000

**Stuttgart** 1 **Club Brugge** 0
Hleb 90 — 34,000

**Denizlispor** 0 **Lyon** 0
15,000

**Lyon** 0 **Denizlispor** 1
29,000 — Ozkan 4

**Hertha Berlin** 2 **Fulham** 1
Beinlich 28, Sava 68 og — Marlet 53
14,477

**Fulham** 0 **Hertha Berlin** 0
15,161

**Malaga** 0 **Leeds** 0
35,000

**Leeds** 1 **Malaga** 2
Bakke 22 — Dely Valdes 13,79
34,123

**PAOK Salonika** 1 **Slavia Prague** 0
Georgiadis 52 — 28,000

**Slavia Prague** 4 **PAOK Salonika** 0
Skacel 13, Vachousek 51, Kuka 88,90 — 8,563

**Paris SG** 2 **Boavista** 1
Nyarko 17, Fiorese 44 — Luiz Claudio 74
30,000

**Boavista** 1 **Paris SG** 0
Silva 55 pen — 14,000
Boavista win on the away goals rule

**Porto** 3 **Lens** 0
Helder Postiga 35, Warmuz 45 og, Jankauskas 87 — 60,000

**Lens** 1 **Porto** 0
Song 27 — 44,505

**Real Betis** 1 **Auxerre** 0
Alfonso 9 pen — 37,800

**Auxerre** 2 **Real Betis** 0
Tainio 19, Lachuer 47 pen — 15,000

**Sturm Graz** 1 **Lazio** 3
Amoah 44 — Chiesa 47, Inzaghi 56,87
15,000

**Lazio** 0 **Sturm Graz** 1
10,000 — Szabics 87

**Slovan Liberec** 2 **Panathinaikos** 2
Zboncak 45, Slovak 85 — Basinas 13 pen, Olisadebe 53
5,805

**Panathinaikos** 1 **Slovan Liberec** 0
Fissas 3 — 13,300

**Vitesse Arnhem** 0 **Liverpool** 1
27,000 — Owen 26

**Liverpool** 1 **Vitesse Arnhem** 0
Owen 20 — 23,576

**Wisla Krakow** 1 **Schalke** 1
Poulsen 39 og — Mpenza 81
10,300

**Schalke** 1 **Wisla Krakow** 4
Hajto 42 — Zurawski 40,86, Uche 51, Kosowski 90
50,000

## 4TH ROUND

| | | |
|---|---|---|
| **Auxerre** 20,452 | **0 Liverpool** | **1** Hyypia 73 |
| **Liverpool** Owen 67, Murphy 72 | **2 Auxerre** | **0** 34,252 |
| **Celtic** Lambert 36, Maloney 45, Petrov 68 | **3 Stuttgart** | **1** Kuranyi 27, 59,000 |
| **Stuttgart** Tiffert 37, Hleb 75, Mutzel 87 | **3 Celtic** | **2** Thompson 12, Sutton 14, 45,000 |
| **Porto** Capucho 49, Derlei 53, Ricardo Costa 66, Jankauskas 69, Deco 73, Alenitchev 82 | **6 Denizlispor** | **1** Kratochvíl 78, 30,000 |
| **Denizlispor** Martin 52, Ozkan 58, 4,300 | **2 Porto** | **2** Derlei 43, Clayton 86 |
| **Hertha Berlin** Alves 15,42, Van Burik 90, 18,000 | **3 Boavista** | **2** Rui Oscar 37, Goulart 80 |
| **Boavista** Avalos 85 | **1 Hertha Berlin** | **0** 5,500 |
| Boavista win on away goals rule | | |
| **Lazio** Lazetic 22, Job 45 og, Chiesa 71 | **3 Wisla Krakow** | **3** Uche 39, Zurawski 49 pen,62 pen, 15,000 |
| **Wisla Krakow** Kuzba 3, 10,000 | **1 Lazio** | **2** Couto 21, Chiesa 54 |
| **Malaga** | **0 AEK Athens** | **0** 15,000 |
| **AEK Athens** 18,000 | **0 Malaga** | **1** Manu 28 |
| **Panathinaikos** Olisadebe 12,74, Liberopoulos 62 | **3 Anderlecht** | **0** |
| **Anderlecht** Jestrovic 69,80 | **2 Panathinaikos** | **0** 14,000 |
| **Slavia Prague** Dosek, T 62 | **1 Besiktas** | **0** |
| **Besiktas** Pancu 41, Ronaldo 61, Dursun 66, Ilhan 70 | **4 Slavia Prague** | **2** Dostalek 77 pen, Hrdlicka 84, 27,500 |

OWEN
10

**Owen struck after 66 minutes** to equal Liverpool's European scoring record with his 22nd goal. Murphy added a second to ensure an away win to go with the Anfield victory over Auxerre.

**The terrific UEFA Cup away form of Celtic** came up trumps again as they ousted Liverpool in style with a 2-0 win at Anfield. Englishman Thompson scored first before Welshman Hartson made sure the Scottish side went through with a stunning strike. "Tonight it was one of those that as I hit it, I knew it was in. You probably get one or two of them in your career," Hartson commented.

**Six second half goals** were shared around the Porto team as they despatched Denizilspor 6-1 to wrap up the tie in the home leg. Capucho's goal opened the floodgates.

SIEMENS
mobile

**Porto needed to win in Greece** after losing 1-0 to Panathinaikos in their home leg. Brazilian Derlei made sure they did with the aggregate equaliser after just 16 minutes. He went one better to hit an extra-time goal to ensure the Portuguese league leaders reached the semi-finals.

**The Italian giants were given it all to do** after Wisla held them 3-3 in Rome. Lazio came through despite Kuzba's 5th-minute effort to win after goals from Couto and Chiesa.

**The fierce marking and chasing of Boavista** knocked Celtic off their stride in the **first leg** of the semi-final at Celtic Park.
The Portuguese side had the undeserved bonus of an away goal when Valgaeren scored in his own net. Larsson equalised minutes later but the chance to take a lead to the away leg was lost when Larsson missed a penalty in the 75th minute.
In a **second leg** of poor quality and spoiling tactics, Larsson's 79th minute goal broke the deadlock to put Celtic in the final.
At last the home side had to go forward and almost levelled but Balde survived a penalty appeal and the more positive side went through.

**Lazio took an away goal lead** through Lopez after only 6 minutes of the **first leg** but were then effectively dismissed from this semi-final tie by four goals from rampant Porto.
Derlei added to his two vital goals in Greece in the previous round with two more here. Maniche and Hélder Postiga added one apiece as the Portuguese side raced to a 4-1 lead by the 58th minute.
The key moment of the **second leg** was López seeing his 57th minute penalty saved by Porto goalkeeper Vítor Baía.
Otherwise it was an even game with Lazio struggling to create chances and Porto missing the ones prompted by the inventive Deco.

## QUARTER FINALS

| | | |
|---|---|---|
| **Celtic** Larsson 2, 59,759 | **1 Liverpool** | **1** Heskey 17 |
| **Liverpool** 44,238 | **0 Celtic** | **2** Thompson 45, Hartson 81 |
| **Lazio** Inzaghi 55 | **1 Besiktas** | **0** 25,000 |
| **Besiktas** Sergen 83, 28,000 | **1 Lazio** | **2** Fiore 5, Castroman 9 |
| **Malaga** Dely Valdes 17 | **1 Boavista** | **0** 15,000 |
| **Boavista** Luiz Claudio 83 | **1 Malaga** | **0** 8,500 |
| Boavista win 4-1 on penalties | | |
| **Porto** 44,310 | **0 Panathinaikos** | **1** Olisadebe 72 |
| **Panathinaikos** 15,000 | **0 Porto** | **2** Derlei 16,103 |
| After extra-time | | |

## SEMI FINALS

| | | |
|---|---|---|
| **Celtic** Larsson 51, 60,000 | **1 Boavista** | **1** Valgaeren 48 og |
| **Boavista** 11,000 | **0 Celtic** | **1** Larsson 78 |
| **Porto** Maniche 10, Derlei 27,50, Helder Postiga 56 | **4 Lazio** | **1** Lopez 5, 45,518 |
| **Lazio** | **0 Porto** | **0** 65,000 |

## THE FINAL

| | | |
|---|---|---|
| **Celtic** Larsson 47,56, 52,972 | **2 Porto** | **3** Derlei 45,115, Alenitchev 54 |

CARLING

**Celtic fell at the very final hurdle** in a brave performance which took them to extra time and almost to penalties against powerful Porto in Seville.
Porto were more at home in the heat of the final and Deco dominated the first half which ended when his Brazilian compatriot Derlei scored in stoppage time.
Larsson hit back for the Scots two minutes into the second half with a terrific far post header.
The two sides exchanged goals again within a few minutes of each other when first Deco pushed Alenichev into space and the Russian slotted home. Larsson sprang again in the 57th minute to equalise from a Thompson corner and Celtic finished stronger over the 90 minutes.
Extra time was dominated by Porto once Balde was dismissed in the 96th minute but they didn't have a chance until a Douglas block fell to Derlei to hit the winner.
It was his 12th goal in this year's competition and he finished the UEFA top scorer ahead of Larsson.

# EUROPEAN LEAGUES ROUND-UP

## STADIUM CAPACITY AND HOME CROWDS

| | | | | | |
|---|---|---|---|---|---|
| 1 | Barcelona | 98600 | 79.01 | 98000 | 48507 |
| 2 | Real Madrid | 87000 | 81.83 | 76300 | 53400 |
| 3 | Inter Milan | 85700 | 68.69 | 78000 | 30000 |
| 4 | AC Milan | 85700 | 66.57 | 78871 | 35000 |
| 5 | Roma | 82307 | 65.59 | 75000 | 43000 |
| 6 | Lazio | 82307 | 58.82 | 80000 | 20000 |
| 7 | Hertha Berlin | 76243 | 51.39 | 59200 | 25000 |
| 8 | Bayern Munich | 69060 | 72.15 | 69000 | 35000 |
| 9 | 1860 Munich | 69060 | 35.88 | 64000 | 10000 |
| 10 | Juventus | 69041 | 59.42 | 65000 | 25000 |
| 11 | Torino | 69041 | 20.77 | 45000 | 300 |
| 12 | B Dortmund | 68600 | 98.22 | 68800 | 64000 |
| 13 | Man Utd | 67750 | 99.78 | 67721 | 67135 |
| 14 | Schalke | 60900 | 99.06 | 60886 | 60000 |
| 15 | Celtic | 60506 | 94.99 | 59027 | 55204 |
| 16 | Marseille | 60000 | 76.67 | 60000 | 10000 |
| 17 | Atl Madrid | 57000 | 85.55 | 57000 | 34200 |
| 18 | Hamburg | 55000 | 81.44 | 55500 | 30000 |
| 19 | Espanyol | 55000 | 60.02 | 49500 | 9900 |
| 20 | Stuttgart | 54267 | 59.56 | 54267 | 19000 |
| 21 | Real Betis | 52500 | 78.76 | 52500 | 18000 |
| 22 | Newcastle | 52200 | 99.47 | 52181 | 51072 |
| 23 | Ajax | 51342 | 91.4 | 50777 | 34434 |
| 24 | Feyenoord | 51177 | 86.04 | 50000 | 40000 |
| 25 | Rangers | 50420 | 96.81 | 49874 | 45992 |
| 26 | Hannover 96 | 50418 | 74.47 | 49800 | 28000 |
| 27 | Valencia | 49092 | 95.69 | 53000 | 37100 |
| 28 | Paris SG | 48712 | 77.68 | 48450 | 22015 |
| 29 | Sunderland | 48300 | 82.19 | 47586 | 34102 |
| 30 | Athl Bilbao | 46500 | 72.35 | 39600 | 20000 |
| 31 | Liverpool | 45000 | 96.09 | 44250 | 41462 |
| 32 | Seville | 45000 | 76.18 | 60000 | 14000 |
| 33 | Chievo | 44758 | 41 | 36000 | 10000 |
| 34 | Nurnberg | 44600 | 61.55 | 44600 | 15000 |
| 35 | Aston Villa | 43275 | 80.82 | 42602 | 25817 |
| 36 | Strasbourg | 43247 | 37.81 | 28000 | 9000 |
| 37 | Chelsea | 42449 | 93.72 | 41911 | 35237 |
| 38 | Lyon | 42000 | 83.86 | 49300 | 20000 |
| 39 | Udinese | 41705 | 41.67 | 32000 | 11000 |
| 40 | Lens | 41649 | 87.2 | 40500 | 24758 |
| 41 | Kaiserslautern | 40600 | 89.48 | 40500 | 31000 |
| 42 | Leeds | 40205 | 97.3 | 40205 | 35537 |
| 43 | Everton | 40200 | 95.75 | 40168 | 32440 |
| 44 | Bologna | 39300 | 61.28 | 37000 | 15000 |
| 45 | Arsenal | 38500 | 98.81 | 38164 | 37878 |
| 46 | Nantes | 38486 | 80.39 | 38000 | 25000 |
| 47 | Malaga | 37151 | 78.68 | 37100 | 15000 |
| 48 | Tottenham | 36214 | 99.12 | 36084 | 34704 |
| 49 | W Bremen | 35800 | 90.83 | 40200 | 24000 |
| 50 | Deportivo | 35600 | 81.53 | 35600 | 14240 |

**Key:** Average. The percentage of each stadium filled in League games over the season (AVE), the stadium capacity and the highest and lowest crowds recorded.

**The fans desert Torino**

Here we chart the power of football to fill stadiums across the seven counties we cover.
The Attendance Table above shows the biggest capacities in those seven countries and the bars give a stark indication of where football still pulls in the crowds.
The largest 50 stadiums are featured and the figure gives the average attendance of each through the season as a percentage of that capacity. We also chart the high and (quite shockingly) low figures recorded in some of Europe's largest cities.

## CLUB STRIKE FORCE

ABN·AMRO

van der Vaart on target for Ajax

| Goals scored in the League | 96 |
|---|---|

**1 Ajax**

| Club Strike Rate (CSR) Average number of minutes between League goals scored by club | 32 |
|---|---|

| | CLUB | LEAGUE GOALS | CSR |
|---|---|---|---|
| 2 | Rangers | 101 | 34 |
| 3 | Feyenoord | 89 | 34 |
| 4 | Celtic | 98 | 35 |
| 5 | PSV Eindhoven | 87 | 35 |
| 6 | Real Madrid | 86 | 40 |
| 7 | Arsenal | 85 | 40 |
| 8 | Bayern Munich | 70 | 44 |
| 9 | Man Utd | 74 | 46 |
| 10 | Real Sociedad | 71 | 48 |
| 11 | Inter Milan | 64 | 48 |
| 12 | Juventus | 64 | 48 |
| 13 | Chelsea | 68 | 50 |
| 14 | Heerenveen | 61 | 50 |
| 15 | Deportivo | 67 | 51 |
| 16 | Monaco | 66 | 52 |
| 17 | Roda JC Kerk | 58 | 53 |
| 18 | Newcastle | 63 | 54 |
| 19 | Athl Bilbao | 63 | 54 |
| 20 | Barcelona | 63 | 54 |

## CLUB DEFENCES

**1 PSV Eindhoven**

| Club Defensive Rate (CDR) Average number of minutes between League goals conceded by club | 153 |
|---|---|

| | CLUB | CONCEDED | CLEAN SH | CDR |
|---|---|---|---|---|
| 2 | Celtic | 26 | 21 | 132 |
| 3 | Bayern Munich | 25 | 17 | 122 |
| 4 | Rangers | 28 | 19 | 122 |
| 5 | Auxerre | 29 | 19 | 118 |
| 6 | Sochaux | 30 | 19 | 114 |
| 7 | B Dortmund | 27 | 14 | 113 |
| 8 | Lens | 31 | 17 | 110 |
| 9 | Nice | 31 | 20 | 110 |
| 10 | Juventus | 29 | 15 | 106 |
| 11 | Monaco | 33 | 12 | 104 |
| 12 | AC Milan | 30 | 14 | 102 |
| 13 | Man Utd | 34 | 13 | 101 |
| 14 | NAC Breda | 31 | 17 | 99 |
| 15 | Valencia | 35 | 15 | 98 |
| 16 | Lazio | 32 | 12 | 96 |
| 17 | Ajax | 32 | 10 | 96 |
| 18 | Celta Vigo | 36 | 16 | 95 |
| 19 | Bordeaux | 36 | 17 | 95 |
| 20 | Marseille | 36 | 17 | 95 |

PHILIPS

PSV defender Andre Ooijer

| Goals conceded Number of goals conceded in League games | 20 |
|---|---|
| Clean Sheets (CS) Number of league games where no goals were conceded | 21 |

## CLUB DISCIPLINARY RECORDS

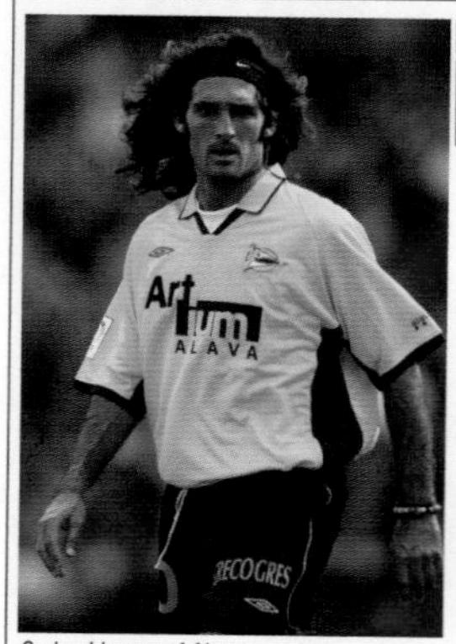
ALAVA

Carlos Llorens of Alaves

| Yellow cards | 13 |
|---|---|
| Red cards | 18 |
| Total | 48 |

**1 Alaves**

| Cards Average in League Average number of minutes between a card being shown of either colour | 25 |
|---|---|

| | CLUB | Y | R | TOTAL | AVE |
|---|---|---|---|---|---|
| 2 | Athl Bilbao | 115 | 10 | 125 | 27 |
| 3 | Atl Madrid | 107 | 7 | 114 | 30 |
| 4 | Barcelona | 105 | 9 | 114 | 30 |
| 5 | Celta Vigo | 102 | 10 | 112 | 31 |
| 6 | Deportivo | 104 | 7 | 111 | 31 |
| 7 | Espanyol | 104 | 7 | 111 | 31 |
| 8 | Malaga | 100 | 10 | 110 | 31 |
| 9 | Motherwell | 97 | 11 | 108 | 32 |
| 10 | Mallorca | 100 | 8 | 108 | 32 |
| 11 | Paris SG | 96 | 12 | 108 | 32 |
| 12 | Montpellier | 97 | 9 | 106 | 32 |
| 13 | Wolfsburg | 92 | 4 | 96 | 32 |
| 14 | Cottbus | 90 | 5 | 95 | 32 |
| 15 | R Vallecano | 98 | 7 | 105 | 33 |
| 16 | R Santander | 95 | 9 | 104 | 33 |
| 17 | Osasuna | 96 | 7 | 103 | 33 |
| 18 | Schalke | 83 | 9 | 92 | 33 |
| 19 | Real Betis | 96 | 6 | 102 | 34 |
| 20 | Bordeaux | 91 | 10 | 101 | 34 |

## CHART-TOPPING MIDFIELDERS

| 1 Jackie McNamara - Celtic | |
|---|---|
| Goals scored in the League | 1 |
| Defensive Rating<br>Av number of mins between League goals conceded while on the pitch | 243 |
| Contribution to Attacking Power<br>Average number of minutes between League team goals while on pitch | 39 |
| Scoring Difference<br>Defensive Rating minus Contribution to Attacking Power | 204 |

| | PLAYER | CLUB | GOALS | DEF R | POWER | SCORE DIFF |
|---|---|---|---|---|---|---|
| 2 | Bah | Guingamp | 1 | 202 | 38 | 164 mins |
| 3 | Guppy | Celtic | 0 | 191 | 31 | 160 mins |
| 4 | Arteta | Rangers | 4 | 189 | 34 | 155 mins |
| 5 | Van Bommel | PSV Eindhoven | 9 | 177 | 35 | 142 mins |
| 6 | Diop | Lens | 3 | 208 | 74 | 134 mins |
| 7 | Jeremies | Bayern Munich | 0 | 162 | 42 | 120 mins |
| 8 | Oruma | Sochaux | 3 | 158 | 54 | 104 mins |
| 9 | Ballack | Bayern Munich | 10 | 141 | 38 | 103 mins |
| 10 | Vogel | PSV Eindhoven | 1 | 140 | 39 | 101 mins |
| 11 | Lennon | Celtic | 0 | 136 | 35 | 101 mins |
| 12 | Maxwell | Ajax | 4 | 132 | 32 | 100 mins |
| 13 | Lambert | Celtic | 3 | 133 | 36 | 97 mins |
| 14 | Petrov | Celtic | 12 | 129 | 33 | 96 mins |
| 15 | de Boer | Rangers | 16 | 127 | 32 | 95 mins |
| 16 | Mostovoi | Celta Vigo | 6 | 156 | 61 | 95 mins |
| 17 | Lee | PSV Eindhoven | 0 | 131 | 36 | 95 mins |
| 18 | Ferguson, B | Rangers | 16 | 126 | 34 | 92 mins |
| 19 | Mjallby | Celtic | 3 | 129 | 37 | 92 mins |
| 20 | van der Vaart | Ajax | 18 | 115 | 28 | 87 mins |

The Divisional Round-up charts combine the records of chart-topping keepers, defenders, midfield players and forwards, from every club in the division.. The one above is for **the Chart-topping Midfielders**. The players are ranked by their Scoring Difference although other attributes are shown for you to compare.

## CHART-TOPPING GOALSCORERS

| 1 Christian Vieri - Inter Milan | |
|---|---|
| Goals scored in the League | 24 |
| Contribution to Attacking Power<br>Average number of minutes between League team goals while on pitch | 49 |
| Player Strike Rate<br>Average number of minutes between League goals scored by player | 78 |
| Club Strike Rate (CSR)<br>Average minutes between League goals scored by club | 48 |

| | PLAYER | CLUB | GOALS | POWER | CSR | S RATE |
|---|---|---|---|---|---|---|
| 2 | Kezman | PSV Eindhoven | 35 | 35 | 35 | 81 mins |
| 3 | van Hooijdonk | Feyenoord | 28 | 33 | 34 | 85 mins |
| 4 | van der Vaart | Ajax | 18 | 27 | 32 | 95 mins |
| 5 | Hartson | Celtic | 18 | 40 | 20 | 96 mins |
| 6 | Ronaldo | Real Madrid | 23 | 43 | 40 | 105 mins |
| 7 | Larsson | Celtic | 28 | 32 | 20 | 106 mins |
| 8 | Makaay | Deportivo | 29 | 52 | 51 | 111 mins |
| 9 | van Nistelrooy | Man Utd | 25 | 45 | 46 | 116 mins |
| 10 | Christiansen | Bochum | 21 | 52 | 56 | 117 mins |
| 11 | Del Piero | Juventus | 16 | 49 | 48 | 117 mins |
| 12 | Prso | Monaco | 12 | 45 | 52 | 118 mins |
| 13 | Nonda | Monaco | 24 | 49 | 52 | 126 mins |
| 14 | Pires | Arsenal | 14 | 37 | 40 | 128 mins |
| 15 | Viduka | Leeds | 20 | 52 | 59 | 129 mins |
| 16 | Nihat | Real Sociedad | 23 | 42 | 48 | 130 mins |
| 17 | Henry | Arsenal | 24 | 39 | 40 | 137 mins |
| 18 | Drogba | Guingamp | 17 | 54 | 58 | 138 mins |
| 19 | Totti | Roma | 14 | 52 | 56 | 138 mins |
| 20 | Anderson | Lyon | 12 | 45 | 54 | 138 mins |

**The Chart-topping Goalscorers** measures the players by Strike Rate. They are most likely to be Forwards but Midfield players and even Defenders do come through the club tables. It is not a measure of the number of League goals scored - although that is also noted - but how often on average they have scored.

## CHART-TOPPING DEFENDERS

| 1 Robert Kovac - Bayern Munich | |
|---|---|
| Goals conceded in the League | 11 |
| Clean Sheets<br>In games when he played at least 70 mins | 15 |
| Defensive Rating<br>Average number of minutes between League goals conceded while on pitch | 191 |
| Club Defensive Rating<br>Average mins between League goals conceded by the club this season | 122 |

| | PLAYER | CLUB | CON: LGE | CS | CDR | DEF RATE |
|---|---|---|---|---|---|---|
| 2 | Muscat | Rangers | 12 | 14 | 71 | 162 mins |
| 3 | Malcolm | Rangers | 12 | 11 | 71 | 160 mins |
| 4 | Mihajlovic | Lazio | 11 | 9 | 96 | 151 mins |
| 5 | Simic | AC Milan | 16 | 14 | 102 | 149 mins |
| 6 | Ndoumbe | Auxerre | 11 | 10 | 118 | 146 mins |
| 7 | Bogelund | PSV Eindhoven | 12 | 12 | 153 | 144 mins |
| 8 | Ooijer | PSV Eindhoven | 20 | 17 | 153 | 139 mins |
| 9 | Brevett | West Ham | 8 | 6 | 58 | 137 mins |
| 10 | Raschke | Sochaux | 11 | 7 | 110 | 135 mins |
| 11 | Balde | Celtic | 24 | 20 | 76 | 134 mins |
| 12 | Moore | Rangers | 23 | 18 | 71 | 134 mins |
| 13 | Faber | PSV Eindhoven | 13 | 10 | 153 | 134 mins |
| 14 | Valgaeren | Celtic | 23 | 19 | 76 | 133 mins |
| 15 | Cobos | Nice | 22 | 19 | 110 | 132 mins |
| 16 | Brouwers | Roda JC Kerk | 8 | 8 | 56 | 131 mins |
| 17 | Marquez | Monaco | 20 | 12 | 104 | 130 mins |
| 18 | Linke | Bayern Munich | 21 | 15 | 122 | 129 mins |
| 19 | Laursen | Celtic | 15 | 13 | 76 | 128 mins |
| 20 | Lachor | Lens | 9 | 7 | 110 | 127 mins |

**The Chart-topping Defenders** are resolved by their Defensive Rating, how often their team concedes a goal while they are playing. All these rightly favour players at the best performing clubs because good players win matches. However, good players in lower-table clubs will chart where they have lifted the team's performance.

## CHART-TOPPING GOALKEEPERS

PHILIPS

| 1 Ronald Waterreus - PSV Eindhoven | |
|---|---|
| Goals conceded in the League | 13 |
| Clean Sheets<br>In games when he played at least 70 mins | 18 |
| Defensive Rating<br>Average number of minutes between League goals conceded while on pitch | 187 |
| Club Defensive Rating<br>Average mins between League goals conceded by the club this season | 48 |

| | PLAYER | CLUB | CON: LGE | C SHEETS | DEF RATE |
|---|---|---|---|---|---|
| 2 | Kahn | Bayern Munich | 22 | 17 | 135 mins |
| 3 | Weidenfeller | B Dortmund | 7 | 5 | 13 mins |
| 4 | Douglas | Celtic | 34 | 12 | 129 mins |
| 5 | Moilanen | Hearts | 11 | 5 | 126 mins |
| 6 | Buffon | Juventus | 23 | 15 | 123 mins |
| 7 | Klos | Rangers | 38 | 19 | 122 mins |
| 8 | Sereni | Brescia | 17 | 13 | 121 mins |
| 9 | Cool | Auxerre | 29 | 19 | 118 mins |
| 10 | Cavallero | Celta Vigo | 27 | 15 | 117 mins |
| 11 | Dida | AC Milan | 23 | 13 | 117 mins |
| 12 | Sylva | Monaco | 9 | 3 | 116 mins |
| 13 | Gregorini | Nice | 29 | 20 | 115 mins |
| 14 | Warmuz | Lens | 13 | 6 | 111 mins |
| 15 | Itandje | Lens | 18 | 11 | 110 mins |
| 16 | Richert | Sochaux | 28 | 16 | 109 mins |
| 17 | Lobont | Ajax | 14 | 5 | 109 mins |
| 18 | Alonzo | Paris SG | 10 | 4 | 108 mins |
| 19 | Lehmann | B Dortmund | 20 | 9 | 106 mins |
| 20 | Roux | Bordeaux | 9 | 4 | 101 mins |

**The Chart-topping Goalkeepers** are positioned by their Defensive Rating. We also show Clean Sheets where the team has not conceded and the Keeper has played all or most (at least 70 minutes) of the game. Now teams use several keepers in a season, not every team will necessarily chart on this page.

## HOW THE TOP TEAMS COMPARE ACROSS EUROPE

| | P | W | D | L | F | A | PTS | AVERAGES W | D | L | F | A | PTS |
|---|---|---|---|---|---|---|---|---|---|---|---|---|---|
| **England** | | | | | | | | | | | | | |
| 1 Man Utd | 38 | 25 | 8 | 5 | 74 | 34 | 83 | 66% | 21% | 13% | 1.95 | 0.89 | 2.18 |
| 2 Arsenal | 38 | 23 | 9 | 6 | 85 | 42 | 78 | 61% | 24% | 16% | 2.24 | 1.11 | 2.05 |
| 3 Newcastle | 38 | 21 | 6 | 11 | 63 | 48 | 69 | 55% | 16% | 29% | 1.66 | 1.26 | 1.82 |
| **France** | | | | | | | | | | | | | |
| 1 Lyon | 38 | 19 | 11 | 8 | 63 | 41 | 68 | 50% | 29% | 21% | 1.66 | 1.08 | 1.79 |
| 2 Monaco | 38 | 19 | 10 | 9 | 66 | 33 | 67 | 50% | 26% | 24% | 1.74 | 0.87 | 1.76 |
| 3 Marseille | 38 | 19 | 8 | 11 | 41 | 36 | 65 | 50% | 21% | 29% | 1.08 | 0.95 | 1.71 |
| **Germany** | | | | | | | | | | | | | |
| 1 Bayern Munich | 34 | 23 | 6 | 5 | 70 | 25 | 75 | 68% | 18% | 15% | 2.06 | 0.74 | 2.21 |
| 2 Stuttgart | 34 | 17 | 8 | 9 | 53 | 39 | 59 | 50% | 24% | 26% | 1.56 | 1.15 | 1.74 |
| 3 B Dortmund | 34 | 15 | 13 | 6 | 51 | 27 | 58 | 44% | 38% | 18% | 1.50 | 0.79 | 1.71 |
| **Holland** | | | | | | | | | | | | | |
| 1 PSV Eindhoven | 34 | 26 | 6 | 2 | 87 | 20 | 84 | 76% | 18% | 6% | 2.56 | 0.59 | 2.47 |
| 2 Ajax | 34 | 26 | 5 | 3 | 96 | 32 | 83 | 76% | 15% | 9% | 2.82 | 0.94 | 2.44 |
| 3 Feyenoord | 34 | 25 | 5 | 4 | 89 | 39 | 80 | 74% | 15% | 12% | 2.62 | 1.15 | 2.35 |
| **Italy** | | | | | | | | | | | | | |
| 1 Juventus | 34 | 21 | 9 | 4 | 64 | 29 | 72 | 62% | 26% | 12% | 1.88 | 0.85 | 2.12 |
| 2 Inter Milan | 34 | 19 | 8 | 7 | 64 | 38 | 65 | 56% | 24% | 21% | 1.88 | 1.12 | 1.91 |
| 3 AC Milan | 34 | 18 | 7 | 9 | 55 | 30 | 61 | 53% | 21% | 26% | 1.62 | 0.88 | 1.79 |
| **Scotland** | | | | | | | | | | | | | |
| 1 Rangers | 38 | 31 | 4 | 3 | 101 | 28 | 97 | 82% | 11% | 8% | 2.66 | 0.74 | 2.55 |
| 2 Celtic | 38 | 31 | 4 | 3 | 98 | 26 | 97 | 82% | 11% | 8% | 2.58 | 0.68 | 2.55 |
| 3 Hearts | 38 | 18 | 9 | 11 | 57 | 51 | 63 | 47% | 24% | 29% | 1.50 | 1.34 | 1.66 |
| **Spain** | | | | | | | | | | | | | |
| 1 Real Madrid | 38 | 22 | 12 | 4 | 86 | 42 | 78 | 58% | 32% | 11% | 2.26 | 1.11 | 2.05 |
| 2 Real Sociedad | 38 | 22 | 10 | 6 | 71 | 45 | 76 | 58% | 26% | 16% | 1.87 | 1.18 | 2.00 |
| 3 Deportivo | 38 | 22 | 6 | 10 | 67 | 47 | 72 | 58% | 16% | 26% | 1.76 | 1.24 | 1.89 |

## PLAYER DISCIPLINARY RECORD

**11 Aliou Cisse - Birmingham**

**Cards Average** — Average number of minutes between a card being shown of either colour: **143**

| | |
|---|---|
| League Yellow | 12 |
| League Red | 1 |
| League Total | 13 |
| All Competitions Yellow | 12 |
| All Competitions Red | 1 |
| TOTAL ALL COMPETITIONS | 13 |

| | PLAYER | LEAGUE | Y | R | TOTAL | AVE |
|---|---|---|---|---|---|---|
| 1 | Battles | Rennes | 8 | 1 | 9 | 119 |
| 2 | Ledesma | Hamburg | 6 | 1 | 7 | 121 |
| 3 | Rool | Lens | 9 | 1 | 10 | 121 |
| 4 | Lopo | Espanyol | 14 | 2 | 16 | 126 |
| 5 | Caracciolo | Perugia | 6 | 1 | 7 | 134 |
| 6 | Alex | Espanyol | 6 | 1 | 7 | 135 |
| 7 | Turiel | Alaves | 8 | 1 | 9 | 136 |
| 8 | Manfredini | Udinese | 11 | 0 | 11 | 136 |
| 9 | Unai | Villarreal | 9 | 1 | 10 | 140 |
| 10 | McLaren | Kilmarnock | 12 | 1 | 13 | 141 |
| 11 | Cisse | Birmingham | 12 | 1 | 13 | 143 |
| 12 | Stehle | Nurnberg | 7 | 0 | 7 | 144 |
| 13 | Gabri | Barcelona | 12 | 1 | 13 | 147 |
| 14 | Iriney | R Vallecano | 6 | 2 | 8 | 148 |
| 15 | Bogusz | Arminia B | 6 | 1 | 7 | 149 |
| 16 | Brouwers | Roda JC Kerk | 6 | 1 | 7 | 149 |
| 17 | Nivet | Troyes | 7 | 1 | 8 | 149 |
| 18 | Sandro | Malaga | 12 | 1 | 13 | 149 |
| 19 | Varela | Real Betis | 18 | 1 | 19 | 149 |
| 20 | Johansen | Marseille | 15 | 1 | 16 | 150 |

## EUROPEAN CHART-TOPPING POINT EARNERS

| | PLAYER | TEAM | GAMES | POINTS | AVE |
|---|---|---|---|---|---|
| 2 | O'Brien | Ajax | 12 | 33 | 2.75 |
| 3 | Lodewijks | Feyenoord | 22 | 60 | 2.73 |
| 4 | van der Vaart | Ajax | 18 | 49 | 2.72 |
| 5 | Malcolm | Rangers | 20 | 53 | 2.65 |
| 6 | Chivu | Ajax | 22 | 58 | 2.64 |
| 7 | Moore | Rangers | 34 | 89 | 2.62 |
| 8 | Lennon | Celtic | 26 | 68 | 2.62 |
| 9 | Laursen | Celtic | 21 | 55 | 2.62 |
| 10 | Agathe | Celtic | 21 | 55 | 2.62 |
| 11 | Arveladze | Rangers | 23 | 60 | 2.61 |
| 12 | de Boer | Rangers | 25 | 65 | 2.6 |
| 13 | Bouma | PSV Eindhoven | 26 | 67 | 2.58 |
| 14 | Valgaeren | Celtic | 34 | 87 | 2.56 |
| 15 | Klos | Rangers | 38 | 97 | 2.55 |
| 16 | Arteta | Rangers | 20 | 51 | 2.55 |
| 17 | Sutton | Celtic | 26 | 66 | 2.54 |
| 18 | Thompson | Celtic | 24 | 61 | 2.54 |
| 19 | Numan | Rangers | 24 | 61 | 2.54 |
| 20 | Balde | Celtic | 36 | 91 | 2.53 |

**1 kevin Muscat - Rangers**

| | |
|---|---|
| **Counting Games** League games where he played at least 70 minutes | 22 |
| **Total League Points** Taken in Counting Games | 61 |
| **Average League Points** Taken in Counting Games | 2.77 |

## TEAM OF THE SEASON

Waterreus
PSV
CG 27 DR 91
Marquez
Monaco
CG 29 DR 130
Campbell
Arsenal
CG 32 DR 92
Kovac
Bayern Munich
CG 23 DR 191
Simic
AC Milan
CG 23 DR 149
Beckham
Man Utd
CG 27 SD 83
Jeremies
Bayern Munich
CG 25 SD 120
Gattuso
AC Milan
CG 27 SD 0
Van Bommel
PSV
CG 26 SD -78
Del Piero
Juventus
CG 20 SR 117
Larsson
Celtic
CG 32 SR 106


**The Team of the Season** in each League's Divisional Round-up is different to those at club level. It doesn't just mirror the Chart-topping performances but highlights Keepers, Defenders, Midfield players and Forwards who are dramatically out-performing their team-mates. We compare their key rating to the club average see below: -

- **The Division Team's goalkeeper** has to be the player with the highest Defensive Rating as he often play most or all the games in a league season.
- **The Division Team's defenders** are also tested by Defensive Rating but against their co-defender's Ratings. We weight it to take into account the fact that differences can fluctuate wildly at the bottom of a division.
- **The Division Team's midfield** all have good Scoring Differences compared to the average Ratings of their colleagues. In all cases these players must have played at least a minimum of Counting Games.
- **The Divisional Team strikeforce** is made up of the two players who have the biggest gap in Strike Rate between themselves and their next forward. These are weighted again, as lower sides may not even have a second charting forward.

# INTERNATIONAL FOOTBALL

Where do the top International players ply their trade in this increasingly global game? The following 15 pages feature the Home Nations and the 25 other sides from the top of the FIFA Coca-Cola World Rankings taken on June 20th 2003.
As well as their results we are charting the globalisation of football by detailing in which leagues the key players in those squads were playing. In the rest of the book current international players of those top 30 ranked teams have their season's caps recorded.

Hughes - manager of the fastest risers.

## TOP RISERS IN EUROPEAN FOOTBALL

| | | Points 02 | Points 03 | Difference | Pos 02 | Pos 03 |
|---|---|---|---|---|---|---|
| 1 | Wales | 440 | 558 | **118** | 96 | 50 |
| 2 | Spain | 713 | 784 | **71** | 8 | 2= |
| 3 | Turkey | 654 | 722 | **68** | 22 | 8 |
| 4 | Germany | 695 | 757 | **62** | 11 | 4 |
| 5 | Denmark | 657 | 715 | **58** | 20 | 10 |
| 6 | Switzerland | 531 | 588 | **57** | 64 | 43 |
| 7 | Estonia | 471 | 528 | **57** | 85 | 61 |
| 8 | Bulgaria | 557 | 611 | **54** | 54 | 35 |
| 9 | Latvia | 435 | 483 | **48** | 99 | 79 |
| 10 | England | 694 | 739 | **45** | 12 | 7 |
| 11 | Holland | 703 | 746 | **43** | 9 | 6 |
| 12 | Czech Republic | 674 | 707 | **33** | 15= | 13 |
| 13 | Israel | 563 | 596 | **33** | 51 | 40 |
| 14 | Liechtenstein | 241 | 274 | **33** | 149 | 148 |
| 15 | Rep of Ireland | 674 | 704 | **30** | 15= | 15 |

### EURO 2004

This page gives the position of the EURO 2004 qualifying tournament across 10 groups of 5 teams each with only 2004 Tournament hosts Portugal already pre-qualified. As well as the group tables and results (up to date as of June 20th) we have the current FIFA World Ranking position and points for each side with a comparison of how that has moved since the June 2002 Rankings. This gives a context for the sides in each group.

## GROUP 1

| | | | | | | | | FIFA RANKING | | RANKING POINTS |
|---|---|---|---|---|---|---|---|---|---|---|
| | Pld | W | D | L | F | A | Pts | 2002 | 2003 | 2003 |
| France | 5 | 5 | 0 | 0 | 19 | 2 | **15** | 1 | 2= | 784 |
| Slovenia | 5 | 3 | 1 | 1 | 10 | 7 | **10** | 25 | 36 | 610 |
| Israel | 5 | 2 | 2 | 1 | 6 | 3 | **8** | 51 | 40 | 596 |
| Cyprus | 6 | 2 | 1 | 3 | 7 | 11 | **7** | 82 | 88 | 463 |
| Malta | 7 | 0 | 0 | 7 | 3 | 22 | **0** | 117 | 128 | 346 |

## GROUP 2

| | | | | | | | | FIFA RANKING | | RANKING POINTS |
|---|---|---|---|---|---|---|---|---|---|---|
| | Pld | W | D | L | F | A | Pts | 2002 | 2003 | 2003 |
| Denmark | 6 | 4 | 1 | 1 | 12 | 6 | **13** | 20 | 10 | 715 |
| Norway | 6 | 3 | 2 | 1 | 8 | 4 | **11** | 33 | 24 | 643 |
| Romania | 6 | 3 | 1 | 2 | 15 | 7 | **10** | 14 | 27 | 631 |
| Bosnia-Herzegovina | 5 | 2 | 0 | 3 | 4 | 7 | **6** | 72 | 72 | 503 |
| Luxembourg | 5 | 0 | 0 | 5 | 0 | 15 | **0** | | | |

## GROUP 3

| | | | | | | | | FIFA RANKING | | RANKING POINTS |
|---|---|---|---|---|---|---|---|---|---|---|
| | Pld | W | D | L | F | A | Pts | 2002 | 2003 | 2003 |
| Czech Republic | 5 | 4 | 1 | 0 | 14 | 1 | **13** | 15= | 13 | 707 |
| Holland | 5 | 4 | 1 | 0 | 11 | 2 | **13** | 9 | 6 | 746 |
| Austria | 6 | 3 | 0 | 3 | 9 | 8 | **9** | 61 | 61= | 528 |
| Belarus | 6 | 1 | 0 | 5 | 2 | 15 | **3** | 88 | 76 | 489 |
| Moldova | 6 | 1 | 0 | 5 | 3 | 13 | **3** | 103 | 115 | 392 |

## GROUP 4

| | | | | | | | | FIFA RANKING | | RANKING POINTS |
|---|---|---|---|---|---|---|---|---|---|---|
| | Pld | W | D | L | F | A | Pts | 2002 | 2003 | 2003 |
| Sweden | 5 | 3 | 2 | 0 | 12 | 2 | **11** | 19 | 20 | 660 |
| Hungary | 6 | 3 | 2 | 1 | 13 | 4 | **11** | 67 | 54 | 544 |
| Latvia | 5 | 3 | 1 | 1 | 6 | 3 | **10** | 99 | 79 | 483 |
| Poland | 5 | 2 | 1 | 2 | 7 | 4 | **7** | 38 | 29 | 627 |
| San Marino | 7 | 0 | 0 | 7 | 0 | 25 | **0** | 159 | 163 | 207 |

## GROUP 5

| | | | | | | | | FIFA RANKING | | RANKING POINTS |
|---|---|---|---|---|---|---|---|---|---|---|
| | Pld | W | D | L | F | A | Pts | 2002 | 2003 | 2003 |
| Germany | 5 | 3 | 2 | 0 | 8 | 3 | 11 | 11 | 4 | 757 |
| Iceland | 5 | 3 | 0 | 2 | 9 | 5 | 9 | 56 | 70 | 509 |
| Scotland | 5 | 2 | 2 | 1 | 7 | 5 | 8 | 54= | 64 | 52 |
| Lithuania | 6 | 2 | 1 | 3 | 4 | 9 | 7 | 98 | 99 | 434 |
| Faeroe Islands | 5 | 0 | 1 | 4 | 4 | 10 | 1 | 119 | 113 | 395 |

## GROUP 6

| | | | | | | | | FIFA RANKING | | RANKING POINTS |
|---|---|---|---|---|---|---|---|---|---|---|
| | Pld | W | D | L | F | A | Pts | 2002 | 2003 | 2003 |
| Greece | 6 | 4 | 0 | 2 | 6 | 4 | **12** | 52 | 45= | 577 |
| Spain | 6 | 3 | 2 | 1 | 10 | 3 | **11** | 8 | 2= | 784 |
| Ukraine | 6 | 2 | 3 | 1 | 10 | 8 | **9** | 44 | 47 | 570 |
| Armenia | 5 | 1 | 1 | 3 | 6 | 11 | **4** | 101 | 105 | 417 |
| Northern Ireland | 5 | 0 | 2 | 3 | 0 | 6 | **2** | 90 | 111 | 399 |

## GROUP 7

| | | | | | | | | FIFA RANKING | | RANKING POINTS |
|---|---|---|---|---|---|---|---|---|---|---|
| | Pld | W | D | L | F | A | Pts | 2002 | 2003 | 2003 |
| Turkey | 6 | 5 | 0 | 1 | 14 | 5 | **15** | 22 | 8 | 722 |
| England | 5 | 4 | 1 | 0 | 10 | 4 | **13** | 12 | 7 | 739 |
| Slovakia | 6 | 2 | 0 | 4 | 8 | 8 | **6** | 49 | 53 | 548 |
| F.Y.R. Macedonia | 6 | 1 | 2 | 3 | 9 | 11 | **5** | 89 | 93 | 446 |
| Liechtenstein | 5 | 0 | 1 | 4 | 2 | 15 | **1** | 149 | 148 | 274 |

## GROUP 8

| | | | | | | | | FIFA RANKING | | RANKING POINTS |
|---|---|---|---|---|---|---|---|---|---|---|
| | Pld | W | D | L | F | A | Pts | 2002 | 2003 | 2003 |
| Bulgaria | 5 | 3 | 2 | 0 | 8 | 3 | **11** | 54= | 35 | 611 |
| Croatia | 5 | 3 | 1 | 1 | 7 | 2 | **10** | 21 | 26 | 640 |
| Belgium | 6 | 3 | 1 | 2 | 7 | 8 | **10** | 23 | 16 | 681 |
| Estonia | 6 | 2 | 2 | 2 | 4 | 2 | **8** | 85 | 61= | 528 |
| Andorra | 6 | 0 | 0 | 6 | 1 | 12 | **0** | 141 | 142 | 297 |

## GROUP 9

| | | | | | | | | FIFA RANKING | | RANKING POINTS |
|---|---|---|---|---|---|---|---|---|---|---|
| | Pld | W | D | L | F | A | Pts | 2002 | 2003 | 2003 |
| Wales | 4 | 4 | 0 | 0 | 10 | 1 | **12** | 96 | 50 | 558 |
| Italy | 5 | 3 | 1 | 1 | 8 | 3 | **10** | 6 | 12 | 709 |
| Finland | 6 | 2 | 0 | 4 | 6 | 8 | **6** | 41 | 45= | 577 |
| Serbia and Mont | 5 | 1 | 2 | 2 | 6 | 8 | **5** | 10 | 22 | 650 |
| Azerbaijan | 6 | 1 | 1 | 4 | 4 | 14 | **4** | 14 | 113 | 395 |

## GROUP 10

| | | | | | | | | FIFA RANKING | | RANKING POINTS |
|---|---|---|---|---|---|---|---|---|---|---|
| | Pld | W | D | L | F | A | Pts | 2002 | 2003 | 2003 |
| Switzerland | 6 | 3 | 3 | 0 | 12 | 7 | 12 | 64 | 43 | 588 |
| Rep of Ireland | 6 | 3 | 1 | 2 | 9 | 8 | 10 | 15= | 15 | 704 |
| Russia | 5 | 2 | 1 | 2 | 11 | 9 | 7 | 27 | 25 | 641 |
| Albania | 6 | 1 | 2 | 3 | 8 | 11 | 5 | 95 | 89 | 458 |
| Georgia | 5 | 1 | 1 | 3 | 3 | 8 | 4 | 58 | 84 | 469 |

# BRAZIL

FIFA/COCA COLA WORLD RANKING: **1st**

**MANAGER:** CARLOS ALBERTO PARREIRA

| | | | | | | |
|---|---|---|---|---|---|---|
| 1 | intnls | **Paraguay** | H | L | 0-1 | |
| 2 | intnls | **South Korea** | A | W | 3-2 | Ronaldo 16,67; Ronaldinho 90 pen |
| 3 | intnls | **China PR** | A | D | 0-0 | |
| 4 | intnls | **Portugal** | A | L | 1-2 | Ronaldinho 65 pen |
| 5 | intnls | **Mexico** | A | D | 0-0 | |
| 6 | intnls | **Nigeria** | A | W | 3-0 | Gil 33; Fabiano 37; Adriano 80 |

**Competition key:** eqg2 = European Qualifying match in Group 2 (g2); Intnls = all other international matches

**Note:** The season of international matches covered includes all games from the end of the 2002 World Cup in June 30th 2002 to June 11th 2003.

## KEY PLAYERS - GOALSCORERS

1 Ronaldo Luiz Nazario de Lima

| | |
|---|---|
| **Goals in Internationals** | 2 |
| **Contribution to Attacking Power** Average number of minutes between team goals while on pitch | 100 |
| Player Strike Rate The total number of minutes he was on the pitch for every goal scored | 151 |
| **Club Strike Rate** Average number of minutes between goals scored by club | 77 |

| | PLAYER | GOALS | ATT POWER | STRIKE RATE |
|---|---|---|---|---|
| 2 | De Assis Moreira Ronaldinho | 2 | 66 | 233 mins |

## TOP PLAYER APPEARANCES

7 Roberto Carlos — Defender

| | |
|---|---|
| **Age** (on 01/07/03) | 30 |
| **Caps this season** | 4 |
| **Total minutes on the pitch** | 305 |
| **Goals** | 0 |
| **Yellow Cards** | 0 |
| **Red Cards** | 1 |
| **Club Side** | Real Madrid |

| | PLAYER | POS | AGE | CAPS | MINS | GOALS | CARDS(Y) | CARDS(R) | CLUB SIDE |
|---|---|---|---|---|---|---|---|---|---|
| 1 | Kleberson | MID | 24 | 6 | 509 | 0 | 0 | 0 | Atletico Paranaense |
| 2 | Ronaldinho | ATT | 23 | 6 | 466 | 2 | 1 | 0 | Paris SG |
| 3 | Nelson Dida | GK | 29 | 5 | 389 | 0 | 0 | 0 | AC Milan |
| 4 | Gilberto Silva | MID | 26 | 6 | 386 | 0 | 1 | 0 | Arsenal |
| 5 | Edmilson | DEF | 26 | 4 | 360 | 0 | 0 | 0 | Lyon |
| 6 | Cafu | DEF | 33 | 4 | 312 | 0 | 0 | 0 | Roma |
| 7 | Roberto Carlos | DEF | 30 | 4 | 305 | 0 | 0 | 1 | Real Madrid |
| 8 | Ronaldo | ATT | 26 | 5 | 302 | 2 | 0 | 0 | Real Madrid |
| 9 | Jose Ze Roberto | MID | 29 | 4 | 292 | 0 | 0 | 0 | Bayern Munich |
| 10 | Marcio Amoroso | MID | 29 | 4 | 236 | 0 | 0 | 0 | B Dortmund |
| 11 | Anderson Correa Polga | DEF | 23 | 3 | 225 | 0 | 0 | 0 | Gremio |
| 12 | Rivaldo | MID | 31 | 3 | 225 | 0 | 0 | 0 | AC Milan |
| 13 | Juliano Hous Beletti | DEF | 27 | 5 | 212 | 0 | 0 | 0 | Sao Paulo |
| 14 | Luizao | ATT | 27 | 3 | 193 | 0 | 0 | 0 | Gremio |
| 15 | Lucimar da Silva Lucio | DEF | 25 | 2 | 180 | 0 | 0 | 0 | B Leverkusen |
| 16 | Emerson | MID | 27 | 5 | 179 | 0 | 0 | 0 | Roma |
| 17 | Ricardo | MID | 27 | 2 | 135 | 0 | 0 | 0 | Corinthians |
| 18 | Marcos Roberto | GK | 29 | 2 | 122 | 0 | 0 | 0 | Palmeiras |
| 19 | Angelo De Sousa Junior | DEF | 30 | 3 | 114 | 0 | 0 | 0 | Parma |
| 20 | Anderson Luisao | MID | 22 | 1 | 90 | 0 | 0 | 0 | Cruzeiro |
| 21 | Silveira dos Santos Juan | DEF | 24 | 2 | 85 | 0 | 0 | 0 | B Leverkusen |

# FRANCE

FIFA/COCA COLA WORLD RANKING: **2nd**

**MANAGER:** JACQES SANTINI

| | | | | | | |
|---|---|---|---|---|---|---|
| 1 | intnls | **Tunisia** | A | D | 1-1 | Silvestre 18 |
| 2 | eqg1 | **Cyprus** | A | W | 2-1 | Cisse 39; Wiltord 52 |
| 3 | eqg1 | **Slovenia** | H | W | 5-0 | Vieira 9; Marlet 34,64; Wiltord 79; Govou 86 |
| 4 | eqg1 | **Malta** | A | W | 4-0 | Carabott 25 og; Henry 36; Wiltord 59; Carriere 84 |
| 5 | intnls | **Serbia & M** | H | W | 3-0 | Carriere 11,49; Kapo 70 |
| 6 | intnls | **Czech Republic** | H | L | 0-2 | |
| 7 | eqg1 | **Malta** | H | W | 6-0 | Wiltord 37; Henry 39,54; Zidane 57 pen,80; Trezeguet 70 |
| 8 | eqg1 | **Israel** | A | W | 2-1 | Trezeguet 23; Zidane 45 |
| 9 | intnls | **Egypt** | H | W | 5-0 | Henry 25,34; Pires 45; Cisse 64; Kapo 79 |

## KEY PLAYERS - GOALSCORERS

1 David Trezeguet

| | |
|---|---|
| **Goals in Internationals** | 2 |
| **Contribution to Attacking Power** Average number of minutes between team goals while on pitch | 26 |
| **Player Strike Rate** The total number of minutes he was on the pitch for every goal scored | 104 |
| **Club Strike Rate** Average number of minutes between goals scored by club | 29 |

| | PLAYER | GOALS | ATT POWER | STRIKE RATE |
|---|---|---|---|---|
| 2 | Thierry Henry | 5 | 25 | 116 mins |
| 3 | Djibril Cisse | 2 | 34 | 120 mins |
| 4 | Sylvain Wiltord | 4 | 24 | 136 mins |
| 5 | Steve Marlet | 2 | 34 | 209 mins |

## TOP PLAYER APPEARANCES

3 Zinedine Zidane — Midfield

| | |
|---|---|
| **Age** (on 01/07/03) | 31 |
| **Caps this season** | 7 |
| **Total minutes on the pitch** | 630 |
| **Goals** | 3 |
| **Yellow Cards** | 0 |
| **Red Cards** | 0 |
| **Club Side** | Real Madrid |

| | PLAYER | POS | AGE | CAPS | MINS | GOALS | CARDS(Y) | CARDS(R) | CLUB SIDE |
|---|---|---|---|---|---|---|---|---|---|
| 1 | Lilian Thuram | DEF | 30 | 8 | 658 | 0 | 0 | 0 | Juventus |
| 2 | Claude Makelele | MID | 30 | 8 | 637 | 0 | 0 | 0 | Real Madrid |
| 3 | Zinedine Zidane | MID | 31 | 7 | 630 | 3 | 0 | 0 | Real Madrid |
| 4 | William Gallas | MID | 25 | 7 | 626 | 0 | 1 | 0 | Chelsea |
| 5 | Mikael Silvestre | DEF | 25 | 8 | 582 | 1 | 0 | 0 | Man Utd |
| 6 | Thierry Henry | ATT | 25 | 8 | 580 | 5 | 0 | 0 | Arsenal |
| 7 | Sylvain Wiltord | ATT | 29 | 8 | 545 | 4 | 0 | 0 | Arsenal |
| 8 | Fabien Barthez | GK | 32 | 6 | 540 | 0 | 1 | 0 | Man Utd |
| 9 | Marcel Desailly | DEF | 34 | 7 | 524 | 0 | 1 | 0 | Chelsea |
| 10 | Patrick Vieira | MID | 27 | 6 | 429 | 1 | 1 | 0 | Arsenal |
| 11 | Steve Marlet | ATT | 29 | 8 | 417 | 2 | 0 | 0 | Fulham |
| 12 | Bixente Lizarazu | DEF | 33 | 4 | 360 | 0 | 0 | 0 | Bayern Munich |
| 13 | Djibril Cisse | ATT | 21 | 6 | 239 | 2 | 0 | 0 | Auxerre |
| 14 | Emmanuel Petit | MID | 32 | 4 | 219 | 0 | 0 | 0 | Chelsea |
| 15 | Benoit Pedretti | MID | 22 | 5 | 209 | 0 | 0 | 0 | Sochaux |
| 16 | David Trezeguet | ATT | 25 | 3 | 208 | 2 | 0 | 0 | Juventus |
| 17 | Gregory Coupet | GK | 30 | 7 | 180 | 0 | 0 | 0 | Lyon |
| 18 | Philippe Christanval | DEF | 24 | 2 | 180 | 0 | 0 | 0 | Barcelona |
| 19 | Willy Sagnol | MID | 26 | 6 | 167 | 0 | 0 | 0 | Bayern Munich |
| 20 | Eric Carriere | ATT | 30 | 4 | 141 | 3 | 0 | 0 | Lyon |
| 21 | Sydney Govou | ATT | 23 | 6 | 137 | 1 | 0 | 0 | Lyon |

# SPAIN

FIFA/COCA COLA WORLD RANKING: 3rd

MANAGER: INAKI SAEZ

| | | | | | | |
|---|---|---|---|---|---|---|
| 1 | intnls | Hungary | A | D | 1-1 | Tamudo 55 |
| 2 | eqg6 | Greece | A | W | 2-0 | Raul 7; Valeron 76 |
| 3 | eqg6 | N Ireland | H | W | 3-0 | Baraja 18,88; Guti 59 |
| 4 | intnls | Paraguay | H | D | 0-0 | |
| 5 | intnls | Bulgaria | H | W | 1-0 | Jose Mari 10 |
| 6 | intnls | Germany | H | W | 2-1 | Raul 30,75 pen; Guti 81 |
| 7 | eqg6 | Ukraine | A | D | 2-2 | Raul 84; Etxeberria 87 |
| 8 | eqg6 | Armenia | H | W | 3-0 | Tristan 61; Helguera 67; Joaquin 90 |
| 9 | intnls | Ecuador | H | W | 4-0 | De Pedro 13; Morientes 19,22,63 |
| 10 | eqg6 | Greece | H | L | 0-1 | |
| 11 | eqg6 | N Ireland | A | D | 0-0 | |

## KEY PLAYERS - GOALSCORERS

1 Fernando Sanchez Morientes

| | |
|---|---|
| **Goals in Internationals** | 3 |
| **Contribution to Attacking Power** Average number of minutes between team goals while on pitch | 60 |
| **Player Strike Rate** The total number of minutes he was on the pitch for every goal scored | 101 |
| **Club Strike Rate** Average number of minutes between goals scored by club | 52 |

| | PLAYER | GOALS | ATT POWER | STRIKE RATE |
|---|---|---|---|---|
| 2 | Raul Gonzalez Blanco | 4 | 53 | 161 mins |
| 3 | Jose Maria Guti | 2 | 56 | 169 mins |
| 4 | Herrera Diego Tristan | 1 | 43 | 262 mins |
| 5 | Ruben Vegas Baraja | 2 | 39 | 280 mins |

## TOP PLAYER APPEARANCES

9 Carlos Puyol — Defender

| | |
|---|---|
| Age (on 01/07/03) | 25 |
| Caps this season | 6 |
| Total minutes on the pitch | 540 |
| Goals | 0 |
| Yellow Cards | 0 |
| Red Cards | 0 |
| Club Side | Barcelona |

| | PLAYER | POS | AGE | CAPS | MINS | GOALS | CARDS(Y) | CARDS(R) | CLUB SIDE |
|---|---|---|---|---|---|---|---|---|---|
| 1 | Michel Salgado | DEF | 27 | 10 | 765 | 0 | 1 | 0 | Real Madrid |
| 2 | Iker Fernandez Casillas | GK | 22 | 10 | 729 | 0 | 0 | 0 | Real Madrid |
| 3 | Rodriguez Vicente | ATT | 21 | 10 | 718 | 0 | 0 | 0 | Valencia |
| 4 | Raul Gonzalez Blanco | ATT | 26 | 8 | 642 | 4 | 0 | 0 | Real Madrid |
| 5 | Carlos Marchena | DEF | 24 | 8 | 618 | 0 | 1 | 0 | Valencia |
| 6 | Sanfelix Raul Bravo | MID | 22 | 10 | 601 | 0 | 0 | 0 | Real Madrid |
| 7 | Ivan Bujia Helguera | MID | 28 | 8 | 584 | 1 | 2 | 0 | Real Madrid |
| 8 | Ruben Vegas Baraja | MID | 27 | 9 | 559 | 2 | 3 | 0 | Valencia |
| 9 | Carlos Puyol | DEF | 25 | 6 | 540 | 0 | 0 | 0 | Barcelona |
| 10 | Joaquin Rodriguez | MID | 22 | 10 | 497 | 1 | 0 | 0 | Real Betis |
| 11 | Juan Carlos Valeron | MID | 28 | 7 | 484 | 1 | 1 | 0 | Deportivo |
| 12 | David Aliques Albelda | MID | 25 | 6 | 425 | 0 | 0 | 0 | Valencia |
| 13 | Xavi Hernandez | MID | 23 | 8 | 423 | 0 | 0 | 0 | Barcelona |
| 14 | Jose Maria Guti | MID | 26 | 9 | 337 | 2 | 0 | 0 | Real Madrid |
| 15 | Joseba Etxeberria Lizardi | ATT | 25 | 6 | 323 | 1 | 1 | 0 | Athl Bilbao |
| 16 | Fernando Morientes | ATT | 27 | 7 | 303 | 3 | 0 | 0 | Real Madrid |
| 17 | Jose Garcia Calvo | DEF | 28 | 5 | 270 | 0 | 0 | 0 | Atl Madrid |
| 18 | Herrera Diego Tristan | ATT | 27 | 5 | 262 | 1 | 0 | 0 | Deportivo |
| 19 | Aranzabal | DEF | 29 | 5 | 254 | 0 | 0 | 0 | Real Sociedad |
| 20 | Martin Villar Cesar | DEF | 26 | 4 | 184 | 0 | 0 | 0 | Deportivo |
| 21 | Gaizka Mendieta | MID | 29 | 5 | 184 | 0 | 1 | 0 | Barcelona |

# GERMANY

FIFA/COCA COLA WORLD RANKING: 4th

MANAGER: RUDI VOLLER

| | | | | | | |
|---|---|---|---|---|---|---|
| 1 | intnls | Bulgaria | A | D | 2-2 | Ballack 23 pen; Jancker 57 |
| 2 | eqg5 | Lithuania | A | W | 2-0 | Ballack 26; Stankevicius 59 og |
| 3 | intnls | Bosnia | A | D | 1-1 | Jancker 56 |
| 4 | eqg5 | Faroe Islands | H | W | 2-1 | Ballack 1 pen; Klose 59 |
| 5 | intnls | Holland | H | L | 1-3 | Bobic 34 |
| 6 | intnls | Spain | A | L | 1-2 | Bobic 38 |
| 7 | eqg5 | Lithuania | H | D | 1-1 | Ramelow 8 |
| 8 | intnls | Serbia & M | H | W | 1-0 | Kehl 59 |
| 9 | intnls | Canada | H | W | 4-1 | Ramelow 40; Freier 53; Bobic 60; Rau 90 |
| 10 | eqg5 | Scotland | A | D | 1-1 | Bobic 23 |
| 11 | eqg5 | Faroe Islands | A | W | 2-0 | Klose 89; Bobic 90 |

## KEY PLAYERS - GOALSCORERS

1 Fredi Bobic

| | |
|---|---|
| **Goals in Internationals** | 5 |
| **Contribution to Attacking Power** Average number of minutes between team goals while on pitch | 54 |
| **Player Strike Rate** The total number of minutes he was on the pitch for every goal scored | 98 |
| **Club Strike Rate** Average number of minutes between goals scored by club | 55 |

| | PLAYER | GOALS | ATT POWER | STRIKE RATE |
|---|---|---|---|---|
| 2 | Michael Ballack | 3 | 58 | 136 mins |
| 3 | Carsten Jancker | 2 | 45 | 158 mins |
| 4 | Tobias Rau | 1 | 49 | 347 mins |
| 5 | Miroslav Klose | 2 | 49 | 349 mins |

## TOP PLAYER APPEARANCES

12 Michael Ballack — Midfielder

| | |
|---|---|
| Age (on 01/07/03) | 26 |
| Caps this season | 5 |
| Total minutes on the pitch | 408 |
| Goals | 3 |
| Yellow Cards | 1 |
| Red Cards | 0 |
| Club Side | Bayern Munich |

| | PLAYER | POS | AGE | CAPS | MINS | GOALS | CARDS(Y) | CARDS(R) | CLUB SIDE |
|---|---|---|---|---|---|---|---|---|---|
| 1 | Carsten Ramelow | MID | 29 | 10 | 810 | 2 | 1 | 0 | B Leverkusen |
| 2 | Bernd Schneider | MID | 29 | 10 | 796 | 0 | 0 | 0 | B Leverkusen |
| 3 | Arne Friedrich | DEF | 24 | 10 | 739 | 0 | 0 | 0 | Hertha Berlin |
| 4 | Torsten Frings | MID | 26 | 8 | 700 | 0 | 2 | 0 | B Dortmund |
| 5 | Miroslav Klose | ATT | 25 | 10 | 698 | 2 | 0 | 0 | Kaiserslautern |
| 6 | Christian Worns | DEF | 31 | 8 | 680 | 0 | 1 | 1 | B Dortmund |
| 7 | Oliver Kahn | GK | 34 | 8 | 630 | 0 | 0 | 0 | Bayern Munich |
| 8 | Jens Jeremies | MID | 29 | 8 | 564 | 0 | 0 | 0 | Bayern Munich |
| 9 | Fredi Bobic | ATT | 31 | 7 | 489 | 5 | 0 | 0 | Hannover 96 |
| 10 | Paul Freier | MID | 23 | 10 | 467 | 1 | 1 | 0 | Bochum |
| 11 | Sebastian Kehl | DEF | 23 | 10 | 456 | 1 | 0 | 0 | B Dortmund |
| 12 | Michael Ballack | MID | 26 | 5 | 408 | 3 | 1 | 0 | Bayern Munich |
| 13 | Tobias Rau | MID | 21 | 5 | 347 | 1 | 2 | 0 | Wolfsburg |
| 14 | Carsten Jancker | ATT | 28 | 4 | 316 | 2 | 1 | 0 | Udinese |
| 15 | Jorg Bohme | MID | 29 | 4 | 302 | 0 | 1 | 0 | Schalke |
| 16 | Frank Baumann | DEF | 27 | 5 | 281 | 0 | 0 | 0 | W Bremen |
| 17 | Dietmar Hamann | MID | 29 | 3 | 270 | 0 | 0 | 0 | Liverpool |
| 18 | Christoph Metzelder | DEF | 22 | 3 | 226 | 0 | 1 | 0 | B Dortmund |
| 19 | Oliver Neuville | ATT | 30 | 7 | 217 | 0 | 0 | 0 | B Leverkusen |
| 20 | Marko Rehmer | DEF | 31 | 6 | 180 | 0 | 0 | 0 | Hertha Berlin |
| 21 | Frank Rost | GK | 30 | 4 | 180 | 0 | 0 | 0 | Schalke |

# ARGENTINA

FIFA/COCA COLA WORLD RANKING: **5th**

**MANAGER:** MARCELO BIELSA

| | | | | | | |
|---|---|---|---|---|---|---|
| 1 | intnls | **Japan** | A | W | 2-0 | Sorin 47; Crespo 49 |
| 2 | intnls | **Honduras** | A | W | 3-1 | Milito, D 15; Gonzalez, L 53; Gonzalez, M 56 |
| 3 | intnls | **Mexico** | A | W | 1-0 | Rodriguez, G 14 |
| 4 | intnls | **United States** | A | W | 1-0 | Gonzalez, L 9 |
| 5 | intnls | **Holland** | A | L | 0-1 | |
| 6 | intnls | **Libya** | A | W | 3-0 | Saviola 30; Riquelme 63; Aimar 87 |
| 7 | intnls | **Japan** | A | W | 4-1 | Saviola 30; Zanetti 45; Romeo 78; Rodriguez, M 82 |
| 8 | intnls | **South Korea** | A | W | 1-0 | Saviola 43 |

## KEY PLAYERS - GOALSCORERS

1 Javier Saviola

Reebok

| | |
|---|---|
| **Goals in Internationals** | 2 |
| **Contribution to Attacking Power** Average number of minutes between team goals while on pitch | 68 |
| **Player Strike Rate** The total number of minutes he was on the pitch for every goal scored | 103 |
| **Club Strike Rate** Average number of minutes between goals scored by club | 53 |

| | PLAYER | GOALS | ATT POWER | STRIKE RATE |
|---|---|---|---|---|
| 2 | Luis Gonzalez | 2 | 53 | 133 mins |
| 3 | Juan Pablo Sorin | 1 | 90 | 180 mins |
| 4 | Mariano Gonzalez | 1 | 42 | 212 mins |
| 5 | Diego Milito | 1 | 45 | 225 mins |

## TOP PLAYER APPEARANCES

1 Cavallero — Goalkeeper

| | |
|---|---|
| **Age** (on 01/07/03) | 29 |
| **Caps this season** | 4 |
| **Total minutes on the pitch** | 360 |
| **Goals** | 0 |
| **Yellow Cards** | 0 |
| **Red Cards** | 0 |
| **Club Side** | Celta Vigo |

| | PLAYER | POS | AGE | CAPS | MINS | GOALS | CARDS(Y) | CARDS(R) | CLUB SIDE |
|---|---|---|---|---|---|---|---|---|---|
| 1 | Cavallero | GK | 29 | 4 | 360 | 0 | 0 | 0 | Celta Vigo |
| 2 | Javier Zanetti | MID | 29 | 4 | 360 | 1 | 0 | 0 | Inter Milan |
| 3 | Facundo Quiroga | DEF | 25 | 4 | 358 | 0 | 0 | 0 | Napoli |
| 4 | Diego Sebastian Saja | GK | 24 | 3 | 270 | 0 | 0 | 0 | San Lorenzo |
| 5 | Nicolas Burdisso | DEF | 22 | 3 | 270 | 0 | 0 | 0 | Boca Juniors |
| 6 | Pablo Guinazu | MID | 24 | 3 | 270 | 0 | 0 | 0 | Toluca |
| 7 | Andres D'Alessandro | MID | 22 | 3 | 269 | 0 | 0 | 1 | River Plate |
| 8 | Luis Gonzalez | MID | 22 | 3 | 265 | 2 | 0 | 0 | River Plate |
| 9 | Federico Insua | ATT | 23 | 3 | 244 | 0 | 0 | 0 | Independiente |
| 10 | Pablo Aimar | MID | 23 | 3 | 229 | 0 | 0 | 0 | Valencia |
| 11 | Sebastian Battaglia | MID | 22 | 3 | 225 | 0 | 0 | 0 | Boca Juniors |
| 12 | Diego Milito | ATT | 24 | 3 | 225 | 1 | 0 | 0 | Racing |
| 13 | Mariano Gonzalez | MID | 22 | 3 | 212 | 1 | 0 | 0 | Racing |
| 14 | Javier Saviola | ATT | 21 | 4 | 205 | 2 | 0 | 0 | Barcelona |
| 15 | Esteban Cambiasso | MID | 22 | 3 | 199 | 0 | 0 | 0 | Real Madrid |
| 16 | Fabricio Coloccini | DEF | 21 | 2 | 180 | 0 | 0 | 0 | Atl Madrid |
| 17 | Diego Placente | DEF | 25 | 2 | 180 | 0 | 0 | 0 | B Leverkusen |
| 18 | Juan Pablo Sorin | MID | 27 | 2 | 180 | 1 | 0 | 0 | Barcelona |
| 19 | Roberto Fabian Ayala | DEF | 30 | 2 | 180 | 0 | 0 | 0 | Valencia |
| 20 | Santiago Hernan Solari | MID | 26 | 4 | 174 | 0 | 0 | 0 | Real Madrid |
| 21 | Ariel Hernan Garce | DEF | 23 | 2 | 168 | 0 | 0 | 1 | River Plate |

# HOLLAND

FIFA/COCA COLA WORLD RANKING: **6th**

**MANAGER:** DICK ADVOCAAT

| | | | | | | |
|---|---|---|---|---|---|---|
| 1 | intnls | **Norway** | A | W | 1-0 | Davids 70 |
| 2 | eqg3 | **Belarus** | H | W | 3-0 | Davids 34; Kluivert 36; Hasselbaink 73 |
| 3 | eqg3 | **Austria** | A | W | 3-0 | Seedorf 16; Cocu 19; Makaay 29 |
| 4 | intnls | **Germany** | A | W | 3-1 | Kluivert 22; Hasselbaink 69; van Nistelrooy 79 |
| 5 | intnls | **Argentina** | H | W | 1-0 | van Bronckhorst 87 |
| 6 | eqg3 | **Czech Republic** | H | D | 1-1 | van Nistelrooy 44 |
| 7 | eqg3 | **Moldova** | A | W | 2-1 | van Nistelrooy 37; Van Bommel 84 |
| 8 | intnls | **Portugal** | H | D | 1-1 | Kluivert 27 |
| 9 | eqg3 | **Belarus** | A | W | 2-0 | Overmars 62; Kluivert 69 |

## KEY PLAYERS - GOALSCORERS

1 Ruud van Nistelrooy

| | |
|---|---|
| **Goals in Internationals** | 3 |
| **Contribution to Attacking Power** Average number of minutes between team goals while on pitch | 49 |
| **Player Strike Rate** The total number of minutes he was on the pitch for every goal scored | 149 |
| **Club Strike Rate** Average number of minutes between goals scored by club | 48 |

| | PLAYER | GOALS | ATT POWER | STRIKE RATE |
|---|---|---|---|---|
| 2 | Patrick Kluivert | 4 | 48 | 181 mins |
| 3 | Roy Makaay | 1 | 48 | 288 mins |
| 4 | Edgar Davids | 2 | 43 | 304 mins |
| 5 | Clarence Seedorf | 1 | 46 | 515 mins |

## TOP PLAYER APPEARANCES

1 Frank de Boer — Defender

| | |
|---|---|
| **Age** (on 01/07/03) | 33 |
| **Caps this season** | 9 |
| **Total minutes on the pitch** | 765 |
| **Goals** | 0 |
| **Yellow Cards** | 1 |
| **Red Cards** | 0 |
| **Club Side** | Barcelona |

| | PLAYER | POS | AGE | CAPS | MINS | GOALS | CARDS(Y) | CARDS(R) | CLUB SIDE |
|---|---|---|---|---|---|---|---|---|---|
| 1 | Frank de Boer | DEF | 33 | 9 | 765 | 0 | 1 | 0 | Barcelona |
| 2 | Boudewijn Zenden | MID | 26 | 9 | 744 | 0 | 1 | 0 | Chelsea |
| 3 | Patrick Kluivert | ATT | 27 | 9 | 722 | 4 | 0 | 0 | Barcelona |
| 4 | Fernando Ricksen | DEF | 26 | 8 | 612 | 0 | 0 | 0 | Rangers |
| 5 | Edgar Davids | MID | 30 | 8 | 607 | 2 | 0 | 0 | Juventus |
| 6 | Mark Van Bommel | MID | 26 | 7 | 589 | 1 | 1 | 0 | PSV Eindhoven |
| 7 | Jaap Stam | DEF | 30 | 7 | 558 | 0 | 0 | 0 | Lazio |
| 8 | Edwin van der Sar | GK | 32 | 6 | 540 | 0 | 0 | 0 | Fulham |
| 9 | Phillip Cocu | MID | 32 | 7 | 531 | 1 | 0 | 0 | Barcelona |
| 10 | Clarence Seedorf | MID | 27 | 6 | 515 | 1 | 1 | 0 | AC Milan |
| 11 | Ruud van Nistelrooy | ATT | 27 | 8 | 446 | 3 | 2 | 0 | Man Utd |
| 12 | Michael Reiziger | DEF | 30 | 7 | 324 | 0 | 0 | 0 | Barcelona |
| 13 | Roy Makaay | ATT | 28 | 7 | 288 | 1 | 0 | 0 | Deportivo |
| 14 | Ronald Waterreus | GK | 32 | 6 | 270 | 0 | 0 | 0 | PSV Eindhoven |
| 15 | Andy van der Meyde | MID | 23 | 3 | 263 | 0 | 0 | 0 | Ajax |
| 16 | Rafael van der Vaart | MID | 20 | 6 | 243 | 0 | 0 | 0 | Ajax |
| 17 | Paul Bosvelt | MID | 33 | 8 | 197 | 0 | 1 | 0 | Feyenoord |
| 18 | G Van Bronckhorst | MID | 28 | 3 | 118 | 1 | 0 | 0 | Arsenal |
| 19 | Wilfred Bouma | MID | 25 | 2 | 112 | 0 | 0 | 0 | PSV Eindhoven |
| 20 | Marc Overmars | ATT | 30 | 2 | 105 | 1 | 0 | 0 | Barcelona |
| 21 | Jimmy-Floyd Hasselbaink | ATT | 31 | 4 | 104 | 2 | 0 | 0 | Chelsea |

# ENGLAND

FIFA/COCA COLA WORLD RANKING: **7th**

**MANAGER:** SVEN GORAN ERIKSSON

| | | | | | | |
|---|---|---|---|---|---|---|
| 1 | intnls | **Portugal** | H | D | 1-1 | Smith 40 |
| 2 | eqg7 | **Slovakia** | A | W | 2-1 | Beckham 65; Owen 82 |
| 3 | eqg7 | **Macedonia** | H | D | 2-2 | Beckham 14; Gerrard 36 |
| 4 | intnls | **Australia** | H | L | 1-3 | Jeffers 69 |
| 5 | eqg7 | **Liechtenstein** | A | W | 2-0 | Owen 28; Beckham 53 |
| 6 | eqg7 | **Turkey** | H | W | 2-0 | Vassell 75; Beckham 90 pen |
| 7 | intnls | **South Africa** | A | W | 2-1 | Southgate 1; Heskey 64 |
| 8 | intnls | **Serbia & M** | H | W | 2-1 | Gerrard 35; Cole, J 82 |
| 9 | eqg7 | **Slovakia** | H | W | 2-1 | Owen 62 pen,73 |

## KEY PLAYERS - GOALSCORERS

1 David Beckham

| | |
|---|---|
| Goals in Internationals | 4 |
| Contribution to Attacking Power<br>Average number of minutes between team goals while on pitch | 48 |
| Player Strike Rate<br>The total number of minutes he was on the pitch for every goal scored | 109 |
| Club Strike Rate<br>Average number of minutes between goals scored by club | 51 |

| | PLAYER | GOALS | ATT POWER | STRIKE RATE |
|---|---|---|---|---|
| 2 | Michael Owen | 4 | 54 | 163 mins |
| 3 | Alan Smith | 1 | 60 | 181 mins |
| 4 | Darius Vassell | 1 | 33 | 201 mins |
| 5 | Steven Gerrard | 2 | 42 | 274 mins |

## TOP PLAYER APPEARANCES

1 Michael Owen — Attacker

| | |
|---|---|
| Age (on 01/07/03) | 23 |
| Caps this season | 9 |
| Total minutes on the pitch | 652 |
| Goals | 4 |
| Yellow Cards | 0 |
| Red Cards | 0 |
| Club Side | Liverpool |

| | PLAYER | POS | AGE | CAPS | MINS | GOALS | CARDS(Y) | CARDS(R) | CLUB SIDE |
|---|---|---|---|---|---|---|---|---|---|
| 1 | Michael Owen | ATT | 23 | 9 | 652 | 4 | 0 | 0 | Liverpool |
| 2 | Paul Scholes | MID | 28 | 8 | 614 | 0 | 1 | 0 | Man Utd |
| 3 | Steven Gerrard | MID | 23 | 8 | 547 | 2 | 1 | 0 | Liverpool |
| 4 | David James | GK | 32 | 9 | 540 | 0 | 0 | 0 | West Ham |
| 5 | Gareth Southgate | DEF | 32 | 7 | 495 | 1 | 0 | 0 | Middlesbrough |
| 6 | David Beckham | MID | 28 | 6 | 434 | 4 | 2 | 0 | Man Utd |
| 7 | Ashley Cole | DEF | 22 | 6 | 405 | 0 | 0 | 0 | Arsenal |
| 8 | Gary Neville | DEF | 28 | 5 | 405 | 0 | 0 | 0 | Man Utd |
| 9 | Emile Heskey | ATT | 25 | 7 | 382 | 1 | 0 | 0 | Liverpool |
| 10 | Wayne Bridge | DEF | 22 | 6 | 328 | 0 | 0 | 0 | Southampton |
| 11 | Rio Ferdinand | DEF | 24 | 5 | 315 | 0 | 0 | 0 | Man Utd |
| 12 | Nicky Butt | MID | 28 | 5 | 302 | 0 | 0 | 0 | Man Utd |
| 13 | Danny Mills | DEF | 26 | 9 | 282 | 0 | 1 | 0 | Leeds |
| 14 | Phil Neville | DEF | 26 | 3 | 267 | 0 | 0 | 0 | Man Utd |
| 15 | Wayne Rooney | ATT | 17 | 5 | 246 | 0 | 0 | 0 | Everton |
| 16 | Frank Lampard | MID | 25 | 6 | 228 | 0 | 0 | 0 | Chelsea |
| 17 | Sol Campbell | DEF | 28 | 3 | 225 | 0 | 0 | 0 | Arsenal |
| 18 | Jonathan Woodgate | DEF | 23 | 5 | 225 | 0 | 0 | 0 | Newcastle |
| 19 | Matthew Upson | DEF | 24 | 4 | 219 | 0 | 0 | 0 | Birmingham |
| 20 | Darius Vassell | ATT | 23 | 8 | 201 | 1 | 0 | 0 | Aston Villa |
| 21 | Owen Hargreaves | MID | 22 | 6 | 188 | 0 | 0 | 0 | Bayern Munich |

# TURKEY

FIFA/COCA COLA WORLD RANKING: **8th**

**MANAGER:** SENOL GUNEZ

| | | | | | | |
|---|---|---|---|---|---|---|
| 1 | intnls | **Georgia** | H | W | 3-0 | Arif Erdem 8; Cihan 51; Nihat 61 |
| 2 | eqg7 | **Slovakia** | H | W | 3-0 | Akin, S 15; Arif Erdem 44,65 |
| 3 | eqg7 | **Macedonia** | A | W | 2-1 | Okan 29; Nihat 53 |
| 4 | eqg7 | **Liechtenstein** | H | W | 5-0 | Okan 7; Umit Davala 15; Ilhan Mansiz 22; Akin, S 82,90 |
| 5 | intnls | **Italy** | A | D | 1-1 | Emre Belozoglu 28 |
| 6 | intnls | **Ukraine** | H | D | 0-0 | |
| 7 | eqg7 | **England** | A | L | 0-2 | |
| 8 | intnls | **Czech Republic** | A | L | 0-4 | |
| 9 | eqg7 | **Slovakia** | A | W | 1-0 | Nihat 12 |
| 10 | eqg7 | **Macedonia** | H | W | 3-2 | Nihat 27; Karadeniz 48; Hakan Sukur 60 |

## KEY PLAYERS - GOALSCORERS

3 Kahveci Nihat

1 Serhat Akin

| | |
|---|---|
| Goals in Internationals | 3 |
| Contribution to Attacking Power<br>Average number of minutes between team goals while on pitch | 29 |
| Player Strike Rate<br>The total number of minutes he was on the pitch for every goal scored | 87 |
| Club Strike Rate<br>Average number of minutes between goals scored by club | 50 |

| | PLAYER | GOALS | ATT POWER | STRIKE RATE |
|---|---|---|---|---|
| 2 | Arif Erdem | 3 | 31 | 135 mins |
| 3 | Kahveci Nihat | 4 | 42 | 150 mins |
| 4 | Umit Davala | 1 | 34 | 241 mins |
| 5 | Buruk Okan | 2 | 49 | 248 mins |

## TOP PLAYER APPEARANCES

10 Emre Belozoglu — Midfielder

| | |
|---|---|
| Age (on 01/07/03) | 22 |
| Caps this season | 7 |
| Total minutes on the pitch | 475 |
| Goals | 1 |
| Yellow Cards | 2 |
| Red Cards | 0 |
| Club Side | Inter Milan |

| | PLAYER | POS | AGE | CAPS | MINS | GOALS | CARDS(Y) | CARDS(R) | CLUB SIDE |
|---|---|---|---|---|---|---|---|---|---|
| 1 | Alpay Ozalan | DEF | 30 | 10 | 863 | 0 | 0 | 0 | Aston Villa |
| 2 | Fatih Akyel | DEF | 25 | 10 | 772 | 0 | 1 | 0 | Fenerbahce |
| 3 | Kerimoglu Tugay | MID | 32 | 10 | 759 | 0 | 0 | 0 | Blackburn |
| 4 | Bulent Korkmaz | DEF | 34 | 10 | 707 | 0 | 1 | 0 | Galatasaray |
| 5 | Recber Rustu | GK | 30 | 8 | 675 | 0 | 0 | 0 | Fenerbahce |
| 6 | Ergun Penbe | DEF | 31 | 8 | 665 | 0 | 0 | 0 | Galatasaray |
| 7 | Kahveci Nihat | ATT | 23 | 8 | 598 | 4 | 0 | 0 | Real Sociedad |
| 8 | Yildiray Basturk | MID | 24 | 8 | 510 | 0 | 1 | 0 | B Leverkusen |
| 9 | Buruk Okan | MID | 29 | 10 | 495 | 2 | 2 | 0 | Inter Milan |
| 10 | Emre Belozoglu | MID | 22 | 7 | 475 | 1 | 2 | 0 | Inter Milan |
| 11 | Arif Erdem | ATT | 31 | 7 | 406 | 3 | 0 | 0 | Galatasaray |
| 12 | Ilhan Mansiz | ATT | 27 | 6 | 371 | 1 | 0 | 0 | Besiktas |
| 13 | Hakan Sukur | ATT | 31 | 4 | 269 | 1 | 0 | 0 | Blackburn |
| 14 | Serhat Akin | ATT | 22 | 6 | 261 | 3 | 0 | 0 | Fenerbahce |
| 15 | Umit Davala | MID | 29 | 6 | 241 | 1 | 1 | 0 | Galatasaray |
| 16 | Hakan Unsal | DEF | 30 | 4 | 211 | 0 | 0 | 0 | Galatasaray |
| 17 | Tayfur Havuctu | MID | 33 | 6 | 203 | 0 | 0 | 0 | Besiktas |
| 18 | Omer Catkic | GK | 28 | 9 | 190 | 0 | 0 | 0 | Gaziantepsor |
| 19 | Uzulmez Ibrahim | MID | 29 | 5 | 171 | 0 | 0 | 0 | Besiktas |
| 20 | Emre Asik | ATT | 29 | 5 | 147 | 0 | 0 | 0 | Galatasaray |
| 21 | Hasan Sas | ATT | 26 | 6 | 147 | 0 | 1 | 0 | Galatasaray |

# MEXICO

FIFA/COCA COLA WORLD RANKING: **9th**

**MANAGER:** RICARDO LAVOLPE

| | | | | | | |
|---|---|---|---|---|---|---|
| 1 | intnls | **Argentina** | H | L | 0-1 | |
| 2 | intnls | **Colombia** | H | D | 0-0 | |
| 3 | intnls | **Bolivia** | H | W | 2-0 | Pardo 27; Olalde 72 |
| 4 | intnls | **Paraguay** | H | D | 1-1 | Paino 72 |
| 5 | intnls | **Brazil** | H | D | 0-0 | |
| 6 | intnls | **United States** | A | D | 0-0 | |

**Competition key:** eqg2 = European Qualifying match in Group 2 (g2); Intnls = all other international matches

**Note:** The season of international matches covered includes all games from the end of the 2002 World Cup in June 30th 2002 to June 11th 2003.

## KEY PLAYERS - GOALSCORERS

2 Pavel Pardo

| 1 Jesus Olalde | |
|---|---|
| **Goals in Internationals** | 1 |
| **Contribution to Attacking Power** Average number of minutes between team goals while on pitch | 94 |
| **Player Strike Rate** The total number of minutes he was on the pitch for every goal scored | 188 |
| **Club Strike Rate** Average number of minutes between goals scored by club | 180 |

| | PLAYER | GOALS | ATT POWER | STRIKE RATE |
|---|---|---|---|---|
| 2 | Pavel Pardo | 1 | 135 | 405 mins |

## TOP PLAYER APPEARANCES

10 Rafael Marquez — Defender

| | |
|---|---|
| **Age** (on 01/07/03) | 24 |
| **Caps this season** | 3 |
| **Total minutes on the pitch** | 251 |
| **Goals** | 0 |
| **Yellow Cards** | 0 |
| **Red Cards** | 0 |
| **Club Side** | Monaco |

| | PLAYER | POS | AGE | CAPS | MINS | GOALS | CARDS(Y) | CARDS(R) | CLUB SIDE |
|---|---|---|---|---|---|---|---|---|---|
| 1 | Duilio Davino | DEF | 27 | 6 | 540 | 0 | 0 | 0 | America |
| 2 | Salvador Carmona | DEF | 27 | 6 | 526 | 0 | 0 | 0 | Toluca |
| 3 | Pavel Pardo | DEF | 26 | 5 | 405 | 1 | 0 | 0 | America |
| 4 | Luis Perez | MID | 22 | 6 | 368 | 0 | 0 | 0 | Rayos del Necaxa |
| 5 | Oswaldo Sanchez | GK | 29 | 4 | 360 | 0 | 0 | 0 | Guadalajara |
| 6 | Omar Briseno | DEF | - | 4 | 331 | 0 | 0 | 0 | UNL |
| 7 | Octavio Valdez | MID | 29 | 4 | 320 | 0 | 0 | 0 | Toluca |
| 8 | Jared Echavarria Borgetti | ATT | 29 | 4 | 315 | 0 | 0 | 0 | Santos Laguna |
| 9 | Hector Altamirano | DEF | 26 | 4 | 274 | 0 | 0 | 0 | Santos Laguna |
| 10 | Rafael Marquez | DEF | 24 | 3 | 251 | 0 | 0 | 0 | Monaco |
| 11 | Ramon Carlos Morales | MID | 27 | 6 | 248 | 0 | 0 | 0 | Guadalajara |
| 12 | Israel Lopez | MID | 28 | 5 | 236 | 0 | 0 | 0 | Toluca |
| 13 | Omar Bravo | ATT | 23 | 4 | 221 | 0 | 0 | 0 | Guadalajara |
| 14 | Johan Alvarez Rodriguez | MID | 27 | 4 | 189 | 0 | 0 | 0 | Santos Laguna |
| 15 | Jesus Olalde | ATT | 29 | 4 | 188 | 1 | 0 | 0 | Tigres |
| 16 | Jose Adolfo Rios | GK | 36 | 2 | 180 | 0 | 0 | 0 | America |
| 17 | Cuauhtemoc Blanco | ATT | 30 | 2 | 160 | 0 | 0 | 0 | America |
| 18 | Jesus Arellano | ATT | 30 | 2 | 143 | 0 | 0 | 0 | Monterrey |
| 19 | Jose Antonio Castro | DEF | 22 | 5 | 128 | 0 | 0 | 0 | America |
| 20 | Braulio Luna | MID | 28 | 2 | 112 | 0 | 0 | 0 | Necaxa |
| 21 | Diego Martinez | DEF | 22 | 1 | 90 | 0 | 0 | 0 | Necaxa |

# USA

FIFA/COCA COLA WORLD RANKING: **10th**

**MANAGER:** BRUCE ARENA

| | | | | | | |
|---|---|---|---|---|---|---|
| 1 | intnls | **El Salvador** | H | W | 2-0 | Olsen 31; Victorine 60 |
| 2 | intnls | **Canada** | H | W | 4-0 | Bocanegra 7; Mathis 31; Klein 32; Ralston 61 |
| 3 | intnls | **Argentina** | H | L | 0-1 | |
| 4 | intnls | **Jamaica** | A | W | 2-1 | Bocanegra 11; Klein 12 |
| 5 | intnls | **Venezuela** | H | W | 2-0 | Kirovski 52; Donovan 76 |
| 6 | intnls | **Mexico** | H | D | 0-0 | |
| 7 | intnls | **Wales** | H | W | 2-0 | Donovan 40 pen; Lewis 60 |
| 8 | intnls | **New Zealand** | H | W | 2-1 | Klein 23; Kirovski 63 |

**Competition key:** eqg2 = European Qualifying match in Group 2 (g2); Intnls = all other international matches

**Note:** The season of international matches covered includes all games from the end of the 2002 World Cup in June 30th 2002 to June 11th 2003.

## KEY PLAYERS - GOALSCORERS

1 Jovan Kirovski

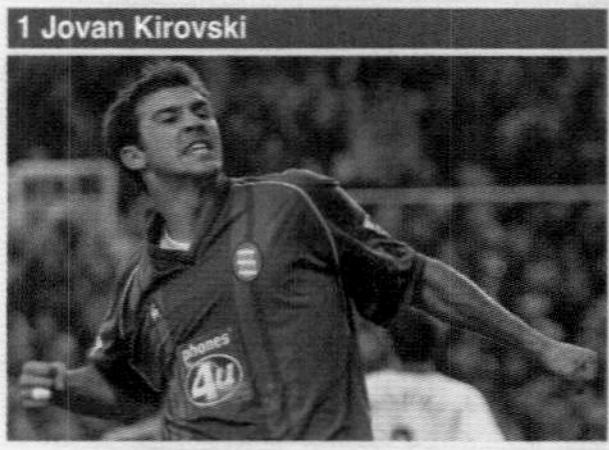

| | |
|---|---|
| **Goals in Internationals** | 2 |
| **Contribution to Attacking Power** Average number of minutes between team goals while on pitch | 47 |
| **Player Strike Rate** The total number of minutes he was on the pitch for every goal scored | 119 |
| **Club Strike Rate** Average number of minutes between goals scored by club | 51 |

| | PLAYER | GOALS | ATT POWER | STRIKE RATE |
|---|---|---|---|---|
| 2 | Chris Klein | 3 | 42 | 126 mins |
| 3 | Ben Olsen | 1 | 55 | 165 mins |
| 4 | Eddie Lewis | 1 | 45 | 180 mins |
| 5 | Sasha Victorine | 1 | 36 | 221 mins |

## TOP PLAYER APPEARANCES

5 Da Marcus Beasley — Midfielder

| | |
|---|---|
| **Age** (on 01/07/03) | 21 |
| **Caps this season** | 6 |
| **Total minutes on the pitch** | 445 |
| **Goals** | 0 |
| **Yellow Cards** | 0 |
| **Red Cards** | 0 |
| **Club Side** | Chigago Fire |

| | PLAYER | POS | AGE | CAPS | MINS | GOALS | CARDS(Y) | CARDS(R) | CLUB SIDE |
|---|---|---|---|---|---|---|---|---|---|
| 1 | Carlos Bocanegra | DEF | 24 | 7 | 600 | 2 | 0 | 0 | Chicago Fire |
| 2 | Landon Donovan | ATT | 21 | 7 | 559 | 2 | 0 | 0 | San Jose Earthquakes |
| 3 | Bobby Convey | ATT | 20 | 7 | 452 | 0 | 0 | 0 | DC United |
| 4 | Dan Califf | DEF | 23 | 5 | 450 | 0 | 0 | 0 | Los Angeles Galaxy |
| 5 | Da Marcus Beasley | MID | 21 | 6 | 445 | 0 | 0 | 0 | Chigago Fire |
| 6 | Pablo Mastroeni | DEF | 26 | 6 | 414 | 0 | 0 | 0 | Colorado Rapids |
| 7 | Clint Mathis | ATT | 26 | 5 | 382 | 1 | 0 | 0 | NY/NJ MetroStars |
| 8 | Chris Klein | MID | 38 | 6 | 378 | 3 | 0 | 0 | Kansas City |
| 9 | Tim Howard | GK | 24 | 5 | 360 | 0 | 0 | 0 | NY/NJ Metrostars |
| 10 | Steve Cherundolo | DEF | 24 | 3 | 245 | 0 | 0 | 0 | Hannover 96 |
| 11 | Ernie Stewart | ATT | 34 | 4 | 239 | 0 | 0 | 0 | NAC Breda |
| 12 | Taylor Twellman | ATT | 23 | 4 | 238 | 0 | 0 | 0 | NE Revolution |
| 13 | Jovan Kirovski | MID | 27 | 3 | 237 | 2 | 0 | 0 | Birmingham |
| 14 | Sasha Victorine | MID | 25 | 3 | 221 | 1 | 0 | 0 | Los Angeles Galaxy |
| 15 | Nick Rimando | GK | 24 | 3 | 180 | 0 | 0 | 0 | DC United |
| 16 | Greg Vanney | DEF | 29 | 2 | 180 | 0 | 0 | 0 | Bastia |
| 17 | Eddie Lewis | MID | 29 | 2 | 180 | 1 | 0 | 0 | Preston |
| 18 | Chris Armas | MID | 30 | 2 | 180 | 0 | 0 | 0 | Chicago Fire |
| 19 | Eddie George Pope | DEF | 29 | 2 | 174 | 0 | 0 | 0 | DC United |
| 20 | Ben Olsen | MID | 26 | 3 | 165 | 1 | 0 | 0 | DC United |
| 21 | Brian McBride | ATT | 31 | 2 | 157 | 0 | 0 | 0 | Columbus Crew |

# DENMARK

FIFA/COCA COLA WORLD RANKING: **11th**

**MANAGER:** MORTEN OLSEN

| | | | | | | |
|---|---|---|---|---|---|---|
| 1 | intnls | **Scotland** | A | W | 1-0 | Sand 9 |
| 2 | eqg2 | **Norway** | A | D | 2-2 | Tomasson 23,73 |
| 3 | eqg2 | **Luxembourg** | H | W | 2-0 | Tomasson 52 pen; Sand 71 |
| 4 | intnls | **Poland** | H | W | 2-0 | Tomasson 22; Larsen 72 |
| 5 | intnls | **Egypt** | A | W | 4-1 | Jensen, C 31,68,70; Poulsen 59 |
| 6 | eqg2 | **Romania** | A | W | 5-2 | Rommedahl 9,90; Gravesen 53; Tomasson 71; Contra 73 og |
| 7 | eqg2 | **Bosnia** | H | L | 0-2 | |
| 8 | intnls | **Ukraine** | H | W | 1-0 | Gravesen 36 |
| 9 | eqg2 | **Norway** | H | W | 1-0 | Gronkjaer 4 |
| 10 | eqg2 | **Luxembourg** | A | W | 2-0 | Jensen, C 21; Gravesen 48 |

## KEY PLAYERS - GOALSCORERS

1 Claus Jensen

hummel
17


| | |
|---|---|
| **Goals in Internationals** | 4 |
| **Contribution to Attacking Power** Average number of minutes between team goals while on pitch | 49 |
| **Player Strike Rate** The total number of minutes he was on the pitch for every goal scored | 136 |
| **Club Strike Rate** Average number of minutes between goals scored by club | 45 |

| | PLAYER | GOALS | ATT POWER | STRIKE RATE |
|---|---|---|---|---|
| 2 | Jon Dahl Tomasson | 5 | 41 | 141 mins |
| 3 | Thomas Roll Larsen | 1 | 78 | 157 mins |
| 4 | Thomas Gravesen | 3 | 41 | 274 mins |
| 5 | Dennis Rommedahl | 2 | 39 | 300 mins |

## TOP PLAYER APPEARANCES

Thomas Gravesen — Midfielder

hummel
7


| | |
|---|---|
| Age (on 01/07/03) | 27 |
| Caps this season | 10 |
| Total minutes on the pitch | 821 |
| Goals | 3 |
| Yellow Cards | 0 |
| Red Cards | 0 |
| Club Side | Everton |

| | PLAYER | POS | AGE | CAPS | MINS | GOALS | CARDS(Y) | CARDS(R) | CLUB SIDE |
|---|---|---|---|---|---|---|---|---|---|
| 1 | Niclas Jensen | DEF | 28 | 10 | 889 | 0 | 0 | 0 | Man City |
| 2 | Thomas Gravesen | MID | 27 | 10 | 821 | 3 | 0 | 0 | Everton |
| 3 | Rene Henriksen | DEF | 33 | 9 | 803 | 0 | 0 | 0 | Panathinaikos |
| 4 | Thomas Sorensen | GK | 27 | 8 | 720 | 0 | 0 | 0 | Sunderland |
| 5 | Jon Dahl Tomasson | ATT | 26 | 8 | 704 | 5 | 0 | 0 | AC Milan |
| 6 | Ebbe Sand | ATT | 30 | 8 | 659 | 2 | 1 | 0 | Schalke |
| 7 | Martin Laursen | DEF | 31 | 7 | 605 | 0 | 2 | 0 | AC Milan |
| 8 | Dennis Rommedahl | ATT | 24 | 10 | 599 | 2 | 0 | 0 | PSV Eindhoven |
| 9 | Claus Jensen | ATT | 25 | 9 | 543 | 4 | 0 | 0 | Charlton |
| 10 | Martin Jorgensen | MID | 27 | 7 | 517 | 0 | 0 | 0 | Udinese |
| 11 | Christian Poulsen | MID | 23 | 6 | 444 | 1 | 0 | 0 | Schalke |
| 12 | Jesper Gronkjaer | ATT | 26 | 7 | 377 | 1 | 0 | 0 | Chelsea |
| 13 | Jan Michaelsen | ATT | 32 | 8 | 377 | 0 | 0 | 0 | Panathinaikos |
| 14 | Thomas Helveg | DEF | 32 | 4 | 360 | 0 | 0 | 0 | AC Milan |
| 15 | Morten Wieghorst | MID | 32 | 8 | 339 | 0 | 1 | 0 | Brondby |
| 16 | Kasper Bogelund | DEF | 22 | 5 | 225 | 0 | 0 | 0 | PSV Eindhoven |
| 17 | Martin Albrechtsen | DEF | 23 | 4 | 180 | 0 | 0 | 0 | FC Copenhagen |
| 18 | Peter Skov-Jensen | GK | 32 | 6 | 180 | 0 | 0 | 0 | Midtjylland |
| 19 | Thomas Roll Larsen | MID | 26 | 6 | 157 | 1 | 0 | 0 | FC Copenhagen |
| 20 | Peter Lovenkrands | ATT | 23 | 4 | 132 | 0 | 0 | 0 | Rangers |
| 21 | Steven Lustu | DEF | 32 | 2 | 97 | 0 | 0 | 0 | FC Copenhagen |

# ITALY

FIFA/COCA COLA WORLD RANKING: **12th**

**MANAGER:** GIOVANNI TRAPATTONI

| | | | | | | |
|---|---|---|---|---|---|---|
| 1 | intnls | **Slovenia** | H | L | 0-1 | |
| 2 | eqg9 | **Azerbaijan** | A | W | 2-0 | Akhmedov 33 og; Del Piero 64 |
| 3 | eqg9 | **Serbia & M** | H | D | 1-1 | Del Piero 39 |
| 4 | eqg9 | **Wales** | A | L | 1-2 | Del Piero 32 |
| 5 | intnls | **Turkey** | H | D | 1-1 | Vieri 38 |
| 6 | intnls | **Portugal** | H | W | 1-0 | Corradi 62 |
| 7 | eqg9 | **Finland** | H | W | 2-0 | Vieri 6,22 |
| 8 | intnls | **Switzerland** | A | W | 2-1 | Legrottaglie 10; Zanetti 76 |
| 9 | intnls | **N Ireland** | H | W | 2-0 | Corradi 31; Delvecchio 67 |
| 10 | eqg9 | **Finland** | A | W | 2-0 | Totti 31; Del Piero 72 |

## KEY PLAYERS - GOALSCORERS

1 Christian Vieri

Kappa


| | |
|---|---|
| **Goals in Internationals** | 3 |
| **Contribution to Attacking Power** Average number of minutes between team goals while on pitch | 45 |
| **Player Strike Rate** The total number of minutes he was on the pitch for every goal scored | 61 |
| **Club Strike Rate** Average number of minutes between goals scored by club | 64 |

| | PLAYER | GOALS | ATT POWER | STRIKE RATE |
|---|---|---|---|---|
| 2 | Alessandro Del Piero | 4 | 67 | 119 mins |
| 3 | Bernardo Corradi | 2 | 49 | 149 mins |
| 4 | Francesco Totti | 1 | 44 | 176 mins |
| 5 | Marco Delvecchio | 1 | 59 | 179 mins |

## TOP PLAYER APPEARANCES

2 Christian Panucci — Defender

| | |
|---|---|
| Age (on 01/07/03) | 30 |
| Caps this season | 8 |
| Total minutes on the pitch | 675 |
| Goals | 0 |
| Yellow Cards | 0 |
| Red Cards | 0 |
| Club Side | Roma |

| | PLAYER | POS | AGE | CAPS | MINS | GOALS | CARDS(Y) | CARDS(R) | CLUB SIDE |
|---|---|---|---|---|---|---|---|---|---|
| 1 | Fabio Cannavaro | DEF | 29 | 9 | 679 | 0 | 1 | 0 | Inter Milan |
| 2 | Christian Panucci | DEF | 30 | 8 | 675 | 0 | 0 | 0 | Roma |
| 3 | Gianluigi Buffon | GK | 25 | 8 | 630 | 0 | 0 | 0 | Juventus |
| 4 | Alessandro Nesta | DEF | 27 | 7 | 630 | 0 | 0 | 0 | AC Milan |
| 5 | Simone Perrotta | MID | 25 | 6 | 506 | 0 | 0 | 0 | Chievo |
| 6 | Alessandro Del Piero | ATT | 28 | 6 | 475 | 4 | 0 | 0 | Juventus |
| 7 | Damiano Tommasi | MID | 29 | 8 | 380 | 0 | 1 | 0 | Roma |
| 8 | Massimo Ambrosini | MID | 26 | 8 | 358 | 0 | 0 | 0 | AC Milan |
| 9 | Cristiano Zanetti | MID | 26 | 4 | 316 | 1 | 1 | 0 | Inter Milan |
| 10 | Bernardo Corradi | ATT | 27 | 5 | 298 | 2 | 0 | 0 | Lazio |
| 11 | Filippo Inzaghi | ATT | 29 | 5 | 279 | 0 | 0 | 0 | AC Milan |
| 12 | Gianluca Zambrotta | MID | 26 | 3 | 270 | 0 | 1 | 0 | Juventus |
| 13 | Luciano Zauri | MID | 25 | 4 | 263 | 0 | 1 | 0 | Atalanta |
| 14 | Gennaro Gattuso | MID | 34 | 4 | 253 | 0 | 0 | 0 | AC Milan |
| 15 | Stefano Fiore | MID | 28 | 5 | 244 | 0 | 0 | 0 | Lazio |
| 16 | Marco Di Vaio | ATT | 26 | 5 | 217 | 0 | 0 | 0 | Juventus |
| 17 | Fabrizio Miccoli | ATT | 24 | 5 | 213 | 0 | 0 | 0 | Perugia |
| 18 | Luigi Di Biagio | MID | 32 | 4 | 202 | 0 | 1 | 0 | Inter Milan |
| 19 | Andrea Pirlo | MID | 24 | 4 | 193 | 0 | 0 | 0 | AC Milan |
| 20 | Nicola Legrottaglie | DEF | 26 | 6 | 188 | 1 | 0 | 0 | Chievo |
| 21 | Christian Vieri | ATT | 29 | 3 | 182 | 3 | 0 | 0 | Inter Milan |

# CZECHOSLOVAKIAN REPUBLIC

FIFA/COCA COLA WORLD RANKING: **13th**

**MANAGER:** KAREL BRUCKNER

| | | | | | | |
|---|---|---|---|---|---|---|
| 1 | intnls | **Slovakia** | H | W | 4-1 | Koller 32,64; Rosicky 71,79 |
| 2 | intnls | **Yugoslavia** | H | W | 5-0 | Smicer 10; Ujfalusi 21,55; Baros 51,80 |
| 3 | eqg3 | **Moldova** | A | W | 2-0 | Jankulovski 70 pen; Rosicky 80 |
| 4 | eqg3 | **Belarus** | H | W | 2-0 | Poborsky 7; Baros 23 |
| 5 | intnls | **Sweden** | H | D | 3-3 | Fukal 8; Vachousek 45; Baros 63 |
| 6 | intnls | **France** | A | W | 2-0 | Grygera 7; Baros 61 |
| 7 | eqg3 | **Holland** | A | D | 1-1 | Koller 68 |
| 8 | eqg3 | **Austria** | H | W | 4-0 | Nedved 19; Koller 32,62; Jankulovski 57 pen |
| 9 | intnls | **Turkey** | H | W | 4-0 | Rosicky 2; Koller 21; Smicer 27; Baros 38 |
| 10 | eqg3 | **Moldova** | H | W | 5-0 | Smicer 42; Koller 73 pen; Stajner 82; Lokvenc 88,90 |

## KEY PLAYERS - GOALSCORERS

1 Milan Baros

| | |
|---|---|
| Goals in Internationals | 6 |
| Contribution to Attacking Power<br>Average number of minutes between team goals while on pitch | 19 |
| Player Strike Rate<br>The total number of minutes he was on the pitch for every goal scored | 81 |
| Club Strike Rate<br>Average number of minutes between goals scored by club | 28 |

| | PLAYER | GOALS | ATT POWER | STRIKE RATE |
|---|---|---|---|---|
| 2 | Jan Koller | 7 | 28 | 91 mins |
| 3 | Vladimir Smicer | 3 | 26 | 140 mins |
| 4 | Tomas Rosicky | 4 | 29 | 163 mins |
| 5 | Jiri Stajner | 1 | 23 | 212 mins |

## TOP PLAYER APPEARANCES

9 Pavel Nedved — Midfield

| | |
|---|---|
| Age (on 01/07/03) | 30 |
| Caps this season | 8 |
| Total minutes on the pitch | 607 |
| Goals | 1 |
| Yellow Cards | 0 |
| Red Cards | 0 |
| Club Side | Juventus |

| | PLAYER | POS | AGE | CAPS | MINS | GOALS | CARDS(Y) | CARDS(R) | CLUB SIDE |
|---|---|---|---|---|---|---|---|---|---|
| 1 | Tomas Ujfalusi | DEF | 25 | 10 | 825 | 2 | 1 | 0 | Hamburg |
| 2 | Petr Cech | GK | 21 | 10 | 767 | 0 | 0 | 0 | Rennes |
| 3 | Zdenek Grygera | DEF | 23 | 10 | 753 | 1 | 1 | 0 | Sparta Prague |
| 4 | Karel Poborsky | MID | 31 | 10 | 737 | 1 | 0 | 0 | Sparta Prague |
| 5 | Rene Bolf | DEF | 29 | 9 | 721 | 0 | 0 | 0 | Sparta Prague |
| 6 | Tomas Galasek | DEF | 30 | 9 | 668 | 0 | 1 | 0 | Ajax |
| 7 | Tomas Rosicky | MID | 22 | 9 | 651 | 4 | 1 | 0 | B Dortmund |
| 8 | Jan Koller | ATT | 30 | 9 | 635 | 7 | 0 | 0 | B Dortmund |
| 9 | Pavel Nedved | MID | 30 | 8 | 607 | 1 | 0 | 0 | Juventus |
| 10 | Marek Jankulovski | MID | 26 | 7 | 597 | 2 | 1 | 0 | Udinese |
| 11 | Milan Baros | ATT | 21 | 9 | 484 | 6 | 0 | 0 | Liverpool |
| 12 | Vladimir Smicer | ATT | 30 | 8 | 419 | 3 | 1 | 0 | Liverpool |
| 13 | Stepan Vachousek | ATT | 23 | 6 | 337 | 1 | 0 | 0 | Slavia Prague |
| 14 | Martin Jiranek | DEF | 24 | 5 | 232 | 0 | 0 | 0 | Reggina |
| 15 | Jiri Stajner | ATT | 27 | 6 | 212 | 1 | 0 | 0 | Hannover 96 |
| 16 | Petr Johana | MID | - | 3 | 210 | 0 | 0 | 0 | Slovan Liberec |
| 17 | Patrick Gedeon | MID | 27 | 6 | 153 | 0 | 0 | 0 | Slavia Prague |
| 18 | Milan Fukal | DEF | 28 | 2 | 134 | 1 | 0 | 0 | Hamburg |
| 19 | Jiri Jarosik | MID | 25 | 5 | 109 | 0 | 2 | 0 | Sparta Prague |
| 20 | Tomas Huebschmann | DEF | 21 | 7 | 94 | 0 | 0 | 0 | Sparta Prague |
| 21 | Vratislav Lokvenc | ATT | 29 | 6 | 90 | 2 | 0 | 0 | Kaiserslautern |

# PORTUGAL

FIFA/COCA COLA WORLD RANKING: **14th**

**MANAGER:** LUIZ FELIPE SCOLARI

| | | | | | | |
|---|---|---|---|---|---|---|
| 1 | intnls | **England** | A | D | 1-1 | Costinha 79 |
| 2 | intnls | **Tunisia** | H | D | 1-1 | Pauleta 3 |
| 3 | intnls | **Sweden** | A | W | 3-2 | Conceicao 34 pen; Romeu 53; Rui Costa 88 |
| 4 | intnls | **Scotland** | H | W | 2-0 | Pauleta 8,17 |
| 5 | intnls | **Italy** | A | L | 0-1 | |
| 6 | intnls | **Brazil** | H | W | 2-1 | Pauleta 8; Deco 82 |
| 7 | intnls | **Macedonia** | H | W | 1-0 | Figo 24 |
| 8 | intnls | **Holland** | A | D | 1-1 | Sabrosa 77 |
| 9 | intnls | **Paraguay** | H | D | 0-0 | |

## KEY PLAYERS - GOALSCORERS

1 Pedro Resendes Pauleta

| | |
|---|---|
| Goals in Internationals | 4 |
| Contribution to Attacking Power<br>Average number of minutes between team goals while on pitch | 79 |
| Player Strike Rate<br>The total number of minutes he was on the pitch for every goal scored | 138 |
| Club Strike Rate<br>Average number of minutes between goals scored by club | 74 |

| | PLAYER | GOALS | ATT POWER | STRIKE RATE |
|---|---|---|---|---|
| 2 | Francisco Rodrigues Costa | 1 | 58 | 290 mins |
| 3 | Simao Sabrosa | 1 | 71 | 357 mins |
| 4 | Luis Madeira Caeira Figo | 1 | 99 | 497 mins |
| 5 | Manuel Rui Costa | 1 | 75 | 527 mins |

## TOP PLAYER APPEARANCES

7 Luis Figo — Midfielder

| | |
|---|---|
| Age (on 01/07/03) | 30 |
| Caps this season | 8 |
| Total minutes on the pitch | 497 |
| Goals | 1 |
| Yellow Cards | 0 |
| Red Cards | 0 |
| Club Side | Real Madrid |

| | PLAYER | POS | AGE | CAPS | MINS | GOALS | CARDS(Y) | CARDS(R) | CLUB SIDE |
|---|---|---|---|---|---|---|---|---|---|
| 1 | Fernando Meira | DEF | 25 | 9 | 768 | 0 | 1 | 0 | Stuttgart |
| 2 | Couto | DEF | 33 | 9 | 757 | 0 | 3 | 0 | Lazio |
| 3 | Sergio Conceicao | MID | 28 | 9 | 603 | 1 | 0 | 0 | Inter Milan |
| 4 | Pereira Ricardo | GK | 27 | 7 | 585 | 0 | 0 | 0 | Boavista |
| 5 | Pauleta | ATT | 30 | 9 | 553 | 4 | 0 | 0 | Bordeaux |
| 6 | Rui Costa | MID | 31 | 9 | 527 | 1 | 0 | 0 | AC Milan |
| 7 | Luis Figo | MID | 30 | 8 | 497 | 1 | 0 | 0 | Real Madrid |
| 8 | Oliveira Sousa Rui Jorge | DEF | 30 | 8 | 487 | 0 | 0 | 0 | Sp Lisbon |
| 9 | Paulo Ferreira | DEF | 24 | 7 | 480 | 0 | 0 | 0 | Porto |
| 10 | Simao Sabrosa | MID | 23 | 5 | 357 | 1 | 0 | 0 | Benfica |
| 11 | Francisco Costa | MID | 28 | 4 | 290 | 1 | 0 | 0 | Porto |
| 12 | Nuno Maniche | MID | 25 | 4 | 277 | 0 | 0 | 0 | Porto |
| 13 | Nuno Valente | DEF | 28 | 4 | 257 | 0 | 0 | 0 | Porto |
| 14 | Cardoso Mendes Tiago | MID | 22 | 3 | 188 | 0 | 0 | 0 | Benfica |
| 15 | Armando Teixeira Petit | MID | 26 | 3 | 187 | 0 | 0 | 0 | Boavista |
| 16 | Nuno Gomes | ATT | 27 | 7 | 181 | 0 | 0 | 0 | Fiorentina |
| 17 | Luis Loureiro | MID | 26 | 5 | 181 | 0 | 2 | 0 | Gil Vicente |
| 18 | Joaquim Quim | GK | 27 | 5 | 178 | 0 | 0 | 0 | Maritimo |
| 19 | Hugo Viana | MID | 20 | 3 | 169 | 0 | 0 | 0 | Newcastle |
| 20 | Anderson Deco | MID | 25 | 4 | 147 | 1 | 0 | 0 | Porto |
| 21 | Ricardo Rocha | DEF | 24 | 3 | 136 | 0 | 1 | 0 | Benfica |

# REPUBLIC OF IRELAND

FIFA/COCA COLA WORLD RANKING: **15th**

**MANAGER:** BRIAN KERR

| | | | | | | |
|---|---|---|---|---|---|---|
| 1 | intnls | **Finland** | A | W | 3-0 | Keane, Robbie 12; Healy 74; Barrett 81 |
| 2 | eqg10 | **Russia** | A | L | 2-4 | Doherty 69; Morrison 76 |
| 3 | eqg10 | **Switzerland** | H | L | 1-2 | Magnin 77 og |
| 4 | intnls | **Greece** | A | D | 0-0 | |
| 5 | intnls | **Scotland** | A | W | 2-0 | Kilbane 9; Morrison 17 |
| 6 | eqg10 | **Georgia** | A | W | 2-1 | Duff 18; Doherty 84 |
| 7 | eqg10 | **Albania** | A | D | 0-0 | |
| 8 | intnls | **Norway** | H | W | 1-0 | Duff 17 |
| 9 | eqg10 | **Albania** | H | W | 2-1 | Keane, Robbie 6; Aliaj 90 og |
| 10 | eqg10 | **Georgia** | H | W | 2-0 | Doherty 43; Keane, Robbie 59 |

## KEY PLAYERS - GOALSCORERS

1 Clinton Morrison

| | |
|---|---|
| **Goals in Internationals** | 2 |
| **Contribution to Attacking Power** Average number of minutes between team goals while on pitch | 38 |
| **Player Strike Rate** The total number of minutes he was on the pitch for every goal scored | 96 |
| **Club Strike Rate** Average number of minutes between goals scored by club | 60 |

| | PLAYER | GOALS | ATT POWER | STRIKE RATE |
|---|---|---|---|---|
| 2 | Gary Doherty | 3 | 43 | 160 mins |
| 3 | Robbie Keane | 3 | 54 | 199 mins |
| 4 | Damien Duff | 2 | 70 | 248 mins |
| 5 | Colin Healy | 1 | 68 | 340 mins |

## TOP PLAYER APPEARANCES

11 Damien Duff — Attacker

| | |
|---|---|
| Age (on 01/07/03) | 24 |
| Caps this season | 7 |
| Total minutes on the pitch | 495 |
| Goals | 2 |
| Yellow Cards | 0 |
| Red Cards | 0 |
| Club Side | Blackburn |

| | PLAYER | POS | AGE | CAPS | MINS | GOALS | CARDS(Y) | CARDS(R) | CLUB SIDE |
|---|---|---|---|---|---|---|---|---|---|
| 1 | Matt Holland | MID | 29 | 10 | 814 | 0 | 0 | 0 | Ipswich |
| 2 | Gary Breen | DEF | 29 | 10 | 808 | 0 | 0 | 0 | West Ham |
| 3 | Kevin Kilbane | MID | 26 | 9 | 710 | 1 | 0 | 0 | Sunderland |
| 4 | Shay Given | GK | 27 | 9 | 704 | 0 | 0 | 0 | Newcastle |
| 5 | Kenny Cunningham | DEF | 32 | 8 | 675 | 0 | 1 | 0 | Birmingham |
| 6 | Mark Kinsella | MID | 30 | 9 | 605 | 0 | 1 | 0 | Aston Villa |
| 7 | Robbie Keane | ATT | 22 | 7 | 598 | 3 | 0 | 0 | Tottenham |
| 8 | Stephen Carr | DEF | 26 | 6 | 540 | 0 | 0 | 0 | Tottenham |
| 9 | John O'Shea | DEF | 22 | 7 | 530 | 0 | 0 | 0 | Man Utd |
| 10 | Lee Carsley | MID | 29 | 9 | 521 | 0 | 0 | 0 | Everton |
| 11 | Damien Duff | ATT | 24 | 7 | 495 | 2 | 0 | 0 | Blackburn |
| 12 | Gary Doherty | DEF | 2004 | 9 | 479 | 3 | 1 | 0 | Tottenham |
| 13 | Ian Harte | DEF | 25 | 7 | 404 | 0 | 0 | 0 | Leeds |
| 14 | Colin Healy | MID | 23 | 10 | 340 | 1 | 0 | 0 | Celtic |
| 15 | Steve Finnan | DEF | 27 | 3 | 211 | 0 | 0 | 0 | Fulham |
| 16 | Clinton Morrison | ATT | 24 | 3 | 192 | 2 | 0 | 0 | Birmingham |
| 17 | Richard Dunne | DEF | 23 | 4 | 190 | 0 | 0 | 0 | Man City |
| 18 | Gary Kelly | DEF | 28 | 3 | 180 | 0 | 0 | 0 | Leeds |
| 19 | Dean Kiely | GK | 32 | 6 | 155 | 0 | 0 | 0 | Charlton |
| 20 | David Connolly | ATT | 26 | 5 | 137 | 0 | 0 | 0 | Wimbledon |
| 21 | Stephen McPhail | MID | 23 | 6 | 135 | 0 | 1 | 0 | Leeds |

# BELGIUM

FIFA/COCA COLA WORLD RANKING: **16th**

**MANAGER:** AIME ANTHUENIS

| | | | | | | |
|---|---|---|---|---|---|---|
| 1 | intnls | **Poland** | A | D | 1-1 | Sonck 42 |
| 2 | eqg8 | **Bulgaria** | H | L | 0-2 | |
| 3 | eqg8 | **Andorra** | A | W | 1-0 | Sonck 61 |
| 4 | eqg8 | **Estonia** | A | W | 1-0 | Sonck 2 |
| 5 | intnls | **Algeria** | A | W | 3-1 | Mpenza, E 1,57; Sonck 6 |
| 6 | eqg8 | **Croatia** | A | L | 0-4 | |
| 7 | intnls | **Poland** | H | W | 3-1 | Sonck 27; Buffel 56; Soetaers 85 |
| 8 | eqg8 | **Bulgaria** | A | D | 2-2 | Kirilov 31 og; Clement 56 |
| 9 | eqg8 | **Andorra** | H | W | 3-0 | Goor 25,68; Sonck 44 |

## KEY PLAYERS - GOALSCORERS

1 Wesley Sonck

| | |
|---|---|
| **Goals in Internationals** | 6 |
| **Contribution to Attacking Power** Average number of minutes between team goals while on pitch | 57 |
| **Player Strike Rate** The total number of minutes he was on the pitch for every goal scored | 126 |
| **Club Strike Rate** Average number of minutes between goals scored by club | 58 |

| | PLAYER | GOALS | ATT POWER | STRIKE RATE |
|---|---|---|---|---|
| 2 | Emile Mpenza | 2 | 85 | 171 mins |
| 3 | Philippe Clement | 1 | 36 | 180 mins |
| 4 | Bart Goor | 2 | 59 | 389 mins |
| 5 | Thomas Buffel | 1 | 46 | 601 mins |

## TOP PLAYER APPEARANCES

8 Daniel Van Buyten — Defender

| | |
|---|---|
| Age (on 01/07/03) | 25 |
| Caps this season | 8 |
| Total minutes on the pitch | 495 |
| Goals | 0 |
| Yellow Cards | 0 |
| Red Cards | 0 |
| Club Side | Marseille |

| | PLAYER | POS | AGE | CAPS | MINS | GOALS | CARDS(Y) | CARDS(R) | CLUB SIDE |
|---|---|---|---|---|---|---|---|---|---|
| 1 | Timmy Simons | MID | 27 | 9 | 793 | 0 | 1 | 0 | Club Brugge |
| 2 | Bart Goor | MID | 30 | 9 | 778 | 2 | 0 | 0 | Hertha Berlin |
| 3 | Wesley Sonck | ATT | 24 | 9 | 753 | 6 | 0 | 0 | Genk |
| 4 | Walter Baseggio | MID | 24 | 8 | 654 | 0 | 0 | 0 | Anderlecht |
| 5 | Geert De Vlieger | GK | 31 | 8 | 652 | 0 | 0 | 0 | Willem II Tilb |
| 6 | Thomas Buffel | MID | 22 | 7 | 601 | 1 | 0 | 0 | Feyenoord |
| 7 | Olivier De Cock | DEF | 27 | 7 | 496 | 0 | 1 | 0 | Club Brugge |
| 8 | Daniel Van Buyten | DEF | 25 | 8 | 495 | 0 | 0 | 0 | Marseille |
| 9 | Peter Van der Heyden | DEF | 26 | 9 | 449 | 0 | 0 | 0 | Club Brugge |
| 10 | Didier Dheedene | DEF | 31 | 5 | 438 | 0 | 0 | 0 | Austria Vienna |
| 11 | Yves Vanderhaeghe | MID | 33 | 5 | 360 | 0 | 0 | 0 | Anderlecht |
| 12 | Emile Mpenza | ATT | 25 | 6 | 342 | 2 | 0 | 0 | Schalke |
| 13 | Mbo Mpenza | ATT | 26 | 5 | 329 | 0 | 0 | 0 | Mouscron |
| 14 | Joos Valgaeren | DEF | 27 | 5 | 308 | 0 | 0 | 0 | Celtic |
| 15 | Gaetan Englebert | MID | 27 | 5 | 288 | 0 | 0 | 0 | Club Brugge |
| 16 | Peter Van Houdt | ATT | 26 | 3 | 182 | 0 | 0 | 0 | B M'gladbach |
| 17 | Philippe Clement | DEF | 29 | 2 | 180 | 1 | 0 | 0 | Club Brugge |
| 18 | Stijn Vreven | DEF | 29 | 2 | 158 | 0 | 0 | 0 | Utrecht |
| 19 | Eric Deflandre | DEF | 29 | 4 | 134 | 0 | 0 | 0 | Lyon |
| 20 | Gaby Mudingayi | MID | 21 | 3 | 90 | 0 | 0 | 0 | Gent |
| 21 | Franck Vandendriessche | GK | 32 | 1 | 90 | 0 | 0 | 0 | Mouscron |

# COSTA RICA

FIFA/COCA COLA WORLD RANKING: **17th**

**MANAGER:** STEVE SAMPSON

| | | | | | | |
|---|---|---|---|---|---|---|
| 1 | intnls | **Ecuador** | H | D | 1-1 | Bryce 53 |
| 2 | intnls | **Ecuador** | A | D | 2-2 | Chinchilla 29; Herron 45 |
| 3 | intnls | **El Salvador** | A | W | 1-0 | Scott 62 |
| 4 | intnls | **Guatemala** | H | D | 1-1 | Scott 24 pen |
| 5 | intnls | **Nicaragua** | H | W | 1-0 | Scott 16 |
| 6 | intnls | **Honduras** | H | W | 1-0 | Bryce 45 |
| 7 | intnls | **Panama** | A | W | 1-0 | Solis 73 |
| 8 | intnls | **Paraguay** | H | W | 2-1 | Parks 36; Benneth 89 |
| 9 | intnls | **Chile** | A | L | 0-1 | |
| 10 | intnls | **Chile** | A | L | 0-1 | |
| 11 | intnls | **Chile** | H | W | 1-0 | Fonseca, R 88 |

## KEY PLAYERS - GOALSCORERS

3 Steven Bryce

| 1 Erick Scott | |
|---|---|
| **Goals in Internationals** | 1 |
| **Contribution to Attacking Power** Average number of minutes between team goals while on pitch | 68 |
| **Player Strike Rate** The total number of minutes he was on the pitch for every goal scored | 136 |
| **Club Strike Rate** Average number of minutes between goals scored by club | 90 |

| | PLAYER | GOALS | ATT POWER | STRIKE RATE |
|---|---|---|---|---|
| 2 | Andy Herron | 1 | 87 | 262 mins |
| 3 | Steven Bryce | 2 | 98 | 393 mins |
| 4 | Try Bennett | 1 | 85 | 427 mins |
| 5 | Rolando Fonseca | 1 | 61 | 427 mins |

## TOP PLAYER APPEARANCES

13 Gilberto Martinez — Defender

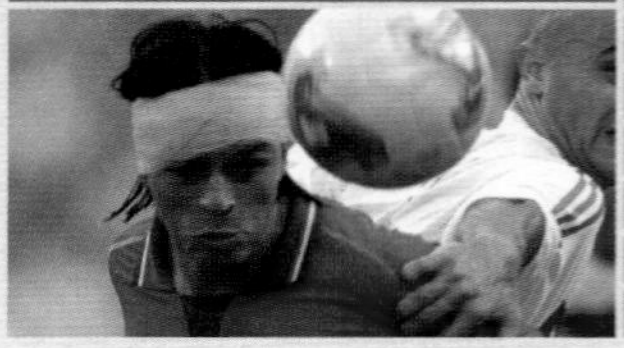

| | |
|---|---|
| Age (on 01/07/03) | 23 |
| Caps this season | 4 |
| Total minutes on the pitch | 360 |
| Goals | 0 |
| Yellow Cards | 0 |
| Red Cards | 0 |
| Club Side | Brescia |

| | PLAYER | POS | AGE | CAPS | MINS | GOALS | CARDS(Y) | CARDS(R) | CLUB SIDE |
|---|---|---|---|---|---|---|---|---|---|
| 1 | Luis Antonio Marin | DEF | 28 | 10 | 900 | 0 | 0 | 0 | Alajuela |
| 2 | Carlos Castro | DEF | 24 | 11 | 786 | 0 | 0 | 0 | Alajuela |
| 3 | Steven Bryce | ATT | 25 | 10 | 786 | 2 | 0 | 0 | Alajuela |
| 4 | Walter Centeno | MID | 28 | 9 | 730 | 0 | 0 | 0 | AEK Athens |
| 5 | Ricardo Gonzalez | GK | 29 | 8 | 720 | 0 | 0 | 0 | LD Alajuelense |
| 6 | Leonardo Gonzalez | DEF | 22 | 8 | 685 | 0 | 0 | 0 | Herediano |
| 7 | Jervis Drummond | DEF | 29 | 7 | 630 | 0 | 0 | 0 | Saprissa |
| 8 | Daniel Vallejos | DEF | 22 | 9 | 580 | 0 | 0 | 0 | Herediano |
| 9 | Pablo Chinchilla | DEF | 24 | 9 | 522 | 1 | 0 | 0 | Alajuela |
| 10 | Rolando Fonseca | MID | 29 | 6 | 427 | 1 | 0 | 0 | Alajuela |
| 11 | Try Bennett | MID | 27 | 8 | 427 | 1 | 0 | 0 | Herediano |
| 12 | Erick Scott | ATT | 22 | 7 | 408 | 3 | 0 | 0 | Alajuelense |
| 13 | Gilberto Martinez | DEF | 23 | 4 | 360 | 0 | 0 | 0 | Brescia |
| 14 | Alvaro Mesen | GK | 30 | 4 | 360 | 0 | 0 | 0 | Alajuela |
| 15 | Mauricio Wright | DEF | 32 | 4 | 360 | 0 | 0 | 0 | AEK Athens |
| 16 | Rodrigo Cordero | MID | 29 | 6 | 280 | 0 | 0 | 1 | Herediano |
| 17 | Andy Herron | ATT | 25 | 5 | 262 | 1 | 0 | 0 | Santos |
| 18 | Alvaro Saborio | ATT | 21 | 4 | 238 | 0 | 0 | 0 | Saprissa |
| 19 | Wilmer Lopez | MID | 31 | 3 | 205 | 0 | 0 | 0 | Alajuela |
| 20 | Jaffet Soto | ATT | 27 | 5 | 200 | 0 | 0 | 0 | Herediano |
| 21 | Alejandro Alpizar | MID | 24 | 4 | 158 | 0 | 0 | 0 | LD Alajuelense |

# CAMEROON

FIFA/COCA COLA WORLD RANKING: **18th**

**MANAGER:** WINFRIED SCHAFER

| | | | | | | |
|---|---|---|---|---|---|---|
| 1 | intnls | **Ivory Coast** | H | L | 0-3 | |
| 2 | intnls | **Madagascar** | H | W | 2-0 | Eto'o 15; Job 43 |

**Marc-Vivien Foe** collapsed and subsequently died during a Confederations Cup semi-final in Lyon France on the 26th June.

The football world mourned a popular footballer who was only 28 and had graced the Premiership in both West Ham and Manchester City colours.

City are retiring shirt number 23, the shirt Foe wore for them in the 2002/3 season when he played on loan from Lyon. He will go down in the club's history as the player who scored the last City goal at their Maine Road stadium. He had 65 caps for Cameroon and was a competitive midfielder with a scoring touch that included 9 goals in 35 appearances for Lyon, where he was set to return next season.

Foe's manager when he was at West Ham was Harry Redknapp, now in charge of Portsmouth. "You couldn't meet a nicer, more fantastic person than Marc Foe. He was a special boy - I just can't believe it."

## KEY PLAYERS - GOALSCORERS

1 Samuel Fils Eto'o

| | |
|---|---|
| **Goals in Internationals** | 1 |
| **Contribution to Attacking Power** Average number of minutes between team goals while on pitch | 89 |
| **Player Strike Rate** The total number of minutes he was on the pitch for every goal scored | 179 |
| **Club Strike Rate** Average number of minutes between goals scored by club | 90 |

## TOP PLAYER APPEARANCES

1 Geremi — Midfielder

| | |
|---|---|
| Age (on 01/07/03) | 24 |
| Caps this season | 2 |
| Total minutes on the pitch | 180 |
| Goals | 0 |
| Yellow Cards | 0 |
| Red Cards | 0 |
| Club Side | Middlesbrough |

| | PLAYER | POS | AGE | CAPS | MINS | GOALS | CARDS(Y) | CARDS(R) | CLUB SIDE |
|---|---|---|---|---|---|---|---|---|---|
| 1 | Geremi | MID | 24 | 2 | 180 | 0 | 0 | 0 | Middlesbrough |
| 2 | Lucien Mettomo | DEF | 26 | 2 | 180 | 0 | 0 | 0 | Man City |
| 3 | Samuel Fils Eto'o | ATT | 22 | 2 | 179 | 1 | 0 | 0 | Mallorca |
| 4 | Rigobert Bahanag Song | DEF | 27 | 2 | 171 | 0 | 0 | 0 | Lens |
| 5 | Eric Djemba-Djemba | MID | 22 | 2 | 138 | 0 | 0 | 0 | Nantes |
| 6 | Idriss Carlos Kameni | GK | 19 | 2 | 135 | 0 | 0 | 0 | Le Havre |
| 7 | Pierre Nlend Wome | DEF | 24 | 2 | 117 | 0 | 0 | 0 | Fulham |
| 8 | Joseph-Desire Job | ATT | 25 | 2 | 92 | 1 | 0 | 0 | Middlesbrough |
| 9 | Salomon Olembe | MID | 29 | 2 | 91 | 0 | 0 | 0 | Marseille |
| 10 | Modeste Mbami | MID | 20 | 1 | 90 | 0 | 0 | 0 | Sedan |
| 11 | Pierre Beaka Njanka | DEF | 28 | 1 | 90 | 0 | 0 | 0 | Sedan |
| 12 | Marc-Vivien Foe | MID | 28 | 1 | 76 | 0 | 0 | 0 | Man City |
| 13 | Tim Atouba | MID | 21 | 2 | 63 | 0 | 0 | 0 | Basle |
| 14 | Perrier Ndoumbe | DEF | 24 | 2 | 56 | 0 | 0 | 0 | Auxerre |
| 15 | Bill Tchato | MID | 28 | 2 | 53 | 0 | 0 | 0 | Kaiserslautern |
| 16 | Ngassam Felami | MID | 29 | 1 | 46 | 0 | 0 | 0 | Steaua Bucarest |
| 17 | Mohamadou Idrissou | ATT | 23 | 1 | 45 | 0 | 0 | 0 | Hannover 96 |
| 18 | Cyrille Bella | ATT | 28 | 1 | 45 | 0 | 0 | 0 | LR Ahlen |
| 19 | Boukar Alioum | GK | 31 | 1 | 45 | 0 | 0 | 0 | Samsunspor |
| 20 | Valery Mezague | MID | 19 | 1 | 44 | 0 | 0 | 0 | Montpellier |
| 21 | Pius Ndiefi | ATT | 28 | 1 | 43 | 0 | 0 | 0 | Sedan |

# PARAGUAY

FIFA/COCA COLA WORLD RANKING: **19th**

**MANAGER:** ANIBAL MUIZ

| | | | | | | |
|---|---|---|---|---|---|---|
| 1 | intnls | **Brazil** | A | W | 1-0 | Cuevas 29 |
| 2 | intnls | **South Africa** | H | W | 2-0 | |
| 3 | intnls | **Iran** | A | L | 3-4* | Bareiros 35 (*on penalties) |
| 4 | intnls | **Spain** | A | D | 0-0 | |
| 5 | intnls | **Mexico** | A | D | 1-1 | Cardozo 74 |
| 6 | intnls | **Costa Rica** | A | L | 1-2 | Caceres 53 |
| 7 | intnls | **Honduras** | A | D | 1-1 | Quintana 55 |
| 8 | intnls | **Honduras** | A | D | 1-1 | Quintana 55 |
| 9 | intnls | **Peru** | A | W | 1-0 | Alvarenga 72 |
| 10 | intnls | **Peru** | A | W | 1-0 | Alvarenga 72 |
| 11 | intnls | **Portugal** | A | D | 0-0 | |
| 12 | intnls | **Japan** | A | D | 0-0 | |

## KEY PLAYERS - GOALSCORERS

2 Nelson Cuevas

| 1 Victor Quintana | |
|---|---|
| Goals in Internationals | |
| Contribution to Attacking Power<br>Average number of minutes between team goals while on pitch | 90 |
| Player Strike Rate<br>The total number of minutes he was on the pitch for every goal scored | 135 |
| Club Strike Rate<br>Average number of minutes between goals scored by club | 144 |

| | PLAYER | GOALS | ATT POWER | STRIKE RATE |
|---|---|---|---|---|
| 2 | Nelson Cuevas | 1 | 341 | 341 mins |
| 3 | Jose Cardozo | 1 | 88 | 354 mins |
| 4 | Julio Caceres | 1 | 136 | 544 mins |

## TOP PLAYER APPEARANCES

| 2 Julio Caceres | Defender |
|---|---|
| Age (on 01/07/03) | 23 |
| Caps this season | 7 |
| Total minutes on the pitch | 544 |
| Goals | 1 |
| Yellow Cards | 0 |
| Red Cards | 0 |
| Club Side | Olimpia |

| | PLAYER | POS | AGE | CAPS | MINS | GOALS | CARDS(Y) | CARDS(R) | CLUB SIDE |
|---|---|---|---|---|---|---|---|---|---|
| 1 | Paulo Da Silva | DEF | 23 | 8 | 631 | 0 | 0 | 0 | Libertad |
| 2 | Julio Caceres | DEF | 23 | 7 | 544 | 1 | 0 | 0 | Olimpia |
| 3 | Angel Ortiz | MID | 25 | 6 | 540 | 0 | 0 | 0 | Guarani |
| 4 | Carlos Bonet | MID | 25 | 5 | 417 | 0 | 0 | 0 | Libertad |
| 5 | Ricardo Tavarelli | GK | 32 | 7 | 405 | 0 | 0 | 0 | Olimpia |
| 6 | Jorge Campos | MID | 32 | 5 | 360 | 0 | 0 | 0 | Univ Catolica |
| 7 | Nestor Isasi | DEF | 30 | 5 | 355 | 0 | 0 | 0 | Olimpia |
| 8 | Jose Cardozo | ATT | 32 | 4 | 354 | 1 | 0 | 0 | Toluca |
| 9 | Nelson Cuevas | ATT | 23 | 4 | 341 | 1 | 0 | 0 | River Plate |
| 10 | Victor Quintana | MID | 27 | 3 | 270 | 2 | 0 | 0 | Porto |
| 11 | Denis Caniza | DEF | 28 | 3 | 270 | 0 | 0 | 0 | Santos Laguna |
| 12 | Ruben Maldonado | DEF | 24 | 3 | 270 | 0 | 0 | 0 | Venezia |
| 13 | Jorge Britez | MID | 22 | 6 | 231 | 0 | 0 | 0 | Libertad |
| 14 | Emilio Martinez | DEF | 22 | 2 | 180 | 0 | 0 | 0 | Libertad |
| 15 | Justo Villar | GK | 26 | 2 | 180 | 0 | 0 | 0 | Libertad |
| 16 | Jose Zorrilla | DEF | - | 2 | 180 | 0 | 0 | 0 | Solde America |
| 17 | Roberto Miguel Acuna | MID | 31 | 2 | 180 | 0 | 0 | 0 | Deportivo |
| 18 | Delio Cesar Toledo | DEF | 26 | 2 | 180 | 0 | 0 | 0 | Real Zaragoza |
| 19 | Carlos Alberto Gamarra | DEF | 32 | 2 | 180 | 0 | 0 | 0 | Inter Milan |
| 20 | Celso Ayala | DEF | 32 | 2 | 180 | 0 | 0 | 0 | River Plate |
| 21 | Carlos Paredes | MID | 26 | 2 | 180 | 0 | 0 | 0 | Porto |

# SWEDEN

FIFA/COCA COLA WORLD RANKING: **20th**

**MANAGER:** LARS LAGERBACK

| | | | | | | |
|---|---|---|---|---|---|---|
| 1 | intnls | **Russia** | A | D | 1-1 | Ibrahimovic 90 |
| 2 | eqg4 | **Latvia** | A | D | 0-0 | |
| 3 | eqg4 | **Hungary** | H | D | 1-1 | Ibrahimovic 76 |
| 4 | intnls | **Portugal** | H | L | 2-3 | Petterson 6; Allback 24 |
| 5 | intnls | **Czech Republic** | A | D | 3-3 | Nilsson, M 29,43; Allback 65 |
| 6 | intnls | **Tunisia** | A | L | 0-1 | |
| 7 | intnls | **Qatar** | H | W | 3-2 | Elmander 16,24; Skoog 82 |
| 8 | intnls | **North Korea** | H | D | 1-1 | Skoog 21 |
| 9 | intnls | **Thailand** | A | W | 4-1 | Thanongsak 47 og; Elmander 63; Farnerud 66; Majastrovic 69 |
| 10 | intnls | **North Korea** | H | W | 4-0 | Skoog 3,77; Grahn 26; Johannesson 56 |
| 11 | eqg4 | **Hungary** | A | W | 2-1 | Allback 34,67 |
| 12 | intnls | **Croatia** | H | L | 1-2 | Ibrahimovic 33 |
| 13 | eqg4 | **San Marino** | A | W | 6-0 | Jonson 16,59,66; Allback 52,84; Ljungberg 55 |
| 14 | eqg4 | **Poland** | H | W | 3-0 | Svensson, A 15,70; Allback 43 |

## KEY PLAYERS - GOALSCORERS

2 Marcus Allback

| 1 Niklas Skoog (played 180 mins) | |
|---|---|
| Goals in Internationals | 3 |
| Contribution to Attacking Power<br>Average number of minutes between team goals while on pitch | 29 |
| Player Strike Rate<br>The total number of minutes he was on the pitch for every goal scored | 60 |
| Club Strike Rate<br>Average number of minutes between goals scored by club | 41 |

| | PLAYER | GOALS | ATT POWER | STRIKE RATE |
|---|---|---|---|---|
| 2 | Marcus Allback | 7 | 37 | 86 mins |
| 3 | Zlatan Ibrahimovic | 3 | 110 | 110 mins |
| 4 | Mattias Jonson | 3 | 26 | 115 mins |
| 5 | Johan Elmander | 3 | 25 | 145 mins |

## TOP PLAYER APPEARANCES

| 8 Erik Edman | Defender |
|---|---|
| Age (on 01/07/03) | 24 |
| Caps this season | 8 |
| Total minutes on the pitch | 527 |
| Goals | 0 |
| Yellow Cards | 0 |
| Red Cards | 0 |
| Club Side | Heerenveen |

| | PLAYER | POS | AGE | CAPS | MINS | GOALS | CARDS(Y) | CARDS(R) | CLUB SIDE |
|---|---|---|---|---|---|---|---|---|---|
| 1 | Andreas Isaksson | GK | 21 | 9 | 765 | 0 | 0 | 0 | Djurgarden |
| 2 | Anders Svensson | MID | 26 | 9 | 727 | 2 | 1 | 0 | Southampton |
| 3 | Olof Mellberg | DEF | 25 | 8 | 675 | 0 | 0 | 0 | Aston Villa |
| 4 | Andreas Jakobsson | DEF | 30 | 9 | 643 | 0 | 1 | 0 | Hansa Rostock |
| 5 | Michael Svensson | DEF | 27 | 9 | 620 | 0 | 2 | 0 | Southampton |
| 6 | Michael Nilsson | MID | 25 | 9 | 609 | 2 | 0 | 0 | IFK Gothenburg |
| 7 | Marcus Allback | ATT | 29 | 9 | 603 | 7 | 0 | 0 | Aston Villa |
| 8 | Erik Edman | DEF | 24 | 8 | 527 | 0 | 0 | 0 | Heerenveen |
| 9 | Teddy Lucic | DEF | 30 | 6 | 505 | 0 | 0 | 0 | Leeds |
| 10 | Kim Kallstrom | MID | 20 | 10 | 489 | 0 | 1 | 0 | Djurgaardens |
| 11 | Johan Elmander | ATT | 22 | 6 | 436 | 3 | 0 | 0 | Djurgarden |
| 12 | Tobias Linderoth | MID | 24 | 4 | 360 | 0 | 1 | 0 | Everton |
| 13 | Niclas Alexandersson | MID | 31 | 5 | 348 | 0 | 0 | 0 | Everton |
| 14 | Mattias Jonson | ATT | 29 | 7 | 345 | 3 | 0 | 0 | Brondby |
| 15 | Fredrik Ljungberg | MID | 26 | 4 | 342 | 1 | 2 | 0 | Arsenal |
| 16 | Zlatan Ibrahimovic | ATT | 21 | 4 | 331 | 3 | 1 | 0 | Ajax |
| 17 | Johan Mjallby | DEF | 32 | 4 | 317 | 0 | 1 | 0 | Celtic |
| 18 | Andreas Andersson | ATT | 29 | 4 | 308 | 0 | 0 | 0 | AIK Solna |
| 19 | Kennedy Bakircioglu | ATT | 22 | 4 | 282 | 0 | 0 | 0 | Hammarby |
| 20 | Daniel Majstorovic | DEF | 26 | 3 | 270 | 1 | 0 | 0 | Malmo |
| 21 | Marcus Johannesson | DEF | 29 | 4 | 261 | 1 | 0 | 0 | Falkenbergs |

# SOUTH KOREA

FIFA/COCA COLA WORLD RANKING: **21st**

**MANAGER:** HUMBERTO COELHO

| | | | | | | |
|---|---|---|---|---|---|---|
| 1 | intnls | **North Korea** | H | D | 0-0 | |
| 2 | intnls | **Brazil** | H | L | 2-3 | Ki-Hyeon 7; Ahn 58 |
| 3 | intnls | **Colombia** | H | D | 0-0 | |
| 4 | intnls | **Japan** | H | L | 0-1 | |
| 5 | intnls | **Japan** | A | W | 1-0 | Ahn 86 |
| 6 | intnls | **Uruguay** | H | L | 0-2 | |
| 7 | intnls | **Argentina** | H | L | 0-1 | |

**Competition key:** eqg2 = European Qualifying match in Group 2 (g2); Intnls = all other international matches

**Note:** The season of international matches covered includes all games from the end of the 2002 World Cup in June 30th 2002 to June 11th 2003.

## KEY PLAYERS - GOALSCORERS

1 Jung-Hwan Ahn

| | |
|---|---|
| Goals in Internationals | 2 |
| Contribution to Attacking Power<br>Average number of minutes between team goals while on pitch | 91 |
| Player Strike Rate<br>The total number of minutes he was on the pitch for every goal scored | 137 |
| Club Strike Rate<br>Average number of minutes between goals scored by club | 210 |

| | PLAYER | GOALS | ATT POWER | STRIKE RATE |
|---|---|---|---|---|
| 2 | Seol Ki-Hyeon | 1 | 53 | 160 mins |

## TOP PLAYER APPEARANCES

2 Tae-Young Kim — Defender

| | |
|---|---|
| Age (on 01/07/03) | 32 |
| Caps this season | 6 |
| Total minutes on the pitch | 540 |
| Goals | 0 |
| Yellow Cards | 0 |
| Red Cards | 0 |
| Club Side | Chunnam Dragons |

| | PLAYER | POS | AGE | CAPS | MINS | GOALS | CARDS(Y) | CARDS(R) | CLUB SIDE |
|---|---|---|---|---|---|---|---|---|---|
| 1 | Woon-Jae Lee | GK | 30 | 7 | 622 | 0 | 0 | 0 | Sangmoo |
| 2 | Tae-Young Kim | DEF | 32 | 6 | 540 | 0 | 0 | 0 | Chunnam Dragons |
| 3 | Sang-Chul Yoo | MID | 31 | 6 | 525 | 0 | 0 | 0 | Kashiwa Reysol |
| 4 | Nam-Il Kim | MID | 29 | 5 | 438 | 0 | 0 | 0 | Excelsior |
| 5 | Byung-Kuk Cho | DEF | 21 | 5 | 405 | 0 | 0 | 0 | Suwon |
| 6 | Chung-Soo Lee | ATT | 21 | 6 | 389 | 0 | 0 | 0 | Ulsan Hyundai |
| 7 | Jung-Hwan Ahn | MID | 27 | 4 | 273 | 2 | 0 | 0 | Perugia |
| 8 | Tae-Uk Choi | ATT | 22 | 4 | 241 | 0 | 0 | 0 | Anyang |
| 9 | Choong-Kyun Park | DEF | 30 | 3 | 224 | 0 | 0 | 0 | Seongnam |
| 10 | Young-Pyo Lee | MID | 26 | 3 | 224 | 0 | 0 | 0 | Anyang |
| 11 | Doo-Ri Cha | ATT | 22 | 4 | 222 | 0 | 0 | 0 | B Leverkusen |
| 12 | Yong-Soo Choi | ATT | 29 | 4 | 211 | 0 | 0 | 0 | JEF United |
| 13 | Sung-Yong Choi | MID | 27 | 3 | 207 | 0 | 0 | 0 | Suwon Blue Wings |
| 14 | Eul-Yong Lee | MID | 27 | 3 | 191 | 0 | 0 | 0 | Pucheon |
| 15 | Jin-Chul Choi | DEF | 32 | 2 | 180 | 0 | 0 | 0 | Chonbuk Hyundai |
| 16 | Lee Young-Pyo | DEF | 26 | 2 | 175 | 0 | 0 | 0 | Anyang |
| 17 | Ki-Hyung Lee | MID | 28 | 3 | 169 | 0 | 0 | 0 | Suwon Samsung |
| 18 | Sung-Kuk Choi | ATT | 20 | 3 | 164 | 0 | 0 | 0 | Korea University |
| 19 | Seol Ki-Hyeon | ATT | 24 | 2 | 160 | 1 | 0 | 0 | Anderlecht |
| 20 | Dong-Gook Lee | ATT | 24 | 2 | 154 | 0 | 0 | 0 | Pohang Steelers |
| 21 | Ki-Hyeon Seol | ATT | 24 | 2 | 135 | 0 | 0 | 0 | Anderlecht |

# SERBIA & MONTENEGRO

FIFA/COCA COLA WORLD RANKING: **22nd**

**MANAGER:** DEJAN SAVICEVIC (Resigned)

| | | | | | | |
|---|---|---|---|---|---|---|
| 1 | intnls | **Czech Republic** | A | L | 0-5 | |
| 2 | e2kq9 | **Italy** | A | D | 1-1 | Mijatovic 28 |
| 3 | e2kq9 | **Finland** | H | W | 2-0 | Kovacevic 56; Mihajlovic 84 pen |
| 4 | intnls | **France** | A | L | 0-3 | |
| 5 | e2kq9 | **Azerbaijan** | H | D | 2-2 | Mijatovic 34 pen; Lazetic 52 |
| 6 | intnls | **Bulgaria** | H | L | 1-2 | Kovacevic 28 |
| 7 | intnls | **Germany** | A | L | 0-1 | |
| 8 | intnls | **England** | A | L | 1-2 | Jestrovic 45 |
| 9 | e2kq9 | **Finland** | A | L | 0-3 | |
| 10 | e2kq9 | **Azerbaijan** | A | L | 1-2 | Boskovic 28 |

## KEY PLAYERS - GOALSCORERS

1 Predrag Mijatovic

| | |
|---|---|
| Goals in Internationals | 2 |
| Contribution to Attacking Power<br>Average number of minutes between team goals while on pitch | 65 |
| Player Strike Rate<br>The total number of minutes he was on the pitch for every goal scored | 196 |
| Club Strike Rate<br>Average number of minutes between goals scored by club | 113 |

| | PLAYER | GOALS | ATT POWER | STRIKE RATE |
|---|---|---|---|---|
| 2 | Darko Kovacevic | 2 | 158 | 237 mins |
| 3 | Sinisa Mihajlovic | 1 | 88 | 264 mins |
| 4 | Danko Boskovic | 1 | 88 | 266 mins |
| 5 | Nikola Lazetic | 1 | 77 | 388 mins |

## TOP PLAYER APPEARANCES

3 Darko Kovacevic — Attacker

| | |
|---|---|
| Age (on 01/07/03) | 29 |
| Caps this season | 3 |
| Total minutes on the pitch | 243 |
| Goals | 0 |
| Yellow Cards | 1 |
| Red Cards | 0 |
| Club Side | Real Sociedad |

| | PLAYER | POS | AGE | CAPS | MINS | GOALS | CARDS(Y) | CARDS(R) | CLUB SIDE |
|---|---|---|---|---|---|---|---|---|---|
| 1 | Dragoslav Jevric | GK | 29 | 10 | 786 | 0 | 0 | 0 | Vitesse Arnhem |
| 2 | Mladen Krstajic | DEF | 29 | 8 | 619 | 0 | 1 | 0 | W Bremen |
| 3 | Igor Duljaj | MID | 23 | 9 | 595 | 0 | 0 | 0 | Partizan Belgrade |
| 4 | Namanja Vidic | DEF | 21 | 6 | 531 | 0 | 2 | 0 | Red Star Belgrade |
| 5 | Darko Kovacevic | ATT | 29 | 7 | 474 | 2 | 1 | 0 | Real Sociedad |
| 6 | Dejan Stankovic | MID | 24 | 6 | 468 | 0 | 1 | 0 | Lazio |
| 7 | Savo Milosevic | ATT | 29 | 10 | 465 | 0 | 1 | 0 | Parma |
| 8 | Zoran Mirkovic | DEF | 31 | 7 | 446 | 0 | 0 | 0 | Red Star Belgrade |
| 9 | Ivica Dragutinovic | DEF | 27 | 5 | 406 | 0 | 0 | 0 | Standard Liege |
| 10 | Predrag Mijatovic | ATT | 34 | 7 | 391 | 2 | 0 | 0 | Levante |
| 11 | Nikola Lazetic | MID | 25 | 6 | 388 | 1 | 1 | 0 | Lazio |
| 12 | Zvonimir Vukic | MID | 23 | 6 | 386 | 0 | 1 | 0 | Partizan Belgrade |
| 13 | Goran Trobok | MID | 28 | 8 | 347 | 0 | 1 | 0 | Partizan Belgrade |
| 14 | Nikola Malbasa | DEF | 25 | 4 | 304 | 0 | 2 | 0 | Hajduk Kula |
| 15 | Nenad Kovacevic | MID | 22 | 6 | 303 | 0 | 0 | 0 | Crvena Zvezda |
| 16 | Nenad Djordjevic | DEF | 23 | 7 | 283 | 0 | 0 | 0 | Obilic Beograd |
| 17 | Mateja Kezman | ATT | 24 | 5 | 271 | 0 | 0 | 0 | PSV Eindhoven |
| 18 | Danko Boskovic | ATT | 23 | 6 | 266 | 1 | 1 | 0 | Kaiserslauten |
| 19 | Sinisa Mihajlovic | DEF | 34 | 4 | 264 | 1 | 2 | 1 | Lazio |
| 20 | Dejan Stefanovic | DEF | 28 | 5 | 170 | 0 | 0 | 0 | Portsmouth |
| 21 | Nenad Brnovic | MID | 23 | 6 | 160 | 0 | 0 | 0 | Zeta Golubovci |

# JAPAN

FIFA/COCA COLA WORLD RANKING: **23rd**

**MANAGER:** ZICO

| | | | | | | |
|---|---|---|---|---|---|---|
| 1 | intnls | **Jamaica** | H | D | 1-1 | Ono 7 |
| 2 | intnls | **Argentina** | H | L | 0-2 | |
| 3 | intnls | **Uruguay** | H | D | 2-2 | Nakamura 23 pen; Inamoto 57 |
| 4 | intnls | **South Korea** | A | W | 1-0 | Nagai 90 |
| 5 | intnls | **South Korea** | H | L | 0-1 | |
| 6 | intnls | **Argentina** | H | L | 1-4 | Akita 55 |
| 7 | intnls | **Paraguay** | H | D | 0-0 | |

**Competition key:** eqg2 = European Qualifying match in Group 2 (g2); Intnls = all other international matches

**Note:** The season of international matches covered includes all games from the end of the 2002 World Cup in June 30th 2002 to June 11th 2003.

## KEY PLAYERS - GOALSCORERS

1 Shunsuke Nakamura

| | |
|---|---|
| **Goals in Internationals** | 1 |
| **Contribution to Attacking Power** Average number of minutes between team goals while on pitch | 142 |
| **Player Strike Rate** The total number of minutes he was on the pitch for every goal scored | 284 |
| **Club Strike Rate** Average number of minutes between goals scored by club | 126 |

| | PLAYER | GOALS | ATT POWER | STRIKE RATE |
|---|---|---|---|---|
| 2 | Junichi Inamoto | 1 | 81 | 324 mins |
| 3 | Yutaka Akita | 1 | 108 | 540 mins |

## TOP PLAYER APPEARANCES

7 Hidetoshi Nakata — Midfielder

| | |
|---|---|
| Age (on 01/07/03) | 26 |
| Caps this season | 4 |
| Total minutes on the pitch | 360 |
| Goals | 0 |
| Yellow Cards | 0 |
| Red Cards | 0 |
| Club Side | Parma |

| | PLAYER | POS | AGE | CAPS | MINS | GOALS | CARDS(Y) | CARDS(R) | CLUB SIDE |
|---|---|---|---|---|---|---|---|---|---|
| 1 | Yutaka Akita | DEF | 32 | 6 | 540 | 1 | 0 | 0 | Kashima |
| 2 | Seigo Narazaki | GK | 27 | 6 | 540 | 0 | 0 | 0 | Nagoya Grampus Eight |
| 3 | Akira Narahashi | DEF | 31 | 6 | 511 | 0 | 0 | 0 | Kashima |
| 4 | Toshihiro Hattori | DEF | 29 | 5 | 450 | 0 | 0 | 0 | Jubilo Iwata |
| 5 | Koji Nakata | DEF | 23 | 7 | 415 | 0 | 0 | 0 | Kashima |
| 6 | Alessandro Santos | MID | 25 | 6 | 390 | 0 | 0 | 0 | Shimizu |
| 7 | Hidetoshi Nakata | MID | 26 | 4 | 360 | 0 | 0 | 0 | Parma |
| 8 | Ryozo Morioka | DEF | 27 | 4 | 360 | 0 | 0 | 0 | Shimizu |
| 9 | Takayuki Suzuki | ATT | 27 | 5 | 346 | 0 | 0 | 0 | Genk |
| 10 | Naohiro Takahara | ATT | 24 | 4 | 345 | 0 | 0 | 0 | Hamburg |
| 11 | Junichi Inamoto | MID | 23 | 4 | 324 | 1 | 0 | 0 | Fulham |
| 12 | Mitsuo Ogasawara | MID | 24 | 4 | 292 | 0 | 0 | 0 | Kashima |
| 13 | Shunsuke Nakamura | MID | 25 | 4 | 284 | 1 | 0 | 0 | Reggina |
| 14 | Takashi Fukunishi | MID | 26 | 5 | 280 | 0 | 0 | 0 | Jubilo Iwata |
| 15 | Masashi Nakayama | ATT | 35 | 4 | 229 | 0 | 0 | 0 | Jubilo Iwata |
| 16 | Naoki Matsuda | DEF | 26 | 2 | 180 | 0 | 0 | 0 | Yokohama |
| 17 | Yoshito Okubo | ATT | 21 | 3 | 160 | 0 | 0 | 0 | Cerezo Osaka |
| 18 | Yasuhito Endo | MID | 23 | 3 | 140 | 0 | 0 | 0 | Gamba Osaka |
| 19 | Shinji Ono | MID | 23 | 2 | 125 | 1 | 0 | 0 | Feyenoord |
| 20 | Nobuhisa Yamada | DEF | 27 | 2 | 119 | 0 | 0 | 0 | Urawa Reds |
| 21 | Keisuke Tsuboi | DEF | 23 | 1 | 90 | 0 | 0 | 0 | Urawa Reds |

# NORWAY

FIFA/COCA COLA WORLD RANKING: **24th**

**MANAGER:** NILS JOHAN SEMB

| | | | | | | |
|---|---|---|---|---|---|---|
| 1 | intnls | **Holland** | H | L | 0-1 | |
| 2 | eqg2 | **Denmark** | H | D | 2-2 | Riise 54; Carew 90 |
| 3 | eqg2 | **Romania** | A | W | 1-0 | Iversen 84 |
| 4 | eqg2 | **Bosnia** | H | W | 2-0 | Lundekvam 6; Riise 27 |
| 5 | intnls | **Austria** | A | W | 1-0 | Kah 82 |
| 6 | intnls | **UAE** | A | D | 1-1 | Helstad 72 |
| 7 | intnls | **Oman** | A | W | 2-1 | Karadas 63; Rushfeldt 82 |
| 8 | intnls | **Greece** | A | L | 0-1 | |
| 9 | eqg2 | **Luxembourg** | A | W | 2-0 | Rushfeldt 58; Solskjaer 74 |
| 10 | intnls | **Rep of Ireland** | A | L | 0-1 | |
| 11 | intnls | **Finland** | H | W | 2-0 | Leonhardsen 21; Flo, T 80 |
| 12 | eqg2 | **Denmark** | A | L | 0-1 | |
| 13 | eqg2 | **Romania** | H | D | 1-1 | Solskjaer 78 pen |

## KEY PLAYERS - GOALSCORERS

1 Thorstein Helstad (played 164 mins)

| | |
|---|---|
| **Goals in Internationals** | 1 |
| **Contribution to Attacking Power** Average number of minutes between team goals while on pitch | 82 |
| **Player Strike Rate** The total number of minutes he was on the pitch for every goal scored | 164 |
| **Club Strike Rate** Average number of minutes between goals scored by club | 84 |

| | PLAYER | GOALS | ATT POWER | STRIKE RATE |
|---|---|---|---|---|
| 2 | Pa Madou-Kah | 1 | 86 | 173 mins |
| 3 | Sigurd Rushfeldt | 2 | 74 | 223 mins |
| 4 | Tore Andre Flo | 1 | 68 | 275 mins |
| 5 | John Alieu Carew | 1 | 195 | 390 mins |

## TOP PLAYER APPEARANCES

3 John Arne Riise — Midfielder

| | |
|---|---|
| Age (on 01/07/03) | 22 |
| Caps this season | 10 |
| Total minutes on the pitch | 870 |
| Goals | 2 |
| Yellow Cards | 1 |
| Red Cards | 0 |
| Club Side | Liverpool |

| | PLAYER | POS | AGE | CAPS | MINS | GOALS | CARDS(Y) | CARDS(R) | CLUB SIDE |
|---|---|---|---|---|---|---|---|---|---|
| 1 | Christer Basma | DEF | 30 | 13 | 1126 | 0 | 0 | 0 | Rosenborg BK |
| 2 | Trond Andersen | MID | 28 | 11 | 905 | 0 | 1 | 0 | Wimbledon |
| 3 | John Arne Riise | MID | 22 | 10 | 870 | 2 | 1 | 0 | Liverpool |
| 4 | Ole Gunnar Solskjaer | ATT | 30 | 10 | 784 | 2 | 0 | 0 | Man Utd |
| 5 | Andre Bergdolmo | DEF | 31 | 8 | 675 | 0 | 1 | 0 | Ajax |
| 6 | Eirik Bakke | MID | 25 | 8 | 664 | 0 | 1 | 0 | Leeds |
| 7 | Claus Lundekvam | DEF | 30 | 10 | 591 | 1 | 0 | 0 | Southampton |
| 8 | Ronny Johnsen | DEF | 34 | 8 | 585 | 0 | 0 | 0 | Aston Villa |
| 9 | Steffen Iversen | ATT | 26 | 8 | 544 | 1 | 0 | 0 | Tottenham |
| 10 | Frode Olsen | GK | 35 | 8 | 540 | 0 | 0 | 0 | Viking |
| 11 | Henning Berg | DEF | 33 | 7 | 534 | 0 | 0 | 0 | Blackburn |
| 12 | Oyvind Leonhardsen | MID | 32 | 8 | 483 | 1 | 0 | 0 | Aston Villa |
| 13 | Sigurd Rushfeldt | ATT | 30 | 9 | 445 | 2 | 0 | 0 | Austria Vienna |
| 14 | Brede Hangeland | MID | 22 | 6 | 405 | 0 | 0 | 0 | Viking |
| 15 | John Alieu Carew | ATT | 23 | 6 | 390 | 1 | 2 | 0 | Valencia |
| 16 | Erik Holtan | GK | 34 | 7 | 315 | 0 | 0 | 0 | Odd Grenland |
| 17 | Tore Andre Flo | ATT | 30 | 6 | 275 | 1 | 0 | 0 | Sunderland |
| 18 | Fredrik Winsnes | MID | 27 | 10 | 268 | 0 | 0 | 0 | Hammarby |
| 19 | Torjus Hansen | DEF | 29 | 6 | 215 | 0 | 0 | 0 | Arminia B |
| 20 | Tomas Pereira | DEF | 30 | 3 | 200 | 0 | 0 | 0 | Viking |
| 21 | Frode Johnsen | ATT | 29 | 8 | 184 | 0 | 0 | 0 | Rosenborg BK |

# RUSSIA

FIFA/COCA COLA WORLD RANKING: **25th**

**MANAGER:** VALERY GAZZAEV

| | | | | | | |
|---|---|---|---|---|---|---|
| 1 | intnls | **Sweden** | H | D | 1-1 | Kerzhakov 56 |
| 2 | eqg10 | **Rep of Ireland** | H | W | 4-2 | Kariaka 20; Beschastnykh 25; Kerzhakov 70; Babb 87 og |
| 3 | eqg10 | **Albania** | H | W | 4-1 | Kerzhakov 3; Semak 41,54; Onopko 52 |
| 4 | intnls | **Cyprus** | A | W | 1-0 | Khokhlov 43 |
| 5 | intnls | **Romania** | H | W | 4-2 | Soavu 31 og; Kariaka 35; Arshavin 42; Gusev 59 |
| 6 | eqg10 | **Albania** | A | L | 1-3 | Semak 76 |
| 7 | eqg10 | **Georgia** | A | L | 0-1 | |
| 8 | eqg10 | **Switzerland** | A | D | 2-2 | Ignashevitch 24,68 pen |

## KEY PLAYERS - GOALSCORERS

2 Serguei Sernak

**1 Alexander Kerzhakov**

| | |
|---|---|
| **Goals in Internationals** | 3 |
| **Contribution to Attacking Power** Average number of minutes between team goals while on pitch | 35 |
| **Player Strike Rate** The total number of minutes he was on the pitch for every goal scored | 130 |
| **Club Strike Rate** Average number of minutes between goals scored by club | 42 |

| | PLAYER | GOALS | ATT POWER | STRIKE RATE |
|---|---|---|---|---|
| 2 | Serguei Semak | 3 | 47 | 160 mins |
| 3 | Vladimir Beschastnykh | 1 | 40 | 161 mins |
| 4 | Andrei Kariaka | 2 | 39 | 218 mins |
| 5 | Sergei Ignashevitch | 2 | 43 | 259 mins |

## TOP PLAYER APPEARANCES

**6 Alexei Smertin** Midfielder

| | |
|---|---|
| Age (on 01/07/03) | 28 |
| Caps this season | 6 |
| Total minutes on the pitch | 476 |
| Goals | 0 |
| Yellow Cards | 0 |
| Red Cards | 0 |
| Club Side | Bordeaux |

| | PLAYER | POS | AGE | CAPS | MINS | GOALS | CARDS(Y) | CARDS(R) | CLUB SIDE |
|---|---|---|---|---|---|---|---|---|---|
| 1 | Gennadi Nizhegorodov | DEF | 26 | 7 | 585 | 0 | 2 | 0 | Lokomotiv Moscow |
| 2 | Yevgeny Aldonin | MID | 23 | 8 | 573 | 0 | 0 | 0 | Rotor Volgograd |
| 3 | Sergei Ignashevitch | DEF | 23 | 6 | 517 | 2 | 0 | 0 | Lokomotiv Moscow |
| 4 | Sergei Ovchinnikov | GK | 32 | 6 | 495 | 0 | 2 | 0 | Porto |
| 5 | Serguei Semak | MID | 27 | 6 | 479 | 3 | 0 | 0 | CSKA Moscow |
| 6 | Alexei Smertin | MID | 28 | 6 | 476 | 0 | 0 | 0 | Bordeaux |
| 7 | Andrei Kariaka | MID | 25 | 7 | 435 | 2 | 0 | 0 | Kryliya SS |
| 8 | Roland Gusev | MID | 25 | 7 | 402 | 1 | 0 | 0 | CSKA Moscow |
| 9 | Alexander Kerzhakov | ATT | 20 | 7 | 389 | 3 | 0 | 0 | Zenit St Petersburg |
| 10 | Dmitri Loskov | MID | 29 | 6 | 388 | 0 | 0 | 0 | Lokomotiv Moscow |
| 11 | Igor Yanovski | MID | 28 | 6 | 365 | 0 | 1 | 0 | CSKA Moscow |
| 12 | Viktor Onopko | DEF | 33 | 5 | 361 | 1 | 0 | 0 | R Vallecano |
| 13 | Andrei Solomatin | MID | 27 | 6 | 332 | 0 | 1 | 0 | CSKA Moscow |
| 14 | Denis Evsikov | DEF | 22 | 4 | 189 | 0 | 0 | 0 | CSKA Moscow |
| 15 | Vasili Berezutsky | DEF | 21 | 5 | 183 | 0 | 0 | 0 | CSKA Moscow |
| 16 | Iouri Kovtun | DEF | 33 | 3 | 180 | 0 | 0 | 0 | Spartak Moscow |
| 17 | Vladimir Beschastnykh | ATT | 29 | 4 | 161 | 1 | 0 | 0 | Spartak Moscow |
| 18 | Veniamin Mandrykin | GK | 21 | 4 | 135 | 0 | 0 | 0 | CSKA Moscow |
| 19 | Dimitri Khokhlov | MID | 27 | 3 | 107 | 1 | 0 | 0 | Real Sociedad |
| 20 | Denis Popov | ATT | 24 | 4 | 106 | 0 | 0 | 0 | CSKA Moscow |
| 21 | Dmitry Sychev | ATT | 19 | 3 | 102 | 0 | 0 | 0 | Spartak Moscow |

# CROATIA

FIFA/COCA COLA WORLD RANKING: **26th**

**MANAGER:** OTTO BARIC

| | | | | | | |
|---|---|---|---|---|---|---|
| 1 | intnls | **Wales** | H | D | 1-1 | Petric 79 |
| 2 | eqg8 | **Estonia** | H | D | 0-0 | |
| 3 | eqg8 | **Bulgaria** | A | L | 0-2 | |
| 4 | intnls | **Romania** | A | W | 1-0 | Maric, T 46 |
| 5 | intnls | **Macedonia** | H | D | 2-2 | Maric, M 35 pen; Andric 72 |
| 6 | intnls | **Poland** | H | D | 0-0 | |
| 7 | eqg8 | **Belgium** | H | W | 4-0 | Srna 9; Prso 53; Maric, T 68; Leko 76 |
| 8 | eqg8 | **Andorra** | H | W | 2-0 | Rapaic 11 pen,43 |
| 9 | intnls | **Sweden** | A | W | 2-1 | Olic 6; Zivkovic 58 |
| 10 | eqg8 | **Estonia** | A | W | 1-0 | Kovac, N 76 |

## KEY PLAYERS - GOALSCORERS

2 Milan Rapaic

**1 Tomislav Maric**

| | |
|---|---|
| **Goals in Internationals** | 2 |
| **Contribution to Attacking Power** Average number of minutes between team goals while on pitch | 47 |
| **Player Strike Rate** The total number of minutes he was on the pitch for every goal scored | 190 |
| **Club Strike Rate** Average number of minutes between goals scored by club | 69 |

| | PLAYER | GOALS | ATT POWER | STRIKE RATE |
|---|---|---|---|---|
| 2 | Milan Rapaic | 2 | 50 | 227 mins |
| 3 | Nico Kovac | 1 | 80 | 241 mins |
| 4 | Marijo Maric | 1 | 69 | 277 mins |
| 5 | Dado Prso | 1 | 42 | 294 mins |

## TOP PLAYER APPEARANCES

**5 Robert Kovac** Defender

| | |
|---|---|
| Age (on 01/07/03) | 29 |
| Caps this season | 6 |
| Total minutes on the pitch | 508 |
| Goals | 0 |
| Yellow Cards | 0 |
| Red Cards | 0 |
| Club Side | Bayer |

| | PLAYER | POS | AGE | CAPS | MINS | GOALS | CARDS(Y) | CARDS(R) | CLUB SIDE |
|---|---|---|---|---|---|---|---|---|---|
| 1 | Stipe Pletikosa | GK | 24 | 10 | 900 | 0 | 0 | 0 | Hajduk Split |
| 2 | Boris Zivkovic | DEF | 27 | 9 | 702 | 1 | 1 | 0 | B Leverkusen |
| 3 | Darijo Srna | MID | 21 | 7 | 540 | 1 | 1 | 0 | Hajduk Split |
| 4 | Ivica Olic | ATT | 23 | 7 | 510 | 1 | 1 | 0 | FC Zagreb |
| 5 | Robert Kovac | DEF | 29 | 6 | 508 | 0 | 0 | 0 | Bayern Munich |
| 6 | Stjepan Tomas | DEF | 27 | 9 | 494 | 0 | 0 | 0 | Como |
| 7 | Josip Simunic | DEF | 25 | 6 | 479 | 0 | 0 | 0 | Hertha Berlin |
| 8 | Dario Simic | DEF | 27 | 7 | 467 | 0 | 1 | 0 | AC Milan |
| 9 | Milan Rapaic | MID | 29 | 7 | 453 | 2 | 0 | 0 | Fenerbahce |
| 10 | Jerko Leko | MID | 23 | 9 | 447 | 1 | 1 | 0 | Dinamo Kiev |
| 11 | Tomislav Maric | ATT | 30 | 7 | 380 | 2 | 0 | 0 | Wolfsburg |
| 12 | Marko Babic | MID | 22 | 9 | 360 | 0 | 0 | 0 | B Leverkusen |
| 13 | Igor Tudor | DEF | 25 | 4 | 318 | 0 | 2 | 0 | Juventus |
| 14 | Dado Prso | ATT | 28 | 4 | 294 | 1 | 0 | 0 | Monaco |
| 15 | Marijo Maric | ATT | 26 | 7 | 277 | 1 | 0 | 0 | Karnten |
| 16 | Mario Tokic | DEF | 27 | 5 | 270 | 0 | 0 | 0 | Grazer AK |
| 17 | Dovani Rosso | MID | 30 | 6 | 251 | 0 | 0 | 0 | Maccabi Haifa |
| 18 | Nico Kovac | MID | 31 | 6 | 241 | 1 | 1 | 0 | Bayern Munich |
| 19 | Davor Vugrinec | ATT | 28 | 3 | 225 | 0 | 0 | 0 | Atalanta |
| 20 | Mario Stanic | MID | 31 | 4 | 201 | 0 | 1 | 0 | Chelsea |
| 21 | Danijel Saric | MID | 30 | 2 | 168 | 0 | 0 | 0 | Panathinaikos |

# ROMANIA

FIFA/COCA COLA WORLD RANKING: **27th**

**MANAGER:** ANGHEL IORDANESCU

| | | | | | | |
|---|---|---|---|---|---|---|
| 1 | eqg2 | **Bosnia** | A | W | 3-0 | Chivu 6; Munteanu, D 8; Ganea 26 |
| 2 | eqg2 | **Norway** | H | L | 0-1 | |
| 3 | eqg2 | **Luxembourg** | A | W | 7-0 | Moldovan 1,4; Radoi 24; Contra 45,47,86; Ghioane 80 |
| 4 | intnls | **Croatia** | H | L | 0-1 | |
| 5 | intnls | **Slovakia** | H | W | 2-1 | Munteanu, D 38; Ganea 41 |
| 6 | intnls | **Russia** | A | L | 2-4 | Tamash 13; Grigorie 71 pen |
| 7 | eqg2 | **Denmark** | H | L | 2-5 | Mutu 5; Munteanu, D 47 |
| 8 | intnls | **Lithuania** | A | W | 1-0 | Bratu 63 |
| 9 | eqg2 | **Bosnia** | H | W | 2-0 | Mutu 46; Ganea 87 |
| 10 | eqg2 | **Norway** | A | D | 1-1 | Ganea 64 |

## KEY PLAYERS - GOALSCORERS

1 Dinu Viorel Moldovan

| | |
|---|---|
| **Goals in Internationals** | 2 |
| **Contribution to Attacking Power** Average number of minutes between team goals while on pitch | 32 |
| Player Strike Rate The total number of minutes he was on the pitch for every goal scored | 82 |
| **Club Strike Rate** Average number of minutes between goals scored by club | 45 |

| | PLAYER | GOALS | ATT POWER | STRIKE RATE |
|---|---|---|---|---|
| 2 | Ioan Vlorel Ganea | 4 | 39 | 137 mins |
| 3 | Florin Bratu | 1 | 92 | 185 mins |
| 4 | Tiberiu Ghioane | 1 | 31 | 186 mins |
| 5 | Dorinel Munteanu | 3 | 41 | 206 mins |

## TOP PLAYER APPEARANCES

7 Ioan Vlorel Ganea — Attacker

| | |
|---|---|
| **Age** (on 01/07/03) | 29 |
| **Caps this season** | 8 |
| **Total minutes on the pitch** | 546 |
| **Goals** | 4 |
| **Yellow Cards** | 1 |
| **Red Cards** | 0 |
| **Club Side** | Stuttgart |

| | PLAYER | POS | AGE | CAPS | MINS | GOALS | CARDS(Y) | (R) | CLUB SIDE |
|---|---|---|---|---|---|---|---|---|---|
| 1 | Cosmin Marius Contra | DEF | 27 | 9 | 760 | 3 | 2 | 0 | Atl Madrid |
| 2 | Mirel Matei Radoi | DEF | 22 | 9 | 759 | 1 | 1 | 0 | Steaua Bucharest |
| 3 | Christian Chivu | DEF | 22 | 8 | 720 | 1 | 1 | 0 | Ajax |
| 4 | Razvan Rat | DEF | 22 | 9 | 638 | 0 | 0 | 0 | Rapid Bucharest |
| 5 | Dorinel Munteanu | MID | 35 | 7 | 619 | 3 | 0 | 0 | Wolfsburg |
| 6 | Adrian Mutu | ATT | 24 | 8 | 599 | 2 | 1 | 0 | Parma |
| 7 | Ioan Vlorel Ganea | ATT | 29 | 8 | 546 | 4 | 1 | 0 | Stuttgart |
| 8 | Daniel Pancu | ATT | 25 | 8 | 452 | 0 | 1 | 0 | Besiktas |
| 9 | Bogdan Lonut Lobont | GK | 25 | 5 | 406 | 0 | 0 | 0 | Ajax |
| 10 | Bogdan Vintila | GK | 31 | 5 | 376 | 0 | 0 | 0 | Nat Bucharest |
| 11 | Iulian Filipescu | DEF | 29 | 4 | 338 | 0 | 0 | 0 | Real Betis |
| 12 | Adrian Iencsi | DEF | 28 | 6 | 334 | 0 | 0 | 0 | Rapid Bucharest |
| 13 | Paul Codrea | MID | 22 | 6 | 332 | 0 | 1 | 0 | Palermo |
| 14 | Adrian Ilie | ATT | 29 | 5 | 304 | 0 | 0 | 0 | Alaves |
| 15 | Gheorghe Popescu | DEF | 35 | 3 | 252 | 0 | 0 | 0 | Hannover 96 |
| 16 | Florin Soava | MID | 24 | 6 | 210 | 0 | 0 | 0 | Rapid Bucharest |
| 17 | Tiberiu Ghioane | MID | 22 | 4 | 186 | 1 | 0 | 0 | Dinamo Kiev |
| 18 | Florin Bratu | ATT | 23 | 7 | 185 | 1 | 0 | 0 | Rapid Bucharest |
| 19 | Gabriel Popescu | MID | 29 | 2 | 180 | 0 | 0 | 0 | Numancia |
| 20 | Dinu Viorel Moldovan | ATT | 31 | 3 | 163 | 2 | 0 | 0 | Nantes |
| 21 | Alin Stoica | MID | 23 | 4 | 154 | 0 | 0 | 0 | Club Brugge |

# WALES

FIFA/COCA COLA WORLD RANKING: **50th**

**MANAGER:** MARK HUGHES

| | | | | | | |
|---|---|---|---|---|---|---|
| 1 | intnls | **Croatia** | A | D | 1-1 | Davies 7 |
| 2 | eqg9 | **Finland** | A | W | 2-0 | Hartson 30; Davies 72 |
| 3 | eqg9 | **Italy** | H | W | 2-1 | Davies 12; Bellamy 73 |
| 4 | eqg9 | **Azerbaijan** | A | W | 2-1 | Speed 8; Hartson 68 |
| 5 | intnls | **Bosnia** | H | D | 2-2 | Earnshaw 8; Hartson 74 |
| 6 | eqg9 | **Azerbaijan** | H | W | 4-0 | Bellamy 1; Speed 40; Hartson 44; Giggs 52 |
| 7 | intnls | **United States** | A | L | 0-2 | |

**Competition key:** eqg2 = European Qualifying match in Group 2 (g2); Intnls = all other international matches

**Note:** The season of international matches covered includes all games from the end of the 2002 World Cup on June 30th 2002 to June 11th 2003.

## KEY PLAYERS - GOALSCORERS

1 John Hartson

| | |
|---|---|
| **Goals in Internationals** | 4 |
| **Contribution to Attacking Power** Average number of minutes between team goals while on pitch | 40 |
| Player Strike Rate The total number of minutes he was on the pitch for every goal scored | 132 |
| **Club Strike Rate** Average number of minutes between goals scored by club | 48 |

| | PLAYER | GOALS | ATT POWER | STRIKE RATE |
|---|---|---|---|---|
| 2 | Craig Bellamy | 2 | 33 | 133 mins |
| 3 | Gary Speed | 2 | 39 | 218 mins |
| 4 | Simon Davies | 3 | 50 | 220 mins |
| 5 | Robert Earnshaw | 1 | 48 | 243 mins |

## TOP PLAYER APPEARANCES

7 Ryan Giggs — Midfielder

| | |
|---|---|
| **Age** (on 01/07/03) | 29 |
| **Caps this season** | 4 |
| **Total minutes on the pitch** | 390 |
| **Goals** | 1 |
| **Yellow Cards** | 0 |
| **Red Cards** | 0 |
| **Club Side** | Manchester United |

| | PLAYER | POS | AGE | CAPS | MINS | GOALS | CARDS(Y) | (R) | CLUB SIDE |
|---|---|---|---|---|---|---|---|---|---|
| 1 | Simon Davies | MID | 23 | 7 | 660 | 3 | 0 | 0 | Tottenham |
| 2 | Andy Melville | DEF | 34 | 7 | 660 | 0 | 0 | 0 | Fulham |
| 3 | John Hartson | ATT | 28 | 6 | 529 | 4 | 1 | 0 | Celtic |
| 4 | Mark Pembridge | MID | 32 | 6 | 527 | 0 | 1 | 0 | Everton |
| 5 | Paul Jones | GK | 36 | 6 | 525 | 0 | 0 | 0 | Southampton |
| 6 | Gary Speed | MID | 33 | 5 | 435 | 2 | 0 | 0 | Newcastle |
| 7 | Ryan Giggs | MID | 29 | 4 | 390 | 1 | 0 | 0 | Man Utd |
| 8 | Mark Delaney | DEF | 27 | 4 | 339 | 0 | 1 | 0 | Aston Villa |
| 9 | Robert Page | DEF | 28 | 4 | 300 | 0 | 1 | 0 | Sheff Utd |
| 10 | Robbie Savage | MID | 28 | 4 | 285 | 0 | 1 | 0 | Birmingham |
| 11 | Daniel Gabbidon | DEF | 23 | 3 | 270 | 0 | 0 | 0 | Cardiff |
| 12 | Craig Bellamy | ATT | 23 | 4 | 265 | 2 | 1 | 0 | Newcastle |
| 13 | Andy Johnson | MID | 29 | 4 | 255 | 0 | 1 | 0 | West Brom |
| 14 | Robert Earnshaw | ATT | 22 | 6 | 243 | 1 | 0 | 0 | Cardiff |
| 15 | Carl Robinson | MID | 28 | 4 | 230 | 0 | 0 | 0 | Portsmouth |
| 16 | Darren Barnard | DEF | 31 | 2 | 178 | 0 | 1 | 0 | Grimsby |
| 17 | John Oster | MID | 24 | 3 | 163 | 0 | 1 | 0 | Sunderland |
| 18 | Rhys Weston | DEF | 22 | 5 | 143 | 0 | 0 | 0 | Cardiff |
| 19 | Jason Koumas | ATT | 23 | 3 | 104 | 0 | 0 | 0 | West Brom |
| 20 | Gareth Taylor | ATT | 30 | 4 | 97 | 0 | 0 | 0 | Burnley |
| 21 | David Vaughan | MID | 20 | 2 | 90 | 0 | 0 | 0 | Crewe |

# SCOTLAND

FIFA/COCA COLA WORLD RANKING: **64th**

**MANAGER: BERTI VOGTS**

| | | | | | | |
|---|---|---|---|---|---|---|
| 1 | intnls | **Denmark** | H | L | 0-1 | |
| 2 | eqg5 | **Faroe Islands** | A | D | 2-2 | Lambert 62; Ferguson, B 83 |
| 3 | eqg5 | **Iceland** | A | W | 2-0 | Dailly 7; Naysmith 63 |
| 4 | intnls | **Canada** | H | W | 3-1 | Crawford 11,73; Thompson 50 |
| 5 | intnls | **Portugal** | A | L | 0-2 | |
| 6 | intnls | **Rep of Ireland** | H | L | 0-2 | |
| 7 | eqg5 | **Iceland** | H | W | 2-1 | Miller, K 12; Wilkie 70 |
| 8 | eqg5 | **Lithuania** | A | L | 0-1 | |
| 9 | intnls | **Austria** | H | L | 0-2 | |
| 10 | intnls | **New Zealand** | H | D | 1-1 | Crawford 11 |
| 11 | eqg5 | **Germany** | H | D | 1-1 | Miller, K 69 |

## KEY PLAYERS - GOALSCORERS

1 Kenny Miller

| | |
|---|---|
| Goals in Internationals | 2 |
| Contribution to Attacking Power<br>Average number of minutes between team goals while on pitch | 96 |
| Player Strike Rate<br>The total number of minutes he was on the pitch for every goal scored | 145 |
| Club Strike Rate<br>Average number of minutes between goals scored by club | 90 |

| | PLAYER | GOALS | ATT POWER | STRIKE RATE |
|---|---|---|---|---|
| 2 | Stevie Crawford | 3 | 63 | **234 mins** |
| 3 | Steven Thompson | 1 | 58 | **349 mins** |
| 4 | Barry Ferguson | 1 | 70 | **424 mins** |
| 5 | Lee Wilkie | 1 | 73 | **517 mins** |

## TOP PLAYER APPEARANCES

5 Paul Lambert — Midfielder

| | |
|---|---|
| Age (on 01/07/03) | 33 |
| Caps this season | 8 |
| Total minutes on the pitch | 644 |
| Goals | 1 |
| Yellow Cards | 1 |
| Red Cards | 0 |
| Club Side | Celtic |

| | PLAYER | POS | AGE | CAPS | MINS | GOALS | CARDS(Y) | CARDS(R) | CLUB SIDE |
|---|---|---|---|---|---|---|---|---|---|
| 1 | Christian Dailly | DEF | 29 | 11 | 945 | 1 | 2 | 0 | West Ham |
| 2 | Gary Naysmith | DEF | 24 | 9 | 790 | 1 | 0 | 0 | Everton |
| 3 | Steven Pressley | DEF | 29 | 8 | 720 | 0 | 2 | 0 | Hearts |
| 4 | Stevie Crawford | ATT | 29 | 10 | 702 | 3 | 1 | 0 | Dunfermline |
| 5 | Paul Lambert | MID | 33 | 8 | 644 | 1 | 1 | 0 | Celtic |
| 6 | Robert Douglas | GK | 31 | 7 | 630 | 0 | 0 | 0 | Celtic |
| 7 | Graham Alexander | DEF | 31 | 10 | 530 | 0 | 1 | 0 | Preston |
| 8 | Lee Wilkie | DEF | 23 | 9 | 517 | 1 | 1 | 0 | Dundee |
| 9 | Paul Devlin | MID | 31 | 9 | 471 | 0 | 2 | 0 | Birmingham |
| 10 | Maurice Ross | DEF | 22 | 9 | 462 | 0 | 2 | 0 | Rangers |
| 11 | Barry Ferguson | MID | 25 | 5 | 424 | 1 | 0 | 0 | Rangers |
| 12 | Steven Thompson | ATT | 24 | 7 | 349 | 1 | 3 | 0 | Rangers |
| 13 | Paul Gallacher | GK | 23 | 9 | 315 | 0 | 0 | 0 | Dundee Utd |
| 14 | Kenny Miller | ATT | 23 | 4 | 289 | 2 | 0 | 0 | Wolverhampton |
| 15 | Andy Webster | DEF | 21 | 3 | 270 | 0 | 1 | 0 | Hearts |
| 16 | Don Hutchison | MID | 32 | 4 | 255 | 0 | 0 | 0 | West Ham |
| 17 | Kevin Kyle | ATT | 22 | 5 | 254 | 0 | 0 | 0 | Sunderland |
| 18 | Jackie McNamara | MID | 29 | 5 | 218 | 0 | 0 | 0 | Celtic |
| 19 | Russell Anderson | DEF | 24 | 4 | 205 | 0 | 0 | 0 | Aberdeen |
| 20 | Scott Dobie | ATT | 24 | 3 | 193 | 0 | 1 | 0 | West Brom |
| 21 | James McFadden | MID | 20 | 4 | 191 | 0 | 0 | 0 | Motherwell |

# NORTHERN IRELAND

FIFA/COCA COLA WORLD RANKING: **111th**

**MANAGER:** SAMMY MCILROY

| | | | | | | |
|---|---|---|---|---|---|---|
| 1 | intnls | **Cyprus** | H | D | 0-0 | |
| 2 | eqg6 | **Spain** | A | L | 0-3 | |
| 3 | eqg6 | **Ukraine** | H | D | 0-0 | |
| 4 | intnls | **Finland** | H | L | 0-1 | |
| 5 | eqg6 | **Armenia** | A | L | 0-1 | |
| 6 | eqg6 | **Greece** | H | L | 0-2 | |
| 7 | intnls | **Italy** | A | L | 0-2 | |
| 8 | eqg6 | **Spain** | H | D | 0-0 | |

**Competition key:** eqg2 = European Qualifying match in Group 2 (g2); Intnls = all other international matches

**Note:** The season of international matches covered includes all games from the end of the 2002 World Cup in June 30th 2002 to June 11th 2003.

**The last Northern Ireland player to score a goal was West Ham's Steve Lomas on 13th Feb 2002 in a 4-1 friendly defeat against Poland. They have since gone ten matches without scoring.**

## TOP PLAYER APPEARANCES

3 Maik Taylor — Goalkeeper

| | |
|---|---|
| Age (on 01/07/03) | 31 |
| Caps this season | 8 |
| Total minutes on the pitch | 640 |
| Goals | 0 |
| Yellow Cards | 0 |
| Red Cards | 0 |
| Club Side | Fulham |

| | PLAYER | POS | AGE | CAPS | MINS | GOALS | CARDS(Y) | CARDS(R) | CLUB SIDE |
|---|---|---|---|---|---|---|---|---|---|
| 1 | Damien Johnson | MID | 24 | 8 | 691 | 0 | 1 | 0 | Birmingham |
| 2 | David Healy | ATT | 23 | 8 | 640 | 0 | 0 | 0 | Preston |
| 3 | Maik Taylor | GK | 31 | 8 | 640 | 0 | 0 | 0 | Fulham |
| 4 | Aaron Hughes | DEF | 23 | 7 | 630 | 0 | 0 | 0 | Newcastle |
| 5 | George McCartney | DEF | 22 | 7 | 605 | 0 | 0 | 0 | Sunderland |
| 6 | Keith Gillespie | MID | 28 | 6 | 515 | 0 | 3 | 1 | Blackburn |
| 7 | Steve Lomas | MID | 29 | 5 | 450 | 0 | 1 | 0 | West Ham |
| 8 | Mark Williams | DEF | 32 | 6 | 447 | 0 | 2 | 0 | Wimbledon |
| 9 | Paul McVeigh | ATT | 25 | 7 | 366 | 0 | 0 | 0 | Norwich |
| 10 | Peter Kennedy | MID | 29 | 4 | 274 | 0 | 0 | 0 | Wigan |
| 11 | James Quinn | ATT | 28 | 4 | 256 | 0 | 0 | 1 | Willem II Tilb |
| 12 | Kevin Horlock | MID | 30 | 3 | 244 | 0 | 0 | 0 | Man City |
| 13 | Daniel Griffin | DEF | 25 | 3 | 225 | 0 | 0 | 0 | Dundee Utd |
| 14 | Stephen Craigan | DEF | 26 | 4 | 205 | 0 | 1 | 0 | Partick |
| 15 | Colin Murdock | DEF | 28 | 3 | 187 | 0 | 0 | 0 | Preston |
| 16 | Grant McCann | MID | 23 | 8 | 181 | 0 | 0 | 0 | Cheltenham |
| 17 | Chris Baird | DEF | 21 | 5 | 180 | 0 | 0 | 0 | Southampton |
| 18 | Andrew Smith | ATT | 22 | 2 | 179 | 0 | 0 | 0 | Glentoran |
| 19 | Phillip Mulryne | MID | 25 | 2 | 179 | 0 | 0 | 0 | Norwich |
| 20 | Tommy Doherty | MID | 24 | 2 | 165 | 0 | 0 | 0 | Bristol City |
| 21 | Michael Hughes | MID | 31 | 3 | 116 | 0 | 1 | 0 | Un-attached |